Quinlan's Film Stars

Fifth Edition

Also by David Quinlan

Quinlan's Film Directors

*Quinlan's Illustrated Directory of Film Character Actors,
Revised Edition*

QUINLAN'S FILM STARS

Fifth Edition

DAVID QUINLAN

Brassey's, Inc
Washington, D.C.

First published 1981
Second Edition 1986
Third Edition 1991
Fourth Edition 1996
Fifth Edition 2000

Typeset by SX Composing DTP, Rayleigh, Essex, UK

Printed in Spain by Bookprint, S.L. Barcelona

ISBN 1-57488-318-6

Brassey's, Inc.
22841 Quicksilver Drive
Dulles, Virginia 20166

Jacket Photos (left to right)

First row: Julia Roberts, Brad Pitt, Robert Redford, Keanu Reeves, Sharon Stone.

Second row: Samuel L Jackson, Catherine Zeta Jones, Sophia Loren, Demi Moore, Uma Thurman.

Third row: Tom Cruise, Ralph Fiennes, Harrison Ford, Robert DeNiro, John Wayne

Fourth row: Marlon Brando, Johnny Depp, Gwyneth Paltrow, Sean Connery, Sigourney Weaver.

To my wife
Still the best backup

ACKNOWLEDGEMENTS

Many readers have continued to write in since the first edition of this book appeared in 1981. Their comments, additions and suggestions have all been eagerly digested and assimilated. My thanks to all of them, but especially Peter Brummell (notably for extending the filmographies of Lynn Bari and Wallace Beery), Alan Frank (for some valuable picture research), Scott Palmer (who corrected some dates of birth), Lionel Perry (who corrected some copyright dates), Geoff Cowling (who thoughtfully supplied film clips to go with his research), David Shaw, co-author of *The Films of Harvey Keitel*, for his help with the Keitel filmography, and to Christopher Glazebrook, Rudy Van Dem Bremt, Henry Rintoul, Jeff Hannay, Lionel Aymes, Allen Dace and Michael Norman for continuing trojan work in the trenches of forgotten films. My thanks also to Tina Persaud and all at Batsford and Chrysalis for continuing tolerance of late deadlines and additions.

Almost all of the photographs in this book were originally issued to publicize or promote films or TV material made and/or distributed by the following companies, past and present, to whom I gratefully offer acknowledgement: Allied Artists, American-International, Anglo-Amalgamated, Artificial Eye, Associate British-Pathé, ATV, Avco-Embassy, BFI, BIP, Brent-Walker, British Screen, British and Dominions, British United Artists, Cannon Classic, Carolco, Cinerama, Columbia, Walt Disney/Buena Vista, Eagle-Lion, Ealing Studios, EMI, Enterprise, Entertainment, Feature Film Co, Filmmakers Associates, FilmFour, First Artists, First National, Gainsborough, Gala, Gaumont, Gaumont-British, Goldwyn, Granada TV, Grand National, Guild, Hammer, HandMade, Hemdale, Icon, Lippert, London Films, LWT, Lorimar, Mayfair, Medusa, Metrodome, Metro-Goldwyn-Mayer, Metro-Tartan, Miracle, Momentum, Monogram, New Line, New World, Optimum, Orion, Palace, Paramount, Pathé, Polygram, PRC, Rank, Rediffusion, Republic, RKO/RKO Radio, Hal Roach, Starlight, Selznivk, Touchstone, Tri-Star, 20th Century Fox, UIP, United Artists, Universal/Universal-International, Vestron, Virgin, Warner Brothers and Yorkshire TV.

A

ABBOTT AND COSTELLO
ABBOTT, Bud
(top) (William Abbott) 1895–1974
COSTELLO, Lou
(Louis Cristillo) 1906–1959

Vaudeville comedians whose brash humour and slick cross-talk attracted immense audiences in the forties. Despite great personal friction (Costello demanded, and got 60% of the take), they stayed together until 1957. Costello died from a heart attack two years later, and a comeback by Abbott with a new partner was not successful. Abbott, a lifetime epileptic, died of cancer after two strokes. Costello was a stunt man on several films of the later twenties, including *Bardelys the Magnificent* (1926), *Taxi Dancer* (1927) and *The Trail of '98* (1928).

1940: *Caribbean Holiday. One Night in the Tropics. Buck Privates (GB: Rookies). In the Navy. 1941: Hold That Ghost. Keep 'Em Flying. *Los Angeles Examiner Benefit. *Meet the Stars No. 4. Ride 'Em Cowboy. 1942: Rio Rita. Pardon My Sarong. Who Done It? 1943: It Ain't Hay (GB: Money for Jam). Hit the Ice. 1944: Lost in a Harem. In Society. 1945: Here Come the Co-Eds. The Naughty Nineties. Bud Abbott and Lou Costello in Hollywood. 1946: Little Giant (GB: On the Carpet). The Time of Their Lives. 1947: Buck Privates Come Home (GB: Rookies Come Home). The Wistful Widow of Wagon Gap (GB: The Wistful Widow). 1948: The Noose Hangs High. Abbott and Costello Meet Frankenstein (GB: Abbott and Costello Meet the Ghosts). 1949: Mexican Hayride. Africa Screams. Abbott and Costello Meet the Killer, Boris Karloff. 1950: Abbott and Costello in the Foreign Legion. 1951:

Abbott and Costello Meet the Invisible Man. Comin' Round the Mountain. 1952: Jack and the Beanstalk. Lost in Alaska. 1953: Abbott and Costello Go to Mars. Abbott and Costello Meet Dr Jekyll and Mr Hyde. 1954: *Screen Snapshots No. 225. 1955: Abbott and Costello Meet the Keystone Kops. Abbott and Costello Meet the Mummy. 1956: Dance with Me, Henry. Costello alone: *1959: The 30 Foot Bride of Candy Rock.* Abbott alone: *1950: The Real McCoy.*

ABRIL, Victoria (V. Rojas) 1959–
Vivacious Spanish actress with fine-boned features, often in controversial or sexually provocative roles. Trained as a dancer, she was acting regularly in Spanish films at 18, but it was in films directed by Pedro Almodóvar that she rose to prominence with a series of uninhibited performances. International ventures have worked out less well, and her best work has continued to be done in Spain.

1875: Obsesión. 1976: Robin and Marian. Esposa y amante. El puente/The Long Weekend. Caperucita y roja. 1977: Cambio de sexo/I Want to be a Woman. Doña Perfecta. Robin, frecce, fagioli e karate/Karate Robin Hood. 1978: El hombre que supo amar. 1979: La muchacha de las bragas de oro/The Girl with the Golden Panties. 1980: Mater amatisima/Clara. Wer spritzt denn da am Mittelmeer? La casa del paraiso. Le coeur a l'envers. 1981: La guérrillera. La batalla del porro. Comin' at Ya! 1982: J'ai épousé une ombre (US: I Married a Dead Man). Sous le signe de poisson. Asesinato en el Comité Central. Entre paréntesis. La colmena/The Beehive. 1983: Las bicicletas son para el verano. The Bastard. The Moon in the Gutter/La lune dans le caniveau. Sem sombra del pecado. 1984: Le voyage. La noche más hermosa. L'addition. Rio abajo/On the Line. 1985: Padre nuestro/Our Father. After Darkness. Rouge-Gorge. La hora bruja. 1986: Nuit d'ivresse. Ternosecco. Vade e torno. Tiempo d silencio. 1987: Barrios altos. El placer de matar. Run for Your Life/El Lute. El juego mas divertido. La ley del deseo (US: Law of Desire). 1988: Bâton rouge. Sans peur et sans reproche. 1989: Si te dicen que caí. Ada in the Jungle. 1990: Sandino. ¡Atame! (GB and US: Tie Me Up! Tie Me Down! O solas contigo. 1991: Amantes/Lovers. Une époque formidable. Tacones lejanos (GB and US: High Heels). 1992: Demasiado corazon. 1993: Intruder/Intruso. Kika. 1994: Casque bleu. Jimmy Hollywood. 1995: Gazon maudit (GB:

French Twist. US: Bushwhacked). Pasion Turca. 1996: Libertarius. 1997: La femme cosmonaute. 1998: Entre las piernas/Between Your Legs. 1999: My Father, My Mother, My Brothers and Sisters. 2000: Semana santa. 101 Reykjavik. 2001: No News from God.

ADAMS, Brooke 1949–
Small, dark, chipper American actress, good at brittle characterizations. An on-stage performer at six, she had made her TV debut at 16 and her first film at 21. But, although given some useful-looking leading roles during a rather spasmodic career thereafter (she did best in the 1978 version of *Invasion of the Body Snatchers*), she never quite became a reason for going to see a film, and was seen in increasingly less commercial ventures after 1980. Married to actor Tony Shalhoub.

1965: OK Crackerby (TV). 1970: Shock Waves/Death Corps (GB: Almost Human. Released 1975). 1974: F Scott Fitzgerald and 'The Last of the Belles' (TV). The Great Gatsby. The Lords of Flatbush. 1975: Murder on Flight 502 (TV). Who is the Black Dahlia? (TV). The Daughters of Joshua Cabe Return (TV). 1976: James Dean: Portrait of a Friend (TV). †Car Wash. 1977: Nero Wolfe (TV). *Minestrone. 1978: Invasion of the Body Snatchers. Days of Heaven. 1979: Cuba. A Man, a Woman and a Bank/A Very Big Withdrawal. 1980: Tell Me a Riddle. 1981: Utilities (released 1983). 1983: Innocents Abroad (TV). The Dead Zone. 1984: Haunted (TV). Special People (TV). Almost You. 1985: Key Exchange. The Stuff. 1987: Man on Fire. The Lion of Africa (TV). 1989: Bridesmaids (TV). 1991: The Unborn. Sometimes They Come Back. 1992: Gas, Food – Lodging. 1993: The Last Hit (TV). 1994: Sleepless (TV). The Fire This Time (narrator only). 1995: The Baby-Sitters' Club. Picture Windows (cable TV).

†*Scene deleted from final release print*

ADAMS, Joey Lauren 1971–
Apple-cheeked, light-haired American actress of cute appeal and engagingly asthmatic voice. After several years in TV series her winning smile and offbeat personality put her consistently near the top of the cast, although the mainstream public is, as yet, still unlikely to add a name to her face. Occasionally credited simply as Joey Adams.

1993: Coneheads. Dazed and Confused. The Program. 1994: S.F.W. Sleep With Me. 1995:

Movie. 1973: Go Ask Alice (TV). 1974: McQ.
1975: The Killer Inside Me. The Wild
McCulloughs. Psychic Killer. 1977: Goodbye,
Franklin High (released 1980). 1980: The
Fifth Floor. 1983: Champions. 1988: ‡Black
Roses. 1989: Backtrack. 1993: King B: A Life
in the Movies. Conviction: The Kitty Dodds
Story (TV).

†As Betty Adams   ‡As Julia Adams

Mallrats. 1996: Chasing Amy. Drawing Flies.
Bio-Dome. Michael. 1997: The Pros & Cons of
Breathing (shot 1994). 1998: A Cool, Dry
Place. 1999: Big Daddy. Bruno. Reaching
Normal. 2000: Beautiful. 2001: Harvard Man.

1952: Somebody Loves Me. 1955: Mister
Roberts. Strange Lady in Town. I Died a
Thousand Times. Rebel Without a Cause.
Picnic. 1956: The Last Wagon. Strange
Adventure. Our Miss Brooks. 1957: Sing, Boy,
Sing. Fury at Showdown. The Troublemakers
(TV). 1958: The FBI Story. No Time for
Sergeants. Teacher's Pet. 1959: Pillow Talk.
1962: The Interns. Hell is for Heroes! 1963:
The Young Lovers. Twilight of Honor (GB:
The Charge is Murder). The Hook. A Girl
Named Tamiko. 1965: Young Dillinger.
Frankenstein Conquers the World. Kaiju
daisenso (US: Monster Zero). 1966: Die,
Monster, Die (GB: Monster of Terror). Don't
Worry, We'll Think of a Title. Willie and the
Yank (TV. GB: cinemas, as Mosby's
Marauders). 1967: Frankenstein Meets the
Giant Devil Fish. Fever Heat. Zettai zetsumei
(US: The Killing Bottle). 1968: Mission
Mars. Los asesinos.

ADAMS, Maud (M. Wikstrum) 1945–
Tall, shapely, tawny-haired, Swedish-born
international model who attracted some
showy big-budget leading roles without quite
having the acting talent to match her
ambitions. Producers seemed more interested
in getting her clothes off, probably the reason
she returned to modelling from time to time
in between films. Best known for her
decorative roles in two James Bond films.
1970: The Christian Licorice Store. The Plastic
Dome of Norma Jean. Mahoney's Estate. The
Boys in the Band. 1971: U-Turn. 1974: Rollerball. The Man with the Golden Gun. The Girl
in Blue. 1975: The Diamond Mercenaries (US:
Killer Force). 1977: L'uomo senza pietà (US:
The Merciless Man). Genova a mano armata.
1978: Big Bob Johnson and His Fantastic Speed
Circus (TV). 1979: Laura – Shades of Summer
(released 1982. GB: Laura). The Hostage
Tower/Alistair MacLean's The Hostage Tower.
1980: Playing for Time (TV). Tattoo. 1982:
Target Eagle. 1983: Octopussy. 1984: Nairobi
Affair (TV). 1985: Blacke's Magic (TV).
1986: Hell Hunters. 1987: Jane and the Lost
City. The Women's Club. 1988: Angel III: The
Final Chapter. Deadly Intent. A Man of
Passion. The Favorite/Intimate Power. 1989:
Ski School. La nuit de sérail. 1990: The Kill
Reflex. Initiation: Silent Night, Deadly Night/
Bugs. 1993: A Perry Mason Mystery: The Case
of the Wicked Wives (TV). 1996: Ringer.

ADAMS, Nick
(Nicholas Adamschock) 1931–1968
Stocky, fair-haired American leading man,
often cast as harebrained, easily led or other
kinds of tearaway. He enjoyed a good period
of popularity from 1959 to 1963 in the TV
series The Rebel and Saints and Sinners (as
crusading gunfighter and crusading reporter
respectively), but never quite made it to the
top in the cinema. Ended by making movies
in far-flung places and was found dead in
1968 from a drug overdose. Oscar nominee
for Twilight of Honor.

ADAMS, Julie (Betty May Adams) 1926–
Striking, jut-jawed brunette whose Hollywood career languished in minor westerns
until Universal signed her up and changed
her name to Julia (the Julie came later). She
remained a reliable, faintly aristocratic
leading lady (though with warmth to spare)
for them for nine years and married another
Universal player, Ray Danton (qv), before
becoming a dialogue coach. Now best
remembered as the girl carried off by the
creature from the Black Lagoon.
1949: Red Hot and Blue. Hostile Country.
†The Dalton Gang. 1950: †Colorado Ranger.
†Crooked River. †Marshal of Heldorado. †For
Heaven's Sake. †Fast on the Draw (later
Sudden Death). †West of the Brazos.
‡Hollywood Story. ‡Bright Victory (GB:
Lights Out). 1951: ‡Finders Keepers. ‡The
Treasure of Lost Canyon. 1952: ‡Bend of the
River (GB: Where the River Bends). ‡Horizons
West. ‡The Lawless Breed. 1953: ‡Mississippi
Gambler. ‡The Man from the Alamo. ‡Wings
of the Hawk. 1954: ‡The Stand at Apache
River. Francis Joins the WACs. The Creature
from the Black Lagoon. 1955: Six Bridges to
Cross. The Looters. One Desire. 1956: The
Private War of Major Benson. Away All Boats.
1957: Slaughter on 10th Avenue. Four Girls in
Town. 1958: Slim Carter. The Dungeon (TV).
Tarawa Beachhead. 1959: Gunfight at Dodge
City. 1960: Raymie. 1962: The Underwater
City. 1965: Tickle Me. 1967: Valley of
Mystery. 1971: The Trackers (TV). The Last

ADAMS, Tom 1938–
Tall, dark, saturnine British leading man who
starred in a series of James Bond spoofs in the
1960s. The budgets of the films were too low
for any large-scale cinema success, and
Adams's personality perhaps too inflexible
for starring roles in bigger movies. Since 1972
he has played 'second lead' roles in TV
dramas, soap operas and serials and cropped
up as an enthusiastic 'salesman' in
commercials.
1962: A Pair of Briefs. Play It Cool. A Prize of
Arms. 1963: The Great Escape. This is My
Street. 1964: *The Peaches. 1965: Licensed to
Kill (US: The Second Best Secret Agent in the
Whole Wide World). 1966: Where the Bullets
Fly. The Fighting Prince of Donegal. 1967:
Somebody's Stolen Our Russian Spy. Fathom.

1968: Subterfuge. Journey into Midnight (TV). 1970: The House That Dripped Blood. 1971: Von Richthofen and Brown (GB: The Red Baron). 1972: Madigan: The Lisbon Beat (TV). 1992: Duel of Hearts (TV).

ADDAMS, Dawn 1930–1985
British-born glamour girl who appeared in some Hollywood films of the 1950s. She was screen-tested for *National Velvet* in 1944, but lost to Elizabeth Taylor, with whom she shared dark hair, dark eyes and a stormy and well-publicized love life which settled down when she married her second husband, a retired businessman. Lived in Malta in the 1970s, in US from 1982. Died from cancer.
1951: Night into Morning. The Unknown Man. 1952: The Hour of 13. Singin' in the Rain. Plymouth Adventure. 1953: The Robe. Young Bess. The Moon is Blue (and German version). Riders to the Stars. Secrets d'alcove (GB and US: The Bed). 1954: The Viscount of Bragelonne (US: Last of the Musketeers). Return to Treasure Island. Khyber Patrol. Mizar (GB: Frogman Spy). 1956: Rommel's Treasure. London Calling North Pole/House of Intrigue. 1957: Four in a Thunderjet. A King in New York. 1958: The Silent Enemy. Il mistero della Pensione Edelweiss. Sursis pour les vivants. The Volga Boatman (GB: The Boatman. US: Prisoners of the Volga). L'île au bout du monde (GB: Temptation Island). 1959: Secret Professional. Voulez-vous danser avec moi? (GB and US: Come Dance With Me). The Treasure of San Teresa (US: Long Distance). The Scarlet Baroness. Geheimaktion schwartze Kapelle (US: Black Chapel). 1960: Die zornigen jungen Männer. The 1,000 Eyes of Dr Mabuse. The Two Faces of Dr Jekyll (US: House of Fright). 1961: Follow That Man. Les menteurs (GB: House of Sin). 1962: L'education sentimentale (GB: Lessons in Love). Come Fly with Me. The £20,000 Kiss. 1963: The Black Tulip. 1964: Ballad in Blue (US: Blues for Lovers). 1966: Where the Bullets Fly. 1969: Zeta One. The Vampire Lovers. Sappho/Sapho. 1973: Vault of Horror.

ADJANI, Isabelle 1955–
Wide-eyed, dark-haired, brittle French actress, at her bewitching best in shallow or sombre roles. Born in Paris to an Algerian father and German mother, she made her film debut during her school holidays and came into demand for international assignments after her Academy Award nomination for *The*

Story of Adèle H. She won a second Oscar nomination for *Camille Claudel*, but has had little luck overall in finding projects that will further her career.
1969: Le petit bougnat. 1971: Faustine et le bel été (GB: Faustine. US: Growing Up/Faustine and the Beautiful Summer). 1974: La gifle (GB and US: The Slap). 1975: The Story of Adèle H. 1976: The Tenant. Barocco. Violette et François. 1978: The Driver (GB: Driver). The Brontë Sisters. 1979: Nosferatu: Phantom der Nacht (GB and US: Nosferatu the Vampyre). 1980: Possession. Clara et les chic types. 1981: Quartet. L'année prochaine si tout va bien. 1982: Tout feu, tout flamme (US: All Fired Up). Antonietta. 1983: L'été meurtrier (GB and US: One Deadly Summer). Mortelle rondonée (US: Deadly Circuit). 1985: Subway. 1986: Maladie d'amour. 1987: Ishtar. Camille Claudel. 1990: Fleur de rubis. Favorita del re. 1991: Lung Ta: Les cavaliers du vent. 1993: Toxic Affair. 1994: La reine Margot. 1996: Diabolique. 1998: Paparazzi. 1999: Passionellement.

ADORÉE, Renée
(Jeanne de la Fonte) 1898–1933
Tiny, brunette French star of Hollywood silent films. Born in a circus tent, she became a Folies Bergères dancer. Found her way (via Australia, and a film debut) to Hollywood by 1920. Big, expressive eyes contributed to her success in silents but ill-health and the advent of the talkies combined to wreck her career. Died from tuberculosis.
1918: £500 Reward. 1920: The Strongest. 1921: Made in Heaven. 1922: Honor First. Daydreams. The Law Bringers. Monte Cristo. A Self-Made Man. West of Chicago. Mixed Faces. 1923: The Eternal Struggle. Six Fifty.

1924: Women Who Give Up. A Man's Mate. The Bandolero. 1925: Exchange of Wives. Excuse Me. Man and Maid. The Big Parade. Parisian Nights. 1926: The Black Bird. Blarney. La Bohème. The Exquisite Sinner. Tin Gods. 1927: Back to God's Country. Heaven on Earth. Flaming Forest. Mr Wu. On Ze Boulevard. The Show. 1928: A Certain Young Man. The Cossacks. Forbidden Hours. The Mating Call. The Michigan Kid. Show People. The Spieler (GB: The Spellbinder). 1929: The Pagan. Hollywood Revue of 1929. Tide of Empire. 1930: Redemption. Call of the Flesh. *Singer of Seville.

AFFLECK, Ben 1972–
Tall, dark, handsome American actor who rose gradually to prominence in films after beginning an acting career as a teenager. Slightly stolid and lacking in personality if still a decent actor, Affleck was on the verge of leading roles by the turn of the millennium without quite developing into a marquee name. Indeed, his was partly fame by association, as he and his rather more charismatic friend and partner Matt Damon (*qv*) took an Oscar for their screenplay for *Good Will Hunting* (in which Affleck gave one of his most relaxed performances). An on-off romance with actress Gwyneth Paltrow (*qv*) helped keep his name in the headlines. His brother Casey Affleck is also an actor.
1986: Wanted: The Perfect Guy (TV). 1987: Hands of a Stranger (TV). 1991: Danielle Steel's 'Daddy' (TV). 1992: Buffy the Vampire Slayer. School Ties. 1993: Dazed and Confused. 1994: A Body to Die For: The Aaron Henry Story (TV). 1995: Mallrats. 1996: Chasing Amy. Glory Daze. 1997: Going All the Way. Phantoms/Dean Koontz's Phantoms. Good Will Hunting. 1998: Big Helium Dog. Armageddon. Shakespeare in Love. 200 Cigarettes. 1999: Forces of Nature. Dogma. 2000: Daddy and Them. Reindeer Games (GB: Deception). Boiler Room. The Third Wheel. Bounce. 2001: Pearl Harbor.

AGAR, John 1921–
Tall, sturdy, fair-haired ex-US Army sergeant who drifted into films after marrying Shirley Temple (*qv*) in 1945 (they divorced in 1949). Lacked the mobility for major films, but sustained his leading man status in co-feature westerns and horrors until the early 1960s. More recently he played bit parts, describing himself as 'poor but happy'.
1948: Fort Apache. 1949: Adventure in

Baltimore (GB: Bachelor Balt). I Married a Communist (GB: The Woman on Pier 13). Sands of Iwo Jima. She Wore a Yellow Ribbon. 1950: Breakthrough. 1951: Along the Great Divide. The Magic Carpet. 1952: Woman of the North Country. 1953: Man of Conflict. 1954: The Rocket Man. The Golden Mistress. Bait. Shield for Murder. 1955: Revenge of the Creature. The Lonesome Trail. Tarantula. 1956: The Flesh and the Spur. Star in the Dust. Hold Back Tomorrow. The Mole People. 1957: Joe Butterfly. Ride a Violent Mile. The Brain from Planet Arous. Daughter of Dr Jekyll. Cavalry Command (released 1965). 1958: Attack of the Puppet People (GB: Six Inches Tall). Frontier Gun. Jet Attack (GB: Through Hell to Glory). 1959: Invisible Invaders. 1960: Raymie. 1961: Lisette. The Hand of Death. Journey to the 7th Planet. 1962: The Young and the Brave. 1963: Of Love and Desire. Law of the Lawless. 1964: Young Fury. 1965: Stage to Thunder Rock. Johnny Reno. Women of the Prehistoric Planet. 1966: The St Valentine's Day Massacre. Waco. Zontar, the Thing from Venus. 1967: The Curse of the Swamp Creature. 1968: Hell Raisers. 1969: Night Fright. The Undefeated. 1971: Chisum. 1972: Big Jake. 1976: King Kong. 1977: How's Your Love Life? 1978: The Amazing Mr No-Legs. 1988: Perfect Victims. Miracle Mile. 1989: Fear (TV). 1990: Nightbreed. 1991: The Perfect Bride (TV). 1992: Invasion of Privacy (TV). 1993: Body Bags (TV).

AGUTTER, Jenny 1952–
Tall, demure-looking, blonde British leading lady, in show business from childhood, from the same ballet school (and mould) as Hayley Mills and Pamela Franklin (both *qv*). Film career faltered after some big hits in the early 1970s when she projected innocence more

convincingly than most, but accelerated again following her British Academy Award for *Equus*. But she seemed to tire of playing roles that required her to be put-on and take her clothes off, and spent most of the 1980s on stage and TV. Now in regal 'older woman' roles.
1964: East of Sudan. 1965: Ballerina. 1966: A Man Could Get Killed. 1968: The Gates of Paradise. Star! 1969: I Start Counting. 1970: The Railway Children. Walkabout. 1971: The Snow Goose (TV). 1972: A War of Children (TV). 1976: Logan's Run. The Eagle Has Landed. The Man in the Iron Mask (TV). 1977: Equus. Sois-belle et tais-toi. 1978: China 9, Liberty 37/Gunfighters (US: Clayton and Catherine). Dominique. The Riddle of the Sands. 1979: Mayflower: the Pilgrims' Adventure (TV). Sweet William. 1980: Miss Right. 1981: The Survivor. Amy. An American Werewolf in London. *Late Flowering Love. 1984: Secret Places. 1985: Silas Marner (TV). 1987: Dark Tower. 1989: King of the Wind. 1990: Child's Play II. The Outsiders (TV). Darkman. 1991: Freddie As FRO 7 (voice only). 1992: Freddie Goes to Washington (voice only. Unfinished). 1995: Blue Juice.

AHERNE, Brian 1902–1986
Matinée idol of the British stage in the twenties. He went to Hollywood in 1933, where his Englishness and lack of dynamism confined him to an interesting variety of lesser roles. A good foil for some powerful American leading ladies of the time. Married to Joan Fontaine (*qv*), 1939–43. Oscar nomination for *Juarez*. Died from heart failure.
1924: The Eleventh Commandment. 1925: King of the Castle. The Squire of Long Hadley. 1926: Safety First. 1927: A Woman Redeemed. 1928: Shooting Stars. 1929: Underground. 1930: The 'W' Plan. 1931: Madame Guillotine. 1933: I Was a Spy. Song of Songs. The Constant Nymph. 1934: What Every Woman Knows. The Fountain. 1935: Sylvia Scarlett. I Live My Life. 1936: Beloved Enemy. 1937: The Great Garrick. 1938: Merrily We Live. 1939: Captain Fury. Juarez. 1940: The Lady in Question. Hired Wife. My Son, My Son. Vigil In the Night. 1941: The Man Who Lost Himself. Skylark. Smilin' Through. 1942: My Sister Eileen. A Night to Remember. 1943: Forever and a Day. First Comes Courage. What a Woman! (GB: The Beautiful Cheat). 1946: The Locket. 1948: Smart Woman. Angel on the Amazon (GB:

Drums Along the Amazon). 1952: I Confess. 1953: Titanic. 1954: Prince Valiant. A Bullet is Waiting. 1956: The Swan. 1959: The Best of Everything. 1961: Susan Slade. 1963: Lancelot and Guinevere. The Waltz King. 1965: The Cavern. 1967: Rosie!

AIMÉE, Anouk (Françoise Sorya) 1932–
Elegant brunette French actress who made her first films billed simply as Anouk. An elfin leading lady of both British and French films while still in her teens, she became a star all over again in her thirties with the international hit *Un homme et une femme*, which won her an Oscar nomination. Married (fourth of five) to Albert Finney from 1970 to 1978.
1947: †La maison sous la mer. La fleur de l'âge. 1948: †Les amants de Verone. 1949: †Golden Salamander. 1951: †Le rideau cramoisi/The Crimson Curtain. †*Conquêtes du froid. †Noche de tormenta. 1952: †La bergère et le ramoneur (voice only). †Nuit d'orage. †The Man Who Watched Trains Go By (US: Paris Express). 1954: Les mauvaises rencontres. Nina. †Forever My Heart. 1955: †Contraband Spain. Ich suche dich. Stresemann. 1956: Pot-bouille (GB: The House of Lovers). 1957: Montparnasse 19 (GB: The Lovers of Montparnasse. Modigliani of Montparnasse). Tous peuvent me tuer (GB: Anyone Can Kill Me). 1958: Carve Her Name with Pride. La tête contre les murs (GB: The Keepers). The Journey. 1959: Las dragueurs (GB: The Young Have No Morals. US: The Chasers). 1960: Le fárceur. Le dolce vita. Le temps d'un reflet. 1961: Lola. Quai Notre Dame. L'imprévisto. Il giudizio universale (US: The Last Judgement). 1962: Eight and a Half/Otto e mezzo. (The Last Days of) Sodom and Gomorrah. Les grands chemins (GB and US: Of Flesh and Blood). 1963: Il successo. Il terrorista. Liola. I giorno più corto (US: The Shortest Day). 1964: Le voci bianche (GB: The Undercover Rogue. US: White Voices). 1965: La fuga. Il morbidone. 1966: Lo scandalo. Le stagioni del nostro amore (GB: A Very Handy Man). Un homme et une femme (GB and US: A Man and a Woman). 1968: Un soir, un train. The Appointment. 1969: Model Shop. Justine. 1977: Si c'était à refaire (GB: Second Chance). 1978: Mon premier amour. Les petits matins. 1980: Salto nel vuoto (US: A Leap in the Dark). 1981: Tragedia di un uomo ridicolo. 1982: Qu'est-ce qui fait courir David? 1983: Il generale dell'armata morta. 1984: Viva la vie. Success is the Best Revenge.

1985: Flagrant Desire. 1986: Un homme et une femme: 20 ans déjà. 1987: La table tournante. Arrivederci e grazie. 1988: The House of the Lord. 1990: Faccia di lepre. Bethune: The Making of a Hero. 1991: Il y a des jours . . . et des lunes. 1992: Voices in the Garden (TV). 1993: Ruptures. Les marmottes. 1994: Scar. Prêt-à-Porter/Ready to Wear. Les cent et une nuits. 1995: Dis moi oui. Noirs désirs. L'univers de Jacques Demy. 1996: Hommes femmes mode d'emploi. 1997: Gueule d'amour. 1998: L.A. Without a Map. Riches, belles et cruelles. 1999: Une pour toutes (US: One 4 All). 1999 Madeleine. 2000: 2000 Eve.

†As Anouk

ALBERGHETTI, Anna Maria 1936–
Dark-haired, Italian-born operatic singer with a sweet, wistful image, who made a big hit in 1953 in *The Stars Are Singing*. Suitable subsequent roles, however, in a Hollywood no longer orientated to musicals, proved difficult to find and she swiftly drifted away from the cinema, appearing on Broadway and in television until the late 1960s. She made a surprise film return in character roles at the turn of the century.
1950: The Medium. 1951: Here Comes the Groom. 1953: The Stars Are Singing. 1955: The Last Command. 1957: 10,000 Bedrooms. Duel at Apache Wells. 1960: Cinderfella. 2000: Friends and Family. The Whole Shebang.

ALBERT, Eddie (E.A. Heimberger) 1908–
Big, gruff, friendly, solidly-built American leading man (and, later, leading character player) with light-brown hair who started in show business in such diverse occupations as radio singer and trapeze artist. He became a

stage actor in light comedy roles in his late twenties, and the Broadway success of *Brother Rat* led him to repeat his role in the 1938 film. He was mainly seen as light lead, hero's friend or comedy relief until the 1950s but after his Oscar nomination for *Roman Holiday* he began to attempt a wider range of roles. Continuing to offer solid, thoughtful performances, even in forgettable films, he was further nominated for an Oscar in *The Heartbreak Kid*. Married actress Margo (Maria Castilla, 1918–1985) in 1945. The actor Edward Albert (1951–) is their son.
1938: Brother Rat. 1939: On Your Toes. Four Wives. 1940: Brother Rat and a Baby (GB: Baby Be Good). An Angel from Texas. My Love Came Back. A Dispatch from Reuter's (GB: This Man Reuter). 1941: Four Mothers. The Wagons Roll at Night. Thieves Fall Out. Out of the Fog. The Great Mr Nobody. 1942: Treat 'Em Rough. Eagle Squadron. 1943: Ladies' Day. Lady Bodyguard. Bombardier. 1945: Strange Voyage. 1946: Rendezvous with Annie. The Perfect Marriage. 1947: Smash-Up (GB: A Woman Destroyed). Time Out of Mind. Hit Parade of 1947. 1948: Every Girl Should be Married. The Dude Goes West. You Gotta Stay Happy. 1950: The Fuller Brush Girl (GB: The Affairs of Sally). USS Teakettle (later and GB: You're in the Navy Now). 1951: Meet Me After the Show. 1952: Actors and Sin. Carrie. 1953: Roman Holiday. 1955: The Girl Rush. Oklahoma! I'll Cry Tomorrow. 1956: Attack! The Teahouse of the August Moon. 1957: The Sun Also Rises. The Joker is Wild. 1958: The Gun Runners. The Roots of Heaven. Orders to Kill. 1959: Beloved Infidel. The Dingaling Girl (TV). 1961: The Young Doctors. The Two Little Bears. 1962: Madison Avenue. The Longest Day. Who's Got the Action? The Party's Over. Miracle of the White Stallions (GB: Flight of the White Stallions). 1963: Captain Newman MD. 1965: Seven Women. 1971: See the Man Run (TV). 1972: Fireball Forward (TV). The Heartbreak Kid. 1974: The Take. McQ. The Borrowers (TV). The Longest Yard (GB: The Mean Machine). Escape to Witch Mountain. 1975: The Devil's Rain. Hustle. Promise Him Anything (TV). Whiffs (GB: C.A.S.H.). Switch (TV). 1976: Birch Interval. 1977: Moving Violation. 1978: Crash (TV). Foolin' Around (released 1980). 1979: Yesterday. The Concorde . . . Airport '79 (GB: Airport '80 . . . the Concorde). 1980: The Fall Guy (TV). How to Beat the High Cost of Living. Scoring. The Border. 1981: Take This Job and Shove It. Goliath Awaits (feature version of TV miniseries). The Oklahoma City Dolls (TV). 1982: Yes, Giorgio. Trouble in the High Timber Country (TV). 1983: The Demon Murder Case (TV). The Act. Dreamscape. 1984: Burning Rage (TV). 1985: In Like Flynn (TV). Stitches. 1986: Turnaround. Head Office. 1987: Brenda Starr (released 1989). Deadly Illusion. 1988: The Big Picture. 1990: Return to Green Acres (TV). 1991: The Girl from Mars (cable TV). 1994: Headless! 1995: The Barefoot Executive (TV). 1997: Illusion Infinity.

ALBRIGHT, Hardie
(Hardy Albrecht) 1903–1975
Tall, fair, beefily handsome American leading

man, built vaguely along Nelson Eddy lines, and at his most popular in the early 1930s, when he successfully tackled several juicy roles. After 1934 the quality of his roles diminished, and he went back to the theatre, later returning to supporting parts in wartime Hollywood films, even appearing in a sex-instruction film. Wrote books on acting and direction. Actress Martha Sleeper was the first (1934–1940) of his two wives. Died from congestive heart failure after pneumonia.
1931: Young Sinners. Hush Money. Heartbreak. Skyline. 1932: A Successful Calamity. So Big. The Crash. Jewel Robbery. The Purchase Price. Three on a Match. This Sporting Age. Cabin in the Cotton. The Match King. 1933: Song of Songs. The Working Man. Three-Cornered Moon. The House on 56th Street. 1934: Nana. Crimson Romance. The Scarlet Letter. White Heat. Beggar's Holiday. Two Heads on a Pillow. Silver Streak. Sing Sing Nights (GB: Reprieved). 1935: Ladies Love Danger. Women Must Dress. Red Salute (GB: Arms and the Girl). Champagne for Breakfast. Calm Yourself. 1940: Granny Get Your Gun. Ski Patrol. Carolina Moon. Flight from Destiny. 1941: Men of the Timberland. Bachelor Daddy. Marry the Boss's Daughter. The Loves of Edgar Allan Poe. 1942: Pride of the Yankees. Lady in a Jam. Captains of the Clouds. 1944: Army Wives. Mom and Dad (GB: A Family Story. Released 1957). 1945: Captain Tugboat Annie. The Jade Mask. Sunset in El Dorado. 1946: Angel on My Shoulder.

ALBRIGHT, Lola 1924–
Blonde ex-typist and telephonist who broke into films in 1948, and was winning leading roles two years later. But she seldom got the

parts that her talent and smouldering personality seemed to warrant, and was lost to TV for long periods, first in *Peter Gunn*, then in *Peyton Place*. Married to Jack Carson (*qv*) 1952–58.

1948: *The Pirate. Easter Parade. Julia Misbehaves.* 1949: *The Girl from Jones Beach. Tulsa. Champion.* 1950: *Bodyhold. Beauty on Parade. When You're Smiling. The Good Humor Man. The Killer That Stalked New York (GB: The Frightened City). Sierra Passage.* 1952: *Arctic Flight.* 1953: *The Silver Whip.* 1954: *The Treasure of Ruby Hills.* 1955: *The Tender Trap. The Magnificent Matador (GB: The Brave and the Beautiful).* 1957: *The Monolith Monsters. Pawnee (GB: Pale Arrow). Oregon Passage. *Jonah and the Highway.* 1958: *Seven Guns to Mesa.* 1961: *A Cold Wind in August.* 1962: *Kid Galahad.* 1964: *Les félins (GB: The Love Cage. US: The Joyhouse).* 1966: *Lord Love a Duck.* 1967: *The Way West. The Helicopter Spies (TV. GB: cinemas). How I Spent My Summer Vacation (TV. GB: cinemas, as Deadly Roulette).* 1968: *Where Were You When the Lights Went Out? The Impossible Years. The Money Jungle.* 1973: *My Secret Mother (TV).* 1975: *The Nurse Killer (TV).* 1976: *Fade In to Murder (TV).* 1977: *Delta County USA (TV). Terraces (TV).*

ALDA, Alan 1936–
Tall, dark-haired, loose-limbed American actor with crooked smile and quiet, wry, dry, sometimes sarcastically humorous personality, the son of Robert Alda (*qv*). He started on the stage in 1953, but his enigmatic, sometimes offhand portrayals have limited his film roles, and he has been seen most successfully on TV, where he seems to find it easier to impose his personality on a show. In 1974, Alda won an Emmy as best actor in a comedy series for the top-rating and much-loved *M*A*S*H*, in which he starred for several seasons. He has written and directed several films in which he has also appeared since 1980, with critically pleasing if undynamic box-office results.

1963: *Gone Are the Days/Purlie Victorious.* 1968: *The Extraordinary Seaman. Paper Lion.* 1970: *Catch 22. The Moonshine War. Jenny.* 1971: *The Mephisto Waltz. To Kill a Clown.* 1972: *The Glass House (TV. GB: cinemas). Playmates (TV).* 1973: *Isn't It Shocking? (TV).* 1977: *Kill Me If You Can/The Caryl Chessman Story (TV).* 1978: *California Suite. Same Time, Next Year.* 1979: *The Seduction*

of Joe Tynan. 1980: †*The Four Seasons.* 1985: †*Sweet Liberty.* 1988: †*A New Life.* 1989: *Crimes and Misdemeanors.* 1990: †*Betsy's Wedding.* 1992: *Whispers in the Dark.* 1993: *Manhattan Murder Mystery. And the Band Played On.* 1994: *White Mile (cable TV).* 1995: *Canadian Bacon. Flirting with Disaster.* 1996: *Everyone Says I Love You. Neil Simon's 'Jake's Women' (TV).* 1997: *Mad City. Murder at 1600.* 1998: *The Object of My Affection. Keepers of the Frame (D).*

†*And directed*

ALDA, Robert
(Alphonso d'Abruzzo) 1914–1986
Hopeful-looking, dark-haired, occasionally moustachioed leading man who started at the top with his portrait of George Gershwin in *Rhapsody in Blue*. A good singer who became a rather stiff actor, he was offered few musical roles except on stage. Later made several films abroad, but never regained his star status in the cinema. Father of Alan Alda (*qv*). Died following a stroke.

1945: *Rhapsody in Blue.* 1946: *Cinderella Jones. Cloak and Dagger. The Beast with Five Fingers. The Man I Love.* 1947: *Nora Prentiss.* 1948: *April Showers.* 1949: *Homicide.* 1950: *Hollywood Varieties. Tarzan and the Slave Girl.* 1951: *Mr Universe. Two Gals and a Guy.* 1955: *La donna più bella del mondo/Beautiful But Dangerous. Assignment Abroad (TV. GB: cinemas). Secret File (TV. GB: cinemas).* 1958: *Gentleman from Second Avenue (TV).* 1959: *Imitation of Life. Un militaro e mezzo. A che sorvonno questi.* 1960: *Sepulchre dei rei (US: Cleopatra's Daughter). Musketeers of the Sea.* 1961: *Force of Impulse.* 1962: *The Devil's Hand. Tote e Peppino, divisi a Berlino.* 1963: *Revenge of the Barbarians.* 1968: *The Girl Who Knew Too Much.* 1973: *Seven Steps from Murder. The Serpent.* 1971: *Cagliostro.* 1975: *Off Shore. Last Hours Before Morning (TV). Won Ton Ton, The Dog Who Saved Hollywood. House of Exorcism. I Will, I Will... for Now.* 1976: *Bittersweet Love.* 1977: *Perfect Gentlemen (TV).* 1978: *River of Promises (TV). Spider Man Strikes Back (TV. GB: cinemas). The Big Rip-Off/The Rip Off (US: The Squeeze). Every Girl Should Have One.* 1979: *Supertrain (TV. Later: Express to Terror).*

ALDON, Mari (Mary Aldon) 1929–
Blonde Canadian, British-educated actress, a former ballerina and singer, whose sweet

personality made a brief impact at Warners in the early 1950s. Within a few years she descended to supporting roles, then retired after marrying director Tay Garnett. They later divorced.

1946: *The Locket.* 1947: *Forever Amber.* 1948: *A Woman's Vengeance.* 1951: *Tomorrow is Another Day. Inside the Walls of Folsom prison. Distant Drums. The Tanks Are Coming.* 1952: *This Woman is Dangerous. Tangier Incident.* 1954: *Mask of Dust (US: Race for Life).* 1955: *The Barefoot Contessa. Summer Madness (US: Summertime).* 1972: *The Mad Trapper.*

ALEXANDER, Jane (J. Quigley) 1939–
Anyone who can be good in such a film as *The Betsy* certainly deserves a place in this book, and this dark-haired, businesslike, un-pretty American actress of warm and individual personality is almost always good, as her record – four Oscar nominations (for *The Great White Hope, All the President's Men, Kramer vs Kramer* and *Testament*) to date and several acclaimed leading roles in TV movies – testifies. In acting since childhood, although I have not been able to ascertain whether she is the child Janie Alexander who appears in *The Naked City* (1948). Married to director Ed(win) Sherin (1930–). Chairperson of the National Endowment of the Arts from 1994.

1970: *The Great White Hope. A Gunfight.* 1971: *Welcome Home, Johnny Bristol (TV).* 1972: *The New Centurions (GB: Precinct 45, Los Angeles Police).* 1973: *Miracle on 34th Street (TV).* 1974: *This is the West That Was (TV).* 1976: *Death Be Not Proud (TV). All the President's Men. Eleanor and Franklin (TV).* 1977: *Eleanor and Franklin: The White*

House Years (TV). A Circle of Children (TV).
1978: The Betsy. A Question of Love (TV).
Lovey – A Circle of Children Part II (TV).
1979: Kramer vs Kramer. 1980: Brubaker.
Playing for Time (TV). 1982: Night Crossing.
In the Custody of Strangers (TV). 1983:
Testament. 1984: When She Says No (TV).
City Heat. Calamity Jane (TV). 1985: Sweet
Country. Malice in Wonderland (TV). 1986:
Square Dance. Jaguar. 1987: In Love and War
(TV). 1988: Open Admissions (TV). A
Friendship in Vienna (TV). 1989: Daughter of
the Streets (TV). An American Place. Glory.
1990: That Magic Moment (TV). 1991: A
Marriage (TV). 1992: Stay the Night (TV).
1993: Le donne non vogliomo piu. 1994:
L'uomo delle stelle (GB: The Starmaker. US:
The Star Man). 1997: Buck and the Magic
Bracelet. 1999: The Cider House Rules.

ALEXANDER, Ross 1907–1937
Tall, dark, liquid-lipped, soulful-looking,
rather gangling American leading man. On
stage from 16, the loose-limbed Alexander
was one of Warners' foremost lighter leading
men in the mid-1930s, especially in college-
style comedies opposite fluffy leading ladies
such as Anita Louise (qv), but is probably
now best remembered as Demetrius in the
1935 A Midsummer Night's Dream. Plagued
with worries that his career was slipping,
Alexander shot himself at 29. He was married
to actress Anne Nagel (also qv).
1932: The Wiser Sex. 1933: Crashing Society.
1934: Flirtation Walk. Gentlemen Are Born.
Loudspeaker Lowdown. Social Register. 1935:
A Midsummer Night's Dream. Captain Blood.
We're in the Money. Shipmates Forever. Apple
Sauce. Going Highbrow. Maybe It's Love.
1936: Brides Are Like That. I Married a
Doctor. Boulder Dam. China Clipper. Hot
Money. Here Comes Carter (GB: The Voice of
Scandal). 1937: Ready, Willing and Able.

ALLAN, Elizabeth 1908–1990
Gracious, genteel, dark-haired English
leading lady, adept at frightened misses early
in her career when, for a while, she was under
contract to M-G-M in Hollywood where she
played well-bred heroines, often in period
dramas. Returning to Britain in 1938 after an
acrimonious dispute with her studio, who had
dropped her from a film, The Citadel, she
appeared as upper-class wives in largely
undistinguished films, but later became
popular in TV panel games.
1931: Alibi. Rodney Steps In. The Rosary.

Black Coffee. Chin Chin Chinaman (US: Boat
from Shanghai). Many Waters. Service for
Ladies (US: Reserved for Ladies). 1932: The
Chinese Puzzle. Michael and Mary. Nine Till
Six. Down Our Street. Insult. The Lodger
(US: The Phantom Fiend). 1933: The
Shadow. The Lost Chord. Ace of Aces. The
Solitaire Man. Looking Forward (GB:
Service). No Marriage Ties. 1934: Java Head.
David Copperfield. The Mystery of Mr X.
Outcast Lady (GB: A Woman of the World).
Men in White. 1935: Mark of the Vampire.
1936: A Woman Rebels. A Tale of Two Cities.
Camille. *The Story of Papworth. 1937: The
Soldier and the Lady (GB: Michael Strogoff).
Slave Ship. 1938: Dangerous Medicine. 1939:
The Girl Who Forgot. Inquest. 1940: Saloon
Bar. 1942: The Great Mr Handel. Went The
Day Well? (US: 48 Hours). 1944: He Snoops
to Conquer. 1949: That Dangerous Age (US:
If This Be Sin). No Highway (US: No
Highway in the Sky). 1952: Folly to be Wise.
1953: Twice Upon a Time. The Heart of the
Matter. Front Page Story. 1955: The Brain
Machine. Born for Trouble. 1958: Grip of the
Strangler (US: The Haunted Strangler).

ALLBRITTON, Louise 1920–1979
Aristocratic but peppy blonde American
leading actress with chiselled features, whose
career in films was almost entirely confined to
the 1940s. Despite often being cast as 'the
other woman', she was poised, witty and had
a great sense of comic timing that might have
made her the successor to Carole Lombard.
Her talents, like Lombard's, certainly looked
at their best in screwball comedy, but she did
not pursue a career with the same single-
mindedness after marriage to news commentator Charles Collingwood in 1946. She

died from cancer.
1942: *Keeping Fit. Parachute Nurse. Danger
in the Pacific. Not a Ladies' Man. Who Done
It? Pittsburgh. 1943: It Comes Up Love. Good
Morning, Judge. Fired Wife. Son of Dracula.
1944: Follow the Boys. This is the Life. Her
Primitive Man. San Diego, I Love You.
Bowery to Broadway. 1945: The Men in Her
Diary. That Night with You. 1946: Tangier.
1947: The Egg and I. 1948: Sitting Pretty.
Walk a Crooked Mile. 1949: Don't Trust Your
Husband. The Doolins of Oklahoma (GB: The
Great Manhunt). 1964: Felicia.

ALLEN, Gracie 1902–1964
Uniquely scatterbrained brunette American
comedienne with plain, strong-chinned
features and squeaky voice, usually seen in
films with husband and partner George
Burns (qv), but most successful on stage and
later, especially, on TV. Began in vaudeville
with her sisters, then teamed with George
and defeated all comers with her own brand
of innocent illogic. The cinema never made
the most of her. She died from a heart attack
at 62.
1929: *Lamb Chops. 1930: *Fit To Be Tied.
*Pulling a Bone. 1931: *The Antique Shop.
*Once Over Light. *One Hundred Percent
Service. 1932: The Big Broadcast. *Hollywood
on Parade A-4. *Oh My Operation. *The
Babbling Book. 1933. *Patents Pending.
International House. College Humor. *Let's
Dance. *Walking the Baby. 1934: We're Not
Dressing. Six of a Kind. Many Happy Returns.
1935: Love in Bloom. Here Comes Cookie
(GB: The Plot Thickens). The Big Broadcast
of 1936. 1936: College Holiday. The Big
Broadcast of 1937. 1937: A Damsel in Distress.
1938: College Swing (GB: Swing, Teacher,
Swing). 1939: The Gracie Allen Murder Case.
Honolulu. 1941: Mr and Mrs North. *Variety
Reel. 1944: Two Girls and a Sailor. 1954:
*Screen Snapshots No. 224.

ALLEN, Joan 1956–
Tall, slender, dark-haired American actress
of pinched attractiveness and patrician
bearing. She was a founding member, along
with John Malkovich (qv), of Chicago's
famous Steppenwolf Theatre Company.
Allen looks good in hats and tailored suits and
has few peers when extracting poignancy
from seemingly ordinary roles – as her
Academy Award nominations for her work in
Nixon and The Crucible testify. There are
fewer films on her record, though, than you

might imagine.

1983: Say Goodnight, Gracie (TV). 1985: Compromising Positions. 1986: Manhunter. All My Sons (TV). Peggy Sue Got Married. 1987: The Room Upstairs (TV). 1988: Tucker The Man and His Dream. 1989: Dominant Fifth. In Country. 1991: Without Warning: The James Brady Story (TV). 1992: Ethan Frome. 1993: Josh and S.A.M. Searching for Bobby Fischer (GB: Innocent Moves). 1995: Nixon. Mad Love. 1996: The Crucible. 1997: Face/Off. The Ice Storm. 1998: Pleasantville. 1999: All the Rage. When the Sky Falls. 2000: The Contender.

ALLEN, Karen 1951–

Personable little blue-eyed Hollywood brunette seen almost exclusively in 'nice-girl' roles. She landed the leading role in the blockbuster *Raiders of the Lost Ark* at the age of 30, then surprised many by declining to star in the sequel. She did well to start an acting career after an attack of kerato conjunctivitis which left her temporarily blind. Keeps looking young for her age, and played some tougher parts in the 1990s.

*1976: The Whidjitmaker. 1977: *The Aftermath. 1978: La grande leche. Lovey: A Circle of Children Part II (TV). National Lampoon's Animal House. 1979: Manhattan. The Wanderers. 1980: A Small Circle of Friends. Cruising. 1981: Raiders of the Lost Ark. Shoot the Moon. 1982: Split Image/Captured! 1983: Until September. 1984: Starman. 1985: Animal Behavior. 1986: Terminus. 1987: The Glass Menagerie. Backfire. Lion of Africa (TV). 1988: Scrooged. 1989: Secret Places of the Heart. Exile. 1990: Challenger (TV). Secret Weapon (TV). 1991: Rapture. Sweet Talker. 1992: Home Fires Burning. Malcolm*

X. 1993: King of the Hill. Voyage. Ghost in the Machine. The Sandlot (GB: The Sandlot Kids). 1994: The Turning. 1996: Hostile Advances: The Kerry Ellison Story (TV). A Reasonable Woman (TV). 'Til There Was You. Ripper. 1997: Crocodile Tears. Wind River. All the Winters That Have Been (TV). 1998: Falling Sky. 1999: The Basket. 2000: The Perfect Storm.

ALLEN, Nancy 1950–

Plump-cheeked, sassy-looking, light-haired American actress who played independent types in her early screen years. Her appearances in films by her then-husband, director Brian de Palma (married 1979, divorced 1984) have been in sexy and outspoken roles, but she remained abrasively personable in anything the 1980s had to offer and also revealed a talent for comedy. Her roles in the past 15 years have been less rewarding and some of the spark seems to have gone out of her after a long stint in the *RoboCop* films.

1973: The Last Detail. 1975: Forced Entry (released 1984 as The Last Victim). 1976: Carrie. 1978: I Wanna Hold Your Hand. 1979: '1941'. 1980: Home Movies. Dressed to Kill. 1981: Blow-Out. 1983: The Buddy System. Strange Invaders. 1984: The Philadelphia Experiment. Terror in the Aisles. Not For Publication. 1986: The Gladiator (TV). Sweet Revenge. 1987: Boogie Woogie. RoboCop. 1988: Poltergeist III. Out of the Dark. 1989: Limit Up. 1990: RoboCop 2. Memories of Murder (TV). 1992: RoboCop 3 (released 1994). 1993: Acting on Impulse (TV. GB: Secret Lies). 1994: Les patriotes. 1995: The Man Who Wouldn't Die (TV). 1997: Quality Time (released 2000). Dusting Cliff Seven. 1998: The Pass. Out of Sight. Secret of the Andes. 1999: Boyd's Out. Kiss Toledo Goodbye. Children of the Corn 666: Isaac's Return (video). 2000: Quality Time.

ALLEN, Tim (T.A. Dick) 1953–

Burly, wavy-haired, rosy-cheeked American comedian of genial appearance, who forsook a career as a scabrous nightclub comedian for television. He turned his image on its head as the do-it-yourself star of the phenomenally successful TV series *Home Improvement*, in which he has appeared since 1991, making himself a multi-millionaire in the process. His film career has been less wildly successful and continues to be a thing of hits and misses since a supersonic start with the surprise

smash-hit *The Santa Clause*. His early credits are sometimes confused with those of an Australian actor with the same name.

1986: Tropical Snow (released 1989). 1988: Comedy's Dirtiest Dozen. What Do You Say to a Naked Lady? 1994: The Santa Clause. 1995: Toy Story (voice only). 1996: Meet Wally Sparks. Jungle 2 Jungle. 1997: For Richer or Poorer. 1999: Toy Story 2 (voice only). Galaxy Quest. 2001: Cletis Tout. Big Trouble.

ALLEN, Woody (Allen Konigsberg) 1935–

Bespectacled, diminutive American writer-director-comedian with a small amount of scruffy hair. He brought the paradoxical combination of shyness, ineptness and obsession with sex to the screen and made it an international hit. Writes and directs most of his own material, which has lately shown a tendency to 'go serious' although mercifully shafts of the lunatic Allen humour keep breaking through. His scant regard for the Establishment was demonstrated when he failed to show up to accept his Oscar for Best Director (on *Annie Hall*) in 1978. The same film also brought him an acting nomination. His bitter court battle with long-time partner Mia Farrow (*qv*) over his relationship with her adopted daughter seemed to have damaged his career; but he bounced back in 1995 with an Oscar nomination for his direction of *Bullets Over Broadway*. Screenplay Oscar nominee for *Deconstructing Harry*.

1965: What's New Pussycat? 1966: What's Up Tiger Lily? 1967: Casino Royale. 1969: †Take the Money and Run. 1971: †Bananas. 1972: †Everything You Always Wanted to Know About Sex . . . But Were Afraid to Ask. Play It Again, Sam. 1974: †Sleeper. 1975: †Love and

Death. 1976: The Front. 1977: †Annie Hall. 1979: †Manhattan. 1980: Stardust Memories. To Woody Allen, from Europe with Love. 1982: †A Midsummer Night's Sex Comedy. 1983: †Zelig. 1984: †Broadway Danny Rose. 1986: †Hannah and Her Sisters. 50 Years of Action! 1987: †Radio Days (narrator only). King Lear. 1989: ‡New York Stories. †Crimes and Misdemeanours. 1991: Scenes from a Mall. †Shadows and Fog. 1992: †Husbands and Wives. 1993: †Manhattan Murder Mystery. 1994: Don't Drink the Water (TV). 1995: The Sunshine Boys (TV). †Mighty Aphrodite. 1996: †Everyone Says I Love You. 1997: Wild Man Blues (doc). †Deconstructing Harry. 1998: Antz (voice only). The Impostors. 1999: Company Man. †Sweet and Lowdown. 2000: Liuret haller mig sallskap (doc).

†And directed ‡And co-directed

Also as director: 1978: Interiors. 1985: The Purple Rose of Cairo. 1987: September. 1988: Another Woman. 1990: Alice. 1994: Bullets Over Broadway. 1998: Celebrity. 2000: Small Time Crooks.

ALLEY, Kirstie 1951–
Tall, elegant, dark-haired American actress of flat-faced prettiness and sea-green eyes. At 30, she decided to quit a high-flying lifestyle (and a cocaine habit) as an interior decorator and become an actress. She got leading roles quite quickly but not many good reviews until someone had the good idea of casting her in comedy as the salty, screwball, extrovert Rebecca (not too far removed from her real-life personality) in the TV series *Cheers*. It suddenly became evident that she was much more effective as a feisty funny-girl and a thumping hit with *Look Who's Talking* brought her big-screen stardom that she did not quite sustain. Married/divorced actor Parker Stevenson.
1981: One More Chance. 1982: Highway Honeys (TV). Star Trek The Wrath of Khan (later Star Trek II The Wrath of Khan). 1983: Masquerade (TV). Champions. 1984: Blind Date. Runaway. Sins of the Past (TV). 1985: The Prince of Bel-Air (TV). A Bunny's Tale (TV). 1986: Stark: Mirror Image (TV). 1987: Infidelity (TV). Summer School. 1988: Shoot to Kill (GB: Deadly Pursuit). 1989: Look Who's Talking. Lover Boy. 1990: Madhouse. Sibling Rivalry. Look Who's Talking Too. 1993: Look Who's Talking Now. 1994: David's Mother (TV). 1995: Peter and the Wolf (voice only). Village of the Damned. It

Takes Two. 1996: Radiant City (TV). Suddenly (TV). When Somebody Loves You (TV). Sticks and Stones. 1997: Nevada. For Richer or Poorer. The Last Don (TV). Deconstructing Harry. Toothless (TV). 1999: Drop Dead Gorgeous. The Mao Game.

ALLYSON, June
(Eleanor 'Ella' Geisman) 1917–
Petite, husky-voiced blonde American actress, singer and dancer with beguilingly dimpled smile – everyone's idea of the girl next door in the forties, everyone's idea of the dutiful wife in the fifties. A sometimes stormy marriage to Dick Powell survived 18 years until his death in 1963. Overcame severe injuries sustained in a childhood fall to become a peroxide blonde Broadway song-and-dance girl before entering 12 popular years at M-G-M with a repeat of her stage success in *Best Foot Forward*.
1937: *All Girl Revue. *Swing for Sale. *Pixilated. *Dime a Dance. *Ups and Downs. 1938: *The Knight is Young. *Dates and Nuts. *The Prisoner of Swing. *Sing for Sweetie. 1939: *Rollin' in Rhythm. 1943: Best Foot Forward. Girl Crazy. Thousands Cheer. 1944: Two Girls and a Sailor. Meet the People. 1945: Her Highness and the Bellboy. The Sailor Takes a Wife. Music for Millions. 1946: Two Sisters from Boston. Till the Clouds Roll By. The Secret Heart. 1947: High Barbaree. Good News. 1948: The Bride Goes Wild. The Three Musketeers. Words and Music. 1949: Little Women. The Stratton Story. The Reformer and the Redhead. 1950: Right Cross. 1951: Too Young to Kiss. 1952: The Girl in White (GB: So Bright the Flame). 1953: Battle Circus. Remains to be Seen. The Glenn Miller Story. 1954: Executive Suite. Woman's World. 1955: Strategic Air Command. The McConnell Story (GB: Tiger in the Sky). The Shrike. 1956: The Opposite Sex. You Can't Run Away from It. 1957: Interlude. My Man Godfrey. 1959: Stranger in My Arms. 1971: See the Man Run (TV). 1972: They Only Kill Their Masters. 1973: Letters from Three Lovers (TV). 1977: Curse of the Black Widow (TV). 1978: Vega$ (TV). Blackout. 1979: Three on a Date (TV). 1982: The Kid with the Broken Halo (TV). 1994: That's Entertainment! III. 2000: Solid Ones.

ALONSO, Maria Conchita 1957–
Comely, fiery, not-too-tall Cuban-born, Venezuelan-raised actress and singer with masses of dark hair and childlike features.

After winning a 'Miss Teenager of the World' contest at 14, she was elected Miss Venezuela four years later and was already a popular singer in her late teens. After four Venezuelan films (not listed below), she went to Hollywood where she enjoyed considerable success as a film star in the mid and late 1980s. In 1985, she won a Grammy as best Latin recording artist. After a pause in film work, she was seen in the 1990s in more subordinate roles.
1984: Moscow on the Hudson. 1985: Fear City. 1986: Touch and Go. A Fine Mess. Blood Ties (TV). 1987: The Running Man. Extreme Prejudice. 1988: Colors. Vampire's Kiss. 1991: Predator 2. McBain. 1992: Teamster Boss: The Jackie Presser Story (TV). 1993: Roosters. The House of the Spirits. MacShayne: The Final Roll of the Dice (TV). 1994: Alejandra (TV). 1995: James A Michener's Texas (TV). 1996: Caught. Yanqui Dollar. Sudden Terror: The Hijacking of Schoolbus No. 17 (TV). Cross Over/Catherine's Grave. 1997: True Blue. 1998: El grito en el cielo. Knockout (released 2000). Exposé. Blackheart. My Husband's Secret Life (TV). For Which He Stands (TV). 2000: Calle ocho. Blind Heat. Best Actress (TV).

AMECHE, Don
(Dominic Amici) 1908–1993
Benign, elegant, likeable American leading man with pencil moustache and a werewolf's quota of dark hair. Often seen as a man-about-town in musicals, he hung on to Hollywood stardom over a surprisingly long period, considering that he was so seldom seen in the comedy roles which enabled him to use the offhand sarcasm which he tempered with charm. Much later, he

returned for the occasional leading character role which he evidently enjoyed. Following his success in *Trading Places* and his Oscar for *Cocoon* (best supporting actor), he became busy in his seventies and eighties before his death from prostate cancer.

1933: *Beauty at the World's Fair. 1935: Clive of India. Dante's Inferno. 1936: Sins of Man. Ramona. Ladies in Love. One in a Million. 1937: Love is News. Fifty Roads to Town. You Can't Have Everything. Love under Fire. 1938: In Old Chicago. Happy Landing. Josette. Alexander's Ragtime Band. Gateway. 1939: The Three Musketeers (GB: The Singing Musketeer). Midnight. The Story of Alexander Graham Bell (GB: The Modern Miracle). Hollywood Cavalcade. Swanee River. 1940: Lillian Russell. Four Sons. Down Argentine Way. 1941: That Night in Rio. Moon over Miami. Kiss the Boys Goodbye. The Feminine Touch. 1942: Confirm or Deny. The Magnificent Dope. Girl Trouble. 1943: Heaven Can Wait. Happy Land. Something to Shout About. 1944: Wing and a Prayer. Greenwich Village. It's in the Bag! (GB: The Fifth Chair). 1945: Guest Wife. 1946: So Goes My Love (GB: A Genius in the Family). 1947: That's My Man (GB: Will Tomorrow Ever Come?). Sleep My Love. 1949: Slightly French. 1952: *Hollywood Night at 21 Club. 1954: Phantom Caravan. Fire One. 1961: A Fever in the Blood. 1966: Rings around the World. Picture Mommy Dead. 1968: Shadow over Elveron (TV). 1970: Suppose They Gave a War and Nobody Came. The Boatniks. 1971: Gidget Gets Married (TV). 1975: Won Ton Ton, The Dog Who Saved Hollywood. 1983: Trading Places. 1985: Cocoon. 1986: A Masterpiece of Murder (TV). Single Room (unfinished). Harry and the Hendersons (GB: Bigfoot and the Hendersons). Pals (TV). 1988: Coming to America. Cocoon: The Return. Things Change. 1990: Odd Ball Hall. 1991: Oscar. 1992: Folks! Sunstroke. 1993: Homeward Bound: The Incredible Journey (voice only). 1994: Corrina, Corrina.*

AMES, Adrienne
See CABOT, Bruce

AMICK, Mädchen 1970–
Spectacularly beautiful, dark-haired American actress, in films as a teenager after leaving her Nevada home at 16 and appearing in commercials and music videos. After several decorative roles, the character of waitress Shelly Johnson in the cult TV series

Twin Peaks jetted her into the public eye. But her subsequent roles have mainly been too bland to consolidate her stardom; she may yet show up best as cool, calculating charmers.

1989: Jury Duty: the Comedy (TV. GB: The Great American Sex Scandal). Baywatch: Panic at Malibu Pier (TV). The Borrower (released 1991). 1990: I'm Dangerous Tonight (TV). Twin Peaks (TV). For the Very First Time. 1991: Till I Kissed Ya (TV). 1992: Sleepwalkers/Stephen King's Sleepwalkers. Don't Tell Her It's Me. Twin Peaks: Fire Walk With Me. 1993: Love, Cheat and Steal. Dream Lover. 1994: Trapped in Paradise. 1995: The Courtyard (cable TV). 1996: French Exit. Wounded. Perfect Crimes. Bombshell. 1997: Heartless (TV). 1998: Twist of Fate. The Black Cat Run (TV). Hunted (TV). 1999: Mr Rock 'n' Roll: The Alan Freed Story (TV). 2000: Hangman. The List.

ANDERS, Merry
(Mary Anderson) 1932–
Blonde American actress, trained (and wasted) by 20th Century-Fox, with pleasant, slow-burning appeal reminiscent of Lola Albright (*qv*). Career-wise, she proved extremely tenacious despite an unassertive talent, continuing to star in 'B' features (some of them quite interesting) right up until the genre vanished.

1952: Belles on Their Toes. Wait 'til the Sun Shines, Nellie. Les Miserables. 1953: Titanic. The Farmer Takes a Wife. How to Marry a Millionaire. 1954: Princess of the Nile. Phffft! Three Coins in the Fountain. 1955: All That Heaven Allows. 1956: The Night Runner. Desk Set (GB: His Other Woman). 1957: The Dalton Girls. No Time to be Young (GB: Teenage Delinquents). Calypso Heatwave. Hear Me Good. Escape from San Quentin. 1958: Death in Small Doses. No Time to be Young. Violent Road. 1959: Five Bold Women. 1960: The Police Dog Story. The Walking Target. The Hypnotic Eye. Young Jesse James. Spring Affair. 1961: 20,000 Eyes. The Gambler Wore a Gun. When the Clock Strikes. The Secret of Deep Harbor. 1962: Air Patrol. Beauty and the Beast. The Case of Patty Smith (GB: The Shame of Patty Smith). FBI Code 98. 1963: House of the Damned. Police Nurse. A Tiger Walks. 1964: The Quick Gun. Raiders from Beneath the Sea. The Time Travelers. Young Fury. 1965: Tickle Me. Women of the Prehistoric Planet. 1967: Flight of the Cougar. 1969: Airport. 1971: Legacy of Blood.

ANDERSON, Gillian 1968–
Diminutive, ginger-haired (originally fair), rarely smiling American actress with questioning lips. Although acting from an early age, she was little known until winning a leading role in the cult TV series *The X-Files*, despite the fact that the producers were looking for an entirely different type. Moving into films, she displayed a cool and capable style that promises a long career in the medium. She may do more comedy in the future (anyone whose favourite film is *The Wrong Trousers* must have a sense of humour).

1992: The Turning. 1997: Chicago Cab/ Hellcab. 1998: The X-Files. The Mighty. Playing by Heart. Princess Mononoke (Voice only: English-language version). 2000: The House of Mirth.

ANDERSON, Rona 1926–
Scottish-born actress, on stage at 16. Came to films at 22 and was often seen as shy or helpless females. Her film career petered out with the demise of the British second-feature, a field in which she had been a regular participant, but she remained active on stage. Married to actor Gordon Jackson (*qv*) from 1951 to his death.

1948: Sleeping Car to Trieste. 1949: Floodtide. Poets' Pub. Torment (US: Paper Gallows). The Twenty Questions Murder Mystery. 1950: Her Favourite Husband (US: The Taming of Dorothy). 1951: Home to Danger. Whispering Smith Hits London (US: Whispering Smith versus Scotland Yard). Scrooge. 1952: Circumstantial Evidence. 1953: Noose for a Lady. Black 13. 1954: Double Exposure. The Black Rider. Shadow of a Man. Little Red Monkey (US: The Case of the Little Red Monkey).

1955: *The Flaw. A Time to Kill. Stock Car.* 1956: *Soho Incident (US: Spin a Dark Web). The Hide-Out.* 1958: *The Solitary Child. Man with a Gun.* 1963: *The Bay of St Michel (US: Pattern for Plunder).* 1964: *Devils of Darkness.* 1967: *River Rivals (serial).* 1968: *Interlude. The Prime of Miss Jean Brodie.*

ANDERSSON, Bibi
(Berit Andersson) 1935–
Blonde Swedish actress with sensitive features, whose best work was all for Ingmar Bergman. Her forays towards international stardom did not pan out well, and she has remained largely in Scandinavian films.
1953: *Dum-Bom.* 1954: *En Natt pu Glim-minghaus. Herr Arnes Penngar (GB and US: Sir Arne's Treasure).* 1955: *Sommarnattens Leende (GB and US: Smiles of a Summer Night). Flickan i Regnet.* 1956: *Sista Paret Ut. Egen Ingang.* 1957: *Det Sjunde Inseglet (GB and US: The Seventh Seal). Sommarnoje Sokes. Smultronstället (GB and US: Wild Strawberries). Nära Livet (GB and US: So Close to Life. US: Brink of Life).* 1958: *Du är mitt äventyr Ansiktet (GB and US: The Face).* 1959: *Den Kära Leken.* 1960: *Bröllopsdagen.* 1961: *Djävulens Oga (GB and US: The Devil's Eye). Karneval. Nasilje na Trgu (US: Square of Violence). Lustgarden.* 1962: *Alskarinnen (GB: The Mistress). Kort är Sommaren.* 1964: *Now about These Women . . . (US: Not to Mention These Women/All These Women). On.* 1965: *Duel at Diablo. Juninatt.* 1966: *Syskonbädd 1782 (GB: My Sister My Love). Persona. Scusi, lei a favorevole a contrario?* 1967: *Le viol (GB: A Question of Rape).* 1968: *Svarta Palmkronor (US: Black Palm Trees). Flickorna (GB and US: The Girls).* 1969: *Taenk pa et Tal. Storia di una Donna (GB: The Story of a Woman). Una estate in quattro. En Passion (GB: A Passion. US: The Passion of Anna). The Kremlin Letter.* 1971: *The Touch.* 1972: *Mannen fran Andra Siden.* 1973: *Scenes from a Marriage.* 1974: *La rivale. The Hour of Parting.* 1975: *It is Raining on Santiago. Blondy (US: Vortex).* 1976: *Mon mari, sa maîtresse et moi. The Hounds of Spring.* 1977: *I Never Promised You a Rose Garden.* 1978: *An Enemy of the People. Justices. Quintet.* 1979: *L'amour en question. The Concorde – Airport '79 (GB: Airport '80 . . . the Concorde). Twee Vrouwen.* 1980: *Barnforbjudet/The Elephant Walk. Prosperous Times. The Marmalade Revolution.* 1981: *Jag Rödnar.* 1982: *Black Crows/Svarte Fugler.* 1983: *Exposed. Berget på Månens Baksida*

(*US: The Hill on the Other Side of the Moon*). 1984: *The Final Game.* 1986: *Huomenna.* 1987: *Babette's Feast. Svart gryning. Los dueños del silencio.* 1988: *Rowing with the Wind. Creditors.* 1989: *Manika, Manika. Fordringsägare.* 1992: *A Passing Season/Una estacion de paso/Whistle Stop.* 1994: *Dromspel/Dream Play. The Dream of the Butterfly/The Butterfly's Dream.* 1996: *I rollerna tre.* 1998: *Little Big Sister (narrator only).* 2000: *Det blir aldrig som man tänkt sig. Liuset haller mig sallskap (doc).*

ANDERSSON, Harriet 1932–
Dark-haired Swedish actress, principally in gloomy, sensual roles in Ingmar Bergman films, the nude scenes in one of which, *Summer with Monica,* quickly brought her into the international limelight. She was whisked from the chorus line into the cinema at 18 and, with her thick lips, soulful eyes and intense style, enjoyed 20 years of great popularity, especially in Scandinavia; international ventures were few and less successful. Married the Finnish-born director Jorn Donner (1933–).
1950: *Medan staden sover (US: While the City Sleeps). Två trappor över garden. Anderssons-kans Kalle. Motorkavaljerer.* 1951: *Biffen och bananen. Puck hete jag. Fränskild. Dårskapens hus (US: House of Folly).* 1952: *Sabotage. U-boat 39. Trots (GB and US: Defiance). Sommaren med Monika (GB: Summer with Monica. US: Monika).* 1953: *Gycklarnas afton (GB and US: Sawdust and Tinsel).* 1954: *En lekyion i kärlek (GB and US: A Lesson in Love).* 1955: *Hoppsan! Kvinnodröm (GB: Journey into Autumn. US: Dreams). Sommarnattens leende (GB and US: Smiles of a Summer Night).* 1956: *Sista paret ut. Nattbarn (GB and US: Children of the Night).* 1957: *Synnöve solbakken.* 1958: *Kvinna I leopard. Flottans överman.* 1959: *Brott I Paradiset (GB: Crime in Paradise). Noc pòslubna.* 1967: *Barbara. Såsom I en spegel (GB and US: Through a Glass Darkly).* 1962: *Siska.* 1963: *Lyckodrommen (GB: Dreams of Happiness). En Söndag I September (GB: One Sunday in September. US: A Sunday in September).* 1964: *För att inte tala om alla dessa kvinnor (GB: Now About These Women. US: Not to Mention These Women/All These Women). Att älska (GB and US: To Love). Loving Couples.* 1965: *För vanskaps skull. Lianbron. Här börjar äventyret.* 1966: *The Deadly Affair. Ormen (GB and US: The Serpent). Tvärbalk.* 1967: *Stimulantia. People Meet and Sweet Music*

Fills the Heart (GB: People Meet). 1968: *Jag älskar, du älskar (GB: I Love, You Love). Flickorna (GB and US: The Girls). The Struggle for Rome.* 1969: *The Struggle for Rome II.* 1970: *Anna.* 1971: *I harsbandet.* 1972: *Cries and Whispers.* 1975: *Den vita väggen (GB: The White Wall). Monismania* 1995. 1977: *Hempas bar (US: Cry of Triumph '57).* 1979: *The Sabina. Linus eller tegelhusets hemlighet.* 1982: *Fanny and Alexander.* 1983: *Raskenstam.* 1986: *De tva saliga (TV).* 1987: *Sommarkväller på jorden (US: Summer Nights).* 1988: *Himmel og Helvede.* 1989: *Kaisa kavat.* 1990: *Blankt Vapen.* 1993: *Beyond the Sky.* 1995: *Love & Hate: European Stories.* 1996: *I rollerna tre.* 1997: *Never Again . . . Selma & Johanna – en roadmovie.* 1998: *Det sjunde skottet.* 1999: *Happy End.* 2000: *Liuset haller mig sallskap (doc).*

ANDES, Keith 1920–
Tall, fair-haired, mild-mannered American actor who came to films (from the stage) too late to make much of an impact. A Universal-International contract from 1955 to 1958 brought him a second-grade stardom, but he lacked the distinctive personality that might have taken him further. Co-starred with Glynis Johns in the TV series *Glynis* but later played bit parts.
1944: *Winged Victory.* 1947: *The Farmer's Daughter.* 1949: *Project X.* 1951: *Clash by Night.* 1952: *Blackbeard the Pirate. Split Second.* 1955: *The Second Greatest Sex. A Life at Stake/Key Man.* 1956: *Away All Boats. Back from Eternity. Pillars of the Sky, (GB: The Tomahawk and the Cross).* 1957: *Interlude. Homeward Borne (TV).* 1958: *The Girl Most Likely. Damn Citizen!* 1959: *Model for Murder. Surrender Hell!* 1964: *The Tattooed Police Horse.* 1968: *Hell's Bloody Devils (released 1970).* 1969: *Smashing the Crime Syndicate.* 1970: *Tora! Tora! Tora!* 1974: *Ordeal (TV).* 1979: *The Ultimate Imposter (TV). . . . And Justice for All.* 1980: *Blinded by the Light (TV).*

ANDRESS, Ursula 1936–
Tigerish Swiss-born blonde star who, after a late introduction to international stardom in *Dr No,* enjoyed 10 years as a top film glamour girl, before her career seemed to submerge beneath her private love life. But she stepped up her work schedule again in the late 1970s, apparently ageless and as sexy as ever. Married to John Derek (*qv*) from 1957 to

1966. Later there was a lengthy liaison with the French star Jean-Paul Belmondo (*qv*) and another with Hollywood star Harry Hamlin (*qv*) that produced a son in 1980.
1954: *Le avventure di Giacomo Casanova (GB: The Loves of Casanova. US: Sins of Casanova). Un Americano a Roma/An American in Rome.* 1955: *La tempesta e passata/The Tempest Has Gone. La catena dell'odio.* 1937: *Anyone Can Play.* 1962: *Dr No.* 1963: *Four for Texas. Nightmare in the Sun. Fun in Acapulco.* 1964: *Toys for Christmas.* 1965: *She. What's New, Pussycat? La decima vittima/The 10th Victim. Les tribulations d'un Chinois en Chine (GB: Up to His Ears. US: Chinese Adventures in China).* 1966: *Once Before I Die. The Blue Max.* 1967: *Casino Royale. Le dolci signore.* 1968: *The Southern Star.* 1970: *Perfect Friday.* 1971: *Red Sun.* 1972: *Five Against Capricorn.* 1973: *The Last Chance (US: Stateline Motel).* 1974: *Colpo in canna (GB: Stick 'Em up, Darlings!).* 1975: *Loaded Guns. Due cuori, una cappella. L'infermiera (GB: I Will If You Will. US: The Sensuous Nurse).* 1976: *Africa Express. Scaramouche/The Loves and Times of Scaramouche. Safari Express.* 1977: *The Fifth Musketeer. Double Murders. Love in Four Easy Lessons.* 1978: *The Mountain in the Jungle (GB: Prisoner of the Cannibal God. US: Primitive Desires).* 1979: *Four Tigers in Lipstick/Letti selvaggi (released 1985). Una strana coppio di gangsters.* 1980: *Nobody's Perfect. Grip.* 1981: *Clash of the Titans. Reporters.* 1982: *Mexico in Flames/Red Bells.* 1985: *Liberté, égalité, choucroute.* 1988: *Big Man.* 1989: *Klassezämekunft. Man Against the Mob: The Chinatown Murders (TV).* 1990: *Another Falling Star (TV).* 1993: *Cave of the Golden Rose III.* 1994: *Cave of the Golden Rose IV.* 1996: *Alles gelogen.* 1997: *Cremaster 5.*

ANDREWS, Anthony 1946–
Fair-haired, blue-eyed, boyish-looking British actor of guileless appearance. His career progressed only slowly until he made an enormous hit in two television series, *Danger UXB* and *Brideshead Revisited.* Subsequently proved the most beautifully cast Sir Percy Blakeney in *The Scarlet Pimpernel* since Leslie Howard 50 years earlier, but found it less easy to make an individual impact in a wider variety of roles. Would also make a good Raffles.
1972: *A War of Children (TV).* 1973: *Take Me High (US: Hot Property).* 1974: *Percy's*

Progress (US: It's Not the Size That Counts). QB VII (TV). 1975: *Operation Daybreak. Les adolescentes.* 1976: *Call Girl.* 1981: *Mistress of Paradise (TV).* 1982: *Ivanhoe (TV).* 1983: *The Scarlet Pimpernel (TV). Sparkling Cyanide/Agatha Christie's Sparkling Cyanide (TV).* 1984: *Under the Volcano. Notes from Under the Volcano. Observations Under the Volcano.* 1985: *The Holcroft Covenant.* 1986: *The Second Victory.* 1987: *The Lighthorsemen. Suspicion (TV).* 1988: *Hanna's War. The Woman He Loved (TV). Bluegrass (TV).* 1989: *Columbo Goes to the Guillotine (TV). The Strange Case of Dr Jekyll and Mr Hyde (TV).* 1990: *Hands of a Murderer (TV).* 1991: *Lost in Siberia.* 1992: *The Law Lords (TV). Jewels (TV).* 1995: *Haunted.*

ANDREWS, Dana
(Carver D. Andrews) 1909–1992
Crackly-voiced, rarely-smiling American actor with dark, crinkly hair, especially prominent in realist thrillers of the post-war years, where he was equally at home projecting quiet sincerity or grim integrity. The son of a minister, he worked for oil companies for some years before getting an acting break. The brother of actor Steve Forrest (*qv*), Andrews overcame alcohol dependency problems to return in later years as a character player. A sufferer from Alzheimer's disease in his last years, he died from pneumonia.
1939: *Lucky Cisco Kid.* 1940: *The Westerner. Sailor's Lady. Kit Carson.* 1941: *Tobacco Road. Belle Starr. Swamp Water (GB: The Man Who Came Back). Ball of Fire.* 1942: *Berlin Correspondent. The Ox-Bow Incident (GB: Strange Incident).* 1943: *December Seventh. Crash Dive. North Star.* 1944: *The*

Purple Heart. Wing and a Prayer. Up in Arms. Laura. 1945: *State Fair. Fallen Angel. A Walk in the Sun. Know Your Enemy: Japan (narrator).* 1946: *Canyon Passage. The Best Years of Our Lives.* 1947: *Boomerang. Night Song. Daisy Kenyon.* 1948: *The Iron Curtain. Deep Waters. No Minor Vices.* 1949: *Britannia Mews (US: Forbidden Street). Sword in the Desert.* 1950: *My Foolish Heart. Where the Sidewalk Ends. Edge of Doom (GB: Stronger Than Fear).* 1951: *The Frogmen. Sealed Cargo. I Want You.* 1952: *Assignment Paris!* 1953: *Elephant Walk.* 1954: *Duel in the Jungle. Three Hours to Kill.* 1955: *Smoke Signal. Strange Lady in Town. While the City Sleeps.* 1956: *Comanche. *Hollywood Goes a-Fishing. Beyond a Reasonable Doubt.* 1957: *Night of the Demon (US: Curse of the Demon). Spring Reunion. Zero Hour.* 1958: *The Fearmakers. Enchanted Island. The Right Hand Man (TV).* 1960: *The Crowded Sky. Alas, Babylon (TV).* 1961: *Madison Avenue.* 1964: *The Satan Bug.* 1965: *Crack in the World. Brainstorm. The Woman Who Wouldn't Die. In Harm's Way. Town Tamer. The Loved One. Battle of the Bulge. Spy in Your Eye/Berlin, appuntamento per le spie.* 1966: *Johnny Reno. Supercolpo da 7 miliardi (GB: The 1,000 Carat Diamond. US: Ten Million Dollar Grab).* 1967: *Hot Rods to Hell. The Frozen Dead. The Cobra. I diamenti che nassuno voleva rubare (US: No Diamonds for Ursula).* 1968: *The Devil's Brigade.* 1971: *The Failing of Raymond (TV).* 1972: *Innocent Bystanders.* 1974: *Airport 1975.* 1975: *The First 36 Hours of Dr Durant (TV). Take a Hard Ride. Shadow in the Streets.* 1976: *The Last Tycoon.* 1977: *Good Guys Wear Black.* 1978: *Born Again. The Last Hurrah (TV).* 1979: *The Pilot.* 1984: *Prince Jack.*

ANDREWS, Dame Julie
(Julia Wells) 1934–
British singer and actress with fresh, healthy looks, on radio as a child. Following stage hits with *The Boy Friend* and *My Fair Lady*, she briefly gained enormous popularity in the cinema of the 1960s; but her antiseptic air soon proved less than popular at the box-office despite strenuous and praiseworthy (if sometimes a trifle desperate) efforts to widen her range. Married to director Blake Edwards (second of two) since 1968, she was frequently seen in his films. Also writes children's stories. An Oscar-winner for *Mary Poppins*, she has also been nominated for *The Sound of Music* and *Victor/Victoria.* Unable

to sing professionally after an operation to remove throat nodes in 1998. Created dame in 2000.

*1952: Rose of Baghdad (voice only). 1956: High Tor (TV). 1958: The Reluctant Debutante (as extra). 1964: Mary Poppins. *Hollywood Goes to a Premiere. The Americanization of Emily. 1965: The Sound of Music. 1966: Torn Curtain. Hawaii. 1967: The Singing Princess (voice only). Thoroughly Modern Millie. 1968: Star! 1969: Darling Lili. 1974: The Tamarind Seed. 1979: '10'. Little Miss Marker. 1981: SOB. 1982: Victor/ Victoria. 1983: The Man Who Loved Women. 1986: Duet for One. 'That's Life!' 1990: Tchin Tchin. 1991: Our Sons (TV). 1992: A Fine Romance. 1999: One Special Night (TV). 2000: Relative Values. 2001: Unconditional Love.*

ANGEL, Heather 1909–1986

After rave reviews in British films, this diffident English actress with clipped tones (her father was an Oxford don) went to Hollywood in 1932, where her best-remembered role proved to be in John Ford's *The Informer*. Later films were less remarkable (although she had a good run as the heroine of Paramount's Bulldog Drummond films), with leads in 'B' films mingling with supporting roles in bigger movies. Married to actor Ralph Forbes (1902–1951) – first of her three husbands – from 1934 to 1942. Died from cancer.

1930: City of Song (US: Farewell to Love). 1931: A Night in Montmartre. Sooky. 1932: The Hound of the Baskervilles. Self-Made Lady. Mr Bill the Conqueror (US: The Man Who Won). Pilgrimage. Men of Steel. After Office Hours. Early to Bed. 1933: Berkeley Square. Frail Women. Charlie Chan's Greatest Case. Orient Express. 1934: Murder in Trinidad. Springtime for Henry. Romance in the Rain. 1935: The Three Musketeers. The Headline Woman (GB: A Woman in the Case). The Informer. The Perfect Gentleman (GB: The Imperfect Lady). The Mystery of Edwin Drood. It Happened in New York. 1936: The Last of the Mohicans. Daniel Boone. 1937: Bulldog Drummond Escapes. Portia on Trial (GB: The Trial of Portia Merriman). The Duke Comes Back (GB: The Call of the Ring). The Bold Caballero (GB: The Bold Cavalier). Western Gold (GB: The Mysterious Stranger). 1938: Bulldog Drummond in Africa. Army Girl (GB: The Last of the Cavalry). Arrest Bulldog Drummond! 1939: Undercover Doctor. Bulldog

Drummond's Bride. Pride and Prejudice. Bulldog Drummond's Secret Police. 1940: Kitty Foyle. Shadows on the Stairs. Half a Sinner. 1941: That Hamilton Woman (GB: Lady Hamilton). Suspicion. Singapore Woman. 1942: Time to Kill. The Undying Monster (GB: The Hammond Mystery). 1943: Lifeboat. Cry Havoc. Three Sisters of the Moors. 1944: In the Meantime, Darling. 1948: The Saxon Charm. 1950: Alice in Wonderland (voice only). 1953: Peter Pan (voice only). 1962: The Premature Burial.

ANGELI, Pier
(Anna Maria Pierangeli) 1932–1971

Tragic, dark-haired, dark-eyed Italian actress in Hollywood films. Initially very popular in M-G-M films, but her fiery emotional entanglements betrayed her gentle screen image and eventually sucked the life out of her career. She ended in sexploitation pictures and committed suicide with barbiturates. Married to singer and sometime film star Vic Damone (Vito Farinola 1928–), first of two husbands, from 1954 to 1958. A passionate affair with James Dean (qv) before her marriages ended with his premature death. Twin sister of actress Marisa Pavan.

1950: †Domani è troppo tardi (GB: Tomorrow is Too Late). 1951: †Domani è un altro giorno (GB: Tomorrow is Another Day). Teresa. The Light Touch. 1952: The Devil Makes Three. 1953: Mam'zelle Nitouche (GB: Oh No, Mam'zelle). The Story of Three Loves. Sombrero. 1954: Flame and the Flesh. The Silver Chalice. 1955: Santarellina. 1956: Meet Me in Las Vegas (GB: Viva Las Vegas!) Somebody Up There Likes Me. Port Afrique. 1957: The Vintage. 1958: Merry Andrew. Bernadette (TV). 1959: The Moon and Sixpence (TV). 1960: The Angry Silence. SOS Pacific. Musketeers of the Sea. 1962: White Slave Ship. (The Last Days of) Sodom and Gomorrah. 1964: †Banco à Bangkok pour OSS 117 (GB: Shadow of Evil). 1965: Battle of the Bulge. †Spy in Your Eye/Berlin, appuntamento per le spie. †MMM 83 (GB: Mission Bloody Mary). 1966: †Per mille dollari al giorno. 1967: †Rose rosse per il Fuhrer (US: Code Name Red Roses). One Step to Hell (US: King of Africa). 1968: La scelta. 1969: †Vive America. †Addio, Alexandra (GB: Love Me, Love My Wife). 1970: †Les enemoniades. Every Bastard a King. 1971: †Nelle pieghe della carne. Octaman.

†As Anna Maria Pierangeli

ANISTON, Jennifer 1969–

Tawny-haired American actress of Greek extraction (the original family name was Anastassakis, changed when her parents came to America). Acting from 18 in off-Broadway productions and from 20 on TV, her career was pretty much summed up by one of her TV series, *Muddling Through*, until she landed a key role as Rachel in the cult TV series *Friends*. Soon a national figure with a much-imitated peek-a-boo hairstyle, she broke into films where her vehicles proved on the whole disappointing, despite her own perky performances. Married Brad Pitt (qv).

*1990: How I Spent My Summer Vacation (TV). 1993: Leprechaun. 1996: 'Til There Was You. She's the One. 1997: Picture Perfect. 1998: Dream for an Insomniac. *Waiting for Woody. The Object of My Affection. 1999: Office Space. The Iron Giant (voice only). 2000: Soapbox Opera.*

ANKERS, Evelyn 1918–1985

Fair-haired, Chilean-born actress and dancer of china doll beauty who, after a beginning in British films, proved one of Hollywood's most effective screamers through a slew of low-budget horror films in the forties. Married to Richard Denning (qv) from 1942 to her death from cancer.

1936: The Bells of St Mary's. Land Without Music (US: Forbidden Music). Rembrandt. 1937: Fire Over England. Knight Without Armour. Wings of the Morning. Over the Moon (released 1939). 1938: The Claydon Treasure Mystery. Murder in the Family. The Villiers Diamond. Second Thoughts. Coming of Age. 1940: Burma Convoy. 1941: Hold That Ghost. Hit the Road. Bachelor Daddy. The Wolf Man. 1942: The Ghost of Frankenstein. Eagle

Squadron. The Great Impersonation. Sherlock Holmes and the Voice of Terror. North to the Klondike. Pierre of the Plains. 1943: Captive Wild Woman. You're a Lucky Fellow, Mr Smith. Hers to Hold. All by Myself. His Butler's Sister. Son of Dracula. Keep 'Em Slugging. The Mad Ghoul. 1944: Ladies Courageous. Jungle Woman. Follow the Boys. The Invisible Man's Revenge. Pardon My Rhythm. The Pearl of Death. Bowery to Broadway. Weird Woman. 1945: The Fatal Witness. The Frozen Ghost. 1946: Black Beauty. The French Key. Queen of Burlesque. Flight to Nowhere. 1947: Last of the Redmen (GB: Last of the Redskins). The Lone Wolf in London. Spoilers of the North. 1949: Parole Inc. Tarzan's Magic Fountain. 1950: The Texan Meets Calamity Jane. 1956: The Empty Room (TV. GB: cinemas). 1957: Clipper Ship (TV). 1960: No Greater Love.

ANNABELLA
(Suzanne Charpentier) 1909–1996

Blonde French star of the twenties and thirties in girl-next-door roles, a favourite of director René Clair, and later in English-speaking films, first in Britain, then (from 1938) in Hollywood. Married (second) Tyrone Power (qv) in 1939, which fatally interrupted her career. When the marriage ended in divorce in 1948, she returned to France. Died from a heart attack.

*1926: Napoleon. 1927: Maldone. 1928: Soir de femme. Barcarole d'amour. 1929: Romance à l'inconnue. Deux fois vingt ans. Trois jeunes filles nues. 1930: La maison de la flèche. Sous les toits de Paris. 1931: Le million. Soir de rafle. Gardez la sourire. Autour d'une enquête. Son altesse d'amour. 1932: Un fils d'Amerique. Paris Mediterranée. Marie, legende Hongroise. Mademoiselle Josette, ma femme. Le quatorze juillet. 1933: La bataille. Sonnenstrahl. 1934: Caravane. Variétés. La Bandera. 1935: Nuits Moscovites. L'équipage/Flight into Darkness. Veille d'armes. 1936: Anne Marie. 1937: La citadella del silence. Hôtel du nord. Under the Red Robe. Dinner at the Ritz. Wings of the Morning. 1938: Suez. The Baroness and the Butler. 1939: Escape from Yesterday. Bridal Suite. 1941: *Stars at Play. 1943: Tonight We Raid Calais. *Screen Snapshots No. 8. Bombers' Moon. 1946: 13 Rue Madeleine. 1947: L'homme qui revient de loin. 1950: *Désordre. Quema el Suelo. 1952: Le plus bel amour de Don Juan.*

ANNIS, Francesca 1944–

Sharp-faced, dark-haired, incisive British actress of pin-up proportions whose tremendous success in television drama series of the 1970s (especially *Lillie*) must have made up for getting into the wrong kind of films to become an international star. In films (she's from an acting family) as a child, she was later the first nude Lady Macbeth in the 1971 film. A better actress than many British-born 'lookers' of recent times, she can count herself unlucky to have missed out on a major star career in the cinema. From the mid 1990s, she made a steady twosome with actor Ralph Fiennes (qv).

1959: The Cat Gang. 1960: His and Hers. The Young Jacobites (serial). No Kidding (US: Beware of Children). 1963: Cleopatra. West 11. Saturday Night Out. Crooks in Cloisters. The Eyes of Annie Jones. 1964: Murder Most Foul. Flipper's New Adventure (GB: Flipper and the Pirates). 1965: The Pleasure Girls. 1966: Run With the Wind. 1970: The Walking Stick. The Sky Pirates. 1971: Macbeth. 1972: Big Truck and Poor Clare. 1973: Penny Gold. 1974: Sign It Death (TV. US: cinemas). 1980: Short Cut to Haifa. Stronger Than the Sun. 1983: Krull. 1984: Dune. Coming Out of the Ice (completed 1982). 1986: The Golden River. Under the Cherry Moon. 1990: Romeo-Juliet (voice only). Onassis: The Richest Man in the World (TV). 1992: Weep No More My Lady (TV). Headhunter. 1994: Doomsday Gun (TV. GB: cinemas). 1999: The Debt Collector. Milk (TV). Onegin.

ANN-MARGRET
(Ann Margaret Olsson) 1941–

Red-haired, feline, Swedish-born singer and dancer who started her Hollywood career in quiet roles. But her extravagant figure soon typecast her as a singing sexpot. Fought back to stardom in the 1970s after a bad accident nearly ended her career and showed improved warmth in her performances, being nominated for an Oscar twice, in *Carnal Knowledge* and *Tommy*. Lately offering uninhibited performances as sexy older women.

*1961: Pocketful of Miracles. 1962: State Fair. *The Ann-Margret Story. 1963: Bye Bye Birdie. 1964: Viva Las Vegas (GB: Love in Las Vegas). Kitten with a Whip. 1965: Bus Riley's Back in Town. The Pleasure Seekers. Once a Thief. 1966: The Cincinnati Kid. Made in Paris. The Swinger. Stagecoach. Murderers' Row. 1967: Il tigre (GB and US: The Tiger and the Pussycat). 1968: Maggie. Sette uomini e un cervello. Rebus. Il profeta (GB and US: Mr Kinky). Il rubamento. 1970: CC and Company. RPM. 1971: Carnal Knowledge. 1972: Un homme est mort (GB and US: The Outside Man). 1973: The Train Robbers. 1975: Tommy. 1976: Joseph Andrews. Folies bourgeoises/The Twist. 1977: The Last Remake of Beau Geste. 1978: Magic. The Cheap Detective. 1979: The Villain (GB: Cactus Jack). Ken Murray Shooting Stars. Middle Age Crazy. 1980: Lookin' to Get Out. 1982: The Return of the Soldier. I Ought to Be in Pictures. 1983: Who Will Love My Children? (TV. GB: cinemas). 1984: A Streetcar Named Desire (TV). 1985: Twice in a Lifetime. 1986: 52 Pick-Up. 1987: A Tiger's Tale. 1988: A New Life. 1991: Newsies (GB: The News Boys). Our Sons (TV). 1993: Grumpy Old Men. 1994: Nobody's Children. Following Her Heart (TV). 1996: Grumpier Old Men. Blue Rodeo (TV). 1997: The Mythfits. 1998: Four Corners (TV). 1999: Any Given Sunday. Happy Face Murders (TV). 2000: The Last Producer.*

ANOUK
See AIMÉE, Anouk

ANSPACH, Susan 1939–

Silky American blonde actress with a penchant for offbeat roles. An under-used talent (also an interesting singer), she has played opposite most of the major male stars of the period in her strangely unfulfilled career. Her first major New York theatre company included Jon Voight, Dustin Hoffman and Robert Duvall; she worked at the Actors' Studio with Al Pacino and Rip Torn and co-starred in films with Jack Nicholson (with whom she has a son), Woody

Allen, Elliott Gould, Richard Dreyfuss, Gene Hackman, Donald Sutherland and Keith Carradine. All this and comparatively little known? Someone missed out somewhere, for her performance in Makaveyev's *Montenegro* was quite remarkable.

1970: The Landlord. Five Easy Pieces. 1972: Play It Again Sam. 1973: Blume in Love. 1975: Nashville. 1976: I Want to Keep My Baby (TV). The Secret Life of John Chapman (TV). 1977: Rosetti and Ryan: Men Who Love Women (TV). Mad Bull (TV). 1978: Blue Collar. Journal (TV). The Big Fix. 1979: The Last Giraffe / Raising Daisy Rothschild (TV). He Wants Her Back. Running. 1980: The Devil and Max Devlin. Gas. Montenegro, or Pigs and Pearls. 1982: Deadly Encounter (TV). 1983: Misunderstood. 1984: Gone Are the Days (cable TV). 1987: Blood Red. Blue Monkey. 1988: Into the Fire / The Legend of Wolf Lodge. 1989: Back to Back. 1990: Killer Instinct. The Rutanga Tapes. 1994: Cagney & Lacey: The Return. 1997: Alien X Factor.

ANTHONY, Lysette (L. Chodzko) 1963–
Lithe, sweet-faced, fair-haired British actress who, despite a number of leading roles and a sharp talent for comedy, hasn't quite made it as a movie star. Acting since childhood (she was carried on to her first TV series at the age of one), she was a National Youth Theatre graduate who switched successfully to modelling ('The Face of the 80s' in 1979) but returned to acting in 1982. She appeared at first as chaste 'ladies fayre' in period dramas and fantasies but later in a better variety of roles. She mixed acting with producing from the mid-1990s.

1982: Ivanhoe (TV). Oliver Twist (TV. GB: cinemas). 1983: Krull. Princess Daisy (TV). 1984: L'étincelle / Tug of Love. Night Train to Murder (TV). 1985: A Drop in the Ocean. 1987: The Emperor's New Clothes. Looking for Eileen. 1988: Without a Clue. Jack the Ripper (TV). 1989: The Lady and the Highwayman (TV). 1990: A Ghost in Monte Carlo (TV). 1991: The Pleasure Principle. Switch. 29 Days in February. 1992: Husbands and Wives. Face the Music. 1993: Hour of the Pig. Save Me. Look Who's Talking Now. A Brilliant Disguise. 1994: Target of Suspicion (cable TV). Dr Jekyll and Ms Hyde. The Hard Truth. 1995: Dead Cold. *Affair Play. Dracula: Dead and Loving It. Robinson Crusoe. 1996: Prince of Lies. Trilogy of Terror II (TV). 1997: Man of Her Dreams / The Fiancé. Misbegotten. 1998: Talos the Mummy. 1999: Dead Man's Gun.

ANWAR, Gabrielle 1969–
Pencil-slim, attractively mannered, dark-haired, British-born Hollywood star of Anglo-Iranian parentage in nineties films, similar in looks to America's Juliette Lewis (*qv*). Acting on British television at 16, Anwar moved to California at 21 and burst into the public eye with one sequence in the award-winning *Scent of a Woman*. Since then, in a mixture of submissive and spirited leads, she has often lacked colour, and has not consolidated her place near the top.

1988: Manifesto. 1991: If Looks Could Kill (GB: Teen Agent). Wild Hearts Can't Be Broken. 1992: The Concierge (later and GB: For Love or Money). Scent of a Woman. 1993: Body Snatchers. The Three Musketeers. Fallen Angels (TV). 1994: Halcyon Days. 1995: In Pursuit of Honor (TV). Innocent Lies. Things to Do in Denver When You're Dead. 1996: The Grave (cable TV). 1997: Crush Depth / Sub Down (TV). Nevada. The Ripper (TV). 1999: Kimberly (TV). The Manor. The Guilty. My Little Assassin (TV). 2000: Stanley's Gig. If You Only Knew.

ARBUCKLE, Roscoe (Fatty) 1887–1933
Popular light-haired American comedian of the silent days, whose plump features could express outrage, tenderness or geniality, and whose attempts at pathos were also more skilful than most. Early vaudeville days were followed by success at Keystone in slapstick shorts, and with his own company, releasing through Paramount. He was moving into features when his career was ruined in 1921 by a scandal (and ensuing court case, which saw him acquitted only after three trials) over one of Arbuckle's orgiastic parties in which a girl died in unpleasant circumstances. He

later directed a few films under the name William Goodrich and had started making sound comedy shorts as star when a heart attack claimed his life at 46. From 1908 to 1925, he was married to actress Minta Durfee (1890–1975), the first of his three wives.

1910: The Sanatarium / The Clinic. 1913: A Small Town Act. Some Never. The Milk We Drink. Prof Bean's Removal. Wine. Safe in Jail. Two Old Tars. The Gangsters. Passions, He Had Three. Help! Help! Hydrophobia! The Waiters' Picnic. A Bandit. For the Love of Mabel. The Tell Tale Light. A Noise from the Deep. Love and Courage. The Riot. Mabel's New Hero. Fatty's Day Off. Mabel's Dramatic Debut. The Gypsy Queen. Mother's Boy. The Faithful Taxicab. A Quiet Little Wedding. Fatty at San Diego. Fatty Joins the Force. The Woman Haters. Fatty's Flirtations. His Sister's Kid. Twixt Love and Fire. A Ride for a Bride. He Would a Hunting Go. 1914: A Misplaced Foot. The Under Sheriff. A Flirt's Mistake. The Bowery Boys. A Bathing Beauty. A Robust Romeo. Lover's Luck. How Hiram Won Out. The Peddler. Peeping Pete. In the Clutches of a Gang. Rebecca's Wedding Day. A Film Johnnie. Tango Tangles. A Rival Demon / A Rural Demon. His Favorite Pastime. Barnyard Flirtations. Chicken Chaser. A Suspended Ordeal. The Water Dog. The Alarm. The Knockout. Fatty and Minnie-Hee-Haw. Our Country Cousin. Fatty and the Heiress. The Sky Pirate. Fatty's Finish. Caught in a Flue. The Baggage Smasher. Those Happy Days. That Minstrel Man. Those Country Kids. Fatty's Gift. The Masquerade. A Brand New Hero. The Rounders. Fatty's Debut. †Fatty Again. Killing Horace. *Tillie's Punctured Romance. Their Ups and Downs. Zip the Dodger. An Incompetent Hero. Lovers' Post Office. The Sea Nymphs. Fatty's Jonah Days. Fatty's Wine Party. 1915: Leading Lizzie Astray. Mabel's Wilful Way. Among the Mourners. Wished on Mabel. Shotguns That Kick. Fatty's Magic Party. Mabel and Fatty's Wash Day. Rum and Wallpaper. Mabel and Fatty's Simple Life. Fatty and Mabel at the San Diego Exposition. Fatty's New Role. Mabel, Fatty and the Law. Colored Villainy. Fatty and Mabel's Married Life. Fatty's Reckless Fling. Fatty's Chance Acquaintance. Love in Armour. Fatty's Faithful Fido. That Little Band of Gold. †When Love Took Wings. Mabel and Fatty Viewing the World's Fair at San Francisco. Miss Fatty's Seaside Lovers. The Little Teacher. Fatty's Plucky Pup. Fatty's Tin Type Tangle. †Fickle Fatty's Fall. 1916: A Reckless Romeo. †His Alibi. †The Village Scandal. Fatty and the Broadway Stars. †Fatty and Mabel Adrift. †He Did and He Didn't. †The Bright Lights. †The Other Man. †His Wife's Mistake. †The Waiters' Ball. †A Creampuff Romance. Rebecca's Wedding Day. 1917: The Late Lamented. †The Butcher Boy. †The Rough House. †His Wedding Night. †Fatty at Coney Island. †A Country Hero. †Oh! Doctor. †Out West. 1918: †The Bell Boy. †Moonshine. †Good Night Nurse. †The Cook. The Sheriff. Camping Out. 1919: †A Desert Hero. †Backstage. †The Garage. †The Hayseed. The Pullman Porter. †Love. The Bank Clerk. 1920: *The Life of the Party. *The Round-Up. *The Traveling Salesman. *Brewster's Millions. *Crazy to Marry. 1921:

*Gasoline Gus. *The Dollar a Year Man. *The Fast Freight. 1922: *Leap Year/Skirt Shy (unreleased in US). 1923: *Hollywood. 1925: *Go West. 1932: Hey, Pop! 1933: How've You Bean? Buzzin' Around. Close Relations. Tomalio. In the Dough.

Also as director: 1916: The Moonshiners. 1925: The Tourist. The Movies. The Fighting Dude. 1926: Cleaning Up. Home Cured. My Stars. His Private Life. Fool's Luck. One Sunday Morning. 1927: Peaceful Oscar. *The Red Mill. *Special Delivery. 1930: Won By A Neck. Three Hollywood Girls. Si Si Senor. Up a Tree. 1931: Crashing Hollywood. The Lure of Hollywood. Windy Riley Goes Hollywood. Queenie of Hollywood. Honeymoon Trio. Ex-Plumber. Pete and Repeat. Marriage Rows. The Back Page. That's My Line. Up Pops the Duke. Beach Pajamas. Take 'Em and Shake 'Em. That's My Meat. One Quiet Night. Once a Hero. The Tamale Vendor. Smart Work. Idle Roomers. 1932: Hollywood Luck. Anybody's Goat. Moonlight and Cactus. Keeping Laughing. Bridge Wives. Mother's Holiday. Niagara Falls. Hollywood Lights. Gigolettes. It's a Cinch.

All shorts except (*) features
†And directed

ARCHER, Anne (A. Bowman) 1945–
Brown-haired, hazel-eyed, full-lipped, athletic-looking American actress who was on the verge of stardom for 25 years without ever quite becoming a major attraction. She contends that she's given good performances in a lot of poor films and narrowly missed out on some plum roles, and that's fair comment. But she also has a screen personality that's a shade dull. An Academy Award nomination as the wronged wife in Fatal Attraction belatedly gave her a boost and was followed by some decent leading roles and good critical notices, especially for her work in 'social conscience' TV movies. The daughter of actors Marjorie Lord (1922–) and John Archer (qv), she is married to actor Terry Jastrow, her co-star in the 1982 film Waltz Across Texas.
1970: The All-American Boy (released 1973). 1972: The Honkers. Cancel My Reservation. 1973: The Blue Knight (TV. GB: cinemas). Trackdown. 1974: The Mark of Zorro (TV). 1975: The Log of the Black Pearl (TV). 1976: Lifeguard. The Dark Side of Innocence (TV). A Matter of Wife . . . and Death/Shamus: A Matter of Wife . . . and Death (TV). 1977:

Good Guys Wear Black. 1978: Paradise Alley. 1980: Hero at Large. Raise the Titanic. 1981: Green Ice. 1982: Waltz Across Texas. 1984: The Naked Face. The Sky's No Limit (TV). 1985: Too Scared to Scream. 1986: The Check is in the Mail. 1987: A Different Affair (TV). Fatal Attraction. 1988: A Leap of Faith (TV). 1989: Love at Large. 1990: Narrow Margin. Eminent Domain. 1991: Family Prayers. 1992: Nails. Body of Evidence. The Last of His Tribe (TV). Patriot Games. 1993: A Question of Faith (TV). Jane's House (TV). Short Cuts. 1994: Clear and Present Danger. Luck, Trust & Ketchup. There Goes My Baby (filmed 1992. Narrator only). Because Mommy Works (TV). 1995: The Man in the Attic (TV). 1996: Mojave Moon. Neil Simon's 'Jake's Women' (TV). 1997: Nico the Unicorn. Indiscretion of an American Wife (TV). 1998: My Husband's Secret Life (TV). 1999: Dark Summer. 2000: The Art of War. Rules of Engagement.

ARCHER, John
(Ralph Bowman) 1915–1999
Big, squarely built American actor with crinkly, reddish hair and crooked grin, who came to Hollywood at 22 after winning a talent contest. Played a few leading roles in his thirties, but his features thickened rather quickly, and the impetus of his career was also somewhat disrupted by war service. Married/divorced actress Marjorie Lord (1922–); the actress Anne Archer (qv) is their daughter. Died from lung cancer.
1938: †Dick Tracy Returns (serial). †Spring Madness. †Overland Stage Raiders. †Flaming Frontier (serial). The Last Gangster. Letter of Introduction. 1939: *Contract. Career. 1940: Barnyard Follies. Scattergood Baines. Curtain Call. 1941: King of the Zombies. Gangs Inc. City of Missing Girls. Mountain Moonlight (GB: Moving in Society). *Sucker List. †Cheers for Miss Bishop. Paper Bullets. 1942: Scattergood Survives a Murder. Bowery at Midnight. Police Bullets. The Moon is Down. Mrs Wiggs of the Cabbage Patch. Hi Neighbor. 1943: Crash Dive. Hello Frisco Hello. The Purple V. Sherlock Holmes in Washington. Shantytown. Guadalcanal Diary. 1944: Roger Touhy – Gangster (GB: The Last Gangster). The Eve of St Mark. 1945: I'll Remember April. 1947: The Lost Moment. 1948: After Nightfall. 1949: White Heat. Colorado Territory 1950: The Great Jewel Robber. Destination Moon. High Lonesome. 1951: Santa Fé. Best of the Badmen. My Favorite

Spy. 1952: The Big Trees. Sea Tiger. Sound Off. A Yank in Indo-China (GB: Hidden Secret). Rodeo. 1953: The Stars Are Singing. 1954: Dragon's Gold. 1955: No Man's Woman. 1956: Rock Around the Clock. Emergency Hospital. 1957: Three Brave Men. Ten Thousand Bedrooms. Affair in Reno. Decision at Sundown. The She-Devil. 1959: City of Fear. 1961: Blue Hawaii. 1964: Apache Rifles. 1965: I Saw What You Did. 1966: Lassie the Voyager (TV. GB: cinemas). 1970: Handford's Point (TV). 1971: How to Frame a Figg. 1974: Thursday's Game (TV). 1976: Amelia Earhart (TV).

†As Ralph Bowman

ARKIN, Alan 1934–
Black-haired, Greek-looking American actor, equally at home with comic or serious characters. Briefly popular in the late 1960s, he proved an insubstantial performer in box office terms and was later seen in co-starring or guest-starring roles; leading parts continued to be commercially unrewarding. Twice nominated for an Academy Award, in The Russians Are Coming, the Russians Are Coming and The Heart is a Lonely Hunter. Also directs. Married actress/writer Barbara Dana (1940–). More recently in cutting cameos.
1957: Calypso Heat Wave. 1962: *That's Me. 1963: *The Last Mohican. 1966: The Russians Are Coming, the Russians Are Coming. 1967: Wait Until Dark. Woman Times Seven. 1968: The Heart is a Lonely Hunter. Inspector Clouseau. 1969: Popi. The Monitors. *People Soup. 1970: Catch 22. 1971: Little Murders. 1972: Last of the Red Hot Lovers. Deadhead Miles. 1974: Freebie and the Bean. 1975: Hearts of the West (GB: Hollywood Cowboy). Rafferty and the Gold Dust Twins. 1976: The Defection of Simas Kudirka (TV). The Seven Per Cent Solution. 1977: Fire Sale. 1978: The Other Side of Hell (TV). The In-Laws. The Magician of Lublin. Improper Channels. 1980: Simon. 1981: Full Moon High. The Last Unicorn (voice only). Chu Chu and the Philly Flash. 1982: The Return of Captain Invincible. 1985: Joshua Then and Now. Bad Medicine. 1986: Big Trouble. A Deadly Business (TV). 1987: Escape from Sobibor (TV). 1988: Necessary Parties (TV). 1989: Coupe de Ville. 1990: Havana. Edward Scissorhands. The Bonfire of the Vanities. 1991: The Rocketeer. 1992: Glengarry Glen Ross. Sessions. 1993: Cooperstown (TV). Taking the Heat. Indian

Summer. So I Married an Axe Murderer. 1994: North. The Jerky Boys. Doomsday Gun (TV. GB: cinemas). 1995: Steal Big, Steal Little. Heck's Way Home (TV). Picture Windows (cable TV). 1996: Mother Night. 1997: Hugo Pool. Four Days in September. Gattaca. Grosse Pointe Blank. 1998: Slums of Beverly Hills. 1999: Jakob the Liar. Magicians. 2000: †Arigo.

†And directed

ARLEN, Richard
(Cornelius R. Van Mattimore) 1899–1976
Hefty, aggressive, ebullient American star who entered films as an extra in 1920. Distinguished by ruddy cheeks, and the just off-centre parting in his dark hair, Arlen remained a second-league star of virile adventure films from 1925 until 1946, when he moved into supporting roles, apart from a few leads in minor British films of the 1950s. Married to actress Jobyna Ralston (second of three) from 1927 to 1945. Died from lung congestion.
1921: †Ladies Must Live. 1922: †The Green Temptation. 1923: †Vengeance of the Deep. †The Fighting Coward. †Quicksands. 1924: Sally. 1925: ‡Coast of Folly. Behind the Front. In the Name of Love. The Enchanted Hill. 1926: Volcano. Padlocked. Old Ironsides. 1927: Figures Don't Lie. Wings. The Blood Ship. Sally in Our Alley. She's a Sheik. Rolled Stockings. Beggars of Life. 1928: Feel My Pulse. Ladies of the Mob. Manhattan Cocktail. The Four Feathers. Under the Tonto Rim. 1929: The Man I Love. Dangerous Curves. Thunderbolt. The Virginian. 1930: Light of Western Stars. *Voice of Hollywood No 2. Burning Up. Paramount on Parade. Dangerous Paradise. The Sea God. The Border Legion. Santa Fé Trail (GB: The Law Rides West). Only Saps Work. 1931: The Conquering Horde. Gun Smoke. The Secret Call. Caught. The Lawyer's Secret. Touchdown (GB: Playing the Game). 1932: Wayward. Sky Bride. Guilty As Hell (GB: Guilty As Charged). Tiger Shark. The All American (GB: Sport of a Nation). Island of Lost Souls. *Hollywood on Parade No. 4. 1933: Song of the Eagle. *Hollywood on Parade No. 6. College Humor. Three-Cornered Moon. Golden Harvest. Alice in Wonderland. Hell and High Water (GB: Cap'n Jericho). Come on Marines. 1934: She Made Her Bed. Ready for Love. 1935: *Hollywood Hobbies. Helldorado. Let 'Em Have It (GB: False Faces). *Screen

Snapshots No. 5. Three Live Ghosts. 1936: The Calling of Dan Matthews. The Mine with the Iron Door. 1937: Artists and Models. Secret Valley (GB: The Gangster's Bride). The Great Barrier (US: Silent Barriers). Murder in Greenwich Village. 1938: No Time to Marry. Call of the Yukon. Straight, Place and Show (GB: They're Off!). 1939: Missing Daughters. Mutiny on the Blackhawk. Tropic Fury. Legion of Lost Flyers. 1940: The Man from Montreal. Danger on Wheels. Hot Steel. The Leather Pushers. Black Diamonds. The Devil's Pipeline. 1941: A Dangerous Game. Lucky Devils. Mutiny in the Arctic. Men of the Timberland. Raiders of the Desert. Forced Landing. Power Dive. Flying Blind. 1942: Torpedo Boat. *A Letter from Bataan. Wrecking Crew. Wildcat. 1943: Alaska Highway. Aerial Gunner. Minesweeper. Submarine Alert. 1944: Timber Queen. Storm over Lisbon. The Lady and the Monster (GB: The Lady and the Doctor). That's My Baby! 1945: Identity Unknown. The Big Bonanza. The Phantom Speaks. 1946: The French Key. Accomplice. 1947: Buffalo Bill Rides Again. 1948: When My Baby Smiles at Me. Speed to Spare. Return of Wildfire (GB: Black Stallion). 1949: Grand Canyon. 1950: Kansas Raiders. 1951: Flaming Feather. Silver City (GB: High Vermilion). 1952: Hurricane Smith. The Blazing Forest. 1953: Sabre Jet. 1954: Devil's Point (US: Devil's Harbor). 1955: Stolen Time (US: Blonde Blackmailer). 1956: Hidden Guns. The Mountain. 1957: Cavalry Command (released 1965). Child of Trouble (TV). 1959: Warlock. 1960: Raymie. 1961: The Last Time I Saw Archie. 1963: The Young and the Brave. The Crawling Hand. Thunder Mountain (GB: Shepherd of the Hills). Law of the Lawless. 1964: The Best Man. Young Fury. 1965: Black Spurs. The Bounty Killer. Town Tamer. The Human Duplicators. 1966: Apache Uprising. Johnny Reno. Road to Nashville. To the Shores of Hell. Waco. 1967: Red Tomahawk. Fort Utah Huntsville/Hostile Guns. 1968: Rogue's Gallery. Buckskin. The Frontiersman. 1970: Sex and the College Girl (completed 1964). 1975: Won Ton Ton, the Dog Who Saved Hollywood. 1976: A Whale of a Tale.

†As Van Mattimore
‡Scenes deleted from final release print

ARLISS, George (G. Andrews) 1868–1946
Dominant, upper-class English stage actor who became a big star on both sides of the Atlantic. His presence and immaculate direction ensured him employment in a serious of portraits of famous men. Won an Academy Award for his second film portrayal of Disraeli. Died from a bronchial ailment. Received an additional Academy Award nomination for The Green Goddess (1930 version). Father of director Leslie Arliss.
1921: The Devil. Disraeli. 1922: The Man Who Played God. 1923: The Green Goddess. The Ruling Passion. 1924: $20 a Week. 1929: Disraeli. 1930: Old English. The Green Goddess. 1931: Millionaire. Alexander Hamilton. 1932: The Man Who Played God (GB: The Silent Voice). A Successful Calamity. 1933: The King's Vacation. The Working Man. Voltaire. The House of Rothschild. 1934: The

Last Gentleman. 1935: Cardinal Richelieu. The Iron Duke. The Tunnel (US: Transatlantic Tunnel). 1936: The Guvnor (US: Mr Hobo). East Meets West. 1937: His Lordship (US: Man of Affairs). Dr Syn.

ARMENDARIZ, Pedro 1912–1963
Swarthy, flashing-eyed, moustachioed Mexican actor with a memorable smile. After years in Mexican films, he went to Hollywood but failed to win a wide variety of roles, spending the greater part of his career as Mexican bandits. Learning that he had terminal cancer, Armendariz shot himself. His son, Pedro Armendariz Jr (1939–) has been playing supporting roles in Mexican and Hollywood films since 1965.
1934: Maria Elena. Bordertown. 1935: Rosario. 1937: Las Cuatro Milpas. Amapola del Camino. Jalisca nunca Pierde. La Adelita. Mi Candidato. 1938: Los Millones de Chafian. La Dama de Rio. El Indio. Canto a Mi Tierra. La China Hilaria. Una Luz en mi Camino. 1939: Con los Dorados de Villa. Borrasca Humana. 1940: Los Olvidados de Diaz. El Charro Negro. Pobre Diablo. Mala Yerba. El Jefe Maximo. El Zorro de Jalisco. El Secreta del Sacerdote. 1941: Ni Sangre ni Arena. La Epapaya del Camino. Simón Bolivar. Del Rancho a la Capital. Alia en el Bajia. La Isla de la Pasión. 1942: Soy Puro Mexicano. Tierra de Pasiónes. 1943: Los Calaveras del Terror. Flor Silvestre. Kangaroja. Guadalajara. Distinto Amanecer. Maria Candelaria. La Guerra de los Pasteles. 1944: El Corsario Negro. Alma de Bronco. La Campana de mi Pueblo. Los Abandonadas. El Capitan Malacara. Entre Hermanos. Bugambilla. 1945: Rayando El Sol. La Perla (GB and US: The Pearl). 1946: Enamorada. 1947: Albur de

Amor. La Casa Colorada. Juan Charras-queado. The Fugitive. 1948: Maclovia. Al Caer la Tarde. En la Hacienda de la Flor. Fort Apache. 3 Godfathers. 1949: Tulsa. La Malquerida. We Were Strangers. The Outlaw and the Lady. Pancho Villa. El Abandonado. Bodas de Fuego. 1950: Rosauro Castro. Tierra Baja. La Loca de La Casa. Por la Puerta Falsa. Camino de Infierno. Nos Veremos en el Cielo. Del Odio Nace el Amor (GB: Bandit General. US: The Torch). 1951: Por Querer a una Mujer. Ella y Yo. La Noche Avanza. 1952: Carne de Presidio. El Rebozo de la Soledad. El Bruto. Les Amants de Tolede (GB: Lovers of Tolèdo. US: Tyrant of Toledo). 1953: Lucretia Borgia. Reportaje. Mate a la Vida. Mulata. 1954: Dos Mundos y Un Amor. La Rebelion de los Colgados. Border River. El Diablo del Desierto (Borderia). 1955: Les Amants du Tage. Tam Tam Mayumba (US: Native Drums. GB: Tom Toms of Mayumba). El Pequeno Proscrito. La Escondida (GB: The Hidden Woman). 1956: The Conqueror. Diane. The Littlest Outlaw. Men and Wolves. Canasta de Cuentos Mexicanos. La Major que no Tuvo Infancia. El Impostor. Viva Revolución. 1957: Flor de Mayo (GB: A Mexican Affair. US: Beyond All Limits). The Big Boodle. Ando Volando Bajo. La Pandilla del Soborno. El Zarco (GB: El Zarco – the Bandit). Asi Era Pancho Villa. Affair in Havana. Manuela (US: Stowaway Girl). 1958: Pancho Villa y la Valentina. Cuando Viva Villa es La Muerte. Café Colón. Spoilers of the Sea. Los Senoritas Vivanco. Los Desarraigados. La Cucaracha (GB: The Bandit). Sed de Amor. 1959: Yo Pecador. El Hombre Nuestro de Cada Dia. Calibre 44. The Wonderful Country. El Pequeno Salvaje. 1960: La Cárcel de Cananco. El Induito. 800 Leguas por el Amazona. Dos Hijos Desobedients. 1961: Los Hermanos del Hierro (US: My Son, the Hero). Los Valientes no Mueren. El Rejedor de Milagros. Francis of Assisi. Arrivani i Titani (GB: Sons of Thunder. US: The Titans). 1962: La Bandida. 1963: Captain Sindbad. From Russia with Love.

ARMSTRONG, Louis
(Daniel L. Armstrong) 1901–1971
Enormously popular and beloved, flat-faced, brow-mopping, beaming black American jazz trumpeter whose relatively few film appearances still managed to convey the obvious pleasure he gained both from playing music and clowning around. There were also memorable vocal duets with such Hollywood stars as Bing Crosby and Danny Kaye.

Known world-wide as Satchmo (Satchel-mouth). Died from heart failure.
1930: Ex-Flame. 1932: *Rhapsody in Black and Blue. 1936: Pennies from Heaven. 1937: Every Day's a Holiday. 1938: Dr Rhythm. Artists and Models. 1941: The Birth of the Blues. 1942: *I'll Be Glad When You're Dead, You Rascal You. *Sleepytime Down South. *Shine. *Swinging on Nothin'. 1943: Cabin in the Sky. *Show Business at War. 1944: Jam Session. Hollywood Canteen. Atlantic City. 1945: Pillow To Post. 1947: New Orleans. 1948: A Song is Born. 1950: Botta e risposta. 1951: The Strip. Here Comes the Groom. 1952: Glory Alley. La route de bonheur. 1953: *Jazz Parade. The Glenn Miller Story. 1956: High Society. 1957: Satchmo The Great. 1959: The Five Pennies. The Beat Generation. 1960: Jazz on a Summer's Day. 1961: Paris Blues. 1965: When the Boys Meet the Girls. 1966: A Man Called Adam. 1968: Jazz: The Intimate Art (TV. GB: cinemas). 1969: Hello, Dolly! 1981: Bix (voice only).

ARMSTRONG, Robert
(Donald R. Smith) 1890–1973
Burly, dark-faced American character star and sometime leading man with rough and ready tones and aggressive style. Remembered by most filmgoers for his Denham in the King Kong films, but often seen as fast-talking men on the make, or crooked politicians. Died from cancer.
1915: The Silent Voice. 1917: War and the Woman. 1921: Boys Will be Boys. Honey Girl. Shavings. Sure Fire. 1924: The Man Who Came Back. 1925: New Brooms. Judy. 1927: Is Zat So? The Main Event. The Leopard Lady. A Girl in Every Port. 1928: Square Crooks. The Cop. Celebrity. The Baby Cyclone. Show Folks. Shady Lady. 1929: The Leatherneck. Ned McCobb's Daughter. The Woman from Hell. Big News. Oh Yeah! (GB: No Brakes). The Racketeer (GB: Love's Conquest). 1930: Big Money. Be Yourself. Danger Lights. Dumbbells in Ermine. Paid (GB: Within the Law). 1931: Easy Money. The Tip-Off (GB: Looking for Trouble). Suicide Fleet. Iron Man. Ex-Bad Boy. 1932: Panama Flo. The Lost Squadron. Is My Face Red. Hold 'em Jail. The Most Dangerous Game (GB: The Hounds of Zaroff). Penguin Pool Murder (GB: The Penguin Pool Mystery). Radio Patrol. 1933: Blind Adventure. The Billion Dollar Scandal. King Kong. I Love That Man. Fast Workers. Above the Clouds (GB: Winged Devils). Son of Kong. 1934:

Search for Beauty. Palooka (GB: The Great Schnozzle). The Hell Cat. She Made Her Bed. Manhattan Love Song. Kansas City Princess. Flirting with Danger. 1935: The Mystery Man. Sweet Music. G Men. Gigolette (GB: Night Club). Remember Last Night? Little Big Shot. 1936: Dangerous Waters. The Ex-Mrs Bradford. Public Enemy's Wife (GB: G-Man's Wife). All American Chump (GB: Country Bumpkin). Without Orders. *Pirate Party on Catalina Isle. 1937: The Three Legionnaires. It Can't Last Forever. Nobody's Baby. The Girl Said No. 1938: She Loved a Fireman. There Goes My Heart. The Night Hawk. 1939: The Flying Irishman. Unmarried (GB: Night Club Hostess). Man of Conquest. Winter Carnival. Flight at Midnight. Call a Messenger. 1940: Framed. Forgotten Girls. Enemy Agent (GB: Secret Enemy). San Francisco Docks. Behind the News. 1941: Mr Dynamite. Citadel of Crime (GB: Outside the Law). Dive Bomber. The Bride Wore Crutches. Sky Raiders (serial). My Favorite Spy. 1942: Baby Face Morgan. Let's Get Tough. It Happened in Flatbush. Gang Busters (serial). 1943: Around the World. The Kansan (GB: Wagon Wheels). Adventures of the Flying Cadets (serial). The Mad Ghoul. 1944: The Navy Way. Action in Arabia. Mr Winkle Goes to War (GB: Arms and the Woman). Belle of the Yukon. 1945: Gangs of the Waterfront. Blood on the Sun. The Falcon in San Francisco. The Royal Mounted Rides Again (serial). Arson Squad. 1946: Gay Blades. Criminal Court. GI War Brides. Blonde Alibi. Decoy. 1947: The Fall Guy. The Fugitive. Exposed. 1948: Return of the Bad Men. The Sea of Grass. The Paleface. 1949: The Lucky Stiff. Crime Doctor's Diary. The Streets of San Francisco. Mighty Joe Young. Captain China. Sons of New Mexico (GB: The Brat). 1950: Destination Big House. 1952: The Pace That Thrills. Cripple Creek. 1955: Las Vegas Shakedown. 1956: The Peacemaker. 1957: The Crooked Circle. 1959: Girl with an Itch. 1963: Johnny Cool. 1964: For Those Who Think Young.

ARNESS, James (J. Aurness) 1923–
Husky 6 ft 8 in American leading man with fair curly hair. With his bear-like build he found difficulty getting a range of roles, but then landed in television's Gunsmoke (GB: Gun Law) as Marshal Matt Dillon, a series that lasted 20 years. Since it ended in 1972, his giant frame, easy-going drawl and rather strained smile have proved just as difficult to cast as before and he was back in the saddle as Marshal Dillon by 1987. Brother of actor

Peter Graves (*qv*).
1947: †*The Farmer's Daughter.* †*Roses Are Red.* 1948: †*The Man from Texas.* 1949: †*Battleground.* 1950: †*Sierra.* †*Two Lost Worlds.* †*Wyoming Mail.* †*Wagonmaster.* †*Double Crossbones. Stars in My Crown.* 1951: *Cavalry Scout. Belle le Grand. Iron Man. The People Against O'Hara. The Girl in White (GB: So Bright the Flame). The Thing from Another World.* 1952: *Carbine Williams. Horizons West. Big Jim McLain. Hellgate.* 1953: *Lone Hand. Ride the Man Down. The Veils of Bagdad. Island in the Sky.* 1954: *Hondo. Her Twelve Men. Them!* 1955: *Many Rivers to Cross. The Sea Chase. Flame of the Islands.* 1956: *The First Traveling Saleslady. Gun the Man Down/Arizona Mission.* 1959: *Alias Jesse James.* 1975: *The MacAhans: How the West Was Won (TV).* 1981: *McClain's Law (TV).* 1987: *The Alamo: 13 Days to Glory (TV). Gunsmoke: Return to Dodge (TV).* 1988: *Red River (TV).* 1990: *Gunsmoke: The Last Apache (TV).* 1991: *Gunsmoke III: To the Last Man (TV).* 1993: *Gunsmoke: The Long Ride (TV).*

†*As James Aurness*

ARNOLD, Edward
(Gunther E.A. Schneider) 1890–1956
Portly, expansive, dark-haired, heavy-headed American character star who started as cowboy heroes in two-reel westerns of the early silent era. After an absence of 12 years on stage, he returned to Hollywood to become famous as Diamond Jim (and detective Nero Wolfe) and other expansive, larger-than-life figures. Later, as his girth widened and his eyes narrowed, Arnold specialized in corrupt politicians and businessmen, remaining a top featured player until his death from a cerebral haemorrhage.
1915: *The Strange Case of Mary Page (serial).* 1916: *When the Man Speaks. The Heart of Virginia Keep. Vultures of Society. The Primitive Strain. The Return of Eve. *The Burning Band. *Dancing With Folly. *Wife in Sunshine.* 1917: *The Slacker's Heart/The Slacker. *The Wide, Wrong Way. *The Sinful Marriage. *The Magic Mirror. *Desertion and Non-Support. *Shifting Shadows. *Ashes on the Hearthstone. *The Extravagant Bride. *The Vanishing Woman. *The Pulse of Madness. *The Wifeless Husband. *The Pallid Dawn. *Meddling with Marriage. *Pass the Hash, Ann.* 1919: *Phil-for-Short. A Broadway Saint.* 1920: *The Cost.* 1927: *Sunrise.* 1932:

Murder in the Pullman. Men of The Nile. Okay America (GB: Penalty of Fame). Three on a Match. Afraid to Talk/Merry-Go-Round. 1933: *Rasputin and the Empress (GB: Rasputin – The Mad Monk). Whistling in the Dark. The White Sister. The Barbarian (GB: A Night in Cairo). Her Bodyguard. Jennie Gerhardt. I'm No Angel. Roman Scandals. Secret of the Blue Room.* 1934: *Sadie McKee. Madame Spy. Thirty Day Princess. Unknown Blonde. Hide-Out. Million Dollar Ransom. Wednesday's Child.* 1935: *The President Vanishes (GB: Strange Conspiracy). Biography of a Bachelor Girl. Cardinal Richelieu. The Glass Key. Diamond Jim. Remember Last Night? Crime and Punishment.* 1936: *Sutter's Gold. Meet Nero Wolfe. Come and Get It.* 1937: *John Meade's Woman. Easy Living. The Toast of New York. Blossoms on Broadway.* 1938: *The Crowd Roars. You Can't Take It With You. Let Freedom Ring.* 1939: *Idiot's Delight. Man about Town. Mr Smith Goes to Washington.* 1940: *The Earl of Chicago. Slightly Honorable. Johnny Apollo. Lillian Russell.* 1941: *Variety Reel. The Penalty. The Lady from Cheyenne. Meet John Doe. Nothing But the Truth. Unholy Partners. Design for Scandal. Johnny Eager. All That Money Can Buy.* 1942: *Eyes in the Night. The War against Mrs Hadley.* 1943: *The Youngest Profession.* 1944: *Ziegfeld Follies (released 1946). Janie. Kismet. Mrs Parkington. Standing Room Only. Main Street After Dark.* 1945: *Weekend at the Waldorf. The Hidden Eye.* 1946: *Janie Gets Married. Three Wise Fools. No Leave, No Love. The Mighty McGurk. My Brother Talks to Horses.* 1947: *Dear Ruth. The Hucksters.* 1948: *Three Daring Daughters (GB: The Birds and the Bees). Big City. Wallflower. Command Decision. Take Me Out to the Ball Game (GB: Everybody's Cheering).* 1949: *John Loves Mary. Big Jack. Dear Wife.* 1950: *The Yellow Cab Man. Annie Get Your Gun. *The Screen Actor. The Skipper Surprised His Wife.* 1951: *Dear Brat.* 1952: *Belles on Their Toes.* 1953: *City That Never Sleeps. Man of Conflict.* 1954: *Living It Up.* 1956: *The Houston Story. The Ambassador's Daughter. Miami Exposé.*

ARNOLD, Tom 1959–
Affable, jolly-looking American writer, comedian and light actor with rubicund cheeks. Often seen as brash, blue-collar characters, Arnold began his career as a stand-up comedian in clubs in his native Iowa. Later he became a writer for the smash-

hit TV comedy series *Roseanne*, joined its cast and married (and divorced) the star, Roseanne Barr. Since the divorce he has enjoyed moderate success in home-grown comedies, but looks more relaxed stealing scenes from stars in bigger films.
1991: *Problem Child 2. Backfield in Motion (TV). Freddy's Dead: The Final Nightmare.* 1992: *Hero (GB: Accidental Hero).* 1993: *Coneheads. Body Bags (TV). The Woman Who Loved Elvis (TV). Undercover Blues.* 1994: *True Lies.* 1995: *Nine Months.* 1996: *The Stupids. Carpool. Big Bully. Touch.* 1997: *McHale's Navy. *Lloyd. Austin Powers: International Man of Mystery. Hacks/Sink or Swim.* 1998: *National Lampoon's Golf Punks. Buster and Chauncey's Silent Night (voice only).* 1999: *The Day October Died. Bar Hopping. End of Innocence. Jackie's Back (TV). I Know What You Screamed Last Summer.* 2000: *Shepherd. Just Sue Me. Animal Factory.*

ARQUETTE, David 1971–
Dark-haired, soldily built, rather diffident-looking American actor, brother of Rosanna and Patricia Arquette. Often in unforceful roles, sometimes as characters of limited intelligence from deprived or depressed backgrounds, Arquette proved a versatile player, but not a movie name until he featured as hapless Deputy Dewey Riley in the very successful *Scream* films. That brought him into the Hollywood social whirl and he became a face the public recognised, especially after his marriage to co-star Courteney Cox.
1992: *Where the Day Takes You. The Webbers/Webbers' World/The Webbers' 15 Minutes. *Halfway House. Cruel Doubt (TV). Buffy the Vampire Slayer.* 1993: *The Killing Box. Grey Knight (director's cut of The Killing Box).* 1994: *Fall Time. Airheads. Roadracers (cable TV). Frank and Jesse. The Road Killer.* 1995: *Johns. Wild Bill.* 1996: *Beautiful Girls. Skin and Bone. Scream.* 1997: *The Alarmist (originally Life During Wartime). Dream With the Fishes. RPM.* 1998: *Scream 2.* 1999: *Ravenous. The Runner (Cable TV). Never Been Kissed. Muppets from Space.* 2000: *Scream 3. The Shrink is In. Kiss & Tell. Ready to Rumble.* 2001: *See Spot Run.*

ARQUETTE, Patricia 1966–
Petite, attractive, rather sombre-looking blonde American actress, the younger sister of Rosanna Arquette (*qv*). Acting professionally as a child, she worked as a teenage

model around Europe before starting an adult acting career in the late 1980s. She was in mainline starring roles by the early 1990s, projecting an appealingly fresh sexiness. Not quite a household name, despite overtaking her sister in popularity, though the quality of her performances declined in the late 1990s. Married to Nicolas Cage (qv). The couple separated in 2000, but reunited the same year.
1986: Pretty Smart. 1987: A Nightmare on Elm Street Part 3: Dream Warriors. Daddy (TV). 1988: Time Out. Far North. 1990: Dillinger (TV). 1991: The Indian Runner. Prayer of the Rollerboys. Wildflower (TV). 1992: Ethan Frome. Trouble Bound. Inside Monkey Zetterland. 1993: Betrayed by Love (TV). True Romance. 1994: Holy Matrimony. The Gold Cup. Ed Wood. 1995: Infinity. Beyond Rangoon. 1996: Flirting With Disaster. The Secret Agent. Lost Highway. 1997: Goodbye Lover. 1998: Nightwatch. The Hi-Lo Country. 1999: Stigmata. Bringing Out the Dead. 2000: In the Boom Boom Room. Little Nicky. 2001: Human Nature.

ARQUETTE, Rosanna 1959–
With her tawny hair, curvy figure, petite stature, real-life salty language and talent for wildcat comedy, this third-generation Hollywood performer could have been the natural successor to Carole Lombard, enjoying a film freedom in which Lombard would have revelled. Granddaughter of comedy character actor Cliff Arquette, she broke through to mainstream stardom in *Desperately Seeking Susan*, but poor scripts and exploitative roles have hampered the progress of a career which has too often seemed to lack dynamism. Sister of actress Patricia Arquette and actors Alexis and David Arquette. Three times married. Recently seen in vicious or conniving roles.
1977: Having Babies II (TV). 1978: Zuma Beach (TV). The Dark Secret of Harvest Home (TV). 1979: More American Graffiti/ The Party's Over/Purple Haze. The Ordeal of Patty Hearst (TV). 1980: Gorp. 1981: SOB. A Long Way Home (TV). The Wall (TV). 1982: The Executioner's Song. Baby It's You. Johnny Belinda (TV). 1983: Off the Wall. One Cooks, the Other Doesn't (TV). 1984: The Parade/Hit Parade (TV). The Aviator. 1985: Survival Guides (TV). Silverado. Desperately Seeking Susan. After Hours. 1986: 8 Million Ways to Die. Nobody's Fool. Amazon Women on the Moon. 1988: The Big Blue. Promised a Miracle (TV). 1989: New York Stories. Black Rainbow. 1990: Wendy Cracked a Walnut. Flight of the Intruder. Sweet Revenge. Separation (TV). 1991: The Linguini Incident. Father and Sons. 1992: The Player. In the Deep Woods (TV). 1993: Nowhere to Run. The Wrong Man. 1994: Pulp Fiction. Search and Destroy. La cité de la peur. une comédie familiale. Nowhere to Hide (TV). 1996: Gone Fishin'. Crash. Stuck. 1997: Do Me a Favor. Love is Murder. Liar/Deceiver. In Defense of Murder. 1998: Hell's Kitchen NYC. Hope Floats. Fait accompli. Pigeonholed (released 1999). I Know What You Did. Buffalo 66. Floating Away. 1999: Palmer's Pick-Up. I'm Losing You. Sugar Town. Switched at Birth (TV). Interview with a Dead Man. 2000: The Whole Nine Yards. Yelling to the Sky. Too Much Flesh. Mistaken Identity (TV).

ARTHUR, Jean
(Gladys Greene) 1905–1991
Fluffily blonde, croaky-voiced (but with piquant sex appeal) American leading actress who started in low-budget westerns, then spent 20 years as a star. She really came into her own in 1930s' comedies and Frank Capra films, which allowed her warm and perky personality full play. Nominated for an Academy Award in *The More the Merrier*. Died from heart failure. Never married.
*1923: *Somebody Lied. Cameo Kirby. 1924: *Spring Fever. *Case Dismissed. *The Powerful Eye. The Temple of Venus. Fast and Fearless. Biff Bang Buddy. Bringin' Home the Bacon. Travelin' Fast. Thundering Romance. 1925: The Fighting Smile. Seven Chances. The Drug Store Cowboy. A Man of Nerve. Tearin' Loose. 1926: *Hello Lafayette. Thundering Through. Born to Battle. *Eight Cylinder Bull. The Hurricane Horseman. The Cowboy Cop (GB: Broke to the Wide). Twisted Triggers. Roaring Rider. The Fighting Cheat. Riding Rivals. The College Boob. Lightning Bill. Double Daring. Under Fire. *The Mad Racer. 1927: The Block Signal. Husband Hunters. The Broken Gate. Horseshoes. *Bigger and Better Blondes. Winners of the Wilderness. The Poor Nut. Flying Luck. The Masked Menace (serial). 1928: Wallflowers. Easy Come, Easy Go. Warming Up. Brotherly Love. Sins of the Fathers. 1929: The Canary Murder Case. The Mysterious Dr Fu Manchu. The Saturday Night Kid. The Greene Murder Case. Halfway to Heaven. Stairs of Sand. 1930: Street of Chance. The Record Run. Young Eagles. Paramount on Parade. The Return of Dr Fu Manchu. Danger Lights. The Silver Horde. 1931: The Gang Buster. The Lawyer's Secret. Virtuous Husband (GB: What Wives Don't Want). Ex-Bad Boy. 1933: Get That Venus. The Past of Mary Holmes. 1934: Whirlpool. The Defense Rests. The Most Precious Thing in Life. The Whole Town's Talking (GB: Passport to Fame). 1935: Public Hero Number One. Party Wire. Diamond Jim. The Public Menace. If You Could Only Cook. 1936: Mr Deeds Goes to Town. The Ex-Mrs Bradford. Adventure in Manhattan (GB: Manhattan Madness). The Plainsman. More Than a Secretary. 1937: History is Made at Night. Easy Living. 1938: You Can't Take It with You. 1939: Only Angels Have Wings. Mr Smith Goes to Washington. 1940: Too Many Husbands (GB: My Two Husbands). Arizona. 1941: The Devil and Miss Jones. 1942: The Talk of the Town. 1943: The More the Merrier. A Lady Takes a Chance. 1944: The Impatient Years. 1948: A Foreign Affair. 1953: Shane.*

ASHCROFT, Dame Peggy 1907–1991
One of Britain's most distinguished actresses through several decades, a diminutive, diffident-looking light-haired lady with something of a Margaret Sullavan (qv) appeal in her earlier days. She appeared only very rarely in films, confining her career almost entirely to the stage – where she became a delicate and distinctive interpreter of Shakespeare – and radio. But her warmth and talent were evident even in unworthy cinematic roles, and she won an Academy Award for her performance in *A Passage to India* at 77. Made Dame Peggy in 1956, she was three times married and divorced. Died following a stroke.
1933: The Wandering Jew. 1935: The 39 Steps.

1936: *Rhodes of Africa (US: Rhodes). 1940:
*Channel Incident. 1941: Quiet Wedding.
1958: The Nun's Story. 1967: Tell Me Lies.
October Revolution (narrator only). 1968:
Secret Ceremony. 1969: Three into Two Won't
Go. 1971: Sunday, Bloody Sunday. 1973: Der
Fussgänger / Le piéton / The Pedestrian. 1976:
Joseph Andrews. 1978: Hullabaloo over
Georgie and Bonnie's Pictures. 1984: A Passage
to India. 1986: When the Wind Blows (voice
only). 1988: Madame Sousatzka. 1989: She's
Been Away (TV).

ASHER, Jane 1946–
Red-haired, delicate-looking, slightly built
British actress, a former child player who
flowered briefly in elfin and usually sensitive
adult roles. Mostly on stage after 1970, she
married the artist and cartoonist Gerald
Scarfe and later became a published expert on
cookery and cake-icing.
1952: Mandy (US: Crash of Silence). 1953:
Third Party Risk. 1954: Dance Little Lady.
Adventure in the Hopfields. 1955: The Quatermass Experiment (US: The Creeping
Unknown). 1956: Charley Moon. 1961: The
Greengage Summer (US: Loss of Innocence).
1962: The Prince and the Pauper. 1963: Girl in
the Headlines (US: The Model Murder Case).
1964: The Masque of the Red Death. 1966:
Alfie. 1968: The Winter's Tale. 1970: The
Buttercup Chain. Deep End. 1972: Henry VIII
and His Six Wives. 1975: *Careless Love.
1981: Hands Up! (mostly shot 1967). 1983:
Runners. 1984: Success is the Best Revenge.
1985: Dream Child. 1988: Paris by Night.
1993: The Volunteer. Closing Numbers (TV).

ASHERSON, Renée (R. Ascherson) 1915–
Brown-haired, large-eyed, London-born
actress who became a specialist in waiting
women and diffident damsels. Her rather
distant and indefinite personality was not
entirely suited to the screen, and she returned
to the stage in the mid-1950s after some
disappointing film roles. Widow of Robert
Donat (qv); married in 1953; they were
separated at the time of his death five years
later.
1944: †The Way Ahead (US: Immortal
Battalion). Henry V. 1945: Caesar and
Cleopatra. The Way to the Stars (US: Johnny
in the Clouds). 1948: Once a Jolly Swagman
(US: Maniacs on Wheels). The Small Back
Room (US: Hour of Glory). 1949: The Cure
for Love. 1950: Pool of London. 1951: The
Magic Box. 1953: Malta Story. 1954: Time is

My Enemy. The Red Dress. 1961: The Day the
Earth Caught Fire. 1965: Rasputin the Mad
Monk. 1969: The Smashing Bird I Used to
Know. 1973: Theatre of Blood. 1979: A Man
Called Intrepid (TV). 1985: Romance on the
Orient Express (TV). 1992: Memento Mori
(TV). 1998: Grey Owl.

†As Renée Ascherson

ASHLEY, Elizabeth (E. Cole) 1939–
Brunette, sharp-featured American actress of
somewhat tart personality, good at vixens and
hard-shelled heroines. Mainly on stage (from
the late 1950s), she was unlucky not to be a
success at her first try in Hollywood, but
picked up some good roles on TV in the
1970s. Married/divorced actors James
Farentino and George Peppard (qv),
1962–1966 and 1966–1972, first and second
of three. Her autobiography, Actress – Postcards from the Road, revealed a traumatic
personal life.
1963: The Carpetbaggers. 1965: Ship of Fools.
The Third Day. 1971: The Face of Fear (TV).
Second Chance (TV). The Marriage of a
Young Stockbroker. Harpy (TV). 1972: Your
Money or Your Wife (TV). When Michael
Calls (TV). 1973: The Magician (TV). The
Heist (TV. GB: Suspected Person). 1974:
Golden Needles. Paperback Hero. Rancho de
Luxe. 1975: One of My Wives is Missing (TV).
92 in the Shade. 1976: The Great Scout and
Cathouse Thursday. 1977: The War Between
the Tates (TV). Coma. 1978: A Fire in the Sky
(TV). 1979: Corky. 1980: Windows. 1981:
Paternity. 1982: Captured! / Split Image.
1983: Svengali (TV). 1986: Stagecoach
(TV). 1987: Warm Hands, Cold Feet (TV).
Dragnet. 1988: Dangerous Curves. A Man of

Passion. Vampire's Kiss. 1989. Lost Memories.
Blue Bayou (TV). 1991: Reason for Living:
The Jill Ireland Story (TV). Love and Curses
... and All That Jazz (TV). 1992: In the Best
Interest of the Children (TV). 1996: Shoot the
Moon. Sleeping Together. 1998: Happiness.
Just the Ticket.

ASKEY, Arthur 1900–1982
Diminutive, much-loved, dark-haired,
bespectacled English music-hall comedian
('Big-Hearted Arthur'), who delighted
audiences with 'silly little songs' and won
enormous success on radio in Band Waggon,
Britain's first comedy series. His films have
not worn too well, but the best are still
sporadically funny. Catchphrases: 'I thank
you', 'Before your very eyes' and 'Hello,
playmates'. Died from gangrene after having
both legs removed.
1937: *Pathe Pictorial No. 115 (The Bee).
Calling All Stars. 1939: Band Waggon. 1940:
Charley's (Big-Hearted) Aunt. 1941: The
Ghost Train. I Thank You. 1942: Back Room
Boy. *The Nose Has It. King Arthur Was a
Gentleman. 1943: Miss London Ltd. 1944:
Bees in Paradise. 1954: The Love Match.
1955: Ramsbottom Rides Again. 1956: *Skilful
Soccer. 1959: Make Mine a Million. Friends
and Neighbours. 1972: The Alf Garnett Saga.
1977: *End of Term. 1978: Rosie Dixon –
Night Nurse. 1982: The Pantomime Dame.

ASKWITH, Robin 1950–
Perky, wide-smiling British actor who, after
an uninteresting apprenticeship, proved
extremely popular in the leading role of the
'Confessions' sex comedies of the 1970s.
When the market for these subsided, he
moved into similar sort of stuff (still vulgar

but slightly laundered) in TV comedy series.

1968: Otley. If . . . 1969: Alfred the Great. Hans Brinker. 1970: Cool It Carol! (US: The Dirtiest Girl I Ever Met). Scramble. †Bartleby. 1971: Nicholas and Alexandra. †The Canterbury Tales. All Coppers Are . . . 1972: Tower of Evil (US: Horror of Snape Island). The Flesh and Blood Show. The Four Dimensions of Greta. Bless This House. Hide and Seek. 1973: Carry On Girls. No Sex Please – We're British. Horror Hospital. 1974: Confessions of a Window Cleaner. 1975: The Hostages. Confessions of a Pop Performer. 1976: Confessions of a Driving Instructor. Stand Up Virgin Soldiers. 1977: Closed Up Tight. Queen Kong. Confessions from a Holiday Camp. Let's Get Laid! 1982: Britannia Hospital. 2000: U-571. The Asylum.

†As Robin Asquith

ASSANTE, Armand 1949–
Wiry, brown-haired American actor with worldly-wise looks, a Latin lover-type in an age where Hollywood no longer needed them. Nonetheless, Assante has got some good film roles down the years in between theatre work, mostly top featured parts, but also some leading roles, notably the older brother in *The Mambo Kings*, which produced his best film performance to date.

1974: The Lords of Flatbush. 1978: Human Feelings (TV). Paradise Alley. Lady of the House (TV). 1979: Prophecy. The Pirate (TV). 1980: Little Darlings. Private Benjamin. Sophia Loren: Her Own Story (TV). Love and Money (released 1982). 1981: I, the Jury. 1983: Unfaithfully Yours. 1984: Why Me? (TV). 1985: Belizaire the Cajun. 1986: A Deadly Business (TV). The Penitent (released 1988). Stranger in My Bed (TV). 1987: Hands of a Stranger (TV). 1988: Jack the Ripper (TV). 1989: Animal Behavior. Passion and Paradise (TV). 1990: Eternity. 1991: Q & A. The Marrying Man (GB: Too Hot to Handle). 1992: The Mambo Kings. Fever. 1492 Conquest of Paradise. Hoffa. 1993: Triple Indemnity. Fatal Instinct. 1994: Trial by Jury. Blind Justice. 1995: Judge Dredd. 1996: Striptease. Kidnapped. Gotti (cable TV). 1997: The Odyssey. 1998: Hunt for the Devil. 1999: Looking for an Echo. The Hunley (cable TV). 2000: The Road to El Dorado (voice only). On the Beach (TV). 2001: After the Storm.

ASTAIRE, Fred (F. Austerlitz) 1899–1987
Pencil-slim, hard-working, innovative dancing star with lean, languid looks and distinctive light singing voice, who made the grinding discipline of constant rehearsal come to the screen as pure poetry. A hit on stage with his sister Adele, then on film with Ginger Rogers. Special Academy Award 1949. Won an Emmy in 1979 for *A Family Upside Down*. Nominated for an Oscar in *The Towering Inferno*. Died from pneumonia.

1932: *Municipal Bandwagon. 1933: Dancing Lady. Flying Down to Rio. 1934: The Gay Divorcee (GB: The Gay Divorce). 1935: Roberta. Top Hat. 1936: Follow the Fleet. Swing Time. 1937: Shall We Dance? A Damsel in Distress. 1938: Carefree. 1939: The Story of Vernon and Irene Castle. 1940: Broadway Melody of 1940. Second Chorus. 1941: You'll Never Get Rich. 1942: Holiday Inn. You Were Never Lovelier. 1943: The Sky's the Limit. 1944: Ziegfeld Follies (released 1946). 1945: Yolanda and the Thief. 1946: Blue Skies. 1948: Easter Parade. 1949: The Barkleys of Broadway. 1950: Three Little Words. Let's Dance. Royal Wedding (GB: Wedding Bells). 1951: The Belle of New York. 1953: The Band Wagon. 1955: Daddy Long Legs. 1956: Funny Face. 1957: Silk Stockings. 1959: On the Beach. 1961: The Pleasure of His Company. 1962: The Notorious Landlady. 1964: Paris When It Sizzles (voice). 1968: Finian's Rainbow. 1969: Midas Run (GB: A Run on Gold). 1971: The Over-the-Hill Gang Rides Again (TV). 1972: Imagine. 1974: The Towering Inferno. That's Entertainment! 1976: That's Entertainment Part Two. 1977: Taxi Mauve (US: Purple Taxi). The Amazing Dobermans. 1979: A Family Upside Down (TV). 1980: The Man in the Santa Claus Suit (TV). 1981: Ghost Story.

ASTHER, Nils 1897–1981
Suave, charismatic and faintly mysterious Swedish-born leading man. During spells in German films, Hollywood (twice) and Britain, he found himself cast as every nationality but his own. Outstanding as the Chinese warlord in Frank Capra's *The Bitter Tea of General Yen*, Asther failed to sustain the impetus of his career in any of its phases, in each of which he eventually regressed to second features. He eventually returned to Sweden in 1959, making a few more films and becoming regarded as something of a father figure in the Swedish cinema.

1916: Vingarne. 1917: Hittebarnet. 1918:

Himmelskibet. De mystiske Fodspar. Solen der draepte. 1920: Gyurkovicsarna. 1922: Vem dömer. 1923: Das Geheimnis der Herzogen. Norrtullsligan. 1924: The Courier of Carl XII. Wienerbarnet. 1925: Briefe, die ihn nicht erreichten. Finale der Liebe. Sveket nej Volontar. Der Mann seiner Frau. 1926: Die drei Kuckucksuhren. Der goldene Schmetterling (US: The Road to Happiness). Das süsse Mädel. Die versunkene Flotte. 1927: Gauner im Frack. Budden Geheimnisse. Hotelratten. Wiener Herzen. Der Mann mit der falschen Banknote. Topsy and Eva. Sorrell and Son. 1928: Hollywood Review. When Fleet Meets Fleet. The Blue Danube. Adventure Mad. Laugh Clown Laugh. The Cossacks. Adrienne Lecouvreur. Loves of an Actress. The Cardboard Lover. Our Dancing Daughters. 1929: Dream of Love. Wild Orchids. Hollywood Revue of 1929. The Single Standard. 1930: The Wrath of the Seas. King of Jazz. The Sea Bat. 1931: But the Flesh is Weak. 1932: Letty Lynton. The Washington Masquerade (GB: Mad Masquerade). 1933: If I Were Free (GB: Behold We Live). The Bitter Tea of General Yen. Storm at Daybreak. The Right to Romance. 1934: By Candlelight. Madame Spy. The Crime Doctor. The Love Captive. Love Time. 1935: Abdul the Damned. 1936: The Marriage of Corbal (US: Prisoner of Corbal). Guilty Melody. 1937: Make Up. 1938: Tea Leaves in the Wind. 1940: The Man Who Lost Himself. 1941: Forced Landing. Flying Blind. Dr Kildare's Wedding Day (GB: Mary Names the Day). The Night Before the Divorce. The Night of January 16th. 1942: Sweater Girl. Night Monster (GB: The Hammond Mystery). 1943: Submarine Alert. Mystery Broadcast. 1944: Alaska. The Hour Before Dawn. The Man in Half Moon Street. Bluebeard. 1945: Love, Honor and Goodbye. Son of Lassie. Jealousy. 1948: The Feathered Serpent. 1953: That Man from Tangier. 1960: När Mörket faller. Svenska Floyd. 1962: Vita frun. 1963: Gudrun (US: Suddenly, a Woman!).

ASTOR, Mary
(Lucille Langhanke) 1906–1987
Wanly beautiful, dark-haired American leading lady, capable of great depths. Despite a quite inflammatory private life, she maintained her star status for more than 20 years. Her best role, in *The Maltese Falcon*, came too late to enable her to become the dominant star she might have been, and she drifted into 'mother' roles. Won an Academy Award in 1941 for *The Great Lie*. Forced to retire after

1965 with a heart condition, she died from respiratory failure.
1921: †Sentimental Journey/Sentimental Tommy. *The Beggar Maid. *Bullets or Ballots. *Brother of the Bear. *My Lady o' the Pines. *The Bashful Suitor. 1922: *The Young Painter. Hope. The Angelus. The Man Who Played God. John Smith. 1923: Second Fiddle. Success. The Scarecrow. The Bright Shawl. Puritan Passions. To the Ladies. The Rapids. The Marriage Maker. Hollywood. Woman Proof. 1924: Beau Brummell. The Fighting Coward. Unguarded Woman. Inez from Hollywood (GB: The Good Bad Girl). The Fighting American (GB: The Fighting Adventurer). The Price of a Party. 1925: Oh, Doctor. Enticement. Playing with Souls. Don Q Son of Zorro. The Pace that Thrills. The Scarlet Saint. 1926: Don Juan. The Wise Guy. Forever After. High Steppers. 1927: The Rough Riders (GB: The Trumpet Calls). The Sea Tiger. Sunset Derby. Rose of the Golden West. Two Arabian Knights. No Place to Go. 1928: Heart to Heart. Sailors' Wives. Dressed to Kill. Three-Ring Marriage. Dry Martini. 1929: Romance of the Underworld. New Year's Eve. Woman from Hell. Ladies Love Brutes. 1930: The Runaway Bride. Holiday. The Lash (GB: Adios). The Royal Bed (GB: The Queen's Husband). 1931: Behind Office Doors. Sin Ship. Other Men's Women. White Shoulders. Smart Woman. 1932: Men of Chance. The Lost Squadron. A Successful Calamity. Those We Love. Red Dust. 1933: The Little Giant. Jennie Gerhardt. The World Changes. Convention City. The Kennel Murder Case. 1934: Easy to Love. Upperworld. *The Hollywood Gad-About. The Man with Two Faces. Return of the Terror. The Case of the Howling Dog. 1935: I Am a Thief. Straight from the Heart. Dinky. Page Miss Glory. Red Hot Tires (GB: Racing Luck). Man of Iron. 1936: The Murder of Dr Harrigan. And So They Were Married. Trapped by Television (GB: Caught by Television). Dodsworth. 1937: The Lady from Nowhere. The Prisoner of Zenda. The Hurricane. 1938: Paradise for Three (GB: Romance for Three). No Time to Marry. There's Always a Woman. Woman Against Woman. Listen, Darling. 1939: Midnight. 1940: Turnabout. Brigham Young – Frontiersman (GB: Brigham Young). 1941: The Maltese Falcon. The Great Lie. 1942: In This Our Life. Across the Pacific. The Palm Beach Story. 1943: Young Ideas. Thousands Cheer. 1944: Meet Me in St Louis. Blonde Fever. 1946: Claudia and David. Cynthia (GB: The Rich, Full Life). 1947: Fiesta.

Desert Fury. Cass Timberlane. 1948: Act of Violence. 1949: Little Women. Any Number Can Play. 1956: *The House Without a Name. A Kiss Before Dying. The Power and the Prize. 1957: The Devil's Hairpin. Mr and Mrs McAdam (TV). The Troublemakers (TV). 1958: This Happy Feeling. The Return of Ansel Gibbs (TV). 1959: Stranger in My Arms. Diary of a Nurse (TV). 1960: Journey to the Day (TV). 1961: Return to Peyton Place. 1964: Youngblood Hawke. Hush . . . Hush, Sweet Charlotte.

†Scenes deleted from final release print

ATTENBOROUGH, Sir Richard
(Lord Attenborough) 1923–
Stocky, buoyant, boyish British actor whose film career has divided itself into four phases: as weak and blustering youths (1942–1953); a genial, faintly roguish leading man (1953–1960); a versatile character star (1961–1970); a workmanlike and occasionally inspired director of daunting prestige subjects. Knighted in 1975. Married to Sheila Sim (1922–) since 1945. Won the best director Oscar in 1983 for Gandhi. A stout campaigner and fighter for the British film industry, he proved its guiding light in the mid-1980s. His on-screen credits were limited to films he directed in the 1980s, but, on turning 70, he returned to acting in crusty character roles. Created Lord Attenborough in 1993.
1942: In Which We Serve. 1943: Schweik's New Adventures. The Hundred-Pound Window. 1945: Journey Together. A Matter of Life and Death (US: Stairway to Heaven). 1946: School for Secrets (US: Secret Flight). 1947: The Man Within (US: The Smugglers). Dancing With Crime. Brighton Rock (US: Young Scarface). 1948: London Belongs to Me (US: Dulcimer Street). The Guinea Pig. 1949: The Lost People. Boys in Brown. 1950: Morning Departure (US: Operation Disaster). 1951: Hell is Sold Out. The Magic Box. 1952: *Sports Page No. 6 – Football. The Gift Horse (US: Glory at Sea). Father's Doing Fine. 1953: Eight O'Clock Walk. 1955: The Ship That Died of Shame (US: PT Raiders). Private's Progress. 1956: The Baby and the Battleship. Brothers-in-Law. 1957: The Scamp. 1958: Dunkirk. Sea of Sand (US: Desert Patrol). The Man Upstairs. 1959: Danger Within (US: Breakout). I'm All Right Jack. Jet Storm. SOS Pacific. The League of Gentlemen. 1960: The Angry Silence. 1961: Only Two Can Play. 1962: All Night Long.

The Dock Brief (US: Trial and Error). 1963: The Great Escape. Seance on a Wet Afternoon. 1964: The Third Secret. *A Boy's Day (narrator). Guns at Batasi. 1965: The Flight of the Phoenix. 1966: The Sand Pebbles. 1968: Dr Dolittle. Only When I Larf. The Bliss of Mrs Blossom. 1969: David Copperfield (TV. GB: cinemas). The Magic Christian. 1970: The Last Grenade (US: Grigsby). A Severed Head. Loot. *Don't Make Me Laugh (narrator). 10 Rillington Place. 1971: Cup Glory (narrator only). 1974: Rosebud. And Then There Were None. 1975: Brannigan. 1976: Conduct Unbecoming. 1977: The Chess Players. 1979: The Human Factor. 1986: Mother Teresa (narrator only). 1993: Jurassic Park. 1994: Miracle on 34th Street. 1995: Wavelength. 1996: Hamlet. 1997: The Lost World: Jurassic Park. 1998: Elizabeth. 2000: Liuset haller mig sallskap (doc).
As director. 1969: 1969: Oh! What a Lovely War. 1971: Young Winston. 1977: A Bridge Too Far. 1978: Magic. 1982: Gandhi. 1985: A Chorus Line. 1987: Cry Freedom. 1993: Shadowlands. 1996: In Love and War. 1998: Grey Owl.

AUMONT, Jean-Pierre
(J-P Salomons) 1909–
Sandy-haired, wry-looking romantic French leading man who never quite realized his potential as an international star. In Hollywood from 1942 to 1948 after distinguished war service. Married (second) to Maria Montez (qv) from 1943 to her death in 1951. In 1956 he married actress Marisa Pavan (1932–) and they have since divorced and remarried. Aumont has also written plays and continued to make international films into the late 1990s. His daughter Tina Aumont has also appeared in films.
1931: Echec et mat. 1932: Faut-il les marier? Jean de la Lune. Eve cherche un père. 1933: Dans les rues. La merveilleuse tragédie de Lourdes. Le voleur. Un jour viendra. 1935: Les yeux noirs. Les beaux jours. Maria Chapdelaine. 1936: Lac aux Dames. La porte du Large. Taras Bulba. L'équipage (US: Flight into Darkness). 1937: Cargaison blanche. Drôle de drame (US: Bizarre Bizarre). Le messager. Cheri-Bibi. Maman Colibri. 1938: La femme du bout du monde. Le paradis du Satan. Hôtel du nord. La belle étoile. 1939: Le deserteur (GB: SOS Sahara. US: Three Hours). Songs of the Street. 1943: Assignment in Brittany. 1944: The Cross of Lorraine. 1946: Heartbeat. 1947: Song of Scheherezade. 1948: Siren of

Atlantis. The First Gentleman (US: Affairs of a Rogue). Hans le marin (GB: The Wicked City). 1949: Golden Arrow/Three Men and a Girl (US: The Gay Adventure. Released 1952). 1950: La vie commence demain. L'homme de joie. L'amant de paille. 1951: La vendetta del corsaro. Ultimo incontro. Les loups chassent la nuit. 1952: Lili. 1953: Königsmark. Moineaux de Paris. 1954: Si Versailles m'était conté (GB: Versailles. US: Royal Affairs in Versailles). 18 heures d'escale. Charge of the Lancers. 1955: Napoléon. Mademoiselle de Paris. 1956: Hilda Crane. 1957: The Seventh Sin. 1958: Word from a Sealed-Off Box (TV). 1959: John Paul Jones. 1960: Una domenica d'estate. The Enemy General. 1961: The Devil at Four O'Clock. Carnival of Crime. 1962: The Blonde of Buenos Aires. Les sept péchés capitaux (GB: The Seven Deadly Sins. US: Seven Capital Sins). Five Miles to Midnight. 1963: The Horse without a Head. Always on Sunday (US: A Summer Sunday). 1964: Vacances portugaises. 1967: Cauldron of Blood (US: Blind Man's Bluff). 1969: Castle Keep. 1972: L'homme au cerveau greffé. 1973: La nuit americaine (GB and US: Day for Night). 1974: Porgi l'altra guancia (US: Turn the Other Cheek). 1975: The Happy Hooker. Mahogany. Catherine and Co. 1976: The Man in the Iron Mask. Des journées entières dans les arbres (GB: Entire Days Among the Trees). 1977: Le chat et le souris (GB: Seven Suspects for Murder. US: Cat and Mouse). 1978: Deux solitudes. Blackout. 1979: Something Short of Paradise. 1980: The Memory of Eva Ryker (TV). 1981: Allons z'Enfants. 1982: Difendimi dalle notte. The Evil Touch. Nana. 1983: Le sang des autres. La Java des ombres. 1985: Sweet Country. 1986: On a volé Charlie Spencer! 1987: Johnny Monroe. 1988: A notre regrettable époux. 1990: A Star for Two. 1991: Becoming Colette. 1994: Giorgino. 1995: Jefferson in Paris. 1996: La propriétaire. 1997: Messieurs les enfants (US: Men Will Be Boys).

AUTEUIL, Daniel 1950–
Dark, brooding, introspective Algerian-born actor, the son of travelling opera singers. He was initially a singer himself before turning to acting and breaking into French films in the mid-1970s. He remained pretty anonymous outside France, though, until his award-winning role as Yves Montand's son Ugolin in *Jean de Florette* and *Manon des Sources* brought him to the attention of international audiences. He rather belatedly tried English-language films in the late 1990s, but his heavy French accent seemed to hamper his performances there. Long romantically associated with French actress Emmanuelle Béart, his co-star in *Manon des Sources* and the almost equally successful *Un coeur en hiver*. The couple are now married.

1975: L'agression (GB: TV, as Aggression. US: Act of Aggression). Attention les yeux (GB and US: Let's Make a Dirty Movie). 1976: L'amour violé (US: Rape of Love). La nuit de Saint-Germain des Prés. 1977: Monsieur Papa. 1978: Les héros n'ont pas froid aux oreilles. 1979: Bête mais discipliné. A nous deux/The Two of Us/An Adventure for Two. 1980: Clara et les chics types. Les sous-doués. La banquière. 1981: Les hommes préfèrent les grosses (US: Men Prefer Fat Girls). Les sous-doués en vacances. 1982: Pour 100 briques t'as plus rien maintenant. Que les gros salaires lèvent le doigt. T'empêches tout le monde de dormir. 1983: Les fauves. L'indic. 1984: L'arbalète. P'tit con. The Beast. 1985: Palace/Paris – Palace Hotel. L'amour en douce. Jean de Florette. 1986: Manon des Sources. Le paltoquet. 1988: Quelques jours avec moi. 1989: Romuald et Juliette. Look Who's Talking (French version. Voice only). 1990: La criminel élégant/Lacenaire. 1991: Ma vie est un enfer. 1992: Un coeur en hiver. 1993: Ma saison préférée. 1994: La séparation. La Reine Margot. 1995: Eine Französische Frau. 1996: Le huitième jour. Afirma Pereira. Les voleurs. 1997: Lucie Aubrac. Le bossu/On Guard! 1998: The Lost Son. La fille sur la pont. 1999: Mauvaise passe (US: The Wrong Blonde). An Interesting State. The Escort. 2000: La veuve de Saint-Pierre. Sade.

AUTRY, Gene (Orvon Autry) 1907– 1998
Genial, stocky cowboy star who turned out second-feature westerns for 20 years. As with Roy Rogers, his films mixed action with song and he was one of the top moneymakers in Hollywood films in the early war years. Usually seen with horse Champion, he became a wealthy businessman in later times. Once said: 'I'm no great actor and I'm no great rider and I'm no great singer. But whatever it is I'm doing, they like it.' Remarried in 1981 after his first wife died.
1934: In Old Santa Fé. Mystery Mountain (serial). 1935: The Phantom Empire (serial. GB: Radio Ranch). Tumbling Tumbleweeds. Melody Trail. Sagebrush Troubador. The Singing Vagabond. 1936: Red River Valley. Comin' Round the Mountain. The Singing Cowboy. Guns and Guitars. Oh, Susannah!

*Ride, Ranger, Ride. The Big Show. The Old Corral (GB: Texas Serenade). 1937: Round-Up Time in Texas. Git Along, Little Dogies (GB: Serenade of the West). Rootin' Tootin' Rhythm (GB: Rhythm on the Ranch). Yodelin' Kid from Pine Ridge (GB: The Hero of Pine Ridge). Public Cowboy No 1. Boots and Saddles. Manhattan Merry-Go-Round (GB: Manhattan Music Box). Springtime in the Rockies. 1938: The Old Barn Dance. Gold Mine in the Sky. Man from Music Mountain. Prairie Moon. Rhythm of the Saddle. Western Jamboree. 1939: Home on the Prairie. Mexicali Rose. Blue Montana Skies. Mountain Rhythm. Colorado Sunset. In Old Monterey. Rovin' Tumbleweeds. South of the Border. 1940: Rancho Grande. Shooting High. Gaucho Serenade. Carolina Moon. *Rodeo Dough. Ride, Tenderfoot, Ride. Melody Ranch. 1941: *Meet Roy Rogers. Ridin' on a Rainbow. *Variety Reel. *Stars at Play. *Stars Past and Present. Back in the Saddle. The Singing Hills. Sunset in Wyoming. Under Fiesta Stars. Down Mexico Way. Sierra Sue. 1942: Cowboy Serenade (GB: Serenade of the West). Heart of the Rio Grande. Home in Wyomin'. Stardust on the Sage. Call of the Canyon. Bells of Capistrano. *Screen Snapshots No 108. 1946: Sioux City Sue. 1947: Trail to San Antone. Twilight on the Rio Grande. Saddle Pals. Robin Hood of Texas. The Last Round-Up. 1948: The Strawberry Roan (GB: Fools Awake). 1949: Loaded Pistols. The Big Sombrero. Riders of the Whistling Pines. Rim of the Canyon. *Screen Snapshots No 179. The Cowboy and the Indians. Riders in the Sky. Sons of New Mexico (GB: The Brat). 1950: Mule Train. Beyond the Purple Hills. Cow Town (GB: Barbed Wire). Indian Territory. The Blazing Sun. 1951: Gene Autry and the Mounties. Texans Never Cry. Whirlwind. Silver Canyon. Hills of Utah. Valley of Fire. 1952: The Old West. Night Stage to Galveston. Apache Country. Wagon Team. Blue Canadian Rockies. Barbed Wire (GB: False News). 1953: Winning of the West. On Top of Old Smoky. Goldtown Ghost Riders. Pack Train. *Memories in Uniform. Saginaw Trial. Last of the Pony Riders. 1954: Hollywood Cowboy Stars. 1959: Alias Jesse James. 1968: Silent Treatment. 1976: It's Showtime.*

AVALON, Frankie
(Francis Avallone) 1939–
Bright, slight, bouncy American actor-singer with dark, curly hair, whose boyish looks and cheerful personality kept him popular with

the teenage audience until the late 1960s, especially in 'beach' movies, which he successfully guyed in 1987's *Back to the Beach*, looking a little more serious but otherwise just the same as ever. He has eight children.

1957: *Jamboree (GB: Disc Jockey Jamboree)*. 1959: *Guns of the Timberland*. 1960: *The Alamo*. 1961: *Alakazam the Great (voice only)*. *Sail a Crooked Ship*. 1962: *The Castilian*. *Panic in Year Zero*. *Voyage to the Bottom of the Sea*. 1963: *Operation Bikini*. *Drums of Africa*. *Beach Party*. 1964: *Bikini Beach*. *Pajama Party*. *Muscle Beach Party*. 1965: *Dr Goldfoot and the Bikini Machine (GB: Dr G. and the Bikini Machine)*. *Beach Blanket Bingo (GB: Malibu Beach)*. *Ski Party*. *How to Stuff a Wild Bikini*. *Sergeant Deadhead*. *I'll Take Sweden*. *Survival*. 1966: *Fireball 500*. *Pajama Party in a Haunted House*. 1967: *The Jet Set*. *Sumuru (GB: The Million Eyes of Sumuru)*. 1968: *Skidoo*. 1969: *Ski Fever*. *The Haunted House of Horror*. 1974: *The Take*. *The Hunters (TV)*. 1978: *Grease*. 1982: *Blood Song*. 1987: *Back to the Beach*. 1989: *Troop Beverly Hills (video clip only)*. 1993: *The Stoned Age*. 1995: *A Dream is a Wish Your Heart Makes: The Annette Funicello Story (TV)*.

AYKROYD, Dan 1951–

Slack-jawed, laconic-looking Canadian comic actor with dark hair flopping forward. He came to films with his TV partner John Belushi (after a minor debut in his native country) providing the same kind of wildly anarchic scatological comedy the pair had pioneered on TV's *Saturday Night Live*. After Belushi's death, Aykroyd paused, then continued making comedy films with other partners (Bill Murray, Eddie Murphy, Chevy Chase). He still prefers working 'in collaboration'. Married to actress Donna Dixon. Oscar nominee for *Driving Miss Daisy*. Gained weight dramatically after the mid 1980s, and became a formidable character star.

1977: *Love at First Sight*. 1979: *Mr Mike's Mondo Video*. 1980: *The Blues Brothers*. 1981: *Neighbors*. 1982: *It Came from Hollywood (video)*. 1983: *Doctor Detroit*. *Trading Places*. *The Twilight Zone (GB: Twilight Zone the Movie)*. 1984: *Ghost Busters*. *Indiana Jones and the Temple of Doom*. *Nothing Lasts Forever*. 1985: *Into the Night*. *Spies Like Us*. 1987: *Dragnet*. *The Couch Trip*. 1988: *My Stepmother is an Alien*. *The Great Outdoors*.

Caddyshack II. 1989: *Loose Cannons*. *Ghostbusters II*. *Driving Miss Daisy*. 1990: *Nothing But Trouble (and directed)*. *Masters of Menace*. 1991: *My Girl*. *This is My Life*. 1992: *Chaplin*. *Sneakers*. 1993: *Coneheads*. 1994: *My Girl 2*. *Exit to Eden*. *North*. 1995: *Getting Away with Murder*. *Rainbow*. *Canadian Bacon*. *Casper*. 1996: *Celtic Pride*. *Sgt Bilko*. *Feeling Minnesota*. *My Fellow Americans*. 1997: *Grosse Pointe Blank*. *The Arrow (TV)*. 1998: *Antz (voice only)*. *Susan's Plan*. 1999: *Diamonds*. 2000: *The House of Mirth*. *Home Brew*. *Hitting the Wall*. *Loser*. *Stardom*. 2001: *Unconditional Love*.

AYRES, Agnes (A. Hinkle) 1896–1940

Petite, dark-haired American leading lady of silent days, whose little-girl-lost, black-eyed appeal kept the men watching while their girlfriends had eyes only for her two-time co-star Rudolph Valentino. Her career was virtually ended by the coming of sound which found her the right age for character roles but unable to mature into them. She died tragically from a cerebral haemorrhage at 44.

1915: **†His New Job*. 1916: *†The Dazzling Miss Davison (GB: Who is She?)*. 1917: *†The Venturers*. *†The Furnished Room*. *†Mrs Belfame*. *†The Mirror*. *†Hedda Gabler*. *†Motherhood*. *†The Debt*. *†Richard the Brazen*. *†The Defeat of the City*. *†The Girl and the Graft*. *†The Purple Dress*. 1918: *The Enchanted Profile*. *The Bottom of the Well*. *$1,000*. 1919: *The Sacred Silence*. *Forbidden Fruit*. 1920: *The Furnace*. *Held by the Enemy*. *A Modern Salome*. *Go and Get It*. *The Inner Voice*. 1921: *The Affairs of Anatol (GB: A Prodigal Knight)*. *The Sheik*. *Cappy Ricks*. *The Love Special*. *Too Much Speed*. 1922: *Clarence*. *The Ordeal*. *The Lane That Had No Turning*. *Bought and Paid For*. **A Trip to Paramount-town*. *Borderland*. *A Daughter of Luxury*. 1923: *The Ten Commandments*. *Tess of the Storm Country*. *Racing Hearts*. *Hollywood*. *The Marriage Maker. (GB: The Faun)*. *The Heart Raider*. 1924: *The Story without a Name (GB: Without Warning)*. *When a Girl Loves*. *Bluff (GB: The Four Flusher)*. *Don't Call It Love*. *The Guilty One*. *Worldly Goods*. 1925: *Tomorrow's Love*. *Morals for Men*. *The Awful Truth*. 1926: *The Lady of Victory*. *Napoleon and Josephine*. *Into the Night*. 1929: *Bye, Bye, Buddy*. *The Donovan Affair*. *Broken Hearted*. 1936: *Small Town Girl*. 1937: **Morning, Judge*. *Souls at Sea*. *Maid of Salem*.

†*As Agnes Ayars*   ‡*As Agnes Eyre*

AYRES, Lew (Lewis Ayer) 1908–1996

Softly spoken, diffident American leading man who, after beginning his career as a danceband musician, became famous both as the young soldier in *All Quiet on the Western Front* and in the *Dr Kildare* series. Career effectively spoiled when he declared himself a conscientious objector during World War II in which he eventually served as a medical orderly. Married to Lola Lane (Dorothy Mullican, 1909–1981) from 1931 to 1933 and to Ginger Rogers (*qv*) from 1934 to 1941, first and second of three wives. Oscar nominee for *Johnny Belinda*. Died in his sleep.

1929: *The Sophomore*. *Big News*. *The Shake-down*. *The Kiss*. 1930: *Compromised*. *All Quiet on the Western Front*. *Common Clay*. *The Doorway to Hell (GB: A Handful of Clouds)*. *East is West*. 1931: *Iron Man*. *Up for Murder*. *Many a Slip*. *Spirit of Notre Dame (GB: Vigour of Youth)*. *Heaven on Earth*. 1932: *The Impatient Maiden*. *Night World*. *Okay America! (GB: Penalty of Fame)*. *The Cohens and Kellys in Hollywood*. 1933: *State Fair*. *Don't Bet on Love*. *My Weakness*. 1934: *Cross Country Cruise*. *She Learned About Sailors*. *Let's Be Ritzy (GB: Millionaire for a Day)*. 1935: *Servants' Entrance*. *Lottery Lover*. *Silk Hat Kid*. *Spring Tonic*. 1936: *The Leathernecks Have Landed (GB: The Marines Have Landed)*. *Panic on the Air (GB: Trapped by Wireless)*. *Shakedown*. *Murder with Pictures*. 1937: *Lady Be Careful*. *The Crime Nobody Saw*. *Last Train from Madrid*. *Hold 'Em Navy (GB: That Navy Spirit)*. 1938: *Scandal Street*. *Holiday (GB: Free to Live/ Unconventional Linda)*. *King of the Newsboys*. *Rich Man – Poor Girl*. *Young Dr Kildare*. 1939: *Ice Follies of 1939*. *Broadway Serenade*. *Calling Dr Kildare*. *These Glamour Girls*. *Remember?* *Secret of Dr Kildare*. *Dr Kildare's Strange Case*. *The Golden Fleecing*. *Crisis*. *Dr Kildare Goes Home*. 1941: *Maisie was a Lady*. *The People versus Dr Kildare (GB: My Life is Yours)*. 1942: *Dr Kildare's Wedding Day (GB: Mary Names the Day)*. *Dr Kildare's Victory (GB: The Doctor and the Debutante)*. *Fingers at the Window*. 1946: *The Dark Mirror*. 1947: *The Unfaithful*. 1948: *Johnny Belinda*. 1950: *The Capture*. 1951: *New Mexico*. 1953: *No Escape*. *Donovan's Brain*. 1956: *The Family Nobody Wanted (TV)*. 1961: *Advise and Consent*. 1963: *The Carpetbaggers*. 1971: *Earth II (TV)*. *The Man*. *The Last Generation*. *She Waits (TV)*. 1972: *The Stranger (TV)*. *The Biscuit Eater*. 1973: *Battle for the Planet of the*

Apes. The Questor Tapes (TV). 1974: Heatwave (TV). 1976: The Last Tycoon. 1977: End of the World. Francis Gary Powers – The True Story of the U2 Incident (TV). 1978: Damien – Omen II. Suddenly Love (TV). Battlestar Galactica (TV. GB: cinemas). 1979: Letters from Frank. Salem's Lot (TV). 1981: Of Mice and Men (TV). 1985: Lime Street (TV). 1986: Under Siege (TV). 1989: Cast the First Stone (TV). 1994: Hart to Hart: Crimes of the Hart (TV).
As director: 1936: Hearts in Bondage.

AZMI, Shabana 1952–

Glowingly, gravely beautiful Indian actress, daughter of the noted poet Kaifi Azmi. Awarded the equivalent of an Indian Oscar in her first film, she has since straddled the three worlds of Indian art cinema, Indian popular cinema and international cinema with remarkable grace and dexterity. After three further Indian Oscars in the 1980s, her talents reached western audiences in such films as Madame Sousatzka and City of Joy.

1974: Ankur/The Seedling. Ishq, Ishq, Ishq. 1975: Nishant/Night's End. Faslah. Kadamberi. Parinay. Sewak. 1976: Fakira. Vishwasghaat. 1977: Aadha din, aadhee raat. The Chess Players/Shatranj ke kilhari. Ek hi rasta. Hira aur Patthar. Parvarish. Amar Akbar Anthony. Chor sipahi. Karm. Khel Khiladi ka. Swami. Zamanat. 1978: Junoon/Obsession. Kanneshwara rama. Shaque/The Trial. Atithee. Devata. Khoon ki pukar. Swarg narak. Toote Khilone. 1979: Amardeep. Bagula bhagat. Ashanti. Lahu ke do rang. Sparsh. 1980: Apne paraye. Jwalamukhi. Ek baar kaho. Yeh kaisa insaaf. Thodisi bewafai. 1981: Shama. Sameera. Why Albert Pinto is Angry/Albert Pinto ko gussa kyon aata hai. Hum paanch. Jeena yahan. Ek hi bhool. 1982: Namkeen. Yeh nazdeekiyan. Raaste Pyare ke. Suraag. Anokha bandhan. 1983: Doosri. Masoom. Doolhan. Mandi/The Marketplace. Arth. Sweekar kiya maine. Log kya kahenge. Khandhar. Pyaasi aankhen. 1984: Itihaas. Aaj ka M.L.A. Ram Avtaar. Bhavna. Libaas. Lorie. Khandar/The Ruins. Kamyaab. 1985: Kamla. Susman/The Essence. Mr X. Paar. Ram tera desh. Rahi badal gaye. Khamosh. Shart. Uttarayan. 1986: Genesis Ek pal. Anjuman. Nasihat. Samay ki dhara. 1987: Itihaas. Jallianwala bagh. 1988: Apne paraye. Pestonjee. Mardon wali baat. Ek din achanak. Madame Sousatzka. The Bengali Night. 1989: Sati. Libaas. Oonch neech beech. Jhoothi sharm. Main azaad hoon. Rakhwala. 1990: Disha/

The Immigrants. Picnic (TV). Ek doktor ki maut. Amba. Muqaddar ka badshah. 1991: Immaculate Conception. 1992: City of Joy. City of Dreams/Dharavie. Adharm. Jhoothi shaan. Antarnaad. 1993: Son of the Pink Panther. In Custody/Hifizaat. 1994: Patang/The Kite. 1996: Fire. 1997: Mrityudand (US: Death Sentence). 1998: Side Streets. Earth (voice only). 1999: Godmother.

AZNAVOUR, Charles
(Shahnour Aznavurjan) 1924–
Tiny, dark-eyed French actor-singer-composer of Armenian origin, self-described as 'a small man with a nose like a can-opener', but the romantic idol of millions, especially singing equally romantic songs. Aznavour, who started out in show business as a dancer, has only toyed with films, but sometimes in unusual and rewarding roles.

1938: Les disparus de Saint-Agil (US: Boys' School). La guerre des gosses. 1945: Adieu Chérie. 1950: Dans la vie tout s'arrange. 1956: Une gosse sans cesse. 1957: Paris Music-Hall. C'est arrivé a 36 chandelles. 1958: Les dragueurs (GB: The Young Have No Morals. US: The Chasers). La tête contre les murs. 1959: La testament d'Orphée. 1960: Tirez sur le pianiste (GB: Shoot the Pianist! US: Shoot the Piano Player). La passage du Rhin (GB: Tomorrow is My Turn). Taxi for Tobruk. 1961: Les lions sont lachés. Les petits matins. Horace '62. 1962: Le rat d'Amérique. Les vierges. Tempo di Roma. Les quatres verités (GB and US: Three Fables of Love). Pourquoi Paris? The Devil and the 10 Commandments. 1964: Alta infidelità (GB and US: High Infidelity). Cherchez l'idole (GB: The Chase). 1965: Le metamorphose des Cloportes. Paris in August. 1966: Le facteur s'en va-t-en guerre. 1967: Caroline Chérie. 1968: Candy. The Games. L'amour. 1969: Le temps des loups. 1970: The Adventurers. Un beau monstre. 1971: Les intrus. La part des lions. 1973: The Blockhouse. 1974: And Then There Were None. 1976: Folies bourgeoises/The Twist. Sky Riders. 1979: The Tin Drum. Ciao, les mecs. 1981: Les fantômes du chapelier (US: The Hatter's Ghost). 1982: Qu'est-ce que fait courir David? Die Zauberberg (US: The Magic Mountain). 1983: Édith et Marcel. Une Jeunesse. 1984: Viva la vie. 1986: Yiddish Connection. 1988: Mangeclous. Migrations. 1989: Il maestro. 1992: Les années campagne. 1997: Sans cérémonie. Pondichéry. Le comédian. 1999: Le messie.

B

BACLANOVA, Olga 1899–1974
Fierce, intense, dark-haired Russian actress (a former ballet dancer) whose Hollywood career as a star was brief, but contains two performances still remembered today – in Josef Von Sternberg's *Docks of New York* and Tod Browning's *Freaks*. She came to America at 24 and stayed for many years (her heavy and inimitable tones hosting radio programmes in the 1930s) before eventually retiring to Switzerland. Sometimes blonde.
1914: *Symphony of Love and Death. When the Strings of the Heart Sound.* 1915: *The Great Magaraz. The Wanderer beyond the Grave.* 1916: *He Who Gets Slapped.* 1917: *The Flowers Are Late.* 1918: *Bread.* 1927: *The Dove.* 1928: *The Street of Sin. Forgotten Faces. The Docks of New York. Avalanche. Three Sinners. The Man Who Laughs.* 1929: *A Dangerous Woman. The Wolf of Wall Street. The Man I Love.* 1930: *Are You There? Cheer Up and Smile.* 1931: *The Great Lover.* *Screen Snapshots No. 4.* 1932: *Freaks. Downstairs.* 1933: *The Billion Dollar Scandal.* 1935: *Broadway Brevities.* *The Telephone Blues.* 1936: *The Double Crossky.* 1943: *Claudia.*

BACALL, Lauren (Betty Perske) 1924–
Tall, slinky, blonde, feline, husky-voiced American leading lady, dubbed 'The Look' who, at 20, co-starred with Humphrey Bogart (*qv*) in her first film, and was married to him from 1945 until his death in 1957. Married to Jason Robards Jnr (also *qv*) from 1961 to 1973. She has made too few films, especially in the late 1940s' period when she was at her best. Later returned in acerbic semi-leads and won an Academy Award nomination for *The Mirror Has Two Faces.*
1944: *To Have and Have Not.* 1945: *Confidential Agent.* 1946: *Two Guys from Milwaukee (GB: Royal Flush). The Big Sleep.* 1947: *Dark Passage.* 1948: *Key Largo.* 1949: *Young Man with a Horn (GB: Young Man of Music).* 1950: *Bright Leaf.* 1953: *How to Marry a Millionaire.* 1954: *Woman's World.* 1955: *The Cobweb.* *Salute to the Theatres. Blood Alley.* 1956: *Written on the Wind.* 1957: *Designing Woman.* 1958: *The Gift of Love.* 1959: *Northwest Frontier (US: Flame over India).* 1964: *Shock Treatment. Sex and the Single Girl.* 1966: *Harper (GB: The Moving Target).* 1974: *Murder on the Orient Express.* 1976: *The Shootist.* 1977: *Perfect Gentlemen (TV).* 1979: *Health.* 1981: *The Fan.* 1988: *Appointment with Death. Mr North. John Huston. Dinner at Eight (TV).* 1989: *The Tree of Hands.* 1990: *Misery. The Actor. A Star for Two.* 1992: *All I Want for Christmas.* 1993: *The Portrait (TV). A Foreign Field (TV. US: cinemas).* 1994: *Prêt-à-Porter (US: Ready to Wear).* 1996: *The Mirror Has Two Faces. My Fellow Americans. Le jour et la nuit.* 1999: *Diamonds. Presence of Mind. The Venice Project.* 2000: *Johnny Hit and Run Pauline.*

BACON, Kevin 1958–
Long-faced, snub-nosed, brown-haired American actor whose truculent good looks seemed to fit him for roles as bullies and psychos. In fact, he's often played straight-A guys, but showed he could be good at being bad in *Criminal Law* and *Sleepers*, and has proved an ace at sadism and sarcasm. Once the youngest student at a Pennsylvania actors' theatre, Bacon is married to actress Kyra Sedgwick.
1978: *National Lampoon's Animal House.* 1979: *The Gift (TV). Starting Over.* 1980:

Friday the 13th. Hero at Large. 1981: *Only When I Laugh (GB: It Hurts Only When I Laugh).* 1982: *Diner. Forty-Deuce.* 1983: *The Demon Murder Case (TV). Enormous Changes at the Last Minute.* 1984: *Footloose. Mister Roberts (TV).* 1986: *Quicksilver.* 1987: *White Water Summer (completed 1985). Lemon Sky (TV). Planes, Trains and Automobiles. End of the Line.* 1988: *She's Having a Baby. The Big Picture. Criminal Law.* 1990: *Tremors. Queens Logic. Flatliners.* 1991: *He Said, She Said. JFK. Pyrates.* 1992: *A Few Good Men.* 1993: *The Air Up There.* 1994: *Murder in the First. The River Wild.* 1995: *Balto (voice only). Apollo 13.* 1996: *Sleepers.* 1997: *Picture Perfect. Telling Lies in America. Digging to China.* 1998: *Wild Things.* 1999: *My Dog Skip. A Stir of Echoes.* 2000: *Hollow Man.*
As director: 1996: *Losing Chase (TV).*

BAKER, Carroll 1931–
Blonde American actress, mainly in 'bitchy' roles. She moved easily from teenage nymphets to faintly overblown blondes with the passing of the years. Something of a sensation in her first major role, as the thumb-sucking Baby Doll, a part that won her an Oscar nomination, she subsequently proved difficult to cast to box-office profitability, sometimes turning to continental sex films to keep her career ticking over. Still around in 'grande dame' roles.
1953: *Easy to Love.* 1956: *Baby Doll. Giant.* 1958: *The Big Country.* 1959: *The Miracle. But Not for Me.* 1961: *Something Wild. Bridge to the Sun.* 1962: *How the West Was Won.* 1963: *Station Six Sahara. The Carpetbaggers.* 1964: *Cheyenne Autumn.* 1965: *Sylvia. The Greatest Story Ever Told. Mr Moses. Harlow.* 1967: *The Harem (US: Her Harem). Jack of Diamonds.* 1968: *Orgasmo (GB: Paranoia). Paranoia (GB: A Quiet Place to Kill). The Sweet Body of Deborah.* 1969: *Con dolce . . . cosi perversa/So Sweet . . . So Perverse.* 1970: *The Spider.* 1971: *At the Bottom of the Pool/The Fourth Mrs Anderson. Captain Apache.* 1972: *The Devil Has Seven Faces. Il cottello di ghiaccio/Behind the Silence. Bloody Mary.* 1973: *Baba Yaga – Devil Witch. The Flower with the Deadly Sting. The Madness of Love.* 1974: *Il corpo (US: The Body. GB: Take This My Body).* 1975: *James Dean – The First American Teenager. The Private Lesson. The Lure. The Sky is Falling. La moglie vergine (GB and US: Virgin Wife).* 1976: *La moglie di mio padre (GB: Confessions of a Frustrated Housewife). Zerschossene Träume. Bad/Andy*

Warhol's Bad. 1977: Cyclone. 1978: Ab Morgen sind wir reich und ehrlich (US: Rich and Respectable). 1979: The World is Full of Married Men. 1981: The Watcher in the Woods. 1983: Red Monarch (TV). The Secret Diary of Sigmund Freud. Star 80. 1985: Hitler's SS: Portrait in Evil (TV. GB: cinemas). What Mad Pursuit? (TV). 1986: Native Son. On Fire (TV). 1987: Ironweed. 1989: Fatal Spell. 1990: Kindergarten Cop. Gipsy Angel. 1991: Blonde Fist. Those Bedroom Eyes (TV). Tales from the Crypt (TV). 1993: Jackpot (US: Cybereden). Men Don't Tell (TV). A Kiss to Die For (TV). Judgment Day: The John List Story (TV). 1995: Desperate Measures. 1996: Skeletons. Just Your Luck/Whiskey Down. 1997: North Shore Fish (TV). The Game. Heart Full of Rain (TV). Silent Hearts (TV). 2000: Another Woman's Husband (TV).

BAKER, Diane 1938–
Demure, sensitive, pretty, dark-haired American actress, capable of projecting great warmth, but not progressing beyond ingenue roles in films. She was often successful, strangely, as outwardly calm characters capable of great spite, as in Hitchcock's *Marnie*. Nice to see her so busy in TV movies in the 1970s, but, in 1980, she became a producer. In the 1990s, she returned to acting roles, looking considerably more mature.
1958: The Diary of Anne Frank. 1959: The Best of Everything. Journey to the Center of the Earth. Della (TV). 1960: Tess of the Storm Country. 1961: The Wizard of Baghdad. 1962: Hemingway's Adventures of a Young Man (GB: Adventures of a Young Man). The 300 Spartans. Nine Hours to Rama. 1963: Stolen Hours. 1964: Straitjacket. The Prize. Marnie. 1965: Mirage. 1966: Sands of Beersheba. The Dangerous Days of Kiowa Jones (TV. GB: cinemas). 1968: The Horse in the Gray Flannel Suit. Krakatoa, East of Java. 1969: Trial Run (TV). The DA: Murder One (TV). The Old Man Who Cried Wolf (TV). Wheeler and Murdock (TV). 1971: The Badge or the Cross (TV). Killer by Night (TV). Congratulations It's a Boy (TV). A Little Game (TV). 1972: The Sagittarius Mine (TV). 1973: Police Story (TV. GB: cinemas). 1974: Half-Way to Danger. A Tree Grows in Brooklyn (TV). Can I Save My Children? (TV). 1975: The Dream Makers (TV). The Last Survivors (TV). 1976: Baker's Hawk. Stigma (TV). Summer of 69 (TV). 1979: The Pilot. 1980: Fugitive Family (TV). 1990: The Silence of the Lambs. 1991: The Closer. The Haunted (TV).

BAKER, George 1929–
Quiet, dark, very tall British leading man (born in Bulgaria of Irish parents), popular for a few years in the late fifties in a good variety of roles. Later played senior civil servants, tried a comedy series on TV and made a series of mystery films for TV in New Zealand. Popular on TV in the 1990s in the 'Ruth Rendell' mysteries. Married (second; first wife died) actress Louie Ramsey, his co-star in that series.
*1953: The Intruder. 1954: Double Exposure. The Dam Busters. 1955: The Ship That Died of Shame (US: PT Raiders). The Woman for Joe. 1956: The Feminine Touch (US: The Gentle Touch). The Extra Day. A Hill in Korea (US: Hell in Korea). 1957: These Dangerous Years (US: Dangerous Youth). No Time for Tears. 1958: The Moonraker. Tread Softly, Stranger. 1963: Lancelot and Guinevere (US: Sword of Lancelot). 1964: The Finest Hours (voice only). The Curse of the Fly. 1967: Mister Ten Per Cent. 1969: Goodbye Mr Chips. Justine. On Her Majesty's Secret Service. 1970: The Executioner. 1972: A Warm December. The Rape. 1973: *The Laughing Girl Murder. 1974: The Firefighters. Three for All. 1975: The Twelve Tasks of Asterix (English-language version, voice only). 1976: Intimate Games. 1977: The Spy Who Loved Me. 1978: Died in the Wool (TV). Colour Scheme (TV). Vintage Murder (TV). Opening Night (TV). The Thirty Nine Steps. 1979: North Sea Hijack (US: ffolkes). 1980: The Biggest Bank Robbery (TV). Hopscotch. 1986: Coast to Coast (TV). 1987: Out of Order. 1988: For Queen and Country.*

BAKER, Joe Don 1936–
Burly, surly, flop-haired, giant-sized American actor who had a habit of crashing his way through tough thrillers. A late starter in films, he unexpectedly became a star of medium-budget mayhem in the 1970s. He was more successful in America than internationally, where his films were less commercial after 1975, and his expanding girth made him ever more fearsome, perhaps more suited to villainy than heroism. There was a

1992: Perry Mason: The Case of the Heartbroken Bride (TV). 1993: Twenty Bucks. The Joy Luck Club. 1994: Imaginary Crimes. 1995: The Net. 1996: The Cable Guy. Courage Under Fire. 1997: Murder at 1600. 1998: About Sarah (TV). 1999: Mulholland Drive (TV). 2001: Hannibal.

TV detective series as the gruff Eischied in the early 1980s; more recently he has been seen in character roles as smiling, untrust-worthy figures of power.
1967: Cool Hand Luke. 1969: Guns of the Magnificent Seven. 1970: Adam at 6 a.m. 1971: Mongo's Back in Town (TV). 1972: Junior Bonner. Wild Rovers. Charley Varrick. Walking Tall. Welcome Home, Soldier Boys. That Certain Summer (TV). 1973: The Outfit. 1974: Golden Needles. 1975: Framed. Mitchell. 1976: Checkered Flag or Crash. 1977: The Pack (GB: The Long Hard Night). The Shadow of Chikara/Wishbone Cutter. Speedtrap. 1978: To Kill a Cop (TV). Streets of Fear (TV). 1979: Power (TV). 1982: Wacko. 1983: Joysticks. 1984: The Natural. The Maltese Connection/Final Justice. 1985: Fletch. 1986: Hostage Dallas. Getting Even. 1987: The Living Daylights. Perfect Stranger. The Abduction of Kari Swenson (TV). The Killing Time. Leonard Part VI. 1988: Criminal Law. Defrosting the Fridge (TV). 1990: The Children. 1991: Cape Fear. 1992: The Distinguished Gentleman. Citizen Cohn (cable TV). 1993: Complex of Fear (TV). Ring of Steel. 1994: Reality Bites. Panther. 1995: GoldenEye. The Underneath. The Grass Harp. 1996: Felony. Mars Attacks! Ruby Ridge: An American Tragedy (TV. GB: The Siege at Ruby Ridge). 1997: Tomorrow Never Dies. George Wallace (TV). 1998: The Man in the Iron Mask (Richert). Poodle Springs (TV). 1999: Forces of Nature. 2001: The Adventures of Joe Dirt.

BAKER, Kathy 1947–
Compactly-built American actress of sensual looks, challenging gaze and a mass of light, curly hair. The daughter of a Texas Quaker family, she has been torn between acting and

cooking for most of her career, studying the former in America, and the latter at the Cordon Bleu school in Paris. Returning to America, she worked as a pastry chef, then ran her own catering business while continuing to act at night. She broke into films in her mid thirties, and although her award-winning performance in *Street Smart* brought her leading roles, her undynamic personality has prevented her achieving her full potential in the medium. She has been in the odd salty character role since the early 1990s.

1983: *The Right Stuff*. 1985: *A Killing Affair (later My Sister's Keeper)*. 1986: *Nobody's Child (TV)*. *Street Smart*. 1988: *Permanent Record*. *Clean and Sober*. *Jacknife*. 1989: *Dad*. *The Image (TV)*. 1990: *Edward Scissorhands*. *Mister Frost*. 1991: *One Special Victory (TV)*. *Article 99*. 1992: *Jennifer Eight*. *Mad Dog and Glory*. *Picket Fences (TV)*. 1993: *Lush Life (cable TV. GB: cinemas)*. 1996: *To Gillian on Her 37th Birthday*. *Inventing the Abbotts*. 1997: *Weapons of Mass Destruction (cable TV)*. *Not in This Town (TV)*. 1998: *Oklahoma City: A Survivor's Story (TV)*. 1999: *The Cider House Rules*. *A Season for Miracles (TV)*. *A.T.F. (TV)*. *Things You Can Tell Just by Looking at Her*. 2000: *Ratz (TV)*.

BAKER, Sir Stanley 1927–1976
Forceful Welsh-born actor (knighted in 1976), whose career progressed predictably from villains-you-love-to-hate to tough and some times crooked central characters. His hard, uncompromising crime films of the early sixties pioneered the way for a new realism – especially in terms of dialogue – in British films of the genre. His star faded in the seventies, and he died from pneumonia after an operation.

1943: *Undercover (US: Underground Guerillas)*. 1948: *All Over the Town*. 1949: *Obsession (US: The Hidden Room)*. 1950: *Something in the City*. *Your Witness (US: Eye Witness)*. *Lilli Marlene*. 1951: *The Rossiter Case*. *Captain Horatio Hornblower RN*. *Home to Danger*. *Cloudburst*. *Whispering Smith Hits London (US: Whispering Smith versus Scotland Yard)*. 1953: *The Cruel Sea*. *The Red Beret (US: Paratrooper)*. **The Tell Tale Heart*. *Hell Below Zero*. 1954: *The Good Die Young*. *Knights of the Round Table*. *Beautiful Stranger (US: Twist of Fate)*. *Helen of Troy*. 1955: *Richard III*. 1956: *Child in the House*. *Alexander the Great*. *A Hill in Korea (US: Hell in Korea)*. *Checkpoint*. 1957: *Hell Drivers*. *Campbell's Kingdom*. *Violent Play-*

ground. 1958: *Sea Fury*. 1959: *The Angry Hills*. *Blind Date*. *Jet Storm*. *Yesterday's Enemy*. 1960: *Hell is a City*. *The Criminal (US: The Concrete Jungle)*. 1961: *The Guns of Navarone*. 1962: *A Prize of Arms*. *The Last Days of Sodom and Gomorrah*. *The Man Who Finally Died*. *In the French Style*. *Eva*. 1963: *Zulu*. 1965: *Dingaka*. **One of Them is Brett (narrator only)*. *Sands of the Kalahari*. *Who Has Seen the Wind? (TV)*. 1967: *Accident*. *Robbery*. *Code Name Heraclitus (TV)*. 1969: *La ragazza con la pistola (US: Girl with a Pistol)*. *Where's Jack?* *The Games*. 1970: *Perfect Friday*. *Popsy Pop (GB: The 21 Carat Snatch*. *US: The Butterfly Affair)*. *The Last Grenade (US: Grigsby)*. 1971: *A Lizard in a Woman's Skin (US: Schizoid)*. 1972: *Innocent Bystanders*. 1975: *Zorro*. *Orzowei*. *Pepita Jiminez/Bride To Be*.

BALDWIN, Alec
(Alexander Baldwin) 1958–
Tall, softly-spoken American actor with thick, dark hair, very handsome in a faintly mean-looking sort of way. From a family of actors – his brothers Stephen, William (both *qv*) and Daniel are all in films – he was stuck in TV soaps for several years, where the contrasting facets of his personality were hardly exploited. Since gaining a foothold in films in the late 1980s, he has proved a hard worker, although most of his starring films in recent times have been less than satisfactory. After a vivid early love life, he married one of his co-stars, Kim Basinger (*qv*), in 1991. One of Hollywood's more politically-minded stars, never afraid to speak his mind: in the mid 1990s, he was considering a full-time entry into politics.

1984: *Sweet Revenge (TV)*. 1985: *Love on the Run (TV)*. 1986: *Forever, Lulu*. 1987: *She's Having a Baby*. *The Alamo: 13 Days to Glory (TV)*. 1988: *Beetlejuice*. *Talk Radio*. *Married to the Mob*. *Working Girl*. 1989: *Miami Blues*. *Great Balls of Fire!* 1990: *The Hunt for Red October*. *The Marrying Man (GB: Too Hot to Handle)*. *Alice*. 1992: *Prelude to a Kiss*. *Glengarry Glen Ross*. 1993: *Malice*. *Earth and the American Dream (voice only)*. 1994: *The Getaway*. *The Shadow*. 1995: *Heaven's Prisoners*. *Two Bits (narrator only)*. *Wild Bill: Hollywood Maverick (narrator only)*. 1996: *Looking for Richard*. *The Juror*. *Ghosts of Mississippi (GB: Ghosts of the Past)*. 1997: *The Edge*. 1998: *Mercury Rising*. *Outside Providence*. *The Confession*. 1999: *Scout's Honor*. *Thick As Thieves*. *Notting Hill*. 2000:

State and Main. *Thomas and the Magic Railroad*. 2001: *Final Fantasy: The Movie (voice only)*. *Pearl Harbor*.

BALDWIN, Stephen 1966–
Long, lean, lounging, fair-haired American actor, often in leering or rebellious roles as unkempt nonconformists. The younger brother of Alec and William Baldwin (both *qv*), but looser-limbed and less conventional, he made a slow start to his film career but had moved forward to co-starring roles by the mid 1990s. Still busy, but mostly on straight-to-video titles.

1988: *The Beast*. *Homeboy*. 1989: *Last Exit to Brooklyn*. *Jury Duty: The Comedy/The Great American Sex Scandal (TV)*. *Born on the Fourth of July*. 1992: *Crossing the Bridge*. 1993: *8 Seconds*. *Threesome*. *Posse*. *Bitter Harvest*. 1994: *A Simple Twist of Fate*. *Fall Time*. *Mrs Parker and the Vicious Circle*. *New Eden*. 1995: *Dead Weekend*. *Under the Hula Moon*. *The Usual Suspects*. 1996: *Sub Down (TV)*. 1998: *One Tough Cop*. *The Object of My Affection*. *Mr Murder (TV)*. *Scarred City*. 1999: *Absence of the Good (TV)*. *Table One*. *Friends & Lovers*. *The Sex Monster*. *Mercy*. 2000: *The Flintstones in Viva Rock Vegas*. *Cutaway*. *Xchange*.

BALDWIN, William or Billy 1963–
Long-faced, dark-haired American actor with confidently knowing smile, often in mischievously sexy roles. The tallest of the four acting Baldwin brothers at 6ft 4in, he graduated from law school, but did modelling and acting in TV commercials before taking acting and dramatic lessons, followed in very short order by leading roles in films. He didn't quite make top-order stardom, though

he counterbalances a tendency to mumble dialogue with considerable personal charm, and can also convey menace when required.
1989: Born on the Fourth of July. The Preppie Murders (TV). 1990: Flatliners. Internal Affairs. 1991: Backdraft. 1993: Three of Hearts. Sliver. G.A.M.M.A. Force (voice only). The Last Party (doc). 1995: A Pyromaniac's Love Story. Fair Game. 1996: Curdled. 1997: Virus (released 1998). 1998: Shattered Image. Bulworth. 1999: Brotherhood of Murder (TV). Informant. 2000: Relative Values. Primary Suspect. 2001: Double Bang.

BALE, Christian 1974–
Youthful, fresh-faced, brown-haired, guileless-looking Welsh actor. Acting since childhood, he got an early taste of leading roles as the 12-year-old central character in Spielberg's *Empire of the Sun*. Although he hasn't displayed a distinct personality in adult roles, he's kept working in leading and semi-leading parts. Looking all the while for a good range, he leapt from playing Jesus Christ in a TV movie to the eponymous lethal nutcase in *American Psycho*.
1986: Mio in the Land of Faraway. Anastasia: The Mystery of Anna (TV). 1987: Empire of the Sun. 1989: Treasure Island (TV. GB: cinemas). Henry V. 1991: A Murder of Quality (TV). 1992: Newsies (GB: Newsboys). 1993: Swing Kids. 1994: Prince of Jutland. Little Women. 1995: Pocahontas (voice only). 1996: The Portrait of a Lady. The Secret Agent (released 1998). 1997: Metroland. 1998: Velvet Goldmine. All the Little Animals. 1999: A Midsummer Night's Dream. Mary, Mother of Jesus/Mary & Jesus (TV). American Psycho. 2000: Villa des Roses. Shaft. 2001: Captain Corelli's Mandolin.

BALFOUR, Betty 1903–1978
With blue eyes, a mass of golden curls and great long pencilled eyebrows, Betty Balfour was Britain's answer to Mary Pickford, and that country's most popular star of the twenties by a wide margin, as her fey, elfin charms and impish humour endeared her to millions. With sound, she slipped into working-class character roles, including a reprise of her biggest hit, as the cockney flower girl Squibs.
1920: Nothing Else Matters. 1921: Mary Find the Gold. Squibs. Mord Em'ly (US: Me and My Girl). 1922: The Wee MacGregor's Sweetheart. Squibs Wins the Calcutta Sweep. 1923: Love, Life and Laughter (US: Tip

Toes). Squibs, MP. Squibs' Honeymoon. 1924: Reveille. 1925: Satan's Sister. Somebody's Darling. The Sea Urchin. Monte Carlo. 1926: Blinkeyes. La petite bonne du palace (GB: Cinders). 1927: Le diable au cœur (GB: Little Devil May Care). Croquette (GB: Monkey Nuts). Die Sieben Töchter der Frau Gyurkovics (GB: A Sister of Six). 1928: A Little Bit of Fluff (US: Skirts). Champagne. Die Regimentstochter (GB: Daughter of the Regiment). Paradise. 1929: The Vagabond Queen. Bright Eyes. 1930: Raise the Roof. The Nipper (later The Brat). 1933: Paddy the Next Best Thing. 1934: Evergreen. My Old Dutch. 1935: Brown on Resolution (later For Ever England. US: Born for Glory). Squibs (remake). 1936: Eliza Comes to Stay. 1945: 29 Acacia Avenue (US: The Facts of Love).

BALK, Fairuza 1974–
Wide-eyed, raven-haired, rebellious-looking American child star who grew up from playing Dorothy in *Return to Oz* and quickly moved into young adult roles, as self-reliant, tough-talking, often gothic types. Most of her characters have, in fact, walked on the wild side, which perhaps accounts for her failure, as yet, to reach top stardom, despite formidable acting abilities.
*1983: The Best Christmas Pageant Ever (TV). 1985: Deceptions (TV). Return to Oz. 1986: The Worst Witch (TV). *Showscan. Discovery. 1988: The Outside Chance of Maximilian Glick. 1989: Valmont. 1991: Deadly Intentions . . . Again? (TV). 1992: Gas Food – Lodging. The Danger of Love (TV). Shame (TV). 1993: Murder in the Heartland (TV). 1994: Tollbooth. Imaginary Crimes. 1995: Fast Sofa. Things to Do in Denver When You're Dead. American Perfekt (released 1997). Shadow of a*

Doubt (TV). 1996: The Craft. The Island of Dr Moreau. Nowhere. 1997: The Maker (TV). 1998: American History X. There's No Fish Food in Heaven. The Water Boy. What Is It? (voice only). 1999: Killer's Head. 2000: Great Sex. Red Letters. Almost Famous. 2001: Deuces Wild.

BALL, Lucille 1911–1989
Red-haired, wide-mouthed, effervescent American comedienne with inimitable, duck-like voice. A former Ziegfeld girl, she survived some striking pieces of miscasting and dozens of indifferent supporting roles to become TV's most popular funny lady in the 1950s, and one of its most powerful producers. Married from 1940 to 1960 to her TV co-star, Cuban-born bandleader Desi Arnaz (1915–1986). Lucie (1951–) and Desi Arnaz Jr (1953-) are their children. Died from a ruptured abdominal aorta following open heart surgery.
*1930: Bulldog Drummond. 1933: Broadway Thru a Keyhole. Blood Money. Roman Scandals. 1934: Moulin Rouge. Nana. Bottoms Up. Hold That Girl. Bulldog Drummond Strikes Back. The Affairs of Cellini. Kid Millions. Broadway Bill (GB: Strictly Confidential). Jealousy. Men of the Night. Fugitive Lady. The Whole Town's Talking (GB: Passport to Fame). *Perfectly Mismated. *Three Little Pigskins. 1935: Carnival (GB: Carnival Nights). Roberta. Old Man Rhythm. Top Hat. The Three Musketeers. I Dream Too Much. *A Night at the Biltmore Bowl. *His Old Flame. 1936: *Dummy Ache. *One Live Ghost. *Swing It. Chatterbox. Follow the Fleet. The Farmer in the Dell. Bunker Bean (GB: His Majesty Bunker Bean). That Girl from Paris. Winterset. *So and Sew. 1937: Don't Tell the Wife. Stage Door. 1938: Joy of Living. Go Chase Yourself. Having Wonderful Time. The Affairs of Annabel. Room Service. The Next Time I Marry. 1939: Annabel Takes a Tour. Beauty for the Asking. Twelve Crowded Hours. Panama Lady. Five Came Back. That's Right, You're Wrong. 1940: The Marines Fly High. You Can't Fool Your Wife. Dance, Girl, Dance. Too Many Girls. 1941: *Stars at Play. A Girl, a Guy and A Gob (GB: The Navy Steps Out). Look Who's Laughing. 1942: Valley of the Sun. The Big Street. Seven Days' Leave. 1943: Dubarry Was a Lady. Best Foot Forward. Thousands Cheer. 1944: Meet the People. Ziegfeld Follies (released 1946). 1945: Without Love. Bud Abbott and Lou Costello in Hollywood. 1946: The Dark Corner. Easy to*

Wed. Two Smart People. Lover Come Back. 1947: Lured (GB: Personal Column). Her Husband's Affairs. 1949: Sorrowful Jones. Easy Living. Miss Grant Takes Richmond (GB: Innocence is Bliss). 1950: A Woman of Distinction. Fancy Pants. The Fuller Brush Girl (GB: The Affairs of Sally). 1951: The Magic Carpet. 1954: The Long, Long Trailer. 1956: Forever, Darling. 1960: The Facts of Life. 1963: Critic's Choice. 1967: A Guide for the Married Man. 1968: Yours, Mine and Ours. 1973: Mame. 1985: Stone Pillow (TV). 1992: The Mambo Kings ('I Love Lucy' TV footage). 1993: Lucy and Desi: A Home Movie (TV).

BANCROFT, Anne
(Anna Maria Italiano) 1931– **2005**
Black-haired, dark-eyed American actress, adept at portraying great depths of passion, hatred or tragedy. Also has a goofy sense of comedy which was only exploited in later years. Acting until 1952 as Anne Marno, she made her Hollywood breakthrough via stage success after years in co-features. Won an Oscar for *The Miracle Worker* and a British Oscar for *The Pumpkin Eater*. Married to director/comedian Mel Brooks (*qv*). Additional Academy Award nominations for *The Pumpkin Eater*, *The Graduate* and *The Turning Point*.
1952: Don't Bother to Knock. Tonight We Sing. 1953: The Treasure of the Golden Condor. The Kid from Left Field. 1954: Demetrius and the Gladiators. The Raid. Gorilla at Large. 1955: A Life in the Balance. New York Confidential. The Naked Street. The Last Frontier. 1956: Walk the Proud Land. Nightfall. 1957: The Restless Breed. Invitation to a Gunfighter (TV). The Girl in Black Stockings. So Soon to Die (TV). 1962: The Miracle Worker. 1963: The Girl of the Via Flaminia. 1964: The Pumpkin Eater. 1965: The Slender Thread. Seven Women. 1967: The Graduate. 1970: Arthur Penn, 1922, Themes and Variants. 1971: Young Winston. 1974: The Prisoner of Second Avenue. 1976: Silent Movie. Jesus of Nazareth (TV). The Hindenburg. Lipstick. 1977: The Turning Point. 1979: Fatso. 1980: The Elephant Man. 1983: To Be or Not to Be. 1984: Garbo Talks! 1985: Agnes of God. 1986: 84 Charing Cross Road. Night, Mother. 1988: Torch Song Trilogy. 1989: Bert Rigby, You're a Fool. 1991: Broadway Bound (TV). 1992: Love Potion No. 9. Honeymoon in Vegas. 1993: Mr Jones. Point of No Return (GB: The Assassin). Malice. 1994: Oldest Living Confederate Widow Tells All (TV). 1995: How to

Make an American Quilt. Home for the Holidays. The Mother (TV). Dracula: Dead and Loving It. 1996: Homecoming (TV). The Sunchaser. 1997: G.I. Jane. Great Expectations. Critical Care. 1998: Mark Twain's America in 3D (narrator only). Antz (voice only). 1999: Deep in My Heart (TV). Up at the Villa. 2000: Keeping the Faith.

BANDERAS, Antonio 1960–
Tall, dark, handsomely round-faced Spanish-born actor who always looks about to perspire even when he's not, but certainly raised a few female temperatures when he moved from TV to films in 1982. He rose to fame in films by cult director Pedro Almodóvar, but it was 1992 before he achieved a crossover to Hollywood with *The Mambo Kings*. Since then he's mostly been seen in dashing action roles. Prolific, too: more than 45 films in 18 years is good going by today's standards, although *Evita*'s long shooting schedule kept him quiet for a while. Divorced from the Spanish actress Aña Leza, he is married to the Hollywood star Melanie Griffith (*qv*).
1982: Laberinto de pasiones/Labyrinth of Passion. Y del seguro . . . libranos señor! Pestañas postizas. 1983: El Señor Galindez. 1984: Los zancos/The Stilts. El Caso Almeria. 1985: Caso Cerrado. La corte de Faraòn. Réquiem por un campesino Español. 1986: 27 horas/27 Hours. Matador. Puzzle. 1987: La ley del deseo/Law of Desire. Asì como habìan sido. El placer de matar/The Pleasure of Killing. 1988: Baton Rouge. Women on the Verge of a Nervous Breakdown. 1989: Si te dicen que cai. 1990: Tie Me Up! Tie Me Down! Contra El Viento. 1991: Terra Nova. Truth or Dare (GB: In Bed With Madonna). La blanca paloma. Cuentos de Borges I. 1992: The Mambo Kings. Una mujer najo la lluvia. Bajarse al moro. 1993: Shoot! Philadelphia. The House of the Spirits. 1994: Miami Rhapsody. Of Love and Shadows (released 1996). Interview with the Vampire. 1995: Desperado. Never Talk to Strangers. Assassins. Young Mussolini (cable TV). Four Rooms. Two Much. 1996: Evita. 1998: The Mask of Zorro. 1999: The White River Kid. The 13th Warrior. Play It to the Bone. 2000: Dancing in the Dark. 2001: Spy Kids.
As Director: *1999: Crazy in Alabama.*

BANKHEAD, Tallulah 1902–1968
Drawling, extravagant, light-haired American leading lady excelling in bitchy roles. Exquisitely pretty in her early days, she

eventually, via a triumphant seven-year sojourn in London, became something of a Bette Davis of the New York stage. Films could rarely find the right material – or directors – for her, and, when not making cutting remarks at show business parties, she remained chiefly in the theatre. At one time married to suave co-star actor John Emery (1905–1964), she died from complications following an attack of Asian 'flu.
*1918: When Men Betray. Thirty a Week. Who Loved Him Best? 1919: The Trap. The Virtuous Vamp. 1928: A Woman's Law. His House in Order. 1929: *Her Cardboard Lover. 1931: Tarnished Lady. My Sin. The Cheat. 1932: Thunder Below. The Devil and the Deep. Faithless. Make Me a Star. 1943: Stage Door Canteen. Lifeboat. 1945: A Royal Scandal (GB: Czarina). 1953: Main Street to Broadway. 1959: The Boy Who Owned a Melephant (voice only). 1964: Fanatic (US: Die! Die! My Darling). 1966: The Day-dreamer (voice only).*

BANKS, Leslie
(James L. Banks) 1890–1952
Taciturn, solid British actor with a distinctive voice, rarely flamboyant but always reliable. Badly wounded in World War I (facial disfigurement converted classic good looks into rugged ones). Banks unexpectedly found himself a star of the British cinema in middle age, after a film debut in Hollywood. In private life a talented painter, he died from a stroke that followed a long illness.
1932: The Most Dangerous Game (GB: The Hounds of Zaroff). Strange Evidence. 1933: The Fire Raisers. 1934: The Night of the Party. Red Ensign. I am Suzanne! The Man Who Knew Too Much. 1935: Sanders of the River.

The Tunnel (US: Transatlantic Tunnel). 1936: Debt of Honour. The Three Maxims (US: The Show Goes On). Fire Over England. 1937: Wings of the Morning. Farewell Again (US: Troopship). 21 Days (US: 21 Days Together). 1938: *Guide Dogs for the Blind. 1939: Jamaica Inn. Dead Man's Shoes. The Arsenal Stadium Mystery. Sons of the Sea. 1940: The Door with Seven Locks (US: Chamber of Horrors). Busman's Honeymoon (US: Haunted Honeymoon). Neutral Port. 1941: *Give Us More Ships. Cottage to Let (US: Bombsite Stolen). Ships with Wings. The Big Blockade. 1942: Went the Day Well? (US: 48 Hours). 1944: Henry V. 1947: Mrs Fitzherbert. 1948: The Small Back Room. 1950: Your Witness (US: Eye Witness). Madeleine.

BANKY, Vilma (V. Lonchit) 1898–1992
Blonde, Budapest-born silent star, publicized as 'The Hungarian Rhapsody'. She made a few films in Hungary and Austria before being 'discovered' by Sam Goldwyn while he was on a European holiday. Had great success in Hollywood, but sound would probably have killed her career: by this time she was more interested in her marriage to fellow star Rod La Rocque (qv), which lasted until his death in 1969. A golf fanatic, she was still playing in her eighties. Died from cardio-respiratory arrest.
1919: Im letzten Augenblick. 1920: Galathea. 1921: Tavasni Szerelem. Veszélyben a Pokol. 1922: Das Auge des Toten. Kauft Mariett-Aktien. Schattenkinder des Glücks. 1923: Die letzte Stunde. 1924: Das schöne Abenteuer (US: The Lady from Paris). Hotel Potemkin. Das verbotene Land. Klown aus Liebe. 1925: Soll man heiraten? L'image. The Dark Angel. The Eagle. 1926: Son of the Sheik. The Winning of Barbara Worth. 1927: The Night of Love. The Magic Flame. 1928: Two Lovers. The Awakening. 1929: This is Heaven. 1930: A Lady to Love (and German version). 1932: The Rebel.

BANNEN, Ian 1928–1999
Black-haired Scottish actor who began his career in gentle roles, largely in comedy, but developed in the mid-1960s into an abrasive character star, fiercely portraying a series of single-minded and even psychotic men. After that time, he was less effective in straight leading roles, but continued to impress when asked to express sourness and cynicism. An Oscar nominee for The Flight of the Phoenix, he was killed in a car crash.

1955: Private's Progress. 1956: The Long Arm (US: The Third Key). 1957: Yangtse Incident (US: Battle Hell). Miracle in Soho. The Birthday Present. 1958: A Tale of Two Cities. She Didn't Say No! Behind the Mask. Carlton-Browne of the FO (US: Man in a Cocked Hat). 1960: On Friday at 11. A French Mistress. Suspect (US: The Risk). 1961: Macbeth. 1962: Station Six – Sahara. 1963: Psyche 59. 1964: Mister Moses. 1965: The Hill. Rotten to the Core. The Flight of the Phoenix. 1966: Penelope. 1967: Sailor from Gibraltar. 1969: Too Late the Hero. Lock Up Your Daughters! 1970: Jane Eyre. The Deserter. 1971: Fright. 1972: Doomwatch. The Offence. 1973: The Mackintosh Man. From Beyond the Grave. 1974: Il viaggio (US: The Voyage). Identikit/The Driver's Seat. 1975: Bite the Bullet. 1976: Sweeney! 1978: The Inglorious Bastards. 1979: Ring of Darkness. 1980: The Watcher in the Woods (shown in revised version 1982). Dr Jekyll and Mr Hyde (TV). 1981: Eye of the Needle. 1982: Night Crossing. 1982: Gandhi. 1983: The Prodigal. Gorky Park. 1985: Defence of the Realm. Lamb. 1987: Hope and Glory. The Courier. 1988: The Match. 1989: The Lady and the Highwayman (TV). Ghost Dad. Witch Story (TV). George's Island. 1990: Perry Mason: The Case of the Desperate Deception (later The Case of the Paris Paradox). The Big Man (US: Crossing the Line). The Cherry Orchard. 1991: The Gamble. Uncle Vanya (TV). 1992: Damage. Common Pursuit (TV). 1994: A Pin for the Butterfly. 1997: Something to Believe In. Waking Ned Devine/Waking Ned. 1999: To Walk with Lions. Best. 2000: The Testimony of Taliesin Jones. Strictly Sinatra/Saracen Street.

BANNON, Jim 1911–1986
Lanky, likeable, red-headed American actor who spent 10 years on radio, including a spell as a sports commentator, before coming to Hollywood to play Red Ryder and other 'B' feature western heroes. Rather surprisingly, the one-time stuntman did not mature into a familiar character actor and was not much seen after the low-budget cowboys ceased to ride the range. Married to actress and cartoon voiceover expert Bea Benaderet (1906–1968). Actor Jack Bannon (1940–) is their son. Besides the list below, Bannon also narrates an obscure 1940 film called I Married Adventure.
1943: Riders of the Deadline. 1944: The Soul of a Monster. Sergeant Mike. The Missing Juror. Tonight and Every Night. 1945: I Love a

Mystery. The Gay Senorita. Out of the Depths. 1946: Renegades. The Devil's Mask. The Unknown. 1947: Johnny O'Clock. Framed (GB: Paula). The Corpse Came COD. The Thirteenth Hour. T-Men. 1948: Miraculous Journey. Dangers of the Canadian Mounted (serial). The Man from Colorado. Frontier Revenge. Trial to Laredo (GB: Sign of the Dagger). 1949: Daughter of the Jungle. Ride, Ryder, Ride. The Fighting Redhead. Roll, Thunder, Roll. 1950: Kill the Umpire! The Cowboy and the Prizefighter. Jiggs and Maggie Out West. The Great Missouri Raid. 1951: Riding the Outlaw Trail. Sierra Passage. Canyon Raiders. Nevada Badmen. Lawless Cowboys. The Redhead and the Cowboy. The Texas Rangers. Stagecoach Driver. Unknown World. Wanted Dead or Alive. 1952: The Black Lash. Rodeo. 1953: Jack Slade (GB: Slade). The Great Jesse James Raid. War Arrow. Phantom from Space. 1954: The Command. 1957: Chicago Confidential. 1959: They Came to Cordura. Inside the Mafia. 1962: 40 Pounds of Trouble. 1963: A Gathering of Eagles. Man's Favorite Sport? 1964: Good Neighbor Sam. 1966: Madame X.

BARA, Theda
(Theodosia Goodman) 1890–1955
Dark-haired, low-eyebrowed American actress who became the screen's first vamp, usually heavy on the soulful stare and eye make-up and extravagantly costumed. Hollywood publicists, who invented places of birth for her such as Egypt or the Sahara Desert, made much of her man-eating qualities on screen. She found enormous success in the early silent days, but it came and went all in a few years. Her image was passé by 1920, and she more or less quit the Hollywood scene

after marrying director Charles J Brabin the following year. It was a marriage that lasted until her death from cancer following a long illness.

1914: *A Fool There Was*. 1915: *The Clemenceau Case (GB: Infidelity)*. *The Devil's Daughter*. *The Kreutzer Sonata (GB: Sonata)*. *Lady Audley's Secret (GB: Secrets of Society)*. *The Two Orphans*. *The Galley Slave*. *Sin*. *Destruction*. *Carmen*. *The Stain*. 1916: *The Serpent (GB: Fires of Hate)*. *Gold and The Woman*. *The Eternal Sappho (GB: Bohemia)*. *East Lynne*. *Her Double Life*. *Romeo and Juliet*. *Under Two Flags*. *The Vixen (GB: The Love Pirate)*. *The Darling of Paris*. *The Tiger Woman (GB: Behind the Throne)*. 1917: *The Light*. *Cleopatra*. *Camille*. *Madame Dubarry*. *Her Greatest Love (GB: Redemption)*. *Heart and Soul*. *The Rose of Blood*. *The Soul of Buddha*. 1918: *Salome*. *Under the Yoke*. *The Forbidden Path*. *When a Woman Sins*. *The She Devil*. *The Message of the Lilies*. *La Belle Russe*. 1919: *Siren's Song*. *When Men Desire*. *A Woman There Was*. *Lure of Ambition*. *Kathleen Mavourneen*. 1921: *The Price of Silence*. *Her Greatest Love*. 1925: *The Unchastened Woman*. **Madame Mystery*. 1926: **45 Minutes from Hollywood*.

BARDOT, Brigitte 1934–
Baby-faced blonde French sex symbol with a figure in a million. Publicized as the 'sex kitten', her steamy pot-boilers of the fifties set innumerable male temperatures rising all over Europe. Responsible almost single-handed for the breakthrough of the continental X film into the international market. Her three husbands included director Roger Vadim, who helped create her image, and actor Jacques Charrier. Later a vigorous campaigner for animal rights.

1952: *Le trou normand (US: Crazy for Love)*. *Manina (GB: The Lighthouse Keeper's Daughter*. *US: The Girl in the Bikini)*. *Les dents longues*. 1953: *Le portrait de son père*. *Act of Love*. *Si Versailles m'était conté (GB: Versailles*. *US: Royal Affairs at Versailles)*. 1954: *Tradita (US: Night of Love)*. *Helen of Troy*. *Le fils de Caroline Chérie*. *Futures vedettes (GB: Sweet Sixteen)*. 1955: *Doctor at Sea*. *Les grandes manoeuvres (GB and US: Summer Manoeuvers)*. *La lumière d'en face (GB and US: The Light Across the Street)*. *Cette sacrée gamine (GB: and US: Mam'zelle Pigalle)*. 1956: *Mio figlio nerone (GB: Nero's Weekend)*. *En effeuillant la Marguerite (GB: Mam'selle Striptease*. *US: Please, Mr*

Balzac). *Et Dieu créa la femme (GB: And Woman . . . Was Created*. *US: And God Created Woman)*. *La mariée est trop belle (GB: and US: The Bride is Too Beautiful)*. 1957: *Une Parisienne (GB and US: Parisienne)*. *Les bijoutiers du clair de lune (GB: Heaven Fell That Night*. *US: The Night Heaven Fell)*. 1958: *En cas de malheur (GB and US: Love Is My Profession)*. *La femme et le pantin (GB: A Woman Like Satan)*. 1959: *Babette Goes to War*. *Le testament d'Orphée*. *Voulez-vous danser avec moi? (GB and US: Come Dance With Me)*. 1960: *L'affaire d'une nuit (GB: It Happened at Night)*. *La vérité (GB and US: The Truth)*. 1961: *La bride sur le cou (GB: Please, Not Now!)*. *Les amours célèbres*. *Vie privée (GB and US: A Very Private Affair)*. 1962: *Le repos du guerrier (GB: Warrior's Rest*. *US: Love on a Pillow)*. 1963: *Le mépris (GB and US: Contempt)*. *Paparazzi*. *Tentazione proibite*. *Une ravissante idiote (GB: A Ravishing Idiot*. *US: Adorable Idiot)*. 1964: *Marie Soleil*. 1965: *Dear Brigitte . . .* *Viva Maria*. 1966: *Masculin-Féminin*. *Two Weeks in September*. 1967: *Histoires extra-ordinaires (GB: Tales of Mystery*. *US: Spirits of the Dead)*. 1968: *Shalako*. 1969: *Les femmes*. 1970: *L'ours et la poupée*. *Les novices*. *Boulevard du rhum (GB: Rum Runner)*. 1971: *Les pétroleuses (GB: The Legend of Frenchie King)*. 1973: *Don Juan 1973 ou Et si Don Juan était une femme (GB: Don Juan, or If Don Juan Were a Woman)*. *Colinot Trousse-Chemise*.

BARI, Lynn (Marjorie Fisher) 1913–1989
Dark-haired, cool-looking American leading lady who emerged from the chorus but never quite made it to the top, although she became deliciously known as 'the Paulette Goddard of the B feature'. Leading roles in bigger films proved too routine to break the image, and she continued as wordly-wise bad girls and 'other women'. Later seen mainly on stage, she eased up on acting assignments after marrying her third husband, a doctor, in 1955. Died 'after a long illness'.

1933: *Dancing Lady*. *Meet the Baron*. 1934: *I Am Suzanne!* *David Harum*. *Handy Andy*. *365 Nights in Hollywood*. *Music in the Air*. *Bottoms Up*. *Coming Out Party*. *Stand Up and Cheer*. *Search for Beauty*. *Caravan*. 1935: *Charlie Chan in Paris*. *Under Pressure*. *Ten Dollar Raise (GB: Mr Faintheart)*. *Spring Tonic*. *Doubting Thomas*. *Ladies Love Danger*. *Orchids to You*. *Charlie Chan in Shanghai*. *Dante's Inferno*. *The Gay Deception*. *Way Down East*. *Metropolitan*. *Welcome Home*.

Lottery Lover. *George White's (1935) Scandals*. *Show Them No Mercy (GB: Tainted Money)*. *The Great Hotel Murder*. *The Man Who Broke the Bank at Monte Carlo*. *Redheads on Parade*. *Thanks a Million*. *Music is Magic*. *My Marriage*. 1936: *It Had to Happen*. *The Song and Dance Man*. *Private Number (GB: Secret Interlude)*. *Poor Little Rich Girl*. *Star for a Night*. *Fifteen Maiden Lane*. *King of Burlesque*. *The Great Ziegfeld*. *Everybody's Old Man*. *Girls' Dormitory*. *Ladies in Love*. *Crack-Up*. *Pigskin Parade (GB: The Harmony Parade)*. *Sing, Baby, Sing*. *36 Hours to Kill*. 1937: *Woman Wise*. *Wake Up and Live*. *Café Metropole*. *She Had to Eat*. *The Lady Escapes*. *Ali Baba Goes to Town*. *45 Fathers*. *Wee Willie Winkie*. *Sing and Be Happy*. *Time Out for Romance*. *This Is My Affair (GB: His Affair)*. *Lancer Spy*. *Love is News*. *Wife, Doctor and Nurse*. *Fair Warning*. *On the Avenue*. *I'll Give a Million*. *Life Begins in College (GB: The Joy Parade)*. *You Can't Have Everything*. 1938: *Josette*. *Rebecca of Sunnybrook Farm*. *Speed to Burn*. *The Baroness and the Butler*. *Walking Down Broadway*. *Love and Hisses*. *Mr Moto's Gamble*. *City Girl*. *Battle of Broadway*. *Always Goodbye*. *Meet the Girls*. *Sharpshooters*. 1939: *Return of the Cisco Kid*. *Chasing Danger*. *News is Made at Night*. *Pack Up Your Troubles (GB: We're in the Army Now)*. *Hotel for Women/Elsa Maxwell's Hotel for Women*. *Charlie Chan in City of Darkness (GB: City of Darkness)*. *Hollywood Cavalcade*. *Pardon Our Nerve*. 1940: *Free, Blonde and 21*. *City of Chance*. *Lillian Russell*. *Earthbound*. *Pier 13*. *Kit Carson*. 1941: *Charter Pilot*. *Blood and Sand*. *Sleepers West*. *We Go Fast*. *Moon over Her Shoulder*. *Sun Valley Serenade*. *The Perfect Snob*. 1942: *Secret Agent of Japan*. *The Night Before the Divorce*. *The Falcon Takes Over*. *The Magnificent Dope*. *Orchestra Wives*. *China Girl*. 1943: *Hello, Frisco, Hello*. 1944: *The Bridge of San Luis Rey*. *Tampico*. *Sweet and Lowdown*. 1945: *Captain Eddie*. 1946: *Shock*. *Home Sweet Homicide*. *Margie*. *Nocturne*. 1948: *The Man from Texas*. *The Amazing Mr X/The Spiritualist*. 1949: *The Kid from Cleveland*. 1951: *I'd Climb the Highest Mountain*. *On the Loose*. 1952: *Sunny Side of the Street*. *Has Anybody Seen My Gal*. 1953: *I Dream of Jeanie*. 1954: *Francis Joins the WACS*. 1955: *Abbott and Costello Meet the Keystone Kops*. 1956: *Women of Pitcairn Island*. *All's Fair in Love (TV. GB: cinemas)*. 1958: *Damn Citizen!* 1962: *Six-Gun Law (TV. GB: cinemas)*. *Trauma*. 1968: *The Young Runaways*.

BARKER, Lex
(Alexander Barker) 1919–1973
Tall, blond and rather stolid American leading man of somewhat cool personality. Picked to take over from Johnny Weissmuller as Tarzan, he quit after five films because of paucity of dialogue, but never rose above action movies. Two of his five marriages were to Arlene Dahl (1951–1952) and Lana Turner (1953–1957). Died of a heart attack.

1946: *Doll Face (GB: Come Back to Me)*. *Do You Love Me*. *Two Guys from Milwaukee (GB: Royal Flush)*. 1947: *The Farmer's Daughter*. *Dick Tracy Meets Gruesome*.

Crossfire. Under the Tonto Rim. Unconquered. 1948: Mr Blandings Builds His Dream House. Return of the Bad Men. The Velvet Touch. 1949: Tarzan's Magic Fountain. 1950: Tarzan and the Slave Girl. 1951: Tarzan's Peril (GB: Tarzan and the Jungle Queen). 1952: Tarzan's Savage Fury. Battles of Chief Pontiac. 1953: Tarzan and the She-Devil. 1954: Thunder Over the Plains. The Yellow Mountain. Vendetta dei Thugs. 1955: The Man from Bitter Ridge. Duel on the Mississippi. Mystery of the Black Jungle (GB: Black Devils of Kali). 1956: The Price of Fear. Away All Boats. 1957: The Girl in the Kremlin. War Drums. Jungle Heat. The Deerslayer. The Girl in Black Stockings. 1958: Strange Awakening (GB: Female Fiends). The Son of the Red Pirate. Killers of the East. 1959: Mission in Morocco. La scimitara de Saraceno. Terror of the Red Mask. Captain Falcon (GB: Robin Hood). The Pirate and the Slave Girl. La dolce vita. 1960: Le secret des hommes bleus. Pirates of the Coast (GB: Pirates of the Barbary Coast). Caravan to Zagota. Il cavaliere dai cento volti (GB: Knight of a Hundred Faces). Robin Hood and the Pirates. 1961: Secret of the Black Falcon. Marco Polo. Le trésor des hommes bleus. The Return of Dr Mabuse. 1962: Frauenarzt Dr Sibelius. Treasure of Silver Lake. The Invisible Dr Mabuse. 1963: Breakfast in Bed. The Mystery of the Indian Temple. Das Todesauge von Ceylon (GB: Storm over Ceylon). The Black Buccaneer. Winnetou I (GB: Winnetou the Warrior. US: Apache Gold). Hangman of Venice (GB: Blood of the Executioner). Kali-Yug, Goddess of Vengeance. 1964: Old Shatterhand (GB: Apaches' Last Battle). Code 7, Victim 5 (GB: Victim Five). $5,000 für den Kopf von Jonny R. 1965: Die Pyramid des Sonnengottes. Winnetou II (GB: Last of the Renegades). Die Hölle von Manitoba (US: The Desperate Trail). Der Schatz der Azteken. Attack of the Kurds (GB: Wild Kurdistan). Im Reiche des silbernen Löwen. 1966: Winnetou III/A Place Called Glory. 24 Hours to Kill. Mister Dynamite (GB: Die Slowly, You'll Enjoy It More). Dynamite al Pentagono. The Shoot (made 1964). Gern hab ich die Frauen gekillt (US: Requiem for a Secret Agent). 1967: Woman Times Seven. Winnetou und das Halbblut Apanatschi. Die Schlangengrube und das Pendel (GB and US: The Blood Demon). 1968: Devil May Care. The Longest Day in Kansas City. Winnetou und Shatterhand im Tal der Toten. 1969: L'uomo dal lungo facile. 1970: Wenn du bei mir bist.

BARKIN, Ellen 1954–

Silkily blonde, close-mouthed, narrow-eyed, distinctive American actress with lopsided smile, often in provocatively independent roles. Her rather passive features resulted in her playing vulnerable and sometimes put-upon women after a late start in films following graduation from the New York High School of Performing Arts. She began getting a more interesting variety of roles (and star billing) in the late 1980s, and her appeal reached a peak with her sexy success in *Sea of Love.* But her tendency to pick poor scripts let her down again in the early 1990s, although the standard of her personal performances remained high. Married/divorced actor Gabriel Byrne (*qv*).

1981: We're Fighting Back (TV). Kent State (TV). 1982: Diner. Parole (TV). Eddie and the Cruisers (released 1984). Tender Mercies. 1983: Daniel. Enormous Changes at the Last Minute. 1984: Harry and Tonto. Terrible Joe Moran (TV). The Adventures of Buckaroo Banzai: Across the Eighth Dimension. In Our Hands. 1985: Terminal Choice. 1986: Desert Bloom. Down by Law. Act of Vengeance (video). The Big Easy. 1987: Made in Heaven. Siesta. 1988: Clinton and Nadine/Blood Money. 1989: Sea of Love. Johnny Handsome. 1990: Switch. 1991: Man Trouble. 1992: Into the West. Mac. 1993: This Boy's Life. 1994: Bad Company. 1995: Wild Bill. 1996: The Fan. Trigger Happy/Mad Dog Time. 1997: Before Women Had Wings (TV). 1998: Fear and Loathing in Las Vegas. 1999: Drop Dead Gorgeous. The White River Kid. Mercy. 2000: Crime and Punishment in Suburbia. In the Boom Boom Room.

BARNES, Barry K.

(Nelson Barnes) 1906–1965

Tall, dark, lean-faced, saturnine British leading man in the John Justin/Michael Rennie mould. Very popular in the late 1930s, especially in Thin Man-style comedy-thrillers, he picked up a mysterious bug in the mid 1940s (probably on war service) which baffled specialists and effectively ended his career, depriving him of 'all power and confidence'. Married to Diana Churchill (*qv*), who looked after him devotedly until his death.

1936: Dodging the Dole. 1937: The Return of the Scarlet Pimpernel. 1938: Who Goes Next? This Man is News. You're The Doctor. Prison without Bars. The Ware Case. 1939: Spies of the Air. This Man in Paris. The Midas Touch.

1940: Two for Danger. Law and Disorder. The Girl in the News. 1946: Bedelia. 1947: Dancing with Crime.

BARNES, Binnie

(Gitelle Barnes) 1903–1998

Sophisticated blonde British-born actress with pencil-line eyebrows, often cast as the 'other woman'. A one-time chorus girl and dance hostess, she started in two-reel comedies, but made over 20 British features before going to Hollywood in 1934. Married producer Mike Frankovich in 1940. He died in 1992.

*1930: *Sugar and Spice (series of shorts). 1931: A Night in Montmartre. Love Lies. Dr Josser KC. Out of the Blue. 1932: Murder at Covent Garden. Partners Please. The Innocents of Chicago (GB: Why Saps Leave Home). Down Our Street. Strip, Strip, Hooray! The Last Coupon. Old Spanish Customers. 1933: Taxi to Paradise. Counsel's Opinion. Their Night Out. Heads We Go (US: The Charming Deceiver). The Private Life of Henry VIII. The Silver Spoon. The Lady is Willing. 1934: Nine Forty-Five. No Escape. The Private Life of Don Juan. Forbidden Territory. Gift of Gab. There's Always Tomorrow. One Exciting Adventure. 1935: Diamond Jim. Rendezvous. *La Fiesta de Santa Barbara. 1936: Sutter's Gold. Small Town Girl. The Last of the Mohicans. The Magnificent Brute. 1937: Three Smart Girls. Breezing Home. Broadway Melody of 1938. 1938: The First Hundred Years. The Adventures of Marco Polo. Holiday (later Unconventional Linda. GB: Free to Live). Getaway. Tropic Holiday. Three Blind Mice. The Divorce of Lady X. Thanks for Everything. Always Goodbye. 1939: Wife, Husband and Friend. The Three Musketeers.*

Frontier Marshal. Daytime Wife. 1940: 'Til We Meet Again. 1941: *Variety Reel. *Stars at Play. *Stars Past and Present. New Wine. This Thing Called Love (GB: Married But Single). Angels with Broken Wings. Tight Shoes. Skylark. Three Girls about Town. 1942: Call Out the Marines. I Married an Angel. In Old California. 1943: The Man from Down Under. 1944: Up in Mabel's Room. The Hour Before the Dawn. It's in the Bag! (GB: The Fifth Chair). 1945: Barbary Coast Gent. The Spanish Main. Getting Gertie's Garter. 1946: The Time of Their Lives. 1948: The Dude Goes West. If Winter Comes. My Own True Love. 1949: The Pirates of Capri (GB: The Masked Pirate). 1950: Shadow of the Eagle. 1951: Fugitive Lady. 1952: Decameron Nights. 1954: Malaga (US: Fire Over Africa). 1966: The Trouble with Angels. 1968: Where Angels Go – Trouble Follows. 1973: Forty Carats.

BARRIE, Wendy
(Margaret Jenkins) 1912–1978
British blonde socialite leading lady, born in Hong Kong, who, after playing Jane Seymour to Charles Laughton's Henry VIII, went to Hollywood and enjoyed a colourful career, including once being engaged to a famous gangster. Film roles mostly 'B' feature leads. Later found renewed success as a popular radio and TV hostess of chat shows.
1931: Collision. 1932: Threads. The Call Box Mystery. Wedding Rehearsal. Where is the Lady? The Barton Mystery. 1933: Cash (US: For Love or Money). It's a Boy. The Private Life of Henry VIII. This Acting Business. The House of Trent. 1934: Murder at the Inn. Without You. The Man I Want. Freedom of the Seas. There Goes Susie (US: Scandals of Paris). Give Her a Ring. 1935: It's a Small World. College Scandal (GB: The Clock Strikes Eight). The Big Broadcast of 1936. A Feather in Her Hat. Millions in the Air. 1936: Love on a Bet. Speed. Ticket to Paradise. Under Your Spell. 1937: Breezing Home. What Price Vengeance? (GB: Vengeance). Wings over Honolulu. Dead End. A Girl with Ideas. Prescription for Romance. 1938: I Am the Law. Pacific Liner. 1939: Newsboys' Home. The Saint Strikes Back. The Hound of the Baskervilles. Five Came Back. The Witness Vanishes. Day-Time Wife. 1940: The Saint Takes Over. Women in War. Cross-Country Romance. Men Against the Sky. Who Killed Aunt Maggie? 1941: Repent at Leisure. The Saint in Palm Springs. The Gay Falcon. Public Enemies. A Dale with the Falcon. Eyes of the

Underworld. 1943: Forever and a Day. Follies Girl. Submarine Alert. 1954: It Should Happen to You. 1963: The Moving Finger.

BARRY, Don 'Red'
(D.B. Da Acosta) 1912–1980
Busy, forceful, intent-looking star of dozens of second-feature westerns in the 1930s and 1940s, including the Red Ryder serial that gave him his nickname – even though he did not have red hair. After finishing with Ryder, Barry tried to widen his range, but the move was not popular with the public. In 1950, he moved into TV, and returned to the cinema four years later as a character actor, often in quite small roles. In August 1980, he shot himself.
1933: This Day and Age. 1934: *Movie Usher. 1936: Night Waitress. Beloved Enemy. 1937: Navy Blue and Gold. The Last Gangster. The Woman I Love (GB: The Woman Between). Born Reckless. Dead End. 1938: Duke of West Point. *Think It Over. There's That Woman Again (GB: What a Woman). Letter of Introduction. Sinners in Paradise. The Crowd Roars. Young Dr Kildare. 1939: Wyoming Outlaw. Saga of Death Valley. Days of Jesse James. SOS Tidal Wave (GB: Tidal Wave). Only Angels Have Wings. Calling Dr Kildare. Panama Patrol. The Secret of Dr Kildare. Calling All Marines. 1940: Sailor's Lady. Jackpot. Frontier Vengeance. The Tulsa Kid. Ghost Valley Raiders. One Man's Law. Texas Terrors. The Adventures of Red Ryder (serial). 1941: A Missouri Outlaw. The Apache Kid. Desert Bandit. Death Valley Outlaws. Phantom Cowboy. Wyoming Wildcat. Two-Gun Sheriff. Kansas Cyclone. 1942: *Army 681 – Keep It Clean. The Cyclone Kid. Red-Headed Justice. Arizona Terrors. Outlaws of Pine Ridge. The Sombrero Kid. The Traitor Within. Remember Pearl Harbor. Stagecoach Express. Jesse James Junior. 1943: The Sundown Kid. Days of Old Cheyenne. Carson City Cyclone. Black Hills Express. Canyon City. Man From Rio Grande. Fugitive from Sonora. Dead Man's Gulch. The Westside Kid. 1944: The Purple Heart. California Joe. My Buddy. Outlaws of Santa Fé. 1945: Bells of Rosarita. The Chicago Kid. 1946: The Plainsman and the Lady. The Last Crooked Mile. Out California Way. 1947: That's My Gal. 1948: Dangers of the Canadian Mounted (serial. Voice only). Madonna of the Desert. Train to Alcatraz. Lightnin' in the Forest. Tough Assignment. Slippy McGee. 1949: Red Desert. The Dalton Gang. Square Dance Jubilee. Ringside. Headin' for Trouble. 1950: Train to

Tombstone. Border Rangers. I Shot Billy the Kid. Gunfire (GB: Frank James Rides Again). 1954: Untamed Heiress. Jesse James' Women. 1955: The Twinkle in God's Eye. I'll Cry Tomorrow. 1956: Seven Men from Now. 1957: Gun Duel in Durango. 1958: China Doll. Andy Hardy Comes Home. Frankenstein 1970. 1959: The Big Operator. The Last Mile. Warlock. Born Reckless. 1960: Walk Like a Dragon. Ocean's Eleven. 1961: The Errand Boy. Buffalo Gun. 1962: A Walk on the Wild Side. Birdman of Alcatraz. 1963: Twilight of Honor (GB: The Charge is Murder). Law of the Lawless. The Carpetbaggers. 1965: Town Tamer. Fort Courageous. Convict Stage. Iron Angel. 1966: Alvarez Kelly. Apache Uprising. War Party. 1967: Shalako. Bandolero! The Shakiest Gun in the West. 1969: The Cockeyed Cowboys of Calico County (GB: TV: A Woman for Charlie). 1970: Hunters Are for Killing (TV). Rio Lobo. Dirty Dingus Magee. 1971: Incident on a Dark Street (TV). Owen Marshall, Counsellor at Law (TV). The Gatling Gun. One More Train to Rob. Johnny Got His Gun. 1972: Junior Bonner. The Eyes of Charles Sand (TV). 1973: Partners in Crime (TV). Showdown. 1974: Big Rose (TV). Punch and Jody (TV). Boss Nigger (GB: The Black Bounty Killer). 1975: Hustle. From Noon Till Three. Whiffs (GB: C.A.S.H.). 1976: Blazing Stewardesses. 1977: Orca, Killer Whale. 1978: Seabo. The Swarm. The Crash of Flight 401/Crash (TV). Kate Bliss and the Tickertape Kid (TV). Buckstone County Prison. 1979: Goldie and the Boxer. (TV). 1981: Back Roads.
As director: 1954: Jesse James' Women.

BARRY, Gene (Eugene Klass) 1921–
Smooth, black-haired American light leading man with plausible smile, good at handsome villains when given the chance. In routine leading roles in the 1950s, he enjoyed enormous personal success as the millionaire Los Angeles chief of detectives Amos Burke in TV's Burke's Law. Afterwards, though, his film roles were, if anything, blander than before, and he returned to television. By the early 1990s, he was playing Amos Burke for the third time.
1952: The Atomic City. The War of the Worlds. 1953: The Girls of Pleasure Island. Those Redheads from Seattle. 1954: Alaska Seas. Red Garters. Naked Alibi. 1955: Soldier of Fortune. The Purple Mask. 1956: The Houston Story. Back from Eternity. 1957: The 27th Day. Ain't No Time for Glory (TV). China Gate. Forty Guns. 1958: Hong Kong Confidential. Thunder

Road. 1967: Prescription Murder (TV). Maroc 7. 1968: Istanbul Express (TV. GB: cinemas). 1969: Subterfuge. 1970: Do You Take This Stranger? (TV). 1971: The Devil and Miss Sarah (TV). A Capital Affair (TV). The Showdown (TV). 1974: The Second Coming of Suzanne. 1977: Ransom for Alice (TV). 1979: Guyana: The Crime of the Century. 1980: A Cry for Love (TV). The Girl, the Gold Watch and Dynamite (TV). 1981: The Adventures of Nelly Bly (TV). 1987: Perry Mason: The Case of the Lost Love (TV). 1989: Turn Back the Clock (TV). 1992: The Gambler Returns: The Luck of the Draw (TV).

BARRYMORE, Drew
(Andrew Barrymore) 1975–
Silkily fair-haired, pouty-mouthed, slinky-eyed American actress, the latest in a long line of acting Drews, Blythes and Barrymores that stretches back to the 19th century. The granddaughter of John Barrymore (qv) and daughter of John Drew Barrymore, she was a chubbily attractive child performer before the family curses of drink and drugs overtook her at an early age. Cleaned up and dried out by 1989, she excited attention as a series of sexual catalysts in provocative teenage roles, posed nude for a magazine, provided hot copy for interviews and married and divorced before she was 20. The 'wild child's work continues to attract good critical notices, and she has even had some solo successes.
1978: Suddenly Love (TV). 1980: Bogie (TV). Altered States. 1982: E.T. The Extra Terrestrial. 1984: Irreconcilable Differences. Firestarter. Cat's Eye. 1986: Babes in Toyland (TV). 1987: Conspiracy of Love (TV). 1988: See You in the Morning. 1989: 15 and Getting Straight (TV). Far from Home. Baby Doll Blues. 1991: No Place to Hide. Tipperary. 1992: Poison Ivy. Sketch Artist (cable TV). Motorama. Waxwork II: Lost in Time. 2000 Malibu Road (TV). Beyond Control: The Amy Fisher Story (TV). Guncrazy. 1993: Doppelganger / Doppelganger: The Evil Within. Wayne's World 2. 1994: Bad Girls. Mad Love. Inside the Goldmine. 1995: Boys on the Side. Batman Forever. 1996: Scream. Everyone Says I Love You. 1997: Home Fries. 1998: The Wedding Singer. Best Men. Ever After. 1999: Never Been Kissed. 2000: Titan AE (voice only). Charlie's Angels. Skipped Parts.

BARRYMORE, Ethel
(E. Blythe) 1879–1956
Dark-haired, stately American leading lady,

sister of John and Lionel, who, after a few rather too regal starring roles in silent films, returned to the stage. In the forties she came back to Hollywood in triumph, winning an Oscar for None But the Lonely Heart and bringing great presence to a series of dowager roles. Died from a heart attack. Received additional Oscar nominations for the The Spiral Staircase, The Paradine Case and Pinky. 1915: The Nightingale. The Final Judgement. 1916: The Kiss of Hate. The Awakening of Helen Richie. 1917: The White Raven. The Greatest Power. The Lifted Veil. The Eternal Mother. An American Widow. The Call of Her People. Life's Whirlpool. 1918: Our Mrs McChesney. 1919: Test of Honor. The Divorcee (GB: Lady Frederick). The Spender. 1933: Rasputin and the Empress (GB: Rasputin the Mad Monk). *All at Sea. 1943: *Show Business at War. 1944: None But the Lonely Heart. 1945: The Spiral Staircase. 1947: The Farmer's Daughter. Moss Rose. Night Song. 1948: The Paradine Case. Moonrise. Portrait of Jennie (GB: Jennie). 1949: The Great Sinner. That Midnight Kiss. The Red Danube. Pinky. 1951: The Secret of Convict Lake. Kind Lady. 1952: It's a Big Country. Deadline – USA (GB: Deadline). Just For You. 1953: The Story of Three Loves. Main Street to Broadway. 1954: Young at Heart. 1956: Eloise (TV). 1957: Johnny Trouble.

BARRYMORE, John (J. Blythe) 1882–1942
Dominant American actor of stern but handsome looks (known as 'The Great Profile'), resonant voice and great presence, the brother of Ethel and Lionel Barrymore. A matinee idol in the 1920s, he had a few striking roles at the beginning of sound, but his career was eventually overtaken by alcohol

and high living, and he ended his days in unworthy, self-mocking roles. Married (third of four) to Dolores Costello (qv) from 1928 to 1935. Actor John Drew Barrymore/John Barrymore Jr (1932–) is their son. Died from pneumonia after collapsing during rehearsal for a radio show.
1914: An American Citizen. The Man from Mexico. 1915: The Dictator. Are You a Mason? The Incorrigible Dukane. 1916: Nearly a King. The Lost Bridegroom. The Red Widow. 1917: Raffles the Amateur Cracksman. 1918: On the Quiet. Here Comes the Bride. 1919: The Test of Honor. 1920: Dr Jekyll and Mr Hyde. 1921: The Lotus Eater. 1922: Sherlock Holmes (GB: Moriarty). 1924: Beau Brummell. 1926: The Sea Beast. 1927: *Life in Hollywood No 4. *Twenty Minutes at Warner Brothers' Studios. When a Man Loves (GB: His Lady). The Beloved Rogue. 1928: Tempest. 1929: Eternal Love. Show of Shows. General Crack. 1930: The Man from Blankley's. Moby Dick. 1931: Svengali. The Mad Genius. 1932: Arsene Lupin. Grand Hotel. A Bill of Divorcement. State's Attorney (GB: Cardigan's Last Case). 1933: Rasputin and the Empress (GB: Rasputin the Mad Monk). Topaze. Reunion in Vienna. Dinner at Eight. Night Flight. Scarlet River. 1934: Counsellor-at-Law. Long Lost Father. Twentieth Century. 1936: Romeo and Juliet. 1937: Maytime. Bulldog Drummond Comes Back. Night Club Scandal. True Confession. Bulldog Drummond's Revenge. 1938: Bulldog Drummond's Peril. Romance in the Dark. Spawn of the North. Marie Antoinette. Hold That Co-Ed (GB: Hold That Gal). The Great Man Votes. 1939: Midnight. 1940: The Great Profile. 1941: Playmates. *Screen Snapshots No. 107.

BARRYMORE, Lionel
(L. Blythe) 1878–1954
Irascible, versatile and popular American character star, the brother of Ethel and John (both qv). A stage actor from his late teens who had at one time ambitions to be an artist, Lionel devoted his later years almost entirely to the cinema. He won an Academy Award in 1931 for A Free Soul, and continued his career despite being disabled by a fall in 1937. Now acting from a wheelchair, he gained renewed popularity as crusty old Dr Gillespie in the M-G-M Kildare/Gillespie series of the 1930s and 1940s. He received an Oscar nomination in the best director category for the 1929 version of Madame X.
1911: *Fighting Blood. *The Miser's Heart.

*The Battle. 1912: *An Adventure in the Autumn Woods. *Brutality. *The Chief's Dilemma. *Friends. *The Chief's Blanket. *A Cry for Help. *Fate. *The God Within. *Gold and Glitter. *Home Folks. *The Informer. *Love in an Apartment Hotel. *The Massacre. *The Musketeers of Pig Alley. *My Baby. *The New York Hat. *Oil and Water. *The One She Loved. *So Near and Yet So Far. *The Burglar's Dilemma. *The Painted Lady. *My Hero. *The Telephone Girl and the Lady. *Three Friends. 1913: *The Battle of Elderbrush Gulch. *Death's Marathon. *The House of Darkness. *Brute Force. *Just Gold. *The Lady and the Mouse. *A Misunderstood Boy. *Near to Earth. *The Mirror. *Red Hicks Defies the World. *In Diplomatic Circles. *The Enemy's Baby. *I Was Meant for You. *The Strong Man's Burden. *All for Science. *The Perfidy of Mary. *The Rancher's Revenge. *The Sheriff's Baby. *The Wrong Bottle. *A Girl's Stratagem. *The Well. *The Crook and the Girl. *The Switch Tower. *A Timely Interception. *The Wanderer. *The Yaqui Cur. *Her Father's Silent Partner. *Pa Says. *A Welcome Intruder. *Woman Against Woman. *The Fatal Wedding. *Father's Lesson. *His Inspiration. *Mister Jefferson Green. *So Runs the Way. *The Suffragette Minstrels. *The Vengeance of Galora. *Classmates. *The House of Discord. *The Power of the Press. *The Stolen Treaty. 1914: Men and Women. The Span of Life. Judith of Bethulia. Strongheart. The Woman in Black. The Seals of the Mighty. Under the Gaslight. 1915: Wildfire. The Romance of Elaine (serial). A Modern Magdalen. The Curious Life of Judge Legarde. The Flaming Sword. Dora Thorne. A Yellow Streak. 1916: Dorian's Divorce. The Quitter. The Upheaval. The Brand of Cowardice. 1917: The End of the Tour. His Father's Son. The Millionaire's Double. Life's Whirlpool. 1919: The Valley of Night. 1920: The Copperhead. The Master Mind. The Devil's Garden. 1921: The Great Adventure. Jim the Penman. 1922: Boomerang Bill. The Face in the Fog. 1923: The Enemies of Women. Unseeing Eyes. 1924: The Eternal City. Decameron Nights. America. Meddling Women. 1925: I am the Man. Die Frau mit dem schlechten Ruf. The Iron Man. Children of the Whirlwind. The Girl Who Wouldn't Work. The Wrongdoers. Fifty-Fifty. The Splendid Road. 1926: The Barrier. *Wife Tamers. Brooding Eyes. The Lucky Lady. Paris at Midnight. The Bells. The Temptress. 1927: The Show. Women Love Diamonds. Body and Soul. The Thirteenth Hour. 1928: Love (GB: Anna Karenina). Sadie Thompson. Drums of Love. West of Zanzibar. The Lion and the Mouse. Road House. The River Woman. 1929: Alias Jimmy Valentine. Hollywood Revue of 1929. Mysterious Island. 1930: Free and Easy. 1931: A Free Soul. The Yellow Ticket (GB: The Yellow Passport). *Jackie Cooper's Christmas (GB: The Christmas Party). Mata Hari. Guilty Hands. 1932: Broken Lullaby (GB: The Man I Killed). Arsene Lupin. Washington Masquerade (GB: Mad Masquerade). Grand Hotel. Rasputin and the Empress (GB: Rasputin the Mad Monk). 1933: Sweepings. Looking Forward (GB: Service). Dinner at Eight. Stranger's Return. Night Flight. One Man's Journey. Scarlet River. The Late Christopher Bean. Should

Ladies Behave? 1934: This Side of Heaven. Carolina (GB: The House of Connelly). Cardboard City. Treasure Island. The Girl from Missouri (GB: 100 Per Cent Pure). 1935: Mark of the Vampire. David Copperfield. The Little Colonel. Public Hero Number One. The Return of Peter Grimm. Ah, Wilderness! 1936: The Voice of Bugle Ann. The Road to Glory. The Devil-Doll. The Gorgeous Hussy. Camille. 1937: A Family Affair. Captains Courageous. Saratoga. Navy Blue and Gold. A Yank at Oxford. 1938: Test Pilot. You Can't Take It With You. Young Dr. Kildare. 1939: Let Freedom Ring. Calling Dr Kildare. On Borrowed Time. Secret of Dr Kildare. 1940: Dr Kildare's Strange Case. Dr Kildare Goes Home. Dr Kildare's Crisis. 1941: The Bad Man (GB: Two-Gun Cupid). The Penalty. *Cavalcade of the Academy Awards. The People versus Dr Kildare (GB: My Life is Yours). Lady Be Good. Dr Kildare's Wedding Day (GB: Mary Names the Day). 1942: Dr Kildare's Victory (GB: The Doctor and the Debutante). Calling Dr Gillespie. Dr Gillespie's New Assistant. 1943: Tennessee Johnson (GB: The Man on America's Conscience). Thousands Cheer. Dr Gillespie's Criminal Case (GB: Crazy to Kill). A Guy Named Joe. *The Last Will and Testament of Tom Smith. 1944: Three Men in White. Dragon Seed (narrator). Since You Went Away. Between Two Women. 1945: The Valley of Decision. 1946: Three Wise Fools. The Secret Heart. It's a Wonderful Life. Duel in the Sun. 1947: Dark Delusion (GB: Cynthia's Secret). 1948: Key Largo. 1949: Down to the Sea in Ships. Malaya (GB: East of the Rising Sun). 1950: Right Cross. *The Screen Actor. 1951: Bannerline. 1952: Lone Star. 1953: Main Street to Broadway.
As director: 1917: Life's Whirlpool. 1929: *Confession. Madame X. His Glorious Night. The Unholy Night. 1930: The Rogue Song. 1931: Ten Cents a Dance.

BARTHELMESS, Richard 1895–1963
Thoughtful, ultra-serious, dark-haired American leading man who came to films straight from college and was used memorably by D.W. Griffith in *Broken Blossoms* and *Way Down East.* Immensely popular in sensitive roles through the 1920s, but his appeal was never quite as strong after the coming of the talkies, when he rarely seemed able to give his lines a completely natural inflexion. Died from cancer. Oscar nominations for *The Noose* and *The Patent Leather Kid.*

1916: War Brides (GB: Motherhood). Snow White. Gloria's Romance (serial). Just a Song at Twilight. 1917: The Seven Swans. The Valentine Girl. Bab's Diary. Camille. The Soul of Magdalen. The Streets of Illusion. Bab's Burglar. Nearly Married. The Moral Code. For Valor. The Eternal Sin. Sunshine Man. 1918: Hit the Trail Holiday. Rich Man, Poor Man. The Hope Chest. Boots. A Wild Primrose. 1919: The Girl Who Stayed Home. Three Men and a Girl. Peppy Polly. Broken Blossoms. I'll Get Him Yet. Scarlet Days. 1920: The Idol Dancer. The Love Flower. Way Down East. 1921: Experience. Tol'able David. 1922: The Seventh Day. Sonny. Fury. The Bond Boy. 1923: The Bright Shawl. The Fighting Blade. 1924: Twenty One. The Enchanted Cottage. Classmates. 1925: New Toys. Soul Fire. Shore Leave. The Beautiful City. 1926: Just Suppose. Ransom's Folly. The Amateur Gentleman. The White Black Sheep. 1927: The Patent Leather Kid. The Drop Kick (GB: Glitter). 1928: The Little Shepherd of Kingdom Come. The Noose. Kentucky Courage. Wheels of Chance. Out of the Ruins. Scarlet Seas. 1929: Weary River. Drag (GB: Parasites). Show of Shows. Young Nowheres. 1930: Son of the Gods. The Dawn Patrol. 1931: The Lash (GB: Adios). The Finger Points. The Last Flight. 1932: *The Stolen Jools (GB: The Slippery Pearls). *The Putter. Alias the Doctor. Cabin in the Cotton. 1933: Central Airport. Heroes for Sale. Massacre. 1934: A Modern Hero. Midnight Alibi. 1935: *Starlight Days at the Lido. A Spy of Napoleon. Four Hours to Kill. 1939: Only Angels Have Wings. 1940: The Man Who Talked Too Much. 1941: *Hollywood Visits the Navy. 1942: The Mayor of 44th Street. The Spoilers.

BARTHOLOMEW, Freddie
(Frederick Llewellen) 1924–1992
Dark-haired, British-born Hollywood child star with appealing round face, mainly in gentle or 'sissified' roles. The subject of many legal tangles between various relations, it was once estimated he had been in court twice a month between 1934 and 1939. In the fifties, he moved to a career in advertising. Died from emphysema.
1930: Toyland. 1931: Fascination. Let's Go Naked. 1932: Lily Christine. 1935: David Copperfield. Anna Karenina. Professional Soldier. 1936: Little Lord Fauntleroy. The Devil is a Sissy (GB: The Devil Takes the Count). Lloyds of London. 1937: Captains Courageous. 1938: Kidnapped. Lord Jeff (GB:

The Boy from Barnardo's). Listen, Darling.
1939: Spirit of Culver (GB: Man's Heritage).
Two Bright Boys. 1940: Swiss Family
Robinson. Tom Brown's Schooldays. 1941:
Naval Academy. 1942: Cadets on Parade. A
Yank at Eton. Junior Army. 1944: The Town
Went Wild. 1947: Sepia Cinderella. 1949:
Outward Bound (TV). 1951: St Benny the Dip
(GB: Escape If You Can).

BARTOK, Eva
(E. Szöke) 1926–1998
Striking, minxish, brunette Hungarian
actress on the international scene who made
more headlines than films, specially in a much
publicized marriage (her fourth) to Curt
Jurgens (1955–1956) and an affair with Frank
Sinatra. Made her debut in Hungary and
claims to have had two lines in a second
Hungarian film, although no trace of this
'appearance' seems to have survived. She left
show business in the sixties for a life of 'peace
and tranquillity' in Indonesia, but by the
nineties was a bag lady in London's Soho.
She died following heart problems.
1947: Mezet Próféta (US: Prophet of the
Fields). 1950: Madeleine. 1951: A Tale of Five
Cities. 1952: Venetian Bird (US: The
Assassin). The Crimson Pirate. 1953: Der letzte
Walzer. Spaceways. Park Plaza 605 (US:
Norman Conquest). Front Page Story. 1954:
Meines Vaters Pferde. Carnival Story (German
version: Rummelplatz der Liebe). Orient
Express. Viktoria und ihr Husar. 1955: Dunja /
Der Postmeister (GB: Her Crime Was Love).
Von Himmel gefallen / Special Delivery. Break
in the Circle. The Gamma People. 1956: Ohne
Dich wird es Nacht. Durch die Wälder, durch
die Auen. 1957: Ten Thousand Bedrooms.
1958: Operation Amsterdam. Der Arzt von
Stalingrad. Madeleine – Tel 136211. 1959:
Operation Caviare. SOS Pacific. Douze heures
d'horloge. 1960: Ein Student ging vorbei.
Beyond the Curtain. 12 Stunden Angst. 1961:
Unter Ausschluss der Öffentlichkeit. Diesmal
muss es Kaviar sein (US: The Reluctant Spy).
The Woman with Red Hair. Es muss nicht
immer Kaviar sein. 1962: Eheinstitut Aurora
(US: Aurora Marriage Bureau). Winter im
Ischia. 1963: Ferien wie noch nie. I'll See You
in Hell. 1964: Sei donne per l'assassino (GB:
Blood and Black Lace). 1965: Savina. 1974:
Pele, King of Football.

BASEHART, Richard 1914–1984
Subdued, introverted, sandy-haired American
actor, much at home with mental anguish,

less at ease in action roles. After winning the
New York Critics' Best Newcomer Award
(1945), he was tipped for top stardom. When
it didn't quite arrive, he went abroad, and
played good roles in some excellent films
until his luck ran out in the late fifties. He
later appeared in a string of unlikely roles.
Long married to Valentina Cortese (qv), but
divorced in 1971. Died after a series of
strokes.
1946: Cry Wolf. 1947: Repeat Performance.
1948: He Walked by Night. 1949: The Black
Book (GB: Reign of Terror). Roseanna
McCoy. Tension. 1950: Outside the Wall.
1951: Fourteen Hours. The House on Telegraph
Hill. Fixed Bayonets. Decision Before Dawn.
1952: Titanic. 1953: The Stranger's Hand.
1954: La strada / The Road. Avanzi di galeria
(US: Jailbirds). The Good Die Young.
Cartouche. 1955: Canyon Crossroads. La veno
d'oro (US: The Golden Touch). Il bidone
(GB: The Spivs. US: The Swindlers). 1956:
The Extra Day. The Intimate Stranger (US:
Finger of Guilt). Moby Dick. 1957: So Soon to
Die (TV). Time Limit. Dimas / Arrivederci,
Dimas. 1958: The Brothers Karamazov. 1959:
The Man Stalin Killed. A Dream of Treason
(TV). Five Branded Women. The Restless and
the Damned (GB: The Climbers. US: The
Ambitious Ones). Jons und Erdman. 1960:
Portrait in Black. The Hiding Place (TV). For
the Love of Mike (GB: None But the Brave).
1961: Passport to China (GB: Visa to
Canton). 1962: Hitler. The Savage Guns.
1963: Kings of the Sun. 1964: Four Days in
November (narrator only). The Satan Bug.
1969: Un homme qui me plaît (GB: A Man I
Like. US: Love is a Funny Thing). The Sole
Survivor (TV). 1971: City Beneath the Sea
(TV. GB: cinemas: One Hour to Doomsday).
The Death of Me Yet (TV). The Birdmen
(TV. GB: cinemas: Escape of the Birdmen).
Chato's Land. 1972: Assignment Munich
(TV). The Bounty Man (TV). Rage. The
Sagittarius Mine. 1973: Dive to Danger
(narrator only). And Millions Must Die.
Maneater (TV). 1974: Valley Forge (TV).
1975: Mansion of the Doomed (GB: The
Terror of Dr Chaney). 1976: 21 Hours at
Munich (TV. GB: cinemas). Flood! (TV. GB:
cinemas). Time Travelers (TV). 1977: The
Island of Dr Moreau. The Great Georgia Bank
Hoax. Stonestreet (TV). 1978: The Court
Martial of Lt William Calley. WEB (TV).
1979: Being There. 1980: Marilyn: the Untold
Story (TV. GB: cinemas). 1981: Knight Rider
(TV).

BASINGER, Kim (Kimila Basinger) 1953–
Willowy (5 ft 7½ in), sultry, full-lipped,
electric-blonde American actress and singer
of calculating gaze. A model, beauty contest
winner, and Playboy centrefold, the girl from
Georgia (pronounce the name Bay-singer, as
in vocalist) hung on to an acting career and
eventually established herself as a lightweight
above-the-title star in her late twenties,
mainly in pallidly sensual roles. Although she
showed no great aptitude for comedy, she
tried several in the late 1980s, but it was in
1990s' drama that she revealed her acting now
carried more bite. One of the few '007' girls to
survive James Bond 'stardom', she hit the
headlines in 1993 when losing a multi-million
lawsuit for withdrawing from a film (Boxing
Helena) just before it started, and was subsequently declared bankrupt. Married actor
Alec Baldwin (qv) in 1991. She won an
Academy Award for L.A. Confidential.
1977: Dog and Cat (TV). 1978: The Ghost of
Flight 401 (TV). Katie: Portrait of a Centerfold (TV). 1981: Hard Country. Killjoy
(TV). 1982: Mother Lode. 1983: Never Say
Never Again. The Man Who Loved Women.
1984: The Natural. 9½ Weeks. 1985: Fool for
Love. 1986: No Mercy. 1987: Blind Date.
Nadine. 1988: My Stepmother is an Alien.
1989: Batman. 1990: The Marrying Man
(GB: Too Hot to Handle). 1991: Final
Analysis. 1992: Cool World. 1993: The Real
McCoy. Wayne's World 2. 1994: The Geta-
way. Prêt-à-Porter (US: Ready to Wear).
1997: L.A. Confidential. 2000: I Dream of
Africa. Bless the Child.

BASSETT, Angela 1958–
Powerful American actress of gaunt beauty
who came lamentably late to leading roles for
the cinema. A resident of the Broadway and
off-Broadway stages in her early years, she
was little seen in films and TV until she had
turned 30. But she really started building up
her small- and big-screen c.v.s in the early
1990s, and was rewarded with the star role in
Tina What's Love Got to Do With It, in which
her shining performance as Tina Turner was
recognised with an Oscar nomination.
Although now established in leading roles, her
age may dictate that her time at the top is
short.
1985: Doubletake (TV). F/X (GB: FX:
Murder by Illusion). 1986: Liberty (TV).
1989: They're Doing My Time (TV). 1990:
Challenger (TV). Perry Mason: The Case of
the Silenced Singer (TV). In the Best Interest

of the Child (TV). 1991: City of Hope. Heroes of Desert Storm. Locked Up: A Mother's Rage (TV. GB: The Other Side of Love). Line of Fire: The Morris Dees Story (TV). Blind Hate (TV). Kindergarten Cop. Fire! Trapped on the 37th Floor (TV). 1992: Critters 4. Innocent Blood. Passion Fish. Malcolm X. 1993: Tina What's Love Got to Do With It. 1995: Strange Days. Vampire in Brooklyn. Waiting to Exhale. Panther. 1997: Contact. 1998: How Stella Got Her Goove Back. 1999: Supernova. Music of the Heart. Wings Against the Wind. 2000: Boesman and Lena. 2001: The Score.

BATES, Alan 1934–

Dark-haired, solid English stage actor who came to the screen with the wave of angry young men in the early 1960s. Adept at playing rough diamonds insensitive to other people's feelings. Bates proved very popular in the middle and late 1960s, after which he got involved in several highly uncommercial enterprises, and concentrated on the theatre until the late 1970s. Further cinema roles continued by and large to be unworthy of his talents. Oscar nomination for *The Fixer*.
1956: *It's Never Too Late*. 1960: *The Entertainer*. 1961: *Whistle Down the Wind*. 1962: *A Kind of Loving*. 1963: *The Running Man*. *The Caretaker* (US: *The Guest*). *Nothing But the Best*. 1964: *Zorba the Greek*. 1965: *Insh'Allah* (narrator only). 1966: *Georgy Girl*. *King of Hearts*. 1967: *Far from the Madding Crowd*. 1968: *The Fixer*. 1969: *Women in Love*. 1970: *Three Sisters*. 1971: *The Go-Between*. *A Day in the Death of Joe Egg*. 1972: *Second Best*. 1973: *Impossible Object / The Story of a Love Story*. 1974: *Mikis Theodorakis: A Profile of Greatness*. *Butley*. *The Story of Jacob and Joseph* (TV). 1975: *In*

Celebration. Royal Flash. 1977: An Unmarried Woman. 1978: The Shout. 1979: The Rose. 1980: Very Like a Whale (TV). Nijinsky. 1981: Quartet. The Trespasser (TV). Rece deo gory / Hands Up! 1982: The Return of the Soldier. Britannia Hospital. 1983: Dr Fischer of Geneva (TV). 1986: Duet for One. 1987: A Prayer for the Dying. Pack of Lies (TV). Force majeure. 1989: We Think the World of You. 1990: Doctor M. Mister Frost. Hamlet. The Cherry Orchard. 1991: 102 Boulevard Haussmann (TV). Secret Friends. Shuttlecock (TV: US: cinemas). 1992: Silent Tongue. 1994: Oliver's Travels (TV). 1995: The Grotesque. 1998: Nicholas' Gift (TV). 1999: The Cherry Orchard. St Patrick The Irish Legend. 2000: Varya.

BAXTER, Anne 1923–1985

Brown-haired American leading actress, particularly good at playing deceptively sweet young things, an outstanding example being her Eve in *All About Eve*, for which she received an Oscar nomination. An attempt to revise her image from dramatic actress to pin-up girl in the fifties proved unsuccessful. The granddaughter of architect Frank Lloyd Wright, she won an Academy Award in 1946 for *The Razor's Edge*. Married to John Hodiak (first of two) 1946–1953. Died following a stroke.
1940: *Twenty Mule Team*. *The Great Profile*. 1941: *Charley's Aunt* (GB: *Charley's American Aunt*). *Swamp Water* (GB: *The Man Who Came Back*). 1942: *The Magnificent Ambersons*. *The Pied Piper*. 1943: *Crash Dive*. *Five Graves to Cairo*. *The North Star*. 1944: *The Sullivans*. *The Eve of St Mark*. *Guest in the House*. *Sunday Dinner for a Soldier*. 1945: *A Royal Scandal* (GB: *Czarina*). *Smoky*. 1946: *Angel on My Shoulder*. *The Razor's Edge*. 1947: *Mother Wore Tights* (narrator only). *Blaze of Noon*. 1948: *Homecoming*. *The Luck of the Irish*. *The Walls of Jericho*. 1949: *Yellow Sky*. *You're My Everything*. 1950: *A Ticket to Tomahawk*. *All About Eve*. 1951: *Follow the Sun*. 1952: *Screen Snapshots No. 206*. *The Outcasts of Poker Flat*. *My Wife's Best Friend*. *O. Henry's Full House* (GB: *Full House*). 1953: *I Confess*. *The Blue Gardenia*. 1954: *Carnival Story / Rummelplatz der Liebe*. 1955: *One Desire*. *The Spoilers*. 1956: *The Come-On*. *The Ten Commandments*. *Three Violent People*. 1958: *The Right Hand Man* (TV). *Chase a Crooked Shadow*. 1960: *Cimarron*. *Summer of the 17th Doll* (US: *Season of Passion*). 1961: *Mix Me a Person*.

1962: *A Walk on the Wild Side*. 1965: *The Family Jewels*. 1966: *The Tall Women*. 1967: *Stranger on the Run* (TV). *The Busy Body*. 1968: *The Challengers* (TV). *Companions in Nightmare* (TV). 1969: *Marcus Welby MD* (TV). 1970: *Ritual of Evil* (TV). 1971: *If Tomorrow Comes* (TV). *Fools' Parade* (GB: *Dynamite Man from Glory Jail*). *The Catcher* (TV). *Lapin 360*. 1972: *The Late Liz* (TV). *Lisa Bright and Dark* (TV). 1977: *Nero Wolfe* (TV). 1978: *Little Mo* (TV). 1980: *Jane Austen in Manhattan* (TV). 1983: *The Architecture of Frank Lloyd Wright* (narrator only). 1984: *The Masks of Death* (TV).

BAXTER, Jane (Feodora Forde) 1909–1996

Unpretty but personable, brown-haired, German-born Jane Baxter had a lovely smile and proved one of Britain's most popular leading ladies in gently upper-crust roles of the mid–1930s. She was Charles Laughton's leading lady in *Down River* and Richard Tauber's in *Blossom Time*. Her limited cinematic appeal soon waned when she reached her thirties, but she continued to appear to good effect on stage. Her first husband, a racing driver, was killed in a crash.
1930: *Bedrock*. *Bed and Breakfast*. 1931: *Down River*. 1932: *Two White Arms* (US: *Wives Beware*). *Flat Number Nine*. 1933: *The Constant Nymph*. 1934: *The Night of the Party*. *The Double Event*. *Girls Please!* *Blossom Time* (US: *April Romance*). *We Live Again*. 1935: *Royal Cavalcade* (US: *Regal Cavalcade*). *Drake of England* (US: *Drake the Pirate*). *The Enchanted April*. *The Clairvoyant*. *Line Engaged*. 1936: *The Man behind the Mask*. *Dusty Ermine* (US: *Hideout in the Alps*). 1937: *Second Best Bed*. 1938: *The Ware Case*. 1939: *Confidential Lady*. *Murder Will Out*. *The Chinese Bungalow* (US: *Chinese Den*). 1940: *The Briggs Family*. 1941: *Ships with Wings*. 1943: *The Flemish Farm*. 1951: *Death of an Angel*. 1953: *All Hallowe'en*.

BAXTER, Warner 1889–1951

Solid, dependable, moustachioed American leading man, whose very seriousness contrasted strangely with his most popular characterization, the Cisco Kid, in which guise he won an Academy Award in 1929. Hollywood's top money-earner in 1936, after which his career gradually declined to lesser films. He had a nervous breakdown in the early 1940s, and suffered from chronic arthritis in later years. Died of bronchial pneumonia.

1914: Her Own Money. 1918: All Woman. 1919: Lombardi Ltd. 1921: Cheated Hearts. First Love. 1922: Her Own Money. The Love Charm. Sheltered Daughters. If I Were Queen. The Girl in His Room. A Girl's Desire. 1923: Blow Your Own Horn. The Ninety and Nine. St Elmo. 1924: Alimony. In Search of a Thrill. Christine of the Hungry Heart. The Female. His Forgotten Wife. Those Who Dance. The Garden of Weeds. 1925: The Golden Bed. The Awful Truth. Welcome Home. Air Mail. A Son of His Father. Mannequin. The Best People. Rugged Water. 1926: Miss Brewster's Millions. The Runaway. Mismates. Aloma of the South Seas. The Great Gatsby. 1927: Drums of the Desert. Singed. The Coward. Telephone Girl. 1928: The Tragedy of Youth. Three Sinners. Ramona. A Woman's Way. Craig's Wife. Danger Street. 1929: Linda. The Far Call. West of Zanzibar. In Old Arizona. Thru Different Eyes. Behind That Curtain. Romance of the Rio Grande. 1930: Happy Days. Such Men Are Dangerous. Arizona Kid. Renegades. Doctors' Wives. 1931: The Squaw Man (GB: The White Man). Daddy Long Legs. Their Mad Moment. The Cisco Kid. Surrender. 1932: Amateur Daddy. *The Stolen Jools (GB: The Slippery Pearls). Man About Town. Six Hours to Live. Dangerously Yours. 1933: Forty-Second Street. I Loved You Wednesday. Paddy the Next Best Thing. Penthouse (GB: Crooks in Clover). 1934: As Husbands Go. Stand Up and Cheer. Such Women Are Dangerous. Grand Canary. Broadway Bill (GB: Strictly Confidential). Hell in the Heavens. 1935: One More Spring. Under the Pampas Moon. King of Burlesque. 1936: *La Fiesta de Santa Barbara. Robin Hood of El Dorado. The Prisoner of Shark Island. The Road to Glory. To Mary – With Love. White Hunter. 1937: Slave Ship. Vogues of 1938. Wife, Doctor and Nurse. Kidnapped. I'll Give a Million. 1939: Wife, Husband and Friend. Return of the Cisco Kid. Barricade. 1940: Earthbound. 1941: Adam Had Four Sons. 1943: The Crime Doctor. The Crime Doctor's Strangest Case (GB: The Strangest Case). 1944: Lady in the Dark. Shadows in the Night. 1945: The Crime Doctor's Courage (GB: The Doctor's Courage). Just Before Dawn. The Crime Doctor's Warning (GB: The Warning). 1946: The Crime Doctor's Man Hunt. 1947: The Millerson Case. The Crime Doctor's Gamble (GB: The Doctor's Gamble). 1948: A Gentleman from Nowhere. Prison Warden. 1949: The Devil's Henchman. The Crime Doctor's Diary. 1950: State Penitentiary.

BEAL, John (James Bliedung) 1909–1997
Dark, compact American leading man of the sincere, sensitive, brooding type, often cast as men wrestling with their own consciences. He enjoyed some good roles at RKO in the 1930s, but failed to prove a dominant enough personality to sustain a star career. In the 1950s, he made some reputation on TV in largely macabre roles. During World War II, he had directed war training films, but never directed a feature film, spending most of the latter part of his career with stage touring companies. Died from complications following a stroke.
1933: Another Language. 1934: Hat, Coat and Glove. The Little Minister. 1935: Les Miserables. Laddie. Break of Hearts. 1936: M'Liss. We Who Are About to Die. 1937: The Man Who Found Himself. Border Café. Danger Patrol. Double Wedding. Madame X. Beg, Borrow or Steal. 1938: Port of Seven Seas. I Am the Law. The Arkansas Traveler. 1939: The Great Conmandment. The Cat and the Canary. 1941: Ellery Queen and the Perfect Crime (GB: The Perfect Crime). Doctors Don't Tell. 1942: Atlantic Convoy. Stand By All Networks. One Thrilling Night. 1943: Edge of Darkness. Let's Have Fun. 1948: Key Witness. So Dear to My Heart. 1949: Alimony. Song of Surrender. Chicago Deadline. 1950: Messenger of Peace. Hit the Deck (TV). 1952: My Six Convicts. 1953: Remains to be Seen. 1954: The Country Parson. 1957: That Night! The Vampire. 1959: The Sound and the Fury. 1960: Ten Who Dared. 1966: The Easter Angel (TV). 1974: The House That Cried Murder. 1975: The Legend of Lizzie Borden (TV). 1977: Eleanor and Franklin: The White House Years (TV). 1979: Jennifer: A Woman's Story (TV). 1983: Amityville 3D. 1988: A Place at the Table (TV). 1990: The Kid Who Loved Christmas (TV). 1993: The Firm.

BEALS, Jennifer 1963–
Tall, willowy, dark-eyed American actress with strong features, 'Latin' looks and a mass of black, curly hair. A successful model thrust into the acting spotlight when given the leading role in Flashdance, her film career nosedived in the years that followed. She surprised many by coming back in 1988 and working hard on lower-profile subjects – for television and overseas producers as well as mainline Hollywood cinema. Married movie director Alexandre Rockwell.
1980: My Bodyguard. 1983: Flashdance. 1985: The Bride. 1988: Layover. Vampire's Kiss. Kid Gloves/Split Decisions. La partita/The Gamble/The Match. 1989: Sons. Rider in the Dark. Jackal's Run. 1990: Doctor M/Club Extinction. Hot House. A Reasonable Doubt. Blood and Concrete, a Love Story. 1991: In the Soup. 1992: Black Wedding/Terror Stalks the Class Reunion. 2000 Malibu Road (TV). Indecency. 1993: Caro diario/Dear Diary. Stress. Le grand pardon 2/Day of Atonement. Red Rain. The Search for James C Hoyt (cable TV. Released in 1996 as The Search for One-Eyed Jimmy). Night Owl (TV). 1994: Dead on Sight. Caro diario/Dear Diary. Mrs Parker & the Vicious Circle. 1995: Let It Be Me. Arabian Knight (voice only). Devil in a Blue Dress. Four Rooms. 1996: The Twilight of the Golds. Deporting California. The Spree (TV). 1997: Prophecy III: Ashtown. 1998: Thursday. The Last Days of Disco. 1999: Turbulence 2: Fear of Flying (TV). Body and Soul (TV). Something More. 2000: A House Divided (TV). Militia.

BEAN, Sean 1958–
Tall, fair-haired, craggily good-looking British actor who has made fewer films than you might think, and several of them as villains. On TV, though, his profile has been higher in several series of the exploits of the heroic Sharpe, as well as in leading roles in such classic dramas as Lady Chatterley's Lover, Clarissa and The Fifteen Streets, plus the US mini-series Scarlett. Sheffield-born, RADA-trained, Bean has continued in leading and semi-leading parts on both sides of the Atlantic, mostly as tough customers. Married/divorced actress Melanie Hill. A passionate supporter of soccer club Sheffield United.
1984: Winter Flight. 1985: Our Exploits at West Poley. 1986: Caravaggio. 1987: My

Kingdom for a Horse. 1988: War Requiem. Stormy Monday. How to Get Ahead in Advertising. 1989: Windprints. 1990: The Field. Lorna Doone (TV). 1991: Tell Me That You Love Me (TV). Prince. 1992: Fool's Gold (TV). Patriot Games. 1993: Shopping. A Woman's Guide to Adultery (TV). 1994: Black Beauty. Jacob (TV). 1995: GoldenEye. When Saturday Comes. 1997: Leo Tolstoy's Anna Karenina. Tarzan & Jane. 1998: Bravo Two Zero (TV). Airborne. The Canterbury Tales (voice only). Ronin. 2000: Essex Boys. 2001: Lord of the Rings: The Fellowship of the Ring. Lord of the Rings: The Two Towers.

BÉART, Emmanuelle 1963–
Wispily fair-haired, delicately attractive, almost other-worldly French actress with fine-boned features. The daughter of singer Guy Béart, her excellent English, the product of several years in Canada, led her to try international films after her first great success as the pivotal figure in *Manon des Sources*, the sequel to *Jean de Florette*. But her film career was disappointingly spotty until a second big hit, with *Un coeur en hiver*, propelled her back into the limelight. Since seen in a more satisfying variety of roles, she dipped her toes into Hollywood waters with a leading part in *Mission: Impossible*. Married actor Daniel Auteuil (*qv*).
1971: La course du lièvre à travers les champs (GB and US: And Hope to Die). 1975: Demain les mômes. 1983: Premiers désirs. 1984: Zacharias. Raison perdue. Un amour interdit. 1985: L'enfant trouvé. L'amour en douce. 1986: Manon des Sources (US: Manon of the Spring). 1987: Date With an Angel. 1989: Les enfants du désordre (US: Children of Chaos). A gauche en sortant de l'ascenseur/Door on Your Left As You Leave the Elevator. 1990: Il viaggio di Capitan Fracassa/Capitaine Fracasse. 1991: La belle noiseuse. J'embrasse pas/I Don't Kiss. 1992: Contre l'oublie. Un coeur en hiver. Ruptures. Le valet de pique. 1993: L'enfer. 1994: Une femme française. Mécaniques célestes. Haute époque. 1995: Nelly et Monsieur Arnaud. L'analphabète. 1996: Mission: Impossible. Le dernier chaperon rouge. 1998: Don Juan. Voleur de vie (US: Stolen Life). 1999: Elephant Juice. Le temps retrouvé. La buche (US: Season's Beatings). 2000: Les déstinées sentimentales.

BEATTY, Robert 1909–1992
Dark-haired Canadian actor, in Britain from the 1930s. He entered films as an extra and

stand-in, but was groomed into a minor star by Ealing Studios from 1943 and remained quite popular in leading parts until the mid–1950s. Also well-liked in radio serials as the detective Philip O'Dell. His velvet tones have been used so frequently in narration, mainly in documentary films, that this part of his work is listed separately here.
1938: Black Limelight. Murder in Soho (US: Murder in the Night). 1940: For Freedom. Mein Kampf – My Crimes. Dangerous Moonlight (US: Suicide Squadron). 1941: 49th Parallel (US: The Invaders). 1942: One of Our Aircraft is Missing. The First of the Few. Flying Fortress. Suspected Person. 1943: San Demetrio London. 1944: It Happened One Sunday. 1946: Appointment with Crime. Odd Man Out. 1947: Green Fingers. 1948: Against the Wind. Counterblast. Another Shore. Portrait from Life (US: The Girl in the Painting). 1949: The Twenty Questions Murder Mystery. 1950: Her Favourite Husband (US: The Taming of Dorothy). 1951: Captain Horatio Hornblower RN. Calling Bulldog Drummond. The Magic Box. 1952: Wings of Danger (US: Dead on Course). The Gentle Gunman. The Net (US: Project M7). The Oracle (US: The Horse's Mouth). 1953: Man on a Tightrope. The Square Ring. The Broken Horseshoe. Albert RN (US: Break to Freedom). 1954: L'amante di Paride (GB: The Face That Launched a Thousand Ships). Out of the Clouds. 1955: Portrait of Alison (US: Postmark for Danger). 1957: Time Lock. Tarzan and the Lost Safari. Something of Value. 1959: The Shakedown. 1961: Tremor. 1962: The Amorous Prawn. 1964: Bikini Paradise. 1965: Die Todesstrahlen des Dr Mabuse. 1967: The 25th Hour. 1968: 2001: a Space Odyssey. Where Eagles Dare. 1972: Sitting Target. 1973: Man at the Top. 1974: The Spikes Gang. 1976: The Pink Panther Strikes Again. 1977: Golden Rendezvous. 1979: The Martian Chronicles (TV). The Spaceman and King Arthur (US: Unidentified Flying Oddball). 1981: The Amateur. 1983: Superman III. 1985: Minder on the Orient Express (TV). 1986: Labyrinth (voice only). 1987: Superman IV: The Quest for Peace. 1988: Diamond High. 1989: The Return of Sam McCloud (TV).
As narrator: 1952: *Spotlight on Reuters. *World of Life (and ensuing series). *The Figurehead. 1953: *Modern Ireland. The Master of Ballantrae. 1954: *Spotlight on Food (and ensuing *Spotlight series). 1955: Paris in London. *Four Legs to Master. 1956: 48

Hours. *Have a Care. *Fur, Feathers and Finery. *Signs of Life. *June in January. 1957: *Operation Universe. The Savage Mountain. *And So Forth. *The Oyster and the Pearl. *Battleground. *Mountain Holiday. 1958: *Pooches on Parade. *Secret World. *Riviera Express. 1959: *Cuckoo Land. *The Isle and the Pussycat. *Wrecker's Coast. 1960: The Mad Twenties. 1962: *Six of the Best. A Short Memory. 1966: One Million Years BC.

BEATTY, Warren
(Henry W. Beaty) 1937–
Boyishly handsome, dark-haired American leading man with a powerful personality and careful preparation of role which tends to show on screen. The brother of Shirley MacLaine (*qv*), his career has varied between immense hits and disastrous flops. In the early 1970s, his prodigious love life won him more headlines than his acting, but when he turned to direction his talent behind the camera was immediately apparent, and he won the 1982 directing Oscar for *Reds*. There have been acting Oscar nominations for *Bonnie and Clyde*, *Heaven Can Wait* and *Reds*. After more than half a lifetime of bachelorhood, he finally married actress Annette Bening (*qv*) in 1992.
1962: Splendor in the Grass. The Roman Spring of Mrs Stone. 1962: All Fall Down. 1964: Lilith. 1965: Mickey One. 1966: Promise Her Anything. Kaleidoscope. 1967: Bonnie and Clyde. 1969: The Only Game in Town. 1970: Arthur Penn, 1922: themes and variants. 1971: $ (GB: The Heist). McCabe and Mrs Miller. 1973: Year of the Woman. 1974: The Parallax View. The Fortune. 1975: Shampoo. 1978: †Heaven Can Wait. 1981: ‡Reds. 1986: Ishtar. 1990: ‡Dick Tracy. 1991: Bugsy. Truth or Dare (GB: In Bed with Madonna). 1994: Love Affair. 1998: Bulworth. 2000: Forever Hollywood (doc). Town and Country.

†And co-directed ‡And directed

BECKINSALE, Kate 1973–
Slim, dark-haired, sharp-featured British actress of pale complexion, who looks as though she would stand less nonsense than Mary Poppins, and has frequently been at her best as bossy or bitchy characters. The daughter of popular TV star Richard Beckinsale (1947–79), she has been in leading roles since she was 20; her ability to assume an immaculate American accent has also undoubtedly furthered her career. She has an

acting sister, Samantha Beckinsale.
1991: One Against the Wind (TV). 1992: Rachel's Dream (TV). 1993: Much Ado About Nothing. 1994: Prince of Jutland (US: Royal Deceit). La tabla de flandes (US: Uncovered). 1995: Cold Comfort Farm (TV. Later: cinemas). Marie-Louise, ou: la permission. Haunted. 1997: Shooting Fish. 1998: The Last Days of Disco. 1999: Brokedown Palace. Alice Through the Looking Glass (TV). 2000: The Golden Bowl. 2001: Pearl Harbor. Serendipity.

BEDELIA, Bonnie (B. B. Culkin) 1946–
A born-again career if ever there were one. A delicately pretty, dark-haired American actress, on stage at 10, Bedelia grew into an attractive performer who made her film debut at 23. She didn't seem to have quite the distinctive qualities for stardom, and drifted into a long run of movies for TV. The film comeback began with her portrayal of a lady racing driver in Heart Like a Wheel, but really blossomed in the late 1980s when she became universally recognised as Bruce Willis' wife in the first two Die Hard films. Aunt of child star Macaulay Culkin (qv).
1969: The Gypsy Moths. They Shoot Horses, Don't They? Then Came Bronson (TV. GB: cinemas). 1970: Lovers and Other Strangers. 1972: Sandcastles (TV. GB: cinemas). The Strange Vengeance of Rosalie. 1973: Hawkins on Murder (TV). Heatwave! (TV). Message to My Daughter (TV). Get Back. 1974: The New Land (TV). 1978: The Big Fix. A Question of Love (TV). 1979: Salem's Lot (TV. Shortened version shown in cinemas). Walking Through the Fire (TV). 1980: Tourist (TV). Fighting Back (TV). 1982: Million Dollar Infield (TV). 1983: Memorial Day (TV). Heart Like a Wheel. 1985: The Lady

from Yesterday (TV). Death of an Angel. Violets Are Blue. 1986: The Boy Who Could Fly. Alex: The Life of a Child (TV). 1987: When The Time Comes (TV). The Stranger. 1988: The Prince of Pennsylvania. Die Hard. 1989: Fat Man and Little Boy (GB: Shadowmakers). 1990: Die Hard 2. Presumed Innocent. Somebody Has to Shoot the Picture (TV). 1991: Switched at Birth (TV). 1992: Shattered Silence (TV). A Mother's Right: The Elizabeth Morgan Story (TV). 1993: Needful Things. The Fire Next Time (TV). Fallen Angels (TV). 1994: Judicial Consent. Shadow of a Doubt (TV). 1995: Speechless. Legacy of Sin: The William Coit Story (TV). 1996: A Season in Purgatory (TV). Homecoming (TV). 1997: Ghost in the Machine/ Bad Manners. Consensual Relations (TV). Her Costly Affair (TV). Any Mother's Son (TV). 1998: There's No Fish Food in Heaven. Gloria. To Live Again. 1999: Anywhere But Here. Locked in Silence (TV). 2000: Sordid Lives. Flowers for Algernon (TV). Picnic (TV).

†Scenes deleted from final release print

BEERY, Wallace 1885–1949
Hollywood's big lummox: a bull in a china shop, whose early serio-comic roles, casting him as the rampaging tough guy, with or without heart of gold, later gave way to figures of outright farce, especially in comedies with Marie Dressler and Marjorie Main. He won an Oscar in 1931 as the washed-up boxer in The Champ (after a nomination for The Big House) and was one of M-G-M's most popular stars in the early 1930s. Married to Gloria Swanson (qv) from 1916 to 1918, the first of two wives. Died from a heart attack at almost the same age as his acting brother Noah Beery Sr. (1883–1946).
1913: *A Successful Failure. *His Athletic Wife. *Sweet Revenge. *Mr Dippy Dipped. *Love Incognito. *Dad's Insanity. *The Usual Way. *Day by Day. *Their Wives Incognito. *Kitty's Knight. *Hello Trouble. *Smithy's Grandma's Party. *At the Old Maids' Ball. 1914: *A Queer Quarantine. *A Foot of Romance. *One-Two-Three. *Looking for Trouble. *Mrs Manley's Baby. *Oh, Doctor. *The Girl, the Cop and the Burglar. *Bargain Hunters. *The Winner. *Three Little Powders. *The Ups and Downs. *The Fable of the Brash Drummer and the Nectarine. *This is the Life. *Actor Finney's Finish. *Grass Country Goes Dry. *The Fable of Napoleon and the Bumpkin. *The Fable of the Higher Education That Was Too Much for

the Old Man. *The Fable of the Coming Champion Who Was Delayed. *Curing a Husband. *The Prevailing Craze. *The Fable of the Busy Business Boy and the Droppers-In. *Sweedie and the Lord. *Sweedie and the Double Exposure. *Sweedie's Skate. *Sweedie Springs a Surprise. *The Fickleness of Sweedie. *The Epidemic. *In and Out. *Topsy-Turvy Sweedie. *Love and Soda. *Rivalry and War. *Sweedie's Clean-Up. *The Laundress. *Three Boiled Down Fables. *Countess Collects for Charity. *Another Sidetrack. *The Fatal Album. *Their Cheap Vacation. *She Landed a Big One. *Sweedie Learns to Swim. *Sweedie and the Trouble Maker. *Sweedie at the Fair. *Madame Double X. *The Plum Tree. *Sweedie the Swatter. *The Fable of the Bush League Lover Who Failed to Qualify. *The Broken Pledge. *Chick Evans Links With Sweedie. 1915: *The Fable of Roystering Blades. *Sweedie's Suicide. *Sweedie and the Dog. *Two Hearts That Beat As Ten. *Sweedie's Hopeless Love. *Sweedie Goes to College. *Love and Trouble. *Sweedie Learns to Ride. *Sweedie's Hero. The Slim Princess. *Sweedie in Vaudeville. *Sweedie's Finish. *The New Teacher. *The Victor. *Sweedie and the Sultan's Present. *A Pound for a Pound. *Father's New Maid. *Ain't It the Truth. *The Bouquet. *Education. *Done in Wax. *The Broken Pledge. 1916: *Just a Few Little Things. *A Capable Lady Cook. *Timothy Dobbs, That's Me (series). *Hearts and Sparks. †*Sweedie and the Janitor. †*The Janitor's Vacation. †*The Janitor. *Teddy at the Throttle. *A Dash of Courage. 1917: *Bombs and Banknotes. *Are Waitresses Safe? *Cactus Nell. *The Clever Dummy. †*A Beach Nut. *Maggie's First False Step. Patria (serial). The Little American. That Night. 1918: *Bathhouse Scandal. Johanna Enlists. 1919: *Only a Janitor. The Love Burglar. The Unpardonable Sin. Life Line. Soldier of Fortune. Behind the Door. Victory. The Virgin of Stamboul. 1920: The Roundup. The Mollycoddle. The Last of the Mohicans. The Rookies Return. 1921: *The Northern Trail. *The Policeman and the Baby. *The Ne'er to Return Road. *The White Mouse. The Four Horsemen of the Apocalypse. 813. Patsy. A Tale of Two Worlds. The Golden Snare. The Last Trail. 1922: Wild Honey. The Man from Hell's River. The Rosary. The Sagebrush Trail. Ridin' Wild. I Am the Law. Robin Hood. Hurricane's Gal. Trouble Associated (GB: Trouble). Only a Shop Girl. 1923: Stormswept. The Flame of Life. Bavu. Ashes of Vengeance. Drifting. The Eternal Struggle. The Spanish Dancer. The Three Ages. Richard, the Lion Hearted. Drums of Jeopardy. White Tiger. 1924: The Sea Hawk. Unseen Hands. Madonna of the Streets. Dynamite Smith (GB: The Side Show). Another Man's Wife. The Red Lily. The Signal Tower. So Big. 1925: Let Women Alone. The Great Divide. Coming Through. The Devil's Cargo. Adventure. The Lost World. The Night Club. Rugged Water. In the Name of Love. Pony Express. 1926: Behind the Front. Volcano. Old Ironsides (GB: Sons of the Sea). We're in the Navy Now. The Wanderer. 1927: Casey at the Bat. Fireman, Save My Child. Now We're in the Air. 1928: Wife Savers. Partners in Crime. The Big Killing. Beggars of Life. 1929: Chinatown

Nights. Stairs of Sand. River of Romance. 1930: Way for a Sailor. Billy the Kid. A Lady's Morals (GB: Jenny Lind). The Big House. Min and Bill. 1931: The Secret Six. Hell Divers. *Jackie Cooper's Christmas (GB: The Christmas Party). The Champ. 1932: Grand Hotel. Flesh. *The Stolen Jools (GB: The Slippery Pearls). 1933: Dinner at Eight. Tugboat Annie. The Bowery. 1934: The Mighty Barnum. Viva Villa! Treasure Island. 1935: *Secrets of Hollywood. West Point of the Air. China Seas. O'Shaughnessy's Boy. Ah, Wilderness! 1936: A Message to Garcia. Old Hutch. 1937: Good Old Soak. Slave Ship. 1938: Bad Man of Brimstone. Port of Seven Seas. Stablemates. 1939: Stand Up and Fight. *Screen Snapshots No. 77. Sergeant Madden. Thunder Afloat. 1940: The Man from Dakota (GB: Arouse and Beware). Twenty Mule Team. Wyoming (GB: Bad Man of Wyoming). 1941: The Bad Man (GB: Two Gun Cupid). Barnacle Bill. The Bugle Sounds. 1942: Jackass Mail. 1943: Salute to the Marines. 1944: Rationing. Barbary Coast Gent. 1945: This Man's Navy. 1945: Bad Bascomb. The Mighty McGurk. 1948: Alias a Gentleman. A Date with Judy. 1949: Big Jack.

†Also directed

Also as director: 1916: Just a Few Little Things. Timothy Dobbs, That's Me. *A Capable Lady Cook.

BELAFONTE, Harry 1927–
Strikingly handsome black American singer/actor with mellifluous light voice who, strangely, didn't do his own singing in his biggest film hit, Carmen Jones. He has remained principally a record star, having several hits with calypso-style ballads, developing later into a portrayer of scruffy types in the occasional film, in contrast to his continuously smooth image as a singer. In 1984, he turned producer with the successful Beat Street. Father of actress Shari Belafonte. 1953: Bright Road. 1954: Carmen Jones. 1957: Island in the Sun. 1959: The World, the Flesh and the Devil. Odds Against Tomorrow. 1970: The Angel Levine. King: a Filmed Record . . . Montgomery to Memphis. 1972: Buck and the Preacher. 1974: Uptown Saturday Night. 1981: Grambling's White Tiger (TV). 1983: The Smoky. 1989: First Look. 1992: The Player. 1994: Prêt-à-Porter (US: Ready to Wear). 1995: White Man's Burden. 1996: Kansas City. Robert Altman's Jazz '34. 1999: Swing Vote (TV).

BEL GEDDES, Barbara 1922–
Round-faced, light-haired American actress of much warmth and appeal, who plays plain, sincere, lovable ladies. She made her stage debut at 17, but her wholesome image never really caught on in the cinema. Her career was also somewhat impaired by ill-health and the McCarthy witch-hunt; thus Hollywood let her best years escape the screen. Nominated for an Oscar in I Remember Mama, she has undoubtedly made too few films, but did become a familiar figure to television audiences of the 1980s as Miss Ellie in Dallas. 1947: The Long Night. The Gangster. 1948: I Remember Mama. Blood on the Moon. 1949: Caught. 1950: Panic in the Streets. 1951: Fourteen Hours. 1958: Rumors of Evening (TV). Vertigo. 1959: The Five Pennies. Five Branded Women. 1961: By Love Possessed. 1971: Summertree. The Todd Killings. 1977: Our Town (TV).

BELL, Tom 1932–
Dark, lean and angry-looking British actor who came to stardom on the wave of 'kitchen sink' dramas of the early 1960s, and quickly gained a reputation for upsetting the 'establishment' which, it was said, cost him much film and television work. As his features became more taut with the years, it was hard to imagine him in comedy – but he built up a formidable range of TV and theatre work without entirely losing his 'stormy petrel' image, having twice refused to appear in sequels to highly successful television series. Now often seen as hard nuts or ruddy-cheeked rurals. 1960: The Criminal (US: The Concrete Jungle). Echo of Barbara. 1961: Payroll. The Kitchen. 1962: HMS Defiant (US: Damn the Defiant!). A Prize of Arms. The L-Shaped Room. 1964: Ballad in Blue (US: Blues for Lovers). 1965: He Who Rides a Tiger. 1966: Sands of Beersheba. 1967: In Enemy Country. 1968: The Long Day's Dying. 1969: Lock Up Your Daughters! The Violent Enemy. All the Right Noises. 1971: Quest for Love. *The Spy's Wife. 1972: Straight on Till Morning. 1975: Royal Flash. 1978: The Sailor's Return. 1980: Stronger Than the Sun. 1985: The Innocent. Summer Lightning (TV). Hard Travelling (TV). 1986: The Magic Toyshop (TV. US: cinemas). 1987: Wish You Were Here. 1988: Resurrected. 1989: Red King, White Knight (TV). 1990: The Krays. Dark River. 1991: Prospero's Books. "Let Him Have It". 1993: Seconds Out. 1994: The Cinder Path. The Great Kandinsky (TV). 1995: The Feast of July. 1996: Bent (released 1998). 1997: Preaching to the Perverted. Swept from the Sea/Amy Foster. The Boxer. 1998: Swing. 1999: The Last Minute. Tube Tales (TV). 2000: Lava.

BELLAMY, Ralph 1904–1991
Tall, heavily-built, fair-haired American actor of genial, resolute features. Beginning on stage, he had his own theatre company at 23, but in films he was generally cast in too many parts which merely required him to be dull and dependable, often as pipe-smoking sleuth, family friend, or guy who fails to get the girl. In later years, he returned to films (after a sojourn on stage) as a redoubtably craggy, often crusty character star, and served four years as the president of Actors' Equity. He was nominated for an Academy Award in The Awful Truth, and was awarded an honourary Oscar in 1987. Four time married including (3rd) organist Ethel Smith, he died from a chronic lung illness. 1931: The Secret Six. The Magnificent Lie. Surrender. West of Broadway. Disorderly Conduct. 1932: Young America (GB: We Humans). Forbidden. Rebecca of Sunnybrook Farm. The Woman in Room 13. Wild Girl (GB: Salomy Jane). Air Mail. Almost Married. 1933: Second Hand Wife (GB: The Illegal Divorce). Parole Girl. Destination Unknown. Picture Snatcher. The Narrow Corner. Below the Sea. Headline Shooter (GB: Evidence in Camera). Blind Adventure. Ace of Aces. Flying Devils (GB: The Flying Circus). 1934: Ever in My Heart. Spitfire. This Man is Mine. Once to Every Woman. One is Guilty. Before Midnight. The Crime of Helen Stanley. Girl in Danger. 1935: Woman in the Dark.

Helldorado. The Wedding Night. Rendezvous at Midnight. Air Hawks. Eight Bells. The Healer. Gigolette (GB: Night Club). Navy Wife. 1936: Hands Across the Table. Dangerous Intrigue. The Final Hour. Roaming Lady. Straight from the Shoulder. Wild Brian Kent. The Man Who Lived Twice. 1937: Counterfeit Lady. The Awful Truth. Let's Get Married. 1938: The Crime of Dr Hallet. Fools for Scandal. Boy Meets Girl. Carefree. Girls' School. Trade Winds. 1939: Let Us Live. Blind Alley. Smashing the Spy Ring. Flight Angels. Coast Guard. His Girl Friday. 1940: Brother Orchid. Queen of the Mob. Dance, Girl, Dance. Public Deb No 1. Ellery Queen, Master Detective. Meet the Wildcat. 1941: Ellery Queen's Penthouse Mystery. Footsteps in the Dark. Affectionately Yours. Ellery Queen and the Perfect Crime (GB: The Perfect Crime). Dive Bomber. Ellery Queen and the Murder Ring (GB: The Murder Ring). The Wolf Man. 1942: The Ghost of Frankenstein. Lady in a Jam. Men of Texas (GB: Men of Destiny). The Great Impersonation. 1943: Stage Door Canteen. 1944: Guest in the House. 1945: Delightfully Dangerous. Lady on a Train. 1955: The Court Martial of Billy Mitchell (GB: One Man Mutiny). 1956: Heritage of Anger (TV). 1960: Sunrise at Campobello. 1966: The Professionals. 1967: Wings of Fire (TV). 1968: Rosemary's Baby. 1969: The Immortal (TV). 1971: Doctors' Wives. 1972: Something Evil (TV). Cancel My Reservation. 1973: Owen Marshall, Counsellor at Law (TV). 1974: Log of the Black Pearl (TV). 1975: Murder on Flight 502 (TV). Adventures of the Queen (TV). Search for the Gods (TV). 1976: McNaughton's Daughter (TV). Nightmare in Badham County (TV). Return to Earth (TV). The Boy in the Plastic Bubble (TV). 1977: Charlie Cobb: Nice Night for a Hanging (TV). The Clone Master (TV). The Millionaire. 1979: The Billion Dollar Threat (TV. GB: cinemas). Power (TV). 1980: The Memory of Eva Ryker (TV). 1983: Trading Places. 1984: Love Leads the Way (TV). 1985: The Fourth Wise Man (TV). 1986: Amazon Women on the Moon. 1987: Disorderlies. 1988: Coming to America. The Good Mother. 1989: Christine Cromwell: Things That Go Bump in the Night (TV). 1990: Pretty Woman. Easy Come, Easy Go (TV).

BELMONDO, Jean-Paul 1933–

The supremely Gallic leading man of the sixties: Belmondo's lazy charm won him an instant international following after his first big success, in Godard's *Breathless*. Thereafter, he tended to trade in on the image. He could be memorable in the right film, but flounder rather badly without a decent script. Like the American Burt Reynolds, Belmondo liked to do his own stunt-work.

1955: *Molière. 1956: Dimanche nous volerons. 1957: A pied, à cheval et en voiture. 1958: Sois belle et tais-toi (GB: Blonde for Danger. US: Be Beautiful and Shut Up). Drôle de Dimanche. Les tricheurs (GB: Youthful Sinners). *Charlotte et son Jules. Les copains de Dimanche. 1959: Mademoiselle Ange. A bout de souffle (GB and US: Breathless). A double tour (GB: Web of Passion. US: Leda). 1960: Moderato contabile (GB: Seven Days . . . Seven

Nights). Lettere di una novizia. La française et l'amour (GB: Love and the Frenchwoman). Les distractions (GB: Trapped by Fear). Classe tous risques (GB: The Big Risk). 1961: La viaccia. La ciociara (GB and US: Two Women). Léon Morin, Priest. Une femme est une femme. Amours célèbres. Un nommé La Rocca. 1962: Un singe en hiver (GB: It's Hot in Hell). Cartouche (GB: Swords of Blood). Le doulos. I Don Giovanni della Costa Azzurra. L'aîné des Ferchaux. 1963: Mere matto. I giorno piu corto . . . (GB and US: The Shortest Day). Dragées au poivre (GB: Sweet and Sour). Peau de banane (US: Banana Peel). 1964: L'homme de Rio (GB: That Man from Rio). Cent mille dollars au soleil. Echappement libre. La chasse à l'homme (GB: The Gentle Art of Seduction). Week-end à Zuydcoote (GB: Weekend at Dunkirk). 1965: Par un beau matin d'été (US: Crime on a Summer Morning). Pierrot le fou. 1966: Les tribulations d'un Chinois en Chine (GB: Up to His Ears. US: Chinese Adventures in China). Is Paris Burning? Tendre voyou. 1967: *La bande à Bébel. Casino Royale. Le voleur (GB and US: The thief). 1968: Ho!/ Ho – Criminal Face. 1969: Dieu a choisi Paris. Le cerveau (GB and US: The Brain). La sirène du Mississippi (GB and US: Mississippi Mermaid). Un homme qui me plaît (GB and US: A Man I Like). 1970: Borsalino. 1971: Les mariés de l'an deux (GB: The Scoundrel). Le casse (GB and US: The Burglars). 1972: Docteur Popaul (GB: Scoundrel in White. US: Tender Scoundrel). La scoumoune. 1973: L'héritier (GB: The Inheritor). 1974: Le magnifique (GB: How to Destroy the Reputation of the Greatest Secret Agent . . .). Stavisky. 1975: Peur sur la ville (GB: Night Caller. US: Fear over the City). 1977: L'animal. Le corps de mon ennemi. 1979: Flic ou voyou. 1980: Le guignolo. I piccioni di Piazza san Marco. 1981: Le professionel. 1982: L'as des as/Ace of Aces. 1983: Le marginal. Les morfalous (US: The Vultures). 1984: Joyeuses pâques/Happy Easter. 1985: Hold-Up. 1986: Le solitaire. 1988: Der Glückspitz. Itineraire d'un enfant gâté. 1994: Les cents et une nuits. 1995: Les misérables/Les misérables du Xxième siècle. Désir/Desire. 1997: Half a Chance/Une chance sur deux. 1999: Peut-être. 2000: Amazon. Les acteurs.

BELUSHI, James or Jim 1951–

Bulldozing, dark-haired, chunkily-built, harsh-voiced American actor with crooked smile, the younger brother of John Belushi (*qv*). Usually seen in light jackets, dark shirts

and colourful ties, as if auditioning for a hard-nosed cop in a TV police series, Belushi treats drama and abrasive comedy alike. After a series of striking rough diamonds, he moved into leading roles in the late 1980s. The 1990s to date have provided him with a variety of starring, co-starring and cameo roles, but he has not become a major box-office draw. Three times married.

1978: The Fury. 1979: Working Stiffs (TV). 1981: Thief (later and GB: Violent Streets). 1983: Trading Places. 1985: The Man with One Red Shoe. Salvador. 1986: 'About Last Night . . .' Little Shop of Horrors. Jumpin' Jack Flash. 1987: Real Men. The Principal. 1988: Red Heat. Homer & Eddie. 1989: K-9. Who's Harry Crumb? Wedding Band. 1990: To Forget Palermo/Dimenticare Palermo/The Palermo Connection. Taking Care of Business (GB: Filofax). Masters of Menace. Curly Sue. Mr Destiny. 1991: Diary of a Hit Man. Only the Lonely. Once Upon a Crime/Criminals. 1992: Traces of Red. 1993: Last Action Hero. 1994: Parallel Lives (TV). Royce. 1995: Destiny Turns on the Radio. Canadian Bacon. Race the Sun. Separate Lives. The Pebble and the Penguin (voice only). Sahara (originally for TV). 1996: Retroactive. Jingle All the Way. Gold in the Streets. 1997: Rake's Progress. Babes in Toyland. *Bad Baby (voice only). Gang Related. Living in Peril (cable TV). Wag the Dog. 1998: Nothing for Nothing/Nothing But Trouble. 1999: The Florentine. Angel's Dance. K-911 (video). Nuttiest Nutcracker. Made Men. 2000: Return to Me. Justice (TV). Who Killed Atlanta's Children? (TV).

BELUSHI, John 1949–1982

Dark, tubby, abrasive American TV comedian and comic actor who made his name, along with such as Chevy Chase and Dan Aykroyd (both *qv*), on the innovative, rule-breaking late-night TV show *Saturday Night Live*. A hard-cursing Lou Costello for modern times, putting audience's backs up or (mostly) having them in stitches. He was mellowing his hard-hitting style towards mainline cinema when high living caught up with him, and his death, from an overdose of cocaine and other drugs, robbed him of intended participation in several major box-office successes, notably *Ghost Busters*.
1975: La honte de la jungle (GB: Jungle Burger. US: Shame of the Jungle. Voice only). 1978: National Lampoon's Animal House. Goin' South. Old Boyfriends. 1979: 1941.

1980: The Blues Brothers. 1981: Neighbors. Continental Divide.

BENDIX, William 1906–1964

Likeable American character star, with fair, wavy hair and soft, Brooklynese voice, built like a barrel, and often cast as amiable, dimwitted thugs. Appeared in a memorable series of Paramount thrillers in the forties, but his later success in comedy meant his virtual loss to TV from 1953 on. Died from lobar pneumonia. Oscar nominee for *Wake Island*.

*1941: Woman of the Year. 1942: McGuerins from Brooklyn. Brooklyn Orchid. Wake Island. The Glass Key. Star Spangled Rhythm. Who Done It? 1943: China. Hostages. The Crystal Ball. Taxi, Mister! Guadalcanal Diary. Lifeboat. 1944: The Hairy Ape. *Skirmish on the Home Front. Abroad with Two Yanks. Greenwich Village. It's in the Bag! (GB: The Fifth Chair). 1945: Duffy's Tavern. Don Juan Quilligan. A Bell for Adano. Calcutta. 1946: Two Years Before the Mast. The Blue Dahlia. The Dark Corner. Sentimental Journey. White Tie and Tails. I'll Be Yours. 1947: Blaze of Noon. Where There's Life. Variety Girl. The Web. 1948: The Time of Your Life. Race Street. The Babe Ruth Story. 1949: The Life of Riley. A Connecticut Yankee in King Arthur's Court (GB: A Yankee in King Arthur's Court). The Big Steal. †Two Knights in Brooklyn/Two Mugs from Brooklyn. Streets of Laredo. Cover Up. Johnny Holiday. 1950: Kill the Umpire! Gambling House. 1951: Submarine Command. Detective Story. 1952: Blackbeard the Pirate. A Girl in Every Port. Macao. 1954: Dangerous Mission. 1955: Crashout. *Hollywood Shower of Stars. 1956: Battle Stations. Going His Way (narrator*

*only). 1958: The Deep Six. 1959: A Quiet Game of Cards (TV). Idle on Parade (US: Idol on Parade). The Rough and the Smooth (US: Portrait of a Sinner). 1961: Johnny Nobody. The Phoney American (GB: It's a Great Life). 1962: Boys' Night Out. *Cash on the Barrel Head. 1963: The Young and the Brave. For Love or Money. Law of the Lawless. 1964: Young Fury.*
†Combined GB version of McGuerins from Brooklyn/Taxi, Mister!

BENING, Annette 1956–

Light-haired, late-flowering American actress whose smile epitomises a warm and attractive personality. For several years an actress with a small San Francisco theatre, Bening landed on Broadway in 1986 and demonstrated an impressive range before marrying (second) Warren Beatty, her co-star in *Bugsy*, in 1992. Since then, her career has taken second place to two children, although her few screen appearances continue to be affairs to remember. Oscar nominee for *The Grifters* and *American Beauty*.
1986: Manhunt for Claude Dallas (TV). 1987: Hostage (TV). 1988: The Great Outdoors. 1989: Valmont. 1990: Postcards from the Edge. The Grifters. Guilty by Suspicion. 1991: Regarding Henry. Bugsy. 1993: Spoils of War (TV). 1994: Love Affair. 1995: The American President. 1996: Richard III. Mars Attacks! 1998: In Dreams/Blue Vision. 1999: American Beauty. Forever Hollywood (doc). 2000: What Planet Are You From?

BENJAMIN, Richard 1938–

Tall, slim, handsome (if too often grouchy-looking) American light actor with black, curly hair, at his most adept with black humour. His career limped along in the 1970s after a dynamic start in films, but his output increased dramatically at the end of the decade. In the 1980s, he became a director, but initial promise was not fulfilled. Married to Paula Prentiss (qv) since 1961.
1969: Goodbye Columbus. 1970: Catch 22. Diary of a Mad Housewife. 1971: The Marriage of a Young Stockbroker. The Steagle. 1972: Portnoy's Complaint. 1973: The Last of Sheila. Westworld. 1975: The Sunshine Boys. 1978: House Calls. No Room to Run. Witches' Brew (released 1985). 1979: Love at First Bite. How to Beat the High Cost of Living. Scavenger Hunt. 1980: The Last Married Couple in America. First Family. 1981: Saturday the 14th. 1983: Packin' It In (TV).

1992: Lift. 1997: Deconstructing Harry. 1998: The Pentagon Wars (cable TV).

As director: *1982: My Favorite Year. 1984: Racing with the Moon. City Heat. 1986: The Money Pit. 1987: Little Nikita/The Sleepers. 1988: My Stepmother is an Alien. 1990: Mermaids. Downtown. 1996: Mrs Winterbourne. 1998: The Pentagon Wars (cable TV).*

BENNETT, Bruce (Herman Brix) 1909–

Tall, taciturn, husky, fair-haired American actor with slow smile. US shot-putt champion from 1928 to 1932, he was introduced to films by Douglas Fairbanks Senior, but badly injured a shoulder while making his first movie, and missed out on the chance to become Tarzan. Resuming an acting career, the soft-voiced star was a serial king before changing his name to Bruce Bennett and becoming a minor-league Gary Cooper. Being resident at Warners, he was always in Cooper's shadow, and never got the parts he seemed to deserve.
1931: †Touchdown (Playing the Game). 1932: †Million Dollar Legs. 1933: †College Humor. 1934: †Student Tour. †Riptide. †Treasure Island. †Death on the Diamond. 1935: †The New Adventures of Tarzan (serial). †The New Adventures of Tarzan (feature version). 1936: †Silks and Saddles. (GB: College Racehorse). †Shadow of Chinatown (serial). 1937: †Blake of Scotland Yard (serial). †Amateur Crook (GB: Crooked but Dumb). †Sky Racket (GB: Flight into Danger). †Million Dollar Racket. †Two Minutes to Play. †Flying Fists. †Danger Patrol. †Tarzan and the Green Goddess (Additional feature from 1935 serial). †The Lone Ranger (serial). †A Million to One. †Land of Fighting Men. †Hawk of the

Wilderness (serial). †*Fighting Devil-Dogs (serial).* 1939: †*Hi-Yo Silver (feature version of The Lone Ranger).* †*Daredevils of the Red Circle (serial).* Café Hostess. My Son is Guilty. (GB: Crime's End). Blondie Brings Up Baby. Invisible Stripes. 1940: Convicted Woman. Island of Doomed Men. Babies for Sale. Blazing Six-Shooters (GB: Stolen Wealth). West of Abilene (GB: The Showdown). The Lone Wolf Meets a Lady. Girls of the Road. The Secret Seven. Before I Hang. *The Heckler. *His Bridal Fright. *The Taming of the Snood. The Phantom Submarine. The Lone Wolf Keeps a Date. The Man with Nine Lives. *Boobs in the Woods. *A Bundle of Bliss. *How High Is Up? *No Census, No Feelings. *The Spook Speaks. 1941: The Officer and the Lady. Honolulu Lu. *So Long, Mr Chumps. *Dutiful But Dumb. Three Girls About Town. Submarine Zone. Two Latins from Manhattan. 1942: Underground Agent. Tramp, Tramp, Tramp. Submarine Raider. Atlantic Convoy. Sabotage Squad. 1943: Frontier Fury. The More the Merrier. Murder in Times Square. Sahara. There's Something About a Soldier. 1944: I'm from Arkansas. U-Boat Prisoner (GB: Dangerous Mists). 1945: Danger Signal. Mildred Pierce. *Beer Barrel Polecats. 1946: The Man I Love. Stolen Life. 1947: Nora Prentiss. Dark Passage. Cheyenne. 1948: The Yellow Phantom (feature version of Shadow of Chinatown). Silver River. Smart Girls Don't Talk. The Treasure of the Sierra Madre. The Younger Brothers. To the Victor. 1949: The House Across the Street. Without Honor. The Doctor and the Girl. Task Force. Undertow. 1950: Mystery Street. Shakedown. The Second Face. 1951: Angels in the Outfield (GB: Angels and the Pirates). The Great Missouri Raid. The Last Outpost. 1952: Sudden Fear. 1953: Dream Wife. Dragonfly Squadron. 1954: Stories of the Century No 1: Quantrill and His Raiders. 1955: Strategic Air Command. Robber's Roost. The Big Tip-Off. 1956: The Bottom of the Bottle (GB: Beyond the River). Love Me Tender. Hidden Guns. Three Outlaws. Daniel Boone – Trail Blazer. Three Violent People. 1957: Ain't No Time for Glory (TV). 1958: The Cosmic Man. Flaming Frontier. 1959: The Alligator People. 1961: The Outsider. Fiend of Dope Island. 1966: Lost Island of Kioga (feature version of Hawk of the Wilderness). 1972: Deadhead Miles. 1973: The Clones (GB: Clones). 1980: Hero's Return.*

†*As Herman Brix*

BENNETT, Constance 1904–1965

Hell-raising, high-powered blonde American leading lady with dainty, calculating features, the older sister of Joan Bennett (qv) and very much her antithesis. Her star career, chiefly distinguished by her performance in *What Price Hollywood?* – the forerunner of *A Star is Born* – soon burned itself out, but she continued in show business and, not surprisingly, ended up as *Auntie Mame* on stage. Died from a cerebral haemorrhage.

*1915: The Valley of Decision. 1920: *Adam and Eve. *Clothes. *Men of the Force. 1921: Reckless Youth. 1922: Evidence. What's Wrong with the Woman? 1924: Cytherea (GB: The Forbidden Way). Into the Net (serial). 1925: The Goose Hangs High. Married? Code of the*

*West. Wandering Fires (GB: Should a Woman Tell?). My Son. My Wife and I. The Goose Woman. Sally, Irene and Mary. The Pinch Hitter. 1929: This Thing Called Love. Rich People. Clothes. 1930: Son of the Gods. Common Clay. Three Faces East. Lazy Lady. Sin Takes a Holiday. 1931: In Deep. The Easiest Way. Born to Love. Adam and Eve. The Common Law. Bought. 1932: Lady With a Past (GB: Reputation). What Price Hollywood? Two Against the World. Rockabye. 1933: Our Betters. Bed of Roses. After Tonight (GB: Sealed Lips). 1934: Moulin Rouge. The Affairs of Cellini. Outcast Lady (GB: A Woman of the World). 1935: After Office Hours. *Starlight Days at the Lido. 1936: Everything is Thunder. Ladies in Love. 1937: Topper. 1938: Merrily We Live. Service De Luxe. 1939: Topper Takes a Trip. Tail Spin. 1941: Submarine Zone. Law of the Tropics. Two-Faced Woman. Wild Bill Hickok Rides. 1942: Sin Town. Madame Spy. 1945: Paris – Underground (GB: Madame Pimpernel). 1946: Centennial Summer. 1947: The Unsuspected. 1948: Smart Woman. Angel on the Amazon (GB: Drums Along the Amazon). 1951: As Young As You Feel. 1953: It Should Happen to You. 1966: Madame X.*

BENNETT, Joan 1910–1990

Exquisitely beautiful, dark-haired (initially blonde) American socialite actress, sister of Constance Bennett. She gave her best performances in several Fritz Lang films of the forties, but her later film appearances were restricted after a shooting scandal involving her agent and her third (of four) husband, Walter Wanger – under whose auspices she did most of her best and most intense work. Died from a heart attack.

*1915: The Valley of Decision. 1923: The Eternal City. 1928: *Alice in Wonderland. 1928: Power. 1929: Three Live Ghosts. Disraeli. The Divine Lady. Mississippi Gambler. 1930: Bulldog Drummond. Puttin' on the Ritz. Crazy That Way. Moby Dick. Maybe It's Love. Scotland Yard (GB: 'Detective Clive' – Bart). 1931: Many a Slip. Doctors' Wives. Hush Money. She Wanted a Millionaire. 1932: Careless Lady. The Trial of Vivienne Ware. Weekends Only. Me and My Gal (GB: Pier 13). Wild Girl (GB: Salomy Jane). Arizona to Broadway. 1933: Little Women. 1934: The Man Who Reclaimed His Head. The Pursuit of Happiness. 1935: Mississippi. Private Worlds. Two for Tonight. The Man Who Broke the Bank at Monte Carlo. She Couldn't Take It*

*(GB: Woman Tamer). 1936: Thirteen Hours by Air. Big Brown Eyes. Two in a Crowd. Wedding Present. 1937: Vogues of 1938. 1938: I Met My Love Again. The Texans. Artists and Models Abroad (GB: Stranded in Paris). Trade Winds. 1939: The Man in the Iron Mask. The Housekeeper's Daughter. 1940: Green Hell. The House Across the Bay. The Man I Married. Son of Monte Cristo. 1941: She Knew All the Answers. Wild Geese Calling. Manhunt. 1942: *White House of Hollywood. Confirm or Deny. Twin Beds. The Wife Takes a Flyer (GB: A Yank in Dutch). Girl Trouble. 1943: Margin for Error. 1944: The Woman in the Window. 1945: Nob Hill. Scarlet Street. Colonel Effingham's Raid (GB: Man of the Hour). 1946: The Macomber Affair. 1948: The Secret Beyond the Door. The Woman on the Beach. Hollow Triumph (GB: The Scar). 1949: The Reckless Moment. 1950: Father of the Bride. For Heaven's Sake. 1951: Father's Little Dividend. The Guy Who Came Back. 1954: Highway Dragnet. 1955: We're No Angels. 1956: There's Always Tomorrow. Navy Wife (GB: Mother – Sir). 1957: The Thundering Wave (TV). 1960: Desire in the Dust. 1970: House of Dark Shadows. Gidget Gets Married (TV). 1972: The Eyes of Charles Sand (TV). 1976: Suspiria. 1978: Suddenly, Love (TV). 1981: This House Possessed (TV). 1982: Divorce Wars (TV).*

BENNY, Jack
(Benjamin Kubelsky) 1894–1974

Uniquely droll, dry-voiced, fiddle-playing American comedian with an air of faint bemusement, a fine sense of timing and a stream of jokes about his own age and parsimoniousness. The cinema never really captured his intimate appeal, mainly because Benny needed an audience off whom to react; but it never quite gave up trying. Married to his radio partner Mary Livingstone (Sadye Marks) from 1927. Died of stomach cancer.

*1928: *Bright Moments. 1929: Hollywood Revue of 1929. *The Songwriters' Revue. 1930: Strictly Modern. *The Rounder. Chasing Rainbows. Medicine Man. 1931: *A Broadway Romeo. *Cab Waiting. *Taxi Tangle. 1933: Mr Broadway. 1934: Transatlantic Merry-Go-Round. 1935: Broadway Melody of 1935. *Broadway Highlights No 1. It's in the Air. 1936: The Big Broadcast of 1937. College Holiday. 1937: Artists and Models. Manhattan Merry-Go-Round (GB: Manhattan Music Box). 1938: Artists and Models Abroad (GB: Stranded in Paris). 1939: Man About Town.*

1940: Buck Benny Rides Again. Love Thy Neighbor. 1941: Charley's Aunt (GB: Charley's American Aunt). 1942: To Be or Not To Be. George Washington Slept Here. The Meanest Man in the World. 1943: *Show Business at War. *Screen Snapshots No 109. 1944: Hollywood Canteen. It's in the Bag! (GB: The Fifth Chair). 1945: The Horn Blows at Midnight. 1946: Without Reservations. 1948: *Screen Snapshots No 166. *Radio Broadcasting Today. 1949: The Lucky Stiff. The Great Lover. *A Rainy Day in Hollywood. 1952: Somebody Loves Me. *Memorial to Al Jolson (narrator only). 1953: *Hollywood's Pair of Jacks. 1954: Susan Slept Here. 1955: The Seven Little Foys. 1957: Beau James. 1958: *Fabulous Hollywood. *The Mouse That Jack Built. 1959: Who Was That Lady? 1962: Gypsy. 1963: It's a Mad, Mad, Mad, Mad World. 1967: A Guide for the Married Man. 1972: The Man.

BENSON, Robby (Robin Segal) 1956–
Precocious, dark-haired, pale-eyed, softly-spoken, eager-looking teenage acting prodigy who later developed into a rather uncharismatic all-rounder who dabbled in writing, directing, singing and even voice-overs for cartoons. The most successful of his early roles were in tear-jerkers, often based on real-life stories; developments in his own life could have almost made one of these when a serious illness in 1984 led to his undergoing open heart surgery. Even after a comeback, he had problems escaping juvenile roles, and he was little seen in movies after 1993. Married actress Karla de Vito.
1972: Jory. 1973: Jeremy. 1974: All the Kind Strangers (TV). The Virginia Hill Story (TV). 1975: Lucky Lady. 1976: Death Be Not

Proud (TV). Ode to Billy Joe. 1977: The Death of Richie (TV). One on One. 1978: The End. Ice Castles. 1979: Walk Proud. 1980: Our Town (TV). Die Laughing. Tribute. The Chosen. 1981: National Lampoon Goes to the Movies (released 1983). 1982: Running Brave (released 1984). Two of a Kind (TV). The Last of Mrs Lincoln (TV). 1984: Harry and Son. City Limits. 1987: Rent-a-Cop. †Crack in the Mirror. 1989: †White Hot. †Modern Love. 1991: Beauty and the Beast (voice only). 1992: Invasion of Privacy. Homewrecker. Betrayal of the Dove (screenplay only). Webber's World/The Webbers/The Webbers' 15 Minutes. 1993: Lethal Exposure. Exosquad. Precious Victims (TV). 1997: Beauty and the Beast: The Enchanted Christmas (V. Voice only). 2000: Dragonheart II (voice only).

†And directed

BENTLEY, John 1916–
Debonair, dark-haired British leading man who didn't film until he had turned 30, but quickly became the second-feature detective par excellence. His raincoated figure was to be seen rescuing heroines and tracking crooks to their lairs throughout the fifties, and he played several sleuths of detective fiction, including Paul Temple and the Toff. A Hollywood contract in the fifties came too late to further his career.
1947: The Hills of Donegal. 1948: Calling Paul Temple. 1949: Torment (US: Paper Gallows). Bait. 1950: The Happiest Days of Your Life. She Shall Have Murder. Paul Temple's Triumph. 1951: Salute the Toff. The Woman's Angle. 1952: Hammer the Toff. The Lost Hours (US: The Big Frame). Tread Softly (US: Tread Softly, Stranger). Paul Temple Returns. 1953: The Black Orchid. Men against the Sun. River Beat. 1954: Double Exposure. Profile. Final Appointment. Golden Ivory (US: White Huntress). The Scarlet Spear. 1955: Confession (US: The Deadliest Sin). Stolen Assignment. The Flaw. Dial 999 (US: The Way Out). Flight from Vienna. Count of Twelve. 1956: Escape in the Sun. 1957: Istanbul. 1958: Submarine Seahawk. 1960: The Singer Not the Song. An heiligen Wassern. 1961: Mary Had a Little. . . The Sinister Man. 1962: The Fur Collar. 1963: Quest of the Damned. Shadow of Treason.

BENTLEY, Wes 1978–
Tall, dark, deep-eyed American actor whom Hollywood seemed to see almost immediately

as a major star – albeit with a sinister slant. The son of Methodist ministers, and described by one of his directors as 'frighteningly mature', he's already played a disturbed Peeping Tom, a youthful serial killer and a vampire.
1998: Three Below Zero. Welcome to Serendipity. Beloved. 1999: American Beauty. The White River Kid. 2000: Kingdom Come. Soul Survivors. 2001: Queen of the Damned. The Four Feathers.

BERENGER, Tom (Thomas Moore) 1949–
American actor with tight, dark, curly hair. His open-faced good looks seemed tinged with humour at the corners of the mouth, and his slight resemblance to Paul Newman (qv) got him cast as the young Butch Cassidy in Butch and Sundance The Early Days. Berenger studied journalism, but took up acting in his early twenties. His career received its biggest boost to date with the scarred psycho he played in Platoon, a performance that won him an Academy Award nomination. He has continued to show up best in rugged, almost primitive roles, albeit in more routine films.
1976: The Sentinel. 1977: Johnny, We Hardly Knew Ye (TV). Looking for Mr Goodbar. 1978: In Praise of Older Women. 1979: Butch and Sundance The Early Days. 1980: The Dogs of War. 1982: Oltre la porta (GB: Beyond the Door. US: Beyond Obsession). Eddie and the Cruisers (released 1984). 1983: Fear City. The Big Chill. 1985: Rustlers' Rhapsody. 1986: If Tomorrow Comes (TV). La sposa americana. Platoon. 1987: Someone to Watch Over Me. Dear America (voice only). 1988: Shoot to Kill (GB: Deadly Pursuit). Last Rites. Betrayed. 1989: Major League. Love at Large. Born on

the Fourth of July. 1990: The Field. 1991: Shattered. At Play in the Fields of the Lord. Sniper. 1993: Sliver. Gettysburg. 1994: Chasers. Major League II. 1995: Last of the Dogmen. Body Language. Avenging Angel. One Man's Hero (released 1998). 1996: The Substitute. An Occasional Hell. 1997: Rough Riders (TV). The Gingerbread Man. 1998: Reasonable Doubt/Shadow of Doubt. A Murder of Crows. 1999: Takedown. In the Company of Spies (TV). Turbulence 2: Fear of Flying. Enemy of My Enemy. 2000: Cutaway. D-Tox/Detox.

BERGEN, Candice 1946–
Tall, icy, light-haired, square-jawed American actress, the daughter of ventriloquist Edgar Bergen (qv). The fervour lacking in her early acting did express itself in her ardent feminism and in her later career as a photojournalist. But her performances improved and she was nominated for an Academy Award for *Starting Over*. She married French director Louis Malle in 1980. In the 1990s, her acting career received fresh impetus with her tremendous success in the TV series *Murphy Brown*. Malle died in 1995.
1966: The Group. The Sand Pebbles. 1967: The Day the Fish Came Out. Vivre pour vivre. 1968: The Magus. 1970: Getting Straight. Soldier Blue. The Adventurers. 1971: Carnal Knowledge. The Hunting Party. 1972: T.R. Baskin (GB: A Date with a Lonely Girl). 1974: 11 Harrowhouse. 1975: Bite the Bullet. The Wind and the Lion. 1976: The Domino Killings/The Domino Principle. 1977: The End of the World, in Our Usual Bed, in a Night Full of Rain. 1978: Oliver's Story. 1979: Starting Over. 1981: Rich and Famous. 1982: Gandhi. 1983: Arthur the King/Merlin & the Sword (TV Released 1985). 1984: Stick. 1986: Murder: By Reason of Insanity (TV). 1995: Tim (TV). 1996: Belly Talkers. Mary and Tim (TV).

BERGEN, Edgar 1903–1978
Dark, dapper, slit-mouthed (probably from concentrating on keeping it closed) American ventriloquist who made a start in vaudeville before finding his greatest success (strange for a ventriloquist, but just like Britain's Peter Brough a decade later) on radio. That led to a few starring films between 1938 and 1944 (one with his radio vis-à-vis W.C. Fields) before nightclub work took over Bergen's career. Father of actress Candice Bergen. His most famous dummy, the smart-

Aleck Charlie McCarthy, still exists, bequeathed to the Smithsonian Institution. Bergen died from a heart attack in his sleep. Received a special Oscar (made of wood) in 1937.
1930: *The Operation. *The Office Scandal. 1931: *The Eyes Have It. *Donkey Business. 1933: *Africa Speaks . . . English. *Free and Easy. 1934: *At the Races. *Pure Feud. 1935: *All American Drawback. *Two Boobs in a Balloon. 1936: *2 Minutes to Play. 1937: *Double Talk. *A Neckin' Party. *Bring on the Girls. 1938: *Hollywood Handicap. The Goldwyn Follies. Letter of Introduction. 1939: Charlie McCarthy, Detective, You Can't Cheat an Honest Man. 1941: Look Who's Laughing. 1942: Here We Go Again. 1943: Stage Door Canteen. 1944: Song of the Open Road. 1947: Fun and Fancy Free. 1948: I Remember Mama. 1949: Captain China. 1950: *Charlie McCarthy and Mortimer Snerd in Sweden. 1953: Mystery Lake. 1964: The Hanged Man (TV. GB: cinemas). 1965: One-way Wahine. 1967: Don't Make Waves. Rogue's Gallery. 1969: The Phynx. 1971: The Homecoming (TV). 1975: Won Ton Ton, The Dog Who Saved Hollywood. 1979: The Muppet Movie.

BERGEN, Polly (Nellie Burgin) 1929–
Pretty, peppy American brunette who became popular as a radio singer in the post-war years and subsequently made a number of films. Although she projected a warm personality, she seemed somewhat difficult to cast, and was most successful on television, where she won an Emmy for her performance in *Helen Morgan*. Married/divorced actor Jerome Courtland (C. Jourolmon, 1926–), first of two husbands.
1949: Champion (voice only). †Across the Rio Grande. 1950: At War With the Army. 1951: That's My Boy. Warpath. 1952: The Stooge. 1953: Arena. Half a Hero. Cry of the Hunted. Fast Company. Escape from Fort Bravo. 1957: Helen Morgan (TV). 1961: Belle Sommers. 1962: Cape Fear. 1963: The Caretakers. Move Over Darling. 1964: Kisses for My President. 1967: A Guide for the Married Man. 1973: Anatomy of Terror (TV). 1974: Death Cruise (TV). 1975: Murder on Flight 502 (TV). Telethon (TV). 1981: The Million Dollar Face (TV). 1987: Making Mr Right. 1988: Addicted to His Love (TV). She Was Marked for Murder (TV). 1989: The Haunting of Sarah Hardy (TV). 1990: Cry-Baby. My Brother's Wife (TV). 1991: Lightning Field (TV). 1992: Lady Against the Odds (TV). 1993: Perry Mason: The Case of the Skin-Deep Scandal (TV). 1994: Leave of Absence (TV). 1995: Dr Jekyll and Ms Hyde. Once Upon a Time . . . When We Were Colored. The Surrogate (TV). 1996: For Hope (TV). In the Blink of an Eye (TV).

†As Polly Burgin

BERGER, Senta 1941–
'One of those 'mittel-European' beauties whom the international cinema snapped up for its epic adventures of the early sixties. With a full-blown prettiness and even fuller-blown bust, Austrian-born Senta could hardly fail. But she seemed to lose some of her ambition after the mid-sixties, and some unworthy Hollywood roles were followed by a return to European features. Only Sam Peckinpah really did her simmering appeal justice, in *Major Dundee*. More recently, a major TV star in Germany.
1957: Die unentschuldige Stunde. Die Lindenwirtin vom Donanstrand. 1958: Der veruntreute Himmel. The Journey. 1959: Katia. Ich heirate herrn Direktor. 1960: The Good Soldier Schweik. O sole mio. 1961: The Secret Ways. Das Wunder des Malachias. Immer Arger mit dem Bett. Eine Hübscher als die Andere. Junge Leute brauchen Liebe. Adieu, Liebewohl, Goodbye. Ramona. Es muss nicht immer Kaviar sein. Diesmal muss es Kaviar Sein (US: The Reluctant Spy). 1962: Das Geheimnis der schwartzen Koffer (GB: Secret of the Black Trunk). Sherlock Holmes and the Deadly Necklace. The Testament of Dr Mabuse. Frauenarzt Dr Sibelius. 1963: The Victors. Jack and Jenny. The Waltz King. Kali-Yug, Goddess of Vengeance. Kali-Yug, Part II (GB: The Mystery of the Indian

Temple). 1964: The Spy With My Face. Full Hearts and Empty Pockets. See How They Run (TV). 1965: Major Dundee. Schüsse in dreivierteltakt. The Glory Guys. 1966: Du suif dans l'orient. Our Man in Marrakesh. The Poppy is Also a Flower. 1967: Peau d'espion (GB and US: To Commit a Murder). Operazione San Gennaro (GB: The Treasure of San Gennaro). The Ambushers. The Miracle of Father Malachios. Paarungen. The Magnificent Thief (TV). Diabolically Yours. 1968: If It's Tuesday, This Must Be Belgium. Istanbul Express (TV. GB: cinemas). 1969: Les étrangers. De Sade. Cuore solitari. 1970: Quando le donne aveano la coda (US: When Women Had Tails). Der Graben/Wer in glashaus liebt. . . Casanova. 1971: L'amante dell' Orsa maggiore. Roma bene. Sancorsiap. Mamma dolce, mamma cara. Un anguilla da trecento milione. Cobra. When Women Lost Their Tails. Causa di divorzio. 1972: The Scarlet Letter. Amore i gimnastica. Die Moral der Ruth Halbfass. 1973: Reigen (GB: Dance of Love. US: Merry-Go-Round). Bisturi, la mafia bianca (US: White Mafia). Di mamma non ce n'è una sola. L'uomo senza memoria. 1974: La bellissima estate. 1975: The Swiss Conspiracy. Il ventro caldo della signora. Mitgift. Lonely Hearts. La guardia del corpo. Progliaccio d'amore. 1976: Das chinesische Wunder. Signore e Signori buonanotte. La padrona e servita (GB: The Mistress). 1977: Una donna di seconda mano. Cross of Iron. Ritratto di Borghesia in Nero/Nest of Vipers. 1978: Sentimenti/Sentiments and Passions. La giaccia verde. 1979: I Miss You, Hugs and Kisses. 1980: Speed Driver. 1984: Fatto su misura. Le due vite di Mattia Pascal (US: The Two Lives of Mattia Pascal). 1985: The Flying Devils. 1986: Killing Cars. L'ultima mazurka. 1987: Urban Animals. Swiss Cheese. 1990: Tre colonne in cronaca. 1995: Bin ich schön? (completed 1998).

BERGIN, Patrick 1952–

Roguish-looking, often moustachioed, rangy Irish actor with dark, curly hair, often seen as eccentric or menacing figures. Bergin's flashing-eyed charm had a decidedly dangerous edge that caused producers to cast him equally as rebels, pioneers or psychos, an unexpected development for a man who had spent five years teaching children with learning disabilities before turning to acting at 29. With or without moustache, Bergin looks not unlike American actor Kevin Kline (qv) and has forged a career in similarly

offbeat roles, though sometimes as men of violence.

1983: Those Glory, Glory Days (TV. Also shown in cinemas). 1984: No Man's Land. 1987: The Courier. 1988: Taffin. 1990: Mountains of the Moon. Sleeping With the Enemy. Morphine and Dolly Mixtures (TV). 1991: Robin Hood (TV. GB: cinemas). Love Crimes. Highway to Hell. 1992: Map of the Human Heart. Patriot Games. Frankenstein – The Real Story (TV). The Hummingbird Tree. 1993: They (TV). 1994: All Things Bright and Beautiful. Raging Earth (TV). Soft Deceit. Double Cross. Twilight Zone: Rod Serling's Lost Classics (TV). 1995: Lawnmower Man 2: Beyond Cyberspace. Triplecross (TV). 1996: The Proposition. Suspicious Minds. 1997: The Ripper (TV). The Apocalypse Witch. The Island on Bird Street. Angela Mooney Dies Again. 1998: Treasure Island. One Man's Hero. Arthur Conan Doyle's The Lost World. Taxman. 1999: The Press Run. Love and Debt. Eye of the Beholder. St Patrick the Irish Legend (TV). When the Sky Falls. 2000: Durango (TV). High Explosive. Cause of Death.

BERGMAN, Ingrid 1914–1982

Square-built blonde Swedish actress who seemed born to play tragic, haunted heroines, never more memorably than in Casablanca, three years after she had gone to Hollywood. Married to director Roberto Rossellini (second of three husbands) from 1950 to 1958, a relationship which, in its premarital state, caused her ostracism from Hollywood in 1948. Three Oscars (for Gaslight, Anastasia and Murder on the Orient Express), plus nominations for For Whom the Bell Tolls, The Bells of St Mary's, Joan of Arc and Autumn Sonata. She died from cancer on her 68th birthday.

1934: Munkbrogreven. 1935: Bränningar. Swedenhielms. Valborgsmässoafton (US: Walpurgis Night). 1936: På Solsidan. Intermezzo. 1937: Juninatten. 1938: En Kvinnas Ansikte (GB and US: A Woman's Face). Die vier Gesellen. Dollar. En Ende Natt. 1939: Intermezzo (GB: Escape to Happiness). 1941: Rage in Heaven. Adam Had Four Sons. Dr Jekyll and Mr Hyde. 1942: Casablanca. 1943: *Swedes in America (GB: Ingrid Bergman Answers). For Whom the Bell Tolls. 1944: Gaslight (GB: The Murder in Thornton Square). 1945: The Bells of St Mary's. Spellbound. Saratoga Trunk. 1946: Notorious. *The American Creed. 1948: Arch of Triumph. Joan of Arc. 1949: Under Capricorn. 1950:

Stromboli. 1951: Europa/The Greatest Love. 1952: Siamo donne (GB: We the Women). 1954: Voyage to Italy (GB: The Lonely Woman. US: The Strangers). Joan at the Stake. Fear. 1956: Elena et les hommes (GB: Elena and Men. US: Paris Does Strange Things). Anastasia. 1958: Indiscreet. The Inn of the Sixth Happiness. 1960: *The Camp (narrator only). 1961: Aimez-vous Brahms? (GB: Goodbye Again). 24 Hours in a Woman's Life (TV). 1964: The Yellow Rolls Royce. The Visit. 1966: Stimulantia. 1967: Fugitive in Vienna. 1969: Cactus Flower. A Walk in the Spring Rain. 1970: Henri Langlois. 1973: From the Mixed-Up Files of Mrs Basil E. Frankweiler (GB: The Hideaways). 1974: Murder on the Orient Express. 1976: A Matter of Time. 1978: Autumn Sonata. 1982: Golda (TV).

BERGNER, Elisabeth (E. Ettel) 1897–1986

Polish-born actress with wispy blonde hair, whose brief popularity in England in the 1930s failed to survive long under the triple strain of her own advancing years, her quickly outdated persona (elfin, fey, almost little-girlish) and the imminence of forties' realism (Margaret Sullavan had much the same trouble). She did her best acting work in later years in the theatre. Married to director Paul Czinner, she was nominated for an Academy Award for her performance in Escape Me Never.

1924: Der Evangelimann. 1925: Nju. 1926: Der Geiger von Florenz. Liebe. 1927: Dona Juana. 1928: Queen Louise. 1929: Fräulein Else (US: Miss Else). 1931: The Loves of Ariane. 1932: Der Träumende Mund. 1934: Catherine the Great. 1935: Escape Me Never. 1936: As You Like It. 1937: Dreaming Lips. 1938: Stolen Life. 1941: Paris Calling. 49th Parallel (US: The Invaders). Die glücklichen Jahre der Thorwalds. 1968: Strogoff/Courier to the Czar. 1970: Cry of the Banshee. 1973: Der Füssgänger/The Pedestrian. 1979: Der Pfingstausflug. 1981: Society Limited. 1982: Feine Gesellschaft – Beschränkte Haftung. 1985: Der Garten.

BERLE, Milton (M. Berlinger) 1908–

Breezy, beaming, black-haired, Broadway-based comedian who never quite made a home for himself in films, even though he made many more movies than most people realise. In vaudeville as a boy, he also made appearances in silents as a child actor, before making a name for himself on stage, radio

and, especially, television, where he was phenomenally successful in the late 1940s and through the 1950s with his own show, when his wit and geniality shone through even poor material and had him dubbed 'Mr Television' or 'Mr Tuesday Night'. His latter years have been mainly spent on the nightclub circuit, although he has continued to do sporadic but typically extrovert cameos in films.

Silents (incomplete). *1911: Betty Becomes a Maid/The Maid's Night Out. 1914: Tess of the Storm Country. The Perils of Pauline (serial). Tillie's Punctured Romance. Bunny's Little Brother. 1915: Fanchon the Cricket. 1916: Easy Street. 1917: Rebecca of Sunnybrook Farm. The Little Brother. 1919: The Wishing Ring Man. Eyes on Youth. 1920: Birthright. The Mark of Zorro. Humoresque. 1921: Love's Penalty. 1922: The Divorce Coupons. The Beauty Shop. Quincy Adams Sawyer. 1923: Ruth of the Range (serial). 1925: Lena Rivers. 1926: Sparrows. Beverly of Graustark.*

Sound (complete). *1932: *Poppin' the Cork. 1934: *Hollywood Hobbies. 1937: New Faces of 1937. 1938: Radio City Revels. 1941: *Los Angeles Examiner Benefit. Tall, Dark and Handsome. Sun Valley Serenade. Rise and Shine. 1942: Whispering Ghosts. A Gentlemen at Heart. 1943: Over My Dead Body. Margin for Error. 1945: The Dolly Sisters. 1949: Always Leave Them Laughing. 1960: Let's Make Love. The Bellboy. 1963: It's a Mad, Mad, Mad, Mad World. 1965: The Loved One. 1966: The Oscar. Don't Worry, We'll Think of a Title. 1967: The Happening. The Silent Treatment. Who's Minding the Mint? 1968: Where Angels Go, Trouble Follows. For Singles Only. 1969: Can Hieronymous Merkin Ever Forget Mercy Humppe and Find True Happiness? Seven in Darkness (TV). The April Fools. 1970: Love, American Style (TV). 1971: Journey Back to Oz (voice only). 1972: Evil Roy Slade (TV). 1974: Lepke. 1975: The Legend of Valentino (TV). Won Ton Ton, the Dog Who Saved Hollywood. 1978: The Muppet Movie. 1979: 'Hey Abbott' (TV). 1980: Off Your Rocker (TV). 1983: Family Business (TV). Smorgasbord. 1985: Pee-wee's Big Adventure. 1988: Side by Side (TV). 1989: Going Overboard/Babes Ahoy. 1991: Autobahn (US: Trabbi Goes to Hollywood). 1994: Storybook.*

BERRY, Halle 1966–

Pretty, personable young American actress who won a string of beauty contests before starting an acting career. After work on TV

soaps and mini-series, she broke through to films at 25, and has shown up well when required to give sensitive, attractive portrayals of ordinary working girls. Attempts at costume drama proved less wise, and her career wavered until she won a clutch of awards at the end of the 1990s for her TV portrait of tragic actress Dorothy Dandridge (qv).

1991: The Last Boy Scout. Jungle Fever. Strictly Business/Go Natalie. 1992: Boomerang. 1993: The Program. 1994: The Flintstones. Father Hood. 1995: Race the Sun. Solomon and Sheba (TV). Losing Isaiah. 1996: Executive Decision. Girl 6. The Rich Man's Wife. 1997: B.A.P.s. The Wedding (TV). 1998: Who Do Fools Fall in Love? Bulworth. 1999: Introducing Dorothy Dandridge (cable TV). 2000: X-Men. 2001: Pluto Nash.

BEST, Edna 1900–1974

Charming, fair-haired, quietly-spoken, very British actress who rose to fame in the stage production of *The Constant Nymph* and continued in unspectacular stage and film roles until going to America in 1939, where she played a few mothers and wives. Married to Herbert Marshall 1928–1940, the second of her three husbands.

1921: Tilly of Bloomsbury. 1923: A Couple of Down and Outs. 1930: Sleeping Partners. Loose Ends. Escape. Beyond the Cities. 1931: Michael and Mary. The Calendar (US: Bachelor's Folly). 1932: The Faithful Heart (US: Faithful Hearts). 1934: The Key. The Man Who Knew Too Much. 1937: South Riding. 1938: Prison Without Bars. 1939: Return to Yesterday. Intermezzo (GB: Escape to Happiness). 1940: Swiss Family Robinson. A

Dispatch from Reuter's (GB: This Man Reuter). 1947: The Late George Apley. The Ghost and Mrs Muir. 1948: The Iron Curtain.

BEY, Turhan (T. Schultavey) 1920–

Austrian-born leading man (of Turkish-Czech parentage) with slick black hair and faintly oriental aspect. His sleekly handsome features flourished in Arabian Nights and other escapist adventures in the war years, but his career foundered after army service (1948–1950) and he became a commercial photographer. Wooed some of Hollywood's most glamorous ladies, but has never married.

1941: Footsteps in the Dark. Raiders of the Desert. Burma Convoy. Shadows on the Stairs. The Gay Falcon. 1942: Junior G-Men of the Air (serial). The Falcon Takes Over. A Yank on the Burma Road (GB: China Caravan). Bombay Clipper. Drums of the Congo. Arabian Nights. Destination Unknown. The Unseen Enemy. The Mummy's Tomb. 1943: Danger in the Pacific. Adventures of Smilin' Jack (serial). White Savage (GB: White Captive). The Mad Ghoul. Background to Danger. 1944: Follow the Boys. The Climax. Dragon Seed. Bowery to Broadway. Ali Baba and the 40 Thieves. 1945: Frisco Sal. Sudan. 1946: A Night in Paradise. 1947: Out of the Blue. 1948: The Amazing Mr X (GB: The Spiritualist). Adventures of Casanova. 1949: Parole Inc. Song of India. 1953: Prisoners of the Casbah. 1994: Healer. The Skateboard Kid 2/The Skateboard Kid: A Magical Moment. 1995: Possessed by the Night. 1996: Virtual Combat (GB: Grid Runners).

BEYMER, Richard
(George Beymer Jr) 1938–
Boyish, dark-haired American leading man

who was in films at 15 and gave some spritely accounts of himself as a teenager. His wooden performance in *West Side Story* effectively torpedoed his Hollywood star career, although he drifted on through a few more films before becoming a producer. Later he worked on documentary films, taught transcendental meditation and returned to the odd acting assignment, especially after 1983.

1953: So Big. Stazione termini/Indiscretion of an American Wife (GB: Indiscretion). 1957: Johnny Tremain. 1958: The Diary of Anne Frank. 1959: Dark December (TV). 1960: High Time. 1961: West Side Story. 1962: Five Finger Exercise. Hemingway's Adventures of a Young Man (GB: Adventures of a Young Man). Bachelor Flat. The Longest Day. 1963: The Stripper (GB: Woman of Summer). 1971: Scream Free! (completed 1969). 1974: †Interview. 1983: Cross Country. 1984: Paper Dolls (II.TV). 1985: Generation (TV). 1989: Silent Night, Deadly Night 3: Better Watch Out. Twin Peaks (TV). 1992: Twin Peaks – Fire Walk with Me. Danger Island (TV). Blackbelt. 1993: My Girl 2. State of Emergency (cable TV). 1995: The Disappearance of Kevin Johnson. The Little Death. 1996: Foxfire. 1997: Elvis Meets Nixon (TV).

†And directed.

BICKFORD, Charles 1889–1967

Rugged, outspoken, curly-haired American star and later leading character player, of Irish ancestry. He never won an Oscar (perhaps because he was one of the banes of the Hollywood establishment), despite gruff, consistently good, characteristically intense performances over 38 years; he was nominated three times – for *The Song of Bernadette, The Farmer's Daughter* and *Johnny Belinda*. Died from emphysema.

1929: Dynamite. South Sea Rose. Hell's Heroes. 1930: Passion Flower. Anna Christie. The Sea Bat. River's End. 1931: East of Borneo. The Squaw Man (GB: The White Man). Pagan Lady. The Men in Her Life. 1932: Thunder Below. Panama Flo. Scandal for Sale. The Last Man. Vanity Street. 1933: No Other Woman. This Day and Age. White Woman. The Red Waggon. Song of the Eagle. 1934: Little Miss Marker (GB: Girl in Pawn). A Wicked Woman. 1935: A Notorious Gentleman. Under Pressure. The Farmer Takes a Wife. East of Java (GB: Java Seas). 1936: Pride of the Marines. Rose of the Rancho. The Plainsman. 1937: Night Club Scandal.

Daughter of Shanghai (GB: Daughter of the Orient). Thunder Trail. 1938: High, Wide and Handsome. Valley of the Giants. Gangs of New York. The Storm. Stand Up and Fight. 1939: Street of Missing Men. Romance of the Redwoods. Our Leading Citizen. One Hour to Live. Mutiny in the Big House. Of Mice and Men. 1940: Thou Shall Not Kill. Girl from God's Country. Queen of the Yukon. South to Karanga. 1941: Burma Convoy. Riders of Death Valley (serial). 1942: Reap the Wild Wind. Tarzan's New York Adventure. 1943: Mr Lucky. The Song of Bernadette. 1944: A Wing and a Prayer. 1945: Captain Eddie. Fallen Angel. 1946: Duel in the Sun. 1947: The Farmer's Daughter. The Woman on the Beach. Brute Force. Four Faces West (GB: They Passed This Way). 1948: The Babe Ruth Story. Johnny Belinda. Command Decision. 1949: Whirlpool. Roseanna McCoy. Guilty of Treason (GB: Treason). 1950: Branded. Riding High. 1951: Jim Thorpe – All American (GB: Man of Bronze). The Raging Tide. Elopement. 1953: The Last Posse. 1954: A Star is Born. 1955: Prince of Players. Not As a Stranger. The Court-Martial of Billy Mitchell (GB: One Man Mutiny). 1956: You Can't Run Away from It. Forbidden Area (TV). Sincerely, Willis Wayde (TV). 1957: Mister Cory. Clipper Ship (TV). Dark Wave (and narrator). 1958: The Big Country. Days of Wine and Roses (TV). Free Week-End (TV). 1959: Out of Dust (TV). Della (TV). The Unforgiven. 1960: Tomorrow (TV). 1962: Days of Wine and Roses. 1966: A Big Hand for the Little Lady (GB: Big Deal at Dodge City).

BIEHN, Michael 1956–

Lean, clean-cut, resolute-looking American actor with dark eyes and light, tufty hair. Biehn's chiselled features looked to have cut him out for heroes when he started acting straight from university. But in fact he's played his fair share of wackos, his eyes conveying unreliability with some skill. An expert in martial arts, he's continued to mix villains with action heroes, starring in lesser films and playing some striking co-star roles in major ones.

1977: Logan's Run. James at 15 (TV). 1978: Grease. A Fire in the Sky (TV). Zuma Beach (TV). Coach. 1979: Steel Town (TV). The Paradise Connection (TV). 1980: Hog Wild. 1981: The Fan. 1982: The Lords of Discipline. 1983: China Rose (TV). 1984: The Terminator. 1985: Deadly Intentions (TV). 1986: Aliens. 1987: Rampage. 1988: In a

Shallow Grave. The Seventh Sign. 1989: The Abyss. 1990: Navy SEALS. 1991: Timebomb. 1992: A Taste for Killing (TV). K-2. 1993: Strapped. Deadfall. The Abyss: Special Edition. Tombstone. 1994: Blood of the Hunter. Deep Red (cable TV). In the Kingdom of the Blind, the Man with One Eye is King. 1995: Jade. Dirty Money/Crash. Conundrum/Frame by Frame (cable TV). 1996: The Rock. Mojave Moon. 1997: Rangers/DMZ. Dead Men Can't Dance. Asteroid (TV). American Dragons. The Magnificent Seven (TV). 1998: The Ride. Susan's Plan. Silver Wolf (TV). 1999: Cherry Falls. Wonderland. 2000: The Art of War. Chain of Command.

BINOCHE, Juliette 1964–

Wistfully attractive, dark-haired French actress, in films after brief dramatic training, and a star at 21. Born in Paris of a playwright mother and stage director father, her cool beauty made rapid inroads into the international scene after her success in *The Unbearable Lightness of Being*. She can be depended on to put heart and soul into a role, and has even survived the discomfort of being cast as a Yorkshire girl in the 1992 version of *Wuthering Heights*. She won an Academy Award for *The English Patient*.

1983: Liberty Belle. 1984: Les nanas. La vie de famille (US: Family Life). Je vous salue, Marie (GB and US: Hail Mary). Adieu Blaireau. 1985: Rendez-vous. Mon beau-frère a tué ma soeur. 1986: The Night is Young. Mauvais sang/Bad Blood. 1987: The Unbearable Lightness of Being. 1988: Un tour de manège. 1991: Women & Men 2: In Love There Are No Rules (TV). Les amants du Pont-Neuf. 1992: Emily Brontë's Wuthering Heights. Damage. 1993: Trois couleurs: bleu/Blue. 1994: Le hussard sur le toît (GB and US: The Horseman on the Roof). 1996: A Couch in New York. The English Patient. 1998: Alice et Martin. 1999: Code Unknown. Les enfants du siècle. Eloge de l'amour. 2000: La veuve de Saint-Pierre. 2001: Chocolat.

BIRCH, Thora 1982–

Perky, outgoing American child player who quit films at 14 to finish her education and came back three years later as a slightly petulant-looking curvaceous brunette who moved quickly into rebel roles. She began her career as a toddler in TV commercials, and was a TV series regular at six, the same year she won a Youth in Film award for her leading role in *Purple People Eater*. The

highest-profile role of her sub-teen years was as Harrison Ford's daughter in two Jack Ryan thrillers.
1988: †Purple People Eater. 1991: Paradise. All I Want for Christmas. 1992: Patriot Games. 1993: Hocus Pocus. 1994: Clear and Present Danger. Monkey Trouble. 1995: Now and Then. 1996: Alaska. 1999: Night Ride Home (TV). American Beauty. Anywhere But Here. 2000: Dungeons and Dragons. The Smokers. Ghost World. 2001: The Hole.

†As Thora

BISHOP, Julie
(Jacqueline Wells Brown) 1914–
Chestnut-haired American actress, the forthright heroine in many a thriller and western, or the girl back home in war films. Made a few films as a child, then acted as Jacqueline Wells from 1931, until she signed for Warner Brothers, who decided to change it to Julie Bishop. After retiring from acting she became a painter of some repute.
1923: ‡Maytime. ‡Bluebeard's Eighth Wife. ‡Children of Jazz. 1924: ‡Captain Blood. ‡Dorothy Vernon of Haddon Hall. 1925: ‡The Golden Bed. ‡The Home Maker. ‡Classified 1926: The Bar-C Mystery (serial). The Family Upstairs (serial). 1931: ‡Pardon Us (GB: Jailbirds). *†Skip the Maloo! †Scareheads (GB: The Speed Reporter). 1932: **Heroes of the West (serial). *†The Knockout. *†Any Old Port. *†In Walked Charley. *†You're Telling Me. 1933: †Clancy of the Mounted (serial). †Tillie and Gus. †Tarzan the Fearless. †Alice in Wonderland. 1934: †The Black Cat (GB: The House of Doom). †Kiss and Make Up. †Happy Landing (GB: Air Patrol). The Square Shooter. †The

Loud Speaker (GB: The Radio Star). 1935: †Coronado. †Night Cargo. 1936: †The Bohemian Girl. 1937: †Frame-Up. †Little Miss Roughneck. †Counsel for Crime. †Paid to Dance. †Girls Can Play. 1938: †She Married an Artist. †When G-Men Step In. †Highway Patrol. †Flight into Nowhere. †My Son is a Criminal. †The Main Event. †The Little Adventuress. †Spring Madness. †Flight to Fame. 1939: †Behind Prison Gates. †Torture Ship. †Kansas Terrors. †My Son is Guilty (GB: Crime's End). 1940: †Young Bill Hickok. †Girl in 313. †Her First Romance. †The Ranger and the Lady. 1941: *Wampas Baby Stars. †Back in the Saddle. The Nurse's Secret. International Squadron. Steel Against the Sky. Wild Bill Hickok Rides. 1942: I Was Framed. The Hidden Hand. Lady Gangster. Busses Roar. Escape from Crime. The Hard Way. 1943: Northern Pursuit. Action in the North Atlantic. Princess O'Rourke. 1944: Hollywood Canteen. 1945: You Came Along. Rhapsody in Blue. 1946: Cinderella Jones. Murder in the Music Hall. Idea Girl. Strange Conquest. 1947: Last of the Redmen (GB: Last of the Redskins). High Tide. 1949: Deputy Marshal. The Threat. Sands of Iwo Jima. 1951: Westward the Women. 1953: Sabre Jet. 1954: Why Men Leave Home. The High and the Mighty. 1955: Headline Hunters. 1956: Survival (TV). 1957: The Big Land (GB: Stampeded!).

‡As Jacqueline Brown †As Jacqueline Wells **As Diane Duval

BISHOP, William 1917–1959
Tall, dark, handsome and virile American leading man who died from cancer at 42. He originally studied to be a lawyer but, after some experience in acting and stage management, he decided to try for a career in films. This had barely got started before he was off on active service in World War Two. His post-war days in Hollywood were spent as cruel, laughing villains in Columbia action films of the late 1940s and 1950s.
1943: Pilot No. 5. Girl Crazy. A Guy Named Joe. Swing Shift Maisie (GB: The Girl in Overalls). Cry Havoc. Swing Fever. Salute to the Marines. The Lost Angel. 1946: Pillow to Post. 1947: Song of the Thin Man. The Romance of Rosy Ridge. The Beginning or the End. Devil Ship. 1948: Thunderhoof (GB: Fury). The Untamed Breed. Adventures in Silverado (GB: Above All Laws). Port Said. Coroner Creek. The Black Eagle. 1949:

Slightly French. Anna Lucasta. The Walking Hills. 1950: The Tougher They Come. Harriet Craig. The Killer That Stalked New York (GB: Frightened City). 1951: Lorna Doone. The Texas Rangers. The Frogmen. The Basketball Fix (GB: The Big Decision). 1952: Breakdown. Cripple Creek. The Raiders/Riders of Vengeance. 1953: The Redhead from Wyoming. Gun Belt. 1954: Overland Pacific. 1955: Top Gun. Wyoming Renegades. 1956: The Boss. The White Squaw. 1957: The Phantom Stagecoach. Short Cut to Hell. The Star-Wagon (TV). 1959: The Oregon Trail.

BISSET, Jacqueline
(Winifred J. Bisset) 1944–
Striking British-born brunette glamour girl and presentable actress in international films who made an unlikely first impact as a spotty schoolgirl in Two for the Road. Her performances tend to be on the grave side but, like Elizabeth Taylor at the same age, she has wisely stayed within her own range. Never quite able to carry a film by herself, although her acting did grow stronger with the years and she is always a pleasure to watch.
1965: †The Knack . . . and how to get it. 1966: †Drop Dead Darling (US: Arrivederci Baby). †Cul-de-Sac. 1967: †Two for the Road. †Casino Royale. The Sweet Ride. The Cape Town Affair. 1968: The Detective. Bullitt. La promesse (GB: Secret World). The First Time (GB: You Don't Need Pyjamas at Rosie's). 1969: Airport. 1970: The Grasshopper. The Mephisto Waltz. 1971: Believe in Me. 1972: Secrets. Stand Up and be Counted. 1973: The Life and Times of Judge Roy Bean. The Thief Who Came to Dinner. La nuit américaine (GB and US: Day for Night). How to Destroy the Reputation of the Greatest Secret Agent/Le magnifique. 1974: Murder on the Orient Express. 1975: The Spiral Staircase. Der Richter und sein Henker/The Judge and His Hangman (GB: Deception. US: End of the Game). 1976: St Ives. The Sunday Woman. 1977: The Deep. 1978: The Greek Tycoon. Who is Killing the Great Chefs of Europe? (GB: Too Many Chefs). 1979: Together?/Amo non amo/I Love You, I Love You Not. 1980: Inchon! When Time Ran Out . . . 1981: Rich and Famous. 1982: Forbidden (cable TV. Originally for cinemas). 1983: Class. 1984: Under the Volcano. Notes from Under the Volcano. Observations Under the Volcano. 1985: Anna Karenina (TV). 1986: Choices (TV). High Season. 1988: La maison de jade. 1989: Amoureuse. Scenes from the Class

Struggle in Beverly Hills. Wild Orchid. 1990: The Maid. 1993: Hoffman's Hunger. Crime Broker. Est & Ouest: les paradis perdus. Les marmottes. 1994: La nonna. Leave of Absence (TV). 1995: La cérémonie/A Judgement in Stone. 1996: End of Summer (TV). Once You meet a Stranger (TV). 1997: The Honest Courtesan (US: Dangerous Beauty). 1999: Refugees from Love. Witch Hunt. New Year's Day. Let the Devil Wear Black (TV). Les gens qui s'aiment. 2000: Sex and Mrs X (TV). Britannic (TV).

BLACK, Karen (K. Ziegler) 1942–
Distinctive, talented and bewitchingly cross-eyed American actress often cast as mischievous or spiteful blondes from the wrong side of the tracks, but capable of a wide range of roles and interpretations, all of which (even flying a crippled plane over a mountain in *Airport 1975*) she seems to enjoy. Although she was Oscar-nominated for *Five Easy Pieces* the quality of her roles – and films (now more than 100) declined after 1985 and she has since then been seen in a bizarre collection of offbeat films.
1959: The Prime Time. 1966: You're a Big Boy Now. 1968: Hard Contract. 1969: Easy Rider. 1970: Five Easy Pieces. A Gunfight. Freedom. 1971: Drive, He Said. Cisco Pike. Born to Win. 1972: Portnoy's Complaint. 1973: Rhinoceros. The Pyx. The Outfit. 1974: Owen. Law and Disorder. Little Laura and Big John. The Great Gatsby. Airport 1975. 1975: The Day of the Locust. Nashville. Crime and Passion/An Ace Up My Sleeve. 1976: Trilogy of Terror (TV). Family Plot. Burnt Offerings. 1977: Capricorn One. The Strange Possession of Mrs Oliver (TV). In Praise of Older Women. 1978: Because He's My Friend. The Big Ripoff/The Rip-Off (US: The Squeeze). Killer Fish. 1979: Mr Horn (TV). The Last Word. Confessions of a Lady Cop/The Other Side of Fear (TV). 1980: Miss Right. Mr Patman. Valentine. Where the Ladies Go (TV). 1981: The Grass is Singing. Separate Ways. Chanel solitaire. 1982: Come Back to the 5 and Dime, Jimmy Dean, Jimmy Dean. 1983: Can She Bake a Cherry Pie? Growing Pains. †Breathless. Full Circle Again (GB: TV). 1984: Bad Manners. Martin's Day. A Stroke of Genius. 1985: Cut and Run. The Flight of the Spruce Goose. Invaders from Mars. Savage Dawn. 1986: The Blue Man. Hostage. It's Alive III: Island of the Alive. 1987: Light in the Afternoon. The Invisible Kid. Hem. Dixie Lanes. 1988: Out of the Dark. Homer and

Eddie. Night Angel. 1989: Dead Girls Don't Dance. Zapped Again. Mirror, Mirror. 1990: Haunting Fear. Night Angel. The Children. Twisted Justice. Club Fed. Evil Spirits. Overexposed (TV). 1991: Children of the Night. Auntie Lee's Meat Pies. Fatal Encounter. The Covenant. Rubin & Ed. Chained Heat II/Caged Fear. Quiet Fire. The Killer's Edge (TV). 1992: The Double-O Kid. The Roller Blade Seven. Final Judgment. Meantime. Tuesday Never Comes. Roller Blade Seven, Part 2. The Player. 1993: The Trust. Bound and Gagged: A Love Story. 1994: Sister Island (released 1996). 1995: The Wacky Adventures of Dr Boris and Nurse Shirley. Death Before Sunrise. Dinosaur Valley Girls. Crimetime. 1996: Dream Catcher. Plan 10 from Outer Space. Cries of Silence (completed 1993). Children of the Corn IV: The Gathering. New York Crossing. 1997: Dogtown. The Underground Comedy Movie. Lightspeed. Men. The Hunger (cable TV). Stir. Conceiving Ada. Invisible Dad. 1998: Malika/Malaika. By the Book. Waiting for Dr McGuffin. Bury the Evidence. I Woke Up Early the Day I Died. Charades. 1999: Red Dirt. Mascara. 2000: Fallen Arches. Hard Luck. Firecracker. The Chosen Ones. The Independent.

†Scenes deleted from final release print

BLACKMAN, Honor 1923–
Blonde British actress whose wartime career as a Home Office dispatch rider seemed to peg her as the adventurous sort. But the Rank Charm School took one look at her china-doll features and cast her as a succession of English roses, whence she slid into heroine roles in numerous second features. TV's *The Avengers* rescued the tiger in her by casting her as a leather-clad, judo-throwing wildcat. Still around, as feline as ever.
1947: Daughter of Darkness. Fame is the Spur. 1948: Quartet. 1949: A Boy, a Girl and a Bike. Conspirator. Diamond City. 1950: So Long at the Fair. Green Grow the Rushes. 1951: Come Die My Love. 1954: The Rainbow Jacket. The Yellow Robe. The Delavine Affair. Diplomatic Passport. 1955: The Glass Cage (GB: The Glass Tomb). 1956: Breakaway. 1957: Suspended Alibi. You Pay Your Money. Account Rendered. *Danger List. 1958: A Night to Remember. The Square Peg. 1961: A Matter of WHO. 1962: Serena. *A Sense of Belonging. 1963: Jason and the Argonauts. 1964: Goldfinger. 1965: Life at the Top. The Secret of My Success. 1966: Moment to

Moment. 1967: A Twist of Sand. 1968: Shalako. The Struggle for Rome. 1969: Twinky. The Struggle for Rome II. 1970: The Virgin and the Gypsy. 1971: The Last Grenade (US: Grigsby). Fright. Something Big. 1976: To the Devil a Daughter. 1977: Summer Rain. Age of Innocence. 1978: The Cat and the Canary. 1985: Minder on the Orient Express (TV). 1998: Talos the Mummy. 1999: To Walk with Lions. 2001: Bridget Jones' Diary.

BLAINE, Vivian (V. Stapleton) 1921–1995
Blonde American band singer whose acerbic personality was somewhat wasted in Fox musicals of the forties. But prolonged Broadway success compensated for a film career whose highlight was a repeat of a stage role – Adelaide in *Guys and Dolls*. Three times married. Died from pneumonia.
1942: Girl Trouble. It Happened in Flatbush. Through Different Eyes. 1943: He Hired the Boss. Jitterbugs. 1944: Greenwich Village. Something for the Boys. 1945: Nob Hill. State Fair. 1946: Doll Face (GB: Come Back to Me). If I'm Lucky. Three Little Girls in Blue. 1952: Skirts Ahoy. 1953: Main Street to Broadway. 1955: Guys and Dolls. 1957: Public Pigeon Number One. 1972: Richard. 1978: The Dark. Katie: Portrait of a Centerfold. 1979: Sooner or Later (TV). Fast Friends (TV). The Cracker Factory (TV). 1982: Parasite. I'm Going To Be Famous.

BLAIR, Betsy (Elizabeth Boger) 1923–
Quiet, intense American actress with silky brown hair whose facial structure and mannerisms made her just as natural for a demented inmate of *The Snake Pit* as for the shy wallflower of *Marty*, for which she won a British Oscar and an Academy Award

nomination. Afterwards she moved to Europe, but was seen only occasionally in films. Married (first and second of three) to actor-dancer Gene Kelly (qv) and director Karel Reisz.

1947: The Guilt of Janet Ames. 1948: A Double Life. Another Part of the Forest. The Snake Pit. 1950: Mystery Street. 1951: Kind Lady. 1955: Marty. Othello. 1956: Calle Mayor. 1957: Il grido (GB: The Cry). The Halliday Brand. 1958: Die Hauptstrasse. 1960: Die Thronfolger. 1961: All Night Long. Senilita. 1968: Mazel Tov ou le mariage (GB and US: Marry Me, Marry Me!). 1973: A Delicate Balance. 1985: The Flight of the Spruce Goose. 1986: Descente aux enfers. 1987: Suspicion (TV). 1988: Betrayed.

BLAIR, Janet (Martha J. Lafferty) 1921–
Vivacious, petite, pretty American 'strawberry blonde, singer-actress with radiant smile whose personality could be alternately sweet and demure, or sharp and peppy. Like Ann Miller later on, she often outshone her co-stars, without ever really becoming a star in her own right. Her brightest performance came in the title role of My Sister Eileen, but she was too often under the shadow of Rita Hayworth at Columbia and, declining the studio's offer of a further contract in 1948, left Hollywood. For many years, though, she did the occasional stint on stage or on TV.

1941: Three Girls about Town. 1942: Two Yanks in Trinidad. Blondie Goes to College. Broadway. *Screen Snapshots No. 103. My Sister Eileen. 1943: Something to Shout About. 1944: Once Upon a Time. Tonight and Every Night. 1946: Tars and Spars. 1947: Gallant Journey. The Fabulous Dorseys. 1948: I Love Trouble. The Fuller Brush Man (GB: That Mad Mr Jones). The Black Arrow (GB: The Black Arrow Strikes). 1957: Public Pigeon Number One. 1962: Night of the Eagle (US: Burn, Witch, Burn). Boys' Night Out. 1968: The One and Only Genuine Original Family Band. 1975: Won Ton Ton, the Dog Who Saved Hollywood.

BLAIR, Linda 1959–
Chubby-faced, light-haired American actress of somewhat pouty prettiness who made an eye-opening start to her major film career by playing the possessed girl in The Exorcist, a performance that won her an Oscar nomination. She then ran the predictable route to Hollywood maturity through the sex-and-drugs-in-the-headlines scene, while

growing into a pneumatic but sparky leading lady. As the 1980s and 1990s progressed, she gave unexpectedly spirited performances in a number of exploitation films, but did not manage to break back into the mainstream.

1970: The Way We Live Now. 1971: The Sporting Club. 1973: The Exorcist. 1974: Born Innocent (TV). Airport 1975. 1975: Sara T: Portrait of a Teenage Alcoholic (TV). Sweet Hostage (TV). Roman Grey (TV. GB: The Art of Crime). 1976: Victory at Entebbe (TV. GB: cinemas). 1977: Exorcist II: The Heretic. 1978: Summer of Fear/Stranger in Our House (TV). 1979: Roller Boogie. Hard Ride to Rantan. Wild Horse Hank. 1980: Ruckus. 1981: Hell Night. 1982: Chained Heat. 1983: Night Fighters (released 1986). Savage Island. 1984: Red Heat. Savage Streets. Night Patrol. 1987: Silent Assassins. SFX Retaliator/The Heroin Deal. 1988: Nightforce. Witchery. 1989: Son/Bad Blood. Up Your Alley. Bail Out. Moving Target. Aunt Millie's Will. Bedroom Eyes II. A Woman Obsessed. The Chilling. Zapped Again. 1990: Repossessed. Dead Sleep. House 5. 1991: Fatal Bond. †Beyond Control. 1992: Calendar Girl, Cop Killer?: The Bambi Bembenek Story (TV). Perry Mason: The Case of the Heartbroken Bride (TV). 1993: *Phone. Double Blast. 1994: Temptress of the Dark/Sorceress. Skins. 1996: Prey of the Jaguar. Scream. 2000: Famous.

†Uncompleted

BLAKE, Robert (Michael Gubitosi) 1933–
Short, chunky, wisecracking, dark-haired Brooklyn-born Hollywood actor who started his screen career at six as a member of Our Gang in their comedy shorts, then moved on to a series of westerns with Wild Bill Elliott

(qv). Following the teenage-drug taking trauma that seems to afflict so many child stars, Blake re-emerged as an adult actor in the late 1950s, had a highly successful TV series called Baretta, and almost (but not quite) became a box-office cinema star.

1939: *†Joy Scouts. *†Auto Antics. *†Captain Spanky's Show Boat. *†Dad for a Day. †Bridal Suite. *†Time Out for Lessons. *†Alfalfa's Double. *†Bubbling Troubles. 1940: *†The Big Premiere. *†All About Hash. *†The New Pupil. *†Goin' Fishing. *†Good Bad Boys. *†Waldo's Last Stand. *†Kiddie Cure. †I Love You Again. *†Fightin' Fools. 1941: *†Baby Blues. *†Ye Olde Minstrels. *†Come Back, Miss Pipps. †*1–2–3, Go! *†Robot Wrecks. *†Helping Hands. †*Wedding Worries. *†Melodies Old and New. 1942: *†Going to Press. *†I Don't Lie. *†Surprised Parties., *†Doin' Their Bit. *†Rover's Big Chance. ‡Mokey. ‡Andy Hardy's Double Life. *‡Mighty Lak a Goat. *‡Unexpected Riches. ‡China Girl. 1943: *‡Benjamin Franklin Jnr. *‡Family Troubles. *‡Election Daze. ‡Lost Angel. *‡Calling All Kids. *‡Farm Hands. *‡Little Miss Pinkerton. *‡Three Smart Guys. ‡Salute to the Marines. ‡Slightly Dangerous. 1944: *‡Radio Bugs. *‡Dancing Romeo. *‡Tale of a Dog. ‡The Cherokee Flash. ‡Tucson Raiders. ‡Marshal of Reno. ‡The Big Noise. ‡The San Antonio Kid. ‡The Woman in the Window. ‡Meet the People. ‡The Seventh Cross. ‡Vigilantes of Dodge City. ‡Cheyenne Wildcat. ‡Sheriff of Las Vegas. ‡The Great Stagecoach Robbery. ‡The Horn Blows at Midnight. ‡Bells of Rosarita. ‡Colorado Pioneers. ‡Wagon Wheels Westward. ‡Lone Texas Ranger. ‡Phantom of the Plains. ‡Dakota. ‡Marshal of Laredo. ‡Pillow to Post. 1946: ‡California Gold Rush. ‡Sante Fé Uprising. ‡Sheriff of Redwood Valley. ‡Stagecoach to Denver. ‡Humoresque. ‡Home on the Range. ‡Sun Valley Cyclone. ‡A Guy Could Change. ‡In Old Sacramento. ‡Out California Way. ‡Homesteaders of Paradise Valley. ‡Conquest of Cheyenne. 1947: ‡Oregon Trail Scouts. ‡Rustlers of Devil's Canyon. ‡Marshal of Cripple Creek. ‡The Last Round-Up. ‡The Return of Rin-Tin-Tin. ‡Vigilantes of Boomtown. 1948: ‡The Treasure of the Sierra Madre. 1950: ‡The Black Rose. ‡Black Hand. 1952: ‡Apache War Smoke. 1953: ‡Treasure of the Golden Condor. ‡The Veils of Bagdad. 1956: ‡Screaming Eagles. ‡Three Violent People. ‡The Rack. Rumble on the Docks. 1957: The Beast of Budapest. The Tijuana Story. 1958: Revolt in the Big House. 1959: Battle Flame. The Purple Gang. Pork Chop Hill. 1961: Town without Pity. 1962: PT 109. The Connection. 1965: The Greatest Story Ever Told. 1966: This Property is Condemned. 1967: In Cold Blood. 1969: Tell Them Willie Boy is Here. 1971: Corky. Ripped Off/The Boxer. 1972: Tough Guy. 1973: Electra Glide in Blue. 1974: Busting. 1978: The Hamster of Happiness (later Second Hand Hearts). 1980: Coast to Coast. The Big Trade (TV). The Big Black Pill (TV). 1981: The Monkey Mission (TV). Of Mice and Men (TV). 1983: Blood Feud (TV). Murder One, Dancer 0 (TV). 1985: Father of Hell Town (TV). The Heart of a Champion: The Ray Mancini Story (TV). 1993: Judgment Day: The John List

Story (TV). 1995: Money Train. 1996: Lost Highway.

†*As Mickey Gubitosi* ‡*As Bobby Blake*

BLANCHARD, Mari

(Mary Blanchard) 1927–1970

Elegant, blonde Californian model whose exotic looks led to her type-casting in a series of 'easterns' and adventure stories, nearly all Technicolor co-features of the mid-fifties. Away from her contract studio, Universal, she was busy at first, but her roles quickly declined when she reached 30. Increasingly ill in later years, she died from cancer.

1950: Mr Music. 1951: On the Riviera. Something to Live For. No Questions Asked. The Unknown Man. Bannerline. Overland Telegraph. Ten Tall Men. 1952: The Brigand. Assignment – Paris! Back at the Front (GB: Willie and Joe in Tokyo). 1953: Abbott and Costello Go to Mars. Veils of Bagdad. 1954: Rails into Laramie. Black Horse Canyon. Destry. 1955: Son of Sinbad. The Return of Jack Slade (GB: Texas Rose). The Crooked Web. 1956: Stagecoach to Fury. The Cruel Tower. 1957: Jungle Heat. She Devil. Machete. 1958: No Place to Land (GB: Man Mad). Escort West. 1962: Don't Knock the Twist. 1963: Twice Told Tales. McLintock!

BLANCHETT, Cate 1969–

Tall Australian actress of rangy prettiness, built along Meryl Streep lines, and similarly dominant at the centre of a film. Despite a formidable stage record in Australia, her film career didn't amount to much until she reached her late twenties. Then she suddenly blossomed as an offbeat leading lady in international films, particularly in the title

role of *Elizabeth* which, despite the faintly bizarre notion of an Australian playing the queen of England (still, Bette Davis had done it, so why not?), won her an Oscar nomination.

1994: Police Rescue (TV). 1996: Parklands. 1997: Paradise Road. Thank God He Met Lizzie. Oscar and Lucinda. 1998: Elizabeth. 1999: Pushing Tin. An Ideal Husband. The Talented Mr Ripley. 2000: The Man Who Cried. The Gift.

BLETHYN, Brenda (B. Bottle) 1946–

British stage actress with large, open features and dark hair who, by one of those quirks of fate not unknown in the film business, quite unexpectedly became a star in middle age and notched up two Oscar nominations. Often seen as loud-mouthed characters with big hearts, she began her off-stage career in TV comedy series and has only attracted top cinema roles since 1996 – but in several high-profile and award-winning subjects. Academy Award nominee for *Secrets and Lies* and *Little Voice*.

1989: The Witches. 1992: A River Runs Through It. 1996: Secrets and Lies. 1997: Remember Me? Girls' Night. 1998: In the Winter Dark. Night Train. Music from Another Room. Little Voice. 1999: Keeping Time. RKO 281 (TV). Saving Grace. 2000: Daddy and Them. 2001: The Sleeping Dictionary

BLONDELL, Joan 1909–1979

Cheerful, big-eyed, wisecracking Hollywood blonde, at her best in the 1930s, especially in films that paired her with James Cagney (*qv*). She held the glamour image until she was past 40, returning in the 1950s to bring a plump, warm brassiness to character roles.

Married to Dick Powell (*qv*) from 1936 to 1945 and producer Mike Todd from 1947 to 1950, second and third of three husbands. Died from leukaemia. Oscar-nominated for *The Blue Veil.*

1930: *Devil's Parade. *Broadway's Like That. The Office Wife. Sinners' Holiday. Other Men's Women/Steel Highway. 1931: Illicit. Millie. My Past. Public Enemy (GB: Too Many Women). Big Business Girl. Night Nurse. The Reckless Hour. Blonde Crazy (GB: Larceny Lane). Union Depot (GB: Gentleman for a Day). 1932: Big City Blues. The Greeks Had a Word for Them. The Crowd Roars. The Famous Ferguson Case. Make Me a Star. Miss Pinkerton. Three on a Match. Central Park. Lawyer Man. 1933: Broadway Bad (GB: Her Reputation). Blondie Johnson. Gold Diggers of 1933. Goodbye Again. Footlight Parade. Havana Widows. Convention City. I've Got Your Number. 1934: Smarty (GB: Hit Me Again). He Was Her Man. Dames. Kansas City Princess. 1935: Traveling Saleslady. Broadway Gondolier. We're in the Money. Miss Pacific Fleet. 1936: Colleen. Sons o' Guns. Bullets or Ballots. Stage Struck. Three Men on a Horse. Gold Diggers of 1937. Talent Scout (GB: Studio Romance). 1937: The King and the Chorus Girl (GB: Romance is Sacred). *A Day at Santa Anita. Back in Circulation. The Perfect Specimen. 1938: Stand-In. There's Always a Woman. 1939: Off the Record. East Side of Heaven. The Kid from Kokomo (GB: The Orphan of the Ring). Good Girls Go to Paris. The Amazing Mr Williams. 1940: Two Girls on Broadway (GB: Choose Your Partner). I Want a Divorce. 1941: *Wampas Baby Stars. Topper Returns. Model Wife. Three Girls About Town. Lady for a Night. 1943: Cry Havoc. 1944: A Tree Grows in Brooklyn. 1945: Don Juan Quilligan. Adventure. 1946: Christmas Eve. 1947: The Corpse Came COD. Nightmare Alley. 1950: For Heaven's Sake. 1951: The Blue Veil. 1956: The Opposite Sex. 1957: Lizzie. This Could be the Night. Child of Trouble (TV). The Desk Set (GB: His Other Woman). Will Success Spoil Rock Hunter (GB: Oh! for a Man). 1959: A Marriage of Strangers (TV). 1960: Angel Baby. 1964: Advance to the Rear (GB: Company of Cowards). 1966: The Cincinnati Kid. Paradise Road. Ride Beyond Vengeance. The Spy in the Green Hat (TV. GB: cinemas). 1967: Waterhole Number 3 (GB: Waterhole 3). Winchester 73 (TV). 1968: Stay Away, Joe. Kona Coast. 1969: The Delta Factor. The Phynx. 1970: Battle at Gannon's Bridge (TV). 1971: Support Your Local Gunfighter. 1974: The Dead Don't Die (TV). 1975: Winner Take All (TV). Big Daddy. Won Ton Ton, the Dog Who Saved Hollywood. 1976: Death at Love House (TV). 1977: Opening Night. 1978: Grease. Battered (TV). 1979: The Champ. Family Secrets (TV). The Glove (released 1981). 1980: The Woman Inside.

BLOOM, Claire (Patricia C. Blume) 1931–

Austerely beautiful dark-haired English actress given her first big film role by Chaplin in *Limelight*. She always seemed too dignified to play comedy, fantasy or sex-drama, although she had a go at all three, sometimes with notable success. But drama is her forte;

although it never made her a box-office attraction, she was, and is, capable of both moving and biting acting. Married to Rod Steiger from 1959 to 1969. Married author Philip Roth in 1990.

*1948: The Blind Goddess. 1952: Limelight. 1953: Innocents in Paris. The Man Between. 1955: Richard III. *Ballet Girl (narrator only). 1956: Alexander the Great. 1958: The Brothers Karamazov. The Buccaneer. 1959: Look Back in Anger. Misalliance (TV). Adventures of Mr Wonderbird (voice only). 1960: Schachnovelle (GB: Three Moves to Freedom. US: The Royal Game). 1961: The Chapman Report. 1962: Wonderful World of the Brothers Grimm. 1963: The Haunting. 80,000 Suspects. Il maestro di Vigevano. 1964: The Outrage. Alta infideltà (GB: High Infidelity). 1965: The Spy Who Came in from the Cold. 1968: Charly. The Illustrated Man. 1969: Three into Two Won't Go. 1970: A Severed Head. 1971: Red Sky at Morning. 1973: A Doll's House (directed by Patrick Garland). 1976: Islands in the Stream. 1981: Clash of the Titans. 1984: Ellis Island (shortened version of TV mini-series). The Ghost Writer (TV). 1985: Always (later Deja Vu). Florence Nightingale (TV). 1987: Beryl Markham: A Shadow on the Sun (TV). Intimate Contact. Sammy and Rosie Get Laid. 1989: The Lady and the Highwayman (TV). Crimes and Misdemeanors. 1991: The Princess and the Goblin (voice only). 1993: It's Nothing Personal (TV). 1995: Mad Dogs and Englishmen (US: Shameless). Mighty Aphrodite. 1996: Daylight. 1998: Wrestling with Alligators. What the Deaf Man Heard (TV). 1999: The Lady in Question (TV).*

BLYTH, Ann 1928–
Diminutive singer-actress who, despite a minxish face, was cast mainly in demure roles. A notable exception was the vindictive daughter in *Mildred Pierce*, a role that won her an Oscar nomination. After a few big (but not good) M-G-M musicals, she suddenly left films at 29. Recovered well after breaking her back in 1945.

*1944: Chip Off the Old Block. The Merry Monahans. Babes on Swing Street. 1945: Bowery to Broadway. Mildred Pierce. 1946: Swell Guy. 1947: Killer McCoy. A Woman's Vengeance. 1948: Another Part of the Forest. Mr Peabody and the Mermaid. 1949: Red Canyon. *The Road to Peace. Once More, My Darling. Top o' the Morning. Free for All. You Can Change the World. 1950: Our Very Own.*

1951: The Great Caruso. Katie Did It. The Golden Horde. Thunder on the Hill (GB: Bonaventure). I'll Never Forget You. 1952: The World in His Arms. Sally and Saint Anne. One Minute to Zero. 1953: All the Brothers Were Valiant. 1954: Rose Marie. The Student Prince. 1955: Kismet. The King's Thief. 1957: Slander. The Buster Keaton Story. The Helen Morgan Story (GB: Both Ends of the Candle).

BOGARDE, Sir Dirk
(Derek Van Den Bogaerde) 1920–1999
Handsome, dark-haired, youthful British leading man, a big box-office attraction in light-hearted star roles, but always at his most interesting as villains, or men of flawed or devious character. These latter parts dominated his career from the early sixties onwards, when he was to be seen in increasingly gloomy roles. Knighted in 1992. Died from a heart attack.

1939: Come on George (as extra). 1947: Dancing with Crime. 1948: Esther Waters. Quartet. Once a Jolly Swagman (US: Maniacs on Wheels). 1949: Dear Mr Prohack. Boys in Brown. The Blue Lamp. 1950: So Long at the Fair. The Woman in Question (US: Five Angles on Murder). Blackmailed. 1951: Hunted (US: The Stranger in Between). 1952: Penny Princess. The Gentle Gunman. Appointment in London. 1953: Desperate Moment. 1954: They Who Dare. Doctor in the House. The Sleeping Tiger. For Better, for Worse (US: Cocktails in the Kitchen). The Sea Shall Not Have Them. Simba. 1955: Doctor at Sea. Cast a Dark Shadow. 1956: The Spanish Gardener. Ill Met by Moonlight (US: Night Ambush). 1957: Doctor at Large. Campbell's Kingdom. 1958: A Tale of Two Cities. The Wind Cannot Read. 1959: The Doctor's Dilemma. Libel!

*1960: Song without End. The Angel Wore Red. The Singer Not the Song. 1961: Victim. 1962: HMS Defiant (US: Damn the Defiant!). The Password is Courage. We Joined the Navy. The Mind Benders. 1963: I Could Go On Singing. Doctor in Distress. Hot Enough for June (US: Agent 8¾). The Servant. 1964: King and Country. The High Bright Sun (US: McGuire, Go Home!). 1965: Darling. 1966: Modesty Blaise. 1967: Accident. Our Mother's House. Sebastian. 1968: The Fixer. *Return to Lochaver. 1969: Oh! What a Lovely War. Justine. La caduta degli dei (GB and US: The Damned). 1970: *Upon This Rock. 1971: Death in Venice. 1973: The Serpent (US: Night Flight from Moscow). 1974: The Night Porter. 1975: Permission to Kill. 1977: Providence. A Bridge Too Far. 1978: Despair. 1981: The Patricia Neal Story (TV). 1987: The Vision (TV). 1990: Daddy Nostalgie (GB: These Foolish Things).*

BOGART, Humphrey 1899–1957
Probably Hollywood's most charismatic and enduring star. Although not an actor of great range, he imposed the sharply-defined lines of his own abrasive but warm personality on every role he played. Oscar for *The African Queen*. Now hero-worshipped to an impossible degree, but imperishably associated with a certain kind of trench-coated, trilby-hatted, cigarette-smoking lone-wolf hero it is no longer possible to portray on today's screens. Died from throat cancer. Married to Lauren Bacall (his fourth wife) from 1945 until his death. Further Oscar-nominated for *Casablanca* and *The Caine Mutiny*.

*1928: *The Dancing Team. 1930: *Broadway's Like That. Up the River. A Devil With Women. 1931: Body and Soul. Bad Sister. Women of All Nations. A Holy Terror. Big City Blues. 1932: Love Affair. Three on a Match. 1934: Midnight. 1935: The Petrified Forest. 1936: Bullets or Ballots. Two Against the World (GB: The Case of Mrs Pembrook). China Clipper. Isle of Fury. Black Legion. The Great O'Malley. 1937: *Swingtime in the Movies. Marked Woman. Kid Galahad. San Quentin. Dead End. Stand-In. Swing Your Lady. 1938: Men Are Such Fools. Crime School. Racket Busters. The Amazing Dr Clitterhouse. Angels with Dirty Faces. 1939: King of the Underworld. The Oklahoma Kid. Dark Victory. You Can't Get Away With Murder. The Roaring Twenties. The Return of Dr X. Invisible Stripes. 1940: Virginia City. It All Came True. Brother Orchid. They Drive By*

ROBERT OSBORNE on
Humphrey Bogart

THAT FACE YOU SEE ON THE COVER of this month's *Now Playing* guide is the same one that graced our very first N.P. cover back in January 1997. It's also the face that has been a cover subject for us the most often since then, this being the seventh time "the Greatest Movie Star of All Time" (as he was declared by *Entertainment Weekly* magazine) and "the Greatest Screen Actor" (as the American Film Institute has called him) has been "covered" by us, either as a solo subject or as part of an ensemble. No one else—not Cary, Clint, Marilyn, the Duke, Kate, Fred and Ginger included—has matched that record. Which, when you think about it, is quite amazing. By any logical yardstick, it's a wonder that Humphrey Bogart, the TCM man of the month for December, managed to became a movie star at all. Once upon a time, and most definitely in Bogie's era, an actor had to be—first and foremost, and with only a few exceptions—tall, dark and handsome to be granted entry behind that velvet rope into the movie pastures where bona fide leading men can roam. Think Clark Gable and Errol Flynn. Think Tyrone Power, Robert Taylor, William Holden. Bogart didn't fit any such Handsome Harry profile. He stood 5 feet 8 inches and possessed a somewhat craggy face with a mouth that curled awkwardly when he spoke. There was even a slight hint of a lisp. Further, that first name did him no favors, "Humphrey" never being a moniker synonymous with toughness, bravado or muscles. But put them all together in the package born December 1899, to a successful New York doctor and his wife, a famous magazine illustrator, and you had

a star as big, magnetic and timeless as Hollywood has ever known. In a profession where the length of popularity has always averaged seven years, the magic of Bogart has lingered for seventy years, with no sign of it ever slowing down. There are as many reasons we're saluting Bogart on his 110th birthday month as there are Bogart movies, and our look back at his career is the most extensive we've ever done on the actor; it may also be the most complete Bogart film retrospective that's been done anywhere. There will be sixty-four Bogart movies, from one of his earliest, 1932's *Love Affair* with Dorothy Mackaill, to his final one, 1956's *The Harder They Fall* with Rod Steiger, along with two documentaries about H.B., plus an additional pair of films in which he makes a guest appearance and a one-hour look on December 16 at trailers from several different Bogart classics. We'll be showing all the usual suspects: *The Maltese Falcon, Casablanca, To Have and Have Not, The Big Sleep, The Treasure of the Sierra Madre, Key Largo, The African Queen* and *The Caine Mutiny,* but also many Bogie blasts from the past you likely have never heard of, much less seen. (Does 1938's *Swing Your Lady* ring a bell? Or 1936's *Isle of Fury* and *One Fatal Hour*?) Do plan to spend quality time with us this month basking in wall-to-wall Bogart, either as the beginning or continuing of a beautiful friendship.

ROBERT OSBORNE
TCM Prime Time Host

Robert O.

www.robertosborne.com

FRANK CAPRA

You Can't Take It with You (1938)

MONDAYS • 23 MOVIES

Frank Capra, the movies' great purveyor of the American Dream, brought to his films, in the words of author Graham Greene, "a kinship with his audience, a sense of common life, a morality." Capra was designated by *Time* magazine the No. 1 director in America during the 1930s, and it is likely that at the time no filmmaker was better loved by the public.

Capra (1897-1991) was born in Bisacquino, Sicily, and came with his family to the U.S. at the age of six. After earning a degree in chemical engineering and serving in the U.S. Army during World War I, he began in films as an extra in 1919 and by 1922 was directing short films. After writing and directing for Harry Langdon and Mack Sennett, he signed with Columbia Pictures, where his early directorial efforts included the silent *Matinee Idol* (1928) and the part-talkie *The Younger Generation* (1929, TCM premiere).

With *Ladies of Leisure* (1930), Capra discovered his muse in Barbara Stanwyck and, with this romantic drama about a "party girl" who poses for an inspirational painting, turned the young stage actress into a movie star. He would make four more films with Stanwyck: *The Miracle Woman* (1931), *Forbidden* (1932), *The Bitter Tea of General Yen* (1932) and *Meet John Doe* (1941).

With his surprise comedy hit *It Happened One Night* (1934), Capra elevated Columbia to

> " IT IS LIKELY THAT AT THE TIME NO FILMMAKER WAS BETTER LOVED BY THE PUBLIC. "

a major studio and took home his first of three Academy Awards® as Best Director. (The others were for *Mr. Deeds Goes to Town*, 1936, and *You Can't Take It with You*, 1938.) *Night* swept all the major awards in its year, also winning Oscars® as Best Picture and for its stars, Clark Gable and Claudette Colbert.

With Gary Cooper in *Mr. Deeds* and, later, James Stewart in *Mr. Smith Goes to Washington* (1939), Capra created a new type of American hero—the shy yet courageous bumbler who lets nothing stand in the way of his ideals. An adept handler of actors, Capra also brought out the best in Ronald Colman (*Lost Horizon*, 1937), Cary Grant (*Arsenic and Old Lace*, 1944) and Katharine Hepburn and Spencer Tracy (*State of the Union*, 1948).

Commissioned as a major in the Army Signal Corps during World War II, Capra directed a series of highly regarded propaganda films for the U.S. Government. Two of his later films were remakes of Capra successes from the 1930s. *Riding High* (1950, TCM premiere), starring Bing Crosby, is a reworking of *Broadway Bill* (1934), starring Warner Baxter. And Capra's final theatrical film, *Pocketful of Miracles* (1961), casts Bette Davis as "Apple Annie," a role originally played by May Robson in *Lady for a Day* (1933).

For complete listings for this month's TCM Spotlight, see pages 18-19.

*Night (GB: The Road to Frisco). 1941: High Sierra. The Wagons Roll at Night. The Maltese Falcon. 1942: Across the Pacific. †In This Our Life. All Through the Night. The Big Shot. Casablanca. 1943: Action in the North Atlantic. *Show Business at War. Thank Your Lucky Stars. Sahara. 1944: Passage to Marseille (GB: Passage to Marseilles). To Have and Have Not. 1945: Conflict. *Hollywood Victory Caravan. Two Guys from Milwaukee (GB: Royal Flush). 1946: The Big Sleep. Dead Reckoning. 1947: The Two Mrs Carrolls. Dark Passage. 1948: Always Together. The Treasure of the Sierra Madre. Key Largo. 1949: Knock on Any Door. Tokyo Joe. 1950: Chain Lightning. In a Lonely Place. The Enforcer (GB: Murder Inc). 1951: Sirocco. The African Queen. 1952: Deadline – USA (GB: Deadline). Battle Circus. 1953: Beat the Devil. The Love Lottery. 1954: The Caine Mutiny. Sabrina (GB: Sabrina Fair). The Barefoot Contessa. We're No Angels. A Star is Born (voice only). 1955: The Left Hand of God. The Desperate Hours. 1956: The Harder They Fall.*

†Scene deleted

BOHRINGER, Romane 1973–
Black-haired, charcoal-eyed, big-bosomed, quite tall French actress whose 'urchin' style appeal is reminiscent of the early Claudia Cardinale. The daughter of actor Richard Bohringer (1942–), she hasn't ventured far outside her native France, but raised her profile by co-starring with such international stars as Leonardo DiCaprio, Gérard Depardieu and Helena Bonham Carter, though perhaps not in their best-remembered roles. She has, however, often out-acted her leading men, and a high-profile role could bring success on a wider stage.
1986: Kamikaze. 1988: Il suffirait d'un pont. 1991: Ragazzi. 1992: L'accompagnatrice. Les nuits fauves (GB and US: Savage Nights). 1993: A cause d'elle. 1994: Mina Tannenbaum. Le Colonel Chabert. 1995: Total Eclipse. Les cent et une nuits/A Hundred and One Nights of Simon Cinema. 1996: L'appartement. Portraits chinois (US: Shadow Play). 1997: Burning Up. Le femme de chambre du Titanic (US: The Chambermaid on the Titanic). Le ciel est à nous (US: Shooting Star). 1998: Vigo – Passion for Life. Quelquechose d'organique. 1999: Rembrandt. 2000: The King is Alive. He Died with a Felafel in His Hand.

BOLES, John 1895–1969
Handsome, affable, dark-haired, moustachioed American actor and singer with a rather stolid acting style. At his best and most popular in such musicals as *The Desert Song*, he also provided competent backup and a comforting shoulder for a number of powerful actresses in successful tear-jerkers of the 1930s. When his movie career flagged, he toured in revivals of stage musicals. Married to the same woman for 51 years, a real rarity in Hollywood, Boles died from a heart attack.
*1924: So This Is Marriage? 1925: Excuse Me. 1927: The Love of Sunya. 1928: The Shepherd of the Hills. We Americans (GB: The Heart of a Nation). The Bride of the Colorado. Fazil. The Water Hole. Virgin Lips. Man Made Woman. Romance of the Underworld. 1929: The Last Warning. Scandal. The Desert Song. Rio Rita. 1930: Song of the West. *Voice of Hollywood No. 1. Captain of the Guard. King of Jazz. One Heavenly Night. 1931: Seed. Resurrection. Good Sport. Frankenstein. 1932: Careless Lady. Back Street. Six Hours to Live. 1933: Child of Manhattan. My Lips Betray. Only Yesterday. Music in the Air. 1934: Beloved. Bottoms Up. I Believed in You. The Life of Vergie Winters. Wild Gold. The Age of Innocence. 1935: *Starlight Days at the Lido. The White Parade. Orchids to You. Curly Top. Redheads On Parade. The Littlest Rebel. 1936: A Message to Garcia. Rose of the Rancho. Craig's Wife. 1937: As Good as Married. Stella Dallas. Fight for Your Lady. 1938: She Married An Artist. Romance in the Dark. Sinners in Paradise. 1942: The Road to Happiness. Between Us Girls. 1943: Thousands Cheer. 1952: Babes in Bagdad.*

BOLGER, Ray 1904–1987
Although immortalized as the Scarecrow in *The Wizard of Oz*, Bolger was never as big a box-office star in the cinema as he had become on the American stage. But, with horsey face, beaming smile and seemingly indiarubber legs, he could be funny, likeable or romantic, as the occasion demanded. He was also capable of some amazing dance routines, and most of his few screen appearances were notable personal successes.
1936: The Great Ziegfeld. 1937: Rosalie. 1938: Sweethearts. †The Girl of the Golden West. 1939: The Wizard of Oz. 1941: Sunny. 1943: Forever and a Day. Stage Door Canteen. 1944: Four Jacks and a Jill. 1945: The Harvey Girls. 1949: Make Mine Laughs. Look for the

Silver Lining. 1952: Where's Charley? 1953: April in Paris. 1961: Babes in Toyland. 1966: The Daydreamer. 1976: The Entertainer (TV). 1979: Just You and Me Kid. Heaven Only Knows (TV). Three on a Date (TV). The Runner Stumbles. 1984: That's Dancing!

†Scenes deleted from final release print

BOND, Derek 1919–
Jovial, Scottish-born actor, mainly in lordly roles. Was effective as officers and gentlemen (although rather less so as Nicholas Nickleby), but his strictly upper-class image could not sustain his stardom beyond the early fifties. From 1959 onwards Bond directed innumerable segments of the Rank Organization's *Look at Life* series of short documentaries; he also wrote several books.
*1946: The Captive Heart. 1947: Nicholas Nickleby. The Loves of Joanna Godden. Uncle Silas (US: The Inheritance). Broken Journey. 1948: The Weaker Sex. Scott of the Antarctic. 1949: Marry Me. Christopher Columbus. Poet's Pub. 1950: Tony Draws a Horse. 1951: The Quiet Woman. 1952: Distant Trumpet. Love's a Luxury (US: The Caretaker's Daughter). The Hour of 13. 1953: Trouble in Store. 1954: Svengali. Stranger from Venus (US: Immediate Decision). A Tale of Three Women. 1953: Three Cornered Fate. 1956: The High Terrace. *Behind the Screen (narrator only). 1957: Rogue's Yarn. 1958: Gideon's Day (US: Gideon of Scotland Yard). Stormy Crossing (US: Black Tide). 1960: The Hand. 1963: Saturday Night Out. 1964: Wonderful Life. 1966: Secrets of a Windmill Girl. Press for Time. 1971: When Eight Bells Toll. 1975: Hijack! Intimate Reflections. 1980: Dangerous Davies – the Last Detective (TV).*

BONHAM CARTER, Helena 1966–
Dark, diminutive, dainty but solidly built Britain actress with wildly straggling brown hair – in looks, a throwback to a pre-Raphaelite age. The great-granddaughter of one-time British prime minister Lord Herbert Asquith, she was a teenage star, but her haunting qualities and unusual looks made her difficult to cast. She seemed ideal as Ophelia in *Hamlet*, but hardly measured up to the role, and it was her impassioned performance in the award-strewn *Howards End* that established her pedigree. Oscar nominee for *The Wings of the Dove*.
1985: Lady Jane. A Room With a View. 1987: Maurice. A Hazard of Hearts (TV). The Vision (TV). 1988: La maschera/The Mask. 1989: Getting It Right. Francesco. 1990: Hamlet. 1991: Howards End. Where Angels Fear to Tread. 1993: Fatal Deception: Mrs Lee Harvey Oswald (TV). 1994: Der Unfisch. Mary Shelley's Frankenstein. *Butter. 1995: Margaret's Museum. Mighty Aphrodite. 1996: Portraits chinois. Twelfth Night. 1997: The Wings of the Dove. The Revenger's Comedies. Keep the Aspidistra Flying. 1998: The Theory of Flight. 1999: Fight Club. Carnivale (voice only). Women Talking Dirty. 2000: *Football. 2001: Till Human Voices Wake Us.

BOONE, Pat (Charles Boone) 1934–
Bland, excessively clean-cut American singer of the fifties who made some popular musicals at Fox before trying hard to escape his own image in the early sixties. But the public wouldn't buy it, and he drifted out of films.
1957: Bernardine. April Love. 1958: Mardi Gras. 1959: Journey to the Center of the Earth. 1961: All Hands on Deck. 1962: State Fair.

1963: The Yellow Canary. The Main Attraction. The Horror of It All. 1964: Never Put It in Writing. Goodbye Charlie. 1965: The Greatest Story Ever Told. 1967: The Perils of Pauline. 1969: The Pigeon (TV). 1970: The Cross and the Switchblade. 1978: Matilda (voice only). 1989: Roger and Me.

BOONE, Richard 1917–1981
Sullen-featured American actor with dark wavy hair – a descendant of Daniel Boone – who looked like a troublemaker and was bad news for movie heroes in the 1950s before huge success in a TV western series, *Have Gun, Will Travel*, brought him better billing. Once a boxer, an oil worker and a navy gunner in World War Two, Boone continued to appear mainly as tough men of action in films and TV until his death from cancer of the throat.
1950: Halls of Montezuma. 1951: Call Me Mister. The Desert Fox (GB: Rommel – Desert Fox). 1952: Kangaroo. Red Skies of Montana. Return of the Texan. 1953: Way of a Gaucho. Beneath the 12-Mile Reef. City of Bad Men. Man on a Tightrope. The Robe. Vicki. 1954: Dragnet. The Raid. The Siege at Red River. 1955: Man Without a Star. Robber's Roost. Ten Wanted Men. The Big Knife (narrator only). 1956: Battle Stations. Away All Boats. Star in the Dust. 1957: Garment Center (GB: The Garment Jungle). Lizzie. The Tall T. 1958: I Bury the Living. 1959: The Tunnel (TV). 1960: The Alamo. Tomorrow (TV). 1961: A Thunder of Drums. 1964: Rio Conchos. 1965: The War Lord. 1966: Hombre. 1968: Kona Coast (TV. GB: cinemas). The Night of the Following Day. The Arrangement. The Kremlin Letter. 1970: Madron. 1971: Big Jake. The Century Turns (TV. GB: Hec Ramsey). In Broad Daylight (TV). 1972: Goodnight My Love (TV). Deadly Harvest (TV). 1974: The Great Niagara (TV). 1976: Against a Crooked Sky. Diamante lobo/God's Gun. The Shootist. 1977: Winter Kills (released 1979). 1978: The Big Sleep. The Last Dinosaur. The Bushido Blade (released 1982). The Hobbit (TV Voice only).

BOOTH, Adrian
(Virginia Pound) 1918–
On the face of it, Ginger Pound, who sang with Roger Pryor's band in the late 1930s, Lorna Gray, the 1940s' serial queen, Adrian Booth, the classy actress from so many of Republic's post-war outdoor adventures, and Mrs Virginia Davis of Southern California

would seem to have had separate careers. But they are all the same person, a gritty auburn-haired lady (and ardent feminist) who frequently lost the hero to the horse, but galloped through more than 70 serials, comedy shorts, musicals and adventures, and seems to have had no lack of variety in her life. Married to David Brian (qv) from 1949. He died in 1993.
1937: Hold 'Em Navy. •Thrill of a Lifetime. 1938: •The Buccaneer. •Scandal Street. •The Big Broadcast of 1938. •Mad About Music. †Red River Range. †Smashing the Spy Ring. †Adventure in Sahara. 1939: †*Three Sappy People. †Mr Smith Goes to Washington. †Flying G-Men (serial). †The Man They Could Not Hang. †The Lone Wolf Spy Hunt (GB: The Lone Wolf's Daughter). †*Pest from the West. †The Stranger from Texas (GB: The Stranger). †Outside These Walls. †Missing Daughters. †Coast Guard. †*Oily to Bed, Oily to Rise. †Café Hostess. †The Amazing Mr Williams. †Good Girls Go to Paris. †Beware Spooks! †Those High Gray Walls (GB: The Gates of Alcatraz). †*Skinny the Moocher. †*Andy Clyde Gets Spring Chicken. 1940: †*Rockin' Through the Rockies. †Drums of the Desert. †Convicted Woman. †Up in the Air. †Deadwood Dick (serial). †*You Nazty Spy! †Bullets for Rustlers (GB: On Special Duty). 1941: †Father Steps Out. †Tuxedo Junction (GB: The Gang Made Good). †City Limits. 1942: †Perils of Nyoka (serial). †Riding Down the Canyon. 1943: †O, My Darling Clementine. †So Proudly We Hail! 1944: †The Girl Who Dared. †Captain America (serial). †Tell It to a Star. 1945: †The Tiger Woman. †Adventures of Kitty O'Day. †Fashion Model. †Dakota. †Federal Operator 99 (serial). 1946: The Invisible Informer. I've Always Loved You. Daughter of Don Q (serial). Valley of the Zombies. Home on the Range. The Man from Rainbow Valley. Out California Way. 1947: Exposed. The Last Frontier (GB: The Last Frontier Uprising). Along the Oregon Trail. Spoilers of the North. Under Colorado Skies. 1948: I, Jane Doe (GB: Diary of a Bride). California Firebrand. The Plunderers. The Gallant Legion. Lightnin' in the Forest. 1949: The Hideout. Brimstone. The Last Bandit. 1950: Rock Island Trail (GB: Transcontinent Express). The Savage Horde. 1951: Oh! Susanna. Yellowfin (GB: Yellow Fin). The Sea Hornet. 1953: Love's A-Poppin (short).

•As Virginia Pound †As Lorna Gray

BOOTH, James

(David Geeves-Booth) 1930–

Slightly lugubrious-looking British actor who had a good run in the sixties with various sharpies, petty gang leaders and men on the make. The public was not attracted to him in leading roles, and he returned to playing rascals. Later lived in America, working mainly as a writer of film and TV scripts.

1956: †The Girl in the Picture. 1959: Jazzboat. 1960: Let's Get Married. The Trials of Oscar Wilde (US: The Man with the Green Carnation). In the Nick. 1961: The Hellions. In the Doghouse. 1962: Sparrows Can't Sing. 1963: Zulu. 1964: 90 Degrees in the Shade. French Dressing. 1965: The Secret of My Success. 1967: Robbery. 1968: The Bliss of Mrs Blossom. Fraulein Doktor. 1969: Adam's Woman. 1970: The Man Who Had Power Over Women. Darker Than Amber. 1971: Revenge. Macho Callahan. 1972: Rentadick. 1973: That'll Be the Day. Penny Gold. 1974: Percy's Progress. Brannigan. 1975: I'm Not Feeling Myself Tonight. 1977: Airport 77. 1978: Murder in Peyton Place (TV). 1979: Jennifer – A Woman's Story (TV). Cabo Blanco. 1980: The Jazz Singer. 1981: Zorro the Gay Blade. 1982: Hotline. 1984: Pray for Death. The Cowboy and the Ballerina (TV). 1986: The Retaliator. 1987: Avenging Force. Programmed to Kill. Moon in Scorpio. Deep Space. 1989: The Lady and the Highwayman (TV). 1991: American Ninja 4: The Annihilation. Gunsmoke: to the Last Man (TV). 1994: Inner Sanctum II.

†As David Geeves

BOOTH, Shirley

(Thelma B. Ford) 1897–1992

Leading American stage actress, a homely-looking, light-haired New Yorker who, after Broadway and radio successes, was widowed in 1951 and became a film star in her middle years, mostly as anguished women trying to hold on to her men. In her first (and best) film, a screen repeat of a stage success, she won an Oscar, but hers was not a popular image and she returned to stage work apart from a fling on television between 1961 and 1966 as star of the comedy series Hazel. At the time of her death, it was revealed that she was 10 years older than most biographies and reference works had ever listed.

1952: Come Back, Little Sheba. 1953: Main Street to Broadway. 1954: About Mrs Leslie. 1957: The Hostess with the Mostess (TV).

1958: Hot Spell. The Matchmaker. 1968: The Smugglers (TV). 1991: A Year Without Santa Claus (voice only).

BOOTHE, Powers 1949–

Powerfully built, large-headed, Texas-born actor with wispy brown hair and heavily charismatic presence. He looked to be a major star in the making when featured in Southern Comfort, but his career in films has perhaps not quite progressed in the right direction and one fears he may be in weighty character roles before long. He did, however, distinguished himself in the theatre and made the best Philip Marlowe for some time in two popular television series from Raymond Chandler's novels.

1977: The Goodbye Girl. 1979: Guyana Tragedy: The Story of Jim Jones (TV). 1980: Cruising. A Cry for Love (TV). The Plutonium Incident (TV). The Cold Eye/My Darling Be Careful. 1981: Skag/The Wildcatters (TV). Southern Comfort. 1984: Red Dawn. A Breed Apart. 1985: The Emerald Forest. 1987: Extreme Prejudice. Into the Homeland (video). 1989: *Sapphire Man. 1990: Grand Tour (TV). By Dawn's Early Light (cable TV). 1991: Blue Sky (released 1994). 1992: Rapid Fire. Wild Card (TV). 1993: Tombstone. 1995: Sudden Death. Bioforce 1. Nixon. Dalva (TV). 1996: The Spree (TV). 1997: U Turn/Stray Dogs. 1999: A Crime of Passion (TV). 2000: Navy Diver.

BORGNINE, Ernest

(Ermes Borgnino) 1915–

Heavy-set American actor whose swarthy scowl was much in evidence as villains in thrillers and westerns after a late debut at 36. Roles for the kindlier image he projected in

Marty (which won him an Oscar) proved difficult to find, and he gradually regressed to aggressive bigots, albeit leavened with humour. Five wives have included Katy Jurado (1959–1964) and Ethel Merman (a few months in 1964). One of the industry's most prodigious workers in the 1970s and 1980s, he even found time to fit in a hit TV series, Airwolf. He survived an air crash in 1996.

1951: China Corsair. The Whistle at Eaton Falls (GB: Richer Than the Earth). The Mob (GB: Remember That Face). 1953: From Here to Eternity. The Stranger Wore a Gun. 1954: Demetrius and the Gladiators. The Bounty Hunter. Johnny Guitar. Vera Cruz. Bad Day at Black Rock. Run for Cover. 1955: Marty. Violent Saturday. The Last Command. The Square Jungle. 1956: Jubal. The Catered Affair (GB: Wedding Breakfast). The Best Things in Life are Free. 1957: Three Brave Men. 1958: The Rabbit Trap. Torpedo Run. The Vikings. 1960: The Badlanders. Pay or Die! Man on a String (GB: Confessions of a Counterspy). Summer of the Seventeenth Doll (US: Season of Passion). 1961: Seduction of the South. Los guerrilleros. Go Naked in the World. Il giudizio universale. Barabbas. 1962: Il re di Poggioreale. 1964: McHale's Navy. 1965: The Flight of the Phoenix. 1966: The Oscar. 1967: The Dirty Dozen. Chuka. 1968: Ice Station Zebra. The Split. The Legend of Lylah Clare. 1969: The Wild Bunch. Vengeance is Mine. Rain for a Dusty Summer. 1970: Suppose They Gave a War and Nobody Came. The Adventurers. A Bullet for Sandoval. 1971: Ripped Off/The Boxer. The Trackers (TV). Bunny O'Hare. Hannie Caulder. Willard. Sam Hill – Who Killed the Mysterious Mr Foster? (TV). 1972: The Revengers. Guns of the Revolution. Tough Guy. The Poseidon Adventure. 1973: Emperor of the North Pole (GB: Emperor of the North). The Neptune Factor. 1974: Law and Disorder. Sunday in the Country. Twice in a Lifetime (TV). 1975: The Devil's Rain. Won Ton Ton, the Dog Who Saved Hollywood. 1976: Future Cop (TV). Shoot. Cleaver and Haven (TV). Hustle. Natale in casa di appuntamento/Holiday Hookers. 1977: Fire! (TV. GB: cinemas). The Prince and the Pauper (US: Crossed Swords). The Greatest. 1978: Convoy. The Double McGuffin. Ravagers. The Cops and Robin (TV). The Ghost of Flight 401 (TV). 1979: The Black Hole. 1980: Super Snooper (US: Super Fuzz). When Time Ran Out. . . All Quiet on the Western Front (TV. GB: cinemas). 1981: Deadly Blessing. High Risk.

Escape from New York. 1982: The Graduates of Malibu High. 1983: Young Warriors. Masquerade (TV). Carpool (TV). Airwolf (TV). 1984: The Last Days of Pompeii (TV). White Stallion (unfinished). Man Hunt Warning (US: The Manhunt). Codename Wildgeese. Love Leads the Way (TV). 1985: The Dirty Dozen: Next Mission (TV). Blood Hunt. 1987: Treasure Island. The Dirty Dozen: The Deadly Mission (TV). Skeleton Coast. Throwback. Qualcuna paghera / The Opponent. 1988: The Dirty Dozen: The Fatal Mission (TV). Any Man's Death. San Francisco Bridge. Spike of Bensonhurst / The Mafia Kid. 1989: Music City Blues. Captain Henkel / Tides of War. Turnaround. Ski School. Moving Target (released 1991). Laser Mission. Jake Spanner – Private Eye (TV). Real Men Don't Eat Gummy Bears. 1990: Appearances (TV). The Last Match. 1992: Mistress. The Burning Shore. 1993: Hunt for the Blue Diamond. 1994: The Legend of O. B. Taggart. Christine. Captiva. 1995: All Dogs Go to Heaven II (voice only). 1996: Merlin's Shop of Mystical Wonders. 1997: All Dogs Go to Heaven 2 (voice only). Gattaca. 1998: Small Soldiers (voice only). 12 Bucks. An All Dogs Christmas Carol (voice only). BASEketball. 1999: Mel. Abilene. The Last Great Ride.

BOTTOMS, Timothy 1949–
Sympathetic-looking, slightly built American actor with a mass of brown curly hair. The best-known and most forthright of a quartet of acting brothers (Ben, Joseph and Sam are the other three), Bottoms started his Hollywood career with a bang in *The Last Picture Show*, but slipped into co-starring roles and was a featured player by the late 1980s.
1971: The Last Picture Show. Johnny Got His Gun. 1972: Look Homeward, Angel (TV). Love and Pain and the whole damn thing. 1973: The Paper Chase. 1974: The White Dawn. The Crazy World of Julius Vrooder / Vrooder's Hooch. 1975: Operation Daybreak. 1976: A Small Town in Texas. 1977: Rollercoaster. A Shining Season (TV). 1978: The Gift of Love (TV). The Other Side of the Mountain – Pt 2. 1979: Hurricane. The First Hello. 1980: The High Country. Escape (TV). 1981: East of Eden (TV). 1983: Hambone and Hillie (GB: The Adventures of Hambone). 1984: Secrets of the Phantom Caverns (later What Waits Below). Love Leads the Way (TV). The Census Taker. 1985: The Sea Serpent. Invaders from Mars. 1986: In the Shadow of

Kilimanjaro. The Fantasist. Perry Mason: The Case of the Notorious Nun (TV). Mio in the Land of Faraway. 1987: Island Sons (TV). 1988: A Case of Honor. Husbands, Wives, Money and Murder. Return from the River Kwai. 1989: Istanbul / Istanbul: Keep Your Eyes Open. The Drifter. 1990: Texasville. Ice Runner. 1991: Picture This. 1993: Digger. 1994: Top Dog. Ava's Magical Adventure (TV). 1995: Hourglass. Misconception. California Roll. 1996: American Hero. Horses and Champions. Uncle Sam. Total Force 2 (TV). Ringer. Third Cowboy on the Right. Death Game. 1997: Mixed Blessings. American Hero. Mr Atlas. Absolute Force. 1998: Monastery: A Ghost Story (completed 1995). Black Sea 213. Illusion Infinity. The Man in the Iron Mask (William Richert version). Tiger. 1999: Little Savages. The Boy with the X-Ray Eyes. The Prince and the Surfer. 2000: Held for Ransom. The Entrepreneurs.

BOUCHEZ, Élodie 1973–
Vivacious, dark-haired, Tunisian-born actress of 'gamine' appeal. Despite enormous personal success in *Wild Reeds*, she had not quite become a name on the international scene when she went from France to America in the late 1990s, producing some of her ventures there without as yet breaking into the mainstream.
1990: Stan the Flasher. 1992: Le cahier volé. 1993: Tango. La lettre inachevée (TV). 1994: Les mots de l'amour. Les roseaux sauvages (GB and US: Wild Reeds). 1995: Le péril jaune. Le plus bel âge. 1996: Mademoiselle Personne. Full Speed / A toute vitesse. The Proprietor. 1997: La petite Lola (GB: Clubbed to Death). La divine poursuite. Le ciel est à nouse (US: Shooting Star). 1998: Flemmen im Paradies / Flames in Paradise. La vie rêvée des anges. Louise (Take 2). J'aimerai pas crever un dimanche (US: Don't Let Me Die on a Saturday). 1999: Zonzon. Les kidnappeurs. 2000: Shooting Vegetarians. Too Much Flesh / Lovers. The Beat Nicks. Meurtre d'une petite grue. La faute à Voltaire.

BOUCHIER, Chili
(Dorothy Boucher) 1909–1999
Sultry in slinky gowns, this brunette bombshell was really too hot for British films to handle. She became known as Britain's 'It' girl, but then walked out on a Hollywood contract, and was 'blacklisted' for a while before resuming her British career. Later developed into a 'grand old gal' of a character

actress, still active on the London stage in her early eighties. Billed as Dorothy Bouchier from 1931 to 1935. The first of her three husbands was revue star Harry Milton (1900–1965).
1927: Mumsie. A Woman in Pawn. 1928: Shooting Stars. Maria Marten. Dawn. Chick. Moulin Rouge. Palais de Dance. You Know What Sailors Are. Warned Off. 1929: The Silver King. City of Play. Downstream. 1930: Enter the Queen. Call of the Sea. Kissing Cup's Race. 1931: Brown Sugar. Carnival. 1932: The Blue Danube. Ebb Tide. 1933: The King's Cup. Summer Lightning. Purse Strings. 1934: It's a Cop. To Be a Lady. The Office Wife. 1935: Death Drives Through. Royal Cavalcade (US: Regal Cavalcade). The Mad Hatters. Honours Easy. Lucky Days. Get Off My Foot. Mr Cohen Takes a Walk. 1936: The Ghost Goes West. Faithful. Where's Sally? Southern Roses. 1937: Gypsy. Mayfair Melody. The Minstrel Boy. Change for a Sovereign. 1938: The Dark Stairway. Mr Satan. The Singing Cop. The Return of Carol Deane. Everything Happens to Me. 1939: The Mind of Mr Reeder (US: The Mysterious Mr Reeder). 1941: My Wife's Family. Facing the Music. 1945: Murder in Reverse. 1946: The Laughing Lady. 1947: Mrs Fitzherbert. 1948: The Case of Charles Peace. 1949: Old Mother Riley's New Venture. 1952: The Wallet. 1956: The Counterfeit Plan. 1956: The Boy and the Bridge. 1960: Dead Lucky. 1987: Catch a Falling Star (TV).

BOW, Clara 1905–1965
Known variously as the 'It' girl, Jazz Baby and the Brooklyn Bonfire, Clara was a vivacious, petite redhead, who typified America in the mid–1920s. Her abrasive love life hardly matched her screen image, which soon palled with the public with the coming of sound. A weight problem (she was always dumpy by modern standards) hastened her early retirement. Married (from 1931) to cowboy star Rex Bell (1905–1962), she was reclusive and in poor health for most of her later life. She died from a heart attack.
1922: Beyond the Rainbow. Down to the Sea in Ships. 1923: Enemies of Woman. Maytime. The Daring Years. 1924: Black Oxen. Poisoned Paradise. Daughters of Pleasure. Wine. Empty Hearts. Grit. Black Lightning. This Woman. 1925: Helen's Babies. Capital Punishment. The Adventurous Sex. My Lady's Lips. Parisian Love. Eve's Lover. Kiss Me Again. The Scarlet West. The Primrose Path. The Plastic Age.

Keeper of the Bees. Lawful Cheaters. Free to Love. The Best Bad Man. 1926: Two Can Play. The Runaway. Mantrap. Kid Boots. The Ancient Mariner. My Lady of Whim. Dancing Mothers. The Shadow of the Law. 1927: Children of Divorce. It. Rough House Rosie. Wings. Hula. Get Your Man. 1928: Red Hair. Ladies of the Mob. The Fleet's In. Three Weekends. 1929: The Wild Party. The Saturday Night Kid. Dangerous Curves. 1930: Paramount on Parade. True to the Navy. Love among the Millionaires. Her Wedding Night. 1931: No Limit. Kick In. 1932: Call Her Savage. 1933: Hoopla.

BOWIE, David
(D. Hayward-Jones) 1947–
Rangy, fair-haired British rock singer and actor of strained, faintly upper-class good looks, and deliberately enigmatic personality and sexuality. Enormously successful on record, he couldn't really get a film career going until Nicolas Roeg asked him to play the title character in The Man Who Fell to Earth, a role entirely suited to his at once magnetic and distant aura. After that he continued to play often unsettling characters with more regularity.
1967: *The Image. 1968: Love You Till Tuesday (unfinished). 1969: The Virgin Soldiers. 1976: The Man Who Fell to Earth. 1978: Just a Gigolo/Arme Gigolo. 1981: Christiane F. 1982: Ziggy Stardust and the Spiders from Mars. Merry Christmas Mr Lawrence. *The Snowman. 1983: The Hunger. Yellowbeard. 1984: Jazzing for Blue Jean (video). 1985: Into the Night. Labyrinth. 1986: Absolute Beginners. 1987: In My Life: The Story of John Lennon. 1988: The Last Temptation of Christ. 1991: The Linguini

Incident. 1992: Twin Peaks – Fire Walk with Me. Travelling Light. 1996: Basquiat. 1997: Closure (v). Inspirations (doc). 1998: Il mio West. 1999: Exhuming Mr Rice/Mr Rice's Secret. Everybody loves Sunshine. The Hunger (TV trilogy).

BOWMAN, Lee 1910–1979
Sleek, gentlemanly, urbane, dark-haired American leading man with razor-thin moustache. From beginnings as a radio singer, he developed into a capable second-rank studio star (often in M-G-M films), even if he was usually to be found playing second-fiddle to someone else. After the 1940s Bowman concentrated on TV, where he made a suave Ellery Queen, and rounded out his career in later years by coaching prominent men in the art of public speaking. With his velvet tones, few were better qualified. He died from a heart attack on Christmas Day, just three days away from his 69th birthday.
1936: Three Men in White. 1937: Swing High, Swing Low. Easy Living. I Met Him in Paris. Internes Can't Take Money (GB: You Can't Take Money). Last Train from Madrid. This Way, Please. Sophie Lang Goes West. 1938: Having Wonderful Time. A Man to Remember. Tarnished Angel. Next Time I Marry. The First Hundred Years. 1939: Society Lawyer. Stronger Than Desire. Fast and Furious. Dancing Co-Ed (GB: Every Other Inch a Lady). The Lady and the Mob. Miracles for Sale. Love Affair. The Great Victor Herbert. 1940: Wyoming (GB: Bad Man of Wyoming). Florian. Gold Rush Maisie. Third Finger, Left Hand. 1941: Buck Privates (GB: Rookies). Model Wife. Washington Melodrama. Married Bachelor. Design for Scandal. 1942: Kid Glove Killer. We Were Dancing. Pacific Rendezvous. Tish. 1943: Bataan. Three Hearts for Julia. 1944: Cover Girl. *Screen Snapshots, Series 24, No 1. Up in Mabel's Room. The Impatient Years. Tonight and Every Night. 1945: She Wouldn't Say Yes. 1946: The Walls Came Tumbling Down. 1947: Smash-Up, the Story of a Woman (GB: A Woman Destroyed). 1949: My Dream is Yours. There's a Girl in My Heart. The House by the River. 1955: Double-Barreled Miracle. 1964: Youngblood Hawke. 1966: Fame is the Name of the Game (TV). 1968: Judd for the Defense: Fall of a Skylark (TV).

BOYD, Stephen
(William Millar) 1928–1977
Handsome, Belfast-born actor with Kirk

Douglas chin. Quickly caught on as an international star after a few roles in British films, but his career fell away in the late sixties after a succession of poor roles in which his performances became progressively less magnetic. Although he was a fitness fanatic, a heart attack killed him while he was playing golf.
1954: Lilacs in the Spring (US: Let's Make Up). 1955: Born for Trouble. An Alligator Named Daisy. 1956: The Man who Never Was. A Hill in Korea (US: Hell in Korea). 1957: Seven Waves Away (US: Abandon Ship!). Island in the Sun. Seven Thunders (US: The Beasts of Marseilles). Les bijoutiers du clair de lune (GB: Heaven Fell That Night. US: The Night Heaven Fell). 1958: The Bravados. 1959: Ben-Hur. A Woman Obsessed. The Best of Everything. 1960: The Big Gamble. To the Sounds of Trumpets (TV). 1962: The Inspector (US: Lisa). Billy Rose's Jumbo. 1963: Imperial Venus. The Fall of the Roman Empire. 1964: The Third Secret. 1965: Genghis Khan. 1966: The Bible . . . in the Beginning. The Poppy is Also a Flower (GB: Danger Grows Wild). The Oscar. Fantastic Voyage. 1967: Assignment K. The Caper of the Golden Bulls (GB: Carnival of Thieves). 1968: Shalako. 1969: Slaves. 1970: Marta. 1971: Hannie Caulder. 1972: Carter's Army (TV). Kill (US: Kill! Kill! Kill!). Bloody Mary. The Hands of Cormac Joyce (TV). Key West (TV). The Big Game. The Devil Has Seven Faces. 1973: The Man Called Noon. 1974: One Man Against the Organization. The Left Hand of the Law. Evil in the Deep/The Treasure of Jamaica Reef. 1975: Of Men and Women II (TV). Those Dirty Dogs. The Lives of Jenny Dolan (TV). 1976: Impossible Love. Potato Fritz/Montana Trap. Lady Dracula. Frauenstation (US: Women in Hospital). 1977: The Squeeze.

BOYD, William 1895–1972
Ohio-born Hollywood star who earned himself security, popularity and a niche in screen history when he started playing the western hero Hopalong Cassidy in 1935. A pillar of respectability and two-fisted justice, Cassidy was perhaps the only cowboy to match white hair with a black outfit. Boyd took the character with him into TV in 1948: Married four times, his last wife (from 1937) being actress Grace Bradley. Died from Parkinson's Disease.
1918: Old Wives for New. 1919: Why Change Your Wife? 1920: Six Best Cellars. City of

Masks. The Jucklins. A City Sparrow. 1921: Brewster's Millions. Moonlight and Honey-suckle. The Affairs of Anatol (GB: A Prodigal Knight). Exit the Vamp. A Wise Fool. 1922: Bobbed Hair. Nice People. The Young Rajah. Manslaughter. On the High Seas. 1923: Enemies of Children. The Temple of Venus. Michael O'Halloran. Hollywood. 1924: Tarnish. Changing Husbands. Triumph. 1925: Forty Winks. The Road to Yesterday. The Golden Bed. The Midshipman. 1926: The Last Frontier. Eve's Leaves. Her Man O' War. The Volga Boatman. Steel Preferred. 1927: Two Arabian Knights. King of Kings. Dress Parade. Wolves of the Air. Jim the Conqueror. Yankee Clipper. 1928: The Night Flyer. Power. Skyscraper. The Cop. 1929: High Voltage (GB: Wanted). Lady of the Pavements (GB: Lady of the Night). The Flying Fool. The Leatherneck. Wolf Song. Locked Door. 1930: Those Who Dance. Officer O'Brien. His First Command. The Storm. 1931: Night Nurse. The Gang Buster. The Painted Desert. Beyond Victory. The Big Gamble. Suicide Fleet. 1932: Carnival Boat. Men of America (GB: Great Decision). The Wiser Sex. Madison Square Garden. 1933: Lucky Devils. Emergency Call. 1934: Port of Lost Dreams. Cheaters. Flaming Gold. 1935: The Lost City. Transatlantic Merry-Go-Round. Night Life of the Gods. Racing Luck. Hop-A-Long Cassidy. Bar 20 Rides Again. Eagle's Brood. Call of the Prairie. Go Get 'Em Haines. 1936: Three on the Trail. Federal Agent. Burning Gold. Heart of the West. Hopalong Cassidy Returns. Trail Dust. Borderland. 1937: Hills of Old Wyoming. North of the Rio Grande. Rustlers' Valley. Hopalong Rides Again. Texas Trail. Partners of the Plains. Cassidy of Bar 20. 1938: Bar 20 Justice. Heart of Arizona. In Old Mexico. The Frontiersman. Pride of the West. Sunset Trail. 1939: Silver on the Sage. Law of the Pampas. Range War. Renegade Trail. 1940: Santa Fé Marshal. Showdown. Hidden Gold. Stagecoach War. Three Men from Texas. 1941: In Old Colorado. Doomed Caravan. Pirates on Horseback. Border Vigilantes. Wide Open Town. Secrets of the Wasteland. Stick to Your Guns. Twilight on the Trail. Outlaws of the Desert. Riders of the Timberline. 1942: Undercover Man. Lost Canyon. 1943: Leather Burners. Hoppy Serves a Writ. Border Patrol. False Colors. Colt Comrades. Bar 20. Riders of the Deadline. 1944: Texas Masquerade. Lumberjack. Forty Thieves. Mystery Man. 1946: The Devil's Playground. Fools' Gold. Unexpected Guest. Dangerous Venture. 1947: Hoppy's Holiday. The Marauders. 1948: Silent Conflict. The Dead

Don't Dream. Strange Gamble. Sinister Journey. False Paradise. Borrowed Trouble. 1951: *Hopalong in Hoppyland. 1952: The Greatest Show on Earth.

BOYER, Charles 1897–1978
The 'great lover' of the screen, every filmgoing lady's ideal of the romantic Frenchman. It was a reputation rendered imperishable by his portrayal of Pepe le Moko in *Algiers*, in which he did *not* ask Hedy Lamarr to 'Come wiz me to de Casbah'. The charm turned deadly to great effect in *Gaslight*: in later years he played equally charming roués. Special Oscar in 1942 for 'cultural achievement'. Committed suicide with barbiturates a few days after the death of his wife, Scottish actress Pat Paterson (born 1911). Their son Michael committed suicide in 1965. Received acting Oscar nominations for *Conquest*, *Algiers*, *Gaslight* and *Fanny*.
1920: L'homme du large. Le grillon du foyer. 1921: Chantelouve. 1922: L'esclave. 1927: La ronde infernale. 1928: Le capitaine Fracasse. 1929: Le procès de Mary Dugan. 1930: Barcarolle d'amour. Révolte dans la prison. 1931: Tumultes. IF.1 reponde pas. The Magnificent Lie. 1932: The Man from Yesterday. Red Headed Woman. 1933: L'épervier. The Only Girl (US: Heart Song. French version: Moi et l'impératrice). Liliom. 1934: The Battle (US: Thunder in the East. French version: La bataille). Caravan (and French version). Le bonheur. 1935: Private Worlds. Break of Hearts. Shanghai. Mayerling. 1936: The Garden of Allah. 1937: Tovarich. Conquest (GB: Marie Walewska). History is Made at Night. Orage. 1938: Algiers. 1939: Love Affair. When Tomorrow Comes. Le corsaire (unfinished). 1940: All This and Heaven Too. The Heart of a Nation (narrator only). 1941: Back Street. Hold Back the Dawn. Appointment for Love. 1942: Tales of Manhattan. 1943: The Constant Nymph. Flesh and Fantasy. *Little Isles of Freedom (narrator only). 1944: Gaslight (GB: The Murder in Thornton Square). Together Again. 1945: Bataille de Russie (narrator only). Le combattant (narrator only). Confidential Agent. 1946: Cluny Brown. 1947: A Woman's Vengeance. 1948: Arch of Triumph. 1949: *On Stage. 1950: *Hollywood-sur-Seine (narrator only). 1951: The First Legion. Thunder in the East. The Thirteenth Letter. 1952: The Happy Time. 1953: Madame de... (US: The Diamond Earrings). 1954: Nana. 1955: The Cobweb. 1956: La fortuna di essera donna (GB and US:

Lucky to be a Woman). Paris–Palace Hôtel. Around the World in 80 Days. 1957: Une Parisienne. C'est arrivé à 36 chandelles. 1958: The Buccaneer. Le grande rencontre (narrator only). Maxime. 1960: Fanny. 1961: The Four Horsemen of the Apocalypse. Les démons de minuit (GB: Demons at Midnight). Adorable Julia. *Son et lumière (narrator only). 1963: Love is a Ball (GB: All This and Money Too). 1965: A Very Special Favor. Is Paris Burning? 1966: How to Steal a Million. 1967: Casino Royale. Barefoot in the Park. 1969: The April Fools. The Madwoman of Chaillot. The Day the Hot Line Got Hot. 1973: Lost Horizon. 1974: Stavisky. 1976: A Matter of Time.

BOYLE, Lara Flynn 1970–
Pale-faced, dark-haired, lissome, impassive American actress who's been in films and TV since she was 15, and plays a mean *femme fatale*. She shot to Hollywood's attention as one of the stars of the cult TV series *Twin Peaks*, and has since done some good work without quite becoming a name and face the public will recognize.
1988: Poltergeist III. 1989: How I Got into College. Terror on Highway 91 (TV). Dead Poets Society. The Preppie Murder (TV). 1990: May Wine. The Rookie. 1991: The Dark Backward (GB: The Man With Three Arms). Mobsters (GB: Mobsters – The Evil Empire). Where the Day Takes You. 1992: Wayne's World. Equinox. Eye of the Storm. Red Rock West. 1993: The Temp. Finnegan's Wake. Past Tense (TV). 1994: Threesome. The Road to Wellville. Jacob (TV). Baby's Day Out. 1995: Farmer and Chase (released 1997). Café Society. 1996: The Sea Change (unreleased). Red Meat (TV. Released 1998). Cannes Man. Body of a Woman/The Big Squeeze. 1997: Afterglow. Dogwater (later Since You've Been Gone). 1998: Happiness. 1999: Susan's Plan. 2000: Chain of Fools. 2001: Speaking of Sex.

BRACCO, Lorraine 1955–
Gutsy, dark-haired, throaty-voiced American actress, adept at down-at-earth characters and less successful with exotic charmers. A fishmonger's daughter, she became a teenage fashion model and worked in Paris from 1974 to 1984, also becoming a disc jockey with Radio Luxembourg and marrying American actor Harvey Keitel (qv) in 1982. Back in America her acting career prospered and she won an Oscar nomination for her performance in *GoodFellas*. Her abrasive style looked good in leading roles, but since 1992 her

performances have been disappointing. The marriage to Keitel ended in 1990 and she is now married to actor Edward James Olmos (1947–). A TV hit in *The Sopranos*.

1979: *Duos sur canapé*. 1980: *Mais qu'est-ce que fait au Bon Dieu pour avoir une femme qui boit dans les cafés avec les hommes?* 1981: *Fais gaffe à la gaffe*. 1985: *Camorra/Un complicato intrig di donne, vicoli e delitti* (GB: *The Naples Connection*. US: *Back Alley of Naples*). 1987: *The Pick-Up Artist. Someone to Watch Over Me*. 1988: *The Dream Team*. 1989: *Sing. GoodFellas. Sea of Love* (scenes deleted. Seen in some TV prints). *On a Moonlit Night/Crystal or Ash, Fire or Wind, As Long as It's Love*. 1990: *Switch*. 1991: *Stranger in the House. Talent for the Game. Radio Flyer. Medicine Man*. 1992: *Traces of Red. Scam. Beyond Suspicion*. 1993: *Even Cowgirls Get the Blues*. 1994: *Getting Gotti* (TV). *Being Human*. 1995: *The Basketball Diaries. Hackers*. 1996: *Lifeline* (TV). *Les menteurs/The Liars*. 1997: *Silent Cradle*. 1998: *The Taking of Pelham One Two Three* (TV). 1999: *Ladies Room*. 2000: *Your Aura is Throbbing*. 2001: *Tangled*.

BRACKEN, Eddie 1920–
This stocky, wavy-haired American comic actor was usually cast as dynamic but dopey sub-Mickey Rooney types whose fast-talking backchat covered their own insecurity. But he did please wartime audiences and was funny in a couple of Preston Sturges' best films. His limited appeal soon faded in postwar years. When business ventures failed, he became a writer and occasional cameo performer. Later, he made film and theatrical comebacks, winning rave reviews for his portrayal of the Wizard of Oz in a 1992 stage musical.

1933: *Secrets*. 1938: *Brother Rat*. 1940: *Too Many Girls*. 1941: *Life With Henry. Caught in the Draft. Reaching for the Sun*. 1942: *The Fleet's In. Sweater Girl. Star Spangled Rhythm*. 1943: *Young and Willing. Happy Go Lucky*. 1944: *The Miracle of Morgan's Creek. Hail the Conquering Hero. Rainbow Island*. 1945: *Bring on the Girls. Duffy's Tavern. Hold That Blonde. Out of This World*. 1946: *Ladies' Man*. 1947: *Fun on a Weekend*. 1949: *The Girl from Jones Beach*. 1950: *Summer Stock* (GB: *If You Feel Like Singing*). 1951: *Two Tickets to Broadway*. **Hollywood on a Sunday Afternoon*. 1952: *We're Not Married. About Face*. 1953: *A Slight Case of Larceny*. 1961: *Wild, Wild World*. 1962: *A Summer Sunday*. 1971: *Shinbone Alley* (voice only). 1983: *National Lampoon's Vacation. The Wind in the Willows* (TV. Voice only). 1991: *Oscar*. 1992: *Home Alone 2: Lost in New York*. 1993: *The American Clock* (TV). *Rookie of the Year*. 1994: *Baby's Day Out. Assault at West Point: The Court Martial of Johnson Whittaker* (TV).

BRADY, Alice 1892–1939
Enchantingly appealing brunette American leading lady of silents, some of which were adaptations of hits she had already had on stage. Left films in 1923, and timed her comeback to Hollywood to perfection, this time in comedy character roles. She had just won an Oscar for a rare dramatic role in *In Old Chicago* (1938), when she learned she had terminal cancer. She died the following year, at 46. Also Oscar-nominated for *My Man Godfrey*.

1914: *As Ye Sow*. 1915: *The Boss. The Lure of Woman. The Cup of Chance*. 1916: *The Rack. The Ballet Girl. La Bohème. The Woman in 47. Then I'll Come Back to You. Tangled Fates. Miss Petticoats. The Gilded Cage* (GB: *The Heart of a Princess*). *Bought and Paid For*. 1917: *A Hungry Heart* (GB: *Frou Frou*). *The Dancer's Peril. Darkest Russia. Maternity. The Divorce Game. A Self-Made Widow. Betsy Ross. A Maid of Belgium. A Woman Alone*. 1918: *The Trap. At the Mercy of Men. The Spurs of Sybil. The Knife. Woman and Wife. Her Silent Sacrifice. The Whirlpool. The Ordeal of Rosetta. The Death Dance. The Better Half. Her Great Chance. In the Hollow of Her Hand*. 1919: *The Indestructible Wife. The World to Live In. Marie Ltd. The Redhead. Her Bridal Night. A Dark Lantern. The Fear Market*. 1920: *Sinners. The New York Idea*. 1921: *Out of the Chorus. The Land of Hope. Dawn of the*

East. *Little Italy. Hush Money*. 1922: **A Trip to Paramounttown. Anna Ascends. Missing Millions*. 1923: *The Snow Bride. The Leopardess*. 1933: *When Ladies Meet. Broadway to Hollywood* (GB: *Ring Up the Curtain*). *Beauty for Sale. Stage Mother. Should Ladies Behave?* 1934: *Miss Fane's Baby is Stolen. The Gay Divorcee* (GB: *The Gay Divorce*). 1935: *Let 'Em Have It* (GB: *False Faces*). *Gold Diggers of 1935. Lady Tubbs* (GB: *The Gay Lady*). *Metropolitan*. 1936: *The Harvester. My Man Godfrey. Go West, Young Man. Mind Your Own Business*. 1937: *Three Smart Girls. Call It a Day. One Hundred Men and a Girl. Mama Steps Out. Mr Dodd Takes the Air. Merry-Go-Round of 1938*. 1938: *Joy of Living. In Old Chicago. Goodbye Broadway*. 1939: *Zenobia* (GB: *Elephants Never Forget*). *Young Mr Lincoln*.

BRADY, Scott (Gerald Tierney) 1924–1985
Rugged, handsome Hollywood leading man with light-brown hair, brother of Lawrence Tierney (*qv*). His forceful early acting promise was dissipated in a series of routine action roles for Universal-International, but he kept busy, in latter days as a pudgy and balding character star. Lost to TV from 1959–1962 as *Shotgun Slade* and from 1974 to 1978 as the barman in *Police Story*. Died from respiratory failure.

1947: *Born to Kill* (GB: *Lady of Deceit*). 1948: *In This Corner. The Counterfeiters* (as Gerald Gilbert). *Canon City. Montana Belle* (released 1952). *He Walked by Night*. 1949: *The Gal Who Took the West. Port of New York. Undertow. I Was a Shoplifter*. 1950: *Kansas Raiders. Undercover Girl*. 1951: *The Model and the Marriage Broker. Untamed Frontier*. 1952: *Yankee Buccaneer. Bronco Buster. Bloodhounds of Broadway*. 1953: *A Perilous Journey. El Alamein* (GB: *Desert Patrol*). *Three Steps to the Gallows* (released 1955. US: *White Fire*). 1954: *The Law versus Billy the Kid. Johnny Guitar*. 1955: *They Were So Young. Gentlemen Marry Brunettes. The Vanishing American*. 1956: *Terror at Midnight. The Maverick Queen. Mohawk*. 1957: *The Storm Rider. Lone Woman* (TV). *The Restless Breed*. 1958: *Ambush at Cimarron Pass. Blood Arrow*. 1959: *Battle Flame*. 1963: *Operation Bikini*. 1964: *Stage to Thunder Rock. John Goldfarb, Please Come Home*. 1965: *Black Spurs. They Ran for Their Lives*. 1966: *Destination Inner Space. Castle of Evil*. 1967: *Red Tomahawk. Fort Utah. Journey to the Center of Time*. 1968: *Arizona Bushwhackers*. 1969: *Nightmare in*

Wax. Cain's Way. The Road Hustlers. Smashing the Crime Syndicate (released 1973). Marooned. The DA: Murder One (TV). 1970: Five Bloody Graves. Satan's Sadists. 1971: Doctors' Wives. The Mighty Gorga. $ (GB: The Heist). Hell's Bloody Devils. 1972: The Loners. The Night Strangler (TV). The Leo Chronicles. Bonnie's Kids. 1975: Wicked, Wicked. Roll, Freddy, Roll (TV). Kansas City Massacre (TV). 1976: Law and Order (TV). 1978: The China Syndrome. Suddenly, Love (TV). Streets of Fear (TV). Pressure Point (TV). When Every Day Was the Fourth Of July (TV). 1979: The Last Ride of the Dalton Gang (TV). 1981: Dead Kids. Shadowland. American Dream (TV). 1983: This Girl for Hire (TV). 1984: Gremlins.

BRANAGH, Kenneth 1960–

Chunky, square-faced, cheery-looking, sandy-haired actor-director, born in Northern Ireland, but raised in England from the age of nine. After a glittering career with the Royal Shakespeare Company, he attempted to bring Shakespeare to the masses much as Sir Laurence Olivier (qv) before him, earning Academy Award nominations both as star and director of his first offering, *Henry V*. Directorial efforts after that had a mixed reception, but his continued to be a name in the news. He married oft-time co-star Emma Thompson (qv), but the couple parted in 1995. Also an Academy Award nominee for the screenplay of *Hamlet*.

1986: High Season. 1987: A Month in the Country. 1989: Henry V. Look Back in Anger (TV). 1991: Dead Again. 1992: Peter's Friends. Swing Kids. 1993: Much Ado About Nothing. 1994: Mary Shelley's Frankenstein. 1995: Othello. 1996: Looking for Richard. Hamlet. 1997: The Proposition. The Gingerbread Man. 1998: The Theory of Flight. Celebrity. Tempting Fate. 1999: Wild Wild West. Alien Love Triangle. Galapagos (narrator only). Love's Labour's Lost. 2000: The Road to El Dorado (voice only). How to Kill Your Neighbor's Dog. As director: *1989: Henry V. 1991: Dead Again. 1992: Peter's Friends. *Swan Song. 1993: Much Ado About Nothing. 1994: Mary Shelley's Frankenstein. 1995: In the Bleak Mid-Winter. 1996: Hamlet. 1999: Love's Labour's Lost.*

BRAND, Neville 1921–1992

A regular army man (the fourth most decorated American soldier of World War II), Brand became interested in acting when

he took part in army training films ('I was always the sergeant, and Charlton Heston the captain'). After leaving the army in 1946, his thick-set scowling, glowering features quickly became a regular feature of the villainy in Hollywood crime films, although some of his best performances (for example, the warder in *Birdman of Alcatraz*) have been in quieter, gently humorous roles. Died from emphysema.

*1949: D.O.A. 1950: Kiss Tomorrow Goodbye. Where the Sidewalk Ends. Halls of Montezuma. 1951: Only the Valiant. The Mob (GB: Remember That Face). Red Mountain. Flame of Araby. *Benjy. 1952: Kansas City Confidential (GB: The Secret Four). The Turning Point. The Man from the Alamo. 1953: Stalag 17. Man Crazy. The Charge at Feather River. Gun Fury. 1954: Prince Valiant. The Lone Gun. Riot in Cell Block 11. Return from the Sea. 1955: The Prodigal. Raw Edge. The Return of Jack Slade (GB: Texas Rose). Bobby Ware is Missing. 1956: Fury at Gunsight Pass. Mohawk. Gun Brothers. Love Me Tender. Three Outlaws. 1957: The Tin Star. The Way to the Gold. The Lonely Man. 1958: Cry Terror! Galvanised Yankee (TV). Badman's Country. 1959: Five Gates to Hell. The Scarface Mob. 1960: The Adventures of Huckleberry Finn. Alcatraz Express (GB: TV). 1961: The Last Sunset. The George Raft Story (GB: Spin of a Coin). 1962: Birdman of Alcatraz. Hero's Island. 1965: That Darn Cat! 1967: Three Guns for Texas (TV). 1968: Backtrack (TV). 1969: The Desperados. 1970: Marriage: Year One (TV). Tora! Tora! Tora! Lock, Stock and Barrel (TV). 1971: Hitched (GB: Westward the Wagon) (TV). Two for the Money (TV). 1972: No Place to Run (TV). The Adventures of Nick Carter (TV). 1973: Cahill, United States Marshal (GB: Cahill). The Deadly Trackers. This is a Hi-Jack. 1974: Killdozer (TV). Death Stalk (TV). Scalawag. The Police Connection. 1975: Psychic Killer. The Mad Bomber. Barbary Coast (TV. GB: In Old San Francisco). 1976: The Quest (TV). Eaten Alive (GB: Death Trap). 1977: Fire! (TV. GB: cinemas). The Mouse and His Child (voice only). Hi-Riders. Captains Courageous (TV). 1978: Seven from Heaven. Five Days from Home. 1979: Angel's Brigade. The Ninth Configuration/Twinkle, Twinkle, Killer Kane. 1980: Without Warning. 1983: Evils of the Night.*

BRANDAUER, Klaus Maria
(K M Steng) 1944–

Brandauer is a homely-looking, round-faced,

Austrian-born character star with wispy brown hair. But the hint of devilment in his eyes gives a hint of the electrifying power and intensity he can bring to top featured and sometimes starring roles. Several of his continental performances have been personal triumphs, but his fires have often been dampened on the international scene and he has continually returned to Europe for more charismatic pivotal roles.

1972: The Salzburg Connection. 1981: Mephisto. 1983: Never Say Never Again. 1984: The Kindergarten. 1985: Colonel Redl. Out of Africa. The Lightship. 1986: Streets of Gold. 1987: Hanussen. Das Spinnennetz. 1988: Hausen der Hellseher. Burning Secret. 1989: The French Revolution. †The Artisan. †Seven Minutes/Georg Elser. 1990: The Last Days of Pompeii (TV). Some Sunny Day. The Russia House. 1994: Mario and the Magician. Das schnarchen Gottes. †Die Wand. Felidae (voice only). 1997: Jedermann's Fest. 1999: Rembrandt. Introducing Dorothy Dandridge (TV). 2000: The Last Story of the Century. The Diver/Dykkaren. Druids/Vercingetorix. Belief, Hope and Blood.

†And directed

BRANDO, Marlon 1924–**2004**

Magnetic, husky American star who created painfully realistic characters that often gripped an audience with their primeval force. His blurred diction was much imitated, he gained a reputation for being 'difficult' and a Brando film was rarely less than controversial. His appeal to women faded in the 1960s, but he returned in triumph a decade later to win his second Oscar for *The Godfather*. His first was for *On the Waterfront*, and there have been six other nominations, for *A Streetcar Named*

Desire, Viva Zapata!, Julius Caesar, Sayonara, Last Tango in Paris and *A Dry White Season*. Married to actresses Anna Kashfi (1957–1959) and Movita (1960–1968), first and second of three, Brando's private life has been traumatic. His daughter Cheyenne committed suicide in 1995, following the arraignment of her half-brother Christian for the murder of her abusive boyfriend.

1950: The Men. 1951: A Streetcar Named Desire. 1952: Viva Zapata! 1953: Julius Caesar. The Wild One. 1954: On the Waterfront. Désirée. 1955: Guys and Dolls. 1956: The Teahouse of the August Moon. 1957: Sayonara. 1958: The Young Lions. 1959: The Fugitive Kind. 1960: One-Eyed Jacks. 1962: Mutiny on the Bounty. 1963: The Ugly American. 1964: Bedtime Story. *Tiger by the Tail. 1965: Morituri (GB: The Saboteur, Code Name Morituri). 1966: The Chase. *Meet Marlon Brando. The Appaloosa (GB: Southwest to Sonora). A Countess from Hong Kong. 1967: Reflections in a Golden Eye. 1968: The Night of the Following Day. Candy. 1969: Burn! (GB: Queimada!). 1971: The Nightcomers. 1972: The Godfather. 1973: Last Tango in Paris. 1976: The Missouri Breaks. 1978: Superman. 1979: Apocalypse Now. Raoni (narrator only). 1980: The Formula. 1988: A Dry White Season. 1990: The Freshman. 1992: Christopher Columbus: The Discovery. 1995: Don Juan DeMarco. 1996: The Island of Dr Moreau. †Divine Rapture. 1997: The Brave (unreleased). 2001: The Score.

As director: *1960: One-Eyed Jacks.*

†Unfinished

BRAZZI, Rossano 1916–1994
A former lawyer who, after 15 years in the Italian cinema, became one of Hollywood's Latin lovers. The light-haired, courteous, romantic Italian he projected with such relaxed ease was perhaps an extension of his own long and happy marriage. Unable or unwilling, however, to change the image, his international appeal decreased after a few years, and he became involved in a succession of increasingly unlikely ventures. Once claimed to have made 200 films. Died (on Christmas Eve) from a virus affecting the nervous system.

1939: Processo e morte di Socrate. Il ponte di vetro. 1940: Kean. Ritorno. La forza bruta. Tosca. 1941: E' caduta una donna. Il re si diverte (US: The King's Jester). Il bravo di Venezia. 1942: Una signora dell'Ovest. I due

Foscari. La Gorgona. Tendenzione. Noi vivi. Addio Kira! Maria Malibran. Il treno crociato. L'accusata. 1943: Baruffe chiozotte. Silenzio si gira! La case senza tempo. Damals. 1945: Le resa di titi (US: The Merry Chase). Malia. I dieci commandamenti/The Ten Commandments. 1946: L'aquila nera (GB; The Black Eagle). La grande aurora. Furia. 1947: Il passatore (US: Bullet for Stefano). I diavolo bianco. Il contrabbandieri del mare. La monaca di Monza. Il corriere del re. Eleanora Duse. 1948: Oliva. The Mistress of Treves. 1949: Little Women. Volcano. 1950: Gli inesorabili. Toselli. Romanzo d'amore. La corona negra. 1951: Incantesimo tragico. Plus fort que la haine. La vendetta di aquila nera. La leggenda di Genoveffa. 1952: La prigioniera della torre di fuoco. L'ingiusta condanna (US: Guilt is Not Mine). La spigolatride di Sapri. La dona che inventò l'amore. Eran trecento. La barriera della legga. Quelli che non muoiono. Il boia di Lilla. Il figlio di Legardère. 1953: C'era una volta Angelo Musco. Carne de horca. Il terrore dell'Andalusia (US: Sierra Moreno). Le chair et le diable (GB and US: Flesh and Desire). 1954: La contessa di Castiglione. Three Coins in the Fountain. Angela. The Barefoot Contessa. 1955: It conte aquila. Summer Madness (US: Summertime). Gli ultimi cinque minuti. Faccia da mascalzone. 1956: Loser Takes All. 1957: Interlude. The Story of Esther Costello (US: Golden Virgin). Legend of the Lost. 1958: South Pacific. A Certain Smile. 1959: Count Your Blessings. L'assedio di Siracusa (GB and US: The Siege of Syracuse). Austerlitz (GB: The Battle of Austerlitz). 1962: The Light in the Piazza. Milady and the Musketeers. Mondo cane. Die Rote. Les quatres vérités (GB and US: Three Fables of Love). Rome Adventure. 1963: Dark Purpose/L'ingorgo. 1964: La ragazza in prestito (US: A Girl for Hire). Il marito latino. 1965: Un amore. The Battle of the Villa Fiorita. Engagement Italiano. 1966: Per amore... per magià... The Christmas That Almost Wasn't. La ragazza del bersagliere. 1967: The Bobo. Woman Times Seven. One Step to Hell. 1968: Sette uomini e un cervelo. Andante. Diario segreto di una minorenne. Krakatoa – East of Java. Salvare la faccia (US: Psychout for Murder). Il rubamento. 1969: The Italian Job. Assignment Istanbul. Honeymoon with a Stranger (TV). 1970: Intimà proibita di una giovane sposa. The Adventurers. 1971: Political Asylum. Il sesso del diavolo. Il giorno del giudizio. 1972: The Great Waltz. Clown. Morir per amar. Detras de esa puerta. De aire y fuego. Il castello di pauro. 1973: Racconti proibiti di nulla vertiti (GB: Master of Love). Mr Kingstreet's War (TV). Frankenstein's Castle of Freaks. 1974: Storia del pugliato degli antichi ad oggi. Drums of Vengeance/Drummer of Vengeance. 1975: Dracula in Brianza. Gli angeli dalle mani bendate. La farina del diavolo. 1976: Tempo d'assassini/Day of the Assassin. I telefoni bianchi. 1977: Maestro d'amore. 1978: Caribia. 1979: Fatti nostri. 1980: The Final Conflict (later Omen III The Final Conflict). Mr Too Little. 1981: Io e Caterina. 1982: Il paramedico (US: The Orderly). La vocazione di Suor Teresa. La voce. 1983: Fear City. 1984: The Maltese Connection/Final Justice. 1985: Formula for a Murder. 1987: Dead-Heat. Devil's Hell. 1988: Ticket to Ride (TV).

Russicum/The Third Solution. 1989: Michelangelo and Me.

As director: *1966: The Christmas That Almost Wasn't. 1968: †Salvare la faccia (US: Psychout for Murder). Il rubamento. †Sette uomini e un cervello. 1972: Cappucetto rosso, cenerentola . . . e voi ci credete.*

†As Edward Ross

BRENT, Evelyn (Mary Riggs) 1899–1975
Dark-haired, oval-faced, sharp-featured American actress who started as a 15-year-old extra and remained popular throughout the silent period on both sides of the Atlantic (especially after making several films in Britain from 1920 to 1922) reaching a peak of achievement in von Sternberg's *Underworld* (1927). Never as popular after sound, she pursued her career doggedly, playing featured roles (albeit in small 'B' pictures) well into her forties. Died from a heart attack.

1914: †A Gentleman from Mississippi. †The Heart of a Painted Woman. †The Pit. 1915: †The Shooting of Dan McGrew. 1916: The Soul Market. The Spell of the Yukon. The Lure of Heart's Desire. The Iron Woman. Playing with Fire. The Weakness of Strength. 1917: Raffles, the Amateur Cracksman. To the Death. Who's Your Neighbor? The Millionaire's Double. 1918: Daybreak. 1919: The Other Man's Wife. Fool's Gold. Help, Help, Police. The Glorious Lady. Border River. Into the River. 1920: The Shuttle of Life. The Law Divine. 1921: Sybil. Demos (US: Why Men Forget). Laughter and Tears. Sonia (US: The Woman Who Came Back). The Door That Has No Key. Circus Jim. 1922: Married to a Mormon. The Experiment. Pages of Life. Spanish Jade. Trapped by the Mormons. 1923: Held to Answer. Loving Lies. 1924: Arizona Express. The Cyclone Rider. The Desert Outlaw. The Lone Chance. My Husband's Wives. Silk Stocking Sal. The Plunderer. Shadow of the East (GB: Shadow of the Desert). 1925: Smooth As Satin. Alias Mary Flynn. The Dangerous Flirt (GB: A Dangerous Flirtation). Broadway Lady. Forbidden Cargo (GB: The Dangerous Cargo). Lady Robin Hood. Midnight Molly. Three Wise Crooks (GB: Three of a Kind). 1926: The Flame of the Argentine. The Impostor. Love 'em and Leave 'em. Queen of Diamonds. The Jade Cup. Secret Orders. 1927: Blind Alley. Love's Greatest Mistake. Woman's Wares. Underworld (GB: Paying the Penalty). 1928: Beau Sabreur. A Night of Mystery. The Dragnet. The Last

Command. The Mating Call. The Showdown. Interference. His Tiger Lady. 1929: Broadway. Darkened Rooms. Fast Company. Woman Trap. Why Bring That Up? 1930: Framed. Madonna of the Streets. Paramount on Parade. Slightly Scarlet. The Silver Horde. 1931: The Mad Parade (GB: Forgotten Women). Traveling Husbands. The Pagan Lady. 1932: High Pressure. Attorney for the Defense. The Crusader. 1933: The World Gone Mad (GB: The Public Be Hanged). 1935: Home on the Range. The Nitwits. Symphony of Living. 1936: It Couldn't Have Happened. The President's Mystery. Hopalong Cassidy Returns. Jungle Jim (serial). Penthouse Party (GB: Without Children). Song of the Trail. 1937: Night Club Scandal. King of the Gamblers. Daughter of Shanghai (GB: Daughter of the Orient). The Last Train from Madrid. 1938: Tip Off Girls. Mr Wong, Detective. The Law West of Tombstone. Sudden Bill Dorn. Speed Limited. 1939: Daughter of the Tong. Panama Lady. The Mad Empress (GB: Carlotta, the Mad Empress). 1941: Forced Landing. Wide Open Town. Dangerous Lady. Emergency Landing. Holt of the Secret Service (serial). Ellery Queen and the Murder Ring (GB: The Murder Ring). 1942: The Wrecking Crew. The Pay-Off. Westward Ho! 1943: The Seventh Victim. Spy Train. Bowery Champs. Silent Witness (GB: The Attorney for the Defence). 1946: Raiders of the South. 1947: Robin Hood of Monterey. 1948: The Mystery of the Golden Eye (GB: The Golden Eye). Stage Struck. 1950: Again, Pioneers.

†As Betty Riggs

BRENT, George
(G. Brendan Nolan) 1904–1979
Irish-born George Brent (he fled to America in the 1922 'troubles' with a price on his head) was a leading man, but never quite a star. He always seemed to be billed beneath the leading lady, most particularly Bette Davis, whom he supported on seven occasions. In the 1930s he moved from rugged action heroes to tender, courteous swains in much the same way as did Rock Hudson in the 1950s. He appeared out of the blue in 1978, playing a judge, but died from emphysema the following year. Married to Ruth Chatterton (1932–1934) and Ann Sheridan (1942–1943), second and fourth of six wives.
1928: The K-Guy. 1930: Those We Love. Love, Honor and Betray. The Big Trail. Under Suspicion. 1931: Lightning Warrior (serial).

Once a Sinner. Fair Warning. Homicide Squad. Charlie Chan Carries On. Ex-Bad Boy. 1932: So Big. Life Begins (GB: The Dawn of Life). The Rich Are Always with Us. Week-End Marriage (GB: Working Wives). Miss Pinkerton. The Purchase Price. The Crash. They Call It Sin (GB: The Way of Life). 1933: 42nd Street. The Keyhole. Luxury Liner. Lilly Turner. Private Detective 62. From Headquarters. Baby Face. Female. 1934: Housewife. Stamboul Quest. Desirable. The Painted Veil. 1935: *A Dream Comes True. Living on Velvet. Front Page Woman. Stranded. The Goose and the Gander. Special Agent. In Person. The Right to Live (GB: The Scared Flame). Snowed Under. The Golden Arrow. The Case Against Mrs Ames. Give Me Your Heart (GB: Sweet Aloes). More Than a Secretary. God's Country and the Woman. 1937: *Swingtime in the Movies. The Go-Getter. Mountain Justice. Submarine D-1. 1938: Jezebel. Racket Busters. Gold Is Where You Find It. 1939: Secrets of an Actress. Dark Victory. The Old Maid. The Rains Came. Wings of the Navy. 1940: The Man Who Talked Too Much. 'Til We Meet Again. The Fighting 69th. Adventure in Diamonds. South of Suez. 1941: Honeymoon for Three. International Lady. They Dare Not Love. The Great Lie. 1942: The Gay Sisters. In This Our Life. Twin Beds. You Can't Escape for Ever. Silver Queen. My Reputation (released 1946). 1944: Experiment Perilous. 1945: The Affairs of Susan. The Spiral Staircase. 1946: Tomorrow is Forever. Lover Come Back. Temptation. 1947: Slave Girl. Out of the Blue. The Corpse Came COD. Christmas Eve. 1948: Luxury Liner (and 1933 film). Angel on the Amazon (GB: Drums Along the Amazon). Montana Belle (released 1952). 1949: Red Canyon. Illegal Entry. The Kid from Cleveland. Bride for Sale. 1951: FBI Girl. 1952: The Last Page (US: Manbait). 1953: Tangier Incident. 1955: †The Rains of Ranchipur. 1956: Death of a Scoundrel. 1978: Born Again.

†Scenes deleted from final release print

BRIAN, David (Brian Davis) 1911–1993
Tall, fair-haired American actor who spent many years on stage (he began as a theatre doorman) before Warners signed him to a contract in 1949. There, his sardonic smile and distinctive voice quickly had him typed as villains in crime movies, especially the melodramas of Joan Crawford. He left Warners after four years, and never seemed as

effective outside their environment. Married to former Republic star Adrian Booth (qv) from 1949. Died of cancer and heart failure.
1949: G Men (new prologue shot for reissue version of 1935 film). Flamingo Road. Beyond the Forest. Intruder in the Dust. 1950: The Damned Don't Cry. Breakthrough. The Great Jewel Robber. 1951: Inside Straight. Fort Worth. Inside the Walls of Folsom Prison. 1952: This Woman is Dangerous. Million Dollar Mermaid (GB: The One Piece Bathing Suit). Springfield Rifle. 1953: Ambush at Tomahawk Gap. A Perilous Journey. 1954: The High and the Mighty. Dawn at Socorro. 1955: Timberjack. 1956: Fury at Gunsight Pass. The First Travelling Saleslady. The White Squaw. No Place to Hide. Accused of Murder. 1958: Ghost of the China Sea. 1959: The Rabbit Trap. 1961: Pocketful of Miracles. 1962: How the West Was Won. 1966: The Rare Breed. Castle of Evil. The Destructors. 1968: The Girl Who Knew Too Much. The Man-hunter (TV). 1969: Childish Things. 1970: Tora! Tora! Tora! 1971: The Seven Minutes. 1972: Confessions of Tom Harris (TV).

BRIAN, Mary (Louise Dantzler) 1908–
Petite, brown-haired, personable Hollywood leading lady with wide blue eyes. She started her career as Wendy in Peter Pan, and was perhaps unfortunately tagged 'the sweetest girl in motion pictures' by fan magazines. Possibly because of this, and despite some good films in Britain, her career petered out earlier than it should have done.
1924: Peter Pan. 1925: The Little French Girl. The Air Mail. The Street of Forgotten Men. A Regular Fellow. 1926: It Must Be Love. Beau Geste. The Enchanted Hill. More Pay – Less Work. The Prince of Tempters. Brown of Harvard. Paris at Midnight. Behind the Front. Stepping Alone. 1927: Running Wild. Two Flaming Youths (GB: The Side Show). Man Power. Knockout Reilly. Her Father Said No. Shanghai Bound. High Hat. 1928: Harold Teen. The Big Killing. Varsity. Under The Tonto Rim. Forgotten Faces. Someone to Love. Partners in Crime. 1929: River of Romance. The Man I Love. The Virginian. The Marriage Playground. Black Waters. 1930: The Light of Western Stars. The Royal Family of Broadway (GB: Theatre Royal). Only Saps Work. The Social Lion. Paramount on Parade. Only the Brave. Burning Up. The Kibitzer (GB: Busybody). *Hollywood Halfbacks. 1931: The Front Page. Gun Smoke. Captain Applejack. *Paramount Pictorial: The Ziegfeld Girls. The

Runaround. Homicide Squad (GB: The Lost Men). 1932: The Unwritten Law. It's Tough to Be Famous. Blessed Event. Manhattan Tower. 1933: Girl Missing. The World Gone Mad (GB: The Public Be Hanged). Hard to Handle. Song of the Eagle. One Year Later. Moonlight and Pretzels (GB: Moonlight and Melody). 1934: Shadows of Sing Sing. Fog. College Rhythm. Monte Carlo Nights. Ever Since Eve. Private Scandal. The Man on the Flying Trapeze (GB: The Memory Expert). 1935: Charlie Chan in Paris. *Star Night at the Cocoanut Grove. 1936: Killer at Large. Spendthrift. Three Married Men. Two's Company. The Amazing Quest of Ernest Bliss (US: Romance and Riches). 1937: Weekend Millionaire. Navy Blues. The Affairs of Cappy Ricks. 1941: Captain of Koepenick (GB: I Was a Criminal). 1942: Dudes Are Pretty People. 1943: I Escaped from the Gestapo (GB: No Escape). Danger! Women at Work. Calaboose. 1947: The Dragnet.

BRIDGES, Beau (Lloyd Bridges III) 1941–
The elder son of Lloyd Bridges (qv), Beau gained some experience as a child actor in the 1940s; but he was older than most people imagined when he made his biggest impact as an innocent abroad, in *Gaily, Gaily* and *The Landlord*. Thereafter, though, his indeterminate features were the subject of much miscasting, and he was always more interesting as devious or low-key characters than as upright heroes. He has also experimented with direction.
1948: No Minor Vices. Force of Evil. 1949: The Red Pony. Zamba (GB: Zamba the Gorilla). 1951: The Company She Keeps. 1961: The Explosive Generation. 1965: Valley of the Giants. 1967: The Incident. Attack on the Iron Coast. 1968: For Love of Ivy. 1969: Gaily, Gaily (GB: Chicago, Chicago). Adam's Woman. 1970: The Landlord. 1971: The Christian Licorice Store. 1972: Hammersmith is Out. Child's Play. 1973: Lovin' Molly. Your Three Minutes Are Up. The Man without a Country (TV). 1974: The Stranger Who Looks Like Me (TV). 1975: Medical Story (TV). The Other Side of the Mountain/A Window to the Sky. 1976: One Summer Love (TV). Swashbuckler (GB: The Scarlet Buccaneer). 1977: Greased Lightning. Behind the Iron Mask (GB: The Fifth Musketeer). 1978: The Four Feathers (US: TV). Two-Minute Warning. Something Light (US: Shimmering Light). The President's Mistress (TV). Norma Rae. 1979: The Runner Stumbles. The Child Stealer (TV).

Silver Dream Racer. 1981: Honky Tonk Freeway. †The Kid from Nowhere (TV). 1982: Night Crossing. Dangerous Company (TV). Love Child. Witness for the Prosecution (TV). 1983: Heart Like a Wheel. 1984: The Hotel New Hampshire. The Red-Light Sting (TV). 1986: Outrage! (TV). A Fighting Choice (TV). †The Thanksgiving Promise (TV). 1987: †Devil's Odds/The Wild Pair. The Killing Time (TV). †Seven Hours to Judgment. Perfect Stranger. 1988: The Iron Triangle. 1989: Signs of Life. The Fabulous Baker Boys. The Wizard. Everybody's Baby: The Rescue of Jessica McClure (TV). Just Another Secret (TV). 1990: Daddy's Dyin' Who's Got the Will? Women & Men: Stories of Seduction (TV). 1991: Married to It. UFO Café. Guess Who's Coming for Christmas (TV). Without Warning: The James Brady Story (TV). Wildflower (TV). 1993: Sidekicks. The Positively True Adventures of the Alleged Texas Cheerleader-Murdering Mom (TV). Elvis and the Colonel: The Untold Story (TV). My Father's Son (TV). The Man with Three Wives (TV). 1994: †Secret Sins of the Father (TV). Vault of Horror. 1995: Hidden in America (TV). The Sandkings (TV). Kissinger and Nixon (TV). 1996: Losing Chase (TV). Jerry Maguire. Nightjohn (cable TV). A Stranger in Love (TV). The Uninvited (TV). Victim of the Haunt (TV). 1997: Space Cadet. The Second Civil War (TV). Rocketman. The Defenders: Playback (TV). 1998: Meeting Daddy. 1999: Inherit the Wind (TV). P T Barnum (TV). 2000: Surfing for Life (doc. Narrator only). Common Ground (TV). Sordid Lives.

†And directed

BRIDGES, Jeff 1949–
More rugged than his brother Beau, Jeff Bridges has also been acting from an early age. Despite a run of critically acclaimed pictures unparalleled in recent times by a young leading man, he doesn't seem quite to have acquired the charisma to become a bankable star. In spite of his versatility, Bridges hit a bad patch with film roles in the late 1970s, but box-office success returned in the early 1980s, and he remains one of the most interesting, if scruffiest of current American stars. Nominated for Academy Awards in *The Last Picture Show, Thunderbolt and Lightfoot* and *Starman*.
1951: The Company She Keeps. 1969: Silent Night, Lonely Night (TV). Halls of Anger. 1970: In Search of America. †The Yin and the Yang of Dr Go. 1971: The Last Picture Show.

Fat City. 1972: Bad Company. 1973: The Last American Hero. Lolly Madonna XXX (GB: The Lolly Madonna War). The Iceman Cometh. 1974: Thunderbolt and Lightfoot. Rancho de Luxe. 1975: Hearts of the West (GB: Hollywood Cowboy). Tilt. 1976: King Kong. Stay Hungry. 1977: Winter Kills (released 1979). 1978: Somebody Killed Her Husband. 1980: Heaven's Gate. Cutter and Bone (later Cutter's Way). The American Success Company (later $uccess). 1981: The Last Unicorn (voice only). 1982: Kiss Me Goodbye. Tron. 1984: Against All Odds. Starman. 1985: 8 Million Ways to Die. Jagged Edge. 1986: The Morning After. 1987: Nadine. The Thanksgiving Promise (TV). 1988: Tucker: The Man and His Dream. See You in the Morning. 1989: Cold Feet. The Fabulous Baker Boys. 1990: Texasville. Capital News (TV). 1991: The Fisher King. 1992: American Heart. The Vanishing. 1993: Fearless. 1994: Blown Away. 1995: Wild Bill. 1996: White Squall. The Mirror Has Two Faces. Hidden in America (TV). 1998: The Big Lebowski. Arlington Road. 1999: The Muse. Simpatico. Forever Hollywood (doc). 2000: The Contender.

†Unreleased

BRIDGES, Lloyd 1913–1998
Tallow-haired Hollywood actor in films after being spotted in off-Broadway plays. Bridges's screen characters were usually unreliable: braggarts who would back down; charmers who would let you down. He had a nice line in cynical sneers, and it was a pity he didn't rise above about fifth place on cast lists until the early fifties. TV gave him his greatest success in an underwater series called *Sea Hunt*, and he continued to work prodigiously in the medium, later blossoming as a comedy actor. Briefly blacklisted 1953/4 after admitting past Communist affiliations, he was the father of actors Beau and Jeff Bridges (both qv). Battling pancreatic cancer in 1998, he died the same year from congestive heart failure.
1936: Dancing Feet. 1941: They Dare Not Love. Honolulu Lu. The Lone Wolf Takes a Chance. Cadets on Parade. Son of Davy Crockett (GB: Blue Clay). I Was a Prisoner on Devil's Island. Here Comes Mr Jordan. The Medico of Painted Springs (GB: Doctor's Alibi). Our Wife. Two Latins from Manhattan. Harmon of Michigan. Three Girls about Town. The Royal Mounted Patrol (GB: Giants A'Fire). Harvard, Here I Come (GB: Here I

Come). You Belong to Me (GB: Good Morning, Doctor). 1942: The Daring Young Man. The Wife Takes a Flyer (GB: A Yank in Dutch). Underground Agent. North of the Rockies (GB: False Clues). West of Tombstone. Blondie Goes to College (GB: The Boss Said No). Sing for Your Supper. Shut My Big Mouth. Canal Zone. Stand By All Networks. Tramp, Tramp, Tramp. Alias Boston Blackie. Hello, Annapolis (GB: Personal Honour). Sweetheart of the Fleet. Meet the Stewarts. Flight Lieutenant. Riders of the Northland (GB: Next in Line). Atlantic Convoy. The Talk of the Town. The Spirit of Stanford. A Man's World. Pardon My Gun. 1943: Commandos Strike at Dawn. Sahara. The Heat's On (GB: Tropicana). Hail to the Rangers (GB: Illegal Rights). *The Great Glover. Passport to Suez. *They Came to Conga/They Stooge to Conga. *His Wedding Scare. *A Rookie's Cookie. The Crime Doctor's Strangest Case (GB: The Strangest Case). Destroyer. 1944: Riding West (GB: Fugitive from Time). Two-Man Submarine. Louisiana Hayride. Once Upon a Time. She's a Soldier Too. The Master Race. Saddle Leather Law (GB: The Poisoner). 1945: A Walk in the Sun. Strange Confession. Secret Agent X-9 (serial). 1946: Miss Susie Slagle's. Abilene Town. Canyon Passage. 1947: Ramrod. The Trouble with Women. Unconquered. 1948: Secret Service Investigator. Sixteen Fathoms Deep. Moonrise. *Mr Whitney Had a Notion. 1949: Red Canyon. Hide-Out. Home of the Brave. Calamity Jane and Sam Bass. Trapped. 1950: Colt 45. Rocketship XM. The White Tower. The Sound of Fury (GB: Try and Get Me). 1951: Little Big Horn (GB: The Fighting 7th). Three Steps North. The Whistle at Eaton Falls (GB: Richer Than the Earth). 1952: High Noon. Plymouth Adventure. Last of the Comanches (GB: The Sabre and the Arrow). The Tall Texan. 1953: City of Bad Men. The Kid from Left Field. The Limping Man. 1954: Pride of the Blue Grass (GB: Prince of the Blue Grass). Third Party Risk (US: The Deadly Game). 1955: Wichita. Apache Woman. 1956: Wetbacks. Heritage of Anger (TV). The Rainmaker. 1957: Ride Out for Revenge. 1958: The Goddess. 1962: Who Killed Julie Greer? (TV). 1966: Around the World Under the Sea. 1967: The Daring Game. Attack on the Iron Coast. 1969: The Happy Ending. Lost Flight (TV). The Love War (TV). The Silent Gun (TV). Silent Night, Lonely Night (TV). 1970: Do You Take This Stranger? (TV). 1971: A Tattered Web (TV). To Find a Man. The Deadly Dream (TV). 1972: Crime Club (TV). Scuba (narrator only). Haunts of the Very Rich (TV). Trouble Comes to Town (TV). 1973: Running Wild. Death Race (TV). 1974: Stowaway to the Moon (TV). Deliver Us from Evil. 1975: The Return of Joe Forrester (TV). 1977: Behind the Iron Mask (GB: The Fifth Musketeer). The Force of Evil (TV). 1978: Something Light (US: Shimmering Light). The Great Wallendas (TV). Telethon (TV). 1979: Disaster on the Coastliner (TV. Later: Express to Terror). Bear Island. Mission Galactica (TV. GB: cinemas). The Critical List (TV). 1980: Airplane! 1982: Airplane II The Sequel. Life of the Party: The Story of Beatrice (TV). 1983: Loving (TV). Grace Kelly (TV). 1984: Paper

Dolls (II. TV). 1985: Weekend Warriors. Hollywood Air Force. 1986: The Thanksgiving Promise (TV). 1987: Devil's Odds/The Wild Pair. 1988: Tucker: The Man and His Dream. Winter People. Cousins. 1990: Joe vs the Volcano. Capital News (TV). Leona Helmsley: The Queen of Mean (TV). 1991: Hot Shots! In the Nick of Time (TV). 1992: Honey, I Blew Up the Kid. Devlin (TV). Run of Hearts. 1993: Hot Shots! Part Deux. Mr Bluesman. Earth and the American Dream (TV). My Father's Son (TV). 1994: Blown Away. The Other Woman (TV). Secret Sins of the Father (TV). 1995: Peter and the Wolf (voice only). The Sandkings (TV). 1996: The Deliverance of Elaine (TV). 1998: MAFIA!/Jane Austen's Mafia! Meeting Daddy. From Russia to Hollywood.

BRITTON, Barbara
(B. Brantingham) 1919–1980

Radiant Hollywood redhead whose blue-eyed charms proved a natural for outdoor action dramas of the forties. Films neglected her natural talent for light comedy and she enjoyed her greatest success on television by a 12-year commercial stint on which she became known as 'the Revlon lady'. Remained active on stage and television, until her early death from gastric cancer.
1941: Secrets of the Wasteland. Louisiana Purchase. 1942: The Fleet's In. Beyond the Blue Horizon. Wake Island. Reap the Wild Wind. Mrs Wiggs of the Cabbage Patch. 1943: Young and Willing. *The Last Will and Testament of Tom Smith. So Proudly We Hail! 1944: The Story of Dr Wassell. Till We Meet Again. 1945: The Great John L (GB: A Man Called Sullivan). Captain Kidd. 1946: The Virginian. The Fabulous Suzanne. They Made Me a Killer. The Return of Monte Cristo (GB: Monte Cristo's Revenge). 1947: Gunfighters (GB: The Assassin). 1948: Albuquerque (GB: Silver City). The Untamed Breed. Mr Reckless. 1949: I Shot Jesse James. Cover-Up. Loaded Pistols. 1950: Champagne for Caesar. Bandit Queen. 1952: The Raiders/Riders of Vengeance. 1953: Ride the Man Down. Bwana Devil. 1954: Dragonfly Squadron. 1955: Ain't Misbehavin'. The Spoilers. Night Freight.

BRODERICK, Matthew 1961–
Fresh-faced, narrow-headed, brown-haired, young-looking American actor, the son of actor James Broderick (1927–1982). Abandoning a baseball career because of a knee injury, he played key roles on Broadway

before chirpily making strides into progressively more mature parts in films. A series of weaker characters made his profile lower in the early 1990s and, perhaps sensing a struggle to get away from such parts, he was directing himself in Infinity by 1995. Married actress Sarah Jessica Parker (qv) in 1997, and found more rewarding roles in the late 1990s.
1983: Max Dugan Returns. War Games. 1984: 1918. LadyHawke. 1985: Master Harold . . . and the Boys (TV). 1986: Ferris Bueller's Day Off. On Valentine's Day. 1987: Project X. 1988: Biloxi Blues. Torch Song Trilogy. 1989: Family Business. Glory. 1990: The Freshman. 1992: Out on a Limb (formerly Welcome to Buzzsaw). 1993: The Night We Never Met. 1994: Mrs Parker and the Vicious Circle. A Life in the Theatre. The Lion King (voice only). The Road to Wellville. 1995: †Infinity. Arabian Knight (voice only). 1996: The Cable Guy. Barefoot in the Park (TV). 1997: Addicted to Love. Godzilla. 1998: Walking to the Waterline. The Lion King 2: Simba's Pride (V. Voice only). 1999: Election. Inspector Gadget. 2000: Rumor of Angels. You Can Count on Me.

†And directed

BROLIN, James (J. Bruderlin) 1940–
Tall, dark-haired, hunk-ish American leading man reminiscent of Clint Walker (qv). He had trouble getting decent roles in Hollywood until television fame as the junior partner in Marcus Welby MD. His cinema portrait of Clark Gable was not a popular success and, after a couple of box-office hits in the late 1970s, he was relegated to tough heroes of minor action films. Father of actor Josh Brolin (1968–). Married Barbra

Streisand (*qv*) in 1998.
1963: Take Her, She's Mine. 1964: Goodbye Charlie. John Goldfarb, Please Come Home. 1965: Von Ryan's Express. Morituri (GB: The Saboteur Code Name Morituri). Our Man Flint. Dear Brigitte. . . 1966: Way . . . Way Out. Fantastic Voyage. 1967: The Cape Town Affair. 1968: The Boston Strangler. 1972: Skyjacked. Westworld. A Short Walk to Daylight (TV). 1973: Trapped (TV. GB: cinemas as Doberman Patrol). Class of '63 (TV). 1975: Gable and Lombard. 1976: The Car. 1977: Capricorn One. 1978: Steel Cowboy (TV). Night of the Juggler. 1979: The Amityville Horror. 1981: High Risk/Big Bucks. Ambush Murders (TV). 1982: Mae West (TV). 1983: White Water Rebels (TV). Cowboy (TV). 1985: Beverly Hills Cowboy Blues (TV. GB: Beverly Hills Connection). Pee-wee's Big Adventure. 1986: Intimate Encounters (TV). 1987: Deep Dark Secrets (TV). 1989: Finish Line (TV). Bad Jim. 1990: Back Stab. Super High Score. Nightmare on the 13th Floor (TV). 1991: Ted and Venus. 1992: Sidney Sheldon's The Sands of Time (TV). Gas Food – Lodging. Twin Sisters. The Last Paesan. City Boy (TV). 1993: Paper Hearts. Gunsmoke – The Long Ride (TV). 1994: Parallel Lives (TV). Relative Fear. Visions of Murder (TV). The Black Curse. The Expert. 1995: Deadly Ambition. Tracks of a Killer (TV). Last Chance (TV). Indecent Behavior II. We the People. 1996: Lewis & Clark & George. Blood Money. Scent of Vengeance. Hijacked: Flight 285 (TV). Cannes Man. 1997: Flashpoint/ My Brother's War (TV. And directed). Goodbye America. City Boy. 1998: Nightwatch. A Marriage of Convenience (TV). 1999: To Love, Honor and Betray (TV). 2001: Traffic.

BRONSON, Charles (C. Buchinski) 1920–
Rugged, hatchet-faced, latterly moustachioed American star, a former juvenile delinquent, miner and boxer who turned to acting after World War II. For many years cast as villains and men of violence, he broke through to stardom only in 1968, after which he played *heroes* and men of violence at just as prolific a rate as before. One of the world's top box-office stars through most of the 1970s, he was married (second) to British-born actress Jill Ireland (*qv*) from 1968 to her death. Kept going in craggy leading roles into his late seventies.
1950: †USS Teakettle (later You're in the Navy Now). 1951: †The People Against
O'Hara. †The Mob (GB: Remember That Face). 1952: †Red Skies of Montana. †My Six Convicts. †The Marrying Kind. †Pat and Mike. †Diplomatic Courier. †Bloodhounds of Broadway. 1953: ‡House of Wax. ‡The Clown. ‡Miss Sadie Thompson. 1954: ‡Crime Wave (GB: The City is Dark). ‡Tennessee Champ. ‡Riding Shotgun. ‡Apache. ‡Vera Cruz. Drum Beat. 1955: Big House USA. Target Zero. 1956: Explosion (TV. GB: cinemas). Jubal. 1957: Run of the Arrow. 1958: Machine Gun Kelly. Gang War. Showdown at Boot Hill. When Hell Broke Loose. Ten North Frederick. 1959: Never So Few. 1960: The Magnificent Seven. 1961: Master of the World. A Thunder of Drums. X–15. 1962: Kid Galahad. This Rugged Land (TV. GB: cinemas). 1963: The Great Escape. Four for Texas. 1964: Guns of Diablo (TV. GB: cinemas). 1965: The Sandpiper. Battle of the Bulge. 1966: This Property is Condemned. 1967: The Meanest Men in the West (TV. Shown in cinemas 1976). The Dirty Dozen. Guns for San Sebastian. 1968: Adieu l'ami (US: Farewell Friend. US: So Long, Pal). Villa Rides! Once Upon a Time . . . in the West. 1969: Twinky (US: Lola). Rider on the Rain. 1970: You Can't Win 'Em All. Violent City (US: The Family). De la part des copains (US: Cold Sweat). Red Sun. 1971: Quelqu'un derrière la porte (GB: Two Minds for Murder. US: Someone behind the Door). Chato's Land. 1972: The Mechanic (later Killer of Killers). The Valachi Papers. 1973: The Stone Killer. Valdez the Halfbreed (GB: The Valdez Horses. US: Chino). 1974: Mr Majestyk. Death Wish. 1975: Breakout. Hard Times (GB: The Streetfighter). From Noon Till Three. 1976: Breakheart Pass. St Ives. Raid on Entebbe (TV. GB: cinemas). 1977: Telefon. The White Buffalo. 1978: Love and Bullets. 1979: Cabo Blanco. 1980: Death Hunt. Borderline (GB: TV). 1981: Death Wish II. 1982: 10 to Midnight. 1983: The Evil That Men Do. 1985: Death Wish 3. Act of Vengeance (TV). 1986: Murphy's Law. Assassination. 1987: Death Wish 4: The Crackdown. 1988: Messenger of Death. 1989: Kinjite/Forbidden Subjects. 1991: The Indian Runner. Yes, Virginia, There is a Santa Claus (TV). 1993: Death Wish V: The Face of Death. Donato and Daughter (TV). The Sea Wolf (TV). 1995: The Brewery (TV). 1996: A Family of Cops (TV). 1997: Breach of Faith: A Family of Cops II (TV). 1998: A Family of Cops III (TV).*

†As Charles Buchinski   ‡As Charles Buchinsky

BROOK, Clive (Clifford Brook) 1887–1974
British-born star of handsome if stern features. The son of an opera singer, Brook became a musician, but turned to acting after being invalided out of World War I in 1918. Equally adept at stiff upper-lip drama and sophisticated comedy, he had no difficulty holding his own in Hollywood (until his age began to tell) after success in home-grown films. After World War II he devoted his time to the stage. Father of actors Faith and Lyndon Brook.
*1920: Trent's Last Case. Kissing Cup's Race. 1921: Her Penalty. The Loudwater Mystery. Daniel Deronda. A Sportman's Wife. Sonia. Christie Johnstone. 1922: *Vanity Fair: extract. *A Tale of Two Cities: extract.*

**Whispering. *The Sheik. Shirley. Married to a Mormon. Stable Companions. *Rigoletto: extract. *La Traviata: extract. The Experiment. *Sir Rupert's Wife. A Debt of Honour. Love and a Whirlwind. *The Parson's Fight. Through Fire and Water. 1923: This Freedom. Out to Win. *The Reverse of the Medal. The Royal Oak. Woman to Woman. The Money Habit. 1924: The White Shadow (US: White Shadows). *The City of Stars. The Wine of Life. The Passionate Adventure. Human Desires. Recoil. Christine of the Hungry Heart. The Mirage. 1925: When Love Grows Cold. Enticement. Seven Sinners. Declassée (GB: The Social Exile). *Peeps into Hollywood No. 9. Playing with Souls. If Marriage Fails. The Woman Hater. Compromise. The Home Maker. The Pleasure Buyers. 1926: Why Girls Go Back Home. For Alimony Only. You Never Know Women. The Popular Sin. Three Faces East. 1927: Afraid to Love. Barbed Wire. Underworld (GB: Paying the Penalty). Hula. The Devil Dancer. French Dressing (GB: Lessons for Wives). 1928: Midnight Madness. The Yellow Lily. The Perfect Crime. Forgotten Faces. The Four Feathers. 1929: Interference. A Dangerous Woman. Charming Sinners. The Return of Sherlock Holmes. The Laughing Lady. 1930: Slightly Scarlet. Paramount on Parade. Sweethearts and Wives. Anybody's Woman. 1931: East Lynne. Tarnished Lady. Scandal Sheet. The Lawyer's Secret. Silence. 24 Hours (GB: The Hours Between). Husband's Holiday. 1932: The Man from Yesterday. Sherlock Holmes. The Night of June 13. Shanghai Express. Make Me a Star. 1933: Gallant Lady. Cavalcade. Midnight Club. 1934: Where Sinners Meet (GB: The Dover Road). If I Were Free (GB: Marriage Symphony). 1935: Dressed to Thrill. The Dictator (US: The Loves of a Dictator). 1936: Love in Exile. The Lonely Road (US: Scotland Yard Commands). 1937: Action for Slander. 1938: The Ware Case. 1939: Return to Yesterday. 1940: Convoy. 1941: Freedom Radio (US: A Voice in the Night). Breach of Promise (US: Adventure in Blackmail). 1943: The Flemish Farm. The Shipbuilders. 1944: †On Approval. 1963: The List of Adrian Messenger.*

†Also directed

BROOK, Lesley (L. Learoyd) 1916–
Quietly pretty, highly animated, sympathetic, dark-haired British actress handed a Warner Brothers contract at 19 (she made several

films for their British arm, but none for Hollywood who would probably have mis-used her in Geraldine Fitzgerald fashion) and a star in her first film. Much seen in both comedies and thrillers of the late 1930s, she drifted away from the cinema soon after World War II.

1937: The Vulture. Side Street Angel. Patricia Gets Her Man. The Man Who Made Diamonds. The Dark Stairway. 1938: Quiet Please! Glamour Girl. The Viper. It's in the Blood. Night Alone. Thistledown. Dead Men Tell No Tales. The Return of Carol Deane. 1939: The Nursemaid Who Disappeared. 1940: The Briggs Family. 1942: Rose of Tralee. Variety Jubilee. 1943: When We Are Married. The Bells Go Down. I'll Walk Beside You. 1944: Twilight Hour. 1945: For You Alone. The Trojan Brothers. 1948: House of Darkness. 1949: The Fool and the Princess.

BROOKE, Hillary
(Beatrice Peterson) 1914–1999
Tall and determined-looking Hollywood blonde who often played predatory women and belongs up there with Lynn Bari, Merry Anders (both *qv*) and all those other actresses who kept their careers going for 20 years or more despite never becoming major stars. Miss Brooke was a first-rate bad girl and occasionally a strong-willed heroine. And, in common with others of her ilk, she had to play a lot of parts that weren't worthy of her talent. Died from a blood clot in the lung.

1937: New Faces of 1937. 1939: Eternally Yours. The Adventures of Sherlock Holmes (GB: Sherlock Holmes). 1940: New Moon. The Philadelphia Story. Two Girls on Broad-way (GB: Choose Your Partner). Florian. 1941: Country Fair. Dr Jekyll and Mr Hyde.

Maisie Was a Lady. Mr and Mrs North. Married Bachelor. Unfinished Business. The Lone Rider Rides On. The Lone Rider in Frontier Fury (GB: Frontier Fury). 1942: Born to Sing. Ship Ahoy. Sleepytime Gal. Wake Island. To the Shores of Tripoli. Counter Espionage. Calling Dr Gillespie. Sherlock Holmes and the Voice of Terror (GB: The Voice of Terror). 1943: Sherlock Holmes Faces Death. The Crystal Ball. Happy Go Lucky. Ministry of Fear. Jane Eyre. 1944: Lady in the Dark. Practically Yours. And the Angels Sing. Standing Room Only. 1945: The Enchanted Cottage. The Crime Doctor's Courage (GB: The Doctor's Courage). The Woman in Green. Road to Utopia. Up Goes Maisie (GB: Up She Goes). 1946: Strange Impersonation. Monsieur Beaucaire. Earl Carroll's Sketchbook (GB: Hats Off to Rhythm). The Strange Woman. The Gentleman Misbehaves. Strange Journey. 1947: Big Town. I Cover Big Town (GB: I Cover the Underworld). Big Town After Dark. 1948: The Fuller Brush Man (GB: That Mad Mr Jones). Big Town Scandal. Let's Live Again. 1949: Alimony. Africa Screams. 1950: Unmasked. The Admiral Was a Lady. Bodyhold. Beauty on Parade. Vendetta. 1951: Lucky Losers. Insurance Investigator. Skip-along Rosenbloom. The Lost Continent. 1952: Confidence Girl. Abbott and Costello Meet Captain Kidd. Never Wave at a WAC (GB: The Private Wore Skirts). 1953: The Lady Wants Mink. Mexican Manhunt. Invaders from Mars. The Maze. 1954: The House Across the Lake (US: Heat Wave). Dragon's Gold. 1955: Bengazi. 1956: The Man Who Knew Too Much. 1957: Spoilers of the Forest.

BROOKS, Albert (A. Einstein) 1947–
Chunky, cheery, boyish-looking American comedy actor/director with a mass of brown curly hair, an incisive and perceptive observer of angst in the modern scene. After cutting his teeth on late-night television comedy satire, Brooks, the son of radio comedian Parkyarkarkus (1904–1958), directed and starred in several comedies about the problems that beset the American male today. Critically well received, they made very little impact on the box-office and, by his own high standards, Brooks fell away in the 1990s. Today, he's probably best remembered as the sweating would-be TV anchorman of *Broadcast News*, a performance that won him an Oscar nomination.

1976: Taxi Driver. 1979: †Real Life/Real People. 1980: Private Benjamin. 1981:

†Modern Romance. 1983: The Twilight Zone (GB: Twilight Zone The Movie). Unfaithfully Yours. 1985: †Lost in America. 1987: Broadcast News. 1991: †Defending Your Life. 1993: I'll Do Anything. 1994: The Scout. 1996: †Mother. 1997: Critical Care. 1998: Out of Sight. Dr Dolittle (vice only). 1999: †The Muse. 2000: My First Mister.

†And directed

BROOKS, Geraldine
(G. Stroock) 1925–1977
Dark-haired, small, pretty American actress of strong personality and performances. Although critics liked most of the few films she did make as a leading lady, she never fulfilled her potential. Later filmed on the continent, became a natural history photographer (a book of her bird studies, *Swan Watch*, was published) and poet, and appeared in the 1970s on television as Dan Dailey's secretary in the feature-length *Faraday and Co* series. Died from cancer. The actress Gloria Stroock is her sister.

1946: Cry Wolf. 1947: Possessed. 1948: Embraceable You. An Act of Murder. 1949: The Younger Brothers. Challenge to Lassie. The Reckless Moment. Volcano. 1950: This Side of the Law. 1951: J'étais une pêcheresse. Ho sognato il paradiso (US: Street of Sorrow). The Green Glove. 1954: La strada (GB: The Road. Dubbed voice only English-language version). 1957: Street of Sinners. 1966: Johnny Tiger. 1973: The Aspern Affair. 1975: Mr Ricco.

BROOKS, Leslie
(Lorraine Gettman) 1922–
Not to be confused with Britain's contem-poraneous Lesley Brook (*qv*), this smart,

attractive, well-groomed, always poised American actress with piled-up blonde hair, was one of the best 'second leads' in the business for all too few years (with some B-feature leading roles thrown in) before retiring on her second marriage.

1941: You're in the Army Now. Ziegfeld Girl. Navy Blues. The Man Who Came to Dinner. 1942: The Talk of the Town. You Were Never Lovelier. Lucky Legs. Underground Agent. Yankee Doodle Dandy. Overland to Deadwood (GB: Falling Stones). 1943: Two Senoritas from Chicago (GB: Two Senoritas). City Without Men. What's Buzzin' Cousin? 1944: Nine Girls. Cover Girl. Tonight and Every Night. 1945: I Love a Bandleader (GB: Memory for Two). It's Great to Be Young. 1946: Secret of the Whistler. The Man Who Dared. 1947: Cigarette Girl. The Corpse Came C.O.D. 1948: Hollow Triumph (GB: The Scar). Romance on the High Seas (GB: It's Magic). Blonde Ice. The Cobra Strikes.

BROOKS, Louise 1906–1985
Black-haired, dark-eyed American leading lady, a former Ziegfeld Follies girl, hailed by some critics as the greatest actress of her generation, derided by others as an over-rated star who could not properly survive sound. Her mask-like face, bobbed hair and luminous personality certainly lend a haunting quality to the two fine films she made in Germany. But she was snubbed on her return to Hollywood, and ended playing western heroines before ignominious retirement. Happily, she became something of a cult figure in later years, always good for a quote on acquaintances from her Hollywood heyday, and wrote a well-received book of memoirs, *Lulu in Hollywood*. At one time (1926–8) married to director A. Edward Sutherland, she died from a heart attack.

*1925: The Street of Forgotten Men. 1926: The American Venus. A Social Celebrity. The Showoff. Love 'Em and Leave 'Em. Just Another Blonde. It's the Old Army Game. 1927: Evening Clothes. Now We're in the Air. The City Gone Wild. Rolled Stockings. 1928: A Girl in Every Port. Beggars of Life. 1929: Die Büchse der Pandora (GB and US: Pandora's Box). The Canary Murder Case. Das Tagebuch einer Verlorenen (GB and US: Diary of a Lost Girl). 1930: Prix de beauté (GB: Miss Europe). 1931: It Pays to Advertise. God's Gift to Women (GB: Too Many Women). The Public Enemy (GB: Enemies of the Public). Other Men's Women / Steel Highway. *Windy*

Riley Goes to Hollywood (GB: The Gas-Bag). 1936: Empty Saddles. 1937: When You're in Love. (GB: For You Alone). †King of Gamblers. 1938: Overland Stage Raiders.

†*Scenes deleted from final release print*

BROOKS, Mel (Melvin Kaminsky) 1926–
Extrovert, enormously self-confident Jewish-American director-comedian who started as a stand-up comic, then switched to comedy writing (first film as writer: *New Faces*, 1954). In the 1970s the immense commercial success of some of his films enabled him to combine both talents in a hit-and-miss series of zany comedies that take satirical sideswipes at everything and range from crude to wittily hilarious. In the 1980s he became increasingly involved with his own film production company. Married to Anne Bancroft (*qv*) since 1964: He won an Academy Award for his screenplay of *The Producers*.

*1963: *The Critic (narrator only). 1967: Putney Swope. 1970: The Twelve Chairs. 1974: Blazing Saddles. 1976: Silent Movie. 1977: High Anxiety. 1978: The Muppet Movie. 1981: History of the World Part I. 1983: To Be or Not To Be. 1987: Spaceballs. 1990: Look Who's Talking Too (voice only). 1991: Life Stinks. 1993: Robin Hood: Men in Tights. 1994: The Silence of the Hams (released 1996). The Little Rascals. 1995: Dracula: Dead and Loving It. 1997: The Prince of Egypt (voice only).*
As director: *1967: The Producers. 1970: The Twelve Chairs. 1974: Blazing Saddles. Young Frankenstein. 1976: Silent Movie. 1977: High Anxiety. 1981: History of the World Part I. 1987: Spaceballs. 1991: Life Stinks. 1993: Robin Hood: Men in Tights. 1995: Dracula: Dead and Loving It.*

BROSNAN, Pierce 1951–
Huskily good-looking, dark-haired, Irish-born actor in international films and TV. Really too handsome for the 1980s (Universal-International would have welcomed him with open arms in the 1950s), Brosnan, who came to England at 11, struggled to make his mark despite extensive London stage experience. But he was successful in elegantly mounted TV series, especially *Remington Steele*, commitment to which prevented him becoming the new James Bond in 1987. In the 1990s, he was drifting into roles as 'the other man' when the chance came up again to play Bond, although he was now slightly too old for

the role, if physically ideal. He married actress Cassandra Harris, but she died from cancer in 1991.

1979: The Long Good Friday. 1980: The Mirror Crack'd. 1985: Nomads. 1987: The Fourth Protocol. 1988: Taffin. The Deceivers. 1989: The Heist (TV). 1990: Mister Johnson. 1991: Murder 101 (TV). Victim of Love (TV). 1992: The Lawnmower Man. Live Wire. Entangled. 1993: Death Train/Alastair MacLean's Death Train (cable TV). Mrs Doubtfire. The Broken Chain (TV). 1994: Love Affair. Don't Talk to Strangers (TV). 1995: Robinson Crusoe. GoldenEye. Alistair MacLean's Night Watch (TV). 1996: The Mirror Has Two Faces. Mars Attacks! Dante's Peak. 1997: The Nephew. The Disappearance of Kevin Johnson (completed 1995). Tomorrow Never Dies. 1998: The Magic Sword: Quest for Camelot (voice only). Grey Owl. 1999: The Thomas Crown Affair. The World is Not Enough. 2000: The Tailor of Panama.

BROWN, Bryan 1947–
Dark-haired, eagle-featured, gimlet-eyed Australian actor, often in aggressive roles. Something like Jason Robards Jr (*qv*) in the way that he can be riveting in some roles and ineffective in others, Brown began his acting career with Britain's National Theatre in 1974. Performances in *Newsfront* and *'Breaker' Morant* brought him to international attention, and he also advanced his standing in the TV series *A Town Like Alice*. British ventures were less successful and he now commutes between Australia and California, where he married the British-born actress Rachel Ward (*qv*) in 1983.

*1975: *The Christmas Tree. 1977: The Love Letters from Teralba Road. 1978: The Irishman. Newsfront. Money Movers. Weekend of Shadows. The Chant of Jimmie Blacksmith. 1979: Cathy's Child. The Odd Angry Shot. Third Person Plural. 'Breaker' Morant. 1980:*

*Palm Beach. *Con Man Harry and the Others. Stir. 1981: The Winter of Our Dreams. 1982: Far East. 1984: Give My Regards to Broad Street. Kim (TV). Bones (later Parker). 1985: Rebel. The Shiralee. F/X (GB: FX: Murder by Illusion). The Empty Beach. 1986: Tai-Pan. The Umbrella Woman (GB and US: The Good Wife). 1988: Cocktail. Gorillas in the Mist. 1989: Sweet Talker (released 1991). 1990: Blood Oath (US: Prisoners of the Sun). 1991: F/X 2: The Deadly Art of Illusion. Blame It on the Bellboy. Dead in the Water (TV). 1992: Day of the Dog. Devlin (TV). 1993: The Last Hit (TV). Age of Treason (TV). 1995: Full Body Massage (cable TV). 1996: Dead Heart. 1997: Dogboys (TV). 1998: On the Border. Dear Claudia. 1999: Journey to the Center of the Earth (TV). Two Hands. Grizzly Falls. 2000: Risk. On the Beach (TV).*

BROWN, Jim 1935–

Squat-faced American former football hero who turned to acting in his thirties, and became popular for a short while as the unlikely black hero of a dozen tough and violent action melodramas. Returned to play featured roles in action movies in the late 1980s.

1964: Rio Conchos. 1967: The Dirty Dozen. 1968: Dark of the Sun (GB: The Mercenaries). The Split. Ice Station Zebra. Riot. 1969: 100 Rifles . . . tick . . . tick . . . tick. 1970: The Grasshopper. Kenner. El Condor. 1972: Black Gunn. Slaughter. 1973: I Escaped from Devil's Island. Slaughter's Big Rip Off. The Slams. 1974: Three the Hard Way. 1975: Take a Hard Ride. 1977: Fingers. Kid Vengeance. Pacific Inferno. 1982: One Down, Two to Go. 1985: Lady Blue (TV). 1987: Slam Dunk. The Running Man. 1988: L.A. Heat. I'm Gonna Git You, Sucka! 1989: Crack House. Twisted Justice. 1991: Divine Enforcer. 1993: Posse. 1995: Hot City (later Original Gangstas). 1996: Mars Attacks! 1998: Small Soldiers (voice only). He Got Game. 1999: Any Given Sunday.

BROWN, Joe E. 1892–1973

Ever-smiling, slick-haired American comedian said to have had the widest mouth in show business. He had long experience in vaudeville dating back to the age of nine, when he began as a boy acrobat. In films, he usually played the innocent abroad and remained very popular from the beginning of sound to the early forties. In his case more than most, his face was his fortune. The 'E'

stood for Evans. Died following a stroke.

*1928: Crooks Can't Win. Road House. Dressed to Kill. The Circus Kid. Hit of the Show. Burlesque. *Don't Be Jealous. Take Me Home. 1929: On With the Show. Painted Faces. *The Dancing Instructor. Sunny Side Up. Molly and Me. My Lady's Past. Sally. The Cock-Eyed World. The Ghost Talks. Protection. 1930: Song of the West. Hold Everything. Top Speed. Lottery Bride. Maybe It's Love. *Screen Snapshots No.5. 1931: Going Wild. Sit Tight. *Screen Snapshots No. 8. Broad Minded. *Practice Shots. Local Boy Makes Good. 1932: Fireman Save My Child. You Said a Mouthful. The Tenderfoot. *The Putter. *The Stolen Jools (GB: The Slippery Pearls). 1933: Elmer the Great. Son of a Sailor. *The Grip. *Hollywood on Parade No. 8. 1934: The Circus Clown. Six-Day Bike Rider. A Very Honorable Guy (GB: A Very Honourable Man). *Hollywood on Parade B.6. 1935: *A Dream Comes True. Alibi Ike. Bright Lights (GB: Funny Face). A Midsummer Night's Dream. 1936: Sons o' Guns. Earthworm Tractors (GB: A Natural Born Salesman). Polo Joe. 1937: When's Your Birthday? Riding on Air (GB: All is Confusion). Fit for a King. 1938: Wide Open Faces. The Gladiator. Flirting with Fate. 1939: A Thousand Dollars a Touchdown. Beware Spooks! 1940: *Rodeo Dough. So You Won't Talk. 1941: *Stars at Play. 1942: Shut My Big Mouth. Joan of Ozark (GB: Queen of Spies). The Daring Young Man. 1943: Chatterbox. 1944: Pin-Up Girl. Hollywood Canteen. Casanova in Burlesque. 1947: The Tender Years. 1951: Show Boat. 1952: *Memories of Famous Hollywood Comedians (narrator only). 1954: *Hollywood Fathers. 1956: Around the World in 80 Days. 1959: Some Like It Hot. 1963: It's a Mad, Mad, Mad, Mad World. The Comedy of Terrors.*

BROWN, Johnny Mack 1904–1974

Husky, square-jawed, dark-haired former All-American football player who came to the screen in the late 1920s and co-starred twice with Greta Garbo (qv). He was also a notable Billy the Kid in 1930. From 1936 to 1952, he starred in almost nothing but 'B' feature westerns, retaining his popularity in the genre throughout that period. Later ran a restaurant. Died from a cardiac condition.

1927: The Bugle Call. Slide, Kelly, Slide. Mockery After Midnight. The Fair Co-Ed (GB: The Varsity Girl). 1928: Our Dancing Daughters. Soft Living. Square Crooks. Play Girl. Annapolis (GB: Branded a Coward). Lady of Chance. The Divine Woman. A

*Woman of Affairs. 1929: Coquette. The Single Standard. The Valiant. Hurricane. Jazz Heaven. 1930: *Voice of Hollywood No.7. Montana Moon. Undertow. Billy the Kid. 1931: *Hollywood Half Backs. The Secret Six. The Great Meadow. Lasca of the Rio Grande. The Last Flight. Laughing Sinners. 1932: Flames. The Vanishing Frontier. 70,000 Witnesses. Malay Nights. 1933: Fighting with Kit Carson (serial). Saturday's Millions. Female. Son of a Sailor. Hollywood on Parade. 1934: Belle of the Nineties. Cross Streets. Marrying Widows. Three on a Honeymoon. 1935: Branded a Coward. St Louis Woman. Between Men. *Star Night at the Cocoanut Grove. The Courageous Avenger. The Rustlers of Red Dog (serial). *Starlight Days at the Lido. The Right to Live. 1936: The Desert Phantom. Rogue of the Range. Riding the Apache Trail. Every Man's Law. Valley of the Lawless. Crooked Trail (GB: Lead Law). Undercover Man. Lawless Land. 1937: *Vitaphone Pictorial Revue No.3. Gambling Terror. Trail Of Vengeance. Bar Z Bad Men. Guns in the Dark. Boot Hill Brigade. A Lawman is Born. Wells Fargo. Wild West Days (serial). 1938: *Screen Snapshots No.4. Flaming Frontiers (serial). Born to the West. Land Of Liberty. 1939: The Oregon Trail (serial). Desperate Trails. Oklahoma Frontier. Chip of the Flying U. 1940: West of Carson City. Riders of Pasco Basin. Bad Man from Red Butte. Son of Roaring Dan. Ragtime Cowboy Joe. Boss of Bullion City. Pony Post. Law and Order (GB: Lucky Ralston). 1941: The Masked Rider. Bury Me Not on the Lone Prairie. Rawhide Rangers. The Man from Montana (GB: Montana Justice). Law of the Range. Arizona Cyclone. Ride 'Em Cowboy. 1942: Fighting Bill Fargo. Deep in the Heart of Texas. The Boss of Hangtown Mesa. Stagecoach Buckaroo. Little Joe the Wrangler. The Silver Bullet. 1943: The Old Chisholm Trail. The Ghost Rider. Raiders of San Joaquin. Six-Gun Gospel. The Texas Kid. Outlaws of Stampede Pass. Tenting Tonight on the Old Camp Ground. Cheyenne Round-Up. The Stranger from Pecos. Lone Star Trail. 1944: Land of the Outlaws. Range Law. West of the Rio Grande. Ghost Guns. Partners of the Trail. They Shall Have Faith (GB: The Right to Live). 1945: Navajo Trail. Gunsmoke. Stranger from Santa Fé. Frontier Feud. Law of the Valley. Raiders of the Border. Law Men. Lost Trail. Flame of the West. 1946: Drifting Along. Under Arizona Skies. The Haunted Mine. Shadows on the Range. Raiders of the South. Gentleman from Texas. Trigger Fingers.*

Silver Range. Border Bandits. 1947: Land of the Lawless. Valley of Fear. Trailing Danger. Flashing Guns. Prairie Express. Code of the Saddle. The Law Comes to Gunsight (GB: Backfire). Gun Talk. 1948: Triggerman. Frontier Agent. Overland Trail. Crossed Trails. The Fighting Ranger. The Sheriff of Medicine Bow. Backtrail. Hidden Danger. Gunning for Justice. 1949: Stampede. Law of the West. West of El Dorado. Trail's End. Range Justice. Western Renegades. 1950: Short Grass. Six Gun Mesa. Law of the Panhandle. Outlaw Gold. Over the Border. West of Wyoming. 1951: Oklahoma Outlaws. Man from Sonora. Colorado Ambush. Montana Desperado. Oklahoma Justice. Texas Lawmen. Blazing Bullets. 1952: Whistling Hills. Dead Man's Trail. Texas City. Canyon Ambush. Man from the Black Hills. 1953: The Marshal's Daughter. 1954: *Hollywood Fathers. 1965: Requiem for a Gunfighter. The Bounty Killer. 1966: Apache Uprising.

BROWN, Tom 1913–1990

Boyish, light-haired, open-faced American actor with eager manner. Upright and solid, Brown looked so good in military uniform that producers couldn't stop putting him in it. He must have played more officer cadets in films than any other actor. Brown, the son of a vaudevillian, had begun in child roles in silent films, but graduated to a series of pleasant all-American boys in the 1930s and early 1940s. A real military uniform put a stopper on his career: he served as a paratrooper in World

War Two and as a lieutenant-colonel in the Korean War. With his undynamic acting style, it was not surprising that he subsequently failed to establish himself as a character player, and his later acting days were spent playing small running roles in television series. Three times married. Died from cancer.
1924: The Hoosier Schoolmaster. 1925: The Wrongdoers. That Old Gang of Mine. Children of the Whirlwind. 1929: The Lady Lies. 1930: Queen High. 1932: Hell's Highway. Tom Brown of Culver. Information Kid / Fast Companions. The Famous Ferguson Case. 1933: Laughter in Hell. Three-Cornered Moon. Central Airport. Destination Unknown. Crossfire. 1934: Anne of Green Gables. Judge Priest. The Witching Hour. This Side of Heaven. Hat, Coat and Glove. Two Alone. 1935: Annapolis Farewell (GB: Gentlemen of the Navy). Mary Jane's Pa (GB: Wanderlust). Bachelor of Arts. Freckles. Black Sheep. Sweepstake Annie (GB: Annie Doesn't

Live Here). 1936: Gentle Julia. And Sudden Death. I'd Give My Life. Rose Bowl (GB: O'Riley's Luck). 1937: Jim Hanvey, Detective. Her Husband Lies. Navy Blue and Gold. The Man Who Cried Wolf. Maytime. That Man's Here Again. 1938: In Old Chicago. The Duke of West Point. Goodbye Broadway. Merrily We Live. Swing That Cheer. The Storm. 1939: Sergeant Madden. Big Town Czar. Ex-Champ (GB: Golden Gloves). These Glamour Girls. 1940: Margie. Sandy is a Lady. Ma, He's Making Eyes at Me. Oh Johnny, How You Can Love. 1941: Niagara Falls. Three Sons o' Guns. Hello Sucker. 1942: Youth on Parade. Hello Annapolis (GB: Personal Honour). Let's Get Tough. Sleepytime Gal. There's One Born Every Minute. 1943: The Payoff. Adventures of Smiling Jack (Serial). 1944: Once Upon a Time. 1945: The House on 92nd Street. 1947: Buck Privates Come Home (GB: Rookies Come Home). 1948: Slippy McGee. 1949: The Duke of Chicago. Ringside. 1950: Operation Haylift. 1954: Fireman Save My Child. 1956: I Killed Wild Bill Hickok. The Naked Gun. 1957: The Quiet Gun. 1958: The Notorious Mr Monks. 1961: The Choppers. 1970: Cutter's Trail (TV).

BRUCE, Brenda 1918–1996

Blonde British actress with distinctive, Scandinavian-type features, often seen with urchin haircut. Originally a dancer, she had her first big success in intimate revue before trying straight acting, demonstrating an unusual gamine appeal. Critics liked her looks and acting ability, but she was perhaps too cool for the public taste and did not become a major star. She played character roles on stage, in films and on TV into her

seventies.
1943: Millions Like Us. 1944: They Came to a City. 1945: I Live in Grosvenor Square (US: A Yank in London). Night Boat to Dublin. 1946: I See a Dark Stranger (US: The Adventuress). Piccadilly Incident. Carnival. While the Sun Shines. 1947: When the Bough Breaks. 1948: My Brother's Keeper. 1949: Marry Me. Don't Ever Leave Me. 1951: Two on the Tiles. 1953: The Final Test. 1958: Law and Disorder. Behind the Mask. 1959: Peeping Tom. 1963: Nightmare. 1964: The Uncle. 1969: The Virgin Soldiers. 1973: That'll Be the Day. 1974: Swallows and Amazons. All Creatures Great and Small. 1976: The Man in the Iron Mask (TV). 1981: Käthe Kollwitz. 1985: Steaming. Time After Time (TV). 1988: The Tenth Man (TV). Little Dorrit I. 1990: Circles of Deceit (TV).

December Bride. Back Home (TV). 1991: Antonia and Jane. 1993: Splitting Heirs.

BRUCE, Virginia

(Helen V. Briggs) 1910–1982
Ultra-blonde American actress, in quiet roles through the 1930s and early 1940s. The private life of this former Ziegfeld girl was less quiet; she married John Gilbert (1932–1934) in the years of his decline. Gilbert died two years after they parted, and her second husband, director J. Walter Ruben, died in 1942. Her third husband, Turkish director Ali Ipar, fell foul of his country's regime and was jailed for 18 months in 1960. They were later divorced.
1929: Fugitives. Blue Skies. Woman Trap. Illusion. The Love Parade. Why Bring That Up? 1930: Safety in Numbers. Only the Brave. Slightly Scarlet. Paramount on Parade. Follow Thru. Whoopee! Raffles. Young Eagles. Lilies of the Field. Social Lion. 1931: Hell Divers. Are You Listening? The Wet Parade. 1932: The Miracle Man. Sky Bride. Downstairs. Kongo. Winner Take All. A Scarlet Week-End. 1934: Jane Eyre. The Mighty Barnum. Dangerous Corner. 1935: Times Square Lady. Society Doctor. Shadow of Doubt. Let 'Em Have It (GB: False Faces). Here Comes the Band. Escapade. Metropolitan. The Murder Man. 1936: The Garden Murder Case. The Great Ziegfeld. *Pirate Party on Catalina Isle. Born to Dance. 1937: Women of Glamour. When Love is Young. Between Two Women. Wife, Doctor and Nurse. 1938: The First Hundred Years. Arsène Lupin Returns. Bad Man of Brimstone. Yellow Jack. Woman Against Woman. There Goes My Heart. There's That Woman Again (GB: What a Woman). 1939: Let Freedom Ring! Society Lawyer. Stranger Than Desire. 1940: Flight Angels. The Man Who Talked Too Much. Hired Wife. 1941: The Invisible Woman. Adventure in Washington (GB: Female Correspondent). 1942: Pardon My Sarong. Butch Minds the Baby. Careful, Soft Shoulders. 1944: Brazil. Action in Arabia. 1945: Love, Honor and Goodbye. 1948: The Night Has a Thousand Eyes. 1949: State Dept – File 649 (GB: Assignment in China). 1953: Istanbul. 1955: The Reluctant Bride (US: Two Grooms for a Bride). 1960: Strangers When We Meet.

BRYNNER, Yul

(Youl Bryner) 1915–1985
Shaven-headed actor of Swiss-Mongolian parentage (born on an island off the coast of Siberia). A former trapeze artist who turned

to acting after being injured in a fall, his subsequent career was inextricably tied up with his portrayals of the King of Siam in *The King and I*, and the mysterious gunfighter in black in *The Magnificent Seven*. His faint accent and clipped tones remained unique, but a further stage stint with *The King and I* in the late seventies signalled his departure from the screen. Married to Virginia Gilmore (*qv*) 1944–1960. Oscar for *The King and I*. Died from lung cancer.

*1949: Port of New York. 1956: The King and I. The 10 Commandments. Anastasia. 1958: The Brothers Karamazov. The Buccaneer. The Journey. 1959: Le testament d'Orphée. Solomon and Sheba. The Sound and the Fury. 1960: Once More with Feeling. *Profile of a Miracle (narrator only). Surprise Package. The Magnificent Seven. 1961: Aimez-vous Brahms? (GB: Goodbye Again). Escape from Zahrain. 1962: Taras Bulba. 1963: Kings of the Sun. 1964: Flight from Ashiya. Invitation to a Gunfighter. 1965: Morituri (GB: The Saboteur Code name Morituri). Is Paris Burning? 1966: Cast a Giant Shadow. Return of the Seven. The Poppy is Also a Flower (GB: Danger Grows Wild). Triple Cross. 1967: The Long Duel. The Double Man. 1968: Villa Rides! 1969: The Picasso Summer. The Battle of Neretva. The File of the Golden Goose. The Magic Christian. The Madwoman of Chaillot. 1970: Indio Black (GB: The Bounty Hunters. US: Adios Sabata). 1971: Romance of a Horsethief. Catlow. The Light at the Edge of the World. 1972: Fuzz. 1973: The Serpent (US: Night Flight from Moscow). Westworld. 1975: The Ultimate Warrior. 1976: Con la rabbia agli occhi (GB: Anger in His Eyes. US: Death Rage). Futureworld.*
As narrator: *1959: *Mission to No Man's Land. 1961: *My Friend Nicholas. 1962: Man is to Man.*

BUCHANAN, Jack
(Walter John Buchanan) 1890–1957
Tall, smooth, stately, sophisticated, Scottish-born musical entertainer with thin lips, dark, curly hair, an impish expression and a dry Martini voice – a British Fred Astaire but with the accent on comedy, indelibly a product of the London stage in the 1920s. A successful screen star as well throughout the 1930s, Buchanan was continually and painfully ill with spinal arthritis in his later years, but made a few very welcome screen reappearances in the 1950s.
1917: Auld Lang Syne. 1919: Her Heritage. 1923: The Audacious Mr Squire. 1924: The

Happy Ending. *1925: Settled Out of Court. *A Typical Budget. Bulldog Drummond's Third Round. *Stage Stars Off Stage. 1927: Confetti. 1928: Toni. 1929: Paris. Show of Shows. 1930: Monte Carlo. *The Glee Quartette. 1931: Man of Mayfair. 1932: Goodnight Vienna (US: Magic Night). ‡Yes Mr Brown. †That's a Good Girl. 1934: Brewster's Millions. Come Out of the Pantry. Limelight (US: Backstage). 1936: When Knights Were Bold. This'll Make You Whistle. 1937: Smash and Grab. The Sky's the Limit. 1938: Break the News. *Cavalcade of the Stars. 1939: The Gang's All Here (US: The Amazing Mr Forrest). The Middle Watch. 1940: Bulldog Sees It Through. 1944: *Some Like It Rough (narrator only). 1951: *A Boy and a Bike. 1952: *Giselle (narrator only). 1953: The Band Wagon. 1955: As Long As They're Happy. Josephine and Men. 1956: The Diary of Major Thompson (US: The French They Are a Funny Race).*

†Also directed ‡Also co-directed

BUCHHOLZ, Horst 1932–
Black-haired, boyishly handsome German leading man who became an international star in the early sixties, but failed to mature well and rang the bell at box-offices for only a few years. Gave all his most charismatic performances in his twenties. Married French film actress Myriam Bru.
1952: Die Spur führt nach Berlin (as extra). 1954: Marianne. Emil and the Detectives. 1955: Himmel ohne Sterne (US: Sky without Stars). 1956: Regine. Die Halbstarken (GB: Wolfpack. US: Teenage Wolfpack). Herrscher ohne Krone (GB: The King in Shadow). 1957: Die Bekenntnisse des Hochstaplers Felix Krull (GB: The Confessions of Felix Krull).

Robinson soll nicht sterben (US: The Legend of Robinson Crusoe). Mompti. Endstation Liebe. 1958: Nasser Asphalt. Resurrection. Das Totenschiff. 1959: Tiger Bay. 1960: The Magnificent Seven. 1961: Fanny. One, Two, Three. 1962: Nine Hours to Rama. 1963: La noia (GB and US: The Empty Canvas). Andorra. 1964: The Fabulous Adventures of Marco Polo (GB: Marco the Magnificent). That Man in Istanbul. 1966: Cervantes, the Young Rebel. Johnny Banco. 1968: L'astragale. Come, quando, perché (GB: How, When and with Whom). 1970: Le sauveur. La columba non deve volare. 1972: The Great Waltz. 1973: Aber Jonny! 1974: Lohngelder für Pitteville. 1975: The Catamount Killing. 1976: Raid on Entebbe (TV. GB: cinemas). The Savage Bees. Frauenstation (US: Women in Hospital). 1977: Dead of Night (TV). 1978: The Amazing Captain Nemo. 1979: Avalanche Express. Da Dunkerque alla vittoria (US: From Hell to Victory). 1981: Aphrodite. 1983: Sahara. Berlin Tunnel 21 (TV). 1984: Wenn Ich Mich fürchte (US: Fear of Falling). 1985: Code Name: Emerald. 1987: And the Violins Stopped Playing. 1990: Fuga dal Paradiso. 1991: Aces: Iron Eagle III. 1993: In weiter Ferne, so nah / Faraway, So Close! 1997: La vita e bella (GB and US: Life is Beautiful). Ptak ohnivak. 1998: Voyage of Terror (TV). 2000: Heller als der Mond. Der Feuervogel.

BUJOLD, Geneviève 1942–
Dark-haired, baby-faced Canadian actress with attractive, very slight French-Canadian accent. After a start in French films, she came on to the international scene when chosen to star as Anne Boleyn in *Anne of the Thousand Days*, a film that won her an Oscar nomination. Since then she has chosen roles that make stern demands of her in all kinds of ways – acting and physical. At her best at the centre of things; least effective when paired with male superstars. Married to director Paul Almond from 1967 to 1973.
*1954: French Can-Can. 1963: Amanita Pestilens. 1964: La terre à boire. La fleur de l'âge ou: les adolescentes. 1965: *Rouli – Roulant (voice only). 1966: La guerre est finie. Le roi de coeur (GB and US: King of Hearts). Le voleur. 1967: The 25th Hour. Isabel. Entre la mer et l'eau douce. 1969: Anne of the Thousand Days. 1970: Act of the Heart. *Marie-Christine. 1971: The Trojan Women. 1972: Epoh / Journey. 1973: Kamouraska. 1974: Earthquake. 1975: Obsession. L'incorrigible. 1976: Swashbuckler (GB: The Scarlet Buccaneer). Alex and the Gypsy. 1977:*

Un autre homme, une autre chance (GB: Another Man, Another Woman. US: Another Man, Another Chance). Coma. 1978: Sherlock Holmes: Murder by Decree (GB: Murder by Decree). 1979: The Last Flight of Noah's Ark. 1980: Final Assignment. 1981: Mistress of Paradise (TV). 1982: Monsignor. 1984: Tightrope. Choose Me. 1985: Trouble in Mind. 1987: The Moderns. 1988: Thank You, Satan. Dead Ringers. Red Earth, White Earth (TV. GB: Snake Treaty). 1989: Secret Places of the Heart. Les noces de papier/Paper Wedding. 1990: False Identity. 1991: Comfort Creek. Rue de Bac. 1992: The Bottom Drawer. 1993: Oh, What a Night. An Ambush of Ghosts. Mon amie Max. 1996: The Adventures of Pinocchio. The House of Yes. 1997: Dead Innocent. 1998: You Can Thank Me Later. Last Night. 1999: Eye of the Beholder. 2001: Sex and a Girl.

BULLOCK, Sandra 1964–
Dark-haired, wide-mouthed (but narrow-featured), friendly-looking, slightly-built American actress with 'Everygirl' qualities. The daughter of German opera singer Helga Bullock, she was raised equally in Austria, Germany and America. Following dramatic training, she got a low-key starring film debut in 1988, followed by the lead role in the shortlived TV series *Working Girl*. She began to build a reputation as heroines who were both independent and in need of protection and burst to prominence in the mid 1990s after great personal successes in *Speed* and *While You Were Sleeping*. Less popular in recent times thanks to poor script choices.
1987: Hangmen. 1988: A Fool and His Money. 1989: The Preppie Murder (TV). The Bionic Showdown: Six Million Dollar Man and the Bionic Woman (TV). Lucky Chances (film version of TV mini-series). Religion Inc. 1990: Who Shot Patakango?/Who Shot Pat? †Memphis Belle. 1991: Fire on the Amazon. 1992: Love Potion No. 9. When the Party's Over. Who Do I Gotta Kill? 1993: Demolition Man. The Vanishing. The Thing Called Love. Wrestling Ernest Hemingway. 1994: Me and the Mob. Speed. 1995: While You Were Sleeping. The Net. Two If by Sea (GB: Stolen Hearts). 1996: A Time to Kill. In Love and War. 1997: Speed 2 Cruise Control. 1998: The Prince of Egypt (voice only). Hope Floats. Practical Magic. 1999: Forces of Nature. Gun Shy. 2000: 28 Days. Miss Congeniality. As Director. 1996: Making Sandwiches.

†*Scenes deleted from final release print.*

BURKE, Kathy 1962–
Abrasive, aggressive, round-faced, rough-toned British actress who won her first success in comic roles on TV, but achieved her cinematic breakthrough in a highly dramatic one, as the much-beaten and abused wife of *Nil by Mouth*, a performance that won her a hatful of awards. She established her versatility as a dying Mary Tudor in *Elizabeth*, and has since brought her generous personality to a variety of roles. She also sings. Her year of birth has proved more closely guarded than the Crown Jewels, so the one above is an educated guess.
*1983: Scrubbers. Forever Young. 1986: Sid and Nancy. 1987: Walker. Eat the Rich. 1989: *Work Experience. 1995: *After Miss Julie. 1997: Nil by Mouth. 1998: Dancing at Lughnasa. Elizabeth. This Year's Love. 1999: Love, Honour & Obey. 2000: Kevin & Perry Go Large. 2001: Tosspot.*

BURNS, Bob 'Bazooka' 1890–1956
Countrified, dark-haired, round-faced American comedian and entertainer, who followed vaudeville and radio success with some cheerful western comedy-musicals of the 1930s and 1940s. Much in the Will Rogers (qv) mould, he was known as The Arkansas Philosopher, and often played guileless rurals whose sheer goodness kept them afloat. Gained his nickname from a musical instrument he played and claimed to have invented.
*1931: Quick Millions. 1935: The Phantom Empire (Serial. GB: Radio Ranch). The Singing Vagabond. *Restless Knights. 1936: The Courageous Avenger. Rhythm on the Range. Guns and Guitars. The Big Broadcast of 1937. 1937: Waikiki Wedding. Wells Fargo. Git Along, Little Dogies (GB: Serenade of the West). Public Cowboy No. 1. Yodelin' Kid*

*from Pine Ridge (GB: The Hero of Pine Ridge). Hit the Saddle. 1938: Mountain Music. Tropic Holiday. Radio City Revels. The Arkansas Traveler. 1939: Our Leading Citizen. I'm from Missouri. Rovin' Tumbleweed. 1940: Alias the Deacon. Prairie Schooners (GB: Through the Storm). Comin' Round the Mountain. 1942: The Hillbilly Deacon. Call of the Canyon. *Soaring Stars. 1944: Belle of the Yukon. Mystery Man.*

BURNS, George
(Nathan Birnbaum) 1896–1996
Cigar-puffing, dark-haired American comedian with wryly poker face and caustic wit, usually the victim of wife and long-time partner Gracie Allen's (they married in 1926 and she died in 1964) harebrained ideas. As a pair, they were more successful in radio and films in the 1930s and television in the 1950s. Burns started a whole new career when he returned to films as a veteran vaudevillian in *The Sunshine Boys* at 79, and won an Academy Award, soon becoming something of a national institution. Even a force to be reckoned with in comedy in his eighties, he died soon after passing his 100th birthday.
*1929: *Lamb Chops. 1930: *Fit to be Tied. *Pulling a Bone. 1931: *The Antique Shop. *Once Over, Light. *One Hundred Percent Service. 1932: The Big Broadcast. *Oh My Operation. *Hollywood on Parade A-2. *The Babbling Book. 1933: International House. College Humor. *Patents Pending. *Let's Dance. *Walking the Baby. 1934: We're Not Dressing. Six of a Kind. Many Happy Returns. 1935: Love in Bloom. Here Comes Cookie (GB: The Plot Thickens). The Big Broadcast of 1936. 1936: College Holiday. The Big Broadcast of 1937. A Damsel in Distress. 1938: College Swing (GB: Swing, Teacher, Swing). 1939: Honolulu. 1941: *Variety Reel. 1954: *Screen Snapshots No. 224. 1956: The Solid Gold Cadillac (narrator only). 1975: The Sunshine Boys. 1977: Oh, God! 1978: Sergeant Pepper's Lonely Hearts Club Band. The Comedy Company (TV). Movie Movie. 1979: Just You and Me, Kid. Going in Style. 1980: Oh, God! Book II. 1983: Two of a Kind (TV). 1984: Oh, God! You Devil. 1988: 18 Again! 1989: George Burns: His Wit and Wisdom (V). 1994: Radioland Murders.*
(V) Video

BURR, Raymond 1917–1993
Tall, dark, heavy, menacing Canadian-born actor with uncompromising mouth who

played Hollywood villains for a decade (including a memorable white-haired maniac in *Rear Window*) before deserting films (and villainy) for such long-running TV series as *Perry Mason* and *A Man Called Ironside*. He returned to Mason with great success in his sixties. Was not lucky in love: twice widowed, once divorced. Died from cancer of the liver: posthumous revelations of his bisexuality hit many headlines.

1940: *Earl of Puddlestone* (GB: *Jolly Old Higgins*). 1946: *San Quentin. Without Reservations.* 1947: *Code of the West. Desperate. Sleep My Love.* 1948: *Pitfall. Ruthless. Raw Deal. Fighting Father Dunne. I Love Trouble. Walk a Crooked Mile. Station West.* 1949: *Adventures of Don Juan* (GB: *The New Adventures of Don Juan*). *Abandoned. Black Magic. Criss Cross. Bride of Vengeance. Red Light. Love Happy* (later *Kleptomaniacs*). 1950: *Unmasked. Borderline. Key to the City.* 1951: *FBI Girl. M. The Magic Carpet. New Mexico. Bride of the Gorilla. His Kind of Woman. A Place in the Sun. The Whip Hand. Meet Danny Wilson.* 1952: *Mara Maru. Horizons West.* 1953: *Tarzan and the She-Devil. Serpent of the Nile. The Blue Gardenia. Fort Algiers. Bandits of Corsica* (GB: *Return of the Corsican Brothers*). *Casanova's Big Night.* 1954: *Khyber Patrol. Gorilla at Large. Rear Window. Passion. Thunder Pass.* 1955: *Double Danger* (TV. GB: cinemas). *They Were So Young. A Man Alone. Count Three and Pray. You're Never Too Young. Godzilla* (US: *Godzilla, King of the Monsters*). 1956: *Great Day in the Morning. A Cry in the Night. The Brass Legend. Secret of Treasure Mountain. Ride the High Iron. Please Murder Me. The Greer Case* (TV). 1957: *Crime of Passion. Affair in Havana. Lone Woman* (TV). 1960: *Desire in the Dust.* 1968: *P.J.* (GB: *New Face in Hell*). 1971: *The Priest Killer* (TV). 1975: *Mallory* (TV). 1976: *The Newspaper Game* (TV). *The Amazing World of Psychic Phenomena* (narrator only). 1977: *Kingston* (TV). *Tomorrow Never Comes.* 1978: *The Jordan Chance* (TV). 1979: *Centennial* (TV). *Love's Savage Fury* (TV). *Disaster on the Coastliner* (TV). 1980: *Out of the Blue. The Night the City Screamed* (TV). 1981: *The Return.* 1982: *Airplane II The Sequel.* 1985: *Godzilla 1985. Perry Mason Returns* (TV). 1986: *Perry Mason: The Case of the Notorious Nun* (TV). *Perry Mason: The Case of the Shooting Star* (TV). 1987: *Perry Mason: The Case of the Lost Love* (TV). *Perry Mason: The Case of the Scandalous Scoundrel* (TV). *Perry*

Mason: The Case of the Sinister Spirit (TV). 1988: *Perry Mason: The Case of the Lady in the Lake* (TV). *Perry Mason: The Case of the Avenging Ace* (TV). 1989: *Perry Mason: The Case of the Lethal Lesson* (TV). *Perry Mason: The Case of the Murder Mystery Murder* (TV). *Perry Mason: The Case of the Sudden Death Play-Off* (TV). *Perry Mason: The Case of the Musical Murder* (TV). *Perry Mason: The Case of the All-Star Assassin* (TV). 1990: *Perry Mason: The Case of the Paris Paradox* (TV). *Perry Mason: The Case of the Defiant Daughter* (TV). *Perry Mason: The Case of the Silenced Singer* (TV). 1991: *Showdown at Williams Creek* (TV). *Delirious. Perry Mason: The Case of the Ruthless Reporter* (TV). *Perry Mason: The Case of the Glass Coffin* (TV). *Perry Mason: The Case of the Reckless Romeo* (TV). *Perry Mason: The Case of the Skin-Deep Scandal* (TV). 1992: *Perry Mason: The Case of the Fatal Framing* (TV). *Perry Mason: The Case of the Heartbroken Bride* (TV). *Perry Mason: The Case of the Maligned Mobster* (TV). *Perry Mason: The Case of the Poisoned Pen* (TV). 1993: *Perry Mason: The Case of the Telltale Talk Show Host* (TV). *Perry Mason: The Case of the Killer Kiss* (TV). *Perry Mason: The Case of the Wicked Wives* (TV). *The Return of Ironside* (TV). *Perry Mason: The Case of the Fatal Fashion* (TV).

BURROWS, Saffron 1969–
Tall, willowy blonde, rather distant-looking British actress, who began her career as a model in Paris, where she became interested in acting, featured in French TV dramas and later enrolled at a London Youth Theatre company. She was one of the three friends in *Circle of Friends*, but co-star Minnie Driver (*qv*) garnered most of the attention from the film and Burrow's film profile was low until Hollywood starring roles in *Wing Commander* and *Deep Blue Sea* brought her box-office success. She lives with director Mike Figgis.
1991: *The Body Beautiful.* 1993: *In the Name of the Father.* 1995: *Circle of Friends. Welcome II the Terrordome.* 1996: *I Bring You Frankincense. Hotel de Love.* 1997: *Love-life. Nevada. One Night Stand. The Match-maker.* 1998: *The Loss of Sexual Innocence.* 1999: *Wing Commander. Deep Blue Sea. Miss Julie.* 2000: *Gangster No. 1. TimeCode.* 2001: *Enigma.*

BURSTYN, Ellen (Edna Gillooley) 1932–
Pretty, butter-haired American actress of much warmth and *joie-de-vivre* who went

through several changes of name before making a reputation on stage and coming to Hollywood in the 1970s. A deserved Oscar for *Alice Doesn't Live Here Any More* did not succeed in making her a bankable star, and she turned her attention to out-of-the-way projects. Also nominated for Academy Awards on *The Last Picture Show, The Exorcist, Same Time, Next Year* and *Resurrection*. A prominent actors' activist, she was president of Actors' Equity from 1982 to 1985, and has also been artistic director at the Actors' Studio.
1964: †*Goodbye Charlie.* †*For Those Who Think Young.* 1969: †*Pit Stop. Tropic of Cancer.* 1970: *Alex in Wonderland.* 1971: *The Last Picture Show.* 1972: *The King of Marvin Gardens.* 1973: *The Exorcist.* 1974: *Harry and Tonto. Thursday's Game* (TV). *Alice Doesn't Live Here Anymore.* 1977: *Providence. A Dream of Passion.* 1978: *Same Time, Next Year.* 1980: *Resurrection. The Silence of the North.* 1981: *Lee Strasberg and the Actors' Studio.* 1982: *The People vs Jean Harris* (TV). 1984: *The Ambassador. In Our Hands.* 1985: *Twice in a Lifetime. Surviving* (TV). *Act of Vengeance* (TV). *Into Thin Air* (TV). 1986: *Brian Walker, Please Call Home* (TV). *Something in Common* (TV). 1987: *Pack of Lies* (TV). *Hello Actors Studio. Dear America* (voice only). 1988: *Hanna's War.* 1990: *When You Remember Me* (TV). 1991: *Mrs Lambert Remembers Love* (TV). *Grand Isle. Dying Young.* 1993: *The Cemetery Club. Earth and the American Dream* (voice only). 1994: *Getting Out* (TV). *When a Man Loves a Woman. Primal Secrets* (TV). *Getting Gotti* (TV). 1995: *Roommates. How to Make an American Quilt. Follow the River* (TV). *The The Baby-Sitters Club.* 1996: *Our Son, the Matchmaker* (TV). *Murder in Mind* (TV). *Timepiece* (TV). 1997: *A Deadly Vision* (TV). *Liar/Deceiver. Flash* (TV). 1998: *You Can Thank Me Later. A Will of Their Own* (TV). *The Patron Saint of Liars* (TV). *Playing by Heart.* 1999: *Walking Across Egypt. Night Ride Home* (TV). *Crime and Punishment in Suburbia.* 2000: *Requiem for a Dream. The Yards.*

†*As Ellen McRae*

BURTON, Richard
(R. Jenkins) 1925–1984
Welsh-born leading actor with rich, resonant speaking voice who went to Hollywood and projected youthful integrity for a few years,

then middle-aged disillusionment. His choice of films in latter times did not always seem wise, but perhaps he was entitled to some degree of disillusion; he was nominated seven times for an Academy Award without winning once. From the 1960s on, his reputation for high living equalled that gained by his better acting performances. Married (second of three wives) to Elizabeth Taylor (*qv*) from 1964 to 1974; briefly remarried her two years later. Died from a cerebral haemorrhage.

*1948: The Last Days of Dolwyn (US: Woman of Dolwyn). 1949: Now Barabbas was a robber... 1950: Waterfront (US: Waterfront Women). The Woman with No Name (US: Her Paneled Door). 1951: Green Grow the Rushes. 1952: My Cousin Rachel. 1953: The Desert Rats. The Robe. 1954: Prince of Players. 1955: The Rains of Ranchipur. *Thursday's Children (narrator only). 1956: Alexander the Great. 1957: Sea Wife. Bitter Victory. 1958: *March to Aldermaston (narrator only). A Midsummer Night's Dream (dubbed voice). 1959: Look Back in Anger. 1960: The Bramble Bush. Ice Palace. 1961: *Dylan Thomas. 1962: The Longest Day. 1963: Cleopatra. The VIPs. Zulu (narrator only). Becket. *Inheritance (narrator only). 1964: The Night of the Iguana. Hamlet. 1965: The Spy Who Came in from the Cold. The Sandpiper. What's New Pussycat? *Eulogy to 5.02 (narrator only). 1966: The Taming of the Shrew. Who's Afraid of Virginia Woolf? 1967: Doctor Faustus. The Comedians. *The Comedians in Africa. 1968: Boom! Candy. A Wall in Jerusalem (narrator only). Where Eagles Dare. The Rime of the Ancient Mariner (narrator only). 1969: Anne of the Thousand Days. Staircase. 1971: Villain. Raid on Rommel. Under Milk Wood (narrator only). 1972: The Assassination of Trotsky. Hammersmith is Out. Bluebeard. 1973: Massacre in Rome. Sujetska (GB: The Fifth Offensive). 1974: Il viaggio (GB and US: The Voyage). The Klansman. 1975: Brief Encounter (TV). 1976: Volcano (voice only). Resistance. 1977: Exorcist II: The Heretic. Equus. 1978: The Medusa Touch. The Wild Geese. California Suite. Absolution (released 1981). 1979: Breakthrough/ Sergeant Steiner, zweite Teil. Tristan and Isolt/Lovespell (unreleased). 1980: Circle of Two. 1982: Wagner (TV). To the End of the Earth (narrator only). 1984: 1984. Ellis Island (TV mini-series shortened for cinemas).*

BYGRAVES, Max
(Walter Bygraves) 1922–

British radio and music-hall comedian with liquid London tones, dark, wavy hair and cheery disposition who, after some character experience, was briefly in starring roles from 1956 to 1961. These parts projected him more as straight actor and singer of some sincerity, and it was on the singing of tried and true sentimental songs that he concentrated the latter stages of his career, in which he was also prominent as a game-show host on television.

*1949: Bless 'Em All. Skimpy in the Navy. Nitwits on Parade. 1951: Tom Brown's Schooldays. 1954: *Harmony Lane. 1956: Charley Moon. 1958: A Cry from the Streets. 1959: Bobbikins. 1961: Spare the Rod. 1972: The Alf Garnett Saga.*

BYRNE, Gabriel 1950–

Dark, brooding, thick-set, heavy-headed, soft-spoken Irish actor, at his best in impassioned roles. A latecomer to acting after five years as a teacher and translator, he made his name at the Abbey Theatre in his native Dublin. Spotted by director John Boorman to play Uther Pendragon in *Excalibur*, Byrne has stayed in films, often billed second or third in the casts of dramas and thrillers, rather too many of which have been unworthy of his talents. He has alternated between heroes and villains in recent times. Married/divorced American actress Ellen Barkin (*qv*).

*1979: The Outsider. 1981: Excalibur. *The Rocking Horse Winner. 1982: Wagner (TV). 1983: Arthur the King (TV. Released 1985). Reflections. The Keep. Hanna K. 1985: Defence of the Realm. Lionheart. 1986: Gothic. 1987: Giulia and Giulia/Julia and Julia.*

Siesta. Hello Again. The Courier. 1988: A Soldier's Tale. 1989: Diamond Skulls (US: Dark Obsession). 1990: Miller's Crossing. Haakon Haakonsen (US: Shipwrecked). 1992: Cool World. Into the West. 1993: A Dangerous Woman. Point of No Return (GB: The Assassin). Prince of Jutland. 1994: All Things Bright and Beautiful (TV). The War. Little Women. Trial by Jury. A Simple Twist of Fate. 1995: The Usual Suspects. Dead Man. Frankie Starlight. 1996: The Last of the High Kings. Somebody is Waiting. Trigger Happy/ Mad Dog Time. The Brylcreem Boys (released 1999). 1997: Smilla's Sense of Snow/Smilla's Feeling for Snow. Polish Wedding. The End of Violence. The Man in the Iron Mask (Randall Wallace version). Weapons of Mass Destruction (cable TV). 1998: The Magic Sword: Quest for Camelot (voice only). Enemy of the State. 1999: Stigmata. End of Days. 2000: Canone Inverso – Making Love.

BYRON, Kathleen 1922–

Fair-haired British actress of slightly forbidding and distinctly dominant personality, which often resulted in her playing schemers. As with others who did not quite make the front rank of stardom, she was drawn into many second-features in the British cinema of the fifties. Two visits to American, from 1943 to 1945 and 1952 to 1954, resulted in only one role – a supporting part in *Young Bess*. Memorable as the mad nun in *Black Narcissus*.

1942: The Young Mr Pitt. 1943: The Silver Fleet. 1946: A Matter of Life and Death (US: Stairway to Heaven). Black Narcissus. 1948: The Small Back Room (US: Hour of Glory). 1949: Madness of the Heart. 1950: The Reluctant Widow. Prelude to Fame. 1951: Tom Brown's Schooldays. Scarlet Thread. Life in Her Hands. Hell is Sold Out. Four Days. The House in the Square (US: I'll Never Forget You). 1952: My Death is a Mockery. The Gambler and the Lady. 1953: Young Bess. 1954: Star of My Night. The Night of the Full Moon. Profile. 1955: Secret Venture. Handcuffs London. 1960: Hand in Hand. 1962: Night of the Eagle (US: Burn Witch Burn). 1968: Hammerhead. 1969: Wolfshead: The Legend of Robin Hood. 1971: Private Road. Twins of Evil. 1972: Nothing But the Night. 1973: Craze. 1974: The Abdication. 1975: One of Our Dinosaurs is Missing. 1980: The Elephant Man. 1981: From a Far Country (GB: TV). 1996: Emma. 1998: Saving Private Ryan. Les Misérables.

C

CAAN, James (J. Cahn) 1938–

Fuzzy-haired American leading man with slow but engaging smile, whose performances on the way to the top were rather better than those he gave when he got there. Capable of excellent work with strong direction, but in lighter roles often appeared to be having more fun than the audience. Oscar nominated for *The Godfather*. Both he and his career hit problems in the 1980s, but a variety of star character parts, often in semi-unsympathetic roles, brought his name back to marquees from 1987 on.

1963: Irma La Douce. 1964: Lady in a Cage. 1965: The Glory Guys. Red Line 7000. 1967: El Dorado. Countdown. Journey to Shiloh. Submarine X-1. Games. 1969: The Rain People. Man Without Mercy (later Gone With the West). 1970: Rabbit Run. 1971: T.R.Baskin (GB: A Date with a Lonely Girl). Brian's Song (TV). The Godfather. 1973: Slither. Cinderella Liberty. 1974: Freebie and the Bean. The Conversation. The Gambler. The Godfather Part II. 1975: Funny Lady. Rollerball. The Killer Elite. 1976: Harry and Walter Go to New York. Silent Movie. 1977: A Bridge Too Far. Un autre homme, une autre chance (GB: Another Man, Another Woman, US: Another Man, Another Chance). 1978: Comes a Horseman. 1979: Chapter Two. 1941. 1980: †Hide in Plain Sight. 1981: Thief (later and GB: Violent Streets). Les uns et les autres (US: The Ins and the Outs). 1982: Kiss Me Goodbye. 1987: Gardens of Stone. 1988: Alien Nation. 1990: Dick Tracy. Misery. 1991: For the Boys. The Dark Backward. 1992: Honeymoon in Vegas. 1993: Flesh and Bone. The Program. Earth and the American Dream (voice only). *1995: A Boy Called Hate. 1996: Eraser. The North Star. Bottle Rocket. Bulletproof. 1998: Poodle Springs (TV). This is My Father. 1999: Mickey Blue Eyes. 2000: The Yards. The Way of the Gun. The Warden (TV). Luckytown. In the Boom Boom Room.*

†*Also directed*

CABOT, Bruce

(Etienne de Bujac) 1903–1972

Tall, taciturn, slick-haired American leading man of French extraction (and education) and a hell-raising private life, in the course of which he found time to marry and divorce three times. His pictures (which included *King Kong*) were almost all action-adventures, with Cabot alternating between hero and villain. Hollywood kept him busy throughout the 1930s, but his career never regained what impetus it had after he returned from active service in World War II. Died from lung cancer. His second wife, actress Adrienne Ames (A. McClure, 1907–1947), also died from cancer.

1931: Confessions of a Co-ed (GB: Her Dilemma). 1932: What Price Hollywood? Lady with a Past (GB: Her Reputation). Roadhouse Murder. 1933: Scarlet River. Lucky Devils. Midshipman Jack. The Great Jasper. Ann Vickers. King Kong. Disgraced! Flying Devils (GB: The Flying Circus). 1934: Shadows of Sing Sing. Murder on the Blackboard. Finishing School. Their Big Moment (GB: Afterwards). His Greatest Gamble. Redhead. Night Alarm. Penthouse Party (GB: Without Children). 1935: Man of the Night. Let 'Em Have It (GB: False Faces). Show Them No Mercy (GB: Tainted Money). Without Children. 1936: Legion of Terror. Three Wise Guys. Fury. Sinner Take All. Don't Gamble with Love. The Last of the Mohicans. Don't Turn 'Em Loose. The Big Game. Robin Hood of Eldorado. 1937: Bad Guy. Love, Takes Flight. 1938: Sinners in Paradise. Bad Men of Brimstone. Smashing the Rackets. Tenth Avenue Kid. 1939: Homicide Bureau. Dodge City. Traitor Spy (US: The Torso Murder Mystery). Mickey the Kid. You and Me. The Mystery of the White Room. My Son is Guilty (GB: Crime's End). 1940: Susan and God (GB: The Gay Mrs Trexel). Girls Under 21. Captain Caution. 1941: The Flame of New Orleans. Sundown. Wild Bill Hickok Rides. 1942: Silver Queen. Pierre of the Plains. The Desert Song. 1945: Divorce. Fallen Angel. Salty O'Rourke. 1946: Smoky. Avalanche. Angel and the Badman. *1947: Gunfighters (GB: The Assassin). 1948: The Gallant Legion. 1949: Sorrowful Jones. 1950: Fancy Pants. Rock Island Trail (GB: Transcontinent Express). 1951: Best of the Badmen. 1952: Lost in Alaska. Kid Monk Baroni (GB: Young Paul Baroni). 1953: William Tell (unfinished). 1956: The Red Cloak. Rommel's Treasure. Toto lascia a raddoppia? 1957: La ragazza del Palio (GB: Girl of the Palio. US: The Love Specialist). 1958: The Sheriff of Fractured Jaw. The Quiet American. 1959: Il terrore dei barbari (GB and US: Goliath and the Barbarians). John Paul Jones. 1961: The Comancheros. 1962: Hatari! 1963: McLintock! Law of the Lawless. Black Spurs. 1965: In Harm's Way. Town Tamer. Cat Ballou. 1966: The Chase. 1967: The War Wagon. 1968: Hellfighters. The Green Berets. 1969: The Undefeated. 1970: WUSA. Chisum. 1971: Big Jake. Diamonds Are Forever.*

CABOT, Susan

(Harriet Shapiro) 1927–1986

Raven-haired, dark-eyed American actress and singer whose ambitions to be another Kathryn Grayson were stillborn at the hands of studios who used her merely as decoration in colourful adventure stories. As a combination of Grayson and Ann Blyth, she was born five years too late and, following a break for marriage and children, appeared in a succession of progressively more unlikely roles that ended her cinema career. Beaten to death by her son.

1947: Kiss of Death (as extra). 1950: On the Isle of Samoa. The Prince Who Was a Thief. Tomahawk (GB: Battle of Powder River). The Enforcer (GB: Murder Inc). 1951: Flame of Araby. 1952: Son of Ali Baba. The Battle at Apache Pass. Duel at Silver Creek. 1953: Gunsmoke! 1954: Ride Clear of Diablo. 1957: Viking Women. One and Only. Sorority Girl (GB: The Bad One). Carnival Rock. 1958: Fort Massacre. War of the Satellites. Machine Gun Kelly. 1959: Surrender Hell! Wasp Woman.

CAESAR, Sid 1922–

Flat-faced, dark-haired, fast-talking American comedian, a sour-looking equivalent of Britain's Bob Monkhouse, and enormously successful in vaudeville, radio and especially television. Attempts to establish him in films were not ambitious enough, and he has been largely confined to guest spots and all-star movies.

1945: *Tars and Spars*. 1947: *The Guilt of Janet Ames*. 1963: *It's a Mad, Mad, Mad, Mad World*. 1966: *The Spirit is Willing. The Busy Body*. 1967: *A Guide for the Married Man*. 1973: *Ten from Your Show of Shows*. 1974: *Airport 1975*. 1976: *Flight to Holocaust* (TV). *Silent Movie*. 1977: *Fire Sale. Barnaby and Me. Curse of the Black Widow* (TV). 1978: *Grease. The Cheap Detective*. 1980: *The Fiendish Plot of Dr Fu Manchu*. 1981: *History of the World Part I. The Munsters' Revenge* (TV). 1982: *Grease 2*. 1983: *Over the Brooklyn Bridge. Cannonball Run II. Found Money* (TV). 1985: *Stoogemania. Love is Never Silent* (TV). 1987: *The Emperor's New Clothes*. 1988: *Freedom Fighter* (TV). *Side by Side* (TV). 1991: *The South Philadelphia Story*. 1995: *The Great Mom Swap* (TV). 1997: *Vegas Vacation*. 1998: *The Wonderful Ice Cream Suit*.

CAGE, Nicolas (N. Coppola) 1964–
Rangy, wild-haired, thick-lipped, sleepy-eyed American actor with fierce eyebrows and leering good looks, the nephew of director Francis (Ford) Coppola. Fear of reflected nepotism could have given him an inferiority complex, but he soon proved more personable and talented than many of the young American actors springing to prominence in the early 1980s, playing vicious, dumb or sensitive characters with equal conviction and offering deeply felt performances in his more emotional roles. In recent times, he has held his position as a middle-to-top bracket star, playing largely blue-collar, often hot-headed characters, and increasingly in downbeat roles. He won an Academy Award for *Leaving Las Vegas*. Married Patricia Arquette (*qv*). The couple

separated in 2000 but later reunited.
1981: †*The Best of Times* (TV). 1982: †*Fast Times at Ridgemont High* (GB: *Fast Times*). *Valley Girl*. 1983: *Racing with the Moon. Rumble Fish*. 1984: *The Cotton Club. Birdy*. 1985: *The Boy in Blue*. 1986: *Peggy Sue Got Married. Raising Arizona*. 1987: *Moonstruck*. 1988: *Vampire's Kiss*. 1989: *Time to Kill/ Short Cut. Industrial Symphony No. 1: The Dream of the Broken Hearted*. 1990: *Wild at Heart. Fire Birds* (GB: *Wings of the Apache*). *Zandalee*. 1992: *Red Rock West. Honeymoon in Vegas. Amos and Andrew*. 1993: *Deadfall. Guarding Tess*. 1994: *It Could Happen to You. Trapped in Paradise. Kiss of Death*. 1995: *Leaving Las Vegas*. 1996: *The Rock*. 1997: *Face/Off. Con Air. City of Angels*. 1998: *Snake Eyes. Welcome to Hollywood. 8MM*. 1999: *Bringing Out the Dead*. 2000: *Gone in Sixty Seconds. Family Man*. 2001: *Captain Corelli's Mandolin*.

†*As Nicolas Coppola*

CAGNEY, James 1899–1986
Short, jaunty, aggressive, gingery-haired Hollywood star, with much-imitated clockwork tippy-toe strut (probably inherited from his Broadway dancing days), rasping speech and truculence of manner. He usually played cocksure, punch-happy characters who rarely bit off more than they could chew, and remains one of the most sharply-defined stars from the American cinema's vintage years. Oscar for *Yankee Doodle Dandy*. Additionally Oscar-nominated for *Angels with Dirty Faces* and *Love Me or Leave Me*. Died from diabetes and circulatory failure.
1930: *Sinner's Holiday. Doorway to Hell* (GB: *A Handful of Clouds*). *Other Men's Women/Steel Highway*. **Intimate Interview*. 1931: *The Millionaire. The Public Enemy* (GB: *Enemies of the Public*). *Smart Money. Blonde Crazy* (GB: *Larceny Lane*). *Taxi! *Practise Shots*. 1932: **James Cagney. The Crowd Roars. Winner Take All. Hard to Handle*. 1933: *Lady Killer. *Hollywood on Parade No.8. Picture Snatcher. The Mayor of Hell. Footlight Parade*. 1934: *Jimmy the Gent. He Was Her Man. *Screen Snapshots No.11. Here Comes the Navy. *The Hollywood Gad-About. The St Louis Kid* (GB: *A Perfect Weekend*). 1935: **A Trip Thru a Hollywood Studio. Devil Dogs of the Air. 'G' Men. The Irish in Us. The Frisco Kid. A Midsummer Night's Dream. Ceiling Zero*. 1936: *Great Guy* (GB: *Pluck of the Irish*). 1937: *Something to

Sing About*. 1938: **For Auld Lang Syne. Boy Meets Girl. Angels with Dirty Faces*. 1939: *The Oklahoma Kid. Each Dawn I Die. The Roaring Twenties*. 1940: *The Fighting 69th. Torrid Zone. City for Conquest*. 1941: *Strawberry Blonde. The Bride Came C.O.D*. 1942: *Captains of the Clouds. Yankee Doodle Dandy*. 1943: **You, John Jones. *Show Business at War. Johnny Come Lately* (GB: *Johnny Vagabond*). 1944: **Battle Stations* (narrator only). 1945: *Blood on the Sun*. 1946: *13 Rue Madeleine*. 1948: *The Time of Your Life*. 1949: *White Heat*. 1950: *Kiss Tomorrow Goodbye. The West Point Story* (GB: *Fine and Dandy*). 1951: *Come Fill the Cup. Starlift*. 1952: *What Price Glory?* 1953: *A Lion is in the Streets*. 1954: *Run for Cover*. 1955: *The Seven Little Foys. Love Me or Leave Me. Mister Roberts. Tribute to a Bad Man*. 1956: *These Wilder Years*. 1957: *Man of a Thousand Faces*. 1958: †*Short Cut to Hell* (introduction only). 1959: *Shake Hands With the Devil. Never Steal Anything Small*. 1960: *The Gallant Hours*. 1961: *One, Two, Three*. 1962: *The Road to the Wall* (narrator only). 1968: *Arizona Bushwhackers* (narrator only). 1981: *Ragtime*. 1984: *Terrible Joe Moran* (TV).

†*Also directed*

CAINE, Sir Michael
(Maurice Micklewhite) 1933–
Whatever qualities Caine has that made him a star, none of them are conventional. Often bespectacled, not especially handsome, with a pronounced London accent and un-fluid acting style, the fair-haired British actor nonetheless took films by storm in 1965, and kept his place as a top box-office star, latterly in more cynical roles, for 25 years – with only a slight dip in the latter half of the 1970s, when he went into all-star films. Nominated for Oscars in *Alfie*, *Sleuth* and *Educating Rita*, he finally won best supporting actor Oscars for *Hannah and Her Sisters* and *The Cider House Rules*. His lectures on acting continue to be admired, even though he has made far too many bad films in the last 25 years of his career. Married/divorced actress Patricia Haines; since 1973 has been married to beauty queen/actress Shakira Baksh. Knighted in 2000.
1956: *A Hill in Korea* (US: *Hell in Korea*). *Sailor Beware!* (US: *Panic in the Parlor*). 1957: *How to Murder a Rich Uncle. The Steel Bayonet*. 1958: *The Key* (scene deleted). *Carve Her Name With Pride. The Two-Headed Spy.*

Blind Spot. A Woman of Mystery. 1959: Danger Within (US: Breakout). Passport to Shame (US: Room 43). 1960: Foxhole in Cairo. The Bulldog Breed. 1961: The Day the Earth Caught Fire. 1962: Solo for Sparrow. The Wrong Arm of the Law. 1963: Zulu. 1965: The Ipcress File. 1966: Gambit. Alfie. The Wrong Box. Funeral in Berlin. Hurry Sundown. 1967: Billion Dollar Brain. Woman Times Seven. Tonite Let's All Make Love in London. Deadfall. 1968: Play Dirty. The Magus. 1969: The Italian Job. Battle of Britain. Too Late the Hero. 1970: The Last Valley. *Simon, Simon. Get Carter. 1971: Zee and Co (US: X, Y and Zee). Kidnapped. 1972: Pulp. Sleuth. 1974: The Marseille Contract (US: The Destructors). The Black Windmill. The Wilby Conspiracy. 1975: The Man Who Would Be King. The Romantic Englishwoman. Peeper. 1976: Harry and Walter Go to New York. The Eagle Has Landed. 1977: A Bridge Too Far. Silver Bears. 1978: The Swarm. California Suite. 1979: Ashanti. Beyond the Poseidon Adventure. 1980: The Island. Dressed to Kill. 1981: The Hand. Escape to Victory (US: Victory). 1982: Deathtrap. 1983: The Jigsaw Man. Educating Rita. Beyond the Limit (GB: The Honorary Consul). Blame it on Rio. 1985: Water. The Holcroft Covenant. Sweet Liberty. 1986: Half Moon Street. The Whistle Blower. Mona Lisa. Hannah and Her Sisters. 1987: Surrender. The Fourth Protocol. Hero (narrator only). Jaws – The Revenge. 1988: John Huston. Without a Clue. Dirty Rotten Scoundrels. 1989: Jekyll and Hyde (TV). 1990: A Shock to the System. Bullseye! Mr Destiny. 1992: Noises Off. Blue Ice. The Muppet Christmas Carol. 1993: On Deadly Ground. 1995: Len Deighton's Bullet to Beijing. Len Deighton's Midnight in St Petersburg. 1996: Blood and Wine. 1997: Mandela and De Klerk (TV). Shadow Run. 1998: Little Voice. 1999: The Debtors. The Cider House Rules. Curtain Call. 2000: Quills. Shiner. Get Carter. Miss Congeniality.

CALHOUN, Rory
(Francis Durgin) 1922–1999
Almost too handsome, black-haired ex-juvenile delinquent, lumberjack, cowboy, miner and firefighter who struggled on his first visit to Hollywood after being discovered by Alan Ladd, then succeeded second time around as the hero of vigorous outdoor action films, and became one of the film world's busiest men about town. Married to actress-singer Lita Baron from 1949 to 1970. He

died from emphysema, pancreatis and diabetes.
1944: †Something for the Boys. †Sunday Dinner for a Soldier. 1945: †The Bullfighters. †Nob Hill. †The Great John L (GB: A Man Called Sullivan). 1947: The Red House. Adventure Island. That Hagen Girl. 1948: Miraculous Journey. 1949: Sand. Massacre River. 1950: A Ticket to Tomahawk. County Fair. I'd Climb the Highest Mountain. Rogue River. Return of the Frontiersman. 1951: Meet Me After the Show. 1952: With a Song in My Heart. Way of a Gaucho. 1953: The Silver Whip. Powder River. How to Marry a Millionaire. 1954: River of No Return. The Yellow Tomahawk. A Bullet is Waiting. Dawn at Socorro. Four Guns to the Border. 1955: The Looters. Ain't Misbehavin'. The Treasure of Pancho Villa. The Spoilers. 1956: Red Sundown. Raw Edge. Flight to Hong Kong. 1957: The Hired Gun. The Domino Kid. Utah Blaine. Ride Out for Revenge. The Big Caper. 1958: Apache Territory. The Saga of Hemp Brown. 1960: The Colossus of Rhodes. Thunder in Carolina. 1961: Marco Polo. The Treasure of Monte Cristo (US: The Secret of Monte Cristo). 1963: A Face in the Rain. The Gun Hawk. The Young and the Brave. 1964: Young Fury. Operation Delilah. Black Spurs. 1965: Apache Uprising. Finger on the Trigger. 1966: Il gioco delle spie (US: Our Men in Bagdad). 1967: La Muchacha del Nilo (GB: The Emerald of Artatama). 1968: Dayton's Devils. 1969: Operation Cross Eagles. 1972: Night of the Lepus. 1973: Blood Black and White. 1975: Mulefeathers/ The West is Still Wild. Won Ton Ton – the Dog Who Saved Hollywood. 1976: Flight to Holocaust (TV). 1977: Kino, the Padre on Horseback. Love and the Midnight Auto Supply. 1978: Bitter Heritage. Flatbed Annie and Sweetiepie: Lady Truckers (TV. GB: Girls of the Road). 1979: Just Not the Same without You. Okinagan's Day. The Main Event. 1980: Running Hot. Motel Hell. 1982: The Circle of Crime. 1983: Angel. 1984: Avenging Angel. 1985: Half Nelson (TV). 1988: Rollerblade/ Rollerblade Warriors. Hell Comes to Frogtown. 1989: Bad Jim. 1992: Pure Country.

†*As Frank McCown*

CALLARD, Kay 1933–
Bright, chirpy, Canadian-born blonde with provocative personality and attractive croaky voice, seen to advantage in leading roles in a number of British second-features of the

1950s which were considerably enlivened by her presence.
1953: They Who Dare. 1954: The Stranger Came Home (US: The Unholy Four). 1955: Final Column. Stolen Assignment. The Reluctant Bride (US: Two Grooms for a Bride). Dial 999 (US: The Way Out). Secret File (TV. GB: cinemas). Joe Macbeth. Assignment Abroad (TV. GB: cinemas). The Price of Greed. 1956: Find the Lady. 1957: West of Suez (US: Fighting Wildcats). The Smallest Show on Earth. The Hypnotist (US: Scotland Yard Dragnet). Man in the Shadow. Cat Girl. The Flying Scot (US: Mailbag Robbery). Undercover Girl. 1958: Escapement (US: Zex/ The Electronic Monster). Intent to Kill. A Woman Possessed. Links of Justice. The Great Van Robbery. 1959: Top Floor Girl. 1961: Freedom to Die.

CALVERT, Phyllis (Phyllis Bickle) 1915–
Dark-haired British leading lady, a former child dancer and actress who only came to star roles in films in her mid-twenties. Her ladylike carriage and upper-class personality proved no bar to popularity and her tremulous lower lip and liquid brown eyes made her a big hit in weepies and regency romance. A trip to Hollywood in the late forties was not successful.
1927: The Land of Heart's Desire/ The Arcadians. 1935: School for Stars. 1938: Inspector Hornleigh. Two Days to Live. 1940: They Came by Night. Let George Do It. Charley's (Big-Hearted) Aunt. Neutral Port. Inspector Hornleigh Goes to It (US: Mail Train). 1941: Kipps (US: The Remarkable Mr Kipps). 1942: The Young Mr Pitt. Uncensored. 1943: The Man in Grey. 1944: Fanny by Gaslight (US: Man of Evil). 2,000 Women. Madonna of the Seven Moons. 1945: They Were Sisters. 1946: Men of Two Worlds. The Magic Bow. 1947: The Root of All Evil. Time Out of Mind. Broken Journey. 1948: My Own True Love. 1949: The Golden Madonna. Appointment with Danger. 1950: The Woman with No Name (US: Her Paneled Door). 1951: Mr Denning Drives North. 1952: Mandy (US: Crash of Silence). The Net (US: Project M-7). 1956: It's Never Too Late. Child in the House. 1958: The Young and the Guilty. Indiscreet. A Lady Mislaid. 1960: Oscar Wilde. 1965: The Battle of the Villa Fiorita. 1968: Twisted Nerve. 1969: Oh! What a Lovely War. 1970: The Walking Stick. 1985: The Death of the Heart. 1988: Across the Lake (TV). 1997: Mrs Dalloway.

CALVET, Corinne (C. Dibos) 1925–
Tawny-haired, sultry-looking Parisienne brought to Hollywood by producer Hal Wallis (after making only four French films) as a kind of combination Lauren Bacall and Rita Hayworth. Calvet didn't quite have that kind of smouldering personality but decorated a number of colourful double-feature films. Married five times, once to actor John Bromfield (1922–).

*1946: La part de l'ombre. Nous ne sommes pas mariés. 1947: Pétrus. Le château de la dernière chance. 1949: *Super Cue Men. Rope of Sand. When Willie Comes Marching Home. 1950: My Friend Irma Goes West. 1951: Quebec. *Hollywood on a Sunday Afternoon. On the Riviera. Peking Express. Sailor Beware. Thunder in the East. 1952: What Price Glory? 1953: Powder River. Flight to Tangier. 1954: The Far Country. So This is Paris. The Adventures of Casanova. The Girls of San Frediano. Four Women in the Night. Bonnes à tuer. 1955: Napoléon. 1958: The Plunderers of Painted Flats. 1960: Bluebeard's Ten Honeymoons. 1962: Hemingway's Adventures of a Young Man (GB: Adventures of a Young Man). 1965: Apache Uprising. 1970: Pound. 1974: The Phantom of Hollywood (TV). 1976: Too Hot to Handle (GB: She's Too Hot to Handle). 1979: She's Dressed to Kill (TV). 1980: Dr Heckyl and Mr Hype. 1982: The Sword and the Sorcerer. 1988: Side Roads. 1996: Big Killing in Little Saigon.*

CAMERON, Rod
(Nathan R. Cox) 1910–1983
Rugged was really the only word for this tall, dark-haired, square-jawed Canadian star, built like a redwood tree, who, after ten years in construction work and a slow start to his

belated film career, played a slew of good-humoured men of action, often in medium-budget westerns, at Universal and Republic in the 1940s and 1950s. Died from cancer.

1939: †The Old Maid. Heritage of the Desert. 1940: If I Had My Way. Rangers of Fortune. Northwest Mounted Police. The Quarterback. Christmas in July. Stagecoach War. Those Were the Days (GB: Good Old Schooldays). 1941: Henry Aldrich for President. The Monster and the Girl. Nothing But the Truth. I Wanted Wings (voice only). Buy Me That Town. Pacific Blackout (GB: Midnight Angel). Among the Living. The Parson of Panamint. The Night of January 16th. No Hands on the Clock. 1942: The Fleet's In. The Remarkable Andrew. Star Spangled Rhythm. Priorities on Parade. Wake Island. True to the Army. The Forest Rangers. 1943: No Time for Love. Gung Ho! The Commandos Strike at Dawn. G-Man versus the Black Dragon (serial). The Good Fellows. Honeymoon Lodge. The Kansan (GB: Wagon Wheels). Secret Service in Darkest Africa (serial. GB: Desert Agent. Riding High (GB: Melody Inn). 1944: Beyond the Pecos (GB: Beyond the Seven Seas). Boss of Boomtown. Mrs Parkington. Trigger Trail. The Old Texas Trail (GB: Stagecoach Line). Renegades of the Rio Grande (GB: Bank Robbery). Riders of the Santa Fé (GB: Mile a Minute). 1945: Frontier Gal (GB: The Bride Wasn't Willing). Salome, Where She Danced. Swing Out, Sister. 1946: The Runaround. 1947: Pirates of Monterey. 1948: River Lady. Panhandle. Strike It Rich. Belle Starr's Daughter. The Plunderers. 1949: Brimstone. Stampede. 1950: Stage to Tucson (GB: Lost Stage Valley). Dakota Lil. Short Grass. 1951: Oh! Susanna. Cavalry Scout. The Sea Hornet. 1952: Ride the Man Down. Woman of the North Country. Wagons West. Fort Osage. 1953: The Jungle. The Steel Lady (GB: Treasure of Kalifa). San Antone. 1954: Southwest Passage (GB: Camels West). Hell's Outpost. 1955: Santa Fé Passage. The Fighting Chance. Headline Hunters. Double Jeopardy (GB: The Crooked Ring). 1956: Passport to Treason. Yaqui Drums. 1957: Spoilers of the Forest. Escapement (later Zex. US: The Electronic Monster). 1958: The Man Who Died Twice. 1963: The Gun Hawk. Bullet and the Flesh. 1964: Las pistoles no discuten/Bullets Don't Argue/Die letzten zwei von Rio Bravo (released 1967). I sentieri dell' odio. 1965: The Bounty Killer. Requiem for a Gunfighter. 1966: Winnetou and His Friend Old Firehand (GB: Thunder at the Border). 1967: Ride the Wind (TV. GB: cinemas). 1971: The Last Movie. Evel Knievel. 1972: Redneck. 1975: The Kirlian Force. Psychic Killer. 1976: Jessie's Girls (GB: Wanted Women). 1977: Love and the Midnight Auto Supply.

†Scenes deleted from final release print

CAMPBELL, Bruce 1957–
Tall, slack-jawed, black-haired American actor, the star of the 'Evil Dead' and 'Maniac Cop' films and a cult figure with horror fans. Campbell describes his characters in these movies, Ash and Mallory, as 'just decent guys trying to stop evil'. Generally speaking, the puzzled-looking Campbell plays straight-forward characters with not too much brain

power, but that's part of their attractiveness. His rough-hewn style has made him a star of horror films, but a supporting player in the few mainstream films he's made. Besides the list below, Campbell says he's been in films called *Cleveland Smith, Torro, Torro, Torro!,* and *The Blind Waiter* in the early 1980s, none of which I can verify.

*1978: *Clockwork. *Within the Woods. 1982: The Evil Dead. 1983: Goin' Back. 1985: Crimewave/Broken Hearts and Noses. 1987: Evil Dead 2/Evil Dead 2: Dead Before Dawn. 1988: Maniac Cop. 1989: Moon Trap. 1990: Darkman. Maniac Cop 2. Sundown – The Vampire in Retreat. 1991: Waxwork II: Lost in Time. Mindwarp. 1992: Lunatics: a Love Story. Army of Darkness: Evil Dead 3/Army of Darkness: The Medieval Dead. 1993: Man With the Screaming Brain. The Hudsucker Proxy. 1995: The Killer Tongue. The Quick and the Dead. 1996: Escape from L.A. Tornado! (TV). In the Line of Duty: Blaze of Glory (TV). 1997: McHale's Navy. Missing Links (TV). Last Chance Love. The Love Bug (TV). Running Time. 1998: Goldrush (TV). 1999: La patinoire. Double Jeopardy. Icebreaker. 2001: Nobody Knows.*

CAMPBELL, Neve 1973–
Dark-haired, dark-eyed, moody-looking, low-voiced Canadian actress often seen as strong-willed characters. The daughter of Scottish-Dutch parents (her father is a drama teacher), she joined the National Ballet School of Canada at the age of nine, but abandoned dancing ambitions after a breakdown at 14 which caused the loss of her hair (it grew back after acupuncture). At 16 she had turned to acting and was soon in the TV series *Catwalk*. Minor film roles

followed, but she broke through to stardom in 1996, most notably with the first of her three portrayals of the beleaguered Sidney in the *Scream* movies. She was also popular in the TV series *Party of Five*.

1994: *The Passion of John Ruskin. Web of Deceit (TV). Northern Passage. The Dark. Paint Cans. The Forget-Me-Not Murders (TV). Baree: The Wolf Dog (TV). 1995: Love Child. 1996: The Craft. The Canterville Ghost (TV). The Witching Hour (TV). Scream. 1997: Scream 2. Simba's Pride (video. Voice only). 1998: 54. Hairshirt. Wild Things. 1999: Three to Tango. Panic. Move. 2000: Drowning Mona. Scream 3.*

CAMPBELL, William 1926–
Black-haired American actor whose youthful looks and smiling sneer qualified him for a good run of sharpies, conceited Romeos and psychopaths in the fifties, ever willing to swap sides at the drop of a dollar. His Death Row study of Caryl Chessman was much admired, but, growing older and heavier without being able to shed the punk image, he regressed to minor roles.

1950: *The Breaking Point. Breakthrough.* 1951: *Inside the Walls of Folsom Prison. Operation Pacific. The People Against O'Hara.* 1952: *Holiday for Sinners.* 1953: *Battle Circus. Small Town Girl. The Big Leaguer. Code Two. Escape from Fort Bravo.* 1954: *The High and the Mighty. The Fast and the Furious.* 1955: *Battle Cry. Running Wild. Cell 2455 – Death Row. Man without a Star. Man in the Vault.* 1956: *Backlash. Love Me Tender. Walk the Proud Land.* 1957: *Eighteen and Anxious.* 1958: *The Naked and the Dead. Money, Women and Guns. The Sheriff of Fractured Jaw.* 1960: *Natchez Train.* 1961: *Night of Evil.* 1963: *The Young Racers. The Secret Invasion. Dementia 13 (GB: The Haunted and the Hunted). Operation Titian (US: Portrait in Terror).* 1964: *Hush . . . Hush, Sweet Charlotte.* 1966: *Blood Bath (revised version of Operation Titian). Track of the Vampire.* 1971: *Pretty Maids All in a Row.* 1972: *Black Gunn.* 1974: *Dirty Mary, Crazy Larry.* 1987: *Return of the Six Million Dollar Man and the Bionic Woman (TV).* 1993: *Gettysburg.*

CANDY, John 1950–1994
Plump, light-haired, eager-looking, fast-talking Canadian comic star, coming to prominence via the late-night TV satire route. Mainly in slobby, low-comedy roles,

he turned the image to his own advantage to give poignant performances in *Planes, Trains and Automobiles* and *Uncle Buck*. A hard worker, he often popped up in cameo and featured roles as well as in his own vehicles. Continual dieting and a voracious appetite, however, affected his health, and he died from a heart attack while making a film in torrid heat in Mexico. Once said: 'A lot of people just see me as the jolly fat guy, but I'd hate to think that was the only reason they were laughing'.

1973: *Class of '44.* 1975: *The Clown Murders.* 1976: *It Seemed Like a Good Idea at the Time. Tunnelvision. Find the Lady.* 1977: *Faceoff.* 1978: *The Silent Partner. The Courage of Kavik, the Wolf Dog (TV).* 1979: *Lost and Found. 1941.* 1980: *Double Negative. The Blues Brothers.* 1981: *Heavy Metal (voice only).* 1982: *It Came from Hollywood (V).* 1983: *Strange Brew. National Lampoon's Vacation. Going Berserk.* 1984: *Splash.* 1985: *Sesame Street Presents: Follow That Bird. Brewster's Millions. Tears Are Not Enough. Volunteers. Summer Rental.* 1986: *The Canadian Conspiracy. Armed and Dangerous. Little Shop of Horrors. Rocket Boy (TV).* 1987: *Spaceballs. Really Weird Tales (TV). Planes, Trains and Automobiles.* 1988: *The Great Outdoors.* 1989: *Who's Harry Crumb? Hot to Trot (voice only). Speed Zone. Uncle Buck.* 1990: *Home Alone. Masters of Menace. The Rescuers Down Under (voice only).* 1991: *Delirious. Nothing But Trouble. Only the Lonely. JFK.* 1992: *Once Upon a Crime. Career Opportunities (later One Wild Night). Bartholomew Vs Neff. Boris and Natasha (cable TV).* 1993: *Cool Runnings. Hostage for a Day (TV. And directed). Rookie of the Year.* 1994: *North (scene deleted). Wagons East.* 1995: *Canadian Bacon.*

CANNON, Dyan
(Samille Friesen, later legally changed) 1937–
Feline American actress whose career as tawny temptresses was swiftly interrupted by meeting Cary Grant, living with him from 1961–1964, being married to him from 1965–1968, then getting a much publicized divorce. She quickly became a star on resumption of her career, but soon tired of playing busty blonde bitches and opted out of films for four years. Her early performances are pure plastic, but she blossomed in comedy in the late seventies. Nominated for Academy Awards in *Bob & Carol & Ted & Alice* and *Heaven Can Wait.*

1959: *This Rebel Breed. The Rise and Fall of Legs Diamond.* 1969: *Bob & Carol & Ted & Alice.* 1970: *Doctor's Wives.* 1971: *The Anderson Tapes. The Love Machine. Le casse (GB and US: The Burglars).* 1972: *Such Good Friends. Shamus.* 1973: *The Last of Sheila.* 1974: *Child Under a Leaf. The Virginia Hill Story (TV).* 1978: *Lady of the House (TV). The Revenge of the Pink Panther. Heaven Can Wait.* 1979: *For the First Time.* 1980: *Coast to Coast. Honeysuckle Rose.* 1982: *Deathtrap. Author! Author! Having It All (TV).* 1983: *Arthur the King (TV Released 1985).* 1984: *Master of the Game (TV).* 1988: *Caddyshack II. Rock 'n' Roll Mom (TV).* 1989: *One Point of View.* 1990: *The End of Innocence.* 1991: *Jailbirds (TV).* 1992: *The Pickle. Christmas in Connecticut (TV).* 1993: *Based on an Untrue Story (TV).* 1995: *The Case of the Jealous Jokester (TV).* 1996: *That Darn Cat. The Rockford Files: If the Frame Fits (TV).* 1997: *Out to Sea. Beverly Hills Family Robinson (TV). 8 Heads in a Duffel Bag.* 1998: *Black Jaq (TV).* 1999: *Kiss of a Stranger.* 2000: *Allie & Me. My Mother the Spy (TV).*

As director: 1975: **Number One.* 1979: *For the First Time.* 1990: *The End of Innocence.*

CANOVA, Judy
(Juliet Canova) 1916–1983
Dark-haired American singer-comedienne with wide grin whose unique brand of scatterbrained hillbilly humour and ear-splitting yodel were enough to keep her going in second-feature comedy films through three decades. The actress Diana Canova, once of TV's *Soap*, is her daughter.

1935: *In Caliente. Going Highbrow. Broadway Gondolier.* 1937: *Artists and Models. Thrill of a Lifetime.* 1940: *Scatterbrain.* 1941: **Variety*

Reel. *Stars Past and Present. Sis Hopkins. Puddin' Head (GB: Judy Goes to Town). *Meet Roy Rogers. 1942: Joan of Ozark (GB: The Queen of Spies). True to the Army. Sleepytime Gal. 1943: Chatterbox. Sleepy Lagoon. 1944: Louisiana Hayride. *Screen Snapshots, series 24, No 1. 1945: Hit the Hay. 1946: Singin' in the Corn. *Famous Hollywood Mothers. *Radio Characters of 1946. 1951: Honeychile. 1952: Oklahoma Annie. 1953: The WAC from Walla Walla (GB: Army Capers). 1954: Untamed Heiress. 1955: Carolina Cannonball. 1956: Lay That Rifle Down. 1960: The Adventures of Huckleberry Finn. 1976: Cannonball (GB: Carquake).

CANTOR, Eddie
(Israel Iskowitz) 1892–1964

Pop-eyed, bushy-browed, black-haired, slightly-built American singer and comedian whose angelic looks of guileless innocence were the centrepiece to some wild and spectacular Hollywood musical comedies of the early 1930s. His appeal surprisingly waned for cinema audiences later in the decade, and the Ziegfeld-trained Cantor returned to stage and radio work. He tried TV variety shows, too, from 1950, but was largely sidelined after his first heart attack in 1952. He received a special Academy Award in 1956, and died from a further heart attack eight years later.

1926: Kid Boots. 1927: *The Speed Hound. Follies. Special Delivery. 1929: *A Ziegfeld Midnight Frolic. Glorifying the American Girl. *That Party in Person. *Getting a Ticket. 1930: *Insurance. Whoopee! 1931: Palmy Days. 1932: The Kid from Spain. 1933: Roman Scandals. 1934: Kid Millions. *Hollywood Cavalcade. *Screen Snapshots No. II. 1936: Strike Me Pink. 1937: Ali Baba Goes to Town. 1940: Forty Little Mothers. 1943: Thank Your Lucky Stars. 1944: Hollywood Canteen. Show Business. 1948: If You Knew Susie. 1952: The Story of Will Rogers. 1953: The Eddie Cantor Story. 1956: Seidman and Son (TV).

CAPSHAW, Kate (Kathleen Nail) 1953–

Quite tall, slightly careworn-looking American actress with masses of brown curly hair. She never quite made top stardom despite coming close on a number of occasions – and has continued to act even after marriage (second) to phenomenally successful director Steven Spielberg. She began her career teaching children with learning disabilities,

switching to acting in her mid twenties.

1982: A Little Sex. Missing Children: A Mother's Story (TV). 1983: Dreamscape. 1984: Windy City. Indiana Jones and the Temple of Doom. Best Defense. 1985: Power. 1986: SpaceCamp. 1987: Code Name Dancer/Her Secret Life (TV). The Quick and the Dead (TV). 1988: Private Affairs. Ti presento un'amica. Internal Affairs (TV). 1989: Black Rain. 1990: Love at Large. 1991: My Heroes Have Always Been Cowboys. 1994: Love Affair. Next Door (TV). 1995: Just Cause. How to Make an American Quilt. *Duke of Groove. 1997: The Locusts. 1998: The Alarmist (formerly Life During Wartime). 1999: The Love Letter.

CAPUCINE
(Germaine Lefebvre) 1931–1990

Elegant, gauntly beautiful, dark-haired French actress who was a top model before beginning a film career in earnest in 1960. Erect and aloof in manner, she was once described by an interviewer as 'haughty as a heron', but unbent delightfully in such 1960s comedies as The Pink Panther. Divorced at 20, she never re-married. Increasingly isolated in later years, she ended her life by hurling herself from the balcony of her eighth-floor apartment in Switzerland.

1949: Rendez-vous de juillet. 1950: Bertrand Coeur de Lion. 1955: Frou-Frou. 1960: Song Without End. North to Alaska. 1961: The Triumph of Michael Strogoff. 1962: I Don Giovanni della Costa Azzurra. A Walk on the Wild Side. The Lion. 1963: The Pink Panther. 1964: The Seventh Dawn. 1965: What's New Pussycat? 1966: Le fate (GB: Sex Quartet). 1967: The Honey Pot. 1968: Fraulein Doktor. Las crueles (US: Exquisite Cadaver). 1969:

Fellini Satyricon. 1970: Ciao Federico. 1971: Red Sun. 1975: Jackpot (uncompleted). Bluff. Ne pas déranger (TV). L'incorrigible. 1976: Per l'amore. La pêche miraculeuse (TV). 1977: Ecce noi per esemprio. Ritratto di borghesia in nero/Nest of Vipers. 1978: Jaguar Lives. Giallo napoletano. Arabian Adventure. 1979: Da Dunkerque alla vittoria (US: From Hell to Victory). 1980: Martin Eden (TV US: cinemas). 1982: Aphrodite. Balles perdues/Stray Bullets. Blackout. Trail of the Pink Panther. 1983: Curse of the Pink Panther. 1984: Honor Thy Father. DeadHeat. 1987: Gila and Rick. Delirium. 1989: Scandalous (TV). My First 40 years.

CARDINALE, Claudia 1938–

Despite a bust best described as generous, an urchin face, an attractively raucous voice and a curriculum vitae that parallels that of Sophia Loren (qv), in that she married the producer who discovered her, the dark-haired, Tunisian-born Cardinale did not make it to the same heights as an international star, lacking in some ways Loren's depth and some of her elegance, and style; also, her English, though as fluent, was less seductive. Still, after a lull in the early 1970s, she keeps busy into her sixties, having produced or co-produced some of her recent films.

1956: *Chaînes d'or. 1957: Goha. 1958: I soliti ignoti (GB: Persons Unknown. US: Big Deal on Madonna Street). Totò e Marcellino. Tre straniere a Roma. La prima notte. 1959: Il magistrato. Un maledetto imbroglio (US: The Facts of Murder). Upstairs and Downstairs. Audace colpo dei soliti ignoti. Vento del sud. Austerlitz (GB: The Battle of Austerlitz). 1960: La ragazza con la valigia. Il bell' Antonio. I delfini. Rocco and His Brothers. 1961: Les lions sont lâchés. Senilità. La viaccia (US: The Love Makers). 1962: Cartouche (GB: Swords of Blood). The Leopard. 1963: Eight and a Half. Time of Indifference. Bebo's Girl. Circus World (GB: The Magnificent Showman). The Pink Panther. 1964: Il magnifico cornuto (US: The Magnificent Cuckold). 1965: Vaghe stelle dell' orsa (GB: Of a Thousand Delights. US: Sandra). 1966: Una rosa per tutti (US: A Rose for Everyone). Le fate (GB: Sex Quartet. US: The Queens). Lost Command. The Professionals. Blindfold. 1967: Don't Make Waves. *Piero Gheradi. Il giorno della civetta (US: Mafia). 1968: The Hell with Heroes. Once Upon a Time . . . in the West. A Fine Pair. 1969: The Red Tent. Nell' anno del signore. The Adventures of Gérard.

Certo, certissimo, anzi . . . probabile. 1970: Popsy Pop (GB: The 21 Carat Snatch. US: The Butterfly Affair). 1971: Les pétroleuses (GB and US: The Legend of Frenchie King). L'udienza. Bello, onesto, emigrato Australia sposerebbe compaesana illibata. 1972: La scoumone. 1973: Libera, amore rio. I guappi. 1974: Il giorna del furore/Un uomo (GB: Fury. US: One Russian Summer). Conversation Piece. 1975: Il profeta di ferro. A mezzanotte va la ronda del piacere (US: The Immortal Bachelor). Beato lore. Il comune senso del pudore. Qui comincia l'avventura (GB: Midnight Pleasures. US: Lucky Girls). 1977: Un jour peut-être à San Pedro ou ailleurs. La part du feu. 1978: Escape to Athena. Good Bye and Amen. L'arma. La petite fille en velours bleu (US: The Girl in Blue Velvet). Cocktails for Three. 1979: L'ingorgo (US: Traffic Jam). Corleone. Si salve chi vuole. 1980: Le cadeau/The Gift. I briganti. 1981: The Salamander. La pelle. 1982: Fitzcarraldo. Burden of Dreams. 1983: The Ruffian. Princess Daisy (TV). Stelle emigranti. Enrico IV. 1984: Claretta. 1985: L'été prochain. La storia (History). The Woman of Wonders. 1987: A Man in Love. 1988: Blu elettrico. Acque di primavera (Torrents of Spring). 1989: The French Revolution. 1990: Hiver 54, l'abbé Pierre. The Battle of the Three Kings. Atto di dolore. 1991: Mayrig/Mother. 1992: 588 Rue Paradis. 1993: Son of the Pink Panther. 1994: Elles ne pensent qu'à ça. 1996: La goulette. 1997: Sous les pieds des femmes. 1998: Riches, belles et cruelles. 1999: Rudy Valentino, il ritorno dello sceicco. Briganti. Mein Liebster Feind (doc).

CAREY, Harry 1878–1947
Grim, unsmiling, light-haired hero of masses of silent westerns, many of them directed by the young John Ford, in which Carey was often the bad guy reformed by the love of the heroine. Left films in 1928 to train his voice for the coming of sound and, on his return in 1931, continued as tough men of action, with sympathetic character roles as the years wore on. Died from a coronary thrombosis. His son Harry Carey Jr (1921–) is the Hollywood character actor. Oscar-nominated for *Mr Smith Goes to Washington*.
1910: *Gentleman Joe. 1911: *Bill Sharkey's Last Game. *Riding de Trail. *The Informer. *Brute Island. *My Hero. 1912: *An Unseen Enemy. *A Cry for Help. *The Musketeers of Pig Alley. *In the Aisles of the Wild. *Two Men of the Desert. *Friends. *Heredity. *The

Unwelcome Guest. *An Adventure in the Autumn Woods. *The Burglar's Dilemma. *The God Within. *A Feud in the Kentucky Hills. *Gold and Glitter. *Brutality. *The Painted Lady. *So Near Yet So Far. *The One She Loved. *Two Daughters of Eve. 1913: *Love in an Apartment Hotel. *Broken Ways. *Pirate Gold. *Three Friends. *Brothers. *The Sheriff's Baby. *The Ranchero's Revenge. *The Left-Handed Man. *The Hero of Little Italy. *Olaf – an Atom. *Oil and Water. *A Chance Deception. *The Wrong Bottle. *A Girl's Stratagem. *Near to Earth. *If Only We Knew. *The Stolen Bride. *The Wanderer. *The Well. *The Switch Tower. *The Sorrowful Shore. *A Gambler's Honor. *The Mistake. *The Mirror. *Under the Shadow of the Law. *Black and White. *The Crook and the Girl. *A Modest Hero. *The Stolen Treaty. *A Tender-Hearted Crook. *Madonna of the Storm. *The Abandoned Well. *A Misappropriated Turkey. *The Tenderfoot's Money. *The Telephone Girl and the Lady. *A Frightful Blunder. *In Diplomatic Circles. *A Dangerous Foe. *The Enemy's Baby. *Red Hicks Defies the World. *When Love Forgives. *The Vengeance of Galora. *The Stopped Clock. *The Van Nostrand Tiara. *The Law and His Son. *I Was Meant for You. *The Detective's Stratagem. *The Strong Man's Burden. *A Gamble with Death. *All for Science. 1914: *The Battle at Elderbush Gulch. *In Prehistoric Days/Wars of the Primal Tribes (later Brute Force). Judith of Bethulia. *Travelin' On. *A Nest Unfeathered. *Her Father's Silent Partner. *McVeagh of the South Seas (GB: Brute Island). 1915: *The Battle of Frenchmen's Run. *The Heart Of a Bandit. *Perils of the Jungle. *The Sheriff's Dilemma. *The Miser's Legacy. *The Gambler's IOU. *A Day's Adventure. *Truth Stranger Than Fiction. *Her Dormant Love. *The Way Out. *Her Convert. *As it Happened. Graft (serial). Judge Not, or The Woman of Mona Diggins. Just Jim. *His Desperate Deed. *Old Offenders. *The Cancelled Mortgage. *A Double Winning. 1916: *A Movie Star. *Stampede in the Night. *The Night Riders. *The Passing of Hell's Crown. *The Committee on Credentials (directed only). *A Woman's Eyes. *Blood Money. *The Bad Man from Cheyenne. *The Jackals of a Great City. *The Wedding Guest. *The Conspiracy. *Stampede in the Night. *The Devil's Own. *Guilty. *A Woman's Eyes (and co-directed). The Three Godfathers. Behind the Lines. A Knight of the Range. Secret Love. 1917: *The Outlaw and the Lady. *Goin' Straight. *The Mysterious Outlaw. *The Texas Sphinx. *Cheyenne's Pal. *Hair-Trigger Burk. The Honor of an Outlaw. A 44-Caliber Mystery. The Golden Bullet. Her Condoned Sin (extended version of Judith of Bethulia). The Wrong Man. Six-Shooter Justice. The Soul Herder. The Almost Good Man. Red Saunders Plays Cupid/The Fighting Gringo. *The Drifter. Beloved Jim. Two Guns. The Secret Man. Straight Shooting. A Marked Man. Bucking Broadway. 1918: Wild Women. Three Mounted Men. Thieves' Gold. The Phantom Riders. Hell Bent. A Regular Fellow. Fighting Through. God's Outlaw. The Mayor of Filbert. The Scarlet Drop (GB: Hillybilly). A Woman's Fool. *Klever Kiddies. 1919:

Roped. Blind Husbands. Bare Fists. Riders of Vengeance. The Outcasts of Poker Flat. A Fight for Love. Ace of the Saddle. A Gun Fightin' Gentleman. Rider of the Law. Marked Men. Sure Shot Morgan. The Fighting Brothers. By Indian Post. The Rustlers. Gun Law. The Gun Packer. The Last Outlaw. 1920: Overland Red. West is West. Sundown Slim. Hitchin' Posts. Human Stuff. Bullet Proof. Blue Streak McCoy. 1921: 'If Only' Jim. The Freeze Out. The Wallop. Hearts Up. Desperate Trails. The Fox. 1922: Man to Man. Canyon of the Fools. The Kickback. Good Men and True. 1923: Crashin' Thru. Desert Driven. The Night Hawk. The Miracle Baby. 1924: The Man from Texas. Roaring Rails. Tiger Thompson. The Lightning Rider. Flaming Frontiers. 1925: Beyond the Border. Soft Shoes. The Texas Trail. The Man from Red Gulch. The Prairie Pirate. The Bad Lands. Wanderer. Silent Sanderson. 1926: Johnny Get Your Hair Cut. Driftin' Thru. Satan Town. The Frontier Trail. The Seventh Bandit. 1927: Slide, Kelly, Slide. A Little Journey. 1928: The Trail of '98. Border Patrol. Burning Bridges. 1931: Trader Horn. Bad Company. The Vanishing Legion (serial). Across the Line. Double Sixes. Horse Hoofs. The Hurricane Rider. 1932: Cavalier of the West. Border Devils. Without Honor. Law and Order. Last of the Mohicans (serial). The Devil Horse (serial). Night Rider. 1933: Man of the Forest. Sunset Pass. 1934: The Thundering Herd. 1935: Rustler's Paradise. Powdersmoke Range. Barbary Coast. Wagon Trail. Wild Mustang. Last of the Clintons. 1936: Sutter's Gold. The Last Outlaw. The Accusing Finger. Valiant is the Word for Carrie. The Prisoner of Shark Island. Little Miss Nobody. The Three Mesquiteers. The Man Behind the Mask. 1937: Ghost Town. Racing Lady. Born Reckless. Kid Galahad. Souls at Sea. Border Café. Annapolis Salute (GB: Salute to Romance). *Lest We Forget. Danger Patrol. Aces Wild. 1938: The Port of Missing Girls. You and Me. The Law West of Tombstone. Gateway. Sky Giant. King of Alcatraz (GB: King of the Alcatraz). 1939: Burn 'Em Up O'Connor. Mr Smith Goes to Washington. Street of Missing Men. Inside Information. Code of the Streets. My Son is Guilty (GB: Crime's End). 1940: Outside the 3-Mile Limit (GB: Mutiny of the Seas). Beyond Tomorrow. They Knew What They Wanted. 1941: Among the Living. Shepherd of the Hills. Sundown. Parachute Battalion. 1942: The Spoilers. 1943: Happy Land. Air Force. 1944: The Great Moment. 1945: China's Little Devils. 1946: Duel in the Sun. Angel and the Badman. 1947: Sea of Grass. Red River. 1948: So Dear to My Heart.

CAREY, Macdonald
(Edward M. Carey) 1913–1994
Bland-looking American leading man, all eyes, eyebrows and lazy smile. His film career, already a late starter, was seriously disrupted by four-year service in the US Marines and, in its latter stages, contained far too many vapid comedies and lukewarm adventure yarns. He was an excellent smiling villain, an ability that remained much underused. An avid writer, he published three volumes of poetry and an autobiography. Died from lung cancer.

1942: Dr Broadway. Take a Letter, Darling (GB: The Green-Eyed Woman). Wake Island. Star Spangled Rhythm. 1943: Shadow of a Doubt. Salute for Three. 1947: Suddenly It's Spring. Variety Girl. 1948: Hazard. Dream Girl. 1949: Streets of Laredo. Bride of Vengeance. The Great Gatsby. Song of Surrender. South Sea Sinner (GB: East of Java). 1950: Comanche Territory. The Lawless (GB: The Dividing Line). Copper Canyon. Mystery Submarine. The Great Missouri Raid. 1951: Excuse My Dust. Meet Me After the Show. Cave of Outlaws. Let's Make It Legal. 1952: My Wife's Best Friend. 1953: Count the Hours (GB: Every Minute Counts). Hannah Lee (later Outlaw Territory). 1954: Malaga (US: Fire over Africa). 1956: Stranger at My Door. In Times Like These (TV. GB: cinemas). Odongo. *Edge of the Law. Miracle on 34th Street (TV. GB: cinemas). 1958: Man or Gun. Natchez (TV). 1959: Blue Denim (GB: Blue Jeans). John Paul Jones. 1961: The Damned (US: These Are the Damned). 1962: Stranglehold. The Devil's Agent. 1963: Tammy and the Doctor. 1965: The Redeemer (voice only). Broken Sabre (TV. GB: cinemas). 1971: Gidget Gets Married (TV). 1973: Ordeal (TV). 1975: Who is the Black Dahlia? (TV). 1977: End of the World. Foes. 1978: Stranger in Our House / Summer of Fear (TV). Pressure Point (TV). 1980: American Gigolo. 1987: Access Code (V. Completed 1984). It's Alive III: Island of the Alive.

CAREY, Phil (Eugene Carey) 1925–
Tall, rugged American actor with brown hair and sympathetic eyebrows whose film career unaccountably went astray after he had proved himself adept at heroes and villains alike. He made an excellent Philip Marlowe in a TV series, but was little seen after 1970. Billed as Philip in some early films.

1949: Daughter of the West. 1950: Operation Pacific. 1951: I Was a Communist for the FBI. Inside the Walls of Folsom Prison. This Woman is Dangerous. The Tanks are Coming. 1952: Springfield Rifle. Cattle Town. The Man Behind the Gun. 1953: Calamity Jane. The Nebraskan. Gun Fury. 1954: Pushover. Massacre Canyon. Outlaw Stallion. They Rode West. The Long Gray Line. 1955: Wyoming Renegades. Three Stripes in the Sun (GB: The Gentle Sergeant). Count Three and Pray. Mister Roberts. 1956: Port Afrique. Wicked As They Come. 1957: The Shadow on the Window. 1958: Screaming Mimi. Return to Warbow. 1959: Tonka. 1960: The Trunk. 1963: Black Gold. 1964: Dead Ringer (GB: Dead Image). FBI Code 98. The Time Travelers. 1965: The Great Sioux Massacre. 1967: Three Guns for Texas. 1968: Backtrack (TV). 1969: Once You Kiss a Stranger. 1970: Sudden Death / The Rebel Rousers. 1971: The Seven Minutes. 1974: Shadow of Fear (TV). Scream of the Wolf (TV). Hard Day at Blue Nose. 1976: Fighting Mad. 1979: Monster.

CARLSON, Richard 1912–1977
Quiet, soft-spoken American leading man who came to Hollywood as a writer, but found himself the juvenile lead in a fistful of films before war service. He failed to regain the same footing from 1947, but looked brainy enough to play the scientist hero of several interesting science-fiction films, having a hand in the writing and direction of some of these, and others. Died from a cerebral haemorrhage.

1935: *Desert Death. 1938: The Young in Heart. Duke of West Point. Little Accident. Dancing Co-Ed (GB: Every Other Inch a Lady). These Glamour Girls. Winter Carnival. 1940: Beyond Tomorrow. Too Many Girls. The Ghost Breakers. No, No, Nanette. The Howards of Virginia (GB: The Tree of Liberty). 1941: West Point Widow. The Little Foxes. Back Street. Hold That Ghost! 1942: My Heart Belongs to Daddy. The Silver Spoon. Fly By Night (GB: Secret of G-32). White Cargo. Highways by Night. The Affairs of Martha (GB: Once Upon a Thursday). The Magnificent Ambersons. 1943: Presenting Lily Mars. Young Ideas. A Stranger in Town. The Man from Down Under. *Suckerbait. 1947: So Well Remembered. 1948: Behind Locked Doors. 1950: Try and Get Me (GB: The Sound of Fury). King Solomon's Mines. 1951: The Blue

Veil. Valentino. A Millionaire for Christy. 1952: Whispering Smith Hits London (US: Whispering Smith versus Scotland Yard). Retreat Hell! 1953: The Magnetic Monster. The Maze. Flat Top (GB: Eagles of the Fleet). All I Desire. Seminole. Riders to the Stars. It Came from Outer Space. 1954: The Creature from the Black Lagoon. 1955: The Last Command. Bengazi. An Annapolis Story (GB: The Blue and the Gold. Narrator only). 1956: Three for Jamie Dawn. 1957: The Helen Morgan Story (GB: Both Ends of the Candle). 1959: Della (TV). 1960: Tormented. 1965: Kid Rodelo. 1966: The Doomsday Flight. 1967: The Power. 1969: The Valley of Gwangi. Change of Habit.

As director: 1953: Riders to the Stars. 1954: Four Guns to the Border. 1958: Appointment with a Shadow (GB: The Big Story). The Saga of Hemp Brown. 1965: Kid Rodelo.

CARLYLE, Robert 1961–
Slightly-built, wiry, dark-haired, narrow-faced, forceful and decisive Scottish actor who only enrolled in acting classes in his early twenties, but 10 years later had founded his own Glasgow theatre company. From the early 1990s he began to make inroads into TV and films. But it was in contrasting roles – an uncharacteristically gentle role as village policeman Hamish Macbeth in the TV series of that title, and the psychopathically violent Begbie in Trainspotting – that he broke through to the top. A worldwide hit with The Full Monty enabled him to pick and choose his projects and he continued in roles as uncultured men of unpredictable and dangerous behaviour.

1990: Silent Scream. Riff-Raff. 1993: Being Human. 1994: Safe. Priest. 1995: Go Now. 1996: Trainspotting. Carla's Song. 1997: The Full Monty. Face. 1999: Ravenous. Plunkett & Macleane. The World is Not Enough. Angela's Ashes. 2000: The Beach. There's Only One Jimmy Grimble.

CARMICHAEL, Ian 1920–
Fair-haired British light comedy actor of the 'I say, old chap' school who was an enormous success in the fifties as the quintessential dithering blunderer, a character once described as 'the muddle-headed pawn in life's game of chess'. Found new fame in the seventies on television as the gentleman sleuth Lord Peter Wimsey, and as P.G. Wodehouse's Bertie Wooster.

1948: Bond Street. 1949: Trottie True (US:

Gay Lady). Dear Mr Prohack. 1952: Time Gentlemen Please! Ghost Ship. Miss Robin Hood. 1953: Meet Mr Lucifer. 1954: The Colditz Story. Betrayed. 1955: Storm over the Nile. Simon and Laura. Private's Progress. 1956: The Big Money. Brothers in Law. 1957: Lucky Jim. Happy is the Bride! 1959: Left, Right and Centre. I'm All Right, Jack. School for Scoundrels. 1960: Light Up the Sky. 1961: Double Bunk. 1962: The Amorous Prawn. 1963: Heavens Above! Hide and Seek. 1964: The Case of the 44s. 1967: Smashing Time. 1971: The Magnificent Seven Deadly Sins. 1973: From Beyond the Grave. 1979: The Lady Vanishes. 1989: Diamond Skulls (US: Dark Obession). 1994: The Great Kandinsky (TV).

CAROL, Martine
(Marie-Louise de Mourer) 1921–1967
Blonde, voluptuous, full-lipped French actress with a mature, Dresden shepherdess-type face. She became the first French post-war sex symbol, and millions flocked to see her as a series of courtesans in films that included *Nana* and the *Caroline Chérie* series. She made one or two international films, but her best roles were behind her when she died from a heart attack at 45. At one time married to director Christian-Jacque, who made several of her most successful films.
1941: Le dernier des six. 1942: Les inconnus dans la maison. 1943: La ferme aux loups. 1945: Bifur III. L'extravagante mission. Trente et quarante. 1946: Voyage surprise. En êtes-vous bien sûr? 1947: La fleur de l'age. Miroir. L'île aux enfants perdus. 1948: Les amants de Vérone. Je n'aime que toi. Les souvenirs ne sont pas à vendre. 1949: Une nuit de noces. Méfiez-vous des blondes. 1950: Caroline Chérie. Nous irons à Paris. 1951: El Deseo y el Amor. 1952:

*Adorables créatures. Une nuit avec Caroline. Les belles de nuit. Lucrezia Borgia. 1953: Un caprice de Caroline Chérie. Destinées (GB: Love, Soldiers and Women. US: Daughters of Destiny). La spiaggia (GB and US: The Beach). 1954: Secrets d'alcove/The Bed. Il letto della Pompadour. Madame DuBarry. 1955: Nana. Lola Montès. 1956: Scandale à Milan/
Defendo il mio amore. The Diary of Major Thompson (US: The French They Are a Funny Race). Around the World in 80 Days. 1957: Nathalie. Action of the Tiger. Au bord du volcan. Nathalie, agent secret (GB: The Foxiest Girl in Paris). 1958: Les noces Venetiennes/La prima notte. Le passager clandéstin (GB: The Stowaway). Ten Seconds to Hell. 1959: Austerlitz (GB: The Battle of Austerlitz). 1960: Love and the Frenchwoman. Operation Gold Ingot. 1961: Le cave se rebiffe (GB: Counterfeiters of Paris. US: The Sucker Strikes Back). Vanina vanini. Un soir sur la plage. En plein cirage. Rape of the Sabines (US: Romulus and the Sabines). 1962: I Don Giovanni della Costa Azzurra (US: Beach Casanova). 1963: Hell is Empty (released 1967).*

CARON, Leslie 1931–
Immensely appealing brunette French gamine, mainly in Hollywood, who could carry a musical with her elegant dancing, or touch the heartstrings in the fifties when, mostly at M-G-M, she produced several performances of tremendous charm. Received Oscar nominations for *Lili* and *The L-Shaped Room*.
1951: An American in Paris. The Man with a Cloak. 1952: Glory Alley. Lili. 1953: The Story of Three Loves. 1954: The Glass Slipper. 1955: Daddy Long Legs. 1956: Gaby. 1958: Gigi. 1959: The Doctor's Dilemma. The Man Who Understood Women. Austerlitz (GB: The Battle of Austerlitz). 1960: The Subterraneans. 1961: Fanny. 1962: Guns of Darkness. The L-Shaped Room. Les quatres vérités (GB: Three Fables of Love). 1964: Father Goose. 1965: A Very Special Favor. Promise Her Anything. Is Paris Burning? 1967: Il padre di famiglia (US: Head of the Family). 1970: Madron. 1971: Chandler. 1972: Purple Night. 1974: QB VII (TV). 1975: James Dean – the First American Teenager. 1976: Sérail. 1977: Valentino. L'homme qui aiment les femmes. 1979: Goldengirl. Tous vedettes. 1980: Kontrakt. 1981: Chanel solitaire. 1982: The Imperative. Die Unerreichbare (TV). 1985: La diagonale du fou (US: Dangerous Moves). Reel Horror.

1987: The Sealed Train. 1989: Courage Mountain. Guerriers et captives. 1990: Blue notte/Dirty Night. 1992: Damage. 1995: Funny Bones. Let It Be Me. 1996: Danielle Steel's The Ring (TV). The Reef/Passioin's Way (TV). 1999: From Russia to Hollywood (doc). 2001: Chocolat.

CARPENTER, Paul
(Patrick P. Carpenter) 1921–1964
A former professional ice-hockey player, then popular band singer, Canadian-born Carpenter's acting career in British films hit fewer headlines than his riotous style of living until he suddenly broke from the ranks of supporting players to become the leading man of a rash of second-features in the fifties. But he regressed to small roles after 1960. Married (2nd) to actress Kim Parker from 1955 to 1958. Collapsed and died in his dressing-room while appearing in a play.
1946: This Man is Mine. School for Secrets (US: Secret Flight). 1948: Uneasy Terms. 1949: Landfall. 1953: Albert RN (US: Break to Freedom). The Weak and the Wicked. 1954: Face the Music (US: The Black Glove). Johnny on the Spot. Duel in the Jungle. The House Across the Lake (US: Heatwave). Mask of Dust (US: Race for Life). The Young Lovers (US: Chance Meeting). The Last Moment. Five Days. Diplomatic Passport. The Stranger Came Home. Night People. The Sea Shall Not Have Them. Shadow of a Man. The Red Dress. 1955: Double Jeopardy. Miss Tulip Stays the Night. One Jump Ahead. The Hornet's Nest. Dust and Gold. Doctor at Sea. The Diamond Expert. Stock Car. 1956: The Narrowing Circle. Women Without Men (US: Blonde Bait). Fire Maidens from Outer Space. Behind the Headlines. The Iron Petticoat. No Road Back. Reach for the Sky. 1957: Murder Reported. The Hypnotist (US: Scotland Yard Dragnet). Black Ice. Les espions. Undercover Girl. 1958: Action Stations. Intent to Kill. 1959: Jet Storm. 1960: The Big Arena (narrator only). Incident at Midnight. I Aim at the Stars. 1962: Dr Crippen. 1963: Panic. Call Me Bwana. Maigret voit rouge. 1964: The Beauty Jungle (US: Contest Girl). First Men in the Moon. Goldfinger.

CARRADINE, David
(John Carradine) 1936–
Tall, heavy-lidded, fair-haired, sulky-looking American actor, son of character star John Carradine (Richmond Carradine 1906–1988). In the 1960s he became best known for his

Gear. The Eliminator/Project: Eliminator. Future Zone. 1991: Dune Warriors. Evil Toons. Midnight Fear. Future Bound. Under the Gun. Omega Cop II. Capital Punishment. First Force. The Gambler Returns: The Luck of the Draw (TV). Deadly Surveillance. 1992: Field of Fire. Roadside Prophets. Double Trouble. Distant Justice. Kill Zone. Animal Instincts. Night Rhythms. Waxwork II: Lost in Time. Crazy Joe. 1993: Frontera Sur. Dragon Cop. The Eagle and the Horse. Karate Cop. 1994: Bitter End. 1996: The Defectors. 1997: The Rage/Plato's Run. Last Stand at Saber River (TV). Full Blast. Crossroads of Destiny/Jailbreak (TV). Lightspeed. 1998: The New Swiss Family Robinson (TV). Shepherd. Children of the Corn V: Fields of Terror. Knocking on Death's Door. 1999: The Puzzel in the Air. American Reel. Dangerous Curves. Zoo. Kiss of a Stranger. Natural Selection. 2000: The Warden (TV).

†And directed ‡Unreleased

CARRADINE, Keith 1949–
Light-haired, gaunt-looking American leading man with cynical smile, the son of John Carradine and younger half-brother of David Carradine (qv). Became early in his career associated with director Robert Altman, and consequently found himself in films that were critically better-received than those of his father and half-brother, if further away from the Hollywood mainline. Also a guitarist, composer and singer. Father of actress Martha Plimpton (1970–).
1970: A Gunfight. 1971: McCabe and Mrs Miller. Man on a String (TV). 1973: Hex. The Emperor of the North Pole (GB: Emperor of the North). Antoine et Sebastian. 1974: You and Me. Thieves Like Us. Idaho Transfer. Run Run Joe. The Godchild (TV). 1975: Nashville. Russian Roulette. 1976: Lumière. Welcome to LA. 1977: Pretty Baby. The Duellists. 1978: Old Boyfriends. Sergeant Pepper's Lonely Hearts Club Band. 1979: An Almost Perfect Affair (released 1983). 1980: The Long Riders. Carradines in Concert. 1981: Southern Comfort. 1984: Maria's Lovers. Choose Me. Scorned and Swindled (TV). 1985: Trouble in Mind. The Tigress. Blackout. 1986: A Winner Never Quits (TV). The Inquiry. 1987: Eye on the Sparrow (TV). The Moderns. Backfire. 1988: Stones for Ibarra (TV). Street of No Return. My Father, My Son (TV). 1989: War Zone. Cold Feet. The Forgotten (TV). The Revenge of Al Capone/Capone Behind Bars

'hippie' lifestyle, and a flagging career was twice saved by TV series – Shane in the mid 1960s, after which he played western villains, and, more recently, Kung Fu. He has since done well as the rakehell hero of way-out action films, but attempts to widen his appeal were not too successful and latterly his performances have been rather better than his films. Perhaps America's busiest actor from the mid 1980s to the early 1990s.
1965: Taggart. Too Many Thieves (TV. GB: cinemas). Bus Riley's Back in Town. 1967: The Violent Ones. Dr Terror's Gallery of Horrors. 1968: Heaven with a Gun. 1969: The Good Guys and the Bad Guys. Young Billy Young. The McMasters . . . Tougher than the West Itself! 1970: Macho Callahan. A Gunfight. Maybe I'll Come Home in the Spring (TV). 1971: McCabe and Mrs Miller. 1972: Boxcar Bertha. 1973: House of Dracula's Daughter. Mean Streets. The Long Goodbye. 1974: ‡Around. †You and Me. 1975: Death Race 2000. Long Way Home (TV). 1976: Cannonball (GB: Carquake). Bound for Glory. 1977: The Serpent's Egg. Gray Lady Down. Thunder and Lightning. 1978: The Silent Flute. Fast Charlie – the Moonbeam Rider. Deathsport 2000. Roger Corman – Hollywood's Wild Angel. 1979: The Perfect Merry-Go Round. ‡Kansas (A Country Mile). Cloud Dancer. Mr Horn (TV). Gauguin – the Savage. 1980: The Long Riders. Carradines in Concert. High Noon: Part II (TV). 1981: Rally (later Safari 3000). †Americana. 1982: 'Q' The Winged Serpent/'Q'/The Winged Serpent. The Bad Seed (TV). Trick or Treat. 1983: Lone Wolf McQuade. Jealousy (TV). 1984: A Distant Scream (TV. Released to US video as The Dying Truth). The Warrior and the Empress (Kain of Dark Planet). On the Line. 1985: Behind Enemy Lines/POW The Escape. 1986: Oceans of Fire (TV). Kung Fu The Movie (TV). The Jade Jungle (later Armed Response). 1987: Wheels of Terror/The Misfit Brigade. Marathon. Six Against the Rock (TV). 1988: Future Force. Warloads. Crime Zone. Animal Protector (later Fatal Secret). I Saw What You Did (TV). Nerds of a Feather. Night Children. Wizards of the Lost Kingdom II. 1989: Beauty and Denise/The Cover Girl and the Cop (TV). C.O.P.S. Sundown: The Vampire in Retreat. Tropical Snow (shot 1986). Back to the Past. Try This On for Size. Future Force II. Ministry of Vengeance. Nowhere to Run. 1990: Think Big (completed 1988). Bird on a Wire. The Secret of Fu Manchu. Sonny Boy. Martial Law. Battle

(TV). Confessional. 1990: Dr Grassler. Judgement (TV). The Bachelor. Daddy's Dyin' – Who's Got the Will? 1991: Crisscross. The Ballad of the Sad Café. Payoff. 1993: Bitter Blood (TV). 1994: André. Mrs Parker & the Vicious Circle. Is There Life Out There? (TV). 1995: Farewell to Paradise. The Tie That Binds. Wild Bill. 1996: Dead Man's Walk (TV). 2 Days in the Valley. Keeping the Promise (TV). Love is All There Is (completed 1994). 1997: A Thousand Acres. Last Stand at Saber River (TV). Prairie Fire. Fast Track (TV). Standoff (TV). The Hunter's Moon. 1998: Special Report: Journey to Mars (TV). 1999: The Virtuoso. Night Ride Home (TV). Out of the Cold. Sirens (TV). A Song from the Heart (TV). Hard Time: Hostage Hotel (TV). 2000: Enslavement.

CARRERA, Barbara 1951–
Tall, olive-complexioned, black-haired, dark-eyed, full-lipped Nicaraguan beauty with feline grace and predatory air, a highly successful model who gradually broke into films in decorative roles. She always seemed to be a must for a James Bond film, and indeed eventually played the luscious Fatima Blush in Never Say Never Again.
1970: Puzzle of a Downfall Child. 1975: The Master Gunfighter. Embryo. 1977: The Island of Dr Moreau. 1978: Centennial (TV). 1980: Masada (TV. GB: cinemas – abridged – as The Antagonists). When Time Ran Out . . . 1981: Condorman. I, the Jury. 1983: Never Say Never Again. Lone Wolf McQuade. 1981: Sins of the Past (TV). 1985: Wild Geese II. 1987: Burnin' Love (Love at Stake). Night School (later The Under-Achievers). 1988: Wicked Stepmother. 1989: The Favorite. The Ambulance. Lover Boy. Murder in Paradise (TV). 1991: A Woman's Secret. 1993: Spanish Rose (later In Too Deep/Point of Impact). 1994: Tryst. 1995: Oh No, Not Her! Night of the Archer. Sawbones. 1996: Love is All There Is. Russian Roulette. Ghost Ships of the Kalahari. 1998: Illusion Infinity. Waking Up Horton. 1999: Alec to the Rescue!

CARREY, Jim 1962–
Dark-haired, sharp-featured, wild-eyed, schoolboy-looking, supercharged, non-stop Canadian comedian with aggressive, on-the-edge style. He failed in his first bid to crack Hollywood, after success in a 1984 TV series, The Duck Factory, but, after another TV series (In Living Colour), he unexpectedly went from zero to hero when his Ace Ventura

Pet Detective proved a massive surprise box-office hit, paving the way for a megastar career that made him one of Hollywood's highest-paid actors inside two years. Married/divorced (2nd) actress Lauren Holly (qv).

1982: *Introducing Janet/Rubberface* (TV. GB: video). 1983: *Club Med/Copper Mountain: A Club Med Experience. All in Good Taste.* 1984: *Finders Keepers.* 1985: *Once Bitten.* 1986: *Peggy Sue Got Married.* 1988: *The Dead Pool. Earth Girls Are Easy.* 1989: *High Strung* (released 1994). *Pink Cadillac. Mickey Spillane's Murder Takes All* (TV). 1992: *Doing Time on Maple Drive* (TV). *The Itsy Bitsy Spider.* 1993: *Ace Ventura Pet Detective.* 1994: *The Mask. Dumb & Dumber.* 1995: *Batman Forever. Ace Ventura – When Nature Calls.* 1996: *The Cable Guy.* 1997: *Liar Liar. The Truman Show.* 1998: *Simon Birch* (and narrator). 1999: *Man on the Moon.* 2000: *Me, Myself & Irene. The Grinch.*

CARROLL, John
(Julian La Faye) 1905–1979
Brawny, handsome, moustachioed singer from New Orleans who led a colourful early life and stayed in Hollywood from the mid-thirties after an abortive first fling there. Carroll didn't make it as a musical star, despite a pleasant voice and personality, but enjoyed a goodish run as a rugged action hero. Married to actress Steffi Duna (1910–1992) from 1936 to 1940, his off-screen amours had the fan magazines buzzing and in 1956 *Confidential* finally, inevitably, 'told all'. Died from leukaemia.
1929: *Devil-May-Care. Hearts in Exile. Marianne.* 1930: *Rogue Song. Doughboys.*

New Moon. Monte Carlo. Reaching for the Moon. 1935: *Go into Your Dance. Hi. Gaucho.* 1936: *Muss 'Em Up* (GB: *House of Fate*). *The Accusing Finger. Murder on the Bridal Path.* 1937: *Zorro Rides Again* (serial). *Death in the Air* (GB: *Murder in the Air*). *Swingtime in the Movies. We Who Are About to Die.* 1938: *Rose of the Rio Grande. I Am a Criminal.* 1939: *Only Angels Have Wings. Wolf Call.* 1940: *Congo Maisie. Phantom Raiders. Susan and God* (GB: *The Gay Mrs Trexel*). *Hired Wife. Go West.* 1941: *This Woman is Mine. Sunny. Lady Be Good.* 1942: *Rio Rita. Pierre of the Plains. Flying Tigers.* 1943: *The Youngest Profession. Hit Parade of 1943.* 1945: *Bedside Manner. A Letter for Evie.* 1947: *Fiesta. Wyoming. The Fabulous Texan. The Flame.* 1948: *I, Jane Doe* (GB: *Diary of a Bride*). *Old Los Angeles. Angel in Exile.* 1950: *The Avengers. Surrender. Hit Parade of 1951.* 1951: *Belle Le Grand.* 1953: *The Farmer Takes a Wife. Geraldine.* 1955: *The Reluctant Bride* (US: *Two Grooms for a Bride*). 1957: *Decision at Sundown.* 1958: *The Plunderers of Painted Flats. Zorro Rides Again.*

CARROLL, Madeleine
(Marie-Madeleine O'Carroll) 1906–1987
Exquisite English blonde actress with glazed china face. Her enormous popularity in British films inevitably led to an exit for Hollywood, but her films there included too few worthy of her beauty and talents. Best remembered as the handcuffed lady in *The 39 Steps* (Hitchcock version), her four marriages included one to actor Sterling Hayden, from 1942 to 1946.
1927: *The Guns of Loos.* 1928: *What Money Can Buy. The First Born. Instinct. *Gaumont Mirror No.82.* 1929: *The Crooked Billet. The American Prisoner. Atlantic.* 1930: *The 'W' Plan. Young Woodley. French Leave. Escape. The School for Scandal. Kissing Cup's Race.* 1931: *Madame Guillotine. Fascination. The Written Law.* 1933: *Sleeping Car. I Was a Spy. *Peace or War?* 1934: *The World Moves On.* 1935: *The Dictator* (US: *Loves of a Dictator*). *The 39 Steps.* 1936: *Secret Agent. *The Story of Papworth. The Case Against Mrs Ames. The General Died at Dawn. Lloyd's of London.* 1937: *On the Avenue. It's All Yours. The Prisoner of Zenda.* 1938: *Blockade.* 1939: *Café Society. Honeymoon in Bali* (GB: *Husbands or Lovers*). *My Son, My Son.* 1940: *Safari. North West Mounted Police.* 1941: *Virginia. One Night In Lisbon. Bahama Passage.* 1942: *My Favorite Blonde.* 1946:

La petite république. 1947: *White Cradle Inn* (US: *High Fury*). 1948: *An Innocent Affair* (later *Don't Trust Your Husband*). 1949: *The Fan* (GB: *Lady Windermere's Fan*).

CARROLL, Nancy
(Ann La Hiff) 1904–1965
Petite, pert, blue-eyed redhead who looked a little like Clara Bow, sang in a tinkly, happy voice and became one of the sound era's first big stars. In recent years, she has built up a cult following. Was discovered dead kneeling in front of her television set. An autopsy yielded no explanation and a verdict of 'natural causes' was returned. Received an Oscar nomination for *The Devil's Holiday*.
1927: *Ladies Must Dress.* 1928: *Abie's Irish Rose. Easy Come, Easy Go. Chicken à la King. The Water Hole. Manhattan Cocktail.* 1929: *The Shopworn Angel. The Wolf of Wall Street. Sin Sister. Close Harmony. The Dance of Life. Illusion. Sweetie.* 1930: *Dangerous Paradise. Paramount on Parade. Follow Thru. The Devil's Holiday. Honey. Laughter. Two Against Death.* 1931: *Stolen Heaven. The Night Angel. Revolt. Personal Maid.* 1932: *Broken Lullaby* (GB: *The Man I Killed*). *Wayward. Scarlet Dawn. Hot Saturday. Undercover Man.* 1933: *Child of Manhattan. The Woman Accused. The Kiss Before the Mirror. I Love That Man.* 1934: *Springtime for Henry. Transatlantic Merry-Go Round. Jealousy. Broken Melody.* 1935: *I'll Love You Always. After the Dance. Atlantic Adventure.* 1938: *There Goes My Heart. That Certain Age.*

CARSON, Jack 1910–1963
Beefy, bulldozing, Canadian-born Hollywood character star, in residence at Warners from 1941 to 1950, often as comedy relief in musicals, or the guy who doesn't get the girl. Elmer was Carson's middle name, and it suited his speciality: happy-go-lucky Joes without too much brain. He made a couple of very funny comedies as star towards the end of the forties, and surprised many by revealing subtler dramatic talents in the fifties. Married four times, once (1952–1958) to actress Lola Albright. Died from stomach cancer.
1935: *Knife No.5. Circle of Death.* 1937: *A Rented Riot. Stage Door. You Only Live Once. Stand-In. It Could Happen to You. Reported Missing. Too Many Wives. On Again, Off Again. †A Damsel in Distress. High Flyers. Music for Madame. The Toast of New York.* 1938: *The Saint in New York. Vivacious Lady.*

Carefree. This Marriage Business. The Girl Downstairs. Condemned Women. Go Chase Yourself. Crashing Hollywood. Law of the Underworld. Everybody's Doing It. Night Spot. Having Wonderful Time. Maid's Night Out. Quick Money. She's Got Everything. Bringing Up Baby. Mr Doodle Kicks Off. 1939: Destry Rides Again. Fifth Avenue Girl. The Kid from Texas. The Escape. The Honeymoon's Over. Mr Smith Goes to Washington. Legion of Lost Flyers. 1940: I Take This Woman. The Girl in 313. Shooting High. Sandy Gets Her Man. Alias the Deacon. Enemy Agent (GB: Secret Enemy). Queen of the Mob. Typhoon. Love Thy Neighbor. Parole Fixer. Lucky Partners. Young As You Feel. I Take This Woman. 1941: Mr and Mrs Smith. Love Crazy. The Strawberry Blonde. The Bride Came COD. Blues in the Night. Navy Blues. 1942: Larceny Inc. Wings for the Eagle. Gentleman Jim. The Hard Way. The Male Animal. 1943: Thank Your Lucky Stars. Princess O'Rourke. Arsenic and Old Lace. 1944: Shine on Harvest Moon. The Doughgirls. Hollywood Canteen. *The Shining Future. Make Your Own Bed. *Road to Victory. 1945: Roughly Speaking. Mildred Pierce. 1946: The Time, the Place and the Girl. One More Tomorrow. Two Guys from Milwaukee (GB: Royal Flush). 1947: Love and Learn. *So You Want to be in Pictures. 1948: Always Together. Two Guys from Texas (GB: Two Texas Knights). Romance on the High Seas (GB: It's Magic). April Showers. 1949: John Loves Mary. My Dream is Yours. It's a Great Feeling. *Rough But Hopeful. 1950: *Hollywood Goes to Bat. Bright Leaf. The Good Humor Man. 1951: The Groom Wore Spurs. Rhubarb. *Hollywood's Pair of Jacks. Mr Universe. 1953: Dangerous When Wet. *Hollywood Goes to Bat. 1954: A Star is Born. Red Garters. Phfffl! *Hollywood Cowboy Stars. 1955: Ain't Misbehavin'. 1956: Magnificent Roughnecks. Bottom of the Bottle (GB: Beyond the River). 1957: The Tattered Dress. Three Men on a Horse (TV). The Tarnished Angels. 1958: Rally 'Round the Flag, Boys! Cat on a Hot Tin Roof. The Long March (TV). 1960: The Bramble Bush. 1961: King of the Roaring Twenties (GB: The Big Bankroll). 1962: Sammy the Way-Out Seal (TV. GB: cinemas).

†Scenes deleted from final release print

CARSON, Jeannie
(Jean Shufflebottom) 1928–
Vivacious red-headed British star, of Scottish parentage, from musicals and revues on stage,

where she made a tremendous hit at only 21 in a show called Love from Judy. British films could never find the right vehicle for her, and she now lives in America with her husband, actor Biff McGuire.
1948: †A Date with a Dream. 1953: †Love in Pawn. 1955: †As Long As They're Happy. †An Alligator Named Daisy. 1958: Rockets Galore (US: Mad Little Island). 1962: Seven Keys.

†As Jean Carson

CARSON, John (J. Carson-Parker) 1927–
Velvet-voiced (aurally a dead ringer for James Mason), suave, dark-haired, Ceylon-born actor who played silky-smooth villains in the 1960s, but has for many years been lost to voice-overs for television commercials. Raised in Ceylon (now Sri Lanka), Oxford University and New Zealand, where he acted until 1955, he now lives in South Africa. Married to actress Luanshya Greer, he has six children.
1955: The Adventures of Quentin Durward (US: Quentin Durward). 1956: Ramsbottom Rides Again. 1958: Intent to Kill. The Lady is a Square. 1959: Beyond This Place (US: Web of Evidence). 1960: Identity Unknown. 1962: Guns of Darkness. Seven Keys. Locker 69. The Set-Up. 1963: Master Spy. Accidental Death. 1964: Act of Murder. Smokescreen. 1965: The Plague of the Zombies. The Night Caller (US: Blood Beast from Outer Space). 1967: Thunderbird 6 (voice only). 1968: The Last Shot You Hear. 1970: The Man Who Haunted Himself. Taste the Blood of Dracula. 1972: Captain Kronos – Vampire Hunter. 1983: City of Blood. 1988: An African Dream. 1989: The Last Warrior. 1990: The Light in the Jungle/Schweitzer. 1991: Au Pair.

1993: Woman of Desire. 1997: Mandela and de Klerk (TV). 1998: Operation Delta Force II: Mayday.

CARTER, Janis (J. Dremann) 1913–1994
Personable, fair-haired American leading lady with bright, cheery smile and attractive personality. Originally a singer in light opera, she enlivened a number of Hollywood second-features in the 1940s, playing good girls and bad girls with equal facility. But she seemed to lack the driving force to move on to bigger things, and retired early after a successful second marriage. Died from a heart attack.
1941: Cadet Girl. 1942: Secret Agent of Japan. Who is Hope Schuyler? Just off Broadway. I Married an Angel. Girl Trouble. Thunder Birds. That Other Woman. 1943: Swing Out the Blues. Lady of Burlesque. The Ghost That Walks Alone. 1944: Girl in the Case (GB: The Silver Key). The Missing Juror. One Mysterious Night. The Mark of the Whistler (GB: The Marked Man). 1945: The Fighting Guardsman. One Way to Love. Power of the Whistler. 1946: Night Editor (GB: The Trespasser). The Notorious Lone Wolf. 1947: I Love Trouble. Framed (GB: Paula). 1949: Miss Grant Takes Richmond (GB: Innocence Is Bliss). Slightly French. And Baby Makes Three. I Married a Communist (GB: The Woman on Pier 13). 1950: A Woman of Distinction. Her Wonderful Lie. 1951: My Forbidden Past. Flying Leathernecks. Santé Fé. 1952: The Half Breed. 1954: Second Face (GB: Double Profile).

CARUSO, David 1956–
Intense, mannered, baby-faced, red-haired American actor, always a supporting player in films (although in quite prominent roles) until stratospheric success in the TV series NYPD Blue in the early 1990s catapulted him into the public eye and on to a thousand magazine covers. Playing with a depth he hadn't been able to show before, Caruso quit the show after a season and a bit, and came to Hollywood a star. His first two top-billed films after that, however, proved disappointing and Caruso's career slid back into television.
1980: Without Warning/Alien Warning. 1981: Crazy Times (TV). An Officer and a Gentleman. 1982: First Blood. 1984: Thief of Hearts. 1986: Crime Story (TV). Blue City. 1987: China Girl. Into the Homeland (TV). 1988: Twins. 1989: King of New York. 1990: Parker

Kane (TV). Rainbow Drive. 1991: Hudson Hawk. Mission of the Shark (TV). 1992: Mad Dog and Glory. 1994: Kiss of Death. 1995: Jade. 1997: Cold Around the Heart. Body Count. Elmore Leonard's Gold Coast (TV). 2000: Deadlocked (TV). 2001: Proof of Life.

CASSAVETES, John 1929–1989

Spare, dark, lean-and-hungry-looking American actor who largely escaped the gangster roles for which his Italianate features seemed to destine him. Also a director of critical acclaim, although his films' public appeal remained limited. His biggest popular success was a TV series, *Johnny Staccato*. He married actress Gena Rowlands (*qv*), subsequent star of many of his films. Oscar-nominated for *The Dirty Dozen*, he died at 59 from complications arising from cirrhosis of the liver.

1951: †Fourteen Hours. 1953: Taxi. 1955: The Night Holds Terror. 1956: Crime in the Streets. 1957: Edge of the City (GB: A Man is 10 Feet Tall). Affair in Havana. 1958: Saddle the Wind. Virgin Island/Our Virgin Island. 1959: Shadows. 1962: The Webster Boy. 1964: The Killers. 1967: The Dirty Dozen. The Devil's Angels. 1968: Rosemary's Baby. Gli intoccabili (GB and US: Machine Gun McCain). Roma coma Chicago (GB: The Violent Four. US: Bandits in Rome). 1969: If It's Tuesday, This Must Be Belgium. 1970: Husbands. 1971: Minnie and Moskowitz. 1975: Capone. 1976: Two-Minute Warning. Mikey and Nicky. 1977: Opening Night. 1978: The Fury. Brass Target. 1979: Flesh and Blood (TV). 1981: Incubus. Whose Life Is It Anyway? 1982: Tempest. 1983: Marvin and Tige. Love Streams. 1984: Like Father and Son. I'm Almost Not Crazy . . .

1993: *Haircut.

As director: *1959: Shadows. 1961: Too Late Blues. 1962: A Child is Waiting. 1968: Faces. 1970: Husbands. 1971: Minnie and Moskowitz. 1974: A Woman Under the Influence. 1976: The Killing of a Chinese Bookie. 1977: Opening Night. 1980: Gloria. 1983: Love Streams. 1986: Big Trouble.*

†*Scene deleted from final release print*

CASSEL, Jean-Pierre

(J.-P. Crochon) 1932–

Tall, sandy-haired, wry-faced French leading man who began as a dancer, and kick-started his film career in a Hollywood movie partly shot in his native Paris. His Gallic good looks faded rather early, but he remained in demand for character roles in both continental and international films until the early 1980s. In style and looks, something of a throwback to the melancholy heroes of the French cinema of the 1930s. Father of actor Vincent Cassel (*qv*).

1950: Pigalle-Saint-Germain-des-Près. 1953: La route du bonheur. 1956: The Happy Road. 1957: A pied, à cheval et en voiture. La peau de l'ours. *Les surmènes. 1958: Le desordre et la nuit. En cas de malheur. Et ta soeur? 1959: Sacrée jeunesse. La marraine de Charley. Les jeux de l'amour (US: The Love Game). 1960: Le farceur (US: The Joker). Candide. 1961: L'amant de cinq jours (US: The Five-Day Lover). Les sept péchés capitaux (GB: The Seven Deadly Sins. US: Seven Capital Sins). La Gamberge. Napoléon II: l'aiglon. 1962: Le caporal epinglé (GB: The Vanishing Corporal. US: The Elusive Corporal). Arsène Lupin contre Arsène Lupin. Cyrano et d'Artagnan. 1963: Nunca pasa nada. Les plus belles escroqueries du monde. *Cabrioles (narrator only). 1964: Alta infidaltà (GB and US: High Infidelity). Un monsieur de compagnie (US: Male Companion). La ronde. 1965: Those Magnificent Men in Their Flying Machines. Les fêtes galantes. Is Paris Burning? 1966: Jeu de massacre (GB: Comic Strip Hero. US: The Killing Game). La dolci signore. 1968: L'ours et la poupée. 1969: Oh! What A Lovely War. L'armée des ombres. 1970: La rupture. 1971: Le bâteau sur l'herbe. Malpertuis. 1972: Baxter! (US: The Boy). Le charme discret de la bourgeoisie (GB and US: The Discreet Charm of the Bourgeoisie). 1973: Il magnate. The Three Musketeers: The Queen's Diamonds. 1974: Le mouton enragé (GB and US: The French Way). Murder on the Orient Express.

The Four Musketeers: The Revenge of Milady. 1975: Docteur Françoise Gailland (US: No Time for Breakfast). That Lucky Touch. 1976: Folies bourgeoises/The Twist. 1978: Les rendez-vous d'Anna. Who is Killing The Great Chefs of Europe? (GB: Too Many Chefs). 1979: Da Dunkerque alla vittoria (US: From Hell to Victory). Superman II. 1980: Alice. Le soleil en face. 1981: La guerillera. La vie continue. 1985: Tranches de la vie. 1986: A Matter Of Convenience (TV). Liberty (TV). 1987: Secret of the Sahara. Casanova (TV). Una moglie. 1988: Chouans! Migrations. Mangeclous. 1989: The Return of the Musketeers. Desperately Julia. Vado a riprendermi il gatto. 1990: Mister Frost. Vincent and Theo. The Fatal Image (TV). 1991: The Maid. The Favour, the Watch and the Very Big Fish. Amor y Deditos del Pie. 1992: Notorious (TV). 1993: Pétain. L'enfer. Metisse. 1994: Coupé shampooing. Casque bleu. Prêt-à-porter (US: Ready to Wear). 1995: Con rabbia e con amore. La cérémonie/A Judgement in Stone. 1996: Amores que matan. (US: Love Kills). Le president et la garde-barriere (TV). 1999: La plus beau pays du monde. La patinoire. 2000: Sade.

CASSEL, Vincent 1967–

Long-faced, horse-headed, nonchalant-looking French actor with dark curly hair and challenging gaze, the son of Jean-Pierre Cassel (*qv*). After studying acting in New York, he returned to France where most of his early career was spent in the theatre. However, the cinema has dominated his life since the mid-1990s, increasingly in international roles, often as abrasive characters and sometimes opposite his long-time girlfriend Monica Bellucci.

1989: Lis cigognes n'en font qu'à leur tête. 1991: Les clés du paradis. 1992: Amour et chocolat/Hot Chocolate. 1993: Métisée/Café au Lait. 1994: Ainsi soient-elles. 1995: Jefferson in Paris. Blood of the Hunter. Adultère, mode d'emploi. La haine. 1996: L'appartement. L'élève. Come mi vuoi (US: As You Want Me). 1997: Dobermann. 1998: Le plaisir (et ses petits tracas). Méditéranées. Elizabeth. 1999: Rembrandt. Guest House Paradiso. The Messenger: The Story of Joan of Arc (GB: Joan of Arc). Femmes enragées. 2000: Les rivières pourpres. Birthday Girl.

CASTLE, Don

(Marion Goodman Jr) 1919–1966

Slim, dark, often moustachioed American actor, a cross between Guy Madison and Don Ameche. His promising career – he was

Horde. *Air Cadet (GB: Jet Men of the Air).
Payment on Demand. 1952: Harem Girl.
Invasion USA. Wagons West. Cow Country.
1953: 99 River Street. Son of Belle Starr. I the
Jury. 1954: The Long Wait. Jesse James'
Women. The Yellow Tomahawk. The White
Orchid. Southwest Passage (GB: Camels
West). Overland Pacific. 1955: Tall Man
Riding. Target Zero. Finger Man. 1956:
Miracle in the Rain. Two Gun Lady.
Oklahoma Woman. Quincannon – Frontier
Scout (GB: Frontier Scout). The Counterfeit
Plan. 1957: Back from the Dead. Hell's
Crossroads. The Beginning of the End. 1958:
The Seven Hills of Rome. The Money.*

†*As Peggy Call*

considered a major star in the making – was
interrupted by war service and his roles
thereafter were confined to leading men in
small second-features. Later became a
producer, but was badly injured in a car
smash. Died from a drug overdose.
*1938: Love Finds Andy Hardy. Rich Man,
Poor Girl. Out West with the Hardys. 1939:
These Glamour Girls. Nick Carter – Master
Detective. Fast and Loose. 1940: The Ghost
Comes Home. I Take This Woman. Northwest
Passage. Susan and God (GB: The Gay Mrs
Trexel). You're the One. 1941: Power Dive.
World Premiere. 1942: Tombstone, the Town
Too Tough to Die. Wake Island. 1946:
Lighthouse. The Searching Wind. Born to
Speed. 1947: The Invisible Wall. Seven Were
Saved. Roses are Red. High Tide. The Guilty.
In Self Defense. 1948: Perilous Waters. I
Wouldn't Be in Your Shoes. Strike it Rich. Who
Killed 'Doc' Robbin? (GB: Sinister House).
1949: Stampede. 1950: Motor Patrol. 1956:
Gunfight at the OK Corral. 1957: The Big
Land (GB: Stampeded!).*

CATES, Phoebe (P. Katz) 1962–
Tallish, pretty, dark-haired, ingenuous-
looking American actress best remembered as
the wide-eyed leading lady in the *Gremlins*
films. The niece of director Gilbert Cates, she
was forced to give up ballet studies after a
knee injury and became a very successful
teenage model before embarking on a
decorative acting career. Refreshing in
ensemble pieces, she proved less than
dynamic when placed in a solo spotlight and
her career faded away in the 1990s. Married
to actor Kevin Kline (*qv*). 'Retired' in 1995.
*1982: Paradise. Fast Times at Ridgemont High
(GB: Fast Times). 1983: Private School. Baby
Sister (TV). 1984: Lace (TV). Gremlins.
1985: Lace II (TV). 1987: Date With an
Angel. 1988: Heartbreak Hotel. Shag. Bright
Lights, Big City. 1989: Heart of Dixie. 1990: I
Love You to Death. Largo Desolato (TV).
Gremlins 2 The New Batch. 1991: Drop Dead
Fred. 1993: Bodies, Rest & Motion. My Life's
in Turnaround. 1994: Princess Caraboo. 1997:
Scratch the Surface (doc).*

CATTRALL, Kim 1956–
Tall, tawny-haired, hazel-eyed, English-born
actress of fresh appeal and cool, calculating
gaze, easily able to sustain roles of characters
much younger than her real age. Brought up
in Canada, she has acted there on stage, as
well as in England and America. That partly
accounts for the sporadic quality of her career
in the cinema, where she has never quite
became a big name. But she had a solidly
successful TV series at the turn of the
century, opposite Sarah Jessica Parker (*qv*) in
Sex and the City.
1972: Deadly Harvest (TV). 1975: Rosebud.

*1977: Good Against Evil (TV). 1978: The
Other Side of the Mountain Part II. How to
Dial a Murder (TV). 1979: The Night Rider
(TV). Crossbar (TV). 1980: Tribute. The
Gossip Columnist (TV). 1981: Ticket to
Heaven. Porky's. 1984: Police Academy. City
Limits. Sins of the Past (TV). 1985: Turk 182!
1986: Holdup. Big Trouble in Little China.
1987: Mannequin. 1988: Masquerade.
Midnight Crossing. Palais Royale. Personal
Choice. 1989: The Return of the Musketeers.
Brown Bread Sandwiches / Good Night,
Michelangelo. 1990: Honeymoon Academy.
Smokescreen. The Bonfire of the Vanities. 1991:
Miracle in the Wilderness (TV). Star Trek VI:
The Undiscovered Country. 1992: Split
Second. Running Delilah (TV). S.I.S. 1993:
Feminine Touch. Double Suspicion / Double
Vision. Cyborg Agent. 1994: Two Golden Balls
(TV). Above Suspicion. Op Center / Tom
Clancy's Op Center (TV). (TV). 1995: Live
Nude Girls. Unforgettable. The Heidi
Chronicles (TV). 1996: Hysteria. Where Truth
Lies. Every Woman's Dream (TV). 1997:
Exception to the Rule. (TV). Robin Cook's
Invasion (TV). 1998: Revenant / Modern
Vampires. Peter Benchley's Creature (TV).
1999: Baby Geniuses. Blood from a Stone. 36
Hours to Die (TV).*

CASTLE, Peggie 1926–1973
Tall, sultry, green-eyed blonde actually
spotted by a talent scout while she was
lunching in a Beverly Hills restaurant. She
was usually somebody's 'woman' rather than
a girl-friend and her career was confined to
colourful co-features. After four years in a
TV western series, she left show business in
1962. Later developed an alcohol problem,
and died from cirrhosis of the liver.
*1947: †When a Girl's Beautiful. 1949: Mr
Belvedere Goes to College. 1950: Shakedown. I
Was a Shoplifter. Bright Victory (GB: Lights
Out). Woman in Hiding. Buccaneer's Girl. The
Prince Who Was a Thief. 1951: The Golden*

CAULFIELD, Joan
(Beatrice J. Caulfield) 1922–1991
Demurely pretty blonde American star, who
came to films via modelling. At her best being
winsomely sexy in light comedies, and,
seemingly not able to provide much depth to
more dramatic characterizations, she had
only a few years at the top. Died from cancer.
*1944: Miss Susie Slagle's (released 1946).
1945: Duffy's Tavern. 1946: Blue Skies.*

*Monsieur Beaucaire. 1947: Welcome Stranger.
Dear Ruth. Variety Girl. The Unsuspected.
1948: The Sainted Sisters. Larceny. 1949:
Dear Wife. 1950: The Petty Girl (GB: Girl of
the Year). 1951: The Lady Says No. 1955:
The Rains of Ranchipur. 1963: Cattle King
(GB: Guns of Wyoming). 1967: Red
Tomahawk. 1968: Buckskin. 1973: The
Magician (TV). 1975: The Hatfields and the
McCoys (TV). 1976: Pony Express Rider.
1977: The Daring Dobermans (TV). 1978:
The Space-Watch Murders (TV).*

CHAKIRIS, George 1933–

Smooth, dark-haired, sharp-featured, boyish
American musical star, first a boy singer, then
dancer in the chorus of fifties' musicals. An
Oscar for *West Side Story* skyrocketed his
career, but his acting proved not quite strong
enough in subsequent dramatic outings.
*1947: †Song of Love. 1951: †The Great
Caruso. 1953: †The 5,000 Fingers of Dr T.
†Give a Girl a Break. Gentlemen Prefer
Blondes. †Second Chance. 1954: White
Christmas. There's No Business Like Show
Business. Brigadoon. 1955: The Girl Rush.
1956: †Meet Me in Las Vegas (GB: Viva las
Vegas!). 1957: †Under Fire. 1961: The
Flower Drum Song. West Side Story. Two and
Two Make Six. 1962: Diamond Head. 1963:
Kings of the Sun. Bebo's Girl. 1964: The High
Bright Sun (US: McGuire, Go Home!). 633
Squadron. Flight from Ashiya. 1965: Is Paris
Burning? Le voleur de la Joconde. 1967: The
Young Girls of Rochefort. 1968: The Day the
Hot Line Got Hot. Sharon in Scarlet. 1969:
The Big Cube. 1979: Why Not Stay for
Breakfast? 1982: Jekyll and Hyde . . . Together
Again. 1991: Pale Blood.*

†As George Kerris

CHAMBERLAIN, Richard
(George R. Chamberlain) 1935–
Fair-haired, boyishly handsome American
actor who achieved immense success as
television's Dr Kildare in the sixties. His
early cinema roles proved too bland for public
taste but, after stage experience, he
established himself as a serious screen actor,
if not quite as a top star. Also sings.
*1960: The Secret of the Purple Reef. 1961: A
Thunder of Drums. 1963: Twilight of Honor
(GB: The Charge is Murder). 1965: Joy in the
Morning. 1968: Petulia. 1969: The Madwoman of Chaillot. 1970: Julius Caesar. The
Music Lovers. 1972: Lady Caroline Lamb.*

*1973: The Three Musketeers. The Woman I
Love (TV). 1974: F Scott Fitzgerald and 'The
Last of the Belles' (TV). The Count of Monte-
Cristo (TV. GB: cinemas). The Towering
Inferno. The Four Musketeers. 1976: The
Slipper and the Rose. The Man in the Iron
Mask (TV). 1977: The Last Wave. 1978: The
Swarm. 1980: Shogun (TV. GB: cinemas in
abbreviated version). 1981: Bells (later Murder
by Phone). 1983: Cook and Peary: The Race to
the Pole (TV). 1984: Wallenberg, the Lost
Hero (TV). 1985: King Solomon's Mines.
1986: Allan Quatermain and the Lost City of
Gold. 1987: Casanova (TV). 1989: The
Return of the Musketeers. 1991: Aftermath: A
Test of Love (TV. GB: The Other Side of
Murder). Night of the Hunter (TV). 1993:
The Grand Defence. Ordeal in the Arctic (TV).
1995: Bird of Prey. 1997: River Made to
Drown In. All the Winters That Have Been
(TV). 1999: The Pavilion.*

CHAMPION, Marge
(Marjorie Belcher) 1921–
Personable blonde American dancer with
lovely legs and a winning smile – not unlike
another musical star, Vera-Ellen (qv), in looks
– who briefly hit the big time in M-G-M
musicals with then-husband Gower. They
were married from 1947 to 1971, and Gower
(1919–1980) turned to directing on the
Broadway stage before dying from a rare
blood cancer. After the divorce, Marge
directed her attentions to choreography,
winning an Emmy for her work on a 1974 TV
movie *Queen of the Stardust Ballroom*. She
married director Boris Sagal, but he was
killed in an accident in 1981. Her son Gregg
has, like Gower, directed a couple of films.
Half-sister of child actress and silent star

Lina Basquette (Lena Baskette, 1907–1994).
A † in the filmography indicates a film in
partnership with Gower.
*1939: ‡The Story of Vernon and Irene Castle.
Sorority House (GB: The Girl From College).
‡Honor of the West. ‡Pinocchio (voice only).
1950: †Mr Music. 1951: †Show Boat. 1952:
†Lovely to Look At. †Everything I Have is
Yours. 1953: †Give a Girl a Break. 1954:
†Three for the Show. 1955: †Jupiter's Darling.
1967: The Swimmer. 1968: The Party. 1969:
The Cockeyed Cowboys of Calico Country
(GB: TV, as A Woman for Charlie).*

‡As Marjorie Bell

CHAN, Jackie (Chan Kwong-Sang) 1954–
Hong Kong-born star of action comedies
who, unlike Bruce Lee (qv), whom he
succeeded in the affections of eastern
audiences, had no instant success in the international market. After upbringing in Hong
Kong and Australia, Chan studied at the
Peking Opera School, where training in
martial arts, acrobatics and comic pantomime
led him to make stunt-filled, but light-
hearted kung-fu films, in which he did all his
own stuntwork, and was often injured in the
process. How-it-went-wrong outtakes are
featured at the end of most of his films. The
durable star had several unsuccessful
attempts at making hit films in Australia and
America, before finally cracking the US box
office with *Rush Hour*.
*1962: Huang tian ba. The World of Suzie
Wong. (And others as child player). 1971:
Little Tiger from Canton (unreleased). 1972:
Fist of Fury (US: The Chinese Connection).
1976: New Fist of Fury. Shaolin Wooden Men.
The Killer Meteors (unreleased). 1977: Snake
and Crane Arts of Shaolin. To Kill with
Intrigue. 1978: Half a Loaf of Kung Fu
(released 1980). Snake in the Eagle's Shadow.
Magnificent Bodyguards. Drunken Monkey in
the Tiger's Eyes/Drunken Master. Spiritual
Kung Fu. 1979: Dragon Fist. The Fearless
Hyena. 1980: The Big Brawl/Battle Creek
Brawl. The Young Master. The Cannonball
Run. 1982: Dragon Lord. Project A. 1983:
Cannonball Run II. Winners and Sinners. The
Fearless Hyena Part II. 1984: Wheels on
Meals. 1985: Heart of the Dragon/First
Mission. My Lucky Stars. Police Story. The
Protector. Twinkle, Twinkle, Lucky Stars.
1986: The Armour of God. 1987: Project A
Part II. 1988: †Police Story Part II. Dragons
Forever. 1989: †Mr Canton and Lady Rose.*

1990: †*Armour of God II: Operation Condor.*
1991: *Island on Fire. Twin Dragons.* 1992:
†*Police Story III: Supercop. Twin Dragons.*
1993: *Crime Story. Project S. City Hunter.*
1994: *Drunken Master II.* 1995: *First Strike.*
Rumble in the Bronx. Thunderbolt. 1996: *The*
Story of the CIA. Master with Crack Fingers.
1997: *Mr Nice Guy. An Alan Smithee Film –*
Burn, Hollywood, Burn. 1998: *Rush Hour.*
Who Am I? 1999: *Gorgeous.* 2000: *The*
Accidental Spy. Shanghai Noon.

†*And directed* ‡*And co-directed*

CHANDLER, Jeff (Ira Grossel) 1918–1961

Square-jawed hero of Hollywood action
yarns of the fifties, with prematurely grey
hair, fierce, scowling features and harsh,
aggressive voice. In early films was often cast
as American Indians – he made his name as
Cochise in three movies – or other dark-
skinned nationals. His death caused something of a scandal as it followed a routine
minor operation in which an artery was
severed. The official cause was blood poison-
ing. He was nominated for an Oscar in *Broken*
Arrow.
1947: *Johnny O'Clock. The Invisible Wall.*
Roses Are Red. 1949: *Mr Belvedere Goes to*
College. Abandoned. Sword in the Desert. 1950:
Deported. Double Crossbones (narrator only).
Two Flags West. Broken Arrow. 1951: *Bird of*
Paradise. Iron Man. Flame of Araby.
Smuggler's Island. Meet Danny Wilson. 1952:
Son of Ali Baba (narrator only). The Battle at
Apache Pass. The Red Ball Express. Yankee
Buccaneer. Because of You. 1953: *East of*
Sumatra. War Arrow. The Great Sioux
Uprising. 1954: *Taza, Son of Cochise.* *Queens*
of Beauty. Yankee Pasha. Sign of the Pagan.
1955: *Foxfire. Female on the Beach. The*
Spoilers. 1956: *Away All Boats. Pillars of the*
Sky (GB: The Tomahawk and the Cross).
The Nat King Cole Musical Story (and
narrator). 1957: *Drango. Toy Tiger. The*
Tattered Dress. Jeanne Eagels. Man in the
Shadow (GB: Pay the Devil). 1958: *The Lady*
Takes a Flyer. Raw Wind in Eden. Ten Seconds
to Hell. 1959: *Thunder in the Sun. Stranger in*
My Arms. The Jayhawkers. 1960: *A Story of*
David. The Plunderers. 1961: *Return to Peyton*
Place. 1962: *Merrill's Marauders.*

CHANEY, Lon
(Alonso Chaney) 1883–1930

American character star known as 'the man
with a thousand faces' because of the ingeni-

ous and sometimes painful make-up devices
with which he changed his appearance from
film to film. The child of deaf-and-dumb
parents, he became a master pantomimist,
bringing great pathos to such creations as
Fagin, Quasimodo and the Phantom of the
Opera. Died from throat cancer.
1913: *The Sea Urchin.* *Poor Jake's Demise.*
The Trap. *Almost an Actress.* *Back to Life.*
Red Margaret – Moonshiner. *Bloodhounds of*
the North. *The Lie.* 1914: *Remember Mary*
Magdalen. *The Honor of the Mounted.*
Discord and Harmony. *The Menace to*
Carlotta. *The Embezzler. The Lamb, the*
Woman and the Wolf. *The End of the Feud.*
The Tragedy of Whispering Creek. *The*
Unlawful Trade. *The Old Cobbler. The Small*
Town Girl. The Forbidden Room. *A Ranch*
Romance. *Her Grave Mistake.* *By the Sun's*
Ray. *A Miner's Romance. The Adventures of*
François Villon (serial). *Her Bounty.* *The*
Pipes of Pan. Richelieu. *Virtue Its Own*
Reward. *Her Life's Story.* *Lights and*
Shadows. *The Lion, the Lamb, the Man.* *A*
Night of Thrills. *Her Escape.* *The Sin of*
Olga Brandt. *The Star of the Sea.* 1915: *The*
Measure of a Man. *The Threads of Fate.*
When the Gods Played a Badger Game. *Such*
is Life. *Where the Forest Ends.* *All for Peggy.*
Outside the Gates. *The Desert Breed.* *Maid*
of the Mist. *The Girl of the Night.* *The Stool*
Pigeon. The Grind. *For Cash.* *Her Chance.*
An Idyll of the Hills. *The Stronger Mind.*
The Oyster Dredger. *The Violin Maker.*
Steady Company. *The Trust. Bound on the*
Wheel. *Mountain Justice.* *Quits.* *The*
Chimney's Secret. *The Pine's Revenge. The*
Fascination of Fleur de Lis. *Alas and Alack.*
A Mother's Atonement. *Lon of Lone*
Mountain. The Millionaire Paupers. Father
and the Boys. *Under a Shadow.* *Stronger*
Than Death. 1916: *Dolly's Scoop. The Grip of*
Jealousy. Tangled Hearts. The Gilded Spider.
Bobbie of the Ballet. Grasp of Greed. The Mark
of Cain. If My Country Should Call. Place
Beyond the Winds. *Felix on the Job. Accusing*
Evidence. The Price of Silence. The Piper's
Price (GB: Storm and Sunshine). 1917: *Hell*
Morgan's Girl. *The Mask of Love. The Girl in*
the Checkered Coat. The Flashlight. A Doll's
House. Vengeance of the West. The Rescue.
Fires of Rebellion. Pay Me. Triumph. The
Empty Gun. Bondage. Anything Once. The
Scarlet Car. 1918: *Broadway Love. The*
Kaiser, the Beast of Berlin. The Grand Passion.
Fast Company. A Broadway Scandal. Riddle
Gawne. That Devil, Bateese. The Talk of the

Town. Danger – Go Slow. 1919: *The Wicked*
Darling. False Faces. Paid in Advance. A
Man's Country. The Miracle Man. When
Bearcat Went Dry. Victory. 1920: *Daredevil*
Jack (serial). Treasure Island. The Gift
Supreme. Nomads of the North. The Penalty.
1921: *Outside the Law. For Those We Love.*
Bits of Life. Ace of Hearts. 1922: *The Trap*
(GB: Heart of a Wolf). Voices of the City.
Flesh and Blood. The Light in the Dark. Oliver
Twist. Shadows. Quincy Adams Sawyer. A
Blind Bargain. 1923: *All the Brothers Were*
Valiant. While Paris Sleeps. The Shock. The
Hunchback of Notre Dame. 1924: *The Next*
Corner. He Who Gets Slapped. 1925: *The*
Monster. The Unholy Three. The Phantom of
the Opera. The Tower of Lies. 1926: *The*
Blackbird. The Road to Mandalay. Tell It to
the Marines. 1927: *Mr Wu. The Unknown.*
Mockery. London after Midnight (GB: The
Hypnotist). 1928: *The Big City. Laugh,*
Clown, Laugh. While the City Sleeps. West of
Zanzibar. 1929: *Where East is East. Thunder.*
1930: *The Unholy Three (re-make).*
As director: 1915: *The Stool Pigeon.* *For*
Cash. *The Oyster Dredger.* *The Violin*
Maker. *The Trust.* *The Chimney's Secret.*

CHANEY, Lon Junior
(Creighton Chaney) 1905–1973

Big, ugly, dark-haired, hulking American
actor, the son of Lon Chaney. A star in horror
films, but a supporting player elsewhere, he
was always best as simple-minded brutes
unable to cope when dramatic events overtook them – whether they took the shape of
men turning into werewolves or worse, or, in
the best performance of his career, the
pitiable Lenny in *Of Mice and Men.* Died
from cancer. His son Lon Ralph Chaney was
killed in a car crash in 1992.
1931: †*The Galloping Ghost (12-part serial).*
1932: †*The Sign of the Cross.* †‡*Girl Crazy.*
†*Bird of Paradise.* †*The Last Frontier (serial).*
1933: †*Lucky Devils.* †*Scarlet River.* †*Son of*
the Border. †*The Three Musketeers (serial).*
1934: †*Girl o' My Dreams (GB: The Love*
Race). †*The Life of Vergie Winters.* †*Sixteen*
Fathoms Deep. 1935: ‡*Captain Hurricane.*
Accent on Youth. Hold 'Em Yale (GB: Uniform
Lovers). Shadow of Silk Lennox. The Marriage
Bargain (GB: Woman of Destiny). Scream in
the Night. 1936: *Rose Bowl (GB: O'Reilly's*
Luck). Undersea Kingdom (serial). The Singing
Cowboy. Killer at Large. The Old Corral (GB:
Texas Serenade). Ace Drummond (serial).
Rhythm on the Range. 1937: *Secret Agent X-9*

(serial). *Midnight Taxi. Angel's Holiday. Wild and Woolly. Wife, Doctor and Nurse. Cheyenne Rides Again. Love is News. Love and Hisses. The Lady Escapes. One Mile from Heaven. This is My Affair (GB: His Affair). City Girl. Second Honeymoon. That I May Live. Born Reckless. Thin Ice (GB: Lovely to Look At). Charlie Chan on Broadway. Slave Ship. Life Begins in College (GB: The Joy Parade). 1938: Mr Moto's Gamble. Straight, Place and Show (GB: They're Off). Walking Down Broadway. Alexander's Ragtime Band. Sally, Irene and Mary. Passport Husband. Road Demon. Submarine Patrol. Speed to Burn. Happy Landing. Josette. 1939: Jesse James. Union Pacific. Frontier Marshal. Charlie Chan in City of Darkness (GB: City of Darkness). Of Mice and Men. 1940: One Million BC (GB: Man and His Mate). Riders of Death Valley (serial). Northwest Mounted Police. 1941: Billy the Kid. San Antonio Rose. Too Many Blondes. Badlands of Dakota. The Wolf Man. Man Made Monster (GB: The Electric Man). 1942: The Ghost of Frankenstein. Overland Mail (serial). North to the Klondike. The Mummy's Tomb. *Keeping Fit. 1943: Frankenstein Meets the Wolf Man. Eyes of the Underworld. Son of Dracula. Frontier Badman. Crazy House. Calling Doctor Death. 1944: Follow the Boys. Ghost Catchers. Weird Woman. Cobra Woman. The Mummy's Ghost. Dead Man's Eyes. The Mummy's Curse. House of Frankenstein. 1945: Here Come the Co-Eds. The Frozen Ghost. House of Dracula. Pillow of Death. Strange Confession. The Daltons Ride Again. 1947: My Favorite Brunette. 1948: 16 Fathoms Deep (and 1934 film). Albuquerque (GB: Silver City). Abbott and Costello Meet Frankenstein (GB: Abbott and Costello Meet the Ghosts). The Counterfeiters. 1949: There's a Girl in My Heart. Captain China. 1950: Once a Thief. 1951: Inside Straight. Only the Valiant. Flame of Araby. Behave Yourself! Bride of the Gorilla. 1952: Thief of Damascus. The Battles of Chief Pontiac. Springfield Rifle. High Noon. The Black Castle. The Bushwhackers (GB: The Rebel). 1953: A Lion is in the Streets. Raiders of the Seven Seas. Casanova's Big Night. 1954: Jivaro (GB: Lost Treasure of the Amazon). Passion. The Boy from Oklahoma. The Big Chase. The Black Pirates. 1955: Big House USA. I Died a Thousand Times. Not As a Stranger. The Indian Fighter. The Silver Star. 1956: Pardners. Manfish (GB: Calypso). The Indestructible Man. Daniel Boone – Trail Blazer. The Black Sleep. 1957: Cyclops. 1958: Money, Women and Guns. The Defiant Ones. 1959: La casa del terror (US: Face of the Screaming Werewolf). The Alligator People. The Devil's Messenger. 1961: The Phantom. Rebellion in Cuba. 1963: The Haunted Palace. Law of the Lawless. 1964: Witchcraft. Stage to Thunder Rock. Young Fury. 1965: Black Spurs. House of the Black Death. Town Tamer. Apache Uprising. Cannibal Orgy (US: Spider Baby). 1966: Johnny Reno. The Vulture. Night of the Beast. Welcome to Hard Times (GB: Killer on a Horse). 1967: Hillybillys in a Haunted House. Dr Terror's Gallery of Horrors. 1968: Buckskin. 1969: The Female Bunch. Jungle Terror (US: Fireball Jungle). 1970: Blood of Frankenstein (US: Dracula versus Frankenstein). Satan's Sadists.*

†*As Creighton Chaney*
‡*Scenes deleted from final release print*

CHANNING, Stockard
(Susan Stockard) 1944–

It seemed that someone was always discovering this dark-haired, cheerful, chubby-cheeked American actress who rocked the critics in her first big movie role, holding her own against Jack Nicholson and Warren Beatty in *The Fortune*. In fact, the 'newcomer' was 30, having struggled for years to get Broadway breaks. Publicists kept her age a big secret for a while, especially when she played a high school queen in *Grease* at 33. Film audiences did not take to her as a star, which was the theatre's gain. Every now and again, though, she has reappeared in films, either in star roles or juicy cameos, and was cinematically busy in the mid-1990s. Four times married. Oscar nominee for *Six Degrees of Separation*.

1971: The Hospital. 1972: Up the Sandbox. 1973: The Girl Most Likely To . . . (TV). 1974: The Fortune. 1976: The Big Bus. Sweet Revenge/Dandy the All-American Girl. 1977: Lucan (TV). 1978: The Cheap Detective. Grease. 1979: The Fish That Saved Pittsburgh. Silent Victory: The Kitty O'Neil Story (TV). 1982: Safari 3000. 1983: Without a Trace. 1984: Table Settings (video). 1985: Not My Kid (TV). 1986: Heartburn. The Men's Club. 1987: A Time of Destiny. The Room Upstairs (TV). 1988: Tidy Endings (TV). 1989: The Perfect Witness (TV). Staying Together. 1991: Meet the Applegates. Married to It. 1992: Bitter Moon. 1994: David's Mother (TV). Six Degrees of Separation. 1995: Smoke. To Wong Foo. Thanks for Everything, Julie Newmar. 1996: Edie and Pen. Moll Flanders. The First Wives Club. Lily Dale (TV). 1997: Twilight. An Unexpected Family (TV). 1998: Lulu on the Bridge. Practical Magic. An Unexpected Life (TV). The Baby Dance (TV). 1999: The Venice Project. Other Voices. Isn't She Great? 2000: The Red Door. Where the Heart Is.

CHAPLIN, Ben 1973–

Tall, dark, soldily built British actor with wavy hair and a big, open, fresh-looking face. After much British television and minor film roles, Chaplin went to America and immediately looked like star material, appearing in a series of high-profile roles, establishing above-the-title credentials while still in his mid twenties. No relation to that *other* Chaplin family.

1991: A Fatal Inversion (TV). 1992: Bye, Bye, Baby (TV). 1993: The Remains of the Day. 1995: Feast of July. 1996: The Truth

About Cats & Dogs. 1997: Washington Square. 1998: The Thin Red Line. 1999: Lost Souls. 2000: Birthday Girl.

CHAPLIN, Sir Charles 1889–1977

British-born pantomimist with dark, curly hair who became the most popular comedian of Hollywood's silent era. His legendary character The Tramp, complete with bowler hat, cane, toothbrush moustache and splay-footed walk, triumphed with great ingenuity and sublime comic timing over life's pitfalls and a mountain of hulking villains. He became less popular after World War II, when his private life did not suit America's tastes, and his films were overtaken by pathos and autocracy. Given special Oscars in 1928 (specifically in connection with *The Circus*) and 1972, he won an Academy Award for his *Limelight* music in 1952. Married four times including (third) Paulette Goddard (*qv*) from 1936 to 1942. Knighted in 1975. Received an acting Oscar nomination for *The Great Dictator*. Father of actors Geraldine Chaplin (*qv*) and Sydney Chaplin (1926–).

1914: Making a Living. Kid Auto Races at Venice. Mabel's Strange Predicament. Between Showers. A Film Johnnie. Tango Tangles. His Favorite Pastime. Cruel, Cruel Love. The Star Boarder. Mabel at the Wheel. Twenty Minutes of Love. The Knockout. †Tillie's Punctured Romance. Caught in a Cabaret. Caught in the Rain. A Busy Day. The Fatal Mallet. Her Friend the Bandit. Mabel's Busy Day. Mabel's Married Life. Laughing Gas. The Property Man. The Face on the Bar-Room Floor. Recreation. The Masquerader. His New Profession. The Rounders. The New Janitor. Those Love Pangs. Dough and Dynamite. Gentlemen of Nerve. His Musical Career. His

*Trysting Place. Getting Acquainted. His Prehistoric Past. 1915: His New Job. A Night Out. The Champion. In the Park. A Jitney Elopement. The Tramp. By the Sea. His Regeneration. Work. A Woman. The Bank. Shanghaied. A Night in the Show. †Carmen/ Charlie Chaplin's Burlesque on Carmen. 1916: Police. The Floorwalker. The Fireman. The Vagabond. One A.M. The Count. The Pawn Shop. Behind the Screen. The Rink. 1917: Easy Street. The Cure. The Immigrant. The Adventurer. 1918: How to Make Movies. The Bond. A Dog's Life. Triple Trouble. †Shoulder Arms. Charles Chaplin in a Liberty Loan Appeal. 1919: Sunnyside. A Day's Pleasure. 1920: †The Kid. †The Mollycoddle. 1921: †The Nut. The Idle Class. 1922: Pay Day. Nice and Friendly. 1923: †The Pilgrim. †Souls for Sale. †A Woman of Paris. 1925: †The Gold Rush. 1926: †A Woman of the Sea. 1927: †The Circus. 1928: †Show People. †The Woman Disputed. 1931: †City Lights. 1933: *Hollywood on Parade No.17. 1936: †Modern Times. 1940: †The Great Dictator. 1947: Monsieur Verdoux. 1951: †Limelight. 1957: †A King in New York. 1966: †A Countess from Hong Kong.*

As narrator of compilation film: *1959: The Chaplin Revue.*

Chaplin directed (or co-directed) all the above except the first 13, plus His Regeneration, The Nut, Souls for Sale and Show People.

All shorts, except (†) features

CHAPLIN, Geraldine 1944–
Wan-faced, toothy, brunette American actress, oldest daughter of Charles Chaplin's fourth marriage. Most of her early performances are as pale as her complexion, and she has never been a power at the box office. But the seventies showed a stronger actress emerging, perhaps through her long personal and working association with the Spanish director Carlos Saura. They split up after 14 years, and she has lived with another Spanish director Paco Castillo, since 1980. Her acting, though, continues to show bite when given the chance.
*1951: Limelight. 1961: *Dernier soir. Par un beau matin d'été. 1965: Doctor Zhivago. Andremo in città. 1966: A Countess from Hong Kong. 1967: I Killed Rasputin. Stranger in the House (US: Cop-Out). Peppermint frappé. 1968: Stres es tres, tres. 1969: La Madriguera (US: The Honeycomb). 1970: El Jardin de las Delicias. The Hawaiians (GB: Master of the*

Islands). Sur un arbre perché. 1971: ZPG (GB: Zero Population Growth). 1972: Innocent Bystanders. La Casa sin Fronteras. 1973: Aña and the Wolves. The Three Musketeers: The Queen's Diamonds. Verflucht, dies Amerika. Y El Projimo? 1974: Le marriage à la mode. The Four Musketeers: The Revenge of Milady. Summer of Silence. 1975: Nashville. The Gentleman Tramp. Cria cuervos (GB: Raise Ravens. US: Cria!). 1976: Elisa, vida mia. Noroît. Buffalo Bill and the Indians. Scrim. Welcome to LA. 1977: Une page d'amour. Roseland. In Memoriam. 1978: The Masked Bride. Remember My Name. L'adoption. Savage Weekend. A Wedding. Los ojos vendados. Mais où et donc ornicar? 1979: Tout est à nous. Mama cumple cien años. La viuda de Montiel. Le voyage en douce. 1980: The Mirror Crack'd. 1981: Les uns at les autres (US: The Ins and the Outs/ Bolero). 1983: La vie est un roman (GB and US: Life is a Bed of Roses). 1984: L'amour par terre (GB: Love on the Ground). The Corsican Brothers (TV). 1985: Hidden Talent. 1987: White Mischief. The Moderns. 1989: The Return of the Musketeers. I Want to Go Home. 1990: The Children. Buster's Bedroom. Gentile Alouette. Duel of Hearts (TV). 1992: Chaplin. La vida lactea/ The Milky Way. Hors saison. 1993: A Foreign Field. The Age of Innocence. 1994: El arbol del Pariso. Words Upon the Window Pane. El canto de los pajaros. 1995: Home for the Holidays. Crimetime. 1996: Les yeux d'Asie. Jane Eyre. 1997: Mother Teresa: In the Name of God's Poor. The Odyssey. 1998: Cousin Bette. Finisterre (Where the World Ends). 1999: Beresina, oder die letzten Tage der Schweitz. Mary, Mother of Jesus (TV). To Walk with Lions. 2000: Y tu que harias por amor? (US: Just Run).

CHAPMAN, Marguerite 1918–1999
Marguerite was a treat in Technicolor. The blue-eyed brunette with the fabulous complexion remained queen of Columbia's double-feature output from 1942 until 1948. But subsequent roles wasted her warmth and latent sensuality and she spent most of the fifties in TV. Later lived in Hawaii, and was occasionally glimpsed in episodes of the television series *Hawaii Five-O.*
*1940: On Their Own. Charlie Chan at the Wax Museum. 1941: Navy Blues. A Girl, A Guy and a Gob (GB: The Navy Steps Out). *West of the Rockies. You're in the Army Now. The Body Disappears. 1942: Submarine Raider. Parachute Nurse. A Man's World. Spy*

Smasher (serial). The Spirit of Stanford. The Daring Young Man. 1943: Murder in Times Square. Appointment in Berlin. My Kingdom for a Cook. Destroyer. One Dangerous Night. 1944: Strange Affair. 1945: Counter Attack. Pardon My Past. One Way to Love. A Thousand and One Nights. 1946: The Walls Came Tumbling Down. 1947: Mr District Attorney. 1948: Relentless. Coroner Creek. The Gallant Blade. 1949: The Green Promise (GB: Raging Waters). 1950: Kansas Raiders. 1951: Flight to Mars. 1952: The Last Page (US: Man Bait). Sea Tiger. Bloodhounds of Broadway. 1955: The Seven Year Itch. 1960: The Amazing Transparent Man.

CHARISSE, Cyd (Tula Finklea) 1921–
Tall, stately, serious-looking American dancing star with lovely legs and a smoulder that only really caught fire in dancing scenes. An elegant, eye-catching partner for both Fred Astaire and Gene Kelly. Since 1948 has been married to second husband Tony Martin, with whom, glamorous as ever, she made night-club and television appearances into the 1990s.
*1941: *Rhumba Serenade. *Poème. *I Knew It Would Be This Way. *Did Anyone Call? 1942: †Something to Shout About. *This Love of Mine. Mission to Moscow. *Magic of Magnolias. 1943: Thousands Cheer. 1944: Ziegfeld Follies (released 1946). 1945: The Harvey Girls. 1946: Three Wise Fools. Till the Clouds Roll By. 1947: Fiesta. The Unfinished Dance. 1948: On an Island with You. Words and Music. The Kissing Bandit. 1949: Tension. East Side, West Side. 1951: Mark of the Renegade. 1952: The Wild North. Singin' In the Rain. 1953: Sombrero. The Band Wagon. Easy to Love. 1954: Deep in My Heart. Brigadoon. 1955: It's Always Fair Weather. 1956: Meet Me in Las Vegas (GB: Viva Las Vegas). 1957: Invitation to the Dance. Silk Stockings. 1958: Twilight for the Gods. Party Girl. 1960: Black Tights. 1961: Five Golden Hours. 1962: Something's Gotta Give (unfinished). Two Weeks in Another Town. 1963: Il segreto del vestito rosso (GB: Assassin ... Made in Italy. US: Assassination in Rome). 1966: The Silencers. Maroc 7. 1972: Call Her Mom (TV). 1975: Won Ton Ton – the Dog Who Saved Hollywood. 1978: Warlords of Atlantis. 1980: Portrait of an Escort (TV). 1989: Swimsuit (TV). Private Screenings. 1994: That's Entertainment! III.*

†As Lily Norwood

CHASE, Chevy (Cornelius Chase) 1943–
Moon-faced American satirist and comic actor with high forehead, dark hair and laconic smile (he looks like a benevolent Henry Silva). Broke into the public limelight with his abrasively aggressive style on a late-night TV satire show, *Saturday Night Live*, along with John Belushi, Dan Aykroyd (*both qv*) and others. Film stardom was longer in coming, but *Fletch* was a personal tour-de-force which established him at the top for a few years. His appeal has waned for film audiences in more recent times after a string of box-office misfires.
1974: The Groove Tube. 1976: Tunnelvision. 1978: Foul Play. 1980: Caddyshack. Oh Heavenly Dog. Seems Like Old Times. 1981: Modern Problems. Under the Rainbow. 1983: Deal of the Century. National Lampoon's Vacation. 1984: Fletch. 1985: National Lampoon's European Vacation. Sesame Street Presents: Follow That Bird. Spies Like Us. 1986: Three Amigos! 1987: Rolling in the Aisles. The Couch Trip. 1988: Funny Farm. Caddyshack II. 1989: Fletch Lives. National Lampoon's Christmas Vacation (GB: National Lampoon's Winter Holiday). 1990: Nothing But Trouble. 1991: L.A. Story. 1992: Memoirs of an Invisible Man. Hero (GB: Accidental Hero). 1993: Last Action Hero. 1994: Cops and Robbersons. 1995: Man of the House. 1997: Vegas Vacation. 1998: Dirty Work. 1999: Snow Day. 2000: Out of Order.

CHATTERTON, Ruth 1893–1961
Pretty, dark-haired American stage star (an immense hit in gamine roles of the 1920s) for whom film talkies came almost too late. She was a major star in them, but for only a few years. Returned to the stage in the late 1930s,

having been nominated for Academy Awards in *Madame X* and *Sarah and Son*. In her later years she became a modestly successful novelist. Married three times, the first two being film stars Ralph Forbes (1924–1932) and George Brent (1932–1934).
1928: Sins of the Fathers. 1929: The Doctor's Secret. The Dummy. Madame X. Charming Sinners. The Laughing Lady. 1930: Sarah and Son. Paramount on Parade. The Lady of Scandal (GB: The High Road). Anybody's Woman. The Right to Love. 1931: Unfaithful. The Magnificent Lie. Once a Lady. 1932: Tomorrow and Tomorrow. The Rich Are Always with Us. The Crash. 1933: Frisco Jenny. Lilly Turner. Female. 1934: Journal of a Crime. 1936: Lady of Secrets. Girls' Dormitory. Dodsworth. 1937: The Rat. 1938: A Royal Divorce.

CHEN, Joan (Chen Chung) 1961–
Slender Chinese actress of strong personality. Born into a family of doctors, Chen made a few films in her native Shanghai before moving to America in the early 1980s. Her career there, though varied, and often in leading roles, was never completely satisfactory, and she moved gradually towards producing and directing in the late 1990s. She's probably still best known for her running role as Josie Packard in the cult TV series *Twin Peaks*.
1977: Qingchun/Youth. 1980: Xiao hua/The Little Flower. 1981: Su xing (US: Awakening). 1984: Dim Sum: A Little Bit of Heart. 1985: †Year of the Dragon. 1986: Tai-Pan. 1987: The Last Emperor. The Night Stalker. 1988: Heartbeat/The Salute of the Jugger. 1989: Twin Peaks (TV). 1991: Strangers. Turtle Beach. Deadlock/Wedlock. 1992: Shadow of a Stranger (TV). Steel Justice (TV). 1993: Heaven & Earth. Golden Gate. You Seng/Temptation of a Monk. 1994: On Deadly Ground. Red Rose, White Rose. Hollywood Zen. Filthy Rich. The Hunted. 1995: Judge Dredd. The Wild Side (released 1999 as Wildside). 1996: Precious Find. 1999: Purple Storm. In a Class of His Own (TV). 2000: What's Cooking?

As director: 1998: Xiu Xiu: The Sent-Down Girl. 2000: Autumn in New York.

†Scenes deleted from final release print

CHER (Cherilyn Sarkisian) 1946–
Dark, bony, rather gloomy-looking, black-haired American entertainer of American

Indian extraction. She came to fame in the mid 1960s with then-husband Sonny Bono as half of the singing partnership Sonny and Cher. They were divorced in 1975, and Cher decided to pursue an acting career. For seven years she 'got nowhere, although I wanted to be an actress all along'. After acting lessons with Lee Strasberg, she belatedly broke through to cinema stardom in 1982, subsequently winning an Oscar nomination for *Silkwood*, and the best actress award four years later for *Moonstruck*. Also famous for the flimsy creations she wears to awards ceremonies, and her well-publicised relationships with younger men.
1965: Wild on the Beach. 1967: Good Times. 1969: Chastity. 1982: Come Back to the 5 and Dime, Jimmy Dean, Jimmy Dean. 1983: Silkwood. 1985: Mask. 1987: The Witches of Eastwick. Moonstruck. Suspect. 1990: Mermaids. 1992: The Player. 1995: Faithful. 1996: If These Walls Could Talk (TV. And co-directed). 1999: Tea with Mussolini.

CHEVALIER, Maurice 1888–1972
French actor and crooner of long stage background and international reputation. With twinkling eyes, Gallic charm and leering lower lip, Chevalier became a big star of early Hollywood musical comedies, especially opposite Jeanette MacDonald (*qv*). Everyone imitated his singing – even the Marx Brothers. Returned in the fifties, still lecherous but more avuncular. Given a special Academy Award in 1958. Died from a heart attack. He was nominated for best actor Oscars in *The Love Parade* and *The Big Pond*.
*1908: *Trop crédule. 1911: *Un marie qui se fait attendre. *La mariée recalcitrante. *Par habitude. 1912: *La valse renversante. 1917:*

Une soirée mondaine. 1921: *Le mauvais garçon.* 1922: **Le match Criqui-Ledoux. Gonzague.* 1923: *L'affaire de la Rue de Lourcine. Jim Bougne, boxeur.* 1924: *Par habitude (remake).* 1928: *Bonjour New York!* 1929: †*Innocents of Paris.* †*The Love Parade.* 1930: †*Paramount on Parade.* †*The Big Pond.* †*Playboy of Paris.* 1931: †*The Smiling Lieutenant.* **El Cliente Seductor.* 1932: †*One Hour With You. Make Me a Star.* **Hollywood on Parade B-5. Love Me Tonight.* **The Stolen Jools (GB: The Slippery Pearls).* **Stopping the Show (voice only).* **Battling Georges.* 1933: *A Bedtime Story.* †*The Way to Love.* 1934: †*The Merry Widow.* 1935: *Folies Bergère (GB: The Man from Folies Bergère).* 1936: †*The Beloved Vagabond. L'homme du jour. Avec le sourire.* 1938: *Break the News.* 1939: *Pièges (US: Personal Column).* 1946: *Paris 1900. Le silence est d'or (US: Man About Town).* 1949: *Le roi (US: A Royal Affair).* 1950: *Ma pomme.* 1952: **Jouons le jeu . . . l'Avarice.* 1953: **Chevalier de Ménilmontant. Schlager-Parade.* 1954: *A Hundred Years of Love. I Had Seven Daughters.* **Caf'Conc.* 1954: **Sur toute la gamme (narrator only).* 1957: *Love in the Afternoon.* **Rendez-vous avec Maurice Chevalier (series). The Heart of Show Business.* 1958: *Gigi.* 1959: *Count Your Blessings. Can-Can. Black Tights. A Breath of Scandal. Pepe.* 1961: *Jessica. Fanny.* 1962: *In Search of the Castaways.* 1963: *Panic Button. A New Kind of Love.* 1964: *I'd Rather Be Rich. La chance et l'amour.* 1967: *Monkeys, Go Home!* 1970: *The Aristocats (voice only).*

†*Also starred in French-language version*

CHONG, Rae Dawn 1960–

Dark-skinned, wild-haired, girlish-looking American actress of mixed extraction, self-described as 'Black, Chinese, French and American', the daughter of TV and film comedian Thomas Chong (half of the Cheech and Chong comedy team). A lull for marriage and a baby (and divorce) restricted her film appearances in her teens and early twenties, but she then proved spirited and sympathetic in both leading and supporting parts and won some good roles. Married/divorced (2nd) actor C. Thomas Howell, her co-star in *Soul Man.* Her girlish looks had disappeared by the mid 1990s and she appeared in character roles.
1978: *Stony Island.* 1981: *Quest for Fire.* 1983: *Fear City.* 1984: *Beat Street. Choose Me. Cheech and Chong's The Corsican Brothers.*

City Limits. 1985: *American Flyers. Running Out of Luck. Commando. The Color Purple. Badge of the Assassin (TV).* 1986: *Soul Man.* 1987: *The Squeeze. The Principal.* 1988: *Loon. Walking After Midnight. Far Out Man.* 1989: *The Borrower (released 1991).* 1990: *Tales from the Darkside. Amazon (released 1992). Curiosity Kills (TV).* 1991: *Chaindance. Common Bonds. Prison Stories: Women on the Inside (TV).* 1992: *When the Party's Over. In Exile. On the Streets of L.A. (TV). The Webbers' 15 Minutes/The Webbers/ Webbers' World. Time Runner.* 1993: *Amberwaves. Starlight (released 1996). Boca. Boulevard (cable TV).* 1995: *Power of Attorney. Hideaway. Crying Freeman. Mask of Death. The Break.* 1996: *Waiting for the Man/Small Time.* 1997: *Goodbye America.* 1998: *Things I Forgot to Remember. Valentine's Day.* 1999: *Dangerous Attraction.* 2000: *The Visit.*

CHOW YUN-FAT 1955–

Impassive, rarely-smiling, solid-headed, squarely built, Hong Kong-born action star, often in brutal or even vicious roles. Immensely popular in films by such successful action directors as John Woo, Chow stayed with Hong Kong mayhem until the mid-1990s, when he surprisingly tried his luck in Hollywood in his early forties. His crime thrillers here were only modestly successful, but he did show an unexpectedly subtler side by giving an exquisite performance as the King of Siam in a sumptuous new version of *Anna and the King.*
1976: *Chi nu/Massage Girls.* 1978: *Miss O. Jing wang shuang xiong (GB: Killers Two).* 1980: *Shi ba (US: See-Bar).* 1981: *Zhi fa zhe (GB: The Executioner. US: Killers Two). Xun cheng ma. Woo Yuet dik goo si.* 1982: *Xue han jin qian (GB and US: Blood Money).* 1983: *Shanghai Beach. Shanghai Beach 2. Lie tou (US: The Head Hunter). Fa sing.* 1984: *Qing cheng zhi lian. Ling qi po ren (US: The Tenant). Dang doi si ming.* 1985: *Nu ren xin. The Nepal Affair. Meigui de gushi (GB: Lost Romance). Gui xin niang.* 1986: *Yuan Zhen xia yu Wei Si Li (US: The Seventh Curse). Yi gai yun tian. Yingxiong bense (GB and US: A Better Tomorrow). Shaqi errenzu/100 Ways to Murder Your Wife. Meng zhong ren. Din lo jing juen. Ni qing wo yuan. Blacklist. Chu yi shi wu. Seiha tsing.* 1987: *Yingxiong bense II (GB and US: A Better Tomorrow II). Long hu feng yun (GB and US: City on Fire). Ying hung ho hon. Xiao sheng meng jing hun. Gong woo ching.*

Jiang hu long hu men/Dragon and Tiger Fight. Liumang daheng. Fu xing jia qi. Gaam yuk fung wan/Prison on Fire. 1988: *Yu Da Fu chuan qi. Zai jian ying xiong. Lo foo chut gang (GB: Tiger on the Beat). Sing si jin jaang. Daai jeung foo yat gei. Gong zi duo qing. Ba xing bao xi. Chang duan jiao zhi lian.* 1989: *Yingxiong bense III (US: A Better Tomorrow 3: Love and Death in Saigon). Wo zai hei she hui de ri zi. Yi hen wu yan. Du shen. Ji xing gong zhao. Diexue shuang xiong (GB and US: The Killer). Ban wo chuang tian ya.* 1990: *Black Vengeance. Diexue jiang nu/No Way Back.* 1991: *Once a Thief. Tao fan (GB: and US: Prison on Fire II). Dou Hap.* 1992: *Xia dao Gao Fei/Full Contact. Hard-Boiled. Wo ai chou wen chai. Du sheng.* 1994: *American Shaolin. Who Do You Think You're Fooling? Du shen xu ji/God of Gamblers Returns.* 1995: *Heping fandian.* 1998: *The Replacement Killers.* 1999: *The Corruptor. Anna and the King. King's Ransom.* 2000: *Crouching Tiger, Hidden Dragon.*

CHRISTIAN, Linda
See POWER, Tyrone
and PURDOM, Edmund

CHRISTIAN, Paul
See HUBSCHMID, Paul

CHRISTIANS, Mady
(Margarethe Christians) 1900–1951
Fluffy Viennese blonde, the Mary Pickford of Austro-German films, in which she commanded a huge and faithful following. Left Germany in 1934, and quickly established herself as a Hollywood character actress, although in later years she seemed to prefer the stage, where she had scored her first US triumph in 1938 as Gertrude in a production of *Hamlet.* Shortly before her death from a cerebral haemorrhage, she was blacklisted in Hollywood during the investigations of the House Un-American Activities Committee.
1916: *Audrey.* 1917: *Das Verlorene Paradies. Die Krone von Kerkyra. Frau Marias Erlebnis.* 1918: *Am andern Ufer. Am Scheidewege. Die Dreizehn. Die Verteidigerin. Nachtschatten.* 1919: *Die Nacht des Grauens. Der goldene Klub. Die Peruanerin. Die Sühne der Martha Marx. Eine junge Dame von Welt. Fidelio.* 1920: *Und Verbrechen. Die Gesunkenen. Wer unter Euch ohne Sünde ist . . . Der Mann ohne Namen.* 1921: *Der Schicksalstag. Das Weib des Pharao (US: The Loves of Pharaoh).* 1922: *Es leuchtet meine Liebe. Kinder der Seit. Ein Glas Wasser.*

Malmaison. 1923: Die Buddenbrooks. Der verlorene Schuh. Der Wetterwart. Die Finanzen des Grossherzogs (US: The Grand Duke's Finances). 1924: Mensch gegen Mensch. Soll und Haben. 1925: Der Abenteurer. Die vom Niederrhein. Der Farmer aus Texas. Ein Walzertraum (GB and US: The Waltz Dream). Die Verrufenen (US: Slums of Berlin). 1926: Die geschiedene Frau. Nanette macht alles. La duchesse de 'Les Folies'/Die Königin vom Moulin Rouge. Die Welt will belogen sein. Wien, wie es weint und lacht. Zopf und Schwert. 1927: Königin Luise (US: Queen Luise). Grand Hotel . . .! Heimveh. Der Sohn der Hagar (US: Out of the Mist). Königin Luise II. 1928: Fräulein Chaffeur. Eine Frau von format. Priscillas Fahrt ins Gluck. Duel. 1929: Das brennende Herz (GB and US: The Burning Heart). Meine Schwester und ich. Dich hab'ich geliebt (US: Because I Loved You). Leutnant warst du einst bei den Husaren. The Runaway Princess. 1931: Das Schicksal der Renate Langen. Die Frau, von der Man spricht. 1932: Der schwartze Husar. Friederike. 1933: Ich und die Kaiserin. The Only Girl (US: Heart Song). Manolescu. Salon Dora Green. 1934: Mon amour. Wicked Woman. 1935: Escapade. Ship Café. 1936: Come and Get It. 1937: Seventh Heaven. Heidi. The Woman I Love. 1943: Tender Comrade. 1944: Address Unknown. 1948: All My Sons. Letter from an Unknown Woman. 1950: The Morning After (TV).

CHRISTIE, Julie 1940–

India-born British actress with corn-coloured hair who suddenly seemed to be the spirit of the swinging sixties. This 'spirit' was rewarded with an Oscar for *Darling* (she was nominated again later for *McCabe and Mrs Miller*), but most of the critics deserted her when she attempted to widen her range, and later performances were felt to lack the passion and colour of the earlier ones. But she returned to something like her best form in *Heaven Can Wait* and stepped up her work-rate in the 1980s, regaining some of her lost standing, if not box-office power, in some prestigious projects. Additional Oscar nomination for *Afterglow*.

*1962: Crooks Anonymous. 1963: The Fast Lady. Billy Liar. 1964: Young Cassidy. 1965: Darling. Doctor Zhivago. 1966: *Star. Fahrenheit 451. 1967: Far from the Madding Crowd. Tonite Let's All Make Love in London. 1968: Petulia. In Search of Gregory. 1970: The Go-Between. 1971: McCabe and Mrs Miller. 1973: Don't Look Now. 1975:*

Shampoo. Nashville. 1977: Demon Seed. 1978: Heaven Can Wait. 1981: Memoirs of a Survivor. Les quarantièmes rugissants (The Roaring Forties). The Animals Film (narrator only). 1982: The Return of the Soldier. 1983: Heat and Dust. The Gold Diggers. 1985: Power. Lillian Alling (doc). 1986: Miss Mary. La mémoir tatouée (US: Secret Obsession). 1988: A Long Way from Home/Dadah is Death/The Control Room (TV). 1990: Fools of Fortune. 1991: The Railway Station Man. 1996: Dragonheart. Hamlet. 1997: Afterglow.

CHURCHILL, Diana 1913–1994

Cool, blonde, elegant, pleasing British leading lady, a resilient wisecracking heroine of some late 1930s' comedy-thrillers, but mostly on stage after World War II. Widow of Barry K. Barnes (*qv*), her one-time co-star, whom she nursed through many years of ill-health until his death in 1965. In 1976 she married actor Mervyn Johns (also *qv*). Died from multiple sclerosis.

1931: Service for Ladies (US: Reserved for Ladies). 1932: Sally Bishop. 1935: Foreign Affaires. 1936: Pot Luck. Dishonour Bright. Sensation! The Dominant Sex. 1937: School for Husbands. 1938: Housemaster. Jane Steps Out. Yes, Madam? 1939: The Spider. Midnight Mall. 1940: Law and Disorder. The Flying Squad. The House of the Arrow (US: Castle of Crimes). 1948: Scott of the Antarctic. 1949: The History of Mr Polly. 1966: The Winter's Tale.

CHURCHILL, Marguerite 1909–2000

Gravely beautiful brown-haired American actress of the 1930s, often seen in spunky roles. Chiefly remembered as John Wayne's leading lady in *The Big Trail*, but her performances almost always had that little extra sparkle. Married to western star George O'Brien (*qv*) from 1933 to 1949 (neither remarried), she interrupted her career after the birth of her first child and retired after the second. Later lived in Portugal, before ending her days in Oklahoma.

1929: The Valiant. Pleasure Crazed. They Had to See Paris. Seven Faces. 1930: Good Intentions. Born Reckless. Harmony at Home. The Big Trail. 1931: Girls Demand Excitement. Charlie Chan Carries On. Quick Millions. Riders of the Purple Sage. Ambassador Bill. 1932: Forgotten Commandments. 1933: Girl without a Room. 1934: Penthouse Party (US: Without Children). 1935: Speed Devils. Man Hunt. 1936: Alibi for

Murder. The Walking Dead. Dracula's Daughter. Murder by an Aristocrat. The Final Hour. Legion of Terror. 1950: Bunco Squad.

CILENTO Diane 1933–

Talented blonde actress (born in New Guinea), principally in British films, with feline smile and stunning figure. Adept at playing tarts with hearts, but born into the wrong era: 20 years earlier in Hollywood she would undoubtedly have become a much bigger star. As it is, she has given some strong performances, but got herself into far too many unworthy films. Married to Sean Connery (*qv*) 1962–1972. Oscar nominated for *Tom Jones*, she is also a novelist. Mother of actor Jason Connery.

1952: Wings of Danger (US: Dead on Course). Moulin Rouge. 1953: Meet Mr Lucifer. All Hallowe'en. 1954: The Angel Who Pawned Her Harp. The Passing Stranger. 1955: Passage Home. The Woman for Joe. 1957: The Admirable Crichton (US: Paradise Lagoon). 1958: The Truth About Women. 1959: Jet Storm. 1961: The Full Treatment (US: Stop Me Before I Kill!). The Naked Edge. 1962: I Thank a Fool. 1963: Tom Jones. 1964: The Third Secret. Rattle of a Simple Man. 1965: The Agony and the Ecstasy. 1966: Hombre. 1968: Negatives. 1972: ZPG (GB: Zero Population Growth). 1973: Hitler: the Last Ten Days. The Wicker Man. 1975: The Tiger Lily. 1981: Duet for Four. 1982: For the Term of His Natural Life (TV). 1985: The Boy Who Had Everything.

CLARK, Dane

(Bernard Zanville) 1913–1998
Grim-faced, wiry American tough-guy actor with light-brown wavy hair, at his peak in

the 1940s (a law graduate in the 1930s, he turned to acting), generally in grouchy roles as guys with chips on their shoulders. Continued in the same morose vein on television, a medium in which he worked solidly from the 1950s to the 1980s. Died from lung cancer.

*1942: †The Glass Key. †Sunday Punch. †Pride of the Yankees. †Tennessee Johnson (GB: The Man on America's Conscience). †Wake Island. 1943: *Rear Gunner. †Heaven Can Wait. †Action in the North Atlantic. Destination Tokyo. 1944: *I Won't Play. The Very Thought of You. Hollywood Canteen. 1945: God is My Co-Pilot. Pride of the Marines (GB: Forever in Love). 1946: Her Kind of Man. A Stolen Life. 1947: That Way with Women. Deep Valley. 1948: Embraceable You. Moonrise. 1949: Without Honor. 1950: Backfire. Barricade. Le traqué (GB: Gunman in the Streets). Highly Dangerous. 1951: Never Trust a Gambler. Fort Defiance. 1952: The Gambler and the Lady. 1954: Go Man Go. Five Days (US: Paid to Kill). Thunder Pass. Port of Hell. 1955: Murder by Proxy (US: Blackout. Completed 1953). Toughest Man Alive. Time Running Out. One Life (TV. GB: cinemas). 1956: The Man is Armed. Massacre. 1957: Outlaw's Son. Reunion (TV). 1966: Flojten. 1969: The McMasters . . . tougher than the west itself! 1971: The Face of Fear (TV). 1972: The Family Rico (TV). Say Goodbye, Maggie Cole (TV). 1974: The Hunters (TV). 1975: Days in My Father's House. The Return of Joe Forester (TV). Murder on Flight 502 (TV). 1976: James Dean (TV). 1978: A Chance to Live (TV). Narc (TV). 1980: The Woman Inside. 1982: Blood Song. 1988: Last Rites.*

†As Bernard Zanville

CLARK, Petula 1932–

Brunette (now blonde) English actress who became a radio star in the war years, having started as a band singer at the age of eight. Played a string of sweet young things as a straight actress, then reverted to singing, most successfully after settling in France. Two big budget musicals in the late 1960s did not lead to a permanent revival of her film career.

*1944: Medal for the General. Strawberry Roan. 1945: Murder in Reverse. I Know Where I'm Going. *Trouble at Townsend. 1946: London Town (US: My Heart Goes Crazy). 1947: Vice Versa. Easy Money. 1948: Here Come the Huggetts. 1949: Vote For Huggett.*

Don't Ever Leave Me. The Huggetts Abroad. The Romantic Age (US: Naughty Arlette). 1950: Dance Hall. 1951: White Corridors. Madame Louise. 1952: The Card (US: The Promoter). Made in Heaven. 1954: The Runaway Bus. The Gay Dog. The Happiness of Three Women. Track the Man Down. 1956: That Woman Opposite (US: City After Midnight). 1958: Six-Five Special. 1963: A couteaux tirés (GB: Daggers Drawn). 1965: Questi pazzi, pazzi Italiani. 1968: Finian's Rainbow. 1969: Goodbye, Mr Chips. 1980: Never Never Land.

CLARK, Susan (Nora Golding) 1940–

Tall, willowy, brunette, Canadian-born leading lady in Hollywood, talented in both comedy and drama, but in a forthright sort of role she was never given until the mid-1970s. In the film capital from 1966, always as a leading lady, but never, despite a warm personality, quite as a marquee name, even after winning an Emmy for the TV film *Babe* in 1975. Married (second) director Alex Karras.

1967: Banning. 1968: The Challengers (TV. GB: cinemas). Something for a Lonely Man (TV). Madigan. Coogan's Bluff. 1969: The Forbin Project. Tell Them Willie Boy is Here. Skullduggery. 1970: Valdez is Coming. 1971: Skin Game. The Astronaut (TV). 1973: Trapped (TV. GB: cinemas as Doberman Patrol). Showdown. 1974: The Midnight Man. The Apple Dumpling Gang. Airport 1975. 1975: Night Games. Babe (TV). 1976: Amelia Earhart (TV). McNaughton's Daughter (TV). 1978: City on Fire. North Avenue Irregulars (GB: Hill's Angels). Sherlock Holmes: Murder by Decree (GB: Murder by Decree). 1979: Promises in the Dark. Double

Negative. 1980: The Choice (TV). 1981: Porky's. Nobody's Perfekt. Jimmy B & André (TV). 1982: Maid in America (TV). 1994: Butterbox Babies (TV). Tonya and Nancy: The Inside Story (TV). 1995: Snowbound: The Jim and Jennifer Stolpa Story (TV).

CLARKE, Mae (Violet Klotz) 1907–1992

American honey-blonde actress who leapt to brief stardom after dancing in the chorus (with Barbara Stanwyck) and became adept at goodtime dames with hearts of gold. She always looked older than her years and after 1931, her peak year (*Frankenstein*, *The Front Page* and getting a grapefruit in the face from Cagney in *The Public Enemy*), her career ran all the way downhill to bit parts, though she kept working into her sixties. Three times married and divorced, she died from cancer.

*1929: Big Time. Nix on Dames (GB: Don't Trust Dames). 1930: The Fall Guy (GB: Trust Your Wife). The Dancers. Men on Call. 1931: *Intimate Interview. Reckless Living. The Front Page. The Good Bad Girl. Waterloo Bridge. The Public Enemy (GB: Enemies of the Public). Frankenstein. 1932: Final Edition (GB: Determination). Night World. Breach of Promise. Penguin Pool Murder (GB: The Penguin Pool Mystery). Impatient Maiden. Three Wise Girls. As the Devil Commands. 1933: Parole Girl. Turn Back the Clock. Penthouse (GB: Crooks in Clover). Fast Workers. 1934: Lady Killer. Flaming Gold. Let's Talk It Over. This Side of Heaven. Nana. The Man with Two Faces. 1935: The Daring Young Man. The Silk Hat Kid. 1936: Hitch Hike Lady (GB: Eventful Journey). Wild Brian Kent. Hats Off. Hearts in Bondage. The House of 1,000 Candles. 1937: Great Guy (GB: Pluck of the Irish). Trouble in Morocco. Outlaws of the Orient. 1940: Women in War. 1941: Sailors on Leave. 1942: Flying Tigers. The Lady from Chungking. 1944: Here Come the Waves. And Now Tomorrow. 1945: Kitty. 1947: Reaching from Heaven. 1948: Daredevils of the Clouds. 1949: Streets of San Francisco. Gun Runner. King of the Rocket Men (serial). 1950: Annie Get Your Gun. Duchess of Idaho. Mrs O'Malley and Mr Malone. Royal Wedding (GB: Wedding Bells). The Yellow Cab Man. 1951: The Unknown Man. Inside Straight. The People Against O'Hara. The Great Caruso. Three Guys Named Mike. Love Is Better than Ever (GB: The Light Fantastic). Mr Imperium (GB: You Belong to My Heart). Callaway Went Thataway (GB: The Star Said No). 1952:*

Thunderbirds. Pat and Mike. Skirts Ahoy! Fearless Fagan. Singin' in the Rain. Horizons West. Because of You. 1953: Confidentially Connie. 1954: Magnificent Obsession. 1955: Wichita. Not As a Stranger. Women's Prison. I Died a Thousand Times. 1956: Come Next Spring. Mohawk. The Catered Affair (GB: Wedding Breakfast). The Desperadoes Are in Town. Ride the High Iron. 1958: The Voice In the Mirror. 1959: Ask Any Girl. 1966: A Big Hand for the Little Lady (GB: Big Deal at Dodge City). 1967: Thoroughly Modern Millie. 1970: Watermelon Man. 1989: Beverly Hills Brats.

CLARKE, Robert 1920–
Moustachioed, solidly-built American actor with dark, curly hair. After getting a break on radio, he began his Hollywood career in small supporting roles. Later, he played leads in several very minor films between 1950 and 1962, showing a liking for frightening slices of science-fiction, occasionally having a hand in writing, producing and directing them. Married one of the King Sisters and later joined The King Family Singing Tour.
*1944: The Falcon in Hollywood. 1945: What a Blonde. Back to Bataan. First Yank into Tokyo (GB: Mask of Fury). The Enchanted Cottage. Zombies on Broadway (GB: Loonies on Broadway). The Body Snatcher. Sing Your Way Home. Man Alive. Radio Stars on Parade. Wanderer of the Wasteland. A Game of Death. Those Endearing Young Charms. 1946: Sunset Pass. Bedlam. San Quentin. Criminal Court. Genius at Work. Step by Step. Lady Luck. The Bamboo Blonde. 1947: *In Room 303. Desperate. Dick Tracy Meets Gruesome (GB: Dick Tracy's Amazing Adventure). Code of the West. The Farmer's Daughter. Under the Tonto Rim. Thunder Mountain. 1948: Return of the Bad Men. If You Knew Susie. Fighting Father Dunne. 1949: The Judge Steps Out. Ladies of the Chorus. Riders of the Range. 1950: Champagne for Caesar. Outrage. A Modern Marriage. 1951: The Valparaiso Story. Hard, Fast and Beautiful. The Man from Planet X. Casa Manana. Pistol Harvest. Street Bandits. 1952: Sword of Venus (GB: Island of Monte Cristo). Tales of Robin Hood. The Fabulous Senorita. Captive Women (GB: 3000 AD). The Sword of D'Artagnan. 1953: Blades of the Musketeers (TV material shown in cinemas). Oil Town USA. Captain John Smith and Pocahontas (GB: Burning Arrows). 1954: The Black Pirates. Man with the Steel Whip (serial). Her Twelve Men. 1955: The Benny*

Goodman Story. †The Hideous Sun Demon (GB: Blood on His Lips. Released 1959). King of the Carnival (serial). 1956: Secret File (TV. GB: cinemas). My Man Godfrey. 1957: The Helen Morgan Story (GB: Both Ends of the Candle). Outlaw Queen. Miss Body Beautiful. The Deep Six. Band of Angels. The Astounding She Monster (GB: The Mysterious Invader). 1958: The Deep Six. Timbuktu. I, Mobster. 1959: A Date with Death. Girl with an Itch. The FBI Story. The Incredible Petrified World. 1960: Beyond the Time Barrier. Cash McCall. 1961: The Last Time I Saw Archie. 1962: Terror of the Bloodhunters. 1964: The Lively Set. 1965: The Restless Ones. Zebra in the Kitchen. 1970: The Brotherhood of the Bell (TV). 1973: Chase (TV). 1977: Where's Willie? 1981: Frankenstein Island. 1986: Midnight Movie Massacre. 1989: What's Up, Hideous Sun Demon? Alienator. 1990: Haunting Fear.

†And directed

CLAYBURGH, Jill 1941–
Tawny-haired American actress with honeyed tones who made no sort of impact on film until she reached 30, remaining very much her own woman in the sorts of parts she would play. Later recognized as a comedienne of Carole Lombard warmth, and a dramatic actress of considerable emotional range, highlighted by her performance in *An Unmarried Woman*, which won her an Oscar nomination. Also Oscar-nominated for *Starting Over*. A long-time relationship with actor Al Pacino ended and she married playwright David Rabe. In much more modest roles in the last decade.
1966: The Wedding Party. 1971: The Telephone Book. 1972: Portnoy's Complaint. The Female Instinct (TV. GB: The Snoop Sisters). 1973: Tiger on a Chain (TV). The Thief Who Came to Dinner. Shock-a-Bye Baby (TV). 1974: The Terminal Man. 1975: Roman Grey (TV. GB: The Art of Crime). Hustling. 1976: Silver Streak. Gable and Lombard. 1977: Semi-Tough. Griffin and Phoenix (GB: Today is Forever. Originally for TV). An Unmarried Woman. 1979: La luna. Starting Over. 1980: It's My Turn. 1981: First Monday in October. 1982: I'm Dancing As Fast As I Can. 1983: Hanna K. 1984: In Our Hands. 1985: Where Are the Children? 1986: Shy People. Miles to Go (TV). 1988: Who Gets the Friends? (TV). 1989: Unspeakable Acts (TV). Fear Stalk (TV). 1990: Beyond

the Ocean. 1991: Pretty Hattie's Baby. Reason for Living: The Jill Ireland Story (TV). 1992: Rich in Love. Sessions. Le grand pardon II/Day of Atonement. Whispers in the Dark. 1993: Naked in New York. 1994: Honor Thy Father and Mother: the True Story of the Menendez Murders (TV). For the Love of Nancy (TV). 1995: The Face on the Milk Carton (TV). 1996: Going All the Way. When Innocence is Lost. 1997: Fools Rush In. Sins of the Mind (TV). Crowned and Dangerous (TV). 1999: My Little Assassin (TV).

CLEESE, John 1939–
Elongated, dark-haired British comedian with grasshopper legs, pained expression and, latterly, moustache – a master of sarcasm and one of the screen's great escalating panickers. Came into show business via university revue, and became a member of *Monty Python's Flying Circus*, where his deadpan expression and cutting, upper-class tones made him a national figure. Most successful of all on TV in the series *Fawlty Towers*. Film roles are mainly cameos, although he successfully essayed comedy leads in the late 1980s. Oscar nominee for the screenplay of *A Fish Called Wanda*.
*1968: Interlude (shown 1967). The Bliss of Mrs Blossom. The Best House in London. 1969: The Magic Christian. 1970: The Rise and Rise of Michael Rimmer. The Statue. 1971: And Now for Something Completely Different. 1972: The Love Ban (originally It's a Two-Foot-Six-Inch-Above-the-Ground World). 1973: *Romance with a Double Bass. 1975: Monty Python and the Holy Grail. 1976: Pleasure at Her Majesty's (US: Monty Python Meets Beyond the Fringe). 1977: The Strange Case of the End of Civilization As We Know It (TV). 1979: Monty Python's Life of Brian. †*Away from It All (narrator only). The Secret Policeman's Ball. 1980: The Taming of the Shrew (TV). 1981: The Great Muppet Caper. Time Bandits. Monty Python Live at the Hollywood Bowl. 1982: The Secret Policeman's Other Ball. Privates on Parade. 1983: Monty Python's Meaning of Life. Yellowbeard. 1985: Silverado. Clockwise. 1987: The Secret Policeman's Third Ball. 1988: A Fish Called Wanda. The Big Picture. 1989: Erik the Viking. 1990: Bullseye! 1991: An American Tail 2. Fievel Goes West (voice only). 1993: Splitting Heirs. 1994: Mary Shelley's Frankenstein. Swan Lake/The Swan Princess (voice only). Richie Rich. Rudyard Kipling's The Jungle Book. 1996: The Wind in the Willows. 1997: Fierce Creatures.*

George of the Jungle (voice only). 1998: Parting Shots. 1999: The Out-of-Towners. The World is Not Enough. Isn't She Great. 2000: Quantum Project. 2001: The Magic Pudding (voice only).

†And co-directed

CLEMENTS, Sir John 1910–1988
Smooth, cheerful British leading man in sterling, upper-class roles, a look-alike for Michael Denison, with whom he shared a preference for the stage. Had some good roles for Alexander Korda in the thirties, but his image quickly palled with the cinemagoing public in post-war years. Long married to Kay Hammond (qv), with whom he became very popular in radio panel games. Knighted in 1968.
*1934: Once in a New Moon. 1935: *No Quarter. The Divine Spark. Ticket of Leave. 1936: Things to Come. Rembrandt. 1937: Knight Without Armour. South Riding. 1938: Star of the Circus (US: Hidden Menace). 1939: The Four Feathers. 1940: Convoy. 1941: This England. Ships with Wings. 1942: Tomorrow We Live (US: At Dawn We Die). 1943: Undercover (US: Underground Guerrillas). 1944: They Came to a City. 1948: †Call of the Blood. 1949: Train of Events. 1958: The Silent Enemy. 1962: The Mind Benders. 1969: Oh! What a Lovely War. 1982: Gandhi. 1983: The Jigsaw Man.*

†And directed

CLIFT, Montgomery
(Edward M. Clift) 1920–1966
Dark, boyish-looking, intense American actor, in soul-searching or romantic roles. On stage as a teenager, but mostly popular in the early

1950s, until a bad car smash changed his facial structure (and, some said, his personality) giving him a more wasted look. Also sustained brain concussion, from which he may never have fully recovered, although the official cause of death was a heart attack. He was nominated for an Academy Award for *The Search, A Place in the Sun, From Here to Eternity* and *Judgment at Nuremberg.*
1948: The Search. Red River. 1949: The Heiress. 1950: The Big Lift. 1951: A Place in the Sun. 1952: I Confess. 1953: From Here to Eternity. 1954: Stazione termini (GB: Indiscretion. US: Indiscretion of an American Wife). 1957: Raintree County. 1958: The Young Lions. 1959: Lonelyhearts. Suddenly Last Summer. 1960: Wild River. 1961: The Misfits. Judgment at Nuremberg. 1962: Freud (GB: Freud – the Secret Passion). 1966: L'espion/The Defector.

CLIVE, Colin (C.C. Greig) 1898–1937
Dark, handsome, but rather worried-looking English actor, often in tortured roles. He went to Hollywood to repeat his stage success in *Journey's End* and stayed to become immortalized for horror fans as Henry Frankenstein in two classic fantasy films. French-born Clive died somewhat mysteriously, apparently from pulmonary tuberculosis. Married to character actress Jeanne de Casalis (1896–1966).
1930: Journey's End. 1931: The Stronger Sex. Frankenstein. 1932: Lily Christine. 1933: Christopher Strong. Looking Forward (GB: Service). 1934: Jane Eyre. The Key. One More River (GB: Over the River). 1935: The Right to Live (GB: The Sacred Flame). Clive of India. Mad Love (GB: The Hands of Orlac). The Girl from Tenth Avenue (GB: Men on Her Mind). The Man Who Broke the Bank at Monte Carlo. Bride of Frankenstein. 1936: The Widow from Monte Carlo. 1937: History is Made at Night. The Woman I Love (GB: The Woman Between).

CLOONEY, George 1961–
Dark-haired (greying early), ruggedly-built, head-tilting, soulful-looking American actor who slaved away for years on TV series and poor exploitation films until TV's medical blockbuster *ER* shot him into the heartthrob class. A university drop-out who worked on his grandfather's tobacco farm before trying acting; his first TV sitcom was, ironically, called *E-R*, 10 years before fame found him with an almost identical title. Now in top

movie action roles as well. Married/divorced from actress Talia Balsam, he is the nephew of singer Rosemary Clooney (1928–) who had a brief film career of her own in the 1950s, and actor Jose Ferrer (qv).

*1982: Grizzly II – The Predator. †And They're Off. 1986: Combat High (GB: Combat Academy). 1987: Return to Horror High. 1988: Return of the Killer Tomatoes. 1990: Sunset Beat (TV). Red Surf. 1992: The Harvest. Unbecoming Age. 1993: Without Warning: Terror in the Towers (TV). 1994: ER (TV). 1996: From Dusk Till Dawn. One Fine Day. 1997: Batman and Robin. The Peacemaker. Full Tilt Boogie. 1998: The Thin Red Line. Out of Sight. *Waiting for Woody. 1999: Three Kings. The Limey. South Park: Bigger, Longer & Uncut (voice only). 2000: The Perfect Storm. Fail Safe (TV). O Brother, Where Art Thou?*

†Unreleased

CLOONEY, Rosemary
See CLOONEY, George

CLOSE, Glenn 1947–
Cornfield-blonde, strong-chinned, porcelain featured, slim-faced American actress, faintly reminiscent of Meryl Streep. A big star on the Broadway stage of the 1970s, she was a late, late comer to films, but quickly moved into showy leading roles. Despite projecting an upper-class image, she has tackled a wide variety of characters, and had huge box-office successes with *Jagged Edge* and *Fatal Attraction.* Academy Award nominations for *The World According to Garp, The Big Chill, The Natural, Fatal Attraction* and *Dangerous Liaisons.* A strong soprano singer, she gained Broadway musical success in the mid 1990s in the leading role of *Sunset Boulevard.*

Strangely, in her only musical film, *Meeting Venus*, her singing voice was dubbed. Played some nastier character roles from 1993 on.
1979: Orphan Train (TV). Too Far to Go (TV). 1982: The World According to Garp. 1983: The Big Chill. Something About Amelia (TV). 1984: The Natural. The Stone Boy. Greystoke: The Legend of Tarzan, Lord of the Apes (dubbed voice only). 1985: Maxie. Jagged Edge. 1987: Fatal Attraction. 1988: Stones for Ibarra (TV). Dangerous Liaisons. 1989. Immediate Family. 1990: Reversal of Fortune. Hamlet. 1991: Meeting Venus. Sarah Plain and Tall (TV). Hook. 1992: Once Upon a Forest (voice only). 1993: The House of the Spirits. Skylark (TV). 1994: The Paper. 1995: Serving in Silence: the Margarethe Cammermeyer Story (TV). Anne Frank Remembered (voice only). 1996: Mary Reilly. One Hundred and One Dalmatians. Paradise Road. Mars Attacks! 1997: Air Force One. In the Gloaming (cable TV). In & Out. 1999: Tarzan (voice only). Cookie's Fortune. Sarah, Plain and Tall: Winter's End (TV). Things You Can Tell Just by Looking at Her. 2000: Joe Gould's Secret. 102 Dalmatians.

CLYDE, June (J. Tetrazini) 1909–1987
Gracious, likeable, sparkling-eyed, peppy blonde American actress, singer and dancer, in vaudeville from seven (as Baby Tetrazini) and films as a regular at 19. She married director Thornton Freeland at 20 (they stayed married until her death) and came to Britain with him in 1934, starring there in several popular light musicals and comedies, and returning to America only with the outbreak of war. The Freelands returned to Britain in 1946, and she played the odd cameo role here and there before retirement.
1920: The Sea Wolf. 1927: Topsy and Eva. 1929: Street Girl. Side Street (GB: Three Brothers). Tanned Legs. Why Bring That Up? 1930: Hit the Deck. The Cuckoos. Midnight Mystery. 1931: The Mad Parade (GB: Forgotten Women). Morals for Women (GB: Farewell Party). Arizona (GB: The Virtuous Wife). Men Are Like That. The Secret Witness. 1932: The All-American (GB: Sport of a Nation). The Cohens and Kellys in Hollywood. Racing Youth. Radio Patrol. Steady Company. The Thrill of Youth. Strange Adventure. Back Street. File 113. Branded Men. 1933: Only Yesterday. Tess of the Storm Country. Her Resale Value. A Study in Scarlet. Hold Me Tight. Forgotten. 1934: I Hate Women. Hollywood Hoodlum (GB: What Price
Fame?). Hollywood Party. 1935: Dance Band. She Shall Have Music. Charing Cross Road. No Monkey Business. 1936: Land Without Music (US: Forbidden Music). Aren't Men Beasts! King of the Castle. 1937: Intimate Relations. School for Husbands. Let's Make a Night of It. Make Up. Sam Small Leaves Town. 1938: Weddings Are Wonderful. His Lordship Goes to Press. 1939: Poison Pen. 1941: Sealed Lips. Unfinished Business. Country Fair. 1942: Hi'Ya Chum (GB: Everything Happens to Us). 1944: Seven Doors to Death. 1945: Hollywood and Vine (GB: Daisy (the Dog) Goes Hollywood). 1946: Behind the Mask. 1951: Night Without Stars. 1952: 24 Hours of a Woman's Life (GB: Affair in Monte Carlo). Treasure Hunt. 1953: The Love Lottery. 1957: The Story of Esther Costello (US: Golden Virgin). After the Ball.

COBB, Lee J. (Leo Jacoby) 1911–1976
Thick-set, mean-looking American actor in tough, growly roles, mostly as bosses, gangsters and men who rode roughshod over the law. Always looked older than his years and so enjoyed a fine run of middle-aged aggressors, topped by his union racketeer in *On the Waterfront*. His thick, crinkly hair hid the reality of a bald head. Died of a heart attack. Oscar-nominated for *On the Waterfront* and *The Brothers Karamazov*.
1934: Vanishing Shadow (serial). 1937: North of the Rio Grande. Rustler's Valley. Ali Baba Goes to Town. 1938: Danger on the Air. 1939: The Phantom Creeps (serial). Golden Boy. 1941: This Thing Called Love (GB: Married But Single). Men of Boys Town. Paris Calling. 1942: How to Operate Behind Enemy Lines. The Moon is Down. 1943: Buckskin Frontier (GB: The Iron Road). Tonight We Raid Calais. The Song of Bernadette. 1944: Winged Victory. 1946: Anna and the King of Siam. 1947: Boomerang. Captain from Castile. Johnny O'Clock. Carnival in Costa Rica. 1948: Miracle of the Bells. Call Northside 777. The Luck of the Irish. 1949: The Dark Past. Thieves' Highway. 1950: The Man Who Cheated Himself. 1951: Sirocco. The Family Secret. 1952: The Fighter. 1953: The Tall Texan. 1954: On the Waterfront. Yankee Pasha. Gorilla at Large. The Day of Triumph. 1955: The Racers (GB: Such Men Are Dangerous). The Road to Denver. The Left Hand of God. 1956: The Man in the Gray Flannel Suit. Miami Exposé. 1957: Twelve Angry Men. The Three Faces of Eve. The Garment Jungle. Panic Button (TV). 1958:
Party Girl. The Brothers Karamazov. Man of the West. The Trap (GB: The Baited Trap). 1959: Green Mansions. Project Immortality (TV). But Not For Me. 1960: Exodus. 1962: The Brazen Bell (TV. GB: cinemas). The Meanest Men in the West (TV). The Four Horsemen of the Apocalypse. How the West Was Won. 1963: Come Blow Your Horn. 1965: Our Man Flint. 1967: The Meanest Men in the West (TV. Shown in cinemas 1976). Il giorno della civetta (US: Mafia). 1968: Mackenna's Gold. Las Vegas 500 milliones (GB and US: They Came to Rob Las Vegas). Coogan's Bluff. 1970: The Liberation of L.B. Jones. Macho Callahan. Lawman. 1971: Heat of Anger (TV). 1973: Double Indemnity (TV). The Man Who Loved Cat Dancing. The Exorcist. La polizia sta a guardare. 1974: Dr Max (TV). The Great Ice Rip-Off (TV). Trapped Beneath the Sea (TV). 1975: Ultimatum alla citta (US: Ultimatum). That Lucky Touch. Venditore di Pallancini (GB: Last Moments. US: The Last Circus Show). Mark il poliziotto (US: Blood, Sweat and Fear). Mark il poliziotto spara per primo. 1976: La legge violenta della squadra anticrimine (GB and US: Cross Shot). Nick the Sting. 1979: Arthur Miller – on Home Ground.

COBURN, Charles 1877–1961
American actor whose paunch, monocle, cigar and thick lips lent superb character to a series of lovable but perceptive upper-class gentlemen with hoarse voices and hearts of pure gold. Like Sydney Greenstreet (*qv*), he did not become a film regular until past 60, but was an instant success with the public and stayed for 20 years, often in near-leading roles. Academy Award in 1943 for *The More the Merrier*. Died of a heart ailment. Also Oscar-nominated for *The Devil and Miss Jones* and *The Green Years*.
*1933: Boss Tweed. 1935: The People's Enemy. 1938: Of Human Hearts. Yellow Jack. Lord Jeff (GB: The Boy from Barnardo's). Vivacious Lady. 1939: Idiot's Delight. Stanley and Livingstone. Made for Each Other. The Story of Alexander Graham Bell (GB: The Modern Miracle). Bachelor Mother. In Name Only. The Captain is a Lady. 1940: *Chinese Garden Festival. The Road to Singapore. Florian. Edison, the Man. 1941: Three Faces West. Our Wife. Kings Row. H.M.Pulham Esq. The Devil and Miss Jones. Unexpected Uncle. The Lady Eve. 1942: In This Our Life. George Washington Slept Here. 1943: The Constant Nymph. Forever and a Day. The More the*

Merrier. Heaven Can Wait. Princess O'Rourke. My Kingdom for a Cook. 1944: Knickerbocker Holiday. Wilson. The Impatient Years. Together Again. 1945: A Royal Scandal (GB: Czarina). Shady Lady. Over 21. Rhapsody in Blue. Colonel Effingham's Raid (GB: Man of the Hour). 1946: The Green Years. 1947: Lured (GB: Personal Column). The Paradine Case. 1948: B.F.'s Daughter (GB: Polly Fulton). Green Grass of Wyoming. 1949: Everybody Does It. The Doctor and the Girl. Yes Sir, That's My Baby. Impact. The Gal Who Took the West. Peggy. 1950: Louisa. Mr Music. 1951: The Highwayman. *Oh Money, Money. 1952: Monkey Business. Has Anybody Seen My Gal. 1953: Trouble Along the Way. Gentlemen Prefer Blondes. 1954: The Rocket Man. The Long Wait. 1955: How to be Very, Very Popular. 1956: Around the World in 80 Days. The Power and the Prize. Town on Trial! 1957: The Story of Mankind. How to Murder a Rich Uncle. 1959: Stranger in My Arms. The Remarkable Mr Pennypacker. John Paul Jones. 1960: Pepe.

COBURN, James 1928–
Lean, gangling American actor with tooth-filled smile whose villainy proved so personable that he made the almost inevitable progression to stardom. His cheetah-like mobility made to him a good bet for 'supermen' spies, but he seemed to prefer more gutsy and offbeat roles. However, he would undoubtedly have sustained top stardom longer with a better choice of scripts. He admitted that he had 'got one right at last' with *Affliction* in 1997, which won him an Academy Award.
1959: Ride Lonesome. Face of a Fugitive. 1960: The Magnificent Seven. 1962: Hell is for Heroes! The Murder Men (TV. GB: cinemas). 1963: The Great Escape. Charade. The Man from Galveston (TV. GB: cinemas). 1964: The Americanisation of Emily. 1965: Major Dundee. A High Wind in Jamaica. The Loved One. Our Man Flint. 1966: What Did You Do in the War, Daddy? Dead Heat on a Merry-Go-Round. 1967: In Like Flint. Waterhole No. 3 (GB: Waterhole 3). The President's Analyst. 1968: Duffy. Candy. Hard Contract. 1969: Last of the Mobile Hot-Shots (later Blood Kin). 1971: Giù la testa (GB: A Fistful of Dynamite. US: Duck, You Sucker!). 1972: The Honkers. The Carey Treatment. A Reason to Live, a Reason to Die (US: Massacre at Fort Holman). 1973: Pat Garrett and Billy the Kid. The Last of Sheila. Harry Never Holds (GB: Harry in Your Pocket). 1974: The Internecine

Project. 1975: Hard Times (GB: The Street-fighter). Bite the Bullet. 1976: Sky Riders. The Last Hard Men. White Rock. A Fast Drive in the Country (and narrator). Midway (GB: Battle of Midway). 1977: Cross of Iron. 1978: The Dain Curse (TV). California Suite. Crimes obscurs en Extrême-Occident. 1979: The Muppet Movie. The Baltimore Bullet. Golden-girl. Firepower. 1980: High Risk. Loving Couples. The Fall Guy (TV). 1981: Looker. 1983: Malibu (TV). Mr Patman/Crossover. Digital Dreams. 1984: Martin's Day. Draw! (TV Originally for cinemas). Sins of the Father. 1986: Death of a Soldier. Phoenix Fire. 1988: Walking After Midnight. 1989: Train to Heaven. 1990: Young Guns II. 1991: Hudson Hawk. Helicon/The Doorman. 1992: Hugh Hefner: Once Upon a Time (narrator only). The Player. Crash Landing: The Rescue of Flight 232 (TV). 1993: Deadfall. The Hit List. Sister Act 2: Back in the Habit. A Christmas Reunion (TV). Greyhounds (TV). 1994: Ray Alexander: A Taste for Justice (TV). Maverick. 1995: Avenging Angel. 1996: Eraser. The Nutty Professor. Skeletons. Third Cowboy on the Right. The Cherokee Kid (TV). Keys to Tulsa. 1997: The Disappearance of Kevin Johnson (completed 1995). Affliction. The Second Civil War (TV). 1998: Mr Murder (TV). Payback. 1999: Intrepid. Noah's Ark (TV). The Good Doctor. 2000: Atticus (TV). Missing Pieces. 2001: Proximity.

COCHRAN, Steve
(Robert Cochran) 1917–1965
Dark, handsome, young-looking American actor whose beetle brows made him slightly menacing, and got him cast as good-looking snakes-in-the-grass, hoodlums with slicked-back hair who were also ladies' men. Never quite made the top, but his off-screen love life, which rivalled that of Errol Flynn, kept him in the public eye. Died of acutely swollen lung tissue sustained aboard his boat when caught in a hurricane with his three-girl crew.
1943: Stage Door Canteen. 1945: Wonder Man. Boston Blackie Booked on Suspicion (GB: Booked on Suspicion). The Gay Senorita. Boston Blackie's Rendezvous (GB: Blackie's Rendezvous). 1946: The Kid from Brooklyn. The Best Years of Our Lives. The Chase. 1947: Copacabana. 1948: A Song is Born. 1949: White Heat. 1950: The Damned Don't Cry. Highway 301. Storm Warning. The West Point Story (GB: Fine and Dandy). Dallas. 1951: Raton Pass (GB: Canyon Pass). The Tanks Are Coming. Inside the Walls of Folsom Prison. Jim

Thorpe – All American (GB: Man of Bronze). Tomorrow is Another Day. 1952: The Lion and the Horse. Operation Secret. 1953: She's Back on Broadway. The Desert Song. Back to God's Country. Shark River. 1954: Carnival Story. Private Hell 36. 1955: Come Next Spring. 1956: Slander. The Weapon. 1957: Il grido (GB: The Cry. US: Outcry). 1958: I, Mobster. Quantrill's Raiders. 1959: The Beat Generation (GB: This Rebel Age). The Big Operator. 1961: The Deadly Companions. 1963: Of Love and Desire. 1964: Tell Me in the Sunlight (and directed). 1965: Mozambique.

COLBERT, Claudette
(Lily Claudette Chauchoin) 1903–1996
Pert, petite and sparkling French-born Hollywood star who excelled in sophisticated comedy, also played Poppaea and Cleopatra and sustained her stardom for over 20 years. All her characters in the thirties were impish and spirited in one way or another, none more so than Ellie Andrews in *It Happened One Night*, which won her an Academy Award. Married (first of two) to actor/director Norman Foster, from 1928 to 1935. Also Oscar-nominated for *Since You Went Away* and *Private Worlds*. She made a rare latter-day appearance in the TV mini-series *The Two Mrs Grenvilles* in 1987.
1927: For the Love of Mike. 1929: The Hole in the Wall. The Lady Lies. 1930: †The Big Pond. Young Man of Manhattan. Manslaughter. L'enigmatique Monsieur Parkes. 1931: †The Smiling Lieutenant. Honor Among Lovers. Secrets Of a Secretary. His Woman. 1932: The Wiser Sex. The Misleading Lady. The Man from Yesterday. Make Me a Star. The Phantom President. The Sign of the Cross. 1933: Tonight is Ours. I Cover the Waterfront. Three Cornered Moon. *Hollywood on Parade No. 13. Torch Singer (GB: Broadway Singer). 1934: Four Frightened People. It Happened One Night. Cleopatra. Imitation of Life. 1935: The Gilded Lily. Private Worlds. She Married Her Boss. The Bride Comes Home. 1936: Under Two Flags. 1937: Maid of Salem. Tovarich. I Met Him in Paris. 1938: Bluebeard's Eighth Wife. Zaza. 1939: Midnight. Drums Along the Mohawk. It's a Wonderful World. 1940: Boom Town. Arise, My Love. 1941: Skylark. Remember the Day. 1942: *White House of Hollywood. The Palm Beach Story. 1943: So Proudly We Hail! No Time for Love. 1944: Since You Went Away. 1945: Practically Yours. Guest Wife. Tomorrow is Forever. 1946: Without Reservations. The Secret Heart. 1947:

The Egg and I. Sleep My Love. 1948: Family Honeymoon. 1949: Bride for Sale. 1950: Three Came Home. The Secret Fury. 1951: Thunder on the Hill (GB: Bonaventure). Let's Make It Legal. 1952: The Planter's Wife (US: Outpost in Malaya). 1953: Destinées (GB: Love and the Frenchwoman. US: Daughters of Destiny). Si Versailles m'était conté (GB: Versailles. US: Royal Affairs in Versailles). 1955: Texas Lady. 1957: One Coat of White (TV). 1961: Parrish.

†And French-language version

COLE, George 1925–

British actor of dark, wavy hair and worried mien who can adapt his cultured tones to cockney or other regional English accents at the drop of a lip. Started in straight roles as a teenager, but soon specialized in shy young bachelors who were all thumbs with girls and life in general, following great personal success in radio's *A Life of Bliss*, and became very popular in 1950s' comedies. Later still he moved to prominence on television, at first with more serious portrayals of middle-aged men, but then back in comedy vein, especially in the hit series *Minder*, which ran for several seasons. Married actresses Eileen Moore (1954–1966) and Penny Morrell (1968 on).
1941: Cottage to Let (US: Bombsite Stolen). 1942: Those Kids from Town. 1943: *Fiddling Fuel. The Demi-Paradise (US: Adventure for Two). 1944: Henry V. 1945: Journey Together. 1948: My Brother's Keeper. Quartet. 1949: The Spider and the Fly. 1950: Morning Departure (US: Operation Disaster). The Happiest Days of Your Life. Gone to Earth (US: The Wild Heart). 1951: Flesh and Blood. Laughter in Paradise. Scrooge (US: A Christmas Carol). Lady Godiva Rides Again. 1952: The Happy Family (US: Mr Lord Says No). Who Goes There! (US: The Passionate Sentry). Top Secret (US: Mr Potts Goes to Moscow). Folly to be Wise. 1953: Will Any Gentleman? The Intruder. Our Girl Friday (US: The Adventures of Sadie). The Clue of the Missing Ape. 1954: An Inspector Calls. Happy Ever After (US: Tonight's the Night). The Belles of St Trinian's. A Prize of Gold. 1955: Where There's a Will. The Constant Husband. The Adventures of Quentin Durward (US: Quentin Durward). 1956: It's a Wonderful World. The Green Man. The Weapon. 1957: Blue Murder at St Trinian's. 1959: Too Many Crooks. Don't Panic Chaps! The Bridal Path. 1960: The Pure Hell of St Trinian's. 1961: The Anatomist. 1963: Dr Syn alias the Scarecrow (US: TV, as the

Scarecrow of Romney Marsh). Cleopatra. 1964: One Way Pendulum. 1965: The Legend of Young Dick Turpin. 1966: The Great St Trinian's Train Robbery. 1968: *The Green Shoes. 1970: The Vampire Lovers. 1971: Fright. 1972: Madigan: The London Beat (TV). 1973: Take Me High. 1976: The Blue Bird. 1983: *Perishing Solicitors. 1985: Minder on the Orient Express (TV). 1996: Mary Reilly.

COLEMAN, Nancy 1912–

Auburn-haired, pretty, round faced, sad-looking American actress in quiet roles, most notably Anne Brontë in *Devotion*. Under contract to Warners for a few years, but married the studio publicity head, had twins and disappointingly worked mostly thereafter (sporadically) for stage and television.
1941: Dangerously They Live. Kings Row. 1942: The Gay Sisters. Desperate Journey. 1943: Devotion (released 1946). Edge of Darkness. 1944: In Our Time. 1946: Her Sister's Secret. 1947: Violence. Mourning Becomes Electra. 1953: That Man from Tangier. 1969: Slaves.

COLLEANO, Bonar
(B. Sullivan II) 1924–1958

Dark-haired, angular-faced, American-born actor in British films, familiar as wisecracking GI or sharpster on the make. From a circus family of acrobats (he was performing with them at five) he had a few semi-leads, but was in supporting roles when killed in a car crash at 34. Married to Susan Shaw (*qv*). Initially billed as Bonar Colleano junior.
1940: Neutral Port. 1943: Starlight Serenade. 1944: *We the People. 1945: The Way to the Stars (US: Johnny in the Clouds). 1946: Wanted for Murder. A Matter of Life and

Death (US: Stairway to Heaven). While the Sun Shines. 1947: Broken Journey. 1948: Merry-Go-Round. One Night with You. Good Time Girl. Sleeping Car to Trieste. Once a Jolly Swagman (US: Maniacs on Wheels). 1949: Give Us This Day (US: Salt to the Devil). 1950: Dance Hall. Pool of London. 1951: A Tale of Five Cities (US: A Tale of Five Women). 1952: Eight Iron Men. 1953: Is Your Honeymoon Really Necessary? Escape by Night. 1954: The Flame and the Flesh. Time is My Enemy. The Sea Shall Not Have Them. 1955: Joe Macbeth. 1956: Stars in Your Eyes. Zarak. 1957: Interpol (US: Pickup Alley). Fire Down Below. Death over My Shoulder. 1958: Them Nice Americans. No Time to Die! (US: Tank Force).

COLLETTE, Toni 1972–

Enthusiastic Australian actress with generous mouth, rosy cheeks and large, expressive features. Nominated for an Australian Academy Award in her first film, she won the award three years later in the international hit *Muriel's Wedding*, then played semi-leads in British and Hollywood films. Her facility with British and American accents and engaging personality should keep her in interesting lead character roles for some time to come. Academy Award nominee for *The Sixth Sense*.
1991: Spotswood. 1993: The Marching Girl Thing. 1994: Muriel's Wedding. 1995: Cosi. Arabian Knight (voice only). 1996: Lillian's Story. Clockwatchers. Emma. The Pallbearer. 1997: Diana & Me. The James Gang. 1998: The Boys. Velvet Goldmine. 1999: The Sixth Sense. Hotel Splendide. 8½ Women. 2000: Shaft. Dead by Monday.

COLLINS, Joan 1933–

A classic example of how to make a provocative face, a stunning figure and a great deal of determination go a very long way. A sultry, dark-haired British actress, she was soon in international films; her temptresses' social standings have improved with the longevity of her career, even if one feels the appeal is still very much on the surface. In the 1980s she became a queen of American soap opera in the series *Dynasty*. Her four marriages, to actors Maxwell Reed and Anthony Newley, producer Ron Kass and playboy Peter Holm, all ended in divorce. Also a best-selling novelist.
1951: Lady Godiva Rides Again. The Woman's Angle. Judgment Deferred. 1952: I Believe in

You. Decameron Nights. Cosh Boy (US: The Slasher). 1953: Turn the Key Softly. The Square Ring. Our Girl Friday (US: The Adventures of Sadie). 1954: The Good Die Young. 1955: Land of the Pharaohs. The Virgin Queen. The Girl in the Red Velvet Swing. 1956: The Opposite Sex. 1957: Sea Wife. Island in the Sun. The Wayward Bus. Stopover Tokyo. 1958: The Bravados. Rally 'round the Flag, Boys! 1959: Seven Thieves. 1960: Esther and the King. 1961: The Road to Hong Kong. 1964: La congiuntura. 1967: Warning Shot. 1968: Subterfuge. Can Hieronymous Merkin Ever Forget Mercy Humppe and Find True Happiness? 1969: Drive Hard, Drive Fast (TV). If It's Tuesday, This Must be Belgium. Breve amore. 1970: Up in the Cellar (GB: Three in the Cellar). The Executioner. 1971: Quest for Love. Revenge (US: Inn of the Frightened People). 1972: Fear in the Night. Tales from the Crypt. 1973: Tales that Witness Madness. Dark Places. 1974: Call of the Wolf. The Referee (later Football Crazy). 1975: Alfie Darling (US: Oh! Alfie). The Bawdy Adventures of Tom Jones. I Don't Want to Be Born. 1977: Fatal Charm. Empire of the Ants. 1978: The Stud. The Big Sleep. Zero to Sixty. 1979: The Bitch. Sunburn. Game for Vultures. 1980: Growing Pains/Homework. 1982: Nutcracker. The Wild Women of Chastity Gulch (TV). Paper Dolls (TV). 1983: Making of a Male Model (TV). 1984: The Cartier Affair (TV). Her Life as a Man (TV). 1986: Monte Carlo (TV). 1993: Decadence. 1995: In the Bleak Mid-Winter. Annie! A Royal Adventure (TV). 1996: Hart to Hart: Two Harts in ¾ Time. 1998: Sweet Deception (TV). 1999: The Clandestine Marriage. 2000: The Flintstones in Viva Rock Vegas.

COLMAN, Ronald 1891–1958

Elegant, strong, moustachioed British-born star who moved easily from Latin lovers of the twenties to men of honour in the thirties. Colman made a few films in England before heading for Hollywood, where he became number one box-office attraction for three consecutive years in the late twenties, and stayed on to star in some of the sound cinema's most beguiling entertainments. Long-deserved Oscar finally won for A Double Life (1948). Married to Benita Hume (second wife) from 1938. Died from pneumonia. Previously nominated for Academy Awards in Bulldog Drummond, Condemned and Random Harvest.

1917: *The Live Wire. 1919: The Toilers. A Daughter of Eve. Sheba. Snow in the Desert. 1920: A Son of David. Anna the Adventuress. The Black Spider. 1921: Handcuffs or Kisses. 1923: The Eternal City. The White Sister. Twenty Dollars a Week. 1924: Tarnish. Her Night of Romance. Romola. A Thief in Paradise. 1925: His Supreme Moment. The Sporting Venus. Her Sister from Paris. The Dark Angel. Stella Dallas. Lady Windermere's Fan. 1926: Kiki. Beau Geste. The Winning of Barbara Worth. 1927: The Night of Love. The Magic Flame. 1928: Two Lovers. 1929: The Rescue. Condemned (GB: Condemned to Devil's Island). 1930: Bulldog Drummond. Raffles. The Devil to Pay. 1931: The Unholy Garden. Arrowsmith. 1932: Cynara. 1933: The Masquerader. 1934: Bulldog Drummond Strikes Back. 1935: Clive of India. The Man Who Broke the Bank at Monte Carlo. A Tale of Two Cities. 1936: Under Two Flags. 1937: Lost Horizon. The Prisoner of Zenda. 1938: If I Were King. 1940: Lucky Partners. The Light That Failed. 1941: My Life with Caroline. 1942: The Talk of the Town. Random Harvest. 1944: Kismet. 1947: The Late George Apley. 1948: A Double Life. 1950: Champagne for Caesar. 1953: *The Globe Playhouse (narrator only). 1956: Around the World in 80 Days. 1957: The Story of Mankind.

COMINGORE, Dorothy 1913–1971

Ethereal-looking, chubby-faced Hollywood blonde whose own rise and fall (she was stuck in bit parts and comedy shorts for years before stardom) so paralleled that of Susan Alexander Kane, whom she played in Citizen Kane, that it was uncanny. Still, she was good when it mattered, unlike poor Mrs K. McCarthy blacklisting finally finished her career in 1951.

1938: †Campus Cinderella. †Comet Over Broadway. †Prison Train. 1939: †Blondie Meets the Boss. †Trade Winds. †Five Little Peppers and How They Grew. †*Oily to Bed, Oily to Rise. †*The Awful Goof. †Good Girls Go to Paris. †North of the Yukon. †Mr Smith Goes to Washington. †Scandal Sheet. †Café Hostess/ Street of Missing Women. 1940: †*The Hecklers. †*Rockin' Through the Rockies. Pioneers of the Frontier (GB: The Anchor). 1941: Citizen Kane. 1944: The Hairy Ape. 1949: Any Number Can Play. 1951: The Big Night.

†As Linda Winters

COMPSON, Betty

(Eleanor Compson) 1896–1974

Petite, blue-eyed, bow-lipped redhead (although her hair colour varies from film to film) popular in early silent comedies, but increasingly accepted as a dramatic actress from 1919 on. Survived the coming of sound to become an equally delightful character actress. Married/divorced director James Cruze (first of three). Academy Award nominee for The Barker.

SHORTS: 1914: Wanted – a Leading Lady. Some Chaperone. Jed's Trip to the Fair. Where the Heather Blooms. Their Quiet Honeymoon. 1915: Heist at Six O'Clock. Love and a Savage. Mingling Spirits. Her Steady Car Fare. When the Losers Won. A Quiet Supper for Four. Her Friend the Doctor. When Lizzie Disappeared. Cupid Trims His Lordship. The Deacon's Waterloo. Love and Vaccination. He Almost Eloped. The Janitor's Busy Day. A Leap Year Tangle. Eddie's Night Out. The Newlywed's Mix Up. Lem's College Career. Potts Bungles Again. He's a Devil. The Wooing of Aunt Jemima. 1916: Her Celluloid Hero. All Over a Stocking. Almost a Widow. Wanted – a Husband. His Baby. The Making Over of Mother. A Brass Buttoned Romance. Some Kid. Cupid's Uppercut. Out for the Coin. Her Crooked Career. Her Friend the Chauffeur. Small Change. Hubby's Night Out. 1917: A Bold Bad Night. As Luck Would Have It. Suspended Sentence. His Last Pill. Those Wedding Bells. Almost a Scandal. Down by the Sea. Won in a Cabaret. Crazy by Proxy. Betty's Big Idea. Love and the Locksmiths. Almost a Bigamist. Almost Divorced. 1918: Betty Makes Up. Nearly a Papa. Betty's Adventure. Their Seaside Tangle. Many a Slip. Whose Wife? Cupid's Camouflage. Somebody's Baby. All Dressed Up. A Seminary Scandal. The Sheriff. FEATURES: Border Raiders. 1919: The

Terror of the Range (serial). The Prodigal Liar. The Miracle Man. The Devil's Trail. The Little Diplomat. Light of Victory. 1921: Prisoners of Love. For Those We Love. Ladies Must Live. At the End of the World. The Little Minister. The Law and the Woman. 1922: *A Trip to Paramounttown. The Green Temptation. Over the Border. Always the Woman. The Bonded Woman. To Have and to Hold. 1923: The White Flower. Kick In. The Rustle of Silk. The Woman with Four Faces. Hollywood. Woman to Woman. The Royal Oak. The Prude's Fall. 1924: The White Shadow (US: White Shadows). The Stranger. Miami. The Enemy Sex. Ramshackle House. The Female. The Garden of Weeds. The Fast Set. 1925: New Lives for Old. Pony Express. Paths to Paradise. Beggar on Horseback. Eve's Secret. Locked Doors. 1926: The Counsel for Defense. The Wise Guy (GB: Into the Light). The Belle of Broadway. The Palace of Pleasure. 1927: Twelve Miles Out. The Ladybird. Temptations of a Shop Girl. Say It with Diamonds. Cheating Cheaters. 1928: Big City. The Desert Bride. Love's Mockery. The Masked Angel (GB: Her Love Cottage). Love Me and the World is Mine. Scarlet Seas. The Docks of New York. Court Martial. The Barker. 1929: Woman to Woman (remake). Weary River. The Time, the Place and the Girl. The Show of Shows. Street Girl. The Great Gabbo. Skin Deep. On with the Show. 1930: The Midnight Mystery. Blaze o' Glory. The Case of Sergeant Grischa. Czar of Broadway. Inside the Lines. Isle of Escape. Boudoir Diplomat. Those Who Dance. The Spoilers. She Got What She Wanted. 1931: *Hollywood Halfbacks. The Lady Refuses. Three Who Loved. Virtuous Husband (GB: What Wives Don't Want). The Gay Diplomat. 1932: The Silver Lining. Guilty or Not Guilty. 1933: Destination Unknown. West of Singapore. Notorious But Nice. 1934: *No Sleep on the Deep. 1935: Manhattan Butterfly. False Pretenses. The Millionaire Kid. August Weekend (GB: Weekend Madness). 1936: Laughing Irish Eyes. Bulldog Edition (GB: Lady Reporter). Hollywood Boulevard. The Dragnet. Killer at Large. 1937: Circus Girl. Federal Bullets. God's Country and the Man. Two Minutes to Play. 1938: Torchy Blane in Panama (GB: Trouble in Panama). A Slight Case of Murder. Port of Missing Girls. Blondes at Work. Two Gun Justice. Under the Big Top (GB: The Circus Comes to Town). Religious Racketeers. 1939: The Mystic Circle Murder. News is Made at Night. Cowboys from Texas. 1940: Mad Youth. Strange Cargo. Laughing at Danger. Texas Terrors. 1941: Mr and Mrs Smith. The Roar of the Press. The Invisible Ghost. Escort Girl. 1943: Danger! Women at Work. Her Adventurous Night. 1946: Claudia and David. 1947: Hard Boiled Mahoney. Second Chance. 1948: Here Comes Trouble.

COMPTON, Fay

(Virginia C. Mackenzie) 1894–1978
Dominant, auburn-haired English actress, sister of novelist Sir Compton Mackenzie. A much-revered figure on the London stage between the two World Wars, she forsook leading roles for some demanding character parts thereafter. Third and fourth marriages were to actors Leon Quartermaine and Ralph Michael.

1914: She Stoops to Conquer. 1917: One Summer's Day. The Labour Leader. 1920: Judge Not. 1921: A Woman of No Importance. The Old Wives' Tale. 1922: The House of Peril. Diana of the Crossways. A Bill for Divorcement. 1923: This Freedom. The Loves of Mary Queen of Scots. 1924: Claude Duval. The Happy Ending. The Eleventh Commandment. 1925: Settled Out of Court. *Stage Stars Off Stage. 1926: London Love. 1927: Robinson Crusoe. Somehow Good. 1928: Zero. 1929: Fashions in Love. 1930: Cape Forlorn (US: The Love Storm). 1931: Uneasy Virtue. Tell England (US: The Battle of Gallipoli). 1934: Waltzes from Vienna (US: Strauss's Great Waltz). Autumn Crocus. The Phantom Light. Song at Eventide. 1936: Wedding Group (US: Wrath of Jealousy). The Mill on the Floss. 1938: *Cavalcade of the Stars. 1939: So This is London. 1941: The Prime Minister. 1946: Odd Man Out. 1947: Nicholas Nickleby. 1948: London Belongs to Me (US: Dulcimer Street). Esther Waters. 1949: Britannia Mews (US: Forbidden Street). 1950: Blackmailed. 1951: Othello. Laughter in Paradise. 1952: I vinti. 1954: Aunt Clara. 1956: Doublecross. Town on Trial! 1957: The Story of Esther Costello (US: Golden Virgin). 1962: In the Cool of the Day. 1963: Uncle Vanya. The Haunting. 1969: I Start Counting. 1970: The Virgin and the Gypsy.

CONNELLY, Jennifer 1970–
Stunning raven-haired American actress, a child and teenage player who grew into a tall, busty beauty almost too lovely to get decent roles, although she's done well when given the chance. Modelling at 10, she retained her childlike facial features in womanhood and has shown signs of fighting to avoid being

seen as mere decoration in glossy action films. *1983: Once Upon a Time in America. 1984: Phenomena/Creepers. 1986: Labyrinth. Seven Minutes in Heaven/This Side of Heaven. 1988: Some Girls (GB: Sisters). 1989: Ballerina/Etoile. 1990: The Hot Spot. 1991: Career Opportunities. The Rocketeer. 1993: Heart of Justice (TV). 1994: Higher Learning. Of Love and Shadows (released 1996). 1995: Mulholland Falls. 1996: Inventing the Abbotts. Mr Spreckman's Boat/Far Harbor. 1997: Dark City. 1998: Waking the Dead (released 2000). 2000: Requiem for a Dream.*

CONNERY, Sir Sean

(Thomas S. Connery) 1930–
Tall, dark, Scottish-born star whose rather bland youthful looks became much more interesting in middle age. Not everyone's ideal James Bond, he created the part on screen in 1962 and quickly made it his own. Has since defied receding hair to continue in a variety of rugged leading roles into his seventies, conveying a number of different nationalities with complete conviction, in spite of a continuing Scottish burr. Married to Diane Cilento (first of two) from 1962 to 1972. An Academy Award winner for *The Untouchables*, he is now one of cinema's most admired actors. Father of actor Jason Connery. Knighted in 2000.

1954: Lilacs in the Spring (US: Let's Make Up). 1956: No Road Back. 1957: Time Lock. Hell Drivers. Action of the Tiger. 1958: Darby O'Gill and the Little People. Another Time, Another Place. A Night to Remember. 1959: Tarzan's Greatest Adventure. 1961: The Frightened City. On the Fiddle (US: Operation Snafu). 1962: The Longest Day. Dr No. 1963: From Russia with Love. 1964: Woman of Straw. Goldfinger. Marnie. 1965: The Hill. Thunderball. 1966: A Fine Madness. 1967: You Only Live Twice. *The Castles of Scotland (narrator only). 1968: Shalako. 1969: The Molly Maguires. The Red Tent. †The Bowler and the Bonnet. 1971: The Anderson Tapes. Diamonds Are Forever. 1972: Something like the Truth (later The Offence). 1973: Zardoz. 1974: Murder on the Orient Express. Ransom (US: The Terrorists). 1975: The Wind and the Lion. The Man Who Would Be King. 1976: Robin and Marian. The Next Man. 1977: A Bridge Too Far. 1978: The First Great Train Robbery. 1979: Meteor. Cuba. 1981: Time Bandits. Outland. 1982: The Man with the Deadly Lens. Five Days One Summer. *Burning (narrator only). 1983: Never Say Never Again.

*Sword of the Valiant. 1985: Highlander. 1986: The Name of the Rose. 1987: The Rose of the Names. The Untouchables. 1988: The Presidio. Memories of Me. 1989: Indiana Jones and the Last Crusade. Family Business. 1990: The Hunt for Red October. The Russia House. Highlander II: The Quickening. *Wake-Up Call. 1991: Robin Hood – Prince of Thieves. Medicine Man. 1993: Rising Sun. A Good Man in Africa. 1995: Just Cause. First Knight. 1996: Dragonheart (voice only). The Rock. 1998: The Avengers. Playing by Heart. 1999: Entrapment. 2001: Unconditional Love. Finding Forrester.*

†Also directed

CONNOLLY, Billy 1942–

Scottish comedian and (much later) dramatic actor with wild hair, bulging eyes and frenzied beard. A big man, Connolly worked as a shipyard welder before his hobby – banjo-playing – led him into show-business where he joined a folk group, The Humblebums. He moved on to become a stand-up comedian who told scabrous stories with lots of bad language. He became a major TV star, and a well-known face in commercials, but acting appearances were hit and miss until he shed the beard at the beginning of the 1990s and began playing men of presence and sometimes menace.

1978: Absolution (released 1981). 1979: The Secret Policeman's Ball. 1981: Concert for Kampuchea. 1982: Blue Money (TV). The Secret Policeman's Other Ball. 1983: Bullshot! 1985: Water. 1986: To the North of Katmandu. 1987: The Hunting of the Snark. 1989: The Return of the Musketeers. 1990: The Big Man (US: Crossing the Line). 1993: Indecent Proposal. 1995: Pocahontas (voice only). 1996: Muppet Treasure Island. 1997: Mrs Brown. Paws (voice only). 1998: The Imposters/Ship of Fools. Middleton's Changeling. Still Crazy. 1999: The Debt Collector. Boondock Saints. Columbo: Murder with Too Many Notes (TV). 2000: Beautiful Joe. An Everlasting Piece. 2001: Cletis Tout.

CONNORS, Chuck

(Kevin Connors) 1921–1992

Big, tall, fair-haired, hatchet-faced American leading man, a former basketball and baseball professional who took up acting when he quit sport. Swiftly in demand for ethnic bad guys, he later became a big star in TV series, but never in films: the title role in *Geronimo* was the nearest he came. Later hung around for the occasional monolithic villain. Married

(second) to actress Kamala Devi 1963–1972. Died from lung cancer.

1952: Pat and Mike. 1953: Trouble along the Way. Code Two. South Sea Woman. 1954: Naked Alibi. Dragonfly Squadron. The Human Jungle. 1955: Target Zero. Good Morning, Miss Dove. Three Stripes in the Sun (GB: The Gentle Sergeant). 1956: Hold Back the Night. Hot Rod Girl. Walk The Dark Street. 1957: Tomahawk Trail. Designing Woman. Death in Small Doses. Old Yeller. The Hired Gun. The Lady Takes a Flyer. 1958: The Big Country. 1962: Geronimo. 1963: Flipper. Move Over, Darling. 1965: Synanon (GB: Get Off My Back). Broken Sabre (TV. GB: cinemas). 1966: Ride Beyond Vengeance. 1968: Captain Nemo and the Underwater City. Kill Them All and Come Back Alone. 1969: The Profane Comedy/Set This Town on Fire (TV). 1970: The Deserter. 1971: Pancho Villa. Support Your Local Gunfighter. The Birdmen (TV. GB: cinemas: Escape of the Birdmen). 1972: Night of Terror (TV). Horror at 37,000 Feet (TV). Embassy. The Proud and the Damned (GB: TV). The Mad Bomber. 1973: Soylent Green. Police Story (TV. GB: cinemas). 1974: 99 and 44/100ths % Dead (GB: Call Harry Crown). Wolf Larsen (US: Sea Wolf). The Police Connection. 1975: Pancho Villa. 1976: Banjo Hackett (TV). Nightmare in Badham County (TV). 1978: Tourist Trap. The Night They Took Miss Beautiful (TV). Standing Tall (TV). 1980: Virus. 1981: Day of the Assassin. Red Alert West. Las mujeres de Jeramias (US: Garden of Venus). The Capture of Grizzly Adams (TV). 1982: Target Eagle. Airplane II The Sequel. 1983: The Vals (released 1985). 1985: Rattlers. Spenser: For Hire (TV). Sakura Killers. Balboa (TV). 1986: Summer Camp Nightmare. 1987: Werewolf (TV). Once Upon a Texas Train (TV). Terror Squad. 1988: Kill and Enjoy/Mania. Trained to Kill. Hell's Heroes. Taxi Killer. 1989: Skinheads. Jump. High Desert Kill (TV). 1990: Critical Action/Three Days to a Kill (released 1992). 1991: Salmonberries. The Gambler Returns: The Luck of the Draw (TV).

CONNORS, Michael

(Kreker Ohanian) 1925–

Dark-haired, heftily built, plastically handsome American star who had a not-too-successful career as a second-league leading man under the name Touch Connors. Then, under his new name, he hit the big time on television, especially in the detective series *Mannix*, which ran from 1967 to 1975. Holly-

wood welcomed him back but continued to give him one-dimensional roles, and he returned to the small screen.

1952: †Sudden Fear. 1953: †Island in the Sky. †The 49th Man. †Sky Commando. 1954: †The Day of Triumph. †Naked Alibi. 1955: †Five Guns West. †Swamp Women. †The Twinkle in God's Eye. 1956: †Oklahoma Woman. †The Day the World Ended. †Jaguar. †Shake, Rattle and Rock. †The Ten Commandments. 1957: Voodoo Woman. 1958: Suicide Battalion. Live Fast, Die Young. 1963: Panic Button. 1964: Good Neighbor Sam. Where Love Has Gone. 1965: Situation Hopeless But Not Serious. Harlow. 1966: Stagecoach. 1967: Kiss the Girls and Make Them Die. 1973: Beg, Borrow or Steal (TV). 1975: The Killer Who Wouldn't Die (TV). 1976: Revenge for a Rape (TV). 1977: Stigma (TV). 1978: Long Journey Back (TV). Cruise Missile. 1979: Avalanche Express. High Midnight (TV). Casino (TV. GB: SS Casino). 1980: The Death of Ocean View Park (TV). NightKill. 1981: Today's FBI (TV). 1984: Too Scared to Scream. 1988: Fistfighter. 1990: Friend to Friend. 1992: Armen and Bullik. 1993: Public Enemy No.2. Hart to Hart Returns (TV). 1994: Downtown Heat. 1995: Wild Bill: Hollywood Maverick. 1996: James Dean – Race with Destiny. (TV. Released 1999). 1999: Gideon (TV).

†As Touch Connors

CONSTANTINE, Eddie 1917–1993 .

Squat, dark, tough-looking American actor and singer, of Russian parentage, who broke into French films after radio and recording success, and was an almost instant hit in Bogart-style private-eye roles, especially as detectives Nick Carter and Lemmy Caution.

Many others (notably George Nader, *qv*) followed his example, but none were as successful. Later widened his range and, although failing to make a decisive mark on the international market, he remained popular in continental pot-boilers. Died (in Germany) from a heart attack.

1953: *Egypt by Three. La môme vert-de-gris (US: Poison Ivy). Cet homme est dangereux. Les femmes s'en balancent.* 1954: *Vote devoué Blake. Avanzi di galeria. Ça va Barder (US: There Goes Barder). Repris de Justice.* 1955: *Vous pigez. Je suis un sentimental (GB: Headlines of Destruction).* 1956: *Les truands. Folies-Bergère. Bonsoir Paris, bonjour l'amour. L'homme et l'enfant.* 1957: *Le grand bluff. Ces dames préfèrent le mambo. Incognito.* 1958: *Hopla jetzt kommt Eddie. Passport to Shame (US: Room 43).* 1959: *The Treasure of San Teresa (US: Long Distance). Du rififi chez les femmes. SOS Pacific. Ravissante.* 1960: *Bomben auf Monte Carlo. Comment qu'elle est? Ne faire ça à moi. Ça va etre ta fête.* 1961: *Le chien de pique. Mani in alto/Hands Up! The Seven Deadly Sins. Bonne chance, Charlie. Lemmy pour les dames. Une grosse tête. Cause toujours, mon lapin. En plein bagarre.* 1962: *Cleo de 5 à 7. Les femmes d'abord (GB: Riff Raff Girls). L'empire de la nuit. Nous irons à Deauville. Comme s'il en pleuvait.* 1963: *Rote Lippen soll man küssen. Comment trouvez-vous ma soeur? Des frissons partout. A toi de faire, Mignonne (US: Your Turn Darling).* 1964: *Lucky Jo (US: Lucky Joe). Nick Carter va tout casser (US: Licence to Kill). Laissez tirer les tireurs. Ces dames s'en mêlent. Alphaville.* 1965: *Feu à volonté. Je vous salue Maffia (US: Hail Mafia). Cartes sur table (US: Attack of the Robots). Nick Carter et le trèfle rouge.* 1967: *Residencia para espias.* 1968: *A tout casser (GB: The Great Chase). Les gros malins.* 1969: *Lions' Love.* 1970: *Malatesta.* 1971: *Warnung vor einen heiligen Nutte (US: Beware of a Holy Whore). Eddie geht weiter/Haytabo.* 1973: *Welt am Draht (TV).* 1974: *Une baleine qui avait mal aux dents.* 1975: *Der zweite Frühling. Souvenir of Gibraltar.* 1976: *Le couple temoin. Raid on Entebbe (TV. GB: cinemas).* 1977: *Mort au sang donneur/Blood-Relations.* 1978: *It Lives Again!* 1979: *Die dritte Generation. The Long Good Friday. Bildnis einer Trinkerin.* 1980: *Box Office. Exit . . . nur keine Panik! Tango durch Deutschland. Rote Liebe. Car Napping.* 1981: *Freak Orlando.* 1983: *Flight to Berlin.* 1984: *J'ai bien l'honneur. Dorian Grey im Spiegel der Boulevardpresse.* 1985: *Tiger – Frühling in Wien. Paul Chevrolet en de ultieme hallucinatie.* 1986: *Frankenstein's Aunt. Macaroni Blues.* 1987: *DeadHeat. Nouvelles brigades du tigre.* 1988: *The Return of Lemmy Caution. Pehavy Max a Strasilda.* 1989: *Europa Abends.* 1990: *Europa.*

CONTE, Richard
(Nicholas Conte) 1910–1975

Dark-haired Italianate American actor, mostly in crime dramas as life's underdogs from the wrong side of the tracks. He had some fine leading roles in realist thrillers at Twentieth Century-Fox in the late forties and, although top stardom had slipped away by the late fifties, he continued working steadily until his early death from a heart attack.

1939: *†Heaven with a Barbed-Wire Fence.* 1943: *Guadalcanal Diary.* 1944: *The Purple Heart.* 1945: *A Bell for Adano. Captain Eddie. The Spider. A Walk in the Sun.* 1946: *Somewhere in the Night. 13 Rue Madeleine.* 1947: *The Other Love. Call Northside 777.* 1948: *Cry of the City.* 1949: *House of Strangers. Thieves' Highway. Whirlpool. Big Jack.* 1950: *The Sleeping City. Under the Gun.* 1951: *Hollywood Story. The Raging Tide.* 1952: *The Fighter. The Raiders.* 1953: *The Blue Gardenia. Desert Legion. Slaves of Babylon. Highway Dragnet.* 1954: *Mask of Dust (US: Race for Life). Little Red Monkey (US: The Case of the Little Red Monkey).* 1955: *New York Confidential. Target Zero. The Big Combo. The Big Tip-Off. Bengazi. I'll Cry Tomorrow.* 1956: *Full of Life. Overnight Haul (TV. GB: cinemas).* 1957: *The Brothers Rico. This Angry Age (GB: The Sea Wall).* 1959: *They Came to Cordura.* 1960: *Ocean's Eleven. Pepe.* 1963: *Who's Been Sleeping in My Bed? The Eyes of Annie Jones.* 1964: *Circus World (GB: The Magnificent Showman).* 1965: *Synanon (US: Get Off My Back). The Greatest Story Ever Told.* 1966: *Assault on a Queen. Hotel.* 1967: *Tony Rome. Death Sentence.* 1968: *Lady in Cement. The Challengers (TV. GB: cinemas).* 1969: *Explosion. Operation Cross Eagles.* 1971: *The Godfather.* 1972: *L'onorata famiglia (Uccidere è Cosa Nostra. US: The Big Family).* 1973: *Tony Arzenta/Big Guns. La polizia vuole giustizia (US: The Violent Professionals). Piazza Pulita (GB and US: Pete, Pearl and the Pole). Il boss (GB: Murder Inferno. US: The New Mafia). My Brother Anastasia. The Inspector is Killed.* 1974: *Il poliziotto è marcio (US: Shoot First, Die Later). Anna quel particolare piacere (GB: Secrets of a Call Girl. US: Anna: the Pleasure, the Torment).* 1975: *No Way Out. Roma violenta (GB: Street Killers). The Spectres. The Evil Eye. Un urlo dalle tenebre (GB: Naked Exorcism. US: Who Are You Satan?). The Citizen Needs Self Protection. The Police Accuse.*

As director: 1969: *Operation Cross Eagles.*

†As Nicholas Conte

CONTI, Tom 1941–

Black-haired (now greying) Scottish actor of wry-faced handsomeness who won praise on television (especially for the series *The Glittering Prizes*) and in the theatre, but had problems finding his slot in films until he played the dissolute lothario poet in

Reuben, Reuben, which won him an Oscar nomination. He still looks uncomfortable, though, playing straightforward leading men, and is best suited to a script on which he can impose his dominant offbeat personality. More lately seen in eccentric cameos.

1974: *Flame. Galileo.* 1976: *Eclipse. Full Circle.* 1977: *The Duellists.* 1980: *Blade on the Feather (TV).* 1981: *The Wall (TV).* 1982: *Reuben, Reuben. Merry Christmas, Mr Lawrence.* 1985: *American Dreamer. Saving Grace.* 1986: *Miracles. Io e D'Annunzio. Nazi Hunter: The Beate Klarsfeld Story (TV. GB: Nazi Hunter: The Search for Klaus Barbie). Heavenly Pursuits.* 1987: *Beyond Therapy. The Quick and the Dead (TV). Roman Holiday (TV).* 1988: *Fatal Judgement (TV). Two Brothers, Running.* 1989: *That Summer of White Roses. Shirley Valentine.* 1990: *Shattered/Voices Within.* 1991: *The Siege of Venice/Caccia alla vedova.* 1995: *Someone Else's America.* 1997: *Crush Depth/Sub Down (TV). Something to Believe In. The Inheritance (TV). Out of Control.* 1998: *Don't Go Breaking My Heart (US: Us Begins with You).*

CONWAY, Tom
(Thomas Sanders) 1904–1967

Russian-born international actor of British parents, brother of George Sanders, whom he followed to Hollywood in 1939. Well remembered as the suave, moustachioed hero of many a minor thriller, most notably as The Falcon, in a series he inherited from his brother. Sustained stardom in black-and-white thrillers until well into his fifties, when high living and heavy drinking took its toll. Died from cirrhosis of the liver.

1940: *Waterloo Bridge (voice only). Sky Murder.* 1941: *The Trial of Mary Dugan. Free* and Easy. The People versus Dr Kildare (GB: My Life Is Yours). Wild Man of Borneo. Mr and Mrs North. Lady Be Good. Tarzan's Secret Treasure. The Bad Man (GB: Two Gun Cupid). 1942: Rio Rita. Grand Central Murder. Mrs Miniver. The Falcon's Brother. Cat People. 1943: The Seventh Victim. I Walked with a Zombie. The Falcon Strikes Back. The Falcon in Danger. The Falcon and the Co-Eds. One Exciting Night. 1944: The Falcon Out West. The Falcon in Hollywood. The Falcon in Mexico. A Night of Adventure. 1945: Two O'Clock Courage. The Falcon in San Francisco. 1946: The Falcon's Alibi. Whistle Stop. Criminal Court. The Falcon's Adventure. Runaway Daughters. 1947: Repeat Performance. Fun on a Week-End. Lost Honeymoon. 1948: The Checkered Coat. The Challenge. Thirteen Lead Soldiers. Bungalow 13. One Touch of Venus. 1949: I Cheated the Law. 1950: The Great Plane Robbery. 1951: Painting the Clouds with Sunshine. Bride of the Gorilla. 1952: Confidence Girl. 1953: Paris Model. Tarzan and the She-Devil. Peter Pan (voice only). Blood Orange. Park Plaza 605 (US: Norman Conquest). 1954: Prince Valiant. Three Stops to Murder. 1955: Barbados Quest (US: Murder on Approval). 1956: Breakaway. The Last Man to Hang? Operation Murder. Death of a Scoundrel. The She-Creature. 1957: Voodoo Woman. 1959: Atomic Submarine. 1960: Twelve to the Moon. 1961: One Hundred and One Dalmatians (voice only). 1964: What a Way to Go!

COOGAN, Jackie 1914–1984

American child star whose floppy fair hair and lovelorn expression endeared him to millions. In the 1930s he was involved in court battles with his parents over earnings (he was left with $125,000 out of an original $4 million) and his unique box-office appeal vanished (so, too, did the hair) with adulthood. After unsuccessful attempts to stay in leading roles, he reappeared in the 1950s as a plump character actor. Married (first of four) to Betty Grable (qv) from 1937 to 1939. Died from a heart ailment.

1916: Skinner's Baby. 1919: A Day's Pleasure. 1920: The Kid. 1921: Peck's Bad Boy. 1922: My Boy. Oliver Twist. Trouble. 1923: Daddy. Circus Days. 1924: Long Live the King. A Boy of Flanders. Little Robinson Crusoe. The Rag Man. 1925: Johnny Get Your Gun. Old Clothes. 1926: Johnny Get Your Hair Cut. 1927: The Bugle Call. Buttons. 1930: *Voice of Hollywood No.2. Tom Sawyer. 1931: Huckle-

berry Finn. 1935: Home on the Range. 1936: *Love in September. 1938: College Swing (GB: Swing, Teacher, Swing). 1939: Million Dollar Legs. Sky Patrol. 1947: Kilroy Was Here. 1948: French Leave (GB: Kilroy on Deck). 1951: Skipalong Rosenbloom. Varieties on Parade. 1952: Outlaw Women. 1953: The Actress. 1954: Mesa of Lost Women/Lost Women. 1956: Forbidden Area (TV). The Proud Ones. 1957: The Buster Keaton Story. The Joker is Wild. The Star-Wagon (TV). Eighteen and Anxious. The Troublemakers. 1958: High School Confidential! Lonelyhearts. No Place to Land (GB: Man Mad). The Space Children. Night of the Quarter Moon. 1959: The Big Operator. The Beat Generation. 1960: Sex Kittens Go to College. Platinum High School (GB: Rich, Young and Deadly). Escape from Terror. 1964: John Goldfarb, Please Come Home. 1965: Girl Happy. 1966: A Fine Madness. 1968: Silent Treatment. Rogue's Gallery. The Shakiest Gun in the West. 1969: Marlowe. 1973: Cahill: United States Marshal (GB: Cahill). 1974: The Phantom of Hollywood (TV). 1975: The Manchu Eagle Murder Caper Mystery. Won Ton Ton, the Dog Who Saved Hollywood. 1976: Sherlock Holmes in New York (TV). 1979: Human Experiments. 1980: Dr Heckyl and Mr Hype. 1982: The Escape Artist. The Specialists (TV). 1983: The Prey.

COOK, Donald 1900–1961

Sturdily-built, round-faced, gentlemanly American actor with florid complexion and low eyebrows. He was a big star on the stage, but his darkly handsome features bore a faint scowl about them that often got him cast as shifty characters during what must have been a faintly frustrating film career. He had a few good leads, notably in Jennie Gerhardt and The Kiss Before the Mirror, yet the role for which he's most remembered was in his familiar let-you-down lover vein: that of Steve in the 1936 Show Boat. He was found dying from a heart attack at 61 after failing to arrive for the performance of a play in which he was starring.

1930: *Roseland. East Side. 1931: The Public Enemy (GB: Enemies of the Public). Party Husband. Side Show. Unfaithful. The Mad Genius. Safe in Hell (GB: The Lost Lady). The Man Who Played God (GB: The Silent Voice). 1932: Taxi! The Trial of Vivienne Ware. The Conquerors. The Heart of New York. Penguin Pool Murder (GB: The Penguin Pool Mystery). New Morals for Old. So Big. Washington Merry-Go-Round (GB: Invisible Power).

1933: Frisco Jenny. Private Jones. The Kiss Before the Mirror. The Circus Queen Murder. Jennie Gerhardt. Baby Face. Brief Moment. The World Changes. The Woman I Stole. Fury of the Jungle (GB: Jury of the Jungle). 1934: Fog. Viva Villa! Long Lost Father. The Ninth Guest. Whirlpool. Jealousy. Most Precious Thing in Life. Fugitive Lady. 1935: The Night is Young. Behind the Evidence. The Casino Murder Case. Ladies Love Danger. Gigolette (GB: Night Club). Murder in the Fleet. Here Comes the Band. Confidential. Motive for Revenge. The Spanish Cape Mystery. 1936: Show Boat. Ring Around the Moon. Can This Be Dixie? The Leavenworth Case. Ellis Island. The Calling of Dan Matthews. The Girl from Mandalay. 1937: Circus Girl. Two Wise Maids. Beware of Ladies. 1944: Bowery to Broadway. Murder in the Blue Room. 1945: Patrick the Great. Here Come the Co-Eds. Blonde Ransom. 1950: Our Very Own.

COOK, Marianne
See KOCH, Marianne

COOK, Rachael Leigh 1979–

Diminutive, delicately beautiful, dark-haired, big-eyed American actress, spectacularly miscast as the school dork in what nonetheless proved to be her breakthrough film She's All That. A child model who turned to acting as a teenager, she's a vegetarian and vigorous anti-drugs campaigner: in a notably successful TV commercial she smashed an egg with a frying pan and told viewers that this was their brain on heroin. Has been quoted as saying: 'If this whole acting thing doesn't work out, I'll just get a talk show.' At the moment, there doesn't look much danger of that.

1994: 26 Summer Street. 1995: The Baby-Sitters Club. Tom and Huck. 1996: Carpool. 1997: The House of Yes. The Eighteenth Angel. The Defenders: Payback (TV). Country Justice (TV). 1998: The Naked Man. Strike! Living Out Loud. 1999: She's All That. The Hi-Line. The Bumblebee Flies Anyway. 2000: Never Better. Texas Rangers. Get Carter. Northanger Abbey. Antitrust. Blow Dry. 2001: Josie and the Pussycats. Tangled.

COOPER, Ben 1930–

Fresh-faced, auburn-haired, pink-cheeked, blue-eyed American actor, usually as brash young cowboys and adventurers. A juvenile player on radio and TV, he progressed quickly to become star or co-star of dozens

(at least, it seemed like dozens) of Republic pictures, and second lead in occasional quality films. Alas, the baby face that had helped shoot him to prominence was also his downfall; the 'young buckaroo' never really graduated to becoming an old buckaroo, and later combined business and acting careers.

1950: Side Street. 1952: Thunderbirds. The Woman They Almost Lynched. 1953: A Perilous Journey. Sea of Lost Ships. 1954: The Outcast (GB: The Fortune Hunter). Johnny Guitar. Jubilee Trail. Flight Nurse. Hell's Outpost. 1955: The Fighting Chance. The Eternal Sea. The Last Command. Headline Hunters. The Rose Tattoo. 1956: A Strange Adventure. Rebel in Town. 1957: Duel at Apache Wells. Outlaw's Son. 1960: Chartroose Caboose. 1963: The Raiders. Gunfight at Comanche Creek. 1965: Arizona Raiders. 1966: Waco. The Fastest Guitar Alive. 1967: Red Tomahawk. 1971: One More Train to Rob. Support Your Local Gunfighter. 1975: The Sky's the Limit. 1994: Lightning Jack.

COOPER, Chris 1951–
Grim-lipped, squarely-built, slightly haunted-looking American actor with thick brown hair. A latecomer to films, but a star in his first, Cooper is often seen as working-class men of great principle, involved in struggles for rights and/or the land. His anguished features, which don't show their age, have been especially effective in films for director John Sayles, for whom he has consistently played star roles while supporting the leading players elsewhere.

1987: Matewan. 1988: Eugene O'Neill:

Journey into Genius (TV). 1990: A Little Piece of Sunshine (TV). *To the Moon Alice. A Thousand Pieces of Gold. 1991: City of Hope. Darrow (TV). Guilty by Suspicion. In Broad Daylight (TV). 1992: Bed of Lies (TV). Ned Blessing: The True Story of My Life/Lone Justice (TV). 1993: This Boy's Life. 1994: One More Mountain (TV). 1995: Money Train. Boys. Pharaoh's Army. 1996: Lone Star. The Deliverance of Elaine (TV). A Time to Kill. 1997: Great Expectations. Breast Men (TV). Horton Foote's Alone (TV). 1998: The Horse Whisperer. 1999: October Sky/The Rocket Boys. The 24-Hour Woman. American Beauty. 2000: Me, Myself & Irene. Patriot.

COOPER, Gary (Frank Cooper) 1901–1961
Gentle-mannered, soft voiced, tall, fair-haired, rather gangling Hollywood superstar with piercing blue eyes. Came to fame in westerns, then moved into comedy and finally back again to the west, where his 'yup' was imitated by a thousand impressionists. His image of the peace-loving man ultimately stirred to action was etched into film history by his Oscars for Sergeant York and High Noon. Was awarded an honorary Oscar in 1960. Died from cancer. Also Oscar-nominated for Mr Deeds Goes to Town, Pride of the Yankees and For Whom the Bell Tolls.

1923: Blind Justice. 1925: Dick Turpin. The Thundering Herd. Wild Horse Mesa. The Lucky Horseshoe. *Tricks. The Eagle. Poverty Row. *Lightnin' Wins. The Vanishing American (GB: The Vanishing Race). The Enchanted Hill. Three Pals. 1926: Watch Your Wife. Old Ironsides. Lightning Justice. The Winning of Barbara Worth. 1927: Arizona Bound. The Last Outlaw. Nevada. Wings. Children of Divorce. It. Quicksands. 1928: Beau Sabreur. The Legion of the Condemned. Half a Bride. The First Kiss. Lilac Time (GB: Love Never Dies). 1929: The Shopworn Angel. Wolf Song. The Betrayal. The Virginian. 1930: Seven Days' Leave (GB: Medals). Only the Brave. Paramount on Parade. The Texan (GB: The Big Race). A Man from Wyoming. The Spoilers. Morocco. 1931: Fighting Caravans. City Streets. I Take This Woman. His Woman. 1932: Make Me a Star. The Devil and the Deep. If I Had a Million. A Farewell to Arms. *Voice of Hollywood. *The Stolen Jools (GB: The Slippery Pearls). *Hollywood on Parade A-Z. 1933: Today We Live. One Sunday Afternoon. Design for Living. Alice in Wonderland. 1934: Operator 13 (GB: Spy

13). *Hollywood Cavalcade. Now and Forever. 1935: *Hollywood on Parade No. 17. The Wedding Night. Lives of a Bengal Lancer. Peter Ibbetson. *La Fiesta de Santa Barbara. *Star Night at the Cocoanut Grove. 1936: Mr Deeds Goes to Town. Hollywood Boulevard. The General Died at Dawn. The Plainsman. 1937: *Lest We Forget. Souls at Sea. 1938: The Adventures of Marco Polo. Bluebeard's Eighth Wife. The Cowboy and the Lady. 1939: Beau Geste. The Real Glory. 1940: The Westerner. Northwest Mounted Police. 1941: Meet John Doe. Sergeant York. Ball of Fire. 1942: The Pride of the Yankees. *Hedda Hopper's Hollywood No. 3. 1943: For Whom the Bell Tolls. 1944: The Story of Dr Wassell. Casanova Brown. *Memo for Joe. 1945: Along Came Jones. Saratoga Trunk. 1946: Cloak and Dagger. 1947: Variety Girl. Unconquered. 1948: Good Sam. 1949: The Fountainhead. It's a Great Feeling. Task Force. *Snow Carnival. 1950: Bright Leaf. Dallas. USS Teakettle (later You're in the Navy Now). 1951: Starlift. It's a Big Country. Distant Drums. 1952: High Noon. Springfield Rifle. 1953: Return to Paradise. Blowing Wild. 1954: Vera Cruz. Garden of Evil. 1955: The Court-Martial of Billy Mitchell (GB: One Man Mutiny). *Hollywood Mothers. 1956: Friendly Persuasion. 1957: Love in the Afternoon. 1958: Ten North Frederick. Man of the West. *Glamorous Hollywood. The Hanging Tree. 1959: Alias Jesse James. They Came to Cordura. The Wreck of the Mary Deare. 1961: The Naked Edge.

COOPER, Jackie
(John Cooperman Jnr) 1921–
Stocky American actor whose blond hair, button nose and appealing surliness made him immensely popular as a Hollywood child star in the early 1930s, after starting in 'Our Gang' shorts. He was nominated for an Oscar in Skippy, a film made by his uncle, director Norman Taurog. Surviving a traumatic growing-up period, Cooper ultimately became, via minor TV stardom in the 1950s, a character actor, producer and director of the 1970s and 1980s. Notable as Perry White in the 'Superman' films.

1929: *Boxing Gloves. *Bouncing Babies. Fox Movietone Follies of 1929. Sunny Side Up. *Moan & Groan Inc. *Shivering Shakespeare. 1930: *The First Seven Years. *When the Wind Blows. *Bear Shooters. *A Tough Winter. *Pups is Pups. *Teacher's Pet.

*School's Out. *Helping Grandma. *Love
Business. 1931: *Little Daddy. *Bargain Day.
Skippy. Sooky. Young Donovan's Kid (GB:
Donovan's Kid). The Champ. *Jackie Cooper's
Christmas (GB: The Christmas Party). 1932:
When a Feller Needs a Friend (GB: When a
Fellow Needs a Friend). *The Stolen Jools
(GB: The Slippery Pearls). Divorce in the
Family. *Hollywood on Parade B-3. 1933:
Broadway to Hollywood (GB: Ring Up the
Curtain). The Bowery. 1934: Lone Cowboy.
Treasure Island. Peck's Bad Boy. 1935: Dinky.
O'Shaughnessy's Boy. 1936: Tough Guy. The
Devil is a Sissy (GB: The Devil Takes the
Count). 1937: Boy of the Streets. 1938: White
Banners. Gangster's Boy. That Certain Age.
1939: Newsboys' Home. Scouts to the Rescue.
Spirit of Culver (GB: Man's Heritage). Streets
of New York. What a Life! Two Bright Boys.
1940: The Big Guy. Seventeen. The Return of
Frank James. Gallant Sons. 1941: Life with
Henry. Ziegfeld Girl. Her First Beau. Glamour
Boy (GB: Hearts in Springtime). 1942:
*Soaring Stars. Syncopation. Men of Texas
(GB: Men of Destiny). The Navy Comes Thru.
1943: Where Are Your Children? 1947: Stork
Bites Man. Kilroy Was Here. 1948: French
Leave (GB: Kilroy on Deck). 1961: Every-
thing's Ducky. 1968: Shadow on the Land
(TV). 1970: Maybe I'll Come Home Again in
the Spring (TV). 1971: The Astronaut (TV).
The Love Machine. 1973: Chosen Survivors.
1974: The Day the Earth Moved (TV). The
Hunters (TV). Of Men and Women (TV).
1975: Mobile Two (TV). News Jungle (TV).
Skin Money (TV). The Invisible Man (TV).
1977: Operation Petticoat (TV). 1978: Super-
man. 1980: Superman II. 1983: Superman III.
1986: Superman IV: The Quest for Peace.
1987: Surrender. 1993: Lucy and Desi: A
Home Movie (TV).
As director: 1972: Stand Up and Be Counted.
1977: Perfect Gentlemen (TV). 1978:
Rainbow (TV). 1979: The White Shadow
(TV). Sex and the Single Parent (TV). 1980:
Marathon. Rodeo Girl (TV). White Mama
(TV). 1981: Leave 'Em Laughing (TV). The
First Nine Months Are the Hardest (TV).
1982: Rosie: The Rosemary Clooney Story
(TV). 1984: The Night They Saved Christmas
(TV). 1985: Izzy and Mo (TV).

CORBETT, Harry H. 1925–1982
Swarthy, dark-haired British leading
character actor and comedy star with beetle
brows and fiercely staring eyes whose career
was conclusively changed from drama to
comedy by his success in the TV series

Steptoe and Son. But with the odd exception
his film comedy roles were extremely dis-
appointing. Born in Burma. Died from a
heart attack.
1952: Never Look Back. 1954: The Passing
Stranger. 1958: Floods of Fear. Nowhere to
Go. 1959: Shake Hands with the Devil. In the
Wake of a Stranger. The Shakedown. 1960:
Cover Girl Killer. The Big Day. The
Unstoppable Man. Marriage of Convenience.
1961: *Wings of Death. 1962: Time to
Remember. Some People. Sparrows Can't Sing.
Sammy Going South. 1963: What a Crazy
World. Ladies Who Do. 1964: The Bargee.
Rattle of a Simple Man. 1965: Joey Boy. 1966:
Carry On Screaming. The Sandwich Man.
*The Vanishing Busker. 1968: Crooks and
Coronets (US: Sophy's Place). 1971: The
Magnificent Seven Deadly Sins. 1972: Steptoe
and Son. 1973: Steptoe and Son Ride Again.
1974: Percy's Progress. 1976: The Chiffy Kids
(serial). 1977: Hardcore. Jabberwocky.
Adventures of a Private Eye. 1978: What's Up
Superdoc? 1980: Silver Dream Racer.

CORDAY, Mara (Marilyn Watts) 1932–
Sultry, statuesque, dark-eyed American
actress with dark chestnut hair, whose rather
forceful style of acting was wasted by
Universal-International in routine leading
roles. Her most effective performances were
often in supporting roles as fiery Latin-
Americans. Her brief film career ended when
she married actor Richard Long but, after his
sudden death in 1974, she returned in
occasional minor film assignments, mostly in
films starring Clint Eastwood, who had played
a small role in her best film, Tarantula!
1951: Two Tickets to Broadway. 1952:
Toughest Man in Arizona. Tarzan's Savage
Fury. Sea Tiger. Bad Men of Marysville (TV.
GB: cinemas). 1953: Tarzan and the She-
Devil. The Lady Wants Mink. Sweethearts on
Parade. Problem Girls/The Velvet Cage.
Playgirl. 1954: Drums Across the River.
Francis Joins the WACs. Dawn at Socorro.
Money from Home. So This is Paris. 1955:
Man Without a Star. Foxfire. Fury at Red
Gulch (TV. GB: cinemas). The Man from
Bitter Ridge. Tarantula! 1956: Naked Gun.
Francis in the Haunted House. A Day of Fury.
Raw Edge. The Quiet Gun. 1957: Crime
Beneath the Sea (GB: Undersea Girl). The
Girl in Death Row. The Giant Claw. The Black
Scorpion. 1958: Girls on the Loose. 1977: The
Gauntlet. 1983: Sudden Impact. 1989: Pink
Cadillac. 1990: The Rookie.

CORDAY, Rita/Paula
(Jeanne Paule Teipotemarga) 1920–1992
Elegant blonde Hollywood leading lady who
had careers (of sorts) under three different
names. Originally thought to be from
Switzerland, she was actually born in Tahiti
of French-Tahitian ancestry. RKO Radio
gave her a contract in the war years and, as
Rita Corday, she played numerous 'B' feature
heroines for them, several of them in the
'Falcon' thrillers (although never as the same
character). In 1947 she attempted to move
up-market as Paule Croset, then put her
career on hold for marriage (and two
children) to producer Harold Nebenzal. She
returned four years later as Paula Corday and
played a few swashbuckling adventuresses
before leaving the movies for good. Died
following gall bladder surgery.
1942: Hitler's Children. 1943: Government
Girl. Mexican Spitfire's Blessed Event.
Gildersleeve on Broadway. The Falcon and the
Co-Eds. Mr Lucky. The Falcon Strikes Back.
1944: Girl Rush. Adventures of a Rookie. The
Falcon in Hollywood. 1945: West of the Pecos.
The Falcon in San Francisco. The Body
Snatcher. 1946: The Truth About Murder. The
Falcon's Alibi. Dick Tracy Vs Cueball. 1947:
The Exile. 1951: Too Young to Kiss. The
Sword of Monte Cristo. 1952: You for Me. The
Black Castle. Because You're Mine. 1953: The
French Line.

COREY, Wendell 1914–1968
Solemn-faced, dark-haired American star who
started his film career late in life and, despite
some decent leading roles, always looked frail
and older than his years. He was best in
cynical roles, failing to project much force as
straightforward heroes. In later years he
became an alcoholic, dying of a liver ailment.

1947: *Desert Fury.* 1948: *I Walk Alone. The Search. Sorry, Wrong Number. The Accused. Man-Eater of Kumaon.* 1949: *Any Number Can Play. Holiday Affair. Thelma Jordon (GB: The File on Thelma Jordon).* 1950: *No Sad Songs for Me. The Furies. Harriet Craig. The Great Missouri Raid.* 1951: *The Wild Blue Yonder (GB: Thunder Across the Pacific). Rich, Young and Pretty.* 1952: *Carbine Williams. My Man and I. The Wild North.* 1953: *Laughing Anne. Jamaica Run.* 1954: *Hell's Half Acre. Rear Window. Fireman Save My Child.* 1955: *The Big Knife.* 1956: *The Killer is Loose. The Bold and the Brave. The Rack. The Rainmaker.* 1957: *Loving You.* 1958: *The Light in the Forest.* 1959: *Alias Jesse James.* 1964: *Blood on the Arrow.* 1965: *Broken Sabre (TV. GB: cinemas). Agent for H.A.R.M.* 1966: *Waco. Women of the Prehistoric Planet. Picture Mommy Dead.* 1967: *Red Tomahawk. Cyborg 2087.* 1968: *Buckskin. The Starmaker. The Astro Zombies.*

CORRI, Adrienne (A. Riccoboni) 1930–
Tempestuous red-headed Scottish-born actress with a reputation for living life to the full. Has, on the whole, not been seen in many films that showcased her particular talent to advantage. Married/divorced actor Daniel Massey (1933–1998).
1949: *The Romantic Age (US: Naughty Arlette).* 1951: *The River. Quo Vadis?* 1953: *The Kidnappers (US: The Little Kidnappers). The Sinners.* 1954: *Devil Girl from Mars. Meet Mr Callaghan. Lease of Life. Make Me an Offer.* 1955: **The Man Who Stayed Alive. Triple Blackmail.* 1956: *The Feminine Touch (US: The Gentle Touch). Behind the Headlines. The Shield of Faith. Three Men in a Boat.* 1957: *Second Fiddle. The Big Chance. The Surgeon's Knife.* 1958: *Corridors of Blood.* 1959: *The Rough and the Smooth (US: Portrait of a Sinner).* 1960: *The Tell-Tale Heart. Sword of Freedom.* 1961: *The Hellfire Club.* 1962: *Dynamite Jack.* 1963: *Lancelot and Guinevere (US: Sword of Lancelot).* 1965: *Bunny Lake is Missing. A Study in Terror (US: Fog). Doctor Zhivago.* 1967: *The Viking Queen. Woman Times Seven. Africa – Texas Style!* 1968: *The File of the Golden Goose. Cry Wolf.* 1969: *Moon Zero Two.* 1971: *A Clockwork Orange. Vampire Circus.* 1974: *Madhouse. Rosebud.* 1978: *Revenge of the Pink Panther.* 1979: *The Human Factor.*

CORTESE, Valentina 1924–
Italian-born (on New Year's Day) actress

whose auburn hair, green eyes and appealing emotional style brought her to the notice of film producers even before she had left Rome's Academy of Dramatic Art. Her international career was fairly brief (1949–1956) but she later proved her talent in more mature roles. Long married to Richard Basehart (*qv*), but divorced in 1971. Surname spelt Cortesa in American films. Oscar-nominated for *Day for Night*.
1940: *Orizzonte dipinto.* 1941: *L'attore scomparso. Il bravo di Venezia. La cena delle beffe. Regina di Navarra. Primo amore.* 1942: *Soltana un bacio. Una signora dell' Ovest. Orizzonte di sangue. Quattro pagina. Giorni felici. L'angelo bianco.* 1943: *Quattro ragazze sognano. Quartien alti. Chi l'ha visto? Nessuno torna indietro.* 1945: *Un americano in vacanza (US: A Yank in Rome). I dieci commandamenti.* 1946: *Roma, città libera.* 1947: *Il passatore. Les misérables. Il corriere del re. L'ebreo errante.* 1948: *Le carrefour des passions (GB: Crossroads of Passion). The Glass Mountain.* 1949: *Donne senza nome (GB: Unwanted Women). Thieves' Highway. Black Magic. Malaya (GB: East of the Rising Sun).* 1950: *Shadow of the Eagle.* 1951: *The House on Telegraph Hill.* 1952: *Secret People. Lulu.* 1953: *La passeggiata. Donne proibite/Forbidden Women (US: Angels of Darkness).* 1954: *Cartouche. The Barefoot Contessa. Il matrimonio. Répris de justice/Avanzi di galera. Addio mia bella signora.* 1955: *Il conte Aquila. Le amiche. Adriana Lecouvreur. Faccia da mascalzone.* 1956: *Magic Fire. Calabuch.* 1957: *Kean.* 1959: *Amore e guai. *Béatrice.* 1961: *Square of Violence. Barabbas.* 1962: *Axel Munthe.* 1963: *The Evil Eye.* 1964: *The Visit.* 1965: *The Possessed. Juliet of the Spirits.* 1966: *Le soleil noir.* 1968: *The Legend of Lylah Clare. Scusi, faciamo l'amore.* 1969: *Toh, é morta la nonna! Les caprices de Marie. The Secret of Santa Vittoria.* 1970: *First Love. Madly.* 1971: *Le bateau sur l'herbe.* 1972: *L'iguana dalla lingua di fuoco. Brother Sun, Sister Moon. Imputazione di omicidio per uno studente. The Assassination of Trotsky.* 1973: *Il bacio. La nuit américaine (GB and US: Day for Night). Franco Zeffirelli: A Florentine Artist.* 1974: *Appassionata. Tendre Dracula. Amore mio non farmi male.* 1975: *La chair de l'orchidée. La città sconvolta – caccia spietata ai rapitori (US: Kidnap Syndicate). Dracula in Brianza.* 1976: *Friends of Nick Hazard. Le grand escogriffe.* 1977: *Nido de viudas/Widow's Nest.* 1978: *Sentimenti e passione. Tanto va la gatta al lardo.* 1980: *When Time Ran Out . . .* 1982: *La Ferdinanda.* 1987:

Monte Napoleone. Blue Tango. 1988: *The Adventures of Baron Munchausen.* 1989: *The Snare. The Betrothed.* 1990: *Buster's Bedroom.* 1994: *Passaggio per il paradiso.*

CORTEZ, Ricardo
(Jacob Krantz) 1899–1977
Black-haired American actor groomed for stardom in the Valentino mould in the twenties. His square, stern and rather immobile features proved more suitable for villainy with the coming of sound and he drifted on in routine roles until giving up the screen for business interests. Married actress Alma Rubens (A. Smith, 1897–1931): she died at 33 from pneumonia.
1923: *Sixty Cents an Hour. Children of Jazz. Hollywood. Call of the Canyon.* 1924: *The Next Corner. A Society Scandal. The Bedroom Window. This Woman. Feet of Clay. The City That Never Sleeps. Argentine Love.* 1925: *The Swan. The Spaniard (GB: Spanish Love). Not So Long Ago. In the Name of Love. The Pony Express.* 1926: *Ibanez's Torrent (GB: The Torrent). The Cat's Pajamas. Volcano. The Sorrows of Satan. The Eagle of the Sea. New York.* 1927: *Mockery. By Whose Hand? The Private Life of Helen of Troy.* 1928: *Ladies of the Night Club. Excess Baggage. Prowlers of the Sea. The Grain of Dust. The Gun Runner.* 1929: *The Younger Generation. Midstream. New Orleans. The Phantom in the House.* 1930: *The Lost Zeppelin. Montana Moon. Her Man. Illicit.* 1931: *Big Business Girl. Ten Cents a Dance. Behind Office Doors. The Maltese Falcon. White Shoulders. Transgression. Bad Company. Reckless Living.* 1932: *Men of Chance. No One Man. Phantom of Crestwood. Flesh. Thirteen Women. Is My Face Red? Symphony of Six Million (GB: Melody of Life).* 1933: *Broadway Bad (GB: Her Reputation). Midnight Mary. Big Executive. Torch Singer (GB: Broadway Singer). The House on 56th Street.* 1934: *The Big Shakedown. Mandalay. Wonder Bar. The Man with Two Faces. Hat, Coat and Glove. The Firebird. Lost Lady (GB: Courageous).* 1935: *Special Agent. The Frisco Kid. Shadow of Doubt. I Am a Thief. White Cockatoo. Manhattan Moon (GB: Sing Me a Love Song).* 1936: *Man Hunt. The Walking Dead. The Murder of Dr Harrigan. Postal Inspector. The Case of the Black Cat. Talk of the Devil.* 1937: *The Californian (GB: Beyond the Law). West of Shanghai. Her Husband Lies. City Girl.* 1939: *Mr Moto's Last Warning. Charlie Chan in Reno.* 1940: *Murder Over New York.* 1941:

Romance of the Rio Grande. A Shot in the Dark. World Premiere. I Killed That Man. 1942: Rubber Racketeers. Who is Hope Schuyler? Tomorrow We Live. 1944: Make Your Own Bed. 1946: The Inner Circle. The Locket. 1947: Blackmail. 1948: Mystery in Mexico. 1950: Bunco Squad. 1958: The Last Hurrah.

As director: *1938: The Inside Story. 1939: Chasing Danger. Heaven with a Barbed Wire Fence. The Escape. City of Chance. 1940: Free, Blonde and 21. The Girl in 313.*

COSTELLO, Dolores 1905–1979

Pale, square-faced, initially dark-haired (later blonde) American actress of fragile appearance, who was married to John Barrymore (*qv*) from 1928 to 1935. Returned to the screen after the break-up of her marriage but soon found that her silent screen image had dated and left films for good in the 1940s. Daughter of early silent actor Maurice Costello, sister of actress Helene Costello (with whom she appeared in films as a child) and mother of actor John Drew Barrymore (John Barrymore Jr). Died from emphysema.
1911: The Meeting of the Ways. His Sister's Children/The Child Crusoes. The Geranium. 1912: A Juvenile Love Affair. Wanted, a Grandmother. Vultures and Doves. Ida's Christmas. The Money King. The Troublesome Stepdaughters. A Reformed Santa Claus. 1913: The Hindoo Charm. Fellow Voyagers. Some Steamer Scooping. 1914: Etta of the Footlights. Too Much Burglar. The Evil Men Do. 1915: How Cissy Made Good. 1923: The Glimpses of the Moon. Lawful Larceny. 1925: Greater Than a Crown. Bobbed Hair. 1926: Mannequin. The Little Irish Girl. The Sea Beast. Bride of the Storm. The Third Degree. 1927: When a Man Loves (GB: His Lady). Old San Francisco. A Million Bid. The Heart of Maryland. The College Widow. 1928: Glorious Betsy. Tenderloin. 1929: Glad Rag Doll. The Redeeming Sin. Madonna of Avenue A. Hearts in Exile. The Show of Shows. Noah's Ark. 1930: Second Choice. 1931: Expensive Women. 1936: Yours for the Asking. Little Lord Fauntleroy. 1938: The Beloved Brat (GB: A Dangerous Age). Breaking the Ice. 1939: Whispering Enemies. Outside These Walls. King of the Turf. 1942: The Magnificent Ambersons. 1943: This is the Army.

COSTNER, Kevin 1955–

Tall, solidly built, taciturn, light-haired, green-eyed American actor who had a hard struggle to the top in terms of roles he didn't

get and ones that ended up on the cutting-room floor. After a brief fling with marketing and finance, he became a stage manager with a film studio for some years before the breaks began to come. Once in star roles, he began to look like a new Gary Cooper, and took the industry by storm in 1991 with the three-hour epic *Dances With Wolves*, which won him a best director Oscar. In the 1990s, however, his success rate thinned along with his hair, his long-standing marriage fell apart and he became better known for an uneven temperament and desire to wrest control of films from their directors.
1981: Shadows Run Black (released 1986). Sizzle Beach, USA. 1982: †Frances. Winning Streak/Stacy's Knights. Night Shift. Table for Five. 1983: Testament. †The Big Chill. The Gunrunner. 1984: Fandango. 1985: American Flyers. Silverado. 1986: Chasing Dreams. 1987: Amazing Stories. The Untouchables. No Way Out. 1988: Bull Durham. 1989: Field of Dreams. Revenge. 1990: Dances With Wolves (and directed). 1991: Robin Hood – Prince of Thieves. Truth or Dare (GB: In Bed With Madonna). JFK. 1992: The Bodyguard. 1993: A Perfect World. 1994: Wyatt Earp. The War. 1995: Waterworld. 1996: Tin Cup. 1997: The Postman (and directed). 1999: Message in a Bottle. Play It to the Bone. For Love of the Game. 2000: Thirteen Days.

†Most scenes deleted from final release print

COTTEN, Joseph 1905–1994

Quiet, taciturn, crinkly-haired American actor with distinctive grating voice, much associated with Orson Welles. Came late to films after drama criticism and stage experience, but thereafter worked steadily in

the medium, most notably in films for Welles and Hitchcock, and in progressively less worthy ones in recent years. Had been married to first wife for 30 years when she died. From 1960, he was married to actress Patricia Medina (*qv*). He recovered from a stroke in 1981 and an operation to remove his larynx in 1990. Died from pneumonia.
1938: Too Much Johnson (unreleased). 1941: Citizen Kane. Lydia. 1942: The Magnificent Ambersons. Journey into Fear. 1943: Hers to Hold. Shadow of a Doubt. 1944: Gaslight (GB: The Murder in Thornton Square). Since You Went Away. I'll Be Seeing You. 1945: Love Letters. 1946: Duel in the Sun. 1947: The Farmer's Daughter. 1948: Portrait of Jennie (GB: Jennie). 1949: The Third Man. Under Capricorn. Beyond the Forest. Walk Softly, Stranger. 1950: Gone to Earth (US: The Wild Heart. Narrator only). Two Flags West. September Affair. 1951: Half Angel. Peking Express. The Man with a Cloak. 1952: Untamed Frontier. The Steel Trap. 1953: Niagara. A Blueprint for Murder. Egypt by Three (narrator only). 1955: Special Delivery/Vom Himmel gefallen. The Killer is Loose. 1956: The Bottom of the Bottle (GB: Beyond the River). *Nobody Runs Away. 1957: The Halliday Brand. Edge of Innocence (TV). 1958: Touch of Evil. From the Earth to the Moon. 1960: The Angel Wore Red. 1961: The Last Sunset. 1964: Hush . . . Hush, Sweet Charlotte. 1965: The Money Trap. The Great Sioux Massacre. Krakatoa (narrator only). 1966: The Oscar. Some May Live (TV. GB: cinemas). Gli uomini dal passo pesante (GB and US: The Tramplers). I crudeli (GB and US: The Hellbenders). Brighty of Grand Canyon. 1967: Jack of Diamonds. 1968: Rio Hondo (GB: White Comanche). Petulia. Gangster '70 (US: Days of Fire). 1969: The Lonely Profession (TV). Cutter's Trail (TV). Latitude Zero. Keene. 1970: The Grasshopper. Tora! Tora! Tora! E venne l'ora della vendetta. Do You Take This Stranger? (TV). Assault on the Wayne (TV). 1971: Lady Frankenstein. The Screaming Woman (TV). The Abominable Dr Phibes. City Beneath the Sea (TV. GB: cinemas: One Hour to Doomsday). 1972: Lo scopone scientifico (US: The Scientific Card-Player). The Devil's Daughter (TV). Doomsday Voyage. Gli orrori del castello di Norimberga (GB: Baron Blood). 1973: Soylent Green. F for Fake. Timber Tramp. 1974: A Delicate Balance. 1975: Il giustiziere sfida la citta (US: Syndicate Sadists). 1976: The Lindbergh Kidnapping Case (TV). A Whisper in the Dark. 1977: Airport 77. Twilight's Last Gleaming. 1978: L'ordre et la sécurité du monde. Caravans. The Fish Men. Return to Fantasy Island (TV). 1979: Guyana: The Crime of the Century. The House Where Death Lives (re-released 1982 as The House Where Evil Dwells). Island of Mutations. Casino (TV. GB: SS Casino). Trauma. The Concorde Affair. 1980: The Hearse. Heaven's Gate. Delusion. 1981: The Survivor. 1982: Screamers (The Fish Men with added footage). Rambo sfida la citta.

COURT, Hazel 1926–

A small, shapely, green-eyed, red-haired British actress with impishly aristocratic looks, Hazel was a Technicolor technician's

dream. Hollywood would have starred her in easterns or earthy period roles, but British films wasted her, as shy sisters and heroines of (black and white!) second-feature crime dramas. A few horror films in the sixties belatedly revealed her as a good Technicolor bad girl. Married to actors Dermot Walsh (1949–1963) and Don Taylor (both *qv*). Widowed in 1998.

1944: Champagne Charlie. Dreaming. 1946: Gaiety George (US: Showtime). Carnival. 1947: Meet Me at Dawn. The Root of All Evil. Dear Murderer. Holiday Camp. 1948: My Sister and I. Bond Street. Forbidden. 1952: Ghost Ship. 1953: Counterspy (US: Undercover Agent). 1954: Devil Girl from Mars. The Scarlet Web. A Tale of Three Women. 1956: The Narrowing Circle. Behind the Headlines. The Curse of Frankenstein. 1957: Hour of Decision. 1958: A Woman of Mystery. 1959: Model for Murder. Breakout. The Man Who Could Cheat Death. The Shakedown. 1960: The Man Who Was Nobody. 1961: Dr Blood's Coffin. Mary Had a Little. 1962: The Premature Burial. 1963: The Raven. 1964: The Masque of the Red Death. 1981: The Final Conflict.

COURTENAY, Tom 1937–
Unhappy-looking British actor briefly in star roles as undernourished working class misfits, but whose working life has been principally committed to the theatre. Oscar-nominated for *Doctor Zhivago* and *The Dresser*.

1962: The Loneliness of the Long Distance Runner. Private Potter. 1963: Billy Liar! 1964: King and Country. 1965: Operation Crossbow (US: The Great Spy Mission). King Rat. Doctor Zhivago. 1966: The Night of the Generals. 1967: The Day the Fish Came Out.

*1968: A Dandy in Aspic. Otley. 1971: Catch Me a Spy. One Day in the Life of Ivan Denisovitch. 1972: *Today Mexico – Tomorrow the World. 1973: I Heard the Owl Call My Name (TV). 1983: The Dresser. 1985: Happy New Year. 1987: Leonard Part VI. 1990: The Last Butterfly. 1991: 'Let Him Have It'. 1996: The Boy from Mercury. 1998: A Rather English Marriage (TV). 1999: Whatever Happened to Harold Smith?*

COURTLAND, Jerome
See BERGEN, Polly

COURTNEIDGE, Dame Cicely
(Esmerelda C. Courtneidge) 1893–1980
Ever-cheerful, much-loved, brown-haired, Australian-born entertainer, a personable comedienne of limitless energy who could sing and dance as well. Her angular features enjoyed their greatest successes on stage but with her husband Jack Hulbert (*qv*) she became very popular for a while in early sound musical comedies, some of which she virtually turned into one-woman shows. Created Dame in 1972.

*1928: *British Screen Tatler No. 10. 1930: Elstree Calling. 1931: The Ghost Train. 1932: Jack's the Boy (US: Night and Day). Happy Ever After. 1933: Soldiers of the King (US: The Woman in Command). Falling for You. Aunt Sally (US: Along Came Sally). 1934: Things Are Looking Up. 1935: Me and Marlborough. The Perfect Gentleman (GB: The Imperfect Lady). 1936: Everybody Dance. 1937: Take My Tip. 1940: Under Your Hat. 1955: Miss Tulip Stays the Night. 1960: The Spider's Web. 1962: The L-Shaped Room. 1965: Those Magnificent Men in Their Flying Machines. 1966: The Wrong Box. 1972: Not Now Darling.*

COWARD, Sir Noël 1899–1973
Multi-talented British playwright and entertainer, noted for his charm and sophisticated wit, and the toast of London's theatreland in the twenties and thirties. His film appearances were as rare as they were often eccentric, but most of his plays were filmed, and enormous successes, encapsulating as they did the mood of Britain at the given time. Knighted in 1970. Died from a heart attack. Special Academy Award 1942.

1918: Hearts of the World. 1935: The Scoundrel. 1942: †In Which We Serve. 1945: Blithe Spirit (narrator only). 1950: The

Astonished Heart. 1956: Around the World in 80 Days. 1959: Our Man in Havana. 1960: Surprise Package. 1963: Paris When It Sizzles. 1965: Bunny Lake is Missing. 1968: Boom! 1969: The Italian Job.

†Also co-directed

COX, Courteney 1964–
Slim, vivacious, dark-haired American actress of slightly cool and brittle personality. After a two-year modelling career in New York, she was seen on screen in a Bruce Springsteen music video, an assignment that led to acting roles in TV series. Her film and TV career, though, was fairly low-key until she became a member of the cast of TV's *Friends*, and created the running role of newsgirl Gale Weathers in the *Scream* films. A six-year relationship with Michael Keaton (*qv*) broke up in 1995. Four years later she married actor David Arquette (also *qv*) and is now billed as Courteney Cox Arquette.

1985: Misfits of Science (TV). 1987: If It's Tuesday, It Still Must Be Belgium (TV). Down Twisted. Masters of the Universe. 1988: I'll Be Home for Christmas (TV). Cocoon The Return. 1989: Judith Krantz's Till We Meet Again (TV). Roxanne: The Prize Pulitzer (TV). 1990: Shaking the Tree. Mr Destiny. Curiosity Kills (cable TV). 1991: Blue Desert. 1992: Battling for Baby (TV). The Opposite Sex (And How to Live With Them) (TV). 1993: Ace Ventura Pet Detective. 1995: Sketch Artist II: Hands That See (TV. GB: A Feel for Murder). 1996: Scream. 1997: Scream 2. Commandments. 1998: Poodle Springs (TV). 1999: Alien Love Triangle. The Runner. 2000: Scream 3. The Shrink Is In.

COYOTE, Peter (P. Cohon) 1941–

Tall, brown-haired, laconic-looking, strong-faced American actor with distinctive speaking voice, seen in dominant leading and semi-leading roles of the 1980s and beyond. A late arrival to cinema screens after a varied early career, Coyote was for many years a leading light in the San Francisco theatre world before bringing his sardonic tones to a wider audience. He proved equally at home in gentle or cruel roles, but remained an offbeat star rather than a major one, and was relegated to fairly minor roles in some late 1990s' films.

1980: Die Laughing. Tell Me a Riddle. In the Child's Best Interest (TV). 1981: Isabel's Choice (TV). The People vs Jean Harris (TV). Southern Comfort. Pursuit/The Pursuit of D. B. Cooper. 1982: E.T. the Extra Terrestrial. Timerider – The Adventure of Lyle Swann. Out. Endangered Species. 1983: Strangers Kiss. Cross Creek. 1984: Scorned and Swindled (TV). Best Kept Secrets (TV). Slayground. 1985: The Legend of Billie Jean. Jagged Edge. Heartbreakers. The Blue Yonder/Time Flyer (TV). 1986: Child's Cry (TV). 1987: Outrageous Fortune. A Man in Love. Season of Dreams/Stacking. Sworn to Silence (TV). 1988: Heart of Midnight. Baja Oklahoma (cable TV/cinemas). Unconquered (TV). The Man Inside. 1990: High Art. 1991: Crooked Hearts. Keeper of the City. A Seduction in Travis County (TV). 1992: Bitter Moon. Exposure. 1993: Earth and the American Dream (voice only). Collage. Kika. 1994: That Eye, the Sky. Breach of Conduct (TV). 1995: Moonlight and Valentino. Cybertech PD. Unforgettable. Dalva (TV). 1996: Perfect Crimes (TV). Seduced by Madness (TV). Seeds of Doubt. 1997: Murder in Mind (TV). Top of the World. Road Ends. Sphere. 1998: Indiscreet. Two for Texas (TV). Route 9. Patch Adams. 1999: More Dogs Than Bones. The Basket. Last Call. Random Hearts. A Murder on Shadow Mountain (TV). 2000: Erin Brockovich. The Wednesday Woman (TV).

CRABBE, Larry 'Buster'
(Clarence Crabbe) 1907–1983

Olympic swimming champion who won a bronze medal for America in 1928 and a gold in 1932, before becoming as famous playing intergalactic heroes Flash Gordon and Buck Rogers as another swimming champ, Johnny Weissmuller (qv) did playing Tarzan. Crabbe became a 'B' western star of the 1940s before moving into business and becoming an

executive in water sports. In 1971 he broke the world 400 metre freestyle record for over-sixties! Died from a heart attack.

*1930: Good News. 1931: Maker of Men. 1932: Island of Lost Souls. The Most Dangerous Game (GB: The Hounds of Zaroff). That's My Boy. 1933: Tarzan the Fearless (serial). King of the Jungle. To the Last Man. Man of the Forest. *Hollywood on Parade (B7). The Sweetheart of Sigma Chi (GB: Girl of My Dreams). The Thundering Herd. 1934: Search for Beauty. You're Telling Me. Badge of Honor. She Had to Choose. We're Rich Again. The Oil Raider. 1935: Hold 'em Yale (GB: Uniform Lovers). Wanderer of the Wasteland. Nevada. 1936: Drift Fence. Desert Gold. Rose Bowl (GB: O'Reilly's Luck). Flash Gordon (serial). Arizona Raiders. Lady, Be Careful. Arizona Mahoney. 1937: Murder Goes to College. Sophie Lang Goes West. Daughter of Shanghai (GB: Daughter of the Orient). King of Gamblers. Forlorn River. Thrill of a Lifetime. 1938: Red Barry (serial). Tip-Off Girls. Hunted Men. Flash Gordon's Trip to Mars (serial). Illegal Traffic. 1939: Unmarried (GB: Night Club Hostess). Million Dollar Legs. Buck Rogers (serial). Colorado Sunset. Call a Messenger. 1940: Sailor's Lady. Flash Gordon Conquers the Universe (serial). 1941: Billy the Kid Wanted. Billy the Kid's Roundup. Jungle Man. 1942: Billy the Kid Trapped. Law and Order (GB: Double Alibi). Jungle Siren. Wildcat. Mysterious Rider. Sheriff of Sage Valley. Billy the Kid's Smoking Guns (GB: Smoking Guns). Queen of Broadway. 1943: The Kid Rides Again. Fugitive of the Plains. Western Cyclone. Devil Riders. The Drifter. The Renegade. Cattle Stampede. Blazing Frontier. 1944: Thundering Gunslingers. Nabonga (GB: The Jungle Woman). Frontier Outlaws. Oath of Vengeance. Fuzzy Settles Down. The Contender. Valley of Vengeance. Rustlers' Hideout. Wild Horse Phantom. 1945: Shadows of Death. Border Badmen. Stagecoach Outlaws. Fighting Bill Carson. Lightning Raiders. Prairie Rustlers. Gangsters' Den. His Brother's Ghost. 1946: Overland Raiders. Outlaws of the Plains. Prairie Badmen. Gentlemen with Guns. Ghost of Hidden Valley. Terrors on Horseback. Swamp Fire. 1947: Last of the Redmen (GB: Last of the Redskins). The Sea Hound (serial). 1948: Caged Fury. 1950: Pirates of the High Seas (serial). Captive Girl. 1952: King of the Congo (serial). 1954: Desert Outpost (TV. GB: cinemas). 1956: Gun Brothers. 1957: The Lawless Eighties. 1958: Badman's Country.*

1960: Gunfighters of Abilene. 1965: The Bounty Killers. Arizona Raiders (and 1936 version). 1971: The Comeback Trail (released 1982). 1979: Swim Team. 1981: The Alien Dead (released 1985).

CRAIG, James (John Meador) 1912–1985

Rugged, black-haired, latterly moustachioed, chubby faced American leading man, a minor-league Clark Gable in tough action roles, with the occasional romantic lead thrown in. A second-line star from 1942 to 1959, following a solid performance in *All That Money Can Buy*, which gave him his first important role, his stormy marriages included one (1959–1962) to actress Jil Jarmyn. Died from lung cancer.

*1937: Sophie Lang Goes West. Born to the West. Thunder Trail. 1938: The Big Broadcast of 1938. The Buccaneer. Pride of the West. 1939: *Trouble Finds Andy Clyde. Blondie Meets the Boss. Blind Alley. The Lone Wolf Spy Hunt (GB: The Lone Wolf's Daughter). North of Shanghai. Romance of the Redwoods. A Woman is the Judge. Café Hostess. *Skinny the Moocher. Good Girls Go to Paris. Missing Daughters. Taming of the West. Flying G-Men (serial). Overland with Kit Carson (serial). Behind Prison Gates. The Man They Could Not Hang. Konga, the Wild Stallion (GB: Konga). 1940: Winners of the West. Black Friday. The House Across the Bay. Zanzibar. Enemy Agent (GB: Secret Enemy). Seven Sinners. Two-Fisted Rangers (GB: Forestalled). Law and Order (GB: Lucky Ralston). South to Karanga. I'm Nobody's Sweetheart Now. Scandal Sheet. Kitty Foyle. 1941: All That Money Can Buy/The Devil and Daniel Webster/Daniel and the Devil. Unexpected Uncle. 1942: Friendly Enemies. The Omaha Trail. Northwest Rangers. Valley of the Sun. Seven Miles from Alcatraz. 1943: Swing Shift Maisie (GB: The Girl in Overalls). The Human Comedy. Lost Angel. The Heavenly Body. 1944: Kismet. Marriage is a Private Affair. Gentle Annie. 1945: Dangerous Partners. Our Vines Have Tender Grapes. She Went to the Races. 1946: Boys' Ranch. Little Mr Jim. 1947: Dark Delusion (GB: Cynthia's Secret). 1948: The Man from Texas. Northwest Stampede. 1949: Side Street. 1950: A Lady without Passport. 1951: The Strip. Drums in the Deep South. 1952: Hurricane Smith. 1953: Code Two. Fort Vengeance. 1955: Last of the Desperadoes. 1956: Women of Pitcairn Island. Massacre. While the City*

Sleeps. 1957: Shootout at Medicine Bend. Cyclops. Ghost Diver. Naked in the Sun. The Persuader. 1958: Man or Gun. 1959: Four Fast Guns. 1967: Fort Utah. Hostile Guns. The Doomsday Machine (released 1973). 1968: The Devil's Brigade. Arizona Bushwhackers. If He Hollers, Let Him Go! 1969: Bigfoot. 1970: The Revenge of Dr X. 1984: The Tormentors.

CRAIG, Michael (M. Gregson) 1928–
Tall, clean-cut, light-haired, British, slightly stuffy actor (born in India) who, through the Rank Organisation, enjoyed a good run of virile leading roles from 1956 to 1963, later giving some interesting performances in character parts. In the middle and late 1970s, was seen in leading roles in Australian films. He has also written screenplays.
1949: †Passport to Pimlico. 1951: The Magic Box. 1952: The Cruel Sea. 1953: Malta Story. 1954: The Love Lottery. Forbidden Cargo. The Embezzler. Svengali. 1955: Passage Home. Handcuffs London. 1956: The Black Tent. Yield to the Night (US: Blonde Sinner). Eyewitness. House of Secrets (US: Triple Deception). 1957: High Tide at Noon. Campbell's Kingdom. 1958: The Silent Enemy. Nor the Moon By Night (US: Elephant Gun). Sea of Sand (US: Desert Patrol). 1959: Life in Emergency Ward 10. Sapphire. Upstairs and Downstairs. 1960: The Angry Silence. Cone of Silence (US: Trouble in the Sky). Doctor in Love. 1961: Payroll. No, My Darling Daughter! A Pair of Briefs. 1962: Mysterious Island. La citta prigioniera (GB: The Captive City. US: The Conquered City). Life for Ruth (US: Walk in the Shadow). The Iron Maiden (US: The Swingin' Maiden). 1963: Stolen Hours. 1965: Vaghe stelle dell'orsa (GB: Of a Thousand Delights). Life at the Top. 1966: Modesty Blaise. Sandra. 1968: Star! 1969: Twinky. The Royal Hunt of the Sun. Country Dance (US: Brotherly Love). 1971: A Town Called Bastard. The Fourth Mrs Anderson. The Night of the Assassin. 1973: Vault of Horror. 1974: Last Rites (TV). Inn of the Damned. 1975: Port Essington. Ride a Wild Pony. 1976: Per amore. The Emigrants. The Fourth Wish. 1977: The Timeless Land (TV). The Irishman. Roses Bloom Twice (TV). 1981: Turkey Shoot. 1983: Stanley. 1988: Appointment with Death.

†As crowd player: and probably more in this capacity

CRAIN, Jeanne 1925–
Green-eyed, auburn-haired, sweet-faced

Wives. The Fan (GB: Lady Windermere's Fan). Pinky. 1950: Cheaper by the Dozen. I'll Get By. 1951: Take Care of My Little Girl. People Will Talk. The Model and the Marriage Broker. 1952: Belles on Their Toes. O Henry's Full House (GB: Full House). 1953: Dangerous Crossing. City of Bad Men. Vicki. 1954: Duel in the Jungle. 1955: Man Without a Star. Gentlemen Marry Brunettes. The Second Greatest Sex. 1956: The Fastest Gun Alive. 1957: The Tattered Dress. The Joker is Wild. 1958: The Great Gatsby (TV). 1959: Meet Me in St Louis (TV). Guns of the Timberland. 1961: With Fire and Sword. Pontius Pilate. Nefertiti, regina del Nilo (GB and US: Queen of the Nile). Twenty Plus Two (GB: It Started in Tokyo). 1962: Madison Avenue. 1964: 52 Miles to Terror (re-released 1967 as Hot Rods to Hell). 1971: The Night God Screamed (GB: Scream). 1972: Skyjacked.

CRAWFORD, Anne
(Imelda Crawford) 1919–1956
Sharply oval-faced, Palestinian-born, cool blonde actress in British films, equally at home as heroines, funny ladies or shrews. Perhaps because of her versatility, she didn't quite find her niche in the cinema, although stealing the notices was possibly reward enough. Died of leukemia at 36.
1938: Prison without Bars. 1940: Ferry Pilot. 1941: They Flew Alone (US: Wings and the Woman). 1942: The Peterville Diamond. The Night Invader. 1943: The Dark Tower. Millions Like Us. Headline. The Hundred Pound Window. 1944: 2,000 Women. 1945: They Were Sisters. 1946: Caravan. Bedelia. 1947: Master of Bankdam. Daughter of Darkness. 1948: Night Beat. The Blind Goddess. It's Hard to be Good. 1950: Tony

Draws a Horse. Trio. 1951: Thunder on the Hill (GB: Bonaventure). 1953: Street Corner (US: Both Sides of the Law). 1954: Knights of the Round Table. Mad About Men.

CRAWFORD, Broderick
(William B. Crawford) 1910–1986
Big, beefy, powerful American actor, the son of Helen Broderick. Began as Damon Runyon-style gangsters and serio-comic western villains, progressing to corrupt politicians and businessman. His career suffered several gradual declines, but he always managed to come back into the limelight. Academy Award for All the King's Men (1949). Very popular in the TV series Highway Patrol. Died following a series of strokes.
1937: Woman Chases Man. Submarine D-1. The Woman's Touch. 1938: Start Cheering. Sudden Money. 1939: Ambush. Undercover Doctor. Island of Lost Men. The Real Glory. Eternally Yours. Beau Geste. 1940: Slightly Honorable. When the Daltons Rode. Trail of the Vigilantes. I Can't Give You Anything but Love, Baby. Seven Sinners. Texas Rangers Ride Again. 1941: The Black Cat. Tight Shoes. South of Tahiti (GB: White Savage). Badlands of Dakota. 1942: Butch Minds the Baby. Broadway. *Keeping Fit. North to the Klondike. Larceny Inc. Men of Texas (GB: Men of Destiny). Sin Town. 1946: The Runaround. The Black Angel. 1947: Slave Girl. The Flame. 1948: The Time of Your Life. Sealed Verdict. Bad Men of Tombstone. 1949: A Kiss In the Dark. Night unto Night. Anna Lucasta. All the King's Men. 1950: Born Yesterday. Cargo to Capetown. Convicted. 1951: The Mob (GB: Remember That Face). 1952: Lone Star. Scandal Sheet (GB: The Dark Page). Last of the Comanches (GB: The Sabre and the Arrow). Stop, You're Killing Me. 1953: The Last Posse. 1954: Night People. Human Desire. Down Three Dark Streets. 1955: New York Confidential. Big House USA. Il bidone (GB and US: The Swindlers). Not As a Stranger. 1956: The Fastest Gun Alive. Between Heaven and Hell. 1958: The Decks Ran Red. 1960: La vendetta di Ercole (GB: Goliath and the Dragon. US: The Revenge of Hercules). 1961: Nasilje na Trgu (GB: Square of Violence). 1962: The Castilian. Convicts Four (GB: Reprieve!). 1964: A House is Not a Home. 1965: Up from the Beach. Kid Rodelo. 1966: The Oscar. El Escuadrón de la Muerte (US: Mutiny at Fort Sharp). The Texican. The Vulture. 1967: Red Tomahawk. 1968: The Fakers. Gregorio and

the Angel. 1969: Smashing the Crime Syndicate (released 1973). 1970: How Did a Nice Girl Like You Get into this Business? Maharlika. The Challenge (TV). 1971: Ransom Money. A Tattered Web (TV). Forbidden Knowledge (TV). 1972: The Candidate (voice only). House of Dracula's Daughter. Embassy. 1973: The Adventures of Nick Carter (TV). Terror in the Wax Museum. 1974: The Phantom of Hollywood (TV). 1975: Won Ton Ton, the Dog Who Saved Hollywood. 1976: Mayday at 40,000 Feet! (TV. GB: cinemas). 1977: Look What's Happened to Rosemary's Baby (TV). Proof of the Man. The Private Files of J. Edgar Hoover. 1979: Supertrain (TV. Later: Express to Terror). Just Not the Same Without You. A Little Romance. Harlequin. There Goes the Bride. 1981: The Upper Crust. Liar's Moon.

CRAWFORD, Joan
(Lucille LeSueur) 1904–1977
Dark-haired (earlier blonde), thick-browed, dominating American actress. After an apprenticeship playing bitchy, hard-headed flappers, the Crawford of the forties and fifties, great haunted eyes and jagged mouth to the fore, excelled as women born to suffer. Still in leading roles when past 50, she remains one of the few actresses to create her own genre, with its ingredients of melodrama, mayhem, murder and mink. Academy Award for Mildred Pierce. Married to actors Douglas Fairbanks Jr (1929–1933), Franchot Tone (1935–1939) and Phillip Terry (1942–1946). Her last husband, a businessman, left her a widow in 1959. Died from a heart attack. Also Oscar-nominated for Possessed (1947 version) and Sudden Fear.
1925: The Midshipman. *Miss MGM. Lady of the Night. Proud Flesh. Pretty Ladies. The Merry Widow. The Circle. The Only Thing (GB: Four Flaming Days). Old Clothes. Sally, Irene and Mary. 1926: The Boob (GB: The Yokel). Paris (GB: Shadows of Paris). Tramp, Tramp, Tramp. 1927: Winners of the Wilderness. The Taxi Dancer. West Point (GB: Eternal Youth). The Understanding Heart. The Unknown. Twelve Miles Out. Spring Fever. 1928: *Voices Across the Sea. The Law of the Range. Rose Marie. Across to Singapore. Dream of Love. Four Walls. 1929: The Duke Steps Out. Our Modern Maidens. Untamed. Hollywood Revue of 1929. 1930: Wir schalten um auf Hollywood! Montana Moon. Our Blushing Brides. Paid (GB: Within the Law). 1931: Dance, Fools, Dance. Laughing Sinners. This Modern Age.

Possessed. 1932: Grand Hotel. *The Stolen Jools (GB: The Slippery Pearls). Letty Lynton. Rain. 1933: Today We Live. Dancing Lady. 1934: Sadie McKee. Forsaking All Others. Chained. 1935: No More Ladies. I Live My Life. 1936: The Gorgeous Hussy. Love on the Run. 1937: The Last of Mrs Cheyney. The Bride Wore Red. Mannequin. 1938: The Shining Hour. 1939: Ice Follies of 1939. The Women. 1940: Strange Cargo. Susan and God (GB: The Gay Mrs Trexel). 1941: When Ladies Meet. A Woman's Face. 1942: They All Kissed the Bride. Reunion/Reunion in France (GB: Mademoiselle France). 1943: Above Suspicion. 1944: Hollywood Canteen. 1945: Mildred Pierce. 1946: Humoresque. 1947: Possessed. Daisy Kenyon. 1949: Flamingo Road. It's a Great Feeling. 1950: The Damned Don't Cry. Harriet Craig. 1951: Goodbye, My Fancy. This Woman is Dangerous. 1952: Sudden Fear. 1953: Torch Song. 1954: Johnny Guitar. 1955: *Hollywood Mothers. Female on the Beach. Queen Bee. 1956: Autumn Leaves. 1957: The Story of Esther Costello (US: Golden Virgin). 1959: The Best of Everything. Della (TV). 1962: What Ever Happened to Baby Jane? 1963: The Caretakers (GB: Borderlines). 1964: Strait-Jacket. 1965: I Saw What You Did. 1967: Berserk! The Karate Killers (TV. GB: cinemas). 1969: Night Gallery (TV). 1970: Trog. 1975: We're Going to Scare You to Death (TV).

CRAWFORD, Michael
(M. Dumble-Smith) 1942–
Light-haired, ingenuous-looking British comedy actor whose early career was spent playing hapless young heroes with two left feet. Broadened his horizons in the seventies and from 1972 to 1980 concentrated entirely on stage and television. Later scored a big personal hit in the leading roles of the stage musicals Barnum and The Phantom of the Opera, which consumed his time in the 1980s.
1957: Soapbox Derby. 1958: Blow Your Own Trumpet. 1960: A French Mistress. 1961: Two Living One Dead. 1962: The War Lover. Two Left Feet. 1965: The Knack . . . and how to get it. 1966: A Funny Thing Happened on the Way to the Forum. The Jokers. 1967: How I Won the War. 1968: The Games. 1969: Hello Dolly! 1970: Hello – Goodbye. 1972: Alice's Adventures in Wonderland. 1981: Condorman. 1993: Once Upon a Forest (voice only).

CRAZY GANG, The
See FLANAGAN, Bud

CREGAR, Laird
(Samuel L. Cregar) 1913–1944
Massively overweight American actor who built up a tremendous reputation in just a few years, after making his name in a stage production of the life of Oscar Wilde. Particularly good at cynics and tormented men of evil, culminating in his portrayals of Jack the Ripper and George Harvey Bone. Died from a heart attack following a crash diet.
1940: Oh, Johnny, How You Can Love! Granny Get Your Gun. Hudson's Bay. 1941: Blood and Sand. Charley's Aunt (GB: Charley's American Aunt). I Wake Up Screaming (GB: Hot Spot). 1942: Joan of Paris. Rings on Her Fingers. This Gun for Hire. The Black Swan. Ten Gentlemen from West Point. 1943: Hello, Frisco, Hello. Holy Matrimony. Heaven Can Wait. 1944: The Lodger. 1945: Hangover Square.

CRENNA, Richard 1926–
Few actors have spent a greater part of their career in television than this quiet, self-effacing, well-weathered American star. Despite several attempts to launch him as a big name in films, his taciturn personality had little box-office drawing power and he always returned to the happy hunting grounds of the small screen.
1951: Red Skies of Montana. 1952: Pride of St Louis. It Grows on Trees. 1955: Our Miss Brooks. 1956: Over-Exposed. 1964: John Goldfarb, Please Come Home. 1965: Made in Paris. 1966: The Sand Pebbles. 1967: Wait Until Dark. 1968: Star! 1969: Midas Run (GB: A Run on Gold). Marooned. 1970: Red Sky at Morning. Doctors' Wives. La spina dorsale del Diavolo/The Deserter. 1971: Catlow. Thief (TV). 1972: Un Flic (GB:

Dirty Money). The Man Called Noon. Footsteps (TV). 1973: Double Indemnity (TV). Nightmare (TV). Jonathan Livingston Seagull (voice only). Shootout in a One-Dog Town (TV). 1974: Honky Tonk (TV). A Girl Named Sooner (TV). 1975: Breakheart Pass. 1977: The War Between the Tates (TV). Cry Demon. 1978: Devil Dog, the Hound of Hell (TV). A Fire in the Sky (TV). First, You Cry (TV). The Evil. 1979: The Sin Sniper. Death Ship. Mayflower: The Pilgrims' Adventure (TV). Wild Horse Hank. 1980: Stone Cold Dead. 1981: Body Heat. The Ordeal of Bill Carney (TV). 1982: Table for Five. First Blood. The Day the Bubble Burst (TV). 1984: Squaring the Circle (narrator only). The Flamingo Kid. Passions (TV). 1985: Double-take (TV). Summer Rental. Rambo: First Blood Part II. The Rape of Richard Beck (TV). 1986: A Case of Deadly Force (TV). 1987: Police Story: The Freeway Killings (TV). Kids Like These (TV). 1988: Rambo III. Plaza Suite (TV). 1989: Leviathan. The Case of the Hillside Stranglers (TV). Janek: Cause of Death (TV). Stuck with Each Other (TV). Montana (TV). 1990: Last Flight Out (TV). Murder Times Seven (TV). Murder in Black and White (TV). 1992: Terror on Track 9 (TV). Intruders (TV). 1993: A Place to be Loved (TV). Hot Shots! Part Deux. 1994: Frame Up (TV). Janek: A Silent Betrayal (TV). Race Against Time: The Search for Sarah (TV). Janek: The Wallflower Murders (TV). 1995: Jade. Sabrina. A Pyromaniac's Love Story. 1996: In the Name of Love: A Texas Tragedy (TV). 20,000 Leagues Under the Sea (TV). Texas Graces (TV). 1997: Heart Full of Rain (TV). Deep Family Secrets (TV). 1998: Wrongfully Accused.

As director: 1979: Better Late Than Never (TV). 1980: Fugitive Family (TV).

CROMWELL, Richard
(Roy Radabaugh) 1910–1960
Blond-haired, lazy-lidded, sensitive-looking, very fresh-faced American actor with the smooth good looks of a 1930s Richard Chamberlain (qv). The son of an inventor, be began his career in Hollywood creating 'masks' of the stars, but his ambitions switched from art to acting, especially when his enthusiasm and boyish appeal won him the leading role in Tol'able David (only his second film). He continued to play youthful and occasionally headstrong roles (most notably as Henry Fonda's brother in Jezebel) through the 1930s, but never really picked up

the threads of his acting career after World War II service with the US Coast Guard, and worked mainly in ceramics before his early death from cancer. Briefly married (1945–46) to Angela Lansbury (qv).

1930: The King of Jazz. Tol'able David. 1931: Fifty Fathoms Deep. Shanghaied Love. Maker of Men. 1932: Age of Consent (GB: Are These Our Children?). The Strange Love of Molly Louvain. That's My Boy. Emma. Tom Brown of Culver. 1933: This Day and Age. Hoopla. Above the Clouds (GB: Winged Devils). 1934: Carolina (GB: The House of Connelly). Among the Missing. Name the Woman. When Strangers Meet. Most Precious Thing in Life. 1935: The Lives of a Bengal Lancer. Life Begins at Forty. McFadden's Flats. Men of the Hour. The Unknown Woman. *Star Night at the Coconut Grove. Annapolis Farewell (GB: Gentlemen of the Navy). 1936: Poppy. 1937: Our Fighting Navy (US: Torpedoed!). The Road Back/Return of the Hero. The Wrong Road. 1938: Jezebel. Come On, Leathernecks! Storm Over Bengal. 1939: Young Mr Lincoln. 1940: Enemy Agent (GB: Secret Enemy). The Villain Still Pursued Her. Village Barn Dance (GB: Dance Your Cares Away). 1941: Parachute Battalion. Riot Squad. 1942: Baby Face Morgan. 1943: Crime Doctor. Cosmo Jones – Crime Smasher (GB: Crime Smasher). 1948: Bungalow 13.

CROSBY, Bing (Harry Crosby) 1901–1977
Fair-haired, sleepy-looking singer with rich, soothing voice whose warm and friendly image, despite an unexceptional talent, made him into one of Hollywood's biggest stars, especially in the forties, when he was No.1 box-office attraction in the country. Won an Oscar for Going My Way (1944), although his best work was in the 'Road' films with Bob Hope and as a dramatic actor in The Country Girl (1954). Married to actresses Dixie Lee (1930–1952) – she died of cancer – and Kathryn Grant (1957 on). So much of Crosby's screen work consisted of gag guest spots in other people's (mostly Hope's) films that such appearances have been marked (G). Died from a heart attack after a round of golf. Also Oscar-nominated for The Bells of St Mary's and The Country Girl.

1930: *Ripstitch the Tailor. *Two Plus Fours. King of Jazz. Check and Double Check. 1931: *I Surrender Dear. *One More Chance. *At Your Command. Reaching for the Moon. Confessions of a Co-Ed (GB: Her Dilemma). 1932: *The Billboard Girl. *Hollywood on

Parade No.2. *Dream House. *Hollywood on Parade No. 4. The Big Broadcast. 1933: *Blue of the Night. *Please. *Sing, Bing, Sing. College Humor. Too Much Harmony. Going Hollywood. 1934: *Just an Echo. We're Not Dressing. Here is My Heart. She Loves Me Not. 1935: *Star Night at the Coconut Grove. Mississippi. Two for Tonight. The Big Broadcast of 1936. 1936: Anything Goes. Rhythm on the Range. Pennies from Heaven. 1937: Waikiki Wedding. Double or Nothing. 1938: Sing You Sinners. *Don't Hook Now. Dr Rhythm. 1939: Paris Honeymoon. The Star Maker. East Side of Heaven. 1940: *Swing with Bing. Rhythm on the River. Road to Singapore. If I Had My Way. 1941: *Stars at Play. Birth of the Blues. Road to Zanzibar. 1942: My Favorite Blonde (G). Holiday Inn. *Angels of Mercy. Road to Morocco. Star Spangled Rhythm. 1943: Dixie. 1944: *The Road to Victory. The Princess and the Pirate (G). The Shining Future. Going My Way. Here Come the Waves. 1945: Road to Utopia. *All Star Bond Rally. *Hollywood Victory Caravan. Duffy's Tavern (G). Out of This World (voice only). The Bells of St Mary's. 1946: Monsieur Beaucaire (G). Blue Skies. 1947: Welcome Stranger. My Favorite Brunette (G). Road to Rio. Variety Girl (G). 1948: The Emperor Waltz. *Rough But Hopeful. 1949: *The Road to Peace. *It's in the Groove. *Honor Caddie. You Can Change the World (G). A Connecticut Yankee in King Arthur's Court (GB: A Yankee in King Arthur's Court). The Adventures of Ichabod and Mr Toad (narrator only). Top o' the Morning. 1950: Riding High. Mr Music. 1951: Here Comes the Groom. Angels in the Outfield (GB: Angels and the Pirates) (G). A Millionaire for Christy (voice only). 1952: The Greatest Show on Earth (G). Son of Paleface (G). Just for You. Road to Bali. 1953: Little Boy Lost. Off Limits (GB: Military Police-men) (G). Scared Stiff (G). *Faith, Hope and Hogan (G). 1954: White Christmas. The Country Girl. 1955: *Bing Presents Oreste. *Hollywood Fathers. 1956: Anything Goes. High Society. High Tor (TV). 1957: The Heart of Show Business (narrator only). Man on Fire. 1958: *Showdown at Ulcer Gulch. 1959: Alias Jesse James (G). *This Game of Golf. *Your Caddie, Sir (G). Say One for Me. 1960: Let's Make Love (G). High Time. Pepe (G). 1961: *Kitty Caddy (voice only). The Road to Hong Kong. 1964: Robin and the Seven Hoods. 1965: Bing Crosby's Cinerama Adventures/Cinerama's Russian Adventure (narrator only). 1966: Stagecoach. 1968: *Bing Crosby's Washington State. 1970: *Golf's Golden Years (narrator only). Goldilocks (TV). Dr Cook's Garden (TV). 1972: Cancel My Reservation (G). 1974: That's Entertainment!

CROSS, Ben (Bernard Cross) 1947–
Dark-haired, frequently unsmiling, hook-nosed, earnest-looking British actor, good-looking in a bony-featured sort of way, who had a hard climb to the top after leaving school at 15 and starting life as a window-cleaner. A personable man with a forthright singing voice, Cross sprang to the attention of major casting directors with his performance in the London cast of the stage musical

Chicago, then successfully projected his own brand of sincerity in such popular TV series as *The Citadel* and *The Far Pavilions*. His film career has been a bit scattered, and by the 1990s he was playing unsympathetic roles, with a career in need of a new direction.
1975: *Great Expectations (TV. GB: cinemas)*. 1977: *A Bridge Too Far*. 1981: *Chariots of Fire*. 1984: *Coming Out of the Ice*. *The Assisi Underground*. 1985: *L'attenzione/The Lie*. 1987: *The Goldsmith's Shop*. *The Seed of Violence*. *The Unholy*. 1988: *Steal the Sky (TV)*. *Paperhouse*. *The House of the Lord*. 1989: *Eye of the Widow*. *Nightlife (TV)*. 1990: *Dark Shadows (TV)*. 1991: *She Stood Alone (TV)*. 1992: *Live Wire*. *The Diamond Fleece (TV)*. 1993: *Cold Sweat*. *Deep Trouble (cable TV)*. *Symphony*. 1994: *Temptress*. *Der Unfisch*. *The Ascent (TV)*. *Honey Sweet Love (released 1999)*. *The House That Mary Bought*. 1995: *First Knight*. 1996: *Robert Ryland's Last Journey*. *The Invader*. *20,000 Leagues Under the Sea (TV)*. *The Criminal Mind*. *Turbulence*. 1997: *Corporate Ladder*. 1998: *Tower of the Firstborn (TV)*. 1999: *The Venice Project*. 2000: *Young Blades*.

CROWE, Russell 1964–
Blue-eyed, fair-haired, taciturn, bow-lipped, unsmiling actor, New Zealand-born, but busy in Hollywood movies since the mid-1990s. The son of film caterers, Crowe acted as a child, but it was singing, composing and playing in a rock band – 'I wanted to be Elvis Presley and still do, a bit' – that occupied his time until he returned to acting in his mid-twenties, now looking something like a latter-day Alan Ladd (only taller). Australian Oscar winner for the controversial *Romper Stomper* and Academy Award nominee for *The Insider*.

1990: *Second Time Lucky*. *Blood Oath (US: Prisoners of the Sun)*. *The Crossing*. 1991: *Spotswood*. *Proof*. 1992: *Romper Stomper*. *Hammers over the Anvil*. *Love in Limbo*. *For the Moment (released 1994)*. 1993: *Red Rain*. *The Silver Brumby*. 1994: *The Sum of Us*. 1995: *The Quick and the Dead*. *Virtuosity*. *Rough Magic*. 1996: *No Way Back (TV)*. 1997: *Breaking Up*. *L.A. Confidential*. *Heaven's Burning*. 1999: *Mystery, Alaska*. *The Insider*. 2000: *Gladiator*. 2001: *Proof of Life*.

CRUDUP, Billy 1968–
Most actors of past decades would have changed this name, so credit to this dark, saturnine, bumpy-nosed American actor, who hung on to the real thing despite making a late start in films at 28. It was only during the previous year that he had reached Broadway, there to win an 'outstanding debut by an actor' award. He still tends to play morose, sometimes tragic roles, but has remained in prestigious leading roles. Romantically involved with Mary-Louise Parker *(qv)* since 1996.
1996: *Sleepers*. *Everyone Says I Love You*. *Inventing the Abbotts*. 1997: *Grind*. *Pre/Without Limits*. 1998: *Monument Ave (formerly Snitch)*. *Princess Mononoke (Voice only, English-language version)*. *The Hi-Lo Country*. 1999: *Jesus' Son*. 2000: *Waking the Dead*. *Almost Famous*.

CRUISE, Tom (T.C. Mapother) 1962–
American actor of medium build, thick dark hair and winningly cocky smile, a charismatic pin-up of the late 1980s who quickly developed into one of the industry's most bankable stars. He has alternated clean-cut heroes with more demanding roles, one of which, the paraplegic Vietnam veteran in *Born on the Fourth of July*, won him an Oscar nomination. He married Mimi Rogers *(qv)*, an actress ten years his senior, in 1987, but this ended in divorce in 1990; in the same year, he married another actress, Nicole Kidman (also *qv*), who has co-starred with him in three films to date. Plans to direct remain largely unfulfilled, although he has proved himself a shrewd businessman in the marketing of his own image. The impetus of his career was somewhat slowed in the late 1990s by the long shooting schedule for *Eyes Wide Shut*, but he has nonetheless notched up further Academy Award nominations for *Jerry Maguire* and *Magnolia*.
1980: *My Bodyguard*. 1981: *Endless Love*. *Taps*. 1983: *The Outsiders*. *Losin' It*. *Risky Business*. 1984: *All the Right Moves*. 1985: *Legend*. 1986: *Top Gun*. *The Color of Money*. 1988: *Young Guns (guest)*. *Cocktail*. *Rain Man*. 1989: *Born on the Fourth of July*. 1990: *Days of Thunder*. 1991: *Far and Away*. 1992: *A Few Good Men*. 1993: *The Firm*. 1994: *Interview with the Vampire*. 1996: *Mission: Impossible*. *Jerry Maguire*. 1999: *Eyes Wide Shut*. *Magnolia*. 2000: *Mission: Impossible 2*.
As co-director: 1993: *Fallen Angels 2 (TV)*

CRUZ, Penélope
(P.C. Sanchez) 1974–
Pretty, rosy-cheeked, dark-haired Spanish actress who came to prominence in films by such award-winning Spanish directors as Pedro Almodóvar and Fernando Trueba, then came into demand for international roles at the end of the 1990s. She trained as a dancer in classical and Spanish ballet, but had started acting in films at 17, her fetching personality soon helping to establish her in leading parts.
1991: *El laberinto griego*. 1992: *Belle Epoque*. *Jamon, jamon*. 1993: *Framed (TV)*. *Per amore, solo per amore (GB and US: For Love, Only for Love)*. *La ribelle*. 1994: *Entre rojas*. *Todo es mentira*. *Allegre ma non troppo*. 1996: *Brujas*. *El amor prejudica seriamente la salud*. *La celestina*. *Más que amor, frenesi*. 1997: *A Corner of Paradise*. *Carne trémula (GB and US: Live Flesh)*. *Abre los ojos*. 1998: *Don Juan*. *Nada en la nevera*. *If Only (US: Twice Upon a Yesterday)*. *The Girl of your Dreams*. *Talk of Angels*. *The Hi-Lo Country*. 1999: *Todo sobre mi madre (GB and US: All About My Mother)*. *Woman on Top*. *En dofi av paradiset*. *Volavérunt*. 2000: *All the Pretty Horses*. *Blow*. *Captain Corelli's Mandolin*.

CRYSTAL, Billy 1947–

Boyish-looking American entertainer with dark frizzy hair, short of stature but handsome in a faintly goofy way, the product of a mixed show-business background. His family owned and operated a jazz record label, but Crystal himself, after graduating from film school in 1970, became a stand-up comedian. TV's *Soap* made him a national name and another TV comedy show, *Saturday Night Live*, persuaded producers to think again of him for the cinema. In the late 1980s, he seemed to have made the breakthrough in terms of film stardom, and established himself in the following decade as faintly frenzied characters in both romantic and action comedies.

1977: Death Flight/SST Death Flight/Disaster in the Sky (TV). 1978: Rabbit Test. Human Feelings (TV). 1979: Breaking Up is Hard to Do (TV). Animalympics (voice only). 1980: Enola Gay: The Men, the Mission, the Atomic Bomb (TV). 1983: This is Spinal Tap. 1986: Running Scared. 1987: The Princess Bride. Throw Momma from the Train. 1988: Memories of Me. 1989: When Harry Met Sally . . . Midnight Train to Moscow (TV). 1991: City Slickers. 1992: Mr Saturday Night. 1994: City Slickers: The Legend of Curly's Gold. 1995: Forget Paris. 1996: Hamlet. 1997: Fathers' Day. Deconstructing Harry. 1998: My Giant. 1999: Analyze This. Get Bruce! (doc). As director: 1992: Mr Saturday Night. Home-run Race (TV). 1995: Forget Paris.

CULKIN, Macaulay 1980–

Fair-haired, ruby-lipped American child star of recent times, with gravely innocent appeal. From an acting family – his aunt (Bonnie Bedelia) and brother (Kieran Culkin) are also in films – he became the highest-paid child star for several decades with his success as the beleaguered Kevin in the *Home Alone* films. But there were quarrels between his father and film-makers and then, inevitably, it was all over in a few short years. By 1994, Culkin was asking eight million dollars a film – but no-one was buying. Adult oblivion followed.

1988: Rocket Gibraltar. See You in the Morning. 1989: Uncle Buck. 1990: Jacob's Ladder. Home Alone. 1991: Only the Lonely. My Girl. 1992: Home Alone 2: Lost in New York. 1993: The Good Son. The Nutcracker/George Balanchine's The Nutcracker. The Pagemaster. 1994: Getting Even With Dad. Richie Rich.

CULP, Robert 1930–

Tall, dark, long-faced American actor, good at cynicism and world-weariness. Has had several good leading roles as well as a top-rating television series (*I Spy*), but his screen personality was not sympathetic or likeable enough to enable him to become a box-office star in the cinema. Much TV work from 1956 to 1961. Married actress France Nuyen (F. Nguyen Vannga. 1939–); later divorced.

1962: PT 109. Sammy the Way Out Seal (TV. GB: cinemas). 1963: Sunday in New York. 1964: Rhino! The Raiders (TV. GB: cinemas). Demon with a Glass Hand. The Hanged Man (TV. GB: cinemas). 1967: The Movie Maker (TV). 1969: †Operation Breadbasket (narrator only). Bob & Carol & Ted & Alice. 1970: †This Land is Mine (narrator only). ‡The Grove. 1971: See the Man Run (TV). Hannie Caulder. 1972: A Cold Night's Death (TV). †Hickey and Boggs. 1973: Outrage (TV). A Name for Evil/The Dead Are Alive (completed 1970). The Lie (TV). 1974: The Castaway Cowboy. Houston, We've Got a Problem (TV). Strange Homecoming (TV). 1975: A Cry for Help (TV). Inside Out. Give Me Liberty. 1976: Sky Riders. Flood! (TV. GB: cinemas). Breaking Point. The Great Scout and Cathouse Thursday. 1977: Spectre (TV). 1978: A Cry for Justice (TV). Last of the Good Guys (TV). Thou Shalt Not Kill (TV). 1979: Goldengirl. Hot Rod (TV). 1980: The Night the City Screamed (TV). Word Games (TV). 1981: Killjoy (TV). The Greatest American Hero. 1982: National Lampoon's Movie Madness. 1984: Her Life As a Man (TV). Turk 182! Calendar Girl Murders (TV). 1985: Brothers-in-law (TV). 1986: The Gladiator (TV). The Blue Lightning. Combat High (TV. GB: Combat Academy). 1987: Big Bad Mama II. 1988: What Price Victory? (TV). 1989: Silent Night Deadly Night 3: Better Watch Out. The Achille Lauro/Voyage of Terror: The Achille Lauro Affair. 1990: Columbo Goes to College (TV). Perry Mason: The Case of the Defiant Daughter (TV). 1991: Murderous Vision (TV). That's Action. Pucker Up and Bark Like a Dog. Timebomb. 1992: Nameless. 1993: The Pelican Brief. 1994: I Spy Returns (TV). 1995: Watch the Skies. Panther. National Lampoon's Favorite Deadly Sins. 1996: Mercenary (TV). Spy Hard. 1997: Most Wanted. Diagnosis Murder (TV). 1998: Wanted (TV). News Break. Dark Summer. 2000: Hunger. Washington Slept Here (TV). 2001: Unconditional Love.

†*Also directed* ‡*Unreleased*

CUMMINGS, Constance

(C.C. Halverstadt) 1910–

Sparkling, sophisticated, brown-haired (often blonde) American leading lady of attractively angular features who, after being sacked from her first film, came back to become not only a thirties' star on both sides of the Atlantic, but a much-respected actress of the London stage (and occasionally screen) through several decades. Married (from 1933 to his death in 1973) to playwright Benn Levy.

1931: The Criminal Code. The Love Parade. Lover Come Back. Guilty Generation. Traveling Husbands. 1932: The Big Timer. Behind the Mask. Movie Crazy. Night after Night. American Madness. The Last Man. Washington Merry-Go-Round (GB: Invisible Power). Attorney for the Defense. 1933: Heads We Go (US: The Charming Deceiver). Channel Crossing. Billion Dollar Scandal. Broadway Thru a Keyhole. The Mind Reader. 1934: Glamour. Looking for Trouble. This Man is Mine. 1935: Remember Last Night? 1936: Seven Sinners (GB: Doomed Cargo). Strangers on a Honeymoon. 1940: Busman's Honeymoon (US: Haunted Honeymoon). 1941: This England. 1942: The Foreman Went to France (US: Somewhere in France) 1945: Blithe Spirit. 1950: Into the Blue (US: The Man in the Dinghy). 1953: Three's Company. 1954: The Scream. 1955: John and Julie. 1956: The Intimate Stranger (US: Finger of Guilt). 1959: The Battle of the Sexes. 1962: Sammy Going South (US: A Boy Ten Feet Tall). 1963: In the Cool of the Day. 1970: Jane Eyre (TV. GB: cinemas). 1986: Dead Man's Folly (TV).

CUMMINGS, Robert

(Clarence R. Cummings) 1908–1990
Perennially young, ever-smiling, black-haired American leading man, most at home in light comedy-romance where his skill at throwaway humour was best displayed. But he could be effectively used in drama, as proved by Sam Wood in *Kings Row* and Hitchcock in *Saboteur*. One of the earliest Hollywood entrants into TV, where he had his own show from 1955 to 1961. Made film debut as crowd player under the name Blade Stanhope Conway. Later billed (after 1962) as Bob Cummings. Suffered from Parkinson's Disease in later years. Died from kidney failure.

1933: *Sons of the Desert (GB: Fraternally Yours)*. 1935: *So Red the Rose. Millions in the Air. The Virginia Judge*. 1936: *Arizona Mahoney. Forgotten Faces. Desert Gold. Border Flight. Three Cheers for Love. Hollywood Boulevard. The Accusing Finger*. 1937: *Wells Fargo. Hideaway Girl. Last Train from Madrid. Souls at Sea*. 1938: *College Swing (GB: Swing, Teacher, Swing). Touchdown Army (GB: Generals of Tomorrow). You and Me. The Texans. I Stand Accused*. 1939: *The Underpup. Rio. Everything Happens at Night. Charlie McCarthy, Detective. Three Smart Girls Grow Up*. 1940: *Spring Parade. Private Affairs. One Night in the Tropics. And One Was Beautiful*. 1941: *The Devil and Miss Jones. Free and Easy. Moon over Miami. It Started with Eve. Kings Row*. 1942: *Saboteur. Between Us Girls*. 1943: *Forever and a Day. Princess O'Rourke. Flesh and Fantasy*. 1945: *You Came Along*. 1946: *The Bride Wore Boots. The Chase*. 1947: *Heaven Only Knows. The Lost Moment. Sleep My Love*. 1948: *The Accused. Let's Live a Little*. 1949: *Free for All. The Black Book (GB: Reign of Terror). Tell It to the Judge*. 1950: *Paid in Full. The Petty Girl (GB: Girl of the Year). For Heaven's Sake*. 1951: *The Barefoot Mailman*. 1952: *The First Time*. 1953: *Marry Me Again*. 1954: *Dial M for Murder. Lucky Me*. 1955: *How to Be Very, Very Popular*. 1958: *Bomber's Moon (TV)*. 1962: *My Geisha*. 1963: *Beach Party*. 1964: *What a Way to Go! The Carpetbaggers*. 1966: *Promise Her Anything. Stagecoach*. 1967: *Five Golden Dragons*. 1969: *Gidget Grows Up (TV)*. 1972: *The Great American Beauty Contest (TV)*. 1973: *Partners in Crime (TV)*.

CUMMINS, Peggy 1925–

Petite Welsh-born Peggy was so pretty of face – plus blonde hair, green bedroom eyes and a

fabulous figure – that no-one minded that she wasn't much of an actress. If she had been, her forties visit to Hollywood might have resulted in her becoming a very big international star. As it was, she graced British and American screens for over 20 years without ever seeming to get any older. Best performance: 1949's *Gun Crazy*.

1939: *Dr O'Dowd*. 1942: *Salute John Citizen. Old Mother Riley – Detective*. 1944: *Welcome Mr Washington. English Without Tears (US: Her Man Gilbey)*. 1946: *The Late George Apley*. 1947: *Moss Rose*. 1948: *Green Grass of Wyoming. Escape*. 1949: *Gun Crazy. That Dangerous Age (US: If This Be Sin)*. 1950: *My Daughter Joy (US: Operation X)*. 1952: *Who Goes There! (US: The Passionate Sentry)*. 1953: *Street Corner (US: Both Sides of the Law). Always a Bride. Meet Mr Lucifer*. 1954: *To Dorothy a Son (US: Cash on Delivery). The Love Lottery*. 1956: *The March Hare*. 1957: *Carry on Admiral (US: The Ship was Loaded). Hell Drivers. Night of the Demon (US: Curse of the Demon)*. 1958: *The Captain's Table*. 1959: *Your Money or Your Wife*. 1960: *Dentist in the Chair*. 1961: *In the Doghouse*.

CURTIS, Jamie Lee

(Jamie Leigh Curtis) 1958–
Lithe, long-legged, light-haired and sumptuously-built American actress, the daughter of Janet Leigh and Tony Curtis (both qv). By no means as pretty as that union would indicate, her unconventional looks, low voice and brooding presence soon boosted her into leading roles, although she found it difficult to escape type-casting: first as a 'screamie' queen in gory horror films, then in roles that traded on her physical assets

– although these also revealed more of the actress beneath the low-lidded gaze. Often doing her own stuntwork in action films, she has showed a pleasing facility in more recent times for abrasive comedy and self-mocking roles. Married to actor Christopher Guest.

1977: *Operation Petticoat (TV). The Bye-Bye, Sky-High, IQ Murder Case (TV)*. 1978: *Halloween*. 1979: *The Fog. Terror Train*. 1980: *Prom Night*. 1981: *Halloween II. Roadgames/Road Games. She's in the Army Now (TV). Death of a Centerfold (TV)*. 1982: *Coming Soon (TV). Money on the Side (TV)*. 1983: *Trading Places. Love Letters/My Love Letters*. 1984: *Grandview USA*. 1985: *Perfect. Annie Oakley (TV)*. 1986: *As Summers Die (TV)*. 1987: *Amazing Grace and Chuck (GB: Silent Voice). A Man in Love*. 1988: *A Fish Called Wanda. Dominick and Eugene (GB: Nicky and Gino)*. 1989: *Blue Steel*. 1990: *Queen's Logic*. 1991: *Tutta colpa di Dio. My Girl*. 1992: *Forever Young*. 1994: *Mother's Boys. My Girl 2. True Lies*. 1995: *House Arrest. The Heidi Chronicles (TV)*. 1997: *Fierce Creatures. Virus (released 1998)*. 1998: *Nicholas' Gift (TV). HomeGrown. Halloween H20 20 Years Later*. 2000: *Drowning Mona. The Tailor of Panama*.

CURTIS, Tony (Bernard Schwartz) 1925–

Bronx-born American actor with a mop of unruly black hair (which thinned as the years wore on) and East Side voice. After World War II service with the US Navy, he became the teenage rage of the early 1950s, baring his chest in a series of lavish sword-and-sandal adventures. Later he proved himself a good actor as well as a pin-up (being nominated for an Oscar in *The Defiant Ones*), but the 1960s heralded a return to the bland comedies in which he had dabbled before, and the downswing of his career. Married (first two of four) to actresses Janet Leigh (1951–1962) and Christine Kaufmann (1963–1967). He played some increasingly undignified roles in his later years. Father of actress Jamie Lee Curtis (qv).

1948: *Criss Cross*. 1949: *City Across the River. Take One False Step. The Lady Gambles. Francis. Johnny Stool Pigeon*. 1950: *Sierra. I Was a Shoplifter. Winchester 73. Kansas Raiders. The Prince Who Was a Thief*. 1951: *Meet Danny Wilson. Flesh and Fury*. 1952: *No Room for the Groom. Son of Ali Baba*. 1953: *All-American (GB: The Winning Way). Forbidden. Houdini*. 1954: *Beachhead. Johnny Dark. The Black Shield of Falworth. So This is Paris*. 1955: *Six Bridges to Cross. The Purple*

Mask. The Square Jungle. 1956: The Rawhide Years. Trapeze. 1957: Mister Cory. The Midnight Story (GB: Appointment with a Shadow). Sweet Smell of Success. 1958: The Vikings. The Defiant Ones. Kings Go Forth. The Perfect Furlough (GB: Strictly for Pleasure). 1959: Some Like It Hot. Operation Petticoat. Who Was That Lady? 1960: Spartacus. Pepe. The Young Juggler (TV). The Rat Race. 1961: The Great Impostor. The Outsider. 1962: 40 Pounds of Trouble. Taras Bulba. 1963: Captain Newman MD. The List of Adrian Messenger. Paris When It Sizzles. 1964: Wild and Wonderful. Goodbye Charlie. Sex and the Single Girl. 1965: The Great Race. Boeing Boeing. 1966: Chamber of Horrors. Not with My Wife, You Don't. Drop Dead Darling (US: Arrivederci Baby). 1967: La cintura di castità (GB: The Chastity Belt. US: A Funny Thing Happened on the Way to the Crusades). Don't Make Waves. 1968: The Boston Strangler. Rosemary's Baby (voice only). 1969: Monte Carlo or Bust! (US: Those Daring Young Men in Their Jaunty Jalopies). 1970: You Can't Win 'Em All. Suppose They Gave a War and Nobody Came. 1973: The Third Girl from the Left (TV). 1974: Lepke. The Count of Monte Cristo (TV. GB: cinemas). 1975: The Big Rip-Off (TV). 1976: The Last Tycoon. 1977: Casanova and Co (GB: The Rise and Rise of Casanova). Sextette. The Manitou. 1978: Vega$ (TV). The Bad News Bears Go to Japan. The Users (TV). It Rained All Night the Day I Left. 1979: Little Miss Marker. The Million Dollar Face (TV). 1980: Title Shot. The Mirror Crack'd. 1981: Inmates: A Love Story (TV). 1982: Brainwaves. Othello the Black Commando. Portrait of a Showgirl (TV). 1984: Where is Parsifal? King of the City (later Club Life). 1985: Insignificance. Half Nelson (TV). Balboa. 1986: Mafia Princess (TV). The Last of Philip Banter. Three-Act Tragedy/ Murder in Three Acts (TV). 1988: Midnight. Der Passagier (US: Welcome to Germany). 1989: Lobster Man from Mars. The High-Flying Mermaid. Tarzan in Manhattan (TV). Walter and Carlo in America. 1990: Thanks-giving Day (TV). 1991: Blood Law. Under Surveillance/Undercover Assassin. Prime Target. 1992: Center of the Web. Christmas in Connecticut (TV). 1993: Naked in New York. Last Action Hero. The Mummy Lives. Bandit 3: Beauty and the Bandit. 1994: A Perry Mason Mystery: The Case of the Grimacing Governor (TV). 1995: The Immortals. Brittle Glory/The Continued Adventures of Reptile Man. The Celluloid Closet. 1997: Star Games. Hardball. Louis & Frank. Elvis Meets Nixon (narrator only). Alien X Factor. 1999: Play It to the Bone.

CUSACK, John 1966–

Taciturn, dark-haired, thin-lipped, plump cheeked, surprised-looking American actor, often seen as non-conformists and drop-outs, but also able to sink himself facelessly into an ensemble of players. He began his career at the age of nine in his native Illinois, and has been writing and directing for the theatre since he was in high school. As the 1990s wore on, he found a good variety of leading and semi-leading roles without quite becoming a box-office force. Brother of character actress Joan Cusack (1962–), son of

screenwriter Dick Cusack.

1983: Class. 1984: Sixteen Candles. Grandview USA. 1985: The Sure Thing. The Journey of Natty Gann. Better Off Dead. 1986: One Crazy Summer. Stand by Me. 1987: *Elvis Stories. Tapeheads. Hot Pursuit. Broadcast News. 1988: Eight Men Out. Say Anything. 1989: Fat Man and Little Boy (GB: Shadow Makers). 1990: The Grifters. 1991: True Colors. 1992: Roadside Prophets. Bob Roberts. Shadows and Fog. Toys. The Player. Map of the Human Heart. 1993: Joey Coyle/The Badger. Money for Nothing. 1994: Flounder-ing. The Road to Wellville. Bullets Over Broadway. 1996: City Hall. 1997: Anastasia (voice only). Grosse Pointe Blank. Con Air. Hellcab/Chicago Cab. Arigo. Midnight in the Garden of Good and Evil. 1998: This is My Father. The Thin Red Line. 1999: The Jack Bull (cable TV). Pushing Tin. Cradle Will Rock. Being John Malkovich. 2000: High Fidelity. Life of the Party. 2001: Serendipity.

CUSHING, Peter 1913–1994

Dark-haired, gaunt-faced British actor with distinctive receding temples and a cold, cultured personality. His career was going nowhere in particular until sudden success in television (British TV Actor of the Year 1955), especially in a production of 1984, launched him into a long run in horror films, chiefly as scientists meddling in things Best Left Alone. Started his film career in Hollywood. Died from cancer.

1939: The Man in the Iron Mask. A Chump at Oxford. 1940: Vigil in the Night. *Dreams. *The Hidden Master. The Howards of Virginia (GB: The Tree of Liberty). Women in War. Laddie. 1941: They Dare Not Love. *We All Help. *The New Teacher. *Safety First. 1947:

*It Might Be You. 1948: Hamlet. 1952: Moulin Rouge. 1954: The Black Knight. The End of the Affair. 1956: Magic Fire. Alexander the Great. Time without Pity. The Curse of Frankenstein. 1957: The Abominable Snowman (US: The Abominable Snowman of the Himalayas). Violent Playground. 1958: Dracula (US: The Horror of Dracula). The Revenge of Frankenstein. 1959: John Paul Jones. The Hound of the Baskervilles. The Mummy. The Flesh and the Fiends (US: Mania). 1960: Suspect (US: The Risk). Cone of Silence (US: Trouble in the Sky). The Brides of Dracula. Sword of Sherwood Forest. 1961: Fury at Smugglers' Bay. The Hellfire Club. The Naked Edge. 1962: Cash on Demand. The Devil's Agent. Captain Clegg (US: Night Creatures). The Man Who Finally Died. 1964: The Evil of Frankenstein. The Gorgon. Dr Terror's House of Horrors. 1965: She. Dr Who and the Daleks. The Skull. 1966: Island of Terror. Some May Live (TV. GB: cinemas). Daleks – Invasion Earth 2150 AD. 1967: Frankenstein Created Woman. Night of the Big Heat (US: Island of the Burning Damned). Torture Garden. Caves of Steel. The Blood Beast Terror (US: The Vampire Beast Craves Blood). The Mummy's Shroud (narrator only). 1968: Corruption. 1969: One More Time. Frankenstein Must Be Destroyed. Scream and Scream Again. 1970: The Vampire Lovers. I, Monster. The House that Dripped Blood. Incense for the Damned (US: Blood-suckers). Death Corps (later Shock Waves. GB: Almost Human). 1971: Twins of Evil. 1972: Fear in the Night. Asylum. Dr Phibes Rises Again. Dracula AD 1972. Nothing But the Night. Tales from the Crypt. The Creeping Flesh. Panico en el Transiberio (GB and US: Horror Express). 1973: The Satanic Rites of Dracula (US: Dracula and His Vampire Bride). Frankenstein and the Monster from Hell. And Now the Screaming Starts. From Beyond the Grave. 1974: The Beast Must Die. The Legend of the Seven Golden Vampires (US: The Seven Brothers Meet Dracula). Madhouse. Tendre Dracula/La grande trouille. The Ghoul. Shatter. Legend of the Werewolf. 1976: The Devil's Men (US: Land of the Minotaur). At the Earth's Core. Trial by Combat (US: Dirty Knight's Work). 1977: The Uncanny. Star Wars. Die Standarte (US: Battle Flag). The Great Houdinis (TV). 1978: Touch of the Sun. *The Detour (narrator only). Hitler's Son. 1979: Arabian Adventure. 1980: Monster Island. 1981: A Tale of Two Cities. (TV. Released 1985). Black Jack. 1982: House of the Long Shadows. 1983: Sword of the Valiant/Sword of the Valiant – The Legend of Gawain and the Green Knight. Helen Keller... The Miracle Continues (TV). 1984: Top Secret! The Masks of Death (TV). 1986: Biggles.

D

DAFOE, Willem
(William Dafoe) 1955–
Sturdily built, fiercely scowling American actor with light tufty hair, whose powerful on-screen presence adapts equally well to heroes or villains. He was with theatre companies (at first in his native Wisconsin, then New York) for several years before starting a screen career, which eventually caught fire in the mid 1980s, especially with his compassionate sergeant in *Platoon*, a role that won him an Oscar nomination. He has not, though, become a box-office force under his own steam. The 'Willem' is a childhood nickname.
1980: Heaven's Gate. 1982: The Loveless. 1983: The Hunger. 1984: Roadhouse 66. New York Nights. Streets of Fire. 1985: To Live and Die in L.A. The Communists Are Comfortable. 1986: Platoon. 1987: Dear America (voice only). Off Limits (GB: Saigon). 1988: The Last Temptation of Christ. Mississippi Burning. 1989: Born on the Fourth of July. Triumph Of the Spirit. 1990: Wild at Heart. Flight of the Intruder. 1991: Light Sleeper. 1992: White Sands. Body of Evidence. 1993: In weiter Ferne, so nah!/Faraway, So Close! 1994: Tom and Viv. Clear and Present Danger. The Night and the Moment. 1995: Victory (released 1997). 1996: The English Patient. Basquiat. 1997: Speed 2: Cruise Control. Affliction. 1998: Waldo's Hawaiian Holiday. Lulu on the Bridge. eXistenZ. New Rose Hotel. 1999: Boondock Saints. Bullfighter. 2000: American Psycho. Shadow of the Vampire. Straight to Hell. Animal Factory. 2001: Gangs of New York. Edges of the Lord.

DAHL, Arlene 1924–
Willowy blue-eyed American redhead of Norwegian ancestry who followed success as an advertising model with a Hollywood career. Here she progressed from pert and saucy girlfriends, through glamour roles to her most successful characterization – the minxish and sometimes unbalanced schemer, before leaving films to become a beauty columnist. Six times married, the first two being actors, Lex Barker (1951–1952) and Fernando Lamas (1954–1960). Mother of action star Lorenzo Lamas (1958–), in whose 1990 film *Night of the Warrior* she made a guest appearance.
1947: Life with Father. My Wild Irish Rose. 1948: The Bride Goes Wild. A Southern Yankee (GB: My Hero). 1949: The Black Book (GB: Reign of Terror). Scene of the Crime. Ambush. 1950: The Outriders. Three Little Words. Watch the Birdie. 1951: Inside Straight. No Questions Asked. 1952: Caribbean (GB: Caribbean Gold). 1953: Desert Legion. Jamaica Run. Sangaree. The Diamond Queen. Here Come the Girls. 1954: Bengal Brigade (GB: Bengal Rifles). Woman's World. 1956: Slightly Scarlet. Wicked As They Come. 1957: Fortune is a Woman (US: She Played With Fire). 1959: Journey to the Centre of the Earth. 1964: Kisses for My President. 1968: Les Poneyettes. 1969: Land Raiders. The Road to Katmandu. 1970: Du blé en liasses. 1972: Sotto a chi tocca! 1989: A Place to Hide. 1990: Night of the Warrior.

DAILEY, Dan 1914–1978
Fair-haired, blue-eyed, cheerful song-and-dance man, at first billed as Dan Dailey Jr. From a family of vaudevillians, he worked in a minstrel show as a boy. He was never the

greatest of musical stars, but the public took a shine to him and kept him at the top for ten good post-war years. His pleasing, often understated acting style was a help. Came to look increasingly cadaverous in later years, and died of anaemia. Three times married and divorced. Nominated for an Oscar in *When My Baby Smiles at Me*, ironically for a rare over-the-top performance.
1939: The Captain is a Lady. 1940: Hullabaloo. Susan and God (GB: The Gay Mrs Trexel). The Mortal Storm. Dulcy. 1941: Ziegfeld Girl. Moon over Her Shoulder. Lady Be Good. The Wild Man of Borneo. Washington Melodrama. The Get-Away. Down in San Diego. 1942: Mokey. Panama Hattie. Sunday Punch. Timber. Give Out, Sister. 1947: Mother Wore Tights. 1948: You Were Meant for Me. Give My Regards to Broadway. Chicken Every Sunday. When My Baby Smiles at Me. 1949: You're My Everything. 1950: When Willie Comes Marching Home. A Ticket to Tomahawk. I'll Get By. My Blue Heaven. 1951: I Can Get It for You Wholesale (GB: This Is My Affair). Call Me Mister. 1952: What Price Glory? Meet Me at the Fair. The Pride of St Louis. 1953: The Girl Next Door. Taxi. The Kid from Left Field. 1954: There's No Business Like Show Business. 1955: It's Always Fair Weather. 1956: Meet Me in Las Vegas (GB: Viva Las Vegas!). The Best Things in Life Are Free. 1957: The Wings of Eagles. Oh, Men! Oh, Women! The Wayward Bus. 1958: Underwater Warrior. 1960: Pepe. 1962: Hemingway's Adventures of a Young Man (GB: Adventures of a Young Man). 1971: Mr and Mrs Bo Jo Jones (TV). 1972: Michael O'Hara the Fourth (TV). 1974: The Daughters of Joshua Cabe Return (TV). 1977: The Private Files of J. Edgar Hoover.

DAINTON, Patricia 1930–
Blue-eyed Dresden china blonde, born in Scotland, and on stage as a teenager. Started as a glamourpuss, following a Rank contract, but did well later on as beleaguered, delicate but resourceful heroines. Seemed to lack the career drive to make herself a big star.
1943: The Bells Go Down. 1947: Dancing with Crime. Uncle Silas (US: The Inheritance). 1948: Love in Waiting/Ladies in Waiting. 1949: Don't Ever Leave Me. 1950: The Dancing Years. 1952: Hammer the Toff. Castle in the Air. Paul Temple Returns. Tread Softly (US: Tread Softly Stranger). 1953: Operation Diplomat. 1956: No Road Back. 1957: The

Passionate Stranger (US: A Novel Affair). At the Stroke of Nine. 1959: Witness in the Dark. 1960: The House in Marsh Road. Ticket to Paradise. 1961: The Third Alibi.

DALE, Jim (James Smith) 1935–
Lanky, cheery, rubber-faced British actor/comedian who stage-managed his film career cleverly without quite reaching the big time. First a stand-up comic, then pop star, he joined the Carry On team, but devoted most of his time from the mid-sixties to (often classical) stage work. A return to films in the seventies included several appearances, with varying success, in Walt Disney productions.
1958: 6.5 Special. 1961: Raising the Wind (US: Roommates). 1962: Nurse on Wheels. The Iron Maiden (US: The Swingin' Maiden). 1963: Carry On Cabby. Carry On Jack. 1964: Carry On Spying. Carry On Cleo. 1965: The Big Job. Carry On Cowboy. 1966: Carry On Screaming. Don't Lose Your Head. The Winter's Tale. 1967: The Plank. Follow That Camel. Carry On Doctor. 1969: Lock Up Your Daughters! Carry On Again, Doctor. 1972: Adolf Hitler – My Part in His Downfall. 1973: Digby – the Biggest Dog in the World. The National Health. 1976: Joseph Andrews. 1977: Pete's Dragon. 1978: Hot Lead and Cold Feet. 1979: The Spaceman and King Arthur (US: Unidentified Flying Oddball). 1983: Scandalous. 1985: The Adventures of Huckleberry Finn (TV). 1992: Carry On Columbus. 1993: The American Clock (TV). 1997: The Hunchback (TV).

DALTON, Timothy 1940–
Brown-haired, serious-looking, narrow-eyed, Welsh-born actor with sharply-defined features. Hailed as the sex symbol of the

1970s and the 'new Olivier' when he played Heathcliff in *Wuthering Heights*, Dalton shied away and went back to the theatre. 'I stayed away from films for three years and when I went back they'd forgotten who I was.' His film career after that was spotty and undistinguished until he was asked to take over the role of James Bond from Roger Moore (*qv*) in 1987. This assignment, however, only lasted two films.
1968: The Lion in Winter. 1970: Cromwell. Wuthering Heights. Giochi particolari/The Voyeur. 1971: Mary, Queen of Scots. 1972: Lady Caroline Lamb. 1975: Permission to Kill. 1976: El hombre que supo amar. 1977: Sextette. 1978: Agatha. 1979: The Flame Is Love (TV). 1980: Flash Gordon. 1981: Chanel solitaire. The Emperor's New Clothes (voice only). 1984: The Master of Ballantrae (TV). 1985: The Doctor and the Devils. Florence Nightingale (TV). 1987: Brenda Starr. The Living Daylights. 1988: Hawks. 1989: Licence to Kill. 1990: The King's Whore. 1991: The Rocketeer. 1993: Naked in New York. Last Action Hero. Sherlock Holmes vs Dracula. 1994: Red Eagle (TV). Lie Down with Lions (TV). 1995: Salt Water Moose. 1996: The Reef/Passion's Way (TV). 1997: The Beautician and the Beast. The Informant/Fields of Blood/Johnny Loves Suzy (cable TV). 1999: Mad Men. 2000: Possessed. Timeshare.

DAMON, Mark (Alan Harris) 1933–
Boyishly handsome, dark-haired American leading man, a chubbier-cheeked version of Robert Wagner. In 1963 he became one of the first Hollywood actors to make a career in the new breed of Italian action film. Without doing a Clint Eastwood he was quite successful. In the seventies he returned to America, later heading a producer sales organization.
1955: Inside Detroit. 1956: Screaming Eagles. Between Heaven and Hell. The Hefferan Family (TV. GB: cinemas). In Times Like These (TV. GB: cinemas). 1957: Young and Dangerous. 1958: Life Begins at 17. The Party Crashers. 1960: This Rebel Breed. The Fall of the House of Usher. 1962: The Longest Day. Beauty and the Beast. The Reluctant Saint. 1963: The Young Racers. Black Sabbath. Sfida al re di Castiglia (GB: Kingdom of Violence. US: The Tyrant of Castile). Mas cornadas da el hombre (US: Wounds of Hunger). 1964: The 100 Horsemen. Son of Cleopatra. Island Affair. Agente 777 – Operazione mistero. 1965: Son of El Cid. 1966: Johnny Oro (GB: Ringo and His Golden Pistol). Il camaleonte d'oro. Johnny

Yuma. 1967: Requiescat. A Train for Durango. Anzio (GB: The Battle for Anzio). Sette vergine per il diavolo (GB and US: The Young, the Evil and the Savage). 1968: Tutto per tutto. Dio cometi amo. 1969: Rassenschande. 1970: Arm of Fire. 1971: The Norman Sword (GB: TV, as the Norman Swordsman). I leoni di Pietroburgo (GB: TV, as The Lions of St Petersburg). 1972: Lo chinamavaño 'Verita'/They Called Him Truth. Crypt of the Living Dead (GB: Vampire Woman). Don't Cry for Me, Little Mother. Byleth. La tumba de la isla maldita. 1973: Il plenilunio della vergini (US: The Devil's Wedding Night). Posate le pistole, reverendo. 1974: A Scaffold for Django. Do I Kill You or Do You Kill Me? 1975: The Scalawag Bunch (completed 1970). 1976: There is No 13. 1982: Stuck on You! 1997: Liar (US: Deceiver).

DAMON, Matt 1970–
Light-haired, snub-nosed, boyish-looking, businesslike American actor, the son of a taxman and a college professor. His parentage perhaps prepared him well for his role as an untaught maths genius in *Good Will Hunting*, a film which won him an Oscar for co-writing its screenplay (and an acting nomination). Despite few film credits in his early acting years – he had one line in his first and extraed in the second – he broke quickly through to stardom after a showy supporting role in *Courage Under Fire* and is now established in the top echelon of younger American stars. At the time of writing, his live-in partner is fellow star Winona Ryder.
1988: Mystic Pizza. The Good Mother. 1990: Rising Son (TV). 1992: School Ties. 1993: Geronimo: An American Legend (and narrated). 1995: The Good Old Boys (TV). 1996: Courage Under Fire. Chasing Amy. Glory Daze. 1997: John Grisham's The Rainmaker. Good Will Hunting. 1998: Saving Private Ryan. Rounders. 1999: Dogma. The Talented Mr Ripley. 2000: Titan A.E. (voice only). All the Pretty Horses. The Third Wheel.

DANCE, Charles 1946–
Tall, debonair, green-eyed, sandy-haired, cool-looking, authoritative British actor with upper-class air, nicknamed 'The Thinking Woman's Crumpet'. Struggled for 15 years before gradually building a reputation in the theatre, mainly in Shakespearian roles. Shot to prominence in the TV series *The Jewel in the Crown*, and came quickly into demand

equally for resolute heroes, callow charmers and sardonic villains.
1977: The Spy Who Loved Me. 1979: Very Like a Whale (TV). 1981: For Your Eyes Only. 1985: The McGuffin (TV). Plenty. 1986: The Golden Child. Good Morning Babylon. 1987: Out on a Limb (TV). White Mischief. Hidden City. 1988: Pascali's Island. 1989: Secret Places of the Heart. Goldeneye (TV). 1991: China Moon (released 1994). Alien 3. Kalkstein/The Valley of Stone. 1993: Century (TV. US: cinemas). Kabloonak (released 1994. US: Nanook). Last Action Hero. 1994: Exquisite Tenderness. Shortcut to Paradise. 1995: Undertow (TV). 1996: Space Truckers. Michael Collins. 1997: In the Prescence of Mine Enemies (TV). The Blood Oranges. 1998: What Rats Won't Do. Hilary and Jackie. Don't Go Breaking My Heart (US: Us Begins with You).

DANDRIDGE, Dorothy 1923–1965
Coffee-coloured American singer and dancer of immense drive who, after a few bit parts, became a successful night-club entertainer in the 1940s. Success in the musical Carmen Jones the following decade (it won her an Oscar nomination) launched her into a different sort of stardom in which suitable film roles proved difficult to find. Seemingly not able to cope with these new stresses, and declared bankrupt in 1962, she was found dead from an overdose of pills mixed with alcohol.
1937: A Day at the Races. 1938: Going Places. 1940: Irene. Four Shall Die. 1941: The Lady from Louisiana. *Easy Street. *Yes, Indeed! *Jungle Jig. *Swing for Your Supper. *Lazybones. Sundown. Sun Valley Serenade. Bahama Passage. 1942: Lucky Jordan. *A

Zoot Suit. *Cow-Cow Boogie. *Paper Doll. *Congo Clambake. *Blackbird Fantasy. Drums of the Congo. 1943: Hit Parade of 1943. 1944: Since You Went Away. Atlantic City. 1945: Pillow to Post. 1947: Ebony Parade. 1951: Tarzan's Peril (GB: Tarzan and the Jungle Queen). The Harlem Globetrotters. 1953: Bright Road. Remains to be Seen. 1954: Carmen Jones. 1956: The Happy Road. 1957: Island in the Sun. 1958: The Decks Ran Red. 1959: Porgy and Bess. Tamango. 1960: Moment of Danger (US: Malaga). 1962: The Murder Men (TV. GB: cinemas).

DANE, Karl (Rasmus Gottlieb) 1886–1934
Tall, hefty, angular Danish actor (on stage in his native country as a juvenile) who became very popular with silent-screen American audiences after his success as Slim in The Big Parade. Later successfully teamed with tiny Briton George K. Arthur (G.K.A. Brest, 1899–1985) in an amusing series of broad comedies for M-G-M. But his career collapsed with the coming of sound (his thick accent did not match his characters) and, after spells as a carpenter and a fast-food operator, Dane shot himself at the age of 47.
1918: My Four Years in Germany. Her Final Reckoning. To Hell with the Kaiser. 1919: Daring Hearts. 1925: Lights of Old Broadway (GB: Merry Wives of Gotham). The Big Parade. La Bohème. His Secretary. The Everlasting Whisper. 1926: Bardelys the Magnificent. Son of the Sheik. The Scarlet Letter. War Paint. Monte Carlo. 1927: The Red Mill. Slide, Kelly, Slide. Rookies. The Enemy. 1928: Show People. The Trail of 98. Detectives. Baby Mine. Brotherly Love. Circus Rookies. Alias Jimmy Valentine. Wyoming. 1929: Speedway. All at Sea. Hollywood Revue of 1929. China Bound. The Duke Steps Out. The Voice of the Storm. The Gob. 1930: Montana Moon. The Big House. Navy Blues. Free and Easy. Numbered Men. Billy the Kid. Crazy House. A Lady's Morals (GB: Jenny Lind). The Rounder. On to Singapore. *The Lease Breakers. *Shove Off. *A Put-Up Job. 1932: Speak Easily. *Summer Daze. Fast Life. 1933: The Whispering Shadow (serial).

DANES, Claire 1979–
Dark-haired, bright-eyed, eager-looking, very slightly built American actress, a star on TV at 15 in the series My So-Called Life. Film-wise, she turned down a role in Schindler's List, but soon made her mark as the ailing Beth in the 1994 Little Women, and

consolidated stardom as Juliet in the innovative 1996 version of William Shakespeare's Romeo & Juliet. She's also a dancer, having studied modern dance since she was six.
1990: Dreams of Love. 1994: More Than Friends: The Coming Out of Heidi Leiter (TV). Little Women. 1995: I Love You, I Love You Not (released 1997). Home for the Holidays. How to Make an American Quilt. 1996: William Shakespeare's Romeo & Juliet. To Gillian on Her 37th Birthday. Verona Beach (D). 1997: U Turn/Stray Dogs. John Grisham's The Rainmaker. 1998: Polish Wedding. Princess Mononoke (Voice only, English-language version). Les Misérables. 1999: The Mod Squad. Brokedown Palace. 2000: Flora Plum. Monterey Pop.

D'ANGELO, Beverly 1951–
Diminutive but exuberant blonde American actress who began her working life at 17 as a cartoonist who wanted to be an animator in films. Sang with a rock band, drifted into acting and excelled in fast-moving, scatterbrained comedy roles with the occasional excursion into heavy drama. Surprised many with her vibrant singing voice as the doomed Patsy Cline in Coal Miner's Daughter.
1976: The Sentinel. Hey Marilyn. 1977: Annie Hall. First Love. 1978: Every Which Way But Loose. 1979: Hair. Highpoint. 1980: Coal Miner's Daughter. 1981: Honky Tonk Freeway. Paternity. 1983: National Lampoon's Vacation. 1984: A Streetcar Named Desire (TV). Finders Keepers. 1985: National Lampoon's European Vacation. Doubletake (TV). Big Trouble. 1986: Slow Burn (TV). The Man Who Fell to Earth (TV). 1987: Maid to Order. Aria. In the Mood (later and GB: The Woo Woo Kid).

Throwback. 1988: Trading Hearts/ Tweeners. High Spirits. 1989: Cold Front. National Lampoon's Christmas Vacation (GB: National Lampoon's Winter Holiday). 1990: Pacific Heights. Daddy's Dyin' – Who's Got the Will? 1991: The Miracle. The Switch (TV). The Pope Must Die (US: The Pope Must Diet). Lonely Hearts. 1992: The Jerry Sherwood Story (TV. GB: A Child Lost Forever). Man Trouble. 1993: Judgment Day: The John List Story (TV). 1994: Lightning Jack. Pterodactyl Woman from Beverly Hills (released 1996). Frame Up (TV). Deadly Games (TV). 1995: How Much Are These Children in the Window?/ Two Much Trouble. Widow's Kiss. Eye for An Eye. 1996: Edie and Pen. Forbidden Love (TV). Sweet Temptation (TV). 1997: Vegas Vacation. Nowhere. Love Always. 1998: American History X. Illuminata. A Rat's Tale. With Friends Like These . . . (released 1999 on cable TV). 1999: *Jazz Night. Lansky (cable TV). Sugar Town. 2000: High Fidelity.

DANIELS, Bebe

(Virginia Daniels) 1901–1971

Dark-haired, effervescent American actress, on stage at three, Dorothy in a film of *The Wizard of Oz* at nine, and a leading lady in Harold Lloyd slapstick silents at 15. Later married actor Ben Lyon, and moved to Britain, where they became one of the entertainment's most popular couples, especially for their radio series *Hi Gang!* in which Bebe blossomed as a singer and comedienne. Another successful series, *Life with the Lyons*, led to a couple of films. Died of a cerebral haemorrhage after a long period of ill-health. 1910: *The Courtship of Miles Standish. *The Common Enemy. The Wizard of Oz. 1911: *Justinian and Theodora. *A Counterfeit Santa Claus. 1914: The Savage. Anne of the Golden West. 1915: Giving Them Fits. 1916: *An Awful Romance. *Luke Laughs Last. *Luke Foils the Villain. *Luke and the Rural Roughnecks. *Luke's Double. *Luke Pipes the Pippins. *Luke and the Bomb Throwers. *Luke's Late Lunches. *Luke's Fatal Flivver. *Luke's Washful Waiting. *Luke Rides Roughshod. *Luke Crystal Gazer. *Luke's Lost Lamb. *Luke Does the Midway. *Luke and the Mermaids. *Luke Joins the Navy. *Luke's Society Mix-Up. *Luke and the Bang-Tails. *Luke's Speedy Club Life. *Luke, the Chauffeur. *Luke's Newsie Knockout. *Luke, Gladiator. *Luke's Preparedness Preparation. *Luke, Patent Provider. *Luke Locates the

Loot. *Luke's Fireworks Fizzle. *Luke's Movie Muddle. *Luke's Shattered Sleep. 1917: *Luke's Busy Days. *Luke's Trolley Trouble. *Lonesome Luke, Lawyer. *Luke's Last Liberty. *Luke Wins Ye Ladye Faire. *Lonesome Luke's Lively Rifle. *Lonesome Luke on Tin Can Alley. *Lonesome Luke's Lively Life. *Lonesome Luke's Honeymoon. *Lonesome Luke, Plumber. *Stop! Luke! Listen! *Lonesome Luke, Messenger. *Lonesome Luke, Mechanic. *Lonesome Luke's Wild Women. *Lonesome Luke Loses Patients. *From London to Laramie. *Over the Fence. *Pinched. *By the Sad Sea Waves. *Birds of a Feather. *Bliss. *Rainbow Island. *Love, Laughs and Lather. *The Flirt. *Clubs Are Trumps. *All Aboard. *We Never Sleep. *Move On. *Bashful. *The Tip. 1918: *The Big Idea. *The Lamb. *Hit Him Again. *Beat It. *A Gasoline Wedding. *Let's Go. *Look Pleasant, Please. *On the Jump. *Here Come the Girls. *Follow the Crowd. *Pipe the Whiskers. *It's a Wild Life. *Hey There! Kicked Out. *The Non-Stop Kid. *Two-Gun Gussie. *Fireman, Save My Child. *That's Him. *The City Slicker. *Sic 'Em Towser. *Somewhere in Turkey. *Bride and Gloom. *Are Crooks Dishonest? *An Ozark Romance. *Kicking the Germ Out of Germany. *Two Scrambled. *Bees in His Bonnet. *Swing Your Partners. *Why Pick on Me? *Nothing But Trouble. *Hear 'Em Rave. *Take a Chance. *She Loves Me Not. 1919: *Wanted: $5,000. *Going! Going! Gone! *Ask Father. *On the Fire. *I'm on My Way. *Look Out Below. *The Dutiful Dub. *Next Aisle Over. *A Sammy in Siberia. *Young Mr Jazz. *Just Dropped In. *Crack Your Heels. *Si, Senor. *Before Breakfast. *The Marathon. *Swat the Cook. *Off the Trolley. *Spring Fever. *Billy Blazes Esquire. *At the Old Stage Door. *A Jazzed Honeymoon. *Chop Suey and Co. *Count Your Change. *Heap Big Chief. *Don't Shove. *Be My Wife. *The Rajah. *He Leads, Others Follow. *Soft Money. *Count the Votes. *Pay Your Dues. *His Only Father. *Never Touched Me. *Just Neighbors. *Bumping Into Broadway. Male and Female (GB: The Admirable Crichton). Everywoman. Captain Kidd's Kids. 1920: Sick Abed. Feet of Clay. Why Change Your Wife? The Dancin' Fool. 1921: The Affairs of Anatol (GB: A Prodigal Knight). Oh Lady, Lady. She Couldn't Help It. One Wild Week. The Speed Girl. Ducks and Drakes. You Never Can Tell. The March Hare. Two Weeks With Pay. 1922: Nancy from Nowhere. The Game Chicken. Nice People. North of the Rio Grande. Singed Wings. Pink Gods. *A Trip to Paramounttown. 1923: The Exciters. The World's Applause. Glimpses of the Moon. His Children's Children. 1924: Sinners in Heaven. Daring Youth. Dangerous Money. Monsieur Beaucaire. Argentine Love. Heritage of the Desert. Unguarded Women. 1925: The Manicure Girl. The Crowded Hour. Wild, Wild Susan. Lovers in Quarantine. Miss Bluebeard. 1926: The Splendid Crime. Stranded in Paris. Mrs Brewster's Millions. The Palm Beach Girl. Volcano. The Campus Flirt (GB: The College Flirt). 1927: She's a Sheik. A Kiss in a Taxi. Senorita. Swim, Girl, Swim. 1928: Feel My Pulse. The Fifty-Fifty Girl. Take Me Home. What a Night! Hot News. 1929: Rio Rita. 1930: Alias French Gertie

(GB: Love Finds a Way). Dixiana. Love Comes Along. Lawful Larceny. 1931: Reaching for the Moon. *Screen Snapshots No. 7. My Past. The Maltese Falcon. Honor of the Family. 1932: Silver Dollar. *Radio Girl. *The Stolen Jools (GB: The Slippery Pearls). 1933: *Hollywood on Parade No. 3. 42nd Street. *Hollywood on Parade No. 7. Cocktail Hour. The Song You Gave Me. A Southern Maid. 1934: Counsellor at Law. Registered Nurse. 1935: Music is Magic. 1936: Not Wanted on Voyage (US: Trickery on the High Seas). 1938: The Return of Carol Deane. 1941: Hi Gang! 1947: The Fabulous Joe. 1953: Life With the Lyons (US: Family Affair). 1954: Adventures With the Lyons (serial). The Lyons in Paris.

DANIELS, Jeff 1955–

Genial, square-jawed, rangy American actor from Georgia who looks at home in a trilby, and indeed has been cast in several period dramas. Educated in Michigan, Daniels left college a year early to begin a career on the New York stage. He was past 30 before film stardom really began to beckon (after he played the actor who steps from the screen in Woody Allen's *The Purple Rose of Cairo*) and still found time for returns to the stage despite being on screen more and more frequently in the late 1980s. Can play reliable, conniving or naive to equal effect but doesn't often pick good scripts. Later played flapping professional men who couldn't get to grips with life.

1981: Ragtime. 1982: An Invasion of Privacy (TV). 1983: Terms of Endearment. 1985: Marie – a True Story. The Purple Rose of Cairo. 1986: Heartburn. Something Wild. 1987: Radio Days. 1988: The House on Carroll Street. The Caine Mutiny Court Martial (TV). Sweet Hearts Dance. Checking Out. 1989: Love Hurts. No Place Like Home (TV). 1990: Welcome Home, Roxy Carmichael. Arachnophobia. 1991: The Butcher's Wife. Timescape/Grand Tour: Disaster in Time (cable TV). 1992: Pay Dirt/There Goes the Neighborhood. Rain Without Thunder. Teamster Boss: The Jackie Presser Story (TV). 1993: Gettysburg. 1994: Speed. Dumb & Dumber. 1995: Redwood Curtain (TV). 1996: Fly Away Home. 2 Days in the Valley. One Hundred and One Dalmatians. 1997: Trial and Error. 1998: My Favorite Martian. Pleasantville. 1999: All the Rage. The Crossing (TV). 2000: Cheaters (TV). Escanaba in da Moonlight.

DANNING, Sybil
(Sybelle Danninger) 1950–

Voluptuous, satin-skinned, Austrian-born blonde glamour star who seemed happy to be regarded as a sex symbol rather than a serious actress – as such a throwback to the bombshells of old, although in less up-market fare. In California for seven years as a child (the explanation of the fluent English), she was a dental assistant in Salzburg when persuaded to appear in soft-porn West German films; rather precariously she made the jump into the international market in the mid–1970s and has since fared best as flashing-eyed wicked women, often in costume spectaculars. A period of ill-health put a stop to her appearances in the early 1990s. She turned producer in 1996, but returned to acting three years later.

1968: Komm nur, mein liebstes Vögelein. 1971: Urlaubsreport (GB: Swedish Love Games). Siegfried und das sagenhafte Liebesleben der Nibelungen (GB: The Erotic Adventures of Siegfried. US: The Long Swift Sword of Siegfried). Das ehrliche Interview. Hausfrauenreport (GB: On the Side). L'amante dell'Orsa maggiore. Paragraph 218 – wir haben abgetrieben, Herr Staatsanwalt. Ehemänner Report (GB: Freedom for Love). Das Mädchen mit der heissen Masche (GB: The Loves of a French Pussycat). L'occhio nel labirinto (GB: Blood). Liebesmarkt in Dänemark (GB: Only in Denmark). 1972: L'émigrante. La dame rossa uccide sette volte. Die liebestollen Apothekerstöchter (GB and US: Passion Pill Swingers). Lorelei. Bluebeard. 1973: The Three Musketeers (The Queen's Diamonds). 1974: †The Odessa File. Joe e Margherito (GB and US: Run Run Joe). The Four Musketeers (The Revenge of Milady). Sam's Song (released 1980 as The Swap). 1975: Der flüsternde Tod (GB: Death in the Sun). Operation Lady Marlene. Der Geheimnistrager. 1976: God's Gun/Diamante lobo (US: The Cop Who Played God). Folies bourgeoises (GB: The Twist). 1977: The Prince and the Pauper (US: Crossed Swords). Entebbe: Operation Thunderbolt. 1979: Cuba Crossing/Kill Castro! The Concorde – Airport '79 (GB: Airport 80 . . . The Concorde). Meteor. Separate Ways (released 1981). 1980: Battle Beyond the Stars. How to Beat the High Cost of Living. The Man With Bogart's Face. 1981: The Day of the Cobra. Julie Darling. NightKill (GB: TV). The Salamander. 1982: S.A.S. San Salvador/S.A.S. Malko. 1983: The Seven Magnificent Gladiators (released 1985). Hercules. Black Diamond. Cat in the Cage/Chained Heat. 1984: Jungle Warriors. They're Playing With Fire. The Wild Life. 1985: The Tomb. Howling II . . . Your Sister is a Werewolf. Malibu Express. Clair/Private Passions. 1986: Pompeii (US: Warrior Queen). Young Lady Chatterley 2 (completed 1984). Reform School Girls. Panther Squad. Amazon Women on the Moon. 1987: Talking Walls (completed 1983). The Phantom Empire. Commando Squad. 1989: L.A. Bounty. 1999: Herbatel. 2000: Ruger: L.A. Bounty 2.

†Most scenes deleted

DANSON, Ted 1947–

Tall, craggy, contented-looking American actor with a mass of brown hair and friendly smile. He studied at the Actors' Institute and made his Broadway stage debut at 24. But film roles were peripheral until his success as the man behind the bar in the TV comedy show Cheers, which ran (with Danson in it) from 1982 to 1994. Since then he has tried drama, comedy and romance in films with fair success. Married (third) actress Mary Steenburgen (qv) in 1995.

1979: The Onion Field. Spider-Man The Dragon's Challenge (TV. GB: cinemas). 1980: The Women's Room (TV). Once Upon a Spy (TV). 1981: Our Family Business (TV). Body Heat. 1982: The Good Witch of Laurel Canyon (TV). Creepshow. 1983: Cowboy (TV). Something About Amelia (TV). 1985: Little Treasure. 1986: Just Between Friends. When the Bough Breaks (TV). A Fine Mess. 1987: We Are the Children (TV). 3 Men and a Baby. 1989: Cousins. Dad. 1990: 3 Men and a Little Lady. 1993: Made in America. 1994: Getting Even With Dad. Pontiac Moon. 1995: Loch Ness. 1998: Jerry and Tom. Saving Private Ryan. Thanks of a Grateful Nation (cable TV). Homegrown. 1999: Mumford.

DANTON, Ray 1931–1992

Narrow-faced, black-haired, snake-eyed (but handsome) American actor (a former child performer) who was a great success in his first film as a smiling villain, and repeated the trick four years later with his portrait of gangster Legs Diamond. Otherwise he perhaps failed to make the most of the chances proffered, although he made a series of colourful adventure yarns on the continent, and later emerged, albeit briefly, as a determined independent director of shockers. Married Julie Adams (qv), though the couple were parted by the time of Danton's death from kidney disease.

1955: The Looters. Chief Crazy Horse (GB: Valley of Fury). The Spoilers. I'll Cry Tomorrow. 1956: Outside the Law. 1957: The Night Runner. 1958: Too Much, Too Soon. Onionhead. Tarawa Beachhead. 1959: The Big Operator. Yellowstone Kelly. The Beat Generation. The Rise and Fall of Legs Diamond. 1960: Ice Palace. A Fever in the Blood. 1961: The George Raft Story (GB: Spin of a Coin). Portrait of a Mobster. A Majority of One. The Chapman Report. 1962: The Longest Day. 1963: Sandokan alla riscossa (GB: Tiger of Terror. US: Sandokan Fights Back). 1964: FBI Code 98. Sandokan Against the Leopard of Sarawak (GB: The Return of Sandokan). 1965: Höllenjagd auf heisse Ware (GB: The Spy Who Went Into Hell). 1966: New York chiama Superdrago. Ballata da milliardo. 1967: Lucky, el intrepido. 1968: The Candy Man. L'ultima mercenario. 1971: Triangle. Banyon (TV). 1972: The Ballad of Billie Blue. A Very Missing Person (TV). 1973: Runaway (TV. GB: cinemas: The Runaway Train). 1974: †Mystic Mountain Massacre. Centerfold Girls. 1976: Our Man Flint Dead on Target (TV). Pursuit (TV). Six-Pack Annie.

As director: 1972: Crypt of the Living Dead (GB: Vampire Woman). 1973: Deathmaster (GB: The Deathmaster). 1975: Psychic Killer. 1986: The Return of Mike Hammer (TV).

†Unreleased

DARBY, Kim (Deborah Zerby) 1947–

Fresh-faced, appealing, girlish (actually married and divorced young) American actress. The daughter of entertainers, she failed to sustain the impression she created as the gutsy young westerner in True Grit, yet still seemed capable of great emotional depths. Hardly seen since 1990: an unlucky career.

1963: Bye Bye Birdie (as extra). 1965: The Restless Ones. Bus Riley's Back in Town. 1967: The Karate Killers (TV. GB: cinemas). Flesh and Blood (TV). 1969: Generation (GB: A Time for Giving). True Grit. 1970: Norwood. The Strawberry Statement. 1971: The Grissom Gang. The People (TV). Red Sky at Morning. 1973: Don't Be Afraid of the Dark (TV). 1974: This is the West That Was (TV). Pretty Boy Floyd (GB: The Story of Pretty Boy Floyd) (TV). 1977: The One and Only. 1978: Flatbed Annie and Sweetiepie: Lady Truckers (TV. GB: Girls of the Road). 1979: The Last Convertible (TV). 1980: The Flight of the Enola Gay (TV). 1981: The Capture of Grizzly Adams (TV). 1983: Summer Girl (TV). Close Ties (TV). 1985: First Steps (TV). Better Off Dead. Embassy (TV). 1987: Teen Wolf Too. 1989: Deadly Embrace. 1995: Halloween 6: The Curse of Michael Myers. 1999: The Last Best Sunday.

DARIN, Bobby
(Robert Walden Cassotto) 1934–1973
Pop star turned actor whose popularity waned along with the collapse of his marriage (1960–1967) to Sandra Dee (*qv*). His intensive, explosive acting style was dissipated in vapid comedies, although not before he had been nominated for an Oscar. Darin remarried and was making a new start to an acting career when he died at 39 following heart surgery. Oscar-nominated for *Captain Newman MD*.

1960: Pepe. Heller in Pink Tights. 1961: Come September. State Fair. Too Late Blues. 1962: Pressure Point. Hell is for Heroes. If a Man Answers. 1963: Captain Newman MD. 1965: That Funny Feeling. 1967: Gunfight in Abilene. Stranger in the House (US: Cop-Out). 1969: The Happy Ending. 1973: Run Stranger Run.

DARNELL, Linda
(Monetta Darnell) 1921–1965
Dark-haired American actress, seldom well cast by her studio, Twentieth Century-Fox, who used her as lovely decoration or (after *Forever Amber*) a lightweight sex symbol. Only occasional films, such as *My Darling Clementine* and *This is My Love*, used properly the qualities of wilfulness, hard-heartedness and deep-seated sexual smoulder that could have made her a tragedienne of the first order. Died in a fire at a friend's home.

Three times married and divorced.

*1939: Elsa Maxwell's Hotel for Women (GB: Hotel for Women). Daytime Wife. 1940: Brigham Young – Frontiersman (GB: Brigham Young). Star Dust. Chad Hanna. The Mark of Zorro. 1941: Blood and Sand. Rise and Shine. 1942: The Loves of Edgar Allan Poe. 1943: City Without Men. The Song of Bernadette. *Show Business at War. 1944: Buffalo Bill. It Happened Tomorrow. Summer Storm. Sweet and Lowdown. 1945: *All-Star Bond Rally. The Great John L (GB: A Man Called Sullivan). Hangover Square. Fallen Angel. 1946: Anna and the King of Siam. Centennial Summer. My Darling Clementine. 1947: Forever Amber. 1948: The Walls of Jericho. Unfaithfully Yours. 1949: A Letter to Three Wives. Everybody Does It. Slattery's Hurricane. 1950: No Way Out. Two Flags West. 1951: The Thirteenth Letter. The Lady Pays Off. The Guy Who Came Back. 1952: Saturday Island (US: Island of Desire). Blackbeard the Pirate. Night Without Sleep. 1953: Donne proibite (GB: Forbidden Women. US: Angels Of Darkness). Second Chance. 1954: This is My Love. 1955: Gli ultimi cinque minuti. 1956: Dakota Incident. 1957: Zero Hour. Homeward Borne (TV). 1963: El Valle de las Espados. 1964: Black Spurs.*

DARRIEUX, Danielle 1917–
For six decades this green-eyed blonde French actress has been staring straight out of the screen, playing pretty well every kind of woman (with perhaps a slight preference. for the experienced woman with something to teach the younger man). Made a star by the first version of *Mayerling*, she has made fewer international appearances than her contemporaries, but that was France's gain, and she remained beautiful into middle age.

1931: Le bal. 1932: Coquecigrole. Le coffret de laque. Panurge. 1933: Château de rêve. L'or dans la rue. 1934: Mauvaise graine. Dedée. La crise est finie (GB: The Slump is Over). Mon coeur t'appelle. Volga en flammes. 1935: Quelle drôle de gosse! J'aime toutes les femmes. La contrôleur des wagon-lits. Le domino vert. Mademoiselle Mozart (US: Meet Miss Mozart). 1936: Mayerling. Tarass Boulba. Port-Arthur (GB: I Give My Life). Club de femmes. Un mauvais garçon. 1937: Abus de confiance. Mademoiselle ma mère. 1938: Katia. Retour à l'aube. The Rage of Paris. 1939: Battement de coeur. 1941: Premier rendez-vous (US: Her First Affair). Caprices. 1942: La fausse maîtresse. 1945: Adieu Chérie. 1946: Au petit bonheur. 1947: Bethsabée. Ruy Blas. 1948: Jean de la Lune. 1949: Occupe-toi d'Amélie (GB: Oh! Amelia). 1950: La ronde. Toselli. 1951: Rich, Young and Pretty. Le plaisir (GB: House of Pleasure). La maison Bonadieu. La vérité sur Bébé Donge. 1952: Five Fingers. Adorables créatures. 1953: Madame de . . . (US: The Diamond Earrings). Le bon Dieu sans confession. Châteaux en Espagne. 1954: Napoléon. Escalier de service. Bonnes à tuer (GB: One Stop to Eternity). Le rouge et le noir. 1955: Lady Chatterley's Lover. Si Paris nous était conté. L'affaire des poisons. 1956: Alexander the Great. Typhon sur Nagasaki. Le salaire du péché. 1957: Pot-Bouille (GB: Lovers Of Paris). Le septième ciel. 1958: Le désordre et la nuit. La vie à deux. Un drôle de dimanche. 1959: Marie-Octobre. Les yeux de l'amour. 1960: L'homme à femmes. Meurtre en 45 tours (GB: Murder at 45 RPM). 1961: The Greengage Summer (US: Loss of Innocence). Les lions sont lâchés. Les bras de la nuit. 1962: Vive Henri IV, vive l'amour. The Devil and the 10 Commandments. Landru (GB: Bluebeard). Le crime ne paie pas. Pourquoi Paris? 1963: Du grabuge chez les veuves. Méfiez-vous, mesdames! 1964: Patate (GB: Friend of the Family). 1965: Le coup de grâce. L'or du Duc. Le dimanche de la vie. 1966: L'homme à la Buick. 1967: The Young Girls of Rochefort. Birds in Peru. 1968: 24 Hours in a Woman's Life. 1969: La maison de campagne. 1972: Roses rouges et piments verts. 1975: Divine. 1976: L'année sainte. 1979: Le cavaleur. 1982: Une chambre de ville. 1983: En haut des marches. 1986: Le lieu du crime. Corps et biens. 1988: Quelques jours avec moi. 1989: Belle en tête. 1990: Le jour des rois. 1992: Las mamies. 1995: L'univers de Jacques Demy (doc). 1996: Les mille et une recettes du cuisinier amoureux.

DARVI, Bella (Bayla Wegier) 1927–1971
Dark-haired, Polish-born actress who was modelling in France when 'discovered' by Darryl F. Zanuck and taken to Hollywood with a Twentieth Century-Fox contract. Things did not go well for Zanuck's protegée and after three films she returned to France, although it was in Monte Carlo at 43 that she committed suicide by gassing herself.
1954: Hell and High Water. The Egyptian. 1955: The Racers (GB: Such Men Are Dangerous). Je suis un sentimental (GB: Headlines of Destruction). 1956: Je reviendra à Kandara. 1957: Le gorille vous salue bien (US: Mask of the Gorilla). Raffles sur la ville (GB:

Trap for a Killer). 1958: Pia de' Tolomei (US: Pia of Ptolemy). 1959: Enigme aux Folies-Bergère. Il rossetto (GB: Red Lips. US: Lipstick). Sinners of Paris. 1960: Le pain de Jules. 1961: L'urlo dei bolidi. 1971: Les petites filles modèles (GB: Good Little Girls).

DAUPHIN, Claude
(C. Franc-Nohan) 1903–1978
Dapper, stocky little French actor, adept at inspectors, doctors and psychiatrists – a more straightforward version of Claude Rains. Dauphin brought an air of relaxed sophistication to all he did and gradually became more in demand internationally after World War II. He started in the theatre as a set designer, but soon started taking acting roles as well. Died from an intestinal occlusion.
1930: Langrevin père et fils. 1931: La fortune. Mondanités. Aux urnes citoyens. Figuration. 1932: Un homme heureux. Faubourg Montmartre. Une jeune fille et un million. Clair de lune. Paris soleil. 1933: L'Abbé Constantin. La fille du régiment. Pas besoin d'argent. Les surprises du Sleeping. Je suis un homme perdu. Maître chez soi. Le billet de mille. Le rayon des amours. 1934: Dédée. Voyage imprévu. Nous ne sommes plus des enfants. D'amour et d'eau fraîche. 1935: Retour au Paradis. Les pantoufles (US: The Slipper Episode). 1936: La route heureuse. Faisons un rêve. 1937: La fessée. Les perles de la couronne. Entrée des artistes (US: The Curtain Rises). Conflit. L'affair Lafont. 1939: Paris – New York. Menaces. Cavalcade d'amour. Le monde tremblera. Battements de coeur. 1940: Les surprises de la radio. 1941: Les petits riens. L'étrange Suzy. Les deux timides. Les hommes sans peur. Une femme dans la nuit. Une femme disparait. Le roman de Renard (voice only).

1942: Promesse à l'inconnue. Félicie Nanteuil. La belle aventure. 1943: The Gentle Sex. 1944: Salut à la France. English without Tears (US: Her Man Gilbey). 1945: Dorothée cherche l'amour. La femme coupée en morceaux. Cyrano de Bergerac. Nous ne sommes pas mariés. 1946: Tombe du ciel. Rendez-vous à Paris. L'eventail (US: Twilight). Parade du rire. 1947: Croisère pour l'inconnu. Route sans issue. La Passion d'Evelyne Cléry. Paris 1900. 1948: L'impeccable Henri. L'inconnue d'un soir. Ainsi finit la nuit. Le bal des pompiers. Jean de la Lune. 1949: La petite chocolatière. La renaissance du rail. 1950: Deported. 1951: Le plaisir. Casque d'or. 1952: April in Paris. Mademoiselle Modiste (US: Naughty Martine). 1953: Little Boy Lost. Innocents in Paris. 1954: Phantom of the Rue Morgue. 1955: Les mauvaises rencontres. 1956: Le temps de l'amour. 1957: Mon coquin de père. 1958: The Quiet American. Pourquoi viens-tu si tard? 1959: Passeport pour le monde (narrator only). 1961: The Full Treatment (US: Stop Me Before I Kill). 1962: The Devil and the 10 Commandments. Tiara Tahiti. 1963: Symphonie pour un massacre. La bonne soupe. 1964: The Visit. 1965: The Sleeping Car Murders. Lady L. Is Paris Burning? 1966: Da Berlino l'Apocalisse (GB: The Spy Pit). Grand Prix. 1967: Two for the Road. L'une et l'autre (US: The Other One). Lamiel. Barbarella. 1968: Adolphe, ou l'âge tendre. Hard Contract. 1969: The Madwoman of Chaillot. 1970: Berlin Affair (TV). 1971: Eglantine. 1972: La piu bella serata della mia vita. Au rendez-vous de la mort joyeuse. 1973: Vogliamo i colonnelli. 1974: L'important c'est d'aimer (US: That Most Important Thing: Love). Rosebud. 1975: La course a l'echalotte. 1976: The Tenant. Mado. 1977: La vie devant soi (GB and US: Madame Rosa). Le point de mire. 1978: Le pion. Les misérables (TV).

DAVIDOVICH, Lolita 1961–
Flame-haired, Canadian-born (of Serbian parentage) Hollywood actress of strong chin and provocative features. Her film career was struggling until cast opposite Paul Newman in the title role of *Blaze*. After initial problems finding suitable parts to follow such a flashy central character, she proved her versatility and settled down as a second-line leading lady capable of poignant performances. Married director Ron Shelton.
1986: †Blindside. †Recruits. 1987: †The Big Town. †Adventures in Babysitting (GB: A Night on the Town). 1989: Blaze. 1991: Prison Stories: Women on the Inside (TV). The Object

of Beauty. The Inner Circle/The Projectionist. JFK. 1992: Raising Cain. Leap of Faith. Keep the Change. 1993: Younger and Younger. Boiling Point. Intersection. 1994: Strange Things. Cobb. 1995: Indictment: The McMartin Case (TV). Salt Water Moose. Now and Then. For Better or Worse. Trial at Fortitude Bay (TV). 1996: Neil Simon's 'Jake's Women' (TV). Harvest of Fire (TV). Touch. Jungle 2 Jungle. Santa Fe. Dead Silence. 1998: Gods and Monsters. Mystery, Alaska. 1999: Shegalla/Touched. No Vacancy. Four Days. Forever Flirt. Play It to the Bone.*

†As Lolita David

DAVIDTZ, Embeth 1966–
Sloe-eyed, dark-haired, slender American actress of serious countenance. Moving to South Africa at nine, she became a member of the National Theatre Company in Johannesburg after taking a Masters degree in drama, and appeared in many classics there. Film appearances, though, were few until she relocated to Los Angeles and won praise for her performance as the Jewish maid and handservant in *Schindler's List*. She hasn't quite become an A-grade star yet but continues to attract leading roles.
*1988: A Private Life. 1989: Night of the Nineteenth. 1990: Sweet Murder. 1992: Deadly Matrimony (TV). Till Death Us Do Part (TV). 1993: Army of Darkness. The Medieval Dead/Army of Darkness: Evil Dead 3. Schindler's List. 1994: *Oh, What a Day. 1995: Feast of July. Murder in the First. 1996: Matilda. 1997: The Garden of Redemption (TV). Fallen. The Gingerbread Man. 1998: Last Rites (TV). 1999: Simon Magus. Mansfield Park. Letters from a Wayward Son. 2000: Bicentennial Man. 2001: Bridget Jones' Diary. The Hole.*

DAVIES, Marion
(Marion Douras) 1897–1961
Bright, chirpy, round-faced Hollywood blonde whose talent for comedy went largely unappreciated in its day because she was the mistress of newspaper magnate William Randolph Hearst whose money kept her in leading roles for 20 years. Nowadays critical opinion, looking objectively at Marion's career, seems to be that the fun-loving girl with the delightful stutter would probably have done very nicely without her protector. Died of cancer.

1917: *Runaway Romany.* 1918: *Cecilia of the Pink Roses. The Burden of Proof.* 1919: *The Cinema Murder. The Dark Star. The Belle of New York. Getting Mary Married.* 1920: *April Folly. Restless Sex.* 1921: *Buried Treasure. Enchantment.* 1922: *The Bride's Play. Beauty's Worth. The Young Diana. When Knighthood Was in Flower.* 1923: *Adam and Eva. Little Old New York.* 1924: *Yolanda. Janice Meredith (GB: The Beautiful Rebel).* 1925: *Zander the Great. Lights of Old Broadway (GB: Merry Wives of Gotham).* 1926: *Beverly of Graustark.* 1927: *Quality Street. The Fair Co-Ed (GB: The Varsity Girl). The Red Mill. Tillie the Toiler.* 1928: *The Patsy (GB: The Politic Flapper). The Cardboard Lover. Show People.* 1929: *Hollywood Revue of 1929. Marianne.* †*The Five O'Clock Girl.* 1930: *Not So Dumb (GB: Dulcy). The Florodora Girl (GB: The Gay Nineties).* 1931: *Bachelor Father. It's a Wise Child. Five and Ten (GB: Daughter of Luxury).* *Jackie Cooper's Christmas (GB: The Christmas Party).* 1932: *Polly of the Circus. Blondie of the Follies. Peg o' My Heart.* 1933: *Going Hollywood.* 1934: *Operator 13 (GB: Spy 13).* 1935: *A Dream Comes True. Page Miss Glory.* 1936: *Hearts Divided. Cain and Mabel.* *Pirate Party on Catalina Isle.* 1937: *Ever Since Eve.*

†*Unreleased*

DAVIS, Bette
(Ruth Elizabeth Davis) 1908–1989
Dark-haired (blonde until 1938), showy, intense American actress with inimitably clipped speech who became one of Hollywood's biggest stars after a long apprenticeship in the early 1930s. Her habit of spitting out her dialogue, or biting off the

ends of her lines, made her the target for a thousand imitators, but few players were as adept as her at expressing a grand passion. Academy Awards in 1935 for *Dangerous* and in 1938 for *Jezebel*. Eight further nominations between 1939 and 1962. Married (fourth of five) to actor Gary Merrill from 1950 to 1960. Died of cancer.
1931: *The Bad Sister. Seed. Waterloo Bridge. Way Back Home (GB: Old Greatheart).* 1932: *Hell's House. So Big. The Dark Horse. The Menace. The Man Who Played God (GB: The Silent Voice). The Rich are Always with Us. Cabin in the Cotton. Three on a Match. 20,000 Years in Sing Sing.* 1933: *Parachute Jumper. Ex-Lady. The Working Man. Bureau of Missing Persons. Fashions/Fashions of 1934 (GB: Fashion Follies of 1934).* 1934: *The Big Shakedown. Jimmy the Gent. Fog Over Frisco. Housewife. Of Human Bondage. Bordertown.* 1935: *A Dream Comes True. Front Page Woman. Special Agent. Dangerous. The Girl from 10th Avenue (GB: Men on her Mind). The Petrified Forest.* 1936: *The Golden Arrow. Satan Met a Lady.* *A Day at Santa Anita.* 1937: *Kid Galahad. Marked Woman. That Certain Woman. It's Love I'm After.* 1938: *Jezebel. The Sisters.* 1939: *The Private Lives of Elizabeth and Essex. Dark Victory. Juarez. The Old Maid.* 1940: *All This and Heaven Too. The Letter.* 1941: *Variety Reel. The Little Foxes. The Great Lie. Shining Victory. The Bride Came COD. The Man Who Came to Dinner.* 1942: *In This Our Life. Now, Voyager.* 1943: *Watch on the Rhine. Thank Your Lucky Stars.* *Show Business at War.* *A Present with a Future.* *Stars on Horseback. Old Acquaintance.* 1944: *Mr Skeffington. Hollywood Canteen.* 1945: *The Corn is Green.* 1946: *A Stolen Life.* 1947: *Deception.* 1948: *Winter Meeting. June Bride.* 1949: *Beyond the Forest.* 1950: *All About Eve.* 1951: *Another Man's Poison. Payment on Demand.* 1952: *Phone Call from a Stranger. The Star.* 1955: *The Virgin Queen.* 1956: *The Catered Affair (GB: Wedding Breakfast). Storm Center.* 1959: *The Scapegoat. John Paul Jones.* 1961: *Pocketful of Miracles.* 1962: *What Ever Happened to Baby Jane?* 1963: *La noia (GB and US: The Empty Canvas).* 1964: *Dead Ringer (GB: Dead Image). Hush . . . Hush, Sweet Charlotte. Where Love Has Gone.* 1965: *The Nanny.* 1967: *The Anniversary.* 1969: *Connecting Rooms.* 1971: *Bunny O'Hare. Madame Sin (TV. GB: cinemas).* 1972: *The Judge and Jake Wyler (TV). The Scientific Card-Player.* 1973: *Scream Pretty Peggy (TV).* 1976: *Burnt Offerings. The Disappearance of Aimee (TV).* 1977: *Return to Witch Mountain.* 1978: *Death on the Nile. The Children of Sanchez.* 1979: *Strangers (TV).* 1980: *White Mama (TV).* 1981: *The Watcher in the Woods. Skyward (TV). Family Reunion (TV). A Piano for Mrs Cimino (TV).* 1982: *Little Gloria – Happy at Last (TV).* 1983: *Right of Way (TV).* 1985: *Murder With Mirrors (TV). As Summers Die (TV).* 1986: *Directed By William Wyler (TV).* 1987: *The Whales of August.* 1988: *Wicked Stepmother.* 1989: *Hairway to the Stars.*

DAVIS, Geena (Virginia Davis) 1957–
Happy-looking, dark-haired American actress with wide, full, distinctive lips and

high cheekbones. Seen mainly in offbeat comedy roles, she has said that she has 'a lot of faith in my comic senses'. One writer dubbed her the Queen of Quirk, but she had the last laugh when collecting an Oscar for her portrait of an eccentric dog-trainer in *The Accidental Tourist*. She was further Oscar-nominated for *Thelma & Louise*. Married (2nd) actor Jeff Goldblum (qv) in 1987, but the couple divorced four years later. She then married Finnish-born director Renny Harlin, but that ended in 1997, seemingly along with her big-star career. One of Hollywood's tallest actresses at six feet..
1982: *Tootsie.* 1984: *Fletch.* 1985: *Sexpionage/Secret Weapons (Video). Transylvania 6-5000.* 1986: *The Fly.* 1987: *Beetlejuice.* 1988: *Earth Girls Are Easy. The Accidental Tourist.* 1990: *Quick Change.* 1991: *Thelma & Louise.* 1992: *A League of Their Own.* 1993: *Hero (GB: Accidental Hero). Angie.* 1994: *Speechless.* 1995: *CutThroat Island.* 1996: *The Long Kiss Goodnight.* 1999: *Stuart Little.*

DAVIS, Jim (Marlin Davis) 1915–1981
Husky, slow-speaking, black-haired, diffident-looking six-footer who was unsuccessful in a star role opposite Bette Davis early in his career, and was thereafter confined to leading parts in 'B' westerns and supporting roles in bigger features. Middle age seemed to suit him, and he gave some good performances in the 1970s. Later still, he became familiar to TV viewers as Jock Ewing of the soap opera *Dallas*, before dying following surgery for a perforated ulcer. Billed in some 1940s' films as James Davis.
1940: *Safari.* 1941: *Revenge of the Zombies.* 1942: *White Cargo.* *Keep 'Em Sailing. Riding Through Nevada. Tennessee Johnson (GB: The*

Man on America's Conscience). Cairo. 1943: Frontier Fury. Salute to the Marines. Swing Shift Maisie (GB: The Girl in Overalls). Pilot No.5. 1944: Cyclone Prairie Rangers. Thirty Seconds Over Tokyo. 1945: What Next, Corporal Hargrove? Up Goes Maisie (GB: Up She Goes). 1946: Gallant Bess. 1947: The Fabulous Texan. Merton of the Movies. The Beginning or the End? The Romance of Rosy Ridge. Louisiana. 1948: Winter Meeting. 1949: Brimstone. Hellfire. Mississippi Rhythm. Yes Sir, That's My Baby. Red Stallion in the Rockies. The Cariboo Trail. 1950: California Passage. The Showdown. Hi-Jacked. Square Dance Katy. The Savage Horde. 1951: Silver Canyon. Oh! Susanna. Cavalry Scout. Little Big Horn (GB: The Fighting Seventh). The Sea Hornet. Three Desperate Men. 1952: Woman of the North Country. Rose of Cimarron. The Big Sky. The Blazing Forest. 1953: The President's Lady. Ride the Man Down. The Woman They Almost Lynched. 1954: The Last Command. The Outcast (GB: The Fortune Hunter). Jubilee Trail. Hell's Outpost. The Big Chase. The Outlaw's Daughter. 1955: Timberjack. Last of the Desperadoes. The Vanishing American. 1956: Blonde Bait (US version of GB film Women without Men). Bottom of the Bottle (GB: Beyond the River). The Maverick Queen. The Wild Dakotas. The Quiet Gun. Frontier Gambler. Duel at Apache Wells. 1957: The Restless Breed. A Lust to Kill. Raiders of Old California. Apache Warrior. Last Stagecoach West. The Monster from Green Hell. The Badge of Marshal Brennan. Guns Don't Argue. 1958: Toughest Gun in Tombstone. Flaming Frontier. Wolf Dog. 1959: Noose for a Gunman. Alias Jesse James. 1961: Frontier Uprising. The Gambler Wore a Gun. 1965: Zebra in the Kitchen. Iron Angel. They Ran for Their Lives (released 1968). 1966: Fort Utah. Jesse James Meets Frankenstein's Daughter. Hondo and the Apaches (TV. GB: cinemas). 1967: Border Lust. El Dorado. 1969: The Road Hustlers. 1970: Blood of Frankenstein (US: Dracula versus Frankenstein). The Gun Riders. Five Bloody Graves. Rio Lobo. Vanished (TV). Monte Walsh. 1971: Big Jake. The Trackers (TV). 1972: High-Flying Spy (TV). The Honkers. Bad Company. 1973: Fire-Eaters. Deliver Us from Evil (TV). One Little Indian. 1974: The Parallax View. 1975: Satan's Triangle (TV). The Runaway Barge (TV). Inferno in Paradise (TV). 1976: The Deputies (TV). 1977: The Choirboys. Just a Little Inconvenience (TV). 1978: Comes a Horseman. Trail of Danger (TV). Stone/Killing Stone (TV). 1979: The Day Time Ended. 1981: Don't Look Back (TV).

DAVIS, Joan (Madonna Davis) 1907–1961

Wide-mouthed, copper-haired, rubber-faced American clown, a rival to Judy Canova (*qv*) in the female B-movie comedy stakes of the forties and early fifties. Crowned her career with phenomenal success in the television comedy series *I Married Joan*. Died from a heart attack.

1935: *Way Up Thar. Millions in the Air. 1936: Bunker Bean (GB: His Majesty Bunker Bean). 1937: The Holy Terror. On the Avenue. Nancy Steele is Missing. The Great Hospital Mystery. Time Out for Romance. Thin Ice

(GB: Lovely to Look At). Life Begins in College (GB: The Joy Parade). Love and Hisses. Angel's Holiday. You Can't Have Everything. Wake Up and Live. Sing and Be Happy. 1938: Hold That Co-Ed (GB: Hold That Girl). Tail Spin. Sally, Irene and Mary. Josette. My Lucky Star. Just Around the Corner. 1939: Day-Time Wife. Too Busy to Work. 1940: Free, Blonde and 21. Sailor's Lady. Manhattan Heartbeat. 1941: Sun Valley Serenade. Hold That Ghost. Two Latins from Manhattan. For Beauty's Sake. 1942: Yokel Boy (GB: Hitting the Headlines). Sweetheart of the Fleet. 1943: He's My Guy. Two Senoritas from Chicago. Around the World. 1944: Beautiful but Broke. Show Business. Kansas City Kitty. 1945: George White's Scandals. She Gets Her Man. 1946: She Wrote the Book. 1948: If You Knew Susie. 1949: Make Mine Laughs. The Traveling Saleswoman. 1950: Love That Brute. 1951: The Groom Wore Spurs. 1952: Harem Girl.

DAVIS, Judy 1955–

Dark-haired, unpretty, sharp-faced Australian actress in strong roles, certainly the most powerful dramatic star to emerge from her native country until the arrival of Nicole Kidman (*qv*). She began her career as a vocalist with a rock band, but switched to acting in her early twenties and, after one line in her first film, burst through to stardom with her second, the well-named *My Brilliant Career*. She later expanded her horizons, and won Academy Award nominations for *A Passage to India* and *Husbands and Wives*. Married Australian actor Colin Friels.

1977: High Rolling (US: High Rolling in a Hot Corvette). 1979: My Brilliant Career. 1981: The Winter of Our Dreams. Heatwave.

Hoodwink. 1982: A Woman Called Golda (TV). 1983: Who Dares Wins (US: The Final Option). 1984: A Passage to India. 1985: Kangaroo. 1986: Rocket to the Moon (TV). 1987: High Tide. 1989: Georgia. 1990: Impromptu. Alice. 1991: One Against the Wind (TV). Naked Lunch. Where Angels Fear to Tread. Barton Fink. 1992: On My Own. Naked Making Lunch. Husbands and Wives. 1994: The New Age. The Ref (GB: Hostile Hostages). †Dark Blood. 1995: Cluck. Serving in Silence: The Margarethe Cammermeyer Story (TV). 1996: Children of the Revolution. Blood and Wine. 1997: Absolute Power. Deconstructing Harry. 1998: The Echo of Thunder (cable TV). Celebrity. 1999: Dash and Lilly (TV). A Cooler Climate (TV). 2000: Gaudi Afternoon.

†Unfinished

DAVIS, Sammy Jr 1925–1990

Dynamic, pint-sized American singer and actor who described himself as 'the first one-eyed Jewish negro' and often gave performances twice as large as the part demanded. On stage as a child, he lost an eye in a car crash in 1954, just before coming to Hollywood. Films could never really restrain him, and he remained at his best as a nightclub performer. Married (second of three) to Swedish actress May Britt (Maj-britt Wilkens 1933–). Died from cancer of the throat.

1933: *Rufus Jones for President. 1934: *Season's Greetings. 1947: Sweet and Low. 1956: The Benny Goodman Story. 1958: Anna Lucasta. 1959: Porgy and Bess. 1960: Ocean's Eleven. Pepe. 1962: The Threepenny Opera/Der Dreigroschenoper. Convicts Four (GB: Reprieve!). Sergeants Three. 1963: Johnny Cool. 1964: Robin and the Seven Hoods. Nightmare in the Sun. 1966: A Man Called Adam. 1968: Salt and Pepper. Sweet Charity. 1969: Man Without Mercy (later Gone with the West). The Pigeon (TV). 1970: One More Time. 1971: The Trackers (TV). Poor Devil (TV). 1973: Save the Children. 1975: James Dean – the First American Teenager. 1978: Sammy Stops the World. 1980: The Cannonball Run. 1981: The Cannonball Run II. 1984: Cry of the City. That's Dancing! 1986: The Perils of P.K. 1988: Moon over Parador. Tap. 1990: The Kid Who Loved Christmas (TV).

DAY, Doris (D. Kappelhof) 1922–

Chirpy blonde American singer with white,

white teeth and an engaging smile. The girl-next-door of Warners' family musicals of the late forties and early fifties, she later became accepted as a competent dramatic actress, and then not only sustained her career but became America's number one box-office star, with a series of fluffy sex comedies from 1958 on. At her best she was endearingly vulnerable. But her finest performances remain in musicals where her characters mixed vivacity with gusto: *The Pajama Game* and *Calamity Jane*. Nominated for an Oscar in *Pillow Talk*.
1941: *My Lost Horizon. *Once Over Lightly. *Is it Love, Or is it Conscription? *Les Brown and His Orchestra (compilation of preceding three shorts). 1948: Romance on the High Seas (GB: It's Magic). 1949: My Dream is Yours. It's a Great Feeling. Young Man with a Horn (GB: Young Man of Music). 1950: The West Point Story (GB: Fine and Dandy). Tea for Two. Storm Warning. 1951: Lullaby of Broadway. Starlift. On Moonlight Bay. I'll See You in My Dreams. 1952: The Winning Team. *Screen Snapshots No. 206. April in Paris. 1953: By the Light of the Silvery Moon. Calamity Jane. *So You Want a Television Set. 1954: Lucky Me. Young at Heart. 1955: Love Me Or Leave Me. 1956: The Man Who Knew Too Much. Julie. 1957: The Pajama Game. 1958: Teacher's Pet. The Tunnel of Love. 1959: It Happened to Jane. Pillow Talk. 1960: Midnight Lace. Please Don't Eat the Daisies. 1961: Lover Come Back. 1962: That Touch of Mink. Billy Rose's Jumbo. 1963: The Thrill of It All. Move Over, Darling. 1964: Send Me No Flowers. 1965: Do Not Disturb. 1966: The Glass Bottom Boat. 1967: Caprice. The Ballad of Josie. 1968: Where Were You When the Lights Went Out? With Six You Get Egg Roll. 1994: Don't Pave Main Street: Carmel's Heritage.*

DAVISON, Bruce 1946–

Fair-haired, pale-eyed American actor of fresh complexion. His film career got off to a notable start with strong leading roles in *Last Summer* and *Willard*, but he then settled down to a mixed bag of a career in a wide range of journeyman roles, from the child molester of *Short Eyes*, through the serial killer of *Live! From Death Row* to more benevolent and less decisive parts in such recent films as *Grace of My Heart* and *Apt Pupil*. He gradually became a face to which you couldn't quite put a name. He gave an award-winning performance on Broadway as *The Elephant Man* and was nominated for an

Oscar in the AIDS drama *Longtime Companion*. He is married (second) to actress Lisa Pelikan, with whom he frequently appears on stage.
1969: Last Summer. 1970: The Strawberry Statement. 1971: Willard. Been Down So Long It Looks Like Up to Me. Owen Marshall, Counsellor at Law (TV). 1972: The Jerusalem File. Ulzana's Raid. 1973: The Affair (TV. GB: cinemas). Mame. 1975: The Last Survivors (TV). 1976: Mother, Jugs and Speed. Grand Jury. 1977: Short Eyes. The Gathering (TV). French Quarter. Portrait of Grandpa Doc. 1978: Brass Target. Summer of My German Soldier (TV). Deadman's Curve (TV). 1979: Mind Over Murder (TV). The Gathering, Part II (TV). 1980: The Lathe of Heaven (TV). 1981: Incident at Crestridge (TV). High Risk. The Wave (TV). 1982: Tomorrow's Child (TV). Kiss My Grits. The Taming of the Shrew. 1983: Ghost Dancing (TV). Summer Heat. Lies. 1984: Crimes of Passion/China Blue. 1985: Spies Like Us. 1986: The Ladies Club. 1987: The Misfit Brigade/Wheels of Terror. 1989: Lady in the Corner (TV). 1990: I Want Him Back! (TV). Steel and Lace. Longtime Companion. 1992: Live! From Death Row (TV). Desperate Choices: To Save My Child (TV). 1993: An Ambush of Ghosts. 6 Degrees of Separation. Short Cuts. A Mother's Revenge (TV). 1994: Luck, Trust & Ketchup (D). Someone Else's Child (TV). The Skateboard Kid 2. 1995: Widow's Kiss (TV). The Cure. Far from Home: The Adventures of Yellow Dog. Down, Out & Dangerous (TV). The Baby Sitters Club. It's My Party. 1996: The Crucible. Grace of My Heart. After Jimmy (TV). Hidden in America (TV). Homage. 1997: Lovelife. Color of Justice (TV). Apt Pupil. 1998: Paulie: A Parrot's Tale. At First Sight. Little Girl Fly Away (TV). 1999: Vendetta. A Memory in My Heart (TV). Locked in Silence (TV). 2000: The King is Alive. X-Men.

DAY, Frances
(F. Schenk) 1907–1984

Blonde, long-nosed, big-busted, minxish American-born musical-comedy star of strong personality, who made her name on the English stage in the late twenties and early thirties, but was not popular with some sections of press and public. Her glamorous image remained most effective on stage and she, too, seemed most at home there. Died from leukemia.
*1928: The Price of Divorce. 1930: *OK Chief.*

Big Business. 1932: The First Mrs Frazer. 1933: The Girl from Maxim's. 1934: Two Hearts in Waltztime. Temptation. 1935: Oh, Daddy! 1936: Public Nuisance No. 1. You Must Get Married. Dreams Come True. 1937: Who's Your Lady Friend? The Girl in the Taxi. 1938: Kicking the Moon Around (US: The Playboy). 1940: Room for Two. 1944: Fiddlers Three. 1949: Scrapbook for 1933. 1952: Tread Softly (US: Tread Softly, Stranger). 1957: There's Always a Thursday. 1960: Climb Up the Wall.*

DAY, Laraine (LaRaine Johnson) 1917–

Quiet, sensitive American actress with demure features and fairish brown hair. A middle-range star from 1939 to 1949, she remains fixed in most minds as Nurse Mary Lamont in the Dr Kildare series, a role she played seven times. She has devoted most of her latter days to the Mormon church into which she was born.
*1937: ‡The Law Commands. ‡Doomed at Sundown. †Stella Dallas. 1938: †Border G-Man. †Scandal Street. †The Painted Desert. 1939: †The Arizona Legion. †Sergeant Madden. †*Think First. Tarzan Finds a Son! Calling Dr Kildare. Secret of Dr Kildare. 1940: My Son, My Son. And One Was Beautiful. Dr Kildare's Strange Case. I Take This Woman. Foreign Correspondent. Dr Kildare Goes Home. Dr Kildare's Crisis. 1941: The Bad Man (GB: Two Gun Cupid). The People Versus Dr Kildare (GB: My Life is Yours). The Trial of Mary Dugan. Unholy Partners. Kathleen. Dr Kildare's Wedding Day (GB: Mary Names the Day). 1942: Journey for Margaret. Fingers at the Window. A Yank on the Burma Road (GB: China Caravan). 1943: Mr Lucky. 1944: The Story of Dr Wassell. Bride by Mistake. 1945: Keep Your Powder Dry. Those Endearing*

Young Charms. 1946: The Locket. 1947: Tycoon. 1948: My Dear Secretary. 1949: I Married a Communist (GB: The Woman on Pier 13). Without Honor. 1954: The High and the Mighty. 1956: Toy Tiger. Three for Jamie Dawn. 1959: The Third Voice. Dark As the Night (TV). 1972: House of Dracula's Daughter. 1975: Murder on Flight 502 (TV).

‡As Lorraine Hayes
†As Laraine Johnson

DAY-LEWIS, Daniel 1957–

Dark-haired, saturnine, bonily handsome Anglo-Irish actor in international films who can play innocent, corrupt or heroic with the change of a tight-lipped smile. A public school image, reinforced by his success on stage in *Another Country*, limited his early screen progress, but his role as the amorous Czech neurosurgeon in *The Unbearable Lightness of Being* opened a good many doors and, after his Academy Award as the disabled artist-writer Christy Brown, he became a busy leading man in films from both sides of the Atlantic. No films in 1994 and 1995 though, which robbed his fans of his talents at a crucial stage. The grandson of film-maker Sir Michael Balcon and son of poet laureate Cecil Day-Lewis, he made his screen debut as a teenager. He received a further Oscar nomination for *In the Name of the Father*. 'Retired' from acting in 1998.

1971: Sunday, Bloody Sunday. 1982: Gandhi. 1984: The Bounty. 1985: My Beautiful Laundrette. A Room With a View. The Insurance Man (TV. US: cinemas). 1986: Nanou. 1987: The Unbearable Lightness of Being. Stars and Bars. 1989: Eversmile New Jersey. My Left Foot. 1992: The Last of the Mohicans. 1993: The Age of Innocence. In the Name of the Father. 1996: The Crucible. 1997: The Boxer. 2001: Gangs of New York.

DEAN, James 1931–1955

Fair-haired American star whose Adonis-like good looks, appeal to the youth market and anguished, intense style of playing shot him to gigantic international stardom in his first leading role, in *East of Eden*. Two films later he was killed in a car crash, and the public sorrow was unequalled since the death of Valentino. Nominated for Academy Awards in *East of Eden* and *Giant*.

1951: Fixed Bayonets! Hill Number One. Sailor Beware. 1952: Has Anybody Seen My Gal. 1953: Trouble Along the Way. 1954: East

of Eden. 1955: Rebel without a Cause. 1956: Giant.

DE CARLO, Yvonne
(Peggy Y. Middleton) 1922–

Pretty Yvonne Middleton from Vancouver, Canada, laboured hard for three years as decoration on the fringe of Hollywood exotica and college comedies. But when they dressed her up in yashmak and bangles, and called her Yvonne de Carlo, she became a star. Although no great actress, she put plenty of fire into a colourful series of easterns and westerns from 1945 to 1960 and even revealed a more delicate shade of beauty in the occasional quieter role.

1941: *I Look at You. Harvard, Here I Come (GB: Here I Come). 1942: *Kink of the Campus. This Gun for Hire. *The Lamp of Memory. Youth on Parade. Road to Morocco. Lucky Jordan. 1943: The Crystal Ball. Rhythm Parade. Salute for Three. For Whom the Bell Tolls. So Proudly We Hail! Let's Face It. True to Life. The Deerslayer. 1944: Practically Yours. Standing Room Only. The Story of Dr Wassell. Kismet. Rainbow Island. *Fun Time. Here Come the Waves. 1945: Bring on the Girls. Salome Where She Danced. Frontier Gal (GB: The Bride Wasn't Willing). 1947: Song of Scheherazade. Slave Girl. Brute Force. 1948: Casbah. River Lady. Black Bart (GB: Black Bart – Highwayman). Criss Cross. 1949: The Gal Who Took the West. Calamity Jane and Sam Bass. 1950: Buccaneer's Girl. The Desert Hawk. Tomahawk (GB: Battle of Powder River). 1951: Hotel Sahara. Silver City (GB: High Vermilion). 1952: The San Francisco Story. Hurricane Smith. Scarlet Angel. 1953: Sea Devils. Sombrero. The Captain's Paradise. Fort Algiers. La contessa di

Castiglione. 1954: Border River. Happy Ever After (US: Tonight's the Night/O'Leary Night). Passion. 1955: Flame of the Islands. Shotgun. 1956: Magic Fire. Raw Edge. The Ten Commandments. Death of a Scoundrel. 1957: Band of Angels. 1958: La spada e la croce. Verdict of Three (TV). 1959: Timbuktu. 1963: McLintock! A Global Affair. Law of the Lawless. 1966: Munster Go Home! 1967: The Power. Hostile Guns/Huntsville. 1968: Arizona Bushwhackers. 1970: The Delta Factor. 1971: The Seven Minutes. 1974: The Girl on the Late, Late Show (TV). The Mark of Zorro (TV). 1975: Arizona Slim. Won Ton Ton, the Dog Who Saved Hollywood. 1976: It Seemed Like a Good Idea at the Time. La casa de las sombras. Blazing Stewardesses. 1977: Satan's Cheerleader. 1978: Nocturna. 1979: Guyana: The Crime of the Century. The Man with Bogart's Face. 1981: The Munsters' Revenge (TV). Liar's Moon. 1982: Play Dead (released 1986). 1983: Vultures in Paradise/Flesh and Bullets. 1986: A Masterpiece of Murder (TV). 1987: American Gothic. 1988: Cellar Dweller. 1989: Mirror, Mirror. 1991: Oscar. 1992: The Naked Truth. Desert Kickboxer. 1993: The Sorority House Murders. Seasons of the Heart. 1995: The Barefoot Executive (TV). Here Come the Munsters (TV).

DEE, Frances (Jean F. Dee) 1907– 2004

Gravely beautiful blue-eyed brunette American actress, noted for her calmness and serenity, who gave many touching and appealing performances without quite making the foremost rank. Married to Joel McCrea from 1933 to his death in 1990. Plucked from the legions of extras by Maurice Chevalier for her first leading role (in *Playboy of Paris*).

1929: Words and Music. 1930: A Man from Wyoming. Follow Thru. Monte Carlo. Manslaughter. Playboy of Paris. Along Came Youth. True to the Navy. 1931: An American Tragedy. Caught. Rich Man's Folly. June Moon. Working Girls. 1932: If I Had a Million. The Strange Case of Clara Deane. Nice Women. Love is a Racket. This Reckless Age. Sky Bride. The Night of June 13th. 1933: The Crime of the Century. King of the Jungle. The Silver Cord. One Man's Journey. Headline Shooter (GB: Evidence in Camera). Blood Money. Little Women. 1934: Keep 'Em Rolling. Finishing School. Coming Out Party. Of Human Bondage. 1935: The Gay Deception. Becky Sharp. 1936: Half Angel. Come and Get It. 1937: Wells Fargo. Souls at

Sea. 1938: If I Were King. 1939: Coast Guard. 1941: So Ends Our Night. A Man Betrayed (GB: Citadel of Crime). 1942: Meet the Stewarts. 1943: I Walked with a Zombie. Happy Land. 1945: Patrick the Great. 1947: The Private Affairs of Bel Ami. Four Faces West (GB: They Passed This Way). 1951: Payment on Demand. Reunion in Reno. 1952: Because of You. 1953: Mr Scoutmaster. 1954: Gypsy Colt.

DEE, Sandra (Alexandria Zuck) 1942–
A petite curvy blonde cosseted by a showbiz mum into becoming Hollywood's first virgin sex-bomb, Sandra Dee grew up seemingly without childhood, married young and seemed to age rather quickly, appearing blowsy and plump in a TV movie of the late sixties with her youthful cinema heyday already over. Married to Bobby Darin (*qv*) from 1960 to 1967. Extremely popular in the early sixties with the youth audience.
1957: Until They Sail. 1958: The Restless Years (GB: The Wonderful Years). The Reluctant Debutante. 1959: A Summer Place. Gidget. Stranger in My Arms. Imitation of Life. The Snow Queen (voice only). The Wild and the Innocent. 1960: Portrait in Black. 1961: Romanoff and Juliet. Tammy Tell Me True. Come September. 1962: If a Man Answers. 1963: Tammy and the Doctor. Take Her, She's Mine. 1964: I'd Rather Be Rich. 1965: That Funny Feeling. 1966: A Man Could Get Killed. 1967: Doctor, You've Got to be Kidding! Rosie! 1968: The Manhunter (TV). 1970: The Dunwich Horror. 1971: Ad est di marsa matruh. 1972: The Daughters of Joshua Cabe (TV). 1974: Houston, We've Got a Problem (TV). 1977: Fantasy Island (TV). 1983: Lost.

DE FUNÈS, Louis
(Carlos L. de F. Galarza) 1908–1983
Staccato, scurrying, ferret-faced and sometimes explosively funny French (of Portuguese parentage) comedian, whose brief burst of popularity outside his native France in the mid-1950s made him an international name, and gained many of his subsequent films a wider distribution. A first acquaintance with De Funès could be quite side-splitting; a little of him, however, went rather a long way. A heart attack in the mid 1970s curtailed his hitherto hectic film schedule.
1945: La tentation de Barloizon. 1946: Six heures à perdre. Dernier refuge. Antoine et Antoinette. 1947: Croiseau pour l'inconnu.

1948: Du Gueslin. Millionaires d'un jour. 1949: Pas de weekend pour notre amour. Un certain monsieur. Je n'aime que toi. Vient de paraître. Ademai au poste frontière. Au revoir, M Grock. Rendez-vous avec la chance. Mission à Tanger. 1950: Le roi du bla-bla-bla. Boniface somnambule (GB: The Sleepwalker). Bibi Fricotin. L'amant de paille. La rue sans loi. Folie douce. La rose rouge. 1951: Pas de vacances pour M le maire. Ma Femme est formidable. Ils etaient cinq. Boîte à vendre. Le poison. Les joueurs. Champions junior. M Leguignon lampist. Les sept péchés capitaux (GB and US: The Seven Deadly Sins). Le dindon. Agence matrimoniale. Un amour de parapluie. 1952: L'amour n'est pas un péché. Le huitième art et la manière. Monsieur Taxi. J'ai été trois fois. Moineaux de Paris. La fugue de M Perle. Légère et court vêtue. Elle et moi. Au diable la vertu. La vie d'un honnête homme (US: The Virtuous Scoundrel). 1953: Dortoir les grandes. Le vire. L'étrange désire de M Bard. Mon frangin du Sénégal. Capitaine Pantoufle. Le blé en herbe (GB: Ripening Seed. US: The Game of Love). Le chevalier de la nuit. Mam'zelle Nitouche (GB: Oh, No, Mam'zelle). Tourments. Innocents in Paris. Le secret d'Hélène Marimon. Faites-moi confiance. Les compagnes de la nuit. Les corsaires du Bois de Boulogne. Les hommes ne pensent qu'à ça. 1954: Les impures. Huis clos. Les pépées font la loi. Les intrigantes. Napoléon. Frou-Frou. Poisson d'avril. La reine Margot. La mouton a cinq pattes (GB and US: The Sheep Has Five Legs). Ah! Les belles bacchantes (GB and US: Peek-a-Boo). Scènes du ménage. Escalier de service. Papa, Mama, the Maid and I. 1955: L'impossible M Pipelet. Geschichtes eines Fotomodells. La bande à Papa. Papa, Mama, My Wife and I. Les hussards. Si Paris nous était conté. Bébés à gogos. La loi des rues. 1956: Courte tête. La traversée de Paris (GB: Pig Across Paris. US: Three Bags Full). Les truands (GB: Lock Up the Spoons). 1957: Ni vu, ni connu (GB: Vive Monsieur Blaireau). Comme un cheveu sur la soupe (GB: A Hair in the Soup. US: Crazy in the Noodle). 1958: Taxi, roulotte et corrida (GB: Taxi). La vie à deux. 1959: Fripouillards et cie. A pied, à cheval et en spoutnik (GB: Hold Tight for the Satellite. US: A Dog, a Mouse and a Sputnik). Mon pote le gitan. Certains l'aiment froide. Toto à Madrid. 1960: Les tortillards. Candide. La capitaine Fracasse. Dans l'eau qui fait des bulles. 1961: La belle americaine. Le crime ne paie pas. Le diable et les dix commandements (GB and US: The Devil and the 10 Command-

ments). La vendetta. Carambolages. Les veinards. Le gentleman d'Epsom/Les grands seigneurs. Nous irons à Deauville. Un clair de lune à mauberge. 1963: Pouic-Pouic. Faites sauter la banque. 1964: Le gendarme de Saint-Tropez. Une souris chez les hommes. 1965: Le corniaud (GB and US: The Sucker). Fantômas se déchaîne (GB: Fantomas Strikes Back). Les bons vivants. A Gendarme in New York. 1966: La grande vadrouille (GB and US: Don't Look Now, We're Being Shot At!). Fantômas contre Scotland Yard. 1967: Les grandes vacances. Le gendarme et les gendarmettes (GB: TV, as The Gendarme Wore Skirts. US: How to Be an Honest Cop). Le grand restaurant. Oscar. Le petit baigneur. 1968: Le gendarme se marie. Le tatoué. 1969: Hibernatus. 1970: L'homme-orchestre. Le gendarme en balade. Sur un arbre perché. 1971: La folie des grandeurs (GB: Delusions of Grandeur). Jo (US: The Gazebo). 1972: Die Dummen streiche der Reichen. 1973: Les aventures de Rabbi Jacob (GB and US: The Mad Adventures of 'Rabbi Jacob'). 1975: L'aile ou la cuisse. 1976: Crocodile. 1977: La zizanie. 1978: Le gendarme et les extra-terrestres (GB: TV, as The Spaceman of St Tropez). 1980: L'avare.

DE HAVEN, Gloria 1924–
Strawberry-blonde (earlier brunette) singer, dancer and light actress, from a vaudeville family. She began as a band singer, but developed into one of the zippiest, bounciest and freshest M-G-M musical co-stars of the forties. Four times married (twice to the same man and once to actor John Payne from 1944 to 1950); later appearances confirmed that she had lost none of her cheeky good looks. Surname sometimes billed DeHaven.
1936: Modern Times. 1940: The Great Dictator. Susan and God (GB: The Gay Mrs Trexel). 1941: Keeping Company. Two-Faced Woman. The Penalty. 1943: Best Foot Forward. Thousands Cheer. 1944: Two Girls and a Sailor. Broadway Rhythm. Step Lively. The Thin Man Goes Home. 1945: Between Two Women. 1947: Summer Holiday (released 1948). 1949: Scene of the Crime. The Doctor and the Girl. Yes, Sir, That's My Baby. 1950: The Yellow Cab Man. Three Little Words. Summer Stock (GB: If You Feel Like Singing). I'll Get By. 1951: Two Tickets to Broadway. 1953: Down Among the Sheltering Palms. 1954: So This is Paris. 1955: The Girl Rush. 1972: Call Her Mom (TV). 1975: Won Ton Ton, the Dog Who Saved Hollywood.

1976: *Who is the Black Dahlia? (TV). Banjo Hackett (TV). 1977: The Cabot Connection (TV). 1978: Sharon: Portrait of a Mistress (TV). A Chance to Live (TV). 1979: Bog. 1984: Off Sides (TV). 1993: †Judge Stone and Family. 1994: The Legend of O B Taggart. 1997: Out to Sea.

†Unfinished

DE HAVILLAND, Olivia 1916–
Tokyo-born sister of Joan Fontaine, this dark-haired actress began her star career at 19 and remained one of the prettiest ladyes fayre in Hollywood action yarns through the thirties and early forties. A commendable fight for better roles gave her some demanding and sometimes harrowing parts in her thirties, resulting in Oscars for *To Each His Own* and *The Heiress*. Middle age became her, but films and TV alike did not make the most of her later years. Also Oscar-nominated for *The Snake Pit*, *Gone With the Wind* and *Hold Back the Dawn*.
1935: *A Dream Comes True. A Midsummer Night's Dream. The Irish in Us. Alibi Ike. Captain Blood. 1936: The Charge of the Light Brigade. Anthony Adverse. *A Day at Santa Anita. 1937: Call It a Day. The Great Garrick. It's Love I'm After. 1938: Gold is Where You Find It. The Adventures of Robin Hood. Hard to Get. Four's a Crowd. 1939: Dodge City. The Private Lives of Elizabeth and Essex. Gone With the Wind. Wings of the Navy. 1940: My Love Came Back. Raffles. Santa Fé Trail. 1941: Strawberry Blonde. They Died With Their Boots On. Hold Back the Dawn. 1942: The Male Animal. In This Our Life. 1943: *Stars on Horseback. Government Girl. Thank Your Lucky Stars. Princess O'Rourke. Devotion (released 1946). 1946: The Well Groomed Bride. The Dark Mirror. To Each His Own. 1948: The Snake Pit. 1949: The Heiress. 1952: My Cousin Rachel. 1953: †Main Street to Broadway. 1955: That Lady. Not As a Stranger. 1956: The Ambassador's Daughter. 1958: The Proud Rebel. 1959: Libel! 1961: The Light in the Piazza. 1964: Lady in a Cage. Hush . . . Hush, Sweet Charlotte. 1970: The Adventurers. 1971: The Screaming Woman (TV). 1972: Pope Joan. 1977: Airport 77. Behind the Iron Mask (GB: The Fifth Musketeer). 1978: The Swarm. 1981: Murder is Easy (TV). 1983: The Devil Imposter. 1984: The Royal Romance of Charles and Diana (TV). 1988: The Woman He Loved (TV).

†Scenes deleted from final release print

DELON, Alain 1935–
Dark-haired, open-faced, boyishly handsome French romantic lead, the successor in that country to Gérard Philipe, but much more successful internationally. His career has had its share of clangers (mainly the films made in Britain and America) but his good looks enabled him to ride them and, after the mid-sixties, he became increasingly involved in the production of his own films, the most successful of which have had a gangster theme. Married to Nathalie Delon (Francine Canovas, 1938–) from 1964 to 1969.
1957: Quand la femme s'en mêle (GB: Send a Woman When the Devil Fails). 1958: Sois belle et tais-toi (GB: Blonde for Danger). Christine. Faible femmes (GB: Women Are Weak. US: Three Murderesses). 1959: Le chemin des écoliers. Plein soleil (GB: Purple Noon). 1960: Rocco and His Brothers. 1961: Che gioia vivere. Les amours célèbres. The Eclipse. 1962: The Devil and the 10 Commandments. Mélodie en sous-sol (GB: The Big Snatch). The Leopard. Marco Polo (unfinished). Carambolages. 1963: The Black Tulip. 1964: Les félins (GB: The Love Cage. US: Joy House). L'insoumis. The Yellow Rolls-Royce. L'amour à la mer. 1965: Once a Thief. Is Paris Burning? 1966: Lost Command. Texas Across the River. Les aventuriers (GB: The Last Adventure). 1967: Le samourai. Histoires extraordinaires (GB: Tales of Mystery. US: Spirits of the Dead). Diabolically Yours. 1968: Girl on a Motorcycle. Adieu l'ami (GB: Farewell Friend. US: So Long, Pal). La piscine (GB: The Sinners). 1969: Jeff. The Sicilian Clan. 1970: Borsalino. Le cercle rouge. Madly. Crepa, padrone, crepa tranquillo (unfinished). 1971: Doucement les basses! Red Sun. Fantasia chez les ploucs. La veuve Couderc. 1972: The Assassination of Trotsky. Un flic (GB: Dirty Money). Le prima notte di quiete. Traitement du choc (GB: The Doctor in the Nude. US: Shock Treatment). Il était une fois un flic. 1973: Tony Arzenta/Big Guns. Deux hommes dans la ville. Les granges brûlées (GB: TV, as The Investigator). 1974: La race des 'Seigneurs'. Les seins de glace. Borsalino & Co (US: Blood on the Streets). Le gifle (US: The Slap). 1975: Zorro. Le gitan. Flic story. Creezy. 1976: Mr Klein. Le gang. Comme un boomerang. 1977: America at the Movies (narrator only). L'homme pressé (GB: TV, as The Hurried Man). Mort d'un pourri. Attention, les enfants regardent. 1978: Le toubib. 1979: Harmonie. The Concorde – Airport '79 (GB: Airport '80 . . . The Concorde). Teheran Incident/Teheran

1943. 1980: Trois hommes à abattre (GB: TV, as Three Men to Kill). 1981: †Pour le peau d'un flic (US: For a Cop's Hide). 1982: Le choc. 1983: Le battant (GB: TV, as the Fighter. US: The Cache). Swann in Love/Un amour de Swann. 1984: Notre histoire (GB: Our Story). Separate Rooms. 1985: The Untouchable. Parôle de flic (US: Cop's Honor). Les mocassins Italiens. 1986: Le passage. 1988: Ne reveillez pas un flic qui dort/Let Sleeping Cops Lie. 1990: Nouvelle vague. 1991: Dancing Machine. 1992: Le retour de Casanova. 1993: Un crime. The Grand Defence. L'orso di peluche/L'ours en peluche. 1994: Les cent et une nuits. 1996: Le jour et la nuit. 1997: Half a Chance/Une chance sur deux. 2000: Les acteurs.

† Also directed

DELPY, Julie 1969–
Tawny-haired French actress with fine-boned features who got her first film role at 15 and has spent much of the past 15 years of her life travelling between (and living in) Paris, New York and California. Despite several leads in Hollywood films, and studies at the Actors' Studio, she has not really become a star name outside France, and her future may lie in direction. In the 1990s, she pursued formal training in directing, graduating first from her class in New York University, and has subsequently helmed a short and two features. Both of her parents are actors.
1985: Detective. 1986: Mauvais sang (GB: The Night is Young. US: Bad Blood). 1987: King Lear. Béatrice. 1988: L'autre nuit. 1989: La noche oscura. 1990: Europa Europa. 1991: Voyager. 1992: Warsaw – Year 5703. 1993: Trois couleurs: bleu/Blue. The Three Musketeers. Trois couleurs: blanc/White. Younger and Younger. Killing Zoë. 1994: Sunny Side Up. Trois Couleurs: rouge/Red. 1995: Before Sunrise. *Blah Blah Blah. 1996: Tykho Moon. Les milles merveilles de l'univers. 1997: An American Werewolf in Paris. The Treat. 1998: L.A. Without a Map. 1999: The Passion of Ayn Rand (cinemas/cable TV). But I'm a Cheerleader. 2000: Sand. Tell Me. 2001: Villa des Roses. Investigating Sex.

As director. 1995: *Blah Blah Blah. 1998: Looking for Jimmy. 2000: Tell Me.

DEL RIO, Dolores (Maria D. Lopez, or Lolita D. Martinez Negrette) 1905–1983
Beautiful, dark-haired, aristocratic-looking

Mexican actress, at her loveliest in exotic roles of the late 1920s and early 1930s. She stayed in the acting profession after her Hollywood days were over and became a much-admired performer in Mexican and international films. Her beauty became graver with the years, but she remained as striking as ever. Died from liver failure.

1925: *Joanna.* 1926: *High Steppers. The Whole Town's Talking. Pals First. What Price Glory?* 1927: *Resurrection. The Loves Of Carmen.* 1928: *The Gateway of the Moon. The Trail of '98. No Other Woman. The Red Dance (GB: The Red Dancer of Moscow). Ramona. Revenge.* 1929: *Evangeline.* 1930: *The Bad One.* 1932: *The Bird of Paradise. The Girl of the Rio (GB: The Dove).* 1933: *Flying Down to Rio.* 1934: *Wonder Bar. Madame Dubarry. *Hollywood on Parade No 13.* 1935: *In Caliente. I Live for Love (GB: I Live for You). *A Trip thru a Hollywood Studio. The Widow from Monte Carlo.* 1936: *Accused.* 1937: *The Devil's Playground. Lancer Spy. Ali Baba Goes to Town.* 1938: *International Settlement.* 1940: *The Man from Dakota (GB: Arouse and Beware). *Chinese Garden Festival.* 1941: *Wampas Baby Stars.* 1942: *Journey Into Fear.* 1943: *Flor silvestre. Maria candelaria (GB and US: Portrait of Maria).* 1944: *Bugambilia. Las abandonas.* 1945: *La selva de fuego.* 1946: *La otra.* 1947: *The Fugitive.* 1948: *Historia de una mala mujer.* 1949: *Le malquerida. La casa chica.* 1950: *Dona perfecta.* 1951: *Deseada.* 1953. *Reportaje. El nino y la niebla.* 1954: *Señor Ama.* 1956: *Torero.* 1958: *La cucuracha (GB: The Bandit). A donde van nuestros hijos.* 1960: *Flaming Star. Pecado de una madre.* 1964: *Cheyenne Autumn.* 1966: *La dama del Alba. Casa de mujeres.* 1967: *C'era una volta / Once Upon a Time (GB: Cinderella Italian Style. US: More Than a Miracle). Rio Blanco.* 1976: *Salsa.* 1978: *The Children of Sanchez.*

DE MARNEY, Derrick 1906–1978

Unforceful British leading man with dark, wavy hair and lantern-shaped face: good-looking but slightly sinister. Kept pretty busy in unmemorable leading roles before World War II. Independent production ventures afterwards were not too successful, and he spent his last few films in small roles. Brother of actor Terence de Marney (1909–1971)

1928: *The Little Drummer Boys. Adventurous Youth. The Forger. Valley of the Ghosts.* 1931: *Shadows. Stranglehold.* 1932: *Laughter of Fools.* 1933: *The Private Life of Henry VIII.*

1934: *Once in a New Moon. Music Hall. The Scarlet Pimpernel.* 1935: *The Immortal Gentleman. Windfall.* 1936: *Things to Come. Café Mascot. Born That Way. Land Without Music (US: Forbidden Music).* 1937: *Victoria the Great. Young and Innocent (US: The Girl Was Young).* 1938: *Sixty Glorious Years (US: Queen of Destiny). Blonde Cheat.* 1939: *Flying Fifty Five. The Spider. The Lion Has Wings.* 1940: *The Second Mr Bush. Three Silent Men.* 1941: *Dangerous Moonlight (US: Suicide Squadron).* 1942: *The First of the Few (US: Spitfire). *The Call of the Sea.* 1945: *Latin Quarter.* 1947: *Uncle Silas (US: The Inheritance).* 1948: *Sleeping Car to Trieste.* 1950: *She Shall Have Murder.* 1954: *Meet Mr Callaghan.* 1955: *Private's Progress.* 1956: *The March Hare.* 1962: *Doomsday at Eleven.* 1966: *The Projected Man.*

DEMONGEOT, Mylène

(Marie-Hélène Demongeot) 1936–

Very slim and shapely French blonde actress with charming smile. More likeable than Bardot and Cardinale and, maybe because of that, not quite so successful as an international star. From 1960 on her peaches-and-cream complexion was seen in less and less interesting roles.

1944: ‡*Les enfants de l'amour.* 1955: ‡*Papa, mama, ma femme et moi.* ‡*Futures vedettes (GB: Sweet Sixteen).* ‡*Frou Frou.* 1956: ‡*Quand vient l'amour.* †*It's a Wonderful World.* 1957: *The Witches of Salem. Une manche et la belle (GB: The Evil That is Eve).* 1958: *Bonjour Tristesse. Sois belle et tais-toi (GB: Blonde for Danger). Cette nuit-là (GB: Night Heat). Faibles femmes (GB: Women Are Weak. US: Three Murderesses).* 1959: *Le vent se lève (GB: Operation Time Bomb). Upstairs*

and Downstairs. The Battle of Marathon (GB: The Giant of Marathon). Entrée de service. 1960: *Under Ten Flags. The Three Musketeers. Un amore a Roma. Les garçons. The Singer Not the Song.* 1961: *Rape of the Sabines (US: Romulus and the Sabines). Le chevalier noir.* 1962: *Copacabana Palace. Gold for the Caesars. L'inassouvie. I Don Giovanni della Costa Azzurra (US: Beach Casanova). A cause d'une femme.* 1963: *Cherchez l'idole (GB: The Chase). Doctor in Distress. L'appartement des filles. Vengeance of the Three Musketeers.* 1964: *Fantômas. Gangster, Gold und flötte Mädchen.* 1965: *Furia a bakla pour OSS 117 (GB: Mission for a Killer). Fantômas revient (GB and US: The Vengeance of Fantomas). Uncle Tom's Cabin. Fantômas se dechaîne (GB and US: Fantomas Strikes Back).* 1966: *Tendre voyou. Fantômas contre Scotland yard.* 1968: *The Private Navy of Sergeant O'Farrell. Une cigarette pour un ingénu.* 1969: *Twelve Plus One (US: The Twelve Chairs).* 1970: *Le champignon (GB: TV, as Fungus).* 1971: *L'explosion.* 1972: *Les pavillons de verre. Quelques arpents de neige / A Few Acres of Snow. Montreal Blues.* 1974: *Les noces de porcelaine.* 1976: *Par le sang des autres.* 1977: *L'echappatoire.* 1979: *Un jour, un tueur.* 1982: *Beruchet, dit la Boulie.* 1983: *Surprise Party. Le bâtard. Retenez-moi, ou je fais un malheur. Flics de choc.* 1984: *Americonga.* 1985: *Paulette.* 1986: *Tenue de soirée.* 1993: *La femme dans le vent.* 1994: *La piste du télégraphe.* 1997: *L'homme idéal.*

†As Mylene Nicole
‡As Mylène-Nicole Demongeot

DeMORNAY, Rebecca (R. George) 1961–

Slim, curvy, cool, demure-looking American actress whose hair colour varies from film to film, although she now seems to have settled on blonde. Born in California but educated in Austria, she studied acting with Lee Strasberg and has tackled a good variety of film roles, from gentle and God-fearing to pert and provocative. As her career progressed, however, she showed up best in icily unsympathetic parts, as typified by her most successful film to date, *The Hand That Rocks the Cradle*, as a psychotic nanny.

1982: *One from the Heart.* 1983: *Risky Business. Testament.* 1985: *The Trip to Bountiful. The Slugger's Wife.* 1986: *Runaway Train. The Murders in the Rue Morgue (TV).* 1987: *And God Created Woman. Beauty and the Beast.* 1988: *Feds.* 1989: *Dealers.* 1990: *By*

Dawn's Early Light (cable TV). 1991: Back-draft. An Inconvenient Woman (TV). 1992: Blind Side (cable TV). The Hand That Rocks the Cradle. 1993: The Three Musketeers. Guilty As Sin. 1994: Getting Out (TV). 1995: The Conversion (TV). Never Talk to Strangers. 1996: The Winner. 1998: The Con (cable TV). 1999: Thick As Thieves. Night Ride Home (TV). A Table for One. 2000: The Right Temptation.

DEMPSEY, Patrick 1966–

Slight, husky-voiced, freckle-faced, black-haired American actor of ingenuous appearance, who usually appeared in (rather too many of) his early films as the centre of oddball happenings on the boy-girl front. A sufferer from dyslexia in boyhood, Dempsey is an expert skier and juggler, the latter talent first leading him into show business. After stock company experience in his native Maine, he made a big impression as an epileptic in his first major part and was in leading roles at 20. Never quite a box-office force, he found himself in too many mediocre movies after a bright start, and was playing supporting roles by the mid 1990s.

1976: Bugsy Malone. 1984: Heaven Help Us (GB: Catholic Boys). 1986: A Fighting Choice (TV). 1987: Meatballs III: Summer Job. In the Mood (later and GB: The Woo Woo Kid). Can't Buy Me Love. 1988: Happy Together. In a Shallow Grave. Some Girls (GB: Sisters). Young Toscanini. 1989: Lover Boy. Coupe de Ville. 1990: Run! 1991: Mobsters (GB: Mobsters: The Evil Empire). 1992: R.S.V.P. (later For Better and For Worse). Face the Music. 1993: Bank Robber. With Honors. JFK: Reckless Youth (TV). 1994: Ava's Magical Adventure (TV. And directed). 1995: Bloodknot. Outbreak. 1996: The Right to Remain Silent (TV). A Season in Purgatory (TV). 1997: The Escape (TV). Hugo Pool. The Treat. 1998: Me & Will (released 1999). There's No Fish Food in Heaven. Jeremiah (TV). Denial. 2000: Scream 3.

DENCH, Dame Judi 1934–

Chubbily pretty, light-haired British actress, most at home on stage, where an amazing variety of work ranges from tragedy to musicals. She has been hardly seen in the cinema, where her sporadic appearances have varied from the distinctive to the disastrous, but a hit comedy series on TV, A Fine Romance, opposite actor-husband Michael Williams, brought her face more to the fore.

Won a British Academy Award for Four in the Morning. Created Dame in 1988. An Academy Award nominee for Mrs Brown, she won an Oscar two years later for Shakespeare in Love.

1964: The Third Secret. 1965: Four in the Morning. A Study in Terror. (US: Fog). He Who Rides a Tiger. 1968: A Midsummer Night's Dream. 1973: Luther. 1974: Dead Cert. 1983: Saigon – Year of the Cat (TV). 1985: Wetherby. The Angelic Conversation (voice only). A Room with a View. 1986: 84 Charing Cross Road. 1988: A Handful of Dust. 1989: Henry V. 1994: Jack and Sarah. 1995: GoldenEye. 1996: Hamlet. 1997: Mrs Brown. Tomorrow Never Dies. 1999: Shakespeare in Love. Tea with Mussolini. The World is Not Enough. 2001: Chocolat.

DENEUVE, Catherine
(Catherine Dorléac) 1943–

Blonde French actress with open, questioning face, the sister of actress Françoise Dorléac (1942–1967). Has worked for most of the major continental directors, plus a few largely fruitful international sorties. With such outward iciness it's surprising she never made a film for Hitchcock, especially as she often exhibits such steel beneath the surface. Still gravely beautiful in her fifties, she won an Academy Award nomination in 1992 for Indochine.

1956: Les collégiennes. 1959: Les petits chats (US: Wild Roots of Love). 1960: L'homme à femmes. Les portes claquent. 1961: Les Parisiennes. 1962: Vice and Virtue. . . .Et Satan conduit le bal. Vacances portugaises. 1963: Les plus belles escroqueries du monde. 1964: Les parapluies de Cherbourg. La chasse à l'homme. Un monsieur de compagnie. Le

costanza della ragione. Repulsion. 1965: Le chant du monde. La vie de château. Das Liebeskarussel (GB: Who Wants to Sleep?). 1966: Les créatures. 1967: Belle de jour. The Young Girls of Rochefort. 1968: Benjamin. Manon 70. Mayerling. La chamade. 1969: The April Fools. Mississippi Mermaid. Don't Be Blue. 1970: Tristana. Peau d'âne (GB: Once Upon a Time. US: The Magic Donkey). Henri Langlois. 1971: Liza. Ça n'arrive qu'aux autres. 1972: Un flic (GB: Dirty Money). Melampo. 1973: L'évènement le plus important depuis que l'homme a marché sur la lune (GB: The Slightly Pregnant Man). Touche pas à la femme blanche. 1974: Fatti di gente perbene / La grande bourgeoise (US: The Murri Affair). Zig-Zig (US: Zig-Zag). La femme aux bottes rouges. 1975: Hustle. Le sauvage (US: Lovers Like Us). L'agression (US: Act of Aggression). 1976: Il cassotto (US: The Beach Hut). Si c'était à refaire (GB: Second Chance). 1977: †Coup de foudre. March or Die! 1978: Ecoute voir. L'argent des autres. Si je suis comme ça, c'est la faute de papa (US: When I was a Kid, I Didn't Dare). Anima persa. 1979: À nous deux (US: An Adventure for Two). Ils sont grands, ces petits. 1980: Courage fuyons. Le dernier métro (GB and US: The Last Metro). Je vous aime. 1981: Le choix des armes. Reporters. Hotel des Amériques. Daisy Chain. 1982: Le choc. L'Africain. 1983: The Hunger. Le bon plaisir. 1984: Fort Saganne. Paroles et musiques. 1985: Let's Hope It's a Girl . . . 1986: La mauvaise herbe. Le lieu de crime. 1987: Agent trouble. Drôle d'endroit pour une rencontre. 1988: Hotel Panique. The Man Who Loved Zoos. Fréquence meurtre. 1989: Helmut Newton: Frames from the Edge. 1991: Indochine. 1992: Ma saison préférée. Contre l'oubli. 1993: Les demoiselles ont eu 25 ans. 1994: La partie d'echecs. Les cent et une nuits. 1995: L'enfant de la nuit. The Convent. L'univers de Jacques Demy. 1996: Les voleurs. L'inconnu. 1997: Généalogies d'un crime. 1998: Place Vendôme. 1999: Le temps retrouvé. Le vent de la nuit. Belle Maman. Pola X. Est-Ouest. 2000: La lettre. Dancer in the Dark.

†Unfinished

De NIRO, Robert 1943–

Lean (later chunky), dark and sallow American actor of great drive and intensity, often seen in explosive Italianate or working-class New Yorker roles. After a slow start, and despite offering a somewhat unvarying performance, he rose quickly to the top following the winning of an Oscar for *The Godfather Part II*. In 1981, he took a second Oscar for his bruising performance in *Raging Bull*, and has been further nominated for *Taxi Driver*, *The Deer Hunter*, *Awakenings* and *Cape Fear*. Much in demand for Mafia sagas, he successfully dabbled in direction in 1993 with *A Bronx Tale*. At one time married to actress Diahnne Abbott (1945–). Remarried in 1997.

1966: Trois chambres à Manhattan. The Wedding Party. 1968: Greetings. 1969: Bloody Mama. 1970: Hi, Mom! 1971: Jennifer on My Mind. The Gang That Couldn't Shoot Straight. Born to Win. 1973: Bang the Drum Slowly. Mean Streets. 1974: Sam's Song (later the Swap). The Godfather Part II. 1976: Taxi Driver. 1900. The Last Tycoon. 1977: New York, New York. 1978: The Deer Hunter. 1980: Raging Bull. 1981: True Confessions. 1982: The King of Comedy. Elia Kazan, Outsider. 1983: Once Upon a Time in America. 1984: Brazil. Falling in Love. 1986: The Mission. 1987: Angel Heart. The Untouchables. Dear America (voice only). Hello Actors Studio. 1988: Midnight Run. Jacknife. 1989: Stanley and Iris. We're No Angels. 1990: Goodfellas. Awakenings. Guilty by Suspicion. 1991: Backdraft. Cape Fear. 1992: Mistress. Blast 'Em (doc). Mad Dog and Glory. 1993: Night and the City. This Boy's Life. †A Bronx Tale. Feeling the Heat (outtake from Falling in Love!). 1994: Mary Shelley's Frankenstein. A Hundred and One Nights. 1995: Casino. Heat. 1996: The Fan. Sleepers. Marvin's Room. 1997: Cop Land. Great Expectations. Wag the Dog. Jackie Brown. Lenny Bruce: Swear to Tell the Truth (doc. Narrator only). 1998: Ronin. 1999: Analyze This. Flawless. 2000: Rocky and Bullwinkle. Navy Diver. 2001: Meet the Parents. The Score.

†And directed

DENISON, Michael 1915–1998
Gently polite but firm upper-class English actor with rich voice, very similar to John Clements, and so popular in British post-war films that it comes as a surprise to find that he made so few. But both he and his wife Dulcie Gray (married 1939) have remained very active in the English theatre. Died from cancer.

1939: Inspector Hornleigh on Holiday (US: Inspector Hornleigh on Leave). 1940: Tilly of Bloomsbury. 1946: Hungry Hill. 1948: My Brother Jonathan. The Blind Goddess. The

*Glass Mountain. 1949: Landfall. 1951: The Franchise Affair. The Magic Box. Angels One Five. 1952: The Importance of Being Earnest. Tall Headlines. There Was a Young Lady. 1955: Contraband Spain. 1958: The Truth about Women. 1960: Faces in the Dark. 1961: *The Friendly Inn (narrator only). 1982: *The Rocking Horse Winner. 1993: Shadowlands.*

DENNING, Richard
(Ludwig, later Louis Denninger) 1914–1998
Tall, fair-haired, breezy, athletic American actor with natural smile who served a crowded apprenticeship before war service, but whose leading man career afterwards was confined almost entirely to second-features. He found some popularity in TV series in the 1950s and later for many years lived in Hawaii. His wife was actress Evelyn Ankers (*qv*) whom he married in 1942. Most recently, he was seen regularly as the Governor in the long-running TV series *Hawaii Five-O*. His later credits sometimes get mixed up with those of a British actor (mainly on stage) of the same name. Died from cardiac arrest.

1937: On Such a Night. Daughter of Shanghai. Hold 'Em Navy (GB: That Navy Spirit). Our Neighbors the Carters. 1938: Give Me a Sailor. King of Alcatraz (GB: King of the Alcatraz). The Texans. Her Jungle Love. The Buccaneer. Touchdown Army (GB: Generals of Tomorrow). College Swing (GB: Swing, Teacher, Swing). Campus Confessions (GB: Fast Play). Illegal Traffic. The Big Broadcast of 1938. The Arkansas Traveler. Say It in French. Ambush. 1939: Grand Jury Secrets. Some Like it Hot. King of Chinatown. Star Maker. Million Dollar Legs. I'm from Missouri. Persons in Hiding. Night of Nights. Television Spy. Geronimo. Zaza. Hotel Imperial. The Gracie Allen Murder Case. Union Pacific. Sudden Money. Disputed Passage. Undercover Doctor. 1940: The Farmer's Daughter. Parole Fixer. Emergency Squad. Golden Gloves. Seventeen. Queen of the Mob. Love Thy Neighbor. Those Were the Days (GB: Good Old Schooldays). Northwest Mounted Police. 1941: Adam Had Four Sons. West Point Widow. Ice Capades. 1942: Calgary Stampede. Star Spangled Rhythm. Quiet Please Murder. Beyond the Blue Horizon. The Glass Key. Ice Capades Revue (GB: Rhythm Hits the Ice). 1946: Black Beauty. The Fabulous Suzanne. 1947: Seven Were Saved. 1948: Unknown Island. Caged Fury. Disaster. Lady at Midnight. When My Baby Smiles at Me. 1950: Double Deal. Harbor of Missing Men.

No Man of Her Own. 1951: Flame of Stamboul. Insurance Investigator. Weekend With Father. 1952: Okinawa. Scarlet Angel. Hangman's Knot. 1953: The 49th Man. The Glass Web. Target Hong Kong. Jivaro (GB: Lost Treasure of the Amazon). 1954: The Creature from the Black Lagoon. Why Men Leave Home. Battle of Rogue River. Target Earth. 1955: The Magnificent Matador (GB: The Brave and the Beautiful). Air Strike. The Creature With the Atom Brain. The Crooked Web. The Gun That Won the West. Day the World Ended. 1956: Decision (TV. GB: cinemas). Naked Paradise. Assignment Redhead (US: Million Dollar Manhunt/ Requirement for a Redhead). Girls in Prison. Oklahoma Woman. 1957: An Affair to Remember. Buckskin Lady. The Black Scorpion. The Lady Takes a Flyer. 1958: Desert Hell. 1960: No Greater Love. 1963: Twice Told Tales. 1968: I Sailed to Tahiti with An All-Girl Crew.

DENNIS, Sandy
(Sandra Dennis) 1937–1992
Toothy, tawny-haired, blue-eyed American actress, mostly in roles which involved much torment of the character's inner self. Her habit of chewing over lines made her a distinctive star, and she had great drive, if at times her all-consuming style could overpower a film. After five years at the top, it seemed that the public tired of her; but in the studio days, she might have been built into a major female star along Bette Davis lines. Academy Award for *Who's Afraid of Virginia Woolf?* Died from ovarian cancer.

*1961: Splendor in the Grass. 1966: The Three Sisters. Who's Afraid of Virginia Woolf? 1967: Up the Down Staircase. The Fox. 1968: Sweet November. *Teach Me! 1969: That Cold Day in the Park. A Touch of Love (US: Thank You All Very Much). 1970: The Out of Towners. The Only Way Out is Dead. 1972: Something Evil (TV). 1975: Mr Sycamore. 1976: Nasty Habits. Demon. The Three Sisters (remake). 1977: Perfect Gentlemen (TV). 1978: Day of Terror, Night of Fear (TV). 1981: The Four Seasons. The Animals Film. 1982: Come Back to the 5 and Dime Jimmy Dean, Jimmy Dean. 1985: The Execution (TV). 1988: Parents. 976-EVIL. Another Woman. 1991: The Indian Runner.*

DEPARDIEU, Gérard 1948–
Dark-haired French actor with easy-going air, a former juvenile delinquent who became France's foremost star in the 1980s, and burst

belatedly through to international prominence the following decade. The energies of
this huge, Punch-chinned actor, who looks
uncomfortable in tweed suits and ties, are
undeniable. He has lumbered his giant
countryman's build through 120 films in 35
years – a phenomenal workrate by today's
standards – quite apart from running his own
wine-making business. Attempting an
astonishing, and sometimes provocative
range of roles, he has looked most relaxed as
figures of history, such as Wajda's *Danton*,
and was wonderfully well cast in *Jean de
Florette* and, most recently, *Le Colonel
Chabert* – if surprisingly less successful as
figures of fun, such as Porthos and Obélix.
Oscar-nominated for *Cyrano de Bergerac*.
1965: *Le beatnik et le minet. A Christmas Carol*
(unfinished). 1967: *Rendez-vous à Badenberg*
(TV). 1970: *Le cri du cormoran, le soir au-
dessus des jonques.* 1971: *Le viager. Le tueur.
Un peu de soleil dans l'eau froide.* 1972:
Nathalie Granger. La scoumoune (GB:
Scoundrel. US: *The Jinx*). *Au rendez-vous de
la mort joyeuse. L'affaire Dominici.* 1973: *Un
monsieur bien rangé* (TV). *Deux hommes dans
la ville. Rude journée pour la reine. Les
Gaspards* (US: *The Holes*). *Les valseuses*
(GB: *Making It.* US: *Going Places*).
L'inconnu (TV). 1974: *Stavisky... La femme
du Gange. Vincent, François, Paul... et les
autres. Pas si méchant que ça* (GB: TV as *This
Wonderful Crook.* US: *The Wonderful Crook*).
1975: *7 morts sur ordonnance. Je t'aime, moi
non plus* (GB: *I Love You, I Don't*). *Bertolucci
secundo il cinéma.* 1976: *Maîtresse. 1900.
L'ultima donna* (GB: *The Last Woman*).
Barocco. René la canne. Baxter – Vera Baxter.
1977: *Le camion. Die linkshändige Frau* (GB:
The Left-Handed Woman). *Dites-lui que j'aime*
(GB: *This Sweet Sickness*). *Préparez vos
mouchoirs* (GB and US: *Get Out Your
Handkerchiefs*). *Violenta. La nuit tous les chats
sont gris.* 1978: *Rêve de singe/Bye Bye
Monkey. Le sucre. Les chiens. Le grand
embouteillage.* 1979: *Loulou. Rosy la
bourrasque. Buffet froid. Mon oncle
d'Amérique.* 1980: *Je vous aime. The Last
Métro. Inspecteur la bavure.* 1981: *La femme
d'à côté* (GB and US: *The Woman Next
Door*). *La chèvre. Le grand frère. Le choix des
armes* (US: *Choice of Arms*). *Trois hommes à
abattre.* 1982: *L'Africain. Danton. Le retour de
Martin Guerre* (GB and US: *The Return of
Martin Guerre*). *Le grand frère.* 1983: *La lune
dans le caniveau* (GB and US: *The Moon in
the Gutter*). 1984: *Fort Saganne.* †*Le tartuffe.*

Les compères (GB: *Father's Day*). 1985: *Une
femme ou deux. Paris Moliers. Police. Rive
droite, rive gauche.* 1986: *Jean de Florette. Rue
de départ. Tenue de soirée. Les fugitifs.* 1987:
The Possessed. Sous le soleil de Satan (GB:
Under Satan's Sun). *Camille Claudel. Drôle
d'endroit pour une rencontre.* 1988: *Deux.*
1989: *I Want to Go Home. Trop belle pour toi.
Cyrano de Bergerac.* 1990: *Green Card.
Shakha Proshakha.* 1991: *Uranus. Welcome to
Veraz. Merci la vie. Mon père ce héros. Tous les
matins du monde.* 1992: *1492 Conquest of
Paradise.* 1993: *Hélas pour moi. François
Truffaut: portraits volés. Germinal.* 1994: *My
Father, the Hero* (US version of 1991 French
film). *Le Colonel Chabert. Una pura
formalità/A Simple Formality. La machine.
Elisa. Les cent et une nuits.* 1995: *L'ange
gardien/Les anges gardiens. Le hussard sur le
toit* (GB: *The Horseman on the Roof*). *Le
garçu.* 1996: *Bogus. The Secret Agent. Unhook
the Stars. Hamlet. Le plus beau métier du
monde.* 1997: *Le gaulois. Que la lumière soit.
'XXL'. The Man in the Iron Mask.* 1998: *Un
pont entre deux rives* (GB: *The Bridge. And co-
directed*). *Asterix & Obélix Contre César* (GB:
Asterix & Obélix Take On Caesar). *La parola
amore esiste/Mots d'amour.* 1999: *Bimboland.
The Mammy. Mirka. Passionément.* 2000:
*Vatel. Town and Country. Les acteurs. Vidocq.
102 Dalmatians. Tutto l'amore. Che c'è. Wings
Against the Wind. Balzac.*

†*And directed*

DEPP, Johnny (John Depp II) 1963–
Slight, dark-haired, moon-faced American
actor of pale complexion, often in childlike or
idiosyncratic roles. A former teenage drug
addict, then rock musician, he decided on an
acting career in his early twenties. He was a
hit in a TV series, *21 Jump Street*, and his
background of drugs, drink, brushes with the
law and several broken engagements to
glamorous actresses contrived to keep his
name in the headlines. He also owns a
controversial nightclub (outside which actor
River Phoenix was to die from a drug overdose), but became equally notorious for his
off-kilter film roles, rarely-smiling portraits
which made him a master of melancholia.
Currently partnered with French actress-
singer Vanessa Paradis.
1984: *A Nightmare on Elm Street.* 1985:
Private Resort. 1986: *Platoon. Slow Burn*
(TV). 1990: *Cry-Baby. Edward Scissorhands.*
1991: *Freddy's Dead: The Final Nightmare.*

1992: *Arizona Dream* (released 1995). *Benny
& Joon.* 1993: *What's Eating Gilbert Grape.*
1994: *Ed Wood. Don Juan De Marco.* 1995:
†*Divine Rapture. Nick of Time. Dead Man.*
1997: *Donnie Brasco.* ‡*The Brave* (unre-
leased). 1998: *Fear and Loathing in Las Vegas.
L.A. Without a Map.* 1999: *The Astronaut's
Wife. Sleepy Hollow. The Ninth Gate. The
Source.* 2000: *The Man Who Cried. Before
Night Falls. Blow.* 2001: *Chocolat. From Hell.*

†*Unfinished* ‡*And directed*

DEREK, Bo (Mary Collins) 1956–
Fair-haired, firm-bodied American actress
with pale blue eyes, facially not unlike Raquel
Welch (*qv*). Married to actor-director John
Derek (also *qv*), who masterminded her
career, she seemed set at one time to become
the cinema's sex symbol for the 1980s, but
films produced by her and directed by her
husband endured stormy passages before
emerging to critical scorn and public apathy.
She was widowed in 1998.
1975: *And Once Upon a Time* (US *Fantasies*).
1977: *Orca – Killer Whale.* 1978: *Love You.*
1979: *'10'.* 1980: *A Change of Seasons.* 1981:
Tarzan the Ape-Man. 1984: *Bolero.* 1990:
Ghosts Can't Do It. 1992: *Chocolate/Hot
Chocolate.* 1993: *Woman of Desire. Sognando
la California/California Dreaming. Shattered
Image* (TV). 1995: *Tommy Boy.* 1998: *Wind
on Water.* 2000: *Family Man. Jack Mize.*

DEREK, John (Derek Harris) 1926–1998
Handsome American leading man with black,
wavy hair, who moved from juvenile delinquents, headstrong pilots and gunslingers to
dashing men of action somewhere between
Cornel Wilde and Tony Curtis (both *qv*). It is

hard to say why Derek did not become a bigger star, unless it was his subservience to the career of his one-time wife Ursula Andress (*qv*), or his partiality for directing, a facet which latterly extended to soft-core exploitation films featuring his fourth and last wife Bo Derek (*qv*). In between, he married actress Linda Evans. Died following heart surgery.

1944: †*Since You Went Away (extra).* †*I'll Be Seeing You. 1948: A Double Life. 1949: Knock on Any Door. All the King's Men. 1950: Rogues of Sherwood Forest. 1951: Saturday's Hero (GB: Idols in the Dust). Mask of the Avenger. Scandal Sheet (GB: The Dark Page). The Family Secret. 1952: Thunderbirds. 1953: Mission Over Korea (GB: Eyes of the Skies). The Last Posse. Prince of Pirates. Ambush at Tomahawk Gap. 1954: Sea of Lost Ships. The Outcast (GB: The Fortune Hunter). The Adventures of Hajji Baba. Run for Cover. Prince of Players. 1955: Annapolis Story (GB: The Blue and the Gold). 1956: *Mr Rhythm's Holiday. The Leather Saint. The Ten Commandments. Massacre at Sand Creek (TV). 1957: Omar Khayyam. Fury at Showdown. The Flesh is Weak. Il corsaro della mezzaluna. 1958: High Hell. Prisoners of the Volga (GB: The Boatmen. US: The Volga Boatman). 1960: Exodus. 1963: Nightmare in the Sun. 1966: Once Before I Die. 1969: Childish Things. 1975: And Once Upon a Time (US: Fantasies). 1978: Love You.*

†*As Derek Harris*

As director: *1966: Once Before I Die. 1969: Childish Things. 1972:* †*Confessions of Tom Harris. 1975: And Once Upon a Time (US: Fantasies). 1978: Love You. 1981: Tarzan the Ape Man. 1984: Bolero. 1990: Ghosts Can't Do It.*

†*Co-directed*

DERN, Bruce 1936–
Tall, gangling American actor with toothy grin who specialized for many years in hairy psychotics, but was such a distinctive performer that leading roles were bound to come eventually. Since stardom caught up with him in the early seventies, he has been seen in a variety of parts, but the more straightforward the role, the less effective he has been, and there is still a hint of madness behind his more compelling characters. Nominated for an Academy Award in *Coming Home*. The father of actress Laura Dern (*qv*),

from his marriage to actress Diane Ladd (Rose D. Ladnier, 1939–), he's still around as wild-eyed eccentrics.

1960: Wild River. 1961: The Crimebusters. 1963: Bedtime Story. 1964: Marnie. Hush . . . Hush, Sweet Charlotte. 1967: The St Valentine's Day Massacre. The War Wagon. The Wild Angels. Waterhole No. 3 (GB: Waterhole 3). Will Penny. The Trip. Rebel Rousers (released 1969). Hang 'Em High. 1968: Psych-Out. Support Your Local Sheriff! Castle Keep. 1969: Number One. They Shoot Horses Don't They? Bloody Mama. 1970: Drive, He Said. The Incredible Two-Headed Transplant. Cycle Savages. 1971: The Cowboys. Sam Hill: Who Killed The Mysterious Mr Foster? (TV). Silent Running. 1972: Thumb Tripping. The King Of Marvin Gardens. The Laughing Policeman (GB: An Investigation of Murder). 1974: The Great Gatsby. Smile. 1975: Posse. Won Ton Ton – the Dog Who Saved Hollywood. 1976: Folies bourgeoises/The Twist. Family Plot. Black Sunday. 1978: Coming Home. The Driver (GB: Driver). 1979: Middle Age Crazy. 1980: Tattoo. 1981: Harry Tracy – Desperado. 1982: That Championship Season. 1984: On The Edge. 1985: Toughlove (TV). 1987: The Big Town. World Gone Wild. Uncle Tom's Cabin (TV). 1988: 1969. The 'burbs. 1989: Trenchcoat in Paradise (TV). 1990: After Dark, My Sweet. The Court-Martial of Jackie Robinson (TV). 1991: Into the Badlands (TV). 1992: Diggstown (GB: Midnight Sting). Carolina Skeletons. 1993: It's Nothing Personal (TV). Dead Man's Revenge (TV). 1994: Amelia Earhart: The Final Flight (TV). 1995: Wild Bill. Mrs Munck. Mother's Prayer (TV). Down Periscope. Mulholland Falls. 1996: Last Man Standing. 1997: Comfort, Texas (TV). 1998: Small Soldiers (voice only). If . . . Dog . . . Rabbit. When the Bough Breaks 2: Perfect Prey (TV). 1999: The Premonition (TV). The Haunting. 2000: All the Pretty Horses. Madison.

DERN, Laura 1966–
Tall, fair-haired American actress whose strong-jawed, slightly sulky looks have helped her show up best in headstrong or resolute roles. The daughter of actors Diane Ladd (1939–) and Bruce Dern (*qv*), she once had the misfortune to be tagged Miss Teenage Meryl Streep, although she doesn't have Streep's range. Hasn't made too many films – 'I have a specific talent and whatever roles are mine will come to me' – even though

she's been acting since childhood. Oscar nominee for *Rambling Rose*.

1973: White Lightning. 1974: Alice Doesn't Live Here Anymore. 1979: Foxes. The Great Rock 'n' Roll Swindle. 1981: Ladies and Gentlemen: The Fabulous Stains. 1983: Happy Endings (TV). 1984: The Three Wishes of Billy Grier (TV). Mask. Teachers. 1985: Smooth Talk. 1986: Blue Velvet. 1987: Sister, Sister. 1988: Haunted Summer. 1989: Fat Man and Little Boy (GB: Shadow Makers). The Strange Case of Dr Jekyll and Mr Hyde (TV). Industrial Symphony No. 1: The Dream of the Broken Hearted. 1990: Wild at Heart. 1991: Rambling Rose. 1992: Afterburn (TV). 1993: Jurassic Park. A Perfect World. Fallen Angels 2 (TV). 1994: The Last Good Time. 1995: Down Came a Blackbird. 1996: Citizen Ruth. Bastard Out of Carolina (TV. Voice only). Ruby Ridge: An American Tragedy (TV. GB: Siege at Ruby Ridge). 1998: The Baby Dance (TV). 1999: October Sky/Rocket Boys. A Season for Miracles (TV). 2000: Daddy and Them. Dr T and the Women.

DE SICA, Vittorio 1894–1974
Distinguished Italian actor and director, a vanguard neo-realist director of the post-war years, a time when he won Oscars for *Shoeshine* and *Bicycle Thieves*. In the thirties he was a charming romantic actor but later, when his dark hair had turned to silver, he was cast in increasingly lightweight and unworthy roles, and all his best post-war work was done from the director's chair. He won two more Academy Awards – for *Yesterday, Today and Tomorrow* and *The Garden of the Finzi-Continis*. Also Oscar-nominated for his performance in *A Farewell to Arms*.

1918: L'affaire Clemenceau. 1926: La bellezza del mondo. 1928: La compagnia dei matti. 1932: La vecchia signora. Gli uomini, che mascalzoni! Due cuori felici. 1933: †*La canzone del sole. La segretaria per tutti. Il signore desidera? Un cattivo soggetto. Lisetta. Passa l'amore. 1934: Tempo massimo. 1935: Amo te sola. Darò un milione. Lohengrin. Non ti conosco più. 1936: Ma non è una cosa seria. L'uomo che sorride. Questi ragazzi. 1937: Il signor Max. Hanno rapito un uomo. Napoli di altri tempi. Le dame i cavalieri. 1938: L'orologio a cucù. Le due madri. La mazurka di papà. Partire.* †*Castelli in aria. Giochi di società. 1939: Napoli che non muore. Grandi magazzini. Finesce sempre così. Ai vostri ordini, signora! 1940: Manon Lescaut. Pazza di gioia.*

La peccatrice. Rose scarlatte/Due dozzine di rose scarlatte. 1941: Teresa Venerdi. Maddalena zero in condotta. L'avventuriera del piano di sopra. 1942: Un garibaldino in convento. Se io fossi onesto. La guardia del corpo. 1943: I nostri sogni. L'ippocampo. Nessuno torna indietro. Dieci minuti di vita (unfinished). 1944: Non sono superstizioso . . . ma! 1945: Lo sbaglio di essere vivo. Il mondo vuole così. 1946: Roma città libera. Abbaso la ricchezza! (US: Peddlin' in Society). 1947: Natale al campo 119. Sperduti nel buio (US: Lost in the Dark). 1948: Lo sconosciuto di San Marino. Cuore. 1950: Domani è troppo tardi (US: Tomorrow is Too Late). 1951: Cameriera bella presenza offresi. Altri tempi (US: Times Gone By). Gli uomini non guardano il cielo. 1952: Buongiorno, elefante! (GB and US: Hello Elephant!). Tempi nostri. 1953: Pane, amore e fantasia (GB and US: Bread, Love and Dreams). Villa Borghese. Il matrimonio. Madame de . . . (US: The Diamond Earrings). Secrets d'alcôve. A Hundred Years of Love. 1954: Pane, amore e gelosia (GB: Bread, Love and Jealousy. US: Frisky). La vergine moderna. L'oro di Napoli. L'allegro squadrone. Peccato che sia una canaglia (GB and US: Too Bad She's Bad). 1955: Il segno di Venere. Gli ultimi cinque minuti. La bella mugnaia. Pane, amore e . . . (GB and US: Scandal in Sorrento). Racconti romani. Il bigamo (US: A Plea for Passion). 1956: Nero's Weekend (US: Nero's Mistress). The Monte Carlo Story. Tempo di villeggiatura. It Happened in Rome. Noi siamo le colonne. Padri e figli. 1957: Amore e chiacchiere. Il conte Max. A Farewell to Arms. Totò, Vittorio e la dottoressa (US: The Lady Doctor). La donna che venne dal mare. Il medico e lo stregone. Vacanze ad Ischia (US: Holiday Island). 1958: Casino de Paris. Anna of Brooklyn (US: Fast and Sexy). Pane, amore e Andalusia. Ballerina e buon Dio (GB and US: Angel in a Taxi). L'ambitieuse. Les noces Venitiennes. Domenica è sempre domenica. Kanonenserenade. La ragazza di piazza San Pietro. Gli zitelloni. La prima notte. 1959: Nel blu dipinto di blu/Volare. Uomini e nobiluomini. Il nemico di mia moglie (US: My Wife's Enemy). Policarpo, uficiale di scrittura. Vacanza d'inverno. The Moralist. Il Generale Della Rovere. Gastone. Ferdinand I, King of Naples. Il mondo dei miracoli. Austerlitz. Three Etcs and the Colonel. 1960: The Angel Wore Red. Fontana di Trevi. Il vigile. It Started in Naples. The Millionairess. The Pillars of Hercules. Un amore a Roma. Gli incensurati. 1961: Il giudizio universale. The Wonders of Aladdin. L'onorata società. Gli attendenti. Lafayette. 1962: The Two Colonels. Boccaccio 70. Vive Henri IV, vive l'amour. 1965: The Amorous Adventures of Moll Flanders. Io, io, io . . . e gli altri. 1966: After the Fox. The Biggest Bundle of Them All. 1967: Caroline Chérie. Un italiano in America. Gli altri, gli altri e noi. 1968: The Shoes of the Fisherman. 1969: If It's Tuesday, This Must Be Belgium. Twelve Plus One (US: The Twelve Chairs). 1970: Cose di 'Cosa Nostra'. 1971: Trastevere. L'ordeur des fauves. Io non vedo, tu none parli, lui non sente. 1972: Snow Job (GB: Ski Raiders). Ettore lo fusto. Pinocchio (TV). Siamo tutti in libertà provvisoria. 1973: Il delitto Matteoli. Small Miracle (TV). Storia de fratelli e de cortelli.

1974: Viaggia, ragazza, viaggia. Andy Warhol's Dracula (GB: Blood for Dracula). C'eravamo tanto amati (US: We All Loved Each Other So Much). Vittorio de Sica: il regista, l'attore, l'uomo (TV).

As director: 1940: Rose scarlatte/Due dozzine di rose scarlatte. Maddalena zero in condotta. 1941: Teresa Venerdi. 1942: Un garibaldino al convento. 1943: The Children Are Watching Us. 1944: La porta del cielo (released 1946). Shoeshine. 1948: Bicycle Thieves. 1950: Miracle in Milan. 1952: Umberto D. 1953: Stazione Termini (GB: Indiscretion. US: Indiscretion of an American Wife). 1954: L'oro di Napoli. 1956: Il tetto. 1961: Il giudizio universale. Two Women. 1962: Boccaccio 70 (episode). The Condemned of Altona. 1963: Il boom. 1964: Yesterday, Today and Tomorrow. Marriage Italian Style. 1965: Un mondo nuovo. 1966: After the Fox. The Witches (episode). 1967: Woman Times Seven. 1968: Amanti/A Place for Lovers. 1969: Sunflower. 1970: Le coppie (episode). 1971: The Garden of the Finzi-Continis. 1972: Lo chiamaremo Andrea. 1973: Una breve vacanza. 1974: The Journey.

†And German version

DEVANE, William 1939–
Dark, square-faced, black-browed American actor, a little like a smaller Dale Robertson (qv), but with distinctive rasping tones and strong acting style. He was a New York stage actor until the seventies when his screen career picked up, at first in TV movies, then when Hitchcock cast him as the villain of Family Plot. Adept at smiling villains and men you can't quite trust. Less prominent since the 1980s.
1967: In the Country. 1970: The Pursuit of Happiness. 1971: The Three Hundred Year Weekend. Lady Liberty. McCabe and Mrs Miller. Glory Boy (GB: My Old Man's Place). Irish Whiskey Rebellion. 1973: The Bait (TV). Crime Club (TV). 1974: The Missiles of October (TV). Operation Undercover (US: Report to the Commissioner). 1975: Fear on Trial (TV). Irish Whiskey Rebellion. 1976: Family Plot. Marathon Man. 1977: Rolling Thunder. Red Alert (TV). The Bad News Bears in Breaking Training. 1978: The Dark. Yanks. 1981: Red Flag: The Ultimate Game (TV). Honky Tonk Freeway. The Fifth Victim (TV). 1982: Hadley's Rebellion. 1983: Jane Doe (TV). Testament. 1984: Intent to Kill (TV. GB: With Intent to Kill). 1986: Timestalkers (TV). 1989: Vital Signs. The Preppie Murder (TV). 1990:

Murder COD (TV). Chips, the War Dog (TV). 1991: Nightmare in Columbia County (TV). 1992: Obsessed (TV). The President's Child (TV). 1993: Prophet of Evil: The Ervil LeBaron Story (TV). Rubdown (TV). 1994: For the Love of Nancy (TV). 1995: Robin Cook's Virus (TV). Freefall: Flight 174 (TV). Alistair MacLean's Night Watch (TV). 1996: Alistair MacLean's Red Alert (TV). The Absolute Truth (TV). 1997: Exception to the Rule (TV). Doomsday Rock/Cosmic Shock (TV). Forgotten Sins (TV). 1998: Payback. 2000: The Hollow Man. Space Cowboys. Goodbye Sunrise. Poor White Trash.

DeVITO, Danny 1944–
Roly-poly, 5ft-tall, moon-faced, balding American actor of Italian origin who usually plays abrasively funny blue-collar characters with short fuses. Struggling for years to make a go of acting – 'I was sure chic Hollywood people gathered round a pool were just waiting for a 5ft Italian to walk into their lives. I was wrong' – he got his feet on the ladder in Romancing the Stone and was one of the cinema's most popular faces by the late 1980s. Married to actress Rhea Perlman (1949–), he has also dabbled several times in direction.
1969: The Sterile Cuckoo (GB: Pookie). 1970: Dreams of Glass. 1971: La mortadella/Lady Liberty. 1973: Scalawag. Hurry Up or I'll Be 30. 1974: *Hot Dogs for Gauguin. 1975: One Flew Over the Cuckoo's Nest. The Money. Deadly Hero. *Minestrone. Deadly Hero. 1976: The Van. Car Wash. 1977: *The Sound Sleeper. The World's Greatest Lover. 1978: Goin' South. 1979: Valentine (TV). 1981: Going Ape. 1983: Terms of Endearment. 1984: Romancing the Stone. †The Ratings Game (TV). Johnny Dangerously. 1985: The Jewel of the Nile. Head Office. 1986: Ruthless People. Wise Guys. My Little Pony (voice only). 1987: Tin Men. †Throw Momma from the Train. 1988: Twins. 1989: †The War of the Roses. 1991: Other People's Money. 1992: †Hoffa. Batman Returns. 1993: Jack the Bear. Look Who's Talking Now (voice only). 1994: Renaissance Man. Junior. 1995: Get Shorty. Felony. 1996: †Matilda. Mars Attacks! 1997: L.A. Confidential. John Grisham's The Rainmaker. Space Jam (voice only). Hercules (voice only). 1998: Living Out Loud. 1999: Man on the Moon. The Big Kahuna/Hospitality Suite. The Virgin Suicides. Stretch Armstrong. 2000: Drowning Mona. Screwed.

†Also directed

DEXTER, Anthony
(Walter Fleischmann) 1919–

Black-haired, aristocratic-looking American actor who, with no previous film experience, was chosen to play Rudolph Valentino in a 1951 biopic. The picture was not terribly successful and – apart from the next one, *The Brigand* – the rest of Dexter's films did little to establish him at the top.

1951: *Valentino*. 1952: *The Brigand*. 1953: *Captain John Smith and Pocahontas* (GB: *Burning Arrows*). 1954: *Captain Kidd and the Slave Girl. The Black Pirates*. 1956: *Fire Maidens from Outer Space. He Laughed Last*. 1957: *The Parson and the Outlaw. The Story of Mankind*. 1960: *Three Blondes in his Life. Twelve to the Moon*. 1962: *Married Too Young. The Phantom Planet*. 1965: *Saturday Night Bath in Apple Valley*. 1967: *Thoroughly Modern Millie*.

DIAZ, Cameron 1972–

Tall, strikingly blue-eyed blonde American actress with mobile features and well-defined bone structure, at her best in comedy but adept in a variety of roles. A much-travelled teenager, she lived in France, Morocco, Australia, Japan and Mexico before returning to her native California and making a career as a model. Auditioning for a small part in the Jim Carrey comedy *The Mask*, she found herself elevated to the lead with no previous acting experience. She soon packed in plenty of that, often in comedy, but sometimes in quite dark and unexpected roles.

1994: *The Mask*. 1995: *The Last Supper*. 1996: *Feeling Minnesota. Head Above Water. She's the One. Keys to Tulsa*. 1997: *My Best Friend's Wedding. A Life Less Ordinary*. 1998: *Very Bad Things. There's Something About Mary. Fear and Loathing in Las Vegas*. 1999: *Being John Malkovich. Man Woman Film. Any Given Sunday. Things You Can Tell Just By Looking at Her*. 2000: *Invisible Circus. Charlie's Angels*.

DiCAPRIO, Leonardo 1974–

Talented, brown-haired American actor with screwed-up, childlike facial features that qualified him for rebel and non-conformist roles. After beginning in commercials and educational films, he soon showed his mettle with an outstanding performance as a retarded youth in *What's Eating Gilbert Grape*, which won him a deserved Oscar nomination. He became one of Hollywood's most popular pin-ups after his worldwide successes in *Romeo & Juliet* and *Titanic*.

1991: *Critters 3*. 1992: *Poison Ivy*. 1993: *This Boy's Life*. *The Foot Shooting Party*. What's Eating Gilbert Grape*. 1994: *Don's Plum. The Basketball Diaries*. 1995: *Total Eclipse. A Hundred and One Nights. The Quick and the Dead*. 1996: *Marvin's Room. William Shakespeare's Romeo & Juliet. Verona Beach* (doc). 1997: *Titanic. The Man in the Iron Mask* (Randall Wallace version). 1998: *Celebrity*. 2000: *The Beach*. 2001: *Gangs of New York. Catch Me If You Can*.

DICKINSON, Angie
(Angeline Brown) 1931–

Long-legged, blonde American actress who entered films via beauty contests. Most film writers patently think Miss Dickinson hard done-by in the cinema but to me she has always been rather plastic, a mould that clearly hardened to polystyrene in her TV series *Policewoman*. It took French director Roger Vadim (in *Pretty Maids All in a Row*) to make her seem really sexy, and she worked regularly in France for a while in the seventies. Married to composer Burt Bacharach 1965–1980. Has lived with singer John Barrowman since 1992.

1954: *Lucky Me*. 1955: *The Man with the Gun* (GB: *The Trouble Shooter*). *The Return of Jack Slade* (GB: *Texas Rose*). *Tennessee's Partner. Hidden Guns*. 1956: *Gun the Man Down. The Black Whip. Tension at Table Rock*. 1957: *Calypso Joe. I Married a Woman. Shoot-Out at Medicine Bend. Run of the Arrow* (voice only). *China Gate*. 1958: *Cry Terror! Frontier Rangers* (TV. GB: cinemas). 1959: *Rio Bravo. The Bramble Bush*. 1960: *A Fever in the Blood. Ocean's Eleven*. 1961: *The Sins of Rachel Cade. I'll Give My Life. Jessica*. 1962: *Rome Adventure* (GB: *Lovers Must Learn*). 1963: *Captain Newman MD*. 1964: *The Killers*. 1965: *The Art of Love*. 1966: *The Chase. Cast a Giant Shadow. The Poppy is Also a Flower* (GB: *Danger Grows Wild*). 1967: *Point Blank. The Last Challenge* (GB: *The Pistolero of Red River*). 1968: *A Case of Libel* (TV). 1969: *Sam Whiskey. The Love War* (TV). *Young Billy Young. Some Kind of a Nut*. 1971: *The Resurrection of Zachary Wheeler* (GB: TV). *Thief* (TV). *See the Man Run* (TV). *Pretty Maids All in a Row*. 1972: *Un homme est mort* (GB: *The Outside Man*). 1973: *The Norliss Tapes* (TV). 1974: *Pray for the Wildcats* (TV). *Big Bad Mama*. 1977: *A Sensitive, Passionate Man* (TV). 1978: *Le labyrinthe* (US: *Labyrinths*). *Overboard* (TV). 1979: *L'homme en colère. Klondike Fever. The Suicide's Wife* (TV). 1980: *Dressed to Kill*. 1981: *Death Hunt. Charlie Chan and the Curse of the Dragon Queen. Dial M for Murder* (TV). 1982: *One Shoe Makes it Murder* (TV). 1983: *Jealousy* (TV). 1984: *A Touch of Scandal* (TV). 1987: *Still Watch* (TV). *Big Bad Mama II. Police Story: The Freeway Killings* (TV). *Once Upon a Texas Train* (TV). 1989: *Prime Target* (TV). *Fire and Rain* (TV). 1992: *Treacherous Crossing* (TV). 1993: *Even Cowgirls Get the Blues*. 1995: *The Maddening. Sabrina*. 1996: *The Sun, the Moon and the Stars. Danielle Steel's Remembrance* (TV). 1997: *Deep Family Secrets* (TV). *National Lampoon's The Don's Analyst* (TV). 1999: *Sealed with a Kiss* (TV). 2000: *Pay It Forward*.

DIETRICH, Marlene
(Maria Magdalene Dietrich) 1900–1992

Alphabetical order ungraciously places two of the best pairs of twentieth-century legs next to each other. Dietrich, a blonde German actress who slaved through a fistful of big parts before being spotted for *The Blue Angel* in 1930, is, next to Garbo, the most magical face and voice from the early sound era. Her ageless charms enabled her to make several comebacks after lulls in her career. And her husky singing voice made her a successful night club entertainer from the fifties on. Towards the end of her life, however, she became a recluse. Received an Oscar nomination for *Morocco*.

1922: *So sind die Männer/Der Kleine Napoleon*. 1923: *Tragödie der Liebe. Der Sprung ins Leben. Der Mensch am Wege*. 1925: *Die freudlose Gasse (GB and US: Joyless Street). Manon Lescaut*. 1926: *Eine DuBarry von Heute (GB: A Modern Dubarry). Madame wünscht keine Kinder (US: Madame Wants No Children). Kopf hoch, Charly! Der Juxbaron*. 1927: *Sein grosster Bluff. Café Electric*. 1928: *Prinzessin Olala*. *Die glückliche Mutter*. 1929: *Die Frau, nach der Man sich sehnt. Ich küsse ihre Hand, Madame. Liebesnächte. Das Schiff der verlorene Menschen*. 1930: *The Blue Angel. Morocco*. 1931: *Dishonored*. 1932: *Shanghai Express. Blonde Venus*. 1933: *Song of Songs*. 1934: *The Scarlet Empress*. 1935: *The Devil is a Woman*. 1936: *Desire. The Garden of Allah. I Loved a Soldier (unfinished)*. 1937: *Knight Without Armour. Angel*. 1939: *Destry Rides Again*. 1940: *Seven Sinners*. 1941: *Manpower. The Flame of New Orleans*. 1942: *The Lady is Willing. The Spoilers. Pittsburgh*. 1943: **Screen Snapshots No. 103. *Show Business at War*. 1944: *Follow the Boys. Kismet*. 1946: *Martin Roumagnac (US: The Room Upstairs)*. 1947: *Golden Earrings*. 1948: *A Foreign Affair*. 1949: *Jigsaw. Stage Fright*. 1951: *No Highway (US: No Highway in the Sky)*. 1952: *Rancho Notorious*. 1956: *Around the World in 80 Days. The Monte Carlo Story*. 1957: *Witness for the Prosecution*. 1958: *Touch of Evil*. 1961: *Judgment at Nuremberg*. 1962: *The Black Fox (narrator only)*. 1963: *Paris When It Sizzles*. 1978: *Just a Gigolo*. 1984: *Marlene*.

DILLER, Phyllis (P. Driver) 1917–

Madcap, crow-voiced, explosive American comedienne with accentuated witch-like looks who followed success on television with a few appearances in films that found it hard to contain her firework style in the framework of a plot. She returned to television and to the nightclub work which had first brought her success. Began her career at 38 after bringing up a family of five.

1961: *Splendor in the Grass*. 1965: *The Fat Spy*. 1966: *Boy, Did I Get a Wrong Number*. **Hollywood Star Spangled Revue*. 1967: *Eight on the Lam (GB: Eight on the Run). Mad Monster Party (voice only)*. 1968: *The Private Navy of Sergeant O'Farrell. Did You Hear the One about the Traveling Saleslady?* 1969: *The Adding Machine*. 1970: *Love American Style (TV)*. 1982: *Pink Motel (GB: Motel)*. 1988: *Dr Hackenstein*. 1990: *The Boneyard. The Nutcracker (voice only). Happily Ever After (voice only)*. 1991: *Pucker Up and Bark like a Dog. Wisecracks*. 1993: *The Perfect Man*. 1994: *The Silence of the Hams (released 1996)*. 1998: *A Bug's Life (voice only)*. 1999: *Everything's Jake. The Debtors*.

DILLMAN, Bradford 1930–

Lean, dark, curly-haired, brooding American actor, mostly in sombre roles, whose career got off to a cracking start in *Compulsion*. But he suffered a few disasters, and was thereafter unable to command the kind of parts he wanted, being seen mainly as bad guys with half a screw loose. Said the once-choosy star in the mid-seventies: 'I'm motivated by financial necessity. I'll accept just about everything I'm offered.' His TV career bears witness to that. Married (second) to ex-actress (and model) Suzy Parker (Cecelia Parker, 1932–) since 1963. Less seen in films and TV since 1980, he has more recently written books on US football history.

1958: *A Certain Smile. In Love and War*. 1959: *Compulsion*. 1960: *Crack in the Mirror. Circle of Deception*. 1961: *Sanctuary. Francis of Assisi*. 1963: *The Case Against Paul Ryker (TV. Released to GB and US cinemas 1968 as Sergeant Ryker). Jane*. 1965: *A Rage to Live*. 1966: *The Plainsman*. 1967: *The Helicopter Spies (TV. GB: cinemas)*. 1968: *Jigsaw*. 1969: *Black Water Gold (TV). The Bridge at Remagen. Fear No Evil (TV)*. 1970: *The Mephisto Waltz. Suppose They Gave a War and Nobody Came. Brother John*. 1971: *Escape from the Planet of the Apes. The Resurrection of Zachary Wheeler (GB. TV). Five Desperate Women (TV). Revenge! (TV)*. 1972: *Moon of the Wolf (TV). The Delphi Bureau (TV). The Eyes of Charles Sand (TV)*. 1973: *Deliver Us from Evil (TV). The Iceman Cometh. The Way We Were*. 1974: *The Disappearance of Flight 412 (TV). Gold. Deborah/A Black Ribbon for Deborah. Murder Or Mercy? (TV). The Last Bride of Salem (TV). 99 and 44/100% Dead (GB: Call Harry Crown)*. 1975: *Widow (TV). Michèle. Bug. Demon, Demon (TV). Force Five (TV). Please Call it Murder (TV). Adventures of the Queen (TV)*. 1976: *The Enforcer. Kingston/The Newspaper Game (TV). Street Killing (TV). Mastermind*. 1977: *The Amsterdam Kill. The Lincoln Conspiracy*. 1978: *Final Judgment (TV). The Swarm. The Hostage Heart (TV). Love and Bullets. Piranha*. 1979: *Guyana: The Crime of the Century. Before and After (TV). The Legend of Walks Far Woman (TV). Jennifer (TV). Running Scared*. 1980: *The Memory of Eva Ryker (TV). Tourist (TV)*. 1983: *Sudden Impact*. 1984: *Covenant (TV). The Treasure of the Amazon/Treasure of Doom*. 1986: *The Tuscaloosan/Man Outside*. 1989: *Lords of the Deep*. 1990: *Heroes Stand Alone*. 1992: *The Heart of Justice (TV)*.

DILLON, Matt 1964–

Long-jawed, slim, dark young American of Bowery-style handsomeness, initially in teenage rebel roles. The great-nephew of cartoonist Alex Raymond, who created the comic strips *Flash Gordon* and *Jungle Jim*, Dillon was in leading roles at 15 and although part of ensemble performances in his first few successes, branched out on his own with *The Flamingo Kid* and subsequent roles. Fared less well towards the end of the 1980s, but scored a critical success in *Drugstore Cowboy*. The brother of actor Kevin Dillon (1965–), he became more of a working actor than a movie megastar in the 1990s; as someone who has always guarded his private life, that's the way he likes it.

1979: *Over the Edge*. 1980: *Little Darlings. My Bodyguard*. 1981: *Liar's Moon*. 1982: *The Great American Fourth of July and Other Disasters (TV). Tex*. 1983: *The Outsiders. Rumble Fish*. 1984: *The Flamingo Kid*. 1985: *Target. Rebel*. 1986: *Native Son*. 1987: *The Big Town. Dear America (voice only)*. 1988: *Kansas. Bloodhounds of Broadway*. 1989: *Drugstore Cowboy*. 1991: *A Kiss Before Dying. Women & Men 2: In Love There Are No Rules (TV)*. 1992: *Malcolm X. Singles. Prufrock (narrator only). Blast 'Em*. 1993: *The Saint of Fort Washington. Mr Wonderful*. 1994: *Golden Gate*. 1995: *To Die For. Frankie Starlight*. 1996: *Beautiful Girls. Albino Alligator. Grace of My Heart. No Vacancy*. 1997: *In & Out*. 1998: *Wild Things. There's Something About Mary*. 2000: *One Night at McCool's*. 2001: *Deuces Wild*.

DIX, Richard (Ernest Brimmer) 1893–1949
Dark-haired, square-faced, usually unsmiling
American leading man, enormously popular
in silents, whose career gradually declined
after the early thirties, when he had been
nominated for an Oscar in *Cimarron*. His
granite features successfully switched from
heroes to unbalanced villains in several of the
offbeat 'Whistler' thrillers of the 1940s. Died
from heart trouble.
*1919: One of the Finest. 1921: The Sin Flood.
Not Guilty. All Fair's in Love. The Old Nest.
The Poverty of Riches. Dangerous Curve Ahead.
1922: The Glorious Fool. Yellow Men and
Gold. The Bonded Woman. The Wallflower.
Fools First. 1923: The Christian. Racing
Hearts. The Woman with Four Faces. The Ten
Commandments. Souls for Sale. The Call of the
Canyon. To the Last Man. Quicksands. 1924:
Sinners in Heaven. Icebound. The Iron Horse.
Manhattan. The Stranger. Unguarded Women.
1925: The Vanishing American. The Shock
Punch. The Lucky Devil. Too Many Kisses. A
Man Must Live. The Lady Who Lied. Men and
Women. 1926: Woman-Handled. The Quarter-
back. Say it Again. Fascinating Youth. Let's
Get Married. 1927: Quicksands (remake).
Knock-Out Reilly. Manpower. Shanghai
Bound. Paradise for Two. 1928: Easy Come,
Easy Go. Moran of the Marines. Sporting
Goods. The Gay Defender. Warming Up. 1929:
Nothing But the Truth. Redskin. The Wheel of
Life. The Love Doctor. Seven Keys to Baldpate.
1930: Lovin' the Ladies. Shooting Straight.
1931: Cimarron. Young Donovan's Kid (GB:
Donovan's Kid). Secret Service. Public
Defender. 1932: The Lost Squadron. Hell's
Highway. *The Stolen Jools (GB: The
Slippery Pearls). Roar of the Dragon. The
Conquerors. Liberty Road. 1933: No Marriage
Ties. The Ace of Aces. The Great Jasper. Day of
Reckoning. Stingaree. West of the Pecos.
His Greatest Gamble. 1935: The Tunnel (US:
Transatlantic Tunnel). The Arizonian. 1936:
The Devil's Squadron. Special Investigator.
Yellow Dust. 1937: The Devil is Driving. It
Happened in Hollywood (GB: Once a Hero).
The Devil's Playground. 1938: Blind Alibi.
Sky Giant. 1939: Man of Conquest. Reno.
Twelve Crowded Hours. Here I Am a Stranger.
1940: The Marines Fly High. Cherokee Strip
(GB: Fighting Marshal). Men Against the
Sky. 1941: The Roundup. Badlands of Dakota.
1942: American Empire (GB: My Son Alone).
Tombstone, The Town Too Tough to Die. 1943:
Buckskin Frontier (GB: The Iron Road). The
Kansan (GB: Wagon Wheels). Eyes of the*

*Underworld. Top Man. The Ghost Ship. 1944:
The Whistler. The Mark of the Whistler (GB:
The Marked Man). 1945: The Power of the
Whistler. 1946: The Voice of the Whistler. The
Mysterious Intruder. The Secret of the Whistler.
1947: The Thirteenth Hour.*

DOLENZ, George 1908–1963
Italian-born leading man with dark, wavy
hair whose handsome but crafty features were
equally well equipped to portray swashbuckling heroes or cunning villains. Once a
tinsmith, he started his show business career
as an opera singer, but enjoyed a fair run of
success in wartime Hollywood in the absence
of more powerful stars. Best remembered in
Britain for his TV series *The Count of Monte-
Cristo*. Father of actor-musician Micky
Dolenz, once of The Monkees. Died from a
heart attack.
*1927: The Ring. 1941: Unexpected Uncle.
Faculty Row. 1942: Take a Letter, Darling
(GB: Green-Eyed Woman). She's for Me.
Calling Dr Death. 1943: No Time for Love.
Young Ideas. Fired Wife. The Strange Death of
Adolf Hitler. Moonlight in Vermont. 1944: In
Society. The Climax. Enter Arsene Lupin.
Bowery to Broadway. 1945: The Royal
Mounted Rides Again (serial). Song of the
Sarong. Easy to Look At. Girl on the Spot.
1946: Idea Girl. A Night in Paradise. 1947:
Song of Scheherezade. 1950: Vendetta. 1952:
My Cousin Rachel. 1953: Wings of the Hawk.
Thunder Bay. Scared Stiff. 1954: Sign of the
Pagan. The Last Time I Saw Paris. 1955: Such
Men Are Dangerous (GB: The Racers). The
Purple Mask. A Bullet for Joey. 1957: The Sad
Sack. 1959: Timbuktu. 1961: Look in Any
Window. 1962: The Four Horsemen of the
Apocalypse.*

DOMERGUE, Faith 1925–1999
Dark-haired, brown-eyed American leading
lady, on the sultry side. She was a protegée of
Howard Hughes, who, after starring her in
one film, kept her under wraps for several
years, then relaunched her in a blaze of Jane
Russell-style publicity. Public and critics did
not take to her, and her star bubble burst
almost at once, although she subsequently
performed competently in a number of
routine thrillers and action films. Married
from 1950 to 1954 to director Hugo
Fregonese. Died from cancer.
*1946: Young Widow. 1950: Where Danger
Lives. Vendetta. 1952: The Duel at Silver
Creek. 1953: The Great Sioux Uprising. 1954:*

*This is My Love. 1955: Cult of the Cobra. This
Island Earth. It Came from Beneath the Sea.
Santa Fé Passage. Timeslip (US: The Atomic
Man). 1956: Soho Incident (US: Spin a Dark
Web). 1957: Man in the Shadow (US: Violent
Stranger). Il cielo brucia. 1958: Live in Fear.
1959: Escort West. 1963: California. 1966:
Prehistoric Planet Women. 1967: Track of
Thunder. 1969: One on Top of the Other. The
Gamblers. Le sorelle / So Evil My Sister. 1970:
L'amore Breve. 1971: Legacy of Blood. L'uomo
dagli occhi di ghiaccio (US: The Man with the
Icy Eyes). 1973: The House of the Seven
Corpses.*

DONAHUE, Troy (Merle Johnson) 1936–
Big, beefy, baby-faced American actor with
butter-coloured hair, the pin-up of a million
teenage girls in the late 1950s and early 1960s.
An attempt to widen his range beyond the
teenage dream was not entirely successful and
after he had left the aegis of his studio,
Warners, he found the going very tough
indeed. He now plays lesser roles but became
one of Hollywood's busiest actors in the late
1980s. Married to Suzanne Pleshette (*qv*) in
1964 and Valerie Allen (from 1966).
*1957: Man Afraid. The Tarnished Angels.
1958: The Voice in the Mirror. Live Fast, Die
Young. This Happy Feeling. Summer Love.
Wild Heritage. Monster on the Campus. The
Perfect Furlough (GB: Strictly for Pleasure).
1959: Imitation of Life. A Summer Place.
1960: The Crowded Sky. 1961: Parrish. Susan
Slade. 1962: Rome Adventure (GB: Lovers
Must Learn). 1963: Palm Springs Weekend.
1964: A Distant Trumpet. 1965: My Blood
Runs Cold. 1967: Rocket to the Moon (US:
Those Fantastic Flying Fools). Come Spy with
Me. 1969: The Lonely Profession (TV). 1971:*

Sweet Saviour. 1973: Seizure. 1974: Born To Kill (GB: Cockfighter). The Godfather Part II. 1977: The Legend of Frank Woods. 1982: Tin Man (TV). 1983: Malibu (TV). 1984: Grandview U.S.A. 1986: Savage Sunday/ Low Blow. 1987: Deadly Prey. Hawk-Eye. 1988: Hollywood Cop. American Rampage. Deadly Diamonds. Dr Alien. 1989: Deadly Spygames. Deadly Embrace. Nudity Required. Son/Bad Blood. Omega Cop. The Chilling. Assault of the Party Nerds. 1990: S.O.S. The Scan. Cry-Baby. Shock 'Em Dead. Terminal Force (completed 1987). 1992: The Pamela Principle. Double Trouble. 1993: Cockroach Hotel. Showdown. 1995: Forever More. 1998: Merchants of Venus. Legion (TV).

DONALD, James 1917–1993

Scottish actor who threw up a university career to join Edinburgh Repertory Company, and thence went into British films where he played serious, thoughtful roles, in keeping with his dark, unsmiling looks. A star from 1948 to 1952, but began to look gaunt in early middle age and was soon in character roles, mostly of dry, literate, office-bound types. Ill-health forced his retirement, and he became a vine-grower in his later years. Died from cancer of the stomach.

*1942: The Missing Million. Went the Day Well? In Which We Serve. 1943: San Demetrio London. 1944: The Way Ahead (US: Immortal Battalion). 1947: Broken Journey. 1948: The Small Voice (US: Hideout). 1949: Edward My Son. Trottie True (US: Gay Lady). 1950: Cage of Gold. 1951: White Corridors. Brandy for the Parson. *The Persian Story (narrator only). 1952: Gift Horse (US: Glory at Sea). The Pickwick Papers. The Net (US: Project M7). 1954: Beau Brummell. 1956: Lust for Life. 1957: The Bridge on the River Kwai. 1958: The Vikings. 1959: Third Man on the Mountain. 1963: The Great Escape. 1965: King Rat. Cast a Giant Shadow. 1966: The Jokers. 1967: Quatermass and the Pit (US: Five Million Miles to Earth). 1968: Hannibal Brooks. 1969: The Royal Hunt of the Sun. David Copperfield (TV. GB: cinemas). Destiny of a Spy (TV). 1975: Conduct Unbecoming. 1978: The Big Sleep.*

DONAT, Robert

(Frederick R. Donat) 1905–1958

Cheerful, chunky, good-looking British leading man who could do very little wrong in films in the thirties. His forthright, pleasing, open acting style endeared him to audiences,

produced a memorable series of characterizations and culminated in his Academy Award for *Goodbye Mr Chips!* Later, blighted by persistent asthma, he was less successful by his own high standards, although his mellifluous voice patterns made him ever-popular on radio. Married (second) to actress Renée Asherson; they were separated at the time of his death from a cerebral thrombosis brought on by chronic bronchial asthma. An Oscar nominee for *The Citadel.*

*1932: Men of Tomorrow. That Night in London (US: Overnight). 1933: Cash (US: For Love Or Money). The Private Life of Henry VIII. 1934: The Count of Monte Cristo. 1935: The 39 Steps. The Ghost Goes West. 1937: Knight without Armour. 1938: The Citadel. 1939: Goodbye Mr Chips! 1941: *Cavalcade of the Academy Awards. The Young Mr Pitt. 1943: The Adventures of Tartu (US: Tartu). 1945: Perfect Strangers (US: Vacation from Marriage). 1947: Captain Boycott. *The British – Are They Artistic? 1948: The Winslow Boy. 1949: †The Cure for Love. 1951: The Magic Box. 1953: *Royal Heritage (narrator only). 1954: Lease of Life. 1956: *The Stained Glass at Fairford. 1958: The Inn of the Sixth Happiness.*

†Also directed

DONLAN, Yolande 1920–

American actress (daughter of character actor James Donlan: 1889–1938) and dancer who slaved away for years on the sidelines in Hollywood before taking them by storm on the London stage as the heroine of *Born Yesterday.* Although her appeal was primarily that of the dizzy blonde, she played some enchanting variations on it in the British

cinema of the late forties and early fifties. Married (second) to British director Val Guest.

1936: Pennies from Heaven. After the Thin Man. 1937: The Champagne Waltz. Rosalie. 1938: Love Finds Andy Hardy. Sweethearts. 1939: The Oklahoma Kid. The Great Man Votes. Idiot's Delight. Man About Town. 1940: I Take This Woman. †Turnabout. †Cross Country Romance. †Dark Streets of Cairo. †The Devil Bat. 1941: †Road Show. †Under Age. †Unfinished Business. 1942: †DuBarry Was a Lady. 1943: †Girl Crazy. 1944: †Meet Me in St Louis. 1949: Traveller's Joy. Miss Pilgrim's Progress. 1950: The Body Said No! Mr Drake's Duck. 1952: Penny Princess. 1955: They Can't Hang Me. 1957: Tarzan and the Lost Safari. 1959: Expresso Bongo. 1962: Jigsaw. 1963: 80,000 Suspects. 1970: The Adventurers. 1976: Seven Nights in Japan.

†As Yvonne Mollot

DONLEVY, Brian

(Grosson B. Donlevy) 1899–1972

Heavy-set, gloweringly handsome, strong, moustachioed, Irish-born Hollywood actor. After an adventurous early life (including World War I service in Lafayette Escadrille) he drifted into acting, although it was 1935 before he settled permanently in Hollywood. A tough villain of the 1930s, he became a popular semi-star of rugged thrillers and action films in the succeeding decade after his success in the title role of *The Great McGinty.* Although Donlevy suffered from drinking problems, his forthright performances remained good value to the end. Died from cancer of the throat. Oscar-nominated for his sadistic sergeant in *Beau Geste.*

*1923: Jamestown. 1924: Monsieur Beaucaire. Damaged Hearts. 1925: School for Wives. 1926: A Man of Quality. 1928: Mother's Boy. 1929: Gentlemen of the Press. 1932: *A Modern Cinderella. 1935: Another Face (GB: It Happened in Hollywood). Barbary Coast. Mary Burns, Fugitive. 1936: Strike Me Pink. High Tension. Crack-Up. Human Cargo. Half Angel. Thirteen Hours by Air. 36 Hours to Kill. 1937: Born Reckless. Midnight Taxi. This Is My Affair (GB: His Affair). 1938: We're Going to be Rich. In Old Chicago. Battle of Broadway. Sharpshooters. 1939: Jesse James. Union Pacific. Behind Prison Gates. Beau Geste. Destry Rides Again. Allegheny Uprising (GB: The First Rebel). 1940: The Great McGinty (GB: Down Went McGinty). Brigham Young Frontiersman (GB: Brigham*

Young). When the Daltons Rode. 1941: I Wanted Wings. Birth of the Blues. Hold Back the Dawn. Billy the Kid. South of Tahiti (GB: White Savage). 1942: The Great Man's Lady. The Remarkable Andrew. A Gentleman After Dark. Wake Island. The Glass Key. Nightmare. Stand by for Action (GB: Cargo of Innocents). Two Yanks in Trinidad. 1943: Hangmen Also Die. The City That Stopped Hitler – Heroic Stalingrad (narrator only). 1944: An American Romance. The Miracle of Morgan's Creek. 1945: Duffy's Tavern. The Trouble with Women (released 1947). 1946: Our Hearts Were Growing Up. The Virginian. Canyon Passage. Two Years Before the Mast. 1947: The Beginning or the End. Song of Scheherezade. Heaven Only Knows. Kiss of Death. Killer McCoy. 1948: A Southern Yankee (GB: My Hero). Impact. Command Decision. 1949: The Lucky Stiff. 1950: Shakedown. Kansas Raiders. 1951: Fighting Coast Guard. Slaughter Trail. 1952: Hoodlum Empire. Ride the Man Down. 1953: The Woman They Almost Lynched. 1954: The Big Combo. 1955: The Quatermass Experiment (US: The Creeping Unknown). 1956: A Cry in the Night. 1957: Quatermass 2 (US: Enemy from Space). 1958: Escape from Red Rock. Cowboy. 1959: Juke Box Rhythm. Never So Few. 1960: The Girl in Room 13. 1961: The Errand Boy. 1962: The Pigeon That Took Rome. 1964: The Curse of the Fly. 1965: Gammera the Invincible. How to Stuff a Wild Bikini. 1966: The Fat Spy. Waco. 1967: Hostile Guns. 1968: Arizona Bushwhackers. Rogue's Gallery. 1969: Pit Stop.

DONOHOE, Amanda 1962–
Honey-blonde, whippily built, sensuous-looking British actress who started her career dangerously by losing her clothes in a series of increasingly absurd films, but gradually improved her acting credentials, especially on a trip to Hollywood which produced a running role in the top TV series L A Law. Making fewer film appearances than her fans would like, she still looked a good bet for wicked ladies of the 1990s in the tradition of Jean Kent, Googie Withers and Margaret Lockwood (all qv), but was sadly relegated to supporting roles by the end of the decade.
1986: Foreign Body. Castaway. 1988: The Lair of the White Worm. An Affair in Mind (TV). 1989: The Rainbow. Tank Malling. Diamond Skulls (US: Dark Obsession). 1990: Paper Mask. 1992: Shame. 1993: It's Nothing Personal (TV). The Substitute (cable TV).

1994: A Woman's Guide to Adultery. The Madness of King George. 1996: Deep Secrets (TV). The Last Day. Shame II: The Secret (TV). 1997: Liar Liar. Stardust Visionaries. One Night Stand. The Real Howard Spitz. 1998: I'm Losing You. A Knight in Camelot (TV). 2000: Thanks for the Memories. Glory Glory. Circus. Wild About Harry.

DORFF, Stephen 1973–
Sharp-faced, deep-eyed, brown-haired, intense-looking American actor, at home in unconventional roles and often as belligerent characters. Acting since childhood, Dorff has been in leading roles for the cinema since the age of 14, and before he was 21 had demonstrated his facility with accents in BackBeat (Liverpudlian) and The Power of One (Afrikaans). Some of his late 1990s parts have been unworthy of his early promise, but he remains an interesting actor in starring roles.
1987: The Gate. In Love and War (TV). 1988: Quiet Victory: The Charlie Wedemeyer Story (TV). 1989: I Know My First Name is Steven (TV). Do You Know the Muffin Man? (TV). 1990: Always Remember I Love You (TV). A Son's Promise (TV). 1992: The Power of One. 1993: BackBeat. Judgment Night. An Ambush of Ghosts. Rescue Me. 1994: SFW. Les cent et une nuits / A Hundred and One Nights of Simon Cinema. 1995: Innocent Lies / Halcyon Days. 1996: I Shot Andy Warhol. Blood and Wine. Reckless (TV). The Audition. 1997: Space Truckers. City of Industry. 1998: Foolish Heart. Blade. 1999: Entropy. Earthly Posessions (cable TV). 2000: Cecil B. DeMented. Quantum Project.

DORLEAC, Françoise 1942–1967
More extrovert sister of Catherine Deneuve,

this dark-haired, rangy French actress with attractive personality was on the verge of becoming as big an international star as her sister when she was killed in a car crash at 25.
1957: *Mensonges. 1959: Les loups dans la bergerie (GB: The Damned and the Daring). 1960: Les portes claquent (US: The Door Slams). 1961: La gamberge. Le jeu da la verité. All the Gold in the World. Ce soir ou jamais. La fille aux yeux d'or (US: The Girl with the Golden Eyes). 1962: Arsène Lupin contre Arsène Lupin. 1964: That Man from Rio. La peau douce (GB: Silken Skin). La Ronde (US: Circle of Love). La chase à l'homme. 1965: Where the Spies Are. Genghis Khan. 1966: Cul-de-sac. 1967: The Young Girls of Rochefort. Billion Dollar Brain.

DORN, Philip
(Hein Van Der Niet) 1901–1975
Dutch stage actor who fled the Germans in 1939 and ended up in Hollywood where, despite his comparative lack of film experience, he was eagerly snapped up for a series of sincere if stolid continentals of varying nationality. He was usually distinctive, however, and occasionally (as in I Remember Mama) quite memorable. A stroke in 1946 disrupted his film career and he was forced to retire in 1955 following an accident in a stage play. Died from a heart attack.
1934: †Op hopp van zegen. 1935: †Op stap. †De big van het regiment. 1936: †De Kribbebyter (GB: The Cross-Patch). †Rubber. 1937: †Der Tiger von Eschnapur. †Das Indische Grabmal. 1938: †Reise nach Tilsit. †Verwehte Spuren. †Immer, wenn ich glücklich bin. †Der Hampelmann. 1939: Confessions of a Nazi Spy. 1940: Ski Patrol. Diamond Frontier. Escape. Enemy Agent (GB: Secret Enemy). 1941: Ziegfeld Girl. Tarzan's Secret Treasure. Underground. 1942: Reunion / Reunion in France (GB: Mademoiselle France). Calling Dr Gillespie. Random Harvest. 1943: Paris After Dark (GB: The Night is Ending). Chetniks. 1944: Passage to Marseille (GB: Passage to Marseilles). Blonde Fever. 1945: Escape in the Desert. Paris Underground (GB: Madame Pimpernel). 1946: Concerto (later and GB: I've Always Loved You). 1948: I Remember Mama. 1949: The Fighting Kentuckian. 1950: Spy Hunt (GB: Panther's Moon). 1951: Sealed Cargo. 1952: Hinter Klostermauern. 1953: Der träumende Mund. 1954: Salto mortale.

†As Fritz Van Dongen

DORNE, Sandra

(Joanna Smith) 1925–1992

Alphabetical order produces more discomfort by squeezing next to one another Britain's two busty blondes from the forties and fifties. For me, Sandra certainly had more sex appeal, if perhaps less acting ability, but was locked away in second-features for three-quarters of her career. And her private life was less sensational than that of La Dors, which meant she hit fewer international headlines. Married to Patrick Holt (qv) from 1954. Later occasionally on TV in plump character roles. Died on Christmas Day.

*1947: Eyes That Kill. 1948: A Piece of Cake. Once a Jolly Swagman (US: Maniacs on Wheels). All Over the Town. Saraband for Dead Lovers (US: Saraband). 1949: Marry Me. Don't Ever Leave Me. Golden Arrow (US: The Gay Adventure). Traveller's Joy. 1950: Don't Say Die. The Clouded Yellow. Helter Skelter. 1951: Happy Go Lovely. 1952: 13 East Street. Hindle Wakes (US: Holiday Week). The Yellow Balloon. Alf's Baby. 1953: Wheel of Fate. The Beggar's Opera. Marilyn/Roadhouse Girl. The Case of Express Delivery. The Weak and the Wicked. The Good Die Young. 1955: Police Dog. The Final Column. Diplomatic Error. 1956: The Gelignite Gang. Alias John Preston. The Iron Petticoat. Operation Murder. 1957: Three Sundays to Live. 1958: Orders to Kill. *Portrait of a Matador. The Bank Raiders. 1960: Not a Hope in Hell. The House in Marsh Road (US: The Invisible Creature). The Malpas Mystery. 1962: The Amorous Prawn (US: The Playgirl and the War Minister). 1963: Devil Doll. 1964: The Secret Door. 1971: All Coppers Are . . . 1976: Joseph Andrews. 1978: The Playbirds. 1987: Eat the Rich.*

DORS, Diana (D. Fluck) 1931–1984

Platinum blonde British actress with sexy smile whose career had as many curves and swerves as her once hourglass figure. One of her first films, *Good Time Girl*, summed up her early career, but she proved herself a real actress in *Yield to the Night*, only to throw the reputation away on an abortive and wildly over-publicized visit to Hollywood. Extremely good in some early 1970s' character roles, she was latterly given less worthy material. Three times married. Died from cancer.

1946: The Shop at Sly Corner. Dancing with Crime. 1947: Holiday Camp. 1948: Good Time Girl. Penny and the Pownall Case. The Calendar. My Sister and I. Oliver Twist. Here Come the Huggetts. 1949: It's Not Cricket. Vote for Huggett. Diamond City. A Boy, a Girl and a Bike. 1950: Dance Hall. 1951: Lady Godiva Rides Again. Worm's Eye View. 1952: The Last Page (US: Manbait). My Wife's Lodger. The Great Game. 1953: Is Your Honeymoon Really Necessary? It's a Grand Life. The Weak and the Wicked (US: Young and Willing). 1955: As Long As They're Happy. A Kid for Two Farthings. Miss Tulip Stays the Night. Value for Money. An Alligator Named Daisy. 1956: Yield to the Night (US: Blonde Sinner). I Married a Woman. 1957: The Unholy Wife. La ragazza del Palio (GB: The Love Specialist. US: Girl of the Palio). The Long Haul. 1958: Tread Softly Stranger. Passport to Shame (US: Room 43). 1960: Scent of Mystery (GB: Holiday in Spain). 1961: On the Double. King of the Roaring Twenties (GB: The Big Bankroll). 1962: Mrs Gibbons' Boys. Encontra a Mallorca. 1963: West 11. 1964: Allez France (US: The Counterfeit Constable). 1966: The Sandwich Man. 1967: Berserk! Danger Route. 1968: Hammerhead. Baby Love. 1970: There's a Girl in My Soup. Deep End. 1971: Hannie Caulder. The Pied Piper. 1972: The Amazing Mr Blunden. Nothing But the Night. 1973: Theatre of Blood. From Beyond the Grave. Steptoe and Son Ride Again. Craze. 1974: The Amorous Milkman. Swedish Wildcats (GB: What the Swedish Butler Saw. US: The Groove Room). Bedtime with Rosie. Three for All. 1975: Adventures of a Taxi Driver. 1976: Keep It Up Downstairs. 1977: Adventures of a Private Eye. 1979: Confessions from the David Galaxy Affair. 1981: Dick Turpin (TV). 1982: Children of the Full Moon. 1984: Steaming.

DOUGLAS, Kirk

(Issur Danielovitch, later Demsky) 1916–

Forceful, fair-haired, powerfully-built American star with dimpled chin and fierce grin, apt to get hold of a role and tear it apart, but a magnetic attraction at the box office from *Champion*, in 1949 – a typical audience-crunching role as a boxer – right up to the early sixties. Father of Michael Douglas (qv). Belatedly turned director, making one disaster and one fairly good western. Nominated for Academy Awards in *Champion*, *The Bad and the Beautiful* and *Lust for Life*. Has also written best-selling novels and an autobiography. Honorary Oscar 1996. The same year he suffered a stroke – but returned to acting at the end of the decade.

*1946: The Strange Love of Martha Ivers. 1947: I Walk Alone. Out of the Past (GB: Build My Gallows High). Mourning Becomes Electra. 1948: My Dear Secretary. The Walls of Jericho. 1949: A Letter to Three Wives. Champion. Young Man with a Horn (GB: Young Man of Music). 1950: The Glass Menagerie. 1951: Along the Great Divide. The Big Carnival (GB: Ace in the Hole). Detective Story. 1952: The Big Sky. The Big Trees. The Bad and the Beautiful. 1953: The Story of Three Loves. The Juggler. Act of Love. Ulysses. 1954: 20,000 Leagues under the Sea. 1955: Man without a Star. The Racers (GB: Such Men Are Dangerous). The Indian Fighter. 1956: Lust for Life. Gunfight at the OK Corral. 1957: Paths of Glory. Top Secret Affair (GB: Their Secret Affair). 1958: The Vikings. 1959: Last Train from Gun Hill. The Devil's Disciple. 1960: Spartacus. Strangers When We Meet. 1961: The Last Sunset. Town without Pity. 1962: Lonely Are the Brave. Two Weeks in Another Town. 1963: The List of Adrian Messenger. For Love Or Money. The Hook. 1964: Seven Days in May. 1965: In Harm's Way. The Heroes of Telemark. Is Paris Burning? 1966: Cast a Giant Shadow. 1967: The Way West. The War Wagon. 1968: A Lovely Way to Die (GB: A Lovely Way to Go). *French Lunch. The Brotherhood. 1969: The Arrangement. 1970: There Was a Crooked Man. A Gunfight. 1971: The Light at the Edge of the World. Catch Me a Spy. 1972: A Man to Respect (US: The Master Touch). 1973: Mousey (TV. GB: cinemas: Cat and Mouse). †Scalawag. 1974: Once is Not Enough. 1975: †Posse. 1976: Victory at Entebbe (TV. GB: cinemas). 1977: Holocaust 2000 (US: The Chosen). 1978: The Fury. 1979: The Villain (GB: Cactus Jack). 1980: Home Movies. Saturn 3. The Final Countdown. Remembrance of Love (TV). 1981: The Man from Snowy River. 1983: Eddie Macon's Run. 1984: Draw! (TV). 1985: Amos (TV). 1986: Tough Guys. 1988: Inherit the Wind (TV). 1991: Oscar. 1992: The Secret (TV). The Lies Boys Tell (TV). 1994: Greedy. 1995: Take Me Home Again (TV). 1999: Diamonds.*

†Also directed

DOUGLAS, Melvyn

(M. Hesselberg) 1901–1981

Elegant American leading man with pencil moustache and a precise sense of romantic comedy (the zanier the comedy, the more at

home he was). His splendidly modulated voice often wittily betrayed the tongue in his cheek. Forsaking Hollywood when his days as a star were over, Douglas spent a rewarding ten years on stage before returning to films as a fine character actor of grouchy but sterling old men. Academy Award for *Hud*, and again in 1980 for *Being There*. Also nominated for *I Never Sang for My Father*. Married (second) actress Helen Gahagan (1900–1980) in 1931. Grandfather of actress Illeana Douglas (1965–).

1931: *Tonight Or Never*. 1932: *Prestige. The Wiser Sex. Broken Wing. The Old Dark House. As You Desire Me*. 1933: *Nagana. The Vampire Bat*. 1934: *Counsellor at Law. Dangerous Corner. Woman in the Dark*. 1935: *Mary Burns – Fugitive. She Married Her Boss. Annie Oakley. People's Enemy*. 1936: *The Lone Wolf Returns. The Gorgeous Hussy. And So They Were Married. Theodora Goes Wild*. 1937: *Angel. Captains Courageous. Women of Glamour. I Met Him in Paris*. 1938: *Arsene Lupin Returns. The Toy Wife (GB: Frou Frou). Fast Company. The Shining Hour. There's Always a Woman. There's That Woman Again (GB: What a Woman). That Certain Age*. 1939: *Good Girls Go to Paris. Tell No Tales. Ninotchka. The Amazing Mr Williams*. 1940: *Too Many Husbands (GB: My Two Husbands). Third Finger, Left Hand. He Stayed for Breakfast*. 1941: *Our Wife. Two Faced Woman. That Uncertain Feeling. This Thing Called Love (GB: Married But Single). A Woman's Face*. 1942: *They All Kissed the Bride. We Were Dancing*. 1943: *Three Hearts for Julia*. 1947: *The Guilt of Janet Ames. Sea of Grass. *Make Way for Youth (narrator only)*. 1948: *Mr Blandings Builds His Dream House. My Own True Love*. 1949: *A Woman's Secret. The Great Sinner*. 1950: *My Forbidden Past*. 1951: *On the Loose*. 1954: *You Can Win Elections (narrator only)*. 1957: *The Greer Case (TV)*. 1958: *The Plot to Kill Stalin. The Return of Ansel Gibbs (TV)*. 1961: **The Highest Commandment (narrator only)*. 1962: *Billy Budd*. 1963: *Hud*. 1964: *Advance to the Rear (GB: Company of Cowards). The Americanization of Emily*. 1965: *Rapture. *The Fast I Have Chosen (narrator only)*. 1966: *Hotel*. 1967: *Companions in Nightmare (TV)*. 1969: *I Never Sang for My Father*. 1970: *Hunters Are for Killing (TV)*. 1971: *Death Takes a Holiday (TV). The Going Up of David Lev (TV)*. 1972: *The Candidate. One is a Lonely Number*. 1973: *Death Squad (TV)*. 1974: *Murder Or Mercy (TV)*. 1975:

Benjamin Franklin: The Statesman (TV). 1976: *The Tenant*. 1977: *Twilight's Last Gleaming. Intimate Strangers (TV)*. 1978: *Battered! (TV)*. 1979: *The Changeling. The Seduction of Joe Tynan. Being There*. 1980: *Tell Me a Riddle*. 1981: *Ghost Story. The Hot Touch*.

DOUGLAS, Michael 1944–

Intense, hard-driving, brown-haired (often centre-parted), green-eyed American actor whose face and distinctive voice both reflect his father, Kirk Douglas (*qv*). He evaded his father's image by playing hippie roles in his early films, then went 'legitimate' as a popular TV cop in *The Streets of San Francisco*. He tried to devote himself to producing in the mid 1970s, but acting wouldn't let him go and the unexpected smash success of *Romancing the Stone* in 1984 pushed him towards superstardom at 40. A long personal relationship with Brenda Vaccaro (*qv*) fell through in 1977 and he later married a non-professional, although this, too, proved stormy and they were divorced in 1999. Since 1985, he has proved one of the box-office's hottest bets in a series of contentious films that have almost always courted controversy in some way. He won an Academy Award in *Wall Street*, and was set to marry Catherine Zeta Jones (*qv*) in 2000.

1968: *The Experiment (TV)*. 1969: *Hail, Hero!* 1970: *Adam at 6am*. 1971: *Summertree. Napoleon and Samantha. When Michael Calls (TV)*. 1972: *The Streets of San Francisco (TV)*. 1977: **Minestrone. Coma*. 1978: *The China Syndrome*. 1979: *Running*. 1980: *It's My Turn. Three Mile Island. Tell Me a Riddle*. 1983: *The Star Chamber*. 1984: *Romancing the Stone*. 1985: *A Chorus Line. The Jewel of the Nile*. 1987: *Fatal Attraction. Wall Street*. 1989: *Black Rain. The War of the Roses*. 1991: *Shining Through*. 1992: *Basic Instinct*. 1993: *Falling Down*. 1994: *Disclosure*. 1995: *The American President*. 1996: *The Ghost and the Darkness*. 1997: *The Game*. 1998: *A Perfect Murder*. 1999: *Forever Hollywood (doc)*. *One Day in September (narrator only)*. 2000: *Wonder Boys. One Night at McCool's. Traffic*.

DOUGLAS, Paul 1907–1959

Big, beaming American sports commentator who found, via stooging for comedians, a talent for acting and excelled as a series of affable, big-hearted, sometimes slow-witted gorillas, both comic and tragic. Also involved with the short series *Paul Douglas' Sports*

Review in the forties, although this may not have included any on-screen appearances. Married (fifth of five) to Jan Sterling (*qv*) from 1950 until his death in 1959 from a heart attack. His fourth wife was actress Virginia Field (*qv*).

1949: *A Letter to Three Wives. It Happens Every Spring. Everybody Does It*. 1950: *The Big Lift. Panic in the Streets. Love That Brute*. 1951: *Fourteen Hours. The Guy Who Came Back. Rhubarb. Angels in the Outfield (GB: Angels and the Pirates)*. 1952: *When in Rome. Clash by Night. We're Not Married. Never Wave at a WAC (GB: The Private Wore Skirts)*. 1953: *Forever Female. *The Javanese Dagger. *The Sable Scarf*. 1954: *Executive Suite. The Maggie (US: High and Dry). Green Fire*. 1955: *Joe Macbeth*. 1956: *The Leather Saint. The Hefferan Family (TV: GB: cinemas). The Solid Gold Cadillac. The Gamma People*. 1957: *This Could Be the Night. Beau James. Fortunella*. 1958: *The Dungeon (TV)*. 1959: *The Raider (TV). The Mating Game. Judgment at Nuremburg (TV)*.

DOUGLAS, Warren 1909–1997

Most of my colleagues in the film world seem not to have heard of Warren Douglas. But 1940s' audiences certainly knew this laughing-eyed, dark-haired American actor as the chunkily-built hero of a fistful of low-budget dramas and thrillers. As his acting career dimmed in the 1950s, Douglas was already turning to writing, producing dozens of screenplays between *Torpedo Alley* (1952) and *The Night of the Grizzly* (1966), before going into television. Died from myocarditis.

1938: *Freshman Year*. 1939: *First Offenders*. 1940: *Northwest Passage*. 1943: *Northern Pursuit. Adventure in Iraq. Murder on the*

Waterfront. Destination Tokyo. Air Force. Mission to Moscow. 1944: The Doughgirls. *I Won't Play. *Proudly We Serve. 1945: *Law of the Badlands. God is My Co-Pilot. Pride of the Marines (GB: Forever in Love). 1946: Below the Deadline. The Man I Love. The Inner Circle. The Pilgrim Lady. The Magnificent Rogue. 1947: *Climbing the Matterhorn. High Conquest. The Trespasser. The Chinese Ring. The Red Hornet. 1948: Homicide for Three (GB: An Interrupted Honeymoon). Incident. Lightnin' in the Forest. The Babe Ruth Story. 1949: Task Force. Post Office Investigator. Homicide. Forgotten Women. 1950: County Fair. Square Dance Katy. The Great Jewel Robber. 1951: Cuban Fireball. Northwest Territory. Yellowfin (GB: Yellow Fin). Secrets of Monte Carlo. 1953: Fangs of the Arctic. 1954: Cry Vengeance. 1955: Double Danger. 1957: The Helen Morgan Story (GB: Both Ends of the Candle). The Deep Six. Dragoon Wells Massacre. 1973: The Red Pony (TV. GB: cinemas, in abridged version).

DOW, Peggy (Margaret Varnadow) 1928–
Spectacularly beautiful green-eyed blonde who swopped medical studies for acting when discovered by Universal. No sooner had she demonstrated a wide range of talents than she retired to marry.
1949: Undertow. Woman in Hiding. 1950: Shakedown. The Sleeping City. Bright Victory (GB: Lights Out). Harvey. 1951: Reunion in Reno. You Never Can Tell (GB: You Never Know). I Want You.

DOWN, Lesley-Anne 1954–
Eye-catching, headline-snatching, dark-haired British actress, in films at 15, at first as schoolgirls, but later as hard-edged decoration in big-budget movies. With her determination to succeed, surface brightness and lack of inhibition about what she tackles, she shows every sign of becoming the Joan Collins of the 1990s and beyond. Married/divorced (2nd) director William Friedkin. A bitter custody battle over their son created many unsavoury headlines.
1969: †The Smashing Bird I Used to Know. All the Right Noises. 1970. Sin un Adios. Countess Dracula. Assault. 1972: Pope Joan. 1973: From Beyond the Grave. Scalawag. 1975: Brannigan. 1976: A Little Night Music. The Pink Panther Strikes Again. 1978: The Betsy. The One and Only Phyllis Dixey (TV). The First Great Train Robbery (US: The Great Train Robbery). 1979: Hanover Street. 1980: Roughcut. Sphinx. 1981: Offbeat. Murder is Easy (TV). 1982: The Hunchback of Notre Dame (TV). 1983: The Devil Impostor. 1984: Arch of Triumph (TV). 1985: Nomads. 1987: Scenes from the Goldmine (TV). 1988: Ladykillers (TV). Indiscreet (TV). 1989: Night Walk (TV). 1992: Antidotus. Over the Line. 1993: Feminine Touch. Death Wish V: The Face of Death. Night Trap/Mardi Gras for the Devil. 1994: Behind Closed Doors (TV). Unfaithful (TV). Munchie Strikes Back. 1996: The Secret Agent Club. Beastmaster III: The Eye of Braxus (TV). A Family of Cops (TV). 1997: Saving Grace. Meet Wally Sparks. 1998: Young Hearts Unlimited/Matchmakers Unlimited (TV). 2000: The King's Guard. The Perfect Wife.

†As Lesley Down

DOWNEY, Robert Jr 1965–
Sad-faced, dark-haired, snub-nosed, not too tall son of independent American director Robert Downey. Has often played tragic if likeable figures, such as wild youths who get hooked on drugs as well as the girl. Voted 'hottest actor of 1988' by a magazine, but his career lacked direction until chosen to play Charlie Chaplin in a 1992 biopic. That won him an Oscar nomination, but did make him a box-office force. Imprisoned for six months on drugs charges in 1997, he was jailed for a further year for probation violation in 1999.
1970: Pound. 1972: Greaser's Palace. 1976: Jive. 1980: Up the Academy. 1982: Baby It's You. 1984: Firstborn. 1985: Weird Science. To Live and Die in LA. Tuff Turf. 1986: America (completed 1982). Back to School. That's Adequate! 1987: The Pick-Up Artist. Less Than Zero. 1988: Johnny Be Good. Rented Lips. '1969'. True Believer (GB: Fighting Justice). 1989: Chances Are. Three of Hearts. 1990: Air America. Too Much Sun. 1991: Soapdish. 1992: Chaplin. 1993: The Last Party (Documentary). Short Cuts. Heart and Souls. 1994: Natural Born Killers. Only You. Hail Caesar. Luck, Trust & Ketchup (doc). 1995: Restoration. Home for the Holidays. Mr Willoughby's Christmas Tree (TV). 1996: Richard III. 1997: Hugo Pool. One Night Stand. The Gingerbread Man. Two Girls and a Guy. 1998: U.S. Marshals. In Dreams/Blue Vision. 1999: Friends & Lovers. Bowfinger. Black & White. 2000: Wonder Boys.

DOWNS, Cathy 1924–1976
A natural, fresh beauty, this brown-haired, blue-eyed American model-turned-actress was starred by John Ford in the title role of My Darling Clementine. But hers was a quiet and unassertive talent, and the rest of her career was a steady downhill slide. Married to actor Joe Kirkwood (1949 on).
1945: The Dolly Sisters. Billy Rose's Diamond Horseshoe (GB: Diamond Horseshoe). State Fair. 1946: The Dark Corner. Do You Love Me? My Darling Clementine. 1947: For You I Die. 1948: The Noose Hangs High. Panhandle. 1949: Massacre River. The Sundowners (GB: Thunder in the Dust). 1950: Short Grass. 1951: Joe Palooka in Triple Cross (GB: The Triple Cross). 1952: Gobs and Gals (GB: Cruising Casanovas). 1953: The Flaming Urge. Bandits of the West. 1955: The Phantom from 10,000 Leagues. Narcotics Squad (released 1957). The Big Tip-Off. 1956: Kentucky Rifle. The She-Creature. Oklahoma Woman. 1957: The Amazing Colossal Man. 1959: Missile to the Moon.

DOWNS, Johnny 1913–1994
Dark-haired, dapper American actor with the looks of a male model. Beginning as a child player in 'Our Gang' comedies, genial Johnny developed into an all-American jack of all trades: light leading man, light dancer, light singer and even light comedian. In the 1930s he was a staple of college comedies, in the 1940s he turned to 'B' movie musicals. He was always welcome if never dynamic. As his movie days dwindled in the 1950s, he became the star-host of a children's TV show that ran, with Downs in it, for 17 years. Latterly combined nightclub and charity work with selling real estate. He died from cancer.
1923: *The Champeen. 1925: *Circus Fever.

*The Love Bug. *Ask Grandma. *Shootin' Injuns. *Official Officers. *Boys Will Be Boys. *Better Movies. *Your Own Back Yard. *One Wild Ride. 1926: *Good Cheer. *Buried Treasure. *Monkey Business. *Baby Clothes. *Thundering Fleas. *Uncle Tom's Uncle. *The Fourth Alarm. *Shivering Spooks. *War Feathers. *Telling Whoppers. 1927: *Seeing the World. *Bring Home the Turkey. *Chicken Feed. Outlaws of Red River. Valley of the Giants. 1928: The Crowd. The Trail of '98. 1934: Babes in Toyland / March of the Wooden Soldiers. 1935: Coronado. College Scandal (GB: The Clock Strikes Eight). So Red the Rose. The Virginia Judge. 1936: *Pirate Party on Catalina Isle. The Arizona Raiders. Everybody's Old Man. College Holiday. The First Baby. Pigskin Parade (GB: The Harmony Parade). 1937: Blonde Trouble. Thrill of a Lifetime. Turn Off the Moon. Clarence. 1938: Hold That Co-Ed (GB: Hold That Girl). Swing, Sister, Swing. Hunted Men. Algiers. 1939: Bad Boy. First Offenders. Hawaiian Nights. Laugh It Off (GB: Lady Be Gay). Parents on Trial. 1940: Melody and Moonlight. I Can't Give You Anything But Love, Baby. A Child is Born. Slightly Tempted. Sing, Dance, Plenty Hot (GB: Melody Girl). 1941: All-American Co-Ed. *Let's Get Away from It All. *Penthouse Serenade. *The Singing Telegram. *I Don't Want to Set the World on Fire. *At a Little Hot Dog Stand. Honeymoon for Three. Adam Had Four Sons. Redhead. Moonlight in Hawaii. Sing Another Chorus. 1942: Freckles Comes Home. Behind the 8-Ball (GB: Off the Beaten Track). The Mad Monster. *Groom and Bored. *Kiss and Wake Up. 1943: Campus Rhythm. Adventures of the Flying Cadets (serial). Harvest Melody. 1944: Trocadero. Twilight on the Prairie. What a Man! Forever Yours / They Shall Have Faith (GB: The Right to Live). 1945: Rhapsody in Blue. 1946: The Kid from Brooklyn. 1949: Square Dance Jubilee. 1950: Hills of Oklahoma. 1953: Column South. Cruisin' Down the River. The Girls of Pleasure Island. Call Me Madam. Here Come the Girls. 1955: Battle Flame.

DRAKE, Charlie (Charles Springall) 1925–
Cherubic, pint-sized British comedian with unruly fair hair and squeaky voice, who, after years as a small-time slapstick comic, hit it big on television in the fifties and followed up his success with three popular film comedies in the early sixties. Later again proved success-ful on television but his popularity fell away

to a degree, and was not helped by a proneness to accidents.
1954: The Golden Link. 1960: Sands of the Desert. 1961: Petticoat Pirates. 1963: The Cracksman. 1967: Mister Ten Per Cent. 1974: Professor Popper's Problem (serial). 1991: Filipina Dreamgirls (TV).

DRAKE, Frances (F. Dean) 1908–2000
No wonder Peter Lorre's Gogol in Mad Love was obsessed by this New York-born beauty with chestnut-coloured hair and ever-open, slightly dismayed, mouth; few lovelier actresses graced the screen. She was raised in Canada from the age of four, but made her name as a dancer in London (where she also filmed for the first time) before becoming a star of Hollywood chillers and thrillers. At 31 she married into the English aristocracy and was seen in only two further films. Died from natural causes.
1933: †Meet My Sister. †The Jewel. 1934: The Trumpet Blows. Ladies Should Listen. Bolero. Forsaking All Others. 1935: Les Miserables. Mad Love (GB: Hands of Orlac). Without Regret. Transient Lady (GB: False Witness). 1936: The Invisible Ray. The Preview Murder Mystery. Florida Special. And Sudden Death. I'd Give My Life. 1937: Midnight Taxi. Love Under Fire. 1938: She Married an Artist. There's Always a Woman. The Lone Wolf in Paris. 1939: It's a Wonderful World. 1940: I Take This Woman. 1942: The Affairs of Martha (GB: Once Upon a Thursday).

†As Frances Dean

DRAKE, Tom
(Alfred Alderdice) 1918–1982
Slight, boyish-looking American actor with

look of innocence, cast to advantage in such 1940s' slices of Americana as Meet Me in St Louis in which, as elsewhere, he was the perennial boy-next-door. After he left MGM in 1949 his career floundered, although he kept working steadily, later in small roles in television series. Died from lung cancer.
1940: †The Howards of Virginia (GB: The Tree of Liberty). 1944: Maisie Goes To Reno (GB: You Can't Do That to Me). Marriage is a Private Affair. Two Girls and a Sailor. Mrs Parkington. Meet Me in St Louis. The White Cliffs of Dover. 1945: This Man's Navy. 1946: Faithful in My Fashion. The Green Years. Courage of Lassie. I'll Be Yours. 1947: Cass Timberlane. The Beginning or the End? 1948: The Hills of Home (GB: Master of Lassie). Alias a Gentleman. Words and Music. 1949: Mr Belvedere Goes to College. Scene of the Crime. 1950: The Great Rupert. 1951: Never Trust a Gambler. Disc Jockey. FBI Girl. 1953: Sangaree. 1955: Sudden Danger. Betrayed Women. The Man Nobody Wanted (TV). 1956: Farewell Appearance (TV). 1957: Cyclops. Date with Disaster. Raintree County. The Brotherhood of the Bell (TV). 1959: Money, Women and Guns. Warlock. 1960: The Bramble Bush. 1965: The Sandpiper. House of the Black Death. 1966: The Singing Nun. Johnny Reno. 1967: Red Tomahawk. 1968: Warkill. 1970: Echo of a Nightmare (TV). The Boy Who Stole the Elephants (TV). 1971: City Beneath The Sea (TV. GB: cinemas, as One Hour to Doomsday). 1972: The Specter of Edgar Allan Poe. 1973: Savage Abduction. 1975: A Matter of Wife and Death (TV). The Return of Joe Forrester (TV). 1976: Mayday at 40,000 Feet! (TV. GB: cinemas). ‡The Keeper.

†As Richard Alden
‡And directed

DRESSLER, Marie
(Leila von Koerber) 1869–1934
Formidable Canadian actress who took to heavyweight harridans in her forties and suddenly became America's number one box-office star in the early thirties, when she used her last two years to build up a little gallery of gargantuan – if sometimes gentle – grotesques. Academy Award for Min and Bill. Additional Oscar nomination for Emma. She died from cancer.
1914: Tillie's Punctured Romance. 1915: *Tillie's Tomato Surprise. 1917: *Tillie Wakes Up. *The Scrublady. 1918: *The Agonies of

Agnes. *The Cross Red Nurse. *Fired! 1926: The Joy Girl. 1927: Breakfast at Sunrise. The Callahans and the Murphys. 1928: The Patsy (GB: The Politic Flapper). Bringing Up Father. 1929: The Vagabond Lover. *Dangerous Females. The Divine Lady. Hollywood Revue of 1929. 1930: Chasing Rainbows. The Girl Said No. One Romantic Night. Let Us Be Gay. Caught Short. Anna Christie. Min and Bill. *The Voice of Hollywood. The Swan. The March of Time (unreleased). Call of the Flesh. Derelict. 1931: Reducing. Politics. *Jackie Cooper's Christmas (GB: The Christmas Party). 1932: Prosperity. Emma. 1933: Tugboat Annie. Dinner at Eight. The Late Christopher Bean. 1934: *Hollywood on Parade No. 13.

DREW, Ellen (Terry Ray) 1915–
Lovely American actress with dark hair, hazel eyes and classic cheekbones who decorated a wide variety of films for over 15 years before virtually leaving the cinema in 1951 when she married for the third time. She was a beauty queen who had small roles on stage before being offered a chance in films by Paramount, with whom she stayed for nine years.
1936: †Yours for the Asking. †College Holiday. †Rhythm on the Range. †The Return of Sophie Lang. †My American Wife. †Hollywood Boulevard. †Lady Be Careful. †Wives Never Know. †Murder with Pictures. †The Big Broadcast of 1937. †Rose Bowl (GB: O'Riley's Luck). 1937: †The Crime Nobody Saw. †Internes Can't Take Money (GB: You Can't Take Money). †Turn Off the Moon. †Murder Goes to College. †Night of Mystery. †Mountain Music. †This Way Please. †Hotel Haywire. †Make Way for Tomorrow. 1938: †Cocoanut Grove. †The Buccaneer. †Blue-

beard's Eighth Wife. †You and Me. †Dangerous to Know. †Scandal Street. If I Were King. Sing You Sinners. 1939: The Lady's from Kentucky. The Gracie Allen Murder Case. Geronimo. French without Tears. 1940: Buck Benny Rides Again. Women Without Names. Christmas in July. The Mad Doctor (GB: A Date with Destiny). 1941: The Monster and the Girl. Texas Rangers Ride Again. Caught in the Draft. Reaching for the Sun. The Parson of Panamint. Our Wife. The Night of January 16th. 1942: The Remarkable Andrew. Ice Capades Revue (GB: Rhythm Hits the Ice). My Favorite Spy. Star Spangled Rhythm. *We Refuse to Die. 1943: Night Plane from Chungking. 1944: The Imposter. Dark Mountain. That's My Baby! 1945: China Sky. Isle of the Dead. Man Alive. 1946: Sing While You Dance. Crime Doctor's Manhunt. 1947: Johnny O'Clock. The Swordsman. 1948: The Man from Colorado. 1949: The Crooked Way. 1950: The Baron of Arizona. Cargo to Capetown. Davy Crockett, Indian Scout (GB: Indian Scout). Stars in My Crown. The Great Missouri Raid. 1951: Man in the Saddle (GB: The Outcast). 1957: Outlaw's Son.

†As Terry Ray

DREYFUSS, Richard 1947–
Chubby, cocksure, curly-haired American star, reminiscent of a smaller Paul Newman (qv), who first came to prominence in the early 1970s as youngsters searching for an identity. He quickly proved himself capable of a wide range of portrayals, mostly leavened with humour, that culminated in his winning an Oscar for The Goodbye Girl. Then his appeal seemed to wane, along with his hair, in the early 1980s, until he overcame a drugs problem and reappeared in leading character roles, mostly as confident wisecrackers. Also Oscar nominated for Mr Holland's Opus.
1967: The Graduate. Valley of the Dolls. 1968: Hello Down There. The Young Runaways. 1971: Two for the Money (TV). 1973: American Graffiti. Dillinger. 1974: The Second Coming of Suzanne. The Apprenticeship of Duddy Kravitz. 1975: Jaws. Inserts. 1976: Victory at Entebbe (TV. GB: cinemas). The Sentinel. 1977: The Goodbye Girl. Close Encounters of the Third Kind. 1978: The Big Fix. 1980: The Competition. 1981: Whose Life Is It, Anyway? 1983: The Buddy System. 1986: Down and Out in Beverly Hills. Stand by Me. 1987: Tin Men. Nuts. StakeOut. 1988: Moon over Parador. 1989: Let it Ride. Always.

1990: Postcards from the Edge. Rosencrantz and Guildenstern are Dead. Once Around. 1991: What About Bob? Prisoner of Honor (cable TV/cinemas). 1993: Lost in Yonkers. Another Stakeout. 1994: The Last Word. Silent Fall. 1995: Mr. Holland's Opus. The American President. 1996: Night Falls on Manhattan. Trigger Happy/Mad Dog Time. James and the Giant Peach (voice only). 1997: Krippendorf's Tribe. Oliver Twist (TV). 1998: A Fine and Private Place. 1999: Lansky (TV). 2000: Fail Safe (TV). The Crew. The Old Man Who Read Love Stories. 2001: Cletis Tout.

DRISCOLL, Bobby 1937–1968
One of Hollywood's saddest ever case histories: an enormously successful child star, awarded a special Oscar in 1949, he was washed up at 15, on heroin and other drugs at 16 and arrested on narcotics and burglary charges in his early twenties. He died alone in an abandoned tenement from hardening of the arteries, the body being identified some months later only by its fingerprints.
1943: Lost Angel. 1944: The Sullivans. Sunday Dinner for a Soldier. Miss Susie Slagle's (released 1946). 1945: Identity Unknown. The Big Bonanza. 1946: From This Day Forward. So Goes My Love (GB: A Genius in the Family). OSS. Song of the South. 1948: If You Knew Susie. So Dear to My Heart. 1949: The Window. 1950: Treasure Island. 1951: When I Grow Up. 1952: The Happy Time. 1953: Peter Pan (voice only). 1955: The Scarlet Coat. 1958: The Party Crashers.

DRIVER, Minnie (Amelia Driver) 1970–
Fairly tall, offbeat British beauty with dimpled smile and festoons of dark, curly

hair. Also a presentable soprano singer (ironically, she had to sing badly for her 'bit' in *GoldenEye*), she was raised in England and Barbados. Her acting career was largely confined to TV sitcom until she broke spectacularly through to top stardom with a fine performance in her first leading role in *Circle of Friends*. Now busily employed in Hollywood, she can assume a very natural-sounding American accent. Academy Award nominee for *Good Will Hunting*.

1992: *God on the Rocks*. 1995: *Cruel Train* (TV). *Circle of Friends*. *GoldenEye*. *Big Night*. 1996: *Sleepers*. 1997: *Grosse Pointe Blank*. *Hard Rain*. *Good Will Hunting*. *The Governess*. 1998: *At Sachem Farm/Trade Winds*. *Princess Mononoke* (English-language version, voice only). 1999: *Tarzan* (voice only). *An Ideal Husband*. *South Park: Bigger, Longer & Uncut* (voice only). 2000: *Slow Burn*. *Return to Me*. *Beautiful*. 2001: *High Heels & Low Lifes*.

DRU, Joanne (J. LaCock) 1922–1996
Striking green-eyed American brunette with high cheekbones and sparkling smile, a former model and showgirl who came to films via her then-husband Dick Haymes, and proved most effective as decorative but resolute heroines of action films. She was in more matronly roles by the later 1950s. Married – first two of three – to Haymes (1941–1949) and John Ireland (1949–1956). Sister of actor/compere Peter Marshall (Pierre LaCock 1924–). Died from respiratory failure.

1946: *Abie's Irish Rose*. 1948: *Red River*. 1949: *She Wore a Yellow Ribbon*. *All the King's Men*. 1950: *Wagonmaster*. *711 Ocean Drive*. 1951: *Vengeance Valley*. *Mr Belvedere Rings the Bell*. 1952: *Return of the Texan*. *The Pride of St Louis*. *My Pal Gus*. 1953: *Thunder Bay*. *Forbidden*. *Outlaw Territory*. 1954: *Duffy of San Quentin* (GB: *Men Behind Bars*). *The Siege at Red River*. *Southwest Passage* (GB: *Camels West*). *Three Ring Circus*. *Day of Triumph*. 1955: *The Dark Avenger* (GB: *The Warriors*). *Sincerely Yours*. *Hell on Frisco Bay*. 1957: *Drango*. *The Blackwell Story* (TV. GB: cinemas). 1958: *The Light in the Forest*. 1959: *The Wild and the Innocent*. 1960: *September Storm*. 1965: *Sylvia*. 1980: *Super Snooper* (US: *Super Fuzz*).

DUCHOVNY, David (D. Ducovny) 1960–
Tall, lithe, light-haired, soft-spoken American actor with smooth but well-defined facial features. A latecomer to acting at 27, he made

a blink-and-you-miss-him film debut the following year, and struggled along in minor roles – apart from a well-played lead in the minor *Julia Has Two Lovers* – before underlining his liking for erotica by narrating the soft-porn series *Red Shoe Diaries* from 1992 to 1997, a number of episodes from which were sewn together for video release. This, however, was soon overtaken in popularity by another TV series, *The X-Files*, which made Duchovny a cult figure and brought him national fame and belated film stardom. Married to actress Téa Leoni, he was blinded in his right eye after a school basketball accident.

1988: *Working Girl*. 1989: *New Year's Day*. 1990: *Bad Influence*. 1991: *Julia Has Two Lovers*. *The Rapture*. *Denial/Loon*. *Don't Tell Mom the Babysitter's Dead*. 1992: *Red Shoe Diaries* (TV). *Ruby*. *Venice/Venice*. *Beethoven*. *Chaplin*. *Red Shoe Diaries 2: Double Dare* (TV). *Baby Snatcher* (TV). 1993: *Red Shoe Diaries 3: Another Woman's Lipstick* (TV). *Kalifornia*. 1994: *Red Shoe Diaries 4: Auto Erotica* (TV). *Red Shoe Diaries 5: Weekend Pass* (TV). 1995: *Red Shoe Diaries 6: How I Met My Husband* (TV). *Red Shoe Diaries 7: Burning Up* (TV). *Red Shoe Diaries 8: Night of Abandon* (TV). 1997: *Playing God*. *Red Shoe Diaries 9: Temple of Flesh* (TV). 1998: *The X-Files*. 2000: *Return to Me*.

DUDLEY-WARD, Penelope 1914–1982
Attractive brunette English actress who proved a useful, highly animated foil for some of Britain's best actors in her few 1930s and 1940s films, but did not return to films in postwar years following her marriage to director Carol Reed. Known to her friends as

Pempie, she was sometimes billed simply as Penelope Ward.

1935: *Escape Me Never*. *Moscow Nights* (US: *I Stand Condemned*). 1938: *The Citadel*. 1939: *Hell's Cargo* (US: *Dangerous Cargo*). 1940: **Dangerous Comment*. *Convoy*. *The Case of the Frightened Lady* (US: *The Frightened Lady*). 1941: *Major Barbara*. 1942: *In Which We Serve*. 1943: †*The Demi-Paradise* (US: *Adventure for Two*). 1944: *The Way Ahead*. †*English Without Tears* (US: *Her Man Gilbey*).

†As Penelope Ward

DUFF, Howard 1913–1990
Wavy-haired, worried-looking, interesting American actor who moved straight into star roles with Universal via radio success as detective Sam Spade. He was often cast as double-shaded characters who died at the end, but his film career nosedived with the end of the studio contract system. Married to Ida Lupino 1951–1968. Died from a heart attack.

1947: *Brute Force*. 1948: *The Naked City*. *All My Sons*. 1949: *Illegal Entry*. *Woman in Hiding*. *Red Canyon*. *Calamity Jane and Sam Bass*. 1950: *Spy Hunt* (GB: *Panther's Moon*). *Shakedown*. 1951: *The Lady From Texas*. *Steel Town*. 1952: *The Roar of the Crowd*. *Models Inc./Call Girl* (later and GB: *That Kind of Girl*). 1953: *Spaceways*. *Tanganyika*. *Jennifer*. 1954: *The Yellow Mountain*. *Private Hell 36*. 1955: *Women's Prison*. *Flame of the Islands*. 1956: *While the City Sleeps*. *Blackjack Ketchum, Desperado*. *The Broken Star*. 1957: *Sierra Stranger*. 1962: *Boys' Night Out*. *Le sette folgori di Assur* (GB: *Thunderbolt. US: War Gods of Babylon*). 1963: *Sardanapalus the Great*. *La congiura dei Borgia*. 1967: *Panic in the City*. 1969: *The DA: Murder One* (TV). 1970: *In Search of America* (TV). 1971: *A Little Game* (TV). 1972: *Snatched* (TV). 1973: *The Heist* (TV. GB: *Suspected Person*). 1974: *Tight As a Drum* (TV). 1977: *The Late Show*. 1978: *A Wedding*. *Battered!* (TV). *In the Glitter Palace* (TV). *Ski Lift to Death* (TV). 1979: *Kramer vs. Kramer*. *Double Negative*. *Family Secrets* (TV). *The Young Maverick* (TV). 1980: *Valentine Magic on Love Island* (TV). *Oh, God! Book II*. *Flamingo Road* (TV). 1982: *The Wild Women of Chastity Gulch* (TV). 1983: *This Girl for Hire* (TV). 1985: *Love on the Run* (TV). 1986: *Monster in the Closet*. 1987: *No Way Out*. 1989: *Settle the Score* (TV). 1990: *Too Much Sun*.

DUKE, Patty (Anna Duke) 1946–
Puffy-cheeked, light-haired American actress who won an Academy award for recreating her stage role as Helen Keller in *The Miracle Worke*r, and had her own television show at 17. After the commercial failure of *Me Natalie* in 1969, she no longer seemed a potential superstar and has been infrequently in films since, although heavily employed in TV movies. Married (third) actor John Astin and from 1973 to 1982 was billed as Patty Duke Astin. Later divorced and remarried. Battling manic depression in recent times.
1955: I'll Cry Tomorrow. 1956: Somebody Up There Likes Me. 1958: The Goddess. Country Music Holiday. 1959: Happy Anniversary. The 4-D Man. 1961: The Power and the Glory (TV. GB: cinemas). 1962: The Miracle Worker. 1965: Billie. 1966: The Daydreamer (voice only). 1967: Valley of the Dolls. 1969: Me Natalie. My Sweet Charlie (TV). 1971: Two on a Bench (TV). If Tomorrow Comes (TV). She Waits (TV). Deadly Harvest (TV). You'll Like My Mother. 1973: Nightmare (TV). 1974: Miss Kline, We Love You (TV). Hard Day at Blue Nose. 1977: Fire! (TV. GB: cinemas). Rosetti and Ryan: Men Who Love Women (TV). Look What's Happened to Rosemary's Baby (TV). The Storyteller (TV). Curse of the Black Widow (TV). 1978: The Swarm. Having Babies III (TV). Killer on Board (TV). 1979: The Miracle Worker (TV). A Family Upside Down (TV). Hanging by a Thread (TV). Before and After (TV). 1980: The Women's Room (TV). The First Nine Months are the Hardest (TV). Mom, the Wolfman and Me (TV). The Babysitter (TV). 1981: By Design. The Violation of Sarah McDavid (TV). 1982: Something So Right (TV). September Gun (TV). 1984: Best Kept Secrets (TV). 1985: A Time to Triumph (TV). 1986: Willy/Milly. 1987: Fight for Life (TV). J.J. Starbuck (TV). Fatal Judgment (TV). Perry Mason: The Case of the Avenging Ace (TV). 1989: The Hitchhikers. Everybody's Baby: The Rescue of Jessica McClure (TV). Amityville: The Evil Escapes (TV). 1990: Call Me Anna (TV). Always Remember I Love You (TV). 1991: Absolute Strangers (TV). 1992: Prelude to a Kiss. Last Wish (TV). Passport to Murder (TV). Grave Secrets: The Legacy of Hilltop Drive (TV). 1993: Final Justice (TV). 1994: Touch of Truth (TV). No Child of Mine (TV). 1995: When the Vows Break (TV). Courting Justice (TV). 1996: To Face Her Past (TV). Harvest of Fire (TV). Race Against Time: The Search for Sarah (TV). 1997: The Disappearing Act (TV). A Christmas Memory (TV). 1998: When He Didn't Come Home (TV). 1999: Still Rockin' in Brooklyn Heights (TV). A Season for Miracles (TV).

DULLEA, Keir 1936–
Lean, good-looking, pale-eyed American leading man, reminiscent of Tab Hunter (*qv*), but generally in more cerebral roles. After a very bright start, his roles have too often seemed ordinary and routine, and his performances have lacked the intensity of earlier years.
1959: Mrs Miniver (TV). 1961: The Hoodlum Priest. 1962: David and Lisa. 1963: Mail Order Bride (GB: West of Montana). 1964: The Thin Red Line. The Naked Hours. 1965: Bunny Lake is Missing. Madame X. 1967: The Fox. 1968: 2001: a Space Odyssey. 1969: De Sade. Black Water Gold (TV). 1972: Paperback Hero. 1973: Il diavolo nel cervello. Last of the Big Guns. 1974: Paul and Michelle. Black Christmas. 1976: Law and Order (TV). Full Circle (US: The Haunting of Julia). 1977: Welcome to Blood City. Leopard in the Snow. 1978: Because He's My Friend (later Love Under Pressure). 1979: The Legend of the Golden Gun (TV). 1980: The Hostage Tower. Brave New World (TV). The Invasion (and other Earthship Ark 'films' originally seen on TV). 1981: No Place to Hide (TV). 1982: The Next One. Brainwaves. 1983: Blind Date. 1984: 2010. 1993: Oh, What a Night. 2000: The Audrey Hepburn Story (TV). Songs in Ordinary Time (TV).

DUNA, Steffi
See CARROLL, John
and O'KEEFE, Dennis

DUNAWAY, Faye
(Dorothy F. Dunaway) 1941–
Blonde American actress with childlike face, horsey smile and purposeful air, not unlike Jane Fonda in acting approach and subsurface smoulder. It's noticeable that both have been successful as gutsy women of pioneer days. Both are also Oscar-winners, Ms (impossible to think of Faye as Miss) Dunaway for her foul-mouthed TV executive in *Network*. Also Oscar-nominated for *Bonnie and Clyde* and *Chinatown*.
1966: The Happening. Hurry Sundown. 1967: Bonnie and Clyde. 1968: The Extraordinary Seaman. The Thomas Crown Affair. Amanti (GB and US: A Place for Lovers). 1969: The Arrangement. 1970: Little Big Man. Puzzle of a Downfall Child. 1971: Doc. The Deadly Trap. 1972: The Woman I Love (TV). 1973: Oklahoma Crude. The Three Musketeers. 1974: The Towering Inferno. The Four Musketeers. Chinatown. 1975: Three Days of the Condor. 1976: The Disappearance of Aimée (TV). Voyage of the Damned. Network. 1978: Eyes of Laura Mars. The Champ. 1979: Arthur Miller – on Home Ground. 1980: The First Deadly Sin. 1981: Mommie Dearest. Evita Peron (TV). 1983: The Wicked Lady. Supergirl. 1984: Ellis Island (TV mini-series shortened for cinemas). Ordeal by Innocence. 1985: Thirteen at Dinner (TV). 1986: Beverly Hills Madam (TV). 1987: Barfly. Casanova (TV). Raspberry Ripple (TV). Midnight Crossing. 1988: Burning Secret. The Match (released 1991 as The Gamble). 1989: Helmut Newton: Frames from the Edge. Wait Until Spring, Bandini. On a Moonlit Night. Cold Sassy Tree (TV). 1990: The Handmaid's Tale. 1991: Scorchers. Silhouette (TV). 1992: Arizona Dream (released 1995). The Temp. 1993: Columbo – It's All in the Game (TV). Double Edge. 1994: Strictly Business. A Family Divided (TV). 1995: Don Juan de Marco. Drunks. Dunston Checks In. 1996: Albino Alligator. The Chamber. The Twilight of the Golds. The People Next Door (TV). 1997: En brazos de la mujer madura. The New Blonde. 1998: Gia (cable TV). A Will of Their Own (TV). 1999: The Thomas Crown Affair (remake). Joan of Arc/The Messenger: The Story of Joan of Arc. 2000: Stanley's Gig. The Yards. Washington Slept Here (TV).

DUNST, Kirsten 1982–
Tall, slim, light-haired, impish-looking American child player now graduating to

adult roles. A child model, she began acting at seven, but it was her role as the strange 12-year-old girl in *Interview With the Vampire* that brought her name to the fore. Her distinctively cutting tones were heard in a star role for the first time in the undervalued satire *Drop Dead Gorgeous*. Known to her friends as Kiki.

1989: New York Stories. High Strung (released 1994). 1990: The Bonfire of the Vanities. 1993: Darkness Before Dawn (TV). 1994: Interview With the Vampire. Little Women. Greedy. 1995: Jumanji. Nothing But Sun (TV. Voice only). 1996: Mother Night. Ruby Ridge: An American Tragedy (TV. GB: The Siege of Ruby Ridge). 1997: Wag the Dog. Tower of Terror (TV). Anastasia (voice only). True Heart. 1998: Small Soldiers. Strike!/ The Hairy Bird. Kiki's Delivery Service (Voice only. US version of 1989 Japanese animated feature). Fifteen and Pregnant (TV). The Animated Adventures of Tom Sawyer (cable TV. Voice only). 1999: Dick. Drop Dead Gorgeous. The Virgin Suicides. The Devil's Arithmetic (cable TV). 2000: The Crow III: Salvation. Deeply. Bring It On. All Forgotten. Luckytown. 2001: Getting over Allison.

DUNN, James 1901–1967
Genial, smooth-faced Hollywood actor of Irish extraction, a lightweight Pat O'Brien who always looked older than his years. Made a sensational debut, played beautifully opposite Shirley Temple and won an Academy Award for *A Tree Grows in Brooklyn*. But there was an awful lot of dross, even after the Oscar. Died after a stomach operation. Married (second of three) to Frances Gifford (*qv*) from 1938 to 1941.

1931: Bad Girl. Sob Sister (GB: The Blonde Reporter). Over the Hill. 1932: Society Girl. Dance Team. Handle with Care. 1933: Hello, Sister! The Girl in 419. Hold Me Tight. Sailor's Luck. Jimmy and Sally. Take a Chance. Arizona to Broadway. 1934: Hold That Girl! Have a Heart. Change of Heart. Stand Up and Cheer. Baby Take a Bow. 365 Nights in Hollywood. Bright Eyes. She Learned About Sailors. 1935: George White's 1935 Scandals. The Pay-Off. Welcome Home. The Daring Young Man. Bad Boy. 1936: Hearts in Bondage. Don't Get Personal. Come Closer, Folks. Two-Fisted Gentleman. 1937: Mysterious Crossing. Living on Love. We Have Our Moments. Venus Makes Trouble. 1938: Shadows Over Shanghai. 1939: Pride of the Navy. Mercy Plane (GB: Wonder Plane).

1940: Son of the Navy. Hold That Woman. A Fugitive from Justice. 1942: The Living Ghost (GB: Lend Me Your Ear). 1943: The Ghost and the Guest. Government Girl. 1944: Leave It to the Irish. A Tree Grows in Brooklyn. 1945: The Caribbean Mystery. 1946: That Brennan Girl. 1947: Killer McCoy. 1948: Texas, Brooklyn and Heaven (GB: The Girl from Texas). 1950: The Golden Gloves Story. 1951: A Wonderful Life. 1960: The Bramble Bush. Journey to the Day (TV). 1962: The Nine Lives of Elfego Baca (TV. GB: cinemas). Hemingway's Adventures of a Young Man (GB: Adventures of a Young Man). Six Gun Law (TV. GB: cinemas). 1966: The Oscar. 1967: The Movie Maker (TV). 1968: Shadow over Elveron (TV).

DUNNE, Irene (I. Dunn) 1898–1990
Ladylike but spunky leading actress, one of Hollywood's brightest stars in the thirties and early forties. Trained as a singer, she came to straight acting with sound, and proved capable of conveying a wide range of moods, from soapy melodrama to lunatic comedy. One of those careers that was unlucky not to have had an Oscar in it along the way: she was nominated five times (*Cimarron, Theodora Goes Wild, The Awful Truth, Love Affair, I Remember Mama*) but never won. Died from heart failure.

*1930: Leathernecking (GB: Present Arms). 1931: Consolation Marriage (GB: Married in Haste). Cimarron. Bachelor Apartment. The Great Lover. 1932: Symphony of Six Million (GB: Melody of Life). Thirteen Women. *The Stolen Jools (GB: The Slippery Pearls). Back Street. 1933: The Secret of Madame Blanche. No Other Woman. The Silver Cord. Ann Vickers. If I Were Free (GB: Behold We Live). 1934: This Man is Mine. Stingaree. The Age of Innocence. 1935: Magnificent Obsession. Sweet Adeline. Roberta. 1936: Show Boat. Theodora Goes Wild. 1937: High, Wide and Handsome. The Awful Truth. 1938: Joy of Living. 1939: Invitation to Happiness. Love Affair. When Tomorrow Comes. 1940: My Favorite Wife. 1941: Penny Serenade. Unfinished Business. 1942: Lady in a Jam. 1943: *Show Business at War. A Guy Named Joe. 1944: Together Again. The White Cliffs of Dover. 1945: Over 21. 1946: Anna and the King of Siam. 1947: Life with Father. 1948: I Remember Mama. 1950: Never a Dull Moment. The Mudlark. 1952: It Grows on Trees.*

DUPREZ, June 1918–1984
Lovely, dark-haired British leading lady who sprang to prominence as Ethne in the 1939 version of *The Four Feathers*. After *The Thief of Bagdad*, also for Alexander Korda, she stayed in Hollywood and made a few more films there before retiring to marry. Daughter of character actor Fred Duprez (1884–1938). Died in her sleep. Some sources suggest she may have been an extra in the 1976 film *The Last Tycoon*.

*1935: The Amateur Gentleman. 1936: The Crimson Circle. The Cardinal. 1939: The Spy in Black (US: U-Boat 29). The Four Feathers. The Lion Has Wings. 1940: The Thief of Bagdad. 1941: Don Winslow of the Coast Guard (serial). 1942: *White House of Hollywood. Little Tokyo USA. They Raid by Night. 1943: Forever and A Day. Tiger Fangs. 1944: None but the Lonely Heart. 1945: The Brighton Strangler. And Then There Were None (GB: Ten Little Niggers). Calcutta. 1946: That Brennan Girl. 1961: The Kinsey Report.*

DURANTE, Jimmy 'Schnozzle'
1893–1980
Big-nosed, gravel-voiced, language-mangling, piano-playing American comedian with a unique repertoire of inspired comic songs. Under contract to M-G-M for many years, but the studio never really projected his personality properly, and he remained at his best in solo spots, night clubs and records. Died from pneumonia.

*1930: Roadhouse Nights. 1931: The Cuban Love Song. The New Adventures of Get-Rich Quick Wallingford. 1932: The Wet Parade. The Passionate Plumber. The Phantom President. Speak Easily. *Hollywood on Parade*

*B-3. Blondie of the Follies. 1933: Hell Below. What! No Beer? Meet the Baron. Broadway to Hollywood (GB: Ring Up the Curtain). 1934: George White's Scandals. She Learned About Sailors. Hollywood Party. Strictly Dynamite. Palooka (GB: The Great Schnozzle). Student Tour. Carnival (GB: Carnival Nights). *Screen Snapshots No. 5. 1936: Land Without Music (US: Forbidden Music). Sally, Irene and Mary. 1938: Start Cheering. Little Miss Broadway. 1940: Melody Ranch. 1941: *Variety Reel. You're in the Army Now. The Man Who Came to Dinner. 1944: Two Girls and a Sailor. Music for Millions. 1946: Two Sisters from Boston. 1947: It Happened in Brooklyn. This Time for Keeps. 1948: On an Island with You. 1950: The Milkman. The Great Rupert. 1957: Beau James. 1960: Pepe. 1961: Il giudizio universale (US: The Last Judgment). 1962: Billy Rose's Jumbo (GB: Jumbo). 1963: It's a Mad, Mad, Mad, Mad World.*

DURBIN, Deanna

(Edna May Durbin) 1921–

Auburn-haired, blue-eyed, oval-faced Canadian songstress with fresh, natural appeal who, almost single-handed, kept her studio (Universal) financially afloat with her appealing charms and lilting soprano until Abbott and Costello came along a few years later. Special Academy Award 1938. Married (third of three) French director Charles David in 1950 and retired to live in France.

*1936: *Every Sunday. Three Smart Girls. 1937: One Hundred Men and a Girl. 1938: That Certain Age. Mad About Music. 1939: Three Smart Girls Grow Up. First Love. 1940: Spring Parade. It's a Date. 1941: *Variety Reel. Nice Girl? It Started with Eve. 1943: The Amazing Mrs Holliday. Hers to Hold. His Butler's Sister. 1944: Christmas Holiday. *The Shining Future. Can't Help Singing. 1945: Lady on a Train. Because of Him. 1946: I'll Be Yours. 1947: Something in the Wind. 1948: Up in Central Park. For the Love of Mary.*

DURYEA, Dan 1907–1968

Tall, fair-haired, lean, laconic, mean-looking American actor who came late to films but quickly made himself a fixture. He was one of the cinema's finest purveyors of nastiness: his villains were vindictive and even his heroes were unscrupulous. Briefly in star roles at the end of the forties, but later mostly as western bad guys with a whining, wheedling charm. Starred in more than 50 episodes of the TV

series *China Smith* from 1952 to 1955. He died from cancer.

1941: The Little Foxes. Ball of Fire. 1942: That Other Woman. The Pride of the Yankees. 1943: Sahara. Ministry of Fear. 1944: Mrs Parkington. None But the Lonely Heart. The Woman in the Window. Main Street After Dark. Man from Frisco. 1945: Scarlet Street. Lady on a Train. Along Came Jones. The Great Flamarion. Valley of Decision. 1946: Black Angel. White Tie and Tails. 1948: Black Bart (GB: Black Bart Highwayman). River Lady. Larceny. Another Part of the Forest. 1949: Criss Cross. Too Late for Tears. Manhandled. Johnny Stool Pigeon. 1950: One Way Street. Winchester 73. The Underworld Story. 1951: Chicago Calling. Al Jennings of Oklahoma. 1953: Sky Commando. Thunder Bay. Ride Clear of Diablo. 1954: World for Ransom. 36 Hours (US: Terror Street). Rails into Laramie. Silver Lode. This is My Love. 1955: Foxfire. The Marauders. Storm Fear. The Burglar. 1956: Smoke Jumpers (TV). 1957: Battle Hymn. Night Passage. Slaughter on 10th Avenue. 1958: Kathy O'. 1959: Showdown at Sandoval (TV. GB: cinemas as Gunfight at Sandoval). 1960: Platinum High School (GB: Rich, Young and Deadly). 1961: Six Black Horses. 1963: He Rides Tall. Walk a Tightrope. 1964: Taggart. Do You Know This Voice? 1965: The Bounty Killer. The Flight of the Phoenix. 1966: Incident at Phantom Hill. Un fiume di dollari (GB: The Hills Run Red). 1967: Five Golden Dragons. Stranger on the Run (TV). Winchester '73 (TV). 1968: The Bamboo Saucer/Collision Course.

DUVALL, Robert 1931–

Slight, balding, generally unsmiling, but forceful and personable American actor with

distinctive thin, outlined lips and pale blue eyes. A Korean War veteran, he turned to acting and could probably have made a lifetime career out of psychotic villains had not a desire for versatility been stronger. In leading roles – with odd little regressions to support or even unbilled guest appearances – since the early 1970s, he was nominated three times for an Academy Award (*The Godfather, Apocalypse Now, The Great Santini*) before winning the Best Actor Oscar for *Tender Mercies*. Additional Oscar nominations for *The Apostle* and *A Civil Action*.

*1960: John Brown's Raid (TV). Destiny's Tot (TV). 1962: To Kill a Mockingbird. 1963: Captain Newman MD. Nightmare in the Sun. 1964: The Inheritors (TV. Later in cinemas as Aliens from Another Planet). 1965: The Chase. 1966: Fame is the Name of the Game (TV). 1967: Cosa Nostra: An Arch Enemy of the FBI (TV. GB: cinemas). 1968: Countdown. Bullitt. The Detective. 1969: True Grit. The Rain People. M*A*S*H. 1970: Lawman. 1971: The Revolutionary. THX 1138. Tomorrow (released 1975). 1972: The Godfather. The Great Northfield Minnesota Raid. Joe Kidd. 1973: Badge 373. Lady Ice. The Outfit. 1974: The Conversation. The Godfather Part II. 1975: Breakout. The Killer Elite. 1976: Network. The Seven Per Cent Solution. The Eagle Has Landed. 1977: The Greatest. 1978: Invasion of the Body Snatchers. The Betsy. 1979: The Great Santini. Apocalypse Now. 1981: True Confessions. The Pursuit of D B Cooper. 1982: Tender Mercies. 1983: The Terry Fox Story (made for TV, but later shown in cinemas). 1984: The Natural. The Stone Boy. 1985: The Lightship. Belizaire the Cajun. 1986: Let's Get Harry. Hotel Colonial. 1988: Colors. The White Crow. 1989: Convicts. 1990: The Handmaid's Tale. A Show of Force. Days of Thunder. 1991: Rambling Rose. Newsies (GB: The News Boys). Hearts of Darkness: A Filmmaker's Apocalypse. 1992: The Plague. Stalin (TV). 1993: Falling Down. Wrestling Ernest Hemingway. Cachao. Geronimo: An American Legend. 1994: The Paper. 1995: The Stars Fell on Henrietta. The Scarlet Letter. Something to Talk About. Sling Blade. 1996: The Man Who Captured Eichmann (TV). 1997: The Apostle. The Gingerbread Man. 1998: A Civil Action. Deep Impact. 2000: Road to Glory/The Cup. Gone in Sixty Seconds. On the Sixth Day. 2001: John Q.*

As director: *1974: We're Not the Jet Set. 1983: Angelo My Love.*

DUVALL, Shelley 1949–

Very thin, dark-haired American actress with huge, brown, bird-like eyes, long thin nose and thick, if attractive, lips: as one might expect, she is good at nervousness and insecurity. Chiefly seen in films by Robert Altman, and especially good in his *Three Women*. Perfectly cast as Olive Oyl in *Popeye*, but too little seen since that film was made in 1980. Became a powerful TV producer in the late 1980s. Returned to acting in the 1990s in a mixture of waspish and mumsy roles.

1970: Brewster McCloud. 1971: McCabe and Mrs Miller. 1974: Thieves Like Us. Un Homme qui dort (voice only). 1975: Nashville. 1976: Buffalo Bill and the Indians, or: Sitting Bull's History Lesson. Bernice Bobs Her Hair.

1977: *Annie Hall*. *Three Women*. 1980: *The Shining*. *Popeye*. 1981: *Time Bandits*. 1984: **Frankenweenie*. 1985: *Annie Oakley* (TV. Narrator only). 1987: *Roxanne*. 1990: *Mother Goose Rock 'n' Rhyme* (TV). 1991: *Suburban Commando*. *Frogs!* (TV). 1995: *The Underneath*. 1996: *The Portrait of a Lady*. *Changing Habits*. 1997: *Rocket Man*. *The Twilight of the Ice Nymphs*. *Shadow Zone: My Teacher Ate My Homework* (TV). *Gay Maddin: Waiting for Twilight* (doc). *Space Cadet*. *Talos the Mummy*. 1998: *Casper Meets Wendy* (TV). *Teen Monster* (TV). 1999: *The 4th Floor*. 2000: *Dreams in the Attic*.

DVORAK, Ann (Anna McKim) 1911–1979 Brunette (later blonde) American actress, daughter of silent actress Anna Lehr. Her prominent nose and slanty green eyes may have been the cause of her getting cast so often (after a brilliant early performance in *Scarface*) in sluttish or spiteful parts. But her career was not helped by her fight with Warners over better roles. Married (first of three) to British-born actor-director Leslie Fenton from 1932 to 1946; she came to Britain with him in the 1940s, made a few films there, and drove an ambulance during the war.

1916: †*Ramona*. 1920: †*The Five Dollar Plate*. 1929: *The Hollywood Revue of 1929*. 1930: *Free and Easy*. *Love in the Rough*. *Way Out West*. *Lord Byron of Broadway* (GB: *What Price Melody?*). 1931: *Son of India*. *Susan Lenox, Her Fall and Rise* (GB: *The Rise of Helga*). *The Guardsman*. *Just a Gigolo* (GB: *The Dancing Partner*). *Politics*. *This Modern Age*. *Dance, Fools, Dance*. *La Sevillana*. 1932: *Sky Devils*. *The Crowd Roars*. *The Strange Love of Molly Louvain*. *Love is a Rocket*. *Scarface*. *Stranger in Town*. *Three on a Match*. *Crooner*. 1933: *The Way to Love*. *College Coach* (GB: *Football Coach*). 1934: *Heat Lightning*. *Massacre*. *Side Streets* (GB: *Woman in Her Thirties*). *Friends of Mr Sweeney*. *Midnight Alibi*. *Housewife*. *I Sell Anything*. *Gentlemen Are Born*. *Murder in the Clouds*. 1935: *Sweet Music*. '*G' Men*. **A Trip thru a Hollywood Studio*. *Bright Lights* (GB: *Funnyface*). *Folies Bergère de Paris* (GB: *The Man from Folies Bergère*). *Dr Socrates*. *Thanks a Million*. 1936: *We Who Are About to Die*. 1937: *Racing Lady*. *Midnight Court*. *Manhattan Merry-Go-Round* (GB: *Manhattan Music Box*). *The Case of the Stuttering Bishop*. *She's No Lady*. 1938: *Merrily We Live*. *Gangs of New York*. 1939: *Blind Alley*. *Café Hostess* (GB: *Street of Missing Women*). *Stronger than Desire*. 1940: *Girls of the Road*. 1941: *Don Winslow of the Navy* (serial). *This Was Paris*. 1942: *Squadron Leader X*. 1943: *Escape to Danger*. *There's a Future in It*. 1945: *Flame of the Barbary Coast*. *Masquerade in Mexico*. *Abilene Town*. 1946: *The Bachelor's Daughters* (GB: *Bachelor Girls*). 1947: *The Long Night*. *The Private Affairs of Bel Ami*. *Out of the Blue*. 1948: *The Walls of Jericho*. 1950: *A Life of Her Own*. *Mrs O'Malley and Mr Malone*. *Our Very Own*. *The Return of Jesse James*. 1951: *The Secret of Convict Lake*. *I Was an American Spy*.

†*As Baby Anna Lehr*

E

Impact. 1984: City Heat. Tightrope. 1985: Pale Rider. 1986: Heartbreak Ridge. 1988: The Dead Pool. 1989: Pink Cadillac. 1990: White Hunter, Black Heart. The Rookie. 1992: Unforgiven. 1993: A Perfect World. In the Line of Fire. 1994: Don't Pave Main Street: Carmel's Heritage (narrator only). 1995: Casper. The Bridges of Madison County. Wild Bill: Hollywood Maverick (doc). 1997: Absolute Power. 1999: True Crime. Forever Hollywood (doc). 2000: Space Cowboys.
As director: 1971: Play 'Misty' for Me. 1972: High Plains Drifter. 1973: Breezy. 1975: The Eiger Sanction. 1976: The Outlaw Josey Wales. 1977: The Gauntlet. 1980: Bronco Billy. 1982: Firefox. 1983: Honkytonk Man. Sudden Impact. 1985: Pale Rider. 1986: Heartbreak Ridge. 1988: Bird. 1990: White Hunter, Black Heart. The Rookie. 1992: Unforgiven. 1993: A Perfect World. 1995: The Bridges of Madison County. 1997: Absolute Power. 1998: Midnight in the Garden of Good and Evil. 1999: True Crime. 2000: Space Cowboys.

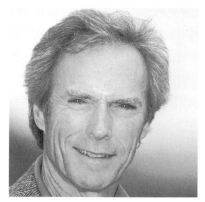

EASTWOOD, Clint 1930–

Tall, dark, tufty-haired American actor with soft, deliberate speech and slow smile who came to fame in the TV western series *Rawhide* (1958–1965), then went to Italy and gained even bigger stardom as ultra-tough, silent western heroes who blew their opponents apart at the twitch of a nostril. Back in Hollywood, he mixed westerners with equally brutish police detectives, but his ventures into direction, although erratic, revealed a more interesting, and talented, side of his nature. He won a directing Oscar for *Unforgiven*, which also gained him an Oscar nomination as best actor.
1955: *A Day in a Hollywood Star Factory. Revenge of the Creature. Francis in the Navy. Lady Godiva (GB: Lady Godiva of Coventry). Tarantula! 1956: Away all Boats. Never Say Goodbye. Star in the Dust. The First Traveling Saleslady. 1957: Escapade in Japan. Lafayette Escadrille (GB: Hell Bent for Glory). 1958: Ambush at Cimarron Pass. 1964: A Fistful of Dollars. 1965: For a Few Dollars More. 1966: The Good, the Bad and the Ugly. The Witches. 1967: Hang 'Em High. 1968: Coogan's Bluff. Where Eagles Dare. 1969: Paint Your Wagon. Two Mules for Sister Sara. 1970: Kelly's Heroes. The Beguiled. 1971: Dirty Harry. Play 'Misty' for Me. 1972: Joe Kidd. High Plains Drifter. 1973: Magnum Force. Breezy. 1974: Thunderbolt and Lightfoot. 1975: The Eiger Sanction. 1976: The Outlaw Josey Wales. The Enforcer. 1977: The Gauntlet. 1978: Every Which Way But Loose. 1979: Escape from Alcatraz. 1980: Bronco Billy. Any Which Way You Can. 1982: Firefox. 1983: Honkytonk Man. Sudden*

EATON, Shirley 1936–

Bright, bouncy British blonde with knowing smile, a teenage sexpot and her own best publicist. A child player, then a sexy stooge on radio at 16, she seemed to be everywhere in the 1950s, singing, dancing, panel-gaming, acting or just being interviewed. The potential to make her into a top star, though, was never quite there, and her appearances had dwindled significantly a decade on. Now best remembered as the girl covered with gold paint in the James Bond film *Goldfinger*. Her autobiography was inevitably called *Golden Girl.*
1949: No Place for Jennifer. 1950: *The Magic Chalks. 1953: A Day to Remember. You Know What Sailors Are. 1954: The Belles of St. Trinian's. Doctor in the House. 1955: The Love Match. 1956: Charley Moon. Sailor Beware! (US: Panic in the Parlor). Three Men in a Boat. 1957: Doctor at Large. Date with Disaster. The Naked Truth (US: Your Past is Showing). 1958: Carry On Sergeant. Further Up the Creek. Life is a Circus. 1959: Carry on Nurse. In the Wake of a Stranger. 1960: Carry on Constable. 1961: A Weekend with Lulu. Nearly a Nasty Accident. Dentist On the Job (US: Get On with It!). What a Carve Up! (US: Home Sweet Homicide). 1963: The Girl Hunters. 1964: Goldfinger. The Naked Brigade. 1965: Around the World Under the Sea. Ten Little Indians. 1966: The Scorpio*

Letters (TV. GB: cinemas). Eight on the Lam (GB: Eight on the Run). 1967: Sumuru (US: The 1,000,000 Eyes of Sumuru). 1968: The Blood of Fu Manchu (US: Kiss and Kill/Fu Manchu and the Kiss of Death). 1969: The Seven Men of Sumuru.

EBSEN, Buddy (Christian Ebsen) 1908–2004

Lanky, dark-haired, disgruntled-looking American actor-dancer who proved extremely tenacious career-wise after he came to Hollywood in 1935 with sister and stage partner Vilma. Specializing in 'countrified characters', Ebsen faltered after war service, then found one profitable slot after another, first playing second-fiddle to Fess Parker in the Davy Crockett series, then on TV as head of *The Beverly Hillbillies*. At 64, he found audience favour again on TV as Barnaby Jones, a sort of elderly Will Rogers type sleuth. 'On TV,' he says, 'they had fat detectives, young detectives, girl detectives – everything but old, tall detectives.' If they ever make a series about an old folks' home, the odds are that Ebsen'll be right in there.
1935: Broadway Melody of 1935. 1936: Captain January. Banjo on My Knee. Born to Dance. 1937: Broadway Melody of 1938. 1938: Yellow Jack. My Lucky Star. The Girl of the Golden West. 1939: Four Girls in White. The Kid from Texas. 1941: Parachute Battalion. They Met in Argentina. 1942: Sing Your Worries Away. 1950: Under Mexicali Stars. 1951: Silver City Bonanza. Thunder in God's Country. Rodeo King and the Senorita. Utah Wagon Train. 1954: Red Garters. Night People. Davy Crockett – King of the Wild Frontier. 1955: Davy Crockett and the River Pirates. 1956: Between Heaven and Hell. Attack! 1958: Frontier Rangers. 1959: Mission of Danger. A Trip to Paradise (TV). Free Weekend (TV). 1961: Breakfast at Tiffany's. 1962: The Interns. 1963: Mail Order Bride (GB: West of Montana). 1968: The One and Only Genuine Original Family Band. 1972: The Daughters of Joshua Cabe (TV). 1973: Horror at 37,000 Feet (TV. GB: cinemas). Tom Sawyer. The President's Plane is Missing (TV). 1976: Smash-Up on Interstate Five (TV). 1978: Leave Yesterday Behind (TV). The Critical List (TV). Final Judgment (TV. Originally material from the 'Barnaby Jones' series). 1979: The Paradise Connection (TV). 1980: Nightmare in Hawaii (TV). 1981: Fire on the Mountain (TV). The Return of the Beverly Hillbillies (TV). 1987: Stone Fox (TV). 1990: Working Trash (TV). 1993: The Beverly Hillbillies.

ECCLESTON, Christopher 1964–
Gaunt, bony-featured, broad-shouldered, jug-eared, earnest-looking British actor, often in roles of stress and anguish. After an early stage career at the Bristol Old Vic and the National Theatre, Eccleston set the tone for his cinema career as the doomed, simple-minded teenager destined to hang in *"Let Him Have It"*. Since then he's looked at ease in doom-and-gloom leading roles; smiles have been few.
1991: "Let Him Have It". 1992: Friday on My Mind. 1994: Anchoress. Shallow Grave. 1995: Hearts and Minds (TV). 1996: Jude. Death and the Compass. 1998: Elizabeth. A Price Above Rubies. 1999: Heart (completed 1997). eXistenZ. Old New Borrowed Blue (US: With or Without You). 2000: Invisible Circus. Gone in Sixty Seconds.

EDDY, Nelson 1901–1967
Very blond, square-shouldered, serious-looking American baritone who, with Jeanette MacDonald (*qv*), became the cinema's most successful singing team in a series of thirties' musicals which, despite phenomenal box-office success and public adulation, brought Eddy a critical panning for his stiff and awkward attempts at dramatic acting. Became a successful nightclub entertainer in later years, and died from a stroke shortly after a performance.
1933: Broadway to Hollywood (GB: Ring Up the Curtain). Dancing Lady. 1934: Student Tour. 1935: Naughty Marietta. 1936: Rose Marie. 1937: Maytime. Rosalie. 1938: Girl of the Golden West. Sweethearts. 1939: Let Freedom Ring. Balalaika. 1940: New Moon. Bitter Sweet. 1941: The Chocolate Soldier. 1942: I Married an Angel. 1943: The

Phantom of the Opera. 1944: Knickerbocker Holiday. 1946: Make Mine Music (voice only). 1947: Northwest Outpost (GB: End of the Rainbow).

EDEN, Barbara
(B. Moorhead, later Huffman) 1934–
Durable blonde American actress and singer with pert face and lithe, curvy figure. Had she been around a decade earlier, Universal would have welcomed her with open arms to their easterns; but in the early sixties at Fox she had difficulty establishing herself. Since then, with the help of a successful TV series – *I Dream of Jeannie* (1965–1969) – and a widening range, she clung tenaciously to her career as a leading actress, playing starring roles in TV movies and series into her early sixties. The Doris Day of TV films, she was married to actor Michael Ansara (1922–) from 1958 to 1973, the first of her three husbands.
1956: Back from Eternity. 1957: Will Success Spoil Rock Hunter? (GB: Oh! for a Man). The Wayward Girl. 1959: A Private's Affair. 1960: The Schnook (GB: Double Trouble). Twelve Hours to Kill. From the Terrace. Flaming Star. 1961: All Hands on Deck. Voyage to the Bottom of the Sea. 1962: Five Weeks in a Balloon. The Interns. Wonderful World of the Brothers Grimm. Swingin' Along (revised version of The Schnook). 1963: The Yellow Canary. 1964: The Brass Bottle. The New Interns. 7 Faces of Dr Lao. Ride the Wild Surf. The Confession (GB: TV as Quick! Let's Get Married). 1970: The Feminist and the Fuzz (TV). 1971: A Howling in the Woods (TV). 1972: The Woman Hunter (TV). 1973: Guess Who's Sleeping in My Bed (TV). 1974: The Stranger Within (TV). 1975: Let's Switch (TV). 1976: How to Break Up a Happy Divorce (TV). 1977: The Amazing Dobermans. Stonestreet (TV). 1978: Harper Valley PTA. 1979: The Girls in the Office (TV). 1981: Return of the Rebels (TV). 1983: Jaws 3-D. 1984: Chattanooga Choo Choo. 1986: I Dream of Jeannie: 15 Years Later (TV). 1987: The Stepford Children (TV). 1988: The Secret Life of Kathy McCormick (TV). 1989: Your Mother Wears Combat Boots (TV. GB: Mom's Army). Brand New Life (TV). 1990: Opposites Attract (TV). Her Wicked Ways (TV. GB: Lethal Charm). 1991: Hell Hath No Fury (TV). I Still Dream of Jeannie (TV). 1993: Visions of Murder (TV). 1994: Visions of Terror (TV). 1995: Dead Man's Island (TV). 1996: A Very Brady Sequel.

EDWARDS, Anthony 1962–
Tall American actor with thinning fair hair and slightly mopy good looks. Part of the upsurge of young Hollywood players in the early 1980s, he attracted attention as the tragic Goose in *Top Gun* but, in spite of three starring roles in a row in 1988, seemed destined for a low-key acting career until his casting as the bespectacled Dr Green in the enormously successful hospital TV series *ER*. Edwards' childhood idols were movie dancers. So far the only steps his lanky legs have danced in films are a few on the ballroom floor in *Mr North*.
1981: The Killing of Randy Webster (TV). 1982: Fast Times at Ridgemont High (GB: Fast Times). 1983: High School USA (TV). Heart Like a Wheel. 1984: Revenge of the Nerds. 1985: Going for the Gold – The Bill Johnson Story (TV). The Sure Thing. Gotcha! 1986: Top Gun. 1987: Revenge of the Nerds II: Nerds in Paradise. Summer Heat. 1988: Hawks. Mr. North. Miracle Mile. 1989: How I Got into College. 1990: El Diablo (TV). Downtown. Hometown Boy Makes Good (TV). 1991: Landslide (TV). 1992: Pet Sematary Two. Delta Heat. 1993: Sexual Healing (TV). 1994: The Client. †Charlie's Ghost (TV). ER (TV). 1998: Don't Go Breaking My Heart (US: Us Begins With You). Playing by Heart.

†And directed

EDWARDS, Henry
(Ethelbert Edwards) 1882–1952
Tall, dark, sober-faced, stalwart British leading man of silent days who also directed many of his films. He married his oft-time co-star Chrissie White (qv), and they became

Britain's most popular film couple of the silent era. After World War II, Edwards began a new career as a character actor, mostly as men of authority, but it was destined to last only a few years.

1914: A Bachelor's Love Story. *Clancarty. 1915: Alone in London. My Old Dutch. Lost and Won/Odds Against. Far from the Madding Crowd. The Man Who Stayed at Home. A Welsh Singer. 1916: Doorsteps. Grim Justice. East is East. 1917: Merely Mrs Stubbs. The Cobweb. The Failure. Broken Threads. Nearer My God to Thee. 1918: The Touch of a Child. The Hanging Judge. *A New Version. *The Message. *Against the Grain. *Anna. *Her Savings Saved. *The Street. *The Refugee. *Tares. Towards the Light. *The Poet's Windfall. *Old Mother Hubbard. *The Inevitable. *What's the Use of Grumbling? 1919: *Broken in the Wars. The Kinsman. Possession. The City of Beautiful Nonsense. His Dearest Possession. 1920: A Temporary Vagabond. Aylwin. The Amazing Quest of Mr Ernest Bliss. John Forrest Finds Himself. 1921: The Bargain. The Lunatic at Large. 1922: Simple Simon. Tit for Tat. 1923: Lily of the Alley. Boden's Boy. The Naked Man. 1924: The World of Wonderful Reality. 1926: *Screen Magazine No. 3. The Flag Lieutenant. 1927: The Fake. Further Adventures of the Flag Lieutenant. 1928: Ein Mödel und drei Clowns. Der Faschingskönig. Indizienbeweiss. Angst. 1929: The Three Kings. Ringing the Changes. 1930: The Call of the Sea. 1931: The Girl in the Night. 1932: The Flag Lieutenant (remake). 1933: General John Regan. 1934: D'Ye Ken John Peel? (US: Captain Moonlight). The Rocks of Valpré (US: High Treason). 1937: Captain's Orders. 1940: East of Piccadilly (US: The Strangler). Spring Meeting. 1946: The Magic Bow. Green for Danger. 1947: Take My Life. 1948: Woman Hater. Oliver Twist. London Belongs to Me (US: Dulcimer Street). Quartet. The Brass Monkey (later Lucky Mascot). All Over the Town. 1949: Dear Mr Prohack. Elizabeth of Ladymead. Golden Salamander. 1950: Double Confession. Madeleine. Trio. 1951: Othello. The Rossiter Case. White Corridors. The Magic Box. The Lady with a Lamp. 1952: Never Look Back. Trent's Last Case. Something Money Can't Buy. The Long Memory.

As director: 1915: A Welsh Singer. 1916: Doorsteps. East is East. 1917: Merely Mrs Stubbs. Dick Carson Wins Through. Broken Threads. 1918: The Hanging Judge. Towards the Light. 1919: His Dearest Possession. The Kinsman. Possession. The City of Beautiful Nonsense. 1920: A Temporary Vagabond. Aylwin. The Amazing Quest of Mr Ernest Bliss. John Forrest Finds Himself. 1921: The Lunatic at Large. The Bargain. 1922: Simple Simon. Tit for Tat. 1923: Lily of the Alley. The Naked Man. Boden's Boy. 1924: The World of Wonderful Reality. 1925: King of the Castle. A Girl of London. One Colombo Night. 1926: The Island of Despair. 1931: The Girl in the Night. Stranglehold. 1932: Brother Alfred. The Flag Lieutenant. The Barton Mystery. 1933: General John Regan. 1934: The Man Who Changed His Name. The Lash. Lord Edgware Dies. Are You a Mason? 1935: The Lad. Vintage Wine. Squibs. Scrooge. The Private Secretary. 1936: Eliza Comes to Stay. In the

Soup. Juggernaut. 1937: Beauty and the Barge. The Vicar of Bray. Song of the Forge.

EDWARDS, Jimmy 1920–1988
Bluff, hearty British comedian with large round face and handlebar moustache, immensely successful on post-war radio after leaving the RAF with the Distinguished Flying Cross. A bombastic stand-up funnyman, in the character of a hectoring schoolmaster ('Wake up at the back there'), he was heard at his best in radio's long-running Take It from Here, followed later by his portrait of the headmaster of Chiselbury School in Whack-O! Films could not cope with his explosive style, but there were some barnstorming latter-day performances, full of ad-libs, for theatre audiences to relish. Died from bronchial pneumonia.

1948: Trouble in the Air. 1949: Murder at the Windmill (US: Murder at the Burlesque). Helter Skelter. 1952: Treasure Hunt. *Sport and Speed. 1953: Innocents in Paris. 1955: An Alligator Named Daisy. 1956: Three Men in a Boat. 1959: Bottoms Up! 1961: Nearly a Nasty Accident. 1967: The Plank. A Ghost of a Chance. 1968: Lionheart. 1969: The Bed Sitting Room. 1970: Rhubarb. 1971: The Magnificent Six and a Half (3rd series). 1972: Anoop and the Elephant.

EDWARDS, Penny
(Millicent Edwards) 1928–1998
As pretty a prairie flower as ever rode the range, Penny Edwards languished in Roy Rogers westerns and made too few films. The blonde American actress and singer was in the Ziegfeld Follies at 12 and films at 19. Fox made a brief attempt to build her into a bigger star, but nothing much seemed to happen.

Her daughter is actress Deborah Winters, who inherited her mother's precocity by marrying at 15. Died from lung cancer two days after her 70th birthday.

1943: *When It Rains. 1947: That Hagen Girl. My Wild Irish Rose. 1948: Adventures of Don Juan (GB: The New Adventures of Don Juan). Two Guys from Texas (GB: Two Texas Knights). Feudin', Fussin' and a Fightin'. 1949: Tucson. 1950: Sunset in the West. North of the Great Divide. Trail of Robin Hood. 1951: Havana Rose. Spoilers of the Plains. Heart of the Rockies. In Old Amarillo. Utah Wagon Train. Missing Women. The Wild Blue Yonder (GB: Thunder Across the Pacific). Million Dollar Pursuit. Street Bandits. 1952: Captive of Billy the Kid. Pony Soldier (GB: MacDonald of the Canadian Mounties). Woman in the Dark. 1953: Powder River. 1957: Ride a Violent Mile. The Dalton Girls. Johnny Bravo (TV. GB: cinemas). The Travellers (TV. GB: cinemas).

EDWARDS, Vince
(Vincento Eduardo Zoino) 1926–1996
Dark, squarely built, thick-haired, slightly soulful-looking American actor who was an Olympic swimming prospect before taking acting lessons in such distinguished company as Grace Kelly, John Cassavetes and Anne Bancroft. His immobile features often got him cast in faintly dangerous roles before success in the title role of television's Ben Casey gave him a softer image and a pin-up's mail-bag. He made films only inconsistently (his main body of work has been for TV), but also had talents as a singer and a photographer. In later years, he complained friends had shunned him because he had gambled away a fortune. Died from pancreatic cancer.
1951: Mr Universe. Sailor Beware. 1952: Hiawatha. 1954: Rogue Cop. 1955: The Night Holds Terror. 1956: The Killing. Serenade. Cell 2455 Death Row. Hit and Run. 1957: The Hired Gun. 1958: Island Women. Ride Out for Revenge. 1959: City of Fear. Murder by Contract. The Scavengers. 1961: The Outsider. 1963: The Victors. 1967: The Devil's Brigade. 1968: Hammerhead. The Marauders (TV). 1969: The Desperados. 1970: Sole Survivor (TV). Dial Hot Line (TV). 1971: Do Not Fold, Spindle or Mutilate (TV). 1972: The Mad Bomber. 1973: Firehouse (TV). 1974: The Police Connection. 1975: Death Stalk (TV). 1977: Cover Girls (TV). 1978: The Courage and the Passion (TV). A Chance to Live (TV). 1981: The Seduction. Knight Rider

(TV). 1983: Space Raiders. 1984: Texas Sno-Line. 1985: The Fix (filmed in 1983 as The Agitators). 1986: Vasectomy, a Delicate Matter. The Return of Mike Hammer (TV). 1987: Return to Horror High. The Dirty Dozen: The Deadly Mission (TV). 1988: Cellar Dweller. The Return of Ben Casey (TV). 1989: The Gumshoe Kid. 1990: Original Intent (released 1992). Dillinger (TV). 1994: Jailbreakers (cable TV). 1995: The Fear.
As co-director: 1979: Mission Galactica – the Cylon Attack (TV. GB: cinemas).

EGAN, Richard 1921–1987
Big, beefy, American leading man with square face and wide, white-toothed smile. At one time spoken of as a successor to Clark Gable but, although he was popular in rugged roles after a good performance in *Split Second*, there was nothing to suggest that Egan possessed Gable's gift for comedy or, indeed, his range, and he slid rapidly into television after the late fifties. Died from prostate cancer.
1949: The Story of Molly X. 1950: Return of the Frontiersman. The Good Humor Man. The Damned Don't Cry. The Killer That Stalked New York (GB: The Frightened City). Wyoming Mail. Kansas Raiders. Undercover Girl. Bright Victory (GB: Lights Out). 1951: Hollywood Story. Up Front. The Golden Horde (GB: The Golden Horde of Genghis Khan). Highway 301. Flame of Araby. 1952: The Battle at Apache Pass. The Devil Makes Three. One Minute to Zero. Cripple Creek. Blackbeard the Pirate. 1953: Split Second. The Glory Brigade. Wicked Woman. The Kid from Left Field. 1954: Gog. Demetrius and the Gladiators. Khyber Patrol. Underwater. 1955: Untamed. Violent Saturday. Seven Cities of Gold. The View from Pompey's Head (GB: Secret Interlude). 1956: The Revolt of Mamie Stover. Love Me Tender. Tension at Table Rock. 1957: Slaughter on 10th Avenue. 1958: These Thousand Hills. Voice in the Mirror. The Hunters. 1959: A Summer Place. 1960: Pollyanna. Esther and the King. 1962: The 300 Spartans. This Rugged Land (TV. GB: cinemas). 1964: Fanfare for a Death Scene (TV). 1966: The Destructors. 1967: Valley of Mystery. 1968: Chubasco. 1969: The Big Cube. 1970: The Day of the Wolves. Moonfire. The House That Would Not Die (TV). 1973: Shoot-Out in a One Dog Town (TV). 1976: Throw Out the Anchor (TV). 1977: The Amsterdam Kill. Kino, the Padre on Horseback. 1978: Ravagers. The Sweet Creek County War.

EGE, Julie 1943–
Shapely, sultry, tawny-haired, Norwegian pin-up girl who decorated the pages of many British newspapers and magazines in various states of undress before bringing her charms to the cinema. A leading role in *Creatures the World Forgot* revealed her acting as too awkward to make her a second Raquel Welch (*qv*), and she moved to decoration in comedies. Eventually she quit acting and became a nurse, but still has a cult following.
1967: Himmel og hav. Robbery. 1969: On Her Majesty's Secret Service. 1970: Every Home Should Have One (US: Think Dirty). Creatures the World Forgot. 1971: Up Pompeii. Rentadick. The Magnificent Seven Deadly Sins. 1972: The Alf Garnett Saga. Go for a Take. Not Now Darling. 1973: The Final Programme (US: The Last Days of Man on Earth). Craze. Kanarifuglen. 1974: Percy's Progress. The Amorous Milkman. The Legend of the Seven Golden Vampires. The Mutations. 1975: Bortreist på ubesemst tid. Den siste flexnes. 1976: Sherlock Jones. Sekretaerena som forsuant. 1988: Fengslender dager for Christina Berg.

EGGAR, Samantha
(Victoria S. Eggar) 1938–
Pretty, chestnut-haired British leading lady of natural, 'outdoor' appeal. Reminiscent of America's Katharine Ross (*qv*), she was mainly seen as resourceful heroines, especially in her earlier days. It's difficult to analyse why she did not progress further up the ladder to international stardom; some of her later performances perhaps reflect her disappointment at not having achieved this, as she mingled TV drama 'guest' spots with some often bizarre motion pictures. Oscar-nominated for *The Collector*.
1961: The Wild and the Willing. 1962: Dr Crippen. 1963: Doctor in Distress. Psyche 59. 1965: Return from the Ashes. The Collector. 1966: Walk Don't Run. 1967: Doctor Dolittle. 1968: The Molly Maguires. 1970: The Walking Stick. The Lady in the Car with Glasses and a Gun. 1971: L'etrusco uccide ancora (US: The Dead Are Alive). The Light at the Edge of the World. 1973: Double Indemnity (TV). A Name for Evil (completed 1970). 1974: All the Kind Strangers (TV). Help on My Terms (TV). 1976: The Seven-Per-Cent Solution. The Killer Who Wouldn't Die (TV). Why Shoot the Teacher? 1977: The Uncanny. Welcome to Blood City. Il grande attacca (US: The Biggest Battle). 1978: Ziegfeld: The Man and His Women (TV). 1979: Hagen (TV). The Brood. Unknown Powers. 1980: The Exterminator. Macabra (US: Demonoid). French Kiss. 1981: The Hot Touch. Curtains (released 1983). 1982: For the Term of His Natural Life (TV). 1986: Directed by William Wyler. 1987: Love Among Thieves (TV). Loner. 1988: Davy Crockett: Rainbow in the Thunder (TV). 1989: Ragin' Cajun (released 1991). 1990: A Ghost in Monte Carlo (TV). 1991: Round Numbers. 1992: Dark Horse. 1993: A Case for Murder (TV). Inevitable Grace. The Magic Voyage (voice only). 1996: The Phantom. 1997: Hercules (voice only). Everything to Gain (TV). 1999: The Astronaut's Wife.

EHLE, Jennifer 1969–
Light-haired, sturdily built, American-born British actress with kindly features and twinkly eyes. Capable of warm and incisive performances, she was entirely seen on television in the early part of her career, and it was that medium that gave her the breakthrough role as Elizabeth Bennet in a series of *Pride and Prejudice*. Daughter of actress Rosemary Harris.
1993: BackBeat. 1997: Wilde. Paradise Road. 1998: Bedrooms & Hallways. A Good Baby. 1999: This Year's Love. Sunshine/The Taste of Sunshine.

EILERS, Sally
(Dorothea Sallye Eilers) 1908–1978
Brunette (blonde from late 1931 on) American actress of Jewish-Irish ancestry who entered Hollywood with schoolfriend Carole Lombard, and led just as active a social life. On screen, she was alternatively seen in romantic or vampish roles. Beset by illness in

later years. Married (first and second of four) to western star Hoot Gibson (1930–1933) and producer Harry Joe Brown (1933–1943). Died from a heart attack.

1927: *The Campus Vamp. *Matchmaking Mammas. Sunrise. Paid to Love. The Red Mill. Slightly Used. 1928: *Johnny of the USA. The Crowd. Cradle Snatchers. Dry Martini. Broadway Daddies (GB: Girl of the Night). The Good-Bye Kiss. 1929: Broadway Babies. Trial Marriage. The Show of Shows. The Long, Long Trail. Sailor's Holiday. 1930: Let Us Be Gay. She Couldn't Say No. Doughboys (GB: Forward March). Trigger Tricks. Roaring Ranch. 1931: Reducing. Quick Millions. The Black Camel. Clearing the Range. Parlor, Bedroom and Bath (GB: Romeo in Pyjamas). Bad Girl. Over the Hill. Dance Team. Holy Terror. 1932: Disorderly Conduct. Hat Check Girl (GB: Embassy Girl). Second Hand Wife (GB: The Illegal Divorce). 1933: State Fair. Made on Broadway (GB: The Girl I Made). I Spy (US: The Morning After). Sailor's Luck. Central Airport. Hold Me Tight. Walls of Gold. 1934: She Made Her Bed. Three on a Honeymoon. 1935: Carnival (GB: Carnival Nights). Pursuit. Alias Mary Dow. Remember Last Night? 1936: Strike Me Pink. Don't Get Personal. Without Orders. Florida Special. 1937: We Have Our Moments. Danger Patrol. Lady Behave. Talk of the Devil. 1938: Condemned Women. The Nurse from Brooklyn. Tarnished Angel. Everybody's Doing It. 1939: They Made Her A Spy. Full Confession. 1941: *Stars Past and Present. *Wampas Baby Stars. I Was a Prisoner on Devil's Island. 1942: *First Aid. 1944: A Wave, a Wac and a Marine. 1945: Out of the Night (GB: Strange Illusion). 1948: Coroner Creek. 1950: Stage to Tucson (GB: Lost Stage Valley).

EKBERG, Anita (Kerstin A. Ekberg) 1931–
Big, tall, sultry-looking Swedish blonde, Miss Sweden of 1951 and subsequently briefly under contract to Howard Hughes. Her buxom and well-publicized charms, during a period in which she was known as The Ice Maiden, proved top box-office from the mid 1950s to the early 1960s. Married to actors Anthony Steel (1956–1962) and Rik Van Nutter (1963–1975). Suffered from on-off weight problems in later years.
1951: Terras forster No. 5. 1953: Abbott and Costello Go to Mars. Take Me to Town. The Golden Blade. Mississippi Gambler. 1955: Blood Alley. Artists and Models. Man in the Vault. 1956: War and Peace. Hollywood or

Bust. Back from Eternity. Zarak. 1957: Interpol (US: Pick-Up Alley). Valerie. 1958: Paris Holiday. Screaming Mimi. The Man Inside. Nel segno di Roma (GB: Sign of the Gladiator). 1959: La dolce vita. Apocalisse sul fiume giallo (GB: Last Train to Shanghai. US: The Dam on the Yellow River). Le tre etcetera del colonnello. 1960: Les cocottes (GB: The Call Girl Business. US: Little Girls and High Finance). A porte chiuse (GB: Behind Closed Doors. US: Behind Locked Doors). 1961: Il giudizio universale (US: The Last Judgement). The Mongols. 1962: Boccaccio 70. 1963: Call Me Bwana. Four for Texas. 1964: L'incastro, Bianco, rosso, giallo, rosa. 1965: Das Liebeskarussel (GB and US: Who Wants to Sleep?). The Alphabet Murders. 1966: Way, Way Out, Scusi, lei e'favorevole o contrario? Come imparai ad amare le donne/Das Gewisse etwas der Frauen (GB: How I Learned to Love Women). 1967: La lunga notte di Tombstone. The Cobra. Woman Times Seven. La sfinga d'oro (GB: The Glass Sphinx). 1968: Malenka, the Vampire's Niece (US: Fangs of the Living Dead). 1969: If It's Tuesday, This Must Be Belgium. Blonde Köder für den Mörder/La morte bussa due volte. Candidate for a Killing. 1970: Il debito coniugale. Quella chiara notte d'ottobre. Il divorzio. The Clowns. 1972: Casa d'appuntamento. North-East of Seoul. La lunga cavalcada della vendetta. 1974: Das Tal der Witwen (US: Valley of the Widows). 1978: Suor omicidio (GB: The Killer Nun). 1979: Gold of the Amazon Women. 1981: Daisy Chain. 1982: Cicciabomba. 1986: Memorie di una ragazza di piacere. 1987: Intervista/The Interview. Dolce pelle di Angela. 1992: Il conte Max. Dov'era lei a quell'ora. Ambrogio. 1993: Cattive ragazze. 1996: Bambola. 1998: Le nain rouge/The Red Dwarf.

EKLAND, Britt
(Britt-Marie Ekland) 1942–
Blonde, kittenish Swedish actress, on the international scene since 1964; better known as the consort of famous men than for her acting ability, although this is not as negligible as some alleged. Her pin-up looks gained her endless newspaper coverage down the years, as well as some interesting roles. Married to Peter Sellers (qv), 1963–1968.
1962: Kort ar Sommaren. 1963: Det är Hos Mig Han Her Varit. Il commandante. Il diavolo. 1964: Carol for Another Christmas (TV). Guns at Batasi. 1965: Too Many Thieves (TV. GB: cinemas). 1966: After the

Fox. 1967: The Double Man. The Bobo. 1968: The Night They Raided Minsky's. 1969: Stiletto. Nell'anno del Signore. Machine Gun McCain. 1970: Percy (US: It's Not the Size that Counts). I cannibali/The Cannibals. Get Carter. Tinto Mara. 1971: Endless Night. Night Hair Child. A Time for Loving. 1972: Asylum. Baxter! 1973: The Wicker Man. 1974: The Man with the Golden Gun. The Ultimate Thrill (US: The Ultimate Chase). 1975: Royal Flash. 1976: High Velocity. 1977: Casanova and Co (GB: The Rise and Rise of Casanova). Slavers. 1978: King Solomon's Treasure. Ring of Passion (TV). The Great Wallendas (TV). 1980: The Monster Club. The Hostage Tower. 1981: Dark Eyes (later Satan's Mistress). Dead Wrong (TV). Greed. 1983: Erotic Images. 1984: Hellhole. 1985: Fraternity Vacation. Marbella. Love Scenes. 1987: Moon in Scorpio. 1988: Scandal. 1989: Beverly Hills Vamp. 1990: The Children. Cold Heat. 1994: The Victim.

ELLIOTT, Sam 1944–
Dark-haired, muscular American leading man with thick moustache, initially seen as faintly roguish types who came out all right in the end. Elliott constantly hovered on the fringe of stardom, despite one outstanding performance in Lifeguard, in which the vulnerability behind his chunky facade was fully exposed. He now plays leathery westerners in a variety of starring and co-starring roles. Long professionally and privately associated with Katharine Ross (qv); the couple married in 1984.
1968: The Games. 1969: Butch Cassidy and the Sundance Kid. 1970: Assault on the Wayne (TV). The Challenge (TV). 1971: Molly and Lawless John. 1972: Frogs. 1973: The Blue

Knight (TV. GB: cinemas). 1975: I Will Fight No More Forever (TV). Evel Knievel (TV). 1976: Lifeguard. 1978: The Legacy. 1979: Wild Times (TV). The Sacketts (TV). The Last Convertible (TV). 1981: Murder in Texas (TV). 1982: The Shadow Riders (TV). 1984: Mask. 1986: Houston: The Legend of Texas (TV). The Blue Lightning. 1987: Fatal Beauty. The Quick and the Dead (TV). 1988: Shakedown (GB: Blue Jean Cop). Road House. 1989: Prancer. 1990: Sibling Rivalry. 1991: Rush. Conagher (TV). 1993: Tombstone. Gettysburg. Fugitive Nights/Danger in the Desert (TV). 1994: The Desperate Trail. 1995: The Final Cut. The Ranger, the Cook and a Hole in the Sky (TV). Blue River (TV). A Woman Undone. 1996: Dog Watch. 1997: Rough Riders (TV). 1998: The Hi-Lo Country. The Big Lebowski. 1999: You Know My Name (TV). 2000: Fail Safe (TV). The Contender.

ELLIOTT, William 'Wild Bill'
(Gordon Nance) 1903–1965
Tall, taciturn western star in the William S. Hart (qv) tradition, with deep-brown voice and purposeful air. A top rodeo rider at 16, he went to Hollywood and won some good featured roles in silents. After a long career in minor and even extra roles in the early sound years, Elliott became a popular star of countless 'B' westerns before being promoted in his mid-forties to leading man in a series of surprisingly high-quality 'A' westerns in the late 1940s. He never did achieve his ambition of starring in the life story of Hart, his idol, and died from cancer at 62.
1925: †The Plastic Age. 1926: †Napoleon Junior. 1927: †The Drop Kick (GB: Glitter). †The Private Life of Helen of Troy. †The Arizona Wildcat. 1928: †Beyond London's Lights. †Valley of Hunted Men. †The Passion Song. †Restless Youth. 1929: †Broadway Scandals. 1930: †The Great Divide. †The Midnight Mystery. †Sunny. †She Couldn't Say No. *†Fast Work. 1931: †God's Gift to Women (GB: Too Many Women). †Born to Love. †Leftover Ladies (GB: Broken Links). *†What a Bozo! †City Streets. †Delicious. †Peach o' Reno. †Palmy Days. †Convicted. †The Magnificent Lie. †Reaching for the Moon. †Platinum Blonde. 1932: †Hat Check Girl (GB: Embassy Girl). Merrily We Go To Hell (GB: Merrily We Go to —). †Night After Night. †Lady with a Past (GB: My Reputation). †One Hour with You. †The Rich Are Always with Us. †Vanity Fair. †Crooner.

†Jewel Robbery. 1933: †Little Giant. †The Keyhole. †Private Detective 62. †Gold Diggers of 1933. †Dancing Lady. 1934: †Registered Nurse. †Wonder Bar. †The Case of the Howling Dog. †Dr. Monica. †Twenty Million Sweethearts. †Here Comes the Navy. †Housewife. †Desirable. †A Modern Hero. †The Secret Bride (GB: Concealment). 1935: †Broadway Hostess. †Living on Velvet. †Page Miss Glory. †Broadway Gondolier. †Dangerous. †Alibi Ike. †Devil Dogs of the Air. †I Live for Love (GB: I Live for You). †Stars over Broadway. †Gold Diggers of 1935. †Doctor Socrates. †Moonlight on the Prairie. †Go Into Your Dance. †A Night at the Ritz. †Bright Lights (GB: Funny Face). †Ceiling Zero. †The Traveling Saleslady. †While the Patient Slept. †The Woman in Red. *†Romance of the West. †The Goose and the Gander. †The Girl from 10th Avenue (GB: Men on Her Mind). †'G'Men. †Man of Iron. 1936: †The Case of the Black Cat. †The Golden Arrow. †China Clipper. †The Case of the Velvet Claws. Romance in the Air. †Trailin' West (GB: On Secret Service). †The Walking Dead. †The Singing Kid. †Bullets or Ballots. †Polo Joe. †Down the Stretch. †Two Against the World (GB: The Case of Mrs Pembrook). †The Story of Louis Pasteur. †Murder by an Aristocrat. †The Big Noise. †The Murder of Dr Harrigan. 1937: †Michael O'Halloran. †Melody for Two. †Midnight Court. †Fugitive in the Sky. †Speed to Spare. †Guns of the Pecos. †Roll Along Cowboy. †Wife, Doctor and Nurse. †Love Takes Flight. †Swing It, Professor (GB: Swing it Buddy). †Boy of the Streets. †Boots and Saddles. †You Can't Have Everything. 1938: †Tarzan's Revenge. †Valley of Hunted Men. †The Devil's Party. †Letter of Introduction. †Lady in the Morgue (GB: The Case of the Missing Blonde). †The Great Adventures of Wild Bill Hickok (serial). **Frontiers of '49. **In Early Arizona. 1939: **Overland with Kit Carson (serial). **Lone Star Pioneers (GB: Unwelcome Visitors). **The Law Comes to Texas. **The Taming of the West. **The Return of Wild Bill (GB: False Evidence). 1940: **Prairie Schooners (GB: Through the Storm). **Pioneers of the Frontier (GB: The Anchor). **The Man From Tumbleweeds. **Beyond the Sacramento (GB: Power of Justice). **Wildcat of Tucson (GB: Promise Fulfilled). 1941: **Across the Sierras (GB: Welcome Stranger). **North from the Lone Star. **Hands Across the Rockies. **King of Dodge City. **Meet Roy Rogers (short). **Roaring Frontiers. **Where Did You Get That Girl? **The Son of Davy Crockett (GB: Blue Clay). **The Return of Daniel Boone (GB: The Mayor's Nest). **Lone Star Vigilantes (GB: The Devil's Price). 1942: **The Valley of the Vanishing Men (serial). **North of the Rockies (GB: False Clues). **Bullets for Bandits. **The Devil's Trail (GB: Rogues Gallery). **Prairie Gunsmoke. **Vengeance of the West. 1943: @Calling Wild Bill Elliott. @The Man from Thunder River. @Wagon Tracks West. @Overland Mail Robbery @Bordertown Gunfighters. @Death Valley Manhunt. 1944: @Mojave Firebrand. @Tucson Raiders. @The San Antonio Kid. @Vigilantes of Dodge City. @Cheyenne Wildcat. @Marshal of Reno. @Hidden Valley Outlaws. @Sheriff of Las Vegas. 1945: @The

Great Stagecoach Robbery. @Lone Texas Ranger. @Phantom of the Plains. @Marshal of Laredo. @Colorado Pioneers. @Wagon Wheels Westward. @Bells of Rosarita. 1946: @California Gold Rush. @Sheriff of Redwood Valley. @Sun Valley Cyclone. @Conquest of Cheyenne. ‡In Old Sacramento. ‡The Plainsman and the Lady. 1947: ‡Wyoming. ‡The Fabulous Texan. 1948: ‡Old Los Angeles. ‡The Gallant Legion. ‡Hellfire. 1949: ‡The Savage Horde. ‡The Last Bandit. 1950: ‡The Showdown. 1951: @The Longhorn. 1952: @Waco (GB: The Outlaw and the Lady). @Fargo. @The Maverick. @Kansas Territory. 1953: @The Homesteaders. @Rebel City. @Topeka. 1954: @Bitter Creek. @Vigilante Terror. @The Forty-Niners. 1955: **Dial Red O. **Sudden Danger. 1956: **Calling Homicide. **Chain of Evidence. 1957: **Footsteps in the Night.

†As Gordon Elliott **As Bill Elliott
@As Wild Bill Elliott ‡As William Elliott

ELLISON, James or Jimmy
(James E. Smith) 1910–1993
Tall, dull, brown-haired American leading man, pleasant enough in routine leading roles, or as youngish western sidekicks, but never seeming to progress to very much more. It seems surprising now that he lasted over 20 years in the Hollywood mill, but in 1952 he gave up acting, apart from sporadic favours for friends, and moved into real estate. Died after breaking his neck in a fall, severing his spinal cord.
1932: Play Girl. 1934: Carolina (GB: The House of Connelly). Death on the Diamond. The Winning Ticket. *Buried Loot. 1935: Reckless. Hop-a-Long Cassidy. The Eagle's Brood. Bar 20 Rides Again. Call of the Prairie. 1936: The Leathernecks Have Landed (GB: The Marines Have Landed.) Three on the Trail. The Plainsman. Hopalong Cassidy Returns. Heart of the West. Trail Dust. Hitch Hike Lady (GB: Eventful Journey). 1937: Borderland. Annapolis Salute (GB: Salute to Romance). 23½ Hours' Leave. The Barrier. 1938: Vivacious Lady. Mother Carey's Chickens. Next Time I Marry? 1939: Zenobia (GB: Elephants Never Forget). Elsa Maxwell's Hotel for Women (GB: Hotel for Women). Fifth Avenue Girl. Almost a Gentleman (GB: Magnificent Outcast). Sorority House (GB: That Girl from College). 1940: You Can't Fool Your Wife. Anne of Windy Poplars (GB: Anne of Windy Willows).

Playgirl. 1941: Charley's Aunt (GB: Charley's American Aunt). Ice-Capades. They Met in Argentina. Lone Star Law Man. 1942: Army Surgeon. Mr District Attorney in the Carter Case (GB: The Carter Case). Careful, Soft Shoulders. The Undying Monster (GB: The Hammond Mystery). 1943: The Gang's All Here (GB: The Girls He Left Behind). Dixie Dugan. I Walked with a Zombie. That Other Woman. 1944: Lady Let's Dance. Johnny Doesn't Live Here Any More. Trocadero. 1945: Hollywood and Vine (GB: Daisy (the Dog) Goes Hollywood). 1946: GI War Brides. 1947: Calendar Girl. The Ghost Goes Wild. 1949: Last of the Wild Horses. Hostile Country. 1950: Crooked River. Marshal of Heldorado. Colorado Ranger. West of the Brazos. Fast on the Draw (later Sudden Death). I Killed Geronimo. The Texan meets Calamity Jane. Everybody's Dancin'. 1951: Texas Lawmen. Oklahoma Justice. Kentucky Jubilee. Whistling Hills. 1952: Texas City. Dead Man's Trail. The Man from the Black Hills. 1956: Ghost Town. 1962: When the Girls Take Over.

ELWES, Cary (Ivan C. Elwes) 1962–
Tall, blond British actor of smooth, upper-crust handsomeness. From an artistic family, he was born in London, but studied drama in America and made his stage debut there before returning to England. Most of his leading film roles have been bland, but he has also shown the ability to poke fun at his own image, as well as play the occasional villain. Reminiscent in looks of a young, more fair-haired Roger Moore (qv). Like Moore on TV, he would make a good 'Saint'.
1984: Another Country. Oxford Blues. 1985: The Bride. Lady Jane. 1986: Maschenka. 1987: The Princess Bride. 1989: Glory. Never on Tuesday. 1990: Days of Thunder. Leather Jackets. 1991: Hot Shots! 1992: Bram Stoker's Dracula. 1993: The Crush. Robin Hood: Men in Tights. 1994: America! The Chase. Rudyard Kipling's The Jungle Book. 1996: Twister. Martin Eden. Ivanhoe. Fields of Blood (TV). 1997: Kiss the Girls. Liar Liar. The Informant (cable TV). 1998: The Magic Sword: Quest for Camelot (voice only). The Last Child. The Pentagon Wars (cable TV). 1999: Cradle Will Rock. 2000: Shadow of the Vampire. Wish You Were Dead. Gabriel's Run.

EMERSON, Faye 1917–1983
Flamboyant, glamorous blonde American actress who came to movies ten years too late

– her natural wit and vivacity would have made her a great wisecracking girl-friend of the thirties. As it was, she was more successful in high society than on the screen, as her studio, Warners, put her into a string of unsuitable roles. But in the fifties she became a popular TV personality, being dubbed 'television's First Lady'. Died from cancer of the stomach.
1941: The Nurse's Secret. Man Power. Blues in the Night. Bad Men of Missouri. Affectionately Yours. Nine Lives Are Not Enough. Wild Bill Hickok Rides. 1942: Murder in the Big House (GB: Human Sabotage). Juke Girl. The Hard Way. Secret Enemies. Lady Gangster. 1943: The Desert Song. Destination Tokyo. Air Force. *We're in the Army Now. Find the Blackmailer. 1944: Hollywood Canteen. The Mask of Dimitrios. Between Two Worlds. The Very Thought of You. In Our Time. Uncertain Glory. Crime by Night. 1945: Hotel Berlin. Danger Signal. 1946: Nobody Lives Forever. Her Kind of Man. 1950: Guilty Bystander. 1953: Main Street to Broadway. 1957: A Face in the Crowd.

ENGLUND, Robert 1947–
Are you ready for Freddy without his make-up on? This happy-looking, lizard-like American actor with fair, curly hair was, though RADA-trained, stuck for years in minor roles as zanies and hoodlums – until cast as Freddy Krueger, the maniac child-murderer who came back to life through dreams in the 'Nightmare on Elm Street' films in which he gradually assumed greater prominence and a wisecracking persona. Lately attempting a wider range of horror roles with variable results.
1974: Buster and Billie. A Star is Born. 1975:

Hustle. 1976: St. Ives. Stay Hungry. Eaten Alive (GB: Death Trap). 1977: Last of the Cowboys (later the Great Smokey Roadblock). Young Joe, the Forgotten Kennedy (TV). 1978: Big Wednesday. Blood Brothers. 1979: The Ordeal of Patty Hearst (TV). Thou Shalt Not Kill (TV). 1980: The Fifth Floor. 1981: Dead and Buried. Galaxy of Terror. Don't Cry, It's Only Thunder. 1982: Thou Shalt Not Kill (TV). Starflight One (TV. GB: cinemas). 1983: Hobson's Choice (TV). I Want to Live! (TV). The Fighter (TV). 1984: A Nightmare on Elm Street. 1985: A Nightmare on Elm Street 2: Freddy's Revenge. 1986: Never Too Young to Die. A Nightmare on Elm Street 3: Dream Warriors. Downtown (TV). 1987: Infidelity (TV). 1988: 976-EVIL (and directed). A Nightmare on Elm Street 4: The Dream Master. 1989: A Nightmare on Elm Street: The Dream Child. Phantom of the Opera. 1990: The Adventures of Ford Fairlane. 1991: Danse Macabre. Freddy's Dead: The Final Nightmare. 1992: Nightmare Café (TV). 1993: Jason Goes to Hell: The Final Friday. Night Terrors/Tobe Hooper's Night Terrors. 1994: Wes Craven's New Nightmare. The Case of the Lethal Lifestyle (TV). Robin Cook's Mortal Fear (TV). 1995: The Unspoken Truth (TV). The Mangler. 1996: The Killer Tongue. The Vampyre Wars. The Paper Brigade. Mind Breakers (TV). 1997: Perfect Target. Wes Craven Presents Wishmaster. 1998: Meet the Deedles. Urban Legend. Dee Snider's Strangeland. Galactic Odyssey (TV). 1999: The Prince and the Surfer. 2000: Wish You Were Dead. Python. Freddy vs Jason.

ERICSON, John (Joseph Meibes) 1926–
Fair-haired German-born leading man, under contract to M-G-M in the fifties, but lacking in sufficient mobility or personality to promote him to the top level. His best screen work was probably the title role of Pretty Boy Floyd, but he remained very active on television in routine action roles.
1950: Saturday's Children (TV). 1951: Teresa. 1954: The Student Prince. Green Fire. Rhapsody. Bad Day at Black Rock. 1955: The Return of Jack Slade (GB: Texas Rose). 1956: The Cruel Tower. Heritage of Anger (TV). 1957: Forty Guns. Oregon Passage. 1958: Day of the Bad Man. The Innocent Sleep (TV). 1960: Under Ten Flags. Pretty Boy Floyd. 1962: Slave Queen of Babylon/I, Semiramis. 1964: 7 Faces of Dr Lao. 1965: Operation Atlantic. 1966: The Destructors. 1967: Odio

per odio. Los Siete de Pancho Villa (GB and US: Treasure of Pancho Villa). 1968:. The Money Jungle. The Bamboo Saucer/Collision Course. 1969: Testa o croce (US: Heads or Tails). 1971: Bedknobs and Broomsticks. 1972: The Bounty Man (TV). 1974: Murder Impossible. Hog Wild (TV). 1975: Alien Zone/House of the Dead. 1976: Hustler Squad (GB: The Dirty Half Dozen). Crash. 1984: Final Mission (released 1986). 1987: The Dream Prince. Genesis of the Vampire. 1988: Primary Target.

ERROL, Leon 1881–1951

Bald, explosive, Australian-born comedian, with indiarubber legs and twitching, lugubrious features, often seen as the hen-pecked drunk, in dozens of short comedies throughout the thirties and forties and popular in the 'Joe Palooka' and 'Mexican Spitfire' series. Died from a heart attack.

1924: Yolanda. 1925: Clothes Make the Pirate. Sally. 1927: The Lunatic at Large. 1929: One Heavenly Night. 1930: *Let's Merge. Paramount on Parade. Queen of Scandal. Only Saps Work. 1931: Her Majesty, Love. *The Master Niblick. Finn and Hattie. *Practice Shots. 1933: Alice in Wonderland. *Poor Fish. *Three Little Swigs. *Hold Your Temper. 1934: We're Not Dressing. The Notorious Sophie Lang. The Captain Hates the Sea. *No More Bridge. *Autobuyography. *Service with a Smile. *Good Morning, Eve. *Perfectly Mismated. *Fixed a Stew. *One Too Many. 1935: Princess O'Hara. Coronado. *Hit and Rum. *Salesmanship Ahoy. *Home Work. *Honeymoon Bridge. *Counselitis. 1936: *Down the Ribber. *Pirate Party on Catalina Isle. *Wholesailing Along. *One Live Ghost. 1937: *Wife Insurance. Make a Wish. *Wrong Romance. *Should Wives Work? *A Rented Riot. *Dummy Owner. 1938: *His Pest Friend. *The Jitters. *Stage Fright. *Major Difficulties. *Crime Rave. *Berth Quakes. 1939: The Girl from Mexico. Career. Dancing Co-Ed (GB: Every Other Inch a Lady). Mexican Spitfire. *Home Boner. *Moving Vanities. *Rung Madness. *Wrong Room. *Truth Aches. *Scrappily Married. 1940: *Bested by a Beard. *He Asked for It. *Tattle Television. *The Fired Man. Pop Always Pays. Mexican Spitfire Out West. The Golden Fleecing. 1941: *Variety Reel. *Stars at Play. Six Lessons from Madame La Zonga. Where Did You Get That Girl? Hurry, Charlie, Hurry. Mexican Spitfire's Baby. Melody Lane. Moonlight in Hawaii. Never Give a Sucker an Even Break (GB: What a Man!). *When Wifie's Away. *A Polo Phony. *A Panic in the Parlor. *Man I Cured. *Home Work (and 1935 film). *Who's a Dummy? 1942: Mexican Spitfire at Sea. *Wedded Blitz. *Hold 'Em Jail. Mexican Spitfire Sees a Ghost. *Framing Father. *Mail Trouble. *Dear! Dear! *Pretty Dolly. Mexican Spitfire's Elephant. 1943: *Double Up. *A Family Feud. *Gem Yams. *Radio Runaround. Cowboy in Manhattan. Strictly in the Groove. *Seeing Nellie Home. *Cutie on Duty. *Wedtime Stories. Mexican Spitfire's Blessed Event. Higher and Higher. Follow the Band. Gals Inc. 1944: Hat Check Honey. The Invisible Man's Revenge. Slightly Terrific. Twilight on the Prairie. Babes on Swing Street. *Say Uncle. *Poppa Knows Worst. *Prices Unlimited. *Girls, Girls, Girls. *Triple Trouble. *He Forgot to Remember. 1945: She Gets Her Man. What a Blonde! Under Western Skies. Mama Loves Papa. *Birthday Blues. *Let's Go Stepping. *It Shouldn't Happen to a Dog. *Double Honeymoon. *Beware of Redheads. 1946: Riverboat Rhythm. *Oh, Professor, Behave. *Maid Trouble. *Twin Husbands. *I'll Take Milk. *Follow That Blonde. Joe Palooka, Champ. Gentleman Joe Palooka. 1947: *Borrowed Blonde. *Wife Tames Wolf. *In Room 303. *Hired Husband. *Blondes Away. Joe Palooka in the Knockout. 1948: The Noose Hangs High. Variety Time. *Bet Your Life. *Don't Fool Your Wife. Joe Palooka in Fighting Mad. *Secretary Trouble. Bachelor Blues. *Uninvited Blonde. *Backstage Follies. 1949: Joe Palooka in the Big Fight. *Dad Always Pays. *Cactus Cut-Up. *I Can't Remember. *Oil's Well That Ends Well. Joe Palooka in the Counterpunch. *Sweet Cheat. *Shocking Affair. Joe Palooka Meets Humphrey. 1950: *High and Dizzy. Joe Palooka in Humphrey Takes a Chance/ Humphrey Takes a Chance. *Texas Tough Guy. *Spooky Wooky. Joe Palooka in the Squared Circle. 1951: *Chinatown Chump. *Punchy Pancho. *One Wild Night. *Deal Me In. *Lord Epping Returns. *Too Many Wives. Footlight Varieties.

ESTEVEZ, Emilio 1962–

Stocky, worried-looking, jaunty young American actor who looks and sounds a lot like his father, Martin Sheen (qv) and seems destined for much the same sort of career pattern. Into TV movies, then films, direct from high school, the talented Estevez has a second string to his bow with writing, contributing the screenplay to his 1985 feature That Was Then, This is Now, and has also tried his hand at directing. He has two acting brothers, Charlie Sheen (qv) and Ramon Estevez, and his plans to play Charley's Aunt on stage seem to reveal an inclination to break away from the family 'seriousness'. And it was action comedies like the 'Stakeout' and 'Mighty Ducks' series that boosted his stock the most with their reliance on his nervous energy. Once engaged to Demi Moore (qv), he married singer Paula Abdul in 1993.

1980: Seventeen Going Nowhere. (TV). 1981: To Climb a Mountain (TV). 1982: Tex. In the Custody of Strangers (TV). 1983: The Outsiders. Nightmares. 1984: Repo Man. The Breakfast Club. 1985: St. Elmo's Fire. That Was Then, This is Now. 1986: Maximum Overdrive. †Wisdom. 1987: Never on Tuesday. StakeOut. 1988: Young Guns. 1989: Nightbreaker (cable TV). †Men at Work. 1990: Young Guns II. 1991: Freejack. 1992: The Mighty Ducks (GB: Champions). 1993: National Lampoon's Loaded Weapon 1. Judgment Night. Another Stakeout. 1994: D2: The Mighty Ducks. 1996: Mission Impossible. D3 The Mighty Ducks/Mighty Ducks 3. †The War at Home. 1997: Sand. Late Last Night. 1998: Waldo's Hawaiian Holiday. †Bang Bang Club. Un dolar pos los muertos/Dollar for the Dead. 1999: Killer's Head. 2000: †Rated X (cable TV).

†Also directed

ETAIX, Pierre 1928–

Mournful-looking, dark-haired, poker-faced, slightly built French comedian of rigid, stick-like gait. After starting his film career on the production side, Etaix worked with Jacques Tati before branching out on his own. At first his character of the man who, riotously, can do no right, was an immense success, but his later films were slower and less popular, and he has not directed one since 1971, occupying his time with his own 'Ecole du Cirque', at which he teaches clowning and mimicry.

1958: Mon oncle. 1959: Pickpocket. 1960: *Le pélerinage. 1961: Tire-au-flanc 62. *†Rupture. *†Happy Anniversary. 1962: †The Suitor/Le soupirant. 1963: Une grosse tête. *†Insomnia. *†Nous n'irons plus au bois. 1964: †Yoyo. 1965: †As Long As You're Healthy. 1966: Le voleur. 1968: †Le grand amour. 1969: *La mayonnaise. 1970: †Pays de cocagne. 1971: The Day the Clown Cried (unfinished). *†La

Polonaise. 1973: ‡Bel ordure. 1974: Sérieux comme le plaisir. 1986: Max mon amour. 1987: L'âge de monsieur est avancé. 1990: Henry and June.

†And directed
‡Scenes deleted from final release print

EVANS, Clifford 1912–1985
Black-haired Welsh actor mainly seen in thoughtful, serious roles who had just worked his way up to star billing in big films when World War II intervened. His film career never had the same momentum afterwards and he was seen mostly in 'B' films as police inspectors or treacherous men of affluence and influence. He had a big hit in the late 1960s with his running role in a successful TV series, *The Power Game.*
*1935: The River House Mystery. 1936: Ourselves Alone (US: River of Unrest). The Tenth Man. Calling the Tune. A Woman Alone. 1937: The Mutiny of the Elsinore. Mademoiselle Docteur. La mort du Sphinx. 1938: 13 Men and a Gun. Luck of the Navy. 1939: His Brother's Keeper. The Proud Valley. At the Villa Rose (US: House of Mystery). 1940: Fingers. The Flying Squad. The House of the Arrow (US: Castle of Crimes). 1941: Freedom Radio. The Saint Meets the Tiger. Love on the Dole. Penn of Pennsylvania (US: The Courageous Mr Penn). 1942: Suspected Person. The Foreman Went to France (US: Somewhere in France). 1943: The Flemish Farm. 1948: The Silver Darlings. While I Live. 1949: The Twenty Questions Murder Mystery. A Run for Your Money. 1952: Escape Route (US: I'll Get You). 1953: Valley of Song (US: Men Are Children Twice). The Straw Man. †The Case of the Marriage Bureau. The Case of Express Delivery. †The Case of Gracie Budd. †The Case of the Last Dance. Point of No Return. The Case of Canary Jones. The Case of the Burnt Alibi. †The Case of the Black Falcon. 1954: Solution by Phone. The Case of Soho Red. The Accused. †The Case of the Second Shot. Companions in Crime. †The Case of Diamond Annie. †The Case of Uncle Henry. *Fool Notions. The Red Dress. The Case of the Bogus Count. The Yellow Robe. 1955: The Gilded Cage. The Diamond Expert. *Ring of Greed. The Case of the Pearl Payroll. 1956: Passport to Treason. 1957: At the Stroke of Nine. Face in the Night (US: Menace in the Night). The Heart Within. Violent Playground. 1958: *Man with a Dog. 1959: SOS Pacific. 1961: The Curse of the Werewolf 1962:*

Kiss of the Vampire (US: Kiss of Evil). 1963: The Long Ships. 1967: A Twist of Sand. 1969: One Brief Summer.

†Three (35-minute) films shown as a single feature on the continent

EVANS, Dale (Frances Smith) 1912–
Red-headed American vocalist who doubtless deserved the luck she had when she met and married Roy Rogers (*qv*) and prolonged her career in his films, for she was a lady with a lot of tragedy in her life. Widowed at 17, she had lost three of her six children before they were 21. Fourteen grandchildren are hopefully some consolation.
*1940: The East Side Kids. 1942: Orchestra Wives. Rhythm Hits the Ice. Girl Trouble. 1943: Here Comes Elmer. Hoosier Holiday (GB: Farmyard Follies). Swing Your Partner. The West Side Kid. In Old Oklahoma (GB: War of the Wildcats). 1944: Casanova in Burlesque. San Fernando Valley. Yellow Rose of Texas. Song of Nevada. The Cowboy and the Senorita. 1945: Utah. Lights of Old Santa Fé. The Big Show-Off. The Man from Oklahoma. Don't Fence Me In. Hitchhike to Happiness. Bells of Rosarita. Sunset in Eldorado. Along the Navajo Trail. 1946: Song of Arizona. My Pal Trigger. Under Nevada Skies. Roll On Texas Moon. Home in Oklahoma. Rainbow over Texas. Out California Way. Heldorado. 1947: Apache Rose. Bells of San Angelo. The Trespasser. 1948: Slippy McGee. 1949: Down Dakota Way. Susanna Pass. *Howdy Podner. The Golden Stallion. 1950: Twilight in the Sierras. Bells of Coronado. Trigger Jr. 1951: South of Caliente. Pals of the Golden West. 1992: Roy Rogers, King of the Cowboys.*

EVANS, Dame Edith 1888–1976
Forthright English actress whose films as a silent screen leading lady were lamentably few, but who touched her every character portrayal in later years with eccentric brilliance. Few could match the richness and resonance of her diction and her indignation as Lady Bracknell in *The Importance of Being Earnest* is one of the cinema's most treasurable occasions. Created Dame in 1946. Died after a short illness following a stroke and heart attack. Oscar-nominated for *Tom Jones, The Chalk Garden* and *The Whisperers.*
1915: A Honeymoon for Three. A Welsh Singer. 1916: East is East. 1948: The Queen of Spades. 1949: The Last Days of Dolwyn (US: Woman of Dolwyn). 1952: The Importance of

Being Earnest. 1958: The Nun's Story. 1959: Look Back in Anger. 1963: Tom Jones. The Chalk Garden. 1964: Young Cassidy. 1966: The Whisperers. 1967: Fitzwilly (GB: Fitzwilly Strikes Back). 1968: Prudence and the Pill. Crooks and Coronets (US: Sophie's Place). 1969: The Madwoman of Chaillot. David Copperfield TV. GB: cinemas). 1970: Scrooge. Upon This Rock. 1973: A Doll's House (Garland). Craze. 1974: QB VII (TV). 1976: The Slipper and the Rose. Nasty Habits.

EVANS, Madge
(Margherita Evans) 1909–1981
Fluffy blonde American actress at her most popular as a child star of the early silent days, when she was known as Baby Madge. As an adult she took glamorous, sophisticated, rather empty roles, and was never more than a second-rank star. After 1938 she deserted the cinema completely for the theatre (she married playwright Sidney Kingsley in 1939), although she was seen occasionally on television in the 1950s. Died from cancer.
1914: †The Sign of the Cross. †Shore Acres. 1915: Zaza. †Alias Jimmy Valentine. †The Garden of Lies. 1916: †Seven Sisters. †Sudden Riches. †Seventeen. †Broken Chairs. †The Hidden Scar. †The Revolt. †Husband and Wife. 1917: †The Little Duchess. †The Volunteer. †The Burglar. †The Little Patriot. †Beloved Adventuress. †The Adventures of Carol. †Maternity. †Web of Desire. †The Corner Grocer. 1918: †Woman and Wife. †Gates of Gladness. †The Power and the Glory. †The Golden Wall. †Stolen Orders. †Neighbors. †Wanted – a Mother. 1919: †The Love Nest. †Home Wanted. †The Love Defender. Seventeen (and 1916 film). 1921:

†*Heidi. 1922: *Neighbor Nellie. 1923: On the Banks of the Wabash. *The Riding Master. 1924: Classmates (GB: Winning Through). 1930: *Envy. *Many Happy Returns. *The Bard of Broadway. 1931: Sporting Blood. Son of India. Guilty Hands. Heartbreak. *Good Times. 1932: Fast Life. Are You Listening? West of Broadway. Lovers Courageous. The Greeks Had a Word for Them. Huddle (GB: Impossible Lover). 1933: Hallelujah, I'm a Bum (GB: Hallelujah, I'm a Tramp). Hell Below. The Nuisance (GB: Accidents Wanted). Dinner at Eight. Broadway to Hollywood (GB: Ring Up the Curtain). Day of Reckoning. Beauty for Sale (GB: Beauty). Mayor of Hell. Made on Broadway (GB: The Girl I Made). 1934: Stand Up and Cheer. The Show Off. Fugitive Lovers. Death on the Diamond (GB: Death on the Sports Field). Grand Canary. What Every Woman Knows. Paris Interlude. 1935: Helldorado. David Copperfield. Age of Indiscretion. Men Without Names. The Tunnel (US: Transatlantic Tunnel). Calm Yourself. 1936: Moonlight Murder. Piccadilly Jim. Exclusive Story. Pennies from Heaven. 1937: Espionage. The Thirteenth Chair. 1938: Army Girl. Sinners in Paradise.

†As Baby Madge

EVANS, Peggy 1924–

Blonde British actress with china doll looks and wide blue, even scared, eyes; on stage from childhood as a dancer, but mainly used in films as gangsters' girls, most notably in *The Blue Lamp*, and despite a spirited showing as a girl investigator in *Penny and the Pownall Case*. Dropped out of show business after a few post-war roles.
1933: Colonel Blood. 1938: The Mikado. 1940: Charley's (Big Hearted) Aunt. 1946: School for Secrets (US: Secret Flight). A Matter of Life and Death (US: Stairway to Heaven). 1947: The Woman in the Hall. Penny and the Pownall Case. 1948: Love in Waiting. Look Before You Love. 1949: The Blue Lamp. 1951: Calling Bulldog Drummond. 1953: Murder at 3 am.

EVERETT, Rupert 1959–

Tall, languidly-handsome, cool, darkly floppy-haired English actor. His sulky good looks got him cast as faintly unpleasant characters with an edge of menace. After a start with Glasgow's Citizens' Theatre, he broke through to film stardom in spectacular

style repeating his stage role in *Another Country*. He roamed the world in search of striking scripts without finding anything to put him back in the public eye, until he broke back to stardom by playing sophisticated gay charmers.
*1981: *Dead on Time. *The Bloody Chamber. 1982: *A Shocking Accident. 1983: Real Life. Arthur the King (TV. Released 1985). 1984: Another Country. Dance with a Stranger. 1986: Chronicle of a Death Foretold. Duet for One. The Right Hand Man. 1987: Hearts of Fire. Gli occhiali d'oro. 1989: Tolérance. 1990: The Comfort of Strangers. 1992: Inside Monkey Zetterland. Quiet Flows the Don. 1993: Remembrance of Things Fast. 1994: Dellamorte, dellamorte. Prêt-à-Porter (US: Ready to Wear). The Madness of King George. 1995: Dunston Checks In. 1997: My Best Friend's Wedding. B Monkey (released 2000). 1998: Shakespeare in Love. 1999: A Midsummer Night's Dream. An Ideal Husband. Inspector Gadget. 2000: The Next Best Thing. Paragraph 175 (narrator only). 2001: Unconditional Love.*

EWELL, Tom
(Samuel Yewell Tornkins) 1909–1994
American actor who played gullible sorts or inept woman chasers, with the occasional wisecracking friend on the side. Not really discovered by Hollywood until into his forties, when his mournful features found their way into several classic comedies. But the qualities of the roles offered fell away, and he returned to his first love, the stage.
*1940: They Knew What They Wanted. 1941: Desert Bandit/The Kansas Kid. 1949: *Caribbean Capers. *Southward Ho! Ho! Adam's Rib. 1950: An American Guerilla in the*

Philippines (GB: I Shall Return). Mr Music. A Life of Her Own. 1951: Up Front. Finders Keepers. 1952: Lost in Alaska. Back at the Front (GB: Willie and Joe in Tokyo). 1955: The Seven Year Itch. The Lieutenant Wore Skirts. 1956: The Great American Pastime. 1957: The Girl Can't Help It. 1958: A Nice Little Bank That Should Be Robbed (GB: How to Rob a Bank). 1961: Tender is the Night. 1962: State Fair. 1965: *Wonders of Kentucky (narrator only). 1970: Suppose They Gave a War and Nobody Came. 1971: To Find a Man. 1972: They Only Kill Their Masters. 1974: †The Great Gatsby. The Spy Who Returned from the Dead. 1975: Promise Him Anything (TV). 1979: Return of the Mod Squad (TV). 1982: Terror at Alcatraz (TV). 1983: Easy Money.*

†Scenes deleted from final version

EYTHE, William 1918–1957
Diffident American leading man whose great promise on stage did not generally reflect itself in his screen performances. His self-opinionated attitudes made him unpopular in Hollywood and his career there petered out after 13 films. Developed an alcohol problem in the fifties and died from complications arising from acute hepatitis.
1942: The Ox-Bow Incident (GB: Strange Incident). 1943: The Song of Bernadette. 1944: The Eve of St Mark. A Wing and a Prayer. Wilson. 1945: The House on 92nd Street. A Royal Scandal (GB: Czarina). Colonel Effingham's Raid (GB: Man of the Hour). 1946: Centennial Summer. 1947: Meet Me at Dawn. 1948: Mr Reckless. 1949: Special Agent. 1950: Customs Agent.

F

FABIAN (F. Forte Bonaparte) 1942–
Beefy, handsome American pop singer with dark, wavy hair. Fox gave him a few semi-leading roles in the sixties on the strength of his popularity as a rockin' teenage idol, and he has continued to crop up from time to time in between night-club engagements.
1959: Rock 'n' Roll. Hound Dog Man. 1960: North to Alaska. High Time. Love in a Goldfish Bowl. 1962: Mr Hobbs Takes a Vacation. The Longest Day. Five Weeks in a Balloon. 1964: Ride the Wild Surf. 1965: Dear Brigitte . . . Ten Little Indians. 1966: Fireball 500. Dr Goldfoot and the Girl Bombs (GB: Dr G and the Love Bomb). 1967: Thunder Alley. 1968: The Devil's Eight. Maryjane. The Wild Racers. 1970: †A Bullet for Pretty Boy. 1972: †Lovin' Man. †Matthew. 1974: †Little Laura and Big John. 1976: †The Day the Lord Got Busted. 1977: Getting Married. 1978: Disco Fever. Katie: Portrait of a Centerfold (TV). 1979: †Crisis in Mid-Air. 1981: †Kiss Daddy Goodbye. 1983: †Get Crazy. 1993: †Rockin' the Joint: The Life and Times of Bill Haley and the Comets. 1994: Runaway Daughters (cable TV). 1996: Up Close & Personal. 1999: Mr Rock 'n' Roll: The Alan Freed Story (TV).

†*As Fabian Forte*

FAHEY, Jeff 1952–
Handsome, rather serious-looking, dark-haired American actor with piercing pale-blue eyes, a former ballet dancer who turned to acting at 30 and made his film debut at 33. Fahey looked set for big-time stardom at the beginning of the 1990s, especially with his charismatic roles in *White Hunter Black Heart*

and *The Lawnmower Man*. That didn't quite work out, but he has continued to work extremely hard in unsmiling leading roles, albeit in material directed at TV, cable or video rather than the cinema – 30 titles altogether since 1994. One of 13 children.
1985: Silverado. The Execution of Raymond Graham (TV). 1986: Psycho III. 1987: Backfire. Riot on 42nd Street. 1988: Split Decisions/Kid Gloves. 1989: True Blood/Edge of Darkness. Out of Time/In Search of the Serpent of Death. Outback/Wrangler/Minnamurra. Parker Kane (TV). 1990: Curiosity Kills (TV). Impulse. Last of the Finest (GB: Blue Heat). White Hunter Black Heart. 1991: Iron Maze. Iran: Days of Crisis (TV). Body Parts. 1992: Blindsided (cable TV). The Lawnmower Man. Sketch Artist. In the Company of Darkness (TV). 1993: Westwind. Quick (GB: Crossfire). Woman of Desire. Hit List. Freefall. 1994: Temptation. Wyatt Earp. Eye of the Wolf. Baree: The Wolf Dog/Northern Passage (TV). 1995: Sketch Artist II: Hands That See (TV. GB: A Feel for Murder). The Sweeper. Addicted to Love/Virtual Seduction (TV). Darkman 2: The Return of Durant (cable TV). Darkman III: Die, Darkman, Die. 1996: Deadly Current/Lethal Tender. Operation Delta Force. Every Woman's Dream (TV). Waiting for the Man/Small Time. Cross Over/Catherine's Grove. 1997: Johnny 2.0 (TV). Down Range. The Underground. Extramarital. Time Under Fire. 1998: On the Line (TV). Detour (GB: Hard to Die). No Tomorrow. When Justice Fails. 1999: The Contract. Revelation. The Newcomers. Hijack. 2000: Spoken in Silence. The Sculptress. Epicenter. Blind Heat.

FAIRBANKS, Douglas Jnr 1909–2000
In films from an early age, this genial spry, light-haired American actor followed his father in swashbuckling mould in several films, although he was a more versatile, if less dominant performer. Gave up movies even earlier than his father and went into production, with just the occasional foray into films or theatre. Married (first of two) to Joan Crawford (*qv*) from 1929 to 1933. Wore a moustache from 1933.
1923: Stephen Steps Out. 1924: The Air Mail. 1925: The American Venus. Wild Horse Mesa. Stella Dallas. 1926: Padlocked. Man Bait. Broken Hearts of Hollywood. 1927: Women Love Diamonds. Is Zat So? A Texas Steer. Dead Man's Curve. 1928: Modern Mothers. The Toilers. The Power of the Press. A Woman of

*Affairs. The Barker. 1929: The Jazz Age. Fast Life. Our Modern Maidens. The Careless Age. The Forward Pass. The Show of Shows. Party Girl. 1930: Loose Ankles. The Little Accident. The Dawn Patrol. The Way of All Men (GB: The Sin Flood). Outward Bound. One Night at Susie's. Little Caesar. 1931: Chances. *Trouble Shots. I Like Your Nerve. L'aviateur. L'athlète malgré lui. 1932: Union Depot (GB: Gentleman for a Day). It's Tough to be Famous. Love is a Racket. Le plombier amoureux. Scarlet Dawn. *Hollywood on Parade B-3. *The Stolen Jools (GB: The Slippery Pearls). 1933: Parachute Jumper. The Life of Jimmy Dolan (GB: The Kid's Last Fight). The Narrow Corner. Captured! Morning Glory. Catherine the Great. 1934: Success At Any Price. 1935: Man of the Moment. The Amateur Gentleman. Mimi. 1936: Accused. 1937: Jump for Glory (US: When Thief Meets Thief). The Prisoner of Zenda. 1938: The Joy of Living. The Rage of Paris. Having Wonderful Time. The Young in Heart. 1939: Gunga Din. The Sun Never Sets. Rulers of the Sea. 1940: Green Hell. Safari. Angels over Broadway. 1941: The Corsican Brothers. 1947: Sinbad the Sailor. The Exile. 1948: That Lady in Ermine. The Fighting O'Flynn. 1950: State Secret (US: The Great Manhunt). Mr Drake's Duck. 1953: Three's Company. The Triangle. The Genie. Thought to Kill (narrator only). 1954: *International Settlement. *The Journey. Destination Milan. Forever My Heart. The Last Moment. 1955: *Hollywood Fathers. 1957: Chase a Crooked Shadow. 1962: The Shadowed Affair (TV). 1967: Red and Blue. The Funniest Man in the World (narrator only). 1972: The Crooked Hearts (TV). 1973: Churchill the Man (narrator only). 1980: The Hostage Tower. 1981: Ghost Story. 1987: Hollywood Uncensored (TV Narrator only). 1996: The Battle Over Citizen Kane. 1998: From Russia to Hollywood (doc).*

FAIRBANKS, Douglas Snr
(D. Ulman) 1883–1939
Florid, moustachioed, ever-cheerful, athletic American actor, one of the biggest stars of the Hollywood silent era, and its swashbuckler par excellence, doing all his own spectacular stunts against equally spectacular sets. When sound came, his time was over. Married to Mary Pickford (second of three) from 1920 to 1936. Father of Douglas Fairbanks Jnr (by first wife). Died from a heart attack. Awarded a special Oscar in 1939.
1915: The Lamb. Double Trouble. 1916: The

Habit of Happiness. His Picture in the Papers. The Good Bad Man. Reggie Mixes In (GB: Mysteries of New York). *The Mystery of the Leaping Fish. The Half-Breed. Flirting with Fate. Manhattan Madness. Intolerance. American Aristocracy. The Matrimaniac. The Americano. 1917: In Again – Out Again. Wild and Wooly. Down to Earth. The Man from Painted Post. Reaching for the Moon. A Modern Musketeer. *War Relief. 1918: Headin' South. Mr Fixit. Say! Young Fellow. He Comes Up Smiling. *Sic 'em Sam! Arizona. *Fire the Kaiser. Bound in Morocco. 1919: The Knickerbocker Buckaroo. His Majesty, the American (GB: One of the Blood). When the Clouds Roll By. 1920: The Mollycoddle. The Mark of Zorro. 1921: The Nut. *Screen Snapshots No. 24. The Three Musketeers. 1922: Robin Hood. 1924: Thief of Bagdad. 1925: Don Q Son of Zorro. 1926: The Black Pirate. 1927: The Gaucho. The Kiss of Mary Pickford (US: Mary Pickford's Kiss). 1928: Show People. 1929: The Iron Mask. The Taming of the Shrew. 1930: *Voice of Hollywood No.2. Reaching for the Moon. 1931: Around the World in 80 Minutes. 1932: Mr Robinson Crusoe. 1934: The Private Life of Don Juan. 1955: *Hollywood Fathers.

FAITH, Adam (Terrence Nelhams) 1940–
Fair-haired, bony-faced, undernourished-looking singer, actor and entrepreneur who has occasionally cropped up in films in anything from comedy (as hapless innocents) to heavy drama (as cockney hardmen or wheeler-dealers). A great pop idol in his day, he was also enormously successful as the central character in the TV series *Budgie*, about a small-time crook, a role he repeated in a stage musical of the late 1980s.

1959: 'Beat' Girl (US: Wild for Kicks). 1960: Never Let Go. 1961: What a Whopper! What a Carve-Up! (US: Home Sweet Homicide). 1962: Mix Me a Person. 1974: Stardust. 1976: McCloud: London Bridges (TV). 1979: Yesterday's Hero. Foxes. 1980: McVicar. 1985: Minder on the Orient Express (TV).

FALK, Peter 1927–
Short, dark, Brooklynese Hollywood star character actor who found it hard to fight clear of the gangster stereotype before his enormous success as television's rumpled, never-fail detective Columbo. Has remained most successful on television despite some promising looking film material in the seventies. A tumour caused the loss of his right eye when he was three. Nominated for Academy Awards in *Murder Incorporated* and *Pocketful of Miracles*. His Columbo creation was still going strong at the turn of the century after more than 60 adventures.
1958: Wind Across the Everglades. 1959: The Bloody Brood. The Rebel Set. Pretty Boy Floyd. 1960: A Death of Princes (TV. GB: cinemas). The Secret of the Purple Reef. Murder Incorporated. 1961: Cry Vengeance (TV). The Million Dollar Incident (TV). Pocketful of Miracles. 1962: Pressure Point. The Balcony. 1963: It's a Mad, Mad, Mad, Mad World. 1964: Robin and the Seven Hoods. Italiano Brava Gente (US: Attack and Retreat). 1965: The Great Race. Too Many Thieves (TV. GB: cinemas). 1966: Penelope. 1967: Luv. 1968: Anzio (GB: The Battle for Anzio). Prescription: Murder (TV). 1969: Rosolino Paterno soldato (US: Operation Snafu). Machine Gun McCain. Castle Keep. 1970: Husbands. A Step Out of Line. (TV). 1971: Ransom for a Dead Man (TV. GB: cinemas). 1972: *The Politics Film (narrator only). 1974: A Woman Under the Influence. 1976: Murder by Death. Mikey and Nicky. Griffin and Phoenix (GB: Today is Forever). 1977: Opening Night. 1978: The Cheap Detective. The Brink's Job. 1979: The In-Laws. 1981: The Great Muppet Caper. All the Marbles (GB: The California Dolls). 1985: Happy New Year. 1986: Big Trouble. 1987: Himmel über Berlin. Vibes. The Princess Bride. 1989: Cookie. In the Spirit. Columbo Goes to the Guillotine. 1990: Aunt Julia and the Scriptwriter (Tune in Tomorrow). Motion and Emotion. Columbo Goes to College (TV). Columbo: Grand Deception (TV). 1991: Caution: Murder Can Be Hazardous to Your Health (TV). Rest in Peace, Mrs Columbo

(TV). 1992: The Player. Columbo: Death Hits the Jackpot (TV). In weiter Ferne, so nah (GB and US: Faraway, So Close!). 1993: Columbo: A Bird in the Hand (TV). Columbo: It's All in the Game (TV). 1994: Columbo: Undercover (TV). Columbo: Butterfly in Shades of Gray (TV). 1995: The Sunshine Boys (TV). Roommates. Columbo: Strange Bedfellows (TV). 1996: Pronto. 1997: Columbo: A Trace of Murder (TV). 1998: Vig. Columbo: Ashes to Ashes (TV). 2000: Enemies of Laughter. Lakeboat. A Storm in Summer. Columbo: Murder with Too Many Notes (TV).

FALKENBURG, Jinx
(Eugenia Falkenburg) 1919–
Tall, attractive, brunette, fresh-looking, Spanish-born actress in Hollywood films. Raised in Chile, she rose to be that country's champion free-style swimmer before becoming America's number one model, her entrée to films. Her vivacious personality and bursting-with-health appearance made her popular in comedies and light musicals of the wartime years. A biography of her eventful life was published as early as 1951.
1936: †Big Brown Eyes. †Strike Me Pink. 1937: †Nothing Sacred. 1938: †Song of the Buckaroo. 1939: †The Lone Ranger Rides Again (serial). †Professional Model. 1941: Sing for Your Supper. 1942: Two Latins from Manhattan. Sweetheart of the Fleet. Lucky Legs. Laugh Your Blues Away. 1943: Two Senoritas from Chicago (GB: Two Senoritas). She Has What It Takes. The Cover Girl. 1944: Nine Girls. Tahiti Nights. 1946: The Gay Senorita. Meet Me on Broadway. Talk about a Lady. 1947: *Brains Can Be Beautiful. 1949: *Straw Hat Cinderella.

FARLEY, Chris 1964–1997
Flabby-featured, sandy-haired, 20-stone American comedian from the famous *Saturday Night Live* stable, who made several films both in partnership with David Spade and as a solo attraction. However, he had perpetual weight, alcohol and drugs problems and was found dead from a drug overdose in December 1997. His frenzied, knockabout style engendered a series of low comedy (but often likeable) characters who triumphed over adversity in the end – unlike the comedian himself.
1992: Wayne's World. 1993: Coneheads. Wayne's World 2. 1994: Airheads. 1995: Tommy Boy. Billy Madison. 1996: Black Sheep. 1997: Beverly Hills Ninja. 1998:

Almost Heroes/ Edwards and Hunt. It's a Dog's Life. Dirty Work. 1999: The Gelfin (voice only).

FARMER, Frances 1910–1970

Determined-looking American actress, a harsher version of Joan Fontaine. She became unpopular in the Hollywood of the thirties, where alcoholism and mental illness put a stop to her career. After seven years in an asylum (1943–1950), she eventually made a comeback in the mid-fifties, and became quite well kown as a TV hostess. Died from cancer of the throat. Married (first of three) to Leif Erickson (William Anderson 1911–1986) from 1936 to 1942. Her harrowing life was filmed several times in the early 1980s.
1936: Too Many Parents. Border Flight. Come and Get It. Rhythm on the Range. 1937: The Toast of New York. Ebb Tide. Exclusive. 1938: Ride a Crooked Mile (GB: Escape from Yesterday). 1940: South of Pago Pago. Flowing Gold. 1941: World Premiere. Badlands of Dakota. Among the Living. 1942: Son of Fury. 1957: Reunion (TV). 1958: The Party Crashers.

FARR, Derek 1912–1986

Quiet, dark, brooding English leading man with distinctive receding hairline, who forsook schoolteaching for acting after work as an extra in films of the late thirties. Usually cast as nice young chaps who were sometimes falsely accused of murder. Maintained leading man status from 1940 to 1951, co-star until 1961, but most latterly in small character roles with bigger parts on TV. Married (second of two) to Muriel Pavlow (qv) from 1947. Died from cancer.
1939: Inspector Hornleigh on Holiday (US:

Inspector Hornleigh on Leave). The Outsider. Q Planes (US: Clouds over Europe). Black Eyes. 1940: Spellbound (US: The Spell of Amy Nugent). 1941: Freedom Radio (US: A Voice in the Night). Quiet Wedding. 1943: *Camouflage. 1946: Quiet Weekend. Wanted for Murder. The Shop at Sly Corner (US: The Code of Scotland Yard). 1947: Teheran (US: The Plot to Kill Roosevelt). 1948: Bond Street. Noose (US: The Silk Noose). The Story of Shirley Yorke. 1949: Silent Dust. Man on the Run. 1950: Double Confession. Murder without Crime. 1951: Young Wives' Tale. Reluctant Heroes. 1952: Little Big Shot. 1953: Front Page Story. Eight O'Clock Walk. 1954: Bang! You're Dead (US: Game of Danger). The Dam Busters. 1955: Value for Money. The Man in the Road. 1956: Town on Trial! 1957: Doctor at Large. The Vicious Circle (US: The Circle). 1958: The Truth about Women. 1961: Attempt to Kill. 1966: The Projected Man. 1967: 30 is a Dangerous Age, Cynthia. 1971: The Johnstown Monster. 1972: Pope Joan.*

FARR, Felicia 1932–

Attractive, tawny-haired, brown-eyed American actress of substantial, warm personality, in star roles from the onset of her film career. She played a few strong-willed heroines in upper-class westerns, but has been only sporadically seen in films and on television since marrying Jack Lemmon (qv) in 1960.
1955: Big House USA. Timetable. 1956: Jubal. The First Texan. Reprisal! 1957: 3:10 to Yuma. The Last Wagon. The Country Husband (TV. GB: cinemas). 1958: Onionhead. 1960: Hell Bent for Leather. 1964: Kiss Me Stupid. 1966: The Venetian Affair. 1967. Asylum for a Spy (TV). 1970: Lock, Stock and Barrel

(TV). 1971: Kotch. 1973: Charley Varrick. 1986: 'That's Life!' 1992: The Player.
†As Randy Farr

FARRAR, David 1908–1995

Strong, silent, dark, saturnine, resolute-looking-British leading man who came late to acting after a spell in journalism, but quickly established himself as stalwart types (including Sexton Blake twice), moving on in postwar years to subtler roles. His decision to go to Hollywood in the early 1950s was an unqualified disaster. He was cast as nothing but villains in increasingly silly costume epics and his special qualities never re-emerged. Retired to South Africa, where he died.
1937: Head Over Heels (US: Head Over Heels in Love). Return of A Stranger. Silver Top. 1938: Sexton Blake and the Hooded Terror. A Royal Divorce. 1941: Danny Boy. Sheepdog of the Hills. Penn of Pennsylvania (US: The Courageous Mr Penn). 1942: Suspected Person. Went the Day Well? (US: 48 Hours). The Night Invader. 1943: The Dark Tower. They Met in the Dark. Headline. The Hundred Pound Window. 1944: For Those in Peril. Meet Sexton Blake. The World Owes Me a Living. 1945: The Echo Murders. The Trojan Brothers. 1946: Lisbon Story. 1947: Black Narcissus. Frieda. 1948: Mr Perrin and Mr Traill. The Small Back Room (US: Hour of Glory). 1949: Diamond City. 1950: Cage of Gold. Gone to Earth (US: revised version: The Wild Heart). 1951: The Late Edwina Black (US: Obsessed). Night without Stars. The Golden Horde (GB: The Golden Horde of Genghis Khan). 1954: Duel in the Jungle. The Black Shield of Falworth. Lilacs in the Spring (US: Let's Make Up). 1955: Escape to Burma. Pearl of the South Pacific. The Sea Chase. Lost (US: Tears for Simon). 1957: Triangle on Safari (US: Woman and the Hunter). I Accuse! 1958: Son of Robin Hood. 1959: John Paul Jones. Watusi. Solomon and Sheba. 'Beat' Girl (US: Wild for Kicks). 1962: The Webster Boy. The 300 Spartans.

FARRELL, Charles 1901–1990

Gentle, tousle-haired, romantic American leading man, now all but forgotten, but immensely popular in the late twenties and early thirties in a series of lyrical love stories opposite Janet Gaynor, one of which, *Seventh Heaven*, won an Academy Award. Left films in 1941 to go into the sports club business, but made a comeback on TV in the fifties. Married to Virginia Valli (V. McSweeney

1895–1968) from 1932 until her death. He died from cardiac arrest.
1923: Rosita. The Cheat. The Hunchback of Notre Dame. The Ten Commandments. 1925: The Love Hour. The Freshman (GB: College Days). Wings of Youth. *The Gosh-darn Mortgage. Clash of Wolves. 1926: Old Ironside (GB: Sons of the Sea). Sandy. A Trip to Chinatown. 1927: The Rough Riders (GB: The Trumpet Call). 7th Heaven. 1928: Street Angel. The Red Dance (GB: The Red Dancer of Moscow). The River. Fazil. 1929: City Girl. Sunny Side Up. Lucky Star. Happy Days. 1930: Liliom. The Princess and the Plumber. The Man Who Came Back. High Society Blues. 1931: Body and Soul. Heartbreak. Merely Mary Ann. Delicious. 1932: After Tomorrow. The First Year. Tess of the Storm Country. Wild Girl (GB: Salomy Jane). 1933: Girl Without a Room. Aggie Appleby, Maker of Men (GB: Cupid in the Rough). The Big Shakedown. 1934: Change of Heart. Falling in Love (US: Trouble Ahead). 1935: *Hollywood Hobbies. Fighting Youth. Forbidden Heaven. 1936: The Flying Doctor. 1937: Moonlight Sonata. Midnight Menace (US: Bombs over London). 1938: Flight to Fame. Just Around the Corner. Tail Spin. 1941: The Deadly Game.

1929: Lucky Boy. 1930: Little Caesar. *The Lucky Break. 1931: Night Nurse. 1932: Three on a Match. *Position and Backswing. Life Begins (GB: The Dawn of Life). The Match King. Scandal for Sale. I Am a Fugitive from a Chain Gang. 1933: The Mystery of the Wax Museum. Central Airport. Girl Missing. Grand Slam. The Keyhole. Gambling Ship. Lady for a Day. Bureau of Missing Persons. Mary Stevens, MD. Man's Castle. Havana Widows. The Mayor of Hell. 1934: I've Got Your Number. Dark Hazard. Kansas City Princess. Hi, Nellie! The Big Shakedown. The Personality Kid/Information Please. The Merry Wives of Reno. Heat Lightning. The Secret Bride (GB: Concealment). 1935: In Caliente. Go Into Your Dance (GB: Casino de Paree). Traveling Saleslady. Gold Diggers of 1935. We're in the Money. Little Big Shot. Miss Pacific Fleet. 1936: Smart Blonde. The Law in Her Hands. Snowed Under. Nobody's Fool. Here Comes Carter! (GB: The Voice of Scandal). High Tension. Gold Diggers of 1937. 1937: Breakfast for Two. Blondes at Work. Hollywood Hotel. Fly-Away Baby. Dance, Charlie, Dance. You Live and Learn. The Adventurous Blonde/Torchy Blane the Adventurous Blonde. 1938: The Road to Reno. Stolen Heaven. Torchy Gets Her Man. Prison Break. Exposed. 1939: Torchy Blane in Chinatown. Torchy Runs for Mayor. 1941: Johnny Eager. 1942: A Night for Crime. The Talk of the Town. Twin Beds. 1943: Klondike Kate. City without Men. 1944: Ever Since Venus. 1947: Heading for Heaven. I Love Trouble. Mary Lou. 1948: Lulu Belle. 1952: Apache War Smoke. 1953: Girls in the Night (GB: Life After Dark). 1954: Secret of the Incas. Susan Slept Here. 1955: The Girl in the Red Velvet Swing. 1959: Middle of the Night. 1964: The Disorderly Orderly. Kissin' Cousins. 1966: Dead Heat on a Merry-Go-Round. 1968: Tiger by the Tail.

FARROW, Mia (Maria Farrow) 1945–
Fair-haired, fragile-looking American actress of expressive brown eyes and fey charm, the daughter of Maureen O'Sullivan (qv) and director John Farrow. She enjoyed something of a reputation as a wild spirit in her younger days, but then gradually came to prominence in the cinema with a series of wistful, vulnerable heroines, sometimes not quite all there. Married to Frank Sinatra (1966–1968) and conductor Andre Previn (1970–1979), she became associated, privately and professionally, with filmmaker Woody Allen (qv) for 10 years from 1982.

During this time, she widened her range as an actress, but the relationship collapsed into a messy court case after she discovered that Allen had been having an affair with her and Previn's adopted Korean-born daughter. Under her own steam, the young-looking Farrow continued to find interesting roles.
1959: John Paul Jones. 1963: *The Age of Curiosity. 1964: Guns at Batasi. 1967: Johnny Belinda (TV). 1968: A Dandy in Aspic. Rosemary's Baby. 1969: Secret Ceremony. John and Mary. 1971: Blind Terror (US: See No Evil). Goodbye Raggedy Ann (TV). Follow Me (US: The Public Eye). 1972: Docteur Popaul (GB and US: Scoundrel in White). 1974: The Great Gatsby. 1975: Peter Pan (TV). 1976: Full Circle. 1978: Death on the Nile. A Wedding. Avalanche. 1979: Hurricane. 1981: The Last Unicorn (voice only). Sarah/The Seventh Match. 1982: A Midsummer Night's Sex Comedy. 1983: Zelig. 1984: Supergirl. Broadway Danny Rose. 1985: The Purple Rose of Cairo. 1986: Hannah and Her Sisters. 1987: Radio Days. 1988: September. Another Woman. 1989: New York Stories. Crimes and Misdemeanors. 1990: Alice. 1991: Shadows and Fog. 1992: Husbands and Wives. 1993: Wolf. Widow's Peak. 1994: Miami Rhapsody. 1996: Reckless (TV). 1997: Private Parts. Angelo Mooney Dies Again/Angela Mooney. Miracle at Midnight (TV). *Redux Riding Hood (voice only). 1999: Coming Soon. Forget Me Never (TV).

FAWCETT, Farrah
(Mary F. Fawcett) 1946–
Lithe, fluffily blonde American actress who rose to the top on the success of a TV series (Charlie's Angels) and her flashing toothpaste smile. Her career seemed to be faltering in the late 1970s, when her private life – married/divorced Lee Majors (qv), then live-in companion of Ryan O'Neal (qv), gained her more notices than her disappointing acting performances. But some courageous portrayals on stage and TV in the 1980s brought her the belated respect of her critics. The relationship with O'Neal also came to an end.
1969: Un homme qui me plaît (US: Love is a Funny Thing). Three's a Crowd (TV). 1970: Myra Breckinridge. The Feminist and the Fuzz (TV). 1972: The Great American Beauty Contest (TV). 1974: Of Men and Women II (TV). The Girl Who Came Gift Wrapped (TV). 1975: Murder on Flight 502 (TV). 1976: Logan's Run. 1978: †Somebody Killed

FARRELL, Glenda 1904–1971
Buoyant, witty, blonde American actress with lived-in charm and long, pencilled eyebrows. Many cinemagoers' favourite wisecracking woman-of-the-world from Hollywood films of the 1930s, she is perhaps most fondly recalled as the intrepid girl reporter Torchy Blane. Was once said to have delivered a 400 word speech in 40 seconds. Won an Emmy in 1963. Died from lung cancer.

Her Husband. 1979: An Almost Perfect Affair. Sunburn. 1980: Saturn 3. The Fall Guy (TV). 1981: The Cannonball Run. Murder in Texas (TV). 1984: The Red-Light Sting (TV). The Burning Bed (TV). 1985: Extremities. 1986: Unfinished Business (TV). Between Two Women (TV). Nazi Hunter: The Beate Klarsfeld Story (TV. GB: Nazi Hunter: The Search for Klaus Barbie). 1987: Poor Little Rich Girl (TV). 1988: See You in the Morning. 1989: Margaret Bourke-White (TV). 1990: Small Sacrifices (TV). 1992: Criminal Behaviour (TV). 1994: The Substitute Wife (TV). 1995: Man of the House. Children of the Dust (TV). Dalva (TV). 1997: The Apostle. The Love Master (released 1999). 1998: Brave Little Toaster Goes to Mars (TV. Voice only). 1999: Silk Hope (TV). 2000: Dr T and the Women.

†As Farrah Fawcett-Majors

FAYE, Alice (A. Leppert) 1912–1998
Blonde, round-faced American singer with a warm smile and voice to match. Starting as a singer with Rudy Vallee's band, she became much in demand for sympathetic roles in musicals of the thirties and early forties, before retiring (too) early to concentrate on consolidating her marriage to Phil Harris (1941 on, her second husband). Harris (1904–1995), a bandleader-singer-actor, and Faye shared a radio show from 1946, and he won renewed popularity doing cartoon voices in Disney features, notably Baloo the bear in The Jungle Book. Her own comeback roles, however, did not showcase her to advantage. Her first marriage (1937–1940) was to singer Tony Martin (qv). Died from cancer.
1934: George White's Scandals. She Learned about Sailors. Now I'll Tell (GB: When New York Sleeps). 365 Nights in Hollywood. 1935: George White's 1935 Scandals. Music is Magic. Every Night at Eight. 1936: Poor Little Rich Girl. Sing, Baby, Sing. King of Burlesque. Stowaway. 1937: On the Avenue. Wake Up and Live. You Can't Have Everything. You're a Sweetheart. 1938: In Old Chicago. Sally, Irene and Mary. Alexander's Ragtime Band. Tail Spin. 1939: Hollywood Cavalcade. Barricade. Rose of Washington Square. 1940: Lillian Russell. Little Old New York. Tin Pan Alley. 1941: That Night in Rio. The Great American Broadcast. Weekend in Havana. 1943: Hello, Frisco, Hello. The Gang's All Here (GB: The Girls He Left Behind). 1944: Four Jills in a Jeep. 1945: Fallen Angel. 1962:

State Fair. 1975: Won Ton Ton – the Dog Who Saved Hollywood. 1978: The Magic of Lassie. Every Girl Should Have One. 1994: Carmen Miranda: Bananas is My Business (doc).

FELDMAN, Marty 1933–1982
Tiny, bug-eyed, hook-nosed British comedian who moved from writing to performing and became a huge success on television in the late 1960s. His film performances did not evoke the same laughter and remained over-indulgent. Died from a heart attack.
1969: The Bed Sitting Room. 1970: Every Home Should Have One (US: Think Dirty). 1971: The Magnificent 7 Deadly Sins. 1974: Young Frankenstein. 1975: The Adventure of Sherlock Holmes' Smarter Brother. 40 gradi all'ombra del lenzuolo (GB and US: Sex with a Smile). 1976: Silent Movie. 1977: †The Last Remake of Beau Geste. 1979: †In God We Trust. 1982: Slapstick/Slapstick of Another Kind. 1983: Yellowbeard.

†Also directed

FENECH, Edwige 1948–
Lovely dark-haired Algerian-born actress and pin-up, probably the most physically beautiful continental star since Hedy Lamarr. Alas, she seemed content to remain lovingly photographed in the shallows of glossy Italian and West German sexploitation films (the English titles speak for themselves), belatedly dipping her toes into international waters with Il grande attacca in 1977. Her prolific apearances in skin-show comedies soon made her a big attraction in Europe, although barely(!) known elsewhere. Like Hedy Lamarr, she failed to mature into older roles, but instead became a powerful producer of

films and TV mini-series in the late 1990s.
1967: Toutes folles de lui. 1968: Madame und ihre Nichte (GB: House of Pleasure). Komme, liebe Maid und mache . . . (GB: Sex is a Pleasure). Il figlio dell Aquila Nera. Frau Wirtin hat auch einen Grafin (GB: Sexy Susan Sins Again. US: Sexy Susan at the King's Court). Samoa, Queen of the Jungle. Sensation!/Top Sensation (US: The Seducers). 1969: Der Mann mit dem goldenen Pinsel. Madame Bovary/Die nächte Bovary (GB: Play the Game or Leave the Bed. US: The Sins of Madame Bovary). Testa o croce. L'année de la contestation. Alle Kätzen naschen gern (GB: Blonde and Black Pussycats). Frau Wirtin hat auch eine Nichte. Die tolldreisten Geschichten des Honoré de Balzac (GB: The Bawdy Women of Balzac). 1970: Swinging Young Seductresses. Le caldi notti de Don Giovanni (GB: Don Giovanni's Hot Nights. US: The Loves of Don Juan). Le Mans, scorciatoia per l'inferno. Cinque bambole per la luna d'agosto (GB and US: Five Dolls for an August Moon). Lo strano vizio della Signora Ward. La tela del ragno. 1971: Deserto di fuoco (US: Desert of Fire). Next Victim. 1972: La bella Antonia (GB: Naughty Nun). Perche quelle strane gocce di sangue sul corpo di Jennifer? (GB: Erotic Blue). Il tuo vizio e una stanza chiusa e solo io ne ho la chiave (GB: Excite Me. US: Eye of the Black Cat). Quando le donne si chiamavano 'Madonne'. Tutti i colori del buio. 1973: Dio, sei proprio un Padreterno (US: Mean Frank and Crazy Tony). Johnny le Fligueur. Fiori uno, sotto un altro, arriva 'Il Passatore'. Quel gran pezzo dell' Ubalda (US: Ubalda, All Naked and Warm). Giovanna coscialunga disonorata con onore. 1974: Anna, quel particolare Piacere (GB: Secrets of a Call Girl. US: Anna: the Pleasure, the Torment). La signora gioca bene a scopa (GB: Poker in Bed. Later: The Good, the Bad and the Sexy). La vedova inconsolabile ringrazia quanti la consolarono (US: The Winsome Widow). Il suo nome faceva tremare . . . Interpol in allarme (US: Power Kill). Innocenza e turbamento. 1975: Il vizio di famiglia (GB and US: Vices in the Family). Grazie nonna (GB: Lover Boy). L'insegnante (GB: Sexy Schoolteacher). La moglie vergine (GB and US: The Virgin Wife). 40 gradi all'ombra del lenzuolo (GB and US: Sex With a Smile). Nude per l'assassino (GB: Strip Nude for Your Killer). La poliziotta fa carriera (US: Confessions of a Lady Cop). 1976: Cattavi pensieri (GB and US: Evil Thoughts). La dottoressa del distretto militare. La pretora. 1977: Taxi Girl. L'insegnante va in collegio. La soldatessa alla visita militare. Gioia/La vergine, il toro e il capricorno (GB: Erotic Exploits of a Sexy Seducer. US: Bull by the Horns). Il grande attacca/The Biggest Battle. 1978: L'insegnante viena a casa. La soldatessa alle grandi manovre. La poliziotta della squadra del buon costume. 1979: The Lady Next Door. My Loves. Il dottore Jeckill Jr (US: Jekyll Junior). Sabato, domenico e venerdi. La patata bollente (US: Hot Potato). Il ladrone (US: The Good Thief). 1980: La moglie in vacanza, l'amante in casa (US: While the Wife's Away . . .). Il ficcanaso. Io sono fotogenico. Zuccero, miele e peperoncino. 1981: Tais-toi quand tu parles! Io a Caterina. Asso. Lo spiritoso. Swing! Ricchi ricchissimi

practicamente in mutande. Cornetti alla crema. 1982: Il paramedico (US: The Orderly). Pizza, prosciutto e fichi. La poliziotta in New York. Roma X112X. L'avventura ideale. 1983: Sballato, gasato, completamente fuso. 1984: Blade of the Ripper. Vacanze in America. 1986: Rimini, Rimini, Rimini. 1987: Nel gorgo del peccato (TV). 1988: Phantom of Death. 1991: Surviving at the Top (TV mini-series shortened for cinemas).

FENN, Sherilyn (Sheryl Ann Fenn) 1965–
Small, apple-cheeked, curvaceous brunette American actress, once memorably described by director David Lynch as 'five feet of heaven in a ponytail' when she starred for him in *Wild at Heart*. Despite Lynch's enthusiasm, she hasn't quite made it to the top, even after interesting star appearances in *Ruby*, *Of Mice and Men* and *Boxing Helena* in the early 1990s. The niece of singer Suzi Quatro, she was once included in a list of the 50 most beautiful people in the world.
1983: Ups and Downs. 1984: The Wild Life. Silence of the Heart (TV). 1985: Out of Control. Just One of the Guys. 1986: The Wraith. Thrashin'. 1987: Zombie High. Power, Passion and Murder (TV). 1988: Two-Moon Junction. Divided We Stand (TV). Crime Zone. A Family Again. 1989: True Blood. 1990: Meridian/Kiss of the Beast. Wild at Heart. Backstreet Strays/Backstreet Dreams. 1991: Dillinger (TV). Diary of a Hit Man. 1992: Ruby. Of Mice and Men. Desire and Hell at the Sunset Motel. 1993: Three of Hearts. Boxing Helena. Fatal Instinct/Triple Indemnity. 1994: Queen of the Galaxy. Spring Awakening (TV). Slave of Dreams. 1995: Liz: The Elizabeth Taylor Story (TV). 1996: A Season in Purgatory (TV). The Assassination File (TV). Lovelife/Friends of Friends. 1997: Just Write. The Shadow Men. National Lampoon's The Don's Analyst (TV). Nightmare Street (TV). 1998: Dangerous Obsession. Outside Ozona. Darkness Falls. 1999: Cement. Johnny Hit.

FERGUSON, Craig 1965–
Tall, ingenuous-looking Scottish actor and comedian with very dark, tangly hair. Not unlike the young Sean Connery (of whom he also does a good impression), Ferguson spent 10 years in TV comedy on both sides of the Atlantic before launching a film career with some success, projecting a quite beguiling personality in light-hearted films of the late 1990s and beyond.

1998: Revenant/Modern Vampyres. 1999: The Big Tease. Saving Grace. 2000: Chain of Fools. Born Romantic.

FERNANDEL
(Fernand Contandin) 1902–1971
This genial, horse-faced French star comedian with the tombstone smile was around from the beginning of sound, but became internationally popular only after World War II. Whether as an unctuous flatterer of ladies, a hapless adventurer or the ubiquitous priest Don Camillo, he was a very funny man. Died from lung cancer.
1930: Le blanc et le noir. *La fine combine. Coeur de lilas. On purge bébé. *La meilleure bobonne. 1931: *Attaque nocturne. Vive la classe. Paris-Béguin. Restez dîner. J'ai quelque chose à vous dire. *Pas un mot à ma femme. *Beau jour de noces. *La veine d'Anatole. *Une brume piquante. *Bric-à-Brac et cie. 1932: Le jugement de minuit Lidoire. Les gaietés de l'escadron. *La claque. Le rosier de Madame Husson (GB: The Virtuous Isadore. US: He). *Cunegorde. *Elle disait non. *Par habitude. Pas de femmes. *Comme une carpe. *Quand tu nous tiens, amour. *La terreur de la Pampa. 1933: L'ordonnance. L'homme sans nom. Le coq du régiment. Adhémar aviateur. *Ça colle. *Restez dîner. 1934: Le garnison amoureuse. Angèle. Ma ruche. Nuit de folies. D'amour et d'eau fraîche. Le chéri de sa concierge. Les bleus de la marine. L'hôtel du libre exchange. 1935: Le train de huit heures. Le cavalier Lafleur. Ferdinand le noceur. Les gaietés de la finance. Jim la Houlette. 1936: Les rois du sport. Les dégourdis de la onzième. François premier. Josette. Un de la légion. 1937: Ignace. Regain. Hercule. Un carnet de bal (US: Life Dances On). Ernest le Rebelle. 1938: Barnabé.

Schpountz. Tricoche et Cacdet. Raphaël le Tatoué. Les cinq sous de Lavarède. 1939: Christine. Berlingot et cie. C'était moi. Fric-Frac. 1940: Monsieur Hector. L'héritier des Montdésir. La fille du puisatier. L'acrobate. Un chapeau de paille d'Italie. L'âge d'or. 1941: La nuit merveilleuse. Le club des soupirants. Les petits riens. Une vie de chien. 1942: La bonne étoile. †Simplet. Ne le criez pas sur les toits. 1943: *Guignol, marinette de France. 1944: Les gueux de paradis. Naïs. *Irma la voyante. 1945: L'adventure de Cabasson. *La carrière du grand café. La mystère Saint-Val. 1946: Pétrus. Coeur de coq. *Comédians ambulants. 1947: Edition spéciale. Emile l'Africain. Escale au soleil. 1948: Si ça peut vous faire plaisir. L'armoire volante. 1949: Je suis de la revue. On demande un assassin. Casimir. L'héroïque Monsieur Boniface. 1950: Topaze. Meutres. Tu m'a sauvé la vie. Botta e riposta. Uniformes et grandes manoeuvres. Boniface somnambule (GB: The Sleepwalker). 1951: The Red Inn. Adhémar. La table aux crevés (GB: Village Feud). The Little World of Don Camillo. 1952: Coiffeur pour dames (GB: An Artist with Ladies). Forbidden Fruit. Le boulanger de Valargue. The Return of Don Camillo. 1953: Carnaval. Santarellina. Mam'zelle Nitouche. Public Enemy No. 1. 1954: The Sheep Has Five Legs. Ali-Baba. Le printemps, l'automne et l'amour. 1955: La grande bagarre de Don Camillo (GB: Don Camillo's Last Round). 1956: Le couturier de ces dames (GB: Fernandel the Dressmaker). El amor de Don Juan (GB: Don Juan. US: Pantaloons). *Le téléphone. L'era de Venerdi 17. Sous le ciel de Provence (US: The Virtuous Bigamist). Honoré de Marseille. Quatre pas dans les nuages. *L'art d'être papa (TV). Around the World in 80 Days. L'homme a l'imperméable. 1957: Ex: fugue pour clarinette. Le chômeur de Clochemerle. Sénéchal the Magnificent. 1958: Paris Holiday. La vie à deux (GB: The Two of Us). La loi c'est la loi. Le grand chef. Le confident de ces dames. The Cow and I. Sous le ciel de Provence. 1959: Crésus. Les vignes du Seigneur. 1960: Le caïd. Cacagne. Dynamite Jack. 1961: Don Camillo Monseigneur. Cet imbécile de Rimoldi. L'assassin est dans l'annaire. Il giudizio universale. 1962: En avant la musique. The Devil and the 10 Commandments. Voyage to Biarritz. 1963: La cuisine au beurre (US: My Wife's Husband). Blague dans le coin. 1964: L'âge ingrat. Relaxe-toi, chérie. Le bon roi Dagobert. 1965: La bourse et la vie. Don Camillo in Moscow. 1966: Le voyage du père. 1967: L'homme à la Buick. 1970: Heureux qui comme Ulysse. 1971: Don Camillo, Peppone e i Giovanni d'oggi (unfinished).

†And directed

FERRER, José
(J. Vicente F. Otero y Cintron) 1908–1992
Glowering, long-faced, thick-lipped Puerto Rican actor who made himself a reputation for versatility in his first few films (which included an Academy Award for *Cyrano de Bergerac*) after coming to the cinema at 40. Later indulged a penchant for direction with variable results. He received additional Academy Award nominations for *Joan of Arc* and *Moulin Rouge*. Marriages to actress Uta Hagen and singer Rosemary Clooney (by whom he had six

children, including actor Miguel Ferrer; 1954–), were among three that ended in divorce. His fourth wife survived him.
1946: *Bolivia (narrator only). 1948: Joan of Arc. 1949: Whirlpool. *The Sydenham Plan (narrator only). 1950: The Secret Fury. Crisis. Cyrano de Bergerac. 1952: Anything Can Happen. Moulin Rouge. *Article 55 (narrator only). 1953: Miss Sadie Thompson. 1954: The Caine Mutiny. Deep in My Heart. 1955: The Shrike. Cockleshell Heroes. 1956: The Great Man. Four Girls in Town. 1957: I Accuse! 1959: The High Cost of Loving. 1961: Forbid Them Not (narrator only). Leggi di guerra. 1962: Lawrence of Arabia. Cyrano and D'Artagnan. Nine Hours to Rama. *Progress for Freedom (narrator only). 1963: Verspätung in Marienborn (GB: Stop Train 349). 1965: The Greatest Story Ever Told. Ship of Fools. 1966: Enter Laughing. 1968: Le avventure e gli amori di Miguel Cervantes (GB: Cervantes. US: Cervantes, the Young Rebel). A Case of Libel (TV). 1969: *The Little Drummer Boy. 1970: The Aquarians (TV). 1971: Banyon (TV). The Cable Car Mystery (later Crosscurrent) (TV). 1973: The Marcus-Nelson Murders (TV). El Clan de los Immorales (GB: Order to Kill). 1974: The Missing Are Deadly (TV). 1975: e'Lollipop (US: Forever Young, Forever Free). Paco. Medical Story (TV). Roman Grey (TV. GB: The Art of Crime). 1976: Crash. The Sentinel. The Big Bus. Voyage of the Damned. 1977: Exo-Man (TV). Who Has Seen the Wind? Behind the Iron Mask (GB: The Fifth Musketeer). Zoltan, Hound of Dracula (US: Dracula's Dog). J. Edgar Hoover, Godfather of the FBI (Later and GB: The Private Files of J. Edgar Hoover) 1978: The Swarm. The Amazing Captain Nemo (TV. GB: cinemas). Fedora. 1979: Natural Enemies. 1980: Bittercreek Brawl/The Big Brawl. The Red Tide (later Blood Tide). Easter Sunday. Pleasure Palace (TV). The Murder That Wouldn't Die (TV). Bloody Birthday. 1981: Berlin Tunnel 21 (TV). 1982: A Midsummer Night's Sex Comedy. 1983: To Be or Not to Be. The Being. This Girl for Hire (TV). Blood Feud (TV). 1984: Dune. The Evil That Men Do. Samson and Delilah (TV). 1985: Hitler's SS: Portrait in Evil (TV. GB: cinemas). Seduced (TV). 1986: The Violins Came with the Americans. 1987: Rosa. The Wind in the Willows (TV. Voice only). 1989: Old Explorers. Mother's Day (TV). 1990: A Life of Sin. The Sun and the Moon. 1991: Primary Motive. The Perfect Tribute (TV). Hired to Kill. 1992: Arrest the Restless.

As director: *1955: The Shrike. Cockleshell Heroes. 1956: The Great Man. 1957: I Accuse! 1958: The High Cost of Loving. 1961: Return to Peyton Place. 1962: State Fair.*

FERRER, Mel (Melchior Ferrer) 1917–
Gaunt, sensitive-looking leading man with receding hair, employed to best advantage in the early fifties, when he proved he could project sensitivity and meanness to equal effect. Went into production (he was a producer-director before acting in films) in the seventies after an increasingly lacklustre series of costume epics. Married to Audrey Hepburn (fourth of five) from 1954 to 1968.
1949: Lost Boundaries. 1950: Born to be Bad. 1951: The Brave Bulls. 1952: Rancho Notorious. Scaramouche. Lili. 1953: Saadia. 1954: Knights of the Round Table. 1955: Proibito (US: Forbidden). Oh, Rosalinda!! 1956: War and Peace. Elena et les hommes (GB and US: Paris Does Strange Things). 1957: The Vintage. The Sun Also Rises. 1958: Fräulein. Mayerling (TV). 1959: The World, the Flesh and the Devil. 1960: The Hands of Orlac. L'homme à femmes. Et mourir de plaisir. 1961: Charge of the Black Lancers. Blood and Roses. 1962: Leggi di guerra/Kriegsgesetz. The Longest Day. The Devil and the 10 Commandments. The Fall of the Roman Empire. 1964: Paris When It Sizzles. Sex and the Single Girl. El Greco. El Señor de la Salle. 1967: Every Day's a Holiday. 1969: Who Are My Own? 1971: Time for Loving. 1975: The Black Pirate. Brannigan. The Girl from the Red Cabaret. 1976: Eaten Alive (GB: Death Trap). Das Netz. The Antichrist (US: The Tempter). 1977: Hi-Riders. Pyjama Girl/La ragazza in pigiama giallo. 1978: The Fish Men. The Amazing Captain Nemo (TV. GB: cinemas). The Norseman. Zwischengleis (US: Yesterday's Tomorrow). Sharon: Portrait of a Mistress (TV). 1979: The Visitor. Top of the Hill (TV). The Fifth Floor. 1980: Sfida all'ultimo paradiso. Avvoltoi sulla city/Vultures over the City. The Memory of Eva Ryker (TV). Nightmare City. Buitres sobre la ciudad. Fugitive Family (TV). Lili Marleen. Mangiati vivi dai cannibali (GB: Eaten Alive. US: Doomed to Die). 1981: Mille milliards de dollars). Die Jäger (US: Deadly Game). 1982: Screamers (The Fish Men, with added footage). One Shoe Makes It Murder (TV). 1984: Lesson in Love (TV). 1985: Seduced (TV). 1986: Outrage! (TV). 1988: Wild Jack (TV). 1989: Christine Cromwell: Things That Go Bump in the Night (TV).

As director: *1945: The Girl of the Limberlost. 1950: The Secret Fury. Vendetta (co-directed). 1958: Green Mansions. 1965: Cabriola (US: Every Day is a Holiday).*

FEUILLÈRE, Edwige
(Caroline E. Cunati-Koenig) 1907–1998
Beautiful, faintly spiteful-looking French actress, only occasionally seen in international roles. In postwar years, she became best known for her parts as sensual, mature women teaching young men about love, or being confounded by fate. Her chestnut haired, brown-eyed loveliness graced the London stage on a number of occasions, although she made just one British film.
1931: *Bric-a-Brac et cie. Cordon-bleu. Mam'zelle Nitouche. *La fine combine. 1932: La perle. Topaze. Monsieur Albert. Maquillage. Une petit femme dans le train. 1933: Toi que j'adore. Les aventures du Roi Pausole. Matricule 33. L'appel de la nuit. Ces messieurs de La Santé. 1934: Le miroir des alouettes. 1935: Lucrecia Borgia. Barcarolle. Stradivarius. Amore. Golgotha. La route heureuse. 1936: Mister Flow (US: Compliments of Mister Flow). 1937: Marthe Richard au service de la France (GB: Au Service de la France). Feu! La dame de Malacca. 1938: J'étais une aventurière. 1939: L'émigrante. Sans lendemain. 1940: De Mayerling à Sarajevo. 1941: Mam'zelle Bonaparte. La Duchesse de Langeais. L'honorable Catherine. 1943: Lucrèce. 1945: Tant que je vivrai. La parte de l'ombre (US: Blind Desire). 1946: L'idiot. Il suffit d'une fois. 1947: L'aigle a deux têtes. 1948: Woman Hater. 1949: Julie de Carneilhan. 1950: Olivia (US: Pit of Loneliness). Souvenirs perdus (GB: Lost Property). 1951: Le Cap de l'Esperance. 1952: Adorables créatures/Adorable Creatures. 1953: Le blé en herbe (GB: Ripening Seed. US: The Game of Love). 1954: Les fruits de l'été (US: Fruits of the Summer). 1957: Quand la femme s'en mêle. Le septième commandment (GB: The Seventh Commandment). 1958: En cas de malheur (GB and US: Love is My Profession). La vie à deux/The Two of Us. 1961: Amours célèbres. 1962: Le crime ne paie pas (GB: The Gentle Art of Murder. US: Crime Does Not Pay). 1964: Aimez-vous les femmes? (GB: Do You Like Women? US: A Taste for Women). 1967: *La route d'un homme (narrator only). 1968: Scusi, facciamo l'amore. 1969: Tous les coups sont bon pour OSS 117. 1970: Le clair de terre. 1974: La chair de l'orchidée. 1981: Le chef de famille.

FIELD, Betty 1918–1973

Neat, versatile American actress, seen in her younger days mostly as girls with some kind of defect, physical or mental, in their make-up. She had some interesting roles (the farm-slut in *Of Mice and Men*; Daisy in the 1949 version of *The Great Gatsby*), but showed preference for the stage and also aged quickly, returning to films from time to time as troubled or repressed women. Died from a cerebral haemorrhage.

1939: What a Life. Of Mice and Men. 1940: Seventeen. Victory. 1941: Shepherd of the Hills. Blues in the Night. 1942: Kings Row. Are Husbands Necessary? 1943: Flesh and Fantasy. 1944: The Great Moment. Tomorrow the World. 1945: The Southerner. 1949: The Great Gatsby. 1955: Picnic. 1956: Bus Stop. 1957: Peyton Place. 1959: Hound Dog Man. 1960: Butterfield 8. 1962: Bird Man Of Alcatraz. 1965: Seven Women. 1968: How to Save a Marriage – and Ruin Your Life. Coogan's Bluff.

FIELD, Sally 1946–

Tiny, pug-faced American actress with silky brown hair and sexy figure who played cute young things in such TV series as *The Flying Nun* throughout the 1960s. Her career seemed to be over by the early 1970s, when, after Actors' Studio training, she suddenly re-emerged as a big star with a series of tough, determined little ladies that only her one previous film appearance had hinted at. Subsequently, she took an Emmy for *Sybil* and Academy Awards for *Norma Rae* and *Places in the Heart*, but became notorious for her gushy speeches of acceptance. Stepdaughter of Jock Mahoney (*qv*) and daughter of actress Margaret Field, later Maggie Mahoney.

1962: Moon Pilot. 1967: The Way West. 1970:

Marriage Year One (TV). Maybe I'll Come Home Again in the Spring (TV). 1971: Hitched (TV. GB: Westward the Wagon). Mongo's Back in Town (TV). 1972: Home for the Holidays (TV). 1976: Bridger (TV). Stay Hungry. Sybil (TV. GB: cinemas). 1977: Smokey and the Bandit. Heroes. 1978: Hooper. The End. Norma Rae. 1979: Beyond the Poseidon Adventure. 1980: Smokey and the Bandit II (GB: Smokey and the Bandit Ride Again). 1981: Back Roads. Absence of Malice. 1982: Kiss Me Goodbye. 1984: Places in the Heart. 1985: Murphy's Romance. 1987: Surrender. 1988: Punchline. 1989: Steel Magnolias. 1990: Not Without My Daughter. 1991: Soapdish. 1993: Homeward Bound: The Incredible Journey (voice only). Mrs Doubtfire. 1994: Forrest Gump. 1996: Homeward Bound II: Lost in San Francisco (voice only). Eye for an Eye. 1999: A Cooler Climate (TV). 2000: Say It Isn't So. Where the Heart Is.
As director: 1996: The Christmas Tree (TV). 2000: Beautiful.

FIELD, Shirley Ann(e)
(S. Bloomfield) 1936

Busty, brunette British actress with cheerful smile and jaunty manner. A multiplicity of pin-up pictures was followed by success as a panellist in the TV quiz game *Yakity Yak*. Her film roles, though increasing in size, remained strictly decorative until 1960, when she surprisingly blossomed as an actress (and added the 'e' to Ann) She was unwisely cast after that, and her career waned, although she came back in TV drama in 1980, looking as ravishing as ever.

1955: Simon and Laura. All for Mary. Lost (US: Tears for Simon). 1956: The Weapon. It's Never Too Late. It's a Wonderful World. Dry Rot. Loser Takes All. The Silken Affair. Yield to the Night (US: Blonde Sinner). 1957: The Flesh is Weak. Seven Thunders (US: The Beasts of Marseilles). The Good Companions. 1959: Horrors of the Black Museum. Upstairs and Downstairs. Once More with Feeling. 'Beat' Girl (US: Wild for Kicks). 1960: And the Same to You. Peeping Tom. The Entertainer. Saturday Night and Sunday Morning. Man in the Moon. 1961: The Damned (US: These Are the Damned). 1962: The War Lover. Lunch Hour. 1963: Kings of the Sun. Hell is Empty (released 1967). 1965: Wedding March. 1966: Doctor in Clover. Alfie. 1969: With Love in Mind. 1970: A Touch of the Other. 1973: House of the Living Dead (GB: Dr Maniac). 1985: My Beautiful Laundrette. 1988: Shag. 1989:

Getting It Right. The Rachel Papers. 1991: Hear My Song. 1993: U.F.O. 1994: Loving Deadly. At Risk. 1999: A Monkey's Tale (voice only). 2000: Christie Malry's Own Double Entry/Christie Malry's Own Double Life.

FIELD, Sid 1904–1950

Crazy, fast-talking British comedian, an immense success in the music-halls, particularly in the provinces, where his cross-talking routines with stooge Jerry Desmonde (especially the famous golfing sketch) frequently brought the house down. His three films tried to do too much with him as a situation-comedy actor and failed to capture his special appeal. Died from a heart attack.

1940: That's the Ticket. 1946: London Town (US: My Heart Goes Crazy). 1948: Cardboard Cavalier.

FIELD, Virginia
(Margaret Field) 1917–1992

Aristocratic, cool-looking, blonde English-born actress of swan-like attractiveness, in Hollywood from 1936. Here, her unmistakeably English tones and poised manner were heard and seen as the heroine of numerous second-feature thrillers. She looked best in smart clothes and pearls and also played 'the other woman' in better-quality features. From 1952, she was furiously busy in television, including several appearances in 'Perry Mason' mysteries. Married three times, the first to actor Paul Douglas (*qv*), the last to actor Willard Parker (*qv*) from 1951 to her death from cancer.

1934: The Merry Widow. The Lady is Willing. The Primrose Path. 1936: Ladies in Love. Career Woman. Lloyds of London. Sing, Baby, Sing. Thank You, Jeeves. 1937: Charlie Chan at Monte Carlo. Lancer Spy. Ali Baba Goes to Town. Think Fast, Mr Moto. London by Night. 1938: Mr Moto Takes a Vacation. 1939: The Cisco Kid and the Lady. Bridal Suite. Eternally Yours. Captain Fury. Mr Moto's Last Warning. The Sun Never Sets. 1940: Hudson's Bay. Dance, Girl, Dance. Waterloo Bridge. 1941: *Stars at Play. Knockout/Right to the Heart. Singapore Woman. 1942: Atlantic Convoy. 1943: The Crystal Ball. Stage Door Canteen. 1946: The Imperfect Lady (GB: Mrs Loring's Secret). The Perfect Marriage. 1947: Christmas Eve. Dream Girl. Ladies' Man. Repeat Performance. Variety Girl. 1948: A Connecticut Yankee in King Arthur's Court (GB: A Yankee in King Arthur's Court). 1949: John Loves Mary. 1950: Dial 1119 (GB: The Violent Hour). 1951: The Lady Pays Off. Week-End With Father. 1953: The Veils of Bagdad. 1956: The Empty Room (TV. GB: cinemas). 1957: Rockabilly Baby. 1958: Appointment With a Shadow (GB: The Big Story). 1961: The Explosive Generation. 1964: The Earth Dies Screaming. 1968: Spara, gringo, spara (GB and US: The Longest Hunt).

FIELDS, Dame Gracie

(Grace Stansfield) 1898–1979

Bubbling, dark-haired British comedienne/singer, whose Lancashire-slanted mixture of comic songs and romantic ballads made her the most popular recording star of her day. Despite coming to films in her thirties, she quickly became Britain's (and, briefly, the world's) highest-paid film star, cruising her chirpy personality through a series of soft-centred, artfully-contrived tragi-comedies. Lost her popularity (and her British film career) when deciding to live abroad during World War II. Married (second of three) director/comedian Monty Banks (1897–1950). Created Dame in 1979. Died from a heart attack.

1931: Sally in Our Alley. 1932: Looking on the Bright Side. 1933: This Week of Grace. 1934: Love, Life and Laughter. Sing As We Go. 1935: Look Up and Laugh. 1936: Queen of Hearts. 1937: The Show Goes On. 1938: We're Going to be Rich. Keep Smiling (US: Smiling Along). 1939: Shipyard Sally. 1943: Stage Door Canteen. Holy Matrimony. 1944: Molly and Me. 1945: Paris Underground (GB: Madame Pimpernel).

FIELDS, W.C.

(William Claude Dukenfield) 1879–1946

Burly, round-faced, red-nosed American

juggler and comedian, with a long history in vaudeville before his serious film career began in the mid-twenties. With sound, his own peculiar, abrasive, embittered, alcohol-oriented delivery really came into its own and, as henpeck or charlatan in turn, he created a series of comedy classics. Wore a fake moustache in films until 1932. Died, from a combination of dropsy, a liver ailment and heart failure, on the day he moaned about more than any other – Christmas Day.

1915: *Pool Sharks. *His Lordship's Dilemma. 1924: Janice Meredith (GB: The Beautiful Rebel). 1925: Sally of the Sawdust. That Royle Girl. 1926: So's Your Old Man. It's the Old Army Game. 1927: The Potters. Running Wild. Two Flaming Youths (GB: The Side Show). 1928: Tillie's Punctured Romance (GB: Marie's Millions). Fools for Luck. 1930: *The Golf Specialist. 1931: Her Majesty Love. 1932: *The Dentist. If I Had a Million. Million Dollar Legs. 1933: *The Fatal Glass of Beer. *The Pharmacist. *Hip Action. *Hollywood on Parade (B7). *The Barber Shop. International House. Tillie and Gus. Alice in Wonderland. 1934: Six of a Kind. You're Telling Me! The Old Fashioned Way. It's a Gift. Mrs Wiggs of the Cabbage Patch. 1935: David Copperfield. Mississippi. The Man on the Flying Trapeze (GB: The Memory Expert). 1936: Poppy. 1938: The Big Broadcast of 1938. 1939: You Can't Cheat an Honest Man. 1940: My Little Chickadee. The Bank Dick (GB: The Bank Detective). 1941: Never Give a Sucker an Even Break (GB: What a Man!). 1942: †Tales of Manhattan. 1944: Follow the Boys. Song of the Open Road. Sensations of 1945.

†Sequences deleted from final release print

FIENNES, Joseph 1970–

Tall, whippy, narrow-faced, dark-haired British actor at his most romantic and charismatic when bearded and moustachioed. Fiennes, brother of actor Ralph Fiennes (qv) and director Martha Fiennes, was rather lost in the shuffle in his first film, but when he grew facial hair and donned doublet and hose for period drama, he looked every inch a star. Unlucky not to be nominated for an Academy Award in Shakespeare in Love, Fiennes looks set for an interesting star career, perhaps as idealists of flawed character.

1995: Stealing Beauty. 1998: Martha, Meet Frank, Daniel and Laurence (US: The Very Thought of You). Elizabeth. Shakespeare in

Love. 1999: Forever Mine. 2000: Enemy at the Gates. Rancid Aluminium. 2001: Dust.

FIENNES, Ralph 1962–

Visionary-looking, brown-haired British actor with fine-grained features. Busy playing Shakespeare on stage through the 1980s, Fiennes was an obvious choice to portray Lawrence of Arabia in a TV film, but less obvious to play Heathcliff in Wuthering Heights, which wasn't a success, or the hideous German officer in Schindler's List, which was, both for the film's makers and for Fiennes, who was nominated for an Academy Award. Winning a second nomination for The English Patient, he quickly settled in as a cool but charismatic leading man in prestige projects. Surname pronounced Fines.

1991: A Dangerous Man: Lawrence After Arabia (TV). 1992: Emily Brontë's Wuthering Heights. 1993: The Baby of Mâcon. Schindler's List. 1994: The Cormorant (TV). Quiz Show. 1995: Strange Days. 1996: The English Patient. 1997: Oscar and Lucinda. 1998: The Prince of Egypt (voice only). The Avengers. 1999: Sunshine. The Miracle Maker (voice only). Onegin. The End of the Affair.

FINCH, Jon 1941–

Dark-haired, handsome, brooding, young-looking British actor who shot to stardom in the early 1970s, especially in the title role of Roman Polanski's Macbeth. But good roles in British films seemed elusive, and he was looking farther afield from the mid-1970s. He did not, however, regain his place at the top in cinematic terms, despite some good supporting roles and one or two further leads.

1970: The Vampire Lovers. The Horror of

Frankenstein. 1971: L'affaire Martine Desclos. Sunday, Bloody Sunday. Macbeth. 1972: Frenzy. Lady Caroline Lamb. 1973: The Final Programme (US: The Last Days of Man on Earth). 1974: Diagnosis: Murder. 1976: Une femme fidèle. The Man with the Green Cross. 1977: El segundo poder. Die Standarte (US: Battle Flag). 1978: El borracho. Death on the Nile. 1979: The Sabina. 1980: Breaking Glass. Gary Cooper, que estas en los cielos. 1981: The Threat. 1982: Giro City (TV. US: And Nothing But the Truth). 1984: Pop Pirates. 1987: Strange. 1988: Streets of Yesterday. 1989: The Voice. La più bella del reame. 1994: Lurking Fear (cable TV). 1996: Darklands.

FINCH, Peter

(Frederick P. Ingle Finch) 1916–1977

Dark-haired, British-born portrayer of strong characters. He made his name in Australia before returning to England where he slowly became much admired as hero, villain and all-round good actor. In the sixties he became an international star, but his roles were less consistently good. A hell-raiser who lived life to the full, he died from a heart attack, and was posthumously given an Oscar for his last film, *Network*. Also Oscar-nominated for *Sunday, Bloody Sunday*.

*1935: †Magic Shoes. 1938: Dad and Dave Come to Town (GB: The Rudd Family Goes to Town). Mr Chedworth Steps Out. 1939: Ants in His Pants. 1940: The Power and the Glory. 1942: Another Threshold. While There's Still Time. 1943: South-West Pacific. Red Sky at Morning (released 1951 as Escape at Dawn). 1944: Rats of Tobruk. *Jungle Patrol (narrator only). 1945: *Indonesia Calling (narrator only). 1946: A Son is Born. *Native Earth (narrator only). 1947: *The Nomads (narrator*

*only). 1948: Eureka Stockade (US: Massacre Hill). The Hunt (narrator only). 1949: *The Corroboree (narrator only). Train of Events. 1950: The Wooden Horse. The Miniver Story. 1952: The Story of Robin Hood and His Merrie Men. 1953: The Story of Gilbert and Sullivan (US: The Great Gilbert and Sullivan). The Heart of the Matter. 1954: Father Brown (US: The Detective). Elephant Walk. Make Me an Offer. 1955: Passage Home. The Dark Avenger (US: The Warriors). Simon and Laura. Josephine and Men. 1956: A Town Like Alice (US: The Rape of Malaya). The Queen in Australia (narrator only). *Melbourne – Olympic City (narrator only). The Battle of the River Plate (US: Pursuit of the Graf Spee). The Royal Tour of New South Wales (narrator only). 1957: The Shiralee. Robbery Under Arms. Windom's Way. 1958: A Far Cry (narrator only). Operation Amsterdam. 1959: The Nun's Story. 1960: The Trials of Oscar Wilde (US: The Man with the Green Carnation). Kidnapped. No Love for Johnnie. 1961: The Sins of Rachel Cade. 1962: I Thank a Fool. 1963: In the Cool of the Day. Girl with Green Eyes. 1964: First Men in the Moon. The Pumpkin Eater. 1965: Judith. The Flight of the Phoenix. 1966: 10.30 p.m. Summer. 1967: Far from the Madding Crowd. 1968: The Legend of Lylah Clare. 1969: The Red Tent. *The Greatest Mother of Them All. 1971: Sunday, Bloody Sunday. Something to Hide. 1972: England Made Me. Lost Horizon. 1973: Bequest to the Nation (US: The Nelson Affair). 1974: The Abdication. 1976: Raid on Entebbe (TV. GB: cinemas). Network.*
As director: *1962: *The Day.*

†*Unreleased*

FINNEY, Albert 1936–

Beefy, scowling, tow-haired British leading actor, one of the original angry young brigade of the early 1960s. His best roles (*Tom Jones, Saturday Night and Sunday Morning, Gumshoe, The Dresser*) have been so good as to make the rest of his film career seem desperately unsatisfactory by comparison. Married to actresses Jane Wenham (1957 to 1961) and Anouk Aimée (*qv*, 1970 to 1978). Nominated for Academy Awards in *Tom Jones, Murder on the Orient Express* and *The Dresser*. In the 1990s, he offered studies of small-town Irish characters among several ruddy-cheeked eccentrics.

1960: The Entertainer. Saturday Night and Sunday Morning. 1963: Tom Jones. The Victors. Night Must Fall. 1967: Two for the

Road. †Charlie Bubbles. 1969: The Picasso Summer. 1970: Scrooge. 1971: Gumshoe. 1972: Alpha Beta (copyrighted and released 1975). 1974: Murder on the Orient Express. 1975: The Adventure of Sherlock Holmes' Smarter Brother. 1977: The Duellists. 1980: Loophole. 1981: Wolfen. Looker. Shoot the Moon. 1982: Annie. 1983: The Dresser. 1984: Under the Volcano. Pope John Paul II (TV). Notes from Under the Volcano. Observations Under the Volcano. 1987: Orphans. 1989: The Image (TV). 1990: Miller's Crossing. Roger Waters The Wall – Live in Berlin. 1991: Der lachende Tod. The Green Man (TV). 1992: The Playboys. Rich in Love. 1993: The Browning Version. 1994: A Man of No Importance. 1995: The Run of the Country. 1997: Washington Square. 1998: Breakfast of Champions. A Rather English Marriage. 1999: Simpatico. 2000: Erin Brockovich. Delivering Milo.

†*And directed*

FIORENTINO, Linda

(Clorinda Fiorentino) 1960–

Dark-haired, dangerous-looking, slender American actress of flat-faced attractiveness. Although she had the leading role in her first film, her acting often bordered on the nondescript and she lit few fires until producing a sensational performance from nowhere at 34 in *The Last Seduction*, a screen-scorching portrayal that won her a hatful of awards. Further roles again disappointed, and two years later she had returned to *Seduction*'s director John Dahl vainly seeking fresh inspiration.

1984: Vision Quest/Crazy for You. 1985: After Hours. Gotcha! 1988: Wildfire. The Moderns. 1989: The Neon Empire. 1990: Queens Logic. 1991: Shout. Strangers (TV). 1992: Chain of Desire. Fixing the Shadow/Beyond the Law. 1993: Acting on Impulse (TV. GB: Secret Lies). 1994: The Desperate Trail. The Last Seduction. Charlie's Ghost (TV). 1995: Jade. Bodily Harm. 1996: Unforgettable. Large Than Life. 1997: Men in Black. Kicked in the Head. Body Count. 1998: Killer's Kiss. 1999: Dogma. Ordinary Decent Criminal. 2000: Where the Money Is. What Planet Are You From?

FIRTH, Colin 1960–

Brown-haired British actor of cocksure, slightly devious-looking handsomeness. He seemed a sound bet for big stardom in the

mid 1980s, but his films and TV after that were not of mainstream appeal and he has not as yet quite made the very front rank. He remains a fascinating actor when in command of his role, and has been impressive in a number of films, among them *Valmont* and *The Hour of the Pig*. But he can sometimes look lost in less well-defined parts. A great success, though, in TV's *Pride and Prejudice*.
1984: *Another Country. Nineteen Nineteen. Camille* (TV). 1985: *Dutch Girls* (TV). *Restless Natives.* 1987: *A Month in the Country. The Secret Garden* (TV). 1988: *Tumbledown* (TV). 1989: *Apartment Zero. Valmont.* 1990: *Wings of Fame.* 1991: *Femme Fatale. Out of the Blue* (TV). 1992: *Hostages* (cable TV). 1993: *The Hour of the Pig/The Advocate.* 1994: *Playmaker.* 1995: *Circle of Friends.* 1996: *The English Patient. Fever Pitch.* 1997: *A Thousand Acres.* 1998: *The Secret Laughter of Women. Shakespeare in Love.* 1999: *My Life So Far.* 2000: *Londinium. Relative Values.* 2001: *Bridget Jones' Diary.*

FISHBURNE, Laurence
(formerly Larry) 1961–
Strong-looking, rarely-smiling American actor, often as powerful, incisive or dangerous characters. An actor since his teens, Fishburne became trained on the classical stage and has often revisited the theatre, resisting conventional film roles throughout his career, probably after becoming tired of saccharine scripts from a long stint on daytime TV soap in his early days. After attention-grabbing performances in *Boyz N the Hood* and *Deep Cover*, he changed his billing to Laurence and promptly won an Academy Award nomination for his finely-shaded portrait of Ike Turner in *Tina*

What's Love Got to Do With It. Still mixes strong lead parts with top supporting roles.
1975: *Cornbread, Earl and Me.* 1979: *Fast Break. Apocalypse Now.* 1980: *Willie and Phil.* 1982: *Death Wish II.* 1983: *For Us the Living* (TV). *Rumble Fish. I Take These Men* (TV). 1984: *The Cotton Club.* 1986: *The Color Purple* (shown 1985). *Quicksilver. Cherry 2000* (released 1988). *A Nightmare on Elm Street 3: Dream Warriors.* 1987: *Gardens of Stone. Band of the Hand.* 1988: *School Daze. Red Heat.* 1989: *The Father Clements Story* (TV). *King of New York.* 1990: *Cadence* (GB: *Stockade*). *Decoration Day* (TV). *Class Action.* 1991: *Hearts of Darkness: A Filmmaker's Apocalypse.* 1992: *Boyz N the Hood.* 1993: *Deep Cover. Searching for Bobby Fischer* (GB: *Innocent Moves*). *Tina What's Love Got to Do With It.* 1994: *Higher Learning. Bad Company.* 1995: *Just Cause. The Tuskegee Airmen* (TV). *Othello.* 1996: *Double Cross. Fled.* 1997: *Hoodlum. Event Horizon.* 1998: *Always Outnumbered* (cable TV). *Welcome to Hollywood* (doc). 1999: *The Matrix. Wilson's Travelling Miles* (doc). 2000: *Cassandra.* †*Riff Raff.* †*Once in the Life.*

†*Also directed.*

FISHER, Carrie 1956–
Diminutive but forceful, dark-haired American actress, daughter of Debbie Reynolds (*qv*) and singer Eddie Fisher, and on stage with her mother at 12. Despite landing the female lead in the *Star Wars* films, she did not quite establish a definite image for herself and her remaining roles don't linger in the mind. Some filmographies credit her with appearances in *I Wanna Hold Your Hand* (1978) and *Wise Blood* (1979), but she doesn't seem to be in either. Married/divorced singer Paul Simon (of Simon and Garfunkel). Also a successful novelist, she wrote the screenplay for the 1990 film of her semi-autobiographical book *Postcards from the Edge*. Since 1992, she has concentrated almost entirely on a writing career that has also involved her working as a 'script doctor' on Hollywood screenplay rewrites.
1975: *Shampoo.* 1977: *Star Wars.* 1978: *Leave Yesterday Behind* (TV). 1979: *Mr Mike's Mondo Video.* 1980: *The Empire Strikes Back. The Blues Brothers.* 1981: *Under the Rainbow.* 1983: *Return of the Jedi.* 1984: *Garbo Talks!* 1985: *Mischief/The Man with the One Red Shoe.* 1986: *Hannah and Her Sisters. Hollywood Vice Squad. Sunday Drive*

(TV). *Liberty* (TV). *Amazon Women on the Moon.* 1987: *The Time Guardian.* 1988: *Appointment with Death. Dead and Married* (later *She's Back*). 1989: *The 'burbs. When Harry Met Sally...* 1990: *Lover Boy. Sweet Revenge* (TV). *Sibling Rivalry.* 1991: *Drop Dead Fred. Soapdish. This is My Life.* 1993: *So I Married an Axe Murderer.* 1997: *Austin Powers: International Man of Mystery.* 2000: *Scream 3. Famous.*

FITZGERALD, Geraldine 1912–
Dark-haired Irish actress with classic 'colleen' complexion and strong personality. She went to Hollywood after a start in British films, but her ideals were too high for Warners, who suspended her a number of times for refusing roles, and her film career stuttered to a halt in the late forties. Latterly became a barnstorming character actress and nightclub singer. Nominated for an Academy Award in *Wuthering Heights*. Mother of director Michael Lindsay-Hogg. Great-aunt of actress Tara Fitzgerald (*qv*).
1934: *Blind Justice. Open All Night.* 1935: *The Lad. The Ace of Spades. Three Witnesses. Lieutenant Daring RN. Turn of the Tide. Radio Parade of 1935. Bargain Basement/Department Store.* 1936: *Debt of Honour. Café Mascot. The Mill on the Floss.* 1939: *Wuthering Heights. Dark Victory.* 1940: *A Child is Born. 'Til We Meet Again.* 1941: *Shining Victory. Flight from Destiny.* 1942: *The Gay Sisters.* 1943: *Watch on the Rhine.* 1944: *Ladies Courageous. Wilson.* 1945: *The Strange Affair of Uncle Harry* (GB: *Uncle Harry*). 1946: *Three Strangers. OSS. Nobody Lives Forever.* 1948: *So Evil My Love.* 1951: *The Late Edwina Black* (US: *Obsessed*). 1958: *10 North Frederick.* 1959: *The Moon and Sixpence* (TV). 1961: *The Fiercest Heart.* 1965: *The Pawnbroker.* 1968: *Rachel, Rachel.* 1971: †*Believe in Me.* 1973: *The Last American Hero.* 1974: *Harry and Tonto.* 1975: *Cold Sweat. Echoes of a Summer.* 1977: *Ciao Male/Bye Bye Monkey!/The Monkey's Uncle. The Mango Tree. Yesterday's Child* (TV). *The Quinns* (TV). 1979: *Tristan and Isolt* (unreleased). 1980: *Arthur.* 1982: *The Link.* 1983: *Kennedy* (TV). *Easy Money.* 1985: *Do You Remember Love?* (TV). 1986: *Poltergeist II. Circle of Violence: A Family Drama* (TV). 1987: *Night of Courage* (TV). 1988: *Arthur 2: On the Rocks.* 1991: *Bump in the Night* (TV).

†*Scenes deleted from release print*

FITZGERALD, Tara 1967–
Chirpy, bright-faced, dark-haired British actress, stepdaughter of actor Norman Rodway and great niece of actress Geraldine Fitzgerald. Although she had trouble keeping her clothes on in early film roles, she looked to be settling in as an in-demand star of British films in the mid-1990s. However, she has chosen TV, the theatre and out-of-the-way film projects since then, few of which have maximised her gamine appeal.
1991: Hear My Song. The Black Candle (TV). 1992: Six Characters in Search of an Author. 1994: A Man of No Importance. Sirens. Fall from Grace (TV). 1995: The Englishman Who Went Up a Hill But Came Down a Mountain. 1996: Brassed Off. 1997: The Student Prince (TV). The Woman in White (TV). 1998: Conquest. Little White Lies (TV). 1999: Frenchman's Creek (TV). New World Disorder. In the Name of Love (TV). 2000: Rancid Aluminium. Villa des Roses. Childhood. Dark Blue World.

FLANAGAN, Bud (Reuben Weintrop, later Robert Winthrop) 1896–1968
Genial Jewish East Londoner who, after music-hall experience as a magician, formed half of a smash-hit comedy team with lean, poker-faced Chesney Allen (1893–1982). Their sense of humour, at once bawdy and lunatic, was amalgamated in the late thirties with fellow comedy teams Nervo and Knox and Naughton and Gold to form the Crazy Gang. Flanagan, customarily in dented porkpie hat and moth-eaten fur coat, led the Gang and also wrote and sang (with Allen) some enormously successful London-based songs. The team ultimately split because of Allen's ill-health but, ironically, it was

Flanagan who died first, from a heart attack.
*1932: *The Bailiffs. 1933: *They're Off. *The Dreamers. 1934: Wild Boy. 1935: A Fire Has Been Arranged. 1937: Underneath the Arches. Okay for Sound. 1938: Alf's Button Afloat. 1939: The Frozen Limits. 1940: Gasbags. 1941: *Listen to Britain. *The Crazy Gang Argue About Lending Money (Gaumont-British newsreel). 1942: We'll Smile Again. 1943: Theatre Royal. 1944: Dreaming. 1945: Here Comes the Sun. 1951: Judgment Deferred. 1958: Dunkirk. Life is a Circus. 1963: The Wild Affair.*

†Without Chesney Allen

FLANERY, Sean Patrick 1965–
Dark, laconic-looking American actor with crooked smile who made his name in the TV series *Young Indiana Jones*, a show that took him to more than 50 countries in four years. Since then, he's attempted a wide variety of leading roles without getting into a big box-office hit.
1987: A Tiger's Tale. 1988: My Life As a Babysitter (TV). Just Perfect (TV). 1993: Kingdom Come. 1994: Frank and Jesse. Lie Down with the Dragon. Guinevere (TV). 1995: The Grass Harp. Mrs Munck. Powder. Raging Angels/The Spirit Realm. 1996: Whiskey Down/Just Your Luck. 1997: Pale Saints. Suicide Kings. Eden. The Method. Best Men. Zack and Reba. 1998: Girl. 1999: Boondock Saints. Simply Irresistible. Body Shots. 2000: Detox. Run the Wild Fields.

FLEMING, Rhonda
(Marilyn Louis) 1922–
So what was wrong with Marilyn Louis? At any rate, the change of name did this stunning, green-eyed American redhead little good until she was selected as Bing Crosby's leading lady in *A Connecticut Yankee in King Arthur's Court*. Then she rapidly became known as Queen of Technicolor in a series of self-reliant, but slightly too self-aware performances in which she never quite seemed to let herself go. Married (fourth of five) to producer-director Hall Bartlett from 1966 to 1971. Joint founder of the Rhonda Fleming Mann Resource Center for Women with Cancer.
*1943: In Old Oklahoma (later War of the Wildcats). 1944: When Strangers Marry (later Betrayed). Since You Went Away. 1945: Spellbound. The Spiral Staircase. Abilene Town. 1947: Adventure Island. Out of the Past (GB: Build My Gallows High). 1949: A Connecticut Yankee in King Arthur's Court (GB: A Yankee in King Arthur's Court). The Great Lover. 1950: The Eagle and the Hawk. The Redhead and the Cowboy. Cry Danger. *Hollywood Goes to Bat. 1951: The Last Outpost. Little Egypt (GB: Chicago Masquerade). Hong Kong. Crosswinds. 1952: The Golden Hawk. Tropic Zone. 1953: Pony Express. Those Redheads from Seattle. Serpent of the Nile. Inferno. 1954: Jivaro (GB: Lost Treasure of the Amazon). Yankee Pasha. The Courtesan of Babylon (GB: The Slave Woman. US: Queen of Babylon). 1955: Tennessee's Partner. 1956: The Killer is Loose. Slightly Scarlet. *Hollywood Beauty. While the City Sleeps. Odongo. *Hollywood Premiere. Gunfight at the OK Corral. 1957: The Buster Keaton Story. Gun Glory. 1958: Bullwhip. Home Before Dark. 1959: Alias Jesse James. The Big Circus. 1960: The Revolt of the Slaves. The Crowded Sky. 1964: The Patsy. Una moglie americana (US: Run for Your Wife). 1968: Backtrack (TV). 1975: Last Hours Before Morning (TV). Won Ton Ton, the Dog Who Saved Hollywood. 1979: Love for Rent (TV). 1980: The Nude Bomb. 1991: Waiting for the Wind (TV).*

FLYNN, Errol 1909–1959
Tasmanian-born star whose colourful early years, spent mainly in various forms of shipping, led him to film in Australia, England and finally Hollywood, where, soon moustachioed, he became the film capital's swashbuckler *par excellence* in a series of expensively-mounted action films. His vivid, womanizing, booze-hitting private life included marriages to actresses Lily Damita (1935–1942) and Patrice Wymore (1950;

separated 1957), first and third of three. Died from a heart attack. Completists claim Flynn may also be glimpsed in 1947's *The Lady From Shanghai*, for which director Orson Welles had hired his yacht.

*1932: Dr. H. Erben's New Guinea Expedition. 1933: In the Wake of the Bounty. 1934: Murder at Monte Carlo. 1935: *A Dream Comes True. The Case of the Curious Bride. Don't Bet on Blondes. Captain Blood. 1936: The Charge of the Light Brigade. *Pirate Party on Catalina Isle. 1937: Green Light. The Prince and the Pauper. Another Dawn. The Perfect Specimen. 1938: The Adventures of Robin Hood. The Sisters. Four's a Crowd. The Dawn Patrol. 1939: Dodge City. The Private Lives of Elizabeth and Essex. 1940: Virginia City. Santa Fé Trail. The Sea Hawk. 1941: Footsteps in the Dark. Dive Bomber. They Died with Their Boots On. 1942: Desperate Journey. Gentleman Jim. 1943: Edge of Darkness. Northern Pursuit. Thank Your Lucky Stars. 1944: Uncertain Glory. 1945: Objective Burma. San Antonio. 1946: Never Say Goodbye. Cry Wolf. Escape Me Never. Always Together. 1948: Silver River. Adventures of Don Juan (GB: The New Adventures of Don Juan). 1949: That Forsyte Woman (GB: The Forsyte Saga). It's a Great Feeling. Montana. 1950: Rocky Mountain. Hello God. Kim. The Adventures of Captain Fabian. 1952: *Cruise of the Zaca. Mara Maru. Against All Flags. *Deep Sea Fishing. 1953: The Master of Ballantrae. Crossed Swords. †William Tell. 1954: Lilacs in the Spring (US: Let's Make Up). 1955: The Dark Avenger (US: The Warriors). 1956: Istanbul. King's Rhapsody. 1956: Istanbul. The Sword of Villon (TV). The Big Boodle (GB: Night in Havana). 1957: The Sun Also Rises. Without Incident (TV). 1958: The Roots of Heaven. Too Much, Too Soon. 1959: Cuban Rebel Girls.*

†Unfinished

FOCH, Nina (N. Fock) 1924–

Aristocratic, cool, resourceful blonde Dutch-born Hollywood actress, the daughter of composer-conductor Dirk Fock and actress Consuelo Flowerton (1900–1965). She gave some excellent performances in the mid-forties that might have set her up for a star career, but she lacked a definitive personality and, after a spell in television and theatre, was confined to top supporting roles. Oscar nominated for *Executive Suite*.

*1943: *Wagon Wheels West. Return of the Vampire. 1944: Cry of the Werewolf. Strange Affair. Nine Girls. She's a Soldier Too. Shadows in the Night. She's a Sweetheart. 1945: Prison Ship. Escape in the Fog. My Name is Julia Ross. I Love a Mystery. A Song to Remember. Boston Blackie's Rendezvous (GB: Blackie's Rendezvous). 1947: The Guilt of Janet Ames. Johnny O'Clock. 1948: The Dark Past. 1949: Johnny Allegro (GB: Hounded). The Undercover Man. 1951: St Benny the Dip (GB: Escape If You Can). An American in Paris. Young Man with Ideas. 1952: Scaramouche. Fast Company. 1953: Sombrero. 1954: Executive Suite. Four Guns to the Border. 1955: One Life (TV. GB: cinemas). You're Never Too Young. Yacht on the High Sea (TV. GB: cinemas). Illegal. 1956: The Ten Commandments. Heritage of Anger (TV). 1957: The Playroom (TV). Three Brave Men. 1958: Free Weekend (TV). 1959: Cash McCall. 1960: Spartacus. 1967: Prescription Murder (TV). 1969: Gidget Grows Up (TV). 1971: Such Good Friends. 1972: Female Artillery (TV). 1973: Salty. 1974: A Little Bit Like Murder (TV). Oh! Baby, Baby, Baby . . . (TV). 1975: Mahogany. 1977: The Great Houdinis (TV). 1978: Jennifer. Ebony, Ivory and Jade (TV). Child of Glass (TV). 1981: Rich and Famous. 1985: Shadow Chasers (TV). 1987: Dixie Lanes. 1988: Outback Bound (TV). 1989: Skin Deep. 1992: In the Arms of a Killer (TV). Sidney Sheldon's The Sands of Time (TV). 1993: Morning Glory. Sliver. 1994: Alien Nation (TV). 1995: It's My Party. 1996: 'Til There Was You. 1998: Hush. Shadow of Doubt. 1999: Family Blessings (and co-directed).*

FONDA, Bridget 1964–

Fair-haired, narrow-faced, darting-eyed American actress with distinctive thin top lip, the daughter of Peter Fonda (*qv*). Sometimes miscast as a femme fatale, she has shown up best as ordinary or lowerclass girls in such films as *It Could Happen to You* and *Single White Female*, where her spiky charm works best. Her pale-green eyes have proved equally confident at projecting toughness and vulnerability, though she doesn't quite yet have the acting depth of her distinguished forebears, Jane and Henry Fonda, her aunt and grandfather. For some years lived with actor Eric Stoltz (*qv*), but the relationship eventually ended.

1969: Easy Rider. 1987: Aria. Out of the Rain (released 1991). 1988: Shag. Scandal. Light Years. You Can't Hurry Love. 1989: Jacob I

Have Loved (TV). Strapless. 1990: Frankenstein Unbound. The Godfather Part III. 1991: Iron Maze. Drop Dead Fred. Doc Hollywood. 1992: Leather Jackets. Singles. Single White Female. Army of Darkness: Evil Dead 3. 1993: Point of No Return (GB: The Assassin). Bodies, Rest & Motion. Little Buddha. 1994: Camilla. It Could Happen to You. The Road to Wellville. 1995: Rough Magic. Balto (voice only). 1996: City Hall. Grace of My Heart. Touch. 1997: Finding Graceland. In the Gloaming (cable TV). Jackie Brown. Mr Jealousy. 1998: The Breakup. A Simple Plan. 1999: Lake Placid. 2000: South from Hell's Kitchen. Monkeybone. Delivering Milo. The Whole Shebang. South of Heaven, West of Hell.*

FONDA, Henry 1905–1982

Dark, handsome, youthful-looking American leading man whose sincerity, sensitivity and memorable speaking voice enabled him to give any number of fine performances in the cinema, amazingly without winning an Academy Award until the year of his death, although nominated for *The Grapes of Wrath* in 1940. His prolific narration is listed separately below. Married (first of five) to Margaret Sullavan (*qv*) from 1931 to 1933. Father of Jane and Peter Fonda (both *qv*). In 1981 Fonda received an honorary Academy Award, then finally won a Best Actor Oscar for *On Golden Pond*, a few months before his death from heart trouble.

*1935: The Farmer Takes a Wife. Way Down East. I Dream Too Much. 1936: The Trail of the Lonesome Pine. Spendthrift. The Moon's Our Home. 1937: Slim. Wings of the Morning. That Certain Woman. You Only Live Once. 1938: Blockade. I Met My Love Again. The Mad Miss Manton. Jezebel. Spawn of the North. 1939: Jesse James. The Story of Alexander Graham Bell (GB: The Modern Miracle). Let Us Live. Drums Along the Mohawk. Young Mr Lincoln. 1940: The Grapes of Wrath. The Return of Frank James. Lillian Russell. Chad Hanna. 1941: *Hollywood Visits the Navy. The Lady Eve. Wild Geese Calling. You Belong to Me (GB: Good Morning, Doctor). 1942: Rings on Her Fingers. The Male Animal. The Magnificent Dope. The Big Street. Tales of Manhattan. The Ox-Bow Incident (GB: Strange Incident). 1943: The Immortal Sergeant. 1946: My Darling Clementine. 1947: The Fugitive. Daisy Kenyon. The Long Night. 1948: Fort Apache. A Miracle Can Happen (later and GB: On Our Merry Way). 1949: Jigsaw. 1953: Main Street* *to Broadway. 1955: Mister Roberts. 1956: 12 Angry Men. The Wrong Man. War and Peace. 1957: The Tin Star. 1958: Stage Struck. *Fabulous Hollywood. 1959: Warlock. The Man Who Understood Women. 1962: Advise and Consent. The Longest Day. How the West Was Won. 1963: Spencer's Mountain. 1964: The Best Man. Fail Safe. Sex and the Single Girl. 1965: The Rounders. In Harm's Way. Battle of the Bulge. La guerre secrète (GB and US: The Dirty Game). 1966: A Big Hand for the Little Lady (GB: Big Deal at Dodge City). Welcome to Hard Times (GB: Killer on a Horse). 1967: Firecreek. Stranger on the Run (TV). All About People. 1968: Yours, Mine and Ours. Madigan. The Boston Strangler. Once Upon a Time in the West. 1969: Too Late the Hero. 1970: There Was a Crooked Man. The Cheyenne Social Club. 1971: Sometimes a Great Notion (GB: Never Give an Inch). Directed by John Ford. 1973: The Serpent (US: Night Flight from Moscow). Ash Wednesday. The Alpha Caper (TV. GB: cinemas, as Inside Job). The Red Pony (TV. GB: cinemas, in abbreviated version). My Name is Nobody. 1974: Mussolini: The Last Act/Mussolini: The Last Four Days. 1976: Midway (GB: Battle of Midway). Collision Course. Tentacles. 1977: Rollercoaster. The Last of the Cowboys (later The Great Smokey Roadblock). Il grande attacca/The Biggest Battle. 1978: The Swarm. Fedora. Wanda Nevada. City on Fire. 1979: Home to Stay (TV). Meteor. 1980: Gideon's Trumpet (TV). The Oldest Living Graduate (TV). 1981: On Golden Pond. Summer Solstice (TV).*

As narrator: 1942: *The Battle of Midway. 1943: *It's Everybody's War. 1950: *Home of the Homeless. 1951: *Grant Wood. *Benjy. *The Growing Years. 1952: The Impressionable Years. 1958: *Reach for Tomorrow. 1963: *Rangers of Yellowstone. 1967: The Golden Flame. 1968: Born to Buck. 1969: *An Impression of John Steinbeck – Writer. 1974: Valley Forge. 1977: *Alcohol Abuse – The Early Warning Signs. 1978: *Big Yellow Schooner to Byzantium. 1979: The Man Who Loved Bears. 1981: America's Sweetheart: The Mary Pickford Story.

†Scenes deleted from final release print.

FONDA, Jane 1937–
Tawny-haired American actress, daughter of Henry Fonda. Started out as bright, knowing city girls, graduated to pin-up roles, then suddenly, at the end of the sixties, burst on the film scene as a fine actress, later picking up Oscars for *Klute* and *Coming Home*. She inherited much of her father's movingly deep sincerity and, given the right role, proved herself one of the best actresses in America. Married (first of two) to director Roger Vadim (1965–1973) and noted for her espousal of women's rights, anti-Vietnam and provocative minority causes. Also Oscar nominated for *They Shoot Horses, Don't They?*, *Julia*, *The China Syndrome*, *On Golden Pond* and *The Morning After*.

1960: Tall Story. 1961: The Chapman Report. A String of Beads (TV). 1962: A Walk on the Wild Side. Period of Adjustment. 1963: In the Cool of the Day. Jane. Sunday in New York. 1964: Les félins (GB: The Love Cage. US: Joyhouse). La ronde. 1965: Cat Ballou. The Chase. 1966: La curée (GB: The Game is Over). Any Wednesday (GB: abridged as Bachelor Girl Apartment). Hurry Sundown. 1967: Barefoot in the Park. Histoires extraordinaires (GB: Tales of Mystery. US: Spirits of the Dead). Barbarella. 1969: They Shoot Horses, Don't They? 1971: Klute. 1972: Steelyard Blues. Tout va bien. FTA. 1973: A Doll's House. *Jane Fonda on Vietnam. 1974: Vietnam Journey. 1976: The Blue Bird. Fun with Dick and Jane. 1977: Sois belle et tais-toi. Julia. 1978: Coming Home. Comes a Horseman. California Suite. The China Syndrome. 1979: The Electric Horseman. 1980: Nine to Five. No Nukes. 1981: On Golden Pond. Lee Strasberg and The Actors' Studio. Roll-Over. 1984: The Dollmaker (TV). 1985: Agnes of God. 1986: The Morning After. 1987: Leonard Part VI. 1989: Old Gringo. Stanley and Iris.
As director: 1974: Vietnam Journey (co-directed).

FONDA, Peter 1939–
Tall, rangy, sensitive-looking American actor, son of Henry Fonda (*qv*). His fair hair and blue eyes at first qualified him for glossily innocuous roles, against which he soon rebelled. His success in *Easy Rider* typecast him again, this time as a bike-riding tearaway, and he has not commanded the same calibre of role maintained by his father and sister Jane. Father of actress Bridget Fonda (*qv*). Academy Award nominee for *Ulee's Gold*.
1963: Tammy and the Doctor. The Victors. 1964: Carol for Another Christmas (TV). The Young Lovers. Lilith. 1965: The Rounders. 1966: The Wild Angels. 1967: The Trip.

Histoires extraordinaires (GB: Tales of Mystery. US: Spirits of the Dead). 1969: Easy Rider. 1971: The Hired Hand. The Last Movie. 1973: *Not So Easy. Motorcycle Safety. Two People. 1974: Open Season. Dirty Mary, Crazy Larry. 1975: 92 in the Shade. Race with the Devil. The Diamond Mercenaries (US: Killer Force). 1976: Fighting Mad. Futureworld. 1977: Outlaw Blues. High-Ballin'. 1978: Roger Corman: Hollywood's Wild Angel. Wanda Nevada. 1980: The Hostage Tower. 1981: The Cannonball Run. Death Bite (later Spasms). 1982: Split Image/Captured!/Dance of the Dwarfs. 1983: Daijoobu, mai furrendo. 1984: Peppermint Frieden/Peppermint Freedom. A Reason to Live (TV). 1985: Certain Fury. Come the Day. 1986: Freedom Fighters (US: Mercenary Fighters). Time of Indifference (TV). Hawken's Breed (released 1990). The Long Voyage. 1988: Sound. Fatal Mission. 1989: The Rose Garden. Montana (TV). 1990: American Express. 1992: South Beach. 1993: Deadfall. Molly & Gina (released 1995). Enemy. Bodies, Rest & Motion. 1994: Love and a 45. Nadja. 1995: Don't Look Back (cable TV). 1996: Escape from L.A. Grace of My Heart (voice only). 1997: Ulee's Gold. Painted Hero/Shadow of the Past. 1998: The Tempest (TV). 1999: The Passion of Ayn Rand (cable TV). Keeping Time. The Limey. 2000: Thomas and the Magic Railroad. South of Heaven, West of Hell. 2001: Second Skin.
As director: 1971: The Hired Hand. 1973: Idaho Transfer.

FONTAINE, Joan (J. de Havilland) 1917–
Purposeful, fair-haired Hollywood actress, born in Japan of English parentage, and the sister of Olivia de Havilland (*qv*). Not such an instant success as her sister, she worked hard in the thirties and early forties to become a star as vulnerable, innocent heroines for whom things ended happily, such as her roles in *Rebecca*, *Suspicion* (for which she won an Oscar) and *Jane Eyre*. As she passed 30 her features hardened, and the quality of her roles fell away fairly rapidly. Married (first of four) to Brian Aherne (*qv*) from 1939 to 1945. Also nominated for Academy Awards in *Rebecca* and *The Constant Nymph*.
1935: †No More Ladies. 1937: Quality Street. Music for Madame. A Damsel in Distress. You Can't Beat Love. 1938: The Man Who Found Himself. Sky Giant. Blonde Cheat. Maid's Night Out. 1939: The Duke of West Point. Gunga Din. Man of Conquest. The Women.

1940: *Rebecca.* 1941: *Suspicion.* 1942: *This Above All.* 1943: *The Constant Nymph.* 1944: *Jane Eyre. Frenchman's Creek.* 1945: *The Affairs of Susan.* 1946: *From This Day Forward.* 1947: *Ivy.* 1948: *Letter from an Unknown Woman. Kiss the Blood Off My Hands (GB: Blood on My Hands). The Emperor Waltz.* 1949: *You Gotta Stay Happy.* 1950: *Born to Be Bad. September Affair.* 1951: *Darling, How Could You? (GB: Rendezvous). Something to Live For.* 1952: *Ivanhoe. Decameron Nights. Othello.* 1953: *Flight to Tangier. The Bigamist. Casanova's Big Night.* 1956: *Serenade. Beyond a Reasonable Doubt.* 1957: *Island in the Sun. Until They Sail.* 1958: *A Certain Smile.* 1961: *Voyage to the Bottom of the Sea. Tender is the Night.* 1966: *The Witches (GB: The Devil's Own).* 1978: *The Users (TV).* 1982: *All by Myself.* 1983: *Dolce cinema.* 1985: *Hitchcock, il brivido del genio.* 1986: *Dark Mansions (TV).* 1994: *Good King Wenceslas (TV).*

†*As Joan Burfield*

FORAN, Dick (John Foran) 1910–1979
Very tall, genial, fair-haired American actor with coat-hanger shoulders. Was once a railroad investigator before becoming a singer, forming his own orchestra and turning film star. From 1936 he was Warners' first (and only) singing cowboy. Later played light 'B' heroes or good guys who didn't get the girl. Died at 69, leaving a wife and four children: in real life, he seems to have been the good guy who did get the girl.
1934: *Change of Heart. Stand Up and Cheer. Gentlemen Are Born.* 1935: *Lottery Lover. One More Spring. It's a Small World. Ladies Love Danger. Moonlight on the Prairie. The Farmer Takes a Wife. Accent on Youth. Shipmates Forever. Dangerous. The Petrified Forest.* 1936: *Song of the Saddle. Treachery Rides the Range. Guns of the Pecos. Trailin' West (GB: On Secret Service). The Case of the Velvet Claws. The Big Noise (GB: Modern Madness). The Golden Arrow. Earthworm Tractors (GB: A Natural Born Salesman). California Mail. Public Enemy's Wife (GB: G-Man's Wife).* 1937: **Vitaphone Pictorial Revue No. 3. Black Legion. Land Beyond the Law. Blazing Sixes. *Sunday Round-up. Devil's Saddle Legion. Empty Holsters. Prairie Thunder. Cherokee Strip (GB: Strange Laws). The Perfect Specimen. She Loved a Fireman. Over the Wall.* 1938: **Screen Snapshots No. 4. Cowboy from Brooklyn (GB: Romance and Rhythm).*

Love, Honor and Behave. Four Daughters. Secrets of a Nurse. Heart of the North. Boy Meets Girl. The Sisters. 1939: *Daughters Courageous. Hero for a Day. Inside Information. I Stole a Million. The Fighting 69th. Four Wives. Private Detective.* 1940: *My Little Chickadee. The House of the Seven Gables. Rangers of Fortune. The Mummy's Hand. Four Mothers. Winners of the West (serial).* 1941: *In the Navy. Horror Island. Mob Town. Ride 'Em Cowboy. Riders of Death Valley (serial). Unfinished Business. The Kid from Kansas. Keep 'Em Flying. Road Agent.* 1942: *The Mummy's Tomb. Butch Minds the Baby. Behind the Eight Ball (GB: Off the Beaten Track). Private Buckaroo. *Keeping Fit.* 1943: *Hi, Buddy. He's My Guy.* 1945: *Guest Wife.* 1947: *Easy Come, Easy Go.* 1948: *Fort Apache.* 1949: *Deputy Marshal. El Paso.* 1951: *Al Jennings of Oklahoma.* 1954: *Treasure of Ruby Hills.* 1955: *Miracle on 34th Street (TV. GB: cinemas).* 1956: *Please Murder Me!* 1957: *Sierra Stranger. Chicago Confidential.* 1958: *Thundering Jets. The Fearmakers. Violent Road.* 1959: *Atomic Submarine. The Sounds of Eden (TV).* 1960: *The Big Night. Studs Lonigan.* 1962: *Donovan's Reef.* 1964: *Taggart.* 1967: *Brighty of Grand Canyon (GB: Brighty).*

FORBES, Bryan (John Clarke) 1926–
Stocky, black-haired, worried-looking English actor whose career as a player never rose above the occasional lead in B-features but who proved himself first as a writer in the mid-fifties, then as a sensitive director in the sixties. An ill-fated spell as head of production for Associated British (1969–1972) heralded a slight falling away from the directorial highpoints of ten years earlier. Married to actresses Constance Smith (1951–1954) and Nanette Newman (1954 on).
1943: **The Tired Man.* 1948: *The Small Back Room (US: Hour of Glory). All Over the Town.* 1949: *Dear Mr Prohack.* 1950: *The Wooden Horse. Saturday Night. Green Grow the Rushes.* 1952: *The World in His Arms. Flesh and Fury. Appointment in London.* 1953: *Sea Devils. Wheel of Fate. The Million Pound Note (US: Man with a Million).* 1954: *An Inspector Calls. The Colditz Story. Up to His Neck.* 1955: *Passage Home.* 1956: *Now and Forever. The Baby and the Battleship. It's Great to be Young. The Extra Day. Satellite in the Sky. The Last Man to Hang?* 1957: *Quatermass 2 (US: Enemy from Space).* 1958: *The Key. I Was Monty's Double.* 1959: *Yesterday's Enemy. The*

League of Gentlemen. 1960: *The Angry Silence.* 1961: *The Guns of Navarone.* 1962: *The L-Shaped Room.* 1964: *A Shot in the Dark. Of Human Bondage.* 1970: *The Raging Moon (US: Long Ago Tomorrow) (voice only).* 1974: *The Stepford Wives.* 1976: *The Slipper and the Rose.* 1978: *International Velvet.* 1984: *The Naked Face.* 1985: *Restless Natives.*
As director: 1961: *Whistle Down the Wind.* 1962: *The L-Shaped Room.* 1963: *Seance on a Wet Afternoon.* 1965: *King Rat.* 1966: *The Wrong Box. The Whisperers.* 1968: *Deadfall.* 1969: *The Madwoman of Chaillot.* 1970: *The Raging Moon (US: Long Ago Tomorrow).* 1974: *The Stepford Wives.* 1976: *The Slipper and the Rose.* 1978: *International Velvet.* 1980 *Sunday Lovers (co-directed).* 1982: *Ménage à trois/ Better Late Than Never.* 1984: *The Naked Face.* 1989: *The Endless Game (TV).*

FORD, Glenn (Gwyllyn Newton) 1916–
Dark-haired, serious-looking Canadian-born actor whose determined style coupled with a lack of warmth caused him to be cast as slightly unsympathetic heroes, notably in films opposite Rita Hayworth. A study of 'method' acting in the early fifties, and a change of hairstyle, enabled Ford to really hit the jackpot and remain one of America's most popular actors, mainly in tortured roles, for almost ten years. Married (first and second of four) to actresses Eleanor Powell (1943–1959) and Kathryn Hays (1966–1968). During World War Two, he served both with the US Marines and the French Foreign Legion.
1937: **Night in Manhattan.* 1939: *Heaven with a Barbed Wire Fence. My Son is Guilty (GB: Crime's End).* 1940: *Convicted Woman. Babies for Sale. Men Without Souls. Blondie Plays Cupid. The Lady in Question.* 1941: **Variety Reel. Texas. So Ends Our Night. Go West, Young Lady.* 1942: *The Adventures of Martin Eden. Flight Lieutenant.* 1943: *Destroyer. Desperadoes. *Hollywood in Uniform.* 1946: *Gilda. A Stolen Life.* 1947: *Gallant Journey. Framed (GB: Paula).* 1948: *The Mating of Millie. The Loves of Carmen. The Return of October (GB: Date with Destiny). The Man from Colorado.* 1949: *The Undercover Man. Lust for Gold. Mr Soft Touch (GB: House of Settlement). The Doctor and the Girl. *Hollywood Goes to Church.* 1950: *The White Tower. Convicted. The Flying Missile. The Redhead and the Cowboy.* 1951: *Follow the Sun. The Secret of Convict Lake. Young Man with Ideas. The Green Glove.* 1952: *Affair in Trinidad.* 1953: *The Man from*

the Alamo. Time Bomb (US: Terror on a Train). Plunder of the Sun. The Big Heat. Appointment in Honduras. 1954: Human Desire. The Americano. City Story (narrator only). 1955: The Violent Men (GB: Rough Company). Interrupted Melody. *Hollywood Fathers. Blackboard Jungle. Trial. Ransom! 1956: Jubal. *Hollywood Goes a-Fishing. The Fastest Gun Alive. The Teahouse of the August Moon. 1957: 3:10 to Yuma. Don't Go Near the Water. 1958: The Sheepman. Cowboy. Torpedo Run. Imitation General. 1959: It Started with a Kiss. The Gazebo. 1960: Cimarron. 1961: Cry for Happy. Pocketful of Miracles. The Four Horsemen of the Apocalypse. 1962: Experiment in Terror (GB: The Grip of Fear). 1963: The Courtship of Eddie's Father. Love is a Ball (GB: All This and Money Too). Advance to the Rear (GB: Company of Cowards). 1964: Fate is the Hunter. Dear Heart. 1965: The Money Trap. The Rounders. Seapower (narrator only). Is Paris Burning? 1966: Rage. 1967: A Time for Killing (GB: The Long Ride Home). The Last Challenge. The Pistolero of Red River. 1968: Day of the Evil Gun. 1969: Smith! Heaven with a Gun. 1970: The Brotherhood of the Bell (TV). 1971: Slayride (TV). 1972: The Gold Diggers (TV). Santee. 1973: Jarrett (TV). 1974: Punch and Jody (TV). The Greatest Gift (TV). The Disappearance of Flight 412 (TV). 1975: Long Way Home (TV). 1976: Midway (GB: The Battle of the Midway). 1977: The 3,000 Mile Chase (TV). 1978: Superman. No Margin for Error (TV). 1979: The Visitor. The Sacketts (TV). The Gift (TV). The Family Holvack (TV). 1980: Virus. 1981: Happy Birthday to Me. Day of the Assassin. 1986: My Town (TV). 1987: Red Riding Hood (TV). 1988: Casablanca Express. 1989: Law at Randado (TV). 1990: Border Shootout. 1991: Raw Nerve (released 1993). Final Version (TV). †JFK. Our Hollywood Education. 1993: Finnegan's Wake.

†Scene deleted from final release print.

FORD, Harrison 1942–
Aggressive, youthful-looking into his forties, light-haired American actor who had several bites at the Hollywood cherry before hitting the big-time as Han Solo in Star Wars. He was billed as Harrison J. Ford until 1970 to avoid any confusion with the silent screen actor of the same name (1892–1957). After settling in as a middle-range star in a variety of popular films, Ford hit the jackpot when he

accepted the role rejected by Tom Selleck (qv) in Raiders of the Lost Ark, and has been in the superstar category since then, often in dour but determined lone-wolf roles. Academy Award nomination for Witness. Romantic scenarios found him less at home. 1966: Dead Heat on a Merry-Go-Round. 1967: Luv. Journey to Shiloh. A Time for Killing (GB: The Long Ride Home). 1970: The Intruders (TV). Zabriskie Point. Getting Straight. 1973: American Graffiti. 1974: The Conversation. 1976: Dynasty (TV). 1977: The Trial of Lt Calley (TV). Star Wars. Heroes. 1978: The Possessed (TV). Force Ten from Navarone. 1979: More American Graffiti/The Party's Over/Purple Haze. Hanover Street. Apocalypse Now. The Frisco Kid. 1980: The Empire Strikes Back. 1981: Raiders of the Lost Ark. 1982: Blade Runner. 1983: Return of the Jedi. 1984: Indiana Jones and the Temple of Doom. 1985: Witness. 1986: The Mosquito Coast. 1987: Frantic. 1988: Working Girl. 1989: Indiana Jones and the Last Crusade. 1990: Presumed Innocent. 1991: Regarding Henry. 1992: Patriot Games. L'envers du décors. Blade Runner: The Director's Cut. 1993: The Fugitive. Earth and the American Dream (voice only). 1994: Clear and Present Danger. Jimmy Hollywood. A Hundred and One Nights. 1995: Sabrina. L'univers de Jacques Demy. 1996: The Devil's Own. 1997: Air Force One. 1998: Six Days Seven Nights. 1999: Random Hearts. 2000: What Lies Beneath.

†Scenes deleted

FORMBY, George
(G. Booth Jnr) 1904–1961
Toothy, ever-grinning, gormless-looking Lancashire comedian who sang smutty songs in between whose verses he frantically strummed a small ukulele. Born blind, the son of another comedian, he recovered his sight in a coughing fit, and went on to become Britain's second biggest box-office star, after Gracie Fields (qv), of the thirties and early forties. Died from a heart attack. The George Formby in No Fool Like an Old Fool (1914) is Formby Senior.
1915: By the Shortest of Heads. 1934: Boots! Boots! 1935: Off the Dole. No Limit. 1936: Keep Your Seats Please. 1937: Keep Fit. Feather Your Nest. 1938: I See Ice. *Cavalcade of the Stars. It's in the Air (US: George Takes the Air). 1939: Come on George. Trouble Brewing. 1940: Let George Do It. Spare a Copper. 1941: Turned Out Nice Again.

South American George. 1942: Much Too Shy. *The Folks at Home. 1943: Bell Bottom George. Get Cracking. 1944: He Snoops to Conquer. 1945: I Didn't Do It. 1946: George in Civvy Street.

FORREST, Frederic 1936–
Light-haired, slightly-built, intense American actor specializing in slightly off-centre characters. Started as a star in his first major film, but was subsequently seen in a mixture of top featured roles, subservient leading roles, or TV movies. His career did not sustain its initial impetus and, although his personal notices have remained good, his did not become a familiar face at the top. Oscar nominee for The Rose.
1969: Futz. 1972: When the Legends Die. 1973: The Don is Dead. 1974: The Dion Brothers (TV. GB: cinemas, as The Gravy Train). The Conversation. Larry (TV). 1975: Permission to Kill. Promise Him Anything (TV). 1976: The Missouri Breaks. 1977: It Lives Again! 1979: The Survival of Dana (TV). The Rose. Ruby and Oswald (TV). Apocalypse Now. 1982: Hammett (completed 1980). One from the Heart. Valley Girl. 1983: Who Will Love My Children (TV. GB: cinemas). Saigon – Year of the Cat (TV). Jealousy (TV). 1984: The Stone Boy. Best Kept Secrets (TV). Calamity Jane (TV). The Parade/Hit Parade (TV). Return! 1985: Right to Kill (TV). The Adventures of Huckleberry Finn (originally for TV). Where Are the Children? 1986: Valentino Returns. 1987: Stacking/Season of Dreams. 21 Jump Street (TV). 1988: Tucker: The Man and His Dream. Little Girl Lost (TV). Gotham (GB: The Dead Can't Lie). Cat Chaser. 1989: Margaret Bourke-White (TV). Music Box. 1990: The Two Jakes. 1991: Twin Sisters. Mirror Image. Hearts of Darkness: A Film-maker's Apocalypse. 1992: Double Exposure. The Habitation of Dragons (TV). Rain Without Thunder. Citizen Cohn (cable TV). 1993: Trauma. Precious Victims (TV). Falling Down. 1994: Before the Night/One Night Stand. Against the Wall (cable TV). Chasers. Hard Evidence. 1995: Lassie. 1996: Double Jeopardy (TV). Black Thunder. Crash Dive (v). Andersonville (TV). 1997: Reasonable Force. Boogie Boy. The End of Violence. The Brave (unreleased). Point Blank. 1998: Implicated. Whatever. The First 9½ Weeks. 1999: Sweetwater (TV). 2000: Shadow Hours. The Spreading Ground. A Piece of Eden.

FORREST, Sally

(Katharine Feeney) 1928–

Appealing American actress with curly blonde hair. She danced away happily in the chorus of M-G-M musicals of the 1940s before Ida Lupino (qv) saw her in a small acting role, 'discovered' her and changed her name. She was much in demand then for two or three years, but appeared to lose her career drive (something she seems in later years to have regretted) after marrying late in 1951.

1946: †Till the Clouds Roll By. 1947: †Fiesta. 1948: †The Pirate. †Easter Parade. †The Kissing Bandit. †Are You With It? †The Daring Miss Jones. 1949: †Mr Belvedere Goes to College. Dancing in the Dark. Take Me Out to the Ball Game (GB: Everybody's Cheering). Not Wanted. Never Fear. 1950: Mystery Street. Vengeance Valley. 1951: Excuse My Dust. Hard, Fast and Beautiful. The Strip. Bannerline. Valentino. The Strange Door. 1953: Code Two. 1955: Son of Sinbad. 1956: While the City Sleeps. Ride the High Iron.

†As Katharine Feeney (when billed)

FORREST, Steve

(William F. Andrews) 1924–

Square-jawed American leading man with fair, curly hair, but less personality than his looks – handsome, mobile features with a hint of a smile – suggested. But he maintained his leading man status, more or less, through the years, largely through working extensively in television from 1957. Brother of Dana Andrews (qv).

1942: †Crash Dive. 1943: †The Ghost Ship. 1951: †Geisha Girl. †Sealed Cargo. 1952: †Last of the Comanches (GB: The Sabre and the Arrow). The Bad and the Beautiful. Dream

Wife. 1953: Battle Circus. The Clown. So Big. Take the High Ground. The Band Wagon. 1954: Rogue Cop. Prisoner of War. Phantom of the Rue Morgue. 1955: Bedevilled. 1957: Clipper Ship (TV). The Living Idol. 1959: It Happened to Jane. 1960: Heller in Pink Tights. Flaming Star. Five Branded Women. 1961: The Second Time Around. 1962: The Longest Day. 1963: The Yellow Canary. 1969: Rascal. 1971: The Wild Country. 1972: The Late Liz. 1973: Chant of Silence (TV). 1974: The Hanged Man (TV). 1975: SWAT Squad (TV). The Hatfields and the McCoys (TV). The Deadly Tide (TV). 1976: The Running Man (TV). The Siege (TV). Wanted: the Sundance Woman (TV). 1977: Last of the Mohicans (TV). 1978: Captain America (TV). Maneaters Are Loose! The Deerslayer (TV). 1979: North Dallas Forty. 1980: Roughnecks (TV). 1981: Mommie Dearest. 1982: Hotline (TV). 1983: Malibu (TV). Sahara. 1984: Finder of Lost Loves (TV). 1985: Spies Like Us. 1986: Amazon Women on the Moon. 1987: Gunsmoke: Return to Dodge (TV). 1992: Storyville. 1993: Columbo: A Bird in the Hand (TV). 1995: Killer: A Journal of Murder.

†As William Andrews

FORSTER, Robert (R. Foster) 1941–

Offbeat American actor in the rebel mould, with tousled dark hair and off-centre gaze. He brought his downtown New York tones to films after a stage career in which he had made a speciality of playing Stanley Kowalski in A Streetcar Named Desire. Subsequently in a variety of 'loner' roles, often as vulnerable heroes. Less effective in top supporting roles, he briefly turned director in the mid-1980s. An Oscar nomination for Jackie Brown briefly revived his career in leading roles.

1967: Reflections in a Golden Eye. 1968: The Stalking Moon. 1969: Justine. Medium Cool. 1970: Pieces of Dreams. Cover Me Babe. 1971: Run Shadow Run. Banyon (TV). The City (TV). 1972: Journey Through Rosebud. 1973: Death Squad (TV). The Don is Dead. 1974: Nakia (TV). 1977: Stunts. 1978: Avalanche. Standing Tall (TV). Pressure Point (TV). 1979: The Black Hole. The Darker Side of Terror (TV). Crunch. Lady in Red. 1980: Royce (TV). Alligator. 1981: Kinky Coaches and the Pom Pom Pussycats. 1982: Vigilante. 1983: Walking the Edge. 1985: †Hollywood Harry/Harry's Machine. 1986: The Delta Force. 1987: Once a Hero (TV). Counterforce.

Esmeralda Bay. 1988: Heat from Another Sun. Committed (released 1991). 1989: Satan's Princess. The Banker. Jesse Hawkes (TV). 1990: Peacemaker. 1991: 29th Street. Diplomatic Immunity. 1992: In the Shadow of a Killer (TV). South Beach. 1993: Midnight Kiss. Sex, Love and Cold. Hard Cash. 1994: Body Chemistry III: Point of Seduction. Scanner Cop 2. Yakuza. 1995: American Perfekt (released 1997). 1996: Hot City (later Original Gangstas). Guns and Lipstick. 1997: Night Vision. The Method. Jackie Brown. Demolition University. 1998: Countdown to Esmeralda Bay. Psycho. Rear Window (TV). Outside Ozona. 1999: Supernova. The Magic of Marciano. Kiss Toledo Goodbye. Family Tree. All the Rage. Mulholland Drive (TV). 2000: Me, Myself & Irene. Lakeboat. Great Sex.

†And directed

FORSYTH, Rosemary 1944–

A sad but classic example of a promising career that went sour. She was feted for her performances in her first two films but, after that, the tall, delicate-looking, blue-eyed Canadian blonde seemed to alienate media and audiences alike. Roles appeared hard to come by and, truth to tell, she was not especially good in them. Her appearance in Gray Lady Down was reduced to a single short scene by the time the film was released. It was her last cinema-film until 1994, when she showed some of her old form as a featured player in Disclosure.

1965: Shenandoah. The War Lord. 1966: Texas Across the River. 1969: Where It's At. Whatever Happened to Aunt Alice? 1970: The Brotherhood of the Bell (TV). How Do I Love Thee? 1971: City Beneath the Sea (TV. GB: cinemas, as One Hour to Doomsday). Triple Play (TV). The Death of Me Yet (TV). 1973: One Little Indian. Black Eye. 1975: My Father's House (TV). 1977: Gray Lady Down. 1984: Call to Glory (TV). 1986: The Gladiator (TV). 1988: Addicted to His Love. (TV). A Friendship in Vienna (TV). 1989: Nashville Beat (TV). 1993: A Case for Murder (TV). 1994: Disclosure. Exit to Eden. The Other Woman (TV). 1995: Melissa. Abandoned and Deceived (TV). 1996: Daylight. 1998: Girl. 1999: Valerie Flake.

FORSYTHE, John (John Freund) 1918–

Solid, dependable American leading man, with dark, wavy hair, at his best as pressurized heroes in films for such directors as

Hitchcock and Robert Wise. Most of his career has been spent on Broadway and in television. A burst of cinematic activity in the fifties seemed to come too late to make him a star. Became a major television personality in the 1980s through the soap opera *Dynasty*.

1943: *Destination Tokyo*. 1952: *The Captive City*. 1953: *It Happens Every Thursday*. *The Glass Web*. *Escape from Fort Bravo*. 1955: *The Trouble with Harry*. 1956: *The Ambassador's Daughter*. *Everything but the Truth*. 1964: *See How They Run (TV)*. 1965: *Kitten with a Whip*. 1966: *Madame X*. *Death Pays in Dollars*. 1967: *In Cold Blood*. 1968: *Shadow on the Land (TV)*. 1969: *Topaz*. *The Happy Ending*. 1971: *Murder Once Removed (TV)*. 1972: *The Letters (TV)*. *Lisa Bright and Dark (TV)*. 1974: *Cry Panic (TV)*. *The Healers (TV)*. *Terror on the Fortieth Floor (TV)*. 1975: *The Deadly Tower (TV)*. 1976: *The Feather and Father Gang (TV)*. *Amelia Earhart (TV)*. *Tail Gunner Joe (TV)*. 1977: *Emily, Emily (TV)*. 1978: *The Users (TV)*. *With This Ring (TV)*. *Good Bye and Amen*. *Cruise into Terror (TV)*. 1979: *. . . And Justice for All*. 1981: *Sizzle (TV)*. 1982: *Mysterious Two (TV)*. 1986: *On Fire (TV)*. 1988: *Scrooged*. 1990: *Opposites Attract (TV)*. 1991: *Stan and George's New Life*. *Dynasty: The Reunion (TV)*. 1992: *The Powers That Be (TV)*. *The Obsessive Doctor (TV)*.

FOSTER, Dianne (D. Laruska) 1928–
Striking, chestnut-haired Canadian actress who started her film career in Britain before she had some success in Hollywood from 1953 to 1958, mainly in westerns and gangland thrillers. Her warm, sympathetic performances in a variety of roles belied her pin-up looks, but she was not quite a strong

enough personality to remain a star.
1951: *The Quiet Woman*. 1952: *The Lost Hours (US: The Big Frame)*. 1953: *The Steel Key*. *Isn't Life Wonderful! Three's Company*. *Bad for Each Other*. 1954: *Drive a Crooked Road*. *Three Hours to Kill*. *The Bamboo Prison*. 1955: *The Violent Men (GB: Rough Company)*. *The Kentuckian*. 1957: *Monkey on My Back*. *Night Passage*. *The Brothers Rico*. 1958: *The Deep Six*. *The Last Hurrah*. *Gideon's Day (US: Gideon of Scotland Yard)*. 1961: *King of the Roaring Twenties (GB: The Big Bankroll)*. 1963: *Who's Been Sleeping in My Bed?*

FOSTER, Jodie (Alicia Foster) 1962–
Fair-haired, blue-eyed, thin-lipped, serious-looking American actress whose rasping tones soon betrayed acerbic edges to the little-girl charm of her early Disney appearances. Before she was 14 she had played a gangster's moll, a murderess and a prostitute. It was no surprise when she blossomed into an intense, deep-thinking adult actress, nor that she soon proved an Academy Award winner, for *The Accused* and *The Silence of the Lambs*, also chalking up Oscar nominations for *Taxi Driver* and *Nell*. What was less expected was that she became a force at the box-office as well, or that it took her until she was 29 to direct her first film. She has her own production company, Smart Egg Productions – but stardom seemed to be drifting away from her at the turn of the century.
1971: *Napoleon and Samantha*. 1972: *Kansas City Bomber*. *Menace on the Mountain (TV. GB: cinemas)*. 1973: *Rookie of the Year (TV)*. *Tom Sawyer*. *One Little Indian*. 1974: *Smile Jenny, You're Dead (TV)*. *Alice Doesn't Live Here Anymore*. 1975: *Echoes of a Summer*. 1976: *Freaky Friday*. *The Little Girl Who Lives Down the Lane*. *Bugsy Malone*. *Taxi Driver*. *Il cassotto (GB: The Beach Hut)*. 1977: *Candleshoe*. *Moi, fleur bleue (US: Stop Calling Me Baby!)*. 1978: *Movies Are My Life*. 1979: *Foxes*. *Carny*. 1981: *O'Hara's Wife*. 1983: *Svengali (TV)*. *Le sang des autres*. 1984: *The Hotel New Hampshire*. *Mesmerized*. 1987: *Siesta*. *Five Corners*. 1988: *The Accused*. *Stealing Home*. 1989: *Backtrack (GB: Catchfire)*. 1990: *The Silence of the Lambs*. 1991: *Little Man Tate (and directed)*. *Shadows and Fog*. 1993: *Sommersby*. *It Was a Wonderful Life (narrator only)*. 1994: *Maverick*. *Nell*. 1997: *Contact*. 1999: *Anna and the King*. 2001: *The Dangerous Lives of Altar Boys*.
Also as director: 1995: *Home for the Holidays*.

FOSTER, Julia 1941–
Fluffily blonde British actress who overcame early roles that required her to look wistful and take her clothes off, to specialize in slightly scatterbrained secretaries and girlfriends. After *Half a Sixpence*, which might have made her an international star but did not, she seemed to turn her back on the cinema and concentrate on theatre and TV.
1962: *Term of Trial*. *The Loneliness of the Long-Distance Runner*. *Two Left Feet*. 1963: *The Small World of Sammy Lee*. 1964: *The System (GB: The Girl Getters)*. *The Bargee*. *One-Way Pendulum*. 1966: *Alfie*. 1967: *Half a Sixpence*. **The Ride of the Valkyrie*. 1970: **Simon, Simon*. *Percy*. 1971: *All Coppers are . . .* 1974: *The Great McGonagall*. 1976: *F. Scott Fitzgerald in Hollywood (TV)*.

FOSTER, Preston 1900–1970
As a boy, I was hopelessly confused between Robert Preston and Preston Foster. Both were dark, well built, often moustachioed and with strong white smiles that qualified them equally for heroes and villains. Foster was the older of the two, a former opera singer who was at his best in films of the early thirties, but continued in middling roles until going into television in 1954.
1928: *Pusher-in-the-Face*. 1929: *Nothing But the Truth*. 1930: *Follow the Leader*. *Heads Up*. 1931: *His Woman*. 1932: *Life Begins (GB: The Dawn of Life)*. *The All American (GB: Sport of a Nation)*. *You Said a Mouthful*. *Two Seconds*. *Doctor X*. *The Last Mile*. *I Am a Fugitive from a Chain Gang*. 1933: *Elmer the Great*. *Ladies They Talk About*. *Corruption (GB: Double Exposure)*. *Danger Crossroads*. *The Man Who Dared*. *Hoopla*. *The Devil's Mate (GB: He Knew Too Much)*. *Sensation*

Hunters. 1934: Heat Lightning. Sleepers East. Wharf Angel. The Band Plays On. 1935: The People's Enemy. Strangers All. *A Night at the Biltmore Bowl. The Informer. Annie Oakley. The Arizonian. The Last Days of Pompeii. 1936: We're Only Human. Love Before Breakfast. The Plough and the Stars. Muss 'Em Up (GB: House of Fate). We Who Are About to Die. 1937: The Outcasts of Poker Flat. Sea Devils. You Can't Beat Love. First Lady. The Westland Case. 1938: Everybody's Doing It. Submarine Patrol. Double Danger. The Lady in the Morgue (GB: The Case of the Missing Blonde). Up the River. The Last Warning. White Banners. Army Girl (GB: The Last of the Cavalry). The Storm. 1939: Twenty Thousand Men a Year. Chasing Danger. Missing Evidence. News is Made at Night. Society Smugglers. 1940: Café Hostess. Geronimo. Moon Over Burma. North West Mounted Police. 1941: The Roundup. Unfinished Business. 1942: Personnel Placement in the Army. Secret Agent of Japan. Little Tokyo USA. A Gentleman After Dark. A Night in New Orleans. American Empire (GB: My Son Alone). Thunder Birds. 1943: My Friend Flicka. Guadalcanal Diary. 1944: Roger Touhy, Gangster (GB: The Last Gangster). Bermuda Mystery. Thunderhead, Son of Flicka. 1945: The Valley of Decision. Abbott and Costello in Hollywood. Twice Blessed. Blonde from Brooklyn. The Harvey Girls. 1946: Inside Job. Tangier. Strange Alibi. 1947: King of the Wild Horses (GB: King of the Wild). Ramrod. 1948: The Hunted. Thunderhoof (GB: Fury). 1949: The Big Cat. I Shot Jesse James. 1950: Tomahawk (GB: Battle of Powder River). The Tougher They Come. 1951: The Big Night. Three Desperate Men. The Big Gusher. 1952: Montana Territory. Face to Face. Kansas City Confidential (GB: The Secret Four). 1953: I, the Jury. Law and Order. The Marshal's Daughter. 1957: Destination 60,000. 1963: Advance to the Rear (GB: Company of Cowards). 1964: The Time Travelers. The Man from Galveston (TV. GB: cinemas). 1967: You've Got to be Smart. 1968: Chubasco.

FOSTER, Susanna
(Susanne Larson) 1924–
Strawberry blonde American singer and actress who starred in operatic chillers and other Universal fol-de-rols of the early forties. Following an acrimonious divorce from fellow-singer Wilbur Evans (her first

and only marriage: 1948–1956) she left show business altogether.
1939: The Great Victor Herbert. 1941: The Hard-Boiled Canary (later There's Magic in Music). Glamour Boy (GB: Hearts in Springtime). 1942: Star Spangled Rhythm. 1943: Phantom of the Opera. Top Man. 1944: Follow the Boys. The Climax. This is the Life. Bowery to Broadway. 1945: Frisco Sal. That Night With You.

FOX, Edward 1937–
Gravely aristocratic English actor, for years under the shadow of his younger brother James. After James temporarily forsook the arts for religion, the fair-haired, blue-eyed Edward scored some notable and deserved critical successes, yet failed to develop into a big box-office star. Married/divorced actress Tracy Reed. Married actress Joanna David.
1962: The Mind Benders. 1965: Morgan – a Suitable Case for Treatment (US: Morgan). 1966: The Frozen Dead. The Jokers. 1967: I'll Never Forget What's 'is Name. The Long Duel. The Naked Runner. 1968: The Breaking of Bumbo. 1969: Battle of Britain. Oh! What a Lovely War. Skullduggery. 1970: The Go-Between. 1973: The Day of the Jackal. 1974: Galileo. A Doll's House (Losey). 1977: The Squeeze. A Bridge Too Far. The Duellists. 1978: The Big Sleep. Survival Run. Force 10 from Navarone. The Cat and the Canary. Soldier of Orange. 1980: The Mirror Cracked. 1982: Gandhi. 1983: The Dresser. Never Say Never Again. 1984: The Bounty. The Shooting Party. 1985: Wild Geese II. 1987: Quartermaine's Terms (TV). A Hazard of Hearts (TV). 1989: Return from the River Kwai. 1990: They Never Slept (TV). Circles of Deceit (TV). 1991: Robin Hood (TV. GB: cinemas). The Crucifer of Blood (TV). 1994: A Month by the Lake. 1995: A Feast at Midnight. 1997: Prince Valiant. Forbidden Territory: Stanley's Search for Livingstone (TV). 1998: Lost in Space.

FOX, James (William Fox) 1939–
British child actor with fair hair and blue eyes, who grew up to play facile, upper-class types. Reached a peak of popularity in the mid–1960s, then turned to evangelism, making only one religion-slanted film in the next 13 years until embarking on a low-key return to mainstream cinema in 1983.
1950: †The Miniver Story. †The Magnet. 1951: †One Wild Oat. †The Lavender Hill Mob. 1958: †Timbuktu. 1960: †The Queen's

Guards. 1961: †The Secret Partner. 1962: †She Always Gets Their Man. †What Every Woman Wants. †The Loneliness of the Long Distance Runner. 1963: Tamahine. The Servant. 1965: Those Magnificent Men in Their Flying Machines. The Chase. King Rat. 1967: Arabella. Thoroughly Modern Millie. 1968: Duffy. Isadora. 1970: Performance. 1978: No Longer Alone. 1983: Runners. Pavlova. 1984: Greystoke: The Legend of Tarzan, Lord of the Apes. A Passage to India. 1986: Absolute Beginners. The Whistle Blower. High Season. 1988: Farewell to the King. 1989: The Boys in the Island. The Mighty Quinn. She's Been Away (TV). 1990: The Russia House. 1991: Afraid of the Dark. A Question of Attribution (TV). 1992: Hostage. 1993: The Remains of the Day. 1994: Heart of Darkness (TV). Doomsday Gun (TV. GB: cinemas). 1996: Never Ever. 1997: Leo Tolstoy's Anna Karenina. Jinnah (released 1998). Shadow Run. 1998: Donald Cammell: The Ultimate Performance (doc). 1999: Mickey Blue Eyes. Up at the Villa. 2000: The Golden Bowl. 2001: The Knights of the Quest.

†As William Fox

FOX, Michael J. (Michael A. Fox) 1961–
Canadian-born actor with brown hair and clean-cut, very boyish looks. A diminutive (5ft 4in) dynamo, he was acting on Canadian TV at 16 before bursting to national fame in the American TV comedy series Family Ties. Young cinemagoers took him to their hearts after he played Marty McFly in Back to the Future, and he remained at his most appealing in comedy, despite creditable attempts at straight dramatic acting. As his popularity wavered in the late 1980s, he made two

sequels to *Back to the Future*. Married actress Tracy Pollan in 1988. He had a successful TV series, *Spin City*, from 1996, but, suffering progressively from Parkinson's Disease, he left the show in 2000.

1979: Letters from Frank. 1980: Midnight Madness. Palmerstown USA (GB: Palmerstown). 1982: Class of 1984. 1983: High School USA (TV). 1984: Poison Ivy (TV). 1985: Back to the Future. Teen Wolf. 1986: Family Ties Vacation (TV). 1987: Light of Day. The Secret of My Success. Dear America (voice only). 1988: Bright Lights, Big City. 1989: Casualties of War. Back to the Future Part II. 1990: The Hard Way. Back to the Future Part III. 1991: Doc Hollywood. 1993: The Concierge/For Love or Money. Life With Mikey. Homeward Bound: The Incredible Journey (voice only). Where the Rivers Run North. 1994: Greedy. Don't Drink the Water (TV). 1995: Coldblooded. The American President. Blue in the Face. 1996: The Frighteners. Homeward Bound II: Lost in San Francisco (voice only). Mars Attacks! 1999: Stuart Little (voice only).

FOX, Sidney (S. Liefer) 1910–1942
One of those 'So what happened?' careers. There certainly weren't many prettier young leading ladies in the Hollywood of the early 1930s, than this tiny (4ft 11in), dark-haired ingénue with an attractively coquettish acting style. She had studied law before turning to acting; she and Bette Davis (*qv*) played sisters in her first film but, whereas Davis's career solidified, Fox's gradually slid away – despite getting good reviews in a wide variety of genres. She married script editor Charles Beahan in 1932; they were divorced in 1934 and remarried in 1935. There was a little theatre, and film projects after 1935 that 'failed to materialize' and then she was found dead at 31, from 'a possible overdose of sleeping pills'.

1931: Bad Sister. Strictly Dishonorable. Six Cylinder Love. 1932: Nice Women. Murders in the Rue Morgue. The Mouthpiece. The Cohens and Kellys in Hollywood. Once in a Lifetime. Le roi pausole (GB and US: The Merry Monarch). Afraid to Talk. 1933: Don Quixote. 1934: Midnight. Down to Their Last Yacht (GB: Hawaiian Nights). 1935: School for Girls.

FRANCIOSA, Anthony or Tony
(A. Papaleo) 1928–
Italianate American actor, lean and ever-smiling with piercing blue eyes. Made a big

reputation on stage before coming to Hollywood where he got some good roles, but showed a certain lack of warmth. After 1963 he was heavily involved with television in less demanding roles, but still profitably stretched his talent in the occasional interesting film, such as *A Man Called Gannon*. Married to Shelley Winters (second of four) from 1957 to 1960. Oscar-nominated for *A Hatful of Rain*.

1957: A Face in the Crowd. This Could Be the Night. A Hatful of Rain. Wild is the Wind. 1958: The Long Hot Summer. The Naked Maja. 1959: The Story on Page One. Career. 1960: Go Naked in the World. Let No Man Write My Epitaph. 1961: Senilità. 1962: Period of Adjustment. 1964: Rio Conchos. 1965: The Pleasure Seekers. 1966: Assault on a Queen. A Man Could Get Killed. The Swinger. Fame is the Name of the Game (TV). 1967: Fathom. The Sweet Ride. 1968: In Enemy Country. A Man Called Gannon. 1971: The Catcher (TV). Dracula im Schloss des Schreckens. Nella stretta morsa del ragno. The Deadly Hunt (TV). Earth II (TV). 1972: Across 110th Street. 1974: Ghost in the Noonday Sun. This is the West That Was (TV). Matt Helm (TV). The Drowning Pool. 1977: Curse of the Black Widow (TV). 1979: Firepower. The World is Full of Married Men. The Concorde Affair. 1980: La cicala. Texas Legend. 1981: Aiutami a sognare (US: Help Me Dream). Side Show (TV). Julie Darling. 1982: Death Wish II. Kiss My Grits. Tenebrae. 1984: Finder of Lost Loves (TV). 1986: Stagecoach (TV). 1987: Blood Vows: The Story of a Mafia Wife (TV). 1988: Death House. La morte e di moda. 1989: Ghostwriter! 1990: Backstreet Dreams. 1992: Double Threat. 1996: City Hall.

FRANCIS, Anne 1930–
Tall, sulky-looking American blonde whose cool talents were ill-used by two studios, Twentieth Century-Fox, who gave her the 'big chance' in the mediocre *Lydia Bailey*, an unsuitable role, and M-G-M, who promoted her as a blonde sexpot to succeed Lana Turner. Low-key drama and sophisticated comedy would have been closer to her abilities, but she rarely got either.

1946: Summer Holiday (released 1948). 1947: This Time for Keeps. 1948: Portrait of Jennie (GB: Jennie). 1950: So Young, So Bad. 1951: Elopement. The Whistle at Eaton Falls (GB: Richer than the Earth.) 1952: Lydia Bailey. Dreamboat. 1953: A Lion is in the Streets.

1954: The Rocket Man. Rogue Cop. Bad Day at Black Rock. Battle Cry. Susan Slept Here. 1955: Blackboard Jungle. The Scarlet Coat. 1956: Forbidden Planet. The Rack. The Great American Pastime. 1957: The Hired Gun. Don't Go Near the Water. 1960: The Crowded Sky. Girl of the Night. 1964: The Satan Bug. 1965: Brainstorm. 1967: The Intruders (TV). 1968: Impasse. Funny Girl. More Dead Than Alive. 1969: Lost Flight (TV). Hook, Line and Sinker. The Love God? 1970: Wild Women (TV). The Intruders (TV). Bourbon in Suburbia. Gun Quest (TV). 1971: The Forgotten Man (TV). Mongo's Back in Town (TV). 1972: Fireball Forward (TV). Pancho Villa. Haunts of the Very Rich (TV). 1973: Night Life (TV). Chant of Silence (TV). 1974: Cry Panic (TV). The FBI versus Alvin Karpis (TV). 1975: The Last Survivors (TV). A Girl Named Sooner (TV). 1976: Banjo Hackett: Roamin' Free (TV). Survival. 1978: Little Mo (TV). Born Again. 1980: Detour to Terror (TV). 1982: Mazes and Monsters/ Rona Jaffe's Mazes and Monsters (TV). 1984: Return! 1986: A Masterpiece of Murder (TV). 1987: Poor Little Rich Girl (TV). Jake and the Fatman (TV). Laguna Heat (TV). 1988: My First Love (TV). 1991: Little Vegas. 1992: Love Can Be Murder (TV). 1993: The Double O Kid. 1996: Lover's Knot. Have You Seen My Son? (TV).

FRANCIS, Kay
(Katharine Gibbs) 1899–1968
Grave, gentle, ladylike, brunette American actress. Essentially a star of the thirties, she starred in some classic light comedies and weepie melodramas, and seemed quite lost in the forties. Some sources give date of birth as 1903, but 1899 seems the most likely. Acted

as Katharine Francis until 1929. Five times married, once (fourth) to actor Kenneth McKellar from 1931 to 1933. Died from cancer – leaving most of her fortune to a seeing eye dogs company.

1929: *Gentlemen of the Press. The Cocoanuts. Dangerous Curves. Illusion. The Marriage Playground. Honest Finder.* 1930: *Behind the Makeup. Paramount on Parade. Raffles. The Children. A Notorious Affair. The Virtuous Sin (GB: Cast Iron). For the Defense. Let's Go Native. Passion Flower. Street of Chance.* 1931: *Scandal Sheet. The Vice Squad. Ladies Man. Guilty Hands. Transgression. The False Madonna (GB: The False Idol). Girls About Town. 24 Hours (GB: The Hours Between).* 1932: *Strangers in Love. Man Wanted. House of Scandal. Jewel Robbery. Street of Women. One-Way Passage. Trouble in Paradise. Cynara.* 1933: *The Keyhole. The House on 56th Street. Mary Stevens MD. I Loved a Woman. Storm at Daybreak.* 1934: *Mandalay. Dr Monica. Wonder Bar. British Agent.* 1935: *Living on Velvet. Stranded. The Goose and the Gander. I Found Stella Parrish.* 1936: *The White Angel. Give Me Your Heart (GB: Sweet Aloes). Stolen Holiday.* 1937: *Another Dawn. First Lady. Confession.* 1938: *My Bill. Women Are Like That. Comet Over Broadway. Secrets of an Actress.* 1939: *In Name Only. King of the Underworld. Women in the Wind.* 1940: *It's a Date. When the Daltons Rode. Little Men.* 1941: *Play Girl. Charley's Aunt (GB: Charley's American Aunt), The Feminine Touch. The Man Who Lost Himself* 1942: *Always in My Heart. Between Us Girls.* 1943: **Show Business at War.* 1944: *Four Jills in a Jeep.* 1945: *Divorce. Allotment Wives (GB: Woman in the Case).* 1946: *Wife Wanted (GB: Shadow of Blackmail).*

FRANCISCUS, James 1934–1991
Handsome, fair-haired American actor with equine, Heston-ish features. He looked to be destined for good things until the disaster of *Youngblood Hawke,* after which he went through a barren patch until settling for routine fodder. But he could still give hints of what might have been when occasionally given the opportunity. He died from emphysema at 57.

1956: *Four Boys and a Gun.* 1958: *The Mugger.* 1959: *I Passed for White.* 1961: *The Outsider.* 1962: *The Miracle of the White Stallions (GB: Flight of the White Stallions).* 1964: *Youngblood Hawke.* 1968: *Operation Deep Yellow (GB: Snow Treasure). Shadow*

over Elveron (TV). Trial Run (TV). Hellboats. 1969: *The Valley of Gwangi. Marooned. Beneath the Planet of the Apes.* 1970: *Cat o' Nine Tails. Night Slaves (TV).* 1973: *The 500 Pound Jerk (GB: The Strong Man) (TV).* 1974: *Aloha Means Goodbye (TV).* 1975: *The Dream Makers (TV). The Trial of Chaplain Jensen (TV). One of My Wives is Missing (TV).* 1976: *The Amazing Dobermans. The Man Inside.* 1978: *Secrets of Three Hungry Wives (TV). The Greek Tycoon. Good Guys Wear Black. City on Fire. Puzzle. Killer Fish. The Pirate (TV).* 1979: *The Concorde Affair.* 1980: *When Time Ran Out.* 1981: *Butterfly. Nightkill. L'ultimo squalo (GB: Shark. US: Great White).* 1982: *Jacqueline Bouvier Kennedy (TV). The Courageous/Heroes.* 1985: *Secret Weapons/ Sexpionage (video).*

FRANKLIN, Pamela 1949–
British actress with dark hair and round, open face, just as well used for spitefulness or innocence. Began as a child star, and, like others of that ilk, seemed anxious to prove herself in 'adult' roles. Although she gave some interesting performances, her films have been few and she did not become any sort of power at the box office. Born in Japan and now lives in America.

1961: *The Innocents.* 1962: *The Lion. The Horse Without a Head.* 1964: *The Third Secret. See How They Run (TV). Flipper's New Adventure (GB: Flipper and the Pirates).* 1965: *The Nanny.* 1967: *Our Mother's House.* 1968: *The Prime of Miss Jean Brodie. The Night of the Following Day.* 1969: *Sinful Davey. David Copperfield (TV. GB: cinemas).* 1970: *And Soon the Darkness.* 1972: *The Letters (TV). Necromancy.* 1973: *The Legend of Hell House. Satan's School for Girls (TV). Ace Eli and Rodger of the Skies.* 1975: *Crossfire (TV).* 1976: *The Food of the Gods. Eleanor and Franklin (TV).*

FRANZ, Arthur 1920–
Curly-haired American leading man whose pleasant features, naturally inclined towards a smile, were mostly seen wearing a thin-lipped, embittered look in roles of tension or neurosis. Had the leading role in his first film, and stayed a minor star, notably in low-budget successes from Stanley Kramer, until 1959, after which he turned to television and the theatre, returning occasionally to films in small character roles. Married/divorced actress Adele Longmire (first of two).

1948: *Jungle Patrol.* 1949: *The Doctor and the Girl. Sands of Iwo Jima. Red Stallion in the Rockies. The Red Light. Roseanna McCoy.* 1950: *Three Secrets. Tarnished.* 1951: *Abbott and Costello Meet the Invisible Man. Submarine Command. Strictly Dishonourable. Flight to Mars.* 1952: *Rainbow 'round My Shoulder. Member of the Wedding. The Sniper. Eight Iron Men.* 1953: *Bad for Each Other. The Eddie Cantor Story. Invaders from Mars.* 1954: *The Caine Mutiny. Flight Nurse. Battle Taxi. Steel Cage.* 1955: *New Orleans Uncensored (GB: Riot on Pier 6). Bobby Ware is Missing.* 1956: *Beyond a Reasonable Doubt. The Wild Party. Running Target.* 1957: *The Devil's Hairpin. The Unholy Wife. Hellcats of the Navy. Back from the Dead.* 1958: *The Young Lions. The Flame Barrier. Monster on the Campus.* 1959: *Atomic Submarine. Woman Obsessed.* 1963: *The Carpetbaggers.* 1966: *Alvarez Kelly.* 1967: *Anzio (GB: The Battle for Anzio). The Sweet Ride.* 1970: *Dream No Evil.* 1973: *So Long, Blue Boy.* 1974: *Murder or Mercy (TV).* 1975: *The 'Human' Factor.* 1976: *Sisters of Death.* 1977: *The Last Hurrah (TV). Jaws of Death.* 1979: *Jennifer: A Woman's Story (TV). Bogie (TV).* 1982: *That Championship Season.*

FRASER, Brendan 1968–
Tall, affable, well-built, open-faced American actor of Canadian parentage who often plays easy-going, laid-back, naive types and says he likes to portray the 'fish out of water'. This facility has mostly been used in comedy, but, once Fraser had achieved the stardom breakthrough in *George of the Jungle* he proved he could be as persuasive in drama with his performance in the award-winning *Gods and Monsters.* He had a massive box-

office hit with the *The Mummy*, but the flop of the follow-up, *Dudley-Do-Right*, showed that Fraser still needed the right vehicle to pull people in. Has several times made unbilled appearances.

1991: ‡*Dogfight*. *Child of Darkness, Child of Light* (TV). *Guilty Until Proven Innocent* (TV. GB: *Presumed Guilty*). 1992: *School Ties*. *Encino Man* (GB: *California Man*). 1993: *Younger and Younger*. *Twenty Bucks*. *With Honors*. *Son in Law*. 1994: *The Passion of Darkly Noon* (released 1996). *Airheads*. *The Scout*. 1995: *Now and Then*. 1996: *Kids in the Hall: Brain Candy*. *The Twilight of the Golds*. *Mrs Winterbourne*. *Glory Daze*. 1997: *Still Breathing*. *George of the Jungle*. 1998: *Gods and Monsters*. 1999: *Blast from the Past*. *The Mummy*. *Sinbad: Beyond the Veil of Mists* (voice only). *Dudley-Do-Right*. 2000: *Monkeybone*. *Bedazzled*. 2001: *The Mummy Returns*.

‡ As Brendon Fraser

FRASER, John 1931–
Fresh-faced, young-looking Scottish actor, a pin-up of the fifties who did not mellow into more mature roles, although he tackled a wider variety of characters than one might think. Divided his time between the cinema and theatre from 1953 to 1965, but afterwards was seen almost entirely in plays, with the occasional foray to films and TV.

1953: *Valley of Song* (US: *Men Are Children Twice*). *The Good Beginning*. 1954: *The Face That Launched a Thousand Ships*. *The Dam Busters*. 1955: *Touch and Go* (US: *The Light Touch*). 1957: *The Good Companions*. 1958: *The Wind Cannot Read*. 1960: *The Trials of Oscar Wilde* (US: *The Man with the Green Carnation*). *Tunes of Glory*. 1961: *Fury at Smuggler's Bay*. *The Horsemasters*. *El Cid*. 1962: *Waltz of the Toreadors*. 1963: *Tamahine*. 1964: *Repulsion*. 1965: *Operation Crossbow* (US: *The Great Spy Mission*). *A Study in Terror* (US: *Fog*). *Doctor in Clover* (US: *Carnaby M.D.*) 1969: *Isadora*. 1972: **The Man and the Snake*. 1976: *Schizo*.

FRASER, Laura 1976–
Small, chirpy Scottish actress bagged for films virtually straight from acting school and a small amount of local theatre. She often subdues her natural prettiness and vivacity to play 'X generation' girls from all regions and walks of life, which bodes well for a distant future in character roles when

her star days are over. *Au naturel*, she has sparkling eyes, a cheeky smile and waif-like appeal.

1995: *Good Day for the Bad Guys*. 1996: *Small Faces*. 1997: *Paris, Brixton*. *Left Luggage*. *The Investigator*. 1998: *Divorcing Jack*. *The Man in the Iron Mask*. *Cousin Bette*. *The Tribe*. 1999: *Virtual Sexuality*. *A Christmas Carol* (TV). *Titus*. *Whatever Happened to Harold Smith?* 2000: *Kevin & Perry Go Large*. *Forgive and Forget*. 2001: *A Knight's Tale*.

FRAZEE, Jane
(Mary J. Frahse) 1918–1985
Sunny, likeable, well-liked strawberry blonde American star with pinchedly pretty face. Contralto, dancer, comedienne and actress, and pretty useful at all four, the sparkling Miss Frazee brightened several minor musicals and comedies of the 1940s, after starting in two-reelers as one of the Frazee Sisters. Her appearances in the Joe McDoakes short comedies of the mid-1950s were a bonus for her fans. Married to comedian Glenn Tryon (the first of four husbands) from 1942 to 1947, she later became a successful businesswoman. Died from pneumonia following strokes that had forced her retirement two years earlier.

1936: **Study and Understudy*. 1939: *Swing Styles. *Arcade Varieties. **Rollin' in Rhythm*. *Pharmacy Frolics. 1940: *Buck Privates* (GB: *Rookies*). *Melody and Moonlight*. 1941: *Moonlight in Hawaii*. *What's Cookin'* (GB: *Wake Up and Dream*). *Hellzapoppin*. *Sing Another Chorus*. *Don't Get Personal*. *Angels with Broken Wings*. *San Antonio Rose*. **Music in the Morgan Manner*. 1942: *Moonlight Masquerade*. *Almost Married*. *Sweetheart of

the Fleet*. *Hi'Ya Chum* (GB: *Everything Happens to Us*). *Get Hep to Love* (GB: *She's My Lovely*). *Moonlight in Havana*. 1943: *Keep 'em Slugging*. *Two Senoritas from Chicago*. *Rhythm of the Islands*. *Beautiful But Broke*. *When Johnny Comes Marching Home*. 1944: *Cowboy Canteen* (GB: *Close Harmony*). *She's a Sweetheart*. *The Big Bonanza*. *Kansas City Kitty*. *Swing in the Saddle* (GB: *Swing and Sway*). *Rosie the Riveter* (GB: *In Rosie's Room*). 1945: *Practically Yours*. *A Guy Could Change*. *Ten Cents a Dance* (GB: *Dancing Ladies*). *Swingin' on a Rainbow*. 1946: *Calendar Girl*. 1947: *Springtime in the Sierras*. *On the Old Spanish Trail*. *The Gay Ranchero*. 1948: *Under California Stars*. *Homicide for Three*. *Grand Canyon Trail*. *Incident*. *Last of the Wild Horses*. 1951: *Rhythm Inn*. 1954: **So You Want to Be Your Own Boss*. **So You Want to Go to a Nightclub*. **So You're Taking in a Roomer*. *Superman and Scotland Yard* (TV. GB: cinemas). 1955: **So You Don't Trust Your Wife*. **So You Want to Be a Gladiator*. **So You Want to Build a Model Railroad*. 1956: **So You Think the Grass is Greener*.

FREDERICK, Pauline
(Beatrice P. Libbey) 1883–1938
Dark-haired, bird-like American actress who started as a chorus girl and developed into one of the *grandes dames* of the Broadway stage. Her best film work came in a series of roles for Samuel Goldwyn, playing strong-willed and sometimes tragic figures, beginning with the definitive version of *Madame X*, which she also played for 10 months on the London stage. Her cinema career was in decline when an acute asthma attack killed her at 55. Five times married.

1915: *The Eternal City*. *Bella Donna*. *Lydia Gilmore*. *Sold*. *Zaza*. 1916: *Her Honor, the Governor*. *The Moment Before*. *The Woman in the Case*. *Audrey*. *The Spider*. *Ashes of Embers*. 1917: *Sleeping Fires*. *Slave Island*. *The Love That Lives*. *Hungry Heart*. 1918: *Fedora*. *Tosca*. *Resurrection*. *Mrs Dane's Defense*. *Her Final Reckoning*. *Madame Jealousy*. 1919: *One Week of Love*. *The Peace of the Roaring River*. *Paid in Full*. *Bonds of Love*. *Out of the Shadow*. 1920: *The Paliser Case*. *Madame X*. *A Slave of Vanity*. 1921: *Mistress of Shenstone*. *Salvage*. *Roads of Destiny*. *The Sting of the Lash*. *The Lure of Jade*. 1922: *The Woman Breed*. *The Glory of Clementina* / *The Glorious Clementina*. *Two Kinds of Women*. 1924: *The Fast Set*. *Smouldering Fires*. *Married Flirts*. *Let No

Man Put Asunder. 1925: The Lady. Three Women. 1926: Devil's Island. Her Honor, the Governor (remake). Josselyn's Wife. The Nest. 1927: Mumsie. 1928: Woman from Moscow. On Trial. 1929: The Sacred Flame. Evidence. 1931: This Modern Age. 1932: Wayward. The Phantom of Crestwood. 1933: Self Defense. 1934: Social Register. 1935: My Marriage. 1936: Ramona. 1937: Thank You, Mr. Moto. 1938: The Buccaneer.

FREEMAN, Mona

(Monica Freeman) 1926–

Pretty, chubby-cheeked, blue-eyed blonde American actress, very popular as brattish kid sisters and teenage spitfires in the forties. She found herself repeating the role well into her twenties and discovered it difficult to settle into routine heroine roles in the fifties.

1944: Double Indemnity. Here Come the Waves. Till We Meet Again. National Velvet. Our Hearts Were Young and Gay. Together Again. 1945: Junior Miss. Roughly Speaking. Danger Signal. 1946: Black Beauty. Our Hearts Were Growing Up. That Brennan Girl. 1947: Mother Wore Tights. Variety Girl. Dear Ruth. 1948: Isn't It Romantic? 1949: Streets of Laredo. The Heiress. Dear Wife. 1950: Branded. I Was a Shoplifter. Copper Canyon. 1951: Dear Brat. Darling, How Could You? (GB: Rendezvous). The Lady from Texas. 1952: Flesh and Fury. Jumping Jacks. Angel Face. The Greatest Show on Earth. Thunderbirds. 1954: Battle Cry. 1955: Before I Wake (US: Shadow of Fear). Dial 999 (US: The Way Out). The Road to Denver. 1956: Men Against Speed (TV. GB: cinemas). Hold Back the Night. Seidman and Son (TV). Huk. 1957: Dragoon Wells Massacre. Three Men on a Horse (TV). 1958: The World Was His Jury. The Long March (TV). 1971: Welcome Home, Johnny Bristol (TV).

FREEMAN, Morgan 1937–

Authoritative, lean-faced, dignified American actor with a low, drawling, persuasive voice, a calming influence in many of his film roles. An early ambition to be a jet pilot led to four years in the US Air Force before he began to study acting. The breakthrough to Broadway roles came at 30 and his became a well-known face (and voice) on the children's TV show The Electric Company from 1971 to 1976, as Easy Reader. Film roles were virtually non-existent until 1980, but he has been able to prove his worth in the past 20 years, chalking up three Oscar nominations

(for Street Smart, Driving Miss Daisy and The Shawshank Redemption) and assuming a progressively higher profile in big-budget films.

1971: Who Says I Can't Ride a Rainbow? (GB: TV, as Barney). 1978: Roll of Thunder, Hear My Cry (TV). 1979: Coriolanus. Hollow Image (TV). 1980: Attica (TV). Brubaker. 1981: Eyewitness (GB: The Janitor). The Marva Collins Story (TV). 1982: Death of a Prophet. 1984: Harry & Son. Teachers. 1985: That Was Then . . . This is Now. Marie – A True Story. The Execution of Raymond Graham (TV). 1986: Resting Place (TV). Street Smart. 1987: Fight for Life (TV). 1988: Clean and Sober. Blood Money/Clinton and Nadine. 1989: Driving Miss Daisy. Lean on Me. Glory. Phantom of the Mall. 1990: The Bonfire of the Vanities. Johnny Handsome. 1991: Robin Hood – Prince of Thieves. Hit Man. 1992: The Power of One. Unforgiven. 1994: The Shawshank Redemption. 1995: Outbreak. Se7en. Moll Flanders. 1996: Chain Reaction. Cosmic Voyage (narrator only). 1997: The Long Way Home (narrator only). Kiss the Girls. Amistad. 1998: Hard Rain. Deep Impact. 1999: Mutiny (TV). Under Suspicion. Water Damage. 2000: Nurse Betty. Along Came a Spider. Long Way to Freedom. Rendezvous with Rama.

FRIEND, Philip 1915–1987

Fresh-faced, youthful-looking British leading man who went to Hollywood in 1946 (on the recommendation of Alfred Hitchcock) and enjoyed middling success there as a dashing adventurer, although he always looked a little too much like Richard Greene (qv) for his own good. Returned to Britain in 1952, but could not regain his place there as a

major star.

1939: The Midas Touch. Inquest. 1940: Old Bill and Son. 1941: Pimpernel Smith (US: Mister V). Dangerous Moonlight (US: Suicide Squadron). Sheepdog of the Hills. 1942: In Which We Serve. Back Room Boy. The Next of Kin. The Day Will Dawn (US: The Avengers). 1943: We Dive at Dawn. The Bells Go Down. Warn That Man. The Flemish Farm. 1944: 2,000 Women. I Want to be an Actress. 1945: Great Day. 1948: My Own True Love. Enchantment. 1949: Sword in the Desert. Buccaneer's Girl. 1950: Spy Hunt (GB: Panther's Moon). 1951: Smuggler's Island. The Highwayman. Thunder on the Hill (GB: Bonaventure). 1953: Desperate Moment. Background (US: Edge of Divorce). 1954: The Diamond (US: Diamond Wizard). Triple Blackmail. 1955: Cloak Without Dagger (US: Operation Conspiracy). 1956: *Dick Turpin – Highwayman. 1957: *Danger List. 1958: The Betrayal. Son of Robin Hood. The Solitary Child. 1959: Web of Suspicion. 1962: Stranglehold. The Fur Collar. 1964: Manutara. 1966: The Vulture.

FROST, Sadie (S. Vaugman) 1967–

Dark-haired, dark-eyed British actress who often plays tough and sultry roles. London born, she was a stage-school child who made her TV acting debut at 18. After her performance as Lucy in Bram Stoker's Dracula, she declined Hollywood offers to stay in England, but her choice of scripts there – apart from Shopping, in which she played a Northern Irish ram-raiding street girl – has not been good enough to keep her in the public eye. She married/divorced singer-actor Gary Kemp and is currently married to actor Jude Law (qv), her Shopping co-star.

1989: Diamond Skulls (US: Dark Obsession). 1990: The Krays. 1992: Paper Marriage. Bram Stoker's Dracula. 1993: Splitting Heirs. Shopping. 1994: The Cisco Kid (TV). Magic Hunter. A Pyromaniac's Love Story. 1996: CrimeTime. Bent. 1997: Flypaper. 1998: Captain Jack. Final Cut. Byron. 1999: An Ideal Husband. The Lake of Darkness (TV). Love, Honour & Obey. 2000: Rancid Aluminium. Presence of Mind.

FULLER, Leslie 1889–1948

Big, aggressive, loud-voiced concert-party comedian whose bull-at-a-gate style rang the British box-office bell in regional comedies of the thirties. His appeal faded rapidly during

the war years and when he died of a heart attack at 59, he was all but forgotten.
1930: *Not So Quiet on the Western Front. Kiss Me Sergeant. Why Sailors Leave Home.* 1931: *Old Soldiers Never Die. Poor Old Bill. Bill's Legacy. What a Night! Tonight's the Night.* 1932: *Old Spanish Customers. The Last Coupon.* 1933: *Hawleys of High Street. The Pride of the Force. A Political Party.* 1934: *The Outcast. Lost in the Legion. Doctor's Orders.* 1935: *Strictly Illegal / Here Comes a Policeman. The Stoker. Captain Bill.* 1936: *One Good Turn.* 1937: *Boys Will be Girls.* 1939: *The Middle Watch.* 1940: *Two Smart Men.* 1941: *My Wife's Family.* 1942: *Front Line Kids.* 1945: *What Do We Do Now?*

FUNICELLO, Annette 1942–
Pretty, ever-smiling, pert and cheerful Disney singer and actress of the 1950s and early 1960s, with tinkling voice, dark hair and dark eyes. Like Kathryn Grayson before her, she played down a formidable bustline to trade in sweetness and light, and had a second career as star of the American-International beach comedy-musicals of the mid–1960s. Began as a child on Disney's *Mickey Mouse Club* TV show. A comeback was announced in *Grease 2* (1982), but it didn't materialize. She did appear, hardly changed and cheerfully guying her own image, in 1987's *Back to the Beach*, but she was stricken by multiple sclerosis in the early 1990s. Founded the Annette Funicello Fund for Neurological Disorders.
1957: *Johnny Tremain.* 1959: †*The Shaggy Dog.* 1961: †*The Horsemasters.* †*Babes in Toyland.* 1962: †*Escapade in Florence (TV. GB: cinemas).* †*Six Gun Law (TV. GB: cinemas).* †*The Golden Horseshoe Revue.*

1963: †*The Misadventures of Merlin Jones. Beach Party.* 1964: *Bikini Beach. Pajama Party. Muscle Beach Party.* 1965: *Dr Goldfoot and the Bikini Machine (GB: Dr G and the Bikini Machine).* †*The Monkey's Uncle.* 1965: *Beach Blanket Bingo (GB: Malibu Beach). How to Stuff a Wild Bikini.* 1966: *Fireball 500. Pajama Party in a Haunted House.* 1967: *Thunder Alley.* 1968: *Head.* 1970: *Divorce American Style (TV).* 1985: *Lots of Luck (TV).* 1987: *Back to the Beach.* 1995: *A Dream is a Wish Your Heart Makes: The Annette Funicello Story (TV).*

†*As Annette*

FURLONG, Edward 1977–
Small, wiry, sharp-featured American actor with 'street-kid' looks and slick dark hair. Brought up by a single-parent mother, he shot to prominence as the boy in *Terminator 2*, and has since maintained his position near the top of casts, mostly as aggressive but unsure and sometimes doomed boys forced to fend for themselves.
1991: *Terminator 2: Judgment Day.* 1992: *American Heart. Pet Sematary Two.* 1993: *A Home of Our Own.* 1994: *Brainscan. Little Odessa.* 1995: *The Grass Harp.* 1996: *Terminator 2 3D: Battle Across Time. Before and After.* 1998: *Pecker. American History X.* 1999: *Detroit Rock City.* 2000: *Animal Factory.* 2001: *I cavalieri che fecero l'impresa.*

FURNEAUX Yvonne (Y. Scatcherd) 1928–
French-born leading lady who spent most of her early life in Britain. Her dark-haired, green-eyed dusky looks qualified her immediately for slave queens of Babylon. British studios knew not what to do with her,

and she spent most of her career roaming Europe in search of decent parts.
1952: *24 Hours in Women's Life (US: Affair in Monte Carlo). Meet Me Tonight.* 1953: *The Beggar's Opera. The Master of Ballantrae. The House of the Arrow.* 1954: *The Genie.* 1955: *Il principe della maschera rossa. The Dark Avenger (US: The Warriors). Cross Channel. L'aigle rouge.* 1956: *Lisbon. Le amiche.* 1959: *The Mummy. La dolce vita.* 1960: *A noi piace freddo . . . ! The Tank of September 8.* 1961: *Dox, caccia all'uomo. The Count of Monte-Cristo. Charge of the Black Lancers. Lui, lei e il nonno. Via Margutta / La rue des amours faciles / Run with the Devil.* 1962: *Io, Semiramide (GB: I, Semiramis. US: Slave Queen of Babylon).* 1963: *Enough Rope / Le meurtrier. Il criminale. I quattro tassisti.* 1964: *The Lion of Thebes. Repulsion.* 1965: *Die Todesstrahlen des Dr Mabuse (US: Dr Mabuse's Rays of Death). Night Train to Milan.* 1966: *Le scandale (GB: The Champagne Murders).* 1971: *In nome del popolo italiano.* 1973: *Versuchung in Sommerwind.* 1983: *Frankenstein's Great Aunt Tillie (released 1985).*

FYFFE, Will 1884–1947
Big, thickly-built Scottish actor, singer and comedian, who was performing at the age of 11 and a music hall star in his twenties, playing the archetypal drunken Scot and singing *I Belong to Glasgow*. He transferred his gruff old Scotsmen to films in the thirties and became a popular character star. Fell to his death from a hotel window in St Andrew's.
1930: *Elstree Calling.* 1933: *Happy.* 1935: *Rolling Home.* 1936: *Debt of Honour. King of Hearts. Love in Exile. Men of Yesterday. Annie Laurie. Well Done Henry.* 1937: *Spring Handicap. Cotton Queen. Said O'Reilly to McNab (US: Sez O'Reilly to McNab). Owd Bob (US: To the Victor).* 1939: *Rulers of the Sea. The Mind of Mr Reeder (US: The Mysterious Mr Reeder). The Missing People.* 1940: *They Came By Night. For Freedom. Neutral Port.* 1941: *The Prime Minister.* **Camp Concert.* 1943: **Scottish Savings No. 2.* 1944: *Heaven is Around the Corner. Give Me the Stars.* 1947: *The Brothers.*

G

GABIN, Jean

(J. Alexis G. Moncourge) 1904–1976

Solidly-built French actor with thick, tousled sandy hair and grimly humorous features who became perhaps more identified with the French cinema of the 1930s, 1940s and 1950s than any other one actor. He began his career with small roles at the Folies Bergère, then appeared in music halls, cafés and the Moulin Rouge before entering films in 1930. His characters always had a certain charm beneath their world-weariness, and he remained immensely popular in tough roles until his death from a heart attack.

*1930: Chacun sa chance. Coeur de lilas. Méphisto. 1931: Paris-Béguin. Tout ça ne vaut pas l'amour. 1932: Les gaietés de l'escadron. La belle marinière. Gloria. La foule hurle. 1933: L'étoile de Valencia. Adieu les beaux jours. Le tunnel. Du haut en bas. 1934: Zouzou. Maria Chapdelaine. La bandera. Variétés. 1936: La belle équipe. Les bas-fonds. Pépé le Moko. 1937: Le messager. La grande illusion. Gueule d'amour. 1938: Quai des brumes. La bête humaine (GB: Judas Was a Woman). 1939: Le jour se lève. La récif de corail. Remorques. 1942: Moontide. 1943: The Imposter. 1946: Martin Roumagnac (GB and US: The Man Upstairs). 1947: Le miroir/ The Mirror. 1948: Au delà des grilles. 1949: La Marie du port. 1950: E più facile che un camelo. 1951: Victor. La nuit est mon royaume. Le plaisir. La vérité sur bébé Donge (GB: The Truth about our Our Marriage). 1952: The Moment of Truth. Bufere. *Echos de plateau. 1953: Leur dernière nuit. La vierge du Rhin. Touchez pas au grisbi (GB: Honour Among Thieves). 1954: L'air de Paris. Napoléon. Le port du désir. French Can Can. Razzia sur la chnouf (GB: Chnouf). 1955: Chiens perdus sans collier. Gas-Oil. Des gens sans importance. Voici le temps des assassins (GB: Twelve Hours to Live). Le sang à la tête. La traversée de Paris (GB: Pig Across Paris. US: Three Bags Full). 1956: Crime and Punishment. The Case of Dr Laurent. 1957: Le rouge est mis. Maigret tend un piège (GB: Maigret Sets a Trap). Les misérables. Le désordre et la nuit. 1958: En cas de malheur (GB and US: Love is My Profession). Les grandes familles. Archimède le clochard. 1959: Maigret et l'affair Saint-Fiacre. Rue des Prairies. 1960: Le baron de l'écluse. Les Vieux de la vieille (GB: The Old Guard). 1961: Le président. Le cave se rebiffe. 1962: Un singe en hiver (GB: It's Hot in Hell). Le gentleman d'Epsom. Mélodie en sous-sol (GB: The Big Snatch). 1963: Maigret voit rouge. 1964: Monsieur. L'âge ingrat. 1965: Le tonnerre de Dieu. Du Rififi à Paname. 1966: Le jardinier d'argenteuil. 1967: Le soleil des voyous (GB and US: Action Man). La pacha. 1968: Sous le signe du taureau/ Fin de journée. Le tatoué. 1969: The Sicilian Clan. Fin de journée. 1970: La Horse. 1971: Le chat. Le drapeau noir flotte sur la marmite. 1972: Le tueur. 1973: L'affaire Dominici. Deux hommes dans la ville. 1974: Verdict. 1976: L'année sainte.*

GABLE, Clark 1901–1960

Jug-eared, moustachioed, smilingly handsome American leading man with dark hair and a great deal of rough, rugged masculine charm. Equally at home in comedy or drama, he became the 'King of Hollywood' in the 1930s, a period in which he won an Oscar for *It Happened One Night*, and which culminated in his triumph (and another Oscar nomination) in *Gone With the Wind*. His rough on-screen treatment of his leading ladies endeared him to his legions of female fans and, although he was never quite the same after the war years, he managed one last great performance in *The Misfits*. Married (third of five) to Carole Lombard (*qv*) from 1939 to her death in 1942. Died from a heart attack.

*1924: Forbidden Paradise. White Man. 1925: The Merry Widow. Déclassée. Ben-Hur. The Merry Pacemakers (serial). 1926: Fighting Blood (series). The Johnstown Flood (GB: The Flood). North Star. The Plastic Age. 1930: The Painted Desert. 1931: The Easiest Way. Dance, Fools, Dance. The Finger Points. Laughing Sinners. The Secret Six. Night Nurse. A Free Soul. Sporting Blood. Susan Lenox, Her Fall and Rise (GB: The Rise of Helga). Possessed. 1932: Hell Divers. Polly of the Circus. Strange Interlude (GB: Strange Interval). Red Dust. No Man of Her Own. Jackie Cooper's Christmas (GB: The Christmas Party). 1933: Hold Your Man. The White Sister. Night Flight. Dancing Lady. *Hollywood on Parade No.6. 1934: Men in White. It Happened One Night. Manhattan Melodrama. Chained. *Hollywood on Parade No. 13. Forsaking All Others. 1935: *Hollywood Hobbies. After Office Hours. Call of the Wild. China Seas. *Starlight Days at the Lido. Mutiny on the Bounty. 1936: Wife Versus Secretary. San Francisco. Cain and Mabel. Love on the Run. 1937: Parnell. Saratoga. 1938: Too Hot to Handle. Test Pilot. 1939: Idiot's Delight. Gone With the Wind. 1940: Strange Cargo. Boom Town. Comrade X. 1941: They Met in Bombay. Honky Tonk. 1942: Somewhere I'll Find You. *Wings Up (narrator only). Aerial Gunner. *Hollywood in Uniform. 1944: Combat America. *Be Careful! (narrator only). 1945: Adventure. 1947: The Hucksters. 1948: Command Decision. Homecoming. 1949: Any Number Can Play. 1950: Key to the City. To Please a Lady. *The Screen Actor. 1951: Across the Wide Missouri. Callaway Went Thataway (GB: The Star Said No!). 1952: Lone Star. 1953: Never Let Me Go. *Memories in Uniform. 1954: Mogambo. Betrayed. 1955: Soldier of Fortune. The Tall Men. 1956: The King and Four Queens. 1957: Band of Angels. 1958: Teacher's Pet. Run Silent, Run Deep. 1959: But Not for Me. 1960: It Started in Naples. 1961: The Misfits.*

GABOR, Eva 1921–1995

Blonde, vivacious, petite Hungarian actress, the younger (and, it must be admitted, prettier) sister of Zsa Zsa Gabor (qv). Teenage ambitions to be a world-class ice skater were soon abandoned in favour of an acting career that never fired on all cylinders. Her films were spasmodic to say the least, and alternated between minor leads and flamboyant cameos. In her forties, however, she became a national celebrity as the star of the wildly successful TV series *Green Acres*, which ran for six years. Later Disney used her distinctive tones for the heroines of several feature cartoons. Two weeks after breaking a hip in a fall, she died from respiratory distress and other infections.

1941: Forced Landing. Pacific Blackout. 1945: A Royal Scandal (GB: Czarina). 1946: Wife of Monte Cristo. 1948: Song of Surrender. 1953: Paris Model. 1954: Captain Kidd and the Slave Girl The Mad Magician. The Last Time I Saw Paris. 1955: Artists and Models. 1957: My Man Godfrey. Don't Go Near the Water. 1958: The Truth About Women. Gigi. 1959: It Started With a Kiss. 1960: Love Island. 1963: A New Kind of Love. 1964: Youngblood Hawke. 1969: Wake Me When the War is Over (TV). 1970: The Aristocats (voice only). 1977: The Rescuers (voice only). 1986: Princess Academy. 1990: Return to Green Acres (TV). 1991: The Rescuers Down Under (voice only).

GABOR, Zsa Zsa (Sari Gabor) 1917–
A former Miss Hungary, Zsa Zsa was (and is!) a slinky-looking blonde who went to Hollywood, called everybody 'darlink' and got into more society columns than films. Someone once described her as a professional guest star and that's about right. Married to George Sanders (third of four) from 1949–1957. Jailed for a few days in 1990 for assaulting a police officer. Older sister of actress Eva Gabor.
1952: We're Not Married. Lovely to Look At. Moulin Rouge. Lili. 1953: The Story of Three Loves. Public Enemy Number 1. 1954: Three Ring Circus. Sang et lumières. Ball der Nationen. 1955: Man of Taste (TV). 1956: Death of a Scoundrel. The Greer Case (TV). 1957: The Girl in the Kremlin. Circle of the Day (TV). The Man Who Wouldn't Talk. 1958: Touch of Evil. Queen of Outer Space. Country Music Holiday. 1959: For the First Time. La contessa azzurra. 1960: Pepe. 1962: Boys' Night Out. 1966: Picture Mommy Dead. Drop Dead Darling (US: Arrivederci, Baby!). 1967: Jack of Diamonds. 1972: Up the Front. 1975: Won Ton Ton, the Dog Who Saved Hollywood. 1978: Every Girl Should Have One. 1983: Frankenstein's Great Aunt Tillie (released 1985). 1986: Smart Alec. 1987: A Nightmare on Elm Street 3: Dream Warriors. Johann Strauss: The King Without a Crown. 1990: Happily Ever After (voice only). 1991: The Naked Gun 2½: The Smell of Fear. 1992: The Naked Truth. 1993: Est & Ouest: les paradis perdus. The Beverly Hillbillies. 1996: A Very Brady Sequel.

GAM, Rita 1927–
Dark-haired, full-lipped American leading lady with challenging gaze, on the slinky side. After theatrical and TV experience, she married director Sidney Lumet (first of three*

– they divorced in 1955) and began a film career as the tenement temptress in the wordless *The Thief*. Finding it hard to break the mould, she seemed to lose interest in the medium. Since 1962, she has only made very rare returns from Broadway for film character roles. In the early 1980s, she became a director of documentaries, but continued sporadically to pursue an acting career.
1952: The Thief. 1953: Saadia. 1954: Night People. Sign of the Pagan. 1956: Magic Fire. Mohawk. 1958: Sierra Baron. 1959: Côte d'Azure (US: Wildcats on the Beach). Hannibal. 1961: King of Kings. 1962: No Exit. 1971: Klute. Shoot Out. 1972: Such Good Friends. 1974: Law and Disorder. 1975: The Gardener (later Seeds of Evil). 1982: Love in the Present Tense (TV). 1987: Distortions. 1988: Midnight. 1993: Deep Trouble (cable TV). 1996: Rowing Through.

GARBO, Greta (G. Gustafsson) 1905–1990
Magnetic, fair-haired Swedish actress whose haunting qualities were especially well employed in tragic situations where she was required, for one reason or another, to forsake her true love. She went to America in 1925 and swiftly became *the* Hollywood love goddess of the twenties and thirties. Later her vehicles became more elaborate and she drifted away from her public and, finally, films themselves, apparently losing confidence in herself, and only remembered by most for her catchphrase 'I want to be alone'. Given a Special Academy Award in 1954. Nominated for best actress Oscars on *Anna Christie, Romance, Camille* and *Ninotchka*. Died from cardiac arrest following treatment for kidney problems.
*1921: *How Not to Dress. Fortune Hunter.*

1922: Our Daily Bread. Peter the Tramp. 1924: Gösta Berlings Saga (GB: The Atonement of Gosta Berling. US: The Story of Gosta Berling). 1925: Die freudlose Gasse (GB: Joyless Street. US: Street of Sorrow). 1926: Ibanez's Torrent (GB: The Torrent). The Temptress. 1927: Flesh and the Devil. 1928: Love (GB: Anna Karenina). The Mysterious Lady. The Divine Woman. A Woman of Affairs. 1929: Wild Orchids. The Single Standard. The Kiss. A Man's Man. 1930: †Anna Christie. Romance. 1931: Susan Lenox – Her Fall and Rise (GB: The Rise of Helga). Inspiration. 1932: Mata Hari. Grand Hotel. As You Desire Me. 1933: Queen Christina. 1934: The Painted Veil. 1935: Anna Karenina. 1936: Camille. 1937: Conquest (GB: Marie Walewska). 1939: Ninotchka. 1941: Two-Faced Woman.

†And German and Swedish versions

GARCIA, Andy
(Andres Garcia-Menendez) 1956–
Dark, low-browed, large-eyed, smooth Cuban-born actor in Hollywood from the late 1970s. His face can look honest or untrustworthy at the lowering of a lid or opening of the eye, and he has seemed most at home in urban crime thrillers on the dark side. After a sketchy early career, he began to make strides as one of *The Untouchables* and did good work in the third 'Godfather' film but, despite exposure in the odd mainstream hit, hasn't quite made it to the very top. Academy Award nomination for *The Godfather Part III*.
1981: Hill Street Blues (TV pilot). 1983: A Night in Heaven. Blue Skies Again. The Lonely Guy. 1984: The Mean Season. 1985: 8 Million Ways to Die. 1987: The Untouchables. 1988: Stand and Deliver. Blood Money/ Clinton and Nadine. American Roulette. 1989: Black Rain. 1990: Internal Affairs. A Show of Force. The Godfather Part III. 1991: Dead Again. 1992: Jennifer Eight. 1993: Hero (GB: Accidental Hero). Cachao (and directed). 1994: When a Man Loves a Woman. 1995: Things to Do in Denver When You're Dead. Steal Big, Steal Little. †Dangerous Minds. 1996: Night Falls on Manhattan. Death in Granada. The Lost City (and directed). 1997: Hoodlum. 1998: Desperate Measures. Just the Ticket. Swing Vote (TV). 2000: Just to be Together.

†Scenes deleted from final release print.

GARDNER, Ava 1922–1990

Strikingly beautiful green-eyed brunette American actress, built by M-G-M into their last great sex symbol. She remained best as characters whose passionate natures ruled their destinies, but was also good at expressing cynicism and world weariness. The glamorous image persisted into her three marriages, all to entertainers: Mickey Rooney (1942–1943), bandleader Artie Shaw (1945–1947) and Frank Sinatra (1951–1957). After her cinema career was over, she appeared in the TV mini-series *A.D.* (1984), *The Long Hot Summer* (1985) and *Harem* (1986). She died from pneumonia.

1941: *Fancy Answers. H.M. Pulham Esq. 1942: Joe Smith – American (GB: Highway to Freedom). We Were Dancing. Sunday Punch. *Mighty Lak a Goat. This Time for Keeps. Kid Glove Killer. *We Do It Because. Calling Dr Gillespie. Reunion/Reunion in France (GB: Mademoiselle France). 1943: Pilot No.5. Hitler's Madman. Ghosts on the Loose (GB: Ghosts in the Night). Young Ideas. Lost Angel. Du Barry Was a Lady. 1944: Swing Fever. Music for Millions. Three Men in White. Blonde Fever. Two Girls and a Sailor. Maisie Goes to Reno (GB: You Can't Do That to Me). 1945: She Went to the Races. 1946: Whistle Stop. The Killers. 1947: Singapore. The Hucksters. 1948: One Touch of Venus. 1949: The Bribe. The Great Sinner. East Side, West Side. 1950: Pandora and the Flying Dutchman. 1951: My Forbidden Past. Show Boat. 1952: Lone Star. The Snows of Kilimanjaro. 1953: Ride, Vaquero! Mogambo. The Band Wagon. 1954: Knights of the Round Table. The Barefoot Contessa. 1956: Bhowani Junction. 1957: The Little Hut. The Sun Also Rises. 1959: On the Beach. 1960: The Angel Wore Red. 1962: 55 Days at Peking. 1964: Seven Days in May. The Night of the Iguana. 1966: The Bible . . . in the beginning. 1968: Mayerling. 1971: Tam Lin (GB: The Devil's Widow). 1972: The Life and Times of Judge Roy Bean. 1974: Earthquake. 1975: Permission to Kill. 1976: The Sentinel. The Cassandra Crossing. The Blue Bird. 1978: City on Fire. 1980: Priest of Love. The Kidnapping of the President. 1982: Roma Regina.

GARFIELD, John

(Jacob Julius Garfinkle) 1912–1952

Dark-haired American actor who played loners, losers and rebels. His 'chip on the shoulder' image was unusual in the late thirties and early forties, and won him great popularity, especially with the younger set. But the Communist witch-hunt of the late forties hit an already wavering career, and he had been virtually out of work for 18 months when he died from a heart attack. Oscar nominee for *Four Daughters* and *Body and Soul*.

1937: *Swingtime in the Movies. 1938: †Secrets of an Actress. Four Daughters. Blackwell's Island. 1939: Juarez. They Made Me a Criminal. Daughters Courageous. Dust Be My Destiny. 1940: *Chinese Garden Festival. Saturday's Children. Flowing Gold. East of the River. Castle on the Hudson (GB: Years Without Days). 1941: The Sea Wolf. Out of the Fog. 1942: Tortilla Flat. Dangerously They Live. 1943: Air Force. Destination Tokyo. Thank Your Lucky Stars. The Fallen Sparrow. 1944: Between Two Worlds. Hollywood Canteen. 1945: Pride of the Marines (GB: Forever in Love). 1946: The Postman Always Rings Twice. Nobody Lives Forever. Humoresque. 1947: Daisy Kenyon. Body and Soul. 1948: Gentleman's Agreement. Force of Evil. 1949: We Were Strangers. Jigsaw. 1950: Under My Skin. The Breaking Point. Difficult Years (narrator only). 1951: He Ran All the Way.

†*Scenes deleted from final release print.*

GARLAND, Beverly (B. Fessenden) 1926–

Brown-eyed blonde American actress of the sultry kind, a sort of cross between Audrey Totter and Gloria Grahame (both *qv*). Allegedly blacklisted in Hollywood for remarks she made about her first film and quarrels with the press, she was more or less out of work for nearly five years, then spent most of her screen time being menaced by mobsters and monsters. Television at least kept this wasted talent fully occupied for 40 years from 1954. Married/divorced actor Richard Garland (1926–1969). Now runs two hotels (Beverly Garland's Holiday Inns) and heads up charity work for needy children.

1949: †DOA. 1950: A Life of Her Own. 1951: Strictly Dishonorable. 1952: Fearless Fagan. 1953: The Glass Web. Problem Girls. 1954: Bitter Creek. The Go-Getter. The Desperado. Two Guns and a Badge. The Rocket Man. The Miami Story. Killer Leopard. 1955: New Orleans Uncensored (GB: Riot on Pier 6). The Desperate Hours. Sudden Danger. 1956: It Conquered the World. Gunslinger. Swamp Woman. Curucu, Beast of the Amazon. The Steel Jungle. 1957: Not of This Earth. The Joker is Wild. Naked Paradise. Badlands of Montana. Chicago Confidential. Bombers B52 (GB: No Sleep Till Dawn). 1958: The Saga of Hemp Brown. 1959: The Alligator People. Gunfight at Sandoval (TV. GB: cinemas). 1963: Twice Told Tales. Stark Fear. 1965: *The Dog That Bit You. 1967: *The Man in the Middle. Trial by Error (TV). 1968: Pretty Poison. 1969: Cutter's Trail (TV). *The Day God Died. The Mad Room. 1972: Say Goodbye, Maggie Cole (TV). The Voyage of the Yes (TV). The Weekend Nun (TV). 1974: Where the Red Fern Grows. The Day the Earth Moved (TV). The Healers (TV). Unwed Father (TV). Airport 1975. 1977: Sixth and Main. 1979: Roller Boogie. 1980: It's My Turn. 1982: Gamble on Love (TV). 1983: This Girl for Hire (TV). 1990: The World's Oldest Living Bridesmaid (TV). *To the Moon, Alice. 1991: Finding the Way Home (TV). 1993: Symphony. King B: A Life in the Movies. 1995: Hellfire.

†*As Beverly Campbell*

GARLAND, Judy

(Frances Gumm) 1922–1969

Small, chubby, dark, peppy and intense American singer and actress with strong, warm, vibrant, throbbing voice. After fantastic success as a teenager (including a special Oscar in 1939, the year she sang 'Over the Rainbow' in *The Wizard of Oz*), her private life buckled under the pressures of her public one, into a mess of pills, psychiatry and attempted suicide. Married to director Vincente Minnelli 1945–1950 (third of five): Liza Minnelli (*qv*) is their daughter. Died from 'an accidental overdose of sleeping pills'. Academy Award nominations for *A Star is Born* and *Judgment at Nuremberg*.

1929: *†The Meglin Kiddie Revue. 1930: *†Holiday in Storyland. *†Bubbles. *†The Wedding of Jack and Jill. 1931: *†The Old Lady in the Shoe. 1935: *†La Fiesta de Santa Barbara. 1936: *Every Sunday. Pigskin Parade (GB: The Harmony Parade). 1937: Broadway Melody of 1938. Thoroughbreds Don't Cry. 1938: Everybody Sing. Love Finds Andy Hardy. Listen, Darling. 1939: The Wizard of Oz. Babes in Arms. 1940: Andy Hardy Meets Debutante. Strike Up the Band. Little Nellie Kelly. 1941: Life Begins for Andy Hardy. Ziegfeld Girl. Babes on Broadway. *Meet the Stars No. 4. *Cavalcade of the Academy Awards. 1942: For Me and My Gal (GB: For Me and My Girl). *We Must Have Music. 1943: Presenting Lily Mars. Girl Crazy. Thousands Cheer. 1944: Ziegfeld Follies (released 1946). Meet Me in St. Louis. 1945: The Clock (GB: Under the Clock). The Harvey Girls. 1946: Till the Clouds Roll By. 1948: The Pirate. Words and Music. Easter Parade. 1949: In the Good Old Summertime. 1950: Summer Stock (GB: If You Feel Like Singing). 1954: A Star is Born. 1960: Pepe (voice only). 1961: Judgment at Nuremberg. 1962: Gay Purr-ee (voice only). 1963: A Child is Waiting. I Could Go on Singing. 1994: That's Entertainment! III (previously unseen footage).

†As one of The Gumm Sisters

GARNER, James (J. Baurngarner) 1928–
Tall, beefy, happy-looking American actor with black curly hair and lopsided grin. Specialized in offbeat heroes who got the better of the villain by means other than muscular. He did not quite make the big time in a cinema unable to pigeonhole him, and returned to television (scene of his greatest success, the western series Maverick) to gain renewed popularity in the mid seventies. Oscar nomination for Murphy's Romance.
1956: Toward the Unknown (GB: Brink of Hell). The Girl He Left Behind. Explosion (TV. GB: cinemas). Decision (TV. GB: cinemas). 1957: Sayonara. Shoot-Out at Medicine Bend. 1958: Darby's Rangers (GB: The Young Invaders). Girl on the Subway (TV. GB: cinemas). 1959: Up Periscope. Alias Jesse James. Cash McCall. 1961: The Children's Hour (GB: The Loudest Whisper). 1962: Boys' Night Out. 1963: The Thrill of It All. Move Over, Darling. The Great Escape. The Wheeler Dealers (GB: Separate Beds). 1964: The Americanization of Emily. 36

Hours. 1965: The Art of Love. Mister Buddwing (GB: Woman without a Face). 1966: A Man Could Get Killed. Duel at Diablo. Grand Prix. 1967: Hour of the Gun. 1968: The Pink Jungle. How Sweet It Is! Support Your Local Sheriff! 1969: Marlowe. 1970: A Man Called Sledge (GB: Sledge). 1971: Skin Game. Support Your Local Gunfighter. 1972: They Only Kill Their Masters. *Just to Prove It (narrator only). 1973: One Little Indian. 1974: The Castaway Cowboy. 1978: The New Maverick (TV). 1979: Young Maverick (TV). Health. The Fan. The Long Summer of George Adams (TV). Bret Maverick (TV). 1982: Victor Victoria. 1983: Tank. 1984. The Glitter Dome (TV. GB: cinemas). Heartsounds (TV). 1985: Murphy's Romance. 1986: Promise (TV). 1988: Sunset. 1989: My Name is Bill W (TV). 1990: Decoration Day (TV). 1992: The Distinguished Gentleman. 1993: Fire in the Sky. Barbarians at the Gate (TV). 1994: Maverick. Breathing Lessons (TV). The Rockford Files: I Still Love LA (TV). 1995: Wild Bill: Hollywood Maverick (doc). The Rockford Files: Blessing in Disguise (TV). 1996: My Fellow Americans. The Rockford Files: Punishment and Crime (TV). The Rockford Files: Friends and Foul Play (TV). The Rockford Files: Godfather Knows Best (TV). The Rockford Files: If the Frame Fits (TV). 1997: Dead Silence. Twilight. The Rockford Files: Murder and Misdemeanors (TV). 1998: Legalese (TV). 1999: One Special Night (TV). The Rockford Files: If It Bleeds, It Leads (TV). 2000: Space Cowboys. 2001: Atlantis (voice only).

GARNER, Peggy Ann 1931–1984
Fair-haired, brown-eyed American actress, outstanding as a child (special Academy Award 1945). She was not given roles that demanded enough of her after that, and her career fell away before she was 21. In later years she made her living selling at first houses, then cars. Married to actor Albert Salmi (1956–1963), second of three. Died from cancer.
1938: Little Miss Thoroughbred. 1939: In Name Only. Blondie Brings Up Baby. 1940: Abe Lincoln in Illinois (GB: Spirit of the People). 1942: The Pied Piper. Eagle Squadron. 1943: Jane Eyre. 1944: The Keys of the Kingdom. 1945: A Tree Grows in Brooklyn. Nob Hill. Junior Miss. 1946: Home Sweet Homicide. 1947: Thunder in the Valley (GB: Bob, Son of Battle). Daisy Kenyon. 1948: The

Sign of the Ram. 1949: The Lovable Cheat. The Big Cat. Bomba the Jungle Boy. 1951: Teresa. 1954: Eight Witnesses. Black Widow. 1955: The Black Forest. 1966: Cat! 1978: A Wedding. Betrayal (TV).

GARR, Teri 1949–
This Hollywood actress of the 1970s and 1980s is facially a throwback to the slinky, sulky film noir blondes of 20 years before – but with a kooky sense of humour which has caused her to be cast successfully in high comedy. The daughter of actor Edward Garr (1900–1956), who made a few films, she combined careers in acting and dancing until 1974, when a big break in Young Frankenstein made her concentrate on the former. She has, alas, subsequently been, as one writer put it, 'cruelly marginalized' in many of her films. Says that, as a teenager, she danced in 'nine Elvis Presley musicals' of the 1960s. Oscar nominee for Tootsie.
1961: †Force of Impulse. 1962: †Gypsy. 1963: †Fun in Acapulco. 1964: †The T.A.M.I Show (GB: Teenage Command Performance). †What a Way to Go. †John Goldfarb, Please Come Home. †Kissin' Cousins. †Pajama Party. †Viva Las Vegas (GB: Love in Las Vegas). †Roustabout. 1966: For Pete's Sake. 1967: Clambake. The Mystery of the Chinese Junk. The Cool Ones. 1968: Head. Maryjane. 1969: Changes/Chances. The Only Game in Town. 1970: The Moonshine War. 1974: For Pete's Sake. Young Frankenstein. The Conversation. 1975: Won Ton Ton, The Dog Who Saved Hollywood. 1976: Law and Order (TV). *The Absent-Minded Waiter. 1977: Oh, God! Close Encounters of the Third Kind. 1978: Once Upon a Brothers Grimm (TV). Witches' Brew (released 1985). 1979: The Black Stallion. Mr Mike's Mondo Video. 1980: Doctor Franken (TV). The Special Edition of Close Encounters of the Third Kind. 1981: Prime Suspect (TV). Honky Tonk Freeway. 1982: The Escape Artist. One from the Heart. Tootsie. 1983: The Sting II. The Black Stallion Returns. Mr Mom (GB: Mr Mum). The Winter of Our Discontent (TV). 1984: To Catch a King (TV). First Born. 1985: After Hours. Intimate Strangers (TV). 1986: Miracles. 1987: Pack of Lies (TV). 1988: Out Cold/Stiffs. Full Moon in Blue Water. 1989: Let it Ride. Waiting for the Light. 1990: Short Time. Mother Goose Rock 'n' Rhyme (TV). A Quiet Little Neighborhood, a Perfect Little Murder (TV. GB: A Perfect Little Murder). 1991: A Stranger in the Family (TV). Tales from the Crypt (TV).

1992: Mom and Dad Save the World. The Player. Deliver Them from Evil: The Taking of Altaview / The Siege at Altaview (TV). 1993: The Whole Shebang (TV). Danger in the Desert (TV). 1994: Perfect Alibi. Prêt-à-Porter (US: Ready to Wear). Dumb & Dumber. 1995: Ronnie and Julie. 1996: Double Jeopardy (TV). Changing Habits. Michael. 1997: The Fairy Godmother / A Simple Wish. Murder Live! (TV). The Definite Maybe. Nightscream (TV). 1998: Casper Meets Wendy (TV). 1999: Life's Little Struggles (TV). Kill the Man. The Sky is Falling. Half a Dozen Babies (TV). Dick.

†As Teri Hope

GARRETT, Betty 1919–

Energetic American singer, dancer and comedienne with dark, curly hair, perky personality and happy, broadly-smiling face, whose musical career was taking great strides to stardom when it was stopped cold by the Communist witch-hunt and never regained impetus. Married to Larry Parks (qv) from 1944 until his death in 1975. Probably best remembered now as Frank Sinatra's taxi-driving love interest in *On the Town*.

1948: The Big City. Words and Music. Take Me Out to the Ball Game (GB: Everybody's Cheering). 1949: Neptune's Daughter. On the Town. 1955: My Sister Eileen. 1957: Shadow on the Window. 1998: The Long Way Home (TV).

GARSON, Greer

(Eileen G. Garson) 1903–1996
Red-haired, Irish-born, ladylike star (known as the Duchess of Garson in her London theatre days). M-G-M took her to Hollywood at the late age of 36, but she quickly became a very big star, winning one Oscar (for *Mrs Miniver*), being nominated for six more, and forming a very successful acting partnership with Walter Pidgeon (qv) which lasted through eight popular films. Married to Richard Ney (1917–, second of three) from 1943 to 1947. Some buffs reckon they can spot an early appearance by Garson in the 1937 (released 1940) film *21 Days* (US: *21 Days Together*). Died from heart failure.

*1932: *St Francis of Assisi. 1939: Goodbye Mr Chips! Remember? 1940: Pride and Prejudice. 1941: *Variety Reel. Blossoms in the Dust. When Ladies Meet. 1942: Mrs Miniver. Random Harvest. 1943: The Youngest Profession. Madame Curie. *A Report from Miss Greer Garson. 1944: Mrs Parkington. *The Miracle of Hickory. 1945: The Valley of Decision. Adventure. 1947: Desire Me. 1948: Julia Misbehaves. 1949: That Forsyte Woman (GB: The Forsyte Saga). 1950: The Miniver Story. 1951: The Law and the Lady. 1952: Scandal at Scourie. 1953: Julius Caesar. 1954: Her Twelve Men. 1955: Strange Lady in Town. 1960: Sunrise at Campobello. Pepe. 1966: The Singing Nun. 1967: The Happiest Millionaire. 1978: Little Women (TV). The Little Drummer Boy (TV Voice only).*

GASSMAN, Vittorio 1922–2000

Dark, sharply-handsome Italian leading man, always more popular – and acclaimed – in his own country, where he received a greater, and more demanding, variety of work. Briefly, but unhappily, under contract to M-G-M in the early fifties. Married to Shelley Winters (qv) 1952–1954. He has an acting son, Alessandro Gassman, from a relationship with the French actress Juliette Mayniel. Died from a heart attack.

1946: Preludio d'amore. 1947: Daniele Cortis. Le avventure di Pinocchio. L'ebreo errante. La figlia del capitano. 1948: Il cavaliere misterioso. 1949: Riso amaro. Lo sparviero del Niro. Il lupo della Sila. 1950: Una voce nel tuo cuòre. No sognato il Paradiso. I fuorillegge. 1951: Il leone di Amalfi. Tradimento. J'étais une pécheresse. Anna. 1952: Il sogno di Zorro. La corona negra. Umanita'. La tratta delle bianchi. 1953: The Glass Wall. Cry of the Hunted. Sombrero. 1954: Rhapsody. 1955: Mambo. La donna più bella del mondo (GB and US: Beautiful But Dangerous). 1956: War and Peace. Difendo il mio amore. 1957: Giovanni dalle bande nere (US: The Violent Patriot). †Kean, Genius or Scoundrel. La ragazza del Palio (GB: The Love Specialist). 1958: Tempest. I soliti ignoti. 1959: The Miracle. La grande guerra. It mattatore. Audace colpo dei soliti ignoti. Le sorprese dell'amore. 1960: La cambiale. Crimen (GB: Killing in Monte Carlo). 1961: Il giudizio universale. I briganti Italiani (GB and US: Seduction of the South). Barabbas. Una vita difficile. 1962: Fantasmi a Roma (GB: Phantom Lovers). Anima nera. Il sorpasso. La smania addosso. La marcia su Roma. Erotica. 1963: The Shortest Day. L'amore difficile. Il successo. I mostri. 1964: Se permettete parliamo di donne. Frenesia d'estate. La congiuntura. 1965: Una vergine per il principe (GB: A Virgin for the Prince). La guerre secrète (GB: The Dirty Game). Slalom. The Devil in Love. Spione unter sich. 1966: L'armata Brancaleone. 1967: Lo scatenato (GB and US: Catch As Catch Can). Woman Times Seven. Il tigre (GB and US: The Tiger and the Pussycat). Le piacevoli notti. 1968: Il profeta (GB and US: Mr Kinky). Ghosts Italian Style. La pecora nera. The Alibi. 1969: Dova vai tutta nuda? (GB and US: Where Are You Going All Naked?). L'arcangelo. Twelve Plus One. La contestazione generale. 1970: Il divorzio. Scipione, detto anche l'Africano. 1971: Brancaleone alle crociate. L'udienza. I fakiri. 1972: In nome delle popolo Italiano. Senza famiglia. 1973: Che c'entriamo noi con la revoluzione. Tosca. 1974: That Female Scent. C'eravamo tanto amati (US: We All Loved Each Other So Much). 1975: A mezzanotte va la ronda del piacere. 1976: Virginity. Signore e signorini, buona notte. Midnight Pleasures. Telefoni bianchi. 1977: Le desert des Tartares. Anima persa. I nuovi mostri. 1978: A Wedding. Quintet. Due pezzi di pane (US: Happy Hobos). Caro padre. 1979: Bugsy. The Immortal Bachelor. The Return of Maxwell Smart (TV). 1980: Io sono fotogenico. La terrazza. 1981: Sharky's Machine. Il turno / Night Shift. Camera d'albergo. 1982: La fuite à Varennes. Tempest. From Father to Son. Il conte Tacchia. 1983: La vie est un roman (GB and US: Life is a Bed of Roses). Benvenuta. 1985: Power of Evil / Le pouvoir du mal. I soliti ignoti 20 anni doppo (US: Big Deal on Madonna Street Update). 1986: La famiglia / Family. 1987: I picari. The Seed of Violence. 1988: The House of the Lord. Lo zio indegno / The Uncle. Mortacci / The Hateful Dead. 1990: To Forget Palermo. Verso sera. Shehérazada. Come un bambino. 1991: The Amusements of Private Life. Tolgo il disturbo / I Won't Disturb You Further. Quando erevamo repressi. 1992: El llarg hivern / The Long Winter. 1994: Tutti gli anni una volta l'anno. Abraham (TV). 1996: Sleepers. 1998: Open Return. La cena / The Dinner. 1999: La bomba.

†Also co-directed

GASTONI, Lisa 1935–

Italian-born actress with sexy smoulder, who became a pin-up blonde of British comedies and light dramas of the 1950s. Returned to Italy in 1961, turned brunette and gained a reputation as a strong actress (after some costume fol-de-rols) in torrid melodramas.

1953: *You Know What Sailors Are.* 1954: *Doctor in the House. The Runaway Bus. They Who Dare. Dance Little Lady. Beautiful Stranger* (US: *Twist of Fate*). 1955: *Man of the Moment. Josephine and Men. Dust and Gold.* 1956: *The Baby and the Battleship. Three Men in a Boat.* 1957: *Face in the Night* (US: *Menace in the Night*). *Second Fiddle. Suspended Alibi. Man from Tangier* (US: *Thunder over Tangier*). *Blue Murder at St Trinian's. The Truth about Women.* 1958: *Family Doctor* (US: *RX Murder*). *The Strange Awakening* (US: *Female Fiends*). *Intent to Kill. Chain of Events. Hello London.* 1959: *The Treasure of San Teresa* (US: *Long Distance*). *Wrong Number.* 1960: *Visa to Canton* (US: *Passport to China*). *The Breaking Point* (US: *The Great Armored Car Swindle*). 1961: *Tharus, Son of Attila. The Adventures of Mary Read* (GB: *Hell Below Deck*). 1962: *Le roi du village. Dicio tenne al sole. RoGoPaG. Duello nella Sila. Eva. Gidget Goes to Rome.* 1963: *Il mito. I maniaca. I piombi di Venezia* (US: *Dungeons of Venice*). *Messalina against the Sons of Hercules. Il monaco di Monza. The Four Musketeers.* 1964: *Il vendicatore mascherato. L'ultimo gladiatore. Beach Party, Italian Style* (US: *18 in the Sun*). *Gli invincibili tre* (GB: *The Three Avengers*). †*The Deadly Diaphanoids.* 1965: *Crimine a due. L'uomo che ride* (GB: *The Man with the Golden Mask*). *I tre centurioni. Callgirls 66.* †*I criminali della galassia* (GB and US: *Wild, Wild Planet*). *The Seven Vipers. Night of Violence.* 1967: *I sette fratelli Cervi. Grazie Zia.* 1968: *La pecora nera.* 1969: *L'amica.* 1970: *Maddalena. L'invasion.* 1973: *Seduction.* 1974: *Amore amaro. Mussolini: The Last Act/Mussolini: The Last Four Days.* 1975: *Scandalo. Labbro di lurido blu.* 1977: *Submission.* 1978: *Perchè Simona? L'immoralità.*

†*As Jane Fate*

GATES, Nancy 1926–

Pretty brown-haired American actress, a radio singer at 13 and under contract to RKO at 15. She broke off her career in 1946 to study for 18 months at university and subsequently found film roles hard to get. It was the mid-fifties before she established herself as a leading lady and after the birth of twins in 1959 she left the cinema to devote more time to her family.
1942: *All I Need is You. *Soundies Song Parade No. 1. The Tuttles of Tahiti. The*

Magnificent Ambersons. Come on, Danger. The Great Gildersleeve. 1943: *Behind the Rising Sun. Hitler's Children. Gildersleeve's Bad Day. This Land is Mine.* 1944: *Bride by Mistake. The Master Race. Nevada. A Night of Adventure.* 1945: *The Spanish Main.* 1947: *Cheyenne Takes Over. Check Your Guns.* 1949: *Roll Thunder Roll.* 1951: *At Sword's Point* (GB: *Sons of the Musketeers*). 1952: *Atomic City. The Greatest Show on Earth. Target Hong King. The Member of the Wedding.* 1953: *Torch Song.* 1954: *Hell's Half Acre. Suddenly. Masterson of Kansas.* 1955: *Top of the World. Stranger on Horseback. No Man's Woman.* 1956: *Bottom of the Bottle* (GB: *Beyond the River*). *Magnificent Roughnecks. The Brass Legend. World without End. Wetbacks. Death of a Scoundrel. The Search for Bridey Murphy.* 1957: *The Rawhide Breed.* 1958: *Some Came Running.* 1959: *Gunfight at Dodge City.* 1960: *Comanche Station.*

GAYE, Lisa
See PAGET, Debra

GAYNOR, Janet (Laura Gainor) 1906–1984
Sweet-faced, tousle-haired, petite American actress and occasional singer – a big star in simple, sentimental, romantic stories of the late 1920s and early 1930s, when she presented a portrait of the ragged-skirted optimist in the midst of the Depression that endeared her to millions. Her image inevitably dated quickly, but it remains a potent one. Married to (Gilbert) Adrian, the M–G–M costumer designer, from 1939 to his death in 1959 (second of three). Oscar as best actress 1927 (the first) for *7th Heaven/ Sunrise/Street Angel.* Never fully recovered from a bad car crash in 1982. Died from

pneumonia. Also Oscar-nominated for *A Star is Born.*
1925: *The Spooney Age. *The Haunted Honeymoon. *The Cloud Rider.* 1926: *The Johnstown Flood* (GB: *The Flood*). *The Shamrock Handicap. The Midnight Kiss. The Blue Eagle. The Return of Peter Grimm.* 1927: *Two Girls Wanted. 7th Heaven. Sunrise.* 1928: *Street Angel. Four Devils. *Fox Talent Movietone.* 1929: *Christina. Lucky Star. Sunny Side Up.* 1930: *Happy Days. High Society Blues. The Man Who Came Back.* 1931: *Daddy Long Legs. Merely Mary Ann. Delicious.* 1932: *Tess of the Storm Country. The First Year. Cardboard City.* 1933: *State Fair. Paddy, The Next Best Thing. Adorable.* 1934: *Carolina* (GB: *The House of Connelly*). *Change of Heart. Servants' Entrance.* 1935: *One More Spring. The Farmer Takes A Wife.* 1936: *Small Town Girl. Ladies in Love.* 1937: *A Star is Born.* 1938: *Three Loves Has Nancy. The Young in Heart.* 1941: *Wampas Baby Stars.* 1957: *Bernardine.*

GAYNOR, Mitzi
(Franceska M. von Gerber) 1930–
Long-legged singing and dancing star with peppy personality and lots of snap and crackle. A teenage stage star, she was signed by Fox at 20, but didn't quite make the top musical rank, despite some fizzy performances. *South Pacific* seemed to give her a second chance, but she was more fizzle than fizz as Nellie Forbush, and thereafter performed mainly for night-clubs and TV. Recently, a racy columnist and commentator on the showbiz nostalgia scene.
1950: *My Blue Heaven.* 1951: *Take Care of My Little Girl. Golden Girl.* 1952: *We're Not Married. Bloodhounds of Broadway.* 1953: *The 'I Don't Care' Girl. Down Among the Sheltering Palms.* 1954: *Three Young Texans. There's No Business Like Show Business.* 1956: *The Birds and the Bees. Anything Goes.* 1957: *The Joker is Wild. Les Girls.* 1958: *South Pacific.* 1959: *Happy Anniversary.* 1960: *Surprise Package.* 1963: *For Love or Money.* 1998: *All About Alfred* (doc).

GAZZARA, Ben (Biago Gazzara) 1930–
Dark, floridly good-looking, Italianate leading actor whose career has been one of much promise but little fulfilment. A critical rave in his first film (unfortunately it was also uncommercial), his best notices since have been won in films with his friends Peter Falk and John Cassavetes. In more commercial

projects, his performances too often smacked of disinterest. Later, he developed a marvellous, grating voice. Married (second of three) to Janice Rule (qv) from 1961 to 1979.
1954: *The Alibi Kid (TV)*. 1957: *The Troublemakers (TV)*. *The Strange One (GB: End As a Man)*. 1958: *The Violent Heart (TV)*. 1959: *Anatomy of a Murder*. 1960: *Risate di gioia (GB: The Passionate Thief)*. 1961: *The Young Doctors*. *Cry Vengeance (TV)*. 1962: *Convicts Four (GB: Reprieve!)*. *La citta prigioniera (GB: The Captive City. US: The Conquered City)*. 1964: *Carol for Another Christmas (TV)*. 1965: *A Rage to Live*. 1966: **Celebration (narrator only)*. 1968: *The Bridge at Remagen*. *If It's Tuesday, This Must Be Belgium*. 1970: *Husbands*. *King: a filmed record, Montgomery to Memphis*. 1971: *When Michael Calls (TV)*. 1972: *Afyon – Opium (US: The Sicilian Connection)*. *Fireball Forward (TV)*. *The Family Rico (TV)*. *Pursuit (TV)*. 1973: *The Neptune Factor*. *Maneater (TV)*. 1974: *QB VII (TV)*. 1975: *Capone*. 1976: *The Death of Ritchie (TV)*. *High Velocity*. *Voyage of the Damned*. *The Killing of a Chinese Bookie*. 1977: *Opening Night*. *The Trial of Lee Harvey Oswald (TV)*. 1979: *Bloodline/Sidney Sheldon's Bloodline*. *Saint Jack*. 1981: *Inchon! They All Laughed*. *Tales of Ordinary Madness*. *A Question of Honor (TV)*. 1982: *La ragazza di Trieste*. 1983: *Boogie Woogie*. *Uno scandalo perbene/ Only for Love*. 1984: *Richie (TV)*. *The Professor/Il camorrista*. *The Woman of Wonders*. 1985: *Figlio mio infinimente caro*. 1986: *An Early Frost (TV)*. *A Letter to Three Wives (TV)*. *La memoire tatouée (US: Secret Obsession)*. 1987: *The Day Before/Control (TV)*. *Downpayment on Murder (TV)*. *Fatale*. *Police Story: The Freeway Killings (TV)*. 1988: *Don Bosco*. *Quicker than the Eye*. *Road House*. *God's Peasant*. 1990: *Beyond the Ocean*. *Silent Memory*. 1991: *Lies Before Kisses (TV)*. *Forever (completed 1988)*. 1992: *Quiet Flows the Don*. *Blindsided (cable TV)*. *Nefertiti, Daughter of the Sun*. 1994: *Parallel Lives (TV)*. *Les hirondelles ne meurent pas à Jerusalem*. *Els de devant (US: The Window Across the Way)*. 1995: *Farmer and Chase*. *Convict Cowboy (cable TV)*. *Fatal Vows: The Alexandra O'Hara Story (TV)*. *The Zone*. *Banditi*. 1996: *Shadow Conspiracy*. *Scene of the Crime (cable TV)*. 1997: *The Spanish Prisoner*. *Vicious Circles*. *Stag*. 1998: *Too Tired to Die*. *Illuminata*. *The Big Lebowski*. *Valentine's Day*. *Happiness*. *Open Return*. *Buffalo 66*. 1999: *Meine erste asche/*

Undertakers' Paradise. *Summer of Sam*. *The Thomas Crown Affair*. *Paradise Cove*. 2000: *Blue Moon*. *Very Mean Men*. *Believe*.
As director: 1974: *Troubled Waters (TV)*. 1975: *A Friend in Deed (TV)*. 1990: *Beyond the Ocean*.

GEESON, Judy 1948–
Fair-haired British actress whose career faltered after she followed the predictable route from stage school through child roles to teenage blonde sex nymphet. Much in demand in the late sixties, when she rarely seemed to be seen with her clothes on, she has had poor roles in horror films and sex farces since then, obtaining much more interesting work on television. Tends to look older than her years. Married actor Kristoffer Tabori in 1985. The couple later parted. Her sister Sally Geeson (1950–) is also an actress.
1963: *Wings of Mystery*. 1966: *To Sir, with Love*. 1967: *Berserk! Here We Go Round the Mulberry Bush*. 1968: *Two Gentlemen Sharing*. *Prudence and the Pill*. *Hammerhead*. 1969: *Three into Two Won't Go*. 1970: *Goodbye Gemini (later Twinsanity)*. *The Executioner*. *10 Rillington Place*. *One of Those Things*. *Nightmare Hotel*. 1971: *Sam Hill – Who Killed the Mysterious Mr Foster? (TV)*. 1972: *Doomwatch*. *Fear in the Night*. 1973: *A Candle for the Devil*. 1974: *Percy's Progress*. *Diagnosis: Murder*. 1975: *Brannigan*. *Adventures of a Taxi Driver*. 1976: *Carry on England*. *The Eagle Has Landed*. 1978: *Dominique*. 1980: *Inseminoid (US: Horror Planet)*. **Towards the Morning*. 1982: *The Plague Dogs (voice only)*. 1988: *The Secret Life of Kathy McCormick (TV)*. 1989: **The Price of Life*. 1991: *Triple Play II (TV)*. 1992: *Young Goodman Brown*. 1996: *To Sir With Love II (TV)*. 1998: *Houdini (TV)*. 1999: *The Duke*.

GELLAR, Sarah Michelle 1977–
Bubbly, diminutive blonde American actress of energetic and outgoing personality. A show-business child, she's been acting in TV commercials and TV drama since she was four, rising to teenage popularity in the daytime soap *All My Children*. In films, her characters always seemed to be killed off, but she got her own back as TV's *Buffy the Vampire Slayer*, a role for which her real-life enthusiasm for martial arts and gymnastics stood her in good stead. She then widened her cinema range with her vindictive conspirator role in *Cruel Intentions*.

1983: *An Invasion of Privacy (TV)*. 1984: *Over the Brooklyn Bridge*. 1988: *Funny Farm*. 1989: *High Stakes*. 1996: *Beverly Hills Family Robinson (TV)*. 1997: *I Know What You Did Last Summer*. *Scream 2*. 1998: *Small Soldiers (voice only)*. 1999: *Cruel Intentions*. *She's All That*. *Simply Irresistible*. 2001: *Harvard Man*.

GENN, Leo 1905–1978
Smooth, urbane, dark-haired British actor who forsook the legal profession in the early thirties. As the forties progressed, he found himself in increasing demand to play confidants, people of calm authority and unflappable officer types. He had some success in Hollywood in the fifties, but, after *Moby Dick* in 1956, his roles grew less interesting and he turned up in an odd bunch of films in his later years. His velvet voice was often heard as narrator in documentaries. Oscar-nominated for *Quo Vadis*. Died from a heart attack.
1935: *The Immortal Gentleman*. 1936: *The Dream Doctor*. 1937: *The Cavalier of the Streets*. *Jump for Glory (US: When Thief Meets Thief)*. *The Squeaker (US: Murder on Diamond Row)*. *The Rat*. 1938: *Consider Your Verdict*. *The Drum (US: Drums)*. *Kate Plus Ten*. *Ripe Earth (narrator only)*. *Governor Bradford*. *Dangerous Medicine*. *Pygmalion*. 1939: *Ten Days in Paris (US: Missing Ten Days)*. 1940: *Law and Disorder*. *The Girl in the News*. *Contraband (US: Blackout)*. 1942: *The Young Mr Pitt*. 1943: *Desert Victory (narrator only)*. *Tunisian Victory (narrator only)*. 1944: *The Way Ahead*. *Return of the Viking*. *Henry V*. 1945: *Julius Caesar*. *Caesar and Cleopatra*. 1946: *Green for Danger*. 1947: *The Velvet Touch*. *Mourning Becomes Elect–*

1948: The Snake Pit. 1949: No Place for Jennifer. 1950: The Undefeated (voice only). The Wooden Horse. The Miniver Story. 1951: The Magic Box. Quo Vadis. 1952: *The Changing Face of Europe (narrator only). *The Good Life (narrator only). Plymouth Adventure. 24 Hours in a Woman's Life (US: Affair in Monte Carlo). 1953: The Girls of Pleasure Island. Elizabeth is Queen (narrator only). The Red Beret (US: Paratrooper). Personal Affair. 1954: The Green Scarf. 1955: The Lowest Crime. Lady Chatterley's Lover. 1956: Beyond Mombasa. Moby Dick. 1957: The Steel Bayonet. Land of Laughter (narrator only). I Accuse! 1958: No Time to Die! (US: Tank Force). *The Immortal Land (narrator only). 1959: *Greek Sculpture (narrator only). Invitation to Monte Carlo (narrator only). Mrs. Miniver (TV). 1960: Era notte a Roma (GB: Wait for the Dawn). Too Hot to Handle (US: Playgirl After Dark). 1961: *Nothing to Eat But Food (narrator only). *The State Opening of Parliament (narrator only). The Life of Hitler (narrator only). 1962: The Longest Day. 55 Days at Peking 1963: Give My Love a Gun. 1965: Ten Little Indians. Circus of Fear (US: Psycho-Circus). Die Todesstrahlen des Dr Mabuse. 1968: Dr Jekyll and Mr Hyde (TV). 1969: Connecting Rooms. 1970: Der Hexentöter von Blackmoor (US: The Bloody Judge). Die Screaming, Marianne. 1971: Endless Night. A Lizard in a Woman's Skin. 1973: The Mackintosh Man. The Silent One. 1974: The Martyr/Sie sind frei, Dr Korczak! Frightmare. 1975: Escape to Nowhere.

GEORGE, Susan 1950–
Another of Britain's stage-school to child actress to blonde sex kitten stars. Her private life pouted and smouldered its way through hundreds of newspapers (one of which made up a 'top eleven' football team of her lovers), but she didn't actually make too many films until a little burst in the early 1980s. Those she has made have usually revealed her as better than her often exploitative material. Screen debut at five in a film whose title she cannot remember. Latterly a producer in collaboration with her husband, actor Simon MacCorkindale, with whom she has also appeared on stage.
1962: The L-Shaped Room. Come Fly With Me. 1965: Cup Fever. Davey Jones' Locker. 1966: *Liz and Sally. 1967: The Sorcerers. Up the Junction. Billion Dollar Brain. 1968: The Strange Affair. All Neat in Black Stockings.

1969: The Looking Glass War. Twinky (US: Lola). Spring and Port Wine. 1970: Eyewitness (US: Sudden Terror). Die Screaming, Marianne. 1971: Fright. Straw Dogs. 1973: Dr Jekyll and Mr Hyde (TV). J and S, a Criminal Story of the Far West (US: Sonny and Jed). 1974: Dirty Mary, Crazy Larry. Mandingo. 1975. Out of Season. 1976: A Small Town in Texas. 1977: Tintorera. The Final Eye (TV). Tomorrow Never Comes. 1978: Blue Orchids. 1981: Venom. Texas Legend. Enter the Ninja. 1982: The House Where Evil Dwells. Kiss My Grits. 1983: The Jigsaw Man. 1986: The White Stallion. 1988: The Lifeguard. 1989: That Summer of White Roses. 1994: The House That Mary Bought.

GERE, Richard 1949–
Fresh-faced, dark-haired (later prematurely greying), youthfully good-looking (if a shade mournful) American actor whose impassioned and charismatic performances in the late 1970s pushed him towards superstar status. He made his first impression in the original stage version of Grease in 1973 and remained prominent in rebel-type roles through to the end of the 1980s. Efforts to extend his range met with varying reward, but he scored two major personal successes in 1990. A forthright spokesman for Buddhist and ecological causes, as well as AIDS awareness. His three-year marriage to model/ actress Cindy Crawford ended in 1995 and he has a child with his present partner, actress Carey Lowell.
1974: Operation Undercover (US: Report to the Commissioner). 1975: *Confusion's Circle. Strike Force (TV). 1976: Baby Blue Marine. 1977: Looking for Mr Goodbar. 1978: Bloodbrothers. Days of Heaven. Yanks. 1979: American Gigolo. 1981: An Officer and a Gentleman. Reporters. 1983: Breathless. Beyond the Limit (GB: The Honorary Consul). 1984: The Cotton Club. 1985: King David. Power. 1986: No Mercy. 1988: Miles from Home. 1990: Internal Affairs. Pretty Woman. Rhapsody in August. 1991: Final Analysis. 1993: Mr. Jones. Sommersby. And the Band Played On. 1994: Intersection. 1995: First Knight. 1996: Primal Fear. 1997: The Jackal. An Alan Smithee Film: Burn, Hollywood, Burn. Red Corner. 1999: Runaway Bride. 2000: Autumn in New York. Dr T. and the Women.

GERRARD, Gene
(Eugene O'Sullivan) 1892–1971
Effervescent, ever-smiling, crinkle-haired

leading man in British musical comedies of the thirties. A former tailor's cutter, he turned to the stage at 18 and made his film debut in an unknown Hepworth film of 1912. Often co-directed and co-wrote his own films and after 1938 went over to direction entirely, mainly on stage.
1931: Let's Love and Laugh (US: Bridegroom for Two). My Wife's Family. Out of the Blue. 1932: Brother Alfred. Lucky Girl. Let Me Explain, Dear. 1933: Leave It to Me. The Love Nest. 1934: There Goes Susie (US: Scandals of Paris). 1935: It's a Bet. Joy Ride. Royal Cavalcade (US: Regal Cavalcade). The Guvnor (US: Mr. Hobo). No Monkey Business. 1936: Faithful. Where's Sally? Such is Life. Wake Up Famous. 1938: Glamour Girl. 1945: Dumb Dora Discovers Tobacco.
As co-director: 1931: Out of the Blue. 1932: Lucky Girl. Let Me Explain, Dear. As director: 1936: Wake Up Famous. 1938: It's in the Blood.

GERSHON, Gina 1962–
Tall, dark-haired American actress of strong personality. An accomplished stage actress whose film career took a long time coming to the boil, and she was in her 30s when roles in such films as Bound (her best work), Showgirls, Face/Off and This World, Then the Fireworks brought her name to the fore. By then she had established her reputation as a femme fatale in the classic Jane Greer tradition.
1986: Pretty in Pink. Stark: Mirror Image (TV). 3:15. 1987: Sweet Revenge. 1988: Red Heat. Cocktail. 1989: Monsters: Jar (TV). Suffering Bastards/Liars Club. 1990: Voodoo Dawn. 1991: Out for Justice. ‡Jungle Fever. City of Hope. 1992: The Player. Miss Rose

White (TV). Joey Breaker. 1993: Love Matters (TV). 1994: Best of the Best 3: No Turning Back. Flinch. 1995: Showgirls. 1996: Bound. Touch. This World, Then the Fireworks. 1997: Face/Off. Original Sin. SK Sunday. Prague Duet/Lies and Whispers. One Tough Cop. 1998: Lulu on the Bridge. Palmetto (Just Another Sucker). Black & White. I'm Losing You. Legalese (TV). 1999: Guinevere. The Insider. 2001: Champs.

‡Scenes deleted

GERTZ, Jami 1965–
Dark, fine-boned, black-eyed, lithe American actress who usually plays characters well able to look after themselves. Acting as a teenager, after initial ambitions to be an ice skater, Gertz was often better than her material, but did not become a name that sells tickets. When she finally got central roles in *Listen to Me* and *Jersey Girl*, the films quickly disappeared to the video stores. She returned to film acting in 1996 after a three-year absence, but has not regained her former footing.
1981: On the Right Track. Endless Love. 1984: Alphabet City. Sixteen Candles. 1985: The Man With One Red Shoe/Mischief 1986: Solarbabies. Crossroads. Quicksilver. 1987: The Lost Boys. Less Than Zero. 1989: Silence Like Glass. Renegades. Listen to Me. 1990: Sibling Rivalry. Don't Tell Her It's Me. 1992: Jersey Girl. Related by Birth (TV). 1993: This Can't Be Love (TV). 1996: Twister. 2000: Seven Girlfriends. Kat and Allison.

GIANNINI, Giancarlo 1942–
Fierce, dark-haired, chunkily built Italian actor with piercing blue eyes, usually seen playing poor-born figures enjoying love-hate relationships with women. Very successful in films by Lina Wertmüller, but his international assignments, seeing him as a sort of sad-eyed Omar Sharif, have not made a good job of showcasing his particular talents. In the mid-1980s he also began showing an interest in direction. Oscar-nominated for *Seven Beauties*. He was in juicy, scene-hogging star cameos by the 1990s.
1965: Fango sulla metropoli. Libido. 1966: Rita la Zanzara. 1967: The Battle for Anzio (GB: Anzio). Arabella. Non stuzzicate la zanzara. Stasere mi butto. 1968: Fräulein Doktor. Stasere mi butto – i due bagnami. 1969: La sorelle/The Sisters. The Secret of Santa Vittoria. Una macchia rosa. 1970: Drama della gelosia (US: The Pizza Triangle). 1971: Mio padre Monsignore. La tarantola del ventre nero (GB and US: The Black Belly of the Tarantula). Mazzabubu . . . quante come stranno quaggiù? Un aller simple. Ettore Lo Fusto. Una prostituta al servizio del pubblico . . . 1972: La prima notte di quiete. Mimi Metallurgico ferito nell' onore (US: The Seduction of Mimi). 1973: Film d'amore e d'anarchia (US: Love and Anarchy). Sono stato io. Paulo il caldo (GB: The Sensual Man. US: The Sensuous Sicilian). Sesso matto. 1974: Il bestione (GB: The 8-Wheeled Beast). Fatti di gente per bene. Travolti da un in soli to destino nell' azzurro mare d'agosto (GB and US: Swept Away). Tutto a posto a niente in ordine (US: All Screwed Up). 1975: A mezzanotte va la ronda del piacere. Pasqualino settebellezze (GB and US: Seven Beauties). 1976: L'innocente (GB and US: The Innocent). How Funny Can Sex Be? 1977: I una notte piena di poggia. The End of the World in Our Usual Bed in a Night Full of Rain. I nuovi mostri. 1978: Vengeance/Revenge. Shimmy, lugano, tarantelle e vino. 1979: Sidney Sheldon's Bloodline/Bloodline. Travels with Anita. The Immortal Bachelor. Suffer or Die. La vita è bella (GB: TV, as They Made Him a Criminal. US: Freedom to Love). 1980: Lili Marleen. 1981: Lovers and Liars. 1982: Bello mio, bellezza mia. 1983: Italia vive. Escape. Where's Picone? 1984: †I capitoni (US: Small Fry and Big Fish). American Dreamer. 1985: Saving Grace. Fever Pitch. 1986: †I numeri del lotto. 1987: I picari. 1988: Snack Bar Budapest. Blood Red. Il male oscuro. Sweet Carioca. Lo zio indegno/The Uncle. 1989: 'O Re. New York Stories. Brown Bread Sandwiches. Tempo di uccidere/Short Cut. 1990: Il sole anche di notte (voice only). 1991: Once Upon a Crime/Criminals. The Amusements of Private Life. Nero come il cuore/Lifeline. 1992: Nel giardino delle rose (US: Age of discretion. Completed 1990). 1993: Culpo di coda/Twist. Il caso Falcone. Pezze di cuore. 1994: Come due coccodrilli. The Bible: Jacob. 1995: A Walk in the Clouds. Palermo Milano (One Way Only). La lupa. 1996: Celluloide. La frontiera. Death in Granada. New York Crossing. Heaven Before I Die. 1997: Mimic. Mas alla del jardin. La stanza dello Scirocco. Una vacanza all'inferno. 1998: Greener Fields (TV). La cena/The Dinner. 1999: Gli indesiderabili. Vuoti a perdere. Terra bruciata. Il ptere della sparanza. 2000: Dolce far niente. The Whole Shebang. Una lunga, lunga, lunga notte d'amore.

GIBSON, Hoot
(Edmund Gibson) 1892–1962
Fair-haired American western star, tagged 'The Smiling Whirlwind' in his heyday. A real-life westerner, Gibson had worked in circuses, Wild West shows and rodeos ('World's All-Round Champion Cowboy' of 1912) and as a law enforcement officer before coming to Hollywood, initially in 1910 and then again in 1914. He got his screen nickname from a passion for hunting owls when a boy. Married to serial queen Helen Gibson (Rose Wegner, 1892–1977) and actress Sally Eilers (qv), first and third of four. Died from cancer.
*1910: *Two Brothers. *Pride of the Range. 1911: *Shotgun Jones. *The New Superintendent. 1912: *His Only Son. 1913: *Cowboy Sports and Pastimes. 1914: *Kid Pink and the Maharajah. *The Man from the East. The Hazards of Helen (serial). 1915: *The Ring of Destiny. *The Man from Texas. Judge Not, or The Woman of Mona Diggins. 1916: A Daughter of Daring (serial). *Night Riders. A Knight of the Range. The Cactus Kid. *The Wedding Guest. *Passing of Hell's Crown. *A Stampede in the Night. 1917: Straight Shooting. *A 44 Calibre Mystery. Voice on the Wire (serial). Shameless Salvation. *The Golden Bullet. The Secret Man. A Marked Man. *The Wrong Man. *The Soul Herder. *Cheyenne's Pal. *The Texas Sphinx. 1918: A Woman in the Web (serial). Danger, Go Slow. *The Midnight Flyer. *The Trail of the Holdup Man. *Play Straight or Fight. *The Double Holdup. Headin' South. *The Branded Man. *The Crow. Ace High. 1919: *Black Jack – Horse Bandit. *Kingdom Come. *The Face in the Watch. Love Letters. *The Jaybird. *The Tell Tale Watch. *The Lone Hand. *West is Best. *Jack o' Hearts. *The Sheriff's Oath. *The Fighting Brothers. *By Indian Post. *The Gun Packer. *Gun Law. *The Four-Bit Man. *The Fighting Heart. 1920: *Saddle King. *Double Danger. *Roaring Dan. *One Law for All. *The Big Catch. *A Gamblin' Fool. *The Shootin' Kid. *Harmony Ranch. *Cinders. *The Champion Liar. *The Smilin' Kid. *Some Shooter. *The Fightin' Terror. *The Rustlers. *The Stranger. *The Marryin' Kid. *The Texas Kid. *Running Straight. *A Nose in a Book. *Hair Trigger Stuff. *Held Up for the Makin's. *The Rattler's Hiss. *The Grinning Granger. *Masked. *The Two-Fisted Lover. *In Wrong Wright. *Fight It Out. *Tipped Off. *The Trail of the Hound. *The Man with the Punch. *Ransom. *Winning a*

Home. *The Shootin' Fool. *The Lone Ranger. 1921: *Superstition. *Teacher's Pet. *The Rustler's Kiss. *A Pair of Twins. *The Marrying Margin. *The Bronco Kid. *Wolf Tracks. *Thieves' Clothes. Action. Red Courage. *Sweet Revenge. *The Driftin' Kid. *The Fighting Fury. *Kickaroo. *Who Was the Man? *The Cactus Kid. *Double Crossers. *The Wild, Wild West. *Crossed Clues. *The Movie Trail. *Bandits Beware. *Beating the Game. *The Man Who Woke Up. *The Winning Trick. *Too Tired Jones. 1922: Surefire. The Bearcat. The Fire Eater. Headin' West. Step On It! Trimmed. The Loaded Doors. The Gallopin' Kid. The Denver Dude. Ridin' Wild. The Lone Hand. 1923: Dead Game. Double Dealing. The Ramblin' Kid. The Gentleman from Arizona/The Gentleman from America. Kindled Courage. Shootin' for Love. Single Handed. *Out of Luck. Blinky. The Thrill Chaser. 1924: Ride for Your Life. The Ridin' Kid from Powder River. *The City of Stars. The Sawdust Trail. Hook and Ladder. Hit and Run. Broadway or Bust. Forty-Horse Hawkins. 1925: *Hollywood Today No. 8. Spook Ranch. Taming the West. Let 'Er Buck. The Hurricane Kid. The Calgary Stampede. The Saddle Hawk. The Arizona Sweepstakes. 1926: Chip of the Flying U. The Phantom Bullet. *The Shoot 'Em Up Kid. The Man in the Saddle. Flaming Frontier. The Buckaroo Kid. The Texas Streak. 1927: Galloping Fury. The Rawhide Kid. The Denver Dude (remake). *The Hawaiian Serenaders. Hero on Horse- back. Hey! Hey! Cowboy. Straight Shootin' (different from 1917 film). The Silent Rider. Painted Ponies. The Prairie King. 1928: The Flyin' Cowboy. Danger Rider. Clearing the Trail. Riding for Fame. A Trick of Hearts. The Wild West Show. 1929: The Lariat Kid. Smilin' Guns. Burning the Wind. King of the Rodeo. The Long, Long Trail. The Winged Horseman. Points West. Courtin' Wildcats. 1930: Roaring Ranch. Trailin' Trouble. Trigger Tricks. Spurs. The Concentratin' Kid. The Mounted Stranger. 1931: Hard Hombre. The Gay Buckaroo. *Screen Snapshots No. 8. Clearing the Range. Wild Horse. 1932: Local Bad Man. Boiling Point. Spirit of the West. A Man's Land. Cowboy Counsellor. 1933: The Dude Bandit. The Fighting Parson. 1935: Powdersmoke Range. Sunset Tango. Rainbow's End. 1936: Frontier Justice. Swifty. The Riding Avenger. Lucky Terror. Cavalcade of the West. Feud of the West (GB: The Vengeance of Gregory Walters). The Last Outlaw. 1937: The Painted Stallion (serial). 1943: Blazing Guns. Wild Horse Stampede. Death Valley Rangers. The Law Rides Again. Westward Bound. 1944: Arizona Whirlwind. The Outlaw Trail. Trigger Law. The Utah Kid. Sonora Stagecoach. Marked Trails. 1946: Flight to Nowhere. 1947: *Hollywood Cow- boys. 1953: The Marshal's Daughter. 1956: *Hollywood Bronc Busters. 1959: The Horse Soldiers. 1960: Ocean's Eleven.

GIBSON, Mel 1956–
Dark-haired, well-built, boyishly-handsome, unsmiling Australian-raised actor whose quiet, brooding, blue-eyed charisma had female temperatures rising in the cinema of the 1980s. Born in New York, one of 11 children, he went to Australia at 12 and made

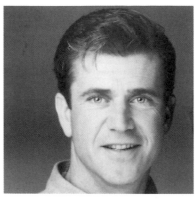

his film debut there, shooting to top stardom as the futuristic desert wanderer in the 'Mad Max' films. Hollywood swooped but made the mistake of pairing him with female stars who provided rather more acting competition that he could yet handle. Back in Australia, he revived his superstar status in a third 'Mad Max' saga, and the Lethal Weapon trilogy made him a major box-office force in his native country. He turned director with some distinction in the 1990s, winning an Oscar for Braveheart. Some sources suggest he was born in 1951.
1977: Summer City. 1978: Tim. 1979: The Chain Reaction. Mad Max. 1980: Attack Force Z. 1981: Gallipoli. Mad Max 2 (US: The Road Warrior). 1982: The Year of Living Dangerously. 1984: The Bounty. The River. Mrs Soffel. 1985: Max Max III (GB and US: Max Mad Beyond Thunderdome). 1987: Lethal Weapon. 1988: Tequila Sunrise. 1989: Lethal Weapon 2. 1990: Bird on a Wire. Hamlet. Air America. 1992: Lethal Weapon 3. Forever Young. 1993: Earth and the American Dream (voice only). The Man Without a Face (and directed). 1994: Maverick. 1995: Casper. Braveheart (and directed). Pocahontas (voice only). 1996: Ransom. 1997: Conspiracy Theory. Fathers' Day. Fairy Tale: A True Story. 1998: Payback. Lethal Weapon 4. 1999: The Million Dollar Hotel. Forever Hollywood (doc). 2000: The Patriot. Chicken Run (voice only). 2001: What Women Want.

GIBSON, Wynne
(Winnifred Gibson) 1899–1987
Fair-haired, square-faced American actress (a chorus girl at 15) who started her film career late in life (although studio biographies advanced her date of birth by varying

numbers of years), but enjoyed a good run of gold digging blondes while with Paramount in the early 1930s. Left acting in the 1950s to become an actor's agent for the remainder of her working life. Died following a stroke.
1929: Nothing But the Truth. 1930: Children of Pleasure. The Fall Guy (GB: Trust Your Wife). 1931: June Moon. City Street. Kick-In. Ladies of the Big House. Man of the World. The Gang Buster. Road to Reno. 1932: If I Had a Million. Night After Night. Lady and Gent. The Strange Case of Clara Deane. The Devil is Driving. Two Kinds of Women. *The Stolen Jools (GB: The Slippery Pearls). 1933: Aggie Appleby, Maker of Men (GB: Cupid in the Rough). Emergency Call. Her Bodyguard. The Television Follies. Crime of the Century. 1934: Gambling. The Crosby Case (GB: The Crosby Murder Case). Sleepers East. The Captain Hates the Sea. 1935: Admirals All. The Crouching Beast. 1936: Come Closer, Folks! 1937: Michael O'Halloran. Trapped by G- Men. Racketeers in Exile. 1938: Flirting with Fate. Gangs of New York. 1939: My Son is Guilty (GB: Crime's End). 1940: Forgotten Girls. Café Hostess. A Miracle on Main Street. 1941: Double Cross. 1942: A Man's World. 1943: The Falcon Strikes Back. Mystery Broadcast.

GIELGUD, Sir John
(Arthur J. Gielgud) 1904–2000
Tall, slim, stern-looking British actor who achieved greatest distinction in Shake- spearian roles on stage. He appeared briefly as an aesthetic leading man in a few pre-war films, but most post-war parts were cameos that were unworthy both of the actor and his reedily mellifluous voice. Knighted in 1953. Won an Academy Award for Arthur. Also nominated for Becket. The longest film career in the history of the British cinema to date.
1924: Who is the Man? 1925: *Romeo and Juliet (extract). 1929: The Clue of the New Pin. 1932: Insult. 1933: The Good Companions. 1936: The Secret Agent. 1937: *Full Fathom Five (voice only). 1939: Hamlet. 1941: The Prime Minister. *An Airman's Letter to His Mother (voice only). 1944: *Unfinished Journey (narrator only). *Shakespeare's Country (voice only). 1945: A Diary for Timothy. 1953: Julius Caesar. 1954: Romeo and Juliet. 1955: Richard III. 1956: Around the World in 80 Days. 1957: The Barretts of Wimpole Street. Saint Joan. 1958: The Immortal Land (narrator only). 1962: To Die in Madrid (narrator only). 1963: Hamlet.

1964: *Becket*. 1965: *The Loved One*. 1966: *Chimes at Midnight* (US: *Falstaff*). 1967: *Sebastian. October Revolution* (narrator only). *Assignment to Kill.* 1968: *The Shoes of the Fisherman. The Charge of the Light Brigade.* 1969: *Oh! What a Lovely War.* 1970: *Julius Caesar. Eagle in a Cage.* 1972: *Lost Horizon. Probe* (TV). 1973: *Frankenstein: the True Story* (TV. GB: cinemas). *Luther.* 1974: *QB VII* (TV). *11 Harrowhouse. Gold. Murder on the Orient Express. Galileo.* 1976: *Aces High. Joseph Andrews.* 1977: *A Portrait of the Artist as a Young Man. Providence.* 1978: *Les Miserables* (TV). *Caligula. Sherlock Holmes: Murder by Decree* (GB: *Murder by Decree*). 1979: *Omar Mukhtar: Lion of the Desert. The Human Factor.* 1980: *Dyrygent/The Conductor. Sphinx. Priest of Love. Arthur.* 1981: *Chariots of Fire. The Elephant Man.* 1982: *The Hunchback of Notre Dame* (TV). *Wagner* (TV). *Gandhi.* 1983: *The Wicked Lady. The Scarlet and the Black* (TV). *Invitation to a Wedding. Scandalous!* 1984: *The Shooting Party. Camille* (TV). *The Master of Ballantrae* (TV). 1985: *Plenty. Romance on the Orient Express* (TV). *Leave All Fair.* 1986: *The Whistle Blower. Time After Time* (TV). *The Canterville Ghost* (TV). 1987: *Quartermaine's Terms* (TV). *Bluebeard, Bluebeard.* 1988: *Appointment with Death. A Man for All Seasons* (TV). *Arthur 2: On the Rocks.* 1989: *Getting It Right. Strike It Rich/Loser Takes All.* 1991: *Prospero's Books.* 1992: *Shining Through. The Power of One. *Swan Song. The Best of Friends* (TV). 1995: *First Knight. Haunted.* 1996: *The Portrait of a Lady. Shine. Looking for Richard. Hamlet. The Leopard Son* (narrator only). *DragonHeart* (voice only). 1998: *The Magic Sword: Quest for Camelot* (voice only). *Elizabeth. The Tichborne Claimant.*

GIFFORD, Frances
(Mary F. Gifford) 1920–1994
Stunning, blue-eyed brunette American actress whose career seemed to be coming to a peak at M-G-M when she suffered serious head injuries in a 1948 car accident from which, despite a couple of minor roles later on, she never really recovered, spending long periods in mental hospitals. Best remembered by nostalgic fans as the screen's first Nyoka in the serial *Jungle Girl*. She died from emphysema. Married to James Dunn (*qv*) from 1938 to 1941.
1937: *Woman Chases Man. New Faces of 1937. Stage Door. The Big Shot. Living on Love.* 1938: *Having Wonderful Time. Sky Giant.* 1939: *Mr Smith Goes to Washington.* 1940: *Mercy Plane. Hold that Woman. A Fugitive from Justice.* 1941: *The Reluctant Dragon. Jungle Girl* (serial). *Border Vigilantes. West Point Widow. Louisiana Purchase.* 1942: *My Heart Belongs to Daddy. American Empire* (GB: *My Son Alone*). *Henry Aldrich Gets Glamour* (GB: *Henry Gets Glamour*). *The Glass Key. Beyond the Blue Horizon. The Remarkable Andrew. Tombstone, the Town Too Tough to Die. Star Spangled Rhythm.* 1943: *Cry Havoc. Tarzan Triumphs.* 1944: *Marriage is a Private Affair.* 1945: *Thrill of a Romance. Our Vines Have Tender Grapes. She Went to the Races.* 1946: *Little Mr Jim.* 1947: *The Arnelo Affair.* 1948: *Luxury Liner.* 1950: *Riding High.* 1953: *Sky Commando.*

GILBERT, John (J. Pringle) 1895–1936
Dashing, moustachioed, rather sharp-faced American actor with very dark hair, an enormous success as a great lover on the silent screen, especially in roles opposite Greta Garbo. His inability to modulate his exaggerated acting style to sound films, coupled with an unappealing voice, led to the rapid decline of his career. He became an alcoholic and died from a heart attack at 40. Besides his well-publicized offscreen affair with Garbo, he was married to actresses Leatrice Joy (1922–1924), Ina Claire (1929–1931) and Virginia Bruce (1932–1934): 2nd, 3rd and 4th of four.
1915: *The Mother Instinct.* 1916: *Hell's Hinges. The Phantom. The Eye of the Night. The Apostle of Vengeance. Bullets and Brown Eyes. Shell 43.* 1917: *Princess of the Dark Happiness. The Millionaire Vagrant. Hater of Men. The Devil Dodger. Doing Her Bit. Golden Rule Kate.* 1918: *Sons of Men. Nancy Comes Home. Three X Gordon. More Trouble. Shackled. Wedlock. The Mask. The Dawn of Understanding.* 1919: *The Busher. Widow by Proxy. Should a Woman Tell? The White Heather. The Red Viper. The Heart o' the Hills.* 1920: *The White Circle. Deep Waters. The Great Redeemer. The Servant in the House.* 1921: *Ladies Must Live. Shame. The Bait. †Love's Penalty.* 1922: *Gleam o' Dawn. The Yellow Stain. Arabian Love. The Count of Monte Cristo. Honor First. The Love Gambler. Calvert's Valley* (GB: *Calvert's Folly*). 1923: *Cameo Kirby. The Exiles. A California Romance. Saint Elmo. Truxton King* (GB: *Truxtonia*). *The Glory of Love. The Madness of Youth. While Paris Sleeps.* 1924: *The Wolf Man. Just Off Broadway. A Man's Mate. Romance Ranch. The Lone Chance. His Hour. The Snob. Wife of the Centaur. He Who Gets Slapped. Married Flirts.* 1925: *The Merry Widow. The Big Parade.* 1926: *La Bohème. Bardelys The Magnificent.* 1927: *The Show. Flesh and the Devil. Twelve Miles Out. Man, Woman and Sin.* 1928: *Love* (GB: *Anna Karenina*). *Four Walls. *Voices across the Sea. The Cossacks. Masks of the Devil.* 1929: *Desert Nights. A Man's Man. Hollywood Revue of 1929. His Glorious Night. A Woman of Affairs.* 1930: *Wir schalten um auf Hollywood! Redemption. Way for a Sailor.* 1931: *Gentleman's Fate. The Phantom of Paris.* 1932: *West of Broadway. Downstairs.* 1933: *Fast Workers. Queen Christina.* 1934: *The Captain Hates the Sea.* 1936: **Pirate Party on Catalina Isle.*

†Also directed

GILMORE, Virginia
(Sherman V. Poole) 1919–1986
Exquisitely pretty brown-eyed blonde American actress (of British parentage) who gave some glowingly warm performances in romantic roles, but lacked a screen personality and was mainly a theatre actress after 1943. Married to Yul Brynner from 1944 to 1960; after their divorce she became a drama coach. Died of complications from emphysema.
1939: *Winter Carnival.* 1939-40: *†Raffles.* 1940: *Laddie. Jennie. Manhattan Heartbeat.* 1941: *Western Union. Swamp Water* (GB: *The Man Who Came Back*). *Mr District Attorney in The Carter Case* (GB: *The Carter Case*). 1942: *Tall, Dark and Handsome. The Loves of Edgar Allan Poe. Orchestra Wives. Berlin Correspondent. Pride of the Yankees. Sundown Jim. That Other Woman.* 1943: *Chetniks.* 1945: *Wonder Man.* 1948: *Close-Up.* 1952: *Walk East on Beacon* (GB: *Crime of the Century*).

†Scenes deleted from final release print

GIRARDOT, Annie 1931–
Dark-haired, personable French actress with impishly angular features, much in demand for romantic roles calling for warmth and depth. Tackled a wide variety of characters following a belated arrival (at 24) on the film scene after five years of dramatic training and some stage work. Her dearth of ventures into the international scene hardly qualifies her

for a place in this book, so the fact that she is the author's favourite continental star will have to suffice. Won an Oscar (French Oscar) in 1976 for *Docteur Françoise Gailland*.

1955: Treize à table. 1956: Le pays d'ou je viens. L'homme aux clés d'or. Réproduction interdite. Le rouge est mis (US: Speaking of Murder). 1957: L'amour est un jeu. Maigret tend un piège (GB: Maigret Sets a Trap. US: Inspector Maigret). 1958: Le desert de Pigalle. 1959: La corde raide (US: Lovers on a Tightrope). 1960: La Française et l'amour (GB and US: Love and the Frenchwoman). Rocco e i suoi fratelli (GB and US: Rocco and His Brothers). Recours en grâce. 1961: La proie pour l'ombre. Le rendezvous. Les amours célèbres. 1962: Pourquoi Paris? Smog. Le bateau d'Emile. Le crime ne paie pas (GB and US: Crime Does Not Pay). 1963: Vice and Virtue. La bonne soupe (US: Careless Love). Il giorno più corto commedia umaristica (US: The Shortest Day). I compagni (US: The Organizer). 1964: Le mari de la femme à barbe (US: The Ape Woman). L'autre femme. Un monsieur de compagnie (US: Male Companion). 1965: L'or du Duc. I fourlegge del matrimonio. La ragazza in prestito. Une voglia di morire. La belle famiglia. Declic et des claques. Guerre secrète (GB and US: The Dirty Game). 1966: Trois chambres à Manhattan. Le streghe (US: The Witches). 1967: Zhurnalist. Vivre pour vivre (GB and US: Live for Life). 1968: Le bande à Bonnot. La vie, l'amour, la mort. Les gauloises bleus. Dillinger is Dead. Erotissimo. 1969: Metti une sera, a cena. Le voleur des crimes. Il seme dell'uomo (US: The Seed of Man). Le clair de terre. Un homme qui me plaît (US: A Man I Like. GB: Love is a Funny Thing). Il pleut dans mon village. The Story of a Woman. 1970: Elle boit pas, elle fume pas, elle drague pas . . . mais elle cause. Les novices. 1971: Mourir d'aimer. La vieille fille. La mandarine. Les feux de la chandeleur. 1972: Elle cause plus . . . . elle flingue. Traitement de choc (GB: The Doctor in the Nude/Shock Treatment. US: Shock!) Il n'y a pas de fumée sans feu (US: Where There's Smoke). 1973: Juliette et Juliette. Missions dans l'italie fasciste. Ursule et Grélu. 1974: Le gifle (US: The Slap). Il sospetto. 1975: It is Raining on Santiago. Il faut vivre dangereusement. Le Gitan. Un cri. D'amour et d'eau fraîche. 1976: Docteur Françoise Gailland (US: No Time for Breakfast). Cours après moi que je t'attrape (US: Run After Me – Until I Catch You!). A chacun son enfer (GB: TV, as To Each His Own Hell). Autopsie d'un monstre. 1977: Le

dernier baiser. Jambon d'Ardenne. La zizanie. Tendre poulet (GB: Dear Detective. US: Dear Inspector). Le point de mire. Le commissaire a de jolies menottes. L'affaire. 1978: La clé sur la porte. Justices. Vas-y maman. Fais-moi rêver. L'ingorgo. 1979: Le cavaleur (US: The Skirt Chaser). L'amour en question. L'embouteillage. Allo, je craque. Bobo Jacco. On a volé la cuisse de Jupiter. 1980: Autres femmes (US: The Mother Beast). Cause toujours . . . tu m'intéresse. Le coeur à l'envers. 1981: All Night Long. La vie continue. 1982: Une robe noire pour un tueur. 1983: Père Noël et fils. La revanche. 1984: Io e Il Duce (US: Mussolini and I). Liste noire/Blacklist. Souvenirs, souvenirs. 1985: Adieu Blaireau. Partir, revenir. Olga e i suoi figli. 1986: Affabulazone L'autre énigma. 1988: Cinq jours en juin. Prisonnières. Trafic jam. 1989: Comédie d'amour. 1990: Il y des jours . . . et des lunes. 1991: Merci la vie. Toujours seuls. 1992: Au bal des grenouilles. 1993: Portagli i mei salutt. Les braqueuses (US: Girls With Guns). 1995: Les misérables (du XXième siècle). 1996: Les bidochons. 1997: Hotel Shanghai. 1998: L'âge de braise (US: When I Will Be Gone). Préférence. 2000: T'aime. 2001: El dia mas joven di mi vida.

GISH, Annabeth (Anne Elizabeth Gish) 1971–

Square-faced, scholarly looking American actress of light hair and attractive plainness. After a remarkable debut as the adolescent girl trying to cope with an abusive stepfather in *Desert Bloom*, her career has been lower in profile than her talent deserved – although she did take time out from acting to study for a degree in English. She was the sensible girl who didn't quite catch the eye in *Shag* and *Mystic Pizza* and has since been in co-starring roles, most notably as Kevin Costner's first wife in *Wyatt Earp* and the treacherous girlfriend in *Double Jeopardy*. No relation to Lillian and Dorothy Gish.

1986: Desert Bloom. Hero in the Family (TV). 1987: Hiding Out. 1988: Shag. Mystic Pizza. 1989: Coupe de Ville. When He's Not a Stranger (TV). 1991: The Last to Go (TV). 1992: Lady Against the Odds (TV). 1993: Silent Cries (TV). 1994: Wyatt Earp. 1995: The Last Supper. Nixon. Don't Look Back (cable TV). 1996: Beautiful Girls. What Love Sees (TV). 1997: Steel. Mayday – Flug in den Tod. 1998: To Live Again (TV). SLC Punk! 1999: Double Jeopardy. No Greater Love (TV). Different (TV). Sealed With a Kiss

(TV. GB: First Comes Love). God's New Plan (TV. GB: No Higher Love). 2000: Morning. Buying the Cow.

GISH, Dorothy (right above)
(D. de Guiche) 1898–1968

Long-faced, solemn, tawny-haired American actress, almost as popular as her prettier sister Lillian at her peak. Played much the same kind of 'sweet girl' roles, but without Lillian's dramatic intensity. Deserted films for the theatre in 1928, but never retired. Died from bronchial pneumonia.

1911: Fate's Turning. 1912: The Informer. Oil and Water. The New York Hat. The Musketeers of Pig Alley. The Painted Lady. An Unseen Enemy. So Near and Yet So Far. Gold and Glitter. My Hero. A Cry for Help. 1913: By Man's Law. The Perfidy of Mary. Just Gold. The Lady and the Mouse. Her Mother's Oath. Almost a Wild Man. Red Hicks Defies the World. Pa Says. The Widow's Kids. The House of Discord. The Lady in Black. The Vengeance of Galora. Those Little Flowers. The Adopted Brother. 1914: †Judith of Bethulia. Her Father's Silent Partner. The Old Man. The Newer Woman. Her Old Teacher. The Mysterious Shot. †The Floor Above. Liberty Belles. †The Mountain Rat. Silent Sandy. The Better Way. Arms and the Gringo (GB: The Rifle Smugglers). The Suffragettes Battle in Nuttyville. †Home Sweet Home. The Painted Lady. The Tavern of Tragedy. The City Beautiful. Their First Acquaintance. The Different Man. Her Mother's Necklace. A Lesson in Mechanics. Granny. His Lesson. †A Fair Rebel. †The Wife. Sands of Fate. Down the Hill to Creditville. The Warning. Back to the Kitchen. The Availing Prayer. The Sisters (GB: A Duel for Love). The Saving Grace. †Man's Enemy. 1915: Minerva's Mission. How Hazel Got Even. The Lost Lord Lowell. An Old-Fashioned Girl. Her Grandparents. †Her Mother's Daughter. †Old Heidelberg. †Bred in the Bone. †Jordan is a Hard Road. The Little Catamount. The Mountain Girl. Victorine. 1916: †Betty of Greystone. †Little Meena's Romance. †Atta Boy's Last Race. Gretchen the Greenhorn. †The Children of the Feud. †Susan Rocks the Boat (GB: Sweet Seventeen). The Little Schoolma'am. 1917: †The Little Yank. †Her Official Fathers. †Stage Struck. 1918: †Hearts of the World. †The Hun Within (GB: The Peril Within). †Battling Jane. 1919: †Boots. †Peppy Polly. †Nugget Nell. †I'll Get Him Yet. †Turning the Tables. †Out of Luck. †The Hope Chest. 1920:

†*Mary Ellen Comes to Town*. †*Little Miss Rebellion*. †*Remodeling Her Husband*. †*Flying Pat*. *1921:* †*The Ghost in the Garret*. †*Oh, Jo!* *1922:* †*Orphans of the Storm*. †*The Country Flapper*. *1923:* †*Fury*. †*The Bright Shawl*. *1924:* †*Romola*. *1925:* †*Night Life of New York*. †*Clothes Make the Pirate*. †*The Beautiful City*. †*Nell Gwyn*. *1926:* †*London* (GB: *Limehouse*). *1927:* †*Madame Pompadour*. †*Tip Toes*. *1930:* †*Wolves* (US: *Wanted Men*). *1944:* †*Our Hearts Were Young and Gay*. *1946:* †*Centennial Summer*. *1951:* †*The Whistle at Eaton Falls* (GB: *Richer Than the Earth*). *1963:* †*The Cardinal*.

All shorts except (†) features

GISH, Lillian (L. de Guiche) 1896–1993

Small, delicately pretty, tawny-haired American actress with heart-shaped face. Became famous with her sister Dorothy in the films of D.W. Griffith and developed into one of Hollywood's finest actresses, not only in silent films but in character roles in talkies following a sojourn in the theatre. Some sources give birthdate as 1893, but this seems unlikely. Special Oscar 1970. Nominated for an Oscar in *Duel in the Sun*. Never married. Died from heart failure.

1912: *Oil and Water. *The New York Hat. **The Musketeers of Pig Alley*. *An Unseen Enemy. *Gold and Glitter. *My Baby. *A Cry for Help. **Two Daughters of Eve*. **In the Aisles of the Wild*. **The Burglar's Dilemma*. **The Unwelcome Guest*. *1913:* *The Stolen Bride. *Just Gold. **The Lady and the Mouse*. **A Misunderstood Boy*. **House of Darkness*. **The Left-Handed Man*. **During the Round-Up*. **The Mothering Heart*. **An Indian's Loyalty*. **The Madonna of the Storm*. **A Woman in the Ultimate*. **A Timely Interception*. *A Modest Hero. **The Battle of Elderbush Gulch*. *1914:* *Judith of Bethulia*. *Home Sweet Home*. **The Green-Eyed Devil*. *The Escape*. *Silent Sandy. *The Tear That Burned*. *The Quicksands*. *The Sisters (GB: *A Duel for Love*). *The Battle of the Sexes*. *Lord Chumley*. *The Hunchback. *Man's Enemy*. *His Lesson*. *The Rebellion of Kitty Belle*. **The Folly of Anne*. *The Wife/A Wife*. **The Angel of Contention*. *1915:* *Enoch Arden* (GB: *As Fate Ordained*). *The Birth of a Nation*. *Captain Macklin*. *The Lost House*. *The Lily and the Rose*. *1916:* *Intolerance*. *Sold for Marriage*. *Flirting with Fate*. *Daphne and the Pirate*. *An Innocent Magdalene*. *Diane of the Follies*. *Pathways of Life*. *The Children Pay*. *1917:* *Souls Triumphant*. *The House Built* Upon Sand. *1918:* *Hearts of the World*. **Buy Liberty Bonds*. *The Great Love*. *The Greatest Thing in Life*. *1919:* *Broken Blossoms*. *True Heart Susie*. *The Greatest Question*. *A Romance of Happy Valley*. *1920:* *Way Down East*. *1922:* *Orphans of the Storm*. *1923:* *The White Sister*. *1924:* *Romola*. *1926:* *La Bohème*. *The Scarlet Letter*. *1927:* *Annie Laurie*. *1928:* *The Enemy*. *The Wind*. *1930:* *One Romantic Night*. *1933:* *His Double Life*. *1942:* *Commandos Strike at Dawn*. *1943:* *Top Man*. *1944:* *Miss Susie Slagle's* (released 1946). *1946:* *Duel in the Sun*. *1948:* *Portrait of Jennie* (GB: *Jennie*). *1955:* *The Cobweb*. **Salute to the Theatres*. *The Night of the Hunter*. *1958:* *Orders to Kill*. *1959:* *The Unforgiven*. *1966:* *Follow Me, Boys! Warning Shot*. *1967:* *The Comedians*. *Arsenic and Old Lace* (TV). *1970:* *Henri Langlois*. *1976:* *Twin Detectives* (TV). *1977:* *Sparrow* (TV). *1978:* *A Wedding*. *1980:* *Thin Ice* (TV). *1983:* *Hobson's Choice* (TV). *Hambone and Hillie* (GB: *The Adventures of Hambone*). *1985:* *The Adventures of Huckleberry Finn* (TV). *Sweet Liberty*. *1987:* *The Whales of August*.

As director: *1920: Remodeling Her Husband*.

GLEASON, Jackie
(Herbert John Gleeson) 1916–1987

Portly American comedian with a nice line in easy-going humour. He played a few small roles as comic relief at the beginning of the 1940s, then made a sensational impact with his first big dramatic role in *The Hustler*, which won him an Academy Award nomination. Disappointingly, he returned to comedy roles and his film career again stuttered, but he was very successful on television. Died from cancer of the liver. Grandfather of actor Jason Patric (*qv*).

1941: Navy Blues. Steel Against the Sky. 1942: Larceny Inc. All Through the Night. Lady Gangster. Escape from Crime. Orchestra Wives. Springtime in the Rockies. 1950: The Desert Hawk. 1961: The Million-Dollar Incident (TV). *The Hustler. 1962: Requiem for a Heavyweight* (GB: *Blood Money*). *Gigot. 1963: Papa's Delicate Condition. Soldier in the Rain. 1968: Skidoo. 1969: Don't Drink the Water. How to Commit Marriage. 1970: How Do I Love Thee? 1977: Mr Billion. Smokey and the Bandit. 1980: Smokey and the Bandit II* (GB: *Smokey and the Bandit Ride Again*). *1982: The Toy. 1983: The Sting II. Smokey and the Bandit – Part 3. 1984: Fools Die. 1985: Izzy and Mo* (TV). *1986: Nothing in Common*.

†*As Jack C. Gleason*

GLENN, Scott 1942–

Lean, laconic, leathery, whippy actor in the James Coburn mould who does all his own stunts and has the reputation of being one of the fittest American actors in films. An ex-marine and one-time reporter, Glenn came up the hard way, not getting his first film role until he was 29 and then having to wait another 10 years for stardom. A real-life hero who saved three children from drowning in 1979, Glenn looks capable of something superior to the action heroes he usually plays, but has only been a featured player in more recent mainstream movies.

1971: The Baby Maker. Angels Hard As They Come. 1972: Gargoyles (TV). *1973: Hex. 1975: Nashville. 1976: Fighting Mad. 1977: She Came to the Valley* (released 1979). *1979: Apocalypse Now. Cattle Annie and Little Britches. More American Graffiti/The Party's Over/Purple Haze. 1980: Urban Cowboy. 1982: The Challenge* (The Equals). *Personal Best. 1983: The Right Stuff. The Keep. 1984: The River. Countdown to Looking Glass* (TV). *1985: Wild Geese II. Silverado. 1986: As Summers Die* (TV). *Gangland: The Verne Miller Story* (TV). *1987: Man on Fire. 1988: Personal Choice. Off Limits* (GB: *Saigon*). *Intrigue* (TV). *1989: Miss Firecracker. The Outside Woman* (TV). *1990: The Hunt for Red October. The Silence of the Lambs. My Heroes Have Always Been Cowboys. 1991: Backdraft. Women and Men 2: In Love There Are No Rules. 1992: The Player. Rope of Sand. 1993: S.I.S./Extreme Justice/Shadow Hunter* (originally for cinemas, but released to cable TV). *Past Tense* (TV). *1994: Night of the Running Man. Flight of the Dove/The Spy Within. 1995: Tall Tale. 1996: Reckless* (TV). *Carla's Song. Edie and Pen. Courage Under Fire. 1997: Absolute Power. Firestorm. Lesser Prophets. 1998: Naked City: Justice with a Bullet* (TV). *Larga distancia. Naked City: A Killer Christmas* (TV). *1999: The Virgin Suicides. The Last Marshal. 2000: The Vertical Limit*.

GODDARD, Paulette
(Pauline G. Levee) 1905–1990

Petite, svelte American brunette who rose from the chorus. One of the few leading ladies 'introduced' by Charlie Chaplin to prove that she could stand on her own feet afterwards. With her verve and vivacity (plus a cute figure), she was equally at home in costume or comedy, as nice girls or minxes. Married to Chaplin (1936–1942), Burgess Meredith (1944–1949) and author Erich Maria

Remarque (1958 on): second, third and fourth of four. Remarque died in 1970. Oscar-nominated for *So Proudly We Hail!* Died from heart failure.

*1929: The Locked Door. *Berth Marks. Rio Rita. 1931: The Girl Habit. City Streets. 1932: The Kid from Spain. Pack Up Your Troubles. *Young Ironsides. *Girl Grief. The Mouthpiece. *Show Business. 1933: *Hollywood on Parade No. 17. Roman Scandals. 1934: Kid Millions. 1936: The Bohemian Girl. Modern Times. 1938: The Young in Heart. Dramatic School. 1939: The Women. The Cat and the Canary. 1940: The Great Dictator. The Ghost Breakers. Northwest Mounted Police. 1941: Second Chorus. Nothing but the Truth. Hold Back the Dawn. Pot o' Gold (GB: The Golden Hour). 1942: The Lady Has Plans. The Forest Rangers. Reap the Wild Wind. Star Spangled Rhythm. 1943: So Proudly We Hail! The Crystal Ball. 1944: Standing Room Only. I Love a Soldier. 1945: Duffy's Tavern. Kitty. 1946: The Diary of a Chambermaid. 1947: Suddenly It's Spring. Variety Girl. Unconquered. 1948: A Miracle Can Happen (later On Our Merry Way). An Ideal Husband. Hazard. 1949: Bride of Vengeance. Anna Lucasta. 1950: The Torch (GB: Bandit General). 1952: Babes in Bagdad. 1953: Vice Squad (GB: The Girl in Room 17). Paris Model. Sins of Jezebel. 1954: Charge of the Lancers. The Stranger Came Home (US: The Unholy Four). 1963: Gli indifferenti (GB and US: Time of Indifference). 1972: The Female Instinct (TV. GB: The Snoop Sisters).*

GOLDBERG, Whoopi
(Caryn Johnson) 1949–
Elastic-featured American comedienne with tousled dreadlocks and the widest smile since

Joe E. Brown (*qv*). After a tough climb to the top, she became a hot cabaret star with her scabrous one-woman comedy shows. She made her major movie entrance in a touching straight acting role, but star comedies were less successful, and she had been doing TV sit-com in the early 1990s when a best supporting actress Academy Award for *Ghost* revived her cinema career. Since then she has worked hard in a variety of starring and guest roles. Additional Oscar nomination for *The Color Purple.*

1982: Citizen (released 1983). 1986: The Color Purple (shown 1985). Jumpin' Jack Flash. 1987: Burglar. The Telephone. Fatal Beauty. 1988: Scared Straight! 10 Years Later (TV). Homer & Eddie. Clara's Heart. 1989: Beverly Hills Brats. Kiss Shot (TV). The Long Walk Home (cable TV). 1990: Ghost. 1991: Soapdish. Wisecracks. House Party 2. 1992: The Player. Sister Act. Sarafina! The Magical World of Chuck Jones. 1993: Naked in New York. Made in America. National Lampoon's Loaded Weapon 1. Sister Act 2: Back in the Habit. 1994: The Pagemaster (voice only). Vault of Horror. The Lion King (voice only). Corrina Corrina. The Little Rascals. Liberation (narrator only). Star Trek Generations. 1995: Boys on the Side. Moonlight and Valentino. T-Rex/Theodore Rex. The Celluloid Closet (doc). The Sunshine Boys (TV). 1996: Bogus. Powder. Eddie. Bordello of Blood. The Associate. Ghosts of Mississippi (GB: Ghosts of the Past). 1997: An Alan Smithee Film: Burn, Hollywood, Burn. In the Gloaming (cable TV). Cinderella (TV). In & Out. 1998: How Stella Got Her Groove Back. Rudolph the Red-Nosed Reindeer (voice only). A Knight in Camelot (TV). The Prince of Egypt (voice only). The Rugrats Movie (voice only). 1999: Deep End of the Ocean. Alice in Wonderland (TV). Get Bruce! (doc). Jackie's Back! (TV). Girl, Interrupted. 2000: More Dogs Than Bones. Monkeybone. Rocky and Bullwinkle.

GOLDBLUM, Jeff 1952–
Dark, spare, cynical-looking American actor with wry smile who broke with tradition by sticking to his obviously Jewish real-life surname and, from a start as callow youths, soon built up a reputation in a formidable variety of roles, usually with a streak of humour in them, before his career lost its way in some ill-chosen scripts and bizarre foreign projects. One of Hollywood's tallest actors at 6ft 4in, he married 6ft actress Geena Davis (*qv*) in 1987, but the union ended after four

years. In the mid 1990s he became a familiar face in TV commercials, as well as in the two *Jurassic Park* films.

*1974: Death Wish. California Split. 1975: Nashville. Next Stop Greenwich Village. 1976: The Sentinel. St Ives. Special Delivery. 1977: Between the Lines. Annie Hall. 1978: Thank God It's Friday. Remember My Name. Invasion of the Body Snatchers. 1980: The Legend of Sleepy Hollow (TV). Tenspeed and Brownshoe (TV). 1981: Threshold. 1982: Rehearsal for Murder (TV). 1983: The Big Chill. The Right Stuff. 1984: Ernie Kovacs: Between the Laughter (TV). The Adventures Of Buckaroo Banzai Across the Eighth Dimension. 1985: Silverado. Into the Night. Transylvania 6-5000. 1986: The Fly. 1987: Beyond Therapy. 1988: Vibes. Earth Girls Are Easy. 1989: The Tall Guy. The Mad Monkey. 1990: Mister Frost. Framed (cable TV). 1991: The Favour, the Watch and the Very Big Fish. Fathers & Sons. 1992: The Player. Deep Cover. Shooting Elizabeth. 1993: Jurassic Park. 1994: Call It Sleep. Lush Life. 1995: Hideaway. Nine Months. *Little Surprises (and directed). 1996: Independence Day. The Great White Hype. Trigger Happy/Mad Dog Time. 1997: The Lost World: Jurassic Park. 1998: Holy Man. The Prince of Egypt (voice only). 1999: Welcome to Hollywood (doc). 2000: Chain of Fools. Auggie Rose.*

GOLINO, Valeria 1966–
The girl in the *Hot Shots!* films who looks like former tennis star Gabriela Sabatini. Italian-born, Greek-raised Golino has untamed dark curly hair, perfect teeth and a smile of eager charm. A teenage model, she was discovered for films by Italian director Lina Wertmüller; so successful was the introduction that Golino had won an Italian Oscar at 21 for her performance in *Storia d'amore.* Since then, her impeccable English has enabled her to easily alternate between Italian and Hollywood pictures.

1983: Scherzo del destino in agguato dietro l'angolo come un brigante si strada/A Joke of Destiny Lying in Wait Around the Corner like a Robber. 1984: Blind Date. 1985: Figlio mio infinamente caro. Piccoli fuochi. Asilo di polizia/Defective Detective/Detective School Dropouts/Dumb Dicks. 1986: Storia d'amore. 1987: Last Summer in Tangiers. Gli occhiali d'oro. 1988: Big Top Pee-wee. Rain Man. Paura e amore/The Three Sisters/Love and Fear. 1989: Torrents of Spring. 1990: The King's Whore. Il y a des jours . . . et des lunes.

Tracce di vita amorosa. 1991: The Year of the Gun. The Indian Runner. Hot Shots! 1992: Puerto escondido. 1993: Hot Shots! Part Deux. 1994: Immortal Beloved. Clean Slate. 1995: Four Rooms. Leaving Las Vegas. 1996: Escape from L.A. The Slaughter of the Cock (completed 1994). Bravo Randy. An Occasional Hell. Perfect Crimes (TV). 1997: Escoriandoli. The Treat. Le acrobate/The Acrobats. 1998: Side Streets. L'albero delle pere (US: Shooting the Moon). 1999: Harem suare. Spanish Judges. Things You Can Tell Just by Looking at Her. 2000: Controvento.

GONG LI 1966–
Resolute-looking Chinese star with big eyes and large, expressive hands, China's best-known actress in history, and the only one to achieve worldwide fame in home-grown films. Originally intending to be a singer, Gong also studied drama, and made a strong and striking debut in *Red Sorghum*, an internationally successful film directed by Zhang Yimou, with whom she was to maintain a personal and professional relationship through the next eight years, and take central roles in many of China's most successful exports. Her profile has been somewhat lower since the break-up of that relationship and her marriage to an industrialist in 1996.

1988: Red Sorghum/Hong gao ling. 1989: A Terra Cotta Warrior/Qin yong. Woman-Demon-Human. 1990: Daihao meizhoubao. Ju Dou. 1991: The Banquet/Haomen yeyan (US: Party of a Wealthy Family). Raise the Red Lantern/Da hong deng long gao gao gua. Du xia II zhi Shang Hai tan du sheng/Back to Shanghai. 1992: Mungsing sifan/The Awakening of Ma Li. The Story of Qui Ju/Qiu Ju da guan si. 1993: Tong bat fu kau Chau Heung. Hau hun/Soul of a Painter/Pan Yi Liang, a Woman Painter. Farewell My Concubine/Ba wang bie ji. 1994: The Great Conqueror's Concubine/Xi chu bawang. The Great Conqueror's Concubine II/Xi chu bawang II. Xin tian long ba bu zhi tian shan tong lao/Dragon Chronicles: The Maidens of Heavenly Mountain. 1995: To Live/Huozhe. Shanghai Triad/Yao a yao yao dao waipo qiao. 1996: Temptress Moon/Feng yue. 1997: Chinese Box. 1998: Ch'in. 1999: The Emperor and the Assassin/Jing ke ci Qin Wang. 2000: Piaoliang mama (US: Breaking the Silence).

GOODING, Cuba Jr 1968–
Round-faced, fast-talking American actor,

often as blustery characters who learn something about themselves in the course of the story. The son of the lead singer with the group The Main Ingredient, Gooding's first claim to fame was breakdancing at the closing ceremony of the 1984 Olympics in Los Angeles. At 20, though, he had launched an acting career, and burst into leading roles three years later with his Tre Styles in *Boyz N the Hood*. He was an Academy Award winner as the sports star in *Jerry Maguire*, turning 'Show me the money!' into a worldwide catchphrase.

*1988: Coming to America. 1989: Sing. 1991: Boyz N the Hood. Gladiator. 1992: A Few Good Men. Murder Without Motive: The Edmund Perry Story (TV). Hitz/Judgement. 1993: Daybreak (TV). Judgment Night. 1994: Lightning Jack. 1995: Outbreak. Losing Isaiah. The Tuskegee Airmen (TV). *The Audition. 1996: Jerry Maguire. 1997: As Good As It Gets. Do Me a Favor. 1998: What Dreams May Come. A Murder of Crows. Welcome to Hollywood. 1999: Chill Factor. Instinct. 2000: Blaze of Glory. Navy Diver. The Gelfin. 2001: Pearl Harbor.*

GOODMAN, John 1952–
A big lug. Bulky, cheerful, fair-haired and flush-faced, Goodman is a throwback to character leads from another era. Thanks to his success on the TV comedy series *Roseanne*, however, the last 10 years have been good to this amiable Missouri-born American actor, mixing juicy supporting roles with the occasional lead. He won an athletics scholarship as a teenager, but soon turned to acting and left his home state for New York at 23. After seven years of dinner theatre, children's theatre, TV commercials

and off-Broadway plays, he began to break through to the big time. He usually plays dim-witted, easy-going buffoons, but has occasionally turned the character over to reveal a darker side.

1978: Jailbait Babysitter. 1983: The Survivors. Eddie Macon's Run. Heart of Steel (TV). The Face of Rage (TV). 1984: CHUD. Revenge of the Nerds. Blind Date. Maria's Lovers. 1985: Sweet Dreams. 1986: True Stories. The Big Easy. 1987: Burglar. Raising Arizona. 1988: The Wrong Guys. Everybody's All-American (GB: When I Fall in Love). Punchline. 1989: Always. Sea of Love. 1990: Stella. Arachnophobia. 1991: Barton Fink. King Ralph. The Babe. 1992: We're Back! A Dinosaur's Story (voice only). 1993: Born Yesterday. Matinee. 1994: The Flintstones. 1995: Kingfish: A Story of Huey P. Long (TV). A Streetcar Named Desire (TV). 1996: Mother Night. Pie in the Sky. 1997: The Borrowers. Fallen. 1998: The Big Lebowski. Blues Brothers 2000. Rudolph the Red-Nosed Reindeer. Dirty Work. 1999: The Runner (cable TV). Bringing Out the Dead. The Jack Bull (cable TV). 2000: What Planet Are You From? One Night at McCool's. Oh Brother, Where Art Thou? Coyote Ugly. Hitting the Wall. My First Mister. 2001: The Emperor's New Groove (voice only).

GORCEY, Leo 1915–1969
Pint-sized, fast-talking (out of the side of his mouth), dark-haired American actor of Swiss parentage, whose round, wise-guy face, Brooklyn voice and success as one of the tough teenagers in the stage and film versions of *Dead End* typed him in the same mould for the rest of his career. A member of the Dead End Kids from 1937–1940, then the East Side Kids from 1940–1945, then leader of the Bowery Boys in a long series of simple comedies which convulsed Americans and proved largely painful to audiences elsewhere. The series soon ended after Gorcey, battling alcoholism, decided to leave in 1956. He died from a liver ailment.

*1937: *Swingtime in the Movies. Portia on Trial (GB: The Trial of Portia Merriman). Headin' East. Dead End. 1938: Crime School. Mannequin. Angels with Dirty Faces. 1939: Hell's Kitchen. Private Detective. Angels Wash Their Faces. The Battle of City Hall. They Made Me a Criminal. The Dead End Kids on Dress Parade. Invisible Stripes. 1940: That Gang of Mine. Gallant Sons. Boys of the City. East Side Kids. Angels with Broken Wings.*

Junior G-Men (serial). Pride of the Bowery (GB: Here We Go Again). 1941: Sea Raiders (serial). Bowery Blitzkrieg (GB: Stand and Deliver). Out of the Fog. Spooks Run Wild. Road to Zanzibar. Down in San Diego. 1942: Mr Wise Guy. Sunday Punch. Smart Alecks. 'Neath Brooklyn Bridge. Let's Get Tough. Born to Sing. Junior G-Men of the Air (serial). Maisie Gets Her Man (GB: She Got Her Man). 1943: Ghosts on the Loose (GB: Ghosts in the Night). Clancy Street Boys. Mr Muggs Steps Out. Destroyer. Follow the Leader. 1944: Block Busters. Bowery Champs. The Million Dollar Kid. 1945: One Exciting Night. Midnight Manhunt. Mr Muggs Rides Again. Docks of New York. Live Wires. Come Out Fighting. 1946: Mr Hex (GB: Pride of the Bowery). In Fast Company. Spook Busters. Bowery Bombshell. 1947: Hard-Boiled Mahoney. News Hounds (GB: News Hound). Pride of Broadway. Bowery Buckaroos. 1948: Jinx Money. So This is New York. Angels' Alley. Trouble Makers. Smugglers' Cove. 1949: Angels in Disguise. Fighting Fools. Master Minds. Hold That Baby. 1950: Blues Busters. Triple Trouble. Blonde Dynamite. Lucky Losers. 1951: Ghost Chasers. Bowery Battalion. Crazy over Horses. Let's Go Navy. 1952: Here Come the Marines. Hold That Line. No Holds Barred. Feudin' Fools. 1953: Jalopy. Loose in London. Clipped Wings. Private Eyes. 1954: Paris Playboys. The Bowery Boys Meet the Monsters. Jungle Gents. 1955: Bowery to Bagdad. High Society. Jail Busters. Spy Chasers. 1956: Dig That Uranium. Crashing Las Vegas. 1963: It's a Mad Mad Mad Mad World. 1965: Second Fiddle to a Steel Guitar. 1969: The Phynx.

1941: The Big Blockade. 1942: The Night Invader. 1943: When We Are Married. 1944: *The True Story of Lilli Marlene. 1945: Night Boat to Dublin. 1946: A Matter of Life and Death (US: Stairway to Heaven). 1947: Take My Life. 1948: The Red Shoes. Mr Perrin and Mr Traill. 1950: Odette. Highly Dangerous. Pandora and the Flying Dutchman. Circle of Danger. 1951: The Magic Box. 1952: So Little Time. Nachts auf den Strassen. The Man Who Watched Trains Go By (GB: Paris Express). Rough Shoot (US: Shoot First). 1953: *The Mirror and Markheim (narrator only). 1955: Break in the Circle. The Adventures of Quentin Durward (US: Quentin Durward). The Barefoot Contessa. 1957: Ill Met by Moonlight (US: Night Ambush). *The Magic Carpet (narrator only). The Truth About Women. The Moonraker. 1958: Family Doctor (US: RX Murder). Son of Robin Hood. I Was Monty's Double (US: Monty's Double). 1959: Whirlpool. The Angry Hills. The Treasure of San Teresa (US: Long Distance). Desert Mice. 1960: Beyond the Curtain. The Unstoppable Man. Exodus. 1961: The Life of Hitler (narrator only). 1962: The Inspector (US: Lisa). The Devil's Daffodil (US: The Daffodil Killer). The Devil's Agent. 1963: This Garden England (narrator only). 1964: The Crooked Road. 1965: Up from the Beach. 1967: The 25th Hour. 1968: Girl on a Motocycle. Subterfuge. 1970: First Love. 1971: Zeppelin. 1978: The Little Girl in Blue Velvet. Meetings with Remarkable Men. 1989: Strike It Rich/Loser Takes All.

Will . . . for Now. Mean Johnny Barrows. 1976: Harry and Walter Go to New York. 1977: A Bridge Too Far. Capricorn One. 1978: The Silent Partner. Matilda. The Muppet Movie. Escape to Athena. 1979: The Lady Vanishes. The Last Flight of Noah's Ark. Falling in Love Again. 1980: Dirty Tricks. The Devil and Max Devlin. A New Life. 1981: The Rules of Marriage (TV). 1983: Over the Brooklyn Bridge. 1984: The Naked Face. The Muppets Take Manhattan. 1985: Inside Out. Dream Chasers. 1986: The Myth. Boogie Woogie. Vanishing Act (TV). 1987: Joker (US: Lethal Obsession). Conspiracy: The Trial of the Chicago 8 (TV). My First 40 Years/Story of a Woman/My Wonderful Life. 1988: The Big Picture. 1989: The Wounded King. Never Cry Devil/Night Visitor. Judgement. The Lemon Sisters. Dead Men Don't Die. Secret Scandal/Scandalo segreto. 1990: I Want Him Back (TV). Beyond Justice. Human Portrait. 1991: Bugsy. I Won't Disturb You Further. 1992: The Player. Exchange Lifeguards (US: Wet and Wild Summer). Somebody's Daughter (TV). 1993: The Last Paesan. Hoffman's Hunger. Amore! (TV). Bloodlines: Murder in the Family (TV). 1994: The Dangerous. The Feminine Touch. The Glass Shield. Naked Gun 33⅓: The Final Insult. Doggin' Around (TV). 1995: A Boy Called Hate. White Man's Burden. Duke of Groove (TV). Let It Be Me. Kicking and Screaming. Johns. 1996: Cover Me. PCH 1 (TV). Busted. *Inside Out. 1997: Hotel Shanghai. Camp Stories. City of Industry. 1998: The Big Hit. American History X. Michael Kael Vs the American News Company. 1999: Two Goldsteins on Acid. Camino dos sonhos. 2000: Playing Mona Lisa. Picking Up the Pieces.

GORING, Marius 1912–1998

Fair-haired, blue-eyed British actor whose suavely sinister looks often got him cast as foreign villains – with the occasional romantic lead thrown in. Attractive but slightly unbalanced characters were also a Goring speciality. He made an excellent Scarlet Pimpernel in a British television series of the 1950s and was also successful later on TV as The Expert, a forerunner of Hollywood's Quincy. Long married (second of three) to actress Lucie Mannheim (1895–1976).

1935: The Amateur Gentleman. 1936: Rembrandt. 1938: Dead Men Tell No Tales. Consider Your Verdict. 1939: The Last Straw. The Spy in Black (US: U-Boat 29). Flying Fifty-Five. 1940: Pastor Hall. The Case of the Frightened Lady (US: The Frightened Lady).

GOULD, Elliott (E. Goldstein) 1938–

Thick-lipped, heavy-featured, mournful-looking American star who can express both cynicism and sincerity. Very popular from 1969 to 1971, but fell victim to his own temperament and was off screen for two years. Later, he returned in more commercial, if less penetrating roles and began working frantically hard in lower-profile assignments from the mid 1980s. Married to Barbra Streisand (first of two) 1963–1969. Received an Academy Award nomination for Bob and Carol and Ted and Alice.

1964: The Confession (GB. TV: Quick, Let's Get Married!). 1968: The Night They Raided Minsky's. 1969: Bob & Carol & Ted & Alice. 1970: M*A*S*H. Getting Straight. I Love My Wife. Move. The Touch. 1971: Little Murders. 1973: The Long Goodbye. Busting. 1974: S*P*Y*S. California Split. Who? 1975: Nashville Whiffs (GB: C*A*S*H). I Will, I

GRABLE, Betty
(Ruth Elizabeth Grable) 1916–1973

Was Betty really a chorus girl at 12 (she was born in December)? Every reference gives the same date of birth, so it must be true: in which case, no wonder she had had enough of powder-puff musicals by the time she was 40. The peaches-and-cream blonde with the healthy, swim-star figure laboured for ten years on the Hollywood scene before a lucky break (Alice Faye's illness) launched her to top stardom in Down Argentine Way. Her 'million-dollar legs' subsequently made her queen of World War II pin-ups. A falling-out with Fox studio boss Darryl F. Zanuck hastened her decline from 1951. Married to

Jackie Coogan (1937–1940) and bandleader Harry James (1943–1965). Died from cancer.
*1929: Happy Days. Let's Go Places (GB: Mirth and Melody). 1930: Fox Movietone Follies of 1930. Whoopee! 1931: Kiki. Palmy Days. *Ex-Sweeties. †*Crashing Hollywood. 1932: †*Hollywood Luck. †*Hollywood Lights. *Lady, Please. *Over the Counter. *The Flirty Sleepwalker. The Greeks Had a Word for Them. Child of Manhattan. Probation (GB: Second Chances). Hold 'Em Jail. The Kid from Spain. The Age of Consent. 1933: *Air Tonic. Cavalcade. The Sweetheart of Sigma Chi (GB: Girl of My Dreams). Melody Cruise. What Price Innocence? (GB: Shall the Children Pay?). 1934: *Elmer Steps Out. *Susie's Affairs. The Gay Divorcee (GB: The Gay Divorce). Student Tour. Hips, Hips, Hooray! By Your Leave. *Love Detectives. *Business is a Pleasure. 1935: The Nitwits. Old Man Rhythm. *A Quiet Fourth. *A Night at the Biltmore Bowl. *Drawing Rumors. *The Spirit of 1976. 1936: Pigskin Parade (GB: The Harmony Parade). Follow the Fleet. Don't Turn 'Em Loose. Collegiate (GB: The Charm School). 1937: This Way Please. Thrill of a Lifetime. 1938: College Swing (GB: Swing, Teacher, Swing). Campus Confessions (GB: Fast Play). Give Me a Sailor. 1939: Man About Town. Million Dollar Legs. The Day the Bookies Wept. 1940: Down Argentine Way. Tin Pan Alley. 1941: A Yank in the RAF. I Wake Up Screaming (GB: Hot Spot). Moon over Miami. 1942: Footlight Serenade. Song of the Islands. Springtime in the Rockies. 1943: Coney Island. Sweet Rosie O'Grady. 1944: Four Jills in a Jeep. Pin-Up Girl. 1945: Billy Rose's Diamond Horseshoe (GB: Diamond Horseshoe). The Dolly Sisters. *All Star Bond Rally. 1946: Do You Love Me. The Shocking Miss Pilgrim. *Hollywood Park. 1947: Mother Wore Tights. 1948: That Lady in Ermine. When My Baby Smiles at Me. 1949: The Beautiful Blonde from Bashful Bend. 1950: Wabash Avenue. My Blue Heaven. 1951: Call Me Mister. Meet Me After the Show. 1953: The Farmer Takes a Wife. How to Marry a Millionaire. 1954: Three for the Show. 1955: How to be Very, Very Popular.*

†As Frances Dean

GRAHAM, Heather 1970–
Tallish, uninhibited American actress with curly blonde hair. She dropped out of university to pursue an acting career, but endured a long apprenticeship in teenage bimbo roles before breaking through to stardom in *Boogie Nights*. Although she's played an even mixture of comedy and light drama, she's proved at her best in the more serious stuff. Her younger sister Aimee Graham is also an actress.
1987: Student Exchange (TV). 1988: Twins. License to Drive. 1989: Drugstore Cowboy. 1990: I Love You to Death. 1991: Guilty as Charged. Shout. 1992: O Pioneers! (TV). Twin Peaks: Fire Walk With Me. Diggstown (GB: Midnight Sting). 1993: Even Cowgirls Get the Blues. The Ballad of Little Jo. 1994: Six Degrees of Separation. Don't Do It. Mrs Parker & the Vicious Circle. 1995: Desert Winds. Tough Guy/Terrified. Let It Be Me. 1996: Entertaining Angels: The Dorothy Day Story (TV). Swingers. 1997: Two Girls and a Guy. Scream 2. Boogie Nights. Nowhere. 1998: Lost in Space. 1999: Austin Powers: The Spy Who Shagged Me. Bowfinger. Kiss & Tell. Committed. 2000: Alien Love Triangle. Say It Isn't So. 2001: When the Cat's Away. Sidewalks of New York. From Hell.

GRAHAME, Gloria
(G.G. Hallward) 1924–1981
Green-eyed blonde of sulky appearance and unique, slightly lisping delivery (reminiscent of Humphrey Bogart, with whom she once co-starred). She painted a superb gallery of bad girls – Oscar-nominated as early as 1947, finally winning best supporting actress for *The Bad and the Beautiful* in 1952 – but could be surprisingly inept when called on to project a sympathetic character. Four times married, including (first) Stanley Clements (1945–1948) and (second) director Nicholas Ray (1948-1952). Died from cancer.
*1943: Cry Havoc. *Oh! Please Tell Me Darling. *Loads of Pretty Women. 1944: Blonde Fever. 1945: Without Love. 1946: It's a Wonderful Life. 1947: It Happened in Brooklyn. Merton of the Movies. Song of the Thin Man. Crossfire. 1948: A Woman's Secret. 1949: Roughshod. 1950: In a Lonely Place. Macao (released 1952). 1952: Sudden Fear. The Greatest Show on Earth. The Bad and the Beautiful. 1953: Man on a Tightrope. The Glass Wall. The Big Heat. Prisoners of the Casbah. 1954: The Good Die Young. Human Desire. Naked Alibi. 1955: Oklahoma! The Cobweb. Not As a Stranger. 1956: The Man Who Never Was. 1957: Ride Out for Revenge. 1959: Odds Against Tomorrow. 1966: Ride Beyond Vengeance. 1971: Blood and Lace. Chandler. The Todd Killings. Black Noon. Escape (TV). 1972: The Loners. Julio and*

Stein. 1973: Tarot. 1974: Mama's Dirty Girls. The Girl on the Late, Late Show (TV). 1975: Mansion of the Doomed (GB: The Terror of Dr Chaney). 1979: Chilly Scenes of Winter/Head Over Heels. The Nesting. 1980: Melvin and Howard. The Biggest Bank Robbery (TV).

GRAHAME, Margot 1911–1982
Britain's first ('aluminium') blonde bombshell. A bright, fluffy-haired blonde (in later years a redhead), she was so successful in British films of the early 1930s that she went to Hollywood, where she started strongly but gradually declined, returning to Britain before the war and latterly appearing more often on the stage than in the cinema. Died from chronic bronchitis.
*1922: Lady of the Camelias. 1930: Rookery Nook (US: One Embarrassing Night). Compromising Daphne (US: Compromised!). To Live Happy. The Love Habit. 1931: Uneasy Virtue. The Rosary. Glamour. Creeping Shadows (US: The Limping Man). Stamboul. 1932: *Postal Orders. A Letter of Warning. Illegal. Innocents of Chicago (US: Why Saps Leave Home). Yes Mr Brown. 1933: Forging Ahead. Timbuctoo. Prince of Arcadia. House of Dreams. Sorrell and Son. I Adore You. 1934: Without You. Easy Money. The Broken Melody. Falling in Love (US: Trouble Ahead). 1935: The Informer. The Arizonian. The Three Musketeers. Two in the Dark. 1936: Falling in Love. Crime over London. Make Way for a Lady. Night Waitress. Counterfeit. 1937: The Soldier and the Lady (GB: Michael Strogoff). Criminal Lawyer. Fight for Your Lady. 1938: The Buccaneer. 1943: The Shipbuilders. 1947: Forever Amber. The Fabulous Joe. Broken Journey. 1949: The Romantic Age (US: Naughty Arlette). Black Magic. 1951: Lucky Nick Cain (GB: I'll Get You for This). 1952: Venetian Bird (US: The Assassin). The Crimson Pirate. 1953: The Beggar's Opera. 1954: Orders Are Orders. 1957: Saint Joan.*

GRANGER, Farley (F. Earle) 1925–
Dark, brooding American leading man with boyish good looks and liquid brown eyes. Signed by Samuel Goldwyn at 18, Granger alternated romantic leads with disturbed youths, but was seen to best advantage as flawed heroes, especially in Hitchcock's *Strangers on a Train*. After a career hiatus, he re-emerged for a few years in the 1970s in Italian exploitation films, mostly as handsome ne'er-do-wells.
1943: North Star. 1944: The Purple Heart.

1947: They Live By Night (released 1949). 1948: Rope. Enchantment. 1949: Roseanna McCoy. 1950: Edge of Doom (GB: Stronger Than Fear). Side Street. Our Very Own. 1951: Strangers on a Train. I Want You. Behave Yourself! 1952: O Henry's Full House (GB: Full House). Hans Christian Andersen . . . and the dancer. 1953: Small Town Girl. The Story of Three Loves. 1954: Senso. 1955: The Naked Street. 1956: The Girl in the Red Velvet Swing. Men Against Speed (TV. GB: cinemas). Seidman and Son (TV). 1957: The Clouded Image (TV). 1967: Laura (TV). Rogue's Gallery. 1968: The Challengers (TV. GB: cinemas). Those Days in the Sun. 1970: Planet Venus. They Call Me Trinity. Qual cosa striscia nel buio (GB: Something Creeping in the Dark. US: Shadows in the Dark). Maharlika. La tela del ragno. 1971: Il posso dell' assassino. Alla ricera del piacere (GB and US: Hot Bed of Sex). 1972: Replica di un delitto (US: Violence). The Serpent (US: Night Flight to Moscow). La rossa dalla pelle che Scotta. Confessions of a Sex Maniac. Amuck. 1973: The Man Called Noon. White Fang. Arnold. 1974: Infamia. The Slasher. The Haunting of Penthouse D (TV). 1975: La polizia chiede auto (US: Co-ed Murders). Death Shall Have Your Eyes. Widow (TV). So Sweet So Dead/ Bad Girls. The Lives of Jenny Dolan (TV). 1981: Rosemary's Killer/ The Prowler. 1984: Deathmask. 1986: The Imagemaker. The Whoopee Boys. Very Close Quarters. 1995: The Celluloid Closet (doc).

GRANGER, Stewart
(James Stewart) 1913–1993
Tall, dark, debonair British actor who, after a hard apprenticeship, was invalided out of war service and promptly shot to stardom

portraying a series of dashing romantic adventurers. He went to Hollywood at the late age of 37, but still enjoyed half-a-dozen good years in bigger-budget M-G-M facsimiles of his British successes. He ended his star career in continental action films. Married to Elspeth March (1939–1949) and Jean Simmons (1950–1960): first and second of three. Died from prostate and bone cancer.
1933: I Spy (US: The Morning After. As stand-in only). A Southern Maid. 1934: Give Her a Ring. Over the Garden Wall. 1937: Mademoiselle Docteur (US: Street of Shadows). 1939: So This is London. 1940: Convoy. 1942: Secret Mission. 1943: Thursday's Child. The Lamp Still Burns. The Man in Grey. 1944: Love Story (US: A Lady Surrenders). Fanny by Gaslight (US: Man of Evil). Madonna of the Seven Moons. Waterloo Road. 1945: Caesar and Cleopatra. 1946: Caravan. The Magic Bow. 1947: Captain Boycott. Blanche Fury. 1948: Saraband for Dead Lovers (US: Saraband). Woman Hater. 1949: Adam and Evelyne. 1950: King Solomon's Mines. 1951: Soldiers Three. The Light Touch. 1952: Scaramouche. The Wild North. The Prisoner of Zenda. 1953: Young Bess. All the Brothers Were Valiant. Salome. 1954: Beau Brummell. Green Fire. 1955: Moonfleet. Footsteps in the Fog. 1956: The Last Hunt. Bhowani Junction. 1957: The Little Hut. Gun Glory. 1958: The Whole Truth. Harry Black (US: Harry Black and the Tiger). 1960: North to Alaska. 1961: The Secret Partner. Swordsman of Siena. 1962: La congiura dei Dieci. The Last Days of Sodom and Gomorrah. 1963: Il giorno piu corto commedia umaristica (US: The Shortest Day). March or Die (GB: The Legion's Last Patrol. US: Commando). 1964: The Secret Invasion. The Crooked Road. Among Vultures (US: Frontier Hellcat). 1965: Der Ölprinz (GB and US: Rampage at Apache Wells). Old Surehand, erste Teil (GB and US: Flaming Frontier). 1966: Das Geheimnis der drei Dschunken (US: Red Dragon). Das Geheimnis der gelben Mönche (US: Target for Killing). Der Chef schickt seinen besten Mann. Gern hab'ich die Frauen gekillt (US: Requiem for a Secret Agent). 1967: The Last Safari. The Trygon Factor. 1969: Any Second Now (TV). 1972: The Hound of the Baskervilles (TV). 1978: The Wild Geese. 1982: The Royal Romance of Charles and Diana (TV). 1986: Hell Hunters. 1987: A Hazard of Hearts (TV). 1988: Oro fino/ Fine Gold. 1989: Chameleons. 1990: Strange Bedfellows (TV).

GRANT, Cary
(Archibald Leach) 1904–1986
Dark-haired, British-born Hollywood star who originally went to America as an acrobat, but stayed to become a top star for over 30 years. His smooth elegance, dry delivery of a line, unique voice, hints of depths (of villainy and heroism) and delicious sense of the absurd built an immensely likeable screen personality apparently at odds with an explosive private life. Married to actresses Virginia Cherrill (1933–1935), Betsy Drake (1949–1960) and Dyan Cannon (1965–1968): first, third and fourth of five. Amazingly never won an Oscar (even his two nominations were not for his best roles); he was

finally given an honorary one in 1969 for 'his unique mastery of the art of screen acting'. Died following a stroke.
*1931: This is the Night. *Singapore Sue. 1932: Merrily We Go to Hell (GB: Merrily We Go To —). Sinners in the Sun. Hot Saturday. The Devil and the Deep. Blonde Venus. Madame Butterfly. 1933: Woman Accused. I'm No Angel. She Done Him Wrong. The Eagle and the Hawk. Gambling Ship. *Hollywood on Parade No. 13. Alice in Wonderland. 1934: Thirty-Day Princess. Born to be Bad. Ladies Should Listen. Kiss and Make Up. Enter Madame. 1935: Wings in the Dark. The Last Outpost. Sylvia Scarlett. 1936: The Amazing Quest of Ernest Bliss (US: Romance and Riches). *Pirate Party on Catalina Isle. Wedding Present. Big Brown Eyes. Suzy. 1937: When You're in Love (GB: For You Alone). The Toast of New York. Topper. The Awful Truth. 1938: Holiday (GB: Free to Live/ Unconventional Linda). Bringing Up Baby. 1939: Only Angels Have Wings. Gunga Din. In Name Only. His Girl Friday. 1940: My Favorite Wife. The Howards of Virginia (GB: The Tree of Liberty). The Philadelphia Story. 1941: Penny Serenade. Suspicion. 1942: The Talk of the Town. Once Upon a Honeymoon. 1943: Mr Lucky. Destination Tokyo. Arsenic and Old Lace. 1944: Once Upon a Time. *Road to Victory. *The Shining Future. None But the Lonely Heart. 1946: Night and Day. Without Reservations. Notorious. 1947: The Bachelor and the Bobby Soxer (GB: Bachelor Knight). 1948: The Bishop's Wife. Mr Blandings Builds His Dream House. Every Girl Should Be Married. 1949: I Was a Male War Bride (GB: You Can't Sleep Here). 1950: Crisis. 1951: People Will Talk. 1952: Room for One More. Monkey Business. 1953: Dream Wife. 1955: To Catch a Thief. 1956: The Pride and the Passion. 1957: An Affair to Remember. Kiss Them for Me. 1958: Indiscreet. Houseboat. 1959: North by Northwest. Operation Petticoat. 1960: The Grass is Greener. 1961: *Captive Islands. 1962: That Touch of Mink. 1963: Charade. 1964: Father Goose. 1966: Walk, Don't Run. 1970: Elvis – That's the Way It Is.*

GRANT, Hugh 1960–
Good-looking, very well-spoken, flop-haired British actor with diffident manner and sheepish smile. He looked a natural for roles as weaklings or wastrels, but his film career seemed shaky until it was seen that he could project shyness and slyness with equal

facility, and perfect casting in *Four Weddings and a Funeral* jetted him to international stardom. His career survived a scandal in 1995 when he was fined for consorting with a prostitute in America, and he portrays bespectacled ineptitude with such conviction that it would be no great surprise in the near future in films to find him hanging from the hands of a giant clock. Lived with actress Elizabeth Hurley (1965–) for 13 years. They parted in 2000. Besides the films below, he also appeared in the US TV miniseries *Jenny's War* in 1985.

1982: †*Privileged.* 1987: *Maurice. White Mischief.* 1988: *The Lair of the White Worm. The Dawning. The Bengali Night.* 1989: *Rowing With the Wind. The Lady and the Highwayman* (TV). *Champagne Charlie* (TV). 1990: *Impromptu. The Big Man* (US: *Crossing the Line*). 1991: *Our Sons* (TV). 1992: *Bitter Moon. Night Train to Venice.* 1993: *Four Weddings and a Funeral. The Remains of the Day. Sirens.* 1994: *The Englishman Who Went Up a Hill But Came Down a Mountain.* 1995: *An Awfully Big Adventure. Nine Months. Sense and Sensibility.* 1996: *Extreme Measures.* 1999: *Notting Hill. Mickey Blue Eyes.* 2000: *Small Time Crooks.* 2001: *Bridget Jones' Diary.*

†*As Hughie Grant*

GRANT, Kirby (K.G. Hoon) 1911–1985
There can't be many bandleaders who became western stars, but this genial, fair-haired actor-musician from the wilds of Montana was certainly one. A child prodigy on the violin, he formed his own dance orchestra in his twenties and made occasional acting appearances before the war years, when spots with his band in low-budget Universal romps brought him back into

demand for films. His acting career seemed to be petering out in the late 1940s, when Poverty Row studio Monogram came along with the offer of a series of films starring Grant as a Canadian Mountie, with a talented white husky as co-star. Several of these rugged little numbers were not at all bad, but with the demise of the second feature market (and his radio and TV series *Sky King*) Grant went touring with a circus. Drowned when his car crashed into a ditch.

1935: *I Dream Too Much.* 1938: *Lawless Valley. Red River Range.* 1939: †*Three Sons.* 1940: †*Bullet Code. The Marines Fly High.* 1941: *Blondie Goes Latin.* 1942: *Hello, Frisco, Hello. My Favorite Blonde. The Stranger from Pecos. Dr Kildare's Victory* (GB: *The Doctor and the Debutante*). 1943: *Bombardier.* 1944: *Rosie the Riveter* (GB: *In Rosie's Room*). *Hi Good Lookin'. Babes on Swing Street. Ghost Catchers. Destination Tokyo. In Society.* 1945: *Trail to Vengeance. I'll Remember April. Penthouse Rhythm. Bad Men of the Border. Code of the Lawless. Easy to Look At.* 1946: *Spider Woman Strikes Back. She Wrote the Book. Gun Town. Gunman's Code. The Lawless Breed. Rustlers' Roundup.* 1948: *Song of Idaho.* 1949: *Black Midnight. Feudin' Rhythm* (GB: *Ace Lucky*). *Trail of the Yukon. Wolf Hunters.* 1950: *Snow Dog. Indian Territory. Call of the Klondike.* 1951: *Comin' Round the Mountain. The Celebrated Jumping Frog (of Calaveras County)* (TV). *Rhythm Inn. Yukon Manhunt. Northwest Territory.* 1952: *Yukon Gold.* 1953: *Cavalcade of America* (TV). *Northern Patrol.* 1954: *Yukon Vengeance.* 1955: *The Court Martial of Billy Mitchell* (GB: *One Man Mutiny*).

†*As Robert Stanton*

GRANT, Lee (Lyova Rosenthal) 1927–
Dark-haired, forceful American actress, on stage at four. Nominated for an Academy Award in her first role, she submerged her handsome looks beneath a series of writhing neurotics. Hollywood could find no niche for her in a career additionally damaged by the McCarthy blacklist, and she spent most of her time on stage and TV. She re-emerged, albeit mainly in character roles, if more commercial ones, into films and TV movies in the late 1960s, finally winning an Oscar for *Shampoo.* Also Oscar-nominated for *The Landlord* and *Voyage of the Damned.* Mother of actress Dinah Manoff (1958–), she has also dabbled in direction with some success: her

1985 documentary *Down and Out in America* was an Academy Award winner.

1951: *Detective Story.* 1955: *Storm Fear.* 1959: *Middle of the Night.* 1962: *The Balcony.* 1963: *Pie in the Sky.* 1965: *An Affair of the Skin.* 1966: *Terror in the City.* 1967: *In the Heat of the Night. Divorce American Style. Valley of the Dolls.* 1968: *Buona Sera Mrs Campbell. The Big Bounce.* 1969: *Perilous Voyage* (TV). *Marooned.* 1970: *There Was a Crooked Man. Night Slaves* (TV). *The Landlord.* 1971: *Plaza Suite. Ransom for a Dead Man* (TV. GB: cinemas). *The Neon Ceiling* (TV). *Portnoy's Complaint.* 1972: *Lt. Schuster's Wife* (TV). 1973: *Partners in Crime* (TV). *What Are Best Friends For?* (TV). 1974: *The Internecine Project.* 1975: *Shampoo. Man Trouble* (TV). 1976: *Voyage of the Damned. Perilous Voyage* (TV). 1977: *Airport 77. The Spell* (TV). 1978: *Damien – Omen II. The Swarm. Thou Shalt Not Kill* (TV). *The Mafu Cage.* 1979: *When You Comin' Back, Red Ryder? You Can't Go Home Again* (TV). *The Million Dollar Face* (TV). 1980: *Little Miss Marker.* 1981: *Charlie Chan and the Curse of the Dragon Queen. For Ladies Only* (TV). *The Fright.* 1982: *Visiting Hours.* 1983: *A Matter of Sex* (TV). 1984: *Trial Run. Teachers. Will There Really Be a Morning?* (TV). *A Billion for Boris* (released 1990). 1985: *Sanford Meisner.* 1986: *Arriving Tuesday.* 1987: *Hello Actors Studio. The Big Town.* 1989: *The Hijacking of the Achille Lauro* (TV). 1990: *Defending Your Life.* 1992: *Stephen Verona: Self Portrait. In My Daughter's Name. Something to Live For: The Alison Gertz Story* (TV. GB: *Fatal Love*). 1993: *Earth and the American Dream* (voice only). *Citizen Cohn* (cable TV). 1994: *Under Heat.* 1995: *It's My Party.* 1966: *The Substance of Fire. Under Heat.* 1999: *Mulholland Drive* (TV). 2000: *The Amati Girls.*

As director: 1976: **The Stranger.* 1980: *Tell Me a Riddle.* 1981: *The Willmar 8.* 1985: *What Sex Am I? Cindy Eller: A Modern Fairy Tale. Down and Out in America.* 1986: *Nobody's Child* (TV). 1988: *Boy's Life. No Place Like Home.* 1989: *Staying Together.* 1990: *Hard Promises* (TV). 1993: *Winter Garden* (TV). 1994: *Seasons of the Heart* (TV). 1995: *Reunion* (TV). *Following Her Heart* (TV). 1997: *Broadway Brawler* (unfinished). 2000: *The Loretta Claiborne Story* (TV).

GRANT, Richard E.
(R. G. Esterhuysen) 1957–
Tall, long-faced, basilisk-eyed, dark-haired, Swaziland-born actor with high forehead, in Britain since 1982 after education and early acting experience in South Africa. His open-mouthed expression can adapt quickly to contempt, menace, determination or self-satisfaction at the drop of a line and, despite several leading roles, he has proved equally if not more adept with top featured roles demanding waspish qualities.

1985: *Honest, Decent and True* (TV). 1986: *Withnail and I.* 1987: *Hidden City.* 1988: *Warlock.* 1989: *How to Get Ahead in Advertising. Killing Dad. Thieves in the Night* (TV). *Mountains of the Moon.* 1990: *Henry and June.* 1991: *L.A. Story. Hudson Hawk.* 1992: *The Player. Bram Stoker's Dracula.*

1993: *Franz Kafka's It's a Wonderful Life (TV). Posse. The Age of Innocence. 1994: Prêt-à-Porter (US: Ready to Wear). *Butter. 1995: The Cold Light of Day. Jack and Sarah. 1996: Twelfth Night. The Portrait of a Lady. 1997: Serpent's Kiss. Food of Love. Keep the Aspidistra Flying. Spice World. 1998: Divorcing Jack. All for Love/St Ives. Cash in Hand. 1999: The Match. A Christmas Carol (TV). The Miracle Maker (voice only). 2000: The Little Vampire.

GRANVILLE, Bonita 1923–1988
Long-nosed, lantern-jawed (but attractive) American actress with light brown hair. Played brats and smart-Alec teenagers through the thirties, most notably the abhorrent Mary in These Three (1936), which won her an Oscar nomination. Her career went slowly downhill in the forties, and she seemed to lose interest in acting after her marriage in 1947, becoming associated with the 'Lassie' TV series for nearly 20 years on the production side. Said to have made small appearances in shorts from 1930 to 1932. Died from cancer.
1932: Westward Passage. Silver Dollar. 1933: Cavalcade. Cradle Song. 1934: The Life of Vergie Winters. Anne of Green Gables. A Wicked Woman. 1935: Ah, Wilderness! 1936: These Three. Song of the Saddle. The Plough and the Stars. The Garden of Allah. 1937: Maid of Salem. Call It a Day. Quality Street. It's Love I'm After. The Life of Emile Zola. 1938: Merrily We Live. White Banners. My Bill. *For Auld Lang Syne. The Beloved Brat (GB: A Dangerous Age). Hard to Get. Nancy Drew, Detective. 1939: Nancy Drew, Reporter. Nancy Drew, Trouble Shooter. Nancy Drew and the Hidden Staircase. Angels Wash Their

Faces. 1940: Those Were the Days (GB: Good Old Schooldays). The Mortal Storm. Forty Little Mothers. Third Finger, Left Hand. Escape. Gallant Sons. 1941: The Wild Man of Borneo. The People vs. Dr Kildare (GB: My Life is Yours). H.M. Pulham Esq. Down in San Diego. 1942: Syncopation. The Glass Key. Now, Voyager. *Soaring Stars. 1943: Seven Miles from Alcatraz. Hitler's Children. What a Woman! (GB: The Beautiful Cheat). 1944: Andy Hardy's Blonde Trouble. Youth Runs Wild. Song of the Open Road. 1945: Senorita from the West. The Beautiful Cheat (GB: What a Woman!). 1946: Love Laughs at Andy Hardy. Breakfast in Hollywood (GB: The Mad Hatter). Suspense. The Truth About Murder (GB: The Lie Detector). 1947: The Guilty. 1948: Strike It Rich. 1950: Guilty of Treason (GB: Treason). 1956: The Lone Ranger. 1958: The Velvet Alley (TV). 1970: Handford's Point (TV). 1981: The Legend of the Lone Ranger.

GRAVES, Peter (P. Aurness) 1925–
Tall, well-built American actor, brother of James Arness. His fair hair, blue eyes and faintly oriental looks seemed to qualify him for a profitable run of handsome villains, especially after his treacherous Price in Stalag 17. But from 1955, he became involved as increasingly artificial men-of-action in such successive TV series as Mission: Impossible. His film leads since then have been largely in 'Z' movies, but, now white-haired, he guyed his own image in the Airplane movies. Began his show business career as a band musician.
1950: Rogue River. 1951: Fort Defiance. 1952: Red Planet Mars. Stalag 17. 1953: East of Sumatra. War Paint. Beneath the 12-Mile Reef. Killers from Space. 1954: The Raid. The Yellow Tomahawk. The Long Gray Line. Black Tuesday. 1955: The Naked Street. Robber's Roost. Wichita. The Night of the Hunter. The Court-Martial of Billy Mitchell (GB: One Man Mutiny). Fort Yuma. 1956: Hold Back the Night. Canyon River. It Conquered the World. 1957: Death in Small Doses. Bayou. The Beginning of the End. 1958: Wolf Larsen. 1959: Stranger in My Arms. 1963: The Case Against Paul Ryker (TV. GB and US cinemas 1968 as Sergeant Ryker). 1965: A Rage to Live. 1966: Texas Across the River. 1967: The Ballad of Josie. Valley of Mystery. 1969: The Five Man Army. Mission Impossible vs. the Mob (TV. GB: cinemas). 1971: The President's Plane is Missing (TV). 1972: Call to Danger (TV). 1974: Sidecar Racers. Where Have All the People Gone?

(TV). The Underground Man (TV). Scream of the Wolf (TV). 1975: Dead Man on the Run (TV). Bigfoot: the Mysterious Monster (narrator only). 1976: Spree. 1977: SST Death Flight (TV). 1978: Missile X. High Seas Hijack. 1979: The Clonus Horror. Death Car on the Freeway (TV). Teheran Incident/Teheran 1943. The Rebels (TV). 1980: Trieste File. Airplane! Survival Run. The Memory of Eva Ryker (TV). 1981: 300 Miles for Stephanie (TV). The Guns and the Fury. 1982: Savannah Smiles. Airplane II The Sequel. 1986: Number One with a Bullet. 1987: The Law & Harry McGraw (TV). Best of Friends (TV). If It's Tuesday, It Must Still Be Belgium (TV). 1993: Addams Family Values. 1999: House on Haunted Hill.

GRAVES, Rupert 1963–
Stocky British actor with dark, wavy hair and soft, upper-class, boyish good looks, often seen as aimless socialites in period dramas, and almost always in roles that require him to keep a serious face. Both a clown in a travelling circus and a holiday camp entertainer in his teenage days, Graves broke into TV in 1980 and film acting, from 1985, via the films of director James Ivory. His career has criss-crossed several times with those of Helena Bonham Carter, James Wilby and Kristin Scott Thomas and he has stayed in leading roles without quite becoming a name the public instantly recognises.
1985: A Room with a View. 1987: Maurice. 1988: A Handful of Dust. 1990: The Children. The Plot to Kill Hitler (TV). 1991: Where Angels Fear to Tread. Una questione privata (TV). 1992: Damage. 1994: Doomsday Gun (TV). The Madness of King George. 1995: Intimate Relations. 1996: The Innocent Sleep. Bent (released 1998). Different for Girls. 1997: Mrs Dalloway. The Revengers' Comedies. 1998: Dreaming of Joseph Lees. 1999: Vsichni moji blizci. 2000: Room to Rent. All My Loved Ones.

GRAY, Coleen (Doris Jensen) 1922–
Petite, full-lipped, showy-looking, fair-haired American actress, always in leading roles, but almost entirely in co-features. Of Danish parentage, she was a relative latecomer to films at 23, but stayed around in a variety of colourful pot-boilers until her late thirties. Most interesting as semi-bad girls, a role in which she wasn't often cast.
1945: State Fair. 1946: Three Little Girls in Blue. 1947: Kiss of Death. Nightmare Alley. 1948: Red River. Fury at Furnace Creek.

1949: *Will James' Sand* (GB: *Sand*). 1950: *Riding High. Father is a Bachelor. The Sleeping City.* 1951: *Apache Drums. Lucky Nick Cain* (GB: *I'll Get You for This*). 1952: *Models Inc* (GB: *That Kind of Girl*). *Kansas City Confidential* (GB: *The Secret Four*). 1953: *The Fake. Sabre Jet. The Vanquished.* 1954: *Arrow in the Dust.* 1955: *Las Vegas Shakedown. The Twinkle in God's Eye. Tennessee's Partner.* 1956: *Star in the Dust. The Wild Dakotas. The Killing. Frontier Gambler. Death of a Scoundrel. The Black Whip.* 1957: *Destination 60,000. The Vampire. Copper Sky. God is My Partner.* 1958: *Hell's Five Hours. Johnny Rocco.* 1959: *The Leech Woman.* 1962: *Phantom Planet.* 1965: *Town Tamer.* 1968: *P.J.* (GB: *New Face in Hell*). 1971: *Ellery Queen: Don't Look Behind You* (TV). 1972: *The Late Liz.* 1979: *The Best Place to Be* (TV). 1986: *Cry from the Mountain.* 1987: *Arriva Frank Capra.*

GRAY, Dulcie (D. Bailey) 1919–
Pretty, appealing, ultra-English brunette actress (actually born in Malaya), never given much chance to realize her capabilities in films, and mostly confined to milk-and-water waiting women. Not surprisingly, she quit films in 1952, and concentrated on dual careers as stage actress and novelist. A great hit as Miss Marple on stage in the seventies. Married to Michael Denison (*qv*) from 1939 to his death.
1941: *Banana Ridge.* 1944: **Victory Wedding. 2,000 Women. Madonna of the Seven Moons.* 1945: *A Place of One's Own. They Were Sisters.* 1946: *Wanted for Murder. The Years Between.* 1947: *A Man About the House. Mine Own Executioner.* 1948: *My Brother Jonathan. The Glass Mountain.* 1951: *The Franchise*

Affair. Angels One Five. 1952: *There Was a Young Lady.* 1966: *A Man Could Get Killed.*

GRAY, Eve 1904–
Blue-eyed blonde known in early sound days as the most beautiful girl in British films. Brought up in Australia (although English-born), she was a big hit on the London stage in the mid-1920s. She turned down Hollywood offers, but did make some films for UFA in Germany. Remaining popular throughout the 1930s, when she concentrated heavily on films, often playing bad girls, she is now best remembered as Errol Flynn's leading lady in his initial British film *Murder at Monte Carlo*.
1927: **A Daughter of the Night. The Silver Lining. Poppies of Flanders. One of the Best.* 1928: *Moulin Rouge. Smashing Through. Lockendes Gift* (GB: *Sweet Pepper*). *Villa Falcionieri. Die Abenteuer GmbH* (GB: *The Secret Adversary*). 1930: *The Loves of Robert Burns. Why Sailors Leave Home. Night Birds.* 1931: *Midnight. The Wickham Mystery.* 1933: *The Flaw. The Bermondsey Kid. Smithy.* 1934: *The Crimson Candle. Guest of Honour. Murder at Monte Carlo. Womanhood. Big Business. What's in a Name?* 1935: *Death on the Set* (GB: *Murder on the Set*). *Just for Tonight. Three Witnesses. Bargain Basement* (later *Department Store*). *Scrooge. The Last Journey.* 1936: *Twice Branded. Such is Life. They Didn't Know. Jury's Evidence. The Happy Family.* 1937: *Pearls Bring Tears. When the Devil Was Well. The Vicar of Bray. The Strange Adventures of Mr Smith. Fifty Shilling Boxer. Who Killed Fen Markham? The Angelus. Silver Blaze* (US: *Murder at the Baskervilles*). 1938: *The Awakening. His Lordship Regrets. His Lordship Goes to Press.* 1951: *One Good Turn.*

GRAY, Lorna
See BOOTH, Adrian

GRAY, Nadia
(Nadja Kujnir-Herescu) 1923–1994
Glamorous, chestnut-haired international leading lady, born in Berlin of Russian parents, and raised in Rumania. After lending her distinctive, spiky personality to films in several European countries over a period of 20 years, she emigrated to America. In the late seventies she launched herself as a nightclub singer. Died following a stroke.
1948: *L'inconnu d'un soir.* 1949: *Monseigneur.*

The Spider and the Fly. 1951: *Night without Stars. Valley of the Eagles.* 1952: *Top Secret* (US: *Mr Potts Goes to Moscow*). 1953: *Gran varietà. Puccini. La vierge du Rhin. Les femmes s'en balancent. Inganno. Moglie per una notte* (GB: *Wife for a Night*). 1954: *Carosello Napoletano* (GB: *Neapolitan Fantasy*). *Crossed Swords. Casta diva. Casa Ricordi. Casanova* (GB: *The Adventures of Casanova.* US: *Sins of Casanova*). *Ivan, il figlio del diavolo bianco.* 1955: *Il falco d'oro. Musik im Blut.* 1956: *Folies-Bergère. Senechal the Magnificent.* 1957: *Il diavolo nero. Une Parisienne* (GB and US: *Parisienne*). *One Week with Love.* 1958: *The Captain's Table.* 1959: *La dolce vita. Vacanze ad Ischia.* 1960: *Candide.* 1961: *Les crouants se porte bien. Le jeu de la vérité. Le pavé de Paris* (GB: *The Pavements of Paris*). *Jeunesse de nuit. Mr Topaze* (US: *I Like Money*). 1962: *Rocambole. Maniac. Adventurer from Tortuga.* 1963: *Zwei Whisky und ein Sofa.* 1964: *Begegnung in Salzburg. The Crooked Road.* 1965: *Up from the Beach.* 1966: *Winnetou und sein Freund Old Firehand* (GB: *Thunder at the Border*). 1967: *The Oldest Profession. The Naked Runner. Two for the Road.* 1976: *Rue Haute.*

GRAY, Sally (Constance Stevens) 1916–
Beautiful British blonde actress with wolf-whistle figure, dancing in a minstrel show at 14 and popular in British films at 19. Suffered a breakdown attributed to overwork in 1941, and retired. Came back in 1946 looking more stunning than ever and made a few more male hearts flutter in the cinema before marrying into the aristocracy in 1953.
1930: *School for Scandal.* 1935: *Radio Pirates. The Dictator* (US: *The Loves of a Dictator*).

Limelight (US: Backstage). Cross Currents. Lucky Days. Checkmate. Marry the Girl. 1936: Olympic Honeymoon. Café Colette (US: Danger in Paris). Cheer Up! Calling the Tune. 1937: Over She Goes. Saturday Night Revue. 1938: Mr Reeder in Room 13 (US: Mystery of Room 13). Hold My Hand. Lightning Conductor. 1939: The Lambeth Walk. The Saint in London. Sword of Honour. A Window in London (US: Lady in Distress). 1940: Honeymoon Merry-Go-Round. 1941: The Saint's Vacation. Dangerous Moonlight (US: Suicide Squadron). 1946: Carnival. Green for Danger. 1947: They Made Me a Fugitive (US: I Became a Criminal). The Mark of Cain. 1948: Obsession (US: The Hidden Room). 1949: Silent Dust. 1952: Escape Route (US: I'll Get You).

GRAYSON, Kathryn
(Zelma K. Hedrick) 1922–
Dark-haired, brown-eyed, almost absurdly pretty American singing star who trilled her coloratura soprano voice across M-G-M sound stages for 13 years and played in some of their best musicals. She played down her sexy hour-glass figure until later in her career, although it was then that she gave two of her most attractive performances – as Magnolia in *Show Boat* and Katherine in *Kiss Me Kate*. Her latter-day appearances showed that the once-svelte star had gained weight dramatically.
1941: Andy Hardy's Private Secretary. The Vanishing Virginian. 1942: Rio Rita. Seven Sweethearts. 1943: Thousands Cheer. 1944: A Century of Cinema. Ziegfeld Follies (released 1946). 1945: Anchors Aweigh. 1946: Two Sisters from Boston. Till the Clouds Roll By. 1947: It Happened in Brooklyn. 1948: The Kissing Bandit. 1949: That Midnight Kiss. 1950: The Toast of New Orleans. Grounds for Marriage. 1951: Show Boat. 1952: Lovely to Look At. 1953: The Desert Song. So This is Love (The Grace Moore Story). Kiss Me Kate. 1956: The Vagabond King. 1957: Lone Woman (TV). 1978: Beverly Hills High (TV). 1994: A Century of Cinema.

GRECO, Juliette 1926–
Dark-haired, dark-eyed French night-club chanteuse who had a sporadic career in French films. Her acerbic songs had made her the darling of Paris Left-Bank existentialist cellars, when she was 'discovered' by Darryl F. Zanuck who put her under contract to Twentieth Century-Fox for five years. She

seemed to lose interest in the cinema from 1966 after marrying (second) French star Michel Piccoli (1925–). But the marriage ended in divorce in 1977, and she later remarried.
1949: Au royaume des ceux. 1950: *Désordre. Orphée. Sans laisser d'adresse. 1951: The Green Glove. 1952: La route de bonheur. 1953: Boum sur Paris! Quand tu liras cette lettre. 1956: La châtelaine du Liban. Elena et les hommes (GB: Paris Does Strange Things). L'homme et l'enfant (GB and US: Man and Child). 1957: C'est arrivé à 36 chandelles. The Sun Also Rises. 1958: The Naked Earth. Roots of Heaven. Bonjour Tristesse. 1959: Whirlpool. 1960: Crack in the Mirror. 1961: The Big Gamble. Maléfices (US: Where the Truth Lies). 1962: Canzoni nel mondo (US: 38-24-36). 1965: Uncle Tom's Cabin. 1966: The Night of the Generals. 1967: Le désordre à 20 ans. 1973: Le far west. 1974: Lily, aime moi. 1997: Jedermann's Fest.

GREENE, Richard 1918–1985
Tall, dark, strongly-built, boyishly handsome British leading man whose acting was somewhat restricted, but who might have become an even bigger Hollywood star had the war not interrupted his career. When he returned to America, he was confined to increasingly minor swashbucklers, but a British television series, *Robin Hood*, was an immense success, made him a household name, and enabled him to retire in middle age. Married to Patricia Medina (first of two) 1941–1951. Never fully recovered from a brain tumour operation in 1982, following injuries sustained in a fall. Some sources suggest he was born in 1914.
1934: †Sing As We Go. 1938: Four Men and a

Prayer. My Lucky Star. Kentucky. Submarine Patrol. 1939: The Hound of the Baskervilles. Stanley and Livingstone. The Little Princess. Here I Am a Stranger. 1940: I Was an Adventuress. Little Old New York. 1942: Unpublished Story. Flying Fortress. 1943: Yellow Canary. 1944: Don't Take It to Heart. 1946: Gaiety George (US: Showtime). 1947: Forever Amber. 1948: The Fighting O'Flynn. 1949: The Fan (US: Lady Windermere's Fan). That Dangerous Age (US: If This Be Sin). Now Barabbas was a robber...1950: My Daughter Joy (US: Operation X). Shadow of the Eagle. The Desert Hawk. 1951: Peter Ibbetson (TV). Lorna Doone. 1952: The Black Castle. 1953: Rogue's March. Captain Scarlett. The Bandits of Corsica (GB: Return of the Corsican Brothers). 1955: Contraband Spain. 1960: Beyond the Curtain. 1961: Sword of Sherwood Forest. 1967: Island of the Lost. 1968: The Blood of Fu Manchu (US: Kiss and Kill/ Fu Manchu and the Kiss of Death). The Castle of Fu Manchu. 1972: Tales from the Crypt. 1984: Special Effects.

†Scenes deleted from final release print

GREENSTREET, Sydney 1879–1954
Huge English actor with impeccable diction and tiny, hostile features above a bulky body that at one time reached 325 pounds. A massive hit in more ways than one as the fat man in *The Maltese Falcon* – his first film at 61 – and a regular in Warner Brothers films after that throughout the forties. Ill-health forced him to retire earlier than the studio would have wished. Most popular of all in films that teamed him with Peter Lorre (*qv*) – a kind of Laurel and Hardy in Hell. He was once a tea planter in Sri Lanka (then Ceylon). Died from Bright's Disease complicated by diabetes. Oscar-nominated for *The Maltese Falcon*.
1941: The Maltese Falcon. They Died with their Boots On. 1942: Across the Pacific. In This Our Life. Casablanca. 1943: Devotion (released 1946). Background to Danger. 1944: Passage to Marseille (GB: Passage to Marseilles). Hollywood Canteen. Between Two Worlds. The Mask of Dimitrios. The Conspirators. 1945: Pillow to Post. Christmas in Connecticut. Conflict. 1946: Three Strangers. The Verdict. 1947: That Way with Women. The Hucksters. The Woman in White. 1948: Ruthless. The Velvet Touch. 1949: Flamingo Road. It's a Great Feeling. Malaya (GB: East of the Rising Sun).

GREENWOOD, Joan 1921–1987
Pixieish, plummy-voiced, green-eyed British blonde, a sort of demure Fenella Fielding. Ideally cast as Lady Caroline Lamb in the otherwise poor *The Bad Lord Byron*, she was mostly seen as *femmes fatales*, although she tried to vary her range and, like most screen bad girls, found it difficult to prolong her film career into her thirties. Married to André Morell (*qv*) from 1960 until his death in 1978. Died from a heart attack.
1940: John Smith Wakes Up. 1941: My Wife's Family. He Found a Star. 1943: The Gentle Sex. 1945: They Knew Mr Knight. Latin Quarter. 1946: A Girl in a Million. 1947: The Man Within (US: The Smugglers). The October Man. The White Unicorn (US: Bad Sister). 1948: Saraband for Dead Lovers (US: Saraband). The Bad Lord Byron. 1949: Whisky Galore! (US: Tight Little Island). Kind Hearts and Coronets. 1950: Le passe-muraille (US: Mr Peek-a-Boo). 1951: Flesh and Blood. Young Wives' Tale. The Man in the White Suit. 1952: The Importance of Being Earnest. 1954: Knave of Hearts (US: Lovers, Happy Lovers). Father Brown ((US: The Detective). 1955: Moonfleet. 1958: Stage Struck. 1962: Mysterious Island. The Amorous Prawn. 1963: Tom Jones. The Moon-Spinners. 1971: Girl Stroke Boy. 1977: The Uncanny. The Hound of the Baskervilles. 1978: The Water Babies. 1979: The Flame is Love (TV). 1984: Ellis Island (TV mini-series shortened for cinema). 1987: Little Dorrit I. Little Dorrit II.

GREER, Jane (Bettejane Greer) 1924–
Strikingly pretty brunette American actress with chiselled features who recovered from Bell's palsy as a child to become a useful

actress who didn't get the breaks to make her a top star. Could be warm and sympathetic or cold and calculating: it was in the latter vein that she did her best film work, at her first studio, RKO, where she had become one of Howard Hughes' protégées in 1943. Married to Rudy Vallee (first of two) 1943–1944.
1945: †Two O'Clock Courage. †Pan-Americana. †George White's Scandals. Dick Tracy (GB: Split Face). 1946: The Falcon's Alibi. The Bamboo Blonde. Sunset Pass. 1947: Sinbad the Sailor. They Won't Believe Me. Out of the Past (GB: Build My Gallows High). 1948: Station West. 1949: The Big Steal. 1950: USS Teakettle (later You're in the Navy Now). 1951: The Company She Keeps. 1952: You for Me. The Prisoner of Zenda. Desperate Search. 1953: The Clown. Down Among the Sheltering Palms. 1955: One Man Missing (TV). 1956: Run for the Sun. 1957: Man of a Thousand Faces. 1958: No Time At All (TV). 1964: Where Love Has Gone. 1965: Billie. 1973: The Outfit. 1982: The Shadow Riders (TV). 1983: Against All Odds. 1986: Something in Common (TV). Just Between Friends. 1990: Immediate Family. 1996: Perfect Mate.

†As Bettejane Greer

GREGSON, John 1919–1975
Diffident, well-liked British star of Irish background, with dark curly hair. Eventually succeeded, after some initial tough times, as shy young heroes with steely inner cores. His film career faded after ten good years, but he found new popularity as a top cop in the succesful TV series *Gideon's Way*. Married for nearly 30 years until his death (from a heart attack) to actress Thea Gregory (1929–).
1948: Saraband for Dead Lovers (US: Saraband). London Belongs to Me (US: Dulcimer Street). Scott of the Antarctic. 1949: The Hasty Heart. Whisky Galore! (US: Tight Little Island). Train of Events. 1950: Treasure Island. Cairo Road. 1951: The Lavender Hill Mob. Angels One Five. 1952: The Brave Don't Cry. The Holly and the Ivy. Venetian Bird (US: The Assassin). 1953: The Titfield Thunderbolt. Genevieve. The Weak and the Wicked (US: Young and Willing). 1954: The Crowded Day. Conflict of Wings. To Dorothy a Son (US: Cash on Delivery). 1955: Above Us the Waves. Three Cases of Murder. Value for Money. 1956: Jacqueline. The Battle of the River Plate (US: Pursuit of the Graf Spee).

True As a Turtle. 1957: Miracle in Soho. 1958: Rooney. Sea of Sand (US: Desert Patrol). The Captain's Table. 1959: SOS Pacific. 1960: Faces in the Dark. Flight from Treason. Hand in Hand. 1961: The Treasure of Monte Cristo (US: The Secrets of Monte Cristo). The Frightened City. 1962: Live Now – Pay Later. Tomorrow at Ten. The Longest Day. 1963: Anatomy of a Disaster (narrator only). 1964: The Yellow Golliwogs. 1966: The Night of the Generals. 1970: 70 Years On (narrator only). 1971: Fright. 1975: The Tiger Lily.

GREY, Anne (Aileen Ewing) 1907–
Tall, dark-haired British actress – a former journalist – with upper-class, Penelope Keith-type looks. Tremendously popular in the early days of sound, she was often cast in aristocratic roles, sometimes as girls of independent spirit, sometimes as 'other women'. Married Lester Matthews (1900–1975) in 1931, and went with him to Hollywood in 1935, making a few films there. Returned to England when the marriage broke up, but could not regain her place in the front rank, and surprisingly did not have a second career as a character player.
1927: The Constant Nymph. 1928: What Money Can Buy. The Warning. Master and Man. 1929: Taxi for Two. The Nipper/The Brat. 1930: The Squeaker. Crossroads. The School for Scandal. Guilt. 1931: The Man at Six (US: The Gables Mystery). Other People's Sins. The Calendar (US: Bachelor's Folly). The Happy Ending. The Old Man. 1932: Murder at Covent Garden. Lily Christine. The Faithful Heart (US: Faithful Hearts). Number Seventeen. Arms and the Man. Leap Year. 1933: She Was Only a Village Maiden. One Precious Year. The Lost Chord. The Golden Cage. The Blarney Stone (US: The Blarney Kiss). The Lure. The Fire Raisers. Just Smith (US: Leave It to Smith). The Wandering Jew. Colonel Blood. The House of Trent. 1934: Borrowed Clothes. The Scoop. Lady in Danger. Road House. The Poisoned Diamond. 1935: Bonnie Scotland. Break of Hearts. 1936: Just My Luck. Too Many Parents. 1937: Dr Sin Fang. 1938: Chinatown Nights.

GREY, Nan (Eschal Miller).1918–1993
Bright, vivacious, Texas-born blonde, kept busy at Universal during her six-year contract with them. Her fresh, breezy personality was seen to best advantage in light roles, such as one of Deanna Durbin's sisters in the *Three*

Smart Girls films. Too often, though, the studio cast her as troubled women and, without an established image she quickly vanished from films once gone from Universal. She came back into the headlines when marrying (second) singer Frankie Laine (*qv*) in 1950. She died on her 75th birthday of natural causes.

1934: *The Firebird. Babbitt.* 1935: *Mary Jane's Pa (GB: Wanderlust). His Night Out. The Great Impersonation. The Affair of Susan.* 1936: *Next Time We Love (GB: Next Time We Live). Dracula's Daughter. Sutter's Gold. Crash Donovan. The Sea Spoilers. Three Smart Girls.* 1937: *Let Them Live! Love in a Bungalow. The Man in Blue. Some Blondes Are Dangerous.* 1938: *The Jury's Secret. The Black Doll. The Storm. Reckless Living. Danger on the Air. Girls' School.* 1939: *Three Smart Girls Grow Up. The Under-Pup. Ex-Champ (GB: Golden Gloves). Tower of London.* 1940: *The Invisible Man Returns. The House of the Seven Gables. Sandy is a Lady. You're Not So Tough. A Little Bit of Heaven. Margie.* 1941: *Under Age.*

GREY, Virginia 1917–
Pretty in a pinched, anguished-looking way, this gentle-mannered, soft-haired American blonde was one of Hollywood's most durable actresses, with a career extending over 40 years, during which time she was a perennial juvenile lead supporting the stars, with one or two better leading roles, although in minor films, in the late forties and early fifties. Long romantically involved with Clark Gable, she lost him to Carole Lombard, and has never married.

1927: *Uncle Tom's Cabin.* 1928: *Heart to Heart. Jazz Mad. The Michigan Kid.* 1931:

Misbehaving Ladies. 1933: *Secrets.* 1934: *Dames. The Firebird. St Louis Kid (GB: A Perfect Weekend).* 1935: *She Gets Her Man. Gold Diggers of 1935.* 1936: *Old Hutch. The Great Ziegfeld. Secret Valley (GB: The Gangster's Bride). *Violets in Spring.* 1937: *Bad Guy. Rosalie.* 1938: *Test Pilot. Dramatic School. *The Canary Comes Across. Shopworn Angel. Youth Takes a Fling. Ladies in Distress. Rich Man, Poor Girl.* 1939: *Thunder Afloat. Broadway Serenade. The Hardys Ride High. Idiot's Delight. The Women. Another Thin Man.* 1940: *Three Cheers for the Irish. The Captain is a Lady. Hullaballoo. The Golden Fleecing.* 1941: *Blonde Inspiration. Keeping Company. Washington Melodrama. The Big Store. Mr and Mrs North. Whistling in the Dark.* 1942: *Tish. Grand Central Murder. Bells of Capistrano. Tarzan's New York Adventure.* 1943: *Idaho. Sweet Rosie O'Grady. Secrets of the Underground. Stage Door Canteen.* 1944: *Strangers in the Night.* 1945: *Blonde Ransom. Flame of the Barbary Coast. Grissly's Millions. The Men in her Diary.* 1946: *Smooth as Silk. Swamp Fire. House of Horrors (GB: Joan Medford is Missing).* 1947: *Unconquered. Wyoming. Glamour Girl (GB: Night Club Girl).* 1948: *So This is New York. Miraculous Journey. Mexican Hayride. When My Baby Smiles at Me. Unknown Island. Who Killed 'Doc' Robbin? (GB: Sinister House). Leather Gloves (GB: Loser Take All).* 1949: *Jungle Jim. The Threat.* 1950: *Highway 301.* 1951: *The Bullfighter and the Lady. Three Desperate Men. Slaughter Trail.* 1952: *Desert Pursuit. The Fighting Lawman.* 1953: *Captain Scarface. A Perilous Journey. Hurricane at Pilgrim Hill.* 1954: *The Forty-Niners. Target Earth.* 1955: *The Eternal Sea. The Last Command. All That Heaven Allows.* 1956: *The Rose Tattoo. Accused of Murder.* 1957: *Crime of Passion. Jeanne Eagels.* 1958: *The Great Gatsby (TV). The Restless Years (GB: The Wonderful Years).* 1959: *No Name on the Bullet.* 1960: *Portrait in Black.* 1961: *Tammy Tell Me True. Bachelor in Paradise. Back Street.* 1963: *Black Zoo.* 1964: *The Naked Kiss. Love Has Many Faces.* 1966: *Madame X.* 1968: *Rosie!* 1969: *Airport.* 1975: *The Lives of Jenny Dolan (TV).*

GRIER, Pam 1949–
Tall, big-busted, straight-backed American actress with challenging gaze and often the hint of a cynical smile. One of four upwardly mobile children of an US Air Force mechanic – her cousin is football star Roosevelt 'Rosey'

Grier, who also made a few films – she gained a foothold in films on the strength of her spectacular figure, but soon attained minor cult stature in violent blaxploitation action films such as *Friday Foster* and *Foxy Brown*. Diagnosed with cancer in 1988 and given 18 months to live, she was in fairly minor roles through the 1980s, but made a triumphant comeback in such box-office hits as *Original Gangstas* and *Jackie Brown*. Never married.

1970: *Beyond the Valley of the Dolls.* 1971: *The Big Doll House. The Big Bird Cage. Women in Cages.* 1972: *Black Mama, White Mama/Women in Chains. Hit Man. Cool Breeze. Twilight People.* 1973: *Coffy. The Arena. Scream, Blacula, Scream.* 1974: *Foxy Brown.* 1975: *Sheba, Baby. Bucktown. Friday Foster.* 1976: *Drum.* 1977: *Greased Lightning. The Night of the High Tide.* 1981: *Fort Apache, The Bronx.* 1982: *Tough Enough/ Tough Dreams.* 1983: *Something Wicked This Way Comes.* 1985: *Stand Alone. On the Edge.* 1986: *Badge of the Assassin (TV). The Vindicator.* 1987: *The Allnighter.* 1988: *Above the Law (GB: Nico).* 1989: *The Package. Class of 1999.* 1991: *Bill and Ted's Bogus Journey.* 1992: *A Mother's Right: The Elizabeth Morgan Story (TV. GB: Shattered Silence).* 1993: *Posse.* 1995: *Serial Killer.* 1996: *Escape from L.A. Original Gangstas/ Hot City. Mars Attacks!* 1997: *Fakin' Da Funk. Woo. Jackie Brown. Strip Search.* 1998: *No Tomorrow.* 1999: *Holy Smoke. Fortress 2. In Too Deep. Jawbreaker. Hayley Wagner, Star (TV). LaVyrle Spencer's Family Blessings (TV).* 2000: *Snow Day.*

GRIFFITH, Andy 1926–
Slow-drawling, light-haired, large-faced, solidly-built American actor and entertainer who made a major impression in his first film role but was thereafter most successful on television, where his 'country-boy' wit and sly charm made him a favourite with his own show from 1960 to 1971, one of the longest runs on record. Later he appeared in a few TV movies as redneck, but warm-hearted sheriffs, preserving his star status well into his sixties with a hit TV series, *Matlock*.

1957: *A Face in the Crowd.* 1958: *No Time for Sergeants. The Male Animal (TV). Onion-head.* 1961: *The Second Time Around.* 1969: *Angel in My Pocket.* 1972: *The Strangers in 7A (TV).* 1973: *Winter Kill (TV).* 1975: *Hearts of the West (GB: Hollywood Cowboy). Adams of Eagle Lake (TV).* 1976: *The Girl in the Empty Grave (TV).* 1977: *The Deadly Game*

(TV). 1978: Salvage-1 (TV). 1981: Murder in Texas (TV). 1983: The Demon Murder Case (TV). Murder in Coweta County (TV). 1985: Rustler's Rhapsody. Crime of Innocence (TV). 1986: Diary of a Perfect Murder (TV). Return to Mayberry (TV). Under the Influence (TV). 1994: The Gift of Love (TV). 1995: Gramps (TV. GB: Lethal Intent). 1996: Spy Hard. 1998: Scattering Dad (TV). 1999: A Holiday Romance (TV). 2000: Daddy and Them.

GRIFFITH, Melanie 1957–

It was a tough road to the top for this bright, bouncy, breathy, round-cheeked blonde with the little girl voice, and a rocky one too. The daughter of Tippi Hedren (qv), and a self-confessed 'wild child' who ran off with her first husband-to-be when only 14, she finally cracked drink and drugs problems and 'started taking acting seriously at 27'. A mixture of secondary and leading roles followed, often brightened by her own brand of naïve vivacity, culminating in star billing in *Working Girl*, which won her an Oscar nomination. In the 1990s, however, she proved increasingly difficult to cast to advantage. Married/divorced actors Don Johnson and Steven Bauer. She remarried Johnson in 1989, but their films together were unsuccessful and the couple had parted again by 1995. Half-sister of actress Tracy Griffith. She married Spanish actor Antonio Banderas (qv) in 1996.

1969: Smith! 1974: Smile. 1975: The Drowning Pool. Night Moves. 1977: Joyride. One on One. 1978: Steel Cowboy (TV). Daddy, I Don't Like It Like This (TV). 1980: Underground Aces. 1981: Golden Gate (TV). She's in the Army Now (TV). Roar. 1983: Fear City. 1984: Body Double. 1985: Alfred Hitchcock Presents (TV). 1986: Something Wild. Cherry 2000 (released 1988). 1988: The Milagro Beanfield War. Stormy Monday. Working Girl. 1989: In the Spirit. 1990: The Bonfire of the Vanities. Pacific Heights. Women & Men: Stories of Seduction (TV). 1991: Paradise. 1992: Shining Through. Born Yesterday. A Stranger Among Us (GB: Close to Eden). 1994: Milk Money. Nobody's Fool. 1995: Two Much. Now and Then. Mulholland Falls. 1996: Lolita. 1997: Reasonable Doubt/Shadow of Doubt. 1998: Another Day in Paradise. Celebrity. 1999: Crazy in Alabama. RKO 281 (cable TV). 2000: Forever Lulu. Cecil B DeMented. Tart. Liuset haller mig sallskap (doc).

GRIFFITHS, Rachel 1968–

Tall, lithe, dark-haired Australian actress who entered films in her native country, caught the eye with an award-winning performance in *Muriel's Wedding*, and soon came into international demand with her ability to move seamlessly into localised British and American accents. At her best as warmly down-to-earth characters, she won an Academy Award nomination for her performance as the put-upon sister in *Hilary and Jackie*.

1993: Feds (TV). 1994: Muriel's Wedding. 1996: Jude. Cosi. To Have & to Hold. Children of the Revolution. 1997: Welcome to Woop Woop. My Best Friend's Wedding. My Son the Fanatic. 1998: Hilary and Jackie. Among Giants. Divorcing Jack. Since You've Been Gone (TV). Amy. 1999: Me Myself I. 2000: Adventures of Tom Thumb and Thumbelina (voice only). Never Better. Pavarotti in Dad's Room. Blow Dry.

As director. 1997: *Tulip.

GRODIN, Charles (C. Grodinsky) 1935–

Diffident, chubby, dark-haired American actor, good at light comedy and comedy-thrillers and seemingly on the verge of stardom in the mid 1970s. But it didn't quite happen and he later seemed content to lend his shuffling cynicism to backing up the stars of the film. A witty raconteur who seems to have found the secret of eternal youth, Grodin has also written screenplays and directed for the stage. He ran a successful talk show on TV in the mid 1990s.

1962/7: The Meanest Men in the West (TV. Shown in cinemas 1976). 1968: Rosemary's Baby. 1970: Sex and the College Girl

(completed 1964). Catch 22. 1973: The Heartbreak Kid. 1974: 11 Harrowhouse. 1976: King Kong. Thieves. 1978: The Grass is Always Greener Over the Septic Tank (TV). Just Me and You (TV). Heaven Can Wait. Sunburn. 1979: Real People/Real Life. 1980: The Incredible Shrinking Woman. It's My Turn. Seems Like Old Times. 1981: The Great Muppet Caper. 1983: The Lonely Guy. 1984: The Woman in Red. 1985: Movers and Shakers (Dreamers). Grown-Ups (TV). 1986: Last Resort. 1987: Ishtar. The Couch Trip. 1988: Midnight Run. You Can't Hurry Love. 1989: *Cranium Command. 1990: Taking Care of Business (GB: Filofax). 1991: Clifford. Beethoven. 1993: Dave. Heart and Souls. Beethoven's 2nd. So I Married an Axe Murderer. 1994: My Summer Story/It Runs in the Family.

GUINNESS, Sir Alec
(A. Guinness de Cuffe) 1914–2000

Fair-haired shy-looking, fresh-faced British actor who made his name as a man of many faces (most notably as eight brothers and sisters in *Kind Hearts and Coronets*), playing mainly lovable scoundrels in a brilliant run of Ealing comedies from the late forties to the late fifties. Later, he continued to tackle off-beat roles as a character star, winning an Oscar (and British Oscar) for *The Bridge on the River Kwai*. Knighted in 1959. Special Academy Award 1980. Received further Oscar nominations for *The Lavender Hill Mob*, *Star Wars* and *Little Dorrit*.

1934: Evensong (as extra). 1946: Great Expectations. 1948: Oliver Twist. 1949: Kind Hearts and Coronets. A Run for Your Money. 1950: Last Holiday. 1951: The Mudlark. The Lavender Hill Mob. The Man in the White Suit. The Card (US: The Promoter). 1953: The Captain's Paradise. Malta Story. 1954: Father Brown (US: The Detective). The Stratford Adventure. To Paris with Love. 1955: The Prisoner. *Rowlandson's England (narrator only). The Lady Killers. 1956: The Swan. 1957. The Bridge on the River Kwai. Barnacle Bill (US: All at Sea). 1958: The Horse's Mouth. 1959: The Scapegoat. Our Man in Havana. 1960: Tunes of Glory. 1961: A Majority of One. 1962: HMS Defiant (US: Damn the Defiant!). Lawrence of Arabia. 1963: The Fall of the Roman Empire. 1965: Situation Hopeless . . . but not serious. Doctor Zhivago. 1966: Hotel Paradiso. The Quiller Memorandum. 1967: The Comedians. 1970: Cromwell. Scrooge. 1972: Brother Sun, Sister

Moon. 1973: Hitler: the Last Ten Days. 1976: Murder by Death. 1977: Star Wars. 1980: The Empire Strikes Back. Raise the Titanic! 1981: Little Lord Fauntleroy. 1983: Lovesick. Return of the Jedi. 1984: A Passage to India. 1987: Little Dorrit I. Little Dorrit II. 1988: A Handful of Dust. 1991: Kafka. 1992: Tales from Hollywood (TV). 1993: A Foreign Field (TV. US: cinemas). 1994: Mute Witness.

GUTTENBERG, Steve 1958–

Well-built, ever-smiling, young-looking American actor with dark, curly hair. Worked his way up from messenger at an actors' agency, through bit parts in the late 1970s, to leading roles in the 1980s, most notably the parking-lot attendant who becomes a police cadet in the *Police Academy* films. His career disappointingly lost its direction in the 1990s.
1977: The Last Chance. Rollercoaster. The Chicken Chronicles. Something for Joey (TV). 1978: The Boys from Brazil. 1979: Players. 1980: Can't Stop the Music. To Race the Wind (TV). 1981: Miracle on Ice (TV). 1982: Diner. 1983: The Day After (TV). The Man Who Wasn't There. 1984: Police Academy. 1985: Police Academy 2: Their First Assignment. Cocoon. Bad Medicine. 1986: Short Circuit. Police Academy 3: Back in Training. Amazon Women on the Moon. 1987: Surrender. The Bedroom Window. Police Academy IV: Citizens on Patrol. 3 Men and a Baby. 1988: High Spirits. Cocoon: The Return. 1990: Don't Tell Her It's Me. 3 Men and a Little Lady. 1992: †Freddie Goes to Washington (voice only). The Magical World of Chuck Jones. 1995: The Big Green. Home for the Holidays. It Takes Two. 1996: Zeus and Roxanne. 1997: Overdrive (TV). Tower of Terror (TV). Casper: A Spirited Beginning (v). 1998: Airborne. 1999: Love & Fear. Home Team. 2001: PS Your Cat is Dead (and directed).

†Unfinished

GWENN, Edmund 1875–1959

Gnome-like Welsh-born character star, often in unsympathetic roles in his British films of the thirties. After some American films, he went permanently to Hollywood in 1940 with retirement vaguely in mind, but they would not hear of it, keeping him exuding testy benevolence as shepherds, scientists and scoundrels, winning a Best Supporting Oscar for his Kris Kringle in *Miracle on 34th Street* (1947), for another 15 years. Further Oscar-

nominated for *Mister 880*.
1916: *The Real Thing at Last. 1920: The Skin Game. Unmarried. 1930: How He Lied to Her Husband. 1931: Hindle Wakes. Money for Nothing. The Skin Game (remake). Frail Women. Condemned to Death. 1932: Love on Wheels. Tell Me Tonight (US: Be Mine Tonight). 1933: The Good Companions. Cash (US: For Love or Money). Early to Bed. I Was a Spy. Channel Crossing. Smithy. Friday the Thirteenth. Marooned. 1934: The Admiral's Secret. Passing Shadows. Waltzes from Vienna (US: Strauss's Great Waltz). Warn London. Java Head. Father and Son. Spring in the Air. 1935: The Bishop Misbehaves (GB: The Bishop's Misadventures). Sylvia Scarlett. 1936: Laburnum Grove. Anthony Adverse. The Walking Dead. All-American Chump (GB: Country Bumpkin). Mad Holiday. 1937: Parnell. South Riding. A Yank at Oxford. 1938: Penny Paradise. 1939: Cheer Boys Cheer. *Happy Families. An Englishman's Home (US: Madmen of Europe). 1940: The Doctor Takes a Wife. The Earl of Chicago. Pride and Prejudice. Foreign Correspondent. 1941: Charley's Aunt. Scotland Yard. Cheers for Miss Bishop. The Devil and Miss Jones. One Night in Lisbon. 1942: A Yank at Eton. *The Greatest Gift. The Meanest Man in the World. 1943: Forever and a Day. Lassie Come Home. 1944: Between Two Worlds. The Keys of the Kingdom. 1945: Bewitched. Dangerous Partners. She Went to the Races. 1946: Of Human Bondage. Undercurrent. 1947: Miracle on 34th Street (GB: The Big Heart). Thunder in the Valley (GB: Bob, Son of Battle). Green Dolphin Street. Life with Father. 1948: Apartment for Peggy. Hills of Home (GB: Master of Lassie). 1949: Challenge to Lassie. 1950: A Woman of Distinction. Mister 880. Pretty Baby. Louisa. For Heaven's Sake. 1951: Peking Express. 1952: Sally and Saint Anne. Bonzo Goes to College. Les Miserables. Something for the Birds. 1953: Mr Scoutmaster. The Bigamist. 1954: Them! The Student Prince. 1955: It's a Dog's Life. The Trouble with Harry. 1956: Calabuch (US: Rocket from Calabuch). 1957: The Greer Case (TV). Winter Dreams (TV).

GWYNNE, Anne

(Marguerite G. Trice) 1918–
The slightly startled look on the face of this willowy ex-model with strawberry-blonde hair and hazel eyes might be attributed to the medley of monsters Universal forced her to meet in the 1940s. She was mainly used as

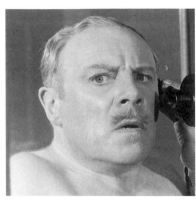

decoration in horror and outdoor films and a return to acting in the late 1960s after an absence of many years did not lead to any meatier roles.
1939: *Swimming Underwater. Charlie McCarthy, Detective. Flash Gordon Conquers the Universe (serial). Oklahoma Frontier. Unexpected Father (GB: Sandy Takes a Bow). The Big Guy. Little Accident. 1940: The Green Hornet (serial). Framed. Bad Man from Red Butte. Black Friday. Sandy is a Lady. Spring Parade. Man from Montreal. Give Us Wings. 1941: Honeymoon Deferred. Jailhouse Blues. The Black Cat. Nice Girl? Washington Melodrama. Give Us Wings. Tight Shoes. Ride 'Em Cowboy. Mob Town. Man Made Monster (GB: The Electric Man). 1942: The Strange Case of Dr RX. Melody Lane. Broadway. Men of Texas (GB: Men of Destiny). Don't Get Personal. Road Agent. *Keeping Fit. You're Telling Me. Sin Town. 1943: We've Never Been Licked (GB: Texas to Tokyo). Top Man. Frontier Bad Men. 1944: Weird Woman. Ladies Courageous. Moon over Las Vegas. South of Dixie. House of Frankenstein. 1945: I Ring Doorbells. Murder in the Blue Room. Babes on Swing Street. 1946: Fear. The Glass Alibi. 1947: The Ghost Goes Wild. Dick Tracy Meets Gruesome (GB: Dick Tracy's Amazing Adventure). Killer Dill. 1948: Panhandle. Arson Inc. 1949: The Enchanted Valley. 1950: The Blazing Sun. Call of the Klondike. 1951: **Dead Man's Voice. **The Man Who Wasn't There. **The Yellow Ticket. **The Innocent Lion. **The Bandaged Hand. **Where Time Stood Still. King of the Bullwhip. 1952: Breakdown. 1955: Phantom of the Jungle. 1957: Teenage Monster (GB: Meteor Monster). 1969: Adam at 6 a.m.

**US TV shorts shown in GB cinemas

GYNT, Greta

(Margrethe Woxholt) 1916–2000
Glamorous Norwegian blonde actress, on stage as teenager, and in British films from 1937, remaining a box-office attraction for 15 years (although her Hollywood chance came too late: she had lost her spark), even if prudes raised eyebrows at her high-flying high-society private life. Although her career lost some of its momentum in the fifties, she worked regularly until 1960. Especially good in strong bad-girl roles.
1934: †Sangen Till Henne. 1935: †It Happened in Paris. 1937: ††Boys Will Be Girls. The Road Back/Return of the Hero. The

Last Curtain. Second Best Bed. 1938: Sexton Blake and the Hooded Terror. The Last Barricade. 1939: Too Dangerous to Live. Dark Eyes of London (US: The Human Monster). The Arsenal Stadium Mystery. The Middle Watch. She Couldn't Say No. 1940: Two for Danger. Bulldog Sees It Through. Room for Two. Crook's Tour. 1941: The Common Touch. 1942: Tomorrow We Live (US: At Dawn We Die). It's That Man Again. 1944: Mr Emmanuel. 1946: London Town (US: My Heart Goes Crazy). 1947: Take My Life. Dear Murderer. Easy Money. 1948: The Calendar. Mr Perrin and Mr Traill. 1950: Shadow of the Eagle. 1951: Lucky Nick Cain (GB: I'll Get You for This). Soldiers Three. Whispering Smith Hits London (US: Whispering Smith versus Scotland Yard). 1952: I'm a Stranger. The Ringer. 1953: Three Steps in the Dark. 1954: Forbidden Cargo. Destination Milan. The Last Moment. Devil's Point (US: Devil's Harbor). 1955: *Dead on Time. See How They Run. Born for Trouble. The Blue Peter (US: Navy Heroes). 1956: Keep It Clean. My Wife's Family. 1957: Fortune is a Woman (US: She Played with Fire). Morning Call (US: The Strange Case of Dr Manning). 1959: The Crowning Touch. The Witness. 1960: Bluebeard's 10 Honeymoons. 1964: The Runaway.

†As Margrethe Woxholt ††As Greta Woxholt

H

1950: *King Solomon's Mines. Vendetta.* 1951: *Pickup. Girl on the Bridge.* 1952: *Strange Fascination.* 1953: *Thy Neighbor's Wife. One Girl's Confession.* 1954: *Bait. The Other Woman.* 1955: *Hold Back Tomorrow. The Tender Trap.* 1956: *Edge of Hell.* 1957: *Hit and Run. Paradise Alley* (released 1962). *Lizzie.* 1959: *Night of the Quarter Moon. Born to be Loved.*
As director: 1937: *Děvčata, nedějte se!* (co-directed). *Bíla Nemoc.* 1938: *Co se Šeptá.* 1939: *Our Combat.* 1951: *Pickup. Girl on the Bridge.* 1952: *Strange Fascination.* 1953: *Thy Neighbor's Wife. One Girl's Confession.* 1954: *Bait. The Other Woman.* 1955: *Hold Back Tomorrow.* 1956: *Edge of Hell.* 1957: *Hit and Run. Lizzie. Paradise Alley* (released 1962). 1959: *Night of the Quarter Moon. Born to be Loved.* 1967: *The Crazy Ones.*

HAAS, Hugo 1901–1968
One of the foremost figures of the Czech cinema in the thirties, Haas never quite recovered from having to leave his homeland when war threatened. Slow to settle in Hollywood, he became a stocky character actor with a guttural accent before writing and directing a series of tawdry moralizing dramas, most (although not all) of which deserved their critical hammering. Was preparing to return to his native land in 1968 when the Russians moved in. Died of heart failure or, as friends put it, 'of a broken heart'.
1925: *Jedenacte Přikazami. Z českych Mlynu.* 1930: *Kariera Pavla Camrdy. Když Struny Lkají.* 1931: *The Good Soldier Schweik. Obrácení Ferdyše Pištory. Muži v Offsidu. Načaderec, Král Kibicü.* 1932: *Sestra Angelika. Zapadlí Vlastenci.* 1933: *Žibot je Pes. Dům na Předměstí. Její Lékař. Madla z Gihelny. Okénko.* 1934: *Poslední muž Mazlicek.* 1935: *Ať žije Neboztík. Jedenácté Přikazání.* 1936: *Velbloud uchem jehly. Ulička v Raji. Švadlenka. Mravnost nade vše. Tri Muži ve Snehu.* 1937: *Kvocna. Tři Vejce do Skla. Děvčata, nedějte se! Bíla Nemoc.* 1938: *Andula Vyhrala. Svět Kde se Žebrá. Go se Šeptá.* 1939: *The Sea in Flames. Our Combat* (narrator). 1940: *Skeleton on Horseback. Documents secrets.* 1943: *Days of Glory.* 1944: *The Princess and the Pirate. Summer Storm. Mrs. Parkington. Strange Affair.* 1945: *A Bell for Adano. Dakota. Jealousy. What Next, Corporal Hargrove?* 1946: *Holiday in Mexico. Two Smart People.* 1947: *Northwest Outpost* (GB: *End of the Rainbow*). *The Foxes of Harrow. Fiesta. The Private Affairs of Bel Ami. Merton of the Movies.* 1948: *Casbah. My Girl Tisa. For the Love of Mary.* 1949: *The Fighting Kentuckian.*

HACKETT, Joan 1934–1983
Brunette American actress who, after years of success on Broadway, made her film debut as one of the girls in *The Group.* In subsequent movies she was normally seen as forthright, independent, strong-willed, unglamorous women; on the whole her screen roles, her character in *Will Penny* apart, were none too rewarding, and she remained primarily a Broadway star. Nominated for an Oscar in *Only When I Laugh.* At one time married to actor Richard Mulligan (1932–). She died from cancer.
1965: †*The Satan Bug.* 1966: *The Group.* 1967: *Will Penny.* 1968: *Assignment to Kill.* 1969: *Support Your Local Sheriff!* 1970: *How Awful About Allan* (TV). *The Other Man* (TV). *The Young Country* (TV). 1971: *Five Desperate Women* (TV). 1972: *The Rivals.* 1973: *The Last of Sheila. Class of 63* (TV). 1974: *Reflections of Murder* (TV). *The Terminal Man.* 1975: *Mackintosh and TJ.* 1976: *Treasure of Matecumbe.* 1977: *Stonestreet* (TV). 1978: *The Possessed* (TV). 1979: *Pleasure Cove* (TV). *Mr Mike's Mondo Video.* 1979: *The North Avenue Irregulars* (GB: *Hill's Angels*). 1980: *One Trick Pony. The Long Days of Summer* (TV). 1981: *Only When I Laugh* (GB: *It Hurts Only When I Laugh*). *The Long Summer of George Adams* (TV). 1982: *The Escape Artist. Paper Dolls* (TV). 1983: *Flicks* (released 1987).

†*Scenes deleted from final release print*

HACKMAN, Gene 1931–
Stocky, curly-haired American actor of unsettling personality who began to get featured roles in Hollywood after an Oscar nomination for *Bonnie and Clyde. The French Connection* (1971) – for which he is said to have been sixth choice but which won him an Oscar – jetted him to stardom and a variety of plum roles for the next four years. His career wavered after poor films in the late seventies but, after two years away, he returned and regained his prestige. Following further Oscar nominations for *I Never Sang for My Father* and *Mississippi Burning,* he won a Best Supporting Actor Oscar for *Unforgiven.* A Spencer Tracy for the modern generation, he has often played villains in recent times.
1961: *Mad Dog Coll.* 1964: *Lilith.* 1966: *Hawaii. Les espions. A Covenant with Death.* 1967: *Banning. First to Fight. Bonnie and Clyde.* 1968: *The Split. Riot. Shadow on the Land* (TV). 1969: *Downhill Racer. The Gypsy Moths. Marooned.* 1970: *I Never Sang for My Father.,* 1971: *Doctors' Wives. The Hunting Party. The French Connection.* 1972: *Cisco Pike. Prime Cut. The Poseidon Adventure.* 1973: *Scarecrow.* 1974: *The Conversation. Young Frankenstein. Zandy's Bride. Bite the Bullet.* 1975: *French Connection II* (GB: *French Connection No.2*). *Lucky Lady. Night Moves.* 1976: *The Domino Killings* (released 1978). 1977: *A Bridge Too Far. March or Die. A Look at Liv.* 1978: *Superman. Speed Fever.* 1980: *Superman II.* 1981: *All Night Long. Reds.* 1982: *Eureka.* 1983: *Misunderstood. Under Fire. Uncommon Valor. Two of a Kind* (voice only). 1985: *Twice in a Lifetime. Target.* 1986: *Power. Hoosiers* (GB: *Best Shot*). *Superman IV: The Quest for Peace.* 1987: *No Way Out. Split Decisions/Kid Gloves.* 1988: *Full Moon in Blue Water. Bat*21. Mississippi Burning. I banchieri di dio. Another Woman.* 1989: *Loose Cannons. The Package.* 1990: *Narrow Margin. Postcards from the Edge. Class Action.* 1991: *Company Business.* 1992: *Unforgiven.* 1993: *The Firm. Earth and the American Dream* (voice only). *Geronimo: An American Legend.* 1994: *Wyatt Earp.* 1995: *Crimson Tide. Get Shorty. The Quick and the Dead.* 1996: *The Birdcage. The Chamber. Extreme Measures.* 1997: *Absolute Power.* 1998: *Twilight. Enemy of the State. Antz* (voice only). 1999: *Hitchcock, Selznick and the End of Hollywood* (doc. Narrator only). *Under Suspicion.* 2000: *The Replacements.* 2001: *Pearl Harbor. The Heartbreakers.*

HAGEN, Jean (Jean Ver Hagen) 1923–1977
Bright, chirpy American blonde actress, equally at home in comedy and drama, although perhaps less happy with

sympathetic roles. Memorable both as the moll in *The Asphalt Jungle* and the squeaky-voiced silent film star in *Singin' in the Rain*, by which time she had become a sort of minor league Judy Holliday. Died from throat cancer. Oscar nominee for *Singin' in the Rain*.

1949: *Side Street. Adam's Rib.* 1950: *The Asphalt Jungle. Ambush. A Life of Her Own.* 1951: *Night into Morning. Shadow in the Sky. No Questions Asked.* 1952: *Singin' in the Rain. Carbine Williams.* 1953: *Arena. Half a Hero. Latin Lovers.* 1955: *The Big Knife.* 1957: *Spring Reunion.* 1959: *The Shaggy Dog.* 1960: *Sunrise at Campobello.* 1962: *Panic in Year Zero.* 1964: *Dead Ringer (GB: Dead Image).* 1977: *Alexander – The Other Side of Dawn (TV).*

HAGERTY, Julie 1955–
Wide-eyed, brown-haired, pencil-slim American actress, still best known as the stewardess from the *Airplane* films. A former model, she was born to a family of musicians, but studied acting for six years before making her debut with her brother's theatre group in New York's Greenwich Village. Best in roles whose inner steel belies her own outward fragility.

1979: *All That Jazz.* 1980: *Airplane! The Day the Women Got Even (TV).* 1982: *A Midsummer Night's Sex Comedy. Airplane II The Sequel.* 1984: *Goodbye New York.* 1985: *Lost in America. Bad Medicine.* 1987: *Beyond Therapy. Aria.* 1988: *Bloodhounds of Broadway.* 1989: *Rude Awakening.* 1990: *Reversal of Fortune.* 1991: *What About Bob?* 1992: *Noises Off.* 1994: *The Wife.* 1996: *Neil Simon's London Suite (TV).* 1997: *U-Turn/Stray Dogs. Boys Will Be Boys (TV).* 1999: *The Story of Us. Mel. Jackie's Back! (TV). Gut Feeling.* 2000: *Held Up.*

HAGMAN, Larry (L. Hageman) 1931–
Wry, dark-haired American actor with large face and small eyes, the son of Mary Martin (*qv*) by her first marriage. In TV programmes as a teenager, he looked at first the natural successor to such actors as Tony Randall (*qv*). He had a good running role in the TV comedy series *I Dream of Jeannie* from 1965 to 1969, but never really made his mark in show business until asked to play the abominable JR in TV's *Dallas*, a persona with which he remained synonymous from 1978 to 1991. He underwent a liver transplant in 1995.

1958: *The Member of the Wedding (TV).* 1960: *Once Around the Block (TV).* 1964: *Ensign Pulver. Fail Safe.* 1965: *In Harm's Way.* 1966: *The Group. The Cavern.* 1969: *Three's a Crowd (TV).* 1970: *Up in the Cellar (GB: Three in the Cellar).* 1971: ††*The Hired Hand.* †*Beware! The Blob (GB: Son of Blob). Vanished (TV). Triple Play (TV). A Howling in the Woods (TV).* 1972: *Getting Away From It All (TV). No Place to Run (TV).* 1973: *The Alpha Caper (TV. GB: cinemas, as Inside Job). Blood Sport (TV). What Are Best Friends For? (TV). Antonio.* 1974: *Sidekicks (TV). Hurricane (TV). Stardust. Harry and Tonto. Mother, Jugs and Speed (released 1976).* 1975: *Sara T: Portrait of a Teenage Alcoholic (TV). The Big Ripoff (TV). The Big Bus. The Eagle Has Landed. Crash. The Return of the World's Greatest Detective (TV).* 1977: *Intimate Strangers (TV).* 1978: *The President's Mistress (TV). Superman. Last of the Good Guys (TV).* 1981: *SOB: Deadly Encounter (TV).* 1992: *Dead Perfect.* 1993: *Staying Afloat (TV).* 1995: *Nixon.* 1996: *Dallas: J R Returns (TV).* 1997: *Orleans (TV).* 1998: *Primary Colors. Dallas: War of the Ewings (TV).*

†*Also directed*
††*Scene deleted: seen in some TV prints*

HALE, Barbara 1921–
Glamorous brunette American star of cheerful and friendly manner who gave some solid performances in juicy roles towards the end of the forties after a small-parts start via the model and beauty queen route. Her looks became motherly rather early (like Rosemary DeCamp), but she found a successful second career as Della Street in the long-running *Perry Mason* series on TV from 1957 to 1965, for which she won an Emmy award in 1959. Married to Bill Williams (*qv*) from 1946. Mother of William Katt (1950–).

1943: *Gildersleeve's Bad Day. Higher and Higher. The Seventh Victim. Mexican Spitfire's Blessed Event. The Iron Major. Gildersleeve on Broadway. Government Girl. Around the World.* 1944: *Goin' to Town.* **Prunes and Politics. Heavenly Days. The Falcon Out West. The Falcon in Hollywood. Belle of the Yukon.* 1945: *West of the Pecos. First Yank into Tokyo (GB: Mask of Fury).* 1946: *Lady Luck.* 1947: *A Likely Story.* 1948: *The Boy with Green Hair.* 1949: *The Clay Pigeon. The Window. Jolson Sings Again.* 1950: *And Baby Makes Three. The Jackpot. Emergency Wedding (GB: Jealousy).* 1951: *Lorna Doone. The First Time.* 1952: *Last of the Comanches (GB: The Sabre and the Arrow).* 1953: *Seminole. Lone Hand. A Lion is in the Streets.* 1955: *Unchained. The Far Horizons. The Country Husband (TV. GB: cinemas).* 1956: *7th Cavalry. The Houston Story.* 1957: *The Oklahoman. Slim Carter.* 1958: *Desert Hell.* 1968: *Buckskin.* 1969: *Airport.* 1971: *Soul Soldier (GB: Men of the Tenth).* 1975: *The Giant Spider Invasion.* 1978: *Big Wednesday.* 1985: *Perry Mason Returns (TV).* 1986: *Perry Mason: The Case of the Notorious Nun (TV). Perry Mason: The Case of the Shooting Star (TV).* 1987: *Perry Mason: The Case of the Lost Love (TV). Perry Mason: The Case of the Scandalous Scoundrel (TV). Perry Mason: The Case of the Sinister Spirit (TV).* 1988: *Perry Mason: The Case of the Avenging Ace (TV). Perry Mason: The Case of the Lady in the Lake (TV).* 1989: *Perry Mason: The Case of the Lethal Lesson (TV). Perry Mason: The Case of the Murder Mystery Murder (TV). Perry Mason: The Case of the Sudden Death Play-Off (TV). Perry Mason: The Case of the All-Star Assassin (TV). Perry Mason: The Case of the Musical Murder.* 1990: *Perry Mason: The Case of the Defiant Daughter (TV). Perry Mason: The Case of the Silenced Singer (TV). Perry Mason: The Case of the Paris Paradox (TV).* 1991: *Perry Mason: The Case of the Ruthless Reporter (TV). Perry Mason: The Case of the Glass Coffin (TV).* 1992: *Perry Mason: The Case of the Fatal Framing (TV). Perry Mason: The Case of the Heartbroken Bride (TV). Perry Mason: The Case of the Poisoned Pen (TV). Perry Mason: The Case of the Maligned Mobster (TV).* 1993: *Perry Mason: The Case of the Reckless Romeo (TV). Perry Mason: The Case of the Skin Deep Scandal (TV). Perry Mason: The Case of the Telltale Talk Show Host (TV). Perry Mason: The Case of the Killer Kiss (TV). Perry Mason: The Case of the Wicked Wives (TV).*

1994: The Case of the Lethal Lifestyle (TV). The Case of the Grimacing Governor (TV). 1995: The Case of the Jealous Jokester (TV).

HALE, Sonnie
(John Robert Hale Monro) 1902–1959

It seems hard to understand now that Britain's small, bespectacled, owlish-looking Sonnie Hale not only had legions of followers as a romantic leading man but wooed and won two of musical comedy's brightest and most beautiful stars. But he had and he did. He also possessed a ready wit, a gift for mimicry, could act and sing with equal facility and write as well. Married to Evelyn Laye from 1926 to 1930 and Jessie Matthews from 1931 to 1944. Died of myelofibrosis, a blood disease.

*1927: On with the Dance. *The Parting of the Ways. 1932: Happy Ever After. Tell Me Tonight (US: Be Mine Tonight). 1933: Friday the Thirteenth. Early to Bed. 1934: Evergreen. Wild Boy. Are You a Mason? My Song for You. My Heart is Calling. 1935: Marry the Girl. First a Girl. 1936: It's Love Again. 1938: The Gaunt Stranger (US: The Phantom Strikes). 1939: Let's Be Famous. 1944: Fiddlers Three. 1946: London Town (US: My Heart Goes Crazy).*

As director: *1937: Head over Heels (US: Head over Heels in Love). Gangway. 1938: Sailing Along.*

HALEY, Jack 1899–1979

Chunky, cheery, dark-haired American musical comedy star of hearty manner, mainly on vaudeville and stage, but quite popular in films from 1935–1945, especially after his performance as the Tin Man in *The Wizard of Oz*. Died from a heart attack.

*1927: Broadway Madness. 1930: *Harlequins. Follow Thru. *The 20th Amendment. 1932: *Sherlock's Home. *The Imperfect Lover. Redheads on Parade. 1933: *Then Came the Yawn. Sitting Pretty. *Wrongorilla. *Nothing But the Tooth. Mr Broadway. 1934: Here Comes the Groom. 1935: The Girl Friend. Coronado. Spring Tonic. 1936: Pigskin Parade (GB: The Harmony Parade). Poor Little Rich Girl. F-Man. Mister Cinderella. 1937: Wake Up and Live. Pick a Star. She Had to Eat. Danger – Love at Work. 1938: Rebecca of Sunnybrook Farm. Alexander's Ragtime Band. Hold That Co-Ed (GB: Hold That Girl). Thanks for Everything. 1939: The Wizard of Oz. 1941: Moon over Miami. Navy Blues. 1942: Beyond the Blue Horizon. 1943: Higher and Higher. 1944: One Body Too Many. Take It Big. 1945: George White's Sandals. People Are Funny. Scared Stiff. Sing Your Way Home. 1946: Vacation in Reno. 1949: Make Mine Laughs. 1958: No Time At All (TV). 1970: Norwood. 1972: Rolling Man (TV). 1977: New York, New York (reissue version only).*

HALL, Huntz (Henry Hall) 1920–1999

Long-faced, pop-eyed, thin-lipped, fair-haired American actor who sprang to prominence as one of the street kids in the stage and film versions of Dead End. Later became the gormless Satch of the Bowery Boys: he was the one who got the laughs while partner Leo Gorcey (qv) expressed exasperation. Hall stayed with the series until the bitter end, and continued working fairly regularly in character roles until the late 1970s. Died from heart failure.

*1937: *Swingtime in the Movies. Dead End. 1938: Crime School. Little Tough Guy. Angels with Dirty Faces. 1939: Hell's Kitchen. Call a Messenger. Angels Wash Their Faces. The Battle of City Hall. The Return of Doctor X. They Made Me a Criminal. The Dead End Kids on Dress Parade. Invisible Stripes. 1940: That Gang of Mine. Give Us Wings. You're Not So Tough. Gallant Sons. Boys of the City. East Side Kids. Angels with Broken Wings. Junior G-Men (serial). Pride of the Bowery (GB: Here We Go Again). 1941: Sea Raiders (serial). Hit the Road. Bowery Blitzkrieg (GB: Stand and Deliver). Zis Boom Bah. Spooks Run Wild. Mob Town. 1942: Junior Army. Private Buckaroo. Mr Wise Guy. Sunday Punch. Tough As They Come. Smart Alecks. 'Neath Brooklyn Bridge. Let's Get Tough. Junior G-Men of the Air (serial). 1943:*

Clancy Street Boys. Mug Town. Kid Dynamite. Mr Muggs Steps Out. Keep 'em Slugging. Ghosts on the Loose (GB: Ghosts in the Night). Follow the Leader. 1944: Block Busters. Bowery Champs. The Million Dollar Kid. 1945: Wonder Man. A Walk in the Sun. Bring on the Girls. Mr Muggs Rides Again. Live Wires. Docks of New York. Come Out Fighting. 1946: Mr Hex (GB: Pride of the Bowery). In Fast Company. Spook Busters. Bowery Bombshell. 1947: Hard-Boiled Mahoney. News Hounds (GB: News Hound). Pride of Broadway. Bowery Buckaroos. 1948: Jinx Money. Angels' Alley. Trouble Makers. Smuggler's Cove. 1949: Angels in Disguise. Fighting Fools. Master Minds. Hold That Baby. 1950: Blues Busters. Triple Trouble. Blonde Dynamite. Lucky Losers. 1951: Ghost Chasers. Bowery Battalion. Crazy over Horses. Let's Go Navy. 1952: Here Come the Marines. Hold That Line. No Holds Barred. Feudin' Fools. 1953: Jalopy. Loose in London. Clipped Wings. Private Eyes. 1954: Paris Playboys. The Bowery Boys Meet the Monsters. Jungle Gents. 1955: Bowery to Bagdad. High Society. Jail Busters. Spy Chasers. 1956: Dig That Uranium. Crashing Las Vegas. Hold that Hypnotist. Hot Shots. Fighting Trouble. 1957: Spook Chasers. Looking for Danger. Up in Smoke. 1958: In the Money. 1965: Second Fiddle to a Steel Guitar. 1967: Gentle Giant. 1969: The Phynx. 1971: Escape (TV). 1974: Herbie Rides Again. The Manchu Eagle Murder Caper Mystery. 1975: Won Ton Ton, the Dog Who Saved Hollywood. 1977: Valentino. 1979: Gas Pump Girls. 1982: The Escape Artist. 1984: The Ratings Game (TV). 1986: Cyclone. 1991: Auntie Lee's Meat Pies.*

HALL, Jon (Charles H. Locher) 1913–1979

The king of the Technicolor, if slightly tatty, eastern (and western) of the 1940s. Husky, dark-haired Hall probably blacked up to play South Sea islander or Arabian adventurer more times than any other Hollywood hero. When his waist thickened, like that of Johnny Weissmuller (qv), Hall, who was the son of Swiss-born character actor Felix Locher (1882–1969), forsook films to devote more time to photography. Married to Frances Langford (1938 to 1955) and Raquel Torres (1959–), second and third of three. After being bedridden for nine months following surgery for bladder cancer, Hall shot himself.

1935: †Here's to Romance. †Women Must Dress. †Charlie Chan in Shanghai. 1936: †The Lion Man. †Winds of the Wasteland. †The

Clutching Hand (serial). †*The Mysterious Avenger.* ††*Mind Your Own Business.* 1937: ††*Girl from Scotland Yard. The Hurricane.* 1940: *South of Pago Pago. Sailor's Lady. Kit Carson.* 1941: *Aloma of the South Seas.* 1942: *The Tuttles of Tahiti. Eagle Squadron. Invisible Agent. Arabian Nights.* 1943: *White Savage (GB: White Captive). Ali Baba and the Forty Thieves.* 1944: *Lady in the Dark. Cobra Woman. Gypsy Wildcat. The Invisible Man's Revenge. San Diego, I Love You.* 1945: *Men in Her Diary. Sudan.* 1947: *Last of the Redmen (GB: Last of the Redskins). The Michigan Kid. The Vigilantes Return (GB: The Return of the Vigilantes).* 1948: *The Prince of Thieves.* 1949: *Zamba (GB: Zamba the Gorilla). The Mutineers. Deputy Marshal.* 1950: *On the Isle of Samoa.* 1951: *When the Redskins Rode. China Corsair. Hurricane Island.* 1952: *Brave Warrior. Last Train from Bombay.* 1953: *White Goddess (GB: Ramar of the Jungle). Eyes of the Jungle (GB: Destination Danger).* 1955: *Phantom of the Jungle. Thunder over Sangoland.* 1957: *Hell Ship Mutiny.* 1958: *Forbidden Island.* 1965: ***The Beachgirls and the Monster/Monster from the Surf.*

†*As Charles Locher* ††*As Lloyd Crane*
**Also directed

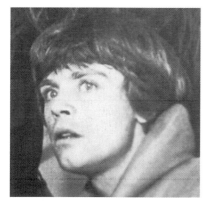

HAMILL, Mark 1951–
Fair-haired, blue-eyed, baby-faced, pocket-sized, energetic American actor who shot to stardom in his first cinema role, as the hero of *Star Wars*, but found a good range of roles hard to come by. Before that, he had been acting since 1969, his light voice gaining him much employment in voice-overs for TV cartoon series. In the 1980s he turned to the stage with noteworthy personal success. His facial features considerably changed by a disfiguring car accident, he returned to film-making in earnest in the 1990s.
1975: *Delancey Street (TV). Mallory (TV). Eric (TV). Sara T: Portrait of a Teenage Alcoholic (TV).* 1977: *Wizards (voice only). The City (TV). Star Wars.* 1978: *Corvette Summer (GB: The Hot One).* 1979: *Samuel Fuller and The Big Red One.* 1980: *The Big Red One. The Empire Strikes Back.* 1981: *The Night the Lights Went Out in Georgia.* 1982: *Britannia Hospital.* 1983: *The Return of the Jedi.* 1988: *The Avalon Awakening.* 1989: *Slipstream.* 1990: *Midnight Ride. Black Magic Woman.* 1991: *Wishman. The Guyver. Earth Angel (TV). Flash 2.* 1992: *In Exile. Time*

Runner. 1993: *Body Bags (TV). Batman: Mask of the Phantasm (voice only).* 1994: *Target Witness. Silk Degrees. The Raffle (released 1997). Wing Comander III: The Heart of the Tiger.* 1995: *Village of the Damned.* 1998: *Hamilton. Watchers Return. Laserhawk.* 1999: *Sinbad: Beyond the Veil of Mists (voice only). Wing Commander (voice only). Walking Across Egypt.*

HAMILTON, George 1939–
Dark, brooding, thick-lipped but extremely handsome American leading man who made a powerful start in his first two films, but was not well served for the remainder of his M-G-M days and had difficulty re-establishing himself as a top star until he hit the jackpot with *Love at First Bite* in 1979. For many years, since his 1975 divorce, he has remained one of Hollywood's most eligible bachelors.
1959: *Crime and Punishment USA.* 1960: *Home from the Hill. All the Fine Young Cannibals. Angel Baby.* 1961: *Where the Boys Are. By Love Possessed. A Thunder of Drums.* 1962: *The Light in the Piazza. Two Weeks in Another Town.* 1963: *The Victors. Act One.* 1964: *The Turncoat (TV). Looking for Love. Your Cheatin' Heart.* 1965: *Viva Maria!* 1966: *That Man George.* 1967: *Doctor, You've Got to be Kidding! The Power. A Time for Killing (GB: The Long Ride Home). Jack of Diamonds.* 1970: *Togetherness. Double Image.* 1972: *The Scorpio Scarab. Evel Knievel.* 1973: *The Man Who Loved Cat Dancing.* 1974: *Medusa. The Dead Won't Die (TV). Once is Not Enough.* 1977: *Sextette. The Happy Hooker Goes to Washington. The Strange Possession of Mrs Oliver (TV).* 1978: *Killer on Board (TV). The Users (TV). The Magnificent Hustle (TV). Institute for Revenge (TV). The Deadly Price of Paradise (TV) (GB: Nightmare at Pendragon's Castle).* 1979: *Supertrain (TV). Da Dunkerque alla vittoria (US: From Hell to Victory). Love at First Bite. The Seekers (TV). Death Car on the Freeway (TV).* 1980: *The Great Cash Getaway (TV).* 1981: *Zorro the Gay Blade.* 1985: *Two Fathers' Justice (TV).* 1986: *Monte Carlo (TV).* 1987: *Poker Alice (TV).* 1990: *Love at Second Bite. The Godfather Part III.* 1991: *Caution: Murder Can Be Hazardous to Your Health (TV). Doc Hollywood. Once Upon a Crime.* 1992: *The House on Sycamore Street (TV).* 1993: *The Last Paesan. Amore! (TV).* 1994: *Double Dragon.* 1995: *Danielle Steel's Vanished (TV).*

Playback. 1996: *Hart to Hart: Till Death Us Do Hart (TV).* 1997: *Meet Wally Sparks. 8 Heads in a Duffel Bag. Rough Riders (TV). The Guilt.* 1998: *Casper Meets Wendy (TV). She's Too Tall. Bulworth.* 1999: *P T Barnum (TV).* 2000: *Pets.* 2001: *Off Key.*

HAMILTON, Linda 1956–
Determined-looking American actress of curly blonde hair and tough femininity, often in roles that call equally for tenderness and resolution. Never quite an 'A' list star, she's best-known as Sarah Conner from the *Terminator* films and for her running role in the popular TV series *Beauty and the Beast*. Married/divorced actor Bruce Abbott and director James Cameron. One of identical twins.
1980: *Reunion (TV).* 1991: *Rape and Marriage: The Rideout Case (TV).* 1982: *Country Gold (TV). Tag: The Assassination Game (TV).* 1983: *Secrets of a Mother and Daughter (TV).* 1984: *The Stone Boy. The Terminator. Children of the Corn.* 1985: *Secret Weapons (TV).* 1986: *Black Moon Rising. King Kong Lives! Club Med (TV).* 1987: *Beauty and the Beast (TV).* 1988: *Go to the Light (TV. GB: Go Towards the Light).* 1989: *Beauty and the Beast: Though Lovers Be Lost (TV).* 1990: *Mr Destiny.* 1991: *Terminator 2: Judgment Day.* 1994: *Silent Fall.* 1995: *Separate Lives. The Way to Dusty Death (TV). A Mother's Prayer (TV).* 1996: *T2 3D: Battle Across Time. Shadow Conspiracy. Dante's Peak.* 1997: *Rescuers: Stories of Courage – Two Couples (TV).* 1998: *On the Line (TV). Point Last Seen (TV). Captured. The Color of Courage (TV).* 1999: *American Pie. The Secret Life of Girls (TV).* 2000: *Unglued. Sex & Mrs X.*

HAMILTON, Neil
(James N. Hamilton) 1899–1984
Stocky, light-haired, boyishly handsome American leading man, especially popular during the latter days of the silent era. Sincerity was his strong point, and his appeal was somewhat akin to a less intense Richard Barthelmess. He seemed to have made the transition to sound stardom, but lacked a definite image and from 1935 he was slipping. Retired in 1969. Died from asthmatic complications.
1918: *The Beloved Imposter.* 1919: *The Great Romance.* 1923: *The White Rose. America.* 1924: *The Side Show of Life. Isn't Life Wonderful?* 1925: *Men and Women. The Little*

French Girl. Street of Forgotten Men. New Brooms. The Golden Princess. The Splendid Crime. 1926: Desert Gold. Beau Geste. Diplomacy. The Great Gatsby. The Music Maker/The Music Master. 1927: 10 Modern Commandments. The Joy Girl. The Spotlight. Shield of Honor. Mother Machree. 1928: The Showdown. Something Always Happens. Don't Marry. The Grip of the Yukon. Hot News. The Patriot. Take Me Home. Three Week-Ends. What a Night! 1929: Why Be Good? A Dangerous Woman. The Studio Murder Mystery. The Insidious Dr Fu Manchu (later The Mysterious Dr Fu Manchu). The Love Trap. Darkened Rooms. 1930: The Kibitzer (GB: Busybody). Anybody's Woman. The Cat Creeps. The Dawn Patrol. The New Adventures of Dr Fu Manchu (later The Return of Dr Fu Manchu). Ladies Must Play. The Widow from Chicago. Ex-Flame (GB: Mixed Doubles). 1931: The Command Performance. Strangers May Kiss. The Sin of Madelon Claudet (GB: The Lullaby). The Great Lover. Laughing Sinners. The Spy. This Modern Age. 1932: Tarzan the Ape Man. The Animal Kingdom (GB: The Woman in His House). Are You Listening? The Wet Parade. Payment Deferred. The Woman in Room 13. What Price Hollywood? Two Against the World. 1933: Terror Abroad. The World Gone Mad (GB: The Public Be Hanged). Ladies Must Love. The Silk Express. One Sunday Afternoon. As the Devil Commands. 1934: Once to Every Bachelor. One Exciting Adventure. Fugitive Lady. Tarzan and His Mate. Here Comes the Groom. Blind Date (GB: Her Sacrifice). By Your Leave. 1935: Keeper of the Bees. The Daring Young Man. 1936: Honeymoon Limited. Mutiny Ahead. Southern Roses. Everything in Life. You Must Get Married. Parisienne Life/La vie Parisienne. 1937: Mr Stringfellow Says No. Secret Lives (US: I Married a Spy). The Gang's All Here (US: The Amazing Mr Forrest). Portia on Trial (GB: The Trial of Portia Merriman). Lady Behave! 1938: Army Girl (GB: The Last of the Cavalry). The Hollywood Stadium Mystery/ The Stadium Murders. 1939: The Saint Strikes Back. 1940: Queen of the Mob. 1941: King of the Texas Rangers (serial). Father Takes A Wife. Federal Fugitives. Dangerous Lady. Look Who's Laughing. They Meet Again. 1942: Too Many Women. X Marks the Spot. The Lady is Willing. 1943: Secrets of the Underground. All by Myself. Bombardier. The Sky's the Limit. 1944: When Strangers Marry/Betrayed. Brewster's Millions. 1961: The Little Shepherd

of Kingdom Come. 1962: The Devil's Hand. 1964: The Patsy. Good Neighbor Sam. Strategy of Terror. 1965: The Family Jewels. 1966: Madame X. Batman. 1970: Which Way to the Front? (GB: Ja, Ja, Mein General! But Which Way to the Front?). Vanished (TV).

HAMLIN, Harry 1951–
Wavily black haired, powerfully built American actor of almost caricature Greek-style handsomeness, never mobile enough to become a big movie star but a king of TV series and TV movies. He's made around 20 TV movies to date, many of them, however, erotic thrillers with Hamlin's morose sex appeal given full play. Probably best remembered for his five-year stint as Michael Kuzak on the TV series *L.A. Law*. Married to actresses Nicollette Sheridan (second of three) and, currently, Lisa Rinna.
1978: Movie Movie. 1981: King of the Mountain. Clash of the Titans. 1982: Making Love. 1983: Blue Skies Again. 1985: Maxie. 1987: Laguna Heat (TV). 1988: Favorite Son (TV). 1989: Dinner At Eight (TV). 1990: Deceptions (TV). 1991: Deadly Intentions . . . Again? (TV). 1992: Deliver Them from Evil: The Taking of Alta View (TV). 1993: Under Investigation (TV). Poisoned by Love: The Kern County Murders (TV). Save Me. 1994: Ebbtide. In the Best Families: Marriage, Pride & Madness (TV). 1995: The Celluloid Closet. Her Deadly Rival (TV). 1996: Badge of Betrayal (TV). One Clean Move. 1997: Allie & Me. 1998: Frogs for Snakes. The Hunted (TV). Stranger in Town (TV). Like Father, Like Santa (TV). 1999: The Christmas Takeover (TV). Silent Predators (TV). Quarantine (TV). 2001: Perfume.

HAMMOND, Kay
(Dorothy Standing) 1909–1980
Glamorous, high-spirited English leading lady with a mass of blonde curls and an attractive, honeyed voice. Particularly effective in comedy, she was popular in British and American films of the early thirties, but won greater fame as a stage and (latterly) radio star. Her later career was dogged by ill-health, and she was forced to retire after a stroke that left her confined to a wheelchair. Daughter of Sir Guy Standing; mother of John Standing (1934–). Married to Sir John Clements (second of two) from 1946.
1929: The Trespasser. Her Private Affair. 1930: Abraham Lincoln. Children of Chance. 1931: Fascination. A Night in Montmartre.

Almost a Divorce. Out of the Blue. Carnival (US: Venetian Nights). The Third String. 1932: A Night Like This. Nine Till Six. Sally Bishop. Money Means Nothing. 1933: Yes, Madam. Sleeping Car. Britannia of Billingsgate. The Umbrella. Bitter Sweet. Racetrack. Double Harness. 1934: Eight Girls in a Boat. By-Pass to Happiness. 1936: Two on a Doorstep. 1941: Jeannie (US: Girl in Distress). 1945: Blithe Spirit. 1948: Call of the Blood. 1961: Five Golden Hours.

HAMPSHIRE, Susan 1937–
Blonde, sweet-faced English leading lady with tip-tilted nose and engaging smile. Throughout her career she has fought enthusiastically against typecasting in milk-and-water roles, winning her biggest audiences in television 'sagas' and becoming a highly-rated star in the seventies. Her lifelong struggle against dyslexia was detailed in her book *Susan's Story*, published in 1982. Married/divorced French director Pierre Granier-Deferre, first of two. Still an engaging presence on British stages.
1947: The Woman in the Hall. 1959: Expresso Bongo. Upstairs and Downstairs. Idle on Parade (US: Idol on Parade). 1961: During One Night. The Long Shadow. 1963: Night Must Fall. The Three Lives of Thomasina. 1964: Wonderful Life (US: Swingers' Paradise). 1965: Paris in August. 1966: The Fighting Prince of Donegal. 1967: The Trygon Factor. 1969: The Violent Enemy. Monte Carlo or Bust! (US: Those Daring Young Men in Their Jaunty Jalopies). David Copperfield (TV. GB: cinemas). 1971: Time for Loving. Baffled! Malpertuis (GB: The Legend of Doom House). 1972: Living Free. Roses rouges et piments verts (US: The Lonely Woman).

Neither the Sea Nor the Sand. 1973: Dr Jekyll and Mr Hyde (TV). 1976: Bang! 1980: Dick Turpin (GB: TV).

HANCOCK, Tony 1924–1968
Lugubrious, dark-haired British comedian with hangdog look, usually seen as aggressive, gullible, self-opinionated loafers. Riotously funny on radio and TV, he led a stormy, alcoholic private life. His intolerance of advice led him to fall fairly flat in films, and his career went downhill rapidly. Committed suicide by taking an overdose of pills.
1954: Orders Are Orders. 1961: The Rebel (US: Call Me Genius). 1962: The Punch and Judy Man. 1965: Those Magnificent Men in Their Flying Machines. 1966: The Wrong Box.

HANDLEY, Tommy 1894–1949
Round-faced British comedian with chorus boy looks and dark, boot-polish hair, who became the country's most popular entertainer in the war years with his radio show *ITMA*. His few films were nowhere near as successful, not capturing the zaniness of his humour. Died after a stroke.
*1928: *Pathe Pictorial No. 548. *Gaumont Mirror No. 94. 1930: Elstree Calling. 1933: *Making a Christmas Pudding. *A Tail of Tails (voice only). This is Paris! That Was!! (narrator only). 1934: *Hot Airman. 1936: *Leslie Jeffries and His Orchestra. 1937: *BBC Musicals No. 2. 1938: Two Men in a Box. 1942: It's That Man Again. 1943: Pictorial Revue of 1943. Time Flies. 1945: *Worker and Warfront Magazine. *Tommy Handley's Victory Song. 1946: *Tom Tom Topia. 1949: Scrapbook for 1933.*

HANKS, Tom 1956–
Tall, gangling American actor with dark, curly hair and clown's smile who soon proved himself the deftest light comedian thrown up by Hollywood since Cary Grant (*qv*), although he has recently tried dramatic roles more serious than those Grant essayed. A self-described 'happy guy', Hanks was praised for his performances in *Big* (an Oscar nomination) and *Punchline* (which showed his darker side). He became Hollywood's hottest box-office bet following back-to-back best actor Academy Awards (the first since Spencer Tracy, in 1937/8, to achieve the feat) for *Philadelphia* and *Forrest Gump*, marred only by his glutinous acceptance speeches. His enthusiasm is infectious in comedy and his forthright sincerity moving in drama. He married (second) actress Rita Wilson, his co-star in an earlier, less auspicious film, in 1988. He looked much older in his forties and took to playing heavier roles, one of which, in *Saving Private Ryan*, won him an additional Oscar nomination.
1980: He Knows You're Alone. 1982: Mazes and Monsters/Rona Jaffe's Mazes and Monsters (TV). 1984: Bachelor Party. Splash. 1985: Volunteers. The Man With One Red Shoe/Mischief. The Money Pit. 1986: Nothing in Common. Every Time We Say Goodbye. 1987: Dragnet. 1988: Big. Punchline. 1989: The 'burbs. Turner & Hooch. 1990: Joe vs the Volcano. The Bonfire of the Vanities. 1992: A League of Their Own. Tales from the Crypt (TV. And co-directed). Radio Flyer. 1993: Sleepless in Seattle. Philadelphia. Fallen Angels (TV. And co-directed). 1994: Forrest Gump. 1995: Apollo 13. The Celluloid Closet. Toy Story (voice only). 1996: †That Thing You Do. 1998: Saving Private Ryan. You've Got Mail. 1999: Toy Story 2 (voice only). 2000: The Green Mile. Cast Away.

†*And directed*

HANLEY, Jimmy 1918–1970
Cherubic, fair-haired British actor who began as a likeable teenage star, then blinked his way myopically through what seemed like dozens of boy-friends, cub reporters and other ranks for the next 20-odd years, before throwing it all up to don his spectacles as the genial, much-liked host of a TV advertising magazine and, later, radio shows. Died from cancer. Married (first of two) to Dinah Sheridan (*qv*) from 1942 to 1953. Their son Jeremy became a Member of Parliament.

Their daughter Jenny is an actress.
*1933: Red Wagon. 1934: Those Were the Days. Little Friend. 1935: Royal Cavalcade (US: Regal Cavalcade). Brown on Resolution/For Ever England (US: Born for Glory). Boys Will be Boys. The Tunnel (US: Transatlantic Tunnel). 1936: Landslide. 1937: Cotton Queen. Night Ride. 1938: Housemaster. Coming of Age. 1939: *Beyond Our Horizon. There Ain't No Justice! 1940: Gaslight (US: Angel Street). 1942: Salute John Citizen. 1943: The Gentle Sex. 1944: The Way Ahead (US: Immortal Battalion). Kiss the Bride Goodbye. Henry V. 1945: For You Alone. 29 Acacia Avenue (US: The Facts of Love). Murder in Reverse. 1946: The Captive Heart. 1947: Holiday Camp. Master of Bankdam. It Always Rains on Sunday. 1948: Here Come the Huggetts. It's Hard to Be Good. 1949: The Huggetts Abroad. Don't Ever Leave Me. Boys in Brown. The Blue Lamp. 1950: Room to Let. 1951: The Galloping Major. 1954: Radio Cab Murder. The Black Rider. 1955: The Deep Blue Sea. 1956: Satellite in the Sky. *Look This Way. 1968: The Lost Continent.*

HANNAH, Daryl 1960–
Long-limbed, narrow-faced, healthy-looking, slightly fretful blonde American actress, of sultry appeal in a fresh kind of way. Throughout the 1980s, she was in demand for offbeat, often outdoor roles that tended to emphasise her rangy physical charms, a period that included her playing a mermaid, a cave girl, a 'replicant' and an Irish ghost! Recently, though, in more subdued roles. Belying her oft-time bimbo image, she directed her first short film in 1992. She remains matrimonially elusive: several high-profile romances have all broken up. Sister of actress Page Hannah

(1964–). Took to modelling underwear in the late 1990s.
1978: *The Fury.* 1981: *Campsite Massacre/ The Final Terror/Three Blind Mice/ Carnivore. Hard Country.* 1982: *Blade Runner. Summer Lovers. Paper Dolls* (TV). 1983: *Reckless.* 1984: *The Pope of Greenwich Village. Splash.* 1985: *The Clan of the Cave Bear.* 1986: *Legal Eagles.* 1987: *Roxanne. Wall Street.* 1988: *High Spirits.* 1989: *Crimes and Misdemeanors. Steel Magnolias.* 1990: *Crazy People.* 1991: *At Play in the Fields of the Lord.* 1992: *Memoirs of an Invisible Man. Blade Runner The Director's Cut.* 1993: *Grumpy Old Men. Attack of the 50 Foot Woman* (cable TV. GB: cinemas). 1994: *The Little Rascals. A Hundred and One Nights.* 1995: *The Tie That Binds. Two Much. Grumpier Old Men.* 1997: *The Last Days of Frankie the Fly. The Gingerbread Man. The Real Blonde. The Last Don* (TV). 1998: *Hi-Life. Addams Family Reunion* (v). 1999: *My Favorite Martian. Speedway Junky. Tripwire. Rear Window* (TV). *Cord. Enemy of My Enemy.* 2000: *Dancing at the Blue Iguana. Cowboy Up/Hearts and Bones.*
As director: 1992: **Last Supper.*

HANNAH, John 1962–
Wry-faced, slightly built Scottish actor with dark curly hair. Once an electrician, he switched to acting at 21 and worked for nearly all Britain's leading repertory companies, hardly attracting film attention at all until his role as Simon Callow's partner in *Four Weddings and a Funeral.* After that, his sly delivery and considered under-acting propelled him into an interesting variety of leading roles.
1987: *Reasonable Force.* 1989: *Kleptophilia.* 1990: *Harbour Beat.* 1991: *Losers' Blues.* 1992: *Joan.* 1993: *Four Weddings and a Funeral.* 1994: *Milner* (TV). *Faith.* 1995: *Madagascar Skin. The Final Cut* (TV). 1996: *The Innocent Sleep. Truth or Dare* (TV). *Romance and Rejection.* 1997: *The James Gang. The Love Bug* (TV). *Sliding Doors. Resurrection Man.* 1998: *So This is Romance?* 1999: *The Mummy. The Intruder. The Hurricane.* 2000: *Circus. Pandemonium.* 2001: *Teeth. The Mummy Returns.*

HARDEN, Marcia Gay 1959–
Wide-mouthed, strong-chinned, very dark-haired American actress, of brittle personality but capable of playing both low comedy and high drama. Born in Japan, she remained a

stage actress until her thirties. Despite a good range of leading roles in the cinema, top stardom has eluded her, but she showed her mettle by stealing scenes in such otherwise dreary pictures as *Meet Joe Black*, and is capable of real warmth.
1990: *Kojak: None So Blind* (TV). *Miller's Crossing.* 1991: *Late for Dinner. In Broad Daylight* (TV). *Fever* (TV). 1992: *Used People.* 1994: *Crush* (completed 1992). *Safe Passage.* 1995: *The Spitfire Grill. Convict Cowboy* (cable TV). 1996: *The First Wives Club. Spy Hard. The Daytrippers. Far Harbor.* 1997: *Flubber. Path to Paradise: The Untold Story of the World Trade Center Bombing* (TV). 1998: *Desperate Measures. Meet Joe Black. Labor of Love* (TV). 1999: *Small Vices* (TV). *Curtain Call.* 2000: *Pollock. Space Cowboys. Gaudi Afternoon.* 2001: *Just Like Mona.*

HARDIN, Ty (Orson Hungerford, later legally changed) 1930–
Fair-haired, blue-eyed, clean-cut, beefy American actor who changed his name from Hungerford to Hardin (the 'Ty' is a boyhood nickname) and became the star of the television western series *Bronco* in the late 1950s and early 1960s. He never managed to impose a personality on his cinema roles and, after being briefly jailed for drug-trafficking in Spain in 1974, became a self-styled minister in 1979, touring America with Bible readings until he ceased active ministry in 1984. Married six times.
1958: †*As Young As We Are.* †*The Space Children.* †*I Married a Monster from Outer Space.* †*The Buccaneer.* 1959: *Last Train from Gun Hill.* 1961: *The Chapman Report.* 1962: *PT 109. Merrill's Marauders.* 1963: *Palm*

Springs Weekend. Wall of Noise. 1964: ††*Boudine. L'uomo della valle muledetta.* 1965: *Battle of the Bulge.* 1966: *Savage Pampas. Custer of the West.* 1967: *Berserk! Ragan/Devil's Angel. One Step to Hell* (US: *King of Africa*). *Bersaglio mobile* (GB and US: *Death on the Run*). 1970: *Sacramento. The Last Rampage/Last Train to Berlin.* 1971: *Acquasanta Joe. The Last Rebel.* 1973: *Vendetta at Dawn.* 1974: *Drums of Vengeance/ Drummer of Vengeance.* 1977: *Fire!* (TV. GB: cinemas). 1981: *Image of the Beast.* 1983: *Rooster: Spurs of Death!* 1985: *The Zoo Gang.* 1988: ††*The Peace Officer. Red River* (TV). 1989: *Bad Jim.* 1990: *Born Killer.* 1993: *Rescue Me.*

†*As Ty Hungerford*
††*Also directed*

HARDING, Ann
(Dorothy Gatley) 1901–1981
Stunning blue-eyed blonde, of genteel manner, good at suffering in thirties' soap operas. Her career suffered from type-casting, also from the fact that she moved over to 'mother' and character roles rather too early. Her throatily attractive voice, however, continued to be heard in the cinema until 1956, and on television until 1965, when she retired. Oscar nomination for *Holiday.*
1929: *Paris Bound. Her Private Affair. Condemned* (GB: *Condemned to Devil's Island*). 1930: *Girl of the Golden West. Holiday.* 1931: *East Lynne. Devotion.* 1932: *Prestige. Westward Passage. The Conquerors. The Animal Kingdom* (GB: *The Woman in His House*). 1933: *When Ladies Meet. Double Harness. Right to Romance. Gallant Lady.* 1934: *The Life of Vergie Winters. The Fountain.* 1935: *Enchanted April. The Flame Within. Peter Ibbetson. Biography of a Bachelor Girl.* 1936: *The Lady Consents. The Witness Chair.* 1937: *Love from a Stranger.* 1942: *Eyes in the Night.* 1943: *Mission to Moscow. North Star.* 1944: *Nine Girls. Janie.* 1945: *Those Endearing Young Charms.* 1946: *Janie Gets Married.* 1947: *Christmas Eve/ Sinners' Holiday. It Happened on Fifth Avenue.* 1950: *The Magnificent Yankee* (GB: *The Man with 30 Sons*). *Two Weeks with Love.* 1951: *The Unknown Man.* 1955: *The Late George Apley* (TV. GB: cinemas). 1956: *I've Lived Before. The Man in the Gray Flannel Suit. Strange Intruder.* 1957: *Young Man from Kentucky* (TV. GB: cinemas).

HARDY, Oliver (Norvell Hardy, later legally changed) 1892–1957
Tie-twiddling, camera-appealing, button-moustached, this ultra-courtly American comedian, the fat half of the Laurel and Hardy team, was in show business from the age of eight (he ran away to sing in a minstrel show). Now rated by many critics as highly as his partner – they teamed in 1927. Died after a stroke.
1913: *Outwitting Dad.* 1914: *Back to the Farm. Pins Are Lucky. The Soubrette and the Simp. The Smuggler's Daughter. The Female Cop. What He Forgot. Cupid's Target. Spaghetti and Lottery. Gus and the Anarchists. Shoddy the Tailor.* 1915: *The Paper Hanger's Helper. Spaghetti a la Mode. Charley's Aunt. Artists and Models. The Tramps. Prize Baby. An Expensive Visit. Cleaning Time. Mixed Flats. Safety Worst. Twin Sister. Baby. Who Stole the Doggies? A Lucky Strike. The New Butler. Matilda's Legacy. Her Choice. The Cannibal King. What a Cinch! The Dead Letter. Avenging Bill. The Haunted Hat. The Simp and the Sophomores. Babe's Schooldays. Ethel's Romeos. A Bungalow Bungle. Three Rings and a Goat. A Rheumatic Joint. Something in Her Eye. A Janitor's Joyful Job. Fatty's Fatal Fun. Ups and Downs. This Way Out. Chickens. A Frenzied Finance. Busted Hearts.* 1916: *He Went and Won. A Special Delivery. A Sticky Affair. Bungles' Rainy Day. The Try Out. One Two Many. Bungles Enforces the Law. The Serenade. Bungles' Elopement. Nerve and Gasoline. Bungles Lands a Job. Their Vacation. Mama's Boys. A Battle Royal. All for a Girl. Hired and Fired. What's Sauce for the Goose. The Brave Ones. The Water Cure. Thirty Days. Baby Doll. The Schemers. Sea Dogs. Hungry Hearts. Edison Bugg's Invention. Never Again. Better Halves. A Day at School. A Terrible Tragedy. Spaghetti. Aunt Bill. The Heroes. It Happened in Pikersville. Human Hounds. Dreamy Knights. Life Savers. Their Honeymoon. An Aerial Joyride. Side Tracked. Stranded. Love and Duty. Artistic Atmosphere. The Reformer. Royal Blood. The Candy Trail. A Precious Parcel. A Maid to Order. Twin Flats. A Warm Reception. Pipe Dreams. Mother's Child. Prize Winners. Ambitious Ethel. The Guilty One. He Winked and Won. Fat and Fickle. Boycotted Baby.* 1917: *Wanted – A Bad Man. The Other Girl. The Love Bugs. Lucky Dog. Back Stage. The Hero. Doughnuts. Cupid's Rival. The Villain. The Millionaire. A Mix-Up in Hearts. The Goat. The Genius. The Stranger. The Fly*

Cop. The Modiste. The Star Boarder. The Chief Cook. The Candy Kid. The Station Master. The Hobo. The Pest. The Prospector. The Bandmaster. 1918: *The Chef. Hello Trouble. Painless Love. The Slave. The Artist. The Barber. King Solomon. The Orderly. His Day Out. The Rogue. The Scholar. The Messenger. The Handy Man. Bright and Early. The Straight and Narrow. Playmates. Freckled Fish.* 1919: *Hop the Bellhop. Lions and Ladies. Mules and Mortgages. Tootsies and Tamales. Healthy and Happy. Flips and Flops. Yaps and Yokels. Mates and Models. Squabs and Squabbles. Bungs and Bunglers. Switches and Sweeties. Dames and Dentists.* 1920: *Maids and Muslin. Squeaks and Squawks. Fists and Fodder. Pals and Pugs. He Laughs Last. Springtime. The Decorator. His Jonah Day. The Back Yard.* 1921: *The Nuisance. The Bellhop. The Bakery. The Blizzard. The Tourist. The Fall Guy. The Sawmill. The Rent Collector.* 1922: *Golf. †Fortune's Masks. The Counter Jumper. †The Little Wildcat.* 1923: *†One Stolen Night. †Three Ages. †The King of the Wild Horses. No Wedding Bells. The Barnyard.* 1924: *†The Girl in the Limousine. Her Boy Friend. Kid Speed.* 1925: *Is Marriage the Bunk? Stick Around. Hop to It! †The Wizard of Oz. Isn't Life Terrible? Yes, Yes, Nanette. Enough to Do. Should Sailors Marry? †The Perfect Clown. †Stop, Look and Listen. Thundering Fleas.* 1926: *A Bankrupt Honeymoon. Madame Mystery. Say It With Babies. Long Fliv the King. †Gentle Cyclone. A Sea Dog's Tale. Along Came Auntie. Crazy Like a Fox. Bromo and Juliet. Be Your Age. 45 Minutes from Hollywood. The Nickel Hopper. Should Men Walk Home?* 1927: *Baby Brother. Why Girls Say No. The Honorable Mr Buggs. †No Man's Law. Crazy to Act. Fluttering Hearts. The Lighter That Failed. Love 'Em and Feed 'Em. Assistant Wives. Duck Soup. Slipping Wives. Love 'Em and Weep. Why Girls Love Sailors. The Rap. With Love and Hisses. Sugar Daddies. Sailors Beware. Call of the Cuckoos. The Second Hundred Years. Flying Elephants. Hats Off. Do Detectives Think? Putting Pants on Philip. Battle of the Century. Let George Do It.* 1928: *Barnum and Ringling Inc. Leave 'Em Laughing. The Finishing Touch. From Soup to Nuts. You're Darn Tootin' (GB: The Music Blasters). Their Purple Moment. Should Married Men Go Home? Early to Bed. Two Tars. Habeas Corpus. We Faw Down (GB: We Slip Up). Liberty.* 1929: *Wrong Again. That's My Wife. Big Business. Unaccustomed as We Are. Double Whoopee. Berth Marks. Men O' War. The Perfect Day. They Go Boom. Bacon Grabbers. The Hoose-Gow. †Hollywood Revue of 1929. Angora Love. The Night Owls.* 1930: *††Blotto. ††Brats. †The Rogue Song. ††Below Zero. ††Hog Wild. ††The Laurel and Hardy Murder Case. ††Another Fine Mess.* 1931: *††Be Big. ††Chickens Come Home. The Stolen Jools (GB: The Slippery Pearls). ††Laughing Gravy. Our Wife. †Pardon Us (GB: Jailbirds). Come Clean. One Good Turn. †††Beau Hunks (GB: Beau Chumps). On the Loose.* 1932: *Helpmates. Any Old Port. The Music Box. The Chimp. Scram. County Hospital. †Pack Up Your Troubles. Their First Mistake. Towed in a Hole.* 1933: *Twice Two. Me and My Pal. †Fra Diavolo/*

The Devil's Brother. The Midnight Patrol. Busy Bodies. Wild Poses. Dirty Work. †Sons of the Desert (GB: Fraternally Yours). Oliver the Eighth (GB: The Private Life of Oliver the Eighth). 1934: *†Hollywood Party. Going Bye Bye. Them Thar Hills. †Babes in Toyland. The Live Ghost. Tit for Tat.* 1935: *The Fixer-Uppers. Thicker Than Water. †Bonnie Scotland.* 1936: *†The Bohemian Girl. On the Wrong Trek. †Our Relations.* 1937: *†Way Out West. †Pick a Star.* 1938: *†Swiss Miss. †Block-Heads.* 1939: *†Zenobia (GB: Elephants Never Forget). †The Flying Deuces.* 1940: *†A Chump at Oxford. †Saps at Sea.* 1941: *†Great Guns.* 1942: *†A-Haunting We Will Go.* 1943: *Tree in a Test Tube. †Air Raid Wardens. †Jitterbugs. †The Dancing Masters.* 1944: *†The Big Noise.* 1945: *†The Bull-fighters. †Nothing But Trouble.* 1949: *†The Fighting Kentuckian.* 1950: *†Riding High.* 1951: *†Atoll K (US: Utopia. GB: Robinson Crusoeland).* 1952: *Meet Bela Lugosi and Oliver Hardy.*

††And foreign language versions
All shorts except (†) features

HARKER, Gordon 1885–1967
Frog-faced British cockney character star (four of his five brothers were scenic painters, like their father) whose lower lip jutted out into a permanent scowl. After his film debut he became a prominent figure in the British cinema, notably in films directed by Alfred Hitchcock or adapted from Edgar Wallace thrillers, and remained a leading film character star until the end of World War II.
1927: *The Ring. The Farmer's Wife.* 1928: *Champagne. The Wrecker.* 1929: *The Return of the Rat. The Crooked Billet. Taxi for Two.* 1930: **All Riot on the Western Front. The 'W' Plan. Elstree Calling. Escape. The Squeaker.* 1931: *Third Time Lucky. The Sport of Kings. The Stronger Sex. Shadows. The Man They Could Not Arrest. The Ringer. The Calendar (US: Bachelor's Folly). The Professional Guilt. Condemned to Death.* 1932: *The Frightened Lady (US: Criminal at Large). Love on Wheels. White Face. Rome Express.* 1933: *Britannia of Billingsgate. Lucky Number. This is the Life. Friday the Thirteenth.* 1934: *My Old Dutch. Road House. Dirty Work. The Phantom Light.* 1935: *The Lad. Admirals All. Squibs. Hyde Park Corner. Boys Will Be Boys. The Amateur Gentleman.* 1936: *Wolf's Clothing. Two's Company. *The Story of Papworth. Millions.* 1937: *Beauty and the*

Barge. *The Frog. 1938: Blondes for Danger. No Parking. Lightning Conductor. The Return of the Frog. Inspector Hornleigh. 1939: *Tommy Atkins. Inspector Hornleigh on Holiday. 1940: Saloon Bar. *Channel Incident. 1941: Inspector Hornleigh Goes to It (US: Mail Train). Once a Crook. 1943: Warn That Man. 1945: 29 Acacia Avenue US: The Facts of Love). 1948: Things Happen at Night. 1950: Her Favourite Husband (US: The Taming of Dorothy). The Second Mate. 1952: Derby Day (US: Four Against Fate). 1954: Bang! You're Dead (US: Game of Danger). 1955: Out of the Clouds. 1956: A Touch of the Sun. 1957: Small Hotel. 1959: Left, Right and Centre.*

HARLOW, Jean
(Harlean Carpentier) 1911–1937
Wisecracking bra-less blonde American actress who started off playing floozies, but developed into a kind of slender Mae West. Alas, by marrying three times and dying young (of uremic poisoning), M-G-M's platinum blonde bombshell set the pattern for several blonde sex symbols to follow in the next 30 years. Real first name pronounced Harley-Ann.
*1928: Moran of the Marines. 1929: *Why is a Plumber? *Thundering Toupees. *Double Whoopee. Fugitives. *Bacon Grabbers. Close Harmony. *Liberty. The Love Parade. *The Unkissed Man. The Saturday Night Kid. *Weak But Willing. New York Nights. This Thing Called Love. 1930: Hell's Angels. 1931: City Lights. Iron Man. Goldie. The Public Enemy (GB: Enemies of the Public). Platinum Blonde. The Secret Six. 1932: Three Wise Girls. The Beast of the City. Red-Headed Woman. Red Dust. 1933: Hold Your Man. Dinner at Eight. Bombshell (GB: Blonde Bombshell). *Hollywood on Parade No. 12. 1934: The Girl from Missouri (GB: 100 Per Cent Pure). 1935: Reckless. China Seas. Riffraff. 1936: Wife versus Secretary. Suzy. Libeled Lady. 1937: Personal Property (GB: The Man in Possession). Saratoga.*

HARMON, Mark
See KNOX, Elyse

HARRELSON, Woody
(Woodrow Harrelson) 1961–
Rangy, strong-jawed and aggressive-looking American actor with receding fair hair and slightly goofy handsomeness. A hit on TV as the dozy barman in *Cheers*, Harrelson looked an unlikely bet for screen stardom. However,

the casual charm of his tough-talking, sometimes violent film characters soon made him a popular middle-range star, especially in films that teamed him with three-time co-star Wesley Snipes (*qv*). Harrelson's parents parted when he was a child (the father was later jailed for murder) and he considered being a minister before turning to acting, making his first film appearance while still studying drama. Also a singer, songwriter and political activist. Academy Award nominee for *The People vs Larry Flynt*.
1978: Harper Valley P.T.A. 1985: Wildcats. 1987: Bay Coven/Bay Cove/Eye of the Demon (TV). 1988: Cool Blue. Killer Instinct (video). 1989: Casualties of War. 1990: Ted & Venus. 1991: L.A. Story. Doc Hollywood. 1992: White Men Can't Jump. 1993: Indecent Proposal. I'll Do Anything. 1994: The Cowboy Way. Natural Born Killers. 1995: Money Train. 1996: Kingpin. The Sunchaser. The People vs Larry Flynt. 1997: Welcome to Sarajevo. Wag the Dog. Kundun. 1998: Palmetto/Just Another Sucker. The Thin Red Line. The Hi-Lo Country. 1999: Ed TV. Austin Powers: The Spy Who Shagged Me. Play it to the Bone. Grass (narrator only). 2000: Enemy at the Gates. American Saint.

HARRIS, Barbara
(Sandra Markowitz) 1935–
Attractive, round-faced, blonde American actress, capable of a wide emotional range. A Tony Award-winner on Broadway, she did not really make her mark in the cinema, despite an Academy Award nomination for *Who Is Harry Kellerman . . .* in 1971. Her face is now beginning to acquire a puckish air and she could well be seen to good advantage in cynical character roles. Recently, however,

she has preferred the theatre.
1965: A Thousand Clowns. 1966: Oh Dad, Poor Dad, Mama's Hung You in the Closet and I'm Feeling So Sad. 1971: Plaza Suite. Who is Harry Kellerman and Why is He Saying Those Terrible Things About Me? 1972: The War Between Men and Women. 1974: Mixed Company. 1975: The Manchu Eagle Murder Caper Mystery. Nashville. 1976: Freaky Friday. Family Plot. 1978: North Avenue Irregulars (GB: Hill's Angels). The Hamster of Happiness (later Second Hand Hearts). Movie Movie. 1979: The Seduction of Joe Tynan. 1985: Night Magic. 1986: Peggy Sue Got Married. 1987: Nice Girls Don't Explode. 1988: The Return of Ben Casey (TV). Dirty Rotten Scoundrels. 1991: The Pamela Principle. 1997: Grosse Pointe Blank.

HARRIS, Ed 1949–
Whippy, thrustful Hollywood actor with very American features, slow grin and thinning ginger-brown hair. He was mostly seen on the Los Angeles stage until director George A. Romero gave him roles in three of his exploitation films; but it was Harris' portrayal of the stuffy John H. Glenn in *The Right Stuff* that made him look like a potential leading man with or without hair. Married two-time co-star Amy Madigan (*qv*) in 1983. Academy Award nominee for *The Truman Show*.
1977: The Amazing Howard Hughes (TV). Coma. 1978: Zombies (GB: Zombies: Dawn of the Dead). 1980: Knightriders. Borderline. 1981: Dream On. 1982: Creepshow. 1983: The Right Stuff. Under Fire. Swing Shift. 1984: Places in the Heart. A Flash of Green. 1985: Sweet Dreams. Alamo Bay. Code Name: Emerald. 1987: Walker. The Last Innocent Man (cable TV). The Suspect. 1988: To Kill a Priest. Jacknife. 1989: The Abyss. 1990: State of Grace. 1991: Paris Trout. China Moon (released 1994). Running Mates (TV). 1992: Glengarry Glen Ross. 1993: Needful Things. The Firm. The Abyss: Special Edition. 1994: Milk Money. 1995: Just Cause. Apollo 13. Nixon. Eye for an Eye. 1996: The Rock. Riders of the Purple Sage (TV). 1997: Absolute Power. The Truman Show. 1998: Stepmom. 1999: The Third Miracle. 2000: †Pollock. The Prime Gig. Enemy at the Gates. Absolute Zero.

†And directed

HARRIS, Julie (Julia Harris) 1925–
Plainish, sad-looking, fair-haired American actress, noted for roles which plumb emo-

tional depths. Has given a number of anguished performances in some powerful films (and won a Tony award on Broadway), but has never become a box-office star. Received an Academy Award nomination for *The Member of the Wedding*. Four times married and divorced.

1952: The Member of the Wedding. 1954: East of Eden. 1955: I Am a Camera. 1958: The Truth About Women. Sally's Irish Rogue (US: The Poacher's Daughter). 1961: The Power and the Glory (TV. GB: cinemas). 1962: Requiem for a Heavyweight (GB: Blood Money). 1963: The Haunting. 1966: Harper (GB: The Moving Target). You're a Big Boy Now. 1967: Reflections in a Golden Eye. 1968: The Split. Journey into Midnight (TV). 1970: The People Next Door. How Awful about Allan (TV). The House on Greenapple Road (TV). 1972: Home for the Holidays (TV). 1974: The Hiding Place (released 1977). The Greatest Gift (TV). 1975: Long Way Home (TV). 1976: Voyage of the Damned. 1978: The Bell Jar. 1982: The Last of Mrs Lincoln (TV). 1983: Brontë. 1986: Leaving Home. Nutcracker, The Motion Picture (voice only). 1988: Gorillas in the Mist. The Woman He Loved (TV). Too Good to be True (TV). The Christmas Wife (cable TV). 1989: Single Women, Married Men (TV). 1991: The Dark Half (released 1993). Paris Trout (cable TV. GB: cinemas). 1992: HouseSitter. 1994: One Christmas/Truman Capote's One Christmas. 1995: Carried Away (GB: Acts of Love). Secrets (TV). Lucifer's Child (TV). 1996: Lift to Heaven/Passage pour le paradis. Ghost in the Machine/Bad Manners. The Christmas Tree (TV). 1997: Ellen Foster (TV). 1998: Frank Lloyd Wright (doc. Voice only). Love is Strange (TV).

HARRIS, Phil
See FAYE, Alice

HARRIS, Richard 1930–
Tall, bony, rangy, aggressive Irish-born star with fair hair, blue eyes and husky voice. A hell-raiser in private (well, hardly private) life, he has been cast in a variety of rugged film roles. A box-office attraction in the late sixties but now a middle-range star. Married (second) to actress Ann Turkel from 1974, but divorced in 1982. Oscar nominations for *This Sporting Life* and *The Field*.

1958: Alive and Kicking. 1959: Shake Hands with the Devil. The Wreck of the Mary Deare. 1960: A Terrible Beauty (US: The Night

*Fighters). The Long and the Short and the Tall. 1961: The Guns of Navarone. 1962: Mutiny on the Bounty. 1963: The Sporting Life. 1964: The Red Desert. Carol for Another Christmas (TV). I tre volti (GB: Three Faces of Love). 1965: Major Dundee. The Heroes of Telemark. 1966: The Bible . . . in the beginning. Hawaii. 1967: Caprice. Camelot. 1968: The Molly Maguires. 1969: A Man Called Horse. †Bloomfield. 1970: Cromwell. 1971: Man in the Wilderness. The Snow Goose (TV). 1972: *Today Mexico, Tomorrow the World. 1973: The Deadly Trackers. 1974: 99 and 44/100 Per Cent Dead (GB: Call Harry Crown). Juggernaut. 1975: Echoes of a Summer. 1976: Robin and Marian. The Return of a Man Called Horse. Gulliver's Travels. The Cassandra Crossing. 1977: Orca . . . Killer Whale. Golden Rendezvous. 1978: The Wild Geese. Ravagers. 1979: The Last Word. Game for Vultures. Highpoint. 1980: Your Ticket is No Longer Valid. 1981: Tarzan the Ape-Man. 1982: Triumphs of a Man Called Horse. 1984: Martin's Day. 1988: The Return. Maigret (TV). 1989: Mack the Knife. King of the Wind. 1990: The Field. 1992: Unforgiven. A Dog of Flanders. Patriot Games. Silent Tongue. 1993: Wrestling Ernest Hemingway. 1994: The Great Kandinsky (TV). Cry, the Beloved Country. Abraham (TV). 1995: Savage Hearts. The Royal Way (released 2000). 1996: This is the Sea. Trojan Eddie. Smilla's Feeling for Snow/Smilla's Sense of Snow. 1997: The Hunchback (TV). 1998: The Barber of Siberia. 1999: To Walk with Lions. Grizzly Falls. 2001: My Kingdom.*

†*Also directed*

HARRISON, Kathleen 1892–1995
Diminutive British character actress with plaintive face (and voice to match) and tight, dark, curly hair. Seen as cockney girl-friends and maids through the thirties, she developed into a popular supporting player, then, with *Holiday Camp* (1947) unexpectedly became a major star of the British cinema for ten years. Extended her star run with a hit TV series in the sixties called *Mrs Thursday*. One of very few actors to pass their 100th birthday.

1915: Our Boys. 1931: Hobson's Choice. 1932: Aren't We All? Happy Ever After. The Man from Toronto. 1933: The Ghoul. 1934: The Great Defender. What Happened Then? 1935: Jury's Evidence. Line Engaged. Dandy Dick. 1936: Broken Blossoms. Everybody Dance. The Tenth Man. Aren't Men Beasts! 1937: Night

*Must Fall. Wanted. Bank Holiday (US: Three on a Weekend). 1938: The Terror. Convict 99. Jane Steps Out. Almost a Gentleman. Lovers' Knot. I've Got a Horse. 1939: Home from Home. A Girl Must Live. I Killed the Count? (US: Who is Guilty?). The Outsider. An Englishman's Home (US: Madmen of Europe). Discoveries. 1940: They Came By Night. Tilly of Bloomsbury. The Flying Squad. Gaslight (US: Angel Street). *Salvage with a Smile. The Girl in the News. 1941: The Ghost Train. Kipps (US: The Remarkable Mr Kipps). The Big Blockade. Once A Crook. Major Barbara. I Thank You. 1942: Much Too Shy. In Which We Serve. 1943: Dear Octopus (US: The Randolph Family). 1944: It Happened One Sunday. Meet Sexton Blake. Waterloo Road. 1945: Caesar and Cleopatra. Great Day. 1946: Wanted for Murder. I See a Dark Stranger (US: The Adventuress). The Shop at Sly Corner (US: The Code of Scotland Yard). 1947: Temptation Harbour. Holiday Camp. 1948: Bond Street. Oliver Twist. The Winslow Boy. Here Come the Huggetts. 1949: Vote for Huggett. Now Barabbas was a robber . . . Landfall. Golden Arrow (US: The Gay Adventure/Three Men and a Girl. Released 1953). The Huggetts Abroad. 1950: Waterfront (US: Waterfront Women). Trio. Double Confession. The Magic Box. Scrooge. 1952: The Happy Family (US: Mr Lord Says No). The Pickwick Papers. 1953: Turn the Key Softly. The Dog and the Diamonds. 1954: Lilacs in the Spring. 1955: Where There's a Will. Cast a Dark Shadow. All for Mary. 1956: It's a Wonderful World. Home and Away. The Big Money. 1957: Seven Thunders (US: The Beasts of Marseilles). 1958: A Cry from the Streets. Alive and Kicking. 1961: On the Fiddle (US: Operation Snafu). 1962: Mrs Gibbons' Boys. The Fast Lady. 1963: West 11. 1969: Lock Up Your Daughters! 1979: The London Connection (US: The Omega Connection).*

HARRISON, Sir Rex
(Reginald Harrison) 1908–1990
Elegant, fair-haired British actor, at first in faintly asinine roles, but rising to stardom as central characters with more than a touch of the rogue about them, especially where ladies were concerned. About this time his much-married private life earned him the nickname 'sexy Rexy'. Career damaged in 1948 by scandal involving Carole Landis' suicide. In 1964 he won an Oscar for repeating his successful stage role, Professor Higgins, in

My Fair Lady. Married to Lilli Palmer (1943–1957), Kay Kendall (1957-1959) and Rachel Roberts (1962–1971), second, third and fourth of six. Also received an Oscar nomination for Cleopatra. Knighted in 1989. Died from pancreatic cancer. Suffered from poor sight in his declining years, but kept working.

*1930: The Great Game. The School for Scandal. 1934: Get Your Man. Leave It to Blanche. 1935: All at Sea. 1936: Men Are Not Gods. 1937: Storm in a Teacup. School for Husbands. Over the Moon. 1938: St Martin's Lane (US: Sidewalks of London). The Citadel. 1939: The Silent Battle (US: Continental Express). Ten Days in Paris (US: Missing Ten Days). 1940: Night Train to Munich (US: Night Train). 1941: Major Barbara. 1945: I Live in Grosvenor Square (US: A Yank in London). Blithe Spirit. Journey Together. The Rake's Progress (US: Notorious Gentleman). 1946: Anna and The King of Siam. 1947: The Ghost and Mrs Muir. The Foxes of Harrow. 1948: Escape. Unfaithfully Yours. 1949: *On Stage. 1951: The Long Dark Hall. 1952: The Four-Poster. 1953: Main Street to Broadway. 1954: King Richard and the Crusaders. 1955: The Constant Husband. 1958: The Reluctant Debutante. 1960: Midnight Lace. 1962: The Happy Thieves. 1963: Cleopatra. 1964: My Fair Lady. The Yellow Rolls-Royce. 1965: The Agony and the Ecstasy. 1966: The Honey Pot. 1967: Dr. Dolittle. 1968: A Flea in Her Ear. 1969: Staircase. 1972: Don Quixote (TV). 1974: Three Faces of Love (TV). 1977: The Prince and the Pauper (US: Crossed Swords). Behind the Iron Mask (GB. TV: The Fifth Musketeer). 1978: Shalimar. 1979: Ashanti. 1980: Seven Graves for Rogan/A Time to Die.*

HART, Ian 1963–

Ginger-haired, underfed-looking British actor of smallish stature, capable of both threatening and conciliatory performances. As soon as Hart got a relatively late-starting film career going, he looked a good all-rounder, a chameleon-like character who proved extremely adaptable and appeared in both leading and supporting roles, escaping typecasting and retaining relative anonymity in the cinema despite a steady output. He has also directed for the theatre in his native Liverpool.

1985: No Surrender. 1992: The Hours and Times. 1993: BackBeat. 1994: Clockwork Mice. 1995: Nothing Personal. Land and Freedom. The Englishman Who Went Up a Hill

*But Came Down a Mountain. Loved Up (TV). 1996: Hollow Reed. Gold in the Streets. Robinson Crusoe. Michael Collins. Still Waters Burn. 1997: Mojo. Snitch/Noose (US: Monument Avenue). The Butcher Boy. 1998: Frogs for Snakes. Enemy of the State. B. Monkey. 1999: *Bait. This Year's Love. Wonderland. The End of the Affair. Spring Forward. The Closer You Get. Best. 2000: Aberdeen. Strictly Sinatra/Saracen Street. Born Romantic.*

HART, William S. 1862–1946

Grim-faced portrayer of upright western heroes who stood up for justice (and oppressed heroines) no matter what the odds, and of good/bad men who saw the light. The tall, sandy-haired performer came to the screen in middle-age but, like John Wayne years later, remained a star of top-class westerns into his sixties. Died after a stroke. The 'S' stood for Surrey.

1913: The Fugitive. 1914: His Hour of Manhood. Jim Cameron's Wife. †The Passing of Two-Gun Hicks. †The Sheriff's Streak of Yellow. †The Scourge of the Desert. The Bargain. †Pinto Ben. 1915: On the Night Stage (Later: The Bandit and the Preacher). †In the Sagebrush Country. †The Man from Nowhere. †The Grudge. †Revolver Bill. †The Taking of Luke McVane. †Mr Silent Haskins. †Cash Parrish's Pal. †The Roughneck. †The Conversion of Frosty Blake. †Keno Bates. Grit. †The Disciple. Liar. †Between Men. The Golden Claw. †The Darkening Trail. †The Tools of Providence. †A Knight of the Trails. 1916: †Bad Buck of Santa Ynez. The Last Act. †The Ruse. †The Aryan. †The Primal Lure. The Captive God. †The Dawn Maker. †The Patriot. †The Apostle of Vengeance. †Hell's Hinges. †The Devil's Double. †The

*Return of Draw Egan. 1917: †Truthful Tulliver. †The Gunfighter. †The Square Deal Man. †The Cold Deck. †The Desert Man. †Wolf Lowry. †The Narrow Trail. †The Silent Man. 1918: †Wolves of the Trail. †Blue Blazes Rawden. †John Petticoats. †The Tiger Man. †Selfish Yates. †Shark Monroe. †Riddle Gawne. †Branding Broadway. †Border Wireless. †*A Bullet for Berlin. *War Relief 1919: †The Poppy Girl's Husband. †Breed of Men. †Square Deal Sanderson. Sand. †The Money Corral. Wagon Tracks. 1920: The Toll Gate. The Cradle of Courage. O'Malley of the Mounted. The Testing Block. 1921: Whistle. Three Word Brand. White Oak. Travelin' On. 1922: The Spoilers. 1923: The Covered Wagon. Hollywood. Wild Bill Hickok. Grit (remake). 1924: Singer Jim McKee. 1925: ††Tumbleweeds. 1928: Show People. 1934: *The Hollywood Gad-About. 1939: Tumbleweeds (reissue with new prologue). 1941: One Foot in Heaven.*

†Also directed ††Also co-directed

HARVEY, Laurence (Hirsch – 'Larushka', later Larry – Skikne) 1927–1973

Auburn-haired, coldly handsome Lithuanian-born leading man, initially in British, later international, films. The cruelty in Harvey's features typed him in caddish roles for a while and, although he had the lead in his second film, it was a fairly slow climb to star parts in bigger movies. After a nomination for an Oscar in *Room at the Top* (1958), he became very popular for a decade as pushy heroes. Married to Margaret Leighton 1957–1961 (first of three). Died from cancer.

1946: Odd Man Out. 1948: House of Darkness. Man on the Run. 1949: The Man from Yesterday. Landfall. The Dancing Years. 1950: Cairo Road. The Black Rose. 1951: There is Another Sun (US: Wall of Death). Scarlet Thread. 1952: A Killer Walks. Women of Twilight (US: Twilight Women). I Believe in You. Decameron Nights. 1953: Innocents in Paris. 1954: The Good Die Young. Romeo and Juliet. King Richard and the Crusaders. 1955: I Am a Camera. Storm over the Nile. 1956: Three Men in a Boat. 1957: After the Ball. 1958: The Truth About Women. Room at the Top. Power Among Men (narrator only). The Silent Enemy. 1959: Expresso Bongo. 1960: Butterfield 8. The Alamo. The Long and the Short and the Tall (US: Jungle Fighters). 1961: Two Loves (GB: Spinster). Summer and Smoke. 1962: Wonderful World of the Brothers

Grimm. The Manchurian Candidate. A Walk on the Wild Side. A Girl Named Tamiko. 1963: The Running Man. The Ceremony. 1964: The Outrage. Of Human Bondage. 1965: Life at the Top. Darling . . . 1966: The Spy with a Cold Nose. The Winter's Tale. 1968: A Dandy in Aspic. Heisses Spiel für harte Männer (US: Rebus). Kampf Um Rom. 1969: He and She. The Deep (unfinished). The Magic Christian. Kampf Um Rom II. 1970: WUSA. 1972: Escape to the Sun. 1973: Welcome to Arrow Ranch (US: Tender Flesh). Night Watch. F for Fake. 1974: The Yellow Headed Summer. As director: 1963: The Ceremony. 1969: He and She. 1973: Welcome to Arrow Beach (US: Tender Flesh).
As co-director: 1968: A Dandy in Aspic.

HARVEY, Lilian (L. Pope) 1906–1968
Tiny, elfin, light-haired British-born dancer, singer and actress with appealingly angular face. Taken to Germany as a child, she became one of that country's biggest stars of the twenties and thirties, with a vivacious sense of comedy and an appeal pitched somewhere between Mary Pickford and Margaret Sullavan. Her British and American films did not quite reach the level of her German ones, and World War II effectively ended her star career.
1925: Der Fluch. Leidenschaft. Liebe und Trompetenblasen. Die Kleine von Bummel. 1926: Princess Trulala. Vater werden ist nicht schwer. Die keusche Susanne. 1927: Die tolle Lola. Ehefrien. 1928: Du sollst nicht stehlen (US: The Love Commandment). Eine Nacht in London. 1929: A Knight in London (English language version of Eine Nacht in London). Ihr dunkler Punkt. Adieu mascotte. Wenn Du einmal Dein Herz verschenkst. 1930: †Liebeswalzer/The Love Waltz. Hokuspokus. The Temporary Widow. †Die Drei von der Tankstelle (GB: Three Men and Lillian). Einbrecher (US: Murder for Sale). 1931: Princesse à vos ordres. Nie wieder Liebe. Calais – Douvres. †Congress Dances. Ihre Hoheit befiehlt. 1932: Zwei Herzen und ein Schlag. La fille et le garçon. †Quick. †Happy Ever After. 1933: †The Only Girl (US: Heart Song). Ich und die Kaiserin. My Lips Betray/Miquette et sa mère. My Weakness. 1934: I Am Suzanne! Let's Live Tonight. 1935: Mein ist die Rache. Did I Betray? (later Black Roses). Invitation to the Waltz. 1936: †Glückskinder. 1937: Sieben Ohrfeigen/Seven Slaps. Fanny Elssler. 1938: Capriccio. 1939: †Castelli in Aria. Frau am Steuer. 1940: Serenade. 1950: Herrliche

Zeiten. 1958: Das gabs nur einmal. 1960: Das kommt nicht wieder.

†Plus French/English/German versions

HASSO, Signe (Signe Larsson) 1910–
Forceful, grave-looking blonde Swedish actress who won the first Swedish 'Oscar' in 1938 for Karriär. Belatedly went to Hollywood in 1942, and biographies for many years gave her date of birth as 1915 to help prolong her career there. She never quite settled in American films, nor did they use her cool, low-key appeal to best advantage. Returned to Sweden in 1950: later divided her acting time between the two countries.
1933: †Tystnadens Hus (US: House of Silence). 1937: Häxnatten. 1938: Karriär. Geld fällt vom Himmel. 1939: Pengar från Skyn. Vi Tra. Emilie Högqvist. 1940: Vildmarkens Sang. Stål. Far och Son. Än en gång Gösta Ekman. Stora Fammen. 1941: Bartard. Den ljusnande Framtid. 1942: Journey for Margaret. 1943: Assignment in Brittany. Heaven Can Wait. 1944: The Story of Dr Wassell. The Seventh Cross. 1945: Dangerous Partners. Johnny Angel. The House on 92nd Street. 1946: Strange Triangle. A Scandal in Paris (GB: Thieves' Holiday). 1947: Where There's Life. Aitanga. 1948: To the Ends of the Earth. A Double Life. 1950: Outside the Wall. Crisis. Sånt Händer inte Här (GB: High Tension). 1953: Maria Johanna. 1954: Die Sonne von St Moritz. Den unter Brara Lognen. Taxi 13. 1955: The True and the False. 1966: Picture Mommy Dead. 1967: Code Name: Heraclitus (TV). 1971: A Reflection of Fear. 1973: The Magician (TV). 1974: QB VII (TV). 1975: Shell Game (TV). 1976: The Black Bird. Sherlock Holmes in New York (TV). 1977: I Never Promised You a Rose Garden. 1985: Mirrors (TV).

†As Signe Larsson

HATFIELD, Hurd
(William H. Hatfield) 1917–1998
Cold, handsome, aloof-looking, ascetic American actor whose career ran sadly downhill in just five years from the leading role in The Picture of Dorian Gray to support in Tarzan and the Slave Girl. In later years he acted mainly on the stage, and still looked absurdly young for many years. 'I guess I must have a portrait in the attic,' he once said. He died (on Christmas Day) in Ireland, his home for the last 25 years of his life.

1944: Dragon Seed. 1945: The Picture of Dorian Gray. 1946: The Diary of a Chambermaid. 1947: The Beginning or the End? The Unsuspected. 1948: The Checkered Coat. Chinatown at Midnight. Joan of Arc. 1950: Tarzan and the Slave Girl. Destination Murder. 1957: The Last Man (TV). 1958: The Left Handed Gun. 1961: King of Kings. El Cid. 1965: Mickey One. Harlow. 1968: The Boston Strangler. The Double-Barrelled Detective Story. 1970: Von Richthofen and Brown (GB: The Red Baron). 1971: Thief (TV). 1973: The Norliss Tapes (TV). 1979: You Can't Go Home (TV). 1985: King David. Lime Street (TV). Waiting to Act. 1986: Crimes of the Heart. 1988: Her Alibi. 1991: Lies of the Twins (TV). 1998: From Russia to Hollywood (doc).

HAUER, Rutger 1944–
Very fair-haired, blue-eyed, unsmiling (except for the occasional sardonic curl of the lip), ambitious Dutch actor who, after becoming known as the 'Paul Newman of Holland', aimed to become an international star, but left it a little late. He seemed most fitted for villainous roles and indeed Hollywood saw him that way at first. Later he widened his range, but even his heroes held tinges of sadism and he did not quite achieve that stature to which he had aspired: many of his latter-day films seem to have had him in action roles calling for a long topcoat and a shotgun, and he has become a man of video rather than a star of the cinema. Started his career in a panto company. Colour-blind.
1973: Repelstweltje. Turks fruit (GB and US: Turkish Delight). 1974: Das Amlett des Todes (GB: Cold Blood). The Wilby Conspiracy. Pusteblume (GB: Hard to Remember). 1975:

Le vent de la violence. Keetje tippel. La donneuse (GB: Naked and Lustful). 1976: Max Havelaar. Het jaar van de kreeft. 1977: Soldier of Orange. 1978: Femme entre chien et loup. Jewel in the Deep. Mysteries. Pastorale 1943. 1981: Nighthawks. Chanel Solitaire. 1982: Blade Runner. Eureka. Grijpstra and De Gier (US: Outsider in Amsterdam). 1983: The Osterman Weekend. Spetters. 1984: A Breed Apart. 1985: Lady Hawke. Flesh and Blood. 1986: The Hitcher. Wanted – Dead or Alive. 1987: Escape from Sobibor (TV). 1988: The Legend of the Holy Drinker. Bloodhounds of Broadway. Blind Fury. 1989: The Salute of the Jugger. On a Moonlit Night. The Edge (cable TV). 1990: Beyond Justice. The Blood of Heroes. 1991: Der lachende Tod. Past Midnight. Wedlock (later Deadlock). 1992: Blade Runner The Director's Cut. Buffy the Vampire Slayer. 1993: Blind Side (cable TV). Voyage. Arctic Blue. 1994: Nostradamus. Surviving the Game. The Malina Brotherhood. The Beans of Egypt, Maine (GB: video, as Forbidden Choices). Amelia Earhart: The Final Flight (TV). Fatherland (TV). 1995: Mr Stitch. Angel of Death. Beyond Forgiveness. Paradise Pages. Mariette in Ecstasy. 1996: Precious Find. Crossworlds (cable TV). Call of the Wild. Blast. Omega Doom. Hemoglobin. 1997: Red Line. Partners in Crime (released 2000). The Ruby Ring (TV). Knockin' on Heaven's Door. Hostile Waters (TV). 1998: Bone Daddy. The Hunter. Tactical Assault. 1999: Simon Magus. New World Disorder. 2000: Lying in Wait. 2001: Ignition. Turbulence 3.

HAVER, June (J. Stovenour) 1925–
Bright, bouncy American singer and actress with pleasing smile and warm personality. A dance band vocalist at 14, her career ran roughly parallel to that of Betty Grable at the same studio (Fox): they actually appeared together in *The Dolly Sisters*. Considered becoming a nun in the early fifties. Married to Fred MacMurray (second) from 1954 to his death in 1991.
1942: *Swing's the Thing. *Trumpet Serenade. 1943: Casanova in Burlesque. The Gang's All Here (GB: The Girls He Left Behind). 1944: Home in Indiana. Irish Eyes are Smiling. 1945: Where Do We Go From Here? The Dolly Sisters. 1946: Three Little Girls in Blue. Wake Up and Dream. 1947: I Wonder Who's Kissing Her Now. 1948: Scudda-Hoo! Scudda-Hay! (GB: Summer Lightning). 1949: Oh, You Beautiful Doll! Look for the Silver Lining. 1950: The

Daughter of Rosie O'Grady. I'll Get By. 1951: Love Nest. 1953: The Girl Next Door.

HAVOC, June (Ellen Hovick) 1916–
Bright, blue-eyed blonde American dancer, singer and later dramatic actress of cool personality, sister of Gypsy Rose Lee (qv). On stage as soon as she could walk. Around 1918, made two or three two-reelers with Harold Lloyd, as Baby June. I have not been able to trace individual titles. Married three times, the first two at 13 and 19. But since 1949, she has been married to director William Spier.
1941: Four Jacks and a Jill. 1942: Powder Town. My Sister Eileen. Sing Your Worries Away. 1943: Hello, Frisco, Hello! No Time for Love. Hi Diddle Diddle. Casanova in Burlesque. 1944: Sweet and Low Down. Timber Queen. Brewster's Millions. 1947: Intrigue. Gentleman's Agreement. 1948: When My Baby Smiles at Me. The Iron Curtain. 1949: The Story of Molly X. Red Hot and Blue. Chicago Deadline. 1950: Mother Didn't Tell Me. Once a Thief. 1951: Follow the Sun. 1952: Lady Possessed. 1956: Three for Jamie Dawn. 1970: The Boy Who Stole the Elephants (TV). 1977: J. Edgar Hoover, Godfather of the FBI (Later and GB: The Private Files of J. Edgar Hoover). 1980: Can't Stop the Music. 1987: Return to Salem's Lot. 1988: The Accidental Tourist.

HAWKE, Ethan 1970–
Dark-haired, fresh-faced, youthful, Texas-born actor, sometimes with goatee beard, who leavened a lack of personality in his early days with the ability to project all-American gaucheness or innocence. Disappointed with filmmaking after a debut at 14, he came back

to the medium five years later and achieved a degree of prominence with a series of sincere if perhaps not penetrating portraits of youth. It's tough to see this sometimes uncharismatic actor developing into a durable leading man, but he has ambitions to direct and, like the similar Ron Howard (qv), his future may lie on the other side of the camera. Married actress Uma Thurman (qv).
1985: Explorers. 1989: Dead Poets Society. Dad. 1991: White Fang. Mystery Date. 1992: *Lions' Den. *Texan. A Midnight Clear. 1993: Rich in Love. Waterland. Alive. 1994: Floundering. Quiz Show. Reality Bites. White Fang 2: Myth of the White Wolf. Search and Destroy. 1995: Before Sunrise. 1997: Gattaca / The Eighth Day. Great Expectations. 1998: The Newton Boys. The Velocity of Gary. 1999: Snow Falling on Cedars. Joe the King / Pleasant View Avenue. 2000: Hamlet. Monterey Pop.

HAWKINS, Jack 1910–1973
Tall, powerful, well-built British actor with square jaw and cheerful grin who emerged in the early fifties from years of solid supporting parts to feature throughout the decade in stiff-upper-lip roles as one of Britain's biggest stars. His finest asset was his rich and fruity voice: sadly this disappeared in 1966 after an operation for throat cancer removed his vocal chords. His death seven years later resulted from haemorrhaging following an operation to implant a 'voice box'. Married (first of two) to Jessica Tandy (1909–1994) from 1932 to 1942.
1930: Birds of Prey (US: The Perfect Alibi). 1932: The Lodger (US: The Phantom Fiend). 1933: The Lost Chord. The Good Companions. I Lived with You. The Jewel. A Shot in the Dark. 1934: Lorna Doone. Autumn Crocus. Death at Broadcasting House. 1935: Peg of Old Drury. 1937: Beauty and the Barge. The Frog. 1938: Who Goes Next? A Royal Divorce. 1939: Murder Will Out. 1940: The Flying Squad. 1942: The Next of Kin. 1948: The Fallen Idol. Bonnie Prince Charlie. The Small Back Room. 1950: The Black Rose. The Elusive Pimpernel (US: The Fighting Pimpernel). State Secret (US: The Great Manhunt). The Adventurers (US: The Great Adventure). 1951: No Highway (US: No Highway in the Sky). Home at Seven (US: Murder on Monday). Angels One Five. 1952: Mandy (US: Crash of Silence). The Planter's Wife (US: Outpost in Malaya). The Cruel Sea. 1953: *Pathway into Light (narrator only). Twice Upon a Time.

*Malta Story. The Intruder. *Prince Philip (narrator only). Front Page Story. 1954: The Seekers (US: Land of Fury). 1955: Land of the Pharaohs. The Prisoner. Touch and Go (US: The Light Touch). 1956: The Long Arm (US: The Third Key). The Man in the Sky (US: Decision Against Time). 1957: *The Battle for Britain (narrator only). Fortune is a Woman (US: She Played with Fire). The Bridge on the River Kwai. 1958: Gideon's Day (US: Gideon of Scotland Yard). The Two-Headed Spy. 1959: Ben-Hur. The League of Gentlemen. 1961: La Fayette. Two Loves (US: Spinster). 1962: Lawrence of Arabia. Five Finger Exercise. Rampage. 1963: Zulu. 1964: The Third Secret. Guns at Batasi. Masquerade. Lord Jim. 1965: Judith. 1966: The Poppy is Also a Flower (GB: Danger Grows Wild). 1967: †Great Catherine. 1968: †Shalako. 1969: †Oh! What A Lovely War. †Monte Carlo or Bust (US: Those Daring Young Men in Their Jaunty Jalopies). †Twinky (US: Lola). †The Adventures of Gerard. 1970: †The Beloved (GB: TV, as Sin). †Jane Eyre (TV. GB: cinemas). †Waterloo. 1971: †When Eight Bells Toll. †Kidnapped. †Nicholas and Alexandra. †Young Winston. 1972: †Escape to the Sun. 1973: †Theatre of Blood. †Tales That Witness Madness. †The Last Lion. 1974: †QB VII (TV).*

†Voice dubbed by other actors (Charles Gray, Robert Rietty)

HAWN, Goldie
(G. Stundlendgehawn) 1945–
Large-eyed, doll-faced, petite, this volatile American actress shot to fame as the daffy, squeaky pin-up of the long-running TV comedy show *Laugh-in*, and plays free-living, lovable scatterbrains. Won an Academy Award (best supporting actress) in her second film, *Cactus Flower*. Also nominated for *Private Benjamin*. Twice married, she has for some years lived with Kurt Russell (qv).
1968: The One and Only Genuine Original Family Band. 1969: Cactus Flower. 1970: There's a Girl in My Soup. 1971: $ (GB: The Heist). 1972: Butterflies Are Free. 1973: The Sugarland Express. 1974: The Girl from Petrovka. 1975: Shampoo. 1976: The Duchess and the Dirtwater Fox. 1978: Foul Play. 1979: Travels with Anita (US: A Trip with Anita). 1980: Private Benjamin. Seems Like Old Times. 1982: Best Friends. 1983: Swing Shift.

1984: Protocol. 1985: Wildcats. 1987: Overboard. 1990: Bird on a Wire. 1991: Criss-Cross. Deceived. 1992: House-Sitter. Death Becomes Her. 1996: Everyone Says I Love You. The First Wives Club. 1999: The Out-of-Towners. 2000: Town and Country. Dr T and the Women.
As director. 1997: Hope (TV).

HAY, Will 1888–1949
Solidly-built, light-haired British music-hall comedian. His chief character, the disreputable (and frequently incompetent) figure of tatty authority, was built up of coughs, grunts and snuffles, plus a pair of pince-nez and a shifty look, and perfected on stage before he launched it on film to provide a series of unparalleled comedy classics, often in partnership with cherubic Graham Moffatt and doddery Moore Marriott. Died after a series of strokes.
1933: *Know Your Apples. 1934: Those Were the Days. Radio Parade of 1935 (US: Radio Follies). 1935: Dandy Dick. Boys Will Be Boys. 1936: Where There's a Will. Windbag the Sailor. 1937: Good Morning, Boys. Oh, Mr Porter. 1938: Convict 99. Hey! Hey! USA. Old Bones of the River. 1939: Ask a Policeman. Where's That Fire? 1941: The Ghost of St Michael's. †The Black Sheep of Whitehall. The Big Blockade. 1942: *Go to Blazes! †The Goose Steps Out. 1943: †My Learned Friend.

†And co-directed

HAWTHORNE, Sir Nigel 1929–
Benevolent-looking English actor with wispy brown hair, a film star in old age after decades in the theatre and in TV. A British TV comedy series, *Yes Minister* (later *Yes Prime Minister*) brought his blink-eyed features into the public domain. An Academy Award nomination for re-creating his stage role in *The Madness of King George* consolidated his belated standing in the cinema, enabling him to tackle a rich variety of ripe cameos and serious leading roles in the next few years. Knighted in 1999.
1971: Young Winston. 1974: S.P.Y.S. 1975: The Hiding Place. 1978: Sweeney 2. The Sailor's Return. Watership Down (voice only). 1980: A Tale of Two Cities (TV). 1981: The Knowledge. Memoirs of a Survivor. History of the World Part 1. 1982: Gandhi. The Plague Dogs (voice only). *Dead on Time. The Hunchback of Notre Dame (TV). World Cup. A Captain's Tale. A Woman Called Golda (TV). Firefox. 1984: Pope John Paul II (TV). 1985: Jenny's War (TV). Turtle Diary. The Chain. The Black Cauldron (voice only). 1989: En händful tid. King of the Wind. 1990: Relatively Speaking. 1991: The Trials of Oz (TV). Freddie as F.R.O.7 (voice only). 1993: Demolition Man. 1994: The Madness of King George. 1995: Richard III. 1996: Inside (cable TV). Twelfth Night. The Fragile Heart (TV). 1997: Murder in Mind. Amistad. Forbidden Territory: Stanley's Search for Livingstone (TV). 1998: Trade Winds/At Sachem Farm. Madeline. The Object of My Affection. 1999: The Winslow Boy. The Clandestine Marriage. Tarzan (voice only). 2000: The Big Brass Ring.

HAYAKAWA, Sessue
(Kintaro Hayakawa) 1889–1973
Good-looking, solidly built Japanese actor who tried his luck in early Hollywood silents, and had a great run of success as sensuous orientals from 1914 until the mid-twenties. After that he made his career mainly on stage, with occasional film forays through the years, mostly as Japanese wartime commanders. Died from cerebral thrombosis complicated by pneumonia. Received an Oscar nomination for *The Bridge on the River Kwai*.
1914: O Mimi San (GB: The Courtship of O'Sann). The Geisha. A Tragedy of the Orient. The Typhoon. The Wrath of the Gods (GB: The Destruction of Sakura Jimo). *The Last of the Line (GB: Pride of Race). *The Vigil. *The Ambassador's Envoy. 1915: The Famine. The Relic of Old Japan. The Cheat. The Chinatown Mystery. The Clue. The Secret Sin. After Five. 1916: Honorable Friend. Alien Souls. The Soul of Kura-San. Temptation. 1917: Forbidden Paths. The Jaguar's Claws. The Debt. Honor

Redeemed (GB: The Victoria Cross). Hashimura Togo. The Bottle Imp. The Call of the East. The Secret Game. Each to His Kind. 1918: Hidden Pearls. The City of Dim Faces. His Birthright. The Temple of Dusk. White Man's Law. The Honor of His House. The Bravest Way. 1919: The Tong Man. The Dragon Painter. Courageous Coward. Heart in Pawn. Gray Horizon (GB: A Dead Line). The Man Beneath. Bonds of Honor. His Debt. The Illustrious Prince. 1920: The Devil's Claim. Li-ting Lang. An Arabian Knight. The Cradle of Courage. The Brand of Lopez. The Beggar Prince. 1921: Black Roses. The First Born. Where Lights Are Low. The Swamp. 1922: The Vermilion Pencil. Five Days to Live. Night Life in Hollywood. 1923: La bataille (GB: The Battle. US: The Danger Line). J'ai tué (GB: The First Born). 1924: The Great Prince Shan. Sen Yan's Devotion. 1925: Loyalty. The Darling of the Gods. 1929: *The Man Who Laughed Last. 1930: *Voice of Hollywood No. 2. 1931: Daughter of the Dragon. 1933: Tohjin Okichi. 1937: Yoshiwara. Die Tochter des Samurai. 1938: Forfaiture. Tempête sur l'Asie. 1939: Macao, l'enfer du jeu (GB: Gambling Hell). 1940: Patrouille blanche. 1941: Le soleil de Miniet. Malaria. Tournavara. 1946: Le cabaret du grand large. Quartier chinois. 1949: Tokyo Joe. 1950: Three Came Home. Les misérables. 1953: Higego no Shogun Yamashita Yasubumi. 1955: House of Bamboo. 1957: The Bridge on the River Kwai. 1958: The Geisha Boy. 1959: Green Mansions. 1960: Swiss Family Robinson. Hell to Eternity. 1962: The Big Wave. 1966: The Daydreamer (voice only).

HAYDEN, Sterling (Christian Walter, later legally changed) 1916–1986
Tall, strong, blond American leading man of Dutch parentage, idyllically good-looking in his early years when he became famous as a sea-going adventurer before taking up the cinema. After a distinguished war career in the Marines, he returned as the strong, silent, sometimes semi-corrupt hero with the occasional plum amidst a waste of routine action films. Quit Hollywood in 1958 and only acted according to financial necessity. Married (first of three) to Madeleine Carroll, 1942–1946. Died from prostate cancer.
1941: †Virginia. †Bahama Passage. 1947: Variety Girl. Blaze of Noon. 1949: El Paso. Manhandled. 1950: The Asphalt Jungle. 1951: Journey into Light. Flaming Feather. 1952: Denver and Rio Grande. The Golden Hawk. Hellgate. Flat Top (GB: Eagles of the Fleet).

1953: Take Me to Town. Kansas Pacific. Fighter Attack. So Big. The Star. Crime Wave (GB: The City is Dark). 1954: Arrow in the Dust. Johnny Guitar. Naked Alibi. Suddenly! Prince Valiant. Battle Taxi. 1955: Timberjack. The Eternal Sea. Shotgun. The Last Command. Top Gun. 1956: The Come-On. The Killing. 1957: Five Steps to Danger. Crime of Passion. The Iron Sheriff. A Sound of Different Drummers (TV). Valerie. Zero Hour. Gun Battle at Monterey. The Last Man (TV). 1958: Terror in a Texas Town. The Long March (TV). Ten Days to Tulara. Old Man (TV). 1963: Dr Strangelove, or: How I Learned to Stop Worrying and Love the Bomb. 1964: Carol for Another Christmas (TV). 1969: Sweet Hunters. Hard Contract. 1970: Loving. 1971: Cobra / Le saut de l'ange. 1972: The Godfather. Le grand départ. 1973: The Long Goodbye. The Final Programme (US: The Last Days of Man on Earth). 1974: Deadly Strangers. 1975: Cry Onion. 1976: 1900. 1977: Winter Kills (released 1979). 1978: King of the Gypsies (released 1980). 1979: The Outsider. 1980: Gas. 9 to 5. 1981: Possession. Charlie Chan and the Curse of the Dragon Queen. Venom. 1983: Leuchtturm des Chaos.

†As Stirling Hayden

HAYEK, Salma (S.H. Jiminez) 1966–
Black-haired, flashing-eyed Mexican fire-brand in the Katy Jurado tradition. Diminutive but curvaceous, she was a popular TV star in her native country for some years before embarking on a film career in her mid twenties. Lacking Jurado's dramatic intensity, she has so far been confined to decorative, if eye-catching roles. Daughter of a Lebanese father and Mexican mother.
1993: Mi vida loca. 1994: Roadracers (TV). 1995: Desperado. Fair Game. El callejan de los milagros / Midaq Alley. Four Rooms. 1996: From Dusk Till Dawn. Fled. Follow Me Home. 1997: Breaking Up. Fools Rush In. The Hunchback of Notre Dame / The Hunchback (TV). Quién diablos es Juliette? Sistole diastole. 1998: The Velocity of Gary. 54. Frida (released 2000). The Faculty. 1999: Wild Wild West. El coronel no tiene quién le escriba. Dogma. Forever Hollywood (D). 2000: Chain of Fools. Timecode. La gran vida.

HAYES, Allison
(Mary Jane Haynes) 1930–1977
Strong, statuesque, chestnut-haired actress who started her professional career as a pianist

with symphony orchestras, but was persuaded to try acting after winning a number of beauty contests. Nowadays has something of a cult following for her performance in Attack of the 50-Foot Woman, one of several chilly, low-budget horror films in which she appeared. Died from blood poisoning.
1954: Francis Joins the WACs. Sign of the Pagan. So This is Paris. The Purple Mask. 1955: Chicago Syndicate. Double Jeopardy (GB: Crooked Ring). Count Three and Pray. 1956: Gunslinger. Mohawk. The Steel Jungle. 1957: The Unearthly. The Disembodied. The Undead. Zombies of Mora Tau (GB: The Dead That Walk). A Lust to Kill. Voodoo Woman. 1958: Attack of the 50-Foot Woman. Wolf Dog. Hong Kong Confidential. 1959: Counterplot. Pier 5 – Havana. 1960: The Hypnotic Eye. The High Powered Rifle. 1963: Who's Been Sleeping in My Bed? The Crawling Hand. 1965: Tickle Me.

HAYES, Helen
(Helen H. Brown) 1900–1993
Fair-haired American child actress who became one of the great Broadway stars of the twenties. Her theatrical style was unsuited to films, nor was she a great film-star beauty, and, despite an Academy Award for The Sin of Madelon Claudet, she soon returned to the stage. Her return to films in later years was more successful, and she won another Academy Award for Airport. Married writer Charles MacArthur (died 1956); actor James MacArthur (qv) is their adopted son. Died from congestive heart disease.
1910: *Jean and the Calico Doll. 1917: The Weavers of Life. 1920: Babs. 1923: Riders of the Range. 1924: A Rodeo Mix-Up. 1928: *The Dancing Team. 1931: The Sin of

Madelon Claudet (GB: The Lullaby).
Arrowsmith. 1932: A Farewell to Arms. The
Son-Daughter. 1933: The White Sister. Another
Language. Night Flight. 1934: What Every
Woman Knows. Crime Without Passion. 1935:
Vanessa, Her Love Story. 1943: Stage Door
Canteen. 1952: My Son John. 1953: Main
Street to Broadway. 1956: Anastasia. 1957:
Four Women in Black (TV). 1959: Third Man
on the Mountain. 1969: Airport. 1972: The
Female Instinct (TV. GB: The Snoop Sisters).
1973: Do Not Fold, Spindle or Mutilate (TV).
Herbie Rides Again. 1975: One of Our
Dinosaurs is Missing. 1976: Victory at Entebbe
(TV. GB: cinemas). 1977: Candleshoe. 1979:
A Family Upside Down (TV). 1981: Hopper's
Silence (voice only). Murder is Easy (TV).
1983: A Caribbean Mystery (TV). 1984:
Highway to Heaven (TV). 1985: Murder with
Mirrors (TV).

HAYMES, Dick 1916–1980
Toothy, light-haired, American singer born
in Argentina, whose fine baritone voice got
him into a succession of film roles in the
forties. In looks, he was rather reminiscent of
Johnnie Ray. The song was fine, but wine,
women and hard living got the better of him
and he declared bankruptcy twice, in 1960
and 1971, before making a night-club comeback in the seventies. Married to Joanne Dru
1941–1949 and Rita Hayworth 1953–1954,
second and fourth of six. Ended his days as an
Irish citizen. Died from lung cancer.
1938: Dramatic School. 1943: Du Barry Was a
Lady. 1944: Four Jills in a Jeep. Irish Eyes
Are Smiling. 1945: State Fair. Billy Rose's
Diamond Horseshoe (GB: Diamond Horse-
shoe). 1946: Do You Love Me? The Shocking
Miss Pilgrim. 1947: Carnival in Costa Rica.
1948: Up in Central Park. 1951: St Benny the Dip (GB: Escape If
You Can). 1953: All Ashore. Cruisin' down the
River. Let's Do It Again! (voice only). 1974:
The Betrayal (TV). 1975: Won Ton Ton, the
Dog Who Saved Hollywood.

HAYWARD, Louis
(Seafield Grant) 1909–1985
Dark-haired, laughing-eyed South African-
born leading man with mocking smile. He
began his career in British films, then went to
Hollywood in 1935, where he played
debonair heroes and was ideally cast as The
Saint. Later, he rather surprisingly became
typed in double-feature swashbucklers, and
drifted out of films in his forties. Married to

Ida Lupino 1939–1945, first of three. A war
hero who won the Bronze Star with the US
marines, he died from lung cancer.
1932: Self Made Lady. 1933: The Thirteenth
Candle. The Man Outside. I'll Stick to You.
Chelsea Life. Sorrell and Son. 1934: The Love
Test. 1935: The Flame Within. A Feather in
Her Hat. 1936: Absolute Quiet. Trouble for
Two (GB: The Suicide Club). Anthony
Adverse. The Luckiest Girl in the World. 1937:
The Woman I Love (GB: The Woman
Between). 1938: Midnight Intruder. The Rage
of Paris. The Saint in New York. Condemned
Women. The Duke of West Point. 1939: The
Man in the Iron Mask. 1940: My Son, My
Son. Dance, Girl, Dance. Son of Monte Cristo.
1941: Ladies in Retirement. 1945: And Then
There Were None (GB: Ten Little Niggers).
1946: Young Widow. The Strange Woman.
The Return of Monte Cristo (GB: Monte
Cristo's Revenge). 1947: Repeat Performance.
1948: Ruthless. The Black Arrow (GB: The
Black Arrow Strikes). Walk a Crooked Mile.
1949: The Pirates of Capri (GB: The Masked
Pirate). The House by the River. 1950: The
Fortunes of Captain Blood. 1951: The Lady
and the Bandit (GB: Dick Turpin's Ride). Son
of Dr Jekyll. 1952: Lady in the Iron Mask.
Captain Pirate (GB: Captain Blood –
Fugitive). 1953: The Saint's Return (US: The
Saint's Girl Friday). Storm over Africa (US:
Royal African Rifles). 1954: Duffy of San
Quentin (GB: Men Behind Bars). 1955: The
Voyage of Captain Tom Jones, Pirate (TV).
1956: The Search for Bridey Murphy. 1967:
Chuka. The Christmas Kid. Electric Man.
1969: The Phynx. 1973: Terror in the Wax
Museum.

HAYWARD, Susan
(Edythe Marrenner) 1917–1975
There was an inner driving force behind the
career of this American star that belied the
pretty face in the chestnut curls and showed
itself in the set of the lips and the look behind
the eyes. It led her swiftly from 'sweet'
heroines to tough ladies in the Stanwyck
mould – but with more problems. First
nominated for an Oscar for her alcoholic in
Smash-Up (a role that set the pace for the
remainder of her career), she was up for the
Academy Award several times after that,
finally winning for *I Want to Live!* ten years
later. Married to actor Jess Barker (first of
two) from 1944 to 1953. Died from a brain
tumour.
1937: Hollywood Hotel. 1938: I Am the Law.

Campus Cinderella. The Sisters. Girls on
Probation. The Amazing Dr Clitterhouse.
Comet over Broadway. 1939: Our Leading
Citizen. $1,000 a Touchdown. Beau Geste.
1941: Adam Had Four Sons. Sis Hopkins.
Among the Living. 1942: Reap the Wild Wind.
*I Married a Witch. Star Spangled Rhythm. *A*
Letter from Bataan. Forest Rangers. 1943: Hit
Parade of 1943/Change of Heart. Young and
Willing. Jack London. 1944: The Fighting
*Seabees. The Hairy Ape. *Skirmish on the*
Home Front. And Now Tomorrow. 1946:
Deadline at Dawn. Canyon Passage. 1947:
Smash-Up, the Story of a Woman (GB: A
Woman Destroyed). The Lost Moment. They
Won't Believe Me. 1948: Tap Roots. The
Saxon Charm. 1949: Tulsa. House of
Strangers. My Foolish Heart. 1950: Rawhide.
1951: I Can Get It For You Wholesale (GB:
This is My Affair). I'd Climb the Highest
Mountain. David and Bathsheba. 1952: With a
Song in My Heart. The Snows of Kilimanjaro.
The Lusty Men. 1953: The President's Lady.
White Witch Doctor. 1954: Demetrius and the
Gladiators. Garden of Evil. 1955: Untamed.
Soldier of Fortune. I'll Cry Tomorrow. 1956:
The Conqueror. 1957: Top Secret Affair (GB:
Their Secret Affair). 1958: I Want to Live!
1959: Woman Obsessed. Thunder in the Sun.
1960: The Marriage-Go-Round. 1961: Ada.
Back Street. 1962: I Thank a Fool. 1963:
Stolen Hours. 1964: Where Love Has Gone.
1966: The Honey Pot. 1967: Valley of the
Dolls. 1971: Heat of Anger (TV). 1972: The
Revengers. Say Goodbye, Maggie Cole (TV).

HAYWORTH, Rita
(Margarita Cansino) 1918–1987
Dark-haired American dancer and actress,
born to show-business parents (and cousin of

Ginger Rogers) and dancing professionally at 14. After a series of minor roles, her wide smile and flashing eyes, allied to a sumptuous figure, propelled her forward as one of the foremost and dreamiest-looking love goddesses of the forties. Her beauty faded with the decade and she lapsed into middle-aged roles as soon as she turned 40. Even so, her appearance in *Gilda* and some of her early musicals can still take the breath away. Married to Orson Welles 1943–1947 and Dick Haymes 1953–1954, second and fourth of five. Died from Alzheimer's disease, a wasting of the brain.

1926: †**La Fiesta.* 1934: †*Cruz Diablo.* 1935: *†*Rose de Francia.* †*Under the Pampas Moon.* †*Dante's Inferno.* †*Charlie Chan in Egypt.* †*In Caliente.* †*Silk Legs.* †*Paddy O'Day.* 1936: †*Human Cargo.* †††*A Message to Garcia.* †*Rebellion.* †*Meet Nero Wolfe.* 1937: †*Hit the Saddle.* †*Trouble in Texas.* †*Old Louisiana (GB: Treason).* *Criminals of the Air.* *The Game That Kills.* *Paid to Dance.* *Girls Can Play.* *The Shadow (GB: The Circus Shadow).* 1938: *There's Always a Woman.* *Who Killed Gail Preston? Juvenile Court.* *Convicted.* *Homicide Bureau.* *Renegade Ranger.* 1939: *The Lone Wolf Spy Hunt (GB: The Lone Wolf's Daughter).* *Only Angels Have Wings.* *Special Inspector (GB: Across the Border).* 1940: **Chinese Garden Festival.* *Music in My Heart.* *Susan and God (GB: The Gay Mrs Trexel).* *Blondie on a Budget.* *The Lady in Question.* *Angels Over Broadway.* 1941: **Stars at Play.* *The Strawberry Blonde.* *Affectionately Yours.* *Blood and Sand.* *You'll Never Get Rich.* 1942: *My Gal Sal.* *Tales of Manhattan.* *You Were Never Lovelier.* 1943: **Show Business at War.* 1944: *Cover Girl.* *Tonight and Every Night.* 1946: *Gilda.* 1947: *Down to Earth.* *The Lady from Shanghai.* 1948: *The Loves of Carmen.* 1952: *Affair in Trinidad.* 1953: *Salome.* *Miss Sadie Thompson.* 1954: *Champagne Safari.* **Screen Snapshots No. 225.* 1957: *Fire Down Below.* *Pal Joey.* 1958: *Separate Tables.* 1959: *They Came to Cordura.* *The Story on Page One.* 1962: *The Happy Thieves.* 1964: *Circus World (GB: The Magnificent Showman).* 1965: *The Money Trap.* 1966: *The Poppy is Also a Flower (GB: Danger Grows Wild).* *L'avventuriero/The Rover.* 1968: *I bastardi/Sons of Satan.* 1970: *The Road to Salina.* 1971: *The Naked Zoo.* 1972: *The Wrath of God.* 1976: *Circle.*

†*As Rita Cansino (when billed)*
††*Scenes deleted from final release print.*

HAZELL, Hy

(Hyacinth Hazel O'Higgins) 1920–1970
Long-legged British musical-comedy star with bubbly blonde hair. Her singing and dancing talents were seldom displayed to advantage in British films, where she was deployed as more of a sex symbol. On stage at seven. Made a great principal boy in panto. She choked to death on a piece of steak.

1943: †*The Dummy Talks.* †*My Learned Friend.* 1947: *Meet Me at Dawn.* *Just William's Luck.* 1949: *Paper Orchid.* *Celia.* 1950: *The Body Said No!* *Dance Hall.* *The Lady Craved Excitement.* 1951: *The Franchise Affair.* 1952: *The Night Won't Talk.* *The Yellow Balloon.*

1953: *Forces' Sweetheart.* 1955: *Stolen Assignment.* 1956: *Up in the World.* *Anastasia.* 1957: *Light Fingers.* *The Key Man.* **The Mail Van Murder.* 1958: *The Whole Truth.* 1960: *Trouble with Eve.* 1961: *Five Golden Hours.* 1962: *What Every Woman Wants.* 1970: *Every Home Should Have One (US: Think Dirty).*

†*As Derna Hazell*

HEADLY, Glenne 1955–

Auburn-haired, perennially young-looking American actress of pixieish attractiveness, trowel-like jaw and high cheekbones, almost always in sympathetic roles, despite capabilities as sharp-tongued harpies. For 10 years a member of Chicago's Steppenwolf Theatre, she married its co-founder John Malkovich (*qv*), the first of her two (divorced) husbands. At her best in the leading roles of *Dirty Rotten Scoundrels* and *Mr Holland's Opus*, but liable to crop up in pretty well any type of film.

1981: *Four Friends (GB: Georgia's Friends).* 1983: *Doctor Detroit.* *Say Goodnight, Grace (TV).* 1984: *Fandango.* 1985: *Eleni.* *The Purple Rose of Cairo.* 1987: *Making Mr Right.* *Nadine.* 1988: *Stars and Bars.* *Dirty Rotten Scoundrels.* *Paperhouse.* 1990: *Dick Tracy.* 1991: *Mortal Thoughts.* *Grand Isle.* 1993: *Ordinary Magic.* *And the Band Played On.* 1994: *Getting Even With Dad.* 1995: *Mr Holland's Opus.* 1996: *Sgt Bilko.* *Bastard Out of Carolina (TV).* *2 Days in the Valley.* 1997: *Pronto (TV).* 1998: *The X Files.* *Winchell (TV).* *My Own Country (TV).* *Babe: Pig in the City (voice only).* *Breakfast of Champions.* 2000: *Timecode.* 2001: *What's the Worst That Could Happen?*

HEARD, John 1945–

American leading man of warmth and versatility, with light brown hair, lantern jaw and laconic good looks slightly along the lines of George Segal (*qv*). After theatrical training in Chicago and New York, he stayed a stage actor until his early thirties; he has not quite fulfilled his first promise in films and now plays featured roles. Very briefly (six days!) married to Margot Kidder (*qv*).

1977: *First Love.* *Between the Lines.* 1978: *On the Yard.* 1979: *Heart Beat.* *Head Over Heels.* 1980: *Misdeal (released 1982).* 1981: *Cutter and Bone (GB: Cutter's Way).* 1982: *Cat People.* 1983: *Legs (TV).* *Best Revenge.* *Will There Really Be a Morning? (TV).* 1984: *C.H.U.D.* *Too Scared to Scream.* 1985: *Heaven Help Us/Catholic Boys.* *After Hours.* *The Trip to Bountiful.* 1986: *Violated.* 1987: *The Telephone.* *Dear America (voice only).* *Necessity (TV).* 1988: *Big.* *The Milagro Beanfield War.* *Betrayed.* *The Seventh Sign.* *Beaches.* 1989: *One Point of View.* *The Package.* 1990: *Mindwalk.* *The End of Innocence.* *Awakenings.* 1991: *Rambling Rose.* *Deceived.* 1992: *Radio Flyer.* *Waterland.* *Home Alone 2: Lost in New York.* *Disaster at Valdez (TV. US: Dead Ahead: The Exxon Valdez Disaster).* *Gladiator.* 1993: *There Was a Little Boy (TV).* *In the Line of Fire.* *Spoils of War (TV).* *The Pelican Brief.* 1994: *Because Mommy Works (TV).* 1995: *John Grisham's The Client (TV).* 1996: *Before and After.* *My Fellow Americans.* 1997: *One Eight Seven.* *Executive Power.* *Men.* *Silent Cradle.* 1998: *There's No Fish Food in Heaven.* *Snake Eyes.* *Desert Blue.* 1999: *Freak Weather.* *Fish Out of Water.* **Jazz Night.* 2000: *Above Ground.* *Pollock.* *Perfect Murder, Perfect Town (TV).* *The Photographer.* *The Wednesday Woman (TV).* '*O*'.

HEARNE, Richard 1908–1979

British circus comedian, acrobatic tumbler and stage actor, of amiable mien, benign expression and fair, wavy hair. In supporting cameos for many years before his character of the doddering, accident-prone Mr Pastry made him a national celebrity on stage and TV. The character even made an appearance in a few, largely quite presentable, low-budget comedy films. Died from a heart attack.

1934: *Give Her a Ring.* 1935: *Dance Band.* *No Monkey Business.* 1936: *Millions.* 1937: *Splinters in the Air.* 1943: *Miss London Ltd.* *The Butler's Dilemma.* 1948: *One Night with You.* *Woman Hater.* 1949: *Helter Skelter.*

Passport to Pimlico. 1950: Something in the City. *Mr Pastry Does the Laundry. 1951: Captain Horatio Hornblower RN. Madame Louise. 1952: *What a Husband. Miss Robin Hood. 1955: The Time of His Life. 1956: Tons of Trouble. 1962: *The King's Breakfast.

HECHE, Anne 1969–

Waif-like blonde American actress of fine-boned face, often seen as women under pressure, and rarely in comedy roles. She first achieved popularity in the daytime TV soap *Another World*, in which she stayed for four years before beginning a cinema career. She appeared, at first, with offbeat performances in supporting parts, but in star roles from 1997. She created some controversy by 'coming out' in one of Hollywood's first openly lesbian relationships (with fellow actress Ellen DeGeneres) but remained modestly popular in leading and semi-leading roles into the new millennium. Surname pronounced Haysh.

1992: An Ambush of Ghosts. O Pioneers! (TV). †Of Mice and Men. 1993: The Adventures of Huck Finn. 1994: Girls in Prison (TV). Against the Wall (TV). I'll Do Anything. Milk Money. †A Simple Twist of Fate. 1995: Pie in the Sky. Kingfish: A Story of Huey P Long (TV). The Wild Side (released 1999 as Wildside). 1996: Walking and Talking. The Juror. If These Walls Could Talk (TV). 1997: Volcano. Wag the Dog. Donnie Brasco. *Stripping for Jesus. I Know What You Did Last Summer. Subway Stories: Tales from the Underground (TV). 1998: Six Days Seven Nights. Return to Paradise. Psycho. 1999: The Third Miracle. One Kill (TV). 2000: Auggie Rose. 2001: John Q.

As director. 1997: *Stripping for Jesus. 1999: If

These Walls Could Talk 2 (TV). 2000: Reaching Normal.

†Scenes deleted from final release print.

HEDLEY, Jack 1929–

Rather solemn-looking British actor with blue eyes and fair, wavy hair: gained a few star roles on the strength of his success as the hero of TV mystery serials by Francis Durbridge. His dour, somewhat colourless acting was not well suited to the cinema, and he has made only a few appearances on the big screen.

1957: The Pack. 1958: Behind the Mask. Room at the Top. 1959: Left, Right and Centre. 1960: Make Mine Mink. Cone of Silence (US: Trouble in the Sky). 1962: Never Back Losers. In the French Style. The Longest Day. Lawrence of Arabia. Nine Hours to Rama. 1963: The Very Edge. The Scarlet Blade. 1964: Witchcraft. Of Human Bondage. The Secret of Blood Island. 1967: How I Won the War. The Anniversary. 1969: Goodbye, Mr Chips. 1975: Brief Encounter (TV). 1977: The Devil's Advocate. Sophia Loren – Her Own Story (TV). 1981: For Your Eyes Only. 1982: The New York Ripper. 1987: Three Kinds of Heat. 1990: The Plot to Kill Hitler (TV). 1997: Karakter / Character.

HEDREN, Tippi (Nathalie Hedren) 1935–

Ultra-slender blonde American model, facially a cross between Grace Kelly and Martha Hyer, and discovered by Alfred Hitchcock for films. Despite extremely interesting performances in *The Birds* and *Marnie* her film roles since then have been very lacklustre. Perhaps it needed Hitchcock to bring out her special disturbing qualities. She became interested in animal welfare –

paticularly of big cats – in later years. Mother of actress Melanie Griffith (qv). Picked up her acting career again in the 1990s.

1950: The Petty Girl (GB: Girl of the Year). 1963: The Birds. 1964: Marnie. 1965: Satan's Harvest. 1966: A Countess from Hong Kong. 1968: Tiger by the Tail. 1969: The Man with the Albatross. 1973: Mister Kingstreet's War (GB: TV). The Harrad Experiment. 1975: Adonde Mucre el Viento. 1980: Roar. 1985: Alfred Hitchcock Presents (TV). 1986: Foxfire Light. 1989: Deadly Spygames. 1990: Return to Green Acres (TV). Pacific Heights. In the Cold of the Night. 1991: Shadow of a Doubt (TV). 1992: Through the Eyes of a Killer (TV). 1993: Inevitable Grace. Perry Mason: The Case of the Skin-Deep Scandal (TV). 1994: The Birds II: Land's End (TV). Teresa's Tattoo. Treacherous Beauties (TV). 1996: Citizen Ruth. 1997: Mulligans! Mind Lies. 1998: The Breakup. I Woke Up Early the Day I Died. Internet Love. 1999: Replacing Dad (TV). Dial H for Hitchcock (doc). The Darklings (TV). 2000: The Hand Behind the Mouse (doc). The Storytellers.

HEFLIN, Van

(Emmet Evan Heflin) 1910–1971

Sandy-haired, square-faced, thin-lipped, friendly-looking American actor and one of Hollywood's most interesting and underrated stars. Not able to bring much to poor leading roles, he often gave quite exceptional performances in meaty, well-written parts. Academy Award 1942 (best supporting actor) in *Johnny Eager*. Died following a massive stroke sustained while swimming. Uncle of director Jonathan Kaplan.

1936: A Woman Rebels. 1937: The Outcasts of Poker Flat. Flight from Glory. Annapolis Salute (GB: Salute to Romance). Saturday's Heroes. 1939: Back Door to Heaven. 1940: Santa Fé Trail. 1941: The Feminine Touch. H.M.Pulham Esq. Johnny Eager. 1942: Seven Sweethearts. Kid Glove Killer. Grand Central Murder. Tennessee Johnson (GB: The Man on America's Conscience). 1943: Presenting Lily Mars. *Hollywood in Uniform. 1946: Till the Clouds Roll By. The Strange Love of Martha Ivers. 1947: Possessed. Green Dolphin Street. 1948: Act of Violence. Tap Roots. B.F.'s Daughter (GB: Polly Fulton). The Three Musketeers. The Secret Land (narrator only). 1949: Madame Bovary. East Side, West Side. 1950: Tomahawk (GB: Battle of Powder River). 1951: The Prowler. Week-End with Father. 1952: My Son John. South of Algiers

*Last. The Lifeguardsman. 1920: *Broken Bottles. Alf's Button. 1924: Tons of Money. 1927: *On with the Dance (series). 1930: A Warm Corner. 1931: The Sport of Kings. 1933: It's a Boy! The Girl from Maxim's. 1935: Oh, Daddy! 1943: The Demi-Paradise (US: Adventure for Two). 1956: Home and Away.*

HENSON, Nicky 1945–
Light-haired, youthful-looking British actor, mostly in light comedy roles calling for dash and aggressive masculinity. Like his father, stage comedian Leslie Henson (qv), he has had leading roles in films, but they have not made him a permanent star of the cinema. In the mid-1970s Henson seemed to be flavour-of-the-month in British films, but it soon melted away. Married to Una Stubbs (1938–) from 1969 to 1975. Later romantically involved with Susan Hampshire (qv) for several years, but this too broke up.
1963: Father Came Too. 1966: Doctor in Clover. 1967: Here We Go Round the Mulberry Bush. 1968: Witchfinder-General (US: The Conqueror Worm). Mosquito Squadron. Crooks and Coronets (US: Sophie's Place). 1970: There's a Girl in My Soup. 1971: All Coppers Are. . . 1972: The Love Ban. Psychomania (US: The Death Wheelers). 1973: Penny Gold. 1974: Vampira (US: Old Dracula). Bedtime with Rosie. 1975: The Bawdy Adventures of Tom Jones. 1977: No 1 of the Secret Service. 1980: L'isola del gabbiano. 1989: Star Trap (TV). 1994: Class Act. 1998: Parting Shots.

HENSTRIDGE, Natasha 1974–
Tall, flaxen-haired, green-eyed model turned actress with a perfect figure and fine bone structure. Born in Newfoundland, but raised

in mainland Canada, she caught the eye as the alien (and her successor) in the *Species* films, but her other movie appearances to date have been less successful. Married/divorced actor Damian Chapa.
1995: Species. Adrenalin: Fear the Rush. 1996: Maximum Risk. 1997: Prairie Fire. Standoff. Kill You Twice. 1998: Bela Donna (formerly White Dunes). Species 2. Dog Park. It Had to Be You. 1999: Caracara/The Last Witness (cable TV). 2000: The Whole Nine Yards. Bounce. A Better Way to Die. 2001: Second Skin. The Ghosts of Mars. Kevin of the North.

HEPBURN, Audrey
(A. Ruston) 1929–1993
Wide-mouthed, dark-eyed, pencil-slim, Belgian-born actress of mixed parentage. She made a few British and continental films before going to Hollywood with her Oscar-winning performance in *Roman Holiday*. Her captivating charm and delivery kept her at the top in a number of glossily successful dramas, comedies and thrillers for the next 15 years. Comebacks after 1967 revealed her aspect as much changed, and were not terribly successful. Married to Mel Ferrer (first of two) from 1954 to 1968. Also Oscar nominated for *Sabrina*, *Breakfast at Tiffany's* and *Wait Until Dark*. Special Oscar 1993. In her latter days, she became a Special Ambassador for UNICEF. Died from colonic cancer.
1948: Nederland in 7 Lessen. 1951: Nous irons à Monte Carlo (GB: Monte Carlo Baby). Laughter in Paradise. One Wild Oat. Young Wives' Tale. The Lavender Hill Mob. 1952: Secret People. 1953: Roman Holiday. 1954: Sabrina (GB: Sabrina Fair). 1956: War and Peace. Funny Face. 1957: Love in the Afternoon. 1958: Mayerling (TV). The Nun's Story. Green Mansions. 1959: The Unforgiven. 1961: Breakfast at Tiffany's. 1962: The Children's Hour (GB: The Loudest Whisper). 1963: Charade. Paris When It Sizzles. 1964: My Fair Lady. 1966: How to Steal a Million. 1967: Two for the Road. Wait Until Dark. 1976: Robin and Marian. 1979: Bloodline/Sidney Sheldon's Bloodline. 1981: They All Laughed. 1986: Directed by William Wyler. 1987: Love Among Thieves (TV). 1989: Always.

HEPBURN, Katharine 1906–
Distinctly individual, copper-haired American actress with attractively grating New England diction and finely-structured features that exude determination and individuality. Usually seen as indomitable feminist aggressors or figures of history but also a whizz at sophisticated screwball comedy. Very choosy about scripts, she has had her ups and downs at the box-office, but gathered four Best Actress Oscars (*Morning Glory*, *Guess Who's Coming to Dinner*, *The Lion in Winter* and *On Golden Pond*) and eight further nominations along the way. For 25 years she was associated publicly and privately with Spencer Tracy, with whom she made eight films. She continued acting for TV and the cinema up to the mid 1990s, despite suffering from an inherited disability superficially similar to Parkinson's Disease.
1932: A Bill of Divorcement. 1933: Christopher Strong. Morning Glory. Little Women. 1934: Spitfire. Break of Hearts. The Little Minister. 1935: Alice Adams. Sylvia Scarlett. 1936: Mary of Scotland. A Woman Rebels. 1937: Quality Street. Stage Door. 1938: Bringing Up Baby. Holiday/Unconventional Linda (GB: Free to Live). 1940: The Philadelphia Story. 1941: Woman of the Year. 1942: Keeper of the Flame. 1943: Stage Door Canteen. Women in Defense (narrator only). 1944: Dragon Seed. 1945: Without Love. 1946: Undercurrent. 1947: Song of Love. Sea of Grass. 1948: State of the Union (GB: The World and His Wife). 1949: Adam's Rib. 1951: The African Queen. 1952: Pat and Mike. 1955: Summer Madness (US: Summertime). 1956: The Rainmaker. The Iron Petticoat. 1957: Desk Set (GB: His Other Woman). 1959: Suddenly Last Summer. 1962: Long Day's Journey into Night. 1967: Guess Who's Coming to Dinner? 1968: The Lion in Winter. 1969: The Madwoman of Chaillot. 1971: The Trojan Women. 1973: The Glass Menagerie (TV). 1974: A Delicate Balance. 1975: Love Among the Ruins (TV. GB: cinemas). Rooster Cogburn. 1978: The

Corn is Green (TV). Olly, Olly, Oxen Free. 1981: On Golden Pond. 1984: The Ultimate Solution of Grace Quigley (GB: Grace Quigley). 1986: Mrs Delafield Wants to Marry (TV). 1987: Guest Appearance (TV). 1988: Laura Lansing Slept Here (TV). 1992: The Man Upstairs (TV). 1994: This Can't Be Love (TV). One Christmas/Truman Capote's One Christmas (TV). Love Affair.

HERLIE, Eileen (E. Herlihy) 1919–
Scottish-born actress with dark hair, twinkling brown eyes, high cheekbones and glowing complexion. She began her career with the Scottish National theatre company and has remained largely a stage star. The British cinema offered her some good roles (to which she brought her own inbuilt warmth), but not a career.
1946: Hungry Hill. 1948: Hamlet. 1950: The Angel with the Trumpet. 1953: The Story of Gilbert and Sullivan (US: The Great Gilbert and Sullivan). Isn't Life Wonderful! 1954: For Better, For Worse (US: Cocktails in the Kitchen). 1958: She Didn't Say No! 1962: Freud (GB: Freud – the Secret Passion). 1964: Hamlet. 1966: Heartbreak House (TV). 1969: The Sea Gull.

HERSHEY, Barbara (B. Herzstein) 1947–
Pretty, smooth-skinned, dark-haired American actress with olive complexion and statuesque figure, at first in Disneyesque roles (e.g. TV's The Monroes), but soon in high drama that called for maximum exposure of her physical assets. Became one of Hollywood's great free spirits, living with David Carradine (qv) from 1969 to 1975. After their break-up, cinema and TV hardly maximised her undoubted talent until she

began to win critical approval in the 1980s, a period which culminated in her winning two best actress awards at the Cannes Film festival in 1987 and 1988. Looking much younger than her years, she prolonged her career with a wide variety of performances as characters alternately down-trodden and sexually aggressive. Finally won a long-overdue Oscar nomination, for The Portrait of a Lady.
1968: With Six You Get Egg Roll. Heaven with a Gun. 1969: Last Summer. The Liberation of L B Jones. 1970: The Pursuit of Happiness. 1971: The Baby Maker. 1972: Boxcar Bertha. Dealing: Or the Berkeley-to-Boston-Forty-Bricks-Lost-Bag Blues. 1973: †Time to Run. 1974: †Vrooder's Hooch/The Crazy World of Julius Vrooder. †You and Me. 1975: †Diamonds. Love Comes Quietly. 1976: Trial by Combat (US: Dirty Knights' Work). The Last Hard Men. Flood! (TV). 1977: In the Glitter Palace (TV). Sunshine Christmas (TV). The Stuntman (released 1980). 1978: Just a Little Inconvenience (TV). 1979: A Man Called Intrepid (TV). 1980: Angel on My Shoulder (TV). 1981: Take This Job and Shove It. Americana. The Entity. 1983: The Right Stuff. 1984: The Natural. 1985: My Wicked, Wicked Ways – The Legend of Errol Flynn (TV). Hannah and Her Sisters. 1986: Passion Flower (TV). Hoosiers (GB: Best Shot). Shy People. 1987: Tin Men. A World Apart. 1988: The Last Temptation of Christ. Beaches. 1989: Defenseless (released 1991). 1990: Aunt Julia and the Scriptwriter. Killing in a Small Town. Evidence of Love (TV). 1991: Paris Trout. 1992: Stay the Night (TV). The Public Eye. Swing Kids. 1993: Falling Down. A Dangerous Woman. Splitting Heirs. 1994: Abraham (TV). 1995: Last of the Dogmen. 1996: The Pallbearer. The Portrait of a Lady. 1998: The Staircase (TV). A Soldier's Daughter Never Cries. Frogs for Snakes. Breakfast of Champions. 1999: Passion. 2000: Drowning on Dry Land.

†As Barbara Seagull

HERSHOLT, Jean 1886–1956
Square-faced Danish actor, sometimes moustachioed, with a bush of dark hair. A handsome leading man (and occasionally villain) of silent films. After he reached the top in the early twenties, his accent and age led him into character roles with sound, and he soon became the screen's best known doctor. His most famous character, Dr Christian, a kindly country physician, was created on

radio, and carried through into films and, later, television. Two special Oscars, one for Motion Picture Relief Fund work, the other for services to the industry. Also has an Oscar – the Jean Hersholt Humanitarian Award – named after him. Uncle of Leslie Nielsen (qv). Died from cancer.
1913: *Short film in Denmark. *Two Men of the Desert. 1915: The Disciple. Don Quixote. *Never Again. 1916: Hell's Hinges. The Aryan. The Deserter. Kinkaid – Gambler. Bullets and Brown Eyes. The Apostle of Vengeance. *As the Candle Burned. *Some Medicine Man. *Scratched. *It's All Wrong. 1917: Love Aflame. The Terror. Southern Justice. The Saintly Sinner. 49 – 17. The Greater Law. Fighting for Love. The Show-Down. The Soul Herder. Black Orchids. *The Clash of Steel. The Townsend Divorce Case. *Her Primitive Man. A Stormy Knight. *Gunman's Gospel. 1918: Princess Virtue. Madame Spy. Smashing Through. The Answer. Little Red Decides. Who is to Blame? 1919: In the Land of the Setting Sun. Whom the Gods Would Destroy. 1920: Merely Mary Anne. The Red Lane. The Servant in the House. The Deceiver. 1921: The Golden Trail. A Certain Rich Man. The Four Horsemen of the Apocalypse. Man of the Forest. The Mysterious Rider. 1922: Tess of the Storm Country. The Gray Dawn. Golden Dreams. When Romance Rides. The Stranger's Banquet. Heart's Haven. 1923: Quicksand. Red Lights. Greed (released 1925). Jazzmania. Torment. 1924: Sinners in Silk. Cheap Kisses. So Big. *The City of Stars. The Woman on the Jury. Her Night of Romance. 1925: A Woman's Faith. If Marriage Fails. Dangerous Innocence. Fifth Avenue Models. Stella Dallas. Don Q Son of Zorro. 1926: My Old Dutch. Flames. The Greater Glory. It Must Be Love. The Old Soak. 1927: The Wrong Mr Wright. 1928: Alias the Deacon. The Student Prince in Old Heidelberg (GB: The Student Prince). The Secret Hour. Jazz Mad. Give and Take. The Battle of the Sexes. 13 Washington Square. 1929: Abie's Irish Rose. The Younger Generation. The Girl on the Barge. Modern Love. You Can't Buy Love. 1930: The Cat Creeps. Hell Harbor. Mamba. The Climax. The Case of Sergeant Grischa. East is West. Third Alarm. Viennese Nights. A Soldier's Plaything (GB: A Soldier's Pay). 1931: Susan Lenox, Her Fall and Rise (GB: The Rise of Helga). The Sin of Madelon Claudet (GB: The Lullaby). Phantom of Paris. Transatlantic. Private Lives. Daybreak. 1932: Beast of the City. Grand Hotel. Are You Listening? Night Court (GB: Justice for Sale). Emma. Skyscraper Souls. New Morals for Old. Hearts of Humanity. Unashamed. Flesh. The Mask of Fu Manchu. 1933: The Crime of the Century. Son of the Eagle. Dinner at Eight. The Late Christopher Bean (GB: Christopher Bean). 1934: Men in White. The Cat and the Fiddle. The Fountain. The Painted Veil. 1935: Break of Hearts. Mark of the Vampire. Murder in the Fleet. 1936: Sins of Man. The Tough Guy. The Country Doctor. Reunion (US: Hearts in Reunion). One in a Million. His Brother's Wife. 1937: Heidi. Seventh Heaven. 1938: I'll Give a Million. Happy Landing. Alexander's Ragtime Band. Five of a Kind. 1939: Mr Moto in Danger Island (GB: Mr Moto on Danger Island). Meet Dr Christian.

1940: *Courageous Dr Christian. Dr Christian Meets the Women. Remedy for Riches.* 1941: *Melody for Three. They Meet Again.* 1943: *Stage Door Canteen.* 1948: **Jean Hersholt Party.* 1949: *Dancing in the Dark.* 1952: **Hollywood Night at 21 Club.* 1954: *Run for Cover.* 1955: **Hollywood Shower of Stars.*

HERVEY, Irene
See JONES, Allan

HESTON, Charlton
(John C. Carter) 1923–
Granite-faced, deep-voiced, light-haired American star, a big man with barrel chest, aquiline nose and noble bearing. He started in outdoor action films, but could express anguish, sincerity and zeal with equal conviction, assets which prompted Cecil B. DeMille to set him up for a lifetime of epic service by casting him as Moses in *The 10 Commandments. Ben-Hur* won him an Academy Award; small-scale successes like *Will Penny* revealed more of the man beneath the muscle. Prolonging his star status past 60 with character leads, he accepted craggy cameos in the 1990s. Married to actress Lydia Clarke since 1944.
1941: *Peer Gynt.* 1949: *Julius Caesar.* 1950: *Dark City. The Greatest Show on Earth. The Savage. Ruby Gentry.* 1953: *Pony Express. The President's Lady. Arrowhead. Bad for Each Other. *Three Lives.* 1954: *Secret of the Incas. The Naked Jungle. The Far Horizons.* 1955: *The Private War of Major Benson. Lucy Gallant.* 1956: *Three Violent People. Forbidden Area (TV). The 10 Commandments.* 1958: *Touch of Evil. Point of No Return (TV). The Buccaneer. The Big Country.* 1959: *The Wreck of the Mary Deare. Ben-Hur.* 1961: *El Cid.* 1962: **Five Cities of June (narrator only). The Pigeon That Took Rome. 55 Days at Peking. Diamond Head.* 1964: *Major Dundee.* 1965: *The Greatest Story Ever Told. The Agony and the Ecstasy. The War Lord. *The Egyptologists (narrator only).* 1966: *Khartoum. *While I Run This Race (narrator only).* 1967: *Counterpoint. All About People. Planet of the Apes. Will Penny.* 1969: *Rowan and Martin at the Movies. Number One. The Heart of Variety. Beneath the Planet of the Apes. The Festival Game.* 1970: *Julius Caesar. King: a Filmed Record . . . Montgomery to Memphis (and narrator). The Hawaiians (GB: Master of the Islands).* 1971: *The Omega Man. †Antony and Cleopatra.* 1972: *Skyjacked. Call of the Wild. *Our Active

Earth (narrator only).* 1973: *Soylent Green. The Three Musketeers (The Queen's Diamonds). *Lincoln's Gettysburg Address (narrator only).* 1974: *Earthquake. The Four Musketeers (The Revenge of Milady).* Airport 1975. 1975: **The Fun of Your Life (narrator only).* 1976: *The Last Hard Men. Two Minute Warning. Midway (GB: Battle of Midway). America at the Movies (narrator only).* 1977: *The Prince and the Pauper (US: Crossed Swords). Gray Lady Down.* 1979: *The Mountain Men.* 1980: *The Awakening.* 1982: *†Mother Lode.* 1984: *Nairobi Affair (TV).* 1986: *Directed by William Wyler.* 1987: *Proud Men (TV).* 1988:*†A Man for All Seasons (TV).* 1989: *Original Sin (TV). Treasure Island (TV. GB: cinemas).* 1990: *Solar Crisis (later Starfire). The Little Kidnappers (TV). Almost an Angel.* 1991: *The Crucifer of Blood (TV).* 1992: *Crash Landing: The Rescue of Flight 232 (TV).* 1993: *Genghis Khan. Tombstone. Wayne's World 2.* 1994: *In the Mouth of Madness. True Lies.* 1995: *Avenging Angel.* 1996: *Alaska. Lord Protector. Hamlet. Third Cowboy on the Right (doc).* 1997: *Hercules (voice only). I Am Your Child (TV).* 1998: *Illusion Infinity. Armageddon (narrator only).* 1999: *Forever Hollywood (doc). Any Given Sunday.* 2000: *Town and Country.*

†And directed

HEWITT, Jennifer Love 1979–
A bouncy, precocious American child actress (sometimes billed as Love Hewitt) who grew into a dark-haired, dark-eyed, not very tall but curvy teenage sex symbol, most notably in the 'I Know What You Did' horror films, in which her bust got more attention from cameramen than the shock special effects. Her figure, indeed, hardly made her ideal casting for a TV biopic on Audrey Hepburn. Still she seems set to decorate magazine covers as well as movies for some time to come. Also popular in the TV series *Party of Five*, and has been singing professionally since the age of four.
1992: *Munchie.* 1993: *Sister Act 2: Back in the Habit. Little Miss Millions.* 1995: *House Arrest.* 1997: *I Know What You Did Last Summer. Trojan War/Rescue Me (TV). The Senior Prom (TV).* 1998: *Can't Hardly Wait. Telling You.* 1999: *I Still Know What You Did Last Summer. The Suburbans.* 2000: *The Audrey Hepburn Story (TV). Adventures of Tom Thumb and Thumbelina (voice only). Bunny.* 2001: *The Heartbreakers.*

HEYWOOD, Anne (Violet Pretty) 1930–
Dark-haired, widely-smiling British actress with distinctive high cheekbones: a beauty contest winner who worked hard to become recognized as a serious actress. Although successful, especially in one film, *The Fox*, she has not often been fortunate in her choice of parts, and has accepted some pretty weird assignments. Still, there can be few better-looking women of her age in the world. Married for more than 30 years to producer Raymond Stross.
1951: *†Lady Godiva Rides Again.* 1956: *Find the Lady. Checkpoint.* 1957: *Doctor at Large. The Depraved. Dangerous Exile. Violent Playground.* 1958: *Floods of Fear.* 1959: *The Heart of a Man. Upstairs and Downstairs. Carthage in Flames.* 1960: *A Terrible Beauty (US: The Night Fighters).* 1961: *Petticoat Pirates. Stork Talk.* 1962: *Vengeance (US: The Brain).* 1963: *The Very Edge.* 1964: *90 Degrees in the Shade.* 1967: *The Fox.* 1968: *The Awful Story of the Nun of Monza.* 1969: *The Chairman (GB: The Most Dangerous Man in the World). Midas Run (GB: A Run on Gold).* 1971: *I Want What I Want.* 1972: *Assassino . . . e al telefono (GB: The Killer is on the Phone).* 1973: *The Nun and the Devil. Trader Horn.* 1975: *Dance in the Open Air Under the Elms.* 1978: *Good Luck, Miss Wyckoff.* 1979: *Ring of Darkness.* 1984: *Secrets of the Phantom Caverns (later What Waits Below).*

†As Violet Pretty

HICKS, Sir Seymour
(Arthur S. Hicks) 1871–1949
British star of stage comedies, an actor-manager who married his oft-time stage

partner, Ellaline Terriss (1871–1971). After a few early silents, he became the first British actor to take a company to the World War I battlefront. With the coming of sound, Hicks, now a character star, transferred several of his stage hits to the screen. Knighted in 1934.
*1907: Seymour Hicks Edits the Tatler. 1913: *Seymour Hicks and Ellaline Terriss. David Garrick. Scrooge. 1914: Always Tell Your Wife. 1915: A Prehistoric Love Story. 1923: Always Tell Your Wife (remake). 1927: Blighty. 1930: *Tell Tales. †Sleeping Partners. The Love Habit. 1931: ††Glamour. Money for Nothing. 1934: The Secret of the Loch. 1935: Royal Cavalcade (US: Regal Cavalcade). Mr What's-His-Name. Vintage Wine. Scrooge (remake). 1936: Eliza Comes to Stay. It's You I Want. 1937: Change for a Sovereign. 1939: The Lambeth Walk. Young Man's Fancy. 1940: Pastor Hall. Busman's Honeymoon (US: Haunted Honeymoon). 1947: Fame is the Spur. 1948: Silent Dust.*

†Also directed ††Also co-directed

HILL, Terence (Mario Girotti) 1939–
German-born star with piercing blue eyes, in Italian films as a teenager. For 15 years he played leads in home produce and supports in international ventures, before a change of hair colour (from dark to fair) and name nudged him to world-wide stardom in spaghetti westerns, often in tandem with burly Bud Spencer (Carlo Pedersoli, 1931–). English-language films oddly did less well, and Hill returned to knockabout action in Italy with Spencer. He took his 'Lucky Luke' film character into a TV series in 1991.
1951: †Vacanze col gangster. †La voca del silenzio. 1953: †Villa Borghese. 1954: †Divisione folgore. 1955: †Gli sbandati. †La vena d'oro. 1956: †Mamma sconosciuta. †Guaglione. †Bambino. 1957: †La grande strada azzurra. †Lazzarella. 1958: †La spada e la croce. 1959: †Hannibal. †Carthage in Flames. †Il padrone delle ferriere. †Cerasella. 1960: †Un militaro e mezzo. †Guiseppe venduto dei fratelli (GB: Sold into Egypt. US: Joseph and his Brethren). 1961: †The Wonders of Aladdin. †Magdalena. †Seven Seas to Calais. 1962: †The Leopard. 1964: †Die Lady (GB: Frustration. US: Games of Desire). †Unter Geiern (GB: Among Vultures. US: Arizona Wildcat). †La rivincita di Ivanhoe. 1965: †Schüsse im Dreivierteltakt. †Der Ölprinz (GB and US: Rampage at Apache Wells). †Old Surehand: erste Teil (GB and US: Flaming Frontier). †Duell vor Sonnenuntergang. †Winnetou II (GB and US: Last of the Renegades). †Du suif dans l'Orient. †Ruf der Wälder. 1966: †La grosse pagaille. †El Misterioso Senor Van Eyck. †Die Nibelungen I – Siegfried. †Die Nibelungen II – Whom the Gods Destroy (GB: Whom the Gods Wish to Destroy). 1967: †Io non protesto, io amo. Dio perdona io no (GB: Blood River). Rita of the West. 1968: Preparati la bara. I quattro dell' Ave Maria (GB: Revenge in El Paso). 1969: Barbaglia. La collina degli stivali (US: Boot Hill). 1970: They Call Me Trinity. The True and the False. La collera del vento. 1971: Trinity is Still My Name. 1972: Baron Blood. E poi lo chiamarono il Magnifico (GB: Man of the East). Piu forte ragazzi (GB: All the Way Boys!). 1973: My Name is Nobody. 1974: Altrimenti ci Arrambiamo (GB: Watch Out, We're Mad!). 1975: Porgi d'altra guancia. Un genio, due compari, un pollo (US: Nobody's the Greatest). 1976: Crime Busters. 1977: Mr Billion. March or Die. 1978: Super Cops. Odds and Evens. 1979: I'm for the Hippopotomus. 1980: Super Snooper (US: Super Fuzz). 1981: The Super Fire Busters. A Friend is a Treasure. 1982: ‡Don Camillo. Hands Off the Island. 1983: Go For It! 1984: The Crew. 1985: Don Camillo II. 1987: Renegade Luke. 1991: ‡Lucky Luke. 1994: ‡The Fight Before Christmas. 1996: Virtual Weapon. 1997: The Flying Dutchman.

†As Mario Girotti ‡And directed

HILLER, Dame Wendy 1912–
Pretty, chestnut-haired British actress with rosy cheeks and fierce eyebrows. Filmed only from time to time, but made her name with an unmistakable voice and a series of determinedly independent heroines. Drifted too soon into a more mature kind of role in which her individual approach was less effective, although she took a Best Supporting Actress Oscar in *Separate Tables*. Created Dame in 1975. Further Oscar-nominated for *Pygmalion* and *A Man for All Seasons*. Around in indomitable cameos until the 1990s.
*1937: Lancashire Luck. 1938: Pygmalion. 1941: Major Barbara. 1945: I Know Where I'm Going. 1951: *To Be a Woman (narrator only). Outcast of the Islands. 1953: Single-Handed (US: Sailor of the King). 1957: How to Murder a Rich Uncle. Something of Value. *Bernard Shaw. 1958: Separate Tables. 1960: Sons and Lovers. 1963: Toys in the Attic. 1966: A Man for All Seasons. 1969: David Copperfield (TV. GB: cinemas). 1974: Murder on the Orient Express. 1976: Voyage of the Damned. 1978: The Cat and the Canary. 1980: The Elephant Man. 1982: Making Love. Witness for the Prosecution (TV). 1983: Attracta (TV). 1985: The Importance of Being Earnest (TV). 1986: The Death of the Heart. 1987: The Lonely Passion of Judith Hearne. 1992: The Best of Friends (TV).*

HINES, Gregory 1946–
Mournful-looking, bag-eyed, narrow-faced American dancer and actor, often with moustache and straggly goatee beard. An innovative tap dancer, he began entertaining with his brother Maurice at five, first as The Hines Kids, then as The Hines Brothers. Later their father, Maurice Sr, joined the act which was billed as Hines, Hines and Dad. Gregory formed a jazz-rock band in the 1970s and concentrated on this and a solo Broadway musical career, before breaking into films at 35. Mainly a co-star rather than a star, he has also choreographed several films and tried his hand at direction.
1981: Wolfen. History of the World Part I. 1983: Deal of the Century. 1984: The Cotton Club. The Muppets Take Manhattan. 1985: White Nights. 1986: Running Scared. 1988: Off Limits (GB: Saigon). 1989: Tap. 1991: Eve of Destruction. A Rage in Harlem. White Lie (released 1994 to cable TV). 1992: T Bone n Weasel (TV). 1994: Dead Air (TV). Renaissance Man. 1995: Waiting to Exhale. A Stranger in Town (TV). The Ox and the Eye/Good Luck/Guys Like Us. 1996: Trigger Happy/Mad Dog Time. The Preacher's Wife. The Cherokee Kid (TV). 1997: The Tic Code (TV. Released 1999). Color of Justice (TV). Subway Stories: Tales from the Underground (TV). 1998: Bohemian Love. 1999: Once in the Life. Things You Can Tell Just by Looking at Her. 2000: Who Killed Atlanta's Children? (TV).

As director: 1994: White Man's Burden. 1996: Magenta.

HOBSON, Valerie 1917–1988
Tall, elegant, full-lipped, long-faced, Irish-born leading lady in British films. Began at 16, spending two years in Hollywood in her teens before returning to Britain, where she remained quite popular, despite limited output, for the next 15 years in upper-bracket roles. In fact, it was a surprise when she retired at 37. Married producer Anthony Havelock-Allan and politician John Profumo.

She spent most of her later time working for Lepra, a leprosy relief charity organization. Died from a heart attack.

1933: For Love of You. Eyes of Fate. 1934: The Path of Glory. Two Hearts in Waltztime Badger's Green. †Great Expectations. The Man Who Reclaimed His Head. Life Returns (released 1938). 1935: Oh, What a Night! Strange Wives. Rendezvous at Midnight. Bride of Frankenstein. The WereWolf of London. The Mystery of Edwin Drood. The Great Impersonation. 1936: August Week-end (GB: Week-End Madness). Chinatown Squad. Tugboat Princess. The Secret of Stamboul. No Escape. 1937: Jump for Glory (US: When Thief Meets Thief). 1938: The Drum (US: Drums). This Man is News. 1939: Q Planes (US: Clouds Over Europe). The Spy in Black (US: U-Boat 29). The Silent Battle (US: Continental Express). This Man in Paris. 1940: Contraband (US: Blackout). 1941: Atlantic Ferry (US: Sons of the Sea). 1942: Unpublished Story. 1943: Adventures of Tartu (US: Tartu). 1946: The Years Between. Great Expectations. 1947: Blanche Fury. 1948: The Small Voice (US: Hideout). 1949: Kind Hearts and Coronets. Train of Events. The Interrupted Journey. The Rocking Horse Winner. 1952: The Card (US: The Promoter). Who Goes There? (US: The Passionate Sentry). Meet Me Tonight. The Voice of Merrill (US: Murder Will Out). 1953: Background. 1954: Knave of Hearts (US: Lovers, Happy Lovers).

†Scenes deleted from final release print

HODIAK, John 1914–1955
Forthright, sincere, often-moustachioed American leading actor with a harsh voice but smoothly ingratiating manner. He tended to be a bit stiff at times, but spent nine quite profitable years at M-G-M, where he made almost all of his films. Married to Anne Baxter 1946–1953. Died from a coronary thrombosis.

1943: A Stranger in Town. I Dood It (GB: By Hook or By Crook). Swing Shift Maisie (GB: The Girl in Overalls). Song of Russia. 1944: Ziegfeld Follies (released 1946). Maisie Goes to Reno (US: You Can't Do That to Me). Lifeboat. Sunday Dinner for a Soldier. Marriage Is a Private Affair. 1945: A Bell for Adano. 1946: The Harvey Girls. Two Smart People. Somewhere in the Night. 1947: Love from a Stranger (GB: A Stranger Walked In). The Arnelo Affair. Desert Fury. 1948: Homecoming. Command Decision. The Bribe. 1949: Malaya (GB: East of the Rising Sun). Battleground. Ambush. 1950: The Miniver Story. A Lady without Passport. 1951: The People against O'Hara. Night unto Morning. Across the Wide Missouri. 1952: The Sellout. *Screen Snapshots No. 206. Battle Zone. 1953: Mission over Korea (GB: Eyes of the Skies). Ambush at Tomahawk Gap. Conquest of Cochise. 1954: Dragonfly Squadron. 1955: Trial. 1956: On the Threshold of Space.

HOFFMAN, Dustin 1937–
Dark-haired, personable, shy-seeming, slightly nasal American actor, short of stature, who burst into the front rank as *The Graduate* and has consistently played people much younger than his real age. In TV series from 1961, he has latterly shown commendable tenacity in hunting for a wide variety of roles. But after his Academy Award for *Kramer vs. Kramer* in 1980, his film schedule slackened dramatically, although he made headlines again as the reluctant female impersonator in *Tootsie*, which won him an Academy Award nomination. Previously Oscar-nominated for *The Graduate, Midnight Cowboy* and *Lenny*. Second Academy Award for *Rain Man*. Further Oscar nomination for *Wag the Dog.*

1966: Un dollaro per sette vigliacci (GB and US: Madigan's Millions). 1967: The Tiger Makes Out. The Graduate. 1969: John and Mary. Midnight Cowboy. 1970: Little Big Man. Arthur Penn. 1922: Themes and Variants *Arthur Penn . . . the Director. 1971: The Point (TV: narrator only). Who is Harry Kellerman and why is he saying these terrible things about me? Alfredo, Alfredo. Straw Dogs. 1973: *Sunday Father. Papillon. 1974: Lenny. 1976: All the President's Men. Marathon Man. 1977: Straight Time. 1978: Agatha. 1979: Kramer vs. Kramer. 1982: Tootsie. 1985: Death of a Salesman (TV). Private Conversations. 1987: Ishtar. 1988: Rain Man. 1989: Family Business. Common Threads (narrator only). 1990: Dick Tracy. 1991: Billy Bathgate. Hook. 1992: Hero (GB: Accidental Hero). 1993: Earth and the American Dream (voice only). 1995: Outbreak. 1996: American Buffalo. Sleepers. 1997: Mad City. Wag the Dog. 1998: Sphere. 1999: The Messenger: The Story of Joan of Arc (GB: Joan of Arc).*

HOFFMANN, Gaby
(Gabriela Hoffman) 1982–
Grave, earnest, dark-haired American child player who grew into a tall, lively, dark-eyed, bright-looking teenage actress. The daughter of underground star and Andy Warhol acolyte Viva (Vivanee Hoffmann, 1948–), Gaby had an unusual childhood, living at the Chelsea Hotel in New York with her mother until she was 11. She was the muse for the children's books her mother co-wrote, *Gaby at the Chelsea*. In commercials at four and films at seven, she started the major part of her acting career in 1992 and soon proved one of Hollywood's most natural and emotionally affecting child players.

1989: Field of Dreams. Uncle Buck. 1992: This is My Life. 1993: Sleepless in Seattle. The Man Without a Face. 1995: Freaky Friday (TV). Whose Daughter is She? (TV. GB: Semi-Precious). Now and Then. 1996: Everyone Says I Love You. 1997: Volcano. 1998: Strike!/ The Hairy Bird. 1999: 200 Cigarettes. Snapped. Coming Soon. Black & White.

HOGAN, Hulk (Terry Bollea) 1953–
Towering American wrestler and actor with wispy golden hair and bandido moustache who brought his formidable frame to films after seven years (1984–1991) as World Wrestling Champion. The films mixed straight action with action comedy and Hogan was briefly a box-office attraction in the early 1990s before spinning off into guest spots and video ventures. Once a hot baseball prospect before turning to the grunt-'n'-grapple game, Hogan regained the world heavyweight wrestling title for a few months in 1998 before losing it again. Sometimes billed as Hollywood Hogan or Terry 'Hulk' Hogan.

1982: Rocky III. 1989: No Holds Barred. 1990: Gremlins 2 The New Batch. 1991: Suburban Commando. 1992: Rough Stuff

(Later and GB: Mr Nanny). 1994: Thunder in Paradise (TV). 1996: The Secret Agent Club (filmed 1993). Santa with Muscles. Spy Hard. 1997: The Ultimate Weapon. Shadow Warriors (later on TV as Assault on Devil's Island). 1998: 3 Ninjas: High Noon at Mega Mountain. Shadow Warriors II: Hunt for the Death Merchant (later on TV as Assault on Death Mountain). 1999: McCinsey's Island. Muppets from Space.

HOGAN, Paul 1939–
Straw-haired Australian comedian with weatherbeaten features. A star on TV in his native country for many years, Hogan became a world star on the strength of one film, Crocodile Dundee, which gave him a funny, likeable, admirable, down-to-earth 'outback' character that worldwide audiences went for in their millions. Hogan's film career has stuttered and almost stopped since then, but he's had a day in the sun many less successful film actors would envy. Married (second) his co-star in the 'Dundee' films, American actress Linda Kozlowski.
1980: Fatty Finn. 1986: Crocodile Dundee (GB and US: 'Crocodile' Dundee). 1988: 'Crocodile' Dundee II. 1990: Almost an Angel. 1994: Lightning Jack. 1996: Flipper. 1998: Floating Away. 2001: Crocodile Dundee in Hollywood.
As director: 1989: The Humpty Dumpty Man.

HOLDEN, William
(W. Beedle) 1918–1981
Smoothly handsome, light-haired American leading man with Bob Hope nose and roguishly charming smile. Although he was popular for a long while, and won an Academy Award for Stalag 17 in 1953 (with

further nominations for Sunset Boulevard and Network), too few films made use of his tremendous talent for portraying charming, callow opportunists, and he was allowed to drift along in a series of stiff roles which demanded and usually got bland performances. Married to Brenda Marshall (qv) from 1941 to 1971. Died from loss of blood after cutting his head in a fall.
1938: Prison Farm. 1939: Each Dawn I Die. Million Dollar Legs. Golden Boy. Invisible Stripes. 1940: Those Were the Days (GB: Good Old School Days). Our Town. Arizona. 1941: *Variety Reel. I Wanted Wings. Texas. 1942: The Remarkable Andrew. Meet the Stewarts. The Fleet's In. 1943: Young and Willing. *Wings Up. 1947: Variety Girl. Blaze of Noon. Dear Ruth. 1948: Apartment for Peggy. The Man from Colorado. Rachel and the Stranger. 1949: *Hollywood Goes to Church. Miss Grant Takes Richmond (GB: Innocence is Bliss). Dear Wife. The Dark Past. Streets of Laredo. 1950: Father is a Bachelor. Born Yesterday. *You Can Change the World. Sunset Boulevard. Union Station. 1951: Submarine Command. Force of Arms. Boots Malone. 1952: The Turning Point. 1953: The Moon is Blue. Stalag 17. Forever Female. Escape from Fort Bravo. 1954: Executive Suite. The Bridges at Toko-Ri. Sabrina (GB: Sabrina Fair). The Country Girl. 1955: Love is a Many-Splendored Thing. Picnic. 1956: Toward the Unknown (GB: Brink of Hell). The Proud and Profane. 1957: The Bridge on the River Kwai. 1958: The Key. 1959: The Horse Soldiers. 1960: The World of Suzie Wong. 1961: The Counterfeit Traitor. 1962: Satan Never Sleeps (GB: The Devil Never Sleeps). The Lion. 1963: Paris When It Sizzles. 1964: The 7th Dawn. 1966: Alvarez Kelly. 1967: Casino Royale. 1968: The Devil's Brigade. 1969: The Christmas Tree. The Wild Bunch. 1971: Wild Rovers. 1972: The Revengers. 1973: The Blue Knight (TV). Breezy. 1974: The Towering Inferno. Open Season. 1976: 21 Hours at Munich. Network. 1978: Damien – Omen II. Fedora. Escape to Athena. 1979: Ashanti. 1980: When Time Ran Out... The Earthling. 1981: SOB. Mysteries of the Sea (TV – narrator only).

HOLLIDAY, Judy
(Judith Tuvim) 1922–1965
Bright, bouncy blonde New Yorker who, after success on Broadway, came to films in her late twenties and played a few memorably dim-witted but lovable dames, revelling in

some witty scripts and winning an Oscar for Born Yesterday. Married jazz musician Gerry Mulligan. Died from cancer of the throat.
1938: †Too Much Johnson. 1944: Winged Victory. Greenwich Village. Something for the Boys. 1949: Adam's Rib. 1950: Born Yesterday. 1952: The Marrying Kind. 1953: It Should Happen to You. 1954: Phffft! *Extra Dollars. 1956: The Solid Gold Cadillac. Full of Life. 1960: Bells Are Ringing.

†Unreleased

HOLLOWAY, Stanley 1890–1982
Big, broad, benign British character star with dark, slicked-back hair, hearty manner and booming tones. Initially a revue artist and monologuist – a side of his talent that remained popular – he made a prolific career in films from 1933, becoming a top star of the British cinema from the mid 1940s to the mid 1950s. Remained an active entertainer well into his eighties. Many of his rich characterizations epitomized the ordinary man. Nominated for an Oscar in My Fair Lady.
1921: The Rotters. 1929: The Co-Optimists. 1933: Sleeping Car. Lily of Killarney (US: Bride of the Lake). The Girl from Maxim's. 1934: Road House. Love at Second Sight (US: The Girl Thief). Sing as We Go. D'Ye Ken John Peel (US: Captain Moonlight). In Town Tonight. 1935: *Sam and His Musket (voice only). Squibs. Play Up the Band. 1936: *Alt! Who Goes There? (voice only). *Sam's Medal (voice only). *Carmen (voice only). *Beat the Retreat (voice only). 1937: Song of the Forge. Our Island Nation. The Vicar of Bray. Sam Small Leaves Town. Cotton Queen. *The Lion and Albert (voice only). *Drummed Out (voice only). *Three Ha'pence a Foot (voice only).

*Gunner Sam (voice only). 1939: *Co-Operette. 1940: *Highlights of Variety No.21. 1941: Major Barbara. 1942: Salute John Citizen. Sabotage at Sea. 1944: This Happy Breed. The Way Ahead. Champagne Charlie. *A Cautionary Tale. 1945: The Way to the Stars (US: Johnny in the Clouds). Brief Encounter. Caesar and Cleopatra. 1946: Wanted for Murder. Carnival. 1947: Meet Me at Dawn. Nicholas Nickleby. 1948: One Night With You. Snowbound. Hamlet. Noose (US: The Silk Noose). Another Shore. The Winslow Boy. 1949: Passport to Pimlico. The Perfect Woman. *A Change for the Better (voice only). 1950: Midnight Episode. 1951: Painter and Poet (narrator only). One Wild Oat. The Lavender Hill Mob. *Sailor's Consolation (voice only). The Magic Box. Lady Godiva Rides Again. 1952: The Happy Family (US: Mr Lord Says No). Meet Me Tonight. 1953: The Beggar's Opera. The Titfield Thunderbolt. A Day to Remember. Meet Mr Lucifer. 1954: Fast and Loose. 1955: Value for Money (voice only). An Alligator Named Daisy. 1956: Jumping for Joy. 1958: Hello London. Alive and Kicking. 1959: No Trees in the Street (US: No Tree in the Street). 1960: No Love for Johnnie. 1961: On the Fiddle (US: Operation Snafu). 1964: My Fair Lady. 1965: In Harm's Way. Ten Little Indians. 1966: The Sandwich Man. 1968: A Little of What You Fancy (voice only). Mrs. Brown, You've Got a Lovely Daughter. 1969: Run a Crooked Mile (TV). How to Make It (GB: Target Harry). 1970: The Private Life of Sherlock Holmes. 1971: Flight of the Doves. 1972: Up the Front. 1976: Journey into Fear.

HOLLY, Lauren 1963–
Dark-haired, narrow-faced, small-chinned American actress of anxious-looking prettiness. Born to teachers, she took a BA in literature, but was already bitten by the acting bug while studying for her degree and was into films at 22. Since then she's played a mixture of leading and supporting roles. Married/divorced actor-producer Daniel Quinn and actor-comedian Jim Carrey. She might have met Carrey earlier, but turned down the lead in Ace Ventura Pet Detective in 1993!
1985: Love Lives On (TV). 1986: Seven Minutes in Heaven/This Side of Heaven. Band of the Hand. 1990: The Adventures of Ford Fairlane. Archie: To Riverdale and Back Again (TV). 1992: Fugitive Among Us (TV). 1993: Dragon: The Bruce Lee Story.

Dangerous Heart (TV). 1994: Dumb and Dumber. 1995: Sabrina. 1996: Beautiful Girls. Down Periscope. 1997: Turbulence. A Smile Like Yours. 1998: No Looking Back. Money Kings/Vig (TV). 1999: Entropy. Any Given Sunday. 2000: The Last Producer. 2001: What Women Want.

HOLM, Celeste 1919–
The nice thing about Celeste Holm is that she actually looks as though she has a marvellous sense of humour. The blue-eyed blonde American actress and singer, of Norwegian parentage, was the original Ado Annie in the stage version of Oklahoma!, but resisted all screen offers until after World War II. After a mixture of musicals, comedies and heavy drama (and an Oscar for Gentleman's Agreement), she became best known in wise-cracking roles, and has improved most of her (too few) films. Also nominated for Academy Awards on All About Eve and Come to the Stable. Married (4th) to actor Wesley Addy (1912–1996) since 1961.
1946: Three Little Girls in Blue. 1947: Carnival in Costa Rica. Gentleman's Agreement. 1948: Road House. The Snake Pit. Chicken Every Sunday. 1949: Come to the Stable. A Letter to Three Wives (voice only). Everybody Does It. 1950: Champagne for Caesar. All About Eve. 1955: The Tender Trap. 1956: High Society. 1961: Bachelor Flat. 1967: Cosa Nostra – an Arch Enemy of the FBI (TV. GB: cinemas). Doctor, You've Got to be Kidding! 1972: The Delphi Bureau (TV). 1973: Tom Sawyer. 1974: The Underground Man (TV). Death Cruise (TV). 1976: Bittersweet Love. 1977: J. Edgar Hoover, Godfather of the FBI (GB: The Private Files of J. Edgar Hoover). The Love Boat 2 (TV). 1981: Midnight Lace (TV). 1983: This Girl for Hire (TV). 1985: Jessie (TV). 1987: 3 Men and a Baby. Marilyn Monroe: Beyond the Legend. Murder by the Book (TV). 1989: Polly (TV). Christine Cromwell: Things That Go Bump in the Night (TV). 1990: Easy Come, Easy Go (TV). Polly – Comin' Home (TV). 1996: Once You Meet a Stranger (TV). 1997: Still Breathing.

HOLM, Sir Ian (I.H. Cuthbert) 1931–
Small, dark, earnest, no-neck British classical actor who, after a sterling career on stage and television, began his film career at 37 with some eye-catching performances, but was too often shunted into unsuitable roles that made the least of his talents. Later he seemed to

have settled for leading roles in the theatre and supporting parts in films, but then thrust his way back to the front in the mid-1980s. Nominated for an Academy Award in Chariots of Fire. Knighted in 1998.
1958: Girls at Sea. 1968: The Fixer. The Bofors Gun. A Midsummer Night's Dream. 1969: Oh! What a Lovely War. 1970: A Severed Head. 1971: Nicholas and Alexandra. Mary, Queen of Scots. Young Winston. 1973: The Homecoming. 1974: Juggernaut. 1976: The Man in the Iron Mask (TV). Robin and Marian. Shout at the Devil. 1977: March or Die. 1978: The Thief of Baghdad. Les Miserables (TV). 1979: Alien. SOS Titanic (TV. GB: cinemas). The Lost Boys (TV. GB: cinemas). All Quiet on the Western Front (TV. GB: cinemas). 1981: Chariots of Fire. Time Bandits. 1982: Return of the Soldier. 1983: Greystoke: The Legend of Tarzan Lord of the Apes. 1984: Brazil. Laughterhouse (later Singleton's Pluck). Dance with a Stranger. 1985: Wetherby. DreamChild. 1988: Another Woman. 1989: Henry V. 1990: Hamlet. 1991: Kafka. Uncle Vanya (TV). Naked Lunch. 1992: Blue Ice. 1993: The Hour of the Pig. 1994: Mary Shelley's Frankenstein. The Madness of King George. 1995: Loch Ness. 1996: Big Night. Night Falls on Manhattan. 1997: The Fifth Element. The Sweet Hereafter. A Life Less Ordinary. Incognito. 1998: King Lear (TV). eXistenZ. 1999: Simon Magus. The Match. Alice Through the Looking Glass. Shergar. The Miracle Maker (voice only). Animal Farm (voice only). 2000: Beautiful Joe. Bless the Child. Wisconsin Death Trip (narrator only). Joe Gould's Secret. 2001: The Lord of the Rings: The Fellowship of the Ring. From Hell. Esther Kahn.

HOLMES, Phillips 1907–1942
Tall, fair-haired, blue-eyed, ultra-handsome American actor, mostly in 'sensitive' roles, the most prominent member of an acting family. The son of character actor Taylor Holmes (1872–1959), he was the leading man in the original version of An American Tragedy – remade 20 years later as A Place in the Sun – but his career waned after that. He was killed in a plane crash while training for service with the Royal Canadian Air Force. Brother Ralph Holmes (1915–1945), also an actor, committed suicide.
1928: †Varsity. †His Private Life. 1929: †The Wild Party. †Stairs of Sand. Pointed Heels. †The Return of Sherlock Holmes. 1930: Only

the Brave. Paramount on Parade. Man to Man. Her Man. The Dancers. The Devil's Holiday. Grumpy. 1931: Confessions of a Co-Ed (GB: Her Dilemma). *Paramount Pictorial: The Ziegfeld Girls. An American Tragedy. Stolen Heaven. The Criminal Code. 1932: Broken Lullaby (GB: The Man I Killed). 70,000 Witnesses. Night Court (GB: Justice for Sale). Make Me a Star. Two Kinds of Woman. 1933: The Secret of Madame Blanche. Men Must Fight. Looking Forward (GB: Service). Storm at Daybreak. Dinner at Eight. The Big Brain (GB: Enemies of Society). Stage Mother. Penthouse (GB: Crooks in Clover). Beauty for Sale (GB: Beauty). 1934: Private Scandal. Nana. Million Dollar Ransom. Great Expectations. Caravan. No Ransom (GB: Bonds of Honour). Casta diva/The Divine Spark. 1935: Ten Minute Alibi. 1936: General Spanky. Chatterbox. The House of a Thousand Candles. 1937: The Dominant Sex. 1938: Housemaster.

†As Phillips R. Holmes

HOLT, Jack (Charles John Holt) 1888–1951
Whippy, dark-haired, moustachioed American leading man whose narrowed eyes and florid complexion suggested villainous types. In fact, he became the cowboy hero of numerous silent westerns before quitting his studio (Paramount) for a wider variety of roles with the arrival of Talkies. Started as a stuntman. Ended his career in smaller roles, but held his popularity with his most loyal fans. Father of western star Tim Holt and actress Jennifer Holt (both qv). Died from a heart attack.
1914: Salomy Jane. 1915: A Cigarette – That's All. Mother Ashton. The Campbells Are

Coming. Jewel. *As the Twig is Bent. *What the River Foretold. The Power of Fascination. The Master Key (serial). The Broken Coin (serial). The Lumber Yard Gang. 1916: The Dumb Girl of Portici. *Behind the Mask. *The Unexpected. *The Wire Pullers. *The Phone Message. Saving the Family Name. Brennon o' the Moor. The Chalice of Sorrow. The Black Sheep of the Family. Born of the People. Liberty – A Daughter of the USA (serial). Naked Hearts. The Madcap Queen of Crona. The Strong Arm Squad. *The Princely Bandit. His Majesty Dick Turpin. The False Part. Her Better Self. The Desperado. The Better Man. 1917: Giving Becky a Chance. The Cost of Hatred. The Call of the East. Patria (serial). The Little American. Sacrifice. Joan the Woman. The Secret Game. The Inner Shrine. Mutiny. The Honor of His House. 1918: Green Eyes. Headin' South. One More American. The Claw. A Desert Wooing. The Marriage Ring. Love Me. Hidden Pearls. The Road through the Dark. White Man's Law. 1919: For Better, For Worse. The Squaw Man. Cheating Cheaters. A Midnight Romance. The Life Line. A Sporting Chance. The Woman Thou Gavest Me. Victory. 1920: Kitty Kelly MD. Crooked Streets. Held by the Enemy. The Best of Luck. Midsummer Madness. The Sins of Rosanne. 1921: After the Show. The Call of the North. The Lost Romance. The Mask. All Souls' Eve. Ducks and Drakes. The Grim Comedian. 1922: North of the Rio Grande. Bought and Paid For. Making a Man. On the High Seas. The Man Unconquerable. While Satan Sleeps. *A Trip to Paramounttown. 1923: The Cheat. Hollywood. A Gentleman of Leisure. Nobody's Money. The Marriage Maker (GB: The Faun). The Tiger's Claw. 1924: North of 36. Wanderer of the Wasteland. The Lone Wolf. Don't Call It Love. Empty Hands. 1925: Eve's Secret. The Thundering Herd. Wild Horse Mesa. The Light of Western Stars. The Ancient Highway. 1926: Born to the West. Man of the Forest. Forlorn River. The Enchanted Hill. Sea Horses. The Blind Goddess. 1927: The Warning. The Mysterious Rider. The Tigress. 1928: The Vanishing Pioneer. Avalanche. The Water Hole. Submarine. Court-Martial. The Smart Set. 1929: Sunset Pass. Father and Son. The Donovan Affair. Flight. 1930: Border Legion. Hell's Island. Vengeance. The Squealer. 1931: White Shoulders. Dirigible. A Dangerous Affair. The Last Parade. Fifty Fathoms Deep. Maker of Men. Subway Express. 1932: Behind the Mask. This Sporting Age. Man Against Woman. War Correspondent. 1933: When Strangers Marry. The Whirlpool. The Wrecker. The Woman I Stole. Master of Men. 1934: The Defense Rests. I'll Fix It! Black Moon. 1935: *Hollywood Hobbies. The Awakening of Jim Burke (GB: Iron Fist). *Screen Snapshots No.5. The Littlest Rebel. Storm over the Andes. The Best Man Wins. Unwelcome Stranger. 1936: San Francisco. Crash Donovan. Dangerous Waters. End of the Trail (GB: Revenge). North of Nome (GB: The Lawless North). 1937: Roaring Timber. Trapped by G-Men. Outlaws of the Orient. Under Suspicion. Trouble in Morocco. 1938: Reformatory. Crime Takes a Holiday. Outside the Law. Making the Headlines. Flight into Nowhere. 1939: Fugitive at Large. Trapped in the Sky. Hidden Power. Whispering Enemies. 1940: Outside the 3-Mile

Limit (GB: Mutiny on the Seas). Passport to Alcatraz (GB: Alien Sabotage). Prison Camp. The Great Plane Robbery. 1941: *Stars at Play. Holt of the Secret Service (serial). The Great Swindle. 1942: Northwest Rangers. Thunder Birds. Cat People. 1943: Customs of the Service. 1944: The Articles of War. 1945: They Were Expendable. 1946: The Chase. My Pal Trigger. Renegade Girl. Flight to Nowhere. 1947: The Wild Frontier. 1948: The Treasure of the Sierra Madre. Arizona Ranger. The Strawberry Roan (GB: Fools Awake). The Gallant Legion. 1949: The Last Bandit. Brimstone. Loaded Pistols. Task Force. Red Desert. 1950: Trail of Robin Hood. Return of the Frontiersman. 1951: King of the Bullwhip. Across the Wide Missouri. 1952: The Daltons' Women.

HOLT, Jennifer
(Elizabeth Holt) 1920–1997
Included here more to complete the Holt family trio than in deference to her acting achievements, the female Holt was a spiky-looking blonde lady who followed her father and brother to Hollywood and seemed to revel in outdoor roles. She was soon elevated to playing female leads in second-feature westerns and spent the whole of her brief film career doing virtually just that. Her looks and style suggested she could have tackled wise-cracking blondes, but she quit the movies in 1948, following the demise of the Eddie Dean oaters for Poverty Row studio PRC. At one time (1947-51) married to actor William Bakewell (1907–1993). He was the second of her eight husbands. She later moved to England, where she died from cancer.
1941: †Mr Dynamite. †San Francisco Docks. †Stick to Your Guns. 1942: †Pardon My Sarong. †Broadway. †Eagle Squadron. Private Buckaroo. The Silver Bullet. Deep in the Heart of Texas. Little Joe, the Wrangler. 1943: Adventures of the Flying Cadets (serial). Cheyenne Roundup. Cowboy in Manhattan. Frontier Law. Raiders of Sunset Pass. Get Going. Hers to Hold. Hi, Buddy! Lone Star Trail. The Old Chisholm Trail. Raiders of San Joaquin. Tenting Tonight on the Old Camp Ground. Oklahoma Raiders (GB: Midnight Raiders). 1944: Marshal of Gunsmoke. Riders of the Santa Fé (GB: Mile a Minute). Beyond the Pecos (GB: Beyond the Seven Seas). Renegades of the Rio Grande (GB: Bank Robbery). Guns of the Law. Outlaw Trail. 1945: Song of Old Wyoming. The Navajo Trail. Under Western Skies. Gun Smoke. The

Lost Trail. 1946: Moon Over Montana. Trigger Fingers. Hop Harrigan (serial). 1947: Pioneer Justice. Over the Santa Fé Trail (GB: No Escape). Where the North Begins. Trail of the Mounties. Buffalo Bill Rides Again. Ghost Town Renegades. The Fighting Vigilantes. Shadow Valley. Stage to Mesa City. 1948: Tornado Range. The Hawk of Powder River. The Tioga Kid. Range Renegades.

†As Jacqueline Holt

HOLT, Patrick (P. Parsons) 1912–1993
Tall British leading man of erect bearing, with dark, curly hair. His aristocratic but sensitive manner made him the Dennis Price of the B film, in many of which he starred between 1948 and 1957, sometimes opposite second wife Sandra Dorne (married 1954). In progressively smaller roles from the late fifties, but he sustained this minor-key career with some tenacity. Gave up an army career for acting; first wife (1947–1953) was actress Sonia Holm (1922–1974). His health deteriorated rapidly after the death of Dorne at Christmas 1992.
1938: The Return of the Frog. 1939: Sword of Honour. 1940: Convoy. *Dangerous Comment. 1946: Hungry Hill. 1947: Master of Bankdam. Frieda. The October Man. When the Bough Breaks. The Mark of Cain. 1948: My Sister and I. Fly Away Peter. Portrait from Life (US: The Girl in the Painting). Good Time Girl. 1949: A Boy, a Girl and a Bike. Marry Me. Boys in Brown. 1950: Guilt is My Shadow. 1951: The Magic Box. 1952: 13 East Street. Ivanhoe. Circumstantial Evidence. Come Back Peter. 1954: The Stranger Came Home (US: The Unholy Four). John Wesley. The Golden Link. The Men of Sherwood Forest. 1955: The Dark Avenger. Miss Tulip Stays the Night. Stolen Assignment. *Diplomatic Error. 1956: The Gelignite Gang. Alias John Preston. Operation Murder. Count of Twelve. The Girl in the Picture. 1957: Suspended Alibi. Fortune is a Woman (US: She Played with Fire). There's Always a Thursday. Murder Reported. 1958: I Was Monty's Double. Further Up the Creek. The Challenge. Too Hot to Handle (US: Playgirl After Dark). 1961: Dentist on the Job (US: Get On With It!). The Frightened City. 1962: Serena. Flight from Singapore. Night of the Prowler. 1963: Girl in the Headlines (US: The Model Murder Case). 1964: Guns at Batasi. 1965: Thunderball. Genghis Khan. 1966: The Vulture. The Fighting Prince of Donegal. 1968:

Hammerhead. 1969: The Magic Christian. 1970: Cromwell. When Dinosaurs Ruled the Earth. No Blade of Grass. 1971: Young Winston. 1972: Diamonds on Wheels. Psychomania. 1974: The Amorous Milkman. Legend of the Werewolf. 1977: Let's Get Laid! 1978: The Wild Geese. 1980: The Sea Wolves. Priest of Love. 1986: Playing Away (TV). The Whistle Blower. 1989: Loser Takes All/Strike It Rich.

HOLT, Tim
(Charles John Holt Jnr) 1918–1973
One of Hollywood's strangest careers: the son of Jack Holt, chunky, gentle-mannered, darkly wavy-haired Tim Holt gave fine performances in major films at periodic intervals, yet spent the vast majority of his career as the hero of 'B' westerns, held back perhaps by his own modesty and lack of stature. Once said 'I made a great picture like The Treasure of the Sierra Madre, then went back to RKO and got more low-budget westerns. I didn't get it.' He wasn't the only one. Died from brain cancer.
1928: The Vanishing Pioneer. 1937: History is Made at Night. Stella Dallas. 1938: Sons of the Legion. Gold is Where You Find It. The Law West of Tombstone. I Met My Love Again. 1939: The Rookie Cop (GB: Swift Vengeance). Spirit of Culver (GB: Man's Heritage). Renegade Ranger. Fifth Avenue Girl. The Girl and the Gambler. Stagecoach. 1940: The Fargo Kid. Wagon Train. Swiss Family Robinson. Laddie. 1941: *Stars at Play. Along the Rio Grande. Cyclone on Horseback. Land of the Open Range. Come On, Danger! Thundering Hoofs. The Bandit Trail. Riding the Wind. Dude Cowboy. Six-Gun Gold. Robbers of the Range. Back Street. 1942: The Magnificent Ambersons. Pirates of the Prairie. Bandit Ranger. 1943: The Avenging Rider. Sagebrush Law. Fighting Frontier. Hitler's Children. Red River Robin Hood. 1946: My Darling Clementine. 1947: Under the Tonto Rim. Wild Horse Mesa. Thunder Mountain. 1948: The Treasure of the Sierra Madre. The Arizona Ranger. Guns of Hate. Gun Smugglers. Western Heritage. Indian Agent. 1949: The Stagecoach Kid. Brothers in the Saddle. Rustlers. Riders of the Range. Masked Raiders. The Mysterious Desperado. Storm over Wyoming. 1950: Dynamite Pass. Rider from Tucson. Rio Grande Patrol. Border Treasure. Law of the Badlands. 1951: Saddle Legion. Gunplay. Pistol Harvest. Hot Lead. Overland Telegraph. His Kind of Woman. 1952: Target. Trail Guide. Desert Passage.

Road Agent. 1957: The Monster That Challenged the World. 1963: The Yesterday Machine. 1971: This Stuff'll Kill Ya!

HOMOLKA, Oscar 1898–1978
Austrian actor with eyebrows as heavy as his Viennese accent and a grating voice which helped him create some formidable characters in Germany, Britain and Hollywood. He was also more than capable of carrying leading roles, notably in Hitchcock's Sabotage, although in latter days he played more than his fair share of German, and later Iron Curtain, spies and commissars. Married (fourth of four) to actress Joan Tetzel (1924–1977) from 1949. Nominated for an Academy Award in I Remember Mama.
1926: Das Abenteuer eines Zehnmarkscheines. Brennende Grenze. Das Mädchen ohne Heimat. 1927: Dirnentragödie. Fürst oder Clown. Die heilige Lüge. Der Kampf des Donald Westhof. Die Leibeigenen. Schinderhannes. Petronella. Regine, die Tragödie einer Frau. 1928: Die Rothausgasse. 1929: Masken. Revolte im Erziehungshaus. 1930: Dreyfus. Hokus Pokus. 1931: Der Weg nach Rio. Im Geheimdienst. Nachtkolonne. 1914 (die letzten Tage von dem Weltbrand). Zwischen Nacht und Morgen (GB: Between Midnight and Dawn). 1932: Die Nächte von Port Said. 1933: Moral und Liebe. Spione am Werk. Unsichtbare Gegner. 1936: Rhodes of Africa (US: Rhodes). Everything is Thunder. Sabotage (US: The Woman Alone). 1937: Ebb Tide. Hidden Power. 1940: Comrade X. Seven Sinners. 1941: The Invisible Woman. Rage in Heaven. Ball of Fire. 1943: Mission to Moscow. Hostages. 1946: The Shop at Sly Corner (US: The Code of Scotland Yard). 1948: I Remember Mama. 1949: Anna Lucasta. 1950: The White Tower. 1951: Der schweigende Mund. 1952: Top Secret (US: Mr Potts Goes to Moscow). 1953: The House of the Arrow. 1954: Prisoner of War. 1955: The Seven Year Itch. 1956: War and Peace. 1957: A Farewell to Arms. 1958: The Plot to Kill Stalin (TV). Tempest. The Key. Heart of Darkness (TV). 1960: In the Presence of Mine Enemies (TV). Assassination Plot at Teheran (TV). Victory (TV). 1961: Mr Sardonicus (GB: Sardonicus). 1962: Boys' Night Out. Wonderful World of the Brothers Grimm. The Mooncussers (TV. GB: cinemas). 1963: The Long Ships. 1964: Joy in the Morning. 1966: Funeral in Berlin. 1967: Billion Dollar Brain. Assignment to Kill. The Happening. Jack of Diamonds. 1968: Dr Jekyll and Mr Hyde

(TV). The Madwoman of Chadlot. 1970: The Executioner. Song of Norway. 1974: The Tamarind Seed. 1975: One of Our Own (TV). The Curse of the Hope Diamond (TV).

HOPE, Bob (Leslie Hope) 1903–
Dark-haired, ski-slope-nosed, English-born Hollywood star comedian, in America from childhood. After a slow start, his film career really blossomed with *The Cat and the Canary* and he remained at his funniest throughout the forties, a period which saw the beginning of his friendly rivalry with Bing Crosby – in and out of the 'Road' films – and made him one of the world's most popular stars, in roles which highlighted his ability to get into situations which exposed the yellow streak running down his back. From the mid-fifties the standard of his material fell away. Special Oscars 1940, 1944, 1952, 1965. He received an honorary British knighthood in 1998.
1934: *Paree, Paree. *Going Spanish. *Soup for Nuts. 1935: *Watch the Birdie. *The Old Grey Mayor. *Double Exposure. 1936: *Calling All Tars. *Shop Talk. 1938: The Big Broadcast of 1938. College Swing (GB: Swing, Teacher, Swing). Give Me a Sailor. Thanks for the Memory. *Don't Hook Now. 1939: Never Say Die. Some Like It Hot. The Cat and the Canary. 1940: Road to Singapore. The Ghost Breakers. 1941: Caught in the Draft. *Cavalcade of the Academy Awards. Road to Zanzibar. Louisiana Purchase. Nothing But the Truth. 1942: Road to Morocco. My Favourite Blonde. Star Spangled Rhythm. They Got Me Covered. 1943: *Welcome to Britain. Let's Face It. *Show Business at War. 1944: The Princess and the Pirate. 1945: *All-Star Bond Rally. Duffy's Tavern. Road to Utopia. *Hollywood Victory Caravan. 1946: Monsieur Beaucaire. 1947: My Favourite Brunette. Variety Girl. Where There's Life. Road to Rio. 1948: *Radio Broadcasting Today. The Paleface. *Screen Snapshots No. 166. *Rough But Hopeful. 1949: *Honor Caddie. Sorrowful Jones. The Great Lover. 1950: Fancy Pants. *On Stage Everybody! 1951: My Favourite Spy. The Lemon Drop Kid. 1952: The Greatest Show on Earth. Son of Paleface. Road to Bali. Off Limits (GB: Military Policemen). *A Sporting Oasis. 1953: Scared Stiff. Here Come the Girls. Casanova's Big Night. 1954: *Screen Snapshots No. 224. 1955: The Seven Little Foys. 1956: That Certain Feeling. The Iron Petticoat. 1957: Beau James. The Heart of Show Business. 1958: Paris Holiday. *Showdown at Ulcer Gulch. 1959: The Five

Pennies. Alias Jesse James. 1960: The Facts of Life. 1961: Bachelor in Paradise. *Kitty Caddy (voice only). The Road to Hong Kong. 1963: Critic's Choice. A Global Affair. Call Me Bwana. 1965: I'll Take Sweden. 1966: The Oscar. Boy, Did I Get a Wrong Number. *Hollywood Star-Spangled Revue. Not With My Wife You Don't. 1967: Eight on the Lam (GB: Eight on the Run). The Movie Maker (TV). 1968: The Private Navy of Sergeant O'Farrell. 1969: How to Commit Marriage. 1972: Cancel My Reservation. 1978: The Muppet Movie. 1979: Ken Murray's Shooting Stars. 1985: Spies Like Us. 1986: A Masterpiece of Murder (TV). 1999: The Source (doc).

HOPKINS, Sir Anthony 1937–
Neatly built, dark-haired, assiduous-looking Welsh actor with distinctive, coaxing voice, capable of playing a wide range of characters and ages. From his beginnings on the London stage in the 1960s, he expressed disinterest in becoming a conventional leading man and showed a preference for the theatre. Still, leading roles pursued and eventually overtook the reluctant star, who has often been at his best as characters under varying kinds of stress beneath an outwardly calm surface. He won an Academy Award for his cannibalistic psycho-killer in *The Silence of the Lambs*, and was nominated again in the very different *The Remains of the Day*, *Nixon* and *Amistad*. Knighted in 1993, he remained busy in intense roles throughout the 1990s.
1963: *Changes. 1968: The Lion in Winter. 1969: Hamlet. The Looking Glass War. 1971: When Eight Bells Toll. Young Winston. 1973: A Doll's House (Garland). 1974: QB VII (TV). Juggernaut. The Girl from Petrovka. All Creatures Great and Small. 1975: Dark Victory (TV). 1976: The Lindbergh Kidnapping Case (TV). Victory at Entebbe (TV. GB: cinemas). 1977: Audrey Rose. A Bridge Too Far. 1978: International Velvet. Magic. 1979: Mayflower: The Pilgrims' Adventure (TV). 1980: A Change of Seasons. The Elephant Man. 1981: The Bunker (TV). Peter and Paul (TV). 1982: The Hunchback of Notre Dame (TV). 1984: Io e il Duce (US: Mussolini and I). Arch of Triumph (TV). The Bounty. 1985: Guilty Conscience (TV). 1986: The Good Father. 84 Charing Cross Road. Blunt (TV). 1988: Across the Lake (TV). Mickey. The Dawning. The Tenth Man (TV). 1989: A Chorus of Disapproval. Face of the Earth (TV). Great Expectations (TV). 1990:

Desperate Hours. The Silence of the Lambs. One Man's War. 1991: Spotswood. Howards End. Freejack. 1992: Bram Stoker's Dracula. 1993: The Innocent. The Trial. The Remains of the Day. Shadowlands. Earth and the American Dream (voice only). 1994: Legends of the Fall. Selected Exits (TV). The Road to Wellville. 1995: August (and directed). Nixon. 1996: Surviving Picasso. 1997: The Edge. Amistad. 1998: Meet Joe Black. The Mask of Zorro. Instinct. 1999: Titus. Siegfried and Roy: The Magic Box (narrator only). 2000: Mission: Impossible 2. 2001: Hannibal.

HOPKINS, Miriam
(Ellen M. Hopkins) 1902–1972
A blue-eyed American blonde who looked just like a thirties version of Cybill Shepherd, Miriam Hopkins was exactly right for her time, her theatrically chic and faintly bitchy sophistication dovetailing beautifully with Lubitsch comedies and other high-gloss offerings to give her star charisma. The passing of the thirties reduced her to ordinariness and she faded from the cinema scene. Married to director Anatole Litvak (1937–1939), third of four. Died from a heart attack. An Oscar nominee for *Becky Sharp*.
1928: *The Home Girl. 1930: Fast and Loose. 1931: The Smiling Lieutenant (and French language version). Twenty Four Hours (GB: The Hours Between). Dr Jekyll and Mr Hyde. 1932: The World and the Flesh. Two Kinds of Women. Trouble in Paradise. Dancers in the Dark. 1933: The Story of Temple Drake. Design for Living. The Stranger's Return. 1934: All of Me. She Loves Me Not. The Richest Girl in the World. 1935: Barbary Coast. Becky Sharp. Splendor. 1936: These Three. Men Are Not Gods. 1937: Woman Chases Man. The Woman I Love (GB: The Woman Between). 1938: Wise Girl. 1939: The Old Maid. 1940: Virginia City. The Lady with Red Hair. 1942: A Gentleman After Dark. 1943: Old Acquaintance. 1944: Skirmish on the Home Front. 1949: The Heiress. 1951: The Mating Season. 1952: Carrie. The Outcasts of Poker Flat. 1962: The Children's Hour (GB: The Loudest Whisper). 1965: Fanny Hill. 1966: The Chase. 1970: Comeback (later copyrighted 1973 as Savage Intruder).

HOPPER, Dennis 1935–
Light-haired, sharp-featured American actor, distantly related to Hedda and William Hopper. Began as bad brothers and whining, wild-eyed psychopaths, then graduated to

hippie heroes. Took the world by storm with *Easy Rider* and, although his pet project *The Last Movie* was less successful, he scored a directing hit with *Colors* in 1987. Oscar nominee for *Hoosiers*. In the 1990s, a series of sadistic, eye-catching villains brought his career full circle. Five times married.

1954: *Johnny Guitar*. 1955: *I Died a Thousand Times. Rebel Without a Cause.* 1956: *The Steel Jungle. Giant. Gunfight at the OK Corral.* 1957: *No Man's Road (TV. GB. cinemas). The Story of Mankind.* 1958: *From Hell to Texas (GB: Manhunt).* 1959: *The Young Land.* 1960: *Key Witness.* 1961: *Night Tide.* 1963: *Tarzan and Jane Regained: Sort of.* 1965: *The Sons of Katie Elder.* 1966: *Planet of Blood.* 1967: *The Glory Stompers. Cool Hand Luke. Panic in the City. Hang 'Em High. The Trip.* 1968: *Head.* 1969: *True Grit.* †*Easy Rider.* 1970: *The American Dreamer.* 1971: †*The Last Movie. Crush Proof.* 1973: *Kid Blue/Dime Box. Hex.* 1975: *James Dean – The First American Teenager. The Sky is Falling.* 1976: *Tracks. Mad Dog Morgan (GB: Mad Dog).* 1977: *The American Friend. Les apprentis sorciers.* 1978: *L'ordre et la securité du monde. Couleur chair. The Human Highway (released 1983).* 1979: *Apocalypse Now. Wild Times (TV).* 1980: *Out of the Blue. King of the Mountain.* 1981: *Reborn.* 1983: *White Star (released 1985). Jungle Warriors. The Osterman Weekend. Rumble Fish.* 1984: *The Utterly Monstrous Mind-Roasting Summer of O C and Stiggs (released 1987). The Inside Man.* 1985: *My Science Project. Running Out of Luck. Stark (TV).* 1986: *The American Way. Blue Velvet. The Texas Chainsaw Massacre Part 2. River's Edge. Hoosiers (GB: Best Shot). Black Widow.* 1987: *Straight to Hell. Blood Red. Colors (directed only). The Pick-Up Artist.* 1989: *Backtrack (GB: Catchfire). Chattahoochee. Flashback.* 1990: *The Hot Spot (directed only). Superstar: The Life and Times of Andy Warhol. Motion and Emotion.* 1991: *Paris Trout (cable TV. GB: cinemas). The Indian Runner. Eye of the Storm. Midnight Heat. Hearts of Darkness: A Filmmaker's Apocalypse. Doublecrossed (video).* 1992: *Nails. Red Rock West. Money Men. Super Mario Bros.* 1993: *Heart of Justice (TV). True Romance. Schneeweiss-Rosenrot. Boiling Point.* 1994: †*Chasers. Witch Hunt (cable TV). Speed. Search and Destroy.* 1995: *Waterworld. Carried Away (GB: Acts of Love).* *A *Hero of Our Time.* 1996: *Basquiat. Space Truckers.* 1997: *The Blackout. Top of the World. The Truman Show. Road Ends. The*

Good Life. The Last Days of Frankie the Fly. Lesser Prophets/The Prophet's Game. 1998: *Me and Will. Meet the Deedles. Lured Innocence.* 1999: *Ed TV. Straight Shooter. The Source (doc). Jesus' Son. Bad City Blues. The Venice Project.* 2000: *Luck of the Draw. The Spreading Ground. Held for Ransom. Knockaround Guys. Listen with Your Eyes.* 2001: *Ticker.*

†*And directed*

HORNE, Lena 1917–
Lithe, dynamic, barnstorming songstress who put more emotion into songs – hot or sweet – than some did into acting. Her splendid voice and pleasant personality made her the first black performer to sign a long-term contract with a major studio (M-G-M), but they frittered her away in all-black films and guest appearances.

1938: *The Duke is Tops.* 1940: *Harlem Hotshots. 1941: *Boogie Woogie Dream. 1942: Harlem on Parade. Panama Hattie. 1943: I Dood It (GB: By Hook or By Crook). Swing Fever. Thousands Cheer. Cabin in the Sky. Stormy Weather. 1944: Ziegfeld Follies (released 1946). We've Come a Long, Long Way. Broadway Rhythm. Two Girls and a Sailor. 1946: Till the Clouds Roll By. *Studio Visit. *Mantan Messes Up. 1948: Words and Music. 1950: Duchess of Idaho. 1956: Meet Me in Las Vegas (GB: Viva Las Vegas!). 1969: Death of a Gunfighter. 1978: The Wiz. 1994: That's Entertainment! III.

HORROCKS, Jane 1964–
Slim, waif-like, dark-haired (later blonde) British actress with downturned mouth. Usually in central roles as much put-upon

working girls, she also has astounding talents in mimicry and an impressive vocal range. These talents, put together, led to her performing one-woman shows in which she impersonates a string of actresses and singers with uncanny accuracy. She was a big success in the play *The Rise and Fall of Little Voice*, which was written for her and led to a hit film version in which she also starred.

1987: *Road.* 1988: *The Dressmaker. The Wolves of Willoughby Chase. No Crying He Makes (TV).* 1989: *The Witches. The Fifteen Streets (TV). Getting It Right. Heartland (TV).* 1990: *Memphis Belle. Life is Sweet.* 1991: *Alive and Kicking (TV).* 1992: *Bad Girl (TV).* 1993: *Deadly Advice. Second Best.* 1994: *Butter. 1995: Some Kind of Life. 1996: Combination Skin (voice only). 1997: Bring Me the Head of Mavis Davis. 1998: Little Voice. 1999: Hunting Venus (TV). 2000: Chicken Run (voice only). The Lion of Oz and the Badge of Courage (voice only). Born Romantic.

HOSKINS, Bob 1942–
Pugnacious British actor with solid build, disappearing dark hair and the voice of a Cockney rough diamond, which can turn convincingly to an assumed American accent. After hard early times, he broke into the public eye with the lead in *The Long Good Friday* as the London gangster, and the TV series *Pennies from Heaven*. Cunningly avoided type-casting as vicious types to hit the jackpot in 1988 as the leading human star in *Who Framed Roger Rabbit*. Still around in a good variety of star character roles, he has also become a familiar face in TV commercials, and tried his hand at direction with varying success. Oscar nominee for *Mona Lisa*.

1972: *Up the Front.* 1973: *The National Health.* 1975: *Royal Flash.* 1976: *Inserts.* 1979: *Zulu Dawn. The Long Good Friday.* 1982: *Pink Floyd the Wall.* 1983: *The Act. Beyond the Limit (GB: The Honorary Consul). Lassiter.* 1984: *Io e Il Duce (US: Mussolini and I/Mussolini: The Decline and Fall of Il Duce). The Cotton Club.* 1985: *Sweet Liberty. Brazil.* *The Woman Who Married Clark Gable. 1986: Mona Lisa. 1987: A Prayer for Dying. The Secret Policeman's Third Ball (voice only). The Lonely Passion of Judith Hearne. 1988: The Raggedy Rawney (and directed). Who Framed Roger Rabbit. 1989: Heart Condition. 1990: The Cherry Orchard. Mermaids. 1991: Shattered. The

Inner Circle/The Projectionist. The Favour, the Watch and the Very Big Fish. Hook. 1992: Blue Ice. Passed Away. 1993: Super Mario Bros. The Big Freeze (unreleased). 1994: Balto (voice only). 1995: Rainbow (and directed). Nixon. 1996: The Secret Agent. Michael. 1997: TwentyFourSeven. Spice World. 1998: Cousin Bette. Parting Shots. Captain Jack/An Inch Over the Horizon. The White River Kid. 1999: Felicia's Journey. A Room for Romeo Brass. Live Virgin. Tube Tales (TV. Co-director only). 2000: Noriega: God's Favorite. Enemy at the Gates. Don Quixote (TV). The Sleeping Dictionary.

HOUSTON, Donald 1923–1991
Handsome golden-haired Welshman who shot to prominence when given the star role in his first film. But his immobile style was of little help in some gloomy melodramas, and he gradually lost his star status as the fifties wore on. Later mixed comedy with men of violence. Brother of actor Glyn Houston (1926–). Married actress Brenda Hogan (1928–).
1949: The Blue Lagoon. A Run for Your Money. 1950: Dance Hall. 1952: My Death is a Mockery. Crow Hollow. 1953: The Red Beret (US: Paratrooper). Small Town Story. The Large Rope. *Point of No Return. The Case of Express Delivery. 1954: Doctor in the House. Devil's Point (US: Devil's Harbor). The Happiness of Three Women (US: Wishing Well). 1955: The Flaw. Doublecross. Return to the Desert. 1956: Find the Lady. The Girl in the Picture. 1957: Yangtse Incident (US: Battle Hell). The Surgeon's Knife. *Every Valley (narrator only). 1958: A Question of Adultery. The Man Upstairs. Room at the Top. 1959: *Jessy. Danger Within (US: Breakout). 1961: The Mark. *A Letter for Wales (and narrator). 1962: The 300 Spartans. Twice Round the Daffodils. The Longest Day. The Prince and the Pauper. Maniac. 1963: Doctor in Distress. Carry On Jack (US: Carry On Venus). 1964: 633 Squadron. 1965: A Study in Terror (US: Fog). 1967: The Viking Queen. 1968: Where Eagles Dare. The Bushbaby. 1969: A Prince for Wales (narrator only). 1970: My Lover, My Son. 1972: Sunstruck. 1973: Tales that Witness Madness. 1976: Voyage of the Damned. 1980: The Sea Wolves. 1981: Clash of the Titans.

HOUSTON, Whitney 1963–
Youthful-looking, pretty American actress and singer, a phenomenally successful recording star with impressive vocal range who decided to try her luck with movies in

the 1990s. Despite a limited acting ability, her first two films were big hits with the paying public, and she looks set to continue mixing her two entertainment worlds.
1992: The Bodyguard. 1995: Waiting to Exhale. 1996: The Preacher's Wife. 1997: Scratch the Surface (doc). Cinderella (TV).

HOWARD, Arliss
See WINGER, Debra

HOWARD, John (J. Cox) 1913–1995
Sturdy and businesslike, oft-moustachioed, brown-haired American actor. He made a forthright Bulldog Drummond in a series of films at Paramount, but his career, not helped by being cast as stuffy 'other men', seemed to be torpedoed by his (distinguished) wartime service. He found it impossible to regain his prewar footing, but did gain a measure of success in two popular television series of the fifties. Died from heart failure.
1935: †Four Hours to Kill. †Car 99. Annapolis Farewell (GB: Gentlemen of the Navy). Millions in the Air. 1936: Soak the Rich. 13 Hours by Air. Border Flight. Easy to Take. Valiant is the Word for Carrie. 1937: Let Them Live! (GB: Let Them Love). Mountain Music. Hold 'Em Navy (GB: That Navy Spirit). Hitting a New High. Penitentiary. Bulldog Drummond Comes Back. Lost Horizon. 1938: Touchdown Army (GB: Generals of Tomorrow). Bulldog Drummond's Revenge. Bulldog Drummond's Peril. Prison Farm. Arrest Bulldog Drummond! Bulldog Drummond in Africa. 1939: Disputed Passage. Bulldog Drummond's Secret Police. Bulldog Drummond's Bride. Grand Jury Secrets. What a Life. 1940: Green Hell. Man from Dakota (GB: Arouse and Beware). Texas Rangers

Ride Again. The Mad Doctor (GB: A Date with Destiny). The Philadelphia Story. 1941: Father Takes a Wife. Tight Shoes. The Invisible Woman. Three Girls About Town. A Tragedy at Midnight. The Man Who Returned to Life. 1942: Submarine Raider. Isle of Missing Men. The Undying Monster (GB: The Hammond Mystery). 1945: The Way to the Stars (US: Johnny in the Clouds). 1946: Le bataillon du ciel. 1947: Love from a Stranger (GB: A Stranger Walked In). 1948: I Jane Doe (GB: Diary of a Bride). 1949: The Fighting Kentuckian. 1950: Experiment Alcatraz. Radar Secret Service. 1951: ‡Dead Man's Voice. ‡The Man Who Wasn't There. ‡The Yellow Ticket. ‡The Innocent Lion. ‡The Bandaged Hand. ‡Where Time Stood Still. 1952: Models Inc (later Call Girl. GB: That Kind of Girl). 1954: Make Haste to Live. The High and the Mighty. 1957: Unknown Terror. 1966: Destination Inner Space. The Destructors. Le sorelle/So Evil My Sister. 1970: The Sky Bike. 1971: Buck and the Preacher. 1975: Capone.

†As John Cox Jr
‡US TV shorts shown in GB cinemas

HOWARD, Leslie (L.H. Stainer, originally possibly Laszlo Horvarth) 1893–1943
Tall, sensitive and intelligent-looking British actor (from a Hungarian family) with unruly fair wavy hair. His faintly distant romantic appeal made him enormously popular in Britain in the 1930s, and he repeated his success in Hollywood, where his youthful looks kept him in important star roles well into his forties. But he was never more happily cast than in Britain as The Scarlet Pimpernel. He went missing on a wartime flight between Portugal and England: his plane was believed shot down. Nominated for Academy Award for Berkeley Square and Pygmalion. Father of Ronald Howard (qv) and brother of character actor Arthur Howard (1910–1995) whose own son Alan is also a prominent actor.
1914: *The Heroine of Mons. 1917: The Happy Warrior. 1918: The Lackey and the Lady. 1920: *Five Pounds Reward. *Bookworms. 1930: Outward Bound. 1931: Never the Twain Shall Meet. A Free Soul. Devotion. Service for Ladies (US: Reserved for Ladies). Five and Ten (GB: Daughter of Luxury). 1932: Smilin' Through. The Animal Kingdom (GB: The Woman in His House). 1933: The Lady is Willing. Secrets. Berkeley Square.

Captured. 1934: British Agent. Of Human Bondage. *Hollywood on Parade No. 13. The Scarlet Pimpernel. 1935: The Petrified Forest. 1936: Romeo and Juliet. 1937: It's Love I'm After. Stand-In. 1938: ‡Pygmalion. 1939: Gone with the Wind. Intermezzo: a Love Story (GB: Escape to Happiness). 1940: *Common Heritage (narrator only). 1941: †Pimpernel Smith (US: Mister V). *From the Four Corners. 49th Parallel (US: The Invaders). *The White Eagle (narrator only). 1942: †The First of the Few (US: Spitfire). 1943: ‡The Gentle Sex.

†Also directed ‡Also co-directed

HOWARD, Ron 1953–

Fresh-faced, fair-haired American actor (and latterly director), in show business from early childhood. He moved from enfants terribles to teenage innocents, then had an enormous hit on TV with *Happy Days*. 'I'm kind of dull' he has said about himself, which is true of Howard the actor and one good reason why he has concentrated more and more on his skills as director, becoming one of Hollywood's hottest behind-the-camera bets in the mid-1980s following his box-office hits with *Splash* and *Cocoon*. He blossomed further as a director of multi-star, high-profile blockbusters in the 1990s and had a big hit with *Apollo 13*.

1956: †Frontier Woman. 1958: †The Journey. 1959: †Black December (TV). 1961: †The Music Man. 1963: †The Courtship of Eddie's Father. 1965: †The Village of the Giants. 1966: †Door-to-Door Maniac. 1967: †A Boy Called Nuthin' (TV). 1970: Smoke (originally for TV). 1971: The Wild Country. 1973: American Graffiti. Happy Mother's Day, Love George/Run, Stranger, Run. 1974: The Spikes Gang. The Migrants (TV). Huckleberry Finn (TV). Locusts (TV). 1975: The First Nudie Musical. 1976: Eat My Dust! The Shootist. 1977: Grand Theft Auto. 1978: Roger Corman: Hollywood's Wild Angel. 1979: More American Graffiti/The Party's Over/Purple Haze. 1980: Act of Love (TV). 1981: Fire on the Mountain (TV). 1982: Bitter Harvest (TV). 1986: Return to Mayberry (TV). 1997: Frank Capra's American Dream (doc. Narrator only).

†As Ronny Howard

As director: *1969: Deed of Derring-Do. 1977: Grand Theft Auto. 1979: Cotton Candy (TV). 1980: Through the Magic Pyramid (TV).*

1981: Skyward (TV). 1982: Night Shift. 1984: Splash. 1985: Cocoon. 1986: Gung Ho. 1998: Willow. 1989: Parenthood. 1991: Backdraft. 1992: Far and Away. 1994: The Paper. 1995: Apollo 13. 1996: Ransom. 1999: Ed TV. 2000: How the Grinch Stole Christmas.

HOWARD, Ronald
(R.H. Stainer) 1916–1996

Suave, scholarly-looking British actor with fair, wavy hair, son of Leslie Howard. He forsook a journalistic career to devote himself full time to acting in the late forties, but was too stolid to have his father's unique appeal and was usually to be found in British 'B' features. Despite presentable performances in a few international incursions (notably *Drango*), he did not become a big name. Mostly seen in later days as ex-Army types.

1941: Pimpernel Smith (US: Mister V). 1946: While the Sun Shines. 1947: My Brother Jonathan. Night Beat. 1948: Bond Street. The Queen of Spades. 1949: Now Barabbas was a robber . . . 1950: Portrait of Clare. Double Confession. 1951: Flesh and Blood. The Browning Version. Assassin for Hire. Night Was Our Friend. 1952: Wide Boy. 1953: *La même route. Black Orchid. Street Corner (US: Both Sides of the Law). Noose for a Lady. Glad Tidings. Flannelfoot. The World's a Stage (series: narrator only). 1954: The Thirteenth Green. 1956: Drango. The Hideout. 1957: Light Fingers. The House in the Woods. I Accuse! 1958: Moment of Indiscretion. Gideon's Day (US: Gideon of Scotland Yard). 1959: No Trees in the Street (US: No Tree in the Street). Man Accused. Babette Goes to War. 1960: The Spider's Web. Compelled. The Malpas Mystery. 1961: The Naked Edge. Murder She Said. Come September. The Monster of Highgate Ponds. Bomb in the High Street. The Spanish Sword. 1962: KIL 1. Fate Takes a Hand. Live Now – Pay Later. Nurse on Wheels. 1963: The Bay of Saint Michel (US: Pattern for Plunder). Siege of the Saxons. 1964: The Curse of the Mummy's Tomb. Week-End à Zuydcoote (GB and US: Weekend at Dunkirk). 1965: You Must Be Joking! 1967: Africa – Texas Style. 1969: Run a Crooked Mile (TV). 1971: The Hunting Party. 1974: Persecution. 1975: Take a Hard Ride. 1980: Act of Love (TV).

HOWARD, Sydney 1884–1946

Portly British comedian whose clenched teeth and twisted expression could as easily express disdain or despair. Popular in concert

parties, he came to films with the beginnings of sound and soon became the star of a number of medium-budget comedies which capitalized on his flapping gestures and dignified panics. He tried top character roles with some success in the war years; a press campaign to have him restored to major comedies in the postwar period was foiled by his early death from a heart attack at 61.

1929: Splinters. 1930: French Leave. 1931: Tilly of Bloomsbury. Almost a Divorce. Splinters in the Navy. Up for the Cup. 1932: The Mayor's Nest. It's a King! 1933: Up for the Derby. Night of the Garter. Trouble. 1934: It's a Cop. Transatlantic Merry-Go-Round. 1935: Where's George?/ The Hope of His Side. 1936: Fame. Chick. 1937: Splinters in the Air. What a Man! 1939: Shipyard Sally. 1940: Tilly of Bloomsbury (remake). 1941: Once a Crook. *Mr Proudfoot Shows a Light. 1943: When We Are Married. 1945: Flight from Folly.

HOWARD, Trevor
(T. Howard-Smith) 1913–1988

Brown-haired, sandpaper-voiced, intensely staring British actor who moved from stage to films in his late twenties, rose rapidly to the top via *Brief Encounter* and proved equally at home as hero or villain in a star run of 20 years. Although there were too many redfaced unworthy cameos in later years, the right part showed that Howard still had the stuff of great acting in him. Married to Helen Cherry (1915–) from 1944. Oscar nominee for *Sons and Lovers*. Died from influenza and bronchitis.

1944: Volga-Volga (dubbed voice). The Way Ahead (US: Immortal Battalion). 1945: The Way to the Stars (US: Johnny in the Clouds). Brief Encounter. 1946: I See a Dark Stranger

(US: *The Adventuress*). *Green for Danger*. 1947: *So Well Remembered*. *They Made Me a Fugitive* (US: *I Became a Criminal*). 1948: *The Passionate Friends* (US: *One Woman's Story*). 1949: *The Third Man*. *Golden Salamander*. 1950: *Odette*. *The Clouded Yellow*. 1951: *Lady Godiva Rides Again*. *Outcast of the Islands*. 1952: *The Gift Horse* (US: *Glory at Sea*). 1953: *The Heart of the Matter*. 1954: *The Stranger's Hand*. *Les Amants du tage* (GB: *The Lovers of Lisbon*). *April in Portugal* (voice only). 1955: *Cockleshell Heroes*. 1956: *Deception* (TV. GB: cinemas). *Around the World in 80 Days*. *Run for the Sun*. 1957: *Interpol* (US: *Pickup Alley*). *Manuela* (US: *Stowaway Girl*). 1958: *The Roots of Heaven*. *The Key*. 1960: *Moment of Danger* (US: *Malaga*). *The Hiding Place* (TV). *Sons and Lovers*. 1962: *Mutiny on the Bounty*. *The Lion*. 1963: *Man in the Middle*. 1964: *Father Goose*. 1965: *Operation Crossbow* (US: *The Great Spy Mission*). *The Liquidator*. *Morituri* (GB: *The Saboteur Code Name Morituri*). *Von Ryan's Express*. 1966: *The Poppy is Also a Flower* (GB: *Danger Grows Wild*). *Triple Cross*. 1967: *The Long Duel*. *Pretty Polly* (US: *A Matter of Innocence*). 1968: *The Charge of the Light Brigade*. 1969: *Battle of Britain*. *Twinky* (US: *Lola*). 1970: *Ryan's Daughter*. 1971: *The Night Visitor*. *Mary, Queen of Scots*. *Catch Me a Spy*. *Kidnapped*. 1972: *Ludwig*. *Pope Joan*. *The Offence*. 1973: *A Doll's House* (*Losey*). *Catholics* (TV). *Craze*. 1974: *11 Harrowhouse*. *Persecution*. *The Count of Monte Cristo* (TV. GB: cinemas). *Who?* 1975: *Hennessy*. *Death in the Sun*. *The Bawdy Adventures of Tom Jones*. *Conduct Unbecoming*. 1976: *Aces High*. 1977: *The Last Remake of Beau Geste*. *Eliza Frazer* (GB: TV as the *Rollicking Adventures of Eliza Frazer*). *Slavers*. 1978: *Die Rebellen/One Take Two* (GB: TV as *Flashpoint Africa*). *Superman*. *Stevie*. *How to Score . . . a Movie*. 1979: *Meteor*. *Night Flight*. *Hurricane*. *The Shillingbury Blowers* (TV). 1980: *Sir Henry at Rawlinson End*. *The Sea Wolves*. *Windwalker*. 1981: *Les années lumières* (GB and US: *Light Years Away*). 1982: *Gandhi*. *Inside the Third Reich* (TV). *The Deadly Game* (TV). *The Missionary*. 1983: *Sword of the Valiant*. *The Devil Impostor*. 1985: *Dust*. *Time After Time* (TV). 1986: *Foreign Body*. *Rumplestiltskin*. *Christmas Eve* (TV). 1987: *White Mischief*. *The Unholy*. 1988: *The Dawning*.

HOWELL, C. Thomas 1966–

Dark, tall, very boyish American actor, in show business from an early age (including a TV debut at five). A keen all-round sportsman, he was a junior rodeo champion at 14, but devoted himself to acting from 1982, and broke through to teen pin-up stardom as Ponyboy in *The Outsiders*. The 'C' stands for Christopher. Married/divorced Rae Dawn Chong (*qv*), first of two. Working hard through the 1990s, but mainly on titles that went straight to video.

1977: *It Happened One Christmas* (TV). 1982: *E.T. The Extra-Terrestrial*. 1983: *The Outsiders*. *Tank*. 1984: *Grandview USA*. 1985: *Red Dawn*. *Secret Admirer*. 1986: *Soul Man*. *The Hitcher*. 1987: *A Tiger's Tale*. *Into*

the Homeland (video). 1988: *Young Toscanini*. *Far Out Man*. 1989: *The Return of the Musketeers*. *Sketches* (released 1992 as *Breaking the Rules*). *The Eyes of the Panther* (TV). 1990: *Kid*. *Sideout*. *Curiosity Kills* (TV). 1991: *Nickel and Dime*. *First Force*. *All Tied Up*. 1992: *To Protect and Serve*. *That Night*. *Kiss and Tell/Tattle Tale*. *Jailbait*. 1993: *Streetwise*. *Natural Selection* (TV). *Gettysburg*. *Treacherous*. *Acting on Impulse* (TV. GB: *Secret Lies*). 1994: *Teresa's Tattoo*. *Power Play/Dangerous Indiscretion*. *Payback*. 1995: *Mad Dogs and Englishmen* (US: *Shameless*). *Suspect Device* (TV). *Sweeper*. *Baby Face Nelson*. *Hourglass*. 1996: *Pure Danger*. *Kindred: The Embraced* (TV). *The Third Force* (TV). *The Big Fall*. *Dead Fire/ Do or Die*. *Last Lives*. 1997: *A Conspiracy Within*. *Burning Down the House*. *Sleeping Dogs*. *Sealed with a Kiss* (TV). *Dilemma*. *Laws of Deception*. 1998: *Matter of Trust*. *Shepherd*. *Fatal Affair* (TV). 1999: *Avalanche*. *Hot Boyz*. *Enemy Action*. *Felons/Charades*. *The Glass Jar*. *Cybermaster*. 2000: *The Million Dollar Kid*.

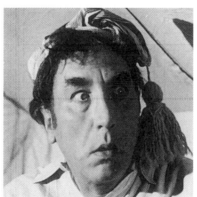

HOWERD, Frankie
(Francis Howard) 1917–1992
Lugubrious, crabbed-looking, purse-lipped, curly-haired British comedian whose unique, audience-belabouring style shot him to radio stardom immediately after World War II. Film roles proved less riotous, but he made invaluable contributions to seemingly unsaveable comedies. Died from a heart attack.

1954: *The Runaway Bus*. 1955: *An Alligator Named Daisy*. *The Ladykillers*. 1956: *Jumping for Joy*. *A Touch of the Sun*. 1958: *Further Up the Creek*. 1959: *Three Seasons*. 1961: *Watch It Sailor!* 1962: *The Fast Lady*. *The Cool*

Mikado. 1963: *The Mouse on the Moon*. 1966: *The Great St Trinian's Train Robbery*. 1967: *Carry On Doctor*. 1969: *Carry On Up the Jungle*. 1971: *Up Pompeii*. *Up the Chastity Belt*. 1972: *Up the Front*. 1973: *The House in Nightmare Park* (US: *Crazy House*). 1978: *Sergeant Pepper's Lonely Hearts Club Band*.

HUBSCHMID, Paul 1917–
Dark-haired, virile, handsome, cheerful-looking Swiss-born leading man whose reputation survived working in German films during World War II sufficiently for him to be offered work in Hollywood in 1949, under a new name – Paul Christian. Although he returned to Germany a few years later, he was for many years still billed as Paul Christian in the English speaking world, on those of his films (mostly swashbuckling adventures) that reached the international market.

1938: *Füsilier Wipf*. 1939: *Der letzte Appel* (unfinished). *Maria Ilona*. 1940: *My Dream*. *Mir lönd nüd lugg*. *Die Missbrauchten/Die missbrauchten Briefe*. 1942: *Der Fall Rainer*. *Meine Freundin Josephine*. *Altes Herz wird wiederung*. 1943: *Liebesbriefe*. *Der gebieterische Ruf*. *Wilder Urlaub*. 1944: *Das Gesetz der Liebe*. 1945: *Das seltsame Fräulein Sylvia*. 1948: *Der himmlische Walzer*. 1949: *Geheimnisvolle Tiefe*. *Gottes Engel sind überall*. *Arlberg Express*. *Bagdad*. 1950: *The Thief of Venice* (released 1953). 1952: *No Time for Flowers*. 1953: *The Beast from 20,000 Fathoms*. *Venus of Tivoli*. *Maske in blau*. *Le mystère de Palace-hotel*. *Musik bei nacht*. *Mit siebzehn beginnt das Leben*. *Les cloches n'ont pas sonné* (US: *Hungarian Rhapsody*). 1954: *Glückliche Reise*. *Schule für Eheglück*. 1955: *Ingrid*. *Die Frau des Botschafters*. *Rommel's Treasure*. 1956: *Heute hieratet mein Mann*. *Du bist Musik*. *Liebe die den Kopf verliert*. *Die goldene Brücke*. 1957: *Salzburger Geschichten*. *Die Zürcher Verlobung*. 1958: *Ihr 106 Geburtstag*. *La morte viene dallo spazio* (GB: *Death Comes from Outer Space*. US: *The Day the Sky Exploded*). *Scampolo*. *Italienreise – Liebe inbegriffen*. *Meine schöne Mama*. *Der Tiger von Eschnapur*. *Das indische Grabmal*. 1959: *Zwei Gitarren*. *Liebe Luft und lauter Lügen*. *Heldinnen*. *Alle Tage ist kein Sonntag*. *Marili*. *Auskunft im Cockpit*. 1960: *Journey to the Lost City*. *The Red Hand*. *Die junge Sünderin*. 1961: *Schwartz Rose, Rosemarie* (US: *Festival*). *Ich bin auch nur eine Frau*. 1963: *Elf Jahre und ein Tag*. *And So to Bed*. 1964: *Die Lady* (GB: *Frustration*. US: *Games of Desire*). *Le grain de sable*. *Die*

*Diamantenhölle am Mekong. Heirate mich, Chérie! 1965: The Devil's Agent. Playgirl (US: That Woman). Ruf der Wälder. Die Herren. Ich suche einen Mann. Der Mann mit den 1,000 Masken. Die schwedische Jungfrau. Die Unmoralischen. Mozambique. 1966: Funeral in Berlin. Caroline und die Männer über vierzig. A belles dents. Upperseven. Ein gewisses Verlangen. 1967: In Enemy Country. Karriere. 1968: Negresco **** Eine tödliche Affaire (GB: My Bed is Not for Sleeping). Manon '70. 1969: Taste of Excitement. Skullduggery. 1973: Versuchung im Sommerwind. 1983: Bolero. 1989: Klassezämekunft. 1991: Linda.*

‡Abridged US version (in one film) of Der Tiger von Eschnapur and Das indische Grabmal.

HUDSON, Rochelle 1914–1972
Pretty, dark-haired, square-faced American actress in films at 16, but mainly as repressed daughters and submissive wives. Stayed an actress all her working life, until illness curtailed her career in her fifties. She worked for US Intelligence in Central America during World War II. Died from pneumonia.
*1930: Laugh and Get Rich. 1931: Fanny Foley Herself (GB: Top of the Bill). Everything's Rosie. The Public Defender. Are These Our Children? 1932: Hell's Highway. Beyond the Rockies. Girl Crazy. Is My Face Red? Penguin Pool Murder (GB: The Penguin Pool Mystery). Liberty Road. Mysteries of the French Police/Secrets of the French Police. 1933: Wild Boys of the Road (GB: Dangerous Days). Love is Like That. She Done Him Wrong. Lucky Devils. The Past of Mary Holmes. Scarlet River. The Savage Girl. Love is Dangerous (GB: Women are Dangerous). Notorious But Nice. Doctor Bull. Mr Skitch. Walls of Gold. 1934: Harold Teen (GB: The Dancing Fool). Bachelor Bait. Judge Priest. *Hollywood Newsreel. The Mighty Barnum. Such Women Are Dangerous. Imitation of Life. 1935: I've Been Around. Life Begins at Forty. Les Miserables. Curly Top. Way Down East. Show Them No Mercy (GB: Tainted Money). 1936: The Music Goes Round. The Country Beyond. Poppy. Everybody's Old Man. Reunion (GB: Hearts in Reunion). 1937: Born Reckless. Woman Wise. That I May Live. She Had to Eat. 1938: Mr Moto Takes a Chance. Rascals. Storm over Bengal. 1939: Pride of the Navy. A Woman is the Judge. Smuggled Cargo. Pirates of the Skies. Missing Daughters. Konga, the Wild Stallion (GB: Konga). 1940:*

Convicted Woman. Babies for Sale. Island of Doomed Men. Men without Souls. Girls under 21. 1941: Meet Boston Blackie. The Stork Pays Off. The Officer and the Lady. 1942: Queen of Broadway. Rubber Racketeers. 1947: Bush Pilot. 1948: The Devil's Cargo. 1949: Sky Liner. 1955: Rebel without a Cause. 1964: Strait-Jacket. 1965: The Night Walker. Broken Sabre (TV. GB: cinemas). 1967: Dr Terror's Gallery of Horrors.

HUDSON, Rock (Roy Scherer) 1925–1985
A gentle giant: a big, beefy American actor with dark, curly hair. His intrinsically quiet and intellectual nature contrasted with the rugged man-of-action roles he was called upon to play in his early Universal-International days, a studio at which he became a star inside three years. Although nominated for an Oscar in *Giant*, he proved to be at his best in a series of smooth, battle-of-the-sexes comedies in the late 1950s and early 1960s in which Doris Day and Paula Prentiss had him looking like a baffled panda. After that good material eluded him and several of his subsequent films were scarcely seen outside America. His losing battle with AIDS made unsavoury headlines in 1985.
*1948: Fighter Squadron. 1949: Undertow. 1950: I Was a Shoplifter. Winchester 73. One Way Street. Peggy. The Desert Hawk. Shakedown. Double Crossbones. Tomahawk (GB: Battle of Powder River). Bright Victory (GB: Lights Out). 1951: Iron Man. The Fat Man. Air Cadet (GB: Jet Men of the Air). 1952: Has Anybody Seen My Gal. Bend of the River (GB: Where the River Bends). Scarlet Angel. Here Come the Nelsons. Horizons West. The Lawless Breed. 1953: Gun Fury. Seminole. The Golden Blade. Back to God's Country. Sea Devils. 1954: Taza, Son of Cochise. Bengal Brigade (GB: Bengal Rifles). Captain Lightfoot. Magnificent Obsession. 1955: All That Heaven Allows. One Desire. 1956: Never Say Goodbye. Written on the Wind. Four Girls in Town. Giant. 1957: Battle Hymn. The Tarnished Angels. A Farewell to Arms. Something of Value. 1958: Twilight for the Gods. 1959: This Earth is Mine. Pillow Talk. 1961: The Last Sunset. Lover Come Back. Come September. 1962: The Spiral Road. 1963: A Gathering of Eagles. Marilyn (narrator only). 1964: Send Me No Flowers. Man's Favorite Sport? 1965: Strange Bedfellows. A Very Special Favor. *The Nurse (narrator only). 1966: Blindfold. Seconds. Tobruk. 1968: Ice*

Station Zebra. 1969: Darling Lili. A Fine Pair. The Undefeated. 1970: Hornet's Nest. 1971: Pretty Maids All in a Row. 1972: Showdown. 1975: Embryo. 1978: Avalanche. 1979: The Martian Chronicles (TV). 1980: The Mirror Crack'd. 1981: The Patricia Neal Story (TV). 1984: The Ambassador. The Vegas Strip War (TV).

HUGHES, Mary Beth 1919–1995
Full-lipped, baby-faced blonde, in films direct from college plays and brief stage experience, in leading roles by the mid-forties, mostly in minor films, and almost equally as good girls and bad girls. Carried on in supporting roles in fifties' films before retiring around 1963. Unexpectedly reappeared in three low-budget seventies' movies and began entertaining in nightclubs as a singer and electric-bass player. Married to actor Ted/Michael North (second of five) from 1943 to 1947.
*1939: Within the Law. Broadway Serenade. Bridal Suite. The Covered Trailer. Dancing Co-Ed (GB: Every Other Inch a Lady). The Women. These Glamour Girls. Fast and Furious. 1940: *Chinese Garden Festival. Free, Blonde and 21. Lucky Cisco Kid. Star Dust. Sleepers West. Four Sons. The Great Profile. 1941: *Los Angeles Examiner Benefit. Ride on, Vaquero. Charlie Chan in Rio. The Cowboy and the Blonde. Dressed to Kill. The Great American Broadcast. Design for Scandal. Blue, White and Perfect. 1942: Over My Dead Body. The Night Before the Divorce. Orchestra Wives. The Ox-Bow Incident (GB: Strange Incident). 1943: Good Morning, Judge. Never a Dull Moment. Melody Parade. Follow the Band. 1944: Men on Her Mind. I Accuse My Parents. Take it Big. Timber Queen. 1945: The Great Flamarion. The Lady Confesses. Rockin' in the Rockies (GB: Partners in Fortune). 1948: Return Of Wildfire (GB: The Black Stallion). Joe Palooka in Winner Take All (GB: Winner Take All). Caged Fury. Waterfront at Midnight. Inner Sanctum. Last of the Wild Horses. 1949: Rimfire. El Paso. Grand Canyon. Riders in the Sky. The Devil's Henchman. Square Dance Jubilee. Young Man with a Horn (GB: Young Man of Music). 1950: Holiday Rhythm. 1951: Passage West (GB: High Venture). Close to My Heart. 1954: Highway Dragnet. Loophole. 1955: Las Vegas Shakedown. 1956: Dig That Uranium. 1957: Gun Battle at Monterey. 1958: No Time at All (TV). 1974: The Working Girls. 1975: Tanya. 1977: How's Your Love Life?*

HULBERT, Claude 1900–1964

Moon-faced, light-haired British comedy star with jutting upper lip, often to be found as blustering, babbling, upper-class 'silly asses' who shared the limelight with, and stole scenes from, the star. A hit on stage in the twenties and thirties: later a useful foil for Will Hay. Married actress Enid Trevor in 1924. Brother of Jack Hulbert (qv). Died in Australia.

1928: Champagne. 1929: Naughty Husbands. 1932: A Night Like This. Thark. The Mayor's Nest. Let Me Explain Dear. The Face at the Window. 1933: Heads We Go (US: The Charming Deceiver). Radio Parade. Their Night Out. The Song You Gave Me. 1934: Love at Second Sight (US: The Girl Thief). The Girl in Possession. A Cup of Kindness. Big Business. Lilies of the Field. 1935: Hello Sweetheart. Man of the Moment. Bulldog Jack (US: Alias Bulldog Drummond). 1936: Where's Sally? Wolf's Clothing. The Interrupted Honeymoon. Hail and Farewell. Olympic Honeymoon (later Honeymoon Merry-Go-Round). Take a Chance. The Vulture. 1937: Ship's Concert. It's Not Cricket. You Live and Learn. 1938: Simply Terrific. It's in the Blood. The Viper. His Lordship Regrets. Many Tanks Mr Atkins. 1940: Sailors Three (US: Three Cockeyed Sailors). 1941: The Ghost of St Michael's. 1943: The Dummy Talks. My Learned Friend. 1946: London Town (US: My Heart Goes Crazy). 1947: The Ghosts of Berkeley Square. 1948: Under the Frozen Falls. 1949: Cardboard Cavalier. 1955: Fun at St Fanny's. 1960: Not a Hope in Hell.

HULBERT, Jack 1892–1978

Jaunty Jack had a chin like a trowel, a prominent nose, a lick of hair and a gap in his teeth. But such was the impact of his happy-go-lucky personality, dry voice and great personal charm that he remained a favourite of London theatregoers, and, later, cinemagoers, as comedian, dancer, singer and light actor for nigh on 30 years. Married his stage partner, Cicely Courtneidge (qv), in 1916.

*1928: *British Screen Tatler No. 10. 1930: Elstree Calling. 1931: The Ghost Train. Sunshine Susie (US: The Office Girl). 1932: Jack's the Boy (US: Night and Day). Love on Wheels. Happy Ever After. 1933: Falling for You. 1934: Jack Ahoy! The Camels Are Coming. 1935: Bulldog Jack (US: Alias Bulldog Drummond). 1936: Jack of All Trades (US: The Two of Us). 1937: Take My Tip. Paradise for Two (US: The Gaiety Girls). 1938: Kate Plus Ten. 1940: Under Your Hat. 1948: *Highwaymen. 1950: Into the Blue (US: The Man in the Dinghy). 1951: The Magic Box. 1955: Miss Tulip Stays the Night. 1960: The Spider's Web. 1972: Not Now Darling. The Cherry Picker.*

HULCE, Tom 1953–

Slightly-built, snub-nosed, faintly apologetic-looking American actor, with dark, curly hair and diffident smile. Has tended to play simple souls, and made his first impact as Peter Firth's successor on Broadway in *Equus*. Didn't make much of a dent in the cinema world until chosen to play the title role in *Amadeus*, which won him an Oscar nomination. Has continued to perform well in offbeat roles, without becoming a solo box-office attraction, but disappeared from films after 1995. Also sings.

1977: 9/30/55 (GB: TV, as September 30, 1955). Emily, Emily (TV). 1978: National Lampoon's Animal House. 1980: Those Lips, Those Eyes. 1984: Amadeus. 1985: Echo Park. 1986: The Rise and Rise of Daniel Rocket (TV). 1987: Slam Dance. 1988: Shadowman. Dominick and Eugene (GB: Nicky and Gino). 1989: Die Dreitseilbahn. Black Rainbow. Parenthood. 1990: Murder in Mississippi (TV). 1991: The Inner Circle/The Projectionist. 1993: Fearless. 1994: Mary Shelley's Frankenstein. Land Mines. 1995: Wings of Courage. The Heidi Chronicles (TV). 1996: The Hunchback of Notre Dame (voice only).

HUME, Benita 1906–1967

Dark, sweetly pretty, serious-looking British leading lady with horizontal eyebrows. In films as a teenager, she became a big star of British films before leaving for Hollywood in

1935, after a visit two years earlier. Her career here was short and sweet: she met and married Ronald Colman (qv) and retired. They were married from 1938 until his death in 1958. In the same year, she married George Sanders (qv). Died from bone cancer.

*1924: The Happy Ending. 1925: *They Wouldn't Believe Me. *Her Golden Hair Was Hanging Down Her Back. 1926: Second to None. 1927: Easy Virtue. The Constant Nymph. 1928: A South Sea Bubble. A Light Woman. The Wrecker. The Lady of the Lake. Balaclava (US: Jaws of Hell). 1929: The Clue of the New Pin. High Treason. 1930: The House of the Arrow. Symphony in Two Flats. 1931: The Flying Fool. *Healthy, Wealthy and Why. A Honeymoon Adventure (US: Footsteps in the Night). The Happy Ending. Service for Ladies (US: Reserved for Ladies). 1932: Women Who Play. Diamond Cut Diamond (US: Blame the Woman). Sally Bishop. Help Yourself. Men of Steel. Lord Camber's Ladies. Discord. 1933: The Little Damozel. Worst Woman in Paris? Clear All Wires. Gambling Ship. Only Yesterday. Looking Forward (GB: Service). 1934: The Private Life of Don Juan. Jew Süss (US: Power). 1935: The Divine Spark. 18 Minutes. The Gay Deception. 1936: The Garden Murder Case. Suzy. Moonlight Murder. Rainbow on the River. Tarzan Escapes! 1937: The Last of Mrs Cheyney. 1938: Peck's Bad Boy with the Circus.*

HUNNICUTT, Gayle 1942–

Chestnut-haired American actress who, after a late start, played strong-nerved heroines in Hollywood, British and French films of the 1970s. Her film career seemed (surprisingly) to go adrift in the later years of the decade. Married to David Hemmings (qv) from 1968 to 1974, she now lives in Britain and works mainly in the theatre. Early 1980s interviews revealed that she had completely lost her American accent.

*1967: The Wild Angels. P.J. (GB: New Face in Hell). 1968: The Smugglers (TV). 1969: Marlowe. Eye of the Cat. 1970: Freelance. Fragment of Fear. 1971: The Love Machine. 1972: *Today Mexico Tomorrow the World. Scorpio. Running Scared. 1973: The Legend of Hell House. Nuits rouges/L'homme sans visage (GB: Shadowman). Voices. 1975: The Sellout. The Spiral Staircase. 1976: Blazing Magnum (US: Strange Shadows in an Empty Room). Tony Saitta/Tough Tony. 1978: Die Rebellen/One Take Two (GB: TV, as Flashpoint Africa). Once in Paris. 1979: The Martian Chronicles (TV). A Man Called Intrepid (TV). The Million Dollar Face (TV). 1980: Kiss of Gold (TV). 1983: Return of the Man from UNCLE (TV). 1985: Target. Dream Lover. 1986: Turnaround. 1987: Hard to be a God. 1989: Silence Like Glass. 1992: Voices in the Garden (TV).*

HUNT, Helen 1963–
This fair-haired, chirpy-looking American actress has been around so long it's almost impossible to believe she's still not hit 40. On TV at 10, she took a long time to crack the big-time in movies, although giving good performances near the top of the cast in several highly-regarded films. She's had several successful TV series, including *Mad About You*, which restricted her other work in the early 1990s. She won an Academy Award for *As Good As It Gets*, after which more high-profile cinema roles came her way. Married actor Hank Azaria (1964–) in 1999.

1973: Pioneer Woman (TV). 1975: Swiss Family Robinson (TV And ensuing series). All Together Now (TV). 1976: Amy Prentiss (TV. And ensuing series). Having Babies (TV). 1977: Rollercoaster. The Spell (TV). 1979: Transplant (TV). 1981: The Miracle of Kathy Miller (TV). Child Bride of Short Creek (TV). Angel Dusted (TV). 1982: Desperate Lives (TV). 1983: Bill: On His Own (TV). Choices of the Heart (TV). Quarterback Princess (TV). 1984: Sweet Revenge/Code of Honor (TV). 1985: Girls Just Want to Have Fun. Trancers/Future Cop. 1986: Peggy Sue Got Married. 1987: Project X. The Frog Prince. 1988: Miles from Home. Incident at Dark River (TV). Stealing Home. Shooter. 1989: Next of Kin. Dark River: A Father's Revenge (TV). 1990: The Hitchhiker (cable

TV). 1991: Into the Badlands (TV). Murder in New Hampshire/Murder in New Hampshire: The Pamela Smart Story (TV). Trancers II: The Return of Jack Deth. 1992: The Waterdance. Mr Saturday Night. In the Company of Darkness (TV). Trancers III: Deth Lives. Only You. 1994: Kiss of Death. 1996: Twister. 1997: As Good As It Gets. 2000: Cast Away. Dr T and the Women. Pay It Forward. 2001: What Women Want.

HUNT, Marsha (Marcia Hunt) 1917–
Pretty, petite brunette American actress who usually played demure but plucky heroines in 'B' movies and gentle or tragic supporting roles in bigger films. She began to get an interesting variety of roles in the late forties, but her career was virtually ended when she was blacklisted in the Communist witch-hunts. Played a few mother roles later on, and remained actively involved in civil rights, the United Nations and charity work. Married director Jerry Hopper (1938–1943) and screenwriter Robert Presnell (1946–).

*1935: The Virginia Judge. 1936: Desert Gold. Gentle Julia. The Accusing Finger. Arizona Raiders. Easy to Take. Hollywood Boulevard. College Holiday. 1937: Annapolis Salute (GB: Salute to Romance). Murder Goes to College. Easy Living. Thunder Trail. Born to the West. 1938: The Long Shot. Come on Leathernecks. 1939: The Hardys Ride High. The Star Reporter. These Glamour Girls. Joe and Ethel Turp Call on the President. Winter Carnival. 1940: *Women in Hiding. Flight Command. Pride and Prejudice. Irene. Ellery Queen, Master Detective. 1941: Blossoms in the Dust. The Trial of Mary Dugan. I'll Wait for You. Cheers for Miss Bishop. The Penalty. Unholy Partners. 1942: Kid Glove Killer. The Affairs of Martha (GB: Once Upon a Tuesday). Seven Sweethearts. Panama Hattie. Joe Smith, American (GB: Highway to Freedom). 1943: Bride by Mistake. Thousands Cheer. The Human Comedy. Pilot No. 5. Lost Angel. Cry Havoc. None Shall Escape. 1944: Music for Millions. 1945: A Letter for Evie. The Valley of Decision. 1947: Smash-Up, the Story of a Woman (GB: A Woman Destroyed). Carnegie Hall. 1948: The Inside Story. Raw Deal. 1949: Jigsaw. Take One False Step. Mary Ryan, Detective. 1952: Actors and Sin. The Happy Time. 1954: Diplomatic Passport. 1956: No Place to Hide. 1957: Man of the Law (TV. GB: cinemas). Bombers B-52 (GB: No Sleep Till Dawn). Back from the Dead. 1959: Blue Denim (GB: Blue Jeans). 1960: The*

Plunderers. 1969: Fear No Evil (TV). 1971: Johnny Got His Gun. 1972: Jigsaw (TV). 1976: The Siege (TV). 1981: Rich and Famous. Terror Among Us (TV).

HUNTER, Holly 1958–
Diminutive but feisty dark-haired American actress, a slightly perter and prettier version of Debra Winger (qv), usually seen as characters younger than her real age. Born in Georgia and raised on a 250-acre cattle farm there, she was a drama school graduate and acting at 16, but waited a long time for a breakthrough in films, which came first with *Raising Arizona*, and then as the news producer in *Broadcast News*, which won her an Oscar nomination. She won an Emmy for TV's *Roe vs Wade*, then an Academy Award for her mute emigrant in *The Piano* which seemed to cement her star status – although there was a long gap before her next film. Also Oscar-nominated for *The Firm*. Married Oscar-winning cinematographer Jonusz Kaminski in 1995.

1981: The Burning. 1983: An Uncommon Love (TV). Swing Shift. Svengali (TV). 1984: Intent to Kill (TV. GB: With Intent to Kill). 1985: Animal Behavior. 1986: Raising Arizona. 1987: A Gathering of Old Men/ Murder in the Bayou (TV). End of the Line. Broadcast News. 1989: Miss Firecracker. Always. Roe vs Wade (TV). 1990: Once Around. 1992: Crazy in Love (TV). 1993: The Firm. The Piano. The Positively True Adventures of the Alleged Texas Cheerleader-Murdering Mom (TV). 1995: Copycat. Home for the Holidays. 1996: Crash. 1997: A Life Less Ordinary. 1998: Living Out Loud. Hurly-burly. 1999: Jesus' Son. Woman Wanted. Things You Can Tell Just by Looking at Her. 2000: Timecode. O Brother, Where Art Thou?

HUNTER, Ian 1900–1975
Tall, solid, pleasant, light-haired South African-born leading man who had long careers in Britain and Hollywood, mostly as quiet dependable types. Although perhaps not dynamic enough to become a top star, his range was wider than his constant casting as 'other men' or members of the aristocracy would suggest and he gave a fascinating performance as the Christ-figure in *Strange Cargo* (1940).

1924: Not for Sale. 1925: Mr Oddy (later Confessions). A Girl of London. 1927: Downhill (US: When Boys Leave Home). Easy Virtue. His House in Order. The Ring.

1928: The Physician. The Thoroughbred. Valley of the Ghosts. 1929: Syncopation. *Highlowbrow. 1930: Cape Forlorn (US: The Love Storm). Escape. 1931: Sally in Our Alley. 1932: The Water Gypsies. The Sign of Four. The Man from Toronto. Marry Me. 1933: Orders is Orders. *Skipper of the Osprey. The Silver Spoon. 1934: The Night of the Party. Something Always Happens. The Church Mouse. No Escape. Death at Broadcasting House. Lazybones. The Phantom Light. 1935: The Morals of Marcus. Jalna. The Girl from 10th Avenue (GB: Men on Her Mind). A Midsummer Night's Dream. I Found Stella Parish. 1936: The White Angel. To Mary, with Love. Stolen Holiday. The Devil is a Sissy (GB: The Devil Takes the Count). 1937: Another Dawn. Confession. Call It a Day. 52nd Street. That Certain Woman. 1938: The Adventures of Robin Hood. Always Goodbye. Secrets of an Actress. The Sisters. Comet over Broadway. 1939: Broadway Serenade. Tarzan Finds a Son! Yes, My Darling Daughter. The Little Princess. Maisie. Tower of London. Bad Little Angel. 1940: Broadway Melody of 1940. Strange Cargo. Bitter Sweet. Dulcy. Gallant Sons. The Long Voyage Home. 1941: Ziegfeld Girl. Billy the Kid. Dr Jekyll and Mr Hyde. Smilin' Through. Come Live with Me. Andy Hardy's Private Secretary. 1942: A Yank at Eton. It Comes Up Love (US: A Date with an Angel). 1943: Forever and a Day. 1946: Bedelia. 1947: White Cradle Inn (US: High Fury). The White Unicorn (US: Bad Sister). 1949: Edward My Son. 1951: Hunted (US: The Stranger in Between). 1952: It Started in Paradise. 1953: Appointment in London. Don't Blame the Stork! Eight O'Clock Walk. 1954: Fire One. 1956: The Battle of the River Plate (US: Pursuit of the Graf Spee). *The Door in the Wall. 1957: Fortune is a Woman (US: She Played with Fire). 1958: Rockets Galore (US: Mad Little Island). 1959: North West Frontier (US: Flame Over India). 1960: The Bulldog Breed. 1961: Dr Blood's Coffin. The Treasure of Monte Cristo (US: The Secret of Monte Cristo). The Queen's Guards. 1962: Guns of Darkness (US: Act of Mercy). 1963: Kali-Yug Goddess of Vengeance. Kali-Yug – the Mystery of the Indian Tomb.

HUNTER, Jeffrey
(Henry McKinnies) 1925–1969

Tall, dark, virile, young-looking American leading man, a favourite target for fan mail throughout the fifties at Twentieth Century-Fox, where his career ran parallel to that of Robert Wagner, with whom he often appeared in films. Away from Fox, Hunter got himself into a variety of out-of-the-way projects, some worthy, some not, that were not given wide distribution, and his name dropped from the popularity polls. Married to Barbara Rush (first of three) from 1950 to 1955. Died after surgery following injuries sustained in a fall.

1948: A Date with Judy. 1949: Julius Caesar. 1951: Call Me Mister. Fourteen Hours. Take Care of My Little Girl. The Frogmen. Red Skies of Montana. 1952: Belles on Their Toes. Dreamboat. Lure of the Wilderness. 1953: Single-Handed (US: Sailor of the King). 1954: Three Young Texans. Princess of the Nile. 1955: White Feather. Seven Angry Men. Seven Cities of Gold. 1956: A Kiss Before Dying. The Empty Room (TV. GB: cinemas). The Proud Ones. The Searchers. Gun for a Coward. The Great Locomotive Chase. Four Girls in Town. 1957: The True Story of Jesse James (GB: The James Brothers). No Down Payment. Count Five and Die. The Way to the Gold. 1958: Mardi Gras. In Love and War. The Last Hurrah. 1960: Key Witness. Hell to Eternity. Sergeant Rutledge. 1961: Man-Trap. King of Kings. The Secret Mission (TV). 1962: No Man is an Island. The Longest Day. Gold for the Caesars. 1963: The Man from Galveston (TV. GB: cinemas). 1964: The Woman Who Wouldn't Die. 1965: Murieta (GB: Vendetta). Brainstorm. 1966: Dimension 5. Witch without a Broom. 1967: The Christmas Kid. A Guide for the Married Man. Custer of the West. Frozen Alive. 1968: The Private Navy of Sergeant O'Farrell. Frau Wirtin hat auch eine Nichte (GB: Sexy Susan Sins Again. US: Sexy Susan at the King's Court). Joe . . . Look for a Place to Die (GB and US: Joe – Find a Place to Die). 1969: Viva America/Mafia Mob. Super Colt 38.

HUNTER, Kim (Janet Cole) 1922–

Sweet-faced, intelligent American actress with dark, coppery hair who sprang to prominence with good performances in low-budget films, was selected by British director Michael Powell to play a 'typical American girl' in 1945, and won a Best Supporting Actress Oscar in 1951 for A Streetcar Named Desire. Despite all that, she never became more than a vaguely familiar name at the box-office, and briefly blacklisted in the McCarthy era. Some filmographies credit her with an appearance in A Canterbury Tale in 1944, but she doesn't appear to be in it.

1943: The Seventh Victim. Tender Comrade. 1944: When Strangers Marry/Betrayed. 1945: You Came Along. A Matter of Life and Death (US: Stairway to Heaven). 1951: A Streetcar Named Desire. 1952: Deadline – USA (GB: Deadline). Anything Can Happen. 1954: Fire One. 1956: Storm Center. The Comedian (TV). Bermuda Affair. 1957: The Young Stranger. The Dark Side of the Earth (TV). 1958: Before I Die (TV). Money, Women and Guns. Free Week-End (TV). 1959: The Sounds of Eden (TV). 1960: Alas, Babylon (TV). 1964: Lilith. 1967: Planet of the Apes. 1968: The Swimmer. The Young Loner (TV). 1969: Beneath the Planet of the Apes. 1970: Dial Hot Line (TV). In Search of America (TV). 1971: Escape from the Planet of the Apes. 1973: The Magician (TV). 1974: Bad Ronald (TV). Born Innocent (TV). Unwed Father (TV). 1975: Ellery Queen: Too Many Suspects (TV). The Impersonation Murder Case (TV). 1976: The Hancocks (TV). The Dark Side of Innocence (TV). 1979: Dark August. The Golden Gate Murders (TV). 1981: Skokie (TV. GB: Once They Marched Through a Thousand Towns). FDR: The Last Year (TV). 1985: Three Sovereigns for Sarah (TV). Private Sessions (TV). 1986: The Kindred. 1988: Drop-Out Mother (TV). 1989: Cross of Fire (TV). Two Evil Eyes. 1993: Triumph Over Disaster: The Hurricane Andrew Story (TV). 1997: Midnight in the Garden of Good and Evil. 1998: A Smaller Place. A Price Above Rubies. 1999: Abilene. Blue Moon (TV). Out of the Cold. 2000: Old Hats.

HUNTER, Tab (Arthur Gelien) 1931–

Tall, rangy actor with close-cropped fair hair, prime teenage bait at Warner Brothers, for whom he became a hot property in the fifties.

Outside their environment, he swam in some strange waters, vainly searching for his former popularity, latterly in continental action films.

1950: †*The Lawless* (GB: *The Dividing Line*). 1952: *Saturday Island* (US: *Island of Desire*). 1953: *The Steel Lady* (GB: *Treasure of Kalifa*). *Gun Belt.* 1954: *Return to Treasure Island.* *Track of the Cat.* 1955: *The Sea Chase.* *Battle Cry.* 1956: *The Burning Hills.* *The Girl He Left Behind.* *Forbidden Area* (TV). 1957: *Lafayette Escadrille* (GB: *Hell Bent for Glory*). 1958: *Portrait of a Murderer* (TV). *Gunman's Walk.* *Damn Yankees* (GB: *What Lola Wants*). 1959: *That Kind of Woman.* *They Came to Cordura.* 1961: *The Pleasure of His Company.* 1962: *The Golden Arrow.* 1963: *Operation Bikini.* 1964: *Ride the White Surf.* *Troubled Waters* (US: *Man with Two Faces*). 1965: *City under the Sea* (GB: *War Gods of the Deep*). *The Loved One.* 1966: *Birds Do It.* 1967: *Hostile Guns.* *The Fickle Finger of Fate/The Cup of San Sebastian.* *Quel maledotto punte sull' Elba* (GB: *The Legion of No Return*). 1968: *Scaccio internationale.* 1970: *San Francisco International Airport* (TV). *La porta del connone.* 1971: *Hacksaw* (TV). *A Kiss from Eddie.* *The Arousers* (GB: *Sweet Kill*). 1972: *The Life and Times of Judge Roy Bean.* 1973: *The Timber Tramp.* 1975: *Won Ton Ton, the Dog Who Saved Hollywood.* 1978: *Katie: Portrait of a Centerfold* (TV). 1979: *The Kid from Left Field* (TV). 1981: *Polyester.* *Thursday the 12th/Pandemonium.* 1982: *Grease 2.* 1984: *Lust in the Dust.* 1987: *Cameron's Closet.* 1988: *Grotesque.* *Out of the Dark.* 1992: *Dark Horse.* 1995: *Wild Bill.* *Hollywood Maverick.*

†*Scenes deleted from final release print*

HUPPERT, Isabelle 1955–
Demure-looking, auburn-haired French actress who seemed resolved to fight off the 'innocent' roles for which her looks qualified her. Despite her performances as tough bitches in later films, her childlike qualities have made her more haunting in sympathetic roles. After the daunting failures of her international ventures (*Rosebud*, *Heaven's Gate*), she has stayed in the more welcoming harbour of her native Paris, busy in films, on stage and in TV. Won best actress at 1978 Cannes festival for *Violette Nozière*.

1971: *Faustine el le bel été* (GB: *Faustine.* US: *Growing Up/Faustine and the Beautiful Summer*). 1972: *César et Rosalie.* *Le Bar de la Fourche.* 1973: *L'ampélopède.* 1974: *Glissements progressifs du plaisir.* *Les valseuses* (GB: *Making It.* US: *Going Places*). *Dupont Lajoie* (US: *Rape of lnnocence*). *Sérieux comme le plaisir.* *Rosebud.* *Le grand délire.* *Aloise.* 1975: *Docteur Françoise Gailland* (US: *No Time for Breakfast*). *Le juge et l'assassin.* *Je suis Pierre Rivière.* *Flash Back.* *Le petit Marcel.* 1976: *La dentellière* (GB and US: *The Lacemaker*). 1977: *Des enfants gâtés* (US: *Spoiled Children*). *Les indiens sont encore loin.* 1978: *Violette Nozière* (US: *Violette*). *Retour à la bien-aimée.* *The Brontë Sisters.* 1979: *Le couleur du temps.* 1980: *Heaven's Gate.* *Sauve qui peut (La vie)/Slow Motion/Every Man for Himself.* *Loulou.* *Le vera storia della signora delle camelie.* *Örökseg* (US: *The Heiresses*). 1981: *Les ailes de la colombe.* *Coup de torchon* (GB and US: *Clean Slate*). *Eaux profondes* (US: *Deep Water*). 1982: *Passion.* *Le truite/The Trout.* 1983: *Coup de foudre* (GB: *At First Sight.* US: *Entre Nous*). *Storia di piera.* *La femme de mon pote* (GB and US: *My Best Friend's Girl*). 1984: *Violences.* *La garce* (GB: TV, as *The Bitch*). 1985: *Signé Charlotte.* *Sac de noeuds* (US: *All Mixed Up*). *Partage de minuit.* 1986: *Cactus.* 1987: *The Possessed.* *The Bedroom Window.* *Chatov et les démons.* *Milan noir.* 1988: *Migrations.* *Une affaire de femmes.* 1989: *Vengeance d'une femme.* *La guerre la plus glorieuse.* 1990: *Malina.* 1991: *Madame Bovary.* 1992: *Après l'amour.* *Contre l'oubli.* 1993: *L'inondation.* 1994: *La séparation.* *Amateur.* 1995: *La cérémonie/A Judgement in Stone.* 1996: *Affinita' elettive.* *Poussières d'amour* (US: *Love's Debris*). 1997: *Rien ne va plus.* *Les palmes de M Schutz* (US: *Pierre and Marie*). 1998: *The Age of the Wolves.* *L'école de la chair.* 1999: *Pas de scandale.* *Saint-Cyr.* 2000: *Les déstinées sentimentales.* *La vie moderne.* *Clara.* *Merci pur le chocolat.* *La fausse suivante.* *Comédie de l'innocence.*

HURLEY, Elizabeth 1965–
Tall, pale, dark-haired, wafer-slim British glamour star, noted for her revealing premiere dresses, her connection with a leading cosmetics company, her reputation as a dynamic hands-on producer and her 13-year partnership with actor Hugh Grant (*qv*), which ended in 2000. In between these things, she's managed to make a good few movies, mostly in drama but probably at her best in tongue-in-cheek comedy roles.

1987: *Aria.* 1988: *Deadline: Madrid* (TV). 1989: *Rowing with the Wind* (completed 1987).

Act of Will (TV). 1990: *The Long Winter.* *The Skipper/Kill Cruise.* 1991: *Orchid House* (TV). 1992: *Passenger 57.* 1993: *Beyond Bedlam* (US: *Nightscare*). 1995: *Mad Dogs and Englishmen* (US: *Shameless*). *The Shamrock Conspiracy* (TV). 1996: *Harrison: Cry of the City* (TV). *Samson and Delilah* (TV). *Dangerous Ground.* 1997: *Austin Powers International Man of Mystery.* 1998: *Permanent Midnight.* 1999: *My Favourite Martian.* *Ed TV.* *Austin Powers: The Spy Who Shagged Me.* 2000: *The Weight of Water.* *Bedazzled.* 2001: *Double Whammy.*

HURST, Veronica
(Patricia Wilmshurst) 1931–
Honey-blonde British actress (born in Malta) with 'English rose' complexion, well thought of in the early fifties. But, lacking the grittiness of her contemporary Virginia McKenna, she was largely confined to gentle leading roles in second-feature adventures. Has remained active on stage and TV. Married William Sylvester (first of two) 1954–1970.

1951: *Laughter in Paradise.* *Here's to the Memory! Angels One Five.* 1952: *The Yellow Balloon.* 1953: *Will Any Gentleman? The Girl on the Pier.* *The Maze.* *Royal African Rifles* (GB: *Storm over Africa*). *Don't Blame the Stork!* 1954: *Bang! You're Dead* (US: *Game of Danger*). 1955: *The Gilded Cage.* 1959: *Peeping Tom.* 1962: *Dead Man's Evidence.* 1963: *Live It Up* (US: *Sing and Swing*). 1965: *The Boy Cried Murder.* *Licensed to Kill* (US: *The Second Best Secret Agent in the Whole Wide World*).

HURT, John 1940–
Serious, rather unusual-looking, slightly-built British leading man and offbeat character star

who can play sneering or sensitive and has certainly mixed triumph with disaster in no uncertain fashion in a sporadic film career. At his best he can give very moving performances; his standing rose dramatically after his Oscar nomination for *The Elephant Man*, and his strained features were put through the mill in other demanding roles. Also nominated for an Oscar in *Midnight Express*, he now plays mainly cynical or corrupt character roles.

1962: *The Wild and the Willing*. 1963: *This is My Street*. 1966: *A Man for All Seasons*. 1967: *The Sailor from Gibraltar*. 1968: *In Search of Gregory*. 1969: *Sinful Davey*. *Before Winter Comes*. 1970: *10 Rillington Place*. 1971: *Mr Forbush and the Penguins* (US: *Cry of the Penguins*). *The Pied Piper*. 1974: *Little Malcolm and his struggle against the eunuchs*. *The Ghoul*. 1975: *The Naked Civil Servant* (TV). 1976: *East of Elephant Rock*. *Stream Line*. 1977: *Spectre* (TV). 1978: *Watership Down* (voice only). *The Shout*. *The Lord of the Rings* (voice only). *Midnight Express*. *The Disappearance*. 1979: *Alien*. 1980: *Heaven's Gate*. *The Elephant Man*. 1981: *History of the World Part I*. *Partners*. 1982: *Night Crossing*. *The Plague Dogs* (voice only). 1983: *The Osterman Weekend*. *Champions*. 1984: *The Hit*. '*1984*'. *Success is the Best Revenge*. 1985: *The Black Cauldron* (voice only). *After Darkness*. 1986: *Jake Speed*. 1987: *From the Hip*. *Rocinante*. *White Mischief*. *Aria*. *Vincent – The Life and Death of Vincent Van Gogh* (voice only). *Hem* (TV). 1988: *Little Sweetheart* (GB: TV, as *Poison Candy*). *Deadline*. 1989: *Scandal*. *The Bengali Night*. 1990: *Frankenstein Unbound*. *The Field*. *Windprints*. 1991: *King Ralph*. *Resident Alien*. *Memory* (US: *Lapse of Memory*). 1992: *L'oeil qui ment*. 1993: *Even Cowgirls Get the Blues*. *Great Moments in Aviation*. *Crime and Punishment*. *Monolith*. *Dark at Noon*. 1994: *Thumbelina* (voice only). *Second Best*. *Wild Bill*. *Betrayal* (narrator only). 1995: *The Adoption* (TV). *Rob Roy*. *Saigon Baby* (TV). *Dead Man*. †*Divine Rapture*. *Picture Windows* (TV). *Prisoners in Time* (TV). 1996: *Love and Death on Long Island*. 1997: *Contact*. *The Commissioner* (cable TV. Released 1999). *Tender Loving Care*. *The Climb*. 1998: *All the Little Animals*. *If . . . Dog . . . Rabbit*. *Bruta/Bandyta*. *Night Train*. 1999: *A Monkey's Tale* (voice only). *You're Dead*. *Lost Souls*. *New Blood*. 2000: *The Tigger Movie* (voice only). 2001: *Captain Corelli's Mandolin*.

†*Unfinished*

HURT, William 1950–

Tall, fair-haired, softly-spoken American actor with enigmatic gaze. Spending his early childhood travelling the South Pacific with his government official father, Hurt studied theology at university, then switched to acting and broke into TV in his mid-twenties. In films he has shown that the more subtleties a role has, the better he likes it. He won an Academy Award for his imprisoned homosexual in *Kiss of the Spider Woman*, and was also nominated for *Children of a Lesser God* and *Broadcast News*. But he seemed too cool to continue in popularity, and played some supporting roles in the 1990s. Married (first of two) to Mary Beth Hurt from 1976–1982.

1978: *Verna the USO Girl* (TV). 1980: *Altered States*. 1981: *Eyewitness* (GB: *The Janitor*). *Body Heat*. 1983: *Gorky Park*. *The Big Chill*. 1985: *Kiss of the Spider Woman*. 1987: *Children of a Lesser God*. *A Time of Destiny*. *Broadcast News*. 1988: *The Accidental Tourist*. 1990: *I Love You to Death*. *Until the End of the World*. *Alice*. 1991: *The Doctor*. 1992: *The Plague*. 1993: *Mr Wonderful*. 1994: *Second Best*. *Trial by Jury*. *Smoke*. 1995: *Les confidences d'un inconnu* (US: *Secrets Shared With a Stranger*). *The Big Nowhere*. 1996: *Jane Eyre*. *A Couch in New York*. 1997: *Loved*. *Michael*. *Dark City*. *The Proposition*. 1998: *Lost in Space*. *One True Thing*. 1999: *The Big Brass Ring*. *Sunshine*. *The 4th Floor*. *The Simian Line*. *The Miracle Maker* (voice only). 2000: *Sebastian's Love*. *The Contaminated Man*. *Do Not Disturb* (TV). *Varian's War*.

HUSSEY, Olivia 1951–

British leading lady (Argentine-born) with dark hair, stunning olive complexion, childlike face and voluptuous figure. A former child player but not a terribly strong adult actress, she, like others before her, could not live up altogether successfully to having been cast as Juliet in *Romeo and Juliet*: even so, she has spasmodically pursued her career.

1965: *The Battle of the Villa Fiorita*. *Cup Fever*. 1968: *Romeo and Juliet*. 1969: *All the Right Noises*. 1971: *The Summertime Killer*. *H-Bomb*. 1972: *Lost Horizon*. 1974: *Black Christmas*. 1976: *Jesus of Nazareth* (TV). 1978: *The Cat and the Canary*. *Death on the Nile*. *The Pirate* (TV). 1979: *The Man with Bogart's Face*. 1980: *Virus*. 1981: *Turkey Shoot*. 1982: *Ivanhoe* (TV). 1984: *The Last Days of Pompeii* (TV). *The Corsican Brothers*

(TV). 1987: *Distortions*. *The Goldsmith's Shop/Bonds of Love*. 1990: *The Undeclared War*. 1991: *Psycho IV: The Beginning* (TV). 1993: *Save Me*. *Quest of the Delta Knights*. 1994: *The Ice Cream Man*. 1996: *Tales of a Son of a Brit*. *Saving Grace*. 1997: *Dead Man's Island* (TV). 1999: *Dead Wrong*. 2000: *Tortilla Heaven*.

HUSSEY, Ruth (R. O'Rourke) 1914–

Chic, rosy-cheeked brunette American actress whose ladylike manner belied her name. She gave sophisticated if largely unmemorable performances in dozens of films and always looked most comfortable in smart suits and mink coats. Her best role was the photographer in *The Philadelphia Story*: it earned her an Oscar nomination.

1937: *The Big City*. *Madame X*. 1938: *Man Proof*. *Judge Hardy's Children*. *Hold That Kiss*. *Marie Antoinette*. *Spring Madness*. *Time Out for Murder*. *Rich Man – Poor Girl*. 1939: *Honolulu*. *Another Thin Man*. *Within the Law*. *Maisie*. *The Women*. *Fast and Furious*. *Blackmail*. 1940: *Northwest Passage*. *Susan and God* (GB: *The Gay Mrs Trexel*). *The Philadelphia Story*. *Flight Command*. 1941: *Free and Easy*. *H.M. Pulham Esq*. *Married Bachelor*. *Our Wife*. 1942: *Pierre of the Plains*. *Tennessee Johnson* (GB: *The Man on America's Conscience*). 1943: *Tender Comrade*. 1944: *The Uninvited*. *Marine Raiders*. 1945: *Bedside Manner*. 1948: *I Jane Doe* (GB: *Diary of a Bride*). 1949: *The Great Gatsby*. 1950: *Louisa*. *Mr Music*. 1951: *Hill Number One*. *That's My Boy*. 1952: *Woman of the North Country*. *Stars and Stripes Forever* (GB: *Marching Along*). 1953: *The Lady Wants Mink*. 1960: *The Facts of Life*. 1973: *My Darling Daughters' Anniversary* (TV).

HUSTON, Anjelica 1951–

Dark, austere, fine-boned, dominant American actress, adept at stealing scenes from the stars since her comeback to films in the mid 1980s. The daughter of John Huston (qv), she began in films as a teenager, but made little impact until past 30, when she re-emerged a stronger actress and took an Academy Award in her father's film *Prizzi's Honor*. Now in demand for juicy star cameos, she has also dabbled in direction. Further Oscar nominations for *Enemies*, *A Love Story* and *The Grifters*. One researcher has claimed that, besides the list of films that follows, she can also be spotted making a tiny appearance in 1969's *Anne of the Thousand Days*.

1969: *Sinful Davey. A Walk with Love and Death. Hamlet. 1976: The Last Tycoon. Swashbuckler (GB: The Scarlet Buccaneer). 1981: The Postman Always Rings Twice. 1982: Frances. 1983: This is Spinal Tap. 1984: The Ice Pirates. The Cowboy and the Ballerina (TV). 1985: Prizzi's Honor. 1986: *Captain Eo. 1987: Gardens of Stone. The Dead. John Huston and the Dubliners. 1988: A Handful of Dust. Mr North. 1989: The Witches. Enemies, a Love Story. Crimes and Misdemeanors. 1990: The Grifters. 1991: The Addams Family. 1992: The Player. †Freddie Goes to Washington (voice only). 1993: Manhattan Murder Mystery. Addams Family Values. And the Band Played On. 1995: Two Deaths. The Perez Family. The Crossing Guard. 1997: Phoenix (cable TV). 1998: Ever After. Buffalo 66. 1999: Agnes Browne. 2000: The Golden Bowl.*
As director: *1994: Maude Gonne. 1996: Bastard Out of Carolina (TV). 1999: Agnes Browne.*

†Unfinished.

HUSTON, John 1906–1987
Tall, grizzled American director with drooping lower lip and rolling eye who became in his later years a leading character actor, presumably to help finance his continuing directing projects. As a director, his films were rich, varied and often formidable – with occasional aberrations. As an actor, he tended to ham. A screenwriter in the 1930s and early 1940s. Academy Awards (direction and screenplay) for *The Treasure of the Sierra Madre.* Son of Walter Huston (*qv*). Received an acting Oscar nomination for *The Cardinal.* Died from emphysema.
*1928: The Shakedown. 1929: *Two Americans.*

1930: *Hell's Heroes. The Storm. 1948: The Treasure of the Sierra Madre. 1949: We Were Strangers. 1963: The List of Adrian Messenger. The Cardinal. 1964: *Return to the Island. 1966: The Bible . . . in the beginning. 1967: Casino Royale. 1968: Candy. Rocky Road to Dublin. 1969: De Sade. A Walk with Love and Death. The Kremlin Letter. 1970: The Deserter. The Bridge in the Jungle. Myra Breckinridge. 1971: Man in the Wilderness. 1972: The Life and Times of Judge Roy Bean. 1973: Battle for the Planet of the Apes. 1974: Chinatown. 1975: Breakout. The Wind and the Lion. The Other Side of the Wind (unfinished). 1976: Hollywood on Trial (narrator only). Sherlock Holmes in New York (TV). Tentacles. 1977: Angela (released 1984). The Hobbit (TV. Voice only). Triangle: The Bermuda Mystery. Il grande attacca/The Biggest Battle. Winter Kills (released 1979). 1978: The Visitor. 1979: Jaguar Lives. Wise Blood. 1980: Head On/Fatal Attraction. Agee. 1982: Cannery Row (voice only). 1983: Lovesick. A Minor Miracle (GB: Young Giants). 1984: Notes from Under the Volcano. Observations Under the Volcano. 1985: Alfred Hitchcock Presents (TV). Momo. 1986: Mr Corbett's Ghost (TV). Directed by William Wyler. 1987: Epic (narrator only). John Huston and the Dubliners.*
As director: *1941: The Maltese Falcon. 1942: In This Our Life. Across the Pacific. 1943: Report from the Aleutians. 1944: The Battle of San Pietro. 1945: Let There Be Light. 1948: The Treasure of the Sierra Madre. Key Largo. 1949: We Were Strangers. 1950: The Asphalt Jungle. 1951: The Red Badge of Courage. The African Queen. 1952: Moulin Rouge. 1953: Beat the Devil. 1956: Moby Dick. 1957: Heaven Knows, Mr Allison. 1958: The Barbarian and the Geisha. The Roots of Heaven. 1959: The Unforgiven. 1961: The Misfits. 1962: Freud (GB: Freud – the Secret Passion). 1963: The List of Adrian Messenger. 1964: The Night of the Iguana. 1966: The Bible . . . in the beginning. 1967: Casino Royale (co-directed). Reflections in a Golden Eye. 1968: Sinful Davey. 1969: A Walk with Love and Death. The Kremlin Letter. 1971: Fat City. 1972: The Life and Times of Judge Roy Bean. 1973: The Mackintosh Man. 1975: The Man Who Would be King. 1976: *Independence. 1979: Wise Blood. 1980: Phobia. 1981: Escape to Victory (US: Victory). 1982: Annie. 1984: Under the Volcano. 1985: Prizzi's Honor. 1987: The Dead.*

HUSTON, Walter
(W. Houghston) 1884–1950
Tall, dark, stiff-legged, authoritative, unhandsome but fascinating Canadian-born actor whose character studies dominated the films he made in Hollywood when he came from Broadway in the late 1920s. Later played old-timers, as one of which (in *The Treasure of the Sierra Madre*) he won a belated Academy Award (having been nominated for *All That Money Can Buy, Yankee Doodle Dandy* and *Dodsworth*). Father of John Huston. Died from an aneurism.
*1929: Gentlemen of the Press. The Lady Lies. *The Bishop's Candlesticks. The Virginian. *Two Americans. *The Carnival Man. 1930: The Virtuous Sin (GB: Cast Iron). The Birth*

of a Nation (new prologue to revised version of 1915 film). Abraham Lincoln. The Bad Man. 1931: The Criminal Code. The Star Witness. The Ruling Voice. 1932: Night Court (GB: Justice for Sale). Kongo. A Woman from Monte Carlo. A House Divided. Law and Order. Beast of the City. American Madness. Rain. The Wet Parade. 1933: Hell Below. The Prizefighter and the Lady (GB: Every Woman's Man). Ann Vickers. *The Spoon. Storm at Daybreak. Gabriel over the White House. 1934: Keep 'Em Rolling! 1935: *Hollywood Hobbies. The Tunnel (US: Transatlantic Tunnel). 1936: Rhodes of Africa (GB: Rhodes). Dodsworth. 1938: Of Human Hearts. 1939: The Light That Failed. 1941: The Maltese Falcon. The Shanghai Gesture. The Outlaw (released 1943). All That Money Can Buy/The Devil and Daniel Webster/Daniel and the Devil. Swamp Water (GB: The Man Who Came Back). 1942: Always in My Heart. Yankee Doodle Dandy. In This Our Life. 1943: Edge of Darkness. *Safeguarding Military Information. Mission to Moscow. North Star (later Armored Attack). 1944: Dragon Seed. 1945: And Then There Were None (GB: Ten Little Niggers). 1946: Dragonwyck. Duel in the Sun. 1947: Summer Holiday (released 1948). 1948: The Treasure of the Sierra Madre. 1949: The Great Sinner. 1950: The Furies.*
*Huston also narrated the following wartime documentaries: 1941: Our Russian Front. 1942: Prelude to War. America Can Give It. 1943: The Nazis Strike. Divide and Conquer. The Battle of Britain. The Battle of Russia. December 7th. *For God and Country. 1944: The Battle of China. Know Your Enemy: Japan. *Suicide Battalion. 1945: War Comes to America. Let There Be Light.*

HUTCHINSON, Josephine 1898–1998
Gracious, gentle-charactered, titian-haired American actress of upright bearing who, had she been born 10 years later, might have become one of Hollywood's best-loved stars. Stage-trained and capable of superior performances laced with her own natural warmth, she was, however, 36 before she arrived in Hollywood. Unlike Greer Garson, who would come at the same age five years later and find the ideal home at M-G-M, Hutchinson was not, on the whole, given roles in the kind of pictures that might have made her a dominant star.
1917: The Little Princess. 1934: Happiness Ahead. 1935: The Right to Live (GB: The Sacred Flame). The Melody Lingers On. Oil

for the Lamps of China. The Story of Louis Pasteur. 1936: I Married a Doctor. 1937: Mountain Justice. The Women Men Marry. 1938: The Crime of Dr Hallett. 1939: Son of Frankenstein. 1940: My Son, My Son. Tom Brown's School Days. 1941: Her First Beau. 1946: Somewhere in the Night. 1947: The Tender Years. Cass Timberlane. 1949: Adventure in Baltimore (GB: Bachelor Bait). 1951: Love is Better than Ever (GB: The Light Fantastic). 1952: Ruby Gentry. 1955: Many Rivers to Cross. 1956: Miracle in the Rain. 1957: Gun for a Coward. 1958: Step Down to Terror (GB: The Silent Stranger). Sing, Boy, Sing. 1959: North by Northwest. 1960: Walk Like a Dragon. The Adventures of Huckleberry Finn. 1965: Baby, the Rain Must Fall. 1966: Nevada Smith. 1968: Shadow over Elveron (TV). 1970: Rabbit Run. 1971: Travis Logan DA (TV). The Homecoming (TV).

HUTTON, Betty
(Elizabeth Thornburg) 1921–
Blonde, blue-eyed, wide-mouthed, tempestuous and temperamental singer, actress, comedienne and all-round female firecracker. Whether belting out a song in loud, if slightly husky, tones, cavorting, clowning or emoting, she grabbed her audience by the scruff of the neck and never let go. Wrecked her film career when she walked out on her Paramount contract in 1952. There have been countless comebacks (and periods of psychiatric treatment) since. Began making Red Tomahawk (1967) but was replaced. Four times married and divorced. Sister of actress-singer Marion Hutton.
1938: *Queens of the Air. 1939: *Vincent Lopez and His Orchestra. *One for the Book. *Headline Bands. *Public Jitterbug Number

One. *Three Kings and a Queen. 1942: The Fleet's In. Star Spangled Rhythm. 1943: Happy Go Lucky. Let's Face It. *Skirmish on the Home Front. 1944: The Miracle of Morgan's Creek. Here Come the Waves. And the Angels Sing. 1945: Incendiary Blonde. Duffy's Tavern. *Hollywood Victory Caravan. The Stork Club. 1946: Cross My Heart. 1947: The Perils of Pauline. Dream Girl. 1949: Red, Hot and Blue. 1950: Annie Get Your Gun. Let's Dance. 1951: Sailor Beware. 1952: The Greatest Show on Earth. Somebody Loves Me. 1957: Spring Reunion. 1990: Preston Sturges: The Rise and Fall of an American Dreamer.

HUTTON, Jim
(Dana James Hutton) 1933–1979
Tall, dark, stringy American actor in the James Stewart mould. His good timing and happy-go-lucky personality provided some good laughs in M-G-M comedies of the early 1960s. Turned to television in the 1970s, but ill-health cut short his career. Father of Timothy Hutton (qv). Died from cancer of the liver.
1958: †A Time to Love and a Time to Die. 1959: Ten Seconds to Hell 1960: The Subterraneans. Where the Boys Are. 1961: Bachelor in Paradise. 1962: Period of Adjustment. The Horizontal Lieutenant. 1964: Looking for Love. 1965: Major Dundee. Never Too Late. The Hallelujah Trail. 1966: Walk, Don't Run. The Trouble with Angels. 1967: Who's Minding the Mint? 1968: The Green Berets. 1969: Hellfighters. 1971: The Deadly Hunter (TV). The Reluctant Heroes (TV. GB: The Reluctant Heroes of Hill 656). They Call It Murder (TV). 1972: Call Her Mom (TV). 1973: Don't Be Afraid of the Dark (TV). 1974: The Underground Man (TV). Nightmare at 43 Hillcrest (TV). 1975: Ellery Queen: Too Many Suspects (TV). Psychic Killer. 1978: Flying High (TV).

†As Dana J. Hutton

HUTTON, Lauren
(Mary Laurence Hutton) 1943–
Tall, tawny-haired, engagingly gap-toothed American actress who, from a swamp urchin's childhood in South Carolina and Florida, worked in a jazz club, then became in turn a Playboy Club bunny and one of America's top models. She had several stabs at establishing herself as a film star from 1968 without demonstrating a strong enough personality to carry a film on her own. She did,

however, widen her range during the 1970s, and scored her biggest box-office American hit as late as 1985 with Once Bitten. She mixed modelling and acting in the 1990s.
1968: Paper Lion. 1970: Pieces of Dreams. Little Fauss and Big Halsy. 1972: Permette? – Rocco Papaleo (US: Rocco Papaleo). 1974: The Gambler. 1976: Gator. Welcome to LA. 1977: Viva Knievel! 1978: A Wedding. Someone is Watching Me! (TV). 1979: Institute for Revenge (TV). 1980: American Gigolo. 1981: Paternity. Zorro the Gay Blade. Hecate et ses chiens. 1982: Starflight One (TV. GB: cinemas). 1983: Tout feu, tout flamme. Lassiter. Cocaine: One Man's Seduction (TV). The Cradle Will Fall. 1985: Once Bitten. Flagrant Desire. Scandal Sheet (TV). 1986: The Return of Mike Hammer (TV). Timestalkers (TV). 1987: Marathon. Malone. 1988: Perfect People (TV). Forbidden Sun. 1989: Fear. 1990: Billions/Milliardi. 1991: Missing Pieces. Guilty As Charged. 1992: Mom and Dad Save the World. 1994: My Father, the Hero. 1996: We the Jury (TV). 1997: Little Warriors (TV). 1998: 54. Beautopia (doc). A Bat's Tale. 1999: Caracara/The Last Witness (cable TV). Just a Little Harmless Sex. The Venice Project. Loser Love.

HUTTON, Robert (R. Winne) 1920–1994
Light-haired, earnest-looking, latterly moustachioed American leading man first seen in fresh-faced 'boy next door' type roles at Warners in the forties. Away from the studio, he regressed quite quickly to small supporting roles, holding up the process at times by playing lead roles in chillers which he sometimes produced himself. Only in very small parts in later years. Wrote the screenplay for 1974's Persecution. Spent his

last days in constant care after breaking his back in a fall.

1943: Northern Pursuit. Destination Tokyo. 1944: Hollywood Canteen. Janie. 1945: Roughly Speaking. Too Young to Know. 1946: Janie Gets Married. 1947: *So You Want to be in Pictures. Always Together. Love and Learn. Time Out of Mind. 1948: Wallflower. Smart Girls Don't Talk. 1949: The Younger Brothers. 1950: And Baby Makes Three. Beauty on Parade. The Man on the Eiffel Tower. 1951: The Racket. New Mexico. The Steel Helmet. Slaughter Trail. 1952: Gobs and Gals (GB: Cruising Casanovas). Tropical Heatwave. *Half Dressed for Dinner. *Three Chairs for Betty. 1953: Paris Model. Casanova's Big Night. 1954: Tales of Adventure. 1955: The Big Bluff. 1956: Scandal Incorporated. Yaqui Drums. 1957: The Man without a Body. Man from Tangier (US: Thunder over Tangier). 1958: The Colossus of New York. Showdown at Boot Hill. Outcasts of the City. 1959: Invisible Invaders. It Started with a Kiss. Wild Youth. 1960: Cinderfella. Jailbreakers. 1962: The Slime People. 1964: The Secret Door. The Sicilians. 1965: Doctor in Clover. Los Novios de Marisol. Busqueme e Esa Chica. 1966: Finders Keepers. The Vulture. 1967: You Only Live Twice. They Came from Beyond Space. Torture Garden. 1968: Can Hieronymous Merkin Ever Forget Mercy Humppe and Find True Happiness? 1970: Cry of the Banshee. Trog. 1972: Tales from the Crypt. 1974: QB VII (TV). 1975: The New Roof.

HUTTON, Timothy 1960–
Tall, intense, sensitive, long-faced, dark-haired American actor, the son of Jim Hutton (*qv*). Starting his major career in TV movies at 18, he won an Academy Award at 20 for his first cinema film, *Ordinary People*. The early Hutton showed a De Niro-like dedication in researching for a role and admitted that 'most of my roles have been rather gruelling'. He tried a change of pace with *Turk 182!*, but it didn't take with the public, and his standing has slipped steadily since the mid 1980s. A talented musician: plays piano and drums. He married Debra Winger (*qv*) in 1986, but the stormy marriage lasted only four years.

1965: Never Too Late. 1978: Zuma Beach (TV). 1979: An Innocent Love (TV). And Baby Makes Six (TV). Friendly Fire (TV). The Best Place to Be (TV). Young Love, First Love (TV). 1980: Father Figure (TV). The Oldest Living Graduate (TV). Ordinary People. 1981: A Long Way Home (TV). Taps.

1983: Daniel. Iceman. 1985: The Falcon and the Snowman. Turk 182! 1986: Made in Heaven. 1987: A Time of Destiny. 1988: Everybody's All American (GB: When I Fall in Love). Betrayed (bit). 1989: Torrents of Spring. 1990: Q & A. 1991: Strangers (TV). 1992: Katya. 1993: The Dark Half (completed 1991). The Temp. Zelda (TV). 1994: Cosa Nostra The Last Word (released 1998). 1995: French Kiss / Paris Match. Land Mines. 1996: Beautiful Girls. The Substance of Fire. City of Industry. Mr and Mrs Loving (TV). 1997: Playing God. Dead by Midnight (TV). 1998: Aldrich Ames: Traitor Within (TV). 1999: The General's Daughter. Deterrence. Just One Night. 2000: The Golden Spiders (TV).

HYAMS, Leila 1905–1977
Vivacious green-eyed blonde of warm personality, the daughter of vaudeville parents. After experience in her parents' act and success as a model, she became a star in her first major role, in *Dancing Mothers*, but with the coming of sound, her career gradually slipped away. Still remembered, though, as the heroine of *Freaks*.

1924: Sandra. 1926: Dancing Mothers. Summer Bachelors. Kick-Off. 1927: The Brute. Bush Leaguer. One Round Hogan. The Wizard. White Pants Willie. The Branded Sombrero. 1928: Crimson City. Honor Bound. Land of the Silver Fox. A Girl in Every Port. 1929: Masquerade. Hurricane. The Thirteenth Chair. Spite Marriage. The Wonder of Women. Alias Jimmy Valentine. The Far Call. The Idle Rich. 1930: Sins of the Children. Part-Time Wife. Way for a Sailor. The Richest Man in the World. Way Out West. The Girl Said No. Flirting Widow. Sweethearts and Wives. The Bishop Murder Case. The Big House. 1931: Men Call It Love. Stepping Out. A Gentleman's Fate. Phantom of Paris. The New Adventures of Get-Rich-Quick Wallingford. *Jackie Cooper's Christmas (GB: The Christmas Party). Surrender. 1932: Red Headed Woman. The Big Broadcast. Freaks. Island of Lost Souls. 1933: The Constant Woman / Auction in Souls. Sing Sinner Sing. Saturday's Millions. Horse Play. 1934: The Poor Rich. Affairs of a Gentleman. No Ransom (GB: Bonds of Honour). 1935: Ruggles of Red Gap. People Will Talk. $1,000 a Minute. 1936: Yellow Dust. 1942: *First Aid.

HYER, Martha 1924–
Brunette (blonde from 1956), alabaster-faced American actress with come-hither looks.

Very gradually rose from small parts to leading roles without ever quite becoming a big star, but pursued her career in films and television with great determination over a remarkable period of almost 30 years without ever seeming to age more than a year or two. She was basically unsympathetic and so best as outright bad girls. Married producer Hal Wallis (second of two) in 1966. Nominated for an Oscar in *Some Came Running*.

1946: The Locket. 1947: Thunder Mountain. Born to Kill (GB: Lady of Deceit). †Woman on the Beach. 1948: The Velvet Touch. Gun Smugglers. The Judge Steps Out (GB: Indian Summer). 1949: Clay Pigeon. Roughshod. The Rustlers. 1950: The Lawless (GB: The Dividing Line). Outcast of Black Mesa (GB: The Clue). Salt Lake Raiders. Frisco Tornado. 1951: Geisha Girl. The Kangaroo Kid. The Invisible Mr Unmei. 1952: Wild Stallion. Yukon Gold. 1953: Abbott and Costello Go to Mars. So Big. 1954: Riders to the Stars. Lucky Me. The Scarlet Spear. Battle of Rogue River. Sabrina (GB: Sabrina Fair). Down Three Dark Streets. Cry Vengeance. 1955: Kiss of Fire. Francis in the Navy. Wyoming Renegades. Paris Follies of 1956. 1956: Red Sundown. Showdown at Abilene. Battle Hymn. 1957: Reunion (TV). Kelly and Me. Mister Cory. My Man Godfrey. The Delicate Delinquent. 1958: Houseboat. Paris Holiday. Once Upon a Horse. Some Came Running. 1959: The Big Fisherman. The Best of Everything. 1960: Ice Palace. Desire in the Dust. Mistress of the World: 1. Mistress of the World: 2. 1961: The Right Approach. The Last Time I Saw Archie. 1962: A Girl Named Tamiko. 1963: The Man from the Diners' Club. Wives and Lovers. 1964: The Carpetbaggers. Pyro (GB: Wheel of Fire). Blood on the Arrow. First Men in the Moon. Bikini Beach. 1965: The Sons of Katie Elder. War Italian Style. 1966: The Chase. The Night of the Grizzly. Picture Mommy Dead. 1967: The Happening. Some May Live. Lo scatenato (GB and US: Catch As Catch Can). 1968: House of 1,000 Dolls. 1969: Crossplot. 1970: Once You Kiss a Stranger. Day of the Wolves (only shown on TV 1973). Another Man's Wife. 1971: The Tyrant.

†Scene deleted from final release print

HYLTON, Jane
(Gwendoline Clark) 1926–1979
Light-haired British actress whose plaintive face and unhappy mouth seemed to doom her to roles of anguish and suffering at both ends

of the social scale. A graduate of Sydney Box's 'company of youth' and the post-war Rank charm school, she had some meaty roles in the forties, but slipped into second-features in the following decade. Long married to actor Peter Dyneley (1921–1977). First husband was producer Euan Lloyd. Died from a heart attack.

1946: †The Years Between. Daybreak. Girl in a Million. 1947: Dear Murderer. The Upturned Glass. Holiday Camp. When the Bough Breaks. It Always Rains on Sunday. Jassy. 1948: My Sister and I. Good Time Girl. My Brother's Keeper. Here Come the Huggetts. 1949: Passport to Pimlico. 1950: Dance Hall. 1951: The Quiet Woman. Out of True. 1952: Tall Headlines. It Started in Paradise. 1953: The Weak and the Wicked (US: Young and Willing). 1954: Burnt Evidence. 1955: Secret Venture. Laughing in the Sunshine. 1957: You Pay Your Money. 1959: Violent Moment. Deadly Record. Devil's Bait. Night Train to Inverness. The Split (US: The Manster). 1960: Circus of Horrors. 1961: House of Mystery. 1963: Bitter Harvest. 1978: The Wild Geese.

†As Gwen Clark

HYSON, Dorothy
See QUAYLE, Anthony

I

fair hair and easy grin. Often seen as sexual predators, he made his first major impact on film in company with his twin brother Llyr in *Twin Town*, but showed he could handle comedy as well when cast as Hugh Grant's scruffy flatmate in *Notting Hill*. A busy part of the British cinema scene at the turn of the century, he has also worked in Hollywood in recent times.

1995: Streetlife (TV). 1996: August. 1997: Twin Town. 1998: Dancing at Lughnasa. 1999: Heart. Notting Hill. You're Dead. Janice Beard 45 WPM. Love, Honour & Obey. 2000: Rancid Aluminium. Kevin & Perry Go Large. The Replacements. Little Nicky. 2001: Human Nature.

Canadian actor who rose nicely from supporting roles, mostly as villains, to star parts, but failed to maintain his expected position at the head of cast lists. A decline into featured parts, or leads in American and British 'B' movies in the 1950s took him into quite small roles in succeeding years. Married (second of three) to Joanne Dru from 1949 to 1958. Half-brother of actor/comedian Tommy Noonan. Nominated for an Oscar in *All the King's Men*. Died from leukemia.

1945: A Walk in the Sun. 1946: Behind Green Lights. It Shouldn't Happen to a Dog. My Darling Clementine. Wake Up and Dream. Somewhere in the Night (voice only). 1947: The Gangster. Railroaded! Red River. I Love Trouble. Repeat Performance (narrator only). 1948: Open Secret. Raw Deal. Joan of Arc. A Southern Yankee (GB: My Hero). 1949: Roughshod. I Shot Jesse James. The Walking Hills. The Doolins of Oklahoma (GB: The Great Manhunt). Mr Soft Touch (GB: House of Settlement). Anna Lucasta. Undercover Man (narrator only). All the King's Men. 1950: Cargo to Capetown. The Return of Jesse James. 1951: Vengeance Valley. The Scarf. Little Big Horn (GB: The Fighting 7th). The Basketball Fix (GB: The Big Decision). The Bushwhackers (GB: The Rebel). Red Mountain. This is Korea (narrator only). 1952: Hurricane Smith. 1953: The 49th Man. Combat Squad. †Hannah Lee (later Outlaw Territory). 1954: The Good Die Young. Security Risk. †The Fast and the Furious. Southwest Passage (GB: Camels West). The Steel Cage. 1955: The Glass Cage (US: The Glass Tomb). Queen Bee. Hell's Horizon. 1956: Gunslinger. Gunfight at the OK Corral. 1957: Without Incident (TV). A Sound of Different Drummers (TV). 1958: Stormy Crossing (US: Black Tide). No Place to Land (GB: Man Mad). Party Girl. 1960: Faces in the Dark. Spartacus. No Time to Kill (released 1963). 1961: Wild in the Country. Return of a Stranger. Brushfire! 1962: 55 Days at Peking. 1963: The Ceremony. The Fall of the Roman Empire. 1965: I Saw What You Did. Day Of the Nightmare. 1966: Fort Utah. 1967: Flight of the Hawk. War Devils. Caxambu! Odio per odio. Dalle Ardenne all' inferno (GB: The Dirty Heroes). Arizona Bushwhackers. 1968: Villa Rides! Corri uomo corri (US: Run, Man, Run). El Chè Guevara (GB: Rebel with a Cause). Sparate è meglio, fidarsi è bene. Tutto per tutto. Una pistola per cento bare. T'ammazzo! – raccomandanti a Dio. 1969: Una sull'altra (GB and US: One on Top of the

ICE CUBE (O'Shea Jackson) 1969–
Burly, round-faced, seldom-smiling rap singer and songwriter with distinctive mutton chop-shaped sideburns who started an acting career just a year after his first big success as a record star. His fast-talking, bouncy and aggressive characters have been seen increasingly more often in movies since the mid-1990s and he made his debut as a director in 1998. Owns his own TV production company called Cubevision.

1991: Boyz N the Hood. 1992: Trespass/The Looters. 1993: CB4. 1994: The Glass Shield. 1995: Higher Learning. 1996: Friday. Dangerous Ground. 1997: Anaconda. 1998: The Players Club. Straight from the Streets. I Got the Hook-up. 1999: Three Kings. Thicker Than Water. Next Friday. 2000: Shadow Man. 2001: The Ghosts of Mars.

IRELAND, Jill 1936–1990
Perky British blonde actress, with distinctive urchin cut in her early days. A favourite magazine pin-up, although saucy rather than sexy, she appeared in supporting parts in British films before going to Hollywood, initially with her first husband, David McCallum (*qv*). Later leading roles with second husband Charles Bronson (also *qv*) revealed her acting as shaky, although she was good in one role – in *The Streetfighter/Hard Times*. Recovered from breast cancer in the mid-1980s, but cancer finally killed her some five years later. She had seven children.

*1955: Oh Rosalinda!! The Woman for Joe. Simon and Laura. 1956: The Big Money. Three Men in a Boat. 1957: There's Always a Thursday. Robbery under Arms. Hell Drivers. 1959: The Desperate Man. *The Ghost Train Murder. Carry on Nurse. 1960: Girls of Latin Quarter. 1961: So Evil, So Young. Raising the Wind. Jungle Street. 1962: Twice round the Daffodils. The Battleaxe. 1967: The Karate Killers (TV. GB: cinemas). 1968: Villa Rides! 1969: Rider on the Rain. 1970: Violent City (US: The Family). 1971: Quelqu'un derrière la porte (GB: Two Minds for Murder). Cold Sweat. 1972: The Mechanic (reissued as Killer of Killers). The Valachi Papers. 1973: Valdez the Halfbreed (GB: The Valdez Horses. US: Chino). 1975: Hard Times (GB: The Streetfighter). Breakheart Pass. From Noon Till Three. Breakout. 1978: Love and Bullets. 1981: Death Wish II. 1983: The Girl, the Gold Watch and Everything (TV). 1986: Assassination. 1987: Caught.*

IRELAND, John 1914–1992
Tough-looking, heavy-browed, slim, narrow-faced, broad-shouldered, very dark-haired

IFANS, Rhys 1967–
Tall, lanky, extrovert Welsh actor with floppy

Other). Rider on the Rain. La sfida dei Mackenna/Badlands Drifter (US: The Challenge of the Mackennas). Zenabel. Femmine insaziabili (US: Carnal Circuit). Quanto costa morire. Quel caldo maledotto giorno di Fuoco. 1970: The Adventurers. 1972: The Mechanic (reissued as Killer of Killers). Escape to the Sun. North-East to Seoul. Der Würger kommt auf leisen Socken (US: The Mad Butcher). 1973: Welcome to Arrow Beach (US: Tender Flesh). The House of the Seven Corpses. 1974: Go for Broke. The Phantom of Hollywood (TV). The Girl on the Late, Late Show (TV). Ten Whites Killed by One Little Indian! 1975: Farewell, My Lovely. The Swiss Conspiracy. La furie du désir. We're No Angels. Il letto in piazza (GB: Sex Diary). 1976: Captain Midnight/On the Air Live with Captain Midnight. Delta Fox. Salon Kitty (US: Madame Kitty). 1977: Assault on Paradise (US: Maniac. GB: TV, as Ransom). The Moon and a Murmur (unfinished). Satan's Cheerleaders. The Perfect Killer. Tomorrow Never Comes. Love and the Midnight Auto Supply. Kino, the Padre on Horseback. 1978: Kavik the Wolf Dog (GB: TV, as The Courage of Kavik the Wolf Dog). The Millionaire (TV). Verano sangrieto. 1979: Crossbar (TV). The Shape of Things to Come. Guyana: The Crime of the Century. 1980: Tourist (TV). Marilyn: The Untold Story (TV). 1981: Incubus. Las majeres de Jeremias/Garden of Venus. 1984: Martin's Day. The Treasure of the Amazon/Treasure of Doom. 1985: The Hitchhiker. Thunder Run. 1986: Cosmos Killer/Miami Golem (released 1988 as Miami Horror). 1988: Bonanza: The Next Generation (TV). Perry Mason: The Case of the Lady in The Lake (TV). Terror Night/Final Curtain. Messenger of Death. 1989: Sundown: The Vampire in Retreat. Big Bad John. 1991: Waxwork II: Lost in Time. 1992: Graveyard Story.

†And co-directed

IRONS, Jeremy 1948–
Tall, slim, erect and handsome in a taut and faintly forlorn-looking kind of way, this romantic British actor (born on the Isle of Wight) played guitar and sang in his early twenties, starting his show business career busking in London's West End. A far cry from the co-starring role with Meryl Streep in The French Lieutenant's Woman and his enormous popular success in the TV series Brideshead Revisited, although Irons's roles since then have been sufficiently off the beaten track for him to have not quite consolidated his position as a leading star of the cinema until the late 1980s. Married actress Sinead Cusack (1948–). Once described as 'the thinking girl's pin-up'. Won an Academy Award in 1991 for Reversal Of Fortune, a role that triggered his playing a whole run of flawed, tormented or sometimes downright villainous characters.
1980: Nijinsky. 1981: The French Lieutenant's Woman. 1982: Moonlighting. The Masterbuilders (narrator only). The Captain's Doll (TV). Betrayal. 1983: The Wild Duck. Un amour de Swann/Swann in Love. 1984: The Lie. 1985: The Statue of Liberty (narrator only). 1986: The Mission. 1988: Dead Ringers. 1989: A Chorus of Disapproval. Danny the Champion of the World (US: TV). Australia. 1990: Reversal of Fortune. 1991: Kafka. 1992: Waterland. Damage. Tales from Hollywood (TV). 1993: M Butterfly. The House of the Spirits. Earth and the American Dream (voice only). 1994: The Lion King (voice only). 1995: Die Hard With a Vengeance. 1996: Stealing Beauty. Lolita. 1997: Chinese Box. The Man in the Iron Mask. 2000: Dungeons and Dragons.

IRVING, Amy 1953–
Petite American actress with a mass of wispy brown hair, steely blue eyes and a slightly cool personality. The daughter of actress Priscilla Pointer, she played a mixture of innocent ingenues and calculating charmers before marrying long-time love Steven Spielberg in 1985. But the couple were in the divorce courts four years later. Nominated for an Academy Award for Yentl, she scored a big personal hit in 1988 with Crossing Delancey. Has also had leads in two major TV miniseries, Anastasia: The Mystery of Anna and The Far Pavilions. Married (second) Brazilian director Bruno Barreto.
1976: Dynasty (TV). James Dean (TV). Panache (TV). Carrie. 1978: The Fury. 1979: Voices. 1980: Honeysuckle Rose. The Competition. 1983: Yentl. 1985: Micki + Maude. 1987: Soft Target. Rumpelstiltskin. 1988: Who Framed Roger Rabbit (voice only). Crossing Delancey. 1990: A Show of Force. 1991: An American Tail 2: Fievel Goes West (voice only). 1993: Benefit of the Doubt. Kleptomania. 1994: Twilight Zone: Rod Serling's Lost Classics (TV). 1995: Carried Away (GB: Acts of Love). Bossa Nova (released 2000). 1996: I'm Not Rappaport. 1997: One Tough Cop. Deconstructing Harry. 1998: The Confession. The Rage: Carrie II. 1999: End of Innocence. Blue Ridge Falls. 2000: Traffic.

IVES, Burl 1909–1995
Genial, jovial American folk singer with tufty dark hair and goatee beard. He won a reputation as a musical story-teller, then made a few appearances in outdoor adventure tales in the 1940s before unexpectedly becoming a dramatic heavyweight, in both senses, in the following decade. Singing remained his first love, but he continued to pop up occasionally in films, mostly as elderly characters as cantankerous as his early portraits had been good-humoured. Oscar (best supporting actor) for The Big Country. Suffered a degenerative bone disease in later years. Died from mouth cancer.
1946: Smoky. *Buckeye Jim. 1948: Green Grass of Wyoming. Station West. So Dear to My Heart. 1950: *Noah Found Grace. Sierra. *Oh Dear, She's Wonderful. 1951: *Darlin Corey. *Cowboy's Lament. 1952: *The Gypsy. *Little White Duck. *The Tailor and the Mouse. *Tell Me Your Story. 1954: East of Eden. 1956: The Power and the Prize. 1957: The Miracle Worker (TV). A Face in the Crowd. 1958: Desire Under the Elms. The Big Country. Cat on a Hot Tin Roof. Wind Across the Everglades. 1959: Our Man in Havana. Day of the Outlaw. 1960: Let No Man Write My Epitaph. 1962: The Flying Clipper (narrator only). The Spiral Road. Summer Magic. 1964: The Brass Bottle. Ensign Pulver. 1965: OK Crackerby (TV). 1966: The Daydreamer (voice only). 1967: Rocket to the Moon/Jules Verne's Rocket to the Moon (US: Those Fantastic Flying Fools). 1968: The Sound of Anger (TV). 1969: The Whole World is Watching (TV). The Only Way Out is Dead (US: TV, as The Man Who Wanted to Live Forever). The McMasters . . . Tougher Than the West Itself! 1976: Baker's Hawk. Hugo the Hippo (voice only). 1978: The Bermuda Depths (TV). The New Adventures of Heidi (TV). Just You and Me, Kid. 1981: Earthbound. 1982: White Dog. 1984: The Ewok Adventure (TV. GB: cinemas, as Caravan of Courage. Narrator only). 1985: Uphill All the Way. 1987: Poor Little Rich Girl (TV). 1988: Two Moon Junction.

J

JACKSON, Anne 1925

Gawky, red-haired, toothy American actress with an easy talent for wisecracks, seen occasionally as ordinary working women. Born ten years too late; a decade earlier, she would have been in hot demand for loveable loyal secretaries and witty best friends. An attempt to make her into a star of the sixties was successful only with the critics. Married to Eli Wallach (*qv*) since 1948.

1950: So Young, So Bad. 1958: The Journey. 1960: Tall Story. 1967: How to Save a Marriage . . . And Ruin Your Life. The Tiger Makes Out. 1968: The Secret Life of An American Wife. 1969: Zigzag (GB: False Witness). 1970: The Angel Levine. Lovers and Other Strangers. Dirty Dingus Magee. 1976: Nasty Habits. Twenty Shades of Pink (TV). 1979: The Bell Jar. The Shining. 1980: Family Man (TV). A Private Battle (TV). Blinded by the Light (TV). 1981: Leave 'Em Laughing (TV). 1984: Sam's Son. 1990: Funny About Love. 1991: Folks! 1997: Rescuers: Stories of Courage – Two Women (TV). 2000: Something Sweet.

JACKSON, Glenda 1936–

Distinctive dark-haired English actress with precise, tart tones who looks as though she would stand no more nonsense than the original Mary Poppins. Remained a stage actress throughout her early career, then suddenly burst on the film scene as tempestuous, destiny-changing females. Won two Oscars in four years (for *Women in Love* and *A Touch of Class*), continued building her stage reputation and endeared herself to British TV millions with her straight-faced sense of comedy on *The Morecambe and Wise Show*. Also nominated for Oscars on *Sunday, Bloody Sunday* and *Hedda*. A staunch Socialist, she became a Labour MP in 1992.

*1963: This Sporting Life. 1966: The Persecution and Assassination of Jean Paul Marat . . . (The Marat/Sade). Benefit of the Doubt. 1967: Tell Me Lies. 1968: Negatives. 1969: Women in Love. 1970: The Music Lovers. 1971: Sunday, Bloody Sunday. The Boy Friend. Mary, Queen of Scots. 1972: The Triple Echo (US: Soldier in Skirts). A Touch of Class. 1973: Bequest to the Nation (US: The Nelson Affair). Il sorriso del grande tentatore (GB: The Tempter. US: The Devil is a Woman). 1974: The Maids. 1975: The Romantic Englishwoman. Hedda. 1976: Nasty Habits. The Incredible Sarah. 1978: House Calls. The Class of Miss MacMichael. Stevie. 1979: Lost and Found. Health. *Build Me a World (narrator only). 1980: Hopscotch. 1981: *Stop Polio. The Patricia Neal Story (TV). 1982: The Return of the Soldier. Giro City (TV. US: And Nothing But the Truth). 1984: Sakharov. 1985: Turtle Diary. 1987: Beyond Therapy. Business As Usual. 1988: Salome's Last Dance. Imago (narrator only). 1989: The Rainbow. King of the Wind. 1990: Doombeach. 1991: The Castle. A Murder of Quality (TV). The House of Bernarda Alba (TV).*

JACKSON, Gordon 1920–1990

Fair-haired, shy-seeming Scottish actor, briefly in engineering before deciding finally on an acting career after service in World War II. Initially as young soldiers and juvenile leads, later in minor leading roles and a good variety of supporting parts in bigger films. Won his greatest popularity in the seventies in the long-running TV series *Upstairs Downstairs*. Married to Rona Anderson (*qv*) from 1951. Died from bone cancer.

*1942: The Foreman Went to France (US: Somewhere in France). Nine Men. 1943: San Demetrio London. Millions Like Us. 1945: Pink String and Sealing Wax. 1946: *Someone Wasn't Thinking. The Captive Heart. 1948: Against the Wind. Eureka Stockade. 1949: Floodtide. Stop Press Girl. Whisky Galore! (US: Tight Little Island). 1950: Bitter Springs. 1951: The Lady with a Lamp. Happy-Go-Lovely. 1952: Castle in the Air. 1953: Malta Story. Death Goes to School. Meet Mr Lucifer. The Love Lottery. 1954: The Delavine Affair. 1955: Passage Home. Windfall. The Quatermass Experiment (US: The Creeping Unknown). 1956: Pacific Destiny. Women without Men (US: Blonde Bait). The Baby and the Battleship. Sailor Beware! (US: Panic in the Parlor). 1957: Seven Waves Away (US: Abandon Ship!). Black Ice. Let's Be Happy. Hell Drivers. Man in the Shadow. 1958: *Scotland Dances (narrator only). Blind Spot. Rockets Galore (US: Mad Little Island). Three Crooked Men. 1959: Yesterday's Enemy. Blind Date. The Bridal Path. Devil's Bait. The Navy Lark. 1960: Cone of Silence (US: Trouble in the Sky). The Price of Silence. Tunes of Glory. Snowball. 1961: Greyfriars Bobby. Two Wives at One Wedding. 1962: Mutiny on the Bounty. 1963: The Long Ships. The Great Escape. 1964: Daylight Robbery. 1965: Cast a Giant Shadow. The Ipcress File. Those Magnificent Men in their Flying Machines. Operation Crossbow. 1966: The Fighting Prince of Donegal. The Night of the Generals. Triple Cross. 1967: Danger Route. 1968: The Prime of Miss Jean Brodie. 1969: On the Run. Run Wild, Run Free. Hamlet. 1970: Scrooge. The Music Lovers. 1971: Kidnapped. Madame Sin (TV. GB: cinemas). 1975: Russian Roulette. 1977: Golden Rendezvous. The Medusa Touch. Spectre (TV). 1979: Raising Daisy Rothschild (GB: TV, as The Last Giraffe). 1984: The Shooting Party. The Masks of Death (TV). 1985: Gunpowder. 1986: The Whistle Blower. My Brother Tom (TV). 1989: The Lady and the Highwayman (TV).*

JACKSON, Samuel L 1948–

Tall, imposing, bony-faced, fast-talking, faintly menacing American actor with receding hair, who overcame a 20-year cocaine habit to keep his career on target and progress to leading roles in his forties after a long run of obscure films and minor parts. Once in star roles, however, Jackson quickly became one of America's most commanding and respected actors. An Academy Award nominee for *Pulp Fiction*, he is married to actress LaTanya Richardson.

1972: *Together for Days*. 1976: *The Displaced Person*. 1978: *The Trial of the Moke* (TV). 1979: *The Rebels* (TV). 1981: *Ragtime*. 1986: *Magic Sticks*. 1987: *Eddie Murphy Raw*. *Uncle Tom's Cabin* (TV). 1988: *Dead Man Walking* (TV. US: *Dead Man Out*). *Coming to America*. *School Daze*. 1989: *Sea of Love*. *Do the Right Thing*. 1990: *Mo' Better Blues*. *Def by Temptation*. *Betsy's Wedding*. *A Shock to the System*. *The Exorcist III*. *GoodFellas*. *The Return of Superfly*. 1991: *Johnny Suede*. *Strictly Business/Go Natalie*. *Jungle Fever*. *Jumpin' at the Boneyard*. *Fathers & Sons*. 1992: *White Sands*. *Juice*. *Amos & Andrew*. *Patriot Games*. 1993: *Menace II Society*. *Jurassic Park*. *Assault at West Point* (TV). *National Lampoon's Loaded Weapon 1*. *True Romance*. *Simple Justice* (TV). 1994: *Hail Caesar*. *The New Age*. *Pulp Fiction*. *Fresh*. *Against the Wall*. (TV). 1995: *Die Hard With a Vengeance*. *Losing Isaiah*. *Kiss of Death*. *Fluke* (voice only). *The Search for One-Eyed Jimmy*. *Mob Justice* (TV). 1996: *Hard Eight/Sydney*. *The Great White Hype*. *The Long Kiss Goodnight*. *Trees Lounge*. *A Time to Kill*. 1997: *187/One Eight Seven*. *Eve's Bayou*. *You're Still Not Fooling Anybody*. *Jackie Brown*. 1998: *Sphere*. *The Negotiator*. *The Red Violin*. *Out of Sight*. 1999: *Star Wars: Episode 1 – The Phantom Menace*. *Deep Blue Sea*. *Rules of Engagement*. *Forever Hollywood* (D). 2000: *Shaft/Shaft Returns*. *51st State*. *Unbreakable*. *Mefisto in Onyx*. *The Caveman's Valentine*.

JACKSON, Sherry 1942–
Another of those snub-nosed tots who, along with Natalie Wood and Gigi Perreau (both *qv*) wormed their ways into all our hearts in the late 1940s and early 1950s. Dark-haired, cubby-cheeked Sherry (stepdaughter of writer Montgomery Pittman) was at her best in near-starring roles of the 1952–53 period, notably *The Miracle of Our Lady of Fatima*. Five years on TV's *The Danny Thomas Show* followed, after which she pursued an adult career for more than 20 years without achieving the breakthrough to big-screen stardom. The actress in such early 1990s films as *Daughters of the Dust* is another Sherry Jackson.
1949: *You're My Everything*. *Ma and Pa Kettle Go to Town* (GB: *Going to Town*). 1950: *A Modern Marriage*. *Covered Wagon Raid*. *Where Danger Lives*. *The Breaking Point*. 1952: *When I Grow Up*. *The Great Caruso*. *Lorna Doone*. *Apache Drums*. *Hello, God*. *Ma*

and Pa Kettle Back on the Farm. 1952: *The Lion and the Horse*. *Ma and Pa Kettle at the Fair*. *This Woman is Dangerous*. *The Miracle of Our Lady of Fatima* (GB: *The Miracle of Fatima*). *Ma and Pa Kettle on Vacation* (GB: *Ma and Pa Kettle Go to Paris*). 1953: *Trouble Along the Way*. 1956: *Come Next Spring*. 1960: *The Adventures of Huckleberry Finn*. 1962: *Frigid Wife*. 1965; *Wild on the Beach*. 1967: *Gunn*. 1968: *The Silent Treatment*. *The Mini-Skirt Mob*. 1969: *The Monitors*. 1970: *Wild Women* (TV). 1973: *Cotter* (TV). 1974: *Hitchhike!* (TV). *The Girl on the Late, Late Show* (TV). 1975: *Returning Home* (TV). 1977: *Bare Knuckles* (released 1984). 1978: *Stingray*. 1979: *Bride of the Incredible Hulk* (TV). 1980: *Casino* (TV).

JACOB, Irène 1966–
Dark-haired, fair-skinned, cool, gracious French actress, often in passive roles. After studying drama in Switzerland and France, she began a film career at 21. Her command of English put her into international films from 1990, although her best performances have been in movies made in her native France. One senses that she needs to get away from playing threatened women to improve her status in the film world.
1987: *Au revoir les enfants*. 1988: *Erreur de jeunesse*. *La veillée*. 1989: *La bande des quatre*. *Le secret de Sarah Tombelaine*. 1990: *Trusting Beatrice*. 1991: *Le double vie de Véronique/ The Double Life of Veronique*. *Enak*. 1992: *Le prédiction/Predskazaniye*. 1993: *La passion Van Gogh/The Van Gogh Wake*. *The Secret Garden*. 1994: *Le moulin de Daudet*. *Trois couleurs: rouge/Red*. 1995: *Victory* (released 1997). *All Men Are Mortal*. *Une fille galante*. *Othello*. *Beyond the Clouds*. *Fugueuses*. 1997: *Incognito*. *Foolish Heart*. 1998: *U.S. Marshals*. *Magic*. *Cuisine Américaine*. 1999: *The Big Brass Ring*. *My Life So Far*. 2000: *History is Made at Night*. *Londinium*. *L'heure d'été*. *L'affaire Marcorelle*.

JACOBSSON, Ulla 1929–1982
Plump-cheeked, light-haired, rather anxious-looking Swedish actress who gained an international reputation of a sort (rather as Hedy Lamarr had done in the 1930s) with her sensational nude scenes in *One Summer of Happiness*. It was 1962, however, before she ventured outside the European film industry, and then she made no sort of impact at all. When she returned to Sweden, her film career tailed away. Died from bone cancer.

1951: *Bärande Har* (US: *The Rolling Sea*). *Hon Dansade en Sommar* (GB and US: *One Summer of Happiness*). 1953: *All Jordens Frojd* (US: *All the Joy of the Earth*). 1954: *. . . und ewig bleibt die Liebe* (US: *Eternal Love*). *Karin Månsdotter*. *Sir Arne's Treasure*. 1955: *Die heilige Lüge* (US: *The Sacred Lie*). *Der Pfarrer von Kirchfeld*. *Sommernattens Leende* (GB: and US: *Smiles of a Summer Night*). 1956: *Crime and Punishment*. *Sangen om den Eldröda Blomman* (US: *Song of the Scarlet Flower*). 1957: *Die letzten Werden die ersten sein*. 1958: *Körkarlen* (US: *The Phantom Carriage*). *Unruhige Nacht* (US: *The Restless Night*). 1959: *Llegaron dos hombres*. *. . .und das am Montagmorgen*. 1960: *Im Name einer Mutter*. 1961: *Una domenica d'estate*. *Riviera Story*. 1962: *The Final Hour*. 1963: *Love is a Ball* (GB: *All This and Money Too*). *Zulu*. 1965: *Nattmara/Nightmare*. *The Heroes of Telemark*. 1967: *Alle Jahre Wieder*. *The Double Man*. 1968: *Bamse* (US: *Teddy Bear*). *Adolphe ou l'âge tendre*. 1969: *The Servant*. 1970: *Atem der Lust*. 1975: *Faustrecht der Freiheit* (GB: *Fox*. US: *Fox and His Friends*).

JAMES, Sidney (S. Cohen) 1913–1976
Dark, crinkly-haired, South African-born character star (in England from 1946) with battered features (a conspiracy between boxing and nature) and distinctive raucous laugh – once also a hairdresser and diamond polisher. Whether as cockney crook or loud-mouthed American, he soon became one of those faces to which one couldn't quite add the name, until TV's *Hancock's Half-Hour* (1956–1960) revealed his facility for comedy. After Tony Hancock broke up the partnership, James became the mainstay of the

'Carry On' films: his Henry VIII is especially treasurable. Died from a heart attack while performing on stage.

1947: Black Memory. The October Man. It Always Rains on Sunday. 1948: No Orchids for Miss Blandish. Night Beat. Once a Jolly Swagman (US: Maniacs on Wheels). The Small Back Room (US: Hour of Glory). 1949: Paper Orchid. The Man in Black. Give Us This Day (US: Salt to the Devil). 1950: Last Holiday. The Lady Craved Excitement. 1951: Talk of a Million (US: You Can't Beat the Irish). Lady Godiva Rides Again. The Lavender Hill Mob. The Magic Box. The Galloping Major. 1952: I Believe in You. Emergency Call (US: Hundred Hour Hunt). Gift Horse (US: Glory at Sea). Cosh Boy (US: The Slasher). Miss Robin Hood. Time Gentlemen Please! Father's Doing Fine. Venetian Bird (US: The Assassin). Tall Headlines. The Yellow Balloon. 1953: The Wedding of Lilli Marlene. Escape by Night. The Titfield Thunderbolt. The Square Ring. Will Any Gentleman? The Weak and the Wicked (US: Young and Willing). Park Plaza 605 (US: Norman Conquest). The Flanagan Boy (US: Bad Blonde). Is Your Honeymoon Really Necessary? Malta Story. 1954: The Rainbow Jacket. The House Across the Lake (US: Heatwave). Father Brown (US: The Detective). Seagulls over Sorrento (US: Crest of the Wave). The Crowded Day. Orders Are Orders. Aunt Clara. For Better, for Worse (US: Cocktails in the Kitchen). The Belles of St Trinian's. The Glass Cage (US: The Glass Tomb). 1955: Out of the Clouds. Joe Macbeth. The Deep Blue Sea. A Kid for Two Farthings. A Yank in Ermine. It's a Great Day. John and Julie. 1956: Ramsbottom Rides Again. The Extra Day. Wicked As They Come. The Baby and the Battleship. The Iron Petticoat. Dry Rot. Trapeze. 1957: Quatermass II (US: Enemy from Space). Interpol (US: Pickup Alley). The Smallest Show on Earth. The Shiralee. Hell Drivers. Campbell's Kingdom. A King In New York. The Story of Esther Costello (US: Golden Virgin). 1958: The Silent Enemy. Another Time, Another Place. Next to No Time! The Man Inside. I Was Monty's Double. The Sheriff of Fractured Jaw. 1959: Too Many Crooks. Make Mine a Million. The 39 Steps. Upstairs and Downstairs. Tommy the Toreador. Desert Mice. Idle on Parade (US: Idol on Parade). 1960: Carry on Constable. Watch Your Stern. And the Same to You. The Pure Hell of St Trinians. 1961: Double Bunk. A Weekend with Lulu. The Green Helmet. What a Carve Up! (US: No Place Like Homicide). Raising the Wind (US: Roommates). What a Whopper! Carry on Regardless. 1962: Carry on Cruising. We Joined the Navy. 1963: Carry on Cabby. 1964: The Beauty Jungle (US: Contest Girl). Carry on Cleo. Three Hats for Lisa. 1965: The Big Job. Carry on Cowboy. 1966: Where the Bullets Fly. Don't Lose Your Head. 1967: Carry on Doctor. 1968: Carry on Up the Khyber. 1969: Carry on Camping. Carry on Again, Doctor. Stop Exchange. Carry on Up the Jungle. 1970: Carry on Loving. Carry on Henry. 1971: Carry on at Your Convenience. Tokoloshe, the Evil Spirit (completed 1964). 1972: Carry on Matron. Bless This House. Carry on Abroad. 1973: Carry on Girls. 1974: Carry on Dick.

JANE, Thomas 1969–

Rugged, fair-haired American actor with Adonis-like good looks who started to break through to stardom in the late 1990s after years of theatre work and smallish parts in films. His performance as Neal Cassady in *The Last Time I Committed Suicide* proved something of a watershed and he was handed action leads in bigger mainstream movies.

1991: Love and Curses . . . and All That Jazz (TV). 1992: I'll Love You Forever . . . Tonight. Buffy the Vampire Slayer. 1993: Nemesis. 1994: At Ground Zero/ Ground Zero. 1996: The Last Time I Commited Suicide. The Crow: City of Angels. 1997: Boogie Nights. Face/ Off. 1998: Thursday. The Velocity of Gary. The Thin Red Line. 1999: Deep Blue Sea. Magnolia. Under Suspicion. 2000: Molly. Dancing in the Dark. The Third Degree.

JANNINGS, Emil
(Theodor E. Janenz) 1882–1950

Big, beefy, glowering, dominant Swiss-born actor whose speciality was great men destined for tragic decline. He became a leading figure in the German cinema in silent days and, when some of his films did well in America, went to Hollywood in 1926. Here, he enjoyed only a few years of popularity, for sound revealed his guttural accent and sent him back to Germany, where his efforts for the Third Reich in wartime led him to spend his final years in virtual exile. Oscar in 1928, jointly for *The Way of All Flesh* and *The Last Command*. Died from cancer.

1914: Arme Eva. Im Banne der Leidenschaft. Im Schützengraben. 1915: Passionels Tagebuch. Frau Eva. 1916: Nächte des Grauens. Stein unter Steinen. Unheilbar. Die Ehe der Luise Rohrbach. Im Angesicht des Toten. Aus Mangel an Beweisen. Der zehnte Pavillon der Zitadelle. Die Bettlerin von St Marien. 1917: Das Leben ein Traum. Der Ring der Giuditta Foscari. Ein fideles Gefängnis. Lulu. Wenn vier dasselbe tun. Das Geschäft. 1918: Nach zwanzig Jahren. Die Augen der Mumie Mâ (GB: The Eyes of the Mummy). Keimendes Leben Part I. Keimendes Leben Part II. 1919: Der Mann der Tat. Die Tochter des Mehemed. Madame Dubarry (US: Passion). Rose Bernd. Kohlhiesels Töchter. 1920: Vendetta. Algol. Anna Boleyn (US: Deception). Colombine. Das grosse Licht. Der Schädel der Pharaonentochter. Der Stier von Oliviera. The Brothers Karamazov. 1921: Danton (US: All for a Woman). Das Weib des Pharao (GB and US: The Loves of Pharaoh). Der Schwur des Peter Hergatz. Die Ratten. 1922: Othello. Peter the Great. Die Gräfin von Paris. 1923: Alles für Geld (US: Fortune's Fool). Tragödie der Liebe. Quo Vadis? 1924: Der letzte Mann (GB and US: The Last Laugh). Nju (US: Husbands or Lovers). Das Wachsfigurenkabinett (GB and US: Waxworks). 1925: Liebe macht blind. Tartüff. Variety (US: Vaudeville). 1926: Faust. 1927: The Way of All Flesh. 1928: The Last Command. The Patriot. Sins of the Fathers. The Street of Sin (GB: King of Soho). 1929: Fighting the White Slave Traffic. Betrayal. 1930: Der blaue Engel/ The Blue Angel. Liebling der Götter. 1931: Stürme der Leidenschaft. 1932: König Pausole (GB: The Merry Monarch). 1934: Der schwarze Walfisch. 1935: Der alte und der junge König. 1936: Traumulus. 1937: Der Herrscher. Der zerbrochene Krug (US: The Broken Jug). 1939: Robert Koch, der Bekämpfer des Todes. 1941: Ohm Krüger. 1942: Die Entlassung. 1943: Altes Herz wird wieder jung. 1945: †Wo ist Herr Belling?

†Unfinished

JANSSEN, David (D. Meyer) 1930–1980

Dark-haired (with distinctive high temples), gravel-voiced, seldom-smiling American actor, in show business as a child. After an apprenticeship at Universal, he became perhaps television's most successful actor ever, especially in the series *Richard Diamond* (1957–1959), *The Fugitive* (1963–1966) and *Harry O* (1973–1975). He exuded cynicism, world-weariness and integrity, and was sometimes quite hypnotic to watch, although not so in films. Died from a heart attack. Has said that he played dozens of walk-on roles as a boy in World War II films, but no records of these seem to exist.

1945: It's a Pleasure. 1946: Swamp Fire. 1952: Untamed Frontier. Yankee Buccaneer. Francis Goes to West Point. No Room for the Groom. Bonzo Goes to College. 1955: Chief Crazy Horse (GB: Valley of Fury). The Private War of Major Benson. Cult of the Cobra. To Hell and Back. Francis in the Navy. The Square Jungle. All That Heaven Allows. 1956: Never Say Goodbye. Away All Boats. Toy Tiger. Francis in the Haunted House. Showdown at Abilene. The Girl He Left Behind. 1957: Lafayette Escadrille (GB: Hell Bent for Glory). Darby's Rangers (GB: The Young Invaders). 1958: The Money. 1960: Hell to Eternity. 1961: Dondi. Twenty Plus Two (GB: It Started in Tokyo). Man-Trap. Ring of Fire. King of the Roaring Twenties (GB: The Big Bankroll). 1962: Belle Sommers. 1963: My Six Loves. 1967: Warning Shot. 1968: The Green Berets. The Shoes of the Fisherman. 1969: Where it's At. Generation (GB: A Time for Giving). Marooned. 1970: Night Chase (TV). Macho Callahan. 1971: Operation Cobra (TV). 1972: The Longest Night (TV). Moon of the Wolf (TV). 1973: Pioneer Woman (TV). Birds of Prey (TV. GB: cinemas). Harry O (TV). Hijack (TV). 1974: Prisoner in the Middle (GB: TV. US: Warhead). Once is Not Enough/Jacqueline Susann's Once Is Not Enough. Smile Jenny, You're Dead (TV). 1975: The Swiss Conspiracy. Fer-de-Lance (TV. GB: cinemas as Death Dive). 1976: Farrell (TV). Two-Minute Warning. Mayday at 40,000 Feet (TV. GB: cinemas). 1977: Golden Rendezvous. A Sensitive, Passionate Man (TV). 1978: Sono stato un agente CIA (US: Covert Action). Stalk the Wild Child (TV). Nowhere to Run (TV). Pressure Point (TV). 1979: Superdome (TV). SOS Titanic (TV. GB: cinemas). Panic on Page One (TV. Later: City in Fear). High Ice. Specter on the Bridge/The Golden Gate Murders (TV). 1980: Inchon!

JANSSEN, Famke 1964–
Dark, dominant, Dutch-born actress, in America since 1985. Her acting career in the US was unspectacular until she landed the role of lascivious villainess Xenia Onatopp in the James Bond adventure *GoldenEye*. She's kept busy since then as tough cookies of various social standings; there haven't been many sympathetic roles.
1991: Fathers & Sons. 1993: Relentless 4: Ashes to Ashes. 1994: Model by Day (video). 1995: Lord of Illusions. GoldenEye. 1996: City of Industry. Dead Girl. 1997: R.P.M. The

Gingerbread Man. 1998: Snitch/Noose/Monument Avenue. Deep Rising (formerly Tentacle). Rounders. Celebrity. The Faculty. The Adventures of Sebastian Cole. 1999: House on Haunted Hill. 2000: Circus. X-Men. Love & Sex. 2001: Made.

JAYNE, Jennifer (J.J. Jones) 1931–
Copper-haired British actress whose film career was undistinguished for ten years. Then she got her first leading role in the same year (1958) as a smash-hit television series, *William Tell*, which she followed with another, *Whiplash*. If her acting was moderate, she was so easy on the eye it was hard to see why success hadn't come earlier. Wrote the screenplay for *Tales That Witness Madness* (1973) under the pseudonym Jay Fairbank.
1948: Once a Jolly Swagman (US: Maniacs on Wheels). 1949: The Blue Lamp. A Boy, a Girl and a Bike. 1950: Trio. 1951: There is Another Sun (later Wall of Death). Black Widow. 1953: It's a Grand Life. 1955: A Yank in Ermine. 1957: The End of the Line. 1958: A Woman of Mystery. Carve Her Name with Pride. Mark of the Phoenix. The Man Who Wouldn't Talk. The Trollenberg Terror (US: The Crawling Eye). 1961: Raising the Wind. 1962: Band of Thieves. On the Beat. 1963: Clash by Night (US: Escape by Night). 1964: Hysteria. Dr Terror's House of Horrors. 1965: The Liquidator. 1967: They Came from Beyond Space. 1978: The Medusa Touch. 1983: The Jigsaw Man. 1985: The Doctor and the Devils.

JEAN, Gloria (G.J. Schoonover) 1928–
Dark-haired American child star and teenage singer and dancer. Gloria Jean was a kind of teenybopper's Diana Lynn. Kept at

Universal as a minor-league rival to Deanna Durbin, Gloria was as pretty as paint and as cute as a button. Her youthful freshness enlivened many a penny-pinching swing session, and she deserved better than her relatively brief career.
1939: The Under-Pup. 1940: If I Had My Way. A Little Bit of Heaven. 1941: *Winter Serenade. Never Give a Sucker an Even Break. 1942: What's Cookin? (GB: Wake Up and Dream). Get Hep to Love (GB: She's My Lovely). It Comes Up Love (GB: A Date with an Angel). When Johnny Comes Marching Home. 1943: Mister Big. Moonlight in Vermont. 1944: Follow the Boys. Ghost Catchers. Destiny. Pardon My Rhythm. The Reckless Age. 1945: Easy to Look At. I'll Remember April. River Gang (GB: Fairy Tale Murder). 1947: Copacabana. 1948: I Surrender, Dear. An Old-Fashioned Girl. 1949: Manhattan Angel. There's a Girl in My Heart. 1950: *Conchita Lopez. *Deep in the Heart of Texas. 1951: *Fools Rush In. *Moon's Song. 1952: *Shrimp Boats. *Soon. 1955: Air Strike. 1961: The Ladies' Man. 1963: The Madcaps.

JEFFREYS, Anne
See STERLING, Robert

JERGENS, Adele 1917–
Forceful, harsh-toned, sturdily built platinum blonde American 'second division' star, tallish for the Forties at 5ft 7in and seemingly a must for saloon gals. A former beauty contest winner, model and chorus girl on Broadway, she was unsuited to demure leading ladies and often portrayed tarts-with-hearts in bigger films, as well as bold heroines in 'B' movies. It was probably a career mistake, though, for her to play Marilyn Monroe's mother at only 31. Married to one-time co-star Glenn Langan (1917–1991) from 1949 until his death from cancer.
1943: Jane Eyre. 1944: Black Arrow (serial). Together Again. Tonight and Every Night. 1945: A Thousand and One Nights. She Wouldn't Say Yes. 1947: Down to Earth. Blondie's Anniversary. When a Girl's Beautiful. The Corpse Came C.O.D. I Love Trouble. 1948: The Fuller Brush Man (GB: That Mad Mr Jones). The Dark Past. Ladies of the Chorus. The Prince of Thieves. The Woman from Tangier. 1949: Law of the Barbary Coast. The Crime Doctor's Diary. The Mutineers. Make Believe Ballroom. The Treasure of Monte Cristo. Slightly French. 1950: Edge of Doom (GB: Stronger Than Fear). Armored

Car Robbery. Beware of Blondie. Everybody's Dancin'. Blonde Dynamite. Blues Busters. Side Street. Radar Secret Service. Try and Get Me (later and GB: The Sound of Fury). Traveling Saleswoman. 1951: Sugarfoot/Swirl of Glory. Abbott and Costello Meet the Invisible Man. Show Boat. 1952: Aaron Slick from Punkin Crick (GB: Marshmallow Moon). Somebody Loves Me. 1954: Overland Pacific. Fireman Save My Child. The Miami Story. The Big Chase. 1955: The Cobweb. Strange Lady in Town. The Lonesome Trail. Outlaw Treasure. 1956: The Day the World Ended. Fighting Trouble. Girls in Prison. 1957: Runaway Daughters.

JOBERT, Marlène 1943–

Red-haired, freckle-faced, green-eyed Algerian-born leading lady in French films, with bonily attractive facial features. She very quickly went into international films, but without noticeable response from the public. In the 1970s she quietly built up a solid reputation with her performances in mainline French pictures.

1965: Masculin féminin. 1966: Martin Soldat (GB: Kiss Me, General). Le voleur (US: The Thief of Paris). 1967: Alexandre le bienheureux (GB: Alexander). 1968: Faut pas prendre les enfants du bon Dieu pour des canards sauvages. Léontine. L'astragale. 1969: Rider on the Rain. Dernier domicile connu (US: Last Known Address). 1970: Les mariés de l'ân II. 1971: Catch Me a Spy. La poudre d'escampette. Le décade prodigieux (and English-language version: Ten Days' Wonder). 1972: Nous ne vieillirons pas ensemble. Représailles. Docteur Popaul (GB: Scoundrel in White). 1973: Juliette et Juliette. 1974: Le secret. Pas si méchant que ça (GB: This Wonderful Crook. US: The Wonderful Crook). 1975: Folle à tuer. Trop ce trop/Touch and Go. Le bon et les méchants (US: The Good and the Bad). 1976: Julie pot de colle/The Chains of Pity. 1977: L'imprécateur. 1978: Va voir maman, papa travaille. 1979: Il giocatto. Grandison. La guerre des polices. 1980: Une sale affaire. 1981: L'amour nu. 1982: Effraction. 1983: Les cavaliers de l'orage. 1984: Souvenirs, souvenirs. 1989: Où est le problème? Les cigognes n'en font qu'à leur tête.

JOHN, Rosamund
(Nora R. Jones) 1913–1998

Grey-eyed British actress with red-blonde hair and gentle, well-bred air. She came to star roles a little late in life, but did give

several compelling performances in the forties before declining into lesser films. Died from 'natural causes'.

1934: The Secret of the Loch. 1942: The First of the Few (GB: Spitfire). 1943: The Gentle Sex. The Lamp Still Burns. 1944: Tawny Pipit. Soldier, Sailor. 1945: The Way to the Stars (US: Johnny in the Clouds). 1946: Green for Danger. 1947: The Upturned Glass. When the Bough Breaks. Fame is the Spur. 1949: No Place for Jennifer. 1950: She Shall Have Murder. 1952: *Sports Pages No. 6 – Football. Never Look Back. Here's to the Memory! 1953: Street Corner (US: Both Sides of the Law). 1956: Operation Murder.

JOHNS, Glynis 1923–

Blue-eyed blonde daughter of Mervyn Johns (qv), born in South Africa. Her direct stare and attractively reedy voice made her a distinctive star of the British cinema: her sex-appeal was apparent even in ordinary roles and she was perfectly cast as Miranda the amorous mermaid. Later career interrupted by illness. Received an Academy Award nomination for The Sundowners.

1937: South Riding. 1938: Murder in the Family. Prison without Bars. 1939: On the Night of the Fire (US: The Fugitive). 1940: The Briggs Family. Under Your Hat. 1941: The Prime Minister. 49th Parallel (US: The Invaders). 1943: Adventures of Tartu (US: Tartu). 1944: Halfway House. 1945: Perfect Strangers (US: Vacation from Marriage). 1946: This Man Is Mine. 1947: Frieda. An Ideal Husband. 1948: Miranda. Third Time Lucky. 1949: Dear Mr Prohack. Helter Skelter. The Blue Lamp. 1950: State Secret (US: The Great Manhunt). 1951: Flesh and Blood. Appointment with Venus (US: Island

Rescue). Encore. The Magic Box. No Highway (US: No Highway in the Sky). 1952: The Card (US: The Promoter). 1953: The Sword and the Rose. Personal Affair. Rob Roy the Highland Rogue. The Weak and the Wicked (US: Young and Willing). 1954: The Seekers (US: Land of Fury). The Beachcomber. Mad About Men. 1955: Josephine and Men. The Court Jester. 1956: Loser Takes All. All Mine to Give (GB: The Day They Gave Babies Away). Around the World in 80 Days. 1958: Another Time Another Place. 1959: Shake Hands with the Devil. Last of the Few. 1960: The Spider's Web. The Sundowners. 1961: The Chapman Report. 1962: The Cabinet of Caligari. 1963: Papa's Delicate Condition. 1964: Mary Poppins. 1965: Dear Brigitte . . . 1967: Don't Just Stand There! 1969: Lock Up Your Daughters! 1971: Under Milk Wood. 1973: Vault of Horror. 1982: Little Gloria – Happy at Last (TV). 1984: Spraggue (TV). 1988: Zelly and Me. Nukie. 1994: The Ref (GB: Hostile Hostages). 1995: While You Were Sleeping. 1999: Superstar.

JOHNS, Mervyn 1899–1992

Chunky, earnest-looking Welsh actor with dark, wavy hair who, in the absence of more high-powered leading men, unexpectedly became a star of the British cinema in the wartime years, doing well in a succession of unusual and rewarding parts. Later dropped back into character roles. His first wife died in 1971 after many years of marriage and, in 1976, he married Diana Churchill (qv). Father of Glynis Johns (qv).

1934: Lady in Danger. 1935: The Tunnel (US: Transatlantic Tunnel). The Guv'nor (US: Mister Hobo). Foreign Affaires. 1936: Everything is Thunder. In The Soup. Pot Luck. Dishonour Bright. 1937: Storm in a Teacup. Song of the Forge. 1938: Almost a Gentleman. 1939: Jamaica Inn. The Midas Touch. 1940: Convoy. Saloon Bar. The Girl in the News. 1942: The Foreman Went to France (US: Somewhere in France). The Next of Kin. Went the Day Well? (US: 48 Hours). 1943: The Bells Go Down. My Learned Friend. San Demetrio London. 1944: Halfway House. Twilight Hour. 1945: They Knew Mr Knight. Dead of Night. Pink String and Sealing Wax. 1946: The Captive Heart. 1947: Captain Boycott. Easy Money. 1948: Quartet. Counter-blast. 1949: Edward My Son. Helter Skelter. Diamond City. 1950: Tony Draws a Horse. 1951: The Magic Box. Scrooge. 1952: Tall Headlines. The Oracle (US: The Horse's

Mouth). 1953: Valley of Song (US: Men Are Children Twice). The Master of Ballantrae. 1954: Romeo and Juliet. 1955: The Blue Peter (US: Navy Heroes). 1984. 1956: The Intimate Stranger (US: Finger of Guilt). The Shield of Faith. Find the Lady. Moby Dick. The Counterfeit Plan. 1957: Doctor at Large. *Danger List. The Vicious Circle (US: The Circle). The Gypsy and the Gentleman. The Surgeon's Knife. 1959: The Devil's Disciple. Once More with Feeling. 1960: Never Let Go. No Love For Johnnie. Echo of Barbara. The Sundowners. 1961: The Rebel. Francis of Assisi. 1962: The Day of the Triffids. 55 Days at Peking. The Old Dark House. 1963: 80,000 Suspects. The Victors. A Jolly Bad Fellow (US: They All Died Laughing). 1965: The Heroes of Telemark. 1966: Who Killed the Cat? 1973: The National Health. 1974: QB VII (TV). 1975: House of Mortal Sin. 1979: Game for Vultures. 1980: Kill and Kill Again. 1989: Ingrid.

JOHNSON, Ben 1918–1996
Fresh-faced, personable dark-haired American western star with rich, slow-drawling voice, a former cowboy, rodeo champion (steer roping) and stunt rider. His career built up in John Ford westerns, but he didn't quite make it as a top star, reappearing in the 1960s as a leathery and weatherbeaten character star. The Academy Award that he won for his role in The Last Picture Show gained him a whole new series of varied and interesting roles. Died from a heart attack.
1939: The Fighting Gringo. 1943: Riders of the Rio Grande. Bordertown Gunfighters. 1944: Nevada. 1945: The Naughty Nineties. Santa Fe Saddlemates. 1946: Badman's Territory. California Gold Rush. Out California Way. 1947: Angel and the Badman. Wyoming. The Fabulous Texan. 1948: The Gallant Legion. Fort Apache. 3 Godfathers. 1949: She Wore a Yellow Ribbon. Mighty Joe Young. 1950: Wagonmaster. Rio Grande. 1951: Fort Defiance. Wild Stallion. 1953: Shane. 1955: Oklahoma! 1956: Rebel in Town. 1957: War Drums. Fort Bowie. Slim Carter. 1960: Ten Who Dared. 1961: Tomboy and the Champ. One-Eyed Jacks. 1964: Cheyenne Autumn. 1966: Major Dundee. The Rare Breed. 1967: Will Penny. Hang 'Em High. 1969: The Wild Bunch. The Undefeated. Ride a Northbound Horse (TV. GB: cinemas). 1970: Chisum. 1971: The Last Picture Show. Something Big. Corky. 1972: Junior Bonner. The Getaway. 1973: Dillinger. Kid Blue.

Bloodsport (TV). Runaway (TV. GB: cinemas, as The Runaway Train). The Train Robbers. The Red Pony (TV. GB: cinemas, in abridged version). 1974: Locusts (TV). The Sugarland Express. 1975: Bite the Bullet. Hustle. 1976: The Savage Bees (TV. GB: cinemas). Breakheart Pass. 1977: The Town That Dreaded Sundown. The Greatest. Grayeagle. 1978: The Swarm. True Grit: A Further Adventure (TV). 1979: The Sacketts (TV). Wild Times (TV). 1980: Ruckus. The Hunter. Soggy Bottom USA. Terror Train. 1981: High Country Pursuit. 1982: Tex. The Shadow Riders (TV). 1983: Champions. 1984: Red Dawn. 1985: Wild Horses (TV). 1986: Cherry 2000 (released 1988). Let's Get Harry. Trespasses. 1988: Dark Before Dawn. Stranger on My Land (TV). 1989: Back to Back. 1990: My Heroes Have Always Been Cowboys. 1991: The Chase (TV). 1992: Radio Flyer. 1993: Bonanza: The Return (TV). 1994: Angels in the Outfield (GB: Angels). The Legend of O B Taggart. 1995: Bonanza: Under Attack (TV). Ruby Jean and Joe. 1996: The Evening Star. Third Cowboy on the Right (doc).

JOHNSON, Dame Celia 1908–1982
Dark-haired (with distinctive wave), pretty but plaintive-looking British actress, almost entirely a stage personality until well into her thirties. Despite her clipped, upper-class tones, she projected real warmth and feeling in several forties' classics, notably Brief Encounter, that confirmed her as one of Britain's leading actresses. With a face that seemed born for suffering, it was much to her credit that she got as many lively roles as she did. Died following a stroke. She received an Oscar nomination for Brief Encounter.
1934: Dirty Work. 1941: *We Serve. *A Letter from Home. 1942: In Which We Serve. 1943: Dear Octopus (US: The Randolph Family). 1944: This Happy Breed. 1945: Brief Encounter. 1950: The Astonished Heart. 1952: I Believe in You. The Holly and the Ivy. 1953: The Captain's Paradise. 1955: A Kid for Two Farthings. 1957: The Good Companions. 1968: The Prime of Miss Jean Brodie. 1978: Les Miserables (TV). 1980: The Hostage Tower.

JOHNSON, Don 1949–
Boyish, tow-haired American actor whose faintly weary good looks appear altogether gentler when he's smiling. He came early to starring roles in films, but won more headlines with his busy love life (married/divorced Melanie Griffith, at one time

engaged to Barbra Streisand) before an enormous success in the TV series Miami Vice brought his acting career back into the public eye. The films that followed, however, did not show Johnson up as a major screen personality. He remarried Griffith (qv) in 1989, but the union was again stormy and they separated twice before parting for good in 1995, by which time Johnson's marital merry-go-round had come full circle and he was (briefly) back with Streisand (also qv) – and a successful TV cop series in Nash Bridges.
1967: Good Morning . . . And Goodbye! (GB: The Lust Seekers). 1970: The Magic Garden of Stanley Sweetheart. 1971: Zachariah. 1973: The Harrad Experiment. 1974: A Boy and His Dog. 1975: Return to Macon County. 1976: The City (TV). Law of the Land (TV). 1977: Cover Girls (TV). 1978: Katie: Portrait of a Centerfold (TV). Amateur Night at the Dixie Bar and Grill (TV). First You Cry (TV). Ski-Lift to Death (TV). The Two-Five (TV). Pressure Point (TV). 1980: Revenge of the Stepford Wives (TV). Soggy Bottom USA. 1981: The Two Lives of Carol Letner (TV). Elvis and the Beauty Queen (TV). 1983: Cease Fire. 1987: G.I. Joe (voice only). 1988: Sweet Hearts Dance. 1989: Dead Bang. 1990: The Hot Spot. 1991: Harley Davidson and the Marlboro Man. Paradise. 1992: Born Yesterday. 1993: Guilty As Sin. 1995: In Pursuit of Honor (TV). 1996: Tin Cup. 1998: Goodbye Lover.

JOHNSON, Kay
(Catherine Townsend) 1904–1975
Fair-haired American actress, notably unpretty, but effective in fragile or genteel roles to which she often brought unexpected

honesty and spirit. Her career got off to a tremendous start in a film on which she had some notable fights with Cecil B. De Mille, but she gradually regressed into supporting parts in a career not well handled either by herself or her studios. Married to director John Cromwell from 1928 to 1948.

1929: *Dynamite*. 1930: *This Mad World. Passion Flower. Billy the Kid. The Ship from Shanghai. The Spoilers. Madam Satan*. 1931: *The Single Sin. The Spy*. 1932: *American Madness. Thirteen Women*. 1934: *Eight Girls in a Boat. Of Human Bondage. This Man is Mine. Their Big Moment*. 1935: *Jalna. Village Tale*. 1938: *White Banners*. 1939: *The Real Glory*. 1942: *Son of Fury*. 1943: *Mr Lucky*. 1944: *The Adventures of Mark Twain*.

JOHNSON, Richard 1927–
Dark, saturnine, smoothly good-looking British actor. He remained a little-known stage player until suddenly bursting into star film roles in the early sixties. Subsequently, his cinema career floundered after he got himself cast in a very high percentage of silly or below-par big-budget films. Divorced from actresses Sheila Sweet and Kim Novak.

1951: *Captain Horatio Hornblower RN. Calling Bulldog Drummond*. 1952: *Lady in the Fog* (US: *Scotland Yard Inspector*). 1953: *Saadia*. 1959: *Never So Few*. 1963: *Cairo. The Haunting. 80,000 Suspects*. 1964: *L'autre femme. The Pumpkin Eater*. 1965: *The Amorous Adventures of Moll Flanders. Operation Crossbow* (US: *The Great Spy Mission*). 1966: *Khartoum. Deadlier than the Male. La strega in amore/The Witch in Love. L'avventuriero/The Rover*. 1967: *Danger Route. A Twist of Sand. Oedipus the King*. 1968: *Lady Hamilton* (GB: *Emma Hamilton*). *Some Girls Do*. 1969: *Gott mit uns*. 1970: *The Beloved* (GB: TV, as *Sin*). *Julius Caesar*. 1971: *The Tyrant*. 1974: *Chi Sei?* (GB: *Devil within Her*. US: *Behind the Door*). 1975: *Hennessy. The Lost Island* (TV). *Night Child/The Cursed Medallion*. 1976: *Aces High. The Message* (narrator only). *Stella*. 1977: *The Comeback*. 1978: *The Fish Men. The Four Feathers*. 1979: *The Delessi Affair. Zombi 2* (GB: *Zombie FleshEaters*. US: *Zombie*). *Island of Mutations. The Biggest Bank Robbery* (TV). *The Flame is Love* (TV). 1980: *The Monster Club*. 1981: *Portrait of a Rebel* (TV). 1982: *Screamers* (*The Fish Men with added footage*). 1983: *The Aerodrome* (TV). 1984: *Secrets of the Phantom Caverns* (later *What Waits Below*). 1985: *Lady Jane.*

Turtle Diary. 1986: *Castaway*. 1988: *A Man for All Seasons* (TV). 1989: *Treasure Island* (TV. GB: cinemas). 1990: *Duel of Hearts* (TV). *The Secret Life of Ian Fleming* (TV). 1991: *Driving In. The Crucifer of Blood* (TV). 1999: *Milk* (TV).

JOHNSON, Rita (R. McSean) 1912–1965
Lovely blonde American actress who despite consistently good critical notices and one outstanding lead performance – as Spencer Tracy's wife in *Edison, the Man* – was not promoted by her studio, M-G-M, as a star. By the middle forties she was typed in 'other woman' roles, and her career was virtually ended after a serious brain operation in 1948 following an accident at home with a hair dryer. Died from a brain haemorrhage.

1931: *The Spy*. 1937: *London by Night. My Dear Miss Aldrich*. 1938: *Man Proof. Rich Man, Poor Girl. Letter of Introduction. Smashing the Rackets*. 1939: *Honolulu. Six Thousand Enemies. They All Come Out. Stronger Than Desire. Within the Law. Broadway Serenade. The Girl Downstairs. Nick Carter, Master Detective*. 1940: *Congo Maisie. The Golden Fleecing. Forty Little Mothers. Edison, the Man*. 1941: *Appointment for Love. Here Comes Mr Jordan*. 1942: *The Major and the Minor*. 1943: *My Friend Flicka*. 1944: *Thunderhead – Son of Flicka*. 1945: *The Naughty Nineties. The Affairs of Susan*. 1946: *The Perfect Marriage. Pardon My Past*. 1947: *They Won't Believe Me. The Michigan Kid*. 1948: *Sleep My Love. The Big Clock. Family Honeymoon. An Innocent Affair* (later *Don't Trust Your Husband*). 1950: *The Second Face*. 1954: *Susan Slept Here*. 1955: *†Unchained*. 1956: *Emergency Hospital. All Mine to Give* (GB: *The Day They Gave Babies Away*).

†*Scenes deleted from final release print*

JOHNSON, Van
(Charles V. Johnson) 1916–
American leading actor whose Swedish ancestry showed in his blue eyes, red-gold hair and boyish, rather hurt-looking expression. He took advantage of the absence of top talent away in wartime (he was himself unfit for service following a car smash which left him with a metal plate in his head) to storm to stardom at M-G-M, where he stayed for 15 years. His boyish charm wore thin in the fifties and he was seen less after 1960.

1940: *Too Many Girls*. 1941: *Murder in the Big House* (GB: *Human Sabotage*). 1942:

For the Common Defense. The War Against Mrs Hadley. Somewhere I'll Find You. Dr Gillespie's New Assistant. 1943: *The Human Comedy. Madame Curie. Dr Gillespie's Criminal Case* (GB: *Crazy to Kill*). *Pilot No. 5. A Guy Named Joe*. 1944: *Ziegfeld Follies* (released 1946). *Three Men in White. Between Two Women. White Cliffs of Dover. Two Girls and a Sailor. Thirty Seconds over Tokyo*. 1945: *Weekend at the Waldorf. Thrill of a Romance*. 1946: *Till the Clouds Roll By. Easy to Wed. No Leave, No Love*. 1947: *High Barbaree. The Romance Of Rosy Ridge*. 1948: *State of the Union* (GB: *The World and His Wife*). *Command Decision. The Bride Goes Wild*. 1949: *Mother is a Freshman* (GB: *Mother Knows Best*). *Battleground. In the Good Old Summertime. Scene of the Crime*. 1950: *Grounds for Marriage. The Big Hangover. Duchess of Idaho*. 1951: *Too Young to Kiss. Go for Broke. It's a Big Country. Three Guys Named Mike. Invitation*. 1952: *Washington Story* (US: *Target for Scandal*). *When in Rome. Plymouth Adventure*. 1953: *Confidentially Connie. Remains to be Seen. Easy to Love*. 1954: *The Caine Mutiny. Men of the Fighting Lady. The Siege at Red River. The Last Time I Saw Paris. Brigadoon*. 1955: *The End of the Affair*. 1956: *23 Paces to Baker Street. The Bottom of the Bottle* (GB: *Beyond the River*). *Slander. Miracle in the Rain*. 1957: *Kelly and Me. Action of the Tiger. The Pied Piper of Hamelin* (TV. GB: cinemas). 1958: *The Last Blitzkrieg. Subway in the Sky*. 1959: *Beyond This Place* (GB: *Web of Evidence*). 1960: *The Enemy General*. 1963: *Wives and Lovers*. 1967: *Divorce American Style. The Doomsday Flight* (TV. GB: cinemas). 1968: *Yours, Mine and Ours. Where Angels Go . . . Trouble Follows*. 1969: *Il prezzo del potere* (GB: *The Price of Power*). *El largo dia Del* (GB: *The Professional*). *La battaglia d'Inghilterra* (GB: *Battle Squadron*. US: *Eagles Over London*). 1970: *Company of Killers* (TV. GB: cinemas). *San Francisco International Airport* (TV). *Wheeler and Murdock* (TV). 1971: *Eye of the Spider*. 1972: *Call Her Mom* (TV). *Man in the Middle* (TV). 1974: *The Girl on the Late, Late Show* (TV). 1977: *Getting Married* (TV). 1979: *From Corleone to Brooklyn. Superdome* (TV). 1980: *The Kidnapping of the President*. 1981: *Absurd!* 1982: *Scorpion with Two Tails*. 1984: *Glitter* (TV). 1985: *The Purple Rose of Cairo*. 1987: *Down There in the Jungle*. 1988: *Killer Crocodile. Taxi Killer*. 1990: *Fuga dal Paradiso. Delta Force, Commando Two*. 1992:

Three Days to a Kill. Clowning Around. 1993: *Lucy and Desi: A Home Movie (TV).*

JOLIE, Angelina (A.J. Voight) 1975–
Darkly sexy American actress with hooded eyes and distinctive tubular lips. The daughter of actor Jon Voight (*qv*), the sharply attractive Jolie can be relied on to strike sparks from pretty well any assignment and awaits only a strong central role to make her into a major star. Also a child player and teenage model in her earlier days, she is divorced from British actor Jonny Lee Miller (also *qv*). Academy Award winner for *Girl, Interrupted*. Married Billy Bob Thornton.
1980: *Lookin' to Get Out (released 1982).* 1993: *Cyborg 2. Glass Shadow.* 1994: *Gathering Evidence.* 1995: *Oh No, Not Her. Hackers.* 1996: *Love is All There Is (completed 1994). Foxfire. Mojave Moon. Without Evidence: A True Story.* 1997: *Wallace (TV). Playing God.* 1998: *Gia (cable TV). Hell's Kitchen. Playing by Heart. Princess Mononoke (English version, voice only).* 1999: *Pushing Tin. The Bone Collector. Girl, Interrupted.* 2000: *Gone in Sixty Seconds. Dancing in the Dark.* 2001: *Tomb Raider.*

JOLSON, Al (Asa Yoelson) 1885–1950
Square-faced, exuberant, larger-than-life Russian-born Hollywood entertainer who made history by starring in the first part-talkie, *The Jazz Singer*. His popularity faded in the thirties, but he came to the fore again with his efforts for Allied troops during World War II, and the smash-hit release of *The Jolson Story* in 1946, for which he supplied the vocals and long-shot dances. Married (third of four) to Ruby Keeler, 1928–1939. Died from a heart attack.

1926: **April Showers.* *A Plantation Act.* 1927: *The Jazz Singer.* 1928: *The Singing Fool.* 1929: *Lucky Boy. New York Nights, Say It with Songs.* 1930: *Mammy. Big Boy. Showgirl in Hollywood.* 1933: *Hallelujah, I'm a Bum (GB: Hallelujah I'm a Tramp).* 1934: *Wonder Bar.* 1935: *Go into Your Dance (GB: Casino De Paree). *Broadway Highlights No. 1. *Kings of the Turf.* 1936: *The Singing Kid.* 1939: *Rose of Washington Square. Hollywood Cavalcade. Swanee River.* 1941: **Cavalcade of the Academy Awards.* 1945: *Rhapsody in Blue.* 1946: *The Jolson Story.* 1948: **Screen Snapshots No. 166.* 1949: *Jolson Sings Again (voice only).*

JONES, Allan 1907–1992
Light-haired American singer, of Welsh parentage and cheerful disposition, a singing straight man for the Marx Brothers and a rival to Nelson Eddy for the screen affections of Jeanette MacDonald. His best role – and performance – came in the 1936 *Show Boat*, but his career nosedived after he fell out with Louis B. Mayer at M-G-M and was forced to work for other studios. Married to Irene Hervey (1909–1998) from 1936 to 1957, the second of his four wives. Father of singer Jack Jones. Died from lung cancer.
1935: *Reckless. A Night at the Opera.* 1936: *The Great Ziegfeld (voice only). Rose Marie. Ramona. Show Boat.* 1937: **Lest We Forget. A Day at the Races. The Firefly.* 1938: *Everybody Sing.* 1939: *Honeymoon in Bali (GB: Husbands or Lovers). The Great Victor Herbert.* 1940: *The Boys from Syracuse. One Night in the Tropics.* 1941: *There's Magic in Music.* 1942: *Moonlight in Havana. True to the Army. When Johnny Comes Marching Home. *Soaring Stars.* 1943: *You're a Lucky Fellow, Mr Smith. Rhythm of the Islands. Larceny with Music. Crazy House.* 1944: *The Singing Sheriff. Sing a Jingle (GB: Lucky Days).* 1945: *Honeymoon Ahead. The Senorita from the West.* 1950: **All My Love. *Donkey Serenade. *The Lonesome Road. *The Monkey and the Organ Grinder.* 1951: **Only a Rose. *Over and Over. *Questa o Quella. *Take Me in Your Arms.* 1952: **The World is Mine Tonight.* 1964: *Stage to Thunder Rock.* 1965: *A Swingin' Summer.* 1971: *Sub Rosa Rising (narrator only).*

JONES, Buck (Charles Gebhardt, later legally changed) 1889–1942
Sharply good-looking, dark-haired American actor, popular for over 20 years in second feature westerns, often featuring himself

providing both the action and 'hick from the sticks' style comedy relief Came from a long background of rodeo shows. Died from burns sustained in a fire while trying to rescue people still trapped.
1913: †*Unidentified '101' Western.* 1917: †*Blood Will Tell.* 1919: *The Speed Maniac. The Sheriff's Son. *When Pals Fall Out. Pitfalls of a Big City. True Blue. Western Blood. The Wilderness Trail. The Rainbow Trail. Riders of the Purple Sage.* 1920: **Desert Rat. *Brother Bill. *The Uphill Climb. *The Two Doyles. The Last Straw. The Cyclone. Forbidden Trails. Square Shooter. Straight from the Shoulder.* 1921: *Just Pals. Two Moons. Firebrand Trevision. The Big Punch. Get Your Man. The One-Man Trail. Sunset Sprague. Riding with Death. To a Finish.* 1922: *Roughshod. Trooper O'Neil. Bells of San Juan. West of Chicago. Bar Nothin'. The Boss of Camp Four. Pardon My Nerve. Western Speed. Fast Mail.* 1923: *Footlight Ranger. Snowdrift. Big Dan. Hell's Hole. The Eleventh Hour. Second Hand Love. Skid Proof. Cupid's Fireman.* 1924: *The Desert Outlaw. The Circus Cowboy. Against All Odds. Western Luck. The Vagabond Trail. Not a Drum Was Heard. Winner Take All.* 1925: *The Trail Rider. The Man Who Played Square. The Timber Wolf. Arizona Romeo. Gold and the Girl. Hearts and Spurs. Lazybones. Durand of the Bad Lands. Good as Gold. The Desert's Price.* 1926: *The Cowboy and the Countess. Desert Valley. The Fighting Buckaroo. A Man Four Square. The Gentle Cyclone. 30 Below Zero. The Flying Horseman (GB: The White Eagle).* 1927: *Black Jack. Chain Lightning. Hills of Peril. *Life in Hollywood No. 4. Whispering Sage. War Horse.* 1928: *Blood Will Tell (remake). The Big Hop. The Branded Sombrero.* 1930: *Stranger from Arizona. The Lone Rider. The Dawn Trail. Shadow Ranch. Men without Law.* 1931: *Fighting Sheriff. South of the Rio Grande. The Texas Ranger. Border Law. Branded. Range Feud. Ridin' for Justice. Desert Vengeance. The Avenger. Sundown Trail.* 1932: *Hello Trouble. White Eagle. McKenna of the Mounted. Deadline. High Speed. One Man Law. Reckless Romance. Riders of Death Valley.* 1933: *Gordon of Ghost City (serial). Unknown Valley. California Trail. Forbidden Trail. Treason. Child of Manhattan. Thrill Hunter. The Sundown Rider.* 1934: *The Red Rider (serial). The Fighting Rangers. The Dawn Trail. Rocky Rhodes. The Man Trailer. The Fighting Code. When a Man Sees Red. Texas Ranger.* 1935: *The Roaring West*

(serial). *Outlawed Guns. Border Brigands. Stone of Silver Creek. The Crimson Trail. The Square Shooter. The Throwback. The Ivory Handled Gun.* 1936: *The Phantom Rider* (serial). *Silver Spurs. Boss Rider of Gun Creek. The Cowboy and the Kid. Sunset of Power. ‡For the Service. Empty Saddles. Ride 'Em Cowboy!* 1937: *Headin' East. Pony Express. ‡Law for Tombstone. Sandflow. Smoke Tree Range. The Left Handed Law. Hollywood Round-Up. ‡Black Aces. Boss of Lonely Valley.* 1938: *Sudden Bill Dorn. Law of the Texan. Overland Express. California Frontier. Stranger from Arizona.* 1939: *Unmarried* (GB: *Night Club Hostess*). 1940: *Wagons Westward.* 1941: *Riders of Death Valley* (serial). *The Gunman from Bodie. Arizona Bound. Forbidden Trails. White Eagle* (serial). 1942: *West of the Law. Ghost Town Law. Down Texas Way. Below the Border. Dawn on the Great Divide. Riders of the West.*

†As Charles Gebhardt
‡And directed

JONES, Carolyn (C. Baker) 1929–1983
Raven-haired American actress with narrow face and unusual, villainess-type features. Attracted a good deal of critical attention in the mid-fifties but her career gradually slid away into television, a medium in which she remained active. Occasionally blonde. Nominated for an Academy Award in *The Bachelor Party*. Known to her friends as Sissy. Married producer Aaron Spelling (first of three). Died from cancer.
1952: *The Turning Point. Road to Bali. Off Limits* (GB: *Military Policemen*). 1953: *House of Wax. The War of the Worlds. The Big Heat. Geraldine.* 1954: *Make Haste to Live. The Saracen Blade. Three Hours to Kill. Shield for Murder. Desirée. East of Eden.* 1955: *Cavalcade* (TV. GB: cinemas). *The Seven-Year Itch. The Tender Trap.* 1956: *The Hefferan Family* (TV. GB: cinemas). *The Man Who Knew Too Much. Invasion of the Body Snatchers. The Opposite Sex.* 1957: *The Bachelor Party. Johnny Trouble. Baby Face Nelson. The Last Man* (TV). 1958: *Marjorie Morningstar. King Creole.* 1959: *A Hole in the Head. Last Train from Gun Hill. Career. The Man in the Net.* 1960: *Ice Palace.* 1961: *Sail a Crooked Ship.* 1962: *How the West Was Won.* 1963: *A Ticklish Affair.* 1966: **Hollywood Star-Spangled Revue.* 1968: *Heaven with a Gun.* 1969: *Color Me Dead.* 1976: *Eaten Alive* (GB: *Death Trap*). 1977: *Little Ladies of the*

Night (TV). 1978: *Good Luck Miss Wyckoff.* 1981: *Midnight Lace* (TV).

JONES, Dean 1930–
Young-looking, brown-haired American comedy actor with wry smile who played bright young chaps on whom fortune never smiled until the happy ending. He had a spotty early career, but from 1965 worked for the Disney studio and made a major contribution – his look of hurt bewilderment was second only to that of James Stewart – to most of their biggest comedy hits. Began his career as a blues singer. In 1978 he became a born-again Christian and left show business to work for the charismatic worship movement. He returned to films in 1991.
1956: *Gaby. These Wilder Years. The Opposite Sex. The Great American Pastime. The Rack. Somebody Up There Likes Me. Tea and Sympathy.* 1957: *Ten Thousand Bedrooms. Designing Woman. Until They Sail. Jailhouse Rock.* 1958: *Handle with Care. Imitation General. Torpedo Run.* 1959: *Night of the Quarter Moon. Never So Few.* 1963: *Under the Yum Yum Tree. The New Interns.* 1964: *Two on a Guillotine.* 1965: *That Darn Cat!* 1966: *Any Wednesday* (GB: abridged, as *Bachelor Girl Apartment*). *The Ugly Dachshund.* 1967: *Monkeys, Go Home. Blackbeard's Ghost.* 1968: *The Horse in the Gray Flannel Suit. The Mickey Mouse Anniversary Show* (narrator only). 1969: *The Love Bug.* 1970: *Mr Superinvisible.* 1971: *Million Dollar Duck. The Great Man's Whiskers* (TV). 1972: *Snowball Express.* 1973: *Guess Who's Sleeping in My Bed* (TV). 1976: *The Shaggy DA.* 1977: *Herbie Goes to Monte Carlo. Once Upon a Brothers Grimm* (TV). 1978: *When Every Day Was the Fourth of July* (TV). *Born Again.* 1980: *The Long Days of Summer* (TV). 1991: *Other People's Money. Beethoven.* 1992: *Saved by the Bell – Hawaiian Style* (TV). 1994: *Clear and Present Danger.* 1995: *The Computer Wore Tennis Shoes* (TV). 1996: *That Darn Cat* (remake). *A spasso nel tempo* (US: *Adrift in Time*). 1997: *The Love Bug* (remake. TV). 1998: *Special Report: Journey to Mars* (TV).

JONES, Emrys
(E. Whittaker-Jones) 1915–1972
Light-haired, quietly-spoken British actor with large, open face, not tall but powerfully built. He built up his career well in the forties, but lacked the strength of personality to become a big star and was soon in some rather glum second-features, whence he did

well to return to, and concentrate on, his stage career. Died from a heart attack.
1942: *One of Our Aircraft is Missing.* 1943: **Tired Man. The Shipbuilders.* 1944: *Give Me the Stars.* 1945: *The Wicked Lady. The Rake's Progress* (US: *Notorious Gentleman*). 1946: *Beware of Pity.* 1947: *Nicholas Nickleby. Holiday Camp.* 1948: *This Was a Woman. The Small Back Room.* 1949: *Blue Scar. Dark Secret. Miss Pilgrim's Progress.* 1953: *Deadly Nightshade.* 1955: *Three Cases of Murder.* 1956: *The Shield of Faith.* 1960: *The Trials of Oscar Wilde* (US: *The Man with the Green Carnation*). *Ticket to Paradise.* 1962: *Serena.* 1963: *On the Run.*

JONES, Griffith 1910–
Light-haired, long-faced, very romantic-looking British actor, at his most appealing in the thirties. His post-war roles were far less interesting and his cinema career tapered off in the fifties with supporting roles and leads in some dreary second-features, when he appeared unsuited to harsher, more modern times. Father of actors Gemma Jones and Nicholas Jones.
1932: *The Faithful Heart. Money Talks.* 1933: *Catherine the Great.* 1934: *Leave It to Blanche.* 1935: *Escape Me Never. First a Girl.* 1936: *The Mill on the Floss. Line Engaged.* 1937: *Wife of General Ling. Return of a Stranger* (US: *The Face Behind the Scar*). *A Yank at Oxford.* 1939: *The Four Just Men* (US: *The Secret Four*). *Young Man's Fancy.* 1941: *Atlantic Ferry* (US: *Sons of the Sea*). *The Big Blockade. This Was Paris.* 1942: *The Day Will Dawn* (US: *The Avengers*). *Uncensored.* 1944: *Henry V.* 1945: *The Wicked Lady. The Rake's Progress* (US: *Notorious Gentleman*). 1947: *They Made Me a*

Fugitive (US: I Became a Criminal). 1948: Miranda. Good Time Girl. Look Before You Love. 1949: Once Upon a Dream. 1951: Honeymoon Deferred. 1954: Star of My Night. The Sea Shall Not Have Them. Scarlet Web. 1957: Face in the Night (US: Menace in the Night). Not Wanted on Voyage. Account Rendered. Kill Her Gently. 1958: The Truth About Women. Hidden Homicide. 1959: The Crowning Touch. 1965: Strangler's Web. 1968: Decline and Fall . . . of a Birdwatcher.

JONES, Jennifer (Phylis Isley) 1919–
It seemed that this dark-haired American actress, with her alabaster beauty, was forever after roles as tempestuous women of destiny (perhaps to escape her saintly Oscar for *The Song of Bernadette*) when what she was best at, in terms of getting an audience to respond to the character, were the Jennies, the Miss Doves and the Cluny Browns of this world. Married to Robert Walker (1939–1945) and David O. Selznick (1949 until his death in 1965). She also received Oscar nominations for *Since You Went Away*, *Love Letters*, *Duel in the Sun* (making four consecutive years) and *Love is a Many-Splendored Thing*. Mother of actor Robert Walker Jr (*qv*).
*1939: †Dick Tracy's G-Men (serial). †The New Frontier. 1940: †The Ranger Rides Again (serial). 1943: The Song of Bernadette. 1944: Since You Went Away. 1945: Love Letters. 1946: Cluny Brown. *The American Creed. Duel in the Sun. 1948: Portrait of Jennie (GB: Jennie). 1949: We Were Strangers. Madame Bovary. 1950: Gone to Earth (US: The Wild Heart). 1952: Carrie. Ruby Gentry. 1953: Stazione termini (GB: Indiscretion. US: Indiscretion of an American Wife). Beat the Devil. 1955: Love is a Many Splendored Thing. Good Morning, Miss Dove. 1956: The Man in the Gray Flannel Suit. 1957: The Barretts of Wimpole Street. A Farewell to Arms. 1961: Tender is the Night. 1966: The Idol. 1969: Angel, Angel, Down You Go/Cult of the Damned. 1974: The Towering Inferno. 1980: Patricia – einmal Himmel und zurück.*

†As Phylis Isley

JONES, Shirley 1933–
Sweet-faced, sweet-voiced, corn-haired American singer who soared to fame in two big Fox musicals of the mid-fifties. Despite her Academy Award as the prostitute in *Elmer Gantry*, she remained underrated and underused as a dramatic actress with warmth

to spare – although she kept busy up to the mid 1980s. The widow of actor-singer Jack Cassidy (1927–1976), who died in a fire, she is also the stepmother of actor David Cassidy and the mother of actor Shaun Cassidy. A hard worker for charity, she became chairman of the US Leukemia Association in the mid-1990s.
1955: Oklahoma! 1956: Carousel. The Big Slide (TV). 1957: April Love. 1959: Never Steal Anything Small. Bobbikins. 1960: Elmer Gantry. Pepe. 1961: Two Rode Together. 1962: The Music Man. 1963: The Courtship of Eddie's Father. A Ticklish Affair. Dark Purpose. 1964: Bedtime Story. 1965: Fluffy. The Secret of My Success. 1969: El golfo. Silent Night, Lonely Night (TV). The Happy Ending. 1970: The Cheyenne Social Club. But I Don't Want to Get Married (TV). 1973: The Girls of Huntingdon House (TV). 1975: The Lives of Jenny Dolan (TV). The Family Nobody Wanted (TV). Winner Take All (TV). 1977: Yesterday's Child (TV). 1978: A Last Cry for Help (TV). 1979: Beyond the Poseidon Adventure. Who'll Save Our Children? (TV). 1980: The Children of An Lac (TV). 1981: Inmates: a Love Story (TV). 1983: Tank. 1985: There Were Times Dear. Charlie (TV). 1994: William Putch: A Life in the Theater. 1995: Cops and Roberts. 1997: Dog's Best Friend (TV). 1999: Gideon (TV). The Adventures of Cinderella's Daughter. 2000: Ping! I Know What You Screamed Last Summer.

JONES, Tommy Lee 1946–
Dark, handsome, gauntly-boned and slightly dangerous-looking American actor who, despite a late start, has tackled some extremely demanding leading roles, as well as proving a

useful sounding-board for some powerhouse leading ladies of the 1970s and 1980s. His unsettling presence makes him something of a lightweight, better-looking Jack Palance (*qv*) but, in the cinema at least, he did not quite find a slot at the top in spite of a best supporting actor Oscar for *The Fugitive*. He followed that achievement with a series of aggressively over-the-top performances, culminating in a successful return to leading roles from 1997.
1970: Love Story. 1972: Life Study. Eliza's Horoscope (released 1977). 1976: Smash-Up on Interstate Five (TV). Charlie's Angels (TV). Jackson County Jail. 1977: Rolling Thunder. The Amazing Howard Hughes (TV). 1978: The Betsy. Eyes of Laura Mars. 1980: Coal Miner's Daughter. 1981: Back Roads. 1982: The Executioner's Song (TV. GB: cinemas in abbreviated version). 1983: Savage Islands/Nate and Hayes. 1984: The River Rat. 1985: Black Moon Rising. The Park is Mine (TV). 1986: Double Image/Yuri Nosenko KGB (TV). 1987: The Big Town. Broken Vows (TV). 1988: Stranger on My Land (TV). Stormy Monday. Gotham (cable TV. GB: cinemas, as The Dead Can't Lie). April Morning (TV). 1989: The Package. 1990: Fire Birds (GB: Wings of the Apache). 1991: Blue Sky (released 1994). JFK. House of Cards/Before I Wake. 1992: Under Siege. 1993: Heaven and Earth. The Fugitive. 1994: Natural Born Killers. The Client. Blown Away. Cobb. 1995: The Good Old Boys (TV. And directed). 1997: Men in Black. Volcano. 1998: U.S. Marshals. Small Soldiers (voice only). 1999: Double Jeopardy. 2000: Rules of Engagement. Space Cowboys.

JORDAN, Richard 1938–1993
Films almost passed up on this chunkily built, blink-eyed, good-looking American actor with tightly curly fair hair and a vague resemblance to the British actor Derren Nesbitt (1935–). A stage actor until he was 32, Jordan was brought to films to play a couple of young western tearaways. A TV series called *Captains and the Kings* brought him more popularity and meatier roles for a short while. After a few years away on stage in the early 1980s, he returned to films a heavier, more menacing actor, to play some plainly dangerous men. Married/divorced actresses Kathleen Widdoes (1939–) and Blair Brown (1948–). Died from a brain tumour.
1970: Valdez is Coming. Lawman. 1971: Chato's Land. 1972: The Trial of the

Catonsville Nine. 1973: Incident at Vichy (TV). The Friends of Eddie Coyle. 1974: The Yakuza. 1975: Rooster Cogburn. Kamouraska. 1976: Logan's Run. 1978: Interiors. Old Boyfriends. The Defection of Simas Kudirka (TV). Les Miserables (TV). 1980: The Biggest Bank Robbery (TV). Raise the Titanic! The French Atlantic Affair (TV). 1981: Washington Mistress (TV). The Bunker (TV). 1984: Dune. A Flash of Green. 1985: The Mean Season. 1986: The Men's Club. Solarbabies (GB: TV, as Solar Warriors). 1987: The Secret of My Success. 1989: Romero. Manhunt: The Search for the Night Stalker (TV). 1990: The Hunt for Red October. 1991: Shout. Heaven is a Playground. Timebomb. 1992: Primary Motive. 1993: Posse. Gettysburg.

JOURDAN, Louis (L. Gendre) 1919–
Debonair, dark-haired French charmer with smilingly handsome face. He was in Hollywood films soon after the end of World War II (during which he worked for the French resistance), but has made fewer than one might think in a 50-year career.
1939: Le corsaire. Félicie Nanteuil. 1940: Untel père et fils. Le comédie du bonheur. 1941: Premier rendez-vous (GB: First Appointment). Nous les jeunes. Parade en sept nuits. 1942: L'arlesienne. La belle aventure. La vie de bohème. 1943: Les petites du quai aux fleurs. 1947: The Paradine Case. 1948: Letter from an Unknown Woman. No Minor Vices. 1949: Madame Bovary. 1951: Bird of Paradise. Anne of the Indies. 1952: The Happy Time. Decameron Nights. 1953: Rue de l'étrapade (GB: Françoise Steps Out). 1954: Three Coins in the Fountain. 1955: The Swan. 1956: Julie. Eloise (TV). La mariée est trop belle (GB and US: The Bride is Too Beautiful). 1957: Escapade. Dangerous Exile. 1958: Gigi. 1959: The Best of Everything. 1960: Can-Can. Les vierges de Rome/The Virgins of Rome. 1961: Dark Journey. Liviathan. Le compte de Monte-Cristo/The Story of the Count of Monte-Cristo. 1962: Le désordre/Disorder. Mathias Sandorf. 1963: The V.I.P.s. 1965: Made in Paris. Les sultans. 1966: Cervantes. 1967: Peau d'espion (GB: To Commit a Murder). 1968: To Die in Paris (TV). A Flea in Her Ear. 1969: Fear No Evil (TV). Run a Crooked Mile (TV). Ritual of Evil (TV). 1972: The Great American Beauty Contest (TV). 1974: The Count of Monte Cristo (TV. GB: cinemas). 1976: The Man in the Iron Mask (TV). 1977: Silver Bears. 1981: Double Deal. 1982: Swamp

Thing. 1983: Octopussy. 1984: Cover-Up. 1986: Beverly Hills Madam (TV). 1987: Counterforce. 1988: Grand Larceny (TV). 1989: The Return of Swamp Thing. Speed Zone. 1992: Year of the Comet.

JOVOVICH, Milla 1975–
Tall, purse-lipped, brown-haired, leggy, lathe-like Hollywood child and teenage model with sea-green eyes, born in the Ukraine. Her acting skills proved rudimentary in her teens, but she began taking drama rather more seriously on her return to films in 1997 after a four-year absence, and she made a brave stab at playing Joan of Arc for her then-husband (second of two), director Luc Besson.
1988: Two Moon Junction. The Night Train to Kathmandu (TV). 1991: Return to the Blue Lagoon. Kuffs. 1992: Chaplin. 1993: Dazed and Confused. 1997: The Fifth Element. 1998: He Got Game. 1999: Jeanne d'Arc (GB: Joan of Arc. US: The Messenger: The Story of Joan of Arc). The Million Dollar Hotel. 2000: The Boathouse. Kingdom Come. 2001: Dummy.

JOYCE, Brenda (Betty Leabo) 1917–
Fresh, bright, athletic, healthy-looking Hollywood blonde of the 1940s. A former model, she showed up well in a number of second leads in 'A' pictures before becoming the screen's second-best-known Jane (in Tarzan films) after Maureen O'Sullivan. She left films when deciding to quit the jungle adventure series in 1949.
1939: Here I Am a Stranger. The Rains Came. 1940: Little Old New York. Maryland. Public Deb No 1. 1941: *Variety Reel. *Stars Past and Present. Private Nurse. Marry the Boss's Daughter. Right to the Heart/Knockout. 1942:

Whispering Ghosts. The Postman Didn't Ring. Little Tokyo USA. 1943: Thumbs Up. 1945: Tarzan and the Amazons. The Enchanted Forest. Pillow of Death. Strange Confession. I'll Tell the World. 1946: Little Giant (GB: On the Carpet). Spider Woman Strikes Back. Tarzan and the Leopard Woman. Danger Woman. 1947: Tarzan and the Huntress. Stepchild. 1948: Tarzan and the Mermaids. Shaggy. 1949: Tarzan's Magic Fountain.

JUDD, Ashley 1968–
Full-lipped, healthy-looking brunette American actress who developed into one of Hollywood's best in the late 1990s and, despite looking like dozens of other actresses, proved something of a box-office force as well. A self-confessed outdoor girl who's uneasy in the film capital, when not working she heads for Tennessee, home of her country-music-singing mother, Wynonna Judd. Her sister Naomi is also a singer and has performed with Wynonna as The Judds.
1992: Kuffs. Till Death Us Do Part/Married for Murder (TV). 1993: Ruby in Paradise. 1994: †Natural Born Killers. 1995: Heat. Smoke. The Passion of Darkly Noon. Naomi & Wynonna: Love Can Build a Bridge (TV. Narrator only). 1996: Normal Life. A Time to Kill. Norma Jean and Marilyn (TV). 1997: The Locusts (GB: A Secret Sin). Kiss the Girls. 1998: Simon Birch. 1999: Double Jeopardy. Eye of the Beholder. 2000: Where the Heart Is. Dexterity. 2001: Animal Husbandry.

†Most scenes deleted from final release print.

JUDD, Edward 1932–
Tall, well-built, gentle-looking, Shanghai-born leading man who had several tiny roles

in British films before being suddenly elevated to stardom in 1961. He surprisingly lasted only six years in star roles, but returned later, balding and seemingly with a tougher streak, in character parts. Married to actresses Gene Anderson (1931–1965) and Norma Ronald.

*1948: The Guinea Pig. Once a Jolly Swagman (US: Maniacs on Wheels). The Small Voice (US: Hideout). 1949: Boys in Brown. 1953: The Large Rope. 1954: Adventure in the Hopfields. The Good Die Young. *Night Plane to Amsterdam. 1956: X the Unknown. Battle of the River Plate (US: Pursuit of the Graf Spee). 1958: I Was Monty's Double. Subway in the Sky. The Man Upstairs. Carry On Sergeant. 1959: The Shakedown. No Safety Ahead. Sink the Bismarck! 1960: Hell is a City. The Challenge. The Criminal (US: The Concrete Jungle). 1961: The Day the Earth Caught Fire. 1962: Mystery Submarine. 1963: The World Ten Times Over (US: Pussycat Alley). Stolen Hours. The Long Ships. 1964: First Men in the Moon. 1965: Strange Bedfellows. Invasion. 1966: Island of Terror. 1968: The Vengeance of She. 1971: Universal Soldier. 1972: Living Free. The Rape. 1973: O Lucky Man! Vault of Horror. Assassin. 1975: Feelings (US: Whose Child Am I?). 1976: The Incredible Sarah. 1979: The House on Garibaldi Street. 1983: The Boys in Blue. The Hound of the Baskervilles. 1984: Night Train to Murder (TV). 1987: The Kitchen Toto.*

JURADO, Katy (Maria J. Garcia) 1924–
Fiery, dark-haired Mexican actress with pouting lips and flashing eyes: with those looks Katy really couldn't have come from anywhere else. Her firecracker acting style brought her to Hollywood, but they were reluctant to let her do much more than toss her curls, wear off-the-shoulder peasant blouses and smoulder. Married to Ernest Borgnine 1959–1963. Nominated for an Academy Award in *Broken Lance*. Later returned to live in Mexico.

1943: No Maturas. 1944: La Vida Inutil de Pito Perez. 1945: La Sombra de Chuco el Roto. El Museo del Crimen. Bartolo Toco la Flauta. Soltera y con Gemelos. 1946: La Viuda Celosa. Rosa del Caribe. 1948: Nosotros los Pobres. Prision de Sueños. 1949: Hay Lugar para Dos. El Seminarista. Mujer de Medica Noche. 1950: Cabellera Blanca. 1951: Cárcel de Mujeres. The Bullfighter and the Lady. 1952: El Bruto. High Noon. 1953: San Antone. Arrowhead. 1954: Broken Lance. Tehuantepec. El Corazón

y la Espada (US: The Sword of Granada). 1955: The Racers (GB: Such Men Are Dangerous). Trial. 1956: The Man from Del Rio. Trapeze. 1957: Dragoon Wells Massacre. Four Women in Black (TV). 1958: The Badlanders. 1960: One Eyed Jacks. 1961: Barabbas. Seduction of the South. 1964: Un Hombre Solo. 1966: Target for Killing. Smoky. A Covenant with Death. 1968: Stay Away Joe. 1969: Any Second Now (TV). 1970: Bridge in the Jungle. 1971: A Little Game (TV). 1973: Pat Garrett and Billy the Kid. 1976: El elegido. 1977: El recurso del metedo. Once Upon a Scoundrel. Los Albaniles. 1978: The Children of Sanchez. 1979: Reasons of State. La Viuda de Montiel. Viva el Dictador! 1981: La Seducción. Distrito federal. Evita Perón (TV). 1984: Under the Volcano. 1985: Lady Blue. 1989: Fearmaker. 1998: Divine/El evangelio de las maravillas. The Hi-Lo Country.

JURGENS, Curt or Curd 1912–1982
Tall, fair-haired, rather stuffy German actor who, after more than 20 years in continental pictures, suddenly blossomed into an international star. Noted for the extravagance of his life-style (he had several homes) and his love life (his five wives included Eva Bartok 1955–1956), he once boasted of making 'probably more bad films than any other actor', which is nice but almost certainly untrue. He portrayed world-weariness better than most. Spent the last year of World War II in a concentration camp for 'political unreliables'. Died from heart failure.

1935: Königswalzer. Hundert tagen. 1936: Die unbekannte. Familienparade. 1937: Liebe kann lügen zu neuen Ufern. 1939: Salonwagen E 417. 1940: Herz ohne Heimat. Operette Weltrekord im Seitensprung. 1942: Stimme des Herzens. Mozart (Wenn die Götter lieben). 1943: Ein glücklicher Mensche. Schule des lebens. Frauen sind keine Engel. 1944: Ein blick zurück. Eine kleine Sommermelodie. 1945: Wiener Mädeln. 1947: Hin und her. Der Wind hat meine Existenze verweht. 1948: Der himmlische Walzer. Hexen. Du dares mich nicht verlassen. Leckerbissen. 1949: Am klingenden Ufern. Das singende Haus. Prämien auf den Tod. Der Engel mit der Posaune (GB: The Angel with the Trumpet). 1950: Lambert fühlt sich bedroht. Küssen ist keine sind. Kuckuckslei. Schuss durchs Fenster. Verlorenes Reunen. Stürm über Alaska. Gute Nacht, Mary. Die gestörte Hochzeitsnacht. 1951: Der schweigende Mund. Das Geheimnis einer Ehe. Kampenfieber. †So ein Theater/Gangsterpremière.

1952: Knall und Fall als Hochstapler. Haus des Lebens. 1 April 2000. Das Leben ist stärker. 1953: Alles für Papa. Du bist die Rose vom Wörthersee. Man nennt es Liebe. Munk bet Nacht. Der letzte Walzer (GB: The Last Waltz). Praterherzen. 1954: Rummelplatz der Liebe/Carnival Story (German version). Lena und Nicoline. Seine dritte Frau. Eine Frau von Heute. Gefangene der liebe. Das Bekenntnis der Ina Kehr (GB: Afraid to Live). Du bist die richtige. Orient Express. 1955: Des Teufels General (GB: The Devil's General). Liebe ohne Illusion. Du mein stilles Tal. Die Ratten. Teufel in Seide/The Devil in Silk. Les héros sont fatigués (GB: The Heroes Are Tired). London Calling North Pole. 1956: Et Dieu créa la femme (GB: Heaven Fell That Night. US: And God Created Woman). Michael Strogoff (GB: Revolt of the Tartars). Oeil pour oeil. Die goldene Brücke. †Ohne dich wird es Nacht (GB: Without You It is Night). 1957: Bitter Victory. The Enemy Below. Les éspions. House of Intrigue. This Happy Feeling. 1958: Tamango. Me and the Colonel. The Inn of the Sixth Happiness. Le vent se lève (GB: Operation Time Bomb). Der Schinderhannes (US: Duel in the Forest). 1959: Ferry to Hong Kong. The Blue Angel. Katja. 1960: I Aim at the Stars. Festival Girls. Schachnovelle (GB: Three Moves to Freedom. US: The Royal Game). Gustav Adolfs Page. 1961: The Triumph of Michael Strogoff. Le désordre (US: Disorder). †Bankraub in der Rue Latour. 1962: The Longest Day. Miracle of the White Stallions (GB: Flight of the White Stallions). The Threepenny Opera. I Don Giovanni della Costa Azzura (US: Beach Casanova). 1963: Of Love and Desire. Les parias de la gloire. Hide and Seek. Château en Suède (US: Naughty, Nutty Chateau). Psyche 59. 1964: Lord Jim. Begegnung in Salzburg. D. M. Killer. 1965: Das Liebeskarussel (GB: Who Wants to Sleep). Der Kongress amüsiert sich. 1966: Le jardinier d'Argenteuil. Das Geheimnis der gelben Mönche (GB and US: Target for Killing). Zwei Girls vom Roten Stern. 1967: Der Lügner und die Nonne. The Karate Killers (TV. GB: cinemas). Dalle Ardenne all'inferno (GB: The Dirty Heroes). 1968: The Battle of Neretva. Der Arzt von St Pauli. The Assassination Bureau. Die Artisten in der Zirkuskuppel: Ratlos. Niete rose per OSS 117 (GB: OSS 117 – Murder for Sale). 1969: Auf der Reeperbahn nachts um halb eins. Ohrfeigen. Cannabis. Battle of Britain. The Invincible Six. La legione dei dannati. 1970: Der Pfarrer von St Pauli. Hello-Goodbye. The Mephisto Waltz. Das Stundenhotel von St Pauli. 1971: Fieras sin Julia. Nicholas and Alexandra. Käpt'n Rauhbein aus St Pauli. 1972: Kill (US: Kill! Kill! Kill!). A la guerre comme à la guerra. Profession: aventuriers. 1973: Vault of Horror. Soft Beds, Hard Battles (US: Undercovers Hero). 1974: Radiografia di una svastika. Cagliostro. Povero cristo. 1975: In Gefahr und grösster not bringt der Mittelweg. La lungo strada senze polvere Danubio. 1976: The Twist/Folies bourgeoises. Auch Mimosen wollen blühen. Nurses for Sale (US: Females for Hire). 1977: U bösser Nacht schleich ich heut Nacht so bang. The Spy Who Loved Me. 1978: Just a Gigolo. Ab Morgen sind wir reich und ehrlich/Rich and Respectable. 1979: Breakthrough/Sergeant Steiner. Goldengirl. Warum die UFOs unseren Salat klauen. Die Patriotin. Teheran incident/Teheran 1943. La guele de l'autre. 1980: The Black Chateau. Checkpoint Charlie. 1981: Daisy Chain. Cruise Missile.

†Also directed

JUSTIN, John (J. Ledsma) 1917–
Tall, straight and almost dauntingly handsome – rather like a gentle-looking Michael Rennie (*qv*) – this light-haired British actor had a few staunch leading roles for the cinema, but remained primarily a man of the stage. Latterly in very small film roles. Married to Barbara Murray (first of two) from 1952 to 1964.
1937: Dark Journey. 1940: The Thief of Bagdad. 1943: The Gentle Sex. 1945: Journey Together. 1948: Call of the Blood. 1950: The Angel with the Trumpet. 1952: The Sound Barrier (US: Breaking the Sound Barrier). Hot Ice. 1953: Melba. King of the Khyber Rifles. 1954: Seagulls Over Sorrento (US: Crest of the Wave). The Teckman Mystery. The Man Who Loved Redheads. The Village. 1955: Untamed. Guilty? 1956: Safari. 1957: Island in the Sun. 1960: The Spider's Web. 1961: Le crime de Dr Chardin. Les hommes veulent vivre. 1962: Candidate for Murder. The Golden Salamander. 1964: Men in Silence (voice only). 1972: Savage Messiah. 1973: Razzia/Barcelona Kill. 1975: Lisztomania. 1977: Valentino. 1978: The Big Sleep. 1980: Very Like a Whale (TV). 1983: Trenchcoat.

K

KANE, Carol (Carolyn Kane) 1950–
Small, waif-like American actress with a mass of light curly hair, who caught the attention in fashionable films of the 1970s. Although mostly in parts calling for suffering and anguish, she has also revealed a pleasing talent for comedy. By the 1980s, though she seemed not to have found an individual identity in the cinema, and roles since then have often been star cameos. Nominated for an Oscar in *Hester Street*.
1970: Is This Trip Really Necessary? 1971: Desperate Characters. Carnal Knowledge. 1973: Wedding in White. The Last Detail. 1974: Hester Street. 1975: Dog Day Afternoon. 1976: Harry and Walter Go to New York. 1977: Annie Hall. Valentino. The World's Greatest Lover. 1978: The Mafu Cage. 1979: The Muppet Movie. When a Stranger Calls. The Sabina. 1980: Les jeux de la comtesse d'Olingen de Gratz Styrie. 1981: Norman Loves Rose. Thursday the 12th/Pandemonium. Keeping On. 1982: An Invasion of Privacy (TV). 1983: Over the Brooklyn Bridge. 1984: The Secret Diary of Sigmund Freud. Burning Rage (TV). 1985: Transylvania 6-5000. 1986: All is Forgiven (TV). Jumpin' Jack Flash. 1987: Ishtar. The Princess Bride. Sticky Fingers. Drop-Out Mother (TV). 1988: Scrooged. Licence to Drive. 1989: The Lemon Sisters. 1990: Flashback. Joe vs the Volcano. My Blue Heaven. 1991: In the Soup. Ted and Venus. 1992: Baby on Board. 1993: Addams Family Values. When a Stranger Calls Back (TV). Even Cowgirls Get the Blues. 1995: How Much Are These Children in the Window?/Two Much Trouble. Dad, the Angel and Me (TV). The Ice Cream Dimension. Big

Bully. Freaky Friday (TV). 1996: The Pallbearer. American Strays. Office Killer. Sunset Park. 1997: Gone Fishin'. 1998: The First Seven Years (v). The Tic Code. 1999: Man on the Moon. Jawbreaker. Beggars and Choosers (TV). 2000: Tomorrow by Midnight/Midnight 5. The Shrink is In. My First Mister.

KARINA, Anna (Hanne Karin Bayer) 1940–
Piquantly pretty Danish-born actress with reddish-chestnut hair, in French and international films, and once described as 'the intellectual's pin-up'. Formerly married (first of three) to French director Jean-Luc Godard, she rose to stardom in his films and has maintained a respected position in the French cinema.
1953: Charlotte et son steak. 1958: *Pingin og Skoene/The Girl and the Shoes. 1960: Le petit soldat. 1961: Ce soir ou jamais. Une femme est une femme. She'll Have to Go (US: Maid for Murder). Le soleil dans l'oeil. 1962: Cléo de 5 à 7. Vivre sa vie. Sheherazade. Le joli mai. Les quatre vérités. 1963: Dragése au poivre (GB: Sweet and Sour). Un mari à prix fixe. 1964: Bande à part. La ronde. Le voleur de Tibidabo. De l'amour. Le soldatesse. Alphaville. 1965: Pierrot le fou. Suzanne Simonin, la religieuse de Diderot (GB: La religieuse). 1966: The Oldest Profession. Made in U.S.A. Tendres réquins. Zärtliche Haie. 1967: Lamiel. Anna (originally for TV). Lo straniero/The Stranger. 1968: The Magus. Michael Kohlhaas. 1969: Laughter in the Dark. Before Winter Comes. Justine. Le temps de mourir. 1970: L'alliance. 1971: Rendezvous à Bray. The Salzburg Connection. 1973: Pane e cioccolata/Bread and Chocolate. L'invenzione di Morel. †Vivre ensemble. 1974: L'assassin musicien. 1975: Les oeufs brouillés. Life. The Two of Us. 1976: Chinese Roulette. Also es war so . . . 1978: Chaussette surprise. Clopin-Clopan. Just Like at Home. 1979: The Story of a Mother. 1982: Roma Regina. 1983: L'ami de Vincent. 1984: Ave Maria. 1986: Treasure Island. Last Song. 1987: Last Summer in Tangiers. Cayenne Palace. 1988: L'oeuvre au noir. 1990: Manden, der ville varer (US: The Man Who Would Be Guilty). 1992: Le bassin de John Wayne. 1995: Haut bas fragile.

†Also directed

KARLOFF, Boris
(William Pratt) 1887–1969
Gaunt, black-haired British actor with massive eyebrows and deep-set eyes. Starting

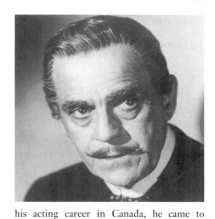

his acting career in Canada, he came to Hollywood in 1919 and struggled for years in small bad-guy roles before being given the role of Frankenstein's creature in 1931. His innate gentleness shone through the masses of makeup to create a pitiable classic (topped by his performance in the 1935 sequel) and the succeeding years made him a legendary star of horror films. Confined to a wheelchair in later years through arthritis, he died from a respiratory ailment. Three times married.
1916: The Dumb Girl of Portici/The Young Girl of Portici. 1917: Wild and Woolly. 1919: Ashes of Desire. His Majesty, the American (GB: One of the Blood). The Prince and Betty. The Lightning Raider (serial). The Masked Raider (serial). 1920: The Deadlier Sex. The Courage of Marge O'Doone. The Last of the Mohicans. The Notorious Miss Lisle. 1921: The Hope Diamond Mystery (serial. GB: The Romance of the Hope Diamond). Without Benefit of Clergy. Cheated Hearts. The Cave Girl. 1922: The Man from Downing Street (GB: The Jade). The Altar Stairs. Omar, the Tentmaker. The Infidel. Nan of the North. 1923: The Woman Conquers. The Prisoner. The Love Brand. The Gentleman from America. 1924: The Hellion. Dynamite Dan. Raiders of the Plains (serial). Parisian Nights. 1925: Lady Robin Hood. Perils of the Wild (serial). Forbidden Cargo (GB: The Dangerous Cargo). The Prairie Wife. Never the Twain Shall Meet. 1926: The Greater Glory. The Eagle of the Sea. Her Honor, the Governor (GB: The Second Mrs Fenway). *The Nickel Hopper. The Golden Web. Old Ironsides (GB: Sons of the Sea). Flames. The Man in the Saddle. Phantoms of the Bat. Flaming Fury. The Bells. Valencia (GB: The Love Song). 1927: The Meddlin' Stranger. Tarzan and the Golden Lion. Let It Rain. The Princess from Hoboken. Phantom Buster. Two Arabian Nights. Soft Cushions. The Love Mart. 1928: Burning Wind. Vultures of the Sea (serial). The Vanishing Rider (serial). The Little Wild Girl. 1929: Phantoms of the North. Behind That Curtain. King of the Kongo (serial). The Fatal Warning (serial). Two Sisters. The Devil's Chaplain. The Unholy Night. Anne Against the World. 1930: Le spectre vert (French-language version of The Unholy Night). The Bad One. The Utah Kid. Mother's Cry. The Sea Bat. King of the Wild (serial). The Criminal Code. 1931: Cracked Nuts. Sous les verrous (French language version of Pardon Us/GB: Jailbirds). I Like Your Nerve. The Public Defender. Young Donovan's Kid (GB: Donovan's Kid).

Smart Money. Business and Pleasure. Graft. The Guilty Generation. The Mad Genius. Dirigible. The Yellow Ticket (GB: The Yellow Passport). The Last Parade. Frankenstein. Tonight Or Never. Five Star Final. 1932: Behind the Mask. Scarface. Alias the Doctor. The Cohens and Kellys in Hollywood. The Miracle Man. Night World. The Old Dark House. The Mask of Fu Manchu. The Mummy. 1933: The Man Who Dared. The Ghoul. The House of Rothschild. 1934: The Lost Patrol. The Black Cat (GB: The House of Doom). Gift of Gab. *Screen Snapshots No. 11. 1935: Bride of Frankenstein. The Black Room. The Raven. *Hollywood Hobbies. 1936: The Invisible Ray. The Man Who Changed His Mind (US: The Man Who Lived Again). Juggernaut (US: The Demon Doctor). The Walking Dead. Charlie Chan at the Opera. 1937: Night Key. West of Shanghai. *Cinema Circus. 1938: The Invisible Menace. Mr Wong, Detective. 1939: Son of Frankenstein. The Mystery of Mr Wong. The Man They Could Not Hang. Mr Wong in Chinatown. Tower of London. Devil's Island. 1940: The Fatal Hour (GB: Mr Wong at Headquarters). British Intelligence (GB: Enemy Agent). Black Friday. The Man with Nine Lives (GB: Behind the Door). Doomed to Die (GB: The Mystery of the Wentworth Castle). Before I Hang. The Ape. You'll Find Out. 1941: *Information Please No. 8. The Devil Commands. *Information Please No. 12. 1942: The Boogie Man Will Get You. 1944: The Climax. House of Frankenstein. 1945: The Body Snatcher. Isle of the Dead. 1946: Bedlam. 1947: The Secret Life of Walter Mitty. Lured (GB: Personal Column). Dick Tracy Meets Gruesome (GB: Dick Tracy's Amazing Adventure). Unconquered. 1948: Tap Roots. 1949: Abbott and Costello Meet the Killer Boris Karloff. 1951: The Strange Door. The Emperor's Nightingale (narrator only). 1952: The Black Castle. 1953: The Hindu (GB: Sabaka). Colonel March Investigates. Abbott and Costello Meet Dr Jekyll and Mr Hyde. Il monstro dell'isola / Monster of the Island. 1956: Rendezvous in Black (TV). 1957: Voodoo Island. *The Juggler of Our Lady (narrator only). 1958: Grip of the Strangler (US: The Haunted Strangler). Frankenstein 1970. Heart of Darkness (TV). Corridors of Blood. 1960: To the Sound of Trumpets (TV). 1963: The Raven. The Terror. Comedy of Terrors. Black Sabbath. *Today's Teens (narrator only). 1964: Bikini Beach. 1965: Monster of Terror (US: Die, Monster, Die). Mondo balordo / Strange World (narrator only). 1966: The Ghost in the Invisible Bikini. The Daydreamer (voice only). The Venetian Affair. The Sorcerers. 1967: Mad Monster Party (voice only). El coleccionista de cadaveras (GB: Cauldron of Blood. US: Blind Man's Buff). 1968: Targets. Curse of the Crimson Altar (US: The Crimson Cult). 1969: Isle of the Snake People / Snake People. The Incredible Invasion. †The Fear Chamber. †House of Evil.

†Unreleased

KATT, William 1950–
Long-faced, diffident, quietly-spoken American leading man with fair, curly hair, the son of actors Bill Williams and Barbara

Hale (both qv). Not dynamic enough to become a big attraction, although smooth and personable, his career has divided itself up into several sections: early days when he looked like a surfing champion; the early 1980s with theatre successes and a TV series; the late 1980s supporting his mother in the 'Perry Mason' revival; and recent times, when he has been making horror, soft-porn and action films of the kind that go straight to video. Best role: The Sundance Kid in the 1979 'Butch and Sundance' film.
1970: Night Chase (TV). 1971: The Late Liz. 1972: The Daughters of Joshua Cabe (TV). 1974: Can Ellen Be Saved? (TV). 1976: Carrie. 1977: First Love. 1978: Big Wednesday. 1979: Butch and Sundance The Early Days. 1981: The Greatest American Hero (TV). Pippin (video). 1984: Baby/ Baby... Secret of the Lost Legend. 1985: Perry Mason Returns (TV). 1986: House. Perry Mason: The Case of the Notorious Nun (TV). Perry Mason: The Case of the Shooting Star (TV). 1987: White Ghost. Perry Mason: The Case of the Scandalous Scoundrel (TV). Perry Mason: The Case of the Sinister Spirit (TV). Perry Mason: The Case of the Lost Love (TV). 1988: Perry Mason: The Case of the Avenging Ace (TV). Perry Mason: The Case of the Lady in the Lake (TV). Perry Mason: The Case of the Murdered Madam (TV). 1989: Swimsuit (TV). Rising Storm. Wedding Band. 1990: Naked Obsession. Last Call. 1991: Desperate Motive. Dark Obsession. 1992: House IV: The Horror Show / House IV. Home Deadly Home. Double X – The Name of the Game. 1993: The Higher Ground. 1994: The Paperboy. Tollbooth. Stranger by Night. Romantic Undertaking (TV). 1995: Blade Boxer II: Blood Masters. Problem Child 3. Piranha (TV). Cyborg 3: The Recycler. 1996: Daddy's Girl. Devil's Food (cable TV). Rattled (TV). 1997: Rough Riders (TV). Mother Teresa: In the Name of God's Poor. 1998: Hyacinth. 1999: Hide and Seek. Jawbreaker. Twin Falls Idaho. 2000: Clean and Narrow.

KAYE, Danny
(David D. Kaminski) 1913–1987
Red-haired, long-legged American zany comedian and singer of tongue-twisting comic songs, almost always on the run from villains and the victim of his own wild imagination. After a big star build-up at the Goldwyn Studio, he made some fun, funny, firecracker, freewheeling entertainments – especially The Secret Life of Walter Mitty,

Wonder Man, Knock on Wood and The Court Jester – before too many of his films somehow began to reflect the dreamy sentimentalism of his much-publicized work for children's charities. Special Oscars 1954 and 1982. Died from a heart attack brought on by hepatitis, after being given contaminated blood during heart bypass surgery.
1937: *Dime a Dance. *Cupid Takes a Holiday. 1938: *Money on Your Life. *Getting an Eyeful. 1942: *Night Shift. 1944: Up in Arms. 1945: Wonder Man. 1946: The Kid from Brooklyn. 1947: *The Secret Life of Walter Mitty. 1948: A Song is Born. 1949: The Inspector General. It's a Great Feeling. 1951: On the Riviera. 1952: Hans Christian Andersen . . . and the dancer. 1953: Knock on Wood. 1954: *Assignment Children. White Christmas. *Hula from Hollywood. 1955: The Court Jester. 1958: Merry Andrew. Me and the Colonel. 1959: The Five Pennies. 1961: On the Double. 1963: The Man from the Diners' Club. 1969: The Madwoman of Chaillot. 1972: *Pied Piper. 1975: Peter Pan (TV). 1977: Pinocchio (TV). 1981: Skokie (TV. GB: Once They Marched Through a Thousand Towns).

KEACH, Stacy
(Walter S. Keach Jr) 1941–
Light-haired (thinning from his twenties) broad-shouldered American actor with slight but distinctive cleft upper lip (latterly covered with moustache); usually seen as slightly off-centre and sometimes downright eccentric characters. He had some powerful leading roles in the early 1970s but by the end of the decade his career seemed, to some observers, to have lost its way. He was jailed in Britain for several months in 1984/1985 on narcotics charges, but soon picked up his career again.

1968: †*The Heart is a Lonely Hunter.* 1969: *End of the Road.* 1970: *The Traveling Executioner.* *Brewster McCloud.* 1971: *Doc. Fat City.* 1972: *The New Centurions (GB: Precinct 45: Los Angeles Police).* *Luther. The Life and Times of Judge Roy Bean. Watched! Orville and Wilbur (TV).* 1973: *Particular Men (TV).* 1974: *The Dion Brothers (TV. GB: cinemas, as the Gravy Train).* *One by One (narrator only). All the Kind Strangers (TV).* 1975: *James Dean – the First American Teenager (and narrator). Conduct Unbecoming.* *†*Hamburger Hamlet. The Killer Inside Me.* 1976: *Dynasty (TV). Gli esecutori (GB: Sicilian Cross. US: Street People). Jesus of Nazareth (TV).* 1977: *The Squeeze. Gray Lady Down. The Duellists (narrator only). Il grande attacca/The Biggest Battle.* 1978: *The Mountain in the Jungle (GB: Prisoner of the Cannibal God. US: Primitive Desires). Deux Solitudes. Up in Smoke.* 1979: *The Search for Solutions (narrator only). The Ninth Configuration/Twinkle, Twinkle, Killer Kane. Diary of a Young Comic (TV).* 1980: *The Long Riders. A Rumor of War (TV).* 1981: *Road Games. Butterfly. Cheech and Chong's Nice Dreams.* 1982: *That Championship Season.* 1983: *Murder Me, Murder You (TV). More Than Murder (TV).* 1984: *Mistral's Daughter (video).* 1985: *Intimate Strangers (TV).* 1986: *The Return of Mike Hammer (TV).* 1989: *The Lover. Class of 1999. The Forgotten (TV).* 1990: *Geliebte Milena. The Mysteries of the Dark Jungle. False Identity.* 1991: *Mission of the Shark (TV).* 1992: *Sunset Grill. Silent Thunder (TV). Revenge on the Highway (TV).* 1993: *Body Bags (TV). Good Cop, Bad Cop. Irresistible Force. Batman: The Mask of Phantasm (voice only). Rio Diablo (TV).* 1994: *Against Their Will (TV). Young Ivanhoe (TV). Trust in Me (TV).* 1995: *James A Michener's Texas (TV). The Pathfinder (TV).* 1996: *Prey of the Jaguar.* 1997: *Murder in My Mind (TV). Jack London's The Sea Wolf. Future Fear. Legend of the Lost Tomb (TV).* 1998: *Birds of Passage. American History X.* 1999: *Icebreaker.* 2000: *Unshackled. Mercy Streets. The Courage to Love (TV).*
As director: 1971: *The Repeater.*

†*As Stacy Keach Junior*

KEATON, Buster
(Joseph Keaton) 1895–1966
Expressionless, dark-haired, soulful-eyed American silent-screen comedian. Dubbed 'The Great Stone Face', he brought the mechanics of visual comedy down to a fine art, but struggled (both with his work and an alcohol problem) with the coming of sound. Much revered in post-war times, especially in Europe, he found fresh inspiration in his last few years. Special Oscar 1959. Died from lung cancer. Married (first of three) silent star Natalie Talmadge (1898–1969).
1917: *A Reckless Romeo. *The Butcher Boy. *The Rough House. *His Wedding Night. *A Country Hero (released 1920). *Coney Island. *Oh Doctor!* 1918: *Out West. *The Bell Boy. *Moonshine. *Good Night Nurse. *The Cook.* 1919: *Love. *A Desert Hero. *Back Stage. *The Hayseed. *The Garage.* 1920: *The Round Up. †*One Week. †*The High Sign. The Saphead. †*The Scarecrow. †*Neighbors.* 1921: †*Convict 13. †*Hard Luck. †*The Goat. †*The Haunted House. †*The Boat. †*The Paleface. †*The Playhouse.* 1922: †*The Electric House. †*The Frozen North. †*My Wife's Relations. †*The Blacksmith. †*Daydreams. †*Cops.* 1923: †*The Balloonatic. *The Love Nest. †The Three Ages. †Our Hospitality.* 1924: ‡*Sherlock Junior. †The Navigator.* 1925: ‡*Seven Chances. ‡Go West.* 1926: †*The General. Battling Butler.* 1927: *College.* 1928: *Steamboat Bill Junior. The Cameraman.* 1929: *Hollywood Revue of 1929 (and German version). Spite Marriage (and French version).* 1930: *Free and Easy (and Spanish version). Doughboys (GB: Forward March).* 1931: *Parlor, Bedroom and Bath (GB: Romeo in Pyjamas. And German and French versions). Sidewalks of New York.* 1932: *Speak Easily. The Passionate Plumber (and French version).* 1933: *Hollywood on Parade A-6. What! No Beer?* 1934: *Le roi des Champs Elysées.* 1935: *L'horloger amoureux. The Invader (US: An Old Spanish Custom). *La Fiesta de Santa Barbara. *Allez-Oop. *The Serenade. *The Gold Ghost. *Palooka from Paducah. *Hayseed Romance. *Stars and Stripes. *The E Flat Man. *One Run Elmer.* 1936: *The Timid Young Man. *Three on a Limb. *Grand Slam Opera. *Blue Blazes. *The Chemist. Three Men on a Horse. *Mixed Magic.* 1937: *Jail Bait. *Ditto. *Love Nest on Wheels.* 1939: *Pest from the West. *Mooching through Georgia. The Jones Family in Hollywood. Hollywood Cavalcade. *Nothing But Pleasure. The Jones Family in Quick Millions.* 1940: *Li'l Abner (GB: Trouble Chaser). The Villain Still Pursued Her. *Pardon My Berth Marks. *The Spook Speaks. *The Taming of the Snood.* 1941: *His Ex Marks the Spot. *General Nuisance. *She's Oil Mine. *So You Won't Squawk.* 1943: *Forever and a Day.* 1944: *San Diego, I Love You. Two Girls and a Sailor.* 1945: *That Night with You. That's the Spirit.* 1946: *God's Country. El moderno Barba Azul (GB: TV, as Boom in the Moon).* 1948: *Un duel à mort.* 1949: *In the Good Old Summertime. The Loveable Cheat. You're My Everything.* 1950: *Sunset Boulevard.* 1951: *Limelight. Paradise for Buster.* 1953: *L'incantevole nemica.* 1956: *Around the World in 80 Days.* 1960: *The Adventures of Huckleberry Finn.* 1962: *Ten Girls Ago (unfinished).* 1963: *It's a Mad, Mad, Mad, Mad World. *The Triumph of Lester Snapwell.* 1964: *Pajama Party.* 1965: *The Railroder. Sergeant Deadhead. Buster Keaton Rides Again. Beach Blanket Bingo (GB: Malibu Beach). *Film. How to Stuff a Wild Bikini. Due Marines e uno generale (US: War Italian Style).* 1966: *A Funny Thing Happened on the Way to the Forum. *The Scribe.*
Also as director: 1938: *Hollywood Handicap. Life in Sometown USA. Streamlined Swing.*

‡*Also directed* †*Also co-directed*

KEATON, Diane (D. Hall) 1946–
Fascinating, bird-like, light-haired American actress and singer, with naturalistic style. She rose to fame in Woody Allen vehicles (and won an Oscar in his *Annie Hall*), but soon proved she could stand on her own feet with a magnetic performance for Richard Brooks in *Looking for Mr Goodbar*. Additionally nominated for an Oscar for *Reds* and *Marvin's Room*, she has also directed several films, with relatively undistinguished results. Also a keen photographer: a number of her portfolios have been published.
1970: *Lovers and Other Strangers.* 1972: *The Godfather. Play It Again Sam.* 1974: *Sleeper. The Godfather Part II.* 1975: *Love and Death. I Will...I Will...For Now.* 1976: *Harry and Walter Go to New York.* 1977: *Annie Hall. Looking for Mr Goodbar.* 1978: *Interiors.* 1979: *Manhattan.* 1981: *Shoot the Moon. Reds.* 1984: *Mrs Soffel. The Little Drummer Girl.* 1986: *Crimes of the Heart.* 1987: *Radio Days. Baby Boom.* 1988: *The Good Mother.* 1989: *The Lemon Sisters.* 1990: *The Godfather Part III.* 1991: *Running Mates (TV). Secret Society. Father of the Bride.* 1993: *Look Who's Talking Now (voice only). Manhattan Murder Mystery.* 1994: *Amelia Earhart: The Final Flight (TV).* 1995: *Father of the Bride 2.* 1996: *Marvin's Room. The First Wives Club.* 1997: *The Only Thrill/Tennessee Valley. Northern Lights (TV).* 1998: *The Other Sister. All About Alfred (doc).* 2000: *Hanging Up. Town and Country.*
As director: 1987: *Heaven.* 1991: *Secret Society. Wildflower (TV).* 1995: *Unstrung Heroes.* 2000: *Hanging Up.*

KEATON, Michael (M. Douglas) 1951–
American light actor of slim build, manic smile and dark, fluffy hair whose comic performances have an edge of nervous intensity missing from those he gives in straight drama. After performing as a club comic and stealing scenes in short-lived TV series, he made a sensational star debut in *Night Shift*. His choice of scripts thereafter

(GB: The Star Said No!). 1952: Lovely to Look At. Desperate Search. I Love Melvin. 1953: Fast Company. Ride, Vaquero! Calamity Jane. Kiss Me Kate. 1954: Rose Marie. Seven Brides for Seven Brothers. Deep in My Heart. 1955: Jupiter's Darling. Kismet. 1958: Floods of Fear. 1959: The Big Fisherman. 1961: Armored Command. 1962: The Day of the Triffids. 1964: The Man from Button Willow (voice only). 1966: Waco. 1967: Red Tomahawk. The War Wagon. 1968: Arizona Bushwackers. 1993: Hart to Hart: Home is Where the Hart Is (TV). 1994: That's Entertainment! III.

†As Harold Keel

was uncertain, but he regained his comic standing in *Beetlejuice*. Although he seemed odd casting as Batman (The Joker might have been more appropriate), the role gave him his only solid box-office hit in recent times; he dropped out of the series after two films but further starring films did only moderately at the box-office. There were a number of separations and reconciliations in his marriage to actress Caroline MacWilliams before the couple finally divorced.
1982: Night Shift. 1983: Mr Mom (GB: Mr Mum). 1984: Johnny Dangerously. 1985: Touch and Go. 1986: Gung Ho. 1987: The Squeeze. 1988: Beetlejuice. Clean and Sober. 1989: The Dream Team. Batman. 1990: Pacific Heights. 1991: One Good Cop. 1992: Batman Returns. 1993: Much Ado About Nothing. My Life. Earth and the American Dream (voice only). 1994: The Paper. Speechless. 1996: Multiplicity. Inventing the Abbotts (narrator only). 1997: Jackie Brown. Out of Sight. 1998: Desperate Measures. Jack Frost. 2000: Road to Glory.

KEEL, Howard (Harold Leek) 1917–
Round-faced American actor with big baritone singing voice and swaggering style. Not too well used by his studio, M-G-M, who cast him in straight roles in second-features as well as some pretty lumpish musicals. He did enjoy a good run in the early fifties with *Kiss Me Kate*, *Calamity Jane* and *Seven Brides for Seven Brothers* but then slipped into routine action films. Later in TV soap.
1948: †The Small Voice (US: Hideout). 1950: Annie Get Your Gun. Pagan Love Song. 1951: Three Guys Named Mike. Texas Carnival. Show Boat. Across the Wide Missouri (narrator only). Callaway Went Thataway

KEELER, Ruby (Ethel Keeler) 1909–1993
Dark-haired Canadian-born star of Hollywood musicals of the thirties, often in tandem with Dick Powell. The famous initial description of Astaire on his arrival in Hollywood – 'Can't act, can't sing, can dance a little' – would have fitted Ruby, though even her clackety-clack dancing was hopeful and energetic rather than hep. Still, she was pretty, and whenever the leading lady broke a leg, Ruby went out there and became a star. Married (first of two) to Al Jolson (qv) from 1928 to 1939. Died from cancer.
1928: *Ruby Keeler. 1933: 42nd Street. Gold Diggers of 1933. Footlight Parade. 1934: Dames. Flirtation Walk. 1935: Go into Your Dance (GB: Casino de Paree). Shipmates Forever. 1936: Colleen. 1937: Ready, Willing and Able. 1938: Mother Carey's Chickens. 1941: Sweetheart of the Campus (GB: Broadway Ahead). 1969: The Phynx. 1989: Beverly Hills Brats.

KEENER, Catherine 1964–
Black-haired, elegant, late-blooming American actress, good in sardonic comedy roles, but mainly on stage and TV until the mid-1990s. She had a leading role opposite Brad Pitt (qv) in the cult hit *Johnny Suede*, but it wasn't until she made a second film for the same director, Tom DiCillo, *Living in Oblivion*, that she got a proper foothold in films and progressed to semi-leading roles in mainstream movies. Married to actor Dermot Mulroney (also qv). Academy Award nominee for *Being John Malkovich*.
1986: The Education of Allison Tate/The Abduction of Allison Tate. 'About Last Night . . .' 1989: Backtrack (GB: Catchfire). Survival Quest. 1991: Switch. Johnny Suede.

1992: The Gun in Betty Lou's Handbag. 1995: Living in Oblivion. 1996: Walking and Talking. The Destiny of Marty Fine. Box of Moon Light. If These Walls Could Talk (TV). Boys. 1997: The Real Blonde. 1998: Out of Sight. Your Friends & Neighbours. 1999: Being John Malkovich. 8 MM. Simpatico. 2000: Spring Forward.

KEITEL, Harvey 1939–
Dark-haired, stockily built, aggressive, dissatisfied looking American actor who began in intense, often violent working-class roles and, after years of near-stardom, has become a cult figure in recent times. The critic who wrote that 'only Keitel could play this part, but then only Keitel would want to' probably encapsulated the Brooklyn-born actor's unique qualities. A sort of Skid Row Fredric March (an actor he also resembles facially), Keitel's unsettling qualities have kept producers queuing for his services in spite of his making often obscure films and foolish comic supporting roles. Still tends to play loners with the cares of the world on their shoulders. One of the screen's hardest-working and furthest-travelled actors: a filmographer's nightmare. Married/divorced actress Lorraine Bracco.
1965: Bring on the Dancing Girls (unfinished). 1968: Who's That Knocking at My Door? 1970: Street Scenes 1970. 1971: A Memory of Two Mondays (TV). 1973: Mean Streets. 1974: Alice Doesn't Live Here Anymore. The Virginia Hill Story (TV). 1975: That's the Way of the World (later Shining Star). 1976: Mother, Jugs and Speed. Taxi Driver. Welcome to LA. Buffalo Bill and the Indians, or: Sitting Bull's History Lesson. 1977: The Duellists. Fingers. 1978: Eagle's Wing. Blue Collar. 1979: Le mort en direct/Death Watch. 1980:

Bad Timing (US: Bad Timing: A Sensual Obsession). Saturn 3. 1981: The Border. 1982: La nuit de Varennes/The New World (GB: That Night in Varennes). 1983: Order of Death/Cop Killer/Corrupt. Une pierre dans la bouche. Exposed. 1984: Falling in Love. Nemo/Dream One (released 1987). 1985: Wiseguys. Camorra/Un complicato intrig di donne, vicoli e delitti (GB: The Naples Connection. US: Back Alley of Naples). El caballero del dragon (US: Star Knight). La sposa americana. 1986: The Men's Club. Off Beat. The Inquiry. Blindside. 1987: Hem. The White Whale. Hello Actors Studio. Maledetto ferragosto/Dark Summer. Dear America (voice only). The Pick-Up Artist. 1988: Down Where the Buffalo Go (TV). Caro Gorbaciov. The Last Temptation of Christ. 1989: The January Man. *This Ain't BeBop. 1990: Two Evil Eyes. The Two Jakes. Il grande cacciatore. Drums of Fire/The Battle of the Three Kings. 1991: Mortal Thoughts. Thelma & Louise. Bugsy. 1992: Reservoir Dogs. Sister Act. Bad Lieutenant. 1993: Rising Sun. The Young Americans. The Piano. Snake Eyes (GB: Dangerous Game). Point of No Return (GB: The Assassin). 1994: Strictly Business. It's Pat. Pulp Fiction. Imaginary Crimes. Le regard d'Ulysse (GB: Ulysses' Gaze). Somebody to Love. Monkey Trouble. 1995: Cluck. Blue in the Face. Smoke. Clockers. Get Shorty. 1996: From Dusk Till Dawn. Head Above Water. City of Industry. 1997: Cop Land. The Miracle of Pelham Bay Park. Dreaming of Julia. Fairytale – A True Story. Full Tilt Boogie. Finding Graceland (released 1999). 1998: Shadrach. Lulu on the Bridge. Three Seasons. Il mio West. 1999: Presence of Mind. Prince of Central Park. Holy Smoke. 2000: Fail Safe (TV). U-571. Texas (The Good War). Little Nicky.

Violent Men (GB: Rough Company). The Bamboo Prison. 1955: Tight Spot. Five Against the House. 1956: Storm Center. Nightfall. 1957: Run of the Arrow. Chicago Confidential. Hell Canyon Outlaws (GB: The Tall Trouble). Dino (GB: Killer Dino). 1958: Sierra Baron. Villa! Violent Road. Fort Dobbs. Appointment with a Shadow (GB: The Big Story). Desert Hell. 1959: The Young Philadelphians (GB: The City Jungle). 1960: Ten Who Dared. 1961: The Parent Trap. The Deadly Companions. 1962: Moon Pilot. 1963: Johnny Shiloh (originally for TV). Savage Sam. A Tiger Walks. 1964: The Tenderfoot (TV. GB: cinemas). The Raiders. Those Calloways. 1965: The Pleasure Seekers. The Hallelujah Trail. 1966: The Russians Are Coming, the Russians Are Coming. The Rare Breed. Way . . . Way Out. Nevada Smith. 1967: Reflections in a Golden Eye. 1968: With Six You Get Eggroll. Krakatoa, East of Java. 1969: Gaily, Gaily (GB: Chicago, Chicago). 1970: Suppose They Gave a War and Nobody Came. The Mackenzie Break. 1971: Scandalous John. Second Chance (TV). Something Big. 1974: The Yakuza. 1975: The Wind and the Lion. 1976: Joe Panther (GB: TV). Nickelodeon. The Quest (TV). 1977: In the Matter of Karen Ann Quinlan (TV). The Loneliest Runner (TV). 1978: Hooper. The Court Martial of George Armstrong Custer (TV). 1979: Meteor. The Mountain Men. 1980: ‡Hammett (released 1982). Charlie Chan and the Curse of the Dragon Queen. The Silent Lovers (TV). 1981: Sharky's Machine. 1982: Cry for the Strangers (TV). 1986: Death Before Dishonor. The B.R.A.T. Patrol (TV). 1987: The Alamo: 13 Days to Glory (TV). 1988: Young Guns. 1989: Welcome Home. Lady in a Corner (TV). Perry Mason: The Case of the Lethal Lesson (TV). 1991: The Gambler Returns: The Luck of the Draw (TV). 1993: Wind Dancer. Walking Thunder. 1995: Entertaining Angels: The Dorothy Day Story. National Lampoon's Favorite Deadly Sins. 1997: Not Your Ordinary Girl/Follow Your Heart.

†As Robert Keith Junior
‡Scenes deleted from final release print

born Keith began to play forceful leading roles from 1982, often as men trapped in some way or another. But he has not had a major success as a solo attraction and his has not become a name audiences would pay to see, although he has remained in or near leading roles. His interest in direction seems to have faded, possibly through lack of opportunity.
1979: Co-Ed Fever (TV). Friendly Fire (TV). The Rose. The Great Santini. 1980: Brubaker. 1981: Back Roads. Take This Job and Shove It. An Officer and a Gentleman. 1982: Independence Day (later Restless). The Lords of Discipline. 1983: The Golden Moment (TV). 1984: Firestarter. Gulag (cable TV. GB: cinemas). 1986: If Tomorrow Comes. †The Further Adventures of Tennessee Buck. 1987: White of the Eye. 1989: Heartbreak Hotel. 1990: Moon Over Miami. The Two Jakes. 1991: Chained Heat II/Caged Fear. Off and Running. Hotel Oklahoma. Desperate Motive. 1992: Liar's Edge. 1993: Distant Cousins/Family Reunion. Good Cop, Bad Cop. Whose Child is This? – The War for Baby Jessica (TV). Temptation. 1994: Major League II. XXXs and 000s. Raw Justice. 1995: The Sisterhood. Till the End of the Night. The Indian in the Cupboard. A Family Thing. Judge and Jury. Deadly Sins (TV). Gold Diggers: The Secret of Bear Mountain. 1996: Red Blooded. From Beyond the Grave. Head Games. Red Blooded 2. Invasion of Privacy. 1997: Burning Down the House. If Looks Could Kill (TV). 1998: Ambushed. Poodle Springs (TV). Secret of the Andes. Perfect Prey (TV). 1999: If . . . Dog . . . Rabbit. A Memory in My Heart (TV). Question of Privilege. 2000: U-571. Navy Diver.
Also as director: 1987: The Well/The Curse.

†And directed

KEITH, Brian
(Robert B. Keith) 1921–1997
Tough-looking, heavy-set American actor with thick mop of light brown hair. The son of Robert Keith (although nothing like his father), he was cast as rugged frontier scouts, grouchy fathers and craggy types with hearts of gold. Became more gruff and granite-like as the years progressed. Dying from lung cancer in June 1997, Keith shot himself.
1924: †Pied Piper Malone. 1947: Boomerang! Kiss of Death. The Naked City. 1948: Portrait of Jennie (GB: Jennie). 1951: Fourteen Hours. 1953: Arrowhead. Jivaro (GB: Lost Treasure of the Amazon). 1954: Alaska Seas. The

KEITH, David 1954–
Pugnacious, strongly-built American actor with wry smile and light, tufty hair. Often in cocksure roles, he can also play sensitive characters when the occasion demands. Similar in looks to Dennis Quaid (qv) and Micky Dolenz of Monkees fame, Tennessee-

KELLER, Marthe (Marte Keller) 1945–
Dark-haired, well-scrubbed, Swiss-born actress whose budding dancing career was cut short by a skiing accident. Turning to acting, she built up a solid reputation on stage before becoming a sporadic visitor to the screen. Hollywood took her up belatedly in 1976, publicists knocking years off her age in trying to present her as a young romantic star. But after six years of American films, she returned to the continent.
1966: Funeral in Berlin. 1967: Wild Reiter GmbH. 1968: Le diable par le queue. 1969: Les caprices de Marie (US: Give Her the Moon).

1971: *La vieille fille. Un cave.* 1972: *Elle court, elle court la banlieue* (GB: TV, as *Love in the Suburbs*). *La raison du plus fou.* 1973: *Toute une vie* (GB and US: *And Now My Love*). *La chute d'un corps.* 1974: *Die Antwort kennt nur der Wind.* 1975: *Par le antiche scale* (GB and US: *Down the Ancient Stairs*). *Le guépier.* 1976: *Marathon Man. Black Sunday.* 1977: *Bobby Deerfield.* 1978: *Fedora.* 1980: *The Formula. Les uns et les autres.* 1981: *The Amateur.* 1982: *Wagner* (TV). 1983: *Femmes de personne.* 1985: *Joan Lui. Rouge baiser.* 1987: *Oci ciornie* (GB and US: *Dark Eyes*). *Una vittoria.* 1989: *The Nightmare Years. Seven Minutes/Georg Elser.* 1991: *Memory* (US: *Lapse of Memory*). 1993: *Mon amie Max.* 1995: *According to Pereira.* 1996: *Seul avec toi. Nuits blanches.* 1997: *'K'.* 1998: *Elles. L'école de la chair.* 1999: *Le derrière.*

KELLERMAN, Sally 1936–
Lanky, braless Hollywood blonde, with gawky gait, distinctive wide mouth and appealingly off-beat personality. Her successful period was limited both by its lateness after disheartening years of struggle, and by the slim number of films she chose to accept after her hit as Lt 'Hot Lips' in *M*A*S*H*, a role which won her an Oscar nomination. Now in character roles, but still an intriguing performer. Also a singer.
1957: *Reform School Girl.* 1960: *Hands of a Stranger* (released 1962). 1965: *The Third Day. The Lollipop Cover* (voice only). *The Movie Maker* (TV). 1968: *The Boston Strangler.* 1969: *The April Fools. M*A*S*H.* 1970: *Brewster McCloud.* 1971: *A Reflection of Fear.* 1972: *Last of the Red Hot Lovers. Lost Horizon.* 1974: *Slither.* 1974: *Rafferty and the Gold Dust Twins.* 1976: *The Big Bus. Welcome to LA.* 1977: *The Mouse and His Child* (voice only). 1978: *She'll Be Sweet/Magee and the Lady.* 1978: *It Rained All Night the Day I Left. Verna the USO Girl* (TV). 1979: *A Little Romance. Foxes.* 1980: *Head On. Serial. Big Blonde* (TV). *Loving Couples. Melvin and Howard.* 1981: *Sweet Sixteen and Pregnant* (TV. Narrator only). 1982: *For Lovers Only* (TV). 1983: *Dempsey* (TV). *September Gun* (TV). 1985: *Secret Weapons/Sexpionage* (video). *Moving Violations. Sesame Street Presents: Follow That Bird* (voice only). 1986: *The Right Hand Man. Back to School. KGB the Secret War/Lethal! 'That's Life!' Meatballs III: Summer Job.* 1987: *Three for the Road. Someone to Love.* 1988: *Skirmish. You Can't Hurry Love. All's Fair.* 1989: *Boris*

& Natasha (released 1992 on TV). *The Secret of the Ice Cave.* 1990: *Boardwalk.* 1991: *Happily Ever After* (voice only). *Drop Dead Georgeous/Victim of Beauty* (TV). 1992: *The Player.* 1993: *Younger and Younger.* 1994: *Prêt-à-Porter* (US: *Ready to Wear*). *Mirror Mirror 2: Raven Dance.* 1995: *It's My Party.* 1996: *The Game.* 1997: *The Lay of the Land. The Maze.* 1998: *Columbo: Ashes to Ashes* (TV). 1999: *Bar Hopping. Live Virgin.*

KELLY, Gene (Eugene Kelly) 1912–1996
Dark-haired American dancer of Irish extraction, who could also sing in a light but distinctive way. Never able to convince purely as an actor, he was one of M-G-M's – and Hollywood's – top stars in musicals from 1945 to 1955 and responsible, with director Stanley Donen, for several memorably innovative entertainments, in most of which he seems, on recollection, to have been a sailor on leave. Astaire's only real rival as a dancing star – though their styles were very different, Kelly's image being much less elegant – he was given a special Oscar in 1951. Married (first of three) to Betsy Blair from 1941 to 1957. His second wife, choreographer Jean Coyne, died in 1973. Oscar nomination for *Anchors Aweigh.* Died after a series of strokes.
1942: *For Me and My Gal* (GB: *For Me and My Girl*). 1943: *Dubarry Was a Lady. Pilot No. 5. Thousands Cheer. The Cross of Lorraine.* 1944: *Cover Girl. Christmas Holiday. Ziegfeld Follies* (released 1946). 1945: *Anchors Aweigh.* 1947: *Living in a Big Way.* 1948: *Words and Music. The Pirate. The Three Musketeers. Take Me Out to the Ball Game* (GB: *Everybody's Cheering*). 1949: *On the Town.* 1950: *Summer Stock* (GB: *If You Feel Like Singing*). *The Black Hand.* 1951: *An American in Paris. It's a Big Country.* 1952: *Singin' in the Rain. The Devil Makes Three. Love is Better Than Ever* (GB: *The Light Fantastic*). 1954: *Seagulls Over Sorrento* (US: *Crest of the Wave*). *Brigadoon. Deep in My Heart.* 1955: *It's Always Fair Weather. Invitation to the Dance.* 1956: *The Happy Road.* 1957: *Les Girls.* 1958: *Marjorie Morningstar.* 1960: *Inherit the Wind. Let's Make Love.* 1964: *What a Way to Go!* 1967: *The Young Girls of Rochefort.* 1973: *40 Carats.* 1974: *That's Entertainment!* 1976: *That's Entertainment Part Two.* 1977: *Viva Knievel!* 1980: *Xanadu.* 1981: *Reporters. America's Sweetheart: the Mary Pickford Story* (narrator only). 1985: *That's Dancing!* 1994: *That's*

Entertainment! III.
As director: 1949: *On the Town* (co-directed). 1952: *Singin in the Rain* (co-directed). 1955: *Invitation to the Dance.* 1956: *The Happy Road.* 1958: *The Tunnel of Love.* 1962: *Gigot.* 1967: *A Guide for the Married Man.* 1969: *Hello, Dolly!* 1970: *The Cheyenne Social Club.* 1975: *Woman of the Year* (TV). 1976: *That's Entertainment Part Two* (new sequences). 1985: *That's Dancing!*

KELLY, Grace 1928–1982
Straight-faced blonde American actress, with peculiarly clipped speech, mostly in strait-laced leading roles, although Alfred Hitchcock did his best to bring out her latent sexuality in her three films for him. Very striking in *High Noon* and strikingly drab in *The Country Girl*, for which she won an Oscar. Her career remained frustratingly unfulfilled, however, when the 'fair Miss Frigidaire' (as Sinatra called her character in *High Society*) married Prince Rainier of Monaco in 1956 and retired. Died from a brain haemorrhage after a car crash. Also received an Oscar nomination for *Mogambo.*
1951: *Fourteen Hours.* 1952: *High Noon.* 1953: *Mogambo.* 1954: *Rear Window. Dial M for Murder. The Country Girl. Green Fire. The Bridges at Toko-Ri.* 1955: *To Catch a Thief.* 1956: *High Society. The Swan.* 1959: *Invitation to Monte Carlo.* 1978: *The Children of Theatre Street* (narrator only).

KELLY, Jack
See KELLY, Nancy

KELLY, Judy 1913–
Australian-born blonde star of British films in the thirties. Never settled down as a top star,

seeming to alternate between leads and supporting roles. Her sophisticated personality often got her cast as 'other women', and with the realism of wartime, her popularity wavered.

1928: Adam's Apple (US: Honeymoon Ahead). 1931: Sleepless Nights. 1932: Money Talks. Lord Camber's Ladies. 1933: Hawleys of High Street. Their Night Out. The Love Nest. The Private Life of Henry VIII. Crime on the Hill. Mannequin. The Black Abbot. Four Masked Men. 1934: Anything Might Happen. Things Are Looking Up. 1935: It's a Bet. Royal Cavalcade (US: Regal Cavalcade). Marry the Girl. Charing Cross Road. Captain Bill. 1936: Under Proof. First Offence. A Star Fell From Heaven. Aren't Men Beasts! 1937: Ship's Concert. Make Up. Boys Will Be Girls. The Price of Folly. Over She Goes. The Last Chance. 1938: Jane Steps Out. Luck of the Navy (US: North Sea Patrol). Première (US: One Night in Paris). Queer Cargo (US: Pirates of the Seven Seas). 1939: Dead Man's Shoes. The Midas Touch. At the Villa Rose (US: House of Mystery). 1940: George and Margaret. Saloon Bar. 1942: Tomorrow We Live (US: At Dawn We Die). 1943: The Butler's Dilemma. 1944: It Happened One Sunday. 1945: Dead of Night. 1947: Dancing with Crime. 1948: Warning to Wantons.

KELLY, Nancy 1921–1995
Dark-haired, ladylike, decorous American actress, often in submissive roles. A child model and occasional actress, she was only really in films from 1938 to 1946, before taking up the stage career upon which she had set her heart. Her brother, Jack Kelly (1927–1992) also had a sporadic film career, winning more success as one of the stars of TV western series Maverick. Nancy was briefly (1941–1942) married to Edmond O'Brien (qv), the first of her three husbands. She died from diabetes complications the day after the death of her third husband. Oscar nominee for The Bad Seed.

1926: The Great Gatsby. Mismates. Untamed Lady. 1929: The Girl on the Barge. 1934: Convention Girl (GB: Atlantic City Romance). 1938: Submarine Patrol. Tailspin. 1939: Jesse James. Frontier Marshal. Stanley and Livingstone. 1940: He Married His Wife. Private Affairs. Sailor's Lady. One Night in the Tropics. 1941: Scotland Yard. A Very Young Lady. Parachute Battalion. 1942: Fly by Night (GB: Secret of G. 32). To the Shores of

Tripoli. Friendly Enemies. 1943: Tornado. Women in Bondage. Tarzan's Desert Mystery. 1944: Show Business. Gambler's Choice. 1945: Song of the Sarong. Betrayal from the East. Double Exposure. The Woman Who Came Back. Follow That Woman. 1946: Murder in the Music Hall. 1956: The Bad Seed. Crowded Paradise. 1975: The Imposter (TV). 1977: Murder at the World Series (TV).

KELLY, Paul 1899–1956
Tall, upright, grim-looking American actor (of Irish parentage), in films as a child. Went grey early – hardly surprising as he was jailed in 1927 for the manslaughter of his mistress's husband (he married her in 1931 and she was killed in a car crash in 1940) after a fight. On his release from prison he became a staunch star of 'B' features and occasional villain of bigger films, but did all his finest work on stage. Died from a heart attack.

1908: *A Good Little Devil. 1911: *Captain Barnacle, Diplomat. *How Milly Became An Actress. 1912: *A Juvenile Love Affair. *Captain Barnacle's Waif. *An Expensive Shine. 1913: *The Mouse and the Lion. *Counsellor Bobby. 1914: *Buddy's First Call. *Buddy's Downfall. *Heartease. Lillian's Dilemma. 1915: *The Jarr Family Discovers Harlem (and subsequent 48-film series). *The Shabbies. *A Family Picnic. 1916: *Myrtle the Manicurist. *Claudia. 1917: Knights of the Square Table. 1918: Fit to Fight. 1919: Anne of Green Gables. 1920: Uncle Sam of Freedom Ridge. 1921: The Old Oaken Bucket. The Great Adventure. 1926: The New Klondike. 1927: Special Delivery. Slide, Kelly, Slide. 1932: The Girl from Calgary. 1933: Broadway thru a Keyhole. 1934: Side Streets (US: Woman in Her Thirties). Blind Date (GB: Her Sacrifice). Death on the Diamond. The Love Captive. School for Girls. 1935: When a Man's a Man. The President Vanishes (GB: Strange Conspiracy). Silk Hat Kid. Speed Devils. Public Hero Number One. Star of Midnight. My Marriage. 1936: Here Comes Trouble. It's a Great Life. The Song and Dance Man. Women Are Trouble. The Accusing Finger. The Country Beyond. Murder with Pictures. 1937: The Frame-Up. Join the Marines. Parole Racket. Fit for a King. Navy Blue and Gold. It Happened Out West (GB: The Man from the Big City). 1938: The Nurse from Brooklyn. Torchy Blane in Panama (GB: Trouble in Panama). Juvenile Court. Island in the Sky. Adventure in Sahara. The Missing Guest. The Devil's Party. 1939: Forged Passport. The

Flying Irishman. Within the Law. 6,000 Enemies. The Roaring Twenties. Invisible Stripes. 1940: The Howards of Virginia (GB: The Tree of Liberty). Girls Under 21. Wyoming (GB: Bad Man of Wyoming). Queen of the Mob. Flight Command. 1941: Ziegfeld Girl. Parachute Battalion. Mystery Ship. I'll Wait for You. Mr and Mrs North. 1942: Call Out the Marines. Tarzan's New York Adventure. Tough As They Come. The Secret Code (serial). Flying Tigers. Gang Busters (serial). Not A Ladies' Man. 1943: The Man from Music Mountain. 1944: The Story of Dr Wassell. Dead Man's Eyes. Faces in the Fog. 1945: China's Little Devils. Grissly's Millions. Allotment Wives (GB: Woman in the Case). San Antonio. 1946: The Cat Creeps. Deadline for Murder. Strange Journey. The Glass Alibi. 1947: Fear in the Night. Spoilers of the North. Adventure Island. Crossfire. 1949: Thelma Jordon (GB: The File on Thelma Jordon). Side Street. There's a Girl in My Heart. 1950: Frenchie. The Secret Fury. Guilty of Treason (GB: Treason). 1951: The Painted Hills. 1952: Springfield Rifle. 1953: Gunsmoke! Split Second. 1954: Duffy of San Quentin (US: Men Behind Bars). Johnny Dark. The High and the Mighty. The Steel Cage. 1955: The Square Jungle. Narcotics Squad. 1956: Storm Center. 1957: Bail Out at 43,000 (GB: Bale Out at 43,000).

KENDALL, Henry 1897–1962
Dark-haired, thickly-built British stage star with distinctive personality and wide range. He became a big star of the British cinema in the thirties, making an enormous number of light comedies and dramas, often as the bespectacled hero who came through half by luck and half by judgment. Returned to the stage in 1938: thereafter only filmed occasionally. Died from a heart attack.

1921: Mr Pim Passes By. Tilly of Bloomsbury. 1930: French Leave. 1931: The House Opposite. The Flying Fool. Rich and Strange (US: East of Shanghai). 1932: Mr Bill the Conqueror (US: The Man Who Won). Watch Beverly. The Innocents of Chicago (US: Why Saps Leave Home). The Iron Stair. 1933: The Shadow. Counsel's Opinion. The Ghost Camera. This Week of Grace. The Flaw. King of the Ritz. Timbuctoo. The Man Outside. Great Stuff. The Stickpin. 1934: Without You. The Girl in Possession. The Man I Want. Death at Broadcasting House. Crazy People. Leave It to Blanche. Sometimes Good. Guest of Honour. 1935: Death on the Set (US: Murder on the

Set). Lend Me Your Wife. Three Witnesses. A Wife Or Two. 1936: Twelve Good Men. The Amazing Quest of Ernest Bliss (US: Romance and Riches). The Mysterious Mr Davis. Take a Chance. 1937: Side Street Angel. It's Not Cricket. The Compulsory Wife. Ship's Concert. School for Husbands. 1943: The Butler's Dilemma. 1945: 29 Acacia Avenue (US: The Facts of Love). 1949: Helter Skelter. 1952: The Voice of Merrill (US: Murder Will Out). 1955: An Alligator Named Daisy. 1961: The Shadow of the Cat. Nothing Barred.

KENDALL, Kay
(Justine Kendall McCarthy) 1926–1959
Effervescent redhead with innate elegance – and a sparkling sense of sophisticated comedy that it took British films a long time to discover (she was a chorus girl at 12, in films at 17). She was just becoming a big international star when struck down by leukemia. Married to Rex Harrison from 1957 to her death.
1944: Fiddlers Three. Champagne Charlie. Dreaming. 1945: Waltz Time. Caesar and Cleopatra. 1946: Spring Song (US: Spring Time). London Town (US: My Heart Goes Crazy). 1950: Night and the City. Dance Hall. Happy Go Lovely. 1951: Lady Godiva Rides Again. 1952: Wings of Danger (US: Dead on Course). Curtain Up. It Started in Paradise. 1953: Mantrap (US: Man in Hiding). Street of Shadows (US: Shadow Man). Genevieve. The Square Ring. Meet Mr Lucifer. 1954: Fast and Loose. Doctor in the House. Abdullah's Harem (GB: Abdullah the Great). 1955: The Constant Husband. Simon and Laura. The Adventures of Quentin Durward (US: Quentin Durward). 1957: Les Girls. 1958: The Reluctant Debutante. 1959: Once More, with Feeling!

KENDALL, Suzy (Frieda Harrison) 1944–
Light-haired, rather sharp-featured, bird-like British leading lady, not unlike Julie Christie to look at. A former fashion model, she matured into a competent enough actress to make one wonder why she disappeared from the film scene. Married/divorced actor comedian-musician Dudley Moore (qv).
1965: The Liquidator. Up Jumped a Swagman. Circus of Fear (US: Psycho-Circus). 1966: The Sandwich Man. To Sir, With Love. 1967: The Penthouse. 30 is a Dangerous Age, Cynthia. Up the Junction. 1968: Fraulein Doktor. 1969: The Gamblers. Color Me Dead. The Bird with the Crystal Plumage (GB: The Gallery Murders). 1970: Assault (US: In The Devil's

Garden). Darker than Amber. 1972: Fear is the Key. 1973: Tales That Witness Madness. Craze. I corpi presentano tracce di violenza carnale / Torso. Storia di una monaca di clasura. 1975: Spasmo. To the Bitter End. 1977: Adventures of a Private Eye. 1987: Aenigma.

KENNEDY, Arthur
(John A. Kennedy) 1914–1990
It's a long way down from City for Conquest and High Sierra to Emmanuelle on Taboo Island, but poor Arthur Kennedy travelled every step of the way. This fair-haired American actor with a slightly fretful look and crooked smile spent six years on stage before deciding on a film career. He became a star without quite heading the cast, was five times Oscar-nominated, and ran up a good row of often likeable western villains. His roles deteriorated in quality from 1958, and in the seventies became increasingly frenzied. Died from a brain tumour.
1940: City for Conquest. Santa Fé Trail. 1941: High Sierra. Knockout. Highway West. Strange Alibi. They Died with their Boots On. Bad Men of Missouri. 1942: Desperate Journey. 1943: Air Force. Devotion (released 1946). 1947: Boomerang! Cheyenne. 1949: The Window. Champion. Too Late for Tears. The Walking Hills. Chicago Deadline. 1950: The Glass Menagerie. Bright Victory (GB: Lights Out). 1951: Red Mountain. 1952: Rancho Notorious. The Girl in White (GB: So Bright the Flame). Bend of the River (GB: Where the River Bends). The Lusty Men. 1954: Impulse. 1955: Crashout. The Man from Laramie. The Naked Dawn. Trial. The Desperate Hours. 1956: The Rawhide Years. 1957: Peyton Place. 1958: Twilight for the Gods. Some Came Running. 1959: A Summer

Place. Home is the Hero. 1960: Elmer Gantry. In the Presence of Mine Enemies (TV). 1961: Claudelle Inglish (GB: Young and Eager). Murder She Said. 1962: Barabbas. Hemingway's Adventures of a Young Man (GB: Adventures of a Young Man). Lawrence of Arabia. 1964: Cheyenne Autumn. Italiano brave gente (GB: Attack and Retreat). 1965: Murieta (GB: Vendetta). Joy in the Morning. 1966: Nevada Smith. Fantastic Voyage. The Brave Rifles (narrator only). 1967: Anzio (GB: The Battle for Anzio). Shark! (released 1970). Il Chica del Lunes (US: Monday's Child). 1968: A Minute to Pray, a Second to Die (GB: Dead or Alive). Day of the Evil Gun. The Prodigal Gun. 1969: Hail Hero. 1970: The Movie Murderer (TV). 1971: Glory Boy (GB: My Old Man's Place). A Death of Innocence (TV). The President's Plane is Missing (TV). 1972: Crawlspace (TV). 1973: Ricco / The Dirty Mob. Baciamo le mane (GB: Family Killer. US: Mafia War). 1974: Nakia (TV). The Living Dead at the Manchester Morgue. The Antichrist (US: The Tempter). 1975: Killer Cop / The Police Can't Move. 1976: The Sentinel. Roma a mano armata (US: Brutal Justice). Nove ospiti per un delitto. 1977: Porco Mondo. Cyclone. The Last Angels. Emmanuelle on Taboo Island. 1978: La cueva de los triburones (GB: The Shark's Cave. US: Cave of Sharks). Ab Morgen sind wir reich und ehrlich / Rich and Respectable. Covert Action / Sono state un agente CIA. 1979: The Humanoid. 1980: Due nelle stelle. 1989: Signs of Life. 1990: Grandpa.

KENNEDY, George 1925–
Scowling, glowering American actor with a powerful build and thinning fair hair. He turned to an acting career after 16 years in the army and surprised many people by becoming a star – mainly on the strength of his Academy Award for Cool Hand Luke in 1967. The transition from villains to good-hearted Joes was almost immediate, but he has been a valuable asset to some poor films.
1957: Will Success Spoil Rock Hunter? (GB: Oh! For a Man). 1961: The Little Shepherd of Kingdom Come. 1962: Lonely Are the Brave. 1963: The Man from the Diners' Club. Charade. 1964: Strait Jacket. Island of the Blue Dolphins. McHale's Navy. Silent Witness. Hush . . . Hush, Sweet Charlotte. 1965: In Harm's Way. Shenandoah. Mirage. The Sons of Katie Elder. The Flight of the Phoenix. See How They Run (TV). 1967: Hurry Sundown. The Dirty Dozen. Cool Hand Luke. The Ballad

of Josie. 1968: Bandolero! The Pink Jungle. The Boston Strangler. The Legend of Lylah Clare. 1969: Guns of the Magnificent Seven. The Good Guys and the Bad Guys. Gaily, Gaily (GB: Chicago Chicago). . . . tick . . . tick . . . tick. Airport. 1970: Zigzag (GB: False Witness). Dirty Dingus Magee. 1971: Fools' Parade (GB: Dynamite Man from Glory Jail). The Badge or the Cross (TV). The Priest Killer (TV). 1972: A Great American Tragedy (TV. GB: Man at the Crossroads). Lost Horizon. 1973: A Cry in the Wilderness (TV). Deliver Us from Evil (TV). Cahill: United States Marshal (GB: Cahill). 1974: Thunderbolt and Lightfoot. Earthquake. Airport 1975. 1975: The Blue Knight 2 (TV). The 'Human' Factor. The Eiger Sanction. 1977: Airport 77. Ningen no shomei. 1978: Brass Target. Death on the Nile. Mean Dog Blues. Search and Destroy (released 1981). 1979: The Double McGuffin. Steel. The Concorde – Airport '79 (GB: Airport '80 . . . the Concorde). Proof of the Man. Never Say Never (TV). 1980: Death Ship. Hotwire. Virus. Just Before Dawn. 1981: Modern Romance. Carnauba/A Rare Breed. The Archer – Fugitive from the Empire (TV). 1982: Wacko. The Jupiter Menace. 1984: Bliss (TV). Bolero. Chattanooga Choo Choo. Radioactive Dreams. Rigged/Hit and Run. 1985: Half Nelson (TV). Savage Dawn. International Airport (TV). 1986: The Delta Force. The Gunfighters (TV). Liberty (TV). 1987: Creepshow 2. Counterforce. Private Roads/No Trespassing. Top Line. Nightmare at Noon (released 1990). 1988: Demonwarp. Uninvited. What Price Victory? (TV). Born to Race. The Naked Gun: From the Files of Police Squad! 1989: The Terror Within. Ministry of Vengeance. 1990: Brain Dead. Mayumi (TV). Good Cops, Bad Cops (TV). 1991: The Naked Gun 2½: The Smell of Fear. Hangfire. Hired to Kill. Autobahn (US: Trabbi Goes to Hollywood). 1992: Distant Justice. Intensive Care. Final Shot: The Hank Getters Story (TV). 1994: Naked Gun 33⅓: The Final Insult. 1996: Cats Don't Dance (voice only). 1998: Dennis the Menace 2/Dennis Strikes Again. Countdown to Esmeralda Bay. Dallas: War of the Ewings (TV). Small Soldiers (voice only). National Lampoon's Men in White (v).
As director: 1965: *Three Songs.

KENNEY, James 1930–1982
Fair-haired British boy actor with clean-cut looks, the son of radio and music-hall comic Horace Kenney. After Cosh Boy, one of the first British films to get an X certificate, he became typed in callow roles. In the sixties he spent four years in Australia and two in America, but after that he was little seen.
1942: The Young Mr Pitt. 1946: London Town (US: My Heart Goes Crazy). 1947: Circus Boy. Vice Versa. 1948: The Guinea Pig. 1949: Trapped by the Terror. 1951: Captain Horatio Hornblower RN. The Magic Box. Outcast of the Islands. 1952: Gift Horse (US: Glory at Sea). Cosh Boy (US: The Slasher). The Gentle Gunman. 1953: Thought to Kill. 1954: The Good Die Young. The Sea Shall Not Have Them. The Red Dress. 1955: The Love Match. Above Us the Waves. Doctor at Sea. 1956: The Gelignite Gang. 1957: Yangtse Incident (US: Battle Hell). Seven Thunders (US: The Beasts of Marseilles). Son of a Stranger. 1958: Hidden Homicide. 1959: No Safety Ahead. 1962: Ambush in Leopard Street. 1966: A Big Hand for the Little Lady (GB: Big Deal at Dodge City).

KENSIT, Patsy 1965–
Very fair-haired, slightly bored-looking, childlike British actress with creamy pale complexion, in show business from early childhood. The cutest of tots, she grew up to have pouty sex-kitten looks, but got solid acting grounding with the Royal Shakespeare Company. The unjustly panned Absolute Beginners looked to have scuppered her adult career, but she foraged away diligently in a variety of roles, and, though not always the strongest of actresses, sometimes stole scenes from the stars when billed lower down the cast. Married/divorced (3rd) singer/musician Liam Gallagher.
1972: For the Love of Ada. 1974: The Great Gatsby. 1975: Alfie Darling (US: Oh! Alfie). 1976: The Blue Bird. 1979: Hanover Street. 1984: The Corsican Brothers (TV). 1985: Silas Marner (TV). 1986: Absolute Beginners. 1988: A Chorus of Disapproval. 1989: Lethal Weapon 2. Chicago Joe and the Showgirl. 1990: The Skipper/Kill Cruise. Bullseye! Blue Tornado. 1991: Twenty One. Beltenebros (GB: Prince of Shadows). Blame It on the Bellboy. Timebomb. Adam Bede (TV). 1992: The Turn of the Screw. Does This Mean We're Married? (TV). 1993: Bitter Harvest. Kleptomania. The Storm. 1994: Full Eclipse. Dream Man. Fall from Grace (TV). Tunnel Vision. 1995: At the Midnight Hour. Angels and Insects. Love and Betrayal – The Mia Farrow Story (TV). 1996: Grace of My Heart. Road to Nowhere. Human Bomb (TV). 1999: Speedway Junky. The Pavilion. Janice Beard 45WPM. Best.

KENT, Jean (Joan Summerfield) 1916–
Strawberry-blonde British actress with knowing smile and faintly haughty mien, in show business at 12. Could play spiteful hussies and femmes fatales with the best of them and in the late forties got typed in the role. Later expressed regret at not having renewed her studio contract in 1952. As a freelance she was never the same force. Active in the theatre into her seventies. Married to Albanian actor Yusuf Ramart from 1946 to his death in 1989.
1934: †The Rocks of Valpré (US: High Treason). 1935: †Who's Your Father? 1939: ‡Frozen Limits. 1940: ‡Hullo Fame! 1942: It's That Man Again. 1943: Miss London Ltd. Warn That Man. 1944: Bees in Paradise. Fanny by Gaslight (US: Man of Evil). Waterloo Road. Champagne Charlie. Soldier, Sailor. 2,000 Women. Madonna of the Seven Moons. 1945: The Wicked Lady. The Rake's Progress (US: Notorious Gentleman). 1946: Carnival. Caravan. The Magic Bow. 1947: The Man Within (US: The Smugglers). The Loves of Joanna Godden. 1948: Good Time Girl. Bond Street. Sleeping Car to Trieste. 1949: Trottie True (US: Gay Lady). 1950: The Woman in Question (US: Five Angles on Murder). Her Favourite Husband (US: The Taming of Dorothy). The Reluctant Widow. 1951: The Browning Version. 1952: The Lost Hours (US: The Big Frame). 1955: Before I Wake (US: Shadow of Fear). 1957: The Prince and the Showgirl. 1958: Bonjour Tristesse. Grip of the Strangler (US: The Haunted Strangler). 1959: Beyond This Place (US: Web of Evidence). Please Turn Over. 1960: Bluebeard's Ten Honeymoons. 1976: Shout at the Devil.

†As Joan Summerfield ‡As Jean Carr

KERR, Deborah (D. Kerr-Trimmer) 1921–
Lovely red-haired Scottish-born leading lady whose angular beauty got her cast in gentle, ladylike roles. A star of the British cinema in only her third film, she went to Hollywood in 1947, where her struggle to break the well-bred image was unsuccessful, despite her torrid love scenes in From Here to Eternity; the vivacious, fun-loving lady of real life remained a suppressed image for the screen, although she did make some extremely good films within that restriction between 1956 and 1961. Nominated six times for the best actress Oscar but never won; perhaps her unluckiest losing performance was in The

Sundowners. Special Oscar, though, in 1994.
1940: †Contraband (US: Blackout). 1941: Major Barbara. Love on the Dole. Hatter's Castle. Penn of Pennsylvania (US: The Courageous Mr Penn). 1942: The Day Will Dawn (US: The Avengers). 1943: The Life and Death of Colonel Blimp (US: Colonel Blimp). 1945: Perfect Strangers (US: Vacation from Marriage). 1946: I See a Dark Stranger (US: The Adventuress). 1947: Black Narcissus. The Hucksters. 1948: If Winter Comes. 1949: Edward My Son. Please Believe Me. 1950: King Solomon's Mines. 1951: Quo Vadis? Thunder in the East (released 1953). 1952: The Prisoner of Zenda. 1953: Julius Caesar. Young Bess. Dream Wife. From Here to Eternity. 1955: The End of the Affair. 1956: The King and I. The Proud and Profane. Tea and Sympathy. 1957: Heaven Knows, Mr Allison. An Affair to Remember. 1958: Separate Tables. Bonjour Tristesse. The Journey. 1959: Count Your Blessings. Beloved Infidel. 1960: The Sundowners. The Grass is Greener. 1961: The Naked Edge. The Innocents. 1963: The Chalk Garden. 1964: The Night of the Iguana. 1965: Marriage on the Rocks. 1966: Eye of the Devil. 1967: Casino Royale. 1968: Prudence and the Pill. 1969: The Arrangement. The Gypsy Moths. 1982: Witness for the Prosecution (TV). 1985: The Assam Garden. Reunion at Fairborough (TV).

†Scenes deleted from final release print

KEYES, Evelyn 1919–
Cat-like American blonde with lithe figure and knowing smile. Mostly played decorative minxes, but was occasionally very good in dramatic roles. A swinger in private life as evidenced by the publication of her somewhat

scarlet memoirs in the seventies. Her first husband shot himself a month after they separated; her second and third, Charles Vidor (1943–1945) and John Huston (1946–1950) were directors. Her fourth husband, in 1957, was eight-times-wed bandleader Artie Shaw.
1937: Artists and Models. 1938: The Buccaneer. Men with Wings. Artists and Models Abroad (GB: Stranded in Paris). Sons of the Legion. Dangerous to Know. 1939: Paris Honeymoon. Union Pacific. Sudden Money. Slightly Honorable. Gone with the Wind. 1940: Before I Hang. Beyond the Sacramento (GB: Power of Justice). The Lady in Question. 1941: The Face behind the Mask. Here Comes Mr Jordan. Ladies in Retirement. 1942: The Adventures of Martin Eden. Flight Lieutenant. 1943: There's Something About a Soldier. Dangerous Blondes. The Desperadoes. *Sweet Kisses. *Stepping Along. 1944: Nine Girls. Strange Affair. 1945: A Thousand and One Nights. 1946: The Jolson Story. Renegades. The Thrill of Brazil. 1947: Johnny O'Clock. 1948: Enchantment. The Mating of Millie. 1949: Mrs Mike. Mr Soft Touch (GB: House of Settlement). 1950: The Killer That Stalked New York (GB: The Frightened City). 1951: Smuggler's Island. Iron Man. The Prowler. 1952: One Big Affair. Rough Shoot (US: Shoot First). 1953: 99 River Street. 1954: Hell's Half Acre. It Happened in Paris. 1955: Top of the World. The Seven Year Itch. 1956: Around the World in 80 Days. 1972: Across 110th Street. 1985: Artie Shaw: Time is All You've Got. 1987: Return to Salem's Lot. 1988: John Huston. Wicked Stepmother.

KIDDER, Margot
(Margaret Kidder) 1948–
Attractively sharp-faced actress with centre-fold figure, wild dark hair and strong personality. The girl from the wilds of Northwest Canada (born in Yellow Knife to a mining engineer) broke into acting when her family moved to Toronto. She had a low-key career as a leading lady before marriage to writer Thomas McGuane brought retirement to a ranch in Montana. After the divorce, she returned to films as Lois Lane in Superman (although she hardly seemed ideal casting). She has on the whole not found roles that extended her undoubted talent. Further married to actor John Heard (qv) for six days and to director Philippe de Broca from 1983. This, too, ended in divorce. Recovered from a severe spinal injury in the early 1990s.

Spent time in a psychiatric hospital in 1996.
1968: The Best Damn Fiddler From Calabogie to Kaladar. 1969: Gaily Gaily (GB: Chicago, Chicago). 1970: Quackser Fortune Has a Cousin in the Bronx. 1971: Suddenly Single (TV). 1972: The Bounty Man (TV). Sisters (GB: Blood Sisters). 1973: A Quiet Day in Belfast/Quiet Days at Belfast. Such Dust as Dreams Are Made On (TV). The Suicide Club (TV). 1974: Honky Tonk (TV). The Dion Brothers (TV. GB: cinemas, as the Gravy Train). The Reincarnation of Peter Proud. Black Christmas. 1975: 92 in the Shade. The Great Waldo Pepper. 1978: Superman. 1979: The Amityville Horror. Mr Mike's Mondo Video. 1980: Miss Right. Willie & Phil. Superman II. 1981: Some Kind of Hero. Shoot the Sun Down (completed 1976). 1982: Heartaches. Trenchcoat. 1983: Louisiana. Superman III. 1984: The Glitter Dome (originally for TV and shown there in 1983). 1985: Little Treasure. Keeping Track (released 1987). 1986: Picking Up the Pieces (TV). GoBots: Battle of the Rock Lords (voice only). Vanishing Act (TV). 1987: Superman IV: The Quest for Peace. The Wonderful Wizard of Oz (voice only). 1988: Body of Evidence (TV). 1989: Mob Story. White Room. 1990: The Dispossessed. 1991: Delirious. 1993: Crime and Punishment. La Florida. 1994: Maverick. Eyes That Went Away. The Pornographer. Windrunner. Under a Killing Moon. Young Ivanhoe (TV). 1995: Henry & Verlin. Bloodknot. 1996: Never Met Picasso. 1997: Twisted. Silent Cradle. The Planet of Junior Brown. 1998: The Clown at Midnight. 1999: †Tail Lights Fade. The Hi-Line. The Annihilation of Fish. Brilliant. The Nightmare Man. Crime in Connecticut: The Story of Alex Kelly (TV). 2000: Someone is Watching (TV). Common Ground (TV). Tribulation.

†Scenes deleted from final release print

KIDMAN, Nicole 1967–
Tall, vixen-like actress with wild red hair, born in Hawaii but raised in Australia. Coming to acting through local theatre groups, she proved an outstanding teenage actress, especially in the mini-series Five-Mile Creek, Vietnam and Bangkok Hilton, and proved equally capable of projecting wholesomeness or devious aggression. The latter of this series (and the suspense movie Dead Calm) brought her to the attention of Hollywood, where, after marrying superstar Tom Cruise (qv), she had difficulty in establishing

herself as an actress of merit until forceful performances as chilling characters in *Malice* and *To Die For* brought her a new respect.
1982: Bush Christmas. 1983: Prince and the Great Race. BMX Bandits. 1985: Archer. The Wacky World of Wills and Burke. 1986: Windrider. 1987: An Australian in Rome. Night Master. The Bit Part. 1988: Dead Calm. 1989: Emerald City. Chase through the Night (TV). Flirting. 1990: Days of Thunder. 1991: Billy Bathgate. 1992: Far and Away. 1993: Malice. My Life. 1995: Batman Forever. To Die For. 1996: The Portrait of a Lady. The Leading Man. 1997: The Peacemaker. 1998: Practical Magic. 1999: Eyes Wide Shut. 2000: Birthday Girl. Moulin Rouge.

KILMER, Val 1959–
Fair-haired American actor with 'lined' lips and pretty-boy looks, a New Year's Eve baby of part Cherokee Indian descent who began as a prospective writer and dramatist before taking a sidestep into acting. After a series of dashing, sometimes arrogant heroes in action and comedy, he tried some more serious stuff. If some performances lacked intensity, this was not true of his portraits of doomed Jim Morrison in *The Doors* and equally doomed Doc Holliday in *Tombstone*. He moved into the mainline movie big league when chosen to replace Michael Keaton (*qv*) in the third Batman film, but remains a nearly-man outside of that image. He married English actress Joanne Whalley (*qv*) in 1988; the couple divorced in 1996.
1984: Top Secret! 1985: One Too Many (TV). Real Genius. 1986: Top Gun. The Murders in the Rue Morgue (TV). 1987: The Man Who Broke 1,000 Chains (TV). 1988: Willow. Gore Vidal's Billy the Kid. 1989: Kill Me Again. 1990: The Doors. 1991: Thunderheart. 1993: True Romance. The Real McCoy. Tombstone. 1994: Dead Girl. 1995: Wings of Courage. Batman Forever. Heat. 1996: The Island of Dr Moreau. The Ghost and the Darkness. 1997: The Saint. The Prince of Egypt (voice only). 1998: At First Sight. 1999: Pleasent View Avenue/Joe the King. 2000: Pollock. Red Planet. 2001: The Salton Sea.

KINGSLEY, Ben (Krishna Banji) 1943–
Small, balding, part-Indian British star actor with distinctive features who, after being chosen from almost nowhere to star as *Gandhi* in 1981 (released 1982) and deservedly winning an Academy Award for his performance, quickly became Britain's most

perceptive and intelligent character star since Alec Guinness (*qv*), offering fully-rounded and amazingly-detailed portraits of everyday men in *Betrayal* and *Turtle Diary*. He continued to attract leading character roles into the 1990s.
1972: Fear is the Key. 1982: Gandhi. 1983: Betrayal. 1984: Camille (TV). 1985: Turtle Diary. Silas Marner (TV). 1986: Harem. 1987: The Sahara Secret. Maurice. Testimony. The Sealed Train. 1988: Pascali's Island. Without a Clue. 1989: Slipstream. The 5th Monkey. Murderers Among Us: The Simon Wiesenthal Story (TV). Cellini: A Violent Life. 1990: The Children. Romeo Juliet (voice only). 1991: The Necessary Love. Bugsy. Freddie as FRO 7 (voice only). 1992: Sneakers. Freddie Goes to Washington (voice only. Unfinished). 1993: Dave. Searching for Bobby Fischer (GB: Innocent Moves). Schindler's List. 1994: Death and the Maiden. The Bible: Joseph. Liberation (narrator only). 1995: Species. 1996: Twelfth Night. 1997: The Assignment. Photographing Fairies. Weapons of Mass Destruction (cable TV). 1998: Parting Shots. The Confession. The Tale of Sweeney Todd (TV). 1999: Spooky House. Alice in Wonderland (TV). The Intruder. A Force More Powerful (narrator only). The Magic of Marciano. 2000: Sexy Beast. What Planet Are You From? Il cielo e sopra di noi. A Storm in Summer. Rules of Engagement. Kingdom Come. As director: 1993: Circle of the White Rose.

KINNEAR, Greg 1963–
Genial, sandy-haired American player of long-faced, laconic good looks. A diplomat's son, Kinnear grew up all over the world (but mainly in Lebanon and Greece) before returning to his native America. He started in

show business by hosting an Athens radio show. In America, he's taken the reverse of many careers, in that he's a successful chat show host who then became a successful actor. Even though he probably plays the unforceful guy who doesn't get the girl a little too often, he's already notched up an Oscar nomination for *As Good As It Gets*.
1990: Murder in Mississippi (TV). 1991: Dillinger (TV). 1993: Based on an Untrue Story (TV). 1994: Blankman. 1995: Sabrina. 1996: Beavis and Butt-head Do America (voice only). Dear God. 1997: A Smile Like Yours. As Good As it Gets. 1998: You've Got Mail. 1999: Mystery Men. 2000: Nurse Betty. What Planet Are You From? Loser. The Gift. 2001: Animal Husbandry.

KINSKI, Nastassja (N. Nakszynski) 1959–
No wonder they cast this dark-haired German actress (daughter of Klaus Kinski) in *Cat People*. She looks cat-like and dangerous. Full-lipped, with tautly attractive features, she was in uninhibited roles from an early age, playing haunted heroines whose sexual magnetism was often the axis on which the plot turned. In the late 1990s, she appeared in more conventional roles. Credited as 'Nastassia' in some early films. Married to jazzman/composer Quincy Jones.
1975: †Falsche Bewegung (GB: Wrong Movement. US: The Wrong Move). 1976: To the Devil a Daughter. 1978: Leidenschaftliche Blumchen (GB: TV, as Passion Flower Hotel. US: Virgin Campus). Cosi come sei (GB and US: Stay As You Are). 1979: Tess. 1982: One from the Heart. Cat People. Reifezeugnis (GB and US: For Your Love Only. Copyrighted 1982, but originally made in 1976 for West German TV). 1983: Frühlings-sinfonie. Exposed. La lune dans le caniveau (GB and US: The Moon in the Gutter). Unfaithfully Yours. 1984: The Hotel New Hampshire. Paris, Texas. Maria's Lovers. 1985: Revolution. 1986: Harem. 1987: Intervista/ The Interview. Maladie d'amour. 1988: Paganini. Torrents of Spring. 1989: '13'. Magdalene. On a Moonlit Night. The Secret. 1990: Il sole anche di notte. 1991: Prospero's Books. Der lachende Tod. The Secret. 1992: L'envers du décors. Night Sun. 1993: In My Room. In weiter Ferne, so nah/Faraway, So Close! 1994: La bionda/The Blonde. Blind Love. Terminal Velocity. 1995: Crackerjack. 1996: The Ring. Somebody is Waiting. One Night Stand. Fathers' Day. Little Boy Blue. Unizhenniei oskorblennie (US: The

Insulted and the Humiliated). Foolish Heart. 1998: Savior. Your Friends & Neighbors. The Lost Son. Susan's Plan. 1999: The Magic of Marciano. The Intruder. Quarantine (TV). 2000: Tuneshare. Town and Country. A Storm in Summer (TV). Kingdom Come.

†*As Nastassja Naksynski*

KIRK, Phyllis (P. Kirkegaard) 1926–
Pencil-slim brunette with chirpy personality who switched from modelling to acting in her early twenties. M-G-M signed her and dropped her; Warners used her as decoration in a variety of colour films; but she was really at her best as the spunky heroine of several low-budget black-and-white thrillers. Played Nora Charles in a TV series of *The Thin Man* from 1957 to 1959. Her acting appearances limited by a hip injury, she made a second career in public relations after 1960.
1950: Our Very Own. Two Weeks with Love. A Life of Her Own. Mrs O'Malley and Mr Malone. 1951: Three Guys Named Mike. 1952: About Face. The Iron Mistress. 1953: House of Wax. Crime Wave (GB: The City is Dark). Thunder over the Plains. 1954: River Beat. 1955: Canyon Crossroads. 1956: Johnny Concho. Back from Eternity. Made in Heaven (TV). That Woman Opposite (US: City after Midnight). 1957: The Sad Sack. Men in Her Life (TV).

KIRKWOOD, Pat 1921–
Raven-haired, strong-voiced, forceful British musical star with seemingly unlimited energy, too much it seemed for films and film audiences, who never really took to her. At first in ingenue roles (including one in Hollywood); later became well known for impersonations of old-time music-hall stars whose traditions she had inherited. Four times married, twice divorced (her second husband died). Her third husband was actor-writer Hubert Gregg (1914–).
1938: Save a Little Sunshine. 1939: Me and My Pal. Come on George. Band Waggon. 1944: Flight from Folly. 1946: No Leave, No Love. 1950: Once a Sinner. 1956: Stars in Your Eyes. 1957: After the Ball. 1977: To See Such Fun (TV).

KITT, Eartha 1927–
Black, feline American nightclub singer (a former Katherine Dunham dancer) who became known as 'That Bad Eartha' from the sexy way she wove her reedy voice through such songs as 'Just an Old-Fashioned Girl', 'I Want to be Evil' and 'Santa Baby'. Most films tried to make her into something other than a sinuous siren, and were notably unsuccessful.
1948: Casbah. 1954: New Faces. 1957: St Louis Blues. 1958: Anna Lucasta. Mark of the Hawk. The Accused. Heart of Darkness (TV). 1961: Saint of Devil's Island. 1965: Uncle Tom's Cabin. Synanon (GB: Get Off My Back). 1971: Up the Chastity Belt. 1972: Lt Schuster's Wife (TV). 1975: Friday Foster. 1978: Streets of Fear (TV). To Kill a Cop (TV). 1982: All by Myself. 1985: The Serpent Warriors. 1986: The Pink Chiquitas (voice only). 1987: Dragonard. Master of Dragonard Hill. 1989: Erik the Viking. Living Doll. 1992: Ernest Scared Stupid. Boomerang. 1993: Fatal Instinct. 1995: Unzipped. 1996: Ill Gotten Gains (released 1998). Harriet the Spy. 1998: Kingdom of the Sun (voice only). I Woke Up Early the Day I Died. 2000: The Emperor's New Groove (voice only).

KLINE, Kevin 1947–
American Shakespearian actor with unkempt brown hair, soulful eyes and, especially when moustachioed, a vague resemblance to Errol Flynn. A big star on stage, he made unsuccessful efforts to break into films (including losing the leading role in *Body Heat*) before the film version of his stage success in *The Pirates of Penzance* did the trick. Not many films since, though. 'I find myself attracted to the offbeat and oddball things, but there are very few about.' He won an Oscar for *A Fish Called Wanda*, although his best performance, and greatest mainstream success, came in the dual leading role of the brilliantly written *Dave*. He married actress Phoebe Cates (*qv*) in 1989.

1982: The Pirates of Penzance. Sophie's Choice. 1983: The Big Chill. 1985: Silverado. 1986: Violets Are Blue. 1987: Cry Freedom. 1988: A Fish Called Wanda. 1989: The January Man. 1990: I Love You to Death. 1991: Soapdish. Grand Canyon. 1992: Chaplin. Consenting Adults. 1993: Dave. 1994: Princess Caraboo. 1995: French Kiss/Paris Match. 1996: The Hunchback of Notre Dame (voice only). Looking for Richard. Shakespeare's Children. 1997: Fierce Creatures. The Ice Storm. In & Out. 1999: A Midsummer Night's Dream. Wild Wild West. 2000: The Road to El Dorado (voice only). 2001: The Anniversary Party.

KNEF, Hildegarde 1925–
Cool, sultry-looking, tallish blonde German actress, cartoonist and writer. Came to international films (where she was billed as Hildegarde Neff) as husky-voiced European ladies with bedroom eyes, often involved in espionage. Returned to German films (and stronger roles) in the fifties, and has sporadically pursued an acting career there since then. Survived numerous operations to remove cancerous growths in the early 1970s.
1945: Fahrt ins Glück. Unter den Brücken. 1946: Die Mörder sind unter uns. Träumerei. 1947: Zwischen Gestern und Morgen. 1948: Film ohne Titel. 1950: Die Sünderin (GB and US: The Sinner). 1951: Es geschehen noch Wunder. Nachts auf den Strassen. Decision before Dawn. 1952: The Snows of Kilimanjaro. Night without Sleep. Diplomatic Courier. La fête à Henriette. Alraune. Illusion in Moll. 1953: The Man Between. Eine Liebegeschichte. 1954: Gestandnis unter vier Augen. Svengali. La fille de Hambour/ The Girl from Hamburg. Madaleine und der Legionär (US: Escape from

Sahara). 1956: Subway in the Sky. 1957: Der Mann, der sich verkanfte. 1959: La strada dei giganti. 1960: Valley of the Doomed. 1962: Landru. Ballade pour un voyou. The Three-penny Opera. Lulu. Catherine of Russia. 1963: Gibraltar (GB: The Spy). And So to Bed/Das Liebeskarussel. 1964: Wartezimmer zum Jeinseits. 1965: Verdamnit zur Sünde. Mozambique. 1968: The Lost Continent. 1975: Jeder stirbt für sich allein (GB. TV: Death Always Comes Alone). 1978: Fedora. 1979: Warum die UFOs unseren Salat klauen. 1980: Checkpoint Charlie. 1984: L'avenir d'Emilie. 1980 Offret/The Sacrifice. 1988: Witchery. 1995: Für mich soll's rote Rosen regnen. 1999: Eine fast perfekte Hochzeit.

KNIGHT, Esmond 1906–1987

Serious and scholarly-looking, dark-haired British actor who progressed to star roles by the mid-thirties, but was blinded on active service during World War II. Partially regained the use of one eye later, and continued his career in stalwart character roles. Long married to his second wife, Nora Swinburne (qv).

*1928: The Blue Peter. 1931: 77 Park Lane. Romany Love. Deadlock. 1933: The Bermondsey Kid. 1934: Waltzes from Vienna (US: Strauss's Great Waltz). Lest We Forget. The Blue Squadron. Womanhood. The King of Wales. Girls Will Be Boys. Father and Son. My Old Dutch. 1935: Dandy Dick. Black Rose. Some Day. Crime Unlimited. 1936: Pagliacci (US: A Clown Must Laugh). Did I Betray? 1937: The Vicar of Bray. 1938: *What Men Live By. Weddings Are Wonderful. The Drum (US: Drums). 1939: The Arsenal Stadium Mystery. 1940: Contraband (US: Blackout). Fingers. 1941: This England. 1943: The Silver Fleet. 1944: Halfway House. A Canterbury Tale. Henry V. 1947: Black Narcissus. Holiday Camp. Uncle Silas (US: The Inheritance). The End of the River. 1948: Hamlet. The Red Shoes. 1950: Gone to Earth (US: The Wild Heart). 1951: The River. 1952: Girdle of Gold. 1953: The Steel Key. 1954: Helen of Troy. 1955: Richard III. 1956: The Battle of the River Plate (US: Pursuit of the Graf Spee). 1957: The Prince and the Showgirl. 1958: Battle of the V1 (US V1/Unseen Heroes). 1959: Sink the Bismarck! 1960: Peeping Tom. 1963: Decision at Midnight. 1965: The Spy Who Came in From the Cold. 1966: The Winter's Tale. 1969: Where's Jack? 1970: Anne of the Thousand Days. 1972: The Boy Who Turned*

Yellow. 1973: Yellow Dog. 1976: Robin and Marian. The Man in the Iron Mask (TV). 1984: Forbrydelsens Element/The Element of Crime. 1987: Superman IV: The Quest for Peace.

KNIGHT, Shirley 1936–

Ethereal, slender blonde American actress who has sought the intelligent roles for which she seemed suited, but has not had a satisfactory screen career, possibly because of her outspoken criticism of Hollywood filmmakers after she had been twice nominated for Academy Awards – in *The Dark at the Top of the Stairs* and *Sweet Bird of Youth*. Married (second) to British dramatist John Hopkins, she was occasionally billed in the 1970s as Shirley Knight Hopkins.

1959: Five Gates to Hell. 1960: Ice Palace. The Dark at the Top of the Stairs. The Shape of the River (TV). 1962: The Couch. Sweet Bird of Youth. House of Women. 1963: Flight From Ashiya. The Group. 1967: The Counterfeit Killer (TV. GB: cinemas). Dutchman. The Outsider (TV). 1968: Shadow Over Elveron (TV). Petulia. 1969: The Rain People. 1971: Secrets. 1974: Juggernaut. 1975: Friendly Persuasion (TV). Medical Story (TV). 1976: Return to Earth (TV). 21 Hours at Munich (TV. GB: cinemas). 1977: Champions, a Love Story (TV). 1978: The Defection of Simas Kudirka (TV). 1979: Beyond the Poseidon Adventure. 1980: Playing for Time (TV). 1981: Endless Love. 1982: The Sender. 1984: With Intent to Kill (TV). 1991: The Gravity of Stars. Prisoners. Bump in the Night (TV). Shadow of a Doubt (TV). A Child for Satan. 1992: Hard Promises. 1993: A Mother's Revenge (TV). 1994: The Secret Life of Houses. A Part of the Family (TV). Color of Night. 1995: Children of the Dust (TV). Stuart Saves His Family. Indictment: The McMartin Trial (TV). Dad, the Angel and Me (TV). 1996: The Uninvited (TV). Mary & Tim (TV). Stolen Memories: Secrets from the Rose Garden/Forbidden Memories (TV). A Promise to Carolyn (TV). Diabolique. If These Walls Could Talk (TV). Change of Heart (TV). Victim of the Haunt (TV). Somebody is Waiting. 1997: Little Boy Blue. Dying to Be Perfect: The Ellen Hart Peña Story (TV). The Wedding (TV). As Good As It Gets. 1998: A Father for Brittany (TV). A Marriage of Convenience (TV). 2000: A House on the Hill. 75 Degrees in July. 2001: Angel Eyes.

KNOTTS, Don

(Jesse Donald Knotts) 1924–

Scrawny, bulbous-eyed, squawk-voiced American cabaret comedian, who moved his 'nervous' character into TV and films in 1958, and starred in a big-budget series of comedies in the sixties that were more popular in America than abroad. Later as comic relief in Disney films, although retaining star billing.

1958: No Time for Sergeants. 1960: Wake Me When It's Over. 1961: The Last Time I Saw Archie. 1963: Move Over, Darling. The Incredible Mr Limpet. It's a Mad, Mad, Mad, Mad World. 1966: The Ghost and Mr Chicken. 1967: The Reluctant Astronaut. I Love a Mystery (TV). 1968: The Shakiest Gun in the West. 1969: The Love God? 1971: How to Frame a Figg. 1974: The Apple Dumpling Gang. 1976: No Deposit, No Return. Gus. 1977: Herbie Goes to Monte Carlo. 1978: Hot Lead and Cold Feet. 1979: The Apple Dumpling Gang Rides Again. The Prize Fighter. 1980: The Private Eyes. 1983: Cannonball Run II. 1986: Return to Mayberry (TV). 1987: Pinocchio and the Emperor of the Night (voice only). 1995: Cats Don't Dance (voice only). 1996: Big Bully. 1998: Pleasantville. 2000: Tom Sawyer (V. Voice only).

KNOWLES, Patric

(Reginald Knowles) 1911–1995

Solidly-built British actor with light, crinkly hair (and moustache to match) who, after five years in British films, decided to take his chances in Hollywood in 1936, and remained a semi-star there in suave roles until the early fifties. Perhaps a little lightweight for the Flynn-type roles for which his looks seemed suited, but a useful foil for some high-powered Hollywood ladies. Died from a cerebral haemorrhage.

1932: Men of Tomorrow. 1934: The Girl in the Crowd. Irish Hearts (US: Norah O'Neale). The Poisoned Diamond. 1935: Abdul the Damned. Royal Cavalcade (US: Regal Cavalcade). The Student's Romance. Honours Easy. The Guvnor (US: Mr Hobo). 1936: The Brown Wallet. Crown v Stevens. Wedding Group (US: Wrath of Jealousy). Two's Company. Fair Exchange. Irish for Luck. Give Me Your Heart (GB: Sweet Aloes). The Charge of the Light Brigade. 1937: It's Love I'm After. Expensive Husbands. 1938: The Patient in Room 18. The Adventures of Robin Hood. Four's a Crowd. Storm Over Bengal. The Sisters. Heart of the North. 1939: Torchy Blane in Chinatown. Beauty for the Asking. Five Came Back. Another Thin Man. The Spellbinder. Two's Company. The Honeymoon's Over. 1940: Married and in Love. A Bill of Divorcement. Women in War. Anne of Windy Poplars (GB: Anne of Windy Willows). 1941: How Green Was My Valley. The Wolf Man. 1942: The Mystery of Marie Roget. The Strange Case of Dr RX. Lady in a Jam. Who Done It? Sin Town. Eyes of the Underworld. 1943: Frankenstein Meets the Wolf Man. Forever and a Day. All By Myself. Hit the Ice. Always a Bridesmaid. Crazy House. 1944: Chip Off the Old Block. This is My Life. Pardon My Rhythm. 1945: Kitty. Masquerade in Mexico. 1946: O.S.S. The Bride Wore Boots. Monsieur Beaucaire. Of Human Bondage. 1947: Variety Girl. Ivy. 1948: Dream Girl. Isn't It Romantic? 1949: The Big Steal. 1950: Three Came Home. 1951: Quebec. 1952: Tarzan's Savage Fury. Mutiny. 1953: Jamaica Run. Flame of Calcutta. 1954: World for Ransom. Khyber Patrol. 1955: No Man's Woman. 1956: The Empty Room (TV. GB: cinemas). 1957: Band of Angels. 1958: From the Earth to the Moon. 1959 Auntie Mame. 1962: Six Gun Law (TV. GB: cinemas). 1967: In Enemy Country. The Way West. 1968: The Devil's Brigade. The DA: Murder One (TV). 1970: Chisum. 1972: The Man. 1973: Terror in the Wax Museum. 1974: Arnold.

KNOX, Alexander 1907–1995
Quietly-spoken, earnest-looking, dark-haired Canadian actor who usually played characters older than his own age. Acted almost exclusively on the British stage throughout the thirties, then went to Hollywood and immediately won leading roles, most notably the title role in *Wilson*, which earned him an Oscar nomination. When his parts grew less interesting, he returned to England, where he was featured mainly in stern supporting roles. The author of several mystery novels, as well as plays and screenplays, he was married to actress Doris Nolan (1916–), who starred in a few minor Hollywood films of the late 1930s. Died from bone cancer.

1931: The Ringer. 1936: Rembrandt. 1938: The Gaunt Stranger (US: The Phantom Strikes). 1939: Cheer Boys Cheer. The Four Feathers. 1940: The Sea Wolf. 1942: Commandos Strike at Dawn. This Above All. 1943: None Shall Escape. 1944: Wilson. 1945: Over 21. 1946: Sister Kenny. 1948: The Sign of the Ram. 1949: The Judge Steps Out (GB: Indian Summer. Completed 1947). Tokyo Joe. 1951: I'd Climb the Highest Mountain. Two of a Kind. Man in the Saddle (GB: The Outcast). Saturday's Hero (GB: Idols in the Dust. Son of Dr Jekyll. 1952: Paula (GB: The Silent Voice). Europa 51. 1954: The Sleeping Tiger. The Divided Heart. 1955: The Night My Number Came Up. 1956: Reach for the Sky. Alias John Preston. 1957: High Tide at Noon. Davy. Hidden Fear. 1958: Chase a Crooked Shadow. The Vikings. Passionate Summer. The Two-Headed Spy. Operation Amsterdam. Intent to Kill. 1959: Crack in the Mirror. The Wreck of the Mary Deare. 1960: Oscar Wilde. 1961: The Damned (US: These Are the Damned). 1962: The Share Out. The Longest Day. In the Cool of the Day. 1963: Man in the Middle. Woman of Straw. 1964: Mister Moses. Bikini Paradise. 1965: Crack in the World. The Psychopath. 1966: Modesty Blaise. Khartoum. 1967: Accident. How I Won the War. The 25th Hour. You Only Live Twice. 1968: Villa Rides! Shalako. Fraulein Doktor. 1969: Run a Crooked Mile (TV). Skullduggery. 1970: Puppet on a Chain. 1971: Nicholas and Alexandra. 1977: Holocaust 2000. 1978: Cry of the Innocent (TV). 1983: Gorky Park. Helen Keller: The Miracle Continues (TV). 1985: Joshua Then and Now.

KNOX, Elyse 1917–
Snappy, vivacious, glamorous blonde American actress who helped breathe life into many an ailing 'B' feature of the 1940s. The daughter of a prominent politician, she worked in the art department of a magazine until modelling, which had given her an isolated film appearance at 19, led to a 10-year film career. The widow of football immortal Tom Harmon, her distinguished family (which calls her 'The Boss') includes actor Mark Harmon (1951–), who has starred in films and TV series, and married actress Pam Dawber, and daughters Kristin (who married singer-actor Rick Nelson) and Kelly, who married automobile tycoon John DeLorean.

1937: Wake Up and Live. 1940: Free, Blonde and 21. Girl in 313. Lillian Russell. Star Dust. The Girl from Avenue A. Youth Will Be Served. 1941: Tanks a Million. Footlight Fever. Sheriff of Tombstone. 1942: Top Sergeant. Arabian Nights. The Mummy's Tomb. Hay Foot. 1943: Hit the Ice. Hi'Ya Sailor. Mr Big. Don Winslow of the Coast Guard (serial). Keep 'Em Slugging. So's Your Uncle. 1944: Moonlight and Cactus. Follow the Boys. A Wave, a Wac and a Marine. Army Wives. 1946: Joe Palooka, Champ. Sweetheart of Sigma Chi. 1947: Black Gold. Joe Palooka in The Knock Out. Linda Be Good. 1948: Fighting Mad (GB: Joe Palooka in Fighting Mad). I Wouldn't Be in Your Shoes. Joe Palooka in Winner Takes All (GB: Winner Take All). 1949: Forgotten Women. Joe Palooka in the Counterpunch. There's a Girl in My Heart.

KOCH, Marianne 1930–
Brown-haired, round-faced German actress (a former medical student) of pleasing personality, very popular in her own country until, amid much publicity, Universal signed her up for Hollywood roles. The 'stardom' lasted two films, and she returned to Germany and parts that made decreasing demands on her ability, seeming to lose interest in the cinema after the mid-1960s. Usually billed in Britain and America as Marianne Cook, she retired in 1970.

1950: Der Mann, der zweimal Leben wollte. Dr Holl/ The Affairs of Dr Holl. 1951: Das Geheimnis einer Ehe. Czardas der Herzen. Mein Freund, der Dieb. 1952: Der keusche Lebemann. Wetterluchten am Dachstein. Skandal in Mädchenpensionat. 1953: Die grosse Schuld. Schloss Hubertus. Der Klösterjäger. Liebe und Trompetenblasen. 1954: Night People. Angelika. Der Schmied von St Bartholomä. Geh mach dein Fensterl auf. 1955: Ludwig II. Zwei blauen Augen. Des Teufels General/ The Devil's General. Und der Himmel lacht dazu. Solange du lebst. Königswalzer. Christine. 1956: Die Ehe des Dr med Danwitz. Wenn wir alle Engel wären. Salzburger Geschichten. Four Girls in Town. 1957: Interlude. Der Stern von Afrika. Vater sein dagegen sehr. Der Fuchs von

Paris/Mission diabolique. Gli italiani sono matti. Die Landärztin. ...und nichts als die Wahrheit. 1959: Frau im besten Mannes alter. 1960: Heldinnen. Mit Himbeergeist geht alles besser. Der Frau am dunkeln Fenster. 1961: Pleins feux sur l'assassin. Unter Ausschluss der Öffentlichkeit. Napoleon II, l'aiglon. 1962: Heisser Hafen Hongkong (GB: Secrets of Buddha). Der schwartze Panther von Ratana. The Devil's Agent. Die Fledermaus. Liebling, ich muss dich erschiessen. 1963: Death Drums Along the River. 1964: Last Ride to Santa Cruz. The Monster of London City. Coast of Skeletons. A Fistful of Dollars. Frozen Alive. Sunscorched. 1965: A Place Called Glory. 1966: Trunk to Cairo. $5,000 für den Kopf von Jonny R. 1968: Schreie in der Nacht. Clint, il solitario. 1969: España, otra vez. Sandy the Seal.

KORTNER, Fritz (F. Kohn) 1892–1970
Suave, stocky, plump-cheeked, brown-haired (going grey early) master character star from Austria, often in insidious roles. An unconventional star of the German theatre in the years following World War I, he fled the country in 1933 and played leading character roles in British and Hollywood films, often as smooth and dispassionate criminals. He returned to Germany in 1948 and soon re-established his reputation on stage, a medium in which he spent most of his later years.
1915: Manya, die Türkin. Das Geheimnis von D 14. Police Nummer 1111. Im Banne der Vergangenheit. Die grosse Gefahr. Sonnwendfeuer. 1916: Das zeite Leben. 1917: Der Brief einer Toten. 1918: Der Stärkere. Der Märtyrer seines Herzens. Das andere Ich. Gregor Marold. Frauenehre. Sonnwendhof. 1919: Elese von Erlenhof. Prinz Kuckuck. Das Auge des Buddha. Ohne Zeugen. Satanas. 1920: Va banque. Gerechtigkeit. Katharina die Grosse/Catherine the Great. Die Brüder Karamasoff/The Brothers Karamazov. Weltbrand. Der Schädel der Pharaonentochter. Die Nacht der Königin Isabeau. 1921: Danton (US: All for a Woman). Die Hintertreppe (US: Backstairs). Die Lieblings Frau des Maharadscha, dritte Teil. Das Haus zum Mond. Das Haus der Qualen. Die Verschwörung zu Genua. Landstrasse und Grosstadt. Am roten Kliff. Die Jagd nach Wahrheit. Aus dem Schwartzbuch eines Polizeikommisars. Der Eisenbahnkönig I. Der Eisenbahnkönig II. 1922: Luise Millerin. Die Mausefalle. Peter der Grosse/Peter the Great. Der Ruf des Schicksals. Der Graf von Esse. Am Rande der Grosstadt. Die Finsternis und ihr

Eigentum. Sterbende Völker I. Sterbende Völker II. 1923: Nora. Der stärkste Trieb. Ein Weib, ein Tier, ein Diamant. Arme Sünderin. Schatten (US: Warning Shadows). 1924: Moderne Ehen. Armes kleines Mädchen. Dr Wislizenus. 1925: Orlacs Hände/The Hands of Orlac. 1926: Dürfen wir schweigen. 1927: Beethoven. Mata Hari/The Red Dancer. Primanerliebe. Alpentragödie. Maria Stuart I. Die Ausgestossenen. Die Geliebte des Gouveneurs. Mein Leben für das Deine. Maria Stuart II. 1928: Frau Sorge. Marquis d'Eon, der Spion der Pompadour. Der Büchse der Pandora/Pandora's Box. Revolutionhochzeit (US: The Last Night). Die Frau auf der Folter (US: A Scandal in Paris). 1929: Die Frau, nach der man sich sehnt (US: Three Loves). Somnambul. Atlantik. Die Frau im Talar. Die Nacht des Schreckens. Giftgas. 1930: Der Andere. Dreyfus (US: The Dreyfus Case). Die grosse Sehnsucht. Menschen im Käfig. 1931: Danton (remake). Der Mörder Dimitri Karamasoff (GB: The Brothers Karamazov. US: The Murderer Dimitri Karamazov. And French-language version). 1934: Chu-Chin-Chow. Evensong. 1935: Abdul the Damned. The Crouching Beast. 1937: Midnight Menace (US: Bombs over London). 1943: The Strange Death of Adolf Hitler. The Purple V. 1944: The Hitler Gang. 1946: The Wife of Monte Cristo. Somewhere in the Night. The Razor's Edge. 1947: The Brasher Doubloon (GB: The High Window). 1948: Berlin Express. 1949: The Last Illusion. 1950: Epilog. 1951: Bluebeard/ Blaubart. 1966: Fritz Kortner spricht Monologe für die Schallplatte.
As director: 1918: Gregor Marold. 1919: Elese von Erlenhoh. 1931: Der brave Sünder (US: The Upright Sinner). 1932: So eine Mädel vergisst man nicht. 1954: Die Stadt ist voller Geheimnisse. 1955: Sarajewo/Sarajevo. 1960: Die Sendung der Lysistrata (TV).

KOSCINA, Sylvia 1933–1994
Brunette (often blonde in films), sexy-looking Yugoslavian actress with pouting lower lip, dazzling smile, very upright carriage and breathtaking figure. She began her 30-year career in Italian films, but was soon in great demand for movies the world over, jetting bewilderingly from one country to another, mainly as lovely decoration, with an equal assortment of heroines and villainesses. Most popular in the mid–1960s. At 25, played the mother of a 16-year-old! She died from heart problems.
1955: Siamo uomini e caporali. 1956: Il

ferroviere (GB: Man of Iron. US: The Railroad Man). Michael Strogoff. Guendalina. 1957: La nonna Sabella (GB: Oh! Sabella). Le fatiche di Ercole (GB and US: Hercules). La Gerusalemme liberata (GB: The Mighty Crusaders. US: The Mighty Invaders). I fidanzati della morte. L'impossibile Isabelle. Femmine tre volte. Ladro lui ladro lei. Giovani mariti. La naif aux quarante enfants. 1958: Ercole e la regina di Lidia (GB: Hercules Unchained. US: Hercules and the Queen of Sheba). La nipote Sabella. Racconti d'estate (GB: Girls for the Summer. US: Love on the Riviera). Le confidant de ces dames. Mogli pericolose. Totò a Parigi/Parisien malgré lui. Totò nella luna. 1959: Erode il grande. Totò innamorato. La cambiale. Poveri millionari. Le sorprese dell' amore. Tempi duri per i vampiri (GB: Uncle Was a Vampire. US: Hard Times for Vampires). L'assedio di Siracusa (GB and US: Siege of Syracuse). I genitori in blue-jeans. 1960: Les distractions (GB: Trapped by Fear). Crimen (GB: Killing in Monte Carlo). Ravissante. Le pillole di Ercole (GB: The Pillars of Hercules). Il sicario. I piaceri dello scapolo. Il vigile. Femmine di lusso (GB: Travelling in Luxury). Mariti in pericolo. 1961: Swordsman of Siena/Le mercenaire. Jessica. 1962: Copacabana Palace (US: Girl Game). Cyrano and D'Artagnan. Les quatres vérités (GB and US: Three Fables of Love). Le massaggiatrici. 1963: Il giorno più corto commedia umoristica (US: The Shortest Day). Hot Enough for June (US: Agent 8¾). Il fornaretto di Venezia. Le monachine (US: The Little Nuns). Judex. Amore in quattro dimensioni (GB: Love in Four Dimensions). L'appartement des filles. 1964: The Dictator's Guns (GB: Guns for the Dictator). Se permettete – parliamo di donne (GB: Let's Talk About Women). Cadavere per signora. Juliet of the Spirits. That Man in Istanbul. L'idea fissa. Gangster, Gold und flotte Mädchen. 1965: Monnaie de singe (GB: Monkey Money). Thrilling. Il morbidone (US: The Dreamer). Made in Italy. Io, io, io . . . a gli altri. I soldi. Baraka sur X 13. 1966: Una storia di notte. Jonny Banco. Three Bites of the Apple. Deadlier than the Male. Layton . . . karatè e bambole. Racconti a due piazze. 1967: The Secret War of Harry Frigg. Das gemüsse etwas der Frauen. 1968: Kampf um Rom. The Battle of Neretva/Battle for Neretva. I protagonisti. A Lovely Way to Die (GB: A Lovely Way to Go). 1969: Kampf um Rom II. L'assoluto naturale/He and She. Justine ovvero le disavventure della virtù. Vendo nudo. 1970: Hornets' Nest. Le modificatioti. Vertige pour un tueur. Mazzabubù . . . quante corna stanno quaggiù? Les jambes en l'air. 1971: Perchè non ci lasciate in pace?/Why Don't You Leave Us in Peace? La colomba non deve volare. Nini Tirabusciò Trittico. Boccaccio. Il sesso del diavolo. 1972: Sette scialli di seta gialla (GB: Crimes of the Black Cat). Uccidere in silenzio. Beati i ricchi. La 'mala' ordina (GB: Manhunt in Milan). Rivelazione di un maniaco al capo della squadra mobile (US: The Slasher/ Confessions of a Sex Maniac). Homo Eroticus (US: Man of the Year). African Story. No desearas la muler de vicino. 1973: La strana legge del Dr Menga. Qualcuno l'ho vista uccidere. Il tuo piacere e il mio. 1974: The Student Connection. So Naked, So Dead (US:

Bad Girls/So Sweet, So Dead). Delitto d'autore. 1975: House of Exorcism (US: Lisa and the Devil). Dracula in Brianza. Un par de Zapatos del '39. Las Corrieras del Visconde Arnau. Clara and Nora. 1977: Casanova & Co (GB: The Rise and Rise of Casanova). 1980: Sunday Lovers/Les séducteurs. 1981: L'asso. 1983: Stelle emigranti. Questo e quello. Mani di fata. 1984: Cinderella '80. 1986: Rimini, Rimini, Rimini. Deadly Sanctuary. 1993: Ricky & Barabba. 1994: C'e Kim Novak al telefono.

KOVACS, Ernie 1919–1962
Black-haired, black-moustached, cigar-chewing, thickly-built American comedian with extravagant lifestyle who played loud-mouthed extroverts, and was very funny indeed in his few Columbia features of the late fifties and early sixties. Married to actress/comedienne Edie Adams (1927). Killed in a car crash.
1957: *It Happened to Ernie. Operation Mad Ball. Topaze (TV). 1958: Bell, Book and Candle. *Showdown at Ulcer Gulch. 1959: It Happened to Jane. Our Man in Havana. 1960: Wake Me When It's Over. Strangers When We Meet. North to Alaska. Pepe. 1961: Five Golden Hours. Sail a Crooked Ship.

KRISTEL, Sylvia 1952–
Dark-haired, sulky-looking Dutch actress, a beauty contest winner who made a few sexploitation films before appearing in the sensational Emmanuelle. Not surprisingly, she became typed as sexual adventuresses. More staid international ventures lit no fires, but she did better at the box-office as experienced women teaching callow youths the facts of life, even if most of these ventures were critical disasters.
1973: Frank and Eva. Naked over the Fence. Because of the Cats (GB: The Rape). 1974: Es war nicht die Nachtigall (GB: Julia. US: Innocence Once Removed). Emmanuelle. Un linceul n'a pas de poches. 1975: Emmanuelle 2. Le jeu avec le feu. 1976: René la canne. La marge (GB: The Streetwalker). Alice ou la dernière fugue. Une femme fidèle (GB: When a Woman in Love . . .). 1977: Die eiserne Maske/Behind the Iron Mask (GB: The 5th Musketeer). Goodbye Emmanuelle. 1978: The Madonna of the Sleeping Cars. Mysteries. Pastorale 1943. 1979: Letti selvaggi (released 1985 as Tigers in Lipstick). The Concorde – Airport '79 (GB: Airport '80 . . . The Concorde). The Million Dollar Face (TV). 1980: Amore in prima classe. Private Lessons. The Nude Bomb. 1981: Lady Chatterley's Lover. 1983: Mata Hari (released 1985). Private School. Emmanuelle IV. 1984: Red Heat. Hot Cruise. 1986: The Big Bet. 1987: Casanova (TV). The Arrogant. 1988: Dracula's Widow. 1990: Hot Blood. 1991: Beauty School. 1992: Emmanuelle 7. Eternelle Emmanuelle (TV). L'amour d'Emmanuelle (TV). Le parfum d'Emmanuelle/Emmanuelle's Revenge. 1993: La magie d'Emmanuelle (TV). 1997: Gaston's War. 1998: An Amsterdam Tale. 1999: Het Been. Film 1.

KRISTOFFERSON, Kris 1936–
Well-built American country-and-western singer who drifted into films in his mid-thirties. Within a couple of years his handsome features, bearded then but later clean-shaven, had made him a world star. In 1978 he declared that he was quitting films to return to full-time music. Although he returned to the cinema some 18 months later, his standing since has not seemed quite the same, even though his looks bely a man of his age, and his performances sometimes seemed to smack of detachment. He kept busy, however, into the 21st century, sometimes finding juicy cameo or semi-leading roles. Married/divorced fellow singer Rita Coolidge.
1971: The Last Movie. 1972: Cisco Pike. 1973: The Gospel Road. Blume in Love. Pat Garrett and Billy the Kid. 1974: Bring Me the Head of Alfredo Garcia. Alice Doesn't Live Here Anymore. 1975: Vigilante Force. 1976: The Sailor Who Fell from Grace with the Sea. A Star is Born. 1977: Semi-Tough. 1978: Convoy. 1979: Freedom Road (longer version serialized on TV). 1980: Heaven's Gate. 1981: Roll-Over. The Million Dollar Face (TV). 1983: The Lost Honor of Kathryn Beck (TV. GB: Acts of Passion). 1984: Flashpoint. 1985: Songwriter. Trouble in Mind. 1986: Stagecoach (TV). The Last Days of Frank and Jesse James (TV). 1988: Dead Or Alive. Big Top Pee-wee. Millennium. The Tracker (TV). 1989: Welcome Home. Ryder. 1990: Original Intent (released 1992). Perfume of the Cyclone. Pair of Aces (TV). Sandino. 1991: Tipperary/No Place to Hide. Another Pair of Aces: Three of a Kind (TV). Miracle in the Wilderness (TV). 1992: Christmas in Connecticut (TV). Knights. 1993: Paper Hearts/Cheatin' Hearts. Trouble Shooters: Trapped Beneath the Earth (TV). Sodbusters. Big Dreams and Broken Hearts: The Dottie West Story (TV). 1994: Fixation. 1995: Tad (TV). Pharaoh's Army. Brothers' Destiny. 1996: Lone Star. Message to Love. Blue Rodeo (TV). 1997: Fire Down Below. Girls' Night. 1998: Blade. A Soldier's Daughter Never Cries. The Long Ride to Justice (TV). Two for Texas (TV). The Land Before Time VI (V. voice only). Dance With Me. Payback. The Joyriders. El largo camino de la venganza/Long Kill. 1999: Molokai – The Story of Father Damien. Limbo. Outlaw Justice (TV). Tom Clancy's Netforce (TV). 2000: D-Tox/Detox. Perfect Murder, Perfect Town (TV). The Ballad of Ramblin' Jack. 2001: Blade 2.

KRÜGER, Hardy
(Franz Eberhard Krüger) 1928–
Very blond, square-faced, young-looking German leading man who marched with Hitler's youth, and began his career in wartime; but he found all doors open to him after his engaging performance as the continually escaping German prisoner-of-war in The One That Got Away. After that, he was seen largely in sympathetic roles in films from many countries.
1944: †Junge Adler. 1949: Das Fräulein und der Vagabond. Diese Nacht vergess ich nie. Kätchen für Alles. 1950: Das Mädchen aus der Südsee. Insel ohne Moral. Schön muss man sein. 1951: Mein Freund, der Dieb. Ich heisse Niki. 1952: Alle Kann ich nicht heiraten. Illusion in Moll. 1953: Die Jungfrau auf dem Dach. Solange du da bist. Ich und Du. The Moon is Blue (German version, released 1958). Muss man such gleich scheiden lassen? 1954: Der letzte Sommer. 1955: Der Himmel ist nie ausverkauft. Alibi. An der schönen blauen Donau. 1956: Die Christel von der Post. Liane

– *Jungle Goddess/Das Mädchen aus dem Urwald. 1957: Monpti. Bankstresor 713. The One That Got Away. 1958: Bachelor of Hearts. Gestehen sie, Dr Corda! (GB: Confess Dr Corda). Mit dem Kopf durch die Wand. Mission diabolique/Der Fuchs von Paris. 1959: Der Rest ist Schweigen (GB and US: The Rest is Silence). Bumerang (GB: Cry Double Cross). Blind Date. Die Gans von Sedan. Die Näckte und der Satan. 1960: Taxi pour Tobruk. 1961: Zwei unter Millionen. Traum von Lieschen Müller. Hatari! 1962: Les dimanches de ville d'Avray/Sundays and Cybèle. Les quatres vérités (GB: Three Fables of Love). 1963: Le gros coup. 1964: Le chant du monde. 1965: The Flight of the Phoenix. Les pianos mécaniques (US: The Uninhibited). 1966: La grande sauterelle. The Defector. 1967: Le Franciscain de Bourges. 1968: Battle for Neretva. The Awful Story of the Nun of Monza. 1969: The Red Tent. The Secret of Santa Vittoria. 1970: El Castillo de la Pureza. 1971: Night Hair Child. Le moine. 1972: Tod eines Fremden (GB: The Execution. US: Death of a Stranger). 1974: Paper Tiger. Un solitaire. 1975: Barry Lyndon. 1976: Autopsie d'un monstre. A chacun son enfer. Potato Fritz/Montana Trap. 1977: A Bridge Too Far. Down. Horizons. 1978: The Wild Geese. Blue Fin. 1981: Society Limited. Feine Gesellschaft – beschränkte Hafnung. 1982: Wrong is Right/The Man with the Deadly Lens. 1984: The Inside Man.*

†As Eberhard Kruger

Angkor – Kampuchea Express (US: Angkor Cambodia Express). 1983: Walking the Edge. The Last Ninja (TV). Fowl Play. 1985: Blade in Hong Kong (TV). 1988: Night Children. 1989: Keys to Freedom. Cold Dog Soup. Stickfighter. 1990: Miracle Landing (TV). Babies (TV). 1993: Dragon: The Bruce Lee Story. 1995: For Life or Death. The Golden Girls. 1997: Soul of the Avenger. 1998: Mr P's Dancing Sushi Bar.

KWAN, Nancy 1938–

Lovely Eurasian leading lady who shot to prominence when Hollywood gave her two plum roles in a row in her first two movies. Despite some appealing performances since then, she has gradually faded from prominence. Born in Hong Kong.

1960: The World of Suzie Wong. 1961: Flower Drum Song. 1962: The Main Attraction. 1963: Tamahine. 1964: Fate is the Hunter. The Wild Affair. Honeymoon Hotel. 1966: Drop Dead Darling (US: Arrivederci, Baby). Lt Robin Crusoe USN. The Peking Medallion (US: The Corrupt Ones). 1967: Nobody's Perfect. 1968: The Wrecking Crew. The Girl Who Knew Too Much. 1969: The McMasters . . . Tougher than the West Itself! The Girl from Peking. 1973: Wonder Women. 1975: Supercock. The Pacific Connection. 1976: Project: Kill. 1978: Devil Cat (US: Night Creature). The Falcon's Ultimatum. 1979: Streets of Hong Kong. 1981:

L

Key. Star Spangled Rhythm. Lucky Jordan. 1943: China. *Hollywood in Uniform. *Letter from a Friend. 1944: *Skirmish on the Home Front. And Now Tomorrow. 1945: Duffy's Tavern. Salty O'Rourke. Calcutta. *Hollywood Victory Caravan. 1946: Two Years Before the Mast. The Blue Dahlia. OSS. 1947: Variety Girl. My Favourite Brunette. Wild Harvest. 1948: Saigon. Beyond Glory. Whispering Smith. 1949: *Eyes of Hollywood. *Variety Club Hospital. Chicago Deadline. The Great Gatsby. Captain Carey USA (GB: After Midnight). 1950: Branded. *The Road to Hope. 1951: Appointment with Danger (completed 1949). Thunder in the East (released 1953). Red Mountain. 1952: The Iron Mistress. *The Sporting Oasis. 1953: Shane. Botany Bay. The Red Beret (US: Paratrooper). Desert Legion. Hell Below Zero. 1954: The Black Knight. Saskatchewan (GB: O'Rourke of the Royal Mounted). Drum Beat. 1955: The McConnell Story (GB: Tiger in the Sky.). Hell on Frisco Bay. 1956: Santiago (GB: The Gun Runner). A Cry in the Night (narrator only). 1957: The Big Land (GB: Stampeded!). Boy on a Dolphin. 1958: The Deep Six. The Proud Rebel. The Badlanders. 1959: The Man in the Net. Guns of the Timberland. 1960: All the Young Men. One Foot in Hell. 1961: Orazi e curiazi/Duel of Champions. 1962: 13 West Street. 1963: The Carpetbaggers.

†Scene deleted from final release print

LADD, Alan 1913–1964

Although born in Hot Springs, Arkansas, Ladd was cool and taciturn – and too short at 5ft 6in for the thirties when he got more work in radio than films. Came the forties (and a second marriage, to an astute agent, Sue Carol) and Ladd suddenly appeared as a kind of fair-haired avenging angel, teaming up with equally pint-sized Veronica Lake, shooting to world stardom in *This Gun for Hire* and making a string of similar tough-guy films. When the genre passed, so did his top stardom and he took to drink in later years, dying in bed from a mixture of medication and alcohol.
*1932: Once in a Lifetime. Island of Lost Souls. Tom Brown of Culver. 1933: Saturday's Millions. No Man of Her Own. 1936: Anything Goes. Pigskin Parade (GB: The Harmony Parade). 1937: Last Train from Madrid. Hold 'Em Navy (GB: That Navy Spirit). All Over Town. Rustlers' Valley. Souls at Sea. 1938: The Goldwyn Follies. Come on Leathernecks. †Born to the West. Freshman Year. The Texans. 1939: The Mysterious Miss X. Rulers of the Sea. *Rita Rio and Her Orchestra. The Green Hornet (serial). Goose Step (GB: Hitler – Beast of Berlin). 1940: Gangs of Chicago. Brother Rat and a Baby (GB: Baby Be Good). Light of Western Stars. The Howards of Virginia (GB: The Tree of Liberty). Her First Romance. In Old Missouri. Meet the Missus. Captain Caution. Wildcat Bus. Those Were the Days (GB: Good Old School Days). Cross Country Romance. 1941: Great Guns. The Parson of Panamint. *I Look at You. Paper Bullets. Petticoat Politics. The Reluctant Dragon. They Met in Bombay. The Black Cat. Cadet Girl. Citizen Kane. 1942: Joan of Paris. This Gun for Hire. The Glass*

LAFONT, Bernadette 1938–

Tall, tough-looking French actress with a sleek figure and challenging gaze, often seen in films by French 'New Wave' directors, especially those of Claude Chabrol. Often in sultry or eccentric roles, she continued her career into her sixties, despite the death of her daughter, actress Pauline Lafont, in a cliff fall at 26 in 1988. Married/divorced (first of two) actor Gérard Blain.
*1957: *Les mistons (GB and US: The Mischief Makers). Giovanni mariti. 1958: Le beau Serge. Bal de nuit. 1959: A double tour (GB: Web of Passion. US: Leda). L'eau à la bouche (US: Game for Six Lovers). 1960: Les mordus. Les bonnes femmes. Les godelureaux. 1961: Tire-au-flanc 62 (US: The Army Game). Me faire ça à moi . . . 1962: . . . Et Satan conduit le bal. Jusqu'à plus soif. Un clair de lune à Maubeuge. 1963: Les femmes d'abord. 1964: La chasse à l'homme. Tous les enfants du monde. *L'avatar botanique de Mademoiselle Flora. 1965: Compartiment tueurs (GB: The Sleeping*

Car Murders. US: The Sleeping Car Murder). Pleins feux sur Stanislas. Les bons vivants. 1966: Le voleur (GB: The Thief. US: The Thief of Paris). *Je ne sais pas. Un idiot à Paris. 1967: Lamiel. 1968: Falak/Walls/Lost Generation. L'amour c'est gai, l'amour c'est triste. Le révélateur. Les idoles. *Le dernier voyage de Commandant Le Bihan. 1969: *Marie et le curé. Piège. Le voleur de crimes. Paul. La fiancée du pirate (US: A Very Curious Girl). Sex Power. Elise, ou: La vraie vie. 1970: Les stances à Sophie. Caïn de nulle part. Valparaiso Valparaiso. 1971: Catch Me a Spy. Out One. La famille. Poulou le Magnificent. L'œuf. What a Flash. Elles plus elles. 1972: Une belle fille comme moi (GB: A Gorgeous Bird Like Me. US: Such a Gorgeous Kid Like Me). Les gants blancs du Diable. Trop jolies pour être honnêtes. 1973: La maman et la putain (GB and US: The Mother and the Whore). Out One: Spectre. Défense de savoir. Colinot Trousse-Chemise. 1974: Zig-Zig. Tendre Dracula. Permiette signora, che ami vostra figlia. 1975: Un divorce heureux. Une baleine qui avait mal aux dents. La ville bidon (originally for TV). Strauberg ist da. 1976: L'ordinateur des pompes funèbres. Un type comme moi ne devrait jamais mourir. Le gaffeur. Noroît. Vincent mit l'âne dans un pré. Qu'il est joli garçon, l'assassin de papa. 1977: Violette Nozière. L'irrévolution. 1978: La tortue sur le dos (GB and US: Like a Turtle on Its Back). Chausette surprise. 1979: Il ladrone. Nous maigrirons ensemble. La gueule de l'autre. Certaines nouvelles. La frisée aux lardons. 1980: Retour en force. Une merveilleuse journée. 1981: Le roi des cons. Si ma gueule vous plaît . . . 1982: On n'est pas sorti de l'auberge. 1983: Cap Canaille. La bête noire. Un bon petit diable. 1984: Dog Day/Canicule. The Perils of Gwendoline in the Land of the Yik Yak. 1985: Charlotte and Lulu. 1986: Masques. 1987: Inspecteur Lavardin. Waiting for the Moon. Babette's Feast. 1988: Les saisons du plaisir. Prisonnières. Une nuit à l'assemblée nationale. 1989: L'air de rien. 1990: Plein fer. Dingo: Dog of the Desert. Boom Boom. 1991: Cherokee. Sissi und der Kaiserkuss. 1992: Sam suffit. Ville à vendre. Sissi la valse des cœurs. 1994: Echec. Seules et abandonées. Personne ne m'aime. Zadoc et le bonheur. 1995: Rainbow pour Rimbaud. Le fils de Gascogne. Tango, mambo et cha-cha-cha (TV). 1997: Généalogies d'un crime. Nous sommes tous encore ici. Love in Ambush. 1998: Rien sur Robert. Sous les pieds des femmes. 1999: Recto/Verso. Les caméléons.*

LAHTI, Christine 1950–

Steeple-tall, sympathetic-looking American actress whose personal warmth has infused any number of productions since her belated debut at 28. Often to be found in concerned or contentious projects with offbeat things to say, Lahti, a surgeon's daughter, studied acting for some years before making her debut with experimental theatre groups and mime troupes. While remaining a force in the theatre, she has never become a box-office attraction in films. Academy Award nomination for *Swing Shift*. Married to director Thomas Schlamme, she herself won a best directing Oscar for the live-action short *Lieberman in Love* in 1996, directing her first feature film four years later.
1978: Dr Scorpion (TV). The Last Tenant

(TV). The Henderson Monster (TV). 1979: . . . And Justice for All. 1981: Ladies and Gentlemen: the Fabulous Stains. Whose Life Is It, Anyway? 1982: The Executioner's Song (TV. GB: cinemas). 1984: Swing Shift. Love Lives On (TV). 1985: Single Bars, Single Women (TV). 1986: Just Between Friends. 1987: Housekeeping. Stacking/Season of Dreams. 1988: Running On Empty. 1989: Miss Firecracker. No Place Like Home (TV). Cross Anatomy/A Cut Above. 1900: Funny About Love. Homeless (TV). 1991: Crazy from the Heart (TV). The Doctor. 1992: The Fear Inside. Leaving Normal. The Good Fight (TV). 1995: Hideaway. Temecula. *Lieberman in Love. The Four Diamonds (TV). A Weekend in the Country. 1996: Pie in the Sky. 1997: Hope (TV). Subway Stories: Tales from the Underground (TV). 1998: Judgment Day: The Ellie Nesler Story (TV). 2000: An American Daughter (TV).
As director: 2000: My First Mister.

LAINE, Frankie
(Francis Lo Vecchio) 1913–
Dark, square faced, beefy, Sicilian-born singer with wide smile whose record sales were third only to Crosby and Sinatra in the 1940s and 1950s. Made several (over-) bright musicals for the Richard Quine-Blake Edwards team at Columbia in the 1950s, but is probably best remembered by filmgoers as the breathy, powerful voice singing theme songs behind the credits to a whole posse of westerns, notably Gunfight at the OK Corral, 3:10 to Yuma and Blazing Saddles. In his youth, a record-breaking marathon dancer! Married to Nan Grey (qv) from 1950 to her death in 1993.
1949: Make-Believe Ballroom. 1950: When

You're Smiling. 1951: Sunny Side of the Street. 1952: Rainbow 'Round My Shoulder. 1955: Bring Your Smile Along. 1956: *Mr Rhythm's Holiday. Meet Me in Las Vegas (GB: Viva Las Vegas!). He Laughed Last. 1957: *Rock 'Em Cowboy.

LAKE, Arthur
(A. Silverlake) 1905–1987
American comic actor with dark, rumpled hair, dumpling face, squeaky voice and a baffled, sometimes desperate expression. His speciality was the all-American idiot, a characterisation that reached its height with his long-running creation of Dagwood Bumstead in the Blondie comedy films that ran from 1938 to 1950. Lake later revived the character on television and said 'When I don't play a dope, I don't work'. In show business from childhood (his father was a circus acrobat), Lake also made two-reel comedies in the late 1920s and early 1930s. Brother of actress Florence Lake (1904–1982).
1917: Jack and the Beanstalk. Aladdin and the Wonderful Lamp. 1925: *A Free Ride. California Straight Ahead. Where Was I? Sporting Life. *Smoked Out. Smouldering Fires. 1926: Skinner's Dress Suit. *A Dumb Friend. *A Swell Affair. *The Village Cut-Up. *Don't Be a Dummy. *A Bedtime Story. *Papa's Mama. *Opery House Tonight. *Wanted – a Bride. *Tiddly Winks. *Business Worries. *Too Much Sleep. *Switching Sleepers. 1927: The Cradle Snatchers. The Irresistible Lover. *Midnight Bum. *A Run for His Money. *Meet the Husband. *Hop Along. *Jailhouse Blues. *In Again, Out Again. 1928: Stop That Man. The Count of Ten. Harold Teen. The Air Circus. Lilac Time. 1929: On With the Show! Dance Hall. Tanned Legs. *Doing His Stuff. *Night Owls. *His Girl's Wedding. 1930: *Some Show. *Her Bashful Beau. *Follow Me. Cheer Up and Smile. She's My Weakness. 1931: Indiscreet. 1933: Midshipman Jack. 1934: The Silver Streak. Girl o' My Dreams (GB: The Love Race). *Hollywood Hobbies. *The Winnah! *Glad to Beat You. 1935: Women Must Dress. Orchids to You. 1936: I Cover Chinatown. 1937: Annapolis Salute (GB: Salute to Romance). 23½ Hours Leave. Topper. Exiled to Shanghai. True Confession. 1938: Double Danger. Everybody's Doing It. There Goes My Heart. Blondie. 1939: Blondie Meets the Boss. Blondie Brings Up Baby. Blondie Takes a Vacation. 1940: Blondie on a Budget. Blondie Has Servant Trouble. Blondie Plays Cupid. 1941:

Blondie Goes Latin (GB: Conga Swing). *Los Angeles Examiner Benefit. Blondie in Society (GB: Henpecked). 1942: Blondie for Victory (GB: Troubles Through Billets). Blondie Goes to College (GB: The Boss Said 'No'). Blondie's Blessed Event (GB: A Bundle of Trouble). The Daring Young Man. 1943: Footlight Glamour. It's a Great Life. 1944: Sailor's Holiday. The Ghost That Walked Alone. Three is a Family. 1945: The Big Show-Off. Life with Blondie. Leave It to Blondie. 1946: Blondie's Lucky Day. Blondie Knows Best. Blondie's Big Moment. 1947: Blondie's Holiday. Blondie in the Dough. Blondie's Anniversary. 1948: Blondie's Secret. Blondie's Reward. 16 Fathoms Deep. 1949: Blondie Hits the Jackpot (GB: Hitting the Jackpot). Blondie's Big Deal (GB: The Big Deal). 1950: Beware of Blondie. Blondie's Hero.

LAKE, Veronica
(Constance Ockleman) 1919–1973
Petite, slinky blonde with sleepy eyes, and unique peek-a-boo hairstyle which, draped over her right eye, swept the country until spoilsports cavilled that factory girls could get such hair caught in machinery. She was highly effective as the icy, husky-voiced femme fatale in night-life thrillers with Alan Ladd, but soon lost her distinctive looks, and Hollywood quickly cast her aside when her peak days were over. Her drink problems were well publicized and she was four times married and divorced, once (1944–1952) to director André de Toth. Died from acute hepatitis.
1939: †All Women Have Secrets. †Sorority House (GB: That Girl From College). †Dancing Co-Ed (GB: Every Other Inch a Lady). ‡*Wrong Room. 1940: †Forty Little Mothers. †Young As You Feel. 1941: I Wanted Wings. Hold Back the Dawn. Sullivan's Travels. 1942: This Gun for Hire. The Glass Key. Star Spangled Rhythm. I Married a Witch. 1943: So Proudly We Hail! 1944: The Hour Before the Dawn. Miss Susie Slagle's (released 1946). 1945: Bring on the Girls. Out of This World. Duffy's Tavern. Hold That Blonde. 1946: The Blue Dahlia. 1947: Variety Girl. Ramrod. 1948: Saigon. The Sainted Sisters. Isn't It Romantic? 1949: Slattery's Hurricane. 1951: Stronghold. 1966: Footsteps in the Snow. 1970: Flesh Feast.

†As Constance Keane
‡As Connie Keane

LAMARR, Hedy
(Hedwig Kiesler) 1913–2000
Perhaps the most beautiful actress ever to appear on screen. A kittenishly pretty face surrounded by raven-black hair, and a sublime figure. Hedy was physical perfection and quite enough to take one's breath away – which she did when sensationally appearing nude in the Czech film *Extase*. She married a millionaire and was out of show business for five years before Louis B. Mayer signed her up for M-G-M – but never really allowed her to let loose the sensuality that played about the lips and could have made her a screen immortal. Ultimately married and divorced six times, including (third) John Loder from 1943 to 1947. Born in Austria. Suffered from poor sight in later years. Co-invented a radar device during World War II. Died 'from natural causes'.
1390: †*Geld auf der Stasse*. 1931: †*Sturm im Wasserglas/Die Blumenfrau von Lindenau*. †*Die Koffer des Herrn O.F. Wir brauchen kein gelt (US: His Majesty King Ballyhoo)*. 1932: †*Extase/Ecstasy*. 1938: *Algiers*. 1939: *Lady of the Tropics*. **Screen Snapshots No. 10*. 1940: *I Take This Woman. Comrade X. Boom Town*. 1941: *Come Live with Me. H.M. Pulham Esq. Ziegfeld Girl*. 1942: *Tortilla Flat. Crossroads. White Cargo*. 1943: **Show Business at War. The Heavenly Body. The Conspirators*. 1944: *Experiment Perilous*. 1945: *Her Highness and the Bellboy*. 1946: *The Strange Woman*. 1947: *Dishonored Lady*. 1948: *Let's Live a Little*. 1949: *Samson and Delilah*. 1950: *A Lady without Passport. Copper Canyon*. 1951: *My Favourite Spy*. 1953: *The Loves of Three Queens/The Love of Three Women*. 1954: *L'amante di Paride/Eterna femmina (GB and US: The Face That Launched a Thousand Ships)*. 1957: *The Story of Mankind. The Female Animal*. ‡*Slaughter on 10th Avenue*. 1990: *Instant Karma*.

†*As Hedy Kiesler*
‡*Scenes deleted from final release print*

LAMAS, Fernando 1915–1982
Slightly cruel-looking in his extremely handsome way, Argentina's Lamas made no Hollywood films until he was 35 and already greying. But his few years with M-G-M gained him a world-wide reputation as a Latin lover and also showed people he could sing. He went into stage musicals from 1956 and later divided his time between per-forming in nightclubs and directing for television. Married (third) Arlene Dahl, 1954–1960, and Esther Williams (fourth) from 1969 (after years of living together) until his death from cancer. Father of actor Lorenzo Lamas (1958–), a star of many straight-to-video action films.
1942: *Frontera Sur. En ul Ultime Piso*. 1945: *Villa Rica del Espiritu Santo*. 1947: *Navidad de los Pobres. Evasion. El Tango Vuelve a Paris*. 1948: *Historia de una Mala Mujer/Lady Windermere's Fan. La Rubia Mireyz. La Otra y Yo*. 1949: *Vidalita. De Padre Desconocido*. 1950: *La Historia del Tango. The Avengers*. 1951: *Rich, Young and Pretty. The Law and the Lady*. 1952: *The Merry Widow. The Girl Who Had Everything*. 1953: *Dangerous When Wet. Jivaro (GB: Lost Treasure of the Amazon). Sangaree. Diamond Queen*. 1954: *Rose Marie*. 1955: *The Girl Rush*. 1960: *The Lost World*. 1961: †*The Magic Fountain*. 1962: *Duello nella Sila*. 1963: *D'Artagnan against the Three Musketeers (US: Revenge of the Musketeers)*. 1967: †*The Violent Ones. Valley of Mystery. Kill a Dragon*. 1968: *Backtrack (TV)*. 1969: *The Lonely Profession (TV). 100 Rifles*. 1970: *Powderkeg (TV. GB: cinemas)*. 1971: *Taxi to Terror*. 1975: *Won Ton Ton, the Dog Who Saved Hollywood. Murder on Flight 502 (TV)*. 1978: *The Cheap Detective*.

†*Also directed*

LAMAS, Lorenzo
See LAMAS, Fernando

LAMBERT, Christopher
(Christophe Lambert) 1957–
Tall, rangy, light-haired actor of quizzical good looks, born in America to a French diplomat and raised in Switzerland. He was set for a career on the London Stock Exchange when he decided to become an actor and, given three years by his parents to make it, moved to Paris to achieve his ambition. But it was his casting as Tarzan in a British film that gave him the breakthrough, his faintly Belmondo-like looks helping him consolidate a middle-range stardom in action films. Married/divorced actress Diane Lane (*qv*), first of two.
1981: *Le bar du téléphone. Putain d'histoire d'amour*. 1983: *Légitime violence*. 1984: *Greystoke – The Legend of Tarzan Lord of the Apes. Paroles et musique/Love Songs*. 1985: *Subway*. 1986: *Highlander. I Love You*. 1987: *The Sicilian. Priceless Beauty*. 1988: *The Yellow Jersey. Love Dream. To Kill a Priest*. †*The Adventures of Baron Munchausen*. 1989: *Why Me? Un plan d'enfer*. 1990: *Highlander II: The Quickening*. 1992: *Knight Moves. Max et Jérémie*. 1993: *Fortress. Tashunga. Do Not Disturb. Roadflower*. 1994: *The Puppet Master. The Hunted. Gunmen*. 1995: *Mortal Kombat. Highlander 3: The Sorcerer. Adrenalin: Fear the Rush*. 1996: *The North Star/Alaska. Fortress 2: Re-Entry. Nirvana. Hercule et Sherlock. Mean Guns*. 1997: *Arlette*. 1999: *Gideon (TV). Resurrection. Operation Splitsville*. 2000: *Druids/Vercingetorix. Highlander: Endgame*.

†*Scenes deleted from final release print*

LAMONT, Molly 1910–
Bright, well-groomed, Transvaal-born actress with light-brown (sometimes blonde) hair and impish personality. A beauty contest winner in South Africa, she came to Britain and was successfully groomed for stardom at Elstree Studios. She went to Hollywood in 1935 but never enjoyed quite the same success, her best roles probably coming as Cary Grant's luckless fiancée in *The Awful Truth* and in the lead of a minor 1943 offering called *A Gentle Gangster*.
1930: *The Black Hand Gang*. 1931: *Uneasy Virtue. Old Soldiers Never Die. What a Night! Shadows. The House Opposite. My Wife's Family. Dr Josser KC*. 1932: *Strictly Business. The Strangler. Lord Camber's Ladies. Brother Alfred. The Last Coupon. Lucky Girl. Josser on the River. His Wife's Mother*. 1933: *Letting in the Sunshine. Leave It to Me. Paris Plane*. 1934: **Wedding Anniversary. White Ensign. Irish Hearts (US: Norah O'Neale). The Third Clue. Murder at Monte Carlo*. 1935: *Oh, What*

a Night! Handle with Care. Rolling Home. Alibi Inn. Another Face (GB: It Happened in Hollywood). Jalna. 1936: Muss 'Em Up (GB: House of Fate). Sylvia Scarlett. A Woman Rebels. Mary of Scotland. The Jungle Princess. 1937: A Doctor's Diary. The Awful Truth. 1942: The Moon and Sixpence. 1943: A Gentle Gangster. 1944: The White Cliffs of Dover. Follow the Boys. Mr Skeffington. Minstrel Man. 1945: The Suspect. 1946: So Goes My Love (GB: A Genius in the Family). The Dark Corner. Scared to Death. 1947: Ivy. Christmas Eve. 1949: South Sea Sinner (GB: East of Java). 1951: The First Legion.

LAMOUR, Dorothy
(Mary D. Slaton) 1914–1996
How anyone so American as dark-haired, sloe-eyed and pencil-eyebrowed Dorothy Lamour could become Hollywood's queen of South Sea Island pictures is a bit of a mystery. But she'll always be remembered as the maiden bursting into sarong and the good-humoured decoration in the 'Road' pictures. Fortunately, she could also sing (rather well, if a bit syrupy) and act (a bit) and so sustained her star career. The public always liked her, and it was a hideous misjudgement of their taste to offer her only a cameo role in the last 'Road' film.
1936: *The Stars Are Singing. *The Stars Can't Be Wrong. *Star Reporter in Hollywood No. 1. College Holiday. The Jungle Princess. 1937: Swing High, Swing Low. High, Wide and Handsome. Last Train from Madrid. The Hurricane. Thrill of a Lifetime. 1938: Her Jungle Love. The Big Broadcast of 1938. Tropic Holiday. Spawn of the North. 1939: St Louis Blues. Man About Town. Disputed Passage. 1940: *Chinese Garden Festival. Typhoon. Johnny Apollo. Moon Over Burma. Road to Singapore. Chad Hanna. 1941: Aloma of the South Seas. Road to Zanzibar. Caught in the Draft. 1942: Beyond the Blue Horizon. Road to Morocco. The Fleet's In. Star Spangled Rhythm. They Got Me Covered. 1943: Dixie. Riding High (GB: Melody Inn). 1944: Rainbow Island. And the Angels Sing. 1945: Road to Utopia. Duffy's Tavern. A Medal for Benny. Masquerade in Mexico. 1947: My Favourite Brunette. Variety Girl. Road to Rio. Wild Harvest. 1948: A Miracle Can Happen (later On Our Merry Way). Lulu Belle. The Girl from Manhattan. 1949: Slightly French. Manhandled. The Lucky Stiff. 1951: Here Comes the Groom. 1952: The Greatest Show on Earth. Road to Bali. *Screen Snapshots No.

205. 1961: The Road to Hong Kong. 1963: Donovan's Reef. 1964: Pajama Party. 1969: The Phynx. 1975: Won Ton Ton, the Dog Who Saved Hollywood. 1976: Death at Love House (TV). 1987: Creepshow 2.

LANCASTER, Burt
(Burton Lancaster) 1913–1994
Muscular, fair-haired American actor with flashing smile tinged with menace. A former circus acrobat – and remarkably nimble for such a big man – he developed a taste for acting in wartime troop shows. Although he started in black thrillers, he became best known in swashbucklers, swinging spectacularly around on ropes. Some regret the drift into excessive seriousness that followed, although he did win an Oscar in 1960 for his fire-eating preacher in Elmer Gantry and was also nominated for From Here to Eternity, Birdman of Alcatraz and, many years later, Atlantic City USA. Died from a heart attack.
1946: The Killers. 1947: Desert Fury. Brute Force. Variety Girl. I Walk Alone. 1948: Sorry Wrong Number. All My Sons. Kiss the Blood Off My Hands (GB: Blood on My Hands). 1949: Cross Cross. Rope of Sand. 1950: The Flame and the Arrow. Mister 880. 1951: Vengeance Valley. Jim Thorpe – All American (GB: Man of Bronze). Ten Tall Men. 1952: The Crimson Pirate. Come Back, Little Sheba. 1953: South Sea Woman. From Here to Eternity. His Majesty O'Keefe. Three Sailors and a Girl. 1954: Apache. Vera Cruz. 1955: †The Kentuckian. The Rose Tattoo. 1956: Trapeze. The Rainmaker. Gunfight at the OK Corral. 1957: Sweet Smell of Success. *Playtime in Hollywood. 1958: Separate Tables. Run Silent, Run Deep. 1959: The Devil's Disciple. The Unforgiven. 1960: Elmer Gantry. 1961: The Young Savages. Judgment at Nuremberg. 1962: A Child is Waiting. Birdman of Alcatraz. The Leopard. 1963: The List of Adrian Messenger. 1964: Seven Days in May. 1965: The Train. The Hallelujah Trail. 1966: The Professionals. 1967: The Swimmer. 1968: The Scalphunters. 1969: Castle Keep. Airport. The Gypsy Moths. 1970: King: A Filmed Record . . . Montgomery to Memphis. Lawman. 1971: Valdez is Coming. 1972: Ulzana's Raid. 1973: Scorpio. 1974: ‡The Midnight Man. Conversation Piece. 1975: Moses. 1976: Buffalo Bill and the Indians. 1900. Victory at Entebbe (TV. GB: cinemas). The Cassandra Crossing. 1977: The Island of Dr Moreau. Twilight's Last Gleaming. Go Tell the Spartans. 1979: Zulu Dawn. 1980: Cattle Annie and Little Britches.

Atlantic City USA (GB and US: Atlantic City). 1981: La pelle. 1983: Local Hero. The Osterman Weekend. 1985: Little Treasure. Scandal Sheet (TV). 1986: Tough Guys. Barnum (TV). 1987: The Day Before/Control (TV). The Suspect. The Goldsmith's Shop. 1988: Robert Gibraltar. 1989: The Betrothed. Field of Dreams. The Achille Lauro (GB: TV, as Voyage of Terror).

†Also directed ‡Also co-directed

LANDI, Elissa
(Elisabeth-Marie-Christine Kühnelt) 1904–1948
Bright, vital, fair-haired, Austrian-born actress and authoress, supposedly the grand-daughter of Elisabeth of Austria. In the late twenties and early thirties she made films in several countries, but was most successful in Hollywood, notably as the haunting heroine of The Sign of the Cross. Died from cancer.
1926: London. 1928: Bolibar. Underground. Le leur su la cime (GB and US: The Betrayal). 1929: Broch och Brett (GB and US: Sin). The Inseparables. 1930: The Parisian (English-language version of Mon gosse de père). Knowing Men. The Price of Things. Children of Chance. 1931: Body and Soul. Always Good-bye. Wicked. The Yellow Ticket (GB: The Yellow Passport). 1932: The Devil's Lottery. The Sign of the Cross. The Woman in Room 13. A Passport to Hell (GB: Burnt Offering). 1933: The Masquerader. The Warrior's Husband. I Loved You Wednesday. 1934: Sisters under the Skin. By Candlelight. Man of Two Worlds. The Count of Monte Cristo. Enter Madame. The Great Flirtation. 1935: Without Regret. Koenigsmark. The Amateur Gentleman. 1936: Mad Holiday. After the Thin Man. 1937: The Thirteenth Chair. 1943: Corregidor.

LANDIS, Carole
(Frances Ridste) 1919–1948
An all-American blonde bombshell, Carole Landis was four times married and divorced, and committed suicide at 29 allegedly from frustration over her desire to marry Rex Harrison (qv). Round-faced, bubbly and as sexy as all-get-out, she was one of the original sweater girls and a favourite pin-up of World War II troops.
1937: A Day at the Races. A Star is Born. The Adventurous Blonde. Over the Goal. Broadway Melody of 1938. The Emperor's Candlesticks. Hollywood Hotel. Varsity Show. The King and the Chorus Girl (GB: Romance is Sacred).

*Blondes at Work. 1938: Alcatraz Island. He Couldn't Say No. Love, Honor and Behave. Gold Diggers in Paris (GB: The Gay Imposters). Over the Wall. Boy Meets Girl. Four's a Crowd. Men Are Such Fools. When Were You Born? Girls on Probation. A Slight Case of Murder. 1939: Daredevils of the Red Circle (serial). Three Texas Steers (GB: Danger Rides the Range). Cowboys from Texas. 1940: One Million BC (GB: Man and His Mate). Mystery Sea Raider. Turnabout. Road Show. 1941: *Hollywood Visits the Navy. Topper Returns. I Wake Up Screaming (GB: Hot Spot). Dance Hall. Moon Over Miami. Cadet Girl. 1942: A Gentleman at Heart. It Happened in Flatbush. Manila Calling. Orchestra Wives. My Gal Sal. 1943: The Powers Girl (GB: Hello! Beautiful). Wintertime. *Screen Snapshots No. 2 (new series). 1944: Secret Command. Four Jills in a Jeep. Having Wonderful Crime. 1946: Behind Green Lights. It Shouldn't Happen to a Dog. Scandal in Paris. 1947: Out of the Blue. 1948: Noose (US: The Silk Noose). The Brass Monkey (US: Lucky Mascot).*

LANE, Abbe 1932–

Vivacious, red-haired American singer of exotic looks, on radio and stage from the age of 14. Married her bandleader, Xavier Cugat (they were later divorced), and decorated a number of American and Italian pictures in 'spitfire' roles, before guesting in TV series and, ultimately, concentrating on a nightclub singing career.

*1952: *Xavier Cugat and His Orchestra. 1953: Wings of the Hawk. Ride Clear of Diablo. 1954: The Americano. 1955: Chicago Syndicate. Donetella. I girovaghi/ The Wanderers. Lo scopolo. 1956: Tempo di villeggiatura.*

Parola di ladro. Sunset in Naples. 1957: Totò, Vittorio e la dottoressa (US: Lady Doctor). 1958: Maracaibo. Sailors, Women – Trouble/ Morinai, donne e guai. Susanna y Yo. 1959: I baccanali di Tiberio (US: Tiberius). 1960: My Friend Jekyll. Caesar Against the Pirates. 1962: Das Feuerschiff. 1983: The Twilight Zone (GB: Twilight Zone – The Movie).

LANE, Allan 'Rocky'
(Harold Albershart) 1904–1973

Allan Lane was tall, dark and handsome, a top American football player who turned to acting when his sporting days were through. He could act enough to make one regret the mediocrity of his roles in the thirties, playing upright juvenile leads in crime films. Suddenly, in the mid-forties, he became the two-fisted star of second-feature westerns, one of the best of his kind. Died from a bone marrow disorder. Some sources are adamant that Lane's year of birth was 1909.

*1929: The Forward Pass. *Knights Out. *Detective Wanted. Not Quite Decent. 1930: Madam Satan. Love in the Rough. 1931: Night Nurse. The Star Witness. *War Mamas. Local Boy Makes Good. Honor of the Family. 1932: The Famous Ferguson Case. Miss Pinkerton. Winner Takes All. One Way Passage. Crooner. It's Tough to be Famous. The Tenderfoot. The Crash. 1933: *Heavens! My Husband. 1936: Stowaway. 1937: Charlie Chan at the Olympics. Laughing at Trouble. Big Business. Fifty Roads to Town. The Duke Comes Back (GB: Call of the Ring). Sing and Be Happy. 1938: Crime Ring. The Law West of Tombstone. Having Wonderful Time. Night Spot. Pacific Liner. Maid's Night Out. Fugitives for a Night. The Marriage Business. 1939: They Made Her a Spy. Panama Lady. Twelve Crowded Hours. Conspiracy. The Spellbinder. 1940: Grand Old Opry. King of the Royal Mounted (serial). 1941: *Coffins on Wheels. All-American Co-Ed. 1942: King of the Mounties (serial. And feature version: Yukon Patrol). 1943: Daredevils of the West (serial). The Dancing Masters. 1944: The Tiger Woman (serial). Call of the South Seas. Stagecoach to Monterey. Sheriff of Sundown. The Silver City Kid. 1945: Don't Fence Me In. Topeka Terror. Bells of Rosarita. Corpus Christi Bandits. Trail of Kit Carson. 1946: Gay Blades. Night Train to Memphis. A Guy Could Change. Out California Way. Stagecoach to Denver. Santa Fé Uprising. 1947: Oregon Trail Scouts. Marshal of Cripple Creek. Bandits of Dark Canyon. Homesteaders of Paradise Valley.*

*Vigilantes of Boomtown. Rustlers of Devil's Canyon. The Wild Frontier. 1948: Oklahoma Badlands. Carson City Raiders. Desperadoes of Dodge City. Sundown in Sante Fé. The Bold Frontiersman. Marshal of Amarillo. The Denver Kid. Renegades of Sonora. 1949: *The American Rodeo. Sheriff of Wichita. Frontier Investigator. Bandit King of Texas. Powder River Rustlers. Death Valley Gunfighters. The Wyoming Bandit. Navajo Trail Raiders. 1950: Gunmen of Abilene. Salt Lake Raiders. Vigilante Hideout. Frisco Tornado. Code of the Silver Sage. Covered Wagon Raid. Rustlers on Horseback. Trail of Robin Hood. 1951: Rough Riders of Durango. Wells Fargo Gunmaster. The Desert of Lost Men. Night Riders of Montana. Fort Dodge Stampede. 1952: Leadville Gunslinger. Thundering Caravans. Black Hills Ambush. Captive of Billy the Kid. Desperadoes' Outpost. 1953: Marshal of Cedar Rock. Bandits of the West. Savage Frontier. El Paso Stampede. 1958: The Saga of Hemp Brown. 1960: Seven Ways from Sundown. Hell Bent for Leather. 1961: Posse from Hell. 1962: Geronimo's Revenge (TV. GB: cinemas).*

LANE, Diane 1965–

Beautiful, silkily dark-haired, slightly petulant young American actress with immaculate complexion. The daughter of a drama coach and a *Playboy* centrefold, she was acting on stage at six. But, although seemingly in the right place at the right time, especially with her films for Francis Ford Coppola, she has not quite become a 'name' star. Her rather hostile personality has tended to get her cast of late in bitchy or unsympathetic roles, and her stripper in *The Big Town* may have been an unwise move for a career whose recent roles have been on the nebulous side. She married actor Christopher Lambert (qv) in 1988, but the couple divorced in 1995.

1979: A Little Romance. 1980: Cattle Annie and Little Britches. Touched by Love. 1981: Child Bride of Short Creek (TV). Ladies and Gentlemen: The Fabulous Stains. 1982: Miss All-American Beauty (TV). Six Pack. National Lampoon Goes to the Movies/ National Lampoon's Movie Madness. 1983: The Outsiders. Rumble Fish. 1984: The Cotton Club. Streets of Fire. 1987: The Big Town. Priceless Beauty. Lady Beware. 1988: Love Dream. 1989: Vital Signs. 1990: Descending Angel (cable TV). 1992: Knight Moves. My New Gun. 1993: Indian Summer. Fallen Angels 2 (TV). Chaplin. Never Talk to Strangers (cable TV). The Setting Sun. 1994: Wild Bill.

1995: Judge Dredd. A Streetcar Named Desire (TV). 1996: Jack. Trigger Happy/Mad Dog Time. 1997: Murder at 1600. The Only Thrill/Tennessee Valley. 1998: Gunshy. A Walk on the Moon. Grace & Glorie (TV). 1999: My Dog Skip. 2000: The Red Door. The Perfect Storm. The Virginian (TV).

LANE, Jackie (later Jocelyn) 1936–

Poutily pretty, dark-haired, dark-eyed starlet, almost a British Bardot. The younger sister of actress Mara Lane, Jackie pursued her career with diligence, appearing mostly in provocative roles, and even changing her name to Jocelyn when she went to Hollywood in 1964. Even so, her acting was never more than adequate – and slightly colourless for a firecracker type – and her films petered out. Later became an actors' agent.

1954: For Better, For Worse (US: Cocktails in the Kitchen). Men of Sherwood Forest. April in Portugal. 1955: Dust and Gold. The Gamma People. 1956: Zarak. 1957: These Dangerous Years (US: Dangerous Youth). The Truth about Women. 1958: Wonderful Things! 1959: The Angry Hills. Jet Storm. 1960: Robin Hood and the Pirates. 1961: Aimez-vous Brahms?/Goodbye Again. Two and Two Make Six. 1962: I tromboni di Fra' Diavolo (US: The Bandits of 'Fra Diavolo'). Mars, God of War. La sette folgori di Assur (GB: 7th Thunderbolt. US: War Gods of Babylon). Operation Snatch. 1963: La congiura die Borgia. 1965: †Tickle Me. †Sword of Ali Baba. 1966: †Bel Ami 2000 (GB: How to Seduce a Playboy). †The Poppy is Also a Flower (GB: Danger Grows Wild). †Incident at Phantom Hill. 1969: †Hell's Belles. †Land Raiders. 1970: †A Bullet for Pretty Boy.

†As Jocelyn Lane

LANE, Priscilla (P. Mullican) 1915–1995

Prettiest, blondest and most personable of five acting sisters, two of whom, Rosemary (1913–1974) and Lola (1909–1981) appeared in films with her. A former dance band singer, she proved equally at ease with romantic or madcap comedy roles, and did all her best work at Warners, where she was under contract from 1937 to 1941.

*1937: *Swingtime in the Movies. Varsity Show. 1938: Love, Honor and Behave. Cowboy from Brooklyn (GB: Romance and Rhythm). Four Daughters. Men Are Such Fools. Brother Rat. 1939: Daughters Courageous. Yes, My Darling Daughter. Dust Be My Destiny. The*

*Roaring Twenties. Four Wives. 1940: Brother Rat and a Baby (GB: Baby Be Good). Three Cheers for the Irish. 1941: Four Mothers. Million Dollar Baby. Blues in the Night. 1942: Saboteur. Silver Queen. The Meanest Man in the World. 1943: *Stars on Horseback. Arsenic and Old Lace. 1947: Fun on a Weekend. 1948: Bodyguard.*

LANG, June (Winifred J. Vlasek) 1915–

Very pretty, delicate-looking American actress with wide blue eyes and auburn hair. Beginning her career as a dancer, she moved on to become a likeably decorative star of light comedies and adventure yarns, much in the Piper Laurie (qv) mould. She might have progressed to more dramatic things, but her studio tore up her contract in 1939 because of her association with convicted criminal John Roselli (they were briefly married from 1940). Miss Lang's career never recovered, although she was quoted as saying in the 1980s that she would 'love to act again'. Also married and divorced (third of three) British actor Joss Ambler (1900–1959).

1931: †Young Sinners. 1932: †Chandu, the Magician. 1933: †I Loved You Wednesday. †The Man Who Dared. 1934: Music in the Air. 1935: Bonnie Scotland. Every Saturday Night. 1936: Captain January. The Country Doctor. The Road to Glory. White Hunter. 1937: Nancy Steele is Missing. Wee Willie Winkie. Ali Baba Goes to Town. 1938: One Wild Night. International Settlement. Meet the Girls. 1939: Captain Fury. Zenobia (GB: Elephants Never Forget). For Love or Money (GB: Tomorrow at Midnight). Forged Passport. 1940: Inside Information. Convicted Woman. 1941: Redhead. The Deadly Game. 1942: Too Many Women. Footlight Serenade. City of Silent

Men. 1943: Stage Door Canteen. Flesh and Fantasy. 1944: Up in Arms. Cookin' Up Trouble/Three of a Kind. 1947: Lighthouse.

†As June Vlasek

LANG, Matheson 1879–1948

Formidable, craggy, heavy-headed, dark-haired star of the British stage who, despite a somewhat theatrical style, became a dominant personality of the British cinema for 20 years between stage runs, mostly in larger-than-life roles that exercised his mastery of disguise. He was born in Canada to a Scottish clergyman, but brought up in Scotland, where he began acting at 18. He spent his later years working on his autobiography (*Mr Wu Looks Back*, a reference to one of his several 'oriental' roles) and in retirement in the Bahamas, where he died.

*1916: The Merchant of Venice. 1917: *Everybody's Business. Masks and Faces. The Ware Case. The House Opposite. 1918: Victory and Peace. 1919: Mr Wu. 1921: Carnival. 1922: Dick Turpin's Ride to New York. A Romance of Old Bagdad. 1923: The Wandering Jew. Guy Fawkes. 1924: White Slippers. Henry – King of Navarre. Slaves of Destiny/Miranda of the Balcony. 1925: The Qualified Adventurer. The Secret Kingdom (US: Beyond the Veil). 1926: Island of Despair. The Chinese Bungalow. 1927: The King's Highway. 1928: The Blue Peter. The Triumph of the Scarlet Pimpernel (US: The Scarlet Daredevil). 1930: The Chinese Bungalow (remake). 1931: Carnival (remake. US: Venetian Nights). 1933: Channel Crossing. 1934: Little Friend. The Great Defender. 1935: Drake of England (US: Drake the Pirate). Royal Cavalcade (US: Regal Cavalcade). 1936: The Cardinal.*

LANGAN, Glenn
See JERGENS, Adele

LANGDON, Harry 1884–1944

Baby-faced, pale-complexioned American silent-screen comedian whose speciality was blank bewilderment at life's vicissitudes. Won great popularity briefly at the end of the twenties, but quarrelled with those around him, failed as his own director and was declared bankrupt in 1931. Although he worked on, he never regained his popularity. Died from a cerebral haemorrhage.

*1918: The Master Mystery (serial). 1923: *Picking Peaches. 1924: *Scarem Much. *Smile Please. *Feet of Mud. *Shanghaied*

Lovers. *Flickering Youth. *The Luck o' the Foolish. *All Night Long. *The Cat's Meow. *His New Mamma. *The First Hundred Years. *The Hansom Cabman. 1925: *Giddap! *Boobs in the Wood. *Plain Clothes. *Lucky Stars. *There He Goes. *The Sea Squawk. *His Marriage Vow. *Remember When? *Horace Greeley Junior. *The White Wing's Bride. 1926: *Saturday Afternoon. *Soldier Man. Fiddlesticks. His First Flame. Ella Cinders. Tramp Tramp Tramp. The Strong Man. 1927: Long Pants. †Three's a Crowd. 1928: †The Chaser. †Heart Trouble. 1929: *Hotter Than Hot. *Shy Boy. *Skirt Shy. 1930: See America Thirst. A Soldier's Plaything (GB: A Soldier's Pay). *Voice of Hollywood No. 9. *The Head Guy. *The Fighting Parson. *The Big Kick. *The King. *The Shrimp. 1932: *The Big Flash. 1933: Hallelujah, I'm a Bum (GB: Hallelujah I'm a Tramp). My Weakness. *Amateur Night. *The Hitch Hiker. *Knight Duty. *Tied for Life. *Hooks and Jabs. *Tired Feet. *Marriage Humor. *The Stage Hand. *Leave It to Dad. 1934: *No Sleep on the Deep. *On Ice. *A Roaming Romeo. *A Circus Hoodoo. *Petting Preferred. *Council on De Fence. *Trimmed in Furs. *Shivers. *Hollywood on Parade B-6. 1935: Atlantic Adventure. *The Leather Necker. *His Marriage Mix-Up. *His Bridal Sweet. *I Don't Remember. 1937: Mad About Money (US: He Loved an Actress). 1938: *A Doggone Mixup. *Sue My Lawyer. There Goes My Heart. 1939: Zenobia (GB: Elephants Never Forget). 1940: *Sitting Pretty. Misbehaving Husbands. *Goodness, a Ghost. *Cold Turkey. 1941: Road Show. *Beautiful Clothes. All-American Co-Ed. Double Trouble. 1942: House of Errors. *What Makes Lizzie Dizzy. *Carry Harry. *Piano Mooner. *A Blitz on the Fritz. *Tireman, Spare My Tires. 1943: Spotlight Scandals. *Here Comes Mr Zerk. *Blonde and Groom. 1944: Defective Detectives. *Mopey Dope. Block Busters. Hot Rhythm. *To Heir is Human. 1945: *Pistol Packin' Nitwits. *Snooper Service. Swingin' on a Rainbow.

†Also directed

As director: 1937: Wise Guys.

LANGE, Hope (H. Ross) 1931–

Square-faced, blonde American actress under contract to Fox in the 1950s. She gave off a warm glow in dramatics (and was nominated for an Academy Award in Peyton Place), later showing a pleasing comedy touch too. Married her first co-star, Don Murray (qv), in 1956 (divorced 1961) and briefly retired after marrying producer-director Alan J. Pakula in 1963. They later divorced, and she remarried in 1986. She has continued to crop up on more recent times, if not as often as one would have liked.

1956: Bus Stop. 1957: The True Story of Jesse James (GB: The James Brothers). Peyton Place. For I Have Loved Strangers (TV). 1958: Point of No Return (TV). The Young Lions. The Innocent Sleep (TV). In Love and War. 1959: The Best of Everything. 1961: Wild in the Country. Pocketful of Miracles. 1963: Love is a Ball (GB: All This and Money Too). 1968: Jigsaw (TV). 1970: Crowhaven Farm (TV). 1972: The 500 Pound Jerk (GB: The Strong Man. TV). That Certain Summer (TV). 1974: Death Wish. I Love You . . . Goodbye (TV). 1975: The Secret Night Caller (TV). Fer de Lance (TV. GB cinemas as Death Dive). The Rivalry (TV). 1979: Like Normal People (TV). 1980: Pleasure Palace (TV). 1981: The Day Christ Died (TV). 1983: I Am the Cheese. 1984: The Prodigal. Finder of Lost Loves (TV). 1985: Private Sessions (TV). A Nightmare on Elm Street Part 2: Freddy's Revenge. 1986: Blue Velvet. 1987: Arriva Frank Capra. 1990: Aunt Julia and the Scriptwriter (Tune in Tomorrow). 1993: Cooperstown (TV). Dead Before Dawn (TV). 1994: Clear and Present Danger. 1995: Just Cause. 1997: Before He Wakes.

LANGE, Jessica 1949–

Faintly fragile-looking blonde American actress with light, slightly sharp voice clearly influenced by her native Minnesota. A former chorus dancer and model, she inherited the Fay Wray role in the 1976 remake of King Kong and had to fight hard to wriggle out of the slot into which it pigeonholed her. Although she proved herself a serious-minded actress with the ability to tackle arduous roles, the films in which she did it were often not popular hits. Won an Academy Award for Tootsie, although her best performance came the same year in Frances. Has lived for some time with actor-writer Sam Shepard (qv). She was further nominated for Academy Awards in Sweet Dreams and Music Box, and took her second Oscar for Blue Sky, even though the film's release had been delayed for three years.

1970: *Home is Where the Heart Is. 1976: King Kong. 1979: All That Jazz. How to Beat the High Cost of Living. 1981: The Postman Always Rings Twice. 1982: Tootsie. Frances. 1984: Country. 1985: Sweet Dreams. 1986: Crimes of the Heart. 1988: Made in Germany. Far North. Everybody's All American (GB: When I Fall in Love). 1989: Men Don't Leave. Music Box. 1991: Blue Sky (released 1994). Cape Fear. 1992: Night and the City. O Pioneers! (TV). 1994: Stick Wife (TV). 1995: Losing Isaiah. Rob Roy. A Streetcar Named Desire (TV). 1996: Kilronan. 1997: A Thousand Acres. 1998: Hush. Cousin Bette. 1999: Titus.

LANGELLA, Frank 1940–

Sleek, dark-haired, panther-like American leading man who, with his dark eyes and 'outlined' lips, made visually the best vampire since Christopher Lee. His career to date has been almost entirely confined to the theatre, with only occasional ventures into cinema and television. Now typecast as faintly dissolute characters.

1965: Benito Creno (TV). 1970: The Twelve Chairs. Diary of a Mad Housewife. 1971: The Deadly Trap. 1972: The Wrath of God. 1974: The Mark of Zorro (TV). 1979: Dracula. 1980: Sphinx. 1981: Those Lips, Those Eyes. 1986: The Men's Club. Liberty (TV). 1987: Masters of the Universe. 1988: And God Created Woman. 1991: True Identity. 1992: Body of Evidence. 1492: Conquest of Paradise. 1993: Dave. 1994: Bad Company. Brainscan. Junior. Doomsday Gun. 1995: CutThroat Island. 1996: Eddie. Lolita. 1998: Alegria. Small Soldiers (voice only). I'm Losing You. 1999: Kilroy (TV). The Ninth Gate. Dark Summer. 2000: 15 Moments/Stardom. Jason and the Argonauts. Sweet November.

LANGFORD, Frances
(F. Newbern) 1914–

Tiny, sweet-faced, even sweeter voiced blonde American singer and light actress who remained one of the world's most popular vocalists over a 20-year period. A major radio star, her film work was minor (often guest spots) in comparison, and she became more famous for World War II (and later Vietnam) troop tours with Bob Hope (qv). Married from 1938 to 1955 to actor Jon Hall (qv), she later married a millionaire and scaled her work rate down from the late 1960s to singing at the nightspot in her own Frances Langford Outrigger Resort in her native Florida. Her second husband died in 1986 and she remarried in 1994.

1935: Broadway Melody of 1936. Every Night at Eight. 1936: Collegiate (GB: The Charm School). Palm Springs (GB: Palm Springs Affair). Born to Dance. 1937: The Hit Parade. Hollywood Hotel. 1940: Dreaming Out Loud. Hit Parade of 1941. Too Many Girls. 1941: Swing It Soldier (GB: Radio Revels of 1942). All American Co-Ed. 1942: Mississippi Gambler. Yankee Doodle Dandy. 1943: Follow the Band. Cowboy in Manhattan. Never a Dull Moment. This is the Army. 1944: The Girl Rush. Career Girl. 1945: Radio Stars on Parade. People Are Funny. Dixie Jamboree. 1946: The Bamboo Blonde. 1947: Beat the Band. 1948: Melody Time. 1949: Deputy Marshal. Make Mine Laughs. 1951: Purple Heart Diary (GB: No Time for Tears). 1953: The Glenn Miller Story.

LANSBURY, Angela 1925–

Blonde, British-born actress and singer, in America from 1940, who always seemed several years older than she was, until she got into her forties. Her petulant prettiness was an invitation to producers to cast her in spiteful or bitchy roles and it was not ignored. But she took Broadway by storm as *Mame* in 1966 and has since commanded a better range of roles and become a bigger name at the box office. In recent times she has played spinster detectives on several occasions with some success. Nominated for the Best Supporting Actress Oscar three times, in *Gaslight*, *The Picture of Dorian Gray* and *The Manchurian Candidate*. Briefly married in 1945–6 (first of two) to actor Richard Cromwell (qv). Much on TV in the 1990s as author-sleuth Jessica Fletcher in the *Murder She Wrote* series.

1944: Gaslight (GB: The Murder in Thornton Square). National Velvet. 1945: The Picture of Dorian Gray. The Harvey Girls. 1946: Till the Clouds Roll By. The Hoodlum Saint. 1947: Tenth Avenue Angel. The Private Affairs of Bel Ami. If Winter Comes. 1948: State of the Union (GB: The World and His Wife). The Three Musketeers. 1949: The Red Danube. Samson and Delilah. 1951: Kind Lady. 1952: Mutiny. 1953: Remains to be Seen. 1955: The Purple Mask. The Court Jester. The Key Man (GB: A Life at Stake). A Lawless Street. 1956: Please Murder Me. 1958: The Reluctant Debutante. The Long Hot Summer. 1960: A Breath of Scandal. The Dark at the Top of the Stairs. Summer of the 17th Doll (US: Season of Passion). 1961: Blue Hawaii. 1962: All Fall Down. The Manchurian Candidate. The Four Horseman of the Apocalypse (voice only). 1963: In the Cool of the Day. 1964: The World of Henry Orient. Dear Heart. 1965: Harlow. The Greatest Story Ever Told. The Amorous Adventures of Moll Flanders. Mister Buddwing (GB Woman without a Face). 1970: Something for Everyone (GB: Black Flowers for the Bride). 1971: Bedknobs and Broomsticks. 1978: Death on the Nile. 1979: The Lady Vanishes. 1980: The Mirror Crack'd. 1981: The Last Unicorn (voice only). 1982: The Pirates of Penzance. Little Gloria – Happy at Last (TV). 1983: The Gift of Love: A Christmas Story (TV). 1984: The Company of Wolves. 1986: A Talent for Murder (TV). 1988: Shootdown (TV). 1990: The Shell Seekers (TV). The Love She Sought (TV. GB: A Green Journey). 1991: †JFK. Beauty and the Beast (Voice only). 1992: Stephen Verona: Self Portrait. Mrs 'Arris Goes to Paris (TV). 1997: Anastasia (voice only). Mrs Santa Claus (TV). Beauty and the Beast: The Enchanted Christmas (V. Voice only). 1999: The Unexpected Mrs Pollifax (TV). Fantasia 2000. Forever Hollywood (doc).

†Scene deleted

LANZA, Mario
(Alfred Cocozza) 1921–1959

Handsome, dark-haired American operatic tenor, enormously popular with audiences and record-buyers alike in the early fifties. After portraying his idol, Caruso, Lanza's career was undone by weight problems and his own temperament. Died from a coronary thrombosis following a crash diet.

1944: Winged Victory. 1949: That Midnight Kiss. 1950: The Toast of New Orleans. 1951: The Great Caruso. 1952: Because You're Mine. 1954: The Student Prince (voice only).

1956: Serenade. 1958: Seven Hills of Rome (and Italian-language version: Arrivederci Roma). 1959: For the First Time.

La PLANTE, Laura
(L. La Plant) 1904–1996

Friendly-looking, square-faced, twinkle-eyed, prettily dimpled blonde American actress and light comedienne with prominent chin and unaffected style. In films at 16, she always performed with charm and to a high standard and was Universal's top female star by 1924. Excellent in the silent version of *The Cat and the Canary*, she appeared in British sound films of the early 1930s produced by her second husband Irving Asher (first husband: director William A. Seiter) but then retired to raise a family. A comeback bid with M-G-M rather fizzled out when Myrna Loy changed her mind about discontinuing her role in 'The Thin Man' films that Miss la Plante was to have taken over in 1944. Died from Alzheimer's Disease.

*1920: *His Four Fathers. 1921: *Back from the Front. *Jiggs in Society. *Father's Close Shave. *Jiggs and the Social Lion. 813. The Old Swimmin' Hole. Big Time Ideas. Play Square. Big Town Roundup (GB: A Fighting Fool). *Should Husbands Do Housework? Old Dynamite. Brand of Courage. *The Alarm. 1922: *A Bottle Baby. *The Deputy's Double Cross. *Fighting Back. *Matching Wits. *The Trail of the Wolf. *Desperation. *The Call of Courage. *A Treacherous Rival. *Society Sailors. *Easy to Cop. *Taking Things Easy. Perils of the Yukon (serial). The Wall Flower. 1923: Around the World in 18 Days (serial). Dead Game. Burning Words. Shootin' for Love. Out of Luck. The Ramblin' Kid. Crooked Alley. The Thrill Chaser. 1924: Sporting Youth. Ride*

for Your Life. Excitement. Young Ideas. The Dangerous Blonde. The Fast Worker. Butterfly. *The City of Stars. The Fatal Plunge. 1925: *Hollywood Today No. 8. Smouldering Fires. Dangerous Innocence. The Teaser. 1926: The Beautiful Cheat. Skinner's Dress Suit. The Midnight Sun. Poker Faces. Her Big Night. Butterflies in the Rain. 1927: The Love Thrill. Beware of Widows. The Cat and the Canary. Silk Stockings. 1928: Thanks for the Buggy Ride. Finders Keepers. Home James. The Last Warning. 1929: Scandal (GB: High Society). Show Boat. The Love Trap. Hold Your Man. 1930: Captain of the Guard. King of Jazz. 1931: Lonely Wives. Meet the Wife. God's Gift to Women (GB: Too Many Women). Men Are Like That (GB: The Virtuous Wife). The Sea Ghost. *Stout Hearts and Willing Hands. 1933: *Lost in Limehouse, or: Lady Esmeralda's predicament. Her Imaginary Lover. 1934: The Girl in Possession. The Church Mouse. Widows Might. 1935: Man of the Moment. 1946: Little Mister Jim. 1956: Spring Reunion.

La ROCQUE, Rod
(Rodrique la Rocque de la Rour) 1896–1969
Light-haired, manly American silent screen star, most memorable in The Ten Commandments, but quite busy throughout the twenties. Made a few sound films as a staunch supporting player, but became a real estate businessman and radio producer and left the cinema in the early forties. Married to Vilma Banky (qv) from 1927.
1914: The Snow Man. 1915: The Alster Case. The Raven. The Primitive Strain. 1916: *The War Bride of Plumville. *The Face in the Mirror. *Destiny. *Sweedie the Janitor. The Lightbearer. 1917: *Much Obliged. *The Girl Who Took Notes and Got Wise and Then Fell Down. *The Fable of the 12-Cylinder Speed of Leisure Class. Efficiency Edgar's Courtship. *The Fable of Back Tracker from the Hot Sidewalks. *The Fable of the Speedy Sprite. *The Fable of the Uplifter and his Dandy Little Opus. *The Fable of What Transpires After the Wind-Up. *Sundaying in Fairview. *Filling His Own Shoes. *The Wandering Boy and the Delinquent Parents. *Would You Believe It? *Vernon the Bountiful. *A Corner in Smiths. *The Long Green Trail. 1918: Ruggles of Red Gap. The Rainbow Box. Sadie Goes to Heaven. The Dream Doll. The Venus Model. Let's Get a Divorce. Money Mad. Hidden Fires. A Perfect 36. A Perfect Lady. 1919: Love and the Woman. The Trap. Miss Crusoe. 1920: Stolen

Kiss. Easy to Get. The Discarded Woman. The Garter Girl. *A Philistine in Bohemia. *Thimble, Thimble. Life. 1921: Suspicious Wives. For Your Daughter's Sake. Paying the Piper. What's Wrong with the Woman? 1922: The Challenge. Notoriety. Slim Shoulders. A Woman's Woman. 1923: Jazzmania. The Ten Commandments. Zaza. The French Doll. 1924: Feet of Clay. Forbidden Paradise. Triumph. Code of the Sea. A Society Scandal. Don't Call It Love. 1925: Braveheart. Phantom Justice. The Golden Bed. Night Life of New York. The Coming of Amos. Wild, Wild Susan. 1926: Red Dice. Bachelor's Brides. The Love Pirate. Gigolo. The Cruise of the Jasper B. 1927: The Fighting Eagle. Resurrection. 1928: Captain Swagger. Hold 'Em Yale. Stand and Deliver. Love Overnight. Our Dancing Daughters. 1929: The Man and the Moment. The One Women Idea. Our Modern Maidens. The Locked Door. The Delightful Rogue. 1930: One Romantic Night. Let Us Be Gay. Beau Bandit. 1931: The Yellow Ticket (GB: The Yellow Passport). 1933: SOS Iceberg. 1935: Mystery Woman. Frisco Waterfront (GB: When We Look Back). Hi, Gaucho! 1936: Taming the Wild (GB: Madcap). The Preview Murder Mystery. The Dragnet. Till We Meet Again. 1937: Clothes and the Woman. The Shadow Strikes. Woman Trap. 1938: International Crime. 1939: The Hunchback of Notre Dame. 1940: Beyond Tomorrow. Dr Christian Meets the Woman. Dark Streets of Cairo. 1941: Meet John Doe.

LARSEN, Keith (K. L. Burt) 1925–
Black-haired, sharp-faced, incisive American actor who turned from professional tennis to acting, and was immediately put to work by Hollywood in leading roles in co-features, several times as Red Indians, and almost entirely for minor studios. Kept busy on television from 1957 onwards, and has occasionally indulged in directing as well, on outdoors adventure films. Married to Vera Miles (qv) from 1960 to 1973.
1951: Flying Leathernecks. The Green Glove. 1952: Flat Top (GB: Eagles of the Fleet). Paula (GB: The Silent Voice). The Rose Bowl Story. Hiawatha. 1953: Fort Vengeance. Son of Belle Starr. War Paint. 1954: Arrow in the Dust. Security Risk. 1955: Dial Red O. Chief Crazy Horse (GB Valley of Fury). Desert Sands. Wichita. Night Freight. 1956: Screaming Eagles. 1957: The Blackwell Story (TV). Last of the Badmen. Badlands of Montana. Apache Warrior. 1959: Frontier

Rangers/Northwest Rangers (TV. GB: cinemas). 1961: Fury River (TV. GB: cinemas). 1965: Women of the Prehistoric Planet. 1967: Caxambu! 1968: Mission Bantangas. The Omegans. 1970: Night of the Witches. 1975: Trap on Cougar Mountain. 1979: Whitewater Sam.
As director: 1968: Mission Batangas. 1970: Night of the Witches. 1974: Run to the High Country. 1975: Trap on Cougar Mountain. 1979: Whitewater Sam.

LAUGHTON, Charles 1899–1962
Seldom if ever can so fat and ugly a man have become so big a star. But this light-haired, rubber-faced, thick-lipped English actor ran up such a string of brilliant characterizations in Hollywood (after winning an Oscar for his British-made Henry VIII) that his precise and plummy tones became the most imitated of all. Captain Bligh, Mr Barrett, Rembrandt, Ruggles of Red Gap, Javert in Les Miserables, Nero and, perhaps best of all, Quasimodo: they were all memorably Laughton. From 1945 till 1953 his overripe performances were the despair of his supporters. But he came good again in his last few films (adding an Oscar nomination for Witness for the Prosecution to the one he had received for Mutiny on the Bounty) before his death from spinal cancer. Married to Elsa Lanchester (1902–1986) from 1929.
1928: *Bluebottles. *Daydreams. 1929: Piccadilly. Comets. 1930: Wolves (US: Wanted Men). 1931: Down River. 1932: The Old Dark House. Payment Deferred. The Devil and the Deep. The Sign of the Cross. If I Had a Million. Island of Lost Souls. 1933: The Private Life of Henry VIII. White Woman. 1934: The Barretts of Wimpole Street. 1935: Ruggles of Red Gap. Mutiny on the Bounty. Les Miserables. 1936: Rembrandt. 1937: I Claudius (unfinished). 1938: Vessel of Wrath (US: The Beachcomber). St Martin's Lane (US: Sidewalks of London). 1939: Jamaica Inn. The Hunchback of Notre Dame. 1940: They Knew What They Wanted. 1941: It Started with Eve. 1942: The Tuttles of Tahiti. Tales of Manhattan. Stand by for Action (GB: Cargo of Innocents). 1943: This Land is Mine. The Man from Down Under. Forever and a Day. 1944: The Canterville Ghost. 1945: The Suspect. Captain Kidd. 1946: Because of Him. 1947: *The Queen's Necklace. 1948: The Paradine Case. Arch of Triumph. The Girl from Manhattan. The Big Clock. 1949: The Bribe. The Man on

the Eiffel Tower. 1951: The Blue Veil. The Strange Door. 1952: O. Henry's Full House (GB: Full House). Abbott and Costello Meet Captain Kidd. 1953: Young Bess. Salome. 1954: Hobson's Choice. 1957: Witness for the Prosecution. 1958: *Fabulous Hollywood. 1960: Under Ten Flags. Spartacus. 1962: Advise and Consent.

As director: 1955: The Night of the Hunter.

LAUREL, Stan
(Arthur S. Jefferson) 1890–1965
Red-haired British comedian from the music-halls, who went to Hollywood in his twenties and eventually became the thin half of the Laurel and Hardy team. The inspiration behind most of their comedy routines, his trade marks included the scratching of his unruly mop of hair, the blank look, the ear-wiggle and dissolving into tears. A man with a somewhat contentious private life (he was fired more than once by his long-time boss, Hal Roach), Laurel was given a special Academy Award in 1960. He died from a heart attack. Foreign-language versions also exist of several of the early 1930s' Laurel and Hardy shorts. Six times married, twice to the same woman.
1917: Lucky Dog. Nuts in May. The Evolution of Fashion. 1918: Hoot Mon. Whose Zoo? Just Rambling Along. Phoney Photos. It's Great To Be Crazy. Hickory Hiram. Huns and Hyphens. No Place Like Jail. Bears and Bad Men. Frauds and Frenzies. Do You Love Your Wife? 1919: Mixed Nuts. Scars and Stripes. Hustling for Health. 1921: The Rent Collector. 1922: The Pest. The Week-End Party. The Egg. Mud and Sand. 1923: When Knights Were Cold. The Noon Whistle. Pick and Shovel. Gas and Air. The Handy Man. A Man About Town. Scorching Sands. Roughest Africa. Mother's Joy. Collars and Cuffs. White Wings. Kill or Cure. Short Orders. The Whole Truth. Save the Ship. Frozen Hearts. Under Two Jags. The Soilers. Oranges and Lemons. 1924: Wild Bill Hiccup/Wide Open Spaces. Detained. Zeb vs. Paprika. Smithy. Near Dublin. Short Kilts. Rupert of Hee-Haw/Rupert of Coleslaw. West of Hot Dog. Postage Due. Brothers Under the Chin. Monsieur Don't Care. 1925: Madam Mix-Up/Mandarin Mix-Up. Pie-Eyed. Navy Blue Days. The Sleuth. Half a Man. Somewhere in Wrong. The Snow Hawk. Twins. Dr Pyckle and Mr Pride. 1926: Atta Boy. On the Front Page (GB: The Editor). Get 'Em Young. 45 Minutes from Hollywood. 1927: Duck Soup. Slipping Wives. Love 'Em and Weep. Eve's

Love Letters. Should Tall Men Marry? Why Girls Love Sailors. With Love and Hisses. Sugar Daddies. Sailors, Beware!/Ship's Hero. Call of the Cuckoos. Flying Elephants. Hats Off. Do Detectives Think? (GB: The Bodyguard). Let George Do It. Putting Pants on Philip. The Second Hundred Years. The Battle of the Century. Now I'll Tell One. Seeing the World. 1928: Leave 'Em Laughing. The Finishing Touch. From Soup to Nuts. You're Darn Tootin' (GB: The Music Blasters). Their Purple Moment. Should Married Men Go Home? Early to Bed. Two Tars. Habeas Corpus. We Faw Down (GB: We Slip Up). 1929: Liberty. Wrong Again. That's My Wife. Big Business. Unaccustomed as We Are. Double Whoopee. Berth Marks. Men o' War/Man o' War. Perfect Day. They Go Boom. Bacon Grabbers. The Hoose-Gow. †Hollywood Revue of 1929. Angora Love. 1930: The Night Owls. Blotto. Brats. †The Rogue Song. Hog Wild (GB: Aerial Antics). The Laurel and Hardy Murder Case. Another Fine Mess. Below Zero. 1931: Be Big. Chickens Come Home. The Stolen Jools (GB: The Slippery Pearls). Laughing Gravy. Our Wife. †Pardon Us (GB: Jail Birds). Come Clean. One Good Turn. †Beau Hunks (GB: Beau Chumps). On the Loose. Helpmates. 1932: Any Old Port. The Music Box. The Chimp. Scram! County Hospital. †Pack Up Your Troubles. Their First Mistake. Towed in a Hole. 1933: Twice Two. Me and My Pal. †The Devil's Brother (GB: Fra Diavolo). The Midnight Patrol. Busy Bodies. Wild Poses. Dirty Work. †Sons of the Desert (GB: Fraternally Yours). 1934: Oliver the Eighth (GB: The Private Life of Oliver the Eighth). †Hollywood Party. Going Bye-Bye! Them Thar Hills. †Babes in Toyland. The Live Ghost. 1935: Tit for Tat. The Fixer Uppers. Thicker Than Water. †Bonnie Scotland. 1936: On the Wrong Trek. †The Bohemian Girl. †Our Relations. 1937: †Way Out West. †Pick a Star. 1938: †Swiss Miss. †Block-Heads. 1939: †The Flying Deuces. †A Chump at Oxford. 1940: †Saps at Sea. 1941: †Great Guns. 1942: †A-Haunting We Will Go. Tree in a Test Tube. 1943: †Air Raid Wardens. †Jitterbugs. †The Dancing Masters. 1944: †The Big Noise. †Nothing But Trouble. 1945: †The Bull Fighters. 1951: †Atoll K (GB: Robinson Crusoeland. US: Utopia).

All shorts except † features

LAURIE, Piper (Rosetta Jacobs) 1932–
Red-haired, a photographer's dream, Piper really was a pretty package, with full lips,

appealing hazel eyes, a cute nose and a figure that set male mouths gaping as it wriggled its way though a maze of iron bars in the easterns with Tony Curtis that made them a hot romantic team. After six years as a Casbah spitfire, Piper went away and gradually proved herself as a serious actress, eventually chalking up three Oscar nominations, for The Hustler, Carrie and Children of a Lesser God. Won an Emmy for the TV movie Promise. Married to film critic Joseph Morgenstern since 1962. Now plays grand old gals.
1950: Louisa. The Milkman. The Prince Who Was a Thief. 1951: Francis Goes to the Races. 1952: Has Anybody Seen My Gal. No Room for the Groom. Son of Ali Baba. 1953: Mississippi Gambler. The Golden Blade. 1954: Dangerous Mission. Johnny Dark. Dawn at Socorro. *Queens of Beauty. 1955: Smoke Signal. Ain't Misbehavin'. 1956: Mr and Mrs McAdam (TV). The Ninth Day (TV). Winter Dreams (TV). 1957: Kelly and Me. Until They Sail. 1958: The Days of Wine and Roses (TV). 1961: The Hustler. 1976: Carrie. 1977: Ruby. In the Matter of Karen Ann Quinlan (TV). 1978: The Boss's Son. Rainbow (TV). Tim. 1980: Skag/The Wildcatters (TV). 1981: The Bunker (TV). 1982: Mae West (TV). 1984: Tender is the Night (TV). 1985: Return to Oz. Toughlove (TV). Love, Mary (TV). 1986: Promise (TV). 1987: Children of a Lesser God. Distortions. Tiger Warsaw. 1988: Appointment with Death. Go Toward the Light (TV). 1989: Dream a Little Dream. Twin Peaks (TV). 1990: Rising Son (TV). *Mother, Mother. 1991: Other People's Money. 1992: Rich in Love. Storyville. Love, Lies & Lullabies (TV). 1993: Wrestling Ernest Hemingway. Trauma. 1994: Shadows of Desire (TV. GB: The Devil's Bed). Fighting for My Daughter: The Annie Dion Story (TV). 1995: Deadly Nightshade (TV). The Crossing Guard. The Grass Harp. 1996: The Road to Galveston (TV). In the Blink of an Eye (TV). 1997: St Patrick's Day. Horton Foote's Alone (TV). A Christmas Memory (TV). Intensity/Dean Koontz's Intensity (TV). 1998: The Faculty. 1999: Palmer's Pick-Up. Inherit the Wind (TV). The Mao Game. 2000: Possessed.

LAVI, Daliah (D. Levenbuch) 1940–
Raven-haired, olive-skinned, flashing-eyed Israeli actress, never as well used as in her first major international film, Lord Jim (supposedly her debut, although she had been in films for quite a few years). Afterwards, she was seen mainly as shapely

decoration in spy thrillers, and never seemed to appear in more serious roles. Pursued a singing career after 1970.

1955: Haemsöborna. 1960: Burning Sands. Candide. 1961: The Return of Dr Mabuse. Un soir sur la plage (GB: Violent Summer). La fête espagnole. Le jeu de la vérité. 1962: The Black, White and Red Four-Poster. Cyrano and D'Artagnan. Le massaggiatrici. Two Weeks in Another Town. 1963: Il demonio. La frustra e il corpo (GB: Night is the Phantom. US: What!). And So to Bed. 1964: Old Shatterhand (GB: Apaches' Last Battle). Lord Jim. Celestina. D.M. – Killer. Ou suif dans l'orient. 1965: Ten Little Indians. Schüsse im dreivierteltakt. 1966: The Silencers. The Spy with a Cold Nose. 1967: Casino Royale. Rocket to the Moon (US: Those Fantastic Flying Fools). 1968: Nobody Runs Forever (US: The High Commissioner). 1969: Some Girls Do. 1971: Catlow. 1993: Magnificat.

LAW, John Phillip 1937–

Tall, fair-haired, well-built, boyish-looking American leading man (actually born in Hollywood) without excessive personality, who has worked equally well in America and Italy. Acting since his early teens (although he studied engineering at university), he was in vogue as a leading man in the late 1960s and early 1970s. In more recent times he has continued to star in action films, albeit of the type more likely to be found on video shelves than cinema screens.

1950: The Magnificent Yankee (GB: The Man with Thirty Sons). 1964: Alta infideltà (GB: High Infidelity). Tre notti di amore. La frustra e il corpo (GB: Night is the Phantom. US: What!). 1966: The Russians Are Coming, the Russians Are Coming. 1967: Death Rides a Horse. Hurry Sundown. Barbarella. Diabolik (GB: Danger: Diabolik). 1968: Skidoo. The Sergeant. 1969: Certo, certissimo, anzi . . . probabile. 1970: The Hawaiians (GB: Master of the Islands). 1971: Von Richthofen and Brown (GB: The Red Baron). The Love Machine. The Last Movie. Michael Strogoff. 1973: The Golden Voyage of Sinbad. 1974: Open Season. Diary of a Telephone Operator. Polvere di Stella. 1975: The Spiral Staircase. Dr Justice. 1976: The Cassandra Crossing. Tigers Don't Cry. Your God and My Hell. A Whisper in the Dark. 1978: The Crystal Man. Der Schimmelreiter. The Devil's Bed. Ring of Darkness. Colpo secco. 1980: Attack Force Z. 1981: Tarzan the Ape-Man. 1982: Tin Man. 1984: Stormrider. No Time to Die (released

1986). 1985: Night Train to Terror. Rainy Day Friends. Die Jagd der goldenen Tiger. 1986: American Ccommandos/Hitman. 1987: Moon in Scorpio. Combat Force/Striker. Johann Strauss: The King Without a Crown. 1988: Space Mutiny. A Case of Honor. Blood Delirium. Nerds of a Feather. 1989: Thunder Warrior 3. Alienator. 1990: Stakes. Cold Heat. 1993: The Day of the Pig. 1994: The Shining Blood. 1995: Angel Eyes. 1996: Hindsight. Like a Cry to Heaven. 1997: Bad Rocks. My Ghost Dog (TV). 1999: Vic/Final Act. Wanted. 2000: Citizens of Perpetual Indulgence.

LAW, Jude 1972–

Fair-haired, sharp-featured, mischievous-looking British actor, equally at home with vicious tormentors and bored socialites. Acting since childhood and a dominant figure in his first leading role at 21, he has often been cast as self-destructive characters with a hint of cruelty in their make-up, and quickly developed into an offbeat leading man. Married actress Sadie Frost (*qv*). Academy Award nominee for *The Talented Mr Ripley*.

1992: *The Crane. 1993: Shopping. 1996: Bent (released 1998). I Love You, I Love You Not. 1997: Music for Another Room. Wilde. Gattaca. Midnight in the Garden of Good and Evil. 1998: The Wisdom of Crocodiles. Final Cut. 1999: eXistenZ. The Talented Mr Ripley. Love, Honour & Obey. 2000: Enemy at the Gates. 2001: A.I.

As co-director: 1999: Tube Tales (cable TV).

LAWFORD, Peter (P. Aylen) 1923–1984

Bland, inoffensive, elegant brown-haired British leading man, a staple ingredient of M-G-M films from 1942 to 1952 as light romantic interest. The thick eyebrows which always made him look a little quizzical became beetling in middle-age, when he became a member of the notorious Sinatra clan and a character actor as benign and lightweight as he had been as a star. An actor since childhood, Lawford died from kidney and liver complications.

1930: Poor Old Bill (US: Old Bill). 1931: A Gentleman of Paris. 1938: Lord Jeff (GB: The Boy from Barnardo's). 1942: Eagle Squadron. Mrs Miniver. Thunder Birds. Junior Army. A Yank at Eton. The London Blackout Murders (GB: Secret Motive). Random Harvest. 1943: Girl Crazy. The Purple V. Pilot No. 5. The Immortal Sergeant. The Man from Down Under. Someone to Remember. Above Suspicion. Sherlock Holmes Faces Death. The Sky's the Limit. Flesh and Fantasy. Corvette K-225 (GB: The Nelson Touch). Assignment in Brittany. Paris After Dark. Sahara. West Side Kid. 1944: The Adventures of Mark Twain. The Canterville Ghost. The White Cliffs of Dover. Mrs Parkington. 1945: The Picture of Dorian Gray. Son of Lassie. 1946: Cluny Brown. My Brother Talks to Horses. Two Sisters from Boston. 1947: It Happened in Brooklyn. Good News. 1948: Easter Parade. Julia Misbehaves. On an Island with You. 1949: Little Women. The Red Danube. 1950: Please Believe Me. Royal Wedding (GB: Wedding Bells). 1952: Just This Once. You for Me. Rogues' March. Kangaroo. The Hour of 13. 1953: It Should Happen to You. 1956: Sincerely, Willis Wayde (TV). 1959: Never So Few. 1960: Ocean's Eleven. Exodus. Pepe. 1962: The Longest Day. Advise and Consent. Sergeants Three. 1964: Dead Ringer (GB: Dead Image). 1965: Sylvia. Harlow. 1966: The Oscar. A Man Called Adam. How I Spent My Summer Vacation (TV. GB cinemas as Deadly Roulette). 1967: Dead Run/Deux billets pour Mexique. 1968: Skidoo. Salt and Pepper. Buona Sera, Mrs Campbell. 1969: The April Fools. The Big Blast. Hook, Line and Sinker. 1970: One More Time. Togetherness. A Step Out of Line (TV). 1971: The Deadly Hunt (TV). Ellery Queen: Don't Look Behind You. (TV). Clay Pigeon (GB: Trip to Kill). Journey Back to Oz (voice only). 1972: They Only Kill Their Masters. 1974: That's Entertainment. Rosebud. The Phantom of Hollywood (TV). 1975: Won Ton Ton, the Dog Who Saved Hollywood. 1977: Fantasy Island (TV). 1978: Seven from Heaven. 1979: Island of Sister Teresa (TV. later: Mysterious Island of Beautiful Women). Angels' Brigade. 1981: Body and Soul. 1983: Where is Parsifal?

LAWRENCE, Delphi 1927–

Tawny blonde, too-cool British actress of Anglo-Hungarian parentage. She gave up an ambition to be a concert pianist to turn to acting, and was quite busy in British films after 1953. Played heroines in 'B' features, and catty, worldy-wise 'other women' in bigger productions. Went to America in 1966 and stayed.

1953: Blood Orange (US: Three Stops to Murder). 1954: Meet Mr Callaghan. Duel in the Jungle. 1955: Murder by Proxy (US: Blackout. Completed 1953). Josephine and Men. Barbados Quest (US: Murder on Approval). The Gold

*Express. 1956: The Feminine Touch (US: The Gentle Touch). Doublecross. It's Never Too Late. 1957: Strangers' Meeting. Just My Luck. 1958: Blind Spot. Son of Robin Hood. 1959: Too Many Crooks. The Man Who Could Cheat Death. 'Beat' Girl (US: Wild for Kicks). 1960: Cone of Silence (US: Trouble in the Sky). 1961: *The Square Mile Murder. The Fourth Square. 1962: Seven Keys. *Dawn Rendezvous. 1963: The List of Adrian Messenger. On the Run. Farewell Performance. 1964: Frozen Alive. 1965: Bunny Lake is Missing. 1967: The Last Challenge (GB: The Pistolero of Red River). 1973: Cops and Robbers.*

LAWRENCE, Gertrude
(G. Lawrence-Klasen) 1898–1952
Jaunty, spring-heeled, irrepressible star of post-World War I revue, the top British star of her type in the twenties, with much of her material written especially for her by Noël Coward. She never came to terms with the cinema any more than it came to terms with her, although Julie Andrews told her story in *Star!* Suffered much from ill-health in later years. Died from cancer of the liver.
*1925: *Stage Stars Off Stage. 1928: *Gertrude Lawrence Singing 'I Don't Know'. 1929: The Battle of Paris. *Early Mourning. 1932: Lord Camber's Ladies. Women Who Play. Aren't We All? 1933: No Funny Business. 1935: Mimi. 1936: Rembrandt. Men Are Not Gods. 1943: Stage Door Canteen. 1950: The Glass Menagerie.*

LAWRENCE, Martin 1965–
Dapper, darting, not too-tall, moustachioed American comedian whose colourful life easily qualified him for the title of his biggest film hit, *Bad Boys*, encompassing brushes

with the law, a ban from TV for a too-rude routine and a period in psychiatric hospital. He won a nationwide comic-talent contest in 1987 and five years later had his own TV show. *Bad Boys* brought him international recognition, but there were a few dips in his career after that before *Blue Streak* gave him another hit in 1999. He had a health scare that year when collapsing into a coma from heat exhaustion, but recovered to resume his career. Born in Germany.
1989: Do the Right Thing. 1990: House Party. 1991: House Party 2. Talkin' Dirty After Dark. 1992: Boomerang. 1994: You So Crazy. 1995: Bad Boys. 1996: †A Thin Line Between Love and Hate. 1997: Nothing to Lose. 1999: Blue Streak. 2000: Big Momma's House. 2001: What's the Worst That Could Happen?
†And directed

LAWSON Sarah 1928–
Warmly attractive, full-lipped redhead equally at home in glamorous or homespun parts. Born in London, she made her acting debut in Edinburgh, then won leading roles almost as soon as she came to films from the repertory company she had formed herself. But her movies were mostly second-features and her career (which might perhaps have blossomed more fully in Hollywood) has long taken second place to that of her husband Patrick Allen (1927–), the Canadian actor she married in 1956.
*1951: The Browning Version. 1952: The Night Won't Talk. 1953: Street Corner (US: Both Sides of the Law). Three Steps in the Dark. Meet Mr Malcolm. You Know What Sailors Are. 1955: The Blue Peter (US: Navy Heroes). 1956: It's Never Too Late. 1958: *Man With a Dog. Links of Justice. Three*

Crooked Men. The Solitary Child. 1962: Night Without Pity. 1963: On the Run. The World Ten Times Over (US: Pussycat Alley). 1967: Night of the Big Heat (US: Island of the Burning Damned). 1968: The Devil Rides Out (US: The Devil's Bride). 1969: Battle of Britain. 1978: The Stud.

LAWSON, Wilfred
(W. Worsnop) 1900–1966
Raucous-voiced, abrasive, distinctive British character star. In spite of alcohol problems that made him difficult to employ, he became a star of the British cinema from 1938 to 1947 (before spending a long sojourn on stage) with fruitful excursions to Hollywood. Even in his last years, he was still capable of stealing scenes from the leading players. Died from a heart attack.
*1931: East Lynne on the Western Front. 1933: Strike It Rich. 1935: Turn of the Tide. 1936: Ladies in Love. White Hunter. 1937: The Man Who Made Diamonds. Bank Holiday (US: Three on a Weekend). 1938: The Terror. Yellow Sands. The Gaunt Stranger (US: The Phantom Strikes). Pygmalion. Stolen Life. 1939: Dead Man's Shoes. Allegheny Uprising (GB: The First Rebel). 1940: The Long Voyage Home. Pastor Hall. Gentleman of Venture (US: It Happened to One Man). The Farmer's Wife. The Man at the Gate (US: Men of the Sea). 1941: Danny Boy. Jeannie. The Tower of Terror. Hard Steel. 1942: The Night Has Eyes (US: Terror House). The Great Mr Handel. 1943: Thursday's Child. 1944: Fanny by Gaslight (US: Man of Evil). 1945: *Macbeth. 1947: The Turners of Prospect Road. 1954: Make Me an Offer. 1955: The Prisoner. An Alligator Named Daisy. 1956: Now and Forever. War and Peace. 1957: Hell Drivers. Miracle in Soho. The Naked Truth (US: Your Past is Showing). Doctor at Large. 1958: Tread Softly Stranger. Room at the Top. 1959: Expresso Bongo. 1961: The Naked Edge. Nothing Barred. Over the Odds. Go to Blazes. 1962: Postman's Knock. 1963: Becket. Tom Jones. 1966: The Wrong Box. 1967: The Viking Queen.*

LAWTON, Frank
(F.L. Mokeley Jnr) 1904–1969
Gentle-looking, light-haired British leading man of some charm, mostly in sensitive roles. Went to Hollywood with *Cavalcade*, and played a few film roles there, then returned to Britain and resumed his stage career. Later a character actor, mostly as upper-class types

of military bearing. Married to Evelyn Laye (*qv*) from 1934.

*1930: Birds of Prey (US: The Perfect Alibi). Young Woodley. 1931: The Skin Game. The Outsider. Michael and Mary. 1932: After Office Hours. 1933: Heads We Go (US: The Charming Deceiver). Friday the Thirteenth. Cavalcade. 1934: One More River. (GB: Over the River). Voice in the Night. 1935: David Copperfield. Bar-20 Rides Again. 1936: The Invisible Ray. The Devil Doll. The Mill on the Floss. 1937: *Secrets of the Stars. 1939: The Four Just Men (US: The Secret Four). Happy Families. 1942: Went the Day Well? (US: 48 Hours). 1948: The Winslow Boy. 1953: Rough Shoot (US: Shoot First). 1956: Doublecross. 1957: The Rising of the Moon. 1958: Gideon's Day (US: Gideon of Scotland Yard). A Night to Remember. 1960: The Queen's Guards.*

LAYE, Evelyn (Elsie E. Lay) 1900–1996
Blue-eyed blonde British singer and musical comedy star, a great success on the London stage in the twenties, but all too rarely seen in the cinema. Married to Sonnie Hale (1926–1931, the divorce case involving Jessie Matthews causing a headline scandal) and Frank Lawton (1934 until his death in 1969). Was known as 'Boo' to her friends. Died from respiratory failure.

*1937: The Luck of the Navy. 1930: Queen of Scandal. 1931: One Heavenly Night. 1933: Waltz Time. 1934: Evensong. The Night is Young. Princess Charming. 1937: *Secrets of the Stars. 1946: I'll Turn to You. 1959: Make Mine a Million. 1965: Theatre of Death (US: Blood Fiend). 1970: Say Hello to Yesterday. Un estate con sentimento (GB: Within and Without). 1980: Never Never Land. 1988: The Woman He Loved (TV).*

LAZENBY, George 1939–
Big, chunky, dark-haired cheerily handsome Australian leading man who blew his big chance as James Bond, failing to correct the impression of an animated puppet from some children's science-fiction series, probably the result of too many years in TV commercials. A few years later he was back in Australia, and later still appeared in featured roles in some eccentric international ventures, including several soft-porn movies for TV.

1969: On Her Majesty's Secret Service. 1971: Universal Soldier. 1972: Who Saw Her Die? 1973: The Dragon Flies. 1974: Stone. 1975: The Man from Hong Kong. 1976: Is Anybody There? (TV). 1977: Cover Girls (TV). Kentucky Fried Movie. Death Dimension. 1978: The Newman Shame (TV). The Falcon's Ultimatum. 1979: Saint Jack. 1981: L'ultimo harem. 1983: The Return of the Man from UNCLE (TV). 1986: Never Too Young to Die. Hell Hunters. 1992: Emmanuelle 7. Eyes of the Beholder. Eternelle Emanuelle (TV). L'amour d'Emmanuelle (TV). Le parfum d'Emmanuelle/Emmanuelle's Revenge (TV). 1993: Gettysburg. Death by Misadventure. La magie d'Emmanuelle (TV). 1995: Life's Little Horrors. The Babysitters. 1999: Gut Feeling. Four Dogs Playing Poker.

LEDERER, Francis
(Frantisek Lederer) 1899–2000
Dark-haired, idyllically handsome Czech-born leading man. After a beginning in German films, he became a Broadway matinee idol. The Hollywood film career that followed was strangely unfulfilling and his looks disappeared as he neared middle age. Three times married, including once to actress Margo (Maria Castilla 1918–) from

1937 to 1940. Billed in his German films as Franz Lederer. Reached his 100th birthday on 6 November 1999.

*1929: Zuflucht. Die Büchse der Pandora (GB and US: Pandora's Box). Die wunderbare Lüge de Nina Petrovna. Atlantik. Ihre Majestät die Liebe. 1930: Maman ceribri. Haitang. 1931: Susanne macht Ordnung. Das Schicksal der Renate Langen. 1934: A Man of Two Worlds. Pursuit of Happiness. Romance in Manhattan. 1935: The Gay Deception. *Starlight Days at the Lido. 1936: My American Wife. One Rainy Afternoon. 1938: It's All Yours. The Lone Wolf in Paris. 1939: Confessions of a Nazi Spy. Midnight. 1940: The Man I Married. 1941: Puddin' Head (GB: Judy Goes to Town). 1944: The Bridges of San Luis Rey. Voice in the Wind. 1946: The Diary of a Chambermaid. The Madonna's Secret. 1948: Million Dollar Week-End. 1949: Captain Carey USA (GB: After Midnight). 1950: Surrender. A Woman of Distinction. 1953: Stolen Identity. 1956: The Ambassador's Daughter. Lisbon. 1958: The Return of Dracula (GB: The Fantastic Disappearing Man). Maracaibo. 1959: Terror is a Man. 1991: Der andere Blick. 1998: Looking for Lulu (doc).*

LEDGER, Heath
(Heathcliffe Ledger) 1979–
Tall, strapping Australian actor with flowing hair and round, impassive features. A prize-winning actor as a teenager, he made an impressive debut in Australian films before being whisked to Hollywood at 20 and immediately placed in significant roles. Quickly proving equally adept at comedy and action, he was soon heading the cast in major movie adventures.

1997: Paws. Blackrock. 1999: Two Hands. 10 Things I Hate About You. 2000: The Patriot. 2001: A Knight's Tale. The Four Feathers.

LEE, Anna (Joanna Winnifrith) 1913–
Diminutive, spirited blonde star of British films in the 1930s. She went to America in 1939 with her then-husband, director Robert Stevenson, and did well during the war years in some strong roles which contrasted with her lightweight British parts. The quality of her roles declined after *Bedlam* in 1946 and she moved rather quickly into middle-aged parts, a number of them small cameos in John Ford films. Goddaughter of Dame Sybil Thorndike (*qv*). Mother of actress, later producer, Venetia Stevenson (1938–).

1932: Ebb Tide. Yes Mr Brown. Say It with

Music. 1933: Mayfair Girl. King's Cup. Chelsea Life. Mannequin. Faces. The Bermondsey Kid. 1934: Lucky Loser. The Camels Are Coming. Rolling in Money. 1935: Heat Wave. The Passing of the Third Floor Back. First a Girl. 1936: The Man Who Changed His Mind (US: The Man Who Lived Again). O.H.M.S. (US: You're in the Army Now). 1937: King Solomon's Mines. Non-Stop New York. 1939: The Four Just Men (US: The Secret Four). Young Man's Fancy. Return to Yesterday. 1940: Seven Sinners. 1941: My Life with Caroline. How Green Was My Valley. 1942: Flying Tigers. Commandos Strike at Dawn. 1943: Hangmen Also Die. Flesh and Fantasy. Forever and a Day. 1944: Summer Storm. Abroad with Two Yanks. 1946: Bedlam. GI War Brides. 1947: High Conquest. The Ghost and Mrs Muir. 1948: Best Man Wins. Fort Apache. 1949: Prison Warden. 1950: Wyoming Mail. 1951: Boots Malone. 1956: Daniel Boone – Trail Blazer. 1958: The Last Hurrah. Gideon's Day (US: Gideon of Scotland Yard). 1959: The Horse Soldiers. Jet over the Atlantic. This Earth is Mine! The Big Night. 1960: The Crimson Kimono. 1961: Jack the Giant-Killer. Two Rode Together. 1962: The Man Who Shot Liberty Valance. What Ever Happened to Baby Jane? 1963: The Prize. 1964: The Unsinkable Molly Brown. For Those Who Think Young. 1965: The Sound of Music. The Movie Maker (TV). 1966: 7 Women. Torn Curtain. Picture Mommy Dead. 1967: In Like Flint. 1968: Star! 1973: My Darling Daughter's Anniversary (TV). 1975: Eleanor and Franklin (TV). 1977: Eleanor and Franklin: The White House Years (TV). 1978: The Beasts Are on the Streets (TV). 1979: The Night Rider (TV). 1980: Scruples. 1984: Clash/Clash. 1987: The Right-Hand Man. 1989: My Name is Bertolt Brecht – Exile in the USA. Listen to Me. Beverly Hills Brats. 1994: What Can I Do?

LEE, Belinda 1935–1961

Sultry British blonde bombshell, a favourite pin-up of fan magazines in the mid-fifties. Taken on by Rank, who gave her a fair range of roles including low-key good-girl parts that revealed her as a capable actress. But she preferred to go to the continent and star in sexy spectaculars, and it was there that she was killed in a car crash.

1954: Life with the Lyons. The Runaway Bus. The Case of Canary Jones. Meet Mr Callaghan. The Belles of St Trinian's. 1955: Murder by Proxy (US: Blackout). Man of the Moment. Footsteps in the Fog. No Smoking. Who Done It? 1956: The Feminine Touch (US: The Gentle Touch). Eyewitness. The Big Money (released 1958). 1957: The Secret Place. Miracle in Soho. Dangerous Exile. La Venere di Cheronea/Aphrodite, Goddess of Love. 1958: Nor the Moon by Night (US: Elephant Gun). Ce corps tant desiré (GB: Way of the Wicked). 1959: Les dragueurs (GB: The Young Have No Morals. US: The Chasers). Brevi amori a Palma di Majorca. I magliari. Le notti di Lucrezia Borgia (GB: Nights of Temptation). Die Wahrheit über Rosemarie (GB: Love Now – Pay Later). Messalina/Messalina venere imperatrice. 1960: Constantine the Great. Il sicario. Femmine di lusso (GB: Travelling in Luxury. US: The Italian Way). Giuseppe venduto dai fratelli (GB: Sold into Egypt). Der Satan lockt mit Liebe. La lunga notte dell 43. Fantasmi a Roma (GB: Phantom Lovers. US: Ghosts of Rome). 1961: Marie des Isles (GB: Marie of the Isles). Visa pour Caracas. Il sicono/Hitman.

LEE, Brandon
See LEE, Bruce

LEE, Bruce (Li Chen-fan) 1940–1973

Slightly-built, very athletic, intensely-staring actor from Hong Kong, who worked for some years in Hollywood, but had to return to his native country to become a world superstar in bone-crunching kung-fu action movies. Died from cerebral oedema while making a film, which was eventually completed some years later using a similar-looking actor. Born in San Francisco. His son Brandon Lee (1964–1993) died in a shooting accident while starring in his fourth major film.

1941: Golden Gate Girl/Tears of San Francisco. 1946: †The Birth of Mankind. 1948: †My Son A-Chen. 1949: †Kid Cheung. 1951: †Infancy. 1953: †A Mother's Tears. †Blame It on Father. †Countless Families. 1954: †In the Face of Demolition. 1955: †An Orphan's Tragedy. †We Owe It to Our Children. †Orphan's Song. 1956: †Those Wise Guys Who Fool Around. †Too Late for Divorce. 1957: †Thunderstorm. 1958: †The Orphan/The Orphan Ah-Sam. 1961: †A Goose Alone in the World. 1969: Marlowe. 1971: The Big Boss (US: Fists of Fury). 1972: Fist of Fury (US: The Chinese Connection). 1973: ‡Way of the Dragon (US: Return of the Dragon). Enter the Dragon. The Unicorn Fist. 1974: Kato and the Green Hornet (TV episodes with added footage). 1978: Game of Death/Bruce Lee's Game of Death.

†As Lee Siu Lung ‡Also directed

LEE, Christopher 1922–

Tall, imposing, dark-haired British actor with faintly contemptuous air and deep, resonant voice. Spent ten years in British films playing relatively minor (often aristocratic) villains, then burst through to stardom with his fine portrayal of Dracula. Has remained happily typed in chillers, with one or two interesting character roles along the way. Still busy in sepulchral star cameos as he nears his eighties.

1948: Corridor of Mirrors. One Night with You. Hamlet. A Song for Tomorrow. Saraband for Dead Lovers (US: Saraband). My Brother's Keeper. Penny and the Pownall Case. The Luck of the Irish. Scott of the Antarctic. 1949: Trottie True (US: Gay Lady). 1950: Prelude to Fame. They Were Not Divided. 1951: Captain Horatio Hornblower R.N. The Valley of Eagles. 1952: Top Secret (US: Mr Potts Goes to Moscow). Babes in Bagdad. Paul Temple Returns. The Crimson Pirate. Moulin Rouge. 1953: Innocents in Paris. The Triangle (US: TV). *The Mirror and Markheim. 1954: Destination Milan (US: TV). The Death of Michael Turbin. 1955: The Dark Avenger (US: The Warriors). That Lady. *Crossroads. The Final Column (US: TV). Storm over the Nile. Man in Demand. Cockleshell Heroes. Police Dog. Stranglehold (US: TV). Private's Progress. 1956: Port Afrique. The Battle of the River Plate (US: Pursuit of the Graf Spee). Beyond Mombasa. Moby Dick (TV). Ill Met by Moonlight (US: Night Ambush). Alias John Preston. The Curse of Frankenstein. 1957: Fortune is a Woman (US: She Played with

Fire). *The Traitor* (US: *The Accused*). *Bitter Victory*. *A Tale of Two Cities*. 1958: *The Truth About Women*. *Battle of the V-1* (US: *V1/Unseen Heroes*). *Dracula* (US: *The Horror of Dracula*). *Corridors of Blood*. 1959: *The Mummy*. *The Hound of the Baskervilles*. *The Man Who Could Cheat Death*. *The Treasure of San Teresa* (US: *Long Distance*). '*Beat' Girl* (US: *Wild for Kicks*). 1960: *City of the Dead* (US: *Horror Hotel*). *The Two Faces of Dr Jekyll* (US: *House of Fright*). *Too Hot to Handle* (US: *Playgirl After Dark*). *The Hands of Orlac* (US: *Hands of a Strangler*). 1961: *Hard Times for Vampires* (US: *Uncle Was a Vampire*). *The Terror of the Tongs*. *Taste of Fear* (US: *Scream of Fear*). *Hercules in the Centre of the Earth* (US: *Hercules in the Haunted World*). *Mystery of the Red Orchid* (US: *Secret of the Red Orchid*). *The Pirates of Blood River*. 1962: *The Devil's Daffodil* (US: *The Daffodil Killer*). *In Namen des Teufels* (GB and US: *The Devil's Agent*). 1963: *La cripta e l'incubo* (GB: *Crypt of Horror*. US: *The Vampire Crypt*). *La vergina di Norimberga* (GB: *Castle of Terror*. US: *Horror Castle*). *The Devil Ship Pirates*. *La frustra e il corpo* (GB: *Night is the Phantom*. US: *What!*). *Catharsis* (US: *Faust '63*). *Sherlock Holmes und das Halsband des Todes* (GB: *Sherlock Holmes and the Deadly Necklace*). 1964: *The Masque of the Red Death* (voice only). *The Gorgon*. *Dr Terror's House of Horrors*. *Castle of the Living Dead*. 1965: *The Face of Fu Manchu*. *She*. *Rasputin the Mad Monk*. *Theatre of Death* (US: *Blood Fiend*). *Circus of Fear* (US: *Psycho-Circus*). *Dracula Prince of Darkness*. *The Skull*. *Ten Little Niggers* (voice only). 1966: *The Brides of Fu Manchu*. 1967: **Victims of Terror* (US: *Victims of Vesuvius*. Narrator only). *Five Golden Dragons*. *The Vengeance of Fu Manchu*. *Die Schlangengrube und das Pendel* (GB: *The Blood Demon*). *Night of the Big Heat* (US: *Island of the Burning Damed*). *The Devil Rides Out* (US: *The Devil's Bride*). 1968: *Dracula Has Risen from the Grave*. *The Castle of Fu Manchu*. *The Face of Eve* (US: *Eve*). *Blood of Fu Manchu* (US: *Kiss and Kill*). *The Curse of the Crimson Altar* (US: *Crimson Cult*). 1969: *The Oblong Box*. *Philosophy in the Boudoir* (US: *Eugenie – the Story of Her Journey into Perversion*). *The Magic Christian*. *Scream and Scream Again*. *One More Time*. 1970: *Taste the Blood of Dracula*. *The Private Life of Sherlock Holmes*. *Der Hexentöter von Blackmoor* (US: *The Bloody Judge*). *Il trono di fuoco* (GB: *Throne of Fire*. US: *Throne of the Blood Monster*). *Julius Caesar*. *The House That Dripped Blood*. *Count Dracula/Bram Stoker's Count Dracula*. *El Umbraculo*. *Scars of Dracula*. *I, Monster*. 1971: *Hannie Caulder*. 1972: *Poor Devil* (TV). *Dracula A.D. 1972*. *Panico en el Transiberio* (GB and US: *Horror Express*). *The Creeping Flesh*. *Death Line* (US: *Raw Meat*). *Nothing But the Night*. 1973: *Dark Places*. *The Satanic Rites of Dracula* (US: *Dracula and His Vampire Bride*). *The Wicker Man*. *Eulalie quitte les champs* (US: *The Star, the Orphan and the Butcher*). *The Three Musketeers – The Queen's Diamonds*. 1974: *The Four Musketeers – the Revenge of Milady*. *The Man with the Golden Gun*. *Diagnosis: Murder*. 1975: *To the Devil . . . a Daughter*.

The Diamond Mercenaries. *The Keeper*. *Revenge of the Dead* (narrator only). *Death in the Sun*. 1976: *Dracula, Father and Son/Père et fils*. 1977: *Airport 77*. *End of the World*. *Meat Cleaver Massacre*. *Starship Invasions/Alien Encounter*. 1978: *Jaguar Lives*. *The Passage*. *Caravans*. *The Pirate* (TV). *Return from Witch Mountain*. *The Silent Flute*. 1979: *Arabian Adventure*. *Bear Island*. 1941: *Nutcracker Fantasy* (voice only). 1980: *Once Upon a Spy* (TV). *Serial*. *Captain America II. Sunday Games* (TV). †*Rollerboy*. 1981: *Goliath Awaits* (feature version of TV mini-series). *The Salamander*. *The Last Unicorn* (voice only). *Rally* (later *Safari 3000*). *An Eye for an Eye*. 1982: *The Return of Captain Invincible*. *House of the Long Shadows*. *Charles and Diana: A Royal Love Story* (TV). 1983: *Massarati and the Brain* (TV). 1984: †*The Bengal Lancers* (TV). *New Magic. 1985: *Mask of Murder*. *The Howling II . . . Your Sister is a Werewolf*. *The Rosebud Beach Hotel*. *Road Trip*. *Jocks*. 1986: *The Disputation*. *Mio in the Land of Faraway*. *The Girl*. *Desperate Moves*. 1987: *Dark Mission: Flowers of Evil*. 1988: *The Avalon Awakening*. *Murder Story*. 1989: *Treasure Island* (TV. GB: cinemas). *La chute des aigles*. *The Return of the Musketeers*. 1990: *The French Revolution*. *Gremlins 2: The New Batch*. *Honeymoon Academy*. *The Care of Time*. *The Rainbow Thief*. *L'avaro* (*The Miser*). *The Monastery*. 1991: *Shogun Mayeda/Journey of Honor*. *Curse III: Blood Sacrifice*. *Sherlock Holmes and the Incident at Victoria Falls* (TV). 1992: *Sherlock Holmes and the Leading Lady* (TV). 1993: *Double Suspicion/Double Vision*. *Jackpot* (US: *Cybereden*). *Death Train/Alistair MacLean's Death Train* (TV). 1994: *Police Academy 7 – Mission to Moscow*. *Funny Man*. 1995: *A Feast at Midnight*. *The Stupids*. 1996: *The Knot*. 1997: *Flesh and Blood*. *Jinnah* (released 1998). *Talos the Mummy*. *The Odyssey*. 1998: *Marco Polo*. 1999: *Sleepy Hollow*. 2001: *The Lord of the Rings: The Fellowship of the Ring*. 2002: *Star Wars: Episode 2*. *The Lord of the Rings: The Two Towers*.

†*Unfinished*
‡*Scenes deleted*

LEE, Gypsy Rose
(R. Louise Hovick) 1913–1970
Slender, long-legged, dark-haired singer, dancer and raconteuse, in show business at six as Baby Rose Louise. Later she became America's most famous stripper and made some sporadic and rather strained film appearances in decorative roles. Also wrote novels and plays, and her autobiography, *Gypsy*, was made into a Broadway musical show which was in turn filmed twice. Sister of June Havoc (*qv*). Died from cancer.
1937: †*You Can't Have Everything*. 1938: †*Sally, Irene and Mary*. †*Ali Baba Goes to Town*. †*The Battle of Broadway*. 1939: †*My Lucky Star*. 1943: *Stage Door Canteen*. 1944: *Belle of the Yukon*. 1952: *Babes in Bagdad*. 1958: *Screaming Mimi*. *Wind Across the Everglades*. 1962: *The Stripper* (GB: *Woman of Summer*). 1965: *Who Has Seen the Wind?* (TV). 1966: *The Trouble with Angels*. 1969: *The Over-the-Hill-Gang* (TV).

†*As Louise Hovick*

LEE, Jason Scott 1966–
Energetic, fit-looking, Hawaiian-raised actor of Chinese descent. So far in a brief, but showy film career, Lee has played an Eskimo, a Polynesian, an Indian and a Hong Kong Chinese. In his spare time, an enthusiastic surfer, gymnast and sketch artist. More action roles followed, but he seemed less in demand as the century passed, and even turned to doing *The King and I* on the London stage.
1987: *Born in East L.A.* 1989: *Back to the Future Part II*. 1990: *Vestige of Honor* (TV). 1991: *The Lookalike* (TV). *Ghoulies 3: American Eyes*. 1992: *Map of the Human Heart*. 1993: *Dragon: The Bruce Lee Story*. *Rapa Nui*. 1994: *Rudyard Kipling's the Jungle Book*. 1995: *Picture Bride*. 1997: *Murder in Mind*. *Talos the Mummy*. 1998: *Soldier*.

LEEDS, Andrea
(Antoinette Lees) 1913–1984
Just like Peggy Dow (*qv*), this American actress rose to the top very quickly, made a deep impression in just a few films, then retired to marry a millionaire. Auburn-haired and dark-eyed with appealingly gentle features, she was at her best in introverted roles, and won an Oscar nomination as the potentially suicidal would-be actress in *Stage Door*. Her husband died in 1962 (she also lost a daughter to cancer a few years later) and she spent the latter years of her working life running a jewellery store that she owned in Palm Springs. Died from cancer.
1935: *Dante's Inferno*. **He Trusted His Wife*. **Life Hesitates at 40*. 1936: *The Bohemian*

Girl. *The Count Takes the Count. Song of the Trail. The Moon's Our Home. Come and Get It. 1937: It Could Happen to You. Stage Door. 1938: Letter of Introduction. The Goldwyn Follies. Youth Takes a Fling. 1939: They Shall Have Music (GB: Melody of Youth). Swanee River. The Real Glory. 1940: Earthbound.*

LEIGH, Janet (Jeanette Morrison) 1927–2004
Fair-haired, prettily minx-faced American actress whose breathtaking figure looked so delicious in clinging period costume that she found it hard to get away from the genre. Making her career secondary to that of then-husband Tony Curtis (third of four marriages, 1951–1962) didn't help – but her later performances, in *Touch of Evil, Psycho* and *The Manchurian Candidate*, are charged with erotic undercurrents, and showed what the cinema missed. Nominated for an Academy Award in *Psycho*. Mother of actress Jamie Lee Curtis (qv).

*1947: The Romance of Rosy Ridge. If Winter Comes. 1948: Words and Music. Hills of Home (GB: Master of Lassie). Act of Violence. 1949: That Forsyte Woman (GB: The Forsyte Saga). The Red Danube. Little Women. The Doctor and the Girl. Holiday Affair. 1950: Jet Pilot (released 1957). 1951: Strictly Dishonorable. Angels in the Outfield (GB: Angels and the Pirates). Two Tickets to Broadway. It's a Big Country. 1952: Just This Once. Scaramouche. Fearless Fagan. 1953: The Naked Spur. Confidentially Connie. *Hollywood Laugh Parade. Houdini. Walking My Baby Back Home. 1954: Prince Valiant. Living It Up. The Black Shield of Falworth. Rogue Cop. 1955: My Sister Eileen. Pete Kelly's Blues. 1956: Safari. 1958: The Vikings. Touch of Evil. The Perfect Furlough (GB: Strictly for*

Pleasure). 1959: Who Was That Lady? 1960: Pepe. Psycho. 1962: The Manchurian Candidate. 1963: Bye Bye Birdie. Wives and Lovers. 1965: Kid Rodelo. 1966: Three on a Couch. Harper (GB: The Moving Target). An American Dream (US: See You in Hell, Darling). 1967: Grand Slam. 1968: Hello Down There. 1969: The Monk (TV). Honeymoon with a Stranger (TV). 1970: The House on Greenapple Road (TV). 1971: The Deadly Dream (TV). 1972: One is a Lonely Number. Night of the Lepus. 1973: Murdock's Gang (TV). 1976: Murder at the World Series (TV). 1977: Telethon (TV). 1979: Boardwalk. 1980: Mirror, Mirror (TV). The Fog. The Fall Guy (TV). 1985: On Our Way (TV). 1992: Stephen Verona: Self Portrait. 1998: Halloween H20: 20 Years Later. 1999: In My Sister's Shadow (TV). Dial H for Hitchcock (doc). 2000: Christmas in the Clouds.

LEIGH, Jennifer Jason
(Jennifer Leigh Morrow) 1962–
Chubby-faced, pert, petite, brown-haired American actress, often in tough roles. Her chameleon-like ability to change her appearance from film to film has attracted admiration from the critics and something of a cult following. At her best as feisty low-lifes; her career faltered slightly in the 1990s when she was asked to play sophisticates, but an Oscar nomination for one of her deeply-felt and carefully-researched performances looks likely soon. The daughter of actor Vic Morrow (qv), she made her theatrical debut as a teenager; insists that her birth year is 1962, and not the widely-quoted 1958, but when she talks of seeing *Tom Jones* at five, you do wonder . . .

1967: Death of a Stranger. 1970: God Bless the Children (TV). 1976: Lialeh. 1977: The Young Runaway (TV). 1979: The Cracker Factory (TV). 1980: Eyes of a Stranger. Angel City (TV). The Promise of Love (TV). 1981: The Best Little Girl in The World (TV). The Killing of Randy Webster (TV). 1982: Fast Times at Ridgemont High (GB: Fast Times). Wrong is Right (GB: The Man With the Deadly Lens). Easy Money. Death Ride to Osaka / Girls of the White Orchid (TV). 1984: Grandview USA. 1985: Flesh and Blood. 1986: The Hitcher. When the Bough Breaks (TV). Picnic (TV). The Men's Club. 1987: Sister, Sister. Under Cover. 1988: Heart of Midnight. The Big Picture. 1989: Last Exit to Brooklyn. Miami Blues. 1990: Fire Princess.

Buried Alive (TV). 1991: Backdraft. Crooked Hearts. Rush. 1992: Single White Female. The Prom. 1993: Short Cuts. The Hudsucker Proxy. 1994: Mrs Parker & the Vicious Circle. Luck, Trust & Ketchup. 1995: Dolores Claiborne. Georgia. 1996: Kansas City. Bastard Out of Carolina (TV). 1997: Washington Square. A Thousand Acres. 1998: The Love Letter (TV). Thanks of a Grateful Nation (cable TV). 1999: eXistenZ. Skipped Parts. 2000: The King is Alive. 2001: The Anniversary Party (and co-directed).

LEIGH, Vivien
(Vivian Hartley) 1913–1967
One of the screen's great beauties. After a fairly ordinary apprenticeship in the British cinema of the 1930s, the Indian-born, dark-haired, blue-eyed vixenish actress went to Hollywood, married Laurence Olivier (second of two, 1940–1960) and won an Oscar as Scarlett O'Hara in *Gone with the Wind*. Her career was dogged by illness, and her striking looks had gone when she took a second Oscar in *A Streetcar Named Desire*. Died from tuberculosis.

*1934: Things Are Looking Up. 1935: The Village Squire. Gentleman's Agreement. Look Up and Laugh. 1936: Fire Over England. 1937: Dark Journey. Storm in a Teacup. 21 Days (US: 21 Days Together). A Yank at Oxford. 1938: St Martin's Lane (US: Sidewalks of London). *Guide Dogs for the Blind. 1939: Gone with the Wind. 1940: Waterloo Bridge. 1941: That Hamilton Woman (GB: Lady Hamilton). *Cavalcade of the Academy Awards. 1945: Caesar and Cleopatra. 1948: Anna Karenina. 1951: A Streetcar Named Desire. 1955: The Deep Blue Sea. 1962: The Roman Spring of Mrs Stone. 1965: Ship of Fools.*

LEIGHTON, Margaret 1922–1976
Aristocratic, long-faced blonde British beauty who had more class than most films could handle. One felt that the elegance amounted almost to disdain for the medium, and she certainly seemed more at home on stage. Married (second and third of three) to Laurence Harvey (1957–1961) and Michael Wilding from 1963. Died from multiple sclerosis. Received an Academy Award nomination for *The Go-Between*.

1948: The Winslow Boy. Bonnie Prince Charlie 1949: Under Capricorn. 1950: The Astonished Heart. The Elusive Pimpernel (US: The Fighting Pimpernel). 1951: Calling Bulldog

Drummond. 1952: *Home at Seven* (US: *Murder on Monday*). *The Holly and the Ivy*. 1954: *The Good Die Young. The Teckman Mystery. Carrington VC* (US: *Court-Martial*). 1955: *The Constant Husband*. 1957: *The Passionate Stranger* (US: *A Novel Affair*). 1958: *The Sound and the Fury*. 1959: *The Second Man* (TV). 1962: *Waltz of the Toreadors*. 1964: *The Best Man*. 1965: *The Loved One*. 1966: *7 Women*. 1969: *The Madwoman of Chaillot*. 1970: *The Go-Between*. 1971: *Zee and Co.* (US: *X, Y and Zee*). 1972: *Lady Caroline Lamb*. 1973: *Bequest to the Nation. From Beyond the Grave. Frankenstein: the True Story* (TV. GB: cinemas). 1974: *Galileo*. 1975: *Great Expectations* (TV. GB: cinemas). 1976: *Trial by Combat* (US: *Dirty Knights' Work*).

LEMMON, Jack 1925–

Dark-haired, diffident-seeming American actor with engaging smile. A late starter, Lemmon only made the Broadway stage at 28, but was quickly a great success in comedy films, either as shy young men to whom Things Just Seemed to Happen, or as human Catherine wheels. Later dedicated himself to winning recognition as a serious actor, and became adept at cynicism and world-weary men. Won Academy Awards in *Mister Roberts* and *Save the Tiger*. Married (second) to Felicia Farr (qv) since 1960. Also Oscar-nominated for *Some Like It Hot, The Apartment, Days of Wine and Roses, The China Syndrome, Tribute* and *Missing*. Father of actor Chris Lemmon (1954–).
1953: *It Should Happen to You*. 1954: *Phffft! Three for the Show*. 1955: *Mister Roberts. My Sister Eileen*. 1956: **Hollywood Bronc Busters. You Can't Run Away from It*. 1957: *Fire Down Below. Operation Mad Ball. The Mystery of 13* (TV). **It Happened to Ernie*. 1958: *Cowboy. Bell, Book and Candle. Face of a Hero* (TV). 1959: *It Happened to Jane/That Jane from Maine. Some Like It Hot*. 1960: *The Wackiest Ship in the Army. The Apartment. Stowaway in the Sky* (narrator only). *Pepe*. 1962: *The Notorious Landlady. Days of Wine and Roses*. 1963: *Irma La Douce. Under the Yum Yum Tree*. 1964: *Good Neighbor Sam. How to Murder Your Wife*. 1965: *The Great Race*. 1966: *The Fortune Cookie* (GB: *Meet Whiplash Willie*). 1967: *Luv. The Odd Couple*. 1968: **There Comes a Day*. 1969: *The April Fools*. 1970: *The Out-Of-Towners*. 1971: *†Kotch* (bit only). 1972: *The War Between Men and Women. Avanti!* 1973: *Save the Tiger*. **Wednesday*. 1974: *The Front Page*. 1975: *The Prisoner of Second Avenue. The Entertainer* (TV). 1976: *Alex and the Gypsy*. 1977: *Airport 77*. 1978: *The China Syndrome*. 1979: *Ken Murray's Shooting Stars*. 1980: *Tribute. Portrait of a 60% Perfect Man*. 1981: *Buddy Buddy*. 1982: *Missing*. 1984: *Mass Appeal*. 1985: *Macaroni*. 1986: *'That's Life!'* 1989: *Dad*. 1991: *JFK*. 1992: *The Player. Glengarry Glen Ross. Father, Son and the Mistress/For Richer, For Poorer* (TV). 1993: *Short Cuts. Grumpy Old Men. Earth and the American Dream* (voice only). 1994: *A Life in the Theater. Luck, Trust & Ketchup*. 1995: *Getting Away With Murder. The Grass Harp. Temecula. Grumpier Old Men*. 1996: *A Weekend in the Country/This Joint is Jumpin'* (TV). *Hamlet. My Fellow Americans*. 1997: *12 Angry Men* (TV). *Out to Sea*. 1998: *The Odd Couple 2/The Odd Couple 2: Travelin' Light. The Long Way Home* (TV). 1999: *Inherit the Wind* (TV). *Tuesdays with Morrie* (TV). *Forever Hollywood* (doc).

†And directed

LENZ, Kay 1953–

Pert, provocative, curvaceous, dark-haired American actress who attracted attention in the late 1970s. She gave some spirited performances, but her choice of roles and films seemed sometimes unwise and her best work so far has been for television, a medium in which she continued to appear to great effect until 1997. Married/divorced singer David Cassidy.
1972: *Lisa Bright and Dark* (TV). *The Weekend Nun* (TV). 1973: *Breezy. A Summer Without Boys* (TV). 1974: *The Underground Man* (TV). *Unwed Father* (TV). *Heart in Hiding* (TV). 1975: *White Line Fever. Journeys from Darkness* (TV). 1976: *Moving Violation. The Great Scout and Cathouse Thursday*. 1977: *The Initiation of Sarah* (TV). 1978: *Mean Dog Blues. The Passage*. 1979: *Girl in the Park/Sanctuary of Fear* (TV). *The Seeding of Sarah Burns* (TV). 1980: *Escape* (TV). *The Hustler of Muscle Beach* (TV). 1981: *Fast-Walking*. 1983: *Prisoners of the Lost Universe. Trial by Terror* (TV). 1985: *House*. 1986: *Stripped to Kill*. 1987: *Heart of the City* (TV). *Death Wish 4: The Crackdown*. 1988: *Flashback. Head-hunter. Fear. Physical Evidence*. 1989: *Hardball* (TV). *Murder by Night* (TV). *Trapped* (TV). 1990: *Streets. Hitler's Daughter* (cable TV). 1991: *Souvenirs/Falling from Grace*. 1994: *Against Their Will* (TV). *Trapped in Space*. 1995: *Gunfighter's Moon*. 1996: *A Gun, a Car, a Blonde. Shame II: The Secret* (TV). 1997: *Journey of the Heart* (TV). 1998: *The Adventures of Ragtime*.

LESLEY, Carole
(Maureen L.C. Rippingdale) 1935–1974
Bubbly British platinum blonde actress, in show business from girlhood. After a pin-up period as Leslie Carol, she was groomed for stardom at the Associated-British studio from the mid-1950s, but did not seem to make a strong enough impression with the public to hold on to stardom after the studio's production schedules slackened. Committed suicide by taking sleeping pills.
1947: *The Silver Darlings*. 1948: *The Brass Monkey/Lucky Mascot*. 1949: *Trottie True* (US: *Gay Lady*). 1954: *The Embezzler*. 1957: *The Good Companions. These Dangerous Years* (US: *Dangerous Youth*). *Woman in a Dressing Gown*. 1958: *No Trees in the Street* (US: *No Tree in the Street*). 1959: *Operation Bullshine*. 1960: *Doctor in Love*. 1961: *Three on a Spree. What a Whopper!* 1962: *The Pot Carriers*.

LESLIE, Joan (J. Brodel) 1925–
Pretty, refreshing, auburn-haired American actress, in films as a girl and adult roles at 16. Although many others, like Joan, were cast as girls next door, she had gentle, radiant beauty – and the spark of personality, offering lively performances until she made the mistake of breaking away from her studio, Warners. Left films to devote more time to her family, and became a successful dress designer.
1936: *†Camille*. 1938: *†Men with Wings*. 1939: *†Two Thoroughbreds. †Nancy Drew,*

Reporter. †Winter Carnival. †Love Affair. 1940: †Susan and God (GB: The Gay Mrs Trexel). †Star Dust. †Military Academy. †Young As You Feel. †High School. †Foreign Correspondent. †Laddie. *Alice in Movieland. 1941: *Wampas Baby Stars. Thieves Fall Out. The Great Mr Nobody. High Sierra. The Wagons Roll at Night. Sergeant York. 1942: Yankee Doodle Dandy. The Male Animal. The Hard Way. 1943: Thank Your Lucky Stars. This is the Army. The Sky's the Limit. 1944: Hollywood Canteen. 1945: Rhapsody in Blue. Too Young to Know. Where Do We Go from Here? 1946: Janie Gets Married. Cinderella Jones. Two Guys from Milwaukee (GB: Royal Flush). 1947: Repeat Performance. 1948: Northwest Stampede. 1950: The Skipper Surprised His Wife. Born to be Bad. 1951: Man in the Saddle (GB: The Outcast). 1952: Hellgate. Toughest Man in Arizona. 1953: The Woman They Almost Lynched. 1954: Flight Nurse. Jubilee Trail. Hell's Outpost. 1956: The Revolt of Mamie Stover. Smoke Jumpers (TV). 1975: The Keegans (TV). 1986: Charley Hannah (TV). 1989: Turn Back the Clock (TV). 1991: Fire in the Dark (TV).

†As Joan Brodel

LESTER, Mark 1958–
Appealing British boy actor with a mop of fair, tousled hair who enjoyed international success as a child star after winning the title role in Oliver! Did not achieve adult stardom to nearly the same degree.
1964: Allez France (US: The Counterfeit Constable). 1965: Spaceflight IC-1. 1966: Fahrenheit 451. Drop Dead Darling (US: Arriverderci, Baby). 1967: Our Mother's House. 1968: Oliver! 1969: Run Wild, Run

Free. 1970: Eyewitness. 1971: Black Beauty. Melody (later S*W*A*L*K). Whoever Slew Auntie Roo? (US: Who Slew Auntie Roo?). Night Hair Child. 1972: Redneck. 1973: Scalawag. 1974: Graduation. †The Dream Time. 1975: Little Adventurer (completed 1972). Dance in the Open Air Under the Elms. 1976: Jungle Boy. 1977: The Prince and the Pauper (US: Crossed Swords).

†Uncompleted

LETO, Jared 1971–
Lanky, brown-haired, boyish-looking American actor, who resembles a sort of serious Jim Carrey (qv) and proved popular in the TV series My So-Called Life, before moving straight away into prominent film roles. Despite title parts in Prefontaine, Basil and Last of the High Kings, Leto hasn't quite made it as a box-office name and in the late 1990s was more newsworthy for dating Cameron Diaz (also qv) than for any of his films. The actress Shannon Leto is his sister.
1994: Cool and the Crazy (cable TV). 1995: How to Make an American Quilt. 1996: The Last of the High Kings. Prefontaine. 1997: Basil. Switchback/Going West in America. 1998: The Thin Red Line. Urban Legend. 1999: Girl, Interrupted. Fight Club. Sunset Strip. Black and White. 2000: American Psycho. Requiem for a Dream. A Leonard Cohen Afterworld.

LEWIS, Jerry (Joseph Levitch) 1926–
Long-faced, crop-haired, harassed-looking American star comedian whose goofy, child-like, disaster-prone comic creation was a tremendous hit in the late forties and fifties, in partnership with Dean Martin. After much

bickering, the partnership split in 1957. Lewis's solo comedy films were excellent value from 1957 to 1964 with often marvellously funny sequences, and the comedian's streak of pathos kept in check. After this, often under his own direction, they became slow, sentimental and self-indulgent, and public support and private backing ran out in 1971. More recently seen in benevolent cameos. Has six children.
1949: My Friend Irma. 1950: My Friend Irma Goes West. At War with the Army. 1951: That's My Boy. *Screen Snapshots No. 197. Sailor Beware. 1952: *Screen Snapshots No. 207. The Stooge. Jumping Jacks. Road to Bali. *Hollywood Fun Festival. 1953: Scared Stiff. The Caddy. 1954: Money from Home. Living It Up. Three Ring Circus. 1955: You're Never Too Young. Artists and Models. 1956: Pardners. Hollywood or Bust. *Hollywood Premiere. The Delicate Delinquent. 1958: The Sad Sack. Rock-a-Bye Baby. The Geisha Boy. 1959: Don't Give Up the Ship. Li'l Abner. 1960: Visit to a Small Planet. †The Bellboy. Cinderfella. 1961: †The Ladies' Man. †The Errand Boy. 1962: It's Only Money. 1963: It's a Mad, Mad, Mad, Mad World. †The Nutty Professor. Who's Minding the Store? 1964: †The Patsy. The Disorderly Orderly. 1965: †The Family Jewels. Boeing-Boeing. 1966: †Three on a Couch. Way . . . Way Out! 1967: †The Big Mouth. Don't Raise the Bridge, Lower the River. 1968: ‡The Silent Treatment. 1969: Hook, Line and Sinker. 1970: †Which Way to the Front? (GB: Ja! Ja! Mein General, But Which Way to the Front?). 1971: †‡The Day the Clown Cried. 1978: ‡Levy Flies Away. 1979: That's Life. Rascal Dazzle (narrator only). 1980: †Hardly Working. 1982: Slapstick (US: Slapstick of Another Kind). The King of Comedy. 1983: †Smorgasbord (completed 1981. Later: Cracking Up). To Catch a . . . Cop! (The Defective Detective). 1984: Par ou t'es rentre, on t'a pas vue sortir? 1987: Fight for Life (TV). 1989: Cookie. 1992: Arizona Dream (released 1994). ‡Freddie Goes to Washington (voice only). Mr Saturday Night. 1995: Funny Bones.

†Also directed ‡Unfinished

Also as director: 1970: One More Time.

LEWIS, Juliette 1973–
Dark-haired American actress of sour prettiness, often in anguished or 'victim' roles. The daughter of character actor Geoffrey Lewis

(1935–), she was in films as a teenager, earning an Oscar nomination at 18 for *Cape Fear*, and quickly moving into uninhibited roles, in several of which she ended up dead. For some years a steady twosome with actor Brad Pitt (*qv*), but the relationship ultimately broke up.

1980: *Any Which Way You Can*. 1987: *Home Fires* (TV). 1988: *My Stepmother is an Alien*. 1989: *National Lampoon's Christmas Vacation* (GB: *National Lampoon's Winter Holiday*). *The Runnin' Kind*. *Meet the Hollowheads*. 1990: *Too Young to Die?* (TV). 1991: *Crooked Hearts*. *Cape Fear*. 1992: *That Night*. *Husbands and Wives*. 1993: *Kalifornia*. *Yesterday*. *Romeo is Bleeding*. *What's Eating Gilbert Grape*. 1994: *Natural Born Killers*. *Mixed Nuts*. 1995: *The Basketball Diaries*. *Strange Days*. 1996: *From Dusk Till Dawn*. *The Audition*. *The Evening Star*. 1997: *Full Tilt Boogie*. 1998: *The Other Sister*. *Girl Talk/Some Girls*. 1999: *The 4th Floor*. 2000: *The Way of the Gun*. *Room to Rent*. *Gaudi Afternoon*.

LEWIS, Ronald 1928–1982
Tall, black-haired, virile Welsh actor, mostly in dashing or forthright parts. When his roles grew less interesting, he returned to the stage and joined the Welsh National Theatre Company. But in 1980 he was declared bankrupt and at 53 committed suicide with sleeping pills.

1953: *Valley of Song* (US: *Men Are Children Twice*). *The Square Ring*. 1954: *The Beachcomber*. *Helen of Troy*. 1955: *The Prisoner*. *Storm over the Nile*. 1956: *Sailor Beware!* (US: *Panic in the Parlor*). *A Hill in Korea* (US: *Hell in Korea*). 1957: *The Secret Place*. *Robbery Under Arms*. 1958: *The Wind Cannot Read*. *Bachelor of Hearts*. 1960: *Conspiracy of Hearts*. 1961: *The Full Treatment* (US: *Stop Me Before I Kill*). *Taste of Fear* (US: *Scream of Fear*). *Mr Sardonicus* (GB: *Sardonicus*). 1962: *Twice Round the Daffodils*. *Jigsaw*. *Billy Budd*. *Nurse on Wheels*. 1963: *Siege of the Saxons*. 1965: *The Brigand of Kandahar*. 1971: *Friends*. 1974: *Paul and Michelle*. 1981: *The John Sullivan Story* (TV).

LIEVEN, Albert (A. Liévin) 1906–1971
Dark, menacing, squat-faced German actor who fled the Nazi regime in 1936, only to be cast in British films as Nazis or other sinister types. He could play sympathetic characters but rarely got the chance. From 1952 he divided his activities between England and

Germany. Four times married and divorced, including actresses Valerie White (1916–1989) and Susan Shaw (*qv*).

1932: *Annemarie, die Braut der Kompagnie*. *Ich bei Tag und Du bei Nacht*. *Kampf um blond*. 1933: *Die vom Niederrhein*. *Reifende Jugend*. *Charley's Aunt*. 1934: *Fin Mödel mit Tempo*. *Eine Siebsehnjährige*. *Hermine und die sieben Aufrechten*. *Fräulein Liselott*. *Glückspilze*. *Krach am Jolanthe*. 1935: *Mach' mich glücklich*. *Die klugen Frauen*. *La kermesse heroique* (GB: *Carnival in Flanders*). 1936: *Eine Frau ohne Bedeutung*. *Kater Lampe*. 1937: *Victoria the Great*. 1939: *Spy for a Day*. 1940: *For Freedom*. *Let George Do It*. *Night Train to Munich* (US: *Night Train*). *Convoy*. *Neutral Port*. 1941: *Jeannie*. **Mr Proudfoot Shows a Light*. *The Big Blockade*. 1942: *The Young Mr Pitt*. 1943: *The Life and Death of Colonel Blimp* (US: *Colonel Blimp*). *The Yellow Canary*. 1944: *English without Tears* (US: *Her Man Gilbey*). 1945: *The Seventh Veil*. 1946: *Beware of Pity*. 1947: *Frieda*. 1948: *Sleeping Car to Trieste*. 1949: *Marry Me*. 1951: *The Dark Light*. *Hotel Sahara*. 1952: *Klettermaxe*. *Fritz und Friederike*. 1953: *Geliebtes Leben*. *Der Rose von Stambul*. *Desperate Moment*. 1954: *Das Bekenntnis der Ina Karr* (GB: *Afraid to Live*). 1955: *Des Teufels General* (GB: *The Devil's General*). 1956: *Die Halbstarken* (GB: *Wolfpack*. US: *Teenage Wolfpack*). *Loser Takes All*. *Nacht der Entscheidung*. 1957: *House of Intrigue/London Calling North Pole*. 1958: *Subway in the Sky*. *Der Fischer von Heiligensee* (GB: *The Big Barrier*). *Es geschah am hellichten Tag* (GB: *Assault in Broad Daylight*). 1960: *Conspiracy of Hearts*. *Foxhole in Cairo*. *Schachnovelle* (GB: *Three Moves to Freedom*. US: *The Royal Game*). 1961: *The Guns of Navarone*. *Brainwashed*. *The Devils' Daffodil* (and German-language version). 1962: *Death Trap*. *In Namen des Teufels* (GB and US: *The Devil's Agent*). *Freddy und das Lied der Südsee*. 1963: *Mystery Submarine*. *The Victors*. *Death Drums along the River*. 1964: *Traitor's Gate*. 1965: *Ride the High Wind*. 1966: *City of Fear* (US: *City of Terror*). 1968: *Der Gorilla von Soho* (US: *The Gorilla Gang*). 1970: *Die Feuerzangenbowle*.

LILLARD, Matthew 1970–
Steeple-tall, gangling, dark-haired American actor (cast as 'Stork' in his first movie) whose crooked smirk has enabled him to play fiends and fools with equal facility. An enthusiastic thespian who has run his own theatre

company twice, Lillard inserted a dangerous edge to most of his roles that soon prompted directors to cast him as borderline psychos when he wasn't contributing comic cameos, or even singing and dancing in *Love's Labour's Lost*. It comes as no surprise to learn that his favourite game is Dungeons and Dragons: one can imagine his demonic gleam participating.

1991: †*Ghoulies 3: Ghoulies Go to College*. 1994: *Serial Mom*. 1995: *Vanishing Son 4* (TV). *Ride for Your Life*. *Mad Love*. *Hackers*. *Animal Room*. 1996: *If These Walls Could Talk* (TV). *Tarantella*. *Scream*. 1997: *The Devil's Child* (TV). *Dead Man's Curve*. 1998: *Senseless*. *Dish Dogs*. *Telling You*. *Without Limits*. *SLC Punk!* 1999: *Wing Commander*. *She's All That*. *Spanish Judges*. *Love's Labours Lost*.

LILLIE, Beatrice 1894–1989
Black-haired, stick-like, Canadian-born wit, star of the British revue stage, comedienne, actress, singer, zany and general law unto herself who contributed her sharp smile and even sharper sense of humour to a few welcome film roles through her many years (on the boards at 16) of stage success.

1925: **Stage Stars Off Stage*. 1926: *Exit Smiling*. 1928: **She's My Baby*. 1929: *The Show of Shows*. 1930: **Beatrice Lillie and Her Boy Friends*. **The Roses Have Made Me Remember*. *Are You There?* 1935: **Broadway Highlights No. 1*. 1938: *Dr Rhythm*. 1943: *Welcome to Britain*. 1944: *On Approval*. 1949: *Scrapbook for 1933*. 1956: *Around the World in 80 Days*. 1967: *Thoroughly Modern Millie*.

LINDFORS, Viveca
(Elsa V. Torstensdötter) 1920–1995

Handsome rather than pretty, but certainly striking, dark-haired Swedish actress. She went to Hollywood in 1947 and stayed, rather surprisingly in view of the fact that the film capital never knew how best to use her strong acting style. Married to director Don Siegel (second of three) from 1949 to 1953. The actor Kristoffer Tabori is her son. Still acting into her seventies, she died of pneumonic complications from rheumatoid arthritis.

1940: Snurriga familjen (GB: The Crazy Family. US: The Spinning Family). 1941: I Paradis . . . Tänk, om jag gifter mig med prasten. 1942: Morgendagens melodi. La donna del peccato. Gula kliniken. Nebbie sul mare. 1943: Anna Lans. Brödernas kvinna. 1944: Appassionata. Jag är eld och luft. 1945: Svarta rosor (US: Black Roses). Maria på kvarngården (US: Marie at the Windmill). Den allvarsamma leken. 1946: I dödens väntrum (US: Interlude). 1947: Night Unto Night. 1948: To the Victor. Adventures of Don Juan (GB: The New Adventures of Don Juan). 1949: Singoalla (and French-language version. GB: The Mask and the Sword. US: The Wind is My Lover). 1950: Backfire. This Side of the Law. No Sad Songs for Me. Dark City. Four in a Jeep. 1951: The Flying Missile. Journey into Light. 1952: The Raiders/Riders of Vengeance. No Time for Flowers. 1954: Run for Cover. 1955: Moonfleet. 1956: The Halliday Brand. 1957: The Last Tycoon (TV). I Accuse! 1958: Tempest. Weddings and Babies. 1960: The Temple of the Swinging Doll. The Story of Ruth. 1961: The Damned (US: These Are the Damned). King of Kings. 1962: No Exit/Huit clos. 1963: An Affair of the Skin. 1964: Fanfare for a Death Scene (TV). 1965: Sylvia. Brainstorm. 1967: El coleccionista de cadaveres (GB: Cauldron of Blood. US: Blind Man's Bluff). 1968: Oscuros sueños de agosta. 1969: Coming Apart. 1970: Puzzle of a Downfall Child. 1972: La casa. 1973: The Way We Were. Campana del infierno (US: A Bell from Hell). 1976: Welcome to LA. 1977: Tabu. 1978: A Question of Guilt (TV). Snorvalpen. Girlfriends. A Wedding. 1979: Voices. Linus. Natural Enemies. 1980: Playing for Time (TV). Marilyn: The Untold Story (TV). Mom, the Wolfman and Me (TV). For Ladies Only. 1981: The Hand. 1982: Creepshow. Divorce Wars (TV). 1983: Dies rigorose Leben/Nothing Left to Lose. Silent Madness. 1984: The Sure Thing. A Doctor's Story (TV). Passions (TV). 1985: Secret Weapons (TV). Yellow Pages (released 1988 as Going Under-

cover). 1986: Frankenstein's Aunt. 1987: Lady Beware. †Unfinished Business. The Ann Jillian Story (TV). 1988: Rachel River. 1989: Forced March. Misplaced (released 1991). 1990: Luba. Zandalee. Goin' to Chicago. The Exorcist III. 1991: Child of Darkness, Child of Light (TV). The Linguini Incident. 1992: North of Pittsburgh. Exiled. 1993: Finnegan's Wake. Zelda (TV). 1994: Stargate. 1995: Last Summer in the Hamptons. 1996: Looking for Richard.

†And directed

LINDSAY, Margaret
(M. Kies) 1910–1981

Engaging, personable, hazel-eyed brunette who could play pretty or plain. Started her career on the English stage, then returned to Hollywood for over 15 years of playing (often spirited) heroines in fairly minor films. Acting was certainly her life and she was delighted to return to it for her closing years in 1974, after 12 years away. Romantically linked with many of Hollywood's most eligible bachelors, but never married. Died from emphysema.

1932: Once in a Lifetime. Afraid to Talk. The All-American (GB: Sport of a Nation). The Fourth Horseman. Okay, America! (GB: Penalty of Fame). 1933: Cavalcade. Christopher Strong. West of Singapore. Baby Face. Captured! Paddy the Next Best Thing. From Headquarters. Private Detective 62. The House on 56th Street. Voltaire. The World Changes. Lady Killer. 1934: The Merry Wives of Reno. The Dragon Murder Case. Gentlemen Are Born. Fog over Frisco. Bordertown. 1935: G-Men. The Florentine Dagger. Frisco Kid. Devil Dogs of the Air. The Case of the Curious Bride. Personal Maid's Secret. Dangerous. 1936: The Law in her Hands. Isle of Fury. The Lady Consents. Sinner Take All. Public Enemy's Wife (GB: G-Man's Wife). 1937: Green Light. Slim. Song of the City. Back in Circulation. 1938: Gold is Where You Find It. When Were You Born? Broadway Musketeers. There's That Woman Again. Jezebel. Garden of the Moon. 1939: Hell's Kitchen. The Under-Pup. 20,000 Men a Year. On Trial. 1940: British Intelligence (GB: Enemy Agent). Double Alibi. The House of the Seven Gables. Ellery Queen, Master Detective. Honeymoon Deferred. Meet the Wildcat. 1941: Ellery Queen and the Murder Ring (GB: The Murder Ring). There's Magic in Music. Ellery Queen's Penthouse Mystery. Ellery Queen and the Perfect Crime (GB: The Perfect Crime). 1942:

The Spoilers. A Close Call for Ellery Queen (GB: A Close Call). A Tragedy at Midnight. Enemy Agents Meet Ellery Queen (GB: The Lido Mystery). A Desperate Chance for Ellery Queen (GB: A Desperate Chance). 1943: Let's Have Fun. The Crime Doctor. No Place for a Lady. 1944: Alaska. 1945: The Adventures of Rusty. Scarlet Street. Club Havana. 1946: Her Sister's Secret. 1947: Seven Keys to Baldpate. Louisiana. Cass Timberlane. The Vigilantes Return (GB: The Return of the Vigilantes). 1948: B.F.'s Daughter (GB: Polly Fulton). 1956: The Bottom of the Bottle (GB: Beyond the River). Emergency Hospital. 1958: The Restless Years (GB: The Wonderful Years). 1959: Jet over the Atlantic. 1960: Please Don't Eat the Daisies. 1963: Tammy and the Doctor. 1974: The Chadwick Family (TV).

LINNEY, Laura 1964–

Lissome, purposeful blonde American actress who often plays professional women. Her talents were unfortunately confined to the stage until her late twenties, but by the end of the 1990s she was settled in to films as a middle-range leading lady. Married to stage actor Christopher Adkins.

1992: Lorenzo's Oil. 1993: Dave. Class of '61 (TV). Searching for Bobby Fischer (GB: Innocent Moves). Blind Spot (TV). 1994: A Simple Twist of Fate. 1995: Congo. 1996: Primal Fear. 1997: Absolute Power. The Truman Show. 1999: Love Letters (TV). 2000: Lush. The House of Mirth. You Can Count on Me. Running Mates (TV).

LIOTTA, Ray 1955–

Strikingly blue-eyed, light-haired American actor who has shown up well in roles of suppressed (and sometimes unsuppressed)

violence, after lean years that delayed the main part of his film career until he was past 30. He can play gentler roles, too, but it's the psychotics that people seem to remember. Also a three-year regular in the TV soap *Another World* in the early days of his career. Has struggled to find high-profile roles since turning 40.

1980: *Hardhat and Legs* (TV). 1981: *Crazy Times* (TV). 1983: *The Lonely Lady*. 1986: *Something Wild*. 1988: *Dominick and Eugene* (GB: *Nicky and Gino*). *Arena Brains*. 1989: *Field of Dreams*. 1990: *GoodFellas*. 1991: *Women and Men 2: In Love There Are No Rules*. *Article 99*. 1992: *Unlawful Entry*. 1994: *No Escape*. *Corrina, Corrina*. 1995: *Dumbo Drop*. 1996: *Unforgettable*. 1997: *Turbulence*. *Cop Land*. *Phoenix* (cable TV). 1998: *The Rat Pack* (TV). 1999: *Muppets from Space*. *Forever Mine*. *Pilgrim*. 2000: *Rumor of Angels*. *Blow Dry*. 2001: *The Heartbreakers*. *Hannibal*. *John Q*.

LISI, Virna (V. Pieralisi) 1936–
Icy Italian blonde, in international films after the wide distribution of *Romulus and Remus*, but not quite in the premier league of continental sex symbols, despite making more American films than most of them, and displaying some sense of comedy. Her career, though, seemed to have dribbled to a halt by 1990, but she made a sensational film comeback in 1994, winning a Cannes best actress award in *La Reine Margot*.

1953: *. . . e Napoli canta*. 1954: *Lettera Napoletana*. *Il vetturale del Moncenisio*. *Cardinal Lambertini*. *La corda d'acciaio*. *Desiderio 'e sole*. *Violenza sul lago*. *Ripudiata*. *Piccola santa*. 1955: *La donna del giorno* (GB and US: *The Doll That Took the Town*). *Les hussards*. *Luna nova*. *Lo scapolo*. *Vendicata*. 1956: *The Teenagers*. *La rossa*. 1957: *Le diciottenni*. *Il conte di materia*. 1958: *Vita perduta*. *Caterina Sforza, leonessa di Romagna*. *Totó, Peppino e la fanatiche*. 1959: *Il padrone delle ferriere*. *Il mondo dei miracoli*. 1960: *Un militare e mezzo*. 1961: *Sua eccellenza si fermò a mangiare*. *Cinque marines per cento ragazze*. *Romulus and Remus* (GB: *Duel of the Titans*). 1962: *Eva* (US: *Eve*). *The Black Tulip*. 1963: *Il giorno più corto* (commedia umoristica) (US: *The Shortest Day*). *Les bonnes causes*/*Don't Tempt the Devil*. *Coplan prend des risques*. 1964: *Casanova 70*. *I complessi*. *How to Murder Your Wife*. 1965: *Signore e signori* (GB: and US: *The Birds, the Bees and the Italians*). *Oggi, domani, dopodomani* (US:

Kiss the Other Sheik). *La donna del lago*/*The Possessed*. *Made in Italy*. *Una vergine per il principe* (GB and US: *A Virgin for the Prince*). *Le bambole* (GB: *Four Kinds of Love*. US: *The Dolls*). *Paranoia*. *La volta buona*. 1966: *Assault on a Queen*. *Not With My Wife, You Don't*. *The Girl and the General*. 1967: *Arabella*. *Meglio vedova* (GB: *Better a Widow*). *Le dolci signore*. *The 25th Hour*. 1968: *Tenderly* (GB: *The Girl Who Couldn't Say No*). 1969: *The Christmas Tree*. *Les temps des loups*. *The Secret of Santa Vittoria*. *If It's Tuesday, This Must Be Belgium*. *Trigon*. 1970: *Giuochi particulari*. *Un beau monstre*. 1971: *Roma bene*. *The Statue*. 1972: *Bluebeard*. *Les galets d'etretat*. 1973: *Le serpent*. 1974: *White Fang*. 1975: *Love Me Strangely*. *Challenge to White Fang*. 1977: *Beyond Good and Evil*. 1978: *Ernesto*. †*Cocktails for Three*. 1979: *Footloose*/*Venetian Lies*. 1980: *La cicala*. *Miss Right*. 1982: *Sapore di mare*. 1983: *Stelle emigranti*. 1984: *Amarsi un po'*. 1987: *I Love N.Y.* 1988: *I ragazzi di via Panisperna*. *No Place Like Home*. *Non se ne voglion o andare*/*. . . And They Don't Want to Leave*. 1989: *Buon natale . . . buon anno joyeux*. 1990: *The Mysteries of the Dark Jungle*. 1994: *La reine Margot*. 1995: *Va dove ti porta il cuore* (US: *Follow Your Heart*). 2000: *Il cielo è sopra di noi*.

†*Unreleased*

LISTER, Moira 1923–
Attractively feline-faced, blue-eyed blonde. Came from her native South Africa to British films during World War II and, with her slim figure and delicately upper-class voice, was cast mostly as sexy society ladies. Still busy on stage in the 1990s.

1943: *The Shipbuilders*. 1944: *Love Story* (US: *A Lady Surrenders*). *My Ain Folk*. *The Agitator*. 1945: *Don Chicago*. 1946: *Wanted for Murder*. 1947: *Mrs Fitzherbert*. 1948: *So Evil My Love*. *Uneasy Terms*. *Another Shore*. *Once a Jolly Swagman* (US: *Maniacs on Wheels*). 1949: *A Run for Your Money*. 1950: *Mon phoque*. *Pool of London*. 1951: *Files from Scotland Yard*. *White Corridors*. 1952: *Something Money Can't Buy*. 1953: *The Cruel Sea*. *Grand National Night* (US: *Wicked Woman*). *The Limping Man*. *Trouble in Store*. 1955: *John and Julie*. *The Deep Blue Sea*. 1957: *Seven Waves Away* (US: *Abandon Ship!*). 1959: *Hiroshima mon amour* (narrator only). 1964: *The Yellow Rolls-Royce*. 1965: *Joey Boy*. 1967: *The Double Man*. *Stranger in the*

House (US: *Cop-Out*). 1972: *Not Now Darling*. 1988: *The Choice*. 1989: *Ten Little Indians*.

LIVESEY, Roger 1906–1976
Cheerful, rich-voiced, solidly-built, Welsh-born actor in British films, as kindly leading man, bluff confidant or versatile character star (especially in *The Life and Death of Colonel Blimp*). Married actress Ursula Jeans (U. McMinn, 1906–1973). Spent more time on stage than filmgoers would have liked. Died from bowel cancer.

1920: *The Old Curiosity Shop*. 1921: *The Four Feathers*. *Where the Rainbow Ends*. 1923: *Married Love*. 1932: *East Lynne on the Western Front*. 1933: *The Veteran of Waterloo*. *A Cuckoo in the Nest*. **The Ace of Trouble*. 1934: *Blind Justice*. *Lorna Doone*. 1935: *The Price of Wisdom*. *Midshipman Easy* (US: *Men of the Sea*). 1936: *Rembrandt*. 1938: *The Drum* (US: *Drums*). *Keep Smiling* (US: *Smiling Along*). *The Rebel Son*/*Taras Bulba*. 1939: *Spies of the Air*. 1940: *The Girl in the News*. 1943: *The Life and Death of Colonel Blimp* (US: *Colonel Blimp*). 1945: *I Know Where I'm Going!* 1946: *A Matter of Life and Death* (US: *Stairway to Heaven*). 1947: *Vice Versa*. 1949: *That Dangerous Age* (US: *If This Be Sin*). 1950: *Green Grow the Rushes*. 1953: *The Master of Ballantrae*. 1956: *The Intimate Stranger* (US: *Finger of Guilt*). 1957: *Le passager clandestin* (GB: *The Stowaway*). 1958: *Es geschah am hellichten tag* (GB: *Assault in Broad Daylight*). 1959: *The League of Gentlemen*. 1960: *The Entertainer*. 1961: *No My Darling Daughter!* 1964: *Of Human Bondage*. 1965: *The Amorous Adventures of Moll Flanders*. 1967: *Oedipus the King*. 1969: *Hamlet*. 1970: *Futtock's End*.

LIVINGSTON, Robert (R. Randall) 1904–1988
Rugged, large-faced American action star with brown wavy hair. Initially a reporter for the *Los Angeles Daily News*, he was led into doing bit parts in movies through his friendships with local actors, and he went over to film acting full time at the age of 30. First seen in dashing romantic leads, Livingston soon became ensconced in westerns, especially 'Three Mesquiteers' adventures, in which he played the character of Stony Brooke more than 30 times between 1936 and 1942. When his days as a western star were through, he played a few leads in crime and horror dramas, then villains in

films featuring Roy Rogers and Gene Autry (both *qv*). More than 20 years after the main body of his career, he made bizarre appearances in three exploitation films of the mid-1970s. Brother of cowboy star Addison 'Jack' Randall (1906–1945), who died from a heart attack at 39.

1929: Rio Rita. 1930: Roaring Ranch. Trigger Tricks. 1921: Dance, Fools, Dance. 1934: Paris Interlude. Death on the Diamond. The Band Plays On. 1935: Mutiny on the Bounty. *Buried Loot. West Point of the Air. *A Thrill for Thelma. Baby Face Harrington (GB: Baby Face). 1936: Three Godfathers. The Bold Caballero (GB: The Bold Cavalier). Small Town Girl. Suzy. Absolute Quiet. Speed. The Three Mesquiteers. Ghost Town Gold. The Vigilantes Are Coming. Roarin' Lead. 1937: Circus Girl. Riders of the Whistling Skull. Larceny on the Air. Come On, Cowboys. Gunsmoke Ranch. Hit the Saddle. Heart of the Rockies. Range Defenders. Wild Horse Rodeo. 1938: The Night Hawk. Orphans of the Street. Federal Man Hunt (GB: Flight from Justice). Ladies in Distress. Call the Mesquiteers. King of the Newsboys. Purple Vigilantes. Outlaws of Sonora. Riders of the Black Hills. Heroes of the Hills. Arson Gang Busters (GB: Arson Racket Squad). 1939: The Lone Ranger Rides Again. The Cowboys from Texas. The Kansas Terrors. Under Texas Skies. 1940: Covered Wagon Days. Rocky Mountain Rangers. The Trail Blazers. Pioneers of the West. Lone Star Raiders. Oklahoma Renegades. Covered Wagon Days. Heroes of the Saddle. 1941: Prairie Pioneers. Pals of the Pecos. Saddlemates. Gangs of Sonora. 1942: Overland Stagecoach. Wolves of the Range. 1943: The Black Raven. Pistol Packin' Mama. Wild Horse Rustlers. Death Rides the Plains. Raiders of Red Gap. 1944: Pride of the Plains. Law of the Saddle. Storm Over Lisbon. Goodnight, Sweetheart. The Laramie Trail. Lake Placid Serenade. The Big Bonanza. Brazil. Beneath Western Skies. 1945: Tell It to a Star. Dakota. The Cheaters. Steppin' in Society. Don't Fence Me In. Bells of Rosarita. 1946: Undecover Woman. Valley of the Zombies. 1948: The Feathered Serpent. Grand Canyon Trail. Daredevils of the Clouds. 1949: Riders in the Sky. The Mysterious Desperado. 1950: Law of the Badlands. Mule Train. 1951: Saddle Legion. 1952: Night Stage to Galveston. Something for the Birds. 1953: Winning of the West. Louisiana Territory. 1958: Once Upon a Horse. 1974: I Spit on Your Corpse. Naughty Stewardesses. Blazing Stewardesses / Texas Layover / Cathouse Callgirls.

LLOYD, Emily (E. Lloyd Pack) 1970–
Bubbly, extrovert, square-faced blonde British actress, the country's first major teenage star since Hayley Mills and Jenny Agutter (both *qv*). The daughter and grand-daughter of actors, she burst on to the international film scene at 16 with her central performance as the rebellious 1950s' teenager in *Wish You Were Here*, dominating many of her elders and betters. She went to Hollywood, but her films there were less than satisfactory. She dropped out of three films in a row in the early 1990s, and has been lost in the shuffle in recent times.

1987: Wish You Were Here. 1989: Cookie. In Country. Chicago Joe and the Showgirl. 1991: Scorchers. 1992: A River Runs Through It. 1994: A Hundred and One Nights. 1995: Under the Hula Moon. When Saturday Comes. *Masculine Mescaline. 1996: Dead Girl. 1997: Welcome to Sarajevo. The Real Thing / Livers Ain't Cheap. 1998: Boogie Boy. Woundings. 2000: Interview with a Dead Man.

LLOYD, Harold 1893–1971
Dark-haired, bespectacled, serious-looking American comedian, the 'boy next door' who lurched anxiously from disaster to disaster in quest of the girl and usually ended up in some hair-raising situation like clinging from the hands of a clock. Special Oscar 1952. Married one of his later co-stars, Mildred Davis (1900–1969). Died from cancer.

1913: †Samson and Delilah. Algy on the Force. The Old Monk's Tale. His Chum the Baron. His Heart, His Hand, His Sword (serial). A Little Hero. Cupid in the Dental Parlor. Hide and Seek. Twixt Love and Fire. 1914: The Wizard of Oz. Willie. Willie's Haircut. From Italy's Shores. Curses! They Remarked. The

Hungry Actors. 1915: Willie at Sea. Willie Runs the Park. Once Every Ten Minutes. Soaking the Clothes. Terribly Stuck Up. Some Baby. Giving Them Fits. Tinkering with Trouble. Ragtime Snap Shots. Ruses, Rhymes, Roughnecks. A One Night Stand. Spit Ball Sadie. Pressing the Suit. A Mix-up for Mazie. Fresh from the Farm. Bughouse Bell Hops. Great While It Lasted. A Foozle at a Tee Party. Peculiar Patient's Pranks. Just Nuts. Lonesome Luke. Lonesome Luke, Social Gangster. Love, Loot and Crash. Miss Fatty's Seaside Lovers. Into the Light. 1916: Lonesome Luke Lolls in Luxury. Luke Lugs Luggage. Lonesome Luke Leans to the Literary. Luke Laughs Out. Luke Foils the Villain. Luke and the Rural Roughnecks. Luke Laughs Last. Luke's Double. Luke Pipes the Pippins. Luke and the Bomb Throwers. Luke's Late Lunchers. Luke's Fatal Flivver. Luke Rides Roughshod. Luke's Washful Waiting. Luke Crystal Gazer. Luke's Lost Lamb. Luke Does the Midway. Luke and the Mermaids. Luke Joins the Navy. Luke's Society Mix-Up. Luke and the Bang-Tails. Luke's Speedy Club Life. Luke, the Chauffeur. Luke's Newsie Knockout. Luke, Gladiator. Luke's Preparedness Preparations. Luke, Patent Provider. Luke Locates the Loot. Luke's Fireworks Fizzle. Luke's Movie Muddle. Luke's Shattered Sleep. Luke the Candy Cut-Up. Lonesome Luke, Circus King. Ice. Them Was the Happy Days! Luke, Rank Impersonator. 1917: Luke's Lost Liberty. Luke's Busy Day. Luke's Trolley Troubles. Luke Wins Ye Lady Fayre. Lonesome Luke, Lawyer. Lonesome Luke's Lively Life. Lonesome Luke on Tin Can Alley. Lonesome Luke, Plumber. Lonesome Luke's Honeymoon. Stop! Luke! Listen! Lonesome Luke, Messenger. Lonesome Luke, Mechanic. Lonesome Luke's Wild Women. Over the Fence. Lonesome Luke Loses Patients. Lonesome Luke from London to Laramie. Drama's Dreadful Deal. Pinched. By the Sad Sea Waves. Bliss. Rainbow Island. Love, Laughs and Lather. The Flirt. Clubs Are Trumps. All Aboard. We Never Sleep. Move On. Bashful. The Tip. Step Lively. 1918: The Big Idea. The Lamb. Hit Him Again. Beat It. A Gasoline Wedding. Let's Go. Look Pleasant, Please. Here Come the Girls. Follow the Crowd. On the Jump. Pipe the Whiskers. It's a Wild Life. Hey There! Kicked Out. The Non-Stop Kid. Two-Gun Gussie. Fireman, Save My Child. That's Him. City Slicker. Sic 'Em Towser. Somewhere in Turkey. Bride and Gloom. Are Crooks Dishonest? An Ozark Romance. Kicking the Germ Out of Germany. Two Scrambled. Bees in His Bonnet. Swing Your Partners. Why Pick on Me? Nothing But Trouble. Hear 'Em Rave. Take a Chance. She Loves Me Not. Wanted: $5000. Going! Going! Gone! Ask Father. On the Fire. 1919: Look Out Below. The Dutiful Dub. Next Aisle Over. A Sammy in Siberia. Young Mr Jazz. Just Dropped In. Crack Your Heels. Si, Senor. Before Breakfast. The Marathon. The Rajah. Swat the Cook. Off the Trolley. Ring Up the Curtain. Back to the Woods. Pistols for Breakfast. Spring Fever. Billy Blazes Esquire. Just Neighbors. At the Old Stage Door. A Jazzed Honeymoon. Chop Suey & Co. Never Touched Me. Count Your Change. Heap Big Chief. Don't Shove. Be My Wife. He Leads, Others Follow. Soft Money. Count the Votes.

Pay Your Dues. Bumping into Broadway. From Hand to Mouth. His Royal Slyness. Captain Kidd's Kids. 1920: Haunted Spooks. An Eastern Westerner. High and Dizzy. Get Out and Get Under. Number, Please. 1921: Now or Never. Among Those Present. I Do. Never Weaken. †A Sailor-Made Man. 1922: †Grandma's Boy. †Doctor Jack. 1923: †Safety Last. †Why Worry? Dogs of War. 1924: †Girl Shy. †Hot Water. 1925: †The Freshman (GB: College Days). 1926: †For Heaven's Sake. 1927: †The Kid Brother. 1928: †Speedy. 1929: †Welcome Danger. 1930: †Feet First. 1931: Screen Snapshots No. 8. 1932: †Movie Crazy. 1934: †The Cat's-Paw. 1936: †The Milky Way. 1938: †Professor Beware! 1946: †The Sin of Harold Diddlebock (later and GB: Mad Wednesday!).

All shorts except (†) features.

LOCKE, Sondra 1945–
Slender blonde American actress who moved in ten years from wan waifs to assertive ladies. Oscar-nominated in her first film, she has not quite fulfilled that early promise despite tackling a variety of genres. Co-starred a number of times with then–partner Clint Eastwood (*qv*) in the late seventies: the break-up between them made bitter headlines. Revealed ambitions to direct in the mid 1980s after their personal and professional relationship ended. Oscar nominee for *The Heart is a Lonely Hunter.*
1968: The Heart is a Lonely Hunter. 1969: Cover Me, Babe. 1970: The Lovemakers. Run, Shadow, Run. 1971: Willard. 1973: A Reflection of Fear. 1974: The Second Coming of Suzanne. 1976: The Outlaw Josey Wales. 1977: The Gauntlet. Death Game. The Shadow of Chikara. 1978: Every Which Way But Loose. 1979: Friendships, Secrets and Lies (TV). 1980: Bronco Billy. Any Which Way You Can. 1982: Rosie: The Rosemary Clooney Story (TV). 1983: Sudden Impact. 1986: †Ratboy. 1999: The Prophet's Game. 2000: Clean and Narrow.

†And directed

As director: 1989: Impulse. 1993: Death in Small Doses (TV). 1997: Do Me a Favor.

LOCKWOOD, Margaret 1911–1990
Dark-haired Indian-born leading lady, with prominent beauty spot by the left eye after 1945. On stage at 16, she came to British films playing fresh young heroines, often in

outdoor settings. Altered her image totally in 1942 to play doxies and villainesses past and present, and became the biggest star of British films in the forties: audiences were scandalized by decolletage that seems quite mild today. A longtime sufferer from middle ear disease.
1934: Lorna Doone. 1935: The Case of Gabriel Perry/Wild Justice. Some Day. Honors Easy. Man of the Moment. Midshipman Easy (US: Men of the Sea). Jury's Evidence. The Amateur Gentleman. 1936: The Beloved Vagabond. Irish for Luck. 1937: The Street Singer. Who's Your Lady Friend? Dr Syn. Melody and Romance. Owd Bob (US: To the Victor). Bank Holiday (US: Three on a Weekend). 1938: The Lady Vanishes. 1939: Rulers of the Sea. Susannah of the Mounties. A Girl Must Live. The Stars Look Down. 1940: Night Train to Munich (US: Night Train). The Girl in the News. 1941: Quiet Wedding. 1942: Alibi. 1943: Dear Octopus (US: The Randolph Family). The Man in Grey. 1944: Give Us the Moon. Love Story (US: A Lady Surrenders). 1945: A Place of One's Own. I'll Be Your Sweetheart. The Wicked Lady. 1946: Bedelia. Hungry Hill. 1947: Jassy. The White Unicorn (US: Bad Sister). 1948: Look Before You Love. 1949: Cardboard Cavalier. Madness of the Heart. 1950: Highly Dangerous. 1952: Trent's Last Case. 1953: Laughing Anne. 1954: Trouble in the Glen. 1955: Cast a Dark Shadow. 1976: The Slipper and the Rose.

LODER, John (J. Lowe) 1898–1988
Square-built, light-haired, cheerfully handsome globe-trotting British actor who began in German films after giving up a military career. Then made films in Britain (four spells), France, Hollywood (two spells), India

and Argentina. Too stiff ever to become a top star, but a useful sounding-board for some dominant leading ladies. Married (third of five) to Hedy Lamarr (*qv*), 1943–1947.
*1926: Madame wünscht keine Kinder (US: Madame Wants No Children). Alraune. Die letzte Walz. The Sinister Man. 1927: Dancing Mad. Der grosse unbekannte. Die Sünderin. Die weisse Spinne. 1928: Casanova's Erbe. Frejwild. Wenn die Mutter und die Tochter . . . The First Born. 1929: Black Waters. Sunset Pass. The Ivory Hunters. The Unholy Night. The Doctor's Secret. The Racketeer (GB: Love's Conquest). Her Private Affair. Rich People. 1930: The Seas Beneath. Lilies of the Field. The Man Hunter. Love's Conquest. The Second Floor Mystery. Sweethearts and Wives. 1931: One Night at Susie's. Hot Dogs. Men of the Sky. 1932: *On the Loose. Wedding Rehearsal. Money Means Nothing. 1933: Money for Speed. The Private Life of Henry VIII. You Made Me Love You. Paris Plane. 1934: Love, Life and Laughter. The Battle (US: Thunder in the East). Rolling in Money. Warn London. Java Head. Sing As We Go. Lorna Doone. My Song Goes Round the World. 1935: The Silent Passenger. It Happened in Paris. 18 Minutes. 1936: Whom the Gods Love (US: Mozart). Queen of Hearts. Ourselves Alone (US: River of Unrest). Sabotage (US: A Woman Alone). The Man Who Changed His Mind (US: The Man Who Lived Again). Guilty Melody. 1937: King Solomon's Mines. Dr Syn. Non-Stop New York. Owd Bob (US: To the Victor). Mademoiselle Docteur. Paix sur le Rhin. Menaces. 1938: Katia. Anything to Declare. 1939: The Silent Battle (US: Continental Express). Confidential Lady. Meet Maxwell Archer (US: Maxwell Archer Detective). Murder Will Out. 1940: Diamond Frontier. Tin Pan Alley. Adventure in Diamonds. 1941: Scotland Yard. One Night in Lisbon. How Green Was My Valley. Confirm or Deny. 1942: *Stars on Horseback. Eagle Squadron. Now, Voyager. Gentleman Jim. The Gorilla Man. 1943: The Mysterious Doctor. Murder on the Waterfront. Old Acquaintance. Adventure in Iraq. 1944: Passage to Marseille (GB: Passage to Marseilles). The Hairy Ape. Abroad with Two Yanks. 1945: The Brighton Strangler. The Fighting Guardsman. A Game of Death. Jealousy. The Woman Who Came Back. 1946: The Wife of Monte Cristo. One More Tomorrow. 1947: Dishonored Lady. 1952: †The Army Story. 1955: *Dead on Time. The Curse of the Cobra. 1957: Woman and the Hunter (GB: Triangle on Safari). The Story of Esther Costello (US: Golden Virgin). Small Hotel. 1958: Gideon's Day (US: Gideon of Scotland Yard). The Secret Man. Josette from New Orleans. 1965: Esquiú. 1970: The Firechasers.*

†Unreleased

LOLLOBRIGIDA, Gina
(Luigina Lollobrigida) 1927–
Raven-haired Italian actress with beauty-queen figure, who became Italy's first post-war sex symbol. A number of home grown films as slinky flirt got her known internationally as 'La Lollo' and appearances in Hollywood movies made her a worldwide

pin-up. Kept going fairly strongly until the early seventies, although long before that overtaken in popularity by Sophia Loren (*qv*). *1946: L'aquila nera. L'elisir d'amore. Lucia di Lammermoor. 1947: Follie per l'opera/Mad about Opera. Il delitto di Giovanni Episcopo. La danse de mort. Il segreto di Don Giovanni. A Man About the House. 1948: I Pagliacci. 1949: Campane a martello. La sposa non puo' attendere. Miss Italia. 1950: Vita da cane. Cuori senza frontiera. Alina. La citta' si defende. 1951: Moglie per una notte/L'ora della fantasia (GB and US: Wife for a Night). Amor non ho, pero'... pero'. Fanfan La Tulipe. Altri tempi (US: As Times Go By). A Tale of Five Cities (US: A Tale of Five Women). Enrico Caruso, leggende di una voce (US: The Young Caruso). Achtung, banditti! 1952: Les belles de nuit (GB and US: Night Beauties). Le infideli. 1953: La provinciale (GB and US: The Wayward Wife). Pane, amore e gelosia/Bread, Love and Jealousy. Pane, amore e fantasia/Bread, Love and Dreams. Crossed Swords. Beat the Devil. 1954: La bella di roma/Woman of Rome. Le grand jeu (GB: The Card of Fate). 1955: La donna più bella del mondo (GB: Beautiful But Dangerous). 1956: Trapeze. The Hunchback of Notre Dame. 1957: Anna of Brooklyn. 1958: La loi (GB: Where the Hot Wind Blows). 1959: Solomon and Sheba. Never So Few. 1961: Go Naked in the World. Come September. 1962: La bellezza d'Ippolito. Mare matto. 1963: Vénus impériale. Woman of Straw. 1964: Strange Bedfellows. 1965: Le bambole (GB: Four Kinds of Love. US: The Dolls). 1966: The Sultans. Io, io, io ... e gli altri. Hotel Paradiso. Cervantes, the Young Rebel. 1967: Le piacevoli notti. La morte ha fatto l'uovo (GB: A Curious Way to Love. US: Plucked). 1968: Buona Sera, Mrs Campbell. The Private Navy of Sgt O'Farrell. Un bellissimo Novembre. 1970: Stuntman. 1971: Bad Man's River. Le avventure di Pinocchio. 1972: Roses rouges et piments verts (US: The Lonely Woman). King, Queen, Knave. 1983: Stelle emigranti. 1985: Deceptions (TV). 1988: La romana. 1994: Les cent et une nuits. 1997: XXL.*

LOM, Herbert

(H. Schluderpacheru) 1917–

Smooth, dark-haired Czech actor who could be romantic, sinister, or even funny. His career hardly got started before he was on the run from the Nazis, landing in British films where his faintly menacing charm had some dubbing him a British Charles Boyer, even

though his characters usually ended up dead. Looked further afield for acting opportunites from 1959, but had a successful British TV series, *The Human Jungle* which cast him in more sympathetic light. Latterly the hapless chief inspector in the 'Pink Panther' films.

1937: Žena pod křížem. 1940: Mein Kampf My Crimes. 1942: The Young Mr Pitt. Secret Mission. Tomorrow We Live (US: At Dawn We Die). 1943: The Dark Tower. 1944: Hotel Reserve. 1945: The Seventh Veil. Night Boat to Dublin. 1946: Appointment with Crime. 1947: Dual Alibi. Snowbound. 1948: Good Time Girl. Portrait from Life (US: The Girl in the Painting). The Brass Monkey/Lucky Mascot. 1949: The Lost People. Golden Salamander. 1950: Night and the City. State Secret (US: The Great Manhunt). The Black Rose. Cage of Gold. 1951: Hell is Sold Out. Two on the Tiles. Mr Denning Drives North. Whispering Smith Hits London (US: Whispering Smith versus Scotland Yard). 1952: The Ringer. The Net (US: Project M7). The Man Who Watched Trains Go By (US: Paris Express). 1953: Rough Shoot (US: Shoot First). The Love Lottery. Star of India. 1954: Beautiful Stranger (US: Twist of Fate). 1955: The Ladykillers. 1956: War and Peace. 1957: Fire Down Below. Hell Drivers. Action of the Tiger. I Accuse! 1958: Chase a Crooked Shadow. The Roots of Heaven. Intent to Kill. 1959: No Trees in the Street (US: No Tree in the Street). The Big Fisherman. Passport to Shame (US: Room 43). Northwest Frontier (US: Flame Over India). Third Man on the Mountain. 1960: I Aim at the Stars. Spartacus. 1961: Mr Topaze (US: I Like Money). El Cid. Mysterious Island. The Frightened City. 1962: The Phantom of the Opera. The Treasure of Silver Lake. Tiara Tahiti. 1963: The Horse without a Head (US: TV). 1964: A Shot in the Dark. 1965: Return From the Ashes. Uncle Tom's Cabin. 1966: Our Man in Marrakesh (US: Bang Bang You're Dead). Gambit. Die Nibelungen (GB: Whom the Gods Wish to Destroy). 1967: Die Nibelungen II. Assignment to Kill. The Karate Killers (TV. GB: cinemas) 1968: The Face of Eve (US: Eve). Villa Rides! 99 Women (US: Island of Despair). 1969: Doppelganger (US: Journey to the Far Side of the Sun). Mister Jericho (US: TV). 1970: Count Dracula. Dorian Gray. Hexen bis aufs Blut geqvält/Mark of the Devil. 1971: Murders in the Rue Morgue. 1972: Asylum. 1973: Dark Places. And Now the Screaming Starts! 1974: The Return of the Pink Panther. And Then There Were None. 1976: The Pink

Panther Strikes Again. 1977: Charleston. 1978: Revenge of the Pink Panther. 1979: The Lady Vanishes. The Man with Bogart's Face. 1980: Peter and Paul (TV). Hopscotch. 1982: Trail of the Pink Panther. 1983: Memed My Hawk. The Dead Zone. Curse of the Pink Panther. 1985: King Solomon's Mines. 1986: Whoops Apocalypse! 1987: African Adventure. Scoop (TV). Skeleton Coast. Master of Dragonard Hill. Going Bananas. 1988: The Crystal Eye. 1989: River of Death. Ten Little Indians. The Masque of the Red Death. 1991: The Sect. The Pope Must Die (US: The Pope Must Diet). 1993: Son of the Pink Panther. 1997: Marco Polo.

LOMBARD, Carole (Jane Peters, later legally changed) 1908–1942

One of Hollywood's most popular blondes. A kind of freewheeling, sophisticated Jean Harlow and good at everything from sensitive drama to screwball comedy. A car crash in 1926 almost ruined her budding career. But she recovered to match wits and words with some of Hollywood's biggest stars. Married to William Powell from 1931–1933 and Clark Gable from 1939 on. Killed in a plane crash. Oscar nominee for *My Man Godfrey*.

*1921: ‡A Perfect Crime. 1924: Gold Heels. 1925: †@Dick Turpin. †Marriage in Transit. †Hearts and Spurs. †Durand of the Badlands. †Gold and the Girl. 1926: †The Road to Glory. †@Half a Bride. 1927: †Smith's Pony. †The Girl from Everywhere. †*Hold That Pose. †*The Campus Vamp. †*The Campus Carmen. †*A Gold Digger of Weepah. †The Fighting Eagle. 1928: †*Run Girl Run. †The Divine Sinner. †*Hubby's Weekend Trip. †*Smith's Restaurant. †*Motorboat Mamas. †*Smith's Army Life. †*The Beach Club. †*The Best Man. †*Matchmaking Mammas. †*The Swim Princess. †*The Bicycle Flirt. †*The Girl from Nowhere. †*His Unlucky Night. †Power. †Show Folks. †Me, Gangster. †Ned McCobb's Daughter. 1929: †High Voltage (GB: Wanted). †Big News. †The Racketeer (US: Love's Conquest). †Don't Get Jealous. †@Dynamite. 1930: †The Arizona Kid. Safety in Numbers. Fast and Loose. 1931: It Pays to Advertise. Ladies' Man! Take This Woman. Up Pops the Devil. Man of the World. 1932: Sinners in the Sun. No One Man. No Man of Her Own. No More Orchids. Virtue. 1933: Supernatural. From Hell to Heaven. The Eagle and the Hawk. White Woman. Brief Moment. 1934: Twentieth Century. Bolero. We're Not Dressing. Now and Forever. The*

Gay Bride. Lady by Choice. 1935: Rumba. Hands Across the Table. 1936: My Man Godfrey. The Princess Comes Across. Love Before Breakfast. 1937: Swing High, Swing Low. True Confession. Nothing Sacred. 1938: Fools for Scandal. 1939: In Name Only. Made for Each Other. 1940: *Picture People No. 4. Vigil in the Night. They Knew What They Wanted. 1941: Mr and Mrs Smith. 1942: To Be or Not To Be. 1943: *Show Business at War.

‡*As Jane Peters* †*As Carol Lombard*
@*Scenes deleted*

LONDON, Julie (J. Peck) 1926–
Acting careers didn't come much more sporadic than that of this tawny-haired American actress. But in the mid-fifties she suddenly became an enormously popular torch-style singer, especially with a million-selling record called *Cry Me a River*. Cropped up much later in a seventies' TV series, looking not a year older. Married to Jack Webb (*qv*) from 1945 to 1953, then to actor/pianist Bobby Troup (1918–1999) to his death.
1944: Nabonga (GB: The Jungle Woman). 1945: On Stage Everybody. Billy Rose's Diamond Horseshoe (GB: Diamond Horseshoe). 1946: Night in Paradise. 1947: The Red House. 1948: Tap Roots. 1949: Task Force. 1950: Return of the Frontiersman. 1951: The Fat Man. 1955: The Fighting Chance. 1956: The Girl Can't Help It. The Great Man. Crime Against Joe. 1957: Without Incident (TV). Drango. Bop Girl. 1958: Saddle the Wind. Man of the West. A Question of Adultery. Voice in the Mirror. 1959: The Third Voice. Night of the Quarter Moon. The Wonderful Country. 1961: The George Raft Story (GB: Spin of a Coin). 1967: The Helicopter Spies (TV. GB: cinemas). 1971: Emergency (TV). 1978: Survival on Charter No. 220.

LONG, Audrey 1923–
Coolly attractive, light-haired (sometimes brunette), hazel-eyed American actress, supposed to have played dozens of walk-ons at Universal and Warners (few records of which seem to exist) before embarking on the major part of her career with RKO. A former model, she was always poised, but her roles were almost entirely confined to chic heroines in second-feature thrillers, and her film career was played out at 29. Married to Leslie Charteris, author of The Saint books, from

1952 to his death in 1993.
1942: The Male Animal. Eagle Squadron. Yankee Doodle Dandy. The Great Impersonation. Pardon My Sarong. 1944: Tall in the Saddle. A Night of Adventure. 1945: Pan-Americana. Wanderer of the Wasteland. A Game of Death. 1946: Perilous Holiday. 1947: Born to Kill (GB: Lady of Deceit). Desperate. In Self Defence. 1948: Song of My Heart. The Adventures of Gallant Bess. Stage Struck. Perilous Waters. Homicide for Three (GB: An Interrupted Honeymoon). Grand Canyon Trail. Miraculous Journey. 1949: The Duke of Chicago. Alias the Champ. Air Hostess. The Red Danube. Post Office Investigator. 1950: Trial without Jury. David Harding, Counterspy. Blue Blood. The Petty Girl (GB: Girl of the Year). 1951: Cavalry Scout. Insurance Investigator. Sunny Side of the Street. 1952: Indian Uprising.

LONG, Nia 1970–
Diminutive but piquant and prettily curvaceous American actress, acting since her early teenage years. After her first major success as Will Smith's fiancée in the TV series *Fresh Prince of Bel Air*, her 'nice girl' looks have mainly confined her to dutiful daughters, wise friends and cute young mothers and she hasn't quite found the right leading role to make her name more familiar.
1986: The B.R.A.T. Patrol (TV). 1990: Buried Alive. 1991: Boyz N the Hood. 1993: Made in America. 1995: Friday. 1997: Love Jones. Soul Food. Hav Plenty. 1998: Black Jaq (TV). Butter. The Secret Laughter of Women. 1999: Stigmata. In Too Deep. Held Up!/Inconvenienced. The Best Man. If These Walls Could Talk 2 (TV). 2000: Boiler Room. The Broken Hearts Club. Big Momma's House.

LONG, Richard
See CORDAY, Mara

LONG, Shelley 1949–
Tall, tawny-haired, prettily spindly, open-eyed American comedienne and light actress, perhaps the most appealing female clown produced by Hollywood since Lucille Ball, and likewise ill-served by her film roles. Like Ball, Long is adept at little bits of comic business, and like Ball she found her greatest success on television, in the long-running comedy series *Cheers*. She seemed to be finding her feet as a funny girl in films, too, but several successive failures in the early 1990s drove her back to TV roles.
1979: The Cracker Factory (TV). 1980: A Small Circle of Friends. The Promise of Love (TV). 1981: The Princess and the Cabbie (TV). Caveman. 1982: Ghost of a Chance (TV). Night Shift. 1983: Losin' It. 1984: Irreconcilable Differences. 1985: The Money Pit. 1987: Outrageous Fortune. Hello Again. 1989: Troop Beverly Hills. 1990: Don't Tell Her It's Me. Shattered/Voices Within: The Lives of Truddi Chase. 1992: Frozen Assets. Fatal Memories (TV). A Message from Holly (TV). 1994: The Women of Spring Break (TV. GB: Welcome to Paradise). 1995: Freaky Friday (TV). The Brady Bunch Movie. 1996: A Very Brady Sequel. Susie Q (TV). A Different Kind of Christmas/The Mom Who Stole Christmas (TV). 1998: The Adventures of Ragtime (TV). 1999: Vanished: Without a Trace (TV). 2000: Dr T and the Women.

LONGDEN, John 1900–1971
Tall, sharp-faced, grave-looking, brown-haired leading man of British films. Born in

the West Indies, the son of a Wesleyan minister, he was a miner for a time before turning to acting, and making a big impact on the British cinema, especially in *Quinneys* and several early Hitchcock films. His career was hit by an alcohol problem and by a visit to Australia that produced only three films in four years. On his return he played a few police inspectors, then dropped to small supporting roles.

*1926: The House of Marney. The Ball of Fortune. 1927: The Arcadians / Land of Heart's Desire. The Flight Commander. The Glad Eye. Quinneys. Bright Young Things. 1928: Mademoiselle Parley-Voo. What Money Can Buy. Palais de Danse. The Last Post. The Flying Squad. 1939: *Memories. Blackmail. Atlantic. Juno and the Paycock (US: The Shame of Mary Boyle). 1930: Elstree Calling. The Flame of Love. Children of Chance. Two Worlds. 1931: The Skin Game. The Singer. Two Crowded Hours. *Healthy, Wealthy and Why. Rynox. The Wickham Mystery. Murder on the Second Floor. 1932: A Lucky Sweep. Born Lucky. 1934: The Silence of Dean Maitland. 1936: It Isn't Done. Thoroughbred. 1937: French Leave. Little Miss Somebody. Jennifer Hale. Young and Innocent (US: The Girl Was Young). Dial 999. 1938: Bad Boy. The Gaunt Stranger (US: The Phantom Strikes). 1939: Q Planes (US: Clouds over Europe). Goodbye Mr Chips! Jamaica Inn. The Lion Has Wings. 1940: Branded. Contraband (US: Blackout). 1941: The Common Touch. Old Mother Riley's Circus. *Post 23. The Tower of Terror. 1942: Unpublished Story. Rose of Tralee. 1943: The Silver Fleet. *Death by Design. The Yellow Canary. 1947: Dusty Bates (serial). The Ghosts of Berkeley Square. 1948: Anna Karenina. The Last Load. Bonnie Prince Charlie. 1949: Trapped by the Terror. 1950: The Lady Craved Excitement. The Elusive Pimpernel (US: The Fighting Pimpernel). Pool of London. 1951: The Dark Light. The Man with the Twisted Lip. Trek to Mashomba. The Magic Box. Black Widow. 1952: The Wallet / Blueprint for Danger. 1954: Dangerous Cargo. Meet Mr Callaghan. 1955: The Ship That Died of Shame (US: PT Raiders). 1956: The Final Column. Alias John Preston. Raiders of the River (serial). Count of Twelve. 1957: Quatermass II (US: Enemy from Space). Three Sundays to Live. 1958: The Silent Enemy. 1959: A Woman's Temptation. *Broad Waterways (narrator only). 1960: An Honorable Murder. 1961: So Evil, So Young. 1963: Lancelot and Guinevere (US: Sword of Lancelot). 1964: Frozen Alive.*
As director: *1932: Come into My Parlour.*

LOPEZ, Jennifer 1970–
Striking, well-groomed American actress of Puerto Rican parentage who progressed to major leading roles in her late twenties after a decade of acting. She then took time out to develop her singing career, but involvement with rap singer Sean 'Puff Daddy' Combs led to a brush with the police that damaged her image in 1999 and she returned to movies. In the same year she had her body insured for $1 billion.

1986: My Little Girl. 1993: Nurses on the Line (TV. GB: Race Against the Dark). 1994: Mi Familia / My Family / East LA. 1995: Money

Train. 1996: Jack. Blood and Wine. 1997: Anaconda. Selena. U Turn / Stray Dogs. 1998: Out of Sight. Antz (voice only). 2000: Thieves. The Cell. The Wedding Planner. 2001: Angel Eyes.

LORD, Jack (John Ryan) 1920–1998
Strapping, square-faced, intent-looking American actor whose film career surprisingly stuttered and stammered without taking off. He was always more successful in television, and in 1968 found a practically permanent niche there as the immaculately-clad, perennially fortyish chief of *Hawaii Five-O*, a crime series which ran for 12 years. Once an artist whose works were exhibited, he returned to that passion in semi-retirement. Made his film debut in 1949's *The Red Menace* under his real name. Died from congestive heart failure.

1949: The Red Menace. Project X. Cry Murder. 1950: The Tattooed Stranger. 1955: The Court Martial of Billy Mitchell (GB: One Man Mutiny). 1956: The Williamsburg Story. The Vagabond King. 1957: Tip on a Dead Jockey (GB: Time for Action). The True Story of Lynn Stuart. Pattern for Violence (TV. GB: cinemas). 1958: Man of the West. God's Little Acre. Reunion (TV). 1959: The Hangman. 1960: Walk Like a Dragon. 1962: Dr No. 1965: The Crime (TV). 1966: The Ride to Hangman's Tree. The Doomsday Flight (TV. GB: cinemas). 1967: The Counterfeit Killer. 1968: The Name of the Game is Kill! 1980: M Station: Hawaii (TV).

LOREN, Sophia (Sofia Scicolone) 1934–
Stunningly beautiful, rich-lipped, full-bosomed, dark-haired Italian star with peasant-style sex appeal. At first in Italian

films, but her looks, attractive English, evident sense of humour and willingness to do her best in almost any genre soon made her a big international name, as popular with women as with men. Retained her following on the continent, especially when teamed with Marcello Mastroianni (*qv*). Academy Award for *Two Women* (1961). Also nominated for *Marriage Italian Style*. Special Oscar 1991. Still glamorous in her sixties.

*1950: †Cuori sul mare. †Luci del varietà. Totò Tarzan. †Il voto. †Io sono il Capataz. †Anna. †Bluebeard's Seven Wives. 1951: ‡Il padrone del vapore. †Lebra bianca. †Milano miliarda. †Il mago per forza. †The Dream of Zorro. †Quo Vadis? ‡E'arrivato l'accordatore. ‡Era lui . . . sì, sì. 1952: La favorita. La tratta delle bianche (GB: Girls Marked Danger). Africa sotto i mari (GB: Woman of the Red Sea). 1953: Carosello Napoletano. Aïda. Ci troviamo in galleria. Tempi nostri (US: Anatomy of Love). Il paese dei campanelli. La Domenica della buona gente. Un giorno in pretura. Two Nights with Cleopatra. Attila the Hun. 1954: Peccato che sia una canaglia (GB: Too Bad She's Bad). Gold of Naples. Woman of the River. Miseria e nobilta. 1955: Pellegrini d'amore. Il segno di Venere / The Sign of Venus. La bella mugnaia. La fortuna di essere donna (GB and US: Lucky to be a Woman). Pane, amore e . . . (GB: Scandal in Sorrento). 1956: The Pride and the Passion. 1957: Boy on a Dolphin. Legend of the Lost. 1958: Desire Under the Elms. Houseboat. The Key. 1959: Black Orchid. That Kind of Woman. 1960: Heller in Pink Tights. It Started in Naples. A Breath of Scandal. The Millionairess. 1961: Madame. El Cid. Two Women. *Captive Island. 1962: Five Miles to Midnight. Boccaccio 70. The Condemned of Altona. 1963: Yesterday, Today and Tomorrow. The Fall of the Roman Empire. 1964: Marriage Italian Style. 1965: Operation Crossbow (US: The Great Spy Mission). Judith. Lady L. 1966: Arabesque. A Countess from Hong Kong. 1967: Cinderella Italian Style (US: More than a Miracle). 1968: Ghosts Italian Style. 1969: Sunflower. 1970: The Priest's Wife. 1971: La mortadella / Lady Liberty. Bianco, rosso e . . . (GB and US: White Sister). 1972: Man of La Mancha. 1974: Il viaggio / The Voyage. Verdict. La pupa del gangster. 1975: Brief Encounter (TV). 1976: The Cassandra Crossing. 1977: Una giornata particolare (GB and US: A Special Day). Angela (released 1984). 1978: Vengeance. Brass Target. 1979: Blood Feud. Shimmy Lugano e tarantelle e tarallucci e vino. Firepower. 1980: Sophia*

Loren: Her Own Story (TV). 1984: Aurora. 1986: Courage (TV). 1988: The Fortunate Pilgrim. 1989: Two Women (TV). 1990: Saturday, Sunday and Monday. 1994: Un bel di'vedremo. Prêt-á-Porter (US: Ready to Wear). 1995: Grumpier Old Men. 1996: Messages. 1997: Soleil. 2000: Destinazione Verna.

†As Sophia Scicolone ‡As Sophia Lazzaro

LORRE, Peter
(Laszlo Löwenstein) 1904–1964
Dark, squat, furtive-looking Hungarian-born actor who made an indelible impression in the German film M as the child murderer. But his wheedling tones and uniquely comic-sinister personality are best remembered from his Hollywood days, as one of life's victims, scuttling from its shadier corners, forever being seized by the lapels by his oft-time cohort, huge Sydney Greenstreet (qv), with whom he became very popular as a sort of unholy Laurel and Hardy, until his career was damaged by the anti-Communist witch-hunts. Married (second of three) actress Kaaren Verne (1918–1967) from 1945 to 1952. Died after a stroke.
1931: Bomben auf Monte Carlo. M. Die Koffer des Herrn O.F. Mann ist mann. 1932: Der weisse Dämon. FP1 antwortet nicht (and French version). Fünf von der Jazzband. Schuss im Morgengrauen. 1933: Was Frauen träumen. Unsichtbare Gegner. Du haut en bas. 1934: The Man Who Knew Too Much. 1935: Mad Love (GB: Hands of Orlac). Crime and Punishment. 1936: Secret Agent. Crack-Up. 1937: Lancer Spy. Nancy Steele is Missing. Thank Fast, Mr Moto. Thank You, Mr Moto. 1938: Mysterious Mr Moto. I'll Give a Million. Mr Moto's Gamble. Mr Moto Takes a Chance. 1939: Mr Moto Takes a Vacation. Mr Moto's Last Warning. Mr Moto in Danger Island (GB: Mr Moto on Danger Island). 1940: Island of Doomed Men. I Was an Adventuress. Strange Cargo. You'll Find Out. Stranger on the Third Floor. 1941: Mr District Attorney. The Maltese Falcon. The Face Behind the Mask. They Met In Bombay. 1942: Invisible Agent. All Through the Night. The Boogie Man Will Get You. Casablanca. In This Our Life. 1943: Background to Danger. The Constant Nymph. The Cross of Lorraine. Arsenic and Old Lace. 1944: Passage to Marseille (GB: Passage to Marseilles). Hollywood Canteen. The Mask of Dimitrios. The Conspirators. 1945: Hotel Berlin. Confi-

dential Agent. 1946: Three Strangers. The Chase. Black Angel. The Verdict. The Beast with Five Fingers. 1947: My Favourite Brunette. 1948: Casbah. 1949: Rope of Sand. 1950: Double Confession. Quicksand. 1951: †Die Verlorene. 1953: Beat the Devil. 1954: 20,000 Leagues Under the Sea. 1956: Seidman and Son (TV). Congo Crossing. Meet Me in Las Vegas (GB: Viva Las Vegas!). Around the World in 80 Days. Operation Cicero (TV). 1957: The Story of Mankind. The Buster Keaton Story. Silk Stockings. The Last Tycoon (TV). The Jet-Propelled Couch (TV). Hell Ship Mutiny. The Sad Sack. 1959: The Big Circus. Thin Ice (TV. GB: cinemas). 1960: The Cruel Day (TV). Scent of Mystery (GB: Holiday in Spain). 1961: Voyage to the Bottom of the Sea. 1962: Tales of Terror. Five Weeks in a Balloon. 1963: The Raven. The Comedy of Terrors. 1964: The Patsy. Muscle Beach Party.

†And directed

LOUISE, Anita
(A.L. Fremault) 1915–1970
Fluffily blonde, delicately beautiful American actress, in leading roles as a teenager, perhaps most notable as Titania in the 1935 A Midsummer Night's Dream. Her vehicles grew less interesting after 1940, but she continued acting, mostly on TV, until the late fifties. Married (first of two) producer Buddy Adler (1909–1960) who left her a widow. Died from a cerebral stroke.
1922: †Down to the Sea in Ships. 1924: †The Sixth Commandment. †Lend Me Your Husband. 1927: †*The Life of Franz Schubert. †The Music Master. 1928: †Four Devils. †A Woman of Affairs. 1929: †The Spirit of Youth. †Wonder of Women. The Marriage Playground. Square Shoulders. 1930: The Florodora Girl (GB: The Gay Nineties). What a Man! (GB: The Gentleman Chauffeur). The Third Alarm. Just Like Heaven. 1931: Millie. The Woman Between (GB: Madame Julie). Heaven on Earth. Everything's Rosie. The Great Meadow. 1932: The Phantom of Crestwood. 1933: Our Betters. 1934: Most Precious Thing in Life. I Give My Love. Judge Priest. The Firebird. Bachelor of Arts. Are We Civilized? Cross Streets. Madame Du Barry. 1935: *A Dream Comes True. Lady Tubbs (GB: The Gay Lady). A Midsummer Night's Dream. Personal Maid's Secret. Apple Sauce. Here's to Romance. 1936: The Story of Louis Pasteur. Anthony Adverse. Brides Are Like That. 1937: Call It a Day. The Go-Getter. That Certain Woman. First Lady. Green Light.

Tovarich. 1938: Going Places. My Bill. The Sisters. Marie Antoinette. 1939: Reno. The Gorilla. The Little Princess. Hero for a Day. Main Street Lawyer (GB: Small Town Lawyer). These Glamour Girls. 1940: Glamour for Sale. The Villain Still Pursued Her. Wagons Westward. 1941: *Wampas Baby Stars. Two in a Taxi. Harmon of Michigan. The Phantom Submarine. 1943: Dangerous Blondes. 1944: Nine Girls. Casanova Brown. *Screen Snapshots, series 24 No. 1. 1945: The Fighting Guardsman. Love Letters. 1946: The Devil's Mask. The Bandit of Sherwood Forest. Shadowed. Personality Kid. 1947: Blondie's Holiday. Bulldog Drummond at Bay. Blondie's Big Moment. 1952: Retreat, Hell! 1957: The Greer Case (TV).

†As Anita Fremault

LOUISE, Tina
(T.L. Blacker) 1934–
Statuesque, titian-haired, whistle-worthy American leading lady who made her first impact on television before being signed up for a notable film starring debut as Grizelda in God's Little Acre. Her career did not progress as it might have done, although she stuck around, kept her figure and developed into a useful supporting actress.
1955: Kismet. 1958: God's Little Acre. The Trap (GB: The Baited Trap). 1959: Day of the Outlaw. The Hangman. Siege of Syracuse. 1960: Garibaldi. Sappho (GB: The Warrior Empress). 1961: Il mantenuto. Armored Command. 1964: Fanfare for a Death Scene (TV). For Those Who Think Young. 1966: Il fischio del naso. 1968: The Wrecking Crew. 1969: House of Seven Joys. The Happy Ending. The Good Guys and the Bad Guys. How to Commit Marriage. 1970: But I Don't Want to Get Married (TV). 1972: Call to Danger (TV). 1974: The Stepford Wives. 1975: Death Scream (TV). 1976: Nightmare in Badham County (TV). 1977: Look What's Happened to Rosemary's Baby (TV). SST – Disaster in the Sky/SST – Death Flight (TV). 1978: Mean Dog Blues. 1979: Friendships, Secrets and Lies (TV). 1980: The Day the Women Got Even (TV). 1981: Advice to the Lovelorn (TV). 1983: Evils of the Night. 1984: Canicule/Dogsday (completed 1982). The Utterly Monstrous Mind-Roasting Summer of O.C. and Stiggs (released 1987). 1985: Hellriders (completed 1983). 1987: The Pool/Miloha. Dixie Lanes. 1991: Johnny Suede. 1993: West from North Goes South. 1997: Welcome to Woop Woop.

LOVE, Bessie (Juanita Horton) 1898–1986
One of the cinema's most indomitable ladies: a tiny blonde American actress with a sweet smile, and a long nose that gave her an old-young face. Started as a teenager with D.W. Griffith in 1916, then became one of the silent screen's great beauties before working hard to make the transition to sound, often in early musicals. Came to Britain in the early thirties and stayed, no longer pursuing her career with such single-mindedness, but playing cameo roles as she chose. In her seventies began a new and successful career as a writer. Nominated for an Academy Award in *The Broadway Melody*.
1916: *Intolerance. Reggie Mixes In (GB: Mysteries in New York). The Aryan. The Flying Torpedo. The Good Bad Man. Hell-to-Pay Austin (GB: Love in the West). A Sister of Six. Acquitted. *The Mystery of the Leaping Fish. Stranded. The Heiress at Coffee Dan's.* 1917: *Wee Lady Betty. Nina, the Flower Girl. Cheerful Givers. Pernickety Polly Ann. A Daughter of the Poor. The Sawdust Ring.* 1918: *How Could You, Caroline? The Great Adventure. Carolyn of the Corners. A Little Sister of Everybody. The Dawn of Understanding.* 1919: *Over the Garden Wall. The Enchanted Barn. A Yankee Princess. Cupid Forecloses. A Fighting Colleen. The Wishing Ring Man. The Little Boss. Pegeen.* 1920: *Bonnie May. The Midlanders.* 1921: *The Spirit of the Lake. Penny of Top Hill Trail. The Sea Lion. The Swamp. The Honor of Ramirez.* 1922: *Bulldog Courage. Deserted at the Altar. Forget-Me-Not. The Vermilion Pencil. Night Life in Hollywood.* 1923: *Three Who Paid. The Village Blacksmith. Souls for Sale. Mary of the Movies. St Elmo. The Adventures of Prince Courageous. Ghost Patrol. Purple Dawn. Human Wreckage. The Eternal Three. Gentle Julia. Slave of Desire.* 1924: *Those Who Dance. A Woman on the Jury. Dynamite Smith (GB: The Agony of Fear). Sundown. The Silent Watcher. Tongues of Flame.* 1925: *A Son of His Father. Soul-Fire. The Lost World. New Brooms. The King on Main Street.* 1926: *Going Crooked. Lovey Mary. The Song and Dance Man. Young April.* 1927: *Rubber Tires (GB: Ten Thousand Reward). *Life in Hollywood No. 4. Dress Parade. The American/The Flag Maker. A Harp in Hock (GB: The Samaritan). *Amateur Night.* 1928: *The Matinee Idol. Sally of the Scandals. Anybody Here Seen Kelly? The Swell Head.* 1929: *The Broadway Melody. Hollywood Revue of 1929. The Girl in the Show. The Idle Rich.* 1930:

Chasing Rainbows. See America Thirst. Good News. They Learned About Women. 1931: *Morals for Women (GB: Farewell Party). Conspiracy. *Screen Snapshots No. 8.* 1936: *Live Again.* 1941: *Atlantic Ferry (US: Sons of the Sea).* 1942: *London Scrapbook.* 1945: *Journey Together.* 1951: *The Magic Box. No Highway (US: No Highway in the Sky).* 1953: *The Weak and the Wicked (US: Young and Willing).* 1954: *The Barefoot Contessa. Beau Brummell.* 1955: *Touch and Go (US: The Light Touch).* 1957: *The Story of Esther Costello (US: Golden Virgin).* 1958: *Nowhere to Go. Next to No Time!* 1959: *Too Young to Love.* 1961: *The Greengage Summer (US: Loss of Innocence).* 1962: *The Roman Spring of Mrs Stone.* 1963: *The Wild Affair. Children of the Damned.* 1964: *I Think They Call Him John (narrator only).* 1965: *Promise Her Anything.* 1967: *Battle Beneath the Earth. I'll Never Forget What's-'is-Name.* 1969: *Isadora. On Her Majesty's Secret Service.* 1971: *Sunday, Bloody Sunday. Catlow.* 1974: *Mousey (TV. GB: cinemas as Cat and Mouse). Vampyres.* 1976: *Gulliver's Travels (voice only). The Ritz.* 1979: *S.O.S. Titanic.* 1981: *Ragtime. Reds. Lady Chatterley's Lover.* 1983: *The Hunger.*

LOVEJOY, Frank 1914–1962
Tough but agreeable-looking, solidly-built American actor with dark curly hair. Acted on radio until his mid-thirties, then quickly rose to third place on film cast lists and stayed there, apart from an occasional, usually unsympathetic leading role in fairly minor films. He had left films again for theatre, TV and radio when he died from a heart attack.
1948: *Black Bart (GB: Black Bart – Highwayman).* 1949: *Home of the Brave. South Sea Sinner (GB: East of Java).* 1950: *In a Lonely Place. Breakthrough. Three Secrets. Try and Get Me (GB: The Sound of Fury).* 1951: *I Was a Communist for the FBI. Starlift. Goodbye, My Fancy. I'll See You in My Dreams.* 1952: *The Winning Team. *Screen Snapshots No. 205. Retreat, Hell!* 1953: *She's Back on Broadway. The Hitch Hiker. The System. House of Wax. The Charge at Feather River.* 1954: *Beachhead. Men of the Fighting Lady. The Americano.* 1955: *Mad at the World. Top of the World. Strategic Air Command. Finger Man. The Crooked Web. Shack Out on 101.* 1956: *Julie. The Country Husband (TV. GB: cinemas).* 1957: *Three Brave Men.* 1958: *Cole Younger, Gunfighter.* 1959: *The Raider (TV).*

LOWE, Edmund 1890–1971
Suave, debonair, latterly moustachioed American actor with sharp, near-Barrymore profile. Mainly on stage until the twenties; then film stardom claimed him, and he enjoyed his best period in the last few years of silents, especially opposite Victor McLaglen in the 'Flagg and Quirt' comedies. Later declined to routine leading roles in crime thrillers, and made several visits to London. Died from a lung ailment. First wife, film actress Lilyan Tashman (1899–1934), died young: subsequently Lowe married and divorced twice.
1915: *The Wild Olive.* 1916: *Zeitungsmaxe and Co.* 1917: *The Spreading Dawn.* 1918: *The Reason Why. Vive La France.* 1919: *Eyes of Youth (GB: The Love of Sunya).* 1920: *The Woman Gives. Madonnas and Men. A Woman's Business. Someone in the House. Devil.* 1921: *Chicken in the Case. My Lady's Latchkey.* 1922: *Living Lies. Peacock Alley.* 1923: *The Silent Command. In the Palace of the King. The White Flower. Wife in Name Only.* 1924: *Honor among Men. Barbara Frietchie. The Brass Bowl. Nellie, The Beautiful Cloak Model.* 1925: *Soul Mates. The Winding Stair. Marriage in Transit. The Kiss Barrier. Greater than a Crown. Ports of Call. East Lynne. The Fool. Champion of Lost Causes. East of Suez.* 1926: *Black Paradise. What Price Glory? Siberia. The Palace of Pleasure.* 1927: *Iz Zat So? Baloo. One Increasing Purpose. The Wizard. Publicity Madness.* 1928: *Happiness Ahead. Outcast. Dressed to Kill.* 1929: *The Cock-Eyed World. In Old Arizona. Making the Grade. Thru Different Eyes. This Thing Called Love.* 1930: *Good Intentions. The Painted Angel. Happy Days. More than a Kiss. Part Time Wife. The Squealer. Born Reckless. The Bad One. Man on Call. Scotland Yard (GB: 'Detective Clive', Bart).* 1931: *Women of All Nations. The Cisco Kid. *Screen Snapshots No. 8. Transatlantic. Don't Bet on Women.* 1932: *Attorney for the Defense. *The Stolen Jools (GB: The Slippery Pearls). Guilty As Hell (GB: Guilty as Charged). American Madness. Chandu, the Magician. The Devil is Driving. The Misleading Lady.* 1933: *Hot Pepper. Her Bodyguard. Dinner at Eight. I Love That Man.* 1934: *Let's Fall in Love. Gift of Gab. Bombay Mail. No More Women.* 1935: *Under Pressure. The Great Hotel Murder. Mr Dynamite. Thunder in the Night. *La Fiesta de Santa Barbara. King Solomon of Broadway. Black Sheep. The Great Impersonation.* 1936: *Seven

Sinners (US: Doomed Cargo). The Garden Murder Case. Mad Holiday. The Grand Exit. The Wrecker. The Girl on the Front Page. 1937: Under Cover of Night. The Squeaker (US: Murder on Diamond Row). Espionage. Every Day's a Holiday. 1938: Secrets of a Nurse. 1939: Our Neighbors, the Carters. Newsboys' Home. The Witness Vanishes. 1940: Honeymoon Deferred. The Crooked Road. I Love You Again. Wolf of New York. Men against the Sky. 1941: *Stars at Play. Flying Cadets. Double Date. 1942: Call Out the Marines. Klondike Fury. 1943: Murder in Times Square. Dangerous Blonde. Oh! What a Night. 1944: The Girl in the Case (GB: The Silver Key). Dillinger. 1945: The Great Mystic. The Enchanted Forest. 1946: The Strange Mr Gregory. 1948: Good Sam. 1955: *The Devil's Bible. 1956: Around the World in 80 Days. 1957: The Wings of Eagles. Execution Night (TV. GB: cinemas). 1958: Plunderers of Painted Flats. The Last Hurrah. 1960: Heller in Pink Tights.

LOWE, Rob 1964–
Dark-haired American actor whose early puppy-dog appeal has now been replaced by a slightly decadent handsomeness. Youthful appeal had him on television as a child before breaking through to adult roles as a 19-year-old in Coppola's The Outsiders. He proved himself more than a pretty face in such off-beat projects as Square Dance and Bad Influence. But the latter title became prophetic when he got involved in unsavoury headlines concerning the alleged corruption of a minor, and his films in the 1990s were of little help in furthering a once-promising career.
1982: Thursday's Child (TV). 1983: The Outsiders. Class. 1984: The Hotel New Hampshire. Oxford Blues. 1985: St Elmo's Fire. 1986: Youngblood. 'About Last Night...' Square Dance. 1987: Illegally Yours. 1988: Masquerade. 1990: Bad Influence. 1991: The Finest Hour/Desert Shield. If the Shoe Fits (later Stroke of Midnight). The Dark Backward (GB: The Man with Three Arms). 1992: Wayne's World. 1993: L'arbre métallique. 1994: Frank and Jesse. 1995: Tommy Boy. First Degree. Mulholland Falls. 1996: Jack Higgins' On Dangerous Ground (TV). The Guardian System. 1997: Contact. Hostile Intent. Living in Peril (cable TV). Crazy Six. Austin Powers International Man of Mystery. 1998: Outrage (TV). One Hell of a Guy. For Hire (TV). 1999: Austin Powers:

The Spy Who Shagged Me. Atomic Train. Dead Silent (TV). The Specials. Statistics. 2000: Under Pressure. Proximity.

LOWERY, Robert
(R.L. Hanke) 1914–1971
Singer, juvenile lead, minor-league star, character player, serial hero and bit parts – this genial-looking American actor, with his mop of light-brown curly hair, did it all. Originally a dance-band singer, he took up acting in his early twenties and became the hero of dozens of second-features in the 1940s. After playing Batman in a serial, his film career gradually drifted away, even though, as his features thickened, he donned a moustache and played villains. Married to Jean Parker (qv) from 1951 to 1957, third of three wives. Died from a heart attack.
1936: Come and Get It. Great Guy (GB: Pluck of the Irish). 1937: The Lady Escapes. Rebecca of Sunnybrook Farm. Big Town Girl. The Jones Family in Hot Water. Charlie Chan on Broadway. City Girl. You Can't Have Everything. Wife, Doctor and Nurse. Second Honeymoon. Life Begins in College (GB: The Joy Parade). Wake Up and Live. 1938: Passport Husband. Tail Spin. Submarine Patrol. Always Goodbye. Alexander's Ragtime Band. Island in the Sky. Happy Landing. One Wild Night. A Trip to Paris. Safety in Numbers. Gateway. Kentucky Moonshine (GB: Three Men and a Girl). Four Men and a Prayer. Josette. 1939: Wife, Husband and Friend. Day-Time Wife. Second Fiddle. Everybody's Baby. Charlie Chan in Reno. The Baroness and the Butler. The Escape. Young Mr Lincoln. Hollywood Cavalcade. Drums Along the Mohawk. Mr Moto in Danger Island (GB: Mr Moto on Danger Island). 1940: City of Chance. Free, Blonde and Twenty-One. Shooting High. Four Sons. Maryland. The Mark of Zorro. Star Dust. Charlie Chan's Murder Cruise. Murder Over New York. 1941: Private Nurse. Ride On, Vaquero! Cadet Girl. Great Guns. 1942: Dawn on the Great Divide. My Gal Sal. Criminal Investigator. Who is Hope Schuyler? She's in the Army. Lure of the Islands. Rhythm Parade. 1943: The Immortal Sergeant. Tarzan's Desert Mystery. So's Your Uncle. The North Star (later Armored Attack). Campus Rhythm. Revenge of the Zombies (GB: The Corpse Vanished). 1944: The Navy Way. Hot Rhythm. A Scream in the Dark (GB: Scream in the Night). Dark Mountain. Dangerous Passage. The Mummy's Ghost. Mystery of the River Boat (serial). 1945:

Homesick Angel. Thunderbolt. Road to Alcatraz. Fashion Model. High Powered. Prison Ship. The Monster and the Ape (serial). 1946: Sensation Hunters. They Made Me a Killer. House of Horrors (GB: Joan Medford is Missing). God's Country. The Lady Chaser. Gas House Kids. 1947: Big Town. Danger Street. I Cover Big Town. Killer at Large. Queen of the Amazons. Jungle Flight. Big Town After Dark. 1948: Death Valley. Heart of Virginia. Mary Lou. Big Town Scandal. Highway 13. 1949: Shep Comes Home. Batman and Robin (serial). Arson Inc. The Dalton Gang. Call of the Forest. 1950: Gunfire (GB: Jesse James Rides Again). Border Rangers. Western Pacific Agent. Train to Tombstone. I Shot Billy the Kid. Everybody's Dancin'. 1951: Crosswinds. 1953: Jalopy. Cow Country. The Homesteaders. 1955: Lay That Rifle Down. 1956: Two-Gun Lady. 1957: The Parson and the Outlaw. 1959: The Rise and Fall of Legs Diamond. 1962: Deadly Duo. When the Girls Take Over. Young Guns of Texas. 1963: McLintock! 1964: Stage to Thunder Rock. 1965: Zebra in the Kitchen. Johnny Reno. 1966: Waco. 1967: The Undertaker (and His Pals). The Ballad of Josie.

LOY, Myrna (M. Williams) 1905–1993
Red-headed Hollywood star of Welsh ancestry who moved from bit parts and oriental vamps to become the 'Queen of Hollywood' by the late 1930s (Clark Gable was voted King). Queen of sophisticated comedy she certainly was, in a dazzling period of success that ran from 1934 to 1941. Her war work for the Red Cross took the sting out of her career and she worked only sporadically after 1941. Four times married and divorced. Amazingly, she was never even nominated for an Academy Award. Special Oscar 1991. Died during surgery.
1925: What Price Beauty? Ben-Hur. Satan in Sables. Pretty Ladies. Sporting Life. 1926: The Wanderer. When a Man Loves (GB: His Lady). Cave Man. The Gilded Highway. Across the Pacific. Don Juan. Why Girls Go Back Home. The Love Toy. The Third Degree. Millionaires. The Exquisite Sinner. So This is Paris. Finger Prints. 1927: Ham and Eggs at the Front (GB: Ham and Eggs). Bitter Apples. The Heart of Maryland. Naughty But Nice. The Jazz Singer. If I Were Single. The Climbers. The Girl from Chicago. Simple Sis. A Sailor's Sweetheart. 1928: A Girl in Every Port. What Price Beauty? Turn Back the Hours (GB: The Badge of Courage). Crimson City.

*State Street Sadie (GB: The Girl from State Street). Beware of Married Men. Midnight Taxi. Pay as You Enter. 1929: Noah's Ark. The Desert Song. Fancy Baggage. The Black Watch (GB: King of the Kyber Rifles). Hardboiled Rose. Evidence. The Show of Shows. The Squall. 1930: Jazz Cinderella (GB: Love is Like That). Cameo Kirby. Isle of Escape. The Bad Man. The Great Divide. Cock o' the Walk. Bride of the Regiment (GB: Lady of the Rose). Last of the Duanes. Under a Texas Moon. Rogue of the Rio Grande. The Truth About Youth. Renegades. The Devil to Pay. 1931: A Connecticut Yankee (GB: The Yankee at King Arthur's Court). Naughty Flirt. Arrowsmith. Consolation Marriage (GB: Married in Haste). Skyline. Rebound. Transatlantic. Hush Money. Body and Soul. 1932: The Wet Parade. The Woman in Room 13. Emma. Love Me Tonight. Thirteen Women. The Animal Kingdom (GB: The Woman in His House). The Mask of Fu Manchu. Vanity Fair. New Morals for Old. 1933: Topaze. Penthouse (GB: Crooks in Clover). The Barbarian (GB: A Night in Cairo). The Prizefighter and the Lady (GB: Everywoman's Man). Night Flight. Scarlet River. When Ladies Meet. 1934: Men in White. Stamboul Quest. Manhattan Melodrama. The Thin Man. Evelyn Prentice. Broadway Bill (GB: Strictly Confidential). 1935: Wings in the Dark. Whipsaw. 1936: Wife vs Secretary. Libeled Lady. After the Thin Man. The Great Ziegfeld. Petticoat Fever. To Mary – with Love. 1937: Parnell. Double Wedding. Man-Proof. 1938: Test Pilot. Too Hot to Handle. 1939: Lucky Night. Another Thin Man. The Rains Came. 1940: Third Finger, Left Hand. I Love You Again. 1941: Shadow of the Thin Man. Love Crazy. 1943: *Show Business at War. 1944: The Thin Man Goes Home. 1946: The Best Years of Our Lives. So Goes My Love (GB: A Genius in the Family). 1947: The Senator Was Indiscreet (GB: Mr Ashton Was Indiscreet). Song of the Thin Man. The Bachelor and the Bobby Soxer (GB: Bachelor Knight). 1948: Mr Blandings Builds His Dream House. 1949: That Dangerous Age (US: If This Be Sin). The Red Pony. 1950: Cheaper by the Dozen. 1952: Belles on Their Toes. 1956: The Ambassador's Daughter. 1958: Lonelyhearts. 1960: From the Terrace. Midnight Lace. 1969: The April Fools. 1971: Death Takes a Holiday (TV). Do Not Fold, Spindle or Mutilate (TV). 1972: The Couple Takes a Wife (TV). 1974: Indict and Convict (TV). Airport 1975. 1975: The Elevator (TV). 1977: It Happened at Lakewood Manor (TV. GB: Panic at Lakewood Manor). 1978: The End. 1979: Just Tell Me What You Want. 1981: Summer Solstice (TV).*

LUCAN, Arthur (A. Towle) 1885–1954

Wry-faced British music-hall comedian who made his name with the creation of Old Mother Riley, a sentimental old harridan of an Irish washerwoman. He paraded the character through 15 barnstorming comedy films and became one of Britain's most popular stars in the wartime years. His daughter on film was played by his real-life wife Kitty McShane (1898–1964). They married in 1913 and their off-stage rows were legendary. He died from a heart attack.

1935: Stars on Parade. 1937: Kathleen Mavourneen (US: Kathleen). Old Mother Riley. 1938: Old Mother Riley in Paris. 1939: Old Mother Riley MP. Old Mother Riley Joins Up. 1940: Old Mother Riley in Society. Old Mother Riley in Business. 1941: Old Mother Riley's Ghosts. Old Mother Riley's Circus. 1942: Old Mother Riley Detective. 1943: Old Mother Riley Overseas. 1945: Old Mother Riley at Home. 1949: Old Mother Riley's New Venture. 1950: Old Mother Riley Headmistress. 1951: Old Mother Riley's Jungle Treasure. 1952: Mother Riley Meets the Vampire (US: Vampire over London).

LUGOSI, Bela (B. Blasko) 1882–1956

Transylvanian-born actor of dominant and rather forbidding personality. After becoming a romantic idol of the Hungarian stage, he fled the country in the face of an oppressive regime and ended in Hollywood, where his performance as Dracula type-cast him in horror for the rest of his career. His later years were dogged by a (finally victorious) battle against drug addiction. Died from a heart attack. Five times married.

1917: Alarscobal. Az elet kiralya. The Leopard. A naszdal. Tavaszi vihar. Az ezredes. 1918: Casanova. Lulu. '99'. Kuzdelem a létért. 1919: Sklaven Fremden Willens. 1920: Der Fluch der Menschen (in two parts). The Head of Janus (GB: Dr Jekyll and Mr Hyde). Die Frau im Delphin. Die Todeskarawane (US: Caravan of Death). Nat Pinkerton in Kampf. Lederstrumpf. Die Teufelsanbeter (US: The Devil Worshipers). 1921: Johann Hopkins III. Der Tanz auf dem Vaulkan (in two parts). 1922: The Last of the Mohicans. 1923: The Silent Command. 1924: The Rejected Woman. 1925: The Midnight Girl. Daughters Who Pay.

*1926: *Punchinello. 1928: How to Handle Women. The Veiled Woman. 1929: Prisoners. The Thirteenth Chair. The Last Performance. Such Men Are Dangerous. 1930: King of Jazz (Hungarian-language version only). Wild Company. Renegades. Viennese Nights. Oh, For a Man. Dracula. 1931: Fifty Million Frenchmen. Women of All Nations. The Black Camel. Broadminded. 1932: The Murders in the Rue Morgue. White Zombie. Chandu, the Magician. The Death Kiss. Island of Lost Souls. 1933: *Hollywood on Parade A-8. Whispering Shadows (serial). International House. Night of Terror. The Devil's in Love. 1934: The Black Cat (GB: The House of Doom). Gift of Gab. The Return of Chandu (serial. And feature version). The Best Man Wins. Chandu on the Magic Isle. *Screen Snapshots No. 11. 1935: The Mysterious Mr Wong. Murder by Television. Mark of the Vampire. The Raven. The Mystery of the Marie Celeste (US: Phantom Ship). The Invisible Ray. 1936: Shadow of Chinatown (serial. GB: The Yellow Phantom). Postal Inspector. 1937: SOS Coastguard (serial). 1939: The Dark Eyes of London (US: The Human Monster. Completed 1936). The Phantom Creeps. (serial). Son of Frankenstein. Ninotchka. The Gorilla. 1940: The Saint's Double Trouble. Black Friday. You'll Find Out. The Devil Bat. 1941: The Invisible Ghost. The Black Cat (and 1934 version). Spooks Run Wild. The Wolf Man. 1942: The Ghost of Frankenstein. Black Dragons. The Corpse Vanishes (GB: The Case of the Missing Brides). Night Monster (GB: House of Mystery). Bowery at Midnight. 1943: Frankenstein Meets the Wolf-Man. The Ape Man (GB: Lock Your Doors). Ghosts on the Loose (GB: Ghosts in the Night). The Return of the Vampire. 1944: Voodoo Man. Return of the Ape Man. One Body Too Many. 1945: The Body Snatcher. Zombies on Broadway (GB: Loonies on Broadway). 1946: Genius at Work. Scared to Death. 1948: Abbott and Costello Meet Frankenstein (GB: Abbott and Costello Meet the Ghosts). 1952: Mother Riley Meets the Vampire (US: Vampire Over London). Bela Lugosi Meets a Brooklyn Gorilla (GB: Monster Meets the Gorilla). *Meet Bela Lugosi and Oliver Hardy. 1953: Glen or Glenda? 1954: Bride of the Monster. 1956: The Black Sleep. 1957: Plan 9 from Outer Space.*

LUKAS, Paul (Pál Lukács) 1887–1971

Smooth, urbane, moustachioed, Hungarian-born leading man, in Hollywood from the late twenties. Seen mostly as villains or continental Romeos at first, but later – after filming in England from 1937 to 1939 – in a more interesting variety of roles, winning an Academy Award in 1943 for *Watch on the Rhine*. It's hard to believe that this most civilized of men was once a wrestler – but he was. Died from heart attack.

1915: A Man of the Earth. 1917: Heartsong. 1918: Udvari Lovegö Sphynx. Vorrei Morir. 1920: Olavi. Névtelen Vár. Masamod. A szürkeruhás Hölgy. The Milliner. Sárga Arnyék. Little Fox. Szinesnö. 1921: Hétszázeves Szerelem. A Telegram from New York/New York Expresz Kábel. 1922: Lady Violette. Samson and Delilah. Eine versunkene Welt. 1923: Das unbekannte Morgen. Az Egyhauszasos Lány. Diadalmas Élet. 1924: Egy Fiunak a Fele. 1928: Woman from Moscow. Two Lovers. Manhattan Cocktail. Three Sinners. Hot News. The Night Watch. Loves of an Actress. 1929: The Wolf of Wall Street. Half Way to Heaven. Illusion. The Shopworn Angel. 1930: Slightly Scarlet. Young Eagles. The Benson Murder Case. Anybody's Woman. Grumpy. The Devil's Holiday. Behind the Make-Up. The Right to Love. 1931: City Streets. The Vice Squad. Strictly Dishonorable. Working Girls. Women Love Once. The Beloved Bachelor. Unfaithful. 1932: No One Man. Tomorrow and Tomorrow. A Passport to Hell (GB: Burnt Offering). Downstairs. Rockabye. Thunder Below. 1933: Grand Slam. Sing Sinner Sing. Secret of the Blue Room. Nagana. Little Women. The Kiss before the Mirror. Captured! 1934: By Candlelight. Glamour. Affairs of a Gentleman. Gift of Gab. The Fountain. The Countess of Monte Cristo. I Give My Love. 1935: Age of Indiscretion. Father Brown – Detective. The Three Musketeers. I Found Stella Parish. The Casino Murder Case. 1936: Dodsworth. Ladies in Love. 1937: Espionage. Brief Ecstasy. The Mutiny of the Elsinore. Dinner at the Ritz. 1938: The Lady Vanishes. Dangerous Secrets. 1939: A Window in London (US: Lady in Distress). The Chinese Bungalow (US: Chinese Den). Confessions of a Nazi Spy. Captain Fury. 1940: Strange Cargo. The Ghost Breakers. 1941: They Dare Not Love. The Monster and the Girl. 1943: Watch on the Rhine. Hostages. 1944: Uncertain Glory. Address Unknown. Experiment Perilous. 1946: Temptation. Deadline at Dawn. 1947: Whispering City. 1948: Berlin Express. 1950: Kim. 1954: 20,000 Leagues Under the Sea. 1958: The Roots of Heaven. 1959: Judgment at Nuremberg (TV). 1960: Tender is the Night. Scent of Mystery (GB: Holiday in Spain). 1962: The Four Horsemen of the Apocalypse. 55 Days at Peking. 1963: Fun in Acapulco. 1964: Lord Jim. 1967: Sol Madrid (GB: The Heroin Gang). 1970: The Challenge (TV).

LUMLEY, Joanna 1946–

Slim, intelligent British leading lady, born in Kashmir, and at her best in bitchy or sardonic roles, in which her curled smile usually precedes the delivery of some whiplash line. Although her film career has been unhappily sketchy, successful TV series (*The New Avengers, Sapphire and Steel, Absolutely Fabulous*) have often triggered mini-revivals in movie roles. Married/divorced actor-writer-comedian Jeremy Lloyd, first of two.

1969: On Her Majesty's Secret Service. Some Girls Do. 1970: Games That Lovers Play. The House That Dripped Blood. 1971: The Breaking of Bumbo. Tam Lin (GB: The Devil's Widow). 1973: Don't Just Lie There, Say Something. 1974: The Satanic Rites of Dracula (US: Count Dracula and His Vampire Bride). 1979: The Plank (TV). 1982: Trail of the Pink Panther. 1983: Curse of the Pink Panther. 1984: The Glory Boys (TV). 1989: Shirley Valentine. 1990: A Ghost in Monte Carlo (TV). 1995: The Forgotten Toys (voice only). Cold Comfort Farm (TV. Later: cinemas). Innocent Lies. 1996: James and the Giant Peach. 1997: Prince Valiant. 1998: A Rather English Marriage (TV). Parting Shots. 1999: Alice in Wonderland (voice only). Mad Cows. 2000: Maybe Baby.

LUND, John 1911–1992

The fair-haired, blue-eyed son of a Norwegian glass-blower who had emigrated to New York, Lund only took up acting in his late twenties. After a good start in films his flair for zany comedy was swiftly shunted aside in favour of stodgy drama, and he soon slid into the almost-permanent role of the slightly dull 'other man' who never got the girl. Died from heart problems.

1946: To Each His Own. 1947: The Perils of Pauline. Variety Girl. 1948: Miss Tatlock's Millions. A Foreign Affair. Night Has a Thousand Eyes. 1949: Bride of Vengeance. My Friend Irma. 1950: No Man of Her Own. Duchess of Idaho. My Friend Irma Goes West. 1951: The Mating Season. Darling, How Could You? (GB: Rendezvous). 1952: Steel Town. Bronco Buster. Just Across the Street. The Battle at Apache Pass. 1953: The Woman They Almost Lynched. Latin Lovers. 1955:

Chief Crazy Horse (GB: Valley of Fury). White Feather. Five Guns West. 1956: Dakota Incident. High Society. Battle Stations! 1957: Affair in Reno. 1960: The Wackiest Ship in the Army. 1962: If a Man Answers.

LUNDGREN, Dolph

(Hans Lundgren) 1959–

Blond, muscular, 6ft 6in tall Swedish-born karate champion, raised in Sweden, Germany and Australia. Coming to America, he was a nightclub bouncer while studying acting. Once into films he soon set out on the body-splitting action movie trail blazed by Chuck Norris, Arnold Schwarzenegger and Jean-Claude Van Damme (all *qv*). Unlike them, though, he also showed an interest in playing the occasional very nasty villain. He did not quite break through into the mainstream, but remains popular in corpse-strewn video mayhem.

1981: For Your Eyes Only. 1985: A View to a Kill. Rocky IV. 1987: Masters of the Universe. 1988: The Punisher. 1989: Red Scorpion. 1990: Dark Angel/I Come in Peace. 1991: Cover-Up. Showdown in Little Tokyo. 1992: Universal Soldier. 1993: Army of One/The Joshua Tree. 1994: Men of War. Meltdown. 1995: Johnny Mnemonic. The Shooter. 1996: The Algonquin Goodbye/Silent Trigger. Hellbent. 1997: The Peacekeeper. The Minion. 1998: Frogs for Snakes. Blackjack/John Woo's Blackjack (TV). Sweepers. 1999: Bridge of Dragons. Storm Catcher. Jill Rips. 2000: The Last Patrol. Captured.

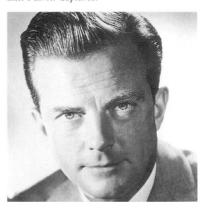

LUNDIGAN, William 1914–1975

Tall, fair-haired American actor, similar in looks to Richard Denning (*qv*). Started as a radio announcer, then turned to acting and developed slowly into a second-line leading man. Briefly in more showy lead roles with Fox in the early fifties, but his career virtually collapsed with the end of the studio system. Died from heart and lung congestion.

*1937: Armored Car. Prescription for Romance. The Lady Fights Back. A Girl with Ideas. 1938: Letter of Introduction. State Police. Freshman Year. Reckless Living. Wives under Suspicion. The Missing Guest. The Black Doll. That's My Story. Danger on the Air. 1939: Dodge City. Legion of Lost Flyers. *Young America Flies. Three Smart Girls Grow Up. The Old Maid. They Asked for It. Forgotten Woman. 1940: The Fighting 69th. The Man Who Talked Too Much. Three Cheers for the Irish. Santa Fé Trail. East of the River. The Sea Hawk. The Case of the Black Parrot. 1941: The Great Mr Nobody. International Squadron. A Shot in the Dark. Sailors on Leave. Highway West. The Bugle Sounds. 1942: The Courtship of Andy Hardy. Sunday Punch. Apache Trail. Northwest Rangers. Andy Hardy's Double Life. 1943: Salute to the Marines. Dr Gillespie's Criminal Case (GB: Crazy to Kill). Headin' for God's Country. 1945: What Next, Corporal Hargrove? 1947: Dishonored Lady. The Fabulous Dorseys. 1948: Inside Story. Mystery in Mexico. 1949: State Department – File 649 (GB: Assignment in China). Follow Me Quietly. Pinky. 1950: Mother Didn't Tell Me. I'll Get By. 1951: The House on Telegraph Hill. I'd Climb the Highest Mountain. Love Nest. Elopement. 1953: Down Among the Sheltering Palms. Inferno. Serpent of the Nile. 1954: Riders to the Stars. Dangerous Voyage (US: Terror Ship). The White Orchid. 1962: Underwater City. 1967: The Way West. Where Angels Go . . . Trouble Follows.*

LUPINO, Ida 1914–1995

Greasepaint ran in these veins all right. The daughter of popular comedian Stanley Lupino (*qv*), and pretty well all her cousins and uncles were music-hall stars. Strangely, the pretty, impish, dark-haired (blonde for a while in the thirties) Ida was not much seen in comedy, starting off as ingenues and frightened ladies, and moving to Hollywood in this mould in 1934. From the early forties she excelled in hard-bitten roles. She also directed a few films, some with controversial themes. Married Louis Hayward (1938–1945) and Howard Duff (1951–1968), first and third of three. Died from cancer of the liver.

*1932: The Love Race. Her First Affaire. 1933: Money for Speed. High Finance. I Lived with You. Prince of Arcadia. The Ghost Camera. 1934: Search for Beauty. Ready for Love. Come on Marines! 1935: Paris in Spring (GB: Paris Love Song). Peter Ibbetson. *La Fiesta de Santa Barbara. Smart Girl. 1936: Anything Goes. The Gay Desperado. One Rainy Afternoon. Yours for the Asking. 1937: Sea Devils. Artists and Models. Let's Get Married. Fight for Your Lady. 1939: The Lone Wolf Spy Hunt (GB: The Lone Wolf's Daughter). The Adventures of Sherlock Holmes (GB: Sherlock Holmes). The Lady and the Mob. The Light That Failed. 1940: They Drive by Night (GB: The Road to Frisco). 1941: The Sea Wolf. High Sierra. Out of the Fog. Ladies in Retirement. 1942: Moontide. Life Begins at 8:30 (GB: The Light of Heart). The Hard Way. 1943: Forever and a Day. Thank Your Lucky Stars. Devotion (released 1946). 1944: Hollywood Canteen. In Our Time. 1945: Pillow to Post. 1946: The Man I Love. 1947: Deep Valley. Escape Me Never. 1948: Road House. 1949: Lust for Gold. 1950: Woman in Hiding. 1951: On Dangerous Ground. 1952: Beware My Lovely. 1953: Jennifer. The Bigamist. 1954: Private Hell 36. 1955: The Big Knife. Women's Prison. 1956: While the City Sleeps. Strange Intruder. 1967: I Love a Mystery (TV). 1968: Backtrack (TV). 1971: Women in Chains (TV). 1972: Female Artillery (TV). Deadhead Miles. Junior Bonner. My Boys Are Good Boys (released 1978). The Letters (TV). The Strangers in 7A (TV). 1975: The Devil's Rain. 1976: The Food of the Gods.*

As director: 1949: Not Wanted (uncredited co-director). 1950: Outrage. Never Fear. 1951: Hard, Fast and Beautiful (and acting 'bit'). 1953: The Bigamist. The Hitch Hiker. 1966: The Trouble with Angels.

LUPINO, Stanley 1892–1942

Dapper, dark-haired, thin-mouthed, wry-faced, London-born farceur, light singer and dancer and confident all-round entertainer. A member of a family who were pretty well all in show business, he was on stage at 17 and a star of revue soon after. His film career, though popular enough, was entirely confined to the 1930s and much restricted by his stage work. Customarily in films he would appear as a breezy young man of faintly working-class origins who got the girl of his dreams after various chicanery from other interested parties. Father of Ida Lupino (*qv*). Died from cancer.

1931: Love Lies. The Love Race. 1932: Sleepless Nights. 1933: King of the Ritz. Facing the Music. You Made Me Love You. Happy. 1935: Honeymoon for Three. 1936: Cheer Up. Sporting Love. 1937: Over She Goes. 1938: Hold My Hand. 1939: Lucky To Me.

LYDON, James 'Jimmy' 1923–

If it weren't for Henry Aldrich, Jimmy Lydon probably wouldn't qualify for this book. But, under the guidance of this red-haired, gangling, dumb-looking young American actor, Henry became the world's second favourite wartime teenager after Andy Hardy. Most of Lydon's other starring roles seem so long ago its hard to believe he's still around. Also a producer and director of TV series in his later days.

*1939: Back Door to Heaven. Middleton Family at the NY World's Fair. Two Thoroughbreds. Racing Luck. 1940: Tom Brown's Schooldays. Little Men. 1941: Naval Academy. Bowery Boy. Henry Aldrich for President. 1942: Cadets on Parade. The Mad Martindales. *A Letter from Bataan. Henry and Dizzy. Star Spangled Rhythm. 1943: Henry Aldrich, Editor. Henry Aldrich Gets Glamour (GB: Henry Gets Glamour). Henry Aldrich Swings It (GB: Henry Swings It). Henry Aldrich Haunts a House (GB: Henry Haunts a House). Henry Aldrich Plays Cupid (GB: Henry Plays Cupid). Aerial Gunner. *The Aldrich Family Gets in the Scrap. 1944: Henry Aldrich Boy Scout (GB: Henry – Boy Scout). My Best Gal. The Town Went Wild. Henry Aldrich's Little Secret (GB: Henry's Little Secret). When the Lights Go on Again. 1945: Out of the Night (GB: Strange Illusion). Twice Blessed. 1946: The Affairs of Geraldine. 1947: Cynthia (GB: The Rich, Full Life). Sweet Genevieve. Life with Father. 1948: The Time of Your Life. Out of the Storm. Joan of Arc. An Old-Fashioned Girl. 1949: Bad Boy. Miss Mink of 1949. Tucson. 1950: Tarnished. When Willie Comes Marching Home. Destination Big House. Hot Rod. September Affair. The Magnificent Yankee (GB: The Man with 30 Sons). Gasoline Alley. 1951: O, Susanna. Corky of Gasoline Alley (GB: Corky). 1953: Island in the Sky. 1954: The Desperado. 1955: Rage at Dawn. 1956: Battle Stations. 1957: Chain of Evidence. 1960: The Hypnotic Eye. I Passed for White. 1961: The Last Time I Saw Archie. 1965: Brainstorm. 1969: Death of a Gunfighter. 1971: Scandalous John. 1972: Bonnie's Kids. 1975: Vigilante Force. Ellery Queen: Too Many Suspects (TV). 1976: The New Daughters of Joshua Cabe (TV). 1977: Peter Lundy and the Medicine Hat Stallion (TV).*

LYNCH, Kelly 1959–
Tall, lithe, leggy, elegant American actress, a top model who only started taking acting seriously in her late twenties. She soon displayed exceptional ability in such films as *Drugstore Cowboy*, but probably changed the course of her career by turning down the Sharon Stone role in *Basic Instinct* in 1992, a year in which she eventually made no films at all. Her profile has been lower since then, although she still managed to shine in some poor films. Not, on the whole, a good chooser of scripts.
1983: *Portfolio*. 1985: *Osa*. 1988: *Bright Lights, Big City. Cocktail*. 1989: *Road House. Drugstore Cowboy. Warm Summer Rain*. 1990: *Desperate Hours*. 1991: *Curley Sue*. 1992: *R.S.V.P. (later: For Better and For Worse)*. 1993: *Three of Hearts*. 1994: *The Beans of Egypt, Maine (GB: video, as Forbidden Choices). Imaginary Crimes*. 1995: *Heaven's Prisoners. Virtuosity. White Man's Burden*. 1996: *Persons Unknown*. 1997: *Mr Magoo. Noose. Cold Around the Heart*. 1998: *Homegrown*. 1999: *Brotherhood of Murder (TV)*. 2000: *Charlie's Angels*.

LYNLEY, Carol (Carolyn Jones) 1942–
Baby-faced American blonde, in films as a teenager, and, as Carolyn Lee, a former model. Like the similar Yvette Mimieux, also trapped in childlike roles, she was a more than competent actress who found herself in progressively less worthy parts. More promising ventures were sunk by inferior scripts and after a slough of 'Z' movies and TV films her chance of big-time stardom slipped away.
1958: *The Light in the Forest*. 1959: *Blue Denim (GB: Blue Jeans). Holiday for Lovers.*

1960: *Hound Dog Man*. 1961: *Return to Peyton Place. The Last Sunset*. 1962: *The Stripper (GB: Woman of Summer)*. 1963: *Under the Yum Yum Tree. The Cardinal*. 1964: *Shock Treatment. The Pleasure Seekers*. 1965: *Harlow (TV). Bunny Lake is Missing*. 1966: *The Shuttered Room*. 1967: *The Helicopter Spies (TV. GB: cinemas). Danger Route*. 1968: *The Smugglers (TV). Shadow on the Land (TV)*. 1969: *The Maltese Bippy. The Immortal (TV). Norwood*. 1970: *Once You Kiss a Stranger. Weekend of Terror (TV)*. 1971: *The Cable Car Mystery (TV. GB: Crosscurrent). The Night Stalker (TV). Beware! The Blob (GB: Son of Blob)*. 1972: *The Poseidon Adventure*. 1973: *Cotter (GB: TV. Completed 1968)*. 1974: *Death Stalk (TV). The Elevator (TV)*. 1975: *The Four Deuces*. 1976: *Flood! (TV). Out of Control (later The Washington Affair)*. 1977: *Bad Georgia Road. Having Babies II (TV). Fantasy Island (TV)*. 1978: *The Cops and Robin (TV). The Cat and the Canary. The Beasts Are in the Streets! (TV)*. 1979: *The Shape of Things To Come. Todos Los Dias un Dia*. 1980: *Lady Doctor (TV). Willow B: Women in Prison (TV)*. 1982: *Vigilante*. 1985: *Balboa*. 1987: *Dark Tower*. 1988: *Blackout*. 1990: *Spirits*. 1991: *Howling VI – The Freaks*. 1992: *Heartfelt*. 1997: *Neon Signs*. 1999: *Vic/Final Act. Drowning on Dry Land.*

LYNN, Ann 1934–
Fair-haired, narrow-faced British actress, granddaughter of Ralph Lynn (qv). Her rather mournful looks got her cast as downtrodden daughters or conniving bitches. She was often the best thing in her films (and was seen in some fairly obscure ones, too), but her unpretty countenance may have given her little chance of becoming a star in the British cinema at the time. Married/divorced Anthony Newley (qv). Granddaughter of Ralph Lynn (qv).
1955: *Johnny, You're Wanted*. 1958: *Moment of Indiscretion*. 1959: *Naked Fury*. 1960: *Piccadilly Third Stop*. 1961: *Strip Tease Murder. Flame in the Streets. The Wind of Change*. 1962: *Strongroom. HMS Defiant (US: Damn the Defiant!). *A Woman's Privilege*. 1963: *The Party's Over. Doctor in Distress*. 1964: *The Black Torment. The System (US: The Girl Getters). A Shot in the Dark. The Uncle*. 1965: *Four in the Morning*. 1967: *Separation. I'll Never Forget What's 'is Name*. 1968: *Baby Love*. 1971: **The Spy's Wife*. 1973: *Hitler: The Last Ten Days*. 1983: *Screamtime (video).*

LYNN, Diana (Dolores Loehr) 1924–1971
As a teenager, light-haired American piano-playing prodigy Diana Lynn was as pretty as any picture. She also had a zany sense of humour and was quite delightful as a series of sassy young sisters in forties' comedies which occasionally used her musical talents as well. In maturity she remained sweet but became a shade dull. Died from a brain haemorrhage.
1939: *†They Shall Have Music (GB: Melody of Youth)*. 1941: *†There's Magic in Music*. 1942: *The Major and the Minor. Star-Spangled Rhythm*. 1943: *Henry Aldrich Gets Glamour (GB: Henry Gets Glamour). Henry Aldrich Plays Cupid (GB: Henry Plays Cupid). *The Aldrich Family Gets in the Scrap*. 1944: *And the Angels Sing. The Miracle of Morgan's Creek. Our Hearts Were Young and Gay*. 1945: *Out of This World. Duffy's Tavern. *Hollywood Victory Caravan*. 1946: *Our Hearts Were Growing Up. The Bride Wore Boots*. 1947: *Easy Come, Easy Go. Variety Girl*. 1948: *Every Girl Should Be Married. Ruthless. Texas, Brooklyn and Heaven (GB: The Girl from Texas)*. 1949: *My Friend Irma*. 1950: *Paid in Full. My Friend Irma Goes West. Rogues of Sherwood Forest. Peggy*. 1951: *The People Against O'Hara. Bedtime for Bonzo*. 1952: *Meet Me at the Fair*. 1953: *Plunder of the Sun*. 1954: *Track of the Cat*. 1955: *Annapolis Story (GB: The Blue and the Gold). You're Never Too Young. The Kentuckian*. 1956: *Forbidden Area (TV)*. 1957: *The Star Wagon (TV). A Sound of Different Drummers (TV)*. 1958: *The Return of Ansel Gibbs (TV)*. 1959: *Marriage of Strangers (TV)*. 1970: *Company of Killers.*

†As Dolly Loehr

LYNN, Jeffrey (Ragnar Godfrey Lind, later legally changed) 1909–1995
Lean-faced, concerned-looking, tall, brown-haired American actor in passive semi-leading roles, perhaps best remembered as the guy who made good while Bogart and Cagney went to the bad in *The Roaring Twenties*. War service disrupted the flow of his career and he was not the same force in post-war years. In the 1960s he gradually drifted out of acting and into selling real estate. Had two children and seven step-children. Began his working career as a teacher.
1938: **Out Where the Stars Begin. The Cowboy from Brooklyn (GB: Romance and Rhythm). When Were You Born? Four*

Lyons in Paris. 1965: The March of the Movies (narrator only).

Daughters. 1939: Yes, My Darling Daughter. Daughters Courageous. Espionage Agent. The Roaring Twenties. Four Wives. 1940: A Child is Born. All This and Heaven Too. The Fighting 69th. It All Came True. My Love Came Back. Money and the Woman. 1941: The Body Disappears. Four Mothers. Law of the Tropics. Flight from Destiny. Million Dollar Baby. Underground. 1948: Black Bart (GB: Black Bart – Highwayman). For the Love of Mary. Whiplash. 1949: A Letter to Three Wives. Strange Bargain. Captain China. 1951: Home Town Story. Up Front. 1953: That I May See. 1958: Lost Lagoon. 1960: Butterfield 8. 1964: Come Thursday. 1967: Tony Rome.

LYNN, Ralph 1881–1962
Dark-haired, monocled, toothy, owl-faced British farceur with idiot grin, a member of the famous trio (with Tom Walls and Robertson Hare) that convulsed audiences at the Aldwych Theatre in Ben Travers farces of the twenties and thirties, and transferred most of their best work on to screen. The archetypal English 'silly ass'. Grandfather of Ann Lynn (qv).
1929: *Peace and Quiet. 1930: Tons of Money. Plunder. Rookery Nook (US: One Embarrassing Night). 1931: Chance of a Night Time. Mischief. 1932: A Night Like This. Thark. Just My Luck. 1933: Summer Lightning. Up to the Neck. Turkey Time. A Cuckoo in the Nest. 1934: A Cup of Kindness. Dirty Work. 1935: Fighting Stock. Foreign Affaires. Stormy Weather. 1936: In the Soup. All In. Pot Luck. 1937: For Valour. 1959: The Adventures of Rex (serial).

LYON, Ben 1901–1979
Genial, avuncular, dark-haired, round-faced

American actor, a popular middle-range star for 15 years in the 1920s and 1930s, best recalled for Hell's Angels, a role which became the subject of a running gag in his popular wartime radio show Hi Gang! after he and his first wife Bebe Daniels (married 1931 to her death in 1971) had come to Britain in the late 1930s and scored an instant personal success. A second radio series, Life with the Lyons, was equally popular, and ran from 1950 to 1961. He married his second wife, ex-actress Marian Nixon (1904–1983), in 1972. Died from a heart attack.
1919: Open Your Eyes. 1921: The Heart of Maryland. 1922: The Custard Cup. Ashes. 1923: Potash and Perlmutter (GB: Dr Sunshine). Flaming Youth. 1924: The White Moth. Painted People. The Wine of Youth. Lily of the Dust. The Wages of Virtue. So Big. 1925: One Way Street. Winds of Chance. The Necessary Evil. The New Commandment. The Pace That Thrills. Bluebeard's Seven Wives. 1926: The Great Deception. The Savage. The Prince of Tempters. The Reckless Lady. 1927: For the Love of Mike. *Life in Hollywood No. 2. The Perfect Sap (GB: The Marriage of Marcia). Dance Magic. The Tender Hour. High Hat. Das tanzende Wien/Dancing Vienna. 1928: The Air Legion. 1929: Quitter. The Flying Marine. 1930: Alias French Gertie (GB: Love Finds a Way). A Soldier's Plaything (GB: A Soldier's Pay). What Men Want. Hell's Angels. Lummox. 1931: Indiscreet. Call of the Rockies. Night Nurse. Aloha (GB: No Greater Love). Hot Heiress. My Past. Misbehaving Ladies. Compromised (GB: We Three). Bought. Her Majesty Love. *Screen Snapshots No. 7. 1932: Lady with a Past (GB: My Reputation). Week-Ends Only. Hat Check Girl (GB: Embassy Girl). By Whose Hand. *Hollywood on Parade No. 3. The Big Timer. The Crooked Circle. *The Stolen Jools (GB: The Slippery Pearls). 1933: I Cover the Waterfront. Girl Missing. The Women in His Life. I Spy (GB: The Morning After). *Hollywood on Parade No. 3. 1934: Crimson Romance. Lightning Strikes Twice. 1935: Frisco Waterfront (GB: When We Look Back). Beauty's Daughter (later Navy Wife). Together We Live. 1936: Dancing Feet. Down to the Sea. 1937: Not Wanted on Voyage. Mad About Money (US: He Loved an Actress). 1939: I Killed the Count (US: Who is Guilty?). Confidential Lady. 1941: Hi Gang! This Was Paris. 1943: The Dark Tower. 1953: Life with the Lyons. (US: Family Affair). 1954: Adventures with the Lyons (serial). The

M

MacARTHUR, James, 1937–

Eager-looking American leading man with fair curly hair, and romantic air, the adopted son of Helen Hayes. Played leading roles in some bland entertainments, but his career was faltering when he became involved with the long-running TV series *Hawaii Five-O*. After ten years he was visibly tiring of the show and taking more interest in his work as explorer and geographer. He left Hawaii and the series in 1979.

1957: The Young Stranger. 1958: The Light in The Forest. 1959: Third Man on the Mountain. 1960: Kidnapped. Swiss Family Robinson. 1962: The Interns. 1963: Cry of Battle. Spencer's Mountain. 1964: The Truth about Spring. 1965: Battle of the Bulge. The Bedford Incident. 1966: Ride Beyond Vengeance. Willie and the Yank (TV. GB: cinemas as Mosby's Marauders). 1967: The Love-Ins. Hang 'Em High. 1968: The Angry Breed. Lassiter (TV). 1979: The Night the Bridge Fell Down (TV). 1980: Alcatraz: the Whole Shocking Story (TV). 1998: Storm Chasers: Revenge of the Twister (TV).

MACCHIO, Ralph 1961–

Slight, very youthful-looking, doe-eyed American actor of olive complexion and 'underdog' appeal. Starting an acting career while still at high school, he broke through to pin-up stardom as *The Karate Kid* and repeated the role, in one guise or another, in several other films. Not surprisingly, his film appeal waned dramatically once he got into his thirties.

1980: Up the Academy. 1982: Dangerous Company (TV). 1983: The Outsiders. 1984: The Karate Kid. The Three Wishes of Billy Grier (TV). Teachers. 1986: Crossroads. Karate Kid II. 1988: Distant Thunder. 1989: The Karate

Kid Part III. 1990: Too Much Sun. Garwood: Prisoner of War – A True Story. 1991: My Cousin Vinny. 1993: Naked in New York. 1998: Can't Be Heaven. Dizzyland. Secret of NIMH 2: Timmy to the Rescue (V. Voice only).

MacDONALD, Jeanette, 1901–1965

Pretty if slightly pasty blond American operetta singer with a lovely sense of comedy all too rarely put to proper use in the cinema. Her early films, with Maurice Chevalier, show her flair for impishly saucy fun to quite good advantage, but it was her musicals with Nelson Eddy – all eight of them – that put her right at the top of the cinema tree. Died from a heart attack after a long battle with a heart ailment. Married Gene Raymond (*qv*) in 1937.

1929: The Love Parade. 1930: The Vagabond King. Let's Go Native. King of Jazz (Spanish-language version only). Oh, for a Man. Monte Carlo. The Lottery Bride. 1931: Annabelle's Affairs. Don't Bet on Women (GB: More Than a Kiss). 1932: †One Hour with You. Love Me Tonight. 1933: *Hollywood on Parade No. 7. 1934: The Cat and the Fiddle. The Merry Widow. 1935: Naughty Marietta. 1936: Rose Marie. San Francisco. 1937: The Firefly. Maytime. 1938: The Girl of the Golden West. Sweethearts. 1939: Broadway Serenade. 1940: New Moon. Bitter Sweet. 1941: Smilin' Through. 1942: I Married an Angel. Cairo. 1944: Follow the Boys. 1948: Three Daring Daughters (GB: The Birds and the Bees). The Sun Comes Up. 1957: Charley's Aunt (TV).

†And French-language version

MACDONALD, Kelly 1979–

Dark-haired, long-nosed, almond-eyed Scottish actress with fresh-looking features, often

seen as girls in need of protection, but also capable of projecting resolution or rebellion. Plucked from an open audition for her first screen role, in *Trainspotting*, she faltered for a while after that, but blossomed at the turn of the century in more sympathetic roles.

1995: Trainspotting. 1996: Flowers of the Forest (TV). *Dancing Some Days. 1997: Stella Does Tricks. *Dead Eye Dick. 1998: Cousin Bette. Elizabeth. The Loss of Sexual Innocence. 1999: My Life So Far. Tube Tales (TV). House! Two Family House. 2000: Splendor. Entropy. Some Voices.

MacDOWELL, Andie

(Rosalie Anderson MacDowell) 1958–

Dark-haired, fragile-looking American model and actress whose Hollywood career looked to have fallen at the first hurdle when her South Carolina accent was dubbed by another actress (Glenn Close) in her first film. To her credit, she fought back to produce some excellent performances in between some rather indifferent ones, but she is good at being lovable and vulnerable, both of which qualities she expressed in one of her most popular films, *Green Card*. Her warmth and brilliant smile stood her in good stead in slightly flaky leading roles through the late 1990s.

1984: Greystoke: The Legend of Tarzan Lord of the Apes. 1985: St Elmo's Fire. 1987: The Sahara Secret (TV). 1989: Sex, Lies and Videotape. 1990: Green Card. 1991: The Object of Beauty. Women & Men 2: In Love There Are No Rules (TV). Hudson Hawk. 1992: The Players. 1993: Groundhog Day. Ruby Cairo. Short Cuts. Four Weddings and a Funeral. 1994: Bad Girls. Luck, Trust & Ketchup. 1995: Unstrung Heroes. 1996:

Multiplicity. Michael. 1997: The End of Violence. 1998: Just the Ticket. Shadrach. 1999: The Muse. Muppets from Space. Reaching Normal. 2000: Town and Country. Harrison's Flowers.

MacGRAW, Ali (Alice MacGraw) 1938–
Impassive-looking, dark-haired, olive-complexioned American leading lady. Certainly one of the Beautiful People, but her acting range on the screen has so far been limited. Has always looked (and played) younger than her age, but has filmed infrequently. Married to Steve McQueen (third) from 1973 to 1978. Received an Oscar nomination for *Love Story*.
1968: A Lovely Way to Die (GB: A Lovely Way to Go). Goodbye Columbus. 1970: Love Story. 1972: The Getaway. 1978: Convoy. Players. 1979: Just Tell Me What You Want. 1983: China Rose (TV). 1985: Murder Elite. 1992: Survive the Savage Sea (TV). 1993: Gunsmoke: The Long Ride (TV). 1994: Natural Causes. 1997: Glam.

MACK, Helen
(Helen McDougall) 1913–1986
Personable, attractive, dark-haired American leading actress, in a couple of films when ten, and vaudeville at 13. Started her adult career in earnest at 18, keeping fairly busy through the thirties, her best-remembered film from which period is *Son of Kong*. Later became a successful radio director, producer and writer. Died from cancer.
1923: Under the Red Robe. Grit. Zaza. Little Red School House (GB: The Greater Law). 1924: Pied Piper Malone. 1931: The Struggle. 1932: Silent Witness. While Pain Sleeps. Fargo Express. 1933: Sweepings. Melody Cruise.

California Trail. Christopher Bean (GB: The Late Christopher Bean). Blind Adventure. Son of Kong. 1934: All of Me. Kiss and Make Up. You Belong to Me. The Lemon Drop Kid. College Rhythm. 1935: Four Hours to Kill. Captain Hurricane. The Return of Peter Grimm. She. 1936: The Milky Way. 1937: You Can't Buy Luck. Last Train from Madrid. Fit for a King. The Wrong Road. 1938: King of the Newsboys. Gambling Ship. I Stand Accused. Secrets of a Nurse. 1939: The Mystery of the White Room. Calling All Marines. 1940: His Girl Friday. Girls of the Road. 1941: Power Drive. 1944: And Now Tomorrow. 1945: Divorce. 1946: Strange Holiday.

MACKINTOSH, Steven 1967–
Fair-haired, broad-shouldered, pale-faced British actor (similar in looks to another British actor, Dennis Waterman (*qv*)), sometimes seen as irresponsible, fly-by-night characters, but capable of a wide variety of performances. Acting since he was a teenager, he built up considerable Shakespearian experience with the National Theatre Company, especially on tours to Russia and Japan, before becoming a familiar member of the British cinema scene from the early 1990s, often in rakish, anti-establishment roles. Married to actress Lisa Jacobs.
1987: Prick Up Your Ears. 1989: Treasure Island (TV. GB: cinemas). 1990: Memphis Belle. 1991: London Kills Me. 1992: The Muppet Christmas Carol. 1993: Safe. 1994: Murder in Mind (TV). Princess Caraboo. Midnight Movie (TV). 1995: The Grotesque (US: Gentlemen Don't Eat Poets). Blue Juice. 1996: Twelfth Night. Different for Girls. House of America. 1997: The Land Girls. 1998: The Ebb-Tide (TV). Lock, Stock & Two Smoking Barrels. 1999: The Criminal.

MacLACHLAN, Kyle 1959–
Tall, dark, dismayed-looking American actor, reminiscent of the young Robert Vaughn (*qv*). Never quite a force in the cinema, he became a cult figure after his appearance as the quirky FBI agent in TV's *Twin Peaks*, whose catchphrase 'Damn fine cup of coffee' went round the world. MacLachlan had also appeared for *Peaks*' director, David Lynch, in *Dune* and *Blue Velvet*. The future of this black-haired actor, though, looks very much as a top character player, dispensing cold sarcasm in the Vaughn mould.
1984: Dune. 1986: Blue Velvet. 1987: The Hidden. 1989: Twin Peaks (TV). 1990: Don't

Tell Her It's Me. 1991: Where the Day Takes You. The Doors. Tales from the Crypt (TV). 1992: Rich in Love. Twin Peaks: Fire Walk With Me. The Trial. 1994: The Flintstones. Against the Wall (cable TV). Roswell (TV). 1995: Showgirls. 1996: The Trigger Effect. Moonshine Highway. 1997: One Night Stand. Route 9 (TV). Jack Higgins' Thunder Point (TV). 1999: Hamlet. 2000: Timecode. The Spring (TV). X Change.

MacLAINE, Shirley
(S. Mclean Beaty) 1934–
Gamine American star with pixieish face, wide clown's smile and short red-brown hair that one critic said 'looks as if it has been combed with an egg-beater.' The sister of actor Warren Beatty (*qv*), she was originally a dancer, but showed a wide range of talents in an enchanting run of successes from 1955 to 1963. After that, things went wrong for her (she was often required to do too much) and she became less of a draw at the box office. An outspoken champion of feminist rights. Academy Award 1984 for *Terms of Endearment*. Previously Oscar-nominated in *Some Came Running, The Apartment, Irma La Douce* and *The Turning Point*.
1955: The Trouble with Harry. Artists and Models. 1956: Around the World in 80 Days. 1958: Hot Spell. The Sheepman. The Matchmaker. Some Came Running. 1959: Ask Any Girl. Career. 1960: Can-Can. Ocean's Eleven. The Apartment. 1961: All in a Night's Work. Two Loves (GB: Spinster). 1962: The Children's Hour (GB: The Loudest Whisper). My Geisha. Two for the Seesaw. 1963: Irma La Douce. 1964: What a Way to Go! John Goldfarb, Please Come Home. The Yellow Rolls Royce. 1966: Gambit. 1967: Woman

Times Seven. 1968: The Bliss of Mrs Blossom. 1969: Sweet Charity. Two Mules for Sister Sara. 1970: Desperate Characters. 1971: The Possession of Joel Delaney. 1977: The Turning Point. Sois belle et tais-toi. 1979: Being There. 1980: Loving Couples. A Change of Seasons. 1983: Terms of Endearment. Cannonball Run II. 1988: Madame Sousatzka. 1989: Steel Magnolias. Waiting for the Light. 1900: Postcards from The Edge. 1991: Defending Your Life. 1992: Used People. 1993: Wrestling Ernest Hemingway. 1994: Guarding Tess. 1995: The Celluloid Closet. Mrs Winterbourne. The West Side Waltz (TV). 1996: The Evening Star. 1997: A Smile Like Yours. 1999: †Bruno. Forever Hollywood (doc).

†Also directed

MacMURRAY, Fred 1907–1991
Bland, agreeable, well-built American actor with dark, wavy hair whose easy grin cruised its way through dozens of light romantic comedies and colourful action films. A former saxophonist, MacMurray got a start in Hollywood at his second attempt, and at one time became its highest-paid actor. He did his best work as plausible guys with feet of clay. Later, he was in some good low-budget westerns in the fifties and a series of gleeful romps for Disney. First wife died in 1953. Married June Haver (qv) the following year. Died from pneumonia.
1929: Girls Gone Wild. Tiger Rose. Glad Rag Doll. 1934: Friends of Mr Sweeney. 1935: Grand Old Girl. Car 99. Alice Adams. Men Without Names. Hands Across the Table. The Bride Comes Home. The Gilded Lady. 1936: The Trail of the Lonesome Pine. The Princess Comes Across. The Texas Rangers. Thirteen Hours By Air. 1937: Swing High – Swing Low. Maid of Salem. True Confessions. Exclusive. Champagne Waltz. 1938: Cocoanut Grove. Men with Wings. Sing, You Sinners. 1939: Café Society. Honeymoon in Bali (GB: Husbands or Lovers). Invitation to Happiness. Remember the Night. 1940: Little Old New York. Too Many Husbands (GB: My Two Husbands). Rangers of Fortune. 1941: Virginia. New York Town. Dive Bomber. One Night in Lisbon. 1942: Star Spangled Rhythm. The Lady is Willing. The Forest Rangers. Take a Letter, Darling (GB: The Green-Eyed Woman). 1943: *The Last Will and Testament of Tom Smith. Above Suspicion. *Show Business at War. No Time for Love. Flight for Freedom. 1944: *Skirmish on the Home Front.

Standing Room Only. Double Indemnity. And the Angels Sing. Murder, He Says. 1945: Where Do We Go From Here? Practically Yours. Captain Eddie. 1946: Smoky. 1947: Singapore. Suddenly It's Spring. The Egg and I. 1948: A Miracle Can Happen (later On Our Merry Way). The Miracle of the Bells. Family Honeymoon. Don't Trust Your Husband. 1949: Father Was a Fullback. Borderline. 1950: Never a Dull Moment. 1951: Callaway Went Thataway (GB: The Star Said No). A Millionaire for Christy. 1953: Fair Wind to Java. The Moonlighter. 1954: The Caine Mutiny. Woman's World. Pushover. The Far Horizons. 1955: There's Always Tomorrow. The Rains of Ranchipur. At Gunpoint (GB: Gunpoint!). 1956: Gun for a Coward. 1957: False Witness (TV). Quantez. Day of the Bad Man. 1958: Good Day for a Hanging. 1959: The Shaggy Dog. Face of a Fugitive. The Oregon Trail. 1960: The Apartment. 1961: The Absent-Minded Professor. 1962: Bon Voyage! *How to Get There When You Want to Go. 1963: Son of Flubber. 1964: Kisses for My President. 1966: Follow Me Boys! 1967: The Happiest Millionaire. 1973: Charley and the Angel. 1974: The Chadwick Family (TV). 1975: Beyond the Bermuda Triangle (TV). 1978: The Swarm.

MacRAE, Gordon 1921–1986
Brown-haired, chubby-cheeked, ingenuous-looking American singer who played bright-eyed young hopefuls opposite Doris Day in some sparkling family musicals during a five-year Warner contract, then won the leading roles in two big musicals from stage successes. Left films for nightclub work when the demand for musicals vanished. At one time an alcoholic, MacRae became Chairman of the National Council of Alcoholism three years before his death from cancer of the mouth and jaw. The actresses Meredith MacRae (1946–2000) and Heather MacRae are his daughters.
1948: The Big Punch. 1949: Look for the Silver Lining. Backfire. 1950: The Daughter of Rosie O'Grady. Tea for Two. Return of the Frontiersman. The West Point Story (GB: Fine and Dandy). 1951: *The Screen Director. Starlift. On Moonlight Bay. 1952: About Face. *Screen Snapshots No. 205. 1953: By the Light of the Silvery Moon. *So You Want a Television Set. The Desert Song. Three Sailors and a Girl. 1955: Oklahoma! 1956: Carousel. The Best Things in Life are Free. 1979: The Pilot.

MADIGAN, Amy 1950–
Husky-voiced, straight-staring American actress whose blonde hair is usually cropped short. Not exactly a star, but a striking co-star, normally playing down-to-earth tough cookies. After nine years studying piano in her native Chicago, she became a rock singer for several years before taking acting classes with Lee Strasberg and making a career of it at 28. Less prominent in the 1990s. Married actor Ed Harris (qv) in 1983.
1981: The Ambush Murders (TV). Crazy Times (TV). Victims (TV). 1982: Love Child. 1983: The Day After. (TV). Love Letters/My Love Letters. Travis McGee (TV). 1984: Streets of Fire. Places in the Heart. 1985: Alamo Bay. Twice in a Lifetime. 1987: Nowhere to Hide. The Laundromat (TV). 1988: The Prince of Pennsylvania. 1989: Field of Dreams. Roe vs Wade (TV). Uncle Buck. 1991: Lucky Day (TV). 1993: The Dark Half (completed 1991). 1994: The Northern Lights. And Then There Was One (TV). 1995: Female Perversions. 1996: Riders of the Purple Sage (TV). Winds of Doctrine. 1997: Loved. 1998: A Bright Shining Lie (cable TV). 1999: With Friends Like These (cable TV). Having Our Say: The Delany Sisters' First 100 Years (TV). 2000: Pollock. In the Name of the People (TV). A Time for Dancing.

MADISON, Guy
(Robert Mosely) 1922–1996
Boyishly handsome, fair-haired, ski-slope-nosed American actor who began in romantic roles but, in an oddly spasmodic film career, was seen from 1949 almost entirely in westerns, most of them big-budget colour productions, if not quite in the Gary Cooper class. He became popular on TV in the 1950s

series *Wild Bill Hickok* (many episodes of which were shown as second-feature films outside America) and very busy during the 1960s in continental westerns and action films. Married to Gail Russell (*qv*) from 1949 to 1954, first of two. Died from emphysema, prompting close friend Rory Calhoun (*qv*) to say that it was 'another empty saddle in the old corral'.

1944: Since You Went Away. 1946: Till the End of Time. 1947: Honeymoon (GB: Two Men and a Girl). 1948: Texas Brooklyn and Heaven (GB: The Girl from Texas). 1949: Massacre River. 1951: Drums in the Deep South. †Behind Southern Lines (TV). 1952: Red Snow. †The Ghost of Crossbones Canyon (TV). †Border City Rustlers (TV). †Two Gun Marshal (TV). †Six Gun Decision (TV). †Arrow in the Dust (TV). 1953: †The Yellow Haired Kid (TV). †Secret of Outlaw Flats (TV). The Charge at Feather River. 1954: The Command. †Titled Tenderfoot (TV). †Timber County Trouble (TV). †Two Gun Teacher (TV). †Danger on the Trail (TV). †Marshals in Disguise (TV). †Outlaw's Son (TV). †Phantom Trails (TV). 1955: †The Match-making Marshal (TV). Five Against the House. The Last Frontier. 1956: Hilda Crane. Reprisal! On the Threshold of Space. The Beast of Hollow Mountain. 1957: The Hard Man. 1958: Bullwhip! 1959: Jet Over the Atlantic. 1960: La Schiava di Roma (GB: Blood of the Warriors. US: Slaves of Rome). 1961: Rosamunda el Alboino (GB and US: Sword of the Conqueror). La prigioniere dell'isola di Diavolo (GB: Women of Devil's Island). 1963: Sandokan the Great. I piombi di Venezia (US: Dungeons of Venice). Il boia di Venezia (GB: Blood of the Executioner. US: Hangman of Venice). 1964: Sandokan alla riscossa (GB: Tiger of Terror. US: Sandokan Strikes Back). Sandokan contro il leopardo di Sarawak (GB: The Return of Sandokan). I misteri della giungla nera (GB: The Mystery of Thug Island. US: Mysteries of the Black Jungle). Old Shatterhand (GB: Appaches' Last Battle. US: Shatterhand). 1965: Adventurer from Tortuga. Sfida a Rio Brave (GB: Duel at Rio Bravo. US: Gunmen of the Rio Grande). 1966: I conque della vendetta (GB and US: Five Giants from Texas). LSD – Flesh of the Devil. 1967: Sette Winchester per un massacro (GB: Payment in Blood. US: Winchester for Hire). The Devil's Man/Devilman Story. The Son of Django. War Devils. Testa di sbarco per otto implacabili (GB: Hell in Normandy). 1968: Il re dei Criminali (GB: Superargo. US: Superargo and the Faceless Giants). I lunghi giorni dell'odio. The Bang Bang Kid. 1969: Un posto all'inferno. La batalla del ultimo Panzer. Commanda all'infierno. 1970: Retroguardia. This Man Can't Die. 1971: Reverendo Colt. 1975: Hatcher Bodine. Won Ton Ton, the Dog Who Saved Hollywood. The Pacific Connection. 1977: Where's Willie? 1988: Red River (TV).

† *Played as films in some countries*

MADONNA (M. Ciccone) 1958–

Platinum blonde (though her hair colour varies) American singer and actress with backstreets looks and voice and blatantly sexy style. Her much-vaunted cinema career

proved a big disappointment, but the determination that made her record megastar from 1982 certainly helped to win her the role of Evita Peron in the film version of the smash stage musical. Married to actor Sean Penn (*qv*) from 1985 to 1991, she remains her own best publicist.

1978: A Certain Sacrifice. 1984: Vision Quest/Crazy for You. 1985: Desperately Seeking Susan. 1986: Shanghai Surprise. 1987: Who's That Girl. 1988: Bloodhounds of Broadway. 1990: Dick Tracy. 1991: Truth or Dare (GB: In Bed with Madonna). Damned in the USA. Shadows and Fog. 1992: A League of Their Own. Body of Evidence. Blast 'Em. 1993: Snake Eyes (later and GB: Dangerous Game). 1995: Four Rooms. Blue in the Face. 1996: Girl 6. Evita. 2000: The Next Best Thing.

MADSEN, Virginia 1963–

It's difficult to pick out Virginia Madsen from movie to movie. She can play sexy or demure, big-city or down-town, glamorous or earthy. But she has always projected both sex appeal and warmth and the quality of her performances has deserved to put her closer on the top. Her lascivious looks have more often than not had her cast as *femmes fatales* in recent times. From a film-making family, she was acting as a teenager. The sister of actor Michael Madsen (1958–). Married/divorced director Danny Huston.

1982: A Matter of Principle (TV). 1983: Class. 1984: Dune. Electric Dreams. 1985: Creator. Mussolini: The Untold Story (TV). The Hearst and Davies Affair (TV). 1986: Fire With Fire. Modern Girls. 1987: Slam Dance. Long Gone (TV). Zombie High. 1988: Hot to Trot. Mr North. Gotham (later and GB: The Dead Can't Lie). 1989: Third Degree

Burn (TV). Heart of Dixie. 1990: The Hot Spot. 1991: Highlander II: The Quickening. Becoming Colette. Ironclads (TV). Victim of Love (TV). Love Kills (TV). 1992: A Murderous Affair: The Carolyn Warmus Story (TV). Candyman (TV). Caroline at Midnight. 1994: Blue Tiger. Bitter Vengeance (TV). 1995: God's Army/The Prophecy. 1996: Whiskey Down/Just Your Luck. 1997: The Apocalypse Watch (TV). The Rainmaker. 1998: Ambushed. Ballad of the Nightingale. 1999: All the Fine Lines. The Florentine. The Haunting. After Sex. 2000: Crossfire Trail (TV). Lying in Wait.*

MAGNANI, Anna 1907–1973

Dark-haired, tempestuous, wild-eyed, angry-looking, Egyptian-born (some sources say Italian-born in 1903 or 1908) actress who, raised in Rome, became Italy's top star in post-war years. Despite a matronly figure, she took Hollywood by storm with the gale-force strength of her impassioned performances. She won an Oscar for *The Rose Tattoo*, and Paramount invited her back twice more. She was Oscar-nominated again for *Wild is the Wind*. Died, amid national mourning in Italy, from complications following a gall-bladder operation.

1928: Scampolo. 1934: La cieca di Sorrento. 1936: Tempo massimo. Cavalleria. Trenta secondi d'amore. 1937: La Principessa Tarakanova. 1939: Una lampada alla finestra. 1940: Finalmente soli. 1941: La fuggitiva. Teresa Venerdi (US: Doctor Beware). 1942: La fortuna viena dal cielo. 1943: L'ultima carrozzella. Campo de fiori (US: The Peddler and the Lady). T'amero sempre. La vita è bella. Abbasso la miseria. 1944: Il fiore sotto gli occhi. 1945: Rome – Open City/Open City. Quartetto Pazzo. 1946: Un uomo ritorna. Il bandito. Abbasso la ricchezza! (US: Peddlin' in Society). Damanti a lui tremava tutta Roma/Tosca. 1947: La sconosciuto di San Marino. L'onorevole Angelina (US: Angelina). 1948: Assunto Spina (US: Scarred). Molti sogni per le strade (GB: Woman Trouble). Amore (GB: Ways of Love. US: The Miracle). 1949: Volcano. 1951: Bellissima. 1952: Camicie rosse/Anita Garibaldi. La carrozza d'oro (GB and US: The Golden Coach). 1953: Siamo donne (GB and US: We the Women). 1955: The Rose Tattoo. 1956: Suor Letizia. 1957: Wild is the Wind. 1958: Nella città l'inferno (GB: Caged. US: And the Wild, Wild Women). 1959: The Fugitive Kind. 1960: Risate di gioia (GB and US: The Passionate

Thief). 1962: *Mamma Roma*. 1963: *La magot de Josèfa*. 1964: *Volles Herz und leere Taschen*. 1965: *Made in Italy*. 1969: *The Secret of Santa Vittoria*. 1972: *1870* (originally TV). *Fellini's Roma*.

MAGUIRE, Tobey
(Tobias Maguire) 1975–

Fresh-faced, ingenuous-looking, flatly dark-haired, boyish American actor, often the picture of innocence abroad. On TV at 15 and in films at 18, he has been in highly prized central roles since his early twenties. Once wanted to be a chef, but soon turned to acting. 1993: *This Boy's Life*. 1994: *Don's Plum* (released 1998). *A Child's Cry for Help* (TV). *Spoils of War* (TV). *S.F.W. Revenge of the Red Baron*. 1995: *Duke of Groove. †*Empire Records*. 1996: *Joyride*. *Seduced by Madness: The Diane Borchardt Story* (TV). 1997: *The Ice Storm*. *Deconstructing Harry*. 1998: *Pleasantville*. *Fear and Loathing in Las Vegas*. 1999: *Ride with the Devil*. *The Cider House Rules*. 2000: *Wonder Boys*. 2001: *Like Cats & Dogs*. *Spider-Man*.

†*Scenes deleted from final release print*

MAHARIS, George
(G. Maharias) 1928–

Dark, taciturn, plastic-looking American actor who had to wait years for his first big success, in the long-running television series *Route 66*. This took him into movies, but these lit no fires, and he continued to be most busy on television. A graduate of the Actors' Studio, though you'd hardly notice if you didn't know.

1960: *A Death of Princes* (TV. GB: cinemas). *Exodus*. 1964: *The Satan Bug*. 1965: *Sylvia*. *Quick Before it Melts*. 1966: *A Covenant with*

Death. 1967: *The Happening*. 1968: *Escape to Mindanao* (TV). *The Desperadoes*. 1969: *Land Raiders*. *The Monk* (TV). *The Last Day of the War*. 1972: *The Victim* (TV). 1974: *Of Men and Women* (TV). *Come Die with Me* (TV). *Death in Space* (TV). 1975: *Murder on Flight 502* (TV). 1977: *Look What's Happened to Rosemary's Baby* (TV). *SST – Death Flight* (TV). 1978: *Crash* (TV). *Return to Fantasy Island* (TV). 1982: *The Sword and the Sorcerer*. 1983: *Doppelganger*.

MAHONEY, Jock
(Jacques O'Mahoney) 1919–1989

Tall, lean, whippy, fair-haired, jut-jawed American actor who gave up a military career to become a film stuntman. Became a featured player in second-feature westerns, and starred in a rip-roaring TV series, *The Range Rider*, then was gradually taken up by bigger studios, notably Universal-International. Played Tarzan in two films, but it seemed the role was his undoing and he faded from the scene. Stepfather of Sally Field (qv). Died after a car crash.

1946: ‡*Son of the Guardsman* (serial). ‡*South of the Chisholm Trail*. ‡*The Fighting Frontiersman* (GB: *Golden Lady*). 1947: ‡*Stranger from Ponca City*. ‡*Out West. 1948: ‡*Trail to Laredo* (GB: *Sign of the Dagger*). ‡*Smokey Mountain Melody*. ‡**Squareheads of the Round Table*. ‡*Blazing Across the Pecos* (GB: *Under Arrest*). ‡*Adventures of Don Juan* (GB: *The New Adventures of Don Juan*). 1949: ‡**Fuelin' Around*. ‡*Cowpunchers. †*The Doolins of Oklahoma* (GB: *The Great Manhunt*). †*Bandits of El Dorado* (GB: *Tricked*). †*The Blazing Trail*. †*Renegades of the Sage* (GB: *The Fort*). †*Rim of the Canyon*. †*Frontier Marshal*. †*Strange Disappearance*. †*Horsemen of the Sierras* (GB: *Remember Me*). 1950: †*The Nevadan* (GB: *The Man from Nevada*). †*David Harding – Counterspy*. †*Cow Town* (GB: *Barbed Wire*). †*Texas Dynamo* (GB: *Suspected*). †*Jolson Sings Again*. †*Pecos River* (GB: *Without Risk*). †*Hoedown*. †*Lightning Guns* (GB: *Taking Sides*). †*Frontier Outpost*. †*Cody of the Pony Express* (serial). 1951: †*The Kangaroo Kid*. †*Santa Fé*. †*The Texas Rangers*. †*Rough Riders of Durango* (serial). †*Roar of the Iron Horse* (serial). 1952: ***The Rough, Tough West*. **Smoky Canyon. **Junction City. ***The Kid from Broken Gun*. ***The Hawk of Wild River*. ***Laramie Mountains* (GB: *Mountain Desperadoes*). 1953: ***Gunfighters of the Northwest* (serial). 1954: **Overland Pacific.

*Knutzy Knights. 1955: *A Day of Fury*. 1956: *Hot Stuff. *Away All Boats*. *I've Lived Before*. *Battle Hymn*. *Showdown at Abilene*. 1957: *Joe Dakota*. *Slim Carter*. *The Land Unknown*. 1958: *Last of the Fast Guns*. *A Time to Live and a Time to Die*. 1959: *Money, Women and Guns*. 1960: *Three Blondes in His Life*. *Tarzan the Magnificent*. 1962: *Tarzan Goes to India*. 1963: *Tarzan's Three Challenges*. *California*. 1964: *Moro Witch Doctor*. *The Walls of Hell*. 1965: *Marine Battleground*. 1966: *Runaway Girl*. 1967: *The Glory Stompers*. 1968: *Bandolero!* 1975: *Tom*. *The Bad Bunch*. 1976: *Their Only Chance*. 1978: *The End*.

‡*As Jacques J. O'Mahoney*
†*As Jock O'Mahoney* **As Jack Mahoney

MAJORS, Lee
(L. Yeary) 1941–

Husky, fair-haired American actor in the Hollywood beefcake tradition. His career has paralleled that of David Janssen (qv), in that he had several hit TV series in a row (*The Big Valley*, *Owen Marshall – Counselor at Law*, *The Six Million Dollar Man* and *The Fall Guy*), while his feature films, though sometimes backed by big budgets, revealed his limited acting and were less successful. Married/divorced Farrah Fawcett (qv), his second wife.

1964: †*Strait-Jacket*. 1967: *Will Penny*. 1969: *The Ballad of Andy Crocker* (TV). *The Liberation of L. B. Jones*. 1970: *Weekend of Terror* (TV). 1971: *Six Million Dollar Man* (TV). 1977: *Gary Francis Powers – The True Story of the U2 Incident* (TV). *Just a Little Inconvenience* (TV. GB: cinemas). 1978: *Killer Fish*. *The Norseman*. 1979: *Steel*. *Ladyfingers*. 1980: *Agency*. *Sharks! The Last Chase*. *Circle of Two*. *High Noon: Part II* (TV). *The Fall Guy* (TV). 1982: *Starflight One* (TV. GB: cinemas). 1984: *The Cowboy and the Ballerina* (TV). 1986: *A Smoky Mountain Christmas* (TV). 1987: *Return of the Six Million Dollar Man and the Bionic Woman* (TV). 1988: *Scrooged*. *Danger Down Under* (TV). 1989: *Travelin'*. *Keaton's Cop*. *The Bionic Showdown* (TV). 1991: *Fire! Trapped on the 37th Floor* (TV). 1992: *Raven* (TV). 1993: *The Cover Girl Murders* (cable TV). 1994: *Bionic Ever After* (TV). 1997: *Trojan War* (TV). *The Protector* (TV). *Lost Treasure of Dos Santos* (TV). 1998: *Musketeers Forever*. 1999: *Chapter Zero*. *Informant*. 2000: *Primary Suspect*.

†*As Lee Yeary*

MALDEN, Karl

(K. Mladen Sekulovich) 1913– 2009
Plum-nosed, rasp-voiced, distinctive and likeable American actor whose receding dark hair was sometimes in latter years covered by a toupee. Used in supporting roles by Fox in their realist thrillers of the late 1940s, but in a variety of leading roles after an Academy Award (best supporting actor) for *A Streetcar Named Desire*. From 1972 to 1977 he became entrenched in a very popular TV crime series *The Streets of San Francisco*. Additional Oscar nomination for *On the Waterfront*. Of Yugoslav parentage, he was president of the US Academy of Motion Picture Arts and Sciences from 1989 to 1993.

*1940: They Knew What They Wanted. 1944: Winged Victory. 1946: 13 Rue Madeleine. 1947: Boomerang! Kiss of Death. 1950: Where the Sidewalk Ends. The Gunfighter. Halls of Montezuma. 1951: The Sellout. A Streetcar Named Desire. 1952: Diplomatic Courier. Ruby Gentry. Operation Secret. 1953: Take the High Ground. I Confess. 1954: Phantom of the Rue Morgue. On the Waterfront. 1956: Baby Doll. 1957: Fear Strikes Out. Bombers B-52 (GB: No Sleep Till Dawn). 1958: The Hanging Tree. 1960: Pollyanna. One Eyed Jacks. The Great Imposter. 1961: Parrish. All Fall Down. 1962: Bird Man of Alcatraz. Gypsy. How the West Was Won. Come Fly with Me. 1964: Dead Ringer (GB: Dead Image). Cheyenne Autumn. 1965: The Cincinnati Kid. The Adventures of Bullwhip Griffin. 1966: Nevada Smith. Murderers' Row. 1967: Hotel. Billion Dollar Brain. 1968: Blue. Hot Millions. 1969: Patton (GB: Patton – Lust for Glory). Cat o' Nine Tails. 1971: Wild Rovers. The Summertime Killer. 1972: The Streets of San Francisco (TV). 1978: Captains Courageous (TV). 1979: Beyond the Poseidon Adventure. Meteor. 1980: The Wildcatters/Skag (TV). 1981: Word of Honor (TV). Miracle on Ice (TV). 1982: Twilight Time. 1983: The Sting II. 1984: Intent to Kill (TV. GB: With Intent to Kill). 1986: Billy Galvin. 1987: Nuts. 1988: My Father, My Son (TV). 1989: The Hijacking of the Achille Lauro (TV). 1990: Call Me Anna (TV). 1991: Absolute Strangers (TV). 1992: Back to the Street of San Francisco (TV). Vanished Without a Trace (TV). Earth and the American Dream (voice only).
As director: 1957: Time Limit.*

MALKOVICH, John 1953–

Craggy, forceful, balding, strong-featured (but slightly dissolute-looking) American actor of Yugoslav descent, at home in

sensitive, aggressive or devious roles. Co-founder of Chicago's innovative Steppenwolf Theatre, Malkovich came to films as the doped-out war photographer in *The Killing Fields*, and wasted little time in establishing a niche for himself as cold, eccentric characters. Nominated for Academy Awards in *Places in the Heart* and *In the Line of Fire*, he has also directed many plays. Married/divorced actress Glenne Headly (*qv*), who has had a modest film career of her own.

1981: Word of Honor (TV). American Dream (TV). 1983: The Killing Fields. Say Goodnight, Gracie (TV). True West (TV. Shown in cinemas 1992). 1984: Places in the Heart. 1985: Eleni. Death of a Salesman (TV. GB: cinemas). 1986: Rocket to the Moon (TV). 1987: The Glass Menagerie. Making Mr. Right. Empire of the Sun. 1988: Miles from Home. Dangerous Liaisons. 1989: Queen's Logic. 1990: The Sheltering Sky. 1991: The Object of Beauty. Shadows and Fog. 1992: Jennifer Eight. Of Mice and Men. We're Back (voice only). 1993: In the Line of Fire. Alive (narrator only). 1994: Heart of Darkness (TV). 1995: Beyond the Clouds. The Convent. Mulholland Falls. 1996: Cannes Man. Mary Reilly. The Ogre/Der Unhold. The Portrait of a Lady. 1997: Con Air. 1998: The Man in the Iron Mask. Rounders. 1999: Joan of Arc/The Messenger: The Story of Joan of Arc. Being John Malkovich. Ladies Room. RKO 281 (cable TV). Le temps retrouvé. 2000: Shadow of the Vampire. Knockaround Guys.

MALONE, Dorothy (D. Maloney) 1925–

Tall, pretty, soulful-looking American leading lady. After 12 years of honest, professional but hardly inspiring performances as brunette nice girls, she turned to blonde floozies and immediately won an Oscar for one such lady in

Written on the Wind. But now she was typed in another sort of role and 'instead of getting better, my parts just got worse.' Married to actor Jacques Bergerac (1927–), first of three, from 1959 to 1964.

*1943: †The Falcon and the Co-Eds. †Gildersleeve on Broadway. †Higher and Higher. 1944: †Step Lively. †Youth Runs Wild. †Show Business. †One Mysterious Night (GB: Behind Closed Doors). †Hollywood Canteen. †Seven Days Ashore. 1945: *Frontier Days. Too Young to Know. 1946: Janie Gets Married. Night and Day. The Big Sleep. 1948: Two Guys from Texas (GB: Two Texas Knights). To the Victor. One Sunday Afternoon. 1949: Flaxy Martin. South of St. Louis. Colorado Territory. 1950: The Nevadan (GB: The Man from Nevada). Mrs O'Malley and Mr Malone. The Killer That Stalked New York (GB: Frightened City). Convicted. 1951: Saddle Legion. The Bushwhackers (GB: The Rebel). 1952: Torpedo Alley. 1953: Scared Stiff. Law and Order. Jack Slade (GB: Slade). 1954: Young at Heart. Pushover. Loophole. Security Risk. Private Hell 36. The Fast and the Furious. Five Guns West. Tall Men Riding. Battle Cry. 1955: Sincerely Yours. Artists and Models. At Gunpoint (GB: Gunpoint!). 1956: Pillars of the Sky (GB: The Tomahawk and the Cross). Tension at Table Rock. Written on the Wind. 1957: Quantez. Man of a Thousand Faces. Tip on a Dead Jockey (GB: Time for Action). The Tarnished Angels. 1958: Too Much, Too Soon. 1959: Warlock. 1960: The Last Voyage. 1961: The Last Sunset. 1963: Beach Party. 1964: Fate is the Hunter. 1969: The Pigeon (TV). Femmine insaziabili (GB: The Insatiables. US: Carnal Circuit). 1970: Excess. 1975: The Man Who Could Not Die (GB: TV). Abduction. 1976: The November Plan. 1977: Golden Rendezvous. Winter Kills (released 1979). Little Ladies of the Night (TV). 1978: Murder in Peyton Place (TV). Katie: Portrait of a Centerfold (TV). Good Luck, Miss Wyckoff. 1979: The Day Time Ended. 1980: Easter Sunday (released 1983 as The Being). Off Your Rocker. 1984: He's Not Your Son! (TV). 1985: Peyton Place: The Next Generation (TV). 1986: Rest in Pieces. 1992: Basic Instinct.*

†As Dorothy Maloney

MANGANO, Silvana 1930–1989

This red-headed Italian sexpot, best remembered for her busty, pouty, thigh-booted paddy-field girl in *Bitter Rice*, stayed in third place behind Loren and Lollobrigida in a hot league, but remained in films. Married top Italian producer Dino de Laurentiis; their son Federico died in a plane crash in 1981 and they separated two years later. A beauty contest winner of English-Sicilian parentage, she eventually proved her ability with some strong performances in later years. Died from a heart attack after an operation for lung cancer.

1946: L'elisir d'amore (GB: Elixir of Love. US: This Wine of Love. 1947: Gli uomini sono nemici. Il delitto di Giovanni Episcopo (US: Flesh Will Surrender). 1948: Le carrefour de passion. 1949: Black Magic. Riso amaro/Bitter Rice. 1950: Il lupo della Sila (GB: The Wolf of Sila. US: Lure of the Sila). Il Brigante Musolino (GB: Fugitive). 1951: Anna. 1953: Ulysses. 1954: Mambo. Il più comico spettacolo del mondo. 1955: L'oro di Napoli (GB: Gold of Naples. US: Every Day's a Holiday). 1956: Uomini e lupi/Men and Wolves. 1958: La diga sul Pacifico (GB: The Sea Wall. US: This Angry Age). Tempest. 1959: La grande guerra (US: The Great War). Five Branded Women. 1960: Crimen (GB: Killing in Monte Carlo. US: . . . And Suddenly It's Murder). 1961: Una vita difficile. Il giudizio universale (US: The Last Judgment). 1962: Il processo di Verona. 1963: La mia signora. 1965: Il disco volante. 1966: Io, io, io . . . e gli altri. Le streghe/The Witches. 1967: Oedipus Rex. Scusi, lei è favorevole o contrario? 1968: Teorema/Theorem. Viaggio di Lavoro. Capriccio all'Italiana. 1971: Morte a Venezia/ Death in Venice. The Decameron. Scipione detto anche l'Africano. 1972: Ludwig/Ludwig II. 1973: The Scientific Cardplayer. D'amor si muore. 1975: Gruppo di famiglia in un interno (GB and US: Conversation Piece). 1984: Dune. 1986: The Good Ship Ulysses. 1987: Oci ciornie/Dark Eyes.

MANSFIELD, Jayne
(Vera Jane Palmer) 1932–1967
Pneumatic American blonde star with little to offer beyond outsize breasts, a cute face and a little-girl voice – enough to propel her to stardom in a few major films at that home of busy blondes through the years, 20th Century-Fox. The seemingly inevitable downward spiral through men, drink, drugs and semi-nude appearances in nightclubs was graphically depicted in a thousand newspaper stories. Died in a car crash.
1950: Prehistoric Women. 1954: Female

Jungle. 1955: Pete Kelly's Blues. Illegal. The Burglar (released 1957). Hell on Frisco Bay. 1956: The Girl Can't Help It. 1957: Will Success Spoil Rock Hunter? (GB: Oh! For a Man). The Wayward Bus. Kiss Them for Me. 1958: The Sheriff of Fractured Jaw. 1960: The Loves of Hercules. The Challenge (US: It Takes a Thief). Too Hot to Handle (US: Playgirl after Dark). 1961: The George Raft Story (GB: Spin of a Coin). 1962: It Happened in Athens. 1963: Promises! Promises! Heimweh nach St Pauli. Panic Button. 1964: When Strangers Meet (US: Dog Eat Dog). L'amore primitivo (GB: Primitive Love). 1965: †The Loved One. Single Room Furnished (released 1967). 1966: The Fat Spy. Las Vegas Hillbillys (GB: Country Music USA). 1967: A Guide for the Married Man. The Wild, Wild World of Jayne Mansfield. Spree. Mondo Hollywood.

†Scene deleted from final release print

MARA, Adele (Adelaida Delgado) 1923–
Slinky, brown-eyed blonde dancer, singer and actress who moved from Columbia to Republic in 1943 and was immediately worked overtime by that studio as the heroine – occasionally bad girl – of numerous second-features throughout the decade. She worked her way slowly up to bigger things by 1948, but disappointed her legions of admirers by drifting out of films and concentrating on marriage to writer-producer Roy Huggins. Later occasionally seen on TV.
*1941: *The Great Glover. Navy Blues. 1942: *Kiss and Wake Up. Shut My Big Mouth. Alias Boston Blackie. You Were Never Lovelier. Blondie Goes to College. Lucky Legs. Vengeance of the West. 1943: *A Rookie's Cookie. *Socks Appeal. *His Girls's Worst Friend. *I Can Hardly Wait. *Farmer for a Day. Reveille with Beverly. Riders of the Northwest Mounted. Redhead from Manhattan. Good Luck, Mr Yates. 1944: Call of the South Seas. San Fernando Valley. The Fighting Seabees. Atlantic City. Faces in the Fog. Thoroughbreds. 1945: Earl Carroll Vanities. The Vampire's Ghost. Flame of the Barbary Coast. Bells of Rosarita. Song of Mexico. The Tiger Woman. Girls of the Big House. Grissly's Millions. A Guy Could Change. 1946: That Brennan Girl. The Invisible Informer. The Inner Circle. I've Always Loved You. Passkey to Danger. The Last Crooked Mile. Night Train to Memphis. The Catman of Paris. Traffic in Crime. The*

Pilgrim Lady. 1947: The Black Widow (serial). The Magnificent Rogue. Exposed. Web of Danger. Campus Honeymoon. Twilight on the Rio Grande. Robin Hood of Texas. Blackmail. The Trespasser. 1948: Nighttime in Nevada. I, Jane Doe (US: Diary of a Bride). Angel in Exile. The Gallant Legion. Wake of the Red Witch. The Main Street Kid. 1949: Sands of Iwo Jima. 1950: Rock Island Trail (GB: Transcontinent Express). California Passage. The Avengers. 1951: The Sea Hornet. 1953: Count the Hours (GB: Every Minute Counts). 1956: The Black Whip. Border Showdown (TV. GB: cinemas). Back from Eternity. 1958: Curse of the Faceless Man. 1959: The Big Circus. 1972: Cool Million (TV).

MARAIS, Jean
(J. Villain-Marais) 1913–1998
Tall, well-built, rather immobile French actor with blond hair and Adonis-like handsomeness, a key figure in French post-war films (when he was for a time France's most popular star), notably those by Jean Cocteau, including *La belle et la bête* and *Orphée*. Although Marais himself had an undoubted affection for these classics, he was equally enthusiastic about the second, and critically less-regarded phase of his career, from the mid 1950s to the late 1960s, in which he played swashbuckling adventurers – 'When I was a boy, my hero was Douglas Fairbanks' – and, in several films, the mysterious modern rogue Fantômas. Seemingly retired from acting, Marais surprisingly reappeared as elderly figures of authority in 1995. He died of pulmonary disease.
*1933: L'épervier. Etienne. Dans les rues. 1934: l'aventurier. Le scandale. 1935: Le bonheur. 1936: Nuits de feu. Les hommes nouveaux. 1937: Abus de confiance. Drôle de drame (US: Bizarre, Bizarre). 1941: La pavilion brûle. 1942: Le lit à colonnes. 1943: L'éternel retour. Carmen. Voyage sans espoir. 1945: La belle et la bête (US: Beauty and the Beast). 1946: Les chouans. 1947: L'aigle a deux têtes (GB: The Eagle Has Two Heads. US: Eagle With Two Heads). 1948: Ruy Blas. Les parents terribles (US: The Storm Within). Aux yeux du souvenir/Souvenir. 1949: Le secret de Mayerling. Leclerc. *Ceux de Tchad. Orphée (GB and US: Orpheus). 1950: Le château de verre. Les miracles n'ont lieu qu'une fois. 1951: Nez de cuir. *Le rendez-vous de Cannes. 1952: La maison du silence. L'appel du destin. 1953: Dortoir des grandes (US: Inside a Girls'*

Dormitory). *Julietta. Les amants de minuit. Le guérisseur. Si Versailles m'était conté (GB: Versailles. US: Royal Affairs in Versailles). 1954: Napoléon. The Count of Monte Cristo. Futures vedettes (GB: Sweet Sixteen). 1955: Goubbiah. Si Paris nous etait conté . . .! Toute la ville accuse. 1956: Typhon sur Nagasaki. S.O.S. Noronha. Elena et les hommes (GB: The Night Does Strange Things. US: Paris Does Strange Things). 1957: Le notti bianche (GB and US: White Nights). Un amour de poche (US: Nude in His Pocket). La Tour, prends garde! Chaque jour a son secret. 1958: La vie à deux/The Two of Us. 1959: Le testament d'Orphée (US: Testament of Orpheus). Le bossu/The King Avenger. 1960: Le capitan/The Captain. La Princesse de Clèves. 1961: Napoleon II, l'Aiglon. Le miracle des loups. Le capitaine Fracasse. The Rape of the Sabines (US: Romulus and the Sabines). Pontius Pilate. 1962: Mysteries of Paris. Le masque de fer/Man in the Iron Mask. 1963: L'honorable Stanislas, agent secret. 1964: Le gentleman de Cocody (GB: Ivory Coast Adventure). Fantômas. Patate. Thomas l'imposteur (narrator only). 1965: Plein feux sur Stanislas. Fantômas se déchaîne (GB: Fantomas Strikes Back). Train d'enfer. 1966: Sept hommes et une garce. Le Saint prend l'affût. 1967: Fantômas contre Scotland Yard. 1968: Le paria. 1969: La provocation. 1970: Peau d'âne (GB: The Magic Donkey. US: Donkey Skin). Le jouet criminel. 1978: Cagliostro in Wien. 1982: *Ombre et secrets. 1985: Parking. 1986: Lien de parenté. 1995: Les misérables. Les misérables du XXième siècle. L'univers de Jacques Demy. Stealing Beauty. 1997: Milice, film noir.

MARCEAU, Sophie (S. Maupu) 1966–
Tall, brown-haired, poutingly pretty French actress with winsome charm and winning smile who got her first role at 14 in a talent competition run by a director looking for fresh faces for a teenage film. Completing her education, she turned professional in earnest at 18 and has been increasingly part of the international scene in recent years. Also a novelist, screenplay writer and director, she lives with director Andrzej Zulawski, who has directed three of her films.
1980: La boum. 1982: La boum 2. 1984: Fort Saganne. Joyeuses Pâques/Happy Easter. 1985: L'amour braque. Police. 1986: Descente aux enfers. 1987: Chouans! 1988: L'étudiante. Mes nuits sont plus belles que vos jours. 1989: Pacific Palissades. 1990: Pour Sacha. 1991: La

note bleue. 1993: Fanfan/Fanfan & Alexandre. 1994: La fille de d'Artagnan/D'Artagnan's Daughter. 1995: Braveheart. Beyond the Clouds. Faire un film pour moi c'est vivre (D). †L'aube à l'envers. 1996: Firelight. 1997: Marquise. Anna Karenina. 1999: Lost & Found. The World is Not Enough. A Midsummer Night's Dream. The Criminal. 2000: La fidélité. 2001: Belphegor.

†And directed

MARCH, Fredric
(Ernest Frederick Bickel) 1897–1975
Dark, stocky American leading man who settled in Hollywood with the coming of sound and remained in top roles for over 20 years, especially in the period between his two Oscars (for *Dr Jekyll and Mr Hyde* and *The Best Years of Our Lives*) when his mellifluous voice and clever, self-effacing style won him a wide variety of roles, and he proved unexpectedly adept at sophisticated comedy. Always, in fact, rather more an actor that a star personality. Married (second of two) Florence Eldridge (F. McKechnie 1901–88) in 1927. He also received Oscar nominations for *A Star is Born*, *The Royal Family of Broadway* and *Death of a Salesman*. Died from cancer.
1920: The Devil. 1921: The Glorious Adventure. Paying the Piper. 1929: Footlights and Fools. The Dummy. The Studio Murder Mystery. Jealousy. The Wild Party. Paris Bound. The Marriage Playground. 1930: Paramount on Parade. Sarah and Son. Manslaughter. The Royal Family of Broadway. Ladies Love Brutes. True to the Navy. 1931: My Sin. Honor among Lovers. The Night Angel. Dr. Jekyll and Mr Hyde. 1932: *Hollywood on Parade No. 1. Strangers in Love. Merrily We Go to Hell (GB: Merrily We Go To –). Make Me a Star. Smilin' Through. The Sign of the Cross. 1933: *Hollywood on Parade No. 17. The Eagle and the Hawk. Tonight is Ours. Design for Living. 1934: Good Dame (GB: Good Girl). All of Me. The Barretts of Wimpole Street. We Live Again. Death Takes a Holiday. The Affairs of Cellini. 1935: Les Miserables. Anna Karenina. The Dark Angel. 1936: Mary of Scotland. The Road to Glory. Anthony Adverse. 1937: Nothing Sacred. A Star is Born. 1938: The Buccaneer. Trade Winds. There Goes My Heart. 1939: The 400 Million (narrator only). 1940: Victory. Susan and God (GB: The Gay Mrs Trexel). *Lights Out in Europe. 1941: So

Ends our Night. One Foot in Heaven. Bedtime Story. *Cavalcade of the Academy Awards. 1942: I Married a Witch. *Lake Carrier. 1944: Tomorrow the World. The Adventures of Mark Twain. *Salute to France. 1946: The Best Years of Our Lives. 1948: An Act of Murder. Another Part of the Forest. 1949: Christopher Columbus. 1950: The Titan – the Story of Michelangelo (and narrator). 1951: Death of a Salesman. It's a Big Country. 1953: Man on a Tightrope. 1954: Executive Suite. The Bridges at Toko-Ri. 1955: The Desperate Hours. 1956: Alexander the Great. The Man in the Gray Flannel Suit. 1957: Albert Schweitzer (narrator only). 1959: Middle of the Night. 1960: Inherit the Wind. 1962: The Condemned of Altona. 1964: Seven Days in May. 1966: Hombre. 1969: . . . tick . . . tick . . . tick. 1973: The Iceman Cometh.

MARGOLIN, Janet 1943–1993
Dark-haired, slim, gravely attractive American actress, too good for Hollywood, who couldn't make her a star in spite of some stunning performances, all the way from her debut as a mental patient in *David and Lisa* (straight from her first Broadway play) to her frighteningly intense murderess in *Last Embrace*. Decent leading roles proved even harder for her to find in the 1980s, and she died from ovarian cancer at 49. Married (second) actor Ted Wass.
1962: David and Lisa. 1964: The Eavesdropper. 1965: Bus Riley's Back in Town. Morituri (GB: The Saboteur – Code Name Morituri). The Greatest Story Ever Told. 1966: Nevada Smith. 1967: Enter Laughing. 1968: Buona Sera, Mrs Campbell. 1969: Take the Money and Run. 1971: The Last Child (TV). 1972: Family Flight (TV). 1973: Your Three Minutes Are Up. 1974: Planet Earth (TV). Pray for the Wildcats (TV). Annie Hall. Sharon: Portrait of a Mistress (TV). 1979: Last Embrace. The Triangle Factory Fire Scandal (TV). 1980: The Plutonium Incident (TV). 1987: The Game of Love. 1988: Distant Thunder. 1989: Ghostbusters II. Murder C.O.D. (TV). 1991: Columbo – Murder in Malibu (TV).

MARLOWE, Hugh (H. Hipple) 1911–1982
Tall, dark-haired, long-faced American actor whose genial good looks could turn shifty and unreliable when the occasion demanded weakness or double-dealing. The most successful of his several stabs at Hollywood stardom was his period at 20th Century-Fox from 1949 to 1952, when he got good roles in

such films as *Twelve O'Clock High*, *All About Eve* and *The Day the Earth Stood Still*. Although never as successful again, the former radio announcer continued alternating leading and supporting roles to the end of his film days. Three times married, all to actresses. Died from a heart attack.

*1936: *The Jonker Diamond. It Couldn't Have Happened. 1937: Married Before Breakfast. Between Two Women. 1943: For God and Country. 1944: Marriage is a Private Affair. Mrs Parkington. Meet Me in St Louis. Murder in the Blue Room. 1945: Identity Unknown. 1949: Come to the Stable. Twelve O'Clock High. 1950: All About Eve. Night and the City. 1951: The Day The Earth Stood Still. Rawhide/Desperate Siege. Mr Belvedere Rings the Bell. 1952: Monkey Business. Wait 'Til the Sun Shines, Nellie. Way of a Gaucho. Bugles in the Afternoon. 1953: The Stand at Apache River. Casanova's Big Night. 1954: Garden of Evil. 1955: Illegal. 1956: World Without End. Earth vs the Flying Saucers. 1957: The Black Whip. 1960: Elmer Gantry. 1961: The Long Rope. 1962: Bird Man of Alcatraz. 1963: 13 Frightened Girls! 1964: Seven Days in May. 1966: Castle of Evil. 1968: The Last Shot You Hear. How to Steal the World (TV. GB: cinemas).*

MARSH, Joan (Nancy Ann Rosher) 1913–2000

Cute, button-nosed, fresh-looking platinum blonde American actress of the 1930s. The daughter of ace cameraman Charles Rosher, she appeared as a young child in several of the films on which he worked, before reappearing at Universal at 17 under the name of Joan Marsh. She never really got a chance to excel at her forte – singing and dancing – and

played a number of ingenues, second-leads and leads in minor films before drifting away from Hollywood after World War II.

*1914: †Hearts Adrift. 1915: †*The Mad Maid of the Forest. 1917: †A Little Princess. 1918: †One Hundred Per Cent American. †Johanna Enlists. †How Could You, Jean? †Women's Weapons. 1919: †Daddy Long Legs. †Captain Kidd Junior. †The Heart o' the Hills. 1920: †Thou Art the Man. †Pollyanna. †Suds. 1921: †Little Lord Fauntleroy. †The Love Light. †Through the Back Door. †Young Mrs Winthrop. 1922: †Tess of the Storm Country. †Hearts Aflame. 1930: The King of Jazz. Little Accident. Eyes of the World. All Quiet on the Western Front. Shipmates. 1931: Inspiration. Meet the Wife. Three Girls Lost. A Tailor Made Man. Dance Fools Dance. Politics. Maker of Men. 1932: Are You Listening? The Wet Parade. Bachelor's Affairs. That's My Boy. The Speed Demon. 1933: *Mark It Paid. Daring Daughters (GB: Behind the Counter). It's Great To Be Alive. The Man Who Dared. High Gear (GB: The Big Thrill). Three-Cornered Moon. Rainbow Over Broadway. 1943: You're Telling Me. Many Happy Returns. We're Rich Again. 1935: Anna Karenina. 1936: Champagne for Breakfast. Dancing Feet. 1937: Charlie Chan on Broadway. Hot Water. Life Begins in College (GB: The Joy Parade). 1938: Brilliant Marriage. The Lady Objects. 1939: Fast and Loose. Idiot's Delight. 1941: Road to Zanzibar. 1942: Police Bullets. Keep 'Em Slugging. The Man in the Trunk. 1943: Mr Muggs Steps Out. Secret Service in Darkest Africa (serial). Follow the Leader. 1945: Mr Muggs Rides Again.*

† As Dorothy Rosher (when billed)

MARSH, Mae (Mary Marsh) 1895–1968

Round-faced, auburn-haired American star with Irish colouring – she would have been perfect for an early Technicolor test – Mae Marsh was one of the foremost actresses of the early silent era (particularly in films by D.W. Griffith, mostly in deglamorized or anguished roles). Retired in 1926 to start a family, but came back in 1931 to play off-and-on character roles in the cinema (frequently for director John Ford) for the rest of her life. Died from a heart attack.

*1910: *Serious Sixteen. 1911: *For the Honor of the Servant. *The Civilian. Fighting Blood. *Home Folks. 1912: *The Old Actor. A Siren of Impulse. *The Lesser Evil. *Lena and the Geese. The New York Hat. Man's Genesis. *One is Business, the Other Crime. *The Sands*

*of Dee. *Brutality. *An Adventure in the Autumn Woods. *When Kings Were Law. *Just Like a Woman. *The Parasite. *Oil and Water. Indian Uprising at Santa Fe. A Temporary Truce. *The Spirit Awakening/*The Spirit Awakened. *The Kentucky Girl. 1913: The Telegraph Girl and the Lady. *A Girl's Stratagem. *If Only We Knew. *Fate. Love in an Apartment Hotel. *The Perfidy of Mary. *The Little Tease. *The Wanderer. *His Mother's Son. *The Reformers. Judith of Bethulia. The Battle at Elderbush Gulch. In Prehistoric Days. *Broken Ways. *The Tender-Hearted Boy. Brothers. Near to Earth. The Lady and the Mouse. *By Man's Law. *Influence of the Unknown. *Two Men of the Desert. *The Primitive Man. One Exciting Night. 1914: The Escape. The Avenging Conscience (GB: Thou Shalt Not Kill). The Great Leap. The Swindlers. Moonshine Molly. The Genius. *Paid With Interest. Home Sweet Home. Down by the Sounding Sea. Big James' Heart. *Brute Force (revised version of In Prehistoric Days). *The Mysterious Shot. *The Tavern of Tragedy. The Birthday Present. *The Great God Fear. 1915: The Birth of a Nation. The Outcast. *The Victim. The Shattered Idol. 1916: Intolerance. Hoodoo Ann. The Wharf Rat. A Child of the Paris Street. The Little Liar. The Marriage of Molly-O. The Wild Girl. 1917: Polly of the Circus. Sunshine Alley. The Cinderella Man. 1918: The Beloved Traitor. All Woman. Spotlight Sadie. The Face in the Dark. Money Mad. Hidden Fires. The Racing Strain. Fields of Honor. The Glorious Adventure. 1919: The Mother and the Law (extended version of episode from Intolerance). The Bondage of Barbara. 1920: The Little 'Fraid Lady. 1921: Nobody's Kid. 1922: Flames of Passion (US: Tides of Passion). 'Till We Meet Again. 1923: The White Rose. Paddy-the-Next-Best-Thing. 1924: Daddies. A Woman's Secret. Arabella. 1925: The Rat. 1927: *Life in Hollywood No. 4. 1928: Racing Through. 1931: Over the Hill. 1932: That's My Boy. Rebecca of Sunnybrook Farm. 1933: Alice in Wonderland. 1934: Little Man, What Now? Bachelor of Arts. 1935: Black Fury. 1936: Hollywood Boulevard. 1939: Drums Along the Mohawk. 1940: The Man Who Wouldn't Talk. The Grapes of Wrath. Young People. 1941: Remember the Day. How Green Was My Valley. Tobacco Road. Belle Starr. Swamp Water (GB: The Man Who Came Back). Great Guns. Blue, White and Perfect. 1942: The Loves of Edgar Allan Poe. Son of Fury. Quiet Please, Murder. Tales of Manhattan. 1943: Dixie Dugan. The Song of Bernadette. Jane Eyre. 1944: The Sullivans. In the Meantime, Darling. 1945: Leave Her to Heaven. A Tree Grows in Brooklyn. The Dolly Sisters. 1946: My Darling Clementine. The Late George Apley. Smoky. 1947: Thunder in the Valley (GB: Bob, Son of Battle). 1948: Apartment for Peggy. The Snake Pit. 3 Godfathers. Fort Apache. Deep Waters. 1949: Impact. A Letter to Three Wives. Everybody Does It. It Happens Every Spring. The Fighting Kentuckian. 1950: When Willie Comes Marching Home. My Blue Heaven. The Gunfighter. The Model and the Marriage Broker. 1951: That's My Boy. 1952: The Quiet Man. Night Without Sleep. 1953: The Sun Shines Bright. Titanic. A Blueprint for*

Murder. The Robe. 1955: Prince of Players. The Tall Men. Good Morning, Miss Dove. Hell on Frisco Bay. 1956: While the City Sleeps. Julie. The Searchers. Girls in Prison. 1957: The Wings of Eagles. 1958: Cry Terror! 1960: From the Terrace. Sergeant Rutledge. 1961: Two Rode Together. 1963: Donovan's Reef. 1964: Cheyenne Autumn. 1967: Arabella (and 1924 film of same title).

MARSH, Marian (Violet Krauth) 1913–
Sweet-faced, blonde, petite leading lady of 1930s Hollywood films who usually played wilting violets or girls in danger. Born in Trinidad of mixed descent, she came to Hollywood at 17 and was almost immediately chosen by John Barrymore to star with him in *Svengali* (as Trilby) and *The Mad Genius*. Her last good leading roles came in 1935 and she retired at 30.
*1929: The Sophomore (GB: Compromised). 1930: †Whoopee! †Hell's Angels. †*Don't Believe It. †*No Brakes. 1931: †*Where Canaries Sing Bass. †*Slow Poison. †*Doomed to Win. Svengali. Five Star Final. The Road to Singapore. The Mad Genius. Under Eighteen. 1932: Beauty and the Boss. Alias the Doctor. Strange Justice. The Sport Parade. 1933: Daring Daughters (GB: Behind the Counter). The Eleventh Commandment. Notorious But Nice. 1934: Der verlorene Sohn (US: The Prodigal Son). A Man of Sentiment. I Like It That Way. Love at Second Sight (US: The Girl Thief). Over the Garden Wall. 1935: In Spite of Danger. A Girl of the Limberlost. Unknown Woman. Crime and Punishment. The Black Room. 1936: Lady of Secrets. Counterfeit. The Man Who Lived Twice. Come Closer Folks. 1937: When's Your Birthday? The Great Gambini. Saturday's Heroes. 1938: Youth on Parole. Prison Nurse. A Desperate Adventure (GB: It Happened in Paris). 1939: Missing Daughters. 1940: Fugitive from a Prison Camp. 1941: Murder by Invitation. 1942: Gentleman from Dixie. House of Errors.*

† As Marilyn Morgan

MARSHALL, Brenda
(Ardis Gaines) 1915–1992
Lovely brunette American actress (actually born in the Philippines) who was a rival to Gene Tierney for sheer facial beauty, and mostly played ladies in danger in colourful adventure stories. She seemed to lose some degree of interest in her film career after marrying William Holden (*qv*) in 1941, but

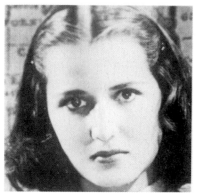

the union eventually ended in divorce 30 years later. Died from throat cancer.
1939: Espionage Agent. 1940: The Man Who Talked Too Much. The Sea Hawk. Money and The Woman. East of the River. South of Suez. 1941: Footsteps in the Dark. Singapore Woman. Highway West. The Smiling Ghost. 1942: Captains of the Clouds. You Can't Escape Forever. 1943: Background to Danger. The Constant Nymph. Paris After Dark (GB: The Night is Ending). 1944: Something for the Boys. 1946: Strange Impersonation. 1948: Whispering Smith. 1950: The Iroquois Trail (GB: The Tomahawk Trail).

MARSHALL, Herbert 1890–1966
Smooth, deliberately-spoken, round-faced, quiet-seeming English actor who diligently pursued his acting career, at first in Britain but soon in Hollywood, despite the loss of a leg in World War I. Came late to films, but made up for it by remaining in star roles until well into his sixties. Equally elegant in comedy or drama, and almost always seen in lounge suit. Married to Edna Best (1928–1940) and Boots Mallory (1946 to her death in 1958) second and fourth of five. Died from a heart attack.
1927: Mumsie. Dawn. 1929: The Letter. 1930: Murder! 1931: Michael and Mary. The Calendar (US: Bachelor's Folly). Secrets of a Secretary. 1932: The Faithful Heart (US: Faithful Hearts). Blonde Venus. Evenings for Sale. Trouble in Paradise. 1933: I Was a Spy. The Solitaire Man. 1934: Outcast Lady (GB: Woman of the World). The Painted Veil. Four Frightened People. Riptide. 1935: The Good Fairy. Accent on Youth. If You Could Only Cook. The Flame Within. The Dark Angel. 1936: Girl's Dormitory. The Lady Consents.

*Make Way for a Lady. A Woman Rebels. Till We Meet Again. Forgotten Faces. 1937: Breakfast for Two. Fight for Your Lady. Angel. 1938: Woman against Woman. Mad about Music. Always Goodbye. Zaza. 1940: The Letter. A Bill of Divorcement / Never to Love. Foreign Correspondent. 1941: The Little Foxes. When Ladies Meet. Kathleen. Adventure in Washington (GB: Female Correspondent). 1942: The Moon and Sixpence. Portrait of a Rebel (narrator only). 1943: Flight for Freedom. Young Ideas. Forever and a Day. 1944: *Shining Future. Andy Hardy's Blonde Trouble. 1945: The Unseen. The Enchanted Cottage. 1946: The Razor's Edge. Crack-Up. Duel in the Sun. 1947: Ivy. The High Wall. 1949: The Secret Garden. 1950: The Underworld Story. Black Jack (US: Captain Black Jack). 1951: Anne of the Indies. 1952: Angel Face. 1954: The Black Shield of Falworth. Gog. Riders to the Stars. 1955: The Virgin Queen. 1956: Wicked As They Come. The Weapon. 1957: The Mystery of 14 (TV). 1958: Stage Struck. The Fly. 1960: Midnight Lace. College Confidential. A Fever in the Blood. 1962: Five Weeks in a Balloon. 1963: The Caretakers (GB: Borderlines). The List of Adrian Messenger. 1965: The Third Day.*

MARSHALL, Zena 1925–
Stunning copper-haired actress in British films, born in Kenya. A little too upper-class and small-voiced for top stardom, she was nonetheless a decorative attraction as heroine of second-features, or the 'other woman' in splashier films, for over 20 years.
*1945: Caesar and Cleopatra. 1947: The End of the River. 1948: Snowbound. Miranda. So Evil My Love. Good Time Girl. Sleeping Car to Trieste. 1949: The Bad Lord Byron. Marry Me. Helter Skelter. The Lost People. Meet Simon Cherry. 1950: Morning Departure (US: Operation Disaster). So Long at the Fair. Soho Conspiracy. Dark Interval. 1951: Hell is Sold Out. Blind Man's Bluff. 1952: Love's a Luxury (US: The Caretaker's Daughter). 1953: Deadly Nightshade. Men Against the Sun. 1954: The Scarlet Web. The Embezzler. 1955: The Price of Greed. Three Cases of Murder. 1956: My Wife's Family. Bermuda Affair. 1957: Let's Be Happy. 1960: A Story of David. 1961: Crosstrap. 1962: Backfire! Dr No. *The Guilty Party. 1963: The Switch. 1964: The Verdict. 1965: Those Magnificent Men in Their Flying Machines. 1967: The Terrornauts.*

MARTIN, Dean
(Dino Crocetti) 1917–1995
Sad-faced, heavy-eyebrowed American crooner and actor who cashed in on his own image as a heavy-drinking ladies' man to make people laugh, then surprised many of them by quitting as straight man to Jerry Lewis (after a partnership lasting from 1946 to 1957) and becoming, after an uncertain start, one of Hollywood's top box-office attractions, and – especially in films between 1958 and 1965 – no mean actor either. Died from acute respiratory failure after suffering for some years with lung cancer. His son Dean Paul Martin, a sometime actor, was killed in an air crash in 1987.
1949: My Friend Irma. 1950: My Friend Irma Goes West. At War with the Army. 1951: That's My Boy. *Screen Snapshots No. 197. Sailor Beware. 1952: *Screen Snapshots No. 207. The Stooge. Jumping Jacks. Road to Bali. *Hollywood Fun Festival. 1953: Scared Stiff. The Caddy. 1954: Money from Home. Living It Up. Three Ring Circus. 1955: You're Never Too Young. Artists and Models. 1956: Pardners. Hollywood or Bust. *Hollywood Premiere. 1957: Ten Thousand Bedrooms. 1958: The Young Lions. Some Came Running. 1959: Career. Rio Bravo. Who Was That Lady? 1960: Bells Are Ringing. Pepe. Ocean's 11. 1961: All in a Night's Work. Ada. 1962: Sergeants Three. The Road to Hong Kong. Who's Got the Action? Canzoni nel mondo/ 38–24–36. †Something's Gotta Give. 1963: Toys in the Attic. Come Blow Your Horn. Who's Been Sleeping in My Bed? Four for Texas. 1964: What a Way to Go! Robin and the Seven Hoods. Kiss Me, Stupid. 1965: The Sons of Katie Elder. Marriage on the Rocks. 1966: The Silencers. Texas across the River. Murderers' Row. 1967: Rough Night in Jericho. The Ambushers. 1968: Bandolero! The Wrecking Crew. Five Card Stud. How to Save a Marriage – and Ruin Your Life. 1969: Airport. 1971: Something Big. 1972: Show-down. 1975: Mr Ricco. 1978: Angels in Vegas (TV). 1981: The Cannonball Run. 1983: The Cannonball Run II. 1985: Half Nelson (TV).

† Uncompleted

MARTIN, Mary 1913–1990
Red-headed, vivacious, energetic musical star never given the chance to dominate a big Hollywood musical in the way she ruled the Broadway stage. After a diet of wartime musical fodder, she went back to the theatre and such successes as South Pacific and The Sound of Music. Recovered from severe injuries sustained in a 1982 auto accident. Mother of Larry Hagman (qv). Died from cancer.
1938: The Rage of Paris. 1939: The Great Victor Herbert. 1940: *Chinese Garden Festival. Love Thy Neighbour. Rhythm on the River. 1941: *Los Angeles Examiner Benefit. *Stars Past and Present. Kiss the Boys Goodbye. Birth of the Blues. New York Town. 1942: Star Spangled Rhythm. Happy Go Lucky. 1943: True to Life. 1946: Night and Day. 1953: Main Street to Broadway. 1979: Valentine (TV).

MARTIN, Steve 1945–
Abrasive, prematurely grey-haired, pale-faced, dark-eyed American 'idiot' comedian who makes a virtue of bad taste and indulges in wild flights of comic fantasy that have moments of genius amid the yawns. A nightclub comedian, he brought his sad/ handsome looks to films in his early thirties and very soon showed some inventively fresh ideas beneath the rudery, notably in the ingenious Dead Men Don't Wear Plaid. His best films are silly, vulgar and rather endearing; his sense of humour creeps up on you. As a straight actor, he has been less effective. Married/divorced actress Victoria Tennant (qv).
1976: *The Absent-Minded Waiter. 1978: Sgt Pepper's Lonely Hearts Club Band. The Kids Are Alright. 1979: The Muppet Movie. The Jerk. 1981: Pennies from Heaven. 1982: Dead Men Don't Wear Plaid. 1983: The Lonely Guy. The Man with Two Brains. 1984: All of Me. 1985: Movers and Shakers (Dreamers). 1986: Little Shop of Horrors. Three Amigos! 1987: Roxanne. Planes, Trains and Automobiles. 1988: Dirty Rotten Scoundrels. 1989: Parenthood. 1990: My Blue Heaven. 1991: L.A. Story. Grand Canyon. Father of the Bride. 1992: Leap of Faith. HouseSitter. 1993: And the Band Played On. 1994: A Simple Twist of Fate. Mixed Nuts. 1995: Father of the Bride 2. 1996: Sgt Bilko. 1997: The Spanish Prisoner. 1998: The Prince of Egypt (voice only). 1999: The Out-of-Towners. Bowfinger. The Venice Project. Fantasia 2000. 2000: Joe Gould's Secret. Novocaine.

MARTIN, Tony (Alvin Maris) 1912–
Craggily handsome, black-haired leading man with a big singing voice. Was a saxo-phonist, bandleader and night-club singer before getting the Hollywood call at 24. Never quite settled in the film city, but did marry two of its most glamorous musical stars, a blonde, Alice Faye (1937–1940) and a brunette, Cyd Charisse (1948–). For many years after their film careers he and Charisse successfully toured night-clubs.
1936: *Educating Father. Pigskin Parade (GB: Harmony Parade). The Farmer in the Dell. Banjo on my Knee. Follow the Fleet. Back to Nature. Sing Baby Sing. 1937: The Holy Terror. Sing and Be Happy. You Can't Have Everything. Life Begins in College (GB: The Joy Parade). Ali Baba Goes to Town. 1938: Sally, Irene and Mary. Kentucky Moonshine (GB: Three Men and a Girl). Thanks for Everything. Up the River. 1939: Winner Take All. 1940: Music in My Heart. 1941: *Stars at Play. Ziegfeld Girl. The Big Store. 1942: *We Must Have Music. 1946: Till the Clouds Roll Bu. 1948: Casbah. 1950: *Hollywood Goes to Bat. 1951: Two Tickets to Broadway. 1953: Easy to Love. 1954: Deep in My Heart. 1955: Hit the Deck. 1956: Meet Me in Las Vegas (GB: Viva Las Vegas!). Quincannon, Frontier Scout (GB: Frontier Scout). 1957: Let's Be Happy. 1979: Todos los Dios un Dia. 1982: Dear Mr Wonderful. 1997: The Interview.

MARTINELLI, Elsa (E. Tia) 1932–
Slinky, very slim Italian leading lady of cat-like qualities. The spitfire in the ex-barmaid was very evident in such early, 'primitive' roles as The Indian Fighter and Manuela, but once part of the international scene she regressed to decoration in cosmopolitan thrillers in which her mind frequently seemed to be on something else.
1954: Le rouge et le noir. 1955: The Indian

Fighter. 1956: La risaia (US: Rice Girl). Donatella. Four Girls in Town. 1957: Manuela (US: Stowaway Girl). La mina. 1958: I battellieri del Volga (GB: The Boatmen. US: Prisoners of the Volga). Tunisi top secret. 1959: Costa Azzura. La notte brava. Le bossu/ The King Avenger. Ciao, ciao, bambina. 1960: Et mourir de plaisir (GB and US: Blood and Roses). Le capitan. Le ménace. Un amore a Roma. I piacere del sabato notte. Il carro armato dell'8 settembre (GB and US: The Tank of 8 September). 1961: Hatari! 1962: The Pigeon That Took Rome. Pelle viva. The Trial/ Le procès. Rampage! 1963: The VIPs. 1964: De l'amour (GB: All About Loving). La fabuleuse aventure de Marco Polo (GB and US: Marco the Magnificent). 1965: La decima vittima (GB and US: The Tenth Victim). Je vous salue, mafia (US: Hail Mafia!). L'or du Duc. Un milliard dans un billard (GB: Diamonds Are Brittle). 1966: Maroc 7. Un dollaro per sette vigliacchi (GB and US: Madigan's Millions). Come imparai ad amare le donne. 1967: The Oldest Profession. Woman Times Seven. Manon 70. Qualcuno ha tradito (US: Requiem for a Rabble). 1968: Belle Starr/ The Belle Starr Story. Candy. Maldonne. 1969: If It's Tuesday, This Must Be Belgium. Una sull'altra (GB and US: One on Top of the Other). Les chemins de Katmandou. L'amica. OSS 117 prend des vacances. 1970: L'araucana massacro degli dei. 1971: La part des lions. 1976: Il garofano rosso. 1986: Barbascio (US: Supernatural Man). 1988: Pygmalion 88. Arrivederci Roma. 1991: Once Upon a Crime.

early fifties as western villains and thuggish gangsters (sometimes in cahoots with Ernest Borgnine, whose career followed a similar pattern). He had progressed to principal villain when a TV series M Squad, promoted him to showier roles, one of which, the drunken gunfighter in Cat Ballou, won him an Oscar and made him a star as a series of powerful, sometimes more sympathetic, protagonists in action films. Died from a heart attack.

1950: Teresa. USS Teakettle (later You're in the Navy Now). 1951: Hong Kong. 1952: We're Not Married. Diplomatic Courier. The Duel at Silver Creek. Eight Iron Men. Hangman's Knot. 1953: Gun Fury. The Stranger Wore a Gun. The Wild One. The Big Heat. The Glory Brigade. Seminole. Down Among the Sheltering Palms. 1954: The Caine Mutiny. The Raid. Gorilla at Large. Bad Day at Black Rock. 1955: Not As a Stranger. A Life in the Balance. Violent Saturday. Pete Kelly's Blues. Shack Out on 101. I Died a Thousand Times. 1956: Pillars of the Sky (GB: The Tomahawk and the Cross). Seven Men from Now. The Rack. Attack! 1957: Raintree County. 1958: The Missouri Traveler. 1961: The Comancheros. 1962: The Man Who Shot Liberty Valance. The Meanest Men in the West (TV). 1963: Donovan's Reef. The Case Against Paul Ryker (TV. GB and US: cinemas, 1968, as Sgt Ryker). 1964: The Killers. 1965: Cat Ballou. Ship of Fools. 1966: The Professionals. 1967: The Meanest Men in the West (TV. Shown in cinemas 1976). Tonite Let's All Make Love in London. Our Time in Hell (narrator only). Point Blank. The Dirty Dozen. 1968: Hell in the Pacific. 1969: Paint Your Wagon. 1970: Monte Walsh. 1971: Pocket Money. 1972: Prime Cut. 1973: The Iceman Cometh. The Emperor of the North Pole (GB: Emperor of the North). 1974: The Spikes Gang. The Klansman. 1976: Shout at the Devil. The Great Scout and Cathouse Thursday. 1979: Samuel Fuller and The Big Red One. Avalanche Express. 1980: Death Hunt. The Big Red One. 1982: Dogsday/ Canicule (released 1984). 1983: Gorky Park. 1985: The Dirty Dozen: Next Mission (TV). 1986: The Delta Force.

quely zany humour developed in vaudeville and was perfected by the time they came to the screen. Zeppo was a singing straight man for the loping, cigar-chewing, eye-rolling, dowager-baiting Groucho whose painted moustache and surface cunning failed to protect him from the fast-talking, Italianate, piano-playing Chico and silent, bewigged, ever-grinning Harpo who chased girls as fast as he could under the burden of an overcoat that could have everything but the kitchen sink inside it. Their films have not dated. A fifth brother, Grummo (1873–1977) – real name: Milton – left them before they moved to Hollywood. Chico died from a heart attack, Harpo after heart surgery, Groucho from pneumonia and Zeppo from cancer. Groucho received a special Oscar in 1973.

1925: Too Many Kisses (H only). 1926: †Humorisk (C, H, G, Z). 1929: The Cocoanuts (C, H, G, Z). 1931: Monkey Business (C, H, G, Z). 1932: *Hollywood on Parade No. 5 (H only). Horse Feathers (C, H, G, Z). 1933: *Hollywood on Parade No. 9 (C only). *Screen Snapshots No. 36 (C, H, G, Z). Duck Soup (C, H, G, Z). *Hollywood on Parade No. 17 (G, C, Z). 1935: *La Fiesta de Santa Barbara (H only). A Night at the Opera (C, H, G). 1936: Yours for the Asking (H, G). 1937: A Day at the Races (C, H, G). 1938: Room Service (C, H, G). 1939: At the Circus (C, H, G). 1940: Go West (GB: The Marx Brothers Go West. C, H, G). 1941: The Big Store (C, H, G). 1943: *Screen Snapshots No. 102 (G only). Stage Door Canteen (H only). *Screen Snapshots No. 110 (C, H, G). 1945: *All-Star Bond Rally (H only). 1946: A Night in Casablanca (C, H, G). 1947: Copacabana (G only). 1949: Love Happy/ Kleptomaniacs (C, H, G). 1950: Mr Music (G only). 1951: Double Dynamite (G only). 1952: A Girl in Every Port (G only). 1957: The Story of Mankind (C, H, G). *Playtime in Hollywood (G only). Will Success Spoil Rock Hunter? (GB: Oh! For a Man. G only). 1958: Next to No Time (TV. C only). *Showdown at Ulcer Gulch (TV. C, H, G). 1959: *The Incredible Jewel Robbery (TV. C, H, G). 1968: Skidoo (G only).

† Unreleased

MARVIN, Lee 1924–1987
Ugly, menacing, tall and gangling American actor with distinctive receding temples to his dark (later silver) hair, furiously busy in the

MARX BROTHERS, The
Chico (Leonard) 1886–1961;
Harpo (Adolph) 1888–1964;
Groucho (Julius) 1890–1977;
Zeppo (Herbert) 1901–1979 (not pictured)
Family of American comedians whose uni-

MASON, James 1909–1984
British leading man with rich, mellow voice and saturnine, sardonic looks. The darker the drama, the more effective he proved, especially as suave villains, men on the run or

characters trapped by circumstance. His scathing comments on the British film industry of the forties ostracized him for a time, and he went to Hollywood where, although alternating quality product with utter tosh, he gradually became one of the world's most respected actors. Died after a heart attack. Oscar nominations for *A Star Is Born*, *Georgy Girl* and *The Verdict*.

1935: *Late Extra*. 1936: *Troubled Waters*. *Twice Branded*. *Blind Man's Bluff*. *Prison Breaker*. *The Secret of Stamboul*. *Fire over England*. *The Mill on the Floss*. 1937: *The High Command*. *Catch as Catch Can*. *The Return of the Scarlet Pimpernel*. 1939: *I Met a Murderer*. 1941: *The Patient Vanishes* (later *This Man is Dangerous*). *Hatter's Castle*. 1942: *The Night Has Eyes* (US: *Terror House*). *Alibi*. *Secret Mission*. *Thunder Rock*. 1943: *The Bells Go Down*. *The Man in Grey*. *They Met in the Dark*. *Candlelight in Algeria*. 1944: *Fanny by Gaslight* (US: *Man of Evil*). *Hotel Reserve*. 1945: *A Place of One's Own*. *They Were Sisters*. *The Seventh Veil*. *The Wicked Lady*. 1946: *Odd Man Out*. 1947: *The Upturned Glass*. 1949: *Caught*. *Madame Bovary*. *The Reckless Moment*. *East Side, West Side*. 1950: *One Way Street*. 1951: *Pandora and the Flying Dutchman*. *The Desert Fox* (GB: *Rommel – Desert Fox*). 1952: *Lady Possessed*. *Five Fingers*. *The Prisoner of Zenda*. *Face to Face*. 1953: *The Man Between*. *Charade*. *The Story of Three Loves*. *The Desert Rats*. *Julius Caesar*. *Botany Bay*. 1954: *Prince Valiant*. *A Star is Born*. *20,000 Leagues Under the Sea*. 1956: *Forever Darling*. *Bigger Than Life*. 1957: *Island in the Sun*. *The Thundering Wave* (TV). 1958: *Not the Glory* (TV). *Cry Terror!* *The Decks Ran Red*. 1959: *North by Northwest*. *Journey to the Center of the Earth*. *The Second Man* (TV). *A Touch of Larceny*. *Big Ben*. 1960: *The Trials of Oscar Wilde*. *John Brown's Raid* (TV). 1961: *The Marriage-Go-Round*. *Escape from Zahrain*. 1962: *Lolita*. *Hero's Island*. *Tiara Tahiti*. *Torpedo Bay/Finche dura la tempesta*. 1963: *The Fall of the Roman Empire*. 1964: *The Pumpkin Eater*. *Lord Jim*. 1965: *Genghis Khan*. *Les pianos mécaniques* (US: *The Uninhibited*). 1966: *The Blue Max*. *Georgy Girl*. *The Deadly Affair*. 1967: *The London Nobody Knows* (and narrator). *Stranger in the House* (US: *Cop Out*). 1968: *Duffy*. *The Legend of Silent Night* (TV). *Mayerling*. 1969: *Age of Consent*. *The Sea Gull*. *Spring and Port Wine*. 1970: *The Yin and the Yang of Dr Go*. 1971: *Cold Sweat*. *Bad Man's River*. 1972: *Kill!* (US: *Kill! Kill! Kill!*). *Child's Play*. *The Wind in the Wires* (narrator only). 1973: *The Last of Sheila*. *The Mackintosh Man*. *Frankenstein: The True Story* (TV. GB: cinemas). 1974: *11 Harrowhouse*. *The Marseille Contract* (US: *The Destructors*). *Trikimia*. *Nostro nero in casa Nichols*. 1975: *Mandingo*. *Inside Out*. *Autobiography of a Princess*. *Great Expectations* (TV. GB: cinemas). *Genti di respetto* (US: *The Flower in His Mouth*). *The Schoolmistress and the Devil*. *La polizia interviene – ordine di uccidere/The Left Hand of the Law* (US: *Roots of the Mafia*). *The Deal*. 1976: *Voyage of the Damned*. *People of the Wind* (narrator only). *Homage to Chagall* (narrator only). *Kidnap Syndicate*. 1977: *Cross of Iron*. *Paura in città*

(US: *Hot Stuff*). 1978: *Heaven Can Wait*. *Sherlock Holmes: Murder by Decree* (GB: *Murder by Decree*). *The Boys from Brazil*. *The Water Babies*. *The Passage*. 1979: *Bloodline/Sidney Sheldon's Bloodline*. *North Sea Hijack* (US: *ffolkes*). *Salem's Lot* (TV). 1981: *Evil Under the Sun*. 1982: *The Verdict*. *Ivanhoe* (TV). *A Dangerous Summer*. 1983: *Yellowbeard*. *Alexandre*. *Dr Fischer of Geneva* (TV). 1984: *The Shooting Party*. *The Assisi Underground*.

As director: 1954: **The Child*.

MASON, Marsha 1940–
Bright-faced American actress with dark, curly hair, the second wife (later divorced) of writer Neil Simon. Almost entirely a stage actress (with ballet training) until the early 1970s, but she has been three times nominated for an Academy Award since then, for warm and deeply-felt performances in *Cinderella Liberty*, *The Goodbye Girl* and *Only When I Laugh*. Surprisingly, her film career was moving in first and starts by the mid-1980s and by the following decade she was in fairly insignificant roles. She has had some success in recent times, however, directing for the stage.

1966: *Hot Rod Hullabaloo*. 1968: *Beyond the Law*. 1973: *Blume in Love*. 1974: *Cinderella Liberty*. 1977: *Audrey Rose*. *The Goodbye Girl*. 1978: *The Cheap Detective*. 1979: *Chapter Two*. 1980: *Promises in the Dark*. 1981: *Only When I Laugh* (GB: *It Hurts Only When I Laugh*). *Lois Gibbs and the Love Canal* (TV). 1983: *Max Dugan Returns*. 1985: *Surviving* (TV). 1986: *Silent Cry* (TV). *Heartbreak Ridge*. *Trapped in Silence* (TV). 1989: *Dinner at Eight* (TV). *The Image* (TV). 1990: *Stella*. 1991: *Drop Dead Fred*. 1994: *I Love Trouble*. 1995: *Broken Trust* (TV). *Nick of Time*. 1996: *2 Days in the Valley*. 1999: *Dead Aviators* (cable TV).

MASSEY, Raymond 1896–1983
Tall, rangy, long-faced Canadian actor with scowling smile and deeply resonant voice. He alternated between British and Hollywood films for ten years before settling in America in 1941 and showing a liking for villains and historical characters. Married actress Adrianne Allen (1907–), second of three; Anna (1937–) and Daniel (1933–1998) are their children. Made fewer films than one might think. Oscar nominee for *Abe Lincoln in Illinois*. Died from pneumonia.

1929: *The Crooked Billet/International Spy*. *High Treason*. 1931: *The Speckled Band*. 1932: *The Face at the Window*. *The Old Dark House*. 1934: *The Scarlet Pimpernel*. 1936: *Things to Come*. *Fire over England*. 1937: *Dreaming Lips*. *Under the Red Robe*. *The Prisoner of Zenda*. *The Hurricane*. 1938: *The Drum* (US: *Drums*). *Black Limelight*. 1940: *Abe Lincoln in Illinois* (GB: *Spirit of the People*). *Santa Fé Trail*. 1941: *49th Parallel* (US: *The Invaders*). *Dangerously They Live*. 1942: *Desperate Journey*. *Reap the Wild Wind*. 1943: *Action in the North Atlantic*. *Arsenic and Old Lace*. 1944: *The Woman in the Window*. 1945: *Hotel Berlin*. *God is My Co-Pilot*. 1946: *A Matter of Life and Death* (US: *Stairway to Heaven*). 1947: *Possessed*. *Mourning Becomes Electra*. 1949: *The Fountainhead*. *Roseanna McCoy*. *Chain Lightning*. 1950: *Barricade*. *Dallas*. 1951: *Sugarfoot*. *Come Fill the Cup*. *David and Bathsheba*. 1952: *Carson City*. 1953: *The Desert Song*. 1954: *East of Eden*. *Prince of Players*. 1955: *The Late George Apley* (TV. GB: cinemas). *Battle Cry*. *Seven Angry Men*. 1957: *Omar Khayyam*. 1958: *The Naked and the Dead*. 1960: *The Great Imposter*. *The Cruel Day* (TV). 1961: *The Fiercest Heart*. *The Queen's Guards*. 1962: *How the West Was Won*. 1963: *Report on China* (narrator only). 1968: *Mackenna's Gold*. 1971: *The President's Plane is Missing* (TV). 1972: *All My Darling Daughters* (TV). 1973: *My Darling Daughters' Anniversary* (TV).

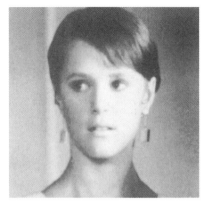

MASTERSON, Mary Stuart 1966–
Slight, sensitive American actress with prominent bone structure, deep brown eyes, light hair and determined chin. The daughter of actors, she has a distinctive dry voice and

the facility of seeming intensely interested in what's going on around her on screen. But she has not quite displayed the strength to become a box-office attraction and, despite some outstanding performances in recent times, seems destined to become a working actress rather than a major star.

1974: *The Stepford Wives*. 1980: *City in Fear/Panic on Page One (TV)*. 1984: *Love Lives On (TV)*. 1985: *Heaven Help Us (later and GB: Catholic Boys. Originally for cable TV)*. *At Close Range*. 1986: *My Little Girl*. 1987: *Gardens of Stone. Some Kind of Wonderful. Amazing Stories (TV. GB: cinemas)*. 1988: *Mr North. Life After Life*. 1989: *Immediate Family. Chances Are*. 1990: *Funny About Love*. 1991: *Married to It. Fried Green Tomatoes (GB: Fried Green Tomatoes at the Whistlestop Café)*. 1992: *Mad at the Moon*. 1993: *Benny & Joon. The Last Party*. 1994: *Bad Girls. Radioland Murders*. 1995: *Heaven's Prisoners*. 1996: *Bed of Roses/Amelia and the King of Plants. Lily Dale (TV)*. 1997: *The Postman. Dogtown. Digging to China. On the 2nd Day of Christmas (TV)*. 1999: *The Book of Stars. The Florentine. Black and Blue (TV)*. 2000: *Grapefruit Moon*.

MASTRANTONIO, Mary Elizabeth
1958–
Reed-like American actress with dark, curly hair and shy smile. She can play both fragile and gentle or tough and tarty, but films have had to compete with her work for the theatre. She trained for the opera, and made her stage debut as Maria in a run of *West Side Story*. As she approached 30, she seemed to take a conscious decision to work more for the cinema, but her output was still not prolific as she passed 40. Married director Pat O'Connor.

1982: †*The King of Comedy*. 1983: *Scarface*. 1985: *Mussolini: The Untold Story (TV)*. 1987: *Slam Dance. The Color of Money*. 1988: *The January Man*. 1989: *The Abyss*. 1990: *Fools of Fortune. Class Action*. 1991: *Robin Hood – Prince of Thieves. Uncle Vanya (TV)*. 1992: *White Sands. Consenting Adults*. 1993: *The Abyss: Special Edition*. 1995: *Two Bits. Three Wishes*. 1998: *My Life So Far (released 2000)*. 1999: *Limbo. Witness Protection (TV)*. 2000: *The Perfect Storm*.

† *Most scenes deleted*

MASTROIANNI, Marcello 1923–1996
Dark-haired, bright-eyed, charming Italian star, not unlike Louis Jourdan (*qv*), but with

more hints of both mischief and melancholy about the eyes. Thus he was equally at home over the years with comedy, romance and emotional torment. From the 1960s he formed something of a latter-day romantic team with Sophia Loren (*qv*): they made several films together. Nominated for Academy Awards in *Divorzio all'Italiana/ Divorce Italian Style*, *Una giornata particolare/A Special Day* and *Oci ciornie/Dark Eyes*. Died from pancreatic cancer.

As extra: 1938: *Marionette*. 1940: *La corona di ferro*. 1942: *Una storia d'amore. I bambini ci guardano*. As actor: 1947: *I miserabili*. 1949: *Cuori sul mare. Vent' anni. Domenica d'Agosto (GB: Sunday in August)*. 1950: *Vita da cane*. 1951: *Atto di accusa. A Tale of Five Cities. Contro la legge. Parigi è sempre Parigi. Sensualita'. Le ragazze di piazza di Spagna (GB: Girls of the Spanish Steps. US: Three Girls from Rome)*. 1952: *L'eterna Catena. Tragico ritorno. Lulu. Gli eroi della Domenica. Penne nere*. 1953: *Il viale della speranza. La valigia dei sogni. Non è mai troppo tardi. Siamo donne (GB and US: We the Women). Cronache di poveri amanti*. 1954: *Tempi nostri (US: The Anatomy of Love). Casa Ricordi. Peccato che sia una canaglia (GB and US: Too Bad She's Bad). Tam-Tam Mayumba. Giorni d'amore. La schiava del peccato. Febbre di vivere*. 1955: *La fortuna di essere donna (GB and US: Lucky to be a Woman). Le bella mugnaia (GB: The Miller's Wife. US: The Miller's Beautiful Wife). La principessa della Canarie*. 1956: *Mädchen und Männer. Il bigamo/The Bigamist*. 1957: *Un ettaro di cielo. Padre e figli (US: A Tailor's Maid). La ragazza della salina. Il momento più bello. Le notti bianche (GB and US: White Nights). Il medico e lo stregone*. 1958: *La loi (GB and US: Where the Hot Wind Blows). Racconti d'estate (GB: Girls for the Summer. US: Love on the Riviera). I soliti ignoti (US: Big Deal on Madonna Street)*. 1959: *Tutti innamorati. Il nemico di mia moglie. Ferdinand of Naples. La dolce vita*. 1960: *La notte. Fantasmi a Roma (GB: Phantom Lovers. US: Ghosts of Rome). Il bell'Antonio. Adua e la compagne (US: Love à la Carte)*. 1961: *l'assassino (US: The Lady Killer from Rome). Vie privée (GB and US: A Very Private Affair). Divorzio all'Italia/ Divorce Italian Style*. 1962: *Cronaca familiare (GB and US: Family Diary). 8½. I compagni (US: The Organizer). Il giorno più corto (US: The Shortest Day). Yesterday, Today and Tomorrow*. 1964: *Marriage, Italian Style*.

1965: *Io, io, io . . . e gli altri. Paranoia (US: Kiss the Other Sheik). The 10th Victim. Casanova 70. The Organiser*. 1966: *The Poppy is Also a Flower (TV. GB: cinemas, as Danger Grows Wild). Shoot Loud . . . Louder, I Don't Understand*. 1967: *Lo straniero/The Stranger*. 1968: *Diamonds for Breakfast. Amanti (GB and US: A Place for Lovers). Questi fantasmi (GB and US: Ghosts Italian Style)*. 1969: *Sunflower*. 1970: *Siochi particolari/The Voyeur. Dramma della gelosia (US: Jealousy Italian Style. US: The Pizza Triangle). Leo the Last. Scipione, detto anche 'l'Africano'. The Priest's Wife*. 1971: *Permette? Rocco Papaleo (US: Rocco Papaleo)*. 1972: *Liza. Mordi e fuggi (US: Bite and Run). What? Ça n'arrive qu'aux autres. 1870. Melampo*. 1973: *La grande bouffe (GB and US: Blow-Out). Rappresaglia (GB and US: Massacre in Rome). Salut l'artiste (GB: The Bit Player). L'évènement le plus important depuis que l'homme a marché sur la lune (GB: The Slightly Pregnant Man. US: A Slightly Pregnant Man)*. 1974: *Touchez pas la femme blanche. C'eravamo tanto amati (GB: We All Loved Each Other So Much). Allosanfan*. 1975: *Culastrisce, nobile veneziano. Down the Ancient Stairs. La divine creatura (US: The Divine Nymph). La donna delle Domenica/ The Sunday Woman*. 1976: *La fantasie amorose di Luca Maria nobile Veneto. Signore e signori buonanotte*. 1977: *Una giornata particolare/A Special Day. Mogliamante (GB and US: Wifemistress). Ciao male/Bye Monkey!/The Monkey's Uncle. Doppo delitto/Double Murders*. 1978: *L'ingorgo (US: Traffic Jam). Vengeance (US: Revenge)*. 1979: *Shimmy Lugano e tarantelle e tarallucci e vino. Blood Feud. Le citta delle donne. Cosi come sei (US: Stay As You Are). L'embouteillage. Giallo Napoletano*. 1980: *Atti atrocissimi di amore e di vendetta. Todo mondo. La terrazza*. 1981: *La pelle. Fantôme d'amour*. 1982: *Revolution. Oltre la porta (GB: Beyond the Door). La nuit de Varennes (US: The New World)*. 1983: *Il generale dell'armata morta. Gabriela. Enrico IV*. 1984: *Il fu Mattia Pascal (US: The Two Lives of Mattia Pascal)*. 1985: *Ginger and Fred. Macaroni. The Legend of the Holy Drinker. I soliti ignoti 20 anni doppo (US: Big Deal on Madonna Street – Update)*. 1986: *The Good Ship Ulysses. Death of a Beekeeper. A Beekeeper Dies – The Other Tale*. 1987: *Oci ciornie/Dark Eyes. I picari. Intervista/The Interview. Miss Arizona*. 1988: *Beyond Obsession. Splendor. Vacanza. Il mitico Gianluca. O samba*. 1989: *Che ore è?/What Time Is It?* 1990: *Tutti stanno bene. Tchin tchin/A Fine Romance. Verso sera*. 1991: *The Broken Flight of the Swan. The Colonel's Children. Le voleur d'enfants*. 1992: *Used People*. 1993: *Do eso no se habla. Un, deux, trois, soleil. Di questo non si parla/We Don't Want to Talk About It*. 1994: *A che punto e la notte. La vera vita di Antonio. H. Prêt-à-porter (US: Ready to Wear). Les cent et une nuits*. 1995: *According to Pereira. Beyond the Clouds*. 1996: *Trois vies et une seule mort*. 1997: *Mi ricordo, si, io mi ricordo. Viagem ao principio do mundo/Journey to the Beginning of the World*.

MATHEWS, Carole (Jean Francis) 1920–
This Hollywood actress with the cynical smile (no wonder) and the piled-high head of

golden hair at least deserves ten out of ten for trying. Miss Chicago of 1938, she played tiny, sometimes even bit parts, on stage and screen from the early forties right through to the fifties. By 1950 she had at least clawed her way up to leading lady in second-features, a position she held on to until the end of the decade. Her performances were almost always better than her roles. Also a torchy singer, she later bred horses and goats and ran a travel agency until retiring in 1987.

1944: Together Again. Girl in the Case (GB: The Silver Key). Swing in the Saddle (GB: Swing and Sway). The Missing Juror. She's a Sweetheart. Strange Affair. Tahiti Nights. 1945: Outlaws of the Rockies (GB: A Roving Rogue). Blazing the Western Trail (GB: Who Killed Waring?). I Love a Mystery. Over 21. A Thousand and One Nights. Sing Me a Song of Texas (GB: Fortune Hunter). Ten Cents a Dance (GB: Dancing Ladies). The Monster and the Ape (serial). 1946: Stars over Texas. 1948: Sealed Verdict. The Accused. 1949: Massacre River. Special Agent. Chicago Deadline. The Great Gatsby. Amazon Quest (GB: Amazon). Cry Murder. 1950: No Man of Her Own. Paid in Full. 1951: The Man with My Face. 1952: Red Snow. Meet Me at the Fair. 1953: Two Gun Marshal (TV. GB: cinemas). City of Bad Men. Shark River. 1954: Port of Hell. Treasure of Ruby Hills. 1955: Betrayed Women. 1956: Assignment Redhead (US: Requirement for a Redhead). Swamp Women. 1957: Showdown at Boot Hill. 1958: Strange Awakening (US: Female Fiends). 1960: 13 Fighting Men. 1961: Tender is the Night. Look in Any Window. 1970: Rabbit, Run.

MATHEWS, Kerwin 1926–

Tall, leanly handsome, clean-cut, quietly spoken American leading man with light wavy hair. He switched from teaching to acting in his late twenties, and unexpectedly became the dashing star of several Dynamation/Arabian Nights adventure tales. But he was only seen in a few oddball adventure yarns after the sixties.

1955: Five Against the House. 1956: The Country Husband (TV. GB: cinemas). 1957: The Garment Jungle. 1958: Tarawa Beachhead. The Last Blitzkrieg. The Seventh Voyage of Sinbad. 1960: The Three Worlds of Gulliver. Sappho (GB: The Warrior Empress). Man on a String (GB: Confessions of a Counterspy). 1961: Jack the Giant Killer. The Devil at Four O'Clock. The Pirates of Blood River. 1962:

Maniac. 1963: OSS 117 se dechaîne. The Waltz King. 1964: Banco à Bangkok pour OSS 117 (GB: Shadow of Evil). 1967: Battle Beneath the Earth. The Viscount. Ghostbreaker (TV). 1968: Faccia d'Angelo/Zucker für den Mörder (GB: The Killer Likes Candy). 1969: Barquero. 1971: Octaman. Death Takes a Holiday (TV). 1973: The Boy Who Cried Werewolf. 1976: Nightmare in Blood.

MATHIS, Samantha 1970–

Pretty blonde (sometimes dark) American actress with wide smile (the daughter of Austrian-born actress Bibi Besch; 1940–1996) who has made strides both as a leading lady and a young character actress since her professional debut at 15. Not too distinctive at times, though: she has not shown up well in leading roles, and done more solid work supporting the stars.

*1987: Aaron's Way (TV). 1988: The Bulldance. 1989: Cold Sassy Tree (TV). 1990: To My Daughter (TV). Pump Up the Volume. 83 Hours 'til Dawn (TV). Extreme Close-Up (TV). 1991: This is My Life. 1992: FernGully The Last Rainforest (voice only). Super Mario Bros. 1993: The Music of Chance. Yesterday. The Thing Called Love. 1994: Jack and Sarah. Little Women. 1995: How to Make an American Quilt. The American President. 1996: Broken Arrow. 1997: Sweet Jane. 1998: *Waiting for Woody. 1999: Freak City (TV). The Simian Line. 2000: American Psycho. Stalk.*

MATTHAU, Walter

(W. Matthow) 1920–2000

Growly, dark-haired, bloodhound-faced, phlegmatic American actor whose mastery of comic timing and crumpled features were at

first hidden behind conventional villain roles. From 1962 to 1965 he stole too many films from the stars to be denied leading parts, and an Oscar for *The Fortune Cookie* clinched his position as an unconventional superstar. Received further Oscar nominations for *Kotch* and *The Sunshine Boys*, both of which foreshadowed the latter part of his career as grouchy eccentrics. Director Charles Matthau is his son. Died from a heart attack.

*1955: The Kentuckian. The Indian Fighter. 1956: Bigger Than Life. 1957: Slaughter on 10th Avenue. Voice in the Mirror. A Face in the Crowd. 1958: Onionhead. King Creole. Ride a Crooked Trail. 1960: ‡The Gangster Story. Strangers When We Meet. 1962: Lonely Are the Brave. Who's Got the Action? 1963: Island of Love. Charade. 1964: Ensign Pulver. Goodbye Charlie. Fail Safe. 1965: Mirage. 1966: The Fortune Cookie (GB: Meet Whiplash Willie). 1967: A Guide for the Married Man. The Odd Couple. 1968: The Secret Life of an American Wife. Candy. 1969: Hello! Dolly. Cactus Flower. 1970: A New Leaf. 1971: Plaza Suite. Kotch. 1972: Pete 'n' Tillie. 1973: Charley Varrick. The Laughing Policeman (GB: An Investigation of Murder). 1974: †Earthquake. The Taking of Pelham 1-2-3. The Front Page. 1975: The Sunshine Boys. The Gentleman Tramp (narrator only). 1976: The Bad News Bears. 1977: Casey's Shadow. 1978: House Calls. California Suite. 1979: Funny Business (narrator only). Little Miss Marker. 1980: Hopscotch. Portrait of a 60% Perfect Man. 1981: *A Change of Heart. Buddy Buddy. First Monday in October. 1982: I Ought to be in Pictures. 1983: The Survivors. 1985: Pirates. Movers and Shakers (Dreamers). 1987: The Couch Trip. 1988: The Little Devil. 1989: The Incident (TV). 1991: JFK. Mrs Lambert Remembers Love (TV). 1993: Dennis the Menace (GB: Dennis). Grumpy Old Men. Incident in a Small Town (TV). 1994: Incident at Christmas (TV). I.Q. 1995: The Grass Harp. Grumpier Old Men. 1996: I'm Not Rappaport. 1997: Out to Sea. 1998: The Odd Couple 2: Travelin' Light/The Odd Couple 2. The Life and Times of Hank Greenberg. The Marriage Fool (TV). 1999: Love After Death (TV). 2000: Hanging Up.*

† As Walter Matuschanskayasky
‡ Also directed

MATTHEWS, Jessie 1907–1981

Dark-haired, sylph-like, big-eyed British singer and dancer with round-faced, little-girl

looks and bell-like voice. She wore sizzling costumes in her musical numbers without losing her winsome appeal and became Britain's only home-grown world star of the thirties. Missed the opportunity of Hollywood stardom in the early thirties, choosing to remain in England for the sake of a (second of three) marriage to Sonnie Hale (in 1931) that would end in 1944. Died from cancer.

*1923: The Beloved Vagabond. This England. 1924: Straws in the Wind. 1931: Out of the Blue. 1932: There Goes the Bride. The Midshipmaid (US: Midshipmaid Gob). The Man from Toronto. 1933: The Good Companions. Friday the Thirteenth. 1934: Waltzes from Vienna (Strauss's Great Waltz). Evergreen. 1935: First a Girl. 1936: It's Love Again. 1937: *Secrets of the Stars. Head over Heels (US: Head over Heels in Love). Gangway. 1938: Sailing Away. Climbing High. 1943: Forever and a Day. 1944: Candles at Nine. 1947: Life is Nothing without Music. Making the Grade. 1958: tom thumb. 1977: The Hound of the Baskervilles.*

As director: *1944: *Victory Wedding (also narrated).*

MATURE, Victor 1913–1999
Big, craggy, black-haired, open-mouthed American star, the forerunner of a new, muscular kind of leading man, who would take over from the lounge lizards of the thirties and be dubbed 'beefcake' by the Press. His Greek-type good looks were mostly seen in open-air action yarns, and he drifted away from films after passing 45. He was often capable of surprisingly subtle and sensitive performances, and generally had more acting talent than his harsher critics

allowed. Five times married. Died from cancer.

1939: The Housekeeper's Daughter. 1940: One Million BC (GB: Man and His Mate). Captain Caution. No, No, Nanette. 1941: The Shanghai Gesture. I Wake Up Screaming (GB: Hot Spot). 1942: Song of the Islands. My Gal Sal. Footlight Serenade. Seven Days' Leave. 1946: My Darling Clementine. 1947: Kiss of Death. Moss Rose. 1948: Fury at Furnace Creek. Cry of the City. 1949: Red, Hot and Blue. Easy Living. Samson and Delilah. 1950: Wabash Avenue. I'll Get By. Gambling House. Stella. 1952: The Las Vegas Story. Androcles and the Lion. Something for the Birds. Million Dollar Mermaid (GB: The One Piece Bathing Suit). 1953: The Glory Brigade. Affair with a Stranger. The Robe. Veils of Bagdad. 1954: Demetrius and the Gladiators. Betrayed. Dangerous Mission. The Egyptian. 1955: Chief Crazy Horse (GB: Valley of Fury). Violent Saturday. The Last Frontier. 1956: Zarak. Safari. The Sharkfighters. 1957: Interpol (US: Pick-Up Alley). The Long Haul. 1958: No Time to Die (US: Tank Force). China Doll. 1959: The Bandit of Zhobe. Escort West. Timbuktu. The Big Circus. 1960: Hannibal. The Tartars. 1966: After the Fox. 1968: Head. 1972: Every Little Crook and Nanny. 1975: Won Ton Ton, the Dog Who Saved Hollywood. 1979: Firepower. 1984: Samson and Delilah (TV).

MAUREY, Nicole 1925–
Auburn-haired, square-jawed French actress who had a middling career in her own country before her selection to co-star with Bing Crosby led to Hollywood. She left Paramount after a couple of films, and made most of her remaining movies in England.
1944: Le cavalier noir. 1948: Les joyeux conscrits. 1949: Blondine. 1950: Le journal d'un curé de campagne (GB and US: Diary of a Country Priest). 1951: Le dernier robin des bois (GB: Smugglers at the Castle). 1952: Opération Magali. Rendez-vous à Grenade. 1953: Les compagnes de la nuit (GB: Companions of the Night). L'ennemi public No. 1 (US: Public Enemy No. 1). L'oeil en coulisses. Little Boy Lost. Si Versailles m'était conté (GB: Versailles. US: Royal Affairs in Versailles). 1954: Secret of the Incas. L'aiglon. 1955: The Constant Husband. 1956: The Weapon. The Bold and the Brave. 1957: Rogue's Yarn. To Catch a Spy. 1958: Me and the Colonel. Paris Streetwalker. 1959: The House of the Seven Hawks. The Scapegoat. The

Jaywalkers. 1960: His and Hers. High Time. 1961: Don't Bother to Knock (US: Why Bother to Knock?). 1962: The Day of the Triffids. 1963: The Very Edge. 1965: Pleins feux sur Stanislaus. 1966: Next Time I'll Kill You. 1977: Gloria. 1981: Chanel solitaire.

MAXWELL, Lois (L. Hooker) 1927–
This durable, much-travelled, tall Canadian actress with light auburn hair and sunny features has had spells in Hollywood and Italy, but spent the majority of her film career in England. Here her pleasant personality was always welcome, if somewhat wasted in playing Miss Moneypenny in the James Bond films for 24 years.
1946: Spring Song (US: Springtime). 1948: Corridor of Mirrors. The Big Punch. That Hagen Girl. The Dark Past. The Decision of Christopher Blake. 1949: The Crime Doctor's Diary. Kazan. 1950: Amore e venene. Domani è troppo tardi (GB: Tomorrow is Too Late). 1951: The Woman's Angle. 1952: Lady in the Fog (US: Scotland Yard Inspector). Women of Twilight (US: Twilight Women). Il filo d'erba. Labra bianca. 1953: Mantrap (US: Woman in Hiding). Aida. 1954: La grande speranza (GB: Torpedo Zone. US: Submarine Attack). The Blue Camellia. 1956: Passport to Treason. The High Terrace. Satellite in the Sky. 1957: Time without Pity. Kill Me Tomorrow. 1959: Face of Fire. 1960: The Unstoppable Man. 1962: Lolita. Dr No. Come Fly with Me. 1963: The Haunting. From Russia with Love. 1964: Goldfinger. 1965: Thunderball. 1967: Operation Kid Brother. You Only Live Twice. 1969: On Her Majesty's Secret Service. 1970: The Adventurers. 1971: Diamonds Are Forever. Endless Night. 1973: Live and Let Die. 1974: The Man with the Golden Gun. 1977: Age of Innocence. The Spy Who Loved Me. 1979: Lost and Found. Moonraker. 1980: Mr Patman. 1981: For Your Eyes Only. 1983: Octopussy. 1985: A View to a Kill. 1986: The Blue Man (later Eternal Evil). 1988: Martha, Ruth and Edie. Rescue Me. 1989: Lady in a Corner (TV). 1998: Hard to Forget (TV).

MAXWELL, Marilyn
(Marvel M. Maxwell) 1921–1972
Blonde American actress and singer, usually in worldly roles. Was a dance-band vocalist at 16, but never really made her mark at M-G-M, where she was under contract for eight years, and her career faded from the early fifties. By the late sixties she was playing in burlesque doing a singing striptease. Died

from a pulmonary ailment. Three times married.

1942: *Stand By for Action!* (GB: *Cargo of Innocents*). *This is No Laughing Matter. *Tea on the Terrace. *Dreamsville, Ohio. *Havin' a Time in Havana. *Goodbye Mama. 1943: Dubarry Was a Lady. Swing Fever. Thousands Cheer. Presenting Lily Mars. Dr Gillespie's Criminal Case (GB: Crazy to Kill). Pilot No. 5. Salute to the Marines. Best Foot Forward. 1944: Three Men in White. Lost in a Harem. Music for Millions. Ziegfeld Follies (released 1946). 1945: Between Two Women. 1946: The Show-Off. 1947: Summer Holiday (released 1948). High Barbaree. 1948: Race Street. 1949: Champion. 1950: Outside the Wall. Key to the City. *Hollywood Goes to Bat. 1951: The Lemon Drop Kid. New Mexico. 1952: Off Limits (GB: Military Policemen). 1953: East of Sumatra. Paris Model. 1955: New York Confidential. 1956: Forever, Darling. Snow Shoes (TV). 1958: Rock-a-Bye Baby. 1963: Critic's Choice. Stage to Thunder Rock. 1964: The Lively Set. 1968: Arizona Bushwhackers. 1969: From Nashville with Music. The Phynx. 1970: Wild Women (TV).

Beautiful Rebel). $50,000 Reward. The Grey Vulture. 1925: The Haunted Ranch. Fighting Courage. The Demon Rider. The Range Fighter (serial: compilation of earlier films). 1926: The Unknown Cavalier. The North Star. Señor Daredevil. 1927: Overland Stage. Land Beyond the Law. The Red Raiders. Gun Gospel. Devil's Saddle. Somewhere in Sonora. 1928: The Upland Rider. Canyon of Adventure. The Glorious Trail. The Wagon Show. The Code of the Scarlet. 1929: Cheyenne. Señor Americano. California Mail. Wagon Master. *The Voice of Hollywood No. 9. The Phantom City. The Lawless Legion. The Royal Rider. 1930: Lucky Larkin. Parade of the West. Song of the Caballero. Sons of the Saddle. Fighting Thru. The Fighting Legion. Mountain Justice. 1931: The Pocatello Kid. Two Gun Man. Arizona Terror. Branded Men. Range Law. Alias – The Bad Man. 1932: False Faces (GB: What Price Beauty?). Texas Gunfighter. Whistlin' Dan. Trail Blazer (serial). Sunset Trail. Hell Fire Austin. Dynamite Ranch. 1933: Phantom Thunderbolt. Drum Taps. Strawberry Roan (GB: Flying Fury). The Lone Avenger. Between Fighting Men. Tombstone Canyon. *Hollywood on Parade B-52. Fargo Express. Come On Tarzan. King of the Arena. The Fiddlin' Buckaroo. 1934: Wheels of Destiny. In Old Santa Fé. Gun Justice. Mystery Mountain (serial). Trail Drive. Smoking Guns (GB: Doomed to Die). Honor of the Range. 1935: Lawless Riders. Western Courage. Western Frontier. Heir to Trouble. The Cattle Thief. Heroes of the Range. The Fugitive Sheriff (GB: Law and Order). Avenging Waters. 1937: Boots of Destiny. Trailing Trouble. 1938: Whirlwind Horseman. Six Shootin' Sheriff. 1939: Flaming Lead. 1940: Death Rides the Range. Phantom Rancher. Lightning Strikes Back. 1942: Road to Morocco. 1943: Wild Horse Stampede. Blazing Guns. Death Valley Rangers. The Law Rides Again. 1944: Westward Bound. Arizona Whirlwind. 1945: Blazing Frontier. Harmony Trail (GB: White Stallion). 1969: Bigfoot. 1972: Buck and the Preacher.

to Michael O'Shea (qv) from 1947 to his death in 1973. Never remarried.

1939: *Gals and Gallons. 1942: Stand by for Action! (GB: Cargo of Innocents). 1943: †Follies Girl. The Adventures of Jack London. †Sweet Rosie O'Grady. Salute to the Marines. Swing Fever. Dr Gillespie's Criminal Case (GB: Crazy to Kill). Hello, Frisco, Hello. 1944: Seven Days Ashore. †Pin-Up Girl. Tonight and Every Night. Three Men in White. Lady in the Death House. Up in Arms. The Princess and the Pirate. 1945: Wonder Man. 1946: The Best Years of Our Lives. The Kid from Brooklyn. 1947: Out of the Blue. The Secret Life of Walter Mitty. 1948: A Song is Born. Smart Girls Don't Talk. 1949: The Girl from Jones Beach. Colorado Territory. Flaxy Martin. White Heat. Always Leave Them Laughing. Red Light. 1950: Backfire. The West Point Story (GB: Fine and Dandy). The Flame and the Arrow. 1951: Along the Great Divide. Captain Horatio Hornblower RN. Starlift. Painting the Clouds with Sunshine. 1952: The Iron Mistress. She's Working Her Way Through College. *Screen Snapshots No. 206. 1953: She's Back on Broadway. South Sea Woman. Devil's Canyon. 1954: The Silver Chalice. 1955: Pearl of the South Pacific. 1956: Great Day in the Morning. Congo Crossing. The Proud Ones. 1957: The Big Land (GB: Stampeded!). The Story of Mankind. The Tall Stranger. Fort Dobbs. Execution Night (TV. GB: cinemas). 1959: Westbound. Jet over the Atlantic. 1960: Revolt of the Mercenaries. 1964: Young Fury. 1966: Castle of Evil. 1967: Fort Utah. 1969: The Haunted. 1975: Won Ton Ton, the Dog Who Saved Hollywood. Fugitive Lovers/ The Runaways. 1976: The Glass Cage. 1977: French Quarter. 1990: Evil Spirits. Midnight Witness.

†Scenes deleted from final release print

McCALLISTER, Lon
(Herbert Alonzo McCallister) 1923–
Dark-haired, earnest, rosy-cheeked, stocky American actor, in films from childhood and boyish-looking to the end of his cinema career. It seems in retrospect that McCallister was always dressed in checked shirt, grooming his horse against some Technicolor background of mountains and pines. But most of his best roles *were* in outdoor dramas and, unable to widen his range, he left show business in the fifties – a pity after working so long to gain a foothold there.

1936: Romeo and Juliet. Let's Sing Again.

MAYNARD, Ken 1895–1973
Dark, handsome, solidly-built American cowboy star of the 1920s and 1930s, a former circus rider and rodeo champion who broke into films as a stuntman and continued to do all his own feats of derring-do in and out of the saddle. Always wore an enormous white stetsons – and could carry a song as well. Died alone in his trailer home from malnutrition.

1923: The Man Who Won. *Somebody Lied. Brass Commandments. The Gunfighter. Cameo Kirby. 1924: Janice Meredith (GB: The

MAYO, Virginia (V. Jones) 1920–
Blonde American dancer and actress of cream-puff complexion who rose quickly from small parts to star roles in Technicolor extravaganzas of every kind. She always gave the impression that there was earthiness lurking beneath the surface of the demurest of her ladies fayre and kept her stardom (and her perfect figure) for a full 15 years. Married

1937: *Internes Can't Take Money* (GB: *You Can't Take Money*). *Stella Dallas. Make a Wish. Souls at Sea.* 1938: *Adventures of Tom Sawyer. Lord Jeff* (GB: *The Boy from Barnardo's*). *Little Tough Guys in Society. That Certain Age. Judge Hardy's Children.* 1939: *Babes in Arms. First Love. Spirit of Culver* (GB: *Man's Heritage*). *Angels Wash Their Faces. Confessions of a Nazi Spy.* 1940: *High School. Joe and Ethel Turp Call on the President. Susan and God* (GB: *The Gay Mrs Trexel*). 1941: †*Henry Aldrich for President.* 1942: †*That Other Woman.* †*Quiet Please Murder.* †*Over My Dead Body. Dangerously They Live. Yankee Doodle Dandy. Gentleman Jim. The Hard Way. Always in My Heart. The Meanest Man in the World.* 1943: *Stage Door Canteen.* 1944: *Winged Victory. Home in Indiana.* 1947: *The Red House. Thunder in the Valley* (GB: *Bob, Son of Battle*). 1948: *Scudda-Hoo! Scudda-Hay!* (GB: *Summer Lightning*). 1949: *The Big Cat.* 1950: *Boy from Indiana* (GB: *Blaze of Glory*). *The Story of Seabiscuit* (GB: *Pride of Kentucky*). 1951: *A Yank in Korea* (GB: *Letter from Korea*). 1952: *Montana Territory.* 1953: *Combat Squad.*

†*As Bud McCallister*

McCALLUM, David 1933–
Blond, youthful-looking, flop-haired Scottish actor in British films, mostly as tearaways and braggarts. Went to America in 1963, and scored a big hit on television as the quietly-spoken Russian agent, Illya, in *The Man from U.N.C.L.E.*, several double-episodes of which went abroad as films. He proved surprisingly colourless in later leading roles, and has only occasionally been effective since. Seen in seedier roles since the mid 1980s. Married (first of two) to Jill Ireland (*qv*) from 1957 to 1967.
1956: *Ill Met by Moonlight* (US: *Night Ambush*). 1957: *The Secret Place. Hell Drivers. Robbery Under Arms. Violent Playground.* 1958: *A Night to Remember.* 1960: *The Long and the Short and the Tall. Carolina.* 1961: *Jungle Street.* 1962: *Billy Budd. Freud* (GB: *Freud – the Secret Passion*). 1963: *The Great Escape.* 1964: *To Trap a Spy* (TV. GB: cinemas). *The Spy with My Face.* 1965: *Around the World under the Sea. The Greatest Story Ever Told. One Spy Too Many* (TV. GB: cinemas). 1966: *The Spy in the Green Hat* (TV. GB: cinemas). *Three Bites of the Apple. One of Our Spies is Missing!* (TV. GB:

cinemas). 1967: *The Karate Killers* (TV. GB: cinemas). *The Helicopter Spies* (TV. GB: cinemas). *Sol Madrid* (GB: *The Heroin Gang*). 1968: *How to Steal the World* (TV. GB: cinemas). *Mosquito Squadron.* 1969: *La cattura/The Ravine. Teacher, Teacher* (TV). 1970: *Hauser's Memory* (TV). 1971: *She Waits* (TV). 1973: *The Screaming Skull* (TV). *Frankenstein: The True Story* (TV. GB: cinemas). 1975: *The Invisible Man* (TV). *The Diamond Hunters* (US: *The Kingfisher Caper*). 1976: *Dogs.* 1978: *King Solomon's Treasure.* 1981: *The Watcher in the Woods.* 1982: *Critical List.* 1983: *The Return of the Man from U.N.C.L.E.* (TV). 1985: *Terminal Choice. OSS* (TV). 1986: *Behind Enemy Lines* (TV). 1987: *The Wind.* 1988: *Freedom Fighter* (TV). 1989: *The Return of Sam McCloud* (TV). 1990: *The Haunting of Morella.* 1991: *Fatal Inheritance. Hear My Song.* 1992: *Dirty Weekend.* 1993: *Shattered Image.* 1994: *Healer.* 1996: *Darkening.* 1997: *Death Game.* 1998: *March in Windy City* (TV). 1999: *Cherry.*

McCALLUM, John 1914–
Handsome, dark-haired Australian leading man who seemed to come to Britain at just the right time (1947), looking as he did like a cross between Stewart Granger and Michael Rennie. He met and married Googie Withers (in 1948) and eight years later returned to Australia with his wife for a long period, having used his casual charm in a variety of British films. Still acting on stage.
1935: *Heritage.* 1936: *South West Pacific. Joe Came Back.* 1946: *A Son is Born. Australia is Like This.* 1947: *Bush Christmas* (narrator only). *The Root of All Evil. The Loves of Joanna Godden. It Always Rains on Sunday.* 1948: *The Calendar. Miranda.* 1949: *A Boy, a Girl and a Bike. Traveller's Joy.* 1950: *The Woman in Question* (US: *Five Angles on Murder*). 1951: *Valley of the Eagles. The Magic Box. Lady Godiva Rides Again.* 1952: *Derby Day* (US: *Four Against Fate*). *Trent's Last Case. The Long Memory.* 1953: *Devil on Horseback. Trouble in the Glen.* 1956: *Port of Escape. Smiley.*
As director: 1956: *Three in One.* 1971: *Nickel Queen.*

McCARTHY, Andrew 1962–
Bushily brown-haired, soft-mouthed American actor of passive personality, who has mostly played shy and sensitive types. Equally at home in light comedy or heavy

drama. Says he likes portraying 'characters at the crossroads' and seemed set for a career in films that depend on dialogue rather than action to get their message across. But by the 1990s, his intriguing but undynamic personality was to be seen, often as weak-willed characters, in a mixture of leading and supporting roles.
1983: *Class.* 1984: *The Beniker Gang.* 1985: *St Elmo's Fire. Heaven Help Us* (GB: *Catholic Boys.* Originally for cable TV). 1986: *Pretty in Pink.* 1987: *Waiting for the Moon. Mannequin. Less Than Zero.* 1988: *Kansas. Fresh Horses. Hot and Cold.* 1989: *Weekend at Bernie's. Dr M* (later *Club Extinction*). 1990: *Quiet Days in Clichy.* 1991: *Year of the Gun. Tales from the Crypt* (TV). 1992: *Only You. Common Pursuit* (TV). 1993: *The Joy Luck Club. Weekend at Bernie's II. Getting In/Student Body.* 1994: *Night of the Running Man. Mrs Parker & the Vicious Circle. Dream Man.* 1995: *Dead Funny. Things I Never Told You. Mulholland Falls. The Courtyard* (cable TV). 1996: *Escape Clause. A Change of Heart* (TV). *Hostile Force. The Christmas Tree* (TV). 1997: *Stag.* 1998: *Perfect Assassins* (TV). *Bela Donna. I'm Losing You. A Father for Brittany* (TV). *I Woke Up Early the Day I Died.* 1999: *New Waterford Girl. New World Disorder. A Twist of Faith. Jump.* 2000: *A Storm in Summer.*

McCARTHY, Kevin 1914–
Big, dark-haired, good-looking (in a slightly shifty, predatory way) American actor, equally convincing as hero or villain. On stage from 1938, TV from 1949, but slow to get into his stride as a film personality. Only had a few years as a leading man, but these included *Invasion of the Body Snatchers*, from

whose aliens he was still on the run in the 1978 remake. He received an Oscar nomination for *Death of a Salesman*.
1944: *Winged Victory*. 1951: *Death of a Salesman*. 1954: *Drive a Crooked Road*. *The Gambler from Natchez*. 1955: *Stranger on Horseback*. *Annapolis Story (GB: The Blue and the Gold)*. 1956: *Nightmare*. *Invasion of the Body Snatchers*. 1957: *City in Flames (TV. GB: cinemas)*. *Diamond Safari*. 1961: *The Misfits*. 1962: *40 Pounds of Trouble*. 1963: *A Gathering of Eagles*. *The Prize*. 1964: *The Best Man*. *An Affair of the Skin*. 1965: *Mirage*. 1966: *Hotel*. *The Three Sisters*. *A Big Hand for the Little Lady (GB: Big Deal at Dodge City)*. 1968: *The Hell with Heroes*. *If He Hollers, Let Him Go! Shadow on the Land (TV)*. *I quattro dell'Ave Maria (GB: Revenge in El Paso)*. 1969: *Operation Heartbeat (TV)*. *Ace High*. 1972: *Richard*. *Kansas City Bomber*. *A Great American Tragedy (TV. GB: Man at the Crossroads)*. 1973: *Alien Thunder (later Dan Candy's Law)*. *El Clan de los Inmorales/Order to Kill*. 1976: *Buffalo Bill and the Indians*. 1977: *Mary Jane Harper Cried Last Night (TV)*. *Exo-Man (TV)*. 1978: *Invasion of the Body Snatchers (remake)*. *Piranha*. 1979: *Hero at Large*. 1980: *The Howling*. *These Lips, Those Eyes*. *Portrait of an Escort (TV)*. *Flamingo Road (TV)*. 1982: *Rosie: The Rosemary Clooney Story (TV)*. *My Tutor*. 1983: *The Twilight Zone (GB: Twilight Zone The Movie)*. *The Making of a Male Model (TV)*. 1984: *Invitation to Hell (TV)*. *The Ratings Game (TV)*. 1985: *The Midnight Hour (TV)*. 1986: *Hostage*. *A Masterpiece of Murder (TV)*. 1987: *Dark Tower*. *InnerSpace*. *LBJ: The Early Years (TV)*. *Poor Little Rich Girl (TV)*. *Love or Money (released 1990)*. *Hostage*. *The Long Journey Home (TV)*. *Once Upon a Texas Train (TV)*. 1988: *In the Heat of the Night (TV)*. *The Sleeping Car*. 1989: *UHF*. 1990: *Eve of Destruction*. 1991: *Ghoulies Go to College/Ghoulies III*. *Final Approach*. *Dead on the Money (TV)*. *Fast Food*. 1992: *Duplicates (cable TV)*. *The Distinguished Gentleman*. 1993: *Matinee*. 1995: *Just Cause*. *Steal Big, Steal Little*. 1996: *The Strange Case of Jekyll & Hyde*. 1997: *The Second Civil War (TV)*. *Elvis Meets Nixon (TV)*. 1998: *Addams Family Reunion (video)*.

McCLURE, Doug 1934–1995
Muscular, fair-haired, blue-eyed American star of action films, equally familiar on TV where he appeared in several successful series, notably the long-running *The*

Virginian. He alleged that his drinking habits got him known as 'Dean Martin on horseback' and was five times married, four divorced. 'My wives were good house-keepers,' he admitted. 'They all kept the house.' Second of them was actress Barbara Luna (1937–). In later years McClure played smaller roles. He died from lung cancer. Father of actress Tane McClure.
1957: *The Enemy Below*. 1958: *South Pacific*. 1959: *Gidget*. *The Unforgiven*. 1960: *Because They're Young*. 1962: *The Brazen Bell (TV. GB: cinemas)*. 1964: *The Lively Set*. 1965: *Shenandoah*. 1966: *Beau Geste*. *The Longest Hundred Miles (TV)*. 1967: *The King's Pirate*. *Nobody's Perfect*. 1968: *Backtrack (TV)*. 1971: *Terror in the Sky (TV)*. *The Birdmen (TV. GB: cinemas as Escape of the Birdmen)*. *The Death of Me Yet (TV)*. *Death Race (TV)*. 1972: *The Judge and Jake Wyler (TV)*. *Playmates (TV)*. 1973: *Shirts/Skins (TV)*. *Die blutigen Geier von Alaska (GB: TV, as The Hellhounds of Alaska)*. 1974: *Adventure in Ventana (narrator only)*. *What Changed Charley Farthing?* 1975: *Satan's Triangle (TV)*. *The Land That Time Forgot*. 1976: *At the Earth's Core*. 1977: *SST Disaster in the Sky/SST Death Flight (TV)*. *The People That Time Forgot*. 1978: *Wild and Wooly (TV)*. *Warlords of Atlantis*. 1980: *Humanoids from the Deep (GB: Monster)*. *The Firebird*. *Nightside (TV)*. 1982: *The House Where Evil Dwells*. 1983: *Cannonball Run II*. 1985: *Half Nelson (TV)*. 1986: *52 Pick-Up*. 1987: *The Omega Syndrome*. *Tapeheads*. 1988: *Dark Before Dawn*. *Prime Suspect*. 1991: *The Gambler Returns: The Luck of the Draw (TV)*. 1994: *Maverick*. 1995: *Slaughter's Gold*. *Riders in the Storm*.

McCONAUGHEY, Matthew 1969–
Quite tall, fair-haired, strikingly blue-eyed American actor with easy grin. Born in Texas, McConaughey has often played men from his birth place or thereabouts since making his debut while still studying film at the University of Texas. The lean, languid and laid-back McConaughey also directed a short film while at university and has plans to do more work behind the camera.
1993: *Dazed and Confused*. *My Boyfriend's Back*. 1994: *Angels in the Outfield (GB: Angels)*. *Return of the Texas Chainsaw Massacre*. 1995: *Boys on the Side*. *Lone Star*. *Judgment/Judgement*. **Submission*. 1996: *Scorpion Spring*. *A Time to Kill*. *Making Sandwiches*. *Larger Than Life*. *Glory Daze*. 1997: *Contact*. *Amistad*. *Texas Chainsaw*

Massacre: The Next Generation (revised version of 1994 film). 1998: *The Newton Boys*. †*The Rebel. 1999: *Ed TV*. 2000: *U-571*. *The Wedding Planner*.

†*And directed*

McCORMACK, Catherine 1972–
Tall, ladylike British actress of Scottish ancestry, with dark, curly hair and determined chin. Often seen as brainy, sensible types, she came to the attention of casting directors straight from drama school and almost immediately made an impact as Mel Gibson's doomed wife in *Braveheart*. Since then she has given feisty performances in a mixture of contemporary and period roles.
1994: *Loaded/Bloody Weekend*. 1995: *The North Star/Tashunga*. *Braveheart*. 1997: *The Land Girls*. *Fathers Day*. 1998: *The Honest Courtesan (US: Dangerous Beauty)*. *Dancing at Lughnasa*. 1999: *This Year's Love*. *The Debtors*. 2000: *Shadow of the Vampire*. *Another Life*. *A Rumor of Angels*. *The Weight of Water*. *Burned to Light*. *Born Romantic*. *The Tailor of Panama*.

McCREA, Joel 1905–1990
Tight-lipped but benign, square-faced and snub-nosed, Joel McCrea was nobody's idea of the all-American boy, but his warmth and cheerful personality radiated from the screen, and he was surprisingly good at light or even zany romantic comedy. After World War II he pursued a grimmer course as an upright western star before retiring to his ranch in the sixties. Married to Frances Dee (*qv*) from 1933. Died from pneumonia.
1927: *The Fair Co-Ed (GB: The Varsity*

Girl). 1928: Freedom of the Press. The Enemy. The Jazz Age. 1929: So This is College. The Five O'Clock Girl. The Single Standard. Dynamite. 1930: The Silver Horde. Lightnin'. Once a Sinner. 1931: Born to Love. Kept Husbands. Girls about Town. 1932: Business and Pleasure. Bird of Paradise. The Lost Squadron. The Sport Parade. The Most Dangerous Game (GB: The Hounds of Zaroff). 1933: The Silver Cord. One Man's Journey. Bed of Roses. Chance at Heaven. Scarlet River. 1934: Half a Sinner. Gambling Lady. The Richest Girl in the World. 1935: Splendor. Barbary Coast. Woman Wanted. 1936: Adventure in Manhattan (GB: Manhattan Madness). Come and Get It. Banjo on My Knee. These Three. Two in a Crowd. 1937: Internes Can't Take Money (GB: You Can't Take Money). Woman Chases Man. Wells Fargo. Dead End. 1938: Three Blind Mice. Youth Takes a Fling. 1939: They Shall Have Music (GB: Melody of Youth). He Married His Wife. Espionage Agent. Union Pacific. 1940: The Primrose Path. Foreign Correspondent. 1941: Reaching for the Sun. Sullivan's Travels. 1942: The Palm Beach Story. The Great Man's Lady. 1943: The More the Merrier. *Stars on Horseback. 1944: The Great Moment. Buffalo Bill. 1945: The Unseen. 1946: The Virginian. 1947: Ramrod. Four Faces West (GB: They Passed This Way). 1949: Colorado Territory. South of St Louis. 1950: Saddle Tramp. The Outriders. Stars in My Crown. 1951: The Hollywood Story. Cattle Drive. 1952: The San Francisco Story. 1953: Lone Hand. Rough Shoot (US: Shoot First). 1954: Border River. Black Horse Canyon. 1955: Wichita. Stranger on Horseback. 1956: The First Texan. 1957: The Oklahoman. Trooper Hook. Gunsight Ridge. The Tall Stranger. 1958: Fort Massacre. Cattle Empire. 1959: The Gunfight at Dodge City. 1961: Ride the High Country (GB: Guns in the Afternoon). 1967: Winchester '73 (TV. Narrator only). 1971: Cry Blood, Apache. 1974: The Great American Cowboy (narrator only). 1976: Mustang Country. 1990: Preston Sturges: The Rise and Fall of an American Dreamer.

McDERMOTT, Dylan
(Mark McDermott) 1961–
Tall, dark, slightly arrogant-looking American actor of great personal charm, who bears a vague resemblance to Richard Gere (qv). The stepson of playwright Eve Ensler (qv), he received much of his own stage tuition from Joanne Woodward (qv), who directed him in several

plays, before branching out into films at 26. Here he mixed leading roles in less popular films with supporting parts in such big mainstream hits as Steel Magnolias and In the Line of Fire. Has also shown up well as dangerous villains.
1987: Hamburger Hill. 1988: The Blue Iguana. 1989: Steel Magnolias. Twister. The Neon Empire (TV). 1990: Hardware. 1991: Where Sleeping Dogs Lie (released 1994). Into the Badlands (TV). 1992: The Fear Inside. Jersey Girl. 1993: In the Line of Fire. 1994: The Cowboy Way. Miracle on 34th Street. 1995: Destiny Turns on the Radio. Home for the Holidays. 1996: 'Til There Was You. 1999: Three to Tango. 2000: Texas Rangers.

McDERMOTT, Hugh 1906–1972
Husky, cheerful-looking Scottish-born actor with ruddy complexion and dark hair. In British films from the mid-1930s, often as Americans, he had his best role as one of Ann Todd's beaux in The Seventh Veil. His career varied from leading parts in minor thrillers to featured or small roles in major films. Later made movies abroad.
1936: David Livingstone. The Captain's Table. Well Done, Henry. 1937: The Wife of General Ling. The Divorce of Lady X. 1938: Hey! Hey! USA. 1939: The Saint in London. Where's That Fire? 1940: Neutral Port. For Freedom. Spring Meeting. 1941: Pimpernel Smith (US: Mister V). 1942: The Young Mr Pitt. 1945: The Seventh Veil. 1946: This Man is Mine. 1948: Good Time Girl. No Orchids for Miss Blandish. 1949: The Huggetts Abroad. 1950: Lilli Marlene. 1951: Two on the Tiles. Four Days. 1952: Trent's Last Case. 1953: The Wedding of Lilli Marlene. The Love Lottery. 1954: Night People. Malaga (US: Fire over Africa). Johnny on the Spot. Devil Girl from Mars. 1955: As Long as They're Happy. 1956: You Pay Your Money. 1957: A King in New York. 1958: The Man Who Wouldn't Talk. 1964: First Men in the Moon. 1966: Bindle (One of Them Days). Delayed Flight. 1968: The Games. The File of the Golden Goose. 1969: Guns in the Heather. The Adding Machine. 1970: Lawman. 1971: Chato's Land. Captain Apache.

McDONNELL, Mary 1952–
Clean, fresh-looking, calm-seeming, dark-haired American actress, whose girlish good looks stood her in good stead when she began a belated film and TV career. Entirely a stage actress until she was in her thirties,

McDonnell sprang to prominence at 38 with an Academy Award nomination as the white woman raised by American Indians in Dances with Wolves. She was an Oscar nominee again for Passion Fish two years later and has enjoyed an interesting range of leading roles without becoming a name to which the general public could add the face.
1982: Money on the Side (TV). 1984: Garbo Talks! 1986: Courage (TV). 1987: Matewan. 1988: Tiger Warsaw. 1990: Dances with Wolves. 1991: O Pioneers! (TV). Grand Canyon. 1992: Passion Fish. Sneakers. 1993: Blue Chips. The American Clock (TV). 1995: A Woman Undone (TV). 1996: Independence Day. Mariette in Ecstasy. 1997: 12 Angry Men (TV). Two Voices (TV). Spanish Fly (voice only). 1998: You Can Thank Me Later. Evidence of Blood (TV). 1999: Mumford. Replacing Dad (TV). Behind the Mask (TV).

McDOWALL, Roddy
(Andrew Roderick McDowall) 1928–1998
Clever and resourceful light-haired British born child actor, in Hollywood from 1940, and popular as the star of boy-and-animal films. Proved ineffectual as a young adult star but after ten years learning his craft in the theatre came back as an astringent and interesting character actor who frequently stole scenes from those billed above him. Won great personal popularity as star of the Apes films. Also a photographer. Died from cancer.
1938: Murder in the Family. Scruffy. Hey! Hey! USA! I See Ice. Convict 99. Yellow Sands. John Halifax, Gentleman. 1939: Just William. Dead Man's Shoes. Poison Pen. Murder Will Out. His Brother's Keeper. The Outsider. 1940: You Will Remember. Saloon

Bar. 1941: This England. Man Hunt. How Green Was My Valley. Confirm or Deny. 1942: The Pied Piper. Son of Fury. On the Sunny Side. 1943: My Friend Flicka. Lassie Come Home. 1944: The Keys of the Kingdom. The White Cliffs of Dover. 1945: Thunderhead, Son of Flicka. Hangover Square (voice only). Molly and Me. 1946: Holiday in Mexico. 1948: Macbeth. Rocky. Kidnapped. 1949: Tuna Clipper. Black Midnight. 1950: Killer Shark. Big Timber. Everybody's Dancin'. 1951: Hill Number One. 1952: The Steel Fist. 1958: Heart of Darkness (TV). 1960: The Subterraneans. Midnight Lace. 1961: The Power and the Glory. (TV. GB: cinemas). 1962: The Longest Day. 1963: Cleopatra. 1964: Shock Treatment. 1965: The Adventures of Bullwhip Griffin. The Greatest Story Ever Told. The Third Day. That Darn Cat! The Loved One. Inside Daisy Clover. Is Paris Burning? 1966: The Defector. Lord Love a Duck. It (US: Return of the Golem). 1967: The Cool Ones. Planet of the Apes. 1968: The Fatal Mistake (TV). Five Card Stud. Hello Down There. 1969: Night Gallery (TV). Midas Run (GB: A Run on Gold). Angel, Angel, Down We Go (US: Cult of the Damned). 1971: Escape from the Planet of the Apes. Terror in the Sky (TV). A Taste of Evil (TV). Corky. Bedknobs and Broosticks. Pretty Maids All in a Row. 1972: The Poseidon Adventure. The Life and Times of Judge Roy Bean. Conquest of the Planet of the Apes. What's a Nice Girl Like You . . .? (TV). 1973: Battle for the Planet of the Apes. Arnold. The Legend of Hell House. 1974: Dirty Mary, Crazy Larry. The Elevator (TV). Miracle on 34th Street (TV). 1975: Funny Lady. Mean Johnny Barrows. Embryo. 1976: Flood! (TV. GB: cinemas). 1977: Sixth and Main. Laser Blast. Circle of Iron/The Silent Flute. 1978: Rabbit Test. The Cat from Outer Space. 1979: The Thief of Bagdad. The Martian Chronicles (TV). Hart to Hart (TV). Nutcracker Fantasy (voice only). Scavenger Hunt. 1980: Charlie Chan and the Curse of the Dragon Queen. The Memory of Eva Ryker (TV). 1981: Kiss of Gold. The Million Dollar Face (TV). Evil Under the Sun (TV). 1982: Class of 1984. Mae West (TV). 1983: The Zany Adventures of Robin Hood (TV). This Girl for Hire (TV). 1985: Deceptions (TV). Fright Night. 1986: GoBots: Battle of the Rock Lords (voice only). Dead of Winter. 1987: The Wind in the Willows (TV. Voice only). Shadow of Death. The Edison Effect. Overboard. 1988: Fright Night Part 2. Carmilla (TV). 1990: Shakma. Dive (later Going Under). 1991: The Color of Evening. Prodigy. Only the Lonely. Under the Gun. Earth Angel (TV). Deadly Game (TV). The Naked Target. 1992: Double Trouble. Sidney Sheldon's The Sands of Time (TV). The Magical World of Chuck Jones. 1993: Home is Where the Hart is (TV). 1994: Fatally Yours. Heads (TV). Of Unknown Origin (GB: Alien Within). 1995: Last Summer in the Hamptons. The Grass Harp. It's My Party. 1996: Dead Man's Island (TV). Unlikely Angel (TV). 1997: Rudyard Kipling's The Second Jungle Book: Mowgli and Baloo. Loss of Faith (TV). Something to Believe In. 1998: A Bug's Life (voice only). 1999: Keepers of the Frame (doc).

As director: 1971: Tam Lin.

McDOWELL, Malcolm
(M. Taylor) 1943–

Slightly-built British actor whose thoughtful features adapted just as easily to cocky grin or worried frown. Starred in a number of controversial commercial successes in his twenties and became a hot property. But the films that followed were too few and did not prove box-office, with his own interpretations sometimes seeming wilfully eccentric. Also, like his contemporary David Hemmings (qv), he aged quite quickly. Married/divorced (2nd) Mary Steenburgen (qv). Has worked non-stop in recent times, often in extravagant roles.

1967: † Poor Cow. 1968: If . . . 1970: Figures in a Landscape. The Raging Moon (US: Long Ago Tomorrow). 1971: A Clockwork Orange. 1973: O Lucky Man! 1975: Royal Flash. 1976: Aces High. Voyage of the Damned. 1977: Caligula (released 1979). 1978: She Fell among Thieves (TV). The Passage. 1979: Time After Time. *Tigers Are Better Looking. 1982: Cat People. Britannia Hospital. Blue Thunder. 1983: Flip Out. Arthur the King (TV. Released 1985). Cross Creek. Get Crazy. 1985: Gulag. 1986: Monte Carlo (TV). 1987: The Caller. Buy and Cell. 1988: Sunset. 1989: Mortacci/ The Hateful Dead. Class of 1999. Musical May. Moon 44. The Maestro. 1990: Schweitzer/The Light in the Jungle. Snake Eyes. Jezebel's Kiss. Happily Ever After (voice only). Disturbed. 1991: The Assassin of the Tsar. 1992: Chain of Desire. The Player. Vent d'est. Night Train to Venice. 1993: Bopha! Le musher. Out of Darkness. 1994: Milk Money. Fatal Pursuit. Star Trek Generations. Dangerous Indiscretion/ Power Play. Seasons of the Heart (TV). Wing Commander III: The Heart of the Tiger. 1995: Exquisite Tenderness. Tank Girl. Fist of the North Star. Kids of the Round Table. The Man Who Wouldn't Die (TV). Yesterday's Target (cable TV). Little Riders (TV). 1996: Hysteria. Amanda's Game. Deadly Wake. Where Truth Lies. Asylum. 1997: Hugo Pool. Mr Magoo. The Fairy King of Ar. 1998: The Gardener. My Life So Far (released 2000). The First 9½ Weeks. Southern Cross. Wing Commander. Y-2-K. Beings. 1999: St Patrick the Irish Legend (TV). 2000: Gangster No. 1. The David Cassidy Story (TV). The Visitors.

†Scenes deleted from final release print

McELHONE, Natascha (N. Taylor) 1971–
Narrow-faced star actress with brown curly hair and wide, expressive mouth. Although

she's mainly played Irish girls on screen, she is in fact English, and has worked alternately in Britain and Hollywood. She showed her developing all-round talent by singing and dancing in Love's Labour's Lost.

1994: A Breed of Heroes. 1996: Surviving Picasso. 1997: Mrs Dalloway. The Devil's Own. The Truman Show. 1998: Ronin. What Rats Won't Do. 1999: Love's Labour's Lost.

McGAVIN, Darren 1922–
Fair-haired American actor in tough-guy roles, adept at dog-eared heroes, slightly corrupt policemen and the occasional smiling villain. Has always shown a preference for theatre and television over films. As early as 1951 was starring in a TV series called Crime Photographer, the type of role that foreshadowed many of his later assignments. Became as familiar on TV in leading roles in his late forties and early fifties as did Gene Hackman (qv) in films.

1945: A Song to Remember. Kiss and Tell. She Wouldn't Say Yes. Counter-Attack (GB: One against Seven). 1946: Fear. 1951: Queen for a Day. 1955: Summer Madness (US: Summertime). The Court Martial of Billy Mitchell (GB: One Man Mutiny). The Man with the Golden Arm. 1957: Beau James. The Delicate Delinquent. 1958: The Case against Brooklyn. 1964: Bullet for a Badman. 1965: The Great Sioux Massacre. Ride the High Wind. 1967: The Outsider (TV). 1968: The Challengers (TV. GB: cinemas). Mission Mars. 1969: Anatomy of a Crime. 1970: The Challenge (TV). Mrs Pollifax – Spy. Berlin Affair (TV). Battle at Gannon's Bridge (TV). Tribes (TV. GB: cinemas as The Soldier Who Declared Peace). The 48 Hour Mile (TV). 1971: The Birdmen (TV. GB: cinemas as Escape of the

Birdmen). Banyon (TV). The Death of Me Yet (TV). The Night Stalker (TV). Say Goodbye, Maggie Cole (TV). The Night Strangler (TV). High Flying Spy (TV). 1973: Smash-Up Alley (TV). 'B' Must Die. †Happy Mother's Day . . . Love George/Run, Stranger, Run. The Petty Story (TV). 1976: No Deposit, No Return. Law and Order (TV). Brink's: the Great Robbery (TV). 1977: Airport 77. 1978: Zero to Sixty. The Users (TV). Donovan's Kid (TV). Hot Lead and Cold Feet. 1979: The Martian Chronicles (TV). Love for Rent (TV). 1980: Waikiki (TV). Hangar 18. 1981: The Firebird. 1983: A Christmas Story. 1984: The Natural. The Return of Marcus Welby MD (TV). The Baron and the Kid (TV). Turk 182! 1985: My Wicked, Wicked Ways: The Legend of Errol Flynn (TV). 1986: Raw Deal. 1987: From the Hip. 1988: Dead Heat. Inherit the Wind (TV). The Diamond Trap (TV). 1989: Captain America. 1990: By Dawn's Early Light (cable TV). Grand Tour: Disaster in Time (cable TV). GB: Timescape). 1991: Blood and Concrete. Clara (TV). Perfect Harmony (TV). 1993: The American Clock (TV). 1995: Billy Madison. Fudge-a-Mania (TV). 1996: Perfect Crimes. Waiting for the Man/Small Time.

†Also directed

McGILLIS, Kelly 1957–
Light-haired, glowingly-attractive, solidly built American actress who jostles with Geena Davis, Mariel Hemingway and Sigourney Weaver among Hollywood's tallest female stars, at 5 feet 11 inches. A doctor's daughter who won an acting award at 15, she made a hesitant start in films, but rose to the top very quickly after her role as the Amish widow in *Witness*. Her career went off the rails again in the 1990s, although she was also busy raising two daughters from her second marriage.
1982: Reuben, Reuben. 1984: Witness. Sweet Revenge (TV). 1985: Private Sessions (TV). 1986: Top Gun. 1987: Once We Were Dreamers. Made in Heaven. 1988: Winter People. The House on Carroll Street. The Accused. Cat Chaser. 1991: Grand Isle. 1992: The Babe. 1993: Bonds of Love (TV). Bitter Blood (TV). 1994: North. Out of Ireland (voice only). 1995: Remember Me (TV). 1996: We The Jury (TV). Prairie Doves. 1997: Painted Angels. 1998: At First Sight. Storm Chasers/Stormchasers: Revenge of the Twister (TV). The Settlement. When the

Bough Breaks 2: Perfect Prey (TV). 1999: Morgan's Ferry. Ground Control. 2000: The Monkey's Mask.

McGOOHAN, Patrick 1928–
American-born, light-haired leading man with cynical smile, laughing eyes and soft, transatlantic voice. Played some interesting roles in the British cinema from 1955 to 1963, often as sadistic villains in the early James Mason mould. Later career engulfed by two TV series, *Danger Man* and *The Prisoner*, the latter a commercial flop but great cult success. Later appeared in, and sometimes directed, 'Columbo' TV films for his close friend Peter Falk.
1954: The Dam Busters. 1955: Passage Home. The Dark Avenger (US: The Warriors). I Am a Camera. 1956: Zarak. 1957: High Tide at Noon. Hell Drivers. The Gypsy and the Gentleman. 1958: Nor the Moon by Night (US: Elephant Gun). 1961: Two Living, One Dead. 1962: Life for Ruth (US: Walk in the Shadow). All Night Long. The Quare Fellow. 1963: Dr Syn – Alias the Scarecrow (US: TV, as The Scarecrow of Romney Marsh). The Three Lives of Thomasina. 1968: Ice Station Zebra. 1970: The Moonshine War. 1971: Mary, Queen of Scots. 1974: Columbo: By Dawn's Early Light (TV). 1975: The Genius/Un genio, due campari e un pollo. Columbo: Identity Crisis (TV). Porgi d'altra guancia/Nobody's the Greatest. 1976: Silver Streak. The Man in the Iron Mask (TV). 1978: Brass Target. 1979: The Hard Way (TV). Escape from Alcatraz. 1980: Scanners. 1981: Kings and Desperate Men. 1983: Jamaica Inn (TV). Finding Katie. 1984: Baby/Baby . . . Secret of the Lost Legend. 1985: Three Sovereigns for Sarah (TV). 1986: Of Pure Blood (TV). 1987: Trespassers. 1990: Columbo: Agenda for Murder (TV). 1992: The Best of Friends (TV). 1995: Braveheart. 1996: A Time to Kill. The Phantom. Hysteria. 1998: Columbo: Ashes to Ashes (TV).

As director: 1973: Catch My Soul. 1975: Columbo: Identity Crisis (TV). 1976: Columbo: Last Salute to the Commodore (TV). 1990: Columbo: Agenda for Murder (TV). 1998: Columbo: Ashes to Ashes (TV). 2000: Columbo: Murder with Too Many Notes (TV).

McGOVERN, Elizabeth 1961–
Chirpy, round-faced American actress, usually with dark, cropped hair and bright lipstick that enhances her twinkling smile. A

major find of the early 1980s after a striking debut at 19, she has proved not quite forceful enough to become a big star. On the tall side, she has been described by one of her directors as 'talented, intelligent, committed and complex' – attributes that should keep her busy even if she's not become a box-office power. She now lives in England and works mainly on stage.
1980: Ordinary People. Heaven's Gate. 1981: Ragtime. 1983: Lovesick. Once Upon a Time in America. 1984: Racing with the Moon. 1986: Native Son. 1987: The Bedroom Window. 1988: She's Having a Baby. 1989: Johnny Handsome. 1990: A Shock to the System. The Handmaid's Tale. Aunt Julia and the Scriptwriter (Tune In Tomorrow). Women & Men: Stories of Seduction (TV). 1991: The Favor (released 1994). 1992: Tales from Hollywood (TV). Me and Veronica. 1993: King of the Hill. 1994: The Changeling (TV). 1995: Wings of Courage. Broken Trust (TV). 1996: The Summer of Ben Tyler (TV). Broken Glass (TV). 1997: The Wings of the Dove. Clover (TV). 1998: The Misadventures of Margaret. The Man with Rain in His Shoes. 1999: Manila. 2000: The House of Mirth.

McGRAW, Charles 1914–1980
Hefty, light-haired American actor with rough-hewn, aggressive features and steely blue eyes. Two first-rate portrayals as leading man in a couple of good low-budget thrillers, *Road Block* and *The Narrow Margin*, surprisingly failed to clinch film stardom, and he moved into television, where he was constantly busy from 1955 to 1973. Later played a variety of tough veterans. Bled to death after falling through a glass shower door.
1938: Angels with Dirty Faces. 1942: The

Undying Monster/The Hammond Mystery. The Moon is Down. 1943: They Came to Blow Up America. The Mad Ghoul. Corvette K-225 (GB: The Nelson Touch). Destroyer. 1944: The Imposter. 1946: The Killers. The Big Fix. 1947: The Long Night. Brute Force. The Farmer's Daughter. The Gangster. Roses Are Red. T-Men. On the Old Spanish Trail. 1948: Hazard. The Hunted. Blood on the Moon. Berlin Express. 1949: Reign of Terror/The Black Book. Border Incident. Once More, My Darling. The Story of Molly X. Side Street. Ma and Pa Kettle Go to Town (GB: Going to Town). 1950: Armored Car Robbery. Double Crossbones. 1951: His Kind of Woman. Road Block. 1952: The Narrow Margin. One Minute to Zero. 1953: Thunder over the Plains. Loophole. War Paint. 1954: The Bridges at Toko-Ri. 1956: Away All Boats. Toward the Unknown (GB: Brink of Hell). The Cruel Tower. Hand of Fate (TV. GB: cinemas). 1957: Joe Dakota. Joe Butterfly. Slaughter on 10th Avenue. 1958: Saddle the Wind. The Defiant Ones. Twilight for the Gods. 1959: The Man in the Net. The Wonderful Country. 1960: Spartacus. Cimarron. 1962: The Horizontal Lieutenant. 1963: It's a Mad, Mad, Mad, Mad World. The Birds. 1965: Nightmare in Chicago. The Busy Body. 1967: Hang 'em High. In Cold Blood. 1968: Pendulum. 1969: Perilous Voyage (TV). Tell Them Willie Boy is Here. 1971: Operation Cobra (TV). Johnny Got His Gun. The Devil and Miss Sarah (TV). The Night Stalker (TV). Chandler. 1972: The Longest Night (TV). 1973: Money to Burn (TV). Death and the Maiden (TV). 1974: A Boy and His Dog. 1975: The Killer Inside Me. 1976: Perilous Voyage (TV). 1977: Twilight's Last Gleaming.

McGREGOR, Ewan 1971–

Jaunty, brown-haired Scottish actor who became British films' star attraction in the second half of the 1990s, a period of success capped by his involvement in the second trilogy of 'Star Wars' films. When his popularity soared following *Shallow Grave* and, particularly, *Trainspotting* (in which he played the toilet-swimming junkie Renton), McGregor became phenomenally busy and, even if the hits (*Brassed Off, Little Voice*) were somewhat outweighed by the misses, his personal profile and popularity remained high. Nephew of actor Denis Lawson.

*1984: A Passage to India (as extra). 1993: Being Human. 1994: Shallow Grave. 1995: Blue Juice. Trainspotting. 1996: The Pillow Book. Brassed Off. Emma. 1997: A Life Less Ordinary. Serpent's Kiss. 1998: *Desserts. Nightwatch. Velvet Goldmine. Little Voice. Rogue Trader. 1999: *Tabula Rasa. Star Wars: Episode 1 – The Phantom Menace. Eye of the Beholder. 2000: Nora. Moulin Rouge. South from Hell's Kitchen. *Anno Domini.*

As co-director: 1999: Tube Tales (TV).

McGUIRE, Dorothy 1916–

Light-haired (she described it as 'burnt blonde') pretty, appealing American actress, mostly in gentle, often downtrodden roles and skilful at manipulating her audience's emotions. Made fewer films as a star than most people think, and moved too swiftly (in 1956) into 'mother' roles, her film career lasting only a few more years. Mother of actress Topo Swope. Nominated for an Academy Award in *Gentleman's Agreement*.

*1943: Claudia. 1944: *Reward Unlimited. A Tree Grows in Brooklyn. 1945: The Enchanted Cottage. The Spiral Staircase. 1946: Claudia and David. Till the End of Time. 1947: Gentleman's Agreement. 1950: Mother Didn't Tell Me. Mister 880. 1951: Callaway Went Thataway (GB: The Star Said No). I Want You. Invitation. 1954: Make Haste to Live. Three Coins in the Fountain. 1955: Trial. 1956: Friendly Persuasion. 1957: Old Yeller. 1959: This Earth is Mine. The Remarkable Mr Pennypacker. A Summer Place. 1960: The Dark at the Top of the Stairs. Swiss Family Robinson. 1961: Susan Slade. 1962: Summer Magic. 1965: The Greatest Story Ever Told. 1971: Flight of the Doves. She Waits (TV). 1973: Jonathan Livingstone Seagull (voice only). 1975: The Runaways (TV). 1978: Little Women (TV). 1979: The Incredible Journey of Dr Meg Laurel (TV). 1983: Ghost Dancing (TV). 1985: Amos (TV). Between the Darkness and the Dawn (TV). 1986: American Geisha (TV). 1987: I Never Sang for My Father (TV). 1990: Caroline? (TV). The Last Best Year (TV).*

McKELLEN, Sir Ian 1935–

Lean-faced British actor with light brown hair, at his best with eccentric or ascetic central roles. A Shakespearian *par excellence*, he made an umpromising start in films and returned to the stage, where he built up an impressive body of work, leading to a knighthood in 1989. As for the impressive resurgence of his movie stardom in late middle age, he has said: 'I deliberately set out

to fashion a film career for myself in the 1990s when I felt I was ready at last to act for the camera.' This successful strategy culminated in an Oscar nomination for *Gods and Monsters*.

1967: The Bells of Hell Go Ting-a-Ling-a-Ling (unfinished). 1969: Alfred the Great. A Touch of Love (US: Thank You All Very Much). The Promise. 1981: Priest of Love. 1982: The Scarlet Pimpernel (TV). 1983: The Keep. Loving Walter (TV). 1984: Walter and June (TV). 1985: Plenty. 1986: Zina. 1988: Windmills of the Gods (TV). 1989: Scandal. 1993: 6 Degrees of Separation. And the Band Played On (TV/cinemas). The Ballad of Little Jo. Last Action Hero. 1994: The Shadow. I'll Do Anything. 1995: Restoration. Thin Ice. Cold Comfort Farm (TV and later cinemas). Jack & Sarah. 1996: Richard III. Bent. Rasputin (TV). 1997: Amy Foster/Swept from the Sea: The Story of Amy Foster. A Bit of Scarlet (narrator only). Apt Pupil. 1998: Gods and Monsters. 2000: X-Men. 2001: The Lord of the Rings: The Fellowship of the Ring.

McKENNA, Virginia 1931–

English-rose type blonde British beauty with super complexion. She had a short but showy star career in British films of the fifties and belied her delicate looks by playing a couple of gutsy war heroines with great spirit and depth of emotion. Married to Denholm Elliott (1954–1956) and Bill Travers (1957 to his death in 1994): her subservience to her husband's career was admirable but something of a loss to the British cinema.

1952: Father's Doing Fine. The Second Mrs Tanqueray. The Oracle (US: The Horse's Mouth). 1953: The Cruel Sea. 1954: Simba. 1955: The Ship That Died of Shame (US: PT

Raiders). 1956: A Town Like Alice (US: The Rape of Malaya). 1957: The Barretts of Wimpole Street. The Smallest Show on Earth (US: Big Time Operators). 1958: Passionate Summer. Carve Her Name with Pride. 1959: The Wreck of the Mary Deare. 1961: Two Living One Dead. 1965: Born Free. 1967: The Lions are Free (TV). 1969: An Elephant Called Slowly. Ring of Bright Water. 1970: Waterloo. 1971: The Lion at World's End (US: Christian the Lion). 1974: Swallows and Amazons. 1976: Beauty and the Beast. 1977: Holocaust 2000 (US: The Chosen). 1978: The Disappearance. 1982: Blood Link. 1990: Duel of Hearts (TV). *Lady in Waiting. 1993: Staggered. 1997: Sliding Doors.

McLAGLEN, Victor 1883–1959

A British-born Wallace Beery. A great cheerful hulk of a man with tousled hair, McLaglen was a soldier, farmer, prospector, boxer (his battered features testified to that) and vaudeville performer before coming to the British cinema and quickly becoming popular by riding roughshod through action roles. Went to Hollywood in 1925, winning an Academy Award ten years later in The Informer but being largely used as aggressive, Irish-biased comedy relief. Also received an Oscar nomination for The Quiet Man. Died from a heart attack.

1920: The Call of the Road. 1921: Carnival. The Prey of the Dragon. The Sport of Kings. Corinthian Jack. The Glorious Adventure. 1922: A Romance of Old Bagdad. A Sailor Tramp. Little Brother of God. The Chinese Circle. The Romany. 1923: M'Lord of the White Road. Heartstrings. In the Blood. The Beloved Brute. 1924: *The Boatswain's Mate. Women and Diamonds. The Gay Corinthians. The Passionate Adventure. 1925: The Fighting Heart (GB: Once to Every Man). The Hunted Woman. Winds of Chance. Percy (GB: Mother's Boy). The Unholy Three. 1926: Beau Geste. What Price Glory? Isle of Retribution. Men of Steel. 1927: Captain Lash. The Loves of Carmen. 1928: Mother Macree. Hangman's House. A Girl in Every Port. The River Pirate. 1929: Strong Boy. Sez You – Sez Me. The Cock-Eyed World. The Black Watch (GB: King of the Khyber Rifles). Hot for Paris. 1930: On the Level. Dust and Sun. Happy Days. Devil with Women. 1931: Dishonored. Annabelle's Affairs. Wicked. Women of All Nations. Not Exactly Gentlemen (GB: Three Rogues). 1932: Devil's Lottery. Guilty as Hell (GB: Guilty As Charged). While Paris Sleeps. Rackety Rax.

*The Stolen Jools (GB: The Slippery Pearls). The Gay Caballero. 1933: Dick Turpin. Laughing at Life. Hot Pepper. 1934: The Lost Patrol. No More Women. Wharf Angel. The Captain Hates the Sea. Murder at the Vanities. 1935: The Informer. Under Pressure. Professional Soldier. The Great Hotel Murder. 1936: Klondike Annie. Under Two Flags. The Magnificent Brute. 1937: This is My Affair (GB: His Affair). Ali Baba Goes to Town. Nancy Steel is Missing. Wee Willie Winkie. Sea Devils. 1938: We're Going to be Rich. Battle of Broadway. The Devil's Party. Captain Fury. Pacific Liner. Full Confession. Gunga Din. The Big Guy. Ex-Champ (GB: Golden Gloves). Let Freedom Ring. Rio. 1940: Diamond Frontier. South of Pago Pago. 1941: Broadway Limited. Call Out the Marines. 1942: China Girl. Powder Town. 1943: Forever and a Day. 1944: Tampico. The Princess and the Pirate. Roger Touhy, Gangster (GB: The Last Gangster). 1945: Love, Honor and Goodbye. Tough and Ready (GB: Men of the Deep). 1946: Whistle Stop. 1947: The Michigan Kid. Calendar Girl. The Foxes of Harrow. 1948: Fort Apache. 1949: She Wore a Yellow Ribbon. 1950: Rio Grande. 1951: *O'Mara's Chain Miracle. 1952: The Quiet Man. 1953: Fair Wind to Java. 1954: Trouble in the Glen. Prince Valiant. 1955: Lady Godiva (GB: Lady Godiva of Coventry). Many Rivers to Cross. City of Shadows. Bengazi. 1956: Around the World in 80 Days. 1957: The Abductors. 1958: Sea Fury. The Italians are Crazy.

McNALLY, Stephen
(Horace McNally) 1911–1994

Dark, confident, slightly oriental-looking American actor, a former lawyer who turned to the theatre in the late thirties, then Hollywood, where he began as earnest clean-cut juveniles. In post-war years he was just as likely to crop up on either side of the law and hovered on the fringe of stardom for ten years. Later he turned up on TV, bigger, balding and blustery, in character roles. Died from heart failure. He had eight children.

1942: †*For the Common Defense. †*The Magic Alphabet. †*Vendetta. †*Inflation. †*Rover's Big Chance. †Grand Central Murder. †The War Against Mrs Hadley. †Eyes in the Night. †For Me and My Gal (GB: For Me and my Girl). †Dr Gillespie's New Assistant. †Keeper of the Flame. 1943: †Air Raid Wardens. †The Man from Down Under. †For God and Country. †Suckerbait. 1944: †An American Romance. †Thirty Seconds Over

Tokyo. 1945: †Bewitched. †Up Goes Maisie (GB: Up She Goes). †Dangerous Partners. †The Harvey Girls. 1946: †Magnificent Doll. 1948: Johnny Belinda. Rogues' Regiment. 1949: City Across the River. Criss Cross. The Lady Gambles. Sword in the Desert. Woman in Hiding. 1950: Winchester 73. No Way Out. Wyoming Mail. 1951: Air Cadet (GB: Jet Men of the Air). Apache Drums. The Iron Man. The Raging Tide. The Lady Pays Off. 1952: Diplomatic Courier. The Duel at Silver Creek. The Black Castle. Battle Zone. 1953: Split Second. The Stand at Apache River. Devil's Canyon. 1954: Make Haste to Live. A Bullet is Waiting. 1955: The Man from Bitter Ridge. Violent Saturday. 1956: Tribute to a Bad Man. 1957: Hell's Crossroads. 1958: The Fiend Who Walked the West. Johnny Rocco. Hell's Five Hours. 1959: Stampede at Bitter Creek (TV. GB: cinemas). 1960: Hell Bent for Leather. 1965: Requiem for a Gunfighter. 1967: Panic in the City. 1969: The Lonely Profession (TV). The Whole World is Watching (TV). 1970: Once You Kiss a Stranger. Vanished (TV). 1972: Black Gunn. Call to Danger (TV). 1974: Nakia (TV). 1975: The Lives of Jenny Dolan (TV). 1976: Most Wanted (TV). 1977: Hi-Riders. Kino, the Padre on Horseback. 1979: Dear Detective (TV).

†As Horace McNally

McNICHOL, Kristy
(Christina McNichol) 1962–

Tawny-haired American juvenile actress with winning smile and enviable talent whose career was torpedoed by ill-health and poor scripts. A child star on television, an Emmy winner as a teenager in the TV series Family and simply tremendous with deeply-felt performances in the TV film Summer of My German Soldier and the movie Little Darlings. Then came a series of flops and half-realized projects, films hardly seen outside preview screens and a period off for 'nervous exhaustion'. Later, her Jane Fonda-style voice was heard in more routine roles. She had a hit television series, Empty Nest, then left it suffering from exhaustion. She quit acting altogether in 1992.

1976: Black Sunday. 1977: The Love Boat II (TV). 1978: Avalanche. Like Mom, Like Me (TV). The End. Summer of My German Soldier (TV). 1980: Blinded by the Light (TV). Little Darlings. 1981: Only When I Laugh (GB: It Hurts Only When I Laugh). The Night the Lights Went Out in Georgia.

1982: *White Dog. My Old Man (TV). The Pirate Movie.* 1983: *I Won't Dance (unfinished).* 1984: *Just the Way You Are. Dream Lover.* 1985: *Love, Mary (TV).* 1986: *Women of Valor (TV).* 1988: *You Can't Hurry Love. Two-Moon Junction.* 1990: *The Forgotten One. Baby of the Bride (TV).* 1991: *Children of the Bride (TV).* 1992: *Mother of the Bride (TV).*

McQUEEN, Steve

(Terence S. McQueen) 1930–1980
Whippy, dynamic American star with close-cropped fair hair and pale blue eyes. Reform school in youth gave him a rough background before he took up acting in his mid-twenties. In leading roles from his third film, he became one of Hollywood's hottest box-office bets, in roles of lean, confident, sometimes psychopathic masculinity, from 1963 through to 1972. After that, he seemed to press the self-destruct button on his career. Married to actresses Neile Adams from 1955 to 1971 and Ali MacGraw (*qv*) from 1973 to 1978. Received an Oscar nomination for *The Sand Pebbles*. Died from a heart attack following surgery for mesothelioma (a cancer of the chest).
1956: †*Somebody Up There Likes Me.* †*Beyond a Reasonable Doubt.* 1958: †*Never Love a Stranger.* †*The Blob.* 1959: *The Great St Louis Bank Robbery. Never So Few.* 1960: *The Magnificent Seven.* 1961: *The Honeymoon Machine.* 1962: *Hell is for Heroes! The War Lover.* 1963: *The Great Escape. Soldier in the Rain.* 1964: *Love with the Proper Stranger.* 1965: *Baby, the Rain Must Fall.* 1966: *The Cincinnati Kid. Nevada Smith. The Sand Pebbles.* 1968: *The Thomas Crown Affair. Bullitt.* 1969: *The Reivers.* 1971: *Le Mans. On Any Sunday.* 1972: *The Getaway. Junior Bonner.* 1973: *Papillon.* 1974: *The Towering Inferno.* 1976: *Dixie Dynamite.* 1977: *An Enemy of the People.* 1980: *Tom Horn. The Hunter.*
†*As Steven McQueen*

McSHANE, Ian 1942–

Alert British leading man with dark, brooding gipsy-like good looks. Started in leading roles, and made an effective Heathcliff for television. Had made himself into a minor international name by the seventies. Married to actress Suzan Farmer (1943–) from 1965 to 1968. The successful TV series *Lovejoy*, in which he played a roguish antiques dealer, kept him busy for 10 years from 1986.

1962: *The Wild and the Willing.* 1965: *The Pleasure Girls. Sky West and Crooked (US: Gypsy Girl).* 1968: *If It's Tuesday, This Must Be Belgium.* 1969: *Battle of Britain.* 1970: *Freelance. Pussycat, Pussycat, I Love You.* 1971: *Tam Lin (GB: The Devil's Widow). Villain.* 1972: *Sitting Target. The Left Hand of Gemini.* 1973: *The Last of Sheila.* 1974: *Ransom.* 1975: *The Lives of Jenny Dolan (TV).* 1976: *Journey into Fear.* 1977: *Behind the Iron Mask (GB: The Fifth Musketeer). Code Name: Diamond Head (TV).* 1978: *The Pirate (TV).* 1979: *Yesterday's Hero. Dirty Money (TV).* 1980: *Cheaper to Keep Her.* 1981: *The Letter (TV).* 1983: *Exposed. Grace Kelly (TV). Torch Light.* 1984: *Ordeal by Innocence. Too Scared to Scream.* 1985: *Braker (TV).* 1986: *The Murders in the Rue Morgue (TV).* 1988: *Grand Larceny (TV). The Great Escape: The Untold Story (TV).* 1989: *Young Charlie Chaplin (TV).* 1990: *Perry Mason: The Case of the Paris Paradox (TV). Rest in Peace, Mrs Columbo (TV).* 1994: *White Goods (TV). Soul Survivors (TV).* 1998: *River of Souls (TV).*

MEDINA, Patricia 1919–

Flashing-eyed British actress with a mass of very dark hair and picture-book beauty. Followed then-husband Richard Greene (*qv*) to Hollywood and became everyone's idea of the swashbuckler's lady fayre. Married to Greene from 1941 to 1951 and Joseph Cotten (*qv*) from 1960, after which she devoted less time to films.
1937: *Dinner at the Ritz.* 1938: *Simply Terrific. Double or Quits.* 1939: *Secret Journey (US: Among Human Wolves).* 1940: *Crooks' Tour.* 1942: *The First of the Few (US: Spitfire). The Day Will Dawn (US: The*

Avengers). 1943: *They Met in the Dark.* 1944: *Hotel Reserve. Kiss the Bride Goodbye. Don't Take It to Heart.* 1945: *Waltz Time. The Secret Heart.* 1947: *Moss Rose. The Foxes of Harrow. The Beginning or the End?* 1948: *The Three Musketeers.* 1949: *The Fighting O'Flynn. Francis. O K Agostina. Children of Chance.* 1950: *Fortunes of Captain Blood. The Jackpot. Abbott and Costello in the Foreign Legion.* 1951: *The Lady and the Bandit (GB: Dick Turpin's Ride). The Magic Carpet. Valentino.* 1952: *Aladdin and His Lamp. Captain Pirate (GB: Captain Blood, Fugitive). Lady in the Iron Mask. Desperate Search.* 1953: *Siren of Bagdad. Botany Bay. Sangaree. Plunder of the Sun.* 1954: *Drums of Tahiti. Phantom of the Rue Morgue. The Black Knight.* 1955: *Pirates of Tripoli. Duel on the Mississippi. Confidential Report (US: Mr Arkadin).* 1956: *Stranger at My Door. Miami Exposé. Uranium Boom. The Beast of Hollow Mountain. The Red Cloak.* 1957: *Buckskin Lady.* 1958: *Battle of the V1 (US: V1/Unseen Heroes/Missiles from Hell).* 1959: *Count Your Blessings.* 1961: *Snow White and the Three Stooges (GB: Snow White and the Three Clowns).* 1968: *The Killing of Sister George.* 1969: *Latitude Zero.* 1973: *The Timber Tramp.*

MEEKER, Ralph

(R. Rathgeber) 1920–1988
Fair-haired, heavily-built American actor often seen as loud-mouthed men of violence. Took over from Marlon Brando (*qv*) in the stage production of *A Streetcar Named Desire* and was much in the same mould, although never in such prestigious films. Grew heavier, like Brando, as the years wore on, and took to playing bragging cowards. Died from a heart attack.
1950: *Four in a Jeep.* 1951: *Teresa. Shadow in the Sky.* 1952: *Glory Alley. Somebody Loves Me.* 1953: *Code Two. Jeopardy. The Naked Spur.* 1955: *Big House USA. Desert Sands. Kiss Me Deadly.* 1956: *A Woman's Devotion (GB: War Shock).* 1957: *Run of the Arrow. The Fuzzy Pink Nightgown. Paths of Glory. Four Women in Black (TV). Deep Water (TV).* 1961: *Ada. Something Wild.* 1963: *Wall of Noise.* 1967: *The Saint Valentine's Day Massacre. The Dirty Dozen. Gentle Giant.* 1968: *The Devil's 8. The Detective.* 1969: *Lost Flight (TV).* 1970: *I Walk the Line.* 1971: *Incident of October 20th. The Anderson Tapes. The Reluctant Heroes (TV. GB: The Reluctant Heroes of Hill 656). The Night Stalker (TV).*

1972: *My Boys Are Good Boys. The Happiness Cage/The Mind Snatchers.* 1973: *Birds of Prey* (TV. GB: cinemas). *Police Story* (TV. GB: cinemas). *You'll Never See Me Again* (TV). 1974: *Cry Panic* (TV). *The Girl on the Late, Late Show* (TV). *Night Games* (TV). *The Dead Don't Die* (TV). 1975: *Johnny Firecloud. Brannigan.* 1976: *Love Comes Quietly. The Food of the Gods.* 1977: *Hi-Riders. Winter Kills* (released 1979). 1980: *Without Warning* (GB: *The Warning*).

MENJOU, Adolphe
(Adolph Menjou) 1890–1963
Dark-haired, moustachioed, supercilious-looking Hollywood charmer, popular as a ladies' man though he always looked older than his years. Later a useful, if not especially biting, character actor in more avuncular roles. Married to actress Verree Teasdale (1904–1987) – third of three – from 1934 to his death from hepatitis. He received an Oscar nomination for *The Front Page*.
1914: *The Man Behind the Door.* 1916: *A Parisian Romance. The Habit of Happiness. Manhattan Madness. Nearly a King. The Crucial Test. The Devil at His Elbow. The Blue Envelope Mystery. The Kiss. The Reward of Patience. The Scarlet Runner* (serial). 1917: *The Amazons. The Moth. The Valentine Girl.* 1920: *What Happened to Rose.* 1921: *The Sheik. The Three Musketeers. Through the Back Door. The Faith Healer* (GB: *Good Heart*). *Courage. Queenie.* 1922: *The Fast Mail. Clarence. Is Matrimony a Failure? Singed Wings. The Eternal Flame. Pink Gods. Head Over Heels* (completed 1920). *Arabian Love.* 1923: *A Woman of Paris. The World's Applause. The Spanish Dancer. Bella Donna. Rupert of Hentzau.* 1924: *The Fast Set. Broadway After Dark. For Sale. The Marriage Cheat. Shadows of Paris. Broken Barriers. Open All Night* (GB: *One Parisian 'Knight'*). *Sinners in Silk.* 1925: *Are Parents People? A Kiss in the Dark. The King on Main Street. Lost – A Wife. The Swan.* 1926: *A Social Celebrity. The Grand Duchess and the Waiter. Fascinating Youth. The Sorrows of Satan. The Ace of Cads.* 1927: *Service for Ladies. A Gentleman of Paris. Blonde or Brunette. Serenade. Evening Clothes.* 1928: *His Tiger Lady. His Private Life. A Night of Mystery.* 1929: *Bachelor Girl. Marquis Preferred. Fashions in Love.* 1930: *Mon gosse de père. Soyons Gais. Wir schalten um auf Hollywood!*

L'enigmatique Monsieur Parkes. The Parisian. New Moon. Morocco. 1931: *The Front Page. Men Call It Love. Friends and Lovers. The Great Lover. The Easiest Way.* 1932: *Two White Arms* (US: *Wives Beware*). *Prestige. Bachelor's Affairs. A Farewell to Arms. Forbidden. Night Club Lady. Diamond Cut Diamond* (US: *Blame the Woman*). 1933: *Worst Woman in Paris? The Circus Queen Murder. Morning Glory. Convention City.* 1934: *The Trumpet Blows. Journal of a Crime. Little Miss Marker* (GB: *Girl in Pawn*). *The Mighty Barnum. The Human Side. The Great Flirtation. Easy to Love.* 1935: *Gold Diggers of 1935. Broadway Gondolier.* 1936: *Sing, Baby, Sing. Wives Never Know. The Milky Way. One in a Million.* 1937: *Café Metropole. A Star is Born. Stage Door. 100 Men and a Girl.* 1938: *Thanks for Everything. The Goldwyn Follies. Letter of Introduction.* 1939: *That's Right – You're Wrong. King of the Turf. Golden Boy. The Housekeeper's Daughter.* 1940: *A Bill of Divorcement. Turnabout. Road Show.* 1941: *Father Takes a Wife.* 1942: *Roxie Hart. Syncopation. You Were Never Lovelier.* 1943: *Sweet Rosie O'Grady. Hi Diddle Diddle.* 1944: *Step Lively.* 1945: *Man Alive.* 1946: *Heartbeat. The Bachelor's Daughters* (GB: *Bachelor Girls*). *I'll Be Yours.* 1947: *The Hucksters. Mr District Attorney.* 1948: *State of the Union* (GB: *The World and His Wife*). 1949: *My Dream is Yours. Dancing in the Dark.* 1950: *To Please a Lady.* 1951: *The Tall Target. Across the Wide Missouri.* 1952: *The Sniper.* *Hollywood's Mr Movies.* 1953: *Man on a Tightrope.* 1954: *Timberjack.* 1956: *Bundle of Joy. The Ambassador's Daughter. I Married a Woman.* 1957: *The Fuzzy Pink Nightgown. Paths of Glory.* 1960: *Pollyanna.*

MERCOURI, Melina
(Anna Amalia Mercouri) 1923–1994
The female equivalent of Anthony Quinn (*qv*): a barnstorming, scene-chewing, throaty-voiced, dominant blonde Greek actress who married director Jules Dassin, achieved world fame in *Never on Sunday* (a performance that won her an Oscar nomination) and swallowed the opposition whole in a number of international films. Later became a force in Greek politics, winning a seat in parliament in 1977 and eventually enjoying two spells as culture minister. Died from lung cancer.
1954: *Stella.* 1956: *Celui qui doit mourir.* 1957: *The Gypsy and the Gentleman.* 1958: *La loi* (GB: *Where the Hot Wind Blows*). 1960:

Never on Sunday. 1961: *Il giudizio universale* (US: *The Last Judgment*). *Phaedra. Vive Henry VI, vive l'amour!* 1962: *Canzoni nel mondo* (US: 38–24–36). 1963: *The Victors.* 1964: *Topkapi.* 1965: *Les pianos mécaniques* (US: *The Uninhibited*). 1966: *A Man Could Get Killed. 10.30 pm Summer.* 1969: *Gaily Gaily* (GB: *Chicago, Chicago*). 1971: *Promise at Dawn.* 1974: *Once is Not Enough/ Jacqueline Susann's Once is Not Enough. †The Rehearsal.* 1976: *Nasty Habits.* 1977: *A Dream of Passion.* 1983: *Keine zufallige geschichte* (US: *Not By Coincidence*).

†Unreleased

MEREDITH, Burgess
(Oliver B. Meredith) 1907–1997
For a man who made virtually nothing for the cinema between 1949 and 1962, this mercurial, tousle-haired American actor must be one of the most difficult tasks for any filmographer: fresh Meredith films, sometimes from the most unlikely places, seem to turn up everywhere one looks. A first-class talent who continually upset Hollywood in his early days, he attacked his parts like a terrier. Four times married, including Paulette Goddard (third) from 1944 to 1949. Long-delayed Academy Award nominations finally came for *Day of the Locust* and *Rocky*. Died from skin cancer and Alzheimer's Disease.
1936: *Winterset.* 1937: *There Goes the Groom.* 1938: *Spring Madness.* 1939: *Idiot's Delight. Of Mice and Men.* 1940: *San Francisco Docks. Castle on the Hudson* (GB: *Years Without Days*). *Second Chorus.* 1941: *That Uncertain Feeling. The Forgotten Village* (narrator only). *Tom, Dick and Harry.* 1942: *Street of Chance.* 1943: *†Welcome to Britain.* 1944: *†Salute to France.* 1945: *The Story of GI Joe/War Correspondent.* 1946: *Magnificent Doll. The Diary of a Chambermaid.* 1947: *Mine Own Executioner.* *A Yank Comes Back.* 1948: *A Miracle Can Happen* (later *On Our Merry Way*). 1949: *†The Man on the Eiffel Tower. Jigsaw. Golden Arrow* (US: *The Gay Adventure.* Released 1953). 1954: *The Sea of Winslow Homer* (voice only). *Screen Snapshots No. 224.* 1957: *Joe Butterfly.* 1961: *Universe* (narrator only). 1962: *Advise and Consent.* 1963: *The Cardinal.* 1964: *Fanfare for a Death Scene* (TV). *Man on the Run/The Kidnappers.* 1965: *In Harm's Way.* 1966: *Crazy Quilt* (narrator only). *A Big Hand for the Little Lady* (GB: *Big Deal at Dodge City*).

Batman. Madame X. 1967: Torture Garden. Hurry Sundown. 1968: Mackenna's Gold. Stay Away, Joe. Skidoo. Hard Contract. 1969: The Reivers (narrator only). 1970: †The Yin and the Yang of Mr Go. There Was a Crooked Man. Lock, Stock and Barrel (TV). 1971: Getting Away from it All (TV). Clay Pigeon (GB: Trip to Kill). The Strange Monster of Strawberry Cove (TV). 1972: The New Healers (TV). Probe (TV). The Man. A Fan's Notes. Such Good Friends. 1973: 'B' Must Die. 1974: Of Men and Women (TV). The Day of The Locust. Golden Needles. Beware! The Blob (GB: Son of Blob). 1975: 92 in the Shade. The Master Gunfighter (narrator only). The Hindenberg. 1976: The Sentinel. Burnt Offerings. Tail Gunner Joe (TV). Rocky. 1977: SST Death Flight (TV). The Wandering Muse of Artemus Flagg. Golden Rendezvous. Remember Those Poker-Playing Monkeys? The Manitou. Johnny, We Hardly Knew Ye (TV). 1978: The Amazing Captain Nemo. Shenanigans (later The Great Georgia Bank Hoax). Foul Play. Magic. Kate Bliss and the Ticker Tape Kid (TV). The Last Hurrah (TV). 1979: *Puff the Magic Dragon (voice only). Rocky II. 1980: When Time Ran Out . . . The Last Chase. Final Assignment. 1981: Clash of the Titans. True Confessions. 1982: Rocky III. 1983: The Twilight Zone (GB: Twilight Zone The Movie. Narrator only). 1984: Wet Gold (TV). 1985: Santa Claus. 1986: Outrage! (TV). Mr Corbett's Ghost (GB: TV). Broken Rainbow (voice only). 1987: GI Joe (voice only). King Lear. 1988: Mr North. John Huston. Full Moon in Blue Water. 1990: Odd Ball Hall. State of Grace. Rocky V. 1993: Grumpy Old Men. 1994: Camp Nowhere. Across the Moon. 1995: Tall Tale. Grumpier Old Men. Wild Bill: Hollywood Maverick.

†Also directed

MERMAN, Ethel
(E. Zimmerman) 1908–1984
Big, bold, brassy American brunette, a successful singer in her early twenties, with pencilled eyebrows, thin, determined lips, a shock of cotton-wool hair and a voice that would still be travelling when it hit the back of the opera house. Hollywood had as little idea of how to cope with her as it did later with Mary Martin (qv), but it did give her a couple of rampaging musical successes in middle age. Married/divorced Ernest Borgnine (fourth husband) in 1964.
1930: Follow the Leader. *Her Future. 1931:

*Devil Sea. *Roaming. *Old Man Blues. 1932: *Time on My Hands (voice only). *Ireno. The Big Broadcast. 1933: *Be Like Me. 1934: We're Not Dressing. Kid Millions. Shoot the Works. 1935: The Big Broadcast of 1936. 1936: Anything Goes. Strike Me Pink. 1938: Happy Landing. Alexander's Ragtime Band. Straight, Place and Show (GB: They're Off). 1943: Stage Door Canteen. 1953: Call Me Madam. 1954: There's No Business Like Show Business. 1963: The Art of Love. It's a Mad, Mad, Mad, Mad, World. 1971: Journey Back to Oz (voice only). 1976: Won Ton Ton, The Dog Who Saved Hollywood. 1979: Rudolph and Frosty's Christmas in July (TV. Voice only). 1980: Airplane!

MERRILL, Gary 1914–1990
Dark-haired, morose-looking American tough-guy actor who often looked as though he needed a shave. At first as unsmiling heroes, not above using dirty methods to get results, later as weary-looking villains. Married to Bette Davis from 1950 to 1960. Died from cancer.
1944: Winged Victory. 1948: The Quiet One (narrator only). 1949: Slattery's Hurricane. Twelve O'Clock High. 1950: Mother Didn't Tell Me. Where the Sidewalk Ends. All About Eve. 1951: The Frogmen. Decision Before Dawn. Another Man's Poison. 1952: The Girl in White (GB: So Bright the Flame). Night Without Sleep. Phone Call from a Stranger. 1953: A Blueprint for Murder. 1954: Witness to Murder. The Black Darkness. The Human Jungle. 1955: Yacht on the High Sea (TV. GB: cinemas). 1956: Navy Wife (GB: Mother – Sir!) Bermuda Affair. 1957: Crash Landing. If You Knew Elizabeth (TV). 1958: The Missouri Traveler. 1959: The Wonderful Country. A Quiet Game of Cards (TV). A Corner of the Garden (TV). The Savage Eye. 1960: The Great Imposter. 1961: Mysterious Island. The Pleasure of His Company. 1962: A Girl Named Tamiko. Hong Kong Farewell/ Hong Kong, un addio. 1963: Catacombs (US: The Woman Who Wouldn't Die). 1965: Run, Psycho, Run. Around the World Under the Sea. The Last Challenge (GB: The Pistolero of Red River). 1966: Ride Beyond Vengeance. Cast a Giant Shadow. The Dangerous Days of Kiowa Jones (TV. GB: cinemas). Hondo and the Apaches. Destination Inner Space. 1967: The Power. Clambake. New York chiama Superdrago. The Incident. 1969: Amarsi male. 1970: Then Came Bronson (TV. GB: cinemas). 1971: Earth II (TV). 1972: The Murderers

(TV). 1973: Pueblo (TV). Murder and the Computer (TV). 1974: Huckleberry Finn. 1976: Thieves. 1979: The Seekers (TV).

MICHAEL, Gertrude
(Lillian G. Michael) 1911–1964
Bright, vivacious, light-haired American star of the 1930s, with wide toothpaste smile and high cheekbones. She was trained for a career as a pianist, but acting successes on stage led to offers from Hollywood, where she remained a second-line lead, although notable as the hazard-prone heroine of the Sophie Lang adventure films. After that series ended in 1937, she moved increasingly into hard-boiled blonde roles and worked hard in TV from the late 1940s. On a slightly macabre note, she died (at only 53) at midnight on the last day of 1964.
1932: Unashamed. Wayward. 1933: Ann Vickers. A Bedtime Story. I'm No Angel. Cradle Song. Night of Terror. Sailor be Good. 1934: Search for Beauty/Beauty. She Was a Lady. I Believed in You. Murder on the Blackboard. Murder at the Vanities. George White's Scandals. Bolero. Cleopatra. The Witching Hour. The Notorious Sophie Lang. Hold That Girl. Menace. 1935: Four Hours to Kill. It Happened in New York. Father Brown, Detective. The Last Outpost. Protegées. 1936: The Return of Sophie Lang. Till We Meet Again. Woman Trap. Make Way for a Lady. Forgotten Faces. Second Wife. 1937: Sins of the Fathers. Mr Dodd Takes the Air. Sophie Lang Goes West. 1938: Star of the Circus (US: The Hidden Menace). Just Like a Woman (released 1940). 1939: Hidden Power. 1940: *Pound Foolish. The Farmer's Daughter. I Can't Give You Anything But Love, Baby. Parole Fixer. Slightly Tempted. 1942: Prisoner of Japan (GB: The Last Command). 1943: Behind Prison Walls (GB: Youth Takes a Hand). Where Are Your Children? Women in Bondage. 1944: Faces in the Fog. 1945: Three's a Crowd. Club Havana. Allotment Wives (GB: Woman in the Case). 1948: That Wonderful Urge. 1949: Flamingo Road. 1950: Caged. 1951: Darling, How Could You? (GB: Rendezvous). 1952: Bugles in the Afternoon. 1953: Major Pauline (TV). No Escape. 1954: Woman Expert (TV). 1955: Women's Prison. 1957: The Traveling Corpse (TV). 1961: The Outsider. 1962: Twist All Night.

MIDLER, Bette 1945–
Diminutive, dynamic, rosy-cheeked, red-haired American entertainer. She grew up (in

Honolulu, Hawaii) from 'a plain, fat, lonely little Jewish kid' into 'The Divine Miss M', a nightclub megastar, combining rude jokes and raunchy songs with powerful renditions of blues numbers. She had mixed luck with films until permitted to use her Mae West-style personality to steal scenes in films not specifically tailored to her. Oscar nominee for *The Rose*. After some moderate 'Mother Earth' roles in the early 1990s, she made a spectacularly successful comeback on stage.
1966: Hawaii. 1968: The Detective. 1969: Goodbye, Columbus. 1974: The Divine Mr J. 1979: The Rose. 1980: Divine Madness. 1982: Jinxed! 1986: Down and Out in Beverly Hills. Ruthless People. 1987: Outrageous Fortune. 1988: Big Business. Oliver and Company (voice only). Beaches. 1990: Stella. 1991: Scenes from a Mall. For the Boys. 1993: Hocus Pocus. Earth and the American Dream (voice only). Gypsy (TV. GB: cinemas). 1995: Get Shorty. 1996: The First Wives Club. That Old Feeling. 1999: Isn't She Great. Get Bruce! (doc). Jackie's Back! (TV). Fantasia 2000. 2000: Drowning Mona. 2001: What Women Want.

MIFUNE, Toshiro 1920–1997
Powerful, fiercely-glowering Japanese actor – the only man to become an international star through Japanese films. He was never as dominant, though, in English-language films, and continued to do his most striking work in home-grown classics, notably movies made by the great Japanese director Akiro Kurosawa. Best recalled as fearsome, fearless, cynical, swashbuckling samurai warrior. Died from organ failure.
1946: Shin Baka Jidai. 1947: Ginrei no Hate. 1948: Yoidore Tenshi. 1949: Datsugoku. Jakoman to Tetsu. Shuban/Scandal. Nora

Inu. Shizu-kanuru Ketto. 1950: Rashomon. Ishinaka – Sensei Gyojoki. Konyaku. Yibiwa. Kaitzoku-Sen. 1951: Bakuro Ichidai. Ai to Nikushimi no Kaneta e Omnago – koro o Dare ga Shiru. Hakuchi/The Idiot. Sasaki Kojiro – kantetsuhen. Ereji. Sengo/Ha Obake. Taikai. 1952: Saikaku Ichidai Omna/Life of O-Haru. Tokyo no Koibito. Sengoku/Burai. Muteki. Gekiryu. Ketto kagiya No Tsuji/Vendetta of Samurai. Minato e Kita Otoko. 1953: Fukeyo Harukaze. Himawari-Misume. Taiheiyo no Washi. Hoyo. 1954: Seven Samurai/Shichi-Nin no Samurai. Shiosai. Muyamoto/ Samurai. 1955: Tenka Tahei. Dansei No. 1. Ikimono no Koroku. Zoku Tenka Tahei. Otoko Arite. Zoku Miyamoto Musashi. Ankoku-Gai. 1956: Aijo no Kessan. Ketto Ganryu-Jima. Narazumono. Tsuma no Kokoro. Kuroobi Sangokushi. Ankoku-Gai. Shujin-Sen. 1957: Throne of Blood/Kumonosu-Jo. Donzoko/The Lower Depths. Yaguy Bugei-Cho (US: Secret Scrolls). Kiken na Eiyu. Shitamachi. Arashi no Naka no Otoko. Kono Futari no Sachi Are. 1958: Tokyo no Kyujitsu. Muhimatsu no Issho/The Rickshaw Man. Yajikita Dochuko. Ninjutsu (US: Secret Scrolls Pt. 2). Jinsei Gekijo Seishin-Han. Kakushi-toride no San Akunin/The Hidden Fortress. 1959: Sengoku Gunto-Den. Ankokugai no Kaoyaku. Dokoritsu Gurentai. Nippon Tanjo. Aru Kengo no Shogai/Samurai Saga/Cyrano de Bergerac. 1960: Otoko tai Otoko. Ankoku-Gai no Taiketsu. Warui-Yatsue hodo Yoko Nemuru/ The Bad Sleep Well. Kunisada Chuji. Taiheiyo no Arashi/I Bombed Pearl Harbor. 1961: Osakajo Monogatari. Animas Trujano. Yojimbo. Gen to Fudo-Myoo. 1962: Sanjuro. Tatsu. Chusingara. 1963: †Goju Man-nin no Isan. Taiheyo no Tsubasa/Attack Squadron. High and Low/Tengoku to Jigoku. Dai-Tozuku/Samurai Pirate/The Lost World of Sinbad. 1964: Dai Tatsumaki. 1965: Sugata Sanshiro. Chi to Suna. Samurai/Samurai Assassin. Red Beard/Akahige. Taiheyo Kiseki no Sakusen Kiska. 1966: Kiganjo no Boken/ Adventures of Takla Makan. Abare Goemen. Grand Prix. Diabosatsu. Doto Ichi Man Kairi. 1967: Joi-Uchi/Rebellion. Nippon no Ichiban Nagai Hi. 1968: Gion Matsuri. Hell in the Pacific. Admiral Yamamoto. Kurobe no Taiyo (GB: Tunnel to the Sun). 1969: Nihonkai Daikaisen. Shinsen Gumi. Furin Kazan. Eiko Eno 5000 Kiro. Aru Heishi no Kake. Akage/ Red Lion. Zatoichi to Yojimbo. 1970: Bakumatsu. Gunbatsu. Machibure. 1971: Red Sun. 1974: Paper Tiger. 1976: Midway (GB: Battle of Midway). 1977: Ningen no Shomei/Proof of the Man. Nippon no Don-Yobohen. Winter Kills (released 1979). 1978: Shogun's Samurai. Inube. Akojo Danzetsu. Lord Incognito. The Don of Japan: the Payoff. The Bushido Blade (released 1982). 1979: Oginsama. 1980: Shogun. Inchon! 1981: The Challenge. 1982: Port Arthur. Seiha. 1983: Umitsubame-jo Nokiseki. 1987: Princess from the Moon/Taketori Monogatari. 1988: Tora-San Goes North. 1989: Sen no Rikyu. Haro Kuru Oni. 1990: Strawberry Road. 1991: Shogun Mayeda/Journey of Honor. Agaguk/ Shadow of the Wolf. 1993: Picture Bride (released 1995). 1995: Fukai kawa/Deep River.

†Also directed

MILES, Sarah 1941–
Puggily pretty, serious-looking, full-lipped, dark-haired British actress with firmly-rounded-figure, usually seen in portraits of repressed sexuality smouldering beneath the surface and bursting forth before the end of the film. Almost a British Bardot, in fact, but in films that strove for great romantic/ erotic cinema. Married/divorced (1967–1975) playwright Robert Bolt. They remarried in 1988 but he died seven years later. Academy Award nomination for *Ryan's Daughter*.
*1962: Term of Trial. 1963: The Servant. *The Six-Sided Triangle. The Ceremony. 1965: Those Magnificent Men in Their Flying Machines. I Was Happy Here (US: Time Lost and Time Remembered). 1966: Blow-Up. 1970: Ryan's Daughter. 1972: Lady Caroline Lamb. 1973: The Hireling. The Man Who Loved Cat Dancing. 1975: Great Expectations (TV. GB: cinemas). Pepita Jimenez/Bride to Be. 1976: The Sailor Who Fell from Grace with the Sea. Dynasty (TV). 1978: The Big Sleep. 1980: Priest of Love. 1981: Venom. 1984: Ordeal by Innocence. Steaming. 1986: †Eat the Peach. 1987: Hope and Glory. White Mischief. 1990: A Ghost in Monte Carlo (TV). 1992: The Silent Touch. 2000: Accidental Detective.*

†Scenes deleted from final release print

MILES. Vera (V. Ralston) 1929–
The American working actress *par excellence*: a pleasant, photogenic, green-eyed blonde who, besides her cinema work, has played over 100 roles on television since 1954. Although taken up by Hitchcock (and missing out on *Vertigo* only through pregnancy) the remainder of her film parts rarely rose above the routine, but she was capable of

very good performances when pushed by her director. Married to Gordon Scott (1956–1959) and Keith Larsen (both qv) from 1960 to 1973, second and third of four.

1950: *When Willie Comes Marching Home.* 1951: *Two Tickets to Broadway. For Men Only/The Tall Lie.* 1952: *The Rose Bowl Story.* 1953: *The Charge at Feather River. So Big.* 1954: *Pride of the Blue Grass (GB: Prince of the Blue Grass).* 1955: *Tarzan's Hidden Jungle. Wichita. Man on the Ledge (TV. GB: cinemas).* 1956: *23 Paces to Baker Street. Autumn Leaves. The Searchers.* 1957: *Beau James. The Wrong Man. Panic Button (TV).* 1959: *Beyond This Place (US: Web of Evidence). The FBI Story. Five Branded Women. A Touch of Larceny.* 1960: *Psycho. The Lawbreakers (TV. GB: cinemas).* 1961: *Back Street.* 1962: *The Man Who Shot Liberty Valance. Recoil (TV. GB: cinemas).* 1963: *The Case against Paul Ryker (TV. GB: cinemas as Sergeant Ryker). A Tiger Walks.* 1964: *Those Calloways. The Hanged Man (TV. GB: cinemas).* 1966: *One of Our Spies is Missing! (TV. GB: cinemas). Follow Me, Boys! The Spirit is Willing.* 1967: *Gentle Giant.* 1968: *Kona Coast. Hellfighters. Mission Batangas.* 1969: *It Takes All Kinds.* 1970: *Goodbye to Yesterday (TV). In Search of America (TV).* 1971: *Owen Marshall – Counselor at Law (TV). Baffled! The Last Generation. The Wild Country. A Howling in the Woods (TV).* 1972: *Jigsaw (TV). Molly and Lawless John. A Great American Tragedy (TV. GB: Man at the Crossroads).* 1973: *Runaway (TV. GB: cinemas as The Runaway Train). One Little Indian.* 1974: *The Castaway Cowboy. Live Again, Die Again (TV). The Underground Man (TV).* 1976: *State Fair (TV). Judge Horton and the Scottsboro Boys (TV). McNaughton's Daughter (TV). Smash-Up on Interstate Five (TV).* 1977: *Fire! (TV. GB: cinemas). †Twilight's Last Gleaming. The Thoroughbreds (later Treasure Seekers).* 1978: *And I Alone Survived (TV).* 1979: *Run for the Roses.* 1981: *Our Family Business (TV).* 1982: *Travis McGee (TV). Brainwaves. Mazes and Monsters/Rona Jaffe's Mazes and Monsters (TV).* 1983: *Psycho II. Helen Keller: The Miracle Continues (TV).* 1984: *The Initiation.* 1985: *International Airport (TV). Into the Night.* 1989: *The Hijacking of the Achille Lauro (TV).* 1994: *Separate Lives.*

†*Scenes deleted from final release print*

MILLAND, Ray
(Reginald Truscott-Jones) 1905–1986
Dark-haired, Welsh-born Hollywood star with round, open face, who, after a start in British films, gave light, good-natured performances in romantic comedies of the thirties and early forties. When it was found that he could project shallowness and other disturbing qualities beneath a surface charm, he was cast as the alcoholic in *The Lost Weekend* (which won him an Oscar) and, later, as the scheming husband in *Dial M for Murder*. At Paramount for 20 years, he was a star for 30. Also an interesting director. He re-emerged as a bald-pated character actor in later years, mainly in testy roles. Died from cancer.

1929: ††*The Plaything.* †*Piccadilly.* †*The Informer (sharpshooter only).* †*The Flying Scotsman.* †*The Lady from the Sea.* 1930: †*Way for a Sailor.* †*Passion Flower.* 1931: †*Strangers May Kiss.* †*Bachelor Father.* †*Just a Gigolo (GB: The Dancing Partner).* †*Ambassador Bill.* †*Bought.* †*Blonde Crazy (GB: Larceny Lane).* 1932: †*The Man Who Played God (GB: The Silent Voice).* †*Polly of the Circus.* †*Payment Deferred.* 1933: *Orders is Orders. This is the Life.* 1934: *Many Happy Returns. Bolero. Charlie Chan in London. We're Not Dressing. Menace.* 1935: *Four Hours to Kill. The Gilded Lily. Alias Mary Dow. One Hour Later. The Glass Key.* 1936: *The Return of Sophie Lang. The Jungle Princess. Next Time We Love (GB: Next Time We Live). The Big Broadcast of 1937.* 1937: *Easy Living. Three Smart Girls. Wise Girl. Ebb Tide. Wings over Honolulu. Bulldog Drummond Escapes.* 1938: *Tropic Holiday. Her Jungle Love. Say It in French. Men with Wings.* 1939: *Hotel Imperial. Everything Happens at Night. Beau Geste. French Without Tears.* 1940: *Untamed. The Doctor Takes a Wife. Irene. Arise, My Love.* 1941: *Skylark. I Wanted Wings.* 1942: *Are Husbands Necessary? Reap the Wild Wind. The Major and the Minor. The Lady Has Plans. Star Spangled Rhythm.* 1943: *The Crystal Ball. Forever and a Day. Ministry of War.* 1944: *Till We Meet Again. The Uninvited. Lady in the Dark.* 1945: *The Lost Weekend. Kitty. The Trouble with Women (released 1947).* 1946: *The Well Groomed Bride. California. The Imperfect Lady (GB: Mrs Loring's Secret).* 1947: *Variety Girl. Golden Earrings.* 1948: *So Evil My Love. Sealed Verdict. The Big Clock. Miss Tatlock's Millions. Alias Nick Beal (GB: The Contact Man).* 1949: *It Happens Every Spring. A Woman of Distinction. Copper Canyon. A Life of Her Own. Circle of Danger.* 1951: *Night into Morning. Close to My Heart. Rhubarb.* 1952: *Something to Live For. The Thief. Bugles in the Afternoon.* 1953: *Jamaica Run. Let's Do It Again.* 1954: *Dial M for Murder.* 1955: ‡*A Man Alone. The Girl in the Red Velvet Swing.* 1956: ‡*Lisbon.* 1957: *The River's Edge. Three Brave Men.* 1958: *High Flight.* ‡*The Safecracker.* 1962: *The Premature Burial.* ‡*Panic in Year Zero.* 1963: *'X' (GB: The Man with the X-Ray Eyes).* 1964: *The Confession (GB: TV as Quick Let's Get Married).* 1967: *Rose rosse per Il Führer.* 1968: ‡*Hostile Witness.* 1969: *Daughter of the Mind (TV). River of Gold (TV). Love Story. Company of Killers.* 1971: *Black Noon*

(TV). 1972: *The Thing with Two Heads. Embassy. Frogs. The Big Game.* 1973: *The House in Nightmare Park. Terror in the Wax Museum.* 1974: *The Student Connection. Gold. Escape to Witch Mountain. The Dead Don't Die (TV).* 1975: *Oil: the Billion Dollar Fire. Ellery Queen: Too Many Suspects (TV). The Swiss Conspiracy.* 1976: *The Last Tycoon. Aces High. Mayday at 40,000 Feet (TV. GB: cinemas).* 1977: *Look What's Happened to Rosemary's Baby (TV). Slavers. The Uncanny. I gabiani volano bassi.* 1978: *Spree. Oliver's Story. Battlestar Galactica. The Darker Side of Terror (TV). Cruise into Terror (TV). Blackout.* 1979: *The Concorde Affair. Game for Vultures. Cave In! (TV). La ragazza in pigiama gialla.* 1980: *The Attic. Survival Run.* 1981: *Our Family Business (TV).* 1982: *Starflight One (TV. GB: cinemas).* 1983: *Cocaine: One Man's Seduction (TV).* 1984: *The Masks of Death (TV).* 1985: *The Sea Serpent. The Gold Key (video).*

†*As Raymond Milland* ††*As Spike Milland*
‡*Also directed*

MILLER, Ann
(Johnnie Lucille Collier) 1919–
Vivacious American dancer with very dark hair and a bright smile. In show business from an early age, she proved the most devastatingly fast tap dancer since Eleanor Powell, with enough vim and verve for the entire cast. One can never remember seeing the Miller waist exposed, but those fabulous legs were almost always in evidence in 20 years of musicals, throughout which she pleased audiences with her own brand of brassy sweetness. Three times married.

1934: *Anne of Green Gables.* 1935: *The Good Fairy.* 1936: *The Devil on Horseback.* 1937: *New Faces of 1937. Life of the Party. Stage Door.* 1938: *Radio City Revels. Having Wonderful Time. Tarnished Angel. You Can't Take It With You. Room Service.* 1940: *Melody Ranch. Too Many Girls. Hit Parade of 1941.* 1941: *Variety Reel. *Stars Past and Present. Go West, Young Lady. Time Out for Rhythm.* 1942: *Priorities on Parade. True to the Army.* 1943: *Reveille with Beverly. What's Buzzin' Cousin?* 1944: *Carolina Blues. Jam Session. Hey, Rookie.* 1945: *Eadie Was a Lady. Eve Knew Her Apples.* 1946: *Thrill of Brazil.* 1948: *Easter Parade. The Kissing Bandit.* 1949: *On the Town.* 1950: *Watch the Birdie.* 1951: *Texas Carnival. Two Tickets to Broadway.* 1952: *Lovely to Look At.* 1953: *Small*

Town Girl. Kiss Me, Kate. 1954: Deep in My Heart. 1955: Hit the Deck. 1956: The Opposite Sex. The Great American Pastime. 1975: Won Ton Ton, the Dog Who Saved Hollywood. 1993: Lucy and Desi: A Home Movie (TV). 1994: That's Entertainment! III. 2000: Mulholland Drive (TV).

MILLER, Jonny Lee 1972–
Dark-haired, strongly built, heavy-headed British actor with slightly sardonic smile, seen in a mixture of rebel roles and sensitive souls in period drama. He started acting in boyhood, one of his earliest roles being in a serialised version of Jane Austen's *Mansfield Park*. Bizarrely, he would play the lead in the film version 16 years later, three years after leaping to stardom as Sick Boy in *Train-spotting*. The grandson of character actor Bernard Lee, he is divorced from the American actress Angelina Jolie (*qv*).
1992: *Dead Romantic. 1995: Hackers. Trainspotting. 1997: Afterglow. Regeneration. 1999: Plunkett & Macleane. Mansfield Park. Complicity. Love, Honor & Obey. 2001: Dracula 2000.*

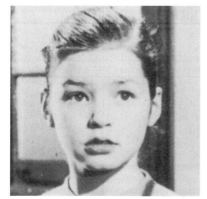

MILLER, Mandy (Carman Miller) 1944–
Sensitive, talented, dark-haired British child star, tear-jerkingly effective in several films, notably as the deaf girl in *Mandy* (after which she was billed simply as 'Mandy' in a couple of films). Grew into a pretty teenager, but sadly decided to leave the business. In 1981, though, she served as presenter with Sea-TV, a station for oil-rig workers. Sister of actress Jan Miller. Aunt of actress Amanda Pays.
1951: The Man in the White Suit. 1952: I Believe in You. Mandy (US: Crash of Silence). 1953: Background. 1954: Adventure

in the Hopfields. Dance Little Lady. 1955: Raising a Riot. The Secret. 1956: The Feminine Touch (US: The Gentle Touch). Child in the House. 1958: The Snorkel. 1962: Kill or Cure.

MILLER, Max
(Thomas Sargent) 1895–1963
Chubby-faced, Roman-nosed, twinkling eyed, dark-haired British music-hall comedian with impish grin and a roistering voice. Dressed in white pork-pie hat and extraordinary loud plus-fours, Miller, who joined a circus as a boy of eight and stayed in showbusiness all his life, would harangue his audiences with rude (well, they were rude then) jokes with double-entendres which he would indignantly deny when the audience started to laugh. Reviled by some as a 'blue' comedian, and tagged 'The Cheeky Chappie'. Miller moved into films, but they were even less able to catch his essence than Hollywood with Mae West. The films simply came across as breathless, rough-and-ready stuff, although Miller did find a good character in the bookmaker 'Educated Evans'. When other character leads proved less successful, he returned to the variety halls.
1933: The Good Companions. Friday the Thirteenth. Channel Crossing. 1934: Princess Charming. 1935: Things Are Looking Up. Get Off My Foot. 1936: Educated Evans. Don't Get Me Wrong. 1937: Take It from Me (US: Transatlantic Trouble). 1938: Thank Evans. Everything Happens to Me. 1939: The Good Old Days. Hoots Mon! 1943: Asking for Trouble.

MILLER, Penelope Ann
(P. Andrea Miller) 1964–
Silky, fresh-faced, vulnerable-looking, well-groomed American actress who acted with

smooth efficiency opposite some of Hollywood's most powerful actors in the early 1990s. Attempts at a top-starring vehicle of her own were less successful, however, and she returned to co-starring roles. She came to prominence on stage playing the role of the prostitute in *Biloxi Blues* that she would later repeat in the successful film version.
1987: Adventures in Babysitting (GB: A Night on the Town). 1988: Miles from Home. Big Top Pee-Wee. Biloxi Blues. 1989: Downtown. Dead Bang. Our Town (TV). 1990: Awakenings. The Freshmen. Kindergarten Cop. 1991: Other People's Money. 1992: Chaplin. Year of the Comet. The Gun in Betty Lou's Handbag. 1993: Carlito's Way. 1994: The Shadow. Witch Hunt (cable TV). 1996: The Relic. The Hired Heart (TV). 1997: Little City. The Last Don (TV). 1998: Ruby Bridges (TV). The Break Up. Outside Ozona. Rhapsody in Bloom. Killing Moon. 1999: Chapter Zero. Rocky Marciano (TV). All-American Girl: The Mary Kay Letourneau Story (TV). 2000: Forever Lulu. Along Came a Spider (TV). A Woman's a Helluva Thing. Famous.

MILLIGAN, Spike
(Terence Milligan) 1918–
Zany, India-born comedian in British films, a law unto himself and likely to ad-lib at the drop of a trouser. Sprang to fame in radio's *The Goon Show*, many of whose scripts he co-wrote, after which films tried in vain to harness his comedy talents, then settled for him as a bearded character actor in a variety of lunatic supporting roles.
1951: Penny Points to Paradise. London Entertains. Let's Go Crazy. 1952: Down Among the Z-Men. 1953: *Super Secret Service. 1954: Calling All Cars (voice only). 1955: *The Case of the Mukkinese Battlehorn. 1960: *The Running Jumping and Standing Still Film. Suspect. Watch Your Stern. 1961: What a Whopper! Invasion Quartet. *Spike Milligan Meets Joe Brown. *Spike Milligan on Treasure Island WC2. 1962: Postman's Knock. 1966: *Fish and Milligan. 1969: The Bed Sitting Room. *The Undertakers. The Magic Christian. 1971: The Magnificent Seven Deadly Sins. 1972: Rentadick. The Adventures of Barry McKenzie. Dot and the Kangaroo (voice only). Adolf Hitler – My Part in His Downfall. Alice's Adventures in Wonderland. 1973: Digby – the Biggest Dog in the World. The Three Musketeers (The Queen's Diamonds). The Cherry Picker. 1974: The*

Great McGonagall. Ghost in the Noonday Sun. Man about the House. 1976: Lost in the Wild. Barney. 1977: The Hound of the Baskervilles. The Last Remake of Beau Geste. 1978: The Prisoner of Zenda. 1979: Monty Python's Life of Brian. 1981: History of the World Part 1. 1983: Yellowbeard.

MILLS, Hayley 1946–
Fair-haired, child-like British actress with baby-blue eyes, the daughter of Sir John Mills (qv) and so appealing in her first British film that she was snapped up by the Disney studio, took a special Oscar in *Pollyanna*, and quickly won an enormous personal following. Although it seemed that Disney kept her too long in juvenile roles, it became apparent that her special drawing-room style of acting, between exaggeration and wistfulness, was unsuited to adult roles. She became equally typed as the virgin-on-the-verge and her film career quietly died. Married/divorced director Roy Boulting. Still busy on stage.
1959: Tiger Bay. 1960: Pollyanna. 1961: Whistle Down the Wind. The Parent Trap. 1962: In Search of the Castaways. Summer Magic. 1963: The Chalk Garden. The Moon-Spinners. 1964: The Truth About Spring. 1965: That Darn Cat! Sky West and Crooked (US: Gypsy Girl). The Trouble with Angels. 1966: The Daydreamer (voice only). The Family Way. 1967: Pretty Polly (US: A Matter of Innocence). Africa – Texas Style! 1968: Twisted Nerve. 1969: Take a Girl Like You. 1971: Mr Forbush and the Penguins (US: Cry of the Penguins). Endless Night. 1974: Deadly Strangers. What Changed Charley Farthing? 1975: The Diamond Hunters (US: The Kingfisher Caper). 1986: Parent Trap II (TV). 1988: Appointment with Death. 1989: Parent Trap III (TV). 1990: Back Home (TV). Parent Trap: Hawaiian Honeymoon (TV). After Midnight (made for cinemas but shown only on TV). 1991: The Last Straw (unreleased). 1994: A Troll in Central Park (voice only).

MILLS, Sir John
(Lewis 'Johnny' Mills) 1908–
Staunch, stocky British leading man, trained in musical comedy, but best recalled for war roles that ran from cockney ratings to stiff-upper-lip officers, and for a series of rural worms-that-turned that culminated in his winning an Oscar for his village grotesque in *Ryan's Daughter*. Sincerity was his best quality, and he projected it throughout the

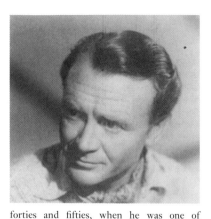

forties and fifties, when he was one of Britain's top box-office stars. Has soldiered on in progressively more unworthy roles. Father of Hayley and Juliet Mills (both qv). Married actresses Aileen Raymond and (from 1941) Mary Hayley Bell, who became a novelist and playwright. Knighted in 1977.
1932: †Words and Music. The Midshipmaid (US: Midshipmaid Gob). 1933: Britannia of Billingsgate. The Ghost Camera. The River Wolves. A Political Party. 1934: The Lash. Those Were the Days. Blind Justice. Doctor's Orders. 1935: Royal Cavalcade (US: Regal Cavalcade). Brown on Resolution (later For Ever England. US: Born for Glory). Car of Dreams. Charing Cross Road. 1936: First Offence. Tudor Rose (US: Nine Days a Queen). OHMS (US: You're in the Army Now). 1937: The Green Cockatoo (US: Four Dark Hours). 1939: Goodbye Mr Chips! *Happy Families. 1940: Old Bill and Son. *All Hands. 1941: Cottage to Let (US: Bombsight Stolen). The Black Sheep of Whitehall. The Big Blockade. 1942: The Young Mr Pitt. In Which We Serve. 1943: We Dive at Dawn. 1944: *Victory Wedding. This Happy Breed. Waterloo Road. 1945: The Way to the Stars (US: Johnny in the Clouds). *The Sky's the Limit. *Total War in Britain (narrator only). 1946: Land of Promise (voice only). Great Expectations. 1947: So Well Remembered. The October Man. 1948: Scott of the Atlantic. 1949: The History of Mr Polly. *Friend of the Family (narrator only). *The Flying Sky-scraper (narrator only). The Rocking Horse Winner. 1950: Morning Departure (US: Operation Disaster). 1951: Mr Denning Drives North. 1952: The Gentle Gunman. The Long Memory. 1954: Hobson's Choice. The Colditz Story. 1955: The End of the Affair. Above Us the Waves. Escapade. 1956: War and Peace. It's Great to be Young. The Baby and the Battleship. Around the World in 80 Days. Town on Trial! 1957: The Vicious Circle (US: The Circle). 1958: Ice-Cold in Alex (US: Desert Attack). I Was Monty's Double. 1959: Tiger Bay. Summer of the Seventeenth Doll (US: Season of Passion). 1960: Tunes of Glory. Swiss Family Robinson. The Singer Not the Song. 1961: Flame in the Streets. The Valiant. 1962: Tiara Tahiti. 1963: The Chalk Garden. 1964: The Truth about Spring. 1965: King Rat. Operation Crossbow (US: The Great Spy Mission). 1966: The Wrong Box. The Family Way. 1967: Chuka. Africa – Texas Style! 1968: Lady Hamilton – zwischen Smach und Liebe (GB and US: Emma Hamilton). La

morte non ha sesso (GB and US: A Black Veil for Lisa). 1969: Oh! What a Lovely War. Run Wild, Run Free. Adam's Woman. 1970: Ryan's Daughter. 1971: Dulcima. Young Winston. 1972: Lady Caroline Lamb. 1973: Oklahoma Crude. 1975: The 'Human' Factor. 1976: Trial by Combat (US: Dirty Knights' Work). 1977: The Devil's Advocate. 1978: The Big Sleep. The Thirty-Nine Steps. Dr Strange (TV). 1979: Zulu Dawn. Quatermass (TV. GB: cinemas as The Quatermass Conclusion). 1982: Gandhi. 1983: Sahara. 1984: The Masks of Death (TV). 1985: Murder with Mirrors (TV). The Adventures of Little Lord Fauntleroy (TV). 1986: When the Wind Blows (voice only). Tribute to Her Majesty. 1987: Who's That Girl. 1989: The Lady and the Highwayman (TV). 1991: The Last Straw (unreleased). 1992: Frankenstein – The Real Story (TV). 1993: The Big Freeze (unreleased). Deadly Advice. 1995: The Grotesque. 1996: Hamlet. 1997: Bean.
As director: 1966: Sky West and Crooked (US: Gypsy Girl).

†16mm record of stage show

MILLS, Juliet 1941–
Tiny, attractive, fizzy, blonde British actress with creamy complexion, the daughter of Sir John Mills (qv). British studios responded to her warm sense of humour by pitching her into 'Carry On'-style comedies. Only Billy Wilder partially exploited the Carole Lombard in her by casting her in *Avanti!*, but it was too little and too late. A talent which deserved more, she won an Emmy for *QB VII*, a 1974 TV film. Not to be confused with French actress Juliette Mills. Married (second) actor Maxwell Caulfield (1959–).
1942: In Which We Serve. 1947: So Well Remembered. The October Man. 1949: The History of Mr Polly. 1961: No, My Darling Daughter. 1962: Twice Round the Daffodils. 1963: Nurse on Wheels. Carry On Jack (US: Carry on Venus). 1965: The Rare Breed. 1967: Wings of Fire (TV). 1968: The Challengers (TV. GB: cinemas). 1969: Oh! What a Lovely War. 1972: Avanti! 1973: Alone with Terror (TV). Letters from Three Lovers (TV). 1974: Jonathan Livingstone Seagull (voice only). Chi sei? (GB: Devil Within Her. US: Behind the Door). Three Faces of Love (TV). QB VII (TV). 1975: Demon, Demon (TV). 1976: The Man with the Green Cross. 1977: Barnaby and Me. Alexander: The Other Side of Dawn (TV). 1979: The Cracker Factory (TV).

1990: Night of the Fox (TV). 1991: The Last Straw (unreleased). Columbo: No Time to Die (TV). 1992: Waxwork II: Lost in Time. A Stranger in the Mirror (TV). 1999: The Other Sister.

MIMIEUX, Yvette 1939–
There was steel behind the delicate appearance of this gossamer Hollywood blonde. It helped her break away from the milk-and-water roles she played at first and prolong her career into her forties with progressively tougher roles, including one TV movie she wrote herself, which cast her as a female assassin. Married/divorced director Stanley Donen.

1960: The Time Machine. Platinum High School (GB: Rich, Young and Deadly). 1961: Where the Boys Are. The Four Horsemen of the Apocalypse. The Light in the Piazza. 1962: Wonderful World of the Brothers Grimm. Diamond Head. 1963: Toys in the Attic. 1964: Looking for Love. 1965: Joy in the Morning. 1966: Monkeys, Go Home! The Reward. 1967: The Caper of the Golden Bulls (GB: Carnival of Thieves). The Mercenaries (GB: Dark of the Sun). 1968: Three in the Attic. 1969: The Picasso Summer. 1971: The Delta Factor. Black Noon (TV). Death Takes a Holiday (TV). The Night of the Assassin. 1972: Skyjacked. 1973: The Neptune Factor. 1974: Hit Lady (TV). 1975: The Legend of Valentino (TV). 1976: Jackson County Jail. Journey into Fear. 1977: Ransom for Alice (TV). Snowbeast (TV). The Busters (TV). 1978: Outside Chance (TV). Devil Dog: The Hound of Hell (TV). 1979: Ladyfingers. The Black Hole. 1980: Mystique/Brainwash/Circle of Power (released 1982). 1982: Forbidden Love (TV). 1983: Night Partners (TV). 1985: Obsessive Love (TV). 1986: The Fifth Missile (TV). 1990: Perry Mason: The Case of the Paris Paradox (TV). 1992: Lady Boss (TV).

MINEO, Sal (Salvador Mineo) 1939–1976
Dark-haired, soulful-eyed, faintly sullen-looking Italianate actor who went to Hollywood after stage success in *The King and I*, and played a variety of voluble (mostly sympathetic) tearaways from the wrong side of the tracks that reflected his own Bronx upbringing. Career faltered after the failure of *The Gene Krupa Story*. Stabbed to death in an alleyway near his home, the killer not being found until two years later. Oscar-nominated for *Rebel Without a Cause* and *Exodus*.

1955: Six Bridges to Cross. The Private War of Major Benson. Rebel Without a Cause. 1956: Giant. Somebody Up There Likes Me. Crime in the Streets. Rock, Pretty Baby. 1957: Dino (GB: Killer Dino). The Young Don't Cry. 1958: Tonka. 1959: A Private's Affair. 1960: The Gene Krupa Story (GB: Drum Crazy). Exodus. 1961: Escape from Zahrain. Cry Vengeance. 1962: The Longest Day. 1964: Cheyenne Autumn. 1965: The Greatest Story Ever Told. 1966: Who Killed Teddy Bear? The Dangerous Days of Kiowa Jones (TV. GB: cinemas). 1967: Stranger on the Run (TV). 1968: The Challengers (TV. GB: cinemas). Krakatoa – East of Java. 1969: 80 Steps to Jonah. 1970: One Day Left Before Tomorrow (TV). In Search of America (TV). 1971: Escape from the Planet of the Apes. 1972: The Family Rico (TV). 1973: Harry O (TV). 1974: The Hunters (TV). 1975: James Dean – The First American Teenager.

MINNELLI, Liza 1946–
Explosive, exhibitionist American singer and actress (the daughter of Judy Garland and director Vincente Minnelli) whose singing voice throbs with the nervous energy she scatters in all directions. Her striking 'Pierrette' looks – black hair, big, dark eyes, full lips and small, rounded face – were seen now and again in films with varying success. After being nominated for an Oscar in *The Sterile Cuckoo*, she won the award for *Cabaret*. She is credited with an appearance in *The King of Comedy*, but seems to appear only as a cardboard cut-out.

1948: Easter Parade. 1949: In the Good Old Summertime. 1954: The Long, Long Trailer. 1967: Charlie Bubbles. 1969: The Sterile Cuckoo (GB: Pookie). Tell Me That You Love Me, Junie Moon. 1971: Journey Back to Oz (voice only). 1972: Cabaret. 1974: That's Entertainment! 1975: Lucky Lady. 1976: A Matter of Time. Silent Movie. 1977: New York, New York. Movies Are My Life. 1980: Arthur. 1982: The King of Comedy. 1984: The Muppets Take Manhattan. 1985: That's Dancing! A Time to Live (TV). 1987: Rent-a-Cop. 1988: Arthur 2: On the Rocks. 1991: Stepping Out. 1994: Parallel Lives (TV). 1995: The West Side Waltz (TV). 1999: Jackie's Back! (TV).

MIRANDA, Carmen
(Maria Do Carmo M. Da Cunha) 1904–1955
Extravagantly made-up, with eyebrows that reached nearly to her black hair, and the widest mouth since Martha Raye, Carmen Miranda could have been made of wood – but when she danced, and sang, you knew she wasn't. Known as 'The Brazilian Bombshell' (although born in Portugal) she spoke wonderful fractured English, and stormed to immense popularity in wartime Hollywood musicals. She was said to have been fired by Fox when they found she wore no knickers beneath her swirling dresses! Died from a heart attack.

*1933: A voz do Carnaval. 1934: Estudiantes. 1935: Alô, Alô, Brazil. 1936: Alô, Alô Carnaval. 1938: Banana da Terra. 1940: Down Argentine Way. 1941: *Hollywood Visits the Navy. That Night in Rio. Week-End in Havana. 1942: Springtime in the Rockies. 1943: The Gang's All Here (GB: The Girls he Left Behind). 1944: Four Jills in a Jeep. Greenwich Village. Something for the Boys. 1945: Hollywood on Parade. *All Star Bond Rally. 1946: Doll Face (GB: Come Back to Me). If I'm Lucky. 1947: Copacabana. 1948: A Date with Judy. 1950: Nancy Goes to Rio. 1953: Scared Stiff.*

MIRREN, Helen (Ilyena Mironoff) 1945–
Forceful blonde British actress (of White Russian descent) with determined features, spectacular figure and classless image. She forsook a possible career as an international sex symbol of the cinema for the calmer waters of the Royal Shakespeare Company, for whom she made a memorable Lady Macbeth. In the late 1970s she returned to films in little clusters, as tarts-with-hearts and allied roles. She enjoyed great success as a tough police inspector in the *Prime Suspect* series on TV in the early 1990s. Oscar nomination for *The Madness of King George*. Married director Taylor Hackford.

1967: Herostratus. 1968: A Midsummer Night's Dream. 1969: Age of Consent. 1972: Savage Messiah. 1973: O Lucky Man! 1976: Hamlet. 1977: Caligula (released 1979). 1979: SOS Titanic (TV. GB: cinemas). Hussy. The Long Good Friday. 1980: The Fiendish Plot of Dr Fu Manchu. 1981: Excalibur. 1984: Cal. 2010. 1985: White Nights. 1986: Heavenly Pursuits. The Mosquito Coast. 1988: When the Whales Came. Pascali's Island. People of the Forest (narrator only). Cause Célèbre (TV). 1989: The Cook, The Thief, His Wife and Her Lover. Red King, White Knight (TV). 1990: The Comfort of Strangers. Bethune: The Making of a Hero. 1991: Where Angels Fear to Tread. 1993: The Hawk. Prince of Jutland. 1994: The Madness of King George. Letters from the East. 1996: Some Mother's Son / Sons and Warriors. Losing Chase (TV). 1997: Critical Care. Painted Lady (TV). 1998: Sidoglio Smithee. The Prince of Egypt (voice only). 1999: Teaching Mrs Tingle. The Passion of Ayn Rand (cable TV). 2000: Green Fingers. The Pledge.

MITCHELL, Cameron
(C. Mizell) 1918–1994
Tough-talking, whippy, curly-haired, bullet-headed American actor. At first he played honest Joes but after coming back to films in 1951 was seen in more aggressive roles. Abroad in the sixties making violent continental thrillers and action yarns and later, as rough-edged as ever, a regular in the TV series *The High Chaparral*. Never quite a top star, but never far away. One of the 1980s' hardest workers. Died from lung cancer.
1945: *The Last Installment. What Next, Corporal Hargrove? They Were Expendable. The Hidden Eye. 1946: The Mighty McGurk.

1947: High Barbaree. Cass Timberlane. Tenth Avenue Angel. 1948: Homecoming. Adventures of Gallant Bess. Leather Gloves (GB: Loser Take All). Command Decision. 1951: Smuggler's Gold. Man in the Saddle (GB: The Outcast). The Sellout. Death of a Salesman. Flight to Mars. Japanese War Bride. 1952: Okinawa. The Outcasts of Poker Flat. Pony Soldier (GB: MacDonald of the Canadian Mounties). Les Misérables. 1953: Man on a Tightrope. How to Marry a Millionaire. Powder River. The Robe (narrator only). 1954: Hell and High Water. Gorilla at Large. Garden of Evil. Désirée. 1955: Strange Lady in Town. Love Me or Leave Me. House of Bamboo. The Tall Men. The View from Pompey's Head (GB: Secret Interlude). Man on the Ledge (TV. GB: cinemas). The Ox-Bow Incident (TV. GB: cinemas). 1956: Carousel. Tension at Table Rock. All Mine to Give (GB: The Day They Gave Babies Away). 1957: Monkey on My Back. No Down Payment. Escapade in Japan. 1959: Pier 5 Havana. Three Came to Kill. Inside the Mafia. Face of Fire. Raubfischer in Hellas (GB and US: As the Sea Rages). 1960: The Unstoppable Man. The House on Airport Drive. The Last of the Vikings. 1961: Fury of the Vikings (US: Eric the Conqueror). 1962: Invasion of the Normans / I Normanni. Caesar the Conqueror. 1963: Girl from La Mancha. 1964: Minnesota Clay. Sei donne per l'assassino (GB and US: Blood and Black Lace). When Strangers Meet (US: Dog Eat Dog). Jim il primo (GB: Killer's Canyon). 1965: Raffica di coltelli. The Treasure of Macuba. 1966: Monster of the Wax Museum (GB: Nightmare in Wax). La Isla de la Muerte (GB: Bloodsuckers. US: Maneater of Hydra). Hombre. 1967: Autopsy of a Ghost. Ride the Whirlwind. Knives of the Avenger. 1969: Rebel Rousers. 1970: The Taste of the Savage. 1971: Thief (TV). The Reluctant Heroes (TV. GB: The Reluctant Heroes of Hill 656). Buck and the Preacher. 1972: Cutter (TV). Political Asylum. The Delphi Bureau (TV). The Rookies (TV). The Big Game. The Stranger (TV). 1974: The Klansman. The Midnight Man. The Hanged Man (TV). The Girl on the Late, Late Show (TV). Hitchhike! (TV). Death in Space (TV). Medusa. 1975: The Swiss Family Robinson (TV). 1976: Flood! (TV). The Taste of the Savage. The Quest (TV). 1977: Slavers. The Tool Box Murders. Return to Fantasy Island (TV). Haunts / The Veil. Viva Knievel! Stigma (TV). 1978: The Fish Men. Texas Detour. The Swarm. The Last Reunion (TV). The Perfect Woman. The Scalp Merchant (TV). The Hostage Heart (TV). 1979: Supersonic Man. Wild Times (TV). The Silent Scream. Hanging by a Thread (TV). 1980: The Boys. Without Warning (GB: The Warning). Turnover Smith (TV). OHMS (TV). 1981: The Demon. Raw Force. Frankenstein Island. The Guns and the Fury. 1982: Texas Lightning. Blood Link. My Favorite Year. Cataclysm. Screamers (The Fish Men with added footage). Kill Squad. 1983: Murder, Baby. Kenny Rogers As The Gambler – The Adventure Continues (TV). 1984: Prince Jack. Go for Gold. Killpoint. 1985: Savage Sunday / Low-Blow / Mission Kill. Night Train to Terror. The Tomb. 1986: From a Whisper to a Scream (later The Offspring). 1987: Ninja vs Nazi.

The Messenger. Killmasters. Night Force. Rage to Kill. Mutant War. Deadly Prey. Codename: Vengeance. 1988: Pop's Oasis. Hollywood Cop. Trapped / Trapped Alive / Forever Mine. Terror Night / Final Curtain. Not My Jurisdiction! Memorial Day. Return to Justice. 1989: Terror in Beverly Hills. Action USA. No Justice. 1990: Crossing the Line. Easy Kill. 1991: Demon Cop. 1995: Jack O'Lantern.

MITCHELL, Yvonne
(Y. Joseph) 1925–1979
Dark-haired, palely attractive British actress, largely in anguished roles. Popular both on television and in films in the fifties (she had made her stage debut at 14), she also wrote books and plays. Died from cancer.
1948: The Queen of Spades. 1949: Children of Chance. 1953: Turn the Key Softly. 1954: The Divided Heart. 1955: Escapade. 1956: Yield to the Night (US: Blonde Sinner). 1957: Woman in a Dressing Gown. 1958: Passionate Summer. 1959: Tiger Bay. Sapphire. 1960: Conspiracy of Hearts. The Trials of Oscar Wilde (US: The Man with the Green Carnation). 1961: Johnny Nobody. 1962: The Main Attraction. 1965: Genghis Khan. 1970: The Corpse (US: Crucible of Horror). 1971: Demons of the Mind. 1971: The Great Waltz. 1976: The Incredible Sarah. 1977: Widow's Nest.

MITCHUM, Robert, 1917–1997
Dark-haired, full-faced, lazy-lidded Hollywood star of powerful build and slow, distinctive speech. He survived the grind of 19 films in his first cinema year (and the narcotics bust that sent him to jail in 1948) to become the star of the firstly RKO *noir* thrillers, then bigger-budget movies of varying quality, and remained at the top of

the tree. Despite a casual acting style that looks more so in rubbish, he proved himself capable, in the right circumstances, of sensitive and haunting performances. Billed as Bob Mitchum until mid-1945. Nominated for an Academy Award in *The Story of GI Joe*. Father of actors Jim Mitchum (1941–) and Christopher Mitchum (1943–). Died from emphysema and lung cancer.

1943: Follow the Band. Bar 20. Hoppy Serves a Writ. Border Patrol. Colt Comrades. We've Never Been Licked (GB: Texas to Tokyo). The Lone Star Trail. False Colors. Corvette K-225 (GB: The Nelson Touch). Riders of the Deadline. Gung Ho! The Leather Burners. The Human Comedy. Beyond the Last Frontier. Doughboys in Ireland. Aerial Gunner. The Dancing Masters. Cry Havoc. Minesweeper. 1944: Mr Winkle Goes to War (GB: Arms and the Woman). When Strangers Marry. Girl Rush. Johnny Doesn't Live Here Any More. Thirty Seconds over Tokyo. Nevada. 1945: West of the Pecos. The Story of GI Joe/War Correspondent. 1946: Till the End of Time. The Locket. Undercurrent. 1947: Pursued. Desire Me. Crossfire. Out of the Past (GB: Build My Gallows High). 1948: Blood on the Moon. 1949: Holiday Affair. The Red Pony. The Big Steal. 1950: Where Danger Lives. 1951: My Forbidden Past. The Racket. His Kind of Woman. 1952: The Lusty Men. One Minute to Zero. Angel Face. 1953: Second Chance. White Witch Doctor. She Couldn't Say No (GB: Beautiful but Dangerous). 1954: Track of the Cat. River of No Return. 1955: The Man with the Gun (GB: The Trouble Shooter). Not As a Stranger. The Night of the Hunter. 1956: Foreign Intrigue. Bandido! 1957: Heaven Knows, Mr Allison. The Enemy Below. Fire Down Below. 1958: Thunder Road. The Hunters. 1959: The Angry Hills. The Wonderful Country. 1960: A Terrible Beauty (US: The Night Fighters). The Sundowners. Home from the Hill. The Grass is Greener. 1961: The Last Time I Saw Archie. 1962: Cape Fear. Two for the Seesaw. The Longest Day. Rampage! 1963: The List of Adrian Messenger. Man in the Middle. 1964: What a Way to Go! 1965: Mr Moses. 1967: Anzio (GB: The Battle for Anzio). The Way West. El Dorado. 1968: Villa Rides! Five Card Stud. Secret Ceremony. 1969: Young Billy Young. The Good Guys and the Bad Guys. 1970: Ryan's Daughter. 1971: Going Home. 1972: The Wrath of God. 1973: The Friends of Eddie Coyle. 1974: The Yakuza. 1975: Farewell, My Lovely. 1976: Midway (GB: Battle of Midway). The Last Tycoon. 1977: The Amsterdam Kill. 1978: Matilda. The Big Sleep. 1979: Breakthrough. 1980: Agency. Nightkill. 1982: That Championship Season. One Shoe Makes It Murder (TV). 1983: A Killer in the Family (TV). 1984: Maria's Lovers. The Ambassador. 1985: Reunion at Fairborough (TV). The Hearst and Davies Affair (TV). 1986: Thompson's Last Run (TV). Promises to Keep (TV). †The Conspiracy. 1987: Marilyn Monroe: Beyond the Legend. 1988: Mr North. Scrooged. John Huston. 1989: Jake Spanner – Private Eye (TV). Believed Violent/Presumé dangereux. 1990: A Family for Joe (TV). 1991: Midnight Ride. Cape Fear (remake). Waiting for the Wind (TV). Tombstone (narrator only). 1993:

Woman of Desire. 1994: Backfire. 1995: The Sunset Boys/Waiting for Sunset (released 1998). Dead Man. Wild Bill: Hollywood Maverick. 1996: James Dean – Race With Destiny (TV).

†*Uncompleted*

MIX, Tom 1880–1940
Dark, hawk-faced American star of silent cowboy films, a former deputy sheriff and rodeo rider who liked to dress flamboyantly in films at his peak but also to do his own stunts. His famous horse, Tony, who outlived him by two years, was almost a popular as his master. After making hundreds of westerns over a 25-year period, Mix's star career was ended in 1933 when he was badly injured in a fall from a horse. In later years he was said to have lost a million dollars backing a circus, and was trying for a comeback as a character actor when he was killed in a car crash. Directed many of his early films from *Local Color* (1913) to *Who's Your Father?* (1918). Five times married.

SHORTS: 1909: On the Little Big Horn. Ranch Life in the Great Southwest. Briton and Boer. An Indian Wife's Devotion. Up San Juan Hill. 1910: The Millionaire Cowboy. The Range Rider. The Long Trail. The Trimming of Paradise Gulch. Taming Wild Animals. Pride of the Range. 1911: Back to the Primitive. The Rose of Old St Augustine. Captain Kate/The Animal Trainer's Daughter. Dad's Girls. The Man from the East. The Totem Mark. In Old California. When the Gringos Came. Kit Carson's Wooing. Lost in the Arctic. The Wheels of Justice. Rescued by Her Lions. Lost in the Jungle. The Schoolmaster of Mariposa. Western Hearts. Why the Sheriff is a Bachelor. In the Days of Gold. A Romance of the Rio Grande. The Telltale Knife. 1912: Days of Daring. The Wagon Trail. Weary Goes Wooing/How Weary Went Wooing. Single Shot Parker. The Sheriff's Girl. Sagebrush Tom. Outlaw Reward. A Reconstructed Rebel. 1913: An Apache's Gratitude. The Range Law. How It Happened. The Sheriff of Yavapai County. The Life Timer. Juggling With Fate. Pauline Cushman, the Federal Spy. The Shotgun Man and the Stage Driver. His Father's Deputy. Religion and Gun Practise. The Wordless Message. The Noisy Six. Sallie's Sure Shot. Songs of Truce. The Marshal's Capture. Made a Coward. The Taming of Texas Pete. The Good Indian. The Stolen Moccasins. Tobias Wants Out. Saved by the Pony Express. Budd

Doble Comes Back. The Escape of Jim Dolan. The Sheriff and the Rustler. A Muddle in Horse Thieves. The Child of the Prairie. A Prisoner of Cabanas. Local Color. The Rejected Lover's Luck. The Cattle Thief's Escape. The Law and the Outlaw. Wilderness Mail. The Stagecoach-Driver and the Girl. 1914: In the Days of the Thundering Herd. Shotgun Jones. The Little Sister. Me an' Bill. The Leopard's Foundling. In Defiance of the Law. The Sheep Runners. Wiggs Takes the Rest Cure. His Fight. Etienne of the Glad Heart. When the Cook Fell Ill. The White Mouse. The Reveler. To Be Called For. Chip of The Flying U. Jim. The Livid Flame. The Lonesome Trail. Hearts and Masks. The Real Thing in Cowboys. Four Minutes Late. Garrison's Finish. The Losing Fight. The Going of the White Swan. Out of Petticoat Lane. If I Were Young Again. The Soul Mate. Your Girl and Mine. Wade Brent Pays. The Flower of Faith. The Lure o' the Windigo. Buffalo Hunting. Picture Cowboy. Ranger's Romance. The Tell-Tale Knife (remake of 1911 film). The Way of the Redman. Jimmy Hayes and Muriel. The Mexican. Why the Sheriff is a Bachelor (remake of 1911 film). The Rival Stage Lines. The Sheriff's Reward. The Man from the East (remake of 1911 film). The Scapegoat. Saved by a Watch. Cactus Jake, Heart-Breaker. A Militant School Ma'am. Arizona Wooing. On the Eagle Trail. 1915: Foreman of the Bar Z. Cactus Jim's Shop Girl. The Puny Soul of Peter Rand. Hearts of the Jungle. Jack's Pals. The Face at the Window. Heart's Desire. The Parson Who Fled West. Bad Man Bobbs. The Grizzly Gulch Chariot Race. The Stagecoach Driver and the Girl. Roping a Bride. Forked Trails. Slim Higgins. The Man from Texas. Bill Haywood, Producer. A Child of the Prairie (remake). Sagebrush Tom (remake). The Legal Light. The Outlaw's Bridge. Ma's Girls. The Conversion of Smiling Tom. Getting a Start in Life. Pals in Blue. A Matrimonial Boomerang. Mrs Murphy's Cooks. The Heart of the Sheriff. Saved by Her Horse. With the Aid of the Law. The Taking of Mustang Pete. The Child, the Dog and the Villain. A Lucky Deal. The Gold Dust and the Squaw. The Auction Sale of Run-Down Ranch. Never Again. The Range Girl and the Cowboy. The Girl and the Mail Bag. The Foreman's Choice. Her Slight Mistake. The Stagecoach Guard. The Brave Deserve the Fair. Athletic Ambitions. The Race for a Gold Mine. The Chef at Circle G. The Tenderfoot's Triumph. The Impersonation of Tom. Lucky Deal. 1916: When Cupid Slipped. The Resurrection of Dan Packard. Along the Border. A Mix-Up in Movies. Making Good. The Passing of Pete. Too Many Chefs. The Desert Calls Its Own. A Five Thousand Dollar Elopement. The Sheriff's Duty. The Man Within. The Cowpuncher's Peril. Going West to Make Good. Crooked Trails. The Girl of Gold Gulch. Taking a Chance. Legal Advice. Some Duel. Shooting Up the Movies. An Angelic Attitude. Local Color on the A-1 Ranch. A Bear of a Story. A Western Masquerade. Tom's Strategy. Roping a Sweetheart. The Taming of Grouchy Bill. The Pony Express Rider. The Raiders. A Corner in Water. The Canby Hill Outlaws. Mistakes Will Happen. Trilby's Love Disaster. A Mistake in Rustlers. An Eventful Evening. Tom's Sacrifice. A Close Call. The Sheriff's Blunder. The

Golden Thought. Twisted Trails. Starring in Western Stuff. In the Days of Daring. Harold's Bad Man. 1917: The Saddle Girth. The Luck That Jealousy Bought. Hearts and Saddles. Six Cylinder Love. A Roman Cowboy. Tom and Jerry Mix. A Soft Tenderfoot. Delayed in Transit. The Law, North of 75. The Rustler's Vindication. FEATURES: The Heart of Texas Ryan. Durand of the Bad Lands. 1918: Ace High. Cupid's Round-Up. Western Blood. *Who's Your Father? Six Shooter Andy. The Rainbow Trail. 1919: Hell-Roarin' Reform. Fame and Fortune. The Coming of the Law. The Wilderness Trail. Fighting for Gold. 1920: The Cyclone. Desert Love. The Terror. Three Gold Coins. Mr Logan USA. Treat 'Em Rough. The Dare-Devil. The Speed Maniac. The Feud. The Untamed. Rough Riding Romance. 1921: Prairie Trails. The Rough Diamond. A Ridin' Romeo. The Texan. The Night Horsemen. Trailin'! Hands Off! The Queen of Sheba. The Road Demon. Big Town Round-Up (GB: A Fighting Fool). After Your Own Heart. 1922: For Big Stakes. Up and Going. Chasing the Moon. Just Tony. Catch My Smoke. Sky High. The Fighting Streak. Do and Dare. Tom Mix in Arabia. 1923: Softboiled (GB: Yes! We Have No Temper). The Lone Star Ranger. Three Jumps Ahead. Romance Land. Stepping Fast. Mile-a-Minute Romeo. 1924: A Golden Thought. Oh! You Tony. Ladies to Board. Eyes of the Forest. The Heart Buster. North of Hudson Bay (GB: North of the Yukon). The Last of the Duanes. Teeth. The Trouble Shooter. The Foreman of Bar Z Ranch. 1925: Law and the Outlaw (remake). Everlasting Whisper. Riders of the Purple Sage. Dick Turpin. A Child of the Prairie. The Lucky Horseshoe. The Best Bad Man. The Rainbow Trail. The Deadwood Coach. 1926: No Man's Gold. The Great K and A Train Robbery. The Canyon of Light. Tony Runs Wild. Hardboiled. The Yankee Senor. My Own Pal. 1927: The Last Trail. Tumbling River. *Life in Hollywood No. 4. Outlaws of Red River. The Circus Ace. Silver Valley. The Bronco Twister. 1928: Hello Cheyenne. The Painted Post. Arizona Wildcat. Daredevil's Reward. King Cowboy (GB: The Cowboy King). A Horseman of the Plains. Son of the Golden West. 1929: Outlawed. Drifter (GB: Two Big Vagabonds). The Big Diamond Robbery. 1930: *Voice of Hollywood No. 1. Under a Texas Moon. *Voice of Hollywood No. 2. 1931: Six Cylinder Love (remake). The Dude Ranch. The Galloping Ghost (serial). 1932: *Hollywood on Parade No. 3. My Pal, the King. The Fourth Horseman. *Hollywood on Parade No. 4. Destry Rides Again. Riders of Death Valley. Texas Bad Man (GB: Defiance). The Cohens and Kellys in Hollywood. 1933: Terror Trail. Flaming Guns (GB: Rough Ridin' Romeo). Hidden Gold. Rustlers' Roundup. 1935: The Miracle Rider (serial).

MODINE, Matthew 1959–

Tall, brown-haired, unsmiling American actor with deep-set eyes and solid features. Often in serious, sensitive roles – in recent times he has also tried light comedy and callow charmers – the limelight avoided him until he took the title role in Birdy. Big commercial successes have evaded the Utah-born actor since then. His performances

have sometimes seemed languid and he has yet to impose his personality on another key role.
1981: Amy and the Angel (TV). 1982: Baby It's You. 1983: Private School. 1984: Vision Quest/Crazy for You. The Hotel New Hampshire. Streamers. 1985: Mrs Soffel. Birdy. 1987: Full Metal Jacket. Orphans. 1988: Married to the Mob. 1989: The Gamble/The Match (released 1991). Gross Anatomy/A Cut Above. 1990: Memphis Belle. Pacific Heights. 1991: Wind. 1992: Equinox. 1993: And the Band Played On. Short Cuts. 1994: The Browning Version. Love, Trust & Ketchup. The Bible: Jacob. 1995: Fluke. Bye, Bye Love. CutThroat Island. 1996: Death in the Afternoon. 1997: The Maker (TV). The Blackout. The Real Blonde. 1998: What the Deaf Man Saw (TV). If . . . Dog . . . Rabbit. 1999: The American. Any Given Sunday. Notting Hill. 2000: Flowers for Algernon (TV). Very Mean Men.

MOL, Gretchen 1973–

Slim, very blonde American actress of pale complexion and Dresden china looks, a sleek sex symbol of the late 1990s. After extensive drama academy training, she was busy on stage for several years before launching an even busier film career, which saw her rise gradually up cast lists from very small beginnings. She made 15 films in the last three years of the 1990s alone.
1996: Girl 6. Calm at Sunset, Calm at Dawn (TV). The Funeral. The Last Time I Committed Suicide. 1997: Subway Stories: Tales from the Underground (TV). Donnie Brasco. Finding Graceland (released 1998). The Deli. Music from Another Room. 1998: Bleach. New Rose Hotel. Rounders. Celebrity.

Too Tired to Die. 1999: Forever Mine. Cradle Will Rock. The Thirteenth Floor. Sweet and Lowdown. 2000: Just Looking. Stalk. Picnic (TV).

MONROE, Marilyn
(Norma Jean Baker) 1926–1962
Blonde sex symbol who became one of the great tragic figures of American cinema. She was sure about her effect on men, but extremely unsure of her talent, which meant that directors had to be increasingly patient with her insecurities in later years. But she could be touching as fading belles (notably in Bus Stop and The Misfits) and winning in musical comedy (especially Gentlemen Prefer Blondes). Fired from her last film because of temperament and impossible timekeeping, she died from a drug overdose, possibly a suicide.
1946: The Shocking Miss Pilgrim. 1947: Dangerous Years. 1948: Scudda-Hoo! Scudda-Hay! (GB: Summer Lightning). Ladies of the Chorus. 1949: Love Happy (later Klepto-maniacs). 1950: The Fireball. Right Cross. A Ticket to Tomahawk. The Asphalt Jungle. All About Eve. 1951: The Hometown Story. Love Nest. Let's Make It Legal. As Young As You Feel. 1952: We're Not Married. Clash by Night. O. Henry's Full House (GB: Full House). Monkey Business. Don't Bother to Knock. 1953: Niagara. Gentlemen Prefer Blondes. How to Marry a Millionaire. 1954: River of No Return. There's No Business Like Show Business. 1955: The Seven Year Itch. 1956: Bus Stop. 1957: The Prince and the Showgirl. 1959: Some Like It Hot. 1960: Let's Make Love. 1961: The Misfits. 1962: Something's Gotta Give (uncompleted).

MONTALBAN, Ricardo 1920–

Smooth Mexican actor with dark hair, oval face and flashing smile. He could sing a bit, dance a little and project dramatic sincerity, qualities that kept him at M-G-M, several times opposite Esther Williams, for seven years. Since then has kept busy in a wide variety of roles, playing, among others, Japanese, Italians, Frenchmen and even American Indians. Married actress Georgiana Young (1923–).
1941: *He's a Latin from Staten Island. 1942: Cinco Fueron Escogidos (released 1945 as Five Were Chosen). El Verdugo de Sevilla. La Razon de la Culpa. *Hi, Neighbor! *El Rancho Grande. 1943: La Fuga. Santa. Fantasia Ranchera. La Casa de la Zorra.

1944: *Cadetes de la Naval. La Hora de la Verdad. Nosotros.* 1945: *Pepita Jimenez.* 1947: *Fiesta.* 1948: *The Kissing Bandit. On an Island with You.* 1949: *Border Incident. Neptune's Daughter. Battleground.* 1950: *Mystery Street. Right Cross. Two Weeks with Love.* 1951: *Across the Wide Missouri. Mark of the Renegade.* 1952: *My Man and I.* 1953: *Sombrero. Latin Lovers.* 1954: *The Saracen Blade. The Courtesan of Babylon (GB: The Slave Woman. US: Queen of Babylon).* 1955: *Sombra Verde. A Life in the Balance. Operation Cicero (TV).* 1956: *Untouched. The Son of the Sheik. Three for Jamie Dawn. Broken Arrow (TV).* 1957: *Child of Trouble (TV). Sayonara.* 1959: *Target for Three (TV).* 1960: *Let No Man Write My Epitaph.* 1961: *Gordon il pirata nero (GB: The Black Buccaneer).* 1962: *The Reluctant Saint. Hemingway's Adventures of a Young Man. (GB: Adventures of a Young Man).* 1963: *Life is a Ball (GB: All This and Money Too).* 1964: *Cheyenne Autumn.* 1965: *The Money Trap.* 1966: *Madame X. The Longest Hundred Miles (TV). The Singing Nun.* 1967: *Code Name: Heraclitus (TV). Sol Madrid (GB: The Heroin Gang).* 1968: *Desperate Mission (TV: released 1975).* 1969: *Black Water Gold (TV). The Pigeon (TV). Blue. Sweet Charity.* 1970: *The Aquarians (TV). La spina dorsale del Diavolo (GB and US: The Deserter).* 1971: *The Badge or the Cross (TV). The Face of Fear (TV). Escape from the Planet of the Apes. Taxi to Terror.* 1972: *Conquest of the Planet of the Apes. The Scorpio Scarab. Fireball Forward (TV).* 1973: *The Last Three Days of Pancho Villa. The Train Robbers.* 1974: *The Mark of Zorro (TV). Wonder Woman.* 1975: *Won Ton Ton, the Dog Who Saved Hollywood. Joe Panther (GB: TV).* 1977: *Fantasy Island (TV). Kino, the Padre on Horseback.* 1978: *Captains Courageous (TV). Return to Fantasy Island (TV).* 1982: *Star Trek II: The Wrath of Khan.* 1983: *Cannonball Run II.* 1988: *The Naked Gun: From the Files of Police Squad!*

MONTAND, Yves (Ivo Livi) 1921–1991
Italian-born actor and singer in French films, usually exuding cynicism and shifty charm, with a perennial cigarette hanging from the corner of the mouth. Not a film regular until the mid-fifties, after *The Wages of Fear* had made his name. Briefly in Hollywood in the early sixties, later a respected senior citizen of French cinema. Long married (from 1951) to Simone Signoret (*qv*). Died from a heart attack.
1945: *Etoile sans lumière.* 1946: *Les portes de la nuit.* 1947: *L'idole.* 1950: *Souvenirs perdus (GB and US: Lost Property).* 1951: *Paris chante toujours.* 1953: *La salaire de la peur (GB and US: The Wages of Fear). Tempi nostri.* 1954: *Napoléon. Une tranche de la vie.* 1955: *Les héros sont fatigués (GB and US: The Heroes Are Tired). Marguerite de la nuit.* 1956: *Uomini e lupi/Men and Wolves. Die vind Rose.* 1957: *Les sorcières de Salem (GB and US: The Witches of Salem). Premier Mai. La grande strada azzurra.* 1958: *La loi (GB and US: Where the Hot Wind Blows).* 1959: *Yves Montand chante . . .* 1960: *Let's Make Love.* 1961: *Sanctuary. Goodbye Again.* 1962: *My Geisha.* 1965: *The Sleeping Car Murders. Is Paris Burning?* 1966: *La guerre est finie.* 1967: *Vivre pour vivre. Grand Prix.* 1968: *Z. Mr Freedom. Un soir . . . un train. Le diable par le queue.* 1969: *Le joli mai (narrator).* 1970: *Le cercle rouge. L'aveu. On a Clear Day You Can See Forever.* 1971: *La folie des grandeurs.* 1972: *Tout ba vien. Le fils. César et Rosalie. Die Dummen streiche der Reichen.* 1973: *Etat de siège/State of Siege.* 1974: *Le hasard et la violence (GB: The Scarlet Room).* 1975: *Vincent, François, Paul et les autres. Le sauvage (US: Lovers Like Us).* 1976: *Police Python 357.* 1977: *Le grand escrogriffe. Flashback. La menace.* 1978: *Les routes du sud.* 1979: *Clair de femme.* 1980: *I comme Icare.* 1981: *Le choix des armes.* 1982: *Tout feu, toute flamme (US: All Fired Up).* 1983: *Garçon!* 1985: *Carné, l'homme à la caméra.* 1986: *Jean de Florette. Manon des sources.* 1988: *Trois places pour le 26.* 1991: *Netchaiev est en retour.* 1992: *IP5: l'île aux pachydermes.*

MONTEZ, Maria (M. Silas) 1918–1951
Exotic brunette leading lady in Hollywood films. Born in the Dominican Republic to a Spanish consulate official, she became the staple ingredient of Universal's Technicolor 'easterns' of the war years until overtaken in popularity by Yvonne De Carlo. Married (second) to Jean-Pierre Aumont (*qv*) from 1943. Drowned in her bath, possibly after a heart attack. Actress Tina Aumont (1946–) is her daughter.
1940: *Boss of Bullion City.* 1941: *Raiders of the Desert. Lucky Devils. The Invisible Woman. That Night in Rio. South of Tahiti (GB: White Savage). Moonlight in Hawaii.* 1942: *The Mystery of Marie Roget. Bombay Clipper. Arabian Nights.* 1943: *White Savage (GB: White Captive). Ali Baba and the Forty Thieves.* 1944: *Cobra Woman. Gypsy Wildcat. Follow the Boys. Bowery to Broadway.* 1945: *Sudan.* 1946: *Tangier.* 1947: *Pirates of Monterey. The Exile.* 1948: *Siren of Atlantis. Hans le marin (US: The Wicked City).* 1949: *Portrait d'un assassin.* 1950: **The Thief of Venice (release 1953). Amore e sangue (US: Sensuality). The Pirate's Revenge.*

MONTGOMERY, Douglass
(Robert D. Montgomery) 1907–1966
Fair-haired American actor of sensitive but cheerful and outgoing personality. Began his career as Kent Douglass to avoid confusion with an already famous Robert Montgomery, but played lacklustre roles largely unworthy of his talents. Became popular in Britain on radio in World War II while serving with the Canadian army, and made several films there but was little seen, even on TV, after the mid-fifties.
1930: †*Paid (GB: Within the Law).* 1931: †*Daybreak.* †*Five and Ten (GB: Daughter of Luxury).* †*A House Divided.* †*Waterloo Bridge.* 1933: *Little Women.* 1934: *Eight Girls in a Boat. Little Man, What Now? Music in the Air.* 1935: *The Mystery of Edwin Drood. Harmony Lane. Lady Tubbs (GB: The Gay Lady).* 1936: *Tropical Trouble. Everything is Thunder.* 1937: *Counsel for Crime. Life Begins with Love.* 1939: *The Cat and the Canary.* 1945: *The Way to the Stars (US: Johnny in the Clouds).* 1946: *Woman to Woman.* 1947: *Sinfonia fatale (GB: When in Rome).* 1948: *Forbidden.* 1949: *Back to Sorrento (narrator only).*

†*As Kent Douglass*

MONTGOMERY, Elizabeth
See MONTGOMERY, Robert

MONTGOMERY, George
(G. M. Letz) 1916–

Few Hollywood heroes were more virile than husky six-footer George Montgomery, who rode the upper-bracket western range (beginning as a stunt man) for more than 20 years, before becoming a star-writer-director of some very presentable action yarns filmed mostly in the Philippines. Married to Dinah Shore (qv) 1943–1960: has never remarried. Once a champion heavyweight boxer.

1935: †Singing Vagabond. 1937: †Conquest (GB: Marie Walewska). †Springtime in the Rockies. 1938: †The Lone Ranger (serial). †Gold Mine in the Sky. †Come on, Rangers. †The Old Barn Dance. †Under Western Stars. †Army Girl (GB: The Last of the Cavalry). †Pals of the Saddle. †Santa Fe Stampede. †Billy the Kid Returns. †Hawk of the Wilderness (serial). †Shine on, Harvest Moon. 1939: †Man of Conquest. †Rough Riders' Round-Up. †Frontier Pony Express. †Wall Street Cowboy. †In Old Caliente. †Hi-Yo Silver (feature version of serial The Lone Ranger). 1939: †The Mysterious Miss X. †I Was a Convict. †The Night Riders. Southward Ho! SOS Tidal Wave (GB: Tidal Wave). New Frontier/Frontier Horizon. Wyoming Outlaw. In Old Monterey. The Arizona Kid. Saga of Death Valley. South of the Border. 1940: Cisco Kid and the Lady. Jennie. Charter Pilot. Young People. Star Dust. 1941: The Cowboy and the Blonde. Last of the Duanes. Riders of the Purple Sage. Cadet Girl. Accent on Love. 1942: Orchestra Wives. Ten Gentlemen from West Point. China Girl. Roxie Hart. 1943: Bombers' Moon. Coney Island. 1946: Three Little Girls in Blue. 1947: The Brasher Doubloon (GB: The High Window). 1948: The Girl from Manhattan. Lulu Belle. Belle Starr's Daughter. 1949: Dakota Lil. 1950: Davy Crockett, Indian Scout (GB: Indian Scout). Iroquois (GB: The Tomahawk Trail). 1951: The Sword of Monte Cristo. The Texas Rangers. 1952: Indian Uprising. Cripple Creek. 1953: Jack McCall, Desperado. The Pathfinder. Fort Ti. Gun Belt. *Hollywood Stuntmen. 1954: The Lone Gun. Battle of Rogue River. 1955: Masterson of Kansas. Robber's Roost. Seminole Uprising. 1956: Huk! Canyon River. 1957: Last of the Badmen. Street of Sinners. Gun Duel at Durango. Pawnee (GB: Pale Arrow). Man from God's Country. 1958: Black Patch. Badman's Country. Toughest Gun in Tombstone. 1959: Watusi. King of the Wild Stallions. 1961: †The Steel Claw. 1962: ‡Samar! 1964: †From Hell

to Borneo. ‡Guerillas in Pink Lace. 1965: Battle of the Bulge. Satan's Harvest. 1966: Outlaw of Red River. 1967: Hostile Guns/Huntsville. Bomb at 10:10. Warkill. 1968: Hallucination Generation. Strangers at Sunrise. 1970: ‡Ride the Tiger. 1971: Daredevil. 1986: Wild Wind. 1988: Ransom in Blood.

†As George Letz ‡Also directed

MONTGOMERY, Robert
(Henry Montgomery) 1904–1981

Dark, debonair American leading man, kept in snappy light comedy roles and romantic leads by M-G-M, although he clearly had a yen for stronger stuff and proved chillingly effective as the killer in Night Must Fall. This got him away from the upper-society-bracket characters with which he had become identified, but he drifted away from show business after the forties and seems little remembered. Father of actress Elizabeth Montgomery (1933–1995). Received Oscar nominations for Night Must Fall and Here Comes Mr. Jordan. A much-decorated war hero, he died from cancer.

1929: The Single Standard. So This is College. Untamed. Three Live Ghosts. 1930: Sins of the Children (GB: The Richest Man in the World). The Divorcee. Their Own Desire. Our Blushing Brides. Love in the Rough. Free and Easy. The Big House. War Nurse. 1931: Inspiration. The Easiest Way. Man in Possession. Shipmates. Private Lives. Strangers May Kiss. 1932: But the Flesh is Weak. Letty Lynton. Lovers Courageous. Faithless. Blondie of the Follies. 1933: Another Language. Hell Below. Night Flight. When Ladies Meet. Made on Broadway (GB: The Girl I Made). 1934: The Mystery of Mr X. Fugitive Lovers. Hideout. Riptide. 1935: Biography of a Bachelor Girl. Forsaking All Others. *Starlight Days at the Lido. No More Ladies. Vanessa. Her Love Story. 1936: Piccadilly Jim. Petticoat Fever. Trouble for Two (GB: The Suicide Club). 1937: Ever Since Eve. Night Must Fall. The Last of Mrs Cheyney. Live, Love and Learn. 1938: Three Loves Has Nancy. The First Hundred Years. Yellow Jack. 1939: Fast and Loose. 1940: Busman's Honeymoon (US: Haunted Honeymoon). The Earl of Chicago. 1941: Rage in Heaven. Mr and Mrs Smith. Unfinished Business. Here Comes Mr Jordan. 1945: They Were Expendable. 1946: Lady in the Lake. 1947: Ride the Pink Horse. 1948: The Secret Land (narrator only). The Saxon Charm. June Bride. 1949: Once More, My Darling. 1950:

Your Witness (US: Eye Witness). 1960: The Gallant Hours (narrator only).
As director: 1946: Lady in the Lake. 1949: Once More, My Darling. 1950: Your Witness (US: Eye Witness). 1960: The Gallant Hours.

MOORE, Clayton
(Jack C. Moore) 1908–1999

Tall, solid, square-faced American action star with brown, wavy hair, a hero of countless 1940s' Saturday morning serials, but now best remembered behind a mask as The Lone Ranger, a role that he played (including two feature film spin-offs from his long-running TV series) from 1949 to 1958. Moore started in films as a stuntman at the advanced age of 29, after years as a circus aerialist. He was soon taking acting roles as well, but there were few leading roles outside serials (he sometimes played the bad guy in minor films) until the Lone Ranger came along: it was a role he continued playing in fairs, rodeos and TV commercials long after his vintage years were over. Married actress Sally Allen in 1943. She died in 1986 and he later married actress Carlita. Died from a heart attack.

1937: †Thunder Trail. 1938: †The Texans. †When Were You Born? †Secrets of an Actress. The Cowboy from Brooklyn (GB: Romance and Rhythm). Go Chase Yourself. Dick Tracy Returns (serial). Daredevils of the Red Circle (serial). 1939: Sergeant Madden. Zorro's Fighting Legion (serial). Mesquite Buckaroo. 1940: Kit Carson. Son of Monte Cristo. 1941: Tuxedo Junction (GB: The Gang Made Good). International Lady. The Corsican Brothers. 1942: Black Dragons. Outlaws of Pine Ridge. Perils of Nyoka (serial). 1946: The Crimson Ghost (serial). The Bachelor's Daughters (GB: Bachelor Girl). Heldorado. Cyclotrode 'X' (feature version of serial The Crimson Ghost). 1947: Jesse James Rides Again (serial). Along the Oregon Trail. 1948: Marshal of Amarillo. Adventures of Frank and Jesse James (serial). The Far Frontier. The Plunderers. G-Men Never Forget (serial). 1949: Frontier Investigator. Sheriff of Wichita. The Cowboy and the Indians. Masked Raiders. The Ghost of Zorro (serial). Riders of the Whistling Pines. Bandits of El Dorado (GB: Tricked). South of Death Valley (GB: River of Poison). Frontier Marshal. Bride of Vengeance. The Gay Amigo. 1950: Sons of New Mexico (GB: The Brat). Flying Disc Man from Mars (serial). 1951: Cyclone Fury. 1952: Night Stage to Galveston. Son of Geronimo (serial). Desert Passage. Barbed Wire (GB: False

News). Mutiny. The Raiders (GB: Riders of Vengeance). Radar Men from the Moon (serial). The Hawk of Wild River. Buffalo Bill in Tomahawk Territory. Captive of Billy the Kid. Montana Territory. 1953: Jungle Drums of Africa (serial). Down Laredo Way. Return of the Corsican Brothers (GB: Bandits of Corsica). Kansas Pacific. Gunfighters of the Northwest (serial). 1954: The Black Dakotas. Titled Tenderfoot (TV). 1955: Apache Ambush. 1956: The Lone Ranger. 1958: The Lone Ranger and the Lost City of Gold. 1959: The Ghost of Zorro (feature version of 1949 serial).

†As Jack Moore

MOORE, Cleo 1928–1973
Statuesque American actress, a minor-league blonde bombshell with handsome, open face. She looked as though she belonged in mink and was alleged to have been discovered by an agent who saw her just that way on someone's arm at a boxing match. Became identified with brassy broads in the seamy melodramas of Hugo Haas, which never rose above B-feature status. Once ran for Governor of Louisiana. Died from a heart attack.
1948: Congo Bill (serial). 1950: The Great Jewel Robber. Dynamite Pass. This Side of the Law. Rio Grande Patrol. Hunt the Man Down. Gambling House. Bright Leaf. 1951: On Dangerous Ground. 1952: The Pace that Thrills. Strange Fascination. 1953: One Girl's Confession. Thy Neighbor's Wife. 1954: Bait. The Other Woman. 1955: Hold Back Tomorrow. Women's Prison. 1956: Over-Exposed. 1957: Hit and Run.

MOORE, Colleen
(Kathleen Morrison) 1900–1988
Cute, chirpy American actress with dark, bobbed hair. Her appeal was somewhat akin to that of Mary Pickford, although she was often to be seen as madcap flappers in frothy comedies. Did not adapt well to sound and, after drifting on for a few years, retired on her second marriage in 1937.
1916: Intolerance (as extra). 1917: Bad Boy. An Old Fashioned Young Man. The Little American. The Savage. Hands Up! 1918: A Hoosier Romance. Little Orphan Annie. 1919: The Busher. The Man in the Moonlight. The Wilderness Trail. The Egg-Crate Wallop (GB: The Knock Out Blow). Common Property. The Cyclone. 1920: *Her Bridal Nightmare. *A Roman Scandal. Dinty. So Long Letty. The

Devil's Claim. When Dawn Came. 1921: The Lotus Eater. His Nibs. Sky Pilot. Broken Hearts of Broadway. 1922: Affinities. Come on Over (GB: Darlin'). Broken Chains. The Wallflower. The Ninety and Nine. Forsaking All Others. 1923: Slippy McGee. Look Your Best. April Showers. The Nth Commandment (GB: The Higher Law). Through the Dark. The Huntress. Flaming Youth. 1924: Painted People. The Perfect Flapper. Flirting with Love. So Big. 1925: Sally. The Desert Flower. We Moderns. 1926: Irene. Ella Cinders. It Must Be Love. 1927: Twinkletoes. Orchids and Ermine. Naughty But Nice. Her Wild Oat. *Life in Hollywood No. 2. 1928: Happiness Ahead. Oh Kay! Lilac Time. Synthetic Sin. Why Be Good? 1929: Smiling Irish Eyes. Footlights and Fools. 1933: The Power and the Glory (GB: Power and Glory). 1934: Success at Any Price. Social Register. The Scarlet Letter. 1970: Voyage à Galveston.

MOORE, Demi
(Demetria Guynes) 1962–
Low-voiced, dark-haired, slightly petulant-looking American actress, a member of the so-called Brat Pack of the 1980s. She made quick strides towards middle-range roles after ditching drug and alcohol habits, and her notorious nude poses for magazines, in and out of pregnancy, made her a headline figure after she married (second) actor Bruce Willis (qv) in 1987. The couple parted in 1998. In the 1990s, boasting a tougher image and fuller figure, she took on more challenging and provocative roles, and soon became one the of the world's highest-paid and powerful female stars. Blind in her left eye.
1981: Choices. 1982: Young Doctors in Love. Parasite. 1983: Blame It on Rio. 1984: No

Small Affair. 1985: St Elmo's Fire. 1986: One Crazy Summer. 'About Last Night . . .' Wisdom. 1988: The Seventh Sign (formerly The Boarder). 1989: We're No Angels. 1990: Ghost. Tales from the Crypt (cable TV). Nothing But Trouble. 1991: Mortal Thoughts. The Butcher's Wife. 1992: A Few Good Men. 1993: Indecent Proposal. 1994: Disclosure. 1995: The Scarlet Letter. Now and Then. 1996: Beavis and Butt-head Do America (voice only). The Juror. Striptease. The Hunchback of Notre Dame (voice only). If These Walls Could Talk (cable TV). 1997: G.I. Jane. Deconstructing Harry. Destination Anywhere (v). 2000: Passion of Mind.

MOORE, Dickie
See POWELL, Jane

MOORE, Dudley 1935–
Tiny, dark-haired, crumple-faced British revue comedian and jazz pianist with ingratiating smile. In partnership with long, lugubrious Peter Cook (1937–1995), he gained great popularity on television in the early 1960s, proving adept at comic voices and funny little men, and even singing soprano. Later he married and divorced (first and second of four) actresses Suzy Kendall and Tuesday Weld (both qv). His popular appeal seemed to have waned when he suddenly hit the big time in Hollywood in his mid forties as a lightly comic leading man. But, after two major hits with '10' and Arthur (the latter winning him an Oscar nomination), roles to keep the diminutive Dud at the top proved too hard to find, although he kept busy for another 10 years.
1964: *The Hat (narrator only). 1966: The Wrong Box. 1967: 30 is a Dangerous Age, Cynthia. Bedazzled. 1969: The Bed Sitting Room. Monte Carlo or Bust (US: Those Daring Young Men in their Jaunty Jalopies). 1972: Alice's Adventures in Wonderland. 1977: The Hound of the Baskervilles. 1978: Foul Play. 1979: '10'. To Russia with Elton (narrator only). 1980: Wholly Moses! Arthur. 1981: Derek and Clive Get the Horn. 1982: Six Weeks. 1983: Lovesick. Unfaithfully Yours. Romantic Comedy! 1984: Best Defence. Micki & Maude. 1985: Santa Claus. 1986: The Adventures of Milo and Otis (narrator, English-language version). 1987: Like Father, Like Son. 1988: Arthur 2: On the Rocks. 1990: Crazy People. 1991: Blame It on the Bellboy. 1993: The Pickle. 1994: Parallel Lives (TV). 1995: The Guv'nor. 1997: The Disappearance

of Kevin Johnson (completed 1995). A Weekend in the Country/ This Joint is Jumpin' (TV).

MOORE, Grace
(Mary G. Moore) 1898–1947

Willowy blonde American opera star, known as 'the Tennessee Nightingale'. She was an obvious choice to feature in early sound musicals, but her early vehicles were not too successful and M-G-M dispensed with her services after she gained weight. A deal with minor studio Columbia seemed to be a step down, but the singer later described it as 'the best contract I ever signed', as she bounced back, won an Oscar nomination for *One Night of Love* and became hugely successful in tailor-made vehicles for a few short years. Her days of cinema stardom had ended when she was killed in a plane crash. Her date of birth, for many years thought to be 1901, was finally revealed to be December 1898.

1930: New Moon. A Lady's Morals (GB: Jenny Lind/ The Soul Kiss). 1934: One Night of Love. 1935: A Dream Comes True. Love Me Forever (GB: On Wings of Song). 1936: The King Steps Out. 1937: I'll Take Romance. When You're in Love (GB: For You Alone). 1939: Louise.

MOORE, Julianne
(Julie Anne Smith) 1960–

Ginger-haired, sharp-chinned American actress of minxish, slightly sad-faced attractiveness and narrow green eyes, English-style features that she has sometimes matched with an impeccable English accent. A self-confessed 'geek' at school – 'small, wears glasses, doesn't do sports' – she took a while to get a toehold in films, but since the mid 1990s has played leading roles in everything from obscure cult movies to big action blockbusters, trying her hand at pretty well every genre. Twice married and divorced, she has a son by her current partner, director Bart Freundlich. Academy Award nominee for *Boogie Nights* and *The End of the Affair*.

1988: Slaughterhouse 2. 1989: Money, Power, Murder (TV). 1990: Tales from the Darkside: The Movie. 1991: Cast a Deadly Spell. The Last to Go (TV). 1992: The Gun in Betty Lou's Handbag. The Hand That Rocks the Cradle. 1993: Short Cuts. Benny & Joon. Body of Evidence. The Fugitive. 1994: Luck, Trust & Ketchup. Safe. Vanya on 42nd Street. 1995: Assassins. Nine Months. Roommates. 1996: Surviving Picasso. The Myth of Fingerprints. 1997: The Lost World: Jurassic Park. Hellcab/Chicago Cab. Boogie Nights. 1998: The Big Lebowski. Psycho. 1999: Cookie's Fortune. An Ideal Husband. A Map of the World. Magnolia. The End of the Affair. 2000: The Ladies' Man. Hannibal.

MOORE, Kieron
(K. O'Hanrahan) 1925–

Dark, brooding, good-looking Irish actor who made a good start in British films, but whose later performances lacked animation. In the late sixties he became very interested in overseas aid development, and subsequently made two documentary films about emergent nations.

1945: †The Voice Within. 1947: A Man About the House. Mine Own Executioner. 1948: Anna Karenina. 1949: Saints and Sinners. Maria Chapdelaine (GB: The Naked Heart). 1951: Honeymoon Deferred. David and Bathsheba. Ten Tall Men. 1953: Mantrap (US: Woman in Hiding). Recoil. 1954: Conflict of Wings. The Green Scarf. 1955: The Blue Peter (US: Navy Heroes). 1956: Satellite in the Sky. 1957: The Steel Bayonet. Three Sundays to Live. 1958: The Key. Darby O'Gill and the Little People. 1959: The Angry Hills. The League of Gentlemen. 1960: The Day They Robbed the Bank of England. The Siege of Sidney Street. 1961: Dr Blood's Coffin. 1962: The Day of the Triffids. I Thank a Fool. The Main Attraction. The 300 Spartans. 1963: Hide and Seek. Girl in the Headlines (US: The Model Murder Case). The Thin Red Line. 1964: Son of a Gunfighter. Bikini Paradise. 1965: Crack in the World. 1966: Arabesque. Run Like a Thief. Custer of The West. As director: 1975: The Progress of Peoples (and narrator). 1979: The Parched Land (and narrator).

†As Kieron O'Hanrahan

MOORE, Mary Tyler 1936–

Bright, pretty, dark-haired American actress, comedienne, singer and dancer who became a television icon over the years in numerous series, but especially *The Dick Van Dyke Show* and *The Mary Tyler Moore Show*. She underwent considerable traumas in her private life as the years went by – including the death of her son from an accidental gunshot wound – and never achieved the same glittering success in films, despite an Oscar nomination for *Ordinary People*. From that time (1980), her natural sparkle was consistently subdued in anguished roles. Three-times married, and co-founder of the powerful MTM Enterprises, which produced many quality TV drama series.

1961: X-15. 1967: Thoroughly Modern Mille. 1968: What's So Bad About Feeling Good? Don't Just Stand There! 1969: Change of Habit. Run a Crooked Mile (TV). 1978: First, You Cry (TV). 1980: Ordinary People. 1982: Six Weeks. 1984: Finnegan Begin Again (TV). Heartsounds (TV). 1986: Just Between Friends. 1988: Gore Vidal's Lincoln. 1990: Thanksgiving Day (TV. GB: The Good Family). The Last Best Year (TV). 1993: Stolen Babies (TV). 1995: Stolen Memories: Secrets from the Rose Garden (TV. GB: Forbidden Memories). 1996: Flirting with Disaster (TV). 1997: Payback (TV). Keys to Tulsa. Reno Finds her Mom. 1998: Three Cats from Miami (TV). 1999: Labor Pains. 2000: Mary & Rhoda (TV). 2001: Cheaters.

MOORE, Owen
See PICKFORD, Mary

MOORE, Roger 1927–

Boyishly-handsome, athletic, well-built British leading man with smooth manner, and suavely cultured voice. Although palpably no great actor, with a limited range, he had an easy presence which disarmed most criticism. After years of struggle, both in Britain and Hollywood, he hit pay dirt with the TV series *The Saint*; later took over from Sean Connery (*qv*) as James Bond. And he occasionally proved himself capable of above-par performances when pushed by a determined director.

1945: Caesar and Cleopatra. Perfect Strangers (US: Vacation from Marriage). 1946: Gaiety George (GB: Showtime). Piccadilly Incident. 1947: Captain Boycott. 1949: Paper Orchid. Trottie True (US: Gay Lady). 1954: The Last Time I Saw Paris. 1955: Interrupted Melody.

The King's Thief. Diane. 1959: The Miracle. 1960: The Sins of Rachel Cade. 1961: Gold of the Seven Saints. Il ratto delle sabine/Rape of the Sabines (US: Romulus and the Sabines). 1962: Un branco di vigliacchi/No Man's Land. 1969: Crossplot. 1970: The Man Who Haunted Himself. 1973: Live and Let Die. 1974: Gold. The Man with the Golden Gun. 1975: That Lucky Touch. 1976: Shout at the Devil. Sicilian Cross (US: Street People). Sherlock Holmes in New York (TV). 1977: The Spy Who Loved Me. 1978: The Wild Geese. Escape to Athena. 1979: Moonraker. North Sea Hijack (US: ffolkes). 1980: The Sea Wolves. Les seducteurs/Sunday Lovers. 1981: The Cannonball Run. For Your Eyes Only. 1983: Octopussy. Curse of the Pink Panther. 1984: The Naked Face. 1985: A View to a Kill. 1987: The Magic Snowman (voice only). 1989: Bed and Breakfast. 1990: Bulls-eye! Fire, Ice and Dynamite. 1995: The Man Who Wouldn't Die (TV). 1996: The Quest. The Saint (voice only). Spice World.

MOORE, Terry (Helen Koford) 1929–
Bright, bubbly, petite, light-haired American actress, a former child model who played several teenage roles before catching the public eye as the girl in *Mighty Joe Young*. She enjoyed a few years of stardom after this before beginning to slip. Received an Oscar nomination for *Come Back, Little Sheba*. Four times married, once to mogul Howard Hughes.
*1940: ‡Maryland. ‡The Howards of Virginia (GB: The Tree of Liberty). 1942: †On the Sunny Side. **A-Haunting We Will Go. **My Gal Sal. 1943: **True to Life. **A Date with Destiny. 1944: **Gaslight. ‡Since You Went Away. ‡Sweet and Lowdown. 1945: ‡Son of Lassie. 1946: ‡Shadows. †Summer Holiday*

(released 1948). 1947: †Devil on Wheels. 1948: The Return of October (GB: A Date with Destiny). 1949: Mighty Joe Young. 1950: The Great Rupert. He's a Cockeyed Wonder. Gambling House. 1951: Two of a Kind. Sunny Side of the Street. The Barefoot Mailman. 1952: Come Back, Little Sheba. 1953: Man on a Tightrope. Beneath the 12-Mile Reef. King of the Khyber Rifles. 1955: Portrait of Alison (US: Postmark for Danger). Shack Out on 101. Daddy Long Legs. 1956: Between Heaven and Hell. The Moneymakers (TV). 1957: The Clouded Image (TV). Bernardine. Peyton Place. 1959: A Private's Affair. Cast a Long Shadow. 1960: Platinum High School (GB: Rich, Young and Deadly). Why Must I Die? (GB: 13 Steps to Death). 1965: Black Spurs. Town Tamer. City of Fear. 1966: Waco. 1967: A Man Called Dagger. 1970: Quarantined (TV). 1971: Daredevil. 1976: Smash Up on Interstate Five (TV). 1977: Death Dimension/Kill Factor. 1984: Hellhole. 1986: W.A.R. 1988: Beverly Hills Brats. 1989: Father's Day. Jake Spanner – Private Eye (TV). 1991: Marilyn and Me (TV). 1996: Speak. 1998: Mighty Joe Young (remake). Second Chances.

‡As Helen Koford. **As Judy Ford
†As Jan Ford

MORE, Kenneth 1914–1982
Square-faced, cheerful British actor with a mop of light wavy hair. A revue artist at 21, he took to films in the late 1940s, at first in quiet supporting roles, but gradually coming to the fore as good-hearted, devil-may-care, ultra-British types with an eye for the ladies. He burst through to stardom in *Genevieve*, and remained one of Britain's most popular stars until the failure of the underrated *The Comedy Man*. Married (third) actress Angela Douglas (1940–). Died from Parkinson's disease.
1935: Look Up and Laugh. 1936: Carry on London. Windmill Revels. Not Wanted on Voyage (US: Treachery on the High Seas). 1946: School for Secrets (US: Secret Flight). 1948: Scott of the Antarctic. 1949: For Them That Trespass. Man on the Run. Now Barabbas was a robber. Stop Press Girl. 1950: Morning Departure (US: Operation Disaster). The Clouded Yellow. Chance of a Lifetime. 1951: No Highway (US: No Highway in the Sky). The Franchise Affair. Appointment with Venus (US: Island Rescue). Brandy for the Parson. 1952: The Yellow Balloon. 1953: Never Let Me Go. Genevieve. Our Girl Friday (US: The Adventures of Sadie). 1954: Doctor in the

House. The Man Who Loved Redheads (narrator only). 1955: Raising a Riot. The Deep Blue Sea. 1956: Reach for the Sky. 1957: The Admirable Crichton (US: Paradise Lagoon). 1958: A Night to Remember. Next to No Time! The Sheriff of Fractured Jaw. 1959: The 39 Steps. Northwest Frontier (US: Flame over India). Sink the Bismarck! 1960: Man in the Moon. 1961: The Greengage Summer (US: Loss of Innocence). 1962: Some People. We Joined the Navy. The Longest Day. 1963: The Comedy Man. 1966: †The Collector. 1967: The Mercenaries (US: Dark of the Sun). 1968: Fraulein Doktor. 1969: Oh! What a Lovely War. Battle of Britain. 1970: Scrooge. 1976: The Slipper and the Rose. Where Time Began. 1977: Leopard in the Snow. 1978: The Silent Witness (narrator only). 1979: The Spaceman and King Arthur (US: Unidentified Flying Oddball). 1981: A Tale of Two Cities (TV).

†Scenes deleted from final release print

MOREAU, Jeanne 1928–
Tight-lipped, sharp-looking brunette French actress, a magnetic screen personality and mistress of high drama. The physical resemblance to Bette Davis cannot be, one feels, entirely insignificant. Once the youngest student at the French National Conservatory of Dramatic Art. Latterly has shown an inclination to direct. She married (second) American director William Friedkin in 1977, but the couple divorced three years later.
1948: Dernier amour. 1950: Pigalle-Saint-Germain-des-Prés. Meurtres. 1951: L'homme de ma vie. 1952: Il est minuit, Docteur Schweitzer. 1953: Julietta. Dortoir des grandes. Secrets d'alcove (GB and US: The Bed). 1954: Touchez pas au grisbi (GB: Grisbi. US: Honor Among Thieves). Les intrigantes. La Reine Margot. 1955: Les hommes en blanc. M'sieur la Caille (GB: The Parasite). Gas-Oil. 1956: Le salaire du péché (US: Wages of Sin). Les louves (GB and US: The She-Wolves). 1957: Jusqu'au dernier. L'étrange Monsieur Stève. Trois jours à vivre. 1958: Ascenseur pour l'échafaud (GB: Lift to the Scaffold. US: Frantic). Le dos au mur (GB and US: Evidence in Concrete). Echec au porteur. Les amants. 1959: Les quatre cents coups (GB and US: The 400 Blows). Les liaisons dangereuses. Five Branded Women. 1960: The Carmelites. Moderato cantabile. 1961: Une femme est une femme. La notte. Jules et Jim. 1962: Eve/Eva. La baie des anges.

1963: Le feu follet (GB: A Time to Live and a Time to Die. US: The Fire Within). The Trial. The Victors. Peau de banane/Banana Peel. 1964: Diary of a Chambermaid. Mata Hari Agent H 21 (GB: Mata Hari). The Yellow Rolls Royce. La peau douce (GB: Silken Skin. Voice only). 1965: The Train. Viva Maria! 1966: Chimes at Midnight (US: Falstaff). Mademoiselle. Sailor from Gibraltar. 1967: The Oldest Profession. 1968: La mariée était en noir/The Bride Wore Black. Great Catherine. The Immortal Story. 1969: Le corps de Diane. The Deep (unfinished). 1970: Monte Walsh. Compte à rebours. 1971: Alex in Wonderland. Cannibales en Sicile. Dead Reckoning. L'humeur vagabonde. Mille baisers de Florence. 1972: Chère Louise. 1973: Le petit théâtre de Jean Renoir (TV. GB and US: cinemas). 1974: Nathalie Granger. Les valseuses (GB: Making It). La race des 'Seigneurs'. Je t'aime. Hu-Man. 1975: Le jardin qui bascule. Souvenirs d'en France (US: French Provincial). 1976: Mr Klein. Lumière. The Last Tycoon. 1980: Your Ticket is No Longer Valid. 1981: La Débandade. Plein Sud/ Southbound. Mille milliards de dollars. La truite/The Trout. 1982: Querelle. 1983: Der Dauer von Babylon. 1986: Le paltoquet. Sauve-toi Lola. 1987: Le simulateur. Le miraculé. La nuit de l'océan. Hôtel Terminus (voice only). 1988: Calling the Shots. 1990: Until the End of the World. Nikita/La Femme Nikita. La femme fardée. Alberto Express. 1991: To meteoro vima to pelargo. Anna Karamozova. La vieille qui marchait dans la mer. 1992: L'amant/The Lover (voice only). Map of the Human Heart. Die Abwesenheit/ L'absence. A demain (US: See You Tomorrow). The Clothes in the Wardrobe (TV. US: cinemas, as The Summer House). 1993: Je m'appelle Victor. A Foreign Field. 1994: Les cent et une nuits. 1995: La propriétaire. I Love You, I Love You Not (released 1997). Beyond the Clouds. L'univers de Jacques Demy. 1996: Tombo. 1997: Amour et confusions. Witch Way Love/Un amour de sorcière. 1998: Ever After. 1999: Princesa. Perdido. 2000: Il manoscritto del principe.

As director: *1976: Lumière. 1978: l'adolescente.*

MORIARTY, Michael 1941–
Tall, round-faced, chubby-cheeked, brown-haired, slightly furtive-looking American actor and jazz pianist. Stage-trained in England, he built up a big reputation on stage back in America, before venturing into films at 30. Despite good beginnings, he never became a cinema 'name' although he continued to pick up awards for TV and theatre performances, and enjoyed success as part of TV's *Law & Order* team in its five most successful years, from 1990 to 1994. Lives in Halifax, Nova Scotia. His busy style has adapted equally well to cops and crooks.

1971: My Old Man's Place (GB: Glory Boy). Hickey & Boggs. 1973: Bang the Drum Slowly. A Summer Without Boys (TV). The Glass Menagerie (TV). The Last Detail. 1974: Shoot It: Black – Shoot It: Blue. 1975: Operation Undercover (US: Report to the Commissioner). 1977: The Deadliest Season (TV). 1978: Who'll Stop the Rain (GB: Dog Soldiers). The Winds of Kitty Hawk (TV). 1979: Too Far to Go (TV). 1981: Reborn. 1982: The Link/Blood Link. Q – The Winged Serpent/Q. The Sound of Murder. 1985: Odd Birds. Troll. Pale Rider. The Stuff. 1987: It's Alive III: Island of the Alive. The Hanoi Hilton. Dark Tower (released 1989). A Return to Salem's Lot. 1988: Nitti (TV). 1989: The Secret of the Ice Cave. Tailspin: Behind the Korean Airliner Tragedy (TV). 1990: Full Fathom Five. 1993: Born Too Soon (TV). 1995: Children of the Dust/A Good Way to Die (TV). 1996: Cagney & Lacey: True Convictions (TV). 1996: Managua. Crime of the Century (TV). Calm at Sunset (TV). Broken Silence (TV). Courage Under Fire. 1997: Shiloh. Major Crime (TV). 1998: Earthquake in New York (TV). The Life and Times of Hank Greenberg (D). 1999: Women Wanted. Shiloh 2: Shiloh Season. The Art of Murder. Bad Faith. 2000: Children of My Heart.

MORELL, André (A. Mesritz) 1909–1978
Staunch, light-haired British actor, in leading roles on stage from the thirties, and on the fringe of cinema stardom for many years without ever becoming a box-office name. In later years, mixed small roles as judges and other figures of authority with leading parts in horror films. Married to Joan Greenwood (*qv*) from 1960.

*1938: Many Tanks Mr Atkins. *The Murdered Constable. *Confidence Tricksters. *Criminals Always Blunder. *Receivers. *The Kite Mob. 13 Men and a Gun. 1939: Ten Days in Paris (US: Missing Ten Days). 1940: Three Silent Men. 1942: Unpublished Story. 1948: Against the Wind. 1949: No Place for Jennifer. 1950: Madeleine. So Long at the Fair. Stage Fright. Seven Days to Noon. The Clouded Yellow. Trio. 1951: Flesh and Blood. High Treason. 1952: Tall Headlines. Stolen Face. 1953: His Majesty O'Keefe. 1954: The Golden Link. The Black Night. 1955: Summer Madness (US: Summertime). Three Cases of Murder. The Secret. They Can't Hang Me. 1956: The Man Who Never Was. The Black Tent. The Baby and the Battleship. Zarak. 1957: Interpol (US: Pickup Alley). Paris Holiday. The Bridge on the River Kwai. Diamond Safari. 1958: The Camp on Blood Island. 1959: The Hound of the Baskervilles. Behemoth the Sea Monster (US: The Giant Behemoth). Ben-Hur. 1960: Cone of Silence (US: Trouble in the Sky). 1961: The Shadow of the Cat. Cash on Demand. 1963: Woman of Straw. 1964: The Moon-Spinners. 1965: Judith. She. The Plague of the Zombies. 1966: The Wrong Box. 1967: The Mummy's Shroud. The Mercenaries (US: Dark of the Sun). 1968: The Vengeance of She. 1970: Julius Caesar. 10 Rillington Place. 1972: Pope Joan. *The Man and the Snake. 1974: QB VII (TV). 1975: Barry Lyndon. 1976: The Slipper and the Rose. The Message. 1978: The Lord of the Rings (voice only). The First Great Train Robbery.*

MORENO, Antonio
(A. Monteagudo) 1886–1967
Dark, Spanish-born Hollywood star of distinguished bearing, a popular leading man in silents for 15 years. The coming of sound coincided naturally with a move into character roles, and he roamed the world in search of interesting material. Later appeared as priests, judges and aristocrats. Died from a stroke.

*1912: *The Voice of the Million. *So Near, Yet So Far. *Two Daughters of Eve. *The Musketeers of Pig Alley. 1913: *No Place for Father. *The House of Discord. *By Man's Law. Judith of Bethulia. 1914: *His Father's House. *Our Mutual Girl. *Too Many Husbands. *The Ladies' War. *The Song of the Ghetto. *The Memories in Men's Souls. *Politics and the Press. *Under False Colors. *The Old Flute Player. *Classmates. *Strongheart. *The Accomplished Mrs Thompson. *The Persistent Mr Prince. *John Rance, Gentleman. *The Hidden Letters. *The Loan Shark King. *The Peacemaker. *Goodbye Summer. 1915: *In the Latin Quarter. *The Quality of Mercy. *The Park Honeymooners. *Love's Way. *The Island of Regeneration. Dust of Egypt. On Her Wedding Night. *Anselo Lee. *Youth. *The Gypsy Trail. *A 'Model' Wife. A Price for Folly. 1916: The Supreme Temptation. Kennedy Square. *Susie, the Sleuth. *She Won the Prize. The Shop Girl. The Tarantula. Rose*

of the South. *By Man's Law. The Devil's Prize. 1917: Her Right to Live. Aladdin from Broadway. The Magnificent Meddler. By Right of Possession. The Mark of Cain. Money Magic. The Captain of the Gray Horse Troop. A Son of the Hills. The Angel Factory. 1918: The First Law. The Naulahka. The Iron Test (serial). The House of Hate. 1919: The Perils of Thunder Mountain (serial). 1920: The Invisible Hand (serial). The Veiled Mystery (serial). 1921: The Secret of the Hills. Three Sevens. 1922: A Guilty Conscience. 1923: My American Wife. Look Your Best. The Trail of the Lonesome Pine. The Spanish Dancer. The Exciter. Lost and Found on a South Sea Island (GB: Lost and Found). 1924: Tiger Love. Flaming Barriers. The Border Legion. The Story without a Name (GB: Without Warning). Bluff (GB: The Four Flusher). 1925: Her Husband's Secret. Learning to Love. One Year to Live. 1926: Mare Nostrum. Beverly of Graustark. The Flaming Forest. The Temptress. Love's Blindness. 1927: Madame Pompadour. It. Venus of Venice. En la Tierra del Sol. 1928: Nameless Men. Come to My House. The Air Legion. Synthetic Sin. The Whip Woman. Midnight Taxi. Adoration. 1929: *Voice of Hollywood. Careers. Romance of the Rio Grande. El Cuerpo del Delita. 1930: Rough Romance. One Mad Kiss. El Hombre Malo. La Voluntad de Muerto. 1931: Los que Danzan. Fin de Fiesta. 1932: *The Wide Open Spaces. Primavera en Otono. La Ciudad de Carton. 1933: Rosa de Francia. Senora Casada. Necisita marido. 1935: Storm over the Andes. 1936: Maria de la O. The Bohemian Girl. 1938: Rose of the Rio Grande. 1939: Ambush. 1940: Seven Sinners. 1941: Two Latins from Manhattan. They Met in Argentina. The Kid from Kansas. 1942: Valley of the Sun. Undercover Man. Fiesta. 1944: Tampico. 1945: The Spanish Main. Sol y Sombra. 1946: Notorious. 1947: Captain from Castile. 1949: Lust for Gold. 1950: Dallas. Crisis. Saddle Tramp. 1951: Mark of the Renegade. 1952: Untamed Frontier. 1953: Thunder Bay. Wings of the Hawk. 1954: The Creature from the Black Lagoon. Saskatchewan (GB: O'Rourke of the Royal Mounted). 1956: The Searchers. 1958: Mr Pharaoh and Cleopatra (US: Catch Me If You Can).
As director: 1931: Santa. 1932: Aguilas Frente al Sol.

from childhood and stealing scenes from stars from the early fifties. Did not become a star cinema attraction, even after an Oscar for West Side Story, but has continued to delight TV and nightclub audiences with her whirling dance routines. Marketed her own fitness video in the 1990s. The only artist ever to win Oscar, Emmy, Tony and Grammy awards, a record that may never be equalled. Films previously credited to her before 1950 now appear to belong to another Rosita Moreno.
1950: †So Young, So Bad. The Toast of New Orleans. Pagan Love Song. 1952: The Fabulous Senorita. The Ring. Singin' in the Rain. Cattle Town. Ma and Pa Kettle on Vacation (GB: Ma and Pa Kettle Go to Paris). 1953: Fort Vengeance. Latin Lovers. Jivaro (GB: Lost Treasure of the Amazon). El Alamein (GB: Desert Patrol). 1954: Garden of Evil. The Yellow Tomahawk. 1955: Untamed. Seven Cities of Gold. 1956: The Vagabond King. The King and I. The Lieutenant Wore Skirts. Broken Arrow (TV). 1957: The Deer-slayer. 1960: This Rebel Breed. Alas, Babylon (TV). 1961: West Side Story. Summer and Smoke. 1962: Samar! 1963: Cry of Battle. 1968: The Night of the Following Day. 1969: Popi. Marlowe. 1971: Carnal Knowledge. Taxi to Terror. 1972: The Voice of La Raza. 1976: The Boss's Son. 1979: Anatomy of a Seduction (TV). 1980: Happy Birthday Gemini. 1981: The Four Seasons. 1982: Portrait of a Showgirl (TV). 1989: B. L. Stryker: The Dancer's Touch (TV). 1991: Life in the Food Chain/ Age Isn't Everything. 1994: Blackout. Italian Movie. I Like It Like That. 1995: Angus. 1996: The Big Spree (TV). The Wharf Rat (TV). 1998: Slums of Beverly Hills. 1999: Carlo's Wake. The Rockford Files: If It Bleeds ... It Leads (TV). Resurrection (TV). 2000: Blue Moon.

†As Rosita Moreno

1935: †I Conquer the Sea. 1936: †Piccadilly Jim. †Suzy. †Old Hutch. †The Great Ziegfeld. †Down the Stretch. 1937: †*Annie Laurie. †Song of the City. †Navy Blue and Gold. †Mama Steps Out. 1938: †Men with Wings. †King of Alcatraz (GB: King of the Alcatraz.) ‡Persons in Hiding. †Illegal Traffic. Waterfront. 1939: *Ride, Cowboy, Ride. *The Singing Dude. The Return of Dr X. No Place to Go. 1940: Three Cheers for the Irish. Tear Gas Squad. River's End. The Fighting 69th. Kitty Foyle. *March on, Marines. Flight Angels. 1941: Bad Men of Missouri. Affectionately Yours. Kisses for Breakfast. 1942: Wings for the Eagle. Captains of the Clouds. In This Our Life. The Hard Way. 1943: Thank Your Lucky Stars. The Desert Song. 1944: Hollywood Canteen. *The Shining Future. Shine on Harvest Moon. The Very Thought of You. 1945: God is My Co-Pilot. Christmas in Connecticut (GB: Indiscretion). 1946: Two Guys from Milwaukee (GB: Royal Flush). One More Tomorrow. The Time, the Place and the Girl. 1947: Cheyenne. My Wild Irish Rose. 1948: Always Together. To the Victor. Two Guys from Texas (GB: Two Texas Knights). One Sunday Afternoon. 1949: It's a Great Feeling. The Lady Takes a Sailor. 1950: Perfect Strangers (GB: Too Dangerous to Love). Raton Pass (GB: Canyon Pass). Pretty Baby. 1951: Painting the Clouds with Sunshine. 1952: This Woman is Dangerous. Cattle Town. 1955: Pearl of the South Pacific. The Gun That Won the West. 1956: Uranium Boom. 1968: Rogue's Gallery. 1975: Won Ton Ton, the Dog Who Saved Hollywood.

†As Stanley Morner ‡As Richard Stanley

MORGAN, Michèle
(Simone Roussel) 1920–
Narrow-faced, golden-haired, green-eyed, sulkily beautiful French actress who has also been a success in British and American films. One of the most sought-after international stars from the early forties to the mid-fifties: the darker the drama, the more haunting her performances became. Still active on the French film and theatre scene. Married to actors William Marshall and Henri Vidal, the latter leaving her a widow in 1959.
1935: †Mademoiselle Mozart. 1936: †Une fille à Papa. †Le mioche. †Mes tantes et moi. †La belle équipe. 1937: Gribouille (US: The Lady in Question). Orage. 1938: Quai des brumes. L'entraîneuse. 1939: Le récif de corail. Les musiciens du ciel. La loi du nord. Remorques.

MORGAN, Dennis
(Stanley Morner) 1909–1994
Fresh-faced, shy-seeming American actor and tenor singer, of Irish parentage. Joined Warners under his new name, and became a likeable part of their product from late 1938 until mid 1952, often in musical tandem with big, brash Jack Carson (qv). Although he played a few action-man roles after this, his rich singing voice ensured that his future would lie in nightclubs. When this career was over he became a rancher. Died from heart problems.

MORENO, Rita (Rosita Alverio) 1931–
Flashing-eyed, fiery, petite, brunette Puerto Rican actress and dancer, in show business

1940: Untel, père et fils. 1942: Joan of Paris. 1943: Two Tickets to London. Higher and Higher. 1944: Passage to Marseille (GB: Passage to Marseilles). 1946: The Chase. La symphonie pastorale. 1948: The Fallen Idol. Fabiola. Aux yeux du souvenir. 1949: La belle que violà. Maria Chapdelaine (GB: The Naked Heart). 1950: Madame X / L'étrange Madame X. Le château de verre. 1951: The Seven Deadly Sins. 1952: La minute de verité / The Moment of Truth. 1953: Destinées (GB: Love and the Frenchwoman. US: Daughters of Destiny). Les orgueilleux (GB: The Proud Ones). 1954: Obsession. Napoléon. 1955: Oasis. Les grandes manoeuvres (GB: Summer Manoeuvres). Marguerite de la Nuit. 1956: Si Paris nous était conté. Marie Antoinette. Les vendangés. 1957: Maxime. The Vintage. Retour de Manivelle (GB and US: There's Always a Price Tag). 1958: Le miroir à deux faces (GB and US: The Mirror Has Two Faces). Pourquoi viens-tu si tard? Racconti d'estate (GB: Girls for the Summer). 1959: Vancanze invierno. Grand Hotel / Menschen im Hotel. 1960: Fortunat. Les scélérats. 1961: Le puits aux trois vérités. Les lions son lâchés. Rencontres. 1962: Le crime ne paie pas. Landru. The Gentle Art of Murder. 1963: Il fornaretto di Venezia. Méfiez-vous mesdames? 1964: Constance aux enfers. 1966: Lost Command. 1968: Benjamin. 1972: Les amis de mon fils. 1975: Le chat et le souris (GB: Seven Suspects to Murder. US: Cat and Mouse). 1978: Robert et Robert. 1986: Un homme et une femme: vingt ans déjà. 1990: Tutti stanno bene. 1997: Des gens si bien élévés.

†As Simone Roussel

MORGAN, Terence 1921–

Darkly sleek British leading man, usually cast as handsome rats. A certain screen charisma helped mask his limited acting ability, and he enjoyed a good variety of leading roles in British films throughout the fifties.

1948: Hamlet. 1950: Shadow of the Past. 1951: Captain Horatio Hornblower RN. Encore. 1952: Mandy (US: Crash of Silence). It Started in Paradise. 1953: Street Corner (US: Both Sides of the Law). The Steel Key. Always a Bride. Turn the Key Softly. 1954: l'amante di paridi / Eterna femmina (GB and US: The Face That Launched a Thousand Ships). I cavalieri dell'illusione. Dance Little Lady. Forbidden Cargo. Svengali. 1955: They Can't Hang Me. 1956: It's a Wonderful World. The March Hare. 1957: The Scamp. 1958: Tread Softly, Stranger. 1959: The Shakedown. 1960: Piccadilly Third Stop. 1964: The Curse of the Mummy's Tomb. 1966: Tiger of the Seven Seas (GB: The Fighting Corsair). La vengeance du Surcouf / Thunder Over the Ocean. 1967: The Penthouse. 1972: Hide and Seek. 1975: The Lifetaker. 1979: Yesterday's Warriors. 1993: The Mystery of Edwin Drood.

MORISON, Patricia
(Eileen P. Morison) 1914–

Dark-haired, pencil-browed, exotic-looking American singer and actress of rather haughty demeanour. Although largely wasted by Hollywood in silly decorative roles, she later achieved great success in Broadway musicals.

*1938: Persons in Hiding. 1939: I'm from Missouri. The Magnificent Fraud. 1940: *Chinese Garden Festival. Rangers of Fortune. Untamed. 1941: Romance of the Rio Grande. The Roundup. One Night in Lisbon. *Stars Past and Present. *Stars at Play. 1942: Beyond the Blue Horizon. Are Husbands Necessary? A Night in New Orleans. 1943: Silver Skates. The Song of Bernadette. Hitler's Madman. The Fallen Sparrow. Calling Doctor Death. Where Are Your Children? 1945: Without Love. Lady on a Train. 1946: Dressed to Kill (GB: Sherlock Holmes and the Secret Code). Danger Woman. 1947: Tarzan and the Huntress. Queen of the Amazons. Song of the Thin Man. †Kiss of Death. 1948: The Prince of Thieves. The Return of Wildfire. Sofia. 1950: *My Foolish Heart. 1953: Eddie Drake Investigates (TV. GB: cinemas). 1960: Song Without End. 1975: Won Ton Ton, the Dog Who Saved Hollywood. 1985: Mirrors (TV).*

†Scenes deleted from final release print

MORLEY, Robert 1908–1992

Large British stage star, film character actor, writer and wit. He often looked as though he had just detected a bad smell (the script, perhaps, in many of his later films) and huffed and puffed to great effect as a comic Sydney Greenstreet. His characters were almost always larger than life and he dominated his films (the earlier ones especially), often to the stars' discomfort. Memorable as W.S. Gilbert, Oscar Wilde and King George III. Nominated for a Best Supporting Actor Oscar in his first film. Died following a stroke.

1938: Marie Antoinette. 1940: You Will Remember. 1941: Major Barbara. The Big

*Blockade. This Was Paris. 1942: The Young Mr Pitt. The Foreman West to France (US: Somewhere in France). *Partners in Crime. 1945: I Live in Grosvenor Square (US: A Yank in London). 1947: The Ghosts of Berkeley Square. 1948: The Small Back Room. 1951: Outcast of the Islands. The African Queen. 1952: Curtain Up. 1953: The Story of Gilbert and Sullivan (US: The Great Gilbert and Sullivan). The Final Test. Beat the Devil. 1954: Beau Brummell. The Good Die Young. The Rainbow Jacket. 1955: The Adventures of Quentin Durward (US: Quentin Durward). 1956: Around the World in 80 Days. Loser Takes All. 1958: Law and Disorder. The Sheriff of Fractured Jaw. The Journey. 1959: The Doctor's Dilemma. Misalliance (TV). Libel. The Battle of the Sexes. 1960: Giuseppe venduto dei fratelli (GB: Sold into Egypt. US: Joseph and his Brethren). Oscar Wilde. 1961: The Young Ones. Go to Blazes. The Road to Hong Kong. 1962: Nine Hours to Rama. The Boys. The Old Dark House. 1963: Murder at the Gallop. Ladies Who Do. Hot Enough for June (US: Agent 8¾). Take Her, She's Mine. 1964: Topkapi. *Rhythm 'n' Greens (narrator only). Of Human Bondage. 1965: Those Magnificent Men in Their Flying Machines. The Alphabet Murders. Genghis Khan. The Loved One. A Study in Terror (US: Fog). Life at the Top. 1966: Hotel Paradiso. Tendre voyou. Way . . . Way Out. Finders Keepers. 1967: Woman Times Seven. The Trygon Factor. 1968: Hot Millions. 1969: Some Girls Do. Sinful Davey. Twinky (US: Lola). 1970: Cromwell. Doctor in Trouble. Song of Norway. 1971: When Eight Bells Toll. 1973: Many Moons (narrator only). Theatre of Blood. 1975: Hugo the Hippo (voice only). Great Expectations (TV. GB: cinemas). 1976: The Blue Bird. 1978: Who is Killing the Great Chefs of Europe? (GB: Too Many Chefs). 1979: The Human Factor. Scavenger Hunt. 1980: Oh Heavenly Dog. 1981: The Great Muppet Caper. 1983: High Road to China. 1984: Second Time Lucky. 1985: Trouble at the Royal Rose / Trouble with Spys. 1987: Little Dorrit I. Little Dorrit II. The Wind. 1989: Istanbul. The Lady and the Highwayman (TV).*

MORRIS, Chester
(John C. Morris) 1901–1970

Grim-faced, square-jawed American actor with long, narrow mouth (almost a serious Joe E. Brown) and liquid eyes. Made a great impact in two dramatic early sound films,

Alibi and *The Big House*, but declined to 'B' features and played the series character Boston Blackie, a resourceful and likeable small-time crook, from 1941 to 1949. Later successful on stage and TV, both as actor and magician. Suffered from ill-health in later years, and was found dead from a drug overdose. Academy Award nominee for *Alibi*. 1917: *An Amateur Orphan*. 1918: *The Beloved Traitor*. 1923: *Loyal Lives*. 1925: *The Road to Yesterday*. 1929: *Fast Life. Woman Trap. The Show of Shows. Alibi*. 1930: *The Big House. Second Choice. She Couldn't Say No. Playing Around. The Case of Sergeant Grisha. The Divorcee*. 1931: *Corsair. The Bat Whispers*. 1932: *Sinners in the Sun. Cock of the Air. Red-Headed Woman. Breach of Promise. The Miracle Man*. 1933: *Tomorrow at Seven. The Infernal Machine. King for a Night. Blondie Johnson. Golden Harvest*. 1934: **Hollywood Cavalcade. Gift of Gab. Embarrassing Moments. The Gay Bride. Let's Talk It Over*. 1935: *Public Hero Number One. Princess O'Hara. Society Doctor. I've Been Around. Frankie and Johnny. Pursuit*. 1936: **Pirate Party on Catalina Isle. Counterfeit. Moonlight Murder. They Met in a Taxi. Three God-fathers*. 1937: *Flight to Glory. I Promise to Pay. The Devil's Playground*. 1938: *Smashing the Rackets. Sky Giant. Law of the Under-ground*. 1939: *Five Came Back. Pacific Liner. Thunder Afloat. Blind Alley*. 1940: *Wagons Westward. The Marines Fly High. The Girl from God's Country*. 1941: *Meet Boston Blackie. No Hands on the Clock*. 1942: *Alias Boston Blackie. Canal Zone. Confessions of Boston Blackie* (GB: *Confessions*). *Wrecking Crew. Boston Blackie Goes to Hollywood* (GB: *Blackie Goes Hollywood*). *I Live on Danger*. 1943: *Aerial Gunner. Tornado. After Midnight with Boston Blackie* (GB: *After Midnight*). *High Explosive. The Chance of a Lifetime*. 1944: *One Mysterious Night* (GB: *Behind Closed Doors*). *Gambler's Choice. Double Exposure. Secret Command*. 1945: *Boston Blackie Booked on Suspicion* (GB: *Booked on Suspicion*). *Rough, Tough and Ready* (GB: *Men of the Deep*). 1946: *One Way to Love. A Close Call for Boston Blackie* (GB: *Lady of Mystery*). *The Phantom Thief. Boston Blackie and the Law* (GB: *Blackie and the Law*). 1947: *Blind Spot*. 1948: *Trapped by Boston Blackie*. 1949: *Boston Blackie's Chinese Venture* (GB: *Chinese Adventure*). 1955: *Unchained*. 1956: *The She-Creature*. 1957: *Child of Trouble* (TV). 1970: *The Great White Hope*.

MORRIS, Lana (Avril Morris) 1930–1998
Striking British actress whose vivid, slightly old-fashioned looks – black hair, dark eyes and a minxish mouth for her deep red lipstick – always suggested that she was capable of interpreting roles with more bite than the milk-and-water misses she actually got from the British cinema of the fifties. A junior-league Margaret Lockwood, perhaps, but her career never veered in that direction. Later a TV panellist. Committed suicide (drug overdose).
1946: †*School for Secrets* (US: *Secret Flight*). 1947: *The Weaker Sex. The Ghosts of Berkeley Square*. 1948: *Spring in Park Lane. It's Hard to be Good. The Chiltern Hundreds* (US: *The Amazing Mr Beecham*). *Trottie True* (GB: *Gay Lady*). 1950: *Morning Departure* (US: *Operation Disaster*). *Guilt is My Shadow. The Reluctant Widow. Trio. The Woman in Question* (GB: *Five Angles on Murder*). 1951: *A Tale of Five Cities* (US: *A Tale of Five Women*). 1953: *The Red Beret* (US: *Paratrooper*). *The Good Beginning. The Straw Man. Trouble in Store. Thought to Kill. Black 13*. 1954: *Radio Cab Murder*. 1955: *Man of the Moment*. 1956: *Home and Away*. 1958: *Moment of Indiscretion*. 1959: *Passport to Shame* (US: *Room 43*). *Jet Storm. No Trees in the Street* (US: *No Tree in the Street*). 1960: *October Moth*. 1969: *I Start Counting*.

†*As Pamela Matthews*

MORRIS, Wayne
(Bert de Wayne Morris) 1914–1959
Big, blond, open-faced American actor who played action heroes, boxers and kind-hearted tough guys. He was prominent in Warners films of the late thirties, but absence

on war service – although he was an air force hero who flew 57 combat missions, shot down several enemy planes and won many medals – badly hit his career, the rest of which was spent in second-features. Died from a heart attack.
1936: *China Clipper. Here Comes Carter* (GB: *The Voice of Scandal*). *King of Hockey* (GB: *King of the Ice Rink*). *Polo Joe. Smart Blonde*. 1937: *Once a Doctor. Land Beyond the Law. Submarine D-1. Kid Galahad. The Kid Comes Back* (GB: *Don't Pull Your Punches*). 1938: *Men Are Such Fools. Love, Honor and Behave. Valley of the Giants. Brother Rat*. 1939: *The Kid from Kokomo* (GB: *The Orphan of the Ring*). *The Return of Dr X*. 1940: *Brother Rat and a Baby* (GB: *Baby Be Good*). *The Quarterback. An Angel from Texas. Ladies Must Live. Gambling on the High Seas. Double Alibi. Flight Angels*. 1941: *Bad Men of Missouri. Three Sons o' Guns. The Smiling Ghost. I Wanted Wings*. 1947: **So You Want to be in Pictures. Deep Valley. The Voice of the Turtle*. 1948: *The Big Punch. The Time of Your Life*. 1949: *The Younger Brothers. A Kiss in the Dark. Task Force. John Loves Mary. The House across the Street*. 1950: *Stage to Tucson* (GB: *Lost Stage Valley*). *Johnny One-Eye. The Tougher They Come*. 1951: *Yellowfin* (GB: *Yellow Fin*). *Sierra Passage. The Big Gusher. The Bushwhackers* (GB: *The Rebel*). 1952: *Arctic Flight. Desert Pursuit*. 1953: *Star of Texas. The Marksman. The Master Plan. The Fighting Lawman. Texas Bad Man*. 1954: *The Green Buddha. Riding Shotgun. The Desperado. Port of Hell. Two Guns and a Badge*. 1955: *Cross Channel. Lord of the Jungle. Lonesome Trail*. 1956: *The Gelignite Gang* (US: *The Dynamiters*). 1957: *The Crooked Sky. Plunder Road. Paths of Glory*. 1958: *Buffalo Gun* (released 1961).

MORROW, Vic 1932–1982
Fair-haired American actor usually cast as characters with a vicious streak. Evidently tired of such aggression by 1961, he devoted himself to directing, on stage, television (where he also played in the series *Combat*) and the occasional film, before returning to acting in 1969, becoming especially prolific in TV movies. In July 1982 a helicopter, filming Morrow for an action scene, was accidentally hit by a 'firebomb' and crashed, killing him instantly. Actress Jennifer Jason Leigh (*qv*) is his daughter.
1955: *Blackboard Jungle*. 1956: *Tribute to a Bad Man*. 1957: *Men in War*. 1958: *God's

Little Acre. Hell's Five Hours. King Creole. 1960: Cimarron. 1961: Portrait of a Mobster. Posse from Hell. 1969: How to Make It (GB: Target: Harry). River of Mystery (TV). 1970: Travis Logan DA. A Step Out of Line. 1972: The Glass House (TV. GB: cinemas). The Weekend Nun (TV). 1973: Police Story (TV. GB: cinemas). Nightmare (TV). 1974: The Take. The California Kid (TV). Death Stalk (TV). Dirty Mary, Crazy Larry. 1975: Wanted: Babysitter. Tom Sawyer (TV). The Night That Panicked America (TV). 1976: Treasure of Matecumbe. The Bad News Bears. Funeral for an Assassin. 1977: The Man with the Power (TV). The Ghost of Cypress Swamp (TV). Curse of the Black Widow (TV). Message from Space. 1978: Wild and Wooly (TV). The Hostage Heart (TV). 1979: The Evictors. Supertrain (TV). Paris (TV). Stone/The Killing Stone (TV). BAD Cats (TV). 1980: Plutonium Incident (TV). Humanoids from the Deep (GB: Monster). 1981: L'ultimo Squalo/Great White (GB: Shark). 1982: The Bronx Warriors. 1983: The Twilight Zone (GB: Twilight Zone The Movie).

As director: 1962: *Last Year at Malibu. 1966: Deathwatch. 1969: Sledge/A Man Called Sledge. 1979: The Evictors.

MORSE, Robert 1931–
Chirpy, rubber-faced American comic actor. Most of his work has been done on Broadway, but he was briefly in vogue in the cinema of the sixties as a kind of thinking Jerry Lewis – like Lewis, mugging gamely and sometimes singing and dancing as well.
1955: The Proud and Profane. 1958: The Matchmaker. 1963: The Cardinal. 1964: Honeymoon Hotel. 1965: Quick Before It Melts. The Loved One. 1966: Oh Dad, Poor Dad, Mama's Hung You in the Closet and I'm Feeling So Sad. How to Succeed in Business without Really Trying. 1967: A Guide for the Married Man. 1968: Where Were You When the Lights Went Out? 1970: The Boatniks. 1984: Calendar Girl Murders (TV). 1987: California Hunk. The Emperor's New Clothes. 1992: Tru (TV). 1995: Here Come the Munsters (TV).

MORTENSEN, Viggo 1958–
Tall, rangy American actor with chiselled features and fair hair often grown lank. After spending the greater part of his childhood in South America (he still speaks fluent Spanish), he launched an acting career in his early twenties, and moved into a series of

leads and semi-leads from 1988. Although never quite an above-the-title name, he has proved a useful foil for some high-powered actresses and was well cast as Aragorn in the 'Lord of the Rings' films of the early 21st century. Also a painter and poet, he is divorced from singer Exene Cervenka and has an actor son, Henry.
1984: Witness. 1985: The Purple Rose of Cairo. CHUD. 1987: Salvation! 1988: Prison. Fresh Horses. 1990: Once in a Blue Moon (TV). Young Guns II. Tripwire. Leatherface: Texas Chainsaw Massacre III. The Reflecting Skin. 1991: The Indian Runner. 1992: Ruby Cairo. Two Small Bodies. 1993: The Young Americans. Desert Lunch. Carlito's Way. The Gospel According to Harry. Boiling Point. 1994: Floundering. American Yakuza. The Crew. 1995: The Passion of Darkly Noon. Crimson Tide. The Prophecy (GB: God's Army). Gimlet. 1996: The Portrait of a Lady. Daylight. Vanishing Point (TV). Albino Alligator. 1997: La pistola de mi hermano (US: My Brother's Gun). G.I. Jane. 1998: A Perfect Murder. Psycho. 1999: A Walk on the Moon. 2000: 28 Days. Dancing in the Dark. 2001: Lord of the Rings: The Fellowship of the Ring. Lord of the Rings: The Two Towers.

MORTIMER, Emily 1972–
Dark-haired, demure British leading lady in the Jean Simmons mould, the daughter of playwright and screenwriter John Mortimer. After studying Russian at university, she spent six months with a Moscow theatre group before returning to England and building up extensive stage experience. Her films in Britain were a curious mixture of leading roles and very small parts and since 1999 she has been working in Hollywood.

1995: The Last of the High Kings. 1996: The Ghost and the Darkness. The Saint. 1998: Elizabeth. 1999: Notting Hill. Love's Labour's Lost. The Miracle Maker (voice only). 2000: Scream 3. The Kid. 2001: The Sleeping Dictionary. Windtalkers.

MORTON, Samantha 1977–
Sleepy-eyed, baby-faced, husky-voiced blonde British actress in the traditions of Joan Greenwood and Susannah York (both qv). A teenage actress on TV since she was 13, her slightly fey charms were soon successful in adult roles and she quickly found leading parts on both sides of the Atlantic. Has a child by her partner, actor Charlie Creed-Miles. Academy Award nomination for Sweet and Lowdown.
1996: The Future Lasts a Long Time. 1997: Under the Skin. 1998: This is the Sea. Dreaming of Joseph Lees. 1999: The Last Yellow. Sweet and Lowdown. Jesus' Son. 2000: Pandemonium.

MOSS, Carrie-Anne 1969–
Tall, curvaceous Canadian actress with short dark hair and decisive way with dialogue. A professional model in Europe at 20, she attracted attention a couple of years later in US TV commercials and began an acting career. This was pretty much low-key until they put her in black leather and introduced her as a romantic action star in The Matrix, ironically also the title of an unsuccessful TV series in which she had appeared six years earlier. She subsequently made other science-fiction films as the century turned.
1993: Doorways (TV). 1994: Flashfire. The Soft Kill. 1995: Terrified/Tough Guy. 1996: Sabotage. Deadly Current/Lethal Tender. 1997: The Secret Life of Algernon. 1999: The

Matrix. New Blood. 2000: The Red Planet. The Crew. Memento. 2001: Chocolat.

MOSTEL, Zero
(Samuel Mostel) 1915–1977
Dark-haired, roly-poly American comic actor with football-shaped face. At first seen in serious roles as swarthy, sweaty, ethnic types, this part of his career was halted by blacklisting at the hands of the Un-American Activities Committee in 1951. After a long sojourn performing on Broadway and in nightclubs and building a reputation as a painter, he returned as a leading comic character actor, firing on all cylinders if you liked that sort of thing. Died from cardiac arrest. Actor Josh Mostel (1946–) is his son.
*1943: DuBarry Was a Lady. 1950: Panic in the Streets. The Enforcer (GB: Murder Inc.). 1951: Sirocco. The Guy Who Came Back. Mr Belvedere Rings the Bell. The Model and the Marriage Broker. 1959: *Zero. 1966: A Funny Thing Happened on the Way to the Forum. 1967: The Producers. Great Catherine. *The Ride of the Valkyrie. 1968: Monsieur Lecoq (unfinished). 1969: The Great Bank Robbery. 1970: The Angel Levine. 1972: The Hot Rock (GB: How to Steal a Diamond in Four Uneasy Lessons). 1973: Rhinoceros. Marco (made for cinemas but shown only on TV). Once Upon a Scoundrel (released 1977). 1974: Foreplay. Journey into Fear (released 1976). 1976: Mastermind (filmed 1969). The Front. Hollywood on Trial. 1978: The Little Drummer Boy (TV. Voice only). Watership Down (voice only). 1979: Best Boy.*

MOUNT, Peggy 1916–
Plain-faced British actress (from 14 years old) whose long stage experience in Yorkshire must have prepared her for all those down-to-earth roles, culminating in her fearsome, stentorian-voiced, mother-in-law, Mrs Hornett, in *Sailor Beware!* which she created on stage and which became her biggest hit.
1954: The Embezzler. 1956: Sailor Beware! (US: Panic in the Parlor). Dry Rot. 1957: The Naked Truth (US: Your Past is Showing). 1960: Inn for Trouble. 1963: Ladies Who Do. 1964: One Way Pendulum. 1966: Hotel Paradiso. Finders Keepers. 1968: Oliver! 1976: The Chiffy Kids (serial). 1992: The Princess and the Goblin (voice only).

MULLEN, Barbara 1914–1979
Tiny blue-eyed blonde purveyor of fey Gaelic charm, actually born in America and a dancer and variety artist for 17 years before coming to the screen in *Jeannie*, a role she repeated on stage and television. Also a writer, but best remembered as the doctors' housekeeper, Janet, in the long-running British television (and later radio) series, *Dr Finlay's Casebook*. Died from a heart attack.
*1941: Jeannie. 1942: Thunder Rock. 1944: Welcome Mr Washington. 1945: A Place of One's Own. The Trojan Brothers. 1948: Corridor of Mirrors. My Sister and I. 1951: Talk of a Million. (US: You Can't Beat the Irish). 1952: So Little Time. The Gentle Gunman. 1953: *The Bosun's Mate. *World of Life (narrator only). 1954: Destination Milan. The Death of Michael Turbin. The Last Moment. *Fool Notions. 1958: Innocent Sinners. 1959: The Siege of Pinchgut. 1960: The Challenge. 1963: The Very Edge. 1966: *Miss Mactaggart Won't Lie Down.*

MULRONEY, Dermot 1963–
Dark, dour American actor of Irish colouring, not quite a top star despite some good leading roles in successful films; the personality-plus factor was never quite there. Acting since childhood, he also has ambitions for a musical career, became a proficient cellist and still plays in an ensemble called The Low & Sweet Orchestra. Married to Catherine Keener (qv).
1986: Sin of Innocence (TV). 1987: Long Gone (TV). Daddy (TV). 1988: Sunset. Young Guns. 1989: Staying Together. Unconquered (TV). Survival Quest. 1990: Longtime Companion. 1991: Career Opportunities/One Wild Night. Bright Angel. Samantha. 1992: Where the Day Takes You. Halfway House. The Heart of Justice (TV). 1993: Silent Tongue. The Thing Called Love. There Goes My Baby. Point of No Return (GB: The Assassin). Family Pictures (TV). 1994: Bad Girls. Angels in the Outfield (GB: Angels). The Last Outlaw (cable TV). 1995: Copycat. Living in Oblivion. How to Make an American Quilt. 1996: Bastard Out of Carolina (originally for TV). Box of Moon Light. Kansas City. The Trigger Effect. 1997: My Best Friend's Wedding. 1998: Goodbye Lover. 2000: Where the Money Is. Trixie. 2001: Investigating Sex.

MUNI, Paul (M. Weisenfreund) 1895–1967
Forceful, mannered, dark-haired, stockily-built Hollywood character star, born in Poland. Came to the fore in Warners' social conscience thrillers of the early thirties, then found his niche playing figures of history, usually under masses of make-up. Many of his performances look artificial by today's standards, but in 1936 he collected an Oscar for *The Story of Louis Pasteur*. Died from heart trouble after deteriorating sight had forced his early retirement. Also nominated for Oscars in *The Valiant, I Am a Fugitive from a Chain Gang, The Life of Emile Zola* and *The Last Angry Man.*
*1929: The Valiant. Seven Faces. 1932: I Am a Fugitive from a Chain Gang. Scarface (The Shame of a Nation). 1933: The World Changes. 1934: Hi Nellie. Bordertown. 1935: Dr Socrates. Black Fury. 1936: The Story of Louis Pasteur. 1937: The Good Earth. The Life of Emile Zola. The Woman I Love (GB: The Woman Between). 1938: *For Auld Lang Syne. 1939: Juarez. We Are Not Alone. 1940: Hudson's Bay. 1942: Commandos Strike at Dawn. 1943: Stage Door Canteen. 1945: Counter-Attack (GB: One Against Seven). A Song to Remember. 1946: Angel on My Shoulder. 1953: Stranger on the Prowl. 1958:*

Last Clear Chance (TV). 1959: The Last Angry Man.

MUNRO, Caroline 1948–

Stunning, dark-haired, dark-eyed, apple-cheeked British actress with whistle-worthy figure. A throwback to the Yvonne de Carlo era, she got into films via eye-catching commercials – then seemed content to appear as slave girls, space maidens, vampires' victims and similar decoration. Male audiences certainly weren't complaining, and it's sad that so few films have found room for her. By the mid-1980s she was hostess on a TV game show.

1969: Where's Jack? A Talent for Loving. 1971: The Abominable Dr Phibes. 1972: Captain Kronos – Vampire Hunter. Dracula AD 1972. 1973: The Golden Voyage of Sinbad. 1975: I Don't Want to be Born. 1976: At the Earth's Core. 1977: The Spy Who Loved Me. 1979: Starcrash. 1980: Maniac. 1982: The Last Horror Film. 1984: Don't Open Until Christmas. 1985: April Fool's Day. 1986: Slaughter High. 1987: El aullido de diablo. 1988: Maigret (TV). Faceless! 1989: The Black Cat. 1993: Night Owl. 1994: To Die For (US: Heaven's a Drag).

MUNRO, Janet 1934–1972

Dark-haired, baby-faced, cuddly British actress who made several films for Walt Disney, but seemed to seek earthier roles back home in Britain. Later appearances restricted by an alcohol problem. Married to Tony Wright, 1956–1961, and Ian Hendry, 1963–1971 (both *qv*). Choked to death while drinking tea.

1957: Small Hotel. 1958: The Young and the Guilty. Darby O'Gill and the Little People. The

Trollenberg Terror (US: The Crawling Eye). 1959: Third Man on the Mountain. Tommy the Toreador. 1960: Swiss Family Robinson. 1961: The Horsemasters. The Day the Earth Caught Fire. 1962: Life for Ruth (US: Walk in the Shadow). 1963: Bitter Harvest. Hide and Seek. A Jolly Bad Fellow (US: They All Died Laughing). 1964: Daylight Robbery. 1967: Sebastian. 1968: Cry Wolf.

MURPHY, Audie 1924–1971

Baby-faced, slightly-built American actor with red-brown hair. America's most-decorated soldier of World War II with 28 medals (an experience from which he never recovered: he always kept a gun under his pillow), he took his light Texan voice and boyish appeal into movies, becoming a prolific star of 80-minute Technicolor westerns in which, he said, 'the scripts were the same – only the horses were changed'. Briefly in 'A' films after the success of the film of his autobiography, *To Hell and Back*. Married to Wanda Hendrix 1949–1950, first of two. Died in a private plane crash.

*1948: Beyond Glory. Texas, Brooklyn and Heaven (GB: The Girl from Texas). 1949: Bad Boy. The Kid from Texas (GB: Texas Kid – Outlaw). 1950: Sierra. Kansas Raiders. 1951: The Red Badge of Courage. The Cimarron Kid. 1952: The Duel at Silver Creek. 1953: Gunsmoke! Column South. Tumbleweed. Ride Clear of Diablo. 1954: Drums Across the River. Destry. *Queens of Beauty. 1955: To Hell and Back. 1956: Walk the Proud Land. World in My Corner. 1957: Joe Butterfly. Night Passage. *Rock 'Em Cowboy. The Guns of Fort Petticoat. 1958: The Quiet American. The Gun Runners. Ride a Crooked Trail. 1959: No Name on the Bullet. The Wild and the Innocent. The Unforgiven. Cast a Long Shadow. 1960: Hell Bent for Leather. Seven Ways from Sundown. 1961: Battle at Bloody Beach (GB: Battle on the Beach). Posse from Hell. 1962: Six Black Horses. 1963: Showdown. Gunfight at Comanche Creek. War is Hell! (on-screen narration). 1964: Bullet for a Badman. The Quick Gun. Apache Rifles. 1965: Arizona Raiders. 1966: Gunpoint. The Texican. Trunk to Cairo. 1967: 40 Guns to Apache Pass. 1969: A Time for Dying.*

MURPHY, Eddie 1961–

Whippy, catlike, black American comedian and actor with slightly menacing air and roguish smile beneath a snappy moustache. After hosting a talent show at 15, he was

performing in nightclubs a year later and a supremely confident star of TV's satirical *Saturday Night Live* before he was 20. His first half-dozen years in films contained some immense personal hits but he came a colossal critical cropper when trying to direct his own film in *Harlem Nights*, and his standing (and box-office appeal) has not been quite the same since. Often cast as the rascal who reforms, he was also quite successful in 'makeup disguise' comedies of the late 1990s.

1982: 48 Hrs. 1983: Trading Places. Delirious (video). 1984: Best Defense. Beverly Hills Cop. 1986: The Golden Child. 1987: Beverly Hills Cop II. 1988: Raw. Coming to America. 1989: Harlem Nights (and directed). Tongues Untied. 1990: Another 48 Hrs. 1992: Boomerang. The Distinguished Gentleman. 1994: Beverly Hills Cop III. 1995: Vampire in Brooklyn. 1996: The Nutty Professor. 1997: Metro. 1998: Dr Dolittle. Holy Man. Mulan (voice only). 1999: Life. Shrek (voice only). Bowfinger. 2000: Nutty Professor 2: The Klumps.

MURPHY, George 1902–1992

American dancer with snub nose, dark, wavy hair and light, pleasant speaking/singing voice. A vigorous hoofer with years of Broadway experience before coming to Hollywood, he soon settled down in films around the top of the second rank of stars. Played a few tough-guy roles after World War II, but left the movies in 1952 for a political career on the Republican side (Congressman for California from 1965 to 1969). Special Oscar 1950. Died from leukemia.

1934: Kid Millions. Jealousy. 1935: Public Menace. I'll Love You Always. After the Dance. 1936: Woman Trap. 1937: London by Night. Top of the Town. You're a Sweetheart.

Women Men Marry. Broadway Melody of 1938. 1938: *Hold That Co-Ed* (GB: *Hold That Girl*). *Little Miss Broadway. Letter of Introduction.* 1939: *Risky Business. Broadway Melody of 1940.* 1940: *Little Nellie Kelly. Two Girls on Broadway* (GB: *Choose Your Partner*). *Public Deb No. 1.* 1941: **Hollywood Visits the Navy. Ringside Maisie* (GB: *Cash and Carry*). *A Girl, a Guy and a Gob* (GB: *The Navy Steps Out*). *Tom, Dick and Harry. Rise and Shine.* 1942: *For Me and My Gal* (GB: *For Me and My Girl*). *Mayor of 44th Street. The Navy Comes Through.* 1943: **Show Business at War. The Powers Girl* (GB: *Hello! Beautiful*). *Bataan. This is the Army.* 1944: *Show Business. Step Lively. Broadway Rhythm.* 1945: *Having Wonderful Crime. Up Goes Maisie* (GB: *Up She Goes*). 1947: *The Arnelo Affair. Cynthia* (GB: *The Rich, Full Life*). 1948: *The Big City. Tenth Avenue Angel.* 1949: *Border Incident. Battleground.* 1951: *No Questions Asked. It's a Big Country.* 1952: *Talk About a Stranger. Walk East on Beacon!* (GB: *The Crime of the Century*).

MURPHY, Mary 1931–
Full-faced, sad-looking brunette American actress of pin-up prettiness who played several small roles before becoming Marlon Brando's leading lady in *The Wild One*. Stardom surprisingly lasted only a few years for her, but she was still seen on and off for many years, mostly on television, in character roles. She married and divorced twice, once to actor Dale Robertson (*qv*), and later ran a Hollywood art gallery.
1951: *The Lemon Drop Kid. Darling, How Could You?* (GB: *Rendezvous*). *When Worlds Collide. Sailor Beware.* 1952: *Carrie. The Turning Point. Come Back, Little Sheba. Plymouth Adventure. Off Limits* (GB: *Military Policemen*). 1953: *Houdini. Main Street to Broadway. The Wild One.* 1954: *Make Haste to Live. The Mad Magician. Sitting Bull. Beachhead.* 1955: *Hell's Island. The Desperate Hours. A Man Alone.* 1956: *The Intimate Stranger* (US: *Finger of Guilt*). *The Maverick Queen.* 1957: *Escapement* (later *Zex*. US: *The Electronic Monster*). 1958: *Live Fast, Die Young.* 1959: *Crime and Punishment USA.* 1962: *Red Hell. 40 Pounds of Trouble.* 1965: *Harlow.* 1972: *Footsteps* (TV). *Junior Bonner.* 1974: *I Love You . . . Goodbye* (TV). *The Stranger Who Looks Like Me* (TV). *Born Innocent* (TV). 1975: *Katherine* (TV).

MURRAY, Barbara 1929–
Sophisticated, very British brunette actress in revue at 17, and, as one of the J. Arthur Rank Charm School, mainly starred in comedies and comedy-thrillers. Ran along Kay Kendall lines but without the Kendall glow. Married to John Justin (first of two) from 1952 to 1964. Still active on stage, latterly as the 21st century's first Miss Marple.
1947: *To the Public Danger.* 1948: *Saraband for Dead Lovers* (US: *Saraband*). *Anna Karenina. Badger's Green.* 1949: *Don't Ever Leave Me. A Boy, a Girl and a Bike. Poet's Pub. Passport to Pimlico. Boys in Brown.* 1950: *Tony Draws a Horse.* 1951: *The Dark Man. Another Man's Poison. Mystery Junction. The Frightened Man.* 1952: *Hot Ice.* 1953: *Street Corner* (US: *Both Sides of the Law*). *Meet Mr Lucifer. Death Goes to School.* 1954: *The Teckman Mystery.* 1957: *Campbell's Kingdom. Doctor at Large.* 1958: *A Cry from the Streets.* 1959: *Operation Bullshine.* 1962: *The Punch and Judy Man.* 1963: *Doctor in Distress.* 1968: *A Dandy in Aspic.* 1970: *Some Will, Some Won't.* 1971: *Up Pompeii.* 1972: *Tales from the Crypt.*

MURRAY, Bill
(William Doyle-Murray) 1950–
Bedraggled-looking, pouch-cheeked American comedy actor with a practical joker's face and a scruff of dark hair. He studied to become a doctor, but graduated instead to the cult TV comedy show, *Saturday Night Live*, along with John Belushi, Chevy Chase, Dan Aykroyd (all *qv*) and others. His laconic sense of humour has been effectively used in films; attempts to go 'straight' as a dramatic actor have been less successful.

1975: *La honte de la jungle* (GB: *Jungle Burger*. US: *Shame of the Jungle*. Voice only). 1976: **The Hat Act.* 1979: *Meatballs. Mr Mike's Mondo Video.* 1980: *Where the Buffalo Roam. Caddyshack.* 1981: *Stripes. Loose Shoes.* 1982: *Tootsie.* 1984: *The Razor's Edge. Ghost Busters. Nothing Lasts Forever.* 1986: *Little Shop of Horrors.* 1987: *Rolling in the Aisles.* 1988: *Scrooged.* 1989: *Ghostbusters II.* 1990: *Quick Change.* 1991: *What About Bob?* 1992: *Mad Dog and Glory.* 1993: *Groundhog Day.* 1994: *Ed Wood.* 1996: *Larger than Life. Kingpin. Space Jam.* 1997: *The Man Who Knew Too Little.* 1998: *Rushmore. Wild Things. With Friends Like These . . .* 1999: *Cradle Will Rock. Hamlet.* 2000: *Charlie's Angels. Michael Jordan to the Max* (doc). 2001: *Veeck as in Wreck. Osmosis Jones. Speaking of Sex.*

MURRAY, Don 1929–
Quiet, self-effacing American actor who was a conscientious objector at the time of the Korean War (something that slowed his career) and has often associated himself with films that expressed noble ideals. His performances are always earnest and sincere, although it is hard to imagine him in comedy. Nominated for a Best Supporting Actor Oscar in *Bus Stop*.
1955: *The Skin of Our Teeth* (TV). 1956: *Bus Stop.* 1957: *The Bachelor Party. A Hatful of Rain. For I Have Loved Strangers* (TV). 1958: *From Hell to Texas* (GB: *Manhunt*). 1959: *Shake Hands with the Devil. These Thousand Hills.* 1960: *One Foot in Hell. Alas, Babylon* (TV). 1961: *The Hoodlum Priest.* 1962: *Advise and Consent. Tunnel 28* (GB and US: *Escape from East Berlin*). 1964: *One Man's Way.* 1965: *Baby, the Rain Must Fall. Kid Rodelo.* 1966: *The Plainsman. Sweet Love Bitter.* 1967: *The Borgia Stick* (TV). *The Viking Queen. Tale of the Cock.* 1969: *Daughters of the Mind* (TV). *Childish Things.* 1970: *The Intruders* (TV). 1971: *Justin Morgan Had a Horse* (TV). 1972: *Conquest of the Planet of the Apes. Happy Birthday Wanda June. Confessions of Tom Harris* (TV). 1973: *Call Me by My Rightful Name. Cotter* (GB: TV). 1974: *The Girl on the Late, Late Show* (TV). *The Sex Symbol* (TV. GB: cinemas). *A Girl Named Sooner* (GB: TV). 1975: *Deadly Hero.* 1978: *Rainbow* (TV). 1979: *The Far Turn* (TV). *The Boy Who Drank Too Much* (TV). *Confessions of a Lady Cop/The Other Side of Fear* (TV). 1980: *If Things Were Different* (TV). *Fugitive Family* (TV). 1981:

Endless Love. Return of the Rebels (TV). 1983: Thursday's Child (TV). Quarterback Princess (TV). I Am the Cheese. License to Kill (TV). 1984: A Touch of Scandal (TV). Radioactive Dreams. 1986: Peggy Sue Got Married. The Summons. Blood Sport (TV). Scorpion. Something in Common (TV). 1987: Still Watch (TV). Made in Heaven. The Stepford Children (TV). Marilyn Monroe: Beyond the Legend. 1989: Score. Brand New Life (TV). 1990: Ghosts Can't Do It. 1996: Hearts Adrift (TV).

MURRAY, Peter 'Pete' 1925–

Fair-haired, long-faced, bland-looking British actor, sporadically in films from 1942, mostly in sensitive juvenile roles. Success as a toothily cheerful disc-jockey, panellist and all-round radio personality in the mid 1950s led him to essay a few minor light comedy leads in films. But his personality remained best projected in sound rather than vision.

1942: The Young Mr Pitt. The Day Will Dawn (US: The Avengers). The First of the Few (US: Spitfire). 1944: Time Flies. 1946: Caravan. Hungry Hill. 1947: Captain Boycott. My Brother Jonathan. 1948: Portrait from Life (US: The Girl in the Painting). 1951: No Highway (US: No Highway in the Sky). 1958: 6-5 Special. 1960: A Taste of Money. Escort for Hire. 1961: Transatlantic. 1962: Behave Yourself. Design for Loving. It's Trad, Dad! (US: Ring-a-Ding Rhythm). 1963: The Cool Mikado. 1968: Otley. 1969: Under the Table You Must Go. 1970: Cool It Carol! (US: The Dirtiest Girl I Ever Met).

MURRAY, Stephen 1912–1983

Serious-looking British actor with dark hair and high forehead. Shakespeare-trained, he moved into leading roles in British films from the early forties, without ever becoming an established star. But he became probably radio's best-known actor with over 400 plays to his credit and, in that medium, appeared as the unlikely star of the long-running comedy series *The Navy Lark*: he did not appear in the film version.

1938: Pygmalion. 1941: The Prime Minister. 1942: The Next of Kin. 1943: Undercover (US: Underground Guerillas). 1947: Master of Bankdam. 1948: My Brother Jonathan. London Belongs to Me (US: Dulcimer Street). Alice in Wonderland (voice only). 1949: *The People Next Door (narrator only). For Them That Trespass. Now Barabbas was a robber . . . Silent Dust. 1950: The Magnet. *Scrapbook for 1933 (narrator only). 1952: 24 Hours in a Woman's Life (US: Affair in Monte Carlo). 1953: Four-Sided Triangle. 1954: *The Heart of England (narrator only). The Stranger's Hand. 1955: The End of the Affair. 1956: *Across Great Waters (narrator only). Guilty? *The Door in the Wall. 1957: At the Stroke of Nine. Any Man's Kingdom (narrator only). 1958: A Tale of Two Cities. The Nun's Story. 1960: Sea Sanctuary (narrator only). The River of Life (narrator only). 1961: *Wild Highlands (narrator only). 1963: Master Spy.

MUTI, Ornella (Francesca Rivelli) 1955–

Dark-haired Italian actress, stunningly beautiful in a slightly pouty way, with a sex-symbol figure that took her into erotic roles at 16 and often saw her cast as slightly off-centre *femmes fatales*. More often seen in semi-international ventures than most present-day Italian stars, she proved a slightly limited actress, but popular enough to run up nearly 50 films before reaching 30.

1969: La moglie più bella. 1970: Un posto ideale per uccidere. 1971: Un solo grande amore/La casa de las palomas. Il sola nella pelle (GB and US: Sun on the Skin). 1972: Fiorina la vacca. 1973: Le monache di Saint' Arcangelo (GB: The Nun and the Devil). Tutti figli di 'Mamma Santissima' (US: Italian Graffiti). Paolo il caldo/The Sensual Man. La seduzione (GB: Seduction). Cebo para una adolescente. Cronace di altre tempe. L'altra faccia del padrino. Amore a morte. 1974: Appassionata. Romanzo populare (US: Come Home and Meet My Wife). Experienze prematrimoniali. Una chica y un señor/L'amante adolescente. 1975: Leonor. La jeune mariée/La joven casada. Mio dio, come cono caduta in basso. 1976: L'ultima donna (GB and US: The Last Woman). Come una rosa al naso (GB: TV, as

Virginity). L'agnese va a morire. 1977: La stanza del vescovo. Mort di una carogna/Mort d'un pourri (GB: TV, as To Kill a Rat). I nuovi mostri. 1978: Primo amore. Ritra ho di Borghesia in nero (US: Nest of Vipers). Eutanasia di un amore. 1979: Giallo Napoleono. La vita è bella/Freedom to Love. 1980: Flash Gordon. Il bribetico domato. Love and Money. 1981: Tales of Ordinary Madness. Nessuno è perfetto. Inamorato pazzo. 1982: Bonnie è Clyde all'Italiana/Bonnie and Clyde Italian style. 1983: The Girl from Trieste. Un provero ricco. Un amour de Swann (GB and US: Swann in Love). 1984: Firebrand – Story of Cellini. Il futura è donna (GB: The Future is Woman). 1985: Tutta colpa di paradiso. 1986: Stregati (US: Bewitched). Chronicle of a Death Foretold. Grandi magazzini. 1987: I picari. Una di queste notti. Casanova (TV). Io e mia sorella. 1988: Codice privato. Frullo del passero. Tough Guys in Marseilles. 1989: Wait Until Spring, Bandini. 'O Re. 1990: Il viaggio di Capitan Fracassa. Tonight at Alice's. 1991: Oscar. Once Upon a Crime. La Domenica specialmente. Max/Il conte Max. 1992: Vacanze di Natale '91. Don't Call Me Omar. 1993: The Bilingual Lover. L'arbre métallique/The Metal Tree. 1994: The Great Fausto. Palermo – Milano (Only One Way). 1995: La muneca rusa. 1996: Mordburo. Somewhere in the City. Pour rire! (US: Just for Laughs). 1997: Widows. 1998: L'inconnu de Strasberg. 1999: Les menus plaisirs. Dirty Linen/Panni sporchi. Tierra del Fuego. 2000: Everybody Dies. Jet Set. Una lunga, lunga, lunga notte d'amore.

MYERS, Mike 1963–

Small, dark, round-faced, sometimes bespectacled, livewire Canadian comic actor with wide grin and impish personality. A stand-up comedian from 19, he often appears as multiple characters and had huge success in the 1990s with the broad and fast-moving 'Wayne's World' and 'Austin Powers' comedies. In private life, an avid collector (and painter) of model soldiers.

1989: Elvis Stories. 1992: Wayne's World. 1993: So I Married an Axe Murderer. Wayne's World 2. 1997: Austin Powers: International Man of Mystery. 1998: 54. 1999: Mystery, Alaska. Austin Powers: The Spy Who Shagged Me. 2000: Meteor/Pete's Meteor (filmed 1998). McClintock's Peach. Sprockets. 2001: Shrek (voice only).

N

aus dem Geigenkasten (GB: Tread Softly). Mordnacht in Manhattan. Um null Uhr schnappt die Falle zu. 1966: Mi Hag Freitag/Operation Hurricane. 1967: House of a Thousand Dolls. Sumuru (US: The Million Eyes of Samuru). 1968: Radhapura – Endstation der Verdammten. Der Tod im roten Jaguar. Dynamit in grüner Seide. 1969: Todeschüsse am Broadway. 1973: Beyond Atlantis. 1974: Nakia (TV).

NAGEL, Anne (Ann Dolan) 1912–1966
Strawberry-blonde American actress with wide blue eyes who played light leading roles, frightened heroines and heroines' friends in Hollywood films of the 1930s and 1940s. Also in serials, notably as the intrepid Miss Case in the *Green Hornet* adventures. In post-war years she was gradually seen in smaller roles. Married (first of two) to Ross Alexander (*qv*) from 1933 to his death in 1937. Died from cancer.
*1932: Hypnotized. 1933: Sitting Pretty. I Loved You Wednesday. College Humor. 1934: Stand Up and Cheer. Search for Beauty. Coming Out Party. She Learned About Sailors. 1935: Doubting Thomas. Music is Magic. Reckless Roads. George White's Scandals. Redheads on Parade. 1936: King of Hockey (GB: King of the Ice Rink). Everybody's Old Man. Down the Stretch. Here Comes Trouble. Bullets or Ballots. Polo Joe. Hot Money. Here Comes Carter (GB: The Voice of Scandal). China Clipper. Love Begins at 20 (GB: All One Night). 1937: Footloose Heiress. The Devil's Saddle Legion. *Romance Road. Guns of the Pecos. The Hoosier Schoolboy (GB: Yesterday's Hero). The Three Legionnaires. The Case of the Stuttering Bishop. Escape by Night. A Bride for Henry. She Loved a Fireman. The Adventurous Blonde/Torchy Blane the Adventurous Blonde. 1938: Saleslady. Gang Bullets (GB: The Crooked Way). Mystery House. Under the Big Top (GB: The Circus Comes to Town). 1939: Call a Messenger. Convicts' Code. Legion of Lost Flyers. Should a Girl Marry? The Girl from Nowhere. The Witness Vanishes. Unexpected Father (GB: Sandy Takes a Bow). 1940: The Green Hornet (serial). Winners of the West (serial). My Little Chickadee. Argentine Nights. Ma, He's Making Eyes at Me. Black Friday. The Green Hornet Strikes Again! (serial). Hot Steel. Diamond Frontier. 1941: *Hollywood Visits the Navy. Meet the Chump. Road Agent. Mutiny in the Arctic. Don Winslow of the Navy (serial). Man-Made*

*Monster (GB: The Electric Man). Never Give a Sucker an Even Break. The Invisible Woman. Sealed Lips. 1942: The Secret Code (serial). Dawn Express. Stagecoach Buckaroo. The Mad Doctor of Market Street. Nazi Spy Ring. The Mad Monster. 1943: Women in Bondage. 1946: Murder in the Music Hall. Traffic in Crime. The Trap (GB: Murder at Malibu Beach). 1947: Blondie's Holiday. The Hucksters. Spirit of West Point. 1948: Every Girl Should Be Married. Homecoming. One Touch of Venus. Family Honeymoon. An Innocent Affair (later Don't Trust Your Husband). *Pal's Return. 1949: Prejudice. The Stratton Story. 1950: *Pal – Fugitive Dog. Armored Car Robbery.*

NADER, George 1921–
Handsome dark-haired American leading man with slow but winning smile and small, well-defined features. Struggled in show business for years before Universal-International gave him a contract, and boosted him to star roles: he was the last of their 'beefcake boys'. Nader hadn't the personality to stay at the top in Hollywood but pursued his career with some determination in overseas movies, becoming popular in Germany as FBI man Jerry Cotton in a series of colourful thrillers. Retired early with eye problems. Some sources suggest his real name may be Georg (or Giorgio) Nardelli. Uncle of Michael Nader (1945–).
1949: Memory of Love. 1950: Rustlers on Horseback. The Prowler. 1951: Two Tickets to Broadway. Han Glomde Henne Aldrig. Overland Telegraph. Take Care of My Little Girl. 1952: Phone Call from a Stranger. Monsoon. 1953: Down Among the Sheltering Palms. Sins of Jezebel. Miss Robin Crusoe. 1954: Robot Monster. Carnival Story. Four Guns to the Border. 1955: Six Bridges to Cross. The Second Greatest Sex. Lady Godiva (GB: Lady Godiva of Coventry). 1956: Away All Boats. Congo Crossing. The Unguarded Moment. Four Girls in Town. 1957: Man Afraid. Joe Butterfly. Flood Tide (GB: Above All Things). 1958: Appointment with a Shadow (GB: The Big Story). The Female Animal. Nowhere to Go. 1962: The Secret Mark of d'Artagnan. 1963: A Walk by the Sea (also directed). Zigzag. 1964: The Great Space Adventure. Alarm on 83rd Street. 1965: The Human Duplicators. Die Rechnung – eiskalt serviert. Der Mörderclub von Brooklyn. Schüsse

NAGEL, Conrad 1896–1970
Tall, fair-haired, long-faced American actor with piercing blue eyes, mostly in very serious roles. A much-respected figure on stage, he never quite achieved the same distinction in films, although busy from 1920 to 1935. Made a few avuncular appearances in post-war years, in between running an acting school. Much involved in film administration, he received a special Academy Award in 1947. Married (third of three) Lynn Merrick (Marilyn Merrick 1919–).
1918: Little Women. 1919: Redhead. The Lion and the Mouse. 1920: Midsummer Madness. The Fighting Chance. Unseen Forces. 1921: Fool's Paradise. What Every Woman Knows. Sacred and Profane Love. The Lost Romance. 1922: Hate. The Impossible Mrs Bellew. Saturday Night. Nice People. The Ordeal. Singed Wings. Pink Gods. 1923: Bella Donna. The Rendezvous. Grumpy. Lawful Larceny. The Eternal Three. 1924: The Snob. Three Weeks (GB: The Romance of a Queen). Name the Man. Tess of the d'Urbervilles. Married Flirts. Sinners in Silk. The Rejected Woman. So This is Marriage. 1925: Cheaper to Marry. Sun-Up. Lights of Old Broadway (GB: Merry Wives of Gotham). The Only Thing (GB: Four Flaming Days). Pretty Ladies. Excuse Me. 1926: The Exquisite Sinner. The Waning Sex. Dance Madness. Tin Hats. There You Are. Memory Lane. 1927: Slightly Used. Quality Street. Heaven on Earth. London After Midnight. The Jazz Singer. The Hypnotist. The Girl from Chicago. 1928: Glorious Betsy. The Mysterious Lady. The Terror. Diamond Handcuffs. State Street Sadie (GB: The Girl from State Street). If I Were Single. Caught in the Fog. Tenderloin. The Michigan Kid. The Divine Woman. 1929: The Idle Rich.

Dynamite. The Kiss. The Sacred Flame. The Redeeming Sin. Hollywood Revue of 1929. Red Wine. Kid Gloves. The Thirteenth Chair. 1930: Numbered Men. DuBarry, Woman of Passion (GB: DuBarry). A Lady Surrenders (GB: Blind Wives). The Divorcee. Ship from Shanghai. Second Wife. One Romantic Night. Free Love. Today. 1931: The Right of Way. Son of India. Bad Sister. Hell Drivers. East Lynne. The Reckless Hour. Three Who Loved. The Pagan Lady. 1932: Kongo. The Man Called Back. Divorce in the Family. Fast Life. 1933: Ann Vickers. The Constant Woman. 1934: The Marines are Coming. Dangerous Corner. 1935: One New York Night (GB: The Trunk Mystery). One Hour Late. Death Flies East. Ball at Savoy. 1936: Yellow Cargo. The Girl from Mandalay. Wedding Present. 1937: The Gold Racket. Navy Spy. 1939: The Mad Empress (GB: Carlotta, the Mad Empress). 1940: I Want a Divorce. One Million BC (GB: Man and His Mate. Narrator only). 1944: Dangerous Money (narrator only). They Shall Have Faith (later Forever Yours. GB: The Right to Live). 1945: The Adventures of Rusty. 1948: Stage Struck. The Vicious Circle (GB: The Woman in Brown). 1949: Dynamite. 1955: All That Heaven Allows. 1956: The Swan. 1957: The Great American Hoax (TV). Hidden Fear. 1959: Stranger in My Arms. The Man Who Understood Women.

As director: 1937: Love Takes Flight.

NARES, Owen (O. Ramsay) 1888–1943
Dark, saturnine, charismatic British leading man and matinee idol of silent screen times. He probably prolonged his leading man status beyond what was good for his career, and failed to mature into the character actor he might have become.
1913: *His Choice. 1914: *Dandy Donovan, the Gentleman Cracksman. 1916: The Real Thing at Last. Milestones. Just a Girl. 1917: The Sorrows of Satan. One Summer's Day. The Labour Leader. Flames. 1918: The Elder Miss Blossom. Tinker, Tailor, Soldier, Sailor. God Bless our Red, White and Blue. Onward Christian Soldiers. The Man Who Won. 1919: Edge o' Beyond. Gamblers All. 1920: A Temporary Gentleman. The Last Rose of Summer. All the Winners. 1921: For Her Father's Sake. 1922: Brown Sugar. The Faithful Heart. 1923: Young Lochinvar. The Indian Love Lyrics. 1924: Miriam Rozella. 1927: His Great Moment (US: Sentence of Death). This Marriage Business. 1930: The

Middle Watch. Loose Ends. The Woman Between (US: The Woman Decides). 1931: Sunshine Susie (US: The Office Girl). Frail Women. 1932: Aren't We All? Women Who Play. The Love Contract. The Impassive Footman (US: Woman in Bondage). There Goes the Bride. Where is This Lady? Discord. *His Great Night. 1933: One Precious Year. 1934: The Private Life of Don Juan. *After Eight. 1935: I Give My Heart. Royal Cavalcade (US: Regal Cavalcade). 1936: Head Office. *The Story of Papworth. 1937: The Show Goes On. 1941: The Prime Minister.

NEAGLE, Dame Anna
(Florence Marjorie Robertson) 1904–1986
Blonde British singer, dancer and actress who rose from the chorus to star in thirties' musicals (1932–1941), as historical heroines (1934–1951) and in a series of frothy post-war comedy-romances with Michael Wilding. Long associated with director Herbert Wilcox, whom she married in 1943. Her career turned full circle in the sixties when she returned to musicals on the London stage. Created Dame in 1969. Suffered for many years from Parkinson's Disease. Died from a brain tumour.
1929: †Those Who Love. 1930: †The School for Scandal. The Chinese Bungalow. Should a Doctor Tell? 1932: Goodnight Vienna (US: Magic Night). The Flag Lieutenant. 1933: Bitter Sweet. The Little Damozel. 1934: The Queen's Affair (US: Runaway Queen). Nell Gwyn. 1935: Peg of Old Drury. Limelight (US: Backstage). 1936: The Three Maxims (US: The Show Goes On). 1937: London Melody (US: Girls in the Street). Victoria the Great. 1938: Sixty Glorious Years (US: Queen of Destiny). 1939: Nurse Edith Cavell. 1940: Irene. No, No, Nanette. 1941: Sunny. They Flew Alone (US: Wings and the Woman). 1943: The Volunteer. Forever and a Day. The Yellow Canary. 1945: I Live in Grosvenor Square (US: A Yank in London). 1946: Piccadilly Incident. 1947: The Courtneys of Curzon Street (US: The Courtney Affair). Royal Wedding (narrator only). 1948: Spring in Park Lane. Elizabeth of Ladymead. 1949: Maytime in Mayfair. 1950: Odette. 1951: The Lady with a Lamp. 1952: Derby Day (US: Four Against Fate). 1954: Lilacs in the Spring (US: Let's Make Up). 1955: King's Rhapsody. My Teenage Daughter (US: Teenage Bad Girl). 1957: No Time for Tears. The Man Who Wouldn't Talk. 1959: The Lady is a Square.

†As Marjorie Robertson

NEAL, Patricia (Patsy Neal) 1926–
Anxious-looking brunette American actress who brought a fresh, sharp approach to roles of angst and was seen in too few films, and even fewer decent ones, before her marriage to writer Roald Dahl in 1953. She won an Academy Award for Hud in 1963, but soon afterwards suffered a paralysing stroke. She made a slow but admirable recovery and returned to acting in the late sixties. She divorced Dahl in 1983. Also received an Oscar nomination for The Subject Was Roses.
1949: John Loves Mary. The Fountainhead. It's a Great Feeling. The Hasty Heart. 1950: Bright Leaf. Three Secrets. The Breaking Point. Raton Pass (GB: Canyon Pass). 1951: Operation Pacific. The Day the Earth Stood Still. Weekend with Father. 1952: Diplomatic Courier. Washington Story (GB: Target for Scandal). Something for the Birds. 1954: Stranger from Venus (US: Immediate Decision). La tua donna. 1957: A Face in the Crowd. The Playroom (TV). 1958: The Gentleman from Seventh Avenue (TV). 1961: Breakfast at Tiffany's. 1963: Hud. 1964: Psyche 59. †The Third Secret. 1965: In Harm's Way. 1968: The Subject Was Roses. 1971: The Homecoming (TV). The Night Digger. 1972: Baxter! 1973: Happy Mother's Day . . . Love George/Run, Stranger, Run. 'B' Must Die. 1974: Things in their Season (TV). 1975: Eric (TV). 1976: Tail Gunner Joe (TV). 1977: A Love Affair – the Eleanor and Lou Gehrig Story (TV). Widows' Nest. 1978: The Passage. 1980: All Quiet on the Western Front (TV. GB: cinemas). 1981: Ghost Story. The Patricia Neal Story (TV). 1984: Shattered Vows (TV). Love Leads the Way (cable TV). Glitter (TV). 1989: Taking Chances: An Unremarkable Life. 1990: Caroline? (TV). 1992: Shattered Silence (TV). 1993: A Mother's Right: The Elizabeth Morgan Story (TV). 1998: From Russia to Hollywood (doc). 1999: Cookie's Fortune.

†Scenes deleted from release print

NEAL, Tom 1914–1972
Shortish, but powerfully-built, dark-haired American actor, moustachioed from 1944. His leading roles were mostly in second-features, although some of them quite highly rated. His spectacular lifestyle – he was several times a headliner in brawls over women, most notably a violent one with Franchot Tone (qv) – finally broke his career when he was arrested for shooting his fourth

wife, and sentenced to 10 years' jail. He was found dead in bed eight months after release from prison, apparently from congestive heart failure. His first and second wives, Vicky Lane and Barbara Payton (qv), were both actresses. His third wife died of cancer.
1938: *The Great Heart. Out West with the Hardys. 1939: Stronger than Desire. Burn 'em up O'Connor. Another Thin Man. Joe and Ethel Turp Call on the President. Within the Law. Honolulu. *Prophet without Honor. Four Girls in White. 6,000 Enemies. They All Come Out. *Help Wanted. *Money to Loan. 1940: *Jack Pot. *Rodeo Dough. Andy Hardy Meets Debutante. The Courageous Dr Christian. Sky Murder. 1941: Jungle Girl (serial). Top Sergeant Mulligan. Under Age. The Miracle Kid. 1942: Pride of the Yankees. Bowery at Midnight. Ten Gentlemen from West Point. China Girl. Flying Tigers. One Thrilling Night. 1943: Behind the Rising Sun. Air Force. She Has What It Takes. No Time for Love. Klondike Kate. *Rear Gunner. There's Something about a Soldier. Good Luck, Mr Yates. 1944: The Unwritten Code. Two-Man Submarine. Throughbreds. The Racket Man. 1945: Club Havana. Crime, Inc. First Yank into Tokyo (GB: Mask of Fury). Detour. 1946: The Unknown. The Brute Man. My Dog Shep. Blonde Alibi. 1947: The Case of the Baby Sitter. The Hat Box Mystery. 1948: Beyond Glory. 1949: Bruce Gentry, Daredevil of the Skies (serial). Amazon Quest (GB: Amazon). Red Desert. Apache Chief. 1950: Radar Secret Service. Joe Palooka in Humphrey Takes a Chance (GB: Humphrey Takes a Chance). Call of the Klondike. Train to Tombstone. Everybody's Dancin'. I Shot Billy the Kid. 1951: King of the Bullwhip. Varieties on Parade. Danger Zone. Navy Bound. GI Jane. Let's Go Navy. Fingerprints Don't Lie. Stop That Cab! 1952: The Dupont Story. The Daltons' Women. 1953: The Great Jesse James Raid.

NEESON, Liam 1952–
Tall, whippy, dark-haired Irish actor with sensitive mouth and small chin. Seen at his best expressing anguish as men with deeply-held convictions, although he has tried comedy and 'would love to make a western'. Started in British-based films, but went to America in the late 1980s and made a surprising impact. Continuing to play patriots and men of conscience, he won an Oscar nomination in 1993 for Schindler's List. Married Natasha Richardson (qv) in 1994.
1981: Excalibur. 1983: Krull. Arthur the King

(TV. Released 1985). 1984: Ellis Island (TV mini-series shortened for cinemas). The Innocent. The Bounty. 1986: Lamb. The Mission. Duet for One. 1987: A Prayer for the Dying. Sweet As You Are. (TV). Sworn to Silence (TV). Suspect. 1988: The Dead Pool. High Spirits. Satisfaction. The Good Mother. 1989: Next of Kin. 1990: The Big Man (US: Crossing the Line). Darkman. 1991: Under Suspicion. 1992: Shining Through. Ruby Cairo. Ethan Frome. Leap of Faith. Husbands and Wives. 1993: Schindler's List. Out of Ireland (voice only). 1994: Nell. 1995: Rob Roy. Before and After. Lumière et cie. 1996: Michael Collins. A Leap of Faith (narrator only. And 1992 film). 1997: Alaska. 1998: Les Misérables. Everest (narrator only). 1999: Star Wars: Episode 1 – The Phantom Menace. The Haunting. 2000: Gun Shy. 2001: Gangs of New York.

NEFF, Hildegarde
See KNEF, Hildegarde

NEGRI, Pola
(Apollonia Chalupec) 1894–1987
Chunky, dark-haired Polish actress who came to Hollywood in 1922, and became one of its most flamboyant but likeable stars. Paraded down Sunset Boulevard with a tiger on a leash, enjoyed tempestuous affairs with Charlie Chaplin and Rudolph Valentino among others, and played vamps wholeheartedly. An unwitting Mae West of the silent screen. Died from pneumonia.
1914: Niewolnicá Zmyslow. 1915: Czarná Ksiazeczka. Pokoj 13. 1916: Jego Ostáni Czyn. Zona. Studenci. Arabella. Die Bestie. 1917: Die toten Augen. Küsse, die man stiehlt im Dunkeln. Niche lange täuschte mich das Glück. Rosen, die

der Sturm entblättert. Zügelloses Blüt (GB and US: Gypsy Passion). 1918: Carmen (US: Gypsy Blood). Der gelbe Schein (GB and US: The Yellow Ticket). Die Augen der Mumie Mâ (GB and US: The Eyes of the Mummy). Camille (US: The Red Peacock). Mania (GB and US: Mad Love). Wenn das Herz in Hass erglüht. 1919: Comptesse Dolly. Karussel des Lebens. Kreuziget sie! Madame Dubarry (US: Passion). 1920: Vendetta. Arme Violetta. Das Martyrium. Die geschlossene Kette. Die Marchesa d'Arminiani. Sumurun (GB and US: One Arabian Night). 1921: Die Bergkatze. Sappho. Die Dame im Glashaus. 1922: Die Flamme (GB and US: Montmartre). 1923: Bella Donna. The Cheat. The Spanish Dancer. Hollywood. 1924: Shadows of Paris. Men. Lily of the Dust. Forbidden Paradise. 1925: East of Suez. The Charmer. Flower of the Night. A Woman of the World. 1926: The Crown of Lilies. Good and Naughty. Hotel Imperial. 1927: Barbed Wire. The Woman on Trial. 1928: The Secret Hour. Three Sinners. Loves of an Actress. The Woman from Moscow. Are Women to Blame? 1929: The Woman He Scorned (US: The Way of Lost Souls). Street of Abandoned Children. 1932: A Woman Commands. 1934: Fanatisme. 1935: Mazurka. 1936: Moskau – Shanghai. 1937: Madame Bovary. Tango notturno. 1938: Die fromme Lüge. Die Nacht der Entscheidung. *Rudolph Valentino. 1943: Hi Diddle Diddle. 1963: The Moon-Spinners.

NEILL, Sam (Nigel Neill) 1947–
Dark and sharply handsome Irish-born, New Zealand-raised actor who had a hard struggle to reach international stardom after a distinguished start in Australian films. He has always seemed to make most impact, however, in roles slightly secondary to another star and, after his seemingly foolproof role in the British TV series Reilly Ace of Spies failed to make him a national figure, he came back strongly in films in which he could steal scenes from those billed above him. Now in a mixture of leading and featured roles. Married actress Lisa Harrow (1945–).
1975: Ashes. Landfall. 1977: Sleeping Dogs. 1979: The Journalist. Out of Reach (US: Just Out of Reach). My Brilliant Career. 1980: Attack Force Z. 1981: From a Far Country: Pope John Paul II. The Final Conflict (later Omen III The Final Conflict). Possession. 1982: Ivanhoe (TV). Enigma. 1983: The Country Girls (TV). 1984: Le sang des autres. 1985: Plenty. Robbery Under Arms. 1986: The

Umbrella Woman (GB and US: The Good Wife). For Love Alone. 1987: Leap of Faith (TV). 1988: A Cry in the Dark. Dead Calm. 1989: The French Revolution. 1990: The Hunt for Red October. Until the End of the World. Death in Brunswick/Nothing to Lose. 1991: Fever (TV). One Against the Wind (TV). 1992: Memoirs of an Invisible Man. Hostage. 1993: The Piano. Jurassic Park. Sirens. 1994: Hostage II. In the Mouth of Madness. Country Life. Rudyard Kipling's The Jungle Book. 1995: Victory (released 1997). Restoration. 1996: Children of the Revolution. Snow White: A Tale of Terror. Forgotten Silver. 1997: Event Horizon. The Revenger's Comedies. 1998: The Horse Whisperer. 1999: Molokai – The Story of Father Damien. Bicentennial Man. My Mother Frank. 2000: Sally Hemmings: An American Scandal (TV). Numero Bruno. 2001: The Magic Pudding (voice only). Jurassic Park 3.

NELLIGAN, Kate (Patricia Nelligan) 1951–

Dark-haired, moist-eyed, Canadian-born actress with full lips who plays independent women and usually gives appealingly emotional performances. In the 1970s and 1980s, she attempted to establish film careers in Britain and then America with only moderate success, considering her talent. Her greatest achievements to date have almost all been on stage. In the cinema, she has been choosy – but not always to her advantage. In the 1990s, she continued to show versatility in a commendable variety of roles in films and TV.

1974: The Count of Monte Cristo (TV. GB: cinemas, released in 1976). The Arcata Promise (TV). 1975: The Romantic Englishwoman. 1977: Bethune (TV). 1979: Dracula. 1980: Midnight Matinee. Mr Patman (released 1983 as Crossover). 1981: Eye of the Needle. Victims (TV). 1983: Without a Trace. 1985: Eleni. 1986: Control/The Day Before (TV). 1987: Kojak: The Price of Justice (TV). 1989: White Room. 1991: Prince of Tides. Frankie & Johnny. Shadows and Fog. Bethune: The Making of a Hero. 1992: The Diamond Fleece (TV). Black Wedding/Terror Stalks the Class Reunion. Liar, Liar (TV). 1993: Fatal Instinct. Spoils of War (TV). 1994: Wolf. 1995: Mother's Prayer (TV). Margaret's Museum. How to Make an American Quilt. 1996: Captive Heart: The James Mink Story (TV). Up Close & Personal. Willam Shakespeare's Romeo & Juliet. 1997: Calm at Sunset (TV). 1998: U.S. Marshals. Boy

Meets Girl. Love is Strange (TV). 1999: The Cider House Rules. Swing Vote (TV).

NELSON, Barry (Robert Nielsen) 1920–
Chunky, cheerful-looking American actor with red-gold hair, under contract to MGM at 21 but never more than a second-line star at a studio he finally left seven years later, achieving more prominence on TV and in stage musicals, which revealed his pleasant singing voice. Later, he won success in several Broadway comedies. He repeated his role in one of them, *Mary, Mary*, in the film version, but it failed to lead to a resumption of his screen career.

1941: Dr Kildare's Victory (GB: The Doctor and the Debutante). Shadow of the Thin Man. Johnny Eager. 1942: The Affairs of Martha (GB: Once Upon a Thursday). Eyes in the Night. Rio Rita. Stand by for Action! (GB: Cargo of Innocents). A Yank on the Burma Road (GB: China Caravan). 1943: A Guy Named Joe. Bataan. The Human Comedy. 1944: Winged Victory. 1947: The Beginning or the End? Undercover Maisie (GB: Undercover Girl). 1948: Tenth Avenue Angel. Command Decision (voice only). 1951: The Man With My Face. 1956: The First Traveling Saleslady. 1963: Mary, Mary. 1967: The Borgia Stick (TV). 1969: †The Only Game in Town. Seven in Darkness (TV). Airport. 1972: Climb an Angry Mountain (TV). Pete 'n' Tillie. 1980: The Shining. 1981: Island Claws (later Night of the Claw).

†Scenes deleted from final release print

NELSON, Gene (G. Berg) 1920–1996
Yellow-haired, long-legged American dancer with ready grin, also a talented swimmer and

skater. Became the male equivalent of Ann Miller in his five years with Warners – although a popular musical star, with a good, light singing voice to match his twinkling feet, and usually billed above the title, he was never given a vehicle of his own. Later made some good low-budget thrillers in Britain, and became a competent director of routine films. Died from cancer.

*1943: This is the Army. 1947: I Wonder Who's Kissing Her Now. 1948: Gentleman's Agreement. Apartment for Peggy. The Walls of Jericho. 1950: The West Point Story (GB: Fine and Dandy). The Daughter of Rosie O'Grady. Tea for Two. 1951: Lullaby of Broadway. Starlift. Painting the Clouds with Sunshine. 1952: She's Working Her Way Through College. 1953: Three Sailors and a Girl. She's Back on Broadway. Crime Wave (GB: The City is Dark). *Hollywood's Great Entertainers. 1954: So This is Paris. 1955: Oklahoma! Timeslip (US: The Atomic Man). Dial 999 (US: The Way Out). 1961: The Purple Hills. 1962: 20,000 Eyes. 1963: Thunder Island. 1972: Family Flight (TV). A Brand New Life (TV). 1981: S.O.B.*

As director: 1962: The Hand of Death. 1963: Hootenanny Hoot. 1964: Kissin' Cousins. Your Cheatin' Heart. 1965: Harum Scarum (GB: Harem Holiday). 1967: The Cool Ones. 1969: Wake Me When the War is Over (TV). 1973: †The Letters (TV).

†Co-directed

NERO, Franco
(Francesco Spartanero) 1941–
Dark, glowering Italian actor with striking light blue eyes – for a long time associated in private life with Vanessa Redgrave (*qv*). He did not quite become an international star, despite several attempts in that direction. His English is not as attractive as that of some continental stars, and he is more interesting in less-than-straightforward roles. Now nudging 60, he continues to be busy in films from assorted countries.

1964: Celestina/Maid at Your Service. 1965: No Tears for a Killer. I criminali della galassia (GB and US: Wild, Wild Planet). Il terzo occhio. The Deadly Diaphanoids/War of the Planets. Io la conoscevo bene. 1966: The Tramplers. Django. The Bible . . . in the beginning. Texas addio (GB: The Avenger). Tecnica di un omicidio (US: Hired Killer). Tempo di massacro (US: The Brute and the Beast). 1967: Il giorno della civetta (US:

Mafia). L'uomo, l'orgoglio, la vendetta. Camelot. La morta viene dal pianeta Aytin. 1968: Il mercenario (GB: A Professional Gun. US: The Mercenary). Sequestro di persona (GB: Island of Crime). A Quiet Place in the Country. Mit Django kam der Tod. The Battle for Neretva/The Battle of Neretva. 1969: Un detective/Detective Belli. Gott mit uns. Sardinia: Ransom! 1970: Compañeros! The Virgin and the Gypsy. Drop Out! Tristana. 1971: Confessions of a Police Commissioner. Giornata nera per i Ariete. L'istruttoria è chiusa: dimentichi. Killer from Yuma/Los guerilleros. 1972: Senza ragione/ Redneck. The Monk. Pope Joan. The Fifth Day of Peace. The Aquarian. Viva la muerte tua. La vacanza. 1973: Los amigos (GB and US: Deaf Smith and Johnny Ears). Il delitto matteotti. High Crime/La polizia incrimina, la legge assolve. 1974: White Fang. I guappi. Il cittadino si ribella. Perchè si uccide un magistrato? Corruzione al Palazzo di Giustizia. 1975: The Legend of Valentino (TV). Gente di rispetto (US: The Flower in His Mouth). Marcia trionfale. Profenzia per un delitto. Scandalo. Cry Onion. The Anonymous Avenger. I quattro dell'apocalisse. Challenge to White Fang. 1976: Un altimo di vita. Il cipollaro. L'ispettore. Autostop rosso sangue (GB: Death Drive). Keoma (GB: The Violent Breed). 21 Hours at Munich (TV. GB: cinemas). 1977: Submission. Django – il grande Titorno. Mussolini: The Last Four Days (completed 1974). 1978: Force Ten from Navarone. The Pirate (TV). 1979: Il grande respiro. The Man with Bogart's Face. The Visitor. Un dramma borghese. 1980: I contrabbandieri. Shark Hunter. Blue-Eyed Bandit. The Day of the Cobra. Danzig Roses. The Falcon. 1981: The Salamander. Sahara Cross. Enter the Ninja. The Day of the Cobra. 1982: Il fioretto. Mexico in Flames/Red Bells. Wagner. Querelle. Grog. 1983: Der Bauer von Babylon. 1984: The Last Days of Pompeii (TV). Un solitario e mezzo. 1985: Sweet Country. Il pentito. Die Förstenbuben. Garibaldi the General. The Girl. 1986: Race to Danger. 1987: Marathon. Django Strikes Again/The Return of Django. Top Line. 1988: Silent Night. Pygmalion 88. Young Toscanini. 1989: Lungo il fiume. 36.15 codice per noele. The Betrothed. The Magistrate. 1990: Die Hard 2. Amelia Lopes O'Neill. Di ceria dell'untore (US: The Plague Soldier). A Double Victory (TV). 1991: Touch and Die. 1992: Prova de memoria. Night of the White Rabbit. Fratelli e sorelle. 1993: I leoni del sol. 1994: La congiura del silenzio. Jonathan of the Bears. The Babylon Project (TV). 1995: Conquest/Honfoglals. The Innocent Sleep. Talk of Angels. Arrivano gli Italiani. Io e il re (US: The King and Me). 1996: La medaglia. 1997: A tres bandas. The Versace Murder. Honfoglalas (US: The Conflict). Talk of Angels. David (TV). 1999: Uninvited. Mirka. 2000: Briganti. La voce del sangue.

NEWLEY, Anthony, 1931–1999

Dark, jaunty, often crop-haired British actor, singer, composer and director from London's East End. He was a memorable teenage Artful Dodger before settling down as a character actor, mostly playing cocky cockneys. Unexpectedly became a pop star after *Idle on*

Parade and enjoyed great success writing stage musicals. He seemed to overreach himself after the late 1960s, and faded to some extent from public favour, although he still cropped up as the star of stage musicals. Married/divorced Ann Lynn and Joan Collins (both *qv*). Died from renal cancer.

1947: Dusty Bates (serial). The Little Ballerina. Vice Versa. 1948: Here Come the Huggetts. Oliver Twist. The Guinea Pig. Vote for Huggett. 1949: A Boy, a Girl and a Bike. Don't Ever Leave Me. Madeleine. 1950: Highly Dangerous. 1952: Those People Next Door. Top of the Form. 1953: The Weak and the Wicked (US: Young and Willing). 1954: Up to His Neck. The Case of the Bogus Count. 1955: Above Us the Waves. The Blue Peter (US: Navy Heroes). The Battle of the River Plate (US: Pursuit of the Graf Spee). Cockleshell Heroes. Port Afrique. 1956: X the Unknown. The Last Man to Hang? 1957: The Good Companions. Fire Down Below. How to Murder a Rich Uncle. High Flight. 1958: No Time to Die! (US: Tank Force). The Man Inside. The Lady is a Square. 1959: The Bandit of Zhobe. Idle on Parade (US: Idol on Parade). The Heart of a Man. Killers of Kilimanjaro. Jazzboat. In the Nick. 1960: Let's Get Married. 1963: The Small World of Sammy Lee. Image of Love (narrator only). 1967: Doctor Dolittle. 1968: Sweet November. Can Hieronymous Merkin Ever Forget Mercy Humppe and Find True Happiness? 1974: Mister Quilp. 1976: It Seemed Like a Good Idea at the Time. 1983: Malibu (TV). 1985: Blade in Hong Kong (TV). 1986: Outrage! (TV). Stagecoach (TV). 1987: The Garbage Pail Kids Movie. 1989: Boris & Natasha (released 1992 on TV). 1990: Coins in the Fountain (TV). Polly – Comin' Home (TV). As director: 1968: Can Hieronymous Merkin . . . ? 1971: Summertree.

NEWMAN, Barry 1940–

Slim-but-craggy, aggressive American actor with dark, curly hair, winning smile and distinctive facial scar. He seemed headed for big things in the early 1970s, but a couple of very routine action films knocked his career off course. He enjoyed a burst of popularity as television's *Petrocelli*, but has only rarely tried again in the cinema.

1959: Pretty Boy Floyd. 1963: The Moving Finger. 1969: The Lawyer. 1971: Vanishing Point. 1972: The Salzburg Connection. Fear is the Key. 1974: Night Games (TV). 1977: Sex and the Married Woman (TV). 1978: Blue

Orchids. City on Fire. Studio Murders/ Fantasies (TV). 1980: King Crab (TV). 1981: Shadow Effects (TV). Amy. Deadline. 1982: Having It All. 1984: Second Sight: A Love Story (TV). 1986: Outrage! (TV). My Two Loves (TV). 1993: Hunt for the Blue Diamond. 1966: Daylight. 1997: Goodbye Lover. 1998: Brown's Requiem. 1999: Bowfinger. The Limey.

NEWMAN, Nanette 1932–

Dark, striking, gentle British leading lady who might have had Jean Simmons–style success had she not chosen to put family before career. Despite winning awards in 1971 for *The Raging Moon*, she has only flirted with films over the years, mainly in husband Bryan Forbes' productions. One applauds the decision, but regrets the waste of talent, especially as she managed to make enough films to emphasize the point. Also writes on cookery and for children.

*1945: *Here We Come Gathering. 1953: Personal Affair. Wheel of Fate. 1955: Triple Blackmail. 1959: The League of Gentlemen. 1960: Faces in the Dark. 1961: The Rebel (US: Call Me Genius). Pit of Darkness. Dangerous Afternoon. House of Mystery. The Painted Smile. 1962: Twice Round the Daffodils. The L-Shaped Room. †Raiders of the Spanish Main. The Wrong Arm of the Law. 1963: Seance on a Wet Afternoon. 1964: Of Human Bondage. 1966: The Whisperers. The Wrong Box. 1967: Deadfall. 1968: Captain Nemo and the Underwater City. 1969: Oh! What a Lovely War. The Madwoman of Chaillot. Journey into Darkness (TV). 1970: The Raging Moon (US: Long Ago Tomorrow). 1972: The Love Ban. 1973: Man at the Top. 1974: The Stepford Wives. 1978: International*

Velvet. 1981: Jessie (TV). 1985: Restless Natives. 1993: The Mystery of Edwin Drood.

†*US cinema release of GB TV material*

NEWMAN, Paul 1925– 9-08

Fair-haired American actor with prominent lips, luminous blue eyes and a boxer's handsomeness who stayed near the top of world popularity despite the occasional disaster – his first film notable among them – for 25 years before his appeal began to fall away. Never less than watchable, he has also been associated with several of Hollywood's biggest-ever box-office hits. Married to Joanne Woodward (*qv*) (second) since 1958, he has directed her several times to good effect. Nominated for an Oscar on seven occasions, Newman finally won for *The Color of Money*. He picked up an honorary Oscar in 1994 for humanitarian work.

1954: The Silver Chalice. 1956: The Rack. Somebody Up There Likes Me. 1957: Until They Sail. The Helen Morgan Story (GB: Both Ends of the Candle). The 80 Yard Run (TV). 1958: Cat on a Hot Tin Roof. Rally 'Round the Flag, Boys! The Long, Hot Summer. The Left-Handed Gun. 1959: The Young Philadelphians (GB: The City Jungle). 1960: From the Terrace. Exodus. 1961: Paris Blues. The Hustler. 1962: Hemingway's Adventures of a Young Man (GB: Adventures of a Young Man). Sweet Bird of Youth. 1963: Hud. A New Kind of Love. The Prize. 1964: What a Way to Go! The Outrage. 1965: Lady L. 1966: Harper (GB: The Moving Target). Torn Curtain. Hombre. 1967: Cool Hand Luke. The Secret War of Harry Frigg. 1969: Winning. Butch Cassidy and the Sundance Kid. 1970: WUSA. King: a Filmed Record . . . Montgomery to Memphis. 1971: Sometimes a Great Notion (GB: Never Give an Inch). Pocket Money. 1972: The Life and Times of Judge Roy Bean. 1973: The Sting. The Mackintosh Man. 1974: The Towering Inferno. 1975: The Drowning Pool. 1976: Silent Movie. Buffalo Bill and the Indians, or: Sitting Bull's History Lesson. 1977: Slap Shot. 1979: Angel Death (narrator only). Quintet. 1980: When Time Ran Out . . . 1981: Fort Apache the Bronx. Absence of Malice. 1982: The Verdict. 1984: Harry and Son. 1986: The Color of Money. 1987: Hello Actors Studio. 1988: John Huston. 1989: Fat Man and Little Boy (GB: Shadow Makers). Blaze. 1990: Mr & Mrs Bridge. 1991: That's Driving. 1993: The Hudsucker Proxy. 1994: Nobody's Fool. 1998:

Twilight. 1999: Message in a Bottle. 2000: Where the Money Is.
As director: *1959: *On the Harmfulness of Tobacco. 1968: Rachel, Rachel. 1971: Sometimes a Great Nation (GB: Never Give an Inch. Co-directed). 1972: The Effect of Gamma Rays on Man-in-the-Moon Marigolds. 1980: The Shadow Box (TV). 1984: Harry and Son. 1987: The Glass Menagerie.*

NEWTON, Robert 1905–1956

Dark, scowling, attention-grabbing British actor of ruddy complexion who mixed rich characterizations with quieter roles – and was effective at both – for the British cinema of the thirties and forties. Despite bouts of alcoholism in later years, his performances remained good value. In 1950 he found his niche as the screen's most memorable Long John Silver and played the role, with variations, for the rest of his career. Died from a heart attack.

*1924: *The Tremarne Case. 1932: Reunion. 1936: Fire over England. 1937: Dark Journey. Farewell Again (US: Troopship). The Squeaker (US: Murder on Diamond Row). The Green Cockatoo. 21 Days (US: 21 Days Together). 1938: Vessel of Wrath (US: The Beachcomber). †I Claudius. Yellow Sands. 1939: Poison Pen. Dead Men are Dangerous. Jamaica Inn. Hell's Cargo (US: Dangerous Cargo). 1940: Bulldog Sees It Through. Busman's Honeymoon (US: Haunted Honeymoon). Gaslight (US: Angel Street). *Channel Incident. 1941: Major Barbara. Hatter's Castle. They Flew Alone (US: Wings and the Woman). 1944: This Happy Breed. Henry V. 1945: Night Boat to Dublin. 1946: Odd Man Out. 1947: Temptation Harbour. 1948: Snowbound. Oliver Twist. Kiss the Blood Off My Hands (GB: Blood on My Hands). Obsession (US: The Hidden Room). 1950: Treasure Island. Waterfront (US: Waterfront Women). 1951: Tom Brown's Schooldays. Soldiers Three. 1952: Blackbeard the Pirate. Les Misérables. 1953: Androcles and the Lion. The Desert Rats. 1954: Long John Silver. The High and the Mighty. The Beachcomber. 1955: Under the Black Flag (TV. GB: cinemas). 1956: Around the World in 80 Days.*

NEWTON, Thandie (Thandiwe Newton) 1970–

Slender, graceful, pretty Zambian-born actress, daughter of an English father and Zimbabwean mother, in England from 11 and originally trained to be a dancer. A back

injury put an end to her dancing ambition, and she made her debut in an Australian film, her quiet but definitive talents later coming into demand in British and international films, although her specific personality has sometimes made her difficult to cast. Married to director Oliver Parker.

1991: Flirting. 1993: The Young Americans. Pirate Prince (TV). 1994: Loaded/Bloody Weekend. Interview with the Vampire. 1995: Jefferson in Paris. The Journey of August King. 1996: The Leading Man. In Your Dreams. 1997: Gridlock'd. 1998: Besieged. Beloved. 2000: Mission: Impossible 2. It Was an Accident.

NICHOLSON, Jack 1937–

Dry-voiced, dark, dynamic American actor with cynical smile. Despite receding hair (and an early career spent in teenage-rebel and horror roles until he was 30) he moved forward, via an Oscar nomination for *Easy Rider*, to become one of America's best actors by the 1970s, winning Academy Awards for *One Flew Over the Cuckoo's Nest* and *Terms of Endearment*, plus eight further nominations. He has also written screenplays and occasionally directs. He won a third Oscar for *As Good As it Gets*.

1958: The Cry Baby Killer. The Wild Ride. 1959: Too Soon to Love (GB: Teenage Lovers). 1960: Studs Lonigan. The Little Shop of Horrors. 1961: The Broken Land. 1963: The Raven. The Terror. 1964: Back Door to Hell. Ensign Pulver. Flight to Fury. 1966: The Shooting. 1967: Ride in the Whirlwind. The St Valentine's Day Massacre. Hell's Angels on Wheels. 1968: Head. Psych-Out. 1969: Rebel Rousers. Easy Rider. 1970: On a Clear Day You Can See Forever. Five Easy Pieces. 1971:

A Safe Place. Carnal Knowledge. 1972: The King of Marvin Gardens. 1973: The Last Detail. 1974: The Fortune. Chinatown. 1975: Tommy. Professione: Reporter/The Passenger. One Flew Over the Cuckoo's Nest. 1976: The Last Tycoon. The Missouri Breaks. 1978: Goin' South. 1980: The Shining. 1981: The Border. The Postman Always Rings Twice. Reds. 1983: Terms of Endearment. 1985: Prizzi's Honor. 1986: Heartburn. 1987: The Witches of Eastwick. Ironweed. Broadcast News. 1989: Batman. 1990: The Two Jakes. 1991: Man Trouble. 1992: Hoffa. A Few Good Men. Blast 'Em (doc). 1994: Wolf. 1995: The Crossing Guard. 1996: Blood and Wine. The Evening Star. Mars Attacks! 1997: As Good As It Gets. 2000: The Pledge.

As director: 1971: Drive, He Said. 1978: Goin' South. 1990: The Two Jakes.

NICOL, Alex 1919–
Fair-haired, coldly handsome American actor, who was usually most effective as vicious, almost sexless villains, although he played a few more routine leading roles in Britain. In acting since 1938, but only signed for films at 31. Later travelled widely, and directed one or two offbeat subjects.
1950: The Sleeping City. Tomahawk (GB: Battle of Powder River). 1951: Target Unknown. Meet Danny Wilson. The Raging Tide. Air Cadet (GB: Jet Men of the Air). 1952: Because of You. Red Ball Express. The Redhead from Wyoming. 1953: Champ for a Day. Law and Order. The Lone Hand. 1954: About Mrs Leslie. Dawn at Socorro. Face the Music (US: The Black Glove). The House Across the Lake (US: Heatwave). The Gilded Cage. 1955: The Man from Laramie. Strategic Air Command. Sincerely Yours. 1956: Great Day in the Morning. 1957: Stranger in Town. 1958: The Screaming Skull. 1959: Five Branded Women. 1960: Then There Were Three (GB: Three Came Back). Under Ten Flags. Tutti a casa. Run with the Devil/Via Margutta/La rue des amours faciles. Il gobbo. 1961: Look in Any Window. A Matter of WHO. 1962: The Savage Guns. 1964: Cavalca e uccidi (GB and US: Ride and Kill). Gunfighters of Casa Grande. 1967: Manila: Open City. 1969: Bloody Mama. 1970: Homer. 1971: The Night God Screamed (GB: Scream). 1973: The Clones (GB: Clones). 1975: Winner Take All (TV). 1976: Woman in the Rain. A*P*E*.
As director: 1958: The Screaming Skull. 1960: Then There Were Three (GB: Three Came

Back). 1971: Point of Terror. 1985: Striker's Mountain (TV).

NIELSEN, Leslie 1922–
Tall, blond-haired (now white) Canadian actor, at his best in early years as treacherous charmers, becoming merely bland when asked to play the hero. A former radio announcer and disc jockey (following war service with the Royal Canadian Air Force), he made his TV debut as an actor in 1949. Becoming one of the medium's most prolific performers, he entered films six years later and did exceptionally well to maintain near-star status in a career that never really went anywhere until he brought his startled stare to zany comedy from 1980. A huge hit in the cult TV comedy series Police Squad, he went on to become an international celebrity as the hapless, poker-faced hero of the Naked Gun films and other wacky spoofs of varying film genres. Nephew of Jean Hersholt (qv).
1955: The Vagabond King. 1956: Forbidden Planet. Ransom! The Opposite Sex. 1957: Hot Summer Night. Tammy and the Bachelor (GB: Tammy). 1958: The Sheepman. The Right Hand Man (TV). 1959: The Velvet Alley (TV). 1964: Night Train to Paris. See How They Run (TV). 1965: Harlow. Dark Intruder. 1966: Beau Geste. The Plainsman. 1967: Gunfight in Abilene. Rosie! The Reluctant Astronaut. Counterpoint. Code Name: Heraclitus (TV). Companions in Nightmare (TV). 1968: Shadow over Elveron (TV). Dayton's Devils. How to Steal the World (TV. GB: cinemas). 1969: Four Rode Out. How to Commit Marriage. Deadlock (TV). Trial Run (TV). 1970: The Aquarians (TV). Hauser's Memory (TV). Incident in San Francisco (TV). Night Slaves (TV). 1971: They Call It Murder (TV). 1972: The Poseidon Adventure. The Letters (TV). Snatched (TV). 1973: And Millions Will Die. The Resurrection of Zachary Wheeler (GB: TV). 1974: Can Ellen Be Saved? (TV). Guadalcanal Odyssey (narrator only). 1975: King of the Underwater World (narrator only). 1976: Day of the Animals. Project: Kill. Brink's: the Great Robbery (TV). The Siege (TV). 1977: Viva Knievel! The Amsterdam Kill. Sixth and Main. Grand Jury (TV). 1978: Institute for Revenge (TV). Little Mo (TV). City on Fire. 1979: The Mad Trapper. RIEL. Cave In! (TV). 1980: Prom Night. OHMS (TV). Airplane! 1981: The Creature Wasn't Nice. A Choice of Two. 1982: Creepshow. Wrong is Right (GB: The Man

with the Deadly Lens). 1985: Reckless Disregard (TV). The Homefront (narrator only). Blade in Hong Kong (TV). Striker's Mountain (TV). 1986: Foxfire Light. The Patriot. Soul Man. Home is Where the Hart Is. 1987: Nuts. Calhoun/Night Stick. Fatal Confession (TV). 1988: Dangerous Curves (TV). The Naked Gun: From the Files of Police Squad! 1990: Repossessed. 1991: The Naked Gun 2½: The Smell of Fear. 1992: All I Want for Christmas. 1993: Surf Ninjas. Digger. 1994: Naked Gun 33⅓: The Final Insult. SPQR: 2000 and a Half Years Ago. 1995: Dracula: Dead and Loving It. Rent-a-Kid. 1996: Spy Hard. Harvey (TV). 1997: Family Plan. Mr Magoo. 1998: Wrongfully Accused. Safety Patrol (TV). 1999: Camouflage. 2000: Santa Who? (TV). 2001: A Space Travesty. 2001: Kevin of the North. Titanic Too: It Missed the Iceberg.

NIGH, Jane (Bonnie Nigh) 1925–1993
Hollywood's red-haired Queen of Cinecolor – a favourite for low-budget outdoors adventures of the late forties and early fifties after she had worked her way up from small roles. Lost to the television series Big Town from 1953, after which her film career never got going again. Died following a stroke.
1944: Something for the Boys. Laura. 1945: State Fair. House of Dracula. Whistle Stop. 1946: Dragonwyck. 1947: Unconquered. 1948: Leather Gloves (GB: Loser Take All). Sitting Pretty. Blue Grass of Kentucky. Give My Regards to Broadway. Cry of the City. 1949: Red Hot and Blue. Captain Carey USA (GB: After Midnight). Zamba (GB: Zamba the Gorilla). Fighting Man of the Plains. 1950: Border Treasure. Rio Grande Patrol. Operation Haylift. Motor Patrol. County Fair. 1951: Blue Blood. Disc Jockey. 1952: Fort Osage. Rodeo. 1956: Hold That Hypnotist.

NIVEN, David
(James D. Niven) 1909–1983
Dark-haired, suave, Scottish-born (some sources say London) international star with impeccable diction, and figure as pencil-slim as his moustache. A witty comedy player, he also showed up well as a stiff-upper-lip Briton in Hollywood epics (having gone there in 1935) and got some meaty dramatic roles on his frequent returns to Britain. Won an Academy Award for his fake major in Separate Tables and later wrote two extremely popular volumes of light-hearted auto-biography. Died from amyotrophic lateral

sclerosis, a motor neurone (wasting) disease. Made film debut in England.

*1932: There Goes the Bride. 1933: Eyes of Fate. 1935: Mutiny on the Bounty. Splendor. Without Regret. A Feather in Her Hat. Barbary Coast. 1936: Palm Springs (GB: Palm Springs Affair). Rose-Marie. Dodsworth. Thank You, Jeeves. The Charge of the Light Brigade. Beloved Enemy. 1937: Dinner at the Ritz. We Have Our Moments. The Prisoner of Zenda. 1938: The Cowboy and the Lady (scenes deleted). Three Blind Mice. Four Men and a Prayer. The Dawn Patrol. Bluebeard's Eighth Wife. 1939: The Real Glory. Wuthering Heights. Bachelor Mother. Eternally Yours. 1939–1940: Raffles. 1942: The First of the Few (US: Spitfire). 1944: The Way Ahead (US: Immortal Battalion). 1946: A Matter of Life and Death (US: Stairway to Heaven). Magnificent Doll. The Perfect Marriage. 1947: The Other Love. The Bishop's Wife. 1948: Bonnie Prince Charlie. Enchantment. 1949: A Kiss for Corliss. A Kiss in the Dark. 1950: The Elusive Pimpernel (US: The Fighting Pimpernel). The Toast of New Orleans. 1951: Happy-Go-Lovely. Appointment with Venus (US: Island Rescue). Soldiers Three. The Lady Says No. 1953: The Moon is Blue. 1954: The Love Lottery. Happy Ever After (US: Tonight's the Night). Carrington VC (US: Court-Martial). 1955: The King's Thief. 1956: The Silken Affair. The Birds and the Bees. Around the World in 80 Days. 1957: Oh, Men! Oh, Women! The Little Hut. My Man Godfrey. 1958: Bonjour Tristesse. *Glamorous Hollywood. Separate Tables. 1959: Happy Anniversary. Ask Any Girl. 1960: Please Don't Eat the Daisies. 1961: The Guns of Navarone. The Best of Enemies. 1962: Guns of Darkness. Road to Hong Kong. La citta prigioniera (GB: The Captive City. US: The Conquered City). 55 Days at Peking. 1963: The Pink Panther. 1964: Bedtime Story. 1965: Where the Spies Are. Lady L. 1966: Eye of the Devil. 1967: Casino Royale. 1968: Prudence and the Pill. The Extraordinary Seaman. The Impossible Years. 1969: Before Winter Comes. The Brain. 1970: The Statue. 1972: King, Queen, Knave. 1974: Paper Tiger. Vampira (US: Old Dracula). 1976: Murder by Death. No Deposit, No Return. 1977: Candleshoe. 1978: Escape to Athena. Death on the Nile. The Billion Dollar Movies (TV. Narrator only). 1979: A Man Called Intrepid (TV). 1980: Rough Cut. The Sea Wolves. The Biggest Bank Robbery (TV). 1982: Ménage à trois/Better Late Than Never. Trail of the Pink Panther. 1983: Curse of the Pink Panther.*

NIVOLA, Alessandro 1973–
Lantern-faced, velvet-voiced, brown-haired American actor of Italian descent and old-fashioned charm who played a good variety of roles in his first Hollywood years, ranging from suave and immaculate to desperate and unkempt. A professional actor at 14, he had an extensive spell of training in England, which also enabled him to turn on an impressive British accent when required.

1996: Inventing the Abbotts. 1997: Face/Off. 1998: Reach the Rock. I Want You. 1999: The Almost Perfect Bank Robbery (TV). Best Laid Plans. Mansfield Park. Love's Labour's Lost. 2000: TimeCode. 2001: Jurassic Park 3.

NOLAN, Lloyd 1902–1985
Skilful and likeable American actor of tough-guy parts, facially not unlike George Raft. Usually billed above the title but behind the stars, but quite capable of carrying a film on his own during his peak period (1935–1949), Nolan was also the star of a presentable little series of crime thrillers about detective Michael Shayne. Remained in occasional character roles until his death from lung cancer.

1935: Stolen Harmony. Atlantic Adventure. One-Way Ticket. She Couldn't Take It (GB: Woman Tamer). G-Men. 1936: You May Be Next! (GB: Panic on the Air). Lady of Secrets. Counterfeit. 15 Maiden Lane. Big Brown Eyes. The Devil's Squadron. The Texas Rangers. 1937: Exclusive. Internes Can't Take Money (GB: You Can't Take Money). Wells Fargo. King of Gamblers. Ebb Tide. Every Day's a Holiday. 1938: Hunted Men. Dangerous to Know. Tip-Off Girls. King of Alcatraz (GB: King of the Alcatraz). Prison Farm. 1939: Undercover Doctor. St. Louis Blues. The Magnificent Fraud. Ambush. 1940: Johnny Apollo. The Man Who Wouldn't Talk. The Man I Married. The Golden Fleecing. Charter Pilot. The House across the Bay. Gangs of Chicago. Pier 13. Behind the News. 1941: Michael Shayne, Private Detective. Dressed to Kill. Sleepers West. Blues in the Night. Blue, White and Perfect. Steel against the Sky. Mr Dynamite. Buy Me That Town. 1942: Just Off Broadway. It Happened in Flatbush. Time to Kill. Apache Trail. Manila Calling. The Man Who Wouldn't Die. 1943: Bataan. Guadalcanal Diary. 1944: A Tree Grows in Brooklyn. 1945: The House on 92nd Street. Circumstantial Evidence. Captain Eddie. 1946: Two Smart People. Lady in the Lake. Somewhere in the Night. 1947: Wild Harvest. 1948: The Street with No Name. Green Grass of Wyoming. 1949: The Sun Comes Up. Bad Boy. Easy Living. 1951: The Lemon Drop Kid. 1953: Island in the Sky. Crazylegs. 1956: Santiago (GB: The Gun Runner). The Last Hunt. Toward the Unknown (GB: Brink of Hell). 1957: Galvanized Yankee (TV). Seven Waves Away (US: Abandon Ship!). Peyton Place. A Hatful of Rain. 1960: Girl of the Night. Portrait in Black. 1961: Susan Slade. 1962: We Joined the Navy. 1963: The Girl Hunters. The Case Against Paul Ryker. (TV. Released 1968 to cinemas as Sergeant Ryker). 1964: Circus World (GB: The Magnificent Showman). 1965: Never Too Late. 1966: An American Dream (GB: See You in Hell, Darling). 1967: The Double Man. Wings of Fire (TV). 1968: Ice Station Zebra. 1969: Airport. 1972: My Boys Are Good Boys. 1973: Isn't It Shocking? (TV). 1974: The Abduction of Saint Anne/They've Kidnapped Anne Benedict (TV). Earthquake. 1976: The November Plan. Flight to Holocaust (TV). 1977: The Mask of Alexander Cross (TV). Fire! (TV. GB: cinemas). J. Edgar Hoover, Godfather of the FBI (later and GB: The Private Files of J. Edgar Hoover). 1979: Valentine (TV). 1980: Galyon. 1984: Prince Jack. It Came Upon the Midnight Clear (TV). 1986: Hannah and Her Sisters.

NOLTE, Nick 1940–
Fair-haired, square-jawed, huskily muscular American leading man of the 1970s who came belatedly to the fore in a TV mini-series, *Rich Man, Poor Man*, one of the most popular of its kind. Following that he showed an interest in tackling film roles that allowed him more depth and width of characterization, although occasionally he over-reached himself in

choosing parts for which he was not entirely suited. Seems to become progressively more gravel-voiced. Oscar nominee for *The Prince of Tides* and *Affliction*. Father of actor Brawley Nolte. Three times married.

1965: *The Feather Farm*. 1974: *The California Kid* (TV). *Winter Kill* (TV). *Death Sentence* (TV). 1975: *Adams of Eagle Lake* (TV). *The Runaway Barge* (TV). *Return to Macon Country* (GB: *Highway Girl*). 1977: *The Deep*. 1978: *Who'll Stop the Rain?* (GB: *Dog Soldiers*). 1979: *Heart Beat*. *North Dallas Forty*. 1982: *48 Hrs*. *Cannery Row*. 1983: *Under Fire*. 1984: *Teachers*. *The Ultimate Solution of Grace Quigley* (GB: *Grace Quigley*). 1985: *Down and Out in Beverly Hills*. 1986: *Extreme Prejudice*. 1987: *Weeds*. 1988: *Farewell to the King*. *Three Fugitives*. 1989: *New York Stories*. 1990: *Everybody Wins*. *Q & A*. *Another 48 Hrs*. 1991: *The Prince of Tides*. *Cape Fear*. 1992: *The Player*. *Lorenzo's Oil*. 1993: *I'll Do Anything*. *Blue Chips*. 1994: *I Love Trouble*. 1995: *Jefferson in Paris*. *Mulholland Falls*. 1996: *Mother Night*. 1997: *Afterglow*. *U Turn*/*Stray Dogs*. 1998: *Nightwatch*. *The Thin Red Line*. 1999: *Simpatico*. *Breakfast of Champions*. *The Best of Enemies*. 2000: *Trixie*. *The Golden Bowl*. 2001: *Investigating Sex*.

NORDEN, Christine
(Mary Thornton) 1924–1988
This green-eyed, slinky blonde siren was literally 'discovered' standing in a cinema queue and groomed by film mogul Alexander Korda to become Britain's most blatant post-war sex symbol before Diana Dors came along in earnest. Later the first actress to appear topless on the Broadway stage! Film career a thing of rags and patches but she certainly smouldered to some effect. The second of her five husbands (1947–1953) was British film director Jack Clayton. Died from lobar pneumonia.
1947: *Night Beat*. *An Ideal Husband*. *Mine Own Executioner*. **A Yank Comes Back*. 1948: *The Idol of Paris*. 1949: *Saints and Sinners*. *The Interrupted Journey*. 1950: *Black Widow*. 1951: *A Case of PC49*. *Reluctant Heroes*. 1958: *Angel's Ransom* (TV. GB: cinemas). 1986: *Little Shop of Horrors*. 1987: *The Wolvercote Tongue* (TV).

NORMAND, Mabel 1892–1930
Bright, bubbling, dark-eyed brunette, the most talented and individual of America's silent screen comediennes, with a great and deservedly devoted public following from

pre-World War I times to the early 1920s. Also directed, or co-directed, often without credit, many of her two-reelers. Loved and lost by slapstick producing kingpin Mack Sennett, she died from tuberculosis, her career already ruined by drug addiction and alleged involvement in a murder. Married actor Lew Cody (Louis Coté, 1884–1934).
1910: *The Indiscretions of Betty*. *Wilful Peggy*. *Over the Garden Wall*. 1911: *Betty Becomes a Maid*. *The Subduing of Mrs Nag*. *When a Man's Married His Troubles Begin*. *Piccioala*. *The Troublesome Secretaries*. *The Changing of Silas Warner*. *The Diving Girl*. *How Betty Won the School*. *His Mother*. *The Baron*. *The Revenue Man and the Girl*. *The Squaw's Love*. *The Making of a Man*. *Her Awakening*. *The Unveiling*. *Italian Blood*. *The Inventor's Secret*. *Their First Divorce Case*. *Through His Wife's Picture*. *A Victim of Circumstances*. *Saved from Himself*. *Why He Gave Up*. 1912: *The Engagement Ring*. *The Brave Hunter*. *The Furs*. *Help! Help!* *The Interrupted Elopement*. *A Dash thru the Clouds*. *The Fickle Spaniard*. *Helen's Marriage*. *Hot Stuff*. *Katchem Kate*. †*Neighbors*. *Oh, Those Eyes*. *Tomboy Bessie*. *The Tourists*. *The Beating He Needed*. *Pat's Day Off*. *The Eternal Mother*. *The Tragedy of a Dress Suit*. *What the Doctor Ordered*. *The Water Nymph*. *The New Neighbor*. *Pedro's Dilemma*. *Stolen Glory*. *The Ambitious Butler*. *The Flirting Husband*. *The Grocery Clerk's Romance*. *Cohen at Coney Island*. *At It Again*. *Mabel's Lovers*. *The Deacon's Trouble*. *A Temperamental Husband*. *The Rivals*. *Mr Fix-It*. *A Desperate Lover*. *Brown's Seance*. *A Family Mix-Up*. *A Midnight Elopement*. *Mabel's Adventures*. *The Duel*. *Mabel's Stratagem*. 1913: *Mabel's Dad*. *The Cure That Failed*. *The Mistaken Masher*. *The Deacon Outwitted*. *Just Brown's Luck*. *The Battle of Who Run*. *Heinze's Resurrection*. *Mabel's Heroes*. *The Professor's Daughter*. *Red-Hot Romance*. *A Tangled Affair*. *The Sleuths at the Floral Parade*. *The Rural Third Degree*. *A Strong Revenge*. *Foiling Fickle Father*. *A Doctor Affair*. *The Rube and the Baron*. *Those Good Old Days*. *Father's Choice*. *The Ragtime Band*. *At 12 O'Clock*. *Her New Boy*. *A Little Hero*. *Mabel's Awful Mistake*. *Hubby's Job*. *The Foreman of the Jury*. *Barney Oldfield's Race for Life*. *The Hansom Driver*. *The Speed Queen*. *The Waiters' Picnic*. *For the Love of Mabel*. *The Telltale Light*. *A Noise from the Deep*. *Love and Courage*. *Professor Bean's Removal*. *The Riot*. *Baby Day*. *Mabel's New Hero*. *The Gypsy Queen*. *Mabel's Dramatic

Career*. *The Faithful Taxicab*. *The Bowling Match*. *Speed Kings*. *Love Sickness at Sea*. *A Muddy Romance*. *Cohen Saves the Day*. *The Gusher*. *Zuzu the Band Leader*. *The Champion*. *Fatty's Flirtation*. 1914: *A Misplaced Foot*. *Mabel's Stormy Love Affair*. *Won in a Closet*. *Mabel's Bare Escape*. *Mabel's Strange Predicament*. *Love and Gasoline*. *Mack At It Again*. *Mabel at the Wheel*. *Caught in a Cabaret*. *Mabel's Nerve*. *The Alarm*. *The Fatal Market*. *Her Friend the Bandit*. *Mabel's Busy Day*. *Mabel's Married Life*. *Mabel's New Job*. *Those Country Kids*. *Mabel's Latest Prank*. *Mabel's Blunder*. *Hello, Mabel!* *Gentlemen of Nerve*. *Lovers' Post Office*. *His Trysting Place*. *How Heroes Are Made*. *Fatty's Jonah Day*. *Fatty's Wine Party*. *The Sea Nymphs*. *Getting Acquainted*. †*Tillie's Punctured Romance*. 1915: *Mabel and Fatty's Washing Day*. *Mabel and Fatty's Single Life*. *Fatty and Mabel at the San Diego Exposition*. *Mabel, Fatty and the Law*. *Fatty and Mabel's Married Life*. *That Little Band of Gold*. *Wished on Mabel*. *Mabel and Fatty Viewing the World's Fair at San Francisco*. *Their Social Splash*. *Mabel's Wilful Way*. *Mabel Lost and Won*. *The Little Teacher*. *My Valet*. *Stolen Magic*. 1916: *Fatty and Mabel Adrift*. *He Did and He Didn't*. *The Bright Lights*. 1917: *Oh! Mabel Behave* (released 1922). 1918: **Stake Uncle Sam to Play Your Hand*. †*Micky*. †*Joan of Plattsburgh*. †*Dodging a Million*. †*The Floor Below*. *Back to the Woods*. †*The Venus Model*. †*Peck's Bad Girl*. †*A Perfect 36*. 1919: †*Sis Hopkins*. †*The Rest*. *When Doctors Disagree*. †*Upstairs*. †*Jinx*. †*Pinto*. 1920: †*The Slim Princess*. †*What Happened to Rosa*. 1921: †*The Last Chance*. †*Arabella Flynn*. †*Molly O*. 1922: †*Head Over Heels*. 1923: †*Suzanna*. 1924: †*The Extra Girl*. 1926: *Raggedy Rose*. *The Nickel Hopper*. *One Hour Married*. *Anything Once*. 1927: *Should Men Walk Home?*

All shorts except † features

NORRIS, Chuck (Carlos Norris) 1939–
Stocky, fair-haired, unsmiling, unhandsome American action hero of few words whose shortness of stature proved no bar to becoming world middleweight karate champion from 1968 to 1974. During this time he taught action stunts to the stars and began a tentative film career, initially purely in kung-fu roles, but later in general action films whose titles spoke for themselves and whose often incredible plots paralleled those of films

made by Charles Bronson (like Norris, a late starter). He became a serviceable actor and a major box-office force in America, while not quite repeating his popularity on the international market. Bearded since 1983.

1968: The Wrecking Crew. 1972: Meng lung kuo chiang (GB: Way of the Dragon. US: Return of the Dragon). 1973: The Student Teachers (GB: Intimate Confessions of the Student Teachers). Slaughter in San Francisco (released 1981). 1977: Breaker! Breaker! Good Guys Wear Black. 1978: Game of Death (GB: Bruce Lee's Game of Death). A Force of One. 1980: The Octagon. 1981: An Eye for an Eye. 1982: Silent Rage. 1983: Forced Vengeance (later Battlerage). Lone Wolf McQuade. 1984: Missing in Action. 1985: Code of Silence. Missing in Action 2 – The Beginning. Invasion USA. 1986: The Delta Force. Firewalker. 1987: Braddock: Missing in Action III. 1988: Hero and the Terror. 1989: Delta Force 2. 1991: 50/50. Hit Man. 1992: Sidekicks. 1993: Walker, Texas Ranger (TV). Hell Bound. 1994: Top Dog. Walker, Texas Ranger: Deadly Reunion (TV). 1996: Forest Warrior. Logan's War: Bound by Honor (TV). 2000: The President's Man (TV).

NORTH, Sheree (Dawn Bethel) 1930–
Angie Dickinson, Dorothy Malone and Stella Stevens all have their supporters; but for me Sheree North is the gamest of all Hollywood's durable blondes. A leggy, curvaceous dancer with well-scrubbed looks, she was dancing professionally at 12, then struggled for years before Fox took her up as bait to get Marilyn Monroe back to work. They dropped her after four years, but she came back in the sixties with a series of vivid, gutsy portrayals of ladies just a little past their prime, but not their pride.

1945: An Angel Comes to Brooklyn. 1951: Excuse My Dust. 1953: Here Come the Girls. 1954: Living It Up. 1955: How to Be Very, Very Popular. The Lieutenant Wore Skirts. 1956: The Best Things in Life Are Free. 1957: The Way to the Gold. No Down Payment. Topaz (TV). 1958: Mardi Gras. In Love and War. 1966: Destination Inner Space. 1967: Code Name: Heraclitus (TV). 1968: Madigan. The Crime (TV). 1969: The Trouble with Girls. The Gypsy Moths. Survival. Then Came Bronson (TV). 1970: Vanished (TV). Lawman. 1971: The Organization. 1972: Key West (TV). Snatched (TV). Trouble Comes to Town (TV). Rolling Man (TV). 1973:

Charley Varrick. The Outfit. Maneater (TV). 1974: Winter Kill (TV). The Cloning of Clifford Swimmer (TV). 1975: Shadow of the Streets (TV). Breakout. 1976: The Shootist. Survival. Most Wanted (TV). 1977: Telefon. 1978: Rabbit Test. The Night They Took Miss Beautiful (TV). Amateur Night at the Dixie Bar and Grill (TV). A Real American Hero (TV). 1979: Only Once in a Lifetime. Portrait of a Stripper (TV). 1980: Marilyn: The Untold Story (TV. GB: cinemas). 1983: Legs (TV). Hard Hat and Legs (TV). 1984: Scorned and Swindled (TV). 1987: Marilyn Monroe: Beyond the Legend. 1988: Maniac Cop. 1989: Jake Spanner – Private Eye (TV). Cold Dog Soup. Defenseless (released 1991). 1991: Dead on the Money (TV). 1998: Susan's Plan.

NORTHAM, Jeremy 1961–
Tall, dark, smooth British actor with authoritative, upper-class personality. A theatre actor for much of his twenties (he won the Olivier Award as the outstanding newcomer of 1990), Northam emerged on the international film scene following Hollywood's desire to cast English actors as villains in its major action films and he appeared opposite Sandra Bullock in *The Net*. His easy charm has since been displayed in a good variety of roles, especially effective when lurking under a moustache.

1987: Suspicion (TV). 1991: A Fatal Inversion (TV). 1992: Wuthering Heights. 1994: A Village Affair. 1995: Carrington. Voices. The Net. 1996: Emma. 1997: Mimic. The Tribe. Amistad. 1998: The Misadventures of Margaret. Gloria. 1999: The Winslow Boy. An Ideal Husband. Happy, Texas. 2000: Sax Rohmer's Fu Manchu. The Golden Bowl. 2001: Enigma. Possession.

NORTH, Ted (Michael)
See HUGHES, Mary Beth

NORTON, Edward 1969–
Light-haired American actor of medium height and build, with easy-going facial features. After a belated film debut at 27, he quickly proved himself capable of striking in-depth performances, and has been twice Oscar-nominated, for *Primal Fear* (his debut) and *American History X*. One of Hollywood's more socially aware actors, he serves on the boards of theatre companies and a foundation dedicated to creating housing for low-income families.

1996: Primal Fear. The People vs Larry Flynt. Everyone Says I Love You. 1997: Out of the Past (voice only). 1998: American History X. Rounders. 1999: Fight Club. Forever Hollywood (D). 2000: †Keeping the Faith. 2001: The Score.

†And directed

NOVAK, Kim (Marilyn Novak) 1933–
There was something more to Kim Novak than a chrysanthemum head of blonde hair and a substantial bust. For a few years in the fifties she was remarkably magnetic with her combination of shyness and sexuality, especially given the right director, such as Hitchcock in *Vertigo*. Fresh in from Chicago to Hollywood with her broad, country-girl build, she played a couple of harem girls before being picked up by Columbia as a sex symbol and continued with them until the sixties, going rather too quickly then into blowsy roles. Married to Richard Johnson 1965–1966 (first of two).

1953: The Veils of Bagdad. 1954: Son of Sinbad. The French Line. Pushover. Phffft! 1955: Five Against the House. Picnic. 1956: The Eddy Duchin Story. The Man with the Golden Arm. 1957: Jeanne Eagels. Pal Joey. 1958: Bell, Book and Candle. Vertigo. 1959: Middle of the Night. 1960: Strangers When We Meet. Pepe. 1962: Boys' Night Out. The Notorious Landlady. 1964: Kiss Me, Stupid. Of Human Bondage. 1965: The Amorous Adventures of Moll Flanders. 1968: The Legend of Lylah Clare. 1969: The Great Bank Robbery. 1973: Third Girl from the Left (TV). Tales That Witness Madness. 1975: Satan's Triangle (TV). 1977: The White Buffalo. 1979: Just a Gigolo. 1980: The Mirror

*Crack'd. 1983: Malibu (TV). 1985: Alfred Hitchcock Presents (TV). 1987: *Es hat mich sehr gefreut. 1990: The Children. 1991: Liebestraum.*

NOVARRO, Ramon

(R. Samaniegos) 1899–1968

Dark-haired, dark-eyed, ultra-handsome Mexican-born leading man, a heart-throb of the silent screen, probably second only in that department to Rudolph Valentino. His biggest hit came with the title role in *Ben-Hur* but then sound erased much of his appeal. In later years he became an alcoholic and in 1968 was murdered by two brothers trying to find out where he kept his money. They were subsequently jailed for life. Also a singer, he began his show-business career as a singing waiter.

1916: †Joan the Woman. 1917: †The Jaguar's Claws. †The Little American. †The Hostage. 1919: †The Goat. 1921: A Small Town Idol. The Four Horsemen of the Apocalypse. The Conquering Power. 1922: Mr Barnes of New York. The Prisoner of Zenda. Trifling Women (GB: The Fatal Orchids). 1923: Where the Pavement Ends. Scaramouche. 1924: The Red Lily. Thy Name is Woman. 1925: A Lover's Oath. The Midshipman. Ben-Hur. 1927: The Student Prince in Old Heidelberg (GB: Old Heidelberg). Lovers? The Road to Romance (GB: Romance). 1928: Forbidden Hours. Across to Singapore. A Certain Young Man. 1929: Devil May Care. The Flying Feet. The Pagan. Wir schalten um auf Hollywood. 1930: In Gay Madrid. Call of the Flesh (and Spanish and French versions). 1931: Son of India. Daybreak. 1932: Mata Hari (GB: Impossible Lover). The Son-Daughter. 1933: The Barbarian (GB: A Night in Cairo). 1934: The Cat and the Fiddle. Laughing Boy. 1935: The Night is Young. 1937: The Sheik Steps Out. 1938: A Desperate Adventure (GB: It Happened in Paris). 1940: La comédie de bonheur. 1942: La Virgen que Forjo una Patria. 1949: We Were Strangers. The Big Steal. 1950: The Outriders. Crisis. 1960: Heller in Pink Tights.

As director: *1930: La Sevillana (Spanish-language version of Call of the Flesh). 1936: Contra la Corriente.*

†As Ramon Samaniegos

NOVELLO, Ivor

(David I. Davies) 1893–1951

Dark, soulful-looking Welsh actor, play-wright and composer with matinee idol-looks, one of the most popular figures in the British theatre over several decades. Also a popular man in British (plus Hollywood, French and German) films for 15 years, but most fondly remembered for such romantic stage musicals as *The Dancing Years* and *Perchance to Dream*. Died from a coronary thrombosis a few hours after appearing on stage.

1919: Call of the Blood (US: Gypsy Passion). 1920: Miarka. 1921: The Bohemian Girl. Carnival. 1923: The White Rose. Bonnie Prince Charlie. The Man without Desire. 1925: The Rat. 1926: The Lodger, a Story of the London Fog (US: The Case of Jonathan Drew). The Triumph of the Rat. 1927: The Constant Nymph. Downhill (US: Why Boys Leave Home). The Vortex. 1928: A South Sea Bubble. Der fesche Husar (GB: The Gallant Hussar). 1929: The Return of the Rat. 1930: Symphony in Two Flats. 1931: Once a Lady. 1932: The Lodger (remake) (US: The Phantom Fiend). 1933: Sleeping Car. I Lived with You. 1934: Autumn Crocus.

NUYEN, France
See CULP, Robert

Call of the Wild. The Big Broadcast of 1936. 1936: The Texas Rangers. Collegiate (GB: The Charm School). Colleen. That Girl from Paris. Florida Special. 1937: The Toast of New York. Champagne Waltz. Hitting a New High. Super Sleuth. Fight for Your Lady. 1938: The Affairs of Annabel. Radio City Revels. Thanks for Everything. Annabel Takes a Tour. 1940: Young People. The Great Dictator. Little Men. Tin Pan Alley. 1941: The Great American Broadcast. *Screen Snapshots No. 87. Rise and Shine. Navy Blues. 1942: Song of the Islands. Iceland (GB: Katina). 1943: Wintertime. Hello, Frisco, Hello. Something to Shout About. 1944: Sweet and Lowdown. It Happened Tomorrow. The Merry Monahans. Bowery to Broadway. 1945: On Stage, Everybody. That's the Spirit. 1946: She Wrote the Book. 1948: Northwest Stampede. When My Baby Smiles at Me. 1949: Thieves' Highway. 1950: Last of the Buccaneers. Tomahawk (GB: Battle of Powder River). 1956: Around the World in Eighty Days. 1959: The Wonderful Country. 1960: The Rat Race. 1961: Lover Come Back.

Head of Alfredo Garcia. 1975: 92 in the Shade. Race with the Devil. Glass Houses. 1976: Drum. Dixie Dynamite. 1977: Prime Time (GB: American Raspberry). Sleeping Dogs. 1978: The Brink's Job. True Grit, a Further Adventure (TV). Day of Terror, Night of Fear (TV). China 9, Liberty 37/Gunfighters (US: Clayton and Catherine). 1979: And Baby Makes Six (TV). 1941. 1980: Baby Comes Home (TV). 1981: The Border. Stripes. 1982: Tough Enough. Blue Thunder. My Old Man (TV).

†Scenes deleted from final release print

OBERON, Merle
(Estelle M. O'Brien Thompson) 1911–1979
Cold-looking, Indian-born brunette beauty of regal bearing who won the heart of British film tycoon Alexander Korda (they married in 1939 and divorced in 1945) and built up a considerable career in his productions, at first in exotic roles. Widened her range in Hollywood (where she married cameraman Lucien Ballard in 1945; divorced 1949), but her looks faded at 40 and later roles were unworthy of her. Nominated for an Academy Award on *The Dark Angel*. Died from a stroke.
1929: The Three Passions (sound version). 1930: A Warm Corner. Alf's Button. 1931: Fascination. Never Trouble Trouble. Service for Ladies (US: Reserved for Ladies). 1932: Ebbtide. For the Love of Mike. Aren't We All? Wedding Rehearsal. Strange Evidence. Men of Tomorrow. 1933: The Private Life of Henry VIII. 1934: The Battle (US: Thunder in the East). The Broken Melody. The Private Life of Don Juan. The Scarlet Pimpernel. 1935: The Dark Angel. Folies Bergère. 1936: These Three. Beloved Enemy. 1937: Over the Moon. The Divorce of Lady X. I Claudius (unfinished). 1938: The Cowboy and the Lady. 1939: Wuthering Heights. The Lion Has Wings. 1940: Till We Meet Again. 1941: Lydia. Affectionately Yours. That Uncertain Feeling. 1943: Forever and a Day. Stage Door Canteen. First Comes Courage. 1944: The Lodger. Dark Waters. 1945: A Song to Remember. This Love of Ours. 1946: A Night in Paradise. Temptation. 1947: Night Song. 1948: Berlin Express. 1949: Dans la vie tout s'arrange. 1951: Pardon My French (GB: The Lady from Boston). 1952: 24 Hours of a Woman's Life (US: Affair in Monte Carlo). 1954: Todo es possible en Grenada. Desiree. Deep in My Heart. 1955: Cavalcade (TV. GB: cinemas). 1956: The Price of Fear. 1963: Of Love and Desire. 1966: The Oscar. Hotel. 1973: Interval.

OAKIE, Jack (Lewis Offield) 1903–1978
Chubby, dark-haired, fast-talking American comedian, short of stature but long on energy. Noted for his facial grimaces, and usually cast as sunny-natured, easy-going guys. At the height of his popularity from 1929 to 1938. When he decided to take a long holiday in 1938 his studio dropped him, Hollywood cold-shouldered him, and his film career never completely recovered. Suffered from deafness in later years. Nominated for an Academy Award in *The Great Dictator*. Died from an aortic aneurysm.
1923: His Children's Children. Big Brother. 1924: Classmates. His Darker Self. 1928: Finders Keepers. The Fleet's In. Sin Town. Road House. Someone to Love. 1929: Close Harmony. Chinatown Nights. The Man I Love. Street Girl. Sweetie. The Wild Party. The Dummy. Fast Company. Hard to Get. 1930: The Social Lion. Paramount on Parade. The Sap from Syracuse (GB: The Sap Abroad). Hit the Deck. Let's Go Native. Sea Legs. 1931: Dude Ranch. The Gang Buster. Touchdown (GB: Playing the Game). June Moon. 1932: *Hollywood on Parade. *The Stolen Jools (GB: The Slippery Pearls). *Cricket Flickers. Make Me a Star. Dancers in the Dark. Madison Square Garden. Once in a Lifetime. Sky Bride. Million Dollar Legs. If I Had a Million. Uptown New York. 1933: The Eagle and the Hawk. Too Much Harmony. *Hollywood on Parade No. 17. From Hell to Heaven. Alice in Wonderland. Sailor Be Good. College Humor. Sitting Pretty. 1934: Shoot the Works (GB: Thank Your Stars). Looking for Trouble. College Rhythm. Murder at the Vanities. *Hollywood Rhythm. 1935: *Star Night at the Coconut Grove. King of Burlesque.

OATES, Warren 1928–1982
Kentucky-born actor with dark, curly hair, who played loutish, countrified villains in his early screen days, but was soon singled out by critics and moved into better roles. When stardom came, he proved distinctly unconventional, mixing such commercial leading roles as *Dillinger* with unshowy secondary parts in other films: he was associated with some quite weird projects in his time. Died from a heart attack.
1958: Up Periscope! 1959: Yellowstone Kelly. Private Property. Seven Against the Wall (TV). 1960: The Rise and Fall of Legs Diamond. 1961: Ride the High Country (GB: Guns in the Afternoon). 1962: Hero's Island. 1963: Mail Order Bride (GB: West of Montana). 1965: †Shenandoah. Major Dundee. 1966: Return of the Seven. The Shooting (released 1971). 1967: Welcome to Hard Times (GB: Killer on a Horse). In the Heat of the Night. 1968: The Split. Something for a Lonely Man (GB: TV). Crooks and Coronets (US: Sophie's Place). 1969: The Wild Bunch. Smith! Barquero. 1970: There Was a Crooked Man. The Movie Murderer (TV). 1971: Chandler. Two-Lane Blacktop. The Reluctant Heroes (TV. GB: The Reluctant Heroes of Hill 656). The Hired Hand. The Showdown (TV). 1973: The Thief Who Came to Dinner. Tom Sawyer. Kid Blue. Dillinger. Badlands. 1974: The White Dawn. Born to Kill (GB: Cockfighter). Bring Me the

O'BRIAN, Hugh (H. Krampe) 1925–
Tall, dark American actor with crooked smile, good-looking in a leathery sort of way. Played mostly lean, grim-faced villains until television success in the title role of *Wyatt Earp* pushed him towards the front rank, a position he never quite consolidated. A vigorous worker for charity in recent times.
1949: DOA. 1950: Never Fear. Rocketship XM. Kansas Riders. Beyond the Purple Hills. The Return of Jesse James. 1951: On the Loose. Buckaroo Sheriff of Texas. Vengeance Valley. Fighting Coast Guard. Cave of Outlaws. Little Big Horn (GB: The Fighting Seventh). The Cimarron Kid. 1952: Red Ball Express. The Battle at Apache Pass. Sally and Saint Anne. Son of Ali Baba. The Raiders/Riders of Vengeance. The Lawless Breed. Meet Me at the Fair. 1953: Seminole. The Man from the Alamo. The Stand at Apache River. Back to God's Country. 1954: Fireman, Save My Child. Saskatchewan (GB: O'Rourke of the Royal Mounted). Drums Across the River. There's No Business Like Show Business. Broken Lance. 1955: White Feather. The Twinkle in God's Eye. 1956: The Brass Legend. 1958: The Fiend Who Walked the West. 1959: Alias Jesse James. 1962: Come Fly with Me. 1963: Assassin... Made in Italy/Assassination in Rome. Il segreto del vestito rosso. 1964: Love Has Many Faces. Strategy of Terror. 1965: In Harm's Way. 10 Little Indians. 1966: Ambush Bay. 1967: Africa – Texas Style! 1970: Wild Women (TV). 1971: Harpy (TV). 1972: Probe (TV). 1975: Killer Force/The Diamond Mercenaries. Murder on Flight 502 (TV). 1976: The Shootist. 1977: Fantasy Island (TV). Murder at the World Series (TV). Benny and Barney: Las Vegas Undercover (TV). 1978: Game of Death. Cruise into Terror (TV). 1987: Doin' Time on Planet Earth. 1988: Twins. 1990: Gunsmoke: The Last Apache (TV). 1992: The Gambler Returns: The Luck of the Draw (TV). 1994: Wyatt Earp: Return to Tombstone (TV).

O'BRIEN, Edmond 1915–1985
Heavy-cheeked, burly, careworn-looking American actor, in leading parts almost from the beginning of his career, who gave everything, and sometimes a little more, to his roles. His career ran in phases: comedy and drama until war service; thrillers from 1946 to 1950; westerns from 1950 to 1953, then more thrillers and a natural sidestep into leading character parts when weight tipped him from the top of the cast. Oscar for *The Barefoot Contessa* (Best Supporting Actor). Also a nomination for *Seven Days in May*. Married to Nancy Kelly (*qv*) from 1941 to 1942 and musical star Olga San Juan (1927–) from 1948; they later divorced after many years. Died from Alzheimer's Disease.
1938: Prison Break. 1939: The Hunchback of Notre Dame. 1941: The Obliging Young Lady. A Girl, a Guy and a Gob (GB: The Navy Steps Out). Parachute Battalion. 1942: Powder Town. 1943: The Amazing Mrs Holliday. 1944: Winged Victory. 1946: The Killers. 1947: The Web. 1948: Another Part of the Forest. An Act of Murder. A Double Life. Fighter Squadron. For the Love of Mary. 1949: DOA. White Heat. Backfire. 1950: 711 Ocean Drive. Between Midnight and Dawn. The Admiral Was a Lady. The Redhead and the Cowboy. 1951: Two of a Kind. Warpath. Silver City (GB: High Vermilion). 1952: Denver and Rio Grande. The Greatest Show on Earth. The Turning Point. 1953: Cow Country. China Venture. Man in the Dark. Julius Caesar. The Hitch-Hiker. The Bigamist. 1954: The Shanghai Story. Shield for Murder. The Barefoot Contessa. 1955: Pete Kelly's Blues. 1984. 1956: A Cry in the Night. D-Day the Sixth of June. The Rack. The Girl Can't Help It. 1957: The Big Land (GB: Stampeded!). The Comedian (TV). Stopover Tokyo. 1958: The World Was His Jury. The Male Animal (TV). Sing, Boy, Sing. Up Periscope! 1959: The Restless and the Damned (GB: The Climbers. US: The Ambitious Ones). The Third Voice. The Blue Men (TV). 1960: The Last Voyage. 1961: The Great Imposter. 1962: The Man Who Shot Liberty Valance. Moon Pilot. Bird Man of Alcatraz. The Longest Day. 1964: Rio Conchos. Seven Days in May. The Hanged Man (TV. GB: cinemas). 1965: Sylvia: Synanon (GB: Get Off My Back). 1966: Fantastic Voyage. 1967: Peau d'espion (GB: To Commit a Murder). The Viscount. The Doomsday Flight (TV. GB: cinemas). The Outsider (TV). 1969: The Wild Bunch. The Love God? 1970: The Intruders (TV). River of Mystery (TV). 1971: What's a Nice Girl Like You? (TV). 1972: They Only Kill Their Masters. Jigsaw (TV). 1973: Isn't It Shocking? (TV). Lucky Luciano. 1974: 99 and 44/100% Dead (GB: Call Harry Crown). 1975: The Other Side of the Wind (uncompleted). 1976: Dream No Evil.
As director: *1954: Shield for Murder (co-directed). 1961: Man-Trap.*

O'BRIEN, George 1900–1985
Rugged, rough-hewn American cowboy star. A one-time boxing champion, he entered films as a stuntman, then featured in some of John Ford's earliest westerns. Settled down into the second-feature corral with the coming of sound, and later played a few character roles for Ford in post-war years, after serving with distinction in the US Navy during World War II. Married to Marguerite Churchill (*qv*) 1933–1948: never remarried. Died following a stroke.
*1922: White Hands. Moran of the Lady Letty. 1923: N'er do Well. Woman Proof. Shadows of Paris/Streets of Paris. The Ghost Breaker. 1924: Painted Lady. The Iron Horse. The Man Who Came Back. The Roughneck (GB: Thorns of Passion). The Sea Hawk. 1925: Fighting Heart (GB: Once to Every Man). The Dancers. Thank You. 1926: Fig Leaves. Havoc. The Johnstown Flood (GB: The Flood). The Blue Eagle. Three Bad Men. The Silver Treasure (GB: Nostromo). Rustlin' for Cupid. 1927: Paid to Love. Is Zat So? East Side, West Side. Sunrise. 1928: Sharpshooters (GB: 3 Naval Rascals). Honor Bound. The Case of Mary Brown. Blindfold. False Colors. 1929: Salute. Noah's Ark. Masked Emotions. True Heaven. *Graduation Daze. 1930: Last of the Duanes. The Lone Star Ranger. Rough Romance. 1931: A Holy Terror. Fair Warning. Riders of the Purple Sage. The Seas Beneath. 1932: Mystery Ranch. The Rainbow Trail. The Gay Caballero. The Golden West. 1933: Life in the Raw. Robbers' Roost. Smoke Lightning. The Last Trail. 1934: The Dude Ranger. Frontier Marshal. Ever Since Eve. 1935: Hard Rock Harrigan. When a Man's a Man. Thunder Mountain. Whispering Smith Speaks. The Cowboy Millionaire. 1936: Daniel Boone. O'Malley of the Mounted. Border Patrolman. 1937: Windjammer. Hollywood Cowboy. Park Avenue Logger (GB: Millionaire Playboy). *Vitaphone Pictorial Revue No. 3. 1938: The Painted Desert. Gun Law. Border G-Man. Lawless Valley. Renegade Ranger. 1939: Arizona Legion. Racketeers of the Range. Trouble in Sundown. The Fighting Gringo. Timber Stampede. 1940: Bullet Code. Marshal of Mesa City. Stage to Chino. Legion of the Lawless. Prairie Law. Triple Justice. 1941: *Hollywood Visits the Navy. 1943: December 7th (narrator only). 1947: My Wild Irish Rose. 1948: Fort Apache. 1949: She Wore a Yellow Ribbon. 1951: Gold Raiders (GB: Stooges Go West). 1964: Cheyenne Autumn.*

O'BRIEN, Margaret

(Angela Maxine O'Brien) 1937–

Dark-haired, appealing and very natural American child star, with big brown eyes and long pigtails, capable of more heart-felt conviction in her performances than most adults. Received a special Oscar in 1944, but when her studio (M-G-M) suspended her in 1950 for refusing to do a planned live-action film of Alice in Wonderland (ironically, never made), her star career was virtually finished. Several comebacks over the years have failed. *1941: †Babes on Broadway. 1942: Journey for Margaret. 1943: Dr Gillespie's Criminal Case (GB: Crazy to Kill). Lost Angel. *You, John Jones. Thousands Cheer. Madame Curie. Jane Eyre. 1944: The Canterville Ghost. Meet Me in St Louis. Music for Millions. 1945: Our Vines Have Tender Grapes. *Victory in Europe. 1946: Three Wise Fools. Bad Bascomb. 1947: Tenth Avenue Angel. The Unfinished Dance. 1948: The Big City. 1949: Little Women. The Secret Garden. 1951: Her First Romance (GB: Girls Never Tell). 1956: Glory. 1957: The Mystery of Thirteen (TV). 1958: Little Women (TV). 1959: Second Happiest Day (TV). 1960: Heller in Pink Tights. 1964: The Turncoat (TV). 1971: Diabolical Wedding. 1972: Annabelle Lee. 1974: Death in Space (TV). 1981: Amy. 1998: Hollywood Mortuary.*

†As Maxine O'Brien

O'BRIEN, Pat

(William P. O'Brien) 1899–1983

Round-faced, dark-haired, solidly-built Hollywood star of the thirties and forties. Pat O'Brien was so Irish that one could hardly believe he actually spoke with an American accent, even if there was a hint of soft Irishness in it. A boyhood friend of Spencer Tracy (qv), he chose acting in preference to the priesthood, but made up for it at Warners by playing priests several times, when he wasn't being fast-talking reporters or happy-go-lucky adventurers. He seemed heavy by the mid-forties and his standing gradually declined, but he kept acting, latterly in character roles. Died from a heart attack.

*1930: Compliments of the Season. *My Mistake. *Crimes Square. *The Nightingale. 1931: The Front Page. Flying High (GB: Happy Landing). Consolation Marriage (GB: Married in Haste). Honor Among Lovers. Personal Maid. 1932: The Strange Case of Clara Deane. The Final Edition (GB: Determination). American Madness. Virtue. Laughter in Hell. Hell's House. Scandal for Sale. Hollywood Speaks. Air Mail. 1933: Bombshell (GB: Blonde Bombshell). The World Gone Mad (GB: The Public Be Hanged). Destination Unknown. Bureau of Missing Persons. College Coach (GB: Football Coach). 1934: I've Got Your Number. Flaming Gold. Here Comes the Navy. I Sell Anything. Gambling Lady. Twenty Million Sweethearts. Personality Kid. Flirtation Walk. 1935: Oil for the Lamps of China. Devil Dogs of the Air. *A Trip thru a Hollywood Studio. Ceiling Zero. The Irish in Us. In Caliente. Page Miss Glory. Stars over Broadway/Stars on Parade. *A Dream Comes True. 1936: China Clipper. I Married a Doctor. Public Enemy's Wife (GB: G-Man's Wife). 1937: *Swingtime in the Movies. San Quentin. The Great O'Malley. Submarine D-1. Slim. Back in Circulation. 1938: Boy Meets Girl. Women Are Like That. *Out Where the Stars Begin. The Cowboy from Brooklyn (GB: Romance and Rhythm). *For Auld Lang Syne. Garden of the Moon. Angels with Dirty Faces. 1939: The Kid from Kokomo (GB: The Orphan of the Ring). Indianapolis Speedway (GB: Devil on Wheels). Off the Record. The Night of Nights. 1940: Castle on the Hudson (GB: Years without Days). Knute Rockne – All American (GB: A Modern Hero). The Fighting 69th. Torrid Zone. Slightly Honorable. Till We Meet Again. Flowing Gold. 1941: Submarine Zone. 1942: Two Yanks in Trinidad. Broadway. The Navy Comes Through. Flight Lieutenant. 1943: The Iron Major. Bombardier. His Butler's Sister. 1944: Marine Raiders. Secret Command. 1945: Man Alive. Having Wonderful Crime. 1946: Perilous Holiday. Crack-Up. 1947: Riffraff. 1948: Fighting Father Dunne. The Boy with Green Hair. *Screen Snapshots No. 166. 1949: *Hollywood Goes to Church. A Dangerous Profession. 1950: The Fireball. Johnny One-Eye. 1951: The People Against O'Hara. Criminal Lawyer. 1952: Okinawa. *Screen Snapshots No. 205. 1954: Jubilee Trail. Ring of Fear. 1955: Inside Detroit. *Hollywood Fathers. 1957: Kill Me Tomorrow. Invitation to a Gunfighter (TV). 1958: The Last Hurrah. 1959: Some Like It Hot. 1965: Town Tamer. The Crime (TV). 1969: The Over-the-Hill Gang (TV). The Phynx. 1971: Welcome Home, Johnny Bristol (TV). 1972: The Adventures of Nick Carter (TV). 1976: Kiss Me, Kill Me (TV). 1977: Billy Jack Goes to Washington. 1978: The End. 1980: Scout's Honor (TV). 1981: Ragtime.*

O'CONNOR, Donald 1925–

Cheerful, slimly-built, non-stop American dancing star and light comedian with a thick bush of brown hair. A child actor of the late 1930s (the offspring of a family vaudeville act), he blossomed in medium-budget musicals at Universal, and later proved a more-than-useful foil for Hollywood's leading musical lights, without quite being able to carry a big film on his own. Was also for many years the master of Francis the talking mule, but his film career faded in the 1950s as musicals fell from fashion, and he embarked on a fresh career as a composer of light symphonic music.

1937: Melody for Two. 1938: Men with Wings. Sing, You Sinners. Tom Sawyer – Detective. Sons of the Legion. 1939: Million Dollar Legs. Unmarried (GB: Night Club Hostess). Boy Trouble. Death of a Champion. Night Work. On Your Toes. Beau Geste. 1941: What's Cookin' (GB: Wake Up and Dream). 1942: Get Hep to Love (GB: She's My Lovely). Give Out, Sisters. It Comes Up Love (GB: A Date with an Angel). When Johnny Comes Marching Home. Private Buckaroo. 1943: Strictly in the Groove. Mister Big. Top Man. 1944: Follow the Boys. This Is the Life. The Merry Monahans. Chip Off the Old Block. Bowery to Broadway. 1945: Patrick the Great. 1947: Something in the Wind. 1948: Feudin', Fussin' and a Fightin'. Are You With It? 1949: Yes, Sir, That's My Baby. Francis. Curtain Call at Cactus Creek (GB: Take the Stage). 1950: The Milkman. Double Crossbones. 1951: Francis Goes to the Races. 1952: Singin' in the Rain. Francis Goes to West Point. I Love Melvin. 1953: Call Me Madam. Walking My Baby Back Home. Francis Covers the Big Town. 1954: There's No Business Like Show Business. Francis Joins the WACs. 1955: Francis in the Navy. 1956: Anything Goes. 1957: The Buster Keaton Story. The Jet-Propelled Couch (TV). 1961: The Wonders of Aladdin. Cry for Happy. 1965: That Funny Feeling. 1966: The Hoofer (TV). 1974: That's Entertainment! 1981: Ragtime. Thursday the 12th/Pandemonium. 1984: Miracle in a Manger (released 1986 as A Time to Remember). 1992: Toys. 1997: Out to Sea.

O'DONNELL, Cathy

(Ann Steely) 1923–1970

Lovely dark-haired American actress of gentle manner, usually in vulnerable roles. Made a tremendous start in The Best Years of Our Lives, but was never a dominant actress,

and had to be content thereafter with what come her way. Died from a cerebral haemorrhage.

1946: The Best Years of Our Lives. 1947: Bury Me Dead. 1948: The Amazing Mr X / The Spiritualist. They Live by Night. 1950: Side Street. The Miniver Story. 1951: Detective Story. Never Trust a Gambler. The Woman's Angle. 1953: Eight O'Clock Walk. 1954: L'amante di paride (GB: The Face That Launched a Thousand Ships). 1955: Mad at the World. The Man from Laramie. 1957: The Deerslayer. The Story of Mankind. 1958: My World Dies Screaming (GB: Terror in the Haunted House). 1959: Ben-Hur.

O'DONNELL, Chris 1970–
Fresh-faced, ingenuous-looking, light-haired American actor, the youngest of seven children. After beating hundreds of applicants for his first film role with little previous acting experience, he progressed cautiously to leading roles by his early twenties, and achieved massive teen popularity by playing Robin in the third and fourth Batman films. He has, however, yet to prove himself more than lightweight.

1989: Men Don't Leave. 1991: Fried Green Tomatoes (GB: Fried Green Tomatoes at the Whistlestop Café). Blue Sky (released 1994). 1992: School Ties. Scent of a Woman. 1993: The Three Musketeers. 1994: Circle of Friends. 1995: Batman Forever. Mad Love. 1996: The Chamber. In Love and War. 1997: Batman and Robin. 1999: Cookie's Fortune. The Bachelor. 2000: Vertical Limit.

O'HARA, Maureen
(M. Fitzsimons) 1920–
Hollywood's favourite red-haired, hazel-eyed

Irish colleen. A strange combination of gentleness and high spirits, she was memorable as staunch wives or spitfire village girls in several John Ford films, but also showed a penchant for action in her many swashbucklers, easterns and westerns, in which her spectacular figure showed to advantage. The story goes that, in one sword-flashing film, as Maureen fought her way to the battlements, jumped down 15 feet from them and carried on fighting without a quiver, the entire unit's stunt team fell to its knees.

1938: †Kicking the Moon Around (US: The Playboy, later Millionaire Merry-Go-Round). †My Irish Molly (US: Little Miss Molly). 1939: Jamaica Inn. The Hunchback of Notre Dame. 1940: A Bill of Divorcement / Never to Love. Dance, Girl, Dance. 1941: They Met in Argentina. How Green Was My Valley. 1942: Ten Gentlemen from West Point. The Black Swan. To the Shores of Tripoli. 1943: The Immortal Sergeant. The Fallen Sparrow. This Land is Mine. 1944: Buffalo Bill. 1945: The Spanish Main. 1946: Sentimental Journey. Do You Love Me? 1947: Sinbad the Sailor. Miracle on 34th Street (GB: The Big Heart). The Foxes of Harrow. The Homestretch. 1948: Sitting Pretty. 1949: Britannia Mews (US: Forbidden Street). Father Was a Fullback. A Woman's Secret. Bagdad. 1950: Comanche Territory. Rio Grande. Tripoli. 1951: Flame of Araby. At Sword's Point (GB: Sons of the Musketeers. Completed 1949). *Australian Diary 144/145. 1952: Kangaroo. The Quiet Man. Against All Flags. The Redhead from Wyoming. 1953: War Arrow. 1954: Malaga (US: Fire over Africa). The Long Gray Line. *The Red, White and Blue Line. 1955: Lady Godiva (GB: Lady Godiva of Coventry). The Magnificent Matador (GB: The Brave and the Beautiful). 1956: Everything But the Truth. Lisbon. 1957: The Wings of Eagles. 1959: Mrs Miniver (TV). Our Man in Havana. 1961: The Deadly Companions. The Parent Trap. 1962: Mr Hobbs Takes a Vacation. 1963: Spencer's Mountain. McLintock! 1965: The Battle of the Villa Fiorita. The Rare Breed. 1970: How Do I Love Thee? 1971: Big Jake. 1973: The Red Pony (TV. GB: cinemas). 1991: Only the Lonely. 1995: The Christmas Box (TV). 1998: Cab to Canada (TV).

†As Maureen Fitzsimmons

O'KEEFE, Dennis
(Edward 'Bud' Flanagan) 1908–1968
Cheery, fast-talking, solidly-built, light-

haired American actor of Irish vaudevillian parents. He laboured for years in tiny roles as Bud Flanagan before making the breakthrough to second-grade stardom. He then moved confidently through a wide range of roles, proving equally at home in light comedy or tough-guy thriller – occasionally taking a hand in the scripts himself. Married (second) to Hungarian actress Steffi Duna (Stephanie Berindey 1913–1992) from 1940. Died from lung cancer.

1931: †Cimarron. †Reaching for the Moon. 1932: †Scarface. †Hat Check Girl (GB: Embassy Girl). †Cabin in the Cotton. †Crooner. †Big City Blues. †Night After Night. †The Man from Yesterday. †Two Against the World. †I Am a Fugitive from a Chain Gang. †A Bill of Divorcement. †Merrily We go to Hell (GB: Merrily We Go to—). †Central Park. 1933: †Broadway thru a Keyhole. †Hello Everybody! †From Hell to Heaven. †Gold Diggers of 1933. †I'm No Angel. †The House on 56th Street. †Torch Singer. †Blood Money. †Girl Missing. †The Eagle and the Hawk. †Too Much Harmony. †Duck Soup. †Lady Killer. 1934: †*In a Pig's Eye. †The Meanest Gal in Town. †The Red Rider (serial). †Jimmy the Gent. †Upper World. †Wonder Bar. †Death on the Diamond. †Desirable. †The Girl from Missouri (GB: 100 Per Cent Pure). †Registered Nurse. †Man with Two Faces. †Lady by Choice. †Transatlantic Merry-Go-Round. †Smarty (GB: Hit Me Again). †He Was Her Man. †Coming Out Party. †Fog Over Frisco. †Madame Du Barry. †College Rhythm. †Imitation of Life. †*Everything's Ducky. †Broadway Bill (GB: Strictly Confidential). 1935: †*A Night at the Biltmore Bowl. †Dante's Inferno. †Devil Dogs of the Air. †The Daring Young Man. †Top Hat. †Burning Gold. †Gold Diggers of 1935. †Anna Karenina. †Let 'em Have It (GB: False Faces). †It's in the Air. †Broadway Hostess. †Doubting Thomas. †Rumba. †The Man Who Broke the Bank at Monte Carlo. †Many Burns, Fugitive. †Biography of a Bachelor Girl. †Mississippi. †Every Night at Eight. †Personal Maid's Secret. †Shipmates Forever. 1936: †The Singing Kid. †Love Before Breakfast. †Anything Goes. †Till We Meet Again. †Three Smart Girls. †13 Hours by Air. †Nobody's Fool. †Rhythm on the Range. †Libeled Lady. †The Accusing Finger. †The Plainsman. †Rose Bowl (GB: O'Riley's Luck). †San Francisco. †The Last Outlaw. †Mr Deeds Goes to Town. †And So They Were Married. †Sworn Enemy. †Yours for the

Asking. †Theodora Goes Wild. †Born to Dance. †Great Guy (GB: Pluck of the Irish). †Piccadilly Jim. 1937: †The Great Gambini. †Married Before Breakfast. †One Mile from Heaven. †When's Your Birthday? †Swing High, Swing Low. †A Star is Born. †The Girl from Scotland Yard. †The Firefly. †Hats Off. †Saratoga. †The Big City. †The Lady Escapes. †Top of the Town. †Captains Courageous. †Parole Racket. †A Yank at Oxford. †Riding on Air. †Easy Living. †Blazing Barriers. 1938: †Vivacious Lady. Bad Man of Brimstone. The Chaser. Hold That Kiss. Vacation from Love. 1939: The Kid from Texas. Unexpected Father (GB: Sandy Takes a Bow). Burn 'em up O'Connor. That's Right – You're Wrong. 1940: Pop Always Pays. Alias the Deacon. La Conga Nights. I'm Nobody's Sweetheart Now. The Lone Wolf Strikes. The Girl from Havana. You'll Find Out. Bowery Boy. Arise, My Love. 1941: Mr District Attorney. Broadway Limited. Week-End for Three. Topper Returns. Lady Scarface. 1942: The Affairs of Jimmy Valentine. Moonlight Masquerade. 1943: Hangmen Also Die. Good Morning, Judge. Tahiti Honey. The Leopard Man. Hi Diddle Diddle. 1944: The Fighting Seabees. Abroad with Two Yanks. The Story of Dr Wassell. Up in Mabel's Room. Sensations of 1945. 1945: Earl Carroll Vanities. The Affairs of Susan. Getting Gertie's Garter. Brewster's Millions. 1946: Doll Face (GB: Come Back to Me). Her Adventurous Night. 1947: Mr District Attorney (remake). Dishonored Lady. T-Men. 1948: Raw Deal. Siren of Atlantis. Walk a Crooked Mile. 1949: Cover Up. Abandoned. The Great Dan Patch. 1950: Woman on the Run. The Company She Keeps. The Eagle and the Hawk. 1951: Follow the Sun. Passage West (GB: High Venture). 1952: One Big Affair, Everything I Have is Yours. 1953: The Lady Wants Mink. The Fake. 1954: The Diamond (US: Diamond Wizard). Drums of Tahiti. ‡Angela. 1955: Chicago Syndicate. Las Vegas Shakedown. 1956: Inside Detroit. 1957: Dragoon Wells Massacre. Sail Into Danger. Lady of Vengeance. Confession (TV). 1958: Graft and Corruption. 1961: All Hands on Deck. 1963: The Flame / The Naked Flame.

†As Bud Flanagan ‡Also directed

OLAND, Warner
(Werner Ölund) 1880–1938
Big, dark, bluff, moustachioed Swedish actor, in Hollywood from the early days. Was seen as shifty foreigners in silent films – notably in

serials – but came into his own when cast in 1931 as the painstaking oriental detective Charlie Chan. Died in his native Sweden from bronchial pneumonia.
1909: Jewels of the Madonna. 1912: The Life of John Bunyan. The Pilgrim's Progress. 1915: Sin. The Unfaithful Wife. 1916: Patria (serial). The Eternal Question/ The Eternal Sappho. The Serpent. Destruction. The Fool's Revenge. The Reapers. The Rise of Susan. 1917: The Fatal Ring (serial). The Cigarette Girl. The Mysterious Client. Convict 993. 1918: The Naulahka. The Yellow Ticket. 1919: The Lightning Raider (serial). Witness for the Defense. Avalanche. Mandarin's Gold. Twin Pawns (GB: The Curse of Greed). The Mad Talon. Roaring Oaks. 1920: The Third Eye (serial). The Phantom Foe (serial). 1921: The Yellow Arm (serial). Hurricane Hutch (serial). 1922: East is West. The Pride of Palomar. 1923: His Children's Children. 1924: Curlytop. One Night in Rome. So This is Marriage. The Fighting American (GB: The Fighting Adventurer). The Throwback. 1925: Flower of Night. Don Q Son of Zorro. The Winding Stair. Riders of the Purple Sage. 1926: Tell It to the Marines. Infatuation. Don Juan. The Marriage Clause. The Mystery Club. Twinkletoes. Man of the Forest. 1927: A Million Bid. The Jazz Singer. Sailor Izzy Murphy. When a Man Loves (GB: His Lady). Good Time Charley. Old San Francisco. What Happened to Father. 1928: The Scarlet Lady. Wheel of Chance. Stand and Deliver. Dream of Love. Tong War. 1929: The Mysterious Dr Fu Manchu. Chinatown Nights. The Mighty. The Studio Murder Mystery. The Faker. 1930: The Return of Dr Fu Manchu. Dangerous Paradise. The Vagabond King. Paramount on Parade. 1931: The Black Camel. Drums of Jeopardy. The Big Gamble. Dishonored. Daughter of the Dragon. Charlie Chan Carries On. 1932: A Passport to Hell (GB: Burnt Offering). Shanghai Express. Charlie Chan's Chance. The Son Daughter. 1933: Charlie Chan's Greatest Case. *Hip Action. Before Dawn. As Husbands Go. 1934: Charlie Chan in London. Mandalay. Bulldog Drummond Strikes Back. The Painted Veil. Charlie Chan's Courage. 1935: Shanghai. The Werewolf of London. Charlie Chan in Paris. Charlie Chan in Egypt. Charlie Chan in Shanghai. 1936: Charlie Chan at the Circus. Charlie Chan at the Race Track. Charlie Chan's Secret. Charlie Chan at the Opera. 1937: Charlie Chan on Broadway. Charlie Chan at the Olympics. Charlie Chan at Monte Carlo.

OLDMAN, Gary (Leonard G. Oldman)
1958–
Small, dark, London-born actor with impish features and considerable presence. After a background in classical stage work, he burst into the public eye with his portraits of Sid Vicious in *Sid and Nancy* and playwright Joe Orton in *Prick Up Your Ears*. Now in international movie assignments, Oldman has been described by one of his directors as 'probably the best actor of his generation'. Would make a dynamically malevolent Puck in *A Midsummer Night's Dream*, but is sometimes in need of strong direction to lend control to his performances. Married/divorced (second) actress Uma Thurman

(qv). Married actress Donya Fiorentino.
1982: Remembrance. Gossip (unfinished). 1983: Meantime (TV. US: cinemas). 1985: Honest, Decent and True (TV). 1986: Sid and Nancy. 1987: Prick Up Your Ears. Track 29. 1988: Criminal Law. The Firm (TV). 1989: We Think the World of You. Chattahoochee. 1990: State of Grace. Rosencrantz and Guildenstern Are Dead. 1991: JFK. Heading Home (TV). 1992: Bram Stoker's Dracula. 1993: Romeo is Bleeding. True Romance. 1994: Leon (US: The Professional). Immortal Beloved. Murder in the First. 1995: The Scarlet Letter. Dead Presidents. 1996: Basquiat. 1997: The Fifth Element. Air Force One. 1998: Lost in Space. The Magic Sword: Quest for Camelot (voice only). 2000: The Contender. Anasazi Moon.

As director. *1997: Nil by Mouth.*

OLIN, Lena 1955–
Lovely, tigerish, red-haired Swedish actress, often in fiercely sensual roles. The daughter of actor Stig Olin (1920–), she, like her father, has worked a great deal with Sweden's most famous director Ingmar Bergman, although primarily on stage. Film credits have been comparatively few since her debut at 20, but she became an international star in 1987 after her success in *The Unbearable Lightness of Being*. Two years later she was nominated for an Academy Award for her portrayal of one of the three wives in *Enemies, a Love Story*, and has continued to mingle Hollywood movies with work in Sweden. Married (second) director Lasse Hallström.
1975: Ansikte mot ansikte (GB and US: Face to Face). 1977: Das Schangenei (GB and US: The Serpent's Egg). Tabu. 1978: The Adventures of Picasso. 1980: Karleken/ Love.

1982: *Fanny and Alexander. Grasanklingar.* 1984: *After the Rehearsal (TV). Wallenberg: The Lost Hero (TV).* 1985: *Flucht in den Norden.* 1986: *Pa liv och dod/A Matter of Life and Death.* 1987: *Hebriana (TV). The Unbearable Lightness of Being. Friends.* 1989: *S/V Gladjen. Enemies, a Love Story.* 1990: *Havana.* 1993: *Mr Jones. Romeo is Bleeding.* 1994: *Call It Sleep. The Night and the Moment.* 1995: *Night Falls on Manhattan.* 1997: *Polish Wedding. The Golden Hour.* 1998: *Commander Hamilton.* 1999: *Titan Æ (voice only). Mystery Men. The Ninth Gate. Dying to Live (TV).* 2000: *Sebastian's Love.* 2001: *Ignition. Chocolat.*

OLIVIER, Sir Laurence
(Lord Olivier) 1907–1989

Dark, dominant, exciting and extremely handsome, Olivier was generally acclaimed as the finest British actor of his generation. Certainly few could be as magnetic when he so chose. Played dashing young characters in the thirties, then slightly wild but intriguing men of mystery in Hollywood, before his Shakespearian triumphs, which won him a special Oscar (1946) for *Henry V* and a best actor Oscar in 1948 for *Hamlet,* although neither was as impressive as his *Richard III.* Tackled offbeat leading roles in the sixties and character roles in later years, when he sadly tended to substitute overacting for characterization. Married to Vivien Leigh from 1940 to 1960 (second). Later married actress Joan Plowright (1929–). Further Special Oscar 1979. Knighted in 1947. Created Lord Olivier in 1970. He received ten Oscar nominations. Stricken in his later years with dermatomyositis, a muscle disease, and with prostate cancer.
1930: *Too Many Crooks. The Temporary Widow.* 1931: *Potiphar's Wife (US: The Strange Desire). The Yellow Ticket (GB: The Yellow Passport). Friends and Lovers. Westward Passage.* 1932: *Perfect Understanding.* 1933: *No Funny Business.* 1935: *Moscow Nights (US: I Stand Condemned). Conquest of the Air.* 1936: *As You Like It. Fire Over England.* 1937: *21 Days (US: 21 Days Together). The Divorce of Lady X.* 1939: *Q Planes (US: Clouds over Europe). Wuthering Heights.* 1940: *Rebecca. Pride and Prejudice.* 1941: *That Hamilton Woman (GB: Lady Hamilton). 49th Parallel (US: The Invaders). *Words for Battle (narrator only).* 1942: *George Cross Island (narrator only).* 1943: *The Demi-Paradise (US: Adventure for Two).*

Malta GC (narrator only). The Volunteer. 1944: ‡*Henry V. This Happy Breed (narrator only).* 1945: *Fighting Pilgrims (narrator only).* 1948: †*Hamlet.* 1951: *The Magic Box.* 1952: *Carrie.* 1953: *The Beggar's Opera. A Queen is Crowned (narrator only).* 1955: ‡*Richard III.* 1957: †*The Prince and the Showgirl.* 1959: *The Devil's Disciple.* 1960: *Spartacus. The Entertainer.* 1961: *The Power and the Glory (TV. GB: cinemas).* 1962: *Term of Trial.* 1963: *Uncle Vanya.* 1965: *Bunny Lake is Missing. Othello.* 1966: *Khartoum.* 1968: *The Shoes of the Fisherman. Romeo and Juliet (narrator only).* 1969: *Oh! What a Lovely War. Battle of Britain. The Dance of Death. David Copperfield (TV. GB: cinemas).* 1970: †*Three Sisters.* 1971: *Nicholas and Alexandra.* 1972: *Lady Caroline Lamb. Sleuth.* 1974: *Love Among the Ruins (TV).* 1975: *The Gentleman Tramp (narrator only).* 1976: *Marathon Man. The Seven-Per-Cent Solution.* 1977: *A Bridge Too Far.* 1978: *The Betsy. The Boys from Brazil.* 1979: *Dracula. A Little Romance.* 1980: *Inchon! The Jazz Singer.* 1981: *Clash of the Titans.* 1983: *The Jigsaw Man.* 1984: *The Bounty. The Last Days of Pompeii.* 1985: *Wild Geese II.* 1986: *Directed by William Wyler. A Talent for Murder (TV).* 1988: *War Requiem.*

†*Also directed* ‡*Also co-directed*

OLSEN and JOHNSON
OLSEN, Ole (John Olsen) 1892–1965
JOHNSON, Chic (Harold Johnson) 1891–1962

Vaudeville comics who, after several false starts, took Hollywood by storm in *Hellzapoppin* with their flair for fast-moving, lunatic comedy with guest stars galore, running gags, a sublime sense of the ridiculous and some hilariously wacky visuals. Olsen was the sad-looking son of Norwegian immigrants and almost always wore smart suits; roly-poly Johnson was a kind of American Bud Flanagan (qv) who looked as though he'd slept in his clothes. The 'Chic' was short for Chicago, where he was born. Both men died from kidney ailments.
1930: *Oh Sailor Behave!* 1931: *Fifty Million Frenchmen. Gold Dust Gertie (GB: Why Change Your Husband?).* 1932: *Hollywood on Parade (A–2).* 1934: *Hollywood on Parade (B–13).* 1937: *All Over Town. County Gentlemen.* 1941: *Hellzapoppin.* 1943: *Crazy House.* 1944: *Ghost Catchers.* 1945: *See My Lawyer.*

OLSON, Nancy 1928–

Pretty, very personable, light-haired American actress with round, fresh-looking face. Came to films straight from college and although soon nominated for an Oscar (in *Sunset Boulevard*) was mostly typed as sensible sorts and waiting wives. In consequence, she made far too few films.
1949: *Canadian Pacific.* 1950: *Sunset Boulevard. Union Station. Mr Music.* 1951: *Submarine Command. Force of Arms.* 1952: *Big Jim McLain.* 1953: *So Big.* 1954: *The Boy from Oklahoma. Battle Cry.* 1956: *High Tor (TV).* 1960: *Pollyanna.* 1961: *The Absent-Minded Professor.* 1963: *Son of Flubber.* 1969: *Smith!* 1972: *Snowball Express.* 1974: *Airport 1975.* 1982: *Making Love.* 1984: *Paper Dolls (II. TV).* 1997: *Flubber.*

ONDRA, Anny
(Aenny Ondráková) 1903–1987

Bubbly, baby-faced, Polish-born, Czech-raised actress with long golden curls. Much adored in Czechoslovakia (in a similar fashion to Mary Pickford in America), where she started her screen career. Became popular in both German and English comedy films of the late twenties before sound put an end to her English-speaking career (she was dubbed in Hitchcock's *Blackmail*). Married boxer Max Schmeling (second husband; Czech director Karel Lamač was her first) and stayed in Germany during World War II and after. Died following a stroke.
1919: †*Zmizele Pismo.* †*Dáma s Malou Nožkou.* †*Nikyho Velevné Dobodružtvi.* 1920: †*Zpěv Zlata/The Song of Gold.* †*Setrele Pismo.* †*Gilly po Prevé v Praze.* †*Dráteniček.* 1921: †*Prichozi z Temnot.* †*Melenky Stareho Kriminalika.* †*Otravene Světlo.* 1922:

†Drvoštěp. †Tam na Horach. †Zigeunerliebe. 1923: †Der Mann ohne Herz. †Unos Bankeře Fuxe. †Muž bez Srdce. †Tu-Ten-Kamen. 1924: †Bily Ráj. †Hricky v Manželstvi. †Chytte Ho! 1925: †Lucerne. †Hraběnka z Podskali. †Karel Havlíček Borovsky. †Šest Mušketýru. Ich Liebe Dich. Do Panskeho Stavu. 1926: Pantáta Bezoušek. Pisně Věznéného. Aničko vrat se! Die Pratermizzi. Velbloud uchem Jehly. Trude, die Sechszehnjährige. 1927: Sladka Josefinka. Kvet ze Sumavy. A Chorus Girl's Romance. 1928: Dcery Eviny. Der erste Küss. Evas Töchter/Eve's Daughters. Saxsophon Susi. God's Clay. Eileen of the Trees/Glorious Youth. 1929: The Manxman. Blackmail. Die Kaviarprinzessin. Das Mädel mit der Peitsche. Sundig und Süss. 1930: Das Mädel aus USA. Sehnsucht. Die vom Rummelplatz. Eine Freundin so goldig wie Du. Die grosse Sehnsucht. 1931: On a Jeho Sestra/Er und seine Schwester. Die Fledermaus. 1932: Mamselle Nitouche. Baby. Die grausame Freundin. Eine Nacht in Paradies. Kiki. Kantor Idél. 1933: Die Regimentstochter. Fräulein Hoffmans Erzählungen. Das verliebte Hotel. Die vertauschte Braut. 1934: Little Dorrit. Polská krev/Polenblut. 1935: Der junge Graf. Grossreinemachen. Knock Out. 1936: Donogoo Tonga. Ein Mädel vom Ballet. Flitterwochen. 1937: Důvod k Rozvodu. Der Scheidungsgrund. Der Unwiderstehliche. Vor Liebe wird gewarnt. 1938: Narrem im Schnee. 1941: Der Gasmann. 1942: Himmel, wir erben ein Schloss. 1950: Schön müss man sein. 1957: Die zürcher Verlorung.

†As Aenny/Anny Ondráková

O'NEAL, Ryan (Patrick R. O'Neal) 1941–
Handsome, if slightly cynical-looking, well-built American leading man with wavy fair hair. Busy in television from 1960, after beginnings as a stuntman, he soon became a favourite pin-up, especially during his run with the series *Peyton Place*. In the 1970s he became one of the world's top superstars, but he attempted some roles outside his range and from the early 1980s he was on the slide. Nominated for an Oscar in *Love Story*, he was formerly married to actresses Joanna Moore and Leigh Taylor-Young, and has a son by longtime companion (now parted) Farrah Fawcett (*qv*). The actors Tatum O'Neal (*qv*) and Griffin O'Neal are children from his first marriage. Has suffered from weight problems in recent times, and film appearances have been few. He was well down the cast in some

1990s films.
1962: *This Rugged Land* (TV. GB: cinemas). 1968: *The Games. The Big Bounce.* 1970: *Love Story. Love Hate Love* (TV). 1971: *The Thief Who Came to Dinner. Paper Moon.* 1975: *Barry Lyndon.* 1976: *Nickelodeon.* 1977: *A Bridge Too Far.* 1978: *Oliver's Story. The Driver* (GB: *Driver*). 1979: *The Main Event.* 1980: *Circle of Two.* 1981: *Green Ice. Partners. So Fine.* 1984: *Irreconcilable Differences.* 1985: *Fever Pitch.* 1987: *Tough Guys Don't Dance.* 1989: *Chances Are.* 1990: *Small Sacrifices* (TV). 1992: *The Man Upstairs* (TV). 1995: *Faithful.* 1997: *Zero Effect. An Alan Smithee Film – Burn, Hollywood, Burn. Hacks.* 1999: *Coming Soon. Gentleman B.* 2000: *The List.*

O'NEAL, Tatum 1962–
Fair-haired, resentful-looking American actress and former child star, the daughter of Ryan O'Neal (*qv*). As a child player, she was nicknamed 'Tantrum' by fellow-workers and the Press, but proved so full of abrasive personality that she collected an Oscar for her first film role at the age of 11. Alas, the cinema career that followed was sporadic in the extreme and her performances as an adult proved no more than ordinary, lacking the strength of her younger days. Married tennis star John McEnroe, but they later divorced and she attempted a seemingly half-hearted and short-lived return to acting.
1973: *Paper Moon.* 1976: *The Bad News Bears. Nickelodeon.* 1978: *International Velvet.* 1980: *Little Darling. Circle of Two.* 1981: *Captured!/Split Image.* 1985: *Certain Fury.* 1989: *15 and Getting Straight* (TV). 1990: *Little Noises.* 1993: *In Between Days. Woman on the Run* (TV). 1996: *Basquiat.*

O'NEILL, Jennifer 1947–
Dark-haired American leading lady coming to prominence in the seventies, so forthright and personable that one sometimes wished there were a greater range of acting talent to go with those finely-structured features. Usually plays an independent woman in a man's world. Born in Brazil. Eight times married.
1968: *For Love of Ivy.* 1969: *Futz.* 1970: *Rio Lobo.* 1971: *Summer of 42.* 1972: *Such Good Friends. The Carey Treatment. Glass Houses* (released 1975). 1973: *Lady Ice.* 1974: *The Reincarnation of Peter Proud.* 1975: *Whiffs* (GB: *C*A*S*H*). *Gente di rispetto* (US: *The Flower in His Mouth*). 1976: *L'innocente/The Innocent.* 1977: *Sette note in nero* (US: *The*

Psychic). 1978: *A Force of One. Caravans.* 1979: *Cloud Dancer. Love's Savage Fury* (TV). *Steel.* 1980: *Scanners.* 1981: *The Other Victim* (TV). 1985: *Chase* (TV). 1986: *Perry Mason: The Case of the Shooting Star* (TV). 1987: *I Love N.Y.* 1988: *The Red Spider* (TV). *Committed* (released 1991). *Glory Days* (TV). *Perfect Family* (TV). 1989: *Full Exposure: The Sex Tapes Scandal* (TV). *Personals* (TV). 1990: *The Raven.* 1992: *Love is Like That* (later *Bad Love*). *Invasion of Privacy. Discretion Assured* (released 1994). 1993: *The Cover Girl Murders* (cable TV). 1994: *Frame Up* (TV). 1996: *Silver Strand.* 1997: *The Corporate Ladder.* 1998: *The Ride.* 1999: *The Prince and the Surfer.*

ORMOND, Julia 1965–
Dark-haired British actress of poised beauty and deliberate speech. She studied art and design, but switched to acting in her early twenties and was rewarded with the London Drama Critics' prize for best newcomer of 1989 after her initial efforts on stage. In the early 1990s, she quickly established herself as a leading lady in films, despite performances that did not always carry conviction. Her speech pattern, though, similar to that of Audrey Hepburn (*qv*), doubtless was a factor in her starring in the remake of *Sabrina*, in which she also displayed some of Hepburn's gamine charm. Her cinema career, though, almost stuttered to a halt in the late 1990s.
1991: *Young Catherine* (TV). 1992: *Stalin* (TV). 1993: *Nostradamus. The Baby of Mâcon.* 1994: *Captives. Legends of the Fall.* 1995: *First Knight. Sabrina.* 1997: *Smilla's Sense of Snow/Smilla's Feeling for Snow.* 1999: *The Barber of Siberia. Animal Farm* (voice only). 2000: *The Gig. Varian's War.*

O'SHEA, Michael
(Edward M. O'Shea) 1906–1973
Smiling, red-haired Hollywood actor who played right guys in the forties after achieving popularity on radio with a crackling voice that held a hint of Irish brogue in its American accent. Once a 'straight man' in circus and vaudeville. Married to Virginia Mayo (*qv*) (second) from 1947. Died from a heart attack.
1943: Jack London. Lady of Burlesque (GB: Striptease Lady). 1944: The Eve of St Mark. Something for the Boys. The Man from Frisco. 1945: Circumstantial Evidence. It's a Pleasure. Where Do We Go from Here? 1947: Mr District Attorney. Violence. Last of the Redmen (GB: Last of the Redskins). 1948: Smart Woman. Parole Inc. 1949: The Big Wheel. The Threat. Captain China. 1950: The Underworld Story. 1951: Fixed Bayonets. Disc Jockey. The Model and the Marriage Broker. 1952: Bloodhounds of Broadway. 1954: It Should Happen to You.

O'SULLIVAN, Maureen 1909–1998
Demure, wistful, dark-haired Irish actress, most often in quiet roles, but carving her special niche in film history as Tarzan's Jane in the thirties. Married to director John Farrow from 1936 to his death in 1963. They had seven children, including actress Mia Farrow (*qv*). In Hollywood from 1930, she was still to be seen in the occasional character role into her eighties. Died from a heart attack.
1930: Song o' My Heart. Just Imagine. So This is London. The Princess and the Plumber. 1931: Skyline. A Connecticut Yankee (GB: The Yankee at King Arthur's Court). The Big Shot (GB: The Optimist). 1932: The Silver Lining. Tarzan the Ape Man. Information Kid/Fast Companions. Skyscraper Souls. Okay America (GB: Penalty of Fame). Payment Deferred.

*Strange Interlude (GB: Strange Interval). 1933: Tugboat Annie. Robbers' Roost. Stage Mother. The Cohens and Kellys in Trouble. 1934: Hideout. *Screen Snapshots No. 11. Tarzan and His Mate. The Barretts of Wimpole Street. The Thin Man. 1935: Cardinal Richelieu. West Point of the Air. Anna Karenina. The Bishop Misbehaves (GB: The Bishop's Misadventures). The Flame Within. Woman Wanted. David Copperfield. 1936: The Voice of Bugle Ann. Tarzan Escapes! The Devil-Doll. 1937: The Emperor's Candlesticks. A Day at the Races. My Dear Miss Aldrich. Between Two Women. A Yank at Oxford. 1938: Port of Seven Seas. The Crowd Roars. Spring Madness. Hold That Kiss. Let Us Live. Tarzan Finds a Son! 1940: Sporting Blood. Pride and Prejudice. 1941: Tarzan's Secret Treasure. Maisie Was a Lady. 1942: Tarzan's New York Adventure. 1947: The Big Clock. 1950: Where Danger Lives. 1952: Bonzo Goes to College. 1953: All I Desire. Mission Over Korea (GB: Eyes of the Skies). 1954: Duffy of San Quentin (GB: Men Behind Bars). The Steel Cage. 1957: The Tall T. Edge of Innocence (TV). 1958: Wild Heritage. 1965: Never Too Late. 1969: The Phynx. 1972: The Crooked Hearts (TV). 1976: The Great Houdinis (TV). 1983: The Doorman. 1984: Too Scared to Scream. 1986: Hannah and Her Sisters. Peggy Sue Got Married. 1987: Stranded. 1988: River Pirates/Good Old Boy (TV). 1992: The Habitation of Dragons (TV). With Savage Intent (TV). 1993: Home is Where the Hart Is (TV).*

O'TOOLE, Annette 1953–
Curvy, red-haired, freckle-faced, friendly-looking actress from Texas. Despite having all the qualifications, including talent, she didn't quite make it as a box-office name, but has been a very pleasurable part of some lively entertainments. Tends to play uncomplicated types whose openness sometimes endangers them. Much in TV movies in the 1990s.
1973: The Girl Most Likely To (TV). 1974: Smile. 1976: The Entertainer (TV). 1977: One on One. The War Between the Tates (TV). 1978: King of the Gypsies (released 1980). Foolin' Around (released 1980). 1979: Love for Rent (TV). 1981: Stand By Your Man (TV). 1982: Cat People. 48 Hrs. 1983: Superman III. 1985: Copacabana (TV). Alfred Hitchcock Presents (TV). 1987: American Date. Broken Vows (TV). Cross My Heart. 1989: Love at Large. 1990: It (TV). A Girl of the Limberlost (TV). The Dreamer of Oz

(TV). 1991: White Lie (TV). 1992: Desperate Justice (TV). Kiss of a Killer (TV). 1993: Love Matters. A Mother's Revenge (TV). 1994: Imaginary Crimes. 1995: The Man Next Door (TV). My Brother's Keeper (TV). 1996: Dead by Sunset. 1997: Keeping the Promise (TV). Final Descent (TV). 1998: Final Justice (TV). 2000: Here on Earth. The Huntress (TV).

O'TOOLE, Peter 1932–
Charismatic, blue-eyed, fair-haired Irish-born actor, typed as idealists or philanderers (occasionally both). Popular in the sixties, when some of his films were enormous commercial successes, but has had little luck at the box-office since 1970. Noted as one of the British 'hell-raising' group in private life: married/divorced actress Siân Phillips. Seven times nominated for an Academy Award (for *Lawrence of Arabia, Becket, The Lion in Winter, Goodbye, Mr Chips, The Ruling Class, The Stuntman* and *My Favorite Year*), he has yet to win. Recently playing eccentric aristocrats.
1959: The Savage Innocents. 1960: Kidnapped. The Day They Robbed the Bank of England. 1962: Lawrence of Arabia. 1963: Becket. 1964: Lord Jim. 1965: What's New Pussycat? The Sandpiper (voice only). 1966: The Bible . . . in the beginning. The Night of the Generals. How to Steal a Million. 1967: Casino Royale. Great Catherine. 1968: The Lion in Winter. 1969: Goodbye, Mr Chips. Country Dance (US: Brotherly Love). 1970: Murphy's War. 1971: Under Milk Wood. The Ruling Class. 1972: Man of La Mancha. 1974: Rosebud. 1975: Man Friday. Foxtrot (later The Far Side of Paradise). 1976: Rogue Male (TV). 1977: Caligula/Gore Vidal's Caligula (released 1979). The Stuntman (released 1980). 1978: Power Play. 1979: Zulu Dawn. 1980: Masada (TV. Shortened for cinemas as The Antagonists). 1982: My Favorite Year. 1983: Svengali (TV). The World of James Joyce (TV). The Sign of Four (voice only). A Study in Scarlet (voice only). The Valley of Fear (voice only). 1984: Kim (TV). Supergirl. Sherlock Holmes and the Baskerville Curse (voice only). 1985: Creator. Club Paradise. Hidden Talent. 1987: The Last Emperor. 1988: High Spirits. 1989: Wings of Fame. On a Moonlit Night. The Pied Piper (TV. US: Crossing to Freedom). 1990: Isabelle Eberhardt. The Nutcracker Prince (voice only). The Rainbow Thief. 1991: King Ralph. 1992: Rebecca's Daughters. The Dark Angel (TV).

1993: The Seventh Coin. 1995: Hob's Grave. Blandings. 1996: Keeping the Promise (TV). 1997: Illumination. Phantoms/Dean Koontz's Phantoms. 1998: Coming Home (TV). 1999: The Manor. Molokai – The Story of Father Damien. 2001: The Final Curtain.

OWEN, Clive 1965–

Big, good-looking, dark-haired, quite boyish British leading man whose TV career has been more fortuitous than his work for the cinema, where he has appeared in a number of often quite good films, which have either not proved popular, or received limited distribution. But he achieved great personal popularity in television's *Chancer* and a big movie break may still be just around the corner.

1988: Vroom. 1990: Lorna Doone (TV). 1991: Close My Eyes. 1992: Class of 61 (TV). 1993: Century. The Magician (TV). 1994: Doomsday Gun (TV/cinemas). The Turn-around. Nobody's Children (cable TV). An Evening with Gary Lineker (TV). The Return of the Native. 1996: Bent (released 1998). The Rich Man's Wife. 1997: Croupier (released 1999). 1998: The Echo (TV). 1999: Split Second (TV). 2000: Green Fingers.

OWENS, Patricia 1925–

It seems improbable that a tall, dark, serious-looking Canadian girl could struggle for 14 years in the British film industry without making barely a dent, and then land a Hollywood contract at 32, star in several big films and become a well-known name. But pretty Pat Owens did it, and all credit to her. She was a capable actress who certainly deserved better than she got in Britain.

1943: Miss London Ltd. 1944: Give Us the Moon. Bees in Paradise. English without Tears (US: Her Man Gilbey). One Exciting Night (US: You Can't Do without Love). 1946: While the Sun Shines. 1948: Panic at Madame Tussaud's. Things Happen at Night. 1949: Bait. I Was a Dancer. Paper Orchid. 1950: Old Mother Riley Headmistress. The Happiest Days of Your Life. 1951: Mystery Junction. 1952: Crow Hollow. Ghost Ship. 1953: House of Blackmail. Colonel March Investigates. 1954: The Good Die Young. Knights of the Round Table. The Stranger Came Home (US: The Unholy Four). A Tale of Three Women. Alive on Saturday (released 1957). 1955: Windfall. 1957: Island in the Sun. No Down Payment. Sayonara. 1958: The Law and Jake Wade. The Fly. The Gun Runners. 1959: These Thousand Hills. Five Gates to Hell. 1960: Hell to Eternity. 1961: Seven Women from Hell. X-15. 1963: Walk a Tight Rope. 1964: Black Spurs. 1966: The Destructors.

P

PACINO, Al (Alfredo Pacino) 1939–
Small, dark, broodingly dynamic, husky-voiced American leading man of Sicilian background who gives explosive, high-decibel performances. He came late to prominence, but always looked and played younger than his yeas, and became a superstar of the 1970s and beyond on the strength of only a few major films. Nominated seven times for an Academy Award – for *The Godfather, Serpico, The Godfather – Part II, Dog Day Afternoon, . . . And Justice for All, Dick Tracy* and *Glengarry Glen Ross*, Pacino finally won the Oscar for *Scent of a Woman*. He has allowed his image to soften a little in some recent films.
1969: *Me Natalie*. 1971: *The Panic in Needle Park*. 1972: *The Godfather*. 1973: *Scarecrow. Serpico*. 1974: *The Godfather – Part II*. 1975: *Dog Day Afternoon*. 1977: *Bobby Deerfield*. 1979: *. . . And Justice for All*. 1980: *Cruising*. 1982: *Author! Author!* 1983: *Scarface*. 1985: *Revolution.* †*The Local Stigmatic (unreleased)*. 1989: *Sea of Love*. 1990: *Dick Tracy. The Godfather Part III*. 1991: *Frankie & Johnny. Truth or Dare (GB: In Bed with Madonna)*. 1992: *Glengarry Glen Ross. Scent of a Woman*. 1993: *Carlito's Way*. 1994: *Two Bits. Jonas in the Desert (doc)*. 1995: *Heat*. 1996: †*Looking for Richard. City Hall*. 1997: *Donnie Brasco. The Devil's Advocate*. 1999: *The Insider. Any Given Sunday*. 2000: *Chinese Coffee*.

†*And directed*

PAGE, Geraldine 1924–1987
This light-haired American lady of the theatre was perhaps unfortunate, as far as her cinema career was concerned, to have the tag 'great actress' pinned on her from the start. Following her stage successes in the works of Tennessee Williams, she tended to be cast as fading southern belles, although eight Oscar nominations (before she finally won the award for *The Trip to Bountiful*) testify to the depth of feeling that went into her work. A personality of her own did not, however, come across on screen. Married (second) to Rip Torn (*qv*) from 1963. Died from a heart attack.
1948: *Out of the Night*. 1953: *Taxi. Hondo*. 1958: *Portrait of a Murderer (TV). Old Man (TV)*. 1961: *Summer and Smoke*. 1962: *Sweet Bird of Youth*. 1963: *Toys in the Attic*. 1964: *Dear Heart*. 1966: *The Three Sisters (released 1976). You're a Big Boy Now. Trilogy/ Truman Capote's Trilogy*. 1967: *La chica del Lunes/Monday's Child. The Happiest Millionaire*. 1969: *Whatever Happened to Aunt Alice?* 1971: *The Beguiled. J.W. Coop*. 1972: *Pete 'n' Tillie*. 1974: *The Day of the Locust. Happy As the Grass Was Green. Live Again, Die Again (TV)*. 1976: *Nasty Habits*. 1977: *The Rescuers (voice only). Something for Joey (TV)*. 1978: *Interiors*. 1980: *Harry's War*. 1981: *Honky Tonk Freeway*. 1982: *I'm Dancing As Fast As I Can*. 1983: *Loving (TV). The Parade/Hit Parade (TV). The Dollmaker (TV)*. 1984: *The Pope of Greenwich Village*. 1985: *Walls of Glass/Flanagan. The Bride. White Nights. The Trip to Bountiful*. 1986: *My Little Girl. Native Son*. 1987: *Nazi Hunter: The Beate Klarsfeld Story (TV. GB: Nazi Hunter – The Search for Klaus Barbie). Single Room (unfinished)*.

PAGET, Debra (Debralee Griffin) 1933–
Although (or perhaps because) copper-haired Debra Paget had the kind of figure that makes men walk into lamp-posts, Twentieth Century-Fox, who signed her at 15, cast her in demure roles. She lacked the animation to make much of these, apart from her Indian girl in *Broken Arrow*, but director Fritz Lang saw her come to life in a harem dance or two, and took her to Germany to play the Indian princess in his two-film saga of 1958, in which she was remarkably effective. Four times married, including (2nd) director Budd Boetticher from 1960 to 1961. Sister of actress Lisa Gaye (L. Griffin, 1935–), a Universal starlet of the 1950s active in films for many years, and of actress Teala Loring.
1948: *Cry of the City*. 1949: *It Happens Every Spring. Mother is a Freshman (GB: Mother Knows Best). House of Strangers*. 1950: *Broken Arrow*. 1951: *Fourteen Hours. Bird of Paradise. Anne of the Indies*. 1952: *Belles on Their Toes. Les Misérables. Stars and Stripes Forever (GB: Marching Along)*. 1954: *Prince Valiant. Demetrius and the Gladiators. Princess of the Nile. The Gambler from Natchez*. 1955: *White Feather. Seven Angry Men*. 1956: *The Last Hunt. The 10 Commandments. Love Me Tender. Gun in His Hand (TV. GB: cinemas)*. 1957: *The River's Edge. Omar Khayyam*. 1958: *From the Earth to the Moon. Der Tiger von Eshnapur. Das Indische Grabmal*. 1960: *Why Must I Die? (GB: 13 Steps to Death). The Highwaymen. Il sepolcro dei re/Cleopatra's Daughter.* †*Journey to the Lost City*. 1961: *The Most Dangerous Man Alive*. 1962: *Tales of Terror. Rome 1585*. 1963: *The Haunted Palace*.

†*Abridged American version (in one film) of Der Tiger von Eshnapur and Das Indische Grabmal*

PAIGE, Janis (Donna Tjaden) 1922–
Red-headed Hollywood musical star with peppy personality and spectacular vocal range. She really needed a vehicle of her own to showcase her talents, but mostly played second fiddle to Dennis Morgan and Jack Carson during her seven-year tenure at Warners. Enjoyed overwhelming stage success in the fifties in *The Pajama Game* and had her best film role in *Silk Stockings*.
1944: *Bathing Beauty. Hollywood Canteen*. 1945: **I Won't Play*. 1946: *Of Human Bondage. Her Kind of Man. Two Guys from Milwaukee (GB: Royal Flush). The Time, the Place and the Girl*. 1947: **So You Want to Be in Pictures. Love and Learn. Cheyenne. Always Together*. 1948: *Wallflower. Winter Meeting. Romance on the High Seas (GB: It's Magic). One Sunday Afternoon*. 1949: *The House across

the Street. The Younger Brothers. 1950: This Side of the Law. 1951: Fugitive Lady. Mr Universe. Two Gals and a Guy. 1957: Silk Stockings. 1960: Please Don't Eat the Daisies. 1961: Bachelor in Paradise. 1963: Follow the Boys. The Caretakers (GB: Borderlines). 1967: Welcome to Hard Times (GB: Killer on a Horse). 1975: The Return of Joe Forrester (TV). 1976: Lanigan's Rabbi (TV). 1980: Angel on My Shoulder (TV). Valentine Magic on Love Island (TV). 1981: Bret Maverick (TV). 1982: Love at the Top (TV). 1983: The Other Woman (TV). 1984: No Man's Land (TV). 1994: Natural Causes.

PAIGE, Robert (John Paige) 1910–1987
Good-natured American leading man, who had a pleasant baritone singing voice, and is now remembered as the rather stiff, ever-smiling young man who backed up Olsen and Johnson, Abbott and Costello, Deanna Durbin and Universal's other top stars in middle-budget comedies and musicals of the war years. Had a talent for zany comedy that was never properly exploited. Became a TV newscaster in the mid-sixties. Died from heart problems.
1935: †Annapolis Farewell (GB: Gentlemen of the Navy). 1936: †Smart Blonde. †Hearts in Bondage. †Cain and Mabel. 1937: †Once a Doctor. †Rhythm in the Clouds. †Melody for Two. *†Murder in Springtime. †Marry the Girl. †Meet the Boy Friend. †The Cherokee Strip (GB: Strange Laws). 1938: The Lady Objects. There's Always a Woman. When G-Men Step In. The Main Event. The Last Warning. The Little Adventuress. Who Killed Gail Preston? Highway Patrol. I Stand Accused. 1939: Flying G-Men (serial). Death of a Champion. Homicide Bureau. 1940: Parole Fixer. Emergency Squad. Golden Gloves. Women without Names. Opened by Mistake. 1941: San Antonio Rose. The Monster and the Girl. Melody Lane. Hellzapoppin. Dancing on a Dime. 1942: What's Cookin'? (GB: Wake Up and Dream). You're Telling Me. Almost Married. Get Hep to Love (GB: She's My Lovely). Pardon My Sarong. Don't Get Personal. Jailhouse Blues. Hi Ya, Chum! (GB: Everything Happens to Us). 1943: Frontier Badmen. Fired Wife. Crazy House. Cowboy in Manhattan. Son of Dracula. Get Going. Hi Buddy! How's About It? Mr Big. Sherlock Holmes in Washington. 1944: Her Primitive Man. Follow the Boys. Can't Help Singing. 1945: Shady Lady. 1946: Tangier. 1947: The Flame. Red Stallion. 1948: Blonde Ice. 1949:

The Green Promise (GB: Raging Waters). 1953: Abbott and Costello Go to Mars. Split Second. 1959: It Happened to Jane. 1960: The Marriage-Go-Round. 1963: Bye Bye Birdie.

†As David Carlyle

PALANCE, Jack (Voladimir, later changed to Walter, Palahnuik) 1919–
Trying to build a Jack Palance filmography is like tracking down a whirlwind. Like some workaholic Jack the Ripper, this American actor of massive physical presence has travelled half the world in search of audiences on whom to impose his fearsome personality. With a face rebuilt by plastic surgery after war burns, and a ferocious acting style, this son of Russian immigrants could hardly fail to dominate his films, and continued to do so, violence smouldering beneath a surface calm, for 40 years. In 1988, his career came full circle with a sadistic western villain in Young Guns. Received Oscar nominations for Sudden Fear and Shane. He finally won an Academy Award many decades later for City Slickers. The actresses Holly and Brooke Palance are his daughters.
1950: †Panic in the Streets. †Halls of Montezuma. 1952: †Sudden Fear. 1953: †Shane. Second Chance. Flight to Tangier. Arrowhead. Man in the Attic. Sign of the Pagan. The Silver Chalice. 1955: Kiss of Fire. The Big Knife. I Died a Thousand Times. 1956: Attack! Requiem for a Heavyweight (TV). 1957: The Last Tycoon (TV). The Lonely Man. House of Numbers. The Death of Manolete (TV). Flor de Mayo (GB: A Mexican Affair. US: Beyond All Limits). 1958: The Man Inside. Ten Seconds to Hell. 1959: Austerlitz (GB: The Battle of Austerlitz). 1960: Revak the Rebel (US. TV, as Rivak the Barbarian/The Barbarians). 1961: Il giudizio universale (US: The Last Judgment). Rosmunda e Alboino/Sword of the Conqueror. The Mongols. La Dernière attaque/La guerra continua. Barabbas. Warriors Five. 1963: Le mépris (GB: Contempt. US: A Ghost at Noon). Il criminale (GB and US: Night Train to Milan). 1965: Once a Thief. 1966: The Spy in the Green Hat (TV. GB: cinemas). The Professionals. 1967: Torture Garden. Kill a Dragon/To Kill a Dragon. 1968: Dr Jekyll and Mr Hyde (TV). Il mercenario (GB and US: A Professional Gun). They Came to Rob Las Vegas/Las Vegas 500 milliones. L'urlo dei giganti (GB: A Bullet for Rommel). The Desperados. 1969: Ché! Marquis de Sade:

Justine/Justine/Justine: le disavventure della virtu. Una ragazza di Eraga. La legione dei dannati (US: Legion of the Damned). The McMasters . . . tougher than the west itself! 1970: Compañeros! Monte Walsh. The Horsemen. 1971: Chato's Land. Si può fare . . . amigo (GB: The Big and the Bad. US: It Can Be Done, Amigo). 1972: Operation: Catastrophe. 1973: The Blu Gang (US: Brothers Blue). Dracula (TV. GB: cinemas). Oklahoma Crude. Craze. Te Deum (GB: The Con Men). 1974: The Godchild (TV). 1975: Bronk (TV). Il richiamo del lupo. L'infermiera (GB: I Will If You Will. US: The Sensuous Nurse). The Hatfields and the McCoys (TV). The Four Deuces. 1976: Africa Express/Safari Express. Eva nera (GB: Erotic Eva). Squadra antiscippo (GB: The Cop in Blue Jeans). Diamante lobo (GB: God's Gun. US: The Cop Who Played God). The Great Adventure. 1977: Sangue di Sbirro (US: Bloody Avenger). Il padrone della città (US: Mister Scarface). Welcome to Blood City. Jimbuck (later Portrait of a Hitman). 1978: Seven from Heaven/Angels Brigade. Dead on Arrival. 1979: Unknown Powers. The Shape of Things to Come. Cocaine Cowboys. The Ivory Ape (TV). The Last Ride of the Dalton Gang (TV). 1980: Hawk the Slayer. Without Warning (GB: The Warning). Ladyfingers. The Golden Moment (TV). 1982: Alone in the Dark. 1983: Evil Stalks the House (TV). 1986: Deadly Sanctuary. 1987: Gor. Out of Rosenheim (GB: Bagdad Café). Outlaw of Gor (released 1989). 1988: Young Guns. 1989: Batman. Tango & Cash. 1990: Solar Crisis (later Starfire). 1991: City Slickers. Radio Flyer. 1992: Keep the Change. 1993: Cyborg 2: Glass Shadow. 1994: Cops and Robbersons. City Slickers: The Legend of Curly's Gold. Natural Born Killers. Twilight Zone: Rod Serling's Lost Classics (TV). The Swan Princess (voice only). 1995: Buffalo Girls (TV). 1997: Marco Polo. Ebenezer (TV). I'll Be Home for Christmas (TV). 1998: Treasure Island. 1999: Sarah, Plain and Tall: Winter's End (TV). 2000: Ready to Rumble.

†As Walter (Jack) Palance

PALMER, Lilli (L. Peiser) 1911–1986
Beautiful, full-lipped, dark-haired German actress (born in Prussia) who began her film career in Britain, offering appealing, emotional performances that usually had more depth than those around her. Went to Hollywood for some years during an eventful

marriage (1943–1957) to first husband Rex Harrison (*qv*). After it was over, she made films in Britain, Germany, France and Spain. Her beauty wore well, and she remained in leading roles into her late forties. Later became a best-selling authoress. Married Argentinian-born actor Carlos Thompson (Juan C. Mundanschaffer, 1916–1990) in 1957. Died from cancer. Her husband shot himself four years after her death.

*1935: Crime Unlimited. 1936: First Offence/ Bad Blood. Wolf's Clothing. Secret Agent. Good Morning, Boys (US: Where There's a Will). 1937: The Great Barrier (US: Silent Barriers). *Secrets of the Stars. Sunset in Vienna (US: Suicide Legion). Command Performance. 1938: Crackerjack (US: The Man with a Hundred Faces). 1939: A Girl Must Live. Blind Folly. 1940: The Door with Seven Locks (US: Chamber of Horrors). 1942: Thunder Rock. 1943: The Gentle Sex. 1944: English without Tears (US: Her Man Gilbey). 1945: The Rake's Progress (US: Notorious Gentleman). 1946: Beware of Pity. Cloak and Dagger. 1947: Body and Soul. 1948: My Girl Tisa. No Minor Vices. Hans le marin (US: The Wicked City). 1951: The Long Dark Hall. 1952: The Four Poster. 1953: Main Street to Broadway. Feuerwerk (GB: Oh! My Papa). 1955: Teufel in Seide/The Devil in Silk. 1956: Anastasia die letzte Zarentochter?/Is Anna Anderson Anastasia? Zwischen Zeit und Ewigkeit/ Between Time and Eternity. Wie ein Sturmwind/The Night of the Storm. 1957: Der gläserne Turm/The Glass Tower. Montparnasse 19/The Lovers of Montparnasse. 1958: Eine Frau die weiss, was sie will. Mädchen in Uniform. La vie à deux (GB: Life Together). 1959: But Not for Me. 1960: Frau Warren's Profession. Conspiracy of Hearts. 1961: The Pleasure of His Company. The Last of Mrs Cheyney. Leviathan. Le rendezvous de minuit. Dark Journey. The Counterfeit Traitor. 1962: The Seduction of Julia/Adorable Julia. Torpedo Bay/Finche dura la tempesta. L'amore difficile (GB: Sex Can Be Difficult). Finden sie, dass Constanze sich richtig verhält? The Miracle of the White Stallions (GB: Flight of the White Stallions). 1963: And So to Bed/Das grosse Liebespiel/The Circular Triangle. 1964: Le grain de sable. 1965: Le tonnerre de Dieu. The Amorous Adventures of Moll Flanders. Operation Crossbow (US: The Great Spy Mission). Le voyage du père. Der Kongress amüsiert sich/An Affair of State. 1966: Zwei Girls vom roten Stern. 1967: Paarungen/ Danse Macabre/The Dance of Death. Oedipus the King. Jack of Diamonds. The Diary of Anne Frank (TV). Sebastian. 1968: Nobody Runs Forever (GB: The High Commissioner). 1969: Le peau de torpédo (GB: Pill of Death. US: Only the Cool). De Sade. Hard Contract. The House That Screamed. 1970: Hauser's Memory (TV). 1971: Night Hair Child (US: What the Peeper Saw). Murders in the Rue Morgue. 1975: Lotte in Weimar. The Other Side of the Wind (uncompleted). 1978: The Boys from Brazil. 1981: Society Limited. 1982: Imaginary Friends (TV). 1985: The Holcroft Covenant.*

PALTROW, Gwyneth 1973–
Sandy-haired, wafer-slim American actress whose naturally smiling features were at first submerged in weepy roles. But when she

revealed her warmth and elegance and a stunning facility for assuming (especially English) accents, she sprang to the top of the Hollywood tree, winning an Academy Award for *Shakespeare in Love* (and accepting it in a notably tear-drenched ceremony). Something of a fashion leader, she's had several romances with top male stars, though none to date has led to marriage. Daughter of actress Blythe Danner.

1991:Shout. Hook. 1992: Cruel Doubt (TV). 1993: Malice. Deadly Relations (TV). Flesh and Bone. 1994: Mrs Parker & the Vicious Circle. 1995: Jefferson in Paris. Moonlight and Valentino. Se7en. 1996: The Pallbearer. Hard Eight. Emma. 1997: Sliding Doors. Great Expectations. 1998: Hush. A Perfect Murder. Out of the Past (voice only). Shakespeare in Love. 1999: The Talented Mr Ripley. 2000: Duets. Bounce. 2001: The Anniversary Party. Possession.

PAQUIN, Anna 1982–
Dark-haired, gravely attractive child and teenage actress, Canadian-born but New Zealand-raised from the age of four. Selected from more than 5,000 girls to play the role of the daughter in *The Piano*, she stunned the film world by winning an Academy Award. When her teacher parents divorced, she relocated with her mother to Los Angeles and now works in Hollywood in a variety of star and semi-star roles.

1993: The Piano. 1996: Fly Away Home. Jane Eyre. 1997: The Member of the Wedding (TV). Amistad. 1998: A Walk on the Moon/The Blouse Man. Hurlyburly. 1999: She's All That. Sleepless Beauty. 2000: All the Rage. X-Men. Almost Famous. 2001: Castle in the Sky (voice only).

PARÉ, Michael 1959–
Tall, dark, good-looking, heftily-built, pale-eyed American actor, who started his career as a professional chef in New York and indeed mixed acting and cooking until he was 24, when star roles in three consecutive films led him to full-time work for the cinema. Unfortunately, most of his movies since those days have been either disappointments or gone straight to video, and it was a surprise to see him make a brief return to mainstream cinema as Sandra Bullock's faithless husband in *Hope Floats* in 1998.

1980: Crazy Times (TV). 1982: Eddie and the Cruisers. 1983: Undercover. 1984: Streets of Fire. The Philadelphia Experiment. 1985: Trackers 2180/Space Rage. 1986: Instant Justice/Marine Issue. Deja View (video). 1987: Houston Knights (TV). The Women's Club. World Gone Wild. 1988: Eddie and the Cruisers II: Eddie Lives! 1989: Moon 44. 1990: Dragonfight. The Dark Sun. 1991: The Last Hour. Midnight Heat. Empire City. Killing Streets. The Closer. 1992: First Light. Into the Sun. 1993: Spanish Rose/Point of Impact. Deadly Heroes. 1994: Lunar Cop. Warriors. The Dangerous. 1995: Village of the Damned. Triplecross (TV). Raging Angels/ The Spirit Realm. Dream Breaker (TV). 1996: The Malibu Branch (TV). The Colony. Thor/Bad Moon. Merchant of Death/ Merchants of Death. Falling Fire. Coyote Run (later on video as Sworn Enemies). 1997: Strip Search. 2103: The Deadly Wake. Men of Means (released 1999). 1998: Bang/October 22. Hope Floats. Back to Even. 1999: Space Fury. Mission of Death (video). 2000: Peril. Sanctimony.

PARKER, Cecil (C. Schwabe) 1897–1971
Aloof British actor who used his upper-class personality, snooty air, piggy eyes and husky voice which had an inborn note of disapproval to good effect in the British cinema for over 40 years. Cast as butlers, aristocrats, statesmen, headmasters and even killers, he propelled himself into star roles by the late forties and never let his supporters down. Largely (at home) in portly comedy roles from 1953.

1928: The Woman in White. 1933: Princess Charming. The Golden Cage. The Silver Spoon. A Cuckoo in the Nest. Flat No. 3. 1934: Nine Forty-Five. Little Friend. Lady in Danger. Dirty Work. The Blue Squadron. The Office Wife. 1935: Foreign Affaires. Me and Marlborough. Crime Unlimited. Her Last

Affaire. 1936: Jack of All Trades (US: The Two of Us). Men of Yesterday. Dishonour Bright. The Man Who Changed His Mind (US: The Man Who Lived Again). 1937: Storm in a Teacup. Dark Journey. Bank Holiday (US: Three on a Weekend). 1938: Housemaster. The Lady Vanishes. The Citadel. Old Iron. 1939: She Couldn't Say No. Sons of the Sea. The Stars Look Down. The Spider. 1940: Two for Danger. Under Your Hat. 1941: Dangerous Moonlight (US: Suicide Squadron). The Saint's Vacation. Ships with Wings. 1945: Caesar and Cleopatra. 1946: The Magic Bow. Hungry Hill. 1947: Captain Boycott. The Woman in the Hall. 1948: The First Gentleman (US: Affairs of a Rogue). Quartet. The Weaker Sex. 1949: Dear Mr Prohack. The Chiltern Hundreds (US: The Amazing Mr Beecham). Under Capricorn. 1950: Tony Draws a Horse. 1951: The Man in the White Suit. The Magic Box. His Excellency. 1952: I Believe in You. 1953: Isn't Life Wonderful! 1954: For Better, For Worse (US: Cocktails in the Kitchen). Father Brown (US: The Detective). 1955: The Constant Husband. The Ladykillers. The Court Jester. 1956: 23 Paces to Baker Street. True As a Turtle. It's Great to Be Young. 1957: The Admirable Crichton (US: Paradise Lagoon). 1958: Happy is the Bride! Indiscreet. I Was Monty's Double (US: Monty's Double). The Wreck of the Mary Deare. A Tale of Two Cities. 1959: The Night We Dropped a Clanger (US: Make Mine a Double). The Navy Lark. 1960: Follow That Horse! Under 10 Flags. A French Mistress. The Pure Hell of St Trinian's. Swiss Family Robinson. 1961: On the Fiddle (US: Operation Snafu). Petticoat Pirates. 1962: The Amorous Prawn. The Iron Maiden (US: The Swingin' Maiden). Vengeance (US: The Brain). 1963: Heavens Above! The Comedy Man. Carry on Jack (US: Carry on Venus). 1964: Guns at Batasi. 1965: The Amorous Adventures of Moll Flanders. A Study in Terror (US: Fog). Circus of Fear (US: Psycho-Circus). Lady L. 1966: A Man Could Get Killed. 1967: The Magnificent Two. 1969: Oh! What a Lovely War.

PARKER, Eleanor 1922–

Warmly upper-bracket American actress with red-gold hair, at her best in films where she had the dominant role or played a strong-willed woman. Less effective as straightforward heroines. In substantial leading roles from 1946 to 1957, surprisingly declining before she was 40. Just the sort of actress one would expect to have won an Oscar, although in fact she hasn't, having been unsuccessfully nominated three times (for *Caged, Detective Story* and *Interrupted Melody*). Four times married.

*1941: †They Died with Their Boots On. 1942: *Soldiers in White. The Big Shot (voice only). *Vaudeville Days. *Men of the Sky. Busses Roar. 1943: *We're in the Army Now. Destination Tokyo. The Mysterious Doctor. Mission to Moscow. 1944: Atlantic City. The Last Ride. Between Two Worlds. Crime by Night. The Very Thought of You. Hollywood Canteen. 1945: Pride of the Marines. 1946: Never Say Goodbye. Of Human Bondage. 1947: The Voice of the Turtle. Escape Me Never. Always Together. The Woman in White. 1949: It's a Great Feeling. 1950: Chain Lightning. Caged. Three Secrets. 1951: Detective Story. Valentino. A Millionaire for Christy. 1952: Scaramouche. Above and Beyond. 1953: Escape from Fort Bravo. 1954: The Naked Jungle. Valley of the Kings. 1955: Many Rivers to Cross. Interrupted Melody. The Man with the Golden Arm. 1956: The King and Four Queens. 1957: Lizzie. 1959: A Hole in the Head. 1960: Home from the Hill. 1961: Return to Peyton Place. 1962: Madison Avenue. 1963: Panic Button. 1965: The Sound of Music. 1966: An American Dream (GB: See You in Hell, Darling). The Oscar. 1967: Il tigre (GB and US: The Tiger and the Pussycat). Warning Shot. 1968: How to Steal the World (TV. GB: cinemas). 1969: Eye of the Cat. 1970: Maybe I'll Come Home Again in the Spring (TV). Vanished (TV). 1972: Home for the Holidays (TV). The Great American Beauty Contest (TV). 1977: Fantasy Island (TV). 1979: She's Dressed to Kill (TV. GB: Someone's Killing the World's Greatest Models). Sunburn. 1980: Once Upon a Spy (TV). Madame X (TV). 1991: Dead on the Money (TV).*

†Scene deleted

PARKER, Fess 1924–

Big, shambling, soft-spoken Texan in small film roles until put under contract by Walt Disney in 1954. As the famous Indian fighter Davy Crockett (whose adventures were first shown on television, then released, with great success, to cinemas), Parker became a national figure, and had a few good years starring in films, before going back to TV in a long-running series as another historic westerner – Daniel Boone. He drifted out of acting in the early 1970s and became a hotelier and vintner in California.

*1952: Springfield Rifle. No Room for the Groom. Untamed Frontier. 1953: Thunder over the Plains. Island in the Sky. The Kid from Left Field. Take Me to Town. 1954: Them! The Bounty Hunter. Davy Crockett – King of the Wild Frontier. Battle Cry. 1955: Davy Crockett and the River Pirates. 1956: The Great Locomotive Chase. Westward Ho! The Wagons. 1957: Old Yeller. 1958: Turn Left at Mount Everest (TV). The Light in the Forest. 1959: The Hangman. Alias Jesse James. The Jayhawkers. 1960: *Saturday Matinee. 1961: Ambush at Wagon Gap (TV). The Secret Mission (TV). 1962: Hell is for Heroes! 1966: Smoky. Daniel Boone – Frontier Trail Rider (TV. GB: cinemas). 1972: Climb an Angry Mountain (TV).*

PARKER, Jean
(Luise-Stephanie Zelinska) 1912–

One of the most dramatic career turnabouts in Hollywood history. In the thirties brown-haired Jean was the cinema's sweet-tempered backwoods girl, at one with nature and radiant in such offerings as *Sequoia* and *Romance of the Redwoods*. She was also Beth in 1933's *Little Women*. After 1940 she suddenly appeared as hard-boiled broads, and became just as typed in this mould as the other. Married to actor Robert Lowery (*qv*) from 1951–1957 – fourth of four husbands.

1932: Divorce in the Family. 1933: Rasputin and the Empress (GB: Rasputin the Mad Monk). Made on Broadway (GB: The Girl I Made). The Secret of Madame Blanche. What Price Innocence? (GB: Shall the Children Pay?). Gabriel over the White House. Little Women. Storm at Daybreak. Lady for a Day.

1934: *Two Alone. A Wicked Woman. Lazy River. Sequoia. Have a Heart. Caravan. You Can't Buy Everything. Operator 13 (GB: Spy 13). Limehouse Blues.* 1935: *Princess O'Hara. Murder in the Fleet. The Ghost Goes West.* 1936: *The Farmer in the Dell. The Texas Rangers.* 1937: *The Barrier. Life Begins with Love.* 1938: *Romance of the Limberlost. The Arkansas Traveler. Penitentiary.* 1939: *Flight at Midnight. Romance of the Redwoods. Zenobia (GB: Elephants Never Forget). Parents on Trial. *Young America Flies. She Married a Cop. The Flying Deuces.* 1940: *Beyond Tomorrow. Sons of the Navy. Knights of the Range.* 1941: *Flying Blind. The Roar of the Press. Power Dive. No Hands on the Clock. The Pittsburgh Kid.* 1942: *Hi, Neighbor. Hello, Annapolis (GB: Personal Honour). Torpedo Boat. The Girl from Alaska. I Live on Danger. The Wrecking Crew. Tomorrow We Live. The Traitor Within.* 1943: *The Deerslayer. Alaska Highway. Minesweeper. High Explosive.* 1944: *Oh! What a Night! Detective Kitty O'Day. Bluebeard. One Body Too Many. Lady in the Death House. The Navy Way. Dead Man's Eyes.* 1945: *The Adventures of Kitty O'Day.* 1946: *Rolling Home.* 1950: *The Gunfighter.* 1952: *Toughest Man in Arizona.* 1953: *Those Redheads from Seattle.* 1954: *Black Tuesday.* 1955: *A Lawless Street.* 1957: *The Parson and the Outlaw.* 1966: *Apache Uprising.* 1972: *Stigma.*

PARKER, Mary-Louise 1964–

Radiantly pretty, dark-haired American star, a respected stage actress whose forays into films were too infrequent until the 1990s. She has not quite reached the top of the cast in movies, but her performances merit more than semi-leading roles. Her lack of dynamism, however, may yet drive her back to the theatre. Romantically involved for some years with actor Billy Crudup (*qv*).

1988: *Too Young the Hero (TV).* 1989: *Signs of Life.* 1990: *Longtime Companion.* 1991: *Fried Green Tomatoes (GB: Fried Green Tomatoes at the Whistlestop Café). Grand Canyon.* 1993: *Naked in New York. Mr Wonderful.* 1994: *A Place for Annie (TV). The Client. Bullets Over Broadway.* 1995: *Boys on the Side. Sugartime (cable TV). Nightwood Bar (TV).* 1996: *The Portrait of a Lady. The Maker (TV). Reckless (TV).* 1997: *Murder in Mind.* 1998: *Goodbye Lover. Saint Maybe (TV). Legalese (TV).* 1999: *The Five Senses. Let the Devil Wear Black (TV). The Simple*

Life of Noah Dearborn (TV). 2000: *Cupid & Cate (TV).*

PARKER, Sarah Jessica 1965–

Honey-blonde American actress of faintly goofy attractiveness who has been in show business since childhood. After a two-year run on Broadway in the title role of *Annie,* Parker, whose vocal talents have been largely ignored in films, gradually began to make inroads into the movie business, showing up best in romantic comedy, but not really blossoming as a star until the early 1990s. Still at her best in light off-centre entertainment: her vigorous witch in *Hocus Pocus* is not untypical of her output. One of nine children, she scored another musical stage hit in 1996 in *How to Succeed in Business Without Really Trying.* Married to actor Matthew Broderick (*qv*), she had a great late-1990s success with the TV series *Sex and the City.*

1979: *Rich Kids.* 1982: *My Body, My Child (TV).* 1983: *Somewhere Tomorrow.* 1984: *Footloose. Firstborn.* 1985: *Girls Just Want to Have Fun.* 1986: *Flight of the Navigator.* 1987: *The Room Upstairs (TV).* 1988: *Dadah is Death (TV).* 1989: *The Ryan White Story (TV). Twist of Fate (TV).* 1991: *L A Story.* 1992: *In the Best Interest of the Children (TV).* 1993: *Honeymoon in Vegas. Striking Distance. Hocus Pocus.* 1994: *Ed Wood. Miami Rhapsody.* 1995: *The Sunshine Boys (TV). If Lucy Fell.* 1996: *The Substance of Fire. 'Til There Was You. The First Wives Club. Mars Attacks! Extreme Measures. Barefoot in the Park (TV).* 1997: *A Life Apart: Hasidism in America (narrator only).* 1999: *Dudley-Do-Right.* 2000: *Isn't She Great. State and Main.*

PARKER, Willard

(Worster Van Eps) 1912–1996

Tall, craggy, sandy-haired American actor whose career was severely disrupted by war service. Took small leading roles thereafter, but never really settled as a star, moving into star-billed supporting roles by the early fifties. He was too stiff to gain a real following, although there were a few more minor leads for him at the beginning of the sixties. Married to actress Virginia Field (*qv*) from 1951. Busy from 1955 to 1959 in the TV series *Tales of the Texas Rangers.* Died from heart failure.

1937: *Over the Goal. Alcatraz Island. Missing Witnesses. That Certain Woman. The Adventurous Blonde/Torchy Blane the Adventurous Blonde. Back in Circulation.*

China Passage. The Devil's Saddle Legion. Love is on the Air (GB: The Radio Murder Mystery). 1938: *Accidents Will Happen. Invisible Menace. A Slight Case of Murder.* 1939: *Zero Hour. The Phantom Creeps (serial).* 1943: *The Fighting Guardsman. What a Woman!* 1946: *One Way to Love. Renegades.* 1948: *The Mating of Millie. Relentless. The Wreck of the Hesperus. You Gotta Stay Happy.* 1949: *Slightly French. Calamity Jane and Sam Bass. David Harding Counterspy. Bodyhold. The Secret Fury. Emergency Wedding (GB: Jealousy). Bandit Queen.* 1951: *Hunt the Man Down. Apache Drums.* 1952: *Caribbean (GB: Caribbean Gold).* 1953: *The Vanquished. Sangaree. Kiss Me Kate.* 1954: *The Great Jesse James Raid.* 1956: *The Naked Gun. Lure of the Swamp.* 1959: *The Lone Texan.* 1960: *Walk Tall. 13 Fighting Men. The High-Powered Rifle. Young Jesse James.* 1962: *Air Patrol.* 1964: *The Earth Dies Screaming.* 1966: *Waco.* 1972: *The Great Waltz.*

PARKS, Larry

(Samuel L. Parks) 1914–1975

Black-haired American actor with open, slightly mischievous looks who, despite a weak heart (from a severe childhood attack of rheumatic fever), maintained a hectic film schedule once signed by Columbia in 1941. His eye-catching performance in *Renegades* came at just the right time and he was chosen for the title role in *The Jolson Story,* which proved a personal triumph (and a box-office gold mine). In 1951, however, he was virtually forced out of films after testifying to the Un-American Activities Committee. Married to Betty Garrett (*qv*) from 1944 to his death from a heart attack. He received an Oscar nomination for *The Jolson Story.*

1935: *Parade of the Maestros. 1941: Honolulu Lu. Mystery Ship. You Belong to Me (GB: Good Morning, Doctor). Harmon of Michigan. Harvard Here I Come (GB: Here I Come). Three Girls About Town. Sing for Your Supper. 1942: Alias Boston Blackie. North of the Rockies (GB: False Clues). Hello Annapolis (GB: Personal Honour). Blondie Goes to College (GB: The Boss Said 'No'). A Man's World. Flight Lieutenant. Atlantic Convoy. You Were Never Lovelier. The Boogie Man Will Get You. They All Kissed the Bride. Submarine Raider. Canal Zone. 1943: Is Everybody Happy? Redhead from Manhattan. Destroyer. That Bedside Manner. The Deerslayer. Power of the Press. Reveille with Beverly. First Comes Courage. 1944: Hey, Rookie. Stars on Parade. The Racket Man. Sergeant Mike. She's a Sweetheart. The Black Parachute. 1945: Counter-Attack (GB: One Against Seven). 1946: Renegades. The Jolson Story. 1947: Down to Earth. The Swordsman. Her Husband's Affairs. 1948: The Gallant Blade. 1949: Jolson Sings Again. 1950: Emergency Wedding (GB: Jealousy). 1951: Love is Better Than Ever (GB: The Light Fantastic). 1955: Tiger by the Tail (US: Crossup). 1962: Freud (GB: Freud – the Secret Passion).

PARRY, Natasha 1930–
Outstandingly pretty brunette British leading lady, in show business from childhood, the daughter of film director Gordon Parry (1908–1981) and a 'Cochran young lady' at 15. Not the world's most wonderful actress, perhaps, but so stunning to look at that one can only regret the paucity of her film output in her peak years: later she appeared in occasional character roles in continental pictures. Married to stage (and occasionally film) director Sir Peter Brook (1925–) since 1951. Actress Irina Brook is their daughter.
1935: Joy Ride. 1949: Trottie True (US: Gay Lady). Golden Arrow (US: Three Men and a Girl/The Gay Adventure. Released 1952). 1950: Midnight Episode. Dance Hall. 1951: The Dark Man. 1952: Crow Hollow. 1954: Knave of Hearts (US: Lovers, Happy Lovers). 1957: Windom's Way. 1959: The Rough and the Smooth (US: Portrait of a Sinner). 1960: Midnight Lace. 1961: The Fourth Square. 1963: Girl in the Headlines (US: The Model Murder Case). 1968: Romeo and Juliet. 1969: Oh! What a Lovely War. 1978: Meetings with Remarkable Men. 1981: La chambre voisine. La fille prodigue. 1982: Le lit/The Bed.

PARTON, Dolly 1945–
Diminutive (well, in height at least), flamboyant, brightly blonde American country and western singer with amazing, Victorian eggtimer-type figure, a sort of Hollywood Barbara Windsor (qv) with vibrantly twangy, powerful singing voice thrown in. Not surprisingly, films paused before casting her in anything, but she has proved she can hold her own as an actress in light comedies and musicals. An obvious contender for a roadshow of Hello, Dolly! in the near future.
1970: The Nashville Sound. 1980: Nine to Five. 1982: The Best Little Whorehouse in Texas. 1984: Rhinestone. 1986: Steel Magnolias. 1991: Wild Texas Wind (TV). 1992: Straight Talk. 1993: The Beverly Hillbillies. 1995: Naomi & Wynonna: Love Can Build a Bridge (TV). Big Dreams and Broken Hearts: The Dottie West Story (TV). 1997: Get to the Heart: The Barbara Mandrell Story (TV). 1999: Jackie's Back! (TV). 2000: Blue Valley Songbird (TV).

PATRIC, Jason (J.P. Miller) 1966–
American actor of dark, curly hair and sullen handsomeness, grandson of Jackie Gleason (qv) and son of actor Jason Miller. During a fairly sparse movie-acting period since 1986, he has had some good leading roles, but sometimes failed to make the most of them and has not quite developed into a name the public will pay to see, although he can be interestingly morose in indifferent parts. Despite some high-profile romances, he remains unmarried at time of writing.
1985: Toughlove (TV). 1986: Solarbabies/Solar Warriors. 1987: The Lost Boys. 1988: The Beast. Loon (released 1991 as Denial). 1989: *Teach 109. 1990: After Dark, My

Sweet. Frankenstein Unbound. 1991: Rush. 1993: Geronimo: An American Legend. 1995: The Journey of August King. 1996: Sleepers. 1997: Incognito. Speed 2: Cruise Control. 1998: Your Friends & Neighbours.

PATRICK, Gail
(Margaret Fitzpatrick) 1911–1980
Tall, straight-faced brunette American actress with honeyed voice, often cast in aristocratic or bitchy roles, but also able to project warmth and sincerity in the right role. Her assignments after 1940 were disappointing, and she later moved into production: her most noteworthy success was the long-running TV series Perry Mason. Died from leukaemia.
1932: If I Had a Million. 1933: The Phantom Broadcast (GB: Phantom of the Air). Pick-Up. The Mysterious Rider. Murder in the Zoo. Cradle Song. Mama Loves Papa. To the Last Man. 1934: Death Takes a Holiday. Wagon Wheels. Take the Stand (GB: The Great Radio Mystery). Murder at the Vanities. The Crime of Helen Stanley. One Hour Late. 1935: Doubting Thomas. Rumba. Smart Girl. Wanderer of the Wasteland. Two Fisted. Mississippi. No More Ladies. The Big Broadcast of 1936. 1936: The Preview Murder Mystery. Two in the Dark. My Man Godfrey. Murder with Pictures. The Lone Wolf Returns. Early to Bed. White Hunter. 1937: John Meade's Woman. Her Husband Lies. Artists and Models. Stage Door. 1938: Wives under Suspicion. Mad about Music. King of Alcatraz (GB: King of the Alcatraz). Dangerous to Know. 1939: Grand Jury Secrets. Man of Conquest. Disbarred. Reno. 1940: My Favorite Wife. Gallant Sons. The Doctor Takes a Wife. 1941: Kathleen. Love Crazy. 1942: We Were Dancing. Tales of Manhattan. Quiet Please Murder. 1943: Hit Parade of 1943. Women in Bondage. 1944: Up in Mabel's Room. 1945: Twice Blessed. Brewster's Millions. 1946: Claudia and David. The Madonna's Secret. Rendezvous with Annie. The Plainsman and the Lady. 1947: Calendar Girl. King of the Wild Horses. 1948: The Inside Story.

PATRICK, Nigel
(N. Wemyss) 1912–1981
Suave, brown-haired British leading man with distinctive receding hairline. Usually cast as men about town and shady smoothies, he was a better actor than most of his contemporaries, but never quite became a big star of the British cinema, and was seen

mostly on stage (where he also directed) after 1961. Married to Beatrice Campbell from 1951 to her death in 1980. Died from lung cancer.
*1939: Mrs Pym of Scotland Yard. 1948: Spring in Park Lane. Noose (US: The Silk Noose). Uneasy Terms. 1949: Silent Dust. The Jack of Diamonds. The Perfect Woman. 1950: Morning Departure (US: Operation Disaster). Trio. 1951: The Browning Version. Pandora and the Flying Dutchman. Encore. Young Wives' Tale. 1952: The Sound Barrier (US: Breaking the Sound Barrier). Who Goes There? (US: The Passionate Sentry). The Pickwick Papers. Meet Me Tonight. 1953: Grand National Night (US: Wicked Woman). 1954: Forbidden Cargo. The Sea Shall Not Have Them. 1955: A Prize of Gold. All for Mary. 1956: Raintree County. 1957: Count Five and Die. *Arriverderci Roma! (narrator only). How to Murder a Rich Uncle. 1958: The Man Inside. 1959: Sapphire. The League of Gentlemen. 1960: The Trials of Oscar Wilde (US: The Man with the Green Carnation). 1961: †Johnny Nobody. 1963: The Informers. 1966: Goal! World Cup 1966 (narrator only). 1969: Battle of Britain. The Virgin Soldiers. 1970: The Executioner. 1972: Tales from the Crypt. The Great Waltz. 1973: The Mackintosh Man. 1977: Silver Bears.*

†Also directed

PATTEN, Luana
See SMITH, John

PAVAN, Marisa
See ANGELI, Pier
and AUMONT, Jean-Pierre

PATTERSON, Lee 1929–
Well-muscled, dark-haired Canadian actor with husky, pop star looks who carved out a busy career for himself as the star of British 'B' film thrillers of the 1950s, some of them well above average. He went to America as the star of a TV series, *Surfslide Six*, in the early 1960s, but his film career subsequently fizzled out, and he appeared mainly on stage in later years.
1953: Malta Story. 1954: The Good Die Young. The Passing Stranger. 36 Hours (US: Terror Street). 1955: The Diamond Expert. Above Us the Waves. 1956: Reach for the Sky. Soho Incident (US: Spin a Dark Web). Checkpoint. Dry Rot. The Counterfeit Plan. 1957: The Key Man. Time Lock. The Story of

Esther Costello (US: Golden Virgin). The Flying Scot (US: Mailbag Robbery). 1958: Bed without Breakfast. The Golden Disc (US: The Inbetween Age). The Spaniard's Curse. Cat and Mouse/The Desperate Ones. Man with a Gun. 1959: Please Turn Over. Breakout. Deadly Record. The White Trap. Jack the Ripper. Third Man on the Mountain. 1960: October Moth. The Three Worlds of Gulliver. 1963: The Ceremony. 1967: Valley of Mystery. Search for the Evil One. 1971: Chato's Land. 1976: Star Street. 1982: Airplane II: The Sequel. 1984: Hunter (TV). 1985: Death Wish 3. 1986: The Last Days of Patton (TV). 1990: Bullseye! 1994: Healer.*

PAVLOW, Muriel 1921–
Petite, light-haired British actress whose clean, girlish good looks enabled her to stay in youthful, albeit fairly tame leading roles for 20 years: a trim, sexy figure and cool, capable acting style certainly helped. Married to Derek Farr from 1947 to his death. Still acting, latterly on TV.
1934: Sing As We Go. 1937: A Romance in Flanders (US: Lost on the Western Front). 1941: Quiet Wedding. 1945: Night Boat to Dublin. 1946: The Shop at Sly Corner (US: The Code of Scotland Yard). 1951: Out of True. 1952: It Started in Paradise. The Net (US: Project M7). 1953: Simon and Laura. 1956: Reach for the Sky. Eyewitness. Tiger in the Smoke. 1957: Doctor at Large. 1958: Rooney. 1959: Whirlpool. 1961: Murder She Said. 1987: Claws (TV). 1992: Memento Mori (TV). 1995: Daisies in December (TV).

PAXTON, Bill 1955–
Soft-faced, boyish, dark-haired American actor equally likely to turn up as law-abiding

or unsavoury characters, as the hero, or in colourful character roles. A film buff from childhood who made his own Super-8 films as a teenager, Paxton came to Hollywood from his native Texas as a set dresser with New World Studios, also getting three lines in one film on which he was working. In 1980, he decided on a permanent switch to acting, but his credits were scarce until the end of the decade, when he broke through to leading and semi-leading roles, showing up strongly in such films as *One False Move, Trespass, Twister* and *A Simple Plan*.
1975: Crazy Mama. 1981: Stripes. 1982: Butcher, Baker, Nightmare Maker/Night Warning. The Lords of Discipline. 1983: Taking Tiger Mountain. 1984: Mortuary. The Terminator. Streets of Fire. Impulse. 1985: Weird Science. An Early Frost (TV). 1986: Aliens. 1987: Near Dark. Pass the Ammo. 1989: Back to Back. Slipstream. Next of Kin. Brain Dead/Paranoia. 1990: The Last of the Finest (GB: Blue Heat). One False Move (released 1994). Predator 2. Navy SEALS. 1991: The Dark Backward (GB: The Man with Three Arms). The Vagrant. 1992: Trespass/The Looters. 1993: Boxing Helena. Indian Summer. Monolith. Tombstone. Future Shock. 1994: True Lies. Frank and Jesse. 1995: Apollo 13. The Last Supper. 1996: Twister. The Evening Star. Traveller. 1997: Titanic. 1998: Mighty Joe Young. A Simple Plan. A Bright Shining Lie (cable TV). 2000: U-571. The Vertical Limit.

PAYNE, John 1912–1989
Dark-haired, tough-looking American actor with fretful expression and slightly husky voice. Always good value as a man of action, his career traced a faintly similar pattern to

that of Dick Powell, in that it followed light musicals (especially opposite Alice Faye and Sonja Henie) with a string of tough-guy roles. Very prolific from 1949 to 1956 when he appeared in a series of thrillers and colourful outdoors action films that were sometimes of quite high quality. Married Anne Shirley (1937–1943) and Gloria De Haven (1944–1950), first and second of three. Died from congestive heart failure.

1936: Dodsworth. 1937: Hats Off. Fair Warning. 1938: College Swing (GB: Swing, Teacher, Swing). Garden of the Moon. Love on Toast. 1939: Indianapolis Speedway (GB: Devil on Wheels). Bad Lands. Wings of the Navy. Kid Nightingale. *Royal Rodeo. 1940: The Great Profile. Tear Gas Squad. Star Dust. Maryland. King of the Lumberjacks. Tin Pan Alley. 1941: Remember the Day. The Great American Broadcast. Week-End in Havana. Sun Valley Serenade. 1942: Iceland (GB: Katina). Springtime in the Rockies. To the Shores of Tripoli. Footlight Serenade. 1943: Hello, Frisco, Hello. 1945: The Dolly Sisters. 1946: Wake Up and Dream. Sentimental Journey. The Razor's Edge. 1947: Miracle on 34th Street (GB: The Big Heart). 1948: Larceny. The Saxon Charm. 1949: The Crooked Way. El Paso. Captain China. 1950: The Eagle and the Hawk. Tripoli. 1951: Passage West (GB: High Venture). Crosswinds. 1952: The Blazing Forest. Caribbean (GB: Caribbean Gold). Kansas City Confidential (GB: The Secret Four). 1953: Raiders of the Seven Seas. The Vanquished. 99 River Street. 1954: Rails into Laramie. Silver Lode. 1955: Hell's Island. Santa Fé Passage. The Road to Denver. Tennessee's Partner. 1956: Slightly Scarlet. The Boss. Rebel in Town. Hold Back the Night. 1957: Bail Out at 43,000 (GB: Bale out at 43,000). 1958: Hidden Fear. 1965: They Ran for Their Lives (and directed). 1968: Gift of the Nile. 1970: The Savage Wild. 1978: Go West, Young Girl (TV).

PAYS, Amanda
See MILLER, Mandy

PAYTON, Barbara 1927–1967
Provocative platinum blonde American actress seen in brassy, man-hungry roles. She made some impressions as harsh, unsympathetic characters in Hollywood (and Britain) in the early Fifties, but much more impression with her explosive private life, which included one actor, Tom Neal, hospitalising another,

Franchot Tone (both qv), in a fistfight over her charms. She lived with Neal and briefly married Tone, before drifting out of films in the mid 1950s. The following decade saw her arrested on drunkenness and prostitution charges, before her early death at 39 'from natural causes', with cirrhosis of the liver a probable factor.

1949: *Silver Butte. Once More, My Darling. Trapped. 1950: Dallas. Kiss Tomorrow Goodbye. 1951: Drums in the Deep South. Only the Valiant. Bride of the Gorilla. 1952: The Great Jesse James Raid. Four-Sided Triangle. 1953: The Flanagan Boy (US: Bad Blonde). Run for the Hills. 1955: Murder is My Beat.

PEARCE, Guy 1967–
English-born (of a New Zealand father killed in an air crash), Australian-raised, dark-haired actor with boyish, cherubic features. Surviving stints on two enormously popular daytime soaps in Australia (Home and Away and Neighbours), he went to Hollywood in the late 1990s and reaped praise for his Depp-like work as a detective in L.A. Confidential. Also a keen musician Pearce sings, plays piano, guitar and saxophone, and pens songs.

1987: Heaven Tonight. 1990: Hunting. 1994: The Adventures of Priscilla, Queen of the Desert. 1996: Flynn. Dating the Enemy. 1997: L.A. Confidential. 1998: Woundings. 1999: Ravenous. A Slipping-Down Life. 2000: Rules of Engagement. Memento. 2001: Till Human Voices Wake Us. The Count of Monte Cristo.

PECK, Gregory (Eldred G. Peck) 1916–
Upright, immensely good-looking, dark-haired, soft-spoken American actor who rose to stardom in his first film and more than almost anyone else suggested (despite his own

sporadic attempts to break the pattern) nobility and incorruptibility just by being on screen. He might have won an Oscar for his cracking-up colonel in 12 O'Clock High (one of four unsuccessful nominations), but Hollywood typically gave him one instead for his tricksy performance under a mound of padding in To Kill a Mockingbird. Peck drifted out of films and into production in the early 1970s. It was a surprise when he returned in big-budget pot-boilers at the end of the decade. Special Oscar 1967. Actress Cecilia Peck (1958–) is his daughter.

1943: Days of Glory. 1944: The Keys of the Kingdom. 1945: The Valley of Decision. Spellbound. 1946: Duel in the Sun. The Yearling. 1947: Gentleman's Agreement. The Macomber Affair. The Paradine Case. 1948: Yellow Sky. 1949: The Great Sinner. 12 O'Clock High. 1950: The Gunfighter. 1951: Captain Horatio Hornblower RN. David and Bathsheba. Only the Valiant. 1952: The Snows of Kilimanjaro. The World in His Arms. 1953: Roman Holiday. The Million Pound Note (US: Man with a Million). 1954: Night People. The Purple Plain. 1956: The Man in the Gray Flannel Suit. Moby Dick. 1957: Designing Woman. 1958: The Bravados. The Big Country. 1959: Beloved Infidel. On the Beach. Pork Chop Hill. 1961: The Guns of Navarone. 1962: Cape Fear. How the West Was Won. 1963: To Kill a Mockingbird. Captain Newman MD. 1964: Behold a Pale Horse. 1965: Mirage. 1966: Arabesque. 1968: Mackenna's Gold. The Stalking Moon. 1969: The Chairman (GB: The Most Dangerous Man in the World). Marooned. 1970: I Walk the Line. 1971: Shoot Out. 1973: Billy Two Hats. 1974: John F. Kennedy, Years of Lightning, Day of Drums (narrator only). 1976: The Omen. 1977: MacArthur (GB: MacArthur the Rebel General). 1978: The Boys from Brazil. 1979: Ken Murray's Shooting Stars. 1980: The Sea Wolves. 1982: The Blue and the Gray (TV). 1983: The Scarlet and the Black (TV). 1986: Directed by William Wyler. 1987: Amazing Grace and Chuck (GB: Silent Voice). 1989: Old Gringo. 1991: Cape Fear (remake). Other People's Money. 1993: The Portrait (TV). 1995: Wild Bill: Hollywood Maverick. 1998: From Russia to Hollywood (doc. Narrator only). 1999: A Conversation with Gregory Peck (doc).

PENN, Sean 1960–
Slim, dark, intense, strong-jawed, seldom-smiling American actor who usually played

rebels against the system in his early films, although his surly good looks often adapted better to villainy. The son of director Leo Penn and brother of actor Christopher Penn (1958–), he led an explosive private life which included marriage and divorce to singer-actress Madonna (*qv*) and a brief prison sentence for assault in 1987. A liaison with actress Robin Wright (*qv*) produced two children: the couple married in 1996 but parted in 2000. Earlier in the decade, he quit acting to concentrate on forging a career as a writer-director. His efforts were moderate and a return to acting was rewarded with Academy Award nominations for *Dead Man Walking* and *Sweet and Lowdown*.

1980: The Killing of Randy Webster (TV). 1981: Hellinger's Law (TV). Taps. 1982: Fast Times at Ridgemount High (GB: Fast Times). Bad Boys. 1983: Crackers. 1984: Racing with the Moon. 1985: The Falcon and the Snowman. At Close Range. 1986: Shanghai Surprise. 1988: Dear America (voice only). Colors. Judgment in Berlin. 1989: Casualties of War. We're No Angels. 1990: State of Grace. 1992: Blast 'Em. 1993: Carlito's Way. Schneeweiss-Rosenrot. The Last Party (documentary). 1995: Dead Man Walking. 1996: Loved. The Bells of Hell. 1997: Hugo Pool. The Game. She's So Lovely. U Turn/Stray Dogs. 1998: The Thin Red Line. Hurlyburly. 1999: Being John Malkovich. Sweet and Lowdown. 2000: Before Night Falls.
As director: *1991: The Indian Runner. 1995: The Crossing Guard. 2000: The Pledge.*

PEPPARD, George 1928–1994
Fair-haired, blue-eyed, hard-headed American actor who looked to be a real find in the early sixties but proved disappointing in the leading roles of several big films (perhaps the wrong kind?) and was shunted into routine action thrillers and westerns. Found belated popularity as leader of TV's *The A-Team*. Married (divorced, re-married and divorced) to Elizabeth Ashley (*qv*) from 1966 to 1972. He married his fifth wife in 1992. Died from pneumonia.
1957: The Strange One (GB: End As a Man). 1959: Pork Chop Hill. 1960: Home from the Hill. The Subterraneans. 1961: Breakfast at Tiffany's. 1962: How the West Was Won. 1963: The Victors. 1964: The Carpetbaggers. 1965: Operation Crossbow (US: The Great Spy Mission). The Third Day. 1966: The Blue Max. 1967: Rough Night in Jericho. Tobruk. 1968: P.J. (GB: New Face in Hell). House of

Cards. Pendulum. What's So Bad About Feeling Good? 1970: The Executioner. Cannon for Cordoba. 1971: One More Train to Rob. The Bravos (TV). 1972: The Groundstar Conspiracy. 1974: Newman's Law. 1975: Guilty or Innocent: the Sam Sheppard Case (TV). One of Our Own (TV). Doctors' Secrets (TV). 1977: Damnation Alley. 1978: †Five Days from Home. 1979: Crisis in Mid-Air (TV). Torn Between Two Lovers (TV. GB: cinemas). Da Dunkerque alla vittoria (US: From Hell To Victory). 1980: Battle Beyond the Stars. Your Ticket is No Longer Valid. 1981: Helicopter. Race for the Yankee Zephyr. 1982: Target Eagle. 1983: The A-Team (TV). 1989: Silence Like Glass. Man Against the Mob (TV. GB: Murder in the City of Angels). The Chinatown Murders (TV). 1990: Night of the Fox (film version of TV mini-series). 1992: The Tigress.

†*And directed*

PEREZ, Rosie (Rosa Perez) 1964–
Petite, volatile, dynamic, wide-mouthed, explosive, fast-talking American actress, dancer and choreographer of Puerto Rican parentage. A delinquent child, she reformed and studied to become a marine biologist. But she was a nightclub dancer when spotted for Hollywood. While displaying a talent for naturalistic acting, she continued her dance work and has since choreographed numerous stage and TV shows as well as music videos. Her habit of chewing her dialogue is irritating or lovable according to taste, but she won an Academy Award nomination for her performance as a bereaved mother in *Fearless*.
1989: Do the Right Thing. 1990: Criminal Justice (TV). 1991: Night on Earth. 1992: White Men Can't Jump. 1993: Fearless. Untamed Heart. 1994: It Could Happen to You. Somebody to Love. 1996: Wishful Thinking. 1977: A Brother's Kiss. Subway Stories: Tales from the Underground (TV). Perdita Durango. 1998: Louis & Frank. The 24-Hour Woman. 2000: The Road to El Dorado (voice only). King of the Jungle.

PERKINS, Anthony 1932–1992
Tall, dark, frail-looking American actor with soft voice, shy smile and coat-hanger shoulders. A teenage pin-up of his time, he proved a useful portrayer of young men defying odds to succeed. *Psycho* brought him a new image, but it proved a hard trick to follow, and the ensuing years were full of

oddball projects and unsuitable roles before he made two further *Psycho* films in the 1980s, directing one himself. The son of character actor Osgood Perkins (1892–1937), he was in 1984 ordained a minister of the Universal Life Church of America. Oscar nominee for *Friendly Persuasion*. Died from AIDS complications.
1953: The Actress. 1956: Friendly Persuasion. 1957: The Lonely Man. Fear Strikes Out. The Tin Star. 1958: Desire under the Elms. This Angry Age (GB: The Sea Wall). The Match-maker. 1959: Green Mansions. On the Beach. 1960: Tall Story. Psycho. 1961: Phaedra. Goodbye Again/Aimez-vous Brahms? 1962: Five Miles to Midnight. The Trial. Le glaive et la balance (GB: Two are Guilty). 1963: Une ravissante idiote (GB: A Ravishing Idiot). 1965: The Fool Killer. Is Paris Burning? 1967: Le scandale (GB and US: The Champagne Murders). 1968: Pretty Poison. 1970: How Awful about Allan (TV). WUSA. Catch 22. 1971: Ten Days' Wonder. Quelqu'un derrière la porte (GB: Two Minds for Murder). 1972: The Life and Times of Judge Roy Bean. Play It As It Lays. 1973: Lovin' Molly. 1974: Murder on the Orient Express. 1975: Mahogany. 1977: Winter Kills (released 1979). 1978: First, You Cry (TV). Remember My Name. Les Misérables (TV). 1979: Twee Vrouwen/Twice a Woman. North Sea Hijack (US: ffolkes). Double Negative. The Horror Show. The Black Hole. Esther, Ruth and Jennifer. 1982: For the Term of His Natural Life (TV). The Sins of Dorian Gray (TV). 1983: Psycho II. 1984: Crimes of Passion. 1986: †Psycho 3. 1988: Lucky Stiff (directed only). Destroyer. 1989: Dr Jekyll and Mr Hyde (later Edge of Sanity). 1990: Daughter of Darkness (TV). I'm Dangerous Tonight (TV). Psycho IV (TV). 1991: A Demon in My View. The Naked Target. 1992: In the Dark Woods (TV).

†*And directed*

PERKINS, Elizabeth
(E. Pisperikos) 1960–
Vivacious, square-faced, dark-haired American actress who likes playing roles 'off the beaten path' and has proved adept on screen in some sexual sparring matches. The daughter of Greek immigrants to America, she has made fewer film appearances than one would have liked, partly because of a late start, and partly through taking a couple of years off after having a baby by her theatre director husband Terry Kinney. Although

she's stolen many a scene, Perkins hasn't quite found her niche in movies, though you suspect that's partly through the choices she herself has made. She has looked much older in more recent roles.

1986: 'About Last Night . . .' 1987: From the Hip. 1988: Sweet Hearts Dance. Big. 1989: Love at Large. *Teach 109. 1990: Enid is Sleeping (later and GB: Over Her Dead Body). Avalon. 1991: He Said, She Said. The Doctor. 1993: Indian Summer. For Their Own Good (TV). 1994: The Flintstones. Miracle on 34th Street. 1995: Land Mines. Moonlight and Valentino. 1997: Cloned (TV). Rescuers: Stories of Courage – Two Women (TV). 1998: Lesser Prophets. I'm Losing You. 1999: Crazy in Alabama. 2000: 28 Days. If These Walls Could Talk 2 (TV).

PERKINS, Millie 1938–
Dark-haired American actress (a former cover-girl model) with dewy-eyed, waif-like appeal. Like the similar Maggie McNamara (1928–1978) a few years earlier, she never came anywhere near matching the success of her first film, The Diary of Anne Frank, once her teenage appeal had faded. Married to Dean Stockwell (qv) from 1960 to 1964, she continues to crop up in occasional mature roles.

1959: The Diary of Anne Frank. 1961: Wild in the Country. 1963: Girl from La Mancha. 1964: Ensign Pulver. 1966: The Shooting. 1967: Ride the Whirlwind. 1968: Wild in the Streets. 1974: Cockfighter / Born to Kill. 1975: Lady Cocoa. The Witch Who Came from the Sea. 1981: A Gun in the House (TV). 1982: Table for Five. Love in the Present Tense (TV). 1983: The Haunting Passion (TV). Licence to Kill (TV). 1985: At Close Range. 1986: The

Other Lover (TV). Penalty Phase (TV). Jake Speed. Slam Dance. The Thanksgiving Promise (TV). 1987: Strange Voices (TV). Wall Street. 1988: Broken Angel (TV). 1989: Two Moon Junction. 1990: Call Me Anna (TV). 1991: Sharkskin. The Pistol: The Birth of a Legend. 1993: Necronomicon. Murder of Innocence (TV). Midnight Run for Your Life (TV). 1995: Bodily Harm. 1996: The Chamber. The Summer of Ben Tyler (TV).

PERREAU, Gigi
(Ghislaine Perreau-Saussine) 1941–
Along with Natalie Wood (qv), this pigtailed charmer with the fresh-faced, well-scrubbed looks was the busiest of non-star child actresses in the 1940s, actually appearing in Hollywood films for 10 years before finishing her schooling and returning in ingenue roles which, like those of Margaret O'Brien (qv) and despite her undoubted talent, were comparatively unsuccessful. Born in America soon after the arrival there of her French parents who had fled from the Nazis. Now combines acting with teaching drama.

1943: Madame Curie. Dear Heart. Abigail. 1944: Lady in the Death House. Dark Waters. San Diego, I Love You. Two Girls and a Sailor. The Master Race. The Seventh Cross. Mr Skeffington. 1945: Yolanda and the Thief. Voice of the Whistler. God is My Co-Pilot. 1946: Alias Mr Twilight. To Each His Own. 1947: Song of Love. High Barbaree. Green Dolphin Street. 1948: Family Honeymoon. Enchantment. The Sainted Sisters. 1949: Roseanna McCoy. My Foolish Heart. Song of Surrender. 1950: Shadow on the Wall. Never a Dull Moment. For Heaven's Sake. 1951: A Weekend with Father. The Lady Pays Off. Reunion in Reno. 1952: Has Anybody Seen My Gal. Bonzo Goes to College. 1956: The Man in the Gray Flannel Suit. There's Always Tomorrow. Dance with Me, Henry. 1958: Wild Heritage. The Cool and the Crazy. 1959: Girls' Town. 1961: Tammy Tell Me True. Look in Any Window. 1967: Hell in the Streets/ Hell on Wheels. Journey to the Center of Time. 1978: High Seas Hijack.

PERRINE, Valerie 1944–
Tall, statuesque, fair-haired, seemingly permanently tanned American leading lady who sprang from showgirl to star at the ripe old age of 28 and almost immediately displayed a talent for affecting seemingly unforced emotion on screen. But producers subsequently concentrated on showcasing her physical

attributes rather than her acting ability. Oscar nominee for Lenny.

1972: Slaughterhouse-Five. The Couple Takes a Wife (TV). 1973: The Last American Hero. 1974: Lenny. 1976: W.C. Fields and Me. 1977: Mr Billion. 1978: Superman. Ziegfeld – the Man and His Women (TV). 1979: The Magician of Lublin. The Electric Horseman. 1980: Can't Stop the Music. Agency. Superman II. 1981: The Border. The Cannonball Run. 1982: Marian Rose White (TV). 1983: When Your Lover Leaves (TV). 1985: Water. Mask of Murder. 1987: Maid to Order. Una casa americana a Roma. 1989: Sweet Bird of Youth (TV). 1990: Bright Angel. 1991: Hit Man. Riflessi in un cielo scuro. 1993: Boiling Point. 1995: The Break. Girl in the Cadillac. 1997: My Girlfriend's Boyfriend. 1998: A Place Called Truth. Brown's Requiem. 54. Shame, Shame, Shame. 1999: Curtain Call. 2000: Picture This.

PESCI, Joe 1943–
Strutting, diminutive, dark-haired American actor with cocky smile and 'wise-guy' looks. Born into the wrong era for his kind of character star, Pesci's career was a struggle until the 1980s. A child entertainer, he was on Broadway at five and a TV variety regular at 10. A nightclub singer in his teens, he cut an album under the name Joe Ritchie. Pesci never quite made it as a singer, though, nor as an actor until cast as Joey, Robert De Niro's brother and manager, in the boxing biopic Raging Bull. That brought Pesci an Oscar nomination, but he stayed in support for another 10 years, finally winning the best supporting actor Oscar for GoodFellas. After that he mixed offbeat character leads with star-billed cameos, notably his white-haired

rascal in the *Lethal Weapon* films. Four times married, Pesci re-married his third wife in 1991. A golf fanatic in private life.

1961: †*Hey, Let's Twist*. 1976: *Death Collector*. 1978: *Family Enforcer (revised version of Death Collector)*. *Don't Go in the House*. 1980: *Raging Bull*. 1981: *I'm Dancing As Fast As I Can*. 1982: *Dear Mr Wonderful*. *Eureka*. 1983: *Easy Money*. *Once Upon a Time in America*. 1984: *Tutti dentro*. 1987: *Man on Fire*. 1988: *Moonwalker (video)*. 1989: *Lethal Weapon 2*. *Backtrack (GB: Catchfire)*. 1990: *Betsy's Wedding*. *GoodFellas*. *Home Alone*. 1991: *My Cousin Vinny*. *JFK*. *The Super*. 1992: *The Public Eye*. *Home Alone 2: Lost in New York*. *Lethal Weapon 3*. 1993: *A Bronx Tale*. *With Honors*. 1994: *Jimmy Hollywood*. *Vault of Horror*. 1995: *Casino*. 1996: *Gone Fishin'*. 1997: *8 Heads in a Duffel Bag*. 1998: *Lethal Weapon 4*.

†*As Joe Ritchie*

PETERS, Jean (Elizabeth J. Peters) 1926–
Dark-haired Hollywood actress with prettily petulant looks. A star in her first film, she played mostly untamed girls and minxes – including a Mexican girl, an Indian and a spitfire pirate – before marriage to film magnate Howard Hughes disappointingly put an end to her career. The marriage, her second, ended in divorce in 1971 after 15 years, and she remarried and resumed acting without making any great impact.

1947: *Captain from Castile*. 1948: *Deep Waters*. 1949: *It Happens Every Spring*. 1950: *Love That Brute*. 1951: *As Young As You Feel*. *Anne of the Indies*. *Take Care of My Little Girl*. 1952: *Viva Zapata!* *Wait 'Til The Sun Shines, Nellie*. *O Henry's Full House (GB: Full House)*. *Lure of the Wilderness*. 1953: *Pickup on South Street*. *Vicki*. *Niagara*. *A Blueprint for Murder*. 1954: *Apache*. *Three Coins in the Fountain*. *Broken Lance*. 1955: *A Man Called Peter*.

PETERS, Susan
(Suzanne Carnahan) 1921–1952
Delicate but determined-looking brunette American actress, capable of projecting great sincerity even from a poor script. M-G-M were building her up into a star when she was paralysed from the waist down in a hunting accident. Appeared in one further film (and a TV series) from a wheelchair before her death from a chronic kidney infection. Married to actor – later director – Richard Quine from

1943 to 1948. She received an Academy Award nomination for *Random Harvest*.

1939: †*Sockaroo*. †*Young America Flies*. 1940: †*Susan and God (GB: The Gay Mrs Trexel)*. †*River's End*. †*The Man Who Talked Too Much*. †*Sante Fé Trail*. †*Money and the Woman*. 1941: †*Here Comes Happiness*. †*Strawberry Blonde*. †*Scattergood Pulls the Strings*. †*Meet John Doe*. †*Three Sons o' Guns*. 1942: †*Escape from Crime (participation disputed)*. *Dr Gillespie's New Assistant*. *The Big Shot*. *Andy Hardy's Double Life*. *Tish*. *Random Harvest*. 1943: *Young Ideas*. *Assignment in Brittany*. *Song of Russia*. *Keep Your Powder Dry (released 1945)*. *The Sign of the Ram*.

†*As Suzanne Carnahan*

PETTET, Joanna 1944–
Fair-haired British-born actress, raised in Canada, who created some glowingly real characters and rose to stardom in Hollywood films. Recent decades have seen her mainly on TV. Married actor Alex Cord (A. Viespi, 1931–) in 1973, but the couple later divorced.

1966: *The Group*. *The Night of the Generals*. 1967: *Casino Royale*. *Robbery*. 1968: *Blue*. *The Best House in London*. 1972: *Footsteps (TV)*. *The Delphi Bureau (TV)*. *The Weekend Nun (TV)*. 1973: *Pioneer Woman (TV)*. *Welcome to Arrow Beach (US: Tender Flesh)*. 1974: *A Cry in the Wilderness (TV)*. 1975: *The Desperate Miles (TV)*. 1976: *The Hancocks (TV)*. *The Dark Side of Innocence (TV)*. 1977: *Sex and the Married Woman (TV)*. 1978: *Cry of the Innocent (TV)*. *The Evil*. 1979: *An Eye for an Eye*. 1980: *The Return of Frank Cannon (TV)*. 1982: *Double Exposure*. *Othello the Black Commando*. 1985: *Sweet Country*. 1990: *Terror in Paradise*.

PFEIFFER, Michelle 1957–
Delicately slinky blonde American actress with svelte figure and upcurled mouth who flitted around for a long time in semi-star roles in films before suddenly becoming an above-the-title name in the late 1980s. One of the current cinema's best-groomed actresses, her acting range has widened noticeably in recent times, giving rise to Academy Award nominations for her performances in *Dangerous Liaisons*, *The Fabulous Baker Boys* and *Love Field*.

1979: *Falling in Love Again*. *The Solitary Man (TV)*. 1980: *Hollywood Knights*. *Charlie Chan and the Curse of the Dragon Queen*. 1981: *Splendor in the Grass (TV)*. *The Children Nobody Wanted (TV)*. *Callie and Son (TV)*. 1982: *Grease 2*. 1983: *Scarface*. 1985: *Lady-Hawke*. *Into the Night*. *Sweet Liberty*. 1986: *Amazon Women on the Moon*. *Power, Passion and Murder (TV)*. 1987: *The Witches of Eastwick*. 1988: *Tequila Sunrise*. *Dangerous Liaisons*. *Married to the Mob*. 1989: *The Fabulous Baker Boys*. 1990: *The Russia House*. 1991: *Frankie & Johnny*. 1992: *Love Field*. *Batman Returns*. 1993: *The Age of Innocence*. 1994: *Wolf*. 1995: *Dangerous Minds*. 1996: *Up Close & Personal*. *To Gillian on Her 37th Birthday*. *One Fine Day*. 1997: *A Thousand Acres*. *The Prince of Egypt (voice only)*. 1998: *The Deep End of the Ocean*. 1999: *A Midsummer Night's Dream*. *The Story of Us*. 2000: *What Lies Beneath*.

PHILIPE, Gérard 1922–1959
Dark, dashing, romantic French actor with sensitively handsome features, the foremost young leading man of the post-war French theatre and cinema. Although he generated warmth from the screen, and could turn his

hand as easily to soulful, sometimes tragic heroes as to swashbuckling amorous adventurers, Philipe had still not quite reached international stardom at the time of his early death from a heart attack.

1943: *Les petites du Quai aux Fleurs*. 1945: *La boîte aux rêves*. *Schéma d'un identification*. *Le pays sans étoiles*. 1946: *L'idiot*. *Ouvert pour cause d'inventaire*. 1947: *Le diable au corps* (US: *Devil in the Flesh*). 1948: *La chartreuse de Parme*. 1949: *Une si jolie petite plage* (US: *Riptide*). *Tous les chemins mênent à Rome* (GB and US: *All Roads Lead to Rome*). 1950: *Juliette, ou la clé des songes*. *La beauté du diable* (GB: *Beauty and the Beast*. US: *Beauty and the Devil*). *La ronde*. *Souvenirs perdus* (GB: *Lost Property*). 1951: *Fanfan la tulipe*. 1952: *Les belles de nuit* (US: *Beauties of the Night*). *Les sept péchés capitaux* (GB and US: *The Seven Deadly Sins*). 1953: *Villa Borghese* (US: *It Happened in the Park*). *Les orgueilleux* (GB: *The Proud Ones*. US: *The Proud and the Beautiful*). *Si Versailles m'était conté* (GB: *Versailles*. US: *Royal Affaires in Versailles*). 1954: *Knave of Hearts* (France: *Monsieur Ripois*. US: *Lovers, Happy Lovers*). *Le rouge et le noir*. 1955: *Si Paris nous était conté*. *La meilleure part*. *Les grandes manoeuvres/ Summer Manoeuvres*. 1956: *Les aventures de Till l'espiègle* (GB: *Till Eulenspiegel*. US: *Bold Adventure*). 1957: *Pot-bouille*. *Montparnasse 19* (GB: *Lovers of Montparnasse*. US: *Modigliani of Montparnasse*). 1958: *La vie à deux*. *Le joueur/The Gambler*. 1959: *Les liaisons dangereuses*. *Los ambiciosos* (US: *Republic of Sin*).

PHILLIPPE, Ryan
(Matthew R. Phillippe) 1974–

Curly-haired, crisply spoken American actor with boyish, faintly cruel-looking facial features who sought a good variety of twentysomething roles in the late 1990s. He first attracted attention as daytime TV's first gay teenager in the soap series *One Life to Live*, and was attracting star film roles by his early twenties. Married to actress Reese Witherspoon (*qv*), he pronounces his surname Phillippay.

1993: *A Perry Mason Mystery: The Case of the Grimacing Governor* (TV). 1994: *Deadly Invasion/Deadly Invasion: The Killer Bee Nightmare* (TV). 1995: *Crimson Tide*. 1996: *White Squall*. *Invader/Lifeform*. 1997: *I Know What You Did Last Summer*. *Nowhere*. 1998: *54*. *Little Boy Blue*. *Homegrown*. *Playing by Heart*. 1999: *Cruel Intentions*.

2000: *Company Man*. *The Way of the Gun*. *Antitrust*.

PHILLIPS, Conrad 1927–

Dark, bequiffed British actor of whippy build and earnest manner. After a few small roles in the early years of his film career, he became probably the last steadily-employed star of British second features from 1957 to 1966, also making a successful TV series, *William Tell*.

1948: *The Gentlemen Go By*. *A Song for Tomorrow*. 1949: *The Temptress*. 1950: *Lilli Marlene*. 1952: *The Last Page* (US: *Manbait*). *It Started in Paradise*. 1953: *Mantrap* (US: *Woman in Hiding*). *The Case of Express Delivery*. 1954: *Johnny on the Spot*. 1955: *Triple Blackmail*. 1956: *The Secret Tent*. *No Road Back*. 1957: *Strangers' Meeting*. *Zarak*. 1958: *A Question of Adultery*. 1959: *The White Trap*. *The Desperate Man*. *Witness in the Dark*. 1960: *Circus of Horrors*. *Sons and Lovers*. *No Love for Johnnie*. 1961: *The Shadow of the Cat*. *The Secret Partner*. *The Fourth Square*. *Murder She Said*. 1962: *The Durant Affair*. *Dead Man's Evidence*. *Don't Talk to Strange Men*. *A Guy Called Caesar*. 1963: *Impact*. *Heavens Above!* *The Switch*. 1964: *Stopover Forever*. 1965: *The Murder Game*. *Dateline Diamonds*. 1966: *Who Killed the Cat?* 1967: *The Ghost of Monk's Island* (serial).

PHILLIPS, Leslie 1923–

Blond British actor with military voice and foxy laugh, in show business from childhood, but not at all well known in films until he brought his successful impersonation of the moustachioed sheep in wolf's clothing (nurtured in radio's very successful *The Navy*

Lark) to the screen in the late fifties. Then enjoyed a very popular run of star parts until 1966 when a cropper with a dramatic role in *Maroc 7* temporarily slowed his career. Married (2nd) to actress Angela Scoular.

1935: *A Lassie from Lancashire*. 1938: *The Citadel*. 1939: *The Four Feathers*. 1943: *Rhythm Serenade*. 1949: *Train of Events*. 1950: *The Woman with No Name* (US: *Her Paneled Door*). 1951: *Pool of London*. *The Galloping Major*. 1952: *The Sound Barrier* (US: *Breaking the Sound Barrier*). 1953: *The Fake*. *The Limping Man*. *Time Bomb* (US: *Terror on a Train*). *You Know What Sailors Are*. 1955: *The Price of Greed*. *Value for Money*. *The Gamma People*. *As Long As They're Happy*. 1956: *The Big Money*. *Brothers in Law*. 1957: *The Barretts of Wimpole Street*. *The Smallest Show on Earth*. *Just My Luck*. *Les Girls*. *High Flight*. 1958: *I Was Monty's Double*. *The Man Who Liked Funerals*. 1959: *Carry on Nurse*. *Ferdinand of Naples*. *The Angry Hills*. *This Other Eden*. *Carry on Teacher*. *Please Turn Over*. *The Night We Dropped a Clanger* (US: *Make Mine a Double*). *The Navy Lark*. 1960: *Inn for Trouble*. *Watch Your Stern*. *Carry on Constable*. *Doctor in Love*. *No Kidding* (US: *Beware of Children*). 1961: *Raising the Wind*. *A Weekend with Lulu*. *In the Doghouse*. *Very Important Person* (US: *A Coming Out Party*). 1962: *Crooks Anonymous*. *The Longest Day*. *The Fast Lady*. 1963: *Father Came Too*. 1965: *You Must Be Joking!* 1966: *Doctor in Clover*. *Zabaglione*. *Maroc 7*. 1970: *Some Will, Some Won't*. *Doctor in Trouble*. 1971: *The Magnificent Seven Deadly Sins*. 1972: *Not Now Darling*. 1973: *Don't Just Lie There, Say Something!* 1975: *Spanish Fly*. 1976: *Not Now, Comrade*. 1979: *The Lion, the Witch and the Wardrobe* (TV. Voice only). 1985: *Out of Africa*. 1986: *Monte Carlo* (TV). 1987: *Empire of the Sun*. 1988: *Scandal*. 1989: *Mountains of the Moon*. 1990: *King Ralph*. 1992: *Carry On Columbus*. 1993: *Bermuda Grace* (TV). 1996: *August*. *The Canterville Ghost* (TV). 1997: *Caught in the Act*. *The Jackal*. 1999: *Mad Cows*. 2000: *Saving Grace*.

PHILLIPS, Lou Diamond (L. D. Upchurch) 1962–

Tall, sullen-looking, dark-skinned, beanpole-slim, Philippines-born actor of mixed heritage. In the Hollywood of 40 years before, he would have been doomed to playing Red Indians, but, although a few native Americans have crept into his CV, after overnight success as the star of *La Bamba*, he's been able to find a satisfying range of roles, albeit sometimes on video. He also writes screenplays, teaches acting techniques and has toured with his own band. Although dubbed in *La Bamba*, he is a reputable singer, and in 1996 undertook a stage run of *The King and I*, scoring a notable personal success.

1984: *Angel Alley. Time Bomb* (TV). *Interface.* 1986: *Harley.* 1987: *Dakota. Trespasses* (completed 1983). *The Three Kings* (TV). *La Bamba.* 1988: *Stand and Deliver. Young Guns. Disorganized Crime.* 1989: *Renegades.* 1990: *The First Power. A Show of Force. Young Guns II.* 1991: *Ambition. The Dark Wind/Cocaine Fever. Agaguk/Shadow of the Wolf.* 1993: *Extreme Justice/S.I.S.* (originally for cinemas, but released on cable TV). †*Dangerous Touch.* 1994: *Teresa's Tattoo.* †*Sioux City* (later on video as *Ultimate Revenge*). *Boulevard* (TV). 1995: *Undertow. Hourglass.* 1996: *Courage Under Fire.* 1998: *The Big Hit. Another Day in Paradise.* 1999: *Supernova. Brokedown Palace. Bats. In a Class of His Own* (TV). 2000: *Hangman. Picking Up the Pieces. A Better Way to Die.*

†*And directed*

PHOENIX, River 1970–1993

Snub-nosed, light-haired, earnest-looking stocky American actor who became prime fan-club bait in the late 1980s. The son of one-time missionaries for a small religious sect, he grew up travelling in South and Central America before the family settled in California. Acting from his early teens, he was an Academy Award nominee for *Running on Empty*. But his career came to an abrupt conclusion when he collapsed and died from a cocaine/heroin overdose. He had acting brothers and sisters called Leaf (now Joaquin), Rainbow (Rain), Summer and Liberty.

1985: *Surviving* (TV). *Explorers.* 1986: *The Mosquito Coast. Circle of Violence: A Family Drama* (TV). *Stand by Me.* 1987: *A Night in the Life of Jimmy Reardon* (GB: *Jimmy Reardon*). *Little Nikita* (GB: TV, in abridged form, as *The Sleepers*). 1988: *Running on Empty.* 1989: *Indiana Jones and the Last Crusade.* 1990: *I Love You to Death.* 1991: *Dogfight. My Own Private Idaho.* 1992: *Sneakers.* 1993: *Silent Tongue. The Thing Called Love.* 1994: *Dark Blood* (unfinished).

PICKFORD, Mary
(Gladys Smith) 1892–1979

Canadian-born star with fluffy fair hair who made her stage debut at five before becoming Hollywood's most famous silent screen actress and 'America's Sweetheart'. Wildly popular in little-girl roles, which she was still playing when past 30. Formed United Artists with Chaplin and Douglas Fairbanks Snr. in 1919, and revealed herself as a formidable business-woman, retiring in 1933 (after an Oscar for *Coquette* in 1929) to concentrate on being a production executive. Married to Owen Moore (1886–1939) from 1909 to 1915, Fairbanks from 1920 to 1936 and Charles 'Buddy' Rogers (1904–1999) from 1937 on. Became a recluse in later years. Special Oscar 1975. Died after a stroke.

1909: *Through the Breakers. Two Memories. Her First Biscuits. The Violin Maker of Cremona. The Son's Return. The Peach Basket Hat. The Necklace. The Country Doctor. The Lonely Villa. The Faded Lilies. The Way of Man. The Mexican Sweethearts. The Cardinal's Conspiracy. The Seventh Day. Sweet and Twenty. They Would Elope. His Wife's Visitor. The Sealed Room. The Little Darling. The Renunciation. A Strange Meeting. The Slave. The Indian Runner's Romance. Oh! Uncle. 1776. In Old Kentucky. The Broken Locket. The Awakening. The Gibson Goddess. His Lost Love. The Light That Came. The Mountaineer's Honor. The Test. Getting Even. What's Your Hurry? The Little Teacher. In the Watches of the Night. The Restoration. A Midnight Adventure. The Trick That Failed. To Save Her Soul.* 1910: *All on Account of the Milk. The Englishman and the Girl. The Thread of Destiny. The Smoker. A Rich Revenge. May and December. The Unchanging Sea. The Woman from Mellon's. The Newlyweds. The Twisted Trail. As It Is in Life. A Romance of the Western Hills. Never Again! Love Among the Roses. Ramona. A Victim of Jealousy. Muggsy's First Sweetheart. The Call to Arms. The Two Brothers. In the Season of Buds. A Child's Impulse. What the Daisy Said. An Arcadian Maid. Muggsy Becomes a Hero. The Sorrows of the Unfaithful. When We Were in Our Teens. Wilful Peggy. Examination Day at School. A Gold Necklace. Waiter No. 5. Lines of White on a Sullen Sea. A Lucky Toothache. Simple Charity. The Masher. The Song of the Wildwood Flute. A Plain Song.* 1911: *White Roses. The Italian Barber. A Decree of Destiny. The Dream. At the Duke's Command. While the Cat's Away.*

Artful Kate. The Message in the Bottle. When a Man Loves. Three Sisters. The First Misunderstanding. Maid or Man. The Mirror. Her Darkest Hour. A Manly Man. The Fishermaid. In Old Madrid. The Stampede. The Fair Dentist. Back to the Soil. The Master and the Man. For the Queen's Honor. Sweet Memories of Yesterday. Second Sight. For Her Brother's Sake. In the Sultan's Garden. Conscience. Her Awakening. The Lighthouse Keeper. A Gasoline Engagement. At a Quarter of Two (GB: *At a Quarter to Two*). *Science. The Skating Bug. The Call of the Song. The Toss of a Coin. The Sentinel Asleep. The Better Way. His Dress Shirt. 'Tween Two Loves. The Rose's Story. From the Bottom of the Sea. The Courting of Mary. Love Heeds Not the Showers. Little Red Riding Hood. The Caddy's Dream.* 1912: *Honor Thy Father. The Female of the Species. Won by a Fish. A Lodging for the Night. Home Folks. The Schoolteacher and the Waif. A Pueblo Legend, The Inner Circle. Friends. A Feud in the Kentucky Hills. My Baby. The Unwelcome Guest. The Mender of Nets. Iola's Promise. Fate's Interception. Just Like a Woman. The Old Actor. A Beast at Bay. Lena and the Geese. An Indian Summer. The Narrow Road. With the Enemy's Help. So Near, Yet So Far. The One She Loved. The Informer. The New York Hat.* 1913: †*In the Bishop's Carriage.* †*Caprice.* 1914: †*A Good Little Devil.* †*Tess of the Storm Country.* †*Hearts Adrift.* †*The Eagle's Mate.* †*Such a Little Queen.* †*Behind the Scenes.* †*Cinderella.* 1915: †*Fanchon the Cricket.* †*Mistress Nell.* †*The Dawn of Tomorrow.* †*Little Pal.* †*Rags.* †*Esmeralda.* †*A Girl of Yesterday.* †*Madam Butterfly.* 1916: †*The Foundling.* †*Poor Little Peppina.* †*Hulda from Holland.* †*The Eternal Grind.* †*Less Than the Dust.* 1917: †*The Pride of the Clan.* †*Poor Little Rich Girl.* †*A Romance of the Redwoods.* †*The Little American.* †*Rebecca of Sunnybrook Farm.* †*A Little Princess.* 1918: †*Stella Maris.* †*Amarilly of Clothes Line Alley.* †*M'Liss.* †*How Could You, Jean?* *One Hundred Per Cent American.* †*Johanna Enlists.* 1919: †*Daddy Long Legs.* †*Captain Kidd Junior.* †*The Hoodlum* (GB: *The Ragamuffin*). †*The Heart o' the Hills.* 1920: †*Pollyanna.* †*Suds.* 1921: †*Little Lord Fauntleroy.* †*The Love Light.* †*Through the Back Door.* 1922: †*Tess of the Storm Country* (remake). 1923: †*Rosita.* 1924: †*Dorothy Vernon of Haddon Hall.* 1925: †*Little Annie Rooney.* 1926: †*Sparrows* (GB: *Human Sparrows*). 1927: †*My Best Girl.* †*The Gaucho.* †*The Kiss of Mary Pickford* (US: *Mary Pickford's Kiss*). 1929: *The Voice of Hollywood No 7.* †*Coquette.* †*The Taming of the Shrew.* 1931: *Screen Snapshots No. 4.* †*Kiki.* 1932: *Hollywood on Parade No. 4.* 1933: †*Secrets. Hollywood on Parade No. 12. Hollywood on Parade No. 17.* 1935: *Star Night at the Cocoanut Grove.* 1940: *Chinese Garden Festival.* 1942: *White House of Hollywood.*

All shorts except †*features*

PIDGEON, Walter 1897–1984

Very tall, dark, conservative-looking Canadian-born actor who started as a singer (and played in some early musicals). His career was going nowhere when he signed an M-G-M contract

at 40, and stayed with them for exactly 20 years, his pipe-and-slippers image boosting him to stardom in the war years when he starred opposite Greer Garson (*qv*) in a series of artfully-contrived box-office smashes. His deep voice stayed with us in character roles until 1977, when he retired at 80 after 53 filming years. Died after a series of strokes. Received Academy Award nominations for *Mrs Miniver* and *Madame Curie*.

1925: Mannequin. 1926: Old Loves and New. The Outsider. Miss Nobody. Marriage License (GB: The Pelican). 1927: The Gorilla. Heart of Salome. The Girl from Rio (GB: Lola). Thirteenth Juror. 1928: Turn Back the Hours (GB: The Badge of Courage). The Gateway of the Moon. Woman Wise. Melody of Love. Clothes Make the Woman. 1929: A Most Immoral Lady. Her Private Life. 1930: Sweet Kitty Bellairs. Bride of the Regiment (GB: Lady of the Rose). Viennese Nights. Show Girl in Hollywood. 1931: Kiss Me Again (GB: The Toast of the Legion). Hot Heiress. Going Wild. The Gorilla (remake). 1932: Rockabye. 1933: The Kiss before the Mirror. 1934: Journal of a Crime. 1935: *Good Badminton. 1936: Big Brown Eyes. Fatal Lady. 1937: As Good As Married. Girl Overboard. A Girl with Ideas. She's Dangerous. Saratoga. My Dear Miss Aldrich. 1938: The Shopworn Angel. Man-Proof. Listen, Darling. Girl of the Golden West. Too Hot to Handle. 1939: Society Lawyer. Stronger Than Desire. 6,000 Enemies. Nick Carter, Master Detective. 1940: Sky Murder. The Dark Command. It's a Date. The House across the Bay. Phantom Raiders. *Chinese Garden Festival. 1941: How Green Was My Valley. Man Hunt. Blossoms in the Dust. *Variety Reel. Flight Command. Design for Scandal. 1942: Mrs Miniver. White Cargo. 1943: The Youngest Profession. Madame Curie. 1944: Mrs Parkington. 1945: Weekend at the Waldorf. 1946: Holiday in Mexico. The Secret Heart. 1947: If Winter Comes. Cass Timberlane. 1948: Julia Misbehaves. Command Decision. 1949: The Red Danube. That Forsyte Woman (GB: The Forsyte Saga). 1950: The Miniver Story. 1951: Soldiers Three. The Unknown Man. Calling Bulldog Drummond. Quo Vadis (narrator only). 1952: The Sellout. Million Dollar Mermaid (GB: The One Piece Bathing Suit). The Bad and the Beautiful. 1953: Scandal at Scourie. 1954: The Last Time I Saw Paris. Men of the Fighting Lady. Deep in My Heart. Executive Suite. 1955: Hit the Deck. The Glass Slipper (narrator only). 1956: Forbidden

Planet. The Rack. These Wilder Years. 1959: Meet Me in St Louis (TV). 1961: Voyage to the Bottom of the Sea. 1962: Advise and Consent. Big Red. The Two Colonels. 1963: Il giorno piu corto commedia umaristica (US: The Shortest Day). 1966: How I Spent My Summer Vacation (TV. GB: cinemas as Deadly Roulette). 1967: Cosa Nostra: an Arch Enemy of the FBI (TV. GB: cinemas). Warning Shot. 1968: Funny Girl. 1969: Rascal (narrator only). The Vatican Affair. 1970: The House on Greenapple Road (TV). The Mask of Sheba (TV). 1971: The Screaming Woman (TV). 1972: Skyjacked. 1973: Harry Never Holds (GB: Harry in Your Pocket). The Neptune Factor. 1974: The Girl on the Late, Late Show (TV). The Yellow Headed Summer. Live Again, Die Again (TV). 1975: You Lie So Deep, My Love (TV). Won Ton Ton, the Dog Who Saved Hollywood. Murder on Flight 502 (TV). 1976: The Lindbergh Kidnapping Case (TV). Mayday at 40,000 Feet (TV. GB: cinemas). Two-Minute Warning. 1977: Sextette.

PILBREAM, Nova
(Margery Pilbream) 1919–

Yet another example of an immensely talented child/teenage actress who never quite made it as an adult star. This silky-haired petite blonde girl's first three performances were her best; after that, her upper-class personality (and marriage to young director Pen Tennyson, tragically killed in 1941) seemed to prevent her acting style moving with the times.

1934: Little Friend. The Man Who Knew Too Much. 1936: Tudor Rose (US: Nine Days a Queen). 1937: Young and Innocent (US: The Girl Was Young). 1939: Cheer Boys Cheer. 1940: Pastor Hall. Spring Meeting. 1941: Banana Ridge. 1942: The Next of Kin. 1943: The Yellow Canary. 1944: Out of Chaos. *Men of Science. 1946: This Man is Mine. 1947: Green Fingers. 1948: The Three Weird Sisters. Counterblast.

PISIER, Marie-France
(Claudia Chauchat) 1944–

Born in Indochina (now Vietnam) and raised in New Caledonia, this small, pretty French brunette hardly caused a ripple on the international scene until she was past 30. Then the worldwide exposure of *Céline et Julie vont en bateau* and *Cousin cousine* (she won a French Oscar for the latter) took her to Hollywood to make (the, as it turned out, disastrous) *The Other Side of Midnight.*

Although that more or less concluded the American connection, her standing in France remained intact on her return. Turned writer, then director, in the late 1980s.

1961: Qui ose nous accuser? 1962: Les saints nitouches (GB: Wild Living). L'amour à vingt ans (GB and US: Love at Twenty). Les amoureux de France. 1963: La mort d'un tueur. Young Girls of Good Families. 1964: Les yeux cernés. Le vampire de Dusseldorf. 1966: Trans-Europ-Express. No sta bene rubare il tesoro. 1967: Baisers volés (GB and US: Stolen Kisses). L'écume des jours. 1968: Nous n'irons plus au bois. 1969: Paulina s'en va. 1971: Le journal d'un suicide. Féminin, féminin. 1974: Céline et Julie vont en bateau (GB and US: Celine and Julie Go Boating). Souvenirs d'en France (GB and US: French Provincial). 1975: Cousin cousine. Sérail. 1976: Barocco. Le corps de mon ennemi. 1977: The Other Side of Midnight. Les apprentis sorciers. 1978: L'amour en fuite (GB and US: Love on the Run). The Brontë Sisters. 1979: French Postcards. 1980: Miss Right (originally begun in 1978). Le banquière. 44, ou les récits de la nuit (released 1985). 1981: The Hot Touch. Chanel solitaire. 1982: Der Zauberberg (US: The Magic Mountain). Meurtres sous protection. Boulevard des assassins. L'as des as. 1983: Le prix du danger (GB and US: The Prize of Peril). Der stille Ozean (US: The Silent Ocean). L'ami de Vincent. 1985: Les nanas/The Chicks. Parking. 1986: L'inconnu de Vienne. 1987: Ou que tu sois. 1988: L'oeuvre au noire. 1991: La note bleue. 1993: François Truffaut: Portraits volés. 1994: Pourquoi Maman est dans mon lit? Tous les jours Dimanche/Seven Sundays. 1995: Le fils de Gasgogne. 1996: Marion. La gazelle. 1998: Pourquoi pas moi? 1999: La patinoire. Le temps retrouvé. 2000: Sur un air de autoroute.

As director: 1990: Le bal du gouverneur.

PITT, Brad
(William Bradley Pitt) 1963–

Fair-haired, dark-eyed, baby-faced, charismatic American actor who has fought hard to avoid the heartthrob image during his film career. Despite his clean-cut looks, he's often been seen as unkempt types since breaking through to the top in *Thelma & Louise* and *Johnny Suede*. In spite of that, his picture was still an adornment for teenage bedroom walls all over the world by the mid 1990s. Tends to overplay the soulful looks and personal charm, but undoubtedly a box-office draw. Several high-profile relationships with

star actresses have not yet resulted in a trip to the altar. Oscar nominee for *Twelve Monkeys*.
1988: *A Stoning in Fulham County (TV)*. 1989: *Cutting Class. Happy Together*. 1990: *Too Young to Die? (TV). The Image (TV)*. 1991: *Across the Tracks. Thelma & Louise. Johnny Suede. Dark Side of the Sun. The Favor (released 1994)*. 1992: *Cool World. *Contact. A River Runs Through It*. 1993: *Kalifornia. True Romance*. 1994: *Interview with the Vampire. Legends of the Fall*. 1995: *Se7en. Twelve Monkeys*. 1996: *The Hamster Factor (doc). Sleepers. Devil's Own*. 1997: *Seven Years in Tibet*. 1998: *Meet Joe Black*. 1999: *Fight Club. Being John Malkovich*. 2000: *Snatch*. 2001: *The Mexican. Ocean's 11. To the White Sea.*

PITT, Ingrid (Ingoushka Petrov) 1937–
Tawny-haired Polish actress who made her film debut in Spain (where she was appearing at the National Theatre) before popping in and out of British films with a trio of lady vampires. She made a name for herself with her ferocious interpretations of these roles, which were heavily laced with sexual content. After a lull she returned in the 1980s with character roles, typically in plunging necklines and subcutaneous trousers, and certainly as sexy as ever. Also writes novels.
1964: *El sonido prehistorico/Sound of Horror*. 1965: *The Splendour of Andalucia. Kiss in the Harbour. Doctor Zhivago*. 1966: *Chimes at Midnight (US: Falstaff). A Funny Thing Happened on the Way to the Forum*. 1968: *The Omegans. Where Eagles Dare*. 1970: *The Vampire Lovers. The House that Dripped Blood. Countess Dracula*. 1971: *Nobody Ordered Love*. 1973: *The Wicker Man*. 1975: *Where the Action Is (TV)*. 1982: *Who Dares*

Wins. 1984: *Bones (later Parker). The House (TV)*. 1985: *Wild Geese II. Underworld*. 1988: *Hanna's War*.

PLEASENCE, Donald 1919–1995
Initially distinctive, later eccentric bald-headed British character star whose pale blue eyes shone psychotically at many a harassed hero in the years following his portrayal of the murderous Dr Crippen. One of filmdom's hardest workers, especially in the early 1960s and from the late 1970s onwards, when he took to playing scientists and detectives compelled by circumstances to believe in the supernatural. The father of actress Angela Pleasence, he died following heart-valve surgery.
1954: *The Beachcomber. Orders Are Orders*. 1955: *Value for Money*. 1984: *The Black Tent*. 1956: *The Man in the Sky (US: Decision Against Time)*. 1957: *Manuela (US: Stowaway Girl). Barnacle Bill (US: All at Sea)*. 1958: *Heart of a Child. A Tale of Two Cities. The Two-Headed Spy. The Man Inside*. 1959: *Killers of Kilimanjaro. Look Back in Anger. The Battle of the Sexes. The Shakedown*. 1960: *Hell is a City. Circus of Horrors. The Flesh and the Fiends. The Big Day. Suspect. Sons and Lovers. The Hands of Orlac. A Story of David. No Love for Johnnie*. 1961: *The Wind of Change. Spare the Rod. The Horsemasters. What a Carve-Up! (US: Home Sweet Homicide)*. 1962: *Dr Crippen. The Inspector (US: Lisa)*. 1963: *The Caretaker. The Great Escape*. 1965: *The Greatest Story Ever Told. The Hallelujah Trail*. 1966: *Fantastic Voyage. Matchless. Cul-de-Sac. Eye of the Devil. The Night of the Generals*. 1967: *You Only Live Twice. Will Penny*. 1968: *Mr Freedom*. 1969: *The Madwoman of Chaillot. Arthur Arthur*. 1970: *Outback. Soldier Blue*. 1971: *The Jerusalem File. Kidnapped. The Pied Piper. THX 1138*. 1972: *Henry VIII and His Six Wives. Innocent Bystanders. Death Line*. 1973: *Wedding in White. The Rainbow Boys. The Seaweed Children. Tales That Witness Madness. From Beyond the Grave*. 1974: *The Mutations. The Black Windmill. Escape to Witch Mountain. The Count of Monte Cristo (TV. GB: cinemas). Altrimenti ci arrabiamo (GB: Watch Out, We're Mad). Barry McKenzie Holds His Own*. 1975: *Hearts of the West (GB: Hollywood Cowboy). I Don't Want to Be Born*. 1976: *The Devil's Men (US: Land of the Minotaur). Journey into Fear. The Eagle Has Landed. The Last Tycoon. Passover Plot. Trial by Combat (US: Dirty Knights' Work)*.

1977: *The Final Eye (TV). The Uncanny. Goldenrod. Blood Relatives. Oh, God! Telefon. Tomorrow Never Comes*. 1978: *The Dark Secret of Harvest Home (TV. Voice only). Devil Cat (US: Night Creature). The Defection of Simas Kudirka. Jaguar Lives. Power Play. L'ordre et la securité du monde. Good Luck, Miss Wyckoff. Halloween. Sergeant Pepper's Lonely Hearts Club Band*. 1979: *Gold of the Amazon Women (TV). Dracula. Labyrinth. L'homme en colère. Out of the Darkness (TV). All Quiet on the Western Front (TV. GB: cinemas). Better Late Than Never (TV)*. 1980: *The Puma Man. Final Eye. Blade on the Feather (TV). The Monster Club. Witch-Hunt*. 1981: *Dick Turpin (GB: TV). Halloween II. Race for the Yankee Zephyr. Escape from New York*. 1982: *Alone in the Dark. Witness for the Prosecution (TV). The Devonville Terror*. 1983: *Warrior of the Lost World (released 1985). Frankenstein's Great Aunt Tillie (released 1985). A Breed Apart. Where is Parsifal?* 1984: *To Kill a Stranger. The Treasure of the Amazon/Treasure of Doom. The Black Arrow (cable TV). The Corsican Brothers (TV)*. 1985: *Operation 'Nam. Reel Horror. Phenomena (GB: Creepers). Sotto il vestito niente (US: Nothing Underneath)*. 1986: *Pompeii (US: Warrior Queen). Honor Thy Father (TV). Rainbow Four. I Love N.Y. Vampire in Venice/Nosferatu in Venice*. 1987: *Ground Zero. Double Target. Scoop (TV). Ghosts. Urban Animals. Prince of Darkness. Gila and Rick. Specters. DeadHeat. Django Strikes Again*. 1988: *Phantom of Death. The Commander. Hanna's War. The Last Platoon. Paganini Horror. Angel Hill. Halloween IV – The Return of Michael Myers. The Great Escape: The Untold Story (TV)*. 1989: *River of Death. Buried Alive. L'avvoltoio puo attendere. Ten Little Indians. The Room. Halloween 5. American Rickshaw. The House of Usher. Casablanca Express*. 1990: *The Raven*. 1991: *Shadows and Fog. Milliardi (Billions). The Great Kandinsky (TV)*. 1992: *Diên Biên Phu*. 1993: *The Hour of the Pig. Femme Fatale (TV). The Big Freeze (unreleased). G.A.M.M.A. Force (voice only)*. 1995: *Safe Haven. Halloween 6: The Curse of Michael Myers*.

PLESHETTE, Suzanne 1937–
Tremendously talented, dark-haired American actress with bedroom smile, sad eyes and sub-surface smoulder. She made it in the movies at her second attempt but later made

some unfortunate choices of script, mainly in rampant melodrama. She was more successful in roles that revealed her zany sense of comedy. Married to Troy Donahue (*qv*) for a few months in 1964. Since remarried, she also now designs sheets and bedwear. Widowed in 2000.
1958: Marjorie Morningstar. The Geisha Boy. 1962: 40 Pounds of Trouble. Rome Adventure (GB: Lovers Must Learn). 1963: Wall of Noise. The Birds. 1964: A Distant Trumpet. Fate is the Hunter. Youngblood Hawke. 1965: A Rage to Live. The Adventures of Bullwhip Griffin (released 1967). Mr Buddwing (GB: Woman Without a Face). 1966: Nevada Smith. The Ugly Dachshund. 1967: Wings of Fire (TV). The Power. 1968: Blackbeard's Ghost. 1969: If It's Tuesday, This Must Be Belgium. How To Make It (GB: Target: Harry). Along Came a Spider (TV). 1970: River of Gold (TV). Hunters Are for Killing (TV). Suppose They Gave a War and Nobody Came. 1971: Support Your Local Gunfighter. In Broad Daylight (TV). A Capitol Affair (TV). 1975: The Legend of Valentino (TV). Beyond the Bermuda Triangle (TV). 1976: The Shaggy DA. Law and Order (TV). 1978: Kate Bliss and the Ticker Tape Kid (TV). 1979: Hot Stuff. Flesh and Blood (TV). 1980: Oh, God! Book II. If Things Were Different (TV). Studio Murders/ Fantasies (TV). 1982: Help Wanted: Male (TV). 1983: DIXIE: Changing Habits (TV). One Cooks, The Other Doesn't (TV). 1984: For Love or Money (TV). 1985: Kojak: The Belarus File (TV). 1987: A Stranger Waits (TV). 1988: Alone in the Neon Jungle/Command in Hell (TV). 1990: Leona Helmsley: Queen of Mean (TV). 1991: Battling for Baby (TV). 1993: A Twist of the Knife (TV). 1998: The Lion King II: Simba's Pride (video, voice only).

PLUMMER, Christopher
(Arthur C. Plummer) 1927–
Finely-boned Canadian actor, a more handsome version of Peter Cushing (*qv*). His sharp features proved equally adaptable to kindliness, literacy, nobility and psychotic villainy. Married/divorced actress Tammy Grimes. Later married English actress Elaine Taylor. Came late to films, although a regular performer on American TV from 1953. Very busy in the 1980s and beyond. Father of actress Amanda Plummer (1957–).
*1958: Wind Across the Everglades. Stage Struck. 1962: The Fall of the Roman Empire. *Trans-Canada Journey (narrator only). 1965: The Sound of Music. Inside Daisy Clover. 1966: The Night of the Generals. Triple Cross. 1967:*

Oedipus the King. 1968: Nobody Runs Forever. 1969: Lock Up Your Daughters! Battle of Britain. The Royal Hunt of the Sun. 1970: Waterloo. 1973: The Pyx. 1974: The Return of the Pink Panther. 1975: Conduct Unbecoming. The Man Who Would Be King. The Spiral Staircase. 1976: Assassination! (US: The Day That Shook the World). Aces High. 1977: Uppdraget (GB: The Assignment). 1978: The Silent Partner. Sherlock Holmes: Murder by Decree (GB: Murder by Decree). International Velvet. The Disappearance. 1979: Hanover Street. Arthur Miller – on Home Ground. Starcrash. RIEL. 1980: Highpoint. Eyewitness (GB: The Janitor). Desperate Voyage (TV). Somewhere in Time. The Shadow Box (TV). 1981: Being Different (narrator only). Dial M for Murder (TV). When the Circus Came to Town (TV). 1982: The Amateur. Little Gloria – Happy at Last (TV). 1983: The Scarlet and the Black (TV). Játszani Kell/Lily in Love/Fitz and Lily. Dreamscape. Prototype (TV). 1984: Ordeal by Innocence. 1985: The Boy in Blue. 1986: An American Tail (voice only). The Boss's Wife. Vampires in Venice/ Nosferatu in Venice. 1987: Dragnet. Spearfield's Daughter. I Love N.Y. A Hazard of Hearts (TV). Souvenir. 1988: Stage Fright. Shadow Dancing. Light Years (voice only). 1989: Mind Field. Where the Heart Is. Kingsgate. 1990: The Dispossessed. Rock-a-Doodle (voice only). Firehead. Red-Blooded American Girl. A Ghost in Monte Carlo (TV). 1991: Bump in the Night (TV). Delusion. Star Trek VI: The Undiscovered Country. A Marriage (TV). Money. The First Circle. Liar's Edge. 1992: Danielle Steel's Secrets (TV). A Stranger in the Mirror (TV). Impolite. Malcolm X. 1994: Wolf. 1995: Dolores Claiborne. Kurt Vonnegut's Harrison Bergeron (TV). Twelve Monkeys. 1996: Crackerjack. Conspiracy of Fear (completed 1994). We the Jury. Skeletons. 1997: An American Affair. The Arrow (TV). 1998: Byron. Blackheart. Winchell (TV). Hidden Agenda. The Clown at Midnight. 1999: All the Fine Lines. The Insider. 2000: Possessed. 2001: Dracula 2000. Lucky Break.

POITIER, Sidney 1927–
Imposingly good-looking black American actor – the first to attract international audiences as a leading man. Although he broke down few actual barriers, he brought dignity to the portrayal of the black man on screen and, more important, played several roles that might have easily been portrayed by a white man. As an actor, most interesting

when being less than saintly; as a director, rather dull. Academy Award for *Lilies of the Field*. Married actress Joanna Shimkus (1943–) in 1976 after the couple had lived together for six years: his second marriage. Also Oscar-nominated for *The Defiant Ones*.
1949: From Whence Cometh My Help. 1950: No Way Out. 1951: Cry the Beloved Country. 1952: Red Ball Express. 1954: Go Man Go! 1955: Blackboard Jungle. 1956: Goodbye My Lady. Edge of the City (GB: A Man is Ten Feet Tall). 1957: Band of Angels. Something of Value. 1958: Mark of the Hawk. The Defiant Ones. Virgin Island/Our Virgin Island. 1959: Porgy and Bess. 1960: All the Young Men. 1961: A Raisin in the Sun. Paris Blues. 1962: Pressure Point. 1963: Lilies of the Field. The Long Ships. 1965: The Greatest Story Ever Told. The Bedford Incident. The Slender Thread. A Patch of Blue. 1966: Duel at Diablo. To Sir, with Love. 1967: In the Heat of the Night. Guess Who's Coming to Dinner. 1968: For Love of Ivy. 1969: The Lost Man. 1970: Brother John. They Call Me MISTER Tibbs! King: A Filmed Record . . . Montgomery to Memphis. 1971: The Organisation. Buck and the Preacher. 1973: A Warm December. 1974: Uptown Saturday Night. The Wilby Conspiracy. 1975: Let's Do It Again. 1977: A Piece of the Action. 1987: Little Nikita (GB: TV, in abridged form, as The Sleepers). 1988: Shoot to Kill (GB: Deadly Pursuit). Separate But Equal (TV). 1992: Sneakers. 1995: Children of the Dust (TV). Wild Bill: Hollywood Maverick. 1996: To Sir, with Love II (TV). 1997: The Jackal. Mandela and de Klerk (TV). 1998: David and Lisa (TV). Park Day. 1999: True Crime. Free of Eden (TV). The Simple Life of Noah Dearborn (TV).
As director: *1971: Buck and the Preacher. 1973: A Warm December. 1974: Uptown Saturday Night. 1975: Let's Do It Again. 1977: A Piece of the Action. 1980: Stir Crazy. 1982: Hanky Panky. 1984: Shootout. 1985: Fast Forward. 1989: Ghost Dad.*

PORTMAN, Eric 1903–
Light-haired British actor with incisive, slightly reedy voice. Rose to stardom in the forties as forthright, hard-headed, occasionally vindictive characters who reflected some of his own Yorkshire bluntness. His image mellowed as he grew into a character actor, but in his last film he was back to his calculating best. Died from a heart ailment.
1933: The Girl from Maxim's. 1935: Abdul the Damned. Old Roses. Maria Marten, or:

Murder in the Red Barn. Hyde Park Corner. 1936: The Cardinal. The Crimes of Stephen Hawke. Hearts of Humanity. The Prince and the Pauper. 1937: Moonlight Sonata. 1941: 49th Parallel. 1942: Uncensored. One of Our Aircraft is Missing. Squadron Leader X. 1943: We Dive at Dawn. Millions Like Us. Escape to Danger. 1944: A Canterbury Tale. 1945: *The Air Plan (narrator only). Great Day. 1946: Wanted for Murder. Men of Two Worlds. Daybreak (released 1948). 1947: Dear Murderer. The Mark of Cain. 1948: Say it with Flowers (narrator only). Corridor of Mirrors. The Blind Goddess. 1949: The Spider and the Fly. 1950: Cairo Road. 1951: The Magic Box. His Excellency. Painter and Poet (narrator only). 1952: South of Algiers (US: The Golden Mask). 1954: The Colditz Story. 1955: The Deep Blue Sea. 1956: Child in the House. 1957: The Good Companions. 1961: The Naked Edge. 1962: Freud (GB: Freud – the Secret Passion). The Man Who Finally Died. 1963: West 11. 1965: The Bedford Incident. 1966: The Spy with a Cold Nose. The Whisperers. 1967: Assignment to Kill. Deadfall.

PORTMAN, Natalie 1981–
Small, very dark-haired, Jerusalem-born Hollywood leading lady of striking, slightly exotic looks. Since an eye-catching film debut at 13, she's become more famous for the roles she's turned down (*The Ice Storm, Lolita, William Shakespeare's Romeo & Juliet, The Horse Whisperer*) than the ones she's fitted in between completing her education. She speaks fluent Hebrew, French and Japanese and says she really wants to be a doctor like her father. Her starring role in the second *Star Wars* trilogy may frustrate that ambition for a few years yet.
1994: Léon. 1995: Developing. 1996: Beautiful Girls. Mars Attacks! Everyone Says I Love You. 1998: The Prince of Egypt (voice only). 1999: Star Wars: Episode I – The Phantom Menace. Anywhere But Here. Better Living Through Circuitry. 2000: Where the Heart Is.

POSEY, Parker 1968–
Dark-haired, angularly attractive American actress with immobile smile and brittle, almost over-bright acting style. Known as the 'queen of the indies' from her appearances in leading roles of independently made films, she dropped out of her acting diploma with three weeks to go to appear for 18 months in a daytime TV soap. However, since then she has largely shied clear of the

mainstream, picking up festival awards but not many roles that the average cinemagoer actually saw.
1991: First Love, Fatal Love (TV). 1992: Joey Breaker. 1993: Dazed and Confused. Coneheads. †Sleepless in Seattle. The Wake. 1994: Sleep with Me. Mixed Nuts. Dead Connection. Opera No. 1. Amateur. 1995: Kicking and Screaming. Party Girl. The Doom Generation. Frisk. Drunks (released 1997). Flirt. The Daytrippers. 1996: Basquiat. Clockwatchers. Waiting for Guffman (released 1999). 1997: SubUrbia. The House of Yes. Dinner at Fred's (released 1999). Henry Fool. 1998: Cross Country. The Misadventures of Margaret. What Rats Won't Do. You've Got Mail. 1999: The Venice Project. 2000: Scream 3. Best in Show. Josie and the Pussycats.

†Scenes deleted from final release print

POTTER, Monica 1971–
Pretty, fragile-looking, gossamer American blonde actress, a pre-teen model and commercials actress. After early marriage and two children, she moved from Ohio to California in 1974 and began to pursue a serious acting career on TV. Films began inauspiciously with a role at the foot of the cast as 'biker's woman' in the bust comedy *Bulletproof*, but, after her performance as Nicolas Cage's wife in *Con Air*, producers began to think of her as a leading lady and she moved into more prominent roles as the century turned.
1996: Bulletproof. 1997: Heaven or Vegas. Con Air. 1998: A Cool, Dry Place. Martha – Meet Frank, Daniel and Laurence (US: The Very Thought of You). Pre/Without Limits. Patch Adams. 2000: Along Came a Spider. Head Over Heels.

POULTON, Mabel 1901–1994
Feisty, mischievous-looking, blonde London-born actress with calculating mouth and come-hither gaze. A teenage typist who turned to acting at 19, she played a couple of supporting roles in pictures starting Betty Balfour (*qv*), then became Balfour's only serious British rival at the end of the 1920s, mostly in rebellious blue-collar roles, as indicated by such titles as *The Alley Cat, The Hellcat* and *Not Quite a Lady*. Sound exposed her cockney vowel sounds and put a stop to her star career: a brief comeback in the mid 1930s was not successful.
1920: Nothing Else Matters. 1921: The Old Curiosity Shop. The God in the Garden. Mary-Find-the-Gold. 1924: *Moonbeam Magic. The Heart of an Actress. 1926: The Ball of Fortune. *Oscillation. 1927: A Daughter in Revolt. The Glad Eye (US: Kiki). 1928: The Constant Nymph. *Knights and Ladies. The Hellcat. Virginia's Husband. Palais de Danse. Not Quite a Lady. Troublesome Wives. 1929: The Alley Cat. Return of the Rat. Taxi for Two. 1930: *Star Impersonations. Children of Chance. Escape. 1931: Number Please. 1935: Pastorale (unreleased). 1936: Crown vs Stevens. Bed and Breakfast. Terror on Tiptoe. 1943: *Pandamonium.

POWELL, Dick 1904–1963
American actor with dimpled smile and light, frizzy hair who spent most of the thirties as the baby-faced crooner (most notably teamed with Ruby Keeler) in Warner Brothers musicals. Seemed washed up in the early forties but then came back (thanks to RKO) as the hero of some tough, hard-hitting and well-made thrillers. A TV regular from 1952 to 1962 in his own drama series. Married to

Joan Blondell (second of three) from 1936 to 1945 and June Allyson (both *qv*) from 1945 on. Died from lymph gland cancer.

*1931: Street Scene. 1932: Big City Blues (voice only). Too Busy to Work. Blessed Event. 1933: The King's Vacation. *The Road is Open Again. *Miss Complexion. Convention City. 42nd Street. Gold Diggers of 1933. College Coach (GB: Football Coach). Footlight Parade. 1934: Twenty Million Sweethearts. Dames. Flirtation Walk. Happiness Ahead. Wonder Bar. 1935: Gold Diggers of 1935. Broadway Gondolier. Shipmates Forever. Page Miss Glory. *A Dream Comes True. A Midsummer Night's Dream. Thanks a Million. 1936: Stage Struck. Colleen. Hearts Divided. Gold Diggers of 1937. 1937: On the Avenue. Varsity Show. The Singing Marine. Hollywood Hotel. 1938: Cowboy from Brooklyn (GB: Romance and Rhythm). *For Auld Lang Syne. Going Places. Hard to Get. 1939: Naughty But Nice. 1940: Christmas in July. I Want a Divorce. 1941: In the Navy. Model Wife. 1942: Star Spangled Rhythm. Happy Go Lucky. 1943: Riding High (GB: Melody Inn). True to Life. 1944: It Happened Tomorrow. Meet the People. 1945: Murder, My Sweet (GB: Farewell, My Lovely). Cornered. 1947: Johnny O'Clock. 1948: Pitfall. To the Ends of the Earth. Station West. Rogues' Regiment. 1949: Mrs Mike. 1950: The Reformer and the Redhead. Right Cross. Cry Danger. 1951: The Tall Target. You Never Can Tell (GB: You Never Know). Callaway Went Thataway (GB: The Star Said No). 1952: The Bad and the Beautiful. 1954: Susan Slept Here.*

As director: *1953: Split Second. 1956: The Conqueror. You Can't Run Away from It. 1957: The Enemy Below. 1958: The Hunters.*

POWELL, Eleanor 1910–1982

Dark-haired American musical star with a happy face. Eleanor Powell was the only female dancer, according to Fred Astaire, who 'put 'em down like a man'. Billed at the time as 'the world's greatest tap dancer', her fast and gutsy dancing looked relaxed and effortless, and she had a run of eight years at M-G-M. Religion later took over her life, and she became an ordained minister of the Unity Church. Married to Glenn Ford from 1943 to 1959. Died from cancer.

1935: George White's 1935 Scandals. Broadway Melody of 1936. 1936: Born to Dance. 1937: Rosalie. Broadway Melody of 1938. 1939: Honolulu. Broadway Melody of 1940. 1941: Lady Be Good. 1942: Ship Ahoy.

1943: I Dood It! (GB: By Hook or by Crook). Thousands Cheer. 1944: Sensations of 1945. 1946: The Great Morgan. 1950: Duchess of Idaho.

POWELL, Jane (Suzanne Burce) 1929–

Sweet-faced American singing star with bubbly blonde hair, the refreshing teenager who gazed at the hero from afar but eventually got him, in M-G-M musicals of the forties and fifties. Her film career suffered with the demise of the original screen musical. She married her fifth husband, former child star Dickie Moore (1925–), in 1988.

1944: Song of the Open Road. 1945: Delightfully Dangerous. 1946: Holiday in Mexico. 1948: Three Daring Daughters (GB: The Birds and the Bees). A Date with Judy. Luxury Liner. 1950: Two Weeks with Love. Nancy Goes to Rio. Royal Wedding (GB: Wedding Bells). 1951: Rich, Young and Pretty. 1953: Small Town Girl. Three Sailors and a Girl. 1954: Seven Brides for Seven Brothers. Athena. Deep in My Heart. 1955: Hit the Deck. 1957: The Girl Most Likely. 1958: The Female Animal. Enchanted Island. 1970: Wheeler and Murdoch (TV). 1972: The Letters (TV). 1976: Mayday at 40,000 Feet (TV. GB: cinemas). 1977: Tubby the Tuba (TV. Voice only).

POWELL, Robert 1944–

Charismatic British leading man with striking blue-green eyes and beguilingly modulated voice, who sprang to prominence in his early twenties (in a TV series, *Doomwatch*) and promised to be one of the few international stars produced by the British cinema of the 1970s. Films cashed in on his other-worldly qualities to cast him in several mystical roles

while, for a television epic series, Franco Zeffirelli made him *Jesus of Nazareth*. As for many another actor, the part seems to have cast something of a hoodoo on his career, for there were few box-office successes for him after that. Recently in TV comedy series.

*1967: Robbery. Far from the Madding Crowd. 1968: Joanna. 1969: The Italian Job. Walk a Crooked Path. 1971: Secrets. 1972: Running Scared. Asylum. The Asphyx (US: Horror of Death). 1974: Mahler. 1975: Tommy. 1977: Beyond Good and Evil. 1978: The Four Feathers (TV. GB: cinemas). Cocktails for Three. The Thirty-Nine Steps. 1979: The Dilessi Affair. Harlequin. 1980: *A Fair Way to Play. Jane Austen in Manhattan (TV). 1981: The Survivor. 1982: The Hunchbank of Notre Dame (TV). The Imperative. 1983: The Jigsaw Man. 1984: Secrets of the Phantom Caverns (later What Waits Below). Frankenstein (TV). 1985: Shaka Zulu (TV). 1987: D'Annunzio and I. Down There in the Jungle. 1990: Romeo-Juliet (voice only). 1991: Once on Chunuk Bair/Chunuk Bair. The First Circle. 1993: The Mystery of Edwin Drood.*

POWELL, William 1892–1984

Suave, moustachioed, droop-eyed American leading man who really hit his stride when joining M-G-M in 1934, and became the epitome of the sophisticate with a cigarette in one hand and a cocktail in the other, in a series of smartly scripted detective stories and screwball comedies, most notably the *Thin Man* series opposite oft-time screen vis-à-vis Myrna Loy. Illness unfortunately curtailed his appearances after 1940. Married to Carole Lombard 1931–1933, second of three. Was going to marry Jean Harlow at the time of her death in 1937. He received Academy Award nominations for *The Thin Man*, *My Man Godfrey* and *Life with Father*. Died from respiratory failure.

1922: When Knighthood Was in Flower. Sherlock Holmes (GB: Moriarty). Spanish Love. Outcast. 1923: The Bright Shawl. 1924: Romola. Under the Red Robe. Dangerous Money. 1925: White Mice. Too Many Kisses. The Beautiful City. Faint Perfume. My Lady's Lips. 1926: The Runaway. Sea Horses. Beau Geste. The Great Gatsby. Desert Gold. Aloma of the South Seas. Tin Gods. 1927: Special Delivery. New York. Paid to Love. Nevada. She's a Sheik. Time for Love. Senorita. Love's Greatest Mistake. 1928: Partners in Crime. Beau Sabreur. The Dragnet. Forgotten Faces. The Last Command. Feel My Pulse. The

Vanishing Pioneer. 1929: The Greene Murder Case. Interference. The Four Feathers. The Canary Murder Case. Charming Sinners. Pointed Heels. 1930: Shadow of the Law. The Benson Murder Case. Street of Chance. Paramount on Parade. Behind the Makeup. For the Defense. 1931: The Road to Singapore. Man of the World. Ladies' Man. 1932: Jewel Robbery. Lawyer Man. High Pressure. One Way Passage. 1933: Private Detective 62. The Kennel Murder Case. Double Harness. Fashions/Fashions of 1934 (GB: Fashion Follies of 1934). 1934: The Key. Manhattan Melodrama. The Thin Man. Evelyn Prentice. 1935: Escapade. Star of Midnight. Reckless. Rendezvous. 1936: My Man Godfrey. The Great Ziegfeld. The Ex Mrs Bradford. After the Thin Man. Libeled Lady. 1937: Double Wedding. The Last of Mrs Cheyney. The Emperor's Candlesticks. 1938: The Baroness and the Butler. 1939: Another Thin Man. 1940: I Love You Again. 1941: Shadow of the Thin Man. Love Crazy. 1942: Crossroads. 1943: The Heavenly Body. The Youngest Profession. 1944: The Thin Man Goes Home. Ziegfeld Follies (released 1946). 1946: The Hoodlum Saint. 1947: Song of the Thin Man. Life with Father. 1948: Mr Peabody and the Mermaid. The Senator Was Indiscreet (GB: Mr Ashton Was Indiscreet). 1949: Take One False Step. Dancing in the Dark. 1951: The Treasure of Lost Canyon. It's a Big Country. 1953: The Girl Who Had Everything. How to Marry a Millionaire. 1955: Mister Roberts.

POWER, Tyrone 1913–1958
One of those seemingly-doomed, Adonis-like leading men that Hollywood has thrown up from time to time, in a long line from Valentino to Christopher Jones. Dark hair, a flashing smile and boyish handsomeness were enough to send a *frisson* up most pre-war female spines, when Power was equally effective as ne'er-do-wells and dashing heroes. When he returned from war service, his face had hardened into earnestness and gravity and he gradually declined, dying of a heart attack on set – just like his actor father. Married to actress Annabella (*qv*), from 1939 to 1948, and Linda Christian (Bianca Welter 1923–), from 1949 to 1955 – first and second of three.
1932: Tom Brown of Culver. 1934: Flirtation Walk. 1935: Northern Frontier. 1936: Girl's Dormitory. Ladies in Love. Lloyds of London. 1937: Thin Ice (GB: Lovely to Look At). Love in News. Café Metropole. Second Honeymoon.

Ali Baba Goes to Town. 1938: Marie Antoinette. In Old Chicago. Alexander's Ragtime Band. Suez. 1939: Jesse James. The Rains Came. Rose of Washington Square. Daytime Wife. Second Fiddle. 1940: Brigham Young – Frontiersman (GB: Brigham Young). The Mark of Zorro. Johnny Apollo. 1941: Blood and Sand. A Yank in the RAF. 1942: This Above All. Son of Fury. The Black Swan. Crash Dive. 1943: *Screen Snapshots No 108. 1946: The Razor's Edge. 1947: Nightmare Alley. Captain from Castile. 1948: That Wonderful Urge. The Luck of the Irish. 1949: Prince of Foxes. 1950: The Black Rose. An American Guerilla in the Philippines (GB: I Shall Return). 1951: Rawhide. The House in the Square (US: I'll Never Forget You). 1952: Diplomatic Courier. Pony Soldier (GB: MacDonald of the Canadian Mounties). 1953: King of the Khyber Rifles. *Memories in Uniform. Mississippi Gambler. 1954: The Long Gray Line. *The Red, White and Blue Line. 1955: Untamed. 1956: The Eddy Duchin Story. 1957: Seven Waves Away (GB: Abandon Ship!). The Rising of the Moon (narrator only). Witness for the Prosecution. The Sun Also Rises.

POWERS, Mala
(Mary Ellen Powers) 1931–
Small, solid, petulant-looking American actress with red-brown hair, a sultry star in her first major film, and best employed as strong-willed central characters. Hollywood never made the most of this forte, and, forced into come-hither decoration, her career declined. A former child player.
1942: Tough As They Come. 1950: Outrage. Edge of Doom (GB: Stronger Than Fear). Cyrano de Bergerac. 1952: Rose of Cimarron. City Beneath the Sea. 1953: City That Never Sleeps. Geraldine. 1954: The Yellow Mountain. 1955: Bengazi. Rage at Dawn. 1957: The Storm Rider. Tammy and the Bachelor (GB: Tammy). Death in Small Doses. The Unknown Terror. Man on the Prowl. 1958: Sierra Baron. Colossus of New York. 1960: Flight of the Lost Balloon. The Warrior's Path (TV). Fear No More. 1967: Rogue's Gallery. Doomsday. 1969: Daddy's Gone a Hunting. 1975: Six Tickets to Hell. 1976: The Siege (TV). 1988: From Russia to Hollywood (doc. Narrator only).

POWERS, Stefanie
(Stefania Federkiewicz) 1942–
Buoyant brunette Hollywood actress with

typically American features. She looked to be a rare find in her early days, but went off the boil after marriage and a flop TV series (The Girl from UNCLE) came all in one year. Still shows flashes of that original talent, but nowadays much lost to TV rubbish. Married to actor Gary Lockwood (John G. Yusolfsky 1937–) from 1966 to 1974. Later was associated for some years with the late William Holden (qv).
1961: Tammy Tell Me True. 1962: The Young Sinner. Experiment in Terror (GB: The Grip of Fear). The Interns. If a Man Answers. 1963: McLintock! Palm Springs Weekend. 1964: The New Interns. Love Has Many Faces. 1965: Fanatic (US: Die, Die, My Darling). 1966: Stagecoach. 1967: Warning Shot. 1969: Crescendo. Man Without Mercy (later Gone With the West). Lancer (TV). 1970: The Boatniks. 1971: Ellery Queen: Don't Look Behind You (TV). Five Desperate Women (TV). Sweet Sweet Rachel (TV). Paper Man (TV). 1972: The Magnificent Seven Ride! No Place to Run (TV). Hardcase (TV). 1973: Herbie Rides Again. Shoot-Out in a One-Dog Town (TV). 1974: Manhunter (TV). Night Games (TV). Skyway to Death (TV). 1975: Sky Heist (TV). 1976: The Feather and Father Gang (TV). Return to Earth (TV). The Man Inside. It Seemed Like a Good Idea at the Time. 1977: The Astral Factor. 1978: Escape to Athena. Death in Canaan (TV). Nowhere to Run (TV). 1979: Hart to Hart (TV). 1984: Mistral's Daughter (video). Family Secrets (TV). Invisible Strangler (revised version of The Astral Factor). 1985: Deceptions (TV). 1987: Beryl Markham: A Shadow on the Sun (TV). 1989: She Was Marked for Murder (TV). Love and Betrayal (TV). Throw-Away Wives (TV). 1990: When Will I Be Loved? (TV). 1991: Night Hunt/Survive the Night (TV). 1992: The Burden of Proof (TV). 1993: Hart to Hart Returns (TV). 1994: Good King Wenceslas (TV). Hart to Hart: Home is Where the Hart Is (TV). Hart to Hart: Crimes of the Hart (TV). Hart to Hart: Old Friends Never Die (TV). 1995: Hart to Hart: Two Harts in ¾ Time (TV). Hart to Hart: Secrets of the Hart (TV). 1996: Hart to Hart: Till Death Us Do Hart (TV). Hart to Hart: Harts in High Season (TV). 1999: Someone is Watching (TV).

PRENTISS, Paula (P. Ragusa) 1939–
Gorgeous, tall, gurgle-voiced, dark-haired American actress, adept from an early age at sophisticated comedy. She seemed quite the

best thing to have hit Hollywood screens in the early sixties, but unfortunately subordinated her career to that of her husband Richard Benjamin (married 1960) and did not succeed in re-establishing herself.

1960: *Where the Boys Are*. 1961: *The Honeymoon Machine*. *Bachelor in Paradise*. 1962: *The Horizontal Lieutenant*. 1963: *Follow the Boys*. 1964: *Looking for Love*. *Man's Favorite Sport?* *The World of Henry Orient*. 1965: *What's New Pussycat?* *In Harm's Way*. 1970: *Catch 22*. *Move*. 1972: *Last of the Red Hot Lovers*. *The Couple Takes a Wife* (TV). 1974: *Crazy Joe*. *The Parallax View*. *The Stepford Wives*. 1977: *Having Babies II* (TV). 1978: *No Room to Run*. 1979: *Top of the Hill* (TV). *Friendships, Secrets and Lies* (TV). 1980: *The Black Marble*. *Lady Doctor* (TV). 1981: *Buddy Buddy*. *Saturday the 14th*. 1982: *El orgasmo y el extasis*. 1983: *Packing' It In* (TV). *MADD: Mothers Against Drunk Drivers* (TV). 1996: *Mrs Winterbourne*.

PRESLE, Micheline (M. Chassagne) 1922–
Light-haired French actress with Claudette Colbert-style personality, in films as a teenager. Briefly but unhappily in Hollywood in post-war years, she has shown up best as older women and is still busy in the French cinema more than 60 years after her debut. Billed as 'Prelle' on her first three Hollywood films. Mother of director Tonie Marshall.

1938: †*Je Chante*. †*Vous seule que j'aime*. †*Petite peste*. 1939: *Jeunes filles en détresse*. *Paradis perdu*. *Fausse alerte*. 1940: *La comédie du bonheur*. *Elles étaient douze femmes*. 1941: *Parade en sept nuits*. *Le soleil a toujours raison*. *Histoire de rire*. 1942: *La nuit fantastique*. *Félicie Nanteuil*. *La belle aventure*. 1943: *Un seul amour*. 1944: *Falbalas*. 1945: *Boule de suif*. 1946: *Le diable au corps*. 1947: *Les jeux sont faits*. *The Last Days of Pompeii*. 1948: *Tous les chemins mènent à Rome*. 1949: *Under My Skin*. 1950: *An American Guerilla in the Philippines* (GB: *I Shall Return*). *The Adventures of Captain Fabian*. 1952: *La dame aux camélias*. 1953: *Si Versailles m'était conté* (US: *Royal Affairs at Versailles*). *L'amour d'une femme*. 1954: *Casa Ricordi*. *Napoléon*. *Les amants de la Villa Borghese*. *Les impures*. *Camille*. 1955: *Treize à table*. *Béatrice Cenci*. 1956: *La mariée est trop belle* (GB and US: *The Bride is Too Beautiful*). 1957: *Les louves*. *Les femmes sont marrantes*. *Le château des amants*. 1958: *Bobosse*. *Christine*. 1959: *Une fille pour l'été* (US: *A Mistress for the Summer*). *Blind Date* (US: *Chance Meeting*). 1960: *Mistress of the World/Il mistero dei tre continenti*. *Le baron de l'écluse*. 1961: *L'amant de cinq jours*. *Les grandes personnes*. *L'assassino*. *I briganti Italiani* (GB: *Seduction of the South*). *The Seven Deadly Sins*. *Infidelity*. *La loi des hommes*. 1962: *The Devil and the 10 Commandments*. *If a Man Answers*. *Coup de bamboo*. 1963: *The Prize*. *Imperial Venus*. *Dark Purpose*. 1964: *Les pieds nickelés*. 1965: *La religieuse*. *Je vous salue Mafia* (US: *Hail Mafia*). *La chasse à l'homme*. 1966: *King of Hearts*. 1968: *To Be a Crook*. 1969: *Le bal du Compte d'Orgel*. *Le clair de terre*. 1970: *Peau d'âne* (GB: *Once Upon a Time*. US: *The Magic Donkey*). 1971: *The Legend of Frenchie King/Les pétroleuses*. *Il diavolo nel cervello*. 1973: *L'événement le plus important depuis que l'homme a marché sur la lune* (GB: *The Slightly Pregnant Man*). *L'oiseau rare*. *Eulalie quitte les champs* (US: *The Star, the Orphan and the Butcher*). *Mords pas, on t'aime*. 1974: *La preda*. *Deux grandes filles dans un pyjama*. 1975: *Trompe-l'oeil*. 1976: *Le diable dans la boîte*. *Néa* (GB: *A Young Emmanuelle*). *Certaines nouvelles*. 1978: *Va voir, Maman, Papa travaille*. *La couleur du temps*. *On efface tout*. 1979: *S'il vous plaît . . . la mer?* *Je te tiens, tu me tiens par La Barbichette*. *Rien ne va plus*. *Tout dépend des filles*. 1980: *La tête à ça*. 1981: *Remueménage*. 1983: *Lili Lamont*. *Thieves After Dark*. *Archipel des amours*. *En haut des marches*. 1984: *Le chien* (released 1986). *Les fausses confidences*. 1986: *Poulet rôti*. *Beau temps, mais orageux enfin de journée*. 1988: *Alouette/Alouette je te plumerai*. *Mignon e'partita*. 1989: *I Want to Go Home*. *La fête des pères*. 1990: *Le jour des rois*. *Après-demain*. 1991: *Der andere Blick*. 1993: *Fanfan*. *Je m'appelle Victor*. 1994: *Pas très catholique* (US: *Something Fishy*). *Les misérables (du XXIème siècle)*. *Casque bleu*. 1995: *Le journal d'un séducteur*. 1996: *Les mille et une recettes du cuisinier amoureux* (US: *A Chef in Love*). *Madame Verdoux*. *Honeymoon for Five* (TV). *Enfants du Salaud* (US: *Bastard Brood*). *Citron Amer*. *Fallais pas . . . !* 1998: *Le voyage à Paris*. 1999: *Vénus beauté institut*. *Bad Company*. 2000: *Charmant garçon*.

†*As Micheline Michel*

PRESLEY, Elvis 1935–1977
Dark, insolent-looking American rock 'n' roll idol who took the world, especially the teenage public, by storm in the mid-fifties and remained the world's top-selling record star for well over a decade. Nicknamed 'Elvis the Pelvis' because of his hip-swivelling gyrations on stage – but films only rarely caught the electric arrogance that set audiences alight. At first he revealed some talent for wacky comedy, but as the sixties progressed both man and films got duller and duller. The end came from drugs and a heart attack.

1956: *Love Me Tender*. 1957: *Loving You*. *Jailhouse Rock*. 1959: *King Creole*. 1960: *Flaming Star*. *GI Blues*. 1961: *Wild in the Country*. *Blue Hawaii*. *Follow That Dream*. 1962: *Kid Galahad*. *It Happened at the World's Fair*. 1964: *Kissin' Cousins*. *Roustabout*. *Viva Las Vegas* (GB: *Love in Las Vegas*). 1965: *Girl Happy*. *Tickle Me*. *Harum Scarum* (GB: *Harem Holiday*). 1966: *Frankie and Johnny*. *Spinout* (GB: *California Holiday*). *Paradise – Hawaiian Style*. 1967: *Easy Come, Easy Go*. *Double Trouble*. *Clambake*. 1968: *Stay Away, Joe*. *Speedway*. *Live a Little, Love a Little*. 1969: *Charro*. *Change of Habit*. *The Trouble with Girls – and How to Get into It*. 1970: *Elvis – That's the Way It Is*. 1972: *Elvis on Tour*. 1981: *This is Elvis*. 1992: *Twist* (archive footage).

PRESTON, Kelly (K. Palzis) 1962–
Bright, fizzy, blonde Hollywood actress with dream figure, but all too often either 'the other woman' or in nebulous leading roles. Born and raised in Hawaii, she also spent much of her youth in Iraq and Australia, before beginning an acting career at 20 in the daytime TV soap *Capitol*. Married/divorced actor Kevin Gage. Married to actor John Travolta (*qv*) since 1991.

1983: *Metalstorm: The Destruction of Jared-Syn*. *Christine*. *For Love and Honor* (TV). *10 to Midnight*. 1985: *Mischief/The Man with*

One Red Shoe. Secret Admirer. SpaceCamp. 1986: 52 Pick-Up. Amazon Women on the Moon. 1987: Burnin' Love. A Tiger's Tale. 1988: The Experts. Witching Hour/ Spellbinder. Twins. 1990: The Perfect Bride (TV). Tales from the Crypt (cable TV). Run! 1992: Only You. 1993: The American Clock (TV). 1994: Love is a Gun. Cheyenne Warrior (TV). Double Cross. 1995: *Little Surprises. Waiting to Exhale. Mrs Munck. 1996: Shattered Image. Precious. Jerry Maguire. From Dusk Till Dawn. Citizen Ruth. Curdled. 1997: Addicted to Love. Nothing to Lose. 1998: Holy Man. Jack Frost. 1999: For Love of the Game. Bar Hopping. 2000: Daddy and Them. Battlefield Earth. 2001: Spy Kids.

PRESTON, Robert
(R. P. Meservey) 1917–1987
Handsome, dark, often moustachioed, solidly-built American actor, much confused with Preston Foster in his earlier days, when he was with Paramount for 12 useful years without quite becoming a big star, getting the girl in B features, and losing her in As. He always looked about 35, and still did when he returned to films in triumph in the sixties after phenomenal musical success as star of Broadway's *The Music Man*. Married to actress Catherine Craig (Kay Feltus 1918–) from 1940. Died from lung cancer. Oscar nominee for *Victor/Victoria*.
1938: King of Alcatraz (GB: King of the Alcatraz). Illegal Traffic. 1939: Union Pacific. Disbarred. Beau Geste. 1940: North West Mounted Police. Moon over Burma. Typhoon. 1941: The Lady from Cheyenne. New York Town. The Night of January 16th. Parachute Battalion. 1942: Wake Island. This Gun for Hire. Pacific Blackout. Star Spangled Rhythm. Reap the Wild Wind. 1943: Night Plane from Chungking. 1947: Variety Girl. The Macomber Affair. Wild Harvest. 1948: Blood on the Moon. Big City. 1949: Whispering Smith. The Lady Gambles. Tulsa. The Sundowners (GB: Thunder in the Dust). 1951: My Outlaw Brother. When I Grow Up. Cloudburst. Best of the Badmen. 1952: Face to Face. 1955: The Last Frontier. 1956: Made in Heaven (TV). Sentinels in the Air (narrator only). 1960: The Dark at the Top of the Stairs. 1961: The Music Man. 1962: How the West Was Won. 1963: Island of Love. All the Way Home. 1972: Junior Bonner. Child's Play. 1974: Mame. 1975: My Father's House (TV). 1977: Semi-Tough. 1979: The Chisholms (TV). 1981: SOB. 1982: Victor/Victoria. Rehearsal for

Murder (TV). 1983: September Gun (TV). 1984: Finnegan Begin Again (GB: TV). The Last Starfighter. 1986: Outrage! (TV).

PRICE, Dennis
(Denniston Rose-Price) 1915–1973
Smooth, devious-looking British actor whose aristocratic charmers were often rotten to the core. When his leading-man career fell away in the fifties, there was a failed suicide bid, but he came back to play a series of sometimes dramatic, sometimes comic characters whose credentials were usually as fake as their smile and old school tie. Married/divorced actress Joan Schofield. Died from cirrhosis of the liver.
1938: No Parking (as extra). 1944: A Canterbury Tale. 1945: A Place of One's Own. The Echo Murders. 1946: Caravan. Hungry Hill. The Magic Bow. 1947: Jassy. Holiday Camp. Master of Bankdam. Dear Murderer. Easy Money. The White Unicorn (US: Bad Sister). 1948: Snowbound. Good Time Girl. The Bad Lord Byron. 1949: Kind Hearts and Coronets. Helter Skelter. The Lost People. 1950: The Dancing Years. Murder without Crime. The Adventurers (US: The Great Adventure). 1951: The Magic Box. The House in the Square (US: I'll Never Forget You). Lady Godiva Rides Again. 1952: Song of Paris (US: Bachelor in Paris). Tall Headlines. 1953: Noose for a Lady. Murder at 3 a.m. The Intruder. 1954: Eight Witnesses (TV. GB: cinemas). Time is My Enemy. For Better, For Worse (US: Cocktails in the Kitchen). 1955: The Price of Greed. Oh Rosalinda!! *Account Closed. That Lady. Private's Progress. 1956: Charley Moon. Port Afrique. A Touch of the Sun. 1957: The Tommy Steele Story (US: Rock Around the World). Fortune is a Woman (US: She Played with Fire). The Naked Truth (US: Your Past is Showing). 1958: Hello London. 1959: Dark As the Night (TV. GB: cinemas). Danger Within (US: Breakout). Don't Panic Chaps! I'm All Right, Jack. School for Scoundrels. 1960: Piccadilly Third Stop. The Millionairess. The Pure Hell of St. Trinian's. Oscar Wilde. Tunes of Glory. No Love for Johnnie. 1961: Five Golden Hours. The Rebel (US: Call Me Genius). Watch It Sailor! Double Bunk! What a Carve Up! (US: No Place Like Homicide). Victim. 1962: The Amorous Prawn. Go to Blazes. Play It Cool. The Pot Carriers. *Behave Yourself. Kill or Cure. The Cool Mikado. The Wrong Arm of the Law. 1963: Doctor in Distress. Tamahine. The Comedy Man. The VIPs. A Jolly Bad Fellow (US: They All Died Laughing). The Horror of

It All. The Cracksman. 1964: The Earth Dies Screaming. Murder Most Foul. Curse of Simba (US: Curse of the Voodoo). 1965: Ten Little Indians. A High Wind in Jamaica. 1966: Just Like a Woman. 1967: Rocket to the Moon (US: Those Fantastic Flying Fools). 1969: The Magic Christian. The Haunted House of Horror (US: Horror House). 1970: Some Will, Some Won't. †Count Downe. Venus in Furs. The Horror of Frankenstein. The Rise and Rise of Michael Rimmer. 1971: Vampyros Lesbos. Twins of Evil. 1972: Pulp. Tower of Evil (US: Horror of Snape Island). Alice's Adventures in Wonderland. That's Your Funeral. Go for a Take. The Adventures of Barry McKenzie. Dracula contro El Doctor Frankenstein (GB: TV, as Dracula, Prisoner of Frankenstein). 1973: Horror Hospital. Theatre of Blood.

†Unreleased

PRICE, Vincent 1911–1993
Tall, handsome but faintly shifty-looking American actor. That slight sneer got him cast in some good forties roles as untrustworthy associates, with a couple of rich accounts of ham actors thrown in. But he was never quite a top-of-the-cast man until he settled into horror films, and became known as the 'Master of Menace', although in truth he rarely seemed in earnest and one was sure there was just a big old softie behind the demonic scowl. Also a cookery and art expert. Married (third) actress Coral Browne (1913–91). Died from lung cancer.
1938: Service De Luxe. 1939: The Private Lives of Elizabeth and Essex. Tower of London. The Invisible Man Returns. 1940: The House of the Seven Gables. Green Hell. Brigham Young – Frontiersman (GB: Brigham Young). Hudson's Bay. 1943: The Song of Bernadette. 1944: Wilson. The Eve of St Mark. Laura. The Keys of the Kingdom. 1945: A Royal Scandal (GB: Czarina). Leave Her to Heaven. 1946: Dragonwyck. Shock. 1947: Moss Rose. The Long Night. The Web. 1948: Abbott and Costello Meet Frankenstein (Voice only. GB: Abbott and Costello Meet the Ghosts). Up in Central Park. Rogues' Regiment. The Three Musketeers. 1949: Bagdad. The Bribe. Curtain Call at Cactus Creek (GB: Take the Stage). 1950: Baron of Arizona. Champagne for Caesar. The Adventures of Captain Fabian. 1951: His Kind of Woman. Pictura: An Adventure in Art. 1952: The Las Vegas Story. 1953: House of Wax. Casanova's Big Night. 1954: The Mad Magician. Dangerous Mission.

1955: Son of Sinbad. *The Story of Colonel Drake. 1956: Serenade. The Ten Commandments. While the City Sleeps. Forbidden Area (TV). 1957: The Story of Mankind. Lone Woman (TV). The Clouded Image (TV). 1958: The Fly. The House on Haunted Hill. 1959: The Bat. The Big Circus. The Tingler. Return of the Fly. 1960: House of Usher (GB: The Fall of the House of Usher). 1961: Master of the World. The Pit and the Pendulum. Nefertite, regina del Nilo (GB and US: Queen of the Nile). Gordon il pirata nero (GB: The Black Buccaneer. US: Rage of the Buccaneer). The Last Man on Earth. Naked Terror (narrator only). 1962: Convicts Four (GB: Reprieve!). Tales of Terror. Tower of London (remake). Confessions of an Opium Eater (GB: Evils of Chinatown). 1963: The Raven. Comedy of Terrors. Twice Told Tales. Diary of a Madman. *Chagall (narrator only). Beach Party. Taboos of the World (narrator only. GB: Tabu). The Haunted Palace. 1964: The Masque of the Red Death. 1965: City under the Sea (US: War Gods of the Deep). Dr Goldfoot and the Bikini Machine (GB: Dr G and the Bikini Machine). The Tomb of Ligeia. 1966: Dr Goldfoot and the Girl Bombs (GB: Dr G and the Love Bomb). 1967: House of 1,000 Dolls. The Jackals. 1968: Witchfinder General (US: The Conqueror Worm). More Dead Than Alive. 1969: The Trouble with Girls . . . and How to Get into It. The Oblong Box. Scream and Scream Again. Cry of the Banshee. 1971: The Abominable Dr Phibes. What's a Nice Girl Like You . . . ? 1972: The Aries Computer. Dr Phibes Rises Again. 1873: Theatre of Blood. 1974: Percy's Progress. Madhouse. 1976: The Butterfly Ball (narrator only). Journey into Fear. 1978: Days of Fury (narrator only). 1979: Scavenger Hunt. 1980: The Monster Club. 1982: House of the Long Shadows. *Vincent (voice only). 1983: Blood Bath at the House of Death. *Michael Jackson's Thriller (video). Praying Mantis (TV. American prologue only). 1984: Pogo for President (voice only). 1986: From a Whisper to a Scream (later The Offspring). The Great Mouse Detective (GB: Basil the Great Mouse Detective. Voice only). 1987: The Little Troll Prince (TV. Voice only). Escapes. The Whales of August. 1988: DeadHeat. 1989: Backtrack (GB: Catchfire). 1990: Edward Scissorhands. 1993: Heart of Justice (TV). 1995: Arabian Knight / The Thief and the Cobbler (voice only).

PRINZE, Freddie Jr 1976–
Tall American actor with dark, wavy hair and slightly goofy good looks, often seen as college boys. The son of a TV star who committed suicide when the boy was one year old, Prinze Jr nonetheless targeted acting as a career from his teens, got his first breaks in television and had moved into starring roles in youth-oriented films in his early twenties.
1996: To Gillian on Her 37th Birthday. Too Soon for Jeff (TV). 1997: The House of Yes. I Know What You Did Last Summer. 1998: Sparkler. Vig/ Money Kings (originally for TV). I Still Know What You Did Last Summer. 1999: She's All That. Wing Commander. 2000: Down to You. Head Over Heels. Boys and Girls.

PROVINE, Dorothy 1937–
Fizzy, impish, pinch-cheeked Hollywood blonde (originally from Deadwood City of Calamity Jane fame), who started in leading roles and enjoyed great success as the Charleston-dancing nightclub entertainer in the television series The Roaring Twenties. She seemed to grow more subdued and less interesting in the 1960s, and her career did not progress. Little seen after 1970. Married director Robert Day in 1969.
1958: The Bonnie Parker Story. Live Fast, Die Young. 1959: Riot in Juvenile Prison. The 30-Foot Bride of Candy Rock. 1963: It's a Mad, Mad, Mad, Mad World. Wall of Noise. 1964: Good Neighbor Sam. 1965: That Darn Cat! The Great Race. One Spy Too Many (TV. GB: cinemas). 1966: Kiss the Girls and Make Them Die. 1967: Who's Minding the Mint? Never a Dull Moment. 1968: The Sound of Anger (TV).

PRYCE, Jonathan 1947–
Offbeat Welsh-born leading man with a scruff of dark hair. His long face can be mournful or menacing at a rearrangement of the mouth and his sprinkling of film appearances to date have been an extraordinary assortment of leads in big films, guest spots, bad guys of one kind or another and unsettling figures on the edge of the action. His preference for the stage kept him from being a major international figure in the cinema, but his unusual presence alone makes his performances fascinating to watch and star roles beckoned again after his triumph in the stage musical Miss Saigon. He continued in theatrical vein by playing Fagin in a revival of Oliver! then stepped back to the screen for another musical, Evita.
1976: Voyage of the Damned. 1979: Breaking Glass. Loophole. 1982: Murder is Easy/ Agatha Christie's Murder is Easy (TV). Something Wicked This Way Comes. 1983: The Ploughman's Lunch. 1984: Brazil. 1985: The Doctor and the Devils. 1986: Haunted Honeymoon. Jumpin' Jack Flash. 1987: Man on Fire. Hotel London. 1988: Consuming Passions. The Adventures of Baron Munchausen. 1989: The Rachel Papers. The Man from the Pru (TV). 1992: Freddie as FR07 (voice only). Glengarry Glen Ross. 1993: Barbarians at the Gate (TV). The Age of Innocence. Shopping. Deadly Advice. Great Moments in Aviation. 1994: Dark Blood (unfinished). A Troll in Central Park (voice only). A Business Affair. 1995: Carrington. 1996: Evita. 1997: Regeneration. David (TV). Tomorrow Never Dies. 1998: Ronin. 1999: Stigmata. Deceit. 2000: Robert Louis Stevenson's The Suicide Club. Very Annie Mary. The Testimony of Taliesin Jones. 2001: Unconditional Love. Bride of the Wind.

PRYOR, Richard 1940–
American nightclub comedian, a black Lenny Bruce who toned down his style to find success in commercial Hollywood films, tried drama without too much effect and showed the world his old scathing and scatological self in films of his nightclub material. Severely burned in an accident in 1980, Pryor never quite realised his full potential for the cinema. He underwent a triple heart bypass operation in 1990; the following year he discovered he was suffering from multiple sclerosis. His last star role to date was yet another (poor) collaboration with his oft-time partner in comic crime, Gene Wilder (qv). Five times married.
1966: The Busy Body. 1968:]The Green Berets. Wild in the Streets. 1969: The Phynx.

The Young Lawyers (TV). 1970: Carter's Army (TV). 1971: Dynamic Chicken. You've Got to Walk It Like You Talk It Or You'll Lose That Beat. Richard Pryor – Live and Smokin'. 1972: Lady Sings the Blues. 1973: Hit! The Mack. Wattstax. Some Call It Loving. 1974: Uptown Saturday Night. 1975: Adios Amigo. 1976: The Bingo Long Traveling All-Stars and Motor Kings. Car Wash. Silver Streak. 1977: Greased Lightning. Which Way Is Up? 1978: The Wiz. The Muppet Movie. Blue Collar. California Suite. 1979: Richard Pryor Live in Concert. In God We Trust. Richard Pryor is Back Live in Concert. 1980: Wholly Moses! Stir Crazy. 1981: Bustin' Loose. Some Kind of Hero. 1982: Richard Pryor Live on the Sunset Strip. The Toy. 1983: Superman III. †Richard Pryor Here and Now. 1985: Brewster's Millions. 1985: †Jo Jo Dancer. 1986: Critical Condition. 1987: Moving. 1989: See No Evil, Hear No Evil. Harlem Nights. 1990: Look Who's Talking Too (voice only). 1991: Another You. 1995: Trial by Fire (TV). 1996: Mad Dog Time / Trigger Happy. 1997: Lost Highway.

‡*As Richard 'Cactus' Pryor*
†*And directed*

PULLMAN, Bill 1954–

Square-jawed, open-faced, very slightly disgruntled-looking American actor who looks a bit like Jeff Daniels (*qv*), and until the mid 1990s played losers – rejected suitors, husbands who have the wool pulled over their eyes, victims of conspiracies, the occult or medical disaster: they're all in Pullman's casebook of men who should have stayed at home. He initially thought of a career in building construction, but switched colleges, graduating in theatre arts and becoming a teacher at the University of Montana, leaving at 27 to pursue an acting career. He soon made his mark as mild-mannered, handsome men of low-level achievement and has rarely looked like bringing home the bacon since his debut as the dim-witted extortionist in *Ruthless People*. He moved into star roles in 1995. *1986: Ruthless People. 1987: Spaceballs. 1988: The Accidental Tourist. The Serpent and the Rainbow. Rocket Gibraltar. 1989: Home Fires Burning (TV). Brain Dead / Paranoia. 1990: Cold Feet. Bright Angel. Sibling Rivalry. 1991: Liebestraum. Going Under. 1992: Newsies (GB: The News Boys). Crazy in Love (TV). Singles. A League of Their Own. Nervous Ticks. 1993: Sommersby. Sleepless in*

Seattle. Malice. Mr Jones. 1994: Wyatt Earp. The Last Seduction. The Favor (completed 1991). 1995: Out There (cable TV). While You Were Sleeping. Casper. 1996: Mr Wrong. Independence Day. Lost Highway. Mistrial (cable TV). Perfect Crimes (TV). 1997: The End of Violence. Zero Effect. 1998: Brokedown Palace. 1999: Lake Placid. Titan AE (voice only). A Man is Mostly Water. 2000: History Is Made at Night. The Guilty. Numbers. Coming to Light: Edward S Curtis and the North American Indians (doc. voice only). The Virginian (TV. And directed). 2001: Ignition.

PURDOM, Edmund 1924–

No more handsome leading man came to Hollywood than this tall, dark Briton, but his rather stiff personality was all at sea in the silly costume epics they gave him, after a much-publicized leap to stardom when Mario Lanza walked out on *The Student Prince*. He offered his best performances later on, in modern dress, as characters of dubious ethics, but there were more frivolities both before and after. Later lived and worked in Italy. Married / divorced (third of three) actress Linda Christian (Bianca Welter, 1923–).
1953: Titanic. Julius Caesar. 1954: The Student Prince. Athena. The Egyptian. 1955: The Prodigal. The King's Thief. 1956: Strange Intruder. 1957: Agguato in Tangeri (GB: Ambush in Tangiers. US: Trapped in Tangiers). 1959: Herod the Great. The Cossacks. Salambò (US: The Loves of Salambo). 1960: Nights of Rasputin. Moment of Danger (US: Malaga). The Last of the Vikings (GB: Fury of the Vikings). 1961: La Fayette. L'ammuti namento (GB and US: White Slave Ship). Nefertite, regina del Nilo (GB and US: Queen of the Nile). Suleiman the Conqueror. 1963: The Comedy Man. 1964: The Beauty Jungle (US: Contest Girl). Last Ride to Santa Cruz. The Charge of the 7th. The Yellow Rolls Royce. 1965: Los cuatreros (US: Texas Jim). L'uomo che ride (GB: The Man with the Golden Mask). 1967: The Black Corsair. 1968: Crisantemi per un branco di carogne. Piluk il Timido. 1969: The Queer . . . the Erotic (narrator only. GB: The Satanists). Naked England (narrator only). 1970: Naked and Violent (narrator only). 1971: Evil Fingers. 1972: The Devil's Lover. 1973: L'onrata famiglia (uccidere è cosa nostra). Frankenstein's Castle of Freaks. 1974: El capitan de quince años. 1975: Night Child / The Cursed Medallion. 1977: Il padrone della città / Mister Scarface. 1978: The New Godfathers. The Sinister Eyes of Dr Orloff.

1979: I Contrabandieri de Santa Lucià 1980: Sophia Loren: Her Own Story (TV). 1981: Greed. Absurd. L'altra donna. 1982: Ator the Fighting Eagle. Pieces. 1983: The Mystery of Gaudo and Matapan. The Scarlet and the Black (TV). 1984: †Don't Open Until Christmas. After the Fall of New York. The Assisi Underground. 1985: Killer vs Killer / Fracchio contro Dracula. 1987: Appuntamento a Trieste. Funny Boy. Don Bosco. 1989: Diritto de vivere. 1990: La grieta.

†*And directed*

PURVIANCE, Edna 1894–1958

Girlish, happy-looking, fair-haired American actress, plump by today's standards, who was discovered by Charlie Chaplin and appeared exclusively in his films. His attempt to make her a world star with the 1923 *A Woman of Paris* was a disaster, she developed an alcohol problem and her career went into stagnation. *1915: A Night Out. The Champion. In the Park. A Jitney Elopement. The Tramp. By the Sea. Work. A Woman. The Bank. Carmen / Charlie Chaplin's Burlesque on Carmen. A Night in the Show. Shanghaied. 1916: Police. The Fireman. The Floorwalker. The Vagabond. The Count. The Pawn Shop. The Rink. Behind the Screen. 1917: Easy Street. The Cure. The Immigrant. The Adventurer. 1918: Triple Trouble. A Dog's Life. *How to Make Movies. †Shoulder Arms. Liberty Loan Appeal / Charles Chaplin in a Liberty Loan Appeal. 1919: Sunnyside. A Day's Pleasure. 1920: †The Kid. 1921: The Idle Class. 1922: Pay Day. 1923: †The Pilgrim. †A Woman of Paris. 1926: ‡A Woman of the Sea / †The Seagull. L'education du prince. 1947: †Monsieur Verdoux. 1951: †Limelight.*

All shorts except †features
‡*Unreleased*

QUAID, Dennis 1954–
Dark-haired, young-looking American actor with jaunty smile and breezy, relaxed personality. The brother of character star Randy Quaid (1948–), he came slowly through to leading roles, but his portrayal of the cocky Gordon Cooper in *The Right Stuff* made his features more familiar, and he was an above-the-title star by the mid-1980s, although his star career went off the rails at the end of the decade. Married/divorced actress P.J. Soles (1955–). Married to actress Meg Ryan (*qv*) since 1991. Has also sung and played with his own rock band. He and Ryan broke up in 2000.
1975: Crazy Mama. 1977: 9/30/55 (GB: TV as 30 September, 1955). I Never Promised You a Rose Garden. 1978: Amateur Night at the Dixie Bar and Grill (TV). The Seniors. Our Winning Season. Are You in the House Alone? (TV). 1979: GORP. Breaking Away. 1980: The Long Riders. 1981: All Night Long. Caveman. The Night the Lights Went Out in Georgia. Bill (TV). 1982: Johnny Belinda (TV). Tough Enough/Tough Dreams. 1983: Jaws 3-D. The Right Stuff. Dreamscape (released 1985). Bill: On His Own (TV). 1985: Enemy Mine. 1986: The Big Easy. 1987: InnerSpace. Suspect. 1988: D.O.A. Everybody's All-American (GB: When I Fall in Love). 1989: Great Balls of Fire. 1990: Postcards from the Edge. Come See the Paradise. 1993: Undercover Blues/Cloak and Diaper. Flesh and Bone. Wilder Napalm. 1994: Wyatt Earp. 1995: Something to Talk About. 1996: Dragonheart. 1997: Savior. Switchback. Gang Related. 1998: The Parent Trap. †Everything That Rises (TV). Playing by Heart. 1999: Any Given Sunday. 2000: Frequency. 2001: Traffic.

†*Also directed*

QUAYLE, Sir Anthony
(John A. Quayle) 1913–1989
Distinguished British stage actor with rounded cheeks, friendly smile, light, curly hair and determined gaze. At 42 he quite unexpectedly became a star of the cinema as well, revealing a pleasing personality that was most seen within men of action, but was adaptable to any kind of role. Character roles in the 1970s were less successful, but he won renewed plaudits on stage. Married actress Dorothy Hyson (D. Heisen, 1914–1996), his second wife. Won an Emmy for 1974's *QB VII*. Nominated for an Oscar for *Anne of the 1,000 Days*. Knighted in 1985. Died from cancer.
1935: Moscow Nights (US: I Stand Condemned). 1938: Pygmalion. 1948: Hamlet. Saraband for Dead Lovers (US: Saraband). 1955: Oh Rosalinda!! 1956: The Battle of the River Plate (US: Pursuit of the Graf Spee). The Wrong Man. 1957: Woman in a Dressing Gown. No Time for Tears. 1958: The Man Who Wouldn't Talk. Ice Cold in Alex (US: Desert Attack). 1959: Tarzan's Greatest Adventure. Serious Charge (US: A Touch of Hell). 1960: The Challenge. 1961: The Guns of Navarone. *Drums for a Queen (narrator only). 1962: HMS Defiant (US: Damn the Defiant!). *This is Lloyd's (narrator only). Lawrence of Arabia. 1963: The Fall of the Roman Empire. 1964: East of Sudan. 1965: Operation Crossbow (US: The Great Spy Mission). A Study in Terror (US: Fog). 1966: The Poppy is Also a Flower (TV. GB: cinemas as Danger Grows Wild). 1967: Incompreso (GB and US: Misunderstood). 1968: Mackenna's Gold. 1969: Destiny of a Spy (TV). *Island Unknown (narrator only). Before Winter Comes. 1970: Anne of the 1,000 Days. 1972: Everything You Always Wanted to Know About Sex**But Were Afraid to Ask. 1973: Bequest to the Nation. Jarrett (TV). 1974: The Tamarind Seed. QB VII (TV). 1975: Moses. Great Expectations (TV. GB: cinemas). 1976: The Eagle Has Landed. 21 Hours at Munich (TV. GB: cinemas). 1977: Holocaust 2000 (US: The Chosen). 1978: Sherlock Holmes: Murder by Decree (GB: Murder by Decree). 1980: Masada (TV. Shortened for cinemas as The Antagonists). 1981: Dial M for Murder (TV). The Manions of America (TV). 1984: The Last Days of Pompeii (TV). 1988: Stille Nacht. Buster. The Bourne Identity (TV). The Legend of the Holy Drinker. 1989: Magdalene. Confessional. King of the Wind.

QUINLAN, Kathleen 1954–
Well, how could I leave out Kathleen (no relation, alas)? This young-looking, dark-haired American actress's moist-eyed appeal got her cast as religious figures and girls in peril of the mind, body and spirit. Her all-stops-out emotional performances won her critical praise in the late 1970s, but she did not become a box-office bet. An all-round athlete, her earliest ambition was to compete in the Olympic Games . . . but acting intervened. In somewhat tougher roles in the 1990s: her career marked time until boosted by her Oscar-nominated performance as Tom Hanks' wife in the award-winning *Apollo 13*. Married actor Bruce Abbott (1954–).
1972: †One is a Lonely Number. 1973: †American Graffiti. 1974: The Abduction of St Anne/They've Kidnapped Anne Benedict (TV). Lucas Tanner (TV). Where Have All the People Gone? (TV). The Missing Are Deadly (TV). Can Ellen Be Saved? (TV). Judgment Day (TV). 1976: Lifeguard. Nightmare in Blood. 1977: Little Ladies of the Night (TV). Airport 77. I Never Promised You a Rose Garden. 1978: The Promise. 1979: The Runner Stumbles. 1980: Les séducteurs/Sunday Lovers. 1981: She's in the Army Now (TV). 1982: Hanky Panky. 1983: Restless/Independence Day. The Twilight Zone (GB: Twilight Zone The Movie). Hakkoref ha' acharon (US: The Last Winter). 1984: When She Says No (TV). 1985: Blackout. Warning Sign. Children of the Night (TV). 1986: Hidden Fear. The Tuscaloosan/Man Outside. 1987: Wild Thing. Dreams Lost, Dreams Found (TV). 1988: Sunset. Clara's Heart. 1989: Trapped (TV). The Operation (TV). 1990: The Doors. 1991: Strays (TV). 1992: Bodily Harm (TV). 1993: Stolen Babies (TV). Last Night (TV). After the Glory (TV). 1994: Trial by Jury. Perfect Alibi. 1995: Apollo 13. Picture Windows (TV). 1996: Zeus and Roxanne. 1997: Breakdown. Lawn Dogs. Event Horizon. 1998: My Giant. A Civil Action. 1999: Today is the Last Day of the Rest of My Life (TV).

†*As Kathy Quinlan*

QUINN, Aidan 1959–
Tight-faced, intense, dark-haired, slightly whimsical-looking Hollywood actor with wide blue eyes and a charming smile he has not been allowed to use too often in films. Born in Chicago, Quinn spent much of his

boyhood (and young manhood) in Ireland, most particularly in Dublin where he aimed to become a writer. Returning to America, he began taking acting classes, had some success on stage, and played the lead in his very first film at the age of 25. Since then he has played heroes competently, but been at his most attractive when acting as top support to the stars, both in sympathetic and unsympathetic roles. Married actress Elizabeth Bracco.

1984: *Reckless.* 1985: *Desperately Seeking Susan. An Early Frost* (TV). 1986: *The Mission. All My Sons* (TV). 1987: *StakeOut.* 1988: *Crusoe.* 1989: *Perfect Witness* (TV). *The Lemon Sisters. The Handmaid's Tale.* 1990: *Avalon.* 1991: *Lies of the Twins* (TV). *At Play in the Fields of the Lord.* 1992: *A Private Matter* (TV). *The Playboys. Benny & Joon. Bodies, Rest and Motion.* 1994: *Blink. Mary Shelley's Frankenstein. Legends of the Fall. Out of Ireland* (voice only). 1995: *Haunted. The Stars Fell on Henrietta.* 1996: *Michael Collins. Commandments. Looking for Richard.* 1997: *The Assignment. The Fairy Godmother. Forbidden Territory: Stanley's Search for Livingstone* (TV). 1998: *This is My Father. Practical Magic.* 1999: *In Dreams. Music of the Heart.* 2000: *Two of Us* (TV). *Night Terrors* (TV). *Songcatcher.*

QUINN, Anthony 1915– 2001

Flamboyant, dark-haired Mexican-born actor, who played Indians and scowling Dago bad guys until his second Oscar, for *Lust for Life* (the first was for *Viva Zapata!*), since when he has lived that title to the hilt playing any number of earth-loving characters of widely varying nationalities. Married (first of three) to actress Katherine DeMille (K. Lester 1911–) from 1937 to 1965. Additional

Oscar nominations for *Wild Is the Wind* and *Zorba the Greek*. Had eight children (one died).

1936: *The Milky Way. Parole! Sworn Enemy. Night Waitress. The Plainsman.* 1937: *Swing High, Swing Low. Waikiki Wedding. Daughter of Shanghai* (GB: *Daughter of the Orient*). *Last Train from Madrid. Partners in Crime.* 1938: *The Buccaneer. Tip Off Girls. Dangerous to Know. King of Alcatraz* (GB: *King of the Alcatraz*). 1939: *Island of Lost Men. King of Chinatown. Union Pacific. Television Spy.* 1940: *Road to Singapore. Parole Fixer. Emergency Squad. City for Conquest. The Ghost Breakers.* 1941: *Thieves Fall Out. Knockout. Texas Rangers Ride Again. Blood and Sand. Bullets for O'Hara. They Died with Their Boots On. The Perfect Snob.* 1942: *The Black Swan. Road to Morocco. The Ox-Bow Incident* (GB: *Strange Incident*). *Larceny Inc.* 1943: *Guadalcanal Diary.* 1944: *Buffalo Bill. Roger Touhy, Gangster* (GB: *The Last Gangster*). *Ladies of Washington. Irish Eyes Are Smiling.* 1945: *Where Do We Go from Here? China Sky. Back to Bataan.* 1946: *California. The Imperfect Lady* (GB: *Mrs Loring's Secret*). 1947: *Sinbad the Sailor. Black Gold. Tycoon.* 1951: *The Brave Bulls. Mask of the Avenger.* 1952: *Viva Zapata! The World in His Arms. The Brigand. Against All Flags.* 1953: *City Beneath the Sea. Seminole. Ride, Vaquero! East of Sumatra. Blowing Wild. Ulysses. Donne proibite* (GB: *Forbidden Women. US: Angels of Darkness*). *Cavalleria Rusticana. Attila the Hun.* 1954: *La strada. The Long Wait. Il più comico spettacolo del mondo.* 1955: *The Magnificent Matador* (GB: *The Brave and the Beautiful*). *The Naked Street. Seven Cities of Gold.* 1956: *The Man from Del Rio. Lust for Life. The Wild Party.* 1957: *The River's Edge. The Ride Back. The Hunchback of Notre Dame. Wild is the Wind.* 1958: *Hot Spell.* 1959: *The Black Orchid. Last Train from Gun Hill. Warlock. The Savage Innocents.* 1960: *Heller in Pink Tights. Portrait in Black.* 1961: *The Guns of Navarone. Barabbas.* 1962: *Requiem for a Heavyweight* (GB: *Blood Money*). *Lawrence of Arabia.* 1964: *The Fabulous Adventures of Marco Polo* (GB: *Marco the Magnificent*). *Behold a Pale Horse. The Visit. Zorba the Greek.* 1965: *A High Wind in Jamaica.* 1966: *Lost Command.* 1967: *The Rover. The 25th Hour. The Happening.* 1968: *Guns for San Sebastian. The Shoes of the Fisherman. The Magus.* 1969: *The Secret of Santa Vittoria. A Dream of Kings. A Walk in the Spring Rain.* 1970: *RPM. Flap* (GB: *The Last Warrior*). *King: a Filmed Record . . . Montgomery to Memphis.* 1971: *Arruza* (narrator only). *The City* (TV). *Forbidden Knowledge* (TV). 1972: *Across 110th Street. The Voice of La Raza* (and narrator). 1973: *Los amigos* (GB and US: *Deaf Smith and Johnny Ears*). *The Don is Dead.* 1974: *The Marseilles Contract* (US: *The Destructors*). 1975: *Bluff. L'eredità Ferramonti* (GB: *The Inheritance*). 1976: *Tigers Don't Cry. The Message.* 1978: *The Greek Tycoon. Caravans. The Children of Sanchez. The Passage.* 1980: *Lion of The Desert/Omar Mukhtar – Lion of the Desert. The Contender.* 1981: *High Risk. The Salamander. Bon Appetit. The Dream of Tangier.* 1982: *Roma Regina. Valentina.*

1983: *1919 – cronica del Alba.* 1984: *The Last Days of Pompeii.* 1986: *Isola del tesoro.* 1988: *Stradivarius. Tough Guys in Marseilles. A Man of Passion.* 1989: *Revenge.* 1990: *The Old Man and the Sea* (TV). *Ghosts Can't Do It. The Actor.* 1991: *Jungle Fever. Mobsters. Only the Lonely.* 1993: *Last Action Hero. Il mago.* 1994: *This Can't Be Love* (TV). *Somebody to Love. Hercules and the Lost Kingdom. Hercules and the Circle of Fire. Hercules in the Maze of the Minotaur. Hercules in the Underworld.* 1995: *A Walk in the Clouds. Hercules and the Amazon Women.* 1996: *The Seven Servants. Il sindaco/The Mayor. Gotti* (cable TV). 1998: *From Russia to Hollywood* (doc). 1999: *Oriundi.*

As director: 1958: *The Buccaneer.*

R

RADFORD, Basil 1897–1952

Amiable, avuncular, moustachioed British actor who looked (and was) a cricket fanatic, a facet of his personality that he put to good use from the late 1930s on, as he and Naunton Wayne (*qv*) gained great popularity in a series of comedy-thrillers in which they played Charters and Caldicot, Englishmen at large more interested in the Test score than in bodies falling all about them. Died from a heart attack.

1929: *Barnum Was Right.* 1930: *Seven Days Leave (GB: Medals).* 1932: *There Goes the Bride.* 1933: *A Southern Maid. Just Smith (US: Leave It to Smith).* 1936: *Broken Blossoms. Dishonour Bright.* 1937: *Jump for Glory (US: When Thief Meets Thief). Captain's Orders. Young and Innocent (US: The Girl Was Young).* 1938: *Climbing High. Convict 99. The Lady Vanishes.* 1939: *Trouble Brewing. Let's Be Famous. The Four Just Men (US: The Secret Four). Spies of the Air. Jamaica Inn. Just William. She Couldn't Say No. Secret Journey (US: Among Human Wolves). The Girl Who Forgot.* 1940: *Room for Two. The Flying Squad. Night Train to Munich (US: Night Train). Crooks' Tour. The Girl in the News.* 1941: **Save Rubber.* 1942: **London Scrapbook. Next of Kin. Unpublished Story. Flying Fortress. *Partners in Crime.* 1943: *Dear Octopus (US: The Randolph Family). Millions Like Us.* 1944: *Twilight Hour. The Way for the Stars (US: Johnny in the Clouds). Dead of Night.* 1946: *The Captive Heart. A Girl in a Million.* 1948: *Quartet. The Winslow Boy. It's Not Cricket.* 1949: *Helter Skelter. Stop Press Girl. Whisky Galore! (US: Tight Little Island).*

The Blue Lamp. Passport to Pimlico. 1950: *Chance of a Lifetime.* 1951: *White Corridors. The Galloping Major.*

RAFFERTY, Chips

(John Goffage) 1909–1971

Tall, lanky, tanned, light-haired, hook-nosed Australian actor, no great looker, but for many years a stalwart, and indeed the epitome of the Australian cinema. Made some British and international films, but always returned to Australia, where he ultimately died from a heart attack.

1939: *Ants in His Pants.* 1940: *Dad Rudd MP. 40,000 Horsemen.* 1944: *Rats of Tobruk (US: The Fighting Rats of Tobruk).* 1946: *The Overlanders.* 1947: *Bush Christmas. The Loves of Joanna Godden.* 1948: *Eureka Stockade (US: Massacre Hill).* 1950: *Bitter Springs.* 1951: **Australian Diary.* 1952: *Kangaroo. The Desert Rats.* 1953: *The Phantom Stockman.* 1954: *Cattle Station. King of the Coral Sea.* 1956: *Smiley. Walk into Paradise.* 1958: *Smiley Gets a Gun.* 1959: **Power with Precision (narrator only).* 1960: *The Sundowners. The Wackiest Ship in the Army.* 1962: *Mutiny on the Bounty.* 1966: *They're a Weird Mob.* 1967: *Double Trouble. Kona Coast.* 1969: *Skullduggery.* 1970: *Outback (US: Wake in Fright).*

RAFFIN, Deborah 1953–

Tall, fair-haired American actress of 'innocent' looks. The daughter of minor 1940s star Trudy Marshall (1922–), she leapt from fashion model to film star at 20 and was immediately cast as virginal daughters. She has tried hard to find interesting roles over the years (and once or twice succeeded), although her acceptance of a role in TV's

Lace 2 made it look as though she might have given up the struggle. Certainly she has led a sporadic acting career to date, the more so in recent times with her involvement in Dove Audio, a successful books-on-tape company she founded with her husband in 1985.

1973: *Forty Carats.* 1974: *The Dove. Once is Not Enough/Jacqueline Susann's Once is Not Enough.* 1976: *Nightmare in Badham County (TV). The Sentinel.* 1977: *Deadly Encounters. Demon/God Told Me To. Maniac/Assault on Paradise (GB: TV, as Ransom).* 1978: *Ski-Lift to Death (TV). How to Pick Up Girls! (TV).* 1981: *Killing at Hell's Gate (TV). Haywire (TV). Mind Over Murder (TV).* 1982: *For Lovers Only (TV). Dance of the Dwarfs/Jungle Heat.* 1983: *Running Out (TV). Sparkling Cyanide/Agatha Christie's Sparkling Cyanide (TV).* 1984: *The Predator.* 1985: *Death Wish 3.* 1986: *Claudia's Story (unreleased).* 1990: *Night of the Fox (TV).* 1991: *Scanners II: The New Order.* 1992: *Sidney Sheldon's The Sands of Time (TV).* 1993: *Morning Glory.* 1994: *A Perry Mason Mystery: The Case of the Grimacing Governor (TV).* 1996: *LaVyrle Spencer's Home Song (TV).*

RAFT, George (G. Ranft) 1895–1980

Silken-smooth, narrow-eyed, rather menacing American actor who slipped from a somewhat dubious background as consort of criminals and nightclub dancers to portray criminals and dancers on screen. Dark hair slicked down, he glided lizard-like through both guises, but it was gangster roles that won him most public favour and he played thriller leads until he was 60. Died from leukaemia.

1929: *Queen of the Night Clubs.* 1931: *Goldie. Quick Millions. Hush Money. Taxi! Palmy Days.* 1932: *Night World. Dancers in the Dark. Night After Night. Scarface. Madame Racketeer (GB: The Sporting Widow). If I Had a Million. Undercover Man. Love is a Racket.* 1933: *The Bowery. Pick Up. *Hollywood on Parade No. 13. Midnight Club. *Hollywood on Parade No. 17.* 1934: *The Trumpet Blows. All of Me. Bolero. Limehouse Blues.* 1935: *Rumba. The Glass Key. She Couldn't Take It (GB: Woman Hater). Every Night at Eight. Stolen Harmony.* 1936: *It Had to Happen. Yours for the Asking.* 1937: *Souls at Sea.* 1938: *You and Me. Spawn of the North. The Lady's From Kentucky.* 1939: *Each Dawn I Die. I Stole a Million. Invisible Stripes.* 1940: *The House Across the Bay. They Drive by Night (GB: The Road to Frisco).* 1941: **Stars* *at Play. Manpower. 1942: Broadway. 1943: Background to Danger. Stage Door Canteen. 1944: Follow the Boys. 1945: Nob Hill. Johnny Angel. 1946: Whistle Stop. Mr Ace. Nocturne. 1947: Christmas Eve. Intrigue. 1948: Race Street. 1949: Outpost in Morocco. Johnny Allegro (GB: Hounded). Nous irons à Paris (GB: Let's Go to Paris). A Dangerous Profession. Red Light. 1951: Lucky Nick Cain (GB: I'll Get You for This). 1952: Loan Shark. Adventure in Algiers/Secret of the Casbah (released 1954). Escape Route (US: I'll Get You). 1953: Man from Cairo (GB: Crime Squad). 1954: Rogue Cop. Black Widow. 1955: A Bullet for Joey. 1956: Around the World in 80 Days. 1959: Jet Over the Atlantic. Some Like It Hot. 1960: Ocean's Eleven. 1961: The Ladies' Man. 1962: Two Guys Abroad (unreleased). 1964: The Patsy. For Those Who Think Young. 1965: Du Rififi à Paname (GB: Rififi in Paris). 1967: Five Golden Dragons. Casino Royale. 1968: Skidoo. The Silent Treatment (unreleased). 1972: Hammersmith is Out. Deadhead Miles.*

RAINER, Luise 1909–

Pretty, doll-like brunette Austrian actress with appealingly expressive face and finely pencilled eyebrows. She won two Oscars in consecutive years after coming to American for *The Great Ziegfeld* and *The Good Earth*, after which too much seemed to be expected of her. M-G-M dropped her after only one more year, and one forties' film was her only remaining screen appearance of note until 1997.

1930: Ja, der Himmel über Wien. 1931: Sehnsucht 202. 1933: Heut' kommt's Drauf an. 1935: Escapade. Wenn die Musik nicht wär. 1936: The Great Ziegfeld. 1937: The Good Earth. The Big City. The Emperor's Candlesticks. 1938: The Great Waltz. The Toy Wife (GB: Frou Frou). Dramatic School. 1943: Hostages. 1960: La dolce vita. 1997: The Gambler.

RAINES, Ella (E. Raubes) 1921–1988

Beautiful, strong-looking American actress with silky brunette hair, just as adept at resourceful heroines as bitchy mistresses, but not well treated by Hollywood who, after a few interesting roles, only offered her nice girls in dull, mediocre films. Died from cancer.

1943: Corvette K-225 (GB: The Nelson Touch). Cry Havoc. 1944: Hail the Conquering Hero. Tall in the Saddle. Phantom Lady.

Enter Arsène Lupin. 1945: The Strange Affair of Uncle Harry/Uncle Harry. The Suspect. 1946: The Runaround. White Tie and Tails. 1947: The Web. Time Out of Mind. Brute Force. 1948: The Senator Was Indiscreet (GB: Mr Ashton Was Indiscreet). 1949: A Dangerous Profession. The Walking Hills. Impact. 1950: Singing Guns. The Second Face. 1951: Fighting Coast Guard. 1952: Ride the Man Down. 1955: The Man in the Road.

RAINS, Claude

(William C. Rains) 1889–1967

Grey-haired (originally dark), stocky British character star who came to Hollywood in young middle age but stayed to become for more than 15 years one of its very best actors. His smooth, relaxed sophistication could just as easily seem chilly or kindly, his clipped tones were inimitable and he was an unselfish and integral part of some very fine films. Four times nominated for the Best Supporting Actor Oscar, he did not win once. Six times married, including (first) actress Isabel Jeans (1892–1985). Died after an intestinal haemorrhage.

1920: Build Thy House. 1933: The Invisible Man. 1934: Crime without Passion. The Man Who Reclaimed His Head. 1935: The Mystery of Edwin Drood. The Clairvoyant. The Last Outpost. 1936: Hearts Divided. Anthony Adverse. The Prince and the Pauper. Stolen Holiday. 1937: They Won't Forget. 1938: The Adventures of Robin Hood. Gold is Where You Find It. Four Daughters. White Banners. 1939: Daughters Courageous. They Made Me a Criminal. Juarez. Mr Smith Goes to Washington. *Sons of Liberty. Four Wives. 1940: The Sea Hawk. Lady with Red Hair. Saturday's

Children. 1941: Four Mothers. The Wolf Man. Here Comes Mr Jordan. Kings Row. 1942: Now, Voyager. Moontide. Casablanca. 1943: Forever and a Day. Phantom of the Opera. 1944: Passage to Marseille (GB: Passage to Marseilles). Mr Skeffington. 1945: Caesar and Cleopatra. This Love of Ours. Strange Holiday (GB: The Day After Tomorrow). 1946: Angel on My Shoulder. Notorious. 1947: Deception. The Unsuspected. 1949: Rope of Sand. Song of Surrender. The Passionate Friends (US: One Woman's Story). 1950: The White Tower. Where Danger Lives. 1951: Sealed Cargo. 1952: The Man Who Watched Trains Go By (US: Paris Express). 1956: Lisbon. 1967: The Pied Piper of Hamelin (TV. GB: cinemas). 1959: Judgement at Nuremberg (TV). This Earth is Mine. 1960: The Lost World. 1961: Battle of the Worlds. 1962: Lawrence of Arabia. 1963: Twilight of Honor (GB: The Charge is Murder). 1965: The Greatest Story Ever Told.

RALSTON, Vera

(V. Hruba) 1919–

Fair-haired (later dark) champion ice-skater from Czechoslovakia, with very Slavic looks – thick lips and even thicker accent – who became an actress and might have done well in sinister roles had she not fallen under the influence of Republic chief Herbert J. Yates, who was determined to groom her as a leading lady (very much a W.R. Hearst-Marion Davies parallel) and eventually married her in 1952. Thus, she was frequently miscast and the public never really took to her.

1941: ‡ Ice-Capades. 1942 ‡Ice-Capades Revue (GB: Rhythm Hits the Ice). 1944: †Storm over Lisbon. †Lake Placid Serenade. †The Lady and the Monster (GB: The Lady and the Doctor). 1945: †Dakota. 1946: †Murder in the Music Hall. The Plainsman and the Lady. 1947: The Flame. Wyoming. 1948: I, Jane Doe (GB: Diary of a Bride). Angel on the Amazon (GB: Drums Along the Amazon). 1949: The Fighting Kentuckian. 1950: Surrender. 1951: Belle le Grand. The Wild Blue Yonder (GB: Thunder Across the Pacific). 1952: Hoodlum Empire. 1953: A Perilous Journey. Fair Wind to Java. 1954: Jubilee Trail. 1955: Timberjack. 1956: Accused of Murder. 1957: Spoilers of the Forest. Gunfire at Indian Gap. 1958: The Notorious Mr Monks. The Man Who Died Twice.

‡ As Vera Hruba †As Vera Hruba Ralston

RAMPLING, Charlotte 1945–

Tall, rangy British actress, noted in her early career for portraits of passionate decadence and rich bitches. From the mid-seventies however, her rather harsh features began to project a more sympathetic image. She maintained her star status over the next two decades, in spite of often appearing in relatively obscure projects. Married to musician/composer of synthesized music Jean-Michel Jarre.

1965: The Knack . . . and how to get it. Rotten to the Core. 1966: Georgy Girl. 1967: The Long Duel. 1968: Sequestro di persona (GB: Island of Crime). Gotterdämmerung/The Damned. 1969: How to Make It (GB: Target: Harry). Three. 1970: †Zabriskie Point. 1971: The Ski Bum. 'Tis Pity She's a Whore. Corky. 1972: Henry VIII and His Six Wives. Asylum. 1973: Zardoz. The Night Porter. Revolt of the City. 1974: Caravan to Vaccares. La chair de l'orchidée. 1975: Farewell, My Lovely. Foxtrot (later The Other Side of Paradise). Yuppi-Du. 1976: Sherlock Holmes in New York (TV). 1977: Taxi Mauve. Orca . . . Killer Whale. 1979: Bugsy. 1980: Stardust Memories. 1982: The Verdict. 1984: Viva la vie. 1985: Tristesse et beauté. On ne meurt que deux fois (GB and US: He Died with His Eyes Open). 1986: Max Mon Amour. 1987: Angel Heart. Mascara. 1988: D.O.A. (GB: Dead on Arrival). Rebus. Paris by Night. 1989: Helmut Newton: Frames from the Edge. Tre colonne in cronaca. 1992: Hammers Over the Anvil. Sacrifice for Love (TV). 1993: Time is Money. 1994: Radetzky March. 1996: La dernière fête (TV). Invasion of Privacy. Head Games. Nid de poules. 1997: The Wings of the Dove. Asphalt Tango. 1999: The Cherry Orchard. 2000: Signs & Wonders. Aberdeen. Sous le sable.

† Scenes deleted from final release print

RANDALL, Tony

(Leonard Rosenberg) 1920–

Dark-haired American comic actor with smooth face and sour mouth. He made no films until his late thirties, then was riotously successful as the lead in satirical comedies at Fox, and as the hero's droll friend in Doris Day fol-de-rols at Universal. After several mediocre mid-sixties films he disappointingly returned to television. Still busy on TV and in the theatre in the 1990s. First wife died; married again and had two children in his seventies.

1957: Will Success Spoil Rock Hunter? (GB:

Oh! For a Man!). No Down Payment. Oh, Men! Oh, Women! The Playroom (TV). 1959: The Mating Game. Second Happiest Day (TV). Pillow Talk. 1960: The Adventures of Huckleberry Finn. Let's Make Love. 1961: Lover Come Back. 1962: Boys' Night Out. 1963: Island of Love. 1964: The 7 Faces of Dr Lao. The Brass Bottle. Send Me No Flowers. 1965: Fluffy. The Alphabet Murders. 1966: Our Man in Marrakesh (US: Bang Bang You're Dead). 1968: Hello Down There. The Littlest Angel (TV). 1972: Everything You Always Wanted to Know About Sex* *But Were Afraid to Ask. 1978: Kate Bliss and the Ticker Tape Kid (TV). Foolin' Around (released 1980). 1979: Scavenger Hunt. 1981: A Girl's Best Friend/Sidney Shorr: A Girl's Best Friend (TV). 1982: The King of Comedy. 1984: Off Sides (TV). 1985: Hitler's SS: Portrait in Evil (TV. GB: cinemas). 1986: That's Adequate! My Little Pony (voice only). Sunday Drive (TV). 1987: It Had to Be You (released 1989). 1988: The Man in the Brown Suit (TV). Save the Dog! (TV). 1990: Gremlins 2: The New Batch (voice only). 1993: Fatal Instinct. The Odd Couple: Together Again (TV).

RANDELL, Ron 1918–

Cheerful-looking Australian leading man with dark, wavy hair who made a strong impression in post-war Australian films before going to Hollywood in 1947 and playing leads in minor features, including such series detectives as Bulldog Drummond and the Lone Wolf. Made his home in Britain for a while, gaining notoriety as a TV panellist who winked at the ladies, before returning to America and small film roles.

1946: Smithy (GB: Southern Cross. US:

Pacific Adventure). A Son is Born. 1947: It Had to be You. Bulldog Drummond at Bay. Bulldog Drummond Strikes Back. 1948: The Sign of the Ram. The Loves of Carmen. The Mating of Millie. 1949: Omoo-Omoo (GB: The Shark God). The Lone Wolf and His Lady. Make Believe Ballroom. 1950: Counterspy Meets Scotland Yard. Tyrant of the Sea. 1951: China Corsair. Lorna Doone. 1952: The Brigand. Captive Women (GB: 3000 AD). 1953: The Girl on the Pier. Mississippi Gambler. Kiss Me Kate. 1954: The Triangle. One Just Man. The Yellow Robe. Three Cornered Fate/The Blue Camellia. 1955: The Diamond Expert. The Man in Demand. The Price of Greed. Triple Blackmail. Desert Sands. I Am a Camera. 1956: Bermuda Affair. Beyond Mombasa. Count of Twelve. The Hostage. The She-Creature. Quincannon, Frontier Scout (GB: Frontier Scout). 1957: The Story of Esther Costello (US: Golden Virgin). Morning Call (US: The Strange Case of Dr Manning). The Girl in Black Stockings. Davy. Man of the Law (TV. GB: cinemas). 1961: King of Kings. The Most Dangerous Man Alive. The Phoney American (GB: It's a Great Life). 1962: Come Fly with Me. The Longest Day. Gold for the Caesars. 1963: Follow the Boys. 1966: Legend of a Gunfighter. Savage Pampas. 1971: The Seven Minutes. Whity. 1983: Exposed.

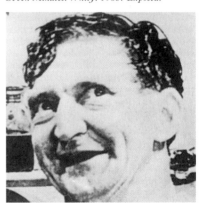

RANDLE, Frank

(Arthur McEvoy) 1901–1957

Big-nosed, toothless, light-haired, abrasive music-hall comedian, fond of disguises and (for their time) rude jokes. Made several low-budget comedies in which one could almost see the cracks in the scenery – but they were immensely popular in his native Lancashire, and didn't do badly elsewhere. Died from gastroenteritis.

1940: Somewhere in England. 1941: Somewhere in Camp. 1942: Somewhere on Leave. 1943: Somewhere in Civvies. 1945: Home Sweet Home. 1946: *Randle and All That. 1947: When You Came Home. 1948: Holidays with Pay. 1949: Somewhere in Politics. School for Randle. 1953: It's a Grand Life.

RATHBONE, Basil

(Philip B. Rathbone) 1892–1967

Suave, sharp-featured, dark-haired, sophisticated British actor, in Hollywood from the late twenties, who proved equally at home with a sword or a witty remark. A sneering dominant villain in thirties' costume pieces, and the screen's best Sherlock Holmes, he

spent his latter days in a weird variety of horror films. Died from a heart attack. Nominated for Academy Awards in *Romeo and Juliet* and *If I Were King*. Born in Transvaal, Southern Africa, to British parents, he made his English stage debut as early as 1911, with roles in British films following 10 years later.

1921: *Innocent. The Fruitful Vine.* 1923: *The Loves of Mary, Queen of Scots. The School for Scandal.* 1924: *Trouping with Ellen.* 1925: *The Masked Bride.* 1926: *The Great Deception.* 1929: *The Last of Mrs Cheyney. Barnum Was Right.* 1930: *The Bishop Murder Case. A Notorious Affair. The Lady of Scandal (GB: The High Road). This Mad World. The Flirting Widow. A Lady Surrenders (GB: Blind Wives). Sin Takes a Holiday.* 1931: *Once a Lady.* 1932: *A Woman Commands. After the Ball.* 1933: *One Precious Year. Loyalties.* 1935: *David Copperfield. Anna Karenina. The Last Days of Pompeii. A Feather in Her Hat. Captain Blood. A Tale of Two Cities.* 1936: *Kind Lady (GB: House of Menace). Private Number (GB: Secret Interlude). Romeo and Juliet. The Garden of Allah.* 1937: *Confession. Love from a Stranger. Make a Wish. Tovarich.* 1938: *The Adventures of Marco Polo. The Adventures of Robin Hood. If I Were King. The Dawn Patrol.* 1939: *Son of Frankenstein. The Hound of the Baskervilles. The Sun Never Sets. The Adventures of Sherlock Holmes (GB: Sherlock Holmes). Rio. Tower of London.* 1940: *Rhythm on the River. The Mark of Zorro. The Mad Doctor (GB: A Date with Destiny).* 1941: *The Black Cat. *Screen Snapshots No 87. International Lady. Paris Calling.* 1942: *Fingers at the Window. Crossroads. Sherlock Holmes and the Voice of Terror. Sherlock Holmes and the Secret Weapon.* 1943: *Sherlock Holmes in Washington. Crazy House. Above Suspicion. Sherlock Holmes Faces Death. Sherlock Holmes and Spider Woman (GB: Spider Woman).* 1944: *The Scarlet Claw. Bathing Beauty. The Pearl of Death. Frenchman's Creek.* 1945: *The House of Fear. The Woman in Green. Pursuit to Algiers.* 1946: *Terror By Night. Heartbeat. Dressed to Kill (GB: Sherlock Holmes and the Secret Code).* 1949: *The Adventures of Ichabod and Mr Toad (narrator only).* 1953: *Casanova's Big Night.* 1955: *We're No Angels. The Court Jester.* 1956: *The Black Sheep.* 1958: *The Last Hurrah.* 1961: *The Magic Sword. Pontius Pilate.* 1962: *Red Hell. Two Before Zero (narrator only). Tales of Terror.* 1963: *The Comedy of Terrors.* 1966: *Planet of Blood/Queen of Blood. Ghost in the Invisible Bikini.* 1967: *Voyage to a Prehistoric Planet (GB: Prehistoric Planet Women). Dr Rock and Mr Roll. Autopsy of a Ghost.* 1968: *Hillbillys in a Haunted House.*

RAY, Aldo (A. de Re) 1926–1991
Bullet-headed, thick-necked, husky-voiced, crew-cut, fair-haired American actor who was a local sheriff before taking up a movie career. At first, amusingly, he was seen in ingenuous roles, but later played sometimes tender-hearted tough guys. A star until 1961, he drifted into some international roles, then returned to Hollywood in the mid-1960s in co-starring parts. Stayed a busy actor, albeit in lesser films – often as men of violence. Once married (1954–6) to actress Jeff Donnell (1921–1988). Died from throat cancer.

1951: *Saturday's Hero (GB: Idols in the Dust). My True Story.* 1952: *Pat and Mike. The Marrying Kind.* 1953: *Let's Do It Again. Miss Sadie Thompson.* 1954: *We're No Angels. Battle Cry.* 1955: *Three Stripes in the Sun (GB: The Gentle Sergeant).* 1956: *Nightfall.* 1957: *Men in War.* 1958: *The Naked and the Dead. God's Little Acre.* 1959: *The Siege of Pinchgut (US: Four Desperate Men).* 1960: *Musketeers of the Sea. The Day They Robbed the Bank of England.* 1961: *Johnny Nobody.* 1963: *Nightmare in the Sun.* 1965: *Sylvia.* 1966: *What Did You Do in the War, Daddy? Dead Heat on a Merry-Go-Round. Welcome to Hard Times (GB: Killer on a Horse).* 1967: *Riot on Sunset Strip. Kill a Dragon/To Kill a Dragon. The Power. The Violent Ones.* 1968: *The Green Berets. The Silent Treatment. Suicide Commandos.* 1969: *Man Without Mercy (later Gone with the West). Deadlock (TV).* 1970: *The Haunted.* 1971: *Angel Unchained.* 1972: *La course du lièvre à travers les champs (GB and US: And Hope to Die).* 1974: *Seven Alone. Centerfold Girls. Stud Brown (GB: The Dynamite Brothers).* 1975: *Promise Him Anything Inside Out. The Man Who Would Not Die. Won Ton Ton, the Dog Who Saved Hollywood. Psychic Killer.* 1976: *Tom/The Bad Bunch.* 1977: *Haunts/The Veil. Kino, the Padre on Horseback. Death Dimension.* 1978: *Sky Dove. Bog.* 1979: *Just Not the Same Without You. Human Experiments. Sanctuary for Evil. When I Am King. The Glove (released 1981).* 1980: *Skycopter Summer. Box Office.* 1981: *Jayne Mansfield – an American Tragedy. Don't Go Near the Park.* 1982: *The Secret of NIMH (voice only). Mongrel. Sweet Sexy Savage. Dark Sanity.* 1983: *Evils of the Night. Frankenstein's Great Aunt Tillie (released 1985). Vultures in Paradise/Flesh and Bullets.* 1984: *To Kill a Stranger. The Executioner Part II.* 1985: *Biohazard (completed 1983). Prison Ship 2005.* 1986: *Red Nights.* 1987: *Terror on Alcatraz. Blood Red. The Sicilian. Terminal Force.* 1988: *Terror Night/Final Curtain. Pop's Oasis. Hollywood Cop.* 1989: *Swift Justice.* 1990: *The Shooters. Shock 'Em Dead.* 1991: *Foreign Agent.*

RAY, René (Irene Creese) 1912–1993
Sharply pretty brunette British actress, on stage from childhood, in films as a teenager. In the thirties her film roles varied bewilderingly from leads to quite small parts: not surprisingly, she didn't settle as a big star. Went to Hollywood after World War II (after a one-film visit in 1938) for a lengthy stay. But it was too late: she only got one film part. Later became a successful novelist, and married into the aristocracy.

1928: *Palais de Danse.* 1929: *Varsity. High Treason. Atlantic.* 1930: *Young Woodley.* 1931: *Keepers of Youth. Peace and Quiet. The Mystery of Marriage. Tonight's the Night.* 1932: *When London Sleeps. Dance Pretty Lady. Born Lucky. *The Changing Year. Two White Arms (US: Wives Beware). Here's George. Smilin' Along. The King's Cup.* 1933: *Excess Baggage. Tiger Bay.* 1934: *Easy Money. Rolling in Money. Nine Forty-Five. Once in a New Moon.* 1935: *Full Circle. Street Song. Royal Cavalcade (US: Regal Cavalcade). The Passing of the Third Floor Back.* 1936: *His Lordship (US: Man of Affairs). Beloved Imposter. Crime over London.* 1937: *Jenifer Hale. Farewell Again (US: Troopship). The Green Cockatoo. The Rat. Bank Holiday (US: Three on a Weekend). Please Teacher.* 1938: *Housemaster. Mountains o' Mourne. That Certain Age. Weddings are Wonderful. The Return of the Frog.* 1939: *Home from Home.* 1940: *The Call for Arms. Old Bill and Son.* 1947: *They Made Me a Fugitive (US: I Became a Criminal). If Winter Comes. *Pathe Pictorial No 132.* 1951: *The Galloping Major.* 1952: *Women of Twilight (US: Twilight Women).* 1954: *The Good Die Young.* 1957: *The Vicious Circle (US: The Circle).*

RAYE, Martha
(Margaret 'Maggie' Reed) 1908–1994
Chasm-mouthed, powerhouse strawberry-blonde American vocalist and comedienne

with the energy of Betty Hutton and a voice that made Ethel Merman sound like Peggy Lee. Mostly on stage, but popular for a while in vigorous screen musicals of the late 1930s and early 1940s. Much later she reappeared, dyspeptically personable, as a housekeeper in the TV series *McMillan*. She was awarded a special Oscar in 1969 for her work entertaining the troops in World War II – facets that may have inspired the Bette Midler character in *For the Boys*, over which Raye unsuccessfully sued. Seven times married, she was in poor health in her last years, suffering a stroke and the amputation of a leg below the knee.

1934: *Nite in a Nite Club. 1936: Rhythm on the Range. College Holiday. The Big Breakfast of 1937. 1937: Mountain Music. Hideaway Girl. Artists and Models. Waikiki Wedding. Double or Nothing. 1938: College Swing (GB: Swing, Teacher, Swing). The Big Broadcast of 1938. Tropic Holiday. Give Me a Sailor. 1939: Never Say Die. $1,000 a Touchdown. 1940: The Boys from Syracuse. The Farmer's Daughter. 1941: Navy Blues. Hellzapoppin. Keep 'Em Flying. 1944: Pin-Up Girl. Four Jills in a Jeep. 1947: Monsieur Verdoux. 1952: *Hollywood Night at 21 Club. 1962: Billy Rose's Jumbo (GB: Jumbo). 1969: The Phynx. 1970: Pufnstuf. 1979: The Concorde – Airport '79 (GB: Airport '80 . . . the Concorde). The Gossip Columnist (TV). 1981: Pippin (video).

RAYMOND, Gene (R. Guion) 1908–1998
Fair-haired, strong-looking American leading man, a former child actor, who won some quite decent leading roles in the Hollywood of the thirties, but is mostly remembered for being married to Jeanette

MacDonald (*qv*) from 1937 to her death in 1965. Died from pneumonia.

1931: Personal Maid. Ladies of the Big House. 1932: Forgotten Commandments. If I Had a Million. Red Dust. The Night of June 13th. 1933: Ann Carver's Profession. Ex-Lady. Brief Moment. Zoo in Budapest. Flying Down to Rio. The House on 56th Street. 1934: Transatlantic Merry-Go-Round. Coming Out Party. I Am Suzanne! Behold My Wife. Sadie McKee. 1935: Transient Lady (GB: False Witness). The Woman in Red. Seven Keys to Baldpate. Hooray for Love. 1936: Walking on Air. Love on a Bet. That Girl from Paris. The Smartest Girl in Town. The Bride Walks Out. 1937: There Goes My Girl. The Life of the Party. 1938: Stolen Heaven. *Hollywood Personalities. She's Got Everything. 1940: Cross-Country Romance. 1941: Me and Mrs Smith. Smilin' Through. 1946: The Locket. 1948: Assigned to Danger. †Million Dollar Week-End. Sofia. 1955: Hit the Deck. 1957: Plunder Road. 1964: The Best Man. I'd Rather Be Rich. The Hanged Man (TV. GB: cinemas). 1970: Five Bloody Graves (narrator only).

†*Also directed*

RAYMOND, Paula
(P. Ramona Wright) 1923–
Tall, slim, glamorous, dark-haired American actress, a model who decided to try a film career in 1948. M-G-M picked her up and gave her some quite good roles but once she left them in 1952 her career slid into second-features and, much later, cheap horror films. Her acting-by-numbers technique did not improve with the years and, while easy on the eye, she never seemed entirely at ease on screen. Recovered from severe facial injuries in a 1962 car crash.

1938: †Keep Smiling. 1944: Experiment Perilous (voice only). 1948: Racing Luck. Rusty Leads the Way. Blondie's Secret. *Powder River Gunfire. 1949: East Side, West Side. Challenge of the Range (GB: Moonlight Raid). Adam's Rib. 1950: Devil's Doorway. Sons of New Mexico (GB: The Brat). Duchess of Idaho. Crisis. Grounds for Marriage. 1951: Inside Straight. The Tall Target. The Sellout. Texas Carnival. 1952: Bandits of Corsica (GB: Return of the Corsican Brothers). 1953: The Beast from 20,000 Fathoms. City That Never Sleeps. 1954: The Human Jungle. King Richard and the Crusaders. 1955: The Gun That Won the West. 1961: Hand of Death. 1962: The Flight That Disappeared. 1964: The Spy with My

Face. 1967: Blood of Dracula's Castle. 1970: Five Bloody Graves. 1993: Mind Twister.

†*As Paula Rae Wright*

REA, Stephen 1942–
Hangdog, unsmiling, bag-eyed Irish actor whose unhappy looks somehow belie his years. Thus, after years on the Irish stage (and a few films in the early 1980s), he was able to start a career as an international leading man in his late forties after an Academy Award nomination for *The Crying Game*. In that, as in others, he played an IRA fighter; in real life, he married former Irish Republican Army member Dolours Price. In the 1990s, he mixed more IRA men with offbeat roles, and showed himself surprisingly adept at warm comedy in *Bad Behaviour*.

1970: Cry of the Banshee. 1973: A Place Called Ardoyne (narrator only). 1978: On a Paving Stone Mounted. 1982: Angel (US: Danny Boy). 1983: Loose Connections. 1984: The Company of Wolves. The House. Four Days in July (TV). 1985: The Doctor and the Devils. Shergar (TV). 1991: Life is Sweet. 1992: The Crying Game. Bad Behaviour. 1993: Angie. 1994: Look Me in the Eye. Princess Caraboo. Prêt-à-Porter (US: Ready to Wear). Interview with the Vampire. 1995: Citizen X (TV). Between the Devil and Deep Blue Sea. All Men Are Mortal. 1996: Crime of the Century (TV). Fever Pitch. Michael Collins. Trojan Eddie. 1997: A Further Gesture (GB: The Break). The Butcher Boy. Double Tap. Hacks (US: The Big Twist). 1998: This is My Father. Still Crazy. In Dreams. 1999: Guinevere. The End of the Affair. The Life Before This. 2000: I Could Read the Sky. The Smiling Suicide Club.

REAGAN, Ronald 1911–
The film career of this brown-haired, friendly-looking American actor bore no hint of his lofty ambition to be US President. He was a loyal servant to Warners for 13 years as easy-going types, without quite getting into the mainstream of their product. When his features hardened with middle age, he played tough westerns for a while before going into politics, becoming Governor of California from 1966 to 1975, and being elected President in 1980. He was re-elected for a further term in 1984. Married to Jane Wyman (*qv*) from 1940 to 1948 and to Nancy Davis (1924–) from 1952 onwards. Suffering from Alzheimer's Disease in recent years.

1937: *Love is on the Air* (GB: *The Radio Murder Mystery*). †*Submarine D-1*. *Hollywood Hotel. Swing Your Lady.* 1938: *Cowboy from Brooklyn. Sergeant Murphy. Brother Rat. Girls on Probation. Boy Meets Girl. Going Places.* *Pictorial Revue No 6*. *Accidents Will Happen.* 1939: *Code of the Secret Service. Dark Victory. Hell's Kitchen. Smashing the Money Ring. Angels Wash Their Faces. Naughty But Nice. Secret Service of the Air.* 1940: *Brother Rat and a Baby* (GB: *Baby Be Good*). *Murder in the Air. Tugboat Annie Sails Again. Knute Rockne – All American* (GB: *A Modern Hero*). *Santa Fé Trail. Angel from Texas.* 1941: *Nine Lives Are Not Enough. The Bad Man* (GB: *Two Gun Cupid*). *Kings Row. International Squadron. Million Dollar Baby.* *How to Improve Your Golf*. 1942: *Mr Gardenia Jones. Juke Girl. Desperate Journey.* 1943: *Rear Gunner*. *Hollywood in Uniform*. *This is the Army.* 1944: *For God and Country.* 1947: *That Hagen Girl. Stallion Road. The Voice of the Turtle. Night unto Night* (released 1949). **So You Want to be in Pictures*. 1948: *Studio Tour*. *OK for Pictures*. 1949: *John Loves Mary. The Girl from Jones Beach. It's a Great Feeling. The Hasty Heart.* 1950: *Louisa. Storm Warning.* 1951: *The Last Outpost. Bedtime for Bonzo. Hong Kong.* 1952: *The Winning Team. She's Working Her Way through College.* 1953: *Law and Order. Tropic Zone.* 1954: *Prisoner-of-War. Cattle Queen of Montana. Beneath These Waters* (TV. GB: cinemas). 1955: *Tennessee's Partner.* 1957: *Hellcats of the Navy.* 1961: *The Young Doctors* (narrator only). 1963: *The Truth about Communism* (narrator only). 1964: *The Killers.*

†*Scenes deleted from final release print*

REASON, Rex 1928–
Chunky, cheerful-looking American actor (born in Germany) with blue eyes and dark wavy hair, who looked a star prospect after playing the leading role in his first film. But a major studio (Universal-International) took him up and seriously disrupted his career by changing his name to Bart Roberts before allowing him too late to revert to the real one. Reason's roles declined towards the end of the 1950s, although he starred in two TV series, *Man Without a Gun* and *The Roaring Twenties*, before dropping from sight in the mid 1960s. His twin brother, Rhodes Reason, was also an actor.
1952: *Storm Over Tibet.* 1953: *Mission Over

Korea (GB: *Eyes of the Skies*). *China Venture. Salome. The Big Heat.* 1954: †*Taza, Son of Cochise.* †*Yankee Pasha.* 1955: †*Kiss of Fire. Lady Godiva* (GB: *Lady Godiva of Coventry*). *Smoke Signal. This Island Earth.* 1956: *The Creatures Walks Among Us. Raw Edge.* 1957: *Badlands of Montana. Band of Angels. Under Fire.* 1958: *The Rawhide Trail. Thundering Jets.* 1959: *The Sad Horse. The Miracle of the Hills.*

†*As Bart Roberts*

REDFORD, Robert
(Charles R. Redford) 1936–
Tall, blond, athletic, hawk-nosed, honest-looking and very handsome American leading man who became one of the great superstar pin-ups of the seventies. His interests – skiing, the American West, climbing, riding – and opinions have often reflected themselves in his acting and writing. Won 1981 Best Director Oscar for *Ordinary People*. Nominated for an acting Oscar in *The Sting*, he is the founder of the Sundance Institute, a training centre for young film-makers.
1960: *In the Presence of Mine Enemies* (TV). 1961: *War Hunt.* 1965: *Situation Hopeless – but not serious. Inside Daisy Clover.* 1966: *The Chase. This Property is Condemned.* 1967: *Barefoot in the Park.* 1969: *Tell Them Willie Boy is Here. Butch Cassidy and the Sundance Kid. The Making of Butch Cassidy and the Sundance Kid. Downhill Racer.* 1970: *Little Fauss and Big Halsy.* 1972: *Jeremiah Johnson. The Candidate. The Hot Rock* (GB: *How to Steal a Diamond in Four Uneasy Lessons*). 1973: *The Way We Were. The Sting.* 1974: *The Great Gatsby.* 1975: *The Great Waldo Pepper. Three Days of the Condor.* 1976: *All

the President's Men. 1977: *A Bridge Too Far.* 1979: *The Electric Horseman.* 1980: *Brubaker.* 1984: *The Natural.* 1985: *Out of Africa.* 1986: *Legal Eagles.* 1990: *Havana.* 1992: *Sneakers. Incident at Oglala* (narrator only). *A River Runs Through It* (narrator only). 1993: *Indecent Proposal.* 1995: *Wild Bill. Hollywood Maverick.* 1996: *Up Close & Personal.* 1998: *The Horse Whisperer. Anthem* (doc). 1999: *Forever Hollywood* (doc). 2000: *The Legend of Bagger Vance.*

As director: 1980: *Ordinary People.* 1988: *The Milagro Beanfield War.* 1992: *A River Runs Through It.* 1994: *Quiz Show.* 1998: *The Horse Whisperer.* 2000: *The Legend of Bagger Vance.*

REDGRAVE, Lynn 1943–
Warm, bouncy, extrovert, tawny-haired British comedy actress, daughter of Sir Michael Redgrave and sister of Vanessa Redgrave (both *qv*). Her appeal was somewhere between Joyce Grenfell (1910–1979) and Pauline Collins (1940–), and her *Georgy Girl*, which won her an Academy Award nomination, was a tragi-comic *tour-de-force*. But after that the cinema seemed to see her as tarts-with-hearts, and she has seldom received roles in films that emphasized her individual appeal. Academy Award nominee for *Gods and Monsters*.
1963: *Tom Jones. Girl with Green Eyes.* 1966: *The Deadly Affair. Georgy Girl.* 1967: *Smashing Time.* 1969: *The Virgin Soldiers. Last of the Mobile Hot-Shots* (later *Blood Kin*). 1971: *Los guerilleros* (US: *Killer from Yuma*). 1972: *Viva la muerte – tua! Everything You Always Wanted to Know about Sex* *But Were Afraid to Ask. Every Little Crook and Nanny.* 1973: *The National Health.* 1974: *The Turn of the Screw* (TV). 1975: *The Happy Hooker. Don't Turn the Other Cheek.* 1976: *The Big Bus.* 1978: *Sooner or Later* (TV). 1979: *Gauguin – the Savage.* 1980: *Sunday Lovers. The Seduction of Miss Leona* (TV). 1982: *The Bad Seed* (TV). *Rehearsal for Murder* (TV). 1985: *Home Front* (released 1978 as *Morgan Stewart's Coming Home*). 1986: *My Two Loves* (TV). 1988: *Death of a Son* (TV). *Midnight.* 1989: *Getting It Right. Jury Duty: the Comedy* (TV. GB: *The Great American Sex Scandal*). 1991: *What Ever Happened to Baby Jane?* (TV). 1996: *Shine.* 1997: *Toothless* (TV). *A Father's Betrayal* (TV). 1998: *Gods and Monsters. Strike!* 1999: *Different* (TV). *Touched/Shegalla. The

Annihilation of Fish. A Season for Miracles (TV). 2000: The Next Best Thing. Deeply. Venus and Mars. The Lion of Oz and the Badge of Courage (TV. Voice only). How to Kill Your Neighbor's Dog. The Simian Line. 2001: Unconditional Love. My Kingdom.

REDGRAVE, Sir Michael 1908–1985

Tall, scholarly-looking British actor with light-brown hair. He switched from teaching to acting in the 1930s, and proved a stalwart servant of the British cinema, often in ideological roles, although also capable of raising a chill. Mainly in guest roles from the late 1950s, he was in very poor health in his last few years. Married to actress Rachel Kempson (1910–), he was the father of actors Lynn, Vanessa (both qv) and Corin Redgrave. Son of British actor Roy Redgrave (1872–1922), who starred in Australian silent films. Nominated for an Oscar in Mourning Becomes Electra, he was knighted in 1959. Died from Parkinson's Disease.

1936: Secret Agent. 1938: The Lady Vanishes. Stolen Life. Climbing High. 1939: A Window in London (US: Lady in Distress). The Stars Look Down. 1941: Kipps (US: The Remarkable Mr Kipps). Jeannie. Atlantic Ferry (US: Sons of the Sea). The Big Blockade. 1942: Thunder Rock. 1945: The Way to the Stars (US: Johnny in the Clouds). Dead of Night. A Diary for Timothy (narrator only). 1946: The Captive Heart. The Years Between. 1947: The Man Within (US: The Smugglers). Fame is the Spur. Mourning Becomes Electra. 1948: Secret Beyond the Door. 1949: *Her Fighting Chance (narrator only). 1951: The Browning Version. Painter and Poet (narrator only). Winter Garden (narrator only). The Magic Box. 1952: The Importance of Being Earnest. 1954: The Sea Shall Not Have Them. The Green Scarf. The Dam Busters. 1955: *The Lake District (narrator only). The Night My Number Came Up. Oh Rosalinda!! 1984: Confidential Report (US: Mr Arkadin). 1956: *Kings and Queens (narrator only). The Happy Road. 1957: Time without Pity. 1958: The Quiet American. Law and Disorder. Behind the Mask. *The Immortal Land (narrator only). 1959: Shake Hands with the Devil. The Wreck of the Mary Deare. 1960: *May Wedding (narrator only). *The Questioning City (narrator only). 1961: No, My Darling Daughter. The Innocents. 1962: The Loneliness of the Long Distance Runner. 1963: Uncle Vanya. 1964: Young Cassidy. 1965: The Hill. The Heroes of Telemark. 1966:

Palaces of a Queen (narrator only). 1967: The 25th Hour. Assignment K. October Revolution (narrator only). 1968: Heidi Comes Home (US: Heidi). 1969: Oh! What a Lovely War. Battle of Britain. Goodbye, Mr Chips. Connecting Rooms. David Copperfield (TV. GB: cinemas). 1970: Goodbye Gemini. The Go-Between. 1971: Nicholas and Alexandra.

REDGRAVE, Vanessa 1937–

Gaunt, fair-haired British actress, daughter of Sir Michael Redgrave and sister of Lynn Redgrave (both qv). Generally well-liked by the critics, she has never become a box-office force, despite her liberated lifestyle and well-publicized espousal of left-wing causes. After unsuccessful Oscar nominations for Morgan – a Suitable Case for Treatment, Isadora and Mary, Queen of Scots, she won a best supporting actress Academy Award (and deservedly so) for Julia. Married/divorced director Tony Richardson. A long association with actor Franco Nero (qv) also came to an end. Additional Oscar nominations for The Bostonians and Howards End.

1958: Behind the Mask. 1961: *The Circus at Clopton Hall (narrator only). 1965: Morgan – a Suitable Case for Treatment. 1966: A Man for All Seasons. Blow-Up. 1967: Tonite Let's All Make Love in London. Red and Blue. Sailor from Gibraltar. Camelot. 1968: The Charge of the Light Brigade. 1969: Isadora. A Quiet Place in the Country. Oh! What a Lovely War. The Sea Gull. 1970: Drop Out! The Body (narrator only). La vacanza. 1971: The Devils. The Trojan Women. Mary, Queen of Scots. 1974: Murder on the Orient Express. 1975: Out of Season. 1976: The Seven Per Cent Solution. 1977: Julia. 1978: Agatha. Yanks. 1979: Bear Island. 1980: Playing for Time (TV). 1982: Wagner. My Body, My Child (TV). 1983: Sing Sing. 1984: The Bostonians. Steaming. 1985: Wetherby. Three Sovereigns for Sarah (TV). 1986: Second Serve (TV). 1987: Prick Up Your Ears. 1988: Consuming Passions. A Man for All Seasons (TV). 1990: Di ceria dell'untore (US: The Plague Sower). Orpheus Descending (TV). Romeo-Juliet (voice only). 1991: The Ballad of the Sad Café. Whatever Happened to Baby Jane? (TV). Howards End. 1993: The House of the Spirits. La Maître Savane. Mother's Boys. Crime and Punishment. Black Flowers. Un muro di silencio. Sparrow. 1994: Great Moments in Aviation (GB: TV). A Month by the Lake. Little Odessa. 1995: Down Came a Blackbird. Mission: Impossible. 1996:

Two Mothers for Zachary (TV). Looking for Richard. 1997: Smilla's Sense of Snow/Smilla's Feeling for Snow. Mrs Dalloway. Déja Vu. Wilde. 1998: Lulu on the Bridge. Deep Impact. 1999: Cradle Will Rock. Toscano. Mirka. Girl, Interrupted. Uninvited. An Interesting State. 2000: If These Walls Could Talk 2. Rumor of Angels. 2001: The Pledge.

REED, Donna (D. Mullenger) 1921–1986

Lovely, dark-haired actress who enjoyed the quietest of Hollywood careers, mainly in nice-girl roles, while gaining a reputation on the other side of the camera as an outspoken critic of directors. Perhaps, in view of the routine nature of her films, it's not surprising. Nor does it say too much for M-G-M, where she spent half her career, that all her best roles (with the possible exception of the later Ransom!) were for other studios, including From Here to Eternity, for which she won a Best Supporting Actress Oscar. Died from cancer of the pancreas.

1941: †Babes on Broadway. †The Get-Away. The Bugle Sounds. Shadow of the Thin Man. 1942: Mokey. Calling Dr Gillespie. Apache Trail. The Courtship of Andy Hardy. Eyes in the Night. 1943: Thousands Cheer. The Human Comedy. Dr Gillespie's Criminal Case (GB: Crazy to Kill). The Man from Down Under. 1944: Gentle Annie. See Here, Private Hargrove. Mrs Parkington. 1945: The Picture of Dorian Gray. They Were Expendable. 1946: Faithful in My Fashion. It's a Wonderful Life. 1947: Green Dolphin Street. 1948: Beyond Glory. 1949: Chicago Deadline. 1951: Scandal Sheet (GB: The Dark Page). Saturday's Hero (GB: Idols in the Dust). 1952: Hangman's Knot. 1953: *Hollywood Laugh Parade. Raiders of the Seven Seas. Trouble Along the Way. The Caddy. From Here to Eternity. Gun Fury. 1954: Three Hours to Kill. The Last Time I Saw Paris. They Rode West. 1955: The Far Horizons. 1956: Ransom! The Benny Goodman Story. Backlash. Beyond Mombasa. 1958: The Whole Truth. 1960: Pepe. 1974: The Yellow Headed Summer. 1979: The Best Place to Be (TV). 1983: Deadly Lessons (TV). 1987: Arriva Frank Capra.

†As Donna Adams

REED, Maxwell 1919–1974

Tall, dark, glowering Irish-born leading man who gained something of a reputation as the wild man of British films before marriage to

Joan Collins (*qv*) in 1952 (they were subsequently divorced). His career ran downhill after the mid-fifties as he looked around for international roles.

1946: No Ladies Please. The Years Between. Gaiety George (US: Showtime). Daybreak. 1947: The Brothers. Dear Murderer. Daughter of Darkness. 1948: Night Beat. 1949: Madness of the Heart. The Lost People. 1950: Blackout. The Clouded Yellow. 1951: The Dark Man. There is Another Sun (US: Wall of Death). Flame of Araby. 1953: Sea Devils. The Square Ring. Marilyn (later Roadhouse Girl). Le corsaire des Caraibes/Captain Phantom. 1954: The Brain Machine. Helen of Troy. 1955: Before I Wake (US: Shadow of Fear). 1961: Pirates of Tortuga. 1962: The Notorious Landlady. Advise and Consent. 1966: Picture Mommy Dead.

REED, Oliver (Robert O. Reed) 1937–1999
Brutish-looking, powerful, heftily-built British actor, much given to sullenness and melodramatics, but also capable of interesting, sometimes touching performances (*The Trap, Hannibal Brooks, Women in Love, Tommy*). The nephew of director Sir Carol Reed, he started as bullies and sneering villains, but powered his way into leading roles by the early sixties and had many female fans breathing heavily before he himself became rather too heavy for romantic roles. Lived a hell-raising, alcoholic private lifestyle. Died in Malta from a heart attack.
1955: Value for Money. 1958: Life is a Circus. Hello London. The Square Peg. The Captain's Table. 1959: Upstairs and Downstairs. Beat Girl (US: Wild for Kicks). The League of Gentlemen. 1960: The Angry Silence. The Two Faces of Dr Jekyll (US: House of Fright).

Sword of Sherwood Forest. His and Hers. No Love for Johnnie. 1961: The Rebel (US: Call Me Genius). The Bulldog Breed. The Curse of the Werewolf. The Pirates of Blood River. 1962: Captain Clegg (US: Night Creatures). The Damned (US: These are the Damned). Paranoiac. The Party's Over. 1963: The Scarlet Blade. 1964: The System (US: The Girl Getters). 1965: The Brigand of Kandahar. 1966: The Trap. The Jokers. 1967: The Shuttered Room. I'll Never Forget What's 'is Name. 1968: Oliver! Hannibal Brooks. The Assassination Bureau. 1969: Women in Love. Take a Girl Like You. 1970: The Lady in the Car with Glasses and a Gun. 1971: The Devils. The Hunting Party. 1972: Sitting Target. Z.P.G. (GB: Zero Population Growth). The Age of Pisces. The Triple Echo (US: Soldier in Skirts). 1973: Mordi e fuggi/Bite and Run. Un Uomo (GB and US: Fury). The Three Musketeers – The Queen's Diamonds. Blue Blood. Revolver. 1974: And Then There Were None. The Four Musketeers – the Revenge of Milady. 1975: Tommy. Lisztomania. Royal Flash. The Sellout. Blood in the Streets. 1976: The Great Scout and Cathouse Thursday. Burnt Offerings. 1977: The Prince and the Pauper (US: Crossed Swords). Tomorrow Never Comes. Assault on Paradise (US: Maniac. GB: TV, as Ransom). 1978: The Big Sleep. The Class of Miss MacMichael. Touch of the Sun. 1979: The Brood. The Mad Trapper (unfinished). 1980: Lion of the Desert/Omar Mukhtar – Lion of the Desert. Dr Heckyl and Mr Hype. 1981: Condorman. Death Bite (later Spasms). Venom. 1982: The Great Question. (Al Mas à la Al Kubra). Clash of Loyalties. Masquerade (TV). 1983: The Sting II. 99 Women. Fanny Hill. Two of a Kind. 1984: The Black Arrow (cable TV). 1986: Captive. Last of the Templars. Castaway. 1987: Wheels of Terror. Gor. Dragonard. Skeleton Coast. Rage to Kill. 1988: Damnation Express. Captive Rage. The Adventures of Baron Munchausen. 1989: The Return of the Musketeers. The Lady and the Highwayman (TV). Treasure Island (TV. GB: cinemas). The Revenger. 1990: A Ghost in Monte Carolo (TV). The House of Usher. Panama Sugar. Master of Dragonard Hill. 1991: Army/Severed Ties. The Pit and the Pendulum. Prisoner of Honor (cable TV). 1992: Hired to Kill. 1995: Funny Bones. 1996: Luise knacht den Jackpot. The Bruce. 1997: Marco Polo. 1998: Parting Shots. Jeremiah (TV). 2000: Gladiator.

REEVE, Christopher 1952–
Strapping young American actor who landed the title role in *Superman*, and surprised many by sustaining the stardom it brought him. Reeve's subtle differentiation between the shy reporter and his alter ego, the Man of Steel, together with subsequent performances in other leading roles, confirmed his talent as being distinctly above the average for portrayers of comic-strip heroes. But his acting career was marking time by the late 1980s, and it was halted in the mid 1990s when he was paralysed from the neck down after a riding fall.
1977: Gray Lady Down. 1978: Superman. 1979: Somewhere in Time. 1980: Superman II. 1981: Deathtrap. 1982: Monsignor. 1983: Superman III. 1984: The Bostonians. The

Aviator. Anna Karenina (TV). 1986: Street Smart. 1987: Superman IV: The Quest for Peace. Switching Channels. 1988: The Great Escape: The Untold Story (TV). 1990: Midnight Spy. So Help Me God! The Rose and the Jackal (TV). 1991: The Horror of Charles Dexter Ward. Bump in the Night (TV). Death Dreams (TV). 1992: Noises Off. The Last Ferry Home (TV). Nightmare in the Daylight (TV). Mortal Sins (TV). 1993: Earth and the American Dream (TV). Black Fox (TV). The Sea Wolf (TV). Blood Horse (TV). Black Fox: Good Men and Bad (TV). The Remains of the Day. Morning Glory. Black Fox: The Price of Peace (TV). 1994: Speechless. Above Suspicion. 1995: Village of the Damned. 1996: A Step Towards Tomorrow (TV). 1997: The Quest for Camelot (voice only). Snakes and Ladders (TV). 1998: Rear Window (TV).
As director: 1997: In the Gloaming (TV).

REEVES, Keanu 1964–
Long-faced, youthful-looking Hollywood actor of cropped dark hair, impassive gaze and tough-talking attitudes. Brought up in Australia, Canada and America, he spent rather too long in the early part of his career playing unkempt boyfriends/sons that only a mother could love. After building up a cult following in both dark drama and daft comedy, the Beirut-born actor (his first name is pronounced Key-Ah-Noo), discarded his scruffy image and had a massive hit with the action film *Speed*. Subsequent ventures, however, were less successful, exposing his limited acting range and difficulty in expressing extreme emotion.
1984: Act of Vengeance (video). 1985: Flying/Dream to Believe. 1986: Under the Influence (TV). Youngblood. Brotherhood of

Justice (TV). Babes in Toyland (TV). 1978: I Wish I Were 18 Again/ Young Again (TV). River's Edge. 1988: Bill and Ted's Excellent Adventure. Permanent Record. The Prince of Pennsylvania. Dangerous Liaisons. The Night Before. 1989: Parenthood. 1990: I Love You to Death. Tune in Tomorrow (GB: Aunt Julia and the Scriptwriter). 1991: My Own Private Idaho. Point Break. Bill and Ted's Bogus Journey. 1992: Bram Stoker's Dracula. 1993: Freaked/Hideous Mutant Freaks. Much Ado About Nothing. Even Cowgirls Get the Blues. Little Buddha. 1994: Speed. 1995: A Walk in the Clouds. Johnny Mnemonic. 1996: Feeling Minnesota. Chain Reaction. The Last Time I Committed Suicide. 1997: The Devil's Advocate. 1998: Me & Will. 1999: The Matrix. 2000: The Replacements. The Watcher. The Gift. Sweet November.

REEVES, Steve 1926–2000

Dark-haired American muscleman who took up acting after winning 'Mr World' and 'Mr Universe' titles and achieved enormous success in Italian sword-and-sandal spectacles, attracting the same kind of queues as would Clint Eastwood with his spaghetti westerns (the first of which Reeves actually turned down) the following decade. Tried without much luck to extend his range and eventually returned to America to run a fruit plantation. Died of complications from lymphoma.

1954: Athena. The Hidden Face/Jail Bait. 1957: The Labours of Hercules (GB: Hercules). 1958: Hercules and the Queen of Sheba (GB: Hercules Unchained). 1959: Il terrore dei barbari (GB and US: Goliath and the Barbarians). The White Devil (GB: The White Warrior). The Giant of Marathon. 1960: The Thief of Baghdad. Morgan the Pirate. 1961: Romulus and Remus (GB: Duel of the Titans). The Trojan War (GB: The Wooden Horse of Troy). The Last Days of Pompeii. 1962: The Legend of Aeneas. Son of Spartacus. 1963: Sandokan the Great. Il giorno piu corto commedia umaristica (US: The Shortest Day). 1964: I pirati della Malesia/ Sandokan and the Pirates of Malaya. 1968: Vivo per la tua morte/A Long Ride from Hell.

REINHOLD, Judge
(Edward Reinhold) 1956–

Tall, lean, sandy-haired, affable-looking American actor, often in comedies as a kind of likeable, ordinary-guy equivalent of Danny Kaye. His childlike qualities and gawky

charms were put to good use in *Vice Versa*, one of a clutch of age-reversal comedies, but a long series of solo misses after that led to his being seen in featured roles again by the mid 1990s, and it seems TV sit-com may be his eventual destination. 'Judge' is a childhood nickname. Very prolific in the late 1990s.

1979: The Survival of Dana (TV). Running Scared. 1981: Stripes. Thursday the 12th (later Pandemonium). 1982: The Lords of Discipline. Fast Times at Ridgemont High (GB: Fast Times). 1983: The Women of Willmar/A Matter of Sex (TV). 1984: Roadhouse 66. Gremlins. Beverly Hills Cop. 1986: Head Office. Ruthless People. Off Beat. 1987: Beverly Hills Cop II. Vice Versa. 1988: A Soldier's Tale. Promised a Miracle (TV). 1989: Rosalie Goes Shopping. Enid is Sleeping (later and GB: Over Her Dead Body). 1990: Daddy's Dyin' – Who's Got the Will? Zandalee. Last Tangle in Paris (US: Near Mrs/Near Misses). 1992: Baby on Board. Black Magic. Four Eyes and Six Guns (TV). 1994: Beverly Hills Cop 3. Bank Robber. The Santa Clause. 1995: Dad, the Angel and Me (TV). As Good As Dead (cable TV). 1996: Crackerjack 2: Hostage Train. The Right to Remain Silent (TV). The Wharf Rat (TV). Last Lives. 1997: Runaway Car (TV). Family Plan. Let's Ruin Dad's Day. 1998: Homegrown. Big Monster on Campus/Teen Monster (TV). Tiger Moth/Floating Away. Santa Fe Tales. Special Report: Journey to Mars (TV). 1999: Walking Across Egypt. News Break. Tom Clancy's Netforce (TV). My Brother the Pig. Puss in Boots. Wild Blue. Redemption High. 2000: Enemies of Laughter. Robot of Mars (voice only). Camp Ninja. Ping! Beethoven's 3rd (v). 2001: No Place Like Home. The Meeksville Ghost.

REMICK, Lee 1935–1991

Cool, blonde American actress with prettily thin features and pale blue eyes. Started her film career playing southern states sexpots, but progressed to more level-headed women, often very much in control of their own fortunes. Lived in Britain for some time in the seventies and was able to turn on an impeccable English accent. Nominated for an Academy Award in *Days of Wine and Roses*, she died from cancer of the liver at 55.

1957: A Face in the Crowd. The Last Tycoon (TV). 1958: Last Clear Chance (TV). The Long, Hot Summer. 1959: These Thousand Hills. Anatomy of a Murder. 1960: Wild River. 1961: Sanctuary. 1962: Experiment in Terror

(GB: The Grip of Fear). Days of Wine and Roses. 1963: The Running Man. The Wheeler Dealers (GB: Separate Beds). 1965: Baby, the Rain Must Fall. The Hallelujah Trail. 1967: No Way to Treat a Lady. 1968: The Detective. Hard Contract. 1970: A Severed Head. Loot. 1971: Sometimes a Great Notion (GB: Never Give an Inch). 1972: Of Men and Women (TV). And No One Could Save Her (TV). 1973: The Blue Knight (TV. GB: cinemas). Touch Me Not. 1974: A Delicate Balance. A Girl Named Sooner (TV). QB VII (TV). 1975: Hustling (TV). Hennessy. The Hunted. 1976: The Omen. 1977: Telefon. 1978: The Medusa Touch. Breaking Up (TV). 1979: The Europeans. Torn Between Two Lovers (TV. GB: cinemas). 1980: Tribute. The Women's Room (TV). The Competition. 1981: The Letter (TV). Haywire (TV). 1983: The Gift of Love: A Christmas Story (TV). 1984: Mistral's Daughter (video). Rearview Mirror (TV). A Good Sport (TV). 1985: Toughlove (TV). 1986: Emma's War. Of Pure Blood (TV). 1987: The Vision (TV). 1988: Jesse (TV). 1989: Bridge to Silence (TV). Dark Holiday (TV).

RENALDO, Duncan
(Renault Renaldo Duncan) 1904–1980

Black-haired, convivial-looking, *very* Latin-American star who became famous the world over as The Cisco Kid in a fistful of 'B' westerns and a long-running TV series which took his career as a cowboy hero with massive sombrero well into his fifties. Never knowing his parents or place of birth (possibly Romania or Spain), Renaldo arrived in America as a stoker on a coal ship. Abandoning early plans to become a painter, he went to Hollywood and began to make inroads as a Latin lover type in between doubling as a producer of shorts. He settled down to 'B' western heroes with the coming of World War Two, first playing The Cisco Kid in 1945. His film and TV careers were over by 1960 and he and his wife retired to their ranch, Rancho Mi Amigo. Also wrote stories and screenplays.

1927: Marchetta. Romany Love. Fifty-Fifty. 1928: The Naughty Duchess. Clothes Make the Woman. 1929: Pals of the Prairie. The Bridge of San Luis Rey. 1931: Trader Horn. 1932: Trapped in Tia Juana (GB: Her Lover's Brother). 1933: Public Stenographer (GB: Private Affairs). 1934: The Moth (GB: Seeing It Through). 1936: Lady Luck. Rebellion. Moonlight Murder. 1937: Jungle Menace (serial). The Painted Stallion (serial). Sky Racket (GB: Flight into Danger). Two Minutes to Play. Crime Afloat. Mile a Minute Love. Zorro Rides Again (serial). Special Agent K-7. 1938: Rose of the Rio Grande. Spawn of the North. Tropic Holiday. Ten Laps to Go. 1939: Cowboys from Texas. The Lone Ranger Rides Again (serial). The Kansas Terrors. The Mad Empress (GB: Carlotta, the Mad Empress). Rough Riders' Roundup. Zaza. South of the Border. 1940: Covered Wagon Days. Heroes of the Saddle. Gaucho Serenade. Oklahoma Renegades. Rocky Mountain Rangers. Pioneers of the West. 1941: Gauchos of El Dorado. Down Mexico Way. Outlaws of the West. South of Panama. King of the Texas Rangers (serial). 1942: We Were Dancing. King of the Mounties (serial). A Yank in Libya. 1943: For Whom the Bell Tolls. Secret Service in Darkest Africa (serial). Around the World. Border Patrol. Hands Across the Border. Mission to Moscow. Tiger Fangs. 1944: Call of the South Seas. The Tiger Woman (serial). The Fighting Seabees. The San Antonio Kid. Sheriff of Sundown. 1945: The Cisco Kid Returns. South of the Rio Grande. In Old New Mexico (GB: The Cisco Kid in Old New Mexico). 1946: Two Years Before the Mast. 1947: Jungle Flight. 1948: The Valiant Hombre. Sword of the Avenger. 1949: The Gay Amigo. The Daring Caballero. Satan's Cradle. 1950: The Capture. The Girl from San Lorenzo. 1951: The Lady and the Bandit (GB: Dick Turpin's Ride). 1959: Zorro Rides Again (feature version of 1937 serial).

mented his earnings as a salesman in the mid-thirties by doing film extra and action stand-in work and had drifted into sufficiently big parts just before World War II service to make acting a full-time career when he returned to civilian life. Became a big star in Britain and went to America in 1951 with some success. Died from heart failure.

1935: Conquest of the Air (released 1940). 1936: The Man Who Could Work Miracles. Gipsy. Secret Agent. 1937: Gangway. The Squeaker (US: Murder on Diamond Row). Bank Holiday (US: Three on a Week-End). 1938: The Divorce of Lady X. 1939: This Man in Paris. 1941: The Patient Vanishes (later This Man is Dangerous). Turned Out Nice Again. Pimpernel Smith (US: Mister V). Dangerous Moonlight (US: Suicide Squadron). Ships with Wings. The Tower of Terror. The Big Blockade. 1945: I'll Be Your Sweetheart. The Wicked Lady. Caesar and Cleopatra. 1947: The Root of All Evil. White Cradle Inn (US: High Fury). 1948: Idol of Paris. Uneasy Terms. 1949: Miss Pilgrim's Progress. The Golden Madonna. 1950: Trio. The Black Rose. The Body Said No! 1951: The House in the Square (US: I'll Never Forget You). The Thirteenth Letter. The Day the Earth Stood Still. 1952: Phone Call from a Stranger. Five Fingers. Les Misérables. 1953: Single-Handed (US: Sailor of the King). The Robe. King of the Khyber Rifles. Dangerous Crossing. 1954: Demetrius and the Gladiators. Princess of the Nile. Desirée. 1955: Mambo. Soldier of Fortune. Seven Cities of Gold. The Rains of Ranchipur. 1956: Teenage Rebel. 1957: Circle of the Day (TV). Island in the Sun. Omar Khayyam. 1958: Battle of the V1 (US: V1/Unseen Heroes). 1959: Third Man on the Mountain. 1960: The Lost World. 1963: Mary, Mary. 1966: Ride Beyond Vengeance. Hondo and the Apaches (TV. GB: cinemas). Hotel. 1967: The Power. Cyborg 2087 (GB: Man from Tomorrow). Sette vergine per il diavolo (US: The Young, the Evil and the Savage). Bersaglio mobile (GB and US: Death on the Run). 1968: Subterfuge. The Search (TV). El Alamein (GB: Desert Tanks). The Devil's Brigade. Scaccio Internazionale. 1969: Operation Terror/Assignment Terror. 1970: Gold Seekers. Dracula versus Frankenstein. 1971: The Last Generation.

in France at 17 and, after getting a start in French films in his early thirties, slaved away for years at a sporadic film career. He gradually achieved recognition in the films of director Luc Besson: *Subway, The Big Blue, Nikita* and, most crucially, *Léon,* as the lone assassin of the title, a performance which has kept his hangdog features in demand for international roles ever since.

1978: L'hypothèse du tableau volé. 1979: Clair de femme. 1980: Voulez-vous un bébé Nobel? 1981: On n'est pas des anges . . . elles non plus. Les Bidasses aux grandes manoeuvres. 1982: La passante de Sans-Souci. Le dernier combat. Signes extérieurs de richesse. 1984: Notre histoire/Separate Rooms. 1985: Strictement personnel. Subway. 1986: I Love You. 1988: The Big Blue. 1989: Nikita (US: La femme Nikita). 1990: L'homme au masque d'or. L'opération corned beef. Zone rouge. 1991: Loulou graffiti. 1992: Les visiteurs. 1993: La vis/The Screw. Flight from Justice. 1994: Léon (US: The Professional). Les truffes. 1995: French Kiss/Paris Match. Two Jerks and a Pig. Beyond the Clouds. 1996: Mission Impossible. Roseanna's Grave/For Roseanna. La jaguar. 1997: Witch Way Love/Un amour de sorcière. Godzilla. 1998: Les visiteurs 2: les couloirs du temps. Ronin. 1999: Tripwire. 2000: The Visitors (US remake of 1992 French film). Les rivières pourpres. 2001: Rollerball.

REYNOLDS, Burt
(Burton Reynolds) 1935–
Round-faced, dark-haired, latterly moustachioed, panther-like American leading man, a superstar of the 1970s and 1980s who, like McQueen and Belmondo, insisted on doing much of action stuntwork. The sense of fun which added a great deal to his appeal lay submerged for years in a slew of poker-faced macho heroes. Later, the relaxed cockiness could turn to alarm with amusing results, which were increasingly overdone in the early 1980s, too many poor scripts devastating a career which had seen him become the world's most popular star for five consecutive years. Promising outings as a director did not lead to a career behind the camera and he has alternated TV series with rather strained leading roles in films in more recent times. Married/divorced actresses Judy Carne and Loni Anderson. Long-time relationships with Dinah Shore and Sally Field (both *qv*) also broke up. Academy Award nominee for *Boogie Nights.*

1960: Angel Baby. Alas, Babylon (TV). 1961:

RENNIE, Michael 1909–1971
Tall, dark British actor, good-looking in a lean-and-hungry sort of way (at times uncannily like John Justin) who supple-

RENO, Jean (Juan Moreno) 1948–
Long-faced, lugubrious-looking, bulge-eyed actor with short, slightly receding dark hair. Morocco-born to Spanish parents, he settled

Armored Command. 1965: Last Message from Saigon (GB: Operation CIA). 1966: Un dollaro a testa (GB and US: Navajo Joe). 1967: Shark! (released 1970). 1968: Impasse. 100 Rifles. Fade In. 1969: Skullduggery. Sam Whiskey. 1970: Run Simon Run (TV). Hunters Are for Killing (TV). 1972. Everything You Always Wanted to Know About Sex ** But Were Afraid to Ask. Deliverance. Fuzz. Shamus. 1973: White Lightning. The Man Who Loved Cat Dancing. 1974: The Longest Yard (GB: The Mean Machine). 1975: WW and the Dixie Dancekings. At Long Last Love. Hustle. Lucky Lady. 1976: Nickelodeon. Silent Movie. †Gator. 1977: Smokey and the Bandit. Semi-Tough. 1978: Hooper. †The End. 1979: Starting Over. 1980: Smokey and the Bandit II (GB: Smokey and the Bandit Ride Again). Roughcut. The Cannonball Run. 1981: †Sharky's Machine. Paternity. 1982: The Best Little Whorehouse in Texas. Best Friends. 1983: Stroker Ace. Cannonball Run II. The Man Who Loved Women. Smokey and the Bandit – Part 3. 1984: †Stick. City Heat. 1985: Uphill All the Way. Sherman's March. 1986: Heat. 1988: Malone. Rent-a-Cop. Switching Channels. 1988: Physical Evidence. All Dogs Go to Heaven (voice only). 1989: Breaking In. B.L. Stryker: The Dancer's Touch (TV. And ensuing series). Modern Love. 1992: The Player. Cop & ½. 1993: †The Man from Left Field (TV). Meet Wally Sparks. Striptease. Mojave Frankenstein / Frankenstein and Me. Citizen Ruth. Raven. Trigger Happy / Mad Dog Time. The Cherokee Kid (TV). 1997: Big City Blues. Boogie Nights. The Hunter's Moon. Crazy Six. Bean. 1998: Waterproof. Mystery, Alaska. Universal Soldier II: Brothers in Arms (TV). Universal Soldier III: Unfinished Business (TV). Stringer. Hard Time (TV). 1999: The Premonition (TV). Hostage Hotel (TV). Pups. 2000: The Crew. †The Last Producer. The Hollywood Sign.

†Also directed

performances and one tour-de-force (in The Unsinkable Molly Brown) before her luck ran out in the mid-sixties. Married to Eddie Fisher (1955-1959), first of three; Carrie Fisher (qv) is their daughter. Nominated for an Academy Award in The Unsinkable Molly Brown. Noted for her indefatigability, she has said: 'I'm going to perform till I drop. Then they can stuff me like Trigger and you'll find me in my own museum. Put a quarter in my mouth and I'll sing Tammy.'

1948: June Bride. 1950: The Daughter of Rosie O'Grady. Mr Imperium (GB: You Belong to My Heart). Three Little Words. Two Weeks with Love. 1952: Skirts Ahoy! Singin' in the Rain. I Love Melvin. 1953: The Affairs of Dobie Gillis. Give a Girl a Break. 1954: Athena. Susan Slept Here. 1955: The Tender Trap. Hit the Deck. 1956: Bundle of Joy. The Catered Affair (GB: Wedding Breakfast). Meet Me in Las Vegas (GB: Viva Las Vegas!). 1957: Tammy and the Bachelor (GB: Tammy). 1958: This Happy Feeling. 1959: The Mating Game. Say One for Me. The Gazebo. It Started with a Kiss. 1960: Pepe. The Rat Race. 1961: The Second Time Around. The Pleasure of His Company. 1962: How the West Was Won. 1963: My Six Loves. Mary, Mary. 1964: Goodbye Charlie. The Unsinkable Molly Brown. 1966: The Singing Nun. 1967: Divorce American Style. 1968: How Sweet It Is! 1971: What's the Matter with Helen? 1972: Charlotte's Web (voice only). 1975: That's Entertainment! 1987: Sadie and Son (TV). 1989: Perry Mason: The Case of the Musical Murder (TV). 1991: Battling for Baby (TV). 1992: The Bodyguard. 1993: Heaven & Earth. 1994: That's Entertainment! III. 1996: Mother. Wedding Belle Blues. 1997: In & Out. Zack and Reba. 1998: Rudolph the Red-Nosed Reindeer (voice only). Kiki's Delivery Service (US version of 1989 Japanese feature. Voice only). The Christmas Wish (TV). Fear and Loathing in Las Vegas (voice only). 1999: Keepers of the Frame (doc). A Gift of Love: The Daniel Huffman Story (TV). 2000: Rugrats in Paris (voice only). Virtual Mom (TV).

decent roles. Played leads in second-features for some years before becoming popular on TV in the mid-fifties as William Bendix's wife in The Life of Riley. Died from congestive heart failure.

1923: Scaramouche. The Broken Wing. 1924: Revelation. 1931: Svengali. 1933: †College Humor. †Wine, Women and Song. 1935: †The Big Broadcast of 1936. 1936: †Collegiate (GB: The Charm School). College Holiday. 1937: Tex Rides with the Boy Scouts. Murder in Greenwich Village. Broadway Melody of 1938. Champagne Waltz. 1938: The Black Bandit. Man's Country. Delinquent Parents. Guilty Trails. Western Trails. Overland Express. Rebellious Daughters. Six-Shootin' Sheriff. 1939: Streets of New York. Tailspin Tommy. Racketeers of the Range. Mr Wong in Chinatown. Gone with the Wind. Mystery Plane. The Phantom Stage. Stunt Pilot. Danger Flight (GB: Scouts of the Air). Timber Stampede. Sky Patrol. 1940: Doomed to Die (GB: The Mystery of the Wentworth Castle). The Fatal Hour (GB: Mr Wong at Headquarters). Midnight Limited. Chasing Trouble. Enemy Agent (GB: Secret Enemy). 1941: Secret Evidence. Robin Hood of the Pecos. Dude Cowboy. Cyclone on Horseback. Up in the Air. The Great Swindle. Tillie the Toiler. Top Sergeant Mulligan. Law of the Timber. 1942: Holiday Inn. Star Spangled Rhythm. 1943: Dixie. Ministry of Fear. 1944: Up in Mabel's Room. Three is a Family. 1945: Bring on the Girls. Duffy's Tavern. 1946: Monsieur Beaucaire. Meet Me on Broadway. The Time of Their Lives. 1947: Heaven Only Knows. 1948: Bad Men of Tombstone. 1949: That Midnight Kiss. 1950: The Great Jewel Robbery. Customs Agent. Rookie Fireman. 1951: The Home Town Story. His Kind of Woman. 1952: Models Inc / Call Girl (later and GB: That Kind of Girl). No Holds Barred. 1955: Mobs Inc. 1959: †Juke Box Rhythm. 1964: The Silent Witness. 1981: All the Marbles (GB: The California Dolls).

†As Marjorie Moore

REYNOLDS, Debbie
(Mary Reynolds) 1932–
Energetic, exuberant, jack-in-the-box, tiny, cute-looking, brown-haired American dancer and light singer, who played refreshingly in several M-G-M musicals (most notably Singin' in the Rain) and comedies of the fifties. She also plays several musical instruments (probably all at once, if she could). Later, there were some appealing acting

REYNOLDS, Marjorie
(née Goodspeed) 1921–1997
Blonde American actress with pert face, who started young and played perky girl-scout types, most notably the intrepid reporter in the Mr Wong series, before Paramout picked her up in 1942 and gave her a more glamorous image – if, Ministry of Fear excepted, few

REYNOLDS, Peter
(P. Horrocks) 1925–1975
A rarity in British films of the fifties: a leading man who played villains. Though Reynolds was tall, blond and good-looking, there was something shifty about the blue-eyed gaze and untrustworthy about the set of the mouth, and he played callous small-time crooks and scheming wastrels, much given to

dark shirts and light ties. Also did well as fast-talking reporters busting crime rings. Went to Australia in the sixties, and died in a fire while acting there.

*1946: The Captive Heart. 1947: The Dark Road. 1948: The Guinea Pig. Things Happen at Night. 1949: Adam and Evelyne (US: Adam and Evalyn). 1950: Guilt is My Shadow. 1951: Smart Alec. Four Days. The Magic Box. The Woman's Angle. 1952: The Last Page (US: Manbait). 24 Hours in a Woman's Life (US: Affair in Monte Carlo). I vinti. I nostri figli. 1953: The Good Beginning. Black 13. 1954: The Delavine Affair. The Accused. Destination Milan. *Little Brother. Devil Girl from Mars. One Just Man. 1955: You Can't Escape. Born for Trouble. 1957: The Long Haul. 1958: The Bank Raiders. 1959: Wrong Number. Shake Hands with the Devil. Your Money or Your Wife. 1960: The Challenge. The Man Who Couldn't Walk. The Breaking Point (US: The Great Armored Car Swindle). 1961: Spare the Rod. A Question of Suspense. Highway to Battle. The Painted Smile. 1962: Gaolbreak. 1963: West 11. 1968: Nobody Runs Forever (US: The High Commissioner). 1972: Private Collection.*

RHYS MEYERS, Jonathan 1977–
Small Irish-born actor (despite the Welsh-Jewish surname!) with unruly hair and Mick Jagger-style looks who quickly scowled his way to stardom in trouble-making 'cat among the pigeons' roles. An actor from his early teens, he just missed out on the leading role of *War of the Buttons* in 1993, but bounced back a few years later to launch a prolific film career and, with his distinctive facial features, looks set to continue in leads and semi-leads for a long time to come. Also sings.

1994: A Man of No Importance. 1995: The Tribe. 1996: Samson and Delilah (TV). The Disappearance of Finbar (released 1998). The Killer Tongue. Michael Collins. 1997: The Governess. Telling Lies in America. The Maker (TV and cinemas). 1998: Velvet Goldmine. B Monkey. The Loss of Sexual Innocence. 1999: Ride with the Devil. Titus. 2001: Tangled.

RICCI, Christina 1980–
Grave-faced, dark-haired, pale-skinned American actress, who grew from the demon child Wednesday in the Addams Family films into a curvaceous teenager player of childlike features who proved popular in comedies and light adventure films in the mid 1990s.

Spotted by a New Jersey theatre critic who, after seeing the precocious Ricci perform in a primary school play, suggested she consider acting as a career.

1990: Mermaids. The Hard Way. 1991: The Addams Family. 1993: The Cemetery Club. Addams Family Values. 1995: Casper. Gold Diggers: The Secret of Bear Mountain. Now and Then. 1996: Last of the High Kings. Bastard Out of Carolina (originally for TV). 1997: That Darn Cat. The Ice Storm. 1998: Little Red Riding Hood. Pecker. Buffalo '66. 200 Cigarettes. Desert Blue. Fear and Loathing in Las Vegas. Small Soldiers (voice only). I Woke Up Early the Day I Died. 1999: Sleepy Hollow. 2000: No Vacancy. Bless the Child. The Man Who Cried. 2001: Prozac Nation.

RICE, Florence 1907–1974
Fair-haired, sloe-eyed American actress of warmth and charm who lacked the forceful personality that might have taken her right to the top. The daughter of sportscaster Grantland Rice, who had his own long-running series of screen shorts, she was a latecomer to films, but popular in pleasant, personable leading roles from 1935 to 1939, often in tandem with Robert Young (qv). Although always competent and well-groomed, she was slipping from 1940 and spent the latter part of her career in second-features. Three times married, once to actor Robert Wilcox (1910–1955), she died in Hawaii from lung cancer.

1932: The Fighting Marshal. 1934: Fugitive Lady. 1935: Carnival (GB: Carnival Nights). Best Man Wins. Under Pressure. Awakening of Jim Burke (GB: Iron Fist). Death Flies East. Guard That Girl. Escape from Devil's Island. Superspeed. 1936: Panic on the Air (GB: Trapped by Wireless). Pride of the Marines. The Longest Night. The Blackmailer. Sworn Enemy. Women are Trouble. 1937: Under Cover of Night. All is Confusion. Beg, Borrow or Steal. Navy Blue and Gold. Man of the People. Riding on Air. Married Before Breakfast. Double Wedding. 1938: Sweethearts. Fast Company. Paradise for Three (GB: Romance for Three). Vacation from Love. 1939: Stand Up and Fight. The Kid from Texas. Four Girls in White. Little Accident. Miracles for Sale. At the Circus. 1940: Girl in 313. Cherokee Strip (GB: Fighting Marshal). Phantom Raiders. Broadway Melody of 1940. The Secret Seven. 1941: Mr District Attorney. Doctors Don't Tell. The Blonde from Singapore (GB: Hot Pearls). Father Takes a Wife. Borrowed Hero. 1942: Let's Get Tough. Tramp, Tramp, Tramp. Boss of Big Town. Stand By All Networks. 1943: The Ghost and the Guest.

RICE, Joan 1930–1997
With so pretty a face and so sumptuous a figure, small wonder this petite brunette beauty contest winner was whisked from waiting at tables to starring in films. She wasn't a terribly strong actress but few red-blooded males minded that and it was a pity her bigger films asked too much of her, hastening her decline. She was certain as pretty and spirited a Maid Marian as ever graced the screen. Died from emphysema.

1950: Blackmailed. 1951: One Wild Oat. 1952: Curtain Up. The Story of Robin Hood and His Merrie Men. Gift Horse (US: Glory at Sea). 1953: His Majesty O'Keefe. The Steel Key. A Day to Remember. 1954: The Crowded Day. One Good Turn. 1955: Police Dog. 1956: Women without Men (US: Blonde Bait). 1958: The Long Knife. 1959: Operation Bullshine. 1961: Payroll. 1970: The Horror of Frankenstein.

RICHARD, Sir Cliff
(Harold Webb) 1939–
British singer who began his days as a hip-wiggling teen idol in white jacket and drain-pies, dark hair dripping with grease. By 1961 he was projecting an image as Mr Clean in a series of musicals that started well, but tailed away. A hard-working spokesman for Christianity, he was knighted in 1995.

1959: Serious Charge (US: A Touch of Hell). 1960: Expresso Bongo. 1961: The Young Ones. 1962: Summer Holiday. 1964: Wonderful Life

(US: *Swingers' Paradise*). 1966: *Finders Keepers*. 1967: *Two a Penny*. 1973: *Take Me High* (US: *Hot Property*).

RICHARDS, Denise 1971–
Cute, candy-floss, dark-haired American actress with pin-up bust and bright smile. Despite lacking animation in her early roles, her looks took her beyond daytime TV soaps and she gave some knowing performances in late 1990s' films, although her Bond girl in *The World is Not Enough* was perhaps a mistake. Male fans should watch out: her favourite sport is kick-boxing.

1993: †*National Lampoon's Loaded Weapon 1*. 1994: *Tammy and the T-Rex*. *Lookin' Italian*. 1995: *919 Fifth Avenue* (TV). *P.C.H*. 1996: *In the Blink of the Eye* (TV). 1997: *Nowhere*. *Starship Troopers*. 1998: *Wild Things*. 1999: *Tail Lights Fade*. *Drop Dead Gorgeous*. *The World is Not Enough*. 2000: *The Third Wheel*. 2001: *Good Advice*. *Valentine*.

†As Denise Lee Richards

RICHARDSON, Joely 1965–
Tall, angular, slightly aloof-looking British actress with brown hair, the daughter of Vanessa Redgrave (*qv*) and director Tony Richardson, and sister of actress Natasha Richardson (*qv*). After a major screen debut playing her mother's character when young in *Wetherby*, she concentrated largely on stage work until the 1990s, when she began to get more prominent roles in mainstream films, also attracting attention in a British TV serialisation of the infamous *Lady Chatterley's Lover*.
1968: *The Charge of the Light Brigade*. 1984: *The Hotel New Hampshire*. 1985: *Wetherby*.

1987: *About That Strange Girl/Body Contact*. 1988: *Drowning by Numbers*. 1991: *Heading Home* (TV). *King Ralph*. 1992: *Hostages* (TV). *Rebecca's Daughters*. *Shining Through*. 1993: *I'll Do Anything*. 1995: *Sister My Sister*. *Loch Ness*. 1996: *Hollow Reed*. *101 Dalmatians*. 1997: *Event Horizon*. *The Tribe*. 1998: *Under Heaven*. *Wrestling with Alligators*. 1999: *Maybe Baby*. 2000: *Return to Me*. *The Patriot*.

RICHARDSON, Miranda 1958–
Fair-haired, intense British actress of pale complexion and pencil-slim build, a star in her first film after extensive stage experience. One of Britain's most versatile performers, she has notched up Academy Award nominations for *Damage* and *Tom and Viv*, making films on both sides of the Atlantic.
1984: *Dance With a Stranger*. 1985: *The Innocent*. *Underworld/Transmutations*. 1986: *The Death of the Heart*. 1987: *Empire of the Sun*. *Sweet As You Are* (TV). *Eat the Rich*. 1988: *After Pilkington* (TV). 1989: *The Mad Monkey/Twisted Obsession*. *Ball Trap on the Cote Sauvage* (TV). 1990: *Broken Skin*. *The Fool*. *The Bachelor*. 1991: *Enchanted April*. 1992: *Damage*. *The Crying Game*. 1993: *Century* (TV. US: cinemas). *The Line, the Cross and the Curve*. *Old Times* (cable TV). 1994: *Tom and Viv*. *The Night and the Moment*. *Fatherland* (TV). 1996: *Kansas City*. *Swann*. *Saint-Ex*. *The Evening Star*. 1997: *The Designated Mourner*. *The Apostle*. 1998: *All for Love/St Ives*. 1999: *Jacob Two Two Meets the Hooded Fang*. *Alice in Wonderland* (TV). *Sleepy Hollow*. 2000: *The Miracle Maker* (voice only). *The King and I* (voice only). *Chicken Run* (voice only). *The Big Brass Ring*. *Get Carter*. 2001: *Johnny Hit and Run*.

RICHARDSON, Natasha 1963–
Big-eyed, brown-haired British actress with large, open face and friendly-looking features. The daughter of Vanessa Redgrave (*qv*) and director Tony Richardson and sister of Joely Richardson (*qv*), she hasn't quite reached the top in films, despite undoubted ability and an uncanny facility for reproducing one of the most convincing-sounding American accents ever heard from a British actress. She married (second) actor Liam Neeson (*qv*) in 1994.
1968: *The Charge of the Light Brigade*. 1984: *Every Picture Tells a Story*. *Ellis Island* (TV mini-series shortened for cinemas). 1986: *Gothic*. 1987: *A Month in the Country*. 1988: *Patty Hearst*. 1989: *Fat Man and Little Boy* (GB: *Shadow Makers*). 1990: *The Handmaid's Tale*. *The Comfort of Strangers*. 1991: *The Favour, the Watch and the Very Big Fish*. *Past Midnight*. 1992: *Hostages* (cable TV). 1993: *Zelda* (cable TV). *Widows Peak*. 1994: *Nell*. 1998: *The Parent Trap*. 1999: *Cotton Mary*. 2000: *Never Better*. *Wakin' Up in Reno*. 2001: *Blow Dry*.

RICHARDSON, Sir Ralph 1902–1983
Solemn-looking, round-faced, beady-eyed British character star with a slick of dark hair that would gradually vanish as he passed through middle age. His careful, well-modulated speech could lend character to men from all walks of life, and he could just as easily be pompous as down-to-earth. At his (considerable) peak from 1937 to 1952, during which time he produced some memorable film performances – for one, in *The Heiress*, he was nominated for an Oscar. First wife died; married actress Meriel Forbes (1913–) in 1944. Knighted in 1947. Died from a virus infection. Additional Oscar nomination for

Greystoke: The Legend of Tarzan Lord of the Apes.
1933: *The Ghoul. Friday the Thirteenth.* 1934: *The King of Paris. Thunder in the Air. The Return of Bulldog Drummond. Java Head.* 1935: *Bulldog Jack (US: Alias Bulldog Drummond).* 1936: *Things to Come. The Man Who Could Work Miracles. Thunder in the City. ‡The Amazing Quest of Ernest Bliss (US: Romance and Riches).* 1937: *South Riding. The Divorce of Lady X.* 1938: **Smith. The Citadel.* 1939: *Q Planes (US: Clouds Over Europe). The Four Feathers. The Lion Has Wings. On the Night of Fire (US: The Fugitive).* 1940: **Health for the Nation (narrator only). *Forty Million People (narrator only).* 1942: *The Day Will Dawn (US: The Avengers).* 1943: *The Silver Fleet. The Biter Bit (narrator only). The Volunteer.* 1946: *School for Secrets (US: Secret Flight).* 1947: *Anna Karenina.* 1948: *The Fallen Idol.* 1949: **Faster Than Sound (narrator only). The Heiress. Come Saturday (narrator only). *Rome and Vatican City (narrator only).* 1950: **Eagles of the Fleet (narrator only).* 1951: **Cricket (narrator only). Outcast of the Islands.* 1952: *†Home at Seven (US: Murder on Monday). The Sound Barrier (US: Breaking the Sound Barrier). The Holly and the Ivy.* 1955: *Richard III.* 1956: *Smiley.* 1957: *The Passionate Stranger (US: A Novel Affair).* 1959: *Our Man in Havana.* 1960: *Exodus. Oscar Wilde.* 1962: *The 300 Spartans. Long Day's Journey into Night.* 1963: *Woman of Straw.* 1965: *Doctor Zhivago.* 1966: *Khartoum. The Wrong Box.* 1969: *Oh! What a Lovely War. Battle of Britain. The Looking Glass War. Midas Run (GB: A Run on Gold). The Bed Sitting Room. David Copperfield (TV. GB: cinemas).* 1970: *Eagle in a Cage.* 1971: *Whoever Slew Auntie Roo? (US: Who Slew Auntie Roo?).* 1972: *Tales from the Crypt. Alice's Adventures in Wonderland. Lady Caroline Lamb.* 1973: *A Doll's House (Garland). O Lucky Man! Frankenstein – the True Story (TV. GB: cinemas, in abridged version).* 1975: *Rollerball.* 1976: *The Man in the Iron Mask (TV). Jesus of Nazareth (TV).* 1978: *Watership Down (voice only).* 1979: *Charlie Muffin (TV).* 1981: *Time Bandits. Dragonslayer.* 1982: *Wagner. Witness for the Prosecution (TV).* 1983: *Invitation to the Wedding.* 1984: *Greystoke: The Legend of Tarzan Lord of the Apes. Give My Regards to Broad Street.* 1986: *Directed by William Wyler.*

† *Also directed*
‡ *Scenes deleted*

RINGWALD, Molly 1968–

Red-haired, very dark-eyed, pouty-mouthed American actress whose unconventional prettiness – long face, spade jaw and overfull lips – would seem to fit her for comedy roles, although in fact she's played mainly fairly heavy drama to date, usually as girls from the wrong side of the tracks. The daughter of a blind jazz musician, she was on stage at six – 'I thought I would grow up to be black and sing in night-clubs' – broke into films at 14, and definitely has a personality of her own which may enable her to survive the slump in her popularity which occurred in the 1990s. Character roles, though, seem more likely.

1982: *P.K. and the Kid (released 1987).* 1983: *Tempest. Packin' It In (TV). Spacehunter: Adventures in the Forbidden Zone.* 1984: *Sixteen Candles.* 1985: *Surviving (TV). The Breakfast Club.* 1985: *Pretty in Pink.* 1987: *The Pick-Up Artist. King Lear. For Keeps? (GB: Maybe Baby).* 1988: *Fresh Horses.* 1989: *Loser Takes All/Strike it Rich.* 1990: *Betsy's Wedding. Women and Men: Stories of Seduction (TV).* 1992: *Something to Live for: The Alison Gertz Story (TV. GB: Fatal Love). Face the Music.* 1993: **Some Folks Call It a Sling Blade.* 1994: *Seven Sundays.* 1995: *Malicious. Baja.* 1996: *Enfants du salaud (US: Bastard Brood). Office Killer.* 1998: *Classy Kill (TV). Twice Upon a Time (TV). Since You've Been Gone (TV).* 1999: *Teaching Mrs Tingle. Kimberly. The Giving Tree.* 2000: *Cowboy Up/Hearts and Bones. Cut. In the Weeds.*

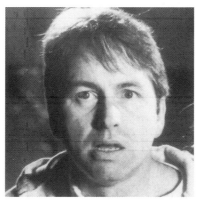

RITTER, John 1948–

Brown-haired, round-faced, rather boyish, expectant-looking American actor, mainly in modest, if sometimes rude comedies, some of which have been unexpected box-office successes. The son of singing cowboy star Tex Ritter (qv), he abandoned a political career in psychology to perform on TV, where he became popular in such series as *The Waltons, Three's Company* and *Hooperman*. Ritter's film career was nothing to write home about until the late 1980s, when he appeared in several popular lowbrow comedies before returning to the small screen. Married/divorced actress Nancy Morgan. Married actress Amy Yasbeck in 1999.
1971: *The Barefoot Executive. Scandalous John.* 1972: *The Other. Evil Roy Slade (TV).*

1973: *The Stone Killer.* 1975: *The Night That Panicked America (TV).* 1976: *Nickelodeon.* 1977: *Breakfast in Bed.* 1978: *Leave Yesterday Behind (TV).* 1979: *Americathon.* 1980: *Hero at Large. Wholly Moses! Comeback Kid (TV).* 1981: *They All Laughed.* 1983: *The Flight of Dragons (TV). In Love With An Older Woman (TV). Pray (TV).* 1983: *Sunset Limousine (TV).* 1984: *Love They Neighbour (TV).* 1986: *Letting Go (TV).* 1986: *The Last Fling (TV). Unnatural Causes: The Agent Orange Story (TV). A Smokey Mountain Christmas (TV). Prison for Children (TV).* 1987: *Real Men.* 1988: *Tricks of the Trade (TV).* 1989: *Skin Deep.* 1990: *Problem Child. My Brother's Wife (TV).* 1991: *Problem Child 2. The Summer My Father Grew Up (TV).* 1992: *Noises Off. Stay Tuned.* 1993: *Danielle Steel's 'Heartbeat' (TV). Grounds for Murder (TV). The Only Way Out (TV).* 1994: *North.* 1995: *Gramps (TV. GB: Lethal Intent). Sling Blade. The Colony (TV). Unforgivable (TV).* 1996: *Mercenary. A Gun, a Car, a Blonde. A Child's Wish/A Fight for Justice (TV).* 1997: *Reasonable Doubt. Loss of Faith (TV). Nowhere. Dead Man's Gun (TV). Hacks/The Big Twist.* 1998: *Montana. It Came from the Sky (TV). Man of Miracles (TV). Chance of a Lifetime (TV). Bride of Chucky. I Woke Up Early the Day I Died.* 1999: *Holy Joe (TV). Panic. Lethal Vows (TV).* 2000: *Terror Tract. Lost in the Pershing Point Hotel. Your Aura is Throbbing. TripFall.*

RITTER, Tex

(Woodward Ritter) 1905–1974
Dark-haired, moon-faced, chubby-cheeked singing cowboy star of the 1930s and 1940s, a country music vocalist from Texas whose acting proved surprisingly competent when thrown into a string of low-budget westerns riding his horse White Flash. Working for 'Poverty Row' studios meant that Ritter never matched the popularity of Roy Rogers and Gene Autry; at bigger studios he was forced to share top billing with such other cowboy stars as William Elliott and Johnny Mack Brown (qv). His starring films dwindled to a halt after 10 years, but his reputation as a balladeer continued to rise, especially after his soundtrack narration for *High Noon*. Once ran unsuccessfully for a US Senate seat in Tennessee. The father of actor John Ritter (qv), he died from a heart attack. Married actress Dorothy Fay (D.F. Southworth, 1915–), one of his co-stars.
1936: *Song of the Gringo (GB: The Old*

Corral). Headin' for the Rio Grande. 1937: Arizona Days. Hittin' the Trail. Sing, Cowboy Sing. Tex Rides With the Boy Scouts. The Mystery of the Hooded Horsemen. 1938: Starlight Over Texas. Frontier Town. Rollin' Plains. The Utah Trail. Where the Buffalo Roam. 1939: Man from Texas. Song of the Buckaroo. Riders of the Frontier. Sundown on the Prairie. Rollin' Westward. Roll, Wagons, Roll. Down the Wyoming Trail. Westbound Stage. 1940: The Golden Trail. Arizona Frontier. Rhythm of the Rio Grande. Pals of the Silver Sage. The Cowboy from Sundown. Take Me Back to Oklahoma. Rainbow Over the Range. 1941: The Pioneers. Rolling Home to Texas. Riding the Cherokee Trail. King of Dodge City. Lone Star Vigilantes (GB: The Devil's Price). Roaring Frontiers. Bullets for Bandits. North of the Rockies (GB: False Clues). Prairie Gunsmoke. Vengeance of the West (GB: The Black Shadow). 1942: Deep in the Heart of Texas. The Devil's Trail (GB: Rogues' Gallery). Little Joe, the Wrangler. The Old Chisholm Trail. Raiders of the San Joaquin. 1943: Tenting Tonight on the Old Camp Ground. The Lone Star Trail. Cheyenne Roundup. Frontier Badmen. Oklahoma Raiders (GB: Midnight Raiders). Arizona Trail. 1944: Marshal of Gunsmoke. Cowboy Canteen (GB: Close Harmony). Dead or Alive. Gangsters of the Frontier. The Whispering Skull. Marked for Murder. 1945: Enemy of the Law. Frontier Fugitives. Three in the Saddle. Flaming Bullets. 1950: Holiday Rhythm. 1952: High Noon (singing narrator only). 1953: The Marshal's Daughter. 1954: The Cowboy (narrator only). 1955: Apache Ambush. Wichita (singing narrator only). 1956: Down Liberty Road. 1957: Trooper Hook (singing narrator only). 1966: Nashville Rebel. Girl from Tobacco Row. What's The Country Coming To? (narrator only). 1967: What Am I Bid? 1971: The Nashville Sound. 1972: Music City, USA (narrator only). The Nashville Story.

THE RITZ BROTHERS (The Joachim Brothers) Al 1901–1965; Jimmy 1903–1985; Harry 1906–1986
Family trio of raucous, long-faced, big-nosed American comedians/comic dancers who provided fun interludes in big-budget musicals, headed up lesser vehicles of their own, were almost as zany as the Marxes and could always be depended on for the unexpected. Al died from a heart attack; Jimmy from heart failure; Harry died from cancer.

1934: *Hotel Anchovy. 1936: Sing Baby Sing. 1937: Life Begins in College (GB: The Joy Parade). One in a Million. On the Avenue. You Can't Have Everything. 1938: Kentucky Moonshine (GB: Three Men and a Girl). The Goldwyn Follies. Straight, Place and Show (GB: They're Off). 1939: The Three Musketeers (GB: The Singing Musketeer). The Gorilla. Pack Up Your Troubles (GB: We're in the Army Now). 1940: Argentine Nights. 1942: Behind the Eight Ball (GB: Off the Beaten Track). Hi Ya, Chum (GB: Everything Happens to Us). 1943: *Screen Snapshots, series 2: No 5. Never a Dull Moment. *Screen Snapshots, series 2: No 8.
Al alone: 1918: The Avenging Trail. Harry and Jimmy: 1975: Won Ton Ton, the Dog Who Saved Hollywood. Blazing Stewardesses. Harry alone: 1976: Silent Movie.

RIX, Sir Brian (Lord Rix) 1924–
Dark-haired British farceur who played gormless idiots in film comedies with Ronald Shiner, gradually becoming the more popular of the two, although not for long. After the early sixties he devoted himself to running and playing in famous farces at London's Whitehall Theatre for more than a decade. In real life he is the most urbane of men, the very opposite of his film and stage self. Married to actress Elspet Gray (1928–) since 1949. Left showbusiness in 1980 to work full-time for the mentally handicapped. Knighted in 1986. Created Lord Rix in 1992.
1951: Reluctant Heroes. 1954: Up to His Neck. What Every Woman Wants. 1956: Dry Rot. 1957: Not Wanted on Voyage. 1959: The Night We Dropped a Clanger (US: Make Mine a Double). 1960: The Night We Got the Bird. And the Same to You. 1961: Nothing Barred. 1973: Don't Just Lie There, Say Something!

ROBARDS, Jason (Jnr) 1920–
Wry, laconic, rasp-voiced American actor with hangdog expression. In semi-star roles for the cinema (after a distinguished stage career) from early middle age. The standard of his performance could vary infuriatingly, but he won two Best Supporting Actor Oscars (for *All the President's Men* and *Julia*) in the 1970s, and was nominated again for *Melvin and Howard*. Married (third of four) to Lauren Bacall (qv) from 1961 to 1973. His father was silent-screen lead and sound character actor Jason Robards Snr (1892–1963). Sons Jason Robards III and Sam Robards have starred in minor films.

1958: The Journey. 1959: For Whom the Bell Tolls (TV). 1961: By Love Possessed. Tender is the Night. 1962: Long Day's Journey into Night. 1963: Act One. 1965: A Thousand Clowns. 1966: Any Wednesday (GB: abridged as Bachelor Girl Apartment). A Big Hand for the Little Lady (GB: Big Deal at Dodge City). 1967: Divorce American Style. Hour of the Gun. The St Valentine's Day Massacre. 1968: The Night They Raided Minsky's. Once Upon a Time . . . in the West. 1969: Isadora. Rosolino Paterno, soldato (US: Operation Snafu). 1970: Tora! Tora! Tora! Julius Caesar. The Ballad of Cable Hogue. Fools. 1971: Murders in the Rue Morgue. Johnny Got His Gun. 1972: The House without a Christmas (TV). Tod eines Fremden (GB: The Execution. US: Death of a Stranger). 1973: Play It As It Lays. Pat Garrett and Billy the Kid. A Boy and His Dog. 1975: Mr Sycamore. The Easter Promise (TV). 1976: All the President's Men. 1977: Julia. L'imprécateur. 1978: Comes a Horseman. A Christmas to Remember (TV). 1979: Hurricane. Cabo Blanco. 1980: Melvin and Howard. Raise the Titanic! Ghosts of Cape Horn (narrator only) 1981: The Legend of the Lone Ranger. FDR: The Last Year (TV). 1982: Burden of Dreams. Something Wicked This Way Comes. 1983: Max Dugan Returns. The Day After (TV). 1984: America and Lewis Hine (voice only). Sakharov (TV). 1985: The Atlanta Child Murders (TV). 1986: Square Dance. Johnny Bull (TV). 1987: Breaking Home Ties (TV). Laguna Heat (TV). 1988: Inherit the Wind (TV). Bright Lights, Big City. The Good Mother. Dream a Little Dream. The Christmas Wife (cable TV). 1989: L'ami retrouvé. Reunion. Black Rainbow. Parenthood. Thomas Hart Benton (narrator only). 1990: Quick Change. 1991: An Inconvenient Woman (TV). Chernobyl: The Final Warning (TV). The Perfect Tribute (TV). Mark Twain and Me (TV). 1992: Storyville. 1993: Philadelphia. The Adventures of Huck Finn. The Trial. 1994: Little Big League. The Paper. The Enemy Within. 1995: My Antonia (TV). Crimson Tide. Journey (TV). 1997: A Thousand Acres. 1998: Enemy of the State. Beloved. Heartwood (TV). 1999: Magnolia. 2000: A Dog of Flanders. Going Home (TV).

ROBBINS, Tim 1958–
Very tall, dark-haired American leading man who has used his gullible good looks to advantage, both in playing characters who are

naïve, and those who pretend to be naïve. The son of a Greenwich Village folk singer (a member of the pop group The Highwaymen), Robbins' chubby-cheeked handsomeness became better known after he played the dim baseball star in *Bull Durham,* and he was near the top of the tree after successes in *The Player, Rob Roberts* and *The Shawshank Redemption.* More recently he seems to have put his acting career in stop-go mode to concentrate on direction. Also a guitarist and singer, he has for some years lived with actress Susan Sarandon (*qv*), by whom he has two children. Oscar nominee as director for *Dead Man Walking.*

1984: No Small Affair. Toy Soldiers. 1985: Fraternity Vacation. The Sure Thing. 1986: Howard the Duck (GB: Howard . . . A New Breed of Hero). Top Gun. 1987: Five Corners. 1988: Tapeheads. Bull Durham. 1989: Miss Firecracker. Twister. Erik the Viking. 1990: Cadillac Man. Jacob's Ladder. 1992: Jungle Fever. The Player. Bob Roberts. 1993: Short Cuts. The Hudsucker Proxy. 1994: I.Q. The Shawshank Redemption. Luck, Trust & Ketchup. Prêt-à-Porter (US: Ready to Wear). 1996: The Typewriter, the Rifle and the Movie Camera. 1997: Nothing to Lose. 1998: Arlington Road. 1999: Austin Powers 2: The Spy Who Shagged Me. Cradle Will Rock (voice only). 2000: Mission to Mars. High Fidelity. Antitrust. 2001: Human Nature.

As director: *1992: Bob Roberts. 1995: Dead Man Walking. 1999: Cradle Will Rock.*

ROBERTS, Eric 1956–
Tall, whippily built, dark-haired American actor of wry-faced handsomeness. The brother of Julia Roberts (*qv*), he began his

career in rebel roles, but there were signs of torment about his good looks that soon caused producers to cast him in anguished or sadistic roles, not always to the benefit of his career. Born in Mississippi, the son of a drama teacher, he was an award-winning child actor at seven and a RADA student in London at 15. After a starring film debut at 22, injuries in a car crash rather slowed the thrust of his career. Despite sometimes undisciplined portrayals in more recent times, he continues to be a striking and prolific performer: 80 films in the past 15 years!

1978: King of the Gypsies. 1980: Paul's Case (TV). 1981: Raggedy Man. 1983: Star 80. Miss Lonelyhearts (TV). 1984: The Pope of Greenwich Village. The Coca Cola Kid. 1985: Runaway Train. 1986: Slow Burn (TV). Nobody's Fool. 1987: Dear America (voice only). 1988: Blood Red (released 1990). To Heal a Nation (TV). Options. Les portes tournantes. 1989: Into Thin Air. Rude Awakening. Best of the Best. 1990: Fire Princess. The Lost Capone (TV). The Ambulance. A Family Matter/Vendetta (TV). Descending Angel (cable TV). 1991: By the Sword. Lonely Hearts (and 1983 film with similar title). Final Analysis. 1992: Fugitive Among Us (TV). Voyage. Best of the Best II. 1993: Love, Cheat and Steal (released 1994). Love, Honor & Obey: The Last Mafia Marriage (TV). Free Fall. 1994: Love is a Gun. The Specialist. Sensation. Babyfever. Nature of the Beast. The Hard Truth. Bad Company. 1995: Saved by the Light (TV). True Killers. Past Perfect. The Immortals. Heaven's Prisoners. It's My Party. 1996: Power 98. The Grave. Public Enemies/Public Enemy No. 1. The Glass Cage. Past Perfect. American Strays. Gudi, El Eñano. The Cable Guy. In Cold Blood (TV). Dark Angel (TV). 1997: Most Wanted. Prophecy II: Ashtown. The Shadow Men. T.N.T. Adam and Smoke. False Pretense. The Odyssey (TV). Death Valley (released 1999 as Facade). 1998: Dead End. Two Shades of Blue. La Cucaracha. Making Sandwiches. Purgatory (TV). 1999: Lansky (cable TV). Heaven's Fire (TV). Restraining Order. The Alternate/Agent of Death. Gabriel's Run. No Alibi. The Hunger (TV). Luck of the Draw. Wildflowers. 2000: The King's Guard. Sanctimony. Mercy Streets. Falcone (TV). Cecil B DeMented. The Beat Nicks. The Flying Dutchman. TripFall. Race against Time (TV).

ROBERTS, Julia (Julie Roberts) 1967–
Tall, attractively angular, dark-haired gamine, Georgia-born American actress with

a wide mouth who emerged as one of the hottest bets for stardom in the 1990s with her delightful performance in *Pretty Woman.* From a family so steeped in acting that 'I was reluctant to admit that I wanted to become an actress', she graduated quickly to leading roles, and tends to play women determined to take charge of their own destinies. Sister of Eric Roberts (*qv*). Oscar nominee for *Steel Magnolias* and *Pretty Woman,* she cancelled her wedding to actor Kiefer Sutherland (*qv*) three days before the ceremony in 1991 and subsequently married (and divorced) rock musician/actor Lyle Lovett. She took a year out from films after these marital traumas, but regained her position as the world's top female star in the late 1990s.

1988: Blood Red (released 1990). Baja Oklahoma (cable TV: also shown in cinemas). Mystic Pizza. Satisfaction. 1989: Steel Magnolias. 1990: Pretty Woman. Flatliners. Sleeping with the Enemy. 1991: Dying Young. Hook. 1992: The Player. 1993: The Pelican Brief. 1994: I Love Trouble. Prêt-à-Porter (US: Ready to Wear). 1995: Something to Talk About. 1996: Mary Reilly. Michael Collins. Everyone Says I Love You. 1997: My Best Friend's Wedding. Conspiracy Theory. 1998: Stepmom. 1999: Notting Hill. Runaway Bride. 2000: Erin Brockovich. 2001: The Mexican. Ocean's 11.

ROBERTS, Lynne
(Theda May Roberts) 1919–1978
Most film buffs seem agreed that this resolute, sweet-faced, blue-eyed, auburn-haired American star, once described as 'button-cute', was probably the best actress never to get out of 'B' pictures. On stage as a child when she and her mother had their own act, she was in films at 17. All she got, though, were frequent name changes and 17 years of sterling service to low-budget westerns and thrillers. After ending in the arms of a man-eating crab in *Port Sinister,* she finally gave up. Who could blame her? Died from a brain haemorrhage. Four times married.

1936: Bulldog Edition (GB: Lady Reporter). 1937: Circus Girl. †Mama Runs Wild. †Stella Dallas. †Dangerous Holiday. 1938: †Call the Mesquiteers (GB: Outlaws of the Wild). †The Hollywood Stadium Mystery. †The Higgins Family. †The Lone Ranger (serial). †Billy the Kid Returns. ‡Come on Rangers. ‡Shine On, Harvest Moon. ‡Dick Tracy Returns (serial). ‡Heart of the Rockies. 1939: ‡Rough Riders' Roundup. ‡Should Husbands Work? †Frontier

Pony Express. ‡Southward Ho. ‡In Old Caliente. ‡The Stadium Murders. ‡The Mysterious Miss X. ‡My Wife's Relatives. ‡Everything's On Ice. 1940: ‡Hi Yo Silver (feature version of serial The Lone Ranger). †Street of Memories. †High School. †Star Dust. †Romance of the Rio Grande. 1941: †Ride on, Vaquero! †The Bride Wore Crutches. †A Yank in the RAF. †Riders of the Purple Sage. †Last of the Duanes. †Moon over Miami. †Sun Valley Serenade. 1942: †Young America. †Dr Renault's Secret. †The Man in the Trunk. †Quiet Please Murder. 1943: †The Ghost That Walks Alone. Three Sisters of the Moors. 1944: Port of 40 Thieves. My Buddy. The Chicago Kid. The Big Bonanza. 1945: Behind the Lights. The Phantom Speaks. Girls of the Big House. The Inner Circle. Sioux City Sue. 1947: The Pilgrim Lady. That's My Gal. The Magnificent Rogue. Robin Hood of Texas. Saddle Pals. Winter Wonderland. 1948: Lightnin' in the Forest. The Timber Trail. Eyes of Texas. Madonna of the Desert. Secret Service Investigator. Trouble Preferred. 1949: Sons of Adventure. A Dangerous Profession. 1950: Dynamite Pass. Call of the Klondike. The Blazing Sun. The Great Plane Robbery. Hunt the Man Down. 1951: Murder Ad Lib (TV. GB: cinemas) 1952: Because of You. The Blazing Forest. 1953: Pattern for Murder. Port Sinister.

‡As Mary Hart †As Lynn Roberts

ROBERTS, Rachel 1927–1980
Mature-looking, dark-haired Welsh actress, mostly on stage until hitting the film big-time as a randy housewife in *Saturday Night and Sunday Morning*. Despite some quieter parts, she found herself typed as blowsy and sexy landladies, to which she gave a strong erotic charge. Later on she was seen in harsher, broader roles. Married/divorced actors Alan Dobie (1932–) and Rex Harrison (*qv*). Received an Academy Award nomination for *This Sporting Life*. Poisoned herself.
1953: Valley of Song (US: Men Are Children Twice). The Limping Man. The Weak and the Wicked. 1954: The Crowded Day. 1957: The Good Companions. Davy. 1959: Our Man in Havana. 1960: Saturday Night and Sunday Morning. 1962: Girl on Approval. 1963: This Sporting Life. 1968: A Flea in Her Ear. 1969: Destiny of a Spy/The Gaunt Woman (TV). The Reckoning. 1970: Doctors' Wives. 1971: Wild Rovers. Baffled! 1973: O Lucky Man! The Belstone Fox. 1974: Murder on the Orient

Express. 1975: Great Expectations (TV. GB: cinemas). Alpha Beta. Picnic at Hanging Rock. 1977: A Circle of Children (TV). 1978: Foul Play. Yanks. 1979: A Man Called Intrepid (TV). When a Stranger Calls. 1980: Charlie Chan and the Curse of the Dragon Queen. The Hostage Tower. 1981: The Wall (TV).

ROBERTS, Tanya
(T. Boum) 1954–
Tall, lissom, light-haired (sometimes dark) knock-out looker whose beauty amply compensated for her moderate acting talent, and almost inevitably got her cast as a James Bond girl in the middle of her career. Acting at 16, she appeared in off-Broadway plays as a decoration in lightweight TV movies being cast as one of *Charlie's Angels* in the last season of that successful TV series. As with so many actresses, the Bond film did little for her career and by the 1990s she was starring in high-gloss soft-porn films aimed at the video market.
1975: The Last Victim (re-released in 1984 as Forced Entry). 1976: The Yum Yum Girls. 1977: The Private Files of J. Edgar Hoover. Fingers. Tourist Trap. 1978: Zuma Beach (TV). Pleasure Cove (TV). Vega$ (TV). 1979: California Dreaming. Racquet. 1980: Waikiki (TV). 1982: The BeastMaster. 1983: Murder Me, Murder You (TV). Sheena/ Sheena, Queen of the Jungle. Hearts and Armour. 1985: A View to a Kill. 1987: Body Slam. 1988: Purgatory. 1989: Demon Hunters. 1990: Night Eyes (TV). Legal Tender. 1991: Almost Pregnant. Inner Sanctum. Down and Dirty. 1992: Sins of Desire. 1993: Deep Down. 1995: National Lampoon's Favorite Deadly Sins.

ROBERTSON, Cliff 1925–
Dark, curly-haired American actor with attractive speaking voice (it's surprising he hasn't been used more for narrations) whose film career had barely got started before he volunteered for service as a merchant seaman. He made a reputation on stage before returning to Hollywood and success as a leading man. After winning an Oscar for *Charly*, he set up a number of his own projects, but these proved largely uncommercial, and he has been most successful with roles that reveal the shadier side to his all-American looks. Married (second) to actress Dina Merrill (1925–) from 1966 to 1989.
1943: Corvette K-225 (GB: The Nelson Touch). We've Never Been Licked (GB: Texas

to Tokyo). 1955: Picnic. 1956: Autumn Leaves. 1957: The Girl Most Likely. 1958: The Naked and the Dead. Natchez (TV). Days of Wine and Roses (TV). 1959: Gidget. Battle of the Coral Sea. As the Sea Rages. 1961: Underworld USA. All in a Night's Work. The Big Show. The Cruel Day (TV). 1962: The Interns. PT 109. 1963: My Six Loves. Sunday in New York. 1964: 633 Squadron. The Best Man. Love Has Many Faces. 1967: The Honey Pot. 1968: The Devil's Brigade. Charly. The Sunshine Patriot (TV). 1969: Too Late the Hero. 1971: †J.W. Coop. 1972: The Great Northfield Minnesota Raid. 1973: Ace Eli and Rodger of the Skies. The Man without a Country (TV). 1974: A Tree Grows in Brooklyn (TV). Man on a Swing. 1975: My Father's House (TV). Three Days of the Condor. Out of Season. 1976: Midway (GB: Battle of Midway). Return to Earth (TV). Obsession. Shoot. 1977: Fraternity Row (narrator only). 1978: Overboard/Dead Reckoning. (TV). Dominique. 1979: †The Pilot. 1981: Brainstorm (released 1983). 1983: Class. Two of a Kind (TV). Star 80. 1985: Shaker Run. 1986: Dreams of Gold: The Mel Fisher Story (TV). 1987: Malone. 1990: Dead Reckoning (TV). 1991: Wild Hearts Can't Be Broken. 1992: Wind. 1994: Renaissance Man. 1995: The Sunset Boys (released 1998 as Waiting for Sunset). Judith Krantz's Dazzle (TV). 1996: Escape from L.A. 1998: Assignment Berlin. Melting Pot. 1999: Family Tree. 2000: Falcon Down.

†Also directed

ROBERTSON, Dale
(Dayle Robertson) 1923–
Tall, dark, rugged, he-man American actor who quit schoolteaching for Hollywood in the

late forties and was soon in leading roles. Did not quite survive a big star build-up from his studio, Fox, as a romantic lead, but remained a respected western star, in regular TV series from 1957. Also a singer. Married/divorced Mary Murphy (*qv*).
1948: *The Boy with Green Hair*. *Johnny Belinda*. 1949: *The Girl from Jones Beach*. *Fighting Man of the Plains*. *Flamingo Road*. 1950: *The Cariboo Trail*. *Two Flags West*. 1951: *Call Me Mister*. *Take Care of My Little Girl*. *Golden Girl*. 1952: *Lydia Bailey*. *Return of the Texan*. *The Outcasts of Poker Flat*. *O. Henry's Full House* (GB: *Full House*). 1953: *The Silver Whip*. *The Farmer Takes a Wife*. *City of Bad Men*. *Devil's Canyon*. 1954: *The Gambler from Natchez*. *Sitting Bull*. 1955: *Top of the World*. *Son of Sinbad*. 1956: *The High Terrace*. *A Day of Fury*. *Dakota Incident*. 1957: *Hell Canyon Outlaws* (GB: *The Tall Trouble*). *Anna of Brooklyn/Fast and Sexy*. *The Still Trumpet* (TV). 1963: *Law of the Lawless*. 1964: *Blood on the Arrow*. *Coast of Skeletons*. *The Man from Button Willow* (voice only). 1966: *The One-Eyed Soldiers*. *Scalplock* (TV). 1974: *Melvin Purvis G-Man* (TV. GB: cinemas as *The Legend of Machine Gun Kelly*). 1975: *Kansas City Massacre* (TV). 1979: *The Last Ride of the Dalton Gang* (TV). 1982: *Matt Houston* (TV). 1987: *J.J. Starbuck* (TV).

ROBESON, Paul 1898–1976
Black American singer and actor with magnificent bass-baritone voice that seemed to come from somewhere near his boots. Made a number of indelible film appearances in the 1930s, mostly as labourers becoming kings of far-off lands, and became famous for his rendition of *Ol' Man River*, but his Communist-influenced political views hampered his later career. Died following a stroke (and a long period of ill-health).
1924: *Body and Soul*. 1930: *Borderline*. 1933: *The Emperor Jones*. 1935: *Sanders of the River* (US: *Bosambo*). 1936: *Show Boat*. *My Song Goes Forth/Africa Looks Up*. *Song of Freedom*. 1937: *Jericho* (US: *Dark Sands*). *Big Fella*. *King Solomon's Mines*. 1939: *The Proud Valley*. 1942: *Tales of Manhattan*. *Native Land* (and narrator). 1955: *Il canto dei grandi fiumi*. 1979: *Paul Robeson: Portrait of an Artist*.

ROBIN, Dany 1927–1995
Charming light-haired French actress, as pretty as her name. Boosted as a new international star in *Act of Love* in the early fifties, she gave an appealing performance,

but preferred to remain in French films, with the occasional overseas venture. Died in a fire.
1946: *Lunegarde*. *Le destin s'amuse*. *Les portes de la nuit*. *Six heures à perdre*. 1947: *Une jeune fille savait*. *L'éventail*. *Le silence est d'or*. *Les amoureux sont seuls au monde*. 1948: *La passagère*. 1949: *Au p'tit zouave*. *Le soif des hommes*. *La voyage inattendue*. 1951: *Deux sous de violettes*. *Le plus joli péché du monde*. *Une historie d'amour*. 1952: *Douze heures de bonheur*. *La fête à Henriette*. 1953: *Julietta*. *Les révoltés de Lomanach*. *Act of Love*. *Tempi nostri*. 1954: *Napoléon*. *Cadet-Rouselle*. 1955: *Escale à Orly/Un soir à Orly*. *Frou-Frou*. *Paris coquin*. 1956: *C'est arrivé à Aden*. *Bonsoir Paris, bonjour l'amour*. *Le coin tranquille*. 1957: *C'est la faute d'Adam*. *Quand sonnera midi*. 1958: *L'école des cocottes*. *Mimi Pinson*. *Les dragueurs* (GB: *The Young Have No Morals*). *Suivez-moi, jeune homme*. 1959: *Le secret du chevalier d'Eon*. 1960: *Love and the Frenchwoman*. *Scheldungsgrund Liebe*. 1961: *Amours célèbres*. *Les Parisiennes*. 1962: *Waltz of the Toreadors*. *Mysteries of Paris*. *Conduite à gauche*. *Mandrin, bandit gentilhomme*. 1963: *Follow the Boys*. *Comment trouvez-vous ma soeur?* 1964: *Sursis pour un espion*. *La corde au cou*. 1966: *Don't Lose Your Head*. 1968: *The Best House in London*. 1969: *Topaz*.

ROBINSON, Edward G.
(Emmanuel Goldenberg) 1893–1973
Squat, wide-mouthed, toad-faced, dark-haired, totally magnetic, Romanian-born Hollywood star who made his name in gangster films and spat out his dialogue like bullets from a machine-gun. Also brought great power to quieter roles. Career somewhat harmed by the Communist witchhunts.

Special Academy Award 1972. In later life an acknowledged art expert (and avid collector). Died from cancer.
1916: *Arms and the Woman*. 1923: *The Bright Shawl*. 1929: *The Hole in the Wall*. 1930: *Outside the Law*. *Night Ride*. *The Widow from Chicago*. *A Lady to Love*. *East is West*. *Little Caesar*. 1931: *Five Star Final*. *Smart Money*. 1932: *Tiger Shark*. **The Stolen Jools* (GB: *The Slippery Pearls*). *Silver Dollar*. **Trouble Shots*. *Two Seconds*. *The Hatchet Man* (GB: *The Honourable Mr Wong*). 1933: *Little Giant*. *I Loved a Woman*. 1934: *The Man with Two Faces*. *Dark Hazard*. *The Whole Town's Talking* (GB: *Passport to Fame*). 1935: *Barbary Coast*. 1936: *Bullets or Ballots*. **A Day at Santa Anita*. *Thunder in the City*. 1937: *The Last Gangster*. *Kid Galahad*. 1938: *I Am the Law*. *The Amazing Dr Clitterhouse*. *A Slight Case of Murder*. 1939: *Confessions of a Nazi Spy*. *Blackmail*. 1940: *Dr Ehrlich's Magic Bullet* (GB: *The Story of Dr Ehrlich's Magic Bullet*). *A Dispatch from Reuter's* (GB: *This Man Reuter*). *Brother Orchid*. 1941: *Manpower*. *The Sea Wolf*. *Unholy Partners*. 1942: *Larceny Inc*. *Tales of Manhattan*. 1943: *Flesh and Fantasy*. *Destroyer*. 1944: *Mr Winkle Goes to War* (GB: *Arms and the Woman*). *Tampico*. *The Woman in the Window*. *Double Indemnity*. 1945: *Scarlet Street*. *Our Vines Have Tender Grapes*. *Journey Together*. 1946: *The Stranger*. 1947: *The Red House*. 1948: *All My Sons*. *Night Has a Thousand Eyes*. *Key Largo*. 1949: *House of Strangers*. *It's a Great Feeling*. 1950: *My Daughter Joy* (US: *Operation X*). 1951: **Hollywood Memories* (narrator only). 1952: *Actors and Sin*. 1953: *The Big Leaguer*. *Vice Squad* (GB: *The Girl in Room 17*). *The Glass Web*. 1954: *Black Tuesday*. *The Violent Men* (GB: *Rough Company*). 1955: *A Bullet for Joey*. *Illegal*. *Hell on Frisco Bay*. *Tight Spot*. 1956: *Nightmare*. *The Ten Commandments*. 1958: *Shadows Tremble* (TV). 1959: *A Hole in the Head*. *Israel* (narrator only). 1960: *Seven Thieves*. *Pepe*. 1962: *My Geisha*. *Two Weeks in Another Town*. *Sammy Going South* (US: *A Boy Ten Feet Tall*). 1963: *The Prize*. 1964: *The Outrage*. *Good Neighbor Sam*. *Robin and the Seven Hoods*. *Cheyenne Autumn*. 1965: *The Cincinnati Kid*. *Who Has Seen the Wind?* (TV). 1966: *The Biggest Bundle of Them All*. 1967: *La blonde de Pékin*. *Never a Dull Moment*. *Grand Slam*. *Operation St Peter's*. 1968: *Uno scacco tutto matto* (GB: *It's Your Move*. US: *Mad Checkmate*). *Mackenna's Gold*. 1969: *UMC* (TV. GB: *Operation Heartbeat*). 1970: *Song of Norway*. *The Old Man Who Cried Wolf* (TV). 1972: *Neither by Day or by Night*. 1973: *Soylent Green*.

ROBSON, Dame Flora 1902–1984
Distinguished British stage actress with dark, tightly-bunched hair and plain, Anne Revere-type looks that often got her cast as (sometimes frustrated) spinsters, but also enabled her to tackle an enviable range of character studies, from queens to killers. In Hollywood 1939–1942. Created Dame in 1960. Nominated for an Academy Award in *Saratoga Trunk*.
1931: *Gentleman of Paris*. 1932: *Dance Pretty Lady*. 1933: *One Precious Year*. *Catherine the Great*. 1936: *Fire over England*. 1937:

Farewell Again (US: Troopship). †I Claudius. 1939: Poison Pen. *Smith. The Lion Has Wings. Wuthering Heights. Invisible Stripes. We Are Not Alone. 1940: The Sea Hawk. 1941: Bahama Passage. 1944: 2,000 Women. 1945: Saratoga Trunk. Great Day. Caesar and Cleopatra. 1946: The Years Between. 1947: Frieda. Black Narcissus. Holiday Camp. 1948: Good Time Girl. Saraband for Dead Lovers (US: Saraband). 1952: Tall Headlines. 1953: Malta Story. *She Shall Be Called Woman (narrator only). 1954: Romeo and Juliet. 1957: High Tide at Noon. The Gypsy and the Gentleman. No Time for Tears. 1958: Innocent Sinners. 1962: 55 Days at Peking. 1963: Murder at the Gallop. 1964: Young Cassidy. Guns at Batasi. 1965: Those Magnificent Men in their Flying Machines. A King's Story (voice only). Seven Women. 1966: Eye of the Devil. Cry in the Wind. 1967: The Shuttered Room. 1970: The Beast in the Cellar. The Beloved (GB: TV, as Sin). Fragment of Fear. 1971: La grande scrofa nera. 1972: Alice's Adventures in Wonderland. 1978: Les Miserables (TV). Dominique. 1979: Gauguin – the Savage. A Man Called Intrepid (TV). 1981: A Tale of Two Cities (TV). Clash of the Titans.

†Unfinished

ROC, Patricia
(Felicia Herold) 1915–
Glamorous, brown-haired (sometimes blonde) British actress, one of the famous Gainsborough (Studios) ladies of the forties, who continually sought to further her career, travelling to France, Italy and Hollywood in search of top star roles, but always returning to Britain. Her fresh looks enabled her to stay in youthful roles until well into her thirties.

Three times married, twice widowed. Latterly living in Switzerland.
1938: The Rebel Son/ Taras Bulba. The Gaunt Stranger (US: The Phantom Strikes). 1939: The Mind of Mr Reeder (US: The Mysterious Mr Reeder). The Missing People. A Window in London (US: Lady in Distress). Dr O'Dowd. 1940: Pack Up Your Troubles. Three Silent Men. Gentleman of Venture (US: It Happened to One Man). 1941: The Farmer's Wife. My Wife's Family. 1942: Let the People Sing. We'll Meet Again. Suspected Person. 1943: Millions Like Us. 1944: 2,000 Women. Madonna of the Seven Moons. Love Story (US: A Lady Surrenders). 1945: The Wicked Lady. Johnny Frenchman. 1946: Canyon Passage. 1947: So Well Remembered, Jassy. The Brothers. Holiday Camp. When the Bough Breaks. 1948: One Night with You. 1949: Retour á la vie. The Perfect Woman. The Man on the Eiffel Tower. 1950: Blackjack (US: Captain Black jack). L'inconnue de Montréal/ Fugitive from Montreal. Circle of Danger. 1952: Something Money Can't Buy. 1953: La mia vita è tua/My Life is Yours. 1954: Cartouche. 1955: La vedova (GB: The Widow). 1957: The Hypnotist (US: Scotland Yard Dragnet). The House in the Woods. 1960: Bluebeard's 10 Honeymoons.

ROCHEFORT, Jean 1930–
Mournfully moustachioed, dark-haired, weathered French star who looks like a *real* Gallic version of Peter Sellers' Inspector Clouseau, and has found himself at the centre of some of the most popular and widely-travelled French entertainments of the past 26 years, without ever leaving his native land. Most of his biggest successes have been in comedy, sometimes of a zany nature, but he has also scored in touching romances and poignant dramas. He won a César (French Oscar) for *Le crabe-tambour*. Started his career as a cabaret performer until films beckoned in his late twenties.
1958: Une balle dans le canon. 1959: 20,000 lieues sur la terre. 1960: Capitaine Fracasse (GB: The Captain). 1961: Le soleil dans l'oeil. 1962: Cartouche (GB: Swords of Blood). Le masque du fer/ The Iron Mask. Fort du fou. 1963: Symphonie pour un massacre. La porteuse de pain. Du grabuge chez les veuves. La foire aux cancres. 1964: Les pieds nickelés. Angélique, Marquise des Anges (GB: Angélique). Le belle famiglie. 1965: Les tribulations d'un Chinois en Chine (GB: Up to His Ears. US: Chinese Adventures in China).

Les dimanches de ma vie. Merveilleuse Angélique. 1966: Qui êtes-vous, Polly Maggoo? A coeur joie (GB and US: Two Weeks in September). Angélique et le roi. 1967: Johnny Banco. Ne jouez pas avec les Martiens. 1968: Pour un amour lointain. Le diable par le queue. 1969: Le temps de mourir. 1970: Céleste. La liberté en croupe. 1971: L'oeuf. 1972: Les feux de la chandelier. Le grand blond avec une chaussure noire (GB: Follow That Guy with the One Black Shoe. US: The Tall Blond Man with One Black Shoe). Le complot (GB and US: The Conspiracy). 1973: L'héritier (GB and US: The Inheritor). Belle ordure. Salut l'artiste! (GB: The Bit Player). Johnny le fligueur. L'horloger de Saint-Paul (GB: The Watchmaker of Saint-Paul. US: The Clockmaker). 1974: Comment réussir dans la vie quand on est C . . . et pleurnichard. Isabelle devant le désir. Nio dio come sono cadutta in basso. Le retour du grand blond (US: The Return of the Tall Blond Man with One Black Shoe). Que la fête commence!/ Let Joy Reign Supreme. Les innocents aux mains sales (GB: Innocents with Dirty Hands. US: Dirty Hands). 1975: Un divorce heureux. 1976: Les magiciens. Calmos (US: Femmes Fatales). Les veces étaient fermés de l'intérieur. Un éléphant ça trompe énormément (GB and US: Pardon Mon Affaire). Le diable dans la boîte. 1977: Le crabe-tambour. Nous irons tous au paradis (GB: Pardon Mon Affaire, Too). 1978: Le cavaleur (GB: The Skirt Chaser. US: Practice Makes Perfect). La grande cuisine/Who is Killing the Great Chefs of Europe? (GB: Too Many Chefs). Les grandissons. 1979: French Postcards. Courage fuyons. Chère inconnue (US: I Sent a Letter to My Love). 1980: Je hais les blondes. Un étrange voyage. 1981: Il faut tuer Birgitt Haas (GB and US: Brigitte Haas Must Be Killed). Le grand frère. 1982: Un dimanche de flic. L'indiscrétion. 1983: L'ami de Vincent. Il cane di gerusalemme. 1984: Frankenstein 90. David, Thomas et les autres. Reveillon chez Bob. 1985: La galette des rois. 1986: Le moustachu. Tandem. 1987: I miei primi quarant' anni/My First 40 Years. 1988: Je suis le seigneur du château. 1989: Le château de ma mère (US: My Mother's Castle). 1990: Amoureux fou. Le mari de la coiffeuse (GB and US: The Hairdresser's Husband). 1991: L'atlantide. Le bal des casse-pieds. Le long hiver '39. 1992: Tango. 1993: Cible émouvante (GB: Wild Target). Va-nu-pieds. 1994: Prêt-à-Porter (US: Ready to Wear). 1995: Tutti gli anni una volta l'anno. 1996: Ridicule. La tournée des grands ducs. 1997: Barracuda. 1998: Rembrandt. El viento se lleveo lo que (US: Wind with the Gone). Le serpent a mangé la grenouille. 1999: Never Ever. 2000: South from Hell's Kitchen. Le placard.

ROGERS, Charles 'Buddy'
See PICKFORD, Mary

ROGERS, Ginger
(Virginia McMath) 1911–1995
Bright, vivacious, likeable blonde American dancer who, after a memorable series of thirties musicals with Fred Astaire, carved herself out a second career as an actress, winning an Oscar for *Kitty Foyle*. Her no-nonsense approach reflected itself in her (still

very feminine) dancing, as well as her acting, and most of her heroines were self-reliant working girls. Married Lew Ayres (*qv*) 1934–1941 and Jacques Bergerac (1927–) 1953–1957, second and fourth of five. Died 'from natural causes' (a diabetic coma).

*1929: *Campus Sweethearts*. *A Night in a Dormitory. *A Day of a Man of Affairs. 1930: *Office Blues. Queen High. *Eddie Cuts In. Young Man of Manhattan. The Sap from Syracuse (GB: The Sap Abroad). Follow the Leader. 1931: Honor Among Lovers. The Tip Off (GB: Looking for Trouble). Suicide Fleet. 1932: The Tenderfoot. Carnival Boat. Hat Check Girl (GB: Embassy Girl). You Said a Mouthful. The Thirteenth Guest. *Hollywood on Parade No 1. *Screen Snapshots No 12. 1933: Broadway Bad (GB: Her Reputation). Professional Sweetheart (GB: Imaginary Sweetheart). A Shriek in the Night. 42nd Street. *Hollywood on Parade No 3. Gold Diggers of 1933. Don't Bet on Love. Sitting Pretty. Flying Down to Rio. Chance at Heaven. 1934: Rafter Romance. Finishing School. Change of Heart. 20 Million Sweethearts. Upperworld. Hollywood on Parade No 13. The Gay Divorcee (GB: The Gay Divorce). Romance in Manhattan. 1935: Star of Midnight. Top Hat. In Person. Roberta. 1936: Follow the Fleet. Swing Time. 1937: *Holiday Greetings. Shall We Dance. Stage Door. 1938: Vivacious Lady. Having Wonderful Time. Carefree. 1939: Bachelor Mother. Fifth Avenue Girl. The Story of Vernon and Irene Castle. 1940: Lucky Partners. The Primrose Path. Kitty Foyle. 1941: Tom, Dick and Harry. 1942: Tales of Manhattan. Once Upon a Honeymoon. Roxie Hart. The Major and the Minor. 1943: Show Business at War. Tender Comrade. *Safeguarding Military Information. 1944: *Battle Stations (narrator only). Lady in the Dark. I'll Be Seeing You. *Ginger Rogers Finds a Bargain. 1945: Weekend at the Waldorf. 1946: Heartbeat. Magnificent Doll. 1947: It Had to Be You. 1949: The Barkleys of Broadway. 1950: Storm Warning. Perfect Strangers (GB: Too Dangerous to Love). 1951: The Groom Wore Spurs. 1952: We're Not Married. Dreamboat. Monkey Business. 1953: Forever Female. *Hollywood's Great Entertainers. 1954: Black Widow. Beautiful Stranger (US: Twist of Fate). 1955: Tight Spot. 1956: The First Traveling Saleslady. Teenage Rebel. 1957: Oh, Men! Oh, Women! 1964: The Confession (GB: TV as Quick! Let's Get Married). 1965: Harlow (TV).*

ROGERS, Jean
(Eleanor Lovegren) 1916–1991

Comely blonde (sometimes red-headed) American actress of much zip and charm who rose to fame in serials of the 1930s – notably two 'Flash Gordon' adventures which cast her as the ever-screaming heroine Dale Arden – and stayed a popular second-feature heroine into her thirties, after originally entering films via the beauty contest route. Modelling and acting in TV commercials into her fifties, she tried to break back into films as a character actress after the death of her husband in 1970 but without success. Died following surgery.

1934: Eight Girls in a Boat. 1935: Manhattan Moon (GB: Sing Me a Love Song). Stormy. Tailspin Tommy in The Great Air Mystery (serial). Fighting Youth. 1936: Don't Get Personal. Ace Drummond (serial). The Adventures of Frank Merriwell (serial). Flash Gordon (serial). My Man Godfrey. Two in a Crowd. Conflict. 1937: Secret Agent X-9 (serial). When Love is Young. Mysterious Crossing. Night Key. Reported Missing. The Wildcatter. 1938: Flash Gordon's Trip to Mars (serial). Always in Trouble. Time Out for Murder. While New York Sleeps. 1939: Hotel for Women/Elsa Maxwell's Hotel for Women. Heaven with a Barbed-Wire Fence. Stop, Look and Love. 1940: Brigham Young – Frontiersman (GB: Brigham Young). The Man Who Wouldn't Talk. Charlie Chan in Panama. Let's Make Music. Yesterday's Heroes. Viva Cisco Kid. 1941: Dr Kildare's Victory (GB: The Doctor and the Debutante). Design for Scandal. 1942: Sunday Punch. Pacific Rendezvous. The War Against Mrs Hadley. 1943: Swing Shift Maisie (GB: The Girl in Overalls). A Stranger in Town. Whistling in Brooklyn. 1945: Rough, Tough and Ready (GB: Men of the Deep). The Strange Mrs Gregory. 1946: Gay Blades. Hot Cargo. 1947: Backlash. Undercover Maisie (GB: Undercover Girl). 1948: Fighting Back. Speed to Spare. 1949: Sky Liner. 1950: The Second Woman (GB: Ellen).

ROGERS, Mimi 1952–
Hollywood never quite discovered this tall, elegant, honey-blonde actress from Florida, even when (indeed, especially when) she married superstar Tom Cruise (*qv*) in 1987. Oddly, she has worked more in films since their 1990 divorce than before it. A late starter in films and TV at 30 – publicists for some time knocked years off her real age –

Rogers has consistently received good reviews for leading roles without breaking into the mainstream, surmounting slightly motherly looks to grab a wide range of characters to play. Even her widest exposure, though – in 1987's *Someone to Watch Over Me* – didn't give her the breakthrough: she made nothing at all for the cinema the following year.

1982: Divorce Wars: A Love Story (TV). Hear No Evil (TV). 1983: The Rousters (TV). Blue Skies Again. 1984: Paper Dolls (TV). 1986: Embassy (TV). Street Smart. Gung Ho. 1987: Someone to Watch Over Me. You Ruined My Life! (TV). 1989: Hider in the House. The Mighty Quinn. 1990: To Forget Palermo/Dimenticare Palermo. Desperate Hours. The Doors. Fourth Story (cable TV. GB: Deadly Identity). 1991: The Rapture. Wedlock (later Deadlock). 1992: White Sands. The Player. Dark Horse. Lady Killer. Shooting Elizabeth. Those Bedroom Eyes. 1993: Pet. Love Most Deadly. Bloodlines: Murder in the Family (TV). 1994: Far From Home: The Adventures of Yellow Dog. Monkey Trouble. Bulletproof Heart (GB: Killer). Wild Bill. Reflections on a Crime. 1995: Full Body Massage (cable TV). 1996: Three Blind Mice. The Mirror Has Two Faces. Trees Lounge. In the Blink of an Eye (TV). Little White Lies. 1997: Austin Powers: International Man of Mystery. Weapons of Mass Destruction (cable TV). Virtual Obsession (TV). Tricks (TV). The Christmas List (TV). 1998: Lost in Space. 1999: Manchester Prep (TV). The Devil's Arithmetic (TV). 2000: Seven Girlfriends. Common Ground (TV). Ginger Snaps.

ROGERS, Roy (Leonard Slye, later legally changed) 1911–1998
Light-haired, slight, faintly oriental-looking American singing cowboy who became for many years the world's number one money-making western star. His medium-budget westerns at Republic were longer (around 75 minutes) than the average and actually burst into colour for a while in the late forties. Also a popular recording star. His horse Trigger (1932–1965) was almost as famous. Married (second; first wife died) to Dale Evans (*qv*), his oft-time leading lady, from 1947. Always signed autographs 'Happy Trails'. Died from congestive heart failure.

*1933: ‡Sailor Be Good. 1935: ‡*Slightly Static. †Way Up Thar. ‡The Old Homestead. **‡Tumbling Tumbleweeds. ‡Gallant*

Defender. 1936: ‡*Lonesome Trailer. ‡The Big Show. ‡Rhythm on the Range. ‡The Mysterious Avenger. ‡The Old Corral (GB: Texas Serenade). 1937: ‡The Old Wyoming Trail. †Wild Horse Rodeo. †The California Mail. 1938: †The Old Barn Dance. Under Western Stars. Come on Rangers. Shine on, Harvest Moon. Billy the Kid Returns. 1939: Rough Rider's Roundup. Frontier Pony Express. Southward Ho. In Old Caliente. Man of Conquest. The Arizona Kid. Wall Street Cowboy. Saga of Death Valley. Days of Jesse James. Jeepers Creepers (GB: Money Isn't Everything). 1940: The Dark Command. The Carson City Kid. The Ranger and the Lady. Colorado. Young Buffalo Bill. *Rodeo Dough. Young Bill Hickok. Border Legion. 1941: Robin Hood of the Pecos. *Meet Roy Rogers. In Old Cheyenne. Arkansas Judge (GB: False Witness). Nevada City. Sheriff of Tombstone. Bad Man of Deadwood. Jesse James at Bay. Red River Valley. 1942: Man from Cheyenne. South of Santa Fé. Sunset on the Desert. Romance on the Range. Sons of the Pioneers. Sunset Serenade. Heart of the Golden West. Ridin' Down the Canyon. 1943: King of the Cowboys. Idaho. Song of Texas. Silver Spurs. Man from Music Mountain. Hands Across the Border. 1944: The Cowboy and the Senorita. The Yellow Rose of Texas. Song of Nevada. San Fernando Valley. Lights of Old Santa Fé. Brazil. Hollywood Canteen. Lake Placid Serenade. 1945: Bells of Rosarita. Utah. Sunset in El Dorado. The Man from Oklahoma. Don't Fence Me In. Along the Navajo Trail. 1946: Song of Arizona. Rainbow over Texas. My Pal Trigger. Under Nevada Skies. Roll on Texas Moon. Home in Oklahoma. Out California Way. Heldorado. 1947: Hit Parade of 1947. Apache Rose. Bells of San Angelo. Springtime in the Sierras. On the Old Spanish Trail. 1948: The Gay Ranchero. Under California Skies. Eyes of Texas. Nighttime in Nevada. Grand Canyon Trail. The Far Frontier. 1949: Susanna Pass. Down Dakota Way. The Golden Stallion. *Howdy Podner. Bells of Coronado. 1950: Twilight in the Sierras. Trigger Jr. Sunset in the West. North of the Great Divide. Trail of Robin Hood. 1951: Spoilers of the Plains. Heart of the Rockies. In Old Amarillo. South of Caliente. Pals of the Golden West. 1952: *Screen Snapshots No 205. Son of Paleface. 1954: *Screen Snapshots No 224. 1956: *Hollywood Bronc Busters. 1959: Alias Jesse James. 1972: Outdoor Rambling. 1975: MacKintosh and T.J. (GB: TV). 1983: Kenny Rogers As The Gambler: The Adventure

Conintues (TV). 1992: Roy Rogers, King of the Cowboys. 1996: The Strange Blues of Cowboy Red (video clips). 1998: All My Friends Are Cowboys.

‡ As Leonard Slye (when billed) †As Dick Weston
**Scene deleted from final release print

ROGERS, Will 1879–1935
Drawling, straw-haired American comedian and entertainer with sagging lower lip, who won the hearts of the nation with his folksy humour, rope-twirling tricks and homespun philosophy. His became a guiding voice during the Depression. His films, once sound came along, were hugely popular, and he was much mourned when killed in a plane crash. His son, Will Rogers Jr. (b1911) had a few starring roles in the early 1950s. He shot himself in 1993.
1918: Laughing Bill Hyde. 1919: Almost a Husband. Jubilo. Water Water Everywhere. 1920: Jes' Call Me Jim. Cupid the Cowpuncher. The Strange Boarder. Scratch My Back. 1921: Boys Will Be Boys. Honest Hutch. Guile of Women. Doubling for Romeo. An Unwilling Hero. 1922: One Glorious Day. The Headless Horseman. A Poor Relation. *Hustling Hank. *The Ropin' Fool. One Day in 365. *Uncensored Movies. 1923: *Jes' Passin' Through. Fruits of Faith. Hollywood. *Gee Whiz, Genevieve. Family Fits. Highbrow Stuff. 1924: *Don't Park There! *The Cake Eater. *Going to Congress. *A Truthful Liar. *Big Moments from Little Pictures. *The Cowboy Sheik. *Jubilo Jr. *Our Congressman. *Two Wagons, Both Covered. 1927: Tiptoes. A Texas Steer. *Winging 'Round Europe *With Will Rogers in Paris. *Reeling Down the Rhine. *Roaming the Emerald Isle. *Hiking Through Holland. *Hunting for Huns in Berlin/Hunting for Germans in Berlin. *Through Switzerland and Bavaria. *Prowling Round France. *Exploring England. 1928: *Over the Bounding Blue. 1929: They Had to See Paris. 1930: So This is London. Happy Days. Lightnin'. 1931: A Connecticut Yankee (GB: The Yankee at King Arthur's Court). Ambassador Bill. Young As You Feel. 1932: Down to Earth. Too Busy to Work. Business and Pleasure. The Plutocrat. 1933: State Fair. Doctor Bull. Mr Skitch. 1934: David Harum. Handy Andy. Judge Priest. *Hollywood on Parade No 13. 1935: The County Chairman. Life Begins at 40. Steamboat 'Round the Bend. Doubting Thomas. In Old Kentucky.

ROLAND, Gilbert
(Luis de Alonso) 1905–1994
Stunningly handsome, moustachioed, black-haired Mexican leading man (from the same town as Anthony Quinn) who kept his good looks until well into middle age, and surprised many by becoming one of Hollywood's most efficient actors in the later stages of his career after proving a dashing Cisco Kid in post-war years. Married (first of two) to Constance Bennett from 1941 to 1946. Died from cancer.
1925: The Lady Who Died. The Plastic Age. 1926: The Blonde Saint. The Midshipman. The Campus Flirt (GB: The College Flirt). 1927: The Love Mart. Camille. The Dove. Rose of the Golden West. 1928: The Woman Disputed. 1929: New York Nights. 1930: Men of the North (and Spanish-language version). 1931: Resurreccion. Hombres en mi Vida. 1932: Call Her Savage. Life Begins (GB: The Dawn of Life). No Living Witness. The Passionate Plumber. A Parisian Romance. The Woman in Room 13. 1933: Our Betters. She Done Him Wrong. Yo, tu y Ella. Una Viuda Romantica. Gigolettes of Paris. Tarnished Youth. After Tonight (GB: Sealed Lips). 1934: Elinor Norton. 1935: Ladies Love Danger. Mystery Woman. *La Fiesta de Santa Barbara. 1936: Julieta Compra un Hijo. 1937: Thunder Trail. Midnight Taxi. Last Train from Madrid. 1938: Gateway. 1939: La Vida Bohemia. Juarez. 1940: The Sea Hawk. Isle of Destiny. Gambling on the High Seas. Rangers of Fortune. 1941: My Life with Caroline. Angels with Broken Wings. 1942: Enemy Agents Meet Ellery Queen (GB: The Lido Mystery). Isle of Missing Men. 1944: The Desert Hawk (serial). 1945: Captain Kidd. 1946: The Gay Cavalier. South of Monterey. Beauty and the Bandit. Le Rebellion de los Fantasmas. 1947: Riding the California Trail. The Other Love. Robin Hood of Monterey. High Conquest. King of the Bandits. Pirates of Monterey. 1948: The Dude Goes West. 1949: Malaya (GB: East of the Rising Sun). We Were Strangers. 1950: The Torch (GB: Bandit General). Crisis. The Furies. 1951: The Bullfighter and the Lady. Ten Tall Men. Mark of the Renegade. 1952: Glory Alley. Apache War Smoke. The Bad and the Beautiful. My Six Convicts. The Miracle of Our Lady of Fatima (GB: The Miracle of Fatima). 1953: Beneath the 12-Mile Reef. The Diamond Queen. Thunder Bay. 1954: The French Line. 1955: Underwater! The Racers (GB: Such Men Are Dangerous). The Treasure of Pancho Villa. That Lady. 1956: Around the

World in 80 Days. Bandido! Three Violent People. 1957: The Midnight Story (GB: Appointment with a Shadow). Invitation to a Gunfighter (TV). 1958: Last of the Fast Guns. Mr Pharaoh and Cleopatra (US: Catch Me If You Can). 1959: The Wild and the Innocent. The Big Circus. Guns of the Timberland. 1962: Samar! 1964: Cheyenne Autumn. 1965: The Reward. 1966: The Poppy is Also a Flower (TV. GB: cinemas as Danger Grows Wild). 1968: Ognuno per se (GB: Every Man for Himself. US: The Ruthless Four). Vado l'ammazzo e torno (GB and US: Any Gun Can Play). Anche nel West, c'era una volta Dio. Quella sproca storia del West. Sartana non pardona (US: Sonora). 1969: Entre Dios y El Diablo. Johnny Hamlet. 1971: The Christian Licorice Store. 1972: Incident on a Dark Street (TV). 1973: Running Wild. 1974: The Mark of Zorro (TV). Deliver Us from Evil. Treasure of Tayopa. 1975: The Black Pearl. The Pacific Connection. The Deadly Tower (TV. Narrator only). 1976: Islands in the Stream. 1977: Infierno en la salva. 1979: The Sacketts (TV). Caco Blanco. 1982: Barbarosa (filmed 1979).

ROLFE, Guy 1911–

Very tall, dark, gaunt, spidery British leading man, popular in serious roles between 1946 and 1960. One was surprised that such skull-like handsomeness was not more often found in horror films of the sixties and seventies than it was. A trip to Hollywood in the early fifties brought scant reward but four decades later, now more skeletal than ever, he made his mark there in four of the popular 'Puppet Master' horror films. A former boxer and racing-car driver, he married actress Jane Aird.

1937: Knight Without Armour. 1938: The Drum (US: Drums). 1946: Old Man Out. Hungry Hill. 1947: Nicholas Nickleby. Meet Me at Dawn. Easy Money. Uncle Silas (US: The Inheritance). Broken Journey. 1948: Saraband for Dead Lovers (US: Saraband). Portrait from Life (US: The Girl in the Painting). 1949: Fools Rush In. The Spider and the Fly. 1950: The Reluctant Widow. Prelude to Fame. 1951: Home to Danger. 1952: Ivanhoe. 1953: Young Bess. The Veils of Bagdad. King of the Khyber Rifles. Operation Diplomat. 1954: Dance Little Lady. 1955: You Can't Escape. 1956: It's Never Too Late. 1958: Girls at Sea. 1959: Yesterday's Enemy. The Stranglers of Bombay. 1960: Revak the Rebel (US: The Barbarian). 1961: King of

Kings. Snow White and the Three Stooges (GB: Snow White and the Three Clowns). 1962: Mr Sardonicus (GB: Sardonicus). Taras Bulba. 1963: The Fall of the Roman Empire. 1965: The Alphabet Murders. 1969: Land Raiders. 1973: Nicholas and Alexandra. 1973: And Now the Screaming Starts! 1979: Bloodline/ Sidney Sheldon's Bloodline. 1983: The Case of Marcel Duchamp. 1984: The Bounty. 1985: The Bride. 1986: The Doll/Dolls. 1991: Puppet Master III: Toulon's Revenge. 1993: Puppet Master Four. 1994: Puppet Master 5: The Final Chapter (video). 1999: Retro Puppet Master.

ROMAIN, Yvonne (Y. Warren) 1938–

Breathtakingly beautiful brunette London-born, French-raised actress, a former photographer's model and in British films as a teenager. Her liquid eyes and stunning figure proved just the ticket for Hammer horror heroines, and she played them with spirit. After the horror vogue waned in the mid 1960s, she was, alas, seldom seen. Long married to composer Leslie Bricusse.

1956: †The Baby and the Battleship. 1957: †Interpol (US: Pick Up Alley). †Action of the Tiger. †Portrait of a Matador. †Seven Thunders (US: The Beasts of Marseilles). 1958: †The Silent Enemy. †Murder Reported. †Corridors of Blood. 1960: Circus of Horrors. 1961: The Curse of the Werewolf. The Frightened City. Village of Daughters. 1962: Captain Clegg (US: Night Creatures). 1963: Return to Sender. The Devil Doll. 1964: Smokescreen. 1965: The Brigand of Kandahar. 1966: The Swinger. Double Trouble. 1973: The Last of Sheila.

†As Yvonne Warren

ROMAN, Ruth

(Norma Roman) 1923–1999

Dark, curvaceous, vividly attractive, if slightly cold-looking American actress who struggled up to stardom through small roles and serials. Her peak starring time was quite short, but she later came back as a mature, but still glamorous, character actress. Ideally cast as the Lady Macbeth figure in Joe Macbeth. Daughter of a circus barker. Died in her sleep.

1943: Stage Door Canteen. 1944: Song of Nevada. Ladies Courageous. White Stallion/ Harmony Trail. Since You Went Away. Storm Over Lisbon. 1945: See My Lawyer. Jungle Queen (serial). The Affairs of Susan. Incendiary Blonde. You Came Along. She Gets

Her Man. 1946: Without Reservations. †A Night in Casablanca. Gilda. 1947: The Web. 1948: Belle Starr's Daughter. The Big Clock. Night Has a Thousand Eyes. Good Sam. 1949: Beyond the Forest. Always Leave Them Laughing. The Window. Champion. 1950: Barricade. Dallas. Three Secrets. Colt 45. 1951: Starlift. Lightning Strikes Twice. Strangers on a Train. Tomorrow is Another Day. *The Screen Director. 1952: Young Man with Ideas. Invitation. Mara Maru. 1953: Blowing Wild. 1954: Tanganyika. The Shanghai Story. The Far Country. Down Three Dark Streets. 1955: Joe Macbeth. La pecatrice del deserto. 1956: The Bottom of the Bottle (GB: Beyond the River). Great Day in the Morning. Rebel in Town. The Sinners. 1957: Five Steps to Danger. 1958: Bitter Victory. 1959: Desert Desperados. 1961: Look in Any Window. Miraglo a los Cobardes. 1964: Love Has Many Faces. 1970: The Old Man Who Cried Wolf (TV). Incident in San Francisco (TV). 1972: The Baby. 1973: The Killing Kind. Go Ask Alice (TV). 1974: Punch and Jody (TV). Impulse. A Knife for the Ladies (later Silent Sentence). 1975: Dead of Night. 1976: Day of the Animals. 1979: The Sacketts (TV). 1980: Echoes (released 1983). 1991: When in Rome.

† Scenes deleted from final release print

ROME, Stewart

(Septimus Ryott) 1886–1965

Tall, dark, airily handsome British leading man of military bearing, one of the first great fan pin-ups of the silent screen. Immensely popular from 1914 to 1924, he soldiered on afterwards as a kind of father-figure to the British cinema, in character roles, mainly as

stern and well-bred as had been his intrepid early heroes.
*1913: *A Throw of the Dice. 1914: *The Price of Fame. *The Whirr of the Spinning Wheel. *Thou Shalt Not Steal. *What the Firelight Showed. *The Girl Who Played the Game. *The Girl Who Lived in Straight Street. *The Guest of the Evening. *The Streets of Circumstance. *Only a Flower Girl. *The Schemers. *Unfit. *The Bronze Idol. *His Country's Bidding. *The Awakening of Nora. *So Much Good in the Worst of Us. *The Quarry Mystery. *Tommy's Money Scheme. *The Double Event. *The Man from India. *They Say – Let Them Say. *John Linworth's Atonement. *The Lie. Justice. The Heart of Midlothian. The Great Poison Mystery. Creatures of Clay. *The Breaking Point. The Terror of the Air. Dr Fenton's Ordeal. The Grip of Ambition. The Chimes. The Brothers. Time, the Great Healer. Despised and Rejected. Life's Dark Road. The Cry of the Captive. The Strength of the Weak. 1915: *The Shepherd of Souls. *The Man with the Scar. *They Called Him Coward. *Schoolgirl Rebels. *The Confession. *Spies. *A Moment of Darkness. *One Good Turn. *Jill and the Old Fiddle. *The Recalling of John Gray. The Canker of Jealousy. Barnaby Rudge. A Lancashire Lass. The Incorruptible Crown. The Curtain's Secret. Court-Martialled. The Bottle. The Baby on the Barge. The Second String. The Sweater. Her Boy. Sweet Lavender. The Golden Pavement. The White Hope. The Nightbirds of London. As the Sun Went Down. Irish. Face to Face. 1916: Sowing the Wind. Trelawney of the Wells. Annie Laurie. The White Boys. Grand Babylon Hotel. Partners. The Marriage of William Ashe. Comin' Thro' the Rye. Molly Bawn. Her Marriage Lines. The House of Fortescue. Love in a Mist. 1917: The Cobweb. The American Heiress. The Man Behind 'The Times'. A Grain of Sand. The Eternal Triangle. 1918: The Touch of a Child. 1919: The Gentleman Rider (US: Hearts and Saddles). A Daughter of Eve. A Great Coup. Snow in the Desert. 1920: The Great Gay Road. The Case of Lady Camber. Her Son. The Romance of a Movie Star. 1921: The Penalty/Her Penalty. Christie Johnstone. The Penniless Millionaire. The Imperfect Lover. In Full Cry. 1922: Son of Kissing Cup. Dicky Monteith. When Greek Meets Greek. The White Hope (remake). 1923: Fires of Fate. The Prodigal Son. The Uninvited Guest. The Woman Who Obeyed. 1924: The Desert Sheik. The Colleen Bawn. The Eleventh Commandment. The Stirrup Cup Sensation. Nets of Destiny. The Shadow of the Morgue. Reveille. 1925: The Silver Treasure. 1926: Thou Fool. 1927: Somehow Good. 1928: The Ware Case. The Passing of Mr Quin. The Man Who Changed His Name. Zero. 1929: The Crimson Circle. Dark Red Roses. 1930: The Last Hour. The Price of Things. Kissing Cup's Race. 1931: The Great Gay Road (remake). Other People's Sins. Deadlock. Rynox. *Sound Cinemagazine No 273. 1932: Reunion. Betrayal. The Marriage Bond. 1933: Song of the Plough. 1934: The Girl in the Flat. Important People. Lest We Forget. Designing Woman. Temptation. 1936: Men of Yesterday. Debt of Honour. 1937: The Squeaker (US: Murder on Diamond Row). Dinner at the Ritz. Wings of the Morning. 1938: The Dance of Death. 1939:

Confidential Lady. The Warning. Shadowed Eyes. 1941: Banana Ridge. 1942: Salute John Citizen. One of Our Aircraft is Missing. 1944: *Tom's Ride. The World Owes Me a Living. 1946: The Magic Bow. 1947: The White Unicorn (US: Bad Sister). Jassy. The Root of All Evil. 1948: My Sister and I. Woman Hater. 1950: Let's Have a Murder.

ROME, Sydne 1946–

So what's a nice Jewish girl from Ohio doing in films like these? At least this bubbly blonde American-born star provided some lively decoration in French and Italian films of the seventies, most noticeably as the seldom-clothed Alice-in-Black-Wonderland heroine of Polanski's *What!* Her name really *is* Sydne Rome.
*1969: Vivi, o preferibilmente morti. Some Girls Do. 1970: Ciao, Gulliver. La ragazza di latta. 1971: Un doppio a metà. 1972: Cosi sia. 1973: What! Order to Kill/ El Clan de los Inmorales. Le ultimo ore di une vergine. L'ospite della notte. Reigen (GB: Dance of Love. US: Merry-Go-Round). La sculacciata. 1974: La race des 'Seigneurs'/Creezy. Nel corpo e nell' anima. Il ragno. Nastro nero in casa Nichols. 1975: Wanted: Babysitter. Sex with a Smile. That Lucky Touch. Il faut vivre dangereusement. 1976: L'immenso è rosso. Shadow of a Killer. The Twist/Folies Bourgeoises. 1977: Pour le corps d'une femme. Moi, fleur bleue (US: Stop Calling Me Baby!). The Fiend/Il mostro. 1978: Just a Gigolo. Speed Fever/Formula 1. 1980: The Puma Man. Los locos vecinos del segundo. 1981: The Couples. Looping. 1982: Red Bells/Ten Days That Shook the World. Red Bells II. Crazy Family/Arrivano i miei. 1986: The Final Romance.

ROMERO, Cesar 1907–1994

Handsome, strong-chinned, black-haired moustachioed American actor of Italian-Mexican parentage, typed as a Latin lover from his earliest Hollywood days, although he had made his reputation as a dancer. For many years the film capital's most eligible bachelor, Romero never married. He won fresh popularity on TV as The Joker in the *Batman* series. Died from blood clot complications after bronchitis. Two years earlier, he had completed 60 years in films.
*1933: The Shadow Laughs. 1934: Cheating Cheaters. The Thin Man. British Agent. 1935: The Good Fairy. Clive of India. Hold 'Em Yale (GB: Uniform Lovers). Diamond Jim.

Rendezvous. Strange Wives. Cardinal Richelieu. The Devil is a Woman. Metropolitan. Show Them No Mercy (GB: Tainted Money). 1936: Nobody's Fool. Fifteen Maiden Lane. Love Before Breakfast. Public Enemy's Wife (GB: G-Man's Wife). 1937: Wee Willie Winkie. She's Dangerous. Dangerously Yours. *Hollywood Screen Test. Armored Car. 1938: Always Goodbye. Happy Landing. My Lucky Star. Five of a Kind. 1939: Return of the Cisco Kid. Charlie Chan at Treasure Island. Wife, Husband and Friend. The Little Princess. Frontier Marshal. 1940: Lucky Cisco Kid. He Married His Wife. Viva Cisco Kid. The Gay Caballero. The Cisco Kid and the Lady. 1941: Ride on, Vaquero! Tall, Dark and Handsome. Dance Hall. The Great American Broadcast. Romance of the Rio Grande. Week-End in Havana. 1942: Tales of Manhattan. Orchestra Wives. A Gentleman at Heart. Springtime in the Rockies. 1943: *Screen Snapshots No 105. Coney Island. Wintertime. 1947: Carnival in Costa Rica. Captain from Castile. 1948: Deep Waters. Julia Misbehaves. That Lady in Ermine. 1949: The Beautiful Blonde from Bashful Bend. 1950: Once a Thief. Love That Brute. 1951: Happy-Go-Lovely. FBI Girl. The Lost Continent. 1952: The Jungle. Lady in the Fog (US: Scotland Yard Inspector). 1953: Prisoners of the Casbah. Street of Shadows (US: Shadow Man). 1954: El Corazon y la Espada (US: The Sword of Granada). Vera Cruz. 1955: *Hollywood Shower of Stars. The Americano. The Racers (GB: Such Men Are Dangerous). 1956: Around the World in 80 Days. Manhattan Tower (TV). *Screen Snapshots No 235. The Leather Saint. *All's Fair in Love (TV. GB: cinemas). 1957: The Story of Mankind. 1958: Villa! 1960: Ocean's Eleven. Pepe. 1961: Seven Women from Hell. 1962: If a Man Answers. The Castilian. 1963: We Shall Return. Donovan's Reef. 1964: A House is Not a Home. Two on a Guillotine. 1965: Sergeant Deadhead. Marriage on the Rocks. Broken Sabre (TV. GB: cinemas). 1966: Batman. 1967: Madigan's Millions. 1968: Hot Millions. A Talent for Loving. Crooks and Coronets (US: Sophie's Place). Skidoo. 1969: Don't Push, I'll Charge When I'm Ready (TV). Latitude Zero. How to Make It (GB: Target: Harry). Midas Run (GB: A Run on Gold). The Computer Wore Tennis Shoes. 1971: Soul Soldier (GB: Men of the Tenth). The Last Generation. 1972: Now You See Him, Now You Don't. The Specter of Edgar Allan Poe. The Proud and the Damned (GB: TV). 1973: Timber Tamp. 1974: The

Strongest Man in the World. 1975: Won Ton Ton, the Dog Who Saved Hollywood. 1977: Kino, the Padre on Horseback. 1979: Monster. 1983: Vultures in Paradise/Flesh and Bullets. 1984: Lust in the Dust. 1988: Mortuary Academy. 1989: Street Law. Judgement Day. 1990: Simple Justice. Preston Sturges: The Rise and Fall of an American Dreamer. 1992: The Player. 1994: Carmen Miranda: Bananas is My Business (doc).

ROONEY, Mickey (Joseph Yule) 1920–
Dynamic, rather light-haired, pocket-sized American star, in films from childhood, after a stage debut at two in his parents' vaudeville act. Rooney could sing, dance, play piano and drums and act in such an engagingly chirpy way that he was soon the favourite of millions. After a career in comedy shorts from the late twenties he joined M-G-M and, whether making The Hardy Family series or teensving musicals with Judy Garland, became the world's number one box-office star for three years from 1939. After war service his star exploded, but he clawed his way back with some gritty acting performances, and still pops up in featured roles. Special Oscars 1938 and 1983. Nominated for Academy Awards in Babes in Arms, The Human Comedy, The Bold and the Brave and The Black Stallion. Nine times married. First wife (1942–1943) was Ava Gardner, third (1949–1951) Martha Vickers. Emmy for TV movie Bill in 1981.
1926: *Not to be Trusted. 1927: †*Mickey's Pals. †*Mickey's Circus. †*Mickey's Eleven. Orchids and Ermine. †* Mickey's Battle. 1928: †*Mickey's Parade. †*Mickey's Little Eva. †*Mickey's Nine. †*Fillum Frolics. †*Mickey's Athletes. †*Mickey's Rivals. †*Mickey in School. †*Mickey in Love. †*Mickey's Triumph. †*Mickey's Movies. †*Mickey's Big Game Hunt. †*Mickey the Detective. †*Mickey's Babies (GB: Baby Show). †*Mickey's Wild West. 1929: †*Rattling Racers. †*Mickey's Surprise. †*Mickey's Big Moment. †*Mickey's Brown Derby. †*Mickey's Explorers. †*Mickey's Great Idea. †*Mickey's Initiation. †*Mickey's Last Chance. †*Mickey's Menagerie. †*Mickey's Northwest Mounted. †*Mickey's Mix-Up. †*Birthday Squeakings. †*Mickey's Midnight Follies. 1930: †*Mickey's Strategy. †*Mickey's Champs. †*Mickey's Luck. †*Mickey's Master Mind. †*Mickey's Musketeers. †*Mickey's Whirlwinds. †*Mickey's Winners. †*Mickey's Warriors. †*Mickey the

Romeo. †*Mickey's Merry Men. †*Mickey's Bargain. 1931: †*Mickey's Rebellion. †*Mickey's Diplomacy. †*Mickey's Thrill Hunters. †*Mickey's Helping Hand. †*Mickey's Stampede. †*Mickey's Crusaders. †*Mickey's Sideline. †*Mickey's Big Business. †*Mickey's Wildcats. 1932: †*Mickey's Travels. †*Mickey's Holiday. †*Mickey's Golden Rule. †*Mickey's Busy Day. †*Mickey's Charity. High Speed. Officer Thirteen. Emma. Information Kid/Fast Companions. My Pal the King. Sin's Pay Day. Beast of the City. 1933: †*Mickey's Ape Man. †*Mickey's Race. †*Mickey's Big Broadcast. †*Mickey's Covered Wagon. †*Mickey's Disguises. †*Mickey's Touchdown. †*Mickey's Tent Show. Broadway to Hollywood (GB: Ring Up the Curtain). The Big Cage. The Chief (GB: My Old Man's a Fireman). The World Changes. The Life of Jimmy Dolan (GB: The Kid's Last Fight). The Big Chance. 1934: The Lost Jungle (serial). †*Mickey's Minstrels. †*Mickey's Rescue. †*Mickey's Medicine Men. Love Birds. Beloved. I Like It That Way. Manhattan Melodrama. Hide-Out. Half a Sinner. Death on the Diamond. Chained. Upper World. Blind Date (GB: Her Sacrifice). 1935: The County Chairman. A Midsummer Night's Dream. The Healer. Reckless. Riff Raff. Ah, Wilderness! 1936: Down the Stretch. *Pirate Party on Catalina Isle. Little Lord Fauntleroy. The Devil is a Sissy (GB: The Devil Takes the Count). 1937: The Hoosier Schoolboy (GB: Yesterday's Hero). Thoroughbreds Don't Cry. Captains Courageous. A Family Affair. Slave Ship. Live, Love and Learn. You're Only Young Once. 1938: Judge Hardy's Children. Hold That Kiss. Love is a Headache. Lord Jeff (GB: The Boy from Barnardos). Love Finds Andy Hardy. Boys Town. Out West with the Hardys. Stablemates. 1939: The Adventures of Huckleberry Finn. The Hardys Ride High. Babes in Arms. Judge Hardy and Son. Andy Hardy Gets Spring Fever. 1940: *Rodeo Dough. Andy Hardy Meets Debutante. Young Tom Edison. Strike Up the Band. Andy Hardy's Private Secretary. 1941: Men of Boys Town. *Cavalcade of the Academy Awards. Life Begins for Andy Hardy. Babes on Broadway. *Meet the Stars No 4 (Los Angeles Examiner Benefit). 1942: The Courtship of Andy Hardy. A Yank at Eton. Andy Hardy's Double Life. 1943: Girl Crazy. Thousands Cheer. The Human Comedy. 1944: National Velvet. Andy Hardy's Blonde Trouble. 1946: Love Laughs at Andy Hardy. 1947: Summer Holiday (released 1948). Killer McCoy. 1948: Words and Music. *Rough but Hopeful. 1949: The Big Wheel. 1950: He's a Cockeyed Wonder. The Fireball. 1951: My Outlaw Brother. The Strip. 1952: †Screen Snapshots No 205. Sound Off. Off Limits (GB: Military Policemen). 1953: A Slight Case of Larceny. *Mickey Rooney – Then and Now. 1954: Drive a Crooked Road. The Bridges at Toko-Ri. The Atomic Kid. 1955: The Twinkle in God's Eye. 1956: The Bold and the Brave. Magnificent Roughnecks. Francis in the Haunted House. 1957: The Comedian (TV). Operation Mad Ball. Baby Face Nelson. *Playtime in Hollywood. 1958: Andy Hardy Comes Home. *Glamorous Hollywood. 1959: A Nice Little Bank That Should Be Robbed. The Last Mile.

The Big Operator. 1960: Platinum High School (GB: Rich, Young and Deadly). The Private Lives of Adam and Eve. 1961: King of the Roaring Twenties (GB: The Big Bankroll). Everything's Ducky. Breakfast at Tiffany's. 1962: Requiem for a Heavyweight (GB: Blood Money). 1963: It's a Mad, Mad, Mad, Mad World. 1964: The Secret Invasion. 1965: How to Stuff a Wild Bikini. The Devil in Love. 24 Hours to Kill. 1966: Ambush Bay. 1968: The Extraordinary Seaman. Skidoo. 1969: 80 Steps to Jonah. The Comic. The Cockeyed Cowboys of Calico County (GB: TV as A Woman for Charlie). 1970: Hollywood Blue. 1971: Evil Roy Slade (TV). Journey Back to Oz (voice only). B.J. Lang Presents. 1972: Pulp. Richard. 1973: The Godmothers. 1974: That's Entertainment! Ace of Aces. Bon Baisers de Hong Kong. Thunder County/It Snows in the Everglades. Cell Block Girls/ Women's Prison Escape. 1975: Rachel's Man. 1976: The Domino Killings/The Domino Principle. Find the Lady. 1977: Pete's Dragon. 1978: The Magic of Lassie. Donovan's Kid (TV). 1979: Rudolph and Frosty's Christmas in July (voice only). Arabian Adventure. The Black Stallion. 1980: My Kidnapper, My Love (TV). Odyssey of the Pacific. 1981: Leave 'Em Laughing (TV). Bill (TV). The Emperor of Peru. The Fox and the Hound (voice only). Senior Trip (TV). 1983: Bill on His Own (TV). 1985: It Came Upon the Midnight Clear (TV). 1985: The Care Bears Movie (voice only). 1986: The White Stallion/Lightning, the White Stallion. The Return of Mike Hammer (TV). Little Spies (TV). 1988: Bluegrass (TV). 1989: Erik the Viking. 1990: My Heroes Have Always Been Cowboys. Home for Christmas. 1991: Silent Night, Deadly Night 5: The Toy Maker. The Gambler Returns: The Luck of the Draw (TV). A Year Without Santa Claus (TV. Voice only). 1992: Maximum Force. The Legend of Wolf Mountain. Sweet Justice. La vida lactea/The Milky Life. Little Nemo: Adventures in Slumberland (voice only). 1993: Judge Stone and Family (unfinished). 1994: The Legend of O.B. Taggart (and screenplay). The Magic Voyage (voice only). That's Entertainment! III. Revenge of the Red Baron. Plane Fear. 1995: He Ain't Heavy/Brothers' Destiny. 1996: Heidi. 1997: Sinbad: The Battle of the Dark Knights. Boys Will Be Boys (TV). Killing Midnight (TV). 1998: The Face on the Barroom Floor. Babe: Pig in the City. Animals (and the Tollkeeper). Michael Kael versus the World News Company. 1999: Internet Love. 2000: The First of May.

As director: 1951: My True Story.
†As Mickey McGuire

ROSS, Katharine 1942–
Attractive, very dark, tart-voiced American actress whose career did not race on at quite the pace expected after three big hits in the late 1960s. Tried (perhaps too hard) to be choosy, but was in routine roles from the early 1970s. Her fifth husband (married since 1984) is actor Sam Elliott (qv). Oscar nominee for The Graduate.
1965: Mr Buddwing (GB: Woman Without a Face). The Singing Nun. Shenandoah. 1966: The Longest Hundred Miles (TV). 1967: The Graduate. Games. 1968: Hellfighters. 1969:

Butch Cassidy and the Sundance Kid. Tell Them Willie Boy is Here. 1970: Get to Know Your Rabbit. Fools. 1972: They Only Kill Their Masters. 1974: Le hasard et le violence (GB: The Scarlet Room). The Stepford Wives. 1976: Wanted: The Sundance Woman (TV). Voyage of the Damned. 1978: The Betsy. The Swarm. The Legacy. 1979: Murder by Natural Causes (TV). 1980: The Final Countdown. Rodeo Girl (TV). 1981: Murder in Texas (TV). 1982: Wrong Is Right (GB: The Man with the Deadly Lens). Pigs (later Daddy's Deadly Darling. Filmed 1972). Travis McGee (TV). The Shadow Riders (TV). Marian Rose White (TV). 1983: Secrets of a Mother and Daughter (TV). 1986: Red-Headed Stranger. Houston: The Legend of Texas (TV). 1988: Mickey. Tattle (TV). A Row of Crows/ A Climate For Killing. 1991: Conagher (TV). 1997: Home Before Dark.

ROSSELLINI, Isabella 1952–
Dark-haired, soulful-faced, Italian-born actress with small, delicate features, still young-looking into her forties, and as likely to turn up as gentle, sensitive characters as in boldly sexual roles. The daughter of Ingrid Bergman (qv) and Italian director Roberto Rossellini, she has also been a teacher, translator, model and journalist, but her acting career was sporadic until the mid 1980s. Married/divorced director Martin Scorsese (first of two). At times still looks uncannily like her mother.
1976: A Matter of Time. 1979: Il prato (US: The Meadow). 1980: Il pap'occhio. 1985: White Nights. 1986: Blue Velvet. 1987: Young Robinson Crusoe. Tough Guys Don't Dance. Red Riding Hood. Siesta. 1988: Zelly and Me. 1989: Cousins. 1990: Wild at Heart. Las dames

galantes. The Last Elephant/Ivory Hunters (TV). 1991: Closet Land. Caccia alla vedova. Lies of the Twins (TV). 1992: Death Becomes Her. 1993: The Innocent. Fearless. The Pickle. Fallen Angels 2 (TV). 1994: Immortal Beloved. Wyatt Earp. 1996: Croce e delizia. Big Night. 1996: The Funeral. Rasputin. Crime of the Century (TV). 1997: The Real Blonde. The Odyssey. Left Luggage. 1998: The Impostors. 1999: Joe Gould's Secret. 2000: Il cielo cade. Don Quixote (TV).

ROTH, Tim 1961–
Abrasive, aggressive-looking, bony-faced, dark-haired British actor who has mostly been seen as tough nuts, bullies and hit men. It was in that image that he made his big break-through as one of the Reservoir Dogs; that prompted a move from Britain to Hollywood where he mixed star roles with eye-catching deviates, most notably his odious villain in Rob Roy, which won him an Oscar nomination.
1983: Made in Britain (TV). Meantime. 1984: The Hit. 1985: Return to Waterloo (TV). Murder With Mirrors (TV). 1987: A World Apart. 1988: To Kill a Priest. 1989: The Cook, the Thief, His Wife and Her Lover. Farend. 1990: Vincent & Theo. Rosencrantz and Guildenstern Are Dead. 1991: Backsliding. Common Pursuit (TV). Reservoir Dogs. 1992: Jumpin' at the Boneyard. 1993: Bodies, Rest & Motion. Pulp Fiction. 1994: Heart of Darkness (TV). Captives. Little Odessa. 1995: Rob Roy. Four Rooms. 1996: Everyone Says I Love You. Gasoline Alley/No Way Home. The Zookeeper. 1997: Gridlock'd. Hoodlum. Liar/ Deceiver. 1998: La leggenda del pianista sull'oceano (shortened and re-released 1999 as The Legend of 1900). 1999: The Million Dollar Hotel. 2000: Numbers. Vatel. 2001: Invincible. Planet of the Apes.

As director: 1998: The War Zone.

ROUNDTREE, Richard 1937–
Tree-like black American actor who came to the fore with his powerhouse portrayal of detective John Shaft in a violent thriller series – James Bond for adults only. Unfortunately, a subsequent Shaft television series and secondary roles in pot-boiler adventures seemed to tame his explosive style. Latterly in featured roles, but still busy.
1969: What Do You Say to a Naked Lady? 1971: Shaft. 1972: Embassy. Shaft's Big Score. Charley One Eye. 1973: Shaft in Africa.

Firehouse (TV). 1974: Earthquake. 1975: Man Friday. Diamonds. 1977: Jimbuck (later Portrait of a Hitman). 1978: Escape to Athena. Heaven Can Wait. 1979: Game for Vultures. 1980: Inchon! 1981: Day of the Assassin. An Eye for an Eye. 1982: 'Q' The Winged Serpent. The Graduates of Malibu High. One Down Two To Go. 1983: The Big Score. Young Warriors. 1984: Killpoint. City Heat. 1985: The Baron and the Kid. Road Trip. 1986: The Fifth Missile (TV). Jocks. Outlaws (TV). 1987: Opposing Force/ Hell Camp (Formerly Clay Pigeons). 1988: Maniac Cop. Angel III: The Final Chapter. Party Line. Emerald Hall. Getting Even. Permanent Justice. American Cops/Miami Cops. 1989: Never Cry Devil/ Night Visitor. Lost Memories. Crack House. The Banker. Bad Jim. 1990: Gypsy Angels. 1991: Inside. A Time to Die. Bloodfist III: Forced to Fight. Nero come il cuore/Lifeline. 1992: Deadly Rivals. Christmas in Connecticut (TV). 1993: Mind Twister. Sins of the Night. Amityville. 1993: The Image of Evil. Body of Influence. Bonanza: The Return (TV). 1994: Shadows of Desire (TV. GB: The Devil's Bed). Ballistic. 1995: T Rex/ Theodore Rex. Deadly Rivals. Once Upon a time . . . When We Were Coloured. 1996: Hot City (later Original Gangstas). 1977: Steel. George of the Jungle. Any Place But Home (TV). 1999: Having Our Say: The Delany Sisters' First 100 Years (TV). 2000: Shaft. 2001: Corky.

ROURKE, Mickey (Philip Rourke) 1950–
Dark-haired, strong-jawed, cynical-looking American actor whose 'Bowery Boy' style good looks and rough-edged tones have often qualified him for criminals, or rebels from the wrong side of the tracks. A former boxer (an activity he continued to pursue sporadically

down the years), he quickly attracted attention after breaking through to featured film roles in his early thirties. He can seize a film by the scruff of the neck and dominate it totally, but got involved with rather too many unworthy projects and eventually saw his career sliding in the 1990s. Married/divorced actress Debra Feuer. He remains something of a law unto himself.

1979: Panic on Page One (TV. Later: City in Fear). '1941'. 1980: Act of Love (TV). Heaven's Gate. Fade to Black. 1981: Body Heat. 1982: Diner. Eureka. 1983: Rumble Fish. Rape and Marriage: The Rideout Case (TV). 1984: The Pope of Greenwich Village. Nine ½ Weeks. 1985: Year of the Dragon. 1987: Angel Heart. Barfly. A Prayer for the Dying. 1988: Homeboy. 1989: Francesco. Johnny Handsome. Wild Orchid. 1990: Desperate Hours. 1991: Harley Davidson and the Marlboro Man. 1992: White Sands. 1994: F.T.W. The Last Outlaw. Fall Time. 1995: Bullet. 1996: Exit in Red. 1997: Double Team/The Colony. Recoil. The Rainmaker. Champions Forever – The Latin Legends. Another 9½ Weeks. Point Blank. 1998: Buffalo '66. Thicker Than Blood (TV). Thursday. 1999: Shades. Cousin Joey. Shergar. Out in 50. A Good Night to Die. 2000: The Last Story of the Century. Animal Factory. The Pledge.

ROWLANDS, Gena
(Virginia Rowlands) 1930–
Cool, blonde American leading lady, mainly on stage and television, and most effective for the cinema in films directed by her husband, actor-director John Cassavetes (*qv*: married 1954 until his death). Increasingly appeared in bravura roles in his films, and has been twice nominated for Academy Awards, for *A Woman under the Influence* and *Gloria*. Won an Emmy for the TV movie *The Betty Ford Story*. Still around in harsh-voiced character leads.

1968: The High Cost of Loving. 1962: A Child is Waiting. Lonely Are the Brave. The Spiral Road. 1967: Tony Rome. 1968: Faces. Gli intoccabili/Machine Gun McCain. 1969: The Happy Ending. 1971: Minnie and Moscowitz. 1974: A Woman under the Influence. 1976: Two-Minute Warning. 1977: Opening Night. 1978: The Brink's Job. A Question of Love (TV). 1979: Strangers: the Story of a Mother and Daughter (TV). 1980: Gloria. 1982: Tempest. 1983: Thursday's Child (TV). Love Streams. 1984: I'm Almost Not Crazy. 1986: The Third Day Comes. An Early Frost (TV).

1987: Light of Day. The Betty Ford Story (TV). Hem. 1988: Another Woman. 1989: Montana (TV). 1990: Once Around. 1991: Night on Earth. Ted and Venus. 1992: Crazy in Love (TV). 1993: Silent Cries (TV). 1994: Parallel Lives (TV). 1995: The Neon Bible. Something to Talk About. 1996: Unhook the Stars. Best Friends for Life (TV. Released 1998). 1997: She's So Lovely. 1998: The Mighty. Hope Floats. Paulie: A Parrot's Tale. Grace and Glorie (TV). Playing by Heart. 1999: The Weekend. 2000: Liuset haller mig sallskap (doc). The Color of Love: Jacey's Story (TV).

RULE, Janice 1931–
Tall, tawny-haired American actress in quiet, well-bred roles. In a spasmodic film career (although she never missed a year on television until 1973), magazines always appeared to be referring to her latest 'comeback'. Yet, even when it gave her sexier roles, the cinema seemed to miss out on her latent warmth. Married to Ben Gazzara (*qv*) from 1961 to 1979. More recently, she has mixed acting with working as a psychoanalyst.

1951: Goodbye My Fancy. Starlift. 1952: Holiday for Sinners. Rogue's March. 1956: A Woman's Devotion (GB: War Shock). Gun for a Coward. 1957: Four Women in Black (TV). 1958: Bell, Book and Candle. 1960: Journey to the Day (TV). The Subterraneans. 1964: Invitation to a Gunfighter. 1966: The Chase. Alvarez Kelly. Welcome to Hard Times (GB: Killer on a Horse). 1967: The Swimmer. The Ambushers. 1968: Shadow on the Land (TV). 1969: Trial Run (TV). 1970: Doctors' Wives. 1971: The Devil and Miss Sarah (TV). Gumshoe. 1973: Kid Blue/Dime Box. 1977: 3 Women. 1982: Missing. 1984: Rainy Day Friends. 1985: American Flyers.

RUSH, Barbara 1927–
There wasn't a prettier actress in the movies in the early fifties than dark-haired, dark-eyed Miss Rush. She had a trim figure, a lovely smile and talent too. As with so many of their latently-talented lovelies, Universal-International didn't treat her too well, keeping her in ingenue roles. She gave her best performance (in *Bigger Than Life*) just after leaving them, and, although not quite a strong enough actress to hold her place at the top, has graced the occasional movie down the years. Married to Jeffrey Hunter (1950 –1955), first of three.

1950: Molly. 1951: The First Legion. Quebec.

When Worlds Collide. Flaming Feather. 1953: Prince of Pirates. It Came from Outer Space. 1954: Taza, Son of Cochise. The Black Shield of Falworth. Magnificent Obsession. Captain Lightfoot. 1955: Kiss of Fire. 1956: World in My Corner. Bigger than Life. Flight to Hong Kong. 1957: Oh Men! Oh Women! No Down Payment. The Troublemakers (TV). 1958: The Young Lions. Harry Black and the Tiger (GB: Harry Black). 1959: The Young Phila-delphians (GB: The City Jungle). 1960: The Bramble Bush. Strangers When We Meet. Alas, Babylon (TV). 1963: Come Blow Your Horn. 1964: Robin and the Seven Hoods. Strategy of Terror (TV. GB: cinemas). 1966: Hombre. 1971: Suddenly Single (TV). The Man. 1972: The Eyes of Charles Sand (TV). Moon of the Wolf (TV). Crime Club (TV). 1973: Cutter (TV). 1974: Superdad. Of Men and Women II (TV). Fools, Females and Fun (TV). 1975: The Last Day (TV). 1976: The Siege (TV). 1979: The Night the Bridge Fell Down (TV. Released 1983). Death Car on the Freeway (TV). 1980: Flamingo Road (TV). Can't Stop the Music. 1982: Summer Lovers. 1983: Between Friends (TV). 1990: Web of Deceit (TV). 1992: Gatta alla pari. 1995: Widow's Kiss (TV). 1999: Walking Across Egypt.

RUSH, Geoffrey 1951–
Tall, faintly sinister, roguish-looking Australian actor with dark wavy hair and rangily broad build. Plucked from the obscurity of the Australian theatre (where he had been a leading light for 15 years), Rush burst into the international spotlight at 45 by winning an Academy Award as pianist David Helfgott in *Shine*. He promptly continued a cinema career, often in extravagant roles in the style of Vincent Price, whom he slightly

resembles. He received a further Oscar nomination for *Shakespeare in Love.*
1981: *Hoodwink.* 1982: *Starstruck.* 1987: *Twelfth Night.* 1995: *On Our Selection (US: Dad and Dave On Our Selection).* 1996: *Shine. Children of the Revolution. Call Me Sal.* 1997: *Oscar and Lucinda (voice only).* 1998: *Elizabeth. Les Misérables. A Little Bit of Soul. Shakespeare in Love.* 1999: *Mystery Men. House on Haunted Hill.* 2000: *Quills. The Tailor of Panama.* 2001: *The Magic Pudding (voice only).*

RUSSELL, Gail 1924–1961

Another of Hollywood's great tragedies: a haunting, beautiful limpid-eyed and gentle-seeming brunette who played helpless heroines beset by problems. In real life she was indeed beset, by the alcoholism that started at an early stage of her career and had ruined it by the early fifties. Found dead on the floor of her apartment 'of natural causes'. Married to Guy Madison 1949–1954.
1943: *Henry Aldrich Gets Glamour (GB: Henry Gets Glamour). Lady in the Dark.* 1944: *Our Hearts Were Young and Gay. The Unseen. Salty O'Rourke.* 1946: *Our Hearts Were Growing Up. The Bachelor's Daughters (GB: Bachelor Girls). Angel and the Badman.* 1947: *Variety Girl.* 1948: *Moonrise. Night Has a Thousand Eyes. Wake of the Red Witch.* 1949: *Song of India. Captain China. El Paso. The Great Dan Patch.* 1950: *The Lawless (GB: The Dividing Line).* 1951: *Air Cadet (GB: Jet Men of the Air).* 1956: *Seven Men from Now.* 1957: *The Tattered Dress.* 1958: *No Place to Land (GB: Man Mad).* 1961: *The Silent Call.*

RUSSELL, Jane
(Ernestine J. Russell) 1921– 2011

A rarity: not only a brunette sex symbol but one who became more fondly regarded by the public as time wore on. She looked as though she liked the cinema to be fun, and her sense of humour and acceptance of her own limited ability lifted more than one of her films. A big, raw-boned lady, she was most enjoyable in her roles opposite Robert Mitchum and Bob Hope – two leading men to whom she obviously responded.
1943: *The Outlaw.* 1946: *Young Widow.* 1948: *The Paleface. Montana Belle (released 1952).* 1950: *Double Dynamite.* *Hollywood Goes to Bat.* 1951: *His Kind of Woman.* 1952: *Road to Bali. Macao. Son of Paleface. The Las Vegas Story.* *Screen Snapshots No 205.* 1953:

Gentlemen Prefer Blondes. 1954: *The French Line.* *Hollywood's Cowboy Stars.* 1955: *Gentlemen Marry Brunettes. Foxfire. Underwater. The Tall Men.* 1956: *Hot Blood. The Revolt of Mamie Stover.* 1957: *Playtime in Hollywood. The Fuzzy Pink Nightgown.* 1964: *Fate is the Hunter.* 1966: *Johnny Reno. Waco.* †*The Honorable Frauds.* 1967: *Born Losers.* 1970: *Darker Than Amber.* 1973: *Cauliflower Cupids.* 1981: *The Jackass Trail.*

†*Unreleased*

RUSSELL, John (William Russell)
1921–1991

Handsome heavies are not exactly a dime-a-dozen, so it's surprising that this clean-looking, very tall, brown-haired American actor, with his quiet menace and sharkish smile, did not become a bigger name, especially during his period with 20th Century-Fox. He had some success on TV in the *Lawman* series, but was seen only sporadically in films and TV after 1960, often in films starring Clint Eastwood. A war hero at the battle of Guadalcanal. Films previously credited to Russell between 1937 and 1940 are almost certainly the work of a different actor, also known as Johnny Russell.
1945: *A Royal Scandal (GB: Czarina). Don Juan Quilligan. A Bell for Adano. Within These Walls.* 1946: *Three Little Girls in Blue. Somewhere in the Night. The Dark Corner. Wake Up and Live.* 1947: *Forever Amber.* 1948: *Sitting Pretty. Yellow Sky. Slattery's Hurricane. The Gal Who Took the West. The Story of Molly X. Undertow.* 1950: *Saddle Tramp. Frenchie.* 1951: *The Fat Man. Fighting Coast Guard. The Barefoot Mailman. Man in the Saddle (GB: The Outcast).* 1952: *Hoodlum Empire.*

Oklahoma Annie. 1953: *The Sun Shines Bright. Fair Wind to Java.* 1954: *Jubilee Trail.* 1955: *Hell's Outpost. The Last Command.* 1957: *Untamed Youth. The Dalton Girls. Hell Bound.* 1958: *Fort Massacre.* 1959: *Rio Bravo. Yellowstone Kelly.* 1965: *Apache Uprising.* 1966: *Fort Utah.* 1967: *Hostile Guns.* 1968: *If He Hollers, Let Him Go! Buckskin.* 1970: *Cannon for Cordoba.* 1971: *Smoke in the Wind. Noon Sunday. Legacy of Blood.* 1975: *Lord Shango. Fugitive Lovers/The Runaways.* 1976: *The Outlaw Josey Wales. Six Tickets to Hell.* 1977: *Kino, the Padre on Horseback.* 1981: *Uncle Scam.* 1982: *Honkytonk Man.* 1985: *Pale Rider.* 1988: *Winter People.* 1989: *Under the Gun (completed 1986).*

RUSSELL, Kurt 1951–

Light-haired, chubby-faced American actor of medium height but thickly built, in bouncy roles as a teenager, then in juvenile leads for the Disney Studio. He also became a minor league baseball star in the 1970s and at one time almost quit acting altogether. But after his striking impersonation of Elvis Presley in a TV movie, he appeared in tougher, more rugged roles and, if not quite in the superstar class, became a major leading man in the 1980s. The son of character actor Bing Russell, he is divorced from actress Season Hubley, and has for some years lived with actress Goldie Hawn (*qv*). Several of his early 1990s' films defied critical dismissal to become popular hits, putting him in the big league.
1961: *The Absent-Minded Professor.* 1963: *It Happened at the World's Fair.* 1965: *Guns of Diablo (TV. GB: cinemas).* 1966: *Follow Me Boys! Willie and the Yank (TV. GB: cinemas, as Mosby's Marauders).* 1968: *The One and Only, Genuine, Original Family Band. The Horse in the Gray Flannel Suit. Guns in the Heather.* 1969: *The Computer Wore Tennis Shoes.* 1970: *Dad, Can I Borrow the Car? (narrator only).* 1971: *Fools' Parade (GB: Dynamite Man from Glory Jail).* 1972: *Now You See Him, Now You Don't.* 1973: *Charley and the Angel.* 1974: *Superdad.* 1975: *The Strongest Man in the World. Search for the Gods (TV). The Deadly Tower (TV).* 1976: *The Quest (TV).* 1977: *Christmas Miracle in Caulfield USA (TV. GB: The Christmas Coal Mine Miracle).* 1979: *Elvis! (TV. GB: cinemas, as Elvis – The Movie).* 1980: *Amber Waves (TV). Used Cars.* 1981: *The Fox and the Hound (voice only). Escape from New York.* 1982: *The Thing.* 1983: *Silkwood.*

Swing Shift. 1985: The Mean Season. The Best of Times. 1986: Big Trouble in Little China. 1987: Overboard. 1988: Tequila Sunrise. Winter People. 1989: Tango & Cash. 1991: Backdraft. 1992: Unlawful Entry. Captain Ron. 1993: Tombstone. 1994: Stargate. 1996: Executive Decision. Escape from L.A. 1997: Breakdown. 1998: Soldier. 2000: 3000 Miles to Graceland.

RUSSELL, Rosalind 1908–1976

Regal American brunette actress who always seemed most at home in tweeds or silk evening gowns, and was often cast as a brisk businesswoman. After her success as the reporter in *His Girl Friday*, she was able to exercise her own (sometimes strange) choice of dominant leading roles, and did not pull out another real plum for herself until her stage mother in *Gypsy*. Four times nominated for an Oscar (in *My Sister Eileen*, *Sister Kenny*, *Mourning Becomes Electra* and *Auntie Mame*), she was given a special Academy Award in 1972 for her charity work. Died from cancer.
1934: Forsaking All Others. Evelyn Prentice. 1935: West Point of the Air. The President Vanishes (GB: Strange Conspiracy). The Casino Murder Case. China Seas. The Night is Young. Reckless. Rendezvous. 1936: Trouble for Two (GB: The Suicide Club). It Had to Happen. Under Two Flags. Craig's Wife. 1937: Live, Love and Learn. Night Must Fall. 1938: Man-Proof. The Citadel. Four's a Crowd. 1939: The Women. Fast and Loose. His Girl Friday. 1940: Hired Wife. *Chinese Garden Festival. No Time for Comedy. 1941: Design for Scandal. This Thing Called Love (GB: Married But Single). They Met in Bombay. The Feminine Touch. 1942: Take a Letter, Darling (GB: The Green-Eyed Woman). My Sister Eileen. 1943: Flight for Freedom. What a Woman! (GB: The Beautiful Cheat). 1945: Roughly Speaking. She Wouldn't Say Yes. 1946: Sister Kenny. 1947: The Guilt of Janet Ames. Mourning Becomes Electra. 1948: The Velvet Touch. 1949: Tell It to the Judge. 1950: A Woman of Distinction. 1952: Never Wave at a WAC (GB: The Private Wore Skirts). 1954: *Screen Snapshots No 222. 1955: The Girl Rush. Picnic. 1958: Auntie Mame. 1961: A Majority of One. 1962: Five Finger Exercise. Gypsy. 1965: The Trouble with Angels. 1966: Oh Dad, Poor Dad, Mama's Hung You in the Closet and I'm Feeling So Sad. 1967: Rosie! 1968: Where Angels Go, Trouble Follows! 1971: Mrs Pollifax – Spy. 1972: The Crooked Hearts (TV).

RUSSELL, Theresa
(T. Paup) 1957–
Slinky, honey-blonde American actress with wide green eyes and petulant mouth, a latter-day Gloria Grahame (*qv*) who, like Grahame, is more effective as complex or fascinatingly bad characters. After two years' study at the Actors' Studio, she made her film debut at 19, but has appeared only sparsely since, often taking time out to raise her two sons by director Nicolas Roeg (her husband since 1982), in whose films she frequently appears.
1976: The Last Tycoon. 1978: Straight Time. 1980: Bad Timing (US: Bad Timing a Sensual Obsession). 1982: Eureka. 1984: The Razor's Edge. 1985: Insignificance. 1987: Aria. Black Widow. 1988: Track 29. Physical Evidence. 1989: Impulse. 1991: Cold Heaven. Kafka. Whore. 1993: A Woman's Guide to Adultery (TV). 1994: Flight of the Dove/The Spy Within. Being Human. 1995: The Grotesque (US: Gentlemen Don't Eat Poets). Trade Off (cable TV). Erotic Tales II: Hotel Paradise. 1996: Public Enemies/Public Enemy No. 1. The Proposition. Once You Meet a Stranger (TV). 1998: The Velocity of Gary. Wild Things. Running Woman. 2000: Luckytown. 2001: The Believer.

RUSSO, René 1954–
American actress of angular jut-chinned beauty and masses of dark hair, a top model for years (famous in TV commercials as The Revlon Girl), who switched to acting at 35 with remarkable success. Inside the past ten years, she has co-starred with such superstar performers as Clint Eastwood, Kevin Costner, Dustin Hoffman, Mel Gibson and John Travolta in major box office hits. If her acting ability is still limited, she brings a striking presence to every role. Sister of actor James Russo (1953–).
1989: Major League. 1990: Mr Destiny. 1991: One Good Cop. Freejack. 1992: Lethal Weapon 3. 1993: In the Line of Fire. 1995: Outbreak. Get Shorty. 1996: Tin Cup. Ransom. 1997: Buddy. 1998: Lethal Weapon 4. 1999: The Thomas Crown Affair. 2000: The Adventures of Rocky and Bullwinkle.

RUTHERFORD, Ann 1917–
Zippy, plumply pretty brunette American actress, in leading roles as a teenager in low budget westerns with John Wayne and Gene Autry. Later won a small slice of screen immortality as Polly, the perennial girlfriend of M-G-M's Andy Hardy series. Mainly in supporting roles after leaving M-G-M in the early forties.
1934: Student Tour. 1935: Waterfront Lady. Melody Trail. The Fighting Marines (serial). The Singing Vagabond. 1936: The Harvester. The Lawless Nineties. Down to the Sea. The Lonely Trail. Doughnuts and Society (GB: Stepping into Society). Comin' round the Mountain. The Oregon Trail. 1937: *Annie Laurie. Public Cowboy No. One. Espionage. The Bride Wore Red. Live, Love and Learn. The Devil is Driving. *Carnival in Paris. 1938: Judge Hardy's Children. Of Human Hearts. A Christmas Carol. Love Finds Andy Hardy. You're Only Young Once. Dramatic School. Out West with the Hardys. 1939: The Hardys Ride High. *Angel of Mercy. Four Girls in White. Dancing Co-Ed (GB: Every Other Inch a Lady). Gone with the Wind. Andy Hardy Gets Spring Fever. These Glamour Girls. Judge Hardy and Son. 1940: Wyoming (GB: Bad Man of Wyoming). Pride and Prejudice. The Ghost Comes Home. Andy Hardy Meets Debutante. 1941: *Variety Reel. Washington Melodrama. Keeping Company. Life Begins for Andy Hardy. Badlands of Dakota. Andy Hardy's Private Secretary. Whistling in the Dark. 1942: Orchestra Wives. The Courtship of Andy Hardy. Whistling in Dixie. Andy Hardy's Double Life. This Time for Keeps. 1943: Happy Land. Whistling in Brooklyn. 1944: Bermuda Mystery. 1945: Bedside Manner. Two O'Clock Courage. 1946: The Madonna's Secret. Murder in the Music Hall. Inside Job. 1947: The Secret Life of Walter Mitty. 1949: Adventures of Don Juan (GB: The New Adventures of Don Juan). 1950: Operation Haylift. 1958: The Male Animal (TV). 1972: They Only Kill Their Masters. 1975: Won Ton Ton, the Dog Who Saved Hollywood.

RUTHERFORD, Dame Margaret
1892–1972

There couldn't have been an actor who didn't tremble in his boots at the thought of having plump, querulous, owl-eyed, round-mouthed, multi-chinned Margaret Rutherford in the same film, knowing that her breathlessly-relaxed delivery and inimitable booming tones would steal every scene. British films used this most British of actresses mostly in comedy as endearing eccentrics; over the years only Alastair Sim and Dame Edith Evans even gave her a run for her money, and she finally won an Academy Award for *The VIPs*. A glorious Miss Marple, she was created Dame in 1967. Married to actor Stringer Davis (1896–1973) from 1954. Died after breaking a hip in a fall.
1936: Dusty Ermine (US: Hideout in the Alps). Troubled Waters. Talk of the Devil. 1937: Missing, Believed Married. Beauty and the Barge. Big Fella. Catch As Catch Can. 1940: Spring Meeting. 1941: Quiet Wedding. 1943: The Yellow Canary. The Demi-Paradise (US: Adventure for Two). 1944: English without Tears (US: Her Man Gilbey). 1945: Blithe Spirit. 1946: While the Sun Shines. 1947: Meet Me at Dawn. 1948: Miranda. 1949: Passport to Pimlico. 1950: The Happiest Days of Your Life. Her Favourite Husband (US: The Taming of Dorothy). 1951: The Magic Box. 1952: Curtain Up. The Importance of Being Earnest. Castle in the Air. Miss Robin Hood. 1953: Innocents in Paris. Trouble in Store. 1954: Aunt Clara. The Runaway Bus. Mad about Men. 1955: An Alligator Named Daisy. 1957: Just My Luck. The Smallest Show on Earth (US: Big Time Operators). 1959: I'm All Right, Jack. 1961: On the Double. Murder She Said. 1963: The Mouse on the Moon. Murder at the Gallop. The VIPs. 1964: Murder Most Foul. 1965: The Alphabet Murders. Murder Ahoy. 1966: Chimes at Midnight (US: Falstaff). A Countess from Hong Kong. The Wacky World of Mother Goose (voice only). 1967: Arabella.

RYAN, Kathleen 1922–1985
Tall, copper-haired Irish actress with lovely complexion and attractively soft speaking voice. She was mostly typed as flowing-haired colleens after a brilliant success in the leading female role of her first film. Consequently, she made too few films and, despite a couple of invitations to Hollywood, her career petered out.
1946: Odd Man Out. 1947: Captain Boycott.

*1948: Esther Waters. 1949: Christopher Columbus. Give Us This Day (US: Salt to the Devil). 1950: Prelude to Fame. Try and Get Me (GB: The Sound of Fury). 1952: The Yellow Balloon. Laxdale Hall (GB: Scotch on the Rocks). 1954: Captain Lightfoot. 1955: *The Clock. 1956: Jacqueline. 1957: Sail into Danger.*

RYAN, Meg (Margaret Hyra) 1961–
Chirpy blonde American actress with wide, saucy smile and busy acting style – usually in spirited, sprightly roles. She studied to be a journalist before drifting into an acting career that stuttered a bit at first, but blossomed spectacularly in the late 1990s. Her endearing qualities took her to big hits in *When Harry Met Sally* and *Sleepless in Seattle*, but began to look more strained in frothy mid-1990s romantic comedies. Married to actor Dennis Quaid (*qv*). They parted in 2000.
1981: Rich and Famous. 1983: Amityville 3D (later Amityville: The Demon). 1985: One of the Boys (TV). 1986: Top Gun. Armed and Dangerous. 1987: Innerspace. Promised Land. 1988: D.O.A. (GB: Dead on Arrival). The Presidio. 1989: When Harry Met Sally. 1990: Joe vs the Volcano. 1991: The Doors. 1992: Prelude to a Kiss. 1993: Sleepless in Seattle. Flesh and Bone. 1994: When a Man Loves a Woman. 1995: I.Q. French Kiss. Restoration. Balto (voice only). 1996: Courage Under Fire. 1997: Anastasia (voice only). Addicted to Love. 1998: City of Angels. You've Got Mail. Hurlyburly. 2000: Hanging Up. 2001: Proof of Life.

RYAN, Peggy (Margaret Ryan) 1924–
Peppy, bow-lipped American dancer and comedienne with attractive dark red-brown hair, usually piled high, in show business

from infancy with her Irish parents, 'The Merry Dancing Ryans'. An electric dancer, she fizzed through a mass of minor musicals for Universal in the forties. Married (second of three) to actor-dancer Ray McDonald (1921–1959) from 1953 to 1957. He committed suicide. Popped up in the late sixties as Jack Lord's secretary in TV's *Hawaii Five-O*.
*1930: *The Wedding of Jack and Jill. 1937: The Women Men Marry. Top of the Town. 1939: She Married a Cop. The Flying Irishman. 1940: The Grapes of Wrath. 1941: Sailor's Lady. 1942: What's Cookin' (GB: Wake Up and Dream). Private Buckaroo. Miss Annie Rooney. Get Hep to Love (GB: She's My Lovely). Give Out, Sisters! Girls' Town. When Johnny Comes Marching Home. 1943: Top Man. Mr Big. 1944: Follow the Boys. The Merry Monahans. Bowery to Broadway. Chip off the Old Block. This is the Life. Babes on Swing Street. 1945: Here Come the Co-Eds. On Stage, Everybody! Patrick the Great. That's The Spirit. Men in Her Diary. 1949: Shamrock Hill. There's a Girl in My Heart. 1953: All Ashore. 1980: Pleasure Palace (TV).*

RYAN, Robert 1909–1973
Tall, lean, dark-haired American actor who, after a spotty early career interrupted by war service, found that his whippy, gritty performances earned him some good leading roles at RKO from 1947 to 1952. After that, often cast as embittered men, he was mostly second or third on the cast list of largely unworthy films, although working steadily. He received an Oscar nomination for his performance in *Crossfire*. Died from cancer.
1940: The Ghost Breakers. Queen of the Mob. Golden Gloves. Northwest Mounted Police.

Texas Rangers Rides Again. 1941: The Feminine Touch. 1943: Gangway for Tomorrow. The Sky's the Limit. Behind the Rising Sun. Bombardier. The Iron Major. Tender Comrade. 1944: Marine Raiders. 1947: Johnny O'Clock. The Woman on the Beach. Trail Street. Crossfire. 1948: Return of the Bad Men. Berlin Express. The Boy with Green Hair. Act of Violence. 1949: Caught. The Set-Up. I Married a Communist (GB: The Woman on Pier 13). 1950: The Secret Fury. Born to Be Bad. 1951: The Racket. Best of the Bad Men. Flying Leathernecks. Hard, Fast and Beautiful (guest). On Dangerous Ground. 1952: Clash by Night. Horizons West. Beware My Lovely. 1953: The Naked Spur. City beneath the Sea. Inferno. 1954: Alaska Seas. About Mrs Leslie. Her Twelve Men. Bad Day at Black Rock. 1955: Escape to Burma. House of Bamboo. The Tall Men. 1956: The Proud Ones. Back from Eternity. 1957: Men in War. 1958: The Great Gatsby (TV). God's Little Acre. Lonelyhearts. 1959: Day of the Outlaw. Odds Against Tomorrow. 1960: Ice Palace. 1961: The Canadians. King of Kings. 1962: Billy Budd. The Longest Day. 1964: The Inheritance (narrator only). The Crooked Road. 1965: La guerre secrète (GB and US: The Dirty Game). Battle of the Bulge. 1966: The Busy Body. The Professionals. Custer of the West. 1967: Hour of the Gun. Anzio (GB: The Battle for Anzio). The Dirty Dozen. 1968: A Minute to Pray, a Second to Die (GB: Dead or Alive). Captain Nemo and the Underwater City. 1969: The Wild Bunch. 1970: Lawman. 1971: The Love Machine. 1972: And Hope to Die. La course du lièvre à travers les champs. 1973: The Iceman Cometh. Executive Action. Lolly Madonna XXX (GB: The Lolly Madonna War). Man without a Country (TV). The Outfit.

RYAN, Sheila
(Katherine McLaughlin) 1921–1975
Lovely dark-haired American actress with large, open face and Irish colouring, the resourceful heroine of numerous second features in the forties. Ended up in Gene Autry westerns – not surprising as she was married to Autry's comic sidekick, Pat Buttram (1915–1994). Died from a lung ailment.
1939: What a Life! 1940: Dancing on a Dime. The Gay Caballero. The Way of All Flesh. 1941: Golden Hoofs. We Go Fast. Dead Men Tell. Sun Valley Serenade. Great Guns. Dressed to Kill. *Wampas Baby Stars. 1942: The Lone Star Rangers. Pardon My Stripes.

Footlight Serenade. Who is Hope Schuyler? A Haunting We Will Go. Careful, Soft Shoulders. 1943: The Gang's All Here (GB: The Girls He Left Behind). Song of Texas. 1944: Something for the Boys. Ladies of Washington. 1945: The Caribbean Mystery. Getting Gertie's Garter. 1946: Slightly Scandalous. Deadline for Murder. The Big Fix. 1947: The Lone Wolf in Mexico. Philo Vance's Secret Mission. Railroaded! Heartaches. 1948: Caged Fury. The Cobra Strikes. 1949: Ringside. Joe Palooka in the Counterpunch. Hideout. The Cowboy and the Indians. 1950: Square Dance Katy. Western Pacific Agent. Mule Train. 1951: Jungle Manhunt. Gold Raiders (GB: Stooges Go West). Mask of the Dragon. Fingerprints Don't Lie. 1953: Pack Train. On Top of Old Smoky. 1954: Crime Squad. 1958: Street of Darkness.

RYDER, Winona
(W. Horowitz) 1971–
A major American teenage star of the later 1980s, with very dark eyes and hair. Petite and pretty in a sharp and positive-looking sort of way. She was named after her home town in Minnesota, but became a misfit at high school – 'I was this really weird kid obsessed with gangster movies' – before enrolling at the Actors' Conservatory Theatre in San Francisco and making a film debut at 15. She's since shown her forthright talent in a good variety of roles, earning Oscar nominations for The Age of Innocence and Little Women as she moved into the upper reaches of Hollywood stars, although her performances since 1996 have been disappointing. Currently lives with actor Matt Damon (qv).
1986: Lucas. 1987: Square Dance. 1988: Beetlejuice. '1969'. 1989: Heathers. Great Balls of Fire! 1990: Welcome Home, Roxy Carmichael. Mermaids. Edward Scissorhands. 1991: Night on Earth. 1992: Bram Stoker's Dracula. 1993: The Age of Innocence. The House of the Spirits. 1994: Reality Bites. Little Women. 1995: How to Make an American Quilt. Boys. 1996: The Crucible. Looking for Richard. 1997: Alien: Resurrection. 1998: Celebrity. 1999: Girl, Interrupted. 2000: Lost Souls. Autumn in New York. 2001: Just to Be Together.

S

SABU (S. Bastagir) 1924–1963

Impish, loveable, slightly-built son of an Indian elephant-driver, snatched from the elephant stables of Mysore by a British film unit in 1936 for his first film, in which his natural charm won the hearts of millions. Made his home in Hollywood after 1940 and appeared entirely in fantasies and jungle films, some of which he journeyed to Europe to make. A war hero with a cluster of medals, he died from a heart attack.

1937: *Elephant Boy*. 1938: *The Drum (US: Drums)*. 1940: *The Thief of Bagdad*. 1942: *Jungle Book. Arabian Nights*. 1943: *White Savage (GB: White Captive). Cobra Woman*. *Screen Snapshots No 103*. *Screen Snapshots No 105*. 1946: *Tangier*. 1947: *Black Narcissus. The End of the River*. 1948: *Man-Eater of Kumaon*. 1949: *Song of India*. 1951: *Savage Drums*. 1952: *Hello Elephant!* 1954: *The Treasure of Bengal (GB: Jungle Boy. US: Jungle Hell)*. 1955: *The Black Panther*. 1956: *Jaguar*. 1957: *Sabu and the Magic Ring*. 1960: *Mistress of the World/Il mistero dei tre continenti (parts one and two)*. 1962: *Rampage!* 1963: *A Tiger Walks*.

SAINT, Eva Marie 1924–

Slender, waif-like blonde American actress seen as harried heroines, or in sympathetic roles. Made her first film at the age of 30 (fortunately she looked very young for her age) and won an Academy Award for it. But proper casting for her has proved elusive, and she has not always made the impact she might.

1954: *On the Waterfront*. 1956: *That Certain Feeling*. 1957: *Raintree County. A Hatful of Rain*. 1959: *North by Northwest*. 1960: *Exodus*. 1962: *All Fall Down*. 1964: *36 Hours. Carol for Another Christmas (TV)*. 1965: *The Sandpiper*. 1966: *The Russians Are Coming, the Russians Are Coming. Grand Prix*. 1968: *The Stalking Moon*. 1969: *A Talent for Loving*. 1970: *Loving*. 1972: *Cancel My Reservation*. 1975: *The McAhans – How the West Was Won (TV)*. 1978: *A Christmas to Remember (TV)*. 1979: *When Hell Was in Session (TV)*. 1981: *Splendor in the Grass (TV). The Best Little Girl in the World (TV)*. 1983: *Jane Doe (TV)*. 1984: *Love Leads the Way (cable TV)*. 1986: *The Last Days of Patton (TV). Nothing in Common*. 1987: *Breaking Home Ties (TV)*. 1988: *I'll Be Home for Christmas (TV)*. 1989: *The Achille Lauro (GB: TV, as Voyage of Terror)*. 1990: *People Like Us (TV)*. 1991: *Danielle Steel's Palomino (TV)*. 1992: *Kiss of a Killer (TV)*. 1995: *My Antonia (TV). Mariette in Ecstasy*. 1996: *After Jimmy (TV)*. 1997: *Time to Say Goodbye? (TV)*. 1999: *Jackie's Back! (TV)*. 2000: *I Dreamed of Africa*.

SANDERS, George 1906–1972

Suave, civilized, cynical, sophisticated, sometimes sinister: Russian-born Sanders, with his heavy head like some huge uncoiled snake, was all of these sibilants. One could almost see the sins beneath the skin. He started in British films, but Hollywood soon seized his rakish charm and gave him an Oscar for *All About Eve*, but few decent parts after that, although no-one was more suited to the voice of Shere-Khan the tiger in *The Jungle Book*. Married to Zsa Zsa Gabor 1949-1957 and Benita Hume 1958 to her death in 1967, third and fourth of five. Committed suicide with barbiturates, leaving behind an aggrieved note complaining of boredom. Brother of Tom Conway (qv).

1934: *Love, Life and Laughter*. 1936: *Find the Lady. Strange Cargo. The Man Who Could Work Miracles. Dishonour Bright. Things to Come. My Second Wife. Lloyd's of London*. 1937: *The Lady Escapes. Love is News. Slave Ship. Lancer Spy*. 1938: *International Settlement. Four Men and a Prayer*. 1939: *Allegheny Uprising (GB: The First Rebel). Mr Moto's Last Warning. So This is London. The Saint Strikes Back. The Outsider. Nurse Edith Cavell. The Saint in London. Confessions of a Nazi Spy*. 1940: *The Saint Takes Over. Green Hell. Bitter Sweet. Foreign Correspondent. Son of Monte Cristo. The Saint's Double Trouble. Rebecca. The House of the Seven Gables*. 1941: *Man Hunt. The Saint in Palm Springs. Rage in Heaven. A Date with the Falcon. Sundown. The Gay Falcon*. 1942: *Her Cardboard Lover. The Black Swan. The Falcon Takes Over. Quiet Please Murder. The Moon and Sixpence. Tales of Manhattan. Son of Fury. The Falcon's Brother*. 1943: *Appointment in Berlin. This Land is Mine. Paris After Dark (GB: The Night is Ending). They Came to Blow Up America*. 1944: *Action in Arabia. The Lodger. Summer Storm*. 1945: *Hangover Square. The Picture of Dorian Gray. Uncle Harry/The Strange Affair of Uncle Harry*. 1946: *A Scandal in Paris. The Strange Woman*. 1947: *The Private Affairs of Bel Ami. Lured (GB: Personal Column). The Ghost and Mrs Muir. Forever Amber*. 1949: *The Fan (GB: Lady Windermere's Fan). Samson and Delilah*. 1950: *All About Eve. Blackjack (US: Captain Blackjack)*. 1951: *I Can Get It For You Wholesale/Only the Best (GB: This is My Affair). The Light Touch*. 1952: *Ivanhoe*. *Screen Snapshots No 205. Assignment–Paris!* 1953: *Call Me Madam. Viaggio in Italia (GB: Voyage to Italy. US: The Strangers)*. 1954: *Witness to Murder. King Richard and the Crusaders*. 1955: *Jupiter's Darling. Laura (TV. GB: cinemas). Moonfleet. The Scarlet Coat. The King's Thief*. 1956: *Death of a Scoundrel. While the City Sleeps. Never Say Goodbye. That Certain Feeling*. 1957: *The Seventh Sin*. 1958: *Rock-a-Bye Baby. The Whole Truth. From the Earth to the Moon*. 1959: *A Touch of Larceny. Solomon and Sheba. That Kind of Woman*. 1960: *Bluebeard's 10 Honeymoons. Cone of Silence (US: Trouble in the Sky). Village of the Damned. The Last Voyage*. 1961: *The Rebel (US: Call Me Genius). Five Golden Hours*. 1962: *Le Rendez-vous. Operation Snatch. In Search of the Castaways*. 1963: *Cairo. The Cracksman. Dark Purpose/L'intrigo. Un aereo per Baalbeck*. 1964: *A Shot in the Dark. The Golden Head*. 1965: *World by Night (narrator only). The Amorous Adventures of Moll Flanders. Trunk to Cairo*. 1966: *The Quiller Memorandum*. 1967: *Warning Shot. Good Times. The Jungle Book (voice only). Laura (TV. Remake). One Step to Hell (US: King of Africa)*. 1968: *The Best House in London. The Candy Man*. 1969: *The Body Stealers. The Seven Men of Sumuru. The Kremlin Letter*. 1971: *Endless Night. The Night of the Assassin*. 1972: *Doomwatch. Psychomania (US: The Death Wheelers)*.

SANDLER, Adam 1966–
Dark-haired, bullet-headed, impish American comedian, actor, singer and writer with goofy good looks. Another graduate of the *Saturday Night Live* TV comedy show, Sandler clowned around in modestly unattractive, low-key fashion for several years in films, until suddenly hitting on a winning formula by turning manic comedy into romantic comedy in *The Wedding Singer* and hiring an actress (Drew Barrymore) capable of upstaging the star. The formula was repeated in a number of slightly less successful (though not at the box office) movies thereafter.
1989: Going Overboard/Babes Ahoy. 1991: Shakes the Clown. 1993: Coneheads. 1994: Airheads. Mixed Nuts. 1995: Billy Madison. 1996: Happy Gilmore. A Very Brady Sequel. Bulletproof. 1998: The Wedding Singer. Dirty Work. The Waterboy. 1999: Big Daddy. 2000: Little Nicky. The Peeper (voice only).

SANDS, Julian 1958–
Languid-looking, lazy-lidded, blond-haired, tall, spare British actor of aristocratic looks who looked born to play roles in white suits and neckerchiefs. Following theatrical training, Sands coached children in drama workshops before embarking on his own acting career, which led to career-forming roles in *The Killing Fields* (as the photographer) and the swain in *A Room With a View*. Since then, he has often been seen in cruel roles, in a mixture of leads and top supporting portraits, sometimes in controversial material.
1981: *Broken English. 1982: Privates on Parade. 1984: The Killing Fields. Oxford Blues. 1985: A Room With a View. After Darkness. The Doctor and the Devils. Romance
on the Orient Express (TV). 1986: Gothic. Harem (TV). 1987: Siesta. 1988: Wherever You Are/Gdzieskolwiek jest, jestis jest. Warlock. Vibes. 1989: Manika: The Girl Who Lived Twice/Manika, Manika (released 1994). Tennessee Nights/Black Water. Murder on the Moon (TV). 1990: Impromptu. Arachnophobia. Il sole anche di notte/Night Sun. 1991: The Friday Villa. Naked Lunch. Wicked. Husband and Lover (US: Husbands and Lovers). Grand Isle. 1992: The Turn of the Screw. Tale of a Vampire. Crazy in Love (TV). 1993: America. Boxing Helena. Warlock: The Armageddon. Lo scambio. 1994: The Browning Version. Mario and the Magician. Witch Hunt (cable TV). 1995: Leaving Las Vegas. The Tomorrow Man. The Great Elephant Escape. 1996: End of Summer (TV). Never Ever. 1997: One Night Stand. 1998: The Phantom of the Opera. Winter. 1999: The Loss of Sexual Innocence. Mercy. Long Time Since (completed 1997). The Million Dollar Hotel. 2000: Timecode. Vatel. Love Me.*

SAN GIACOMO, Laura 1961–
Dark, diminutive, sultry, spirited American actress briefly in vogue for leading roles after her high-profile success in *Sex, Lies and Videotape*. In the 1980s, the fast-talking San Giacomo ran up many theatre credits, and has turned again to the medium since the fires of her film career have burned less brightly in the mid 1990s: it could be moviegoers' loss, as her dynamic performance in *Quigley Down Under* showed. But she was rarely allowed such three-dimensional characters in her brief stay at the top.
1988: Miles from Home. 1989: Sex, Lies and Videotape. 1990: Pretty Woman. Vital Signs (TV). Quigley Down Under. Once Around. 1991: Where the Day Takes You. Under Suspicion. 1992: For Their Own Good (TV). 1993: Nina Takes a Lover. 1994: The Two Fridas. 1995: Stuart Saves His Family. 1996: The Right to Remain Silent (TV). 1997: Eat Your Heart Out. Suicide Kings. The Apocalypse. 1999: With Friends Like These (cable TV). 2000: A House on the Hill.

SARANDON, Susan
(S. Tomalin) 1946–
Light-haired, rosy-cheeked, squirrel-eyed, piquant American actress, pretty in a stringy sort of way, who looked born to play women trodden down by the land, but in fact has played a bright variety of uninhibited roles.

Trained for ballet, she turned to acting instead, married/divorced actor Chris Sarandon and has won critical approval for her performances without quite becoming a major star. Once an enthusiastic amateur racing driver. Oscar nominee for *Atlantic City USA*, *Thelma & Louise*, *Lorenzo's Oil* and *The Client*. She finally won the award for *Dead Man Walking*, and continues to defy her age in meaty leading roles. Lives with actor Tim Robbins (qv).
1970: Joe. 1971: Lady Liberty/La mortadella. Owen Marshall – Counsellor at Law (TV). 1972: Walk Away Madden. 1973: Lovin' Molly. 1974: The Front Page. F. Scott Fitzgerald and 'The Last of the Belles' (TV). 1975: The Rocky Horror Picture Show. The Great Waldo Pepper. 1976: The Other Side of Midnight. Dragonfly/One Summer's Love. 1977: The Last of the Cowboys (later The Great Smokey Roadblock). Checkered Flag or Crash. 1978: Pretty Baby. King of the Gypsies. 1979: Something Short of Paradise. 1980: Loving Couples. Atlantic City USA (GB and US: Atlantic City). 1981: Who Am I This Time? (TV). 1982: The Hunger. Tempest. 1983: The Buddy System. 1984: Eyes. In Our Hands. Io e Il Duce (US: Mussolini and I). 1985: Compromising Positions. Women of Valor (TV). 1987: The Witches of Eastwick. 1988: Da grande. Sweet Hearts Dance. Bull Durham. The January Man. 1989: A Dry White Season. 1990: White Palace. Through the Wire (narrator only). 1991: Thelma & Louise. Light Sleeper. 1992: Lorenzo's Oil. Bob Roberts. The Player. 1994: The Client. Safe Passage. Little Women. 1995: Dead Man Walking. The Celluloid Closet. 1996: James and the Giant Peach (voice only). 1998: Twilight. Illuminata. Stepmom. 1999: Cradle Will Rock. Anywhere But Here. Earthly Possessions (cable TV). 2000: Baby's in Black. Rugrats in Paris (voice only). Joe Gould's Secret. Livset haller mig sallskap (doc). 2001: Time of Our Lives. Like Cats and Dogs.

SARRAZIN, Michael
(Jacques Sarrazin) 1940–
Good-looking, dark-haired Canadian-born actor with deep-set eyes, lined lips and guileless look. Often cast as younger men undergoing initiation at the hands of older men. Despite leading roles opposite Jane Fonda, Barbra Streisand and Julie Christie (or perhaps because of them) he did not quite hold his place at the front of things.
1966: Gunfight in Abilene. The Doomsday

Flight (TV. GB: cinemas). 1967: The Flim Flam Man (GB: One Born Every Minute). The Sweet Ride. Journey to Shiloh. 1968: A Man Called Gannon. 1969: In Search of Gregory. They Shoot Horses Don't They? Eye of the Cat. The Pursuit of Happiness. 1971: Believe in Me. Sometimes a Great Notion (GB: Never Give an Inch). 1972: The Groundstar Conspiracy. 1973: Frankenstein: the True Story (TV. GB: cinemas). Harry Never Holds (GB: Harry in Your Pocket). 1974: The Reincarnation of Peter Proud. For Pete's Sake. 1976: The Gumball Rally. Scaramouche. 1978: Caravans. 1979: Double Negative. 1981: The Seduction. 1982: Fighting Back (GB: Death Vengeance). 1983: The Train Killer. 1985: Joshua Then and Now. Keeping Track (released 1987). 1987: Mascara. Fate of a Hunter. Captive Hearts. 1989: Malarek: a Street Kid Who Made It. The Phone Call (TV). 1990: Rose Against the Odds. 1991: Lena's Holiday. 1993: La Florida. 1995: Midnight Man (TV). Len Deighton's Bullet to Beijing. Len Deighton's Midnight in St Petersburg. 1996: Thunder Point (TV). Crackerjack 2: Hostage Train. 1997: The Peacekeeper. 1998: The Second Arrival.

The Killing Kind. 1974: The Sister-in-Law. All the Kind Strangers (TV). Lenny. 1975: The Turning Point of Jim Malloy/Gibbsville (TV). Eric (TV). 1978: The Deer Hunter. 1979: Hair. The Onion Field. 1980: Cattle Annie and Little Britches. Inside Moves. 1981: The Amateur. 1982: Coming Out of the Ice (originally for TV. Released 1984). 1983: The Long Ride/Brady's Escape. 1984: Nairobi Affair (TV). Maria's Lovers. Vengeance of a Soldier. 1985: The Little Sister (TV). Salvador. 1986: Silent Witness (TV). 1987: The Beat. Dear America (voice only). Beauty and the Beast. Desperate (TV). Hotel Colonial. 1988: Caribe. Any Man's Death. 1989: Do the Right Thing. Hunting (released 1991). 1990: The Godfather Part III. Voice in the Dark. War Shepherds/Point of View. Ottobre rosa all'Arbat. 1991: Le porte del silenzio. Mountain of Diamonds. Buck ai confini del cielo. 1992: Primary Motive. Daybreak (TV). Favola crudele. 1993: Il caso bianco, Berlino 39. CIA: Target Alexa. Children of the Silent One. My Forgotten Man. The Accident. 1994: Red Scorpion 2. La congiura del silenzio. The Takeover (cable TV). Tuono do proiettile/Deadly Weapon. Killing Obsession. The Dangerous. Shattered Image (TV). 1995: From the Edge. White Squall. Tom Clancy's Op Center (TV). The Crossing Guard. Firestorm. Carnosaur 2. 1996: Hysteria. American Strays. Flynn. Where Truth Lies. The Guardian System. The Mouse. Amnesia (released 1997). Managua. 1997: Hostile Intent. Little Boy Blue. Club Vampire. Hollywood Safari. Before Women Had Wings (TV). A Corner of Paradise. 1998: Burning Down the House/Snide and Prejudice. Front Line. Centurion Force. Nightworld: Lost Souls (TV). The Thin Red Line. 1999: Message in a Bottle. The Jack Bull (cable TV). Summer of Sam. 2000: Bombshell. Redemption of the Ghost. They Nest. The Virginian (TV).

for an Academy Award in *Birdman of Alcatraz*. Died from prostate cancer.

*1961: The Young Savages. Mad Dog Coll. The Young Doctors. 1962: Birdman of Alcatraz. Cape Fear. The Interns. 1963: Love is a Ball (GB: All This and Money Too). The Man from the Diners' Club. Johnny Cool. 1964: The New Interns. Fanfare for a Death Scene (TV). 1965: The Greatest Story Ever Told. Battle of the Bulge. The Slender Thread. Genghis Khan. 1966: Beau Geste. 1967: The Dirty Dozen. The Karate Killers (TV. GB: cinemas). Cosa Nostra, an Arch Enemy of the FBI (TV. GB: cinemas). Sol Madrid (GB: The Heroin Gang). 1968: The Scalphunters. Buona Sera, Mrs Campbell. The Assassination Bureau. Mackenna's Gold. Crooks and Coronets (US: Sophie's Place). 1969: Land Raiders. On Her Majesty's Secret Service. 1970: Violent City. Kelly's Heroes. 1971: A Town Called Bastard (US: A Town Called Hell). Mongo's Back in Town (TV). Pretty Maids All in a Row. Pancho Villa. Clay Pigeon (GB: Trip to Kill). 1972: The Lost World of Libra. A Reason to Live, a Reason to Die. Assassino è al telefono (GB: The Killer Is on the Phone). Panico en al Transiberio (GB: Horror Express). Red Neck. Visions (TV). I familiari delle vittime non saranno avertiti. 1973: She Cried Murder (TV). J and S, a Criminal Story of the Far West (US: Sonny and Jed). The Marcus-Nelson Murders (TV). 1975: The Diamond Mercenaries. Inside Out. House of Exorcism (US: Lisa and the Devil). 1976: Crime Boss. †Mati (released 1985 as Beyond Reason). 1977: Capricorn One. 1978: The Muppet Movie. Escape to Athena. 1979: Beyond the Poseidon Adventure. 1980: Alcatraz: The Whole Shocking Story (TV). The Border. Hellinger's Law (TV). 1981: *Telly Savalas Looks at Birmingham. *Telly Savalas Looks at Portsmouth. *Telly Savalas Looks at Aberdeen. 1982: Fake-Out. My Palikari (TV). 1983: Cannonball Run II. 1984: The Cartier Affair (TV). 1985: Kojak: The Belarus File (TV). 1987: The Sahara Secret. The Dirty Dozen: The Deadly Mission (TV). Kojak: The Price of Justice (TV). 1988: The Dirty Dozen: The Fatal Mission (TV). 1989: The Hollywood Detective (TV). Kojak: Ariana (TV. And ensuing series of TV movies). 1990: Stakes. 1993: Mind Twister. Vengeance/The Set Up. 1994: Backfire.*

†And directed

SAVAGE, John (J. Youngs) 1949–
Stocky, sturdy, tufty-haired American actor, an up-and-coming star for the first 10 years of his career (when he was in such films as *Bad Company*, *The Deer Hunter* and *The Onion Field*), but more of a journeyman actor for the past 20 years. In the late 1990s, he enjoyed something of a cult resurgence with his appearances in *The Thin Red Line* and *Summer of Sam*, and continues to be busy. Brother of actor Jim Youngs, father of actress Jennifer Youngs.

1972: Bad Company. Steelyard Blues. 1973:

SAVALAS, Telly
(Aristotle Savalas) 1922–1994
Shaven-headed, strong-faced and grinning American character star of Greek parentage. He switched from being a TV executive to an actor in the late 1950s. His slightly unbalanced features got him cast as psychopathic villains, and it was only with his great personal success as the tough detective in the TV series *Kojak* that he managed to break the mould. His attempts at direction on that series were very promising, but his one film as director proved disappointing. Nominated

SAXON, John
(Carmen Orrico) 1935–
Very dark-haired American actor of baby-faced handsomeness. Of Italian parentage, he started his career as a teenage rave, but soon veered into off-centre roles. Spent some time in Italy in the sixties, and re-emerged on the international scene with hair receding, but as a much harder actor with terse delivery who frequently played nasty characters.

1953: It Should Happen to You. 1955: Running Wild. 1956: The Unguarded Moment. Rock, Pretty Baby. 1957: Summer Love. 1958: The Reluctant Debutante. The Restless Years (GB: The Wonderful Years). This Happy Feeling. 1959: Portrait in Black. The Unforgiven. Cry Tough. The Big Fisherman. 1960: The Plunderers. 1961: Posse from Hell.

War Hunt. 1962: *La ragazza che sapeva troppa / The Girl Who Knew Too Much (GB: The Evil Eye). Agostino. Mr Hobbs Takes a Vacation.* 1963: *The Cardinal.* 1964: *The Cavern.* 1965: *The Ravagers. The Night Caller (US: Blood Beast From Outer Space).* 1966: *The Appaloosa (GB: Southwest to Sonora). The Doomsday Flight (TV. GB: cinemas). Planet of Blood / Queen of Blood.* 1967: *The Magnificent Thief (TV). Winchester 73 (TV).* 1968: *For Singles Only. Istanbul Express (TV. GB: cinemas). Vado, vedo e sparo.* 1969: *Death of a Gunfighter.* 1970: *Company of Killers. The Intruders (TV).* 1972: *Joe Kidd. Snatched (TV).* 1973: *Mr Kingstreet's War (GB: TV). Linda (TV). Enter the Dragon. Baciamo len mani (US: Mafia War).* 1974: *Black Christmas. Can Ellen Be Saved? (TV). Planet Earth (TV).* 1975: *The Swiss Conspiracy. Mitchell. Strange New World (TV). Crossfire (TV).* 1976: *Family Killer. Moonshine County Express. La legge violenta della squadra anticrimine (GB and US: Cross Shot). Raid on Entebbe (TV. GB: cinemas). Blazing Magnum (US: Strange Shadows in an Empty Room). Napoli violenta (GB: Death Dealers). Italia a mano armata (GB: Special Cop in Action).* 1977: *House Made of Dawn (completed 1972). E specialista di 44. Tre soldi e la donna di classe.* 1978: *The Bees. Fast Company. Shalimar.* 1979: *The Glove. The Electric Horseman.* 1980: *Savage Apocalypse (US: Cannibals in the Streets). Battle Beyond the Stars. Blood Beach (filmed 1978). Golden Gate (TV).* 1981: *Beyond Evil.* 1982: *Wrong is Right / The Man with the Deadly Lens. Tenebrae.* 1983: *Desire. Prisoners of the Lost Universe. Hardcastle and McCormick (TV). The Big Score.* 1984: *A Nightmare on Elm Street. Half-Slave, Half-Free (TV).* 1985: *Brothers-in-Law (TV). Fever Pitch.* 1986: *Hands of Steel / Atomic Cyborg.* 1987: *A Nightmare on Elm Street 3: Dream Warriors.* 1988: †*Death House. Tunnels (later Criminal Act). Welcome to Spring Break.* 1989: *My Mom's a Werewolf. Blood Salvage. Aftershock. Nightmare Beach. The Last Samurai.* 1990: *The Final Alliance. Crossing The Line. The Arrival.* 1991: *Payoff. Soul Stealer. Blackmail (TV).* 1992: *Maximum Force. Animal Instincts. No Escape No Return. Frame-Up II: The Cover-Up.* 1993: *Genghis Khan. The Baby Doll Murders.* 1994: *Killing Obsession. Beverly Hills Cop III. Wes Craven's New Nightmare.* 1995: *Jonathan of the Bears. The Killers Within. Liz: The Elizabeth Taylor Story (TV).* 1996: *From Dusk Till Dawn.* 1997: *Party Crashers*

(released 1999). 1998: *Guardian / Lancelot, Guardian of Time. Joseph's Gift.*

†*And directed*

SCACCHI, Greta (G. Gracco) 1958–
Flaxen-haired beauty with challenging, come-hither gaze, very busy on the international scene in the late 1980s, when film-makers sometimes seemed more anxious to get her clothes off on screen then to display her considerable acting talent. Born in Milan of an Italian father and English mother, she was educated in Britain and Australia, before embarking on a stage, TV and film career that has taken her all over the world.

1981: *Dead on Time.* 1982: *Der Zweiter Gesicht.* 1983: *Heat and Dust. Dr Fischer of Geneva (TV). The Ebony Tower (TV).* 1984: *The Coca Cola Kid. Camille (TV).* 1985: *Burke and Wills. Defence of the Realm.* 1986: *Good Morning, Babylon.* 1987: *A Man in Love. White Mischief.* 1988: *La donna della luna. Paura e amore / Love and Fear / The Three Sisters.* 1990: *Presumed Innocent.* 1991: *Shattered. Fires Within. Turtle Beach.* 1992: *The Player.* 1993: *The Browning Version. Salt on Our Skin.* 1994: *Omero. Country Life.* 1995: *Jefferson in Paris. Cosi.* 1996: *Bravo Randy. Emma. Rasputin.* 1997: *The Serpent's Kiss. The Odyssey.* 1998: *The Red Violin. Love and Rage / Lynchehaun. Tom's Midnight Garden. The Power Lakes.* 1999: *The Manor. Cotton Mary. Looking for Alibrandi. Ladies Room.* 2000: *One of the Hollywood Ten.*

SCHEIDER, Roy 1932–
Dark, thin-faced American leading man with hard-driving acting style that was chiefly employed in thrillers, but ultimately proved

adaptable to other genres. He made the most of his late chance at film stardom after coming to prominence in his late thirties. Nominated for Academy Awards in *The French Connection* and *All That Jazz.*

1963: †*The Curse of the Living Corpse.* 1968: *Paper Lion. Star!* 1969: *Stiletto.* 1970: *Puzzle of a Downfall Child. Loving.* 1971: *Klute. The French Connection.* 1972: *L'attentat (GB: Plot. US: The French Conspiracy). Un homme est mort (GB and US: The Outside Man). Assignment Munich (TV).* 1973: *The Seven-Ups.* 1975: *Jaws. Sheila Levene is Dead and Living in New York.* 1976: *Marathon Man.* 1977: *Sorcerer (GB: Wages of Fear).* 1978: *Jaws 2.* 1979: *Last Embrace. All That Jazz.* 1982: *Still of the Night. Blue Thunder.* 1983: *Tiger Town. Jacobo Timmerman / Prisoner without a Name, Cell Without a Number (TV).* 1984: *2010. In Our Hands.* 1985: *Mishima (narrator only).* 1986: *The Men's Club. 52 Pick-Up.* 1988: *Cohen & Tate.* 1989: *Night Game. Listen to Me. The Fourth War.* 1990: *The Russia House. Somebody Has to Shoot the Picture (TV).* 1991: *Naked Lunch.* 1993: *SeaQuest DSV (TV). Romeo is Bleeding.* 1994: *Assault in Broad Daylight / Es geschah am hellichten Tag.* 1996: *Money Plays (TV). The Myth of Fingerprints. Plato's Run. The Rage. The Peacekeeper / Hellbent.* 1997: *Executive Target. The Rainmaker. The Definite Maybe.* 1998: *Silver Wolf (TV). Better Living. Love and Rage. The White Raven. Evasive Action.* 1999: *Falling Through. RKO 281 (cable TV).* 2000: *The Doorway. Chain of Command. Daybreak. Angels Don't Sleep Here. Better Living.*

†*As Roy R. Scheider*

SCHELL, Maria (Margarete Schell) 1926–
Wispily-blonde, Austrian-born leading lady (of Swiss nationality), who rarely smiled in mostly red-eyed roles across Europe, Britain and Hollywood. Could give very touching performances, but did not quite have the stamp of an international star. Sister of Maximilian Schell (*qv*).

1941: *Quarry / Steinbruch.* 1943: *Maturareise.* 1948: *Nach dem Sturm. Wiener Kavalkade.* 1949: *Der Engel mit der Posaune / The Angel with the Trumpet. Der Angeklagte hat das Wort. Marosi.* 1950: *Es kommt ein Tag. The Affairs of Dr Holl.* 1951: *The Magic Box.* 1952: *So Little Time. The Heart of the Matter. Der träumende Mund (US: Dreaming Lips). Bis wir uns Wiedersehen.* 1953: *Tagebuch einer*

Verliebten. Die letzte Brücke/The Last Bridge. Solange du da Bist. 1954: Angelika. Napoléon. 1955: Uragano sul Po. Gervaise. Die Ratten. Herr über Leben und Tod. 1956: Liebe/Love. 1957: Rose Bernd. White Nights/Le notti bianchi. Ungarn in Flammen (narrator only). 1958: Une vie. The Brothers Karamazov. The Hanging Tree. Word from a Sealed-Off Box (TV). Der Schinderhannes (US: Duel in the Forest). 1959: Raubfischer in Hellas (GB and US: As the Sea Rages). For Whom the Bells Toll (TV). 1960: Cimarron, 1961: Das Riesenrad. The Mark. 1962: Ich bin auch nur eine Frau (US: Only a Woman). 1963: L'assassin connait la musique. Zwei Whisky und ein Sofa (US: Rendezvous in Trieste). 1965: Who Has Seen the Wind? 1968: 99 Women (US: Island of Despair). Heidi Comes Home (US: Heidi). 1969: Le diable par le queue. La provocation. 1970: Der Hexentöter von Blackmoor (US: The Bloody Judge). 1971: Such a Pretty Cloud. Dans la poussière du soleil/Lust in the Sun. 1972: Chamsin. Die Pfarrhauskomödie. 1974: The Odessa File. Change. 1975: The Quack. So oder so ist das Leben. 1976: Voyage of the Damned. Folies Bourgeoises/The Twist. 1978: Just a Gigolo. Die erste Polka. Superman. 1979: Christmas Lilies of the Field (TV). 1981: La passante de Sans-Souci. 1982: Inside the Third Reich (TV). 1984: Samson and Delilah (TV). 1919. King Thrushbeard.

SCHELL, Maximilian 1930–
Dark-haired, long-faced Austrian actor, brother of Maria Schell (qv). His features adapted equally well to kindliness and fanaticism, and it was with a mixture of both that he won his reputation in TV and film versions of *Judgment at Nuremberg*, the film of which won him an Oscar. But his roles gradually deteriorated to the point where he started directing his own films. Additional Oscar nomination for *Julia*.
1955: Kinder, Mütter und ein General. Ein Mädchen aus Flandern. 1956: Der 20 Juli. Reifende Jügend. Ein Herz kehrt Heim. Die Ehe des Dr Med Donwitz. 1957: Taxi-Chauffeur Bartz. Die Letzten werden die Ersten sein. 1958: Ein wunderbaren Sommer. The Young Lions. 1959: Judgment at Nuremberg (TV). Child of Our Time (TV). 1960: The Fifth Column (TV). Hamlet. 1961: Judgment at Nuremberg. 1962: Five Finger Exercise. The Reluctant Saint. 1963: The Condemned of Altona. 1964: Topkapi. 1965: Return from the Ashes. 1966: The Deadly Affair. 1967:

Counterpoint. 1968: The Desperate Ones. Krakatoa – East of Java. Heidi Comes Home (US: Heidi). 1969: The Castle. L'assoluto naturale/He and She. Simon Bolivár. 1970: First Love. 1971: Trotta. 1972: Pope Joan. 1973: Paulina 1880. Der Fussgänger/Le piéton. 1974: The Odessa File. 1975: The Man in the Glass Booth. 1976: Assassination! (US: The Day That Shook the World). St Ives. 1977: Julia. Cross of Iron. A Bridge Too Far. 1978: Avalanche Express. 1979: The Black Hole. Together/I Love You, I Love You Not. Players. 1980: Diary of Anne Frank (TV). 1981: The Chosen. Les îles. 1983: Phantom of the Opera (TV). 1984: Morgen in Alabama (US: A German Lawyer). The Assissi Underground. 1986: †Laughter in the Dark. 1989: The Rose Garden. 1990: The Freshman. An American Place. Labyrinth. 1992: Miss Rose White (TV). A Far Off Place. Stalin (TV). 1993: Justiz. 1994: Abraham (TV). Little Odessa. 1996: The Vampyre Wars. Through Roses. 1997: The Eighteenth Angel. Der Feuervogel. Telling Lies in America. Left Luggage. 1998: John Carpenter's Vampires. Deep Impact. 1999: Wer liebt, dem wachsen Fluegel. Wings of Love (TV). Fisimatenten. 2000: Just Messing About.
As director: 1969: The Castle. 1970: First Love. 1973: Der Fussgänger/Le piéton. 1976: End of the Game. 1979: Tales from the Vienna Woods. 1980: Diary of Anne Frank (TV). 1984: Marlene. 1990: An American Place.

†Unfinished

SCHNEIDER, Romy
(Rosemarie Albach-Retty) 1938–1982
Tartly attractive brunette Austrian actress, in films as a teenager, at first as pretty apple dumplings in frothily empty fifties' concoctions; but when she came back to films in 1961 after two years away there was much more bite to her work and she quickly became an international star in demand. Died from a heart attack.
1953: Wenn der weisse Flieder Blüht. 1954: Feuerwerk (GB: Oh! My Papa). Der Zigeunerbaron. Mädchenjahre einer Königin. 1955: Die Deutschmeister. Der letzte Mann. Sissi. 1956: Kitty. Sissi die junge Kaiserin. 1957: Robinson soll nicht sterben. Monpti. Scampolo. Sissi – Schicksalsjahre einer Kaiserin. 1958: Mädchen in Uniform. Christine. Die Halbzarte. †Forever My Love. 1959: Mademoiselle Ange (US: Angel on Earth). Die schöne Lügnerin. Katia. Plein soleil. 1961: Le combat dans l'île.

Die Sendung der Lysistrata. 1962: Boccaccio 70. The Legend of Robinson Crusoe. The Trial. 1963: The Victors. The Cardinal. 1964: Good Neighbor Sam. 1965: What's New, Pussycat? 1966: 10.30 p.m. Summer. La voleuse. Triple Cross. 1968. Otley. La piscine (GB: The Sinners). 1969: Les choses de la vie (GB: The Things of Life. US: These Things Happen). My Lover, My Son. Bloomfield. 1970: Que? (GB: TV, as Who Are You? US: The Sensuous Assassin). Don't You Cry. 1971: La califfa. Max et les ferailleurs. The Assassination of Trotsky. 1972: Ludwig. César et Rosalie. 1973: Le train. Un amour de pluie. Le mouton enragé (GB: The French Way). 1974: Le trio infernal. L'important c'est d'aimer (US: That Most Important Thing: Love!). Innocents with Dirty Hands. 1975: Le vieux fusil (GB: The Hidden Gun). 1976: Une femme à sa fenêtre. Mado. Portrait de groupe avec dame/Gruppenbild mit Dame. 1978: Une histoire simple. 1979: Clair de femme. Lo sconosciuto. La mort en direct/Deathwatch. Bloodline/Sidney Sheldon's Bloodline. 1980: La banquière. 1981: Fantôme d'amour. Garde à vue (GB: The Inquisitor. US: The Grilling). La passante du Sans-Souci.

†Combined GB version of the three 'Sissi' films

SCHREIBER, Liev
(Isaac L. Schreiber) 1967–
Tall, thin-lipped American actor with tight curly hair and aggressively inquisitive features. Following a colourful childhood, he and his four half-brothers at one time living as squatters in an abandoned building while their mother drove a cab, he was a late graduate from drama school at 25, but has since proved one of America's most prolific players, with 30 films and a string of theatrical appearances to his credit in the last seven years. Despite such feverish activity, he's probably still best-known as the dodgy Cotton Weary in the 'Scream' horror films. Christian name pronounced Lee-ev.
1994: Mixed Nuts. Janek: The Silent Betrayal (TV). 1995: Mad Love. Party Girl. The Sunshine Boys (TV). Buffalo Girls (TV). The Daytrippers (released 1997). 1996: Denise Calls Up. Scream. Ransom. *Baggage. Walking and Talking. Big Night. 1997: Scream 2. Since You've Been Gone/Dogwater (TV). His and Hers. Phantoms/Dean Koontz's Phantoms. 1998: Sphere. Over the Moon. Desert Blue (TV. Voice only). Babe Ruth (TV. Narrator only). Twilight. 1999: Jakob the Liar. A Walk on the Moon. The Hurricane. RKO 281 (cable TV).

Hamlet. 2000: *Spring Forward. Scream 3. Pay It Forward*. 2001: *Dial 9 for Love*.

SCHRODER, Rick(y) 1970–

Angelic, golden-haired and appealingly talented American child actor to whom adulthood gave less sympathetic facial features. Rick (then Ricky) broke a million hearts as the boxer's son in *The Champ*, but his adult career has been more of a struggle, sunk in the anonymity of leading roles in a fistful of TV movies, with the odd supporting part in feature films. He was catapulted back into the public eye in 1998, when he took over from Jimmy Smits (*qv*) as the leading younger cop in the successful TV series *NYPD Blue*. Happily married since 1992, the child player now has three kids of his own.

1979: †*The Champ*. 1980: †*Little Lord Fauntleroy* (TV. GB: cinemas). †*The Last Flight of Noah's Ark*. †*The Earthling*. 1982: †*Something So Right* (TV). 1983: †*Two Kinds of Love* (TV). 1984: †*A Reason to Live* (TV). 1988: †*Too Young the Hero* (TV). 1989: †*Terror on Highway 91* (TV). *Out on the Edge* (TV). 1990: *The Stranger Within* (TV). *A Son's Promise* (TV). 1991: *Across the Tracks. My Son Johnny* (TV). *Blood River* (TV). *Miles from Nowhere* (TV). 1993: *Call of the Wild* (TV). 1994: *There Goes My Baby. Texas* (TV). *To My Daughter with Love* (TV). 1995: *Crimson Tide*. 1996: *Innocent Victims* (TV). 1997: *Detention: The Siege at Johnson High* (TV. GB: *Target for Rage*). *Ebenezer* (TV). *Heart Full of Rain* (TV). *Too Close to Home* (TV). 1998: *I Woke Up Early the Day I Died. What We Did That Night* (TV. GB: *Murder at Devil's Glen*).

† *As Ricky Schroder*

SCHWARZENEGGER, Arnold 1947–

Austrian muscleman, bodybuilder and, latterly, actor, with solid features, gap-toothed smile and a surprisingly subtle sense of humour. A five times Mr Universe, Schwarzenegger's boyhood idol was Steve Reeves (*qv*); after a stop-go start in films, the scale of the action in his violent adventure movies rapidly pushed him up towards the top of the league of Hollywood's most bankable stars. His crowd-pleasing personality has enabled him to try more comedy in recent years. For the record, he's 6ft 2in, weighs 240lbs and has a 57-inch chest! Resumed career after heart-bypass surgery in 1998.

1969: †*Hercules Goes Bananas (later Hercules*

in New York). 1973: †*The Long Goodbye*. 1976: *Stay Hungry*. 1977: *Pumping Iron*. 1979: *Scavenger Hunt. The Villain* (GB: *Cactus Jack*). 1981: *Conan the Barbarian. The Jayne Mansfield Story* (TV). 1984: *Conan the Destroyer. The Terminator*. 1985: *Red Sonja. Commando*. 1986: *Raw Deal*. 1987: *The Running Man. Predator*. 1988: *Red Heat. Twins*. 1990: *Total Recall. Kindergarten Cop*. 1991: *Terminator 2: Judgment Day*. 1992: *Beretta's Island*. 1993: *Last Action Hero. Dave*. 1994: *True Lies. Junior*. 1996: *Eraser. Jingle All the Way*. 1997: *Batman and Robin*. 1998: *Billion Dollar Funfairs* (doc). 1999: *End of Days*. 2000: *On the Sixth Day*. 2001: *Collateral Damage*.

As co-director: 1990: *Tales from the Crypt* (TV). As director: 1992: *Christmas in Connecticut* (TV).

†*As Arnold Strong*

SCHYGULLA, Hanna 1943–

Polish-born, Bavarian-raised, sultry-looking, square-built blonde actress with faintly mysterious air. Studied to be a teacher, but instead joined Munich's offbeat 'action theatre' where she met director Rainer Werner Fassbinder (together with others they founded the city's famous 'anti-theatre'), in whose films she would rise to stardom. She gained international prominence belatedly with *Lili Marleen*, but after Fassbinder's death in 1982 her career faltered.

1968: **Der Bräutigam, die Komödiantin und der Zuhälter* (GB: *The Bridegroom, the Comedienne and the Pimp*). 1969: *Liebe ist kälter als der Tod. Katzelmacher. Götter der Pest* (GB and US: *Gods of the Plague*).

Jagdzenen aus Niederbayern. Baal (TV). 1970: *Rio das Mortes* (TV). *Niklaushauserer Fahrt. Pioniere in Ingolstadt* (TV). *Das Kaffeehaus* (TV). *Kuckucksei im Gangsternest*. 1971: *Whity. Warnung vor einer heiligem Nutte* (GB: *Warning of a Holy Whore*. US: *Beware the Holy Whore*). *Der Händler der vier Jahreszeiten* (GB and US: *The Merchant of Four Seasons*). *Jacob Von Guten*. 1972: *Die bitteren Tränen der Petra von Kant* (GB and US: *The Bitter Tears of Petra von Kant*). *Wildwechsel* (GB: *Wild Game*. US: *Jail Bait*). *Das Haus am Meer*. 1974: *Fontane: Effi Brest* (GB and US: *Effi Brest*). 1975: *Falsche Bewegung* (GB: *Wrong Movement*. US: *The Wrong Move*). *Ansichten eines Clowns. Der Stumme*. 1977: *Die Dämonen. Die Heimkehr des alten Herrn*. 1978: *Aussagen nach einer Verhaftung* (TV). *Die grosse Flatter. Die Ehe der Maria Braun* (GB and US: *The Marriage of Maria Braun*). 1979: *Berlin-Alexander Platz* (originally series for TV). 1980: *Lili Marleen*. 1981: *Die Fälschung* (GB and US: *Circle of Deceit*). 1982: *Passion. Revolution. La nuit de Varennes. La storia di Piera. Antonieta*. 1983: *Heller Wahn* (GB: *Friends and Husbands*. US: *A Labour of Love*). 1984: *The Future is Woman. Eine Liebe in Deutschland* (GB and US: *A Love in Germany*). 1985: *Sheer Madness*. 1986: *Storm Over Venice/Storm in Venice. The Delta Force. Forever, Lulu. Barnum* (TV). 1987: *The Summer of Miss Forbes. Casanova* (TV). *Miss Arizona*. 1989: *The Adventures of Catherine C. Abraham's Gold*. 1991: *Dead Again*. 1992: *The Down Bearer. Warszawa* (US: *Warsaw–Year 5703*). *Golem, l'esprit d'exil*. 1993: *Aux petits bonheurs* (US: *Life's Little Treasures*). *Petrified Garden. Mavi surgun* (US: *The Blue Exile*). 1994: *Ich will nicht nur, dass ihr mich liebt. Les cent et une nuits*. 1995: *Hey Stranger. The Sunset Boys* (released 1998 as *Waiting for Sunset*). *Die Nacht der Regisseure*. 1996: *Black-Out. Lea. Milim/Words*. 1997: *Chronique*. 1998: *Life, Love and Celluloid* (doc). *La Niña de tus ogos*. 2000: *Werckmeister Harmoniak*.

SCIORRA, Annabella 1964–

Dark-haired, thickly-eyebrowed American actress of peasant-style prettiness. She formed her own theatre company at 20, but, on entering films four years later, found herself cast almost entirely as working-class Italian-Americans, despite a quite upper-class upbringing (her mother is French, her father Cuban-Italian). Hit movies and good performances didn't seem to make her a

familiar star name, and she may be destined to play out her career in middle-bracket fare.
1988: *Mario Puzo's The Fortunate Pilgrim (TV)*. *True Love*. 1990: *Cadillac Man*. *Internal Affairs*. *Reversal of Fortune*. 1991: *Jungle Fever*. *The Hard Way*. *Prison Stories: Women on the Inside (TV)*. 1992: *The Hand That Rocks the Cradle*. *Whispers in the Dark*. 1993: *Mr Wonderful*. *Romeo is Bleeding*. *The Night We Never Met*. *The Addiction*. 1995: *The Cure*. *The Innocent Sleep*. *National Lampoon's Favorite Deadly Sins*. 1996: *Underworld*. *The Funeral*. 1997: *Cop Land*. *Little City*. *Mr Jealousy / Highball*. *Destination Anywhere (video)*. *Lesser Prophets*. 1998: *What Dreams May Come*. *New Rose Hotel*. 1999: *Once in the Life*. 2000: *King of the Jungle*. *Above Suspicion*. *One of the Hollywood Ten*. *Domenica*.

SCOFIELD, Paul
(David P. Scofield) 1922–
Light-haired, intelligent-looking, quietly-spoken British actor who has been too little seen in films. Acclaimed for his performance as Sir Thomas More in *A Man for All Seasons*, which won him an Academy Award, he still preferred to return to the theatre. The cinema claimed a fairer share of his time from the 1980s, when he began playing weathered character roles, one of which, in *Quiz Show*, won him a further Oscar nomination.
1955: *That Lady*. 1958: *Carve Her Name with Pride*. 1965: *The Train*. 1966: *A Man for All Seasons*. *The Other World of Winston Churchill (narrator only)*. 1967: *Tell Me Lies*. 1970: *King Lear*. *Bartleby*. 1972: *Scorpio*. 1974: *A Delicate Balance*. 1983: *Ill Fares the Land (TV. Voice only, uncredited)*. 1984: '1919'. 1985: *Summer Lightning (TV)*. 1986: *The Conspiracy*. *Mr Corbett's Ghost (TV)*. 1987: *The Attic: The Hiding of Anne Frank (TV)*. 1989: *When the Whales Came*. *Henry V*. 1990: *Hamlet*. 1992: *UTZ*. 1994: *London (narrator only)*. *Quiz Show*. *The Bible: Genesis (narrator only)*. 1995: *The Little Riders (TV)*. 1996: *The Crucible*. 1997: *Robinson in Space (narrator only)*. 1999: *Animal Farm (voice only)*.

SCOTT, Dougray (Stephen Scott) 1965–
Smooth but burly Scottish actor of wry smile and untamed hair. He trained at the Welsh College of Music and Drama, where he was named most prominent student, but he spent years working in regional theatre before his performance as the corrupt policeman in

Twin Town brought his face to the attention of film producers. He consolidated his arrival on the international scene by playing the villain in *Mission: Impossible II*.
1994: *Princess Caraboo*. 1997: *Another 9½ Weeks*. *Twin Town*. *Regeneration*. 1998: *Deep Impact*. *Ever After*. 1999: *This Year's Love*. *Gregory's Two Girls*. *The Miracle Maker (voice only)*. 2000: *Arabian Nights (TV)*. *Mission: Impossible II*. 2001: *Enigma*.

SCOTT, George C. 1925–1999
Craggy, rasp-voiced American whose earthy arrogance dominated his films but rarely over-balanced them. He won notoriety as the first actor to refuse to accept an Oscar (awarded for *Patton*), but by and large his roles have not been worthy of his larger-than-life talents. Married (fourth) to Trish Van Devere (Patricia Dressel, 1943–). Also Oscar-nominated for *Anatomy of a Murder*, *The Hustler* and *The Hospital*. Later became bogged down in Dickensian roles. Father of actor Campbell Scott (1962–). Died following a series of heart attacks.
1958: *The Hanging Tree*. 1959: *Anatomy of a Murder*. *Target for Three (TV)*. 1961: *The Power and the Glory (TV. GB: cinemas)*. *The Hustler*. 1962: *The Brazen Bell (TV. GB: cinemas)*. 1963: *The List of Adrian Messenger*. *Dr Strangelove, or: How I Learned to Stop Worrying and Love the Bomb*. 1964: *The Yellow Rolls Royce*. 1966: *The Bible . . . in the beginning*. *Not with My Wife, You Don't! Shadow on the Land (TV)*. 1967: *The Flim Flam Man (GB: One Born Every Minute)*. 1968: *Petulia*. 1969: *Patton (GB: Patton–Lust for Glory)*. 1970: *Jane Eyre (TV. GB: cinemas)*. 1971: *They Might Be Giants*. *The Hospital*. *The Last Run*. 1972: *The New*

Centurions (GB: Precinct 45: Los Angeles Police). *Rage*. 1973: *Oklahoma Crude*. *The Day of the Dolphin*. 1974: *Bank Shot*. *The Savage is Loose*. 1975: *The Hindenberg*. *Fear on Trial (TV)*. 1976: *Islands in the Stream*. *Beauty and the Beast*. 1977: *The Prince and the Pauper (GB: Crossed Swords)*. 1978: *Movie Movie*. *Hardcore (GB: The Hardcore Life)*. 1979: *Arthur Miller–On Home Ground*. *The Changeling*. 1980: *The Formula*. 1981: *Taps*. 1982: *Oliver Twist (TV. GB: cinemas)*. 1983: *China Rose (TV)*. 1984: *Firestarter*. *A Christmas Carol (TV. GB: cinemas)*. 1985: *The Indomitable Teddy Roosevelt (narrator only)*. 1986: *The Last Days of Patton (TV)*. *Choices (TV)*. *The Murders in the Rue Morgue (TV)*. 1987: *Pals (TV)*. 1989: *The Ryan White Story (TV)*. 1990: *The Exorcist III*. *The Rescuers Down Under (voice only)*. *Descending Angel (cable TV)*. 1991: *Finding the Way Home (TV)*. 1993: *Curacao*. *Malice*. 1994: *The Whipping Boy / Prince Brat and the Whipping Boy (TV)*. 1995: *Angus*. *Tyson (TV)*. 1996: *Family Rescue (TV)*. 1997: *12 Angry Men (TV)*. 1998: *Gloria*. 1999: *Rocky Marciano (TV)*. *Inherit the Wind (TV)*.
As director: 1972: *Rage*. 1974: *The Savage is Loose*.

SCOTT, Gordon (G. Werschkul) 1927–
Muscular, fair-haired American leading man whisked from his job as a lifeguard to become the screen's new Tarzan in 1955. Unwisely gave up the role five years (and several above-average Tarzan films) later, and went into Italian muscleman epics. Not heard from since the mid-sixties. Married to Vera Miles (1955–1959), third of four wives.
1955: *Tarzan's Hidden Jungle*. 1957: *Tarzan and the Lost Safari*. 1958: *Tarzan's Fight for Life*. *Tarzan and the Trappers*. 1959: *Tarzan's Greatest Adventure*. 1960: *Tarzan the Magnificent*. 1961: *Romulus and Remus (GB: Duel of the Titans)*. *Maciste against the Vampires (GB: Goliath against the Vampires)*. *Maciste alla corte del Gran Kan (GB: Samson and the Seven Miracles)*. 1962: *A Queen for Caesar*. *The Gladiator of Rome (GB: Battles of the Gladiators)*. *Son of the Sheik*. *Hero of Babylon (GB: Goliath–King of the Slaves)*. *Coriolanus*. 1963: *Zorro and the Three Musketeers*. *Hercules against Moloch (GB: Hercules Attacks)*. *The Lion of St Mark*. *Il giorno piu corto commedia umaristica (US: The Shortest Day)*. *Thunder of Battle (US: Hero of Rome)*. *Arrow of the Avenger*. *Conquest of Mycene*. *Goliath and the Black Hercules*. 1964:

Buffalo Bill, Hero of the Far West. Arm of Fire. The Tyrant of Lydia against the Son of Hercules. The Colossus of Rome. 1966: The Tramplers. Segretissimo (US: Top Secret). 1967: Nest of Spies.

SCOTT, Janette (Thora J. Scott) 1938–
Talented, brown-haired, pigtailed British child star who broke a million hearts in *No Place for Jennifer*. Tried hard to make a go of an adult career, but never seemed completely at ease. Daughter of actress Thora Hird (1913–). Married to Mel Tormé (1923–1999), second of three, from 1966 to 1977.
1942: Went the Day Well? (US: 48 Hours). 1943: The Lamp Still Burns. 1944: 2,000 Women. Medal for the General. 1949: Conspirator. No Place for Jennifer. 1951: The Magic Box. The Galloping Major. No Highway (US: No Highway in the Sky). 1953: Background (US: Edge of Divorce). 1954: Helen of Troy. 1955: As Long As They're Happy. 1956: Now and Forever. 1957: The Good Companions. Happy is the Bride! 1959: The Lady is a Square. The Devil's Disciple. School for Scoundrels. 1960: His and Hers. 1961: Double Bunk. Two and Two Make Six. 1962: The Day of the Triffids. Paranoiac. The Old Dark House. 1963: Siege of the Saxons. 1964: The Beauty Jungle (US: Contest Girl). Bikini Paradise. 1965: Crack in the World.

SCOTT, Lizabeth (Emma Matzo) 1922–
Sultry blonde American actress of husky voice and strong personality, initially billed as 'The Threat'. Usually in grim-faced roles as tough babes who ended up with no more than they deserved. Has never married.
1945: You Came Along. 1946: The Strange Love of Martha Ivers. Dead Reckoning. 1947:

Desert Fury. I Walk Alone. Variety Girl. 1948: Pitfall. 1949: Too Late for Tears. Easy Living. 1950: Dark City. Paid in Full. 1951: Two of a Kind. The Company She Keeps. The Racket. Red Mountain. 1952: Stolen Face. 1953: Scared Stiff. Bad for Each Other. 1954: Silver Lode. 1956: Overnight Haul (TV. GB: cinemas). The Weapon. 1957: Loving You. 1972: Pulp.

SCOTT, Martha 1914–
Appealing strawberry blonde American actress who always seemed to be required to age in her films: ironically, her youthful looks faded fast and she had a very short star career, although she continued to crop up through the years in mother roles. She received an Oscar nomination for *Our Town*.
*1940: The Howards of Virginia (GB: The Tree of Liberty). Our Town. 1941: Cheers for Miss Bishop. One Foot in Heaven. They Dare Not Love. *Variety Reel. 1943: Hi Diddle Diddle. In Old Oklahoma/War of the Wildcats. Stage Door Canteen. 1947: So Well Remembered. 1949: Strange Bargain. 1951: When I Grow Up. 1955: The Desperate Hours. 1956: The Ten Commandments. 1957: Sayonara. Eighteen and Anxious. 1959: Ben-Hur. A Trip to Paradise (TV). 1972: Charlotte's Web (voice only). 1973: Sorority Kill (TV). 1974: Airport 1975. The Devil's Daughter (TV). Thursday's Game (TV). The Abduction of Saint Anne/They've Kidnapped Anne Benedict (TV). 1975: Medical Story (TV). 1977: The Turning Point. 1979: Charleston (TV). 1980: Father Figure (TV). 1983: Adam (TV). Summer Girl (TV). 1986: Adam: His Song Continues (TV). 1987: Doin' Time on Planet Earth. 1989: Love and Betrayal (TV). Daughter of the Streets (TV).*

SCOTT, Randolph
(George R. Crane Scott) 1898–1987
Sandy-haired, light leading man of the twenties and thirties who developed in post-war years into Hollywood's number one westerner. Grim-faced, quietly spoken and two-fisted, he played men of rigid integrity who pursued single-minded courses for what they thought was right. Always looked around 45, and appeared consistently in high-budget colour westerns while almost every other cowboy star was in black-and-white 'B's. At his death from heart trouble, Scott was one of Hollywood's wealthiest stars.
1928: Sharp Shooters. 1929: The Far Call.

*The Black Watch. The Virginian. Dynamite. 1931: The Women Men Marry. Sky Bride. 1932: Hot Saturday. Island of Lost Souls. Heritage of the Desert. A Successful Calamity. 1933: Supernatural. When the West Was Young. Murders in the Zoo. Wild Horse Mesa. Cocktail Hour. To the Last Man. The Thundering Herd. Hello, Everybody! Sunset Pass. Man of the Forest. Broken Dreams. 1934: Wagon Wheels. The Last Round-Up. The Lone Cowboy. 1935: Home on the Range. The Rocky Mountain Mystery. She. Roberta. Village Tale. So Red the Rose. 1936: And Sudden Death. Follow the Fleet. The Last of the Mohicans. Go West, Young Man. *Pirate Party on Catalina Isle. 1937: High, Wide and Handsome. 1938: The Texans. Rebecca of Sunnybrook Farm. Road to Reno. 1939: Jesse James. Susannah of the Mounties. Frontier Marshal. 20,000 Men a Year. Coast Guard. 1940: When the Daltons Rode. Virginia City. My Favourite Wife. 1941: Paris Calling. Western Union. Belle Starr. 1942: Pittsburgh. To the Shores of Tripoli. The Spoilers. 1943: Bombardier. Gung Ho! The Desperadoes. Corvette K-225 (GB: The Nelson Touch). 1944: Follow the Boys. Belle of the Yukon. 1945: China Sky. Captain Kidd. 1946: Home Sweet Homicide. Abilene Town. Badman's Territory. 1947: Gunfighters (GB: The Assassin). Christmas Eve. Trail Street. 1948: Coroner Creek. Albuquerque (GB: Silver City). Return of the Bad Men. 1949: The Doolins of Oklahoma (GB: The Great Manhunt). The Walking Hills. Canadian Pacific. Fighting Man of the Plains. 1950: The Nevadan (GB: The Man from Nevada). The Cariboo Trail. Colt 45. 1951: Sugarfoot. Santa Fé. Starlift. Fort Worth. Man in the Saddle (GB: The Outcast). 1952: Carson City. Hangman's Knot. The Man Behind the Gun. 1953: Thunder over the Plains. The Stranger Wore a Gun. 1954: Riding Shotgun. The Bounty Hunter. 1955: Ten Wanted Men. Tall Man Riding. Rage at Dawn. A Lawless Street. 1956: 7th Cavalry. Seven Men from Now. 1957: The Tall T. Shoot Out at Medicine Bend. Decision at Sundown. 1958: Buchanan Rides Alone. 1959: Ride Lonesome. Westbound. 1960: Comanche Station. 1961: Ride the High Country (GB: Guns in the Afternoon).*

SCOTT, Zachary 1914–1965
Treachery was Zachary Scott's stock-in-trade: This dark-haired, moustachioed American actor with a way of looking sideways at his fellow-players was almost exclusively cast as scoundrels or powerful

criminals, all of them used to a high standard of living. He was capable of a good range – as *The Southerner* showed – but sneers and hollow laughter prevailed. Died from a brain tumour. He began his acting career on stage in England.

1944: The Mask of Dimitrios. Hollywood Canteen. 1945: The Southerner. Mildred Pierce. Danger Signal. 1946: Her Kind of Man. 1947: Cass Timberlane. Stallion Road. The Unfaithful. 1948: Whiplash. Ruthless. Flaxy Martin. 1949: South of St Louis. Flamingo Road. One Last Fling. 1950: Guilty Bystander. Shadow on the Wall. Born to Be Bad. Colt 45. 1951: Let's Make it Legal. The Secret of Convict Lake. Lightning Strikes Twice. 1952: Wings of Danger (US: Dead on Course). 1953: Appointment in Honduras. 1954: The Treasure of Ruby Hills. 1955: Shotgun. Flame of the Islands. 1956: Bandido. The Counterfeit Plan. 1957: Man in the Shadow (US: Violent Stranger). Flight into Danger. 1960: Natchez Trace. 1961: The Young One (GB: Island of Shame). 1962: It's Only Money.

SCOTT THOMAS, Kristin 1960–
Cool, elegant, dark-haired British actress with gravely calm features. Trained in drama, she married a Frenchman and moved to France, making her film debut there in Prince's infamous *Under the Cherry Moon*. She improved her image via a series of French and British films, finally winning a British Oscar for *Four Weddings and a Funeral*. The bilingual actress now alternates French and British films, and is growing in stature.

1986: Under the Cherry Moon. Chameleon/La tricheuse (TV). 1987: Djamal et Juliette.

L'agent Troubé. 1988: A Handful of Dust. La Méridienne. The Tenth Man (TV). Force majeure. 1989: Bille en tête. Le bal du gouverneur. 1990: Spymaker: The Secret Life of Ian Fleming (TV). The Bachelor. Framed (cable TV). 1992: Weep No More My Lady (TV). Bitter Moon. 1993: Four Weddings and a Funeral. 1994: Aux yeux du monde/Autobus. Un été inoubliable. 1995: Le confessionel. Angels and Insects. En mai fais ce qu'il te plaît/Mayday. Plaisir d'offrir. Richard III. Les milles. 1996: The Pompatus of Love. Microcosmos (narrator, English version only). The English Patient. Mission: Impossible. 1997: Amour et confusion. 1998: The Revenger's Comedies. The Horse Whisperer. 1999: Random Hearts. Up at the Villa.

SEAGAL, Steven 1950–
Tall, dark, impassive, narrow-eyed, harshly-spoken, often pony-tailed American action star who forsook careers running security operations and martial arts academies to move, via training actors in stuntwork, into a series of exceptionally violent action films in which the object often seemed to be to inflict death in as many different painful ways as possible during the course of the plot. His films, though, did on the whole do well at the box-office, notably the 'Under Siege' adventures, until his fortunes dipped in the late 1990s. Married/divorced (second of two) actress Kelly LeBrock.

1988: Above the Law (GB: Nico). 1990: Hard to Kill. Marked for Death. 1991: Out for Justice. 1992: Under Siege. 1993: †On Deadly Ground. 1995: Under Siege 2/Under Siege: Dark Territory. 1996: Executive Decision. The Glimmer Man. 1997: Fire Down Below. 1998: The Patriot. My Giant. 1999: Blood on the Moon. Get Bruce! (doc). 2001: Ticker. Exit Wounds.

†And directed

SEBERG, Jean 1938–1979
Blonde American acress who brought warmth, vitality and emotional appeal to French films of the early sixties after a shaky start in her own country in *Saint Joan*. Later films never trained her abilities along the right lines and, although she continued to look better in French films than those of Hollywood, her film career had ground to a halt some years before she committed suicide with barbiturates. Married to writer-director Romain Gary (b1914) from 1963 to 1970. He shot himself in 1980.

*1957: Saint Joan. 1958: Bonjour tristesse. 1959: The Mouse That Roared. A bout de souffle/Breathless. 1960: Let No Man Write My Epitaph. La recréation (GB and US: Playtime). Les grandes personnes (GB: A Taste of Love). L'amant de cinque jours (GB: Infidelity). 1961: Congo Vivo (GB: Eruption). 1962: In the French Style. 1963: Les plus belles escroqueries du monde. *Le grand escroc. 1964: Lilith. Echappement libre (US: Backfire). 1965: Un milliard dans un billard (GB: Diamonds Are Brittle). Moment to Moment. 1966: Estouffade à la Caraïbe (GB: The Looters). A Fine Madness. La ligne de démarcation. 1967: The Road to Corinth. 1968: Pendulum. Birds in Peru/Birds Come to Die in Peru. 1969: Paint Your Wagon. Airport. A Bullet for Rommel. Ondata di calore. 1970: Macho Callahan. 1971: Questa specie d'amore. Kill. 1972: L'attentat (GB: Plot). The Corruption of Chris Miller (US: Behind the Shutters). Camorra. 1973: Mousey (TV. GB: cinemas, as Cat and Mouse). 1974: Les hautes solitudes. Bianchi cavalli d'Agosto. 1975: Le grand délire. 1976: The Wild Duck.*

As director: 1974: Ballad for the Kid.

SECOMBE, Sir Harry 1921–
Explosive, ebullient, crinkly-haired Welsh zany comedian and singer, forever giggling between singing operatic arias, and an integral part of the success of the innovative British 1950s' radio comedy programme *The Goon Show*. His plumpness increased with the years – he should have played Tweedledum and Tweedledee – until a peritonitis attack caused the emergence of a new slimline Secombe. Films featuring him as star have by and large not been popular successes. Knighted in 1981.

1948: *Hocus Pocus.* 1949: *Helter Skelter.* 1950: *Fake's Progress (narrator only).* 1951: *London Entertains. Penny Points to Paradise.* 1952: *Down Among the Z Men.* 1953: *Forces' Sweetheart.* 1954: *Svengali.* 1957: *Davy.* 1959: *Jet Storm.* 1968: *Oliver!* 1969: *The Bed Sitting Room.* 1970: *Song of Norway. Rhubarb. Doctor in Trouble.* 1971: *The Magnificent Seven Deadly Sins.* 1972: *Sunstruck.* 1980: **A Fair Way to Play.*

SEDGWICK, Kyra
See BACON, Kevin

SEGAL, George 1934–
American leading man with fair hair and lived-in face; his wry, sly sense of fun permeated most of his best work and, coupled with a naturalistic acting style, allowed him to be cast as an assortment of dog-eared heroes, frayed charmers and potential losers destined to win by sheer, dogged peristence. A star of the cinema until 1980 – he made rather too many comedies in the late 1970s – he reappeared from 1983 in a variety of out-of-the-way roles. Oscar nominee for *Who's Afraid of Virginia Woolf?*
1961: *The Young Doctors.* 1962: *The Longest Day.* 1963: *Act One.* 1964: *Invitation to a Gunfighter. The New Interns.* 1965: *King Rat. Ship of Fools.* 1966: *Lost Command. Who's Afraid of Virginia Woolf? The Quiller Memorandum.* 1967: *The St Valentine's Day Massacre. No Way to Treat a Lady.* 1968: *Bye Bye Braverman. Tenderly/The Girl Who Couldn't Say No. Unstrap Me.* 1969: *The Southern Star. The Bridge at Remagen.* 1970: *Loving. Where's Poppa? The Owl and the Pussycat.* 1971: *Born to Win.* 1972: *A Touch of Class. The Hot Rock (GB: How to Steal a Diamond in Four Uneasy Lessons).* 1973: *Blume in Love.* 1974: *The Terminal Man. California Split.* 1975: *The Black Bird. Russian Roulette.* 1976: *The Duchess and the Dirtwater Fox. Fun with Dick and Jane.* 1977: *Rollercoaster.* 1978: *Who is Killing the Great Chefs of Europe? (GB: Too Many Chefs).* 1979: *Lost and Found. Arthur Miller on Home Ground.* 1980: *The Last Married Couple in America. Carbon Copy.* 1983: *The Cold Room. The Zany Adventures of Robin Hood (TV). Trackdown: Finding the Goodbar Killer (TV).* 1984: *Stick.* 1985: *Not My Kid (Video). Who's in the Closet? Killing 'Em Softly (filmed 1982 as The Man in 5A).* 1986: *Many Happy Returns.* 1987: *Marathon.* 1988: *All's Fair. Skirmish.* 1989: *Look Who's Talking.* 1991:

The Clearing. For the Boys. 1992: *Me, Myself and I. A Bear Named Arthur.* 1993: *The Joshua Tree/Army of One.* 1993: *Deep Down. Taking the Heat. Direct Hit.* 1994: *Following Her Heart (TV). The Feminine Touch. Seasons of the Heart (TV).* 1995: *To Die For. It's My Party. Picture Window (cable TV). The Babysitter.* 1996: *The Cable Guy. The Mirror Has Two Faces. The Last Day. Flirting with Disaster. The Paul Fleiss Story (TV).* 1998: *Houdini (TV).* 2000: *The Linda McCartney Story (TV).*

SELLARS, Elizabeth 1923–
Cool, elegant, brunette British actress of slightly discontented prettiness. She was cast as a neurotic young girl in her first film, and thereafter often found herself in roles of anguish, latterly as unsympathetic wives. Built up a wider range on stage and TV.
1946: *Floodtide.* 1950: *Madeleine. Guilt is My Shadow.* 1951: *Cloudburst. Night Was Our Friend.* 1952: *Hunted (US: The Stranger in Between). The Gentle Gunman. The Long Memory.* 1953: *Three's Company. The Broken Horseshoe. Recoil.* 1954: *Forbidden Cargo. Desiree. *Conscience. The Barefoot Contessa.* 1955: *Three Cases of Murder. Prince of Players.* 1956: *The Last Man to Hang? The Man in the Sky (US: Decision against Time).* 1957: *The Shiralee.* 1958: *Law and Disorder.* 1959: *Jet Storm.* 1960: *The Day They Robbed the Bank of England. Never Let Go.* 1962: *55 Days at Peking. The Webster Boy.* 1963: *The Chalk Garden.* 1967: *The Mummy's Shroud.* 1973: *The Hireling.* 1990: *A Ghost in Monte Carlo (TV).*

SELLECK, Tom 1945–
Big, dark, heavily-moustached, bearlike

American actor of seemingly gentle disposition. In minor leading roles in his twenties, his career seemed to go backwards after that until it took off again with his casting as the detective in the TV series *Magnum PI*; to do the series he had to turn down the leading role in *Raiders of the Lost Ark.* His bulk, all 6' 4" of it, and good looks, kept him going as tough action heroes into the 1990s, with a few fair forays into light comedy. From 1991, though, his faint lack of personality and increasingly hangdog features consigned him to lesser fare.
1969: *Judd for the Defense: The Holy Ground (TV).* 1970: *Myra Breckinridge. The Movie Murderer (TV).* 1971: *The Seven Minutes.* 1972: *Daughters of Satan.* 1973: *Terminal Island (GB: Knuckle-Men).* 1974: *Washington Affair. A Case of Rape (TV).* 1975: *Returning Home (TV).* 1976: *Bunco (TV). Most Wanted (TV. Later: Killer). Midway (GB: Battle of Midway).* 1977: *Coma.* 1978: *Superdome (TV). The Gypsy Warriors.* 1979: *The Sacketts (TV). Concrete Cowboys (TV).* 1982: *Divorce Wars (TV). The Shadow Riders (TV). The Chinese Typewriter (TV).* 1983: *High Road to China. Lassiter.* 1984: *Runaway.* 1986: *Sullivan's Travels (TV).* 1987: *3 Men and a Baby.* 1988: *Her Alibi.* 1989: *An Innocent Man.* 1990: *Quigley Down Under. 3 Men and a Little Lady.* 1992: *Mr Baseball/ Tokyo Diamond. Folks! Christopher Columbus: The Discovery.* 1994: *Open Season.* 1995: *Ruby Jean and Joe. Broken Trust (TV).* 1997: *In & Out. Last Stand at Saber River (TV).* 1999: *The Love Letter.* 2000: *Running Mates (TV). The Crossfire Trail (TV).*

SELLERS, Peter
(Richard Sellers) 1925–1980
Plump-faced, dark-haired, apprehensive-looking British comic actor who sprang to fame as a man of many funny voices on radio, then hit his stride in an hilarious series of comedies from 1957 to 1963, before his talent began to overreach itself. Recovered from a serious heart attack in 1964, but only occasionally regained his old brilliance. Married to Britt Ekland 1963–1968 and Lynne Frederick (1954–) from 1977, second and fourth wives, and suffered several minor heart attacks before another major one killed him. Oscar nominee for *Dr Strangelove* and *Being There.*
1951: *Penny Points to Paradise. Let's Go Crazy. London Entertains. Burlesque on Carmen (sound reissue, narrator only).* 1952: *Down Among the Z Men.* 1953: **The Super*

Secret Service. Our Girl Friday (US: The Adventures of Sadie: voice only). 1954: Orders Are Orders. 1955: John and Julie. The Ladykillers. *The Case of the Mukkinese Battlehorn. 1956: The Man Who Never Was (voice only). 1957: *Insomnia is Good for You. *Cold Comfort. The Smallest Show on Earth. *Dearth of a Salesman. The Naked Truth (US: Your Past is Showing). 1958: Up the Creek. tom thumb. 1959: Carlton-Browne of the FO (US: Man in a Cocked Hat). The Battle of the Sexes. I'm All Right, Jack. The Mouse That Roared. Two-Way Stretch. 1960: Climb Up the Wall. *The Running, Jumping and Standing Still Film. Never Let Go. The Millionairess. 1961: Only Two Can Play. †Mr Topaze (US: I Like Money). Lolita. 1962: The Waltz of the Toreadors. The Road to Hong Kong. The Dock Brief (US: Trial and Error). The Wrong Arm of the Law. 1963: Heavens Above! Dr Strangelove, or: How I Learned to Stop Worrying and Love the Bomb. The Pink Panther. 1964: A Shot in the Dark. A Carol for Another Christmas (TV). The World of Henry Orient. 1965: What's New Pussycat? 1966: After the Fox. The Wrong Box. *Birds, Bees and Storks (narrator only). 1967: Woman Times Seven. The Bobo. Casino Royale. 1968: The Party. I Love You, Alice B. Toklas. 1969: The Magic Christian. 1970: Hoffman. *Simon, Simon. There's A Girl in My Soup. A Day at the Beach. 1971: Where Does it Hurt? 1972: Alice's Adventures in Wonderland. 1973: Soft Beds, Hard Battles (US: Undercovers Hero). The Optimists of Nine Elms. The Blockhouse. 1974: The Return of the Pink Panther. Ghost in the Noonday Sun. The Great McGonagall. 1976: Murder By Death. The Pink Panther Strikes Again. 1978: Revenge of the Pink Panther. The Prisoner of Zenda. The Great Pram Race (voice only). 1979: Being There. 1980: The Fiendish Plot of Dr Fu Manchu. 1982: Trail of the Pink Panther.

†Also directed

SEVIGNY, Chloë 1974–
Fair-haired, clear-faced American fashion designer turned actress. She began her career working as a fashion assistant on a New York magazine, then got into show business via her appearances in music videos. She began to make strides towards the front rank of Hollywood actresses after her Academy Award nomination for *Boys Don't Cry*. A long-term relationship with director Harmony Korine (she was both

actress and costume designer on his film *Gummo*) eventually broke up.
1995: Kids. 1996: Trees Lounge. 1997: Gummo. 1998: The Last Days of Disco. Palmetto/Just Another Sucker. 1999: Julien Donkey-Boy. Boys Don't Cry. A Map of the World. 2000: If These Walls Could Talk 2 (TV). American Psycho.

SEWELL, Rufus 1967–
Brooding, curly-haired, dark-eyed, unsmiling British leading man of medium height, plus a smouldering personality that seemed to qualify him for playing roles like *Lady Chatterley's Lover*. Only in *Cold Comfort Farm*, though, has he really been trapped in that image, and has in fact found a good range of roles in his 10 years in the cinema, although he has always been most successful playing slightly dubious characters.
1991: Twenty One. The Last Romantics (TV). 1992: Dirty Weekend. 1994: A Man of No Importance. 1995: Cold Comfort Farm (TV. Later: cinemas). Victory (released 1997). Carrington. 1996: Hamlet. 1997: Dark City. 1998: The Woodlanders. Martha – Meet Frank, Daniel and Laurence (US: The Very Thought of You). Dangerous Beauty (GB: The Honest Courtesan). At Sachem Farm/Trade Winds. Illuminata. 1999: In a Savage Land. 2000: Bless the Child. 2001: A Knight's Tale.

SEYMOUR, Jane
(Joyce Frankenberger) 1951–
Strikingly lovely British brunette actress whose career faltered after she was cast as the heroine in a James Bond film. She later seemed typed as high-born ladies and painted dolls but, right at the end of the 1970s and in between cosmetics commercials, signs of real

talent began to emerge and she gave notable performances in *Somewhere in Time* and the TV mini-series and movie *East of Eden* and *Dark Mirror*. But she has been seen in increasingly shallow roles in more recent times and became a prolific TV movie star. Her TV western series *Dr Quinn Medicine Woman* was a great success in the mid 1990s. Married (fourth of four) to actor-director James Keach.
1969: Oh! What a Lovely War. 1970: Oktober-Dage (GB: The Only Way). 1972: Young Winston. 1973: Frankenstein–The True Story (TV. GB: cinemas in abridged version). Live and Let Die. 1974: The Hanged Man (TV). 1976: Morir . . . dormir . . . tal vez soñar. 1977: Sinbad and the Eye of the Tiger. Benny and Barney: Las Vegas Undercover (TV). Killer on Board (TV). 1978: Battlestar Galactica (TV. GB: cinemas). The Four Feathers (TV. GB: cinemas). Matilda. Dallas Cowboy Cheerleaders (TV). Love's Dark Ride (TV). 1979: The Pirate (TV). 1980: Oh Heavenly Dog. Somewhere in Time. 1981: East of Eden (TV). 1982: Phantom of the Opera (TV). 1983: Lassiter. Jamaica Inn. The Haunting Passion (TV). The Scarlet Pimpernel (TV). 1984: Dark Mirror (TV). 1985: Obsessed with a Married Woman (TV). The Sun Also Rises (TV). 1986: Head Office. 1987: The Tunnel. 1988: The Woman He Loved (TV). 1989: Keys to Freedom. 1990: The French Revolution. Angel of Death (TV). Matters of the Heart. Onassis: The Richest Man in the World (TV). 1991: Memories of Midnight. 1992: Are You Lonesome Tonight? (TV). Sunstroke. Dr Quinn Medicine Woman (TV). 1993: Praying Mantis (TV). Quest for Justice (TV). 1996: The Absolute Truth (TV). 1997: Spin (TV). 1998: The New Swiss Family Robinson. The Magic Sword: Quest for Camelot (voice only). A Marriage of Convenience (TV). 1999: A Memory in My Heart. 2000: Murder in the Mirror (TV). Enslavement: The True Story of Fanny Kemble (TV). 2001: Blackout (TV).

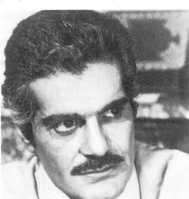

SHARIF, Omar (Michel Shalhoub) 1932–
Black-haired Egyptian actor with flashing dark eyes and faintly bogus smile. Built up a reputation as the number one male pin-up of the Egyptian cinema from 1954 to 1961 before venturing into international films. Was cast almost entirely in blockbuster epics, and found, in the seventies, that the public were less willing to accept him in smaller-scale dramas. Later in co-starring roles, and con-

centrating on his first love – bridge. Nominated for an Academy Award in *Lawrence of Arabia*. Also a former Egyptian soccer international! Married (first of two) to Egyptian-born star Faten Hamama (1931–) from 1955 to 1974.

*1954: ‡The Blazing Sun. ‡Our Happy Days. ‡Devil of the Sahara. 1955: ‡Struggle on the Pier. ‡Land of Peace. 1956: ‡No Sleep. †La chatelaine du Liban. 1957: †Shore of Secrets. †My Lover's Mistake. †Goha. 1958: †For the Sake of a Woman. †The Lady of the Castle. †Rendezvous with a Stranger. †Scandal at Zamalek. 1959: †We The Students. †Struggle on the Nile. 1960: †Love Rumour. †The Beginning and the End. †The Agony of Love. †River of Love. †The Mamelukes (GB: Revolt of the Mamelukes). †I Love My Boss. †My Only Love. 1961: †A Man in Our House. 1962: Lawrence of Arabia. 1963: The Fall of the Roman Empire. 1964: The Fabulous Adventures of Marco Polo (GB: Marco the Magnificent). Behold a Pale Horse. The Yellow Rolls Royce. 1965: Genghis Kahn. Doctor Zhivago. 1966: The Night of the Generals. The Poppy is Also a Flower (TV. GB: cinemas as Danger Grows Wild). 1967: C'era una volta/ Once Upon a Time (GB: Cinderella Italian Style. US: More Than a Miracle). 1968: Funny Girl. Mayerling. Mackenna's Gold. 1969: The Appointment. Che! 1970: *Simon, Simon. The Horsemen. The Last Valley. 1971: Le casse (GB and US: The Burglars). 1972: Elle lui chrait dans l'île/The Right to Love (GB: TV, as Brainwashed). 1973: The Mysterious Island of Captain Nemo. 1974: Juggernaut. The Tamarind Seed. 1975: Funny Lady. Crime and Passion. 1976: The Pink Panther Strikes Again. 1979: Ashanti. Bloodline/Sidney Sheldon's Bloodline. S*H*E*. The Baltimore Bullet. 1980: Oh Heavenly Dog. Pleasure Palace (TV). 1981: Chanel solitaire. Green Ice. 1984: Ayoub (TV). Top Secret! 1987: La novice. Chatov et les démons. The Possessed. 1988: Grand Larceny (TV). Les pyramides bleues. 1989: Keys to Freedom. Michelangelo and Me. 1990: The Rainbow Thief (unreleased). Beyond Justice. 1991: The Castle. Viaggio d'amore. Al moaten al myssri (US: War in the Land of Egypt). Memories of Midnight. Mayrig/ Mother. 1992: 588 Rue Paradis. Mrs 'Arris Goes to Paris (TV). 1993: Tengoku no taizai/Sin of Heaven. 1994: The Will in Sand. Red Eagle (TV). 1996: Heaven Before I Die. Umm Kulthum. A Voice Like Egypt. 1999: The 13th Warrior. 2000: Mysteries of Egypt.*

‡As Omar el Cherif
†As Omar Cherif

SHATNER, William 1931–

Solidly-built Canadian actor with dark, curly hair and easy smile. After a start in repertory in his native Montreal, he broke into American television in 1956, films from 1958. Despite a promising start in *The Brothers Karamazov*, Shatner's film career faltered during the 1960s and it took a successful TV series, *Star Trek*, to make his name and face familiar. Film assignments, however, continued to be largely outside the mainstream, but he had another hit television series in the 1980s with *T J Hooker*, and

appeared in a number of successful *Star Trek* films. Three times married.

1957: The Defenders (TV). No Deadly Medicine (TV). 1958: A Town Has Turned to Dust (TV). The Brothers Karamazov. 1961: Judgment at Nuremberg. The Intruder (GB: The Stranger). The Explosive Generation. 1964: The Outrage. 1968: Hour of Vengeance. 1969: Sole Survivor. 1971: Vanished (TV). Owen Marshall, Counsellor at Law (TV). 1972: The People (TV). The Hound of the Baskervilles (TV). 1973: Incident on a Dark Street (TV). Go Ask Alice (TV). The Horror at 37,000 Feet (TV). Pioneer Woman (TV). 1974: Dead of Night. Indict and Convict (TV). Big Bad Mama. Pray for the Wildcats (TV). 1975: Impulse. Barbary Coast (TV. GB: In Old San Francisco). The Devil's Rain. 1976: Perilous Voyage (TV). A Whale of a Tale. 1977: Kingdom of the Spiders. 1978: Land of No Return (released 1981). Little Women (TV). The Third Walker. Crash (TV). 1979: Riel. Star Trek The Motion Picture. The Kidnapping of the President. 1980: The Babysitter (TV). 1981: Visiting Hours. 1982: Star Trek The Wrath of Khan. Airplane II: The Sequel. 1984: Secrets of a Married Man (TV). Star Trek III: The Search for Spock. 1985: North Beach and Rawhide (TV). 1986: The Voyage Home Star Trek IV. Blood Sport (TV). 1988: Broken Angel (TV). 1989: †Star Trek V: The Final Frontier. 1991: Star Trek VI: The Undiscovered Country. 1993: Family of Strangers (TV). National Lampoon's Loaded Weapon 1. Warriors. Janek: A Silent Betrayal (TV). 1994: †Tekwar (TV). Star Trek Generations. 1995: Dead Man's Island (TV). 1996: The Prisoner of Zenda Inc (TV). Project ALF (TV). 1998: Free Enterprise. Land of the Free. 1999: The First Men on the Moon (video). 2000: Osmosis Jones (voice only). Miss Congeniality. 2001: Falcon Down.

†And directed

SHAW, Robert 1927–1978

Wide-faced, forceful British actor who made his name as a man of action in a fifties' TV series, *The Buccaneers*, moved into more thoughtful roles, then eventually returned to adventures. Powered his way into world stardom by the seventies, but was killed by a heart attack. Married to Mary Ure (second of three) from 1963 to her death in 1975. Also a best-selling writer. Nominated for an Academy Award in *A Man for All Seasons*.
1951: The Lavender Hill Mob. 1954: The Dam

*Busters. 1956: Doublecross. A Hill in Korea (US: Hell in Korea). 1958: Sea Fury. 1959: Libel. 1961: The Valiant. 1962: Tomorrow at Ten. 1963: The Cracksman. The Caretaker. From Russia with Love. *North to the Dales (narrator only). 1964: The Luck of Ginger Coffey. Carol for Another Christmas (TV). 1965: Battle of the Bulge. 1966: A Man for All Seasons. Custer of the West. 1969: Battle of Britain. The Royal Hunt of the Sun. The Birthday Party. 1970: Figures in a Landscape. 1971: A Town Called Bastard (US: A Town Called Hell). Young Winston. A Reflection of Fear. 1973: The Hireling. The Sting. 1974: The Taking of Palham 1-2-3. 1975: Diamonds. Jaws. The Judge and His Hangman (US: End of the Game. Later: Deception). 1976: Robin and Marian. Swashbuckler (GB: The Scarlet Buccaneer). Black Sunday. 1977: The Deep. 1978: Force Ten from Navarone. 1979: Avalanche Express.*

SHAW, Susan (Patsy Sloots) 1929–1978

Lovely British blonde actress, on stage as a teenager, who came up through the Rank 'Charm School' of the forties, and played working-class glamour girls. Married to Albert Lieven 1949–1953 and Bonar Colleano (both *qv*) 1954 to his death in 1958, first and second of three. Later fell on hard times, and died in poverty from cirrhosis of the liver, her funeral being paid for by Rank.
1946: London Town (US: My Heart Goes Crazy). Walking on Air. 1947: The Upturned Glass. Jassy. Holiday Camp. It Always Rains on Sunday. 1948: To the Public Danger. My Brother's Keeper. London Belongs to Me (US: Dulcimer Street). Quartet. Here Come the Huggetts. 1949: It's Not Cricket. Vote for Huggett. Marry Me. The Huggetts Abroad.

Train of Events. 1950: Waterfront (US: Waterfront Women). The Woman in Question (US: Five Angles on Murder). Pool of London. 1951: There is Another Sun (US: Wall of Death). 1952: Wide Boy. A Killer Walks. 1953: Small Town Story. The Large Rope. The Intruder. 1954: The Good Die Young. Devil's Point (US: Devil's Harbor). Time is My Enemy. 1955: Stolen Time (US: Blonde Blackmailer). Stock Car. 1956: Fire Maidens from Outer Space. 1957: Davy. 1958: Diplomatic Corpse. Girls at Sea. Chain of Events. 1959: Carry on Nurse. 1960: The Big Day. 1962: Stranglehold. 1963: The Switch.

SHEARER, Norma
(Edith N. Fisher) 1900–1983
Brown-haired Canadian actress who married M-G-M's top producer of the twenties and thirties, Irving Thalberg, and became the studio's first lady until his death in 1936. Her well-bred looks and ultra-smart wardrobe made her a byword for chic sophistication, although she sometimes could not stay away from roles from which she was too old. Academy Award for *The Divorcee*. Also nominated for Academy Awards on *Their Own Desire*, *The Barretts of Wimpole Street*, *Romeo and Juliet*, *A Free Soul* and *Marie Antoinette*. Died from bronchial pneumonia.
*1920: Way Down East. The Flapper. The Stealers. The Restless Sex. 1921: The Sign on the Door. *The End of the World. Torchy's Millions. 1922: The Bootleggers. The Devil's Partner. Channing of the Northwest. The Man Who Paid. The Leather Pushers (serial). 1923: Pleasure Mad. A Clouded Name. Man and Wife. The Wanters. Lucretia Lombard. 1924: Blue Waters. Broadway After Dark. Empty Hands. He Who Gets Slapped. Married Flirts. Trail of the Law. The Wolf Man. Broken Barriers. The Snob. 1925: Pretty Ladies. Lady of the Night. The Tower of Lies. His Secretary. A Slave of Fashion. Excuse Me. Waking Up the Town. 1926: Upstage (GB: The Mask of Comedy). The Devil's Circus. The Waning Sex. 1927: The Student Prince. The Demi-Bride. After Midnight. 1928: Lady of Chance. The Latest from Paris. The Actress (GB: Trelawney of the Wells). *Voices Across the Sea. 1929: Hollywood Revue of 1929 (and German version). The Trial of Mary Dugan. The Last of Mrs Cheyney. 1930: Let Us Be Gay. The Divorcee. Their Own Desire. 1931: Private Lives. Strangers May Kiss. A Free Soul. *Jackie Cooper's Christmas (GB: The Christmas Party). 1932: Smilin' Through.*

*The Stolen Jools (GB: The Slippery Pearls). Strange Interlude (GB: Strange Interval). 1934: Riptide. *Hollywood on Parade No 13. The Barretts of Wimpole Street. 1936: Romeo and Juliet. 1938: Marie Antoinette. 1939: The Women. Idiot's Delight. *Screen Snapshots, Series 18, No. 8. 1940: Escape. 1941: *Cavalcade of the Academy Awards. 1942: We Were Dancing. Her Cardboard Lover.*

SHEEDY, Ally (Alexandra Sheedy) 1962–
Dark-haired, chirpy-looking American actress, dancer, poetess and all-round child prodigy who somehow contrives to look quite different in every film in which she appears. She had a children's book published at 12 and reviewed children's literature for the *New York Times* the following year. At 15 she was acting in TV commercials and had a leading role in a TV movie at 18. Filmwise, she became part of the then-current 'youth ensemble' pictures and soon demonstrated the ability to touch the emotions. She overcame problems with drugs, alcohol and bulimia in the 1980s, but her films have been mostly video fodder for the past 10 years.
1980: The Best Little Girl in the World (TV). 1981: The Day the Loving Stopped (TV). Splendor in the Grass (TV). 1982: Deadly Lessons (TV). 1983: Bad Boys. WarGames. 1984: Oxford Blues. The Breakfast Club. 1985: St Elmo's Fire. Twice in a Lifetime. 1986: Blue City. Short Circuit. 1987: Maid to Order. We Are the Children (TV). 1989: Heart of Dixie. 1990: Fear. Betsy's Wedding. The Lost Capone (TV). 1991: Only the Lonely. 1992: Tattle Tale/Kiss and Tell. Home Alone 2: Lost in New York. 1993: Man's Best Friend. Lethal Exposure (TV). The Pickle. Chantilly Lace (TV). 1994: One Night Stand/Before the Night. Parallel Lives (TV). Ultimate Betrayal (TV). The Haunting of Seacliff Inn (TV). Red Shoe Diaries 4: Auto Erotica (video). 1995: The Tin Soldier (TV). 1996: Hijacked: Flight 285 (TV). Amnesia. 1997: Myth America. Crossroads of Destiny/Jailbreak (TV). The Definite Maybe. Highball/Mr Jealousy. Groupies. Amnesia. Family Rescue (TV). Buried Alive II (cable TV). 1998: High Art. The Autumn Heart. 1999: The Fury Within (TV). Sugar Town. Our Guys (TV). I'll Take You There.

SHEEN, Charlie (Carlos Estevez) 1965–
Square-faced, thickly dark-haired American leading man, only of average height, but solidly built and with an air of sharp aggres-

siveness. The brother of Emilio Estevez and son of Martin Sheen (both *qv*), he's been acting since boyhood, and has now toned down a wild lifestyle to present a more powerful image. A top pin-up of the late 1980s. Billed as Charles Sheen in some recent films, he seems to have lost his place in the mainstream cinema.
1974: The Execution of Private Slovik (TV). 1982: Grizzly II: The Predator. 1984: Red Dawn. Silence of the Heart (TV). The Boys Next Door. 1985: Three for the Road (released 1987). Out of the Darkness (TV). The Fourth Wise Man (TV). 1986: Lucas. The Wraith. Ferris Bueller's Day Off. Platoon. Wisdom. 1987: Wall Street. No Man's Land. 1988: Eight Men Out. Johnny Utah (unfinished). Young Guns. Never on a Tuesday. 1989: Major League. Courage Mountain. Backtrack (GB: Catchfire). A Tale of Two Sisters (narrator only). 1990: Men at Work. Cadence (GB: Stockade). Navy SEALS. The Rookie. 1991: Hot Shots! Stop at Nothing. 1992: Fixing the Shadow/Beyond the Law. 1993: Deadfall. Hot Shots! Part Deux. Frame by Frame. National Lampoon's Loaded Weapon 1. The Three Musketeers. 1994: The Chase. Major League II. Terminal Velocity. 1995: Martin Eden. Wings of Courage. 1996: All Dogs Go to Heaven II (voice only). Shadow Conspiracy. The Arrival/Shockwave. 1997: Loose Women. Bad Day on the Block. Money Talks. 1998: Postmortem. No Code of Conduct. Five Aces. Free Money. A Letter from Death Row. 1999: Being John Malkovich. 2000: Rated X (cable TV). Famous. 2001: Good Advice.

SHEEN, Martin (Ramon Estevez) 1940–
Good-looking, brooding, tight-lipped, dark-

haired American actor, perhaps the first star of the seventies to be made by TV work. In the theatre since 1960, but it was 10 years before films and TV caught up with his talent, and then his youthful looks enabled him to play men in their early twenties. He has been in two or three of the best TV movies ever made, but his film work – apart from *Badlands* – has been disappointingly routine. Three sons, Emilio Estevez, Charlie Sheen (both *qv*) and Ramon Sheen are also actors. Won an Emmy for directing the TV special *Babies Having Babies* in 1986. He made more than 50 films and TV movies in the 1990s.
1967: The Incident. 1968: The Subject Was Roses. Then Came Bronson (TV. GB: cinemas). 1970: †When the Line Goes Through. The Andersonville Trial (TV). Catch 22. 1971: †The Forests Are Nearly All Gone. Welcome Home, Johnny Bristol (TV). Mongo's Back in Town (TV). Goodbye, Raggedy Ann (TV). No Drums, No Bugles. 1972: Rage. Crime Club (TV). Pursuit (TV). That Certain Summer (TV). Pick Up on 101 (GB: Echoes of the Road). 1973: Message to My Daughter (TV). Letters from Three Lovers (TV). Catholics (TV). Harry O (TV). A Prowler in the Heart (TV). The Execution of Private Slovik (TV). Badlands. 1974: Pretty Boy Floyd (TV). The Missiles of October (TV). The California Kid (TV). 1975: The Legend of Earl Durand. Roman Gray (TV. GB: The Art of Crime). Sweet Hostage (TV). The Last Survivors (TV). 1976: The Cassandra Crossing. The Little Girl Who Lives Down the Lane. 1978: Eagle's Wing. 1979: Apocalypse Now. 1980: The Final Countdown. Loophole. 1981: Blind Ambition (TV). 1982: Gandhi. In the Custody of Strangers (TV). Enigma. That Championship Season. *No Place to Hide (narrator only). In The King of Prussia. Man, Woman and Child. 1983: Kennedy (TV). The Dead Zone. Choices of the Heart (TV). 1984: Firestarter. The Atlanta Child Murders (TV). ‡ Listen to the City. The Guardian (TV). 1985: Consenting Adults (TV). In the Name of the People (narrator only). Shattered Spirits (TV). The Fourth Wise Man (TV). Out of the Darkness (TV). A State of Emergency. 1986: News at Eleven (TV). Samaritan: The Mitch Snyder Story (TV). Broken Rainbow (voice only). 1987: The Believers. Wall Street. Judgment in Berlin. Conspiracy: The Trial of the Chicago 8 (TV). Siesta. Dear America (voice only). Da. 1989: Beverly Hills Brats. Walking After Midnight. Cold Front. Nightbreaker (TV). Marked for Murder. Beyond the Stars. 1990: Cadence (GB: Stockade. And directed). Original Intent. The Maid. 1991: Limited Time. Another Time, Another Place. Hearts of Darkness: A Filmmaker's Apocalypse. JFK (narrator only). Presumed Guilty (TV). Touch and Die. 1992: Garwood: Prisoner of War – A True Story (completed 1990). Running Wild. The Water Engine (TV). 1993: Finnegan's Wake. Two Rivers. Hear No Evil. My Home, My Prison (narrator only). Reason to Believe. When the Bough Breaks. The Killing Box/Ghost Brigade. Hot Shots! Part Deux. Gettysburg. Final Justice (TV). Guns of Honor. Fortunes of War. Trigger Fast. 1994: The Break. Hits! One of Our Own/One of Her Own (TV). Roswell (TV). Gospa. A Hundred and

One Nights. Boca. 1995: Sacred Cago. Captain Nuke & the Bomber Boys. Dillinger and Capone. Dead Presidents. The American President. Entertaining Angels: The Dorothy Day Story (TV). 1996: The War at Home. Project ALF (TV). The Elevator. Crystal Care (TV). 1997: Spawn. Act of Conscience (narrator only). Hostile Waters (TV). Truth or Consequences, N. M. Tudjman (narrator only). 1998: A Stranger in the Kingdom. Voyage of Terror (TV). River of Souls (TV). Free Money. Family Attraction. Snitch/Monument Avenue. No Code of Conduct. Noose. A Letter from Death Row. 1999: Seeing in the Dark. Storm (TV). A Texas Funeral. Lost & Found. Forget Me Never (TV). The Time Shifters (cable TV). D.R.E.A.M. Team (TV). The Darklings (TV). Ninth Street. 2000: 'O'. Mexico (narrator only).

†Unreleased
‡Scene deleted from final release print

SHEFFIELD, Johnny 1931–
A freckle-faced American boy actor with fair, curly hair who played Tarzan's son, and then, when he grew up, Bomba the Jungle Boy. Sheffield quit films at the age of 25, and, for many years, made his career in real estate. Son of Reginald Sheffield (1901–1957), a child star of the silents in his native Britain, who came to America in the 1920s and, after taking the lead in *David Copperfield* (1923), played mainly character roles until his death.
1939: Tarzan Finds a Son! Babes in Arms. 1940: Little Orvie. Lucky Cisco Kid. Knute Rockne – All American (GB: A Modern Hero). 1941: Million Dollar Baby. Tarzan's Secret Treasure. 1942: Tarzan's New York Adventure. 1943: Tarzan Triumphs. Tarzan's Desert Mystery. 1944: The Great Manhunt. Our Hearts Were Young and Gay. The Man in Half Moon Street. Wilson. 1945: Roughly Speaking. Tarzan and the Amazons. 1946: Tarzan and the Leopard Woman. 1947: Tarzan and the Huntress. 1949: Bomba the Jungle Boy. Bomba on Panther Island. 1950: The Lost Volcano. Bomba and the Hidden City. 1951: The Lion Hunters (GB: Bomba and the Lion Hunters). Bomba and the Elephant Stampede. 1952: African Treasure (GB: Bomba and the African Treasure). Bomba and the Jungle Girl. 1953: Safari Drums (GB: Bomba and the Safari Drums). 1954: The Golden Idol. Killer Leopard. 1955: Lord of the Jungle. 1956: The Black Sleep. 1960: Midnight Lace.

SHEFFIELD, Reginald
See SHEFFIELD, Johnny

SHELLEY, Barbara (B. Kowin) 1933–
Lovely brunette British leading lady of porcelain beauty who spent the first three years of her career in Italian films, then came home to become the first lady of British horror films, proving a match for, and sometimes even turning into, things that went bump in the House of Hammer.
1953: †Mantrap (US: Woman in Hiding). 1954: Ballata tragica/Love without Tomorrow. The Barefoot Contessa. 1955: La crime di spora. Luna nuova. Motivo in maschera. I quattro del getto tonante/Four in a Thunderjet. 1956: Destinazione Piovarolo. Suprema confessione. The Little Hut. Mio figlio Nerone/Nero's Weekend. 1957: Cat Girl. The End of the Line. 1958: The Camp on Blood Island. The Solitary Child. Blood of the Vampire. 1959: Deadly Record. Bobbikins. Murder at Site Three. 1960: A Story of David. Village of the Damned. 1961: The Shadow of the Cat. 1962: Death Trap. Postman's Knock. Stranglehold. 1963: Blind Corner. 1964: The Secret of Blood Island. The Gorgon. 1965: Dracula – Prince of Darkness. Rasputin the Mad Monk. 1967: Quatermass and the Pit (US: 5,000,000 Miles to Earth). 1969: The Spy Killer (TV). 1974: Ghost Story (US: Madhouse Mansion). 1988: Maigret (TV). 1992: More Than a Messiah.

†As Barbara Kowin

SHELTON, Joy (Joyce Shelton) 1922–2000
Dark-haired British actress with gentle, refined features and faintly old-fashioned looks. A RADA scholarship winner at 15. Played a good variety of wives, waifs and (not

always willingly) waiting women in films, and became much loved on radio as the girlfriend of the bungling PC49 in a long-running comedy-thriller series, a role she later repeated on film. From the mid-1950s she worked mostly in the theatre. Married to actor Sydney Tafler (b1916) from 1944 to his death in 1979. Died from emphysema.

1943: Millions Like Us. 1944: Bees in Paradise. Waterloo Road. 1946: Send for Paul Temple. 1948: Uneasy Terms. *Designing Women. No Room at the Inn. 1950: The Golden Age (narrator only). Midnight Episode. Once a Sinner. 1951: A Case for PC49. 1952: Emergency Call (US: Hundred Hour Hunt). 1953: Park Plaza 605 (US: Norman Conquest). 1955: Impulse. 1960: No Kidding (US: Beware of Children). 1961: The Greengage Summer (US: Loss of Innocence). Five Golden Hours. 1962: HMS Defiant (US: Damn the Defiant!).

SHEPARD, Sam (S.S. Rogers) 1943–
Lean-faced (it seems somehow permanently in shadow), dark-haired, soft-spoken American Pulitzaer Prize-winning playwright and on-off actor and singer. The son of an Air Force man who retired to be a farmer, Shepard is a country-loving man reclaimed by acting (in which he made his show-business start) after big writing successes off and on Broadway. Now combines the two careers. Has lived for some years with actress Jessica Lange (*qv*). Nominated for an Academy Award for his performance in *The Right Stuff*, his characters exude quiet charisma and authority. The secret of directing successful films, however, has so far eluded him.

1969: Easy Rider (voice only). 1977: Renaldo and Clara. 1978: Days of Heaven. 1980: Resurrection. 1981: Raggedy Man. 1982: Frances. 1983: The Right Stuff. 1984: Country. 1985: Fool for Love. 1986: Crimes of the Heart. 1987: Baby Boom. 1989: Steel Magnolias. 1990: Defenseless. Bright Angel. 1991: Voyager. 1992: Thunderheart. 1993: The Pelican Brief. 1994: Safe Passage. The Northern Lights. 1995: The Good Old Boys (TV). 1996: Lily Dale (TV). 1997: The Only Thrill/Tennessee Valley. 1998: Purgatory (TV). 1999: One Kill (TV). Curtain Call. Snow Falling on Cedars. Dash and Lily (TV). 2000: One Kill (TV). All the Pretty Horses. The Pledge. 2001: Just to Be Together.
As director: *1988: Far North. 1993: Silent Tongue.*

SHEPHERD, Cybill 1949–
Blonde, forties-style Hollywood beauty, who plays characters who cock a snook at conventions. Was for several years associated with director Peter Bogdanovich, and appeared in a number of his films. Her career faltered when the relationship broke up. But she had the talent to survive, and certainly scored a big personal success in the 1980s with the TV series *Moonlighting*. She was out of the big time again by the early 1990s but back to TV success, with *Cybill*.

1971: The Last Picture Show. 1972: The Heartbreak Kid. 1974: Daisy Miller. 1975: At Long Last Love. 1976: Taxi Driver. Special Delivery. 1977: Silver Bears. Aliens from Spaceship Earth. 1978: A Guide for the Married Woman (TV). 1979: The Lady Vanishes. 1981: The Return. 1984: Secrets of a Married Man (Video). 1985: Moonlighting (TV) Seduced (TV). 1989: Chances Are. 1990: Texasville. Alice. 1991: Married to It. Which Way Home? (TV). Once Upon a Crime. Picture This. 1992: Memphis (TV). Stormy Weathers (TV). Telling Secrets (TV). 1993: There Was a Little Boy (TV). 1994: The Last Word. While Justice Sleeps (TV). 1995: Baby Brokers (TV). 1996: Journey of the Heart (TV). 1999: The Muse. 2000: Marine Life.

SHERIDAN, Ann
(Clara Lou Sheridan) 1915–1967
Tough but hopeful: those were the characters that this fair-haired American actress played in her heyday, even before she became world famous as the 'oomph girl'. She'd been kicked around, but was still an optimist: the mould suited the wartime years, and the wide-faced, mockingly-smiling star herself, who had appeared in numerous small roles before

hitting the big time. Married to Edward Norris (1910–) from 1936–1939 and George Brent (*qv*) from 1942–1943, first and second of three. Died from cancer.

1933: †Search for Beauty. 1934:†The Lemon Drop Kid. †One Hour Late. †Ready for Love. †Ladies Should Listen. †Murder at the Vanities. †Bolero. †Shoot the Works (GB: Thank Your Stars). †Mrs Wiggs of the Cabbage Patch. †You Belong to Me. †Come on, Marines. †Kiss and Make Up. †The Notorious Sophie Lang. †College Rhythm. †Wagon Wheels. †Limehouse Blues. 1935: Hollywood Extra Girl. †Rumba. †Enter Madame. †Home on the Range. Rocky Mountain Mystery. Behold My Wife. The Glass Key. Fighting Youth. *Star Night at the Cocoanut Grove. Mississippi. Car 99. The Crusades. Red Blood of Courage. 1936: Black Legion. Sing Me a Love Song (GB: Come Up Smiling). 1937: Wine, Women and Horses. The Great O'Malley. Footloose Heiress. San Quentin. 1938: The Patient in Room 18. Alcatraz Island. Cowboy from Brooklyn (GB: Romance and Rhythm). She Loved a Fireman. Mystery House. Little Miss Thoroughbred. Broadway Musketeers. Letter of Introduction. Angels with Dirty Faces. 1939: Naughty But Nice. The Angels Wash Their Faces. They Made Me a Criminal. Indianapolis Speedway (GB: Devil on Wheels). Winter Carnival. Dodge City. 1940: Torrid Zone. Castle on the Hudson (GB: Years without Days). City for Conquest. It All Came True. They Drive by Night (GB: The Road to Frisco). 1941: Honeymoon for Three. Kings Row. Navy Blues. The Man Who Came to Dinner. 1942: George Washington Slept Here. Juke Girl. Wings for the Eagle. 1943: Thank Your Lucky Stars. Edge of Darkness. 1944: The Doughgirls. Shine On, Harvest Moon. 1946: One More Tomorrow. 1947: Nora Prentiss. The Unfaithful. 1948: The Treasure of the Sierra Madre. Silver River. Good Sam. 1949: I Was a Male War Bride (GB: You Can't Sleep Here). 1950: Stella. Woman on the Run. 1952: Steel Town. Just Across the Street. 1953: Take Me to Town. Appointment in Honduras. 1955: Come Next Spring. 1956: The Opposite Sex. 1957: Triangle on Safari (US: Woman and the Hunter). Without Incident (TV).

†As Clara Lou Sheridan

SHERIDAN, Dinah (D. Mec) 1920–
Although fondly remembered from *Genevieve*, this fair-haired, grey-eyed, very

lovely British actress with smiling mouth and high cheekbones made only 25 films in nearly 20 years, and enjoyed just a few years as a star before retiring (too early) to marry her second husband (actor Jimmy Hanley was the first). A lone appearance in the seventies showed that she had lost none of her grace and charm and she later returned to try comedy and drama on TV.

1934: *I Give My Heart*. 1935: *Music Hath Charms*. 1936: *Irish and Proud of It*. *Landslide*. 1937: *Father Steps Out*. *Behind Your Back*. *Wings of the Morning*. 1938: *Merely Mr Hawkins*. 1939: *Full Speed Ahead*. 1942: *Salute John Citizen*. 1943: *Get Cracking*. *The Gentle Sex*. 1945: *29 Acacia Avenue* (US: *The Facts of Life*). *For You Alone*. *Murder in Reverse*. 1947: *The Hills of Donegal*. 1948: *Calling Paul Temple*. 1949: *The Story of Shirley Yorke*. *The Huggetts Abroad*. *Dark Secret*. 1950: *No Trace*. *Paul Temple's Triumph*. *Blackout*. 1951: *Where No Vultures Fly* (US: *Ivory Hunter*). 1952: *The Sound Barrier* (US: *Breaking the Sound Barrier*). *Appointment in London*. 1953: *The Story of Gilbert and Sullivan* (US: *The Great Gilbert and Sullivan*). *Genevieve*. 1970: *The Railway Children*. 1980: *The Mirror Crack'd*.

SHIELDS, Brooke
(Christa B. Shields) 1965–
Leggy, dark-haired, striking American actress with heavy eyebrows and lips. A child model, she started a whole new look in fashion modelling, as well as launching an acting career, principally with her role as a child prostitute in *Pretty Baby*. But she seemed unprepared or unable to offer more than a surface performance in later films, and the scripts were little help. Married/divorced tennis star André Agassi.

1976: *Communion/Alice Sweet Alice*. 1977: †*Morning, Winter and Night*. *The Prince of Central Park* (TV). 1978: *Pretty Baby*. *Wanda Nevada*. *King of the Gypsies*. *Tilt*. 1979: *Just You and Me Kid*. *An Almost Perfect Affair*. 1980: *The Blue Lagoon*. 1981: *Endless Love*. 1983: *Sahara*. 1984: *Wet Gold* (TV). *The Muppets Take Manhattan*. 1987: *Brenda Starr* (released 1989). 1988: *Young Guns* (gag bit). *The Diamond Trap* (TV). 1989: *Speed Zone*. 1990: *The Actor*. *Backstreet Dreams*. 1992: *An American Love*. 1993: *L'arbre métallique*. *Stalking Laura* (TV). *Freaked*. 1994: *Seventh Floor*. 1995: *Running Wild* (TV). *Vault of Love* (TV). 1996: *Freeway*. *The Almost Perfect Bank Robbery* (TV). 1997: *Scratch the Surface*

(doc). 1998: *The Misadventures of Margaret*. 1999: *The Weekend*. *Black and White*. 2000: *The Bachelor*. *After Sex*. 2001: *Mayor of the Sunset Strip* (doc).

†*Unfinished*

SHIMKUS, Joanna
See POITIER, Sidney

SHINER, Ronald 1903–1966
Raucous-voiced, beady-eyed, dark-haired British comedy actor who played dozens of cockney character parts before a repeat of a successful stage role (in *Worm's Eye View*) catapulted him to stardom. Once he reached the top he insured his substantial nose for £20,000. The 1950s saw him in a series of broad but at first very popular comedies (several of them remakes of 1930s' successes), before his popularity faded again late in the decade. He was a Mountie in his twenties. Forced to retire at 60 through ill-health, he died three years later from heart problems brought on by chronic bronchitis.

1934: *My Old Dutch*. *Doctor's Orders*. 1935: *Gentleman's Agreement*. *It's a Bet*. *Limelight* (US: *Backstage*). *Squibs*. *Royal Cavalcade* (US: *Regal Cavalcade*). *Once a Thief*. *Line Engaged*. *Escape Me Never*. *The Clairvoyant*. *While Parents Sleep*. 1936: *Excuse My Glove*. *King of Hearts*. 1937: *London Melody* (US: *Girls in the Street*). *Our Fighting Navy* (US: *Torpedoed!*). *Silver Blaze/Murder at the Baskervilles*. *Dreaming Lips*. *The Black Tulip*. *Farewell Again* (US: *Troopship*). *Dinner at the Ritz*. *Beauty and the Barge*. *A Yank at Oxford*. 1938: *Prison Without Bars*. *They Drive by Night*. *St Martin's Lane* (US: *Sidewalks of London*). 1939: *The Spider*. *Flying Fifty Five*. *The Mind of Mr Reeder* (US: *The Mysterious Mr Reeder*). *I Killed the Count* (US: *Who is Guilty?*). *Discoveries*. *The Middle Watch*. *Trouble Brewing*. *The Missing People*. *The Gang's All Here* (US: *The Amazing Mr Forrest*). *The Lion Has Wings*. *Come on George*. 1940: *'Bulldog' Sees It Through*. **Salvage with a Smile*. *Spare a Copper*. *Let George Do It*. *The Case of the Frightened Lady* (US: *The Frightened Lady*). *Old Bill and Son*. 1941: *The Black Sheep of Whitehall*. *South American George*. *The Seventh Survivor*. *Major Barbara*. *The Big Blockade*. *They Flew Alone* (US: *Wings and the Woman*). 1942: *The Young Mr Pitt*. *Sabotage at Sea*. *The Balloon Goes Up*. *Those Kids from Town*. *King Arthur Was a*

Gentleman. *The Night Invader*. *Unpublished Story*. *Squadron Leader X*. 1943: *The Gentle Sex*. *Get Cracking*. *Thursday's Child*. *Miss London Ltd*. *My Learned Friend*. *The Butler's Dilemma*. 1944: *Bees in Paradise*. 1945: *I Live in Grosvenor Square* (US: *A Yank in London*). *Caesar and Cleopatra*. *The Way to the Stars* (US: *Johnny in the Clouds*). 1946: *George in Civvy Street*. 1947: *Dusty Bates* (serial). *The Man Within* (US: *The Smugglers*). *The Ghosts of Berkeley Square*. *Brighton Rock* (US: *Young Scarface*). 1948: *Forbidden*. *Rise and Shiner*. 1951: *The Magic Box*. *Worm's Eye View*. *Reluctant Heroes*. 1952: *Little Big Shot*. *Top of the Form*. 1953: *Innocents in Paris*. *Laughing Anne*. 1954: *Aunt Clara*. *Up to His Neck*. 1955: *See How They Run*. 1956: *Keep It Clean*. *Dry Rot*. *My Wife's Family*. 1957: *Carry On Admiral* (US: *The Ship Was Loaded*). *Not Wanted on Voyage*. 1958: *Girls at Sea*. 1959: *Operation Bullshine*. *The Navy Lark*. 1960: *The Night We Got the Bird*.

SHIRE, Talia (née Coppola) 1945–
Petite, toothily pretty American actress with very dark hair, the sister of director Francis (Ford) Coppola. Usually plays 'ordinary' girls. After a few minor roles she had her first part of consequence in her brother's *The Godfather*, but has remained best known as Sylvester Stallone's girlfriend/wife in the *Rocky* films. Nominated for Academy Awards on *The Godfather Pt II* and *Rocky*. Turned producer in 1985 and made her first film as director 1994, later returning to acting.

1963: †*'X'* (GB: *The Man with the X-Ray Eyes*). 1966: †*You're a Big Boy Now*. 1968: †*The Wild Racers*. 1969: †*Don't Push, I'll Charge When I'm Ready* (TV). 1970: †*The Dunwich Horror*. †*Gas-s-s-s –or– It Became Necessary to Destroy the World in Order to Save It*. 1971: †*The Christian Licorice Store*. *The Godfather*. 1972: *Un homme est mort* (GB and US: *The Outside Man*). 1974: *The Godfather Pt II*. 1975: *Foster and Laurie* (TV). *Doctors' Secrets* (TV). 1976: *Rocky*. 1977: *Kill Me If You Can/The Caryl Chessman Story* (TV). 1978: *Old Boyfriends*. *Daddy, I Don't Like It Like This* (TV). 1979: *Rocky II*. *Corky*. *Prophecy*. 1980: *Windows*. 1982: *Rocky III*. 1983: *The Butcher*. *Rocky IV*. *Reel Horror*. 1986: *Rad*. *Hyper Sapien*. 1987: *Blood Vows: The Story of a Mafia Wife* (TV). 1989: *New York Stories*. *Bed and Breakfast*. 1990: *The Godfather Part III*.

Rocky V. 1992: Father, Son and the Mistress/ For Richer, For Poorer (TV). Mark Twain and Me (TV). Cold Heaven. 1993: Deadfall. Chantilly Lace (TV). 1997: Born into Exile (TV). River Made to Drown In. 1998: Can I Play? The Landlady. 1999: Palmer's Pick-Up. Divorce. Lured Innocence. Caminho dos sonhos. 2000: The Whole Shebang. The Visit. Your Aura is Throbbing.

As director: 1994: Before the Night/One Night Stand.

†*As Talia Coppola*

SHIRLEY, Anne
(Dawn Paris) 1918–1993

Pretty-as-a-picture auburn-haired child actress of the twenties (under the name Dawn O'Day) who, when she grew into a teenager, proved perfect casting for *Anne of Green Gables*, legally changing her name to that of the heroine in that film. Her films were too lachrymose for her to last, though she was a charming purveyor of sweetness-and-light through the tears. Married to John Payne 1937–1943, first of three. Nominated for an Academy Award on *Stella Dallas*. Died from lung cancer.

*1922: †The Hidden Woman. †Moonshine Valley. 1923: †The Spanish Dancer. †The Rustle of Silk. 1924: †The Fast Set. †The Man Who Fights Alone. 1925: †Riders of the Purple Sage. 1926: †*Alice's Mysterious Mystery (and subsequent series). 1927: †The Callahans and the Murphys. †Night Life. 1928: †Mother Knows Best. †Sins of the Father. 1929: †Four Devils. 1930: †City Girl. †Liliom. 1931: †Rich Man's Folly. 1932: †Young America (GB: We Humans). †Emma. †So Big. †The Purchase Price. †Three on a Match. 1933: †The Life of Jimmy Dolan (GB: The Kid's Last Fight). †Rasputin and the Empress (GB: Rasputin – the Mad Monk). 1934: †The Key. †*Picture Palace. †This Side of Heaven. †*Private Lessons. †Finishing School. †School for Girls. Anne of Green Gables. 1935: Steamboat 'Round the Bend. *A Night at the Biltmore Bowl. Chasing Yesterday. 1936: Make Way for a Lady. Chatterbox. M'Liss. 1937: Meet the Missus. Too Many Wives. Stella Dallas. 1938: Law of the Underworld. Condemned Women. Mother Carey's Chickens. Girls' School. A Man to Remember. 1939: Sorority House (GB: That Girl from College). Career. Boy Slaves. 1940: Anne of Windy Poplars (GB: Anne of Windy Willows). Vigil in the Night. Saturday's Children. 1941:*

Unexpected Uncle. West Point Widow. All That Money Can Buy/The Devil and Daniel Webster. Four Jacks and a Jill. 1942: Mayor of 44th Street. 1943: Lady Bodyguard. The Powers Girl (GB: Hi! Beautiful). Bombardier. Government Girl. 1944: Man from Frisco. Music in Manhattan. 1945: Murder, My Sweet (GB: Farewell, My Lovely).

†*As Dawn O'Day*

SHORE, Dinah
(Frances Shore) 1917–1994

Sweet-faced, strawberry-blonde, healthy-looking American singing star (a child entertainer, as Fanny Rose), whose rich, melodious adult voice captivated record buyers and radio audiences in the early 1940s. Her special appeal never came across in her few films. Married to George Montgomery (*qv*) from 1943 to 1960. A long association with Burt Reynolds (also *qv*) a decade later was eventually broken off. Died from cancer.

1943: Thank Your Lucky Stars. 1944: Up in Arms. Follow the Boys. Belle of the Yukon. 1946: Make Mine Music (voice only). Till the Clouds Roll By. 1947: Fun and Fancy Free. 1952: Aaron Slick from Punkin Crick (GB: Marshmallow Moon). 1977: Oh, God! 1979: Health. Death Car on the Freeway (TV).

SHUE, Elisabeth 1963–

Friendly-looking, square-featured American actress with light curly hair, whose sparse output for the cinema is partially accounted for by studies at Harvard University and work for the theatre. Known as '100 per cent Shue' to some of her fellow film workers for

the effort she puts into her roles, Shue found that, after some success in *Cocktail* and *Adventures in Babysitting*, 100 per cent was not enough by itself to make her a box-office name. The standard of her roles after that was disappointing until 1995's *Leaving Las Vegas* showed that she was indeed one of America's best young dramatic actresses and won her an Oscar nomination. Since then, however, her choice of scripts has been highly questionable.

1983: Call to Glory (TV). 1984: The Karate Kid. 1986: Link. Double Switch (TV). 1987: Adventures in Babysitting (GB: A Night on the Town). 1988: Cocktail. 1989: Back to the Future Part II. Howling V: The Rebirth. 1990: Back to the Future Part III. 1991: The Marrying Man (GB: Too Hot to Handle). Soapdish. 1993: Heart and Souls. Twenty Bucks. Teresa's Tattoo. 1994: Radio Inside. Blind Justice. 1995: Leaving Las Vegas. The Underneath. 1996: The Trigger Effect. 1997: The Saint. 1998: Cousin Bette. Palmetto/Just Another Sucker. Deconstructing Harry. 1999: Molly/Rescue Me. 2000: Hollow Man.

SIDNEY, Sylvia (Sophia Kosow) 1910–1999

Pretty, plaintive-looking, dark-haired American actress who played plucky working girls battling against environmental odds, and only sometimes winning. Her naturalistic acting style made her one of Paramount's biggest stars of the thirties, but her decision to do stage work in 1939 came at the wrong time in her career, and a film comeback in the mid-forties failed. In the seventies she unexpectedly returned, playing elderly character roles. Has written a book on needlepoint. Married to Luther Adler (1903–1984) from 1938 to 1946, second of three. Nominated for an Academy Award on *Summer Wishes, Winter Dreams*. Died from throat cancer.

*1927: Broadway Nights. 1929: Thru Different Eyes. 1930: *Five Minutes from the Station. 1931: Confessions of a Co-Ed (GB: Her Dilemma). An American Tragedy. Ladies of the Big House. City Streets. Street Scene. 1932: The Miracle Man. Merrily We Go to Hell (GB: Merrily We Go to –). Madame Butterfly. Make Me a Star. 1933: Jennie Gerhardt. Pick-Up. 1934: Behold My Wife. Good Dame (GB: Good Girl). Thirty Day Princess. 1935: Accent on Youth. Mary Burns, Fugitive. 1936: Sabotage (US: The Woman Alone). Fury. Trail of the Lonesome Pine. 1937: Dead End. You Only Live Once. 1938: You and Me. 1939: One Third of a Nation. 1941: The*

Wagons Roll at Night. 1945: Blood on the Sun. 1946: The Searching Wind. Mr Ace. 1947: Love from a Stranger (GB: A Stranger Walked In). 1952: Les Misérables. 1955: Man on the Ledge (TV. GB: cinemas). Violent Saturday. 1956: Behind the High Wall. 1957: Helen Morgan (TV). 1958: The Gentleman from Seventh Avenue (TV). 1971: Do Not Fold, Spindle or Mutilate (TV). 1973: Summer Wishes, Winter Dreams. 1975: Winner Take All (TV). The Secret Night Caller (TV). 1976: Raid on Entebbe (TV. GB: cinemas). Demon/God told Me To. Death at Love House (TV). 1977: I Never Promised You a Rose Garden. Snowbeast (TV). Perfect Gentlemen (TV). 1978: Damien – Omen II. Siege (TV). 1979: The Gossip Columnist (TV). 1980: Hammett (shown and later copyrighted 1982). The Shadow Box (TV). 1981: A Small Killing (TV). FDR: The Last Year (TV). 1982: Having It All. 1983: Order of Death. 1984: Finnegan Begin Again (GB: TV). 1986: An Early Frost (TV). 1987: Pals (TV). 1988: Beetlejuice. 1990: The Exorcist III. André's Mother (TV). The Witching of Ben Wagner (TV). 1992: Used People. 1996: Mars Attacks!

chante . . . 1960: Le joli mai (narrator only). Les mauvais coups. Adua e la compagne (GB: Hungry for Love). 1961: Les amours célèbres. 1962: Le jour et l'heure. Term of Trial. 1963: Dragées au poivre (GB: Sweet and Sour). Il giorno piu corto commedia umaristica (US: The Shortest Day). 1965: Ship of Fools. Is Paris Burning? Compartiment tueurs/The Sleeping Car Murders. 1966: The Deadly Affair. 1967: Games. 1968: The Seagull. Mr Freedom. 1969: L'Américain. L'armée des ombres. 1970: Le rose et le noir. L'aveu. Compte à rebours. 1971: Le chât. La veuve Couderc. 1973: Les granges brûlées (GB: TV, as The Investigator). 1974: Rude journée pour la reine. La chair de l'orchidée. Défense de savoir. 1975: Madame le juge (TV. And ensuing series). 1976: Police Python 357. 1977: La vie devant soi (GB: Madame Rosa). 1978: Une femme dangereuse. L'adolescente. 1979: Judith Therpauve. Je t'ai écrit une lettre d'amour/Chère inconnue (US: I Sent a Letter to My Love). 1980: L'étoile du nord. 1981: Gina. 1982: Guy de Maupassant. 1983: Des 'Terroristes' à la retraite (narrator only).

World. 1966: A Funny Thing Happened on the Way to the Forum. 1967: Follow That Camel. 1968: Buona Sera, Mrs Campbell. 1970: The Boatniks. 1975: The Deadly Tide (TV). The Strongest Man in the World. Won Ton Ton, the Dog Who Saved Hollywood. All Trails Lead to Las Vegas (TV). 1976: Murder by Death. 1977: The Chicken Chronicles. The New Love Boat (TV). 1978: Racquet. The Night They Took Miss Beautiful (TV). The Cheap Detective. 1979: Hey Abbott! (TV). Goldie and the Boxer (TV). 1980: The Happy Hooker Goes to Hollywood. Hollywood Blue.

†Scene deleted from final release print

SILVERSTONE, Alicia 1976–
Slim, blonde, smily-faced, innocent-looking American teenage star of British parentage. After a stage debut at 16, she branched out into TV movies and then films, starring in one of the sleeper successes of 1995, Clueless, as the air-headed central character. Since then, though, she has struggled to shine in fully-fledged adult roles.
1992: Scattered Dreams (TV). 1993: Torchsong (TV). The Crush. 1994: True Crime. Le nouveau monde. The Cool and the Crazy (TV). 1995: Hideway. The Babysitter. Clueless. 1996: Excess Baggage. 1997: Batman and Robin. 1998: Blast from the Past. 1999: Love's Labour's Lost.

SIGNORET, Simone
(S. Kaminker) 1921–1985
Blonde French actress (born in Germany), mostly in moody roles. In her youth she was prettily comely and sensual but even in early middle age her features had turned heavier and this led to some fairly gloomy film roles. Academy Award for Room at the Top (she also won three British Academy Awards, plus an Oscar nomination for Ship of Fools). Married/divorced director Yves Allégret. Married to Yves Montand (qv) from 1951 to her death from cancer. Failing sight put an end to her acting career in the early 1980s, but she found new success as a writer.
1942: Le prince charmant. Boléro. Les visiteurs du soir. 1943: La boîte aux rêves. Adieu Léonard. 1944: Béatrice devant le désir. 1945: Les démons de l'aube. Le couple idéal. 1946: Macadam. 1947: Dédée d'Anvers (GB and US: Dédée). Fantômas. 1948: Against the Wind. L'impasse aux deux anges. 1949: Manège. 1950: Four Days' Leave. Le traqué/Gunman in the Streets. La ronde. 1951: Ombre et lumière. 1952: Casque d'or. 1953: Thérèse Raquin. 1954: Les diaboliques/The Fiends. 1956: La muerte en este jardin (GB: Evil Eden. US: Death in the Garden). Die Windrose. 1957: The Witches of Salem. 1958: Room at the Top. 1959: Yves Montand

SILVERS, Phil
(P. Silversmith) 1911–1985
Explosive, bespectacled American comedian whose vigorous shirkers entertained wartime film audiences before he returned to vaudeville and stage shows. In the mid-1950s he re-emerged on television as one of the world's most popular comedians, playing the bald, scheming army sergeant Bilko in the long-running You'll Never Get Rich. Film appearances afterwards did not repeat that success, and he was in poor health for some years before his death.
1937: *Here's Your Hat. *Ups and Downs. 1938: *The Candid Kid. 1940: Hit Parade of 1941. †Strike Up the Band. †Pride and Prejudice. 1941: †Ball of Fire. The Penalty. The Wild Man of Borneo. Ice-Capades. Tom, Dick and Harry. Lady Be Good. You're in the Army Now. 1942: Roxie Hart. All Through the Night. †Tales of Manhattan. My Gal Sal. Footlight Serenade. Just Off Broadway. 1943: Coney Island. A Lady Takes a Chance. 1944: Cover Girl. Four Jills in a Jeep. Something for the Boys. Take It or Leave It. 1945: Billy Rose's Diamond Horseshoe (GB: Diamond Horseshoe). A Thousand and One Nights. 1946: If I'm Lucky. 1950: Summer Stock (GB: If You Feel Like Singing). 1952: Top Banana. 1954: Lucky Me. 1962: 40 Pounds of Trouble. 1963: It's a Mad, Mad, Mad, Mad

SIM, Alastair 1900–1976
Long-faced, tombstone-toothed Scottish-born character star, bald from an early age, whose expressions of ghoulish glee, doleful dithering and agonized anguish, coupled with uniquely gurgling diction, were associated

with much that was best in British comedies and comedy-thrillers from the late 1930s to the mid-1950s. The cinema let him go too early at 60. An incomparable Scrooge. Died from cancer.

*1935: The Case of Gabriel Perry. The Riverside Murder. A Fire Has Been Arranged. The Private Secretary. Late Extra. 1936: Wedding Group (US: Wrath of Jealousy). Troubled Waters. Keep Your Seats Please. The Mysterious Mr Davis (US: My Partner Mr Davis). The Big Noise. The Man in the Mirror. She Knew What She Wanted. Strange Experiment. 1937: The Squeaker (US: Murder on Diamond Row). Clothes and the Woman. Melody and Romance. Gangway. A Romance in Flanders (US: Lost on the Western Front). 1938: Alf's Button Afloat. Sailing Along. The Terror. Climbing High. This Man is News. Inspector Hornleigh. 1939: This Man in Paris. Inspector Hornleigh on Holiday. 1940: Law and Disorder. *Her Father's Daughter. 1941: Cottage to Let (US: Bombsight Stolen). Inspector Hornleigh Goes to It (US: Mail Train). 1942: Let the People Sing. 1943: *Fiddling Fuel. 1944: Waterloo Road. 1945: Journey Together. 1946: Green for Danger. 1947: Hue and Cry. Captain Boycott. 1948: London Belongs to Me (US: Dulcimer Street). 1950: The Happiest Days of Your Life. Stage Fright. 1951: Laughter in Paradise. Lady Godiva Rides Again. Scrooge (US: A Christmas Carol). 1952: Folly to Be Wise. 1953: Innocents in Paris. 1954: The Belles of St Trinian's. An Inspector Calls. 1955: Escapade. *Festival in Edinburgh (narrator only). Geordie (US: Wee Geordie). 1956: The Green Man. 1957: Blue Murder at St Trinian's. 1959: The Doctor's Dilemma. Left, Right and Centre. School for Scoundrels. 1960: The Millionairess. 1961: The Anatomist. *A Christmas Carol (voice only). 1971: The Ruling Class. 1975: Royal Flash. 1976: Rogue Male (TV). Escape from the Dark (US: The Littlest Horse Thieves).*

Academy Awards on *Hamlet* and *The Happy Ending*.

*1944: Give Us the Moon. Mr Emmanuel. Kiss the Bride Goodbye. Meet Sexton Blake. 1945: *Sports Day. The Way to the Stars (US: Johnny in the Clouds). Caesar and Cleopatra. 1946: Great Expectations. Hungry Hill. 1947: Black Narcissus. Uncle Silas (US: The Inheritance). The Woman in the Hall. 1948: Hamlet. The Blue Lagoon. 1949: Adam and Evelyne (US: Adam and Evalyn). 1950: Trio. So Long at the Fair. Cage of Gold. The Clouded Yellow. 1952: Androcles and the Lion. Angel Face. 1953: She Couldn't Say No (GB: Beautiful But Dangerous). Young Bess. Affair with a Stranger. The Actress. The Robe. 1954: The Egyptian. Desiree. A Bullet is Waiting. 1955: Footsteps in the Fog. Guys and Dolls. 1956: Hilda Crane. 1957: This Could Be the Night. Until They Sail. 1958: Home Before Dark. The Big Country. 1959: This Earth is Mine. 1960: Elmer Gantry. Spartacus. 1961: The Grass is Greener. 1963: All the Way Home. 1965: Life at the Top. Mr Buddwing (GB: Woman without a Face). 1967: Rough Night in Jericho. Divorce American Style. 1968: Heidi Comes Home (US: Heidi). 1969: The Happy Ending. 1970: Decisions! Decisions! (TV). Say Hello to Yesterday. 1975: Mr Sycamore. The Easter Promise (TV). 1978: The Dain Curse (TV). Dominique. 1981: A Small Killing (TV). Golden Gate (TV). 1983: Robin Hood (TV). 1984: Midas Valley (TV). 1985: Yellow Pages (released 1988 as Going Undercover). 1987: Perry Mason: The Case of the Lost Love (TV). 1988: The Dawning. A Friendship in Vienna (TV. Narrator only). Inherit the Wind (TV). 1989: Great Expectations (TV). 1990: People Like Us (TV). Sensibility and Sense (TV). The Laker Girls (TV). Dark Shadows (TV). 1994: One More Mountain (TV). 1995: How to Make an American Quilt. Daisies in December (TV). 1998: Her Own Rules (TV).*

SIMMONS, Jean 1929–
Britain never sent a prettier actress to Hollywood (and few more talented): all the more pity the film capital did so little with her. The demure-looking brunette with oval face and stunning figure had done rather well in Britain, but had to wait 10 years for comparable American roles. In leading roles as a teenager. Married to Stewart Granger (*qv*) 1950–1960. A later marriage to director Richard Brooks also ended. Nominated for

sauvé de eaux, remade many years later by Hollywood as *Down and Out in Beverly Hills*. Sometimes he appeared to be a continental Charles Laughton, although the roles he played were often more reminiscent of those of Lon Chaney Sr. His output was restricted after 1957 by an accident that partially paralysed his face and body. Died from heart failure.

1924: La galérie des monstres. 1925: La puissance du travail (US: The Vocation of André Carrel). Feu Mathias Pascal. 1926: L'inconnue des six jours. 1927: Casanova. 1928: Tire-au-flanc. La Passion de Jeanne d'Arc. 1929: Pivoine. 1930: L'enfant de l'amour. 1931: On purge Bébé. Baleydier. La Chienne. Jean de la Lune. 1932: Boudu sauvé des eaux. 1933: Du haut en bas (GB and US: High and Low). Léopold le bien-aimé. Miquette et sa mère. 1934: Lac aux Dames. L'Atalante. Le bonheur. 1935: Amants et voleurs. Ademï au Moyen-Age. Le bébé de l'escadron. 1936: Moutonnet. Sous les yeux d'occident. Le mort en fuite. Les jumeaux de Brighton. Jeunes filles de Paris. 1937: Faisons un rêve. Drôle de drame (US: Bizarre, Bizarre). La bataille silencieuse. Naples au baiser de feu/ Kiss of Fire. Si tu m'aimes. Le choc en retour. Boulot aviateur. 1938: Quai des brumes (US: Port of Shadows). Les disparus de Saint-Agil/ Boys' School. Les nouveaux riches. La chaleur de sein. Le ruisseau. Belle étoile. Noix de coco. 1939: Le dernier tournant. Le fin du jour. Eusèbe député. Cavalcade d'amour. Circonstances atténuantes. Derrière la façade. Fric-Frac. Les musiciens du ciel. Paris-New York. 1940: La Tosca. La comédie du bonheur. 1941: Il re se diverte (US: The King's Jester). 1942: La dame de l'ouest. 1943: Au bonheur des dames (US: Shop Girls of Paris). Vautrin (US: Vautrin the Thief). 1945: Un ami viendra ce soir. 1946: Panique/ Panic. La taverne du poisson couronné. Non coupable/ Not Guilty. 1947: Les amants de Pont Saint-Jean. La carcasse et le Tord-Cou. 1948: Fabiola. 1950: Le beauté du Diable (GB: Beauty and the Beast. US: Beauty and the Devil). Les deux vérités. 1951: Le poison. Vedettes sans maquillage. La cité du midi. Le due verità. 1952: Monsieur Taxi. La fille au fouet. Brelan d'as. Le chemin de Damas. Le rideau rouge. Le vie d'un honnête homme (GB and US: The Virtuous Scoundrel). The Merchant of Venice. Femmes de Paris. 1953: L'étrange désire de M Bard. Par ordre du Tsar. Saadia. Quelques pas dans la vie. 1954: Les cloches n'ont pas sonnées/ Hungarian Rhapsody. Tempi nostri (US: The Anatomy of Love). 1955: Les mémoires d'un flic. L'impossible M Pipelet. 1956: La joyeuse prison. 1957: Les trois font la paire. Un certain Monsieur Jo. 1958: It Happened in Broad Daylight. 1959: Simenon (D). The Head. Austerlitz. 1960: Candide. Pierrot la Tendresse. Mon ami Lazlo. 1961: Le bateau d'Emile. 1962: The Devil and the Ten Commandments. 1963: Cyrano et D'Artagnan. 1964: Michel Simon (D). Steinlein. 1965: The Train. Deux heures à tuer. 1966: Le vieil homme et l'enfant (GB and US: The Two of Us). 1967: Ce sacré grand-père (GB: The Marriage Came Tumbling Down). 1968: Ecce homo. 1970: La maison. Contestation générale. 1971: Blanche. 1972: La più bella serata della mia vita. 1973: Eulalie quitte les champs/ The Star, the Orphan and the Butcher. 1975: L'ibis rouge.

SIMON, Michel
(François Simon) 1895–1975
Hulking, undeniably ugly, flat-nosed, flour-faced Swiss-born character star, not always a lovable brute but sometimes as odious types who dominated their surroundings (and the supporting cast). As evidenced by the battered features, Simon was once a boxer, but had turned to acting at 23 and started making films at 30. With the coming of sound, he soon established himself as a gravel-voiced, unforgettable presence, especially in *Boudu*

SIMON, Simone 1910–

Pert, mercurial, dark-haired French actress with childlike face (and voice to match). Producer Darryl F. Zanuck brought her to Hollywood in 1935, but only one or two films – *Seventh Heaven, Cat People* – capitalized on her special appeal, and her best work was done in her native France, where she now lives.

1931: *Le chanteur inconnu. Mam'zelle Nitouche. Le père sans douleur. La petite chocolatière.* 1932: *Un fils d'Amérique. Le roi des palaces. L'étoile de Valance. Prenez garde de la peinture.* 1933: *Le voleur. Tire-au-flanc.* 1934: *Lac-aux-dames.* 1935: *Les yeux noirs. Les beaux jours.* 1936: *Girls' Dormitory. Ladies in Love.* 1937: *Love and Hisses. Seventh Heaven.* 1938: *Josette. La bête humaine.* 1941: *All That Money Can Buy/The Devil and Daniel Webster.* 1942: *Cat People.* 1943: *Tahiti Honey.* 1944: *Johnny Doesn't Live Here Anymore. The Curse of the Cat People. Mademoiselle Fifi.* 1946: *Petrus.* 1947: *Temptation Harbour.* 1949: *Donna senze nome.* 1950: *Olivia (US: Pit of Loneliness). La ronde.* 1951: *Le plaisir.* 1954: *I tre ladri.* 1955: *Double Destiny.* 1956: *The Extra Day.* 1973: *La femme en bleu.*

SINATRA, Frank (Francis Sinatra) 1915–1998

Slightly-built, dark-haired American singer and actor, *the* romantic crooner of the forties (and idol of screaming teenage millions) who developed into the supreme song stylist of the fifties and sixties. His appeal as a star of musicals faded with the end of the forties, but an Oscar for *From Here to Eternity* opened up a new field for him as a dramatic actor, especially in films which cashed in on his own cynical persona. Four times married,

including Ava Gardner (second 1951–1957) and Mia Farrow (third 1966–1968). Also nominated for an Academy Award for *The Man with the Golden Arm.* Special Oscar 1970. Died from a heart attack.

1935: **Major Bowes' Amateur Theatre of the Air.* 1941: *Las Vegas Nights (GB: The Gay City).* 1942: *Ship Ahoy.* 1943: *Reveille with Beverly. *Show Business at War. Higher and Higher.* 1944: *Step Lively. *The Shining Future.* 1945: *Anchors Aweigh. *All Star Bond Rally. *The House I Live In.* 1946: *Till the Clouds Roll By.* 1947: *It Happened in Brooklyn.* 1948: *The Miracle of the Bells. The Kissing Bandit. Take Me Out to the Ball Game (GB: Everybody's Cheering).* 1949: *On the Town.* 1951: *Double Dynamite. Meet Danny Wilson.* 1952: **Screen Snapshots No 206.* 1953: *From Here to Eternity.* 1954: *Suddenly. Young at Heart.* 1955: *Not As a Stranger. The Tender Trap. Guys and Dolls. The Man with the Golden Arm.* 1956: *Meet Me in Las Vegas (GB: Viva Las Vegas!). Johnny Concho. High Society. Around the World in 80 Days. The Pride and the Passion.* 1957: *The Joker is Wild. Pal Joey.* 1958: *Kings Go Forth. Some Came Running.* 1959: *A Hole in the Head. Never So Few. Invitation to Monte Carlo.* 1960: *Can-Can. Ocean's Eleven. Pepe. Love in Monaco.* 1961: *The Devil at Four O'Clock.* 1962: *The Road to Hong Kong. Sergeants Three. The Manchurian Candidate.* 1963: *The List of Adrian Messenger. Come Blow Your Horn. Four for Texas.* 1964: *Robin and the Seven Hoods.* 1965: *†None but the Brave. Von Ryan's Express. Marriage on the Rocks.* 1966: *The Oscar. Cast a Giant Shadow. Assault on a Queen.* 1967: *Tony Rome. The Naked Runner.* 1968: *Lady in Cement. The Detective.* 1970: *Dirty Dingus Magee.* 1974: *That's Entertainment!* 1977: *Contract on Cherry Street (TV).* 1980: *The First Deadly Sin.* 1983: *Cannonball Run II.* 1988: *Who Framed Roger Rabbit (voice only).* 1990: *Places You Find Love. Listen Up.* 1995: *Young at Heart (TV).*
†Also directed

SINDEN, Sir Donald 1923–

Hearty, strongly-built, dark-haired British actor with rich, fruity voice. Became a star in his first major role and then played a variety of leading parts, usually as men with a roving eye, until 1962. Returned in occasional character roles from the late sixties, but has concentrated largely on building up his reputation in the theatre. Also popular as the butler in the long-running British TV series,

Two's Company. His actor son Jeremy died from cancer in 1996. Knighted in 1997.

1948: *Portrait from Life (US: The Girl in the Painting).* 1952: *The Cruel Sea.* 1953: *A Day to Remember. Mogambo. You Know What Sailors Are.* 1954: *The Beachcomber. Doctor in the House. Mad About Men. Simba.* 1955: *Above Us the Waves. Josephine and Men. An Alligator Named Daisy.* 1956: *Tiger in the Smoke. Eyewitness. The Black Tent.* 1957: *Doctor at Large.* 1958: *The Captain's Table. Rockets Galore (US: Mad Little Island).* 1959: *Operation Bullshine. Your Money or Your Wife.* 1960: *The Siege of Sidney Street.* 1962: *Twice Round the Daffodils. Mix Me a Person.* 1968: *Decline and Fall . . . of a Bird-watcher.* 1971: *Villain.* 1972: *Rentadick. Father Dear Father.* 1973: *The Day of the Jackal. The National Health. The Island at the Top of the World.* 1975: *That Lucky Touch.* 1981: *Helicopter.* 1990: *The Children.* 1995: *Balto (voice only).* 1996: *The Canterville Ghost (TV).* 1997: *The Treasure Seekers.* 1999: *Alice in Wonderland (TV, voice only).* 2000: *Accidental Detective.*

SINGLETON, Penny

(Mariana Dorothy McNulty) 1908–

American singer, dancer and comedienne who dyed her dark hair blonde in 1938 to play the dizzy housewife heroine of strip-cartoons, Blondie, and remained in the role for 13 years and 28 films. When the series was done she returned to stage musicals. Later active in show-business union politics.

1929: *†*Belle of the Night.* 1930: *†Good News. †Love in the Rough.* 1936: *†After the Thin Man.* 1937: *†Vogues of 1938. †Sea Racketeers.* 1938: *Men Are Such Fools. Outside of Paradise. Mr Chump. Garden of the Moon. Hard to Get. Swing Your Lady. *Campus Cinderella. Boy Meets Girl. The Mad Miss Manton. Secrets of an Actress. Blondie. Racket Busters.* 1939: *Blondie Meets the Boss. Blondie Brings up Baby. Blondie Takes a Vacation.* 1940: *Blondie on a Budget. Blondie Has Servant Trouble. Blondie Plays Cupid.* 1941: *Blondie Goes Latin (GB: Conga Swing). Blondie in Society (GB: Henpecked). Go West, Young Lady.* 1942: *Blondie for Victory (GB: Troubles through Billets). Blondie Goes to College (GB: The Boss Said 'No'). Blondie's Blessed Event (GB: A Bundle of Trouble).* 1943: *Footlight Glamour. It's a Great Life.* 1945: *Leave It to Blondie. Life with Blondie.* 1946: *Blondie's Lucky Day. Blondie Knows Best. Young Widow. Blondie's Big Moment.*

1947: Blondie's Holiday. Blondie in the Dough. Blondie's Anniversary. 1948: Blondie's Secret. Blondie's Reward. 1949: Blondie Hits the Jackpot (GB: Hitting the Jackpot). Blondie's Big Deal (GB: The Big Deal). 1950: Beware of Blondie. Blondie's Hero. 1964: The Best Man. The Jetsons Meet the Flintstones (TV, voice only). 1990: Jetsons: The Movie (voice only).

†As Dorothy McNulty

SKELTON, Red (Richard Skelton) 1910–1997
Red-haired, rubber-faced, elastic-mouthed American comedian, the son of a circus clown, who usually wore clothes slightly too big, and mugged madly through M-G-M comedies and musicals for 14 years, whether as leading man or in black and white comedies or comic relief in big colour musicals. It's said that he was at his best as a radio comedian: certainly his visual style has dated. His TV show, though, which started in 1951, ran for 20 years. Died from pneumonia.
1938: Having Wonderful Time. 1939: *Seein' Red. *Broadway Buckaroo. 1940: Flight Command. 1941: The People vs Dr Kildare (GB: My Life is Yours). Dr Kildare's Wedding Day (GB: Mary Names the Day). Lady Be Good. Whistling in the Dark. 1942: Maisie Gets Her Man (GB: She Got Her Man). Panama Hattie. Ship Ahoy. Whistling in Dixie. 1943: DuBarry Was a Lady. I Dood It (GB: By Hook or by Crook). Thousands Cheer. Whistling in Brooklyn. 1944: Bathing Beauty. Ziegfeld Follies (released 1946:). *Radio Bugs (voice only). 1946: The Show-Off. *Luckiest Guy in the World (voice only). 1947: Merton of the Movies. 1948: A Southern Yankee (GB: My Hero). The Fuller Brush Man (GB: That Mad Mr Jones). 1949: Neptune's Daughter. 1940: The Yellow Cab Man. The Fuller Brush Girl (GB: The Affairs of Sally). Three Little Words. Duchess of Idaho. Watch the Birdie. 1951: Excuse My Dust. Texas Carnival. 1952: Lovely to Look At. The Clown. 1953: Half a Hero. The Great Diamond Robbery. 1954: Susan Slept Here. 1956: Around the World in 80 Days. The Big Slide (TV). 1957: Public Pigeon No 1. 1960: Ocean's Eleven. 1965: Those Magnificent Men in their Flying Machines.

SKERRITT, Tom 1933–
Big, shambling, often bearded, happy-go-lucky-looking American actor, facially not unlike Britain's Bill Travers (qv). After years

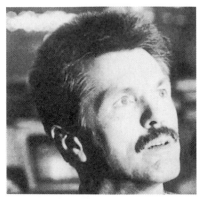

of anonymous slog in TV, the theatre and a few films, he played one of the three zany Army surgeons in Altman's *M*A*S*H*. Stardom reached for the others, Elliott Gould and Donald Sutherland both (qv), but Skerritt somehow got left by the way. Since then his performances have invariably been better than his films, but even the doomed captain in *Alien* did not make him a bankable star; an unlucky film career. He won an Emmy in 1993 for his work on the TV series *Picket Fences*.
1961: War Hunt. 1964: One Man's Way. Those Callaways. 1969: M*A*S*H. 1971: The Birdmen (TV. GB: cinemas, as Escape of the Birdmen). Wild Rovers. 1972: Fuzz. 1974: The Last Day (TV). Run Run Joe. Big Bad Mama. Thieves Like Us. 1975: Maneaters Are Loose! (TV). The Devil's Rain. 1976: La Madama. 1977: The Turning Point. 1978: Ice Castles. Up in Smoke. 1979: Alien. 1980: The Silence of the North. 1981: Savage Harvest. 1982: A Dangerous Summer/The Burning Man. Fighting Back (GB: Death Vengeance). 1983: The Dead Zone. 1984: A Touch of Scandal (TV). Calendar Girl Murders (TV). 1986: SpaceCamp. Top Gun. Wisdom. Miles to Go (TV). 1987: Maid to Order. The Big Town. Parent Trap II (TV). Opposing Force/ Hell Camp (formerly Clay Pigeons). Poker Alice (TV). 1988: Poltergeist III. Nightmare at Bitter Creek (TV). Moving Target (TV). 1989: Steel Magnolias. Red King, White Knight (TV). Honor Bound. Big Man on Campus. The Heist (TV). 1990: The China Lake Murders. The Rookie. Child in the Night (TV). She'll Take Romance (TV). 1991: Knight Moves. Blue Movie Blue (later Wild Orchid II: Two Shades of Blue). Poison Ivy. 1992: A River Runs Through It. In Sickness and In Health (TV). Singles. Picket Fences (TV). 1996: †Divided by Hate (TV). 1997: What the Deaf Man Heard (TV). Contact. 1998: The Other Sister. Two for Texas(TV). Smoke Signals. 1999: The Hunt for the Unicorn Killer. 2000: High Noon (TV). Texas Rangers. An American Daughter (TV).

†And directed

SLATER, Christian (C. Hawkins) 1969–
Dark-haired, dynamic American teenage actor of wry good looks and mocking smile, who grew into a slightly less dynamic and more serious adult actor. The son of an actor and a casting director, he began acting on TV at seven years old. Films followed a decade

later although, after a youthful starring role opposite Sean Connery, his talent took a while to assert itself. He moved into strongly offbeat leading roles in the late 1980s, but his recent work has been slightly more routine. He was jailed for three months (with three months' drug rehab) after assault charges in 1997.
1983: Living Proof: The Hank Williams Jr Story (TV). 1985: The Legend of Billie Jean. 1986: The Name of the Rose. Twisted. Cry Wolf (TV). 1987: The Rose of the Names. 1988: Tucker: The Man and His Dream. Gleaming the Cube. 1989: Personal Choice (later Beyond the Stars). Heathers. Desperate for Love (TV). The Wizard. 1990: Tales from the Darkside/Tales from the Darkside: The Movie. Young Guns II (GB: Young Guns II: Blaze of Glory). Pump Up the Volume. 1991: Robin Hood – Prince of Thieves. Mobsters (GB: Mobsters The Evil Empire). Kuffs. Star Trek VI: The Undiscovered Country. Where the Day Takes You. 1992: Untamed Heart. FernGully . . . The Last Rainforest (voice only). 1993: True Romance. The Last Party. 1994: Murder in the First. Jimmy Hollywood. Interview With the Vampire. 1996: Bed of Roses/Amelia and the King of Plants. Broken Arrow. 1997: Julian Po. Hard Rain. Basil. Austin Powers International Man of Mystery. 1998: Very Bad Things. 1999: Love Stinks. 2000: The Contender. 3000 Miles to Graceland. 2001: Cletis Tout. Windtalkers.

SLAUGHTER, Tod
(N. Carter Slaughter) 1885–1956
Big, beefy, brown-haired, barnstorming British actor-manager who toured the country giving over-the-top renditions of lurid Victorian melodramas, most of which

proved quite popular with the public (if not the critics) when brought to the screen; *The Greed of William Hart* (based on Burke and Hare) was his best. The forerunner of such flamboyant figures as Robert Newton and Donald Wolfit (both *qv*), he remained active until his death.

1935: *Maria Marten: or Murder in the Red Barn.* 1936: *Sweeney Todd, The Demon Barber of Fleet Street. The Crimes of Stephen Hawke.* 1937: *It's Never Too Late to Mend. Song of the Road. Darby and Joan. The Ticket of Leave Man.* 1938: *Pathe Pictorial No 131. Sexton Blake and the Hooded Terror.* 1939: *The Face at the Window.* 1940: *Crimes at the Dark House.* 1942: *Soldiers without Uniform.* 1945: *Bothered by a Beard.* 1946: *The Curse of the Wraydons.* 1948: *The Greed of William Hart.* 1952: *King of the Underworld. *Murder in the Strand.* 1953: *Murder at Scotland Yard. *A Ghost for Sale. *Murder at the Grange.* 1954: *Puzzle Corner No 14.*

SMITH, Alexis
(Gladys Smith) 1921–1993
Blonde Canadian actress whose height (5ft 10in) and square, determined features got her cast as adventuresses of one kind or another, sometimes spirited, sometimes scheming. Also a dancer and light singer. Resident at Warners throughout the forties. Married to Craig Stevens (*qv*) from 1944. Died from cancer.

1940: *Lady with Red Hair.* 1941: *Three Sons o' Guns. Affectionately Yours. Passage from Hong Kong. Steel against the Sky. Singapore Woman. Dive Bomber. She Couldn't Say No. Flight from Destiny. The Smiling Ghost.* 1942: *Gentleman Jim.* 1943: *Thank Your Lucky Stars. The Constant Nymph. *Show Business at War.* 1944: *Hollywood Canteen. The Dough-girls. The Adventures of Mark Twain.* 1945: *San Antonio. Conflict. Rhapsody in Blue. The Horn Blows at Midnight.* 1946: *One More Tomorrow. Of. Human Bondage. Night and Day.* 1947: *So You Want to be in Pictures. Always Together. The Two Mrs Carrolls. Stallion Road. The Woman in White.* 1948: *Whiplash.* 1949: *One Last Fling. South of St Louis. Any Number Can Play.* 1950: *Montana. Wyoming Mail. Undercover Girl.* 1951: *Here Comes the Groom. Cave of Outlaws.* 1952: *The Turning Point.* 1953: *Split Second.* 1954: *The Sleeping Tiger.* 1955: *The Eternal Sea.* 1956: *The Hefferan Family (TV. GB: cinemas).* 1957: *Beau James.* 1958: *This Happy Feeling.* 1959: *The Young Philadelphians (GB: The*

City Jungle). 1974: *Once is Not Enough/ Jacqueline Susann's Once is Not Enough.* 1976: *The Little Girl Who Lives Down the Lane.* 1977: *Casey's Shadow.* 1981: *La truite/The Trout.* 1986: *Tough Guys.* 1988: *Hothouse (TV). A Holiday Affair (TV).* 1993: *The Age of Innocence.*

SMITH, Constance 1929–
Dark-haired, blue-eyed Irish actress whose colourful personal life overshadowed her acting career. After a beginning in British films, she landed a Hollywood contract with Twentieth Century-Fox, for whom she starred competently in a good variety of movies. Later went to Italy. Married to Bryan Forbes (*qv*) 1951–1954.

1946: *Material Evidence.* 1947: *Easy Money. Brighton Rock (US: Young Scarface). Jassy.* 1948: *The Calendar. Saraband for Dead Lovers (US: Saraband).* 1949: *Murder at the Windmill. Trottie True (US: Gay Lady). The Perfect Woman. Now Barabbas was a robber . . .* 1950: *Room to Let. Don't Say Die. Blackmailed. The Mudlark.* 1951: *I'll Get You for This (US: Lucky Nick Cain). The Thirteenth Letter.* 1952: *Red Skies of Montana. Lure of the Wilderness.* 1953: *Taxi. Treasure of the Golden Condor. Man in the Attic.* 1955: *Impulse. Tiger by the Tail (US: Crossup). Un po' di cielo. The Big Tip-Off.* 1957: *Giovanni dalle bande nere (GB: TV, as John of the Black Gang. US: The Violent Patriot). Addio per sempre.* 1958: *La conguira dei Borgia (released 1963). Il cavaliere senza terra.*

SMITH, John
(Robert Van Orden) 1931–1995
Fresh-faced, fair-haired, boyish-looking American actor, a favourite pin-up of the

1950s who never really rose above being a co-star in big films and an action hero of minor ones. A talented singer, he began his show business career as a boy soloist in The Mitchell Choir, appearing with them in one or two popular films. In the early 1950s, he legally changed his name to John Smith over the protests of his agent. He had a good run on TV as one of the two heroes of the western series *Laramie* (1959–1963), but further leading roles in films proved hard to find. Married/divorced fellow child/teenage player Luana Patten (1938–1996). Died from cirrhosis and heart problems.

1944: *Going My Way.* 1946: *The Bells of St Mary's.* 1950: *A Woman of Distinction.* 1951: *The Guy Who Came Back.* 1952: *Carbine Williams.* 1954: *The High and the Mighty. We're No Angels.* 1955: *Desert Sands. Seven Angry Men. Wichita.* 1956: *The Bold and the Brave. Friendly Persuasion. Ghost Town. Hot Rod Girl. Quincannon, Frontier Scout (GB: Frontier Scout). Rebel in Town. The Tomahawk Trail (GB: Mark of the Apache).* 1957: *The Money. The Kettles on Old McDonald's Farm. Fury at Sundown. The Lawless Eighties. Women of Pitcairn Island. The Crooked Circle.* 1958: *Handle With Care.* 1959: *Island of Lost Women.* 1964: *Circus World (GB: The Magnificent Showman).* 1966: *Waco. Hondo and the Apaches.* 1971: *Legacy of Blood. Justin Morgan Had a Horse.* 1982: *Personal Best.* 1984: *Purple Hearts: A Vietnam Love Story.* 1985: *Star Crystal.*

SMITH, Kent (Frank K. Smith) 1907–1985
Quiet, square-faced American actor of serious aspect. Came to films in his mid-thirties and after a few useful leads in 'B' pictures went grey early and slipped into unshowy supporting roles, often playing upright but rather dull sticks who saw the girl snatched from under their noses. His authoritative acting style later served him well as a character player. Married (second of two) actress Edith Atwater (1911–1986). Died from congestive heart failure.

1936: *The Garden Murder Case.* 1942: *Cat People. Hitler's Children.* 1943: *Three Russian Girls (GB: She Who Dares). Forever and a Day. This Land is Mine.* 1944: *Youth Runs Wild. The Curse of the Cat People.* 1945: *The Spiral Staircase.* 1947: *Magic Town. Nora Prentiss. The Voice of the Turtle.* 1948: *Design for Death (narrator only).* 1949: *My Foolish Heart. The Fountainhead.* 1950: *This Side of the Law. The Damned Don't Cry.* 1952: *Paula*

(GB: *The Silent Voice*). 1956: *Comanche*. 1957: *Sayonara*. 1958: *The Mugger. The Badlanders. Party Girl. Imitation General*. 1959: *This Earth is Mine*. 1960: *Strangers When We Meet*. 1961: *Susan Slade*. 1962: *Moon Pilot*. 1963: *The Balcony*. 1964: *A Distant Trumpet. The Young Lovers. Youngblood Hawke*. 1965: *The Trouble with Angels*. 1967: *Games. A Covenant with Death. Assignment to Kill*. 1968: *Kona Coast. The Money Jungle*. 1969: *The Games. Death of a Gunfighter. How Awful About Allan (TV)*. 1971: *The Night Stalker (TV). The Last Child (TV)*. 1972: *Probe (TV). The Judge and Jake Wyler (TV). Pete 'n' Tillie. The Female Instinct (TV. GB: The Snoop Sisters). The Crooked Hearts (TV). Lost Horizon*. 1973: *The Affair (TV. GB: cinemas). Maurie. The Cat Creature (TV)*. 1974: *Murder or Mercy? (TV). The Disappearance of Flight 412 (TV)*.

SMITH, Dame Maggie 1934–
Red-haired, sharply-spoken, extremely dominant British actress, mostly seen in the theatre. For a while her film roles were softer than the parts she played on the stage, until she began to go in for acidulous spinsters. Married/divorced actor Robert Stephens (1931–95). Actor Toby Stephens is their son. Academy Awards for *The Prime of Miss Jean Brodie* and *California Suite*. Also nominated for Oscars on *Othello, Travels with My Aunt* and *A Room with a View*. Created Dame in 1989.
1956: *Child in the House*. 1958: *Nowhere to Go*. 1962: *Go to Blazes*. 1963: *The VIPs*. 1964: *Young Cassidy. The Pumpkin Eater*. 1965: *Othello*. 1966: *The Honey Pot*. 1968: *Hot Millions. The Prime of Miss Jean Brodie*. 1969: *Oh! What a Lovely War*. 1972: *Love and Pain and the whole damn thing. Travels with My Aunt*. 1976: *Murder by Death*. 1978: *Death on the Nile. California Suite*. 1981: *Clash of the Titans. Quartet*. 1982: *Evil Under the Sun. Ménage à Trois/Better Late Than Never. The Missionary*. 1983: *Fitz and Lily/Jatsani kell/Lily in Love*. 1984: *A Private Function*. 1985: *A Room with a View*. 1987: *The Lonely Passion of Judith Hearne*. 1990: *Romeo-Juliet (voice only). The Cherry Orchard*. 1991: *Hook*. 1992: *Sister Act. Memento Mori (TV). The Secret Garden*. 1993: *Sister Act 2: Back in the Habit*. 1995: *Richard III*. 1996: *The First Wives Club*. 1997: *Washington Square*. 1999: *Tea with Mussolini. The Last September. Curtain Call*.

SMITH, Will (Willard Smith Jr) 1968–
Tall, stringy, narrow-headed, jug-eared, fast-talking American rap star and light leading man, very popular in the late 1990s in smooth, self-confident roles. A rap music sensation with hs partner Jeff Townes as DJ Jazzy Jeff and The Fresh Prince, he soon turned to acting as well, appearing in the hit TV comedy series *The Fresh Prince of Bel-Air*. Early film success eluded him until *Bad Boys*, the first of a string of popular hits that took him into the top 10 of actors guaranteed to ensure box-office success. Married (second) actress Jada Pinkett in 1997.
1992: *Where the Day Takes You*. 1993: *Made in America*. 1994: *Six Degrees of Separation*. 1995: *Bad Boys*. 1996: *Independence Day*. 1997: *Men in Black*. 1998: *Welcome to Hollywood (D). Enemy of the State*. 1999: *Wild Wild West*. 2000: *The Legend of Bagger Vance*. 2001: *Men in Black: Alien Attack*.

SMITS, Jimmy 1955–
Dark-eyed, very tall (6ft 5in), Hispanic-looking American actor of concerned features: sincerity has been his strongpoint in a series of conscientious roles following dodgy early casting as drug dealers. After a leading role in the TV series *L.A. Law*, Smits tried co-starring roles in films with moderate success. Sensibly, he returned to small-screen action with another hugely successful series, *NYPD Blue*, proving himself a major star in the medium, though he made little impact on a second return to films. He began his working life as a community organiser before turning to the theatre.
1984: *Miami Vice (TV pilot)*. 1986: *Rockabye (TV). Running Scared*. 1987: *The Believers. Dangerous Affection (TV). Stamp of a Killer*

(TV). 1988: *The Highwayman (TV). Glitz (TV)*. 1989: *Old Gringo*. 1990: *Vital Signs (TV)*. 1991: *Switch. Fires Within*. 1992: *The Broken Cord (TV)*. 1993: *Gross Misconduct (TV)*. 1994: *The Cisco Kid (TV). Mi Familia/My Family/East L.A.* 1995: *Solomon and Sheba (TV)*. 1996: *Marshal Law*. 1997: *Murder in Mind*. 1998: *Lesser Prophets*. 1999: *The Million Dollar Hotel*. 2000: *Price of Glory. Bless the Child*.

SNIPES, Wesley 1962–
Fast-talking, good-looking, solidly-built American actor with prominent mouth and wide features, often in tough roles, but surprisingly effective in quieter stuff too. Brought up in a tough South Bronx district, he became an expert martial artist and fencer, then worked three years as a puppeteer before breaking into films, after one or two false starts, as an actor. Although the quality of his vehicles has been variable, he quickly became a popular star, and the marquee value of his name is still high, especially in harness with Woody Harrelson (*qv*) in buddy-buddy action films.
1985: *Wildcats*. 1986: *Streets of Gold*. 1987: *Bad (video). Critical Condition*. 1988: *Vietnam War Stories (TV)*. 1989: *Major League*. 1990: *King of New York. The H.E.L.P. (TV). Mo' Better Blues*. 1991: *New Jack City. Jungle Fever*. 1992: *White Men Can't Jump. Passenger 57. The Waterdance*. 1993: *Boiling Point. Rising Sun. Demolition Man. Sugar Hill*. 1994: *Drop Zone*. 1995: *To Wong Foo Thanks for Everything, Julie Newmar. Money Train. Waiting to Exhale*. 1996: *John Henrik Clarke: A Great and Mighty Walk (narrator only). The Fan. Sandblast. America's Dream (TV)*. 1997: *One Night Stand. Murder at 1600. Futuresport (TV)*. 1998: *Blade. Down in the Delta (cable TV/cinemas). U.S. Marshals*. 1999: *Play It to the Bone*. 2000: *The Art of War. Disappearing Acts. Blade 2: Bloodhunt*.

SOBIESKI, Leelee (Liliane Sobieski) 1982–
Tawny-haired American actress of smooth, patrician features who looks sensible and intelligent and was often cast that way in her films as a teenager. However, she looked a good bet for all-round stardom after her award-winning performance as Joan of Arc in a 1999 TV mini-series. Born in France, she was discovered in her New York City school and had launched an acting career at 12. Her father is the painter Jean Sobieski.
1994: *Reunion (TV). A Horse for Danny*

(TV). 1997: Jungle 2 Jungle. 1998: Deep Impact. A Soldier's Daugher Never Cries. 1999: Never Been Kissed. Eyes Wide Shut. 2000: Here on Earth. My First Mister. Squelch. 2001: The Glass House.

SOMMER, Elke (E. Schletz) 1940–
Baby-faced, very blonde West German star with provocative figure, usually in impishly sexy roles. In international films from the early sixties and, considering how many bad ones she has made, has lasted (and worn) remarkably well. Later divided her time between acting and painting, and held her first exhibition in 1978.
1958: Das Totenschiff. 1959: Lampenfieber. Am Tag, als der Regen kam (US: The Day It Rained). Uomini e nobiluomini. Freund von der Jaguar. Ragazzi del Juke-Box. Ti diro . . . che tu mi piaci. La pica sul Pacifico. 1960: Femmine lusso (US: Traveling in Luxury). Himmel, amor und Zwirn (US: Heaven and Cupid). Urlatori alla sbarra. 1961: Don't Bother to Knock! (US: Why Bother to Knock?). Douce violence (GB and US: Violent Ecstasy). Du quoi tu te mêles, Daniela? (GB and US: Daniela by Night). Les mutins de Yorik. Zarte haut in schwartzer Seide . . . und so was nennt sich leben. Geliebte Hochstaplerin. 1962: Les bricoleurs (GB: Who Stole the Body?). Auf wiedersehen. Café Oriental. Nachts ging des Telefon (US: The Phone Rings Every Night). Caprici Borghesi. Das Mädchen und der Staatsanwalt. Un chien dans un jeu de guilles. Bahia de Palma. 1963: The Victors. Denn die Musik und die Liebe in Tirol. Verführung am Meer Ostrva (GB and US: Island of Desire). The Prize. 1964: Unter Geiern (GB: Among Vultures. US: Frontier Hellcat). Le bambole (GB: Four Kinds of Love). A Shot in the Dark.

Seven Tons of Gunfire. 1965: The Art of Love. The Money Trap. Hotel der toten Gäste. Wenn man baden geht auf Teriffa. 1966: The Peking Medallion (US: The Corrupt Ones). The Oscar. Boy, Did I Get a Wrong Number. Deadlier than the Male. The Venetian Affair. 1967: The Wicked Dreams of Paula Schultz. 1968: The Invincible Six. Las Vegas 500 milliones (GB and US: They Came to Rob Las Vegas). 1969: The Wrecking Crew. 1970: Percy. 1971: Zeppelin. 1972: Probe (TV). Baron Blood. 1973: Die Reise nach Wien. Einer von uns Beiden. 1974: Ein unbekannten rechnet ab. And Then There Were None. Percy's Progress. 1975: The Swiss Conspiracy. Carry on Behind. House of Exorcism (US: Lisa and the Devil). 1976: Das Netz. On a Dead Man's Chest. 1977: The Thoroughbreds (later Treasure Seekers). The Astral Factor. 1978: I Miss You, Hugs and Kisses. Fantastic Seven/ Stunt Seven. The Double McGuffin. The Prisoner of Zenda. 1979: Top of the Hill (TV). 1980: Exit Sunset Boulevard. The Biggest Bank Robbery/A Nightingale Sang in Berkeley Square (TV. Originally for cinemas). 1981: Der Mann in Pyjama. 1983: Fitz and Lily/ Jatsani kell/Lily in Love. 1984: Invisible Strangler (revised version of The Astral Factor). 1985: Niemand weint für immer. 1986: Death Stone/In der Hitze des Dschungels. Neat and Tidy (TV). 1989: Himmelsheim. 1991: Army/Severed Ties. 1996: Das Fest. Dangerous Cargo. 1997: Alles nur Tarnung (US: Life is a Bluff). 2000: Take Out. Flashback.

SORVINO, Mira 1967–
Tall, dark-haired (sometimes blonde) American actress of snappy, faintly Latino attractiveness and sparkling eyes. Her career has followed a somewhat similar pattern to that of her contemporary Marisa Tomei (qv), with an Oscar for an eye-catching early performance (in Mighty Aphrodite), followed by starring roles in a string of ill-chosen, unworthy, unlucky or disappointing projects. The daughter of character star Paul Sorvino (1939–), she's a brainbox who graduated magna cum laude from Harvard in East Asian Studies and speaks fluent Mandarin Chinese.
1993: Amongst Friends. Tales of Erotica. *The Second Greatest Story Ever Told. *The Obit Writer. 1994: Barcelona. Parallel Lives (TV). Quiz Show. 1995: *The Dutch Master. NY Cop (GB: New York Cop). Mighty Aphrodite. Sweet Nothing. Blue in the Face. Tarantella. 1996: Norma Jean and Marilyn (TV). Neil

Simon's 'Jake's Women' (TV). Beautiful Girls. 1997: Romy and Michele's High School Reunion. Mimic. 1998: The Replacement Killers. Too Tired to Die. Lulu on the Bridge. Money Talks/Free Money. At First Sight. 1999: Summer of Sam. 2000: The Grreat Gatsby (TV). Joan of Arc: The Virgin Warrior. Famous.

SOTHERN, Ann (Harriette Lake) 1909–
Likeable, small but spirited Hollywood blonde with the 'hard-boiled Brooklyn dame' look (thin upper lip, full lower lip, arched eyebrows) who, after ingenue roles in the thirties, wisecracked her way through the forties, notably as a heart-of-gold adventuress called Maisie. Following a good run on TV in her own shows (1953–1961) she came back plump and blowsy, in character roles. Her first husband was actor Roger Pryor (1901–1974). Married (second) to Robert Sterling (qv) from 1943 to 1949; has not remarried. Oscar nominee for The Whales of August.
1927: Broadway Nights. 1929: The Show of Shows. Hearts in Exile. 1930: Doughboys (GB: Forward March). Hold Everything. 1933: Broadway thru a Keyhole. 1934: Let's Fall in Love. The Party's Over. Blind Date. (GB: Her Sacrifice). Kid Millions. Melody in Spring. Hell Cat. 1935: Hooray for Love. Eight Bells. Grand Exit. Folies Bergère (GB: The Man from the Folies Bergère). The Girl Friend. 1936: Don't Gamble with Love. You May Be Next! (GB: Panic on the Air). My American Wife. Hell Ship Morgan. Walking On Air. The Smartest Girl in Town. 1937: Ali Baba Goes to Town. There Goes My Girl. Dangerous Number. Danger–Love at Work. There Goes the Groom. Super Sleuth. Fifty Roads to Town. 1938: Trade Winds. She's Got Everything. 1939: Joe and Ethel Turp Call on the President. Hotel for Women/Elsa Maxwell's Hotel for Women. Fast and Furious. Maisie. 1940: Congo Maisie. Brother Orchid. Gold Rush Maisie. Dulcy. 1941: Maisie Was a Lady. Lady Be Good. Ringside Maisie (GB: Cash and Carry). 1942: Maisie Gets Her Man. (GB: She Gets Her Man). Panama Hattie. 1943: *You, John Jones. Swing Shift Maisie (GB: The Girl in Overalls). Cry Havoc. Thousands Cheer. Three Hearts for Julia. 1944: Maisie Goes to Reno (GB: You Can't Do That to Me). 1945: Up Goes Maisie (GB: Up She Goes). 1947: Undercover Maisie (GB: Undercover Girl). 1948: Words and Music. April Showers. The Judge Steps Out (GB:

Indian Summer). 1949: A Letter to Three Wives. 1950: Nancy Goes to Rio. Shadow on the Wall. 1953: The Blue Gardenia. 1964: Lady in a Cage. The Best Man. 1965: Sylvia. 1967: The Outsider (TV). 1968: Chubasco. 1971: Congratulations, It's a Boy (TV). A Death of Innocence (TV). The Great Man's Whiskers (TV). 1972: The Weekend Nun (TV). 1973: The Killing Kind. 1974: Golden Needles. 1975: Crazy Mama. 1977: The Manitou. 1980: The Little Dragons. 1985: A Letter to Three Wives (TV). 1987: The Whales of August.

SPACEK, Sissy

(Mary Elizabeth Spacek) 1949–

Small, fair-haired, freckled, childlike American actress whose large, pale eyes looked made for weeping and, in films, often were. Usually cast several years younger than her real age, she has offered striking performances in some very successful films of the 1970s and 1980s. Also sings. Won an Oscar for *Coal Miner's Daughter* and has also been nominated for *The River*, *Carrie*, *Missing*, and *Crimes of the Heart*. Married art director and sometime film director Jack Fisk in 1974. Cousin of Rip Torn (*qv*).

1970: Trash (as extra). 1972: Prime Cut. 1973: Badlands. Ginger in the Morning (GB: (TV). The Girls of Huntingdon House (TV). 1974: The Migrants (TV). 1975: Katherine (TV). 1976: Carrie. Welcome to L.A. 1977: 3 Women. 1979: Heart Beat. 1980: Coal Miner's Daughter. 1981: Raggedy Man. 1982: Missing. 1983: The Man with Two Brains (voice only). 1984: The River. 1985: Violets Are Blue. Marie – A True Story. 1986: 'Night, Mother. Crimes of the Heart. 1989: The Long Walk Home. 1991: Hard Promises. JFK. 1992: A Private Matter (TV). 1993: Trading Mom. A Place for Annie (TV). 1995: The Good Old Boys (TV). The Grass Harp. 1996: Beyond the Call (TV). If These Walls Could Talk (cable TV). 1997: Affliction. 1998: Blast from the Past. 1999: The Straight Story.

SPADER, James 1960–

This American actor is a smooth, fair-haired smiler who played oily villains for most of his first decade in the cinema, selling the hero or heroine down the river while pretending to be a nice guy. The only actor in a family of teachers, Spader began to find a wider variety of roles on offer after his Best Actor award for *Sex, Lies and Videotape* at the Cannes Film Festival. But the failure of other out-of-the-

way projects has made his profile lower in recent times.

*1978: Team-Mates. 1981: Endless Love. 1982: Cocaine: One Man's Seduction (TV). 1983: A Killer in the Family (TV). 1984: Family Secrets (TV). 1985: Tuff Turf. The New Kids. Starcrossed (TV). 1986: Pretty in Pink. 1987: Baby Boom. Less Than Zero. Mannequin. Wall Street. 1988: Jack's Back. *Greasy Lake. 1989: The Rachel Papers. Sex, Lies and Videotape. 1990: Bad Influence. White Palace. True Colors. 1992: Storyville. Bob Roberts. 1993: The Music of Chance. Dream Lover. 1994: Wolf. Stargate. 1996: Driftwood. 2 Days in the Valley. Crash. Keys to Tulsa. 1997: Critical Care. 1999: Supernova. Slow Burn. Curtain Call. 2000: The Watcher.*

SPACEY, Kevin (K.S. Fowler) 1959–

American actor of medium height and build with calm, relaxed features, slightly thinning dark hair and soothing tones. He opted for acting after being thrown out of military academy and rapidly established a reputation in the theatre. In films and on TV, however, his darting eyes and ironic mouth often had him cast as shady characters, but he took on a wider range after his Academy Award (Best Supporting Actor) for *The Usual Suspects* and is now considered one of Hollywood's most skilled performers. He won the Best Actor Oscar for his performance in *American Beauty*.

1986: Heartburn. 1987: The Murder of Mary Phagan (TV). Wiseguy (TV). Long Day's Journey into Night (TV). 1988: Working Girl. Rocket Gibraltar. 1989: Dad. See No Evil, Hear No Evil. 1990: Henry and June. A Show of Force. When You Remember Me (TV). 1991: Fall from Grace (TV). 1992: Con-

*senting Adults. Glengarry Glen Ross. Darrow (TV). 1993: Tribeca (TV). 1994: Iron Will. Doomsday Gun (TV). The Ref (GB: Hostile Hostages). Swimming with Sharks. 1995: The Usual Suspects. Outbreak. Se7en. 1996: Albino Alligator (directed only). A Time to Kill. Looking for Richard. 1997: L.A. Confidential. 1998: Midnight in the Garden of Good and Evil. Hurlyburly. The Negotiator. A Bug's Life (voice only). 1999: The Big Kahuna/ Hospitality Suite. *It's Tough to be a Bug. American Beauty. Ordinary Decent Criminal. Forever Hollywood (D). 2000: Pay It Forward.*

STACK, Robert (R. Modini) 1919–

Fair-haired American star of open, immobile features, hard, clipped tones and slightly crooked smile. Although good-looking and personable, he often seemed rather distant, those pale blue eyes not quite concentrating on the matter in hand. These facets of his character had him cast either as strong and dashing heroes or (best) men with weak links in their make-up, as in *The Tarnished Angels* or *Written on the Wind*. Later, a very successful TV star. Married actress Rosemarie Bowe. Oscar nominee for *Written on the Wind*.

*1939: First Love. 1940: A Little Bit of Heaven. The Mortal Storm. When the Daltons Rode. 1941: Nice Girl? Badlands of Dakota. *Variety Reel. 1942: Men of Texas (GB: Men of Destiny). To Be or Not To Be. *Keeping Fit. Eagle Squadron. 1948: Miss Tatlock's Millions. Fighter Squadron. A Date with Judy. 1950: Mr Music. 1951: My Outlaw Brother. The Bullfighter and the Lady. 1953: Bwana Devil. Sabre Jet. Conquest of Cochise. War Paint. 1954: The High and the Mighty. The Iron Glove. 1955: Good Morning, Miss Dove. House of Bamboo. Laura (TV. GB: cinemas). 1956: Great Day in the Morning. Written on the Wind. 1957: The Tarnished Angels. Panic Button (TV). 1958: The Gift of Love. 1959: John Paul Jones. The Scarface Mob (TV. GB: cinemas). 1960: The Last Voyage. Alcatraz Express (TV). 1963: The Caretakers (GB: Borderlines). 1965: Is Paris Burning? 1966: The Peking Medallion (US: The Corrupt Ones). 1967: Le soleil de voyous (GB and US: Action Man). Asylum for a Spy (TV). The Pill Caper (TV). 1969: Storia di una donna (GB and US: The Story of a Woman). 1970: Battle at Gannon's Bridge (TV). 1975: Adventures of the Queen (TV). Murder on Flight 502 (TV). The Strange and Deadly Occurrence (TV). 1976: Most Wanted (TV). 1978: Un second* souffle. Check Up. 1979: 1941. My Undercover Years with the KKK (TV. Voice only). 1980: Airplane! My Kidnapper, My Love (TV). 1983: Uncommon Valor. 1984: Big Trouble. Lusitano (narrator only). 1986: The Transformers (voice only). 1987: Perry Mason: The Case of the Sinister Spirit (TV). Korea: The Forgotten War (Cable TV. Narrator only). 1988: Dangerous Curves. Caddyshack II. Plain Clothes. 1990: Joe vs the Volcano. 1991: The Return of Eliot Ness (TV). 1995: Wild Bill: Hollywood Maverick. 1996: Beavis and Butt-head Do America (voice only). 1998: From Russia to Hollywood (doc). BASEketball. 1999: Mumford. Sealed with a Kiss (TV). Totally Irresponsible.

STALLONE, Sylvester 1946–
Muscular, surly-looking, dark-haired American actor with big ambitions who, after early struggles, shot into the superstar bracket with *Rocky*, an old-fashioned entertainment movie which he wrote himself. The film won an Oscar as Best Picture (Stallone received a Best Actor nomination), but its star has had to work hard to stay at the top. The characters of Rocky and, later, Vietnam veteran Rambo, enabled him to brush aside failures in other directions and stay in the superstar class. Known to his friends as 'Sly'. Married/divorced (second of three) actress Brigitte Nielsen.
1970: Party at Kitty and Studs (later re-released as The Italian Stallion). Lovers and Other Strangers. 1971: Bananas. Klute. 1972: No Place to Hide. The Prisoner of Second Avenue. 1974: The Lords of Flatbush. 1975: Farewell, My Lovely. Capone. Death Race 2000. 1976: Cannonball (GB: Carquake). Rocky. 1978: F.I.S.T. †Paradise Alley. 1979: †Rocky II. 1981: Nighthawks. Escape to Victory (US: Victory). 1982: First Blood. †Rocky III. 1983: Rebel (revised version of No Place to Hide). Later: A Man Called Rainbo). †Staying Alive. 1984: Rhinestone. 1985: Rambo: First Blood Part II. †Rocky IV. 1986: Cobra. 1987: Over the Top. 1988: Rambo III. 1989: Lock Up. Tango & Cash. 1990: Rocky V. 1991: Oscar. 1992: Stop, Or My Mom Will Shoot. Stephen Verona: Self Portrait. 1993: Cliffhanger. Demolition Man. 1994: The Specialist. 1995: Judge Dredd. Assassins. 1996: Daylight. 1997: Cop Land. An Alan Smithee film – Burn, Hollywood, Burn 1998: Antz (voice only). 2000: D-Tox/Detox. Get Carter. 2001: Champs.

†Also directed

STAMP, Terence 1939–
Pale-eyed, clear-faced, unsmiling British leading man. A sensation in his first two films, but a star career has gradually drifted away from him, though he came back to leading roles in the 1990s. Most recently seen as men of mystery and menace, he still remains one of filmland's most eligible bachelors. Oscar nominee for *Billy Budd*.
1962: Term of Trial. Billy Budd. 1964: The Collector. 1966: Modesty Blaise. 1967: Far from the Madding Crowd. Poor Cow. Histoires Extraordinares (GB: Tales of Mystery). 1968: Theorem/Teorema. Blue. 1969: The Mind of Mr Soames. 1971: Una stagione all' inferno. 1974: Hu-man. 1975: La divina creatura (US: The Divine Nymph). 1976: Striptease. 1978: Meetings with Remarkable Men. The Thief of Bagdad. Superman. 1979: Amo non amo/I Love You I Love You Not! Together. 1980: Superman II. Monster Island. 1981: Morte in Vaticano. 1984: The Hit. The Company of Wolves. 1985: Link. 1986: Under the Cherry Moon. Legal Eagles. Directed by William Wyler. Hud/Skin. 1987: The Sicilian. Wall Street. 1988: Young Guns. Alien Nation. 1990: Genuine Risk. 1991: Stranger in the House (and directed). Beltenebros (GB: Prince of Shadows). 1993: The Real McCoy. 1994: Priscilla Queen of the Desert. 1995: Uri. Bliss (released 1997). 1996: Limited Edition/Tire à part. 1997: The Bitter End. The Hunger (cable TV). 1998: Love Walked In. 1999: Bowfinger. The Limey. Star Wars: Episode 1 – The Phantom Menace. Kiss the Sky (TV). 2000: Mars/The Red Planet. La soutane écarlate.

STAMP-TAYLOR, Enid 1904–1946
British blonde actress with finely-boned features, a beauty contest winner who, after a shaky transition to sound, moved on to be a busy minor leading lady of the thirties, mostly in comedy. She was playing character roles as 'other woman' deserted by the hero for someone younger, when she died at 41 from a cerebral haemorrhage following injuries sustained in a fall.
1927: Land of Hope and Glory. Easy Virtue. Remembrance. 1928: A Little Bit of Fluff (US: Skirts). Yellow Stockings. Cocktails. 1929: Broken Melody. 1933: Meet My Sister. A Political Party. 1934: The Feathered Serpent. Virginia's Husband. Gay Love. 1935: Mr What's-His-Name. Radio Pirates. While Parents Sleep. So You Won't Talk? Jimmy Boy. Two Hearts in Harmony. 1936: Queen of Hearts. Blind Man's Bluff. House Broken. 1937: Underneath the Arches. Take a Chance. Talking Feet. Feather Your Nest. Okay for Sound. Action for Slander. 1938: Old Iron. Blondes for Danger. Stepping Toes. Climbing High. 1939: The Lambeth Walk. The Girl Who Forgot. 1940: The Farmer's Wife. Spring Meeting. Big Ben Calling (shortened version of Radio Pirates). 1941: Hatter's Castle. South American George. 1942: Alibi. 1943: Candlelight in Algeria. 1945: The Wicked Lady. 1946: Caravan.

STANWYCK, Barbara (Ruby Stevens, later legally changed) 1907–1990
Although it has been made before, the comparison between the real and assumed names of this tough, well-liked Hollywood lady (perhaps the best actress never to win an Oscar) is inescapable. So many of her characters were women, good or bad, struggling to escape the Ruby Stevens image and cross to Barbara Stanwyck on the glamorous side of the tracks. Often, their efforts ended in violence and tragedy. But whatever else, Stanwyck (who was also nifty in comedy) grabbed her films by the scruff of their necks, and left an indelible imprint. And she always insisted on doing her own stunt-work. Married (second) to Robert Taylor 1939–1951; never remarried. Special Academy Award 1982, following four unsuccessful nominations (*Stella Dallas*; *Ball of Fire*; *Double Indemnity*; *Sorry, Wrong Number*). Died from congestive heart failure following treatment for chronic bronchitis.
1927: Broadway Nights. 1929: The Locked Door. Mexicali Rose (GB: The Girl from Mexico). *The Voice of Hollywood. 1930: Ladies of Leisure. 1931: Illicit. Ten Cents a Dance. The Miracle Woman. *Screen Snapshots No 4. Night Nurse. 1932: Forbidden.

Shopworn. So Big. The Purchase Price. 1933: Baby Face. The Bitter Tea of General Yen. Ladies They Talk About. Ever in My Heart. *Hollywood on Parade A-11. 1934: A Lost Lady (GB: Courageous). Gambling Lady. The Secret Bride (GB: Concealment). 1935: Red Salute (GB: Arms and the Girl). The Woman in Red. Annie Oakley. 1936: The Bride Walks Out. A Message to Garcia. The Plough and the Stars. His Brother's Wife. Banjo on My Knee. 1937: Internes Can't Take Money (GB: You Can't Take Money). This is My Affair (GB: His Affair). Stella Dallas. Breakfast for Two. 1938: The Mad Miss Manton. Always Goodbye. 1939: Union Pacific. Golden Boy. Remember the Night. 1941: You Belong to Me (GB: Good Morning, Doctor). Ball of Fire. The Lady Eve. Meet John Doe. 1942: The Gay Sisters. The Great Man's Lady. 1943: Lady of Burlesque (GB: Striptease Lady). Flesh and Fantasy. 1944: Hollywood Canteen. Double Indemnity. My Reputation (released 1946). 1945: *Hollywood Victory Caravan. Christmas in Connecticut (GB: Indiscretion). 1946: The Bride Wore Boots. California. The Strange Love of Martha Ivers. 1947: The Two Mrs Carrolls. Variety Girl. The Other Love. Cry Wolf. 1948: BF's Daughter (GB: Polly Fulton). Sorry, Wrong Number. 1949: Thelma Jordon (GB: The File on Thelma Jordon). East Side, West Side. The Lady Gambles *Eyes of Hollywood. 1950: To Please a Lady. The Furies. No Man of Her Own. 1951: The Man with a Cloak. 1952: Clash by Night. 1953: All I Desire. Titanic. Jeopardy. The Moonlighter. Blowing Wild. 1954: Witness to Murder. Executive Suite. Cattle Queen of Montana. The Violent Men (GB: Rough Company). 1955: Escape to Burma. 1956: The Maverick Queen. These Wilder Years. There's Always Tomorrow. 1957: Crime of Passion. Forty Guns. Trooper Hook. 1962: A Walk on the Wild Side. 1964: Roustabout. 1965: The Night Walker. 1970: The House That Wouldn't Die (TV). 1971: A Taste of Evil (TV). 1972: The Letters (TV).

STARRETT, Charles 1904–1986
Well-built, dark-haired, square-jawed American leading man (a former star footballer) who played handsome, rocklike juvenile leads until he started making westerns in 1936. The rugged Starrett quickly became one of America's most popular 'B' western stars, especially in those dust-rousers which featured him as the Durango Kid. Some of the title changes in this list are quite extraordinary. He died from cancer.

1926: The Quarterback. 1930: The Royal Family of Broadway. Fast and Loose. 1931: Touchdown (GB: Playing the Game). The Viking. Silence. The Age for Love. Damaged Love. Sky Bride. 1932: Lady and Gent. The Mask of Fu Manchu. 1933: The Return of Casey Jones (GB: Train 2419). Our Betters. Mr Skitch. The Jungle Bride. The Sweetheart of Sigma Chi (GB: Girl of My Dreams). 1934: Murder on the Campus (GB: On the Stroke of Nine). This Man is Mine. Desirable. Gentlemen Are Born. Call It Luck. Green Eyes. The Silver Streak. One in a Million. Three on a Honeymoon. Stolen Sweets. 1935: What Price Crime? Sons of Steel. Make a Million. The Gallant Defender. A Shot in the Dark. One New York Night (GB: The Trunk Mystery). So Red the Rose. 1936: Stampede. Along Came Love. Code of the Range. Dodge City Trail. The Mysterious Avenger. The Cowboy Star. Secret Patrol. 1937: Westbound Mail. Two-Gun Law. One Man Justice. Outlaws of the Prairie. Old Wyoming Trail. Two Fisted Sheriff. Trapped. 1938: Law of the Plains. Start Cheering. Colorado Trail. South of Arizona. West of the Santa Fé. Cattle Raiders. West of Cheyenne. Call of the Rockies. Rio Grande. 1939: The Man from Sundown (GB: A Woman's Vengeance). Spoilers of the Range. Texas Stampede. The Stranger from Texas (GB: The Stranger). North of the Yukon. Western Caravans (GB: Silver Sands). Riders of Black River. Outpost of the Mounties (GB: On Guard). The Thundering West. 1940: Two-Fisted Rangers. Bullets for Rustlers (GB: On Special Duty). West of Abilene (GB: The Showdown). Thundering Frontier. Blazing Six-Shooters (GB: Stolen Wealth). Texas Stagecoach (GB: Two Roads). The Durango Kid (GB: The Masked Stranger). 1941: The Medico of Painted Springs (GB: Doctor's Alibi). Outlaws of the Panhandle (GB: Faro Jack). Thunder over the Prairie. Royal Mounted Patrol (GB: Giants A'Fire). The Pinto Kid (GB: All Square). The Prairie Stranger (GB: The Marked Bullet). Riders of the Badlands. 1942: Down Rio Grande Way (GB: The Double Punch). West of Tombstone. Bad Men of the Hills (GB: Wrongly Accused). Riding through Nevada. Lawless Plainsmen (GB: Roll On). Riders of the Northland (GB: Next in Line). Overland to Deadwood (GB: Falling Stones). Pardon My Gun. 1943: Robin Hood of the Range. The Fighting Buckaroo. Hail to the Rangers (GB: Illegal Rights). Cowboy in the Clouds. Frontier Fury. Law of the Northwest. 1944: Sundown Valley. Riding West (GB: Fugitive From Time). Cyclone Prairie Rangers. Cowboy Canteen (GB: Close Harmony). Cowboy from Lonesome River. Saddle Leather Law (GB: The Poisoner). 1945: Both Barrels Blazing (GB: The Yellow Streak). Rough Ridin' Justice (GB: Decoy). Rustlers of the Badlands (GB: By Whose Hand?). Outlaws of the Rockies (GB: A Roving Rogue). Sagebrush Heroes. Return of the Durango Kid (GB: Stolen Time). Blazing the Western Trail (GB: Who Killed Waring?). Lawless Empire (GB: Power of Possession). Texas Panhandle. 1946: Roaring Rangers (GB: False Hero). Frontier Gun Law (GB: Menacing Shadows). Two-Fisted Stranger. Heading West (GB: The Cheat's Last Throw). Terror Trail (GB: Hands of Menace).

Gunning for Vengeance (GB: Jail Break). Galloping Thunder (GB: On Boot Hill). The Desert Horseman (GB: Checkmate). Landrush (GB: The Claw Strikes). The Fighting Frontiersman (GB: Golden Lady). South of the Chisholm Trail. 1947: The Lone Hand Texan (GB: The Cheat). Prairie Raiders (GB: The Forger). The Buckaroo from Powder River. Riders of the Lone Star. West of Dodge City (GB: The Sea Wall). Law of the Canyon (GB: The Price of Crime). The Stranger from Ponca City. The Last Days of Boot Hill. 1948: Whirlwind Raiders (GB: State Police). Phantom Valley. Blazing across the Pecos (GB: Under Arrest). El Dorado Pass (GB: Desperate Men). West of Sonora. Six Gun Law. Trail to Laredo (GB: Sign of the Dagger). Quick on the Trigger (GB: Condemned in Error). 1949: Desert Vigilante. Challenge of the Range (GB: Moonlight Raid). Horsemen of the Sierras (GB: Remember Me). Bandits of El Dorado (GB: Tricked). The Blazing Trail (GB: The Forged Will). South of Death Valley (GB: River of Poison). Laramie. Renegades of the Sage (GB: The Fort). 1950: Trail of the Rustlers (GB: Lost River). Outcasts of Black Mesa (GB: The Clue). Across the Badlands (GB: The Challenge). Raiders of Tomahawk Creek (GB: Circle of Fear). Texas Dynamo (GB: Suspected). Streets of Ghost Town. Lightning Guns (GB: Taking Sides). Frontier Outpost. 1951: Fort Savage Raiders. Prairie Roundup. Bonanza Town (GB: Two-Fisted Agent). The Kid from Amarillo (GB: Silver Chains). Riding the Outlaw Trail. Snake River Desperadoes. Cyclone Fury. Pecos River (GB: Without Risk). 1952: Junction City. Smoky Canyon. The Hawk of Wild River. The Rough, Tough West. Laramie Mountains (GB: Mountain Desperadoes). The Kid from Broken Gun.

STEEL, Anthony 1919–
Strongly-built, smiling boyish, light-haired British leading man, trained for stardom by the Rank Organization, and the number one 'beefcake' pin-up of the British cinema from 1951 to 1956. Broke with Rank after marrying (1956–1962) Anita Ekberg, and resumed his career in Italy, but did not regain his former eminence with the British public. Much later played elder statesmen in sexploitation movies.

1948: Quartet. To the Public Danger. My Brother's Keeper. Saraband for Dead Lovers (US: Saraband). Portrait from Life (US: The Girl in the Painting). A Piece of Cake.

1949: *The Blue Lamp. Once Upon a Dream. Marry Me. Helter Skelter. Poet's Pub. Don't Ever Leave Me. The Chiltern Hundreds (US: The Amazing Mr Beecham). Trottie True (US: Gay Lady). Christopher Columbus.* 1950: *Trio. The Wooden Horse. The Mudlark.* 1951: *Another Man's Poison. Laughter in Paradise. Where No Vultures Fly (US: Ivory Hunter). Emergency Call (US: Hundred Hour Hunt).* 1952: *Something Money Can't Buy. The Planter's Wife (US: Outpost in Malaya).* 1953: *Malta Story. Albert RN (US: Break to Freedom). The Master of Ballantrae.* 1954: *West of Zanzibar. The Sea Shall Not Have Them.* 1955: *Out of the Clouds. Passage Home. Storm over the Nile.* 1956: *Checkpoint. The Black Tent.* 1957: *Valerie.* 1958: *Harry Black (US: Harry Black and the Tiger). A Question of Adultery.* 1959: *The Man in the Middle. Honeymoon. Forty Eight Hours to Live.* 1960: *Revenge of the Barbarians.* 1961: *Vacanze alla baia d'argento.* 1962: *Tiger of the Seven Seas.* 1963: *The Switch. A Matter of Choice. Hell is Empty (released 1967).* 1965: *Winnetou II (GB: Last of the Renegades).* 1966: *Le fate (GB: Sex Quartet). Zwei Girls vom Roten Stern (US: An Affair of State).* 1967: *Anzio (GB: The Battle for Anzio). War Devils.* 1968: *A Case for Inspector Blomfeld.* 1969: *Funkstreife XY. Häschen in der Grube.* 1973: *Massacre in Rome.* 1975: *Run, Rabbit, Run.* 1976: *The Night of the High Tide. The Story of O.* 1977: *Hardcore. Let's Get Laid!* 1978: *Indagine su un delitto perfetto.* 1979: *The World is Full of Married Men.* 1980: *The Mirror Crack'd. The Monster Club.*

STEELE, Barbara 1937–

Hauntingly beautiful, black-haired British actress with startlingly large brown eyes and unsettling presence. She went to Italy in 1960 (after a variety of small roles in Britain and Hollywood), where her strong, chilling performances in tales of fright earned her the title 'queen of horror films'. 'I had a marvellous time making them,' she once said, 'but I'm never going to climb out of another coffin as long as I live.' She disappeared in the late 1960s, before re-emerging for a while in Canadian and American films, older but still disturbingly watchable. Married/divorced playwright-screenwriter James Poe. Later, she became a producer.
1958: *Bachelor of Hearts. Houseboat.* 1959: *Sapphire. The 39 Steps. Upstairs and Downstairs. Your Money or Your Wife.* 1960:

Mask of the Demon (GB: Black Sunday). 1961: *The Iron Captain. The Pit and the Pendulum.* 1962: *Revenge of the Mercenaries. 8½. L'orrible segreto del Dr Hichcock (GB: The Terror of Dr Hichcock. US: The Horrible Dr Hitchcock). Le coup. Amour sans lendemain/Un tentativo sentimentale. Danse macabre (GB and US: Castle of Blood).* 1963: *Lo spetro (GB: The Spectre. US: The Ghost). The Hours of Love. Le voci bianche/Le sexe des anges. Les baisers (US: White Voices). I maniaci (US: The Maniacs). The Long Hair of Death. Amore facile. Le monocle rit jaune. El ataco (US: The Road to Violence).* 1965: *I soldi. L'armata Brancaleone. Cinque tombe per un medium (GB and US: Terror-Creatures from the Grave). Gli amanti d'oltre tomba (GB: The Faceless Monster. US: Nightmare Castle). La sorella di Satana (GB: Revenge of the Blood Beast. US: The She Beast).* 1966: *Young Törless. Un angelo per Satan/An Angel for Satan. For Love and Gold.* 1967: *Fermato il mondo . . . voglio scenere.* 1968: *Handicap. Curse of the Crimson Altar (US: Crimson Cult).* 1969: *Honeymoon with a Stranger (TV).* 1974: *The Parasite Murders (GB: Shivers. US: They Came from Within). Caged Heat.* 1977: *I Never Promised You a Rose Garden.* 1978: *Piranha. Pretty Baby. La clé sur la porte. The Space Watch Murders (TV).* 1979: *The Silent Scream.* 1990: *Dark Shadows (TV).* 1994: *Deep Above.* 1998: *Donald Cammell: The Ultimate Performance.* 1999: *The Prophet.*

STEELE, Tommy
(T. Hicks) 1936–
Cheerful, energetic, fair-haired, eager-to-please British entertainer who began as a rock 'n' roll star but soon enlarged his range, becoming a dancer and comedy actor, and bringing his chirpy cockney personality and engaging grin to several films. Entirely a stage star in the seventies and beyond.
1957: *Kill Me Tomorrow. The Shiralee (voice only). The Tommy Steele Story (US: Rock Around the World).* 1958: *The Duke Wore Jeans.* 1959: *Tommy the Toreador.* 1960: *Light Up the Sky.* 1963: *It's All Happening (US: The Dream Maker).* 1967: *The Happiest Millionaire. Half a Sixpence.* 1968: *Finian's Rainbow.* 1969: *Where's Jack?*

STEENBURGEN, Mary 1952–
Vivacious, wide-smiling American actress (also a useful singer), with dark, curly hair, warm, slightly offbeat personality and

deliberate speaking voice. A late arrival on the movie scene, she has somehow seemed difficult to cast and therefore made too few films, despite an Academy Award for her performance in *Melvin and Howard*. Married to actors Malcolm McDowell (from 1980 to 1990) and Ted Danson (both *qv*) from 1995.
1978: *Goin' South.* 1979: *Time After Time.* 1980: *Melvin and Howard.* 1981: *Ragtime.* 1982: *A Midsummer Night's Sex Comedy.* 1983: *Cross Creek. Romantic Comedy!* 1985: *One Magic Christmas.* 1986: *Dead of Winter.* 1987: *The Attic: The Hiding of Anne Frank (TV). End of the Line. The Whales of August.* 1989: *Miss Firecracker. Parenthood.* 1990: *Back to the Future Part III. The Long Walk Home.* 1991: *Clifford (released 1994). The Butcher's Wife.* 1992: *Best Interests.* 1993: *Philadelphia. What's Eating Gilbert Grape. Earth and the American Dream (voice only).* 1994: *My Summer Story/It Runs in the Family. Wyatt Earp. Pontiac Moon.* 1995: *Mi Famiglia/My Family/East L.A. Nixon. The Grass Harp. Powder.* 1998: *About Sarah (TV).* 1999: *Witness Protection (TV).* 2000: *Wish You Were Dead. Absolute Zero. Picnic (TV). Anasazi Moon.*

STEWART, Patrick 1940–
Bald British character star with small eyes, assertive features and rich, Shakespearian voice. Despite a distinguished theatrical career, those ringing tones were largely confined to glorified cameos in films until he was seconded to US TV in 1987 to play Captain Jean-Luc Picard in a revived *Star Trek* format. Although he quickly gathered a large fan following, it was another seven years before the franchise made its way to the big screen at a late stage in his career. It was only

then that he was able to begin a profitable period as a TV and film character star, with an impressive range of roles.

1975: Hedda. Hennessy. 1976: The Madness (TV). 1980: Little Lord Fauntleroy (TV. GB: cinemas). 1981: Excalibur. 1982: The Plague Dogs (voice only). 1983: Uindii. 1984: Dune. Pope John Paul II (TV). 1985: LifeForce. Lady Jane. Wild Geese II. 1991: L.A. Story. 1993: Alistair MacLean's Death Train (TV). Robin Hood: Men in Tights. 1994: Gunmen. In Search of Dr Seuss (TV). Star Trek Generations. 1995: Jeffrey. Let It Be Me. 1996: Star Trek: First Contact. The Canterville Ghost (TV). 1997: Masterminds/ Smart Alec. Conspiracy Theory. Dad Savage. 1998: Star Trek: Insurrection. Moby Dick (TV). The Prince of Egypt (voice only). 1999: A Safe House (TV). Animal Farm (voice only). A Christmas Carol (TV). 2000: X-Men.

STEIGER, Rod (Rodney Steiger) 1925–
Stocky, intense American actor whose ranting, raving, chew-up-the-scenery style based on 'The Method' made him one of the few latter-day acting targets for impressionists. In time, his performances grew less mannered and more enjoyable. Won an Oscar in 1967 for *In the Heat of the Night*. Married (second of four) to Claire Bloom from 1959 to 1969. Additional Oscar nominations for *On the Waterfront* and *The Pawnbroker*. Still around, often in very effective cameos.

1951: Teresa. 1954: On the Waterfront. 1955: The Big Knife. Oklahoma! The Court-Martial of Billy Mitchell (GB: One Man Mutiny). 1956: The Harder They Fall. Back from Eternity. Jubal. 1957: The Unholy Wife. Run of the Arrow. Across the Bridge. 1958: A Town Has Turned to Dust (TV). Cry Terror! 1959: Al Capone. 1960: Seven Thieves. 1961: The Mark. On Friday at 11. 1962: Convicts Four (GB: Reprieve!). 13 West Street. The Longest Day. 1963: Gli indifferenti (GB and US: Time of Indifference). Hands across the City. 1964: E venne un uomo/A Man Named John. 1965: The Pawnbroker. The Loved One. Doctor Zhivago. 1967: In the Heat of the Night. The Girl and the General. The Movie Maker (TV). No Way to Treat a Lady. 1968: The Sergeant. The Illustrated Man. Three into Two Won't Go. 1970: Waterloo. 1971: A Fistful of Dynamite/Duck You Sucker. Happy Birthday Wanda June. 1972: The Heroes. 1973: Lucky Luciano. Lolly Madonna XXX (GB: The Lolly Madonna War). 1974: Innocents with

Dirty Hands. 1975: Hennessy. 1976: W.C. Fields and Me. 1977: Jimbuck/Portrait of a Hitman. Mussolini: the Last Four Days. 1978: Love and Bullets. Wolf Lake (released 1984). F.I.S.T. 1979: Breakthrough/Sergeant Steiner. The Amityville Horror. Cattle Annie and Little Britches. 1980: Klondike Fever. Lion of the Desert/Omar Mukhtar Lion of the Desert. The Lucky Star. 1981: The Chosen. 1982: Der Zauerberg (US: The Magic Mountain). 1983: Mafia Kingpin. Cook and Peary: The Race to the Pole (TV). 1984: The Naked Face. 1986: Feel the Heat. The Kindred. Sword of Gideon (TV). 1987: American Gothic. Hello Actors Studio. 1988: Desperado: Avalanche at Devil's Ridge (TV). The January Man. Ice Runner. Celluloid. 1989: Passion and Paradise (TV). That Summer of White Roses. Tennessee Nights. 1990: Men of Respect. The Exiles. 1991: The Ballad of the Sad Café. In the Line of Duty: The Twilight Murders (TV). The Final Contract (TV). Guilty As Charged. 1992: The Player. Genghis Khan. 1993: The Neighbor. Earth and the American Dream (voice only). Taking Liberties. 1994: La congiura del silenzio. Seven Sundays. The Last Tattoo. The Specialist. Op Center (TV). 1995: In Pursuit of Honor (TV). Dalva (TV). Powder. Out There (cable TV). 1996: Livers Ain't Cheap/The Real Thing. Carpool. Mars Attacks! Truth or Consequences, N.M. Shiloh. 1997: The Kid (TV). Incognito. Cypress Edge (TV). Animals (and the Tollkeeper). The Flying Dutchman. 1998: Legacy. Revenant/ Modern Vampires. 1999: Crazy in Alabama. End of Days. The Hurricane. Shiloh 2: Shiloh Season. Body and Soul (TV). 2000: Wish You Were Dead. The Red Door. The Last Producer. The Hollywood Sign. Spoken in Silence.

STEN, Anna (Anjuschka Stenskaya Sujakevich) 1908–1993
Attractive, sympathetic, blonde Ukrainian actress who inherited her silky good looks from her Swedish mother. Imported by Samuel Goldwyn to Hollywood in 1933, following beginnings in Russian and German films, she was not a hit with the ticket-buying American public, although she was effective at portraying earth-rooted girls doomed to tragic romance. Stayed in America and became a painter in the 1960s and held several exhibitions. Married/divorced Russian director Fedor Ozep (first of two), she still lived in Manhattan at the time of her death from a heart attack.

1927: Zluta Knizka/The Yellow Ticket. Devushka a Korobkoi /The Girl with the Hatbox. 1928: Popmok Chingis-Khana (GB and US: Storm over Asia). Moskva v Okjabre (GB: Moscow Laughs and Cries. US: When Moscow Laughs). Belyi Orel (GB: The White Eagle. US: The Lash of the Czar). The House on Trubnaya Square. 1929: Moj Syn. Zolotoj Kljuw. 1930: Lohnbuchhalter Kremke. 1931: Bomben auf Monte Carlo. Der Mörder Dimitri Karamasoff/ The Brothers Karamazov. Salto Mortale (US: Trapeze). Stürme der Leidenschaft. 1934: Nana. We Live Again. 1935: The Wedding Night. 1936: A Woman Alone (US: Two Who Dared). 1939: Exile Express. 1940: The Man I Married. 1941: So Ends Our Night. 1943: They Came to Blow Up America. Chetniks. 1944: Three Russian Girls (GB: She Who Dares). 1948: Let's Live a Little. 1955: Soldier of Fortune. 1956: Runaway Daughters. 1957: Heaven Knows, Mr Allison. 1962: The Nun and the Sergeant.

STEPHEN, Susan 1931–2000
Demurely pretty British actress, her fair hair usually cropped short, with pin-up figure and attractively semi-husky speaking voice, in appealing leading roles within months of leaving RADA. Her roles after 1956 were disappointing. Married/divorced (second) cinematographer (now director) Nicolas Roeg.

1951: His Excellency. 1952: Stolen Face. Treasure Hunt. Fanciulle di lusso/Luxury Girls. Father's Doing Fine. 1953: The Red Beret (US: Paratrooper). The Case of the Studio Payroll. 1954: The House across the Lake (US: Heatwave). For Better, For Worse (US: Cocktails in the Kitchen). Dangerous Cargo. Golden Ivory (US: White Huntress). 1955: As Long As They're Happy. Value for Money. 1956: It's Never Too Late. Pacific Destiny. 1957: Carry on Nurse. 1960: Operation Stogie. 1961: The Court Martial of Major Keller. Return of a Stranger. 1962: Three Spare Wives.

STEPHENSON, James 1903–1941
One of the cinema's more extraordinary figures. A dark, moustachioed, tautly handsome British actor who made no films until his mid-thirties, he went to Hollywood in 1938, and, at Warners, advanced slowly to leading roles, revealing a talent and presence that had not been evident in his British films. Then, after only a handful of star parts, he dropped dead from a heart attack. Nominated

for an Academy Award on *The Letter*. Some sources give date of birth (a continuing controversy) as 1888 or 1889.

1937: The Man Who Made Diamonds. Dangerous Fingers (US: Wanted by Scotland Yard). The Perfect Crime. Take It From Me. You Live and Learn. 1938: The Dark Stairway. It's in the Blood. Mr Satan. Cowboy from Brooklyn (GB: Romance and Rhythm). Heart of the North. When Were You Born? White Banners. Nancy Drew, Detective. Boy Meets Girl. 1939: The Private Lives of Elizabeth and Essex. The Old Maid. On Trial. Torchy Blane in Chinatown. *Sons of Liberty. Espionage Agent. Secret Service of the Air. We Are Not Alone. Adventures of Jane Arden. Confessions of a Nazi Spy. Beau Geste. King of the Underworld. 1940: *The Monroe Doctrine. Wolf of New York. Devil's Island. Murder in the Air. Calling Philo Vance. A Dispatch from Reuter's (GB: This Man Reuter). The Letter. The Sea Hawk. South of Suez. River's End. 1941: Shining Victory. Flight from Destiny. International Squadron.

STERLING, Jan (Jane S. Adriance) 1923– Thin-faced, pencil-slim blonde American actress. Her looks got her cast as bitches, but her warm personality sometimes saw her through to more sympathetic roles. A solid dramatic performer whose considerable comedy talents were under-used. Married (second) to Paul Douglas from 1950 to his death in 1959. Later lived (in London) with actor Sam Wanamaker (1919–1993). Nominated for an Academy Award on *The High and the Mighty*.

1947: †Tycoon. †The Unfinished Dance. 1948: Johnny Belinda. 1950: The Skipper Surprised His Wife. Mystery Street. Caged. Union

Station. 1951: Appointment with Danger. The Big Carnival (GB: Ace in the Hole). The Mating Season. Rhubarb. 1952: Flesh and Fury. Sky Full of Moon. 1953: Pony Express. Split Second. The Vanquished. 1954: Alaska Seas. The High and the Mighty. The Human Jungle. Return from the Sea. 1955: The Man with the Gun (GB: The Trouble Shooter). Women's Prison. Female on the Beach. 1984. 1956: The Harder They Fall. Requiem for a Heavyweight (TV). 1957: Slaughter on Tenth Avenue. Clipper Ship (TV. GB: cinemas). 1958: Kathy O'. The Female Animal. High School Confidential! 1961: Love in a Goldfish Bowl. 1967: The Incident. 1968: The Angry Breed. 1969: The Minx. 1976: Sammy Somebody. Having Babies (TV). 1980: My Kidnapper, My Love (TV). 1981: First Monday in October. 1982: Dangerous Company (TV).

†As Jane Adrian

STERLING, Robert (William Hart) 1917– Brown-haired, boyish, blandly handsome American leading man; busy in the early war years, he rose slowly to co-star status, but found rewarding roles difficult to come by after returning from war service as an army pilot instructor. Chiefly noteworthy for marrying two glamorous actresses – Anne Sothern (*qv*) 1943–1949 and Anne Jeffreys (1923–) from 1951 on. With Jeffreys he had some success in the TV series *Topper*, but eventually quit show business to go into computer software. Father of actress Tisha Sterling.

1939: The Amazing Mr Williams. Blondie Brings Up Baby. Blondie Meets the Boss. *Charles Goodyear. Golden Boy. The Man They Could Not Hang. Mr Smith Goes to Washington. My Son is Guilty (GB: Crime's End). Those High Gray Walls (GB: The Gates of Alcatraz). Beware Spooks! Only Angels Have Wings. First Offenders. Good Girls Go to Paris. Missing Daughters. Outside These Walls. A Woman is the Judge. Romance of the Redwoods. 1940: *The Heckler. *Nothing But Pleasure. Yesterday's Heroes. Scandal Sheet. The Gay Caballero. Manhattan Heartbeat. 1941: The Getaway. The Penalty. Two-Faced Woman. Ringside Maisie. Johnny Eager. Dr Kildare's Victory (GB: The Doctor and the Debutante). I'll Wait for You. 1942: This Time for Keeps. Somewhere I'll Find You. 1946: The Secret Heart. 1949: The Sundowners (GB: Thunder in the Dust). Roughshod. 1950: Bunco

Squad. 1951: Show Boat. 1953: Column South. 1961: Return to Peyton Place. Voyage to the Bottom of the Sea. 1963: A Global Affair.

STEVENS, Andrew 1955–
Light-haired American actor of boyish handsomeness and clean-cut appeal, the son of Stella Stevens (*qv*). After dramatic training, he looked an up-and-comer in the 1970s, but never quite reached the top in films. In TV series and mini-series, though, he was a star and, despite limited ability, established a dominant presence in several of them through the early 1980s. From the middle of the decade, he began to make straight-to-video movies, some of which he directed himself, very varied in quality and content: everything from soft-core sexploitation to action films and children's entertainments. Entirely a producer since 1997.

1975: The Last Survivors (TV). Shampoo. Vigilante Force. 1976: Massacre at Central High. The Oregon Trail (TV. And ensuing series). The Quest (TV). The Day of the Animals. Las Vegas Lady (TV). 1977: Secrets (TV). The Boys in Company C. 1978: The Fury. 1979: The Rebels (TV). Topper (TV). Women at West Point (TV). 1980: Death Hunt. 1981: Miracle on Ice (TV). Code Red (TV. And ensuing series). The Seduction. 1982: Forbidden Love (TV). 10 to Midnight. 1985: Tusks (released 1990). 1986: Scared Stiff. 1987: Counterforce. 1988: Deadly Innocents/ Deadly Innocence (TV). Oro fino/Fine Gold. The Terror Within. 1989: The Ranch. Down the Drain. 1990: Night Eyes. Red-Blooded American Girl. †The Terror Within 2. 1991: Munchie. Night Eyes 2. Columbo: Murder in Malibu (TV). 1992: Deadly Rivals. Double Threat. Eyewitness to Murder. 1993: †Illicit Dreams. †Night Eyes 3. A Woman Scorned. 1994: Body Chemistry 3: Point of Seduction. Munchie Strikes Back. †The Skateboard Kid 2. 1995: A Woman Scorned 2. Night Eyes 4. Body Chemistry 4: Full Exposure. 1996: Subliminal Seduction (TV). 1997: The Shooter.

†And directed

STEVENS, Connie (Concetta Ingolia) 1938–
Bright, busy American leading lady who flourished briefly in the cinema as a kind of cross between Sandra Dee and Connie Francis. Usually in innocent roles that belied her looks. Only very sporadically seen in the cinemas after the mid-sixties. Married to

actor James Stacy and singer Eddie Fisher (both ended in divorce). Mother of actresses Tricia Leigh Fisher and Joely Fisher.
1957: Eighteen and Anxious. Young and Dangerous. 1958: Rock-a-Bye Baby. Dragstrip Riot. The Party Crashers. 1961: Susan Slade. Parrish. 1963: Palm Springs Weekend. 1964: Two on a Guillotine. 1965: Never Too Late. 1967: Way . . . Way Out. 1969: Mr Jerico. The Littlest Angel (TV). 1971: The Grissom Gang. The Last Generation. 1972: Call Her Mom (TV). Playmates (TV). Every Man Needs One (TV). 1974: The Sex Symbol (TV. GB: cinemas) 1976: Scorchy. 1978: Sergeant Pepper's Lonely Hearts Club Band. 1979: Love's Savage Fury (TV). 1980: Murder Can Hurt You! 1981: Side Show (TV). 1982: Grease 2. 1987: Back to the Beach. Tapeheads. 1988: Bring Me the Head of Dobie Gillis (TV). 1993: King B: A Life in the Movies. 1995: Oh No, Not Her! 1996: James Dean – Race with Destiny (TV. Released 1999). Love is All There Is.

STEVENS, Craig (Gail Shikles) 1918–2000
Tall, broad-shouldered American leading man with wavy, brown hair who played solid, reliable types in largely undistinguished films and was much more successful on television, especially from 1958 in the series Peter Gunn, a private eye he later recreated on screen. Married to Alexis Smith (qv) from 1944 to her death in 1993. Died from cancer. One source gives date of birth as 1910.
1939: Mr Smith Goes to Washington. 1941: *At the Stroke of Twelve. The Body Disappears. Law of the Tropics. Affectionately Yours. Dive Bomber. Steel against the Sky. 1942: Secret Enemies. Now, Voyager. Spy Ship. The Hidden Hand. 1943: *Jap Zero. *Three Cadets. This is the Army. 1944:

Resisting Enemy Interrogation. Hollywood Canteen. The Doughgirls. Since You Went Away. 1945: God is My Co-Pilot. Roughly Speaking. Too Young to Know. 1946: The Man I Love. Humoresque. 1947: That Way with Women. Love and Learn. 1948: *Melodies of Memory Lane. 1949: The Lady Takes a Sailor. Night Unto Night. 1950: Where the Sidewalk Ends. Blues Busters. 1951: Katie Did It. The Lady From Texas. Drums in the Deep South. 1952: Phone Call from a Stranger. 1953: Murder without Tears. Abbott and Costello Meet Dr Jekyll and Mr Hyde. 1954: The French Line. 1955: Duel on the Mississippi. 1956: Forbidden Planet. 1957: The Deadly Mantis. 1958: Buchanan Rides Alone. 1967: Gunn. 1968: The Limbo Line. McCloud: Who Killed Miss USA? (TV). 1972: The Female Instinct (TV. GB: The Snoop Sisters). 1974: The Killer Bees (TV). 1975: The Elevator (TV). Nick and Nora (TV). 1977: The Cabot Connection (TV). 1978: Secrets of Three Hungry Wives (TV). 1981: SOB. La truite/The Trout. 1986: Condor (TV). 1988: A Holiday Affair (TV). Supercarrier (TV).

STEVENS, Inger (I. Stensland). 1934–1970
Swedish-born actress in Hollywood, whose smooth, enigmatic, high-cheekboned prettiness somehow gave hints of great sex appeal smouldering below the surface. Had a tough time in the mid-sixties when many would-be employers apparently ostracized her after she married a black musician. Committed suicide with sleeping pills.
1957: Man on Fire. 1958: Cry Terror! The Buccaneer. 1959: The World, the Flesh and the Devil. Diary of a Nurse (TV). 1964: The New Interns. 1967: A Guide for the Married Man. The Borgia Stick (TV). A Time for Killing (GB: The Long Ride Home). Firecreek. 1968: Madigan. Hang 'Em High. House of Cards. Five Card Stud. 1969: A Dream of Kings. 1970: Run, Simon, Run (TV). The Mask of Sheba (TV).

STEVENS, Mark
(Richard Stevens) 1915–1994
Dark-haired American actor of serious personality who began his career in Canada, then came to Hollywood in 1941 to play small roles as Stephen Richards. Did his best work as fatalistic heroes in noir thrillers; later directed a few of his own films, proving quite efficient at manipulating suspense. Died in Spain.
1941: †Two-Faced Woman. 1943: †Destination Tokyo. †Background to Danger. †Northern

Pursuit. 1944: †Passage to Marseilles. †The Doughgirls. †Hollywood Canteen. 1945: †Objective Burma. †Pride of the Marines (GB: Forever in Love). †Roarin' Guns. †Rhapsody in Blue. †God is My Co-Pilot. Within These Walls. 1946: From This Day Forward. The Dark Corner. 1947: I Wonder Who's Kissing Her Now? 1948: The Street With No Name. The Snake Pit. 1949: Will James's Sand (GB: Sand). Oh, You Beautiful Doll. Dancing in the Dark. 1950: Please Believe Me. Between Midnight and Dawn. 1951: Target Unknown. Katie Did It. Reunion in Reno. Little Egypt (GB: Chicago Masquerade). 1953: Mutiny. Torpedo Alley. The Lost Hours (US: The Big Frame). 1952: Jack Slade (GB: Slade). 1954: ‡Cry Vengeance. 1955: ‡Timetable. 1957: Gunsight Ridge. ‡Gun Fever. 1958: Gunsmoke in Tucson. 1960: September Storm. 1964: ‡Escape from Hell Island. Fate is the Hunter. Frozen Alive. 1965: ‡Vergeltung in Catano (GB and US: Sunscorched). 1969: España otra vez. 1970: Lola, dicen que no vive sola. 1971: Es usted mi padre? 1972: La furia del hombre lobo.

†As Stephen Richards ‡Also directed.

STEVENS, Stella
(Estelle Eggleston) 1936–
Another of Hollwood's gutsy blondes, still in there working as she pushes on into her sixties. With rosebud lips, turned-up nose and a figure that would look good in a sack, Stella found herself mostly used in films as lightweight decoration, but she also had lots of personality, spirit and too-rarely-tapped acting ability, only Too Late Blues and The Ballad of Cable Hogue bringing out anything like the best in her. The thoughtfulness behind the ingenuously sexy surface appeal

was underlined when she directed a feature documentary in 1980. But she was seen mainly in undignified sex and horror straight-to-video films in the run-up to her sixties, sometimes in movies directed by Andrew Stevens (qv), her actor son.

1959: Say One for Me. The Blue Angel. Li'l Abner. 1961: Mantrap. Too Late Blues. 1962: Girls! Girls! Girls! 1963: The Courtship of Eddie's Father. The Nutty Professor. Advance to the Rear (GB: Company of Cowards). 1965: Synanon (GB: Get Off My Back). The Secret of My Success. 1966: The Silencers. Rage (Glenn Ford). 1967: How to Save a Marriage . . . and Ruin Your Life. Sol Madrid (GB: The Heroin Gang). 1968: Where Angels Go . . . Trouble Follows. The Mad Room. 1970: The Ballad of Cable Hogue. 1971: A Town Called Bastard (US: A Town Called Hell). Stand Up and Be Counted. In Broad Daylight (TV). 1972: The Poseidon Adventure. Rage (George C. Scott). Climb an Angry Mountain (TV). Slaughter. 1973: Arnold. Linda (TV). 1974: The Day the Earth Moved (TV). Honky Tonk (TV). 1975: Cleopatra Jones and the Casino of Gold. The New Original Wonder Woman (TV). 1976: Las Vegas Lady. Wanted: The Sundance Woman (TV). Nickelodeon. Kiss Me, Kill Me (TV). 1977: Charlie Cobb: Nice Night for a Hanging (TV). The Manitou. The New Love Boat (TV). 1978: The Jordan Chance (TV). The Hostage Heart (TV). Cruise into Terror (TV). The Deadly Price of Paradise (TV. GB: Nightmare at Pendragon's Castle). Murder in Peyton Place (TV). 1979: Supertrain (TV. Later: Express to Terror). Hart to Hart (TV). Friendship, Secrets and Lies (TV). The Night They Took Miss Beautiful (TV). 1980: Make Me an Offer (TV). 1981: Twirl (TV). Mister Deathman. 1982: Children of Divorce (TV). Wacko. 1983: Women of San Quentin (TV). 1984: Amazons (TV). No Man's Land (TV). 1985: The Long Shot. 1986: Monster in the Closet. A Masterpiece of Murder (TV). Neat and Tidy (TV). 1987: Fatal Confession (TV). 1988: The Ranch. 1989: Mom. Down the Drain. Jake Spanner – Private Eye (TV). Man Against the Mob (TV. GB: Murder in the City of Angels). 1990: Last Call. 1991: The Terror Within II. 1992: The Nutty Nut. Exiled / Exiled in America. South Beach. 1993: Eye of the Stranger. Illicit Dreams. 1994: Hard Drive. Attack of the 5' 2" Woman. F.T.W. Body Chemistry III: Point of Seduction. 1995: The Granny. Blood Relative. Molly & Gina. Body Chemistry 4: Full Exposure. Star Hunter (V). Invisible Mom. 1996: Virtual Combat. Sublimal Seduction (TV). In Cold Blood (TV). 1997: Bikini Hotel. The Christmas List (TV). The Dukes of Hazzard Reunion! (TV). As director: 1980: The American Heroine. 1988: The Ranch.

STEWART, Alexandra 1939–

Tall, cool, sandy-haired Canadian actress who began her career in France, and has filmed all over the world without quite becoming an international star. Tackled all kinds of cinema, but (perhaps because of this) there was little consistency to her work: Truffaut one moment, Emmanuelle the next.

1958: Le bel âge (GB: Love is Where You find It). 1959: L'eau à la bouche (GB: The Game

of Love). Les motards. Deux hommes dans Manhattan. Liaisons dangereuses. 1960: Merci natercia (released 1962). 1960: La mort de belle. The Season for Love. Les distractions (GB: Trapped by Fear). Tarzan the Magnificent. Exodus. 1961: Une grosse tête. Naked Autumn. Les mauvais coups. Rendezvous de minuit. 1962: Humenaje a la hora de la siesta (US: Four Women for One Hero). Violenza secreta. Die Dekenntnisse eines möblierten Heern. Climats. Rogopag. 1963: And So to Bed / Das grosse Liebesspiel. Dragées au poivre (GB: and US: Sweet and Sour). Le feu follet (GB: A Time to Live and a Time to Die. US: Will o' the Wisp). The Passion of Slow Fire. 1964: Die endlose Nacht. The Man Called Gringo / Sie nannten ihn, Gringo. Volles Herz und leere Taschen. 1965: Thrilling. Wedding March. Mickey One. La Ley del Forastero. 1966: Maroc 7. 1967: La loi du survivant. L'écume des jours. 1968: Waiting for Caroline. Only When I Larf. La mariée était en noir / The Bride Wore Black. Bessen – das Lock in der Wand. 1969: Ohrfeigen. Bye Bye Barbara. Umano no umano. 1970: The Man Who Had Power over Women. Le ciel est bleu. Ils. 1971: Valparaiso, Valparaiso. Zeppelin. Ou est passé, Tom? 1972: Les soleils de l'île de Pâques. The Rape. 1973: La nuit Américaine (GB and US: Day for Night). Bingo. The Heatwave Lasted Four Days. 1974: The Marseilles Contract (US: The Destructors). 1975: Black Moon. Un animal odue de déraison. 1977: Goodbye Emmanuelle. Julie Pot-de-Cole / The Chains of Pity. The Uncanny. In Praise of Older Women. 1978: The Little Girl in Blue Velvet. 1980: Agency. The Last Chase. Your Ticket is No Longer Valid. Phobia. Le soleil en face. Final Assignment. 1981: Chanel solitaire. Madame Claude 2 (later and US: Intimate Moments. GB: The Girls of Madame Claude). Aiutami e sognare (US: Help Me Dream). Chassé-croisé. La guerillera. Les uns et les autres / Boléro. 1982: L'imposteur. Le jour le plus court. 1983: Sans soleil (narrator only). Le sang de autres / The Blood of Others. Femmes. Charlots Connection. Le bon plaisir. 1984: Kusameikyu (narrator of English version only). Mistral's Daughter (Cable TV). L'herbe rouge. 1985: Le matou (US: The Alley Cat). 1986: Under the Cherry Moon. Peau d'ange (filmed 1983). 1987: Frantic. 1988: Der Passagier (US: Welcome to Germany). 1989: Champagne Charlie (TV). Monsieur. 1995: Le fils de Gascogne. 1996: Seven Servants. 1997: La Candide. Madame Duff.

STEWART, James 1908–1997

Tall, slim, long-faced, dark-haired, much-loved American leading man with a slow bumbling drawl which reflected those qualities of thoughtfulness and honesty which he projected in so many of his roles and which made him the target for a million drawing-room impressionists. His best roles (pre-war) cast him as one man against the system, or (post-war) one man against the odds in westerns and suspense thrillers. Only his later comedies are consistently less successful: but even in films as late as Firecreek and The Magic of Lassie, his sincerity is still capable of raising a lump in the throat. Oscar for The Philadelphia Story. Also nominated for Academy Awards on Mr Smith Goes to Washington, It's a Wonderful Life!, Harvey and Anatomy of a Murder. Died from a lung embolism.

*1934: *Art Trouble. 1935: *Important News. The Murder Man. 1936: Next Time We Love (GB: Next Time We Live). Rose Marie. Wife vs. Secretary. Small Town Girl. Speed. Born to Dance. The Gorgeous Hussy. After the Thin Man. 1937: Seventh Heaven. The Last Gangster. Navy Blue and Gold. 1938: Of Human Hearts. The Shopworn Angel. Vivacious Lady. You Can't Take It with You. 1939: Ice Follies of 1939. It's a Wonderful World. Made for Each Other. Destry Rides Again. Mr Smith Goes to Washington. 1940: No Time for Comedy. The Shop Around the Corner. The Mortal Storm. The Philadelphia Story. 1941: Ziegfeld Girl. Come Live with Me. Pot o' Gold (GB: The Golden Hour). 1942: *Screen Snapshots No 103. *Fellow American. *Winning Your Wings. 1946: *American Brotherhood Week. It's a Wonderful Life! 1947: Thunderbolt (narrator only). Magic Town. Call Northside 777. 1948: A Miracle Can Happen (later: On Our Merry Way). Rope. You Gotta Stay Happy. *10,000 Kids and a Cop. 1949: The Stratton Story. Malaya (GB: East of the Rising Sun). 1950: *And Then There Were Four (narrator only). The Jackpot. Winchester '73. Broken Arrow. Harvey. 1951: No Highway (US: No Highway in the Sky). 1952: The Greatest Show on Earth. Bend of the River (GB: Where the River Bends). Carbine Williams. 1953: Thunder Bay. *Hollywood Laugh Parade. The Naked Spur. The Glenn Miller Story. 1954: Rear Window. The Far Country. 1955: Strategic Air Command. The Man from Laramie. 1956: The Man Who Knew Too Much. 1957: Night Passage. The Spirit of St Louis. 1958: Bell,*

Book and Candle. Vertigo. 1959: The FBI Story. Anatomy of a Murder. 1960: The Mountain Road. 1961: Two Rode Together. X-15 (narrator only). 1962: The Man Who Shot Liberty Valance. Mr Hobbs Takes a Vacation. How the West Was Won. 1963: Take Her, She's Mine. 1964: Cheyenne Autumn. 1965: Dear Brigitte. . . The Flight of the Phoenix. Shenandoah. The Rare Breed. 1966: *Hollywood Star-Spangled Revue. 1967: Firecreek. 1968: Bandolero! 1970: The Cheyenne Social Club. 1971: Fools' Parade (GB: Dynamite Man from Glory Jail). 1973: Hawkins on Murder (TV). 1974: That's Entertainment! 1976: The Shootist. 1977: Airport 77. 1978: The Big Sleep. The Magic of Lassie. Mr Kreuger's Christmas (TV). 1981: The Green Horizon/A Tale of Africa. 1983: Right of Way (TV). 1991: An American Tail 2: Fievel Goes West (voice only).

STILLER, Ben 1965–
Rather sullen-looking American actor-comedian-writer-director with dark curly hair. After playing some minor roles and directing a short film, he was hired by the cult TV comedy show Saturday Night Live as a writer-performer and soon had his own TV show. Film success as a performer and director has proved more elusive, but he has built up an interestingly varied gallery of performances and his best film as director, The Cable Guy, was better than most critics allowed. After showing well as a comic performer in There's Something About Mary and Mystery Men, Stiller tried direction again with What Makes Sammy Run. Son of actress-writer Anne Meara. Married to actress Christine Taylor.
1987: The House of Blue Leaves (TV). *The Hustler of Money. Empire of the Sun. Hot Pursuit. 1988: Fresh Horses. 1989: *Elvis Stories. Next of Kin. 1990: Stella. 1991: Working Trash. Highway to Hell. 1994: Reality Bites. 1995: Heavyweights. 1996: Flirting with Disaster. Happy Gilmore. If Lucy Fell. The Cable Guy. 1997: Zero Effect. 1998: There's Something About Mary. Your Friends & Neighbors. Permanent Midnight. 1999: The Suburbans. Black & White. Mystery Men. 2000: The Independent. Keeping the Faith. 2001: Meet the Parents. Zoolander.
As director. 1987: *The Hustler of Money. 1989: *Elvis Stories. 1994: Reality Bites. 1996: The Cable Guy. 2000: What Makes Sammy Run.

STING (Gordon Sumner) 1951–
Tall, slim, fair-haired, waspish-looking British singer and, latterly, actor. Rising to fame as lead singer with the pop group Police (after beginning his career as a teacher), Sting moved into movies, but soon showed he needed casting with care to get the most out of his unusual and faintly unsettling personality. Brilliantly effective in Brimstone and Treacle, he sounded far less happy in The Bride, but chose more wisely after that. In the mid nineties he hit more headlines for his courtroom battles with his former accountant than for his acting or music. Married/divorced actress Frances Tomelty. Later married actress Trudie Styler.
1979: Quadrophenia. Radio On.1981: Urgh – A Music War. 1982: The Secret Policeman's Other Ball. Brimstone and Treacle. 1984: Dune. 1985: The Bride. Plenty. Bring On the Night. 1987: Giulia and Giulia. 1988: Stormy Monday. The Adventures of Baron Munchausen. 1990: Resident Alien. 1992: The Music Tells You. 1995: The Grotesque (US: Gentlemen Don't Eat Poets). 1998: Lock, Stock & Two Smoking Barrels. 2001: All Access.

ST JOHN, Jill
(J. Oppenheim) 1940–
Red-headed American actress with sumptuous figure and headline-hitting private life. Had a surprised sort of face and usually played slightly daffy but likeable heroines. Whatever her merits as an actress, she was a performer of some spirit, notably in her intrepid heroine of Diamonds Are Forever and swashbuckling spitfire of The King's Pirate, the latter proving she could have filled Maureen O'Hara boots had not the time for the genre long passed. Married/divorced singer Jack Jones. Married Robert Wagner (qv) in 1990, her fourth husband.
1953: Thunder in the East (completed 1951). 1957: Summer Love. 1959: The Remarkable Mr Pennypacker. Holiday for Lovers. 1960: The Lost World. 1961: The Roman Spring of Mrs Stone. Tender is the Night. 1963: Who's Been Sleeping in My Bed? Who's Minding the Store? Come Blow Your Horn. 1964: Honeymoon Hotel. 1965: The Liquidator. 1966: The Oscar. Fame is the Name of the Game (TV). How I Spent My Summer Vacation (TV. GB: cinemas as Deadly Roulette). 1967: Banning. Eight on the Lam (GB: Eight on the Run). The King's Pirate. Tony Rome. 1969: Foreign Exchange (TV). The Spy Killer (TV). 1971: Decisions, Decisions! (TV). Diamonds are Forever. 1972: Sitting Target. 1974: Brenda Starr, Girl Reporter (TV). 1978: Telethon (TV). 1979: Hart to Hart (TV). 1982: Rooster (TV). The Concrete Jungle. The Act. Matt Houston (TV). 1983: 99 Women. 1992: The Player. 1995: Out There (cable TV). 1997: Something to Believe In.

STOCKFELD, Betty 1905–1966
This light-haired Australian actress with square chin and friendly eyes wasn't exactly pretty, but she had a forthright personality that endeared her to British audiences of the 1930s and she made the majority of her screen career in that country, mostly as girls of strong character. There was also a debut film in Hollywood and a few forays to France. In billing, her surname was sometimes (erroneously) spelt Stockfield. She died from cancer.
1926: What Price Glory? 1930: City of Song (US: Farewell to Love). 1931: Captivation. 77 Park Lane. 1932: Life Goes On/Sorry You've Been Troubled. Money for Nothing. The Impassive Footman (US: Woman in Bondage). The Maid of the Mountains. Women in Chains. 1933: King of the Ritz. Lord of the Manor. Anne One Hundred. 1934: The Man Who Changed His Name. The Battle (US: Thunder in the East). Brides to Be. 1935: The Lad. Runaway Ladies. 1936: Under Proof. Beloved Vagabond. Dishonour Bright. 1937: Who's Your Lady Friend? L'ange du foyer. Club de femmes (US: Girls' Club). 1938: I See Ice. The Slipper Episode. 1939: Ils étaient douze femmes. Derrière la façade. 1942: Hard Steel. Flying Fortress. 1949: The Girl Who Couldn't Quite. 1950: Édouard et Caroline. 1955: The Lovers of Lisbon. 1956: Guilty? True As a Turtle. 1957: Le désir interdit.

STOCKWELL, Dean
(Robert D. Stockwell) 1936–
Appealing American boy actor with dark, curly hair. As a young adult, he offered two excellent performances, in *Compulsion* and *Sons and Lovers*, but his star career got away from him in the sixties: some said he was too choosy. Maybe he is just a clever actor who lacks the strength and stature of a superstar. Married to Millie Perkins 1960–1964. An Oscar nominee for *Married to the Mob*, he won renewed popularity in the 1990s in the TV series *Quantum Leap*. Brother of actor Guy Stockwell.
*1945: The Valley of Decision. Abbott and Costello in Hollywood. Anchors Aweigh. 1946: Home Sweet Homicide. The Green Years. *A Really Important Person. 1947: Song of the Thin Man. The Mighty McGurk. The Arnelo Affair. The Romance of Rosy Ridge. Gentleman's Agreement. 1948: Down to the Sea in Ships. The Secret Garden. 1950: The Happy Years. Stars in My Crown. Kim. 1951: Cattle Drive. 1956: Gun for a Coward. 1957: Horsepower (TV). The Careless Years. 1959: Made in Japan (TV). Compulsion. 1960: Sons and Lovers. 1962: Long Day's Journey into Night. 1965: Rapture. 1968: Psych-Out. 1970: †Ecstasy 70. The Dunwich Horror. 1971: The Last Movie. The Failing of Raymond (TV). Paper Man (TV). 1972: The Loners. The Adventures of Nick Carter (TV). 1973: The Werewolf of Washington. 1974: Another Day at the Races (GB: Win, Place or Steal). Edweard Muybridge, Zoopraxographer (narrator only). 1975: Won Ton Ton, the Dog Who Saved Hollywood. The Pacific Connection. The Return of Joe Forrester (TV). 1976: Tracks. 1977: The Killing Affair (TV). 1979: She Came to the Valley (uncompleted). 1981: Born to be Sold (TV. GB: The Baby Brokers). 1982: Wrong is Right/The Man with the Deadly Lens. Human Highway. 1983: Alsino y El Condor. 1984: To Kill a Stranger. Dune. Paris, Texas. 1985: The Legend of Billy Jean. Papa Was a Preacher. To Live and Die in L.A. 1986: Blue Velvet. Banzai Runner. 1987: Gardens of Stone. Beverly Hills Cop II. The Blue Iguana. 1988: Tucker: The Man and His Dream. Buying Time. Married to the Mob. Palais Royale. The Time Guardian. 1989: Backtrack (GB: Catchfire). Limit Up. Jorge um Brasiliero. Quantum Leap (TV). The Long Haul. Stickfighter. 1990: Smokescreen. Sandino. 1992: Shame (cable TV). The Player. Friends and Enemies. 1993: Bonanza: The Return (TV). 1994: Chasers. The*

Innocent (TV). The Langoliers (TV). Madonna: Innocence Lost (TV). 1995: Naked Souls. 1996: Mr Wrong. Midnight Blues. Twilight Man. Unabomber: The True Story (TV). 1997: McHale's Navy. Air Force One. Living in Peril (cable TV). Sinbad: The Battle of the Dark Knights. Shadow Men. 1998: Water Damage. Rites of Passage. 1999: The Venice Project. What Katy Did (TV). Restraining Order. 2000: They Nest.

†Unreleased

STOLTZ, Eric 1961–
Slight, auburn-haired, shyly-smiling diffident-seeming, chipmunk-like Hollywood jack-of-all trades actor, born in American Samoa, who has done pretty well everything without making much of an individual mark. He's been fine at burying himself in ensemble casts, rather too much so perhaps, especially as he was literally buried beneath mounds of makeup in two of his highest-profile roles, in *Mask* and *The Fly II*. In other roles, he's just as likely to be anonymous as perceptive and touching, and a career in featured roles beckons. For some time lived with actress Bridget Fonda (*qv*).
1981: The Violation of Sarah McDavid (TV). 1982: Fast Times at Ridgemont High (GB: Fast Times). Paper Dolls (TV). 1983: Thursday's Child (TV). A Killer in the Family (TV). 1984: Surf 2. Running Hot. The Wild Life. 1985: Mask. The New Kids. Code Name: Emerald. 1986: Some Kind of Wonderful. 1987: Lionheart. Sister, Sister. 1988: Haunted Summer. Manifesto. 1989: The Fly II. Say Anything. 1990: Memphis Belle. 1991: The Widow Clare. A Woman at War (TV). 1992: The Waterdance. Singles. 1993: Bodies, Rest and Motion. Naked in New York. Heart of Justice (TV). Killing Zoë. Foreign Affairs (TV). 1994: Roommates (TV). Sleep With Me. Pulp Fiction. Little Women. 1995: Don't Look Back (cable TV). Fluke. God's Army. Rob Roy. Kicking and Screaming. 1996: 2 Days in the Valley. Inside (cable TV). Grace of My Heart. Perfect Crimes (TV). Jerry Maguire. Keys to Tulsa. 1997: Mr Jealousy/Highball. Anaconda. 1998: A Murder of Crows. Blackout Effect (TV). Hi-Life (TV). 1999: The Passion of Ayn Rand (cable TV). One Kill (TV). Our Guys (TV). 2000: The House of Mirth. The Lot (TV). The Simian Line. The Last Dance (TV). Common Ground (TV).

STONE, Sharon (Sherrie Stone) 1958–
Not many actresses hit the big-time at 34 after 12 years of trying, but, at least for the feistiest of her performances in a series of unrewarding roles, this spicy American blonde deserved it. A bright, open-faced beauty who won both scholarships and beauty contests as a teenager, she worked in TV commercials before breaking into films at 22. Although she shone when given the chance, it wasn't until she took a very uninhibited role, in the sensationalistic *Basic Instinct*, that producers saw her as true star material. Success seemed to have put out the fire in the Stone after that, and she was dull in some dull films until her striking performance in *Casino* restored her standing in the industry and won her an Oscar nomination. Three times married.
1980: Stardust Memories. 1981: Bay City Blues (TV). Deadly Blessing. Bolero/Les uns et les autres. 1982: Not Just Another Affair (TV). 1984: Irreconcilable Differences. Calendar Girl Murders (TV. Video title: Victimised). The Vegas Strip Wars (TV). 1985: King Solomon's Mines. 1986: Allan Quartermain and the Lost City of Gold. 1987: Police Academy 4: Citizens on Patrol. Action Jackson. 1988: Tears in the Rain (TV). Above the Law (GB: Nico). 1989: Personal Choice/Beyond the Stars. Blood and Sand. 1990: Total Recall. 1991: Year of the Gun. Scissors. He Said, She Said. Sleeping Dogs (released 1994. GB: Where Sleeping Dogs Lie). 1992: Diary of a Hitman. Basic Instinct. 1993: Sliver. Intersection. Last Action Hero. 1994: The Specialist. 1995: The Quick and the Dead. Casino. 1996: Catwalk. Diabolique. Last Dance. 1998: The Mighty. Sphere. Gloria. Antz (voice only). 1999: The Muse. Simpatico. Forever Hollywood (doc. Narrator only). 2000: If These Walls Could Talk 2 (TV). Picking Up the Pieces. Beautiful Joe.

STOOGES, The Three
FINE, Larry (Laurence Feinburg)
1902–1974 (bottom)
HOWARD, Curly (Jerome Horowitz)
1903–1952 (top)
HOWARD, Moe (Moses Horowitz)
1895–1975 (centre)
HOWARD, Shemp (Shmuel Horowitz)
1891–1955
Pie-in-the-face group of American comedians who humour was very basic, but who made millions of children laugh in scores of shorts throughout the 1930s, 1940s and 1950s. They

whacked each other on the head, kicked each other's ankles and poked their fingers in each other's eyes; the soundtracks of their films seemed very noisy. Larry, Curly and Moe were the Stooges from 1933 to 1946. Shemp, who had left in 1933, rejoined in 1946, replacing an ailing Curly. Vaudeville comedians Joe Besser and Joe de Rita were later Stooges. Curly died from a stroke, Shemp from a coronary occulsion, Larry (the one with the wild hair) from a stroke and Moe (the leader, the one with the pudding-basin haircut) from cancer. One of their early two-reelers, *Men in Black*, was nominated for an Academy Award. Shemp Howard's solo credits from 1933 to 1946 can be found in our companion volume, *Quinlan's Illustrated Directory of Character Actors*.

1930: ‡*Hollywood on Parade*. ‡*Soup to Nuts*. 1933: †*Dancing Lady*. †*Turn Back the Clock*. †*Meet the Baron*. †*Fugitive Lovers*. †*Myrt and Marge* (GB: *Laughter in the Air*). 1934: †*Hollywood Party*. †*The Captain Hates the Sea*. †*Gift of Gab*. *Hello Pop*. *Plane Nuts*. *The Big Idea*. *Beer and Pretzels*. *Woman Haters*. *Punch Drunks*. *Men in Black*. *Three Little Pigskins*. 1935: *Pop Goes the Easel*. *Horses' Collars*. *Restless Knights*. *Hoi Polloi*. *Uncivil Warriors*. *Screen Snapshots No 6*. *Pardon My Scotch*. *Three Little Beers*. 1936: *Half-Shot Shooters*. *A Pain in the Pullman*. *Whoops I'm an Indian*. *Ants in the Pantry*. *Movie Maniacs*. *Disorder in the Court*. *False Alarms*. *Slippery Silks*. 1937: *Three Dumb Clucks*. *Grips, Grunts and Groans*. *Back to the Woods*. *Playing the Ponies*. *Dizzy Doctors*. *Goofs and Saddles*. *Cash and Carry*. *The Sitter-Downers*. 1938. †*Start Cheering*. *Termites of 1938*. *Tassels in the Air*. *Three Missing Links*. *Mutts to You*. *Wee Wee Monsieur*. *Healthy, Wealthy and Dumb*. *Violent is the Word for Curly*. *Flat Foot Stooges*. 1939: *A Ducking They Did Go*. *Three Little Sew and Sews*. *Saved by the Belle*. *Oily to Bed, Oily to Rise*. *We Want Our Mummy*. *Yes We Have No Bonanza*. *Calling All Curs*. *Three Sappy People*. 1940: *A-Plumbing We Will Go*. *You Natzy Spy!* *Nutty But Nice*. *No Census No Feeling*. *Boobs in Arms*. *How High is Up?* *Cuckoo Cavaliers*. *Rockin' Through the Rockies*. 1941: †*Time Out for Rhythm*. *All the World's a Stooge*. *So Long, Mr Chumps*. *An Ache in Every Stake*. *Some More of Samoa*. *In the Sweet Pie and Pie*. *Dutiful But Dumb*. *I'll Never Heil Again!* *Loco Boy Makes Good*. 1942: †*My Sister Eileen*. *Matri-Phony*. *Cactus Makes Perfect*. *Even as IOU*. *Sock-a-Bye Baby*. *What's the Matador?* *Three Smart Saps*.

1943: *Spook Louder*. *They Came to Conga*. *Three Little Twerps*. *I Can Hardly Wait*. *Phony Express*. *Dizzy Detectives*. *Back from the Front*. *Higher Than a Kite*. *Dizzy Pilots*. *A Gem of a Jam*. 1944: *The Yoke's on Me*. *Crash Goes the Hash*. *Gents without Cents*. *Busy Buddies*. *Idle Roomers*. *No Dough, Boys*. 1945: †*Rockin' in the Rockies* (and 1940 short with similar title. GB: *Partners in Crime*). *Idiots Deluxe*. *Three Pests in a Mess*. *Micro Phonies*. *If a Body Meets a Body*. *Booby Dupes*. 1946: †*Swing Parade of 1946*. *Uncivil Warbirds*. *Beer Barrel Polecats*. *Monkey Businessmen*. *G I Wanna Go Home*. *Three Little Pirates*. *A Bird in the Head*. *The Three Troubledoers*. *Three Loan Wolves*. *Rhythm and Weep*. 1947: *Out West*. *Half Wits' Holiday*. *Brideless Groom*. *All Gummed Up*. *Fright Night*. *Hold That Lion*. *Sing Me a Song of Six Pants*. 1948: *Squareheads of the Round Table*. *Shivering Sherlocks*. *Heavenly Daze*. *I'm a Monkey's Uncle*. *Crime on Their Hands*. *Pardon My Clutch*. *Fiddlers Three*. *Hot Scots*. *Mummy's Dummies*. 1949: *The Ghost Talks*. *Hocus Pokus*. *Who Done It?* *Fuelin' Around*. *Vagabond Loafers*. *Malice in the Palace*. *Dunked in the Deep*. 1950: *Dopey Dicks*. *Punchy Cowpunchers*. *Love at First Bite*. *Three Hams on Rye*. *Slap Happy Sleuths*. *Hugs and Mugs*. *Self Made Maids*. *Studio Stoops*. *A Snitch in Time*. 1951: †*Gold Raiders* (GB: *Stooges Go West*). *Don't Throw That Knife*. *Three Arabian Nuts*. *Merry Mavericks*. *Hula La-La*. *Baby Sitters' Jitters*. *Scrambled Brains*. *The Tooth Will Out*. *The Pest Man Wins*. 1952: *Corny Casanovas*. *Gents in a Jam*. *Cuckoo on a Choo-Choo*. *Three Dark Horses*. *He Cooked His Goose*. *Listen, Judge*. *A Missed Fortune*. 1953: *Loose Loot*. *Up in Daisy's Penthouse*. *Spooks*. *Rip, Sew and Stitch*. *Goof on the Roof*. *Booty and the Beast*. *Tricky Dicks*. *Pardon My Backfire*. *Bubble Trouble*. 1954: *Pals and Gals*. *Income Tax Sappy*. *Shot in the Frontier*. *Knutzy Knights*. *Scotched in Scotland*. *Musty Musketeers*. 1955: *Gypped in the Penthouse*. *Fling in the Ring*. *Stone Age Romeos*. *Hot Ice*. *Of Cash and Hash*. *Bedlam in Paradise*. *Wham-Bam-Slam*. *Blunder Boys*. 1956: *Flagpole Sitters*. *Husbands Beware*. *Rumpus in the Harem*. *Scheming Schemers*. *Creeps*. *For Crimin' Out Loud*. *Hot Stuff*. *Commotion on the Ocean*. 1957: *A Merry Mix-Up*. *Hoofs and Goofs*. *Space Ship Sappy*. *Horsing Around*. *Outer Space Jitters*. *Muscle Up a Little Closer*. *Gun a-Poppin'*. *Rusty Romeos*. 1958: *Pies and Guys*. *Quiz Whiz*. *Flying Saucer Daffy*. *Fifi Blows Her Top*. *Sweet and Hot*. *Oil's Well That Ends Well*. 1959: †*Have Rocket, Will Travel*. *Triple Crossed*. *Sappy Bullfighters*. 1960 †*Three Stooges Scrapbook*. †*Stop! Look! And Laugh!* 1961: †*Snow White and the Three Stooges* (GB: *Snow White and the Three Clowns*). 1962: †*The Three Stooges in Orbit*. †*The Three Stooges meet Hercules*. 1963: †*It's a Mad, Mad, Mad, Mad World*. †*The Three Stooges Go Around the World in a Daze*. †*Four for Texas*. 1964: †*The Outlaws is Coming*. 1968: †*Star Spangled Salesman*.

Moe alone: 1958: †*Space Master X-7*. 1966: †*Don't Worry, We'll Think of a Title*. 1973: †*Dr Death – Seeker of Souls*.

All shorts except †*features*
‡*As The Racketeers*

STORM, Gale (Josephine Cottle) 1922–
Small, sturdy, resilient American actress with lovely, round face and light auburn hair who was also a lively singer. Her pert peppiness presumably helped her maintain her popularity through a host of minor films until television swallowed her up in 1952 for her own show, which ran, under various titles, for the remainder of the fifties. Later worked in insurance. Married actor Lee Bonnell (1918–1986), first of two. Twice widowed.

1940: *Tom Brown's School Days*. *One Crowded Hour*. 1941: *Saddlemates*. **I Know Somebody Who Loves You*. **Penthouse Serenade*. **Let's Get Away from It All*. *Let's Go Collegiate* (GB: *Farewell to Fame*). *Jesse James at Bay*. *Gambling Daughters*. *City of Missing Girls*. *Red River Valley*. **Merry-Go-Roundup*. 1942: *Rhythm Parade*. **He Plays Gin Rummy*. *Smart Alecks*. *Lure of the Islands*. *Foreign Agent*. *The Man from Cheyenne*. *Freckles Comes Home*. 1943: **Glamour Girl*. **Shy Guy*. *Where Are Your Children? Cosmo Jones – Crime Smasher* (GB: *Crime Smasher*). *Nearly Eighteen*. *Campus Rhythm*. *Revenge of the Zombies* (GB: *The Corpse Vanished*). 1944: *They Shall Have Faith/Forever Yours* (GB: *The Right to Live*). 1945: *GI Honeymoon*. *Sunbonnet Sue*. 1946: *Swing Parade of 1946*. 1947: *It Happened on Fifth Avenue*. 1948: *The Dude Goes West*. 1949: *Stampede*. *The Kid from Texas* (GB: *Texas Kid – Outlaw*). *Abandoned*. *Curtain Call at Cactus Creek* (GB: *Take the Stage*). 1950: **Almost Like Being in Love*. **Are You from Dixie?* *The Underworld Story*. *Between Midnight and Dawn*. **Between the Devil and the Deep Blue Sea*. 1951: **Papa, Won't You Dance With Me?* *Al Jennings of Oklahoma*. *The Texas Rangers*. **Swinging on a Star*. **Waiting for the Robert E Lee*. **When a Lady Meets a Gentleman Down South*. 1952: **Ain't Misbehavin'*. **I Been Down to Texas*. **Isn't It Romantic? Woman of the North Country*.

STOWE, Madeleine 1958–
Doe-eyed, dark-haired, liquid-voiced, elegantly sensual American actress. She was spotted while still at university, starred in one TV movie and featured in another, all that same year. Her star career in films, though, took a long while to get going; it took a showy role in the successful *StakeOut* nine years later to do the trick. Now in a variety of largely independent-minded leading roles. Married to actor Brian Benben.

1978: *The Deerslayer* (TV). *The Nativity*

(TV). 1981: Gangster Wars (TV). 1983: Amazons (TV). 1986: Tropical Snow (released 1989). 1987: StakeOut. 1989: Worth Winning. Revenge. 1990: The Two Jakes. 1991: China Moon (released 1994). Closet Land. 1992: The Last of the Mochicans. Unlawful Entry. 1993: Short Cuts. 1994: Luck, Trust & Ketchup. Blink. Another Stakeout. Bad Girls. 1995: Twelve Monkeys. 1996: The Hamster Factor (doc). 1998: The Proposition. Playing by Heart. 1999: The General's Daughter. 2000: Impostor/Alien Love Triangle.

STRASBERG, Susan 1938–1999
Tiny, dark-haired American actress who, after an auspicious debut, was looked on as a great star in the making in the late fifties. Alas, her career followed a similar pattern to that of Dean Stockwell (qv): she did not seem to come to terms with mainstream American cinema and was soon in continental dramas and American-International youth movies. Daughter of acting teacher/actor Lee Strasberg, who founded The Method. Married/divorced actor Christopher Jones (1941–). Died from breast cancer.
1955: Picnic. The Cobweb. 1957: Stage Struck. 1960: Kapo. 1961: Taste of Fear (US: Scream of Fear). 1962: Désordre/Disorder. Hemingway's Adventures of a Young Man (GB: Adventures of a Young Man). 1963: Il giorno più corto commedia unmaristica (US: The Shortest Day). 1964: The High Bright Sun (US: McGuire Go Home!) 1967: The Trip. Cosa Nostra, an Arch Enemy of the FBI (TV. GB: cinemas). 1968: Chubasco. Psych-Out. The Name of the Game is Kill! The Brotherhood. 1969: Le sorelle/So Evil My Sister. Sweet Hunters. 1970: Hauser's Memory (TV). 1971: Mr and Mrs Bo Jo Jones (TV).

1972: Toma (TV. GB: Man of Many Faces). 1973: And Millions Will Die. Frankenstein (TV). 1974: Who Fears the Devil? Best of All the Safecrackers (TV). 1975: The Other Side of the Wind (unfinished). 1976: Sammy Somebody. 1977: SST Disaster in the Sky/SST Death Flight (TV). The Manitou. Tre soldi e la donna di classe. Rollercoaster. In Praise of Older Women. 1980: Bloody Birthday. 1981: Sweet Sixteen. Lee Strasberg and the Actor's Studio. 1982: Mazes and Monsters/Rona Jaffe's Mazes and Monsters (TV). 1983: The Returning. 1986: The Delta Force. 1987: Marilyn Monroe: Beyond the Legend. 1988: Prime Suspect. 1989: The Runnin' Kind. 1990: Schweitzer/The Light in the Jungle/Out of Darkness. 1992: The Cherry Orchard. 1993: Trauma.

STREEP, Meryl
(Mary Louise Streep) 1949–
Fair-haired, freckle-faced American actress whose determined features and naturalistic style initially took her into fairly unsympathetic roles as ambitious bitches. Later she played tormented women. An Academy Award for Kramer vs Kramer pushed her forward towards superstar status, which she consolidated with another Oscar for Sophie's Choice. Also nominated for Oscars on The Deer Hunter, The French Lieutenant's Woman, Silkwood, Out of Africa, Ironweed, A Cry in the Dark, Postcards from the Edge, The Bridges of Madison County, One True Thing and Music of the Heart.
1976: Everybody Rides a Carousel (voice only). 1977: Julia. The Deadliest Season (TV). 1978: The Deer Hunter. 1979: Manhattan. The Seduction of Joe Tynan. Kramer vs Kramer. 1981: The French Lieutenant's Woman. 1982: Still of the Night. Sophie's Choice. Alice at the Palace (TV). 1983: Silkwood. 1984: In Our Hands. Falling in Love. 1985: Plenty. Out of Africa. 1986: Heartburn. Directed by William Wyler. 1987: Ironweed. 1988: A Cry in the Dark. 1989: She Devil. 1990: Postcards from the Edge. 1991: Defending Your Life. 1992: Death Becomes Her. 1993: The House of the Spirits. 1994: The River Wild. 1995: The Bridges of Madison County. Before and After. 1996: Marvin's Room. First Do No Harm (TV). 1998: Dancing at Lughnasa. One True Thing. 1999: Music of the Heart.

STREISAND, Barbra
(Barbara Steisand) 1942–
Dark-haired (although it got lighter through

the years), sexy, aggressive American singer and actress whose prominent nose and clown's smile sit well with her talent for comedy. Her larger-than-life personality and magical singing voice – all throb and passion – grabbed her an Oscar for Funny Girl. She was further nominated for The Way We Were. Her sense of throwaway comedy remains pleasing, but she can over-dominate a film and after a series of dispiriting misfires, proved in 1983 with Yentl that she was in her element when producing, directing and starring all at once. Married/divorced actor Elliott Gould (qv). Currently married to actor James Brolin (also qv).
1968: Funny Girl. 1969: Hello, Dolly! 1970: On a Clear Day You Can See Forever. The Owl and the Pussycat. 1972: What's Up Doc? Up the Sandbox. 1973: The Way We Were. 1974: For Pete's Sake. 1975: Funny Lady. 1976: A Star is Born. 1979: The Main Event. 1981: All Night Long. 1983: †Yentl. 1987: Nuts. 1990: Places You Find Love. Listen Up. 1991: †The Prince of Tides. 1996: †The Mirror Has Two Faces.

†And directed

STRIBLING, Melisa 1927–1992
Blonde, blue-eyed Scottish actress whose calculating looks suggested that she would make a good villainess along the lines of Kathleen Byron (qv). But producers only rarely gave her a chance, and she remains best remembered as the frightened heroine in Hammer's Dracula, a role for which she was not ideally cast. Started as an assistant in the cutting room at Ealing Studios. Married director Basil Dearden. He was killed in a 1971 car crash.

played gentler roles with equal success. Left home at 15, married at 20 and became a father at 21! Divorced at 23, he almost married Julia Roberts (*qv*) in 1991. His career looked to be losing some of its impetus in the 1990s, and he tried his hand at direction. In private life, an enthusiastic rodeo competitor.

1983: *Max Dugan Returns*. 1984: *The Bay Boy*. 1985: *At Close Range*. 1986: *Trapped in Silence* (TV). *Brotherhood of Justice* (TV). *Crazy Moon*. *Stand by Me*. 1987: *Amazing Stories* (TV. GB: cinemas). *The Killing Time*. *The Lost Boys*. *Promised Land*. 1988: *Bright Lights, Big City*. *'1969'*. 1989: *Renegades*. *Chicago Joe and the Showgirl*. 1990: *Flash-back*. *The Nutcracker* (voice only). *Flatliners*. *Young Guns II*. (GB: *Young Guns II – Blaze of Glory*). 1991: *Article 99*. 1992: *Teresa's Tattoo*. *A Few Good Men*. *Twin Peaks – Fire Walk with Me*. *The Vanishing*. 1993: *The Three Musketeers*. †*Last Light* (TV). 1994: *The Cowboy Way*. 1995: *Double Cross*. *Hourglass*. *Duke of Groove*. 1996: *Eye for an Eye*. *Freeway*. *Frankie the Fly*. *Perfect Crimes* (TV). *A Time to Kill*. 1997: *The Last Days of Frankie the Fly*. †*Truth or Consequences, N.M.* *Dark City*. 1998: *The Breakup*. *A Soldier's Sweetheart*. 1999: †*Woman Wanted*. *Ground Control*. 2000: *Picking Up the Pieces*. *Hearts and Bones/Cowboy Up*. *After Alice*. *Beat*. *Desert Saints*. *The Right Temptation*. *To End All Wars*.

SVENSON, Bo 1941–
Fair-haired, tree-like, Swedish-born Hollywood leading man who crashed his way through the star roles of a number of action films in the 1970s. Has travelled widely searching for heroes who combined brain with brawn, although he has largely settled for the same sort of monolithic career as Chuck Connors (*qv*).

1971: *The Bravos* (TV). 1973: *You'll Never See Me Again* (TV). *Maurie* (later *Big Mo*. TV). *Frankenstein* (TV). 1975: *The Great Waldo Pepper*. *Target Risk* (TV). *Part Two Walking Tall* (GB: *Legend of the Lawman*). 1976: *Breaking Point*. *Special Delivery*. 1977: *Snowbeast* (TV). *Jimbuck/Portrait of a Hitman*. *Final Chapter Walking Tall*. 1978: *The Inglorious Bastards*. *Our Man in Mecca*. 1979: *Gold of the Amazon Women* (TV). *North Dallas Forty*. 1980: *Due nelle stelle*. *Virus*. 1981: *Thrilled to Death*. 1982: *Butcher, Baker, Nightmare Maker*. 1983: *Thunder Warrior*. *Jealousy*. 1984: *Crossfire*. *Man Hunt Warning* (US: *The Manhunt*). 1985: *Wizards*

of the Lost Kingdom (filmed 1983 as *Wizard Wars*). 1986: *Brothers in Blood*. *On Dangerous Ground*. *Delta Force Kommando* (released 1990). *Choke Canyon*. *Deadly Impact*. *Heartbreak Ridge*. 1987: *Thunder Warrior 2*. *White Phantom*. *Double Target*. *Crack Down*. *The Dirty Dozen: The Deadly Mission* (TV). *Deep Space*. 1988: *Kill and Enjoy/Mania*. *Strangers in a Strange Land*. *Primal Rage*. 1989: *Running Combat*. *Captain Henkel/Tides of War*. *Curse II: The Bite*. *The Train*. *The Kill Reflex*. 1990: *Justice Done*. *A Spirit Rebellious* (and directed). *Andy Colby's Incredible Video Adventure* (V). *Critical Action*. 1991: *Walking Tall*. *The Ultimate Walk*. 1992: *Three Days to Kill*. 1994: *Steel Frontier*. *Savage Land*. 1995: *Private Obsession*. 1997: *Speed 2*. *Cruise Control*. *Heartless* (TV). 2000: *Crackerjack 3*.

SWANSON, Gloria
(G. Swenson) 1899–1983
Dark-haired, highly mannered American star and (very) dramatic actress. Progressed from being a Mack Sennett bathing beauty at 16 to the silent screen's adventuress *par excellence*, moving chicly through a new-found sexual freedom. Never really cashed in her abilities as a comedienne, and her career foundered with the coming of sound, although she made one remarkable comeback appearance in *Sunset Boulevard*. Married to Wallace Beery (*qv*) 1916–1918, first of six. Oscar nominee for *Sadie Thompson*, *The Trespasser* and *Sunset Boulevard*. Died following heart surgery.

1915: *The Romance of an American Duchess*. *At the End of a Perfect Day*. *Broken Pledge*. *The Ambition of the Baron*. *The Fable of Elvira and Farina and the Meal Ticket*. *His New Job*. 1916: *Sweedie Goes to College*. *A Dash of Courage*. *Girls' Dormitory*. *Hearts and Sparks*. *A Social Club*. *Haystacks and Steeples*. *Love on Skates*. *Danger Girl*. *The Nick-of-Time Baby*. *Teddy at the Throttle*. 1917: *Baseball Madness*. *Whose Baby?* *The Pullman Bride*. *The Sultan's Wife*. *Dangers of a Bride*. 1918: *Her Decision*. *You Can't Believe Everything*. *Society for Sale*. *Station Content*. *Shifting Sands*. *The Secret Code*. *Everywoman's Husband*. *Wife or Country*. 1919: *Don't Change Your Husband*. *Male and Female* (GB: *The Admirable Crichton*). *For Better, For Worse*. 1920: *Why Change Your Wife?* *Something to Think About*. 1921: *The Affairs of Anatol* (GB: *A Prodigal Knight*). *The Great Moment*. *Under the Lash* (GB: *The Shulamite*). *Don't Tell Everything*. 1922: *Her*

Husband's Trademark. *Beyond the Rock*. *Her Gilded Cage*. *The Impossible Mrs Bellew*. *My American Wife*. 1923: *Bluebeard's Eighth Wife*. *Prodigal Daughters*. *Hollywood*. *Zaza*. 1924: *Manhandled*. *The Humming Bird*. *The Wages of Virtue*. *A Society Scandal*. *Her Love Story*. 1925: *Madame Sans Gêne*. *The Coast of Folly*. *Stage Struck*. 1926: *The Untamed Lady*. *Fine Manners*. 1927: *The Loves of Sunya*. 1928: *Queen Kelly*. *Sadie Thompson*. 1929: *The Trespasser*. 1930: *What a Widow!* 1931: *Indiscreet*. *Tonight or Never*. *Screen Snapshots No 4*. 1932: *Perfect Understanding*. 1934: *Music in the Air*. 1941: *Father Takes a Wife*. 1950: *Sunset Boulevard*. 1952: *Three for Bedroom C*. 1956: *Mio Figlio Nerone* (GB: *Nero's Weekend*. US: *Nero's Mistress*). 1974: *The Killer Bees* (TV). *Airport 1975*.

SWANSON, Kristy 1969–
Single-minded – at 16 she sued for emancipation from her parents to help set up a show business career – American blonde actress of 'college student' appeal and pin-up proportions. Her dazzling good looks moved her forward to leading roles by the early 1990s, but her acting abilities have so far looked merely competent, and she seems destined to appear in mainly light action films and comedies that go straight to video.

1986: *Miracle of the Heart: A Boys Town Story* (TV). *Pretty in Pink*. *Ferris Bueller's Day Off*. *Mr Boogedy* (TV). *Deadly Friend*. 1987: *Flowers in the Attic*. *Bride of Boogedy* (TV). *Not Quite Human* (TV). 1988: *Nightingales* (TV). 1989: *B L Stryker: The Dancer's Touch* (TV). 1990: *Diving In*. *Dream Trap*. 1991: *Mannequin on the Move/Mannequin Two: On the Move*. *Hot Shots!* *Highway to Hell*. 1992: *Buffy the Vampire Slayer*. 1993: *The Program*. *Getting In/Student Body*. 1994: *The Chase*. *Higher Learning*. 1996: *The Phantom*. *Marshal Law*. 1997: *8 Heads in a Duffel Bag*. *Self-Storage*. *Lover Girl*. *Bad to the Bone* (TV). 1998: *Meeting Daddy*. *Ground Control* (TV). 1999: *Big Daddy*. *Supreme Sanction* (TV). 2001: *Dude, Where's My Car?*

SWAYZE, Patrick 1952–
Tall, lithe, broad-shouldered, dark-haired American actor, singer, dancer and songwriter with 'backstreets' good looks. The son of a choreographer, he trained as a dancer in ballet and tap and made his Broadway debut in musicals. Turned to straight acting in the late 1970s, and became associated with the so-

called 'Brat Pack' through his appearance in *The Outsiders*, although much older than his youthful co-stars. Their careers seemed to be moving faster than his until his meteoric success in *Dirty Dancing*. Married to actress Lisa Niemi, his co-star in *Steel Dawn*. Surname pronounced Swayzy.

1979: Skatetown USA. 1980: The Comeback Kid (TV). 1981: Return of the Rebels (TV). 1982: The Renegades (TV). 1983: The Outsiders. The New Season (TV). Uncommon Valor. 1984: Pigs vs Freaks/Off Sides (TV). Grandview USA. Red Dawn. 1986: Call to Action. Youngblood. 1987: In Love and War (TV). Steel Dawn (filmed 1985 as Desert Warrior). Dirty Dancing. Tiger Warsaw. 1988: Road House. 1989: Next of Kin. 1990: Ghost. 1991: Point Break. City of Joy. 1992: The Player (scene deleted). 1993: Father Hood. 1995: Tall Tale. To Wong Foo Thanks for Everything, Julie Newmar. Three Wishes. 1997: Letters from a Killer. 1998: Black Dog. 1999: Without a Word. 2000: Forever Lulu. Wakin' Up in Reno. The Green Dragon.

SWEET, Blanche
(Sarah B. Sweet) 1895–1986
Light-haired, appealing, bow-lipped American silent star who forged her career playing intrepid heroines facing dangers in a man's world, mostly in films by D.W. Griffith. In acting from childhood, often billed as Baby Blanche or Little Blanche, she began making films at 13, and broke through to stardom two years later in the title role of *The Lonedale Operator*, as a girl who foils a gang of western outlaws. Sound and her age eventually ended her star success in films and she built a new career on stage. Married director Marshall Neilan (1922–29) and stage/sometime screen

actor Raymond Hackett (1902–1958) from 1936 on. Died following a stroke.

1909: A Man With Three Wives. Choosing a Husband. A Corner in Wheat. The Day After. 1910: All on Account of the Milk. The Rocky Road. A Romance of the Western Hills. 1911: Was He a Coward? The Lonedale Operator. The Country Lovers. The Miser's Heart. Heartbeats of Long Ago. The White Rose of the Wild. How She Triumphed. The Last Drop of Water. A Smile of a Child. The Blind Princess and the Poet. Out from the Shadow. The Long Road. The Making of a Man. The Battle. Love in the Hills. A Woman Scorned. Through Darkened Vales. The Primal Call. †Fighting Blood. A Country Cupid. The Stuff Heroes Are Made Of. 1912: Under Burning Skies. The Transformation of Mike. The Eternal Mother. For His Son. The Punishment. The Goddess of Sagebrush Gulch. The Lesser Evil. The Outcast Among Outcasts. One is Business, the Other Crime. A Temporary Truce. Man's Lust for Gold. The Spirit Awakened. With the Enemy's Help. The Painted Lady. A Change of Spirit. The Chief's Blanket. Blind Love. The God Within. A Sailor's Heart. 1913: Oil and Water. Pirate Gold. Three Friends. Broken Ways. A Chance Deception. The Stolen Bridge. The Hero of Little Italy. Love in an Apartment Hotel. Classmates. Death's Marathon. If We Only Knew. The Mistake. The Coming of Angelo. The House of Discord. Two Men on the Desert. Ashes of the Past. Her Wedding Bell. Near to Earth. The Vengeance of Galora. 1914: Strongheart. The Massacre. The Sentimental Sister. The Soul of Honor. Men and Women. The Second Mrs Roebuck. Her Awakening. For Those Unborn. The Tear That Burned. For Her Father's Sins. The Little Country Mouse. The Odalisque. †Judith of Bethulia. The Old Maid. †The Escape. †Home Sweet Home. †The Avenging Conscience (GB: Thou Shalt Not Kill). 1915: †The Warrens of Virginia. †Stolen Goods. †The Captive. †The Secret Orchard. †The Clue. †The Case of Becky. †The Secret Sin. 1916: †Blacklist. †The Ragamuffin. †The Sowers. †The Dupe. †The Thousand-Dollar Husband. †The Storm. †Public Opinion. †Unprotected. 1917: †Those Without Sin. †The Evil Eye. †The Silent Partner. †The Tides of Barnegat. 1919: †A Woman of Pleasure. †Fighting Cressy. †The Unpardonable Sin. †The Hushed Hour. 1920: †Simple Souls. †The Deadlier Sex. †Help Wanted – Male. †The Girl in the Web. †Her Unwilling Husband. 1921: †That Girl Montana. 1922: †Quincy Adams Sawyer. 1923: †Anna Christie. †The Meanest Man in the World. †In the Palace of the King. † Souls for Sale. 1924: †Those Who Dance. †Tess of the d'Urbervilles. 1925: †Why Women Love. †The New Commandment. †His Supreme Moment. †The Sporting Venus. 1926: †The Lady from Hell (GB: The Interrupted Wedding). †Bluebeard's Seven Wives. †The Far Cry. †Diplomacy. 1927: †Singed. 1929: †The Woman in White. †Always Faithful. 1930: †The Woman Racket (GB: Lights and Shadows). †Show Girl in Holywood. †The Silver Horde. 1959: The Five Pennies. 1982: Before the Nickelodeon: The Early Cinema of Edwin S Porter (narrator only).

All shorts except †features

SWINBURNE, Nora
(Elinor S. Johnson) 1902–2000
Cool, pretty, blonde English actress of delicate features, a former dancer, of faintly genteel personality, who danced for World War One troops at 16, filmed fairly regularly from 1920, and continued in character roles from 1942. Long married to Esmond Knight (*qv*), her third husband, who died in 1987. Died from natural causes.

*1920: Saved from the Sea. Branded. 1921: The Fortune of Chirstina McNab. The Autumn of Pride. 1922: The Wee McGregor's Sweetheart. 1923: Hornet's Nest. 1924: The Unwanted. His Grace Gives Notice. 1925: One Colombo Night. A Girl of London. 1930: Caste. Alf's Button. 1931: Potiphar's Wife (US: Her Strange Desire). Alibi. *Sound Cinemagazine No 273. Man of Mayfair. These Charming People. 1932: White Face. A Voice Said Goodnight. Mr Bill the Conqueror (US: The Man Who Won). Perfect Understanding. 1933: Too Many Wives. 1934: The Office Wife. Boomerang. 1935: Lend Me Your Husband. Jury's Evidence. 1936: The Gay Adventure. The Lonely Road (US: Scotland Yard Commands). 1937: Dinner at the Ritz. Lily of Laguna. 1938: The Citadel. 1940: Gentleman of Venture (US: It Happened to One Man). The Farmer's Wife. 1941: They Flew Alone (US: Wings and the Woman). 1943: The Man in Grey. Dear Octopus (US: The Randolph Family). 1944: Fanny by Gaslight (US: Man of Evil). 1945: They Knew Mr Knight. 1947: Jassy. 1948: Good Time Girl. The Blind Goddess. Saraband for Dead Lovers (US: Saraband). Quartet. 1949: The Bad Lord Byron. Fools Rush In. Marry Me. Christopher Columbus. Landfall. 1950: My Daughter Joy (US: Operation X). 1951: The River. Quo Vadis. 1954: Betrayed. Helen of Troy. 1955: The End of the Affair. 1958: Strange Awakening (US: Female Fiends). 1959: Third Man on the Mountain. 1960: Conspiracy of Hearts. 1963: Decision at Midnight. 1967: Interlude. 1970: Anne of the Thousand Days. 1971: Up the Chastity Belt.*

SWINTON, Tilda 1960–
Bony, ascetic, red-haired British actress with almost translucent skin, often seen in parts of sexual ambivalence: in more than one film she's played both a woman and a man, or characters who 'swing both ways'. After a period as a member of the Royal Shakespeare Company on stage, she entered films, mixing blue-stocking roles with some controversial

*Alf Garnett Saga. 1973: Theatre of Blood. 1982: *It's Your Move. 1983: The Boys in Blue. 1983: Gabrielle and the Doodleman. 1986: Absolute Beginners. 1988: Mr H is Late (TV). 1993: ‡†The Big Freeze (unreleased). Splitting Heirs.*

†Also directed
‡ Unreleased

and provocative work for director Derek Jarman. Tall and heron-like, she also attracted attention posing for a week in a glass case at a London gallery. Her first really mainstream role was as the island community leader in *The Beach*.

1986: Caravaggio. Egomania – Insel ohne Hoffnung. 1987: Aria. The Last of England. Friendship's Death. 1989: War Requiem. 1990: The Garden. 1991: Edward II. The Party: Nature Morte. 1992: Man to Man. Orlando. 1993: Blue (voice only). Wittgenstein. Remembrance of Things Fast. 1994: Glitterbug. 1996: Female Perversions. Die totale Therapie. 1997: Conceiving Ada. 1998: Love is the Devil. The Protagonists. 1999: The War Zone. 2000: The Beach. Possible Worlds.

SYKES, Eric 1923–
Long, lean, dark, mournful-looking British comedian and comic actor who began as a scriptwriter for radio comedy programmes, had some interesting leading roles at the beginning of the sixties, then settled down to stealing scenes in all-star comedies, and to working on his own long-running television show in partnership with Hattie Jacques (1924–1980)

*1954: Orders Are Orders. 1956: Charley Moon. 1959: Tommy the Toreador. 1960: Watch Your Stern. 1961: Very Important Person. Invasion Quartet. Village of Daughters. 1962: Kill or Cure. 1963: Heavens Above! 1964: One Way Pendulum. The Bargee. 1965: Those Magnificent Men in Their Flying Machines. Rotten to the Core. The Liquidator. 1966: The Spy with a Cold Nose. 1967: †*The Plank. 1968: Shalako. 1969: Monte Carlo or Bust! (US: Those Daring Young Men in Their Jaunty Jalopies). 1970: †Rhubarb. 1972: The*

SYLVESTER, William 1922–1995
American actor with dark, curly hair, resident in Britain since coming to study at RADA in 1946. In the fifties became familiar as the resolute hero of some intelligently constructed and above-average second-features. Returned to America in 1968, but was rarely seen on screen thereafter. Married (second) to Veronica Hurst from 1954 to 1970.

1949: Give Us This Day/Salt to the Devil. 1950: They Were Not Divided. 1952: The Yellow Balloon. Appointment in London. 1953: House of Blackmail. Albert RN (US: Break to Freedom). 1954: What Every Woman Wants. The Stranger Came Home (US: The Unholy Four). 1955: Portrait of Alison (US: Postmark for Danger). 1957: High Tide at Noon. 1958: Dublin Nightmare. 1959: Whirlpool. 1960: Offbeat. Gorgo. 1961: Information Received. 1962: Incident at Midnight. 1963: The Devil Doll. Blind Corner. Ring of Spies. 1964: Devils of Darkness. 1966: The Hand of Night. 1967: The Last Safari. Red and Blue. 1968: 2001: a Space Odyssey. The Syndicate. The Challengers (TV. GB: cinemas). The Lawyer. 1973: Busting. Don't Be Afraid of the Dark (TV). 1975: The Hindenburg. Guilty or Innocent: The Sam Sheppard Murder Case (TV). 1978: Heaven Can Wait. 1979: Sharks!

SYMS, Sylvia 1934–
Blonde British actress with long face and sexy mouth, good at expressing emotions, a star in her first film and 'hot' in the British cinema from 1956 to 1963, tackling a wide variety of roles. Seemed to become more ordinary after 1964 and has been mostly seen recently in repertory. Her daughter, Beatie Edney, is also an actress.

1955: My Teenage Daughter (US: Teenage Bad Girl). 1957: The Birthday Present. No Time for Tears. Woman in a Dressing Gown. 1958: Bachelor of Hearts. The Moonraker. Ice Cold in Alex (US: Desert Attack). 1959: No Trees in the Street (US: No Tree in the Street). Ferry to Hong Kong. Expresso Bongo. 1960: Conspiracy of Hearts. Les vierges de Rome/The

*Virgins of Rome. The World of Suzie Wong. 1961: Flame in the Streets. Victim. 1962: The Quare Fellow. The Punch and Judy Man. 1963: The World Ten Times Over (US: Pussycat Alley). 1964: East of Sudan. 1965: Operation Crossbow (US: The Great Spy Mission). The Big Job. 1967: Danger Route. 1968: Hostile Witness. 1969: Run Wild, Run Free. The Desperados. 1972: Asylum. 1974: The Tamarind Seed. 1978: Give Us Tomorrow. 1979: There Goes the Bride. 1982: *It's Your Move. 1986: Absolute Beginners. 1987: Intimate Contact. 1988: A Chorus of Disapproval. 1989: Shirley Valentine. 1992: Shining Through. 1993: Dirty Weekend. Staggered. 1997: Food of Love. The House of Angels (TV).*

T

TALBOTT, Gloria 1931–

Snub-nosed, dark-haired, slightly-built American actress of waif-like appeal, a former child player. She could project determination well, but usually played girls in need of protection, especially the one who married a monster from outer space! After experience in high school plays and repertory, she was a television regular at 18 (often in the *Wild Bill Hickok* series, some episodes of which were pasted together to make films for overseas). But she never quite got into the class of film which would have made her a name with the public.

1937: Maytime. 1943: Sweet and Lowdown. 1945: A Tree Grows in Brooklyn. 1947: ‡Hollywood Barn Dance. 1952: Border City Rusters. 1953: Desert Pursuit. Northern Patrol. 1954: We're No Angels. 1955: Crashout. Lucy Gallant. All That Heaven Allows. 1956: The Cyclops. The Young Guns. Strange Intruder. The Oklahoman. 1957: Daughter of Dr Jekyll. The Kettles on Old MacDonald's Farm. Taming Sutton's Gal. 1958: Cattle Empire. I Married a Monster from Outer Space. 1959: Alias Jesse James. Girls' Town. The Oregon Trail. The Leech Woman. 1960: Oklahoma Territory. 1961: The Crimebusters. 1965: Arizona Raiders. 1966: An Eye for an Eye. 1985: Attack of the B-Movie Monster (V).

‡As Lori Talbot

TALMADGE, Norma 1893–1957

There were few prettier silent screen actresses than this dark-haired, dark-eyed charmer, popular in romance but with a keen sense of comedy. But her Brooklyn accent

was not able to survive the coming of sound. Her sisters Constance (1898–1973) and Natalie (1897–1969) were also silent screen players. Died from a cerebral stroke after contracting pneumonia.

1910: *Uncle Tom's Cabin. Heart o' the Hill. *A Dixie Mother. *The Love of the Chrysanthemums. Murder by Proxy. *The Household Pest (GB: The Four-Footed Pest). 1911: *Mrs 'Enery 'Awkins. A Tale of Two Cities. Nellie the Model. *The Four Poster Pest. Forgotten. The Wildcat. Her Sister's Children. *Sky Pilot. *Paola and Francesca. *In Neighboring Kingdoms. *Her Hero. The Convict's Child. *The Child Crusoes. *The Thumb Print. A Broken Spell. *The General's Daughter. 1912: *Mr Butler Buttles. *Lovesick Maidens of Cuddleton. The Fortune in a Teacup. *The First Violin. *Fortunes of a Composer. Mrs Carter's Necklace. Mr Bolter's Sweetheart. The Extension Table. *Captain Barnacle's Messmate. *The Troublesome Stepdaughter. *Captain Barnacle's Reformer. *Omens and Oracles. *The Midget's Revenge. *O'Hara Helps Cupid. *Squatter and Philosopher. *Captain Barnacle's Waif. 1913: The Blue Rose. The Other Woman. *Under the Daisies. Counsel for the Defense. The Silver Cigarette Case. *Fanny's Conspiracy. Plot and Counterplot. Sleuthing. Getting Up a Practise. Keeping Husbands Home. Extremities. The Kiss of Retribution. Let 'Em Quarrel. Officer John Donovan. Country Barber. An Old Man's Love Story. Solitaires. *His Official Appointment. *His Silver Bachelorhood. *Casey at the Bat. Wanted – a Strong Hand. *He Fell in Love with His Mother-in-Law. *'Arriet's Baby. *The Doctor's Secret. *Father's Hatband. A Lady and her Maid. The Sacrifice of Kathleen. His Little Page. *O'Hara as a Guardian Angel. The Tables Turned. *Just Show People. The Varasour Ball. *O'Hara's Godchild. The Honorable Algernon. An Elopement at Home. 1914: Sawdust and Salome. The Hero. Cupid vs Money. John Rance, Gentleman. *The Loan Shark King. *Goodbye Summer. *Memories in Men's Souls. *The Peacemaker. The Curing of Myra May. The Mill of Life. A Wayward Daughter. Old Reliable. The Helpful Sisterhood. *Mr Murphy's Wedding Present. *Politics and the Press. *A Question of Clothes. Sunshine and Shadows. The Hidden Letters. The Right of Way. *Under False Colors. A Daughter of Israel. Fogg's Millions. Etta of the Footlights. Dorothy Danebridge, Militant. 1915: Elsa's Brother. The Barrier of Faith. The Criminal. The Battle Cry of Peace. Janet of the Chorus. A

Daughter's Strange Inheritance. The Pillar of Flame. The Captivating Mary Carstairs. 1916: Martha's Vindication. The Missing Links. The Honorable Algy (and 1913 film of similar title). The Devil's Needle. Fifty-Fifty. The Crown Prince's Double. The Children in the House. Going Straight (GB: Corruption). The Social Secretary. 1917: The Secret of Storm Country. Panthea. The Moth. Under False Colors. Poppy. The Law of Compensation. The Lone Wolf. 1918: The Ghost of Yesterday. The Forbidden City. De Luxe Annie. The Heart of Wetona. The Safety Curtain. By Right of Purchase. Her Only Way. Salome. 1919: The New Moon. The Probation Wife. The Way of a Woman. The Isle of Conquest. 1920: A Daughter of Two Worlds. The Right of Way. Yes or No. The Loves and Lies. The Branded Woman. The Woman Gives. 1921: Love's Redemption. The Passion Flower. The Sign on the Door. The Wonderful Thing. 1922: Smilin' Through. Foolish Wives. The Eternal Flame. Branded! 1923: Ashes of Vengeance. The Song of Love. Dust of Desire. The Voice from the Minaret. Within the Law. Sawdust. 1924: Secrets. The Only Woman. In Hollywood with Potash and Perlmutter (GB: So This is Hollywood). 1925: Graustark. The Lady. 1926: Kiki. 1927: Camille. The Dove. 1928: The Woman Disputed. Show People. 1929: New York Nights. 1930: Du Barry, Woman of Passion (GB: Du Barry).

TAMBLYN, Russ

(Russell Tamblyn) 1934–

Slight, springy, ginger-haired American star with winning smile – first a boy actor, then a dancing star with spectacular high leaps, just about M-G-M's last such animal before their musicals dwindled to a halt. Tamblyn's career dwindled, too, without the electric spark he gave to dancing, and he was little seen until a burst of activity in the late 1980s. Nominated for an Oscar in *Peyton Place*. Lately combining film and cabaret work with a painting career.

1948: †The Boy with Green Hair. 1949: †Reign of Terror / The Black Book. †Deadly is the Female (later Gun Crazy). †The Kid from Cleveland. †Captain Carey USA (GB: After Midnight). †Samson and Delilah. 1950: †The Vicious Years. †Father's Little Dividend. 1951: †Father's Little Dividend. †As Young As You Feel. †Cave of Outlaws. 1952: The Winning Team. Retreat Hell! 1953: Take the High Ground. 1954: Seven Brides for Seven Brothers. Deep in My Heart. 1955: Many Rivers to

Cross. *Hit the Deck.* 1956: *The Last Hunt. The Fastest Gun Alive. The Young Guns.* 1957: *Don't Go Near the Water. Peyton Place.* 1958: *High School Confidential! tom thumb.* 1960: *Cimarron.* 1961: *West Side Story.* 1962: *Wonderful World of the Brothers Grimm. How the West Was Won.* 1963: *Follow the Boys. The Haunting. The Long Ships.* 1964: *Son of a Gunfighter.* 1966: *War of the Gargantuas.* 1970: *Dracula vs Frankenstein (GB: Blood of Frankenstein). Satan's Sadists.* 1971: *Scream Free! The Last Movie.* 1974: *Another Day at the Races (GB: Win, Place or Steal).* 1976: *Black Heat.* 1982: *Human Highway.* 1986: *Les monjes sangrientōs (US: Blood Screams). Cyclone.* 1987: *The Phantom Empire. Commando Squad.* 1988: *B.O.R.N.* 1989: *Aftershock. Necromancer. Demon Sword. Twin Peaks (TV).* 1991: *Wizards of the Demon Sword.* 1992: *Twin Peaks – Fire Walk With Me. Running Mates (TV).* 1993: *Cabin Boy. Little Devils. The Birth.* 1995: *Invisible Man (TV). Attack of the 60ft Centerfold.* 1996: *Johnny Mysto – Boy Wizard.* 1997: *My Ghost Dog/My Magic Dog (TV). Invisible Dad (TV). Little Miss Magic.*

†*As Rusty Tamblyn*

TANI, Yoko 1932–1999
Very pretty, full-lipped, petite, Paris-born Japanese leading lady whose father was attached to the Japanese embassy in Paris. Completing her education in Japan, she returned to Paris to train as a dancer, but began playing small acting roles in films from the mid-1950s. Quickly breaking through to leading roles, she showed herself capable of very touching performances (especially in *The Wind Cannot Read* and *The Savage Innocents*), but was too often caught up in international hotch-potches about secret agents. Died from cancer.
1954: *Ali-Baba.* 1956: *Mannequins de Paris.* 1957: *Les oeufs de l'autriche. La fille de feu (GB: Fire in the Flesh). The Quiet American.* 1958: *The Wind Cannot Read.* 1959: *The Savage Hordes. US: Tartar Invasion).* 1960: *Piccadilly Third Stop. First Spaceship on Venus.* 1961: *Samson and the Seven Miracles of the World/Maciste alla corte del Gran Kan/Samson and the Seven Miracles. Ursus e la ragazza tartara (GB: The Savage Hordes. US: Tartar Invasion).* 1962: *My Geisha. Marco Polo. The Sweet and the Bitter.* 1963: *Who's Been Sleeping in My Bed? Un aereo per Baalbeck. The Partner.* 1964: *Agent 225 – Desperate Mission. Bianco, rosso,*

giallo, rosa. 1965: *OSS 77, Operation Lotus Flower. Die Toddesstrahlen des Dr Mabuse (US: Dr Mabuse's Rays of Death).* 1966: *Goldsnake. Invasion. Le spie amano i fiori.* 1967: *Seven Golden Chinamen. The Power.* 1978: *Tilt/Ça fait tilt.*

TASHMAN, Lilyan
See LOWE, Edmund

TATI, Jacques (J. Tatischeff) 1908–1982
Tall, gangling French pantomomist, writer, comic actor and director who invented the great, hulking, mournful Monsieur Hulot, a continual catalyst of disaster, and played him in several very successful post-war comedies whose gentle humour, visual invention and explosive belly-laughs sometimes reduced audiences to tears. Unfortunately he was (as a film-maker) almost as disorganized as his creation. His last announced project, *Confusion* in 1977, was all too aptly titled and did not materialize. Died from a pulmonary embolism.
1932: **Oscar, champion de tennis.* 1934: **On demande une brute.* 1935: **Gai Dimanche.* 1936: **Soigné ton gauche.* 1938: *Retour à la terre.* 1945: *Sylvie et le fantôme (US: Sylvia and the Ghost).* 1946: *Le diable au corps (GB: and US: Devil in the Flesh).* 1947: **L'école des facteurs.* 1949: *Jour de fête.* 1951: *Monsieur Hulot's Holiday.* 1956: *Mon oncle/My Uncle.* 1967: *Playtime. *Cours du soir.* 1970: *Domicile conjugal (GB and US: Bed and Board).* 1971: *Trafic/Traffic.* 1974: *Parade (TV).*
As director: 1947: **L'école des facteurs (co-directed).* 1949: *Jour de fête.* 1951: *Monsieur Hulot's Holiday.* 1956: *Mon oncle/My Uncle.* 1967: *Playtime.* 1971: *Traffic.* 1974: *Parade (TV).*

TAYLOR, Alma 1895–1974
Brown-haired, blue-eyed, round-faced British actress of great charm who started as a child in early silents, and continued in child-like roles into her late teens. Best remembered for her roles in the long-running 'Tilly the Tomboy' series. Her output and popularity began to fall away in the twenties (she first lost star billing in 1928), but she kept working, often, in later times, on TV.
1907: *His Daughter's Voice.* 1908: *The Little Flower Girl.* 1909: *The Little Milliner and the Thief. The Story of a Picture.* 1910: *Tilly the Tomboy Goes Boating. The Burglar and Little Phyllis. Tilly the Tomboy Buys Linoleum. A New Hat for Nothing. Tilly the Tomboy Visits*

the Poor. Tilly at the Election. 1911: *Evicted. Tilly's Party. Tilly's Unsympathetic Uncle. When Tilly's Uncle Flirted. Tilly – Matchmaker. Tilly and the Mormon Missionary. Tilly and the Fire Engines. A Wilful Maid. Envy, Hatred and Malice. For a Baby's Sake. Tilly at the Seaside. The Veteran's Pension. A Fight with Fire. The Smuggler's Stepdaughter. A Seaside Introduction. Tilly and the Smugglers.* 1912: *Bill's Reformation. The Curfew Must Not Ring Tonight. †Oliver Twist. King Robert of Sicily. The Curate's Bride. Winning His Stripes. Tilly and the Dogs. Tilly Works for a Living. Tilly in a Boarding House. The Dear Little Teacher. For Love and Life. The Real Thing. The Tailor's Revenge.* 1913: *The Lover Who Took the Cake. The Mill Girl. Petticoat Perfidy. Partners in Crime. Adrift on Life's Tide. A Little Widow is a Dangerous Thing. A Midnight Adventure. †The Old Curiosity Shop. Blind Fate. The Whirr of the Spinning Wheel. Tried in the Fire. Paying the Penalty. Tilly's Breaking Up Party. Her Little Pet. The Girl at Lancing Mill. †David Copperfield. †The Cloister and the Hearth. The Broken Oath. Justice. The Price of Fame.* 1914: *†The Heart of Midlothian. An Engagement of Convenience. Over the Garden Wall. The Kleptomaniac. The Hills Are Calling. His Country's Bidding. The Awakening of Nora. Time, the Great Healer. His Great Opportunity. Oh My Aunt! The Canker of Jealousy. Tilly at the Football Match. By Whose Hand? The Girl who Lived in Straight Street. The Schemers, or: The Jewels of Hate. The Basilisk. In the Shadow of Big Ben. Aladdin, or: a Lad Out. Morphia the Death Drug. The Double Event.* 1915: *Spies. The Painted Lady Betty. A Moment of Darkness. Tilly and the Nut. The Passing of a Soul. †The Man Who Stayed at Home. The Outrage. Love in a Mist. A Lancashire Lass. Alma Taylor. Jill and the Old Violin/Jill and the Old Fiddle. Court-Martialled! The Baby on the Barge. †Sweet Lavender. †The Golden Pavement. †Iris. The Man at the Wheel.* 1916: *†Annie Laurie. †Trelawney of the Wells. †The Grand Babylon Hotel †Molly Bawn. †Sowing the Wind. †The Marriage of William Ashe. †Comin' Through the Rye. The Cobweb.* 1917: *†Nearer My God to Thee. The American Heiress. †Merely Mrs Stubbs.* 1918: *The W.L.A. Girl. †The Touch of a Child. The Refugee. †Boundary House. A New Version. The Leopard's Spots. Tares. Broken in the Wars.* 1919: *†Sheba. †The Nature of the Beast. †The Forest on the Hill. †Sunken Rocks.* 1920: *†Helen of Four Gates. †Anna the*

Adventuress. †*Alf's Button.* †*Mrs Erricker's Reputation.* 1921: †*Dollars in Surrey.* †*The Tinted Venus.* †*Tansy.* †*The Narrow Valley.* 1923: †*Strangling Threads.* †*The Pipes of Pan.* †*Comin' thro' the Rye* (remake). †*Mist in the Valley.* 1924: †*The Shadow of Egypt.* 1926: †*The House of Marney.* 1927: †*Quinneys.* 1928: †*Two Little Drummer Boys.* †*The South Sea Bubble.* 1931: †*Deadlock.* 1932: †*Bachelor's Baby.* 1933: †*House of Dreams.* 1934: †*Things Are Looking Up.* 1936: †*Everybody Dance.* 1954: †*Lilacs in the Spring* (US: *Let's Make Up*). 1955: †*Stock Car.* †*Lost* (US: *Tears for Simon*). 1957: †*Blue Murder at St Trinian's.*

All shorts except †*features*

TAYLOR, Don 1920–1998
Genial, red-haired American leading man who displayed some warmth in playing pleasant fellows for 10 years or so, but turned to direction in the late fifties, and made some very competent features without setting the screen on fire. Married (third) to Hazel Court (*qv*) from 1964. Died from heart failure.
1943: *The Human Comedy. Thousands Cheer. Girl Crazy. Swing Shift Maisie* (GB: *The Girl in Overalls*). *Salute to the Marines.* 1944: *Winged Victory.* 1945: *The Red Dragon.* 1947: *Song of the Thin Man.* 1948: *The Naked City. For the Love of Mary.* 1949: *Battleground. Ambush.* 1950: *Father of the Bride.* 1951: *Flying Leathernecks. Target Unknown. Father's Little Dividend. Submarine Command. The Blue Veil.* 1952: *Japanese War Bride.* 1953: *The Girls of Pleasure Island. Destination Gobi. Stalag 17.* 1954: *Johnny Dark. Men of Sherwood Forest.* 1955: *I'll Cry Tomorrow.* 1956: *The Bold and the Brave.* 1957: *Love Slaves of the Amazon/ Lost Slaves of the Amazon. Ride the High Iron.* 1962: *The Savage Guns.* 1973: *Tom Sawyer.*
As director: 1961: *Everything's Ducky.* 1964: *Ride the Wild Surf.* 1967: *Jack of Diamonds.* 1968: *Something for a Lonely Man* (TV). 1969: *The Five Man Army. The Man Hunter* (TV). 1970: *Wild Women* (TV). 1971: *Escape from the Planet of the Apes.* 1972: *Heat of Anger* (TV). 1973: *Tom Sawyer.* 1974: *Honky Tonk* (TV). *Night Games* (TV). 1975: *Echoes of a Summer* (US: *The Last Castle*). 1976: *The Great Scout and Cathouse Thursday.* 1977: *A Circle of Children* (TV). *The Island of Dr Moreau.* 1978: *Damien – Omen II.* 1979: *The Gift* (TV). 1980: *The Final Countdown.* 1981: *Broken Promise*

(TV). *The Red Flag.* 1982: *A Change of Heart* (TV). *Listen to Your Heart* (TV). 1983: *Spetember Gun* (TV). 1984: *He's Not Your Son* (TV). 1985: *Going for the Gold: The Bill Johnson Story* (TV). *Sexpionage* (V). 1986: *Classified Love* (TV). 1987: *Ghost of a Chance* (TV). 1988: *The Diamond Trap* (TV).

TAYLOR, Dame Elizabeth 1932– 2o4
Raven-haired child star who developed into a breathtaking beauty and highly professional actress, if with a limited range. However, she did win Academy Awards for *Butterfield 8* and *Who's Afraid of Virginia Woolf?*, and was further Oscar-nominated for *Raintree County, Cat on a Hot Tin Roof* and *Suddenly Last Summer.* Eight times married (seven divorces and once widowed), including (second) Michael Wilding (*qv*) 1952–1957; (fourth) singer Eddie Fisher 1959–1964, and (fifth and sixth) Richard Burton (*qv*) 1964–1974 and briefly remarried 1976. Created Dame in 2000.
1942: **Man or Mouse. One Born Every Minute.* 1943: *Lassie Come Home. Jane Eyre.* 1944: *The White Cliffs of Dover. National Velvet.* 1946: *Courage of Lassie.* 1947: *Cynthia* (GB: *The Rich, Full Life*). *Life with Father.* 1948: *A Date with Judy. Julia Misbehaves.* 1949: *Little Women. Conspirator.* 1950: *The Big Hangover. Father of the Bride.* 1951: *Love is Better than Ever* (GB: *The Light Fantastic*). *A Place in the Sun. Father's Little Dividend. Quo Vadis. Callaway Went Thataway* (GB: *The Star Said No*). 1952: *Ivanhoe.* 1953: *The Girl Who Had Everything.* 1954: *The Last Time I Saw Paris. Rhapsody. Beau Brummell. Elephant Walk.* 1956: *Giant.* 1957: *Raintree County.* 1958: *Cat on a Hot Tin Roof.* 1959: *Suddenly Last Summer.* 1960: *Butterfield 8. Scent of Mystery* (GB: *Holiday in Spain*). 1963: *Cleopatra. The VIPs.* 1965: *The Sandpiper. What's New Pussycat?* 1966: *Who's Afraid of Virginia Woolf?* 1967: *The Taming of the Shrew. The Comedians. Reflections in a Golden Eye.* 1968: *Dr Faustus. Boom. Secret Ceremony.* 1969: *Anne of the Thousand Days. The Only Game in Town.* 1971: *Zee and Co* (US: *X, Y and Zee*). *Under Milk Wood.* 1972: *Hammersmith is Out.* 1973: *Night Watch. Ash Wednesday.* 1974: *The Driver's Seat/ Identikit. That's Entertainment!* 1976: *Victory at Entebbe* (TV. GB: *Cinemas*). *The Blue Bird.* 1977: *A Little Night Music. Winter Kills* (released 1979). 1978: *Return Engagement* (TV). 1980: *The Mirror Crack'd.* 1981: *Genocide* (narrator only). 1983:

Between Friends (TV). 1985: *Malice in Wonderland* (TV). 1986: *There Must Be a Pony* (TV). 1987: *Poker Alice* (TV). 1988: *Young Toscanini.* 1989: *Sweet Bird of Youth* (TV). 1994: *The Flintstones.*

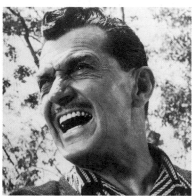

TAYLOR, Kent (Louis Weiss) 1906–1987
Perhaps this smooth, dark-haired, moustachioed American actor lacked the variety of expression to become a top star, but he deserves some kind of award for his longevity as a second-feature hero, keeping his ranking in the genre from 1932 to 1963 but spending his last film years in a bizarre collection of horror films. Died following a heart operation.
1931: *Road to Reno.* 1932: *Dancers in the Dark. Forgotten Commandments. Two Kinds of Women. Husband's Holiday. The Devil and the Deep. Merrily We Go to Hell* (GB: *Merrily We Go to—*). *The Sign of the Cross. Make Me a Star. If I Had a Million. Sinners in the Sun. Blonde Venus.* 1933: *Mysterious Rider. A Lady's Profession. The Story of Temple Drake. Sunset Pass. I'm No Angel. White Woman. Cradle Song. Under the Tonto Rim.* 1934: *Death Takes a Holiday. Many Happy Returns. David Harum. Double Door. Mrs Wiggs of the Cabbage Patch. Limehouse Blues.* 1935: *The County Chairman. College Scandal* (GB: *The Clock Strikes Eight*). *Smart Girl. Without Regret. Two-Fisted. My Marriage.* 1936: *The Sky Parade. Florida Special. Ramona. The Accusing Finger.* 1937: *When Love is Young. Wings Over Honolulu. The Lady Fights Back. A Girl with Ideas. Prescription for Romance. Love in a Bungalow.* 1938: *The Jury's Secret. The Last Express.* 1939: *Four Girls in White. Pirates of the Skies. The Gracie Allen Murder Case. Five Came Back. Three Sons. Escape to Paradise.* 1940: *I Take This Woman. Sued for Libel. Two Girls on Broadway* (GB: *Choose Your Partner*). *The Girl in 313. Men Against the Sky. I'm Still Alive. The Girl from Avenue A.* 1941: *Washington Melodrama. Repent at Leisure.* 1942: *Mississippi Gambler. Tombstone, the Town Too Tough to Die. Army Surgeon. Half Way to Shanghai. Frisco Lil. Gang Busters* (serial). 1943: *Bombers' Moon.* 1944: *Roger Touhy, Gangster* (GB: *The Last Gangster*). *Alaska.* 1945: *The Daltons Ride Again.* 1946: *Smooth as Silk. Young Widow. Tangier. Deadline for Murder. Dangerous Millions* (GB: *The House of Tao Ling*). 1947: *Second Chance. The Crimson Key.* 1948: *Half Past Midnight.* 1950: *Federal Agent at Large. Western Pacific Agent. Trial without Jury.* 1951: *Payment on Demand.* 1954: *Playgirl.*

Track the Man Down. 1955: Secret Venture. Ghost Town. The Phantom from 10,000 Leagues. 1956: Slightly Scarlet. Frontier Gambler. 1957: The Iron Sheriff. 1958: Fort Bowie. Gang War. 1960: Walk Tall. 1961: The Purple Hills. 1962: The Broken Land. The Firebrand. 1963: The Day Mars Invaded Earth. Harbor Lights. Law of the Lawless. The Crawling Hand. 1965: Fort Courageous. 1968: Brides of Blood. 1969: Smashing the Crime Syndicate (released 1973). 1970: Satan's Sadists. The Last Escape. Hell's Bloody Devils. 1971: The Mighty Gorga. Angels' Wild Women. 1972: Blood of Ghastly Horror. Brain of Blood. 1974: Girls for Rent/ I Spit on Your Corpse.

TAYLOR, Lili 1967–

An icon of American independent movies, Lili Taylor's career might have been different had she been the one of the three girls in Mystic Pizza to attract all the attention rather than Julia Roberts. But that probably wouldn't have pleased this brown-haired, slightly downcast-looking and other-worldly actress who has said that 'I like to play women who are a little crazy.' She's certainly fulfilled that ambition in a Julie Harris-style career that even saw her inheriting Harris' old role in a remake of The Haunting. She is also a prominent figure in local theatre, especially involving young people's projects.

1987: Night of Courage (TV). 1988: Mystic Pizza. She's Having a Baby. 1989: Born on the Fourth of July. Say Anything. 1990: Family of Spies (TV). 1991: Bright Angel. Dogfight. 1992: Arizona Dream (released 1995). 1993: Watch It. Short Cuts. Rudy. Household Saints. 1994: Luck, Trust & Ketchup (D). Mrs Parker & the Vicious Circle. Prêt-à-Porter (US: Ready to Wear). Touch Base. Cold Fever. 1995: Four Rooms. Things I Never Told You. The Addiction. Killer: A Journal of Murder. 1996: Girls' Town. I Shot Andy Warhol. Ransom. Illtown. *Plain Pleasures. Cosas que nunca te dije. 1997: Subway Stories: Tales from the Underground (TV). Letters Not About Love (voice only). Kicked in the Head. 1998: O.K. Garage. Pecker. The Impostors/ Ship of Fools. 1999: A Slipping Down Life. The Haunting. Janis. 2000: Spring Forward. High Fidelity. Gaudi Afternoon. 2001: Julie Johnson.

TAYLOR, Robert
(Spangler Brugh) 1911–1969
Tall, dark and, in his twenties, idyllically handsome American star who grew a

moustache to escape the 'pretty-boy' image and stayed at or near the top for 25 years. Although his features hardened quickly after return from war service, his career was prolonged by several first-class slices of historical adventure in the early fifties. Married to Barbara Stanwyck from 1939 to 1952 and Ursula Thiess (1929–) from 1954 on. Died from lung cancer.

1934: Handy Andy. A Wicked Woman. There's Always Tomorrow. *The Spectacle Maker. *Buried Loot. 1935: Society Doctor. Murder in the Fleet. West Point of the Air. Times Square Lady. Magnificent Obsession. *La Fiesta de Santa Barbara. Broadway Melody of 1936. Only Eight Hours. 1936: His Brother's Wife. Small Town Girl. Private Number (GB: Secret Interlude). The Gorgeous Hussy. Camille. 1937: Personal Property (GB: The Man in Possession). This is My Affair. (GB: His Affair). Broadway Melody of 1938. *Lest We Forget. A Yank at Oxford. 1938: The Crowd Roars. Three Comrades. 1939: Lady of the Tropics. Remember? Stand Up and Fight. Lucky Night. 1940: Escape. Waterloo Bridge. Flight Command. 1941: Billy the Kid. When Ladies Meet. 1942: Her Cardboard Lover. Johnny Eager. Stand by for Action! (GB: Cargo of Innocents). 1943: The Youngest Profession. Bataan. Song of Russia. 1945: The Fighting Lady (narrator only). 1946: Undercurrent. 1947: The High Wall. 1948: The Secret Land (narrator only). The Bribe. 1949: Ambush. Conspirator. 1950: Devil's Doorway. 1951: *Challenge in the Wilderness. Quo Vadis. Westward the Women. 1952: Above and Beyond. Ivanhoe. I Love Melvin. 1953: All the Brothers Were Valiant. Ride, Vaquero! 1954: Knights of the Round Table. Rogue Cop. Valley of the Kings. 1955: The Adventures of Quentin Durward (US: Quentin Durward). Many Rivers to Cross. 1956: The Last Hunt. The Power and the Prize. D-Day the Sixth of June. 1957: Tip on a Dead Jockey (GB: Time for Action). 1958: Party Girl. Saddle the Wind. The Law and Jake Wade. 1959: The House of the Seven Hawks. The Hangman. Killers of Kilimanjaro. 1962: Recoil (TV. GB: cinemas) Miracle of the White Stallions. Flight of the White Stallions). 1963: Cattle King (GB: Guns of Wyoming). 1964: A House is Not a Home. 1965: The Night Walker. 1966: Savage Pampas. Johnny Tiger. Return of the Gunfighter. Hondo and the Apaches (TV. GB: cinemas). 1967: The Glass Sphinx. Where Angels Go . . . Trouble Follows. 1968: The Day the Hot Line Got Hot. Devil May Care.

TAYLOR, Rod
(Robert Taylor) 1926–
Chunky, jut-jawed, light-haired Australian actor who came to Hollywood in 1954 to establish himself. Once in leading roles, he showed genuine warmth, charm and forcefulness, although only a top star from 1963–1968; producing his own films at this stage proved rather a mistake in terms of his box-office popularity, which should have solidified, but instead ebbed away.

1951: †The Sturt Expedition. 1954: †Long John Silver. King of the Coral Sea. 1955: The Virgin Queen. Hell on Frisco Bay. Top Gun. 1956: The Rack. The Catered Affair (GB: Wedding Breakfast). Giant. World without End. 1957: Raintree County. 1958: Step Down to Terror (GB: The Silent Stranger). Separate Tables. Verdict of Three (TV). The Great Gatsby (TV). Ask Any Girl. Misalliance (TV). Queen of the Amazons (GB: Colossus and the Amazon Queen). 1960: The Time Machine. 1961: One Hundred and One Dalmatians (voice only). Seven Seas to Calais. 1963: Sunday in New York. A Gathering of Eagles. The Birds. The V.I.P.s. 1964: Fate is the Hunter. Thirty-Six Hours. Young Cassidy. 1965: Do Not Disturb. The Liquidator. 1966: The Glass Bottom Boat. Hotel. 1967: The Mercenaries (US: Dark of the Sun). Chuka. 1968: The Hell with Heroes. Nobody Runs Forever. 1969: Zabriskie Point. 1970: The Man Who Had Power over Women. Darker than Amber. 1971: Powderkeg (TV. GB: cinemas). 1972: Family Flight (TV). The Heroes. 1973: The Train Robbers. Trader Horn (GB: TV). The Deadly Trackers. 1974: Partizan (US: Hell River). 1975: Blondy (US: Vortex). Shamus (TV. GB: A Matter of Wife and Death). 1976: The Oregon Trail (TV). 1977: The Picture Show Man. The Thoroughbreds (later Treasure Seekers). 1978: Cry of the Innocent (TV). An Eye for an Eye. 1980: Seven Graves for Rogan. Hellinger's Law (TV). 1982: Jacqueline Bouvier Kennedy (TV). Charles and Diana – a Royal Love Story (TV). On the Run. 1983: Masquerade (TV). 1985: Marbella. Half Nelson. Mask of Murder. 1986: Outlaws (TV). 1991: Danielle Steel's Palomino (TV). 1994: Open Season (released 1996). 1995: Underground Love. Point of Betrayal. 1987: Welcome to Woop Woop.

†As Rodney Taylor

TEMPLE, Shirley 1928–

There never has been a child star to compare with Shirley Temple. An adorable golden-haired child, with the timing, reactions, know-how and sly wit of an adult, she appeared completely natural on screen, and quite beguiling. The combination of these factors was irresistible, and she was an above-the-title star at six. She couldn't really sing, but did, delightfully; and danced with the confidence of a Kelly. She was America's top star from 1935 to 1938, having taken a special Oscar in 1934. One could wish she had persevered a little more with her adult career: instead she became a diplomat. Married John Agar (qv) 1945–1949, first of two.

1932: *War Babies. *Glad Rags to Riches. *Pie Covered Wagon. *The Runt Page. Red-Haired Alibi. *1933:* *Polly-Tix in Washington. *Kid 'n' Hollywood. *Kid 'n' Africa. To the Last Man. *Kid's Last Night. *Merrily Yours. *Dora's Dunkin' Donuts. Out All Night. *1934:* *Pardon My Pups. *Managed Money. Mandalay. New Deal Rhythm. Carolina (GB: The House of Connelly). Stand Up and Cheer. Now I'll Tell (GB: When New York Sleeps). Change of Heart. Little Miss Marker (GB: Girl in Pawn). Baby, Take a Bow. Now and Forever. Bright Eyes. *Hollywood Cavalcade. *1935:* Curly Top. The Little Colonel. Our Little Girl. The Littlest Rebel. *1936:* Captain January. Dimples. Poor Little Rich Girl. Stowaway. *1937:* Wee Willie Winkie. Heidi. Ali Baba Goes to Town. *1938:* Rebecca of Sunnybrook Farm. Little Miss Broadway. Just Around the Corner. *1939:* The Little Princess. Susannah of the Mounties. *1940:* The Blue Bird. Young People. *1941:* Kathleen. *1942:* Miss Annie Rooney. *1944:* Since you Went Away. I'll Be Seeing You. *1945:* Kiss and Tell. *1947:* Honeymoon (GB: Two Men and a Girl). The Bachelor and the Bobby-Soxer (GB: Bachelor Knight). That Hagen Girl. *1948:* Fort Apache. *1949:* Mr Belvedere Goes to College. A Kiss for Corliss. Adventure in Baltimore (GB: Bachelor Bait). The Story of Seabiscuit (GB: Pride of Kentucky).

TENNANT, Victoria 1948–

Blonde British leading lady of the genteel type, with impeccable pedigree and facial features, but the limited ability common to many 'gracious' English actresses from her era. Daughter of ballerina Irina Baronova and goddaughter of Laurence Olivier (qv), she was hailed as a new talent on her starring film debut at 22, but it was some years before she

projected anything but an unsympathetic personality. Films in Poland and Germany did little for her, but 1980 was the lowpoint: minor roles in three films, two of them abysmal. She went to America and her career picked up. She achieved popularity in TV mini-series, such as The Winds of War, War and Remembrance, Chiefs and Act of Will, and performed adequately in some feature films. In 1986 she married (first of two) actor-comedian Steve Martin (qv). The couple divorced in 1994. Her first screenplay, Edie & Pen, was filmed in 1996.

1972: The Ragman's Daughter. *1975:* The Speckled Band. Nullpunkt. *1977:* The Killing. *1980:* The Dogs of War. Sphinx. La guerre des insects. Inseminoid (US: Horror Planet). *1983:* Dempsey (TV). Strangers Kiss. *1984:* All of Me. *1985:* The Holcroft Covenant. *1986:* Under Siege (TV). Best Seller. *1987:* Flowers in the Attic. *1988:* Maigret (TV). *1989:* Fool's Mate. Zugzwang. *1990:* The Handmaid's Tale. *1991:* L.A. Story. Whispers. *1992:* The Plague. *1996:* Edie & Pen. *1997:* Legend of the Mummy.

TERRY-THOMAS

(Thomas Terry Hoar-Stevens) 1911–1990
Gap-toothed, dark-haired, moustachioed British comedian whose exaggerated upper-crust accent, benign but foxy expression and long cigarette holder were all part of the act. He started as a dance extra, but in post-war years gained a reputation as a stand-up comic (always prefacing his act with 'How do you do') before successfully tackling character comedy on film, alternately playing bluster-ing idiots and wily rogues. In poor health in his last years. Died from Parkinson's Disease.
1936: It's Love Again. Rhythm in the Air. This'll Make You Whistle. *1937:* Rhythm

Racketeer. *1940:* For Freedom. Under Your Hat. *1947:* The Brass Monkey/Lucky Mascot. *1948:* A Date with a Dream. *1949:* Helter Skelter. Melody Club. *1951:* *Cookery Nook. *The Queen Steps Out. *1955:* Private's Progress. *1956:* The Green Man. Brothers in Law. *1957:* Blue Murder at St Trinian's. Lucky Jim. The Naked Truth (US: Your Past is Showing). *1958:* Happy is the Bride. tom thumb. *1959:* Too Many Crooks. Carlton-Brown of the F.O. (US: Man in a Cocked Hat). I'm All Right, Jack. School for Scoundrels. *1960:* Make Mine Mink. His and Hers. *1961:* A Matter of WHO. *1962:* Operation Snatch. Bachelor Flat. Kill or Cure. Wonderful World of the Brothers Grimm. *1963:* It's a Mad, Mad, Mad, Mad World. Mouse on the Moon. *1964:* The Wild Affair. *1965:* Strange Bedfellows. Those Magnificent Men in Their Flying Machines. You Must Be Joking! *1966:* The Daydreamer (voice only). Our Man in Marrakesh (US: Bang Bang You're Dead). Operation Paradise. The Sandwich Man. Munster Go Home. Kiss the Girls and Make Them Die. La grande vadrouille (GB: Don't Look Now, We're Being Shot At). *1967:* Rocket to the Moon (US: Those Fantastic Flying Fools). Arabella. Bandidos. I Love a Mystery (TV). The Karate Killers (TV. GB: cinemas). The Perils of Pauline. A Guide for the Married Man. Top Crack. Diabolik (GB: Danger: Diabolik). *1968:* Don't Raise the Bridge, Lower the River. Uno scacco tutto matto (US: Mad Checkmate). Sette volte sette/Seven Times Seven. How Sweet It Is! Where Were You When The Lights Went Out? *1969:* †Arthur, Arthur, 2,000 Years Later. Monte Carlo or Bust! (US: Those Daring Young Men in their Jaunty Jalopies). Twelve Plus One/una su Zradici. *1970:* Le mur de l'Atlantique. The Abominable Dr Phibes. *1972:* The Cherrypicker. The Heroes. Dr Phibes Rises Again. *1973:* Vault of Horror. Robin Hood (voice only). *1974:* Who Stole the Shah's Jewels? *1975:* Side by Side. The Bawdy Adventures of Tom Jones. Spanish Fly. *1977:* The Hound of the Baskervilles. The Last Remake of Beau Geste. *1981:* Happy Birthday Harry!

†Unreleased

THAXTER, Phyllis 1921–

Pretty, brown-haired American actress who tended to play nice girls and women who wrung their hands and waited, but her performances were spirited enough to bring an extra dimension to such roles. The impetus of her career was badly hit by an attack of infantile paralysis in 1952, but she continued to act, latterly in character roles. Mother of actress Skye Aubrey (1945–).

1944: *Thirty Seconds over Tokyo*. 1945: *Bewitched*. *Weekend at the Waldorf*. 1947: *Sea of Grass*. *Living in a Big Way*. 1948: *The Sign of the Ram*. *Act of Violence*. *Tenth Avenue Angel*. *Blood on the Moon*. 1950: *No Man of Her Own*. *The Breaking Point*. 1951: *Come Fill the Cup*. *Fort Worth*. *Jim Thorpe – All American* (GB: *Man of Bronze*). 1952: *She's Working Her Way Through College*. *Springfield Rifle*. *Operation Secret*. 1955: *Women's Prison*. 1957: *Man Afraid*. 1960: *The Cruel Day* (TV). 1964: *The World of Henry Orient*. 1971: *Incident in San Francisco* (TV). 1972: *The Longest Night* (TV). 1978: *Superman*. 1985: *Three Sovereigns for Sarah* (TV).

THERON, Charlize 1975–
Serene, sylph-like blonde South African actress with green-eyes and alabaster features. A teenage model and ballerina in her native country, she sustained a knee injury which ended her dancing career and decided to try acting in Hollywood. 'I had enough cash for about six weeks, then it would have been back to South Africa.' Fortunately, she landed a role in a video horror film 'that will probably come back to haunt me' and puts her subsequent rapid rise to star billing down to a combination of luck and hard work. Can be affectingly natural in the right role.

1996: *Children of the Corn IV: The Gathering* (video). *2 Days in the Valley*. *That Thing You Do!* 1997: *The Devil's Advocate*. *Trial and Error*. *Hollywood Confidential* (TV). 1998: *Mighty Joe Young* (GB: *Mighty Joe*). *Celebrity*. 1999: *The Astronaut's Wife*. *The Cider House Rules*. 2000: *Reindeer Games/ Deception*. *The Yards*. *Navy Diver*. *The Legend of Bagger Vance*. *Sweet November*. 2001: *Wakin' Up in Reno*. *Chicago*. *The Husband*.

THOMAS, Jameson 1889–1939
Dark, dominant, moustachioed, somewhat severe-looking, smoothly-groomed British actor who looked born to play nasty pieces of work, but was equally adept as heroes and became a big star of British films in the years immediately preceding sound, which revealed his crackling tones. He went to America as early as 1930 but after a couple of leading roles gradually regressed to handsome lotharios and

'other men'. Increasingly ill in his later years, he died at 49 from tuberculosis.

1923: *Chu Chin Chow*. 1924: *The Drum*. *The Cavern Spider*. *Decameron Nights*. *The Sins Ye Do*. *Chester Forgets Himself*. 1925: *Daughter of Love*. *The Apache*. *Afraid of Love*. *The Gold Cure*. 1926: *The Brotherhood*. *Jungle Woman*. *Pearl of the South Seas*. 1927: *Blighty*. *As We Lie*. *Roses of Picardy*. *Poppies of Flanders*. 1928: *The White Sheik* (US: *King's Mate*). *The Farmer's Wife*. *Tesha* (US: *A Woman in the Night*). *The Rising Generation*. *Weekend Wives*. 1929: *Piccadilly*. *Power Over Men*. *The Feather*. *Memories*. *High Treason*. *The Hate Ship*. 1930: *Night Birds*. *Elstree Calling*. *Extravagance*. 1931: *Lover Come Back*. *Convicted*. *Night Life in Reno*. 1932: *Three Wise Girls*. *The Trial of Vivienne Ware*. *The Phantom President*. *No More Orchids*. *Escapade*. 1933: *Brief Moment*. *The Invisible Man*. *Bombay Mail*. *Self Defense*. 1934: *A Lost Lady* (GB: *Courageous*). *The Scarlet Empress*. *It Happened One Night*. *Now and Forever*. *The Man who Reclaimed His Head*. *Beggers in Ermine*. *Sing Sing Nights* (GB: *Reprieved*). *Stolen Sweets*. *The Moonstone*. *Jane Eyre*. *A Woman's Man*. *A Successful Failure*. 1935: *Lives of a Bengal Lancer*. *The World Accuses*. *Rumba*. *Mr Dynamite*. *Coronado*. *The Lady in Scarlet*. *Charlie Chan in Egypt*. *Crimson Romance*. *The Last Outpost*. 1936: *Mr Deeds Goes to Town*. *Lady Luck*. 1937: *House of Secrets*. *The League of Frightened Men*. *The Man Who Cried Wolf*. *100 Men and a Girl*. *Girl Loves Boy*. 1938: *Death Goes North*.

THOMAS, Richard 1951–
Young-looking, light-haired American actor who became immensely popular on TV as

John Boy in the long-running series *The Waltons*. In films as a teenager, he has played several sensitive roles and (rather more effectively) one or two nasty ones. But he has, on the whole, not made the strides that one might have hoped for and, although still in leading roles, has been seen mostly in TV movies and the theatre in recent times.

1969: †*Winning*. *Last Summer*. 1970: *Cactus in the Snow*. *The Todd Killings*. *You Can't Have Everything*. 1971: *The Homecoming* (TV). *Red Sky at Morning*. 1972: *You'll Like My Mother*. 1974: *The Red Badge of Courage* (TV). 1975: *The Silence* (TV). 1977: *Getting Married* (TV). *9–30–55* (GB: TV, as *30 September, 1955*). 1979: *No Other Love* (TV). 1980: *All Quiet on the Western Front* (TV. GB: cinemas). *Battle Beyond the Stars*. *To Find My Son* (TV). 1981: *Berlin Tunnel 28* (TV). 1982: *Johnny Belinda* (TV). 1983: *Living Proof: The Hank Williams Jr Story* (TV). *Hobson's Choice* (TV). 1984: *The Master of Ballantrae* (TV). 1985: *Final Jeopardy* (TV). 1986: *Welcome to Our Night* (TV). 1989: *Glory! Glory!* (cable TV). 1990: *André's Mother* (TV). *It* (TV). 1991: *Yes, Virginia, There is a Santa Claus* (TV). *Mission of of the Shark* (TV). 1992: *Crash Landing: The Rescue of Flight 232* (TV). 1993: *Linda* (TV). *Stalking Laura* (TV). *Precious Victims* (TV). 1994: *A Walton Reunion* (TV). *A Walton Wedding* (TV). 1995: *The Christmas Box* (TV). *Death in Small Doses* (TV). 1996: *What Love Sees* (TV). *Timepiece* (TV). 1997: *Promised Land* (TV). *Narrow Escape*. *A Walton Easter* (TV). *A Thousand Men and a Baby* (TV). 1998: *Big and Hairy* (TV). 1999: *In the Name of the People* (TV). *Beyond the Prairie* (TV). *The Million Dollar Kid* (TV). 2000: *Wonder Boys*.

†As Richard Thomas Jr

THOMPSON, Carlos
See PALMER, Lilli

THOMPSON, Emma 1959–
Drawlingly-voiced, multi-talented, brown-haired (though often lighter in recent films) British actress, singer, comedienne and writer. After stage and television successes, she married sometime co-star Kenneth Branagh (*qv*) and made a delayed entry to films at 30. Triumphs in this medium were not long in coming: she won an Academy Award for *Howards End*, and was Oscar-nominated for her performances in *The*

Remains of the Day, Sense and Sensibility and *In the Name of the Father*. Further awards followed her first venture into screenwriting with *Sense and Sensibility*: its screenplay won her another Academy Award. Her marriage to Branagh, however, foundered, and the couple parted in 1995. Now partnered with actor Greg Wise.

1989: The Tall Guy. Henry V. 1990: Impromptu. 1991: Dead Again. Howards End. 1992: Peter's Friends. 1993: The Remains of the Day. Much Ado about Nothing. In the Name of the Father. 1994: The Blue Boy (TV). My Father the Hero. Junior. 1995: Carrington. Sense and Sensibility. 1997: The Winter Guest. 1998: Primary Colors. Judas Kiss (US: TV). 1999: Maybe Baby.

THOMPSON, Marshall
(James M. Thompson) 1925–1992

Tall, unassuming, sandy-haired American actor who played quiet juvenile roles at M-G-M for eight years before carrying on his career as a third-line leading man in equally unspectacular fashion. But his most successful period was yet to come, starting with the film *Clarence the Cross-Eyed Lion*, which led to the long-running TV animal-clinic series *Daktari*. He continued his association with wildlife producer Ivan Tors into the seventies. Died from congestive heart failure.

1944: The Purple Heart. Reckless Age. Blonde Fever. 1945: The Valley of Decision. The Clock (GB: Under the Clock). Twice Blessed. They Were Expendable. 1946: The Cockeyed Miracle (GB: Mr Griggs Returns). Bad Bascomb. The Show Off. Gallant Bess. The Secret Heart. 1947: The Romance of Rosy Ridge. 1948: Homecoming. B.F.'s Daughter (GB: Polly Fulton). Words and Music. Command Decision. 1949: Battleground. Roseanna McCoy. 1950: Mystery Street. Devil's Doorway. Dial 1119 (GB: The Violent Hour). 1951: The Tall Target. The Basketball Fix (GB: The Big Decision). 1952: My Six Convicts. The Rose Bowl Story. 1953: The Caddy. 1954: Port of Hell. Battle Taxi. 1955: Cult of the Cobra. Crashout. Good Morning, Miss Dove. To Hell and Back. 1956: La grande caccia. 1957: Lure of the Swamp. Young Man from Kentucky (TV. GB: cinemas). The Blackwell Story (TV). 1958: Fiend without a Face. IT! The Terror from Beyond Space. The Secret Man. 1959: First Man into Space. 1961: Flight of the Lost Balloon. 1962: No Man is an Island (GB: Island Rescue). East of Kilimanjaro/The Big Search. 1964: †A Yank in Viet-Nam. The

Mighty Jungle. 1965: Clarence the Cross-eyed Lion. Zebra in the Kitchen. 1966: To the Shores of Hell. Around the World Under the Sea. 1970: George! 1977: The Turning Point. 1978: Cruise into Terror (TV). Bog. 1980: ‡The Formula. 1982: White Dog. 1986: Dallas: the Early Years (TV).

†*Also directed*
‡*Scenes deleted from final release print*

THORBURN, June 1931–1967

Pretty, rose-cheeked, fair-haired British actress, born in Kashmir. A former junior skiing champion, her cinema course was from second-features into major films – and back again. She retired to concentrate on married life in 1964, but was killed in a plane crash.

1952: The Pickwick Papers. The Cruel Sea. 1953: The Triangle. 1954: Fast and Loose. Delayed Action. Orders Are Orders. Children Galore. The Death of Michael Turbin. 1955: The Hornet's Nest. Touch and Go (US: The Light Touch). 1956: True as a Turtle. 1958: Rooney. tom thumb. 1959: Broth of a Boy. 1960: The Price of Silence. The Three Worlds of Gulliver. Escort for Hire. 1961: Fury at Smuggler's Bay. Don't Bother to Knock! (US: Why Bother to Knock?). Transatlantic. The Spanish Sword. 1962: Design for Loving. 1963: The Scarlet Blade. Master Spy.

THORNDIKE, Dame Sybil
(Agnes S. Thorndike) 1882–1976

Distinguished British stage actress of upright bearing – a memorable St Joan in her late youth. Made a few film appearances in between a string of stage triumphs – mostly in old age. Married to equally distinguished stage actor Sir Lewis Casson (1876–1969).

Made a Dame in 1931. Died from a heart attack.

*1921: Moth and Rust. 1922: *Nancy. Bleak House. *Macbeth: extract. *Jane Shore. *The Lady of the Camelias: extract. *The Merchant of Venice: extract. *Esmeralda. *The Scarlet Letter: Extract. 1927: *Saint Joan: extract. 1928: Dawn. 1929: To What Red Hell. 1931: Hindle Wakes. A Gentleman of Paris. 1936: Tudor Rose (US: Nine Days a Queen). 1941: Major Barbara. 1947: Nicholas Nickleby. 1949: Britannia Mews (US: Forbidden Street). 1950: Stage Fright. Gone to Earth (US: The Wild Heart). 1951: The Magic Box. The Lady with a Lamp. 1953: Melba. The Weak and the Wicked. 1957: *Bernard Shaw. The Prince and the Showgirl. 1958: Smiley Gets a Gun. Alive and Kicking. 1959: Shake Hands with the Devil. Jet Storm. 1960: Hand in Hand. The Big Gamble. 1963: Uncle Vanya.*

THORNTON, Billy Bob 1955–

Tall, dark, taciturn American actor with lopsided grin and Arkansas drawl. A singer and drummer in his young days, he decided to try an acting career in the 1980s, but was stuck in 'backwoods' roles until he wrote himself an eye-catching featured part in *One False Move* in 1991. An Oscar nominee for *Sling Blade* and *A Simple Plan*, he won an Academy Award for his *Sling Blade* screenplay, and was moving towards direction at the turn of the century. Sometimes called 'the hillbilly Orson Welles', he married (5th) Angelina Jolie in 2000.

*1986: Hunter's Blood. 1987: The Man Who Broke 1000 Chains (cable TV). South of Reno. 1989: Going Overboard/Babes Ahoy. Chopper Chicks in Zombietown. 1990: Trouble Bound (released 1992). 1991: For the Boys. One False Move. 1992: Living and Working in Space: The Countdown Has Begun (video). 1993: The Killing Box/Ghost Brigade. Indecent Proposal. Bound by Honor (GB: Blood In . . . Blood Out). Tombstone. *Some Folks Call It a Sling Blade. 1994: On Deadly Ground. Floundering. 1995: A Family Thing. Don't Look Back (cable TV). Out There (cable TV). Dead Man. The Stars Fell on Henrietta. 1996: The Winner. Sling Blade. A Gun, a Car, a Blonde (released 1998). 1997: The Apostle. U Turn/ Stray Dogs. An Alan Smithee Film – Burn, Hollywood, Burn. 1998: Princess Mononoke (English-language version, voice only). Home-grown. Primary Colors. Armageddon. A Simple Plan. 1999: Pushing Tin. The Million Dollar Hotel. 2000: Daddy and Them. South of*

Heaven, West of Hell. 2001: Wakin' Up in Reno. The Barber Movie. Bandits.

As director: 1996: Sling Blade. 2000: Daddy and Them. All the Pretty Horses.

THULIN, Ingrid 1929–
Cool, long-necked Swedish actress whose bleak blonde beauty has been best used in the films of Ingmar Bergman. Elsewhere she has made some strange movies that sometimes border on sexploitation, but proved herself a fine stage actress in her native country.
1948: *Känn dej som Hemma. Dit vindarna Bär.* 1949: *Havets Son. Kärlekan Segrar.* 1950: *Hajarter Knekt. När Kärlekan Kom till byn.* 1951: *Leva pa 'Hoppet'.* 1952: *Möte med Livet. Kalle Karlsson fran Jularbo.* 1953: *En Skärgardsnatt. Goingehovdingen.* 1954: *Tva Sköna Juveler. I Rök och Dans.* 1955: *Hoppsan! Danssalongen.* 1956: *Foreign Intrigue.* 1957: *Smultronstället / Wild Strawberries. Aldrig i Livet.* 1958: *Nära Livet / So Close to Life. Ansiktet / The Face.* 1960: *Domaren.* 1961: *The Four Horsemen of the Apocalypse.* 1962: *Agostino.* 1963: *Nattvardsgästerna / Winter Light. Tystnaden / The Silence.* 1964: *Die Lady (GB: Frustration). Der Film den Niemand sieht. Sekstet.* 1965: †*Hängivelse. Return from the Ashes. La guerre est finie.* 1966: *Night Games.* 1967: *Domani non siamo più qui.* 1968: *Vargtimmen / Hour of the Wolf. Adelaide (GB: The Depraved). Badarna (GB and US: I, a Virgin).* 1969: *Ritten / The Rite. Un Diablo bajo la Almohada. La caduta degli dei (GB and US: The Damned).* 1970: *Deux affreux sur le sable.* 1971: *N.P. il segreto. Malastrana.* 1972: *La sainte famille. Cries and Whispers / Viskingar och rop.* 1973: *En Handful Kärlek (GB: TV: A Handful of Love).* 1974: *Monismanien.* 1975: *La cage (GB: TV). Moses.* 1976: *The Cassandra Crossing. Salon Kitty (US: Madame Kitty).* 1977: *En och en. Il viaggio nella vertigini.* 1980: *It Rained All Night the Day I Left.* 1981: *Brustel himmel (GB: Broken Sky. Directed only).* 1984: *After The Rehearsal (TV).* 1986: *Control (TV).* 1987: *Orn. Il giorno primo.* 1988: *Il cuore di mamma. La casa del sorriso.* 1990: *Faccia di lepre.*

†Also directed

THURMAN, Uma 1970–
Tall, lithely curvaceous light-haired, distinctively large-lipped Hollywood actress of Swedish-American parentage. After a start as a teenage model, she brought her wistful

beauty and gawky elegance to starring roles at 17. Still not quite a name the public will pay to see, although her acting has steadily improved, and she notched up an Oscar nomination for *Pulp Fiction*. Married/ divorced actor Gary Oldman (*qv*). Her father, a college professor who taught Buddhism, named her after a Hindu goddess. Currently married to actor Ethan Hawke (*qv*).
1987: *Kiss Daddy Good Night.* 1988: *Johnny Be Good. The Adventures of Baron Muchausen. Dangerous Liaisons.* 1990: *Henry & June. Where the Heart Is.* 1991: *Final Analysis. Dylan. Robin Hood (TV. GB: cinemas).* 1992: *Jennifer Eight. Mad Dog and Glory.* 1993: *Even Cowgirls Get the Blues.* 1994: *Pulp Fiction.* 1995: *A Month by the Lake. *Duke of Groove.* 1996: *Beautiful Girls. Marlene. The Truth About Cats & Dogs.* 1997: *Gattaca. Batman and Robin.* 1998: *The Avengers. Les Misérables.* 1999: *Sweet and Lowdown.* 2000: *Vatel. The Golden Bowl.*

TIERNEY, Gene 1920–1991
Dark-haired, glowingly beautiful American star, probably the most strikingly lovely Hollywood actress of the forties. She enjoyed a good variety of attractive star roles, before her beauty, health, career and marriage all began to fade in the late forties. There was a nervous breakdown and a rather half-hearted comeback in the early sixties. She received an Academy Award nomination for *Leave Her to Heaven*. Died from emphysema.
1940: *The Return of Frank James. Hudson's Bay.* 1941: *Sundown. Tobacco Road. The Shanghai Gesture. Belle Starr.* 1942: *Thunder Birds. Rings on Her Fingers. Son of Fury. China Girl.* 1943: *Heaven Can Wait.* 1944: *Laura.* 1945: *Leave Her to Heaven. A Bell for*

Adano. 1946: *Dragonwhyck. The Razor's Edge.* 1947: *The Ghost and Mrs Muir.* 1948: *The Iron Curtain. That Wonderful Urge.* 1949: *Whirlpool.* 1950: *Night and the City. Where the Sidewalk Ends.* 1951: *On the Riviera. The Mating Season. Close to My Heart. The Secret of Convict Lake.* 1952: *Plymouth Adventure. Way of a Gaucho.* 1953: *Never Let Me Go. Personal Affair.* 1954: *The Egyptian. Black Widow.* 1955: *The Left Hand of God.* 1962: *Advise and Consent.* 1963: *Toys in the Attic.* 1964: *The Pleasure Seekers.* 1969: *Daughter of the Mind (TV).*

TIERNEY, Lawrence 1919–
Grim-looking, square-faced, light-haired American 'tough-guy' actor, brother of Scott Brady (*qv*). The title role in *Dillinger* was his biggest break, and he infused it with menace and sub-surface violence. But Tierney was unable to follow through to all-round stardom. He worked for minor studios, and still plays small parts, bald now but as threatening as ever, even in old age.
1943: *Government Girl. The Ghost Ship. Gildersleeve on Broadway.* 1944: *Youth Runs Wild. The Falcon Out West.* 1945: *Sing Your Way Home. Mama Loves Papa. *Birthday Blues. Dillinger. Those Endearing Young Charms. Back to Bataan.* 1946: *San Quentin. Badman's Territory. Step by Step.* 1947: *The Devil Thumbs a Ride. Born to Kill (GB: Lady of Deceit).* 1948: *Bodyguard.* 1950: *Kill or Be Killed. Shakedown.* 1951: *The Hoodlum. Best of the Badmen. The Bushwhackers (GB: The Rebel).* 1952: *The Greatest Show on Earth.* 1954: *The Steel Cage.* 1956: *Singing in the Dark. Female Jungle.* 1962: *A Child is Waiting.* 1966: *Custer of the West.* 1971: *Such Good Friends.* 1973: *Exorcism at Midnight (US version of 1966 GB film Naked Evil).* 1975: *Abduction.* 1976: *Bad / Andy Warhol's Bad.* 1978: *The Kirlian Witness.* 1980: *Never Pick Up a Stranger / Bloodrage. Gloria. Arthur.* 1981: *Rosemary's Killer.* 1982: *Midnight.* 1985: *Prizzi's Honor. Silver Bullet.* 1986: *Murphy's Law. From a Whisper to a Scream.* 1987: *Tough Guys Don't Dance.* 1988: *The Horror Show. The Naked Gun: From the Files of Police Squad!* 1989: *Why Me?* 1990: *The Runestone. Dillinger (TV).* 1991: *Wizards of the Demon Sword. Reservoir Dogs.* 1992: *Casualties of Love: The 'Long Island Lolita' Story (TV).* 1993: *The Death Merchant. Eddie Presley.* 1994: *Junior. A Kiss Goodnight (TV). Social Club.* 1995: *Fatal Passion.* 1996: *Big Killing in Little Saigon.*

Speak. 2 Days in the Valley. Third Cowboy on the Right. 1997: American Hero. Brass Ring. Portrait in Red. 1998: Corpus Christy. Southie. Armageddon. 2000: Juan-a-Be.com.

TILLY, Meg 1960–
Dark-haired, American-born, Canadian-raised, delicate-looking actress with faintly oriental features. Originally a dancer whose career was ended by a back injury (she can be glimpsed in the background of Alan Parker's *Fame*), she soon proved herself a sensitive actress and, despite another accident which took her out of the Oscar-laden *Amadeus*, won an Oscar nomination for *Agnes of God*. Marriage to producer Tim Zinnemann (her first, his fourth) and two children restricted her appearances until the late 1980s. Later the couple parted and she married a Sony studio executive, having been overtaken in popularity by her sister, Jennifer Tilly (1958–).
1980: Fame. 1982: Tex. One Dark Night. Psycho II. 1983: The Big Chill. 1984: Impulse. 1985: Agnes of God. 1986: Off Beat. 1987: Schweigen wie Glas. 1988: The Girl on a Swing. Masquerade. 1989: Carmilla. Valmont. Threepenny Opera. 1990: The Two Jakes. Under Cover. In the Best Interest of the Child (TV). 1992: Leaving Normal. 1993: Body Snatchers (later: Body Snatcher: The Invasion Continues). Fallen Angels (TV). 1994: Primal Secrets (TV). Sleep With Me. Double Cross. 1995: Journey (TV).

TOBIN, Genevieve 1899–1995
Sophisticated, blue-eyed, effervescent, platinum blonde American actress with beestung lips. Coming to Hollywood at 31 with a formidable stage reputation, she found her-self all too often cast as the 'other woman' and entrapped many a hapless hero with her terrific figure and low-lidded gaze. In real life she proved a hard girl to catch, but eventually married director William Keighley in 1938. He died in 1984. A sort of high-class Gloria Grahame (*qv*) in her film characters, though their cynicism was often sugared with her personal charm. Died 'from natural causes'.
1923: No Mother to Guide Her. 1930: Free Love. A Lady Surrenders (GB: Blind Wives). 1931: Seed. Up for Murder. The Gay Diplomat. 1932: One Hour with You. Hollywood Speaks. The Cohens and Kellys in Hollywood. Perfect Understanding. 1933: Infernal Machine. Pleasure Cruise. The Wrecker. Golden Harvest. Goodbye Again. I Loved a Woman. 1934: The Ninth Guest. Easy to Love. Dark Hazard. Uncertain Lady. Success at Any Price. By Your Leave. Kiss and Make Up. 1935: The Woman in Red. The Goose and the Gander. Here's to Romance. The Case of the Lucky Legs. Broadway Hostess. 1936: The Petrified Forest. Snowed Under. The Man in the Mirror. 1937: The Great Gambini. The Duke Comes Back (GB: The Call of the Ring). 1938: Kate Plus Ten (US: The Queen of Crime). Dramatic School. Zaza. 1939: Yes, My Darling Daughter. Our Neighbors, The Carters. 1940: No Time for Comedy.

TODD, Ann 1909–1993
Glacial British blonde actress whose porcelain features and set expression helped keep her in leading roles for a long time. Her career was severely disrupted in the early thirties by a car accident, but in the mid-forties she became one of Britain's most popular stars, married (third) director David Lean (1949–1957) and appeared in several of his films. Later directed a few critically praised documentary films. In 1992, she popped up as a dotty bird fancier in the pilot to the British TV series *Maigret*, but died the following year after a stroke.
1931: Keepers of Youth. The Ghost Train. These Charming People. 1932: The Water Gipsies. 1934: The Return of Bulldog Drummond. 1936: Men of Yesterday. Things to Come. 1937: Action for Slander. The Squeaker (US: Murder on Diamond Row). South Riding. 1939: Poison Pen. 1941: Danny Boy. Ships with Wings. 1945: Perfect Strangers (US: Vacation from Marriage). The Seventh Veil. 1946: Gaiety George (US: Showtime). Daybreak. 1947: The Paradine Case. 1948: So Evil My Love. 1949: The Passionate Friends (US: One Woman's Story). 1950: Madeleine. 1952: The Sound Barrier (US: Breaking the Sound Barrier). 1954: The Green Scarf. 1957: Time without Pity. 1961: Taste of Fear (US: Scream of Fear). 1963: The Son of Captain Blood. 1965: Ninety Degrees in the Shade. 1971: The Fiend. 1979: The Human Factor. 1985: The McGuffin (TV). Hitchcock, il brivido del genio.
As director: 1965: *Thunder in Heaven. 1966: *Thunder of the Gods. 1967: *Thunder of the Kings.

TODD, Richard
(R. Palethorpe-Todd) 1919–
Dark-haired, boyish-looking Irish-born actor who, despite a lack of stature, was plucked from repertory work at 30, and became a major star of the British cinema almost at once. His performance as the dying Scot in *The Hasty Heart* made him an international name and, with varying success, he appeared in several films for Warners, Fox and Disney. His standing slipped away in the sixties and in the following decade he was back appearing regularly in repertory, one of the first big names in the British cinema to do so. Oscar-nominated for *The Hasty Heart*.
1949: For Them That Trespass. The Interrupted Journey. The Hasty Heart. 1950: Portrait of Clare. Stage Fright. 1951: Lightning Strikes Twice. Flesh and Blood. 1952: Elstree Story. The Story of Robin Hood and his Merrie Men. 24 Hours of a Woman's Life (US: Affair in Monte Carlo). Venetian Bird (US: The Assassin). 1953: The Sword and the Rose. Rob Roy the Highland Rogue. Secrets d'alcove (GB and US: The Bed). 1954: A Man Called Peter. The Dam Busters. 1955: *People and Places. The Virgin Queen. 1956: D-Day the Sixth of June. Marie Antoinette. 1957: Yangtse Incident (US: Battle Hell). Saint Joan. 1958: Chase a Crooked Shadow. The Naked Earth. Intent to Kill. 1959: Danger Within (US: Breakout). 1960: Never Let Go. The Long and the Short and the Tall (US: Jungle Fighters). 1961: Don't Bother to Knock! (US: Why Bother to Knock!). The Hellions. 1962: Le crime ne paie pas (GB: The Gentle Art of Murder). The Boys. The Longest Day. 1963: The Very Edge. Death Drums Along the River. 1964: Coast of Skeletons. 1965: Operation Crossbow (US: The Great Spy Mission). The Battle of the Villa Fiorita. 1967: The Love-Ins. 1968: Subterfuge. The Last of the Long-Haired Boys. 1970: Dorian Gray. 1972: Asylum. The Aquarian. 1977: No 1 of the Secret Service.

1978: *The Big Sleep. Home Before Midnight.* 1982: *House of the Long Shadows.* 1988: *Murder One* (TV). 1991: *Sherlock Holmes and the Incident at Victoria Falls* (TV).

TODD, Thelma 1905–1935
Tall, funny, blonde American character comedienne with pencilled eyebrows and happy, expressive face. A former beauty contest winner, she stooged for almost all the great early thirties comedians, including the Marx Brothers and Laurel and Hardy, and proved herself a funny lady in her own right in a long series of two-reelers with ZaSu Pitts (*qv*) and Patsy Kelly. Died from carbon monoxide poisoning, in her garaged car. The subsequent enquiry never determined whether it was murder, suicide or accident. Half a century later, it was revealed that she had been murdered by gangsters.
1926: *God Gave Me Twenty Cents. Fascinating Youth. The Popular Sin.* 1927: *Rubber Heels. Nevada. The Shield of Honor. The Gay Defender. Fireman, Save My Child.* 1928: *The Haunted House. Vamping Venus. Seven Footprints to Satan. The Crash. Heart to Heart. The Noose.* †*Hell's Angels. Naughty Baby* (GB: *Reckless Rosie*). 1929: *Trial Marriage. Bachelor Girl. Careers. House of Horror. Her Private Life.* *Look Out Below. *Snappy Sneezer. *Crazy Feet. *Stepping Out. *Unaccustomed As We Are. *Hurdy Gurdy. *Hotter than Hot. Shy Boy. *The Head Guy. *The Real McCoy.* 1930: *Follow Thru* (GB: *Follow Through*). *Swanee River. No Limit. Her Man.* *Whispering Whoopee. *Another Fine Mess. *All Teed Up. *Dollar Dizzy. *Looser than Loose. *High Cs. *The Fighting Parson. *The Shrimp. *The King.* 1931: *The Command Performance. Aloha* (GB: *No Greater Love*). *The Hot Heiress. Broad-Minded.* ‡*Corsair. Monkey Business. The Maltese Falcon. Beyond Victory. This is the Night.* *Catch as Catch Can. *Love Fever. *Let's Do Things. *Voice of Hollywood. *Chickens Come Home. *Rough Seas. *The Pip from Pittsburgh. *The Pajama Party. *War Mamas.* 1932: *Klondike* (GB: *The Doctor's Sacrifice*). *Speak Easily. Call Her Savage. Horse Feathers. Big Timer. No Greater Love.* *The Nickel Nurser. *Seal Skins. *On the Loose. *Cauliflower Alley. *Strictly Unreliable. *Red Noses. *Alum and Eve. *The Old Bull. *Show Business. *The Soilers.* 1933: *The Devil's Brother* (GB: *Fra Diavolo*). *Air Hostess. Mary Stevens M.D. Sitting Pretty. Deception. Cheating Blondes.* (GB: *House of*

Chance). *Counsellor-at-Law. Son of a Sailor.* *Maids à la Mode. *Sneak Easily. *One Track Minds. *Asleep in the Fleet. *Bargain of the Century. *Air Fright. *Beauty and the Bus. *Backs to Nature. You Made Me Love You.* 1934: *Palooka* (GB: *The Great Schnozzle*). *Bottoms Up. Hips, Hips, Hooray. Cockeyed Cavaliers. The Poor Rich. Take the Stand* (GB: *The Great Radio Mystery*). *Maid in Hollywood. *Babes in the Goods. *Three Chumps Ahead. *Opened by Mistake. *Bum Voyage. *Soup and Fish. *I'll Be Suing You. *One Horse Farmers. *Done in Oil.* 1935: *Two for Tonight. Lightning Strikes Twice. After the Dance.* *The Tin Man. *Treasure Blues. *Slightly Static *Twin Triplets. *Top Flat. *Sing, Sister, Sing. *The Misses Stooge. *Hot Money. *All American Toothache.* 1936: *The Bohemian Girl.*

†*Silent version only (never shown)*
‡*As Alison Loyd*

TOLER, Sidney 1874–1947
Dark-haired, heavy-set American character actor who staked his claim to a niche in the Hollywood Hall of Fame when he took over the role of Charlie Chan, the wily oriental detective, from Warner Oland (*qv*), when the latter died in 1938. Toler played the role for nine years (he never looked his age) before he too died, and Roland Winters (1904–1989) took over the declining series.
1929: *In the Nick of Time. Madame X.* 1930: *Strictly Dishonourable.* 1931: *White Shoulders.* *The Devil's Parade.* 1932: *Speak Easily.* *Over the Counter. *Union Wages. Tom Brown of Culver. Strangers in Love. Is My Face Red? Blondie of the Follies. The Phantom President. Blonde Venus. Radio Patrol.* 1933: *The Way to Love.* *Ducky Dear. He Learned About Women. Billion Dollar Scandal. King of the Jungle. The World Changes. The Narrow Corner.* 1934: *Registered Nurse. Dark Hazard. Romance in Manhattan. Upper World. Operator 13* (GB: *Spy 13*). *Massacre. Spitfire. The Trumpet Blows. Here Comes the Groom.* 1935: *Orchids to You. Call of the Wild. This is the Life. The Daring Young Man. Champagne for Breakfast.* 1936: *The Longest Night. Three Godfathers. Give Us This Night. Our Relations. The Gorgeous Hussy.* 1937: *Double Wedding. That Certain Woman. Quality Street.* 1938: *Up the River. Gold is Where You Find It. If I Were King. Three Comrades. One Wild Night. The Mysterious Rider. Charlie Chan in Honolulu. Wide Open Faces.* 1939: *The Kid from Kokomo*

(GB: *The Orphan of the Ring*). *Charlie Chan in Reno. Disbarred. Law of the Pampas. Charlie Chan at Treasure Island. King of Chinatown. Charlie Chan in City in Darkness. Heritage of the Desert. Broadway Cavalier.* 1940: *Charlie Chan in Panama. Charlie Chan's Murder Cruise. Murder over New York. Charlie Chan at the Wax Museum.* 1941: *Dead Men Tell. Charlie Chan in Rio.* 1942: *Castle in the Desert. The Adventures of Smilin' Jack* (serial). *A Night to Remember.* 1943: *Isle of Forgotten Sins. White Savage* (GB: *White Captive*). *Charlie Chan in the Secret Service.* 1944: *Black Magic. Charlie Chan in the Chinese Cat. The Scarlet Clue. It's in the Bag!* (GB: *The Fifth Chair*). 1945: *The Jade Mask. The Shanghai Cobra. The Red Dragon.* 1946: *Shadows over Chinatown. Dark Alibi. Dangerous Money. The Trap* (GB: *Murder at Malibu Beach*).

TOMEI, Marisa 1964–
Raven-haired, flashing-eyed, pigeon-cheeked, volatile-looking American actress who won an Academy Award for *My Cousin Vinny*, but has searched in vain for successes to match it. Her film career was sporadic at best in the 1980s, when she got more work in daytime TV serials. From 1986, however, she received consistently good notices for her stage performances and came back to films in the 1990s. Good material, though, only occasionally came her way, and she needs the successes her ability deserves to raise the profile of her career.
1984: *The Flamingo Kid.* 1986: *Playing for Keeps.* 1989: *Parker Kane* (TV). 1991: *Oscar. My Cousin Vinny.* 1992: *Equinox. Zandalee. Chaplin. Untamed Heart.* 1994: *Only You. The Paper.* 1995: *The Perez Family. Four Rooms.* 1996: *Unhook the Stars.* 1997: *A Brother's Kiss. Welcome to Sarajevo. Reflections of Eden* (TV). 1998: *Slums of Beverly Hills. Since You've Been Gone* (TV). *My Own Country* (TV). *Only Love* (TV). 1999: *Dirk & Betty. Happy Accidents.* 2000: *King of the Jungle. The Watcher.* 2001: *What Women Want.*

TOMLIN, Lily (Mary Tomlin) 1939–
Slim, loose-limbed, dark-haired American comedy star with goofy grin and infectious sense of physical comedy. Although a star on TV, where she made her name as the zany switchboard operator in *Rowan and Martin's Laugh In*, and an Oscar nominee in her first film, her film comedies, though often colourful and idiotic, were not as popular as

they deserved to be. She returned to stage work and TV specials, although in the 1990s she was busy in the cinema again, this time mainly in guest roles. Also a singer and composer, she often works in collaboration with writer-director Jane Wagner.

1975: Nashville. 1977: The Late Show. 1978: Moment by Moment. 1980: Nine to Five. 1981: The Incredible Shrinking Woman. 1984: All of Me. 1986: Lily Tomlin. 1988: Big Business. 1991: The Search for Signs of Intelligent Life in the Universe. Shadows and Fog. 1992: The Player. 1993: Even Cowgirls Get the Blues. Short Cuts. And the Band Played On. The Beverly Hillbillies. 1994: Luck, Trust & Ketchup. 1995: Blue in the Face. The Celluloid Closet (narrator only). Getting Away with Murder. 1996: Flirting with Disaster. 1997: Krippendorf's Tribe. Reno Finds Her Mom. 1999: Get Bruce! (doc.). Tea with Mussolini. 2000: The Kid. Picking Up the Pieces.

TOMLINSON, David 1917–2000
Dark-haired, crumple-faced British comic actor, the archetypal 'silly ass' of his day. Because of the variety of roles he played in post-war years, it took him a while to come into his own, but he enjoyed a good star run in scatty comedies from 1951–1960, later registering well in character roles for the Disney studios. Died in his sleep.

*1940: *Name, Rank and Number. Garrison Follies. 1941: Quiet Wedding. My Wife's Family. Pimpernel Smith (US: Mister V). 1945: The Way to the Stars (US: Johnny in the Clouds). Journey Together. 1946: I See a Dark Stranger (US: The Adventuress). School for Secrets (US: Secret Flight). 1947: Master of Bankdam. Easy Money. Fame is the Spur. Broken Journey. 1948: Love in Waiting.*

Miranda. Here Come the Huggetts. My Brother's Keeper. Sleeping Car to Trieste. Warning to Wantons. 1949: Helter Skelter. Vote for Huggett. Landfall. Marry Me. The Chiltern Hundreds (US: The Amazing Mr Beecham). 1950: So Long at the Fair. The Wooden Horse. 1951: The Magic Box. Hotel Sahara. Calling Bulldog Drummond. 1952: Castle in the Air. Made in Heaven. 1953: Is Your Honeymoon Really Necessary? 1955: All for Mary. 1956: Three Men in a Boat. 1957: Carry on Admiral (US: The Ship Was Loaded). 1958: Up the Creek. Further Up the Creek. 1960: Follow that Horse! 1963: Tom Jones. 1964: Mary Poppins. The Truth about Spring. 1965: City Under the Sea (US: War Gods of the Deep). The Liquidator. 1968: The Love Bug. 1971: Bedknobs and Broomsticks. 1974: Bon Baisers de Hong Kong. 1977: Wombling Free. 1978: Dominique. The Water Babies. 1980: The Fiendish Plot of Dr Fu Manchu.

TONE, Franchot
(Stanislas F. Tone) 1905–1968
Smooth, brown-haired American actor, adept at callow charmers, and too often employed in that mould, or as lounge lizards, or best friends not strong enough to get the girl. When handed unusual assignments he became much more interesting, and did some good character work in his later years. Married/divorced Joan Crawford (1935–1939) and three blonde starlets: Jean Wallace (*qv*) from 1941 to 1948, Barbara Payton (*qv*) from 1951 to 1952, and Dolores Dorn (1935–) from 1956 to 1959. Oscar-nominated in the Best Actor category in *Mutiny on The Bounty*, Tone might well have won an Academy Award had the category of best supporting actor been brought in a year earlier. Died from lung cancer.

1932: The Wiser Sex. 1933: Today We Live. Gabriel over the White House. Bombshell (GB: Blonde Bombshell). Midnight Mary. Dancing Lady. Stage Mother. The Stranger's Return. 1934: Straight is the Way. Moulin Rouge. The Girl from Missouri (GB: 100 Per Cent Pure). The World Moves On. Gentlemen Are Born. Sadie McKee. 1935: Reckless. Lives of a Bengal Lancer. Dangerous. Mutiny on the Bounty. No More Ladies. One New York Night (GB: The Trunk Mystery). 1936: The Unguarded Hour. Exclusive Story. The King Steps Out. The Gorgeous Hussy. Suzy. Love on the Run. 1937: They Gave Him a Gun. Between Two Women. Quality Street. The

Bride Wore Red. 1938: Man-Proof. Three Comrades. The Girl Downstairs. Love is a Headache. Three Loves Has Nancy. 1939: Thunder Afloat. Fast and Furious. 1940: Trail of the Vigilantes. 1941: Nice Girl? She Knew All the Answers. This Woman is Mine. 1942: Star Spangled Rhythm. The Wife Takes a Flyer (GB: A Yank in Dutch). 1943: True to Life. His Butler's Sister. Pilot No 5. Five Graves to Cairo. 1944: Phantom Lady. The Hour Before the Dawn. Dark Waters. 1945: That Night with You. 1946: Because of Him. 1947: Honeymoon (GB: Two Men and a Girl). Her Husband's Affairs. Lost Honeymoon. 1948: Every Girl Should be Married. I Love Trouble. 1949: Jigsaw. Without Honor. The Man on the Eiffel Tower. 1951: Here Comes the Groom. 1957: The Thundering Wave (TV). 1958: †Uncle Vanya. 1959: A Quiet Game of Cards (TV). Hidden Image (TV). 1960: The Shape of the River (TV). 1962: Advise and Consent. 1963: La bonne soupe (US: Careless Love). 1964: See How They Run (TV). 1965: In Harm's Way. Mickey One. 1968: Nobody Runs Forever (US: The High Commissioner). Shadow over Elveron (TV).

†Also co-directed

TOREN, Marta (Märta Torén) 1925–1957
Tall, dark, sultry Swedish actress who always seemed to pose with her eyes half-closed, and her full lips in a semi-pout. Hollywood liked what it saw and signed her up even though she had made only one film in Sweden. She returned from America in 1952, but seemed to be losing her appetite for films when she was killed by a rare brain disease.

1947: Eviga Länkar. 1948: Casbah. Rogues' Regiment. 1949: Illegal Entry. Sword in the Desert. 1950: One-Way Street. Spy Hunt (GB: Panther's Moon). Deported. Mystery Submarine. 1951: Sirocco. 1952: The Man Who Watched Trains Go By (US: Paris Express). Assignment – Paris! Puccini, une vie de l'amour. 1953: Maddalena. 1954: Casa ricordi. L'ombra. 1955: La vena d'oro. 1956: Carta a Sara. L'ultima notte d'amore (GB: Femme Fatale. US: Fatal Rendezvous). Tormento d'amore. 1957: La puerta abierta.

TORN, Rip (Elmore Torn) 1931–
Mean-looking, dynamic, dark-haired, thin-faced American actor who has made the stage the major part of his career, but appeared spasmodically in films, mainly in unsympathetic but eye-catching roles. Married to

Geraldine Page from 1963 to her death in 1987. Cousin of Sissy Spacek (*qv*). Oscar nominee for *Cross Creek*.

1956: Baby Doll. 1957: Time Limit. A Face in the Crowd. 1958: Cat on a Hot Tin Roof. Bomber's Moon (TV). Face of a Hero (TV). 1959: The Tunnel (TV). Pork Chop Hill. 1961: King of Kings. 1962: Sweet Bird of Youth. Hero's Island. 1963: Critic's Choice. 1965: One Spy Too Many (TV. GB: cinemas). The Cincinnati Kid. 1966: You're a Big Boy Now. 1967: Beach Red. Sol Madrid (GB: The Heroin Gang). 1968: Beyond the Law. Coming Apart. 1969: The Rain People. Tropic of Cancer. One P.M. 1970: Maidstone. 1971: The President's Plane is Missing (TV). 1972: Slaughter. 1973: Payday. Cotter (GB: TV). 1974: Crazy Joe. 1975: Attack on Terror (TV). The Man Who Fell to Earth. 1976: Birch Interval. Nasty Habits. 1977: J. Edgar Hoover, Godfather of the F.B.I. (Later and GB: The Private Files of J. Edgar Hoover). Coma. 1978: Betrayal (TV). Steel Cowboy (TV). 1979: A Shining Season (TV). The Wobblies (voice only). The Seduction of Joe Tynan. Heartland. 1980: Sophia Loren – Her Own Story (TV). One Trick Pony. Rape and Marriage: The Rideout Case (TV). First Family. 1981: Blind Ambition (TV). A Stranger is Waiting. 1982: Jinxed! Airplane II the Sequel. The BeastMaster. Scarab. 1983: Cross Creek. Misunderstood. 1984: When She Says No (TV). Flashpoint. City Heat. Songwriter. 1985: The Execution (TV). The Atlanta Child Murders (TV). Summer Rental. Beer. 1986: Extreme Prejudice. Manhunt for Claude Dallas (TV). 1987: J. Edgar Hoover (TV). Destination: America (TV). Nadine. Laguna Heat (TV). The King of Love (TV). 1988: Hit List. April Morning (TV). 1989: Cold Feet. Silence Like Glass. Beautiful Dreamers. Grand Tour (TV). Sweet Bird of Youth (TV). 1990: Pair of Aces (TV). Defending Your Life. By Dawn's Early Light (cable TV). 1991: Dolly Dearest. Hard Promises. Another Pair of Aces: Three of a Kind (TV). Kojak: None So Blind (TV). Columbo: Death Hits the Jackpot (TV). 1992: T Bone n Weasel (TV). Shattered Silence (TV). Disaster at Valdez (TV. US: Dead Ahead: the Exxon Valdez Disaster). Fixing the Shadow/Beyond the Law. Robocop 3. 1993: Where the Rivers Flow North. A Mother's Right: The Elizabeth Morgan Story (TV). 1995: She Stood Alone: The Tailhook Scandal (TV). Canadian Bacon. How to Make an American Quilt. Letter to My Killer (TV). For

Better or Worse. 1996: The Mouse. Down Periscope. 1997: Trial and Error. Hercules (voice only). Men in Black. 1998: Senseless. Seasons of Love (TV). Balloon Farm (TV). 1999: Passing Glory (TV). The Insider. 2000: A Vision of Murder: The Story of Danielle (TV). Wonder Boys. 2001: Men in Black: Alien Attack.
As director: *1987: The Telephone.*

TOTTER, Audrey 1918–

American actress with narrow features, reddish-blonde hair and petite sexy figure. Well known on radio as 'the girl with a thousand voices' before being whisked of by M-G-M who made use of her talent for accents. Later her looks got her cast as hard-boiled, flint-hearted types. Tended to play leads in co-features and top supporting roles in big productions.

1944: Ziegfeld Follies (released 1946. Voice only). Main Street After Dark. 1945: Bewitched (voice only). The Sailor Takes a Wife. The Hidden Eye. Her Highness and the Bellboy. Adventure. Dangerous Partners. 1946: The Postman Always Rings Twice. The Cockeyed Miracle (GB: Mr Griggs Returns). The Secret Heart. Lady in the Lake. 1947: The Beginning or the End? The High Wall. The Unsuspected. 1948: Tenth Avenue Angel. The Saxon Charm. Alias Nick Beal (GB: The Contact Man). 1949: The Set-Up. Any Number Can Play. Tension. 1950: Under the Gun. 1951: The Blue Veil. The Sellout. FBI Girl. 1952: My Pal Gus. Assignment–Paris! 1953: Man in the Dark. The Woman They Almost Lynched. Cruisin' Down the River. Mission over Korea (GB: Eyes of the Skies). Champ for a Day. 1954: Massacre Canyon. 1955: Women's Prison. A Bullet for Joey. One Life (TV. GB: cinemas). The Vanishing American. 1957: Ghost Diver. 1948: Jet Attack (GB: Through Hell to Glory). Man or Gun. 1963: The Carpetbaggers. 1965: Harlow (TV). 1967: The Outsider (TV). 1968: Chubasco. 1975: The Fourth Sex (TV. Formerly episodes of Medical Center series). 1978: The Magnificent Hustle (TV). 1979: The Apple Dumpling Gang Rides Again. 1984: City Killer (TV).

TRACY, Lee

(William L. Tracy) 1898–1968
Stocky, bouncy, light-haired American actor, possibly the screen's fastest talker. Very popular in the early thirties as a wisecracking reporter, but became so stereotyped in the

image that eventually it was used as light relief in serious stuff. His appeal dated and faded quickly (he had also upset M-G-M's Louis B. Mayer), and he was little seen when the thirties were through. Died from cancer of the liver. Oscar nominee for *The Best Man*.

*1929: Big Time. 1930: Liliom. She Got What She Wanted. Born Reckless. 1931: On the Level. 1932: Blessed Event. The Strange Love of Molly Louvain. Night Mayor. The Half-Naked Truth. Love is a Racket. Doctor X. Washington Merry-Go-Round (GB: Invisible Power). 1933: The Nuisance (GB: Accidents Wanted). Clear All Wires. Turn Back the Clock. Advice to the Lovelorn. Private Jones. Dinner at Eight. Bombshell (GB: Blonde Bombshell). Phantom Fame. 1934: The Lemon Drop Kid. I'll Tell the World. You Belong to Me. 1935: Carnival (GB: Carnival Nights). Two-Fisted. 1936: Sutter's Gold. *Pirate Party on Catalina Isle. Wanted – Jane Turner. 1937: Behind the Headlines. Criminal Lawyer. 1938: Crashing Hollywood. 1939: Fixer Dugan (GB: Double Daring). Spellbinder. 1940: Millionaires in Prison. 1942: The Payoff. 1943: Power of the Press. 1945: Betrayal from the East. I'll Tell the World (remake). 1947: High Tide. 1964: The Best Man.*

TRACY, Spencer 1900–1967

Rugged, thick-set, brown-haired American star with un-handsome but determined and sympathetic features, now generally acknowledged to have been Hollywood's best actor from the early thirties to the early fifties. Certainly, few were more successful at compelling total audience belief, thanks to a naturalistic approach to acting that always made him seem sincere. Two Academy Awards (for *Captains Courageous* and *Boys'*

Town) and seven nominations. Also noted for a series of salty battle-of-the-sexes comedies opposite Katharine Hepburn, with whom he was long professionally and privately associated. Died from a heart attack.

1930: *Taxi Talks. *The Strong Arm. *The Hard Guy. Up the River. 1931: Quick Millions. Six Cylinder Love. Goldie. 1932: She Wanted a Millionaire. Sky Devils. Disorderly Conduct. Young America (GB: We Humans). Society Girl. The Painted Woman. Me and My Gal (GB: Pier 13). 20,000 Years in Sing Sing. 1933: The Face in the Sky. Shanghai Madness. The Power and the Glory. The Mad Game. Man's Castle. 1934: Bottoms Up! The Show-Off. Looking for Trouble. Now I'll Tell (GB: When New York Sleeps). Marie Galante. 1935: It's a Small World. Dante's Inferno. The Murder Man. Whipsaw. Riffraff. 1936: San Francisco. Fury. Libeled Lady. 1937: They Gave Him a Gun. Captains Courageous. The Big City. Mannequin. 1938: Boys Town. Test Pilot. 1939: Stanley and Livingstone. 1940: I Take This Woman. Northwest Passage. Edison the Man. Boom Town. 1941: Men of Boys Town. Dr Jekyll and Mr Hyde. Woman of the Year. 1942: Tortilla Flat. Ring of Steel (narrator only). Keeper of the Flame. 1943: A Guy Named Joe. *US War Bonds Trailer. 1944: The Seventh Cross. Thirty Seconds over Tokyo. *Battle Stations (narrator only). 1945: Without Love. 1947: The Sea of Grass. Cass Timberlane. 1948: State of the Union (GB: The World and His Wife). 1949: Edward My Son. Adam's Rib. Malaya (GB: East of the Rising Sun). 1950: Father of the Bride. 1951: The People Against O'Hara. Father's Little Dividend. 1952: Pat and Mike. Plymouth Adventure. 1953: The Actress. 1954: Broken Lance. Bad Day at Black Rock. 1956: The Mountain. 1957: Desk Set (GB: His Other Woman). 1958: The Last Hurrah. The Old Man and the Sea. 1960: Inherit the Wind. 1961: The Devil at Four O'Clock. Judgment at Nuremberg. 1962: How the West Was Won (narrator only). 1963: It's a Mad, Mad, Mad, Mad World. 1967: Guess Who's Coming to Dinner.

sixties he became much more interested in animals and nature films than commercial stardom. Married (second) to Virginia McKenna (*qv*) from 1957: they appeared in several wildlife movies together.

1949: Conspirator. 1950: Trio. The Wooden Horse. 1951: The Browning Version. 1952: The Story of Robin Hood and His Merrie Men. Hindle Wakes (US: Holiday Week). It Started in Paradise. The Planter's Wife (US: Outpost in Malaya). 1953: Mantrap (US: Woman in Hiding). Street of Shadows (US: Shadow Man). The Genie. Counterspy (US: Undercover Agent). The Square Ring. 1954: Romeo and Juliet. 1955: Footsteps in the Fog. Geordie (US: Wee Geordie). 1956: Bhowani Junction. 1957: The Barretts of Wimpole Street. The Seventh Sin. The Smallest Show on Earth (US: Big Time Operators). 1958: Passionate Summer. 1959: The Bridal Path. 1960: Gorgo. 1961: Two Living One Dead. The Green Helmet. Invasion Quartet. 1965: Born Free. 1966: Duel at Diablo. 1967: The Lions Are Free (TV). 1968: A Midsummer Night's Dream. 1969: Ring of Bright Water. An Elephant Called Slowly. 1970: Boulevard du rhum (US: Rum Runner). 1971: The Lion at World's End (US: Christian the Lion). 1973: The Belstone Fox. 1979: Bloody Ivory (TV). 1984: Dream One (TV).

TRAVERS, Linden
(Florence Lindon-Travers) 1913–
Florid, sharp-faced British brunette actress (occasionally blonde), sister of Bill Travers (*qv*). Usually seen in vivid, brittle portrayals, often as women whose mental makeup rendered them not to be trusted.

1935: Children of the Fog. 1936: Wednesday's Luck. 1937: Brief Ecstasy. Double Alibi. The Last Adventurers. Against the Tide. Bank Holiday (US: Three on a Week-End). London Melody (US: Girls in the Street). 1938: The Terror. Almost a Honeymoon. The Lady Vanishes. 1939: The Stars Look Down. Inspector Hornleigh on Holiday. 1941: The Ghost Train. South American George. The Seventh Survivor. 1942: The Missing Million. 1946: Beware of Pity. 1947: Jassy. Master of Bankdam. 1948: No Orchids for Miss Blandish. Quartet. 1949: The Bad Lord Byron. Christopher Columbus. Don't Ever Leave Me. 1955: *The Schemer.

TRAVIS, Nancy 1961–
Feisty little American actress with a determined set of the mouth and a bundle of light-

brown hair. She made a high-profile starring debut in the 1986 TV mini-series *Harem*, but since then she has mostly been the girl billed just after the male stars. Although very good in such indifferent entertainments as *Greedy* and *The Vanishing*, she failed to make much of an individual mark and moved into TV sitcom in 1996.

1985: Malice in Wonderand (TV). 1988: I'll Be Home for Christmas (TV). Eight Men Out. 3 Men and a Baby. Married to the Mob. 1989: Loose Cannons. Internal Affairs. 1990: 3 Men and a Little Lady. Air America. 1992: Passed Away. The Vanishing. Chaplin. 1993: So I Married an Axe Murderer. Fallen Angels 2 (TV). 1994: Greedy. 1995: Body Language. Destiny Turns on the Radio. Fluke. 1996: Bogus. Almost Perfect (TV). 1999: To Live For (TV). My Last Love (TV). 2000: Auggie Rose. Running Mates (TV).

TRAVERS, Bill
(William Lindon-Travers) 1921–1994
Dark, tall, taciturn British actor, quietly-spoken brother of Linden Travers (*qv*). Took up acting after war service, and progressed very gradually to leading roles by 1955: studio handouts often chopped several years off his age at the time. However, after the early

TRAVOLTA, John 1954–
Thickly black-haired American actor, dancer and singer whose rather surly and aggressive good looks could break into arrogant, charismatic smiles and, coupled with his dynamic, loose-limbed dancing, made him a teenage favourite in the late 1970s, when he was nominated for an Academy Award for his performance in the abrasive *Saturday Night Fever*. His star career sagged in the mid 1980s and beyond (despite an unexpected comedy success with *Look Who's Talking*) until someone had the bright idea of turning his sullen features towards less sympathetic roles. This resulted in a further Oscar nomination for *Pulp Fiction*, and a career reborn to such an extent that he was Hollywood's highest paid actor by 1995. Married actress Kelly Preston (*qv*).

1975: *The Devil's Rain.* 1976: *Carrie. The Boy in the Plastic Bubble* (TV). 1977: *Saturday Night Fever.* 1978: *Grease. Moment by Moment.* 1980: *Urban Cowboy.* 1981: *Blow Out.* 1983: *Staying Alive. Two of a Kind.* 1985: *Perfect.* 1988: *The Experts.* 1989: *Boris & Natasha* (released 1992 on cable TV). *Look Who's Talking.* 1990: *Chains of Gold. Eyes of an Angel/The Tender. Look Who's Talking Too.* 1991: *Cold Heaven. Shout.* 1993: *Look Who's Talking Now.* 1994: *Pulp Fiction.* 1995: *White Man's Burden. Get Shorty.* 1996: *Broken Arrow. Phenomenon. Michael.* 1997: *She's De Lovely/Call It Love. Mad City. Face/Off.* 1998: *Primary Colors. The Thin Red Line. Welcome to Hollywood. A Civil Action.* 1999: *The General's Daughter. Forever Hollywood* (doc.) 2000: *Battlefield Earth. Numbers.* 2001: *Swordfish.*

TREVOR, Claire (C. Wemlinger) 1909–2000

This blonde American actress with the direct stare certainly looked in films as though she had knocked about a bit (or even been knocked about a bit). Small wonder, then, that this quality saw her spending half a lifetime as molls, broads, floozies, showgirls and whores: for 25 years if there was a saloon in town, the odds were that Claire Trevor would have a hand in running it. Stayed in leading roles to her late forties. Oscar for *Key Largo.* Also Oscar-nominated in *Dead End* and *The High and the Mighty.* Died from respiratory ailments.

1933: *Life in the Raw. Jimmy and Sally. The Last Trail. The Mad Game.* 1934: *Hold That Girl. Baby Take a Bow. Elinore Norton. Wild Gold.* 1935: *Dante's Inferno. Spring Tonic. Navy Wife. Black Sheep.* 1936: *Human Cargo. My Marriage. The Song and Dance Man. To Mary – With Love. 15 Maiden Lane. Career Woman. Star For a Night.* 1937: *One Mile from Heaven. Time Out for Romance. Second Honeymoon. Big Town Girl. Dead End. King of Gamblers.* 1938: *The Amazing Dr Clitterhouse. Walking Down Broadway. Valley of the Giants. Two of a Kind.* 1939: *I Stole a Million. Stagecoach. Allegheny Uprising* (GB: *The First Rebel).* 1940: *The Dark Command.* 1941: *Texas. Honky Tonk.* 1942: *Street of Chance. The Adventures of Martin Eden. Crossroads.* 1943: *Woman of the Town. The Desperados. Good Luck, Mr Yates.* 1945: *Murder, My Sweet* (GB: *Farewell, My Lovely). Johnny Angel.* 1946: *Crack-Up. The Bachelor's Daughters* (GB: *Bachelor Girls).* 1947: *Born*

to *Kill* (GB: *Lady of Deceit).* 1948: *The Velvet Touch. Raw Deal. Key Largo. The Babe Ruth Story.* 1949: *The Lucky Stiff.* 1950: *Borderline.* 1951: *Hard, Fast and Beautiful. Best of the Badmen.* 1952: *Hoodlum Empire. My Man and I. Stop, You're Killing Me.* 1953: *The Stranger Wore a Gun.* 1954: *The High and the Mighty.* 1955: *Man without a Star. Lucy Gallant.* 1956: *The Mountain.* 1957: *If You Knew Elizabeth* (TV). 1958: *Marjorie Morningstar.* 1962: *Two Weeks in Another Town. The Stripper* (GB: *Woman of Summer).* 1965: *How to Murder Your Wife.* 1967: *The Cape Town Affair.* 1982: *Kiss Me Goodbye.* 1987: *Breaking Home Ties* (TV).

TRINDER, Tommy 1909–1989

Long-chinned, slyly smiling, dark-haired (often hidden under pork-pie hat) British music-hall comedian, very popular in film comedies from 1938 to the end of the war, later equally successful as a master of ceremonies in TV variety shows. Catchphrase: 'you lucky people'. Died from heart problems.

1938: *Almost a Honeymoon. Save a Little Sunshine.* 1939: *She Couldn't Say No. Laugh It Off.* 1940: *Sailors Three* (US: *Three Cockeyed Sailors).* 1941: **Eating Out with Tommy.* 1942: *The Foreman Went to France* (US: *Somewhere in France).* 1943: *The Bells Go Down.* 1944: *Fiddlers Three. Champagne Charlie.* 1946: **Staggered Holidays.* 1947: **Family Guide.* 1950: *Bitter Springs.* 1955: *You Lucky People.* 1959: *Make Mine a Million.* 1964: *The Beauty Jungle* (US: *Contest Girl).* 1969: *Under the Table You Must Go.* 1974: *Barry McKenzie Holds His Own.*

TRINTIGNANT, Jean-Louis 1930–

Quiet, introspective, dark-haired, slightly fretful-looking French actor. A romantic figure in his wryly Gallic way. Trintignant, who threw up a legal career to take up acting, became a star in his first year in French films, and has since enjoyed international hits too, none more so than *Un homme et une femme,* to which he made a sequel 20 year later. He has also had some famous romances of his own, including a much-publicized liaison with Brigitte Bardot. His first wife was actress Stephane Audran (1932–), his second is director Nadine Trintignant. The son of motor-racing ace Maurice Trintignant, Jean-Louis himself escaped a 200mph crash in the 1980 Le Mans endurance race.

1955: **Pechinef. Si tous les gars du monde* (GB: *Race for Life).* La loi des rues. 1956: *Et Dieu créa la femme* (GB: *And Woman . . . Was Created.* US: *And God Created Woman). Club des femmes.* 1959: *Les liaisons dangereuses. L'estate violente. Austerlitz* (GB: *The Battle of Austerlitz).* La millième fenêtre. 1960: *Pleins feux sur l'assassin. Le coeur battant* (US: *The French Game).* 1961: *L'Atlantide* (GB: *Atlantis, The Lost Continent/The Lost Kingdom.* US: *Journey Beneath the Desert).* Le jeu de la verité. Le combat dans l'île. Horace '62. Les sept péchés capitaux (GB: *The Seven Deadly Sins.* US: *Seven Capital Sins).* 1962: *Il successo. Il sorpasso* (US: *The Easy Life).* 1963: *Château en Suède* (US: *Naughty, Nutty Chateau).* 1964: *Les pas perdus. La bonne occase. Mata Hari – Agent H 21. Angélique, Marquise des Anges* (GB: *and US: Angelique). Io uccido, tu uccidi.* 1965: **Un jour à Paris. Merveilleuse Angélique* (GB: *Angelique: The Road to Versailles). Compartiment tueurs* (GB *and US: The Sleeping Car Murder). Is Paris Burning?* 1966: *Meurtre à l'Italienne* (US: *Murder Italian Style). La longue marche. Le dix-septième ciel. Un homme et une femme* (GB *and US: A Man and a Woman). Safari-diamants.* 1967: *Trans-Europ Express. Enigma. Col cuoror al gola* (US: *Deadly Sweet). L'homme qui ment. Mon amour . . . mon amour. La morte ha fatto l'ouvo* (GB: *A Curious Way to Love.* US: *Plucked). *Fragilité ton nom est femme. Les biches* (US: *The Does).* 1968: *La matriarcha* (US: *The Libertine). Il grande silenzio. Le voleur des crimes.* 1969: *Z. Ma nuit chez Maud* (GB: *My Night with Maud.* US: *My Night at Maud's). Metti una sera a cena* (US: *The Love Circle). Cosi dolce, cosi perversa/So Sweet . . . So Perverse. L'Américain. Il conformista* (GB and US: *The Conformist). Las secretas intenciones. L'opium et le bâton.* 1970: *Le voyou* (GB: *Simon the Swiss.* US: *The Crook/The Criminal). Par le sang versé le bâteau.* 1971: *La course du lièvre à travers les champs* (GB and US: *And Hope to Die). Sans mobile apparent* (GB: *and US: Without Apparent Motive).* 1972: *L'homme aux cerveaux greffés. l'attentat* (GB: *Plot.* US: *The French Conspiracy). Une homme est mort* (GB and US: *The Outside Man).* 1973: *†Une journée bien remplie* (GB: *TV, as A Full Day's Work). Défense de savoir* (US: *Forbidden to Know). Le train* (GB: *TV, as The Last Train).* 1974: *Les violons du bal. Glissements progressifs du plaisir. Le mouton enragé* (GB: *The French Way.* US: *Love at the Top). Le secret. L'escapade. Le jeu avec le feu* (US: *Playing*

with Fire). 1975: La donna della domenica. L'agression. Flic Story. Il pleut sur Santiago. Le voyage de noces. 1976: L'ordinateur des pompes funèbres (GB: TV, as The Probability Factor). Le desert des Tartares. Les passagers (GB: Shattered). 1977: Repérages (US: Faces of Love). L'affaire. 1978: †Le maître-nageur (GB and US: The Lifeguard). L'argent des autres. 1979: Melancholy Baby. La terrazza. 1980: La banquière. Je vous aime. Malville/Malevil. 1981: Un assassin qui passe. Passione d'amore. Une affaire d'homme. Eaux profondes. Le grand pardon. Boulevard des assassins. Le nuit de Varennes. 1982: Colpire al cuore. Under Fire. Meurtres sous protection. 1983: Vivement dimanche (GB: Finally Sunday! US: The Long Saturday Night). Le bon plaisir, la crime (US: Cover-Up). Credo (TV). 1984: Femmes de personne. Viva la vie. 1985: Partir, revenir. David, Thomas, et les autres. Rendezvous. L'été prochaine. L'homme aux yeux d'argent. Sortuz egy fekete bivalyert. 1986: Vingt ans déjà (Un homme et une femme II). La femme de ma vie. Quinzième août. 1987: Le moutachu (US: The Field Agent). La vallée fantôme. 1989: Bunker Palace Hotel. 1990: Pour un oui ou pour un non. 1991: Merci la vie. 1992: L'oeil écarlate. 1993: Fraternité. Regarde les hommes tomber (GB and US: See How They Fall). 1994: Trois couleurs: rouge/Red. 1995: Fiesta. Jardins secrets. La cité des enfants perdus (voice only). 1996: Tykho Moon. Un héros très discret (GB and US: A Self-Made Hero). Les bidochons. Un homme est tombé dans la rue. C'est jamais loin. 1998: Ceux qui m'aiment prendront le train.

†And directed

TRIPPLEHORN, Jeanne 1963–
Winsome, dark-haired American actress with old-fashioned 'star' looks, slightly reminiscent of Gene Tierney (qv). She started a late screen career at 28, but quickly attracted attention as the 'other' girl in Basic Instinct, and has since played a number of romance-driven characters, although she has not been able to sustain a film on her own.
1991: The Perfect Tribute (TV). 1992: Basic Instinct. 1993: The Firm. The Night We Never Met. 1994: Reality Bites. 1995: Waterworld. 1996: 'Til There Was You. Office Killer. 1997: Old Man (TV). Sliding Doors. 1998: Very Bad Things. Snitch (later Monument Avenue). 1999: Mickey Blue Eyes. Abbie! 2000: Steal This Movie. Relative Values. Timecode. Paranoid. 2001: Dial 9 for Love.

TRYON, Tom 1925–1991
Tall, brooding American leading man, a handsomer version of John Travolta (qv). Boosted as a new star in his first film (at 31, after an eventful early life), he played rugged roles in westerns and other action films, but was a little too unbending for top stardom. In any case he didn't need it, forsaking acting to become the best-selling author of epic novels, a couple of which were filmed. Died from cancer.
1956: The Scarlet Hour. Screaming Eagles. Three Violent People. 1957: The Unholy Wife. Young Man from Kentucky (TV. GB: cinemas). Charley's Aunt (TV). 1958: I Married a Monster from Outer Space. Texas John Slaughter (TV. GB: cinemas). 1959: Gunfight at Sandoval (TV. GB: cinemas). 1960: Geronimo's Revenge (TV. GB: cinemas). The Story of Ruth. 1961: Showdown at Bitter Creek (TV. GB: cinemas). Marines, Let's Go. 1962: Moon Pilot. The Longest Day. 1963: The Cardinal. 1965: In Harm's Way. The Glory Guys. 1967: The Narco Men. Winchester '73 (TV). 1969: Color Me Dead.

TUCKER, Forrest 1915–1986
Very tall, rugged American actor with pugnacious good looks and wavy blond hair, persuaded to try his luck in films in 1940 while on holiday in California. He started well but war service came along, and his career never quite retained its drive thereafter, although he remained in leading roles until the late fifties. He died from cancer of the throat.
1940: The Westerner. The Howards of Virginia (GB: The Tree of Liberty). 1941: Emergency Landing. New Wine (GB: The Great Awakening). Honolulu Lu. Canal Zone. *Camp

Nuts. 1942: Tramp, Tramp, Tramp. Shut My Big Mouth. Parachute Nurse. The Spirit of Stanford. Keeper of the Flame. Boston Blackie Goes Hollywood (GB: Blackie Goes Hollywood). My Sister Eileen. Submarine Raider. Counter Espionage. 1946: The Man Who Dared. Talk About a Lady. Renegades. Dangerous Business. Never Say Goodbye. The Yearling. 1947: Gunfighters (GB: The Assassin). 1948: Adventures in Silverado (GB: Above All Laws). The Plunderers. Montana Belle (released 1952). Coroner Creek. Two Guys from Texas (GB: Two Texas Knights). 1949: The Big Cat. Brimstone. The Last Bandit. Sands of Iwo Jima. Hellfire. 1950: The Nevadan (GB: The Man from Nevada). Rock Island Trail (GB: Transcontinental Express). California Passage. 1951: Fighting Coastguard. O, Susanna. Crosswinds. The Wild Blue Yonder (GB: Thunder Across the Pacific). Flaming Feather. Warpath. 1952: Hoodlum Empire. Bugles in the Afternoon. Hurricane Smith. Ride the Man Down. 1953: Pony Express. San Antone. Flight Nurse. 1954: Jubilee Trail. Laughing Anne. Trouble in the Glen. Break in the Circle. 1955: Rage at Dawn. Finger Man. The Vanishing American. Night Freight. Paris Follies of 1956. 1956: Stagecoach to Fury. Three Violent People. The Quiet Gun. 1957: The Deerslayer. The Abominable Snowman. Girl in the Woods. 1958: The Strange World of Planet X (US: Cosmic Monsters). The Trollenberg Terror (US: The Crawling Eye). Auntie Mame. Gunsmoke in Tucson. Fort Massacre. 1959: Counterplot. 1966: Don't Worry, We'll Think of a Title. 1968: The Silent Treatment. The Night They Raided Minsky's. 1969: Barquero. 1970: Chisum. 1971: Welcome Home, Johnny Bristol (TV). 1972: Footsteps (TV). The Incredible Rocky Mountain Race (TV). Cancel My Reservation. 1973: Jarrett (TV). 1975: The Wild McCullochs. 1976: The Wackiest Wagon Train in the West. 1977: Final Chapter Walking Tall. 1978: The Adventures of Huckleberry Finn (TV). A Real American Hero (TV). 1981: Carnauba. 1983: Blood Feud (TV). 1985: Thunder Run. Outtakes. 1986: Timestalkers (TV).

TUFTS, Sonny
(Bowen Tufts III) 1911–1970
Strapping blond American actor and light singer, a success at Paramount in the war years. His high-spirited, hell-raising, heavy-drinking lifestyle put an end to his marriage and, after 1950, his career, although there were periodic comeback roles in the best of

which (*The Gift Horse, Come Next Spring*) he was almost back to his old, likeable, buoyant self. Died from pneumonia.

*1939: Ambush. 1943: So Proudly We Hail! Government Girl. 1944: I Love a Soldier. Here Come the Waves. In the Meantime, Darling. Miss Susie Slagle's (released 1946). 1945: Bring on the Girls. Duffy's Tavern. 1946: The Virginian. The Well-Groomed Bride. Swell Guy. 1947: Easy Come, Easy Go. Variety Girl. Blaze of Noon. Cross My Heart. 1948: The Untamed Breed. 1949: The Crooked Way. Easy Living. 1950: *Hollywood Goes to Bat. 1952: The Gift Horse (US: Glory at Sea). 1953: No Escape. Run for the Hills. Cat Women of the Moon. 1954: Serpent Island. 1955: The Seven Year Itch. Come Next Spring. 1956: *Hollywood Goes a-Fishing. 1957: The Parson and the Outlaw. 1965: Town Tamer. 1967: Cottonpickin' Chickenpickers.*

TURNER, Kathleen
(Mary K. Turner) 1954–

Tall, tawny-haired, smooth-moving American actress with purring voice and challenging eyes, slightly reminiscent of Lauren Bacall (*qv*). Although physically no great beauty, she was often cast in steamy roles calling for great erotic charge. She was more than adequate at supplying that, although she has also been very effective in frenetic comedy roles. Her time at the very top was brief (1984–1989) and she was in featured roles by the mid 1990s. Oscar nominee for *Peggy Sue Got Married*. She caused a stir by appearing nude in a 2000 London stage production of *The Graduate*.

*1982: Body Heat. 1983: The Man With Two Brains. 1984: Romancing the Stone. A Breed Apart. Crimes of Passion/China Blue. 1985: Prizzi's Honor. The Jewel of the Nile. 1986: Peggy Sue Got Married. 1987: Giulia and Giulia. Switching Channels. Dear America (voice only). Who Framed Roger Rabbit (voice only). The Accidental Tourist. 1989: *Tummy Trouble (voice only). The War of the Roses. 1990: *Roller Coaster Rabbit (voice only). 1991: V.I. Warshawski. House of Cards/ Before I Wake. 1993: Naked in New York. Undercover Blues/Cloak and Diaper. Serial Mom. 1995: Moonlight and Valentino. 1996: Friends at Last (TV). 1997: A Simple Wish. The Real Blonde. Lion King 2: Simba's Pride (voice only. Video). 1998: Legalese (TV). 1999: Prince of Central Park. The Virgin Suicides. Baby Geniuses. 2000: Love and Action in Chicago. Cinderella (TV). Beautiful. 2001: The Amati Girls.*

TURNER, Lana
(Julia 'Judy' Turner) 1920–1995

Blonde (originally auburn) American actress and sex symbol, dubbed 'The Sweater Girl' and later a shimmering platinum queen of melodrama, who lived the film star image to the hilt and married seven times, including (fourth) Lex Barker from 1953 to 1957. Weathered various unpalatable headline stories to extend her star run to 25 years. Oscar-nominated for *Peyton Place*. Died from throat cancer.

*1937: A Star is Born. Topper. The Great Garrick. They Won't Forget. 1938: †The Chaser. Four's a Crowd. *Pictorial Revue No 6. The Adventures of Marco Polo. Dramatic School. Love Finds Andy Hardy. Rich Man, Poor Girl. 1939: Dancing Co-Ed (GB: Every Other Inch a Lady). Calling Dr Kildare. Those Glamour Girls. *Rhumba Rhythm. 1940: Two Girls on Broadway (GB: Choose Your Partners). We Who Are Young. 1941: Dr Jekyll and Mr Hyde. Ziegfeld Girl. *Stars at Play. Johnny Eager. Honky Tonk. 1942: Somewhere I'll Find You. 1943: *Show Business At War. Slightly Dangerous. DuBarry Was a Lady. The Youngest Profession. 1944: Marriage is a Private Affair. 1945: Weekend at the Waldorf. Keep Your Powder Dry. 1946: The Postman Always Rings Twice. 1947: Green Dolphin Street. Cass Timberlane. 1948: Homecoming. The Three Musketeers. 1950: A Life of Her Own. Mr Imperium (GB: You Belong to My Heart). 1952: The Merry Widow. The Bad and the Beautiful. 1953: Latin Lovers. 1954: Flame and the Flesh. Betrayed. 1955: The Prodigal. The Sea Chase. Diane. The Rains of Ranchipur. 1957: Peyton Place. 1958: The Lady Takes a Flyer. Another Time, Another Place. 1959: Imitation of Life. 1960: Portrait in Black. 1961: Bachelor in Paradise. By Love Possessed. 1962: Who's Got the Action? 1964: Love Has Many Faces. 1966: Madame X. 1969: The Big Cube. 1974: Persecution. 1976: Bittersweet Love. 1978: Witches' Brew (released 1985).*

†*Most scenes deleted from final release print*

TUSHINGHAM, Rita 1940–

Dark-haired, big-eyed, waif-like British Actess with appealing 'ugly duckling' looks. Has given several very affecting performances, if her output has been a little disappointing – only just over one film a year. Took a British Academy Award for her very first film role, but the lack of suitable parts had taken her

abroad by the early 1970s. More recently back in Britain trying situation comedy on TV.

1961: A Taste of Honey. 1963: The Leather Boys. A Place to Go. Girl with Green Eyes. 1965: The Knack . . . and how to get it. Doctor Zhivago. 1966: The Trap. 1967: Smashing Time. 1968: Diamonds for Breakfast. The Guru. 1969: The Bed Sitting Room. 1972: Straight on Till Morning. The Case of Laura C. Where Do You Go From Here? 1973: Situation (TV). 1974: Instant Coffee. 1975: Rachel's Man. The 'Human' Factor. Ragazzo di borgata. 1976: The Search for Green Eyes (TV). 1977: Slaughter Day. Gran bollito. 1978: Sotto choc. Mysteries/Knut Hamsum's Mysteries. 1982: Spaghetti House. 1984: Dream to Believe/Flying. 1986: A Judgement in Stone (later The Housekeeper). 1987: Hem (originally for TV). 1988: Resurrected. Hard Days, Hard Nights. 1991: Paper Marriage. 1992: Rapture of Deceit. 1993: Desert Lunch. 1995: An Awfully Big Adventure. 1996: The Boy from Mercury. 1997: Under the Skin. 1998: Swing. 1999: Out of Depth.

TWEED, Shannon 1957–

Golden-blonde, tall, big-busted, predatory-looking Canadian-born pin-up and actress, a former *Playboy* centrefold (Playmate of the Year 1982) whose film career was spotty at best until she started a long series of soft-porn video thrillers spiced with lengthy sex scenes. Although most of these were derivative, all of them were glossily made – some directed by Tweed's oft-time co-star Andrew Stevens (*qv*) – and had made Tweed a very rich woman by the mid 1990s. As the decade progressed, she diversified into tough action films, also aimed at the home-screen market. Once memorably described by a critic as 'the vixen of video', she is divorced from actor/singer Gene Simmons.

1982: Drop-Out Father (TV). 1983: Hot Dog . . . The Movie. Of Unknown Origin. 1984: The Surrogate. 1986: Hitchhiker 4 (TV). The Last Fling (TV). 1987: Dragnet. Meatballs III: Summer Job. Steele Justice. Codename: Vengeance. 1988: Lethal Woman. Piranha Women/Cannibal Women in the Avocado Jungle of Death. Longarm (TV). 1989: Desperado: The Outlaw Wars. Night Visitor. Twisted Justice. 1990: Last Call. In the Cold of the Night. 1991: The Firing Line. The Last Hour. Night Eyes 2. 1992: The Naked Truth. Tell Me Your Secrets. No Contest. Liar's Edge. Night Eyes 3. Sexual Response. 1993: Extreme. Cold Sweat. Possessed by the Night. Sexual Revenge. A Woman Scorned. Model by Day. Illicit Dreams. Indecent Behavior. 1994: Night Fire. Victim of Desire/Implicated. Vegas Vice/ Hard Vice. Body Chemistry IV: Full Exposure. 1995: Indecent Behavior II. Electra. Indecent Behavior 3. Dark Dancer. 1996: White Cargo. No Contest II. Desires/Indecent Behavior 4. 1997: Assault on Devil's Island/Shadow Warriors (shown on TV as Assault on Death Mountain). Naked Lies. 1998: Dead by Dawn. Shadow Warriors II: Hunt for the Death Merchant. 1999: Singapore Sling. Detroit Rock City. Powerplay. 2000: Diaries of Darkness. The Rowdy Girls.

TWELVETREES, Helen (nee Jurgens) 1907–1958
This blonde American weepie queen of the Depression era with the swooping pencilled eyebrows never looked far from tears. In films she played fallen women and long-suffering girlfriends. Millions wept with her through the early 1930s, but the popularity of her image faded with more prosperous times and she was out of films by the end of the decade. Her personal life had its traumas too: her first husband, an alcoholic, died young, and there were violent repercussions to the break-up of her second marriage. Her third seemed happy enough and she played the lead in *A Streetcar Named Desire* on stage in the early 1950s. But in February 1958 she died from an overdose of sleeping pills at the age of 50.

1929: The Ghost Talks. Blue Skies. Words and Music. 1930: The Grand Parade. The Cat Creeps. Swing High. Her Man. 1931: The Painted Desert. A Woman of Experience. Millie. Bad Company. 1932: Young Bride. Panama Flo. State's Attorney (GB: Cardigan's Last Case). Is My Face Red? Unashamed. 1933: A Bedtime Story. Disgraced! My Woman. King for a Night. 1934: All Men Are Enemies. Now I'll Tell (GB: When New York Sleeps). She Was a Lady. One Hour Late. 1935: Times Square Lady. She Gets Her Man. The Spanish Cape Mystery. Frisco Waterfront (GB: When We Look Back). 1936: Thoroughbred. 1937: Hollywood Round-Up. 1939: Persons in Hiding. Unmarried (GB: Night Club Waitress).

TWIGGY (Lesley Hornby) 1946–
Blonde British fashion model of wide-eyed, waif-like appeal and friendly London accent. She had a few fairly indifferent tries at star film roles, did better on stage in song and dance shows, and looked like developing into a useful star character actress in the late 1980s. Married/divorced actor Michael Witney (1931–1983). Currently married to actor Leigh Lawson (1943–).

1971: The Boy Friend. 1974: 'W'. 1979: There Goes the Bride. 1980: The Blues Brothers. 1985: The Doctor and the Devils. 1986: Club Paradise. 1988: The Diamond Trap (TV). Madame Sousatzka. 1989: Istanbul. Young Charlie Chaplin (TV). 1993: Body Bags (TV). 1997: Something Borrowed, Something Blue (TV). 1998: †Woundings. †Edge of Seventeen.

†As Twiggy Lawson

TYLER, Liv 1976–
Very dark-haired, long-legged, ruby-lipped American actress of picture-book beauty. The daughter of the lead singer of the band Aerosmith, she was briefly a model (she's 5' 10") before turning to acting at 18 and swiftly moving into leading roles. She continued to attract graceful star parts into the 21st century.

1994: Silent Fall. 1995: Heavy. Empire Records. 1996: Stealing Beauty. That Thing You Do! Inventing the Abbotts. †Everyone Says I Love You. 1997: U Turn/Stray Dogs. 1998: Armageddon. Can't Hardly Wait (voice only). 1999: Plunkett & Macleane. Cookie's Fortune. Onegin. 2000: The Little Black Book. One Night at McCool's. Dr T and the Women. 2001: Lord of the Rings: The Fellowship of the Ring. 2002: Lord of the Rings: The Two Towers.

†Scenes deleted from final release print

U

Shadow/The Prodigal Son. 1993: Zorn (released 1995). 1994: Dream Play/Dromspel. 1995: Jag är Nyfiken. Film. Lumière et cie. 2000; Liuset haller mig sallskap (doc.).

As director: 1982: †Love. 1992: Sofie. 1995: Kristen Lavransdatter. 1996: Enskilda Samtal/Private Confessions. 2000: Faithless/Troloesa.

†Co-directed

ULRICH, Skeet (Bryan Ulrich) 1969–
Dark, deep-eyed, soulful, bedraggled American actor in rebel roles. Despite a late start to a film-acting career at 26, he was soon tagged as a budding cult sensation in the James Dean mould. Subsequent roles have been too far away from the mainstream to justify the build-up, and he needs to get into more powerful central roles to solidify his stardom. Married English actress Georgina Cates (Clare Woodgate 1975–).
1995: Boys. 1996: Last Dance. Scream. Albino Alligator. Touch. The Craft. 1997: As Good As It Gets. 1998: The Newton Boys. A Soldier's Sweetheart. 1999: Ride With the Devil. Chill Factor. Takedown. 2000: Anasazi Moon. 2001: Kevin of the North.

UNDERDOWN, Edward 1908–1989
Tall, erect, stick-like British actor who also pursued a successful career as a steeplechase jockey. Came to prominence in films when in his 40s, but his dour mien and diffident acting style (and some dull roles) pushed him back down the cast list. Subsequently, he was often seen in quite small roles.
1934: The Warren Case. Girls Please! 1935: Annie, Leave the Room! 1937: Wings of the

ULLMANN, Liv 1939–
Sandy-haired, Japan-born, Norwegian-raised star actress whose strained expression seemed made for anguish. All her best roles have so far been for director Ingmar Bergman (with whom she was associated for many years, and by whom she has a child). Her international ventures were sad misfires, and, declining to try Hollywood again after such daunting failures, she carved out a new career for herself as a director. Received Academy Award nominations for *The Emigrants* and *Face to Face*.
1957: Fjol til Fjells. 1959: Ung Flukt (GB: The Wayward Girl). 1962: Tonny. Kort är Sommaren. 1965: De Kalte Ham Skarven. 1966: Persona. 1968: Skammen/The Shame. Vargtimmen/Hour of the Wolf. 1969: An-Magritt. En Passion/A Passion (US: The Passion of Anna). Cold Sweat. 1971: The Night Visitor. The Emigrants. 1972: Pope Joan. The New Land. Cries and Whispers. 1973: *Foto: Sven Nykvist. Lost Horizon. Forty Carats. 1974: Scenes from a Marriage (TV). The Abdication. Zandy's Bride. 1975: Face to Face. 1976: Leonor. 1977: The Serpent's Egg. A Bridge Too Far. 1978: Autumn Sonata. Coleur chair. 1979: Players. 1980: The Gates of the Forest. 1981: Richard's Things (TV). 1983: The Wild Duck. Jacobo Timmerman/Prisoner Without a Name, Cell Without a Number (TV). 1984: The Bay Boy. 1985: La diagonale du fou (US: Dangerous Moves). 1986: Let's Hope It's a Girl. 1987: Moscow Goodbye. Moon Circus. Time of Indifference (TV). Gaby – a True Story. 1988: La amiga. 1989: The Rose Garden. 1990: Mindwalk. 1991: The Ox. 1992: The Long

Morning. 1938: The Drum (US: Drums). Inspector Hornleigh. 1940: Inspector Hornleigh Goes to It (US: Mail Train). 1947: The October Man. The Woman in the Hall. 1948: The Brass Monkey/Lucky Mascot. 1949: Man on the Run. 1950: They Were Not Divided. The Woman with No Name (US: Her Paneled Door). 1951: The Dark Man. The Woman's Angle. 1952: The Voice of Merrill (US: Murder Will Out). 1953: Street of Shadows (US: Shadow Man). Recoil. Beat the Devil. 1954: The Rainbow Jacket. 1958: The Camp on Blood Island. The Two-Headed Spy. Heart of a Child. 1961: The Day the Earth Caught Fire. The Third Alibi. Information Received. 1962: Locker 69. Dr Crippen. 1963: The Bay of Saint Michel (US: Pattern for Plunder). Man in the Middle. Woman of Straw. 1964: Dr Terror's House of Horrors. Traitor's Gate. 1965: Thunderball. 1966: Khartoum. The Hand of Night. Triple Cross. 1968: The Great Pony Raid. 1969: The Magic Christian. 1971: The Last Valley. 1972: Running Scared. 1973: Digby – The Biggest Dog in the World. 1974: The Abdication. 1978: Tarka the Otter.

UNGER, Deborah Kara 1966–
Tall, golden-blonde, wide-smiling, Canadian-born, Australia-raised actress with warm and friendly personality, seemingly on course for stardom from her first film but, despite a move to Hollywood and a variety of roles, not quite a top attraction. Besides the credits listed below, she made her first impact in the 1989 TV mini-series Bangkok Hilton. Billed in her first film (and on and off ever since) as Deborah Unger.
1990: Blood Oath (US: Prisoners of the Sun). Breakaway. 1991: Till There Was You. 1992: Hotel Room (cable TV). Whispers in the Dark. 1994: State of Emergency (cable TV). 1995: Highlander 3: The Sorcerer. 1996: No Way Home/Gasoline Alley. Crash. 1997: Keys to Tulsa. The Game. 1998: Payback. Luminous Motion/The History of Luminous Motion. The Rat Pack (TV). 1999: The Weekend. The Hurricane. Sunshine. 2000: Youri. Signs and Wonders. 2001: The Salton Sea.

URE, Mary 1933–1975
Slim, cool, sleek, blonde Scottish-born actress who was acting at 17 and on the London stage at 21. The major part of her career, in fact, was for the theatre, although the cinema was lucky enough to get her in the occasional leading role, often in projects which involved her first husband, playwright

John Osborne, or her second (married 1963), film actor Robert Shaw (*qv*). She died tragically, from an accidental mixture of champagne and barbiturates, after celebrating her successful opening in a new play.
1955: Storm Over the Nile. 1957: Windom's Way. 1959: Look Back in Anger. 1960: Sons and Lovers. 1962: The Mind Benders. 1964: The Luck of Ginger Coffey. 1966: Custer of the West. 1968: Where Eagles Dare. 1973: A Reflection of Fear.

URQUHART, Robert 1921–1995
Fresh-faced, dark-haired, frail-looking Scottish actor. Briefly popular in leading roles in the British cinema around 1953–1958, but seemed to age quickly. Perhaps it was being nearly throttled by the Frankenstein monster that did it. Died following open heart surgery.
*1952: You're Only Young Twice. Tread Softly (US: Tread Softly, Stranger). Paul Temple Returns. 1953: The House of the Arrow. Isn't Life Wonderful! 1954: Happy Ever After (US: Tonight's the Night/O'Leary Night). Knights of the Round Table. Golden Ivory (US: White Huntress). 1955: The Dark Avenger (US: The Warriors). You Can't Escape. 1956: The Curse of Frankenstein. 1957: Yangtse Incident (US: Battle Hell). 1958: Dunkirk. 1960: Trouble with Eve. Foxhole in Cairo. Danger Tomorrow. Murder in Mind. The Bulldog Breed. 1962: The Break. 55 Days at Peking. 1962: Murder at the Gallop. 1968: The Syndicate. The Limbo Line. Mosquito Squadron. 1969: The Looking Glass War. Country Dance (US: Brotherly Love). 1980: The Dogs of War. 1981: A Tale of Two Cities. *The Dollar Bottom. 1982: P'Tang Yang Kipperbang (TV. Later shown in cinemas). 1984: Sharma and Beyond*

(TV). 1985: Restless Natives. Hitler's S S: Portrait in Evil (TV. GB: cinemas). 1986: Playing Away (TV). 1987: The Kitchen Toto. Testimony. 1993: The Long Roads (TV).

USTINOV, Sir Peter 1921–
Heavily-built, shambling British actor-writer-director-raconteur with mop of hair and mellifluous, drawling voice, a treasured after-dinner speaker and sometimes hilarious supporting player in his own films. Something of a juvenile prodigy, he wrote his first screenplay at 23 and directed his first film at 25. Two Academy Awards as best supporting actor – for *Spartacus* and *Topkapi*. Also nominated for an Oscar in *Quo Vadis*. He has more recently several times played Agatha Christie's master-sleuth Hercule Poirot. Knighted in 1990. Married to actress Suzanne Cloutier (1927–) from 1954 to 1971.
*1940: Hullo Fame! Mein Kampf, My Crimes. 1942: The Goose Steps Out. One of Our Aircraft is Missing. Let the People Sing. 1944: The Way Ahead (US: Immortal Battalion). 1945: The True Glory. 1947: Vice Versa. 1949: Private Angelo. 1950: Odette. 1951: Hotel Sahara. The Magic Box. Quo Vadis. 1954: Beau Brummell. The Egyptian. We're No Angels. 1955: I girovaghi/The Wanderers. Lola Montès. 1957: Les espions. Un angelo è sceso a Brooklyn/The Man Who Wagged His Tail. 1959: Adventures of Mr Wonderbird (voice only). 1960: Spartacus. The Sundowners. 1961: Romanoff and Juliet (US: Dig That Juliet). 1962: Billy Budd. 1964: *The Peaches (narrator only). John Goldfarb, Please Come Home. Topkapi. 1965: Lady L. 1967: The Comedians. Blackbeard's Ghost. 1968: Hot Millions. 1970: Viva Max! A Storm in Summer (TV). 1972: Hammersmith is Out. Big Mack and Poor Clare. 1973: Robin Hood (voice only). 1975: One of Our Dinosaurs is Missing. 1976: Logan's Run. Treasure of Matecumbe. 1977: Doppio delitto/Double Murders. Taxi Mauve/Purple Taxi. The Last Remake of Beau Geste. The Mouse and His Child (voice only). 1978: The Thief of Bagdad. Death on the Nile. Tarka the Otter (narrator only). 1979: Ashanti. Nous maigrirons ensemble. Players. Winds of Change (narrator only). 1980: Charlie Chan and the Curse of the Dragon Queen. Short Cut to Haifa. 1981: Grendel Grendel Grendel (voice only). The Great Muppet Caper. Evil Under the Sun. 1983: Memed My Hawk. 1985: Thirteen at Dinner (TV). 1986: Dead Man's Folly (TV). Three Act Tragedy/Murder in Three Acts*

*(TV). Ferdinand (narrator only). 1988: Appointment with Death. *Peep and the Big Wide World. 1989: The French Revolution. Grandpa (voice only). 1990: Chera un castello con 40 cani. 1992: Lorenzo's Oil. Arnold Böcklin (narrator only). 1993: The Dancer. 1994: Phoenix and the Magic Carpet. 1996: Stiff Upper Lips. 1999: Alice in Wonderland (TV). Animal Farm (voice only). The Bachelor.*

As director: *1946: School for Secrets (US: Secret Flight). 1947: Vice Versa. 1949: Private Angelo (co-directed). 1961: Romanoff and Juliet (US: Dig That Juliet). 1962: Billy Budd. 1965: Lady L. 1972: Hammersmith is Out. 1983: Memed My Hawk.*

V

VALENTINO, Rudolph (Rodolpho di Valentino d'Antonguolla) 1895–1926

Dark-eyed Italian dancer and actor with slicked-back hair who became the great lover of Hollywood's silent screen and the idol of worshipping female millions. He played mysterious, dominant men, usually from other, far-flung parts of the world, who swept the heroine off to their tent/temple/palace. He died from peritonitis brought on by a perforated ulcer and was mourned by vast crowds amid a lying-in-state.

1914: My Official Wife. 1916: Patria. Isle of Love. Ambition. 1918: Alimony. All Night. A Society Sensation (GB: The Little Duchess). 1919: The Delicious Little Devil. A Rogue's Romance. The Homebreaker. The Big Little Person. Out of Luck. Virtuous Sinners. Eyes of Youth (GB: The Love of Sunya). 1920: The Cheater. The Married Virgin (later Frivolous Wives). Once to Every Woman. Passion's Playground. An Adventuress (later The Isle of Love). Stolen Moments. The Wonderful Chance. 1921: The Conquering Power. The Four Horsemen of the Apocalypse. Uncharted Seas. Camille. The Sheik. 1922: Moran of the Lady Letty. Beyond the Rocks. Blood and Sand. The Young Rajah. 1924: Monsieur Beaucaire. A Sainted Devil. 1925: Cobra. The Eagle. 1926: Son of the Sheik.

VALLEE, Rudy (Hubert Vallee) 1901–1986

Before Presley there was Sinatra; before Sinatra there was Crosby; and before Crosby there was Rudy Vallee – and his megaphone. With round face, brown hair parted just left of centre and appealing blue eyes, Vallee was the crooning idol of thousand of flappers as he led his band, the Connecticut Yankees, through the jazz era. In the late thirties he

became a useful comic character actor, usually as the ineffectual suitor who didn't get the girl. Married Jane Greer (second of three) 1943–1945. Died from a heart attack.

1929: *Radio Rhythm. *Rudy Vallee and his Connecticut Yankees. Vagabond Lover. Glorifying the American Girl. 1930: *Campus Sweethearts. 1931: *Musical Justice. 1932: *The Musical Doctor. *Rudy Vallee Melodies. *Knowmore College. 1933: International House. George White's Scandals of 1934. 1935: Sweet Music. *A Trip Thru a Hollywood Studio. *Broadway Highlights No 1. 1938: *For Auld Lang Syne. Gold Diggers in Paris (GB: The Gay Imposters). 1939: Second Fiddle. 1941: Time Out for Rhythm. Too Many Blondes. *Lydia. *Take Me Back to My Boots and Saddle. 1942: The Palm Beach Story. 1943: Happy Go Lucky. 1944: It's in the Bag! (GB: The Fifth Chair). 1945: Man Alive. 1946: People Are Funny. The Fabulous Suzanne. The Sin of Harold Diddlebock (later/GB: Mad Wednesday). 1947: The Bachelor and the Bobby-Soxer (GB: Bachelor Knight). 1948: I Remember Mama. So This is New York. My Dear Secretary. Unfaithfully Yours. 1949: Mother is a Freshman (GB: Mother Knows Best). The Beautiful Blonde from Bashful Bend. Father Was a Fullback. 1950: The Admiral Was a Lady. 1954: Ricochet Romance. 1955: Gentlemen Marry Brunettes. 1957: The Helen Morgan Story (GB: Both Ends of the Candle). 1967: How to Succeed in Business Without Really Trying. The Night They Raided Minsky's (narrator only). 1968: The Silent Treatment. Live a Little Love a Little. 1969: The Phynx. 1974: Sunburst. 1975: Won Ton Ton, the Dog who Saved Hollywood. 1978: The Perfect Woman.

VALLI, Alida (A. Altenburger) 1921–

It's hard to reconcile the Valli (as she was known in her English-speaking films of the forties and fifties) of the later years – the hardened, square face looks type-cast for a prison governess and indeed is usually seen in severe roles – with the lovely, soulful, shiningly dark-haired creature of *The Third Man*. How green was our Valli then. Still, the facial structure was always there, emphasizing the enigma of *The Paradise Case*, too, and at least this talented and gentle Italian actress has kept very busy, even if in decreasingly worthwhile roles.

1935: Il capello a tre punte. 1936: I due sergenti. 1937: Il feroce Saladino. L'ultima nemica. Sono stato io! 1938: Ma l'amor mio non muore. L'ha

VACCARO, Brenda 1939–

Dark-haired, chubby-faced, personable American actress with throaty voice, mostly in toughly independent roles, but hot on the wisecracks when needed. She was acting busily on TV from the early 1960s; Hollywood obviously missed out on a good thing (and anyone who can get nominated for an Oscar from a film like *Once is Not Enough* has to be a class act), before John Schlesinger found her for *Midnight Cowboy*. Although she did not become a box-office star, she can often be an oasis of talent amid scriptural wastes.

1969: Midnight Cowboy. Where It's At. 1970: I Love My Wife. Travis Logan DA (TV). 1971: Summertree. What's A Nice Girl Like You . . . ? (TV). Going Home. 173: Honor Thy Father (TV. GB: cinemas). Sunshine (TV. GB: cinemas). 1974: Once is Not Enough/ Jacqueline Susann's Once is Not Enough. 1976: The House by the Lake (GB: and US: Death Weekend). 1977: Airport 77. Capricorn One. 1978: Fast Charlie . . . The Moonbeam Rider. 1979: Dear Detective (TV). 1980: The First Deadly Sin. Guyana Tragedy: The Story of Jim Jones (TV). 1981: Chanel Solitaire. A Long Way Home (TV). Zorro the Gay Blade. The Pride of Jesse Hallam (TV). 1984: Paper Dolls (H. TV). Supergirl. 1985: Deceptions (TV). Water. 1986: The White Stallion. 1988: Heart of Midnight. For Keeps? (GB: Maybe Baby). 1989: Cookie. Ten Little Indians. The Masque of the Red Death. Lethal Games. 1990: I Want Him Back (TV). Columbo: Murder in Malibu (TV). 1992: Red Shoe Diaries (TV). 1994: Love Affair. Following Her Heart (TV). 1996: The Mirror Has Two Faces. 1998: When Husbands Cheat (TV).

fatto una signore. La casa del peccato. Mille lire al mese. 1939: Assenza ingiustificata. Manon Lescaut. Ballo al castello. Taverna rossa/The Red Inn. 1940: Oltre l'amore. La prima donna che passa. Piccolo mondo antico. Luce nelle tenebre. 1941: L'amante segreta. Ore nove lezione di chimica. 1942: Cantene invisibili. Noi vivi. Addio Kira! Le due orfanelle. I Pagliacci. Strasera niente di nuovo. 1943: Apparizione. T'amero' sempre. 1945: Circo equestre za bum. La vita ricominicia (US: Life Begins Anew). Giovanna. Il canto della vita. 1946: La vita continua. Eugénie Grandet. 1947: †The Paradine Case. 1948: †The Miracle of the Bells. 1949: †The Third Man. Les miracles n'ont lieu qu'une fois. 1950: Ultimo incontro. †Walk Softly Stranger. †The White Tower. 1952: †The Lovers of Toledo. 1953: Siamo donne (GB and US: We the Woman). Senso (GB: and US: The Wanton Countess). Il mondo le condanna. 1954: †The Stranger's Hand. 1957: Les bijoutiers du clair de lune (GB: Heaven Fell that Night US: The Night Heaven Fell). Il grido. La grande strada azzurra. 1958: †This Angry Age (GB: The Sea Wall). Tal Vez Mañana/L'uomo dai Calzoni Corit. 1959: L'assegno/Il peccato degli Anni Verdi. Le dialogue des Carmélites. Arsène Lupin et la toison d'or. Les yeux sans visage/Eyes Without a Face. 1960: Le gigolo. Treno di natale. 1961: Une aussi longue absence. 1962: The Happy Thieves. La fille du torrent. Homenaje a la Hora de la Siesta/Four Women for One Hero. Al otro lado de la ciudad. Il disordine (GB: Disorder). The Castilian. Ophèlia. 1963: El Hombre de Papel. 1964: L'autre femme. 1965: Umorismo nero. 1967: Oedipus Rex. 1970: Le champignon. The Spider's Stratagem (TV. GB and US: cinemas). 1971: Concerto per pistola solista. L'occhio nel labirinto. 1972: La prima notte di quiete. Diario di un Italiano. 1974: La grande trouille. Tendre Dracula. No es nada Mama, solo un Juego. La chair de l'orchidée. 1975: House of Exorcism (US: Lisa and the Devil). Ce cher Victor (US: Cher Victor). Il caso Raoul. 1976: The Antichrist (GB: The Tempter). Suspiria. Le jeu de solitaire. 1990: The Cassandra Crossing. 1977: Berlinguer, ti voglio bene. Cuore semplice. 1978: Zoo/Zéro. Indagine su un delitto perfetto. 1979: Porco mondo. La Luna. Suor omicida (GB: The Killer Nun). 1980: Inferno. Aquella casa en las Afeuras. Puppenspiel mit toten Augen. 1981: La caduta degli Angeli Ribelli. Sezona mira u Parizu. 1982: Aspern. Sogni mostruosamente proibiti. 1985: Segreti, segreti. Il brivido del genio. 1987: Le jupon rouge. 1988: A notre regrettable époux. Noi vivi. 1991: Zitti e mosca (US: The Party's Over). 1993: Il lungo silenzio. 1994: A Month by the Lake. The Seventh Room. 1996: Fatal Frames. 1998: Probably Love. 1999: Il dolce rumore della vita.

†As Valli

VALLONE, Raf (Raffaele Vallone) 1916– Good-natured, dark-haired, thick-set Italian actor, persuaded to give up a career as a reporter in the late forties in favour of acting. Usually seen in sweaty, earthy roles, he got his best parts in the late fifties and early sixties. After this he went international, only to be handed increasingly silly assignments from which he did not re-emerge as the powerful actor he could be.

1948: Bitter Rice/Riso amaro. 1949: Non c'è pace fra gli ulvi. Vendetta. 1950: Cuori senza frontier. Il cammino della speranza. Il bivio. 1951: Anna. Cristo proibito. 1952: Camicie rosa. Roma ore II. Mandrin. Carne inquieta/Restless. Uomini senza pace. Gli eroi della Domenica. Perdonami. 1953: Domanda di grazia. Los Ojos dejan Huellas. Delirio. La spiaggia. Thérèsa Raquin. Destinées. 1954: Human Torpedoes. The Sign of Venus. 1955: Uragano sul Po. Andrea Chenier. Obsession. Siluri umani. 1956: Les possédés. Le secret de Soeur Angèle. Liebe. Guendalina. 1957: Rose Bernd. 1958: La venganza. Le piège. La violetera. 1960: Recours en grâce. La garçonnière. 1961: Two Women/La ciociara. El Cid. Phaedra. A View from the Bridge. 1963: The Cardinal. 1964: The Secret Invasion. Una voglia da morire. La scoperta dell'America. 1965: Harlow. 1966: Nevada Smith. Volver a vivir. Kiss the Girls and Make Them Die. 1968: The Desperate Ones. Sharaz. 1969: The Italian Job. The Kremlin Letter. 1970: La morte risale a ieri sera. Cannon for Cordoba. A Gunfight. 1971: Summertime Killer. Perchè non ci lasciate in pace?/Why Don't You Leave Us in Peace? La villa. 1973: Honor Thy Father (TV. GB: cinemas). Small Miracle (TV). Catholics (TV). Grazie, amore mio. 1974: Rosebud. L'histoire de l'oeil. 1975: That Lucky Touch. The 'Human' Factor. 1977: The Other Side of Midnight. The Devil's Advocate. 1978: The Greek Tycoon. 1979: Retour à Marseille. An Almost Perfect Affair. 1980: Seven Graves for Rogan. Lion of the Desert/Omar Mukhtar Lion of the Desert. 1981: Senzona mira u parizu. A Tale of Africa. 1983: The Scarlet and the Black (TV). 1985: Power of Evil/Le pouvoir du mal. 1986: The Conspiracy. La nuit de l'océan. 1990: Der Bierkönig. The Godfather Part III. La Leyenda del Cura de Bargota. 1991: Julianus barát I. Julianus barát II. Julianus barát III. 1992: Torn Between Two Hearts (TV). 1999: Toni.

VAN CLEEF, Lee 1925–1989 Lean, mean-looking, dark-haired, narrow-eyed American actor of faintly oriental aspect, almost entirely confined to westerns. After he switched to acting instead of taking over his father's accountancy business, he spent more than a decade in films as ugly villains (with the occasional American Indian thrown in) with itchy trigger fingers. Then he lost his hair, grew a moustache and, recovered from a severe car crash in 1959, pleasantly surprised his fans by becoming a star of spaghetti westerns in the wake of Clint

Eastwood (qv). Died from a heart attack. 1950: The Showdown. 1952: Untamed Frontier. High Noon. Kansas City Confidential (GB: The Secret Four). The Lawless Breed. 1953: Arena. The Bandits of Corsica (GB: The Return of the Corsican Brothers). Tumbleweed. The Beast from 20,000 Fathoms. Vice Squad (GB: The Girl in Room 17). The Nebraskan. Private Eyes. White Lightning. Jack Slade (GB: Slade). 1954: Arrow in the Dust. Gypsy Colt. Dawn at Socorro. Princess of the Nile. The Desperado. The Yellow Tomahawk. Rails into Laramie. The Big Combo. 1955: Ten Wanted Men. I Cover the Underworld. Man Without a Star. The Naked Street. The Road to Denver. The Vanishing American. A Man Alone. The Treasure of Ruby Hills. The Kentuckian. 1956: The Conqueror. Tribute to a Bad Man. Red Sundown. Pardners. Accused of Murder. It Conquered the World. Backlash. The Quiet Gun. Gunfight at the OK Corral. 1957: Last Stagecoach West. The Lonely Man. Joe Dakota. Gun Battle at Monterey. The Badge of Marshal Brennan. The Tin Star. 1958: Raiders of Old California. China Gate. The Bravados. Day of the Bad Man. Machete. The Young Lions. 1959: Ride Lonesome. Guns, Girls and Gangsters. 1961: Posse from Hell. 1962: The Man Who Shot Liberty Valance. How the West Was Won. 1965: For a Few Dollars More. 1966: Call to Glory. The Good, the Bad and the Ugly. 1967: The Big Gundown. Death Rides a Horse. Day of Anger. 1968: Above the Law/Die letzte Rechnung zählst du selbst. Commandos (US: Sullivan's Marauders). Der Tod ritt Dienstages. A Mercenary for Any War. 1969: Sabata! A Professional Gun. Creed of Violence. Bite the Dust. Barquero. 1970: El Condor. 1971: Captain Apache. Bad Man's River. Return of Sabata. 1972: The Grand Duel. The Magnificent Seven Ride! Drei Vaterunser für vier Halunken. 1973: The Gun. Mean Frank and Crazy Tony. 1974: Blood Money. 1975: Take a Hard Ride. Power Kill. The Stranger and the Gunfighter. Crime Boss. 1976: Vendetta. Diamante lobo/God's Gun. Dio sei proprio un padveterno/Gangster Story. 1977: The Perfect Killer. Nowhere to Hide. Kid Vengeance. 1978: The Big Rip-Off (US: The Squeeze). 1979: The Hard Way (TV). 1980: The Octagon. Trieste File. 1981: Escape from New York. 1984: Codename Wildgeese. 1985: Captain Yankee and the Jungle Raiders (US: Jungle Raiders). 1986: Killing Machine (made 1983). The Jade Jungle (later Armed Response). 1988: The Commander. 1989: Speed Zone. 1990: Thieves of Fortune.

VAN DAMME, Jean-Claude
(J-C Van Varienberg) 1960–

Tight-lipped, impassive, light-haired Belgian karate and kickboxing expert, known as 'The Muscles from Brussels', who became a star of martial arts-slanted action films in the late 1980s. In real life his own best publicist, Van Damme has normally been seen on screen as the unassuming type out for revenge for the death or immobilisation of a friend or relation. He sought a slightly wider range in the following decade and proved to have some appeal for mainstream audiences. His fans, though, demanded little more than to see him breaking bones and crushing skulls and attempts to project a more romantic or humorous image placed too great a strain on his limited acting ability. Married (third of four) bodybuilding star Gladys Portugues. Remarried her in 1999.

1983: Rue Barbar (US: Street of the Damned). 1984: Breakin' (GB: Breakdance). Missing in Action (stunts only). 1985: Monaco Forever. No Retreat, No Surrender. 1987: Predator. Bloodsport. 1988: Dusted. Black Eagle. 1989: Kickboxer. Cyborg. 1990: Death Warrant. A.W.O.L./Lionheart. 1991: Double Impact. 1992: Universal Soldier. 1993: Hard Target. Nowhere to Run. Last Action Hero. 1994: Time Cop. Street Fighter. 1995: Sudden Death. 1996: The Quest. Maximum Risk. 1997: Double Team. 1998: Legionnaire. Knock Off. 1999: Inferno. Universal Soldier: The Return. 2000: Replicant.

VAN DEVERE, Trish
See SCOTT, George C.

VAN DIEN, Casper 1968–

Tall, square-shouldered, fair-haired American actor who looks like one of the *Thunderbirds* puppets. He was perhaps predictably stuck in such daytime TV soaps as *One Life to Live* for the first five years of his acting career. After landing the star part in *Starship Troopers* in 1997 he was seen in other roles that demanded physical presence rather than acting range and looks set for a solid future in straight-to-video action flicks. Married/divorced actress Carrie Mitchum (granddaughter of actor Robert Mitchum). Currently married to actress Catherine Oxenberg (1961–).

1995: P.C.H. Night Eyes 4. Beastmaster 3: The Eye of Braxus. 1996: Orbit. James Dean: Race with Destiny (released 1997). 1997: Casper: A Spirited Beginning (V). Starship Troopers. Nightscream (TV). 1998: Modern Vampires/ Revenant. On the Border. Dream True. Tarzan

and the Lost City. 1999: Shark Attack. The Collectors. Sleepy Hollow. Chasing Destiny. The Time Shifters (TV). Meltdown. The Omega Code. Romantic Moritz. The Collectors. 2000: Partners. Python. Sanctimony. Cutaway. The Tracker.

VAN DOREN, Mamie
(Joan Olander) 1931–

Petite, voluptuous plantinum blonde American actress with moon-shaped face and come-hither dark eyes. She failed in her first attempt to break into films, as a teenager, then, after she had become a dance band vocalist, Universal signed her up, but never did more than make her the sex-bomb of the double-feature, a niche in which she found herself stuck. Later followed Jayne Mansfield's route by taking her clothes off in sexploitation comedies. Made a surprise comeback to acting in the 1980s.

1950: †Jet Pilot (released 1957). 1951: †His Kind of Woman. †Two Tickets to Broadway. †Footlight Varieties. 1952: †Hawaiian Nights. 1953: Forbidden. The All-American (GB: The Winning Way). 1954: Yankee Pasha. Francis Joins the WACs. 1955: Ain't Misbehavin'. The Second Greatest Sex. Running Wild. 1956: Star in the Dust. 1957: Untamed Youth. The Girl in Black Stockings. 1958: High School Confidential! Teacher's Pet. Guns, Girls and Gangsters. Le bellissime gambe di Sabrina. 1959: Born Reckless. The Beat Generation. Girls' Town. The Big Operator. 1960: Vice Raid. College Confidential. Sex Kittens Go to College. The Private Lives of Adam and Eve. 1964: The Sheriff Was a Lady/ Freddy und das Lied der Prairie. Three Nuts in Search of a Bolt. The Candidate. 1965: The Navy vs. the Night Monster (GB: Monsters of the Night).

1966: Women of the Prehistoric Planet/ Voyage to the Planet of Prehistoric Women. Las Vegas Hillbillys. 1967: You've Got to Be Smart. 1971: The Arizona Kid. 1985: ‡The Tomb. 1986: Boarding School (later Free Ride).

†As Joan Olander ‡Scenes deleted

VAN DYKE, Dick 1925–

Long-jawed, gangling, widely-smiling, fair-haired American funny-man of great visual comic talents. His television show was enormously popular from 1961 to 1966; the brightest of the films that sprang from it were those that appealed to juvenile audiences. His much-publicized but finally triumphant battle with alcohol may have damaged his career in the seventies, when he seemed to feel the need to prove his worth as a serious actor. He settled into a comfortable TV career as a sleuthing doctor in the 1990s.

1963: Bye Bye Birdie. 1964: What a Way to Go! Mary Poppins. 1965: The Art of Love. 1966: Lt Robin Crusoe USN. 1967: Divorce American Style. Fitzwilly (GB: Fitzwilly Strikes Back). Never a Dull Moment. 1968: Chitty Chitty Bang Bang. 1969: The Comic. 1970: Some Kind of Nut. 1971: Cold Turkey. 1974: The Morning After (TV). 1977: Tubby the Tuba (TV. Voice only). 1979: The Runner Stumbles. 1982: Drop-out Father (TV). 1983: Found Money (TV). 1987: Ghost of a Chance (TV). 1990: Dick Tracy. 1991: Daughters of Privilege (TV). Diagnosis of Murder (TV). 1992: †Freddie Goes to Washington (voice only). The House on Sycamore Street (TV). 1993: A Twist of the Knife. (TV).

†Unfinished.

VAN PEEBLES, Mario
(Mario Peebles) 1957–

Young-looking American actor, writer, director and songwriter, son of veteran director Melvin Van Peebles. He studied economics and began his career as a budget analyst in government administration before turning seriously to an acting career in his late twenties. Although he has remained a prolific on-screen performer, his talents as a director probably outweigh his acting abilities. So far the achievements of this jack-of-all-trades have not quite been the sum of his ambitions, and he remains at his best in the staging of dynamic action scenes. Born in Mexico.

1971: Sweet Sweetback's Baadasssss Song. The Cable Car Murder (TV. GB: Crosscurrent).

1981: *Sophisticated Gents* (TV). 1984: *The Cotton Club. Exterminator 2. Delivery Boys.* 1985: *Children of the Night* (TV). *Rappin'. South Bronx Heroes* (GB: *Revenge of the Innocents*). 1986: *Heartbreak Ridge. 3:15. Last Resort* (GB: *She Knew No Other Way*). *L.A. Law* (TV). 1987: *Jaws: The Revenge/Jaws 4. The Facts of Life Down Under* (TV). *Hotshot.* 1988: *The Child Saver* (TV). 1989: †*Juliet.* 1990: *Blue Bayou* (TV). *Identity Crisis.* 1991: †*New Jack City. A Triumph of the Heart: The Ricky Bell Story* (TV). 1992: *In the Line of Duty: Street War* (TV. GB: *In the Line of Duty: Urban Crossfire*). *Stompin' at the Savoy* (TV). 1993: †*Posse.* 1994: *Full Eclipse* (cable TV). *Gunmen. Highlander 3: The Sorcerer.* 1995: †*Panther.* 1996: ‡*Gang in Blue* (TV). *Riot* (cable TV. Later on video as *Riot in the Streets*). *Solo.* 1997: *Stag. Los Locos* (TV). 1998: *Mama Flora's Family* (TV). *Killers in the House* (TV). †*Love Kills. Valentine's Day* (TV). *Crazy Six.* 1999: *Raw Nerve. Blowback. Judgment Day.* 2000: *Sally Hemings: An American Scandal* (TV).

†And directed ‡And co-directed
Also as director. 1999: *Standing Knockdown.*

VARNEY, Jim 1949–2000
Rubber-necked, goggle-eyed American comedian, all eyebrows, teeth and nose. Performing professionally at 17 he was, for a while, associated as much with country music as with comedy, but his creation Ernest P. Worrell, an amiable oaf who acted like a bull in a china shop and trod on everyone's corns, brought him to national comic stardom after he tried the character out in scores of regional commercials. 'Ernest' hit the big screen in 1987 in a long series of lowbrow comedies

that appalled the critics but pleased children and family audiences outside the big cities, performed well on video and would doubtless still be going on but for Varney's early death from lung cancer.
1977: *Operation Petticoat* (TV). 1983: *The Rousters* (TV). 1986: *Dr Otto and the Riddle of the Gloom Beam.* 1987: *Ernest Goes to Camp.* 1988: *Ernest Saves Christmas.* 1989: *Fast Food.* 1990: *Ernest Goes to Jail.* 1991: *Ernest Scared Stupid.* 1992: **Mr Bill Goes to Washington.* 1993: *Ernest Rides Again. Wilder Napalm. The Beverly Hillbillies.* 1994: *Ernest Goes to School. The Expert. Your World As I See It. XXX's & 000's* (TV). 1995: *Toy Story* (voice only). *Slam Dunk Ernest.* 1996: *Snowboard Academy.* 1997: *Ernest Goes to Africa. 100 Proof.* 1998: *Ernest in the Army/Stormin' Ernest. Annabelle's Wish* (voice only). *Pirates of the Plain. 3 Ninjas: High Noon on Mega Mountain.* 1999: *Existo. Ernest and the Mummy's Curse. Treehouse Hostage. Toy Story 2* (voice only). 2000: *Daddy and Them. Atlantis* (voice only).

VARSI, Diane 1937–1992
Sweet-faced American actress with light-brown hair, one of Fox's big new young stars of the late fifties. Briefly a singer and drummer, she won an Academy Award nomination in her first film, but left the studio after only three more, and was unable to get back into films for several years thereafter because she had broken her contract. Even so, she had seemed to have sufficient talent to survive as an actress, but later screen appearances were sporadic and undistinguished. She died from Lyme Disease and respiratory problems.
1957: *Peyton Place.* 1958: *Ten North Frederick. From Hell to Texas* (GB: *Manhunt*). 1959: *Compulsion. The Dingaling Girl* (TV). 1966: *Sweet Love Bitter.* 1967: *Roseanna.* 1968: *Wild in the Streets. Killers Three.* 1969: *Bloody Mama.* 1971: *Johnny Got His Gun. The People* (TV). 1977: *I Never Promised You a Rose Garden.*

VAUGHAN, Frankie (F. Abelsohn) 1928–1999
Handsome, black-haired, thick-lipped British singer, a great showman. Seemed to be everybody's favourite – even Hollywood's – in the late fifties and early sixties, and co-starred with Monroe. But the bubble burst, and suddenly he was back on the stage, wowing the mums with the high kicks, winks and

waves of the staw hat and cane. Died from complications following heart operations.
1956: *Escape in the Sun* (singing commentary only). *Ramsbottom Rides Again.* 1957: *These Dangerous Years* (US: *Dangerous Youth*). 1958: *Wonderful Things!* 1959: *The Lady is a Square. The Heart of a Man.* 1960: *Let's Make Love.* 1961: *The Right Approach.* 1963: *It's All Over Town.*

VAUGHN, Robert 1932–
Dark-haired, cold-eyed, superior-looking American actor with metallic, calculating voice. He had already caught the eye as shifty, upper-class villains (typically the gone-to-the-bad scion of a good family) before sensational success in the James Bond-style TV series *The Man from UNCLE* – several double-episodes of which were released as films outside America – as the smooth-as-silk agent Napoleon Solo. Alas, he got rather better film roles before the series than after it, and has recently been seen happily playing thoroughly nasty, conniving villains again. One of Hollywood's more politically-minded actors; nominated for an Oscar in *The Young Philadelphians*.
1956: *The Ten Commandments.* 1957: *Hell's Crossroads. The Trouble Makers* (TV). *No Time To Be Young* (GB: *Teenage Deliquents*). 1958: *Teenage Caveman* (GB: *Out of the Darkness*). *Unwed Mother. A Good Day for a Hanging.* 1959: *The Young Philadelphians* (GB: *The City Jungle*). *Made in Japan* (TV). 1960: *The Magnificent Seven.* 1961: *The Big Show.* 1963: *The Caretakers* (GB: *Borderlines*). 1964: *To Trap a Spy* (TV. GB: cinemas). *Honeymoon Hotel. The Spy with My Face.* 1965: *One Spy Too Many* (TV. GB: cinemas). 1966: *One of Our Spies is Missing!*

(TV. GB: cinemas). The Venetian Affair. The Spy in the Green Hat (TV. GB: cinemas). The Glass Bottom Boat. 1967: The Karate Killers (TV. GB: cinemas). The Helicopter Spies (TV. GB: cinemas). 1968: Bullitt. How to Steal the World (TV. GB: cinemas). The Bridge at Remagen. If It's Tuesday, This Must Be Belgium. 1969: The Mind of Mr Soames. 1970: Julius Caesar. 1971: Clay Pigeon (GB: Trip to Kill). The Statue. 1972: The Woman Hunter (TV). 1974: The Towering Inferno. 1975: Wanted: Babysitter. 1976: Kiss Me, Kill Me (TV). 1977: Demon Seed (voice only). Starship Invasions. 1978: Good Luck, Miss Wyckoff. The Islander (TV). Brass Target. The Deadly Price of Paradise (TV. GB: Nightmare at Pendragon's Castle). 1979: Panic on Page One/City in Fear (TV). The Gossip Columnist (TV). 1980: Cuba Crossing. Virus. Batle Beyond the Stars. Hangar 18. Doctor Franken (TV). Mirror, Mirror (TV). Studio Murders/Fantasies (TV). 1981: SOB. A Question of Honor (TV). 1982: The Courageous. The Day the Bubble Burst (TV). 1983: Superman III. The Return of the Man from UNCLE (TV). Intimate Agony (TV). Full Circle Again (GB: TV). 1984: Atraco en la jungla (completed 1978). 1985: The Hitch-hiker. Black Moon Rising. Private Sessions (TV). International Airport (TV). Murrow (TV). 1986: The Delta Force. That's Adequate! Prince of Bel Air (TV). Hour of the Assassin. 1987: Night Stick/Calhoun. Skeleton Coast. Desperado (TV). Renegade Luke. 1988: Kid McCoy (US: Brutal Glory). Killing Birds. Captive Rage. The Emissary. Another Way. 1989: Buried Alive. River of Death. Nobody's Perfect. Transylvania Twist. 1990: Dive/Going Under. Twilight Blue. Perry Mason: The Case of the Defiant Daughter (TV). Dark Avenger (TV). 1991: Little Devils. 1992: Blind Vision. 1993: Witch Academy. 1994: Dust to Dust. 1995: Dancing in the Dark (TV). Escape to Witch Mountain (TV). Joe's Apartment. 1996: Visions. Milk & Money. Menno's Mind. 1997: Vulcan. The Sender. Diagnosis Murder (TV). Motel Blue. An American Affair. 1998: BASEketball. Virtual Obsession (TV). McCinsey's Island (TV).

VAUGHN, Vince 1970–
Tall (6ft 5in), curly-haired, rugged American actor, a bigger version of Michael Keaton, with deep-set eyes. A TV actor at 19, his film career was sketchy until he made an impression in *Swingers* in 1996. He was in

leading roles two years later, although the indifferent performance of the new version of *Psycho* denied him major stardom. He also has plans to write and direct his own projects.
1991: For the Boys. 1993: Rudy. 1994: At Risk. 1996: Just Your Luck (video). Swingers. 1997: The Locusts (GB: A Secret Sin). The Lost World: Jurassic Park. 1998: A Cool, Dry Place. Return to Paradise. Psycho. Clay Pigeons. 2000: The Cell. The Prime Gig. South of Heaven, West of Hell. The Gelfin. 2001: Made.

As director. *2000: Marshall of Revolution.*

VEIDT, Conrad
(Hans Konrad Weidt) 1893–1943
Dark, fine-boned German actor with piercing gaze and considerable presence. Handsome in a slightly sinister way, he was a key figure in the early German cinema, seeming to be in on many of its most striking and/or innovative films. Left Germany in 1934 (after a visit to Hollywood in the late twenties), and his remaining roles in Britain and America were mostly as clever enemy agents that you more or less loved to hate. Died from a heart attack while playing golf.
1916: Der Spion. Der Weg des Todes. 1917: Das Rätsel vom Bangalor. Wenn Tote sprechen. Die Seeschlacht. Es werde Licht. Die Claudi von Geiserhot. Furcht. 1918: Colomba das Dreimäderlhaus. Das Tagebuch einer Verlorenen (parts 1 and 2). Henriette Jacoby. Jettchen gebert. Dida Ibsens Geschichte. Nocturno der Liebe. Opfer der Gesellschaft. Peer Gynt. Opium. Die Serenyi. Die Japanerin. 1919: Anders als die Andern. Chopin. Die Prostitution (parts 1 and 2). The Cabinet of Dr Caligari. Around the World in 80 Days. Die nacht auf Goldenhall. Die Okarina. Die Mexikanerin. Unheimliche Geschichten. Die sich verkaufen. Prinz Kuckuck. Santanas. Washsinn. Gewitter im Mai. 1920: Abend-Nacht-Morgen. Das Geheimnis von Bombay. Der Gang in die Nacht. Der Graf von Cagliostro. Der Januskopf/Dr Jekyll and Mr Hyde. Der Reigen/Merry-Go-Round. Die Augen der Welt. Künstlerlaunen. Kurfürsten-dam. Menschen im Rausch. Liebestaumel. Manolescus Memoiren (GB: The Memoirs of Manolescu). Morituris. Nachtsgestalten. Patience. Sehnsucht. Weltbrand. 1921: Christian Wahnschaffe/Die Flucht aus dem goldenen Kerker. Das Indische Grabmal (parts 1 and 2). Der Leidensweg der Inge Krafft. Die Liebschafen des Hektor Dalmore. Lady Hamilton. Landstrasse und Grosstadt. Sündige

Mütter. 1922: Lukrezia Borgia. Danton. 1923: Glanz gegen Glück. Paganini. Wilhelm Tell. 1924: Carlos und Elisabeth. Nju (GB: and US: Husbands or Lovers). Orlacs Hände (GB and US: The Hands of Orlac) Schicksal/Fate. Das Wachsfigurenkabinet (GB and US: Three Wax Men). 1925: Graf Kostja/Le comte Kostja. Liebe macht blind. Ingmarsarvet (GB: in Dalarna and Jerusalem). 1926: Die Brüder Schellenberg. Durfen wir schweigen? Die Fluch in die Nacht. Der Geiger von Florenz (GB: Impetuous Youth). Kreuzzug des Weibes. Der Student von Prag (GB: The Student of Prague. US: The Man Who Cheated Life). 1927: Enrico IV. Jerusalem. Les maudits. The Beloved Rogue. The Man Who Laughs. A Man's Past. Husbands or Lovers. 1928: Two Brothers. 1929: Das Land ohne Frauen. Last Performance (GB: The Last Call). 1930: Die Grosse Sehnsucht. Die letzte Compagnie (and English version. US: 13 Men and a Girl). Menschen im Käfig/Cape Forlorn. Bride 68. 1931: Der Mann, der den Mord beging. Nachte am Bosporus. Die ändere Seite. Die Nachte der Entscheidung. Congress Dances. 1932: Rome Express. Rasputin. Ich und die Kaiserin. Der schwarze Husar. 1933: Wilhelm Tell (remake). FP.1. I Was a Spy. The Wandering Jew. 1934: Bella Donna. Jew Süss (US: Power). 1935: The Passing of the Third Floor Back. King of the Damned. 1937: Dark Journey. Under the Red Robe 1938: Tempête sur l'Asie/Storm over Asia. Joueur d'echecs (GB: The Chess Player. US: The Devil is an Empress). 1939: The Spy in Black (US: U-Boat 29). 1940: Contraband (US: Blackout). The Thief of Bagdad. Escape. 1941: A Woman's Face. Whistling in the Dark. The Men in Her Life. 1942: Nazi Agent. All Through the Night. Casablanca. 1943: Above Suspicion.

As director: *1919: Die Nacht auf Goldenhall. 1922: Lord Byron.*

VELEZ, Lupe
(Guadelupe V. De Villalobos) 1908–1944
Tiny, curvaceous, dark-haired, tempestuous Mexican actress who lived life to the full and seemingly had enough energy for a dozen of her kind. As volatile in life as on the screen – where she is best remembered from the Mexican Spitfire comedies – she was married to Johnny Weissmuller (qv) from 1933 to 1939. Committed suicide with sleeping pills.
*1927: *What Women Did for Me. The Gaucho. *Sailors, Beware! 1928: Stand and Deliver. 1929: Lady of the Pavements (GB: Lady of the Night). Wolf Song. Tiger Rose. Where East is*

East. 1930: †East is West. Hell Harbor. *Voice of Hollywood No 1. The Storm. 1931: †Resurrection. Cuban Love Song. The Squaw Man (GB: The White Man). Hombres en mi Vida. 1932: The Half-Naked Truth. The Broken Wing. Kongo. 1933: Hot Pepper. Mr Broadway. 1934: Palooka (GB: The Great Schnozzle). Hollywood Party. Laughing Boy. Strictly Dynamite. 1935: The Morals of Marcus. 1936: Gypsy Melody (US: Under Your Spell). 1937: High Flyers. La Zandunga. Mad about Money (US: He Loved an Actress). 1939: The Girl from Mexico. Mexican Spitfire. 1940: Mexican Spitfire Out West. 1941: Six Lessons from Madame La Zonga. Honolulu Lu. Mexican Spitfire's Baby. Playmates. 1942: Mexican Spitfire at Sea. Mexican Spitfire Sees a Ghost. Mexican Spitfire's Elephant. 1943: Mexican Spitfire's Blessed Event. Ladies' Day. Rehead from Manhattan. 1944: Nana.

†And Spanish version

VENABLE, Evelyn 1913–1993
Dark-haired, doll-like, demure American actress, the daughter of a college lecturer and star of some big films in the early 1930s after brief theatrical experience. But the standard of her roles fell away disastrously in the latter half of the decade and she retired from acting in 1943 to raise the five children of herself and husband Hal Mohr, an Oscar-winning cinematographer to whom she was married from 1934 to his death in 1974. She later became a teacher at UCLA. Died from cancer.
1933: Cradle Song. 1934: Death Takes a Holiday. David Harum. Double Door. Mrs Wiggs of the Cabbage Patch. 1935: The County Chairman. Alice Adams. Harmony Lane. Streamline Express. The Little Colonel. Vagabond Lady. 1936: Star for a Night. 1937: North of Nome. Happy-Go-Lucky. Racketeers in Exile. 1938: The Frontiersman. Female Fugitive. Hollywood Stadium Mystery. My Old Kentucky Home. 1939: Heritage of the Desert. The Headleys at Home. 1940: Lucky Cisco Kid. Pinocchio (voice only). 1943: He Hired the Boss.

VERA-ELLEN
(Vera-Ellen Rohe) 1920–1981
Peppy, pert, petite blonde American dancing star with cute figure, engaging smile, rosy cheeks and sexily muscular calves. Usually played the little girl from the sticks who somehow kept the wolves at bay while becoming a star. Retired too soon, even though studio publicity for years hid her real

age. Dancing from the age of 10, although one report, of a film debut in 1935 in the short Major Bowes' Amateur Theatre of the Air, remains unconfirmed. Died from cancer.
1945: Wonder Man. 1946: The Kid from Brooklyn. Three Little Girls in Blue. 1947: Carnival in Costa Rica. 1948: Words and Music. 1949: Love Happy (later Kleptomaniacs). On the Town. 1950: Three Little Words. 1951: Happy-Go-Lovely. 1952: The Belle of New York. 1953: Call Me Madam. Big Leaguer. 1954: White Christmas. 1956: Let's Be Happy.

VERSOIS, Odile
(Katiana de Poliakoff-Baidarov) 1930–1980
Gentle blonde French star, a ballet dancer-turned actress and a far cry from her sultry sister Marina Vlady (qv). Won acting awards at two festivals for her first film, and scored a big hit in Britain (where she filmed several times) in The Young Lovers. Her fragile beauty did not wear too well, and she was much beset by illness to her later years.
1947: Les dernières vacances. 1948: Fantômas contre Fantômas. 1949: Orage d'été. 1950: Francesca di Rimini. Bel amour. Les anciens de Saint-Loup. Mademoiselle Josette, ma femme. *Désordre. Into the Blue (US: The Man in the Dinghy). 1951: Domenica. 1953: A Day to Remember. 1954: The Young Lovers (US: Chance Meeting). To Paris with Love. 1955: Les insoumises. 1956: Checkpoint. 1957: Herrscher ohne Krone. 1958: Night is Not for Sleep. Passport to Shame (US: Room 43). 1959: Toi, le venin (GB and US: Nude in a White Car). 1960: La dragée haute. 1961: Le rendez-vous. Le trésor des hommes bleus. Cartouche (GB: Swords of Blood). 1962: A cause, à cause d'une femme. Transit à Saigon. 1964: Le dernier tiercé. 1968: Benjamin. 1972:

Eglantine. 1975: Stationschef Fallmerayer. 1977: Le crabe-tambour.

VICKERS, Martha
(M. MacVicar) 1925–1971
Minxish brunette American actress, a good bad girl (especially when playing sulky and spoiled) who could also sing and dance a little. Her biggest success came early – as the nymphomaniac Carmen Sternwood in the 1946 version of The Big Sleep. Marriage to Mickey Rooney (second of three) from 1949 to 1951 virtually finished her big-screen career, and she died young after a lengthy illness.
1943: †Frankenstein Meets the Wolf Man. †Hi'Ya Sailor. †Captive Wild Woman. †Top Man. 1944: †Marine Raiders. †The Mummy's Ghost. †This is the Life. †The Falcon in Mexico. 1946: The Big Sleep. The Time, the Place and the Girl. The Man I Love. 1947: That Way with Women. Love and Learn. *So You Want to be in Pictures. 1948: Ruthless. 1949: Alimony. Bad Boy. Daughter of the West. 1955: The Big Bluff. The Burglar (released 1957). 1959: Four Fast Guns.

†As Martha MacVicar

VINCENT, Jan-Michael 1944–
Fresh-faced, youthful, strongly-built, fair-haired American actor in leading roles from 1970. Despite being photogenic and personable, and continuing to star in action films, he did not quite make the big-budget film and superstar bracket. But he scored major personal successes on television in the 1980s both in the mini-series The Winds of War and the action series Airwolf. Much later seen as seedy businessmen in exploitation videos. Suffered a broken neck in a 1996 car crash.

1966: †Bandits/ Los bandidos. 1967: †Journey to Shiloh. 1969: †The Undefeated. 1970: Tribes (TV. GB: cinemas, as The Soldier Who Declared Peace). 1971: The Catcher (TV). Going Home. 1972: Sandcastles. The Mechanic (later Killer of Killers). 1973: The World's Greatest Athlete. Deliver Us from Evil (TV). 1974: Buster and Billie. 1975: Bite the Bullet. White Line Fever. Vigilante Force. 1976: Baby Blue Marine. Shadow of the Hawk. 1977: Damnation Alley. Big Wednesday. 1978: Hooper. 1979: Defiance. 1980: Hard Country. 1981: The Return. 1983: Last Plane Out. Airwolf (TV). 1987: Six Against the Rock (TV). Enemy Territory. 1988: Born in East L.A. Hit List. 1989: Deadly Embrace. Heartstone. 1990: Haunting Fear. Tarzan in Manhattan (TV). Midnight Witness. Alienator. 1991: Team 6. Xtro II. Raw Nerve. Beyond the Call of Duty. Hangfire. Divine Enforcer. 1992: Deadly Exposure. Animal Instincts. Sins of Desire. In Gold We Trust. 1993: Indecent Behavior. Deadly Heroes. Rage. Extreme. Ipi Tombi. 1994: Singapore Sling (TV). The Ice Cream Man. The Silencer. Abducted II: The Reunion. 1995: Redline. Vital Contact. 1996: Russian Roulette. Lethal Orbit (GB: Orbit). 1997: Body Count. 1998: No Rest for the Wicked. Buffalo 66. 1999: White Boy. 2000: Escape to Grizzly Mountain. The Thundering 8th.

†As Michael Vincent

My Way to the Crusades, I Met a Girl Who . . . / A Funny Thing Happened on the Way to the Crusades). Ti ho sposata per allegria (US: I Married You for Fun). 1968: La femme écarlate. Le ragazza con la pistola. 1969: Amore mio, aiutami (US: Help Me, Darling). Vedo nudo. 1970: Le coppie/ The Couples. Nini Tirabuscio, la donna che inventò la mossa. Dramma della gelosia (GB: Jealousy Italian Style. US: The Pizza Triangle). 1971: La pacifista. Lei. La supertestimone. Noi donne siamo fate cosi. 1972: Gli ordini sono ordini. Teresa la ladra. 1973: Tosca. 1974: The Phantom of Liberté. Polvere di Stelle. 1975: Qui comincia l'avventura (US: Lucky Girls). A mezzanotte va la ronda del piacere (GB and US: Midnight Pleasures). Canard à l'orange/ L'antra all'arancia. 1976: Mimi Bluette. La goduria. Basta che non si sappia in giro. 1977: L'altra meta del cielo. 1978: La raison d'état. Amori miei/ My Loves. Per vivere meglio/ The Good Life. 1979: The Mystery of Krantz. An Almost Perfect Affair. Take Two. Letti selvaggi/ Tigers in Lipstick (released 1985). 1980: The Mystery of Oberwald. Camera d'albergo. 1981: Appuntamento d'amore. Tango della gelosia. 1982: Infedelmente tua. I Know That You Know That I Know. Scusa se e poco. 1983: Flirt. When Veronica Calls. Trenta minuti d'amore. 1986: Francesco e mia. 1989: †Scandalo secreto.

†And directed

VITTI, Monica (Maria Ceciarelli) 1931–
Wispily delicate blonde Italian actress, at her haunting best in films by Antonioni, four in all. Subsequent international ventures leaned too heavily on her physical attractions and alleged gift for comedy and were less than successful. She continued, however, to prosper in Italian films and even tried direction.
1955: Ridere, ridere, ridere. Adriana Lecouvreur. 1956: Una pelliccia di visone. 1957: Il grido/ The Cry (voice only). 1958: Le dritte (US: Smart Girls). 1960: L'avventura. La notte. 1962: L'eclisse (GB: and US: Eclipse). 1963: Les quatres vérités (GB and US: Three Fables of Love). Château en Suède (US: Naughty, Nutty Chateau). Dragées au poivre (GB: Sweet and Sour). 1964: The Red Desert. Alta infedeltà (GB and US: High Infidelty). Il disco volante. Le bambole (GB: Four Kinds of Love. US: The Dolls). 1966: Le fate (GB: Sex Quartet. US: The Queens). Modesty Blaise. Fai in fretta ad uccidermi . . . ho freddo! 1967: The Chastity Belt (US:

VLADY, Marina
(M. de Poliakoff-Baidarov) 1937–
Seemingly doomed throughout her career to playing tawny temptresses, this light-haired French actress of brooding nature, sister of Odile Versois (qv), was a sex-kitten (of a more tigerish variety) second only to Bardot, after tremendous international impact in *The Wicked Go To Hell*. Her name continued to have marquee value outside the continent, although she never really made an international career. She did, however, develop into a stronger actress than many of her contemporaries. Married/divorced French actor Robert Hossein (R. Hosseinoff. 1927–). Became very busy again in movie roles in the mid 1980s.
1949: Orage d'été. Due sorelle amano. 1952: Franciulle di lusso (GB: and US: Luxury Girls). Grand gala. Penne nere. Le infedeli. La figlia del diavolo. 1953: Canzoni, canzoni, canzoni (US: Cavalcade of Song). L'âge de l'amour. Avant le déluge. Des gosses de riches.

L'età dell'amore. 1954: Le avventure di Giacomo Casanova/ Casanova (GB: The Adventures of Casanova. US: Sins of Casanova). Le crâneur. Mosoduro. Giorno d'amore. Sinfonia d'amore – Schubert. 1955: Les salauds vont en enfer (GB and US: The Wicked Go to Hell). Sie/ Her. Sophie et le crime (US: The Girl on the Third Floor). La sorcière (GB and US: The Sorceress). 1956: Crime and Punishment. Pardonnez nos offences. 1957: Symphonie inachevée. La liberté surveillée. 1959: Toi, le venin (GB and US: Nude in a White Car). La sentence. La nuit des espions (US: Night Encounter). Les canailles. 1960: La fille dans la vitrine. La princesse de Clèves. 1961: Adorable menteuse. La steppa. Les sept péchés capitaux (GB: The Seven Deadly Sins. US: Seven Capital Sins). 1962: Climatis (US: Climates of Love). La cage. Le meutrier (GB and US: Enough Rope). 1963: Les bonnes causes (GB: and US: Don't Tempt the Devil). Dragées au poivre (GB and US: Sweet and Sour). Ape Regina (GB: Queen Bee. US: The Conjugal Bed). 1965: On a volé La Joconde. Run for Your Wife. 1966: Chimes at Midnight (US: Falstaff). Mona, pour une étoile sans nom. A tout coeur à Tokyo pour OSS 117 (GB and US: Terror in Tokyo). 1967: Deux ou trois choses que je sais d'elle/ One or Two Things I Know About Her. 1968: Le temps à vivre. 1969: Sirokko (GB: Winter Sirocco. US: Winter Wind). Siuzhet dlya nebolshova rass kaza (US: Theme for a Short Story). Le temps des loups (US: The Last Shot). 1970: La nuit Bulgare. Contestazione generale. Sapho/ Sappho/ Sex is My Game. 1972: Tout le monde il est beau, tout le monde il est gentil. 1973: Le complot. 1974: Que le fête commence (US: Let Joy Reign Supreme). 1975: Sept morts sur ordonnance. 1977: Ok ketten (GB: and US: The Two of Them). The Bermuda Traingle. 1978: The Thief of Baghdad (TV. GB: cinemas). 1979: Il malato immaginario (US: The Hypochondriac). 1980: L'oeil du maître. 1981: Les jeux de la comtesse Dolingen de Gratz/ Styrie. L'ogre de Barbarie. 1982: Duo sur canapé. 1985: Tangos – l'exil de Gardel. Bordello. 1986: An Island. Il sapore del grano (US: The Flavor of Corn). Boogie Woogie. Twist Again à Moscou. Laughter in the Dark. Una casa in bilico (US: Tottering Lives). 1987: Les exploits d'un jeune Don Juan. 1988: Migrations. Splendor. Notes pour Debussy. 1989: Follow Me. 1991: Mountain of Diamonds. Kodayu. 1995: Le fils de Gascogne. 1996: Animos stin poli (US: Wind Over the City). Veter nad gorodom.

VOIGHT, Jon 1938–
Fair-haired, flush-cheeked, tall, boyish-looking American leading man of Czech descent who, after early struggles, broke through to stardom in *Midnight Cowboy*. After that he chose his roles carefully, with the accent on painful realism, both mental and physical. He maintained his major stardom for almost two decades thereafter, despite an output that was never more than meagre. Academy Award for *Coming Home*; further nominations for *Midnight Cowboy* and *Runaway Train*. In 1995, he both reappeared in featured roles after an absence of some years on stage, and tried his hand at directing a TV movie. Married (first of two) actress

Lauri Peters. The actress Angelina Jolie (*qv*) is his daughter.
1967: *The Hour of the Gun.* 1968: *Fearless Frank (completed 1964).* 1969: *Out Of It. Midnight Cowboy.* 1970: *Catch 22. The Revolutionary. The All American Boy (released 1973).* 1972: *Deliverance.* 1974: *The Odessa File. Conrack.* 1975: *The Judge and His Hangman (US: End of the Game. later: Deception).* 1978: *Coming Home. The Champ.* 1980: *Lookin' to Get Out.* 1982: *Table for Five.* 1985: *Runaway Train.* 1986: *Desert Bloom.* 1990: *Eternity.* 1991: *Chernobyl: The Final Warning (TV).* 1992: *The Last of His Tribe.* 1995: *Heat. Convict Cowboy (TV). The Tin Soldier (TV).* 1996: *Rosewood. Mission: Impossible. Anaconda.* 1997: *Boys Will Be Boys (TV). John Grisham's The Rainmaker. Most Wanted. U-Turn/Stray Dogs.* 1998: *Enemy of the State. The General.* 1999: *Varsity Blues.* 2000: *A Dog of Flanders. Second String (TV).* 2001: *Pearl Habor.*

As director: 1995: *The Tin Soldier (TV).*

VON STROHEIM, Erich
(Hans E.S. von Nordenwall, or E. Oswald Stronheim) 1885–1957
Egocentric Austrian actor and director with a death's head countenance and aristocratic manner, qualifying him for villainous ladies' men. As a director he proved impossibly extravagant, a quality which led to several projects being taken out of his hands by studios, and the eventual cessation of his directing career. Acting in sound films, he built up a new reputation as 'The Man You Love to Hate'. Oscar-nominated as an actor for *Sunset Boulevard.* Died from a spinal ailment.
1914: *Captain McLean.* 1915: *The Birth of a Nation. Old Heidelberg. A Bold Impersonation. The Failure. Ghosts.* 1916: *Intolerance. His Picture in the Papers. Macbeth. The Social Secretary. Less than the Dust.* 1917: *For France. Reaching for the Moon. In Again, Out Again. Sylvia of the Secret Service. Panthea.* 1918: *Hearts of the World. Hearts of Humanity. The Unbeliever. The Hun Within (GB: The Peril Within).* 1919: *Blind Husbands.* 1921: *Foolish Wives.* 1928: *The Wedding March.* 1929: *The Great Gabbo.* 1930: *Three Faces East.* 1931: *Friends and Lovers.* 1932: *The Lost Squadron. As You Desire Me.* 1934: *Crimson Romance. House of Strangers. The Fugitive Road.* 1935: *The Crime of Dr Crespi.* 1936: *Marthe Richard au service de la France.* 1937: *Mademoiselle docteur. La grande illusion. Between Two Women. Les pirates due rail. L'alibi.* 1938: *L'affaire Lafarge. Les disparus de Saint-Agil (US: Boys' School). Gibraltar.* 1939: *Tempête sur Paris/Thunder over Paris. Derrière la façade. Rappel immédiat/Instant Recall. Macao – l'enfer du jeu (GB: and US: Gambling Hell). Paris-New York. Pièges (US: Personal Column). Le monde tremblera.* 1940: *I Was an Adventuress. Ultimatum.* 1941: *So Ends Our Night.* 1943: *Storm over Lisbon. Five Graves to Cairo. North Star.* 1944: *Armored Attack. The Lady and the Monster (GB: The Lady and the Doctor). 32 Rue de Montmartre.* 1945: *Scotland Yard Investigator. The Great Flamarion.* 1946: *The Mask of Diijon. La foire aux chimères (GB: The Fair Angel. US: The Devil and the Angel). On ne meurt pas comme ça. La danse de mort.* 1948: *Le signal rouge.* 1949: *Portrait d'un assassin. Le diable et l'ange.* 1950: *Sunset Boulevard.* 1952: *La maison du crime. Altraune.* 1953: *Alert au sud. L'envers du paradis. Minuit – Quai de Bercy.* 1954: *Napoléon. Série noire.* 1955: *La modone des sleepings.* 1956: *L'homme aux cent visages/Man of 100 Faces.*

As director: 1919: *Blind Husbands.* 1920: *The Devil's Pass Key.* 1921: *Foolish Wives.* 1923: *†Merry-Go-Round.* 1924: *†Greed.* 1925: *The Merry Widow.* 1928: *The Wedding March. †Marriage du prince. †Queen Kelly.* 1933: *†Hello Sister/Walking Down Broadway.*

†Taken out of director's hands before issue of release print

VON SYDOW, Max
(Carl Von Sydow) 1929–
Tall, blonde Swedish actor of austere countenance, ideal for the gloom of Ingmar Bergman's films (he has been in 10 to date) and seized on as an international utility player from the mid-sixties, in which capacity his sombre expression and tones – although initially seen as Christ, and as the missionary in *Hawaii* (his best English-speaking performance) – have mostly loomed up as double agents and master spies. Oscar nominee for *Pelle the Conqueror.*
1949: *Bara en Mor.* 1951: *Miss Julie.* 1953: *Ingen Mans Kvinna.* 1956: *Rätten att Älska.* 1957: *Det Sjunde Inseglet (GB: and US: the Seventh Seal). Prästen I Uddarbo. Smultronstället (GB and US: Wild Strawberries).* 1958: *Nära Livet (GB: So close to Life. US: Brink of Life). Spion 503. Ansiktet (GB and US: The Face).* 1960: *Jungfrukällen (GB and US: The Virgin Spring). Bröllopsdagen.* 1961: *Såsom I en Spegel (GB and US: Through a Glass Darkly).* 1962: *Nils Holgeressons Underbara Resa. Älskarinnen. Nattvardsgästerna (GB and US: Winter Light).* 1965: *4 × 4/ Uppehåll i Myrlandet. The Greatest Story Ever Told. The Reward.* 1966: *Hawaii. The Quiller Memorandum.* 1968: *Vargtimmen (GB and US: Hour of the Wolf). Här Här Du Ditt Liv (GB: Here is Your Life). Svarta Palmkronor. Skammen (GB and US: The Shame)).* 1969: *Made in Sweden. A Passion/En Passion (US: The Passion of Anna). The Kremlin Letter.* 1971: *The Night Visitor. The Touch. The Emigrants. Äppelkriget. I hasbandet.* 1972: *Embassy. The New Land.* 1973: *The Exorcist.* 1974: *Steppenwolf. Äägget är löst (GB: Egg! Egg! A Hardboiled Story).* 1975: *Foxtrot (later The Other Side of Paradise). Illustrious Corpses. Three Days of the Condor. The Ultimate Warrior. Cuore di cane.* 1976: *Voyage of the Damned.* 1977: *Le désert des Tartares. Exorcist II: The Heretic. March or Die. La signora della orrori (US: Black Journal).* 1978: *Brass Target. Gran bolitto.* 1979: *Hurricane. Deathwatch/Le mort en direct. Footloose/Venetian Lies.* 1980: *Flash Gordon.* 1981: *Flight of the Eagle. Escape to Victory (US: Victory). Coñan the Barbarian.* 1982: *Target Eagle. She Dances Alone.* 1983: *Strange Brew. Never Say Never Again. Cercel es passions. Dreamscape.* 1984: *Dune. Samson and Delilah (TV).* 1985: *Kojak: The Belarus File (TV). Il pentito. Code Name: Emerald.* 1986: *The Second Victory. Duet for One. Hannah and Her Sisters. Oviri (US: The Wolf at the Door).* 1987: *Pelle Erobreren/Pelle the Conqueror.* 1989: *Cellini: A Violent Life. Red King, White Knight (TV).* 1990: *Dr Grassler. Father. Until the End of the World. Awakenings. The Bachelor.* 1991: *A Kiss Before Dying. Hiroshima: Out of the Ashes (TV). Europa (narrator only). The Ox.* 1992: *A Dog of Flanders. The Silent Touch. Den goda viljan (GB and US: The Best Intentions). Zentropa.* 1993: *Needful Things. Time is Money. Morfars resa (US: Grandfather's Journey). The Last Good Time.* 1994: *A Che punto e la notte. Radetzky March.* 1995: *Judge Dredd. Citizen X (TV).* 1996: *Depth Solitude. Jerusalem.* 1997: *Hostile Witness (TV). Private Confessions.* 1998: *What Dreams May Come. Their Frozen Dream (doc. Narrator only).* 1999: *Snow Falling on Cedars.* 2000: *I Can't Sleep. Druids/Vercingetorix.*

As director: 1988: *Katinka.*

W

WAGNER Robert 1928–
Boyish, cherubically handsome, dark-haired American actor, a good bet at the box-office for Fox in the fifties, when he was one of the prime targets for teenage fanmail. He tried to improve his range after 1960, but the end product did not always match his ambition, and he wisely became one of the first big stars to move positively into TV, where he has exuded bland masculinity for the last 30 years. Married to Natalie Wood (*qv*) 1957–1963; remarried her 1972, with another marriage in between. Widowed in 1981. Married Jill St John (*qv*) in 1990.
1950: The Happy Years, Halls of Montezuma. 1951: Let's Make It Legal. The Frogmen. 1952: With a Song in My Heart. What Price Glory? Stars and Stripes Forever (GB: Marching Along). 1953: Titanic. The Silver Whip. Beneath the 12-Mile Reef. 1954: Prince Valiant. Broken Lance. 1955: White Feather. The Ox-Bow Incident (TV. GB: cinemas). 1956: A Kiss before Dying. Gun in His Hand (TV. GB: cinemas). The Mountain. Between Heaven and Hell. 1957: The True Story of Jesse James (GB: The James Brothers). Stopover Tokyo. 1958: The Hunters. Mardi Gras. In Love and War. 1959: Say One for Me. 1960: All the Fine Young Cannibals. 1961: Sail a Crooked Ship. 1962: The Longest Day. The War Lover. The Condemned of Altona. 1963: The Pink Panther. 1966: How I Spent My Summer Vacation. (TV. GB: cinemas, as Deadly Roulette). Harper (GB: The Moving Target). 1967: The Magnificent Thief (TV). Banning. 1968: Don't Just Stand There. The Biggest Bundle of Them All. 1969: Winning. 1971: City Beneath the Sea (TV. GB:

cinemas, as One Hour to Doomsday). Killer by Night (TV). The Cable Car Mystery (TV. GB: Crosscurrent). Madame Sin (TV. GB: Cinemas). 1972: The Street of San Francisco (TV). 1973: The Affair (TV. GB: Cinemas). 1974: The Towering Inferno. The Abduction of St Anne (TV). 1975: Switch (TV). 1976: Death at Love House (TV). Midway (GB: Death of Midway). 1978: The Critical List (TV). 1979: The Concorde – Airport '79 (GB: Airport '80 . . . the Concorde). Hart to Hart (TV). 1983: Curse of the Pink Panther. I Am the Cheese. 1984: To Catch a King (TV). 1985: Lime Street (TV). 1986: There Must Be a Pony (TV). 1987: Love Amongst Thieves (TV). 1988: Indiscreet (TV). 1990: This Gun for Hire (TV). 1991: False Arrest (TV). Delirious P.S.I. LUV U (TV). 1992: The Player. 1993: Deep Trouble (cable TV). Dragon: The Bruce Lee Story. Hart to Hart Returns (TV). 1994: Parallel Lives (TV). Hart to Hart: Home is Where the Hart Is (TV). Hart to Hart: Crimes of the Hart (TV). Hart to Hart: Old Friends Never Die (TV). 1995: Hart to Hart: Two Harts in ¾ Time (TV). Hart to Hart: Secrets of the Hart (TV). 1996: Hart to Hart: Till Death Us Do Hart (TV). Hart to Hart: Harts in High Season (TV). 1997: Something to Believe In. Austin Powers: International Man of Mystery. Overdrive (TV). 1998: Wild Things. 1999: Crazy in Alabama. Fatal Error (TV). Austin Powers: The Spy Who Shagged Me. Play It to the Bone. The Kidnapping of Chris Burden. 2000: No Vacancy. Ties That Bind – A Chicago Fable. Becoming Dick (TV).

WAHLBERG, Mark 1971–
Brown-haired American actor with cheeky, boyish features. One of nine children, he was a juvenile delinquent who joined his older brother Donnie (now also an actor) in the pop group New Kids on the Block and became rap star Marky Mark. Although not very tall at 5ft 7in, his intense acting style took him quickly into leading roles. His bad boy image in the days as a music star, when he dropped his pants on stage, were soon forgotten. He has also made such unreleased short films as *Chippendale* and *Damn Van Damme*, and plans to turn one of his projects into a full-length film.
1993: The Substitute (cable TV. As Marky Mark). 1994: Renaissance Man. 1995: The Basketball Diaries. 1996: Fear. 1997: Traveller. Boogie Nights. 1998: The Big Hit. Out on My Feet. 1999: The Corruptor. Three

Kings. 2000: The Yards. The Perfect Storm. Metal God. 2001: Planet of the Apes.

WALBROOK, Anton
(Adolf A. Wohlbrück) 1900–1967
Stylish, dark-haired, moustachioed, dashing Austrian actor. From a family of circus clowns, he rose to fame in German operettas of the early thirties, but, leaving Germany in 1936, soon revealed himself to be a sound dramatic actor (notably in the British *Gaslight* and in *The Queen of Spades*) in both British and American films. He died from a heart attack.
1915: Marionetten. 1922: Mater Dolorosa. 1925: Der Fluch der bösen Tat. Das Geheimnis auf Schloss Elmshoh. 1931: Der Stolz der dreiter Kompanie. Salto Mortale. 1932: Baby. Cinq gentilhommes maudits. Drei von der Stempenstelle. Melodie der liebe. 1933: Keine Angst vor Liebe. Viktor and Viktoria. Walzerkrieg. Mond über Marokko. 1934: Die englische Heirat. Die vertauschte Barut. Eine Frau, die weiss, was sie will. Maskerade (GB: Masquerade in Vienna). Regina. 1935: Der Student von Prag/The Student of Prague. Ich war Jack Mortimer. Zigeunerbaron. 1936: Allotria. Der Kurier des Zaren. Port Arthur (and English, French and Czech versions). 1937: Victoria the Great. The Rat. The Soldier and the Lady (GB: Michael Strogoff). 1938: Sixty Glorious Years (US: Queen of Destiny). 1940: Gaslight (US: Angel Street). Dangerous Moonlight (US: Suicide Squadron). 1941: 49th Parallel. 1943: The Life and Death of Colonel Blimp (US: Colonel Blimp). 1945: The Man from Morocco. 1948: The Red Shoes. 1949: The Queen of Spades. 1950: La ronde. 1951: Wien tanzt (US: Vienna Waltz). 1953: L'affaire Maurizius (GB: On Trial). 1955: Oh Rosalinda!! Lola Montès. 1956: König für eine Nacht. 1957: St Joan. I Accuse!

WALKEN, Christopher
(Ronald Walken) 1943–
Tall, blond, handsome American actor, reminiscent of the late 1920s and early 1930s in looks, and often cast in unsmiling or tormented roles, sometimes as man on the edge of sanity, and alternating sympathetic with unsympathetic roles. He had one or two showy parts before a supporting Oscar for *The Deer Hunter* made him a star at 35, a position he has never quite consolidated, although he has continued to show up well in offbeat leading roles and unsettling top featured parts.
1968: Me and My Brother. 1971: The Anderson

Tapes. 1972: The Happiness Cage (later The Mind Snatchers). 1975: Next Stop, Greenwich Village. 1976: The Sentinel. 1977: Annie Hall. Roseland. 1978: The Deer Hunter. 1979: Last Embrace. 1980: Heaven's Gate. The Dogs of War. Shoot the Sun Down. 1981: Brainstorm (released 1983). Pennies from Heaven. Who Am I This Time? (TV). 1983: The Dead Zone. 1985: A View to a Kill. 1986: At Close Range. The Conspiracy. River of Death. War Zone. 1987: Puss in Boots. Biloxi Blues. Deadline. 1988: Via dal freddo/In from the Cold. The Milagro Beanfield War. Homeboy. 1989: Communion. King of New York. 1990: The Comfort of Strangers. 1991: McBain. Sarah Plain and Tall (TV). 1992: Batman Returns. All-American Murder. Day of Atonement/La grande pardon II. Mistress. Scam. 1993: True Romance. Skylark (TV) Sherlock Holmes vs Dracula. Wayne's World 2. 1994: A Business Affair. Search and Destroy. God's Army. Pulp Fiction. The Addiction. 1995: Romance in Time. Galatea. The Wild Side (released 1999 as Wildside). Things to Do in Denver When You're Dead. Nick of Time. 1996: Darkening. Last Man Standing/Welcome to Jericho. Celluloid. Touch. Basquiat. The Funeral. 1997: Excess Baggage. Prophecy II: Ashtown. MouseHunt. Suicide Kings. 1998: New Rose Hotel. Trance. Antz (voice only). Blast from the Past. Illuminata. 1999: Vendetta. Sleepy Hollow. Prophecy 3: The Ascent. Sarah, Plain and Tall: Winter's End (TV). 2000: Kiss Toledo Goodbye. The Opportunists.

WALKER, Clint (Norman Walker) 1927–
Big, husky, dark-haired, deep-voiced American actor, a major part of whose career was taken up by a television western series called *Cheyenne*, which ran from 1955 to 1963. In the cinema he had a few leading roles in colourful adventure dramas, and one or two interesting supporting parts that guyed his own giant he-man image.
1949: ‡*Mighty Joe Young.* 1954: †*Jungle Gents.* 1956: *The Ten Commandments. Border Showdown (TV. GB: cinemas). The Storm Raiders (TV. GB: cinemas). Julesburg (TV. GB: cinemas). The Argonauts (TV. GB: cinemas). The Outlander (TV. GB: cinemas). Decision (TV. GB: cinemas). The Last Train West (TV. GB: cinemas).* 1957: *The Travellers (TV. GB: cinemas). Fort Dobbs.* 1959: *Yellowstone Kelly.* 1961: *Gold of the Seven Saints.* 1964: *Send Me No Flowers.* 1965: *None But the Brave.* 1966: *Night of the Grizzly. Maya.* 1967: *The Dirty Dozen.* 1968: *Sam Whiskey. More Dead Than Alive.* 1969: *The Great Bank Robbery. The Phynx.* 1971: *Yuma (TV). Pancho Villa.* 1972: *Hardcase (TV). The Bounty Man (TV).* 1974: *Killdozer (TV). Scream of the Wolf (TV).* 1975: *Death Harvest.* 1976: *Baker's Hawk.* 1977: *Snowbeast (TV). The White Buffalo.* 1979: *Island of Sister Teresa/Mysterious Island of Beautiful Woman (TV).* 1982: *Hysterical.* 1983: *The Golden Viper.* 1985: *The Serpent Warriors.* 1987: *Legend of Grizzly Adams.* 1991: *The Gambler Returns: The Luck of the Draw (TV).* 1998: *Small Soldiers (voice only).*

†*As Jett Norman* ‡ *As Norman Walker*

WALKER, Robert 1914–1951
Solidly-built, brown-haired American actor with clear-cut features. The turmoil in this unhappy man's private life finally reflected itself in his roles, as he moved from sensitivity and sincerity to mania lurking beneath an over-bright surface – brilliantly effective though this was in *Strangers on a Train*. Married Jennifer Jones in 1939, but lost her to David O. Selznick by 1945; a second marriage was disastrous. There was a period in a psychiatric clinic and a conviction for drunken driving. Death came from respiratory failure after a dose of sedatives.
1939: *Dancing Co-Ed (GB: Every Other Inch a Lady). These Glamour Girls. Winter Carnival.* 1940: *Pioneer Days.* 1941: *I'll Sell My Life.* 1943: *Bataan. Madame Curie.* 1944: *See Here, Private Hargrove. Thirty Seconds over Tokyo. Since You Went Away.* 1945: *What Next, Corporal Hargrove? Her Highness and the Bellboy. The Sailor Takes a Wife. The Clock (GB: Under the Clock).* 1946: *Till the Clouds Roll By.* 1947: *The Sea of Grass. The*
Beginning or the End? Song of Love. 1948: *One Touch of Venus.* 1950: *Please Believe Me. The Skipper Surprised His Wife.* 1951: *Vengeance Valley. Strangers on a Train.* 1952: *My Son John.*

WALKER, Robert Jr 1940–
Underfed-looking, light-haired, pale-eyed American actor, son of Robert Walker (qv). After a bright start he was often seen in dreamy, moody, introspective or even mystic roles, almost always the oppressed rather than oppressor. Performed steadily on TV from 1961, but has never entered the Hollywood mainstream.
1963: *The Hook. Ceremony.* 1964: *Ensign Pulver.* 1966: *The Happening.* 1967: *The War Wagon.* 1968: *The Savage Seven. Killers Three. The Face of Eve (US Eve).* 1969: *Easy Rider. Young Billy Young. Man Without Mercy (later Gone With the West). Agilok and Blubbo.* 1970: *The Road to Salina. The Man from ORGY.* 1971: *Beware! The Blob (GB Son of Blob).* 1972: *The Spectre of Edgar Allan Poe. Prelude to Taurus.* 1973: *Hex. Don Juan, or If Don Juan Were a Woman.* 1974: *God Bless Dr Shagetz/God Damn Dr Shagetz.* 1976: *The Passover Plot.* 1978: *The Deadly Price of Paradise (TV. GB: Nightmare at Pendragon's Castle).* 1981: *Angkor (US Angkor-Cambodia Express). Olivia/Double Jeopardy. (later A Taste of Sin).* 1983: *Hambone and Hillie (GB: The Adventures of Hambone). The Devonsville Terror.* 1984: *The Jungle.* 1985: *Heated Vengeance.* 1987: *Evil Town.* 1992: *Fatal Charm (TV).*

WALLACE, Jean (J. Walasek) 1923–1990
Platinum blonde American actress of clear complexion and slinky looks. At first she

played *femmes fatales* in comedies, but later revealed herself capable of stronger and more sensitive portrayals. Stormily married (1941–1948) to Franchot Tone, then from 1951 to 1983 to Cornel Wilde (both *qv*) and from the 1950s appeared exclusively in Wilde's films. Died from a gastro-intestinal haemorrhage.

1941: Louisiana Purchase. Ziegfeld Girl. 1944: You Can't Ration Love. 1946: It Shouldn't Happen to a Dog. 1947: Blaze of Noon. 1948: When My Baby Smiles at Me. 1949: Jigsaw. The Man on the Eiffel Tower. 1950: The Good Humor Man. 1951: Native Son. 1952: Star of India. 1954: The Big Combo. 1955: Storm Fear. 1957: The Devil's Hairpin. 1958: Maracaibo. 1963: Lancelot and Guinevere (US: The Sword of Lancelot). 1967: Beach Red. 1970: No Blade of Grass.

WALLACE STONE, Dee
(Deanna Bowers) 1948–
So what was wrong with Deanna Bowers? This fair-haired, regretful-looking, slightly built American actress and dancer decided on a change of name when she branched out from TV commercials into dramatic acting. Few saw her, though, on any sort of screen, until participation in the controversial hit *The Hills Have Eyes* made her a prominent heroine of fantasy, horror and science-fiction movies for the next decade. Her profile was never high enough for top-flight stardom when that ended, but she has developed into a consummate working actress in the Vera Miles (*qv*) tradition. Billed as Dee Wallace until she married actor Christopher Stone (her co-star in *Cujo*) in 1985. He died from a heart attack in 1995.

1971: Terror in the Sky (TV). 1974: The Stepford Wives. 1977: The Hills Have Eyes. 1979: '10'. Young Love, First Love (TV). 1980: The Howling. The Secret War of Jackie's Girls (TV). A Whale for the Killing (TV). 1971: Jimmy the Kid. The Five of Me (TV). Child Bride of Short Creek (TV). 1982: E.T. The Extra Terrestrial. I Take These Men (TV). Skeezer. 1983: Cujo. Happy (TV). 1984: The Sky's No Limit (TV). 1985: Club Life (released 1987 as King of the City). Shopping Maul. Secret Admirer. Hostage Flight (TV). White Dragon/Legend of the White Horse. 1986: Critters. Shadow Play. Sin of Innocence (TV). 1987: Bushfire Moon/Miracle Down Under/Christmas Visitor. 1988: Stranger on my Land (TV). Addicted to His Love (TV). 1989: Wait 'Til Your Mother Gets Home (TV). 1990: Popcorn. Alligator II: The

Mutation. I'm Dangerous Tonight (TV). Rock-a-Doodle (voice only). 1991: Rescue Me (released 1993). P.S.I LUV U (TV). 1992: Huck and the King of Hearts. Discretion Assured (released 1994). 1993: Lightning in a Bottle. My Family Treasure. Search and Rescue (TV). Prophet of Evil: The Ervil LeBaron Story. 1994: Witness to the Execution (TV). Phoenix and the Magic Carpet. Runaway Daughters (cable TV) Cradle of Conspiracy (TV). The Skateboard Kid II/The Skateboard Kid: A Magical Moment. Temptress. 1995: He Ain't Heavy/Brothers' Destiny. Invisible Man (TV). Cops n Roberts. Lightning in a Bottle. 1996: The Frighteners. 1997: Nevada. Black Circle Boys. The Perfect Mother. Swearing Allegiance (TV). Mutual Needs. 1998: Love's Deadly Triangle: The Texas Cadet Murder (TV). Flamingo Dreams. Illusion Infinity. Bad As I Wanna Be: The Dennis Rodman Story (TV). 1999: To Love, Honor and Betray TV). Deadly Delusions. Pirates of the Plain. Invisible Mom II (TV). 2000: '18'. Killer Instinct.

WALLACH, Eli 1915–
Dark-haired, plum-nosed American actor who always looked about to say something forceful, even when he wasn't. Started sensationally in *Baby Doll* (after nearly 20 years as a stage actor), then played extrovert villains, with some nicely-played light comedy roles thrown in, sometimes opposite his wife, Anne Jackson (married 1948). The rasping voice is redolent of his native Brooklyn.

1952: Danger (TV. Available on video). 1956: Baby Doll. 1958: The Plot to Kill Stalin (TV). The Line Up. 1959: For Whom the Bells Toll (TV). Seven Thieves. 1960: A Death of Princes (TV. GB: cinemas). The Magnificent Seven. 1961: The Misfits. 1962: Hemingway's Adventures of a Young Man (GB: Adventures of a Young Man). How the West Was Won. 1963: Act One. The Victors. The Moon-Spinners. 1964: Kisses for My President. Lord Jim. 1965: Genghis Khan. 1966: The Poppy is Also a Flower (TV. GB: cinemas, as Danger Grows Wild). The Good, the Bad and the Ugly. How to Steal a Million. 1967: The Tiger Makes Out. How to Save a Marriage . . . and Ruin Your Life. 1968: Mackenna's Gold. A Lovely Way to Go. I quattro dell' Ave Maria (GB: Revenge in El Paso). 1969: The Brain. Ace High. 1970: Zigzag (GB: False Witness). The Angel Levine. The People Next Door. The Adventures of Gérard. 1971: Romance of a Horsethief. Los Guerilleros (US: Killer from

Yuma). 1973: A Cold Night's Death (TV). The Last Chance (US: Stateline Motel). 1974: Indict and Convict (TV). Crazy Joe. Cinderella Liberty. Samurai. 1975: Don't Turn the Other Cheek (completed in 1972). Attente al buffone!/Eye of the Cat. Viva la muerte . . . tua! 1976: E tanta paura. *Independence. The Domino Killings/The Domino Principle (released 1978). Nasty Habits. Twenty Shades of Pink. The Sentinel. 1977: The Deep. Winter Kills (released 1979). The Silent Flute/Circle of Iron. 1978: Girl Friends. Movie Movie. Squadra antimafia (US: Little Italy). 1979: Firepower. 1980: The Hunger. Fugitive Family (TV). 1981: The Salamander. The Wall (TV). The Pride of Jesse Hallam (TV). Skokie (TV. GB: Once They Marched Through 1,000 Towns). 1982: The Executioner's Song (TV. GB: cinemas). Alby and Elizabeth. 1984: Anatomy of an Illness (TV). Sam's Son. 1985: Our Family Honor (TV). 1986: Murder: By Reason of Insanity (TV). Tough Guys. Rocket to the Moon (TV). Something in Common (TV). 1987: Nuts. The Impossible Spy (TV). Hello Actors Studio. 1989: Terezin Diary. Rosengarten. 1990: Smoke. The Two Jakes. The Godfather Part III. 1991: Article 99. Legacy of Lies (TV). 1992: Mistress. Teamster Boss: The Jackie Presser Story (TV). Night and the City. 1994: La congiura del silenzio. 1995: Honey Sweet Love (released 1999). Two Much. 1996: The Associate. 1998: Naked City: Justice with a Bullet (TV). 1999: Uninvited. 2000: Keeping the Faith. The Bookfair Murders (TV).

WALLS, Tom 1883–1949
Bluff, dark-haired, dark-complexioned British farceur, guiding light behind London's famous Aldwych Theatre farces, most of which he transferred to the screen. During the war years he found a new career as a forceful dramatic character star.

1930: †Rookery Nook (US: One Embarrassing Night). †Canaries Sometimes Sing. On Approval. †Plunder. 1932: †Thark. †A Night Like This. †Leap Year. 1933: †Turkey Time. †Just Smith. †The Blarney Stone (US: The Blarney Kiss). †A Cuckoo in the Nest. 1934: †A Cup of Kindness. †Lady in Danger. 1935: †Fighting Stock. Me and Marlborough. †Stormy Weather. †Foreign Affaires. 1936: †Dishonour Bright. †Pot Luck. 1937: †Second Best Bed. †For Valour. 1938: †Old Iron. Strange Boarders. Crackerjack (US: Man with a Hundred Faces). 1943: Undercover (US: Underground Guerillas). They Met in the

Dark. 1944: *Halfway House. Love Story (US: A Lady Surrenders).* 1945: *Johnny Frenchman.* 1945: *This Man is Mine.* 1947: *Master of Bankdam. While I Live.* 1948: *Spring in Park Lane.* 1949: *Maytime in Mayfair. The Interrupted Journey.*

†*Also directed*

Also as director: 1930: *Tons of Money.* 1934: *Dirty Work.*

WALSH, Dermot 1924–
Handsome dark-haired Irish actor with grey streak in his hair, quickly in leading roles in the British cinema after the war, then lost to the theatre for a few years. Returned to become one of Britain's busiest B-feature leads, belted raincoat at the ready, with occasional small parts in major films. Later on television. Married to Hazel Court (*qv*) from 1949–1963; they appeared a number of times together in low-budget thrillers. Busy on the stage since 1963, where he stayed in leading roles. Actress Elisabeth Dermot-Walsh is his daughter.
1946: *Bedelia. Hungry Hill.* 1947: *Jassy. The Mark of Cain.* 1948: *My Sister and I. To the Public Danger. Third Time Lucky.* 1949: *Torment (US: Paper Gallows).* 1952: *The Frightened Man. Ghost Ship.* 1953: *Counterspy (US: Undercover Agent). The Blue Parrot. The Straw Man. The Floating Dutchman.* 1954: *The Night of the Full Moon (released 1956).* 1956: *Bond of Fear. The Hideout.* 1957: *At the Stroke of Nine. Chain of Events. A Woman of Mystery. Sea Fury. Sea of Sand.* 1959: *Crash Drive. Make Mine a Million. The Bandit of Zhobe. The Crowning Touch. The Witness.* 1960: *The Flesh and the Fiends (US: Mania). The Clock Struck Three. The Challenge. The Tell-Tale Heart. The Trunk. The Breaking Point (US: The Great Armored Car Swindle).* 1961: *Shoot to Kill. Tarnished Heroes. Out of the Shadow (US: Murder on the Campus).* 1962: *Emergency. The Cook Mikado.* 1963: *The Switch. Echo of Diana.* 1966: **Infamous Conduct.* 1983: *The Wicked Lady.* 1995: *Arabian Knight / The Thief and the Cobbler (voice only).*

WALSH, Kay 1914–
Fair-haired British leading lady with the common touch. A former dancer, she proved bright and popular in the thirties, although her career was marred by ill-health. But she has made useful contributions as a character actress. Also a writer. Married director David

Lean, later divorced.
1934: *How's Chances? Get Your Man.* 1935: *The Luck of the Irish. Smith's Wives.* 1936: *All That Glitters. If I Were Rich. The Secret of Stamboul.* 1937: *Keep Fit. The Last Adventurers.* 1938: *I See Ice. Meet Mr Penny.* 1939: *The Mind of Mr Reeder (US: The Mysterious Mr Reeder). All at Sea. Sons of the Sea. The Missing People. The Middle Watch. The Chinese Bungalow (US: Chinese Den).* 1940: *The Second Mr Bush.* 1942: *In Which We Serve.* 1944: *This Happy Breed.* 1947: *Vice Versa. The October Man.* 1948: *Oliver Twist.* 1950: *Last Holiday. Stage Fright. The Magnet.* 1951: *The Magic Box. Encore.* 1952: *Hunted (US: The Stranger in Between). Meet Me Tonight.* 1953: *Young Bess. Gilbert Harding Speaking of Murder.* 1954: *The Rainbow Jacket. Lease of Life.* 1955: *Cast a Dark Shadow.* 1956: *Now and Forever.* 1958: *The Horse's Mouth.* 1960: *Tunes of Glory.* 1961: *Greyfriars Bobby.* 1962: *Lunch Hour. Reach for Glory.* 1963: *80,000 Suspects. Dr Syn – Alias the Scarecrow.* 1964: *Circus World (GB: The Magnificent Showman). The Beauty Jungle (US: Contest Girl). Bikini Paradise.* 1965: *A Study in Terror (US: Fog). He Who Rides a Tiger.* 1966: *The Witches (US: The Devil's Own).* 1969: *Taste of Excitement. Connecting Rooms.* 1970: *The Virgin and the Gypsy. Scrooge.* 1971: *The Ruling Class.* 1982: *Night Crossing.*

WALTER, Jessica 1940–
Striking, dark-haired American leading lady, usually in strong roles. Despite one or two vividly effective performances for the cinema – notably her psychopath in *Play 'Misty' for Me* – her talents have mostly been consigned to television in less interesting roles. Married

to actor Ron Leibman.
1964: *Lilith.* 1966: *Grand Prix. The Group.* 1968: *Bye Bye Braverman.* 1969: *Number One. The Immortal (TV). Three's a Crowd (TV).* 1971: *Women in Chains (TV). The Showdown (TV). They Call It Murder (TV). Play 'Misty' For Me.* 1972: *Home for the Holidays (TV).* 1974: *Hurricane (TV).* 1976: *Having Babies (TV). Victory at Entebbe (TV. GB: cinemas). Amy Prentiss (TV).* 1977: *Black Market Baby (TV).* 1978: *Wild and Wooly (TV). Secrets of Three Hungry Wives (TV). Dr Strange (TV).* 1979: *Vampire (TV). She's Dressed to Kill (TV. GB: Someone's Killing the World's Greatest Models). Goldengirl (TV version only).* 1981: *Scruples (TV). Going Ape! Miracle on Ice (TV).* 1983: *Spring Fever.* 1984: *The Flamingo Kid.* 1985: *The Execution (TV).* 1986: *Killer in the Mirror (TV).* 1987: *Tapeheads.* 1988: *Jenny's Song.* 1992: *The Round Table (TV).* 1993: *Ghost in the Machine.* 1994: *PCU. Temptress. Leave of Absence (TV).* 1997: *Cosmic Shock / Doomsday Rock (TV). Mother Knows Best (TV).* 1998: *Slums of Beverly Hills.*

WALTERS, Julie 1950–
Bubbly, extrovert British actress and comedienne with a mass of light-brown hair who, after years as a cabaret entertainer providing faintly risqué jokes and songs with long-time partner Victoria Wood, burst upon the acting scene with her stage and film performances in *Educating Rita.* Somewhat typecast as sex-minded scatterbrains, she projects the image of someone who refuses to take life seriously. In the 1990s, she widened her range with a series of often controversial roles. Oscar nominee for *Educating Rita.*
1976: *Occupy!* 1983: *Educating Rita.* 1984: *Unfair Exchanges. She'll Be Wearing Pink Pyjamas.* 1985: *Car Trouble. Dreamchild (voice only).* 1986: *Personal Services.* 1987: *Prick Up Your Ears.* 1988: *Buster.* 1989: *Mack the Knife. Killing Dad.* 1991: *Stepping Out.* 1992: *Just Like a Woman. Clothes in the Wardrobe (TV. US: cinemas, as The Summer House).* 1993: *Wide-Eyed and Legless (TV. US: cinemas, as The Wedding Gift). Getaway.* 1994: *Rebuilding Coventry. Bambino Mio (TV). Pat and Margaret (TV). Requiem Apache (TV).* 1995: *Sister My Sister. Intimate Relations.* 1996: *Brazen Hussies (TV).* 1997: *Girls' Night.* 1998: *Titanic Town.* 2000: *Dancer (later Billy Elliot). All Forgotten.*

WARD, Fred 1942–

Stockily-built, dark, taciturn, squatly good-looking American actor, partly of Cherokee Indian descent, usually in tough roles, sometimes with a quirky vein of humour running through them. After throwing over an Air Force career to study acting, Ward roamed the world in search of decent chances. But it was a Hollywood role, as Clint Eastwood's partner in *Escape from Alcatraz*, that gave him the breakthrough. Since 1985, he has played a mixture of often offbeat leading and character parts, often as weathered men of violence.

*1971: No Available Witness. 1973: L'eta di Cosimo de' Medici (originally for TV). 1974: Descartes (originally for TV). 1979: Escape from Alcatraz. 1980: Carny. Tilt. Belle Starr (TV). 1981: Cardiac Arrest. Southern Comfort. 1982: Timerider: The Adventures of Lyle Swann. 1983: Uncommon Valor. The Right Stuff. Silkwood. Swing Shift. 1984: Secret Admirer. Uforia 84 (filmed 1980). 1985: Remo Williams: The Adventure Begins (GB: Remo: Unarmed and Dangerous). Noon Wine (TV). 1986: Florida Straits (cable TV). 1988: Saigon (GB: Off Limits). Big Business. The Prince of Pennsylvannia. 1989: Backtrack (GB: Catchfire). Miami Blues. *The Prince of Life. 1990: Henry and June. Tremors. 1991: The Dark Wind. Cast a Deadly Spell. 1992: The Player. Thunderheart. Equinox. Bob Roberts. Four Eyes and Six Guns (TV). 1993: Short Cuts. Two Small Bodies. 1994: Naked Gun 33⅓: The Final Insult. Luck, Trust & Ketchup. Un bruit qui rend fou (US: The Blue Villa). 1995: Tremors 2 / Tremors 2: Aftershock. 1966: Chain Reaction. First Do No Harm (TV). 1997: Independence. 1998: The Honest Courtesan (US: Dangerous Beauty). The Vivero Letter. 1999: The Crow III: Salvation. All the Fine Lines. Chaos Factor. 2000: Circus. Road Trip. Ropewalk.*

WARD, Rachel 1957–

Brown-haired British beauty, model and actress of aristocratic background. A classic looker somewhere between Brigitte Bardot and Elizabeth Taylor (both *qv*), she has been hampered by a limited acting talent, but nonetheless made great public impact in the early 1980s – especially in the TV series *The Thorn Birds* – and courageously attempted a series of roles whose range was often beyond her. She gave an interesting featured performance as the mad mother in *Wild Sargasso Sea*, but since then most roles have called for

her to be little more than decorative. Married to Australian actor Bryan Brown (*qv*).

1980: Nightschool (GB: Terror Eyes). 1981: Campsite Massacre / Three Blind Mice / Carnivor. Sharky's Machine. 1982: Dead Men Don't Wear Plaid. 1984: Against All Odds. 1985: Fortress (TV). 1986: The Umbrella Woman (GB and US: The Good Wife). Hotel Colonial. 1987: Hem (TV). 1989: How to Get Ahead in Advertising. 1990: After Dark, My Sweet. 1991: Best Interests. 1992: Wide Sargasso Sea. Christopher Columbus: The Discovery. Double Jeopardy (cable TV). Black Magic. 1994: The Ascent (TV). 1996: Love, Murder and Deceit (TV). 1998: Seasons of Love (TV). 2001: Children of the Night.

WARD, Simon 1941–

Boyish, diffident, fair-haired British actor who, after a few small roles, was thrust into the limelight as Winston Churchill. Not surprisingly, that proved a hard act to follow, and Ward was not exactly charismatic. But, to his credit, he continued to graft away in top supporting and minor leading roles in films until the mid-1980s. Father of actress Sophie Ward.

1968: If . . . 1969: Frankenstein Must Be Destroyed. I Start Counting. 1971: Quest for Love. Young Winston. 1973: Hitler: The Last Ten Days. The Three Musketeers: the Queen's Diamonds. Dracula (TV. GB: cinemas). 1974: All Creatures Great and Small. Deadly Strangers. The Four Musketeers: the Revenge of Milady. 1975: Valley Forge (TV). 1976: Aces High. 1977: Die Standarte / Battle Flag. Holocaust 2000 (US: The Chosen). Children of Rage. 1978: The Four Feathers (TV. GB: cinemas). Dominique. 1979: Raising Daisy Rothschild (US: TV, as The Last Giraffe).

Zulu Dawn. The Sabina. 1980: Supergirl. L'étincelle (US: Tug of Love). The Corsican Brothers (TV). 1985: Leave All Fair. 1992: Double X – The Name of the Game. Wuthering Heights. 1995: Nightshade (TV).

WARNER, David 1941–

Tall, fair-haired, raw-boned, harassed-looking British actor. After early struggles as a book salesman, he made his name in Shakespearean roles on stage, but started in mournful comedies for the cinema. Later he played men desperate in one way or another, and drifted into leading character roles. His success as Heydrich in the TV series *Holocaust* (1978) saw him cast in a succession of 'evil' roles, often in war, fantasy or horror films.

*1962: The Loneliness of the Long Distance Runner. *The King's Breakfast. 1963: Tom Jones. 1965: A King's Story (voice only). Morgan – a Suitable Case for Treatment (US: Morgan). 1966: The Deadly Affair. 1967: Work is a Four-Letter Word. 1968: A Midsummer Night's Dream. The Fixer. The Bofors Gun. 1969: The Seagull. Michael Kohlhaas. 1970: The Engagement. Perfect Friday. The Ballad of Cable Hogue. 1971: Straw Dogs. 1972: A Doll's House (Losey). From Beyond the Grave. 1974: Mr Quilp. Little Malcolm and his Struggle Against the Eunuchs. 1976: The Omen. 1977: The Disappearance. Cross of Iron. Age of Innocence. Silver Bears. Providence. 1978: The Thirty Nine Steps. 1979: S.O.S. Titanic (TV. GB: cinemas). Time After Time. Nightwing. The Concorde – Airport '79 (GB: Airport '80 . . . the Concorde). 1980: The Island. †William and Dorothy. Masada (TV. GB: cinemas in abridged version as the Antagonists). 1981: Time Bandits. The French Lieutenant's Woman. 1982: Tron. 1983: The Man with Two Brains. 1984: Charlie (TV). The Company of Wolves. A Christmas Carol (TV. GB: cinemas). 1985: Hitler's SS: Portrait of Evil (TV. GB: cinemas). 1986: Hansel and Gretel. 1987: Pulse Pounders. Desperado (TV) 1988: Mr North. Waxwork. Hanna's War. Office Party. My Best Friend is a Vampire. 1989: S.P.O.O.K.S. Keys to Freedom. Magdalene. Star Trek V: The Final Frontier. Mortal Passions. Trip Wire. 1990: Grave Secrets. The Secret Life of Ian Fleming (TV). Blue Tornado. 1991: Uncle Vanya (TV). Teenage Mutant Ninja Turtles II: The Secret of the Ooze. Drive. Star Trek VI: The Undiscovered Country. Cast a Deadly Spell. 1992: The*

Unnamable Returns. The House on Sycamore Street (TV). L'oeil qui ment. 1993: Necronomicon. Le terreur de midi/Dark at Noon. Body Bags (TV). Piccolo grande amour (US: Pretty Princess). 1994: Tryst. Taking Liberty. Quest for the Delta Knights. In the Mouth of Madness. Inner Sanctum II. The Ice Cream Man. Loving Deadly. 1995: Felony. Naked Souls. Danielle Steel's Zoya (TV). Final Equinox. 1996: The Leading Man. Beastmaster III: The Eye of Braxus. Seven Servants. Rasputin (TV). 1997: Titanic. The Lost World: Jurassic Park. Money Talks. Pooh's Grand Adventure: The Search for Christopher Robin (TV). Scream 2. 1998: The Last Leprechaun. Babe: Pig in the City (voice only). Houdini (TV). 1999: Wing Commander. Shergar. 2000: Cinderella (TV). The Code Conspiracy.

†Unreleased.

WARNER, Jack (John Waters) 1894–1981
Good-natured, square-faced, brown-haired brother of comediennes Elsie and Doris Waters, and on stage from the twenties as a monologuist and comedian (best-known catchphrase 'Mind my bike!'). Quite unexpectedly became a film character star in the immediate post-war years, portraying more successfully than anyone else the common man and, although never a romantic figure, remaining a major star of the British cinema throughout his fifties. Later popular on TV as 'the world's oldest copper' in the long running Dixon of Dock Green, based on a character he himself created in The Blue Lamp. Died from pneumonia after a stroke.
1943: The Dummy Talks. 1946: The Captive Heart. 1947: Hue and Cry. Easy Money. It Always Rains on Sunday. Holiday Camp. Dear Murderer. 1948: Against the Wind. Here Come the Huggetts. My Brother's Keeper. 1949: Vote for Huggett. Train of Events. The Huggetts Abroad. The Blue Lamp. Boys in Brown. 1951: Talk of a Million (US: You Can't Beat the Irish). Valley of Eagles. Scrooge. 1952: Emergency Call (US: Hundred Hour Hunt). Le dernier robin des bois (GB: Smugglers at the Castle. Narrator English version only). Meet Me Tonight. Those People Next Door. 1952: Albert RN (US: Break to Freedom). The Final Test. The Square Ring. 1954: Bang! You're Dead (US: Game of Danger). Forbidden Cargo. 1955: The Quatermass Xperiment (US: The Creeping Unknown). The Ladykillers. 1956: Home and Away. Now and Forever.

1958: Carve Her Name with Pride. 1962: Jigsaw. 1978: Dominique.

WARREN, Lesley Ann 1946–
Spirited, sad-faced American actress and singer with tousled brown hair. A teenage music prodigy and the youngest student in her day to be accepted at the Actors' Studio. A star on Broadway but a co-star in films, Warren has jumped too much from one medium to the other over the years for her image to settle. Apart from the films and TV movies below, she has appeared in TV mini-series, many stage musicals and even spent a year in the cult TV series Mission Impossible. Oscar nominee for Victor/Victoria, but film roles generally disappointing. Married/divorced (first of two) producer Jon Peters.
1964: Cinderella (TV). 1967: The Happiest Millionaire. 1968: The One and Only Genuine, Original Family Band. 1969: Seven in Darkness (TV). 1971: Love Hate Love (TV). 1972: The Daughters of Joshua Cabe (TV). Pickup on 101/Where the Eagle Flies (GB: Echoes of the Road). Assignment: Munich (TV). 1973: The Letters (TV). 1975: The Legend of Valentino (TV). 1976: Harry and Walter Go to New York. 1978: Betrayal (TV). 1979: Portrait of a Stripper (TV). 1981: Race for the Yankee Zephyr. 1982: Portrait of a Showgirl (TV). Victor/Victoria. 1983: A Night in Heaven. 1984: Choose Me. Songwriter. 1985: Clue. 1986: Apology for Murder (TV). A Fight for Jenny (TV). 1987: Burglar. Cop. 1988: Baja Oklahoma (TV). Blood on the Moon. 1989: Worth Winning. 1991: A Seduction in Travis County (TV). Hearts on Fire (TV). Life Stinks. Blind Judgement (TV). 1992: Pure Country. 1993: Desperate Justice (TV). A Mother's Revenge (TV). 1994: Color of Night. 1995: Joseph (TV). Bird of Prey. 1996: Natural Enemy. Going All the Way. 1997: Diary of an American Family. 1998: Love Kills. All of It. Richie Rich's Christmas Wish (V). Twin Falls Idaho. 1999: The Limey. Teaching Mrs Tingle. 2000: Trixie. Spoken in Silence. Ropewalk. 2001: The Quickie. Losing Grace.

WASHINGTON, Denzel 1954–
Authoritative New York-born star, at home in both leading and leading character roles, and perhaps the most handsome and imposing black American actor since Sidney Poitier. All the same, success did not come quickly and Washington, who thought of careers in journalism and medicine before

opting for acting, only came to national and international attention when he played for several years in the TV series St Elsewhere as Dr Chandler. The role of Steven Biko in Cry Freedom revived a meandering film career which blossomed spectacularly after a best supporting actor Oscar for his performance in Glory. He was now established in the top echelon, and won further Academy Award nominations for his title roles in Malcolm X and The Hurricane. Often plays thinking men of action beset by personal demons.
1977: †Wilma (TV). 1981: Carbon Copy. 1983: Licence to Kill (TV). 1984: A Soldier's Story. 1985: Power. 1986: The George McKenna Story (TV). 1987: Cry Freedom. 1988: For Queen and Country. 1989: The Mighty Quinn. Glory. Heart Condition. 1990: Mo' Better Blues. 1991: Mississippi Masala. Ricochet. 1992: Malcolm X. Liberators (TV). 1993: Much Ado About Nothing. Philadelphia. The Pelican Brief. 1995: Crimson Tide. Virtuosity. Devil in a Blue Dress. 1996: Courage Under Fire. The Preacher's Wife. 1997: Fallen. 1998: He Got Game. The Siege. 1999: The Hurricane. The Bone Collector. 2000: Remember the Titans. 2001: John Q.

†As Denzel Washington Jr

WASSON, Craig 1952–
Stocky American actor with homely face and fair, wavy, flowing hair, especially good at worried, desperate or small-town characters. On his way to accept a drama scholarship, he auditioned for the national touring company of Hair and landed a leading role. He never took up the scholarship, but made his Broadway debut in 1975 and started playing leading roles in films (after one bit part) from 1977.

His roles were nearly always sympathetic, often as men trapped in circumstances beyond their control. In the 1990s, he was seen more on TV, often as less pleasant characters.

1977: Rollercoaster. The Boys in Company C. Go Tell the Spartans. 1979: The Outsider. 1980: Thornwell (TV). Carny. Schizoid. 1981: Ghost Story. Skag/The Wildcatters (TV). Four Friends (GB: Georgia's Friends). 1982: Second Thoughts. 1983: The Innocents Abroad (TV). 1984: Body Double. Why Me? (TV). 1986: The Men's Club. 1987: A Nightmare on Elm Street 3: Dream Warriors. 1988: Bum Rap. 1989: The Trackers. 1991: Midnight Fear. 1993: Strapped. 1994: Trapped in Space. 1995: The Sister-in-Law. (TV). The Tomorrow Man. 1996: Harvest of Fire (TV). I Shot a Man in Vegas. 1998: Velocity Trap. Yellow Wedding. 1999: The Last Best Sunday/The Pornographer. 2000: Escape Under Pressure. The Storytellers.

WATERMAN, Denis 1948–
Pugnacious, fair-haired British actor, who started playing cheeky kids, notably television's *Just William*, then moved on to adult roles that by and large reflected his own South London background. Career seemed to be faltering in the early seventies, when he had an enormous hit with the TV series *The Sweeney*, following it with the equally successful *Minder*. Also a singer.

*1959: Night Train for Inverness. 1960: Ali and the Camel (serial. Voice only). Snowball. 1961: The Pirates of Blood River. 1962: Crooks Anonymous. 1963: Go Kart Go! 1967: Up the Junction. 1969: The Smashing Bird I Used to Know. A Promise of Bed. I Can't . . . I Can't (GB: Wedding Night). 1970: My Lover, My Son. The Scars of Dracula. 1971: Fright. Man in the Wilderness. 1972: Alice's Adventures in Wonderland. 1973: The Belstone Fox. 1976: Sweeney! 1978: Sweeney 2. 1985: Minder on The Orient Express (TV). 1986: *A Dog's Day Out. 1987: The First Kangaroos (TV). 1990: Cold Justice/Father Jim. 1996: The Wedding Vol-au-Vent/Vol-au-Vent.*

WATERSTON, Sam 1940–
Dark-haired, slightly-built, languid American actor who, like so many of his generation, only came to film prominence in his thirties. He has tackled a good range of parts, but seems to lack that inner drive that creates charisma, and his Anthony Perkins-like personality did not settle into a star niche. His Academy Award

nomination for *The Killing Fields* may have come too late to make him a box-office force, but was a welcome recognition of consistent talent, intelligently applied.

1966: †The Plastic Dome of Norma Jean. 1967: Fitzwilly (GB: Fitzwilly Strikes Back). 1969: Three. Generation (GB: A Time for Giving). 1970: Cover Me Babe. 1971: Who Killed Mary What's Her Name? 1972: Savages. 1973: A Delicate Balance. The Glass Menagerie. 1974: The Great Gatsby. Reflections of Murder (TV). Rancho de Luxe. 1976: Dandy, the All American Girl (GB: Sweet Revenge). Journey Into Fear. 1977: Coup de foudre. Capricorn One. 1978: Interiors. Eagle's Wing. 1979: Sweet William. Friendly Fire (TV). 1980: Hopscotch. Heaven's Gate. 1971: QED (TV). 1982: Games Mother Never Taught You (TV). 1983: In Defence of Kids (TV). Dempsey (TV). 1984: Finnegan Begin Again (GB: TV). The Killing Fields. 1985: Love Lives On (TV). Something in Common. Flagrant Desire. Warning Sign. 1986: Just Between Friends. Hannah and Her Sisters. The Fifth Missile (TV). 1987: The Devil's Paradise. Terrorist on Trial (TV). The Room Upstairs (TV). Swimming to Cambodia. 1988: September. 1989: Welcome Home. The French Revolution. Lantern Hill (TV). The Teddy Bear Habit. The Nightmare Years. A Walk in the Woods (TV). Crimes and Misdemeanors. 1990: Mindwalk. A Captive in the Land. 1991: The Man in the Moon. I'll Fly Away (TV). 1993: Earth and the American Dream (voice only). Serial Mom. Conduct Unbecoming: The Court Martial of Johnson Whittaker (TV). Assault at West Point (TV). 1994: David's Mother (TV). The Enemy Within. 1995: The Journey of August King. Nixon. 1996: Shadow Conspiracy. The Proprietor. 1997: Miracle at Midnight (TV). 1998: Exiled (TV). 2000: A House Divided (TV).

†Unreleased

WATSON, Emily 1967–
Tall, pretty, brown-haired, dainty-looking British actress with 'Scottish' complexion. Born in London, she made a belated film bow at 29 after years on stage with the Royal Shakespeare Company. Her debut was as a Scots lass in *Breaking the Waves* – and it won her the first of two Academy Award nominations. An additional Oscar nomination came two years later for *Hilary and Jackie*.

1996: Breaking the Waves. 1997: Metroland. The Mill on the Floss. The Boxer. 1998: Hilary

and Jackie. 1999: Cradle Will Rock. Angela's Ashes. Trixie. 2000: The Luzhin Defence. 2001: Librium.

WAYNE, David
(W.D. McMeekan) 1914–1995
Despite an oddball face, a slight build and a lack of stature, Wayne had so much talent that he almost made it as a star, after coming to Hollywood from the theatre in the late forties. Three of his performances, in *M, Tonight We Sing* and the underrated *Wait 'Til the Sun Shines, Nellie,* are among the best early fifties acting from Hollywood. But the fair-haired, close-cropped American actor slipped back into top supporting roles, and rightly judged he would be more gainfully employed in the theatre. Died from lung cancer.

1948: Portrait of Jennie (GB: Jennie). 1949: Adam's Rib. 1950: The Reformer and the Redhead. My Blue Heaven. Stella. 1951: M. Up Front. As Young As You Feel. 1952: With a Song in My Heart. O. Henry's Full House (GB: Full House). We're Not Married. Wait 'Till the Sun Shines, Nellie. 1953: Down Among the Sheltering Palms. The 'I Don't Care' Girl. Tonight We Sing. How to Marry a Millionaire. 1954: Hell and High Water. 1955: The Tender Trap. 1956: The Naked Hills. 1957: The Sad Sack. The Three Faces of Eve. 1959: The Last Angry Man. 1960: The Big Gamble. 1968: Holloway's Daughters (TV). 1970: The Andromeda Strain. The Boy Who Stole the Elephants (TV). 1971: The Catcher. King Elephant (narrator only). 1974: The Front Page. Huckleberry Finn. Return of the Big Cat. The Apple Dumpling Gang. The FBI Versus Alvin Karpis (TV). 1975: Ellery Queen (TV). 1977: In the Glitter Palace (TV).

Tubby the Tuba (TV. Voice only). 1978: Murder at the Mardi Gras (TV). The Girls in the Office (TV). The Gift of Love (TV). It's Bird, It's a Plane, It's Superman (TV). 1979: The Prize Fighter. An American Christmas Carol (TV). Lassie: The New Beginning (TV). 1984: Finders Keepers. 1987: The Survivalist. Poker Alice (TV).

WAYNE, John

(Marion Morrison) 1907–1979

Giant-sized, slow-spoken, brown-haired American star with twinkling smile, whom one could always depend upon to be himself on screen. Started as a football player turned actor and had some good leading roles in the early thirties, notably in *The Big Trial* and *Baby Face*. Slipped into low-budget and singing-cowboy westerns until rescued by *Stagecoach* in 1939, after which he rode increasingly tall in the saddle, gradually becoming an American institution, as the solitary, basically friendless, almost allegorical man of action. His last performance is possibly his best. Died from complications arising from the treatment of cancer. Academy Award for *True Grit*. Also Oscar-nominated for *Sands of Iwo Jima*.

*1926: Brown of Harvard. 1927: The Drop Kick (GB: Glitter). Mother Machree. 1928: Hangman's House. Four Sons. 1929: Salute. Words and Music. 1930: Cheer Up and Smile. Men without Women. The Big Trail. Born Reckless. Rough Romance. 1931: Arizona (GB: The Virtuous Wife). Men Are Like That. The Deceiver. *Voice of Hollywood. Girls Demand Excitement. Range Feud. Three Girls Lost. 1932: The Hurricane Express (serial). Maker of Men. *The Hollywood Handicap. Texas Cyclone. Ride Him Cowboy (GB: The Hawk). The Big Stampede. Shadow of the Eagle (serial). Two Fisted Law. Lady and Gent/The Challenger. *Station S.T.A.R. Haunted Gold. 1933: The Telegraph Trail. The Three Musketeers (serial). Central Airport. The Sagebrush Trail. The Life of Jimmy Dolan (GB: The Kid's Last Fight). The Man from Monterey. College Coach (GB: Football Coach). His Private Secretary. Baby Face. Somewhere in Sonora. Riders of Destiny. 1934: Lucky Texan. West of the Divide. Randy Rides Alone. The Trail Beyond. Blue Steel. The Man from Utah. The Star Packer. Neath Arizona Skies. 1935: Lawless Range. Texas Terror. Paradise Canyon. Westward Ho! The Lawless Frontier. Rainbow Valley. The Dawn Rider. Desert Trail. New Frontier. 1936: The Lawless*

*Nineties. King of the Pecos. The Oregon Trail. Winds of the Wasteland. The Sea Spoilers. The Lonely Trail. Conflict. 1937: California Straight Ahead. I Cover the War. Idol of the Crowds. Adventure's End. Born to the West/ Hell Town. 1938: Pals of the Saddle. Overland Stage Raiders. Red River Range. Santa Fé Stampede. 1939: The Night Riders. Three Texas Steers (GB: Danger Rides the Range). Wyoming Outlaw. Stagecoach. The New Frontier/Frontier Horizon. Allegheny Uprising (GB: The First Rebel). 1940: Dark Command. Three Faces West. Seven Sinners. The Long Voyage Home. 1941: Lady for a Night. The Shepherd of the Hills. The Lady from Louisiana. A Man Betrayed (GB: Citadel of Crime). 1942: Reunion/Reunion in France (GB: Mademoiselle France). In Old California. Pittsburgh. Reap the Wild Wind. The Spoilers. Flying Tigers. 1943: In Old Oklahoma (GB: War of the Wildcats). A Lady Takes a Chance. 1944: The Fighting Seabees. Tall in the Saddle. 1945: Flame of the Barbary Coast. They Were Expendable. Back to Bataan. Dakota. 1946: Without Reservations. Angel and the Badman. 1947: Tycoon. 1948: Wake of the Red Witch. 3 Godfathers. Red River. Fort Apache. 1949: *Hollywood Rodeo. Sands of Iwo Jima. She Wore a Yellow Ribbon. The Fighting Kentuckian. 1950: Rio Grande. *Reno's Silver Spurs Award. Jet Pilot (released 1957). 1951: Flying Leathernecks. Operation Pacific. 1952: The Quiet Man. Big Jim McLain. 1953: Island in the Sky. Trouble along the Way. Hondo. 1954: The High and the Mighty. *Hollywood Cowboy Stars. 1955: Blood Alley. The Sea Chase. 1956: The Searchers. The Conqueror. 1957: The Wings of Eagles. Legend of the Lost. I Married a Woman. 1958: The Barbarian and the Geisha. 1959: Rio Bravo. The Horse Soldiers. 1960: North to Alaska. †The Alamo. 1961: The Comancheros. Hatari! 1962: The Man Who Shot Liberty Valance. The Longest Day. How the West Was Won. 1963: Donovan's Reef. McLintock! 1964: Circus World (GB: The Magnificent Showman). 1965: In Harm's Way. The Sons of Katie Elder. The Greatest Story Ever Told. 1966: Cast a Giant Shadow. *The Artist and the American West. 1967: El Dorado. The War Wagon. 1968 ‡ The Green Berets. Hellfighters. 1969: The Undefeated. True Grit. 1970: Rio Lobo. Chisum. 1971: Big Jake. The Cowboys. No Substitute for Victory (narrator only). 1972: Cancel My Reservation. 1973: The Train Robbers. Cahill: United States Marshal (GB: Cahill). 1974: McQ. Brannigan. 1975: Rooster Cogburn. 1976: The Shootist.*

†Also directed ‡ Also co-directed.

WAYNE, Naunton (N. Davies) 1901–1970

Dapper, round-faced, Welsh-born light actor in British films, with dark, boot-polish hair and a casual way with a funny line. Most successful in company with Basil Radford (qv), with whom he was felicitously teamed in *The Lady Vanishes*. They became the archetypal cricket-loving Englishmen abroad, and made several more engaging films (and many radio serials) together before Radford's early death broke the partnership. *1932: The First Mrs Fraser. 1933: Going Gay (US: Kiss Me Goodbye). For Love of You.*

*1938: The Lady Vanishes. 1939: A Girl Must Live. 1940: Night Train to Munich (US: Night Train). Crooks' Tour. 1942: *Partners in Crime. Next of Kin. 1943: Millions Like Us. 1945: Dead of Night. 1946: A Girl in a Million. 1948: Quartet. 1949: It's Not Cricket. Passport to Pimlico. Obsession (US: The Hidden Room). Stop Press Girl. Helter Skelter. 1950: Trio. Double Confession. Highly Dangerous. Circle of Danger. 1952: Tall Headlines. Treasure Hunt. The Happy Family (US: Mr Lord Says No). 1953: The Titfield Thunderbolt. You Know What Sailors Are. 1959: Operation Bullshine. 1961: Double Bunk. Nothing Barred.*

WEAVER, Dennis (Billy D. Weaver) 1924–

Laconic, slant-faced, brown-haired, twangily-spoken American actor who, after an apprenticeship with Universal-International, mostly as villains, was involved in several hit series on TV from 1955, most notably as the limping deputy Chester in *Gunsmoke*, and the bulldozing marshal at large in city life in *McCloud*. Has also starred in some above-average TV movies.

1952: The Raiders/Riders of Vengeance. Horizons West. The Lawless Breed. 1953: The Redhead from Wyoming. Mississippi Gambler. Law and Order. Column South. It Happens Every Thursday. The Man from the Alamo. The Golden Blade. The Nebraskan. 1954: War Arrow. Dangerous Mission. Dragnet. 1955: Ten Wanted Men. The Bridges at Toko-Ri. Seven Angry Men. Chief Crazy Horse (GB: Valley of Fury). Storm Fear. 1958: Touch of Evil. The Dungeon (TV). 1960: The Gallant Hours. 1966: Duel at Diablo. Way . . . Way Out. 1967: Gentle Giant. 1968: Mission Batangas. 1970: Sledge (GB: A Man Called Sledge).

*McCloud: Who Killed Miss USA? (TV).
1971: The Great Man's Whiskers (TV). The
Forgotten Man (TV). What's the Matter with
Helen? 1972: Duel (TV. GB: cinemas).
Rolling Man (TV). Female Artillery (TV).
1973: Terror on the Beach (TV). 1977: Ishi:
The Last of His Tribe (TV). 1978: A Cry for
Justice (TV). Battered! (TV). The Islander
(TV). 1979: The Ordeal of Patty Hearst
(TV). Stone/The Killing Stone (TV). 1980:
Amber Waves (TV). The Ordeal of Dr Mudd
(TV). 1981: The Day the Loving Stopped
(TV). 1982: Cocaine: One Man's Poison
(TV). Don't Go to Sleep (TV). 1985: Going
for the Gold: The Bill Johnson Story (TV).
1986: The Best Christmas Pageant Ever (TV).
1987: Bluffing It (TV). 1988: Walking After
Midnight. Disaster at Silo 7 (TV). 1989: The
Return of Sam McCloud (TV). 1993: Earth
and the American Dream (voice only).
Greyhounds (TV). 1995: Two Bits and Pepper.
1997: Seduction in a Small Town (TV). Stolen
Women, Captured Hearts (TV). 1998: Escape
from Wildcat Canyon (TV). 2000: High Noon
(TV). The Virginian (TV).*

WEAVER, Marjorie 1913–1994
Dark-haired, apple-cheeked, round-faced,
healthy-looking American actress. A former
beauty contest winner, she modelled, went to
dancing school and became a dance-band
vocalist. She also gained acting experience in
touring companies. Although 20th Century-
Fox put her under contract for six years, they
almost never gave her the musical-oriented
roles that might have established her as a top
star. Instead she was mostly seen as the bright
heroine of minor mysteries. Died following a
stroke.
*1934: Transatlantic Merry-Go-Round. 1936:
China Clipper. Here Comes Carter (GB: The
Voice of Scandal). Gold Diggers of 1937. 1937:
This is My Affair (GB: His Affair). Life
Begins in College (GB: The Joy Parade). The
Californian (GB: Beyond the Law). Big
Business. Hot Water. Second Honeymoon.
1938: Sally, Irene and Mary. Kentucky
Moonshine (GB: Three Men and a Girl). I'll
Give a Million. Three Blind Mice. Hold That
Co-Ed (GB: Hold That Girl). 1939: Chicken
Wagon Family. Young Mr Lincoln. The
Honeymoon's Over. 1940: The Cisco Kid and
the Lady. Charlie Chan's Murder Cruise.
Murder Over New York. Shooting High.
Maryland. 1941: Michael Shayne, Private
Detective. Murder Among Friends. For
Beauty's Sake. Man at Large. 1942: The Man*

*Who Wouldn't Die. Just Off Broadway. The
Mad Martindales. 1943: Let's Face It. 1944:
You Can't Ration Love. Pardon My Rhythm.
Shadow of Suspicion. The Great Alaskan
Mystery (serial). 1945: Fashion Model. Leave
It to Blondie. 1952: We're Not Married.*

WEAVER, Sigourney
(Susan Weaver) 1949–
Energetic, lithe, tall American actress with
mass of dark-brown hair and wide-eyed,
challenging gaze. She has always looked
younger than her age, yet naturally brought a
maturity to her roles that often set her above
her fellow-players, most notably in *Alien*, in
which her forthright astronaut landed her on
the front covers of many magazines. But her
films to follow this were surprisingly less than
smash-hits and by 1986, in need of a career
boost, she was back fighting aliens in outer-
space in her old role. Niece of character actor
Doodles Weaver (Winstead Weaver, 1911–
1983). Oscar nominee for *Aliens, Gorillas in
the Mist* and *Working Girl*.
*1977: Annie Hall. 1978: Camp 708/Madman/
Tribute to a Madman. 1979: Alien. 1981:
Eyewitness (GB: The Janitor). 1982: The
Year of Living Dangerously. 1983: Deal of the
Century. 1984: Ghost Busters. 1985: Une
femme ou deux. 1986: Half Moon Street.
Aliens. 1988: Gorillas in the Mist. Working
Girl. 1989: Ghostbusters II. Helmut Newton:
Frames from the Edge. 1992: Alien 3. Blast
'Em. 1942 Conquest of Paradise. 1993: Dave.
1994: Death and the Maiden. Jeffrey. 1995:
Copycat. 1996: Snow White: A Tale of Terror
(cable TV. GB: cinemas). 1997: The Ice
Storm. Alien: Resurrection. 1999: Get Bruce!
Galaxy Quest. A Map of the World. 2000:
Company Man. 2001: The Heartbreakers.*

WEBB, Clifton
(W. Hollenbeck) 1889–1966
Tall, thin, light-haired, moustachioed American star with superior expression, a former
exhibition dancer and Broadway musical star
who came back to films in the forties, and
played punctilious, aesthetic narcissists who
hated women and children. This pose was
equally successful in drama and comedy, and
Webb became a highly-rated star with Fox for
the next 15 years, appearing in some beguiling
entertainments. Died from a heart attack.
Three times Oscar-nominated, for *Laura, The
Razor's Edge* and *Sitting Pretty*.
*1920: Polly with a Past. 1924: Let Not Man
Put Asunder. New Toys. 1925: The Heart of a*

*Siren. 1926: *Still Alarm. 1944: Laura. 1946:
The Razor's Edge. The Dark Corner. 1948:
Sitting Pretty. 1949: Mr Belvedere Goes to
College. 1950: Cheaper by the Dozen. For
Heaven's Sake. 1951: Mr Belvedere Rings the
Bell. Elopement. 1952: Dreamboat. Stars and
Stripes Forever (GB: Marching Along). 1953:
Titanic. Mr Scoutmaster. 1954: Woman's
World. Three Coins in the Fountain. 1956: The
Man Who Never Was. 1957: Boy on a Dolphin.
1959: The Remarkable Mr Pennypacker.
Holiday for Lovers. 1962: Satan Never Sleeps.*

WEBB, Jack 1920–1982
Dark-haired American actor with 'honest
Joe' face who, after a few variable supporting
roles in films, moved into TV in 1951 and
became one of the most successful of early
television stars with his series *Dragnet* and the
catchphrase: 'My name's Friday, I'm a cop'.
When later careers as film actor-director and
head of Warner TV did not open out as he
had hoped, he returned, in 1967, to a new
series of *Dragnet*. Directed his last six films.
Married (first of three) to Julie London (*qv*)
from 1945 to 1953. Died from a heart attack.
*1948: He Walked by Night. Hollow Triumph
(GB: The Scar). 1949: Appointment with
Danger. 1950: Halls of Montezuma. The Men.
Dark City. Sunset Boulevard. USS Teakettle
(later You're in the Navy Now). 1954:
Dragnet. 1955: Pete Kelly's Blues. 1957: The
DI. 1959: -30- (GB: Deadline Midnight).
1961: The Last Time I Saw Archie. 1969:
Dragnet (TV. GB: The Big Dragnet).*

WEISSMULLER, Johnny
(Janos Weissmuller) 1904–1984
Tall, powerfully-built, light-haired,
Romanian-born, American-raised Holly-

wood actor, a former Olympic swimming champion (he won five gold medals at the 1924 and 1928 games) who became the screen's best-known and longest-serving Tarzan, bringing a human touch to the jungle adventures, the earlier of which, at M-G-M, were extremely well made. When his features hardened and his waist thickened, he played another long-running character, Jungle Jim. But he suffered from poor health throughout the last decade of his life and died following a series of strokes. He married Lupe Velez (qv, third of six). Cheta (born 1931), the chimpanzee in the Tarzan films, still lives!
1929: *Glorifying the American Girl*. 1930: **Grantland Rice's Swim Shorts (series)*. 1931: **The Big Splash*. 1932: *Tarzan the Ape-Man*. 1934: *Tarzan and His Mate*. *Hollywood Party*. 1935: *Tarzan Escapes!* 1939: *Tarzan Finds a Son!* 1940: **Rodeo Dough*. 1941: *Tarzan's Secret Treasure*. 1942: *Tarzan's New York Adventure*. 1943: *Stage Door Canteen*. *Tarzan Triumphs*. *Tarzan's Desert Mystery*. 1945: *Tarzan and the Amazons*. 1946: *Swamp Fire*. *Tarzan and the Leopard Woman*. 1947: *Tarzan and the Huntress*. 1948: *Tarzan and the Mermaids*. *Jungle Jim*. 1949: **Sports Serenade*. *The Lost Tribe*. 1950: *Captive Girl*. *Mark of the Gorilla*. *Pigmy Island*. 1951: *Fury of the Congo*. *Jungle Manhunt*. 1952: *Voodoo Tiger*. *Jungle Jim in the Forbidden Land*. 1953: *Savage Mutiny*. *Valley of the Headhunters*. *Killer Ape*. 1954: *Jungle Man-Eaters*. *Cannibal Attack*. 1955: *Jungle Moon Men*. *Devil Goddess*. 1969: *The Phynx*. 1975: *Won Ton Ton, the Dog Who Saved Hollywood*.

WEISZ, Rachel 1970–
Raven-haired, kittenish, square-faced British actress of plaintive prettiness, who won best

newcomer awards for her stage work before making a starring film debut in a Hollywood action movie. She then came back home to play largely upper-class roles in largely indifferent films. Another Hollywood blockbuster, *The Mummy*, with its promises of equally profitable sequels, restored her to the 'A' list.
1995: *Death Machine*. 1996: *Stealing Beauty*. *Chain Reaction*. *Bent (released 1998)*. 1997: *Swept from the Sea/Amy Foster*. *Going All the Way*. *The Land Girls*. 1998: *I Want You*. *My Summer with Des (TV)*. 1999: *Tube Tales (TV)*. *The Mummy*. *Sunshine/The Taste of Sunshine*. 2000: *Enemy at the Gates*. 2001: *Beautiful Creatures*. *The Mummy Returns*.

WELCH, Raquel
(R. Tejada) 1940–
Chestnut-haired, open-mouthed, big-busted American actress, *the* sex symbol of the late 1960s, with a personality that was winning or irritating, according to taste. Later she showed a talent for warm comedy, but it was insufficiently exploited. Unexpectedly faded from (or turned her back on) the cinema scene in the late 1970s, even though she had more ability than her critics allowed. She proved her durability in the 1980s when she became a Broadway musical star, nightclub attraction and best-selling author of fitness courses. Mother of actress Tahnee Welch. Four times married.
1964: *Roustabout*. *A House is Not a Home*. 1965: *Do Not Disturb*. *A Swinging Summer*. 1966: *One Million Years BC*. *Fantastic Voyage*. *The Biggest Bundle of Them All*. *Le fate (GB: Sex Quartet*. *US: The Queens)*. *Shoot Loud . . . Louder, I Don't Understand*. 1967: *Fathom*. *The Oldest Profession*. *Bedazzled*. 1968: *Bandolero!* *Lady in Cement*. *100 Rifles*. 1969: *Flareup*. *The Magic Christian*. 1970: *Myra Breckinridge*. *The Beloved (GB: TV, as Sin)*. 1971: *Hannie Caulder*. 1972: *Kansas City Bomber*. *Bluebeard*. *Fuzz*. 1973: *The Last of Sheila*. *The Three Musketeers: the Queen's Diamonds*. 1974: *The Four Musketeers: the Revenge of Milady*. *The Wild Party*. 1976: *Mother, Jugs and Speed*. 1977: *The Prince and the Pauper (US: Crossed Swords)*. *L'animal*. 1979: *The Legend of Walks Far Woman (TV)*. 1987: *Right to Die (TV)*. 1988: *Scandal in a Small Town (TV)*. 1989: *Trouble in Paradise (TV)*. 1993: *Tainted Blood (TV)*. *Torchsong (TV)*. 1994: *Naked Gun 33⅓: The Final Insult*. 1998: *Chairman of the Board*. *What I Did for Love/Folle d'elle*.

WELD, Tuesday (Susan Weld) 1943–
Dark-eyed, fair-haired, baby-faced American actress, in show business from childhood (once described by Danny Kaye as '14 going on 27'), who moved from knowing blonde nymphets to the darker side of emotional disturbance. But she did not seem fashionable in the seventies and, considering the depth of which she is capable, the cinema has made remarkably little of her. An Academy Award nominee for her performance in *Looking for Mr Goodbar*, she was once married to Dudley Moore (qv), second of three husbands.
1956: *The Wrong Man*. *Rock, Rock, Rock*. 1958: *Rally 'Round the Flag, Boys!* 1959: *The Five Pennies*. 1960: *Because They're Young*. *High Time*. *Sex Kittens Go to College*. *The Private Lives of Adam and Eve*. 1961: *Return to Peyton Place*. *Wild in the Country*. 1962: *Bachelor Flat*. 1963: *Soldier in the Rain*. 1965: *I'll Take Sweden*. *The Cincinnati Kid*. 1966: *Lord Love a Duck*. 1968: *Pretty Poison*. 1970: *I Walk the Line*. 1971: *A Safe Place*. 1973: *Play It As It Lays*. 1974: *Reflections of Murder (TV)*. 1976: *F. Scott Fitzgerald in Hollywood (TV)*. 1977: *Looking for Mr Goodbar*. 1978: *Who'll Stop the Rain? (GB: Dog Soldiers)*. *A Question of Guilt (TV)*. 1980: *Serial*. *Madame X (TV)*. 1981: *Thief (later and GB: Violent Streets)*. *Mother and Daughter – The Loving War (TV)*. 1982: *Author! Author!* 1983: *Once Upon a Time in America*. *The Winter of Our Discontent (TV)*. 1984: *Scorned and Swindled (TV)*. 1986: *Circle of Violence: A Family Drama (TV)*. *Something in Common (TV)*. 1988: *Heartbreak Hotel*. 1993: *Falling Down*. 1996: *Feeling Minnesota*.

WELLER, Peter 1947–
Thin-faced American actor with pale blue eyes and fair, tousled hair. He seemed to have

missed his chances of stardom until cast at 40 in the title role of *RoboCop*, confirming his position as a leading man in mainline films in the years that followed, although his profile has been lower since 1991. The son of an Army helicopter pilot from Wisconsin, he's also an enthusiastic jazz trumpeter in his spare time. Plays figures of authority but often uncertain stability.

1979: Butch and Sundance – The Early Days. Just Tell Me What You Want. TED. 1981: Shoot the Moon. 1983: Two Kinds of Love (TV). Kentucky Woman (TV). Of Unknown Origin. 1984: Firstborn. The Adventures of Buckaroo Banzai Across the Eighth Dimension. 1985: A Killing Affair (released 1989 as My Sister's Keeper). 1986: Apology – for Murder (TV). 1987: The Tunnel. RoboCop. 1988: Shakedown (GB: Blue Jean Cop). Cat Chaser. 1989: Leviathan. 1990: Rainbow Drive. RoboCop 2. Women & Men: Stories of Seduction (TV). 1991: Naked Lunch. 1992: Road to Ruin. Sunset Grill. 1994: The New Age. The Substitute Wife (TV). 1995: Decoy. Screamers. Mighty Aphrodite. Beyond the Clouds. 1996: End of Summer (TV). 1997: Top of the World. 1998: Tower of the Firstborn (TV). 1999: Enemy of My Enemy. Falling Through. 2000: Shadow Hows. Ivansxtc. The Contaminated Man. 2001: Vlad the Impaler. As director: 1992: *Partners. 1996: Incognito. 1997: Elmore Leonard's Gold Coast (TV).

WELLES, Orson
(George O. Welles) 1915–1985
Tall, brooding, intense, dark-haired American actor-director with uniquely soft, resonant voice. Came to Hollywood after building a formidable reputation as a maverick genius with his Mercury Theatre company, and opened more than a few critical eyes with his memorably innovative *Citizen Kane*. After this, Welles proved an elusive wanderer, forever in search of another masterpiece and although there were directorial highspots, he was more impressive as an actor, lending his dominant, larger-than-life and increasingly overweight style to projects which he often seemed to mock. Academy Award 1941 for co-writing script of *Citizen Kane*. Special Oscar 1970. Collapsed and died at home after a long battle with heart trouble and diabetes. Married/divorced Rita Hayworth (*qv*), second of three.

1934: *The Hearts of Age. 1938: †Too Much Johnson. 1940: Swiss Family Robinson (narrator only). 1941: Citizen Kane. 1942:

The Magnificent Ambersons (narrator only). Journey into Fear. 1943: *Show Business at War. Jane Eyre. 1944: Follow the Boys. 1945: Tomorrow is Forever. 1946: Duel in the Sun (narrator only). The Stranger. 1947: The Lady from Shanghai. 1948: Macbeth. 1949: The Third Man. Black Magic. Price of Foxes. 1950: *Désordre. The Black Rose. 1951: Othello. *Return to Glennauscaul. 1952: Trent's Last Case. Man, Beast and Virtue. 1953: Si Versailles m'était conté. 1954: Napoléon. Trouble in the Glen. 1955: Three Cases of Murder. Confidential Report (US: Mr Arkadin). 1956: Moby Dick. 1957: Man in the Shadow (GB: Pay the Devil). 1958: The Vikings (narrator only). South Seas Adventure (narrator only). Lords of the Forest (narrator only). Touch of Evil. The Long, Hot Summer. The Roots of Heaven. 1959: Ferry to Hong Kong. High Journey (narrator only). Compulsion. Crack in the Mirror. Austerlitz (GB: The Battle of Austerlitz). 1960: The Mongols. The Tartars. David and Goliath. Masters of the Congo Jungle (narrator only). 1961: La Fayette. King of Kings (narrator only). 1962: The Trial. River of the Ocean (narrator only). RoGoPaG. 1963: The VIPs. 1964: The Finest Hours (narrator only). The Fabulous Adventures of Marco Polo (GB: Marco the Magnificent). 1965: Is Paris Burning? 1966: A Man for All Seasons. Chimes at Midnight (US: Falstaff). 1967: Casino Royale. Sailor from Gibraltar. I'll Never Forget What's-'is-Name. Oedipus the King. 1968: House of Cards. Kampf um Rom. The Immortal Story. Tepepa. 1969: Twelve Plus One/Una su tradici. The Southern Star. Kampf un Rom II. The Battle of Neretva. Start the Revolution without Me. The Kremlin Letter. Barbed Water (narrator only). 1971: La décade prodigieuse (GB and US: Ten Days' Wonder). Malpertuis. Happiness in 20 Years (narrator only). Treasure Island. A Safe Place 1972: Necromancy. Kelly Country (narrator only). 1973: F for Fake. 1974: And Then There Were None (voice only). 1975: Bugs Bunny, Superstar (narrator only). 1976: Voyage of the Damned. 1977: Hot Tomorrows (narrator only). It Happened One Christmas (TV). 1978: The Muppet Movie. Filming Othello. A Woman Called Moses (narrator only). The Late, Great Planet Earth. Future Shock (TV. And narrator). Mysterious Castles of Clay (narrator only). 1980: Never Trust an Honest Thief (later Hot Money). The Secret of Nikola Tesla. Shogun (narrator only). The Man Who Saw Tomorrow (and narrator). 1981: History of the World Part I. Butterfly. Genocide (narrator only). 1982: Slapstick (voice only. US: Slapstick of Another Kind). 1983: Where is Parsifal? 1984: Almonds and Raisins (narrator only). In Our Hands. 1986: The Transformers (voice only). 1987: Someone to Love.
As director: *1934: *The Hearts of Age (co-directed). 1938: †Too Much Johnson. 1941: Citizen Kane. 1942: The Magnificent Ambersons. Journey into Fear (co-directed). ‡It's All True. 1946: The Stranger. 1947: The Lady from Shanghai. 1948: Macbeth. 1951: Othello. 1955: Confidential Report (US: Mr Arkadin). 1958: Touch of Evil. 1962: The Trial. 1966: Chimes at Midnight (US: Falstaff). 1968: Immortal Story. The Deep (unfinished). 1973:*

F for Fake.

Welles had also been working on the unfinished film 'The Other Side of the Wind' on and off from 1975, and on the unfinished 'Don Quixote' for several years from 1955.

†unreleased ‡ Uncompleted

WELLS, Jacqueline
See BISHOP, Julie

WERNER, Oskar
(O. Bschliessmayer) 1922–1984
Baby-faced, fair-haired, blue-eyed, innocent-looking Austrian actor who always appeared years younger than his real age. Despite a memorable performance in his first Hollywood film, *Decision Before Dawn*, he did not break through to international stardom. It found him in the mix-sixties, but somehow slipped through his fingers, and he went back to the theatre. An Oscar nominee for *Ship of Fools*, he became a recluse in his later years and died from a heart attack.

1938: Geld fällt vom Himmel. 1949: The Angel with the Trumpet. 1950: Eroica. 1951: The Wonder Kid. Ruf aus dem Aether. Ein Lächeln in Sturm. Das gesothlene Jahr. Decision before Dawn. 1955: Der letzte Akt (GB: Ten Days to Die. US: The Life of Hitler). Spionage. Lola Montès. 1956: The Life of Mozart. 1961: Jules et Jim. 1965: Ship of Fools. The Spy Who Came in from the Cold. 1966: Fahrenheit 451. 1967: Interlude. 1968: The Shoes of the Fisherman. 1972: Ludwig. 1976: Voyage of the Damned.

WEST, Mae (Mary Jane West) 1892–1980
Plumply sexy, stylish, fruity and scandalous blonde American entertainer who sidled

along like a predatory costumed lobster casting her eyes (and antennae) over the men most likely to. Wrote most of her own material – a stream of clever *double-entendre* one-liners with the accent on sex – and took Hollywood by storm after successful stage excesses, proving conclusively that 'When women go wrong, men go right after 'em'. The Hays Office's censors put an end to the best of her badinage, and latter-day appearances were sadly unnecessary. Died from complications following a stroke.

1930: *An unidentified 'Screen Snapshots'. 1932: Night after Night. 1933: She Done Him Wrong. *Hollywood on Parade No. 17. I'm No Angel. 1934: Belle of the Nineties. 1935: Goin' to Town. 1936: Klondike Annie. Go West, Young Man. 1938: Every Day's a Holiday. 1940: My Little Chickadee. 1943: The Heat's On (GB: Tropicana). 1970: Myra Breckinridge. 1977: Sextette.

WHALEN, Michael
(Joseph Shovlin) 1902–1974
Genial, tall, dark-haired, well-built American leading man who came to Hollywood after becoming a well-known voice in radio drama series (occasionally he sang too). A useful second-line star with his husky charm and solid presence, he played heroes in second-features (or second fiddle to Shirley Temple). War service disrupted his career, and he was too old to regain his place in the line-up of things on his return – although there were one or two more leads in 'B' thrillers. Died from bronchial pneumonia.

1935: Professional Soldier. 1936: The Man I Marry. The Song and Dance Man. Poor Little Rich Girl. Career Woman. The Country Doctor. Sing, Baby, Sing. White Fang. 1937: The Lady Escapes. Woman Wise. Time Out for Romance. Wee Willie Winkie. Ali Baba Goes to Town. 1938: Time Out for Murder. Walking Down Broadway. Speed to Burn. Inside Story. Meridian 7 – 1212. Change of Heart. Island in the Sky. While New York Sleeps. Pardon Our Nerve. 1939: The Mysterious Miss X. They Asked For It. Outside These Walls. 1940: Ellery Queen, Master Detective. 1941: Sign of the Wolf. I'll Sell My Life. 1942: Nazi Spy Ring. Tahiti Honey. 1947: Gas House Kids in Hollywood. 1948: Blonde Ice. Shep Comes Home. Highway 13. Thunder in the Pines. 1949: Omoo Omoo (GB: The Shark God). Sky Liner. Son of a Badman. Treasure of Monte Cristo. Tough Assignment. Parole Inc. Batman and Robin (serial). 1950: Sarumba.

Everybody's Dancin'. 1951: Mask of the Dragon. According to Mrs Hoyle. Kentucky Jubilee. Fingerprints Don't Lie. GI Jane. 1952: Waco (GB: The Outlaw and the Lady). King of the Bullwhip. 1955: The Silver Star. Outlaw Treasure. The Phantom from 10,000 Leagues. 1957: She Shoulda Said No. 1958: Missile to the Moon. 1960: Elmer Gantry.

WHALLEY-KILMER, Joanne
(J. Whalley) 1964–
Dark, diminutive, darting-eyed, icily attractive British actress, often as spiteful or wayward characters. An actress on TV from the age of 12, her performances, though well received, were more often on stage until marriage to American star Val Kilmer (*qv*) in 1988 prompted a move to Hollywood. Her work here, often in inferior material, was less satisfactory, her output decreased by the birth of two sons. The marriage came to an end in 1995.

1982: †Pink Floyd The Wall. 1984: †A Christmas Carol ((TV). GB: cinemas). 1985: †Dance with a Stranger. †No Surrender. 1986: †The Good Father. 1987: †Will You Love Me Tomorrow? (TV). 1988: †Scandal. †Willow. †To Kill a Priest/Popelusko. 1989: Kill Me Again. 1990: The Big Man (US: Crossing the Line). Navy SEALS. 1991: Shattered. 1992: Storyville. 1993: The Secret Rapture. Mother's Boys. A Good Man in Africa. 1994: Trial by Jury. 1996: †Look Me in the Eye. 1997: †The Man Who Knew Too Little. 1999: †A Texas Funeral. †The Guilty. 2000: †Breathtaking. †Run the Wild Fields.

†As Joanne Whalley

WHEELER and WOOLSEY
WHEELER, Bert 1895–1968
WOOLSEY, Robert 1889–1938
American knockabout vaudeville comedy team whose slap-happy minor comedies proved popular with audiences (if not critics) in the thirties: their run was broke by Woolsey's early death from a kidney disease. He was the one who looked a bit like George Burns, and sported large spectacles and a stream of cigars. Wheeler had dark, wavy hair, a fresh face and seemingly endless teeth. He died from an emphysema.

1929: Rio Rita. 1930: The Cuckoos. Half-Shot at Sunrise. Hook, Line and Sinker. Dixiana. 1931: *Oh! Oh! Cleopatra. Cracked Nuts. Caught Plastered. Peace O'Reno. 1932: *The Stolen Jools (GB: The Slippery Pearls).

*Hollywood on Parade (B-3). Girl Crazy. Hold 'Em Jail. 1933: So This is Africa. Diplomaniacs. 1934: Hips! Hips! Hooray! Cockeyed Cavaliers. Kentucky Kernels (GB: Triple Trouble). 1935: The Nitwits. The Rainmakers. 1936: Silly Billies. Mummy's Boys. 1937: On Again, Off Again. High Flyers.
Wheeler alone: *1922: Captain Fly-by-Night. 1929: *Small Timers. *The Voice of Hollywood. 1931: Too Many Cooks. 1932: *Hollywood Handicap. 1935: *A Night at the Biltmore Bowl. 1939: Cowboy Quarterback. 1941: Las Vegas Nights (GB: The Gay City). 1950: *Innocently Guilty. 1951: *The Awful Sleuth.*
Woolsey alone: *1930: *The Voice of Hollywood (2nd series). 1931: Everything's Rosie. 1933: Hollywood on Parade (B-7).*

WHELAN, Arlene 1914–1993
Feisty red-haired American actress with demurely beautiful features, at first as appealing ingenues, but later in tougher roles, though she never lost her innate elegance. Supposedly discovered for the screen in a Hollywood beauty parlour, she had a surprisingly sporadic 20-year career which never quite gave her the breakthrough to top roles; and, strangely for a redhead, she only made two colour films. Three times married, once to actor Alex D'Arcy, she died following a stroke.

1938: Kidnapped. Gateway. Thanks for Everything. 1939: Boy Friend. Sabotage (GB: Spies at Work). Young Mr Lincoln. 1950: Young People. Charter Pilot. 1941: Charley's Aunt (GB: Charley's American Aunt). 1942: Castle in the Desert. Sundown Jim. 1943: Stage Door Canteen. 1947: Suddenly It's Spring. Ramrod. Variety Girl. The Senator Was

*Indiscreet (GB: Mr Ashton Was Indiscreet).
1948: That Wonderful Urge. 1949: Dear Wife.
1951: Passage West (GB: High Venture).
Flaming Feather. 1952: Never Wave at a
WAC (GB: The Private Wore Skirts). 1953:
San Antone. The Sun Shines Bright. 1957: The
Badge of Marshal Brennan. Women of Pitcairn
Island. Raiders of Old California.*

WHITE, Carol (Carole White) 1941–1991
Impish British child actress who grew up into
a big, busty blonde. Had some promising
ingenue roles in the early 1960s, but her
career seemed to be fading away when she
made a sensational comeback in a television
play, *Cathy Come Home*, and proved very
effective in a few more films as working-class
girls whose bodies ruled their destinies. Her
autobiography revealed a traumatically
unhappy private life, and her battles with
drink and drugs problems ended with her
death from liver failure at 49.
*1954: The Belles of St Trinian's. Doctor in the
House. A Prize of Gold. 1955: Doctor at Sea.
An Alligator Named Daisy. 1956: Moby Dick.
Around the World in 80 Days. Circus Friends.
1957: Blue Murder at St Trinian's. 1959: The
39 Steps. Web of Suspicion. Carry on Teacher.
'Beat' Girl (US: Wild for Kicks). 1960:
Surprise Package. Never Let Go. Linda. 1961:
The Man in the Back Seat. A Matter of WHO.
Village of Daughters. 1962: All Night Long.
The Boys. Gaolbreak. Bon Voyage! 1963:
Ladies Who Do. 1964: A Hard Day's Night.
1966: Slave Girls (US: Prehistoric Women).
1967: Poor Cow. I'll Never Forget What's -'is-
Name. 1968: The Fixer. 1969: Daddy's Gone
a-Hunting. 1970: The Man Who Had Power
over Women. 1971: Something Big. Dulcima.
1972: Made. 1973: Some Call It Loving.
1977: The Squeeze. 1982: Nutcracker.*

WHITE, Chrissie (Ada White) 1894–1989
Light-haired teenage actress from the early
days of the British cinema, with which, for
many years, she was the sole surviving link.
The peak of her popularity came with Alma
Taylor (qv) in the 'Tilly the Tomboy' series.
She grew into a delicately pretty star, but
disappointed her admirers by retiring in the
early 1920s, with only a couple of appearances
thereafter. Married her co-star and sometime
director, Henry Edwards (qv). Rode to the
studios on a bicycle in her early years as a star.
*1908: For the Little Lady's Sake. 1909: The
Jewel Thieves. The Little Milliner and the
Thief. The Cabman's Good Fairy. The Girl*

*Who Joined the Bushrangers. 1910: The
Sheriff's Daughter. Over the Garden Wall.
Tilly the Tomboy Goes Boating. Tilly the
Tomboy Buys Linoleum. 1911: A Sprained
Ankle. Gipsy Nan. When Tilly's Uncle Flirted.
Tilly's Party. Tilly at the Seaside. Tilly Match-
maker. Tilly and the Mormon Missionary.
Janet's Flirtation. Wealthy Brother John (US:
Our Wealthy Nephew John). Tilly and the Fire
Engine. The Greatest of These. The Reclama-
tion of Sharky. In Jest and Earnest. The
Fireman's Daughter. Tilly and the Smugglers.
1912: Love in a Laundry. Her Only Pal. A
Curate's Love Story. The Mermaid. The
Lieutenant's Bride. Tilly and the Dogs. The
Deception. Tilly Works for a Living. Her 'Mail'
Parent. A Man and a Serving Maid. Tilly in a
Boarding House. The Unmasking of Maud. A
Harlequinade Let Loose. Plot and Pash. 1913:
Held for Ransom. The Curate's Bride. The Real
Thing. At the Foot of the Scaffold. Love and a
Burglar. The Defecting Detective. Blood and
Bosh. Drake's Love Story. The Mysterious
Philanthropist. All's Fair. The Man or His
Money. Her Crowning Glory. Tilly's Breaking
Up Party. Captain Jack VC. The Dogs and the
Desperado. The Inevitable. Peter's Little Picnic.
The Promise. The Old Nuisance. Kissing Cup.
Look Before You Leap. Dr Trimball's Verdict.
The Red Light. Lt Pie's Love Story. The Gift
†The Vicar of Wakefield. For the Honour of the
House. One Fair Daughter. A Damp Deed. For
Marion's Sake. †Shadows of a Great City. For
Love of Him. †David Garrick. Deceivers Both.
†The Lady of Lyons. 1914: The Sneeze. The
Curtain. Misleading Miss. Judged by
Appearances. The Jealous Count. The Girl Who
Played the Game. Two of a Kind. The Girl
Who Lived in Straight Street. The Breaking
Point. Only a Flower Girl. Dr Fenton's Ideal. A
Knight of the Road. Rhubarb and Rascals.
Lucky Jim. Simpkins Gets the War Scare. The
Basilisk. The Unseen Witness. Wildflower. Pals.
Time the Great Healer. Getting His Own Back.
The Lie. Despised and Rejected. Tilly at the
Football Match. John Linworth's Atonement.
1915: A Losing Game. †Barnaby Rudge. The
Little Mother. The Man with the Scar.
Coward! (US: They Called Him Coward).
One Good Turn. Tilly and the Nut. Sister
Susie's Sewing Shirts for Soldiers. Phyllis and
the Foreigner. Behind the Curtain. †The
Incorruptible Crown. The Sweater. The Second
String. †The Man Who Stayed at Home. †Her
Boy. †Sweet Lavender. Wife, the Weaker
Vessel. †The Nightbirds of London. The
Recalling of John Grey. †As the Sun Went*

*Down. The Painted Lady Betty. Schoolgirl
Rebels. The Confession. Marmaduke and His
Angel. 1916: Who's Your Friend? Miggles'
Maid. Face to Face. †A Bunch of Violets. †The
White Boys. †Sowing the Wind. Partners.
Tubby's Spanish Girls. Tubby's Bungle-Oh!
Tubby's Good Work. †Comin' thro' the Rye.
†The Man Behind 'The Times'. †Carrots.
†The Eternal Triangle. †The Failure. A Grain
of Sand. The Countess of Summacount.
Lollipops and Poses. Neighbours. The Joke that
Failed. †The Blindness of Fortune. †The
Failure. †Broken Threads. †Dick Carson Wins
Through. 1918: †The Hanging Judge. The
Message. Against the Grain. Anna. Her
Savings Saved. The Poet's Windfall. What's
the Use of Grumbling? The Secret. The Refugee.
†Towards the Light. 1919: Broken in the Wars.
†His Dearest Possession. †The Kinsman.
†Possession. †The City of Beautiful Nonsense.
1920: †A Temporary Vagabond. †Aylwin.
†The Amazing Quest of Ernest Bliss. †John
Forrest Finds Himself. 1921: †The Lunatic at
Large. †Wild Heather. †The Bargain. 1922:
†Simple Simon. †Tit for Tat. 1923: †Lily of
the Alley. †Boden's Boy. †The Naked Man.
1924: †The World of Wonderful Reality. 1930:
†The Call of the Sea. 1933: †General John
Regan.*
All shorts except †features

WHITE, Pearl 1889–1938
Round-faced, resolute-looking, auburn-
haired American star, an ex-circus performer
who began as a stunt girl, then became the
queen of the silent serials, in a series of hair-
raising chapter plays, at the end of each
episode of which she would be left in some
quite inextricable predicament. Her name
survives in memory more than many of her
more distinguished contemporaries. She quit
Hollywood in the 1920s and went to live in
France, but died there of a liver ailment at 49.
*1910: The Life of Buffalo Bill. *The Missing
Bridegroom. *Tommy Gets His Sister Married.
*Her Photograph. When the World Sleeps.
*The New Magdalene. *The Hoodoo. *The
Girl from Arizona. *A Summer Flirtation.
*The Maid of Niagara. *The Yankee Girl.
*Sunshine in Poverty Row. The Woman Hater.
1911: *The Lost Necklace. *Helping Him Out.
*Angel of the Slums. *Home Sweet Home. *For
the Honor of the Name. The Power of Love.
Through the Window. *The Motor Friend.
*How Rastus Gets His Turkey. *The Stepsister.
*Love's Renunciation. *Her Little Slipper. The
Count of Monte Cristo. Memories of the Past.*

*The Reporter. *The Unforeseen Complication. *The Quarrel. *The Coward. *Honoring a Hero. *Winonah's Vengeance. *The Flaming Arrow. *For Massa's Sake. *Love Molds Labor. *A Daughter of the South. *Message of the Arrow. *The Rival Brother's Patriotism. *Gun o' Gunga Din. *Prisoner of the Mohican. *The Compact. *The Governor's Double. 1912: Mayblossom. *The Gipsy Flirt. *The Girl in the Next Room. *Her Dressmaker's Bills. *Locked Out. *His Birthday. *The Chorus Girl. *Oh Such a Night! *The Arrowmaker's Daughter. A Pair of Fools. Her Visitor. *His Wife's Stratagem. A Tangled Marriage. Bella's Beau. The Mind Cure. *Her Twin Brother. *The Bunch That Failed. *Pearl and the Burglars. *Cops is a Business. *Her Necklace. *The Book Agents. *The Manic's Desire. *The Tell Tale Brother. 1913: *Girls Will Be Boys. *The Convict's Daughter. *The Cabaret Singer. *Heroic Harold. *The Girl Reporter. *Pearl's Mistake. *Where Charity Begins. *Pearl's Hero. The Women and the Law. *Hubby's New Coat. *Hearts Entangled. *Dress Reform. *Robert's Lesson. *His Rich Uncle. *A Woman's Revenge. *A Dip into Society. *That Other Girl. *Pearl As a Detective. *Pearl and the Tramp. *Pearl and the Poet. *Oh, You Pearl! *Accident Insurance. *Her Kid Sister. *Pearl's Admirers. *With Her Rival's Help. *Strictly Business. *A Night in Town. *Who is the Goat? *Knights and Ladies. *Lovers Three. *The Drummer's Note Book. *Our Parents-in-Law. *Pearl as a Clairvoyant. The Veiled Lady. Two Lunatics. Forgetful Flossie. His Awful Daughter. When Love is Young. *A Call from Home. *Homlock Shermes. Toodleums. The New Typist. Will Power. Who is in the Box? Muchly Engaged. *An Hour of Terror. *True Chivalry. *Pearl's Dilemma. *College Chums. *The Hall Room Girls. The Broken Spell. The Paper Doll. *Starving for Love. *What Papa Got. *A Child's Influence. *Oh! You Scotch Lassie. Caught in the Act. *His Aunt Emma. That Crying Baby. Much Ado about Nothing. A Greater Influence. The Hand of Providence. Lost in the Night. Pleasing Her Husband. A News Item. Misplaced Love. His Lost Gamble. Willie's Great Scheme. A Hidden Love. The Fatal Plunge. Out of the Grove. When Duty Calls. *Pals. Daisy Wins the Day. At the Burglar's Command. Her Secretaries. Out of the Grave. *First Love. The Lifted Veil. The Soubrette. *The Heart of an Artist. Lure of the Stage. The Kitchen Mechanic. 1914: *Shadowed. The Perils of Pauline (serial). The Exploits of Elaine (serial). The Shadow of Crime. *The Ring. *Lizzie and the Ice Man. Willie's Disguise. It May Come to This. A Father's Devotion. *Oh! You Puppy. *A Grateful Outcast. *What Didn't Happen to Mary. For a Woman. *Getting Reuben Back. A Sure Cure. *McSweeney's Masterpiece *Going Some. *The Lady Doctor. *Get Out and Get Under. *A Telephone Engagement. *The Mashers. The Dancing Craze. *Easy Money. *The Girl in Pants. *Her New Hat. *What Pearl's Pearls Did. *East Lynne in Bugville. Some Collectors. Oh! You Mummy. *Detective Swift. *The Ticket of Leave Man. *The Stolen Birth Right. *The Warning. *The Phantom Thief. *The Hand of Destiny. *The House of Mystery. *Detective Craig's Coup. *A Pearl of

the Punjab. 1915: The New Exploits of Elaine (serial). The Romance of Elaine (serial). New York Lights. A Lady in Distress. Mayblossom (remake). 1916: *Annabel's Romance. Pearl of the Army (serial). The Iron Claw (serial. The King's Game. Hazel Kirke. 1917: The Fatal Ring (serial). 1918: The House of Hate (serial). 1919: The Black Secret (serial). The Lightning Raider (serial). 1920: The White Moll. Black is White. The Dark Mirror. 1921: A Virgin Paradise. Know Your Men. The Thief. Beyond Price. Tiger's Cub. The Mountain Woman. Singing River. 1922: Any Wife. The Broadway Peacock. Without Fear. 1923: Plunder (serial). 1924: Parisian Nights. 1925: Perils of Paris/Terreur (serial).

WHITELAW, Billie 1932–
Tawny, tigerish British actress, often in strongwilled roles: can play tough, sexy or friendly. A familiar radio voice from an early age, notably as 'Henry' in the long-running Norman and Henry Bones series for children, she has since made shamefully few films, and it is some mystery why she did not make the front rank. Still occasionally seen, though, in much-relished cameos. Married/divorced Peter Vaughan (P. Ohm 1923–).
1953: The Fake. 1954: Companions in Crime. The Sleeping Tiger. 1955: Room in the House. 1957: Small Hotel. Miracle in Soho. 1958: Gideon's Day (US: Gideon of Scotland Yard). Carve Her Name with Pride. 1959: Bobbikins. 1960: The Flesh and the Fiends (US: Mania). Hell is a City. Make Mine Mink. No Love for Johnnie. 1961: Mr Topaze (US: I Like Money). Payroll. 1962: The Devil's Agent. 1963: The Comedy Man. Becket. 1967: Charlie Bubbles. 1968: Dr Jekyll and Mr Hyde (TV). Twisted Nerve. 1969: The Adding Machine. Start the Revolution without Me. 1970: Gumshoe. 1972: Frenzy. 1973: Night Watch. 1976: The Omen. 1977: Leopard in the Snow. 1978: The Water Babies. 1981: A Tale of Two Cities (TV). An Unsuitable Job for a Woman. 1982: The Dark Crystal (voice only). 1983: Tangier. Slayground. 1984: Camille (TV). 1986: The Chain. Shadey. Murder Elite. 1987: Maurice. The Secret Garden (TV). 1988: The Dressmaker. 1989: Joyriders. 1990: The Krays. Duel of Hearts (TV). Lorna Doone (TV). 1991: Freddie as F.R.O.7. (voice only). A Murder of Quality (TV). 1993: Deadly Advice. 1994: Skallagrigg (TV). 1996: Jane Eyre. Breaking Free (TV). 1998: The Lost Son. The Canterbury Tales (voice only). 2000: Quills.

WHITMAN, Stuart 1926–
Black-haired, craggy-faced, disgruntled-looking American leading man who played a lot of very small roles before breaking into the big time via a Fox contract. These years at the studio (1958–1965) were his only ones as a top Hollywood star, and contain his best performances. After that he remained a regular, if somewhat immobile, second-line leading man and, latterly, veteran character star. Won an Oscar nomination for The Mark. 1951: When Worlds Collide. The Day the Earth Stood Still. 1952: Barbed Wire (GB: False News). One Minute to Zero. 1953: The All-American (GB: The Winning Way). All I Desire. The Veils of Bagdad. Appointment in Honduras. 1954: Rhapsody. Silver Lode. Brigadoon. Passion. 1955: Interrupted Melody. King of the Carnival (serial). Diane. 1956: Seven Men from Now. Crime of Passion. 1957: Bombers B-52 (GB: No Sleep Till Dawn). Johnny Trouble. Hell Bound. The Girl in Black Stockings. War Drums. Darby's Rangers (GB: The Young Invaders). 1958: Ten North Frederick. The Decks Ran Red. China Doll. 1959: These Thousand Hills. The Sound and the Fury. Hound Dog Man. 1960: Murder Inc. The Story of Ruth. 1961: The Mark. The Fiercest Heart. Francis of Assisi. The Comancheros. 1962: Convicts Four (GB: Reprieve!). The Longest Day. Le jour et l'heure. 1964: Signpost to Murder. Shock Treatment. Rio Conchos. 1965: Those Magnificent Men in Their Flying Machines. Sands of the Kalahari. 1966: An American Dream (GB: See You in Hell, Darling). 1968: The Last Escape. The Invincible Six. 1969: Sweet Hunters. Four Rode Out. The Only Way Out is Dead (US: TV. as The Man Who Wanted to Live Forever). 1970: The Man Who Died Twice (TV). 1971: City Beneath the Sea (TV. GB: cinemas, as One Hour to Doomsday). Captain Apache. Revenge! (TV). The Last Generation. Breakout. 1972: The Woman Hunter (TV). Seeta the Mountain Lion (GB: Run Cougar Run). Night of the Lepus. The Lost World of Libra. High Flying Spy (TV). The Heroes. 1973: The Cat Creature (TV). Welcome to Arrow Beach (US: Tender Flesh). 1974: Shatter (US: Call Him Mr Shatter). 1975: Las Vegas Lady. Mean Johnny Barrows. Oil: The Billion Dollar Fire. Crazy Mama. 1976: Blazing Magnum/Strange Shadows in an Empty Room. Delta Fox. Eaten Alive (GB: Death Trap). Tony Saitta/Tough Tony. 1977: The White Buffalo. Assault on Paradise (GB: Maniac.

Later on TV, as Ransom). Ruby. The Thoroughbreds/On a Dead Man's Chest (later Treasure Seekers). 1978: Go West Young Girl (TV). Woman from the Torrid Land. Run for the Roses. 1979: Guyana: The Crime of the Century. When I Am King. The Seekers (TV). 1980: Cuba Crossing. Macabra (US: Demonoid). Hostages. The Monster Club. 1981: Greed. Butterfly. Magnum Thrust. High Country Pursuit. 1982: Sweet Dirty Tony. 1983: Vultures in Paradise/Flesh and Bullets. 1984: Treasure of the Amazon/Treasure of Doom. 1985: First Strike. Deadly Intruder. Beverley Hills Cowboy Blues (TV. GB: Beverly Hills Connection). 1987: Still Watch (TV). Once Upon a Texas Train (TV). †SilverHawk. 1989: Deadly Embrace. Omega Cop. Moving Target. †Score. Deadly Reactor. 1990: Mob Boss. Ten to chi to/Heaven and Earth (narrator only). Smooth Talker. The Color of Evening (released 1994). 1991: Common Ground. True Colors. 1993: Lightning in a Bottle (TV). Private Wars. The Adventures of Brisco County Jr (TV). 1994: Improper Conduct. Trial by Jury. 1995: Land of Milk and Honey. Wounded Heart (TV). 1997: Two Weeks from Sunday. 1998: 2nd Chances. 2000: The President's Man (TV).

†Unreleased

WIDMARK, Richard 1914–
Fair-haired, pale-faced, grey-eyed American actor with distinctive metallic voice. Began his career as a teacher, and Hollywood failed to discover him until he was 32. In the late forties he played frightening urban villains, the unique product of immediate post-war times. From 1950 he cornered the market in unpopular commanders, all the way from *Halls of Montezuma* to *The Bedford Incident* in 1965. But danger always lurked behind the smile that could twist into a sneer, and his later reversion to villains was taken with obvious relish. Won an Academy Award nomination for *Kiss of Death*.
1947: Kiss of Death. 1948: Road House. The Street with No Name. Yellow Sky. 1949: Down to the Sea in Ships. Slattery's Hurricane. 1950: Night and the City. Panic in the Streets. Halls of Montezuma. No Way Out. 1951: The Frogmen. 1952: Red Skies of Mantana. Don't Bother to Knock. O. Henry's Full House (GB: Full House). My Pal Gus. *Screen Snapshots No 206. 1953: Take the High Ground. Destination Gobi. Pickup on South Street. 1954: Hell and High Water. Garden of Evil.

Broken Lance. 1955: A Prize of Gold. The Cobweb. 1956: Backlash. Run for the Sun. The Last Wagon. 1957: Saint Joan. Time Limit. 1958: The Law and Jake Wade. The Tunnel of Love. The Trap (GB: The Baited Trap). 1959: Warlock. 1960: The Alamo. 1961: The Secret Ways. Two Rode Together. Judgment at Nuremberg. 1962: How the West Was Won. *On the Highway. 1963: The Long Ships. 1964: Flight from Ashiya. Cheyenne Autumn. 1965: The Bedford Incident. 1966: Alvarez Kelly. 1967: The Way West. 1968: Madigan. A Talent for Loving. 1969: Death of a Gunfighter. 1970: The Moonshine War. Vanished (TV). 1972: Brock's Last Case (TV). When the Legends Die. 1974: Murder on the Orient Express. 1975: The Sellout. The Last Day (TV). 1976: To the Devil a Daughter. The Domino Killings/The Domino Principle (released 1978). 1977: Twilight's Last Gleaming. Rollercoaster. Coma. 1978: The Swarm. Dinero Maldito. 1979: Mr Horn (TV). Bear Island. 1980: A Whale for the Killing (TV). All God's Children (TV). 1981: National Lampoon Goes to the Movies/National Lampoon's Movie Madness (released 1983). 1982. Hanky Panky. Who Dares Wins. Lady of the Sea. 1983: Against All Odds. 1985: Blackout. 1987: A Gathering of Old Men (TV). Once Upon a Texas Train (TV). 1989: Cold Sassy Tree (TV). 1991: True Colors. 1995: Wild Bill: Hollywood Maverick.

WILBY, James 1958–
Tall, aristocratic-looking British actor (born in Burma) with fair, wavy hair. Going straight from drama school into film and theatre work, Wilby found himself cast in much the same sort of roles James Fox (qv) had been playing 30 years earlier – uppercrust characters with weaknesses that would often prove their downfall. But he could turn the weak smile into an equally weak scowl and play deceitfully nasty pieces of work.
1982: Privileged. 1985: Dutch Girls. Dream Child. 1987: Maurice. 1988: A Handful of Dust. 1989: A Summer Story. 1991: Caccia alla vedova/The Siege of Venice. 1992: Immaculate Conception. Howards End. 1994: La partie d'échecs. 1997: Regeneration. 1998: Tom's Midnight Garden. 1999: An Ideal Husband. The Dark Room (TV). Cotton Mary.

WILCOXON, Henry 1905–1984
Tall, dark, sternly handsome British leading man (born in the West Indies) who went to

America as a Broadway star in the early thirties and made occasional films there, becoming associated with Cecil B. DeMille. After war service he returned to America, and acted little after 1950, serving instead as an executive producer for DeMille. Resumed his acting career in 1965. Died from congestive heart failure.
1931: †The Perfect Lady. 1932: †Self Made Lady. †The Flying Squad. 1933: †Taxi to Paradise. †Lord of the Manor. 1934: †Princess Charming. Cleopatra. 1935: The Crusades. 1936: The Last of the Mohicans. A Woman Alone (US: Two Who Dared). The President's Mystery (GB: One for All!). 1937: Jericho (US: Dark Sands). Souls at Sea. 1938: Keep Smiling (GB: Miss Fix-It). Prison Nurse. Mysterious Mr Moto. Five of a Kind. Arizona Wildcat. If I Were King. 1939: Woman Doctor. Chasing Danger. Tarzan Finds a Son! 1940: Free, Blonde and 21. The Crooked Road. Earthbound. Mystery Sea Raider. 1941: Scotland Yard. That Hamilton Woman (GB: Lady Hamilton). The Lone Wolf Takes a Chance. The Corsican Brothers. South of Tahiti (GB: White Savage). 1942: Mrs Miniver. The Man Who Wouldn't Die. Johnny Doughboy. 1947: The Dragnet. Unconquered. 1949: A Connecticut Yankee in King Arthur's Court (GB: A Yankee in King Arthur's Court). Samson and Delilah. 1950: The Miniver Story. 1952: The Greatest Show on Earth. Scaramouche. 1956: The Ten Commandments. 1958: The Buccaneer. 1965: The War Lord. 1967: Doomsday. 1968: The Private Navy of Sergeant O'Farrell. 1971: Man in the Wilderness. The Badge or the Cross (TV). 1974: The Log of the Black Pearl (TV). The Tribe (TV). 1975: Won Ton Ton, the Dog Who Saved Hollywood. 1976: Against a Crooked Sky. Pony Express Rider. 1978: F.I.S.T. When Every Day Was the Fourth of July (TV). 1979: The Two Worlds of Jenny Logan (TV). The Man with Bogart's Face. 1980: Caddyshack. Enola Gay: The Men, the Mission, the Atomic Bomb (TV). 1981: Sweet Sixteen.

†As Harry Wilcoxon

WILDE, Cornel
(Cornelius Wilde) 1915–1989
Hungarian-born, New York-raised Hollywood star actor with very dark, curly hair, idyllically handsome in his younger days and later an intriguing director who pared subjects down to basic emotions. As he was an

Olympic fencer, it was surprising that Hollywood did not launch him as a swash-buckling star. Instead, he had to fight his way up through small parts before the fan mail convinced the film capital it had a photogenic superstar and passable leading actor. Married to Patricia Knight (1918–) from 1939 to 1951, and to Jean Wallace (*qv*) from 1951 to 1983. Received an Oscar nomination for *A Song to Remember*. Died of leukemia.

1940: The Lady with Red Hair. 1941: Right to the Heart (GB: Knockout). Kisses for Breakfast. The Perfect Snob. High Sierra. 1941: Manila Calling. Life Begins at 8:30 (GB: The Light of Heart). 1943: Wintertime. 1944: Guest in the House. 1945: A Song to Remember. A Thousand and One Nights. Leave Her to Heaven. 1946: Centennial Summer. The Bandit of Sherwood Forest. 1947: Forever Amber. The Homestretch. It Had to Be You. 1948: Road House. The Walls of Jericho. 1949: Shockproof. *Stairway for a Star. Four Day's Leave. 1950: Two Flags West. 1951: At Sword's Point (GB: Sons of the Musketeers). 1952: The Greatest Show on Earth. California Conquest. Operation Secret. 1953: Treasure of the Golden Condor. Main Street to Broadway. Saadia. Star of India. 1954: Passion. Woman's World. The Big Combo. 1955: The Scarlet Coat. Storm Fear. 1956: Hot Blood. Beyond Mombasa. 1957: The Devil's Hairpin. Omar Khayyam. 1958: Maracaibo. 1959: Edge of Eternity. 1960: Constantine the Great. 1963: Lancelot and Guinevere (US: The Sword of Lancelot). 1966: The Naked Prey. 1967: Beach Red. 1969: The Comic. 1972: Gargoyles (TV). 1975: Shark's Treasure. 1977: Behind the Iron Mask (GB: The Fifth Musketeer). 1978: The Norseman. 1983: Vultures in Paradise / Flesh and Bullets.
As director: *1955: Storm Fear. 1958: Maracaibo. 1963: Lancelot and Guinevere (US: The Sword of Lancelot). 1966: The Naked Prey. 1967: Beach Red. 1970: No Blade of Grass. 1975: Shark's Treasure. 1983: Vultures in Paradise / Flesh and Bullets.*

WILDER, Gene (Jerome Silberman) 1934–
Quirky American comedian with unruly ginger hair and beguiling personality, somewhere between Danny Kaye and Woody Allen, but with his own brand of manic panic. Once a fencing instructor, he came to prominence in the firecracker comedies of Mel Brooks, then tried his hand at directing vehicles for himself, with variable results. Oscar-nominated for *The Producers*, Wilder

married (third of four) star comedienne Gilda Radner in 1984, but she died from cancer in 1989.

1967: Bonnie and Clyde. 1968: The Producers. 1969: Start the Revolution Without Me. 1970: Quackser Fortune Has a Cousin in the Bronx. 1971: Willy Wonka and the Chocolate Factory. 1972: The Scarecrow (TV). The Trouble with People (TV). Everything You Always Wanted to Know About Sex ** But Were Afraid to Ask. 1973: Rhinoceros. 1974: The Little Prince. Thursday's Game (TV). Blazing Saddles. Young Frankenstein. 1975: †The Adventure of Sherlock Holmes' Smarter Brother. 1976: Silver Streak. 1977: †The World's Greatest Lover. 1979: The Frisco Kid. 1980: Stir Crazy. Les séducteurs / Sunday Lovers. 1982: Hanky Panky. 1984: †The Woman in Red. 1986: †Haunted Honeymoon. 1987: Grandpère. Hello Actors Studio. 1989: See No Evil, Hear No Evil. 1990: Funny About Love. 1991: Another You. 1998: Murder in a Small Town (TV). 1999: Alice in Wonderland (TV). The Lady in Question (TV).

†Also directed.

WILDING, Michael 1912–1979
Debonair brown-haired English leading man with high forehead and handsomely 'upper-class' looks. After a varied apprenticeship, he became a tremendous British box-office star opposite Anna Neagle in an immediate post-war series of elegant society romantic comedies. Made the mistake of going to Hollywood in the wake of then-wife Elizabeth Taylor (1952–1957, second of four) and looked all too embarrassed in the tosh they gave him. Did not revive his star career on his return to England. Married to

Margaret Leighton (*qv*) from 1963. Died from a brain haemorrhage following a fall.

1933: Bitter Sweet (as extra). Heads We Go (US: The Charming Deceiver). 1934: Wild Boy (as extra). 1935: Pastorale. Late Extra. 1936: Wedding Group (US: Wrath of Jealousy). 1939: There Ain't No Justice! Black Eyes. 1940: Tilly of Bloomsbury. Convoy. Sailors Don't Care. Sailors Three (US: Three Cockeyed Sailors). The Farmer's Wife. Spring Meeting. 1941: Kipps (US: The Remarkable Mr Kipps). Cottage to Let (US: Bombsight Stolen). Ships with Wings. The Big Blockade. *Mr Proudfoot Shows a Light. 1942: Secret Mission. In Which We Serve. 1943: Undercover (US: Underground Guerillas). Dear Octopus (US: The Randolph Family). 1944: English without Tears (US: Her Man Gilbey). 1946: Carnival. Piccadilly Incident. 1947: The Courtneys of Curzon Street (US: The Courtney Affair). An Ideal Husband. 1948: Spring in Park Lane. 1949: Maytime in Mayfair. Under Capricorn. 1950: Stage Fright. Into the Blue (US: The Man in the Dinghy). 1951: The Lady with a Lamp. The Law and the Lady. 1952: Derby Day (US: Four Against Fate). Trent's Last Case. 1953: Torch Song. 1954: The Egyptian. The Glass Slipper. 1955: The Scarlet Coat. Cavalcade (TV. GB: cinemas). 1956: Stranger in the Night (TV. GB: cinemas). Zarak. 1957: Verdict of Three (TV). 1958: Hello London. 1959: Danger Within (US: Breakout). Dark as the Night (TV). 1960: The World of Suzie Wong. 1961: The Naked Edge. The Best of Enemies. 1962: A Girl Named Tamiko. 1967: The Sweet Ride. Rose rosse per il Führer / Code Name Red Roses. 1970: Waterloo. 1972: Lady Caroline Lamb. 1973: Frankenstein: the True Story (TV. GB: cinemas).

WILLIAM, Warren
(W.W. Krech) 1895–1948
Smooth, dark-haired, moustachioed American leading man with Barrymore-like profile, a frequent co-star of Bette Davis in her early years at Warners. Busy throughout the 1930s, William was often seen as such famous sleuths of fiction as Philo Vance, Perry Mason, Arsene Lupin and the Lone Wolf, but also as Julius Caesar in the 1934 *Cleopatra*. He died from multiple myeloma, a form of bone cancer.

1914: The Perils of Pauline (serial). 1920: The Town That Forgot God. 1923: Plunder (serial). 1927: Twelve Miles Out. 1930: Let Us Be Gay. 1931: Those Who Love. Expensive Women. Honor of the Family. 1932: The Dark

Horse. *The Woman from Monte Carlo. Skyscraper Souls. The Match King. Beauty and the Boss. Under 18. The Mouthpiece. Three on a Match. 1933: The Great Jasper. The Mind Reader. Goodbye Again. Gold Diggers of 1933. Employees' Entrance. Lady for a Day. 1934: Smarty (GB: Hit Me Again). Upper World. The Case of the Howling Dog. Bedside. The Dragon Murder Case. Cleopatra. The Secret Bride (GB: Concealment). Dr Monica. Imitation of Life. 1935: The Case of the Lucky Legs. Living on Velvet. The Case of the Curious Bride. Don't Bet on Blondes. *A Dream Comes True. 1936: Stage Struck. The Widow from Monte Carlo. Times Square Playboy (GB: His Best Man). The Case of the Velvet Claws. Satan Met a Lady. Go West, Young Man. 1937: The Firefly. Outcast. Madame X. Midnight Madonna. 1938: Wives under Suspicion. Arsene Lupin Returns. The First Hundred Years. 1939: The Man in the Iron Mask. The Lone Wolf Spy Hunt (GB: The Lone Wolf's Daughter). The Gracie Allen Murder Case. Daytime Wife. 1940: The Lone Wolf Meets a Lady. Lillian Russell. Trail of the Vigilantes. Arizona. The Lone Wolf Strikes. 1941: Wild Geese Calling. The Lone Wolf Takes a Chance. The Wolf Man. The Lone Wolf Keeps a Date. Secrets of the Lone Wolf (GB: Secrets). 1942: Wild Bill Hickok Rides. Counter Espionage. Eyes of the Underworld. 1943: Passport to Suez. One Dangerous Night. 1945: Out of the Night (GB: Strange Illusion). 1946: Fear. 1947: The Private Affairs of Bel Ami.*

The Stratton Story. Fighting Man of the Plains. Range Justice. A Dangerous Profession. 1950: Blue Grass of Kentucky. The Cariboo Trail. Operation Haylift. Rookie Fireman. The Great Missouri Raid. 1951: The Last Outpost, Blue Blood. Havana Rose. Return of Trigger Dawson (TV. GB: cinemas). 1952: The Murango Story (TV. GB: cinemas). Roaring Challenge (TV. GB: cinemas). Ticket to Mexico (TV. GB: cinemas). Law of the Six Gun (TV. GB: cinemas). The Pace That Thrills. Bronco Buster. Torpedo Alley. Son of Paleface. Rose of Cimarron. 1953: The Range Masters (TV. GB: Cinemas). Riders of Capistrano (TV. GB: cinemas). The Teton Tornado (TV. GB: cinemas). 1954: Racing Blood. Thunder Over Inyo (TV. GB: cinemas). The Outlaw's Daughter. 1955: Apache Ambush. Hell's Horizon. 1956: The Broken Star. Wiretapper. The Wild Dakotas. The Halliday Brand. 1957: The Storm Rider. Slim Carter. Pawnee (GB: Pale Arrow). 1958: Space Master X-7. Legion of the Doomed. 1959: The Scarface Mob. Stampede at Bitter Creek (TV. GB: cinemas). Alaska Passage. 1960: Hell to Eternity. Oklahoma Territory. 1961: The Sergeant Was a Lady. A Dog's Best Friend. 1963: Law of the Lawless. †Creatures of Darkness. 1965: Tickle Me. The Hallelujah Trail. Space Flight IC-1. 1966: Curse of the Swamp Creature. 1967: Trial by Error. 1968: Buckskin. 1969: The Divorcee/ Frustrations. 1970: Rio Lobo. 1971: Scandalous John. 1974: The Phantom of Hollywood (TV). 1975: The Giant Spider Invasion. 1976: Flight of the Grey Wolf (TV). 1977: 69 Minutes. 1978: A Fire in the Sky (TV). 1980: Moon Over the Alley. 1981: Goldie and the Boxer Go to Hollywood (TV). Night of the Zombies.*

†*Also directed*

WILLIAMS, Bill
(Herman Katt) 1914–1992

American leading man with laughing, boyish looks and fair, curly hair, an adagio dancer for several years who decided to take up acting after being invalided out of the war in 1944. Played a few years in co-features, and was sometimes the good-bad guy who gets killed at the end trying to atone for his treachery. Had some success on TV in the *Kit Carson* series. Married to Barbara Hale from 1946; father of William Katt (*qv*). Died after a long illness.

1944: *He Forgot to Remember. Murder in the Blue Room. Thirty Seconds over Tokyo. Those Endearing Young Charms. 1945: Sing Your Way Home. The Body Snatcher. Back to Bataan. Johnny Angel. West of the Pecos. 1946: Deadline at Dawn. Till the End of Time. 1947: Smoky River Serenade. A Likely Story. 1949: A Woman's Secret. The Clay Pigeon.*

WILLIAMS, Billy Dee
(William December Williams) 1937–

Cheerful but determined-looking black American star who has been acting on and off since the age of seven. Also interested in painting, he won an art scholarship but plumped for acting, although he was in his thirties before he really made the leap from stage to screen. In leading roles from the early 1970s, he reached a wider viewing public than hitherto with his portrayal of the effervescent Lando Calrissian in two *Star Wars* films.

1959: The Last Angry Man. 1969: The Out of Towners. Carter's Army (TV). 1970: Lost Flight. 1971: Brian's Song (TV). 1972: Lady*

Sings the Blues. The Final Comedown/ Blast. The Glass House (TV. GB: cinemas). 1973: Hit! 1974: The Take. 1975: Mahogany. 1976: Scott Joplin. The Bingo Long Traveling All Stars and Motor Kings. 1977: Com-Tac 303 (unfinished). 1980: The Empire Strikes Back. The Hostage Tower (TV. GB: cinemas). 1981: Nighthawks. 1982: Children of Divorce (TV). 1983: Marvin and Tige. Shooting Stars (TV). Fear City. Return of the Jedi. 1984: Time Bomb (TV). The Imposter (TV). Like Father and Son. 1986: Number One with a Bullet. Courage (TV). Oceans of Fire. 1987: Hot and Deadly. Deadly Illusion. 1988: The Return of Desperado (TV). 1989: Batman. Dangerous Passion (TV). Secret Agent Double-O Soul. 1991: Autobahn (US: Trabbi Goes to Hollywood. Later: Driving Me Crazy). The Pit and the Pendulum. 1992: Giant Steps. Percy & Thunder (cable TV). 1993: Alien Intruder. Deadly Ice. 1995: Pistol Blues. Falling for You (TV). Mask of Death. Triplecross (TV). 1996: Steel Sharks. Moving Target. 1997: The Prince. 1998: Woo. The Contract (TV). Hard Time (TV). 1999: The Visit. 2000: The Ladies' Man.*

WILLIAMS, Emlyn
(George E. Williams) 1905–1987

Welsh writer, actor and director with black unruly hair, an unconventional matinee idol of the thirties, two of whose plays, *Night Must Fall* (twice) and *The Corn is Green* (twice) have been filmed. Also an eye-catching featured player. Died from cancer.

1932: The Frightened Lady (US: Criminal at Large). Sally Bishop. Men of Tomorrow. 1933: Friday the Thirteenth. 1934: Road House. My Song for You. Evensong. The Iron Duke. 1935: The Dictator (US: The Loves of a Dictator). The City of Beautiful Nonsense. 1936: Broken Blossoms. 1937: ‡I Claudius. 1938: A Night Alone. Dead Men Tell No Tales. The Citadel. They Drive by Night. 1939: The Stars Look Down. Jamaica Inn. 1940: The Girl in the News. *Mr Borland Thinks Again. You Will Remember. 1941: This England. Major Barbara. Hatter's Castle. 1949: †The Last Days of Dolwyn (US: Woman of Dolwyn). 1950: Three Husbands. 1951: The Scarf. The Magic Box. Another Man's Poison. 1952: Ivanhoe. 1955: The Deep Blue Sea. 1958: I Accuse! 1959: Beyond This Place (US: Web of Evidence). The Wreck of the Mary Deare. 1952: The L-Shaped Room. 1966: Eye of the Devil. 1969: David Copperfield (TV. GB: cinemas). 1970: The Walking Stick.*

†*Also directed* ‡ *Unfinished.*

WILLIAMS, Esther 1922–

Cheerful, light-haired American star of brisk manner, a member of the abortive US Olympic team for 1940 who turned to films and swam her way into the world's box-office top ten in a stunningly-mounted series of M-G-M aqua-musicals. Married to Fernando Lamas (third of four) from 1969 to his death in 1982. Has visiting cards which read 'Yes, I still swim'.

*1942: Andy Hardy's Double Life. *Inflation. 1943: A Guy Named Joe. 1944: Bathing Beauty. Ziegfeld Follies (released 1946). 1945: Thrill of a Romance. 1946: The Hoodlum Saint. Easy to Wed. Till the Clouds Roll By. 1947: Fiesta. This Time for Keeps. 1948: On an Island with You. Take Me Out to the Ball Game (GB: Everybody's Cheering). 1949: Neptune's Daughter. 1950: *The Screen Actor. Duchess of Idaho. Pagan Love Song. 1951: Texas Carnival. Callaway Went Thataway (GB: The Star Said No!). 1952: Skirts Ahoy! Million Dollar Mermaid (GB: The One Piece Bathing Suit). 1953: Dangerous When Wet. Easy to Love. 1955: Jupiter's Darling. 1956: The Unguarded Moment. 1958: Raw Wind in Eden. 1961: The Big Show. The Magic Fountain. 1994: That's Entertainment! III.*

WILLIAMS, Hugh
(Brian Williams) 1904–1969

Dark, moustachioed, impeccably-groomed and spoken British actor who played strong, silent types in the thirties, and made a couple of visits to Hollywood. Had supporting roles in post-war British films, but became increasingly interested in writing and, in his later days, was best known as a playwright, writing often in collaboration with his second wife, Margaret Vyner (married 1940). She

died in 1993. He died following surgery.
1930: Charley's Aunt. 1931: In a Monastery Garden. A Night in Montmartre. A Gentleman of Paris. 1932: White Face. Insult. Down Our Street. After Dark. Rome Express. 1933: Sorrell and Son. Bitter Sweet. The Jewel. This Acting Business. 1934: All Men are Enemies. Elinor Norton. Outcast Lady (GB: A Woman of the World). 1935: David Copperfield. Let's Live Tonight. Lieutenant Daring R.N. The Last Journey. The Amateur Gentleman. Her Last Affaire. 1936: The Man behind the Mask. The Happy Family. Gypsy. 1937: The Perfect Crime. Side Street Angel. The Dark Stairway. The Windmill. Brief Ecstasy. Bank Holiday (US: Three on a Weekend). 1938: Dead Men Tell No Tales. His Lordship Goes to Press. Premiere (US: One Night in Paris). Inspector Hornleigh. 1939: Wuthering Heights. The Dark Eyes of London (US: The Human Monster. Completed 1936). 1941: Ships with Wings. 1942: One of our Aircraft is Missing. The Day Will Dawn (US: The Avengers). Talk about Jacqueline. Secret Mission. 1946: A Girl in a Million. 1947: Take My Life. An Ideal Husband. 1948: The Blind Goddess. Elizabeth of Ladymead. 1949: Paper Orchid. The Romantic Age (US: Glory at Sea). The Holly and the Ivy. 1953: The Fake. Twice Upon a Time. The Intruder. 1954: Star of My Night. 1966: Khartoum. 1967: Doctor Faustus.

WILLIAMS, JoBeth 1951–

Vivacious, slightly-built American actress with copper-coloured hair and concerned features, from a varied theatrical and TV background. She sprang to the attention of filmgoers as the mother fighting tooth and nail to protect her children in *Poltergeist*. She has also displayed a pleasing sense of knock-about comedy, but hasn't become a major box-office name. Married director John Pasquin.

1979: Kramer vs Kramer. 1980: The Dogs of War. Stir Crazy. Fun and Games (TV). 1981: The Big Black Pill (TV). 1982: Fun and Games II (TV). Poltergeist. Endangered Species. 1983: Adam (TV). The Day After (TV). The Big Chill. 1984: Teachers. 1985: American Dreamer. Kids Don't Tell (TV). 1986: Poltergeist II. Desert Bloom. Adam: His Song Continues (TV). 1988: Just You, Just Me. Memories of Me. 1989: Welcome Home. My Name is Bill W (TV) 1990: Child in the Night (TV). 1991: Switch. Victim of Love (TV). Dutch (GB: Driving Me Crazy). Stop! Or My Mom Will Shoot. 1992: Me, Myself

and I. Jonathan: The Boy Nobody Wanted (TV). 1993: Chantilly Lace (TV). Sex, Love and Cold, Hard Cash. 1994: Wyatt Earp. Lying in Wait/Final Appeal. Parallel Lives (TV). 1995: Ruby Jean and Joe. John Grisham's The Client (TV). 1996: Shattering the Silence (TV). 1997: Jungle 2 Jungle. Breaking Through (TV). Little City. When Danger Follows You Home (TV). 1998: It Came from the Sky (TV). A Chance of Snow (TV). 1999: Jackie's Back! (TV). 2000: Trapped in a Purple Haze (TV). Justice (TV).

WILLIAMS, Kenneth 1926–1988

Snooty-looking, brown-haired British comic actor whose contortions with his mouth in the 'Carry On' films may have stemmed from his radio days as a man of many outrageous voices, from devilish imps to haughty aristocrats, all of them guaranteed to annoy the hapless hero (usually Tony Hancock). A formidable raconteur and radio panellist. Died from a drug overdose.

*1952: Trent's Last Case. 1953: Innocents in Paris. Valley of Song (US: Men Are Children Twice). The Beggar's Opera. 1954: The Seekers (US: Land of Fury). 1958: Carry on Sergeant. 1959: Carry on Nurse. Tommy the Toreador. Carry on Teacher. 1960: Make Mine Mink. Carry on Constable. His and Hers. 1961: Carry on Regardless. Raising the Wind (US: Roommates). 1962: *Love Me, Love Me, Love Me (Narrator only). Carry on Cruising. Twice Round the Daffodils. 1963: Carry on Jack (US: Carry on Venus). 1964: Carry on Spying. Carry on Cleo. 1965: Carry on Cowboy. 1966: Don't Lose Your Head. Carry on Screaming. 1967: Follow That Camel. Carry on Doctor. 1968: Carry on Up the Khyber. 1969: Carry on Camping. Carry on Again, Doctor. 1970: Carry on Loving. Carry on Henry. 1971: Carry on at Your Convenience. 1972: Carry on Matron. Carry on Abroad. 1974: Carry on Dick. 1975: Carry on Behind. 1977: The Hound of the Baskervilles. That's Carry On. 1978: Carry on Emmannuelle.*

WILLIAMS, Robin 1951–

Wide-mouthed, chestnut-haired, manic American comedian, light dramatic actor and specialist in offbeat star roles, with friendly features that you might mistake at a passing glance for some Australian sportsman. A stand-up comedian from his early twenties, Williams broke into the TV big-time as the star of *Mork and Mindy*. Cinema proved a

posure: The Sex Tapes Scandal (TV). Under the Gun. 1990: The Kid Who Loved Christmas (TV). Perry Mason: The Case of the Silenced Singer (TV). 1991: Harley Davidson and the Marlboro Man. Another You. 1992: The Jacksons: An American Dream (TV). Stompin' at the Savoy (TV). 1995: Bye Bye Birdie (TV). 1996: Eraser. 1997: Hoodlum/Hoods. The Odyssey (TV). Soul Food. 1998: Dance with Me. Futuresport (TV). 1999: Light It Up. The Adventures of Elmo in Grouchland. Prisoner of Love. 2000: Shaft. The Courage to Love (TV). Playing with Fire (TV). Don Quixote (TV). 2001: The Powder Heart (TV). Baby of the Family.

harder nut to crack, but then *Good Morning, Vietnam* brought him an Academy Award nomination and world-wide recognition. Still occasionally demonstrates his scathing one-man humour on the stage. Further Oscar nomination for *Dead Poets Society* was followed by *tour-de-force* performances, in drag as *Mrs Doubtfire*, and as the voice of the genie in Disney's *Aladdin*. One unconfirmed source suggests that his real name may be Ralph Lipschitz. He finally won an Oscar for *Good Will Hunting*, but his starring roles in recent times have been over-sentimental.

1977: Can I Do It 'Till I Need Glasses? 1980: Popeye. 1982: The World According to Garp. 1983: The Survivors. 1984: Moscow on the Hudson. 1985: The Best of Times. Club Paradise. 1986: Seize the Day (originally for (TV). Robin Williams Live at the Met (video). 1987: Dear America (voice only). Good Morning, Vietnam. 1988: The Adventures of Baron Munchausen. Portrait of a White Marriage (TV). 1989: Dead Poets Society. 1990: Awakenings. Cadillac Man. 1991: The Fisher King. Hook. Dead Again. Shakes the Clown. 1992: FernGully the Last Rainforest (voice only). Toys. Aladdin (voice only). 1993: Being Human. Mrs Doubtfire. 1995: Jumanji. To Wong Foo Thanks for Everything, Julie Newmar. Nine Months. 1996: Aladdin and the King of Thieves (voice only). The Birdcage. The Secret Agent. Hamlet. Jack. 1997: Fathers Day. Flubber. Good Will Hunting. Deconstructing Harry. 1998: What Dreams May Come. 1999: Jakob the Liar. Get Bruce! (doc). Patch Adams. Bicentennial Man 2000: The Interpreter. Don't Worry, He Won't Get Far on Foot.

WILLIAMS, Treat

(Richard Williams) 1951–

Dark, taciturn, well-built, thickly black-haired American actor very much in the Vince Edwards (*qv*) mould, who brought presence if not much in the way of expression to his roles. Despite coming to the public eye first in *Hair*, his close-set features have seemed most at home in intensely serious roles. Since his rather stolid showing in *Prince of the City*, he has been stuck in co-starring film roles, alternating with leads in TV movies.

1975: Deadly Hero. 1976: The Ritz. The Eagle Has Landed. 1979: Hair. 1941. 1980: Why Would I Lie? 1981: The Pursuit of D B Cooper/Pursuit. Prince of the City. 1983: Dempsey (TV). Once Upon a Time in America.

1984: Flashpoint. A Streetcar Named Desire (TV). 1985: Club Paradise. Smooth Talk. 1986: The Men's Club. 1987: The Well. Sweet Lies (released 1989). Boogie Woogie. J. Edgar Hoover (TV). The Night of the Sharks (released 1990). 1988: Dead Heat. Viper. The Third Solution/Russicum. 1989: Third Degree Burn (TV). Heart of Dixie. Max and Helen (TV). 1990: Beyond the Ocean. Burro! 1992: Till Death Us Do Part (TV). Tales from the Crypt (TV). The Water Engine (TV). 1993: Where the Rivers Flow North. Bonds of Love (TV). 1994: Parallel Lives (TV). Handgun. Johnny's Girl (TV). 1995: In the Shadow of Evil (TV). Things to Do in Denver When You're Dead. 1996: The Late Shift (TV). The Phantom. Cannes Man. Mulholland Falls. 1997: The Substitute 2: School's Out. The Devil's Own. 1998: Deep Rising. Frogs for Snakes. Escape: Human Cargo (TV). 1999: The Deep End of the Ocean. 36 Hours to Die (TV). Substitute 3: Winner Takes All (TV). 2000: Blood from a Stone. Journey to the Center of the Earth (TV).
As director. 1992: *Texan.

WILLIAMS, Vanessa L. 1963–

Tall, lithe American beauty queen, dancer, singer and actress who has decorated a number of films, but never quite achieved the breakthrough that at times she seemed she might. The daughter of music teachers, her career got off to a sensational start when she became Miss America 1984, then lost the title when nude photographs of her appeared in a men's magazine. She took up acting in 1987, but took periods off to have children (she has four), and she was 33 when she got her highest-profile role, opposite Arnold Schwarzenegger (*qv*) in *Eraser*.

WILLIAMSON, Fred 1938–

Towering, formidably built black American sportsman and actor who graduated from college with a degree in business administration, but became a pro football player instead. After 10 years at the top, Williamson turned to acting and forced himself into leading roles in exploitation action movies almost right away, in macho roles. He had the misfortune to be making Bronson/Norris/Schwarzenegger-type paeans of violence some 10 years before the genre became fashionable and so, despite directing several of his own films, has never exceeded a limited if tenaciously sustained stardom.

1969: M*A*S*H. Deadlock (TV). Tell Me That You Love Me, Junie Moon. 1972: Hammer. The Legend of Nigger Charley. 1973: That Man Bolt. Black Caesar (GB: The Godfather of Harlem). Black Eye. The Soul of Nigger Charley. Hell Up in Harlem. Three Tough Guys. 1974: Three the Hard Way. Crazy Joe. 1975: Boss Nigger (GB: The Black Bounty Hunter). Bucktown/Darktown. Take a Hard Ride. 1976: †Mean Johnny Burrows. †Adios Amigo. †Death Journey. †No Way Back. 1977: †Joshua. †Destinazione Roma (US: Mr Mean). 1978: The Inglorious Bastards. 1979: Supertrain (TV. Later shown on GB TV as Express to Terror). 1980: Due nelle stelle. Fist of Fear, Touch of Death. 1981: Il capotto di legno. 1982: Vigilante. Bronx Warrior. The New Barbarians/Warriors of the Wasteland. 1983: White Fire (released 1985). Blind Rage (filmed 1977). The Centurions. Warrior of the Lost World (released 1985). †The Last Fight. †The Big Score. 1984: Snowballs. Half Nelson (TV). 1986: †Foxtrap. Delta Force Kommando (released 1990). Deadly Impact (completed 1984). 1987:

†*The Messenger. Rome 2072 AD – The New Gladiators (completed 1983). The Black Cobra. 1988: Deadly Intent. Hell's Heroes. 1989: The Black Cobra 2. †The Kill Reflex. 1990: Justice Done. Critical Action. Delta Force, Commando Two. 1991: Black Cobra 3: Manila Connection. 1992: Three Days to a Kill. South Beach. †Steele's Law. 1993: State of Mind. Deceptions. 1994: Silent Hunter (directed only). 1995: Hot City (later Original Gangstas). 1996: From Dust Till Dawn. Silent Hunter 2: The Standoff. 1997: Night Vision. Fast Track (TV). Full Tilt Boogie. 1998: Blackjack. Ride! Children of the Corn V: Fields of Terror. 1999: Active Stealth. Whatever It Takes. 2000: The Independent.*

†*And directed*

WILLIAMSON, Nicol 1938–
Big, raw-boned, sandy-haired Scottish actor whose sexual bull on the rampage became a fashionable and popular image at the end of the sixties. Was pleasingly effective in much quieter roles in the latter half of the next decade, although he has remained distinctive in all he does.
*1963: *The Six-Sided Triangle. 1968: Inadmissable Evidence. The Bofors Gun. 1969: Hamlet. Laughter in the Dark. The Reckoning. 1971: The Jerusalem File. 1972: The Monk. 1974: The Wilby Conspiracy. 1976: Robin and Marian. The Seven Per Cent Solution. 1977: The Goodbye Girl. 1978: The Cheap Detective. 1979: The Human Factor. 1981: Excalibur. Venom. 1982: I'm Dancing As Fast As I Can. 1984: Sakharov. 1985: Return to Oz. 1986: Passion Flower (TV). 1987: Black Widow. Apt Pupil. 1988: Berlin Blues. 1990: The Exorcist III. 1993: The Hour of the Pig. 1996: The Wind in the Willows. 1997: Spawn.*

WILLIS, Bruce
(Walter B. Willis) 1955–
Chunkily-built, chubby-faced, Germany-born American actor with cynical curving smile, long gap 'twixt nose and lip, twinkling personal charm and much publicised receding hairline. He struggled for years in small roles and minor plays before leaping to stardom as a fast-talking, wisecracking detective in the hit TV series *Moonlighting*. After an uncertain start, his subsequent cinema career took off in style with the *Die Hard* films. Since then, he has unusually mixed tough action heroes with offbeat character leads. His wife in a high-profile

marriage that survived several stormy patches was the actress Demi Moore (*qv*). The couple finally parted in 1998.
1978: Ziegfield – The Man and His Women (TV). 1980: The First Deadly Sin. 1981: Prince of the City. 1982: The Verdict. 1985: Moonlighting (TV). 1986: That's Adequate! 1987: Blind Date. 1988: Sunset. Die Hard. 1989: In Country. Look Who's Talking (voice only). 1990: Die Hard 2. The Bonfire of the Vanities. 1991: Mortal Thoughts. Hudson Hawk. Look Who's Talking Too (voice only). Billy Bathgate. The Last Boy Scout. 1992: Death Becomes Her. The Player. 1993: Striking Distance. National Lampoon's Loaded Weapon 1. 1994: North. Color of Night. Pulp Fiction. Nobody's Fool. 1995: Die Hard With a Vengeance. Four Rooms. Twelve Monkeys. 1996: Last Man Standing. The Hamster Factor (doc). Beavis and Butt-head Do America (voice only). The Jackal. The Fifth Element. Broadway Brawler (unfinished). 1998: Armageddon. The Siege. Mercury Rising. 1999: The Story of Us. Breakfast of Champions. The Sixth Sense. 2000: The Whole Nine Yards. The Kid. 2001: Unbreakable. Bandits.

WILSON, Marie
(Katherine White) 1916–1972
Platinum blonde, wide-mouthed, high-cheekboned, almost too bright American comedienne, a Broadway dancer who became adept at 'dumb blondes', especially in the 'Irma' films, and fashioned a whole career out of it. Died from cancer. Married (first and second of three) to director Nick Grindé and actor Allan Nixon.
*1934: *My Girl Sally. Down to Their Last Yacht (GB: Hawaiian Nights). Babes in Toyland. 1935: Slide, Kelly, Slide. Ladies*

Crave Excitement. Broadway Hostess. The Girl Friend. Stars over Broadway. Miss Pacific Fleet. 1936: *Slide, Nelly, Slide. Satan Met a Lady. The Great Ziegfeld. Colleen. King of Hockey (GB: Modern Madness). China Clipper. 1937: Melody for Two. The Great Garrick. Without Warning. Public Wedding. 1938: The Invisible Menace. Fools for Scandal. *For Auld Lang Syne. *Pictorial Revue No 6. Boy Meets Girl. Broadway Musketeers. 1939: Cowboy Quarterback. Sweepstakes Winner. Waterfront. Should Husbands Work? 1941: Rookies on Parade. Virginia. Flying Blind. Harvard Here I Come (GB: Here I Come). 1942: Broadway. She's in the Army. 1944: Shine on Harvest Moon. Music for Millions. You Can't Ration Love. 1946: No Leave, No Love. Young Widow. 1947: The Private Affairs of Bel Ami. Linda Be Good. The Fabulous Joe. 1949: My Friend Irma. 1950: My Friend Irma Goes West. 1951: *Hollywood on a Sunday Afternoon. A Girl in Every Port. 1952: Never Wave at a WAC (GB: The Private Wore Skirts). 1953: Marry Me Again. 1957: The Story of Mankind. 1962: Mr Hobbs Takes a Vacation.*

WINDSOR, Barbara (B. Deeks) 1937–
Pint-sized, bubbly, squeaky-voiced British comedienne with hour-glass figure and blonde hair piled high. Came to prominence via the theatre, playing cockneys, and was soon a regular member of the 'Carry On' comedy team, usually losing most of her clothes during the films, but never her smile. More recently busy on TV soap.
1954: The Belles of St Trinian's. 1955: Lost (US: Tears for Simon). 1959: Make Mine a Million. 1960: Too Hot to Handle (US: Playgirl After Dark). 1961: On the Fiddle (US: Operation Snafu). Flame in the Streets. Hair of the Dog. 1962: Death Trap. Sparrows Can't Sing. 1963: Crooks in Cloisters. 1964: Carry on Spying. 1965: San Ferry Ann. A Study in Terror (US: Fog). 1967: Carry on Doctor. 1968: Chitty Chitty Bang Bang. 1969: Carry on Camping. Carry on Again, Doctor. 1970: Carry on Henry. 1971: The Boy Friend. 1972: Carry on Matron. Carry on Abroad. Not Now Darling. 1973: Carry on Girls. 1974: Carry on Dick. 1977: That's Carry On. 1986: Comrades. 1987: It Couldn't Happen Here.

WINDSOR, Marie
(Emily M. Bertelson) 1922–
Auburn-haired (though often much darker in films) former beauty queen who became

nearly everybody's favourite B-feature bad girl. Considering that most of the parts she played were Jezebel and Lucretia Borgia rolled into one, the 5ft 9in Miss Windsor, who looked like Jane Wyman gone to the bad, generated surprising warmth in her more sympathetic (if never ingenuous) characters.

1941: All American Co-Ed. Weekend for Three. Playmates. 1942: *The Lady or the Tiger. Parachute Nurse. Call Out the Marines. †George Washington Slept Here. The Big Street. Smart Alecks. Eyes in the Night. 1943: Let's Face It. Chatterbox. Three Hearts for Julia. Pilot No 5. 1947: Song of the Thin Man. The Hucksters. The Romance of Rosy Ridge. The Unfinished Dance. *I Love My Wife, But! 1948: On an Island with You. The Kissing Bandit. The Three Musketeers. 1949: The Beautiful Blonde from Bashful Bend. Force of Evil. Outpost in Morocco. The Fighting Kentuckian. Hellfire. 1950: Dakota Lil. The Showdown. Double Deal. Frenchie. 1951: Little Big Horn (GB: The Fighting Seventh). Two Dollar Bettor (GB: Beginner's Luck). Hurricane Island. 1952: The Narrow Margin. Japanese War Bride. The Jungle. The Sniper. Outlaw Women. 1953: The Tall Texan. City That Never Sleeps. Trouble Along the Way. The Eddie Cantor Story. So This is Love (GB: The Grace Moore Story). Cat Women of the Moon. 1954: Hell's Half Acre. The Bounty Hunter. The Silver Star. 1955: Abbott and Costello Meet the Mummy. Stories of the Century No 1 – Belle Starr. No Man's Woman. Two-Gun Lady. 1956: The Killing. Swamp Woman. The Unholy Wife. 1957: The Girl in Black Stockings. The Story of Mankind. The Parson and the Outlaw. 1958: Day of the Bad Man. Island Women. 1962: Paradise Alley. 1963: Critic's Choice. The Day Mars Invaded Earth. Mail Order Bride (GB: West of Montana). 1964: Bedtime Story. 1966: Chamber of Horrors. 1969: The Good Guys and the Bad Guys. 1970: Wild Women (TV). 1971: Support Your Local Gunfighter. One More Train to Rob. 1973: Cahill: United States Marshal (GB: Cahill). The Outfit. Manhunter (TV). 1974: The Apple Dumpling Gang. 1975: Hearts of the West (GB: Hollywood Cowboy). 1975: Freaky Friday. Stranded (TV). 1978: The Perfect Woman. 1979: Salem's Lot (TV). 1983: Lovely But Deadly. 1985: JOE and the Colonel (TV). 1987: Commando Squad.

†Scenes deleted from final release print

WINGER, Debra (Mary D. Winger) 1955–
Small, dark, dynamic, fiery-looking American actress with husky voice (so low she was used as the voice of E.T. in 1982) who sprang to prominence by stealing scenes from macho male stars, but upset the Hollywood establishment with her forthright, go-it-alone attitudes. She was nominated for Academy Awards in *An Officer and a Gentleman* and *Terms of Endearment*, but a severe back injury deprived audiences of her talent for some time in the mid-1980s. After a number of headline romances, she married Timothy Hutton (*qv*) in 1986. The couple later divorced and she married actor Arliss Howard (Leslie Howard. 1954–) in 1996. Winger was further Oscar-nominated for her performance in *Shadowlands*.

1976: Slumber Party '57. 1978: Special Olympics (TV). Thank God It's Friday. 1979: French Postcards. 1980: Urban Cowboy. 1981: An Officer and a Gentleman. 1982: E.T. The Extra Terrestrial (voice only). Cannery Row. Mike's Murder (released 1984). 1983: Terms of Endearment. 1986: Legal Eagles. 1987: Made in Heaven. Black Widow. 1988: Betrayed. 1990: Everybody Wins. The Sheltering Sky. 1992: Leap of Faith. 1993: Wilder Napalm. Shadowlands. A Dangerous Woman. 1995: Forget Paris. †Divine Rapture.

†Unfinished.

WINNINGHAM, Mare
(Mary Winningham) 1959–
Slight, fair-haired, plaintive-looking American actress, a TV movie specialist who has made 30 of them since her acting debut straight from graduation. Amazingly, she's also made quite a few films, although, as on TV, almost always

seen as women pressured or getting a raw deal from life. In 1995, she gave an award-winning performance in the film *Georgia*. She also sings with her acoustic folk-rock band The Waybacks in between acting and raising a family. One of five children, she now has four of her own. Oscar nominee for *Georgia*.

1978: Special Olympics/A Special Kind of Love (TV). 1979: The Death of Ocean View Park (TV). 1980: One-Trick Pony. Off the Minnesota Strip (TV). Amber Waves (TV). The Women's Room (TV). 1981: Threshold (released 1983). Freedom (TV). A Few Days at Weasel Creek (TV). 1982: Missing Children: A Mother's Story (TV). 1983: Helen Keller: The Miracle Continues (TV). 1984: St Elmo's Fire. 1985: Love is Never Silent (TV). Single Bars, Single Women (TV). 1986: Nobody's Fool. Shy People. 1987: Eye on the Sparrow (TV). Made in Heaven. Who is Julia? (TV). A Winner Never Quits (TV). 1988: Miracle Mile. God Bless the Child (TV). 1989: The Pied Piper (TV). Turner & Hooch. 1990: Love and Lies (TV. GB: True Betrayal). True Texas Blue/True Blue (TV). 1991: She Stood Alone (TV). Fatal Exposure (TV). Hard Promises. 1992: Intruders (TV). 1993: Better Off Dead (TV). Betrayed by Love (TV). Sexual Healing (TV). 1993: Wyatt Earp. The War. 1995: Georgia. Letter to My Killer (TV). 1996: The Boys Next Door (TV). Bad Day on the Block. The Deliverance of Elaine (TV). 1997: Wallace (TV). 1998: Little Girl Fly Away (TV). 1999: Everything That Rises (TV). 2000: Sharing the Secret (TV). Sally Hemings: An American Scandal (TV).

WINSLET, Kate 1975–
Full-lipped, chunkily built, feisty-looking British actress with harvest-gold hair and open, handsome face. A talented singer, she was in stage musicals as a teenager, and did her own singing as one of the youthful murderesses in *Heavenly Creatures*, her film debut. An uninhibited adult performer who sought roles as independent spirits and has never been afraid of nudity, she won an Academy Award nomination in her second film, *Sense and Sensibility*, and was further nominated for *Titanic*.

1994: Heavenly Creatures. 1995: Sense and Sensibility. 1996: A Kid in King Arthur's Court. Jude. Hamlet. 1997: Titanic. 1998: Hideous Kinky. 1999: Holy Smoke. 2000: Quills. 2001: Therese Raquin. Enigma. A Christmas Carol (voice only).

WINSTONE, Ray 1957–

Chunky, ebullient, dark-haired, roughly spoken, powerful British actor, a dead ringer for the former England soccer manager Terry Venables. A talented amateur boxer who won more than 80 medals and trophies, he began an acting career in juvenile-delinquent-type leading roles, making a big impression in the films *Scum* and *Quadrophenia*. However, his career marked time for many years after that until he sprang back into the limelight as the abusive husband in the hard-hitting *Nil by Mouth*. Since then he has worked non-stop as an integral part of the 'in' British movie scene. Has made some very bad movies – and some very good ones too. Also a restaurateur and soccer enthusiast.

1979: Scum. That Summer! Quadrophenia. 1981: Ladies and Gentlemen: The Fabulous Stains. 1988: Tank Malling. 1994: Ladybird Ladybird. 1997: Nil by Mouth. Face. Yellow. Dangerous Obsession. Our Boy. 1998: Woundings. Final Cut. Martha, Meet Frank, Daniel and Laurence (US: The Very Thought of You). The Sea Change. Darkness Falls. The War Zone. 1999: Fanny & Elvis. Agnes Browne. Tube Tales (TV). Love, Honour and Obey. Last Christmas (TV). 2000: There's Only One Jimmy Grimble. Sexy Beast. Five Seconds to Spare. 2001: Salami Man.

WINTERS, Shelley

(Shirley Schrift) 1922–

American actress with frothy blonde hairdo and the common touch that could make her characters at once comic and moving. After a long tussle with very small roles, she got to the top and stayed there, playing working-class girls who were no better than they ought to be, usually through no fault of their own. Retained the glamour touch until well into her forties, then put on weight and took on more extravagant roles. Academy Awards for *The Diary of Anne Frank* and *A Patch of Blue*; further nominated for *A Place in the Sun* and *The Poseidon Adventure*. Married to Vittorio Gassman (qv) from 1952 to 1954 and to Anthony Franciosa (qv) from 1957 to 1960 (second and third of three). The first title in this list sums her up.

*1943: What a Woman! (GB: The Beautiful Cheat). †The Racket Man. 1944: †Two-Man Submarine. Sailor's Holiday. She's a Soldier Too. †Nine Girls. Cover Girl. There's Something About a Soldier. Knickerbocker Holiday. Together Again. Tonight and Every Night. 1945: A Thousand and One Nights. Dancing in Manhattan. Escape in the Fog. 1946: Suspense. 1947: New Orleans. Killer McCoy. Living in a Big Way. The Gangster. 1948: Larceny. Cry of the City. Red River. A Double Life. 1949: The Great Gatsby. Johnny Stool Pigeon. Take One False Step. South Sea Sinner (GB: East of Java). 1950: Winchester '73. Frenchie. 1951: The Raging Tide. A Place in the Sun. Meet Danny Wilson. He Ran All the Way. Behave Yourself! 1952: Phone Call from a Stranger. My Man and I. Untamed Frontier. 1954: Playgirl. Saskatchewan (GB: O'Rourke of the Royal Mounted). To Dorothy A Son (US: Cash on Delivery). Tennessee Champ. Executive Suite. 1955: I Am a Camera. Mambo. The Night of the Hunter. I Died a Thousand Times. The Treasure of Pancho Villa. The Big Knife. 1957: Beyond This Place (TV). 1959: Odds Against Tomorrow. The Diary of Anne Frank. 1960: Let No Man Write My Epitaph. 1961: The Young Savages. The Chapman Report. 1962: Lolita. 1963: The Balcony. Gli indifferenti (GB: and US: Time of Indifference). Wives and Lovers. 1964: A House is Not a Home. 1965: The Greatest Story Ever Told. A Patch of Blue. 1966: Alfie. Harper (GB: The Moving Target). 1967: Enter Laughing. 1968: The Scalphunters. Wild in the Streets. The Mad Room. Buona Sera, Mrs Campbell. 1969: *The Greatest Mother of Them All. ‡Arthur Arthur. Bloody Mama. 1970: How Do I Love Thee. What's the Matter with Helen? 1971: Whoever Slew Auntie Roo? (US: Who Slew Auntie Roo?). Revenge! (TV). A Death of Innocence (TV). 1972: The Poseidon Adventure. Something to Hide. The Devil's Daughter (TV). The Adventures of Nick Carter (TV). 1973: Blume in Love. Cleopatra Jones. 1974: Big Rose (TV). Poor Pretty Eddie. The Sex Symbol (TV. GB: cinemas). 1975: Diamonds. That Lucky Touch. Next Stop Greenwich Village. 1976: The Tenant. Tentacles. The Scarlet Dahlia. Mimi Bluette. The Three Sisters. Journey Into Fear. 1977: Gran bollito. The Initiation of Sarah (TV). Un borghese piccolo piccolo. Pete's Dragon. La signore degli orrori (US: Black Journal). 1978: City On Fire. King of the Gypsies. 1979: The Visitor. Rudolph and Frosty's Christmas in July (voice only). Elvis the Movie. The Magician of Lublin. Redneck County Rape/Girl in the Web. 1981: SOB. My Mother, My Daughter. Looping. 1983: Fanny Hill. Over the Brooklyn Bridge. Ellie. 1986: Always/Deja Vu. Witchfire. 1986: Very Close Quarters. The Delta Force. 1987: Hello Actors Studio. Marilyn Monroe: Beyond the Legend.*

1988: The Order of Things. Purple People Eater. 1989: Taking Chances: An Unremarkable Life. 1990: Touch of a Stranger. 1991: †The Linguini Incident. Stepping Out. 1992: Weep No More My Lady (TV). 1993: The Pickle. Searching for Bobby Fischer (GB: Innocent Moves). 1994: The Silence of the Hams (released 1996). The Spirit Realm/ Raging Angels. Backfire. Heavy. 1995: Jury Duty. Mrs Munck. 1996: The Portrait of a Lady. 1999: Gideon. La bomba.

†*Scenes deleted from final release print*
‡ *Unreleased*

WISDOM, Sir Norman 1915–

Small, dark-haired, cloth-capped British comedian, very fond of too-tight suits and tumbles downstairs; portrayed the willing trier for whom absolutely nothing goes right. Much helped in his rapid early fifties' rise to stardom by his stiff-faced straight man Jerry Desmonde (1908–1967) at whose coat-tails Wisdom would invariably tug appealingly at the end of each new disaster. His first starring comedy, *Trouble in Store*, provoked such massive country-wide queues that he was able to make roughly one comedy a year for Rank for the next 14 years. Knighted in 2000.

1948: A Date with a Dream. 1953: Meet Mr Lucifer. Trouble in Store. 1954: One Good Turn. 1955: As Long as They're Happy. Man of the Moment. 1956: Up in the World. 1957: Just My Luck. 1958: The Square Peg. 1959: Follow a Star. 1960: There Was a Crooked Man. 1961: The Bulldog Breed. 1962: The Girl on the Boat. On the Beat. 1963: A Stitch in Time. 1965: The Early Bird. 1966: The Sandwich Man. Press for Time. 1968: The Night they Raided Minsky's. 1969: What's Good for the Goose. 1992: Double X – The Name of the Game.

WITHERS, Googie

(Georgette Withers) 1917–

Titian-haired (initially blonde) British actress of minxish looks, a professional dancer at 14 who served a long apprenticeship in supporting roles in the cinema before breaking through to stardom in the early forties, and quickly becoming known as the best bad girl in British films. Lost to Britain when she decided to go to Australia with her husband John McCallum; in the seventies made a comeback on British TV as a prison governess in the long-running *Within These Walls*. Born in India.

1934: The Girl in the Crowd. The Love Test. 1935: All at Sea. Windfall. Dark World. Her Last Affaire. 1936: She Knew What She Wanted. Crown v Stevens. Crime Over London. King of Hearts. Accused. 1937: Action for Slander. Pearls Bring Tears. Paradise for Two (US: The Gaiety Girls). The Green Cockatoo. 1938: Kate Plus Ten (US: The Queen of Crime). Paid in Error. Convict 99. You're the Doctor. If I Were Boss. Strange Boarders. The Lady Vanishes. Murder in Soho (US: Murder in the Night). 1939: Dead Men are Dangerous. She Couldn't Say No. Trouble Brewing. The Gang's All Here (US: The Amazing Mr Forrest). 1940: Bulldog Sees It Through. Busman's Honeymoon (US: Haunted Honeymoon). 1941: Jeannie. 1942: One of Our Aircraft is Missing. Back Room Boy. 1943: The Silver Fleet. 1944: On Approval. They Came to a City. Natasha (Dubbed voice only). 1945: Dead of Night. Pink String and Sealing Wax. 1947: The Loves of Joanna Godden. It Always Rains on Sunday. 1948: Miranda. 1949: Once Upon a Dream. Traveller's Joy. 1950: Night and the City. 1951: White Corridors. The Magic Box. Lady Godiva Rides Again. 1952: Derby Day (US: Four Against Fate). 1954: Devil on Horseback. 1956: Port of Escape. 1970: The Nickel Queen. 1985: Time After Time (TV). Hôtel du Lac (TV). 1987: Northanger Abbey (TV). 1994: Country Life. 1996: Shine.

WITHERS, Jane 1926–
Dark-haired, pudge-faced, multi-talented American child star, the contemporary and antithesis of Shirley Temple, and, in the mid-thirties, almost as popular. While Shirley charmed and do-gooded, Jane howled and scratched and kicked, and was generally awful. In later years she suffered from ill

health and personal tragedy (her second husband was killed in a plane crash in 1968) but has kept acting on and off. Nickname as a child: Dixie's Dainty Dewdrop.
1932: Handle With Care. 1933: Zoo in Budapest. *Hollywood on Parade A-11. 1934: It's a Gift. *Hollywood Hobbies. Imitation of Life. Bright Eyes. 1935: This is the Life. Ginger. The Farmer Takes a Wife. Paddy O'Day. The Good Fairy. 1936: Pepper. Gentle Julia. Little Miss Nobody. Can This Be Dixie? 1937: Wild and Woolly. The Holy Terror. Checkers. Angel's Holiday. Forty-Five Fathers. 1938: Always in Trouble. Rascals. Keep Smiling (GB: Miss Fix-It). Arizona Wildcat. 1939: Pack Up Your Troubles (GB: We're in the Army Now). The Chicken Wagon Family. Boy Friend. 1940: Youth Will Be Served. Shooting High. High School. The Girl from Avenue A. *Chinese Garden Festival. 1941: Her First Beau. *Stars at Play. Golden Hoofs. A Very Young Lady. Small Town Deb. 1942: The Mad Martindales. Young America. Johnny Doughboy. 1943: The North Star. 1944: My Best Gal. Faces in the Fog. 1946: The Affairs of Geraldine. 1947: Danger Street. 1956: Giant. *Hollywood Small Fry. 1961: The Right Approach. 1963: Captain Newman M.D. 1975: All Together Now (TV). 1996: The Hunchback of Notre Dame (voice only).

WITHERSPOON, Reese
(Laura R. Witherspoon) 1976–
Petite, pretty, bow-lipped, blonde American actress who moved easily from teenage to adult roles and can turn her all-American looks with equal ease to nice or nasty characters. She received praise for her self-centred college girl in Election, although she obviously didn't like teen horror films, having turned down roles in Scream, I Know What You Did Last Summer and Urban Legend! Married to actor Ryan Phillippe (qv). 1991: The Man in the Moon. Wildflower (TV). 1992: Desperate Choices: To Save My Child (TV. GB: Solomon's Choice). 1993: A Far Off Place. Jack the Bear. 1994: SFW. 1996: Fear. Freeway. 1997: Overnight Delivery. 1998: Twilight. Pleasantville. 1999: Best Laid Plans. Cruel Intentions. Election. 2000: American Psycho. Slow Motion. Little Nicky. 2001: Legally Blonde.

WOLFIT, Sir Donald
(D. Woolfitt) 1902–1968
Dark, glowering, ruddy-cheeked, beetle-browed British actor, a formidable Thespian

and interpreter of Shakespeare who later gave some richly melodramatic performances on film to become the Tod Slaughter of his day. Knighted in 1957. Died from a heart attack.
1931: Down River. 1934: Death at Broadcasting House. *The Wigan Express. *Inasmuch. 1935: Sexton Blake and the Bearded Doctor. Drake of England (US: Drake the Pirate). Late Extra. Checkmate. The Silent Passenger. Hyde Park Corner. 1936: Calling the Time. 1937: Knight without Armour. 1952: The Pickwick Papers. The Ringer. 1953: Isn't Life Wonderful! 1954: Svengali. 1955: A Prize of Gold. The Man in the Road. 1956: *A Man on the Beach. Guilty? Satellite in the Sky. 1957: The Traitor (US: The Accused). I Accuse! 1958: Room at the Top. Blood of the Vampire. 1959: The Angry Hills. The Rough and the Smooth (US: Portrait of a Sinner). The House of the Seven Hawks. 1960: The Hands of Orlac. 1961: The Mark. 1962: Lawrence of Arabia. Dr Crippen. 1963: Becket. 1964: 90 Degrees in the Shade. 1965: Life at the Top. 1966: The Sandwich Man. 1968: Decline and Fall . . . of a Birdwatcher. The Charge of the Light Brigade.

WONG, Anna May
(Wong Liu Tsong) 1907–1961
Delicately-boned American actress of Chinese parentage, a great success on stage and screen on both sides of the Atlantic in the early thirties. Within the restrictions imposed by being Oriental, she managed to give some haunting performances, and was also an admirable villainess. Never married. The Anna May Wong who appears in The Savage Innocents (1959) and Just Joe (1960) is not the same actress. Died from a heart attack.
1919: The Red Lantern. 1921: Shame. The

First Born. Bits of Life. Dinty. 1922: The Toll of the Sea. Thundering Dawn. 1923: Drifting. 1924: The Alaskan. Lilies of the Field. The 40th Door. Peter Pan. The Thief of Bagdad. 1925: Forty Winks. 1926: The Desert's Toll. A Trip to Chinatown. Fifth Avenue. The Dragon Horse. 1927: Old San Francisco. Mr Wu. Driven from Home. Streets of Shanghai. The Chinese Parrot. The Devil Dancer. 1928: Across to Singapore. The Crimson City. Chinatown Charlie. Song. 1929: Grossstadt-schmetterling (GB: and US: The City Butterfly). Piccadilly. 1930: Elstree Calling. The Flame of Love (and French and German versions). On the Spot. 1931: Daughter of the Dragon. 1932: Shanghai Express. *Hollywood on Parade B-3. 1933: A Study in Scarlet. Tiger Bay. 1934: Chu Chin Chow. Java Head. Limehouse Blues. 1937: Daughter of Shanghai (GB: Daughter of the Orient). 1938: When Were You Born? Dangerous to Know. 1939: Island of Lost Men. King of Chinatown. 1940: *Chinese Garden Festival. 1941: Ellery Queen's Penthouse Mystery. 1942: Bombs over Burma. The Lady from Chungking. 1949: Impact. 1960: Portrait in Black.

WOOD, Elijah 1981–

Dark-haired, chipmunk-faced American actor, short on stature, but long on talent, and generally acknowledged to have been Hollywood's best child player of the 1990s. He began as a child model, but his resolute and un-showy style of acting soon won him film roles, even if his profile was never as high as that of the more distinctive-looking Macaulay Culkin (qv). Wood moved closer to adult stardom when he was selected to play the hobbit hero in the ambitious three-film adaption of J. R. R. Tolkien's Lord of the Rings.

1989: Back to the Future Part II. 1990: Child in the Night (TV). Avalon. Internal Affairs. 1991: Paradise. 1992: Forever Young. Radio Flyer. 1993: The Good Son. The Adventures of Huck Finn. 1994: *Witness. The War. North. 1996: Flipper. 1997: The Ice Storm. Oliver Twist (TV). 1998: Deep Impact. The Faculty. 1999: The Bumblebee Flies Anyway. Black and White. 2000: Chain of Fools. The Adventures of Tom Thumb and Thumbelina (voice only). 2001: Lord of the Rings: The Fellowship of the Ring. 2002: Lord of the Rings: The Two Towers.

WOOD, Natalie

(Natasha Virapaeff, later Gurdin) 1938–1981 Delicately pretty, dark-haired American

child star, of Russian parentage. She grew into a petite but talented actress who reached the top of the tree with some memorable dramatic performances (she was less successful in comedy), then inexplicably drifted out of film at the peak of her ability, playing only five starring roles for the cinema in her last 15 years. Three times nominated for an Academy Award, on Rebel Without a Cause, Splendor in the Grass and Love with the Proper Stranger. Married to Robert Wagner (qv) 1957–1963, she remarried him in 1972 after another, intervening marriage. Afraid of water all her life, she drowned in a boating accident.

1943: †Happy Land. 1945: Tomorrow is Forever. 1946: The Bride Wore Boots. 1947: Driftwood. Miracle on 34th Street (GB: The Big Heart). The Ghost and Mrs Muir. 1948: Scudda-Hoo! Scudda-Hay! (GB: Summer Lightning). Chicken Every Sunday. 1949: The Green Promise (GB: Raging Waters). Father Was a Fullback. 1950: The Jackpot. Our Very Own. Never a Dull Moment. No Sad Songs for Me. 1951: Dear Brat. The Blue Veil. 1952: The Star. Just For You. The Rose Bowl Story. 1954: The Silver Chalice. 1955: One Desire. Rebel Without a Cause. 1956: The Searchers. The Burning Hills. The Girl He Left Behind. A Cry in the Night. 1957: Bombers B-52 (GB: No Sleep Till Dawn). 1958: Marjorie Morningstar. Girl on the Subway (TV. GB: cinemas). Kings Go Forth. 1959: Cash McCall. 1960: All the Fine Young Cannibals. 1961: Splendor in the Grass. West Side Story. 1962: Gypsy. 1963: Love with the Proper Stranger. 1964: Sex and the Single Girl. 1965: The Great Race. Inside Daisy Clover. 1966: This Property is Condemned. Penelope. 1969: Bob & Carol & Ted & Alice. 1972: The Candidate. 1973: The Affair (TV. GB: cinemas). 1975: James Dean – the First American Teenager. Peeper. 1979: The Cracker Factory (TV). Meteor. †Hart to Hart (TV). 1980: The Last Married Couple in America. The Memory of Eva Ryker (TV). Willie and Phil. 1981: Brainstorm (released and copyrighted 1983).

†As Natasha Gurdin

WOODS, Donald (Ralph Zink) 1904–1998

Quiet, neat Canadian-born leading man with dark, wavy hair. He came to Hollywood after a stage career, but never really rose to being more than a leading man in co-features. Just the sort of actor you'd expect to find in a low-budget detective series, although in reality

even that didn't come Woods' way, apart from one (miscast) go at Perry Mason in an already dying 1930s series. Later played a few kindly fathers, did some television (his soothing tones proving ideal for host or narrator chores) and even sold real estate.

1934: Charlie Chan's Courage. As the Earth Turns. The Merry Wives of Reno. Sweet Adeline. Fog Over Frisco. She Was a Lady. 1934: The Case of the Curious Bride. The Frisco Kid. Stranded. The Florentine Dagger. A Tale of Two Cities. Anna Karenina. 1936: Anthony Adverse. The Story of Louis Pasteur. Isle of Fury. A Son Comes Home. Road Gang (GB: Injustice). The White Angel. 1937: Big Town Girl. Once a Doctor. Charlie Chan on Broadway. Talent Scout (GB: Studio Romance). Sea Devils. The Case of the Stuttering Bishop. 1938: I Am the Law. The Black Doll. Romance on the Run. Danger on the Air. 1939: Heritage of the Desert. Beauty for the Asking. The Girl from Mexico. Mexican Spitfire. 1940: Mexican Spitfire Out West. Forgotten Girls. City of Chance. Love, Honor and Oh, Baby! If I Had My Way. *Young America Flies. 1941: Bachelor Daddy. I Was a Prisoner on Devil's Island. Sky Raiders (serial). 1942: The Gay Sisters. Thru Different Eyes. 1943: Corregidor. Hi'Ya Sailor! So's Your Uncle. Watch on the Rhine. 1944: The Bridge of San Luis Rey. Hollywood Canteen. The Life of Goebbels. Enemy of Women. 1945: God is My Co-Pilot. Wonder Man. Roughly Speaking. *Star in the Night. Voice of the Whistler. 1946: Night and Day. Never Say Goodbye. *The Jade Lady. The Time, the Place and the Girl. 1947: The Return of Rin Tin Tin. Bells of San Fernando. Stepchild. 1949: Daughter of the West. Barbary Pirate. Scene of the Crime. Free for All. 1950: The Lost Volcano. Mr Music. Johnny One-Eye. 1951: All That I Have. 1953: The Beast from 20,000 Fathoms. Born to the Saddle. 1959: I'll Give My Life. 1960: Thirteen Ghosts. 1961: Five Minutes to Live. 1964: Kissin' Cousins. The Satan Bug. 1966: Dimension 5. Moment to Moment. 1967: Express (TV. GB: cinemas). A Time to Sing. 1969: True Grit.

WOODS, James 1947–

Skull-faced, dark-haired, faintly oriental-looking American actor with thick, curling lips and an air of sub-surface menace. Woods seemed built for psychotic villains from the start, but has made some interesting attempts to break free of the mould, even if most of his portraits seemed still to be of characters living

near the edge of themselves in one way or another. Playing leading and supporting roles with equal success, he remains one of the most distinctive Hollywood players of the 1970s and 1980s. Oscar nominee for *Salvador* and *Ghosts of Mississippi*. Emmy winner for the TV movie *Promise*.

1971: *The Visitors. Home Free.* 1972: *Hickey and Boggs. Footsteps* (TV). *A Great American Tragedy* (TV. GB: *Man at the Crossroads*). 1973: *The Way We Were.* 1974: *The Gambler.* 1975: *Night Moves. Foster and Laurie* (TV). *Distance.* 1976: *F. Scott Fitzgerald in Hollywood* (TV). *The Disappearance of Aimee* (TV). *Raid on Entebbe* (TV. GB: cinemas). *Alex and the Gypsy.* 1977: *The Choirboys.* 1978: *The New Maverick* (TV). *The Gift of Love* (TV). 1979: *The Incredible Journey of Dr Meg Laurel* (TV). *The Onion Field. And Your Name is Jonah* (TV). 1980: *The Black Marble.* 1981: *Eyewitness* (GB: *The Janitor*). *Fast-Walking.* 1982: *Split Image/Captured! Videodrome.* 1983: *Once Upon a Time in America.* 1984: *Against All Odds. Cat's Eye.* 1985: *Joshua Then and Now. Salvador. Badge of the Assassin* (TV). 1986: *Good Morning Babylon. Best Seller. Promise* (TV). 1987: *In Love and War* (TV). *Cop.* 1988: *The Boost. True Believer/Fighting Justice.* 1989: *Immediate Family. My Name is Bill W* (TV). 1990: *The Hard Way. Women & Men: Stories of Seduction* (TV). *The Guys* (later on TV as *The Boys*). 1992: *Straight Talk. Diggstown* (GB: *Midnight Sting*). *Chaplin. Citizen Cohn* (cable TV). 1993: *Blue. Jane's House* (TV). *The Getaway. Fallen Angels 2* (TV). 1994: *Curse of the Starving Class. The Specialist. Next Door* (TV). *Stranger Things.* 1995: *Casino. Indictment: The McMartin Trial* (cable TV). *Killer: A Journal of Murder. For Better or Worse.* 1996: *The Summer of Ben Tyler* (TV). *Ghosts of Mississippi* (GB: *Ghosts of the Past*). 1997: *Kicked in the Head. Contact. Hercules* (voice only). 1998: *John Carpenter's Vampires. Another Day in Paradise.* 1999: *True Crime. The Virgin Suicides. Play It to the Bone. Any Given Sunday. The General's Daughter.* 2000: *Dirty Pictures. Race to Space. Final Fantasy: The Movie* (voice only). 2001: *John Q.*

WOODWARD, Edward 1930–
Bullet-headed, trustworthy-looking, light-haired British actor whose career went nowhere much for 15 years until tremendous success as a lone wolf secret agent in the TV series *Callan*. His film appearances have not

equalled that success, although some have been interesting. He enjoyed latter-day TV fame as the star of the series *The Equaliser*.

1955: *Where There's A Will.* 1960: *Inn For Trouble.* 1963: *Becket.* 1968: *The File of the Golden Goose.* 1970: *Incense for the Damned.* 1971: *Young Winston. Hunted.* 1972: *Sitting Target.* 1973: *The Wicker Man.* 1974: *Callan. Three for All.* 1977: *Stand Up Virgin Soldiers.* 1980: *'Breaker' Morant.* 1981: *The Appointment.* 1982: *Who Dares Wins. Comeback.* 1983: *Champions. Arthur the King* (TV. Released 1985). *Love is Forever* (TV). 1984: *A Christmas Carol* (TV). 1985: *King David.* 1987: *Uncle Tom's Cabin* (TV). 1988: *The Man in the Brown Suit* (TV). 1990: *Mister Johnson. Hands of a Murderer* (TV). *Over My Dead Body* (TV). 1993: *Deadly Advice. A Christmas Reunion/Tan ar y comin* (TV). 1995: *The Shamrock Conspiracy* (TV). 1996: *Harrison: Cry of the City* (TV). 1997: *The House of Angelo.*

WOODWARD, Joanne 1930–
Offbeat American actress with oft-cropped blonde hair. Soon showed a liking for meaty drama and won an Academy Award as the schizophrenic in *The Three Faces of Eve*. Although difficult to cast, she has sustained her career with an interesting variety of portraits, mostly of women under pressure, sometimes in films directed by her husband Paul Newman (*qv*; married 1958). Received other Oscar nominations for *Rachel Rachel* and *Summer Wishes, Winter Dreams*. Took an Emmy for *See How She Runs* in 1978.

1955: *Count Three and Pray. The Late George Apley* (TV. GB: cinemas). 1956: *A Kiss Before Dying.* 1957: *The Three Faces of Eve. No Down Payment.* 1958: *The Long, Hot*

Summer. Rally 'Round the Flag, Boys. The 80 Yard Run (TV). 1959: *The Sound and the Fury. The Fugitive Kind.* 1960: *From the Terrace.* 1961: *Paris Blues.* 1962: *The Stripper* (GB: *Woman of Summer*). 1963: *A New Kind of Love.* 1964: *Signpost to Murder.* 1966: *A Big Hand for the Little Lady* (GB: *Big Deal at Dodge City*). *A Fine Madness.* 1968: *Rachel Rachel.* 1969: *Winning.* 1970: *WUSA. King: A Filmed Record . . . Montgomery to Memphis.* 1971: *They Might be Giants.* 1972: *The Effect of Gamma Rays on Man-in-the-Moon Marigolds.* 1973: *Summer Wishes, Winter Dreams.* 1975: *The Drowning Pool.* 1977: *Sybil* (TV. GB: cinemas). 1978: *The End. See How She Runs* (TV). *The Melodeon* (TV). *A Christmas to Remember* (TV). 1979: *Angel Dust/Angel Death* (TV Narrator only). *Streets of L.A.* (TV). 1980: *Crisis at Central High* (TV). *The Shadow Box* (TV). 1984: *Harry and Son. Passions* (TV). 1985: *Do You Remember Love?* (TV). 1987: *The Glass Menagerie.* 1990: *Mr and Mrs Bridge.* 1993: *Philadelphia. Foreign Affairs* (TV). *Blind Spot* (TV). *The Age of Innocence* (voice only). 1994: *Breathing Lessons* (TV).

WOOF, Emily 1968–
Light-haired British actress, performance artist and aerialist with resolute 'country girl' looks that adapt well to period costume. She started her scantily clad, one-woman shows on sex while still at university, then did additional training in France with a physical theatre company and a circus school, where she became an expert on the trapeze. Diminutive in stature, she didn't make her film debut until she was 29, but made up for it with eight leading roles in four years, as well as star parts in three TV mini-series, *Killer Net, Oliver Twist* and *Daylight Robbery*. 1997: *The Full Monty. Photographing Fairies. The Woodlanders.* 1998: *Velvet Goldmine. Fast Food.* 1999: *This Year's Love. Passion: The Story of Percy Grainger/Passion.* 2000: *Pandaemonium.*

WOOLLEY, Monty
(Edgar Montillion Woolley) 1888–1963
Big, bluff, bearded American actor, a former university professor who roared to film stardom in his fifties as the irascible international wit Sheridan Whiteside in *The Man Who Came to Dinner*, and remained popular for another decade in big-budget, laughter-and-tears stuff. Received two Oscar nominations, for *The Pied Piper* and *Since*

You Went Away. Died from a kidney ailment.
1936: *Ladies in Love*. 1937: *Live, Love and Learn*. *Nothing Sacred*. 1938: *Arsene Lupin Returns*. *Everybody Sing*. *Girl of the Golden West*. *Lord Jeff* (GB: *The Boy from Barnardo's*). *Artists and Models Abroad* (GB: *Stranded in Paris*). *Three Comrades*. *Young Doctor Kildare*. *Vacation from Love*. *Zaza*. 1939: *Midnight*. *Never Say Die*. *Man About Town*. **See Your Doctor*. *Honeymoon in Bali* (GB: *Husbands or Lovers*). *Dancing Co-Ed* (GB: *Every Other Inch a Lady*). 1941: *The Man Who Came to Dinner*. 1942: *Life Begins at 8:30* (GB: *The Light of Heart*). *The Pied Piper*. 1953: *Holy Matrimony*. 1944: *Irish Eyes Are Smiling*. *Since You Went Away*. 1945: *Molly and Me*. 1946: *Night and Day*. 1957: *The Bishop's Wife*. 1948: *Miss Tatlock's Millions*. *Paris 1900* (narrator only). 1951: *As Young As You Feel*. 1955: *Kismet*. 1956: *Eloise* (TV).

WOOLSEY, Robert
See WHEELER and WOOLSEY

WRAY, Fay (Vina F. Wray) 1907–
Canadian actress with red-brown hair and attractive almond eyes, a great beauty adrift in westerns when whisked to stardom by Erich von Stroheim in *The Wedding March*. Immortalized a few years later as the girl admired by *King King*, she gained a reputation as the great screaming heroine of thirties' horror films. Retiring on marrying her second husband, writer-producer Robert Riskin, in 1942, but he died in 1955. Later wrote a play, and a perceptive memoir called *On the Other Hand*.
1923: **Gasoline Love*. 1925: *What Price Goofy?* **No Father to Guide Her*. *The Coast*

Patrol. *A Cinch for the Gander*. 19265: *Wild Horse Stampede*. *Don't Shoot*. *Lazy Lightning*. *The Man in the Saddle*. *A One-Man Game*. **One Wild Time*. *The Saddle Tramp*. *Loco Luck*. 1927: *Spurs and Saddles*. 1928: *The Wedding March*. *Legion of the Condemned*. *The First Kiss*. *The Streets of Sin*. *The Four Feathers*. 1929: *Pointed Heels*. *Thunderbolt*. 1930: *Captain Thunder*. *Behind the Make-Up*. *The Sea God*. *The Border Legion*. *Paramount on Parade*. *The Texan* (GB: *The Big Race*). 1931: *Not Exactly Gentlemen* (GB: *The Three Rogues*). *The Finger Points*. *The Lawyer's Secret*. *The Conquering Horde*. **The Stolen Jools* (GB: *The Slippery Pearls*). *Dirigible*. *The Unholy Garden*. 1932: *The Most Dangerous Game* (GB: *The Hounds of Zaroff*). *Stowaway*. *Doctor X*. 1933: *Below the Sea*. *King Kong*. *The Woman I Stole*. *The Vampire Bat*. *Ann Carver's Profession*. *The Big Brain* (GB: *Enemies of Society*). *The Mystery of the Wax Museum*. *One Sunday Afternoon*. *The Bowery*. *Master of Men*. *Shanghai Madness*. 1934: *The Countess of Monte Cristo*. *Madame Spy*. *The Affairs of Cellini*. *The Richest Girl in the World*. *Woman in the Dark*. *Once to Every Woman*. *Viva Villa!* *Black Moon*. *Cheating Cheaters*. *White Lie*. 1935: *Bulldog Jack* (US: *Alias Bulldog Drummond*). *Come Out of the Pantry*. *The Clairvoyant*. *Mills of the Gods*. 1936: *When Knights Were Bold*. *They Met in a Taxi*. *Roaming Lady*. 1937: *Murder in Greenwich Village*. *It Happened in Hollywood* (GB: *Once a Hero*). 1938: *The Jury's Secret*. *Smashing the Spy Ring*. 1939: *Navy Secrets*. 1940: *Wildcat Bus*. 1941: **Wampas Baby Stars*. **Stars at Play*. *Adam Had Four Sons*. *Melody for Three*. 1942: *Not a Ladies' Man*. 1953: *Small Town Girl*. *Treasure of the Golden Condor*. 1955: *The Cobweb*. *Queen Bee*. *Hell on Frisco Bay*. 1956: *In Times Like These* (TV. GB: cinemas). 19657: *Rock Pretty Baby*. *Crime of Passion*. *Tammy and the Bachelor* (GB: *Tammy*). *Dragstrip Riot* (GB: *The Reckless Age*). *Summer Love*. 1959: *Second Happiest Day* (TV). 1980: *Gideon's Trumpet* (TV).

WRIGHT, Robin 1966–
Blonde American actress of rather plain attractiveness, which has enabled her to play both country and city girls since she abandoned teenage modelling for an acting career at 18. Her output since then has been too sparse for her fans' liking. 'Good roles only come along once or twice a year,' she explains, 'and, if I can't get one, I'd rather not

work.' This situation was exacerbated by having two children from her long time relationship with actor Sean Penn (qv), but she has increased her workload since the mid-1990s. She and Penn married in 1996 but separated in 2000.
1986: *Hollywood Vice Squad*. 1987: *The Princess Bride*. 1988: *Loon* (video title: *Denial*). 1990: *State of Grace*. 1992: *The Playboys*. *Toys*. 1994: *Forrest Gump*. 1995: *The Crossing Guard*. 1996: *Moll Flanders*. 1997: *†She's So Lovely*. *†Loved*. 1998: *†Hurlyburly*. 1999: *†Message in a Bottle*. 2000: *How to Kill Your Neighbor's Dog*. *The Pledge*. 2001: *Unbreakable*.

†As Robin Wright-Penn

WRIGHT, Teresa
(Muriel T. Wright) 1918–
Small, slight, gentle-mannered American actress with reddish-brown hair, an Oscar winner in her second film (*Mrs Miniver*) but, seen far too early in mother roles (the first in 1953), she faded from the film scene and has spent most of her later years on stage. Married (second) to playwright Robert Anderson in 1959. They later divorced and remarried. Also received Oscar nominations for *The Little Foxes* and *Pride of the Yankees*.
1941: *The Little Foxes*. 1942: *Pride of the Yankees*. *Mrs Miniver*. 1943: *Shadow of a Doubt*. 1944: *Casanova Brown*. 1945: *The Trouble with Women* (released 1947). 1946: *The Best Years of Our Lives*. *The Imperfect Lady* (GB: *Mrs Loring's Secret*). 1947: *Pursued*. 1948: *Enchantment*. 1950: *The Capture*. *The Men*. 1952: *Something to Live For*. *California Conquest*. *The Steel Trap*. 1953: *The Actress*. *Count the Hours* (GB: *Every Minute Counts*). 1954: *Track of the Cat*. 1955: *Miracle on 34th Street* (TV. GB: cinemas). 1956: *The Search for Bridey Murphy*. 1957: *The Miracle Worker* (TV). *Escapade in Japan*. *Edge of Innocence* (TV). 1958: *The Restless Years* (GB: *The Wonderful Years*). 1969: *Hail Hero!* *The Happy Ending*. 1972: *Crawlspace* (TV). 1974: *The Elevator* (TV). 1975: *Flood!* (TV). 1977: *Roseland*. 1980: *Somewhere in Time*. *The Rocking Chair Rebellion*. 1983: *Bill: On His Own* (TV). 1986: *Morning Star/Evening Star*. 1988: *The Good Mother*. 1990: *Perry Mason: The Case of the Desperate Deception* (TV). 1991: *Lethal Innocence* (TV). 1993: **The Red Coat*. 1997: *John Grisham's The Rainmaker*. 1999: *Dial H for Hitchcock* (doc).

WRIGHT, Tony 1925–1986

Fair-haired British actor who had his first success in French films (after a varied early career including whaling in the Antarctic, and repertory in South Africa), then, for a few brief years, became the 'beefcake boy' of British films. Hadn't quite the acting range required for permanent stardom but he remained a working actor, latterly in small parts on television. Died from multiple injuries after a fall.

1953: The Flanagan Boy (US: Bad Blonde). 1954: A toi de jouer, Callaghan (GB: The Amazing Mr Callaghan). 1955: Plus de whisky pour Callaghan. 1956: Et par ici la sortie. Jumping for Joy. Jacqueline. Tiger in the Smoke. 1957: Seven Thunders (US: The Beast of Marseilles). *The Stars Don't Shine. 1958: The Spaniard's Curse. 1959: Broth of a Boy. In the Wake of a Stranger. The Rough and the Smooth (US: Portrait of a Sinner). 1960: Faces in the Dark. And the Same to You. The House in Marsh Road (US: The Invisible Creature). 1961: Attempt to Kill. Callaghan remet ça. 1962: Journey to Nowhere. 1965: The Liquidator. 1970: The Man Who Haunted Himself. 1971: All Coppers Are . . . Clinic Xclusive. The Magnificent Six and a Half (third series). Kidnapped. 1972: The Creeping Flesh. 1975: Hostages. 1979: Can I Come Too?

WYATT, Jane 1911–

It rhymes with 'quiet' and that's just the impression one gets from this small, pretty, brown-haired American actress capable on occasions of such glowing warmth that it was a shame her film career was largely limited to waiting women. Still, she did rather better on stage, and won three Emmys for the long-running TV series Father Knows Best in the fifties.

1934: One More River (GB: Over the River). Great Expectations. 1936: We're Only Human. The Luckiest Girl in the World. 1937: Lost Horizon. 1940: The Girl from God's Country. 1941: Kisses for Breakfast. Hurricane Smith. Week-End for Three. 1942: Army Surgeon. The Navy Comes Through. 1943: Buckskin Frontier (GB: The Iron Road). The Kansan (GB: Wagon Wheels). 1944: None But the Lonely Heart. 1946: Strange Conquest. The Bachelor's Daughters (GB: Bachelor Girls). 1947: Gentlemen's Agreement. Boomerang. 1948: Pitfall. No Minor Vices. 1949: Task Force. Bad Boy. Canadian Pacific. 1950 Our Very Own. House By the River. My Blue Heaven. The Man Who Cheated Himself. 1951: Criminal Lawyer. 1957: Interlude. 1961: The Two Little Bears. 1964: See How They Run (TV). 1965: Never Too Late. 1970: Weekend of Terror (TV). 1973: You'll Never See Me Again (TV). 1976: Tom Sawyer (TV). Katherine (TV). 1976: Treasure of Matecumbe. Amelia Earhart (TV). 1977: The Father Knows Best Christmas Reunion (TV). A Love Affair: The Eleanor and Lou Gehrig Story (TV). 1978: Superdome (TV). The Millionaire (TV). The Nativity (TV). 1982: Missing Children: A Mother's Story (TV). 1986: Star Trek IV: The Voyage Home. 1989: Amityville: The Evil Escapes (TV).

WYMAN, Jane (Sarah J. Faulks) 1914–2007

Brunette (earlier blonde) American actress, singer, dancer, painter and designer who served 10 years as girlfriends in routine thrillers and comedies before getting a reward for perseverance with the lead in The Lost Weekend. That led to Johnny Belinda (an Oscar as a deaf mute) and a lushly-mounted series of films known as Wyman weepies, in which she plucked at the heartstrings of the world as she suffered in poverty and luxury alike. Married (second of four) to Ronald Reagan (qv) 1940 to 1948. Also nominated for Academy Awards on The Yearling, The Blue Veil and Magnificent Obsession.

1932: †The Kid from Spain. 1933: †Elmer the Great. 1934: †College Rhythm. 1935: †Rumba. †All the King's Horses. †Stolen Harmony. †King of Burlesque. 1936: †Polo Joe. †Anything Goes. Cain and Mabel. Gold Diggers of 1937. ‡My Man Godfrey. Smart Blonde. Stage Struck. 1937: Slim. The King and the Chorus Girl (GB: Romance is Sacred). Public Wedding. Ready, Willing and Able. The Singing Marine. Mr Dodd Takes the Air. 1938: Wide Open Faces. The Spy Ring. Brother Rat. The Crowd Roars. He Couldn't Say No. Fools for Scandal. Tailspin. 1939: The Kid from Kokomo (GB: Orphan of the Ring). Private Detective. Torchy Plays with Dynamite. Kid Nightingale. 1940: Brother Rat and a Baby (GB: Baby Be Good). Flight Angels. Tugboat Annie Sails Again. *The Sunday Round-Up. An Angel from Texas. My Love Came Back. Gambling on the High Seas. 1941: The Body Disappears. Bad Men of Missouri. You're In The Army Now. 1942: Footlight Serenade. Larceny Inc. My Favorite Spy. 1943: Princess O'Rourke. 1944: The Doughgirls. Make Your Own Bed. Hollywood Canteen. Crime By Night. 1945: The Lost Weekend. 1946: One More Tomorrow. Night and Day. The Yearling. 1947: Magic Town. Cheyenne. 1948: Johnny Belinda. 1949: The Lady Takes a Sailor. A Kiss in the Dark. It's a Great Feeling. Stage Fright. 1950: The Glass Menagerie. 1951: The Blue Veil. Three Guys Named Mike. Starlift. Here Comes the Groom. 1952: Just For You. The Will Rogers Story (GB: The Story of Will Rogers). 1953: Let's Do It Again. So Big. 1954: Magnificent Obsession. 1955: All That Heaven Allows. Lucy Gallant. Miracle in the Rain. 1959: Holiday for Lovers. 1960: Pollyanna. 1962: Bon Voyage! 1969: How to Commit Marriage. 1971: The Failing of Raymond (TV). 1978: The Outlanders. 1979: The Incredible Journey of Dr Meg Laurel (TV). 1996: Wild Bill: Hollywood Maverick.

†As Sarah Jane Faulks (when billed)
‡Scene deleted from final release print

WYMORE, Patrice 1926–

Tall, tawny but not too terrific, this reddish-blonde, hazel-eyed singer and dancer from Kansas was brought by Warner Brothers to Hollywood at 23 as a sort of female equivalent to their Gene Nelson. She was Errol Flynn's leading lady in her second film and became his third wife, but, even before she left films to look after their baby daughter, her cool, Alexis Smith-style personality had demoted her to 'other women' in musicals and her only other leading roles were, like the first, in westerns.

1950: Tea for Two. Rocky Mountain. 1951: Starlift. I'll See You in My Dreams. 1952: The Big Trees. She's Working Her Way Through College. The Man Behind the Gun. 1953: She's Back on Broadway. 1955: King's Rhapsody. 1959: The Sad Horse. 1960: Ocean's Eleven.

1966: Chamber of Horrors. 1977: The Thoroughbreds/On a Dead Man's Chest (later: Treasure Seekers).

WYNTER, Dana

(Dagmar Spencer-Marcus) 1927–2011

Raven-haired, pale-faced, coolly glamorous, British-born, South African-raised leading lady, at first in small roles in British films but then enjoying a few years of Hollywood stardom (she stayed in America) as a Fox contractee.

1951: †White Corridors. †Lady Godiva Rides Again. †The Woman's Angle. 1952: †The Crimson Pirate. †Something Money Can't Buy. †It Started in Paradise. 1953: †Colonel March Investigates. †Escape by Night. Knights of the Round Table. 1955: Laura (TV. GB: cinemas). The View from Pompey's Head (GB: Secret Interlude). 1956: Invasion of the Body Snatchers. D-Day the Sixth of June. 1957: Winter Dreams (TV). Something of Value. Diamond Safari. 1958: The Violent Heart (TV). Fraulein. In Love and War. Wings of the Dove (TV). 1959: Shake Hands with the Devil. Sink the Bismarck! 1961: On the Double. 1963: The List of Adrian Messenger. 1966: Danger Has Two Faces (TV). 1968: If He Hollers, Let Him Go! Companions in Nightmare (TV). The Crime (TV). 1969: Airport. Any Second Now (TV). 1971: Triangle. Owen Marshall – Counsellor at Law (TV). 1972: Santee. 1973: The Connection (TV). The Questor Tapes (TV). 1975: The Lives of Jenny Dolan (TV). Le sauvage (US: Lovers Like Us). 1980: M Station: Hawaii (TV). 1985: The Royal Romance of Charles and Diana (TV). 1993: The Return of Ironside (TV).

†As Dagmar Wynter

WYNYARD, Diana

(Dorothy Cox) 1906–1964

Fair-haired, personably attractive British actress who went to Hollywood in 1932, but returned after only seven feature films there and went back to the stage. Fortunately, the British cinema persuaded her to try another little burst of films, including the brilliant *Gaslight,* before her star days were over. Married/divorced director Carol Reed. Received an Academy Award nomination for *Cavalcade.* Died from a kidney ailment.

*1933: Rasputin and the Empress (GB: Rasputin the Mad Monk). Cavalcade. Men Must Fight. Reunion in Vienna. 1934: Where Sinners Meet (GB: The Dover Road). *Hollywood on Parade No 13. One More River (GB: Over the River). Let's Try Again (GB: Marriage Symphony). 1939: On the Night of the Fire (US: The Fugitive). 1940: Gaslight (US: Angel Street). 1941: Freedom Radio (US: A Voice in the Night). The Prime Minister. Kipps (US: The Remarkable Mr Kipps). 1947: An Ideal Husband. 1951: Tom Brown's Schooldays. 1956: The Feminine Touch (US: The Gentle Touch). 1957: Island in the Sun. 1959: The Second Man (TV).*

Y

Return of the Musketeers. The Lady and the Highwayman (TV). Midnight Cop. 1990: Duel of Hearts (TV). 1991: Elina Vere. 1992: The Four Minute Mile. Wide Sargasso Sea. The Long Shadow. La vida lactea/The Milky Life. Shadow of a Kiss. †Discretion Assured. 1994: L'enigma di un giorno. L'ombra abitata. Gospa. 1996: The Ring. 1997: Goodbye America. Austin Powers: International Man of Mystery. The Ripper (TV). Dark Planet. 1998: Wrongfully Accused. One Hell of a Guy, '54'. Merchant of Venus. The Treat. A Knight in Camelot (TV). 1999: Henry James' The Ghostly Rental. The Omega Code. Austin Powers: The Spy Who Shagged Me. Puss in Boots. 2000: Borstal Boy.

†Unreleased

YORK, Michael, (M. York-Johnson) 1942–
Fair-haired British actor with gentle, refined voice whose almost impossibly boyish good looks were fortunately tempered and toughened by a broken nose. Usually seen as callow aristocrats, he has hinted that he could also play comedy better than most. One of Britain's busiest actors in the 1970s, but his box-office success faltered after 1978 and, although he has kept busy (often in overseas films), he has not regained the limelight.
1962: The Mind Benders. 1966: The Taming of the Shrew. 1967: Smashing Time. Confessions of a Loving Couple. Accident. Red and Blue. 1968: The Guru. Romeo and Juliet. The Strange Affair. 1969: Justine. Alfred the Great. 1970: Something for Everyone (GB: Black Flowers for the Bride). 1971: Zeppelin. 1972: Cabaret. England Made Me. Lost Horizon. 1973: The Three Musketeers: The Queen's Diamonds. 1974: Murder on the Orient Express. The Four Musketeers: the Revenge of Milady. 1975: Great Expectations (TV. GB: cinemas). Conduct Unbecoming. Touch and Go. 1976: Seven Nights in Japan. Logan's Run. 1977: The Island of Dr Moreau. The Last Remake of Beau Geste. 1978: Death on the Nile. The Riddle of the Sands. Fedora. 1979: A Man Called Intrepid (made for cinemas but shown only on TV). 1980: Final Assignment. 1981: The White Lions (released 1983). 1982: Phantom of the Opera (TV). 1983: For Those I Loved/Au nom de tous les miens. Le sang des autres. 1984: Success is the Best Revenge. The Master of Ballantrae (TV). 1985: L'aube. 1986: Dark Mansions. Sword of Gideon (TV). 1987: Joker (US: Lethal Obsession). 1988: Phantom of Death. City Blue. 1989: A proposito di quelle strana ragazza. The

YORK, Susannah (S. Fletcher) 1939–
Beguiling, baby-faced, charismatic star actress, another in the long line of plummy-voiced British blondes. At first in appealing ingenue roles, she then played anything from English roses to boldly sexual roles, without compromising her popularity, which lasted until near the end of the 1970s. Also a writer of children's books, she won an Oscar nomination for *They Shoot Horses, Don't They?*
*1960: Tunes of Glory. There Was a Crooked Man. 1961: The Greengage Summer. 1962: Freud (GB: Freud – the Secret Passion). 1963: Tom Jones. 1964: The Seventh Dawn. *Scene Nun, Take One. 1965: *Scruggs. Sands of the Kalahari. 1966: Kaleidoscope. A Man for All Seasons. 1967: Sebastian. 1968: Duffy. The Killing of Sister George. 1969: They Shoot Horses, Don't They? Lock Up Your Daughters! Oh! What a Lovely War. Battle of Britain. Country Dance (US: Brotherly Love). 1970: Jane Eyre (TV. GB: cinemas). 1971: Zee and Co. (US: X, Y and Zee). Happy Birthday, Wanda June. 1972: Images. 1974: Gold. The Maids. 1975: Conduct Unbecoming. Sky Riders. That Lucky Touch. 1977: Eliza Fraser (GB: TV, as The Rollicking Adventures of Eliza Fraser). 1978: The Shout. Long Shot. The Silent Partner. Superman. 1979: The Specter on the Bridge/The Golden Gate Murders (TV). Falling in Love Again (released 1981). 1980: The Awakening. Alice. Loophole. *Late Flowering Love. Superman II. 1983: Yellow-beard. 99 Women. Nelly's Version. 1984: A Christmas Carol (TV. GB: cinemas). 1986: Mio in the Land of Faraway. 1987: PrettyKill. Bluebeard, Bluebeard. The Apple Tree. Super-man IV: The Quest for Peace (voice only). 1988:*

Just Ask for Diamond. A Summer Story. American Roulette. 1989: Melancholia. A Handful of Time. The Man from the Pru (TV). 1990: Fate. 1992: Illusions. 1993: The Higher Mortals. Piccolo, grande amore (US: Pretty Princess). 1996: La propriétaire. Loop/You Can Keep the Animals. 1997: Romance and Rejection. Diana and Me. 1998: So This is Romance? 1999: St Patrick the Irish Legend.

YOUNG, Gig (Byron Barr) 1913–1978
Sardonically-smiling, dark-haired American leading man, mainly in comedy in his latter days, although an Academy Award winner in 1969 in a dramatic role (*They Shoot Horses, Don't They?*). Started as a moustachioed romantic lead, but soon became known as the amiable guy who didn't get the girl, notably in Doris Day comedies of the late fifties and early sixties. He didn't get the girl in real life, either: of his five marriages, four ended in divorce (his second wife died), including the third, to actress Elizabeth Montgomery (1933–1993). He received additional Oscar nominations for *Come Fill the Cup* and *Teacher's Pet*. A lifelong alcoholic, he committed suicide (shot himself).
1940: †Misbehaving Husbands. 1941: †One Foot in Heaven. †Here Come the Cavalry. †Dive Bomber. †The Man Who Came to Dinner. †You're in the Army Now. †Sergeant York. †They Died with Their Boots On. †Navy Blues. 1942: †The Male Animal. †Captains of the Clouds. †The Gay Sisters. 1943: Old Acquaintance. Air Force. 1947: Escape Me Never. The Woman in White. 1948: Wake of the Red Witch. The Three Musketeers. 1949: Tell It to the Judge. Lust for Gold. 1950: Hunt the Man Down. 1951: Target Unknown. Too Young to Kiss. Come Fill the Cup. Only the Valiant. Slaughter Trail. 1952: Holiday for Sinners. You for Me. 1953: City That Never Sleeps. The Girl Who Had Everything. Arena. Torch Song. 1954: Young at Heart. 1955: The Desperate Hours. 1957: Desk Set (GB: His Other Woman). 1958: Teacher's Pet. The Tunnel of Love. 1959: Ask Any Girl. The Story on Page One. 1962: That Touch of Mink. Kid Galahad. Five Miles to Midnight. 1963: For Love or Money. A Ticklish Affair. 1965: Strange Bedfellows. 1966: The Shuttered Room. 1968: Companions in Nightmare (TV). 1969: They Shoot Horses, Don't They? 1970: Lovers and Other Strangers. 1971: The Neon Ceiling (TV). 1974: The Great Ice Rip-Off (TV). Bring Me the Head of Alfredo Garcia. Deborah/A Black Ribbon for Deborah. 1975:

The Hindenberg. Michèle. The Killer Elite.
1976: Sherlock Holmes in New York (TV).
1977: Spectre (TV). 1978: Game of Death.

†*As Byon Barr*

YOUNG, Karen 1958–
Elfin, wide-mouthed American actress with urchin-cut fair hair and charming gap in her teeth. Such vulnerable prettiness has been, surprisingly, largely employed in playing touch cookies who have taken a few knocks in life. Her first film could have made her a big star, but it didn't quite come off. Since then she's looked in vain for another major break, but remains an interesting screen personality.
1982: Handgun (US: Deep in the Heart).
*1984: Almost You. Birdy. 9½ Weeks. 1985: The Execution of Raymond Graham (TV). 1986: The High Price of Passion (TV). Heat. 1987: Jaws the Revenge. 1988: Wild Things (TV). Torch Song Trilogy. Criminal Law. Poison Candy (TV). 1989: Night Game. *To the Moon, Alice. 1991: Line of Duty. The 10 Million Dollar Getaway (TV). The Summer My Father Grew Up (TV). The Boy Who Cried Bitch. 1992: Drug Wars II: The Cocaine Cartel (TV). Hoffa. 1994: The Wife. 1996: Daylight. 1997: On the Edge of Innocence (TV). 1998: Pants on Fire. 1999: Joe the King. Mercy.*
As director: *1992: *A Blink of Paradise.*

YOUNG, Loretta
(Gretchen Belzer) 1913–2000
Blue-eyed brunette (sometimes blonde in earlier days) American actress with liquid lips who was both pretty and glamorous and stayed at the top (admittedly in mostly mediocre films) for more than 20 years before calling it a

day. Best roles came in the early thirties and late forties (during which latter period she won an Oscar for *The Farmer's Daughter*). Married Grant Withers (1904–1959) from 1930 to 1931, first of three. She married Oscar-winning costume designer Jean-Louis in 1993: he died in 1997. She was also an Oscar nominee for *Come to the Stable*. Three of her sisters were also actresses: Polly Ann Young (1908–1997), Sally Blane (Elizabeth Belzer, 1910–1997) and Georgiana Young (1923–). She died from ovarian cancer.
*1917: †The Only Way. 1919: †Sirens of the Sea. 1921: †The Sheik. 1927: Naughty But Nice. 1928: The Magnificent Flirt. Whip Woman. Scarlet Seas. Laugh, Clown, Laugh. The Head Man. 1928: Her Wild Oat. The Fast Life. The Squall. The Show of Shows. The Girl in the Glass Cage. The Careless Age. The Forward Pass. 1930: Show Girl in Hollywood. The Man from Blankley's. The Second Floor Mystery. Loose Ankles. Kismet. The Devil to Pay. Road to Paradise. The Truth about Youth. 1931: Three Girls Lost. Beau Ideal. Big Business Girl. Platinum Blonde. The Right of Way. Too Young to Marry. I Like Your Nerve. Taxi! The Ruling Voice. 1932: Play Girl. Life Begins (GB: The Dawn of Life). The Hatchet Man (GB: The Honourable Mr Wong). Week-End Marriage (GB: Working Wives). They Call It Sin (GB: The Way of Life). 1933: Employee's Entrance. The Life of Jimmy Dolan (GB: The Kid's Last Fight). *Hollywood on Parade No. 17. Grand Slam. Zoo in Budapest. Midnight Mary. The Devil's in Love. Man's Castle. Heroes for Sale. She Had to Say Yes. The House of Rothschild. 1934: Bulldog Drummond Strikes Back. The White Parade. Born to be Bad. Caravan. 1935: Call of the Wild. Clive of India. Shanghai, The Crusades. 1935: Ramona. The Unguarded Hour. Private Number (GB: Secret Interlude). Ladies in Love. 1937: Love under Fire. Love is News. Second Honeymoon. Café Metropole. Wife, Doctor and Nurse. 1938: Suez. Four Men and a Prayer. Kentucky. Three Blind Mice. 1939: Eternally Yours. The Story of Alexander Graham Bell (GB: The Modern Miracle). Wife, Husband and Friend. 1940: The Doctor Takes a Wife. He Stayed for Breakfast. 1941: Bedtime Story. The Lady from Cheyenne. The Men in Her Life. 1942: A Night to Remember. 1943: China. *Show Business at War. 1944: And Now Tomorrow. Ladies Courageous. 1945: Along Came Jones. 1946: The Stranger. The Perfect Marriage. 1947: The Farmer's Daughter. The Bishop's Wife. 1948: Rachel and the Stranger. The Accused. 1949: Mother is a Freshman (GB: Mother Knows Best). Come to the Stable. 1950: Key to the City. 1951: Half Angel. Cause for Alarm. 1952: Paula (GB: The Silent Voice). Because of You. 1953: It Happens Every Thursday. 1960: The Immaculate Road (TV. GB: cinemas). 1986: Christmas Eve (TV). 1989: Lady in a Corner (TV).*

†*As Gretchen Young*

YOUNG, Robert 1907–1998
Quiet, round-faced, dark-haired, well-groomed American star with ready faint smile. After many years of charming blandness (he once described himself in Hollywood

in the early sound days as 'an introvert in a field of extroverts'), he surprisingly developed into a solid actor, defeated alcoholism, and made almost all his best films in a very good run from 1941 to 1948. From 1949 to 1961, first on radio, then on TV, he starred in the phenomenally successful series *Father Knows Best*, winning two Emmys along the way. Another successful TV series, *Marcus Welby MD*, followed from 1969 to 1975. Died from respiratory failure.
1931: The Sin of Madelon Claudet (GB: The Lullaby). The Black Camel. Hell Divers. Guilty Generation. 1932: New Morals for Old. The Wet Parade. The Kid from Spain. Strange Interlude (GB: Strange Interval). Unashamed. 1933: Men Must Fight. Today We Live. Saturday's Millions. Tugboat Annie. Right to Romance. Hell Below. The House of Rothschild. 1934: Cardboard City. Spitfire. Hollywood Party. Paris Interlude. The Band Plays On. Carolina (GB: The House of Connelly). Lazy River. Whom the Gods Destroy. Death on the Diamond. 1935: Calm Yourself. West Point of the Air. The Bride Comes Home. Vagabond Lady. Red Salute (GB: Arms and the Girl). Remember Last Night? 1936: It's Love Again. Secret Agent. Sworn Enemy. The Longest Night. Three Wise Guys. The Bride Walks Out. Stowaway. 1937: The Emperor's Candlesticks. Dangerous Number. The Bride Wore Red. I Met Him in Paris. Married Before Breakfast. Navy Blue and Gold. 1938: The Toy Wife (GB: Frou-Frou). Paradise for Three (GB: Romance for Three). Rich Man, Poor Girl. Josette. Three Comrades. The Shining Hour. 1939: Maisie. Honolulu. Miracles for Sale. Bridal Suite. 1940: The Mortal Storm. Florian. Sporting Blood. Dr Kildare's Crisis. Northwest Passage. 1941: Lady Be Good. The Trial of Mary Dugan. Married Bachelor. Western Union. H.M. Pulham Esq. 1942: Joe Smith, American (GB: Highway to Freedom). Cairo. Journey for Margaret. 1943: Sweet Rosie O'Grady. Slightly Dangerous. Claudia. 1944: The Canterville Ghost. 1945: Those Endearing Young Charms. The Enchanted Cottage. 1946: Lady Luck. Claudia and David. The Searching Wind. 1947: Crossfire. They Won't Believe Me. 1948: Relentless. Sitting Pretty. 1949: Bride for Sale. Adventure in Baltimore (GB: Bachelor Bait). That Forsyte Woman (GB: The Forsyte Saga). 1950: And Baby Makes Three. The Second Woman (GB: Ellen). 1951: Goodbye, My Fancy. 1952: The Half-Breed. 1954: The Secret of the Incas. 1968: Holloway's Daughters (TV). Marcus Welby MD/A Matter of

Humanities (TV). 1970: Vanished (TV). 1972: All My Darling Daughters (TV). 1973: My Darling Daughters' Anniversary (TV). 1977: The Father Knows Best Christmas Reunion (TV). 1978: Little Women (TV). 1984: The Return of Marcus Welby MD (TV). 1986: Mercy or Murder? (TV). 1987: Conspiracy of Love (TV). 1988: A Holiday Affair (TV).

YOUNG, Sean (Mary S. Young) 1959–
Fiery, controversial, headline-grabbing, lithe, dark-haired, Kentucky-born American actress with sensual mouth and deep brown eyes. Often plays women with hints of danger in them: you never know quite what to expect when a Sean Young character's on the screen. She studied dance at college and was briefly a model, then made her first film at 20. It's been an in-out career since. Back injury cost her the female lead in *Batman* and, according to her own accounts, she has lost more roles by refusing affairs with stars and producers than most actresses around! She returned to star billing in the 1990s in spite of choosing some of the worst projects going.
1980: Jane Austen in Manhattan (TV). 1981: Stripes. 1982: Blade Runner. Young Doctors in Love. 1983: Quarter Till . . . 1984: Dune. Baby/Baby . . . Secret of the Lost Legend. 1985: Under the Biltmore Clock. 1987: No Way Out. Wall Street. 1988: Arena Brains. The Boost. 1989: Cousins. 1990: Fire Birds (GB: Wings of the Apache). 1991: A Kiss Before Dying. Love Crimes. Once Upon a Crime. 1992: Blade Runner: The Director's Cut. Hold Me, Thrill Me, Kiss Me (released 1995). Sketch Artist (cable TV). Blue Ice. Forever. 1993: Even Cowgirls Get the Blues. Fatal Instinct. Model by Day. 1994: Ace Ventura Pet Detective. Smoke. Witness to the Execution (TV). 1995: Bolt. Dr Jekyll and Ms Hyde. Mirage. 1996: La propriétaire/The Proprietor. Evil Has a Face (TV). The Invader. Barbara Taylor Bradford's Everything to Gain (TV). Starchild. 1997: Exception to the Rule (TV). Men. Out of Control. Motel Blue. 1998: Armstrong. The Cowboy and the Movie Star/Love on the Edge (TV). 1999: The Calling/Special Delivery. 2000: Goodbye Sunrise. Death Game. Secret Cutting (TV). The Amati Girls. 2001: Poor White Trash.

Z

ZADORA, Pia (P. Schipani) 1954–
Petite, pouting, peek-a-boo blonde American entertainer who promoted herself as a Bardot-style sexpot in the early 1980s. Her first vehicles were star-studded and impressively mounted, but she was no match for Bardot and the characters she was given were always faintly ludicrous, if less so than those of taller rival Bo Derek (*qv*). Pia, though, was more fun, and continued her career as a singer in night-clubs, also proving a popular chat-show guest on television. Has been in show business since childhood.
1964: Santa Claus Conquers the Martians. 1981: Butterfly. 1982: Fake-Out. 1983: The Lonely Lady. 1985: Voyage of the Rock Aliens. 1986: Feel the Motion. 1988: Hairspray. 1984: Troop Beverly Hills. 1994: Naked Gun 33⅓: The Final Insult. 1995: National Lampoon's Favorite Deadly Sins.

ZANE, Billy 1966–
Wiry American actor with dark, fluffy, receding hair and slightly cruel pretty-boy facial features. Often seen in roles that carry a dangerous edge, Zane's played an amazing number of villains and psychotics for such a good-looking actor. Perhaps best remembered in this little gallery was his ocean-bound killer in *Dead Calm*. He has an acting sister, Lisa Zane.
1985: Back to the Future. 1986: Critters. The Brotherhood of Justice (TV). 1988: Police Story: Monster Manor (TV). Dead Calm. 1989: The Case of the Hillside Stranglers/The Hillside Stranglers (TV). Going Overboard/ Babs Away. Back to the Future Part II. 1990: Memphis Belle. Megaville. Blood and Concrete, a Love Story. 1991: Miliardi/Billions/Millions.

Femme Fatale. 1992: Betrayal of the Dove. Running Delilah (TV). 1993: Lake Consequence. Orlando. Sniper. Poetic Justice. Posse. Tombstone. 1994: Reflections on a Crime. Only You. Demon Knight/Tales from the Crypt Presents Demon Knight. Flashfire. The Silence of the Hams (released 1996). 1995: The Set Up. Danger Zone. 1996: Head Above Water. The Phantom. This World, Then the Fireworks. 1997: Titanic. 1998: I Woke Up Early the Day I Died. Susan's Plan. Pocahontas II: Journey to a New World (V. Voice only). 1999: Taxman. Morgan's Ferry.

ZELLWEGER, Renée 1969–
Appealing, husky-voiced, sleepy-eyed light-haired American actress of Swiss-Norwegian parentage. She attracted little attention in her first few years in films and TV until 1996, when she made the success *The Whole Wide World* and especially *Jerry Maguire*, in which she won all hearts with her romance with Tom Cruise. Yet to prove a solo attraction, although that might happen with her 'Bridget Jones' project in 2001.
1992: A Taste for Killing (TV). 1993: Dazed and Confused. My Boyfriend's Back. Murder in the Heartland (TV). 1994: Love and a .45. Shake, Rattle and Rock! (cable TV). The Return of the Texas Chainsaw Massacre. Reality Bites. Low Life. 8 Seconds. 1995: Empire Records. 1996: The Whole Wide World. Jerry Maguire. 1997: Texas Chainsaw Massacre: The Next Generation (revised version of 1994 film). Liar (US: Deceiver). 1998: A Price Above Rubies. One True Thing. 1999: The Bachelor. 2000: Nurse Betty. Me, Myself and Irene. 2001: Bridget Jones' Diary.

ZETA JONES, Catherine (C. Jones) 1969–
Stunning raven-haired Welsh-born actress, a

classic beauty of the screen, first popular in the British TV series *The Darling Buds of May*. Strangely, her early film career was of little consequence, even in Hollywood, where she struggled for a couple of years until finding her breakthrough role in *The Mask of Zorro*. At the turn of the century, her affair with Michael Douglas (*qv*) made more headlines than her acting achievements, and the couple had a child together in 2000.
1990: Les 1001 nuits. 1991: Out of the Blue (TV). 1992: Christopher Columbus: The Discovery. 1993: Splitting Heirs. 1994: The Return of the Native (TV). 1995: Blue Juice. 1996: The Phantom. 1998: The Mask of Zorro. 1999: Entrapment. The Haunting. 2000: High Fidelity. Traffic. Lulu/Amazon.

ZETTERLING, Mai 1925–1994
Blonde Swedish actress with waif-like qualities but sexy sea-green eyes. Came to Britain after the international success of *Frenzy* and brought grace, intelligence and a sense of humour to assignments that were often rather dreary or mere decoration. Remained a major star until the late fifties, then became a director for a few years, with considerable critical success. Died from cancer.
1941: Lasse-Maja. 1943: Jag Dräpte. 1944: Hets/Frenzy. Prins Gustaf. 1946: Iris och Löjtnantschjärta (GB: Iris). Driver Dagg, Faller Regn. 1947: Frieda. Musuk: Mörker (GB: Night is My Future). 1948: Nu Börjar Livet. Quartet. Portrait from Life (US: The Girl in the Painting). 1949: The Bad Lord Byron. The Lost People. The Romantic Age (US: Naughty Arlette). 1950: Blackmailed. 1951: Hell is Sold Out. 1952: Tall Headlines. The Ringer. 1953: Desperate Moment. Knock on Wood. Dance Little Lady. 1954: A Prize of Gold. 1956: Ent Dockhem. 1957: Seven Waves Away (US: Abandon Ship!). Giftas. 1958:

The Truth about Women. Lek på Regnbågen (GB: The Rainbow Game). 1959: Jet Storm. 1960: Faces in the Dark. Piccadilly Third Stop. Offbeat. 1961: Only Two Can Play. 1962: The Man Who Finally Died. The Main Attraction. 1963: The Bay of Saint Michel (US: Pattern for Plunder). 1965: Lianbron. 1976: We har manje namn. 1989: The Witches. 1990: Hidden Agenda. 1993: Morfars resa (US: Grandfather's Journey). 1994: The Woman Who Cleaned the World.

As director: 1963: The War Game. 1964: Älskande Par/Loving Couples. 1966: Night Games. 1967: Doktor Glas. 1968: The Girls/ Flickorna. 1972: Vincent the Dutchman. 1973: Visions of Eight (co-directed). We har manje namn. 1982: Scrubbers. 1986: Amarosa. 1990: Sunday Pursuit.

ZIEMANN, Sonja 1925–

Vivaciously pretty, dark-haired German actress who came to films as a teenager, survived working during the Nazi years, and later made several forays into the international market, most notably when she was recruited by Britain's Rank Organization to play a sexy *Hungarian* maid in *Made in Heaven*. The British connection didn't last, and she was based in Germany for the remainder of her career.

1942: Ein Windstross. 1943: Die Jungfern vom Bischofsberg. Geliebte Schatz. 1944: Eine kleine Sommermelodie. Freunde. Hundstage. Spuk im Schloss. 1945: Eine reizende Familie. Liebe nach Noten. 1946: Sag' die Wahrheit. 1947: Herzkönig. Wege im Zwielicht. 1948: Nichts als Zufälle. 1949: Die Freunde meine Frau. Nach Regen scheint Sonne. Nächte am Nil. Um eine Nasenlänge. Eine Nacht in Séparée. 1950: Maharadscha wider Willin. Schwarzwaldmädel/Girl of the Black Forest. Die lustigen Weiber von Windsor/The Merry Wives of Windsor. Schön muss man sein. Die Frauen des Herrn S. 1951: Grün ist die Heide. Johannes und die 13 Schönkeitsköniginnen. 1952: Die Diebin von Bagdad. Alle kann ich nicht heiraten. Am Brunnen vor dem Tore. Made in Heaven. 1953: Mit 17 beginnt das Leben. Die Privatsekretärin. Hollandmädel. 1954: Bei Dir war es immer so schön. Die sieben Kleider der Katrin. La tzarévitch. Meine Schwester und Ich/My Sister and I. 1955: Liebe ohne Illusion. Grosse Stern-Parade. Ich war ein hässliches Mädchen. Mädchen ohne Grezen. 1956: Das Bad auf der Tenne. Dany, bitte schreiben sie. Opernball. Nichs als Ärger mit der Liebe. Kaiserball. 1957: Die Zürcher Verlobung. Frühling in Berlin. Tabarin. Die grosse Sünde. Frauenarzt Dr Bertram. 1958:

Der achte Wochentag (GB: Eighth Day of the Week). Hunde, wollt ihr ewig leben! (GB: Battle Inferno). Glie italiani sono matti. Serenade au Texas. 1959: Liebe auf Krummen Beinen. Menschen im Hotel. Abschied von den Wolken. Strafbataillon 999 (GB: March to the Gallows). 1960: Nacht viel über Gotenhafen. Au voleur. 1961: The Secret Ways. A Matter of WHO. Affaire Nabob. Denn das Weib ist schwach. Traum von Lieschen Müller. 1962: Journey into Nowhere. Ihr Schönster Tag. Axel Munthe, der Arzt von San Michèle. Der Tod fahrt mit. 1964: Frühstück mit dem Tod. 2 × 2 im Himmelblatt. 1965: Murder by Proxy. 1968: The Bridge at Remagen. 1969: De Sade.

ZIMBALIST, Efrem Jr 1918–

Dark, well-built American actor who plays solid, reliable (even a shade dull) types. The son of a famous concert violinist, his early acting career was interrupted by distinguished war service and the death of his first wife, as well as a period devoted to writing and researching musicology. From the late 1950s there were a few films as he returned to acting full time, but much TV as leading man, including 16 consecutive seasons on the two crime series *77 Sunset Strip* and *The FBI*. Father of actress Stephanie Zimbalist.

1949: House of Strangers. 1957: Bombers B-52 (GB: No Sleep Till Dawn). Band of Angels. Execution Night (TV. GB: cinemas). 1958: The Deep Six. Violent Road. Girl on the Run. Hell's Highway. Home Before Dark. Too Much, Too Soon. 1960: The Crowded Sky. 1961: A Fever in the Blood. By Love Possessed. The Chapman Report. 1965: The Reward. Harlow (Carol Lynley version). 1967: Cosa Nostra: an Arch Enemy of the FBI (TV GB: cinemas). Wait Until Dark. 1974: Airport 1975. 1975: Who is the Black Dahlia? (TV). 1979: Terror Out of the Sky (TV). A Family Upside Down (TV). The Gathering, Part One (TV). 1980: The Gathering Part Two (TV). 1983: Shooting Stars (TV). The Avenging. Baby Sister (TV). 1989: Elmira. 1991: Hot Shots! 1993: Batman: The Mask of Phantasm (voice only). 1998: Sub Zero (V. Voice only). Cab to Canada (TV).

ZUCCO, George 1886–1960

Staring-eyed, bushy-browed, balding British actor who played uninteresting supporting roles in early British sound films and went to Hollywood in 1936, where his deep, mellifluous voice and air of faintly seedy upper-class menace very soon made him the Boris Karloff of the 'B' feature. His characters frequently

dabbled in things best left alone, and from 1938 (Charlie Chan in Honolulu) to 1948 (Who Killed 'Doc' Robbin?), he became associated with a whole run of doomed medical ventures. Died from pneumonia after years in a psychiatric hospital.

*1930: The 'W' Plan. 1931: Dreyfus (US: The Dreyfus Case). 1932: There Goes the Bride. The Midshipmaid (US: Midshipmaid Gob). The Man from Toronto. 1933: The Good Companions. 1934: Autumn Crocus. What Happened Then? What's in a Name? 1935: It's a Bet. Abdul the Damned. 1936: The Man Who Could Work Miracles. After the Thin Man. Sinner Takes All. 1937: Saratoga. Parnell. The Firefly. Madame X. Conquest (GB: Marie Walewska). Souls at Sea. London by Night. The Bride Wore Red. Rosalie. 1938: Lord Jeff (GB: The Boy from Barnardo's). Arsene Lupin Returns. Vacation from Love. Suez. Marie Antoinette. Fast Company. Three Comrades. Charlie Chan in Honolulu. 1939: Arrest Bulldog Drummond! The Adventures of Sherlock Holmes (GB: Sherlock Holmes). The Magnificent Fraud. The Cat and the Canary. Captain Fury. Here I Am, a Stranger. The Hunchback of Notre Dame. 1940: Dark Streets of Cairo. New Moon. Arise My Love. The Mummy's Hand. 1941: International Lady. The Monster and the Girl. Ellery Queen and the Murder Ring. (GB: The Murder Ring). A Woman's Face. Topper Returns. 1942: Dr Renault's Secret. Half Way to Shanghai. My Favourite Blonde. The Mummy's Tomb. The Mad Monster. The Black Swan. 1943: The Black Raven. Sherlock Holmes in Washington. Holy Matrimony. The Mad Ghoul. Song of Russia. Dead Men Walk. Never a Dull Moment. 1944: The Mummy's Ghost. One Body Too Many. †The Return of the Ape Man (GB: Lock Your Doors). The Seventh Cross. Voodoo Man. Shadows in the Night. House of Frankenstein. 1945: Sudan. Hold That Blonde. Confidential Agent. Week End at the Waldorf. Midnight Manhunt. Having Wonderful Crime. *Watchtower over Tomorrow. Fog Island. One Exciting Night. The Woman in Green. 1946: The Imperfect Lady (GB: Mrs Loring's Secret). The Flying Serpent. Scared to Death. 1947: Captain from Castile. Where There's Life. Lured (GB: Personal Column). Desire Me. Moss Rose. 1948: Secret Service Investigator. Tarzan and the Mermaids. The Pirate. Joan of Arc. Who Killed 'Doc' Robbin? (GB: Sinister House). 1949: The Barkleys of Broadway. Madame Bovary. The Secret Garden. 1950: Let's Dance. Harbor of Missing Men. 1951: David and Bathsheba. The First Legion. Flame of Stamboul.*

†Participation (some scenes as the ape-man) disputed.